THE POLITICAL HISTORY OF THE UNITED STATES OF AMERICA DURING THE GREAT REBELLION 1860–1865

A Da Capo Press Reprint Series

STUDIES IN AMERICAN HISTORY AND GOVERNMENT

GENERAL EDITOR: LEONARD W. LEVY

Claremont Graduate School

THE POLITICAL HISTORY OF THE UNITED STATES OF AMERICA DURING THE GREAT REBELLION 1860–1865

BY EDWARD McPHERSON

New Introduction by Harold M. Hyman, *Rice University*
and Hans L. Trefousse, *Brooklyn College, CUNY*

DA CAPO PRESS · NEW YORK · 1972

Library of Congress Cataloging in Publication Data

McPherson, Edward, 1830-1895.
The political history of the United States of America during the Great Rebellion, 1860-1865.
(Studies in American history and government)
On spine: Political history of the great rebellion, 1860-1865.
Reprint, with a new introd., of the 2d ed., enl., published in 1865.
1. U. S. — Politics and government — Civil War.
I. Title. II. Title: Political history of the great rebellion, 1860–1865.
E458.M16 1972 320.9′73′07 73-127287
ISBN 0-306-71207-5

This Da Capo Press edition of *The Political History of the United States of America During the Great Rebellion* is an unabridged republication of the second edition, enlarged, published in Washington, D.C., in 1865.

A Subsidiary of Plenum Publishing Corporation
227 West 17th Street, New York, New York 10011

Manufactured in the United States of America

INTRODUCTION

EDWARD MCPHERSON'S *Political History of the United States of America During the Great Rebellion* has long been known to scholars as an indispensable tool for research in the era of the Civil War. A unique compilation of facts, documents, and statistics first published in 1864, and, with appropriate additions, republished in 1865 in a second edition, it was an almost immediate success.[1] Eagerly sought after by statesmen, journalists, and politicians, the *Political History* turned out to be the beginning of a publishing venture that was to last for almost thirty years. First annually, and then biennially, many Americans came to await the appearance of a new handbook of politics edited by McPherson.[2] Although the original *Political History* has long been out of print, its value has never diminished. As it was over a hundred years ago, it remains today a reference work of the highest utility.

Curiously, despite growing interest among modern historians in the pioneers of their profession, McPherson has remained a shadowy figure. This is the more remarkable in light of the significant political-constitutional episodes in which he played important roles. In many ways McPherson was the prototype of the men who founded the Republican party and directed its course during the first half-century of its existence. A firm believer in nationalism, individualism, and private enterprise, he detested slavery and the evils springing from it. Republicanism was to him more than a mere political affiliation; it represented a way of life appropriate to America's past and promise. Like his fellow-Pennsylvanian, great friend, and mentor, Thaddeus Stevens, McPherson preached indefatigably the advantages of an individualistic society in which every citizen, equal in the sense of the absence of restraints, would enjoy opportunity to make the most of his

[1] Edward McPherson, *The Political History of the United States of America During the Great Rebellion* (Washington: Philp & Solomons, 1864); 2d ed., enl. (Washington: Philp & Solomons, 1865).

[2] A.K. McClure, *Old-Time Notes of Pennsylvania* (Philadelphia: The John C. Winston Co., 1905), I:339; James G. Blaine, *Twenty Years of Congress* (Norwich, Conn.: The Henry Bill Publishing Co., 1884), II:543; Augustus Frank to McPherson, November 29, 1866, and Theophilus Parsons to McPherson, November 25, 1865, both McPherson Papers, Library of Congress.

particular endowments. He believed that these advantages were linked indissolubly with the financial, legal, and political environments developed within the firm union of the states. To be sure, the excesses of predatory economic opportunists saddened him, for they clouded the happy horizons he foresaw for America, but he never lost his basic belief in the rectitude of his opinions or the redeemability of his nation's institutions. His fellow townsmen honored him for what he was, the incarnation of their ideas of American progress.[3] Leading members of the party with which he identified so closely appreciated his services and elected him Clerk of the House of Representatives for eight terms.

McPherson's career was closely connected with the development of his native Gettysburg. Born on July 31, 1830, the son of a prominent local banker, he enjoyed the advantages of wealth and an established position in society. His paternal ancestors had long been active in the affairs of the colony and commonwealth.[4] Public service was expected of this favored youth. Leisured, literate, and energetic, McPherson nevertheless needed direction beyond his family's sympathies toward the Whig party.

McPherson's convictions and the tenacity with which he defended them probably owed much to the influence of his father's friend, Thaddeus Stevens. After graduating in 1848 from Pennsylvania (now Gettysburg) College, young McPherson read law in Stevens' office, and it was Stevens' example that he sought to follow. The famous radical remained his idol throughout his life, and it later became McPherson's fondest hope to be his biographer.[5]

McPherson did not finish his legal studies. Finding himself drawn toward journalism, he became a reporter of legislative proceedings at Harrisburg, where in 1851 he also edited the Harrisburg *Daily American.* Later that year, in Stevens' interest, he took over as editor of the Lancaster *Independent,* a position he continued to hold until 1854. The next year, however, after a brief connection with the Pittsburgh *Daily Times,* he gave up his editorial work, presumably because of bad health, and returned to Gettysburg to devote himself to farming.[6]

But not to isolation. In addition to continuing communications with "Thad" Stevens, young McPherson took every opportunity to exchange ideas with some of the best literary and scholarly lights the nation boasted. In 1857, for example, he struck up a correspondence with German-born Francis Lieber. That was the year the United States Supreme Court issued

[3] Edward McPherson, *The Growth of Individualism: From the Annual Address Delivered Before the Alumni of Pennsylvania College, Gettysburg, Pa., September 17, 1856* (Gettysburg, 1857); Gettysburg *Star & Sentinel,* December 17, 1865; August 16, 1867; April 29 and August 5, 1890. For McPherson's fear of corruption, see *Remarks of Edward McPherson, Chief of the Bureau of Engraving and Printing, Before the Committee on Banking and Currency, House of Representatives, on H.R. Bill No. 1808, February 6, 1878* (Washington: Government Printing Office, 1878).

[4] *History of Cumberland and Adams Counties, Pennsylvania* (Chicago: Warner, Beers & Co., 1886), pt. III:364–66.

[5] Gettysburg *Star & Sentinel,* August 5, 1890; William M. Hall, *Reminiscences and Sketches, Historical and Biographical* (Harrisburg: Meyers Printing House, 1890), p. 3.

[6] J.M. Morrison to McPherson, April 28, 1883, McPherson Papers, Library of Congress; *History of Cumberland and Adams Counties,* pt. III:365–66.

its tragically misdirected decision in the case of the slave, Dred Scott, in which Chief Justice Roger B. Taney, a Marylander, concluded that Congress could not constitutionally contain slavery by prohibiting its entry into national territories (the basic position of the new Republican party was that Congress must do precisely what the Court said was impermissible), and that Negroes never had been, were not, and never could be equal persons or citizens under United States law. Lieber's criticisms of Taney's opinion, published first in newspapers, won McPherson's praise. Fourteen years later, McPherson was delighted to quote to Lieber phrases from an 1859 lower court decision by Taney in which the jurist contradicted his own *Dred Scott* position, stating that "the word person is used in the Constitution to describe slaves as well as freemen."[7]

As the 1850's drew to a close, McPherson found ways to present his ideas to wider audiences than the readers of local newspapers. Asked to deliver the annual address to the alumni of Pennsylvania College, he chose "The Growth of Individualism" as his topic. Individualism was the measure of the progress of mankind, he asserted. Its success in antiquity had been impossible because of the absence of Christianity, so that it had really developed only in modern times, particularly with the spread of Protestantism. But its greatest triumph, he believed, was destined to be in the United States. Only one obstacle still marred its complete ascendency—the continued existence of slavery, which, McPherson was certain, must pass away. Scoffing at the notion that liberty could be confined to white men alone, he pointed out that at one time not too far back in history, poor whites had been treated much like Negroes in his day. In other addresses during the Civil War and Reconstruction decades, McPherson stressed similar ideas, developing further the influence of the "Christian principle" and of the family upon the state.[8]

With principles of this type, it was natural for young McPherson to become active in the political struggles of his native state. The newly formed Republican party was the obvious vehicle for his exertions, not only because of his friendship with Stevens, but also because it stood for the ideas in which he himself believed.

McPherson's first major political battle involved the question of public or private ownership of the state's system of public transportation. As a heritage from the Age of Jackson, Pennsylvania owned an extensive network of railroads and canals. McPherson, devoted to individual enterprise and appalled at the mismanagement of the state system, advocated its sale to private interests, a measure he popularized in 1857 in letters to the Philadelphia *Evening Bulletin* which he later reprinted in pamphlet form. His recommendations were carried out the next year, and he promptly advocated the sale of the branch canals as well. The young Republican had made a name for himself, and he has been credited with formulating in terms appropriate for America's way of economic capitalism, political democracy,

---

[7] McPherson to Lieber, May 13, 1857, and April 13, 1871, Lieber Papers, Huntington Library.

[8] McPherson, *The Growth of Individualism; History of Cumberland and Adams Counties*, pt. III:365.

and plural governments, *laissez-faire* doctrines which the Supreme Court later elaborated for the protection of great corporations.[9] McPherson believed in the absence of restraints with respect to enterprise as well as to bondage.

Thaddeus Stevens was not unmindful of his protégé's progress. When in 1858 the antislavery leader sought to return to Congress, he urged McPherson to run as well. Originally Stevens had sought to induce Alexander K. McClure, the experienced Harrisburg editor, to seek the local seat and thus add weight to his own candidacy; but finding his first choice unavailable, he turned instead to his Gettysburg friend. McPherson accepted, while McClure finally consented to run for the state assembly in order to help the district's newly-organized Republican party in an overall campaign to defeat the Democrats in incumbent President Buchanan's home state. Both McPherson and McClure were elected.[10]

The Congress in which the freshman representative took his seat in 1859 was torn by dissension. The slavery issue had become pervasive; John Brown had recently staged his raid upon Harper's Ferry and found immortality on Virginia's gallows; and southern delegates were in an ugly mood. The continued existence of the Union seemed in doubt.

In this atmosphere, McPherson lined up with the "radical" Republicans who stood four-square against backtracking on the slave extension issue, as had occurred in 1820, 1850, and 1854. In his first speech, on February 24, 1860, he severely castigated southern congressmen for threatening disunion during heated floor debates. Slaveholders' threats to secede if a Republican president was elected were particularly reprehensible to McPherson. Pennsylvania was ever loyal to the Union, he said, and as for him, "the cardinal doctrine" of his political faith was "the maintenance of the Union of the States."

As in his home state, McPherson sought to limit governmental expenses and to expand individual enterprise. Hence he offered a resolution instructing the Committee on Printing to inquire into the expediency of abandoning the existing system of public printing in favor of a method favoring the highest bidder. Apparently his constituents appreciated his efforts. In 1860 they returned him to his seat.[11]

Before McPherson could begin his new term, Lincoln's election triggered secession in the states of the Deep South. Not only was the Union breaking up, but lame-duck President Buchanan remained immobile, saying only that although the withdrawal of states was unconstitutional, the United States government had no way to prevent it. In Washington, McPherson watched, despondent, as democracy and federalism took the path toward self-destruction. "Sometimes in thinking over the possible . . . future, I have

---

9 *History of Cumberland and Adams Counties,* pt. III:365; Louis Hartz, *Economic Policy and Democratic Thought: Pennsylvania, 1776–1860* (Cambridge: Harvard University Press, 1948), pp. 167, 315.

10 McClure, *Old-Time Notes of Pennsylvania,* I:335-38; Richard N. Current, *Old Thad Stevens: A Story of Ambition* (Madison: University of Wisconsin Press, 1942), pp. 109–110.

11 *Congressional Globe,* 36th Congress, 1st Session, pp. 796, 880–83; Blaine, *Twenty Years of Congress,* I:327.

grown almost sick, but have tried to feel deep faith in the inherent... [soundness?] of our institutions, & the virtue of our people," he wrote Lieber during the depths of the secession winter. For the nation to accept more contumely without retaliating amounted to heaping further "reproach upon [the] Constitution."[12]

Then war came. Animated by the patriotic wave sweeping the North, McPherson served briefly as captain of a company of Pennsylvania reserves. He was mustered out to attend the special session of Congress in July and August, but after adjournment, he returned to military duty as a volunteer aide on the staff of General George A. McCall, a position which gave him some insight into the problems of the armed forces.[13]

During his second congressional term, McPherson continued the general lines of policy he had previously pursued. In February, 1862 he delivered a ringing patriotic address avowing that the entire rebellion was an insurrection against popular government on the part of those who believed in aristocracy—an assault upon American government which must be resisted to the utmost. But even in the midst of war, he had not forgotten his concern for fiscal conservatism. Speaking against a bill proposing an increase in the staffs of division commanders, he contended that the measure was too costly. In addition, he feared that it would tend to discriminate against officers in the field, for commanding generals were likely to choose civilians for their staffs. His objections were incorporated in the law.[14]

But Representative McPherson was to become known for more than Unionism and frugality. From the beginning of his congressional career, McPherson had made himself acquainted with the details of parliamentary procedure. As the journalist Benjamin Perley Poore pointed out, he was "a man of facts and figures, blindly devoted to his party, [who] was ever ready to spring some ingenious parliamentary trap for the discomfiture of its opponents." It was this interest in the rules of order which in later years was to make him significant in politics and lend such authority to his compilations.[15]

McPherson's service as a member of Congress was cut short by the Republican setbacks in 1862. Because his district's boundaries had been changed, he found it impossible to prevail against the general Democratic tide and was defeated for reelection. In April, 1863, upon the recommendation of Secretary of the Treasury Salmon P. Chase, he was appointed Deputy Commissioner of Internal Revenue, but his tenure in that office was brief. With the aid of his friend Stevens, he soon was elected to the office of Clerk of the House of Representatives, a position he was to hold intermittently for the next three decades.[16]

McPherson had now found his real niche in politics. The House Clerk dispensed patronage, kept the records of the House, and called the roll of

---

12 To Lieber, January 7, 1861, Lieber Papers, Huntington Library.

13 Gettysburg *Star & Sentinel*, December 17, 1895; McPherson to "Aunts," August 28, 1861, McPherson Papers, Library of Congress.

14 *Congressional Globe*, 37th Congress, 2nd Session, pp. 835–38, 1098–1100.

15 Ben. Perley Poore, *Perley's Reminiscences of Sixty Years in the National Metropolis* (Philadelphia: Hubbard Bros., 1886), II:102.

16 Gettysburg *Star & Sentinel*, December 17, 1895; Current, *Old Thad Stevens*, pp. 187–88.

the members-elect. The new incumbent's parliamentary skill made him a perfect choice for the post, and his loyalty to the Republican party was useful for its leaders. A powerful man, expert in the office's potential, could make the Clerk's role muscular and vital.

According to a custom dating back to the Continental Congress, the Clerk performed a particularly important function prior to the election of a Speaker: he was empowered to read the roll of the members-elect who would then choose the Speaker. For many years the question of who was on the roll and who was not had engendered partisan controversy. In order to make certain that the incumbent Republican Clerk would retain the power of decision, Congress, on March 3, 1863, enacted a law reaffirming the right of the Clerk of the preceding House to draw up a list of members-elect, such list to include only those whose credentials showed that they had been regularly chosen.[17] The first time McPherson would have to exercise these powers would be in December of 1865. By that time, entirely unforeseen, the fate of President Andrew Johnson's Reconstruction arrangements in the crumpled Confederate states depended upon the admission of newly-elected southern delegates to the Thirty-ninth Congress. History's outworkings contrived events so that McPherson would have a decisive role to play.

He played it perfectly. Loyal to Stevens and the radical wing of the Republican party, McPherson stated publicly before Congress met that he would "not put on the rolls of the new House, nor call the names of persons claiming to be representatives from States that have been in rebellion."[18] On December 2, 1865, he did what he had promised, the wonder being not that he did so, but that southern delegates-elect assumed that he would not. Reading names of members-elect, he omitted deliberately from the roll all from the former Confederate states, including even Horace Maynard, like President Johnson a Tennessee Unionist of undoubted loyalty. When Maynard sought to protest, McPherson cut him short. "The clerk cannot be interrupted while ascertaining whether a quorum is present," he said, and the roll call went on. Not one of the representatives from states reconstructed by Andrew Johnson was admitted. The President had lost an important round in his still ill-defined augmenting struggle with Congress.[19]

As the Reconstruction proceeded, McPherson's influence increased. In 1867, Congress passed a bill giving the Clerk power to select local newspapers in which to publish the laws. Editors eagerly sought the valuable privilege, and McPherson was thus able to dispense patronage to the Republicans' advantage.[20]

He caught the public eye once again on February 24, 1868, when the House of Representatives was considering the motion to impeach the President. Stevens, too ill to finish his speech calling for the removal of his enemy, Andrew Johnson, handed the manuscript to the Clerk, who com-

---

17 De Alva Stanwood Alexander, *History and Procedure of the House of Representatives* (Boston: Houghton, Mifflin, 1916), pp. 12ff., 22.

18 New York *Times*, November 14, 1865.

19 *Congressional Globe*, 39th Congress, 1st Session, p. 3.

20 W. Hartshoon to McPherson, March 25, 1867, and J.F. Chews to McPherson, April 1, 1867, both McPherson Papers, Library of Congress.

pleted reading it—the final address before the House proceeded to take the vote, which carried by a strict party division.[21]

This was one of the last services McPherson was able to render to Stevens. In August, 1868, the Commoner, as he was called, died. Pennsylvania had lost its most effective radical leader, McPherson a life-long friend and protector. What could be more fitting than that he should prepare Stevens' biography? He began to collect material. Assembling documents, reminiscences, and momentos of the Commoner, McPherson let it be known that he intended to write a book on the life of the man he admired, and for the next twenty-five years he labored intermittently on the project. Despite his enthusiasm, however, he never finished the biography. Whether pressure of time or ill health prevented him from doing so is difficult to determine; it may be that he overresearched it and never felt ready to proceed. But the collection of material which he assembled, the short articles he published in the Gettysburg *Star and Sentinel,* and the brief draft he wrote (now in the Stevens Papers) have long been useful to historians.[22]

McPherson did not neglect the duties of his office. Reelected Clerk for as long as the Republicans retained the power to elect one, he succeeded in impressing friends and opponents alike with his talents. "As clerk of the House of Representatives," commented the sympathetic Philadelphia *City Item* in the fall of 1867, "none of Mr. McPherson's predecessors have been more faithful and efficient. That love of order and system which is one of his characteristics places the clerical offices under his easy control. He rarely appears officially upon the floor of the House unless at the beginning of the session or to read Executive messages or vetoes, which he delivers with such cleartoned precision as to give these documents a force that of late they have not possessed inherently."[23] The Democratic Philadelphia *Age* was almost as complimentary. "If a Democrat cannot be chosen," it conceded in March, 1871, "the Radical party can furnish no better man than Mr. McPherson. He is, in the execution of his duties, and in his personal character, one of the most satisfactory officers that his party has ever chosen."[24]

On extraordinary occasions, McPherson's rhetorical ability added excitement to the proceedings of the House. When, during the investigation of the *Crédit Mobilier* scandal, Oakes Ames, the Congressman whose activities had brought about the disgrace of many of his colleagues, was given the floor, he asked the clerk to read his statement. According to the New York *Independent,* McPherson "read it for him with a point, a pathos, a power which he could not possibly have commanded for himself. Mr. McPherson has a ringing, sympathetic voice, and if the appeal had been from his own

21 Fawn M. Brodie, *Thaddeus Stevens, Scourge of the South* (New York: W.W. Norton Co., 1959), pp. 335–36.

22 Gettysburg *Star & Sentinel,* August 14, 1868; August 16, 1887; April 29, 1890; January 13, 1891; Hall, *Reminiscences,* pp. 3, 23; J.A. Murray to McPherson, January 13, 1869; C.E. Phelps to McPherson, January 13, 1869; Gerrit Smith to McPherson, February 13, 1869; Thomas Cochran to McPherson, May 6, 1875; Benson Lossing to McPherson, March 13, 1872; and A.K. McClure to McPherson, July 8, 1873, constitute examples of his efforts available in the McPherson Papers, Library of Congress; unsigned memorandum, Stevens Papers, Library of Congress, XVI:55309–55323.

23 Philadelphia *City Item,* quoted in Gettysburg *Star & Sentinel,* October 16, 1867.

24 Philadelphia *Age,* quoted in Gettysburg *Star & Sentinel,* March 10, 1871.

heart, instead of the written address of another, he could not possibly have uttered every syllable with more effect."[25]

As a representative of the Republican party, with whose leaders he was intimately acquainted, the Clerk was doing an excellent job. "Suppose our new Congress ... were composed of the peers of the Hon. Edward McPherson?" queried the Philadelphia *Press* in December, 1873, while bemoaning the general corruption in Washington. "The blush of shame would no longer crimson the national cheek."[26]

McPherson's political activities during the Grant era were not merely confined to his role as Clerk. Highly respected at home, he served on local Republican committees; when his health permitted, he campaigned actively for his party in state and national contests; and in 1868 he had hopes of a cabinet post.[27] In 1873, his close friendship with James G. Blaine enabled him to play an important role in the negotiations which led to the appointment of various House committees.[28] In addition, he had become one of the owners of the Gettysburg *Star and Sentinel,* which he used as a mouthpiece for radical views.[29] And although he lost his position as Clerk after the Democratic victory in the 1874 congressional balloting, he continued to take active interest in the affairs of his party and of his friend Blaine. The upshot was that McPherson became Permanent Chairman of the Republican National Convention in 1876.[30]

In this unaccustomed post, McPherson did not show the same skill that had marked his tenure as House Clerk. Blaine's candidacy was contested by the former Speaker's numerous enemies. He was accused of graft, suspected of ill health too profound to allow him to run, and considered unfit by the Stalwart faction of the party. McPherson had been selected by Blaine's supporters, who were in control of the national committee. At first he seemed to fulfill their expectations. For example, his decision against the unit rule allowed convention delegates to cast individual votes, and this appeared to favor Blaine, although McPherson always insisted that he had given the ruling on principle and precedent. Blaine received 285 votes on the first ballot; on the sixth, his total had climbed to 308. But at this point, McPherson faltered. By permitting a temporary recess, he gave the anti-Blaine elements a chance to combine, and Rutherford B. Hayes was nominated instead.[31] McPherson was severely criticized for his action,[32] but

---

[25] New York *Independent,* quoted in Gettysburg *Star & Sentinel,* March 12, 1873.

[26] Philadelphia *Press,* quoted in Gettysburg *Star & Sentinel,* December 3, 1873.

[27] Gettysburg *Star & Sentinel,* August 7, 1867; July 17, 1868; October 30, 1868; August 4, 1871; September 12, 1872; October 7 and 14, 1875; Buehler to McPherson, December 8, 1868, McPherson Papers, Library of Congress.

[28] J.G. Blaine to McPherson, November 17 and 22, 1873, McPherson Papers, Library of Congress.

[29] Gettysburg *Star & Sentinel,* July 10, 1867. The weekly issues of the paper faithfully reflected the party's position.

[30] *Ibid.,* March 12, September 30, 1875; March 30, April 6, 1876; New York *Times,* June 15, 1876.

[31] *Proceedings of the Republican National Convention of 1876* (Concord: Republican Press Association, 1876), pp. 29–30, 83ff.; New York *Times,* June 15 and 17, 1876; David Saville Muzzey, *James G. Blaine, A Political Idol of Other Days* (New York: Dodd, Mead & Co., 1935), pp. 104, 115.

[32] Theron Clark Crawford, *James G. Blaine* (New York: Edgewood Publishing Co., 1893),

whether he could in any event have overcome the powerful opposition to the "Plumed Knight" is doubtful. Regardless, he loyally supported the party's nominee and campaigned strenuously for the Republican cause. Hayes did not forget his services, and in April, 1877, appointed him Chief of the Bureau of Printing and Engraving.[33]

In his new office, McPherson found himself in a peculiar position. Although he had long argued against government interference in business, he was now the head of a federal bureau engaged in work which some Congressmen felt might better be performed by private enterprise. But having convinced himself of the need for the agency, McPherson became its enthusiastic supporter and sought to streamline its operations. When he found that some of the work formerly done by private bank note companies could be handled more economically by his bureau, he discontinued the practice of letting out contracts and thus effected sizable savings. And when the operations of the bureau were attacked by those favoring private interests, he promptly testified in its favor. In a lengthy argument before the House Committee on Banking and the Currency, he sought to show that the agency was not only efficient and performed services which private operators could not duplicate, but that there was no civilized country in which the same functions were not performed by the government. The argument was convincing. Congress refused to abolish the bureau, and a pamphlet containing McPherson's remarks was printed and widely distributed.[34] When government operation was clearly more efficient than private enterprise, especially in activities traditionally associated with the state, McPherson's financial conservatism overrode his devotion to *laissez-faire.*

In the long run, however, McPherson was not anxious to remain the head of a government agency. In 1878, after thoroughly reorganizing the Bureau, he resigned his position. He preferred newspaper work, and a splendid opportunity was beckoning.[35]

The new enterprise which attracted McPherson was the editorship of the Philadelphia *Press,* a major metropolitan newspaper. For a man of his tastes, the challenge was great, and he accepted the offer, moving to Philadelphia.[36] But his editorial career in the Quaker City was a stormy one. The *Press* was owned by Calvin Wells, a Pittsburgh iron master whose concepts of running a newspaper did not coincide with those of his new editor. Admonishing McPherson to secure more competent reporters, criticizing him

---

pp. 383, 391; Charles Edward Russell, *Blaine of Maine* (New York: Cosmopolitan Book Corp., 1931), p. 314.

33 Gettysburg *Star & Sentinel,* September 14, October 26, November 9, 1876; New York *Tribune,* October 21, 1876; New York *Times,* October 21, 1876; April 27, 1877.

34 Gettysburg *Star & Sentinel,* July 5 and 15, October 5, 1877; April 12, September 20, November 20, 1878; *Remarks of Edward McPherson . . . Before the Committee on Banking and Currency, passim.*

35 New York *Times,* September 20, 1878; C.C. Buehler to McPherson, September 19, 1878, and John Sherman to McPherson, September 19, 1878, both McPherson Papers, Library of Congress.

36 Gettysburg *Star & Sentinel,* September 26, 1878.

for content and lay-out, and interfering in the day-to-day operations of the journal, Wells proved to be a difficult superior.[37] The publishing enterprise began to experience financial difficulties, and in February, 1880, Wells finally decided to let McPherson go. "The simple fact is the paper is not doing well," he explained to the editor. "You have some very brilliant qualifications for political editorial work but for general editorial management you appear to me to lack necessary training and experience."[38] Arranging for a dignified exit for the editor—McPherson became Secretary of the Republican Congressional Committee—the iron master severed the mutually trying relationship. McPherson's only remaining journalistic venture was the Gettysburg *Star and Sentinel.*[39]

Because 1880 was a presidential year, McPherson's new position was important. The Republican Congressional Committee was responsible for protecting the party's interests in each of the congressional districts and played a significant part in the organization of the campaign.[40] In spite of his initial doubts about Blaine's chances—he tended to favor John Sherman—McPherson rallied to his friend's standard. As the Republican politician William E. Chandler pointed out, an all-out effort for Blaine was necessary in order to prevent Don Cameron's bid to hitch the Pennsylvania delegation on the third-term movement for Grant.[41] When Blaine again failed to obtain the nomination, McPherson loyally supported James A. Garfield, the convention's choice.

In his official capacity, McPherson circulated nationally pamphlets pointing out the shortcomings of the Democrats.[42] His services helped to structure the Republican victory. In the November elections, the Republicans won not only the presidency, but control of Congress as well. Although Cameron sought revenge by attempting to block the way, McPherson's friends succeeded in reelecting him to his old post as Clerk of the House. For the seventh time, he had secured the office with which he had become increasingly identified.[43]

McPherson's reputation as one of the country's leading parliamentarians was firm and enduring. He received frequent inquiries about points of parliamentary law from "old" Republicans and from newer breeds as well. Among these was a letter from Theodore Roosevelt, who wanted to run for Congress although he was not yet twenty-five years old. Would he be eligible, he wanted to know, since he would be of age by March 4? By the time the Clerk had supplied a precedent for him, young Roosevelt had decided

---

37 Calvin Wells to McPherson, March 5 and 8, April 17, June 5, July 2 and 10, August 6, October 24 and 28, November 26 and 30, 1879; all McPherson Papers, Library of Congress.

38 Wells to McPherson, February 18, 1880, McPherson Papers, Library of Congress.

39 Wells to McPherson, February 27, 1880, and Jay A. Hubbell to McPherson, March 2, 1880, both McPherson Papers, Library of Congress.

40 Gettysburg *Star & Sentinel,* March 4 and 11, 1880.

41 Wells to McPherson, January 10, 1880; W.E. Chandler to McPherson, January 30, 1880; Wells to McPherson, February 26, 1880; all McPherson Papers, Library of Congress.

42 Correspondence of Republican Congressional Committee in McPherson Papers, Library of Congress, 1880; New York *Times,* August 5, 1880.

43 New York *Times,* December 4, 1881; J.M. Scovel to McPherson, December 9, 1881, McPherson Papers, Library of Congress.

not to seek office. "I feel as if I had lost the great chance of my life," he wrote, "as it has always been my greatest ambition to go to Congress."[44]

In 1884, when Blaine finally won the nomination he had been seeking for so long, McPherson served again as Secretary of the Republican Congressional Committee.[45] His party's lack of success in the election did not discourage McPherson—he had lost his own job, House Clerk, to the Democrats two years before—and he returned to Gettysburg. There he devoted himself to local concerns, including the history of Adams County.[46] But he never gave up his interest in politics. Actively participating as Secretary of the Republican Congressional Committee in local and national campaigns, he was to be Clerk of the House one more time. In 1888, when Benjamin Harrison defeated Grover Cleveland and the Republicans recaptured the House, McPherson sought an eighth term. This time his ambitions were seriously contested. The activities of the Republican Congressional Committee had come under criticism, and the candidate's age and uncertain health spoke against him. But since he was able to secure the support of Pennsylvania's powerful leader, Senator Matthew Quay, he triumphed once again. For two years more he occupied the office in which he had served so long, and it was widely conceded that he had earned the honor.[47]

During his last term, the Clerk was interviewed by the Cincinnati *Enquirer.* Describing McPherson's office in the room in the old part of the Capitol to which John Quincy Adams had been brought after his collapse in the House—a bust of "Old Man Eloquent" stood in the room—the reporter dwelled on the Clerk's close relationship with Stevens. The achievement of which McPherson was still proudest, however, was his advocacy in the 1850's of the sale of the publicly-owned transportation enterprise of Pennsylvania. He "says he regards as the most useful thing he ever did agitating . . . for the sale of those public works," wrote the reporter. The Clerk was still an individualist.[48]

When the Democrats took over the House in 1893, McPherson retired permanently to Gettysburg. His remaining years were uneventful. He continued his interest in the Gettysburg *Star and Sentinel,* although in 1893 he sold his shares to his son. His obituary of Blaine was a tribute to the man he called "the greatest of Americans," and his faithfulness to the party remained constant. Active in the affairs of his native town, he was a director of the Battlefield Memorial Association, served as president of various local

---

44 N.B. Nettleton to McPherson, July 19, 1882; Roosevelt to McPherson, October 2, 13, and 24, 1882; all McPherson Papers, Library of Congress.

45 Gettysburg *Star & Sentinel,* February 12, August 5, September 9, 1884.

46 Gettysburg *Star & Sentinel,* May 11, 1886; June 14, July 12, August 2, September 6 and 20, October 11, November 15, 1886; February 7, 13, and 19, July 16, August 6, 1887; Edward McPherson, *The Story of the Creation of Adams County, Pennsylvania, and the Selection of Gettysburg as Its Seat of Justice. An Address Before the Historical Society of Adams County, on Its First Anniversary, May 6, 1889* (Lancaster, Pa.: Inquirer Printing Co., 1889).

47 New York *Times,* November 3 and 30, 1889; Gettysburg *Star & Sentinel,* October 16, 1888; December 3 and 10, 1889; form letter, McPherson to Republican leaders, October 8, 1889, McPherson Papers, Library of Congress.

48 Gettysburg *Star & Sentinel,* August 5, 1890.

corporations, and maintained his connection with the local college, both as member of the board of trustees and as president of the alumni association.[49] In December, 1895, thinking that he was taking his usual tonic prescription, he swallowed a teaspoon of a powerful emetic instead. Although the family doctor attempted to save his life, the strain proved too great. "Gettysburg's greatest son," as the local paper called him, was no more.[50]

McPherson's death also brought to an end an editorial enterprise which had almost become an American institution. His famous yearbooks had appeared with unfailing regularity ever since in 1864 he had published his *Political History of the United States During the Great Rebellion.* In addition, he had edited for a number of years the New York *Tribune Almanac* and served as American representative for the *Almanach de Gotha,* the handbook of European nobility.[51] Compiling facts in book form was McPherson's forte, and his reputation must rest on these editorial services. Because his official positions allowed him access to documents others viewed only belatedly or in inadequate and incorrect form, his compilations are more accurate and more detailed than others. Furthermore, McPherson's keen insights into political realities made him sensitive to the significance of documents which other editors, compilers, and scholars passed over or misinterpreted.

Consider in this connection the first of the author's compilations, *The Political History of the United States of America During the Great Rebellion.* A truly remarkable volume, its timely collection of public acts, records, bills, treaties, conventions, public papers, correspondence, reports, and historical surveys was so skillfully arranged that in some ways it surpassed the originals in usefulness. By following carefully the progress of important measures through both Houses of Congress, the author saved readers hours of hard work in the pages of the *Congressional Globe,* and his competence, thoroughness, and awareness of the relationships of men and measures made his volume more informative than the official records themselves. He always indicated party membership of those voting on bills, highlighted the most important ayes and nays, and brought to light almost inaccessible state proceedings to document the controversies of the time. In addition, he facilitated research by means of an excellent index and the inclusion of statistical information. The result was that virtually every important scholarly work dealing with the period has had to rely on McPherson's *Political History of . . . the Great Rebellion.* The book was successful enough to call for a second edition the next year containing additional material

---

49 Gettysburg *Star & Sentinel,* January 31, May 16, July 18, 1893; June 26, 1894; May 14, December 17, 1895.

50 New York *Tribune,* December 15, 1895; Gettysburg *Star & Sentinel,* December 17, 1895; New York *Times,* December 15, 1895.

51 *The American Annual Cyclopaedia and Register of Important Events of the Year 1895* (New York: Appleton & Co., 1896), p. 581; New York *Tribune,* November 23, 1876; Whitelaw Reid to McPherson, December 9, 1881; October 3, 1882; September 8, 14, and 21, 1876; Redaktion des Gothaischen Hofkalenders to McPherson, July 7, 1871; all McPherson Papers, Library of Congress.

dealing with events since the appearance of the first. Many additional printings followed during the next two decades.[52]

From the very beginning, *The Political History of . . . the Great Rebellion* was well received. "Your Political History of the Rebellion must be indispensable . . . to one who would understand that tremendous conflict," wrote the famous Harvard lawyer, Theophilus Parsons. "You give its details with accuracy, & present and group them in such a way as to make them illustrate each other. . . . And for the comprehension of its character, your book . . . must be used."[53] The *North American Review* considered the volume "of great value for reference and consultation," and predicted that it would "be found a desirable, almost an indispensable, supplement to the methodical histories of the Rebellion."[54] In November, 1865, Charles Sumner expressed the opinion that it was the best history of the war that had yet appeared.[55]

Events bore out the predictions of success. McPherson was so satisfied with the response that he resolved to continue the work begun during the war. After adding the material for the second edition,[56] he began to compile documents for a new work. Calling it *A Political Manual for 1866,* he advertised it as "an Indispensable Handbook for Politicians, Full, Accurate, and Impartial." It included "a Classified Summary of the Important Executive, Legislative, and Politico-Military Facts of the Period, From President Johnson's Accession, April 15, 1865 to July 4, 1866," and contained what he maintained was a "Full Record of the Action of Each Branch of the Government on Reconstruction."[57] Much shorter than its predecessor, the *Political Manual* was equally well received, and in the following year, the author edited a new volume, *A Political Manual for 1867*, which brought the story up to April 1, 1867.[58] Similar *Political Manuals* for 1868, 1869, and 1870 followed. The 1868 volume, including not only the important docu-

52 Eventually, a total of fourteen editions appeared, the last, in 1882, published in Washington by J.J. Chapman.

53 Theophilus Parsons to McPherson, November 25, 1865, McPherson Papers, Library of Congress.

54 *North American Review,* VI (January, 1865):241-2.

55 Theophilus Parsons to McPherson, November 25, 1865, McPherson Papers, Library of Congress.

56 The second edition contains the following additions: "an Appendix Containing the Principal Political Facts of the Campaign of 1864, a Chapter on the Church and the Rebellion, and the Proceedings of the 2d Session of the 38th Congress."

57 Flyer with advertisement in McPherson Papers, Library of Congress; McPherson, *A Political Manual for 1866* (Washington: Philp & Solomons, 1866).

58 James G. Blaine to McPherson, August 22, 1866, and Benson Lossing to McPherson, July 3, 1866, both McPherson Papers, Library of Congress. The New York *Tribune* undertook to distribute it. Samuel Sinclair to McPherson, August 17, 1866, and Horace Greeley to McPherson, August 21, 1866, both McPherson Papers, Library of Congress. McPherson, *A Political Manual for 1867, Including a Classified Summary of the Important, Executive, Legislative, Judicial and Politico-Military Facts of the Period from July 4, 1866, to April 1, 1867, Including the Late Action of Congress on Reconstruction* (Washington: Philp & Solomons, 1867).

ments pertaining to the impeachment of President Johnson and the record of General Grant's achievements, but also all national party platforms between 1852 and 1868, was particularly notable.[59]

The *Political Manuals* proved as popular as *The Political History of . . . the Great Rebellion.* Public figures wrote in praise, although occasionally some, like Horace Greeley, were disturbed that only excerpts of an important piece of legislation, like the Legal Tender Act, appeared in the volumes. McPherson corresponded with experts all over the country in order to insure accuracy, and by and large he succeeded.[60] When some of his acquaintances suggested that he combine the books in order to obviate the necessity for procuring several small ones, he complied. Having already combined the 1866 and 1867 volumes, in 1868 McPherson published a *Handbook of Politics for 1868* which consisted of the *Manuals* for 1866, 1867, and 1868. Two years later, he put out a *Handbook of Politics for 1870* combining the 1869 and 1870 *Manuals.* Finally, he revised, reedited, and bound together all five *Manuals* to produce a second major work, *The Political History of the United States of America During the Period of Reconstruction, From April 15, 1865, to July 15, 1870.* This volume appeared in April, 1871, and, like its predecessor, went through several editions.[61]

While the new book was not as original as the old, it nevertheless proved as useful. As the editor stated in the introduction:

> This volume takes up the thread where it was dropped by that on the Rebellion, and it is naturally a companion to it. That gives the record of the steps by which Secession was accomplished and Disunion attempted, as well as of those by which Secession was resisted and Disunion defeated. This gives the equally portentious record of the means by which, the War over, the Government and people of the United States reaped its fruits, and especially the memorable steps by which four millions of slaves, formerly known as chattels, became incorporated, first into the civil, and next into the political, body.

McPherson apologized for the work's organization, based upon subdivisions according to separate years, but expressed hope that his index would make

---

59 Edward McPherson, *A Political Manual for 1868, . . . from April 1, 1867 to July 15, 1868* (Washington: Philp & Solomons, 1868) ; *A Political Manual for 1869, . . . from July 15, 1868 to July 15, 1869* (Washington: Philp & Solomons, 1869); *A Political Manual for 1870, . . . from July 15, 1869 to July 15, 1870* (Washington: Philp & Solomons, 1870).

60 Joseph R. Hawley to McPherson, August 23, 1866; Thomas Nast to McPherson, April 1, 1867, and June 16, 1868; J.L.M. Curry to McPherson, April 10, 1867; William D. Kelley to McPherson, March 10, 1876; Carl Schurz to McPherson, June 27, 1867; L. Fairchild to McPherson, July 13, 1867; Horace Greeley to McPherson, September 4, 1868; all McPherson Papers, Library of Congress.

61 George H. Pendleton to McPherson, July 15, 1869, McPherson Papers, Library of Congress; McPherson, *A Political Manual for 1866 and 1867* (Washington: n.p., 1867) ; *A Handbook of Politics for 1868* (Washington: Philp & Solomons, 1868); *A Handbook of Politics for 1870* (Washington: Philp & Solomons, 1870); *The Political History of the United States of America During the Period of Reconstruction* (Washington: Philp & Solomons, 1871). The second edition of this work was published by Solomons & Chapman in 1875 and the third by James J. Chapman in 1880, both in Washington.

up for this inconvenience.[62] Like its predecessor, *The Political History of ... Reconstruction* has been invaluable to historians.

By the time the new work appeared, McPherson's *Political Manuals* had become so widely known that the Clerk determined to continue them. After 1870, he changed the name permanently to *A Handbook of Politics,* and all subsequent issues appeared with the new title. Following the *Handbook ... for 1870,* the volumes appeared biennially, at first covering the two years between July 15 of the initial year and July 15 of the terminal one. Between 1878 and 1880, the editor substituted July 1, and afterward, July 31. (In 1888, he chose August 31 as the final date.) The last volume appeared in 1894.[63]

Throughout the years of their appearance, the *Handbooks* were eagerly awaited by subscribers and generally received favorable notices. "As a means of informing American citizens of the really vital legislation that has been enacted by Congress during the past two years, the ... work deserves the highest commendation," wrote the New York *Times* in 1872. Its reviewer admired McPherson's impartiality as well as his industry and expressed the conviction that both parties would benefit from its perusal.[64] Even the violently Democratic New York *World* was impressed. It expressed approbation of the arrangement, the table of contents, and "the very full index." "The campaign speaker, to whichever party he may belong," it commented, "will find McPherson's *Hand Book of Politics for 1872* of infinite service to him."[65] In 1876, the New York *Tribune* called the book a "Citizen's Vade Mecum"; in 1884, the New York *Times* found it "very well calculated for the needs of the political man, the politician, and the journalist"; and in 1892 the Gettysburg *Star and Sentinel* was justified in referring to the whole series as "an authority equally for all parties."[66] Summing up the editor's contributions, Alexander K. McClure, who had not always agreed with his policies, concluded: "He was known in Washington as the best informed in political history of any of the members of the House, and the most valuable records of his highly creditable career remain in his *History of the Great Rebellion,* his *History of Reconstruction,* and his political manuals, issued every two years. . . ."[67] Nothing like the series had ever existed in the United States before, nor has there been anything like it since. Long out of print, the volumes have been very difficult to obtain. Therefore they are now reprinted.

Hans L. Trefousse
Brooklyn College

Harold M. Hyman
Rice University

---

62 McPherson, *The Political History ... of Reconstruction,* p. v.

63 McPherson, *A Handbook of Politics for 1872* [to 1894], 12 vols. (Washington: Philp & Solomons, 1872; Solomons & Chapman, 1874–1878; J.J. Chapman, 1880–1892, R. Beall, 1894).

64 Francis Lieber to McPherson, June 5, 1872, McPherson Papers, Library of Congress; New York *Times,* August 25, 1872.

65 New York *World,* quoted in Gettysburg *Star & Sentinel,* September 5, 1872.

66 New York *Tribune,* September 9, 1876; New York *Times,* October 19, 1884; Gettysburg *Star & Sentinel,* July 26, 1892.

67 McClure, *Old-Time Notes of Pennsylvania,* I:339.

THE POLITICAL HISTORY OF THE UNITED STATES OF AMERICA DURING THE GREAT REBELLION 1860–1865

THE POLITICAL HISTORY

OF THE

UNITED STATES OF AMERICA,

DURING

THE GREAT REBELLION,

INCLUDING

A CLASSIFIED SUMMARY OF THE LEGISLATION OF THE SECOND SESSION OF THE THIRTY-SIXTH CONGRESS, THE THREE SESSIONS OF THE THIRTY-SEVENTH CONGRESS, THE FIRST SESSION OF THE THIRTY-EIGHTH CONGRESS, WITH THE VOTES THEREON,

AND THE IMPORTANT

EXECUTIVE, JUDICIAL, AND POLITICO-MILITARY FACTS OF THAT EVENTFUL PERIOD;

TOGETHER WITH THE

ORGANIZATION, LEGISLATION, AND GENERAL PROCEEDINGS OF THE REBEL ADMINISTRATION;

AND

AN APPENDIX

CONTAINING THE PRINCIPAL POLITICAL FACTS OF THE CAMPAIGN OF 1864 A CHAPTER ON THE CHURCH AND THE REBELLION, AND THE PROCEEDINGS OF THE SECOND SESSION OF THE THIRTY-EIGHTH CONGRESS.

BY EDWARD McPHERSON,

OF GETTYSBURG, PENNSYLVANIA,

CLERK OF THE HOUSE OF REPRESENTATIVES OF THE U. S.

SECOND EDITION.

WASHINGTON, D. C.:

PHILP & SOLOMONS.

1865.

Stereotyped by
McGILL & WITHEROW,
Washington, D. C.

PREFACE.

This volume is intended to be a Record of the Legislation, and the general Political History of the United States, for the last four years—a period of unexampled activity and of singularly deep interest and inportance, whether reference be had to the vast material interests involved in the stupendous struggle, or the precedents, principles, and measures which the Convulsion has produced. It is further intended to be a Record rather of those salient facts which embody or illustrate principles, than of those which relate to men or parties, and hence have transient and inferior significance.

So abundant have been the materials, that compression has been a necessity. Selection has been made with the purpose of presenting, fully and fairly, the facts as they are, and the agencies by which they came—viewing all else as subordinate.

The first Ninety pages are devoted to the period of Secession, and contain a narrative of the successive steps in the movement in each State, in chronological order; also, the elaborate justifying papers of the South Carolina Convention, with counter-selections from other authorities; together with a condensation of the various propositions of Adjustment made in or out of Congress and the vote upon each taken in either body, and the various Official Papers of the day tending to show the relations of the parties, the wrongs complained of, and the remedies proposed. Closely examining this Record, it is difficult for a candid person to escape the conviction that Adjustment was hopeless—Revolution having been the pre-determined purpose of the reckless men who had obtained control of the State machinery of most of the slaveholding States. This conviction will be strengthened by study of what has since transpired.

It will be remembered that the Thirty-Sixth Congress proposed permanently to settle the security of slavery in the slaveholding States by an amendment of the Constitution, which was adopted by a two-thirds vote in each House. And that it completely disposed of the Territorial feature of the difficulties by agreeing upon, and almost unanimously passing, bills organizing Territories covering the entire area owned by the Government. The record of these two important historical facts is given within. They have great significance in establishing the character of the Rebellion.

The copy of the Constitution of the United States is believed to be *strictly accurate* in text and punctuation, which, it is understood, can be said of only one other copy in print—that in the work known as Hickey's Constitution. The statement of the differences between it and the Rebel Constitution has been made with extreme care. The common index to the two instruments shows, at a glance, wherein they differ, and will be found both interesting and convenient—the whole chapter possessing special value to large classes of persons.

In presenting the facts upon each subject of legislation, the general plan has been: first, to state the result reached, with the final votes; and, then, such proceedings, in the intermediate stages, as are of adequate importance, or necessary to explain the position of Members. This preparation involved constant selection, concerning which there may be differences of opinion—some thinking that too much detail on one subject is given; others, too little of another. In all cases the rule stated, governed. As far as it has been possible to obtain the Rebel legislation on the same or corresponding subjects, it has been added, with such of their orders and proclamations as were connected with them. A comparison of the two, and the dates of enactment or issue, will prove of service in dispelling delusions and correcting general misconceptions.

Besides the legislation proper, the volume contains, in a classified form, all the Messages, Proclamations, Orders, Correspondence, and Addresses of the President; the Diplomacy of the Secretary of State; valuable letters and papers from the Secretaries of the Treasury, of War, of the Navy, of the Interior, and from the Postmaster General; Opinions of the Attorney General upon commanding public questions; those of the Orders of Commanding Officers which are within the scope of the work; the Decisions of the Courts; and such other data as properly belong therein—the whole forming a multitudinous mass of facts, to any one of which the classification adopted, and the copious index appended, will, it is hoped, make it easy to refer.

The votes by Yeas and Nays have been carefully compared with the Official Journals of Congress. In preparing these lists, the names of those persons have, for comparison's sake, been *italicised*, who were elected by, or were at the time generally co-operating with, the Democratic party. All others are in roman.

Under "Our Foreign Relations" will be found much of permanent value, as well as of current interest and dispute.

The chapter on the "Conspiracy of Disunion" contains several very interesting documents, chief of which are the extract from U. S. Senator Maclay's journal of 1789, recording, probably, the first threat of disunion uttered in Congress, and upon a subject which remained a matter of complaint in some quarters down to the period of Secession; and the Minutes of the Proceedings of the Police Commissioners of Baltimore in 1861, one of the most flagrant as well as one of the latest outbursts of treason. Other portions of this chapter will richly bear examination. I greatly regret that want of space has required the omission of many other facts, gathered from our political history, tending to reveal the true character of this foul conspiracy against Liberty, this crime against humanity.

The lists of the organization of the Rebel "Provisional" and "Permanent" Government have been made up from every accessible source, and, though not complete, are more nearly so than any other yet published north of the Potomac, and as nearly so as present facilities afford. They are the result of careful and extensive examination. As a matter of interest, the names of those of the conspirators who were once members of the Congress of the Union have been put in *italic*.

This work was undertaken a few months ago without a realizing sense of the labor it involved. I can scarcely hope to have escaped errors, both of omission and commission, but have striven to make it fair, impartial, and truthful. It deals with the most momentous events of this Century, which will be studied while civil Government exists. I trust that the volume will be of service to those consulting it, and that its general effect will be to help strengthen the purpose of the American people to maintain their Unity, their Freedom, and their Power.

EDWARD McPHERSON.

August 11, 1864.

PREFACE TO THE SECOND EDITION.

I have revised the entire work, and corrected every error ascertained. The Appendix has expanded greatly beyond the original design. Much of the matter in it is quite inaccessible, and the delays and uncertainties of procuring it led almost insensibly to an enlargement, and also somewhat disturbed the methodical arrangement elsewhere preserved. The historic papers of the South Carolina Convention, as now printed, are from official copies, and differ very suggestively from current versions, in numerous material points. The votes on Secession Ordinances, and subsequently on the Extinction of Slavery, in several of the rebellious States, form a pleasing contrast.

The copious chapter on "The Church and the Rebellion" has been gathered with great care, and will serve to show their mutual relations and influence, as well as the singularly diverse views which have prevailed in Church courts. The contributions from the Bureau of Military Justice illustrate the practical working of the Emancipation policy, and will amply justify attention. To the action of the last session of Congress, and the record of the Presidential canvass which preceded it—of the result of which an official tabular statement is furnished—every student of American politics will have constant occasion to refer. On the great unsettled question of Reconstruction, the full record is presented.

It would be improper, in issuing this enlarged, and it is hoped improved edition, not to express my thanks for the kind reception given the first by the Press and the Public.

March 24, 1865. EDWARD McPHERSON.

TABLE OF CONTENTS.

RESULT OF THE PRESIDENTIAL ELECTION OF 1860.

STATES.	ELECTORAL VOTE.				POPULAR VOTE.			
	Lincoln.	Bell.	Douglas.	Breckinridge.	Lincoln.	Bell.	Douglas	Breckinridge.
Maine	8				62,811	2,046	26,693	6,368
New Hampshire	5				37,519	441	25,881	2,112
Massachusetts	13				106,533	22.331	34,372	5,939
Rhode Island	4				12,244		*7,707	
Connecticut	6				43,792	3,291	15,522	14,641
Vermont	5				33,808	1,969	6,849	218
New York	35				362,646		*312,510	
New Jersey	4		3		58,324		*62,801	
Pennsylvania	27				268,030	12,776	16,765	*178,871
Delaware				3	3,815	3,864	1,023	7,337
Maryland				8	2,294	41,760	5,966	42,482
Virginia		15			1,929	74,681	16,290	74,323
North Carolina				10		44,990	2,701	48,539
South Carolina				8		No	popular	vote.
Georgia				10		42,886	11,590	51,889
Kentucky		12			1,364	66,058	25,651	53,143
Tennessee		12				69,274	11,350	64,709
Ohio	23				231,610	12,194	187,232	11,405
Louisiana				6		20,204	7,625	22,681
Mississippi				7		25,040	3,283	40,797
Indiana	13				139,033	5,306	115,509	12,295
Illinois	11				172,161	4,913	160,215	2,404
Alabama				9		27,875	13,651	48,831
Missouri			9		17,028	58,372	58,801	31,317
Arkansas				4		20,094	5,227	28,732
Michigan	6				88,480	405	65,057	805
Florida				3		5,437	367	8,543
Texas				4		*15,438		47,548
Iowa	4				70,409	1,763	55,111	1,048
Wisconsin	5				86,110	161	65,021	888
California	4				39,173	6,817	38,516	34,334
Minnesota	4				22,069	62	11,920	748
Oregon	3				5,270	183	3,951	5,006
Total	180	39	12	72	1,866,452	590,631	1,375,157	847,953

Lincoln over Douglas 491,295

" " Breckinridge 1,018,499

" " Bell 1,275,821

Other candidates over Lincoln 947,289

* Fusion.

SECESSION MOVEMENT DEVELOPED.

IMMEDIATELY thereupon, and clearly by concert of action previously arranged, various disunion Governors hastily took steps to procure the passage of ordinances of secession by Conventions of their States, artfully using the unsettled excitements of the Presidential canvass to that end.

These proceedings in brief were as follows:

SOUTH CAROLINA.

November 6th, 1860. Legislature met to choose Presidential electors, who voted for Breckinridge and Lane for President and Vice President. Gov. WILLIAM H. GIST recommended in his message that in the event of ABRAHAM LINCOLN's election to the Presidency, a convention of the people of the State be immediately called to consider and determine for themselves the mode and measure of redress. He expressed the opinion that the only alternative left is the "secession of South Carolina from the Federal Union."

7th. United States officials resigned at Charleston.

10th. U. S. Senators JAMES H. HAMMOND and JAMES CHESNUT, Jr., resigned their seats in the Senate. Convention called to meet Dec. 17th. Delegates to be elected Dec. 6th.

13th. Collection of debts due to citizens of non-slaveholding States stayed. FRANCIS W. PICKENS elected Governor, who appointed a cabinet consisting of A. G. MAGRATH Secretary of State, DAVID F. JAMISON Secretary of War, C. G. MEMMINGER Secretary of Treasury, W. W. HARLLEE P. M. General, ALBERT C. GARLINGTON Secretary of Interior.

17th. Ordinance of Secession adopted unanimously.

21st. Commissioners appointed (BARNWELL, ADAMS, and ORR) to proceed to Washington to treat for the possession of U. S. Government property within the limits of South Carolina. Commissioners appointed to the other Slaveholding States. Southern Congress proposed.

24th. Representatives in Congress withdrew.

Gov. PICKENS issued a proclamation "announcing the repeal, Dec. 20th, 1860, by the good people of South Carolina," of the Ordinance of May 23d, 1788, and "the dissolution of the union between the State of South Carolina and other States under the name of the United States of America," and proclaiming to the world "that the State of South Carolina is, as she has a right to be, a separate, sovereign, free and independent State, and, as such, has a right to levy war, conclude peace, negotiate treaties, leagues, or covenants, and to do all acts whatsoever that rightfully appertain to a free and independent State.

"Done in the eighty-fifth year of the sovereignty and independence of South Carolina."

Jan. 3d, 1861. South Carolina Commissioners left Washington.

4th. Convention appointed T. J. Withers, L. M. Keitt, W. W. Boyce, Jas. Chesnut, Jr., R. B. Rhett, Jr., R. W. Barnwell, and C. G. Memminger, delegates to Southern Congress.

5th. Convention adjourned, subject to the call of the Governor.

14th. Legislature declared that any attempt to reinforce Fort Sumter would be considered an open act of hostility and a declaration of war. Approved the Governor's action in firing on the *Star of the West*. Accepted the services of the Catawba Indians.

27th. Received Judge Robertson, Commissioner from Virginia, but rejected the proposition for a conference and co-operative action.*

---

* The resolutions are:

Resolved unanimously, That the General Assembly of South Carolina tenders to the Legislature of Virginia their acknowledgment of the friendly motives which inspired the mission entrusted to Hon. Judge Robertson, her Commissioner.

Resolved unanimously, That candor, which is due to the long-continued sympathy and respect which has subsisted between Virginia and South Carolina, induces the Assembly to declare with frankness that they do not deem it advisable to initiate negotiations, when they have no desire or intention to promote the ultimate object in view. That object is declared, in the resolution of the Virginia Legislature, to be the procurement of amendments to, or new guarantees in, the Constitution of the United States.

March 26th. Convention met in Charleston.

April 3d. Ratified "Confederate" Constitution—yeas 114, nays 16. (See p. 398)

8th. Transferred forts, etc. to "Confederate" government.

GEORGIA.

November 8th, 1860. Legislature met pursuant to previous arrangement.

18th. Convention called. Legislature appropriated $1,000,000 to arm the State.

Dec. 3d. Resolutions adopted in the Legislature proposing a Conference of the Southern States at Atlanta, Feb. 20th.

January 17th, 1861. Convention met. Received Commissioners from South Carolina and Alabama.

18th. Resolutions declaring it the right and duty of Georgia to secede, adopted—yeas 165, nays 130.

19th. Ordinance of Secession passed—yeas 208, nays 89.

21st. Senators and Representatives in Congress withdrew.

24th. Elected Delegates to Southern Congress at Montgomery, Alabama.

28th. Elected Commissioners to other Slaveholding States.

29th. Adopted an address "to the South and the world."

March 7th. Convention reassembled.

16th. Ratified the "Confederate" Constitution—yeas 96, nays 5.

20th. Ordinance passed authorizing the "Confederate" government to occupy, use and possess the forts, navy yards, arsenals, and custom houses within the limits of said State.

April 26th. Governor Brown issued a proclamation ordering the repudiation by the citizens of Georgia of all debts due Northern men.

Resolved unanimously, That the separation of South Carolina from the Federal Union is *final, and she has no further interest in the Constitution of the United States;* and that the only appropriate negotiations between her and the Federal Government are as to their *mutual relations* as foreign States.

Resolved unanimously, That this Assembly further owes it to her friendly relations with the State of Virginia to declare that they have no confidence in the Federal Government of the United States; that the most solemn pledges of that government have been disregarded; that under pretence of preserving property, hostile troops have been attempted to be introduced into one of the fortresses of this State, concealed in the hold of a vessel of commerce, with a view to subjugate the people of South Carolina, and that even since the authorities at Washington have been informed of the present mediation of Virginia, a vessel of war has been sent to the South, and troops and munitions of war concentrated on the soil of Virginia.

Resolved unanimously, That in these circumstances this Assembly, with renewed assurances of cordial respect and esteem for the people of Virginia, and high consideration for her Commissioner, decline entering into the negotiations proposed.

The Charleston *Mercury* of an earlier date thus alluded to Border State embassies:

"Hear them, if you please; treat them with civility; feed them, and drench them in champagne—and let them go! Let us act as if they had never come, as if they had not spoken, as if they did not exist; and let them seek to preserve their Treasury pap through some more supple agency than ours. The time has gone by when the voice of a Virginia politician, though he coo like a dove, should be heard in the land of a patriotic people."

MISSISSIPPI.

November 26th, 1860. Legislature met Nov. 26th, and adjourned Nov. 30th. Election for Convention fixed for Dec. 20th, Convention to meet Jan. 7th. Convention bills and secession resolutions passed unanimously. Commissioners appointed to other Slaveholding States to secure "their co-operation in effecting measures for their common defence and safety."

Jan. 7th, 1861. Convention assembled.

9th. Ordinance of Secession passed—yeas 84, nays 15.

In the ordinance the people of the State of Mississippi express their consent to form a federal union with such of the States as have seceded or may secede from the Union of the United States of America, upon the basis of the present Constitution of the United States, except such parts thereof as embrace other portions than such seceding States.

10th. Commissioners from other States received. Resolutions adopted, recognizing South Carolina as sovereign and independent.

Jan. 12th. Representatives in Congress withdrew.

19th. The committee on the Confederacy in the Legislature reported resolutions to provide for a Southern Confederacy, and to establish a provisional government for seceding States and States hereafter seceding.

21st. Senators in Congress withdrew.

March 30th. Ratified "Confederate" Constitution—yeas 78, nays 7.

FLORIDA.

November 26th, 1860. Legislature met. Governor M. S. Perry recommended immediate secession.

Dec. 1st. Convention bill passed.

Jan. 3d, 1861. Convention met.

7th. Commissioners from South Carolina and Alabama received and heard.

10th. Ordinance of Secession passed—yeas 62, nays 7. (See p. 399.

18th. Delegates appointed to Southern Congress at Montgomery.

21st. Senators and Representatives in Congress withdrew.

Feb. 14th. Act passed by the Legislature declaring that after any actual collision between Federal troops and those in the employ of Florida, the act of holding office under the Federal government shall be declared treason, and the person convicted shall suffer death. Transferred control of government property captured, to the "Confederate" government.

LOUISIANA.

December 10th, 1860. Legislature met.

11th. Convention called for Jan. 23d. Military bill passed.

12th. Commissioners from Mississippi received and heard. Governor instructed to communicate with Governors of other southern States.

January 23d, 1861. Convention met and organized. Received and heard Commissioners from South Carolina and Alabama.

25th. Ordinance of Secession passed—yeas 113, nays 17. Convention refused to submit the ordinance to the people by a vote of 84 to 45.

The statement in the first edition that this action was re-considered, and the Ordinance submitted, is incorrect. It was not voted upon by the people.

Feb. 5th. Senators withdrew from Congress, also the Representatives, except John E. Bouligny. State flag adopted. Pilots at the Balize prohibited from bringing over the bar any United States vessels of war.

March 7th. Ordinance adopted in secret session transferring to "Confederate" States government $536,000, being the amount of bullion in the U. S. mint and customs seized by the State.*

16th. An ordinance voted down, submitting the "Confederate" Constitution to the people—yeas 26, nays 74.

21st. Ratified the "Confederate" Constitution—yeas 101, nays 7. Governor authorized to transfer the arms and property captured from the United States to the "Confederate" Government.

27th. Convention adjourned *sine die.*

ALABAMA.

January 7th, 1861. Convention met.

8th. Received and heard the Commissioner from South Carolina.

11th. Ordinance of Secession passed in secret session—yeas 61, nays 39. Proposition to submit ordinance to the people lost—yeas 47, nays 53.

14th. Legislature met pursuant to previous action.

19th. Delegates elected to the Southern Congress.

21st. Representatives and Senators in Congress withdrew.

26th. Commissioners appointed to treat with United States Government relative to the United States forts, arsenals, etc., within the State.

The Convention requested the people of the States of Delaware, Maryland, Virginia, North Carolina, South Carolina, Florida, Georgia, Mississippi, Louisiana, Texas, Arkansas, Tennessee, Kentucky and Missouri to meet the people of Alabama by their delegates in Convention, February 4th, 1861, at Montgomery, for the purpose of consulting as to the most effectual mode of securing concerted or harmonious action in whatever measures may be deemed most desirable for their common peace and security.—Military Bill passed. Commissioners appointed to other Slaveholding States.

March 4th. Convention re-assembled.

13th. Ratified "Confederate" Constitution, yeas 87, nays 6. Transferred control of forts, arsenals, etc., to "Confederate" Government

ARKANSAS.

January 16th, 1861. Legislature passed Convention Bill. Vote of the people on the Convention was 27,412 for it, and 15,826 against it.

February 18th. Delegates elected.

March 4th. Convention met.

18th. The Ordinance of Secession defeated—yeas 35, nays 39. The Convention effected a compromise by agreeing to submit the question of co-operation or secession to the people on the 1st Monday in August.

May 6th. Passed Secession Ordinance—yeas 69, nays 1. Authorized her delegates to the Provisional Congress, to transfer the arsenal at Little Rock and hospital at Napoleon to the "Confederate" Government.

TEXAS.

January 21st, 1861. Legislature met.

28th. People's State Convention met.

29th. Legislature passed a resolution declaring that the Federal Government has no power to coerce a Sovereign State after she has pronounced her separation from the Federal Union.

February 1st. Ordinance of Seeession passed in Convention—yeas 166, nays 7. Military Bill passed.

7th. Ordinance passed, forming the foundation of a Southern Confederacy. Delegates to the Southern Congress elected. Also an act passed submitting the Ordinance of Secession to a vote of the people.

23d. Secession Ordinance voted on by the people; adopted by a vote of 34,794 in favor, and 11,235 against it.

March 4th. Convention declared the State out of the Union. Gov. Houston issued a proclamation to that effect.

16th. Convention by a vote of 127 to 4 deposed Gov. Houston, declaring his seat vacant. Gov. Houston issued a proclamation to the people protesting against this action of the Convention.

20th. Legislature confirmed the action of the Convention in deposing Gov. Houston by a vote of 53 to 11. Transferred forts, etc., to "Confederate" Government.

23d. Ratified the "Confederate" Constitution—yeas 68, nays 2.

NORTH CAROLINA.

November 20th, 1860. Legislature met. Gov. Ellis recommended that the Legislature invite a conference of the Southern States, or failing in that, send one or more delegates to the neighboring States so as to secure concert of action. He recommended a thorough reorganization of the militia, and the enrolment of all persons between 18 and 45 years, and the organization of a corps of ten thousand men; also, a Convention, to assemble immediately after the proposed consultation with other Southern States shall have terminated.

---

* March 14th, 1861. The "Confederate" Congress passed a resolution accepting these funds, with "a high sense of the patriotic liberality of the State of Louisiana."

December 9th. Joint Committee on Federal Relations agreed to report a Convention Bill.

17th. Bill appropriating $300,000 to arm the State, debated.

18th. Senate passed above bill—yeas 41, nays 3.

20th. Commissioners from Alabama and Mississippi received and heard—the latter, J. Thompson, by letter.

22d. Senate Bill to arm the State failed to pass the House.

22d. Adjourned till January 7th.

January 8th, 1861. Senate Bill arming the State passed the House, yeas 73, nays 26.

30th. Passed Convention Bill—election to take place February 28th. No Secession Ordinance to be valid without being ratified by a majority of the qualified voters of the State.

31st. Elected Thos. L. Clingman United States Senator.

February 13th. Commissioners from Georgia publicly received.

20th. Mr. Hoke elected Adjutant General of the State. Military Bill passed.

28th. Election of Delegates to Convention took place.

28th. The vote for a Convention was 46,671; against 47,333—majority against a Convention 661.

May 1st. Extra session of the Legislature met at the call of Gov. Ellis. The same day they passed a Convention Bill, ordering the election of delegates on the 13th.

2d. Legislature adjourned.

13th. Election of delegates to the Convention took place.

20th. Convention met at Raleigh.

21st. Ordinance of Secession passed; also the "Confederate" Constitution ratified.

June 5th. Ordinance passed, ceded the arsenal at Fayetteville, and transferred magazines, etc., to the "Confederate" Government.

TENNESSEE.

January 6th, 1861. Legislature met.

12th. Passed Convention Bill.

30th. Commissioners to Washington appointed.

February 8th. People voted no Convention: 67,360 to 54,156.

May 1st. Legislature passed a joint resolution authorizing the Governor to appoint Commissioners to enter into a military league with the authorities of the "Confederate" States.

7th. Legislature in secret session ratified the league entered into by A. O. W. Totten, Gustavus A. Henry, Washington Barrow, Commissioners for Tennessee, and Henry W. Hilliard, Commissioner for "Confederate" States, stipulating that Tennessee until she became a member of the Confederacy placed the whole military force of the State under the control of the President of the "Confederate" States, and turned over to the "Confederate" States all the public property, naval stores and munitions of war. Passed the Senate, yeas 14, nays 6, absent and not voting 5; the House, yeas 42, nays 15, absent and not voting, 18.* Also a Declaration of Independence and Ordinance dissolving the Federal relations between Tennessee and the United States, and an ordinance adopting and ratifying the Confederate Constitution, these two latter to be voted on by the people on June 8th, were passed.

June 24th. Gov. Isham G. Harris declared Tennessee out of the Union, the vote for Separation being 104,019 against 47,238.

VIRGINIA.

January 7th, 1861. Legislature convened.

8th. Anti-coercion resolution passed.

9th. Resolution passed, asking that the *status quo* be maintained.

10th. The Governor transmitted a despatch from the Mississippi Convention, announcing its unconditional secession from the Union, and desiring on the basis of the old Constitution to form a new union with the seceding States. The House adopted—yeas 77, nays 61,—an amendment submitting to a vote of the people the question of referring for their decision any action of the Convention dissolving Virginia's connection with the Union, or changing its organic law. The Richmond *Enquirer* denounced "the emasculation of the Convention Bill as imperilling all that Virginians hold most sacred and dear."

16th. Commissioners Hopkins and Gilmer of Alabama received in the Legislature.

17th. Resolutions passed proposing the Crittenden resolutions as a basis for adjustment, and requesting General Government to avoid collision with Southern States. Gov. Letcher communicated the Resolutions of the Legislature of New York, expressing the utmost disdain, and saying that "the threat conveyed can inspire no terror in freemen." The resolutions were directed to be returned to the Governor of New York.

18th. $1,000,000 appropriated for the defence of the State.

19th. Passed resolve that if all efforts to reconcile the differences of the country

---

* The following is the vote in the Senate on the adoption of the league:

YEAS.—Messrs. Allen, Horn, Hunter, Johnson, Lane, Minnis, McClellan, McNeilley, Payne, Peters, Stanton, Thompson, Wood, and Speaker Stovall. NAYS.—Messrs. Boyd, Bradford, Hildreth, Nash, Richardson and Stokes. *Absent and not voting*—Messrs. Bumpass, Mickley, Newman, Stokely, and Trimble.

The following is the vote in the House:

YEAS.—Messrs. Baker of Perry, Baker of Weakley, Bayless, Bicknell, Bledsoe, Cheatham, Cowden, Davidson, Davis, Dudley, Ewing, Farley, Farrelly, Ford, Frazie, Gantt, Guy, Havron, Hart, Ingram, Jones, Kenner, McCabe, Morphies, Nall, Hickett, Porter, Richardson, Roberts, Shield, Smith, Sewel, Trevitt, Vaughn, Whitmore, Woods, and Speaker Whitthorne. NAYS.—Messrs. Armstrong, Brazelton, Butler, Caldwell, Gorman, Greene, Morris, Norman, Russell, Senter, Strewsbury, White of Davidson, Williams of Knox, Wisener, and Woodard. *Absent and not voting*—Messrs. Barksdale, Beaty, Bennett, Britton, Critz, Doak, East, Gillespie, Harris, Hebb, Johnson, Kincaid of Anderson, Kincaid of Claiborne, Trewhitt, White of Dickson, Williams of Franklin, Williams of Hickman, and Williamson.

fail, every consideration of honor and interest demands that Virginia shall unite her destinies with her sister slaveholding States. Also that no reconstruction of the Union can be permanent or satisfactory, which will not secure to each section self-protecting power against any invasion of the Federal Union upon the reserved rights of either. (See Hunter's proposition of adjustment.)

21st. Replied to Commissioners Hopkins and Gilmer, expressing inability to make a definite response until after the meeting of the State Convention.

22d. The Governor transmitted the resolutions of the Legislature of Ohio, with unfavorable comment. His message was tabled by a small majority.

30th. The House of Delegates to-day tabled the resolutions of the Pennsylvania Legislature, but referred those of Tennessee to the Committee on Federal Relations.

February 20th. The resolutions of the Legislature of Michigan were returned without comment.

28th. Ex-President Tyler and James A. Seddon, Commissioners to the Peace Congress, presented their report, and denounced the recommendation of that body as a delusion and a sham, and as an insult and an offense to the South.

Proceedings of Virginia Convention.

February 4th. Election of delegates to the Convention.

13th. Convention met.

14th. Credentials of John S. Preston, Commissioner from South Carolina, Fulton Anderson from Mississippi, and Henry L. Benning from Georgia, were received.

18th. Commissioners from Mississippi and Georgia heard; both pictured the danger of Virginia remaining with the North; neither contemplated such an event as reunion.

19th. The Commissioner from South Carolina was heard. He said his people believed the Union unnatural and monstrous, and declared that there was no human force —no sanctity of human touch,—that could re-unite the people of the North with the people of the South—that it could never be done unless the economy of God were changed.

20th. A committee reported that in all but sixteen counties, the majority for submitting the action of the Convention to a vote of the people was 52,857. Numerous resolutions on Federal Relations introduced, generally expressing attachment to the Union, but denouncing coercion.

26th. Mr. Goggin of Bedford, in his speech, denied the right of secession, but admitted a revolutionary remedy for wrongs committed upon a State or section, and said wherever Virginia went he was with her.

March 2d. Mr. Goode of Bedford offered a resolution that, as the powers delegated to the General Government by Virginia had been perverted to her injury, and as the Crittenden propositions as a basis of adjustment had been rejected by their Northern confederates, therefore every consideration of duty, interest, honor and patriotism requires that Virginia should declare her connection with the Government to be dissolved.

5th. The thanks of the State were voted to Hon. John J. Crittenden, by yeas 107, nays 16, for his efforts to bring about an honorable adjustment of the national difficulties. Mr. Harvie of Amelia offered a resolution, requesting Legislature to make needful appropriations to resist any attempt of the Federal authorities to hold, occupy or possess the property and places claimed by the United States in any of the seceded States, or those that may withdraw or collect duties or imposts in the same.

9th. Three reports were made from the Committee on Federal Relations. The majority proposed to submit to the other States certain amendments to the Constitution, awaiting the response of non-slaveholding States before determining whether "she will resume the powers granted by her under the Constitution of the United States, and throw herself upon her reserved rights; meanwhile insisting that no coercion be attempted, the Federal forts in seceded States be not reinforced, duties be not collected, etc.," and proposing a Convention at Frankfort, Kentucky, the last Monday in May, of the States of Delaware, Maryland, North Carolina, Tennessee, Kentucky, Missouri and Arkansas. Henry A. Wise differed in details, and went further in the same direction. Messrs. Lewis E. Harvie, Robert L. Montague and Samuel C. Williams recommended the immediate passage of an Ordinance of Secession. Mr. Barbour of Culpeper insisted upon the immediate adoption by the non-slaveholding States of needed guarantees of safety, and provided for the appointment of three Commissioners to confer with the Confederate authorities at Montgomery.

19th. Committee on Federal Relations reported proposed amendments to the Constitution, which were the substitute of Mr. Franklin of Pa, in "Peace Conference," changed by using the expression "involuntary servitude" in place of "persons held to service." The right of owners of slaves is not to be impaired by congressional or territorial law, or any pre-existing law in territory hereafter acquired.

Involuntary servitude, except for crime, to be prohibited north of 36° 30′, but shall not be prohibited by Congress or any Territorial legislature south of that line. The third section has some verbal alterations, providing somewhat better security for property in transit. The fifth section prohibits the importation of slaves from places beyond the limits of the United States. The sixth makes some verbal changes in relation to remuneration for fugitives by Congress, and erases the clause relative to the securing of privileges and immunities. The seventh forbids the granting of the elective franchise and right to hold office to persons of the African race. The eighth provides that none of these amendments, nor the third paragraph of the second section of the first article of the Constitution, nor the third paragraph of the second section of the fourth article thereof, shall be amended or abolished without the consent of all the States.

25th. The Committee of the Whole refused (yeas 4, nays 116) to strike out the majority report and insert Mr. Carlile's "Peace Conference" substitute.

26th. The Constitution of the "Confederate" States, proposed by Mr. Hall as a substitute for the report of the committee, rejected—yeas 9, nays 78.

28th. The first and second resolutions reported by the committee adopted.

April 6th. The ninth resolution of the majority report came up. Mr. Bouldin offered an amendment striking out the whole, and inserting a substitute declaring that the independence of the seceded States should be acknowledged without delay, which was lost —yeas 68, nays 71.

9th. Mr. Wise's substitute for the tenth resolution, to the effect that Virginia recognizes the independence of the seceding States, was adopted—yeas 128, nays 20.

April 17. Ordinance of Secession passed in secret session—yeas 88, nays 55, one excused, and eight not voting.*

Same day the Commissioners adopted and ratified the Constitution of the Provisional Government of the "Confederate" States of America, this ordinance to cease to have legal effect if the people of Virginia voting upon the Ordinance of Secession should reject it.*

---

* The injunction of secrecy has never been removed from this vote, but the tally was recently discovered among the papers of Lewis T. Kinser, Esq., deceased, former law partner of George W. Brent, delegate from Alexandria, Va., and is as follows, as published in the Washington *Star :*

YEAS.—Wm. M. Ambler, Wm. B. Aston, Jas. Barbour, Angus R. Blakey, George Blow, Jr., James Boisseau, Peter B. Boost, Wood Bouldin, Wm. W. Boyd, Thomas Branch, James C. Bruce, Fred. M. Cabell, John A. Campbell, Allen T. Caperton, William P. Cicil, John R. Chambliss, Manilus Chapman, Sam'l A. Coffman, Raphael M. Conn, James H. Cox, Richard H. Cox, John Crither, Harvy Deskins, James B. Dorman, John Echols, Miers W. Fisher, Thos. S. Flournoy, Wm. W. Forbes, Napoleon B. French, Sam'l M. Garland, H. L. Gillespie, Sam'l L. Graham, Fendall Gregory, Jr., Wm. L. Goggin, John Goode, Jr., Thos. F. Goode, F. L. Hale, Cyrus Hall, L. S. Hall, Lewis E. Harvie, James P. Holcombe, John N. Hughes, Eppa Hunton, Lewis D. Isbell, Marmaduke Johnson, Peter C. Johnston, Robert C. Kent, John J. Kindred, James Lawson, Walter D. Leake, Wm. H. McFarland, Charles K. Mallory, Jas. B. Mallory, John L. Mayre, Sr., Fleming B. Miller, Horatio G. Moffett, Robert L. Montague, Edward T. Morris, Jeremiah Morton, William J. Neblett, Johnson Orrick, Wm. C. Parks, Wm. Ballard Preston, George W. Randolph, George W. Richardson, Timothy Rives, Robert E. Scott, William C. Scott, John T. Seawell, James W. Sheffey, Charles R. Slaughter, Valentine W. Southall, John M. Speed, Sam'l G. Staples, James M. Strange, Wm. T. Sutherlin, George P. Tayloe, John T. Thornton, Wm M. Treadway, Robert H. Turner, Franklin P. Turner, John Tyler, Edward Waller, Robert H. Whitfield, Sam'l C. Williams, Henry A. Wise, Sam'l Woods, Benjamin F. Wysor—88.

NAYS.—Edward M. Armstrong, John B. Baldwin, Geo. Baylor, Geo. W. Berlin, Caleb Boggess, Geo. W. Brent, Wm. G. Brown, John S. Burdett, James Barley, Benj. W. Byrne, John S. Carlile, John A. Carter, Sherrard Clemens, C. B. Conrad, Robert Y. Conrad, James H. Couch, W. H. B. Custis, Marshal M. Dent, Wm. H. Dulany, Jubal A. Earley, Colbert C. Fugate, Peyton Gravely, Algernon S. Gray, Ephraim B. Hall, Allen C. Hammond, Alpheus F. Haymond, James W. Hodge, J. G. Holladay, Chester D. Hubbard, George W. Hall, John J. Jackson, John F. Lewis, Wm. McComas, James C. McGrew, James Marshall, Henry M. Masters, Samuel McD. Moore, Hugh M. Nelson, Logan Osburn, Spicer Patrick, Edmund Pendleton, George McC. Porter, Samuel Price, David Pugh, John D. Sharp, Thomas Sitlington, Burwell Spurloch, Alexander H. H. Stuart, Chapman J. Stuart, Geo. W. Summers, Campbell Tarr, William White, William C. Wickham, Waitman T. Willey, John Janney (President)—55.

Excused—Benjamin Wilson.

The following members appear not to have been present, as there is no tally opposite their names in the list from which we quote:

Alfred Barbour, Robert E. Grant, Addison Hale, John R. Kilby, Paul McNeil, John Q. Marr, Thomas Martin, Peter Saunders, Sen.

*Pending the vote on ratifying the Ordinance of Secession, senator J. M. Mason published the following letter:

Winchester, Virginia, May 16, 1861.

To the Editor of the Winchester Virginian:

The question has been frequently put to me, what position will Virginia occupy should the Ordinance of Secession be rejected by the people at the approaching election? And the frequency of the question may be an excuse for giving publicity to the answer.

The Ordinance of Secession withdrew the State of Virginia from the Union, with all the consequences resulting from the separation. It annulled the Constitution and the laws of the United States within the limits of this State, and absolved the citizens of Virginia from all obligations of obedience to them.

Hence it follows, if this Ordinance be rejected by the people, the State of Virginia will remain in the Union, and the people of the State will remain bound by the Constitution of the United States, and obedience to the Government and laws of the United States will be fully and rightfully enforced against them.

It follows, of course, that in the war now carried on by the Government of the United States against the seceded States, Virginia must immediately change sides, and under the orders of that Government turn her arms against her southern sisters.

From this there can be no escape. As a member of the Union, all her resources of men and money will be at once at the command of the Government of the Union.

Again: for mutual defence, immediately after the Ordinance of Secession passed, a treaty or "military league" was formed by the convention, in the name of the people of Virginia, with the "Confederate States" of the South, by which the latter were bound to march to the aid of our State against the invasion of the Federal Government. And we have now in Virginia, at Harper's Ferry and at Norfolk, in face of the common foe, several thousand of the gallant sons of South Carolina, of Alabama, of Louisiana, Georgia, and Mississippi, who hastened to fulfil the covenant they made, and are ready and eager to lay down their lives, side by side with our sons, in defence of the soil of Virginia.

If the Ordinance of Secession is rejected, not only will this "military league" be annulled, but it will have been made a trap to inveigle our generous defenders into the hands of their enemies.

Virginia remaining in the Union, duty and loyalty to her obligations to the Union will require that those southern forces shall not be permitted to leave the State, but shall be delivered up to the government of the Union; and those who refuse to do so will be guilty of treason, and be justly dealt with as traitors.

Treason against the United States consists as well "in adhering to its enemies and giving them aid," as in levying war.

If it be asked, What are those to do who in their consciences cannot vote to separate Virginia from the United States? the answer is simple and plain. Honor and duty alike require that they should not vote on the question; and if they retain such opinions, they must leave the State.

None can doubt or question the truth of what I have written, and none can vote against the Ordinance of Secession who do not thereby (whether ignorantly or otherwise) vote to place himself and his State in the position I have indicated. J. M. MASON.

25th. A Convention was made between Commissioners of Virginia, chosen by the Convention, and A. H. Stephens, Commissioner for "Confederates," stipulating that Virginia until she became a member of the Confederacy should place her military force under the direction of the President of the "Confederate" States; also turn over to "Confederate" States all her public property, naval stores, and munitions of war. Signed by J. Tyler, W. B. Preston, S. McD. Moore, Jas. P. Holcombe, Jas. C. Bruce, Lewis E. Harvie—for Virginia; and A. H. Stephens for "Confederate" States.

June 25th. Secession vote announced as 128,884 for, and 32,134 against.

July. The Convention passed an ordinance to the effect, that any citizen of Virginia holding office under the Government of the United States after the 31st of July, 1861, should be forever banished from the State, and be declared an alien enemy. Also that any citizen of Virginia, hereafter undertaking to represent the State of Virginia in the Congress of the United States, should in addition to the above penalties be considered guilty of treason and his property be liable to confiscation. A provision was inserted exempting from the penalties of the act all officers of the United States outside of the United States, or of the Confederate States, until after July 1st, 1862.

KENTUCKY.

December 12th, 1860. Indiana militia offer their services to quell servile insurrection. Gov. Magoffin declines accepting them.

January 17th, 1861. Legislature convened.

22d. The House by a vote of 87 to 6 resolved to resist the invasion of the South at all hazards.

27th. Legislature adopted the Virginia resolutions requiring the Federal Government to protect Slavery in the Territories and to guarantee the right of transit of slaves through the Free States.

February 2d. The Senate passed by a vote of 25 to 11, resolutions appealing to the Southern States to stop the revolution, protesting against Federal coercion and providing that the Legislature reassemble on the 24th of April to hear the responses from sister States, also in favor of making an application to call a National Convention for proposing amendments to the Constitution of the United States, also by a vote of 25 to 14 declared it inexpedient at this time to call a State Convention.

5th. The House by a vote of 54 to 40 passed the above resolutions.

March 22d. State Rights Convention assembled. Adopted resolutions denouncing any attempt on the part of the Government to collect revenue as coercion; and affirming that, in case of any such attempt, the border States should make common cause with the Southern Confederacy. They also recommended a border State Convention.

April 24th. Gov. Magoffin called an extra session of the Legislature.

May 20th. Gov. Magoffin issued a neutrality proclamation.

September 11th. The House of Representatives by a vote of 71 to 26, adopted a resolution directing the Governor to issue a proclamation ordering the Confederate troops to evacuate Kentucky soil. The Governor vetoed the resolution, which was afterwards passed over his veto, and accordingly he issued the required proclamation.

October 29th. Southern Conference met at Russellville. H. C. Burnett elected Chairman, R. McKee Secretary, T. S. Bryan Assistant Secretary. Remained in secret session two days and then adjourned *sine die*. A series of resolutions reported by G. W. Johnson were adopted. They recite the unconstitutional and oppressive acts of the Legislature, proclaim revolution, provide for a Sovereignty Convention at Russellville, on the 18th of November, recommend the organization of county guards, to be placed in the service of and paid by the Confederate States Government; pledge resistance to all Federal and State taxes, for the prosecution of the war on the part of the United States; and appoint Robert McKee, John C. Breckinridge, Humphrey Marshall, Geo. W. Ewing, H. W. Bruce, Geo. B. Hodge, Wm. Preston, Geo. W. Johnson, Blanton Duncan, and P. B. Thompson to carry out the resolutions.

November 18th. Convention met and remained in session three days.

20th. It passed a Declaration of Independence and an Ordinance of Secession. A Provisional Government consisting of a Governor, Legislative Council of ten, a Treasurer, and an Auditor were agreed upon. Geo. W. Johnson was chosen Governor. Legislative Council were: Willie B. Machen, John W. Crockett, James P. Bates, Jas. S. Chrisman, Phil. B. Thompson, J. P. Burnside, H. W. Bruce, J. W. Moore, E. M. Bruce, Geo. B. Hodge.

MARYLAND.

November 27th, 1860. Gov. Hicks declined to call a special session of the Legislature, in response to a request for such convening from Thomas G. Pratt, Sprigg Harwood, J. R. Franklin, N. H. Green, Llewellyn Boyle, and J. Pinkney.

December 19th. Gov. Hicks replied to A. H. Handy, Commissioner from Mississippi, declining to accept the programme of Secession.

20th. Wm. H. Collins, Esq., of Baltimore, issued an address to the people, in favor of the Union, and in March a second address.

31st. The "Clipper" denied the existence of an organization in Maryland to prevent the inauguration of President Lincoln.

A. H. Handy of Mississippi addressed citizens of Baltimore in favor of disunion.

January 3d, 1861. Henry Winter Davis issued an address in favor of the Union.

3d. Numerous Union meetings in various parts of the State. Gov. Hicks issued an address to the people against secession.

11th. John C. Legrand in a letter to Hon. Reverdy Johnson replied to the Union speech of the latter.

14th. James Carroll, former Democratic candidate for Governor, announced his desire to go with the seceding States.

16th. Wm. A. Spencer, in letter to Walter S. Cox, Esq., declared against the right of Secession but for a Convention.

16th. Marshal Kane, in a letter to Mayor Berrett, denied that any organization exists to prevent the inauguration of President Lincoln, and said that the President elect would need no armed escort in passing through or sojourning within the limits of Baltimore and Maryland.

24th. Coleman Yellott declared for a Convention

30th. Messrs. John B. Brooke, President of the Senate, and E. G. Kilbourn, Speaker of the House of Delegates, asked the Governor to convene the Legislature in response to public meetings. Senator Kennedy published his opinion that Maryland must go with Virginia.

February 18th. State Conference Convention held, and insisted upon a meeting of the Legislature. At a meeting in Howard Co., which Speaker E. G. Kilbourn addressed, a resolution was adopted that "immediate steps ought to be taken for the establishment of a Southern Confederacy, by consultation and co-operation with such other Southern and Slave-States as may be ready therefor."

April 21st. Gov. Hicks wrote to Gen. Butler, advising that he do not land his troops at Annapolis. Butler replied that he intended to land there and march thence to Washington. Gov. Hicks protested against this and also against his having taken forcible possession of the Annapolis and Elkridge railroad.

24th. A special election of ten delegates to the Legislature took place at Baltimore. The total vote cast in all the wards was 9,249. The total vote cast at the Presidential election in November, 1860, was 30,148.

26th. Legislature reassembled at Frederick, Annapolis being occupied by Union troops.

29th. Gov. Hicks sent a message to the Legislature communicating to them the correspondence between himself and Gen. Butler and the Secretary of War relative to the landing of troops at Annapolis.

The House of Delegates voted against Secession, 53 to 13. Senate unanimously.

May 2d. The Committee on Federal Relations, "in view of the seizure of the railroads by the General Government and the erection of fortifications," presented resolutions appointing Commissioners to the President to ascertain whether any becoming arrangements with the General Government are practicable, for the maintenance of the peace and honor of the State and the security of its inhabitants. The report was adopted, and Otho Scott, Robt. M. McLane, and Wm. J. Ross were appointed such Commissioners.

Mr. Yellott in the Senate introduced a bill to appoint a Board of Public Safety. The powers given to the Board included the expenditure of the two millions of dollars proposed by Mr. Brune for the defence of the State, and the entire control of the military, including the removal and appointment of commissioned officers. It was ordered to a second reading by a vote of 14 to 8. The Board was to consist of Ezekiel F. Chambers, Enoch Louis Lowe, John V. L. MacMahon, Thomas G. Pratt, Walter Mitchell, and Thomas Winans. Gov. Hicks was made *ex-officio* a member of the Board. This measure was strongly pressed by the Disunionists for a long time, but they were finally compelled to give way, and the bill never passed.

6th. The Commissioners reported the result of their interview with the President, and expressed the opinion that some modification of the course of the General Government towards Maryland ought to be expected.

10th. The House of Delegates passed a series of resolutions reported by the Committee on Federal Relations by a vote of 45 to 12. The resolutions declare that Maryland protests against the war, and does earnestly beseech and implore the President of the United States to make peace with the "Confederate" States; also, that "the State of Maryland desires the peaceful and immediate recognition of the independence of the Confederate States." Those who voted in the negative are Messrs. Medders, Lawson, Keene, Routzahn, Naill, Wilson of Harford, Bayless, McCoy, Fiery, Stake, McCleary, and Gorsuch.

13th. Both Houses adopted a resolution providing for a committee of eight members, (four from each House) to visit the President of the United States and the President of the Southern Confederacy. The committee to visit President Davis were instructed to convey the assurance that Maryland sympathizes with the Confederate States, and that the people of Maryland are enlisted with their whole hearts on the side of reconciliation and peace.

June 11th. Messrs. McKaig, Yellott and Harding, Commissioners to visit President Davis, presented their report; accompanying which is a letter from Jefferson Davis, expressing his gratification to hear that the State of Maryland was in sympathy with themselves, was enlisted on the side of peace and reconciliation, and avowing his perfect willingness for a cessation of hostilities, and a readiness to receive any proposition for peace from the United States Government.

20th. The House of Delegates, and June 22d, the Senate adopted resolutions unqualifiedly protesting against the arrest of Ross Winans and sundry other citizens of Maryland, as an "oppressive and tyrannical assertion and exercise of military jurisdiction within the limits of Maryland, over the persons and property of her citizens, by the Government of the United States."

MISSOURI.

January 15th, 1861. Senate passed Convention Bill—yeas 31, nays 2. Passed House also.

February 28th. Convention met; motion to go into secret session, defeated. A resolution requiring members to take an oath to support the Constitution of the United States and the State of Missouri, was lost—65 against 30.

March 4th. Resolution passed, 64 yeas, 35 nays, appointing committee to notify Mr. Glenn, Commissioner of Georgia, that the Convention was ready to hear any communication from his State. Mr. Glenn was introduced, read Georgia's articles of secession, and made a speech urging Missouri to join her.

5th. Resolutions were read, ordering that the protest of St. Louis against coercion be reduced to writing, and a copy sent to the President of the United States; also, resolutions were adopted informing Commissioner from Georgia that Missouri dissented from the position taken by that State, and refused to share the honors of secession with her.

6th. Resolutions were offered by several members and referred, calling a Convention of the Southern States which have not seceded, to meet at Nashville, April 15th, providing for such amendments to the Constitution of the United States as shall secure to all the States equal rights in the Union, and declaring strongly against secession.

9th. The Committee on Federal Relations reported a series of resolutions, setting forth that at present there is no adequate cause to impel Missouri to leave the Union, but that on the contrary she will labor for such an adjustment of existing troubles as will secure peace and the rights and equality of all the States; that the people of Missouri regard the amendments to the Constitution proposed by Mr. Crittenden, with their extension to territory hereafter to be acquired, a basis of adjustment which would forever remove all difficulties; and that it is expedient for the Legislature to call a Convention for proposing amendments to the Constitution.

The Senate passed resolutions that their Senators be instructed, and their Representatives requested, to oppose the passage of all acts granting supplies of men and money to coerce the seceding States into submission or subjugation; and that, should such acts be passed by Congress, their Senators be instructed, and their Representatives requested, to retire from the halls of Congress.

16th. An amendment to the fifth resolution of the majority report of the Committee on Federal Relations, asserting that Missouri would never countenance nor aid a seceding State in making war upon the General Government, nor provide men and money for the purpose of aiding the General Government to coerce a seceding State, was voted down.

27th. The following resolution was passed by a vote in the House of 62 against 42:—

Resolved, That it is inexpedient for the General Assembly to take any steps for calling a National Convention to propose amendments to the Constitution, as recommended by the State Convention.

July 22d. The Convention reassembled.

23d. Resolution passed, by a vote of 65 to 21, declaring the office of President, held by General Sterling Price at the last session of the Convention, vacant. A committee of seven were appointed to report what action they deem it advisable to take in the dislocated condition of the State.

25th. The committee presented their report. It alludes at length to the present unparalleled condition of things, the reckless course of the recent Government, and flight of the Governor and other State officers from the capital. It declares the offices of Governor, Lieutenant-Governor, and Secretary of State vacant, and provides that their vacancies shall be filled by the Convention, the officers so appointed to hold their positions till August, 1862, at which time it provides for a special election by the people. It repeals the ninth section of the sixth article of the Constitution, and provides that the Supreme Court of the State shall consist of seven members; and that four members, in addition to the three now comprising the Court, shall be appointed by the Governor chosen by this Convention to hold office till 1862, when the people shall decide whether the change shall be permanent. It abolishes the State Legislature, and ordains that in case, before the 1st of August, 1862, the Governor chosen by this Convention shall consider that the public exigencies demand, he shall order a special election for members of the State Legislature. It recommends the passage of an ordinance repealing the following bills, passed by the Legislature in secret session, in May last: The military fund bill, the bill to suspend the distribution of the school fund, and the bill for cultivating friendly relations with the Indian tribes. It repeals the bill authorizing the appointment of one major-general of the Missouri militia, and revives the militia law of 1859.

A resolution was passed that a committee of seven be appointed by the President to prepare an address to the people of the State of Missouri.

November 26th. Jefferson Davis transmitted to the "Confederate" Congress a message concerning the secession of Missouri. It was accompanied by a letter from Governor Jackson, and also by an act dissolving the union with the United States, and an act ratifying the Constitution of the Provisional Government of the Confederate States; also, the Convention between the Commissioners of Missouri and the Commissioners of the Confederate States. Congress unanimously ratified the Convention entered into between the Hon. R. M. T. Hunter for the rebel Government and the Commissioners for Missouri.

Inter-State Commissioners.

The seceding States, as part of their plan of operation, appointed Commissioners to visit other slaveholding States. They were as follows, as announced in the newspapers:

SOUTH CAROLINA.

To Alabama, A. P. Calhoun.
To Georgia, James L. Orr, Ex-M.C.
To Florida, L. W. Spratt.
To Mississippi, M. L. Bonham, Ex-M. C.
To Louisiana, J. L. Manning.
To Arkansas, A. C. Spain.
To Texas, J. B. Kershaw.
To Virginia, John S. Preston.

ALABAMA.

To North Carolina, Isham W. Garrett.
To Mississippi, E. W. Pettus.
To South Carolina, J. A. Elmore.
To Maryland, A. F. Hopkins.
To Virginia, Frank Gilmer.
To Tennessee, L. Pope Walker.
To Kentucky, Stephen F. Hale.
To Arkansas, John Anthony Winston.

GEORGIA.

To Missouri, Luther J. Glenn.
To Virginia, Henry L. Benning.

MISSISSIPPI.

To South Carolina, C. E. Hooker.
To Alabama, Jos. W. Matthews, Ex-Gov.
To Georgia, William L. Harris.
To Louisiana, Wirt Adams.
To Texas, H. H. Miller.
To Arkansas, George R. Fall.
To Florida, E. M. Yerger.
To Tennessee, T. J. Wharton, Att'y-Gen.
To Kentucky, W. S. Featherstone, Ex-M.C.
To North Carolina, Jacob Thompson, Ex-M. C.
To Virginia, Fulton Anderson.
To Maryland, A. H. Handy, Judge.
To Delaware, Henry Dickinson.
To Missouri, —— Russell.

Southern Congress. (See p. 400)

This body, composed of Deputies elected by the Conventions of the Seceding States, met at Montgomery, Alabama, February 4th, 1861, to organize a Southern Confederacy. Each State had a representation equal to the number of members of the Thirty-sixth Congress. The original members were:

SOUTH CAROLINA.

Robert W. Barnwell, Ex-U. S. Senator.
R. Barnwell Rhett, " " "
James Chesnut, Jr., " " "
Lawrence M. Keitt, Ex-M. C.
William W. Boyce, " "
Wm. Porcher Miles, " "
C. G. Memminger.
Thomas J. Withers.

ALABAMA.

W. P. Chilton.
Stephen F. Hale.
David P. Lewis.
Thomas Fearn.
Richard W. Walker.
Robert H. Smith.
Colin J. McRae.
John Gill Shorter.
J. L. M. Curry, Ex-M. C.

FLORIDA.

J. Patten Anderson, Ex-Delegate from Washington Territory.
Jackson Morton, Ex-U. S. Senator.
James B. Owens.

MISSISSIPPI.

W. S. Wilson.
Wiley P. Harris, Ex-M. C.
James T. Harrison.
Walter Brooke, Ex-U. S. Senator.
William S. Barry, Ex-M. C.
A. M. Clayton.

GEORGIA.

Robert Toombs, Ex-U. S. Senator.
Howell Cobb, Ex-M. C.
Martin J. Crawford, " "
Augustus R. Wright, " "
Augustus H. Kenan.
Benjamin H. Hill.
Francis S. Bartow.
E. A. Nisbet.
Thomas R. R. Cobb.
Alexander H. Stephens, Ex-M. C.

LOUISIANA.

Duncan F. Kenner.
Charles M. Conrad, Ex-U. S. Senator.
Henry Marshall.
John Perkins, Jr.
G. E. Sparrow.
A. de Clouet.

TEXAS.—(Admitted March 2d, 1861.)

Louis T. Wigfall, Ex-U. S. Senator.
John Hemphill, " " "
John H. Reagan, Ex-M. C
T. N. Waul.
John Gregg.
W. S. Oldham.
W. B. Ochiltree.

Proceedings of the Southern Congress.

February 4th, 1861. Howell Cobb of Georgia elected President, Johnson J. Hooper of Alabama, Secretary. Mr. Cobb announced that secession "is now a fixed and irrevocable fact, and the separation is perfect, complete and perpetual."

6th. David L. Swain, M. W. Ransom and John L. Bridgers, were admitted as Commissioners from North Carolina, under resolutions of the General Assembly of that State, passed January 29, 1861, "to effect an honorable and amicable adjustment of all the difficulties that disturb the country, upon the basis of the Crittenden resolutions, as modified by the Legislature of Virginia," and to consult with the delegates to the Southern Congress for their "common peace, honor and safety."

7th. Congress notified that the State of Alabama had placed $500,000 at its disposal, as a loan to the provisional government of the Confederacy of Seceding States.

8th. The Constitution of the Provisional Government adopted.*

9th. Jefferson Davis of Mississippi, elected Provisional President of the Confederate States of America, and Alexander H. Stephens of Georgia, Vice President. The question of attacking Fort Sumter has been referred to the Congress.

11th. Mr. Stephens announced his acceptance. Committee appointed to prepare a permanent Constitution.

12th. The Congress assumed "charge of all questions and difficulties now existing between the sovereign States of this Confederacy and the Government of the United States, relating to the occupation of forts, arsenals, navy yards, custom-houses, and all other public establishments." The resolution was directed to be communicated to the Governors of the respective States of the Confederacy.

15th. Official copy of the Texas Ordinance of Secession presented.

16th. President Davis arrived and received with salute, etc.

18th. President Davis inaugurated.

19th. Tariff law passed.

21st. Robert Toombs appointed Secretary of State; C. G. Memminger, Secretary of the Treasury; L. Pope Walker of Alabama, Secretary of War; Stephen R. Mallory, Secretary of the Navy; Judah P. Benjamin, Attorney-General, and John H. Reagan, Postmaster-General; Philip Clayton of Georgia appointed Assistant Secretary of the Treasury, and Wm. M. Browne, late of the Washington *Constitution*, Assistant Secretary of State.

March 2d. The Texas Deputies received.

The Justifying Causes of Secession.

In justification of the passage of an ordinance of Secession, the Convention of South Carolina adopted two papers, one reported by Mr. R. B. Rhett, being styled "The Address of the people of South Carolina, assembled in Convention, to the people of the Slaveholding States of the United States," and the other, reported by Mr. C. G. Memminger, being styled "Declaration of the causes which justify the Secession of South Carolina from the Federal Union." As these official papers have historic value, they are inserted in full.

The former of these two papers is as follows:

It is seventy-three years, since the Union between the United States was made by the Constitution of the United

---

* The Provisional Constitution adopted by the Seceded States differs from the Constitution of the United States in several important particulars. The alterations and additions are as follows:

ALTERATIONS.

1st. The Provisional Constitution differs from the other in this: That the legislative powers of the Provisional Government are vested in the Congress now assembled, and this body exercises all the functions that are exercised by either or both branches of the United States Government.

2d. The Provisional President holds his office for one year, unless sooner superseded by the establishment of a permanent Government

3d. Each State is erected into a distinct judicial district, the judge having all the powers heretofore vested in the district and circuit courts; and the several district judges together compose the supreme bench—a majority of them constituting a quorum.

4th Wherever the word "Union" occurs in the United States Constitution the word "Confederacy" is substituted.

THE FOLLOWING ARE THE ADDITIONS.

1st. The President may veto any separate appropriation without vetoing the whole bill in which it is contained.

2d. The African slave-trade is prohibited.

3d. Congress is empowered to prohibit the introduction of slaves from any State not a member of this Confederacy.

4th. All appropriations must be upon the demand of the President or heads of departments.

OMISSIONS.

1st. There is no prohibition on members of Congress holding other offices of honor and emolument under the Provisional Government.

2d. There is no provision for a neutral spot for the location of a seat of government, or for sites for forts, arsenals, and dock-yards; consequently there is no reference made to the territorial powers of the Provisional Government.

3d. The section in the old Constitution in reference to capitation and other direct tax is omitted; also, the section providing that no tax or duty shall be laid on any exports.

4th. The prohibition on States keeping troops or ships of war in time of peace is omitted.

5th. The Constitution being provisional merely, no provision is made for its ratification.

AMENDMENTS.

1st. The fugitive slave clause of the old Constitution is so amended as to contain the word "slave," and to provide for full compensation in cases of abduction or forcible rescue on the part of the State in which such abduction or rescue may take place.

2d. Congress, by a vote of two-thirds, may at any time alter or amend the Constitution.

TEMPORARY PROVISIONS.

1st. The Provisional Government is required to take immediate steps for the settlement of all matters between the States forming it and their other late confederates of the United States in relation to the public property and the public debt.

2d. Montgomery is made the temporary seat of government.

3d. This Constitution is to continue one year, unless altered by a two-thirds vote or superseded by a permanent Government.

States. During this time, their advance in wealth, prosperity and power, has been with scarcely a parallel in the history of the world. The great object of their Union, was defence against external aggressions; which object is now attained, from their mere progress in power. Thirty-one millions of people, with a commerce and navigation which explore every sea, and with agricultural productions which are necessary to every civilized people, command the friendship of the world. But unfortunately, our internal peace has not grown with our external prosperity. Discontent and contention have moved in the bosom of the Confederacy, for the last thirty-five years. During this time, South Carolina has twice called her people together in solemn Convention, to take into consideration, the aggressions and unconstitutional wrongs, perpetrated by the people of the North on the people of the South. These wrongs, were submitted to by the people of the South, under the hope and expectation, that they would be final. But such hope and expectation, have proved to be vain. Instead of producing forbearance, our acquiescence has only instigated to new forms of aggressions and outrage; and South Carolina, having again assembled her people in Convention, has this day dissolved her connection with the States, constituting the United States.

The one great evil, from which all other evils have flowed, is the overthrow of the Constitution of the United States. The Government of the United States, is no longer the Government of Confederated Republics, but of a consolidated Democracy. It is no longer a free Government, but a Despotism. It is, in fact, such a Government as Great Britain attempted to set over our Fathers; and which was resisted and defeated by a seven years' struggle for independence.

The Revolution of 1776, turned upon one great principle, self-government,—and self-taxation, the criterion of self-government. Where the interests of two people united together under one Government, are different, each must have the power to protect its interests by the organization of the Government, or they cannot be free. The interests of Great Britain and of the Colonies, were different and antagonistic. Great Britain was desirous of carrying out the policy of all nations towards their Colonies, of making them tributary to her wealth and power. She had vast and complicated relations with the whole world. Her policy towards her North American Colonies, was to identify them with her in all these complicated relations; and to make them bear, in common with the rest of the Empire, the full burden of her obligations and necessities. She had a vast public debt; she had an European policy and an Asiatic policy, which had occasioned the accumulation of her public debt; and which kept her in continual wars. The North American Colonies saw their interests, political and commercial, sacrificed by such a policy. Their interests required, that they should not be identified with the burdens and wars of the mother country. They had been settled under Charters, which gave them self-government; at least so far as their property was concerned. They had taxed themselves, and had never been taxed by the Government of Great Britain. To make them a part of a consolidated Empire, the Parliament of Great Britain determined to assume the power of legislating for the Colonies in all cases whatsoever. Our ancestors resisted the pretension. They refused to be a part of the consolidated Government of Great Britain.

The Southern States, now stand exactly in the same position towards the Northern States, that the Colonies did towards Great Britain. The Northern States, having the majority in Congress, claim the same power of omnipotence in legislation as the British parliament. "The General Welfare," is the only limit to the legislation of either; and the majority in Congress, as in the British parliament, are the sole judges of the expediency of the legislation, this "General Welfare" requires. Thus, the Government of the United States has become a consolidated Government; and the people of the Southern States, are compelled to meet the very despotism, their fathers threw off in the Revolution of 1776.

The consolidation of the Government of Great Britain over the Colonies, was attempted to be carried out by the taxes. The British parliament undertook to tax the Colonies, to promote British interests. Our fathers, resisted this pretension. They claimed the right of self-taxation *through their Colonial Legislatures*. They were not represented in the British parliament, and, therefore, could not rightly be taxed by its legislation. The British Government, however, offered them a representation in parliament; but it was not sufficient to enable them to protect themselves from the majority, and they refused the offer. Between taxation without any representation, and taxation without a representation adequate to protection, there was no difference. In neither case would the Colonies tax themselves. Hence, they refused to pay the taxes laid by the British parliament.

And so with the Southern States, towards the Northern States, in the vital matter of taxation. They are in a minority in Congress. Their representation in Congress, is useless to protect them against unjust taxation; and they are taxed by the people of the North *for their benefit*, exactly as the people of Great Britain taxed our ancestors in the British parliament for their benefit. For the last forty years, the taxes laid by the Congress of the United States, have been laid with a view of subserving the interests of the North. The people of the South have been taxed by duties on imports, not for revenue, but for an object inconsistent with revenue—to promote, by prohibitions, Northern interests in the productions of their mines and manufactures.

There is another evil, in the condition of the Southern towards the Northern States, which our ancestors refused to bear towards Great Britain. Our ancestors not only taxed themselves, but all the taxes collected from them, were expended amongst them. Had they submitted to the pretensions of the British Government, the taxes collected from them, would have been expended in other parts of the British Empire. They were fully aware of the effect of such a policy in impoverishing the people from whom taxes are collected, and in enriching those who receive the benefit of their expenditure. To prevent the evils of such a policy, was one of the motives which drove them on to Revolution. Yet this British policy, has been fully realized towards the Southern States, by the Northern States. The people of the Southern States are not only taxed for the benefit of the Northern States, but after the taxes are collected, three-fourths of them are expended at the North. This cause, with others, connected with the operation of the General Government, has made the cities of the South provincial. Their growth is paralyzed; they are mere suburbs of Northern cities. The agricultural productions of the South are the basis of the foreign commerce of the United States; yet Southern cities do not carry it on. Our foreign trade, is almost annihilated. In 1740, there were five ship yards in South Carolina, to build ships to carry on our direct trade with Europe. Between 1740 and 1779, there were built in these yards, twenty-five square rigged vessels, besides a great number of sloops and schooners, to carry on our coast and West India trade. In the half century immediately preceding the Revolution, from 1725 to 1775, the population of South Carolina, increased sevenfold.

No man can for a moment believe, that our ancestors intended to establish over their posterity, exactly the same sort of Government they had overthrown. The great object of the Constitution of the United States, in its internal operation, was, doubtless, to secure the great end of the Revolution—a limited free Government—a Government limited to those matters only, which were general and common to all portions of the United States. All sectional or local interests, were to be left to the States. By no other arrangement, would they obtain free Government, by a Constitution common to so vast a Confederacy. Yet by gradual and steady encroachments on the part of the people of the North, and acquiescence on the part of the South, the limitations in the Constitution have been swept away; and the Government of the United States has become consolidated, with a claim of limitless powers in its operations.

It is not at all surprising, such being the character of the Government of the United States, that it should assume to possess power over all the institutions of the country. The agitations on the subject of slavery, are the natural results of the consolidation of the Government. Responsibility, follows power; and if the people of the North, have the power by Congress—"to promote the general welfare of the United States," by any means they deem expedient—why should they not assail and overthrow the institution of slavery in the South? They are responsible for its continuance or existence, in proportion to their power. A majority in Congress, according to their interested and perverted views, is omnipotent. The inducements to act upon the subject of slavery, under such circumstances, were so imperious, as to amount almost to a moral necessity. To make, however, their numerical power available to rule the Union, the North must consolidate their power. It would not be united, on any matter common to the whole Union—in other words, on any constitutional subject—for on such subjects divisions are as likely to exist in the North as in the South. Slavery was strictly, a sectional interest. If this could be made the criterion of parties at the North, the North could be united in its power; and thus carry out its measures of sectional ambition, encroachment, and aggrandizement. To build up their sectional predominance in the Union, the Constitution must be first abolished by constructions; but that being done, the consolidation of the North, to rule the South, by the tariff and slavery issues, was in the obvious course of things.

The Constitution of the United States, was an experiment. The experiment consisted, in uniting under one Government, peoples living in different climates, and having different pursuits and institutions. It matters not, how carefully the limitations of such a Government be laid down in the Constitution,—its success must at least depend, upon the good faith of the parties to the constitutional compact, in enforcing them. It is not in the power of human language, to exclude false inferences, constructions and perversions, in any Constitution; and when vast sectional interests are to be subserved, involving the appropriation of countless millions of money, it has not been the usual experience of mankind, that words on parchments can arrest power. The Constitution of the United States, irrespective of the interposition of the States, rested on the assumption, that power would yield to faith,—that integrity would be stronger than interest; and that thus, the limitations of the Constitution would be observed. The experiment, has been fairly made. The Southern States, from the commencement of the Government, have striven to keep it, within the orbit prescribed by the Constitution. The experiment, has failed. The whole Constitution, by the constructions of the Northern people, has been absorbed by its preamble. In their reckless lust for power, they seem unable to comprehend that seeming paradox—that the more power is given to the General Government, the weaker it becomes. Its strength, consists in the limitation of its agency to objects of common interest to all sections. To extend the scope of its power over sectional or local interests, is to raise up against it, opposition and resistance. In all such matters, the General Government must necessarily be a despotism, because all sectional or local interests must ever be represented by a minority in the councils of the General Government—having no power to protect itself against the rule of the majority. The majority, constituted from those who do not represent these sectional or local interests, will control and govern them. A free people, cannot submit to such a Government. And the more it enlarges the sphere of its power, the greater must be the dissatisfaction it must produce, and the weaker it must become. On the contrary, the more it abstains from usurped powers, and the more faithfully it adheres to the limitations of the Constitution, the stronger it is made. The Northern people have had neither the wisdom nor the faith to perceive, that to observe the limitations of the Constitution was the only way to its perpetuity.

Under such a Government, there must, of course, be many and endless "irrepressible conflicts," between the two great sections of the Union. The same faithlessness which has abolished the Constitution of the United States, will not fail to carry out the sectional purposes for which it has been abolished. There must be conflict; and the weaker section of the Union can only find peace and liberty, in an independence of the North. The repeated efforts made by South Carolina, in a wise conservatism, to arrest the progress of the General Government in its fatal progress to consolidation, have been unsupported, and she has been denounced as faithless to the obligations of the Constitution, by the very men and States, who were destroying it by their usurpations. It is now too late, to reform or restore the Government of the United States. All confidence in the North, is lost by the South. The faithlessness of the North for a half century, has opened a gulf of separation between the North and the South which no promises nor engagements can fill.

It cannot be believed, that our ancestors would have assented to any Union whatever with the people of the North, if the feelings and opinions now existing amongst them, had existed when the Constitution was framed. There was then, no Tariff—no fanaticism concerning negroes. It was the delegates from New England, who proposed in the Convention which framed the Constitution, to the delegates from South Carolina and Georgia, that if they would agree to give Congress the power of regulating commerce *by a majority*, that they would support the extension of the African Slave Trade for twenty years. African slavery, existed in all the States, but one. The idea, that the Southern States would be made to pay that tribute to their Northern confederates, which they had refused to pay to Great Britain; or that the institution of African slavery, would be made the grand basis of a sectional organization of the North to rule the South, never crossed the imaginations of our ancestors. The Union of the Constitution, was a union of slaveholding States. It rests on slavery, by prescribing a Representation in Congress, for three-fifths of our slaves. There is nothing in the proceedings of the Convention which framed the Constitution, to shew, that the Southern States would have formed any other Union; and still less, that they would have formed a Union with more powerful non-slaveholding States, having majority in both branches of the Legislature of the Government. They were guilty of no such folly. Time and the progress of things, have totally altered the relations between the Northern and Southern States, since the Union was established. That identity of feelings, interests and institutions, which once existed, is gone. They are now divided, between agricultural—and manufacturing, and commercial States; between slaveholding, and non-slaveholding States. Their institutions and industrial pursuits, have made them, totally different peoples. That Equality in the Government between the two sections of the Union which once existed, no longer exists. We but imitate the policy of our fathers in dissolving a union with non-slaveholding confederates, and seeking a confederation with slaveholding States.

Experience has proved, that slaveholding States cannot be safe, in subjection to non-slaveholding States. Indeed, no people can ever expect to preserve its rights and liberties, unless these be in its own custody. To plunder and oppress, where plunder and oppression can be practiced with impunity, seems to be the natural order of things. The fairest portions of the world elsewhere, have been turned into wildernesses; and the most civilized and prosperous communities, have been impoverished and ruined by anti-slavery fanaticism. The people of the North have not left us in doubt, as to their designs and policy. United as a section in the late Presidential election, they have elected as the exponent of their policy, one who has openly declared, that all the States of the United States, must be made *free States* or *slave States*. It is true, that amongst those who aided in his election, there are various shades of anti-slavery hostility. But if African slavery in the Southern States, be the evil their political combination affirms it to be, the requisitions of an inexorable logic, must lead them to emancipation. If it is right, to preclude or abolish slavery in a Territory,—why should it be allowed to remain in the States? The one is not at all more unconstitutional than the other, according to the decisions of the Supreme Court of the United States. And when it is considered, that the Northern States will soon have the power to make that Court what they please, and that the Constitution never has been any barrier whatever to their exercise of power—what check can there be, in the unrestrained counsels of the North, to emancipation? There is sympathy in association, which carries men along without principle; but when there is principle—and that principle is fortified by long-existing prejudices and feelings, association is omnipotent in party influences. In spite of all disclaimers and professions, there can be but one end by the submission of the South, to the rule of a sectional anti-slavery government at Washington; and that end, directly or indirectly, must be—the emancipation of the slaves of the South. The hypocrisy of thirty years—the faithlessness of their whole course from the commencement of our union with them, shew that the people of the non-slaveholding North, are not, and cannot be safe associates of the slaveholding South, under a common Government. Not only their fanaticism, but their erroneous views of the principles of free governments, render it doubtful whether, if separated from the South, they can maintain a free government amongst themselves. Numbers with them, is the great element of free government. A majority, is infallible and omnipotent. "The right divine to rule in kings," is only transferred to their majority. The very object of all Constitutions, in free popular Government, is to restrain the majority. Constitutions, therefore, according to their theory, must be most unrighteous inventions, restricting liberty. None ought to exist; but the body politic ought simply to have a political organization, to bring out and enforce the will of the majority. This theory may be harmless in a small community, having identity of interests and pursuits; but over a vast State—still more, over a vast Confederacy, having various and conflicting interests and pursuits, it is a remorseless despotism. In resisting it, as applicable to ourselves, we are vindicating the great cause of free government, more important, perhaps, to the world, than the existence of all the United States. Nor in resisting it, do we intend to depart from the safe instrumentality, the system of government we have established with them, requires. In separating from them, we invade no rights—no interest of theirs. We violate, no obligation or duty to them. As separate, independent States in Convention, we made the Constitution of the United States with them; and as separate independent States, each State acting for itself, we adopted it. South Carolina acting in her sovereign capacity, now thinks proper to secede from the Union. She did not part with her Sovereignty, in adopting the Constitution. The last thing, a State can be presumed to have surrendered, is her Sovereignty. Her Sovereignty, is her life. Nothing but a clear, express grant, can alienate it. Inference is inadmissible. Yet it is not at all surprising, that those who have construed away all the limitations of that Constitution, should also by construction, claim the annihilation of the Sovereignty of the States. Having abolished barriers to their omnipotence, by their faithless constructions in the operations of the General Government, it is most natural that they should endeavor to do the same towards us, in the States. The truth is, they, having violated the express provisions of the Constitution, it is at an end, as a compact. It is morally obligatory only on those, who choose to accept its perverted terms. South Carolina, deeming the compact not only violated in particular features, but virtually abolished by her Northern confederates, withdraws herself as a party, from its obligations. The right do do so, is denied by her Northern confederates. They desire to establish a sectional despotism, not only omnipotent in Congress, but omnipotent over the States; and as if to manifest the imperious necessity of our secession, they threaten us with the sword, to coerce submission to their rule.

Citizens of the slaveholding States of the United States! Circumstances beyond our control, have placed us in the van of the great controversy between the Northern and Southern States. We would have preferred, that other States should have assumed the position we now occupy. Independent ourselves, we disclaim any design or desire, to lead the counsels of the other Southern States. Providence has cast our lot together, by extending over us an identity of pursuits, interests and institutions. South Carolina, desires no destiny, separate from yours. To be one of a great Slaveholding Confederacy, stretching its arms over a territory larger than any power in Europe possesses—with a population, four times greater than that of the whole United States, when they achieved their independence of the British Empire—with productions, which make our existence more important to the world, than that of any other people inhabiting it—with common institutions to defend, and common dangers to encounter—we ask your sympathy and confederation. Whilst constituting a portion of the United States, it has been *your* statesmanship which has guided it, in its mighty strides to power and expansion. In the field, as in the cabinet, *you* have led the way to its renown and grandeur. You have loved the Union, in whose service your great statesmen have labored, and your great soldiers have fought and conquered—not for the material benefits it conferred, but with the faith of a generous and devoted chivalry. You have long lingered in hope over the shattered remains of a broken Constitution. Compromise after compromise, formed by your concessions, has been trampled under foot, by your Northern confederates. All fraternity of feeling between the North and the South is lost, or has been converted into hate; and we, of the South, are at last driven together, by the stern destiny which controls the existence of nations. Your bitter experience, of the faithlessness and rapacity of your Northern confederates, may have been necessary, to evolve those great principles of free government, upon which the liberties of the world depend, and to prepare you for the grand mission of vindicating and re-establishing them. We rejoice, that other nations should be satisfied with their institutions. Contentment, is a great element of happiness, with nations as with individuals. We, are satisfied with ours. If they prefer a system of industry, in which capital and labor are in perpetual conflict—and chronic starvation keeps down the natural increase of population—and a man is worked out in eight years—and the law ordains, that children shall be worked only *ten hours a day*—and the sabre and bayonet are the instruments of order—be it so. It is their affair, not ours. We prefer, however, our system of industry, by which labor and capital are identified in interest, and capital, therefore, protects labor—by which our population doubles every twenty years—by which starvation is unknown, and abundance crowns the land—by which order is preserved by an unpaid police, and many fertile regions of the world, where the white man cannot labor, are brought into usefulness by the labor of the African, and the whole world is blessed by our productions. All we demand of other peoples is, to be let alone, to work out our own high destinies. United together, and we must be the most independent, as we are among the most important of the nations of the world. United together, and we require no other instrument to conquer peace, than our beneficent productions. United together, and we must be a great, free and prosperous people, whose renown must spread throughout the civilized world, and pass down, we trust, to the remotest ages. We ask you to join us, in forming a Confederacy of Slaveholding States.

The latter paper is as follows:

DECLARATION OF THE IMMEDIATE CAUSES WHICH INDUCE AND JUSTIFY THE SECESSION OF SOUTH CAROLINA FROM THE FEDERAL UNION.

The people of the State of South Carolina, in convention assembled, on the 26th day of April, A. D., 1852, declared that the frequent violations of the constitution of the United States by the federal government, and its encroachments upon the reserved rights of the states, fully justified this state in then withdrawing from the Federal Union; but in deference to the opinions and wishes of the other slaveholding states, she forebore at that time to exercise this right. Since that time, these encroachments have continued to increase, and further forbearance ceases to be a virtue.

And now the State of South Carolina having resumed her separate and equal place among nations, deems it due to herself, to the remaining United States of America, and to the nations of the world, that she should declare the immediate causes which have led to this act.

In the year 1765, that portion of the British Empire embracing Great Britain, undertook to make laws for the government of that portion composed of the thirteen American colonies. A struggle for the right of self-government ensued, which resulted on the 4th of July, 1776, in a declaration by the colonies, "that they are, and of right ought to be, FREE AND INDEPENDENT STATES: and that as free and independent states, they have full power to levy war, conclude peace, contract alliances, establish commerce, and to do all other acts and things which independent states may of right do."

They further solemnly declared that whenever any "form of government becomes destructive of the ends for which it was established, it is the right of the people to alter or abolish it, and to institute a new government." Deeming the government of Great Britain to have become destructive of these ends, they declared that the colonies "are absolved from all allegiance to the British crown, and that all political connection between them and the State of Great Britain is, and ought to be totally dissolved."

In pursuance of this Declaration of Independence, each of the thirteen states proceeded to exercise its separate sovereignty; adopted for itself a constitution, and appointed officers for the administration of government in all its departments—legislative, executive and judicial. For purposes of defence, they united their arms and their counsels; and, in 1778 they entered into a league known as the articles of confederation, whereby they agreed to entrust the administration of their external relations to a common agent, known as the Congress of the United States, expressly declaring in the first article, "that each state retains its sovereignty, freedom and independence, and every power, jurisdiction and right which is not, by this confederation, expressly delegated to the United States in Congress assembled."

Under this confederation the war of the revolution was carried on, and on the 3d September, 1783, the contest ended, and a definitive treaty was signed by Great Britain, in which she acknowledged the independence of the colonies in the following terms:

"*Article I.*—His Britanic Majesty acknowledges the said United States, viz: New Hampshire, Massachusetts Bay, Rhode Island and Providence Plantations, Connecticut, New York, New Jersey, Pennsylvania, Delaware, Maryland, Virginia, North Carolina, South Carolina and Georgia, to be FREE, SOVEREIGN AND INDEPENDENT STATES; that he treats with them as such; and for himself, his heirs and successors, relinquishes all claims to the government, proprietary and territorial rights of the same and every part thereof."

Thus were established the two great principles asserted by the colonies, namely: the right of a state to govern itself; and the right of a people to abolish a government when it becomes destructive of the ends for which it was instituted. And concurrent with the establishment of these principles, was the fact that each colony became, and was recognized by the mother country as a FREE, SOVEREIGN AND INDEPENDENT STATE.

In 1787, deputies were appointed by the states to revise the articles of confederation, and on the 17th of September, 1787, these deputies recommended for the adoption of the states, the articles of union known as the Constitution of the United States.

The parties to whom this constitution was submitted, were the several sovereign states; they were to agree or disagree, and when nine of them agreed, the compact was to take effect among those concurring; and the general government, as the common agent, was then to be invested with their authority.

If only nine of the thirteen states had concurred, the

other four would have remained as they then were—separate, sovereign states, independent of any of the provisions of the constitution. In fact, two of the states did not accede to the constitution until long after it had gone into operation among the other eleven; and during that interval they each exercised the functions of an independent nation.

By this constitution, certain duties were imposed upon the several states, and the exercise of certain of their powers was restrained, which necessarily implied their continued existence as sovereign states. But to remove all doubt, an amendment was added, which declared that the powers not delegated to the United States by the constitution, nor prohibited by it to the states, are reserved to the states, respectively, or to the people. On 23d May, 1788, South Carolina, by a convention of her people, passed an ordinance assenting to this constitution, and afterwards altered her own constitution, to conform herself to the obligations she had undertaken.

Thus was established, by compact between the states, a government, with defined objects and powers, limited to the express words of the grant. This limitation left the whole remaining mass of power subject to the clause reserving it to the states or to the people, and rendered unnecessary any specification of reserved rights.

We hold that the government thus established is subject to the two great principles asserted in the Declaration of Independence; and we hold further, that the mode of its formation subjects it to a third fundamental principle, namely: the law of compact. We maintain that in every compact between two or more parties the obligation is mutual; that the failure of one of the contracting parties to perform a material part of the agreement, entirely releases the obligations of the other; and that where no arbiter is provided, each party is remitted to his own judgment to determine the fact of failure, with all its consequences.

In the present case, the fact is established with certainty. We assert that fourteen of the states have deliberately refused for years past, to fulfil their constitutional obligations, and we refer to their own statutes for the proof.

The constitution of the United States, in its 4th article, provides as follows:

"No person held to service or labor, in one state, under the laws thereof, escaping into another, shall, in consequence of any law or regulation therein, be discharged from such service or labor, but shall be delivered up on claim of the party to whom such service or labor may be due."

This stipulation was so material to the compact, that without it that compact would not have been made. The greater number of the contracting parties held slaves, and they had previously evinced their estimate of the value of such a stipulation by making it a condition in the ordinance for the government of the territory ceded by Virginia, which now composes the states north of the Ohio river.

The same article of the constitution stipulates also for the rendition, by the several states, of fugitives from justice from the other states.

The general government, as the common agent, passed laws to carry into effect these stipulations of the states. For many years these laws were executed. But an increasing hostility on the part of the non-slaveholding states to the institution of slavery has led to a disregard of their obligations, and the laws of the general government have ceased to effect the objects of the constitution. The States of Maine, New Hampshire, Vermont, Massachusetts, Connecticut, Rhode Island, New York, Pennsylvania, Illinois, Indiana, Michigan, Wisconsin and Iowa have enacted laws which either nullify the acts of Congress or render useless any attempt to execute them. In many of these states the fugitive is discharged from the service or labor claimed, and in none of them has the state government complied with the stipulation made in the constitution. The State of New Jersey, at an early day, passed a law in conformity with her constitutional obligation; but the current of anti-slavery feeling has led her more recently to enact laws which render inoperative the remedies provided by her own law and by the laws of Congress. In the State of New York even the right of transit for a slave has been denied by her tribunals; and the States of Ohio and Iowa have refused to surrender to justice fugitives charged with murder, and with inciting servile insurrection in the State of Virginia. Thus the constitutional compact has been deliberately broken and disregarded by the non-slaveholding states, and the consequence follows that South Carolina is released from her obligation.

The ends for which this constitution was framed are declared by itself to be "to form a more perfect union, establish justice, insure domestic tranquility, provide for the common defence, promote the general welfare, and secure the blessings of liberty to ourselves and our posterity."

These ends it endeavored to accomplish by a federal government, in which each state was recognized as an equal, and had separate control over its own institutions. The right of property in slaves was recognized by giving to free persons distinct political rights, by giving them the right to represent, and burthening them with direct taxes for three-fifths of their slaves; by authorizing the importation of slaves for twenty years, and by stipulating for the rendition of fugitives from labor.

We affirm that these ends, for which this government was instituted, have been defeated, and the government itself has been made destructive of them by the action of the non-slaveholding states. Those states have assumed the right of deciding upon the propriety of our domestic institutions; and have denied the rights of property established in fifteen of the states and recognized by the constitution; they have denounced as sinful the institution of slavery; they have permitted the open establishment among them of societies, whose avowed object is to disturb the peace and to eloign the property of the citizens of other states. They have encouraged and assisted thousands of our slaves to leave their homes, and those who remain have been incited by emissaries, books and pictures to servile insurrection.

For twenty-five years this agitation has been steadily increasing, until it has now secured to its aid the power of the common government. Observing the *forms* of the constitution, a sectional party has found within that article establishing the executive department the means of subverting the constitution itself. A geographical line has been drawn across the Union, and all the states north of that line have united in the election of a man to the high office of President of the United States, whose opinions and purposes are hostile to slavery. He is to be entrusted with the administration of the common government, because he has declared that that "government cannot endure permanently half slave, half free," and that the public mind must rest in the belief that slavery is in the course of ultimate extinction.

This sectional combination for the subversion of the constitution, has been aided in some of the states by elevating to citizenship, persons, who, by the supreme law of the land, are incapable of becoming citizens; and their votes have been used to inaugurate a new policy, hostile to the South, and destructive of its peace and safety.

On the 4th of March next this party will take possession of the government. It has announced that the South shall be excluded from the common territory; that the judicial tribunals shall be made sectional, and that a war must be waged against slavery until it shall cease throughout the United States.

The guaranties of the constitution will then no longer exist; the equal rights of the states will be lost. The slaveholding states will no longer have the power of self-government, or self-protection, and the federal government will have become their enemy.

Sectional interest and animosity will deepen the irritation, and all hope of remedy is rendered vain, by the fact that public opinion at the North has invested a great political error with the sanctions of a more erroneous religious belief.

We, therefore, the people of South Carolina, by our delegates, in convention assembled, appealing to the Supreme Judge of the world for the rectitude of our intentions, have solemnly declared that the union heretofore existing between this state and the other states of North America, is dissolved, and that the State of South Carolina has resumed her position among the nations of the world, as a separate and independent state, with full power to levy war, conclude peace, contract alliances, establish commerce, and do all other acts and things which independent states may of right do.

The debate on the adoption of these papers discloses some interesting facts, and is subjoined.

Upon Mr. Memminger's declaration being read, Mr. Furman and Mr. Inglis raised questions as to the accuracy of certain statements, the former as to whether New-Jersey had, as alleged, voted for a "sectional candidate," and the latter as to the allegation that Pennsylvania had on her statute-book a "personal liberty law."

Mr. Inglis said: They (Pennsylvania) have what they call a law to prevent kidnapping, nearly similar to the law of Virginia, which law, owing to the condition of public sentiment in Pennsylvania, has no doubt been perverted to this purpose. A document of this kind, and proceeding from a body like this, ought to be exactly accurate in its statements. I should like to ask the Chairman of the Committee if he has satisfied himself with regard to the fact that there is any such law as this on the statute-book of Pennsylvania? If he has, why then I am satisfied.

Mr. MEMMINGER. In reply to the gentleman I would say that I hold in my hand an elaborate report made on this point by a Committee of the Legislature of Virginia in which the laws of each State are professed to be correctly stated.

Mr. INGLIS. Will the gentleman give me the date of that report?

Mr. MEMMINGR. It was made at the last session, January 26th, 1860.

Mr. INGLIS. To what law do they refer? for Pennsylvania has recently revised her criminal code, and, I understand, has omitted some portion of that law.

Mr. MEMMINGER. This is all the information I have on the subject. It confirms what is stated in the report.

Mr. ENGLISH read from DeBow's Review an article [a very erroneous one] in support of the assertion contained in the Declaration, that nearly all the Free States had refused to sustain the Constitution.

Mr. MAXCY GREGG. The gentleman who just resumed his seat, has pointed out in detail the various questions referred to in this report. He has shown that things have been said there which ought not to to have been said, and of the correctness of which we have not sufficient evidence. But my objection to the paper is greater than this. It is that, as a State paper, to go out as a new Declaration of Independence, it is entirely defective and imperfect. It purports to be a declaration of the causes which justify the Secession of South Carolina from the Federal Union. The causes! And yet in all this declaration not one word is said about the tariff, which for so many years caused a contest in this State against the Federal Government. Not one word is said about the violations of the Constitution in expenditures not authorized by that instrument; but the main stress is laid upon an incomparably unimportant point relative to fugitive slaves, and the laws passed by Northern States obstructing the recovery of fugitive slaves. Mr. President, if we undertake to set forth a declaration of the causes which justify our Secession, we ought to publish a complete document —a document which might vie in its completeness with that which was adopted in 1776—not that I mean to say that that is a model cause! that would be to say a good deal too much. This declaration might be put forth by gentlemen who had no objection whatever to the lavish and unconstitutional expenditures which have been made by the Federal Government for forty years past. This is not the sort of paper which, in my opinion, ought to go forth to justify our action. A correct designation of this paper would be a declaration of some of the causes which justify the secession of South Carolina from the Federal Union. If it is proper to set forth in a solemn declaration some of the causes, why let the title be altered, and, if the Convention think proper, let it go forth; but if we undertake to set forth all the causes, do we not dishonor the memory of all the statesmen of South Carolina, now departed, who commenced forty years ago a war *against the tariff and against internal improvements*, saying nothing of the *United States Bank* and other measures which may now be regarded as obsolete. Many of the acts of the non-slaveholding States obstructing the recovery of fugitive slaves have been passed since 1852—I think the majority of them; *but I do not regard it as a matter of any importance.* But when the people of South Carolina, eight years since, declared that the causes then existing fully justified the State in seceding, did they confine themselves to these miserable fugitive slave laws? No! Sir, I regard it as unworthy of the State of South Carolina to send forth a new declaration now, and in it to say nothing about any other cause justifying their action but fugitive slaves. I am in favor of laying this report on the table, or recommitting it.

Mr. KEITT. I agree with the gentleman that the power of taxation is the central power of all Governments. If you put that into my hands, I do not care what the form of Government may be, I will control your people through it. But that is not the question in this address. We have instructed the Committee to draw up a statement of the reasons which influenced us in the present case in our withdrawal. *My friend suggests that sufficient notice has not been paid to the tariff. Your late Senators, and every one of your members of the House of Representatives voted for the present tariff. If the gentleman had been there he would also have voted for it.* [Laughter.] The question of the tariff did agitate us in 1832, and did array this State against the Federal Government. And I maintain that this State did triumph then. Mr. Clay said, before the nullification, that the tariff system had been established for all time. After the nullification ordinance Mr. Clay said that that ordinance abolished the American system, and that the State had triumphed. It is true that we were cheated in the compromise. *The tariff is not the question which has brought us up to our present attitude.* We are giving a list of the causes to the world—to the Southern States. Let them not quarrel with us now, when we are brought up to a dissolution of the Union, by the discussion of debatable and doctrinal points. The Whig party, throughout all the States, have been protective tariff men, and they cling to that old issue with all the passion incident to the pride of human opinions. Are we to go off now, when other Southern States are bringing their people up to the true mark—are we to go off on debatable and doctrinal points? Are we to go back to the consideration of this question, of this great controversy; go back to that party's politics around which so many passions cluster? Names, sir, are much. Opinions, prejudiced passions, cluster around names. Our people have come up to this great act. *I am willing in this issue to rest disunion upon the question of slavery. It is the great central point from which we are now proceeding.* I believe, sir, that the reference to other States in this address is all correct. The gentleman from Chesterfield says that a certain construction of one act of the Pennsylvania code is denied by the citizens of that State. *I myself have very great doubts about the propriety of the fugitive slave law.* The Constitution was, in the first place, a compact between the several States, and in the second a treaty between the sections; and, I believe the fugitive slave law was a treaty between sections. It was the act of sovereign States as sections; and I believe, therefore, and have very great doubts whether it ought not to have been left to the execution of the several States, and, failing of enforcement, I believe it should have been regarded as a *casus belli*. I go for the address because I believe it does present succinctly and conspicuously what are the main primary causes.

Mr. GREGG. If this address was to be a declaration of the immediate causes which produced the secession of South Carolina, what the gentleman had said might be applicable, but its title does not say so. Another document has been submitted to this body—an Address to the Southern States. This is inconsistent with the other. In the latter address all the causes are stated in full. *If we wish to find the immediate cause of the secession of South Carolina, the immediate cause of all is the election of Lincoln.*

Mr. INGLIS. Will the gentleman inform us whether the statutes of Virginia do not contain a paragraph relating to kidnapping, precisely similar to that of Pennsylvania?

A VOICE. It is the case with Georgia.

Mr. KEITT. It may be so, sir, but I do not know.

Mr. INGLIS. I say, Mr. President, I make no attack upon this report; but I propose to amend it by striking out the word "fifteen" and inserting "many" instead; and then to strike out the sentence which contains the enumeration of States. It will not disturb the order to omit that.

Mr. DARGAN. I confess my difficulty results from the same sources as the gentleman from Richland. Let me express also my earnest conviction of the eminent propriety of obtaining a concurrence and symmetry in the declaration of the causes which led to the secession of South Carolina, and in the sentiments enunciated in the Address to the Southern States; and as the Address to the Southern States, which was read here to-day, was made the special order for to-morrow, I move that this document be also made the special order at the same time and in connection with that subject.

Mr. MIDDLETON. They are very different matters —the one an address to the Southern people and the other an address to the world.

Mr. DARGAN. The subject-matter is the same.

The PRESIDENT. The question will be on making the report of the Committee declaring Secession the special order for one o'clock to-morrow, in connection with the report of the Committee on Slaveholding States upon the same subject.

The question was taken and the motion was agreed to.

On Monday, December 24th, 1860, the Convention proceeded to consider both the Address and the Declaration, when further debate ensued.

Many verbal amendments having been made to the latter,

Mr. J. J. P. Smith moved to adopt the former for the present, and table the latter.

A DELEGATE. I second the motion, and call for the previous question.

Mr. LOUIS WARDLAW. I trust that this Convention is not going to act hastily. Whatever is done should be done well. This address will reach no one of the Southern States before the elections, unless it be the State of Georgia. There is, therefore, no special need of hurrying the reference. There is not one single sentence of that address to which I do not heartily subscribe. It is an able and admirable exposition of the structure of our Government and its general operation. And yet I do not think it is exactly that which an address to our Southern sisters should be. I think it treats too much upon some subjects, and does not touch others that are very important. From the beginning I have been very anxious that these two papers should be consistent one with the other, and contain all those matters which we confess should operate either upon the opinion of the Southern people or the opinion of the world. Now, sir, my objection to the address to the Southern people is that it does not dilate as it should upon matters connected with the immediate cause of our secession, *but on matters connected with slavery.* My objection to the other address is, that it dwells too much upon those fugitive slave laws and those personal liberty bills, *which give it too much the appearance of special pleading.* The address which we have under consideration does not set off to the Southern people, as it should, our defenceless condition. Already our adversaries have the House of Representatives; they will soon have the Senate, and then they can make the Judiciary what they please, and thus have entire power over the Government. It does not set forth, as I think it should, that the election of Lincoln is, in fact, an edict of emancipation. It does not set forth what would be the deleterious effects of emancipation; that emancipation would be destruction to the blacks and degradation to the whites. Nor does this address set forth the shameless hypocrisy of the North, who, whilst they cry out against what they call the sin of slavery, do not choose to relieve themselves of that which they assert is an evil by withdrawing from the Confederacy. When these addresses go forth, they go forth as solemn State papers, by which we must be able to stand. For this reason, every word should be most carefully considered, and nothing superfluous should be contained in them; nothing important should be omitted.

Mr. MEMMINGER next took the floor and defended the address to the nations of the world, which was reported by himself. After reciting its points and the principles it enunciated, he said: We show by law of compact that we are entitled to leave this Government. My friend from Abbeville says, in this regard, he does not exactly approve this document. Allow me to say to the honorable gentlemen that when you take the position that you have a right to break your faith, to destroy an agreement which you have made, to tear off your seal from the document to which it is affixed, you are bound to justify yourself fully to all the nations of the world; for there is nothing that casts such a stain upon the escutcheon of a nation as a breach of faith. Therefore the document shows fully that both in measure and in spirit our co-States have broken the Constitution and the Union. Not only in letter has this been done, but also in spirit. The common agent which should have acted for our common good has been converted into an instrument for our destruction. And now as a consummating act a sectional President has been elected, whose chief recommendation was that he desires to see slavery abolished. The great objection that we raise is not to Abraham Lincoln himself, but because he is the representative of a hostile opinion, destructive of every interest of the South.

Mr. RHETT next spoke in explanation of the Address to the Southern States, which was reported by himself. This committee, he said, determined that whilst setting forth the immediate cause which induced South Carolina to secede, it was not improper to go into previous causes which led to that result. *The secession of South Carolina is not an event of a day. It is not anything produced by Mr. Lincoln's election, or by the non-execution of the fugitive slave law. It has been a matter which has been gathering head for thirty years.* The election of Lincoln and Hamlin was the last straw on the back of the camel. But it was not the only one. The back was nearly broken before. The point upon which I differ from my friend is this: He says he thought it expedient for us to put this great question before all the world upon this simple matter of wrongs on the question of slavery, and that question turned upon the fugitive slave law. *Now, in regard to the fugitive slave law, I myself doubt its constitutionality*, and I doubted it on the floor of the Senate, when I was a member of that body. The States, acting in their sovereign capacity, should be responsible for the rendition of fugitive slaves. That was our best security. This report has proceeded upon the elaborate discussion of a constitutional question, about which the very ablest men in this State have doubted. When we go before the world, if we put it upon mere matter of this kind, we do not do justice to our cause. Sir, to whom are we to speak? Is it simply to the North? We are about to sunder our relations with that section, and I trust forever. Our treaties, I suppose, will be with the nations of Europe. Do you suppose the nations of Europe will have any sympathy with us, or confidence, or affection, because of the violation of the fugitive slave law? Germany, and France, and England, what do they all say? Sir, in setting up our independence we are not to narrow it down simply to the question of slavery. We do not do ourselves justice. The aggression upon slavery is the last consequence of a great cause, and that great cause is the dissolution of the Constitution of the United States by the agents of the North. It is that which led them to the aggressions upon the taxing power. It is that which led to the aggressions upon the appropriation power. It is that which led to the aggressions on slavery in the District of Columbia. And now the great cause is, that we do not live in a free Government.

Mr. MEMMINGER. The gentleman who has just taken his seat is not as familiar with this document as I am, or he would have been saved the necessity of a good deal he has said. I entirely concur in the opinion that the Constitution of the United States requires the rendition of slaves by the States and not by the General Government; and if any one will read this report he will perceive that that is precisely the ground upon which it proceeds. We there complain that the States have not fulfilled their constitutional obligations—not that the Federal Government has not done its duty. We there complain that when the Federal Government undertakes to do that which the States had obligated themselves to do, they interfere to prevent its faithful execution.

Judge WITHERS said: I have not much to say to this Convention, but the first thing which I desire to submit to them is this: that the addresses which are now upon your table, and which are the subject-matter of a motion for further reference to the two committees reporting them, are, in my understanding, diplomatic papers. I profess not to be much of a diplomat myself, yet I profess to have a desire that this Convention shall confine itself to the object which it prescribes to itself.

What is the object of the Address to the Southern People? Is it not to conciliate the Southern States towards the purposes of a Southern Confederacy; and, as far as we can, to persuade them to enter into a compact with South Carolina? Is that the object of the Address to the Slaveholding States? If not, why should it be issued?

It is said in the discussion that the Address to the Slaveholding States should descant upon the taxing power and the power to lay duties upon imports, as well as the expenditures of money in undue proportion upon the part of the Federal Government among the Free States, as matters of grievances of the greatest importance; that such topics ought to be found in this paper setting forth the causes of Secession. Well, in an Address to the People of the Slaveholding States is it expedient to dwell and insist upon a topic which will not find favor with all the Southern States? I submit to the experience of the able gentleman who prepared that address to say whether, if we declared that we separated from the Confederacy because of the tariff of protection to domestic manufactures, he will find that, be it ever so true, a sentiment corresponding to public opinion in Louisiana, Missouri, or Kentucky?

All this matter of the tariff has been enacted while the Confederacy existed, and with South Carolina as a party to the transaction. When it begun in 1816, who was it voted for a tariff highly protective to domestic manufactures? Did not that great man whom we all reverence, both living and dead—I mean Mr. Calhoun—vote for this measure? Did not the Representative in the House from the Congressional district including Richland vote for the tariff of 1816? Has there ever been a time when Louisiana, Missouri, and Kentucky were not in favor of a protective tariff; not only for protection of domestic manufactures, but for protection on the products of sugar and hemp? Are you sure they will join you in saying they should dissolve the Union on account of the existing tariff giving protection to domestic manufactures? You believe, and so do I, that there has been a perversion of the Constitution in relation to imposts for the purpose of protection to domestic manufactures. I know of no time, from the period of my entering college in 1823, that I did not believe it was a bold and daring invasion of the Constitution of the United States. Undoubtedly this is my opinion, undoubtedly this is the opinion of South Carolina. Then if I had to draw these papers, if I should present my views and opinions in a common address to the Slaveholding States, I should suggest the propriety of leaving out all topics of that description, when I believe that three of these States differ in sentiment with South Carolina. It appears to me, therefore, we have not exactly hit upon the matter which is the most expedient and proper in an Address to the People of the Slaveholding States. It is a diplomatic document. I shall vote for it. But at the same time I do not think as a diplomatic paper, that with respect to the levying of duties on imports, it is likely to find favor with all our slaveholding friends for whom this tariff was designed as well as for the North.

In regard to expenditures by the Federal Government of its income, we all know very well that the great bulk has gone within the Northern States—that there have been, on the part of the Federal Government, favorite States.

When we complain in the aggregate, or in general terms, when we say that the grievances of South Carolina are found in the fact that the Treasury has been depleted by illegal means, and in undue proportion administered to the North, I question whether we are quite safe in alleging that as a grievance of South Carolina, without qualification. There has been an unfaithful execution of the Constitution on the part of its own general agent in that respect. But let us not forget to confess the truth under any and all circumstances. What have we ourselves been doing? And in the city of Charleston, too, where have you bought your supplies, and with whom do you trade? Where has the great surplus of your money been necessarily spent? Where has it gone to? Has it not gone to these people who have received the Federal money? Government and individuals have sought the same market. Why? Because nobody else could furnish the articles each wanted. Can you say, therefore, that the Federal Government is to be blamed for spending a large amount of money in the non-slaveholding States? Where was the Federal Government obliged to get its necessary support for the army and navy? Where could the Federal Government fill up the ranks of its army and navy? Will you not allow the Government to buy of its own citizens, as we have all done? If by the cunning of these men in the non-slaveholding States they have been able to present to the Government inducements to obtain their supplies, can we complain? Where else could they have been procured? So far, the Government has been obliged to spend its money among the people of the North and Northwest for bacon, lard, and all the supplies of the army and navy. I submit these views for the purpose of drawing the attention of the Convention to the fact that we may go too far in this document, and use assertions too strong.

In respect to the argument of the fugitive slave law, I concur fully. I heard something said here questioning the Constitutionality of the fugitive slave law, as it is called. This is a difficult question. In the case of Prigg and the Commonwealth of Pennsylvania, all the Judges of the United States Court but two declared that Congress, and Congress alone, could provide legislation to execute the fourth article of the Constitution of the United States. Immediately after that decision the astute Legislatures of the New England States seized upon that decision and passed their liberty laws, invoking the doctrine announced in the case of Prigg vs. the Commonwealth of Pennsylvania. Could any man say that South Carolina should separate from the United States in consequence of the Congress of the United States passing such a law? A like law was passed in 1793. Did our people object to it then? I confess I have a reverence for antiquity. I profess to have a veneration of the men of 1793—Christopher Gadsden, John Rutledge, the Pinckneys, and others. I profess to believe that they were as patriotic as I profess to be. If we made no objection at that time to the power of Congress to pass a fugitive slave law, under the fourth article of the Constitution of the United States, I hold it would be unsafe for the Convention of South Carolina to say that that is a cause for which she separates from the United States. It was a matter, as long ago as 1643, of stipulation between Massachusetts, Rhode Island, and another colony, that they should deliver each other's fugitive slaves. It was a matter between the colonies that each colony should deliver fugitives. As long ago as that period Congress did exercise this power, and we did acquiesce and never voted against it.

If I were to stand here and declare the various causes which led me to subscribe my name to the Act of Secession, I should insist on some other considerations besides those suggested by this address. I would have said that when a citizen of Maryland went to Pennsylvania to recover his fugitive under an act of Congress they murdered him, and his murderer* escaped from justice in the court of Pennsylvania. Then was the time for Maryland to have demanded justice under the compact. It was then I would have stood up for the rights of that slaveholder. If I chose further to afflict this Convention I could bring before them a long catalogue of grievances. I think if every *member of the Convention should draw up an indictment against the people of the unfaithful confederate States*, and you might have any number of addresses upon that subject, *you would probably find no two very nearly alike*. Since, therefore, every one's taste and judgment cannot be answered, if there be no substantial objection to the addresses before us, as I think there is not, it is proper to vote for them, and I shall do so.

The papers were both adopted.

A third report was made to the Convention by Judge Withers from the Committee on Relations with the Slaveholding States of North America, which should be included, to make the catalogue complete:

The committee on "relations with the slaveholding states of North America," beg leave to report that they have carefully considered the three several propositions contained in the resolutions referred to them, which were submitted in convention by three several members from St. Phillip's and St. Michael's. All the resolutions referred to the committee look to the purpose of confederate relations with our sister states of the South, having common interests with us, and every cause, as we trust, to indulge towards us common sympathies and to contract cordial relations. In such a purpose the committee entirely and unanimously concur, and they recommend that every proper measure be adopted to accomplish such an end. Upon this subject so much unanimity prevails, and has long prevailed in this state, that an argument thereupon would be wholly superfluous. All seem to agree that the first step proper to be taken for the purpose of promoting and securing the confederation we seek, is the appointment of commissioners, by the authority of this convention, to such states of the South as may call conventions to consider and determine their future political relations.

The committee advise that such steps be taken by this convention, hoping and believing that our sister states of the South will correctly interpret our action in taking the initiative as arising, by no means, from any presumptuous arrogance, but from the advance position which circumstances have given to this state in the line of procedure for the great design of maintaining the rights, the security and the very existence of the slaveholding South.

It has been a subject of anxious consideration with the committee whether the commissioners, whose appointment they recommend, should be instructed to tender any basis of a temporary or provisional government to the states to which they may be accredited.

The instrument called the constitution of the United States of America, has been suggested as a suitable and proper basis to be offered for a provisional government.

The suggestion has been commended to the committee by various considerations, which cannot now be set forth in full or at large. Among these are:

That the said instrument was the work of minds of the first order, in strength and accomplishment.

That it was most carefully constructed by comprehensive views and careful examinations of details.

That experience has proved it to be a good form of government for those sufficiently virtuous, intelligent and patriotic to cause it to be fairly and honestly construed and impartially administered.

That the settled opinion of this state has never been adverse to that plan of government of confederated states, on account of anything in its structure; but the dissatisfaction is attributable to the false glosses, and dangerous misinterpretation, and perversion of sundry of its provisions, even

* In 1847.

to the extent, in one particular, of so covering up the real purposes of certain legislation, (meant to protect domestic manufactures in one section), as to estop the supreme court in its opinion, from judicially perceiving the real design.

That it presents a complete scheme of confederation, capable of being speedily put into operation; familiar by long acquaintance with its provisions, and their true import to the people of the South, many of whom are believed to cherish a degree of veneration for it, and would feel safe under it, when in their own hands, for interpretation and administration, especially as the portions that have been, by perversion, made potent for mischief and oppression in the hands of adverse and inimical interests, have received a settled construction by the South. That a speedy confederation by the South is desirable in the highest degree, which, it is supposed, must be temporary at first, (if accomplished as soon as it should be), and no better basis than the constitution of the United States is likely to be suggested or adopted for temporary purposes.

That the opinions of those to whom it is designed to offer it, would be conciliated by the testimony the very act itself would carry, that South Carolina meant to seek no selfish advantage, nor to indulge the least spirit of dictation.

That such form of government is more or less known to Europe, and, if adopted, would indicate abroad that the seceding southern states had the foresight and energy to put into operation forthwith, a scheme of government and administration competent to produce a prompt organization for internal necessities, and a sufficient protection of foreign commerce directed hither, as well as to guarantee foreign powers in the confidence that a new confederacy had immediately arisen, quite adequate to supercede all the evils, internal and external, of a partial or total interregnum.

That its speedy adoption would work happily as a revivifying agency in matters financial and commercial between the states adopting it, and between them as a united power and foreign commercial nations, and at the same time would combine, without delay, a power touching purse and sword, that might bring to a prudent issue the reflections of those who may perchance be contemplating an invasion, or to an issue disastrous to them, the attempted execution of such unholy design.

Such are some of the considerations, very rapidly stated, which address themselves to this subject. It is contended that some limitation of the power to levy duties, and that to regulate commerce, (and perhaps other provisions of the said constitution), may be desirable, and are in fact so, to some of the committee, yet these modifications may be safely left to a period when the articles of a permanent government may be settled, and that, meantime, the constitution referred to will serve the purpose of a temporary confederation, which the committee unite in believing ought to be sought, through all proper measures, most earnestly.

It is also submitted, that if the tender of the said constitution, even as a provisional government, should, in the opinion of the convention, be accompanied by a condition that it be subject to specific limitations, expositions of ambiguities, or modifications, the committee would respectfully refer to the convention itself such matters; and this is done, not because the committee would not willingly consider and report upon such subject, but because they deem it due to the convention and the public interest that they should now lay before the convention the resolutions, which the majority of the committee recommend to the convention as fit to be adopted, viz:

Resolved, First. That this convention do appoint a commissioner to proceed to each of the slaveholding states that may assemble in convention, for the purpose of laying our ordinance of secession before the same, and respectfully inviting their co-operation in the formation with us of a southern confederacy.

Second. That our commissioners aforesaid, be further authorized to submit, on our part, the federal constitution, as the basis of a provisional government for such states as shall have withdrawn from their connection with the government of the United States of America: *Provided*, That the said provisional government, and the tenures of all officers and appointments arising under it, shall cease and determine in two years from the 1st day of July next, or when a permanent government shall have been organized.

Third. That the said commissioners be authorized to invite the seceding states to meet in convention, at such time and place as may be agreed upon, for the purpose of forming and putting in motion such provisional government, and so that the said provisional government shall be organized and go into effect at the earliest period previous to the 4th day of March, 1861, and that the same convention of seceded states shall proceed forthwith to consider and propose a constitution and plan for a permanent government for such states, which proposed plan shall be referred back to the several state conventions for their adoption or rejection.

Fourth. That eight deputies shall be elected by ballot by this convention, who shall be authorized to meet in convention such deputies as may be appointed by the other slaveholding states who may secede from the Federal Union, for the purpose of carrying into effect the foregoing resolutions; and that it be recommended to the said states that each state be entitled to one vote in the said convention, upon all questions which may be voted upon therein; and that each state send as many deputies as are equal in number to the number of senators and representatives to which it was entitled in the Congress of the United States.

On the question of sending copies of the Ordinance and the accompanying Declaration of Causes and the Address, to the Governors of the slaveholding States, there was a debate, in which Mr. Dargan urged the propriety of notifying the authorities of all the States, which being objected to,

Mr. Dargan said: A statement of the reasons is required, as well as the Ordinance of Secession. Courtesy to our late Confederates, whether enemies or not, calls for the reasons that have actuated us. It is not true, in point of fact, that all the Northern people are hostile to the rights of the South. *We have a Spartan band in every Northern State. It is due to them they should know the reasons which influence us.* According to our apprehensions the necessity which exists for our immediate withdrawal from association with the Northern States is that this hostile Abolition party have the control of the Government, and there is no hope of redress for our grievances.

Speech of Alexander H. Stephens, November 14th, 1860.

As against these allegations, we insert the speech of Hon. Alexander H. Stephens of Georgia, before the Legislature of Georgia, November 14th, 1860, and an extract from his speech in the Convention of Georgia, of January, 1861:

Fellow-Citizens:—I appear before you to-night, at the request of members of the Legislature and others, to speak of matters of the deepest interest that can possibly concern us all of an earthly character. There is nothing—no question or subject connected with this life—that concerns a free people so intimately as that of the government under which they live. We are now, indeed, surrounded by evils. Never, since I entered upon the public stage, has the country been so environed with difficulties and dangers that threatened the public peace, and the very existence of society, as now. I do not now appear before you at my own instance. It is not to gratify a desire of my own that I am here. Had I consulted my own ease and pleasure I should not be before you; but, believing that it is the duty of every good citizen to give his counsels and views whenever the country is in danger, as to the best policy to be pursued, I am here. For these reasons, and these only, do I bespeak a calm, patient and attentive hearing.

My object is not to stir up strife, but to allay it; not to appeal to your passions, but to your reason. Good governments can never be built up or sustained by the impulse of passion. I wish to address myself to your good sense, to your good judgment, and if, after hearing, you disagree, let us agree to disagree, and part as we met, friends. We all have the same object, the same interest. That people should disagree, in republican governments, upon questions of public policy, is natural. That men should disagree upon all matters connected with human investigation, whether relating to science or human conduct, is natural. Hence, in free governments, parties will arise. But a free people should express their different opinions with liberality and charity, with no acrimony toward those of their fellows when honestly and sincerely given. These are my feelings to-night.

Let us, therefore, reason together. It is not my purpose to say aught to wound the feelings of any individual who may be present; and if, in the ardency with which I shall express my opinions, I shall say any thing which may be deemed too strong, let it be set down to the zeal with which I advocate my own convictions. There is with me no intention to irritate or offend.

The first question that presents itself is, shall the people of the South secede from the Union in consequence of the election of Mr. Lincoln to the Presidency of the United States? My countrymen, *I tell you frankly, candidly and earnestly, that I do not think that they ought.* In my judgment the election of no man, constitutionally chosen to that high office, is sufficient cause for any State to separate from the Union. It ought to stand by and aid still in maintaining the Constitution and the country. To make a point of resistance to the government, to withdraw from it because a man has been constitutionally elected, puts us in the wrong. We are pledged to maintain the Constitution. Many of us have sworn to support it. Can we, therefore, for the mere election of a man to the Presidency, and that too in accordance with the prescribed forms of the Constitution, make a point of resistance to the government without becoming the breakers of that sacred instrument ourselves—withdraw ourselves from it? Would we not be in the wrong? Whatever fate is to befall this country, let it never be laid to the charge of the people of the South, and especially to the people of Georgia, that we were untrue to our national engagements. Let the fault and the wrong rest upon others. If all our hopes are to be blasted, if the Republic is to go down, let us be found to the last moment standing on the deck, with the Constitution of the United States waving over our heads. Let the fanatics of the North break the Constitution, if such is their fell purpose. Let the responsibility be upon them. I shall speak presently more of their acts; but let not the South—let us not be the ones to commit the aggression. We went into the election with this people. The result was different from what we wished; but the election has been constitutionally held. Were we to make a point of resistance to the Government and go out of the Union on that account, *the record would be made up hereafter against us.*

But it is said Mr. Lincoln's policy and principles are against the Constitution, and that if he carries them out it will be destructive of our rights. Let us not anticipate a threatened evil. If he violates the Constitution, then will come our time to act. Do not let us break it because, forsooth, he may. If he does, that is the time for us to strike. I think it would be injudicious and unwise to do this sooner. I do not anticipate that Mr. Lincoln will do any thing to jeopard our safety or security, whatever may be his spirit to do it; for he is bound by the constitutional checks which are thrown around him, which at this time render him powerless to do any great mischief. This shows the wisdom of our system. The President of the United States is no Emperor, no dictator—he is clothed with no absolute power. He can do nothing unless he is backed by power in Congress. The House of Representatives is largely in the majority against him.

In the Senate he will also be powerless. There will be a majority of four against him. This, after the loss of Bigler, Fitch, and others, by the unfortunate dissensions of the National Democratic party in their States. Mr. Lincoln cannot appoint an officer without the consent of the Senate. He cannot form a cabinet without the same consent. He will be in the condition of George III. (the embodiment of Toryism), who had to ask the whigs to appoint his ministers, and was compelled to receive a cabinet utterly opposed to his views; and so Mr. Lincoln will be compelled to ask of the Senate to choose for him a cabinet, if the Democracy of that body choose to put him on such terms. He will be compelled to do this or let the government stop, if the National Democratic men—for that is their name at the North—the conservative men in the Senate, should so determine. Then how can Mr. Lincoln obtain a cabinet which would aid him, or allow him to violate the Constitution?

Why, then, I say, should we disrupt the ties of this Union when his hands are tied, when he can do nothing against us? I have heard it mooted that no man in the State of Georgia, who is true to her interests, could hold office under Mr. Lincoln. But, I ask, who appoints to office? Not the President alone; the Senate has to concur. No man can be appointed without the consent of the Senate. Should any man then refuse to hold office that was given to him by a Democratic Senate? [Mr. Toombs interrupted, and said if the Senate was Democratic it was for Mr. Breckinridge.] Well, then, continued Mr. S., I apprehend no man could be justly considered untrue to the interests of Georgia, or incur any disgrace, if the interests of Georgia required it, to hold an office which a Breckinridge Senate had given him, even though Mr. Lincoln should be President.

I trust, my countrymen, you will be still and silent. I am addressing your good sense. I am giving you my views in a calm and dispassionate manner, and if any of you differ with me, you can, on any other occasion, give your views as I am doing now, and let reason and true patriotism decide between us. In my judgment, I say, under such circumstances, there would be no possible disgrace for a Southern man to hold office. No man will be suffered to be appointed, I have no doubt, who is not true to the Constitution, if Southern Senators are true to their trusts, as I cannot permit myself to doubt that they will be.

My honorable friend who addressed you last night (Mr. Toombs), and to whom I listened with the profoundest attention, asks if we would submit to Black Republican rule? I say to you and to him, as a Georgian, I never would submit to any Black Republican *aggression* upon our constitutional rights. I will never consent myself, as much as I admire this Union for the glories of the past, or the blessings of the present—as much as it has done for the people of all these States—as much as it has done for civilization—as much as the hopes of the world hang upon it, I would never submit to aggression upon my rights to maintain it longer; and if they cannot be maintained in the Union, standing on the Georgia platform, where I have stood from the time of its adoption, I would be in favor of disrupting every tie which binds the States together.

I will have equality for Georgia and for the citizens of Georgia, in this Union, or I will look for new safeguards elsewhere. This is my position. The only question now is, can they be secured in the Union? That is what I am counseling with you to-night about. Can it be secured? In my judgment it may be, but it may not be; but let us do all we can, so that in the future, if the worst come, it may never be said that we were negligent in doing our duty to the last.

My countrymen, I am not of those who believe this Union has been a curse up to this time. True men, men of integrity, entertain different views from me on this subject. I do not question their right to do so; I would not impugn their motives in so doing. Nor will I undertake to say that this government of our fathers is perfect. There is nothing perfect in this world of a human origin—nothing connected with human nature, from man himself to any of his works. You may select the wisest and best men for your judges, and yet how many defects are there in the administration of justice? You may select the wisest and best men for your legislators, and yet how many defects are apparent in your laws? And it is so in our Government.

But that this government of our fathers, with all its defects, comes nearer the objects of all good governments than any other on the face of the earth is my settled conviction. Contrast it now with any on the face of the earth. [England, said Mr. Toombs.] England, my friend says. Well, that is the next best, I grant; but I think we have improved upon England. Statesmen tried their apprentice hand on the government of England, and then ours was made. Ours sprung from that, avoiding many of its defects, taking most of the good and leaving out many of its errors, and from the whole constructing and building up this model Republic—the best which the history of the world gives any account of.

Compare, my friends, this Government with that of Spain, Mexico, the South American Republics, Germany, Ireland—are there any sons of that down-trodden nation here to-night?—Prussia, or, if you travel further east, to Turkey or China. Where will you go, following the sun in its circuit round our globe, to find a government that better protects the liberties of its people, and secures to them the blessings we enjoy? I think that one of the evils that beset us is a surfeit of liberty, an exuberance of the priceless blessings for which we are ungrateful. We listened to my honorable friend who addressed you last night (Mr. Toombs) as he recounted the evils of this Government.

The first was the fishing bounties, paid mostly to the sailors of New England. Our friend stated that forty-eight years of our government was under the administration of Southern Presidents. Well, these fishing bounties began under the rule of a Southern President, I believe. No one of them during the whole forty-eight years ever set his administration against the principle or policy of them. It is not for me to say whether it was a wise policy in the beginning; it probably was not, and I have nothing to say in its defence. But the reason given for it was to encourage our young men to go to sea and learn to manage ships. We had at the time but a small navy. It was thought best to encourage a class of our people to become acquainted with seafaring life, to become sailors—to man our naval ships. It requires practice to walk the deck of a ship, to furl the sails, to go aloft, to climb the mast; and it was thought, by offering this bounty, a nursery might be formed in which young men would become perfected in these arts, and it applied to one section of the country as well as to any other.

The result of this was, that in the war of 1812 our sailors, many of whom came from this nursery, were equal to any that England brought against us. At any rate, no small part of the glories of that war were gained by the veteran tars of America, and the object of these bounties was to foster that branch of the national defence. My opinion is that whatever may have been the reason at first, this bounty ought to be discontinued—the reason for it at first no longer exists. A bill for this object did pass the Senate the last Congress I was in, to which my honorable friend contributed greatly, but it was not reached in the House of Representatives. I trust that he will yet see that he may with honor continue his connection with the government, and that his eloquence, unrivalled in the Senate, may hereafter, as heretofore, be displayed in having this bounty, so obnoxious to him, repealed, and wiped off from the statute book.

The next evil which my friend complained of, was the tariff. Well, let us look at that for a moment. About the time I commenced noticing public matters, this question was agitating the country almost as fearfully as the slave question now is. In 1832, when I was in college, South Carolina was ready to nullify or secede from the Union on this account. And what have we seen? The tariff no longer distracts the public counsels. Reason has triumphed! The present tariff was voted for by Massachusetts and South Carolina. The lion and the lamb lay down together—every man in the Senate and House from Massachusetts and South Carolina, I think, voted for it, as did my honorable friend himself. And if it be true, to use the figure of speech of my honorable friend, that every man in the North that works in iron, and brass and wood, has his muscle strengthened by the protection of the government, that stimulant was given by his vote, and I believe every other Southern man. So we ought not to complain of that.

Mr. Toombs. The tariff assessed the duties.

Mr. Stephens. Yes, and Massachusetts with unanimity voted with the South to lessen them, and they were made just as low as Southern men asked them to be, and that is the rate they are now at. If reason and argument, with experience, produced such changes in the sentiments of Massachusetts from 1832 to 1857, on the subject of the tariff, may not like changes be effected there by the same means—reason and argument, and appeals to patriotism on the present vexed question? And who can say that by 1875 or 1890 Massachusetts may not vote with South Carolina and Georgia upon all those questions that now distract the country and threaten its peace and existence. I believe in the power and efficiency of truth, in the omnipotence of truth, and its ultimate triumph when properly wielded.

Another matter of grievance alluded to by my honorable friend was the Navigation Laws. This policy was also commenced under the Administration of one of these Southern Presidents who ruled so well, and has been continued through all of them since. The gentleman's views of the policy of these laws and my own do not disagree. We occupied the same ground in relation to them in Congress. It is not my purpose to defend them now. But it is proper to state some matters connected with their origin.

One of the objects was to build up a commercial American marine by giving American bottoms the exclusive carrying-trade between our own ports. This is a great arm of national power. This object was accomplished. We have now an amount of shipping, not only coastwise, but to foreign countries, which puts us in the front rank of the nations of the world. England can no longer be styled the Mistress of the Seas. What American is not proud of the result? Whether those laws should be continued is another question. But one thing is certain: no President, Northern or Southern, has ever yet recommended their repeal. And my friend's efforts to get them repealed were met with but little favor, North or South.

These, then, were the true main grievances or grounds of complaint against the general system of our Government and its workings—I mean the administration of the Federal Government. As to the acts of the Federal States I shall speak presently; but these three were the main ones used against the common head. Now, suppose it be admitted that all of these are evils in the system; do they overbalance and outweigh the advantages and great good which this same government affords in a thousand innumerable ways that cannot be estimated? Have we not at the South, as well as the North, grown great, prosperous, and happy under its operations? Has any part of the world ever shown such rapid progress in the development of wealth, and all the material resources of national power and greatness, as the Southern States have under the General Government, notwithstanding all its defects?

Mr. Toombs. In spite of it.

Mr. Stephens. My honorable friend says we have, in spite of the General Government; that without it, I suppose he thinks, we might have done as well, or perhaps better, than we have done this in spite of it. That may be and it may not be; but the great fact that we have grown great and powerful under the Government as it exists—there is no conjecture or speculation about that; it stands out bold, high, and prominent, like your Stone Mountain, to which the gentleman alluded in illustrating home facts in his record—this great fact of our unrivalled prosperity in the Union as it is admitted; whether all this is in spite of the Government—whether we of the South would have been better off without the Government—is, to say the least, problematical. On the one side we can only put the fact against speculation and conjecture on the other. But even as a question of speculation I differ with my distinguished friend.

What we would have lost in border wars without the Union, or what we have gained simply by the peace it has secured, no estimate can be made of. Our foreign trade, which is the foundation of all our prosperity, has the protection of the navy, which drove the pirates from the waters near our coast, where they had been buccaneering for centuries before, and might have been still had it not been for the American Navy, under the command of such spirits as Commodore Porter. Now that the coast is clear, that our commerce flows freely outwardly, we can not well estimate how it would have been under other circumstances. The influence of the Government on us is like that of the atmosphere around us. Its benefits are so silent and unseen that they are seldom thought of or appreciated.

We seldom think of the single element of oxygen in the air we breathe, and yet let this simple, unseen and unfelt agent be withdrawn, this life-giving element be taken away from this all-pervading fluid around us, and what instant and appalling changes would take place in all organic creation.

It may be that we are all that we are in "spite of the General Government," but it may be that without it we should have been far different from what we are now. It is true there is no equal part of the earth with natural resources superior perhaps to ours. That portion of this country known as the Southern States, stretching from the Chesapeake to the Rio Grande, is fully equal to the picture drawn by the honorable and eloquent Senator last night, in all natural capacities. But how many ages and centuries passed before these capacities were developed to reach this advanced age of civilization? There these same hills, rich in ore, same rivers, same valleys and plains, are as they have been since they came from the hand of the Creator; uneducated and uncivilized man roamed over them for how long no history informs us.

It was only under our institutions that they could be developed. Their development is the result of the enterprise of our people, under operations of the Government and institutions under which we have lived. Even our people, without these, never would have done it. The organization of society has much to do with the development of the natural resources of any country or any land. The institutions of a people, political and moral, are the matrix in which the germ of their organic structure quickens into life—takes root, and develops in form, nature, and character. Our institutions constitute the basis, the matrix, from which spring all our characteristics of development and greatness. Look at Greece. There is the same fertile soil, the same blue sky, the same inlets and harbors, the same Ægean, the same Olympus; there is the same land where Homer sung, where Pericles spoke; it is in nature the same old Greece—but it is living Greece no more.

Descendants of the same people inhabit the country; yet what is the reason of this vast difference? In the midst of present degradation we see the glorious fragments of ancient works of art—temples, with ornaments and inscriptions that excite wonder and admiration—the remains of a once high order of civilization, which have outlived the language they spoke—upon them all, Ichabod is written—their glory has departed. Why is this so? I answer, their institutions have been destroyed. These were but the fruits of their forms of government, the matrix from which their grand development sprung; and when once the institutions of a people have been destroyed, there is no earthly power that can bring back the Promethean spark to kindle them here again, any more than in that ancient land of eloquence, poetry, and song.

The same may be said of Italy. Where is Rome, once the mistress of the world? There are the same seven hills now, the same soil, the same natural resources; nature is the same, but what a ruin of human greatness meets the eye of the traveller throughout the length and breadth of that most down-trodden land! Why have not the people of that Heaven-favored clime the spirit that animated their fathers? Why this sad difference?

It is the destruction of her institutions that has caused it; and, my countrymen, if we shall in an evil hour rashly pull down and destroy those institutions which the patriotic band of our fathers labored so long and so hard to build up, and which have done so much for us and the world, who can venture the prediction that similar results will not ensue? Let us avoid it if we can. I trust the spirit is among us that will enable us to do it. Let us not rashly try the experiment, for, if it fails, as it did in Greece and Italy, and in the South American Republics, and in every other place wherever liberty is once destroyed, it may never be restored to us again.

There are defects in our government, errors in administration, and short-comings of many kinds; but in spite of these defects and errors, Georgia has grown to be a great State. Let us pause here a moment. In 1850 there was a great crisis, but not so fearful as this; for, of all I have ever passed through, this is the most perilous, and requires to be met with the greatest calmness and deliberation.

There were many among us in 1850 zealous to go at once out of the Union, to disrupt every tie that binds us together. Now, do you believe, had that policy been carried out at that time, we would have been the same great people that we are to-day? It may be that we would, but have you any assurance of that fact? Would you have made the same advancement, improvement, and progress in all that constitutes material wealth and prosperity that we have?

I notice, in the Comptroller-General's report, that the taxable property of Georgia is $670,000,000 and upward, an amount not far from double what it was in 1850. I think I may venture to say that for the last ten years the material wealth of the people of Georgia has been nearly if not quite doubled. The same may be said of our advance in education and every thing that marks our civilization. Have we any assurance that, had we regarded the earnest but misguided patriotic advice, as I think, of some of that day, and disrupted the ties which bind us to the Union, we would have advanced as we have? I think not. Well, then, let us be careful now before we attempt any rash experiment of this sort. I know that there are friends—whose patriotism I do not intend to question—who think this Union a curse—and that we would be better off without it. I do not so think, if we can bring about a correction of those evils which threaten—and I am not without hope that this may yet be done. This appeal to go out, with all the provisions for good that accompany it, I look upon it as a great and I fear a fatal temptation.

When I look around and see our prosperity in every thing, agriculture, commerce, art, science, and every department of education, physical and mental, as well as moral advancement, and our colleges, I think, in the face of such an exhibition, if we can, without the loss of power, or any essential right or interest, remain in the Union, it is our duty to ourselves and to posterity to—let us not too readily yield to this temptation—do so. Our first parents, the great progenitors of the human race, were not without a like temptation when in the garden of Eden. They were led to believe that their condition would be bettered—that their eyes would be opened—and that they would become as gods. They in an evil hour yielded—instead of becoming gods, they only saw their own nakedness.

I look upon this country with our institutions as the Eden of the world, the paradise of the universe. It may be that out of it we may become greater and more prosperous, but I am candid and sincere in telling you that I fear if we rashly evince passion, and without sufficient cause shall take that step, that instead of becoming greater or more peaceful, prosperous, and happy—instead of becoming gods, we will become demons, and at no distant day commence cutting one another's throats. This is my apprehension. Let us, therefore, whatever we do, meet those difficulties, great as they are, like wise and sensible men, and consider them in the light of all the consequences which may attend our action. Let us see first clearly where the path of duty leads, and then we may not fear to tread therein.

I come now to the main question put to me, and on which my counsel has been asked. That is, what the present Legislature should do in view of the dangers that threaten us, and the wrongs that have been done us by several of our confederate States in the Union, by the acts of their legislatures nullifying the fugitive slave law, and in direct disregard of their constitutional obligations. What I shall say will not be in the spirit of dictation; it will be simply my own judgment for what it is worth. It proceeds from a strong conviction that according to it our rights, interests and honor—our present safety and future security—can be maintained without yet looking to the last resort, the "*ultima ratio regum.*" That should not be looked to until all else fails. That may come. On this point I am hopeful, but not sanguine. But let us use every patriotic effort to prevent it while there is ground for hope.

If any view that I may present in your judgment be inconsistent with the best interests of Georgia, I ask you, as patriots, not to regard it. After hearing me and others whom you have advised with, act in the premises according to your own conviction of duty as patriots. I speak now particularly to the members of the legislature present. There are, as I have said, great dangers ahead. Great dangers may come from the election I have spoken of. If the policy of Mr. Lincoln and his Republican associates shall be carried out, or attempted to be carried out, no man in Georgia will be more willing or ready than myself to defend our rights, interests and honor, at every hazard and to the last extremity.

What is this policy? It is, in the first place, to exclude us, by an act of Congress, from the Territories with our slave property. He is for using the power of the General Government against the extension of our institutions. Our position on this point is, and ought to be, at all hazards, for perfect equality between all the States, and the citizens of all the States, in the Territories, under the Constitution of the United States. If Congress should exercise its power against this, then I am for standing where Georgia planted herself in 1850. These were plain propositions, which were then laid down in her celebrated platform as sufficient for the disruption of the Union if the occasion should ever come. On these Georgia has declared that she will go out of the Union; and for these she would be justified by the nations of the earth in so doing.

I say the same; I said it then; I say it now—if Mr. Lincoln's policy should be carried out. I have told you that I do not think his bare election sufficient cause: but if his policy should be carried out in violation of any of the principles set forth in the Georgia platform, that would be such an act of aggression which ought to be met as therein provided for. If his policy shall be carried out in repealing or modifying the fugitive slave law so as to weaken its efficacy, Georgia has declared that she will, in the last resort, disrupt the ties of the Union—and I say so too. I stand upon the Georgia platform, and upon every plank, and say, if these aggressions therein provided for take place—I say to you and to the people of Georgia, keep your powder dry, and let your assailants then have lead, if need be. I would wait for an act of aggression. This is my position.

Now upon another point, and that the most difficult, and deserving your most serious consideration, I will speak. That is the course which this State should pursue towards those Northern States, which by their legislative acts have attempted to nullify the fugitive slave law. I know that in some of these States their acts pretend to be based upon the principles set forth in the case of PRIGG against Pennsylvania. That decision did proclaim the doctrine that the State officers are not bound to carry out the provisions of a law of Congress—that the Federal Government can not impose duties upon State officials—that they must execute their own laws by their own officers. And this may be true. But still it is the duty of the States to deliver fugitive slaves, as well as the duty of the General Government to see that it is done.

Northern States, on entering into the Federal compact, pledged themselves to surrender such fugitives; and it is in disregard of their obligations that they have passed laws which even tend to hinder or obstruct the fulfilment of that obligation. They have violated their plighted faith what ought we to do in view of this? That is the question. What is to be done? By the law of nations you would have a right to demand the carrying out of this article of agreement, and I do not see that it should be otherwise with respect to the States of this Union; and, in case it be not done, we would, by these principles, have the right to commit acts of reprisal on these faithless governments, and seize upon their property, or that of their citizens, wherever found. The States of this Union stand upon the same footing with foreign nations in this respect. But, by the law of nations, we are equally bound, before proceeding to violent measures, to set forth our grievances before the offending Government, to give them an opportunity to redress the wrong. Has our State yet done this? I think not.

Suppose it was Great Britain that had violated some compact of agreement with the General Government, what would be first done? In that case our Minister would be directed, in the first instance, to bring the matter to the attention of that Government, or a Commissioner be sent to that country to open negotiations with her, ask for redress, and it would only be when argument and reason had been exhausted, that we should take the last resort of nations. That would be the course toward a foreign government, and toward a member of this Confederacy I would recommend the same course.

Let us, therefore, not act hastily in this matter. Let your Committee on the State of the Republic make out a bill of grievances; let it be sent by the Governor to those faithless States, and if reason and argument shall be tried in vain—all shall fail to induce them to return to their constitutional obligations—I would be for retaliatory measures, such as the Governor has suggested to you. This mode of resistance in the Union is in our power. It might be effectual, and, if in the last resort, we would be justified in the eyes of nations, not only in separating from them, but by using force.

[Some one said the argument was already exhausted.]

MR. STEPHENS continued. Some friend says that the argument is already exhausted. No, my friend, it is not. You have never called the attention of the Legislatures of those States to this subject that I am aware of. Nothing has ever been done before this year. The attention of our own people has been called to this subject lately.

Now, then, my recommendation to you would be this: In view of all these questions of difficulty, let a convention of the people of Georgia be called, to which they may be all referred. Let the sovereignty of the people speak. Some think that the election of Mr. Lincoln is cause sufficient to dissolve the Union. Some think those other grievances are sufficient to dissolve the same, and that the Legislature has the power thus to act, and ought thus to act. I have no hesitancy in saying that the Legislature is not the proper body to sever our Federal relations, if that necessity should arise. An honorable and distinguished gentleman, the other night (Mr. T. R. R. Cobb), advised you to take this course—not to wait to hear from the cross-roads and groceries. I say to you, you have no power so to act. You must refer this question to the people, and you must wait to hear from the men at the cross-roads and even the groceries; for the people in this country, whether at the cross-roads or the groceries, whether in cottages or palaces, are all equal, and they are the sovereigns in this country. Sovereignty is not in the Legislature. We, the people, are the sovereigns. I am one of them and have a right to be heard, and so has any other citizen of the State. You, legislators—I speak it respectfully—are but our servants. You are the servants of the people, and not their masters. Power resides with the people in this country.

The great difference between our country and all others, such as France and England and Ireland, is, that here there is popular sovereignty while there sovereignty is exercised by kings and favored classes. This principle of popular sovereignty, however much derided lately, is the foundation of our institutions. Constitutions are but the channels through which the popular will may be expressed. Our Constitution came from the people. They made it, and they alone can rightfully unmake it.

Mr. Toombs. I am afraid of conventions.

Mr. Stephens. I am not afraid of any convention legally chosen by the people. I know no way to decide great questions affecting fundamental laws except by representatives of the people. The Constitution of the United States was made by the representatives of the people. The Constitution of the State of Georgia was made by representatives of the people chosen at the ballot-box. But do not let the question which comes before the people be put to them in the language of my honorable friend who addressed you last night: Will you submit to abolition rule or resist?

Mr. Toombs. I do not wish the people to be cheated.

Mr. Stephens. Now, my friends, how are we going to cheat the people by calling on them to elect delegates to a convention to decide all these questions without any dictation or direction? Who proposes to cheat the people by letting them speak their own untrammelled views in the choice of their ablest and best men, to determine upon all these matters involving their peace?

I think the proposition of my honorable friend had a considerable smack of unfairness, not to say cheat. He wished to have no convention, but for the Legislature to submit their vote to the people—submission to abolition rule or resistance? Now who, in Georgia, would vote "submission to abolition rule?"

Is putting such a question to the people to vote on a fair way of getting an expression of the popular will on all these questions? I think not. Now, who in Georgia is going to submit to abolition rule?

Mr. Toombs. The convention will.

Mr. Stephens. No, my friend, Georgia will never do it. The convention will never secede from the Georgia Platform. Under that there can be no abolition rule in the General Government. I am not afraid to trust the people in convention upon this and all questions. Besides, the Legislature were not elected for such a purpose. They came here to do their duty as legislators. They have sworn to support the Constitution of the United States. They did not come here to disrupt this Government. I am therefore for submitting all these questions to a convention of the people. Submit the question to the people, whether they would submit to an abolition rule or resist, and then let the Legislature act upon that vote? Such a course would be an insult to the people. They would have to eat their platform, ignore their past history, blot out their records, and take steps backward, if they should do this. I have never eaten my record or words, and never will.

But how will it be under this arrangement if they should vote to resist, and the Legislature should reassemble with this vote as their instruction? Can any man tell what sort of resistance will be meant? One man would say secede; another pass retaliatory measures; these are measures of resistance against wrong--legitimate and right—and there would be as many different ideas as there are members on this floor. Resistance don't mean secession—that, in no proper sense of the term, is resistance. Believing that the times require action, I am for presenting the question fairly to the people, for calling together an untrammelled convention, and presenting all the questions to them whether they will go out of the Union, or what course of resistance in the Union they may think best, and then let the Legislature act, when the people in their majesty are heard; and I tell you now, whatever that Convention does, I hope and trust our people will abide by. I advise the calling of a convention with the earnest desire to preserve the peace and harmony of the State. I should dislike, above all things, to see violent measures adopted, or a disposition to take the sword in hand, by individuals, without the authority of law.

My honorable friend said last night: "I ask you to give me the sword, for if you do not give it to me, as God lives, I will take it myself."

Mr. Toombs. I will.

Mr. Stephens. I have no doubt that my honorable friend feels as he says. It is only his excessive ardor that makes him use such an expression; but this will pass off with the excitement of the hour. When the people in their majesty shall speak, I have no doubt that he will bow to their will, whatever it may be, upon the "sober second thought."

Should Georgia determine to go out of the Union—I speak for one, though my views might not agree with them—whatever the result may be, I shall bow to the will of her people. Their cause is my cause, and their destiny is my destiny; and I trust this will be the ultimate course of all. The greatest curse that can befall a free people is civil war.

But, as I said, let us call a convention of the people; let all these matters be submitted to it, and when the will of a majority of the people has thus been expressed, the whole State will present one unanimous voice in favor of whatever may be demanded; for I believe in the power of the people to govern themselves, when wisdom prevails and passion is silent.

Look at what has already been done by them for their advancement in all that ennobles man. There is nothing like it in the history of the world. Look abroad from one extent of the country to the other—contemplate our greatness. We are now among the first nations of the earth. Shall it be said, then, that our institutions, founded upon principles of self-government, are a failure?

Thus far it is a noble example, worthy of imitation. The gentleman, Mr. Cobb, the other night said it had proven a failure. A failure in what? In growth? Look at our expanse in national power. Look at our population and increase in all that makes a people great. A failure? Why, we are the admiration of the civilized world, and present the brightest hopes of mankind.

Some of our public men have failed in their aspirations; that is true, and from that comes a great part of our troubles.

No, there is no failure of this Government yet. We have made great advancement under the Constitution, and I cannot but hope that we shall advance higher still. Let us be true to our cause.

Now, when this convention assembles, if it shall be called, as I hope it may, I would say in my judgment, without dictation, for I am conferring with you freely and frankly, and it is thus that I give my views, I should take into consideration all those questions which distract the public mind; should view all the grounds of secession so far as the election of Mr. Lincoln is concerned, and I have no doubt they would say that the constitutional election of no man is a sufficient cause to break up the Union, but that the State should wait until he at least does some unconstitutional act.

Mr. Toombs. Commit some overt act.

Mr. Stephens. No, I did not say that. The word overt is a sort of technical term connected with treason, which has come to us from the mother country, and it means an open act of rebellion. I do not see how Mr. Lincoln can do this unless he should levy war upon us. I do not, therefore, use the word overt. I do not intend to wait for that. But I use the words unconstitutional act, which our people understand much better, and which expresses just what I mean. But as long as he conforms to the Constitution, he should be left to exercise the duties of his office.

In giving this advice I am but sustaining the Constitution of my country, and I do not thereby become a Lincoln aid man either but a Constitutional aid man. But this matter the Convention can determine.

As to the other matter, I think we have a right to pass retaliatory measures, provided they be in accordance with the Constitution of the United States, and I think they can be made such. But whether it would be wise for this Legislature to do this now is the question. To the Convention, in my judgment, this matter ought to be referred. Before we commit reprisals on New England we should exhaust every means of bringing about a peaceful solution of the question.

Thus did General Jackson in the case of the French. He did not recommend reprisals until he had treated with France, and got her to promise to make indemnification, and it was only on her refusal to pay the money which she had promised that he recommended reprisals. It was after negotiation had failed. I do think, therefore, that it would be best, before going to extreme measures with our Confederate States, to make a presentation of our demands, to appeal to their reason and judgment to give us our rights. Then, if reason should not triumph, it will be time enough to commit reprisals, and we should be justified in the eyes of a civilized world. At least, let the States know what your grievances are, and if they refuse, as I said, to give us our rights under the Constitution of our country, I should be willing, as a last resort, to sever the ties of this Union.

My own opinion is, that if this course be pursued, and they are informed of the consequences of refusal, these States will secede; but if they should not, then let the consequences be with them, and let the responsibility of the consequences rest upon them. Another thing I would have that Convention to do. Reaffirm the Georgia platform with an additional plank in it. Let that plank be the fulfilment of the obligation on the part of those States to repeal these obnoxious laws as a condition of our remaining in the Union. Give them time to consider it, and I would ask all States South to do the same thing.

I am for exhausting all that patriotism can demand before taking the last step. I would invite, therefore, South Carolina to a conference. I would ask the same of all the other Southern States, so that if the evil has got beyond our control, which God, in his mercy, grant may not be the case let us not be divided among ourselves, but, if possible, secure the united co-operation of all the Southern States; and then, in the face of the civilized world, we may justify our action; and, with the wrong all on the other side, we can appeal to the God of battles to aid us in our cause. But let us not do any thing in which any portion of our people may charge us with rash or hasty action. It is certainly a matter of great importance to tear this Government asunder. You were not sent here for that purpose. I would wish the whole South to be united if this is to be done; and I believe if we pursue the policy which I have indicated, this can be effected.

In this way our sister Southern States can be induced to act with us, and I have but little doubt that the States of New York, and Pennsylvania, and Ohio, and the other Western States, will compel their Legislatures to recede from their hostile attitudes if the others do not. Then with these we would go on without New England if she chose to stay out.

[A voice in the assembly. "We will kick them out."]

Mr. STEPHENS. I would not kick them out. But if they chose to stay out, they might. I think, moreover, that these Northern States, being principally engaged in manufactures, would find that they had as much interest in the Union under the Constitution as we, and that they would return to their constitutional duty—this would be my hope. If they should not, and if the Middle States and Western States do not join us, we should at least have an undivided South I am, as you clearly perceive, for maintaining the Union as it is, if possible. I will exhaust every means thus to maintain it with an equality in it. My principles are these:

First, the maintenance of the honor, the rights, the equality, the security, and the glory of my native State in the Union; but if these cannot be maintained in the Union, then I am for their maintenance, at all hazards, out of it. Next to the honor and glory of Georgia, the land of my birth, I hold the honor and glory of our common country. In Savannah I was made to say, by the reporters—who very often make me say things which I never did say—that I was first for the glory of the whole country, and next for that of Georgia.

I said the exact reverse of this. I am proud of her history, of her present standing. I am proud even of her motto, which I would have duly respected at the present time by all her sons—Wisdom, Justice, and Moderation. I would have her rights and that of the Southern States maintained now upon these principles. Her position now is just what it was in 1850, with respect to the Southern States. Her platform then has been adopted by most, if not all, the other Southern States. Now I would add but one additional plank to that platform, which I have stated, and one which time has shown to be necessary.

If all this fails, we shall at least have the satisfaction of knowing that we have done our duty and all that patriotism could require.

From Mr. STEPHENS's speech in the State Convention of Georgia:

This step (of secession) once taken, can never be recalled; and all the baleful and withering consequences that must follow, will rest on the convention for all coming time. When we and our posterity shall see our lovely South desolated by the demon of war, WHICH THIS ACT OF YOURS WILL INEVITABLY INVITE AND CALL FORTH: when our green fields of waving harvest shall be trodden down by the murderous soldiery and fiery car of war sweeping over our land; our temples of justice laid in ashes; all the horrors and desolations of war upon us; WHO BUT THIS CONVENTION WILL BE HELD RESPONSIBLE FOR IT? and who but him who shall have given his vote for this unwise and ill-timed measure, as I honestly think and believe, SHALL BE HELD TO STRICT ACCOUNT FOR THIS SUICIDAL ACT BY THE PRESENT GENERATION, AND PROBABLY CURSED AND EXECRATED BY POSTERITY FOR ALL COMING TIME, for the wide and desolating ruin that will inevitably follow this act you now propose to perpetrate? Pause, I entreat you, and consider for a moment what reasons you can give that will even satisfy yourselves in calmer moments—what reasons you can give to your fellow-sufferers in the calamity that it will bring upon us. WHAT REASONS CAN YOU GIVE TO THE NATIONS OF THE EARTH TO JUSTIFY IT? They will be the calm and deliberate judges in the case; and what cause or one overt act can you name or point, on which to rest the plea of justification? WHAT RIGHT HAS THE NORTH ASSAILED? What interest of the South has been invaded? What justice has been denied? and what claim founded in justice and right has been withheld? Can either of you to-day name one governmental act of wrong, deliberately and purposely done by the government of Washington, of which the South has a right to complain? I challenge the answer. While, on the other hand, let me show the facts (and believe me, gentlemen, I am not here the advocate of the North; but I am here the friend, the firm friend, and lover of the South and her institutions, and for this reason I speak thus plainly and faithfully for yours, mine, and every other man's interest, the words of truth and soberness), of which I wish you to judge, and I will only state facts which are clear and undeniable, and which now stand as records authentic in the history of our country. When we of the South demanded the slave-trade, or the importation of Africans for the cultivation of our lands, did they not yield the right for twenty years? When we asked a three-fifths representation in Congress for our slaves, was it not granted? When we asked and demanded the return of any fugitive from justice, or the recovery of those persons owing labor or allegiance, was it not incorporated in the Constitution, and again ratified and strengthened by the Fugitive Slave Law of 1850? But do you reply that in many instances they have violated this compact, and have not been faithful to their engagements? As individual and local communities, they may have done so; but not by the sanction of Government; for that has always been true to Southern interests. Again, gentlemen, look at another act: when we have asked that more territory should be added, that we might spread the institution of slavery, have they not yielded to our demands in giving us Louisiana, Florida and Texas, out of which four States have been carved, and ample territory for four more to be added in due time, if you by this unwise and impolitic act do not destroy this hope, and, perhaps, by it lose all, and have your last slave wrenched from you by stern military rule, as South America and Mexico were; *or by the vindictive decree of a universal emancipation, which may reasonably be expected to follow?*

But, again, gentlemen, what have we to gain by this proposed change of our relation to the General Government? We have always had the control of it, and can yet, if we remain in it, and are as united as we have been. We have had a majority of the Presidents chosen from the South; as well as the control and management of most of those chosen from the North. We have had sixty years of Southern Presidents to their twenty-four, thus controlling the Executive department. So of the Judges of the Supreme Court, we have had eighteen from the South, and but eleven from the North; although nearly four-fifths of the judicial business has arisen in the Free States, yet a majority of the Court has always been from the South. This we have required so as to guard against any interpretation of the Constitution unfavorable to us. In like manner we have been equally watchful to guard our interests in the Legislative branch of Government. In choosing the presiding Presidents (*pro tem.*) of the Senate, we have had twenty-four to their eleven. Speakers of the House, we have had twenty-three, and they twelve. While the majority of the Representatives, from their greater population, have always been from the North, yet we have so generally secured the Speaker, because he, to a great extent, shapes and controls the legislation of the country. Nor have we had less control in every other department of the General Government. Attorney-Generals we have had fourteen, while the North have had but five. Foreign ministers we have had eighty-six, and they but fifty-four. While three-fourths of the business which demands diplomatic agents abroad is clearly from the Free States, from their greater commercial interests, yet we have had the principal embassies so as to secure the world-markets for our cotton, tobacco, and sugar on the best possible terms. We have had a vast majority of the higher offices of both army and navy, while a larger proportion of the soldiers and sailors were drawn from the North. Equally so of Clerks, Auditors, and Comptrollers filling the Executive department, the records show for the last fifty years that of the three thousand thus employed, we have had more than two-thirds of the same, while we have but one-third of the white population of the Republic.

Again, look at another item, and one, be assured, in which we have a great and vital interest; it is that of revenue, or means of supporting Government. From official documents, we learn that a fraction over three-fourths of the revenue collected for the support of Government has uniformly been raised from the North.

Pause now while you can, gentlemen, and contemplate carefully and candidly these important items. Look at another necessary branch of Government, and learn from stern statistical facts how matters stand in that department. I mean the mail and Post-Office privileges that we now enjoy under the General Government as it has been for years past. The expense for the transportation of the mail in the Free States was, by the report of the Postmaster-General for the year 1860, a little over $13,000,000, while the income was $19,000,000. But in the Slave States the transportation of the mail was $14,716,000, while the revenue from the same was $8,001,026, leaving a deficit of $6,704,974, to be supplied by the North for our accommodation, and without it we must have been entirely cut off from this most essential branch of Government.

Leaving out of view, for the present, the countless millions of dollars you must expend in a war with the North; with tens of thousands of your sons and brothers slain in battle, and offered up as sacrifices upon the altar of your ambition—and for what, we ask again? Is it for the overthrow of the American Government, established by our common ancestry, cemented and built up by their sweat and blood, and founded on the broad principles of *Right, Justice* and *Humanity?* And, as such, I must declare here, as I have often done before, and which has been repeated by the greatest and wisest of statesmen and patriots in this and other lands, that it is the best and freest Government—the most equal in its rights, the most just in its decisions, the most lenient in its measures, and the most aspiring in its principles to elevate the race of men, that the sun of heaven ever shone upon. Now, for you to attempt to overthrow such a Government as this, under which we have lived for more than three-quarters of a century—in which we have gained our wealth, our standing as a nation, our domestic safety while the elements of peril are around us, with peace and tranquillity accompanied with unbounded prosperity and rights unassailed—is the height of *madness, folly,* and *wickedness,* to which I can neither lend my sanction nor my vote.

In strong contrast with the doleful narrative of the South Carolina Secessionists, are the following extracts touching the point of the security and prosperity of the Slave system:

From the speech of Hon. JAMES H. HAMMOND, U. S. Senator from South Carolina, delivered at Barnwell Court House, October 27, 1858.

From the time that the wise and good Las Casas first introduced into America the institution of African slavery—I say institution, because it is the oldest that exists, and will, I believe, survive all others that now flourish—it has had its enemies. For a long while they were chiefly men of peculiar and eccentric religious notions. Their first practical and political success arose from the convulsions of the French revolution, which lost to that empire its best colony. Next came the prohibition of the slave-trade, the excitement of the Missouri compromise in this country, and then the deliberate emancipation of the slaves in their colonies by the British Government in 1833–'34. About the time of the passage of that act the abolition agitation was revived again in this country, and Abolition societies were formed. I remember the time well, and some of you do also.

And what then was the state of opinion in the South? Washington had emancipated his slaves. Jefferson had bitterly denounced the system, and had done all that he could to destroy it. Our Clays, Marshalls, Crawfords, and many other prominent Southern men, had led off in the colonization scheme. The inevitable effect in the South was that she believed slavery to be an evil—weakness—disgraceful—nay, a sin. She shrunk from the discussion of it. She cowered under every threat. She attempted to apologize, to excuse herself under the plea—which was true—that England had forced upon her: and in fear and trembling she awaited a doom that she deemed inevitable. But a few bold spirits took the question up: they compelled the South to investigate it anew and thoroughly, and what is the result? Why it would be difficult to find now a Southern man who feels the system to be the slightest burden on his conscience; who does not, in fact, regard it as an equal advantage to the master and the slave elevating both, as wealth, strength, and power, and as one of the main pillars and controlling influences of modern civilization, and who is not now prepared to maintain it at every hazard. *Such have been for us the happy results of this abolition discussion. So far our gain has been immense from this contest, savage and malignant as it has been.* Nay, we have solved already the question of emancipation by this re-examination and exposition of the false theories of religion, philanthropy, and political economy which embarrassed our fathers in their day.

With our convictions and our strength, emancipation here is simply an impossibility to man, whether by persuasion, purchase, or coercion. The rock of Gibraltar does not stand so firm on its basis as our slave system. For a quarter of a century it has borne *the brunt of a hurricane as fierce and pitiless as ever raged.* At the North and in Europe they cried "havoc," and let loose upon us all the dogs of war. And how stands it now? Why, in this very quarter of a century *our slaves have doubled in numbers and each slave has more than doubled in value.* The very negro who as a prime laborer would have brought $400 in 1828, would now, with thirty more years upon him, sell for $800. What does all this mean? Why, that we ourselves have settled this question of emancipatoin against all the world, in theory and in practice, and the world must accept our solution.

From the carefully-prepared speech of Hon. ALEX. H. STEPHENS of Georgia, in July, 1859, after his retirement from Congress, and in review of his political course:

Nor am I of the number of those who believe that we have sustained any injury by those agitations. It is true, we were not responsible for them. We were not the aggressors. We acted on the defensive. We repelled assault, calumny, and aspersion, by argument, by reason and truth. But so far from the institution of African slavery in our section being weakened or rendered less secure by the discussion, *my deliberate judgment is, that it has been greatly strengthened and fortified*—strengthened and fortified not only to the opinions, convictions, and consciences of men, *but by the action of the Government.*

From the Charlottesville (Va.) speech of Hon. ROBERT M. T. HUNTER, U. S. Senator from Virginia, at the Breckinridge Democratic State Convention, 1860:

When I first entered the Federal councils, which was at the commencement of Mr. Van Buren's administration, the moral and political status of the slavery question was very different from what it now is. Then the Southern men themselves, with but few exceptions, admitted slavery to be a moral evil, and palliated and excused it upon the plea of necessity. Then there were few men of any party to be found in the non-slaveholding States who did not maintain both the constitutionality and expediency of the anti-slavery resolution, now generally known as the Wilmot Proviso. Had any man at that day ventured the prediction that the Missouri restriction would ever be repealed, he would have been deemed a visionary and theorist of the wildest sort. What a revolution have we not witnessed in all this! The discussion and the contest on the slavery question have gone on ever since, so as to absorb almost entirely the American mind. *In many respects the results of that discussion have not been adverse to us. Southern men no longer occupy a deprecatory attitude upon the question of negro slavery in this country.* While they by no means pretend that slavery is a good condition of things, under any circumstances and in all countries, they do maintain that, under the relations that the two races stand to each other here, it is best for both that the inferior should be subjected to the superior. The same opinion is extending even to the North, where it is entertained by many, although not generally accepted. As evidence, too, of the growing change on this subject of the public sentiment of the world, I may refer to the course of France and Great Britain in regard to the coolie and the African apprenticeship system introduced into their colonies. That they are thus running the slave-trade in another form is rarely denied. It is not to be supposed that these Governments are blind to the real nature of this coolie-trade; and the arguments by which they defend it already afford an evidence of a growing change in their opinions upon slavery in general.

From the appeal for recognition, made to Earl Russell, by WM. L. YANCEY, P. A. ROST and A. DUDLEY MANN, Rebel Commissioners, dated:

No. 15 *Half Moon Street, London*, August 14th, 1861.

It was from no fear that the Slaves would be liberated that secession took place. The very party in power has proposed to guarantee slavery forever in the States, if the South would but remain in the Union. Mr. Lincoln's message proposes no freedom to the slave, but announces subjection of his owner to the will of the Union, in other words to the will of the North. Even after the battle of Bull Run, both branches of the Congress at Washington passed resolutions that the war *is only waged in order to uphold that* (*Pro-Slavery*) *Constitution, and to enforce he laws* (many of them Pro-Slavery), and out of 172 votes in the lower House they received all but two, and in the Senate all but one vote. As the army commenced its march, the commanding-general issued an order that no slaves should be received into, or allowed to follow, the camp.

The great object of the war, therefore, as now officially announced, is not to free the slave, but to keep him in subjection to his owner, and to control his labor through the legislative channels which the Lincoln Government designs to force upon the master. The undersigned, therefore, submit with confidence that as far as the anti-slavery sentiment of England is concerned, it can have no sympathy with the North; nay, it will probably become disgusted with a canting hypocrisy which would enlist those sympathies on false pretences. The undersigned are, however, not insensible to the surmise that the Lincoln Government may, under stress of circumstances, change its policy, a policy based at present more upon a wily view of what is to be its effect in rearing up an element in the Confederate States favorable to the reconstruction of the Union than upon any honest desire to uphold a Constitution, the main provisions of which it has most shamelessly violated. But they confidently submit to your Lordship's consideration that success in producing so abrupt and violent a destruction of a system of labor which has reared up so vast a commerce between America and the great States of Europe, which, it is supposed, now gives bread to 10,000,000 of the population of those States, which, it may be safely assumed, is intimately blended with the basis of the great manufacturing and navigating prosperity that distinguishes the age, and probably not the least of the elements of this prosperity, would be visited with results disastrous to the world, as well as to the master and slave.

These Commissioners made a verbal statement to Earl Russell, May 4th, 1861, as appears from the despatch of the Earl to Lord Lyons:

Foreign Office, May 11th, 1861.

My Lord:—On Saturday last I received at my house Mr. Yancey, Mr. Mann, and Judge Rost, the three gentlemen deputed by the Southern Confederacy to obtain their recognition as an independent State.

One of these gentlemen, speaking for the others, dilated on the causes which had induced the Southern States to secede from the Northern. *The principal of these causes, he said, was not slavery, but the very high price which, for the sake of protecting the Northern manufacturers, the South were obliged to pay for the manufactured goods which they required.* One of the first acts of the Southern Congress was to reduce these duties, and to prove their sincerity he gave as an instance that Louisiana had given up altogether that protection on her sugar which she enjoyed by the legislation of the United States. As a proof of the riches of the South, he stated that of $350,000,000 of exports of produce to foreign countries, $270,000,000 were furnished by the Southern States.

I said that I could hold no official communication with the delegates of the Southern States. That, however, when the question of recognition came to be formally discussed, there were two points upon which inquiry must be made—first, whether the body seeking recognition could maintain its position as an independent State; secondly, in what manner it was proposed to maintain relations with foreign States.

After speaking at some length on the first of these points, and alluding to the news of the secession of Virginia and other intelligence favorable to their cause, these gentlemen called my attention to the article in their constitution prohibiting the slave-trade. I said that it was alleged very currently that if the Slave States found that they could not compete successfully with the cotton of other countries they would revive the slave-trade for the purpose of diminishing the cost of production. They said this was a suspicion unsupported by any proof. The fact was, that they had prohibited the slave-trade, and did not mean to revive it. They pointed to the new tariff of the United States as a proof that British manufacturers would be nearly excluded from the North, and freely admitted in the South. Other observations were made, but not of very great importance.

The delegates concluded by stating that they should remain in London for the present, in the hope that the recognition of the Southern Confederacy would not be long delayed. I am, etc., J. RUSSELL.

To all these arguments and suggestions, the Earl was deaf, and the Confederate States of America are still unrecognized

---

Seizures and Surrenders, From November 4, 1860, to March 4, 1861.

SOUTH CAROLINA.

December 27th, 1860. Fort Moultrie and Castle Pinckney, light-house tender and schooner William Aiken, surrendered by Captain Coste of South Carolina.

31st. U. S. Arsenal, Post-Office, and Custom-House in Charleston; arsenal containing seventy thousand stand of arms, and other stores.

January 9th, 1861. Steamer Marion at Charleston. Star of the West fired upon.

April 13th. Fort Sumter surrendered.

GEORGIA.

January 2d, 1861. Forts Pulaski and Jackson and United States Arsenal, by State troops, under advice from Georgia members of Congress.

24th. Arsenal at Augusta, containing two 12-pound howitzers, two cannon, 22,000 muskets and rifles, and large stores of powder, balls, grape, etc. U. S. steamer Ida seized.

February 8th. Brig W. R. Kibby, and four other New York vessels, estimated at $50,000, seized by order of the Governor of Georgia, to be held until certain guns on board the Monticello, seized by the police of New York, shall be delivered to the agents of Georgia. Collector of the port of Savannah ordered by the Governor of Georgia to retain all moneys from customs in his possession, and make no payment on account of the Federal Government.

21st. Three New York vessels seized at Savannah by order of the Governor.

FLORIDA.

January 12th, 1861. The Navy Yard, and Forts Barrancas and McRae, taken by Florida and Alabama troops. Jan. 7, Fort Marion and the arsenal at St. Augustine. The Chattahoochee arsenal taken, containing 500,000 rounds of musket cartridges, 300,000 rifle cartridges, and 50,000 pounds of gunpowder, but no arms. Coast survey schooner F. W. Dana seized.

ALABAMA.

January 4th, 1861. Fort Morgan seized by Mobile troops, containing about 5,000 shot and shell. Also Mt. Vernon Arsenal, containing 20,000 stand of arms, 1,500 barrels of powder, (150,000 pounds), some pieces of cannon, and large amount of munitions of war. Captain Morrison, of the revenue cutter Lewis Cass, surrendered his vessel on the demand of the collector of Mobile, and subsequently took command of it under authority of the State.

MISSISSIPPI.

January 20th, 1861. Fort at Ship Island seized, and the U. S. Hospital on the Mississippi river.

LOUISIANA.

January 11th, 1861. Forts Jackson and St. Philip, on the Mississippi, and Fort Pike, on Lake Pontchartrain, and the arsenal at Baton Rouge, seized by State troops. The arsenal contained 50,000 small arms, 4 howitzers, 20 heavy pieces of ordnance, 2 batteries, 300 barrels of powder, etc. Also, U. S. hospital at New Orleans.

12th. The entire armament of the revenue cutter Lewis Cass stored at Bellville Iron Works.

28th. All quartermasters' and commissary stores in possession of U. S. officials. Revenue cutter McClelland surrendered by Captain Breshwood.

February 1st. Mint and Custom-House containing $599,303 in gold and silver.

TEXAS.

January 10th, 1861. U. S. guns and stores seized on steamship Texas by Galveston troops.

February 20th. Forts Chadbourne and Belknap seized by Texans, with all the property of the Overland Mail Company.

25th. General Twiggs surrendered all Government stores in his command, after hearing that he had been superseded in command by Colonel Waite. The stores estimated at $1,300,000 in value, consisting of $55,000 in specie, 35,000 stand of arms, 26 pieces of mounted artillery, 44 dismounted, ammunition, horses, wagons, forage, etc.

March 2d. Revenue cutter Dodge seized by Texas authorities, in Galveston bay.

6th. Fort Brown surrendered.

ARKANSAS.

February 8th, 1861. Arsenal at Litttle Rock seized, containing 9,000 small arms, 40 cannon, and quantities of ammunition, etc.

NORTH CAROLINA.

January 8th, 1861. Forts Johnson and Caswell seized by the State militia. Governor Ellis ordered them to be surrendered to the United States authorities, with an intimation to the President that if any attempt should be made to reinforce them, they would be again seized and held by the State.

—

Governor Letcher of Virginia, in his annual message of December 31st, 1861, thus alluded to Fortress Monroe:

"It is to be regretted that Fortress Monroe is not in our possession; that it was not as easily captured as the Navy Yard and Harper's Ferry. *As far back as the 8th of January last,* I consulted with a gentleman whose position enabled him to know the strength of that fortress, and whose experience in military matters enabled him to form an opinion as to the number of men that would be required to capture it. He represented it to be one of the strongest fortifications in the world, and expressed his doubts whether it could be taken, unless assailed by water as well as by land, and simultaneously. He stated, emphatically and distinctly, that with the force then in the fortress, it would be useless to attempt its capture without a large force thoroughly equipped and well appointed. At no time previous to the secession of Virginia had we a military organization sufficient to justify an attempt to take it, and events since that occurrence demonstrate very clearly that with our military organization since, and now existing, it has not been deemed prudent to make the attempt."

Mr. Buchanan's Cabinet.

December 12th, 1860. Lewis Cass resigned as Secretary of State, because the President declined to reinforce the forts in Charleston harbor. December 17th. Jeremiah S. Black was appointed his successor.

December 10th. Howell Cobb resigned as Secretary of the Treasury—"his duty to Georgia requiring it." December 12th. Philip F. Thomas appointed his successor, and resigned, January 11th, 1861, because differing from the President and a majority of the cabinet, "in the measures which have been adopted in reference to the recent condition of things in South Carolina," especially "touching the authority, under existing laws, to enforce the collection of the customs at the port of Charleston." January 11th, 1861. John A. Dix appointed his successor.

29th. John B. Floyd resigned as Secretary of War, because, after the transfer of Major Anderson's command from Fort Moultrie to Fort Sumter, the President declined "to withdraw the garrison from the harbor of Charleston altogether."

December 31st. Joseph Holt, Postmaster-General, was entrusted with the temporary charge of the War Department, and January 18th, 1861, was appointed Secretary of War.

January 8th, 1861. Jacob Thompson resigned as Secretary of the Interior, because "additional troops, he had heard, have been ordered to Charleston" in the Star of the West.

December 17th, 1860. Jeremiah S. Black resigned as Attorney-General, and Edwin M. Stanton, December 20th, was appointed his successor.

January 18th, 1861. Joseph Holt resigned as Postmaster-General, and Horatio King, February 12th, 1861, was appointed his successor.

Correspondence between President Buchanan and the "Commissioners" of South Carolina.

The "Commissioners" to the President.

Washington, Dec. 28th, 1860.

SIR: We have the honor to transmit to you a copy of the full powers from the Convention of the people of South Carolina, under which we are "authorized and empowered to treat with the Government of the United States for the delivery of the forts, magazines, lighthouses, and other real estate, with their appurtenances, in the limits of South Carolina; and also for an apportionment of the public debt, and for a division of all other property held by the Government of the United States as agent of the Confederated States of which South Carolina was recently a member, and generally to negotiate as to all other measures and arrangements proper to be made and adopted in the existing relation of the parties, and for the continuance of peace and amity between this Commonwealth and the Government at Washington."

In the execution of this trust, it is our duty to furnish you, as we now do, with an official copy of the Ordinance of Secession by which the State of South Carolina has resumed the powers she delegated to the Government of the United States, and has declared her perfect sovereignty and independence.

It would also have been our duty to have informed you that we were ready to negotiate with you upon all such questions as are necessarily raised by the adoption of this ordinance, and that we were prepared to enter upon this negotiation with the earnest desire to avoid all unnecessary and hostile collision, and so to inaugurate our new relations as to secure mutual respect, general advantage, and a future of good-will and harmony beneficial to all the parties concerned. But the events of the last twenty-four hours render such an assurance impossible.

We came here the representatives of an authority which could, at any time within the past sixty days, have taken possession of the forts in Charleston harbor, but which, upon pledges given in a manner that we cannot doubt, determined to trust to your honor rather than to its own power. Since our arrival here, an officer of the United States, acting, as we are assured, not only without, but against your orders, has dismantled one fort and occupied another; thus altering, to a most important extent, the condition of affairs under which we came.

Until the circumstances are explained in a manner which relieves us of all doubt as to the spirit in which these negotiations shall be conducted, we are forced to suspend all discussion as to any arrangements by which our mutual interests might be amicably adjusted.

And, in conclusion, we would urge upon you the immediate withdrawal of the troops from the harbor of Charleston. Under present circumstances they are a standing menace which renders negotiation impossible, and, as our recent experience shows, threatens speedily to bring to a bloody issue questions which ought to be settled with temperance and judgment.

We have the honor to be, very respectfully, your obedient servants,

R. W. BARNWELL,
J. H. ADAMS,
JAMES L. ORR,
Commissioners.

To the President of the United States.

The President to the "Commissioners."

Washington, December 30th, 1860.

GENTLEMEN: I have had the honor to receive your communication of the 28th inst., together with a copy of "your full powers from the Convention of the people of South Carolina," authorizing you to treat with the Government of the United States on various important subjects therein mentioned, and also a copy of the Ordinance, bearing date on the 20th inst., declaring that "the Union now subsisting between South Carolina and other States, under the name of the United States of America, is hereby dissolved."

In answer to this communication, I have to say that my position as President of the United States was clearly defined in the message to Congress on the 3d inst. In that I stated that "apart from the execution of the laws, so far as this may be practicable, the Executive has no authority to decide what shall be the relations between the Federal Government and South Carolina. He has been invested with no such discretion. He possesses no power to change the relations heretofore existing between them, much less to acknowledge the independence of that State. This would be to invest a mere executive officer with the power of recognizing the dissolution of the Confederacy among our thirty-three sovereign States. It bears no resemblance to the recognition of a foreign *de facto* Government, involving no such responsibility. Any attempt to do this would, on his part, be a naked act of usurpation. It is, therefore, my duty to submit to Congress the whole question in all its bearings."

Such is my opinion still. I could, therefore, meet you only as private gentlemen of the highest character, and was entirely willing to communicate to Congress any proposition you might have to make to that body upon the subject. Of this you were well aware. It was my earnest desire that such a disposition might be made of the whole subject by Congress, who alone possess the power, as to prevent the inauguration of a civil war between the parties in regard to the possession of the Federal forts in the harbor of Charleston, and I therefore deeply regret that, in your opinion, "the events of the last twenty-four hours render this impossible."

In conclusion, you urge upon me the "immediate withdrawal of the troops from the harbor of Charleston," stating that "under present circumstances they are a standing menace which renders negotiation impossible, and, as our recent experience shows, threatens speedily to bring to a bloody issue questions which ought to be settled with temperance and judgment."

The reason for this change in your position is, that since your arrival in Washington, "an officer of the United States, acting, as we, (you) are assured, not only without, but against your (my) orders, has dismantled one fort and occupied another—thus altering to a most important extent the condition of affairs under which we (you) came." You also allege that you came here "the representatives of an authority which could, at any time within the past sixty days, have taken possession of the forts in Charleston harbor, but which, upon pledges given in a manner that we (you) cannot doubt, determined to trust to your (my) honor rather than to its power."

This brings me to a consideration of the nature of those alleged pledges, and in what manner they have been observed.

In my message of the 3d of December last, I stated, in regard to the property of the United States in South Carolina, that it "has been purchased for a fair equivalent, by the consent of the Legislature of the State," for the erection of forts, magazines, arsenals, &c., and over these the authority "to exercise exclusive legislation" has been expressly granted by the Constitution to Congress. It is not believed that any attempt will be made to expel the United States from this property by force; but if in this I should prove to be mistaken, the officer in command of the forts has received orders to act strictly on the defensive. In such a contingency, the responsibility for consequences would rightfully rest upon the heads of the assailants.

This being the condition of the parties, on Saturday, 8th December, four of the Representatives from South Carolina called upon me and requested an interview. We had an earnest conversation on the subject of these forts, and the best means of preventing a collision between the parties, for the purpose of sparing the effusion of blood. I suggested, for prudential reasons, that it would be best to put in writing what they said to me verbally. They did so accordingly, and on Monday morning, the 10th instant, three of them presented to me a paper signed by all the Representatives from South Carolina, with a single exception, of which the following is a copy:

Washington, December 9th, 1860.

"*To His Excellency James Buchanan, President of the United States:*

"In compliance with our statement to you yesterday, we now express to you our strong convictions that neither the constituted authorities, nor any body of the people of the State of South Carolina, will either attack or molest the United States forts in the harbor of Charleston, previously to the action of the Convention, and we hope and believe not until an offer has been made through an accredited representative to negotiate for an amicable arrangement of all matters between the State and the Federal Government; provided that no reinforcements shall be sent into those forts and their relative military status shall remain as at present.

John McQueen,
M. L. Bonham,
W. W. Boyce,
Lawrence M. Keitt."

And here I must, in justice to myself, remark that at the time the paper was presented to me I objected to the word "provided," as it might be construed into an agreement on my part, which I never would make. They said that nothing was farther from their intention; they did not so understand it, and I should not so consider it. It is evident they could enter into no reciprocal agreement with me on the subject. They did not profess to have the authority to do this, and were acting in their individual character. I considered it as nothing more, in effect, than the promise of highly honorable gentlemen to exert their influence for the purpose expressed. The event has proven that they have faithfully kept this promise, although I have never since received a line from any one of them nor from any member of the Convention on the subject. It is well known that it was my determination, and this I freely expressed, not to reinforce the forts in the harbor, and thus produce a collision, until they had been actually attacked or until I had certain evidence that they were about to be attacked. This paper I received most cordially, and considered it as a happy omen that peace might be still preserved, and that time might be thus given for reflection. This is the whole foundation for the alleged pledge.

But I acted in the same manner as I would have done had I entered into a positive and formal agreement with parties capable of contracting, although such an agreement would have been on my part, from the nature of my official duties, impossible. The world knows that I have never sent any reinforcements to the forts in Charleston harbor, and I have certainly never authorized any change to be made "in their relative military status." Bearing upon this subject, I refer you to an order issued by the Secretary of War, on the 11th instant, to Major Anderson, but not brought to my notice until the 21st instant. It is as follows:

"*Memorandum of verbal instructions to Major Anderson, First Artillery, commanding Fort Moultrie, South Carolina.*

"You are aware of the great anxiety of the Secretary of War that a collision of the troops with the people of this State shall be avoided, and of his studied determination to pursue a course with reference to the force and forts in this harbor which shall guard against such a collision. He has therefore carefully abstained from increasing the force at this point, or taking any measure which might add to the present excited state of the public mind, or which would throw any doubt on the confidence he feels that South Carolina will not attempt by violence to obtain possession of the public works, or interfere with their occupancy.

"But, as the counsel and acts of rash and impulsive persons may possibly disappoint these expectations of the Government, he deems it proper that you should be prepared with instructions to meet so unhappy a contingency. He has, therefore, directed me verbally to give you such instructions.

"You are carefully to avoid every act which would needlessly tend to provoke aggression, and for that reason you are not, without necessity, to take up any position which could be construed into the assumption of a hostile attitude; but you are to hold possession of the forts in this harbor, and, if attacked, you are to defend yourself to the last extremity. The smallness of your force will not permit you, perhaps, to occupy more than one of the three forts; but an attack on or attempt to take possession of either of them will be regarded as an act of hostility, and you may then put your command into either of them which you may deem most proper to increase its power of resistance. You are also authorized to take similar steps whenever you have tangible evidence of a design to proceed to a hostile act. D. P. BUTLER,

"Assistant Adjutant-General.

"*Fort Moultrie,* (*S. C.*) Dec. 11th, 1860.

"This is in conformity to my instructions to Major Buell.

"JOHN B. FLOYD, Secretary of War."

These were the last instructions transmitted to Major Anderson before his removal to Fort Sumter, with a single exception, in regard to a particular which does not in any degree affect the present question.

Under these circumstances it is clear that Major Anderson acted upon his own responsibility, and without authority,—unless, indeed, he "had tangible evidence of a design to proceed to a hostile act" on the part of the authorities of South Carolina, which has not yet been alleged. Still he is a brave and honorable officer, and justice requires that he should not be condemned without a fair hearing.

Be this as it may, when I learned that Major Anderson had left Fort Moultrie and proceeded to Fort Sumter, my first promptings were to command him to return to his former position, and there to await the contingencies presented in his instructions. This could only have been done with any degree of safety to the command by the concurrence of the South Carolina authorities. But before any step could possibly have been taken in this direction, we received information that the "Palmetto flag floated out to the breeze at Castle Pinckney, and a large military force went over last night (the 27th) to Fort Moultrie." Thus the authorities of South Carolina, without waiting or asking for any explanations, and doubtless believing, as you have expressed it, that the officer had acted not only without but against my orders, on the very next day after the night when the removal was made, seized, by a military force, two of the three Federal forts in the harbor of Charleston, and have covered them under their own flag instead of that of the United States.

At this gloomy period of our history, startling events succeed each other rapidly. On the very day, the 27th instant, that possession of these two forts was taken, the Palmetto flag was raised over the Federal custom-house and post-office in Charleston; and on the same day every officer of the customs—Collector, Naval Officer, Surveyor and Appraiser—resigned their offices. And this, although it was well-known from the language of my message that as an executive officer I felt myself bound to collect the revenue at the port of Charleston under the existing laws. In the harbor of Charleston we now find three forts confronting each other, over all of which the Federal flag floated four days ago; but now, over two of them this flag has been supplanted, and the Palmetto flag has been substituted in its stead.

It is under these circumstances that I am urged immediately to withdraw the troops from the harbor of Charleston, and I am informed that without this negotiation is impossible. This I cannot do; this I will not do. Such an idea was never thought of by me in any possible contingency. No such allusion had been made in any communication between myself and any human being.

But the inference is that I am bound to withdraw the troops from the only fort remaining in the possession of the United States in the harbor of Charleston, because the officer there in command of all the forts thought proper, without instructions, to change his position from one of them to another.

At this point of writing, I have received information by telegraph from Capt. Humphreys, in command of the arsenal at Charleston, that "it has to-day (Sunday, the 30th) been taken by force of arms." It is estimated that the munitions of war belonging to the United States in this arsenal are worth half a million of dollars.

Comment is needless. After this information, I have only to add that, whilst it is my duty to defend Fort Sumter as a portion of the public property of the United States against hostile attacks, from whatever quarter they may come, by such means as I may possess for this purpose, I do not perceive how such a defence can be construed into a menace against the city of Charleston.

With great personal regard, I remain yours, very respectfully,

JAMES BUCHANAN.

To Honorable Robert W. Barnwell, James H. Adams, James L. Orr.

January 1st, 1861. The "Commissioners" replied at length, alleging, with reference to the President's declaration, that he could not withdraw the troops from Charleston harbor, that he had in conversation left a different impression upon their minds and the minds of others who had approached him on that subject, and generally reflecting upon the motives of the President. This paper, Mr. BUCHANAN "declined to receive." In the State Convention of South Carolina, December 19th, 1860, upon a proposition of Mr. MAGRATH to appoint a committee to consider the relations of the State to the forts, Mr. W. PORCHER MILES alluded to the interview between the President and the South Carolina representatives in Congress relative to the forts, and "expressed his solemn opinion that the President was not going to attempt to reinforce those forts." Subsequently Mr. MILES and Mr. KEITT made to the Convention a written statement sustaining the offensive allegations of the Commissioners as to the President's good faith to them. These papers are too long for insertion, and have but limited importance.

Further demand of South Carolina for Fort Sumter.

January 11th, 1861. F. W. Pickens, Governor of South Carolina, demanded of Major Anderson the surrender of Fort Sumter to the authorities of the State of South Carolina, to prevent a "waste of life." Same day Major Anderson replied, announcing his refusal, but suggesting that if at any time prior to a resort to arms, the Governor should deem fit to "refer this matter to Washington," he could with much pleasure depute one of his officers to accompany the Governor's messenger. Same day, Governor Pickens deputed Hon. Isaac W. Hayne, Attorney-General of the State, to proceed to Washington, and demand from the President the delivery of Fort Sumter to the constituted authorities of South Carolina, adding:

"The demand I have made of Major Anderson, and which I now make of you, is suggested because of my earnest desire to avoid the bloodshed which a persistence in your attempt to retain possession of that fort will cause, and which will be unavailing to secure you that possession, but induce a calamity most deeply to be deplored. If consequences so unhappy shall ensue, I will secure for this State, in the demand which I now make, the satisfaction of having exhausted every attempt to avoid it.

"In relation to the public property of the United States within Fort Sumter the Hon. I. W. HAYNE, who will hand you this communication, is authorized to give you the pledge of the State that the valuation of such property will be accounted for by this State, upon the adjustment of its relations with the United States, of which it was a part.

"F. W. PICKENS.

"To the President of the United States."

Upon Colonel Hayne's arrival, ten U. S. Senators "from States which have already seceded from the United States, or will have done so before the first of February next,"* requested that he should not present his demand until these States should have formed a Confederacy. Meanwhile, they offered to propose to the President, that Fort Sumter should not be reinforced in the meantime. To this Colonel Hayne consented, and the Senators proposed this arrangement, which the President declined through Hon. JOSEPH HOLT, Secretary of War, as follows:

War Department, January 22d, 1861.

To the Honorable Benjamin Fitzpatrick, S. R. Mallory and John Slidell.

GENTLEMEN: The President has received your communication of the 19th instant, with the copy of a correspondence between yourselves and others, "representing States which have already seceded from the United States, or will have done so before the first of February next," and Colonel Isaac W. Hayne, of South Carolina, in behalf of the Government of that State, in relation to Fort Sumter; and you ask the President "to take into consideration the subject of that correspondence." With this request he has complied, and has directed me to communicate his answer.

In your letter to Col. Hayne of the 15th instant, you propose to him to defer the delivery of a message from the Governor of South Carolina to the President, with which he has been entrusted for a few days, or until the President and Col. Hayne shall have considered the suggestions which you submit. It is unnecessary to refer specially to these suggestions, because the letter addressed to you by Col. Hayne, of the 17th instant, presents a clear and specific answer to them. In this he says: "I am not clothed with power to make the arrangement you suggest; but provided you can

* Being:

Louis T. Wigfall, John Hemphill, } Texas.
D. L. Yulee, S. R. Mallory, } Florida.
Jefferson Davis, Mississippi,
C. C. Clay, Jr., Benjamin Fitzpatrick } Ala.
A. Iverson, Georgia.
John Slidell, J. P. Benjamin, } La.

get assurances, with which you are entirely satisfied, that no reinforcements will be sent to Fort Sumter in the interval, and that the public peace will not be disturbed by any act of hostility towards South Carolina, I will refer your communication to the authorities of South Carolina, and, withholding the communication with which I am at present charged, will await further instructions."

From the beginning of the present unhappy troubles, the President has endeavored to perform his Executive duties in such a manner as to preserve the peace of the country and to prevent bloodshed. This is still his fixed purpose. You, therefore, do him no more than justice in stating that you have assurances (from his public messages, I presume) that "notwithstanding the circumstances under which Major Anderson left Fort Moultrie and entered Fort Sumter with the forces under his command, it was not taken and is not held with any hostile or unfriendly purpose towards your State, but merely as property of the United States, which the President deems it his duty to protect and preserve," you have correctly stated what the President deems to be his duty. His whole object now is and has been, to act strictly on the defensive, and to authorize no movement against the people of South Carolina, unless clearly justified by a hostile movement on their part. He could not have given a better proof of his desire to prevent the effusion of blood than by forbearing to resort to the use of force under the strong provocation of an attack (happily without a fatal result) on an unarmed vessel bearing the flag of the United States.

I am happy to observe that, in your letter to Col. Hayne, you express the opinion that it is "especially due from South Carolina to our States, to say nothing of other slaveholding States, that she should, as far as she can consistently with her honor, avoid initiating hostilities between her and the United States, or any other Power." To initiate such hositilities against Fort Sumter would, beyond question, be an act of war against the United States.

In regard to the proposition of Col. Hayne, "that no reinforcements will be sent to Fort Sumter in the interval, and that the public peace will not be disturbed by any act of hostility towards South Carolina," it is impossible for me to give you any such assurances. The President has no authority to enter into such an agreement or understanding. As an executive officer, he is simply bound to protect the public property, so far as this may be practicable; and it would be a manifest violation of his duty to place himself under engagements that he would not perform this duty either for an indefinite or a limited period. At the present moment, it is not deemed necessary to reinforce Major Anderson, because he makes no such request, and feels quite secure in his position. Should his safety, however, require reinforcements, every effort will be made to supply them.

In regard to an assurance from the President "that the public peace will not be disturbed by any act of hostility towards South Carolina," the answer will readily occur to yourselves. To Congress, and to Congress alone, belongs the power to make war, and it would be an act of usurpation for the Executive to give any assurance that Congress would not exercise this power, however strongly it may be convinced that no such intention exists.

I am glad to be assured from the letter of Col. Hayne, that "Major Anderson and his command do now obtain all necessary supplies, including fresh meat and vegetables, and, I believe, fuel and water, from the city of Charleston, and do now enjoy communication, by post and special messenger, with the President, and will continue to do so, certainly until the door to negotiation has been closed." I trust that these facilities may still be afforded to Major Anderson. This is as it should be. Major Anderson is not menacing Charleston; and I am convinced that the happiest result which can be attained is, that he and the authorities of South Carolina shall remain on their present amicable footing, neither party being bound by any obligation whatever except the high Christian and moral duty to keep the peace and to avoid all causes of mutual irritation.

Very respectfully,
Your obedient servant,
J. Holt,
Secretary of War.

January 31st, 1861. Col. Hayne, having received additional instructions from Governor Pickens, reciting the correspondence between the President and the ten Senators, and expressing his dissatisfaction with the terms of the latter's reply, demanded possession of Fort Sumter "as the legal officer of the State, asserting its undoubted right of eminent domain."

February 6th. The President replied, through Secretary Holt, asserting the title of the United States to Fort Sumter as complete and incontrovertible, and declining the demand, as, "whatever may be the claim of South Carolina to this fort, he has no constitutional power to cede or surrender it." The closing paragraph of the President's reply is as follows:

"If the announcement so repeatedly made of the President's pacific purpose in continuing the occupation of Fort Sumter until the question shall be settled by competent authority, has failed to impress the Government of South Carolina, the forbearing conduct of the Administration for the last few months should be received as conclusive evidence of his sincerity. And if this forbearance, in view of the circumstances which have so severely tried it, be not accepted as a satisfactory pledge of the peaceful policy of this Administration towards South Carolina, then it may be safely affirmed that neither language nor conduct can possibly furnish one. If, with all the multiplied proofs which exist of the President's anxiety for peace, and of the earnestness with which he has pursued it, the authorities of that State shall assault Fort Sumter, and peril the lives of the handful of brave and loyal men shut up within its walls, and thus plunge our common country into the horrors of civil war, then upon them and those they represent, must rest the responsibility."

"Commissioner from Alabama."

February 1st, 1861. Hon. C. C. CLAY, Jr., Senator from Alabama, addressed the President, informing him that Hon. THOMAS J. JUDGE of Alabama had arrived, "duly commissioned to negotiate with the Government of the United States in reference to the forts, arsenals and custom-houses in that State, and the debt of the United States," and desiring when he might have an audience "to present his credentials and enter upon the proposed negotiations."

2d. The PRESIDENT replied, stating that he would be happy to receive Mr. JUDGE as a "distinguished citizen of Alabama," and that, in his judgment, he had no power to recognize him in the character ascribed to him. Mr. CLAY, under date of February 5th, volunteered to give the President his views of men and things, in an excited epistle, which scarcely deserves preservation, either for intrinsic merit of style or thought for historical value.

Transfer of U. S. Arms South in 1859-60.

REPORT (Abstract of) made by Mr. B. Stanton, from the Committee on Military Affairs, in House of Representatives, Feb. 18th, 1861:

The Committee on Military Affairs, to whom was referred the resolution of the House of Representatives of 31st of December last, instructing said committee to inquire and report to the House, how, to whom, and at what price, the public arms distributed since the 1st day of January, A. D. 1860, have been disposed of; and also into the condition of the forts, arsenals, dock-yards, etc., etc., submit the following report:

That it appears from the papers herewith submitted, that Mr. Floyd, the late Secretary of War, by the authority or under color of the law of March 3d, 1825, authorizing the Secretary of War to sell any arms, ammunition, or other military stores which should be found unsuitable for the public service, sold to sundry persons and States 31,610 flint-lock muskets, altered to percussion, at $2.50 each, between the 1st day of January, A. D. 1860, and the 1st day of January, A. D. 1861. It will be seen from the testimony of Colonel Craig and Captain Maynadier, that they differ as to whether the arms so sold had been found, "upon proper inspection, to be unsuitable for the public service."

Whilst the Committee do not deem it important to decide this question, they say, that in their judgment it would require a very liberal construction of the law to bring these sales within its provisions.

It also appears that on the 21st day of November last, Mr. Belknap made application to the Secretary of War for the purchase of from one to two hundred and fifty thousand United States muskets, flint-locks and altered to percussion, at $2.15 each; but the Secretary alleges that the acceptance was made under a misapprehension of the price bid, he supposing it was $2.50 each, instead of $2.15.

Mr. Belknap denies all knowledge of any mistake or misapprehension, and insists upon the performance of his contract.

The present Secretary refuses to recognize the contract, and the muskets have not been delivered to Mr. Belknap.

Mr. Belknap testifies that the muskets were intended for the Sardinian government.

It will appear by the papers herewith submitted, that on the 29th of December, 1859, the Secretary of War ordered the transfer of 65,000 percussion muskets, 40,000 muskets altered to percussion, and 10,000 percussion rifles, from the Springfield Armory and the Watertown and Watervliet Arsenals, to the Arsenals at Fayetteville, N. C., Charleston, S. C., Augusta, Ga., Mount Vernon, Ala., and Baton Rouge, La., and that these arms were distributed during the spring of 1860 as follows:

	Percussion muskets.	Altered muskets.	Rifles.
To Charleston Arsenal,	9,280	5,720	2,000
To North Carolina Arsenal,	15,480	9,520	2,000
To Augusta Arsenal,	12,380	7,620	2,000
To Mount Vernon Arsenal,	9,280	5,720	2,000
To Baton Rouge Arsenal,	18,580	11,420	2,000
	65,000	40,000	10,000

All of these arms, except those sent to the North Carolina Arsenal,* have been seized by the authorities of the several States of South Carolina, Alabama, Louisiana and Georgia, and are no longer in possession of the United States.

It will appear by the testimony herewith presented, that on the 20th of October last the Secretary of War ordered forty columbiads and four thirty-two pounders to be sent from the Arsenal at Pittsburg to the fort on Ship Island, on the coast of Mississippi, then in an unfinished condition, and seventy columbiads and seven thirty-two pounders to be sent from the same Arsenal to the fort at Galveston, in Texas, the building of which had scarcely been commenced.

This order was given by the Secretary of War, without any report from the Engineer department showing that said works were

* These were afterwards seized

ready for their armament, or that the guns were needed at either of said points.

It will be seen by the testimony of Captain Wright, of the Engineer department, that the fort at Galveston cannot be ready for its entire armament in less than about five years, nor for any part of it in less than two; and that the fort at Ship Island will require an appropriation of $85,000 and one year's time before it can be ready for any part of its armament. This last named fort has been taken possession of by the State authorities of Mississippi.

The order of the late Secretary of War (Floyd) was countermanded by the present Secretary (Holt) before it had been fully executed by the shipment of said guns from Pittsburg.*

It will be seen by a communication from the Ordnance office of the 21st of January last, that by the last returns there were remaining in the United States arsenals and armories the following small arms, viz:

Percussion muskets and muskets altered to percussion of calibre 69,	499,554
Percussion rifles, calibre 54	42,011
Total	541,565

Of these 60,878 were deposited in the arsenals of South Carolina, Alabama, and Louisiana, and are in the possession of the authorities of those States, reducing the number in possession of the United States to 480,687.

Since the date of said communication, the following additional forts and military posts have been taken possession of by parties acting under the authority of the States in which they are respectively situated, viz:

Fort Moultrie, South Carolina.
Fort Morgan, Alabama.
Baton Rouge Barracks, Louisiana.
Fort Jackson, Louisiana.
Fort St. Philip, "
Fort Pike, Louisiana.
Oglethorpe Barracks, Georgia.

And the department has been unofficially advised that the arsenal at Chattahoochee, Forts McRea and Barrancas, and Barrancas Barracks, have been seized by the authorities of Florida.

To what further extent the small arms in possession of the United States may have been reduced by these figures, your committee have not been advised.

The whole number of the sea-board forts in the United States is fifty-seven; their appropriate garrison in war would require 26,420 men; their actual garrison at this time is 1,334 men, 1,308 of whom are in the forts at Governor's Island, New York; Fort McHenry, Maryland; Fort Monroe, Virginia, and at Alcatraz Island, California, in the harbor of San Francisco.

From the facts elicited, it is certain that the regular military force of the United States is wholly inadequate to the protection of the forts, arsenals, dock-yards, and other property of the United States in the present disturbed condition of the country. The regular army numbers only 18,000 men when recruited to its maximum strength, and the whole of this force is required for the protection of the border settlements against Indian depredations. Unless it is the intention of Congress that the forts, arsenals, dock-yards, and other public property, shall be exposed to capture and spoliation, the President must be armed with additional force for their protection.

In the opinion of the Committee the law of February 28th, 1795, confers upon the President ample power to call out the militia to execute the laws and protect the public property. But as the late Attorney-General has given a different opinion, the Committee, to remove all doubt upon the subject, report the accompanying bill, etc.

OTHER ITEMS.

Statement of Arms distributed by Sale since the first of January, 1860, to whom sold, and the place whence sold.

To whom sold.	*No.*	1860. *Date of sale.*	*Arsenals Where sold.*
J. W. Zacharie & Co.	4,000	Feb. 3	St. Louis.
James T. Ames	1,000	Mar. 14	New York.
Captain G. Barry	80	June 11	St. Louis.
W. C. N. Swift	400	Aug. 31	Springfield.
Do	80	Nov. 13	Do.
State of Alabama	1,000	Sep. 27	Baton Rouge.
Do	2,500	Nov. 14	Do.
State of Virginia	5,000	Nov. 6	Washington.
Phillips county, Ark	50	Nov. 16	St. Louis.
G. B. Lamar	10,000	Nov. 24	Watervliet.

The arms were all flint-lock muskets altered to percussion, and were all sold at $2.50 each, except those purchased by Captain G. Barry and by the Phillips county volunteers, for which $2 each were paid.

The Mobile *Advertiser* says: "During the past year 135,430 muskets have been quietly transferred from the Northern arsenal at Springfield alone, to those in the Southern States. We are much obliged to Secretary Floyd for the foresight he has thus displayed in disarming the North and *equipping the South for this emergency.* There is no telling the quantity of arms and munitions which were sent South from other Northern arsenals. There is no doubt but that every man in the South who can carry a gun can now be supplied from private or public sources. The Springfield contribution alone would arm all the militiamen of Alabama and Mississippi."

General Scott, in his letter of December 2d, 1862, on the early history of the Rebellion, states that "Rhode Island, Delaware and Texas had not drawn, at the end of 1860, their annual quotas of arms for that year, and Massachusetts, Tennessee, and

* The attempted removal of these heavy guns from Allegheny Arsenal, late in December, 1860, created intense excitement. A monster mass meeting assembled at the call of the Mayor of the city, and citizens of all parties aided in the effort to prevent the shipment. Through the interposition of Hon. J. K. Moorhead, Hon. R. McKnight, Judge Shaler, Judge Wilkins, Judge Shannon, and others, inquiry was instituted, and a revocation of the order obtained. The Secessionists in Congress bitterly complained of the "mob law" which thus interfered with the routine of governmental affairs.

Kentucky only in part; Virginia, South Carolina, Georgia, Florida, Alabama, Louisiana, Mississippi and Kansas were. by order of the Secretary of War, supplied with their quotas for 1861 in advance, and Pennsylvania and Maryland in part."

This advance of arms to eight Southern States is in addition to the transfer, about the same time, of 115,000 muskets to Southern arsenals, as per Mr. Stanton's report.

Governor Letcher of Virginia, in his Message of December, 1861, says, that for some time prior to secession, he had been engaged in purchasing arms, ammunition, etc.; among which were 13 Parrott rifled cannon, and 5,000 muskets. He desired to buy from the United States Government 10,000 more, when buying the 5,000, but he says "the authorities declined to sell them to us, although five times the number were then in the arsenal at Washington." Had Jefferson Davis' bill relative to the purchase of arms become a law, the result might have been different.

Sale of Arms to States.

January 9th, 1860. Mr. Jefferson Davis of Mississippi introduced to the Senate a bill "to authorize the sale of public arms to the several States and Territories, and to regulate the appointment of Superintendents of the National Armories."

18th. He reported it from the Military Committee without amendment.

February 21st. Mr. Davis. I should like the Senate to take up a little bill which I hope will excite no discussion. It is the bill to authorize the States to purchase arms from the National Armories. *There are a number of volunteer companies wanting to purchase arms*, but the States have not a sufficient supply. I move to take up the bill.

The motion was agreed to.

The bill is as follows:—

Section 1. That the Secretary of War be, and he is hereby authorized to issue to any State or Territory of the United States, on application of the Governor thereof, arms made at the United States Armories, to such extent as may be spared from the public supplies without injury or inconvenience to the service of the General Government, upon payment therefor, in each case, of an amount sufficient to replace, by fabrication at the national armories, the arms so issued.

Section 2. That so much of the act approved August 5th, eighteen hundred and fifty-four, as authorizes the appointment of a civilian as superintendent of each of the national armories be, and the same is hereby repealed, and that the superintendents of these armories shall hereafter be selected from officers of the ordnance corps.

After a brief discussion, it was made a special order for February 23d.

23d. Its consideration was resumed. Mr. Fessenden calling for an explanation of the reasons upon which the first section is founded,

Mr. Davis said: "It is, that the volunteer companies of the States desiring arms, may purchase them of the Government manufacture. It is a long settled policy—and I think a wise one on the part of the United States—to furnish arms, of the approved pattern for the public service, to the militia. The appropriation which is made to supply the militia with arms, has not been found sufficient. There are constant applications for arms beyond the quota. The Secretary of War has no authority to issue them beyond the fixed allowance to each State, being its *pro rata* share of the arms which may be made with $200,000. The Secretary of War, under that pressure, has this year recommended that the appropriation for the arming of the militia should be increased. In the meantime, there are volunteer companies with State appropriations anxious to obtain arms if they will be furnished. If the Congress thinks proper to exclude them from the purchase of arms from the armories, then they must go to private establishments, and get patterns which are not those established by the Government, arms which I believe to be inferior; and arms which, if they were brought into the service of the United States, in the event of the country being involved in war, would not receive the ammunition which the Government supplies. If they are to buy arms at all, it is therefore advantageous that they should buy the Government pattern."—*Congressional Globe*, 1st *Session*, 36*th Congress*, *Part* 1, *p.* 862.

March 1st. Its consideration was resumed.

On motion of Mr. Trumbull of Illinois, an amendment was inserted in the first section, requiring the payment "in cash, at the time of delivery." It was debated further, without a vote.

5th. Mr. Fessenden moved to add the following to the first section:

Provided, That the whole number of arms which may be sold, as aforesaid, shall be ascertained and determined in each year by the Secretary of War, and no State or Territory shall be allowed to purchase a number of arms bearing a greater proportion to the whole number so ascertained and determined, than the Federal population of such State or Territory bears to the aggregate Federal population of all the States and Territories of the Union, according to the census of the United States next preceding such purchase.

16th. Mr. Davis of Mississippi moved the following as a substitute for the above proviso:

"That the sales of each year shall not exceed the increased manufacture which may result from said sales; and that the whole number to be sold, if less than the requisitions made, shall be divided between the States applying to purchase, *pro rata*, as arms furnished by the United States are now distributed."

Which was agreed to—yeas 28, nays 18, as follows:

YEAS.—Messrs. Benjamin, Bigler, Bragg, Bright, Brown, Clay, Clingman, Crittenden, Davis, Fitch, Fitzpatrick, Green, Gwin, Hammond, Hunter, Iverson, Johnson of Arkansas, Johnson of Tennessee, Kennedy, Latham, Mallory, Nicholson, Pearce, Powell, Sebastian, Thomson, Toombs, and Wigfall—28.

NAYS.—Messrs. Anthony, Bingham, Chandler, Clark, Collamer, Dixon, Doolittle, Fessenden, Foot, Foster, Grimes, Hamlin, Harlan, Ten Eyck, Trumbull, Wade, Wilkinson, and Wilson—18.

A party vote, Democrats in affirmative—Republicans in negative.

The amendment as amended was then adopted.

A motion to strike out the first section was lost—yeas 20, nays 28.

March 26th. The bill passed—yeas 29, nays 18.

NAYS.—Anthony, Bingham, Cameron, Chandler, Clark, Collamer, Doolittle, Durkee, Fessenden, Foot, Grimes, Hamlin, Harlan, King, Simmons, Sumner, Ten Eyck, and Wade.

During the debate, on March 28th, between Mr. Simmons of Rhode Island, and Mr. Davis of Mississippi, the latter made these remarks:

"The Senator runs into *an error which I find very often prevails, that the militia of the States are not a part of the Army of the United States.* It is our glory that the defence of the country rests upon the people. He proposes, then, to arm the militia in time of peace with a weapon which they will not use in time of war."—*Congressional Globe, 1st Session, 36th Congress, Part 2, p.* 1351.

In the House, the bill was referred to the Committee on Military Affairs, and was not reported.

How the Telegraph was made to aid in effecting Secession.

Senator TOOMBS has publicly declared in Georgia that he would, under no circumstances, serve in the Senate after the inauguration of Mr. Lincoln. He said the same thing in the following telegraphic despatch to Mr. KEITT:

"*Macon*, November 14th, 1860.

"To Hon. L. M. KEITT: I will sustain South Carolina in secession. I have announced to the Legislature that I will not serve under Lincoln. If you have the power to act, act at once. We have bright prospects here.

"R. TOOMBS."

—

SOUTHERN MANIFESTO.

Washington, December 13th.

At the request of Hon. REUBEN DAVIS of Mississippi, member of the Committee of States, the Southern members of Congress assembled at his rooms to-night and adjourned at eleven o'clock, at which the following declaration was made and signed by those present. It had already been presented to the Committee of Thirty-three:

Washington, December 13th, 1860.

To our Constituents: The argument is exhausted. All hope of relief in the Union, through the agency of committees, Congressional legislation, or constitutional amendments, is extinguished, and we trust the South will not be deceived by appearances or the pretence of new guarantees. The Republicans are resolute in the purpose to grant nothing that will or ought to satisfy the South. We are satisfied the honor, safety, and independence of the Southern people are to be found only in a Southern Confederacy—a result to be obtained only by separate State secession—and that the sole and primary aim of each slaveholding State ought to be its speedy and absolute separation from an unnatural and hostile Union.

Signed by J. L. Pugh, David Clopton, Sydenham Moore, J. L. M. Curry, and J. A. Stallworth of Alabama; Alfred Iverson, J. W. H. Underwood, L. J. Gartrell, and Jas. Jackson, (Senator Toombs is not here, but would sign), John J. Jones, and Martin J. Crawford of Georgia; Geo. S. Hawkins of Florida. It is understood Mr. Yulee will sign it. T. C. Hindman of Arkansas. Both Senators will also sign it. A. G. Brown, Wm. Barksdale, O. R. Singleton, and Reuben Davis of Mississippi; Burton Craige and Thos. Ruffin of North Carolina; J. P. Benjamin and John M. Landrum of Louisiana. Mr. Slidell will also sign it. Senators Wigfall and Hemphill of Texas, will sign it.

Mr. Davis made the following statement to the caucus:

Being a member of the Committee of Thirty-three, I state that the above witnessed despatch was communicated to the committee this evening, and a resolution passed proposing no specific relief, eight Northern States dissenting, avowedly intended to counteract the effect of the above despatch, and, as I believe, to mislead the people of the South. From information derived from Republican members of the committee and other Northern Representatives, I fully concur in the above despatch.

REUBEN DAVIS.

The manifesto will be immediately communicated to the several constituencies of the gentlemen named by telegraph.

A TELEGRAPHIC MANIFESTO FROM SENATOR TOOMBS.

The Savannah *News* of Monday, December 24th, publishes the following address to the people of Georgia, telegraphed from Washington, on Saturday, December 22d:

Fellow-Citizens of Georgia: I came here to secure your constitutional rights, or to demonstrate to you that you can get no guarantees for these rights from your Northern Confederates.

The whole subject was referred to a committee of thirteen in the Senate yesterday. I was appointed on the committee and accepted the trust. I submitted propositions, which, so far from receiving decided support from a single member of the Republican party on the committee, were all treated with either derision or contempt. The vote was then taken in committee on the amendments to the Constitution proposed by Hon. J. J. CRITTENDEN of Kentucky, and each and all of them were voted against, unanimously, by the Black Republican members of the committee.

In addition to these facts, a majority of the Black Republican members of the committee declared distinctly that they had no guarantees to offer, which was silently acquiesced in by the other members.

The Black Republican members of this Committee of Thirteen are representative men of their party and section, and to the extent of my information, truly represent the Committee of Thirty-three in the House, which on Tuesday adjourned for a week without coming to any vote, after solemnly pledging themselves to vote on all propositions then before them on that date.

That committee is controlled by Black Republicans, your enemies, who only seek to amuse you with delusive hope until your election, in order that you may defeat the friends of secession. If you are deceived by them, it shall not be my fault. I have put the test fairly and frankly. It is decisive against you; and now I tell you upon the faith of a true man that all further looking to the North for security for your constitutional rights in the Union ought to be instantly abandoned. It is fraught with nothing but ruin to yourselves and your posterity.

Secession by the fourth of March next should be thundered from the ballot-box by the unanimous voice of Georgia on the second day of January next. Such a voice will be your best guarantee for LIBERTY, SECURITY, TRANQUILLITY and GLORY.

ROBERT TOOMBS.

IMPORTANT TELEGRAPHIC CORRESPONDENCE.

Atlanta, Georgia, December 26th, 1860.

Hon. S. A. Douglas or Hon. J. J. Crittenden:

Mr. TOOMBS's despatch of the 22d inst. unsettled conservatives here. Is there any hope for Southern rights in the Union? We are for the Union of our fathers, if Southern rights can be preserved in it. If not, we are for secession. Can we yet hope the Union will be preserved on this principle? You are looked to in this emergency. Give us your views by despatch, and oblige

WILLIAM EZZARD.
ROBERT W. SIMS.
JAMES P. HAMBLETON.
THOMAS S. POWELL.
S. G. HOWELL.
J. A. HAYDEN.
G. W. ADAIR.
R. C. HONLESTER.

—

Washington, December 29th, 1860.

In reply to your inquiry, we have hopes that the rights of the South, and of every State and section, may be protected within the Union. Don't give up the ship. Don't despair of the Republic.

J. J. CRITTENDEN.
S. A. DOUGLAS.

From the Raleigh Standard Extra of January 2d.

The *State Journal* of to-day, one of the organs of the disunionists, contains a telegraphic despatch calculated, and no doubt intended, to inflame the public mind and to precipitate North Carolina into revolution. This despatch, most probably sent here from the *Journal* Office, Wilmington, is as follows:

IMPORTANT !—IMMEDIATE RETURN OF LEGISLATORS TO THEIR POSTS.

Wilmington, Dec. 31st, 8½ P.M.

The following is the substance of a despatch received here this evening:

"Cabinet broken up in a row; Floyd, Thompson and Thomas have resigned; the President has gone over to the North. Federal troops on their way South. Our fort at the mouth of Cape Fear will shortly be occupied by troops for coercion. The citizens of North Carolina call upon the Legislature for advice and assistance."

The above produced great excitement in our community. As soon as we saw it we telegraphed to a well-informed and reliable friend in Washington city, whose reply is as follows:

"No troops ordered South. No new ground for excitement known."

Special Despatch to the Republican.

Augusta, Ga., Jan. 1st.

A special despatch to the *True Democrat,* of this city, dated at Washington, 3 o'clock, P.M., to-day, says:

"The cabinet is broken up, Mr. Floyd, Secretary of War, and Mr. Thompson, Secretary of the Interior, having resigned. A coercive policy has been adopted by the Administration. Mr. Holt, of Kentucky, our bitter foe, has been made Secretary of War. Fort Pulaski is in danger. The Abolitionists are defiant."

This despatch is signed "Robert Toombs"

This spurious and inaccurate despatch had a great influence, it is said, in deciding the wavering vote of Georgia on the question of union or disunion.

The Macon (Georgia) *Telegraph* of the 2d instant, contains the following sensation despatch from the President of the South Carolina Convention. Of course it obtained immediate currency throughout the Southern States:

Charleston, January 1st, 1861.

Mayor of Macon: The Convention of South Carolina have directed me to send you the following telegram just received from our Commissioners at Washington:

"Holt has been appointed Secretary of

War. He is for *coercion*, and war is inevitable. We believe reinforcements are on the way. Prevent their entrance into the harbor at every hazard.

"D. F. Jamison,
"President South Carolina Convention."

From the Neu Orleans Delta.

THE SOUTH CAROLINA CONVENTION TO THE CITY OF NEW ORLEANS.

The following highly-important despatch from the President of the South Carolina Convention, has been furnished to us for publication by Mayor Monroe, to whom it was addressed:

Charleston, January 1st.

To the Hon. John T. Monroe, Mayor of New Orleans: The Convention of South Carolina has directed me to send you the following telegram, just received from our Commissioners at Washington:

"Holt has been appointed Secretary of War. He is for coercion, and war, we believe, is inevitable. We believe reinforcements are on the way. We shall prevent their entrance into the harbor at every hazard.

"D. F. Jamison,
"President South Carolina Convention."

From the National Intelligencer.

In January, when the Crittenden plan of adjustment was voted down in the Senate, rather because of the absence of Southern Senators than by the strength of its opponents, we find from the St. Louis journals, that a despatch was reported to have been straightway sent from Washington to that city by Senators Polk and Green, representing as follows:

"The Crittenden resolutions were lost by a vote of 25 to 23. A motion of Mr. Cameron to reconsider was lost; and thus ends all hope of reconciliation. Civil war is now considered inevitable, and late accounts declare that Fort Sumter will be attacked without delay. *The Missouri delegation recommend immediate secession.*"

We need not say that no such despatch was ever sent by these gentlemen. Yet, says the St. Louis *Republican*, "all over the city (St. Louis) it was spoken of as the despatch from Messrs. Green and Polk."

The temporary rejection of the Crittenden plan was in like manner pressed into the service of the Secessionists in order to accelerate the pace of grave, deliberate, and patriotic North Carolina. The Raleigh *Register* of the 19th instant contains the following despatch, under the signature of Mr. Crittenden himself, published to counteract the disturbing effect of the exaggerated rumors which had been put in circulation from this city:

"*Washington*, January 17th, 9 P. M.

"In reply, the vote against my resolutions will be reconsidered. *Their failure was the result of the refusal of six Southern Senators to vote.* There is yet good hope of success."

"John J. Crittenden."

Senate, January 25th, 1861.

My Dear Sir: Mr. Crittenden is not present, but I can say with confidence that there is hope of adjustment, and the prospect has never been better than now since we first assembled.

Very truly, your friend,
S. A. Douglas.

We concur in the opinion that there is hope of an adjustment.

J. J. Crittenden,
A. R. Boteler,
John T. Harris.

Hon. James Barbour.

In addition to the foregoing testimony on the subject, we insert an extract of a letter from the Hon. John S. Millson to Mr. Barbour to the same effect:

"For myself, I say that I have never had so confident an expectation *as I have at this time*, of such a termination of the present controversy as would be satisfactory to me, and, I believe, to a large majority of the people of Virginia."

TO THE PEOPLE OF VIRGINIA.

We deem it our duty, as your Representatives at Washington, to lay before you such information as we possess in regard to the probable action of Congress in the present alarming condition of the country.

At the beginning of this session, now more than half over, committees were appointed, in both Houses of Congress, to consider the state of the Union. Neither committee has been able to agree upon any mode of settlement of the pending issues between the North and the South.

The Republican members in both committees rejected propositions acknowledging the right of property in slaves, or recommending the division of the Territories between the slaveholding and non-slaveholding States by a geographical line.

In the Senate, the propositions commonly known as Mr. Crittenden's were voted against by every Republican Senator; and the House, on a vote by ayes and noes, refused to consider certain propositions, moved by Mr. Etheridge, which were even less favorable to the South than Mr. Crittenden's.

A resolution giving a pledge to sustain the President in the use of force against the seceding States, was adopted in the House of Representatives by a large majority; and in the Senate every Republican voted to substitute for Mr. Crittenden's propositions resolutions offered by Mr. Clark of New Hampshire, declaring no new concessions, guarantees, or amendments to the Constitution were necessary; that the demands of the South were unreasonable, and that the remedy for the present danger was simply to enforce the laws; in other words, coercion and war.

In this state of facts, our duty is to warn you that it is vain to hope for any measures of conciliation or adjustment (from Congress) which you could accept. We are also satisfied that the Republican party designs, by civil war alone, to coerce the Southern States, under the pretext of enforcing the laws, unless it shall become speedily apparent that the seceding States are so numerous, determined and united, as to make such an attempt hopeless.

We are confirmed in these conclusions by our general intercourse here; by the speeches of the Republican leaders here and elsewhere; by the recent refusals of the Legislatures of Vermont, Ohio and Pennsylvania, to repeal their obnoxious Personal Liberty Laws; by the action of the Illinois Legislature on resolutions approving the Crittenden propositions, and by the adoption of the resolutions in the New York and Massachusetts Legislatures (doubtless to be followed by others) offering men and money for the war of coercion.

We have thus placed before you the facts and conclusions which have become manifest to us from this post of observation where you have placed us. There is nothing to be hoped from Congress—the remedy is with you alone, when you assemble in sovereign Convention.

We conclude by expressing our solemn conviction that prompt and decided action, by the people of Virginia in Convention, will afford the surest means under the Providence of God, of averting an impending civil war, and preserving the hope of reconstructing a Union already dissolved.

J. M. Mason,
R. M. T. Hunter,
D. C. De Jarnette,
M. R. H. Garnett,
Shelton F. Leake,
E. S. Martin,
H. A. Edmundson,
Roger A. Pryor,
Thos. S. Bocock,
A. G. Jenkins.

Washington City, January 26th, 1861.

[Owing to the detention of Ex-Governor Smith, at his home in Virginia, by sickness, this address could not be presented to him for his signature. There is no doubt he would have joined in it, if present.]

STIRRING THE FIRES.

The Richmond *Examiner* of Friday last contains the following despatch, intended to "operate" on the election to be held in Virginia to-day:

"The following despatch fully explains itself. The voters of Virginia cannot now fail to perform their duty:

"'*Charleston*, January 30th, 1861.

"'*To Judge Hopkins, Richmond, Virginia:* Reinforcements have been ordered to Fort Sumter and elsewhere. Will not Virginia, by her Legislature, interpose to prevent coercion? It will be too late when her Convention meets.

"J. S. Preston.'"

The Richmond *Whig* states that a similar despatch was received by another distinguished member of the Legislature, "to which, after consultation with many leading members of the Legislature, a reply was made to the effect that we, here, had heard of no attempt at coercion, but that the President was exerting himself to preserve peace."

IN FEBRUARY.

From the Nashville Union of February 6th.

Virginia Despatches.—Our special despatch with regard to the Virginia election is direct from Richmond, and is from the Editors of the Richmond *Enquirer*. Of course it is more reliable than the despatch sent by the Associated Press of the same date.

Special Despatch to Union and American.

Richmond, (*Va.*) Feb. 5th.—Resistance men have carried the Convention overwhelmingly. Submission Unionists, not twenty elected Enquirer.

From another column of the same paper.

THE OLD DOMINION!—ALL HAIL!

A voice, as from the grave of the immortal Washington, tells us that Virginia will be true to her ancient, ever glorious, historical renown. Throughout the length of her immense territories only twenty Submissionist Union men have been elected. Virginia will before the 4th of March declare herself absolved from all further obligation to a Government, etc. It is eminently proper that the State which was the leader in the Revolution, and the first to proclaim the great doctrine of State-rights in 1799, should lead the column of the Border States.

From the Nashville Union of February 7th.

IMPORTANT DESPATCHES!

Listen to the following glorious news from old Virginia:

Richmond, Feb. 6th.—To Wm. Williams: The Submissionists will not number thirty in the Convention. The Resistance men have more than one hundred elected. The action of the Convention will be prompt as soon as the Washington Conference adjourns. Enquirer.

Will Tennessee elect members to her Convention that wish to wait, wait, wait until Black Republicanism trample us in the dust or kick us out?

We are indebted (says the Charlotte *Bulletin*) to our much-esteemed Senator, the Hon. T. L. Clingman, for the following highly important-information, by telegraph, dated:

Washington, Feb. 18th, 1861.

Editor Bulletin: There is no chance whatever for Crittenden's proposition. North Carolina must secede, or aid Lincoln in making war on the South.

T. L. Clingman.

SMASHING OF THE PEACE CONFERENCE.

The following is part of a special telegram to the Charleston *Mercury*, dated at Washington, Feb. 21st:

"The only hope now is in the smashing up of the Peace Congress and getting Virginia out."

False Despatches.— The Fayetteville (North Carolina) *Observer*, referring to false telegraphic despatches sent out from Charleston, says: "They are of a piece with the stories circulated in Georgia to affect the election in that State; that which preceded the mission of the Wilmington Committee to Raleigh; and that which resulted in the treasonable seizure of Fort Caswell, whither no troops have been or will be ordered. It does not answer the purposes of those engaged in disunion schemes to allow any period of rest from excitement. The 'Southern heart' must be 'fired,' that the South may be 'precipitated into secession.'"

Other Secessions Proposed.

December 24th, 1860.

Mr. John C. Burch offered the following resolution, which was referred to the Committee on Military affairs:

That the Secretary of War be, and is hereby, directed and required to issue to the State of California quotas of arms for the years 1850 and 1851, equal to the quota issued to said State for the year 1852, of such description as the authorities of said State may require.

From California.

Fort Kearney, Feb. 5th.—The Pony Express from California on the 19th has arrived. The Governor's message is strong for the Union. The letters from Congressmen Scott and Burch, advocating a Pacific Republic, are severely denounced by the papers.

From California.

Fort Kearney.—The Pony Express, bringing California news as late as the 29th ultimo, has arrived.

Senator Latham's declaration that California will remain with the Union of the Northern and Western States is generally commended by the newspapers. They undoubtedly present a correct representation of a vast majority of the people of the State.

From the California correspondent of the New York *World*, written in the winter of 1860:

CALIFORNIA FOR THE UNION.

On Friday last the Assembly passed a series of most warm and decided Union resolutions, declaring the rebellion in the South to be treasonable, and recommending the use of such force as may be found necessary to vindicate the laws and preserve the Union. The final vote was, ayes 40, nays 22. The official synopsis of the resolutions is as follows:

Resolved, By the Assembly, the Senate concurring, *First*. The withdrawal of a State from its membership and obligations in the Federal Union, in defiance of the General Government, can only be accomplished by a successful resistance to the whole power of the United States. *Second*. Decent respect to the opinions of the people of the civilized world, and the instinct of self-preservation demands that the United States Government should use all the power necessary to enforce obedience to its laws and to protect its property. *Third*. The people of the State of California will sustain and uphold the constitutionally-elected officers of the United States Government, in all constutional efforts to preserve the integrity of the Union, and to enforce obedience to the acts of Congress and the decisions of the courts. After the laws have been enforced, and the power and authority of the Constitution and Government of the United States recognized and acknowledged, every feeling of nationality and brotherhood demand that such compromises as are consistent with justice shall be made for the purpose of restoring that harmony which should characterize the people of a common country.

The majority vote was given by moderate Douglas Democrats and Republicans, the minority by Breckenridge men, who did not conceal, but on the contrary loudly boasted their approval of the secession of the South, and spoke with the utmost enthusiasm of the Southern Confederacy and President Davis. The conflict of feeling on this subject in California is more intense than elsewhere, because it is between Northern and Southern men who are contending for ascendancy in the State. Many of the latter, however, refuse to accept the disunion issue, and declare their intention to fight the battle of the South in the Union.

The result was received with most hearty applause, proving the devotion of our people to the Union, and their love of country. Considering the outrageously-treasonable speeches that have been made during the sessions, and the symptoms of approval elicited by them, chiefly from secessionists in the employ of the State, this evidence of patriotic feeling is especially gratifying.

A Pacific Repubplic.—The Shasta *Herald*, of Saturday, in discussing political matters, says:

"If disunion does come, neither North nor South need look for aid and comfort from the Pacific coast. The Almighty has piled up the elements along these shores for a great empire, and if it needs he can make it one. We have no such interest that would demand an alliance with either of the belligerents upon the other side. We are, and have been for ten years, as fully separated from them as though we were but a foreign colony. This coast can stand alone, and if disunion between North and South ever comes, it will stand alone and independent. When that day comes—if unfortunately it should ever come—then 'Long live the Pacific Republic!'"

To which the San Francisco *Bee* responded in opposition:

We have frequently mentioned the existence of an organization in California, having for its object the establishment of a Pacific Republic on this coast, in accordance with the treasonable recommendations of Scott and Burch. We should have taken some pains to learn the names of the leaders of the movement, that they might be held up to the scorn and ridicule of a union-loving people, had we not been satisfied, as we now are, that the scheme would be frowned down the moment it was openly advocated. But two of the ninety journals in California have ventured to offer a word in favor of the movement, and they were actuated, we imagine, more by a spirit of bravado than a hope of success. Aside from a few disappointed office-seekers, there are not to be found to-day in California, outside of the State prison, a thousand voices to give encouragement to the treason. With less to thank the Union for than any other portion of the Confederacy, the people of the Pacific are prepared to make any sacrifice to maintain it—to suffer every neglect rather than sever their connection with it. Still a Pacific Republic is talked of, *and a conspiracy*, with the focus in San Francisco, *is poisoning the land.* One of its leading branches, we learn by the *Appeal*, is in Marysville. It is a secret organization, and is "forming," says the journal, "in a section of country lying back of the Buttes, with a view to establish a military company, pledged to the maintainance of a Pacific Republic. They will apply to *the State for arms* under the covert pretence of an organization under the State militia law. These misguided men have been deluded into the belief by their leaders that the Union is irretrievably gone to pieces, and the only hope for California is the immediate establishment of an independent government." The raising of the "bear flag," at Stockton, some days since, was probably a part of the programme. We are anxious to see the faces of some of these revolutionists—to note the mark with which treason brands its votaries.—*San Francisco Mirror.*

SOUTH AND NORTHWEST.

The Cincinnati *Gazette*, in the winter of 1860, states:

We are most reliably informed that there are agents of the Gulf States now in the city endeavoring to create a sentiment among business men favorably to the establishment of a Confederacy composed of the Northern and Southwestern States. A well-known leader among the democracy has been approached, our information goes to show, within the past two or three days, by these agents, with a view of obtaining his influence, but he declined to have any thing to do with so traitorous a scheme, as he is a staunch Union man. The object is to make free-trade the basis of the confederacy—to cut off New York, Pennsylvania, New Jersey, and all the New England States, which are so wedded to a protective tariff. These Southern gentlemen state that there are agents of the Gulf States throughout all the northwestern States, who are making similar overtures, and that it is their aim to spring the issue soon among the citizens of those States.

MAYOR WOOD'S RECOMMENDATION OF THE SECESSION OF NEW YORK CITY, JANUARY 6TH, 1861.

To the Honorable the Common Council:

GENTLEMEN: We are entering upon the public duties of the year under circumstances as unprecedented as they are gloomy and painful to contemplate. The great trading and producing interests of not only the city of New York, but of the entire country, are prostrated by a monetary crisis; and although similar calamities have before befallen us, it is the first time that they have emanated from causes having no other origin than that which may be traced to political disturbances. Truly, may it now be said, "We are in the midst of a revolution *bloodless* AS YET." Whether the dreadful alternative implied as probable in the conclusion of this prophetic quotation may be averted, "no human ken can divine." It is quite certain that the severity of the storm is unexampled in our history, and if the disintegration of the Federal Government, with the consequent destruction of all the material interests of the people shall not follow, it will be owing more to the interposition of Divine Providence, than to the inherent preventive power of our institutions, or the intervention of any other human agency.

It would seem that a dissolution of the Federal Union is inevitable. Having been formed originally on a basis of general and mutual protection, but separate local independence—each State reserving the entire and absolute control of its own domestic affairs, it is evidently impossible to keep them together longer than they deem themselves fairly treated by each other, or longer than the interests, honor and fraternity of the people of the several States are satisfied. Being a Government created by *opinion*, its continuance is dependent upon the continuance of the sentiment which formed it. It cannot be preserved by coercion or held together by force. A resort to this last dreadful alternative would of itself destroy not only the Government, but the lives and property of the people.

If these forebodings shall be realized, and a separation of the States shall occur, momentous considerations will be presented to the corporate authorities of this city. We must provide for the new relations which will necessarily grow out of the new condition of public affairs.

It will not only be necessary for us to settle the relations which we shall hold to other cities and States, but to establish, if we can, new ones with a portion of our own State. Being the child of the Union, having drawn our sustenance from its bosom, and arisen to our present power and strength through the vigor of our mother—when deprived of her maternal advantages, we must rely upon our own resources and assume a position predicated upon the new phase which public affairs will present, and upon the inherent strength which our geographical, commercial, political, and financial pre-eminence imparts to us.

With our aggrieved brethren of the Slave States, we have friendly relations and a common sympathy. We have not participated in the warfare upon their constitutional rights or their domestic institutions. While other portions of our State have unfortunately been imbued with the fanatical spirit which actuates a portion of the people of New England, the city of New York has unfalteringly preserved the integrity of its principles in adherence to the compromises of the Constitution and the equal rights of the people of all the States. We have respected the local interests of every section, at no time oppressing, but all the while aiding in the development of the resources of the whole country. Our ships have penetrated to every clime, and so have New York capital, energy and enterprise found their way to every State, and, indeed, to almost every county and town of the American Union. If we have derived sustenance from the Union, so have we in return disseminated blessings for the common benefit of all. Therefore, New York has a right to expect, and should endeavor to preserve a continuance of uninterrupted intercourse with every section.

It is, however, folly to disguise the fact that, judging from the past, New York may have more cause of apprehension from the aggressive legislation of our own State than from external dangers. We have already largely suffered from this cause. For the past five years, our interests and corporate rights have been repeatedly trampled upon. Being an integral portion of the State, it has been assumed, and in effect tacitly admitted on our part by non-resistance, that all political and governmental power over us rested in the State Legislature. Even the common right of taxing ourselves for our own government, has been yielded, and we are not permitted to do so without this authority. * * *

Thus it will be seen that the political connection between the people of the city and the State has been used by the latter to our injury. The Legislature, in which the present partizan majority has the power, has become the instrument by which we are plundered to enrich their speculators, lobby agents, and Abolition politicians. Laws are passed through their malign influence by which, under forms of legal enactment, our burdens have been increased, our substance eaten out, and our municipal liberties destroyed. Self-government, though guaranteed by the State Constitution, and left to every other county and city, has been taken from us by this foreign power, whose dependents have been sent among us to destroy our liberties by subverting our political system.

How we shall rid ourselves of this odious and oppressive connection, it is not for me to determine. It is certain that a dissolution cannot be peacefully accomplished, except by the consent of the Legislature itself. Whether this can be obtained or not, is, in my judgment, doubtful. Deriving so much advantage from its power over the city, it is not probable that a partizan majority will consent to a separation—and the resort to force by violence and revolution must not be thought of for an instant. We have been distinguished as an orderly and law-abiding people. Let us do nothing to forfeit this character, or to add to the present distracted condition of public affairs.

Much, no doubt, can be said in favor of the justice and policy of a separation. It may be said that secession or revolution in any of the United States would be subversive of all Federal authority, and, so far as the Central Government is concerned, the resolving of the community into its original elements—that, if part of the States form new combinations and Governments, other States may do the same. California and her sisters of the Pacific will no doubt set up an independent Republic and husband their own rich mineral resources. The Western States, equally rich in cereals and other agricultural products, will probably do the same. Then it may be said, why should not New York city, instead of supporting by her contributions in revenue two-thirds of the expenses of the United States, become also equally independent? As a free city, with but nominal duty on imports, her local Government could be supported without taxation upon her people. Thus we could live free from taxes, and have cheap goods nearly duty free. In this she would have the whole and united support of the Southern States, as well as all the other States to whose interests and rights under the Constitution she has always been true.

It is well for individuals or communities to look every danger square in the face, and to meet it calmly and bravely. As dreadful as the severing of the bonds that have hitherto united the States has been in contemplation, it is now apparently a stern and inevitable fact. We have now to meet it with all the consequences, whatever they may be. If the Confederacy is broken up the Government is dissolved, and it behooves every distinct community, as well as every individual, to take care of themselves.

When Disunion has become a fixed and certain fact, why may not New York disrupt the bands which bind her to a venal and corrupt master—to a people and a party that have plundered her revenues, attempted to ruin her commerce, taken away the power of self-government, and destroyed the Confederacy of which she was the proud Empire City? Amid the gloom which the present and prospective condition of things must cast over the country, New York, as a *Free City*, may shed the only light and hope of a future reconstruction of our once blessed Confederacy.

But I am not prepared to recommend the violence implied in these views. In stating this argument in favor of freedom, "peaceably if we can, forcibly if we must," let me not be misunderstood. The redress can be found only in appeals to the magnanimity of the people of the whole State. The events of the past two months have no doubt effected a change in the popular sentiment of the State and National politics. This change may bring us the desired relief, and we may be able to obtain a repeal of the law to which I have referred, and a consequent restoration of our corporate rights.

Fernando Wood, Mayor.

January 6th, 1861.

Personal Liberty Laws.

Among the grievances mentioned by the South Carolina Convention was the existence in Northern States of "Personal Liberty Laws." We give from the *National Intelligencer* of December 11th, 1860, a summary of these laws, except that of Massachusetts, which has been condensed more accurately than was there published:

MAINE.

The laws of this State provide that no sheriff, deputy sheriff, coroner, constable, jailer, justice of the peace, or other officer of the State, shall arrest or detain or aid in so doing, in any prison or building belonging to this State, or in any county or town, any person on account of a claim on him as a fugitive slave, under a penalty not exceeding one thousand dollars, and make it the duty of all county attorneys to repair to the place where such person is held in custody, and render him all necessary and legal assistance in making his defence against said claim.

NEW HAMPSHIRE.

The law of the State declares that slaves, coming or brought into the State, by or with the consent of the master, shall be free; declares the attempt to hold any person as a slave within the State as a felony, with a penalty of imprisonment of not less than one nor more than five years; provided, that the provisions of this section shall not apply to any act lawfully done by any officer of the United States, or other person, in the execution of any legal process.

VERMONT.

This State, by her several acts of 1843, 1850 and 1858, provides that no court, justice of the peace or magistrate, shall take cognizance of any certificate, warrant, or process under the fugitive slave law; provides that no officer, or citizen of the State, shall arrest, or aid, or assist in arresting, any person for the reason that he is claimed as a fugitive slave; provides that no officer or citizen shall aid or assist in the removal from the State of any person claimed as a fugitive slave; provides a penalty of one thousand dollars, or imprisonment five years in State prison for violating this act. This act, however, shall not be construed to extend to any citizen of the State acting as a Judge of the Circuit or District Court of the United States, or as Marshal or Deputy-Marshal of the District of Vermont, or to any person acting under the command or authority of said Courts or Marshal. Requires the State's attorneys to act as counsel for alleged fugitives; provides for issuing *habeas corpus* and the trial by jury of all questions of fact in issue between the parties; and ordains that every person who may have been held as a slave, who shall come, or be brought, or be in the State, with or without the consent of his or her master or mistress, or who shall come, or be brought, or be involuntarily, or in any way, in this State, shall be free. It is also provided that every person who shall hold, or attempt to hold, in this State, in slavery, or as a slave, any person mentioned as a slave in the section of this act, relating to fugitive slaves, or any free person in any form, or for any time, however short, under the pretence that such person is or has been a slave, shall, on conviction thereof, be imprisoned in the State prison for a term not less than one year nor more than fifteen years, and be fined not exceeding two thousand dollars.

MASSACHUSETTS.

That of 1860.

The Governor to appoint commissioners in each county to defend alleged fugitives from service or labor, who shall secure to them impartial trials by jury: and the alleged fugitives may have the services of any attorney whose assistance may be desired.

All the expenses of the defence of alleged fugitives to be paid by the commonwealth.

Persons holding office under this State not to issue process for the arrest of alleged fugitives, nor to serve the same, nor to do any official act in furtherance of the execution of the fugitive slave law of 1793 or that of 1850. Any justice of the peace offending against this provision to forfeit not exceeding one thousand dollars, or be imprisoned, in jail, not exceeding one year, for each offence.

The jails and other prisons of the State not to be used for the detention or imprisonment of any person accused or convicted of any offence created by either of the said acts of Congress; or accused or convicted of resisting any process issued under either of them, or of rescuing or attempting to rescue any person detained under the provisions of either of said acts; nor for the imprisonment of a person arrested on mesne process or execution in a suit for damages in consequence of aid rendered to any fugitive escaping from service or labor.

Whoever removes from this State or assists in so doing, or comes into the State with the intention of removing or assisting in the removing therefrom, or procures or assists in procuring to be so removed, any person who is not "held to service or labor" by the "party" making "claim," or has not "escaped" from the "party" making "claim" or whose "service or labor" is not "due" to the party making "claim" within the meaning of the words of the Constitution of the United States, or the pretence that such person is so held or has escaped or that his "service or labor" is so "due" or with the intent to subject him to such "service or labor," shall be punished by fine not less than one thousand nor exceeding five thousand dollars, and by imprisonment in the State prison not less than one nor more than two years.

And any person sustaining wrong or injury by any proceedings punishable as aforesaid, may maintain an action and recover damages therefore.

Sheriffs, deputy-sherffs and others, state, county, city, district and town officers, and officers of the volunteer militia forbidden to arrest, imprison, detain, or return, or aid in so doing, any person for the reason that he i claimed or adjudged to be a fugitive from service or labor, shall be punished by fine not less than one thousand and not exceeding two thousand dollars, and by imprisonment in the State prision not less than one nor exceeding two years.

The volunteer militia not to aid in the seizure, detention or rendition of a person for the reason that he is claimed or adjudged to be a fugitive from service or labor. Any member thereof offending against this provision, to be punished by fine not less than one thousand nor more than two thousand dollars, and by imprisonment in the State prison for not less than one nor more than two years.

The penalties prescribed by the two preceding sections not to apply to any act of military obedience performed by an officer or private of the militia.

The preceding sections not to apply to fugitives from justice. United States judicial officers not to hold any judicial office under the constitution and laws of this State, except that of justice of the peace.

No justice of the peace, while holding the office of a Commissioner of the United States Circuit Court, shall have authority to grant any warrant or to issue any process, civil or criminal, other than summons to witnesses, or hear and try any cause, civil or criminal, under the laws of this State.

ACT APPROVED MARCH 25TH, 1861.

Sec. 1. Writ of *habeas corpus* returnable before the Supreme Judicial Court except in cases mentioned in Sections 30 and 32, Chap. 144 of General Statutes.

Sec. 2. On a trial upon a writ of *habeas corpus*, under sec. 19 of same act, issues to be framed under direction of the court, and rules of evidence, etc., to be those of the common law.

Sec. 3. A person not to be taken by writ of *habeas corpus* out of the custody of the U. S. Marshal, or his deputy, holding him by legal process issued by court of competent jurisdiction, *provided*, that the Supreme Judicial Court may investigate and determine upon the validity and legal effect of any process which may be relied upon to defeat the writ, or any other matter properly arising.

Sec. 4. No person to be punished, who, without any false pretence or unlawful intent, claims another person as a fugitive from service or labor.

Sec. 5. The right of any officer or court to call out the militia for the prevention or suppression of any riot or mob, is not prohibited by the 144th chapter aforesaid; the officers or members of the volunteer militia not excused from obeying any lawful order, or liable to any penalty for executing the same; *provided*, that the militia shall not be used to hinder the service of any lawful process of this commonwealth.

CONNECTICUT.

The State of Connecticut provides that every person who shall *falsely* and *maliciously* declare, represent, or pretend that any free person *entitled to freedom* is a slave, or owes service or labor to any person or persons, with intent to procure or to aid or assist in procuring the forcible removal of such free person from this State as a slave, shall pay a fine of $5,000 and be imprisoned five years in the Connecticut State prison; requires two witnesses to prove that any person is a slave or owes labor; denounces a penalty of $5,000 against any person seizing or causing to be seized *any free person* with intent to reduce him to slavery; depositions not to be admitted as evidence; witnesses testifying falsely, liable to $5,000 fine and five years imprisonment.

RHODE ISLAND.

This State by her legislation forbids the carrying away of any person by force out of the State; forbids any judge, justice, magistrate, or court from officially aiding in the arrest of a fugitive slave under the fugitive slave law of 1793 or 1850; forbids any sheriff or other officer from arresting or detaining and person claimed as a fugitive slave; provides a penalty of $500, or imprisonment not exceeding six months, for violating the act; denies the use of her jails to the United States for the detention of fugitive slaves.

NEW YORK.

The State of New York has passed no laws having relation to the United States fugitive slave act of 1850. Though pressed frequently upon the Legislature, they have always failed of adoption. The old and obsolete act of 1840, entitled "An act to extend the right of trial by jury," extends the trial by jury to the cases of persons arrested as fugitive slaves; but in the fourth edition of the laws of the State, as prepared and published by Hon. Hiram Denio, at present Chief Justice of the Court of Appeals, may be found appended to the chapter containing this law the following note:

"*An Act to Extend the Right of Trial by Jury, passed May 6th*, 1840.—The decision of the Supreme Court of the United States, in Prigg *vs.* the Commonwealth of Pennsylvania, 16 Peters' R. 539, establishes the doctrine that all State laws calculated to interfere with the third subdivision of section 2, article 4, of the Constitution of the United States are unconstitutional. Since that decision the fugitive slave law (Laws of Congress, 1850, chap. 60) has been passed, containing provisions repugnant to the whole of this act. It is therefore of no force; but, as it never has been repealed, it is here inserted."

NEW JERSEY.

The State of New Jersey has no statutes bearing on this subject save those which enjoin upon her State officers the duty of aiding in the recovery of fugitive slaves. Persons temporarily residing in the State are also permitted to bring with them and retain their domestic slaves.

PENNSYLVANIA.

The State of Pennsylvania has not formally and specially legislated at all against the United States fugitive slave law of 1850, though there was an old statute of 1847 which prohibited any judge, justice of the peace, or alderman from taking cognizance of the case of any fugitive from labor, "under a certain act of Congress passed on the 12th day of February, 1793." During the last session of her Legislature the Commissioners appointed to revise and amend the Penal Laws of Pennsylvania (John C. Knox, Edward King, and David Webster) made a report to the Legislature that they had completed their labors, and the result was presented in the shape of a bill entitled "An act to consolidate, revise and amend the Penal Laws of this Commonwealth." That report, on the thirty-first day of March, 1860, was enacted into a law, and by the ninety-fifth section it is enacted as follows:

"No Judge of any of the Courts of this Commonwealth, nor any Alderman or Justice of the Peace of said Commonwealth, shall have jurisdiction or take cognizance of the case of any fugitive from labor from any of the United States or Territories under any act of Congress, nor shall any such Judge, Alderman, or Justice of the Peace of this Commonwealth issue or grant any certificate or warrant of removal of any such fugitive from labor, under any act of Congress; and if any Alderman or Justice of the Peace of this Commonwealth shall take cognizance or jurisdiction of the case of any such fugitive, or shall grant or issue any certificate or warrant of removal, as aforesaid, then, and in either case, he shall be deemed guilty of a misdemeanor in office, and shall, on conviction thereof, be sentenced to pay, at the discretion of the Court, any sum not exceeding one thousand dollars, the one-half to the party prosecuting for the same, and the other half to the use of this Commonwealth."

The theory of this law, it will be seen, is founded strictly on the decision of the Supreme Court of the United States in the Prigg case, and does not interfere with the functions of the Commissioner appointed under the United States law.

MICHIGAN.*

The law of this State requires State's attorneys to act as counsel for fugitive slaves; secures to persons arrested as fugitive slaves the benefits of the writ of *habeas corpus*, and trial by jury; denies use of State jails for detention of alleged fugitives; requires that identity of fugitive slaves shall be proved by two credible witnesses, or by legal evidence equivalent thereto, and provides a fine of not less than five hundred nor more than one thousand dollars, and imprisonment in State prison for five years, for forcibly seizing, or causing to be seized, *any free person*, with intent to have such person held in slavery.

IOWA.

This State has no legislation on the subject.

* March, 1861. A bill to repeal this was indefinitely postponed in the House by a vote of 43 to 24

WISCONSIN.

The law of this State enjoins on the district attorneys the duty of acting as counsel for alleged fugitive slaves; secures to such persons the benefits of the writ of *habeas corpus;* provides for appeal to be taken to next stated term of the Circuit Court; secures trial by jury; enjoins a penalty of one thousand dollars and imprisonment of not more than five nor less than one year on all who "falsely and maliciously represent any free person to be a slave"; identity of alleged fugitive slave to be proved by two credible witnesses; no deposition to be received in evidence. It is also provided that—

"No judgment recovered against any person or persons for any neglect or refusal to obey, or any violations of, the act of Congress commonly termed the 'Fugitive Slave Act,' approved September eighteenth, one thousand eight hundred and fifty, or any of the provisions thereof, shall be a lien on any real estate within this State, nor shall any such judgment be enforcable by sale or execution of any real or personal property within this State; but all such sales shall be absolutely void; and in case of seizure or sale of any personal property, by virtue of any execution issued on such judgment, the defendant in said execution may maintain an action in replevin, or other action to secure possession thereof, in the manner provided by law for such actions, on affidavit filed as required by law, and a further statement therein that said execution issued in a judgment rendered under the provisions of the act of Congress aforesaid; and the provisions of this section shall also apply to judgments heretofore rendered."

OHIO, INDIANA, ILLINOIS, MINNESOTA, CALIFORNIA AND OREGON.

We cannot find that these States have any laws in force on the subject.

Notes.

In VERMONT Legislature, Nov., 1860, a majority of the Committee of House of Representatives reported in favor of the repeal of the above law, but their proposition was rejected by a vote of two to one.

In MAINE, a repealing bill passed the Senate—yeas 17, yeas 10, and failed in the House.

In MASSACHUSETTS, a modifying bill was passed. For detail, see under "Massachusetts."

In RHODE ISLAND, a repealing bill passed the Senate—yeas 21, nays 9; the House—yeas 49, nays 18.

In MICHIGAN, a repealing bill was indefinitely postponed in the House—yeas 43, nays 24.

In PENNSYLVANIA, a repealing bill was introduced into the House, but was not reached, in the course of business, when the firing on Sumter opened the war. A majority of each House was understood to be in favor of it. This law was first passed in 1847, after the Prigg decision; and one section prohibiting the use of State jails was repealed in 1852.

U. S. Senator Simmons of Rhode Island, in one of his speeches, made these remarks:

"Complaint had been made of personal liberty bills. Now, the Massachusetts personal liberty bill was passed by a Democratic House, a Democratic Senate, and signed by a Democratic Governor, a man who was afterwards nominated by Mr. Polk for the very best office in New England, and was unanimously confirmed by a Democratic United States Senate. Further than this, the very first time the attention of the Massachusetts Legislature was called to the propriety of a repeal to this law was by a Republican Governor, Governor Banks. Now, on the other hand, South Carolina had repealed a law imprisoning British colored sailors, but retained the one imprisoning those coming from States inhabited by her own brethren."

THE PROCEEDINGS OF THE GOVERNMENT IN RELATION TO THE SECESSION MOVEMENT.

Meeting and Proceedings of Congress.

THIRTY-SIXTH CONGRESS—SECOND SESSION.

Congress met on the first Monday of December, 1860, and was composed of the following persons:—

SENATE.

JOHN C. BRECKINRIDGE of Kentucky, *Vice President.*

MAINE—H. Hamlin,* W. P. Fessenden.

NEW HAMPSHIRE—John P. Hale, Daniel Clark.

VERMONT—Solomon Foot, J. Collamer.

MASSACHUSETTS—Henry Wilson, Charles Sumner.

RHODE ISLAND—James F. Simmons, H. B. Anthony.

CONNECTICUT—L. S. Foster, Jas. Dixon.

NEW YORK—Wm. H. Seward, Preston King.

NEW JERSEY—J. C. Ten Eyck, J. R. Thomson.

PENNSYLVANIA—S. Cameron, Wm. Bigler.

DELAWARE—J. A. Bayard, W. Saulsbury.

MARYLAND—J. A. Pearce, A. Kennedy.

VIRGINIA—R. M. T. Hunter, James M. Mason.

SOUTH CAROLINA—James Chesnut,† Jas. H. Hammond.†

NORTH CAROLINA—Thomas Bragg, T. L. Clingman.

ALABAMA—B. Fitzpatrick, C. C. Clay, Jr.

MISSISSIPPI—A. G. Brown, Jeff. Davis.

LOUISIANA—J. P. Benjamin, John Slidell.

TENNESSEE—A. O. P. Nicholson, A. Johnson.

ARKANSAS—R. W. Johnson, W. K. Sebastian.

KENTUCKY—L. W. Powell, J. J. Crittenden.

MISSOURI—Jas. S. Green, Trusten Polk.

OHIO—B. F. Wade, Geo. E. Pugh.

INDIANA—J. D. Bright, G. N. Fitch.

ILLINOIS—S. A. Douglas, L. Trumbull.

MICHIGAN—Z. Chandler, K. S. Bingham.

FLORIDA—D. L. Yulee, S. R. Mallory.

GEORGIA—Alfred Iverson, Robt. Toombs.

TEXAS—John Hemphill, L. T. Wigfall.

WISCONSIN—Charles Durkee, J. R. Doolittle.

IOWA—J. W. Grimes, Jas. Harlan.

CALIFORNIA—M. S. Latham, William M. Gwin.

* Resigned January 17th, 1861, and succeeded by Hon. Lot M. Morrill.

† Did not attend.

MINNESOTA—H. M. Rice, M. S. Wilkinson.

OREGON—Joseph Lane, Edward D. Baker.

HOUSE OF REPRESENTATIVES.

WILLIAM PENNINGTON of New Jersey, *Speaker.*

MAINE—D. E. Somes, John J. Perry, E. B. French, F. H. Morse, Israel Washburn, Jr.,‡ S. C. Foster.

NEW HAMPSHIRE—Gilman Marston, M. W. Tappan, T. M. Edwards.

VERMONT—E. P. Walton, J. S. Morrill, H. E. Royce.

MASSACHUSETTS—Thos. D. Eliot, James Buffinton, Charles Francis Adams, Alexander H. Rice, Anson Burlingame, John B. Alley, Daniel W. Gooch, Charles R. Train, Eli Thayer, Charles Delano, Henry L. Dawes.

RHODE ISLAND—C. Robinson, W. D. Brayton.

CONNECTICUT—Dwight Loomis, John Woodruff, Alfred A. Burnham, Orris S. Ferry.

DELAWARE—W. G. Whiteley.

NEW YORK—Luther C. Carter, James Humphrey, Daniel E. Sickles, W. B. Maclay, Thos. J. Barr, John Cochrane, George Briggs, Horace F. Clark, John B. Haskin, Chas. H. Van Wyck, Wm. S. Kenyon, Chas. L. Beale, A'bm. B. Olin, John H. Reynolds, Jas. B. McKean, G. W. Palmer, Francis E. Spinner, Clark B. Cochrane, James H. Graham, Richard Franchot, Roscoe Conkling, R. H. Duell, M. Lindley Lee, Chas. B. Hoard, Chas. B. Sedgwick, M. Butterfield, Emory B. Pottle, Alfred Wells, Wm. Irvine, Alfred Ely, Augustus Frank, Edwin R. Reynolds, Elbridge G. Spaulding, Reuben E. Fenton.

NEW JERSEY—John T. Nixon, John L. N. Stratton, Garnett B. Adrain, Jetur R. Riggs, Wm. Pennington (Speaker.)

PENNSYLVANIA—Thos. B. Florence, E. Joy Morris, John P. Verree, Wm. Millward, John Wood, John Hickman, Henry C. Longnecker, Jacob K. McKenty, Thaddeus Stevens, John W. Killinger, James H. Campbell, George W. Scranton, William H. Dimmick, Galusha A. Grow, James T. Hale, Benjamin F. Junkin, Edward McPherson, Samuel S. Blair, John Covode, William Montgomery, James K. Moorhead, Robert McKnight, William Stewart, Chapin Hall, Elijah Babbitt.

‡ Resigned and succeeded January 2d, 1861, by Hon. Stephen Coburn.

MARYLAND—Jas. A. Stewart, J. M. Harris, H. W. Davis, J. M. Kunkel, G. W. Hughes.

VIRGINIA—John S. Millson, Muscoe R. H. Garnett, Daniel C. De Jarnette, Roger A. Pryor, Thomas S. Bocock, William Smith, Alex. R. Boteler, John T. Harris, Albert G. Jenkins, Shelton F. Leake, Henry A. Edmundson, Elbert S. Martin, Sherrard Clemens.

SOUTH CAROLINA—John McQueen, Wm. Porcher Miles, Lawrence M. Keitt, Milledge L. Bonham, John D. Ashmore, Wm. W. Boyce.

NORTH CAROLINA—W. N. H. Smith, Thos. Ruffin, W. Winslow, L. O'B. Branch, John A. Gilmer, Jas. M. Leach, Burton Craige, Z. B. Vance.

GEORGIA—Peter E. Love, M. J. Crawford, Thos. Hardeman, Jr., L. J. Gartrell, J. W. H. Underwood, James Jackson, Joshua Hill, John J. Jones.

ALABAMA—Jas. L. Pugh, David Clopton, Sydenh. Moore, Geo. S. Houston, W. R. W. Cobb, J. A. Stallworth, J. L. M. Curry.

MISSISSIPPI—L. Q. C. Lamar, Reuben Davis, William Barksdale, O. R. Singleton, John J. McRae.

LOUISIANA—John E. Bouligny, Miles Taylor, T. G. Davidson, John M. Landrum.

OHIO—G. H. Pendleton, John A. Gurley, C. L. Vallandigham, William Allen, James M. Ashley, Wm. Howard, Thomas Corwin, Benj. Stanton, John Carey, C. A. Trimble, Chas. D. Martin, Saml. S. Cox, John Sherman, H. G. Blake, William Helmick, C. B. Tompkins, T. C. Theaker, S. Edgerton, Edward Wade, John Hutchins, John A. Bingham.

KENTUCKY—Henry C. Burnett, Green Adams, S. O. Peyton, F. M. Bristow, W. C. Anderson, Robert Mallory, Wm. E. Simms, L. T. Moore, John Y. Brown, J. W. Stevenson.

TENNESSEE—T. A. R. Nelson, Horace Maynard, R. B. Brabson, William B. Stokes, Robert Hatton, James H. Thomas, John V. Wright, James M. Quarles, Emerson Etheridge, Wm. T. Avery.

INDIANA—Wm. E. Niblack, Wm. H. English, Wm. M'Kee Dunn, Wm. S. Holman, David Kilgore, Albert G. Porter, John G. Davis, James Wilson, Schuyler Colfax, Chas. Case, John U. Pettit.

ILLINOIS—E. B. Washburne, J. F. Farnsworth, Owen Lovejoy, Wm. Kellogg, I. N. Morris, John A. McClernand, James C. Robinson, P. B. Fouke, John A. Logan.

ARKANSAS—Thomas C. Hindman, Albert Rust.

MISSOURI—J. R. Barrett, T. L. Anderson, John B. Clark, James Craig, S. H. Woodson, John S. Phelps, John W. Noell.

MICHIGAN—William A. Howard, Henry Waldron, F. W. Kellogg, De W. C. Leach.

FLORIDA—George S. Hawkins.

TEXAS—John H. Reagan, A. J. Hamilton.

IOWA—S. R. Curtis, Wm. Vandever.

CALIFORNIA—Charles L. Scott, John C. Burch.

WISCONSIN—John F. Potter, C. C. Washburn, C. H. Larrabee.

MINNESOTA—Cyrus Aldrich, Wm. Windom.

OREGON—Lansing Stout.

KANSAS—Martin F. Conway, (sworn Jan. 30th, 1861).

President Buchanan's Last Annual Message.

It was delivered on Tuesday, December 4th, 1860.

Mr. Buchanan alluded to the distracted condition of the country, and appealed to the American people. He declared that the election of any one of our fellow-citizens to the office of President does not, of itself, afford just cause for dissolving the Union; and that, to justify a revolutionary resistance the Federal Government must be guilty of "a deliberate, palpable, and dangerous exercise" of powers not granted by the Constitution—which, he alleged, and proceeded to prove, was not at all the case. He denied that "secession" could be justified as a Constitutional remedy, and asserted that the "principle is wholly inconsistent with the history, as well as the character, of the Federal Constitution;" and claimed that such a proposition was not advanced until many years after the origin of the Federal Government, and that then it was met and refuted by the conclusive arguments of General Jackson. He held that this Government is invested with all the attributes of sovereignty over the special subjects to which its authority extends, and then discussed, in the following language, what he denominated

THE POWER TO COERCE A STATE.

The question, fairly stated, is: Has the Constitution delegated to Congress the power to coerce a State into submission which is attempting to withdraw or has actually withdrawn from the Confederacy? If answered in the affirmative, it must be on the principle that the power has been conferred upon Congress to declare and to make war against a State. After much serious reflection I have arrived at the conclusion that no such power has been delegated to Congress nor to any other department of the Federal Government. It is manifest, upon an inspection of the Constitution, that this is not among the specific and enumerated powers granted to Congress; and it is equally apparent that its exercise is not "necessary and proper for carrying into execution" any one of these powers. So far from this power having been delegated to Congress, it was expressly refused by the Convention which framed the Constitution. It appears, from the proceedings of that body, that on the 31st May, 1787, the clause "*authorizing an exertion of the force of the whole against a delinquent State*" came up for consideration. Mr. Madison opposed it in a brief but powerful speech, from which I shall extract but a single sentence. He observed: "The use of force against a State would look more like a declaration of war than an infliction of punishment, and would probably be considered by the party attacked as a dissolution of all previous compacts by which it might be bound." Upon his motion the clause was unanimously postponed, and was never, I believe, again presented. Soon, afterwards, on the 8th June, 1787, when incidentally adverting to the subject, he said: "Any Government for the United States, formed on the supposed practicability of using force against the unconstitutional proceedings of the States, would prove as visionary and fallacious as the government of Congress," evidently meaning the then existing Congress of the old Confederation.

Without descending to particulars, it may be safely asserted that the power to make war against a State is at variance with the whole spirit and intent of the Constitution. Suppose such a war should result in the conquest of a State, how are we to govern it afterwards? Shall we hold it as a province and govern it by despotic power? In the nature of things we could not, by physical force, control the will of the people, and compel them to elect Senators and Representatives to Congress, and to perform all the other duties depending upon their own volition, and required from the free citizens of a free State as a constituent member of the Confederacy.

But, if we possessed this power, would it be wise to exercise it under existing circumstances? The object would doubtless be to preserve the Union. War would not only present the most effectual means of destroying it, but would banish all hope of its peaceable reconstruction. Besides, in the fraternal conflict a vast amount of blood and treasure would be expended, rendering future reconciliation between the States impossible. In the meantime who can foretell what would be the sufferings and privations of the people during its existence?

The fact is, that our Union rests upon public opinion, and can never be cemented by the blood of its citizens shed in civil war. If it cannot live in the affections of the people, it must one day perish. Congress possesses many means of preserving it by conciliation; but the sword was not placed in their hand to preserve it by force.

In this connexion, I shall merely call attention to a few sentences in Mr. Madison's justly celebrated report, in 1799, to the Legislature of Virginia. In this he ably and conclusively defended the resolutions of the preceding Legislature against the strictures of several other State Legislatures. These were mainly founded upon the protest of the Virginia Legislature against the "alien and sedition acts," as "palpable and alarming infractions of the Constitution." In pointing out the peaceful and constitutional remedies, and he referred to none other to which the States were authorized to resort on such occasions, he concludes by saying, "that the Legislatures of the States might have made a direct representation to Congress with a view to obtain a rescinding of the two offending acts, or they might have represented to their respective Senators in Congress their wish that two-thirds thereof would propose an explanatory amendment to the Constitution, or two-thirds of themselves, if such had been their option, might, by an application to Congress, have obtained a Convention for the same object."

This is the very course which I earnestly recommend in order to obtain an "explanatory amendment" of the Constitution on the subject of slavery. This might originate with Congress or the State Legislatures, as may be deemed most advisable to attain the object.

The explanatory amendment might be confined to the final settlement of the true construction of the Constitution on three special points:

1. An express recognition of the right of property in slaves in the States where it now exists or may hereafter exist.

2. The duty of protecting this right in all the common Territories throughout their territorial existence, and until they shall be admitted as States into the Union, with or without slavery, as their constitutions may prescribe.

3. A like recognition of the right of the master to have his slave, who has escaped from one State to another, restored and "delivered up" to him, and of the validity of the fugitive-slave law enacted for this purpose, together with a declaration that all State laws impairing or defeating this right are violations of the Constitution, and are consequently null and void.

It may be objected that this construction of the Constitution has already been settled by the Supreme Court of the United States, and what more ought to be required? The answer is, that a very large proportion of the people of the United States still contest the correctness of this decision, and never will cease from agitation and admit its binding force until established by the people of the several States in their sovereign character. Such an explanatory amendment would, it is believed, forever terminate the existing dissensions and restore peace and harmony among the States.

It ought not to be doubted that such an appeal to the arbitrament established by the Constitution itself would be received with favor by all the States of the Confederacy. In any event, it ought to be tried in a spirit of conciliation before any of these States shall separate themselves from the Union.

Opinion of Attorney-General Black upon the Powers of the President.

ATTORNEY-GENERAL'S OFFICE,
November 20, 1860.

SIR: I have had the honor to receive your note of the 17th, and I now reply to the grave questions therein propounded as fully as the time allowed me will permit.

Within their respective spheres of action the Federal Government and the Government of a State are both of them independent and supreme, but each is utterly powerless beyond the limits assigned to it by the Constitution. If Congress would attempt to change the law of descents, to make a new rule of personal succession, or to dissolve the family relations existing in any State, the act would be simply void, but not more void than would be a State law to prevent the recapture of fugitives from labor, to forbid the carrying of the mails, or to stop the collection of duties on imports. The will of a State, whether expressed in its constitution or laws, cannot, while it remains in the Confederacy, absolve her people from the duty of obeying the just and constitutional requirements of the Central Government. Nor can any act of the Central Government displace the jurisdiction of a State, because the laws of the United States are supreme and binding only so far as they are passed *in pursuance of the Constitution.* I do not say what might be effected by mere revolutionary force. I am speaking of legal and constitutional right.

This is the view always taken by the Judiciary, and so universally adopted that the statement of it may seem common-place. The Supreme Court of the United States has declared it in many cases. I need only refer you to the *United States* vs. *Booth* where the present Chief Justice, expressing the unanimous opinion of himself and all his brethren, enunciated the doctrine in terms so clear and full that any further demonstration of it can scarcely be required.

The duty which these principles devolve not only upon every officer, but every citizen, is that which Mr. Jefferson expressed so compendiously in his first inaugural, namely, "to support the State Governments in all their rights, as the most competent administrations for their domestic concerns, and the surest bulwarks against anti-republican tendencies," combined with "the preservation of the General Government, in its whole constitutional vigor, as the sheet-anchor of our peace at home and safety abroad."

To the Chief Executive Magistrate of the Union is confided the solemn duty of seeing the laws faithfully executed. That he may be able to meet this duty with a power equal to its performance, he nominates his own subordinates and removes them at his pleasure. For the same reason the land and naval forces are under his orders as their commander-in-chief. But his power is to be used only in the manner prescribed by the legislative department. He cannot accomplish a legal purpose by illegal means, or break the laws himself to prevent them from being violated by others.

The acts of Congress sometimes give the President a broad discretion in the use of the means by which they are to be executed, and sometimes limit his power so that he can exercise it only in a certain prescribed manner. Where the law directs a thing to be done, without saying how, that implies the power to use such means as may be necessary and proper to accomplish the end of the Legislature. But where the mode of performing a duty is pointed out by statute, that is the exclusive mode, and no other can be followed. The United States have no common law to fall back upon when the written law is defective. If, therefore, an act of Congress declares that a certain thing shall be done by a particular officer, it cannot be done by a different officer. The agency which the law furnishes for its own execution must be used, to the exclusion of all others. For instance, the revenues of the United States are to be collected in a certain way, at certain established ports, and by a certain class of officers; the President has no authority, under any circumstances, to collect the same revenues at other places by a different sort of officers, or in ways not provided for. Even if the machinery furnished by Congress for the collection of the duties should by any cause become so deranged or broken up that it could not be used, that would not be a legal reason for substituting a different kind of machinery in its place.

The law requires that all goods imported into the United States within certain collection-districts shall be entered at the proper port, and the duty thereon shall be received by the Collector appointed for and residing at that port. But the functions of the Collector may be exercised anywhere at or within the port. There is no law which confines him to the custom-house, or to any other particular spot. If the custom-house were burnt down, he might remove to another building; if he were driven from the shore, he might go on board a vessel in the harbor. If he keeps within the port he is within the law. A port is a place to which merchandize is imported, and from whence it is exported. It is created by law. It is not merely a harbor or haven, for it may be established where there is nothing but an open roadstead, or on the shore of a navigable river, or at any other place where vessels may arrive and discharge or take in their cargoes. It comprehends the city or town which is occupied by the mariners, merchants, and others who are engaged in the business of importing and exporting goods, navigating the ships and furnishing them with provisions. It includes also so much of the water adjacent to the city as is usually occupied by vessels discharging or receiving their cargoes, or lying at anchor and waiting for that purpose.

The first section of the act of March 2d, 1833, authorized the President in a certain contingency to direct that the custom-house for any collection district be established and kept *in any secure place within some port or harbor of such district*, either upon land or on board any vessel. But this provision was temporary, and expired at the end of the session of Congress next afterwards. It conferred upon the Executive a right to remove the site of the custom-house, not merely to any secure place within the legally-established port of entry for the district—that right he had before—but it widened his authority so as to allow the removal of it to any *port or harbor* within the whole district. The enactment of that law and the limitation of it to a certain period of time now past, is not therefore, an argument against the opinion above expressed that you can now if necessary, order the duties to be collected on board a vessel inside of any established port of entry. Whether the first and fifth sections of the act of 1833, both of which were made temporary by the eighth section, should be re-enacted, is a question for the legislative department.

Your right to take such measures as may seem to be necessary for the protection of the public property is very clear. It results from the proprietary rights of the Government as owner of the forts, arsenals, magazines, dock-yards, navy-yards, custom-houses, public ships, and other property which the United States have bought, built, and paid for. Besides, the Government of the United States is authorized by the Constitution (Art. I, Sec. 8) to "exercise exclusive legislation in all cases whatsoever . . over all places purchased by the consent of the Legislature of the State in which the same shall be for the erection of forts, magazines, arsenals, dock-yards, and other needful buildings." It is believed that no important public building has been bought or erected on ground where the Legislature of the State, in which it is, has not a passed a law consenting to the purchase of it and ceding the exclusive jurisdiction. This Government, then, is not only the owner of those buildings and grounds, but, by virtue of the supreme and paramount law, it regulates the action and punishes the offences of all who are within them. If any one of an owner's rights is plainer than another, it is that of keeping exclusive possession and repelling intrusion. The right of defending the public property includes also the right of recapture after it has been unlawfully taken by another. President Jefferson held the opinion, and acted upon it, that he could order a military force to take possession of any land to which the United States had title, though they had never occupied it before, though a private party claimed and held it, and though it was not then needed nor proposed to be used for any purpose connected with the operations of the Government. This may have been a stretch of Executive power; but the right of retaking public property in which the Government has been carrying on its lawful business, and from which its officers have been unlawfully thrust out, cannot well be doubted; and when it was exercised at Harper's Ferry in October, 1859, every one acknowledged the legal justice of it.

I come now to the point in your letter which is probably of the greatest practical importance. By the act of 1807 you may employ such parts of the land and naval forces as you shall judge necessary for the purpose of causing the laws to be duly executed, in all cases where it is lawful to use the militia for the same purpose. By the act of 1795 the militia may be called forth "whenever the laws of the United States shall be opposed or the execution thereof obstructed in any State by combinations too powerful to be suppressed by the ordinary course of judicial proceedings, or by the power vested in the marshals." This imposes upon the President the sole responsibility of deciding whether the exigency has arisen which requires the use of military force; and in proportion to the magnitude of that responsibility will be his care not to overstep the limits of his legal and just authority.

The laws referred to in the act of 1795 are manifestly those which are administered by the judges and executed by the ministerial officers of the courts for the punishment of crime against the United States, for the protection of rights claimed under the Federal Constitution and laws, and for the enforcement of such obligations as come within the cognizance of the Federal Judiciary. To compel obedience to these laws, the Courts have authority to punish all who obstruct their regular administration, and the marshals and their deputies have the same powers as sheriffs and their deputies in the several States in executing the laws of the States. These are the ordinary means provided for the execution of the laws, and the whole spirit of our system is opposed to the employment of any other except in cases of extreme necessity, arising out of great and unusual combinations against them. Their agency must continue to be used until their incapacity to cope with the power opposed to them shall be plainly demonstrated. It is only upon clear evidence to that effect that a military force can be called into the field. Even then its operations must be purely defensive. It can suppress only such combinations as are found directly opposing the laws and obstructing the execution thereof. It can do no more than what might and ought to be done by a civil posse, if a civil posse could be raised large enough to meet the same opposition. On such occasions especially the military power must be kept in strict subordination to the civil authority, since it is only in aid of the latter that the former can act at all.

But what if the feeling in any State against the United States should become so universal that the Federal officers themselves (including judges, district-attorneys, and marshals) would be reached by the same influences, and resign their places? Of course the first step would be to appoint others in their stead, if others could be got to serve. But, in such an event, it is more than probable that great difficulty would be found in filling the offices. We can easily conceive how it might become altogether impossible. We are therefore obliged to consider what can be done in case we have no courts to issue judicial process, and no ministerial officers to execute it. In that event troops would certainly be out of place, and their use wholly illegal. If they are sent to aid the courts and marshals, there must be courts and marshals to be aided. Without the exercise of those functions, which belong exclusively to the civil service, the laws cannot be executed in any event, no matter what may be the physical strength which the Government has at its command. Under such circumstances, to send a military force into any State with orders to act against the people would be simply making war upon them.

The existing laws put and keep the Federal Government strictly on the defensive. You can use force only to repel an assault on the public property, and aid the courts in the performance of their duty. If the means given you to collect the revenue and execute the other laws be insufficient for that purpose, Congress may extend and make them more effectual to that end.

If one of the States should declare her independence, your action cannot depend upon the rightfulness of the cause upon which such declaration is based. Whether the retirement of a State from the Union be the exercise of a right reserved in the Constitution or a revolutionary movement, it is certain that you have not in either case the authority to recognize her independence or to absolve her from her Federal obligations. Congress or the other States in convention assembled must take such measures as may be necessary and proper. In such an event I see no course for you but to go straight onward in the path you have hitherto trodden, that is, execute the laws to the extent of the defensive means placed in your hands, and act generally upon the assumption that the present constitutional relations between the States and the Federal Government continue to exist until a new order of things shall be established, either by law or force.

Whether Congress has the constitutional right to make war against one or more States, and require the Executive of the Federal Government to carry it on by means of force to be drawn from the other States, is a question for Congress itself to consider. It must be admitted that no such power is expressly given; nor are there any words in the Constitution which imply it. Among the powers enumerated in article I. section 8, is that "to declare war, grant letters of marque and reprisal, and to make rules concerning captures on land and water." This certainly means nothing more than the power to commence and carry on hostilities against the foreign enemies of the nation. Another clause in the same section gives Congress the power "to provide for calling forth the militia," and to use them within the limits of the State. But this power is so restricted by the words which immediately follow, that it can be exercised only for one of the following purposes: 1. To execute the laws of the Union; that is, to aid the Federal officers in the performance of their regular duties. 2. To suppress insurrections against the States; but this is confined by article IV. section 4, to cases in which the State herself shall apply for assistance against her own people. 3. To repel the invasion of a State by enemies who come from abroad to assail her in her own territory. All these provisions are made to protect the States, not to authorize an attack by one part of the country upon another; to preserve their peace, and not to plunge them into civil war. Our forefathers do not seem to have thought that war was calculated "to form a more perfect union, establish justice, insure domestic tranquility, provide for the common defence, promote the general welfare, and secure the blessings of liberty to ourselves and our posterity." There was undoubtedly a strong and universal conviction among the men who framed and ratified the Constitution, that military force would not only be useless, but pernicious as a means of holding the States together.

If it be true that war cannot be declared, nor a system of general hostilities carried on by the central government against a State, then it seems to follow that an attempt to do so would be *ipso facto* an expulsion of such State from the Union. Being treated as an alien and an enemy, she would be compelled to act accordingly. And if Congress shall break up the present Union by unconstitutionally putting strife and enmity, and armed hostility, between different sections of the country, instead of the "domestic tranquillity" which the Constitution was meant to insure, will not all the States be absolved from their Federal obligations? Is any portion of the people bound to contribute their money or their blood to carry on a contest like that?

The right of the General Government to preserve itself in its whole constitutional vigor by repelling a direct and positive aggression upon its property or its officers, cannot be denied. But this is a totally different thing from an offensive war to punish the people for the political misdeeds of their State governments, or to prevent a threatened violation of the Constitution, or to enforce an acknowledgment that the government of the United States is supreme. The States are colleagues of one another, and if some of them shall conquer the rest and hold them as subjugated provinces, it would totally destroy the whole theory upon which they are now connected.

If this view of the subject be as correct as I think it is, then the Union must utterly perish at the moment when Congress shall arm one part of the people against another for any purpose beyond that of merely protecting the General Government in the exercise of its proper constitutional functions. I am, very respectfully, yours, etc.,

J. S. Black.

To the President of the United States.

Committee of Thirty-three.

December 4th. In the House of Representatives, Mr. Boteler of Virginia moved that so much of the President's message as relates to the present perilous condition of the country be referred to a special committee of one from each State, which was agreed to—yeas 145, nays 38, as follows:

Yeas—Messrs. Adams of Massachusetts, Adams of Ky., *Adrain*, Aldrich, *Allen*, Alley, Anderson of Ky., *Anderson*, of Missouri, *Avery*, Babbitt, *Barr*, *Barrett*, *Bocock*, Boteler, Bouligny, *Branch*, Brayton, Briggs, Bristow, *Brown*, *Burch*, *Burnett*, Campbell, Carter, *Clark* of N. Y., *Clark* of Mo., *Cobb*, *John Cochrane* of N. York, Colfax, Conkling, Corwin, Covodo, *Cox*, Curtis, Davis of Md., *Davis* of Ind., *Davis*, of Miss., *De Jarnette*, Dolano, Duell, Dunn, *Edmundson*, Eliot, Ely, *English*, Etheridge, Ferry, *Florence*, Foster, *Fouke*, Frank, French, Gilmer, Gooch, Graham, Gurley, Hale, Hall, *Hardeman*, Harris of Md., *Harris* of Va., *Haskin*, Hatton, Helmick, Hill, Hoard, *Holman*, *Houston*, *Howard* of Ohio, *Hughes*, Humphrey, *Jenkins*, Junkin, Kellogg of Illinois, Kenyon, Kilgore, Killinger, *Kunkel*, *Larrabee*, Leach of N. Carolina, *Leake*, *Logan*, Longnecker, *Love*, *Maclay*, *Martin* of Ohio, *Martin*, of Va., Maynard, *McClernard*, *McKenty*, McPherson, *Millson*, Moore of Ky., Moorhead, Morrill, Morris of Penn., *Morris* of Ill., Nelson, *Niblack*, Nixon, *Noell*, Palmer, *Pendleton*, Pettit, *Peyton*, *Phelps*, Porter, *Pryor*, Quarles, Reynolds, Rice, *Riggs*, Robinson of R. I., Robinson of Illinois, Royce, *Rust*, *Sickles*, *Smith* of Va., Smith of N. C., Somes, Spaulding, Spinner, *Stevenson*, *Stewart* of Md., Stewart of Pa., Stokes, *Stout*, Stratton, Thayer, Theaker, *Thomas*, Train, Trimble, *Vallandigham*, Vance, Vandever, Verree, Walton, Washburn of Me., Webster, *Whiteley*, Windom, *Winslow*, Wood, Woodruff—145.

Nays—Messrs. Ashley, Beale, Bingham, Blair, Blake, Buffinton, Burlingame, Burnham, Carey, Case, Edgerton, Fenton, Grow, Hickman, Howard of Mich., Hutchins, Irvine, Kellogg of Mich., Leach of Mich., Lee, Loomis, Lovejoy, McKean, McKnight, Morse, Perry, Potter, Pottle, Sedgwick, Sherman, Stanton, Stevens, Tappan, Tompkins, Wade, Washburn of Wis., Washburne of Ill., Wells—38.

During the vote, Mr. Singleton of Mississippi, said he declined to vote because he had not been sent here to make any compromise or patch up existing difficulties, and that a Convention of the people of Mississippi would consider and decide the subject.

Mr. HAWKINS of Florida, said the day of compromise had passed, and that he was opposed, and he believed his State was opposed, to all and every compromise.

Mr. CLOPTON of Alabama, believed in the right of a State to secede, considered that the only remedy for present evils, and would not hold out any delusive hope, or sanction any temporizing policy.

Mr. MILES of South Carolina, said their delegation had not voted on the question because they conceived they had no interest in it. They considered their State as already withdrawn from the Confederacy in every thing except form.

Mr. PUGH of Alabama, said that State intended following South Carolina out of the Union by the 10th of January next, and he paid no attention to any action taken in this body. The Committee consisted of

Mr. Corwin of Ohio.
Mr. Millson of Virginia.
Mr. Adams of Massachusetts.
Mr. Winslow of North Carolina.
Mr. Humphrey of New York.
Mr. Boyce of South Carolina.
Mr. Campbell of Pennsylvania.
Mr. Love of Georgia.
Mr. Ferry of Connecticut.
Mr. Davis of Maryland.
Mr. Robinson of Rhode Island.
Mr. Whiteley of Delaware.
Mr. Tappan of New Hampshire.
Mr. Stratton of New Jersey.
Mr. Bristow of Kentucky.
Mr. Morrill of Vermont.
Mr. Nelson of Tennessee.
Mr. Dunn of Indiana.
Mr. Taylor of Louisiana.
Mr. Reuben Davis of Mississippi.
Mr. Kellogg of Illinois.
Mr. Houston of Alabama.
Mr. Morse of Maine.
Mr. Phelps of Missouri.
Mr. Rust of Arkansas.
Mr. Howard of Michigan.
Mr. Hawkins of Florida.
Mr. Hamilton of Texas.
Mr. Washburn of Wisconsin.
Mr. Curtis of Iowa.
Mr. Burch of California.
Mr. Windom of Minnesota.
Mr. Stout of Oregon.

Messrs. Hawkins and Boyce asked to be excused from service on the Committee, but the House refused.

Propositions Submitted to the Committee.

By Mr. THAYER of Massachusetts. A series of resolutions to the effect that the representatives of the people should devote themselves to the cause of the country, in the spirit of the fathers of the Republic; that the people should be true to their constitutional obligations; that as our differences had arisen mainly from the acquisition of new territory, no more territory ought ever to be acquired; affirming the right of self-government in the Territories as independent of Congress or the President; in favor of admission of new States with a population equal to the ratio of representation; that the Government of the United States should never own any more territory, and that annexation of territory in the future should only be by consent of the States; that there should be no Congressional legislation whatever on the subject of slavery, and that every Congressional District should in future be an Electoral District, entitled every four years to elect one Presidential elector.

By Mr. JOHN COCHRANE of New York. A preamble and resolution to the effect that the decision of the Supreme Court in the Dred Scott case should be received as a settlement of the questions therein discussed and decided; also, in favor of amending the Constitution so as to give a right to Congress to establish territorial governments; providing for admission of new States with a population equal to the Federal ratio of representation, with or without slavery, and prohibiting Congress and the people of the territory from impairing the right of property in slaves during its existence as a territory.

Mr. JOHN COCHRANE of New York, also offered amendments to the Constitution in favor of a division of territory on the line of thirty-six degrees thirty minutes; in favor of admission of new States with or without slavery; to prohibit Congress from abolishing the inter-State slave-trade; reaffirming the obligation of the fugitive slave law; guaranteeing a right of transit in free States of persons with slaves, and declaring void all nullifying acts of State or Territorial Legislatures.

Mr. JOHN COCHRANE of New York, also offered a preamble and resolutions to the same effect, as regards the question of slavery in the territories, with his proposition to amend the Constitution, just cited, and coupled with a resolution declaring that the Constitution of the United States existed only by agreement of sovereign States, and that any attempt of the Federal Government to coerce a sovereign State into the observance of the Constitutional compact, would be to levy war upon a substantial power and precipitate a dissolution of the Union.

Mr. HASKIN offered as a substitute to the above, a resolution directing the Committee on the Judiciary to inquire and report as to what action Congress should take in regard to enforcing the Constitution and laws in South Carolina, and what was the duty of the Executive in this regard.

By Mr. MALLORY of Kentucky. Instructing the Committee of Thirty-three in favor of a division of territory on line of thirty-six degrees thirty minutes, and admission of new States with a population equal to the Federal ratio of representation, with or without slavery, and to prohibit Congress from abolishing slavery in any places within its jurisdiction, or from abolishing the inter-State slave-trade.

By Mr. STEVENSON of Kentucky. To so amend the fugitive slave law as to make it felony to resist the execution of said law

By Mr. ENGLISH of Indiana. That said committee be instructed to inquire into the expediency of settling all matters of controversy upon the following basis: 1. Division of Territory between the free and slave States, with provision for admission of new States with a population equal to the Federal ratio of representation. 2. Prohibiting Congress from impairing the right of property in slaves. 3. Making the city, county, or township liable in double the value of fugitive slaves forcibly rescued, etc.

By Mr. KILGORE of Indiana. To give the right of trial by jury, where a fugitive slave claims to be free, with right of appeal on writ of error to either party. Monied compensation in case of rescue by force, etc., and making it a criminal offence to resist the enforcement of the fugitive slave law.

By Mr. HOLMAN of Indiana. Resolutions opposing the right of secession, declaring the duty of the General Government to enforce with temperate firmness and in good faith the provisions of the Constitution, and instructing the Committee of Thirty-three to inquire and report what legislation is needed to thwart any attempted nullification.

By Mr. NIBLACK of Indiana. That the committee be instructed to inquire and report whether Congress has power to provide by law for a payment of money to the owner of a fugitive slave prevented by violence from recapturing him.

By Mr. JOHN A. MCCLERNAND of Illinois To same effect, and further to inquire and report as to the expediency of establishing a *special* Federal police to execute the laws of the United States, and prevent opposition thereto.

By Mr. NOELL of Missouri. That said Committee be instructed to inquire and report as to the expediency of abolishing the office of President of the United States, and establishing in lieu thereof an Executive Council of three members to be elected by districts composed of contiguous States as nearly as possible—each member to be armed with a veto power; and also as to whether the equilibrium of free and slave States in the United States Senate can be restored and preserved, particularly by a voluntary division of some of the slave States into two or more States.

By Mr. HINDMAN of Arkansas. In favor of amending the Constitution as follows:

1st. An express recognition of slavery in the States where it exists, and prohibition of right of Congress to interfere therewith or with the inter-State slave-trade.

2d. Expressly requiring Congress to protect slavery in the territories, and in all places under its jurisdiction.

3d. For admission of new States, with or without slavery, as their Constitutions should provide.

4th. Right of transit for persons with slaves through the free States.

5th. To prohibit a right of representation in Congress to any States passing laws to impair the obligations of the fugitive slave law until such acts shall have been repealed.

6th. Giving the slave States a negative upon all acts of Congress relating to slavery.

7th. Making the above amendments, and all provisions of the Constitution relative to slavery unamendable.

8th. Granting to the several States authority to appoint all Federal officers within their respective limits.

By Mr. LARRABEE of Wisconsin. Recommending the several States to call a Convention of all the States to adopt such measures as the existing exigency required.

By Mr. ANDERSON of Missouri. In favor of a joint resolution to refer the questions at issue between the free and slave States to the Supreme Court of the United States for their opinion, and when obtained, that Congress should pass all necessary laws for giving effect to the opinion of said court.

By Mr. SMITH of Virginia. In favor of declaring out of the Union every State which shall aim by legislation to nullify an act of Congress.

By Mr. SICKLES of New York. To amend the Constitution so as to provide, that whenever a Convention of delegates chosen in any State by the people thereof under a recommendation of its Legislature, shall rescind its ratification of the Constitution, the President shall appoint, with consent of the Senate, three Commissioners to agree with such State regarding the disposition of the public property therein, and the proportion of the public debt which such State ought to assume, which being approved by the President and two-thirds of the Senate, he shall by proclamation declare the assent of the United States to the withdrawal of any such State from the Union.

By Mr. DUNN of Indiana. A resolution in favor of a more effectual execution of the 2d Section of the 4th Article of the Constitution to secure the personal rights of citizens of any State, travelling or sojourning in any other State.

By Mr. ADRAIN of New Jersey. A series of resolutions in substance as follows: Declaring the doctrine of non-intervention of Congress in the territories; the right of the people to be admitted as a State, either with or without slavery, as its Constitution should provide; in favor of the repeal of all enactments of State Legislatures which conflicted with acts of Congress, or the Constitution, affirming the constitutionality of the fugitive slave law; inculcating a kind and fraternal spirit among the people of the different States, and deprecating any interference with the domestic institutions of one another, and declaring that the Constitution could only be preserved by the same spirit of compromise that had governed its formation.

By Mr. MORRIS of Pennsylvania. Instructing the Committee of Thirty-three to report if there are any personal liberty bills of any State in conflict with the fugitive slave law, and to inquire and report if the fugitive slave law is not susceptible of amendment so as to prevent kidnapping, and render more certain the ascertainment of the true character of the fugitive.

By Mr. STEWART of Maryland. A lengthy preamble reciting to the effect that the States were sovereign, independent political organizations originally, and had united from time to time under such form of association or union as was deemed expedient—which form of association had been from time to time changed peaceably as circumstances required; that it was the deliberate opinion of many of the people that our present form of government, from causes either resulting from or in violation of the Constitution, was inadequate for the purposes for which it was created; that certain States were threatening to withdraw their allegiance; and that we had reached a crisis in our history which required an alteration of the present form of government; and he followed with a resolution instructing the committee on the President's message to inquire if any measures could be adopted for preserving the rights of all the States under the Union, and if not, to then inquire as to the best mode of adjusting the rights of the several States in a dissolution of the Union.

By Mr. LEAKE of Virginia. A resolution in favor of the amendment of the Constitution in the following particulars: Making it the duty of Congress to pass laws to protect slavery where it exists; taking away all territorial jurisdiction over the matter; guaranteeing the right of transit for persons with their slaves in any State; reaffirming the fugitive slave clause, with additional provision for compensation in case of failure to return the fugitive.

By Mr. JENKINS of Virginia. A resolution directing the Committee of Thirty-three to inquire into the best mode of amending the fugitive slave law so as to adequately punish its infraction and render compensation when the slave should not be restored; also as to whether the election of a President hostile to the slaveholding interest was not a sufficient reason to justify the slaveholding States to require that their concurrent sanction should be separately given to every act of the Federal Government, or whether there should be a dual Executive or a dual Senate, or the assent of a majority of the Senators from each section necessary to pass any law, or what other measures were needed for the protection of the slaveholding States.

By Mr. COX of Ohio. A resolution directing the Committee of Thirty-three to inquire what additional legislation was necessary to enforce the provisions of the Constitution relative to rendition of fugitives, and that such inquiry should be made with special reference to punishing all judges, attorney-generals, executives, and other State officers who should oppose its execution.

By Mr. HUTCHINS of Ohio. A resolution directing said committee to inquire what legislation was needed to give effect to section two of article four of the Constitution, granting to "the citizens of each State all the privileges and immunities of citizens in the several States," and to secure to all the people the full benefit of article four of amendments to the Constitution, which guarantees exemption from unreasonable searches and seizures, etc.

By Mr. SHERMAN of Ohio. A series of resolutions to the effect that the only remedy for existing dissensions was to be found in a faithful observance of all the compromises of the Constitution and the laws made in pursuance thereof; instructing the Committee of Thirty-three to inquire whether any State or the people thereof have failed of their duty in this regard, and if so what remedy should be made therefor, and directing said committee to divide the remaining Territories into States of convenient size with a view to their immediate admission into the Union.

By Mr. BINGHAM of Ohio. A resolution directing the committee to report such additional legislation as might be needed to put down armed rebellion and protect the property of the United States from seizure, and the citizens thereof from unlawful violence.

OTHER PROPOSITIONS SUBMITTED TO THE HOUSE.

Mr. ETHERIDGE of Tennessee proposed a series of amendments to the Constitution, in substance as follows:

That Congress shall not interfere with slavery in the States, nor in any forts, arsenals, etc., ceded to the United States by a slave State, nor in the District of Columbia, without the consent of Maryland, Virginia, and the inhabitants of the District, nor without making compensation; nor with the inter-State slave-trade. Foreign slave-trade prohibited. In regard to slavery in Territories, a provision similar to that proposed by Mr. Cochrane, before cited. No foreign territory to be acquired except on a concurrent two-thirds vote of both houses of Congress or by a treaty ratified by two-thirds of the members of the Senate; and an amendment in reference to rendition of fugitives from justice.

Mr. DAVIS of Indiana. A preamble and resolution reciting the Ordinance of Secession of South Carolina, and directing the Committee on the Judiciary to inquire and report what legislation had been rendered necessary in consequence thereof.

Mr. HOLMAN of Indiana, offered a series of resolutions, denying the right of secession, affirming it to be the duty of the General Government to collect the revenue and protect the public property, and instructing the Committee on the Judiciary to inquire and report what legislation is needed to enable the Government to discharge its constitutional duty in these regards.

Mr. FLORENCE of Pennsylvania, offered as a substitute for the report of the Committee of Thirty-three a series of amendments to the Constitution, in substance as follows:

1st. Granting the right to hold slaves in all territory south of 36° 30′, and prohibiting Congress and the Territorial Legislature from interfering with it therein, or in any other place within the jurisdiction of the United States, without the consent of all the slave States.

2d. Admitting States into the Union with a population equal to the ratio of representation, with or without slavery, as their Constitution shall prescribe.

3d. Prohibiting any alteration of the present basis of representation—declaring the slavery question to be one exclusively for each State; but with proviso that this amendment shall not be construed so as to release the General Government from its obligations to suppress domestic insurrection in any State.

4th. Giving the right to abolish slavery in the District of Columbia exclusively to the State of Maryland.

5th. Prohibiting any State from passing laws to obstruct the rendition of fugitive slaves.

6th. Granting the right of transit with slaves through all the States.

7th. Declaring all slaves brought into any State by permission thereof, and escaping, to be fugitives from labor.

8th. Prohibiting the African slave-trade, and also prohibiting persons of African descent from becoming citizens.

9th. Making all acts of any inhabitants of the United States tending to incite slaves to insurrection, penal offences.

10th. Making the county in which any fugitive slave shall be rescued, liable to pay the value thereof.

11th. Prohibiting slavery in territory north of 36° 30′.

12th. Giving returned fugitive slaves a trial by a jury in the place to which they shall have been returned.

13th. Provides for rendition of fugitives from justice.

14th. Declaring inviolable the rights of the citizens of any State sojourning in another State.

15th. No State shall retire from the Union without the consent of three-fourths of all the States.

16th. Giving full power to three-fourths of the States at any time to call a Convention to amend or abolish the Constitution.

17th. Declares articles 8, 9 and 10 of these amendments to be unalterable, unless by consent of all the slave States.

Mr. FENTON of New York, offered as a substitute for the report of the Committee of Thirty-three a preamble and resolution, reciting the conflicting differences of opinion as to the causes of the present disturbances, and favoring the calling of a Convention of delegates from the several States.

Mr. KELLOGG of Illinois. As a substitute for the report of the Committee, amendments to the Constitution in substance as follows: Prohibiting slavery in territory north of 36° 30′, and permitting it south of that line, and providing for its admission as States with a population equal to the ratio of representation, with or without slavery, as its Constitution should prescribe; prohibiting any interference by Congress with the subject in the States, either to abolish or establish slavery; affirmatory of the fugitive slave-clause of the Constitution, with amendment providing for compensation, and prohibiting the foreign slave-trade.

By Mr. VALLANDIGHAM of Ohio, the following preamble and resolution:

JOINT RESOLUTION PROPOSING AMENDMENTS TO THE CONSTITUTION.

WHEREAS, the Constitution of the United States is a grant of specific powers delegated to the Federal Government by the people of the several States, all powers not delegated to it nor prohibited to the States being reserved to the States respectively, or to the people: and whereas it is the tendency of stronger Governments to enlarge their powers and jurisdiction at the expense of weaker Governments, and of majorities to usurp and abuse power and oppress minorities, to arrest and hold in check which tendency compacts and Constitutions are made; and whereas the only effectual constitutional security for the rights of minorities, whether as people or as States, is the power expressly reserved in Constitutions of protecting those rights by their own action; and whereas this mode of protection, by checks and guarantees, is recognized in the Federal Constitution, as well in the case of the equality of the States in representation and in suffrage in the Senate, as in the provision for overruling the vote of the President, and for amending the Constitution, not to enumerate other examples; and whereas, unhappily, because of the vast extent and diversified interests and institutions of the several States of the Union, sectional divisions can no longer be suppressed; and whereas it concerns the peace and stability of the Federal Union and Government that a division of the States into mere slaveholding and non-slaveholding sections, causing hitherto, and from the nature and necessity of the case, inflammatory and disastrous controversies upon the subject of slavery, ending already in present disruption of the Union, should be forever hereafter ignored: and whereas this important end is best to be attained by the recognition of other sections without regard to slavery neither of which sections shall alone be strong enough to oppress or control the others, and each be vested with the power to protect itself from aggressions: Therefore,

Be it resolved by the Senate and House of Representatives of the United States of America in Congress assembled, (two-thirds of both Houses concurring,) That the following articles be and are hereby proposed as amendments to the Constitution of the United States, which shall be valid to all intents and purposes as part of said Constitution when ratified by Conventions in three-fourths of the several States:

ARTICLE XIII. SEC. 1. The United States are divided into four sections, as follows:

The States of Maine, New Hampshire, Vermont, Massachusetts, Rhode Island, Connecticut, New York, New

Jersey, and Pennsylvania, and all new States annexed and admitted into the Union, or formed or erected within the jurisdiction of any of said States, or by the junction of two or more of the same or of parts thereof, or out of territory acquired north of said States, shall constitute one section, to be known as the NORTH.

The States of Ohio, Indiana, Illinois, Michigan, Wisconsin, Minnesota, Iowa, and Kansas, and all new States annexed or admitted into the Union, or erected within the jurisdiction of any of said States, or by the junction of two or more of the same or of parts thereof, or out of territory now held or hereafter acquired north of latitude 36° 30′ and east of the crest of the Rocky Mountains, shall constitute another section, to be known as the WEST.

The States of Oregon and California, and all new States annexed and admitted into the Union, or formed or erected within the jurisdiction of any of said States, or by the junction of two or more of the same or of parts thereof, or out of territory now held or hereafter acquired west of the crest of the Rocky Mountains and of the Rio Grande, shall constitute another section to be known as the PACIFIC.

The States of Delaware, Maryland, Virginia, North Carolina, South Carolina, Georgia, Florida, Alabama, Mississippi, Louisiana, Texas, Arkansas, Tennessee, Kentucky, and Missouri, and all new States annexed and admitted into the Union, or formed or erected within the jurisdiction of any of said States, or by the junction of two or more of the same or of parts thereof, or out of territory acquired east of the Rio Grande and south of latitude 36° 30′, shall constitute another section, to be known as the SOUTH.

SEC. 2. On demand of one-third of the Senators of any one of the sections on any bill, order, resolution, or vote, to which the concurrence of the House of Representatives may be necessary, except on a question of adjournment, a vote shall be had by sections, and a majority of the Senators from each section voting shall be necessary to the passage of such bill, order, or resolution, and to the validity of every such vote.

SEC. 3. Two of the electors for President and Vice President shall be appointed by each State in such manner as the Legislature thereof may direct for the State at large. The other electors to which each State may be entitled shall be chosen in the respective Congressional districts into which the State may at the regular decennial period have been divided, by the electors of each district having the qualifications requisite for electors of the most numerous branch of the State Legislature. A majority of all the electors in each of the four sections in this article established shall be necessary to the choice of President and Vice President; and the concurrence of a majority of the States of each section shall be necessary to the choice of President by the House of Representatives, and of the Senators from each section to the choice of Vice President by the Senate, whenever the right of choice shall devolve upon them respectively.

SEC. 4. The President and Vice President shall hold their offices each during the term of six years; and neither shall be eligible to more than one term except by the votes of two-thirds of all the electors of each section, or of the States of each section, whenever the right of choice of President shall devolve upon the House of Representatives, or of the Senators from each section whenever the right of choice of Vice President shall devolve upon the Senate.

SEC. 5. The Congress shall by law provide for the case of a failure by the House of Representatives to choose a President, and of the Senate to choose a Vice President, whenever the right of choice shall devolve upon them respectively, declaring what officer shall then act as President; and such officer shall act accordingly until a President be elected. The Congress shall also provide by law for a special election for President and Vice President in such case, to be held and completed within six months from the expiration of the term of office of the last preceding President and to be conducted in all respects as provided for in the Constitution for regular elections of the same officers, except that if the House of Representatives shall not choose a President, should the right of choice devolve upon them, within twenty days from the opening of the certificates and counting of the electoral votes, then the Vice President shall act as President as in the case of the death or other constitutional disability of the President. The term of office of the President chosen under such special elections shall continue six years from the 4th day of March preceding such election.

ARTICLE XIV. No State shall secede without the consent of the Legislatures of all the States of the section to which the State proposing to secede belongs. The President shall have power to adjust with seceding States all questions arising by reason of their secession; but the terms of adjustment shall be submitted to the Congress for their approval before the same shall be valid.

ARTICLE XV. Neither the Congress nor a Territorial Legislature shall have power to interfere with the right of the citizens of any of the States within either of the sections to migrate upon equal terms with the citizens of the States within either of the other sections, to the Territories of the United States; nor shall either have power to destroy or impair any rights of either person or property in the Territories. New States annexed for admission into the Union, or formed or erected within the jurisdiction of other States, or by the junction of two or more States or parts of States, and States formed with the consent of the Congress out of any territory of the United States, shall be entitled to admission upon an equal footing with the original States, under any constitution establishing a Government republican in form, which the people thereof may ordain, whenever such States shall contain, within an area of not less than thirty thousand square miles, a population equal to the then existing ratio of representation for one member of the House of Representatives.

Report of the Committee of Thirty-three.

January 14th, 1861. Mr. CORWIN reported a series of propositions, with a written statement in advocacy thereof, which closes with the remark that "the Committee were not unanimous on all the resolutions and bills presented, but a majority of a quorum was obtained on them all."

Mr. CHARLES FRANCIS ADAMS of Massachusetts, made a separate report, which closes thus: "The general conclusion to which the subscriber has arrived from a close observation of the action of the Committee, is this: That no form of adjustment will be satisfactory to the recusant States which does not incorporate into the Constitution of the United States a recognition of this obligation to protect and extend slavery. On this condition, and on this alone, will they consent to withdraw their opposition to the recognition of the constitutional election of the Chief Magistrate. Viewing the matter in this light, it seems unadvisable to attempt to proceed a step further in the way of offering unacceptable propositions. He can never give his consent to the terms demanded.

"For this reason it is that, after having become convinced of this truth, he changed his course and declined to recommend the very measures which he in good faith had offered. It certainly can be of no use to propose as an adjustment that which has no prospect of being received as such by the other party. Hence he feels it his duty now to record his dissent from the action of a majority of his colleagues in introducing any measures whatever for the consideration of the House."

Mr. C. C. WASHBURN of Wisconsin, and Mr. MASON W. TAPPAN of New Hampshire, also submitted a minority report, concluding with this resolution:

Resolved, That the provisions of the Constitution are ample for the preservation of the Union and the protection of all the material interests of our country; that it needs to be obeyed rather than amended; and that our extrication from our present difficulties is to be looked for in efforts to preserve and protect the public property and enforce the laws, rather than in new guarantees for particular interests, or compromises or concessions to unreasonable demands.

Messrs. TAYLOR of Louisiana, PHELPS of Missouri, RUST of Arkansas, WHITELEY of Delaware, and WINSLOW of North Carolina, also submitted a minority report, arguing that the present difficulties can only be remedied by amendments to the Constitution, and suggesting the Crittenden proposition. If that cannot be adopted, they recommend a Convention of the States, with a view, if no adjustment can be effected, to peaceable separation, by providing for a partition of the common property of the United States, settling the terms on which the social and commercial intercourse between the separated States shall be conducted, and making a permanent arrangement with respect to the navigation of the Mississippi river.

Messrs. BURCH of California and STOUT of Oregon submitted a separate report, sustaining the propositions submitted by Mr. CORWIN, but urging, in addition, the assembling of a National Constitutional Convention to consider the whole subject matter of the difficulties.

Mr. NELSON of Tennessee made a report, arguing in favor of the establishment of the line of 36° 30′, north of which slavery shall be prohibited, and south of which it shall be protected until any territory shall contain the population requisite for a member of Congress, when, if its form of government be republican, it shall be admitted into the Union, with or without slavery, as the Constitution of such new State may provide. He dissented from the proposition to admit New Mexico, opposed the proposed change of the fugitive slave law, and recommended the Crittenden proposition.

Messrs. LOVE of Georgia, and HAMILTON of Texas, dissented from the majority report, and recommended the Crittenden proposition.

Mr. FERRY was unable to concur in the report made by MR. CORWIN, and made a statement of his position.

VOTE ON THE FIRST PROPOSITION OF THE COMMITTEE OF THIRTY-THREE, FEB. 27TH, 1861.

DECLARATORY RESOLUTIONS.

Resolved by the Senate and House of Representatives of the United States of America in Congress assembled, That all attempts on the part of the Legislatures of any of the States to obstruct or hinder the recovery and surrender of fugitives from service or labor, are in derogation of the Constitution of the United States, inconsistent with the comity and good neighborhood that should prevail among the several States, and dangerous to the peace of the Union.

Resolved, That the several States be respectfully requested to cause their statutes to be revised, with a view to ascertain if any of them are in conflict with or tend to embarrass or hinder the execution of the laws of the United States, made in pursuance of the second section of the fourth article of the Constitution of the United States for the delivery up of persons held to labor by the laws of any State and escaping therefrom; and the Senate and House of Representatives earnestly request that all enactments having such tendency be forthwith repealed, as required by a just sense of constitutional obligations, and by a due regard for the peace of the Republic; and the President of the United States is requested to communicate these resolutions to the Governors of the several States, with a request that they will lay the same before the Legislatures thereof respectively.

Resolved, That we recognize slavery as now existing in fifteen of the United States by the usages and laws of those States; and we recognize no authority, legally or otherwise, outside of a State where it so exists, to interfere with slaves or slavery in such States, in disregard of the rights of their owners or the peace of society.

Resolved, That we recognize the justice and propriety of a faithful execution of the Constitution, and laws made in pursuance thereof on the subject of fugitive slaves, or fugitives from service or labor, and discountenance all mobs or hindrances to the execution of such laws, and that citizens of each State shall be entitled to all the privileges and immunities of citizens in the several States.

Resolved, That we recognize no such conflicting elements in its composition, or sufficient cause from any source, for a dissolution of this Government; that we were not sent here to destroy, but to sustain and harmonize the institutions of the country, and to see that equal justice is done to all parts of the same; and finally, to perpetuate its existence on terms of equality and justice to all the States.

Resolved, That a faithful observance, on the part of all the States, of all their constitutional obligations to each other and to the Federal Government, is essential to the peace of the country.

Resolved, That it is the duty of the Federal Government to enforce the Federal laws, protect the Federal property, and preserve the Union of these States.

Resolved, That each State be requested to revise its statutes, and, if necessary, so to amend the same as to secure, without legislation by Congress, to citizens of other States travelling therein, the same protection as citizens of such State enjoy; and also to protect the citizens of other States travelling or sojourning therein against popular violence or illegal summary punishment, without trial in due form of law, for imputed crimes.

Resolved, That each State be also respectfully requested to enact such laws as will prevent and punish any attempt whatever in such State to recognize or set on foot the lawless invasion of any other State or Territory.

Resolved, That the President be requested to transmit copies of the foregoing resolutions to the Governors of the several States, with a request that they be communicated to their respective Legislatures.

YEAS—Messrs. Charles F. Adams, Green Adams, *Adrain*, Aldrich, William C. Anderson, Babbitt, *Barrett*, Beale, Boteler, Brabson, Brayton, Briggs, Bristow, *Brown*, *Burch*, Burnham, Butterfield, Campbell, Carter, *John B. Clark*, Coburn, Clark B. Cochrane, *John Cochrane*, Colfax, Conkling, Corwin, Covode, *Cox*, *James Craig*, H. Winter Davis, *John G. Davis*, Delano, *Dimmick*, Dunn, Edwards, Ely, *English*, Etheridge, Farnsworth, Ferry, *Florence*, Foster, *Fouke*, French, Gilmer, Graham, Grow, Gurley, Hale, Hall, *Hamilton*, J. Morrison Harris, *John T. Harris*, *Haskin*, Hatton, Helmick, Hoard, *Holman*, *William Howard*, William A. Howard, Humphrey, Irvine, Junkin, Francis W. Kellogg, William Kellogg, Kenyon, Kilgore, Killinger, *Larrabee*, James M. Leach, Lee, *Logan*, Longnecker, Loomis, *Maclay*, Mallory, Marston, *Charles D. Martin*, Maynard, *McClernand*, McKean, *McKenty*, McKnight, McPherson, *Millson*, *Montgomery*, Laban T. Moore, Moorhead, Morrill, Edward Joy Morris, *Isaac N. Morris*, Morse, Nelson, *Niblack*, Nixon, *Noell*, Olin, Palmer, Perry, Pettit, *Peyton*, *Phelps*, Porter, Pottle, Quarles, John H. Reynolds, Rice, *Riggs*, Christopher Robinson, *James C. Robinson*, Royce, Scranton, Sherman, *Sickles*, *Simms*, William N. H. Smith, Spaulding, Stanton, *Stevenson*, William Stewart, Stokes, *Stout*, Stratton, Thayer, Tompkins, Train, Trimble, *Vallandigham*, Vance, Verree, Waldron, Walton, Webster, Wilson, Windom, Wood, Woodruff—137.

NAYS—Messrs. Alley, Ashley, *Avery*, Bingham, Blair, Blake, *Bocock*, *Branch*, Buffinton, Burlingame, *Burnett*, Carey, Case, Conway, *Burton Craige*, Dawes, *De Jarnette*, Duell, *Edmundson*, Eliot, Fenton, *Garnett*, Gooch, Hickman, *Hindman*, *Hughes*, Hutchins, *Jenkins*, De Witt C. Leach, *Leake*, Lovejoy, *Elbert S. Martin*, Potter, *Pryor*, Edwin R. Reynolds, *Ruffin*, *Rust*, Sedgwick, *William Smith*, Somes, Spinner, Stevens, *James A. Stewart*, Tappan, *Thomas*, Vandever, Van Wyck, Wade, Cadwalader C. Washburn, Wells, *Whiteley*, *Winslow*, *Woodson*—53.

So the joint resolution was passed.

VOTE ON SECOND PROPOSITION.

CONSTITUTIONAL AMENDMENT.

Be it resolved by the Senate and House of Representatives of the United States of America in Congress assembled, two-thirds of both Houses concurring, That the following article be proposed to the Legislatures of the several States as an amendment to the Constitution of the United States, which, when ratified by three-fourths of said Legislatures, shall be valid, to all intents and purposes, as a part of the said Constitution, namely:

ART. XII. No amendment of this Constitution having for its object any interference within the States with the relation between their citizens and those described in section second of the first article of the Constitution as "all other persons," shall originate with any State that does not recognize that relation within its own limits, or shall be valid without the assent of every one of the States composing the Union.

Before the vote was taken Mr. CORWIN offered the following substitute for the above article:

ART. XII. No amendment shall be made to the Constitution which will authorize or give to Congress the power to abolish or interfere, within any State, with the domestic institutions thereof, including that of persons held to labor or service by the laws of said State.

Which was agreed to, yeas 120, nays 61, as follows:

YEAS—Messrs. Charles F. Adams, Green Adams, Aldrich, William C. Anderson, *Avery*, Babbitt, *Barr*, *Barrett*, *Bocock*, Boteler, Brabson, Briggs, Bristow, *Brown*, *Burch*, *Burnett*, Butterfield, Campbell, *Horace F. Clark*, *John B. Clark*, Coburn, Clark B. Cochrane, *John Cochrane*, Colfax, Corwin, *Cox*, *James Craig*, H. Winter Davis, *John G. Davis*, Dawes, *De Jarnette*, Delano, *Dimmick*, Dunn, *Edmundson*, *English*, Etheridge, *Florence*, *Fouke*, Gilmer, Hale, Hall, *Hamilton*, J. Morrison Harris, *John T. Harris*, Hatton, Helmick, Hoard, *Holman*, *William Howard*, William A. Howard, *Hughes*, Humphrey, *Jenkins*, Junkin, Francis W. Kellogg, William Kellogg, Kenyon, Kilgore, Killinger, *Kunkel*, *Larrabee*, James M. Leach, *Leake*, *Logan*, Mallory, Marston, *Charles D. Martin*, *Elbert S. Martin*, Maynard, *McClernand*, *McKenty*, McKnight, McPherson, *Millson*, *Montgomery*, Laban T. Moore, Moorhead, Morrill, Edward Joy Morris, *Isaac N. Morris*, Nelson, *Niblack*, Nixon, *Noell*, Olin, Palmer, *Peyton*, *Phelps*, Porter, *Pryor*, Quarles, John H. Reynolds, Rice, *Riggs*, Christopher Robinson, *James C. Robinson*, *Ruffin*, *Rust*, Scranton, *Sickles*, *Simms*, William N. H. Smith, Spaulding, Stanton, *Stevenson*, *James A. Stewart*, Stokes, *Stout*, Stratton, Thayer, *Thomas*, Trimble, Vance, Verree, Walton, Webster, Windom, *Woodson*, *Wright*—120.

NAYS—Messrs. Alley, Ashley, Beale, Bingham, Blair, Blake, Brayton, Buffinton, Burlingame, Burnham, Carey, Carter, Case, Conkling, Conway, Duell, Edgerton, Edwards, Eliot, Ely, Fenton, Ferry, Foster, Frank, Gooch, Graham, Grow, Hickman, *Hindman*, Hutchins, Irvine, De Witt C. Leach, Lee, Longnecker, Loomis, Lovejoy, McKean, Perry, Pettit, Potter, Pottle, Edwin R. Reynolds, Royce, Sedgwick, Somes, Spinner, Stevens, William Stewart, Tappan, Tompkins, Train, Vandever, Van Wyck, Wade, Waldron, Cadwalader C. Washburn, Ellihu B. Washburne, Wells, Wilson, *Winslow*, Woodruff—61.

The resolution as amended was then negatived, yeas 120, nays 71, two-thirds not voting in the affirmative, as follows:

YEAS—Messrs. Charles F. Adams, Green Adams, *Adrain*, William C. Anderson, *Avery*, Babbitt, *Barr*, *Barrett*, *Bocock*, Boteler, Bouligny, Brabson, *Branch*, Briggs, Bristow, *Brown*, *Burch*, *Burnett*, Campbell, *Horace F. Clark*, *John B. Clark*, Clark B. Cochrane, *John Cochrane*, Colfax, Corwin, *Cox*, *James Craig*, *Burton Craige*, H. Winter Davis, *John G. Davis*, *De Jarnette*, Delano, *Dimmick*, Dunn, *Edmundson*, *English*, Etheridge, *Florence*, *Fouke*, *Garnett*, Gilmer, Hale, Hall, *Hamilton*, J. Morrison Harris, *John T. Harris*, Hatton, Helmick, Hoard, *Holman*, *Wm. Howard*, William A. Howard, *Hughes*, Humphrey, *Jenkins*, Junkin, William Kellogg, Kenyon, Killinger, *Kunkel*, *Larrabee*, James M. Leach, *Leake*, *Logan*, *Maclay*, Mallory, *Charles D. Martin*, *Elbert S. Martin*, Maynard, *McClernand*, *McKenty*, McKnight, McPherson, *Millson*, *Montgomery*, Laban T. Moore, Moorhead, Morrill, Edward Joy Morris, *Isaac N. Morris*, Nelson, *Niblack*, Nixon, *Noell*, Olin, *Peyton*, *Phelps*, Porter, *Pryor*, Quarles, John H. Reynolds, Rice, *Riggs*, Christopher Robinson, *James C. Robinson*, *Ruffin*, *Rust*, Scranton, *Sickles*, *Simms*, William N. H. Smith, Spaulding, Stanton, *Stevenson*, *James A. Stewart*, Stokes, *Stout*, Thayer, *Thomas*, Trimble, *Vallandigham*, Vance, Verree, Webster, *Whiteley*, Windom, *Winslow*, Wood, *Woodson*, *Wright*—120.

NAYS—Messrs. Aldrich, Alley, Ashley, Beale, Bingham, Blair, Blake, Brayton, Buffinton, Burlingame, Burnham, Butterfield, Carey, Carter, Case, Coburn, Conkling, Conway, Covode, Dawes, Duell, Edgerton, Edwards, Eliot, Ely, Farnsworth, Fenton, Ferry, Foster, Frank, Gooch, Graham, Grow, Gurley, Hickman, Hutchins, Irvine, Francis W. Kellogg, Kilgore, De Witt C. Leach, Lee, Longnecker, Loomis, Lovejoy, Marston, McKean, Morse, Perry, Pettit, Potter, Pottle, Edwin R. Reynolds, Royce, Sedgwick, Somes, Spinner, Stevens, William Stewart, Tappan, Tompkins, Train, Vandever, Van Wyck, Wade, Waldron, Walton, Cadwalader C. Washburn, Ellihu B. Washburne, Wells, Wilson, Woodruff—71.

Mr. KILGORE entered a motion to re-consider.

February 28th. This motion was carried, yeas 125, nays 68, and the joint resolution then passed, yeas 133, nays 65, as follows:

YEAS—Messrs. Charles F. Adams, Green Adams, *Adrain*, Aldrich, William C. Anderson, *Avery*, Babbitt, *Barr*, *Barrett*, *Bocock*, Boteler, Bouligny, Brabson, *Branch*, Briggs, Bristow, *Brown*, *Burch*, *Burnett*, Butterfield, Campbell, *Horace F. Clark*, *John B. Clark*, *Clemens*, Clark B. Cochrane, *John Cochrane*, Colfax, Corwin, *Cox*, *James Craig*, *Burton Craige*, H. Winter Davis, *John G. Davis*, *De Jarnette*, Delano, *Dimmick*, Dunn, *Edmundson*, *English*, Etheridge, *Florence*, *Fouke*, French, *Garnett*, Gilmer, Hale, Hall, *Hamilton*, J. Morrison Harris, *John T. Harris*, *Haskin*, Hatton, Helmick, Hoard, *Holman*, *William Howard*, William A. Howard, *Hughes*, Humphrey, *Jenkins*, Junkin,

William Kellogg, Kenyon, Kilgore, Killinger, *Kunkel*, *Larrabee*, James M. Leach, *Leake*, *Logan*, *Maclay*, Mallory, *Charles D. Martin*, *Elbert S. Martin*, Maynard, *McClernand*, *McKenty*, McKnight, McPherson, *Millson*, *Montgomery*, Laban T. Moore, Moorhead, Morrill, Edward Joy Morris, *Isaac N. Morris*, Morse, Nelson, *Niblack*, Nixon, *Noell*, Olin, Palmer, *Pendleton*, *Peyton*, *Phelps*, Porter, *Pryor*, Quarles, John H. Reynolds, Rice, *Riggs*, Christopher Robinson, *James C. Robinson*, *Ruffin*, *Rust*, *Scott*, Scranton, Sherman, *Sickles*, *Simms*, William N. H. Smith, Spaulding, Stanton, *Stevenson*, *James A. Stewart*, Stokes, *Stout*, Stratton, Thayer, Theaker, *Thomas*, Trimble, *Vallandigham*, Vance, Verree, Webster, *Whiteley*, Windom, *Winslow*, Wood, *Woodson*, *Wright*—133.

NAYS—Messrs. Alley, Ashley, Beale, Bingham, Blair, Blake, Brayton, Buffinton, Burlingame, Burnham, Carey, Carter, Case, Coburn, Conkling, Conway, Dawes, Duell, Edgerton, Edwards, Eliot, Ely, Farnsworth, Fenton, Ferry, Foster, Frank, Gooch, Grow, Gurley, Hickman, *Hindman*, Hutchins, Irvine, Francis W. Kellogg, DeWitt C. Leach, Lee, Longnecker, Loomis, Lovejoy, Marston, McKean, Pettit, Potter, Pottle, Edwin R. Reynolds, Royce, Sedgwick, Somes, Spinner, Stevens, William Stewart, Tappan, Tompkins, Train, Vandever, Van Wyck, Wade, Waldron, Walton, Cadwalader C. Washburn, Ellihu B. Washburne, Wells, Wilson, Woodruff—65.

March 2d. The joint resolution passed the Senate, yeas 24, nays 12, as follows:

YEAS—Messrs. Anthony, Baker, *Bigler*, *Bright*, Crittendon, Dixon, *Douglas*, Foster, Grimes, *Gwin*, Harlan, *Hunter*, *Johnson* of Tennessee, *Kennedy*, *Latham*, *Mason*, Morrill, *Nicholson*, *Polk*, *Pugh*, *Rice*, *Sebastian*, Ten Eyck, *Thomson*—24.

NAYS—Messrs. Bingham, Chandler, Clark, Doolittle, Durkee, Foot, King, Sumner, Trumbull, Wade, Wilkinson, Wilson—12.

So the joint resolution was agreed to, by both Houses.*

VOTE ON THIRD PROPOSITION.

FOR THE ADMISSION OF NEW MEXICO INTO THE UNION, MARCH 1, 1861.

Whereas, by the act of Congress approved on the 9th of September, in the year 1850, it was provided that the people of New Mexico, when admitted as a State, shall be received into the Union with or without slavery, as their constitution may provide at the time of their admission; and whereas the population of said Territory is now sufficient to constitute a State government: Therefore,

Be it enacted by the Senate and House of Representatives of the United States of America in Congress assembled, That the inhabitants of the Territory of New Mexico, including therein the region called Arizona, be, and they are hereby, authorized to form for themselves a constitution of State government by the name of the State of New Mexico; and the said State, when formed, shall be admitted into the Union upon the same footing with the original States in all respects whatever. And said constitution shall be formed by a convention of the people of New Mexico, which shall consist of twice the number of members now by law constituting the House of Representatives of the Territory; each representative district shall elect two members to said convention for every member now by law elected in such district to the Territorial House of Representatives; and in such election only those persons shall vote for such delegates as are, by the laws of said Territory now in force, entitled to vote for members of the Territorial House of Representatives. The election for the convention shall be held on the 5th day of August, 1861, by the same officers who would hold an election for members of the said House of Representatives; and those officers shall conform to the law now in force in said Territory for election for members of said House of Representatives in all respects, in holding the election, receiving and rejecting votes, and making the returns of the election for the convention. The convention shall assemble at the city of Santa Fé, on the 2d day of September, 1861, and continue its sessions at that place until its deliberations shall be closed. The constitution agreed on by the convention shall be submitted to the people of the Territory for their approval or rejection as a whole; at such election on the constitution, all those and others shall be entitled to vote who are now entitled to vote for members of the House of Representatives of said Territory; and such election shall be held by the same officers who conduct, by the present laws, the election for members of the House of Representatives of the Territory, at the same places for voting, and in the same manner in all respects; and such election shall be held on the 4th day of November, 1861, and the returns thereof made to the Governor of the Territory, who shall forthwith sum up and declare the result, and shall send a certificate thereof, together with a copy of the constitution, to the President of the United States. The said State shall be entitled to one member of the House of Representatives of the United States of America, held until the apportionment under the next census.

Mr. HICKMAN moved to lay the bill on the table; which was agreed to, yeas 115, nays 71, as follows:

YEAS—Messrs. Aldrich, Alley, Ashley, *Avery*, Babbitt, Beale, Bingham, Blair, Blake, *Bocock*, Boteler, Bouligny, Brabson, *Branch*, Brayton, Buffinton, Burlingame, *Burnett*, Burnham, Carey, Carter, Case, Coburn, Colfax, Conway, Covode, *Burton Craige*, *John G. Davis*, Dawes, *De Jarnette*, Duell, Edgerton, *Edmundson*, Edwards, Eliot, Ely, Farnsworth, Fenton, Ferry, *Florence*, Foster, Frank, *Garnett*, Gooch, Graham, Grow, Hale, *Haskin*, Hatton, Hickman, *Hindman*, Hoard, William A. Howard, Humphrey, Hutchins, Irvine, *Jenkins*, Francis W. Kellogg, De Witt C. Leach, Jas. M. Leach, *Leake*, Lee, Longnecker, Loomis, Lovejoy, *Maclay*, Marston, *Elbert S. Martin*, Maynard, McKean, Morrill, Morse, Nelson, *Niblack*, Olin, Palmer, Perry, *Phelps*, Potter, Pottle, *Pryor*, Quarles, Edwin R. Reynolds, John H. Reynolds, Christopher Robinson, *James C. Robinson*, Royce, Sedgwick, William N. H. Smith, Somes, Spinner, Stevens, William Stewart, Tappan, *Thomas*, Tompkins, Train, Trimble, *Vallandigham*, Vance, Vandever, Van Wyck, Wade, Waldron, Walton, Cadwalader C. Washburn, Ellihu B. Washburne, Wells, *Whiteley*, Wilson, Windom, *Winslow*, Woodruff, *Woodson*, *Wright*—115.

NAYS—Messrs. Chas. F. Adams, Green Adams, *Adrain*, William C. Anderson, *Barr*, Briggs, Bristow, *Brown*, *Burch*, Butterfield, Campbell, *Horace F. Clark*, *John B. Clark*, *Clemens*, Clark B. Cochrane, *John Cochrane*, Conkling, Corwin, *Cox*, *James Craig*, H. Winter Davis, Delano, *Dimmick*, Dunn, *English*, Etheridge, *Fouke*, Gilmer, J. Morrison Harris, *John T. Harris*, *Holman*, *William Howard*, *Hughes*, Junkin, William Kellogg, Kenyon, Kilgore, Killinger, *Kunkel*, *Larrabee*, *Logan*, Mallory, *Chas. D. Martin*, *McClernand*, *McKenty*, McKnight, McPherson, *Millson*, Laban T. Moore, Moorhead, Edward Joy Morris, *Isaac N. Morris*, Nixon, *Noell*, *Pendleton*, Pettit, *Peyton*, Porter, Rice, *Riggs*, *Sickles*, *Simms*, Spaulding, Stanton, *Stevenson*, *James A. Stewart*, Stokes, Stratton, Thayer, Webster, Wood—71.

---

* The Legislatures of Ohio and Maryland agreed to the amendment promptly.

FOURTH PROPOSITION.

AMENDMENT OF FUGITIVE SLAVE LAW, MARCH 1.

Be it enacted by the Senate and House of Representatives of the United States of America in Congress assembled, That every person arrested under the laws of Congress for the delivery up of fugitives from labor shall be produced before a court, judge, or commissioner, mentioned in the law approved the 18th of September, 1850, for the State or Territory wherein the arrest may be made; and upon such production of the person, together with the proofs mentioned in the sixth or the tenth section of the said act, such court, judge, or commissioner, shall proceed to hear and consider the same publicly; and if such court, judge, or commissioner, is of opinion that the person arrested owes labor or service to the claimant according to the laws of any other State, Territory, or District of Columbia, and escaped therefrom, the court, judge, or commissioner shall make out and deliver to the claimant, or his agent, a certificate stating those facts; and if the said fugitive shall, upon the decision of the court, judge, or commissioner being made known to him, aver that he is free, and does not owe service or labor according to the law of the State or Territory to which he is to be returned, such averment shall be entered upon the certificate, and the fugitive shall be delivered by the court, judge, or commissioner to the marshal, to be by him taken and delivered to the marshal of the United States for the State or district from which the fugitive is ascertained to have fled, who shall produce said fugitive before one of the judges of the Circuit Court of the United States for the last mentioned State or district, whose duty it shall be, if said alleged fugitive shall persist in his averment, forthwith, or at the next term of the Circuit Court, to cause a jury to be impanelled and sworn to try the issue whether such fugitive owes labor or service to the person by or on behalf of whom he is claimed, and a true verdict to give according to the evidence, on which trial the fugitive shall be entitled to the aid of counsel and to process for procuring evidence at the cost of the United States; and upon such finding the judge shall render judgment, and cause said fugitive to be delivered to the claimant, or returned to the place where he was arrested, at the expense of the United States, according to the finding of the jury; and if the judge or court be not satisfied with the verdict, he may cause another jury to be impanelled forthwith, whose verdict shall be final. And it shall be the duty of said marshal so delivering said alleged fugitive, to take from the marshal of the State from which said fugitive is alleged to have escaped, a certificate acknowledging that said alleged fugitive had been delivered to him, giving a minute description of said alleged fugitive, which certificate shall be authenticated by the United States district judge, or a commissioner of a United States Court for said State from which said fugitive was alleged to have escaped, which certificate shall be filed in the office of the United States District Court for the State or district in which said alleged fugitive was seized, within sixty days from the date of the arrest of said fugitive; and should said marshal fail to comply with the provisions of this act, he shall be deemed guilty of a misdemeanor, and shall be punished by a fine of $1,000 and imprisoned for six months, and until his said fine is paid.

SEC. 2. *And be it further enacted,* That no citizen of any State shall be compelled to aid the marshal or owner of any fugitive in the capture or detention of such fugitive, unless when force is employed or reasonably apprehended to prevent such capture or detention, too powerful to be resisted by the marshal or owner; and the fees of the commissioners appointed under the act of 18th of September, 1850, shall be ten dollars for every case heard and determined by such commissioner.

Which was passed, yeas 92, nays 83, as follows:

YEAS—Messrs. Green Adams, *Adrain*, Aldrich, William C. Anderson, Babbitt, *Barr*, Blair, Brayton, Briggs, Bristow, *Burch*, Burlingame, Burnham, Butterfield, Campbell, Carter, Case, *Clemens*, Coburn, *John Cochrane*, Colfax, Conkling, Corwin, Covode, H. Winter Davis, *John G. Davis*, Delano, *Dimmick*, Dunn, Edwards, Ely, Ferry, *Fouke*, French, Gurley, Hale, Hall, J. Morrison Harris, Hatton, Helmick, Hoard, *William Howard*, William A. Howard, Humphrey, Junkin, Francis W. Kellogg, William Kellogg, Kenyon, Kilgore, Killinger, Lee, Longnecker, Loomis, Marston, *Chas. D. Martin*, *McClernand*, McKean, *McKenty*, McKnight, McPherson, Millward, Moorhead, Morrill, Edw. Joy Morris, *Isaac N. Morris*, Nixon, Olin, Palmer, Perry, Pettit, Porter, Pottle, John H. Reynolds, Rice, *Riggs*, Christopher Robinson, *James C. Robinson*, Scranton, *Sickles*, Spaulding, Spinner, Stanton, Stratton, Thayer, Theaker, Tompkins, Train, Trimble, Walton, Windom, Wood, Woodruff—92.

NAYS—Messrs. Ashley, *Avery*, *Barrett*, Beale, Bingham, Blake, *Bocock*, Boteler, Bouligny, Brabson, *Branch*, *Brown*, Buffinton, *Burnett*, Carey, *Horace F. Clark*, *John B. Clark*, Conway, *Burton Craige*, Dawes, Duell, Edgerton, *Edmundson*, Eliot, Farnsworth, Fenton, *Florence*, Foster, Frank, *Garnett*, Gilmer, Gooch, Grow, *John T. Harris*, Hickman, *Hindman*, *Hughes*, Hutchins, Irvine, *Jenkins*, *Kunkel*, De Witt C. Leach, James M. Leach, *Leake*, Lovejoy, *Maclay*, Mallory, *Elbert S. Martin*, Maynard, *Millson*, Laban T. Moore, Nelson, *Niblack*, *Noell*, *Pendleton*, *Peyton*, *Phelps*, Potter, Quarles, *Reagan*, Royce, *Ruffin*, Sedgwick, *Simms*, Somes, Stevens, *Stevenson*, Stokes, Tappan, *Thomas*, *Vallandigham*, Vance, Van Wyck, Wade, Waldron, Cadwalader C. Washburn, Ellihu B. Washburne, Wells, *Whiteley*, Wilson, *Winslow*, *Woodson*, *Wright*—83.

FIFTH PROPOSITION.

AMENDMENT OF THE ACT FOR THE RENDITION OF FUGITIVES FROM JUSTICE, MARCH 1.

Be it enacted by the Senate and House of Representatives of the United States of America in Congress assembled, That every person charged, by indictment or other satisfactory evidence, in any State, with treason felony, or other crime, committed within the jurisdiction of such State, who shall flee or shall have fled from justice and be found in another State, shall, on demand of the executive authority of the State from which he fled upon the district judge of the United States of the district in which he may be found, be arrested and brought before such judge, who, on being satisfied that he is the person charged, and that he was within the jurisdiction of such State at the time such crime was committed, of which such charge shall be *prima facie* evidence, shall deliver him up to be removed to the State having jurisdiction of the crime; and if any question of law shall arise during such examination, it may be taken on exceptions by writ of error to the Circuit Court.

Which was rejected, yeas 48, nays 125, as follows:

YEAS—Messrs. Green Adams, *Adrain*, William C. Anderson, *Barr*, *Barrett*, Bouligny, Brabson, Briggs, Bristow, *Burch*, *John B. Clark*, *Clemens*, *John Cochrane*, Corwin, *Cox*, H. Winter Davis, *John G. Davis*, Etheridge, *Fouke*, Gilmer, *Hamilton*, J. Morrison Harris, *John T. Harris*, Hatton, *Holman*, *William Howard*, *Hughes*, *Larrabee*, James M. Leach, *Logan*, Mallory, *Charles D. Martin*, Maynard, *McClernand*, *McKenty*, *Millson*, Laban T. Moore, Moorhead, Nelson, Nixon, *Phelps*, *Riggs*, *James C. Robinson*, Scranton, *Sickles*, Stokes, Webster, Wood—48.

NAYS—Messrs. Charles F. Adams, Alley, Ashley, *Avery*, Babbitt, Beale, Bingham, Blair, Blake, *Bocock*, Boteler, *Branch*, Brayton, *Brown*, Buffinton, Burlingame, *Burnett*, Burnham, Butterfield, Campbell, Carey, Carter, Case, *Horace F. Clark*, Coburn, Colfax, Conkling, Conway, Covode, *Burton Craige*, Dawes, *De Jarnette*, Delano, Duell, Dunn, Edgerton, Edwards, Eliot, Ely, Farnsworth, Fenton, Ferry, *Florence*, Foster, Frank, French, *Garnett*, Gooch, Graham, Grow, Hale, Hall, Helmick, Hickman, *Hindman*, Hoard, William A. Howard, Humphrey, Hutchins, Irvine, *Jenkins*, F. W. Kellogg, Kenyon, Kilgore, *Kunkel*, *Leake*, Longnecker, Loomis, Lovejoy, Marston, *Elbert S. Martin*, McKean, McKnight, McPherson, Morrill, Edward Joy Morris, *Isaac N. Morris*, Morse, Palmer, *Pendleton*, *Peyton*, Porter, Potter, Pottle, *Pryor*, Quarles, Edwin R. Reynolds, John H. Reynolds, Christopher Robinson, Royce, *Ruffin*, Sedgwick, Sherman, *Simms*, William H. N. Smith, Somes, Spinner, Stanton, Stevens, *Stevenson*, *James A. Stewart*, William Stewart, Stratton, Tappan, Theaker, *Thomas*, Tompkins, Train, Trimble, *Vallandigham*, Vance, Vandever, Van Wyck, Wade, Waldron, Walton, Cadwalader C. Washburn, Ellihu B. Washburne, Wells, *Whiteley*, Wilson, Windom, *Winslow*, Woodruff, *Woodson*—125.

Neither of these propositions was considered in the Senate, except the proposed Constitutional amendment, which was passed. For vote, see page 60.

Pending this report in the House of Representatives,

A CONVENTION.

February 27th. Mr. BURCH moved to add to the declaratory resolutions, one recommending to the several States that they, through their legislatures, request Congress to call a Convention of all the States, to amend it "in such manner with regard to such subjects as will more adequately respond to the wants, and afford more sufficient guarantees to the diversified and growing interests of the Government and of the people composing the same; which was rejected, yeas 74, nays 109, as follows:

YEAS—Messrs. Green Adams, *Garnett B. Adrain*, W. C. Anderson, Babbitt, *Barr*, Boteler, Brabson, Briggs, Bristow, *Burch*, Burnham, Campbell, Coburn, Clark B. Cochrane, *John Cochrane*, Colfax, *Cox*, Curtis, Duell, Etheridge, Ferry, *Fouke*, Gilmer, Hall, J. Morrison Harris, *John T. Harris*, Hatton, Helmick, Hoard, *Holman*, *Wm. Howard*, *Hughes*, Humphrey, Junkin, Wm. Kellogg, Kenyon, Killinger, *Larrabee*, J. M. Leach, *Logan*, Loomis, Mallory, *Chas. D. Martin*, Maynard, *McClernand*, *McKenty*, McPherson, *Millson*, *Montgomery*, Moore, Edward Joy Morris, *Isaac N. Morris*, Nixon, *Noell*, Palmer, Porter, Quarles, John H. Reynolds, *Riggs*, *J. C. Robinson*, Scranton, Sedgwick, Stanton, *James A. Stewart*, Wm. Stewart, Stokes, Stout, Stratton, Thayer, Waldron, Webster, Wells, Wood, Woodruff—74.

NAYS—Messrs. Chas. F. Adams, Aldrich, Alley, *T. L. Anderson*, Ashley, *Avery*, *Barrett*, Beale, Bingham, Blair, Blake, *Bocock*, *Branch*, Brayton, *Brown*, Buffinton, Burlingame, *Burnett*, Butterfield, Carey, Carter, Case, *John B. Clark*, Corwin, Covode, *Jas. Craig*, *Burton Craige*, H. Winter Davis, *J. G. Davis*, Dawes, *De Jarnette*, Delano, *Dimmick*, Dunn, Edgerton, *Edmundson*, Edwards, Eliot, Ely, *English*, Farnsworth, Fenton, *Florence*, Frank, French, *Garnett*, Gooch, Graham, Haskin, Hickman, *Hindman*, W. A. Howard, Hutchins, Irvine, *Jenkins*, F. W. Kellogg, Kilgore, *Kunkel*, D. C. Leach, *Leake*, Lee, Longnecker, Lovejoy, Marston, *Elbert S. Martin*, McKean, McKnight, Moorhead, Morrill, Morse, Nelson, *Niblack*, Olin, Perry, Pettit, *Peyton*, *Phelps*, Potter, Pottle, *Pryor*, E. R. Reynolds, Rice, C. Robinson, *Ruffin*, *Sickles*, *Simms*, W. H. N. Smith, Somes, Spaulding, Spinner, Stevens, *Stevenson*, Tappan, *Thomas*, Tompkins, Train, Trimble, *Vallandigham*, Vance, Wade, Walton, C. C. Washburn, E. B. Washburne, *Whiteley*, Wilson, Windom, *Winslow*, *Woodson*, *Wright*—109.

Same day. Mr. KILGORE moved to lay the whole subject on the table; which was rejected—yeas 14, nays 179. The yeas were

Messrs. Alley, Beale, Buffinton, Carey, Eliot, Farnsworth, Grow, Kilgore, Potter, Sedgwick, Somes, Waldron, Cadwalader C. Washburn, Windom—14.

Same day. The House came to a vote on the following substitute for it, offered by Mr. WM. KELLOGG, of Illinois:

Strike out all after the word "that," and insert:

The following articles be, and are hereby, proposed and submitted as amendments to the Constitution of the United States, which shall be valid, to all intents and purposes, as part of said Constitution, when ratified by conventions of three-fourths of the several States.

ART. 13. That in all the territory now held by the United States situate north of latitude 36° 30′, involuntary servitude, except in the punishment for crime, is prohibited while such territory shall remain under a territorial government; that in all the territory now held south of said line, neither Congress nor any Territorial Legislature shall hinder or prevent the emigration to said territory of persons held to service from any State of this Union, when that relation exists by virtue of any law or usage of such State, while it shall remain in a territorial condition; and when any territory north or south of said line, within such boundaries as Congress may prescribe, shall contain the population requisite for a member of Congress, according to the then Federal ratio of representation of the people of the United States, it may, if its form of government be republican, be admitted into the Union on an equal footing with the original States, with or without the relation of persons held to service or labor, as the constitution of such new State may provide.

ART. 14. That nothing in the Constitution of the United States, or any amendment thereto, shall be so construed as to authorize any department of the Government to, in any manner, interfere with the relation of persons held to service in any State where that relation exists, nor in any manner to establish or sustain that relation in any State where it is prohibited by the laws or constitution of such State. And that this article shall not be altered or amended without the consent of every State in the Union.

ART. 15. The third paragraph of the second section of the fourth article of the Constitution shall be taken and construed to authorize and empower Congress to pass laws necessary to secure the return of persons held to service or labor under the laws of any State, who may have escaped therefrom, to the party to whom such service or labor may be due.

Art. 16. The migration or importation of persons held to service or involuntary servitude, into any State, Territory, or place within the United States, from any place or country beyond the limits of the United States or Territories thereof, is forever prohibited.

Art. 17. No territory beyond the present limits of the United States and the Territories thereof shall be annexed to, or acquired by the United States, unless by treaty, which treaty shall be ratified by a vote of two-thirds of the Senate.

This was disagreed to—yeas 33, nays 158.

The Yeas were—Messrs. *Adrain*, *Barr*, Briggs, *Burch*, *Horace F. Clark*, *John Cochrane*, *Cox*, *John G. Davis*, *English*, Etheridge, *Fouke*, Gilmer, J. Morrison Harris, *Holman*, *William Howard*, Junkin, William Kellogg, *Larrabee*, *Logan*, *Charles D. Martin*, *McClernand*, *McKenty*, *Montgomery*, *Isaac N. Morris*, Nelson, *Niblack*, *Riggs*, *James C. Robinson*, *Sickles*, Stokes, *Stout*, *Vallandigham*, Webster—33.

MR. CLEMENS'S RESOLUTION.

Mr. Sherrard Clemens of Virginia, then offered a substitute for it, being Mr. Crittenden's proposition as amended on motion of Mr. Powell, with these additions:

Art. 7. *Section* 1. The elective franchise and the right to hold office, whether Federal, State, Territorial, or Municipal, shall not be exercised by persons who are, in whole or in part, of the African race.

Section 2. The United States shall have power to acquire, from time to time, districts of country in Africa and South America, for the colonization, at the expense of the Federal Treasury, of such free negroes and mulattoes as the several States may wish to have removed from their limits, and from the District of Columbia, and such other places as may be under the jurisdiction of Congress. And the substitution of the words: "*the Southern boundary of Kansas and the Northern boundary of New Mexico*," for the words: "*latitude* 36° 30′," in the first sentence of Article 1.

Which was negatived, yeas 80, nays 113, as follows:

Yeas—Messrs. *Adrain*, William C. Anderson, *Avery*, *Barr*, *Barrett*, *Bocock*, Boteler, Bouligny, Brabson, *Branch*, Briggs, Bristow, *Brown*, *Burch*, *Burnett*, *Horace F. Clark*, *John B. Clark*, *John Cochrane*, *Cox*, *James Craig*, *Burton Craige*, *John G. Davis*, *De Jarnette*, *Dimmick*, *Edmundson*, *English*, *Florence*, *Fouke*, *Garnett*, Gilmer, *Hamilton*, J. Morrison Harris, *John T. Harris*, Hatton, *Holman*, *Wm. Howard*, *Hughes*, *Jenkins*, *Kunkel*, *Larrabee*, James M. Leach, *Leake*, *Logan*, *Maclay*, Mallory, *Charles D. Martin*, *Elbert S. Martin*, Maynard, *McClernand*, *McKenty*, *Millson*, *Montgomery*, Laban T. Moore, *Isaac N. Morris*, Nelson, *Niblack*, *Noell*, *Peyton*, *Phelps*, *Pryor*, Quarles, *Riggs*, *Jas. C. Robinson*, *Rust*, *Sickles*, *Simms*, *William Smith*, William N. H. Smith, *Stevenson*, *James A. Stewart*, Stokes, *Stout*, *Thomas*, *Vallandigham*, Vance, Webster, *Whiteley*, *Winslow*, *Woodson*, and *Wright*—80.

Nays—Messrs. Charles F. Adams, Aldrich, Alley, Ashley, Babbitt, Beale, Bingham, Blair, Blake, Brayton, Buffinton, Burlingame, Burnham, Butterfield, Campbell, Carey, Carter, Case, Coburn, Clark B. Cochrane, Colfax, Conkling, Conway, Corwin, Covode, H. Winter Davis, Dawes, Delano, Duell, Dunn, Edgerton, Edwards, Eliot, Ely, Etheridge, Farnsworth, Fenton, Ferry, Foster, Frank, French, Gooch, Graham, Grow, Hale, Hall, Helmick, Hickman, *Hindman*, Hoard, William A. Howard, Humphrey, Hutchins, Irvine, Junkin, Francis W. Kellogg, William Kellogg, Kenyon, Kilgore, Killinger, De Witt C. Leach, Lee, Longnecker, Loomis, Lovejoy, Marston, McKean, McKnight, McPherson, Moorhead, Morrill, Morse, Nixon, Olin, Palmer, Perry, Pettit, Porter, Potter, Pottle, Edwin R. Reynolds, Rice, Christopher Robinson, Royce, Scranton, Sedgwick, Sherman, Somes, Spaulding, Spinner, Stanton, Stevens, William Stewart, Stratton, Tappan, Thayer, Theaker, Tompkins, Train, Trimble, Vandever, Van Wyck, Verree, Wade, Waldron, Walton, Cadwalader C. Washburn, Ellihu B. Washburne, Wells, Wilson, Windom, Wood, and Woodruff—113.

Votes in the Senate.

During the pendency, in the Senate, of the Constitutional amendment reported from the House Committee of Thirty-three, and adopted by the House, Mr. Pugh, of Ohio, offered a substitute, which was the same as Mr. Crittenden's* (as amended by Mr. Powell) with the omission of the preamble and four resolutions, and the addition of the following at the close of Article 4:

But the African slave trade shall be forever suppressed, and it shall be the duty of Congress to make such laws as shall be necessary and effectual, to prevent the migration and importation of slaves, or persons owing service or labor into the United States from any foreign country, place, or jurisdiction whatever.

Section 2. That persons committing crimes against the rights of those who hold persons to service or labor in one State, and fleeing to another, shall be delivered up in the same manner as persons committing other crimes; and that the laws of the States from which such persons flee shall be the test of criminality.

Section 3. Congress shall pass efficient laws for the punishment of all persons in any of the States, who shall in any manner aid and abet invasion or insurrection in any other State, or commit any other act tending to disturb the tranquillity of its people, or government of any other State.

And the insertion of a new article:

Art. 7. *Section* 1. The elective franchise and the right to hold office, whether Federal, State, Territorial, or Municipal, shall not be exercised by persons who are, in whole or in part, of the African race.

MR. DOOLITTLE'S ON THE RIGHT OF SECESSION.

Mr. Doolittle, of Wisconsin, offered as a substitute for the above the following:

"Under this Constitution, as originally adopted, and as it now exists, no State has power to withdraw from the jurisdiction of the United States; but this Constitution, and all laws passed in pursuance of its delegated powers, are the supreme law of the land, any thing contained in any constitution, ordinance, or act of any State, to the contrary notwithstanding."

March 2, 1861. This was rejected—yeas 18, nays 28, as follows:

* See page 64.

YEAS—Messrs. Bingham, Chandler, Clark, Collamer, Doolittle, Durkee, Fessenden, Foot, Grimes, Hale, Harlan, King, Morrill, Simmons, Trumbull, Wade, Wilkinson, and Wilson—18.

NAYS—Messrs. Anthony, Baker, *Bayard*, *Bigler*, *Bragg*, *Bright*, Cameron, *Clingman*, Crittenden, Dixon, *Douglas*, Foster, *Gwin*, *Hemphill*, *Hunter*, *Johnson* of Tennessee, *Kennedy*, *Lane*, *Latham*, *Mason*, *Nicholson*, *Pearce*, *Powell*, *Pugh*, *Rice*, *Sebastian*, Ten Eyck, and *Wigfall*—28.

VOTE ON MR. PUGH'S.

The substitute of Mr. PUGH was then rejected—yeas 14, nays 25, as follows:

YEAS—Messrs. *Bayard*, *Bright*, *Gwin*, *Hunter*, *Johnson* of Arkansas, *Kennedy*, *Lane*, *Mason*, *Nicholson*, *Polk*, *Powell*, *Pugh*, *Thomson*, and *Wigfall*—14.

NAYS—Messrs. Anthony, Baker, *Bigler*, Bingham, Chandler, Clark, Crittenden, Dixon, Doolittle, *Douglas*, Fessenden, Foot, Foster, Grimes, Harlan, *Johnson* of Tennessee, King, *Latham*, Morrill, *Rice*, *Sebastian*, Sumner, Ten Eyck, Wilkinson, and Wilson—25.

MR. BINGHAM'S PROPOSITION.

Mr. BINGHAM, of Michigan, offered the following substitute, which was rejected—yeas 13, nays 24, as follows:

"That the provisions of the Constitution are ample for the preservation of the Union, and the protection of all the material interests of the country: that it needs to be obeyed rather than amended; and that an extrication from our present dangers is to be looked for in strenuous efforts to preserve the peace, protect the public property, and enforce the laws, rather than in new guarantees for particular interests, compromises for particular difficulties, or concessions to unreasonable demands.

"*Resolved*, That all attempts to dissolve the present Union, or overthrow or abandon the present Constitution, with the hope or expectation of constructing a new one, are dangerous, illusory, and destructive; that in the opinion of the Senate of the United States no such reconstruction is practicable; and therefore, to the maintenance of the existing Union and Constitution should be directed all the energies of all the departments of the Government, and the efforts of all good citizens.

YEAS—Messrs. Bingham, Chandler, Clark, Doolittle, Durkee, Fessenden, Foot, King, Sumner, Trumbull, Wade, Wilkinson, and Wilson—13.

NAYS.—Messrs. Anthony, Baker, *Bigler*, *Bright*, Crittenden, Dixon, *Douglas*, Foster, *Gwin*, Harlan, *Hunter*, *Johnson* of Arkansas, *Johnson* of Tennessee, *Kennedy*, *Lane*, *Latham*, *Mason*, *Nicholson*, *Polk*, *Pugh*, *Rice*, *Sebastian*, Ten Eyck, and *Thomson*—24.

A CONVENTION.

Mr. GRIMES, of Iowa, offered the following substitute:

"The Legislatures of the States of Kentucky, New Jersey and Illinois, have applied to Congress to call a Convention for proposing amendments to the Constitution of the United States: therefore,

"*Be it Resolved by the Senate and House of Representatives of the United States of America in Congress assembled*, That the Legislatures of the other States be invited to take the subject of such a Convention into consideration, and to express their will on that subject to Congress, in pursuance of the fifth article of the Constitution."

Which was rejected—yeas 14, nays 25 as follows:

YEAS—Messrs. Bingham, Chandler, Clark, Doolittle, Fessenden, Foot, Grimes, King, Morrill, *Pugh*, Sumner, Trumbull, Wilkinson, and Wilson—14.

NAYS—Messrs. Anthony, Baker, Bigler, *Bright*, Crittenden, Dixon, *Douglas*, Durkee, Foster, *Gwin*, Harlan, *Hunter*, *Johnson* of Arkansas, *Johnson* of Tennessee, Kennedy, *Lane*, *Latham*, *Mason*, *Nicholson*, *Polk*, *Rice*, *Sebastian*, Ten Eyck, *Thomson*, and Wade—25.

THE PEACE CONFERENCE.

The Peace Conference propositions offered by Mr. JOHNSON, of Arkansas, were then considered as a substitute, and rejected—yeas 3, nays 34.

The joint resolution of the House of Representatives was then passed.

NOTE.—During the above votes, several Senators said in explanation of their negative votes upon propositions, that they had determined to vote against all substitutes for the House proposition, and for it, believing it to be the only measure practicable at so late a period in the session. Mr. DOUGLAS, of Illinois, and Mr. TEN EYCK, and others, made this statement.

Vote on the Crittenden Resolutions, January 16, 1861.

A JOINT RESOLUTION (S. NO. 50) PROPOSING CERTAIN AMENDMENTS TO THE CONSTITUTION OF THE UNITED STATES.

WHEREAS, serious and alarming dissensions have arisen between the Northern and Southern States, concerning the rights and security of the rights of the slaveholding States, and especially their rights in the common territory of the United States; and whereas it is eminently desirable and proper that these dissensions, which now threaten the very existence of this Union, should be permanently quieted and settled by constitutional provisions, which shall do equal justice to all sections, and thereby restore to the people that peace and good-will which ought to prevail between all the citizens of the United States: Therefore,

Resolved by the Senate and House of Representatives of the United States of America in Congress assembled (two-thirds of both Houses concurring), That the following articles be, and are hereby, proposed and submitted as amendments to the Constitution of the United States, which shall be valid to all intents and purposes, as part of said Constitution, when ratified by conventions of three-fourths of the several States:

ARTICLE 1. In all the territory of the United States now held, or hereafter acquired, situate north of latitude 36° 30′, slavery or involuntary servitude, except as a punishment for crime, is prohibited while such territory shall remain under territorial government. In all the territory south of said line of latitude, slavery of the African race is hereby recognized as existing, and shall not be interfered with by Congress, but shall be protected as property by all the departments of the territorial government during its continuance. And when any Territory, north or south of said line, within such boundaries as Congress may prescribe, shall contain the population requisite for a member of Congress according to the then Federal ratio of representation of the people of the United States, it shall, if its form of government be republican, be admitted into the Union, on an equal footing with the original States, with or without slavery, as the constitution of such new State may provide.

ART. 2. Congress shall have no power to abolish slavery in places under its exclusive jurisdiction, and situate within the limits of States that permit the holding of slaves.

ART. 3. Congress shall have no power to abolish slavery within the District of Columbia, so long as it exists in the adjoining States of Virginia and Maryland, or either, nor without the consent of the inhabitants, nor without just compensation first made to such owners of slaves as do not consent to such abolishment. Nor shall Congress at any time prohibit officers of the Federal Government, or members of Congress, whose duties require them to be in said District, from bringing with them their slaves, and holding them as such during the time their duties may require them to remain there, and afterwards taking them from the District.

ART. 4. Congress shall have no power to prohibit or

hinder the transportation of slaves from one State to another, or to a Territory in which slaves are by law permitted to be held, whether that transportation be by land, navigable rivers, or by the sea.

ART. 5. That in addition to the provisions of the third paragraph of the second section of the fourth article of the Constitution of the United States, Congress shall have power to provide by law, and it shall be its duty so to provide, that the United States shall pay to the owner who shall apply for it, the full value of his fugitive slave in all cases when the marshal or other officer whose duty it was to arrest said fugitive was prevented from so doing by violence or intimidation, or when, after arrest, said fugitive was rescued by force, and the owner thereby prevented and obstructed in the pursuit of his remedy for the recovery of his fugitive slave under the said clause of the Constitution and the laws made in pursuance thereof. And in all such cases, when the United States shall pay for such fugitive, they shall have the right, in their own name, to sue the county in which said violence, intimidation, or rescue was committed, and to recover from it, with interest and damages, the amount paid by them for said fugitive slave. And the said county, after it has paid said amount to the United States, may, for its indemnity, sue and recover from the wrong-doers or rescuers by whom the owner was prevented from the recovery of his fugitive slave, in like manner as the owner himself might have sued and recovered.

ART. 6. No future amendment of the Constitution shall affect the five preceding articles; nor the third paragraph of the second section of the first article of the Constitution; nor the third paragraph of the second section of the fourth article of said Constitution; and no amendment shall be made to the Constitution which shall authorize or give to Congress any power to abolish or interfere with slavery in any of the States by whose laws it is, or may be, allowed or permitted.

And whereas, also, besides these causes of dissension embraced in the foregoing amendments proposed to the Constitution of the United States, there are others which come within the jurisdiction of Congress, and may be remedied by its legislative power; and whereas it is the desire of Congress, as far as its power will extend, to remove all just cause for the popular discontent and agitation which now disturb the peace of the country, and threaten the stability of its institutions: Therefore,

1. *Resolved by the Senate and House of Representatives of the United States of America in Congress assembled*, That the laws now in force for the recovery of fugitive slaves are in strict pursuance of the plain and mandatory provisions of the Constitution, and have been sanctioned as valid and constitutional by the judgment of the Supreme Court of the United States; that the slaveholding States are entitled to the faithful observance and execution of those laws, and that they ought not to be repealed, or so modified or changed as to impair their efficiency; and that laws ought to be made for the punishment of those who attempt by rescue of the slave, or other illegal means, to hinder or defeat the due execution of said laws.

2. That all State laws which conflict with the fugitive slave acts of Congress, or any other constitutional acts of Congress, or which, in their operation, impede, hinder, or delay the free course and due execution of any of said acts, are null and void by the plain provisions of the Constitution of the United States; yet those State laws, void as they are, have given color to practices, and led to consequences which have obstructed the due administration and execution of acts of Congress, and especially the acts for the delivery of fugitive slaves, and have thereby contributed much to the discord and commotion now prevailing. Congress, therefore, in the present perilous juncture, does not deem it improper, respectfully and earnestly to recommend the repeal of those laws to the several States which have enacted them, or such legislative corrections or explanations of them as may prevent their being used or perverted to such mischievous purposes.

3. That the act of the 18th of September, 1850, commonly called the fugitive slave law, ought to be so amended as to make the fee of the commissioner, mentioned in the eighth section of the act, equal in amount, in the cases decided by him, whether his decision be in favor of or against the claimant. And to avoid misconstruction, the last clause of the fifth section of said act, which authorizes the person holding a warrant for the arrest or detention of a fugitive slave, to summon to his aid the *posse comitatus*, and which declares it to be the duty of all good citizens to assist him in its execution, ought to be so amended as to expressly limit the authority and duty to cases in which there shall be resistance or danger of resistance or rescue.

4. That the laws for the suppression of the African slave-trade, and especially those prohibiting the importation of slaves in the United States, ought to be made effectual, and ought to be thoroughly executed; and all further enactments necessary to those ends ought to be promptly made.

MR. POWELL moved to amend by inserting in article 1, after the word "territory," in the second sentence, the words "now held or hereafter to be acquired," so that the clause will read: "In all the territory now held or hereafter to be acquired south of said line of latitude, slavery of the African race is hereby recognized, etc.," which was agreed to as follows:

YEAS—Messrs. Baker, *Bayard*, *Benjamin*, *Bigler*, *Bragg*, *Bright*, *Clingman*, Crittenden, *Douglas*, *Fitch*, *Green*, *Gwin*, *Hemphill*, *Hunter*, *Iverson*, *Johnson* of Tennessee, *Kennedy*, *Lane*, *Mason*, *Nicholson*, *Pearce*, *Polk*, *Powell*, *Pugh*, *Rice*, *Saulsbury*, *Sebastian*, *Slidell*, and *Wigfall*—29.

NAYS—Messrs. Anthony, Bingham, Cameron, Chandler, Clark, Collamer, Dixon, Doolittle, Durkee, Fessenden, Foot, Foster, Grimes, Hale, Harlan, King, *Latham*, Seward, Simmons, Sumner, Ten Eyck, Trumbull, Wade, and Wilson—24.

MR. CLARK of New Hampshire offered an amendment to strike out the preamble, and all the resolutions after the word "resolved," and insert: "That the provisions of the Constitution are ample for the preservation of the Union, and the protection of all the material interests of the country; that it needs to be obeyed rather than amended; and that an extrication from our present danger is to be looked for in strenuous efforts to preserve the peace, protect the public property and enforce the laws, rather than in new guarantees for particular interests, compromises for particular difficulties, or concessions to unreasonable demands.

"*Resolved*, That all attempts to dissolve the present Union, or overthrow or abandon the present Constitution with the hope or expectation of constructing a new one, are dangerous, illusory and destructive; that in the opinion of the Senate of the United States no such reconstruction is practicable; and therefore, to the maintenance of the existing Union and Constitution should be directed all the energies of all the departments of the Government, and the efforts of all good citizens."

Which was agreed to:

YEAS—Messrs. Anthony, Baker, Bingham, Cameron, Chandler, Clark, Collamer, Dixon, Doolittle, Durkee, Fessenden, Foot, Foster, Grimes, Hale, Harlan, King, Seward, Simmons, Sumner, Ten Eyck, Trumbull, Wade, Wilkinson, and Wilson—25.

NAYS—Messrs. *Bayard*, *Bigler*, *Bragg*, *Bright*, *Clingman*, Crittenden, *Fitch*, *Green*, *Gwin*, *Hunter*, *Johnson* of Tennessee, *Kennedy*, *Lane*, *Latham*, *Mason*, *Nicholson*, *Pearce*, *Polk*, *Powell*, *Pugh*, *Rice*, *Saulsbury*, and *Sebastian*—23.

Messrs. BENJAMIN of Louisiana, DOUGLAS of Illinois, HEMPHILL of Texas, IVERSON of Georgia, JOHNSON of Arkansas, SLIDELL of Louisiana, and WIGFALL of Texas, who voted on the next preceding question, did not vote on this. MR. DOUGLAS stated afterwards in open Senate that he was accidentally absent in one of the retiring rooms, and asked to record his vote, but was refused permission.

January 18th, 1861.—MR. CAMERON'S motion to reconsider the vote adopting Mr. Clark's amendment, was agreed to:

YEAS—Messrs. *Bayard*, *Bigler*, *Bragg*, *Bright*, *Clingman*, Crittenden, *Douglas*, *Fitch*, *Green*, *Gwin*, *Hemphill*, *Hunter*, *Johnson* of Arkansas, *Johnson* of Tennessee, *Kennedy*, *Lane*, *Latham*, *Mason*, *Nicholson*, *Pearce*, *Polk*, *Powell*, *Pugh*, *Rice*, *Saulsbury*, *Sebastian*, and *Slidell*—27.

NAYS—Messrs. Anthony, Baker, Bingham, Cameron, Chandler, Clark, Collamer, Dixon, Doolittle, Fessenden, Foot, Foster, Grimes, Hale, Harlan, King, Seward, Simmons, Sumner, Ten Eyck, Wade, *Wigfall*, Wilkinson, and Wilson—24.

March 2d. After the adoption of the House resolution proposing an amendment to the Constitution relative to slavery in the States, the Senate returned to the consideration of the Crittenden proposition,—the question being on the amendment offered by MR. CLARK of New Hampshire, once adopted and then reconsidered, [for which see above vote,] which was rejected—yeas 15, nays 22, as follows:

YEAS—Messrs. Bingham, Chandler, Clark, Doolittle, Durkee, Fessenden, Foot, Harlan, King, Morrill, Sumner, Trumbull, Wade, Wilkinson, and Wilson—15.

NAYS—Messrs. Anthony, Baker, *Bayard*, *Bigler*, *Bright*, Crittenden, Dixon, *Douglas*, Foster, *Gwin*, *Hunter*, *Johnson* of Tennessee, *Kennedy*, *Lane*, *Latham*, *Mason*, *Nicholson*, *Polk*, *Pugh*, *Rice*, *Sebastian*, and Ten Eyck—22.

The Senate adopted, without a division, the amendments offered by Mr. Powell in the Committee of the whole, and agreed to as follows: Insert after "territory," in second sentence in first article, the words "now held or to be hereafter acquired," and add to article fourth the words "But the African slave trade shall be forever suppressed; and it shall be the duty of Congress to make such laws as shall be necessary and effectual to prevent the migration or importation of slaves, or persons owing service or labor, into the United States from any foreign country, place, or jurisdiction whatever.

SEC. 2. That persons committing crimes against the rights of those who hold persons to service or labor in one State, and fleeing to another, shall be delivered up in the same manner as persons committing other crimes; and the laws of the State from which such persons flee shall be the test of criminality.

SEC. 3. Congress shall pass efficient laws for the punishment of all persons in any of the States who shall in any manner aid and abet invasion or insurrection in any other State, or commit any other act tending to disturb the tranquillity of its people, or government of any other State."

Mr. CRITTENDEN moved to substitute for his proposition that recommended by the Peace Conference, which was rejected—yeas 7, nays 28. (For vote, see p. 69.)

The Crittenden proposition, as amended, was then rejected—yeas 19, nays 20, as follows:

YEAS—Messrs. *Bayard*, *Bigler*, *Bright*, Crittenden, *Douglas*, *Gwin*, *Hunter*, *Johnson* of Tennessee, *Kennedy*, *Lane*, *Latham*, *Mason*, *Nicholson*, *Polk*, *Pugh*, *Rice*, *Sebastian*, *Thomson*, and *Wigfall*—19.

NAYS—Messrs. Anthony, Bingham, Chandler Clark, Dixon, Doolittle, Durkee, Fessenden, Foot, Foster, Grimes, Harlan, King, Morrill, Sumner, Ten Eyck, Trumbull, Wade, Wilkinson, and Wilson—20.

It was not voted upon in the House of Representatives, except as far as it was embodied in the proposition offered by Mr. Clemens of Virginia—for which, see p. 63.

Respecting the vote of January 16th, on the Crittenden proposition in the Senate, ANDREW JOHNSON, Senator from Tennessee, in his speech on the expulsion of Jesse D. Bright, Senator from Indiana, delivered January 31st, 1862, made these remarks. When the six Senators refused to vote on Senator Clark's amendment,* Senator Johnson says:

"I sat right behind Mr. Benjamin, and I am not sure that my worthy friend, (Mr. LATHAM,) was not close by, when he refused to vote, and I said to him, 'Mr. Benjamin, why do you not vote? Why not save this proposition, and see if we cannot bring the country to it?' He gave me rather an abrupt answer, and said he would control his own action without consulting me or anybody else. Said I, 'Vote and show yourself an honest man.' As soon as the vote was taken, he and others telegraphed South, 'We cannot get any compromise.' Here were six Southern men refusing to vote, when the amendment would have been rejected by four majority if they had voted. Who, then, has brought these evils on the country? Was it Mr. CLARK? He was acting out his own policy; but with the help we had from the other side of the chamber, if all those on this side had been true to the Constitution, and faithful to their constituents, and had acted with fidelity to the country, the amendment of the Senator from New Hampshire could have been voted down, the defeat of which the Senator from Delaware says would have saved the country. Whose fault was it? Who is responsible for it? I think that it is not only getting the nail through, but clinching it on the other side, and the whole staple commodity is taken out of the speech. Who did it? Southern traitors, as was said in the speech of the Senator from California. They did it. They wanted no compromise. They accomplished their object by withholding their votes; and hence the country has been involved in the present difficulty. Let me read another extract from the speech of the Senator from California, [Mr. LATHAM]:

"'I recollect full well the joy that pervaded the faces of some of those gentlemen at the result, and the sorrow manifested by the venerable Senator from Kentucky, [MR. CRITTENDEN.] The record shows that Mr. Pugh, from Ohio, despairing of any compromise between the extremes of ultra Republicanism and disunionists, working manifestly for the same end, moved, immediately after the vote was announced, to lay the whole subject on the table. If you will turn to page 443, same volume, you will find, when at a late period, Mr. Cameron, from Pennsylvania, moved to reconsider the vote, appeals having been made to sustain those who were struggling to preserve the peace of the country, that vote *was* reconsidered; and when, at last, the Crittenden propositions were submitted on the 2d day of March, these Southern States having nearly all se-

* See Mr. Crittenden's despatch to Raleigh, January 17th, page 39.

ceded, they were then lost by but one vote. Here is the vote:

YEAS—Messrs. Bayard, Bigler, Bright, Crittenden, Douglas, Gwin, Hunter, Johnson of Tennessee, Kennedy, Lane, Latham, Mason, Nicholson, Polk, Pugh, Rice, Sebastian, Thomson, and Wigfall—19.

NAYS—Messrs. Anthony, Bingham, Chandler, Clark, Dixon, Doolittle, Durkee, Fessenden, Foot, Foster, Grimes, Harlan, King, Morrill, Sumner, Ten Eyck, Trumbull, Wade, Wilkinson, and Wilson—20.

"'If these seceded Southern States had remained, there would have passed, by a large vote, (as it did without them,) an amendment, by a two-third vote, forbidding Congress ever interfering with slavery in the States. The Crittenden proposition would have been indorsed by a majority vote, the subject finally going before the people, who have never yet, after consideration, refused justice, for any length of time, to any portion of the country.

"'I believe more, Mr. President, that these gentlemen were acting in pursuance of a settled and fixed plan to break up and destroy the Government.'

"When we had it in our power to vote down the amendment of the Senator from New Hampshire, and adopt the Crittenden resolutions, certain Southern Senators prevented it; and yet, even at a late day of the session, after they had seceded, the Crittenden proposition was only lost by one vote. If rebellion and bloodshed and murder have followed, to whose skirts does the responsibility attach? I summed up all these facts myself in a speech during the last session, but I have preferred to read from the speech of the Senator from California, he being better authority, and having presented the facts better than I could."

Mr. Lincoln's Opinions on a Compromise.

From the *N. Y. Tribune of Jan. 30th*, 1861.

"We do not hesitate to say that these statements are false and calumnious. We have the best authority for saying that Mr. Lincoln is opposed to all concessions of the sort. We *know* that his views are fully expressed in his own language as follows:

"'I will suffer death before I will consent or advise my friends to consent to any concession or compromise which looks like buying the privilege of taking possession of the Government to which we have a constitutional right; because, whatever I might think of the merit of the various propositions before Congress, I should regard any concession in the face of menace as the destruction of the government itself, and a consent on all hands that our system shall be brought down to a level with the existing disorganized state of affairs in Mexico. But this thing will hereafter be, as it is now, in the hands of the people; and if they desire to call a convention to remove any grievances complained of, or to give new guarantees for the permanence of vested rights, it is not mine to oppose.'"

The "Peace Conference" and its Proposition.

Commissioners composing the "Peace Conference," held at the request of the Legislature of Virginia, met in Washington, February 4th, 1861, and adjourned February 27th. The following gentlemen represented their States, under appointment of the Governors or Legislatures thereof:

DELEGATES.

Maine.—William P. Fessenden, Lot M. Morrill, Daniel E. Somes, John J. Perry, Ezra B. French, Freeman H. Morse, Stephen Coburn, and Stephen C. Foster.

New Hampshire.—Amos Tuck, Levi Chamberlain, and Asa Fowler.

Vermont.—Hiland Hall, Levi Underwood, H. Henry Baxter, L. E. Chittenden, and B. D. Harris.

Massachusetts.—John Z. Goodrich, John M. Forbes, Richard P. Waters, Theophilus P. Chandler, Francis B. Crowninshield, Geo. S. Boutwell, and Charles Allen.

Rhode Island.—Samuel Ames, Alexander Duncan, William W. Hoppin, George H. Browne, and Samuel G. Arnold.

Connecticut.—Roger S. Baldwin, Chauncey F. Cleveland, Charles J. McCurdy, James T. Pratt, Robbins Battelle, and Amos Treat.

New York.—David Dudley Field, Wm. Curtis Noyes, James S. Wadsworth, James C. Smith, Amaziah B. James, Erastus Corning, Greene C. Bronson, William E. Dodge, John A. King, and John E. Wool.

New Jersey.—Charles S. Olden, Peter D. Vroom, Robert F. Stockton, Benjamin Williamson, Joseph F. Randolph, Fred. T. Frelinghuysen, Rodman M. Price, William C. Alexander, and Thomas J. Stryker.

Pennsylvania.—Thomas White, James Pollock, Wm. M. Meredith, David Wilmot, A. W. Loomis, Thomas E. Franklin, and William McKennan.

Delaware.—George B. Rodney, Daniel M. Bates, Henry Ridgely, John W. Houston, and William Cannon.

Maryland.—John F. Dent, Reverdy Johnson, John W. Crisfield, Augustus W. Bradford, Wm. T. Goldsborough, J. Dixon Roman, and Benjamin C. Howard.

Virginia.—John Tyler, William C. Rives, John W. Brockenbrough, George W. Summers, and James A. Seddon.

North Carolina.—George Davis, Thomas Ruffin, David S. Reid, D. M. Barringer, and John M. Morehead.

Tennessee.—Samuel Milligan, Josiah M. Anderson, Robert L. Caruthers, Thomas Martin, Isaac R. Hankins, A. O. W. Totten, Robert J. McKinney, Alvin Cullom, Wm. Hickerson, Geo. W. Jones, F. K. Zollicoffer, and William H. Stevens.

Kentucky.—William O. Butler, James B. Clay, Joshua F. Bell, Charles S. Morehead, James Guthrie, and Charles A. Wickliffe.

Missouri.—John D. Coalter, Alexander

M. Doniphan, Waldo P. Johnson, Aylett H. Buckner, and Harrison Hough.

Ohio.—John C. Wright,* Salmon P. Chase, William S. Groesbeck, Franklin T. Backus, Reuben Hitchcock, Thomas Ewing, and V. B. Horton.

Indiana.—Caleb B. Smith, Pleasant A. Hackleman, Godlove S. Orth, E. W. H. Ellis, and Thos. C. Slaughter.

Illinois.—John Wood, Stephen T. Logan, John M. Palmer, Burton C. Cook, and Thomas J. Turner.

Iowa.—James Harlan, James W. Grimes, Samuel R. Curtis, and William Vandever.

The officers were:

JOHN TYLER of Virginia, President; CRAFTS J. WRIGHT of Ohio, Secretary; JAMES M. TOWER of New Jersey, J. HENRY PULESTON of Pennsylvania, WM. M. HOPPIN of Rhode Island, JOHN STRYKER of New York, assistants.

They recommended that the following be proposed to the several States as amendments to the Constitution of the United States:

ARTICLE 13. SEC. 1. In all the present territory of the United States, north of the parallel of 36° 30′ of north latitude, involuntary servitude, except in punishment of crime, is prohibited. In all the present Territory south of that line, the *status* of persons held to involuntary service or labor, as it now exists, shall not be changed: nor shall any law be passed by Congress or the Territorial Legislature to hinder or prevent the taking of such persons from any of the States of this Union to said Territory, nor to impair the rights arising from said relation; but the same shall be subject to judicial cognizance in the Federal courts, according to the course of the common law. When any Territory north or south of said line, within such boundary as Congress may prescribe, shall contain a population equal to that required for a member of Congress, it shall, if its form of Government be republican, be admitted into the Union on an equal footing with the original States, with or without involuntary servitude, as the constitution of such State may provide.

SEC. 2. No Territory shall be acquired by the United States, except by discovery and for naval and commercial stations, depots, and transit routes, without the concurrence of a majority of all the Senators from States which allow involuntary servitude, and a majority of all the Senators from States which prohibit that relation; nor shall Territory be acquired by treaty, unless the votes of a majority of the Senators from each class of States hereinbefore mentioned be cast as a part of the two-thirds majority necessary to the ratification of such treaty.

SEC. 3. Neither the Constitution nor any amendment thereof shall be construed to give Congress power to regulate, abolish, or control, within any State the relation established or recognized by the laws thereof touching persons held to labor or involuntary service therein, nor to interfere with or abolish involuntary service in the District of Columbia without the consent of Maryland and without the consent of the owners, or making the owners who do not consent just compensation; nor the power to interfere with or prohibit Representatives and others from bringing with them to the District of Columbia, retaining, and taking away, persons so held to labor or service; nor the power to interfere with or abolish involuntary service in places under the exclusive jurisdiction of the United States within those States and Territories where the same is established or recognized; nor the power to prohibit the removal or transportation of persons held to labor or involuntary service in any State or Territory of the United States to any other State or Territory thereof where it is established or recognized by law or usage, and the right during transportation, by sea or river, of touching at ports, shores, and landings, and of landing in case of distress, shall exist; but not the right of transit in or through any State or Territory, or of sale or traffic, against the laws thereof. Nor shall Congress have power to authorize any higher rate of taxation on persons held to labor or service than on land. The bringing into the District of Columbia of persons held to labor or service, for sale, or placing them in depots to be afterwards transferred to other places for sale as merchandize, is prohibited.

SEC. 4. The third paragraph of the second section of the fourth article of the Constitution shall not be construed to prevent any of the States, by appropriate legislation, and through the action of their judicial and ministerial officers, from enforcing the delivery of fugitives from labor to the person to whom such service or labor is due.

SEC. 5. The foreign slave trade is hereby forever prohibited; and it shall be the duty of Congress to pass laws to prevent the importation of slaves, coolies, or persons held to service or labor, into the United States and the Territories from places beyond the limits thereof.

SEC. 6. The first, third, and fifth sections, together with this section of these amendments, and the third paragraph of the second section of the first article of the Constitution, and the third paragraph of the second section of the fourth article thereof, shall not be amended or abolished without the consent of all the States.

SEC. 7. Congress shall provide by law that the United States shall pay to the owner the full value of his fugitive from labor, in all cases where the marshal or other officer, whose duty it was to arrest such fugitive, was prevented from so doing by violence or intimidation from mobs or riotous assemblages, or when, after arrest, such fugitive was rescued by like violence or intimidation, and the owner thereby deprived of the same; and the acceptance of such payment shall preclude the owner from further claim to such fugitive. Congress shall provide by law for securing to the citizens of each State the privileges and immunities of citizens in the several States.

Section 1 was first lost, yeas 8, nays 11, then re-considered, and agreed to, yeas 9, (Delaware, Illinois, Kentucky, Maryland, New Jersey, Ohio, Pennsylvania, Rhode Island, Tennessee,) nays 8, (Connecticut, Iowa, Maine, Massachusetts, North Carolina, New Hampshire, Vermont, Virginia.)

Section 2 was agreed to, yeas 11, (Delaware, Indiana, Kentucky, Maryland, Missouri, New Jersey, Ohio, Pennsylvania, Rhode Island, Tennessee, Virginia,) nays 8, (Connecticut, Illinois, Iowa, Maine, Massachusetts, North Carolina, New Hampshire, Vermont.)

Section 3 was agreed to, yeas 12, (Delaware, Illinois, Kentucky, Maryland, Missouri, New Jersey, North Carolina, Ohio, Pennsylvania, Rhode Island, Tennessee, Virginia,) nays 7, (Connecticut, Indiana, Iowa, Maine, Massachusetts, New Hampshire, Vermont.)

Section 4 was agreed to, yeas 15, (Connecticut, Delaware, Illinois, Indiana, Kentucky, Maryland, Missouri, New Jersey, North Carolina, Ohio, Pennsylvania, Rhode Island, Tennessee, Vermont, Virginia,) nays 4, (Iowa, Maine, Massachusetts, New Hampshire.)

Section 5 was agreed to, yeas 16, (Connecticut, Delaware, Illinois, Indiana, Kentucky, Maryland, Missouri, New Jersey, New York, New Hampshire, Ohio, Pennsylvania, Rhode Island, Tennessee, Vermont, Kansas,) nays 5, (Iowa, Maine, Massachusetts, North Carolina, Virginia.)

Section 6 was agreed to, yeas 11, (Delaware, Illinois, Kentucky, Maryland, Missouri, New Jersey, Ohio, Pennsylvania, Rhode Island, Tennessee, Kansas,) nays 9, (Connecticut, Indiana, Iowa, Maine, Massachusetts, North Carolina, New Hampshire, Vermont, Virginia.) New York was divided.

Section 7 was agreed to, yeas 12, (Dela-

* Died during the session, and succeeded by C. P. Wolcott.

ware, Illinois, Indiana, Kentucky. Maryland, New Jersey, New Hampshire, Ohio, Pennsylvania, Rhode Island, Tennessee, Kansas,) nays 7, (Connecticut, Iowa, Maine, Missouri, North Carolina, Vermont, Virginia.) New York was divided.

By a vote of 12 to 7, (New York divided,) the resolution offered by Mr. FRANKLIN of Pennsylvania, after the adoption of the above proposition, to the effect that no State of this Union has any constitutional right to secede therefrom, or to absolve its citizens from their allegiance to the Government of the United States, was indefinitely postponed, yeas 10, (Delaware, Kentucky, Maryland, Missouri, New Jersey, North Carolina, Ohio, Rhode Island, Tennessee, Virginia,) nays 7, (Connecticut, Illinois, Indiana, Iowa, Maine, Massachusetts, Pennsylvania.)

Pending the vote in the Conference on these propositions,

Mr. DAVID DUDLEY FIELD, of New York, moved to substitute for Section 7, a provision that "no State shall withdraw from the Union without the consent of all the States, given in a Convention of the States, convened in pursuance of an act passed by two-thirds of each house of Congress;" which was rejected—yeas 10, nays 11, as follows:

YEAS — Connecticut, Illinois, Indiana, Iowa, Maine, Massachusetts, New York, New Hampshire, Vermont, Kansas—10.

NAYS—Delaware, Kentucky, Maryland, Missouri, New Jersey, North Carolina, Ohio, Pennsylvania, Rhode Island, Tennessee, Virginia—11.

Mr. BALDWIN, of Connecticut, moved a substitute recommending that Congress call a Convention for proposing amendments to the Constitution of the United States; which was lost—yeas 8, nays 13, as follows:

YEAS—Connecticut, Illinois, Iowa, Maine, Massachusetts, New York, New Hampshire, Vermont—8.

NAYS—Delaware, Indiana, Kentucky, Maryland, Missouri, New Jersey, North Carolina, Ohio, Pennsylvania, Rhode Island, Tennessee, Virginia, Kansas—13.

Mr. SEDDON's project—securing in addition to the Crittenden proposition, the right of transit for slaves through Free States—excluding from the elective franchise, or the right to hold Federal, State, Territorial or Municipal office, all persons who are in whole or part of the African race—and in a modified form recognizing the right of peaceable State secession,—was also offered, and was lost—yeas 4, nays 16, as follows:

YEAS—Kentucky, Missouri, North Carolina and Virginia.

NAYS—Connecticut, Delaware, Illinois, Indiana, Maine, Massachusetts, Maryland, New Jersey, New York, New Hampshire, Ohio, Pennsylvania, Rhode Island, Tennessee, Vermont, and Kansas—16.

Mr. JAMES B. CLAY's substitute (much like Mr. Seddon's) was also lost—yeas 5 (Tennessee, besides those above), nays 14 (same as above with Tennessee and Kansas out).

Mr TUCK's substitute, denying the power of Congress, or any branch of the Federal Government, to interfere in any manner with slavery in any of the States, and that either of the great political organizations of the country contemplates a violation of the Constitution, and recommending a Convention to propose amendments to the Constitution of the United States for the redress of whatever grievances exist, was also rejected—yeas 9, nays 11, as follows:

YEAS—Connecticut, Illinois, Indiana, Iowa, Maine, Massachusetts, New York, New Hampshire, Vermont—9.

NAYS — Delaware, Kentucky, Maryland, Missouri, New Jersey, North Carolina, Ohio, Pennsylvania, Rhode Island, Tennessee, Virginia—11.

There were 133 members present upon the adoption of the report, representing

Maine, Massachusetts, New York, Delaware, North Carolina, Missouri, New Hampshire, Rhode Island, New Jersey, Maryland, Tennessee, Ohio, Vermont, Connecticut, Pennsylvania, Virginia, Kentucky, Indiana, Illinois, Iowa, Kansas.

NOTE.—Michigan, Wisconsin, California and Oregon, of the loyal States, were not represented in the Conference.

These propositions were offered to the Senate by Mr. JOHNSON of Arkansas, March 2d, pending the House resolution proposing an amendment of the Constitution, and they were rejected—yeas 3, nays 34, as follows:

YEAS—Messrs. Foot, *Nicholson*, and *Pugh*—3.

NAYS—Messrs. Anthony, Baker, *Bigler*, Bingham, *Bright*, Chandler, Clark, Crittenden, Dixon, Doolittle, *Douglas*. Durkee, Fessenden, Foster, Grimes, Harlan, *Hunter*, *Johnson* of Arkansas, *Johnson* of Tennessee, *Kennedy*, King, *Latham*, *Mason*, Morrill, *Polk*, *Rice*, *Sebastian*, Sumner, Ten Eyck, Trumbull, Wade, *Wigfall*, Wilkinson, and Wilson —34.

Subsequently (March 2d) they were offered to the Senate by Mr. CRITTENDEN of Kentucky, after the adoption of the House constitutional amendment, and pending the Crittenden propositions, and they were rejected, yeas 7, nays 28, as follows:

YEAS—Messrs. Crittenden, *Douglas*, Harlan, *Johnson* of Tennessee, *Kennedy*, Morrill, and *Thomson*—7.

NAYS—Messrs. *Bayard*, *Bigler*, Bingham, *Bright*, Chandler, Clark, Dixon, Fessenden, Foot, Foster, Grimes, *Gwin*, *Hunter*, *Lane*, *Latham*, *Mason*, *Nicholson*, *Polk*, *Pugh*, *Rice*, *Sebastian*, Sumner, Ten Eyck, Trumbull, Wade, *Wigfall*, Wilkinson, and Wilson—28.

March 1st, 1861. Mr. MCCLERNAND moved to suspend the rules for the purpose of receiving the recommendation of the Peace Congress, which was rejected, yeas 93, nays 67, as follows:

YEAS—Messrs. Charles F. Adams, Green Adams, *Adrain*, Aldrich, William C. Anderson, *Avery*, *Barr*, *Barrett*, *Bocock*, Boteler, Brabson, *Branch*, Briggs, Bristow, *Brown*, *Burch*, *Burnett*, Campbell, *Horace F. Clark*, *John B. Clark*, *John Cochrane*, Corwin, *James Craig*, *John G. Davis*, *De Jarnette*, Dunn, Etheridge, *Florence*, Foster, *Fouke*, *Garnett*, Gilmer, Hale, Hall, *Hamilton*, J. Morrison Harris, *John T. Harris*, *Haskin*, Hatton, Hoard, *Holman*, *William Howard*, *Hughes*, *Jenkins*, Junkin, W. Kellog, Killinger, *Kunkel*, *Larrabee*, J. M. Leach, *Leake*, *Logan*, *Maclay*, Mallory, *Chas. D. Martin*, Maynard, *McClernand*, *McKenty*, McKnight, McPherson, *Millson*, Millward, Laban T. Moore, Moorhead, Edward Joy Morris, Nelson, *Niblack*, Nixon, Olin, *Pendleton*, Peyton,

Phelps, Porter, *Pryor*, Quarles, John H. Reynolds, Rice, *Riggs*, *James C. Robinson*, *Sickles*, *Simms*, Wm. N. H. Smith, Spaulding, *Stevenson*, William Stewart, Stokes, *Thomas*, Vance, Webster, *Whiteley*, *Winslow*, *Woodson*, and *Wright*—93.

NAYS—Messrs. Alley, Ashley, Bingham, Blair, Brayton, Buffinton, Burlingame, Burnham, Carey, Case, Coburn, Colfax, Conway, *Burton Craige*, Dawes, Delano, Duell, Edgerton, Eliot, Ely, Fenton, Ferry, Frank, Gooch, Graham, Grow, Gurley, Helmick, Hickman, *Hindman*, William A. Howard, Hutchins, Irvine, Francis W. Kellogg, Kenyon, Loomis, Lovejoy, McKean, Morrill, Morse, Palmer, Perry, Potter, Pottle, Christopher Robinson, Royce, *Ruffin*, Sedgwick, Sherman, Somes, Spinner, Stanton, Stevens, Tappan, Tompkins, Train, Vandever, Van Wyck, Wade, Waldron, Walton, Cadwalader C. Washburn, Ellihu B. Washburne, Wells, Wilson, Windom, and Woodruff—67.

When the report was presented to the Senate and a motion made to fix a time to consider it,

Mr. THOS. L. CLINGMAN of North Carolina, said he was "utterly opposed to the proposition," but was willing to give it the direction its friends desired.

Mr. MILTON S. LATHAM of California, said he "had no confidence in this thing," but would vote for the motion.

When it was presented to the House,

Mr. SAML. H. WOODSON of Missouri, said he would vote to receive it, but was against the proposition.

Mr. BURTON CRAIGE of North Carolina, said he was "utterly opposed to any such wishy-washy settlement of our National difficulties."

Mr. SHELTON F. LEAKE "regarded this *thing* as a miserable abortion, forcibly reminding one of the old fable of the mountain and the mouse; nevertheless, he was willing to let the mouse in, in order to have the pleasure of killing it."

Mr. THOS. C. HINDMAN of Arkansas, believed the report "to be unworthy of the vote of any Southern man."

Mr. MUSCOE R. H. GARNETT of Virginia, "intending and desiring to express my abhorrence of these insidious propositions, conceived in fraud and born of cowardice, by giving a direct vote against them, yet from respect for the conference which reported them" was willing to receive them.

The above were the only votes taken upon the recommendation. That in the House was not a test, as some voted to receive who were opposed to the adoption of the report, and probably *vice versâ*.

Senate Committee of Thirteen.

December 18th, 1860. On motion of Mr. POWELL, a Committee of Thirteen were authorized to consider the condition of the country; which consisted of

Mr. Powell, Mr. Seward, Mr. Collamer, Mr. Bigler, Mr. Hunter, Mr. Toombs, Mr. Davis, Mr. Rice, Mr. Crittenden, Mr. Douglas, Mr. Wade, Mr. Doolittle, Mr. Grimes.

Dec. 31st. The chairman reported that the Committee had not been able to agree upon any general plan of adjustment.

PROCEEDINGS OF THE COMMITTEE.

Dec. 22d, 1860, it was agreed that no proposition shall be reported as adopted, unless sustained by each of the two classes of Senators of the Committee—Senators of the Republican party to constitute one class, and Senators of other parties to constitute the other.

Mr. CRITTENDEN offered his amendments.

The first article was lost—yeas 6, nays 7:

YEAS—Messrs. *Bigler*, Crittenden, *Douglas*, *Hunter*, *Powell*, *Rice*—6.

NAYS—Messrs. Collamer, *Davis*, Doolittle, Grimes, Seward, *Toombs*, Wade—7.

The second was lost *under the rule*—yeas 8, nays 5. The nays were Messrs. Collamer, Doolittle, Grimes, Seward, and Wade.

The third, fourth, and fifth articles were lost by a similar vote; also the sixth, except that Mr. Grimes did not vote.

Mr. CRITTENDEN then submitted a Joint Resolution, containing four propositions:

1. That the Fugitive Slave law is in strict pursuance of the plain and mandatory provisions of the Constitution, and has been sanctioned as valid and constitutional by the judgment of the Supreme Court of the United States, that the slave-holding States are entitled to its faithful execution, and laws should be made to punish those who attempt, by rescue or other illegal means, to hinder or defeat its execution.

2. Congress recommends the repeal of those State laws which conflict with the Fugitive Slave law or other constitutional acts of Congress, or impede, hinder or delay its free course and execution, or such modification of them as may prevent their being used or perverted to such mischievous purposes.

3. The Fugitive Slave law should be so amended as to make the fee of the Commissioner equal, whether his decision be for or against the claimant, and the authority to call the *posse comitatus* to his aid should be limited to cases of resistance, or danger of resistance or rescue.

4. The laws for the suppression of the African slave trade should be made effectual and thoroughly executed.

The *first* was lost *under the rule*—yeas 8, nays 3—Messrs. Doolittle, Grimes and Wade, voting nay; Mr. Collamer and Mr. Seward not voting.

The *second* was lost *under the rule*—yeas 7, nays 4—Messrs. Collamer, Doolittle, Seward, and Wade, voting nay; Mr. Grimes not voting.

The *third* was unanimously agreed to—yeas 13; also the *fourth*.

Mr. DOOLITTLE moved that the laws should secure to the alleged fugitive slave, when he shall claim that he is not a fugitive slave, a jury trial before he shall be delivered to the claimant.

Mr. TOOMBS moved to amend by adding the words, "*in the State from which he fled.*" Agreed to, yeas 7, nays 5.

Mr. CRITTENDEN moved to limit this right to cases "where he shall have been out of the possession of the claimant for more than two years." Lost—yeas 6, nays 6. Mr. Toombs' motion was then lost—yeas 3 (Bigler, Crittenden, Grimes), nays 9.

Dec. 24th, 1860. Mr. SEWARD submitted these Resolutions:

1. No amendment shall be made to the Constitution which will authorize or give to Congress the power to abolish or interfere, within any State, with the domestic institutions thereof, including that of persons held to labor or service by the laws of said State.

2. The Fugitive Slave act of 1850 shall be so amended as to give to the alleged fugitive a jury trial.

3. The Legislatures of the several States shall be respectfully requested to review all of their legislation affecting the right of persons recently resident in other States, and to repeal or modify all such acts as may contravene the provisions of the Constitution of the United States, or any laws made in pursuance thereof.

The *first* was agreed to—yeas 11, nays 2 (*Rice* and *Toombs.*)

Mr. TOOMBS moved to add to the second the words, "*in the State from which he fled.*" Agreed to—yeas 7, nays 5. The resolution as amended was disagreed to—yeas 6, nays 7.

YEAS—Messrs. Collamer, Doolittle, *Douglas*, Grimes, Seward, Wade.

NAYS—Messrs. *Bigler*, Crittenden, *Davis, Hunter, Powell, Rice, Toombs.*

The *third* was lost, *under the rule*—yeas 7, nays 5.

YEAS—Messrs. *Bigler*, Collamer, Crittenden, Doolittle, Grimes, Seward, Wade.

NAYS — Messrs. *Davis, Hunter, Powell Rice, Toombs.*

Mr. TOOMBS'* propositions were then negatived.

* They were—1st. The people of the United States shall have an equal right to emigrate to, and settle in, the present or any future acquired territories, with whatever property they may possess (including slaves), and be securely protected in its peaceable enjoyment, until such Territory may be admitted as a State in the Union, with or without slavery, as she may determine, on an equality with all existing States. *Lost under the rule*—yeas 7, nays 5 (the Republican members).

2. That property in slaves shall be entitled to the same protection from the Government of the United States in all of its departments, everywhere, which the Constitution confers the power upon it to extend to any other property—this not to interfere with the right of every State to prohibit, abolish, or establish, and protect slavery within its limits. *Lost under the rule* by the same vote.

3. Persons committing crimes against slave property in one State and fleeing to another, shall be delivered up as other criminals. Lost by the same vote.

4. Congress to pass laws punishing persons engaged in invasion or insurrection, or other act tending to disturb the tranquillity of any other State. Lost, 6 to 4.

5. Fugitive slaves not to have benefit of writ of *habeas corpus* or trial by jury. Lost, 7 to 5, as before.

6. Congress to pass no law in relation to slavery in the States or Territories or elsewhere, without the consent of a majority of the Senators and Representatives of the slaveholding States. Amended, on motion of Mr. HUNTER, so as to add: "*and also a majority of the Senators and Representatives of the non-slaveholding States,*" and then lost—yeas 5, nays 6.

7. None of these provisions, or others in the Constitution relating to slavery (except the African slave trade), to be altered without the consent of all the States in which slavery exists. Lost, 6 to 5 (the Republican members).

Dec. 26, 1860. Mr. SEWARD moved, That under the 4th section of the 4th article of the Constitution, Congress should pass an efficient law for the punishment of all persons engaged in the armed invasion of any State from another, by combinations of individuals, and punishing all persons in complicity therewith, on trial and conviction in the State or district where their acts of complicity were committed, in the Federal courts.

Mr. TOOMBS moved to add: "*And also all attempts to excite insurrection in any State by the people of any other State.*" Agreed to—yeas 8, nays 5 (Collamer, Doolittle, Grimes, Seward, Wade).

Mr. DOUGLAS moved to add: "*And for the suppression and punishment of conspiracies or combinations, in any State or Territory, with intent to invade, assail, or molest the government, inhabitants, property, or institutions of any other State or Territory of the Union.*" Agreed to.

On the resolution as amended, the question was divided, and the proposition offered by Mr. Seward was agreed to—yeas 9, nays 3 (*Rice, Toombs*, Wade); that offered by Mr. Toombs was agreed to; that offered by Mr. Douglas was lost—yeas 6, nays 6 (Collamer, *Davis*, Doolittle, Grimes, Seward, Wade). The resolution as amended by Mr. Toombs was then lost, *under the rule*—yeas 7, nays 5 (Collamer, Doolittle, Grimes, Seward, Wade).

MR. DAVIS submitted a proposition, that it shall be declared, by amendment of the Constitution, that property in slaves, recognized as such by the local laws of any of the States in the Union, shall stand on the same footing in all constitutional and federal relations as any other species of property so recognized, and like other property shall not be subject to be divested or impaired by the local law of any other State, either in escape thereto or of transit or sojourn of the owner therein; and in no case whatever shall such property be subject to be divested or impaired by any legislative act of the United States, or any of the territories thereof. This was lost—yeas 6, nays 6.

YEAS.—Messrs. *Bigler, Davis, Hunter, Powell, Rice, Toombs.*

NAYS. — Messrs. Collamer, Crittenden, Doolittle, Grimes, Seward, Wade.

December 28th, 1860. Mr. CRITTENDEN submitted a proposition relative to New Mexico, which was lost—yeas 2, (Crittenden and *Douglas*,) nays 11.

Mr. BIGLER submitted a proposition, proposing *seven* amendments to the Constitution.

1st. Dividing the territory now owned by the United States by a line from east to west on the parallel of 36° 30′.

2d. Dividing the territory south into four territories, the territory north into eight.

3d. Congress to provide governments when the inhabitants become sufficiently numerous, and when the *bona fide* inhabitants in any one shall be equal to the ratio of representation in Congress, it shall be the duty of the President, by proclamation, to announce the admission of such State into the Union.

4th. In territory south, involuntary servitude, as it now exists in the States south of Mason and Dixon's line, shall be recognized and protected by all the departments of the Territorial Governments; and in all territories north, involuntary servitude except as a punishment of crime shall be prohibited.

5th. Congress shall be denied power to abolish slavery in places now under its jurisdiction within slave States and the District of Columbia, while slavery may exist in Virginia or Maryland.

6th. Non-slaveholding States shall provide efficient laws for the delivery of fugitives from labor to the persons to whom such service or labor may be due.

7th. Neither these amendments nor the third paragraph of the second section of the first article of the Constitution, nor the third paragraph of the second section of the fourth article of the Constitution, shall be liable to further amendment.

This proposition was determined in the negative without a division.

Mr. DOUGLAS's propositions were then considered. They were:

1st. Congress shall make no law in regard to slavery or servitude in the territories, but the status of such territory in this respect to remain as at present; and that every territory might form a Constitution when its population should be fifty thousand, and exercise all the rights of self-government; and that such State should be admitted into the Union on an equal footing with the original States, with or without slavery, as its Constitution should provide, when such State should contain a population to entitle it to a representation, according to the federal ratio of representation.

2d. No more territory to be acquired except on a vote of two-thirds of both branches of Congress, and the status thereof as to servitude to remain as at the time of its acquisition, until altered by the people in framing a Constitution as aforesaid.

3d. Area of future States to contain not less than 60,000, nor more than 80,000 square miles.

4th. Extending provisions of the fugitive slave law to the new States and Territories.

5th. Extending the judicial power of the United States to the new States and Territories.

6th. Forbidding the exercise of the elective franchise to persons of the African race, in whole or in part.

7th. Giving power to Congress to acquire territory in Africa or South America for colonization of free blacks.

8th. Prohibiting Congress from abolishing slavery in any places in any slave State without the consent of such State.

9th. Prohibiting Congress from abolishing slavery in the District of Columbia without the consent of Maryland, or preventing persons having business in the District from bringing their slaves with them and taking them away again.

10th. Prohibits Congress from interfering with the inter-State slave-trade.

11th. Provides a payment in cash for any fugitive slave who cannot be arrested by the marshal through fear of mob violence, etc.

12th. Provides that these amendments and the third paragraph of the second section of the first article, and the third paragraph of the second section of the fourth article of the Constitution, shall never be amended, and prohibits any amendment authorizing Congress ever to abolish slavery in the States.

Mr. DOUGLAS's propositions were negatived. The vote on the *first* was, yeas 2 (Crittenden and Douglas,) nays 11. On the *second*, yeas 1, nays 10. On the *third*, yeas 2, nays 11. On the *fourth*, lost *under the rule*, yeas 8, nays 5 (the Republican members). The *fifth* was lost, *nem con.* The *sixth*, lost *under the rule*, yeas 8, nays 5 (the Republican members). The *seventh* was adopted, yeas 10, nays 3 (Davis, Hunter, Toombs). The *eighth* and *ninth* were lost, *nem con.* The *tenth* was amended, and negatived *under the rule*, yeas 8, nays 5 (the Republican members). The *eleventh* and *twelfth* were negatived, *nem con.*

Mr. RICE offered a proposition to settle the territorial question by admitting at once into the Union as a State all the territory lying north of 36° 30′ to be called the State of Washington, and all the territory lying south of 36° 30′ to be called the State of Jefferson; and in each case, whenever any portion of said States shall contain, within an area of not less than 60,000 square miles, 130,000 inhabitants, a new State may be formed—all acts organizing territorial governments to be repealed, and Congress to appropriate money to pay the expenses of the convention to form constitutions.

Mr. SEWARD moved to amend by adding: "*except so much of the Territory of Kansas as is contained in the proposed boundary of the Wyandot Constitution.*" Lost—yeas 6, nays 6, *Douglas* voting aye with the Republican members.

Mr. RICE's resolution was lost—yeas 3 (*Bigler*, *Davis*, *Rice*), nays 10 (Collamer, Crittenden, Doolittle, *Douglas*, Grimes, *Hunter*, *Powell*, Seward, *Toombs*, Wade).

On motion of Mr. TOOMBS, the committee then agreed to report to the Senate, with their journal, the fact that they had not been able to agree upon any general plan of adjustment.

Other Propositions of Adjustment.

Other propositions were made, which do not appear to have been voted on in either House, or a committee of either:

Mr. JOSEPH LANE, Senator from Oregon,

offered a preamble and resolutions reciting the irreconcilable differences which had arisen between the North and South on the question of slavery in the Territories, and the measures that had been from time to time adopted to settle the difficulties; that the Southern States had resolved to dissolve the Union rather than submit to the principles embodied in the Chicago platform, and that the mode of amendment to the Constitution prescribed by that instrument itself was inadequate to the emergency. And he proposed to the several States to send delegates to a general convention to devise a new form of government and requesting the delegates of the Southern States to first meet in convention, being the aggrieved party, to confer and submit their conclusions to the delegates from the Northern States, and declaring it contrary and abhorrent to the religion and civilization of the age to prevent by force any State from taking such course as her safety and prosperity might require.

Mr. ANDREW JOHNSON, Senator from Tennessee, submitted a joint resolution proposing amendments to the Constitution in substance as follows:

1st. To apportion each State into as many districts as should be equal in number to the whole number of Senators and Representatives in Congress to which such State should be entitled, and that in every such district the persons receiving the highest number of votes for President and Vice President should be holden to have received one vote; that the persons receiving the vote of a majority of the districts, provided it should be a majority of the whole number of votes given, should be President and Vice President, but that if no person had received a majority of the whole number of votes as aforesaid, then a second election should be held between the two persons having the highest number of votes at the first election, and providing further for the election of a President from the free States and Vice President from a slave State, and *vice versâ*, every four years.

2d. Providing for an election of United States Senators by the people instead of by the State Legislatures.

3d. Limiting the tenure of office of the Judges of the Supreme Court of the United States to twelve years, and providing for an election of one-third of said Judges every fourth year.

Mr. JOHNSON also offered a resolution instructing the Committee of Thirteen to inquire into the expediency of amending the Constitution, so as to establish a division line in the Territories; to repeal the legislation of Congress relative to the return of fugitive slaves, and require each State to return them or pay their cash value to the owner; allowing the question of slavery in dock-yards, arsenals, etc., to be regulated by the States in which such places were located; restricting Congress from abolishing slavery in the District of Columbia without the consent of Maryland, and making compensation to the owners; and also from interfering with the three-fifths representation of slaves or the inter-State trade; and declaring that these amendments should never be amended.

THE BORDER STATES PROPOSITION.

At a meeting of Senators and Representatives from the fourteen border free and slave States, at which about seventy-five gentlemen were present, Mr. CRITTENDEN acting as President, and Messrs. COLFAX and BARRETT as Secretaries, the following propositions were submitted:

By Mr. BARRETT of Missouri. Eleven amendments to the Constitution on the slavery question.

By Mr. PRYOR of Virginia. That an attempt to preserve the Union between the States of this Confederacy by force would be equally unconstitutional, impolitic, and destructive of Republican liberty.

By Mr. VALLANDIGHAM. The Crittenden resolutions.

By Mr. COLFAX. That the laws of the Union should be enforced and the Union of the States maintained; and that it is the duty of the Executive to protect the property of the United States with all the power placed in his hands by the Constitution.

By Mr. MORRIS of Illinois. That in the maturing any plan for adjusting the existing difficulties of the country we will keep steadily in view the preservation of the Union under the Constitution as a paramount consideration.

All of the above propositions after some discussion were referred to a committee consisting of Messrs. CRITTENDEN of Kentucky, HARRIS of Maryland, SHERMAN of Ohio, NIXON of New Jersey, SAULSBURY of Delaware, GILMER of North Carolina, HATTON of Tennessee, PETTIT of Indiana, HARRIS of Virginia, MCCLERNAND of Illinois, BARRETT of Missouri, SEBASTIAN of Arkansas, VANDEVER of Iowa, and HALE of Pennsylvania.

The committee after consultation adopted the following propositions:

Recommending a repeal of all personal liberty bills.

An efficient amending of the fugitive slave law, preventing kidnapping, equalizing commissioners' fees, etc.

Amending the Constitution so as to prohibit interference by Congress with slavery in the States, or abolishing it in any places within its jurisdiction without the consent of the State in which such places are located.

Or with the inter-State slave trade.

Perpetual prohibition of the African slave trade.

Division of territory into free and slave on the line of 36° 30′, prohibiting Congress or the Territorial Legislature from abolishing or interfering with slavery south of that line, and providing for admission of new States with population sufficient for one member of Congress and 60,000 square miles of area.

OTHER PROPOSITIONS.

Proposition to the Hon. JAMES HUMPHREY, member of the Committee of Thirty-three from the State of New York, signed by JOHN COCHRANE, WILLIAM B. MACLAY, DANIEL E. SICKLES, GEORGE BRIGGS, THOMAS J. BARR, and HORACE F. CLARK, members of Congress from said State:

1st. Recommending the territorial line of 36° 30′.

2d. Non-interference of Congress with slavery in any places within the jurisdiction of Congress without the consent of the States in which such places are located.

3d. Change in the mode of electing President, by the adoption of the single electoral district system for the election of Presidential electors, with two electors at large for each State; with provision for a second election between the two highest candidates in case no one had received a majority on the first vote.

4th. Limiting the eligibility to the Presidency to one term, and recommending a change in the fugitive slave law so as to provide for the delivery of the fugitive, not to his master, but to the marshal of the district in which the claimant resided, there to be tried as to the right of ownership; and in case of unlawful rescue, etc., his value to be paid by the State or county in which such rescue occurred.

A "distinguished gentleman of Kentucky" proposed to so amend the Constitution as to restrain Congress from passing any law to interfere with slavery in territory south of 36° 30′, or to interfere with the inter-State slave trade, or to abolish slavery in places belonging to the General Government within the limits of a slave State, or to permit the reopening of the slave trade, or to interfere with slavery in the States by unequal taxation or otherwise, but authorizing Congress to regulate the transit of slaves through free States, and to authorize the recapture of slaves escaping in such transit, and to give compensation to the owner of the slave in case of violent rescue, etc., making it compulsory to admit new States with slave constitutions, and to prevent and punish unlawful invasions of any State with a design to excite slave insurrections.

Mr. A. H. H. STUART offered a series of resolutions in the Senate of Virginia to the effect that the slaveholding States should be created trustees of the territory south of 36° 30′, and the free States trustees of the territory north of that line, with the right to regulate the question of slavery in either case respectively.

The *National Intelligencer* of January 12th, 1861, proposed a plan of compromise by amendments to the Constitution and Congressional legislation substantially as follows:

To prohibit Congress from interfering with slavery in the States, in places under Federal jurisdiction within the limits of a slave State, or in the District of Columbia, or with the inter-State slave trade, or to reopen the slave trade; from acquiring any additional territory except by a concurrent vote of two-thirds of both Houses of Congress, or by treaty ratified by two-thirds of the Senate, and to adopt the single electoral district system, with two electors at large for each State.

Also, to so amend the fugitive slave law as to give the same compensation to the Commissioner whether the slave was given up or not, and making the State liable for all extraordinary expenses attending the capture of fugitive slaves, and for compensation to the owner in case of violent rescue, etc. To admit all the territory north of 36° 30′ at once into the Union as a State to be called "Washington," and all south of that line as a State to be called "Jefferson," with provision for the sub-division of said States into two or more States.

Governor LETCHER, of Virginia, in his message to the Legislature, proposed in substance the following plan: To appoint Commissioners to visit each Northern State that had passed personal liberty bills and urge their repeal, guarantee slavery in the District of Columbia, equal rights in the Territories, free transit for slave property, and the inter-State slave trade, punishment of persons aiding in any way in inciting slave insurrections, and deprive the General Government of the power to appoint to office in slave States persons hostile to the institution of slavery. He also declared strongly against the right of coercion, and that the passage of Federal troops across Virginia for such purpose would be repelled, and expressed his willingness that New England and Western New York should be sloughed off and permitted to ally themselves with Canada.

The *Albany Evening Journal* proposed the following as a basis of settlement:

1. The passage of an efficient but not revolting fugitive slave law.
2. The repeal of personal liberty laws.
3. Non-intervention by Congress with slavery in the Territories.
4. The admission of Territories as States with or without slavery, as they may decide, whenever they have a population entitling them to a Representative in Congress.
5. Or if the two last propositions are inadmissible, then the restoration of the Missouri compromise line.

Hon. JOSEPH W. TAYLOR of Alabama proposed the following:

1st. That every Southern State should meet in Convention and adopt a platform expressive of their views and wishes in the present crisis, and then that they should all meet in a Southern Convention and adopt a platform setting forth all that they had to demand, with a request that the people of the Northern States should meet in a similar Convention to consider said demands.

The New York *Sun* published as its plan of settlement:

1st. The prompt excision by amendment of the Constitution, of any State which shall within the next ten years, elect by vote of two-thirds of her inhabitants to secede from the Union.

2d. The adoption of State and Federal laws for the indemnification of owners of slaves who should be rescued by force or otherwise unlawfully.

In an article in the *Baltimore Exchange* of January 7th, 1861, it was proposed as a settlement of the territorial question, to admit New Mexico and Arizona as a State, and then amend the Constitution so as to absolutely prohibit the acquisition in the future of any additional territory whatever, the author strongly alleging that Republican Governments had more to fear from the expansion of territory than from any other cause whatever.

BY A DISTINGUISHED CITIZEN OF NORTH CAROLINA.

An amendment of the Constitution in regard to the election of a President and Vice President, providing for a vote of the people throughout each State directly for President and Vice President; then ascertain the number to which the popular vote ought to be increased by reason of the slave population, and let that be divided *pro rata* between the several sets of electors according to their respective strength, then let the majority of each set of electors cast the popular vote for President and Vice President of their choice.

A writer in the *National Intelligencer* proposed the following: That Congress, by joint resolution, should declare that the personal liberty bills are unconstitutional, and the States should repeal them; that Congress should not interfere with slavery in the States; that no more territory should be acquired except by consent of three-fourths of the States, and that the Dred Scott decision should govern all our present territory.

In a letter published in the *New York Herald*, purporting to have been written at Lexington, Kentucky, it was asserted that JOHN C. BRECKINRIDGE was in favor of the Crittenden Compromise, and that the Crittenden amendment had actually been drawn up by Mr. Breckinridge and a Mr. M. C. Johnson of Lexington, prior to Mr. Breckinridge's departure for Washington.

Miscellaneous Resolutions.

ON UNCONSTITUTIONAL STATE LAWS.

December 17, 1860. Mr. ADRAIN, of New Jersey, offered the following:

"Whereas the Constitution of the United States is the supreme law of the land, and its ready and faithful observance the duty of all good and law-abiding citizens,—

"*Resolved*. That we deprecate the spirit of disobedience to the Constitution, wherever manifested, and we earnestly recommend the repeal of all statutes, including personal liberty bills, so called, enacted by State Legislatures, which are in conflict with and in violation of that sacred instrument, and of the laws of Congress made in pursuance thereof."

Which was agreed to—yeas 154, nays 14, as follows:

YEAS—Messrs. Adams of Ky., *Adrain*, Aldrich, Allen, *Anderson* of Missouri, Anderson of Ky., Ashley, *Avery*, Babbitt, *Barr*, *Barrett*, Beale, Bingham, Blair, Blake, *Bocock*, Boteler, Bouligny, *Branch*, Brayton, Briggs, *Brown*, Buffinton, Burlingame, *Burnett*, Burnham, Butterfield, Campbell, Carter, Case, *Horace F. Clark*, *Clark* of Missouri, *Cobb*, *John Cochrane*, Colfax, Conkling, Covode, *Cox*, *Craig* of Missouri, *Craige* of North Carolina, *Crawford*, *Davis* of Indiana, Dawes, *De Jarnette*, Delano, Duell, Dunn, *Edmundson*, Ely, *English*, Etheridge, Farnsworth, Fenton, *Florence*, *Fouke*, Frank, *Garnett*, Gilmer, Gooch, Graham, Grow, Hale, Hall, *Hardeman*, Harris of Md., *Harris* of Va., Hatton, Helmick, Hill, *Hindman*, *Holman*, *Houston*, *Howard* of Ohio, *Hughes*, Humphrey, Irvine, *Jenkins*, Jones, Junkin, Kellogg of Michigan, Kenyon, Kilgore, Killinger, *Landrum*, *Larrabee*, Leach of N. Carolina, *Leake*, Lee, *Logan*, Longnecker, Loomis, Lovejoy, *Maclay*, Mallory, *Martin* of Ohio, *Martin* of Va., Maynard, *McClernand*, McKean, *McKenty*, McKnight, McPherson, Millward, *Montgomery*, Moore of Ky., Moorhead, Morris of Penn'a, *Morris* of Ill., *Niblack*, Nixon, *Noell*, Olin, Palmer, *Pendleton*, Pettit, *Peyton*, Porter, Pottle, *Pryor*, Quarles, *Reagan*, J. H. Reynolds, Rice, *Riggs*, *Robinson*, Royce, *Ruffin*, *Scott*, Scranton, Sherman, *Sickles*, *Simms*, Smith of N. C., Spaulding, Stanton, *Stevenson*, Stewart of Pa., Stokes, Thayer, *Thomas*, Tompkins, Train, Trimble, Vance, Verree, Wade, Waldron, Walton, Washburne of Ill., Webster, Wilson, Wood, *Woodson*, *Wright*—154.

NAYS—Messrs. Alley, Carey, Edwards, Eliot, Hutchins, Potter, E. R. Reynolds, Sedgwick, Spinner, Tappan, Vandever, Washburn of Wisconsin, Washburn of Maine, Wells—14.

The preamble was agreed to—yeas 156, nays none.

ON THE UNION.

Mr. MORRIS, of Illinois, offered the following:

"*Resolved, &c.*, That we properly estimate the immense value of our National Union to our collective and individual happiness; that we cherish a cordial, habitual, and immovable attachment to it; that we will speak of it as of the palladium of our political safety and prosperity; that we will watch its preservation with jealous anxiety; that we will discountenance whatever may suggest even a suspicion that it can in any event be abandoned, and indignantly frown down the first dawning of every attempt to alienate any portion of our country from the rest, or enfeeble the sacred ties which now link together the various parts; that we regard it as a main pillar of the edifice of our real independence, the support of our tranquillity at home, our peace abroad, our safety, our prosperity, and that very liberty which we so highly prize; that we have seen nothing in the past, nor do we see any thing in the present, either in the election of Mr. Lincoln to the Presidency of the United States, or from any other existing cause, to justify its dissolution; that we regard its perpetuity as of more value than the temporary triumph of any party or any man; that whatever evils or abuses exist under it ought to be corrected within the Union, in a peaceful and Constitutional way; that we believe that it has sufficient power to redress every wrong and enforce every right growing out of its organization or pertaining to its proper functions; and that it is a patriotic duty to stand by it, as our hope in peace and our defence in war."

Which was agreed to—yeas 115, nays 44, as follows:

YEAS—Messrs. Adams of Kentucky, *Adrain*, Aldrich, *Allen*, Alley, Anderson of Kentucky, Ashley, Babbitt, Beale, Bingham, Blair, Blake, Brayton, Briggs, Buffinton, Burlingame, Burnham, Butterfield, Campbell, Carey, Carter, Case, Colfax, Conkling, Covode, *Cox*, *Davis* of Indiana, Dawes, Delano, Duell, Dunn, Edgerton, Edwards, Eliot, Ely, *English*, Etheridge, Farnsworth, Fenton, Foster, Frank, French, Gooch, Graham, Grow, Hale, Hall, Harris of Md., Helmick, Hickman, Hoard, Holman, *Howard* of Ohio, Humphrey, Hutchins, Irvine, Junkin, Kellogg of Mich., Kenyon, Kilgore, Killinger, Leach of Mich., Lee, *Logan*, Longnecker, Loomis, Lovejoy, *Martin* of Ohio, *McClernand*, McKean, *McKenty*, McKnight, McPherson, *Montgomery*, Moorhead, Morris of Pa., *Morris* of Illinois, *Niblack*, Nixon, Olin, Palmer, Perry, Pettit, Porter, Potter, Pottle, E. R. Reynolds, J. H. Reynolds, Rice, *Riggs*, *Robinson* of Ill., Royce, Scranton, Sedgwick, Sherman, Spaulding, Spinner, Stanton, Stewart of Pa., Stokes, Tappan, Thayer, Tompkins, Train, Trimble, Vandever, Verree, Wade, Waldron, Walton, Washburne of Ill., Washburn of Maine, Wells, Wilson, Wood—115.

NAYS—Messrs. *Anderson* of Missouri, *Avery*, *Barksdale*, Bouligny, *Branch*, *Burnett*, *Clark* of Missouri, *Clopton*, *Cobb*, *Crawford*, *Curry*, *De Jarnette*, *Edmundson*, *Florence*, *Garnett*, *Gartrell*, *Hardeman*, Hill, *Hindman*, *Hughes*, *Jackson*, *Jenkins*, *Jones*, *Landrum*, Leach of N. C., *Leake*, *Martin* of Virginia, *Moore* of Alabama, *Noell*, *Pryor*, Quarles, *Reagan*, *Ruffin*, *Scott*, *Sickles*, *Singleton*, *Smith* of Va., *Stallworth*, *Stevenson*, *Thomas*, *Underwood*, Vance, Webster, *Wright*—44.

THE CONSTITUTION AND SLAVERY.

Mr. CRAWFORD, of Georgia, offered the following:

"*Resolved*, That the Constitution of the United States recognizes property in slaves. That the Congress of the United States has passed laws to aid slaveholders in recapturing their slaves whenever they escape and make their way into the free States. That the Supreme Court of the United States have decided that negroes were not included either in the Declaration of Independence or in the Constitution of the United States except as slaves; and that they cannot become citizens of the United States. And we, the members of this House, hereby sustain and will support this construction of the Constitution, the laws, and said decisions of the Supreme Court."

Dec. 18th. Mr. SHERMAN moved to lay the resolution on the table, which was rejected —yeas 89, nays 92. Subsequently a motion was made to reconsider this vote, and the House refusing—yeas 87, nays 91—to lay the motion to reconsider on the table, the motion of Mr. Sherman to lay the resolution on the table was agreed to—yeas 88, nays 81, as follows:

YEAS—Messrs. Aldrich, *Allen*, Alley, Babbitt, Beale, Bingham, Blair, Blake, Brayton, Buffinton, Burlingame, Butterfield, Carey, Carter, Case, Colfax, Conkling, Covode, Curtis, Dawes, Delano, Duell, Edgerton, Edwards, Eliot, Ely, Farnsworth, Fenton, Foster, Frank, Gooch, Graham, Grow, Gurley, Hale, Hall, Helmick, Hickman, Hoard, Hutchins, Irvine, Junkin, Francis W. Kellogg, Kenyon, Kilgore, Killinger, De Witt C. Leach, Lee, Longnecker, Loomis, Lovejoy, McKean, McKnight, McPherson, Millward, Moorhead, Edward Joy Morris, Morse, Perry, Pettit, Porter, Pottle, Edwin R. Reynolds, John H. Reynolds, Rice, Royce, Sedgwick, Sherman, Spaulding, Spinner, Stanton, William Stewart, Tappan, Theaker, Tompkins, Train, Trimble, Vandever, Verree, Wade, Waldron, Walton, Cadwalader C. Washburn, Ellihu B. Washburne, Israel Washburn, Wells, Wilson, Wood—88.

NAYS—Messrs. Green Adams, *Adrain*, *Thomas L. Anderson*, Ashley, *Barksdale*, *Barrett*, *Bocock*, Boteler, *Boyce*, Briggs, *Brown*, *Burnett*, *Horace F. Clark*, *John B. Clark*, *Clemens*, *Clopton*, *Cobb*, *John Cochrane*, *Cox*, *James Craig*, *Burton Craige*, *Crawford*, *Curry*, *John G. Davis*, *De Jarnette*, *Edmundson*, *English*, *Florence*, *Fouke*, *Gartrell*, Gilmer, *Hardeman*, J. Morrison Harris, *John T. Harris*, Hatton, Hill, *Hindman*, *Holman*, *Hughes*, *Jackson*, *Jones*, *Kunkel*, *Landrum*, *Larrabee*, Jas. M. Leach, *Leake*, *Logan*, *Maclay*, Mallory, *Elbert S. Martin*, *McClernand*, *McKenty*, *Montgomery*, Laban T. Moore, *Sydenham Moore*, *Isaac N. Morris*, *Niblack*, *Noell*, *Pendleton*, *Peyton*, *Pryor*, *Pugh*, Quarles, *Reagan*, *Riggs*, *Scott*, *Sickles*, *Simms*, *Singleton*, *Wm. Smith*, Wm. N. H. Smith, *Stallworth*, *Stevenson*, *James A. Stewart*, Stokes, *Thomas*, *Underwood*, Vance, Webster, *Woodson*, *Wright*—81.

APPROVAL OF MAJOR ANDERSON'S COURSE.

In the House of Representatives, January 7th, 1861, this resolution was offered by Mr. ADRAIN, of New Jersey, and adopted—yeas 125, nays 56.

"*Resolved*, That we fully approve the bold and patriotic act of Major Anderson in withdrawing from Fort Moultrie to Fort Sumter, and of the determination of the President to maintain that fearless officer in his present position; and that we will support the President in all constitutional measures to enforce the laws and preserve the Union."

VOTE.

YEAS—Messrs. Charles F. Adams, Green Adams, *Adrain*, Aldrich, *Allen*, Alley, W. C. Anderson, Ashley, Babbitt, Beale, Bingham, Blair, Blake, Brayton, Briggs, Buffinton, Burlingame, Campbell, Carey, Carter, *Clemens*, Coburn, *J. Cochrane*, Colfax, Corwin, Covode, *Cox*, Curtis, *H. W. Davis*, *J. G. Davis*, Dawes, Delano, *Dimmick*, Duell, Dunn, Edgerton, Edwards, Eliot, Ely, Etheridge, Farnsworth, Fenton, Ferry, Foster, *Fouke*, Frank, French, Gooch, Grow, Gurley, Hale, Hall, *Haskin*, Helmick, Hickman, Hoard, *Holman*, *William Howad*, William A. Howard, Humphrey, Hutchins, Irvine, Junkin, Francis W. Kellogg, William Kellogg, Kenyon, Kilgore, *Larrabee*, De Witt C. Leach, *Logan*, Longnecker, Loomis, Lovejoy, *Maclay*, Marston, *Charles D. Martin*, *McClernand*, McKean, *McKenty*, McKnight, McPherson, Millward, *Montgomery*, Moorhead, Morrill, Edward Joy Morris, Morse, Nixon, Olin, Palmer, Perry, Pettit, Porter, Pottle, Edwin R. Reynolds, Rice, *Riggs*, Christopher Robinson, *James C. Robinson*, Royce, Sedgwick, Sherman, *Sickles*, Spaulding, Spinner, Stanton, Stevens, William Stewart, Stratton, Tappan, Thayer, Theaker, Tompkins, Train, Trimble, Vandever, Wade, Waldron, Walton, Cadwalader C. Washburn, Ellihu B. Washburne, Wells, Wilson, Windom, Wood—125.

NAYS—Messrs. *Thomas L. Anderson*, *Avery*, *Barksdale*, *Barrett*, *Bocock*, Bouligny, *Branch*, *Brown*, *Burch*, *Burnett*, *John B. Clark*, *Clopton*, *Cobb*, *James Craig*, *Crawford*, *De Jarnette*, *Florence*, *Garnett*, *Gartrell*, Gilmer, *Hamilton*, *Hardeman*, *John T. Harris*, Hatton, *Hawkins*, Hill, *Hindman*, *Houston*, *Hughes*, *Jones*, *Kunkel*, *Landrum*, James M. Leach, *Love*, Mallory, *Elbert S. Martin*, Maynard, *McRae*, Laban T. Moore, *Sydenham Moore*, *Peyton*, *Phelps*, *Pryor*, Quarles, *Reagan*, *Rust*. *Scott*, *Simms*, *Singleton*, William N. H. Smith, *Stevenson*, Stokes, *Vallandigham*, Vance, Webster, *Wright*—56.

COERCION.

December 31st. Mr. PRYOR offered the following resolution:

Resolved, That any attempt to preserve the Union between the States of this Confederacy by force would be impracticable and destructive to republican liberty.

Mr. STANTON moved to lay this upon the table, which was agreed to—yeas 98, nays 55, as follows:

YEAS—Messrs. Adams of Mass., Adams of Ky., *Adrain*, Aldrich, *Allen*, Babbitt, Beale, Bingham, Blair, Blake, Brayton, Briggs, Buffinton, Burlingame, Burnham, Campbell, Carey, Case, *Clemens*, Colfax, Conkling, *Cox*, *Davis* of Ind., Dawes, Duell, Edgerton, Eliot, Ely, Etheridge, Farnsworth, Fenton, Foster, *Fouke*, French, Gooch, Grow, Hale, Harris of Md., Hatton, Helmick, Hill, *Holman*, *Howard* of Ohio, Howard of Michigan, Humphrey, Hutchins, Junkin, Kellogg of Mich., Kenyon, Kilgore, *Larrabee*, Leach of Mich., Lee, Longnecker, Loomis, Lovejoy, Marston, *Martin* of Ohio, Maynard, McKean, *McKenty*, McKnight, McPherson, *Montgomery*, Moore of Ky., Morris of Pa., *Morris* of Ill., Morse, *Noell*, Olin, Palmer, *Pendleton*, Perry, Pettit, Porter, Quarles, Reynolds, Robinson of Rhode Island, *Robinson* of Ill., Royce, Sherman, Spaulding, Stanton, Stevens, Stokes, Tappan, Thayer, Theaker, Vance, Vandever, Verree, Wade, Walton, Washburn of Wisconsin, Washburne of Illinois, Webster, Wilson, Windom—98.

NAYS—Messrs. Alley, *Anderson* of Mo., Ashley, *Avery*, *Barksdale*, *Barrett*, *Bocock*, *Branch*, *Burch*, *Clark* of Mo., *Clopton*, *Cobb*, *John Cochrane*, *Craig* of Mo., *Crawford*, *Curry*, Curtis, *De Jarnette*, Dunn, *Edmundson*, *Florence*, *Garnett*, *Gartrell*, *Hardeman*, *Harris* of Va., *Hindman*, *Houston*, *Hughes*, *Jackson*, *Jenkins*, *Jones*, Leach of N. C., *Logan*, *Love*, *Martin* of Va., *McClernand*, *McRae*, *Moore* of Ala., *Niblack*, *Peyton*, *Pryor*, *Pugh*, *Riggs*, *Rust*, *Scott*, *Sickles*, *Singleton*, Spinner, *Thomas*, *Vallandigham*, Wells, *Whiteley*, *Winslow*, *Woodson*, *Wright*—55.

NON-INTERFERENCE WITH SLAVERY IN THE STATES.

February 11th, 1861. Mr. SHERMAN of Ohio, offered the following:

Resolved, That neither the Congress of the United States, nor the people or governments of the non-slaveholding States have the constitutional right to legislate upon or interfere with slavery in any of the slaveholding States in the Union.

Which were agreed to—yeas 162, nays none.

YEAS—Messrs. Charles F. Adams, Green Adams, Aldrich, *Allen*, *Thomas L. Anderson*, William C. Anderson, *Avery*, Babbitt, *Barr*, *Barrett*, Bingham, Blair, Blake, *Bocock*, Boteler, Brabson, Brayton, Briggs, Bristow, *Brown*, Buffinton, *Burch*, Burlingame, *Burnett*, Butterfield, Campbell, Carey, Carter, Case, *Horace F. Clark*, *John B. Clark*, Coburn, *John Cochrane*, Colfax, Conkling, Corwin, Covode, *Cox*, *Jas. Craig*, Curtis, Dawes, Delano, *Dimmick*, Duell, Dunn, *Edmundson*, Edwards, Eliot, Ely, *English*, Etheridge, Farnsworth, Ferry, *Florence*, Foster, Frank, French, *Garnett*, Gilmer, Gooch, Graham, Grow, Gurley, Hall, *Hamilton*, J. Morrison Harris, *John T. Harris*, Haskin, Hatton, Helmick, Hoard, *Holman*, *William Howard*, William A. Howard, *Hughes*, Humphrey, Hutchins, Irvine, *Jenkins*, Junkin, Francis W. Kellogg, Kenyon, Killinger, *Larrabee*, *Leake*, Lee, Lovejoy, *Maclay*, Mallory, Marston, *Elbert S. Martin*, Maynard, *McClernand*, McKean, *McKenty*, McKnight, McPherson, *Millson*, Millward, *Montgomery*, Laban T. Moore, Moorhead, Morrill, Edward Joy Morris, *Isaac N. Morris*, Morse, Nelson, *Niblack*, Nixon, *Noell*, Palmer, Perry, Pettit, *Peyton*, *Phelps*, Porter, Potter, Pottle, *Pryor*, Quarles, John H. Reynolds, Rice, *Riggs*, Christopher Robinson, Royce, Scranton, Sedgwick, Sherman, *Sickles*, William N. H. Smith, Spaulding, Spinner, Stanton, *Stevenson*, William Stewart, Stokes, *Stout*, Stratton, Tappan, Thayer, Theaker, *Thomas*, Tompkins, Train, Trimble, *Vallandigham*, Vance, Vandever, Van Wyck, Verree, Wade, Waldron, Walton, Cadwalader C. Washburn, Elihu B. Washburne, Webster, Wells, *Whiteley*, Wilson, Windom, *Winslow*, *Woodson*—162.

NAYS—None.

BILL TO RE-ORGANIZE THE MILITIA OF THE DISTRICT OF COLUMBIA.

January 28th, 1860. Mr. STANTON of Ohio, reported from the Military Committee a bill providing that every officer, non-commissioned officer, musician, and private of the militia of the District of Columbia, shall take and subscribe to the oath required by the eighteenth section of the act approved January 11, 1812, the name of any person refusing to be stricken from the roll, or if an officer his commission to be forfeited.

The rules were suspended—yeas 116, nays 41, to permit its introduction, and it was finally passed—yeas 120, nays 42, as follows:

YEAS—Messrs. Charles F. Adams, Green Adams, *Adrain*, Aldrich, Alley, William C. Anderson, Ashley, Babbitt, Beale, Bingham, Blair, Blake, Brayton, Briggs, Bristow, Buffinton, Burnham, Butterfield, Campbell, Carey, Case, Coburn, Colfax, Conkling, Covode, Curtis, H. Winter Davis, *John G. Davis*, Dawes, Delano, Duell, Edgerton, Eliot, Etheridge, Fenton, Foster, Frank, French, Gilmer, Gooch, Grow, Gurley, Hale, J. Morrison Harris, Helmick, Hoard, *Holman*, *William Howard*, William A. Howard, Humphrey, Hutchins, Irvine, Junkin, Francis W. Kellogg, William Kellogg, Kenyon, Killinger, De Witt C. Leach, Lee, Longnecker, Loomis, Lovejoy, Mallory, Marston, *Charles D. Martin*, *McClernand*, McKean, McKnight, McPherson, *Montgomery*, Laban T. Moore, Moorhead, Morrill, Edward Joy Morris, *Isaac N. Morris*, Morse, Nelson, *Niblack*, Nixon, Olin, Palmer, Perry, Potter, Pottle, Edwin R. Reynolds, John H. Reynolds, Rice, *Riggs*, Christopher Robinson, Royce, Scranton, Sedgwick, Sherman, Somes, Spaulding, Spinner, Stanton, Stevens, Wm. Stewart, Stokes, Stratton, Tappan, Thayer, Theaker, Tompkins, Train, Trimble, Vandever, Van Wyck, Wade, Waldron, Walton, Cadwalader C. Washburn, Elihu B. Washburne, Webster, Wells, Wilson, Windom, Wood, Woodruff—119.

NAYS—Messrs. *Avery*, *Bocock*, Boteler, *Branch*, *Brown*, *Burnett*, *Horace F. Clark*, *John B. Clark*, *James Craig*, *Burton Craige*, *De Jarnette*, *Edmundson*, *Florence*, *Fouke*, *Garnett*, *John T. Harris*, Hatton, *Hindman*, *Hughes*, *Kunkel*, James M. Leach, *Leake*, *Logan*, *Maclay*, *Elbert S. Martin*, Maynard, *McKenty*, *Millson*, *Pendleton*, *Peyton*, *Pryor*, Quarles, *James C. Robinson*, *Scott*, *Simms*, William N. H. Smith, *Stevenson*, *Thomas*, Vance, *Whiteley*, *Winslow*, *Wright*—42.

The bill was debated in the Senate, recommitted, re-reported, but objected to by Mr. Mason, Mr. Green, and others, and not finally disposed of.

BILL TO SUPPRESS INSURRECTION.

February 18th. Mr. STANTON of Ohio, reported from the Committee on Military affairs a bill enacting:

That the provisions of an act approved the 28th day of February, in the year 1795, entitled "An act to provide for calling forth the militia to execute the laws of the Union, suppress insurrections, and repel invasions, and to repeal the act now in force for those purposes," and of the act approved the 3d day of March, in the year 1807, entitled "An act authorizing the employment of the land and naval forces of the United States in cases of insurrections," are hereby extended to the case of insurrections against the authority of the United States.

That the President in any case in which it may be lawful to use either the militia or the military and naval force of the United States for the purpose aforesaid, may accept the services of such volunteers as may offer their services, as cavalry, infantry, or artillery, organized in companies of the maximum standard, squadrons and regiments, respectively, according to the mode prescribed for the organization of the respective arms in the military establishment of the United States; and it shall be lawful for the President to commission the officers of such companies, battalions, squadrons, and regiments, in their respective grades, to continue till discharged from the service of the United States; and such volunteers, while in the service of the United States, shall be subject to the rules and articles of war, and shall be entitled to same pay and emoluments as officers and soldiers of the same grade in the regular service.

A motion to reject the bill was negatived—yeas 68, nays 109, as follows:

YEAS—Messrs. *Thomas L. Anderson*, William C. Anderson, *Avery*, *Barr*, *Barrett*, *Bocock*, Bouligny, Brabson, *Branch*, Bristow, *Brown*, *Burch*, *Burnett*, *Horace F. Clark*, *John B. Clark*, *John Cochrane*, *Cox*, *James Craig*, *Burton Craige*, *John G. Davis*, *De Jarnette*, *Edmundson*, *English*, Etheridge, *Florence*, *Garnett*, Gilmer, J. Morrison Harris, *John T. Harris*, Hatton, *Hindman*, *William Howard*, *Hughes*, *Kunkel*, *Larrabee*, James M. Leach, *Leake*, *Logan*, *Maclay*, Mallory, Maynard, *McKenty*, *Millson*, Laban T. Moore, *Isaac N. Morris*, Nelson, *Niblack*, *Noell*, *Peyton*, *Phelps*, *Pryor*, Quarles, *James C. Robinson*, *Ruffin*, *Rust*, *Scott*, *Sickles*, *Simms*, William N. H. Smith, Stokes, *Stout*, *Thomas*, *Vallandigham*, Vance, Webster, *Winslow*, *Woodson*, *Wright*—68.

NAYS—Messrs. Charles F. Adams, *Adrain*, Aldrich, *Allen*, Alley, Ashley, Babbitt, Bingham, Blair, Blake, Brayton, Briggs, Buffinton, Burlingame, Burnham, Butterfield, Campbell, Carey, Carter, Case, Colfax, Conkling, Conway, Corwin, Covode, H. Winter Davis, Dawes, Delano, Duell, Dunn, Edgerton, Edwards, Eliot, Ely, Farnsworth, Fenton, Frank, French, Graham, Grow, Gurley, Hale, Hall, Helmick, Hickman, Hoard, William A. Howard, Hutchins, Irvine, Junkin, Francis W. Kellogg, William Kellogg, Kenyon, Kilgore, Killinger, De Witt C. Leach, Lee, Longnecker, Loomis, Lovejoy, Marston, McKean, McKnight, McPherson, *Montgomery*, Moorhead, Morrill, Morse, Nixon, Olin, Palmer, Perry, Pettit, Porter, Potter, Pottle, Edwin R. Reynolds, John H. Reynolds, Rice, *Riggs*, Christopher Robinson, Royce, Scranton, Sedgwick, Sherman, Somes, Spaulding, Spinner, Stevens, William Stewart, Stratton, Tappan, Thayer, Theaker, Tompkins, Train, Trimble, Vandever, Van Wyck, Wade, Waldron, Walton, Cadwalader C. Washburn, Ellihu B. Washburne, Wells, Wilson, Windom, Wood, Woodruff—109.

19th. A motion to lay it on the table was negatived—yeas 68, nays 105. The yeas were:

YEAS—Messrs. *Adrain*, *Allen*, *Thomas L. Anderson*, Wm. C. Anderson, *Avery*, *Barr*, *Bocock*, Boteler, Bouligny, Brabson, *Branch*, Bristow, *Burch*, *Burnett*, *Horace F. Clark*, *John B. Clark*, *John Cochrane*, *Cox*, *James Craig*, *Burton Craige*, *John G. Davis*, *De Jarnette*, *Edmundson*, *English*, Etheridge, *Florence*, *Fouke*, *Garnett*, Gilmer, *Hamilton*, J. Morrison Harris, *John T. Harris*, Hatton, *Hindman*, *Wm. Howard*, *Hughes*, *Kunkel*, *Larrabee*, James M. Leach, *Leake*, *Maclay*, Mallory, *Charles D. Martin*, *Elbert S. Martin*, Maynard, *McKenty*, *Millson*, Laban T. Moore, Nelson, *Niblack*, *Noell*, *Peyton*, *Pryor*, Quarles, *Riggs*, *James C. Robinson*, *Ruffin*, *Rust*, *Scott*, *Simms*, Stokes, *Stout*, *Thomas*, *Vallandigham*, Vance, *Winslow*, *Woodson*, *Wright*—68.

26th. On motion of Mr. CORWIN of Ohio, the bill was postponed till the 28th, to take up the report of the Committee of Thirty-three, which was agreed to—yeas 100, nays 74, as follows:

YEAS—Messrs. Green Adams, *Adrain*, *Thos. L. Anderson*, Wm. C. Anderson, *Avery*, *Barr*, *Barrett*, *Bocock*, Boteler, Bouligny, Brabson, *Branch*, Briggs, Bristow, *Brown*, *Burch*, *Burnett*, Campbell, *Horace F. Clark*, *John B. Clark*, *John Cochrane*, Corwin, *Cox*, *Jas. Craig*, *Burton Craige*, H. Winter Davis, *John G. Davis*, *De Jarnette*, *Edmundson*, Etheridge, *Florence*, *Fouke*, *Garnett*, Gilmer, Hale, Hall, *Hamilton*, J. Morrison Harris, *Jno. T. Harris*, Hatton, *Holman*, *Wm. Howard*, *Hughes*, *Jenkins*, Junkin, W. Kellogg, Kilgore, *Kunkel*, *Larrabee*, James M. Leach, *Leake*, *Logan*, *Maclay*, Mallory, *Charles D. Martin*, *Elbert S. Martin*, Maynard, *McClernand*, *McKenty*, McKnight, McPherson, *Millson*, Millward, *Montgomery*, Laban T. Moore, Moorhead, Edward Joy Morris, *Isaac N. Morris*, Nelson, *Niblack*, Nixon, *Noell*, Peyton, *Phelps*, *Pryor*, Quarles, John H. Reynolds, *Riggs*, *James C. Robinson*, *Ruffin*, Scranton, *Sickles*, *Simms*, William N. H. Smith, *Stevenson*, *James A. Stewart*, Wm. Stewart, Stokes, *Stout*, Stratton, Thayer, *Thomas*, *Vallandigham*, Vance, Verree, Webster, *Winslow*, Wood, *Woodson*, *Wright*—100.

NAYS—Messrs. Charles F. Adams, Alley, Ashley, Babbitt, Beale, Bingham, Blair, Blake, Brayton, Buffinton, Burlingame, Burnham, Butterfield, Carey, Carter, Case, Coburn, Colfax, Conkling, Curtis, Delano, Duell, Edgerton, Edwards, Eliot, Ely, Farnsworth, Fenton, Ferry, Gooch, Grow, Gurley, *Haskin*, Hickman, Hoard, William A. Howard, Hutchins, Francis W. Kellogg, Kenyon, De Witt C. Leach, Lee, Longnecker, Loomis, Lovejoy, Marston, Morrill, Morse, Olin, Palmer, Porter, Potter, Pottle, Edwin R. Reynolds, Christopher Robinson, Royce, Sedgwick, Spaulding, Spinner, Stanton, Stevens, Tappan, Theaker, Tompkins, Train, Trimble, Wade, Waldron, Walton, Cadwalader C. Washburn, Ellihu B. Washburne, Wells, Wilson, Windom, Woodruff—74.

The bill was not again reached.

BILL TO PROVIDE FOR THE COLLECTION OF DUTIES ON IMPORTS.

January 3d, 1860. Mr. BINGHAM of Ohio, reported from the Committee on the Judiciary a bill providing—

That whenever by reason of unlawful obstructions, combinations or assemblages of persons, it shall become impracticable, in the judgment of the President, to execute the revenue laws and collect the duties on imports in the ordinary way in any collection district, it shall be lawful for the President to direct that the custom-house for such district be established and kept in any secure place within some port or harbor of such district, either upon land or on board any vessel; and that, in that case, it shall be the duty of the collector to reside at such place, and there to detain all vessels and cargoes arriving within the district until the duties imposed on the cargoes by law are paid in cash, any thing in the laws of the United States to the contrary notwithstanding; and that, in such cases, it shall be unlawful to take the vessel or cargo from the custody of the proper officer of the customs unless by process from some court of the United States; and that, in case of any attempt otherwise to take such vessel or cargo by any force, or combination, or assemblage of persons, too great to be overcome by the officers of the customs, it shall be lawful for the President of the United States or such person or persons as he shall have empowered for that purpose, to employ such part of the land or naval forces, or militia of the United States, as may be deemed necessary for the purpose of preventing the removal of such vessel or cargo, and protecting the officers of the customs in retaining the custody thereof.

March 2d. On a motion to take up the bill, by a suspension of the rules, the yeas were 103, the nays 62, as follows:

YEAS—Messrs. Charles F. Adams, *Adrain*, Aldrich, Alley, Ashley, Babbitt, Beale, Bingham, Blake, Brayton, Briggs, Buffinton, Burlingame, Butterfield, Carey, Carter, Coburn, Colfax, Conkling, Conway, Covode, Dawes, Delano, Duell, Dunn, Edgerton, Eliot, Ely, Farnsworth, Fenton, Ferry, Foster, Frank, French, Gooch, Graham, Grow, Gurley, Hale, Hall, *Haskin*, Helmick, Hickman, Hoard, *Holman*, Humphrey, Hutchins, Irvine, Junkin, Francis W. Kellogg, William Kellogg, Kenyon, Kilgore, Killinger, De Witt C. Leach, Lee, Longnecker, Loomis, Lovejoy, Marston, McKean, McKnight, McPherson, Millward, Edward Joy Morris, Nixon, Olin, Palmer, Pettit, Porter, Potter, Pottle, Rice, Christopher Robinson, Royce, Sedgwick, Sherman, Somes, Spaulding, Spinner, Stanton, Stevens, William Stewart, Stratton, Tappan, Thayer, Theaker, Tompkins, Train, Trimble, Vandever, Van Wyck, Verree, Wade, Waldron, Walton, Cadwalader C. Washburn, Ellihu B. Washburne, Wells, Wilson, Windom, Wood, Woodruff—103.

NAYS—Messrs. William C. Anderson, *Barr*, *Barrett*, Brabson, *Branch*, Bristow, *Brown*, *Burch*, *Burnett*, *Horace F. Clark*, *John B. Clark*, *Clemens*, *John Cochrane*, Corwin, *Cox*, *James Craig*, *John G. Davis*, *De Jarnette*, *Edmundson*, Etheridge, *Florence*, *Fouke*, *Garnett*, Gilmer, *Hamilton*, J. Morrison Harris, *John T. Harris*, Hatton, *William Howard*, *Hughes*, *Kunkel*, *Larrabee*, James M. Leach, *Leake*, Mallory, *Charles D. Martin*, *Elbert S. Martin*, Maynard, *McKenty*, *Millson*, Laban T. Moore, Nelson, *Niblack*, *Pendleton*, *Peyton*, *Phelps*, *Pryor*, Quarles, *Riggs*, *James C. Robinson*, *Simms*, William N. H. Smith, *James A. Stewart*, Stokes, *Thomas*, *Vallandigham*, Vance, Webster, *Whiteley*, *Winslow*, *Woodson*, *Wright*—62.

Two-thirds not having voted in the affirmative, the bill was not taken up, nor was it again reached.

January 30th, 1861. Mr. JOHN COCHRANE from the Select Committee on the President's message reported a bill for the "Collection of Duties on Imports," which was ordered to be printed and re-committed to the committee. It was not again heard from. His views of the subject were expressed as follows:

While fully concurring with the President in the opinion that no State possesses, under and by virtue of the Federal Constitution, any right or authority to secede, or withdraw, or separate itself from the Federal Union, I am equally convinced that, not having been prohibited, the justification of the exercise of such right is referable to the nature and extent of those rights reserved to the States or the people thereof. Therefore all the acts and ordinances of secession which have been or may be enacted by any State or States, acting separately, in my opinion, are, in as far as the same may be carried into effect, to be considered as revolutionary infractions of the supreme law of the land, however they may be regarded as the proper exercise of an indefeasible right of "resisting acts' which are plainly unconstitutional and too oppressive to be endured."

I also concur with the President that the Federal Constitution has abstained from conferring upon the Federal Government, or any department thereof, authority to declare and wage oppressive war against a seceding State, in order to coerce the repeal of any act or ordinance of secession which she may have passed, or the renunciation of any purpose of secession which she may entertain, or to compel her to remain nominally, as well as in fact, a member of the Federal Union. On the contrary, the plenary power of offensive war and reprisals, conferred by the Constitution upon Congress, is, in my judgment, designed exclusively to authorize and empower such war by the Federal Government, in its discretion, against such governments and communities as may be rightfully considered foreign to the United States. States which profess to have seceded from the Federal Union, by their separate State action, cannot, in my opinion, be rightfully so considered; and, therefore, a just conception of the constitutional authority of Congress combines with other and, if possible, higher and more commanding motives to prescribe other measures than aggressive and coercive war to remedy the grave inconveniences, perils, and evils of such secession.

It is, on the other hand, entirely manifest that the Federal Government, throughout the whole extent of its constitutional jurisdiction, both territorial and maritime, is vested with powers which it cannot surrender, and charged with trusts and duties which it must perform. It holds valuable property in every part of the territory over which its jurisdiction has been, by the solemn mandate of the people of all the States, extended; and it holds every article of this property as the common trustee of all the people of all the States for their common use and benefit; and to them, and to all of them, it is directly responsible for the safe keeping and protection of such property. By constitutional legislation, supreme in its character and irrepealable except by the authority which created it, the Federal Government has established a system of revenue laws which it is bound to maintain, and against all obstructions to the execution of which it is equally bound adequately to provide. No extra constitutional action of any State can possibly release the Federal Government in any of its departments from this imperative obligation.

It is to this aspect of the duty of Congress in the unfortunate and unexampled state of facts presented for its consideration by the President, in his late message, that the attention of the committee has been specially directed, and they report herewith a bill designed, as is believed, peaceably and in a spirit of moderation and forbearance fully to protect the entire revenue system of the United States from all the unconstitutional and unlawful obstructions and disturbances with which it is now or may be hereafter threatened.

In framing this measure there has been kept steadily in view, first, the obstacles of every character which oppose any attempt by the Federal Government to coerce a State; and, secondly, the principle upon which, as is conceived, the whole coercive action of our revenue system has, from its inception, been founded.

The just and rightful coercion exercised under the Constitution by the Federal Government in the collection of its revenue from foreign commerce is a coercion, not directed against State authority, nor even against unlawful action by assemblages of persons within any State. That coercion on the contrary, applies itself directly to the bulk and body of the foreign importations upon which the revenue is chargeable, and to the vessels and the agents by which they are brought into our ports, opened to such commerce only under the protection and by the regulation of the Federal law.

The well-understood and just assumption upon which all this foreign commerce proceeds is, that the Federal Government provides for it ports of entry and delivery in which it may be entered and delivered, and in which the lawful duties chargeable upon it shall be collected and paid to the Federal Government, whose laws have, for that very consideration, established and protected and regulated such entry and delivery. The failure to observe those regulations is, by our whole code of revenue law, visited in penalties upon the agents by whom the merchandise is transported, the vessels in which it is carried, and finally in the form of seizure and forfeiture upon the merchandise itself. All this is a coercion of law upon foreign commerce, and not a coercion of force upon any State to which it may be bound. No State can rightfully expect that the United States shall permit foreign commerce to be carried on in ports and places open to it only under their authority, without compliance with the constitutional conditions under which those ports or places have been thus opened. It is in this view that the bill proposes that vessels from a foreign port bound to a port within the scope of its provisions shall, with its foreign cargo, be liable to seizure and condemnation, and in the same view of applying its restrictions only to foreign commerce on which revenue is by law collected, all vessels lawfully engaged in the coastwise trade are exempted from the operation of its purely remedial and defensive provisions.

REPORTS RELATIVE TO MILITARY AND NAVAL MATTERS.

January 8th, 1861. The President sent a message relative to the condition of the country, urging upon Congress to devote itself exclusively to the question how the Union can be preserved in peace, and recommending the establishment of a line and "letting the North have exclusive control of the Territory above it, and giving Southern institutions protection below it." He transmits copies of the correspondence between himself and the "commissioners" of South Carolina, pledges himself to preserve the public peace in the District of Columbia, warns his countrymen of the dangers which now surround us, and says that he shall carry to his grave the consciousness that he at least meant well for his country.

9th. Mr. HOWARD of Michigan, offered the following resolution:

Resolved, That the message be referred to a special committee of five members of this House, and that they be instructed to report on the same as early as possible; and that said committee make immediate inquiry, and report:

1st. Whether any executive officer of the United States has been or is now treating or holding communication with any person or persons concerning the surrender of any forts, fortresses, or public property of the United States, and whether any demand for such surrender has been made, when and by whom, and what answer has been given.

2d. Whether any officer of this Government has at any time entered into any pledge, agreement, or understanding, with any person or persons, not to send reinforcements to the forts of the United States in the harbor of Charleston, and the particulars of such agreement, pledge, or understanding; when, where, and with whom it was made, and on what consideration.

3d. What demand for reinforcements of the said forts has been made, and for what reason such reinforcements have not been furnished.

4th. Where the ships of the United States are now stationed, with what commands, and with what orders.

5th. Whether the custom-house, post-office, arsenal, and other public buildings of the United States at Charleston have been seized and are held in possession by any person or persons, and the particulars of such seizure and possession.

6th. Whether any revenue cutter of the United States has been seized and is now held in possession by any person or persons, and the particulars thereof; and whether any efforts have been made by the head of the Treasury Department to recapture or recover possession of said vessel.

That the committee have power to send for persons and papers, to take testimony, and report from time to time, as facts material to the national safety and national honor may be disclosed by the evidence.

Which was adopted—yeas 133, nays 62, as follows:

YEAS—Messrs. Charles F. Adams, Green Adams, *Adrain*, Aldrich, *Allen*, Alley, William C. Anderson, Ashley, Babbitt, Beale, Bingham, Blair, Blake, Brayton, Briggs, Bristow, Buffinton, *Burch*, Burlingame, Burnham, Butterfield, Campbell, Carey, Carter, *Clemens*, Coburn, *John Cochrane*, Colfax, Covode, *Cox*, Curtis, *John G. Davis*, Dawes, Delano, Duell, Dunn, Edgerton, Edwards, Eliot, Ely, Etheridge, Farnsworth, Fenton, Ferry, Foster, *Fouke*, Frank, French, Gilmer, Gooch, Grow, Gurley, Hale, Hall, *Hamilton*, *Haskin*, Helmick, Hickman, Hoard, *Holman*, *Wm. Howard*, Wm. A. Howard, Humphrey, Hutchins, Irvine, Junkin, Francis W. Kellogg, Wm. Kellogg, Kenyon, Kilgore, *Larrabee*, De Witt C. Leach, Lee, *Logan*, Longnecker, Loomis, Lovejoy, *Maclay*, Marston, *McClernand*, McKean, McKnight, McPherson, Millward, *Montgomery*, Moorhead, Morrill, Edward Joy Morris, Morse, Nelson, Nixon, *Noell*, Olin, Palmer, Perry, Pettit, Porter, Pottle, Edwin R. Reynolds, John H. Reynolds, Rice, *Riggs*, Christopher Robinson, *James C. Robinson*, Royce, Scranton, Sedgwick, Sherman, Somes, Spaulding, Spinner, Stanton, Stevens, Wm. Stewart, Stokes, Stratton, Tappan, Thayer, Theaker, Tompkins, Train, Trimble, Vandever, Wade, Waldron, Cadwalader C. Washburn, Ellihu B. Washburne, Webster, Wells, Wilson, Windom, Wood, Woodruff—133.

NAYS—Messrs. *Thomas L. Anderson*, *Avery*, *Barksdale*, *Barrett*, *Bocock*, Boteler, Bouligny, *Branch*, *Brown*, *Burnett*, *John B. Clark*, *Clopton*, *Cobb*, *Crawford*, *De Jarnette*, *Dimmick*, *Edmundson*, *English*, *Florence*, *Garnett*, *Gartrell*, *Hardeman*, *John T. Harris*, Hatton, *Hawkins*, Hill, *Houston*, *Hughes*, *Jones*, *Kunkel*, *Landrum*, James M. Leach, *Leake*, *Love*, Mallory, *Charles D. Martin*, *Elbert S. Martin*, Maynard, *McKenty*, *McRae*, *Millson*, Laban T. Moore, *Sydenham Moore*, *Niblack*, *Pendleton*, *Peyton*, *Phelps*, *Pryor*, Quarles, *Reagan*, *Rust*, *Sickles*, *Simms*, *Wm. Smith*, Wm. N. H. Smith, *Taylor*, *Vallandigham*, Vance, *Whiteley*, *Winslow*, *Woodson*, *Wright*—62.

January 10th. The Committee was announced, consisting of Messrs. HOWARD of Michigan, BRANCH of North Carolina, JOHN COCHRANE of New York, DAWES of Massachusetts, and HICKMAN of Pennsylvania. Mr. Hickman was subsequently excused from serving, and Mr. JOHN H. REYNOLDS of New York, was substituted.

SECRET ORGANIZATION TO ATTACK THE CAPITAL.

February 14th. The committee reported unanimously that "the evidence produced before them does not prove the existence of a secret organization, here or elsewhere, hostile to the Government, that has for its object, upon its own responsibility, an attack upon the Capital, or any of the public property here, or an interruption of any of the functions of the Government."

The majority of the committee, however, state that certain organizations in the District and in Maryland, formerly political clubs have since become military and are drilling, expecting arms from State authorities or private subscriptions; but that, while they sympathize strongly with secession, there is no proof that they intend to attack the Capital or the District, "unless the surrender should be demanded by a State to which they profess a higher degree of allegiance." "Some of these companies in Baltimore profess to be drilling for the sole purpose of preventing other military companies from passing through the State of Maryland." These clubs are, in no proper sense, secret, and hence not such as are contemplated in the resolution of the House.

Mr. BRANCH of North Carolina, added a brief minority report, chiefly to the point that Lieutenant-General Scott has seven companies of artillery, and one company of sappers and miners of the regular army ordered to and quartered in the City of Washington, and closing with this resolution, which he offered:

Resolved, That the quartering of troops of the regular army in this District and around the Capitol, when not necessary for their protection from a hostile enemy and during the session of Congress, is impolitic and offensive, and, if permitted, may be destructive of civil liberty; and, in the opinion of this House, the regular troops now in this city ought to be forthwith removed therefrom.

On motion of Mr. JOHN COCHRANE, this resolution was laid on the table—yeas 125, nays 35, as follows:

YEAS—Messrs. Charles F. Adams, Green Adams, Aldrich, *Allen*, Alley, William C. Anderson, Ashley, Babbitt, Beale, Bingham, Blair, Blake, Brayton, Briggs, Bristow, Buffinton, Burlingame, Butterfield, Campbell, Carter, Case, *Horace F. Clark*, Coburn, *John Cochrane*, Colfax, Conkling, Conway, Covode, *Cox*, Curtis, H. Winter Davis, *John G. Davis*, Dawes, Duell, Dunn, Edgerton, Eliot, Ely, Etheridge, Farnsworth, Fenton, Ferry, Foster, *Fouke*, Frank, French, Gilmer, Gooch, Graham, Grow, Hale, Hall, *Haskin*, Hatton, Helmick, Hoard, *Holman*, W. A. Howard, Humphrey, Hutchins, Irvine, Junkin, F. W. Kellogg, W. Kellogg, Kenyon, Kilgore, *Larrabee*, De Witt C. Leach, Lee, *Logan*, Longnecker, Loomis, Lovejoy, Mallory, Marston, *McClernand*, McKean, *McKenty*, McKnight, McPherson, *Millson*, Laban T. Moore, Moorhead, Morrill, Edward Joy Morris, *Isaac N. Morris*, Morse, Nelson, *Niblack*, Nixon, Palmer, Perry, Porter, Potter, Pottle, Edwin R. Reynolds, Rice, Christopher Robinson, *James C. Robinson*, Royce, Scranton, Sedgwick, Sherman, *Sickles*, Spaulding, Spinner, Stevens, William Stewart, Stokes, Stratton, Tappan, Theaker, Tompkins, Train, Vandever, Van Wyck, Wade, Waldron, Walton, Cadwalader C. Washburn, Ellihu B. Washburne, Webster, Wells, Wilson, Woodruff—125.

NAYS—Messrs. *Avery*, *Barr*, *Barrett*, *Bocock*, Boteler, Bouligny, Brabson, *Branch*, *Burch*, *Burnett*, *John B. Clark*, *Burton Craige*, *De Jarnette*, *English*, *Florence*, *Garnett*, *John T. Harris*, *Hindman*, *Hughes*, *Kunkel*, *Maclay*, *Elbert S. Martin*, Maynard, *Peyton*, *Phelps*, *Pryor*, Quarles, *Rust*, *Scott*, William N. H. Smith, *Stevenson*, *Thomas*, *Whiteley*, *Winslow*, *Wright*—35.

6

SECRETARY HOLT'S REPORT.

On this subject, the Secretary of War, under date of February 18th, 1861, made report upon a resolution of inquiry passed by the House of Representatives:

This resolution having been submitted to this Department for consideration and report, I have the honor to state, that the body of troops temporarily transferred to this city is not large, as is assumed by the resolution, though it is a well-appointed corps and admirably adapted for the preservation of the public peace. The reasons which led to their being assembled here will now be briefly stated.

I shall make no comment upon the origin of the revolution which for the last three months has been in progress in several of the Southern States, nor shall I enumerate the causes which have hastened its advancement or exasperated its temper. The scope of the question submitted by the House will be sufficiently met by dealing with the facts as they exist, irrespective of the cause from which they have proceeded. That revolution has been distinguished by a boldness, and completeness of success, rarely equalled in the history of civil commotions. Its overthrow of the Federal authority has not only been sudden and wide-spread, but has been marked by excesses which have alarmed all, and been sources of profound humiliation to a large portion of the American people. Its history is a history of surprises and treacheries, and ruthless spoliations. The forts of the United States have been captured and garrisoned, and hostile flags unfurled upon their ramparts. Its arsenals have been seized, and the vast amount of public arms they contained appropriated to the use of the captors; while more than half a million dollars, found in the mint at New Orleans, has been unscrupulously applied to replenish the coffers of Louisiana. Officers in command of revenue cutters of the United States have been prevailed on to violate their trusts and surrender the property in their charge; and instead of being branded for their crimes, they and the vessels they betrayed have been cordially received into the service of the seceded States. These movements were attended by yet more discouraging indications of immorality. It was generally believed that this revolution was guided and urged on by men occupying the highest positions in the public service, and who, with the responsibilities of an oath to support the Constitution still resting upon their consciences, did not hesitate secretly to plan and openly to labor for the dismemberment of the Republic whose honors they enjoyed, and upon whose treasury they were living. As examples of evil are always more potent than those of good, this spectacle of demoralization on the part of States and statesmen could not fail to produce the most deplorable consequences. The discontented and the disloyal everywhere took courage. In other States, adjacent to and supposed to sympathize in sense of political wrong with those referred to, revolutionary schemes were set on foot, and forts and arms of the United States seized. The unchecked prevalence of the revolution, and the intoxication which its triumphs inspired, naturally suggested wilder and yet more desperate enterprises than the conquest of ungarrisoned forts or the plunder of an unguarded mint. At what time the armed occupation of Washington city became a part of the revolutionary programme, is not certainly known. More than six weeks ago the impression had already extensively obtained that a conspiracy for the accomplishment of this guilty purpose was in process of formation, if not fully matured. The earnest endeavors made by men known to be devoted to the revolution to hurry Virginia and Maryland out of the Union, were regarded as preparatory steps for the subjugation of Washington. This plan was in entire harmony with the aim and spirit of those seeking the subversion of the Government, since no more fatal blow at its existence could be struck than the permanent and hostile possession of the seat of its power. It was in harmony too with the avowed designs of the revolutionists, which looked to the formation of a confederacy of all the slave States, and necessarily to the conquest of the capital within their limits. It seemed not very indistinctly prefigured in a proclamation made upon the floor of the Senate, without qualification, if not exultingly, that the Union was already dissolved—a proclamation which, however intended, was certainly calculated to invite, on the part of men of desperate fortunes, or of revolutionary States, a raid upon the capital. In view of the violence and turbulent disorders already exhibited in the South, the public mind could not reject such a scheme as at all improbable. That a belief in its existence was entertained by multitudes, there can be no doubt, and this belief I fully shared. My conviction rested not only on the facts already alluded to, but upon information, some of which was of a most conclusive character, that reached the Government from many parts of the country, not merely expressing the prevalence of the opinion that such an organization had been formed, but also often furnishing the plausible grounds on which the opinion was based. Superadded to these proofs were the oft-repeated declarations of men in high political positions here, and who were known to have intimate affiliations with the revolution, if indeed they did not hold its reins in their hands—to the effect that Mr. Lincoln would not, or should not, be inaugurated at Washington. Such declarations from such men could not be treated as empty bluster. They were the solemn utterances of those who well understood the import of their words, and who, in the exultation of the temporary victories gained over their country's flag in the South, felt assured that events would soon give them the power to verify their predictions. Simultaneously with these prophetic warnings, a Southern journal of large circulation and influence, and which is published near the city of Washington, advocated its seizure as a possible political necessity.

The nature and power of the testimony thus accumulated may be best estimated by the effect produced upon the popular mind. Apprehensions for the safety of the capital were communicated from points near and remote, by men unquestionably reliable and loyal. The resident population became disquieted, and the repose of many families in the city was known to be disturbed by painful anxieties. Members of Congress too, men of calm and comprehensive views and of undoubted fidelity to their country, frankly expressed their solicitude to the President and to this Department, and formally insisted that the defences of the capital should be strengthened. With such warnings, it could not be forgotten that, had the late Secretary of War heeded the anonymous letter which he received, the tragedy at Harper's Ferry would have been avoided; nor could I fail to remember that, had the early admonitions which reached here in regard to the designs of lawless men upon the forts of Charleston harbor been acted on by sending forward adequate reinforcements before the revolution began, the disastrous political complications that ensued might not have occurred.

Impressed by these circumstances and considerations, I earnestly besought you to allow the concentration at this city of a sufficient military force to preserve the public peace from all the dangers that seemed to threaten it. An open manifestation on the part of the Administration of a determination, as well as of the ability, to maintain the laws, would, I was convinced, prove the surest, as also the most pacific means of baffling and dissolving any conspiracy that might have been organized. It was believed, too, that the highest and most solemn responsibility resting upon a President, withdrawing from the Government, was to secure to his successor a peaceful inauguration. So deeply in my judgment did this duty concern the whole country, and the fair fame of our institutions, that to guarantee its faithful discharge I was persuaded no preparation could be too determined or too complete. The presence of the troops alluded to in the resolution is the result of the conclusion arrived at by yourself and Cabinet, on the proposition submitted to you by this Department. Already this display of life and loyalty on the part of your Administration has produced the happiest effects. Public confidence has been restored, and the feverish apprehension which it was so mortifying to contemplate has been banished. Whatever may have been the machinations of deluded, lawless men, the execution of their purpose has been suspended, if not altogether abandoned, in view of preparations which announce, more impressively than words, that this Administration is alike able and resolved to transfer in peace, to the President elect, the authority that under the Constitution belongs to him. To those, if such there be, who desire the destruction of the Republic, the presence of these troops is necessarily offensive; but those who sincerely love our institutions cannot fail to rejoice that by this timely precaution they have possibly escaped the deep dishonor which they must have suffered had the capital, like the forts and arsenals of the South, fallen into the hands of the revolutionists, who have found this great Government weak only because in the exhaustless beneficence of its spirit it has refused to strike, even in its own defence, lest it should wound the aggressor.

I have the honor to be, very respectfully, your obedient servant,

J. HOLT,
Secretary of War.

The President.

ON THE DISPOSITION OF UNITED STATES VESSELS.

February 21st. Mr. DAWES from the committee made a report upon the fourth item of investigation, furnishing these statements:

Dismantled ships 28, mounting 874 guns; none could be repaired under several weeks, and many would require six months. No orders have been issued to put any of them in readiness.

The vessels in the East India, Brazil, Pacific, Mediterranean, African, and Home Squadrons are named, with those on special service, and on the way to stations, and the committee then say:

That the entire naval force available for the defence of the whole Atlantic coast, at the time of the appointment of this committee, consisted of the steamer Brooklyn, twenty-five guns, and the store-ship Relief, two guns; while the former was of too great draught to permit her to enter Charleston harbor with safety, except at spring tides, and the latter was under orders to the coast of Africa with stores for the African squadron. Thus the whole Atlantic seaboard has been to all intents and purposes without defence during all the period of civil commotion and lawless violence, to which the President has called our attention as "of such vast and alarming proportions" as to be beyond his power to check or control.

It further appears that of the vessels which might have been available for protection or defence in case of any sudden emergency arising at home, now at stations in distant seas, or on the way thither, on the 13th of October last the Richmond left our coast to join the Mediterranean squadron; the Vandalia left on the 21st of December to join the East India squadron; and about the same time the Saratoga to join the African squadron, and others to join the Home squadron, then in the harbor of Vera Cruz supporting one of the revolutionary governments of Mexico.

* * * * * * * *

To the Committee, this disposition of the naval force at this critical time seems most extraordinary. The permitting of vessels to depart for distant seas after these unhappy difficulties had broken out at home; the omission to put in repair, and commission ready for orders, a single one of the twenty-eight ships dismantled and unfit for service in our own ports, and that too while $646,639.79 of the appropriations for repairs in the Navy the present year remained unexpended, were in the opinion of the committee grave errors in the administration of the Navy Department—the consequences of which have been manifest in the many acts of lawless violence to which they have called attention. The Committee are of opinion that the Secretary had it in his power, with the present naval force of the country at his command, and without materially impairing the efficiency of the service abroad, at any time after the settled purpose of overthrowing the government had become manifest, and before that purpose had developed itself in overt acts of violence, to station at anchor, within reach of his own orders, a force equal to the protection of all the property and all the rights of the government and the citizen, as well as the flag of the country, from any outrage or insult, at any point on the entire Atlantic seaboard. The failure to do this is without justification or excuse.

The committee proceed respecting the acceptance of resignations in the navy:

The attention of the Committee was also drawn to the resignations which have taken place among the officers in the Navy, caused by the political troubles in which the country is now involved, and the course pursued by the Navy department in reference thereto. It will appear from a "List of resignations" furnished by the Department, and which accompanies this report, that since the election twenty-nine officers in the Navy, citizens of the southern disaffected States, have tendered their resignations to the Secretary, all of which have been forthwith and without inquiry accepted by him. The circumstances under which these resignations have been received and accepted, and the effect of that acceptance, deserves especial notice. That these officers have sought to resign and relieve themselves from the obligation to the government imposed by their commissions, because of disaffection, and a desire to join, and in many instances to lead insurgent forces against that government, is notorious. One of them, Lieut. J. R. Hamilton, a citizen of South Carolina, forwarded his resignation from on board the Wyoming, at Panama, dated December 1st, 1860. It did not reach the Department until the 15th of the same month, and without inquiry into his conduct, his purpose in resigning, his loyalty, or any circumstances connected with so unusual a proceeding at such a time, his resignation was accepted the same day. He immediately, from Charleston, South Carolina, issued a letter addressed to all the officers in the Navy from Southern States, urging them to resign and join a hostile force against the government, and that those of them in command should bring with them their vessels into Southern ports and surrender them to the traitors already in arms, taking new commissions under their authority, and then turning their guns upon their own flag.

Such conduct is nothing less than treason, and has no parallel since the attempt of Benedict Arnold to deliver over important military posts to the enemies of his country. Had the Secretary declined to accept the resignation thus tendered, this man would have been subject to the trial and punishment of a court-martial, according to the rules which govern the service, and would have met the fate of a traitor. This extraordinary letter was published throughout the United States. After its circulation in the public prints in Washington, V. M. Randolph, a captain in the Navy, a citizen of Alabama, who had been excused from active service for two or three years, because of alleged ill-health, on the 10th of January, 1861, forwarded from Montgomery, Alabama, his resignation to the Secretary. Before twelve o'clock at noon of the 12th, and before his resignation had reached Washington, and while he was still a captain in the Navy, he appeared at the gates of the Pensacola navy-yard, in Florida, at the head of an insurgent force, and demanded its surrender. The yard, with whatever of force it had and the United States stores and other property to a vast amount therein, was unconditionally surrendered to him; and he is now its commandant, occupying the quarters of its late commandant, and granting paroles of honor to such of his prisoners of war as have desired to depart, and not serve under him. The despatch from the late commandant, then a prisoner of war, informing the Secretary of this ignominious surrender, was received at the Department on the evening of the 13th of January; and the resignation of Captain Randolph, who, on the 12th, was the leader of the insurgents, did not reach the Secretary till the 14th, when, without inquiry or delay, it was immediately accepted.

E. Farrand, commander in the Navy, and also a citizen of Alabama, was the second in command at the Pensacola navy-yard, the executive officer of the yard. When the attack was made upon the yard, Farrand met the assailants at the gates by previous understanding, admitted them to the yard, and conducted their leader to the commanding officer, participated in the formal capitulation, and immediately engaged in service under the new commandant of the yard. This was done while he still held in his possession his commission as a commander in the Navy. On the 13th or 15th of January, (the Department does not know which,) Farrand forwarded his resignation to the Secretary, but it did not reach him till the 21st of the same month, seven days after official notice of the surrender had been received at the Department. Yet this resignation was immediately, and without inquiry, accepted.

F. B. Renshaw, a lieutenant in the Navy, and a citizen of Florida, was the first lieutenant of the yard, and actively engaged in securing its surrender. It was by his order that the flag was hauled down amid the jeers and shouts of a drunken rabble. He immediately enrolled himself under the leader of the insurgents, and present commandant of the yard, and from the day of its surrender has continued under him to discharge the duties of first lieutenant, as before under the United States. Yet he continued to hold his commission as a lieutenant in the Navy till the 16th of January, and the resignation did not reach the Secretary until the 22d, when, like the others, it was, without inquiry or delay, accepted.

The conduct of these officers plainly comes within the constitutional definition of treason against the United States, namely: "Levying war against them, or in adhering to their enemies, giving them aid and comfort." And so long as their resignations were unaccepted by the Secretary, they could be tried and punished by a court-martial as traitors. From this they have been relieved by the Secretary himself. To have done this with a knowledge of their acts, would have been to have involved himself in their crime; would have been to have committed treason himself. To have done it without inquiry, and without reason to know that they have committed no offence, shows a want of that solicitude for the honor and efficiency of the service which is indispensable to its just administration. Yet the resignation of Farrand and Renshaw, and also those of the other officers resigning at the Pensacola navy-yard, were all received and accepted after the Secretary had already been officially informed that they had surrendered to a lawless band of insurgents, and he had detached them to await orders, having "neither approved nor disapproved of their conduct, and not proposing to do so, without full information touching their conduct in the surrender of the yard." Why, after having been thus warned, and having taken his position, the Secretary did not wait for this "information," the committee cannot understand.

Several other resignations of officers who do not appear to have engaged in actual war against the United States before tendering the same, were nevertheless accepted by the Secretary, with an unnecessary haste which neither the purpose of the resignation nor the times would justify or excuse. Some of them were even accepted by telegraph, when it was perfectly apparent that the object in resigning was to relieve themselves, as early as possible, from embarrassment and the obligation of the oath of office, as well as summary trial and punishment by a court-martial, previous to joining insurgent forces against the constituted authorities of their country. These resignations, thus accepted, have been followed by immediate engagement in a service hostile to the Government.

One man, holding the office of civil engineer in the Pensacola navy-yard at the time of its surrender, forwarded his resignation on that day to the Secretary, inclosed in a letter to Senator Mallory, in which he expressly states the reason of his resignation to be because he is prevented from acting against the Government by the obligations of his commission. The letter of resignation, and the one inclosing it stating this reason, were both laid before the Secretary on the 24th of January; yet the Secretary not only accepted the resignation at once, and thus relieved him from the obligation imposed on him by his commission not to act against the Government, but caused the acceptance to take effect "from the 12th of January, the day of the surrender of the yard," twelve days anterior to the time of its date. The reason given for thus making this acceptance retroactive in its effect, namely, to stop his pay from that time, did not appear, under any extraordinary circumstances by which it was surrounded, at all satisfactory to the committee.

The resignation of the officer in charge of the marine hospital at Pensacola was accepted by telegraph, and he was thereby enabled to take upon himself the same position under the insurgent force without any interruption. And that of Lieutenant R. T. Chapman, dated on board the Brooklyn, when about to sail under orders, was likewise accepted by telegraph, and he was thus relieved of any inconvenience he would otherwise have experienced in being carried to sea against his wishes.

The course pursued by the Secretary, in thus accepting these resignations, appears, under the circumstances, to be most extraordinary. No custom of the Department, in ordinary times, could justify it. No want of confidence in the loyalty of these officers can excuse it; for, if their previous conduct had justified any such suspicion, it also demanded investigation beforehand, which would, as to some of them, have disclosed to the Secretary their complicity in treason, calling for court-martial rather than honorable discharge. A prudent regard for the public safety would no doubt have justified, if not imperiously demanded, that some of these officers should have been early removed from delicate and responsible positions of trust, by the substitution of others more reliable. But these very considerations appear to the committee to have forbidden the furnishing of any such facilities for engaging in hostilities against the Government, as the relief from the summary trial and punishment of a court-martial, secured by an acceptance of their resignations.

The course pursued by the Secretary has resulted in furnishing those engaged in an attempt to overthrow the Government, with the skill, experience, and discipline which education at the expense of the Government, and a long service in the Navy have conferred upon our own officers. The committee cannot understand how this course is consistent with a proper discharge of the duties of his office by the Secretary, in this critical juncture of affairs. It appears to them to have been attended with consequences the most serious to the service and the country. They can find no excuse or justification in the claim set up in behalf of the Secretary, that these resignations have been accepted in ignorance of any misconduct, for no resignation should at any time be accepted until there is reason to know at least that the officer tendering it had been guilty of no unofficerlike conduct deserving a court-martial.

But the circumstances connected with these resignations, the apparent purpose for which they were made, and the hostile attitude which the manner of their tender clearly disclosed, called upon the Secretary to refrain from that haste in their acceptance which permitted of neither delay nor inquiry. The committee cannot approve, but are compelled to condemn such a failure in the discharge of public duty, and they therefore recommend the adoption of the following resolution:

Resolved, That the Secretary of the Navy, in accepting without delay or inquiry, the resignations of officers of the Navy, who were in arms against the Government when tendering the same, and of those who sought to resign, that they might be relieved from the restraint imposed by their commissions upon engaging in hostilities to the constituted authorities of the nation, has committed a grave error, highly prejudicial to the discipline of the service, and injurious to the honor and efficiency of the Navy, for which he deserves the censure of this House.

Mr. Branch made a minority report, as follows:

An examination of the table accompanying the report, marked "List of the vessels of the United States Navy in commission on the 16th of January, 1861," will disclose the fact that, so far from there being any ground to believe that the ships of the Navy have been purposely placed out of reach, the foreign squadrons are unusually weak, in proportion to the whole force of the Navy, and the home squadron unprecedentedly strong. In his annual report of 3d December, 1857, the Secretary of the Navy said:

"The home squadron, under the command of its flag-officer, Hiram Paulding, has consisted of the steam-frigates Wabash and Roanoke, the sloops-of-war Saratoga and Cyane, and the war steamers Susquehanna and Fulton. The unsatisfactory state of affairs in New Grenada and portions of Central America required the increase of this squadron, and the almost constant presence of a considerable force in the neighborhood, both in the Atlantic and the Pacific."

From which it will be seen that, at that time, six ships were considered so large a force for the home squadron as to call for an explanation from Congress.

The same squadron, on the 16th of January, 1861, consisted of eleven ships, of which seven were steamers; of the eleven, eight were on the coast, or under orders for the coast, and have since arrived. It is difficult to perceive from what portion of the testimony the committee have reached the conclusion that the only ships available for the defence of the coast are the Brooklyn and one other. It is true, they were on the 16th of January the only vessels in our harbors; but the House need not be informed that vessels in commission are not allowed to lie idle in the harbors, but are required to cruise on their stations, coming in occasionally for supplies and for orders. The home squadron, as its name imports, is mainly intended to guard and protect our own coasts, and on comparatively short notice it could be concentrated for service at a given point.

It will be seen from the abstract of orders issued from the Navy Department, furnished to the committee, and dated 24th January, that not a single ship has been ordered to any foreign station since the date of the Presidential election; every order since that date has been to increase the force at home.

The second ground on which the committee condemn the action of the Secretary is, that a large number of ships are dismantled and not ready for immediate service.

It is well known that, from the very nature of the service, only a portion of even the serviceable ships can be kept in commission. In the midst of a foreign war with a naval power, some of the vessels of the Navy will always be in ordinary. There is nothing in the testimony to show that the number in ordinary at the present time is unusually large. If, however, it is unusually large, both the testimony and the records of the House furnish a sufficient reason for it. It is stated in the following extract from the paper already alluded to, dated 24th January:

"2. All the vessels above named, except the Pawnee and the Constitution, are dismantled. Vessels of war are nearly always dismantled immediately after their arrival in port, at the termination of a cruise. It is also customary to commence repairing them as soon as possible after their return, if the appropriations and other work will permit. The appropriations were reduced $1,000,000 below the estimates of the Department; and of the whole sum appropriated ($1,523,000) for repairs, etc., for the fiscal year ending June 30, 1861, there remained on the 1st January, the close of the first half of the fiscal year, the sum of $646,639.79 for the remaining half."

The Secretary stated to the Committee that he deemed it his duty to conform to the action of Congress, and that in addition, having already expended more than half the appropriation in half the year, he did not think it just to his successor that he should continue expenditures until 4th March on the same scale, much less to increase them.

A large majority of the members of this House voted at the last session to reduce the appropriation; and of course those who thus voted will not unite with the committee in censuring the Secretary for the inevitable consequence of their own act.

Another equally satisfactory reason for not placing more ships in commission, is found in the letter of 24th January, as follows:

"The other vessels mentioned in the list have not been put in condition for immediate service within the last month, because the number of vessels in commission is governed by the numerical strength of the officers and seamen of the Navy."

And again, in a communication from the Navy Department dated February 4th, 1861:

"In reply to the second inquiry, there are enough captains, commanders, surgeons, chaplains. In the other grades there are not, nor is there a sufficient number of seamen."

It will be remembered that the number of both officers and seamen to be employed is limited by law, and the Secretary of the Navy cannot exceed that limit.

The Secretary deserves no censure; but should receive the highest commendation for inflexibly obeying the law in the administration of his Department. Every attempt at retrenchment and economy is defeated because heads of Departments will not themselves conform to the law and compel their subordinates to do the same. The facility with which Congress supplies deficiencies created by disregarding the law, has encouraged such practices; and it would be mournful indeed, if in the first well-authenticated case in which a head of Department has faithfully and sternly conformed his expenditures to so radical a reduction of his estimates, the officer should receive a vote of censure instead of a vote of thanks.

The Navy seems to have been adequate for all the demands made upon it by the wise and peace-preserving policy of the President. If the President who goes into office on the 4th March desires to engage in civil war, he will have an ample naval force with which to begin, even so early as the 5th of March; and there will probably be abundant time for increasing it before the war closes.

II. RESIGNATION OF OFFICERS.

A list of all the officers of the Navy who have resigned,* between the 11th of November and the 24th January, was furnished to the Committee, and the chief clerk of the Navy Department was fully examined as to the circumstances attending each resignation. The whole number was fifty-six, including eleven from the Naval Academy.

It is known that in many, if not most of these cases, the officers, in resigning, have not only given up an honorable profession for which alone they were fitted by education and habits, but have reduced themselves and families to penury. Some powerful motive must have actuated them. If it was selfish, let any one point out a possible advantage they could promise themselves personally. It could not be that they aimed to recommend themselves to the favor and patronage of the southern confederacy, for that government does not possess a ship, and cannot, for a long time, provide itself with a navy. When it has done so, it cannot be expected that the officers will be in any better situation with reference to their personal interests than they would have been if they had remained in the Navy of the United States.

It is evident that in resigning they have been actuated by a high sense of duty to the States of which they were respectively citizens; and that, in the time and manner of tendering their resignations, they have consulted a nice sense of honor. In a few instances they have engaged in the military service of their States; but not until they had resigned their commissions in the Navy of the United States. In no instance does it appear that one of them has betrayed the trust reposed in him by this government, or engaged in any hostile service until he had discharged himself of all the responsibilities imposed by his commission. The testimony taken before the committee, partial and limited as it is on this point, is confidently appealed to for the correctness of this statement.

The undersigned would gladly pursue this subject, grateful as it is to him to vindicate, against the very harsh aspersions cast upon them by the committee, the characters of the honorable body of men who have so long and so gallantly borne the flag of the Republic. But it is foreign to the inquiry the committee were instructed to make, and will for that reason be dismissed, except in so far as it is the basis of the resolution reported. The censure of the Secretary seems to be based principally, if not entirely, on his acceptance of the resignations of Captain Randolph and the two lieutenants on duty at the Pensacola navy-yard at the time of its surrender.

Captain Randolph's resignation was dated at Montgomery, Alabama, on the 10th of January, was received at the Department on the 14th, and accepted on the 14th. The Pensacola navy-yard was surrendered on the 12th, and Captain Armstrong immediately sent the following telegraphic despatch, which was received by the Secretary of the Navy on the 13th, at eight o'clock, P.M.:

Hon. Isaac Toucey, Secretary of the Navy:

Commissioners appointed by the Governor of Florida, with a regiment of armed men at the gate, demanded the surrender of this navy-yard, having previously taken possession of the magazines. I surrendered the place and struck my flag at half-past one o'clock this day. The store-ship Supply sailed for Vera Cruz the moment the yard flag was lowered.

JAMES ARMSTRONG,
Captain U. S. Navy, late Commandant Navy Yard.

The testimony shows that this was the only information received by the Department previous to the 24th.

It is evident, from this statement of facts and dates, that at the time Captain Randolph's resignation was accepted, and for at least ten days thereafter, the Department was totally ignorant of his participation in the Pensacola expedition. Even if we were at liberty to infer that the Secretary had seen his name connected with the expedition in the newspapers earlier than the 24th, we cannot suppose that it had been seen before the 14th, the day on which the resignation was accepted, for it would be impossible for even flying newspaper reports to reach this city from Pensacola in so short a time. Lieutenant Farrand, who was first lieutenant and executive officer of the navy-yard, resigned on the 13th January, and his resignation was accepted on the 21st. Lieutenant Renshaw resigned on the 16th, and it was accepted on the 22d.

The testimony discloses nothing on which the Secretary could have refused to accept these resignations, if all the testimony taken before the committee had been in his possession at the time he acted. But by a comparison of dates it will be seen that they were received, and in due course of business acted on before he had any intelligence from Pensacola except the telegraphic despatch already set forth.

The undersigned would hold the Secretary, who should accept the resignation of an officer who before resigning had been guilty of any conduct unbecoming an officer, amenable to the severest censure. An acceptance of a resignation is an honorable discharge from service, which should only be given to him who has acquitted himself with fidelity and honor, but one who has thus acquitted himself is entitled to be discharged without question as to what he intends to do thereafter.

The base man would hold his commission and seek an opportunity to betray his Government, so that the fruits of his treason might purchase for him favor and reward. Such was the conduct of Arnold.

The pure man, who, compelled to select between two claims to his allegiance, chooses that which promises least personal advantage, scrupulously discharges all existing obligations, then voluntarily and openly renounces a cherished commission from a sense of duty to his native State, gives the highest proof of devotion to principle and obedience to the dictates of honor. Such men cannot be regarded as traitors; and to call them so is to arraign manly virtue in the name of patriotism.

It has been the proud boast of the American Navy that it has never contained a traitor in its ranks. Will it be credited that it has suddenly become a hot-bed from which has sprung such a bountiful crop of traitors? Such a supposition would discredit the whole body of its officers; for it could only consist with the existence of some poisonous and traitorous influence pervading all its ranks and corrupting all its members.

The chief clerk of the Navy Department testified that there has been nothing unusual in the course recently pursued in regard to resignations; and that the uniform course, from time immemorial, has been to act promptly on resignations, unless some special reason existed for taking a case out of the routine of current business. The orderly conduct of business necessitates prompt action on each case in its turn; and in an ill-organized Department, or in one in which the force is insufficient, affairs will soon fall into inextricable confusion. No consideration of convenience, nor the maintenance of any mere system of business, should be allowed to interfere with the substantial demands of justice and public interest. But in the absence of any reason for deviating from the usual course (and the undersigned says confidently that in the present case no such reason existed), the head of an Executive Department is not censurable for requiring all its business to be regularly and promptly despatched.

The undersigned can find in the testimony nothing to detract from the high reputation always borne by the present Secretary for integrity and patriotism; and therefore I cannot concur with the committee in recommending the passage of a resolution of censure.

March 2d. The resolution appended to the majority report, was agreed to—yeas 95, nays 62, as follows:

YEAS—Messrs. Charles F. Adams, Aldrich, Alley, Ashley, Beale, Bingham, Blair, Blake, Brayton, Buffinton, Burlingame, Butterfield, Campbell, Carey, Carter, Case, Coburn, Colfax, Conway, Covode, H. Winter Davis, Dawes, Delano, Duell, Edgerton, Edwards, Eliot, Ely, Farnsworth, Fenton, French, Gooch, Grow, Gurley, Hale, Haskin, Helmick, Wm. A. Howard, Humphrey, Hutchins, Irvine, Junkin, Francis W. Kellogg, Wm. Kellogg, Kenyon, Killinger, De Witt C. Leach, Lee, Longnecker, Lovejoy, Marston, McKean, McKnight, McPherson, Millward, Moorhead, Morrill, Edward Joy Morris, *Isaac N. Morris*, Nixon, Olin, Palmer, Perry, Pettit, Potter, Pottle, Edwin R. Reynolds, Rice, Christopher Robinson, Royce, Sedgwick, Sherman, Somes, Spaulding, Spinner, Stanton, Stevens, Wm. Stewart, Stratton, Tompkins, Train, Trimble, Vandever, Van Wyck, Verree, Wade, Waldron, Walton, Cadwalader C. Washburn, Ellihu B. Washburne, Wells, Wilson, Windom, Wood, Woodruff—95.

NAYS—Messrs. *Adrain*, Wm. C. Anderson, *Barr*, *Barrett*, Boteler, Brabson, *Branch*, *Brown*, *Burch*, *Burnett*, *John B. Clark*, *Clemens*, *John Cochrane*, *Cox*, *James Craig*, *Burton Craige*, *John G. Davis*, *De Jarnette*, *English*, Ferry, *Florence*, *Fouke*, *Garnett*, *Hamilton*, *John T. Harris*, Hatton, *Hindman*, *Holman*, *Wm. Howard*, *Hughes*, Kilgore, *Kunkel*, *Larrabee*, James M. Leach, *Leake*, *Charles D. Martin*, *McKenty*, *Millson*, *Montgomery*, Nelson, *Niblack*, *Pendleton*, *Peyton*, *Phelps*, *Pryor*, *Quarles*, *Riggs*, *James C. Robinson*, *Ruffin*, *Sickles*, *Simms*, William N. H. Smith, *Stevenson*, *James A. Stewart*, Stokes, *Thomas*, *Vallandigham*, Vance, *Whiteley*, *Winslow*, *Woodson*, *Wright*—62.

January 30th. Mr. JOHN H. REYNOLDS made the majority report, and L. O'B. BRANCH the minority report, upon the bill to authorize the President to call out the militia, which was ordered to be printed and recommitted to the committee.*

February 27th. The majority of the committee presented a report reviewing the correspondence, communicated by the President January 8th, between himself and Isaac W. Hayne, "Special Envoy" of South Carolina, and concluding with a resolution that in the opinion of the House, "the President had no constitutional power to negotiate with the representatives of the State of South Carolina for the surrender of any public property within the limits of that State." Messrs. COCHRANE and BRANCH, as a minority, made a report of dissent. Both reports were ordered to be printed and recommitted, and the subject was not resumed.

28th. Mr. HOWARD of Michigan, made the closing report, on the general subject of Secession. Mr. COCHRANE and Mr. BRANCH gave notice of their dissent, and obtained leave to make a minority report.

WITHDRAWAL OF UNITED STATES TROOPS.

January 2d, 1861. Mr. JEFFERSON DAVIS of Mississippi offered this joint resolution, which was read and ordered to be printed:

* Mr. John Cochrane expressed his dissent from the measure "at this particular time."—*Congressional Globe, Seond Session, 36th Congress, p.* 646.

Joint Resolution in relation to the Militia of the States, the condition of forts, magazines, arsenals and dock-yards; military power; withdrawal of troops from garrisons on the application of a State; and the recognition of the right of a State to keep troops and ships of war by proclamation of the President.

Whereas, by the second and third articles of amendment of the Constitution, it is declared that a well regulated Militia is the security of a free State, and that no soldier shall, in time of peace, be quartered in any house without the consent of the owner; and whereas, by the second and third clauses of the tenth section of the first article of the Constitution, it is indirectly provided that a State may, with the consent of Congress, keep troops and ships of war in time of peace; and whereas, by the seventeenth clause of the eighth section of the first article of the Constitution, the exclusive jurisdiction of the Federal Government over forts, magazines, arsenals, dock-yards, and so forth, is limited to places purchased by the consent of the Legislature of the State in which the same shall be; and whereas, the military powers delegated by the States to the Federal Government were designed for the purposes stated generally, in the preamble to the Constitution, namely: to insure domestic tranquillity, and provide for the common defence; therefore, *Be it resolved by the Senate and House of Representatives, etc.*, that upon the application of a State, either through a Convention or Legislature thereof, asking that the Federal forces of the Army and Navy may be withdrawn from its limits, the President of the United States shall order the withdrawal of the Federal garrisons, and take the needful security for the safety of the public property which may remain in said State.

Sec. 2. *And be it further resolved*, That whenever a State Convention, duly and lawfully assembled, shall enact that the safety of the State requires it to keep troops and ships of war, the President of the United States be, and he is hereby, authorized and directed to recognize the exercise of that power by the State, and by proclamation to give notice of the fact for the information and government of all parties concerned.

SUSPENDING CERTAIN LAWS IN SECEDED STATES.

January 19th, 1861. Mr. Mason of Virginia offered the following resolution, which was printed:

"It appearing to Congress that the State of South Carolina has, by an ordinance of the people of that State, in Convention assembled, declared the State separated from the United States, and from the Government thereof, as established under the Constitution; and it further appearing, that by reason of such declared separation, there are no officers of the United States acting under the authority thereof, in the judiciary department of this Government, or under the laws for the collection of the revenues of the United States; whereby, and in consequence whereof, the laws of the United States are in fact suspended within the limits of said State; therefore, to avoid any hostile collision that might arise between the authorities of the United States and of the State aforesaid, in the attempt to execute laws of the United States, in the absence of those officers required by law to administer and execute said laws:

"*Be it resolved by the Senate and House of Representatives*, That from and after the passage of this joint resolution, all laws of the United States directing the mode in which the Army and Navy and other public force of the United States shall be used by the President of the United States, in aid of the civil authorites in executing the laws and authorizing the same, and all laws for the collection of revenue shall be, and the same are hereby suspended, and made inoperative in the State of South Carolina for the time being; and should it be made to appear hereafter by the executive authority of any other State or States, that a like ordinance has been passed by the people of any State, declaring such State or States separated from the United States, then it shall be the duty of the President of the United States to announce such separation by his proclamation, and all the laws of the United States shall, in like manner, be suspended and rendered inoperative in such State last aforesaid."

RETROCESSION OF FORTS AND ARSENALS.

January 2d, 1861. Mr. Hunter offered in the Senate this resolution, upon which, on the 11th of January, he gave his opinion on the condition of the country and the needed remedies:

Whereas certain forts, magazines, arsenals, dock-yards, and other needful buildings have been placed under the exclusive jurisdiction of the United States by a cession to that effect from certain States, and it may be the desire of one or more of these States to resume the jurisdiction thus ceded: Now, therefore—

Be it Resolved, That the President of the United States ought to be authorized by law, upon the application of the Legislature or of a regular Convention of the people of any such State, to retrocede this jurisdiction to such States, upon taking proper security for the safe-keeping and return of all the property of the United States, or for paying for the value of the same, if destroyed or injured by the act of any of the States making such application.

MR. HUNTER'S PLAN OF ADJUSTMENT.

In his speech, Mr. Hunter indicated the points of adjustment which he considered indispensable

He thought the Southern people were bound to withdraw from the Government unless they can get constitutional guarantees, which shall provide: first, that Congress shall have no power to abolish slavery in the States, in the District of Columbia, in the dock-yards, forts, and arsenals of the United States; second, that it shall not abolish, tax, or obstruct the slave trade between the States; third, that it shall be the duty of each of the States to suppress combinations within their jurisdiction for armed invasions of another; fourth, that States shall be admitted with or without slavery, according to the election of the people; fifth, that it shall be the duty of the States to restore fugitive slaves when within their borders, or to pay the value of the same; sixth, that fugitives from justice shall be deemed all those who have offended against the laws of a State within its jurisdiction, and who have escaped therefrom; seventh, that Congress shall recognize and protect as property whatever is held to be such by the laws or prescriptions of any State within the Territories, dock-yards, forts, and arsenals within the United States, and wherever the United States has exclusive jurisdiction; with the following exceptions: First, it may leave the subject of slavery or involuntary servitude to the people of the Territories when a law shall be passed to that effect with the usual sanction, and also with the assent of a majority of the Senators from the slaveholding States, and a majority of the Senators from the non-slaveholding States. That exception is designed to provide for the case where we might annex a territory almost fully peopled, and whose people ought to have the right of self-government, and yet might not be ready to be admitted as a State into the Union.

The next exception is that "Congress may divide the territories to the effect that slavery or involuntary servitude shall be prohibited in one portion of the territory, and recognized and protected in another; provided the law has the sanction of a majority from each of the sections as aforesaid," and that exception is designed to provide for the case where an unpeopled territory is annexed, and it is a fair subject of division between the two sections.

In addition to these "guarantees of principles," there should be "guarantees of power," without which he did not think permanent peace could be secured. He indicated these as the best: *First*, the dual Executive, not in the form proposed by Mr. Calhoun, but in one less fairly open to objections. He would provide:

That each section shall elect a President, to be called the first and second President: the first to serve for four years as President, the next to succeed him at the end of four years, and to govern for four other years, and afterwards to be re-eligible.

That during the term of service of the first President, the second should be President of the Senate, with a casting vote in case of a tie; and that no treaty should be valid which did not have the signatures of both Presidents, and the assent of two-thirds of the Senate.

That no law should be valid which did not have the assent of both Presidents, or in the event of a veto by one of them, the assent of a majority of the Senators of the section from which he came.

That no person should be appointed to a local office in the section from which the second President was elected, unless the appointment had the assent of that President, or, in the event of his veto, the assent of a majority of the Senators from the section from which he came.

He proposed to change the mode of electing these Presidents as follows:

I would provide that each State should be divided into Presidential electoral districts; that each district should elect one man, and that these representatives from the whole United States should meet in one chamber, and that the two men who, after a certain number of ballots, received the highest number of votes, should be submitted as the candidates to the people, and he should be declared as President who received a majority of the districts—the districts each voting singly. I would do this to destroy the opportunities which are given under our present system of nomination to the formation of corrupt combinations for purposes of plunder and of patronage. I would substitute this instead of the National Conventions, which have already done so much harm in our system.

Further:

I would also diminish the temptation to such corrupt combinations for spoils and patronage by the fact that the President, after the first election, would be elected four years before he commenced his service as President, and in the meantime he would be training as a second President at the head of the Senate, and exercising the veto power. The fact that he was elected four years beforehand would do much to prevent such combinations; but, further than this, the effect of such a division of the Executive power would be to destroy, to a great extent, the miserable system of rotation in office which exists at present, and to make merit the test of the fitness for office, and a guarantee for his permanence in place; for, as the second President would probably keep those in office during his term of President whom he had protected by his veto power before, if they were worthy of the place, the effect would be, at least if this system were introduced, that the rotation principle would be applied, if at all, not once in four years, but once in eight years.

But this plan would have another good effect. It would save us from most of those agitations attending a Presidential election which now disturb the country, which unsettle public affairs, and which are doing so much to demoralize and corrupt the people. The election would take place in one section at a time; it would take place in each section but once in eight years, and in this way we would escape those disturbances which are now dividing and destroying us.

Further, "to secure the proper enforcement of rights which are now without remedies," he proposed "that the Supreme Court should also be adjusted. It should consist of ten judges—five from each section—the Chief Justice to be one of the five. I would allow one State to cite another State before this tribunal to charge it with having failed to perform its constitutional obligations; and if the court decided a State thus cited to be in default, then I would provide, if it did not repair the wrong it had done, that any State might deny to its citizens within its jurisdiction the privileges of citizens in all the States; that it might tax its commerce and the property of its people until it ceased to be in default. Thus I would provide a remedy without bringing the General Government into collision with the States, and without bringing the Supreme Court into collision with them. Whenever international stipulations in regard to the duties imposed on the States, as laid down in the Constitution, are violated, I would remedy the wrong by international remedies. I would give a State the right, in such cases, after the adjudication of the court, to deny to the offending State the performance of the mutual obligations which had been created for its benefit. In this way I believe that these wrongs might be remedied without producing collision in the system. A self-executing process would thus provide a remedy for the wrong, without a jar to the machinery of Government. In order to make this check efficient, it should be provided that the Judges of the Supreme Court in each section shall be appointed by the President from that section, and this is the only original appointing power which I would give to the second President."

In consideration of these changes, he expressed his willingness "to regulate the right of Secession, *which I hold to be a right not given in the Constitution, but resulting from the nature of the compact*. I would provide that, before a State seceded, it should summon a Convention of the States in the section to which it belonged, and submit to them a statement of its grievances and wrongs. Should a majority of the States in such Convention decide the complaint to be well founded, then the State ought to be permitted to secede in peace. For, whenever a majority of States in an entire section shall declare that good cause for secession exists, then who can dispute that it ought to take place? Should they say, however, that no good cause existed, then the moral force of such a decision, on the part of confederates of those who are bound to the complaining State by identical and homogeneous interests, would prevent it from prosecuting the claim any further. I believe that the system thus adjusted would give us a permanent Union, an efficient, a useful, and just Government. I think our Government would then rank among the most permanent of human institutions. It is my honest opinion that, with a Government thus balanced, and with such capacities for empire as our people possess, we should build up a political system whose power and stability and beneficial influences would be unparalleled in all the history of the past."

He believed "this scheme afforded the best basis of settlement which has yet been devised. There are other schemes upon which I would settle. I would settle upon something which would give only a truce, provided it promised to be a long truce, and then trust to public opinion and the progress of truth to remedy future evils when they might arise. But I would prefer, when we do settle, after all this turmoil and confusion, that we should do so upon some principle which promises us a permanent adjustment, a constant and continuing peace, a safe, an efficient, and a stable Government."

At the close of Mr. Hunter's speech, this significant colloquy took place:

Mr. BAKER. I desire to ask the gentleman from Virginia, if he will allow me, and consider it respectful, one question.

Mr. HUNTER. What is the question?

Mr. BAKER. It is this: If a majority of this branch of Congress—the constitutional majority, and a majority of the other branch, also the constitutional majority—shall pass constitutional amendments, to be submitted according to the forms of the Constitution for the consent and approbation of the people, in that event, if they be such as substantially meet the views of the gentlemen on the other side, will the Senator from Virginia, so far as he can, throw the weight of Virginia, and especially the weight of his own individual character, to maintain the Constitution as it is, the Government as it is, the laws as they now are, with the power of the Government, until the people of the States shall have decided upon those amendments?

Mr. HUNTER. The Senator has asked me some questions which I cannot answer. I cannot answer for Virginia; I am not authorized to do so. I can only say this: that I will vote for the propositions of the Senator from Kentucky which were presented in committee; and other gentlemen declared that they believed they would be satisfactory; but whether the people, who are now seceding and getting in line together for purposes of common defence, would wait to ascertain whether the State would adopt them, I am not authorized to say.

Mr. BAKER. That is not quite it: I do not make myself understood by the gentleman. Will the gentleman himself, as a Senator——

Mr. HUNTER. If the Senator is not satisfied I cannot satisfy him.

Mr. BAKER. Ah!

For speech and colloquy, see *Congressional Globe*, second session, 36th Congress, pages 328–332.

No vote was taken upon the resolution.

CONSTRUCTION OF SCREW SLOOPS OF WAR.

February 11th. The Senate, as in Committee of the Whole, adopted an amendment to the Naval Appropriation bill, providing for the construction of seven steam screw sloops of war of the second class, with full steam power, whose greatest draught of water shall not exceed 14 feet, and appropriating $1,200,000 for the purpose. The vote was, yeas 30, nays 18, as follows:

YEAS—Messrs. Anthony, Baker, *Bigler*, Bingham, Cameron, Chandler, Clark, Collamer, Doolittle, Durkee, Fessenden, Foot, Grimes, Hale, Harlan, *Johnson* of Tennessee, *Kennedy*, King, *Latham*, Morrill, *Sebastian*, Seward, Simmons, Sumner, Ten Eyck, *Thomson*, Trumbull, Wade, Wilkinson, and Wilson—30.

NAYS—Messrs. *Bayard*, *Bragg*, *Bright*, *Clingman*, Crittenden, *Fitch*, *Gwin*, *Hemphill*, *Hunter*, *Lane*, *Mason*, *Nicholson*, *Pearce*, *Polk*, *Powell*, *Rice*, *Saulsbury*, and *Wigfall*—18.

12th. The amendment made in Senate as in Committee of the Whole, was agreed to, yeas 27, nays 17.

20th. The House adopted the amendment, yeas 114, nays 38, as follows:

YEAS—Messrs. Charles F. Adams, *Adrain*, Aldrich, *Allen*, Alley, Wm. C. Anderson, Ashley, *Barr*, Bingham, Blake, Brayton, Briggs, Bristow, Buffinton, Burlingame, Burnham, Butterfield, Campbell, Carey, Carter, Case, Coburn, C. B. Cochrane, *John Cochrane*, Colfax, Conkling, Conway, *Cox*, Curtis, Dawes, Delano, Duell, Dunn, Edgerton, Edwards, Eliot, Ely, Farnsworth, Fenton, Ferry, *Florence*, Frank, French, Gooch, Graham, Grow, Gurley, Hall, *Hamilton*, J. Morrison Harris, Helmick, Hoard, *Holman*, *William Howard*, Humphrey, Hutchins, Irvine, Junkin, Francis W. Kellogg, Wm. Kellogg, Kenyon, Killinger, *Larrabee*, De Witt C. Leach, Lee, Longnecker, Loomis, Lovejoy, Marston, McKean, *McKenty*, McKnight, McPherson, *Millson*, Millward, Laban T. Moore, Moorhead, Morrill, Edward Joy Morris, *Isaac N. Morris*, Morse, Nixon, Olin, Palmer, Porter, Potter, Pottle, Edwin R. Reynolds, Rice, Christopher Robinson, Royce, Scranton, Sedgwick, *Sickles*, Spaulding, Spinner, Stanton, Stevens, Wm. Stewart, Stratton, Tappan, Theaker, Tompkins, Van Wyck, Verree, Wade, Waldron, Cadwalader C. Washburn, Ellihu B. Washburne, Webster, Wells, Wilson, Windom, Woodruff—114.

NAYS—Messrs. *Avery*, *Barrett*, *Bocock*, *Branch*, *Brown*, *Burch*, *Burnett*, *John B. Clark*, *Burton Craige*, *John G. Davis*, *De Jarnette*, *Edmundson*, Etheridge, *Garnett*, *John T. Harris*, Hatton, *Hindman*, *Hughes*, James M. Leach, *Elbert S. Martin*, Nelson, *Niblack*, *Phelps*, Quarles, *Riggs*, *James C. Robinson*, *Rust*, *Scott*, Sherman, *Simms*, Wm. N. H. Smith, *Stevenson*, Stokes, *Thomas*, *Vallandigham*, Vance, *Winslow*, and *Wright*—38.

RECOGNITION OF THE SOUTHERN CONFEDERACY.

February 11, 1861. Mr. BURTON CRAIGE of North Carolina, offered in the House of Representatives, the following resolution, which was referred to the Committee on Foreign Affairs, on his motion:

Whereas, the States of South Carolina, Florida, Alabama, Georgia, Mississippi, and Louisiana have seceded from the Confederacy of the United States, and have established a Government under the name of "the Confederacy of the United States South;" and whereas it is desirable that the most amicable relations should exist between the two Governments, and war should be avoided as the greatest calamity which can befall them:

Resolved by the Senate and House of Representatives of the United States of America in Congress assembled, That the President of the United States be, and is hereby, required to acknowledge the independence of said government as soon as he is informed officially of its establishment; and that he receive such envoy, embassador, or commissioner as may or shall be appointed by said government for the purpose of amicably adjusting the matters in dispute with said Government.

It was not reported from the Committee.

THE TERRITORIAL DIFFICULTIES SETTLED BY CONGRESS.

Congress passed and the President approved bills to provide temporary governments for Colorado, February 28th, Nevada, March 2d, and Dakotah, March 2d, 1861.

These three Territories cover the entire region owned by the United States and not included within the States.

The sixth and sixteenth sections of each bill are as follows:

"That the legislative power of the Territory shall extend to all rightful subjects of legislation consistent with the Constitution of the United States and the provisions of the act; but no law shall be passed interfering with the primary disposal of the soil; no tax shall be imposed upon the property of the United States; nor shall the lands or other property of non-residents be taxed higher than the lands or the property of residents; nor shall any law be passed impairing the right of private property; nor shall any discrimination be made in taxing different kinds of property; but all property subject to taxation shall be in proportion to the value of the property taxed.

"That the Constitution and all laws of the United States, which are not locally inapplicable, shall have the same force and effect within the said Territory of Dakotah as elsewhere within the United States."

The ninth section contains this provision:

"And each of the said District Courts shall have and exercise the same jurisdistion in all cases arising under the Constitution and laws of the United States as is vested in the Circuit and District Courts of the United States; and the said Supreme and District Courts of the said Territory, and the respective judges thereof, shall and may grant writs of *habeas corpus* in all cases in which the same are grantable by the judges of the United States in the District of Columbia."

The provisions of these bills were, as was announced in debate, agreed upon by Mr. GREEN of Missouri, Chairman of the Senate Committee on Territories, and Mr. GROW of Pennsylvania, Chairman of the House Committee on Territories, Mr. Wade and others in consultation, and the bills passed without material opposition in either House. The Colorado bill passed the Senate February 4th, without a division, and the House, February 18th, by a vote of 90 yeas to 44 nays as follows:

YEAS—Messrs. Charles F. Adams, Aldrich, Alley, Bingham, Blair, Blake, Brayton, Buffinton, Burlingame, Burnham, Butterfield, Campbell, Carey, Carter, Case, Colfax, Conkling, Conway, Covode, Dawes, Delano, Duell, Edgerton, Edwards, Eliot, Ely, Farnsworth, Fenton, *Florence*, Frank, French, Gooch, Graham, Grow, Gurley, Hale, Hall, Helmick, *William Howard*, William A. Howard, Humphrey, Hutchins, Irvine, Junkin, Francis W. Kellogg, William Kellogg, Kenyon, Killinger, De Witt C. Leach, Lee, Longnecker, Loomis, Lovejoy, Marston, McKean, *McKenty*, McKnight, McPherson, Moorhead, Morrill, Edward Joy Morris, *Isaac N. Morris*, Morse, Nixon, Palmer, Porter, Potter, Pottle, Edwin R. Reynolds, Rice, Christopher Robinson, Royce, Scranton, Sedgwick, Spinner, Stanton, Stevens, Tappan, Tompkins, Train, Vandever, Wade, Waldron, Walton, Cadwalader C. Washburn, Ellihu B. Washburne, Wells, Windom, Wood, Woodruff—90.

NAYS—Messrs. *Adrain, Allen*, W. C. Anderson, *Avery, Barrett, Bocock, Burch, Burnett, Horace F. Clark, Jno. B. Clark, Jno. Cochrane*, Corwin, *Cox, Burton Craige, Jno. G. Davis, De Jarnette, Edmundson, Garnett*, Gilmer, *John T. Harris*, Hatton, *Hindman, Holman, Hughes, Leake, Logan*, Maynard, *McClernand, Millson*, Laban T. Moore, Nelson, *Niblack*, Pettit, *Phelps, Pryor*, Quarles, *James C. Robinson, Ruffin, Sickles, Simms*, William N. H. Smith, *Stevenson*, Stokes, *Thomas*—44.

The Nevada bill was passed by the House, March 1st—yeas 91, nays 32, and the Dakotah, same day, without a division.

ON PROTECTING SLAVERY IN THE TERRITORIES.

During the consideration of the Davis resolutions in the United States Senate in May, 1860,

Mr. THOMAS L. CLINGMAN of North Carolina, May 24th, offered an amendment to add to the fourth resolution the following:

"*Resolved*, That the existing condition of the Territories of the United States does not require the intervention of Congress for the protection of property in slaves."

Mr. ALBERT G. BROWN of Mississippi, moved to strike from the amendment the word "not," so as to assert that the existing condition of the Territories of the United States *does* require the intervention of Congress for the protection of property in slaves.

Which was rejected May 25th—yeas 5, nays 43, as follows:

YEAS—Messrs. *Brown, Clay, Iverson, Johnson* of Arkansas, *Yulee*—5.

NAYS—Messrs. *Benjamin, Bigler*, Bingham, *Bragg, Bright*, Chandler, *Chesnut*, Clark, *Clingman*, Collamer, Crittenden, *Davis*, Dixon, Doolittle, *Fitzpatrick*, Foot, *Green, Gwin*, Hale, Hamlin, *Hammond, Hemphill, Hunter, Johnson* of Tennessee, *Kennedy, Lane, Latham, Mallory, Mason, Nicholson, Pearce, Polk, Powell, Pugh, Rice, Sebastian, Slidell*, Ten Eyck, *Toombs*, Trumbull, Wade, *Wigfall*, Wilson—43.

The question recurring on Mr. CLINGMAN's amendment,

Mr. COLLAMER of Vermont, moved to amend it so as to make it read:

Resolved, That the existing condition of the Territories of the United States does not, and in our opinion never will, require, etc.

Which was rejected—yeas 16, nays 33, as follows:

YEAS—Messrs. Bingham, Chandler, Clark, Collamer, Crittenden, Dixon, Doolittle, Foot, Hale, Hamlin, Harlan, Simmons, Ten Eyck, Trumbull, Wade, Wilson—16.

NAYS—Messrs. *Benjamin, Bigler, Bragg, Bright, Brown, Chesnut, Clay, Clingman, Davis, Fitzpatrick, Green, Hammond, Hemphill, Hunter, Iverson, Johnson* of Arkansas, *Johnson* of Tennessee, *Lane, Latham, Mallory, Mason, Nicholson, Pearce, Polk, Powell, Pugh, Rice, Saulsbury, Sebastian, Slidell, Toombs, Wigfall, Yulee*—33.

The motion of Mr. CLINGMAN was then agreed to—yeas 26, nays 23, as follows:

YEAS—Messrs. *Bigler*, Bingham, *Bragg*, Chandler, Clark, *Clingman*, Collamer, Crittenden, Dixon, Doolittle, Foot, Grimes, Hale, Hamlin, Harlan, *Johnson* of Tennessee, *Kennedy, Latham, Polk, Pugh*, Simmons, Ten Eyck, *Toombs*, Trumbull, Wade, Wilson—26.

NAYS—Messrs. *Benjamin, Bright, Brown, Chesnut, Clay, Davis, Fitzpatrick, Green, Hammond, Hunter, Iverson, Lane, Mallory, Mason, Nicholson, Pearce, Powell, Rice, Saulsbury, Sebastian, Slidell, Wigfall, Yulee*—23.

When the fifth resolution was pending,

Mr. CLINGMAN moved to amend by adding, as follows:

"*Provided*, That it is not hereby intended to assert the duty of Congress to provide a system of laws for the maintenance of slavery."

Which was rejected—yeas 12, nays 31, as follows:

YEAS—Messrs. Clark, *Clingman*, Dixon, Foot, Foster, Hale, Hamlin, *Latham, Pugh*, Ten Eyck, Trumbull, Wilson—12.

NAYS—Messrs. *Benjamin, Bragg, Bright, Brown, Chesnut, Clay, Davis, Fitzpatrick, Green, Hammond, Hemphill, Hunter, Iverson, Johnson* of Arkansas, *Johnson* of Tennessee, *Kennedy, Lane, Mallory, Mason, Nicholson, Pearce, Polk, Powell, Rice, Saulsbury, Sebastian, Slidell, Thomson, Toombs, Wigfall, Yulee*—31.

Mr. BROWN of Mississippi, then offered a substitute for the fifth resolution, as follows:

"That experience having already shown that the Constitution and the common law, unaided by statutory enactment, do not afford adequate and sufficient protection to slave property—some of the Territories having failed, others having refused to pass such enactments—it has become the duty of Congress to interpose and pass such laws as will afford to slave property in the Territories that protection which is given to other kinds of property."

Which was rejected—yeas 3, nays 42, as follows:

YEAS—Messrs. *Brown, Johnson* of Arkansas, *Mallory*—3.

NAYS—Messrs. *Benjamin, Bigler, Bragg, Bright, Chesnut*, Clark, *Clay, Clingman*, Crittenden, *Davis*, Dixon, Doolittle, *Fitzpatrick*, Foot, Foster, *Green*, Grimes, *Gwin*, Hamlin, Harlan, *Hemphill, Hunter, Iverson, Johnson* of Tennessee, *Lane, Latham, Mason, Nicholson, Pearce, Polk, Powell, Pugh, Rice, Sebastian, Slidell*, Ten Eyck, *Thomson, Toombs*, Trumbull, *Wigfall*, Wilson, *Yulee*—42.

CONSTITUTION OF THE UNITED STATES,

AND OF THE

"CONFEDERATE" STATES.

WITH AN INDEX TO BOTH.

Constitution of the United States of America.

We the People of the United States, in order to form a more perfect Union, establish Justice, insure domestic Tranquillity, provide for the common defence, promote the general Welfare, and secure the Blessings of Liberty to ourselves and our Posterity, do ordain and establish this Constitution for the United States of America.

ARTICLE I.

SECTION I.

All legislative Powers herein granted shall be vested in a Congress of the United States, which shall consist of a Senate and House of Representatives.

SECTION II.

The House of Representatives shall be composed of Members chosen every second Year by the People of the several States, and the Electors in each State shall have the Qualifications requisite for Electors of the most numerous Branch of the State Legislature.

No Person shall be a Representative who shall not have attained to the Age of twenty five Years, and been seven Years a Citizen of the United States, and who shall not, when elected, be an Inhabitant of that State in which he shall be chosen.

Representatives and direct Taxes shall be apportioned among the several States which may be included within this Union, according to their respective Numbers, which shall be determined by adding to the whole Number of free Persons, including those bound to Service for a Term of Years, and excluding Indians not taxed, three fifths of all other Persons. The actual Enumeration shall be made within three Years after the first Meeting of the Congress of the United States, and within every subsequent Term of ten Years, in such Manner as they shall by Law direct. The Number of Representatives shall not exceed one for every thirty Thousand, but each State shall have at Least one Representative; and until such enumeration shall be made, the State of New Hampshire shall be entitled to chuse three, Massachusetts eight, Rhode Island and Providence Plantations one, Connecticut five, New York six, New Jersey four, Pennsylvania eight, Delaware one, Maryland six, Virginia ten, North Carolina five, South Carolina five, and Georgia three.

When vacancies happen in the Representation from any State, the Executive Authority thereof shall issue Writs of Election to fill such Vacancies.

The House of Representatives shall chuse their Speaker and other Officers; and shall have the sole Power of Impeachment.

SECTION III.

The Senate of the United States shall be composed of two Senators from each State, chosen by the Legislature thereof, for six Years; and each Senator shall have one Vote.

Immediately after they shall be assembled in Consequence of the first Election, they shall be divided as equally as may be into three Classes. The Seats of the Senators of the first Class shall be vacated at the Expiration of the second Year, of the second Class at the Expiration of the fourth Year, and of the third Class at the Expiration of the sixth Year, so that one-third may be chosen every second Year; and if Vacancies happen by Resignation, or otherwise, during the Recess of the Legislature of any State, the Executive thereof may make temporary Appointments until the next Meeting of the Legislature, which shall then fill such Vacancies.

No Person shall be a Senator who shall not have attained to the Age of thirty Years, and been nine Years a Citizen of the United States, and who shall not, when elected, be an Inhabitant of that State for which he shall be chosen.

The Vice President of the United States shall be President of the Senate, but shall have no Vote, unless they be equally divided.

The Senate shall chuse their other Officers, and also a President pro tempore, in the Absence of the Vice President, or when he shall exercise the Office of President of the United States.

The Senate shall have the sole Power to try all Impeachments. When sitting for that Purpose, they shall be on Oath or Affirmation. When the President of the United States is tried, the Chief Justice shall preside: And no Person shall be convicted without the Concurrence of two thirds of the Members present.

Judgment in Cases of Impeachment shall not extend further than to removal from Office, and

Disqualification to hold and enjoy any Office of honour, Trust or Profit under the United States: but the Party convicted shall nevertheless be liable and subject to Indictment, Trial, Judgment and Punishment, according to Law.

SECTION IV.

The Times, Places and Manner of holding Elections for Senators and Representatives, shall be prescribed in each State by the Legislature thereof; but the Congress may at any time by Law make or alter such Regulations, except as to the places of chusing Senators.

The Congress shall assemble at least once in every Year, and such Meeting shall be on the first Monday in December, unless they shall by Law appoint a different Day.

SECTION V.

Each House shall be the Judge of the Elections, Returns and Qualifications of its own Members, and a Majority of each shall constitute a Quorum to do Business; but a smaller Number may adjourn from day to day, and may be authorized to compel the Attendance of absent Members, in such Manner, and under such Penalties as each House may provide.

Each House may determine the Rules of its Proceedings, punish its Members for disorderly Behaviour, and, with the Concurrence of two thirds, expel a Member.

Each House shall keep a Journal of its Proceedings, and from time to time publish the same, excepting such Parts as may in their Judgment require Secrecy; and the Yeas and Nays of the Members of either House on any question shall, at the Desire of one fifth of those Present, be entered on the Journal.

Neither House, during the Session of Congress, shall, without the Consent of the other, adjourn for more than three days, nor to any other Place than that in which the two Houses shall be sitting.

SECTION VI.

The Senators and Representatives shall receive a Compensation for their Services, to be ascertained by Law, and paid out of the Treasury of the United States. They shall in all Cases, except Treason, Felony and Breach of the Peace, be privileged from Arrest during their Attendance at the Session of their respective Houses, and in going to and returning from the same; and for any Speech or Debate in either House, they shall not be questioned in any other Place.

No Senator or Representative shall, during the Time for which he was elected, be appointed to any civil Office under the Authority of the United States, which shall have been created, or the Emoluments whereof shall have been encreased during such time; and no Person holding any Office under the United States, shall be a Member of either House during his Continuance in Office.

SECTION VII.

All Bills for raising Revenue shall originate in the House of Representatives; but the Senate may propose or concur with Amendments as on other Bills.

Every Bill which shall have passed the House of Representatives and the Senate, shall, before it become a Law, be presented to the President of the United States; If he approve he shall sign it, but if not he shall return it, with his Objections to that House in which it shall have originated, who shall enter the Objections at large on their Journal, and proceed to reconsider it. If after such Reconsideration two thirds of that House shall agree to pass the Bill, it shall be sent, together with the Objections, to the other House, by which it shall likewise be reconsidered, and if approved by two thirds of that House, it shall become a Law. But in all such Cases the Votes of both Houses shall be determined by yeas and Nays, and the Names of the Persons voting for and against the Bill shall be entered on the Journal of each House respectively. If any Bill shall not be returned by the President within ten Days (Sundays excepted) after it shall have been presented to him, the Same shall be a law, in like Manner as if he had signed it, unless the Congress by their Adjournment prevent its return, in which Case it shall not be a Law.

Every Order, Resolution, or Vote to which the Concurrence of the Senate and House of Representatives may be necessary (except on a question of Adjournment) shall be presented to the President of the United States; and before the Same shall take Effect, shall be approved by him, or being disapproved by him, shall be repassed by two thirds of the Senate and House of Representatives, according to the Rules and Limitations prescribed in the Case of a Bill.

SECTION VIII.

The Congress shall have Power

To lay and collect Taxes, Duties, Imposts and Excises, to pay the Debts and provide for the common Defence and general Welfare of the United States; but all Duties, Imposts and Excises shall be uniform throughout the United States;

To borrow Money on the credit of the United States;

To regulate Commerce with foreign Nations, and among the several States, and with the Indian Tribes;

To establish an uniform Rule of Naturalization, and uniform Laws on the subject of Bankruptcies throughout the United States;

To coin Money, regulate the Value thereof, and of foreign Coin, and fix the Standard of Weights and Measures;

To provide for the Punishment of counterfeiting the Securities and current Coin of the United States;

To establish Post Offices and post Roads;

To promote the progress of Science and useful Arts, by securing for limited Times to Authors and Inventors the exclusive Right to their respective Writings and Discoveries;

To constitute Tribunals inferior to the supreme Court;

To define and punish Piracies and Felonies committed on the high Seas, and Offences against the Law of Nations;

To declare War, grant Letters of Marque and Reprisal, and make Rules concerning Captures on Land and Water;

To raise and support Armies, but no Appropriation of Money to that Use shall be for a longer Term than two Years;

To provide and maintain a Navy;

To make Rules for the Government and Regulation of the land and naval Forces;

To provide for calling forth the Militia to execute the Laws of the Union, suppress Insurrections and repel Invasions;

To provide for organizing, arming, and disciplining, the Militia, and for governing such Part of them as may be employed in the Service of the United States, reserving to the States respectively, the Appointment of the Officers, and the Authority of training the Militia according to the Discipline prescribed by Congress;

To exercise exclusive Legislation in all Cases whatsoever, over such District (not exceeding ten Miles square) as may, by Cession of particular States, and the Acceptance of Congress, become the Seat of the Government of the United States, and to exercise like Authority over all Places purchased by the Consent of the Legislature of the State in which the Same shall be, for the Erection of Forts, Magazines, Arsenals, Dock-Yards, and other needful Buildings;—And

To make all Laws which shall be necessary and proper for carrying into Execution the foregoing Powers, and all other Powers vested by this Constitution in the Government of the United States, or in any Department or Officer thereof.

SECTION IX.

The Migration or Importation of such Persons as any of the States now existing shall think proper to admit, shall not be prohibited by the Congress prior to the Year one thousand eight hundred and eight, but a Tax or Duty may be imposed on such Importation, not exceeding ten dollars for each Person.

The Privilege of the Writ of Habeas Corpus shall not be suspended, unless when in Cases of Rebellion or Invasion the public Safety may require it.

No Bill of Attainder or ex post facto Law shall be passed.

No Capitation, or other direct, Tax shall be laid, unless in Proportion to the Census or Enumeration herein before directed to be taken.

No Tax or Duty shall be laid on Articles exported from any State.

No Preference shall be given by any Regulation of Commerce or Revenue to the Ports of one State over those of another: nor shall Vessels bound to, or from, one State, be obliged to enter, clear, or pay Duties in another.

No Money shall be drawn from the Treasury, but in Consequence of Appropriations made by Law; and a regular Statement and Account of the Receipts and Expenditures of all public Money shall be published from time to time.

No Title of Nobility shall be granted by the United States: and no Person holding any Office of Profit or Trust under them, shall, without the Consent of the Congress, accept of any present, Emolument, Office, or Title, of any kind whatever, from any King, Prince, or foreign State.

SECTION X.

No State shall enter into any Treaty, Alliance, or Confederation; grant Letters of Marque and Reprisal; coin Money; emit Bills of Credit; make any Thing but gold and silver Coin a Tender in Payment of Debts; pass any Bill of Attainder, ex post facto Law, or Law impairing the Obligation of Contracts, or grant any Title of Nobility.

No State shall, without the consent of the Congress, lay any Imposts or Duties on Imports or Exports, except what may be absolutely necessary for executing it's inspection Laws: and the net Produce of all Duties and Imposts, laid by any State on Imports or Exports, shall be for the Use of the Treasury of the United States; and all such Laws shall be subject to the Revision and Controul of the Congress.

No State shall, without the Consent of Congress, lay any Duty of Tonnage, keep Troops, or Ships of War in time of Peace, enter into any Agreement or Compact with another State, or with a foreign Power, or engage in War, unless actually invaded, or in such imminent Danger as will not admit of Delay.

ARTICLE II.

SECTION I.

The executive Power shall be vested in a President of the United States of America. He shall hold his Office during the Term of four Years, and, together with the Vice President, chosen for the same Term, be elected, as follows

Each State shall appoint, in such Manner as the Legislature thereof may direct, a Number of Electors, equal to the whole Number of Senators and Representatives to which the State may be entitled in the Congress: but no Senator or Representative, or Person holding an Office of Trust or Profit under the United States, shall be appointed an Elector.

[The Electors shall meet in their respective States, and vote by Ballot for two Persons, of whom one at least shall not be an Inhabitant of the same State with themselves. And they shall make a List of all the Persons voted for, and of the Number of Votes for each; which List they shall sign and certify, and transmit sealed to the Seat of the Government of the United States, directed to the President of the Senate. The President of the Senate shall, in the Presence of the Senate and House of Representatives, open all the Certificates, and the Votes shall then be counted. The Person having the greatest Number of Votes shall be the President, if such Number be a Majority of the whole Number of Electors appointed; and if there be more than one who have such Majority, and have an equal Number of Votes, then the House of Representatives shall immediately chuse by Ballot one of them for President; and if no Person have a Majority, then from the five highest on the List the said House shall in like Manner chuse the President. But in chusing the President, the Votes shall be taken by States, the Representation from each State having one Vote; A Quorum for this Purpose shall consist of a Member or Members from two-thirds of the States, and a Majority of all the States shall be necessary to a Choice. In every Case, after the Choice of the President, the Person having the greatest Number of Votes of the

Electors shall be the Vice President. But if there should remain two or more who have equal Votes, the Senate shall chuse from them by Ballot the Vice President.*]

The Congress may determine the Time of chusing the Electors, and the Day on which they shall give their Votes; which Day shall be the same throughout the United States.

No Person except a natural born Citizen, or a Citizen of the United States, at the time of the Adoption of this Constitution, shall be eligible to the Office of President; neither shall any Person be eligible to that Office who shall not have attained to the Age of thirty five Years, and been fourteen Years a Resident within the United States.

In Case of the Removal of the President from Office, or of his Death, Resignation, or Inability to discharge the Powers and Duties of the said Office, the same shall devolve on the Vice President, and the Congress may by Law provide for the Case of Removal, Death, Resignation, or Inability, both of the President and Vice President, declaring what Officer shall then act as President, and such Officer shall act accordingly, until the Disability be removed, or a President shall be elected.

The President shall, at stated Times, receive for his Services, a Compensation, which shall neither be encreased nor diminished during the Period for which he shall have been elected, and he shall not receive within that Period any other Emolument from the United States, or any of them.

Before he enter on the Execution of his Office, he shall take the following Oath or Affirmation:—

"I do solemnly swear (or affirm) that I will faithfully execute the Office of President of the United States, and will to the best of my Ability, preserve, protect and defend the Constitution of the United States."

SECTION II.

The President shall be Commander in Chief of the Army and Navy of the United States, and of the Militia of the several States, when called into the actual Service of the United States; he may require the Opinion, in writing, of the principal Officer in each of the executive Departments, upon any Subject relating to the Duties of their respective Offices, and he shall have Power to grant Reprieves and Pardons for Offences against the United States, except in Cases of Impeachment.

He shall have Power, by and with the Advice and Consent of the Senate, to make Treaties, provided two thirds of the Senators present concur; and he shall nominate, and by and with the Advice and Consent of the Senate, shall appoint Ambassadors, other public Ministers and Consuls, Judges of the supreme Court, and all other Officers of the United States, whose Appointments are not herein otherwise provided for, and which shall be established by Law: but the Congress may by Law vest the Appointment of such inferior Officers, as they think proper, in the President alone, in the Courts of Law, or in the Heads of Departments.

The President shall have Power to fill up all Vacancies that may happen during the Recess of the Senate, by granting Commissions which shall expire at the End of their next Session.

SECTION III.

He shall from time to time give to the Congress Information of the State of the Union, and recommend to their Consideration such Measures as he shall judge necessary and expedient; he may, on extraordinary Occasions, convene both Houses, or either of them, and in Case of Disagreement between them, with Respect to the Time of Adjournment, he may adjourn them to such Time as he shall think proper; he shall receive Ambassadors and other public Ministers; he shall take Care that the Laws be faithfully executed, and shall Commission all the officers of the United States.

SECTION IV.

The President, Vice President and all civil Officers of the United States, shall be removed from Office on Impeachment for, and Conviction of, Treason, Bribery, or other high Crimes and Misdemeanors.

ARTICLE III.

SECTION I.

The judicial Power of the United States, shall be vested in one supreme Court, and in such inferior Courts as the Congress may from time to time ordain and establish. The Judges, both of the supreme and inferior Courts, shall hold their Offices during good Behavior, and shall, at stated Times, receive for their Services, a Compensation, which shall not be diminished during their Continuance in Office.

SECTION II.

The judicial Power shall extend to all cases, in Law and Equity, arising under this Constitution, the Laws of the United States, and Treaties made, or which shall be made, under their Authority;—to all Cases affecting Ambassadors, other public Ministers, and Consuls;—to all Cases of admiralty and maritime Jurisdiction;—to Controversies to which the United States shall be a Party;—to Controversies between two or more States;—between a State and Citizens of another State;—between Citizens of different States,—between Citizens of the same State claiming Lands under Grants of different States, and between a State, or the Citizens thereof, and foreign States, Citizens or Subjects.

In all Cases affecting Ambassadors, other public Ministers and Consuls, and those in which a State shall be Party, the supreme Court shall have original Jurisdiction. In all the other Cases before mentioned, the supreme Court shall have appellate Jurisdiction, both as to Law and Fact, with such Exceptions, and under such Regulations as the Congress shall make.

The Trial of all Crimes, except in Cases of Impeachment, shall be by Jury; and such Trial shall be held in the State where the said Crimes shall have been committed; but when not committed within any State, the Trial shall be at such Place or Places as the Congress may by Law have directed.

---

* This clause of the Constitution has been annulled. See twelfth article of the amendment, page 96.

SECTION III.

Treason against the United States, shall consist only in levying War against them, or in adhering to their Enemies, giving them Aid and Comfort. No Person shall be convicted of Treason unless on the Testimony of two Witnesses to the same overt Act, or on Confession in open Court.

The Congress shall have Power to declare the Punishment of Treason, but no Attainder of Treason shall work Corruption of Blood, or Forfeiture except during the Life of the Person attainted.

ARTICLE IV.

SECTION I.

Full Faith and Credit shall be given in each State to the public Acts, Records, and judicial Proceedings of every other State. And the Congress may by general Laws prescribe the Manner in which such Acts, Records and Proceedings shall be proved, and the Effect thereof.

SECTION II.

The Citizens of each State shall be entitled to all Privileges and Immunities of Citizens in the several States.

A Person charged in any State with Treason, Felony, or other Crime, who shall flee from Justice, and be found in another State, shall on Demand of the executive Authority of the State from which he fled, be delivered up, to be removed to the State having Jurisdiction of the Crime.

No Person held to Service or Labour in one State, under the Laws thereof, escaping into another, shall, in Consequence of any Law or Regulation therein, be discharged from such Service or Labour, but shall be delivered up on Claim of the Party to whom such Service or Labour may be due.

SECTION III.

New States may be admitted by the Congress into this Union; but no new State shall be formed or erected within the Jurisdiction of any other State; nor any State be formed by the Junction of two or more States, or Parts of States, without the Consent of the Legislatures of the States concerned as well as of the Congress.

The Congress shall have Power to dispose of and make all needful Rules and Regulations respecting the Territory or other Property belonging to the United States; and nothing in this Constitution shall be so construed as to Prejudice any Claims of the United States, or of any particular State.

SECTION IV.

The United States shall guarantee to every State in this Union a Republican Form of Government, and shall protect each of them against Invasion; and on Application of the Legislature, or of the Executive (when the Legislature cannot be convened) against domestic Violence.

ARTICLE V.

The Congress, whenever two thirds of both Houses shall deem it necessary, shall propose Amendments to this Constitution, or, on the Application of the Legislatures of two thirds of the several States, shall call a Convention for proposing Amendments, which, in either Case, shall be valid to all Intents and Purposes, as Part of this Constitution, when ratified by the Legislatures of three fourths of the several States, or by Conventions in three fourths thereof, as the one or the other Mode of Ratification may be proposed by the Congress; Provided that no Amendment which may be made prior to the Year one thousand eight hundred and eight shall in any Manner affect the first and fourth Clauses in the Ninth Section of the first Article; and that no State, without its Consent, shall be deprived of its equal Suffrage in the Senate.

ARTICLE VI.

All Debts contracted and Engagements entered into, before the Adoption of this Constitution, shall be as valid against the United States under this Constitution, as under the Confederation.

This Constitution, and the Laws of the United States which shall be made in Pursuance thereof; and all Treaties made, or which shall be made, under the authority of the United States, shall be the supreme Law of the Land; and the Judges in every State shall be bound thereby, any Thing in the Constitution or Laws of any State to the Contrary notwithstanding.

The Senators and Representatives before mentioned, and the Members of the several State Legislatures, and all executive and judicial Officers, both of the United States and of the several States, shall be bound by Oath or Affirmation, to support this Constitution; but no religious Test shall ever be required as a Qualification to any Office or public Trust under the United States.

ARTICLE VII.

The Ratification of the Conventions of nine States, shall be sufficient for the Establishment of this Constitution between the States so ratifying the Same.

DONE in Convention by the Unanimous Consent of the States present the Seventeenth Day of September in the Year of our Lord one thousand seven hundred and Eighty seven and of the Independance of the United States of America the Twelfth In Witness whereof We have hereunto subscribed our Names,

G°: WASHINGTON,

Presidt and Deputy from Virginia

NEW HAMPSHIRE.
John Langdon,
Nicholas Gilman.

MASSACHUSETTS.
Nathaniel Gorham,
Rufus King.

CONNECTICUT.
Wm. Saml. Johnson,
Roger Sherman.

NEW YORK.
Alexander Hamilton.

NEW JERSEY.
Wil: Livingston,
David Brearley,
Wm. Paterson,
Jona. Dayton.

PENNSYLVANIA.
B. Franklin,
Thomas Mifflin,
Robt. Morris,
Geo: Clymer,
Tho: Fitzsimons,
Jared Ingersoll,
James Wilson,
Gouv: Morris.

DELAWARE.
Geo: Read,
Gunning Bedford, Jun'r,
John Dickinson,
Richard Bassett,
Jaco: Broom.

MARYLAND.
James McHenry,
Dan: of St. Thos. Jenifer,
Danl. Carroll.

VIRGINIA.
John Blair,
James Madison, Jr.,

NORTH CAROLINA.
Wm. Blount,
Rich'd Dobbs Spaight,
Hu. Williamson.

SOUTH CAROLINA.
J. Rutledge,
Charles Cotesworth Pinckney
Charles Pinckney,
Pierce Butler,

GEORGIA.
William Few,
Abr. Baldwin.

Attest: WILLIAM JACKSON, *Secretary.*

Amendments.

ARTICLE I.

Congress shall make no law respecting an establishment of religion, or prohibiting the free exercise thereof; or abridging the freedom of speech, or of the press; or the right of the people peaceably to assemble, and to petition the Government for a redress of grievances.

ARTICLE II.

A well regulated Militia, being necessary to the security of a free State, the right of the people to keep and bear Arms, shall not be infringed.

ARTICLE III.

No Soldier shall, in time of peace be quartered in any house, without the consent of the Owner, nor in time of war, but in a manner to be prescribed by law.

ARTICLE IV.

The right of the people to be secure in their persons, houses, papers, and effects, against unreasonable searches and seizures, shall not be violated, and no Warrants shall issue, but upon probable cause, supported by Oath or affirmation, and particularly describing the place to be searched, and the persons or things to be seized.

ARTICLE V.

No person shall be held to answer for a capital, or otherwise infamous crime, unless on a presentment or indictment of a Grand Jury, except in cases arising in the land or naval forces, or in the Militia, when in actual service in time of War or public danger; nor shall any person be subject for the same offence to be twice put in jeopardy of life or limb; nor shall be compelled in any Criminal Case to be a witness against himself, nor be deprived of life, liberty, or property, without due process of law; nor shall private property be taken for public use, without just compensation.

ARTICLE VI.

In all criminal prosecutions, the accused shall enjoy the right to a speedy and public trial, by an impartial jury of the State and district wherein the crime shall have been committed, which district shall have been previously ascertained by law, and to be informed of the nature and cause of the accusation; to be confronted with the witnesses against him; to have Compulsory process for obtaining Witnesses in his favour, and to have the Assistance of Counsel for his defence.

ARTICLE VII.

In Suits at common law, where the value in controversy shall exceed twenty dollars, the right of trial by jury shall be preserved, and no fact tried by a jury shall be otherwise reexamined in any Court of the United States, than according to the rules of the common law.

ARTICLE VIII.

Excessive bail shall not be required, nor excessive fines imposed, nor cruel and unusual punishments inflicted.

ARTICLE IX.

The enumeration in the Constitution, of certain rights, shall not be construed to deny or disparage others retained by the people.

ARTICLE X.

The powers not delegated to the United States by the Constitution, nor prohibited by it to the States, are reserved to the States respectively, or to the people.

ARTICLE XI.

The Judicial power of the United States shall not be construed to extend to any suit in law or equity, commenced or prosecuted against one of the United States by Citizens of another State, or by Citizens or Subjects of any Foreign State.

ARTICLE XII.

The Electors shall meet in their respective states, and vote by ballot for President and Vice President, one of whom, at least, shall not be an inhabitant of the same state with themselves; they shall name in their ballots the person voted for as President, and in distinct ballots the person voted for as Vice-President, and they shall make distinct lists of all persons voted for as President, and of all persons voted for as Vice-President, and of the number of votes for each, which lists they shall sign and certify, and transmit sealed to the seat of the government of the United States, directed to the President of the Senate;—The President of the Senate shall, in presence of the Senate and House of Representatives, open all the certificates and the votes shall then be counted;—The person having the greatest number of votes for President, shall be the President, if such number be a majority of the whole number of Electors appointed; and if no person have such majority, then from the persons having the highest numbers not exceeding three on the list of those voted for as President, the House of Representatives shall choose immediately, by ballot, the President. But in choosing the President, the votes shall be taken by states, the representation from each state having one vote; a quorum for this purpose shall consist of a member or members from two thirds of the states, and a majority of all the states shall be necessary to a choice. And if the House of Representatives shall not choose a President whenever the right of choice shall devolve upon them, before the fourth day of March next following, then the Vice-President shall act as President, as in the case of the death or other constitutional disability of the President. The person having the greatest number of votes as Vice-President, shall be the Vice-President, if such number be a majority of the whole number of Electors appointed, and if no person have a majority, then from the two highest numbers on the list, the Senate shall choose the Vice-President; a quorum for the purpose shall consist of two-thirds of the whole number of Senators, and a majority of the whole number shall be necessary to a choice. But no person constitutionally ineligible to the office of President shall be eligible to that of Vice-President of the United States.

PROCEEDINGS OF THE CONVENTION WHICH FORMED THE CONSTITUTION.

IN CONVENTION.

MONDAY, *September* 17, 1787.

Resolved, That the preceding Constitution be laid before the United States in Congress assembled: and that it is the opinion of this Convention that it should afterwards be submitted to a convention of delegates, chosen in each State by the people thereof, under the recommendation of its legislature, for their assent and ratification; and that each convention assenting to and ratifying the same should give notice thereof to the United States in Congress assembled.

Resolved, That it is the opinion of this Convention that, as soon as the conventions of nine States shall have ratified this Constitution, the United States in Congress assembled should fix a day on which electors should be appointed by the States which shall have ratified the same, and a day on which electors should assemble to vote for the President, and the time and place for commencing proceedings under this Constitution; that after such publication, the electors should be appointed, and the Senators and Representatives elected; that the electors should meet on the day fixed for the election of the President, and should transmit their votes, certified, signed, sealed, and directed, as the Constitution requires, to the Secretary of the United States in Congress assembled; that the Senators and Representatives should convene at the time and place assigned; that the Senators should appoint a President of the Senate, for the sole purpose of receiving, opening, and counting the votes for President; and that, after he shall be chosen, the Congress, together with the President, should, without delay, proceed to execute this Constitution.

By the unanimous order of the Convention:

G°: WASHINGTON, *President.*

WILLIAM JACKSON, *Secretary.*

LETTER OF THE CONVENTION TO THE OLD CONGRESS.

IN CONVENTION.

SEPTEMBER 17, 1787.

SIR: We have now the honor to submit to the consideration of the United States in Congress assembled, that Constitution which has appeared to us the most advisable.

The friends of our country have long seen and desired that the power of making war, peace, and treaties; that of levying money, and regulating commerce, and the correspondent executive and judicial authorities, should be fully and effectually vested in the General Government of the Union; but the impropriety of delegating such extensive trust to one body of men is evident; hence results the necessity of a different organization.

It is obviously impracticable in the federal government of these States to secure all rights of independent sovereignty to each, and yet provide for the interest and safety of all. Individuals entering into society must give up a share of liberty to preserve the rest. The magnitude of the sacrifice must depend as well on situation and circumstance as on the object to be obtained. It is at all times difficult to draw with precision the line between those rights which must be surrendered and those which may be reserved; and on the present occasion, this difficulty was increased by a difference among the several States as to their situation, extent, habits, and particular interests.

In all our deliberations on this subject, we kept steadily in our view that which appears to us the greatest interest of every true American—the consolidation of our Union—in which is involved our prosperity, felicity, safety, perhaps our national existence. This important consideration, seriously and deeply impressed on our minds, led each State in the Convention to be less rigid on points of inferior magnitude than might have been otherwise expected; and thus the Constitution which we now present is the result of a spirit of amity and of that mutual deference and concession which the peculiarity of our political situation rendered indispensable.

That it will meet the full and entire approbation of every State is not, perhaps, to be expected; but each will doubtless consider that, had her interest been alone consulted, the consequences might have been particularly disagreeable or injurious to others. That it is liable to as few exceptions as could reasonably have been expected, we hope and believe. That it may promote the lasting welfare of that country so dear to us all, and secure her freedom and happiness, is our most ardent wish.

With great respect, we have the honor to be, sir, your excellency's most obedient, humble servants.

By unanimous order of the Convention:

G°: WASHINGTON, *President.*

His Excellency the PRESIDENT OF CONGRESS.

PROCEEDINGS IN THE OLD CONGRESS.

UNITED STATES IN CONGRESS ASSEMBLED.

FRIDAY, *September* 28, 1787.

Present—New Hampshire, Massachusetts, Connecticut, New York, New Jersey, Pennsylvania, Delaware, Virginia, North Carolina, South Carolina, and Georgia; and from Maryland, Mr. Ross.

Congress having received the report of the Convention lately assembled in Philadelphia—

Resolved, unanimously, That the said report, with the resolutions and letter accompanying the same, be transmitted to the several legislatures, in order to be submitted to a convention of delegates chosen in each State by the people thereof, in conformity to the resolves of the Convention made and provided in that case.

CHARLES THOMSON, *Secretary.*

Constitution of the "Confederate" States.

In framing the Constitution of the so-called "Confederate States of America," its authors, in nearly all its parts, have adopted the precise language of the Constitution of the United States, and have followed the same order of arrangement in its articles and sections throughout. The two Constitutions, however, differ in many particulars, and it is designed, in this chapter, to exhibit clearly the points of difference between them.

The preamble is changed in the following respects: the words "*United States,*" near the beginning, are stricken out, and the following words inserted in their place: "*Confederate States, each State acting in its sovereign and independent character;*" also, the words "*more perfect union*" are stricken out, and the words "*permanent federal government*" inserted in their place; also, the following words are omitted: "*provide for the common defence, promote the general welfare;*" also, after the word "*posterity,*" the following words are inserted: "*invoking the favor and guidance of Almighty God;*" also, the word "*Confederate*" takes the place of "*United,*" preceding the word "*States.*" This last change takes place throughout the entire instrument, with a single exception, which will be noted in the appropriate place.

ARTICLE I.

SECTION 1. The word "*granted*" is stricken out, and the word "*delegated*" inserted in its place; also, the word "*United,*" preceding the word "*States,*" is stricken out, and the word "*Confederated*" inserted in its place.

SECTION 2. This section is changed as follows: in the first paragraph, after the words "*in each State shall,*" the following words are inserted: "*be citizens of the Confederate States, and*"; also, the following words are added to this paragraph: "*but no person of foreign birth, and not a citizen of the Confederate States, shall be allowed to vote for any officer, civil or political, State or federal.*"

In the second paragraph, the words "*been seven years a citizen of the United*" are stricken out, and the words "*be a citizen of the Confederate*" inserted in place of them.

In the third paragraph the word "*Union*" is stricken out, and the word "*Confederacy*" substituted; also the words "*other persons*" are stricken out, and the word "*slaves*" substituted; also, the word "*thirty,*" preceding the word "*thousand,*" is stricken out, and the word "*fifty*" substituted; also, all the words in this paragraph after the words "*the State of*" are stricken out, and the following words substituted: "*South Carolina shall be entitled to choose six, the State of Georgia ten, the State of Alabama nine, the State of Florida two, the State of Mississippi seven, the State of Louisiana six, and the State of Texas six.*"

No change is made in the fourth paragraph, and the fifth paragraph is changed by adding the following words: "*except that any judicial or other federal officer resident and acting solely within the limits of any State, may be impeached by a vote of two thirds of both branches of the Legislature thereof.*"

SECTION 3. In the first paragraph, after the words "*thereof for six years,*" the words "*at the regular session next immediately preceding the commencement of the term of service*" are inserted.

No change is made in the second paragraph. In the third paragraph the words "*been nine years a citizen of the United*" are stricken out, and the words "*be a citizen of the Confederate*" substituted.

SECTION 4. The first paragraph of this section is changed by inserting the words "*subject to the provisions of this Constitution*" between the word "*thereof*" and the word "*but.*" Also, the words "*times and*" are inserted near the close, before the word "*places.*"

SECTION 5. In the second paragraph of this section, the words "*of the whole number*" are inserted, between the word "*two-thirds*" and the word "*expel.*"

SECTION 6. This section is changed by striking out the word "*felony*" after the word "*treason*" in the first paragraph.

The second paragraph is changed by adding thereto the following words: "*But Congress may, by law, grant to the principal officer in each of the executive departments a seat upon the floor of either House, with the privilege of discussing any measures appertaining to his department.*"

SECTION 7. The following changes are made in this section: In the second paragraph the words "*the House of Representatives and the Senate,*" are stricken out, and the words "*both Houses*" substituted; also the word "*such*" is inserted between the word "*all*" and the word "*cases;*" also the following words are added to the end of this paragraph: "*The President may approve any appropriation and disapprove any other appropriation in the same bill. In such case he shall, in signing the bill, designate the appropriations disapproved, and shall return a copy of such appropriations, with his objections, to the House in which the bill shall have originated; and the same proceedings shall then be had as in case of other bills disapproved by the President.*"

The third paragraph is changed by striking out the words "*The Senate and House of Representatives*" in both places where they occur, and inserting in their places, in both cases, the words "*both Houses;*" also by substituting the word "*may*" for the word "*shall*" after the words "*disapproved by him.*"

SECTION 8. In the first paragraph, after the word "*excises*" the words "*for revenue necessary*" are inserted; also the word "*and*" after the word "*debts*" is omitted; also the words "*and general welfare of the United States; but*" are stricken out, and the following words substituted: "*and carry on the government of the Confederate States; but no bounties shall be granted from the treasury, nor shall any duties or taxes on importations from foreign nations be laid to promote or foster any branch of industry; and*"

The third paragraph is changed by adding thereto the following words: "*but neither this, nor any other clause contained in the Constitution, shall ever be construed to delegate the power to Congress to appropriate money for any internal improvement intended to facilitate commerce; except for the purpose of furnishing lights, beacons, and buoys, and other aids to navigation upon the coasts, and the improvement of harbors, and the removing of obstructions in river navigation; in all such cases such duties shall be laid on the navigation facilitated thereby, as may be necessary to pay the costs and expenses thereof.*"

The fourth paragraph is changed by adding thereto the following words: "*but no law of Congress shall discharge any debt contracted before the passage of the same.*"

The seventh paragraph is changed as follows: the last word "*roads*" is changed to "*routes,*" and the following words added thereto: "*but the expenses of the Post-office Department, after the first day of March, in the year of our Lord eighteen hundred and sixty-three, shall be paid out of its own revenues.*"

In the fifteenth paragraph, the word "*Union*" is stricken out, and the words "*the Confederate States*" substituted.

SECTION 9. The whole of the first paragraph is stricken out, and the following words substituted therefor: "*The importation of negroes of the African race from any foreign country other than the slaveholding States or territories of the United States of America is hereby forbidden; and Congress is required to pass such laws as shall effectually prevent the same. Congress shall also have power to prohibit the introduction of slaves from any State not a member of, or territory not belonging to, this Confederacy.*"*

In the third paragraph, after the word "*law,*" the words "*or law denying or impairing the right of property in negro slaves*" are inserted.

The fifth paragraph is changed by adding thereto the following words: "*except by a vote of two thirds of both Houses.*"

The sixth paragraph is changed by the omission of all, after the word "*another.*"

The following clauses are inserted after the seventh paragraph: "*Congress shall appropriate no money from the Treasury except by a vote of two thirds of both Houses, taken by yeas and nays, unless it be asked and estimated for by some one of the heads of departments and submitted to Congress by the President; or for the purpose of paying its own expenses and contingencies; or for the payment of claims against the Confederate States, the justice of which shall have been judicially declared by a tribunal for the investigation of claims against the Government, which it is hereby made the duty of Congress to establish.*"

"*All bills appropriating money shall specify in Federal currency the exact amount of each appropriation and the*

---

* This provision is said to have been adopted as a part of the Permanent Constitution, by the vote of the States of Georgia, Alabama, Louisiana, and Mississippi, against that of South Carolina and Florida.

purposes for which it is made; and Congress shall grant no extra compensation to any public contractor, officer, agent, or servant, after such contract shall have been made or such service rendered."

This section is further changed by adding to it the first eight amendments to the Constitution of the United States, followed by this paragraph: "*Every law or resolution having the force of law, shall relate to but one subject, and that shall be expressed in the title.*"

SECTION 10. The first paragraph is changed by striking out the following words: "*emit bills of credit;*" also by inserting the word "*or*" between the word "*attainder*" and the words "*ex post facto.*"

The third paragraph is changed by inserting after the word "*tonnage,*" the following words: "*except on seagoing vessels, for the improvement of its rivers and harbors navigated by the said vessels; but such duties shall not conflict with any treaties of the Confederate States with foreign nations; and any surplus of revenue thus derived shall, after making such improvement, be paid into the common Treasury; nor shall any State*". Also the following clause is added to this paragraph: "*But when any river divides or flows through two or more States, they may enter into compacts with each other to improve the navigation thereof.*"

ARTICLE II.

SECTION 1. The first paragraph is so altered as to read as follows: "*The executive power shall be vested in a President of the Confederate States of America. He and the Vice President shall hold their offices for the term of six years; but the President shall not be re-eligible. The President and Vice President shall be elected as follows:*"

The third paragraph is stricken out, and the twelfth article of the amendments to the Constitution of the United States substituted.

The fifth paragraph is changed in the following respects: the words "*or a citizen of the United States*" are stricken out, and the words "*of the Confederate States, or a citizen thereof*" substituted; also after the word "*Constitution,*" the following words are inserted: "*or a citizen thereof born in the United States, prior to the 20th of December, 1860;*" also the words "*United States*" at the close of the paragraph, are stricken out, and the words "*limits of the Confederate States, as they may exist at the time of his election*" are substituted.

The eighth paragraph is changed by substituting the word "*enters*" for the word "*enter.*"

The last paragraph is changed by striking out the words "*of the United States*" at the close, and substituting the word "*thereof.*"

SECTION 2. The second paragraph is changed by adding thereto the words following: "*The principal officer in each of the executive departments, and all persons connected with the diplomatic service, may be removed from office at the pleasure of the President. All other civil officers of the executive department may be removed at any time by the President, or other appointing power, when their services are unnecessary, or for dishonesty, incapacity, inefficiency, misconduct, or neglect of duty; and when so removed, the removal shall be reported to the Senate, together with the reasons therefor.*"

The third paragraph is changed by dropping the word "*up*" after the word "*fill.*"

SECTION 3. This section is changed in the following respects: the first word "*He*" is stricken out and the words "*The President*" substituted; also the word "*Union*" is stricken out and the word "*Confederacy*" substituted.

ARTICLE III.

SECTION 1. In this section the word "*supreme*" is stricken out and the word "*Superior*" substituted in the first sentence of the first paragraph.

SECTION 2. This section is changed as follows: after the clause "*citizens of another State,*" the following clause is inserted: "*where the State is plaintiff;*" also the next simple sentence is changed by inserting the words "*claiming lands under grants*" between the word "*citizens*" and the word "*of;*" also the following clause is stricken out: "*between citizens of the same State claiming lands under grants of different States;*" also the following clause is added to the first paragraph: "*but no State shall be sued by a citizen or subject of any foreign State;*" also in the first part of this paragraph the following clauses: "*in law and equity,*" and "*arising under this Constitution,*" are transposed.

In the third paragraph, in the clause "*where the said crimes shall have been committed,*" the word "*crimes*" is changed to the word "*crime.*"

ARTICLE IV.

SECTION 1. No change.

SECTION 2. The first paragraph is changed by adding thereto the following clauses: "*and shall have the right of transit and sojourn in any State of this Confederacy, with their slaves and other property; and the right of property in such slaves shall not be thereby impaired.*"

The third paragraph is changed in the following respects: after the first word "*No*" the words "*slave or*" are inserted; also the words "*one State*" are stricken out, and the words "*any State or Territory of the Confederate States*" are substituted; also, after the word "*escaping*" the words "*or lawfully carried into*" are inserted; also the words "*slave belongs, or to whom such*" are inserted between the word "*such*" and the word "*service,*" near the close of the paragraph.

SECTION 3. The first paragraph is changed by striking out all the words to and including the word "*Union,*" and substituting the words "*Other States may be admitted into this Confederacy by a vote of two thirds of the whole House of Representatives and two thirds of the Senate, the Senate voting by States.*"

The second paragraph is changed by striking out all after the word "*regulations*" and inserting the following clauses: "*concerning the property of the Confederate States, including the lands thereof.*"

"*The Confederate States may acquire new territory, and Congress shall have power to legislate and provide governments for the inhabitants of all territory belonging to the Confederate States lying without the limits of the several States, and may permit them, at such times and in such manner as it may by law provide, to form States to be admitted into the Confederacy. In all such territory the institution of negro slavery as it now exists in the Confederate States shall be recognized and protected by Congress and by the territorial government, and the inhabitants of the several Confederate States and territories shall have the right to take to such territory any slaves lawfully held by them in any of the States or Territories of the Confederate States.*"

SECTION 4. This section is changed as follows: the words "*in this Union*" are stricken out, and the words "*that now is, or hereafter may become, a member of this Confederacy*" inserted; also, after the word "*Legislature,*" the words "*cannot be convened*" are dropped, and the words "*is not in session,*" substituted; also this entire section is omitted, as a section, and placed at the end of section 3, as a paragraph thereof.

ARTICLE V.

This article is stricken out entirely, and the following substituted: "*Upon the demand of any three States, legally assembled in their several Conventions, the Congress shall summon a Convention of all the States, to take into consideration such amendments to the Constitution as the said States shall concur in suggesting at the time when the said demand is made; and should any of the proposed amendments to the Constitution be agreed on by the said Convention—voting by States—and the same be ratified by the Legislatures of two-thirds of the several States, or by Conventions in two-thirds thereof—as the one or the other mode of ratification may be proposed by the general Convention—they shall henceforward form a part of this Constitution. But no State shall, without its consent, be deprived of its equal representation in the Senate.*"

ARTICLE VI.

This article is preceded by the following paragraph: "*The Government established by this Constitution is the successor of the Provisional Government of the Confederate States of America, and all laws passed by the latter shall continue in force until the same shall be repealed or modified; and all the officers appointed by the same shall remain in office until their successors are appointed and qualified or the offices abolished.*"

The first paragraph is changed by striking out the word "*Confederation*" and substituting the words "*Provisional Government.*"

In the second paragraph, the words "*which shall be*" following the word "*States*" are stricken out.

This article is also changed by adding thereto the 9th and 10th articles of the Amendments to the Constitution of the United States, as two additional paragraphs, after adding to the 9th Article the words: "*of the several States.*"

ARTICLE VII.

The first paragraph is changed by substituting the word "*five*" for the word "*nine*" preceding the word "*States.*"

Also the following paragraph is added to the foregoing as amended:

"*When five States shall have ratified this Constitution, in the manner before specified, the Congress under the Provisional Constitution shall prescribe the time for holding the election of President and Vice President; and for the meeting of the electoral college; and for counting the votes and inaugurating the President. They shall also prescribe the time for holding the first election of members of Congress under this Constitution, and the time for assembling the same. Until the assembling of such Congress, the Congress under the provisional Constitution shall continue to exercise the legislative powers granted them, not extending beyond the time limited by the Constitution of the Provisional Government."*

The final paragraph: "*Done in convention by the unanimous consent,*" &c., is omitted, and the words following substituted: "*Adopted unanimously, March* 11, 1861."

Index to the Constitution of the United States, and of the "Confederate" States.

	U. S.		"C." S.	
	Art.	Sec.	Art.	Sec.
Senators shall not be elector	2	1	2	1
Senators and Representatives, election of, how prescribed	1	4	1	4
Slaves, their importation may be prohibited after 1808	1	9		
their importation prohibited, no law to be passed impairing right of property in	......	......	1	9
right of transit and sojourn with, in any State, guarantied	......	......	4	2
introduction of, from any State not a member of the Confederacy, may be prohibited by Congress	......	......	1	9
Soldiers not to be quartered on citizens	3 A	m'd.	1	9
Speaker, how chosen	1	2	1	2
Speech, freedom of	1 A	m'd.	1	9
States prohibited from—				
entering into treaty, alliance, or confederation	1	10	1	10
granting letters of marque	1	10	1	10
coining money	1	10	1	10
emitting bills of credit	1	10		
making anything a tender but gold and silver	1	10	1	10
passing bills of attainder, *ex post facto* laws, or laws impairing contracts	1	10	1	10
granting titles of nobility	1	10	1	10
laying duties on imports and exports	1	10	1	10
laying duties on tonnage	1	10	1	10
may lay tonnage duty on sea-going vessels for the improvement of rivers, &c.	......	......	1	10
keeping troops or ships of war in time of peace	1	10	1	10
entering into any agreement or compact with another State or foreign Power	1	10	1	10
may enter into compact for improvement of certain rivers	......	......	1	10
engaging in war	1	10	1	10
States, new, may be admitted into the Union (or Confederacy)	4	3	4	3
new, may be admitted upon two-thirds vote of both Houses, the Senate voting by States	......	......	4	3
may be formed within the jurisdiction of others, or by the junction of two or more, with the consent of Congress and the Legislatures of the States concerned	4	3	4	3
State judges bound to consider treaties, the Constitution, and the laws under it, as supreme	6	1	6	1
State, every, guarantied a republican form of government, protected by the United (or Confederate) States	4	4	4	4
Supreme Court—(See Court and Judiciary.)				
Suits at Common Law, proceedings in	7 A	m'd.	1	9
T				
Tax, direct, according to representation	1	2	1	2
shall be laid only in proportion to census	1	9	1	9
on exports prohibited	1	9		
except by vote of two-thirds of both Houses	......	......	1	9
Tender, what shall be a legal	1	10	1	10
Territory, or public property, Congress may make rules concerning	4	3		
Test, religious, shall not be required	6	1	6	1
Titles, (see Nobility.)				
Title from foreign State prohibited	1	9	1	9
Treason, defined	3	3	3	3
two witnesses, or confession, necessary for conviction	3	3	3	3
punishment of, may be prescribed by Congress	3	3	3	3
Treasury, money drawn from only by appropriation	1	9	1	9
Treaties, how made	2	2	2	2
the supreme law	6	1	6	1
States cannot make	1	10	1	10
V.				
Vacancies happening during the recess may be filled temporarily by the President	2	2	2	2
Vacancies in representation in Congress, how filled	1	2	1	2
Veto of the President, effect of and proceedings on	1	7	1	7
Vice-President to be President of the Senate	1	3	1	3
how elected	2	1	2	1
also, Amendment	12			
shall in certain cases discharge the duties of President	2	1	2	1
may be removed by impeachment	2	4	2	4
Vote of one house requiring the concurrence of the other	1	7	1	7
W.				
War, Congress to declare	1	8	1	8
Warrants for searches and seizures, when and how they shall issue	4 A	m'd.	1	9
Witness in criminal cases, no one compelled to be against himself	5 A	m'd.	1	9
Weights and Measures, standard of	1	8	1	8
Y.				
Yeas and Nays entered on journal, and published	1	5	1	5

THEIR CONSTITUTION AS INTERPRETED BY THE "CONFEDERATE" VICE PRESIDENT.

1861, March 21, ALEX. H. STEPHENS delivered a speech at Savannah, in explanation and vindication of the Constitution, from which this is a well known extract:

"The new Constitution has put at rest forever all the agitating questions relating to our peculiar institutions—African slavery as it exists among us—the proper status of the negro in our form of civilization. *This was the immediate cause of the late rupture and present revolution. Jefferson, in his forecast, had anticipated this as the 'rock upon which the old Union would split.'* He was right. What was conjecture with him, is now a realized fact. But whether he fully comprehended the great truth upon which that rock stood and stands, may be doubted. The prevailing ideas entertained by him and most of the leading statesmen at the time of the formation of the old Constitution, were that the enslavement of the African was in violation of the laws of nature: that it was wrong in principle, socially, morally, and politically. It was an evil they knew not well how to deal with, but the general opinion of the men of that day was, that somehow or other, in the order of Providence, the institution would be evanescent and pass away. This idea, though not incorporated in the Constitution, was the prevailing idea at the time. The Constitution, it is true, secured every essential guarantee to the institution while it should last, and hence no argument can be justly used against the constitutional guarantees thus secured, because of the common sentiment of the day. Those ideas, however, were fundamentally wrong. They rested upon the assumption of the equality of races. This was an error. It was a sandy foundation, and the idea of a government built upon it; when the 'storm came and the wind blew, it fell.'

"Our new Government is founded upon exactly the opposite idea; its foundations are laid, its corner stone rests upon the great truth that the negro is not equal to the white man. That slavery—subordination to the superior race, is his natural and normal condition. This, our new Government, is the first, in the history of the world, based upon this great physical and moral truth. This truth has been slow in the process of its development, like all other truths in the various departments of science. It has been so even amongst us. Many who hear me, perhaps, can recollect well, that this truth was not generally admitted, even within their day. The errors of the past generation still clung to many as late as twenty years ago. Those at the North who still cling to these errors, with a zeal above knowledge, we justly denominate fanatics. * * *

"In the conflict thus far, success has been, on our side, complete throughout the length and breadth of the Confederate States. It is upon this, as I have stated, our actual fabric is firmly planted; and I cannot permit myself to doubt the ultimate success of a full recognition of this principle throughout the civilized and enlightened world.

"As I have stated, the truth of this principle may be slow in development, as all truths are, and ever have been, in the various branches of science. It was so with the principles announced by Galileo—it was so with Adam Smith and his principles of political economy—it was so with Harvey and his theory of the circulation of the blood. It is stated that not a single one of the medical profession, living at the time of the announcement of the truths made by him, admitted them. Now they are universally acknowledged. May we not, therefore, look with confidence to the ultimate universal acknowledgment of the truths upon which our system rests. It is the first government ever instituted upon principles of strict conformity to nature, and the ordination of Providence, in furnishing the materials of human society. Many governments have been founded upon the principle of certain classes; but the classes thus enslaved, were of the same race, and in violation of the laws of nature. Our system commits no such violation of nature's laws. The negro, by nature, or by the curse against Canaan, is fitted for that condition which he occupies in our system. The architect, in the construction of buildings, lays the foundation with the proper materials, the granite; then comes the brick or the marble. The substratum of our society is made of the material fitted by nature for it, and by experience we know that it is best, not only for the superior, but for the inferior race that it should be so. It is, indeed, in conformity with the ordinance of the Creator. It is not for us to inquire into the wisdom of His ordinances, or to question them. For His own purposes He has made one race to differ from another, as He has made 'one star to differ from another star in glory.'

"The great objects of humanity are best attained when conformed to His laws and decrees, in the formation of governments, as well as in all things else. Our Confederacy is founded upon principles in strict conformity with these laws. This stone which was first rejected by the first builders 'is become the chief stone of the corner' in our new edifice.

"The progress of disintegration in the old Union may be expected to go on with almost absolute certainty. We are now the nucleus of a growing power, which, if we are true to ourselves, our destiny, and high mission, will become the controlling power on this continent. To what extent accessions will go on in the process of time, or where it will end, the future will determine."

ADMINISTRATION OF ABRAHAM LINCOLN.

Abraham Lincoln's Inaugural Address, March 4, 1861.

Fellow-citizens of the United States: In compliance with a custom as old as the Government itself, I appear before you to address you briefly, and to take in your presence the oath prescribed by the Constitution of the United States to be taken by the President "before he enters on the execution of his office."

I do not consider it necessary at present for me to discuss those matters of administration about which there is no special anxiety or excitement.

Apprehension seems to exist among the people of the Southern States that by the accession of a Republican Administration their property and their peace and personal security are to be endangered. There has never been any reasonable cause for such apprehension. Indeed, the most ample evidence to the contrary has all the while existed and been open to their inspection. It is found in nearly all the published speeches of him who now addresses you. I do but quote from one of those speeches when I declare that "I have no purpose, directly or indirectly, to interfere with the institution of slavery in the States where it exists. I believe I have no lawful right to do so, and I have no inclination to do so." Those who nominated and elected me did so with full knowledge that I had made this and many similar declarations, and had never recanted them. And more than this, they placed in the platform for my acceptance, and as a law to themselves and to me, the clear and emphatic resolution which I now read:

"*Resolved*, That the maintenance inviolate of the rights of the States, and especially the right of each State to order and control its own domestic institutions according to its own judgment exclusively, is essential to the balance of power on which the perfection and endurance of our political fabric depend, and we denounce the lawless invasion by armed force of the soil of any State or Territory, no matter under what pretext, as among the gravest of crimes."

I now reiterate these sentiments; and, in doing so, I only press upon the public attention the most conclusive evidence of which the case is susceptible, that the property, peace, and security of no section are to be in anywise endangered by the now incoming Administration. I add, too, that all the protection which, consistently with the Constitution and the laws, can be given, will be cheerfully given to all the States when lawfully demanded, for whatever cause — as cheerfully to one section as to another.

There is much controversy about the delivering up of fugitives from service or labor. The clause I now read is as plainly written in the Constitution as any other of its provisions:

"No person held to service or labor in one State, under the laws thereof, escaping into another, shall, in consequence of any law or regulation therein, be discharged from such service or labor but shall be delivered up on claim of the party to whom such service or labor may be due."

It is scarcely questioned that this provision was intended by those who made it for the reclaiming of what we call fugitive slaves; and the intention of the law-giver is the law. All members of Congress swear their support to the whole Constitution—to this provision as much as any other. To the proposition, then, that slaves, whose cases come within the terms of this clause, "shall be delivered up," their oaths are unanimous. Now, if they would make the effort in good temper, could they not, with nearly equal unanimity, frame and pass a law by means of which to keep good that unanimous oath?

There is some difference of opinion whetner this clause should be enforced by national or by State authority; but surely that difference is not a very material one. If the slave is to be surrendered, it can be of but little consequence to him, or to others, by which authority it is done. And should any one, in any case, be content that his oath shall go unkept, on a merely unsubstantial controversy as to *how* it shall be kept?

Again, in any law upon this subject, ought not all the safeguards of liberty known in civilized and humane jurisprudence to be introduced, so that a free man be not, in any case, surrendered as a slave? And might it not be well at the same time to provide by law for the enforcement of that clause in the Constitution which guaranties that "the citizens of each State shall be entitled to all privileges and immunities of citizens in the several States?"

I take the official oath to-day with no mental reservations, and with no purpose to construe the Constitution or laws by any hypercritical rules. And while I do not choose now to specify particular acts of Congress as proper to be enforced, I do suggest that it will be much safer for all, both in official and private stations, to conform to and abide by all those acts which stand unrepealed, than to violate any of them, trusting to find impunity in having them held to be unconstitutional.

It is seventy-two years since the first inauguration of a President under our National Constitution. During that period fifteen different and greatly distinguished citizens have, in succession, administered the Executive branch of the Government. They have conducted it through many perils, and generally with great success. Yet, with all this scope for precedent, I now enter upon the same task for the brief constitutional term of four years under great and peculiar difficulty. A disruption of the Federal Union, heretofore only menaced, is now formidably attempted.

I hold that, in contemplation of universal law, and of the Constitution, the Union of these States is perpetual. Perpetuity is implied, if not expressed, in the fundamental law of all National Governments. It is safe to assert that no Government proper ever had a provision in its organic law for its own termination. Continue to execute all the express provisions to our National Constitution, and the Union will endure forever—it being impossible to destroy it, except by some action not provided for in the instrument itself.

Again, if the United States be not a Government proper, but an association of States in the nature of the contract merely, can it, as a contract, be peaceably unmade by less than all the parties who made it? One party to a contract may violate it—break it, so to speak; but does it not require all to lawfully rescind it?

Descending from these general principles, we find the proposition that, in legal contemplation, the Union is perpetual, confirmed by the history of the Union itself. The Union is much older than the Constitution. It was formed in fact by the Articles of Association in 1774. It was matured and continued by the Declaration of Independence in 1776. It was further matured, and the faith of all the then thirteen States expressly plighted and engaged that it should be perpetual, by the Articles of Confederation in 1778. And, finally, in 1787, one of the declared objects for ordaining and establishing the Constitution was "*to form a more perfect union.*"

But if destruction of the Union, by one, or by a part only, of the States, be lawfully possible, the Union is *less* perfect than before, the Constitution having lost the vital element of perpetuity.

It follows, from these views, that no State, upon its own mere motion, can lawfully get out of the Union; that *resolves* and *ordinances* to that effect are legally void, and that acts of violence, within any State or States, against the authority of the United States, are insurrectionary or revolutionary, according to circumstances.

I, therefore, consider that, in view of the Constitution and the laws, the Union is unbroken, and, to the extent of my ability, I shall take care, as the Constitution itself expressly enjoins upon me, that the laws of the Union be faithfully executed in all the States. Doing this I deem to be only a simple duty on my part; and I shall perform it, so far as practicable, unless my rightful masters, the American people, shall withhold the requisite means, or, in some authoritative manner, direct the contrary. I trust this will not be regarded as a menace, but only as a declared purpose of the Union that it *will* constitutionally defend and maintain itself.

In doing this there need be no bloodshed or violence; and there shall be none, unless it be forced upon the national authority. The power confided to me will be used to hold, occupy, and possess the property and places belonging to the Government, and to collect the duties and imposts; but, beyond what may be necessary for these objects, there will be no invasion, no using of force against or among the people anywhere. Where hostility to the United States, in any interior locality, shall be so great and universal as to prevent competent resident citizens from holding the Federal offices, there will be no attempt to force obnoxious strangers among the people for that object. While the strict legal right may exist in the Government to enforce the exercise of these offices, the attempt to do so would be so irritating, and so nearly impracticable with all, I deem it better to forego, for the time, the uses of such offices.

The mails, unless repelled, will continue to be furnished in all parts of the Union. So far as possible, the people everywhere shall have that sense of perfect security which is most favorable to calm thought and reflection. The course here indicated will be followed, unless current events and experience shall show a modification or change to be proper, and in every case and exigency my best discretion will be exercised, according to circumstances actually existing, and with a view and a hope of a peaceful solution of the national troubles, and the restoration of fraternal sympathies and affections.

That there are persons in one section or another who seek to destroy the Union at all events, and are glad of any pretext to do it, I will neither affirm nor deny; but if there be such I need address no word to them. To those, however, who really love the Union, may I not speak?

Before entering upon so grave a matter as the destruction of our national fabric, with all its benefits, its memories, and its hopes, would it not be wise to ascertain precisely why we do it? Will you hazard so desperate a step while there is any possibility that any portion of the ills you fly from have no real existence? Will you, while the certain ills you fly to are greater than all the real ones you fly from—will you risk the commission of so fearful a mistake?

All profess to be content in the Union, if all constitutional rights can be maintained. Is it true, then, that any right, plainly written in the Constitution, has been denied? I think not. Happily the human mind is so constituted that no party can reach to the audacity of doing this. Think, if you can, of a single instance in which a plainly written provision of the Constitution has ever been denied. If, by the mere force of numbers, a majority should deprive a minority of any clearly written constitutional right, it might, in a moral point of view, justify revolution—certainly would if such right were a vital one. But such is not our case. All the vital rights of minorities and of individuals are so plainly assured to them by affirmations and negations, guarantees and prohibitions in the Constitution, that controversies never arise concerning them. But no organic law can ever be framed with a provision specifically applicable to every question which may occur in practical administration. No foresight can anticipate, nor any document of reasonable length contain express provisions for all possible questions. Shall fugitives from labor be surrendered by National or by State authority? The Constitution does not expressly say. *May* Congress prohibit slavery in the Territories? The Constitution does not expressly say. *Must* Congress protect slavery in the Territories? The Constitution does not expressly say.

From questions of this class spring all our constitutional controversies, and we divide upon them into majorities and minorities. If the minority will not acquiesce the majority must, or the Government must cease. There is no other alternative; for continuing the Government is acquiescence on one side or the other. If a minority in such case will secede rather than acquiesce they make a precedent which, in turn, will divide and ruin them; for a minority of their own will secede from them whenever a majority refuses to be controlled by such minority. For instance, why may not any portion of a new Confederacy, a year or two hence, arbitrarily secede again, precisely as portions of the present Union now claim to secede from it? All who cherish disunion sentiments are now being educated to the exact temper of doing this.

Is there such perfect identity of interests among the States to compose a new Union, as to produce harmony only, and prevent renewed secession?

Plainly, the central idea of secession is the essence of anarchy. A majority held in restraint by constitutional checks and limitations and always changing easily with deliberate changes of popular opinions and sentiments, is the only true sovereign of a free people. Whoever rejects it, does, of necessity, fly to anarchy or to despotism. Unanimity is impossible; the rule of a minority, as a permanent arrangement, is wholly inadmissible; so that, rejecting the majority principle, anarchy or despotism in some form is all that is left.

I do not forget the position assumed by some, that constitutional questions are to be decided by the Supreme Court; nor do I deny that such decision must be binding, in any case, upon the parties to a suit, as to the object of that suit, while they are also entitled to very high respect and consideration in all parallel cases by all other departments of the Government. And while it is obviously possible that such decision may be erroneous in any given case, still the evil effect following it, being limited to that particular case, with the chance that it may be overruled, and never become a precedent for other cases, can better be borne than could the evils of a different practice. At the same time the candid citizen must confess that if the policy of the Government upon vital questions, affecting the whole people, is to be irrevocably fixed by decisions of the Supreme Court, the instant they are made in ordinary litigation between parties in personal actions the people will have ceased to be their own rulers, having to that extent practically resigned their government into the hands of that eminent tribunal.

Nor is there in this view any assault upon the Court or the Judges. It is a duty from which they may not shrink to decide cases properly brought before them, and it is no fault of theirs if others seek to turn their decisions to political purposes. One section of our country believes slavery is *right*, and ought to be extended, while the other believes it is *wrong*, and ought not to be extended. This is the only substantial dispute. The fugitive slave clause of the Constitution, and the law for the suppression of the foreign slave trade, are each as well enforced, perhaps, as any law can ever be in a community where the moral sense of the people imperfectly supports the law itself. The great body of the people abide by the dry legal obligation in both cases, and a few break over in each. This, I think, cannot be perfectly cured; and it would be worse in both cases *after* the separation of the sections than before. The foreign slave trade, now imperfectly suppressed, would be ultimately revived without restriction in one section; while fugitive slaves, now only partially surrendered, would not be surrendered at all, by the other.

Physically speaking, we cannot separate. We cannot remove our respective sections from each other, nor build an impassable wall between them. A husband and wife may be divorced, and go out of the presence and beyond the reach of each other; but the different parts of our country cannot do this. They cannot but remain face to face; and intercourse, either amicable or hostile, must continue between them. Is it possible, then, to make that intercourse more advantageous or more satisfactory *after* separation than *before*? Can aliens make treaties easier than friends can make laws? Can treaties be more faithfully enforced between aliens than laws can among friends? Suppose you go to war, you cannot fight always; and when after much loss on both sides, and no gain on either, you cease fighting, the indentical old questions, as to terms of intercourse, are again upon you.

This country, with its institutions, belongs to the people who inhabit it. Whenever they shall grow weary of the existing Government they can exercise their *constitutional* right of amending it, or their *revolutionary* right to dismember or overthrow it. I cannot be ignorant of the fact that many worthy and patriotic citizens are desirous of having the National Constitution amended. While I make no recommendation of amendments, I fully recognize the rightful authority of the people over the whole subject, to be exercised in either of the modes prescribed in the instrument itself; and I should under existing circumstances, favor rather than oppose a fair opportunity being afforded the people to act upon it. I will venture to add that to me the convention mode seems preferable, in that it allows amendments to originate with the people themselves, instead of only permitting them to take or reject propositions originated by others, not especially chosen for the purpose, and which might not be precisely such as they would wish to either accept or refuse. I understand a proposed amendment to the Constitution—which amendment, however, I have not seen—has passed Congress, to the effect that the Federal Government shall never interfere with the domestic institutions of the States, including that of persons held to service. To avoid misconstruction of what I have said, I depart from my purpose not to speak of particular amendments so far as to say that, holding such a provision now to be implied constitutional law, I have no objection to its being made express and irrevocable.

The Chief Magistrate derives all his authority from the people, and they have conferred none upon him to fix terms for the separation of the States. The people themselves can do this also if they choose; but the Executive, as such, has nothing to do with it. His duty is to administer the present Government, as it came to his hands, and to transmit it, unimpaired by him, to his successor.

Why should there not be a patient confidence in the ultimate justice of the people? Is there any better or equal hope in the world? In our present differences is either party without faith of being in the right? If the Almighty Ruler of Nations, with his eternal truth and justice, be on your side of the North, or on yours of the South, that truth and that justice will surely prevail, by the judgment of this great tribunal of the American people.

By the frame of the Government under which we live, this same people have wisely given their public servants but little power for mischief; and have, with equal wisdom, provided for the return of that little to their own hands at very short intervals. While the people retain their virtue and vigilance, no Administration, by any extreme of weakness or folly, can very seriously injure the Government in the short space of four years.

My countrymen, and all, think calmly and *well* upon this whole subject. Nothing valuable can be lost by taking time. If there be an object to hurry any of you, in hot haste, to a step which you would never take *deliberately*, that object will be frustrated by taking time; but no good object can be frustrated by it. Such of you as are now dissatisfied, still have the old Constitution unimpaired, and, on the sensitive point, the laws of your own framing under it; while the new Administration will have no immediate power, if it would, to change either. If it were admitted that you who are dissatisfied hold the right side in the dispute, there still is no single good reason for precipitate action. Intelligence, patriotism, christianity, and a firm reliance on Him who has never yet forsaken this favored land, are still competent to adjust, in the best way, all our present difficulty.

In *your* hands, my dissatisfied fellow-countrymen, and not in *mine*, is the momentous issue of civil war. The Government will not assail *you*. You can have no conflict without being yourselves the aggressors. *You* have no oath registered in Heaven to destroy the Government, while I shall have the most solemn one to "preserve, protect, and defend it."

I am loth to close. We are not enemies, but friends. We must not be enemies. Though passion may have strained, it must not break our bonds of affection. The mystic chords of memory, stretching from every battle-field and patriot grave to every living heart and hearthstone, all over this broad land, will yet swell the chorus of the Union, when again touched, as surely they will be, by the better angels of our nature.

PRESIDENT LINCOLN'S CABINET.

Secretary of State—WILLIAM H. SEWARD, of New York.

Secretary of the Treasury—SALMON P. CHASE, of Ohio; succeeded July 5, 1864, by WM. PITT FESSENDEN, of Maine.

Secretary of War—SIMON CAMERON, of Pennsylvania; succeeded January 11, 1862, by EDWIN M. STANTON, of Ohio.

Secretary of the Navy—GIDEON WELLES, of Connecticut.

Secretary of the Interior—CALEB B. SMITH, of Indiana; succeeded January 8, 1863, by JOHN P. USHER, of Indiana.

Attorney General—EDWARD BATES, of Missouri; succeeded December 14, 1864, by JAMES SPEED, of Kentucky.

Postmaster General—MONTGOMERY BLAIR, of Maryland; succeeded October 1, 1864, by WILLIAM DENNISON, of Ohio.

MR. SEWARD AND "THE COMMISSIONERS OF THE SOUTHERN CONFEDERACY."

[Memorandum.] DEPARTMENT OF STATE,
WASHINGTON, *March* 15, 1861.

Mr. John Forsyth, of the State of Alabama, and Mr. Martin J. Crawford, of the State of Georgia, on the 11th instant, through the kind offices of a distinguished Senator, submitted to the Secretary of State their desire for an unofficial interview. This request was, on the 12th instant, upon exclusively public considerations, respectfully declined.

On the 13th instant, while the Secretary was preoccupied, Mr. A. P. Banks, of Virginia, called at this Department and was received by the Assistant Secretary, to whom he delivered a sealed communication, which he had been charged by Messrs. Forsyth and Crawford to present to the Secretary in person.

In that communication Messrs. Forsyth and Crawford inform the Secretary of State that they have been duly accredited by the Government of the Confederate States of America as Commissioners to the Government of the United States, and they set forth the object of their attendance at Washington. They observe that seven States of the American Union, in the exercise of a right inherent in every free people, have withdrawn, through conventions of their people, from the United States, reassumed the attribute of sovereign power, and formed a Government of their own, and that those Confederate States now constitute an independent nation *de facto* and *de jure*, and possess a Government perfect in all its parts, and fully endowed with all the means of self-support.

Messrs. Forsyth and Crawford, in the aforesaid communication, thereupon proceed to inform the Secretary that, with a view to a speedy adjustment of all questions growing out of the political separation thus assumed, upon such terms of amity and good will as the respective interests, geographical contiguity, and the future welfare of the supposed two nations might render necessary, they are instructed to make to the Government of the United States overtures for the opening of negotiations, assuring this

Government that the President, Congress, and people of the Confederate States earnestly desire a peaceful solution of these great questions, and that it is neither their interest nor their wish to make any demand which is not founded in strictest justice, nor to do any act to injure their late confederates.

After making these statements, Messrs. Forsyth and Crawford close their communication, as they say, in obedience to the instructions of their Government, by requesting the Secretary of State to appoint as early a day as possible in order that they may present to the President of the United States the credentials which they bear, and the objects of the mission with which they are charged.

The Secretary of State frankly confesses that he understands the events which have recently occurred, and the condition of political affairs which actually exists in the part of the Union to which his attention has thus been directed, very differently from the aspect in which they are presented by Messrs. Forsyth and Crawford. He sees in them not a rightful and accomplished revolution and an independent nation, with an established Government, but rather a perversion of a temporary and partisan excitement to the inconsiderate purpose of an unjustifiable and unconstitutional aggression upon the rights and the authority vested in the Federal Government, and hitherto benignly exercised, as from their very nature they always must be so exercised, for the maintenance of the Union, the preservation of liberty, and the security, peace, welfare, happiness, and aggrandizement of the American people.

The Secretary of State, therefore, avows to Messrs. Forsyth and Crawford that he looks patiently but confidently for the cure of evils which have resulted from proceedings so unnecessary, so unwise, so unusual, and so unnatural, not to irregular negotiations, having in view new and untried relations with agencies unknown to and acting in derogation of the Constitution and laws, but to regular and considerate action of the people of those States, in co-operation with their brethren in the other States, through the Congress of the United States, and such extraordinary Conventions, if there shall be need thereof, as the Federal Constitution contemplates and authorizes to be assembled. It is, however, the purpose of the Secretary of State on this occasion not to invite or engage in any discussion of these subjects, but simply to set forth his reasons for declining to comply with the request of Messrs. Forsyth and Crawford.

On the 4th of March instant the then newly elected President of the United States, in view of all the facts bearing on the present question, assumed the Executive administration of the Government, first delivering, in accordance with an early and honored custom, an inaugural address to the people of the United States. The Secretary of State respectfully submits a copy of this address to Messrs. Forsyth and Crawford. A simple reference to it will be sufficient to satisfy those gentlemen that the Secretary of State, guided by the principles therein announced, is prevented altogether from admitting or assuming that the States referred to by them, have, in law or in fact, withdrawn from the Federal Union, or that they could do so in the manner described by Messrs. Forsyth and Crawford, or in any other manner than with the consent and concert of the people of the United States, to be given through a National Convention, to be assembled in conformity with the provisions of the Constitution of the United States. Of course the Secretary of State cannot act upon the assumption, or in any way admit that the so-called Confederate States constitute a foreign Power, with whom diplomatic relations ought to be established.

Under these circumstances the Secretary of State, whose official duties are confined, subject to the direction of the President, to the conducting of the foreign relations of the country, and do not at all embrace domestic questions or questions arising between the several States and the Federal Government, is unable to comply with the request of Messrs. Forsyth and Crawford, to appoint a day on which they may present the evidences of their authority and the object of their visit to the President of the United States. On the contrary, he is obliged to state to Messrs Forsyth and Crawford that he has no authority, nor is he at liberty to recognize them as diplomatic agents, or hold correspondence or other communication with them.

Finally, the Secretary of State would observe that, although he has supposed that he might safely and with propriety have adopted these conclusions without making any reference of the subject to the Executive, yet so strong has been his desire to practice entire directness and to act in a spirit of perfect respect and candor towards Messrs. Forsyth and Crawford, and that portion of the people of the Union in whose name they present themselves before him, that he has cheerfully submitted this paper to the President, who coincides generally in the views it expresses, and sanctions the Secretary's decision declining official intercourse with Messrs. Forsyth and Crawford.

APRIL 8, 1861.

The foregoing memorandum was filed in this Department on the 15th of March last. A delivery of the same, however, to Messrs. Forsyth and Crawford was delayed, as was understood, with their consent. They have now, through their secretary, communicated their desire for a definitive disposition of the subject. The Secretary of State therefore directs that a duly verified copy of the paper be now delivered.

A true copy of the original, delivered to me by Mr. F. W. Seward, Assistant Secretary of State of the United States, on April 8th, 1861, at 2.15 P. M., in blank envelope.

ATTEST: J. T. PICKETT,
Secretary to the Commissioners.

The Commissioners in reply to Mr. Seward.

WASHINGTON, *April* 9, 1861.

Hon. WM. H. SEWARD, *Secretary of State of the United States, Washington.*

The "memorandum," dated Department of State, Washington, March 15, 1861, with postscript under date of 8th instant, has been received through the hands of Mr. J. T. Pickett, secretary to this commission, who, by the instructions of the undersigned, called for it on yesterday at the Department.

In that memorandum you correctly state the purport of the official note addressed to you by the undersigned on the 12th ultimo. Without repeating the contents of that note in full, it is enough to say here that its object was to invite the Government of the United States to a friendly consideration of the relations between the United States and the seven States lately of the Federal Union, but now separated from it by the sovereign will of their people, growing out of the pregnant and undeniable fact that those people have rejected the authority of the United States and established a Government of their own. Those relations had to be friendly or hostile. The people of the old and new Governments, occupying contiguous territories, had to stand to each other in the relation of good neighbors, each seeking their happiness and pursuing their national destinies in their own way, without interference with the other, or they had to be rival and hostile nations. The Government of the Confederate States had no hesitation in electing its choice in this alternative. Frankly and unreservedly, seeking the good of the people who had entrusted them with power, in the spirit of humanity, of the Christian civilization of the age, and of that Americanism which regards the true welfare and happiness of the people, the Government of the Confederate States, among its first acts, commissioned the undersigned to approach the Government of the United States with the olive branch of peace, and to offer to adjust the great questions pending between them in the only way to be justified by the consciences and common sense of good men who had nothing but the welfare of the people of the two Confederacies at heart.

Your Government has not chosen to meet the undersigned in the conciliatory and peaceful spirit in which they are commissioned. Persistently wedded to those fatal theories of construction of the Federal Constitution always rejected by the statesmen of the South, and adhered to by those of the Administration school, until they have produced their natural and often predicted result of the destruction of the Union, under which we might have continued to live happily and gloriously together had the spirit of the ancestry who framed the common Constitution animated the hearts of all their sons, you now, with a persistence untaught and uncured by the ruin which has been wrought, refuse to recognize the great fact presented to you of a completed and successful revolution; you close your eyes to the existence of the Government founded upon it, and ignore the high duties of moderation and humanity which attach to you in dealing with this great fact. Had you met these issues with the frankness and manliness with which the undersigned were instructed to present them to you and treat them, the undersigned had not now the melancholy duty to return home and tell their Government and their countrymen that their earnest and ceaseless efforts in behalf of peace had been futile, and that the Government of the United States meant to subjugate them by force of arms. Whatever may be the result, impartial history will record the innocence of the Government of the Confederate States, and place the responsibility of the blood and mourning that may ensue upon those who have denied the great fundamental doctrine of American liberty, that "Governments derive their just powers from the consent of the governed," and who have set naval and land armaments in motion to subject the people of one portion of this land to the will of another portion. That that can never be done while a freeman survives in the Confederate States to wield a weapon, the undersigned appeal to past history to prove. These military demonstrations against the people of the seceded States are certainly far from being in keeping and consistency with the theory of the Secretary of State, maintained in his memorandum, that these States are still component parts of the late American Union, as the undersigned are not aware of any constitutional power in the President of the United States to levy war, without the consent of Congress, upon a foreign people, much less upon any portion of the people of the United States.

The undersigned, like the Secretary of State, have no purpose to "invite or engage in discussion" of the subject on which their two Governments are so irreconcilably at variance. It is this variance that has broken up the old Union, the disintegration of which has only begun. It is proper, however, to advise you that it were well to dismiss the hopes you seem to entertain that, by any of the modes indicated, the people of the Confederate States will ever be brought to submit to the authority of the Government of the United States. You are dealing with delusions, too, when you seek to separate our people from our Government and to characterize the deliberate, sovereign act of that people as a "perversion of a temporary and partisan excitement." If you cherish these dreams you will be awakened from them and find them as unreal and unsubstantial as others in which you have recently indulged. The undersigned would omit the performance of an obvious duty were they to fail to make known to the Government of the United States that the people of the Confederate States have declared their independence with a full knowledge of all the responsibilities of that act, and with as firm a determination to maintain it by all the means with which nature has endowed them as that which sustained their fathers when they threw off the authority of the British crown.

The undersigned clearly understand that you have declined to appoint a day to enable them to lay the objects of the mission with which they are charged before the President of the United States, because so to do would be to recognize the independence and separate nationality of the Confederate States. This is the vein of thought that pervades the memorandum before us. The truth of history requires that it should distinctly appear upon the record that the undersigned did not ask the Government of the United States to recognize the independence of the Confederate States. They only asked audience to adjust, in a spirit of amity and peace, the new relations springing from a manifest and accomplished revolution in the Government of the late Federal Union. Your refusal to entertain these overtures for a peaceful solution, the active naval and military preparation of this Government, and a formal notice to the commanding general of the Confederate forces in the harbor of Charleston that the President intends to provision Fort Sumter by forcible means, if necessary, are viewed by the undersigned, and can only be received by the world, as a declaration of war against the Confederate States; for the President of the United States knows that Fort Sumter cannot be provisioned without the effusion of blood. The undersigned, in behalf of their Government and people, accept the gage of battle thus thrown down to them, and, appealing to God and the judgment of mankind for the righteousness of their cause, the people of the Confederate States will defend their liberties to the last against this flagrant and open attempt at their subjugation to sectional power.

This communication cannot be properly closed without adverting to the date of your memorandum. The official note of the undersigned, of the 12th March, was delivered to the Assistant Secretary of State on the 13th of that month, the gentleman who delivered it informing him that the Secretary of this commission would call at twelve o'clock, noon, on the next day for an answer. At the appointed hour Mr. Pickett did call, and was informed by the Assistant Secretary of State that the engagements of the Secretary of State had prevented him from giving the note his attention. The Assistant Secretary of State then asked for the address of Messrs. Crawford and Forsyth, the members of the Commission then present in this city, took note of the address on a card, and engaged to send whatever reply might be made to their lodgings. Why this was not done it is proper should be here explained. The memorandum is dated March 15, and was not delivered until April 8. Why was it withheld during the intervening twenty-three days? In the postscript to your memorandum you say it "was delayed, as was understood, with their (Messrs. Forsyth and Crawford's) consent." This is true; but it is also true that on the 15th of March Messrs. Forsyth and Crawford were assured, by a person occupying a high official position in the Government, and who, as they believed, was speaking by authority, that Fort Sumter would be evacuated within a very few days, and that no measure changing the existing status prejudicially to the Confederate States, as respects Fort Pickens, was then contemplated, and these assurances were subsequently repeated, with the addition that any contemplated change as respects Fort Pickens would be notified to us. On the 1st of April we were again informed that there might be an attempt to supply Fort Sumter with provisions, but that Governor Pickens should have previous notice of this attempt. There was no suggestion of a reinforcement. The undersigned did not hesitate to believe that these assurances expressed the intention of the Administration at the time, or at all events of prominent members of the Administration. This delay was assented to for the express purpose of attaining the great end of the mission of the undersigned, to wit, a specific solution to existing complications. The inference deducible from the date of your memorandum that the undersigned had, of their own volition and without cause, consented to this long hiatus in the grave duties with which they were charged is therefore not consistent with a just exposition of the facts of the case.

The intervening twenty-three days were employed in active unofficial efforts, the object of which was to smooth the path to a pacific solution, the distinguished personage alluded to co-operating with the undersigned, and every step of that effort is recorded in writing, and now in possession of the undersigned and of their Government. It was only when all these anxious efforts for peace had been exhausted, and it became clear that Mr. Lincoln had determined to appeal to the sword to reduce the people of the Confederate States to the will of the section or party whose President he is, that the undersigned resumed the official negotiation temporarily suspended, and sent their secretary for a reply to their official note of March 12.

It is proper to add that, during these twenty-three days, two gentlemen of official distinction as high as that of the personage hitherto alluded to, aided the undersigned as intermediaries in these unofficial negotiations for peace.

The undersigned, Commissioners of the Confederate States of America, having thus made answer to all they deem material in the memorandum filed in the Department on the 15th of March last, have the honor to be,

JOHN FORSYTH,
MARTIN J. CRAWFORD,
A. B. ROMAN.

A true copy of the original by one delivered to Mr. F. W. Seward, Assistant Secretary of State of the United States, at eight o'clock in the evening of April 9, 1861.

Attest: J. T. PICKETT, *Secretary, &c.*

Mr. Seward in reply to the Commissioners.

DEPARTMENT OF STATE,
WASHINGTON, *April* 10, 1861.

Messrs. Forsyth, Crawford, and Roman, having been apprized by a memorandum which has been delivered to them that the Secretary of State is not at liberty to hold official intercourse with them, will, it is presumed, expect no notice from him of the new communication which they have addresssed to him under date of the 9th instant, beyond the simple acknowledgment of the receipt thereof, which he hereby very cheerfully gives.

A true copy of the original received by the Commissioners of the Confederate States this 10th day of April, 1861.

Attest: J. T. PICKETT, *Secretary, &c.*

JUDGE CAMPBELL'S STATEMENT RESPECTING HIS PART IN THE NEGOTIATION.

WASHINGTON CITY, *April* 13, 1861.

SIR: On the 15th of March ultimo I left with Judge Crawford, one of the Commissioners of the Confederate States, a note in writing to the effect following:

"I feel entire confidence that Fort Sumter will be evacuated in the next five days. And this measure is felt as imposing great responsibility on the Administration.

"I feel entire confidence that no measure changing the existing status, prejudicially to the Southern Confederate States, is at present contemplated.

"I feel an entire confidence that an immediate demand for an answer to the communication of the Commissioners will be productive of evil and not of good. I do not believe that it ought at this time to be pressed."

The substance of this statement I communicated to you the same evening by letter. Five days elapsed and I called with a telegram from General Beauregard to the effect that Sumter was not evacuated, but that Major Anderson was at work making repairs.

The next day, after conversing with you, I communicated to Judge Crawford, in writing, that the failure to evacuate Sumter was not the result of bad faith, but was attributable to causes consistent with the intention to fulfill the engagement, and that, as regarded Pickens, I should have notice of any design to alter the existing status there. Mr. Justice Nelson was present at these conversations, three in number, and I submitted to him each of my written communications to Judge Crawford, and informed Judge C. that they had his (Judge Nelson's) sanction. I gave you, on the 22d of March, a substantial copy of the statement I had made on the 15th.

The 30th of March arrived, and at that time a telegram came from Governor Pickens inquiring concerning Colonel Lamon, whose visit to Charleston he supposed had a connection with the proposed evacuation of Fort Sumter. I left that with you, and was to have an answer the following Monday, (1st of April.) On the 1st of April I received from you the statement in writing: "I am satisfied the Government will not undertake to supply Fort Sumter without giving notice to Governor P." The words "I am satisfied" were for me to use as expressive of confidence in the remainder of the declaration.

The proposition as originally prepared was, "The President *may desire* to supply Sumter, but will not do so," &c., and your verbal explanation was that you did not believe any such attempt would be made, and that there was no design to reinforce Sumter.

There was a departure here from the pledges of the previous month, but, with the verbal explanation, I did not consider it a matter then to complain of. I simply stated to you that I had that assurance previously.

On the 7th of April I addressed you a letter on the subject of the alarm that the preparations by the Government had created, and asked you if the assurances I had given were well or ill-founded. In respect to Sumter your reply was, "Faith as to Sumter, fully kept—wait and see." In the morning's paper I read, "An authorized messenger from President Lincoln informed Governor Pickens and General Beauregard that provisions will be sent to Fort Sumter—peaceably, or *otherwise by force*." This was the 8th of April, at Charleston, the day following your last assurance, and is the evidence of the full faith I was invited to wait *for* and *see*. In the same paper, I read that intercepted dispatches disclosed the fact that Mr. Fox, who had been allowed to visit Major Anderson, on the pledge that his purpose was pacific, employed his opportunity to devise a plan for supplying the fort by force, and that this plan had been adopted by the Washington Government, and was in process of execution. My recollection of the date of Mr. Fox's visit carries it to a day in March. I learn he is a near connexion of a member of the Cabinet. My connection with the Commissioners and yourself was superinduced by a conversation with Justice Nelson. He informed me of your strong disposition in favor of peace, and that you were oppressed with a demand of the Commissioners of the Confederate States for a reply to their first letter, and that you desired to avoid it if possible at that time."

I told him I might perhaps be of some service in arranging the difficulty. I came to your office entirely at his request and without knowledge of either of the Commissioners. Your depression was obvious to both Judge Nelson and myself. I was gratified at the character of the counsels you were desirous of pursuing, and much impressed with your observation that a civil war might be prevented by the success of my mediation. You read a letter of Mr. Weed to show how irksome and responsible the withdrawal of troops from Sumter was. A portion of my communication to Judge Crawford on the 15th March was founded upon these remarks, and the pledge to evacuate Sumter is less forcible than the words you employed. These words were: Before this letter reaches you (a proposed letter by me to President Davis) Sumter will have been evacuated.

The Commissioners who received those communications conclude they have been abused and overreached. The Montgomery Government hold the same opinion. The Commissioners have supposed that my communications were with you, and upon the hypothesis were prepared to arraign you before the country in connection with the President. I placed a peremptory prohibition upon this as being contrary to the term of my communications with them. I pledged myself to them to communicate information upon what I considered as the best authority, and they were to confide in the ability of myself, aided by Judge Nelson, to determine upon the credibility of my informant.

I think no candid man who will read over what I have written, and considers for a moment what is going on at Sumter, but will agree that the equivocating conduct of the Administration, as measured and interpreted in connection with these promises, is the proximate cause of the great calamity.

I have a profound conviction that the telegrams of the 8th of April of General Beauregard, and of the 10th of April of General Walker, the Secretary of War, can be referred to nothing else than their belief that there has been systematic duplicity practiced on them through me. It is under an oppressive sense of the weight of this responsibility that I submit to you these things for your explanation.

Very respectfully, JOHN A. CAMPBELL,
Associate Justice of the Supreme Court U. S.
Hon. WILLIAM H. SEWARD, *Secretary of State.*

Dispatches.

CHARLESTON, *April* 8, 1861.
To L. P. WALKER, *Secretary of War.*

An authorized message from President Lincoln* just informed Governor Pickens and myself that provisions will be sent to Fort Sumter peaceably, or otherwise by force.
G. T. BEAUREGARD.

MONTGOMERY, *April* 10, 1861.
GEN. G. T. BEAUREGARD.

If you have no doubt as to the authorized character of the agent who communicated to you the intention of the Washington Government to supply Fort Sumter by force, you will at once demand its evacuation, and if this is refused proceed in such manner as you may determine to reduce it.
L. P. WALKER.

Judge Campbell to the Secretary of State.

WASHINGTON, *April* 20, 1861.

SIR: I inclose you a letter, corresponding very nearly with one I addressed to you one week ago, (13th April,) to which I have not had any reply. The letter is simply one of inquiry in reference to facts concerning which, I think, I am entitled to an explanation. I have not adopted any opinion in reference to them which may not be modified by explanation; nor have I affirmed in that letter, nor do I in this, any conclusion of my own unfavorable to your integrity in the whole transaction. All that I have said and mean to say is, that an explanation is due from you to myself. I will not say what I shall do in case this request is not complied with, but I am justified in saying that I shall feel at liberty to place these letters before any person who is entitled to ask an explanation of myself.

Very respectfully, JOHN A. CAMPBELL,
Associate Justice of the Supreme Court U. S.
Hon. WM. H. SEWARD, *Secretary of State.*

April 24, 1861.—No reply has been made to this letter.

Judge Campbell to General Davis.

MONTGOMERY, (ALA.,) *May* 7, 1861.

SIR: I submit to you two letters that were addressed by me to the Hon. W. H. Seward, Secretary of State of the United States, that contain an explanation of the nature and result of an intervention by me in the intercourse of the Commissioners of the Confederate States with that officer. I considered that I could perform no duty in which the entire American people, whether of the Federal Union or of the Confederate States, were more interested than that of promoting the counsels and the policy that had for their object the preservation of peace. This motive dictated my intervention. Besides the interview referred to in these letters, I informed the Assistant Secretary of State of the United States, (not being able to see the Secretary,) on the 11th of April ultimo, of the existence of a telegram of that date from Gen. Beauregard to the Commissioners, in which he informed the Commissioners that he had demanded the evacuation of Sumter, and if refused he would proceed to reduce it. On the same day I had been told that President Lincoln had said that none of the vessels sent to Charleston were war vessels, and that force was not to be used in the attempt to supply the fort. I had no means of testing the accuracy of this information, but offered that, if the information was accurate, I would send a telegram to the authorities at Charleston, and it might prevent the disastrous consequences of a collision at that fort between the opposing forces. It was the last effort that I would make to avert the calamities of war. The Assistant Secretary promised to give the matter attention, but I had no other intercourse with him or any other person on the subject, nor have I had any reply to the letters submitted to you.

Very respectfully, JOHN A. CAMPBELL.
Gen. DAVIS, President of the Confederate States.

In an article of Mr. THURLOW WEED, in the *Albany Evening Journal* of May 30, 1861, we find the following statements respecting Judge Campbell's publication:

"If the Secretary of State were at liberty to reply to ex-Judge Campbell, revealing all that passed between them on several occasions, not only no imputation of insincerity would rest upon the Secretary, but the facts would seriously affect Judge Campbell's well established reputation for candor and frankness. The revelations would furnish no evidence of either the falsehood or the duplicity of Governor Seward, for there was nothing of either in his conversations.

"We violate no confidence in saying that Judge Campbell balanced long between loyalty and secession, the preponderance, up to a late day, being in favor of the Union.

* See President Lincoln's First Message to Congress, July 4, 1861.

"If he at any time looked with favor or satisfaction upon secession, he was much and generally misunderstood. If he did not seriously contemplate remaining in the Union and upon the Bench, he was misunderstood.

"If during that period of mental trial, he was acting in harmony with the leading enemies of the Union, he was grossly misunderstood.

"That Gov. Seward conversed freely with Judge Campbell, we do not deny, nor do we doubt, that in these conversations, at one period, he intimated that Fort Sumter would be evacuated.

"He certainly believed so, founding his opinion upon a knowledge of Gen. Scott's recommendation.

"Subsequently, the President deemed it his duty to authorize an effort to reinforce and provision that fortress. We do not know whether Gov. Seward met Judge Campbell after that change of purpose; but he was not at liberty, if they did meet, to reveal what was so well kept.

"But, whatever Gov. Seward said or intimated to Judge Campbell was true at the time it was said.

"That Judge Campbell reported to the Confederate President half that he said or intimated, is more than doubtful."

PRESIDENT LINCOLN'S ANSWER TO THE DELEGATES FROM VIRGINIA.

April 13, 1861. The PRESIDENT had an interview with Wm. Ballard Preston, Alexander H. H. Stuart, and George W. Randolph, who were appointed by the Convention of Virginia then in session, under a resolution recited in the President's reply, which was as follows:

Hon. Messrs. Preston, Stuart, and Randolph:

GENTLEMEN: As a committee of the Virginia Convention, now in session, you present me a preamble and resolution in these words:

"Whereas, in the opinion of this Convention, the uncertainty which prevails in the public mind as to the policy which the Federal Executive intends to pursue toward the seceded States is extremely injurious to the industrial and commercial interests of the country, tends to keep up an excitement which is unfavorable to the adjustment of pending difficulties, and threatens a disturbance of the public peace: Therefore,

"*Resolved*, That a committee of three delegates be appointed to wait on the President of the United States, present to him this preamble and resolution, and respectfully ask him to communicate to this Convention the policy which the Federal Executive intends to pursue in regard to the Confederate States."

In answer I have to say, that, having at the beginning of my official term expressed my intended policy as plainly as I was able, it is with deep regret and some mortification I now learn that there is great and injurious uncertainty in the public mind as to what that policy is, and what course I intend to pursue.

Not having as yet seen occasion to change, it is now my purpose to pursue the course marked out in the inaugural address. I commend a careful consideration of the whole document as the best expression I can give of my purposes. As I then and therein said, I now repeat:

"The power confided to me will be used to hold, occupy, and possess the property and places belonging to the Government, and to collect the duties and imposts; but beyond what is necessary for these objects there will be no invasion, no using of force against or among the people anywhere."

By the words "property and places belonging to the Government" I chiefly allude to the military posts and property which were in the possession of the Government when it came to my hands.

But if, as now appears to be true, in pursuit of a purpose to drive the United States authority from these places, an unprovoked assault has been made upon Fort Sumter, I shall hold myself at liberty to repossess, if I can, like places which had been seized before the Government was devolved upon me. And, in any event, I shall, to the best of my ability, repel force by force.

In case it proves true that Fort Sumter has been assaulted, as is reported, I shall perhaps cause the United States mails to be withdrawn from all the States which claim to have seceded, believing that the commencement of actual war against the Government justifies and possibly demands it.

I scarcely need to say that I consider the military posts and property situated within the States which claim to have seceded as yet belonging to the Government of the United States as much as they did before the supposed secession.

Whatever else I may do for the purpose, I shall not attempt to collect the duties and imposts by any armed invasion of any part of the country—not meaning by this, however, that I may not land a force deemed necessary to relieve a fort upon the border of the country.

From the fact that I have quoted a part of the inaugural address, it must not be inferred that I repudiate any other part, the whole of which I reaffirm, except so far as what I now say of the mails may be regarded as a modification.

WHY AND HOW WAR WAS MADE UPON THE UNITED STATES.

In January, the rebel leaders then in Washington prevented an attack upon the forts in Charleston harbor and at Pensacola.

War not breaking out, the conspiracy weakened, and, as expressed by the Mobile *Mercury* in discussing the position of affairs in those harbors:

"The country is sinking into a fatal apathy, and the spirit and even the patriotism of the people is oozing out under this do-nothing policy. If something is not done pretty soon, decisive, either evacuation or expulsion, the whole country will become so disgusted with the sham of southern independence that the first chance the people get at a popular election they will turn the whole movement topsy-turvy so bad that it never on earth can be righted again."

On Wednesday, April 10, 1861, Roger A. Pryor, of Virginia, was serenaded in Charleston, and spoke as follows, as reported in the *Mercury:*

"Gentlemen, I thank you, especially that you have at last annihilated this accursed Union, [applause,] reeking with corruption, and insolent with excess of tyranny. Thank God, it is at last blasted and riven by the lightning wrath of an outraged and indignant people. [Loud applause.] Not only is it gone, but gone forever. [Cries of 'You're right,' and applause.] In the expressive language of Scripture, it is water spilt upon the ground, which cannot be gathered up. [Applause.] Like Lucifer, son of the morning, it has fallen, never to rise again. [Continued applause.] *For my part, gentlemen, if Abraham Lincoln and Hannibal Hamlin to-morrow were to abdicate their offices and were to give me a blank sheet of paper to write the condition of reannexation to the defunct Union, I would scornfully spurn the overture.* * * * * * I invoke you, and I make it in some sort a personal appeal—personal so far as it tends to our assistance in Virginia—I do invoke you, in your demonstrations of popular opinion, in your exhibitions of official intent, to give no countenance to this idea of reconstruction. [Many voices, emphatically, 'Never,' and applause.] In Virginia they all say, if reduced to the dread dilemma of this memorable alternative, they will espouse the cause of the South as against the interest of the Northern Confederacy, but they whisper of reconstruction, and they say Virginia must abide in the Union, with the idea of reconstructing the Union which you have annihilated. *I pray you, gentlemen, rob them of that idea.* Proclaim to the world that upon no condition, and under no circumstance, will South Carolina ever again enter into political association with the Abolitionists of New England. [Cries of 'Never,' and applause.]

"Do not distrust Virginia. As sure as to-morrow's sun will rise upon us, just so sure will Virginia be a member of this Southern Confederation. [Applause.] *And I will tell you, gentlemen, what will put her in the Southern Confederation in less than an hour by Shrewsbury clock*—STRIKE A BLOW! [Tremendous applause.] *The very moment that blood is shed, old Virginia will make common cause with her sisters of the South.* [Applause.] It is impossible she should do otherwise."

Hon. JEREMIAH CLEMENS, formerly United States Senator from Alabama, and a member of the Alabama Seceding Convention who resisted the movement until adopted by the body, at an adjourned Reconstruction meeting held at Huntsville, Ala., March 13, 1864, made this significant statement:

Mr. Clemens, in adjourning the meeting, said he would tell the Alabamians how their State was got out of the Union. "In 1861," said Mr. C., "shortly after the Confederate Government was put in operation, I was in the city of Montgomery. One day I stepped into the office of the Secretary of War, General Walker, and found there, engaged in a very excited discussion, Mr. Jefferson Davis, Mr. Memminger, Mr. Benjamin, Mr. Gilchrist, a member of our Legislature from Loundes county, and a number of other prominent gentlemen. They were discussing the propriety of immediately opening fire on Fort Sumter, to which General Walker, the Secretary of War, appeared to be opposed. Mr. Gilchrist said to him, 'Sir, unless you sprinkle blood in the face of the people of Alabama they will be back in the old Union in less than ten days!' The next day General Beauregard opened his batteries on Sumter, and Alabama was saved to the Confederacy."

CORRESPONDENCE PRECEDING BOMBARDMENT.

CHARLESTON, *April* 8, 1861.

To Hon. L. P. WALKER, *Secretary of War, Montgomery:*

An authorized messenger from President Lincoln* has just informed Gov. Pickens and myself that provisions will be sent to Fort Sumter peaceably, or otherwise by force.

G. T. BEAUREGARD.

MONTGOMERY, *April* 10, 1861.

To Gen. BEAUREGARD, *Charleston:*

If you have no doubt of the authorized character of the agent who communicated to you the intention of the Washington Government to supply Fort Sumter by force, you will at once demand its evacuation, and, if this is refused, proceed in such manner as you may determine to reduce it. L. P. WALKER.

CHARLESTON, *April* 10, 1861.

To Hon. L. P. WALKER:

The demand will be made to-morrow at 12 o'clock.

G. T. BEAUREGARD,
Brigadier General.

MONTGOMERY, *April* 10, 1861.

To Gen. BEAUREGARD, *Charleston:*

Unless there are special reasons connected with your own condition, it is considered proper that you should make the demand at an earlier hour.

L. P. WALKER.

CHARLESTON, *April* 10, 1861.

To Hon. L. P. WALKER:

The reasons are special for 12 o'clock.

G. T. BEAUREGARD.

CHARLESTON, *April* 11, 1861.

To Hon. L. P. WALKER:

The demand was sent at 2 p. m., and until 6 was allowed for the answer. G. T. BEAUREGARD.

MONTGOMERY, *April* 11, 1861.

Gen. BEAUREGARD, *Charleston:*

Telegraph the reply of Major Anderson.

L. P. WALKER.

CHARLESTON, *April* 11, 1861.

To Hon. L. P. WALKER:

Major Anderson replies: "I have the honor to acknowledge the receipt of your communication demanding the evacuation of this fort, and to say in reply thereto that it is a demand with which I regret that my sense of honor and of my obligation to my Government prevent my compliance." He adds, verbally, "*I will await the first shot, and, if you do not batter us to pieces, we will be starved out in a few days.*" G. T. BEAUREGARD.

MONTGOMERY, *April* 11, 1861.

To General BEAUREGARD:

Do not desire needlessly to bombard Fort Sumter. If Major Anderson will state the time at which, as indicated by himself, he will evacuate, and agree that, in the mean time, he will not use his guns against us unless ours should be employed against Fort Sumter, you are authorized thus to avoid the effusion of blood. If this or its equivalent be refused, reduce the fort, as your judgment decides to be the most practicable. L. P. WALKER.

HEADQUARTERS PROVISIONAL ARMY C. S. A.,
CHARLESTON, (S. C.) *April* 11, 1861, 2 p. m.

Maj. ROBERT ANDERSON,
Commanding at Fort Sumter, Charleston Harbor, S. C.:

SIR: The Government of the Confederate States has hitherto forborne from any hostile demonstration against Fort Sumter, in the hope that the Government of the United States, with a view to the amicable adjustment of all questions between the two Governments, and to avert the calamities of war, would voluntarily evacuate it.

There was reason at one time to believe that such would be the course pursued by the Government of the United States, and, under that impression, my Government has refrained from making any demand for the surrender of the fort. But the Confederate States can no longer delay assuming actual possession of a fortification commanding the entrance of one of their harbors, and necessary to its defence and security.

I am ordered by the Government of the Confederate States to demand the evacuation of Fort Sumter. My aids, Col. Chesnut and Capt. Lee, are authorized to make such demand of you. All proper facilities will be afforded for the removal of yourself and command—together with company arms and property, and all private property—to any post in the United States which you may elect. The flag which you have upheld so long, and with so much fortitude, under the most trying circumstances, may be saluted by you on taking it down.

Col. Chesnut and Capt. Lee will, for a reasonable time, await your answer.

I am, sir, very respectfully, your obedient servant,
G. T. BEAUREGARD, *Brig. Gen. Commanding.*

HEADQUARTERS FORT SUMTER, S. C.,
April 11, 1861.

To Brig. Gen. G. T. BEAUREGARD,
Commanding Provisional Army C. S. A.:

GENERAL: I have the honor to acknowledge the receipt of your communication demanding the evacuation of this fort, and to say in reply thereto that it is a demand with which I regret that my sense of honor and my obligation to my Government prevent my compliance.

Thanking you for the fair, manly, and courteous terms proposed, and for the high compliment paid me, I remain, General, very respectfully, your obedient servant,

ROBERT ANDERSON,
Major U. S. Army, Commanding.

HEADQUARTERS PROV'L ARMY C. S. A.,
CHARLESTON, (S. C.) *April* 11, 1861, 11 P. M.

Major ROBERT ANDERSON,
Commanding at Fort Sumter, Charleston Harbor, S. C.:

MAJOR: In consequence of the verbal observations made by you to my aids, Messrs. Chesnut and Lee, in relation to the condition of your supplies, and that you would in a few days be starved out if our guns did not batter you to pieces, or words to that effect, and desiring no useless effusion of blood, I communicated both the verbal observation and your written answer to my communication to my Government.

If you will state the time at which you will evacuate Fort Sumter, and agree that in the mean time you will not use your guns against us unless ours shall be employed against Fort Sumter, we shall abstain from opening fire upon you. Col. Chesnut and Capt. Lee are authorized by me to enter into such an agreement with you. You are, therefore, requested to communicate to them an open answer.

I remain, Major, very respectfully, your obedient servant,

G. T. BEAUREGARD,
Brigadier General Commanding.

HEADQUARTERS FORT SUMTER, S. C.
2.30 A. M., *April* 12, 1861.

To Brig. Gen. G. T. BEAUREGARD,
Commanding Provisional Army C. S. A.:

GENERAL: I have the honor to acknowledge the receipt of your second communication of the 11th instant, by Col. Chesnut, and to state in reply, that, cordially uniting with you in the desire to avoid the useless effusion of blood, I will, if provided with the necessary means of transportation, evacuate Fort Sumter by noon on the 15th instant, should I not receive prior to that time, controlling instructions from my Government, or additional supplies, and that I will not in the mean time open my fire upon your forces, unless compelled to do so by some hostile act against this fort or the flag of my Government, by the forces under your command, or by some portion of them, or by the perpetration of some act showing a hostile intention on your part against this fort or the flag it bears.

I have the honor to be, General, very respectfully, your obedient servant, ROBERT ANDERSON,
Major U. S. A. Commanding.

FORT SUMTER, S. C.,
April 12, 1861, 3.20 A. M.

MAJOR ROBERT ANDERSON, *United States Army,*
Commanding Fort Sumter:

SIR: By authority of Brigadier General Beauregard, Commanding the Provisional Forces of the Confederate States, we have the honor to notify you that he will open the fire of his batteries on Fort Sumter in one hour from this time.

We have the honor to be, very respectfully, your obedient servants,

JAMES CHESNUT, Jr.,
Aid-de-Camp.
STEPHEN D. LEE,
Captain S. C. Army and Aid-de-Camp.

* See his first message, July 4, 1861, page 124.

CHARLESTON, *April* 12, 1861.

To Hon. L. P. WALKER:
He would not consent. I write to-day.
G. T. BEAUREGARD.

CHARLESTON, *April* 12, 1861.

To Hon. L. P. WALKER:
We opened fire at 4.30. G. T. BEAUREGARD.

NOTE.—Intercepted despatches disclose the fact that Mr. Fox, who had been allowed to visit Major Anderson on the pledge that his purpose was pacific, employed his opportunity to devise a plan for supplying the fort by force, and that this plan had been adopted by the Washington Government, and was in process of execution.

REPORT OF MAJOR ANDERSON TO THE SECRETARY OF WAR.

STEAMSHIP BALTIC, OFF SANDY HOOK,
April 18, 1861, 10.30 *A. M., via New York.*

Having defended Fort Sumter for thirty-four hours, until the quarters were entirely burnt, the main gates destroyed by fire, the gorge walls seriously injured, the magazine surrounded by flames, and its door closed from the effects of heat; four barrels and three cartridges of powder only being available, and no provisions remaining but pork, I accepted terms of evacuation offered by General Beauregard—being the same offered by him on the 11th instant, prior to the commencement of hostilities—and marched out of the Fort on Sunday afternoon, the 14th instant, with colors flying and drums beating, bringing away company and private property, and saluting my flag with fifty guns.

ROBERT ANDERSON,
Major 1st Artillery, commanding.

Hon. SIMON CAMERON,
Secretary of War, Washington.

After the surrender, and while the tidings were received throughout the South with joy, Davis and his associates were serenaded, salvos of artillery were fired, and the whole population seemed to be in an exstacy of triumph. The rebel Secretary of War, L. Pope Walker, defiantly said:

"No man can foretell the events of the war inaugurated; but I will venture to predict that the flag which now floats on the breeze" (that was his miserable secession flag) "will, before the first of May, float over the dome of the old Capitol at Washington, and if they choose to try Southern chivalry, and test the extent of Southern resources, will eventually float over Faneuil Hall, in Boston.

The idea spread throughout the South, and such paragraphs as these abounded:

[*From the Richmond Enquirer, April* 13, 1861.]

"ATTENTION, VOLUNTEERS!—Nothing is more probable than that President Davis will soon march an army through North Carolina and Virginia to Washington. Those of our volunteers who decide to join the Southern Army as it shall pass through our borders, had better organize at once for that purpose, and keep their arms, accoutrements, uniforms, ammunition, and knapsacks in constant readiness."

[*From the New Orleans Picayune, April* 18.]

"The first fruits of a Virginia secession will be the removal of Lincoln and his cabinet, and whatever he can carry away, to the safer neighborhood of Harrisburg or Cincinnati—perhaps to Buffalo or Cleveland."

[*From the Richmond Examiner, April* 28.]

"There never was half the unanimity among the people before, nor a tithe of the zeal upon any subject, that is now manifested to take Washington. From the mountain tops and valleys to the shores of the sea, there is one wild shout of fierce resolve to capture Washington city at all and every human hazard."

THE "WAR POWER CALLED OUT."

April 15, 1861. The PRESIDENT issued his proclamation for seventy-five thousand troops, as follows:

"Whereas the laws of the United States have been for some time past, and now are opposed, and the execution thereof obstructed, in the States of South Carolina, Georgia, Alabama, Florida, Mississippi, Louisiana, and Texas, by combinations too powerful to be suppressed by the ordinary course of judicial proceedings, or by the powers vested in the marshals by law; now, therefore, I, ABRAHAM LINCOLN, President of the United States, in virtue of the power in me vested by the Constitution and the laws, have thought fit to call forth, and hereby do call forth, the militia of the several States of the Union to the aggregate number of 75,000, in order to suppress said combinations, and to cause the laws to be duly executed.

"The details for this object will be immediately communicated to the State authorities through the War Department. I appeal to all loyal citizens to favor, facilitate, and aid this effort to maintain the honor, the integrity, and existence of our national Union, and the perpetuity of popular government, and to redress wrongs already long enough endured. I deem it proper to say that the first service assigned to the forces hereby called forth, will probably be to repossess the forts, places, and property which have been seized from the Union; and in every event the utmost care will be observed, consistently with the objects aforesaid, to avoid any devastation, any destruction of, or interference with property, or any disturbance of peaceful citizens of any part of the country; and I hereby command the persons composing the combinations aforesaid, to disperse and retire peaceably to their respective abodes, within twenty days from this date.

"Deeming that the present condition of public affairs presents an extraordinary occasion, I do hereby, in virtue of the power in me vested by the Constitution, convene both Houses of Congress. The Senators and Representatives are, therefore, summoned to assemble at their respective chambers at twelve o'clock, noon, on Thursday, the 4th day of July next, then and there to consider and determine such measures as, in their wisdom, the public safety and interest may seem to demand.

"In witness whereof I have hereunto set my hand, and caused the seal of the United States to be affixed.

"Done at the city of Washington, this fifteenth day of April, in the year of our Lord one thousand eight hundred and sixty-one, and of the independence of the United States the eighty-fifth.

"By the President: "ABRAHAM LINCOLN.
"WILLIAM H. SEWARD, *Secretary of State.*"

The Governors of all the northern States responded with alacrity.

Governor BURTON, of Delaware, issued a proclamation, April 26, recommending the formation of volunteer companies for the protection of the lives and property of the people of Delaware against violence of any sort to which they may be exposed, the companies not being subject to be ordered by the Executive into the United States service, the law not vesting him with such authority, but having the option of offering their services to the General Government for the defence of its capital and the support of the Constitution and laws of the country.

Governor HICKS, of Maryland, May 14, issued a proclamation for the troops, stating that the four regiments would be detailed to serve within the limits of Maryland or for the defence of the capital of the United States.

Governor LETCHER, of Virginia, replied that

"The militia of Virginia will not be furnished to the powers at Washington for any such use or purpose as they have in view. Your object is to subjugate the southern States, and a requisition made upon me for such an object—an object, in my judgment, not within the purview of the Constitution or the act of 1795—will not be complied with. You have chosen to inaugurate civil war, and having done so we will meet it in a spirit as determined as the Administration has exhibited toward the South."

Governor ELLIS, of North Carolina, replied April 15:

"Your dispatch is received, and, if genuine—which its extraordinary character leads me to doubt—I have to say in reply that I regard the levy of troops made by the Administration, for the purpose of subjugating the States of the South, as in violation of the Constitution and a usurpation of power. I can be no party to this wicked violation of the laws of the country, and to this war upon the liberties of a free people. You can get no troops from North Carolina. I will reply more in detail when your call is received by mail."

Governor MAGOFFIN, of Kentucky, replied, April 15:

"Your dispatch is received. In answer I say emphatically, Kentucky will furnish no troops for the wicked purpose of subduing her sister Southern States."

Governor HARRIS, of Tennessee, replied, April 18:

"Tennessee will not furnish a single man for coercion, but fifty thousand, if necessary, for the defence of our rights or those of our southern brethren."

Governor JACKSON, of Missouri, replied:

"Your requisition is illegal, unconstitutional, revolutionary, inhuman, diabolical, and cannot be complied with."

Governor RECTOR, of Arkansas, replied, April 22:

"None will be furnished. The demand is only adding insult to injury."

May 3, 1861—The President called for thirty-nine volunteer regiments of infantry and one regiment of cavalry, with a minimum aggregate of 34,506 officers and enlisted men, and a maximum of 42,034; and for the enlistment of 18,000 seamen.

May 3, 1861—The President directed an increase of the regular army by eight regiments of infantry, one of cavalry, and one of artillery—minimum aggregate, 18,054; maximum, 22,714.

August 6—Congress legalized this increase, and all the acts, orders, and proclamations respecting the Army and Navy.

July 22 and 25, 1861—Congress authorized the enlistment of 500,000 volunteers.

September 17, 1861—Commanding officer at Hatteras Inlet, N. C., authorized to enlist a regiment of loyal North Carolinians.

November 7, 1861—The Governor of Missouri was authorized to raise a force of State militia for State defence.

December 3, 1861—The Secretary of War directed that no more regiments, batteries, or independent companies be raised by the Governors of States, except upon the special requisition of the War Department.

July 2, 1862—The President called for three hundred thousand volunteers.

Under the act of July 17, 1862,

August 4, 1862—The President ordered a draft of three hundred thousand militia, for nine months unless sooner discharged; and directed that if any State shall not, by the 15th of August, furnish its quota of the additional 300,000 authorized by law, the deficiency of volunteers in that State will also be made up by special draft from the militia. Wednesday, September 3, was subsequently fixed for the draft.

May 8, 1863—Proclamation issued, defining the relations of aliens to the conscription act, holding all aliens who have declared on oath their intention to become citizens and may be in the country within sixty-five days from date, and all who have declared their intention to become citizens and have voted.

June 15, 1863—One hundred thousand men, for six months, called to repel the invasion of Maryland, West Virginia, Ohio, and Pennsylvania.

October 17, 1863—A proclamation was issued for 300,000 volunteers, to serve for three years or the war, not, however, exceeding three years, to fill the places of those whose terms expire "during the coming year," these being in addition to the men raised by the present draft. In States in default under this call, January 5, 1864, a draft shall be made on that day.

February 1, 1864—Draft for 500,000 men for three years or during the war, ordered for March 10, 1864.

March 14, 1864—Draft for 200,000 additional for the army, navy and marine corps, ordered for April 15, 1864, to supply the force required for the navy and to provide an adequate reserve force for all contingencies.

April 23, 1864—85,000 one hundred day men accepted, tendered by the Governors of Ohio, Indiana, Illinois, Iowa, and Wisconsin; 30,000, 20,000, 20,000, 10,000, and 5,000 being tendered respectively. (see page 270.)

Our Military Legislation.

1861, July 22—The President was authorized to accept the services of volunteers, not exceeding five hundred thousand, for a period not exceeding three years. July 27, this authority was duplicated.

1861, July 27—Nine regiments of infantry, one of cavalry, and one of artillery, added to the regular army.

August 5—Passed bill approving and legalizing the orders of the President respecting the army and navy, issued from 4th of March to that date.

1862, July 17—Authorized the President, when calling forth the militia of the States, to specify the period of such service, not exceeding nine months; and if by reason of defects in existing laws or in the execution of them, it shall be found necessary to provide for enroling the militia, the President was authorized to make all necessary regulations, the enrolment to include all able bodied male citizens between eighteen and forty-five, and to be apportioned according to representative population. He was authorized, in addition to the volunteers now authorized, to accept 100,000 infantry, for nine months; also, for twelve months, to fill up old regiments, as many as may be presented for the purpose.

1863, February 7—Authorized the Governor of Kentucky, by the consent and under the direction of the President, to raise twenty thousand volunteers, for twelve months, for service within the limits of the State, for repelling invasion, suppressing insurrection, and guarding and protecting the public property—two regiments to be mounted riflemen. With the consent of the President, these troops may be attached to, and become a part of, the body of three years' volunteers.

1863, March 3—The enrollment act passed. It included as part of the national forces, all able bodied male citizens of the United States, and persons of foreign birth who shall have declared on oath their intention to become citizens under and in pursuance of the laws thereof, between the ages of twenty-one and forty-five years, except such as are rejected as physically or mentally unfit for the service; also, the Vice President, the judges of the various courts of the United States, the heads of the various executive departments of the Government, and the Governors of the several States; also, the only son liable to military service, of a widow dependent upon his labor for support; also, the only son of aged or infirm parent or parents, dependent upon his labor for support; also, where there are two or more sons of aged or infirm parents, subject to draft, the father, or if he be dead, the mother, may elect which son shall be exempt; also, the only brother of children not twelve years old, having neither father nor mother, dependent upon his labor for support; also, the father of motherless children under twelve years of age, dependent upon his labor for support; also, where there are a father and sons in the same family and household, and two of them are in the military service of the United States as non-commissioned officers, musicians, or privates, the residue of such family; provided that no person who has been convicted of any felony shall be enrolled or permitted to serve in said forces. It divided the forces into two classes: 1st, those between twenty and thirty-five and all unmarried persons above thirty-five and under forty-five; 2d, all others liable to military duty. It divided the country into districts, in each of which an enrolment board was established. The persons enrolled were made subject to be called into the military service for two years from July 1, 1863, and to continue in service for three years. A drafted person was allowed to furnish an acceptable substitute, or pay $300, and be discharged from further liability under that draft. Persons failing to report, to be considered deserters. All persons drafted shall be assigned by the President to military duty in such corps, regiments, or branches of the service as the exigencies of the service may require.

1864, Feb. 24—Provided for equalizing the draft by calculating the quota of each district or precinct and counting the number previously furnished by it. Any person enrolled may furnish an acceptable substitute who is not liable to draft, nor, at the time, in the military or naval service of the United States; and such person so furnishing a substitute shall be exempt from draft during the time for which such substitute shall not be liable to draft, not exceeding the time for which such substitute shall have been accepted. If such substitute is liable to draft, the name of the person furnishing him shall again be placed on the roll and shall be liable to draft in future calls, but not until the present enrollment shall be exhausted. The exemptions are limited to such as are rejected as physically or mentally unfit for the service; to persons actually in the military or naval service of the Government, and all persons who have served in the military or naval service two years during the present war and been honorably discharged therefrom.

The separate enrolment of classes is repealed and the two classes consolidated.

Members of religious denominations, who shall by oath or affirmation declare that they are conscientiously opposed to the bearing of arms, and who are prohibited from doing so by the rules and articles of faith and practice of said religious denomination, shall when drafted, be considered non-combatants, and be assigned to duty in the hospitals, or the care of freedmen, or shall pay $300 to the benefit of sick and wounded soldiers, if they give proof that their deportment has been uniformly consistent with their declaration.

No alien who has voted in county, State, or Territory shall, because of alienage, be exempt from draft.

"All able-bodied male colored persons between the ages of twenty and forty-five years, resident in the United States, shall be enrolled according to the provisions of this act, and of the act to which this is an amendment, and form part of the national forces; and when a slave of a loyal master shall be drafted and mustered into the service of the United States, his master shall have a certificate thereof; and thereupon such slave shall be free, and the bounty of one hundred dollars, now payable by law for each drafted man, shall be paid to the person to whom such drafted person was owing service or labor at the time of his muster into the service of the United States. The Secretary of War shall appoint a commission in each of the slave States represented in Congress, charged to award to each loyal person to whom a colored volunteer may owe service a just compensation, not exceeding three hundred dollars, for each such colored volunteer, payable out of the fund derived from commutations, and every such colored volunteer on being mustered into the service shall be free. And in all cases where men of color have been heretofore enlisted, or have volunteered in the military service of the United States, all the provisions of this act so far as the payment of bounty and compensation are provided, shall be equally applicable, as to those who may be hereafter recruited. But men of color, drafted or enlisted, or who may volunteer into the military service, while they shall be credited on the quotas of the several States, or sub-divisions of States, wherein they are respectively drafted, enlisted, or shall volunteer, shall not be assigned as State troops, but shall be mustered into regiments or companies as United States colored troops."

1864, Feb. 29—Bill passed reviving the grade of Lieutenant General in the army, and Major General Ulysses S. Grant was appointed March 2d.

1864, June 15—All persons of color shall receive the same pay and emoluments, except bounty, as other soldiers of the regular or volunteer army from and after Jan. 1, 1864, the President to fix the bounty for those hereafter mustered, not exceeding $100.

1864, June 20—The monthly pay of privates and non-commissioned officers was fixed as follows, on and after May 1:

"Sergeant majors, twenty-six dollars; quartermaster and commissary sergeants of Cavalry, artillery, and infantry, twenty-two dollars; first sergeants of cavalry, artillery, and infantry, twenty-four dollars; sergeants of cavalry, artillery, and infantry, twenty dollars; sergeants of ordnance, sappers and miners, and pontoniers, thirty-four dollars; corporals of ordnance, sappers and miners, and pontoniers, twenty dollars; privates of engineers and ordnance of the first class, eighteen dollars, and of the second class, sixteen dollars; corporals of cavalry, artillery, and infantry, eighteen dollars; chief buglers of cavalry, twenty-three dollars; buglers, sixteen dollars; farriers and blacksmiths of cavalry, and artificers of artillery, eighteen dollars; privates of cavalry, artillery, and infantry, sixteen dollars; principal musicians of artillery and infantry, twenty-two dollars; leaders of brigade and regimental bands, seventy-five dollars; musicians, sixteen dollars; hospital stewards of the first class, thirty-three dollars; hospital stewards of the second class, twenty-five dollars; hospital stewards of the third class, twenty-three dollars."

July 4—This bill became a law:

Be it enacted, &c. That the President of the United States may, at his discretion, at any time hereafter call for any number of men as volunteers for the respective terms of one, two, and three years for military service; and any such volunteer, or, in case of draft, as hereinafter provided, any substitute, shall be credited to the town, township, ward of a city, precinct, or election district, or of a county not so subdivided towards the quota of which he may have volunteered or engaged as a substitute; and every volunteer who is accepted and mustered into the service for a term of one year, unless sooner discharged, shall receive, and be paid by the United States, a bounty of one hundred dollars; and if for a term of two years, unless sooner discharged, a bounty of two hundred dollars; and if for a term of three years, unless sooner discharged, a bounty of three hundred dollars; one third of which bounty shall be paid to the soldier at the time of his being mustered into the service, one-third at the expiration of one-half of his term of service, and one-third at the expiration of his term of service. And in case of his death while in service, the residue of his bounty unpaid shall be paid to his widow, if he shall have left a widow; if not, to his children; or if there be none, to his mother, if she be a widow.

SEC. 2. That in case the quota, or any part thereof, of any town, township, ward of a city, precinct, or election district, or of any county not so subdivided, shall not be filled within the space of fifty days after such call, then the President shall immediately order a draft for one year to fill such quota, or any part thereof, which may be unfilled; and in case of any such draft no payment of money shall be accepted or received by the Government as commutation to release any enrolled or drafted man from personal obligation to perform military service.

SEC. 3. That it shall be lawful for the executive of any of the States to send recruiting agents into any of the States declared to be in rebellion, except the States of Arkansas, Tennessee, and Louisiana, to recruit volunteers under any call under the provisions of this act, who shall be credited to the State, and to the respective subdivisions thereof, which may procure the enlistment.

SEC. 4. That drafted men, substitutes, and volunteers, when mustered in, shall be organized into, or assigned to, regiments, batteries, or other organizations of their own States, and, as far as practicable, shall, when assigned, be permitted to select their own regiments, batteries, or other organizations from among those of their respective States which at the time of assignment may not be filled to their maximum number.

SEC. 5. That the twentieth section of the act entitled "An act to amend an act entitled 'An act for enrolling and calling out the national forces, and for other purposes,'" approved February twenty-four, eighteen hundred and sixty-four, shall be construed to mean that the Secretary of War shall discharge minors under the age of eighteen years under the circumstances and on the conditions prescribed in said section; and hereafter, if any officer of the United States shall enlist or muster into the military service any person under the age of sixteen years, with or without the consent of his parent or guardian, such person so enlisted or recruited shall be immediately discharged upon repayment of all bounties received; and such recruiting or mustering officer who shall knowingly enlist any person under sixteen years of age shall be dismissed the service, with forfeiture of all pay and allowances, and shall be subject to such further punishment as a court-martial may direct.

SEC. 6. That section three of an act entitled "An act to amend an act entitled 'An act for enrolling and calling out the national forces, and for other purposes,'" approved February twenty-four, eighteen hundred and sixty-four, be, and the same is hereby, amended, so as to authorize and direct district provost marshals, under the direction of the Provost Marshal General, to make a draft for one hundred per centum in addition to the number required to fill the quota of any district as provided by said section.

SEC. 7. That instead of travelling pay, all drafted persons reporting at the place of rendezvous shall be allowed transportation from their places of residence; and persons discharged at the place of rendezvous shall be allowed transportation to their places of residence.

SEC. 8. That all persons in the naval service of the United States who have entered said service during the present rebellion, who have not been credited to the quota of any town, district, ward, or State, by reason of their being in said service and not enrolled prior to February twenty-four, eighteen hundred and sixty-four, shall be enrolled and credited to the quotas of the town, ward, district, or State, in which they respectively reside, upon satisfactory proof of their residence made to the Secretary of War.

SEC. 9. That, if any person duly drafted shall be absent from home in prosecution of his usual business, the provost marshal of the district shall cause him to be duly notified as soon as he may be, and he shall not be deemed a deserter, nor liable as such, until notice has been given him, and reasonable time allowed for him to return and report to the provost marshal of his district; but such absence shall not affect his liability under this act.

SEC. 10. That nothing contained in this act, shall be construed to alter or in any way affect the provisions of the seventeenth section of an act approved February twenty-fourth, eighteen hundred and sixty-four, entitled "An act to amend an act entitled 'An act for enrolling and calling out the national forces, and for other purposes,'" approved March third, eighteen hundred and sixty-three.

SEC. 11. That nothing contained in this act shall be construed to alter or change the provisions of existing laws relative to permitting persons liable to military service to furnish substitutes.

"Confederate" Military Legislation.

February 28, 1861, (four days before the inauguration of Mr. Lincoln)—The "Confederate" Congress passed a bill providing—

1st. To enable the Government of the Confederate States to maintain its jurisdiction over all questions of peace and war, and to provide for the public defence, the President be, and he is hereby authorized and directed to assume control of all military operations in every State, having reference to a connection with questions between the said States, or any of them, and Powers foreign to them.

2d. The President was authorized to receive from the several States the arms and munitions of war which have been acquired from the United States.

3d. He was authorized to receive into Government service such forces in the service of the States, as may be tendered, in such number as he may require, for any time not less than twelve months, unless sooner discharged.

March 6, 1861—The President was authorized to employ the militia, military and naval forces of the Confederate States to repel invasion, maintain rightful possession of the territory, and secure the public tranquillity and independence against threatened assault, to the extent of 100,000 men, to serve for twelve months.

May 4, 1861—One regiment of Zouaves authorized.

May 6, 1861—Letters of marque and reprisal authorized.

1861, August 8—The Congress authorized the President to accept the services of 400,000 volunteers, to serve for not less than twelve months nor more than three years after they shall be mustered into service, unless sooner discharged.

The Richmond *Enquirer* of that date announced that it was ascertained from official data, before the passage of the bill, that there were not less than 210,000 men then in the field.

August 21—Volunteers authorized for local defence and special service.

1862, January—Publishers of newspapers, or other printed matter, are prohibited from giving the number, disposition, movement, or destination of the land or naval forces, or description of vessel, or battery, fortification, engine of war, or signal, unless first authorized by the President or Congress, or the Secretary of War or Navy, or commanding officer of post, district, or expedition. The penalty is a fine of $1,000 and imprisonment not over twelve months.

1862, February—The Committee on Naval Affairs were instructed to inquire into the expediency of placing at the disposal of the President five millions of dollars to build gunboats.

1862—Bill passed to "regulate the destruction of property under military necessity," referring particularly to cotton and tobacco. The authorities are authorized to destroy it to keep it from the enemy; and owners, destroying it for the same purpose, are to be indemnified upon proof of the value and the circumstances of the destruction.

1862, April 16—The first "conscription"

bill became a law. The *Richmond Enquirer*, of April 23, gives this abstract of it:

To the law of Congress, as published, there were subsequently passed several amendments or auxiliary laws. We present the following synopsis of the law as thus modified:

The conscription law places in the service of the Confederate States, for three years, unless the war sooner ends, *all white men between eighteen and thirty-five years of age, resident in the Confederate States, and not legally exempt from service.*

The law is silent as to exemptions; but an act defining the class of exempts has since been passed, which embraces generally those hitherto exempt, with some additions.

All twelve months' men between the prescribed ages, are continued in service for two years from the expiration of their present term, should the war continue so long; and all those under eighteen and over thirty-five, are to be retained for ninety days after their term expires, unless their places are sooner supplied by recruits.

The twelve months' men between eighteen and thirty-five, who are retained beyond their term of enlistment, and who have not yet received bounty and furlough, shall receive both; the furloughs, however, to be granted in such numbers and at such times as the Secretary of War may deem most compatible with the public interest; and the men may receive in lieu of furlough, the commutation value in money of the transportation granted to furloughed men by the act.

The term of service of those who originally enlisted for the war, or who have since re-enlisted for that period, is not affected by the law.

Men now in service are not permitted to re-enlist in other organizations than those to which they now belong; and all re-enlistments that have been made from one existing company to another, or into a new company, where the re-enlistment has not been perfected by actual transfer, are in effect canceled.

Companies, battalions, and regiments of twelve months' men, retained in service by the act, shall be entitled, within forty days from the date of the act, on a day to be fixed by the commander of the brigade, to reorganize by electing all their officers whom they had a right heretofore to elect.

Companies, battalions, squadrons, or regiments organized, or in process of organization, by authority from the Secretary of War, which may, within thirty days from the passage of the act, have the whole number of men necessary to complete their organization actually enrolled, *not including, however, in that number persons now in service*, shall be mustered into the service of the Confederate States, and be received in that arm of the service in which they were authorized to organize, and elect their company, battalion, and regimental officers.

To enroll the persons contemplated by the act, and not now in service, the President may, with the consent of the Governors of the States, employ State officers; if such consent cannot be obtained, Confederate officers shall be appointed by the President.

Persons not now in service, who shall be enrolled, shall be assigned by the Secretary of War to the different companies of the State from which such persons are drawn, until each company is filled to its maximum number.

Seamen and ordinary seamen, enrolled under the act, may, on application of the Secretary of the Navy, be transferred to the naval service.

If, after filling up the companies, regiments, battalions, and squadrons from any State, there shall remain any of the enrolled men, the excess shall be kept as a reserve; and at stated intervals, not exceeding three months, details, to be made by lot, shall be drawn from the reserve to keep the companies as nearly full as practicable. The persons so reserved remain at home until called into service, and receive no pay until actually mustered in.

They are not, while at home in reserve, subject to the rules and articles of war, except that if they wilfully refuse to obey a call of the President, they shall be held as deserters, and punished as such.

Whenever the President shall think that the exigencies of the service require it, he may call into active service the entire reserve, or as much as may be necessary, and they shall be organized under such rules as the Secretary of War may adopt, and shall elect their field and company officers.

The reserves from each State, when thus called out, shall be organized separately.

Every man mustered into service, who shall bring with him a musket, shot gun, rifle or carbine accepted as an efficient weapon, shall receive the value of it as ascertained by the mustering officer under such regulations as the Secretary of War may prescribe, or if the owner be unwilling to sell, he shall receive $1 a month for the use of such arm.

Persons not liable to duty may be received as substitutes, under such regulations as the Secretary of War may prescribe.

Vacancies may be filled by the President from the company, battalion, squadron or regiment in which such vacancies occur, by promotion according to seniority, except in cases of disability or other incompetency.

The President may, however, fill a vacancy by promoting any officer of the company, battalion, squadron, or regiment, who may have been distinguished in the service by valor and skill, without reference to seniority. Vacancies in the lowest grade of commissioned officers of a company shall be filled by election, or the President may promote to such vacancies non-commissioned officers who have distinguished themselves by skill and valor in the service. Persons *not* now in service may, before being enrolled, volunteer with existing companies now in service.

—

DAVIS'S CONSCRIPTION PROCLAMATION.

[*From the Richmond Enquirer, July* 18, 1863.]

PROCLAMATION BY THE PRESIDENT.

Whereas, It is provided by an act of Congress, entitled "An Act to further provide for the public defence," approved on the 16th day of April, 1862, and by another act of Congress, approved on the 27th September, 1862, entitled "An Act to amend an act antitled 'An Act to provide further for the public defence,'" approved 16th April, 1862, that the President be authorized to call out and place in the military service of the Confederate States, for three years, unless the war shall have been sooner ended, *all white men who are residents of the Confederate States between the ages of* 18 *and* 45 *years, at the time the call may be made, and who are not at such time legally exempted from military service*, or such part thereof as in his judgment may be necessary to the public defence; and

Whereas, in my judgment the necessities of the public defence require that every man capable of bearing arms, between the ages aforesaid, should now be called out to do his duty in the defence of his country, and in driving back the invaders now within the limits of the Confederacy:

Now, therefore, I, Jefferson Davis, President of the Confederate States of America, do, by virtue of the powers vested in me as aforesaid, call out and place in the military service of the Confederate States all white men residents of said States, between the ages of eighteen and forty-five years, not legally exempted from military service; and I do hereby order and direct that all persons subject to this call, and not now in the military service, do, upon being enrolled, forthwith repair to the conscript camps established in the respective States of which they may be residents, under pain of being held and punished as deserters in the event of their failure to obey this call, as provided in said laws.

And I do further order and direct that the enrolling officers of the several States proceed at once to enroll all persons embraced within the terms of this proclamation, and not heretofore enrolled.

And I do further order that it shall be lawful for any person embraced within this call to volunteer for service before enrollment, and that persons so volunteering be allowed to select the arm of service and the company which they desire to join, provided such company be deficient in the full number of men allowed by law for its organization.

Given under my hand and the seal of the Confederate States of America, at the City of Richmond, on this 15th day of July, in the year of our Lord 1863.

JEFFERSON DAVIS.

By the President: J. P. BENJAMIN, *Sec. of State.*

ORDERS UNDER THE CONSCRIPTION ACT.

ADJUTANT AND INSPECTOR GENERAL'S OFFICE, RICHMOND, *July* 20, 1863.—*General Orders, No.* 98.—I. All white male residents of the Confederate States, between the ages of eighteen and forty-five, not exempted by law, and not already in the service, will be enrolled. Persons liable to enrollment may be enrolled wherever they may be found.

II. The first paragraph of General Order No. 86, current series, is so amended as to read as follows: companies, battalions and regiments composed of persons not within the age of conscription, (eighteen and forty-five,) will be accepted as volunteers throughout the Confederacy, under the act of August 21, 1861, (No. 209,) for local defence and special service. Those persons belonging to such organizations, who are of conscript age, and neither exempted by law, nor already in the service, will be discharged, and reported to the bureau of conscription for enrollment.

III. The following regulation will be in addition to those heretofore published in regard to substitutes: Hereafter every person furnishing a substitute, in accordance with existing regulations, shall become liable to, and be immediately enrolled for military duty, upon the loss of the services of the substitute furnished by him from any cause other than the casualties of war.

By order, S. COOPER,
Adjutant and Inspector General.

1864, February. The second conscription bill became a law.

The Richmond Sentinel of February 17, 1864, contains a synopsis of what is called the military bill, heretofore forbidden to be printed:

The first section provides that all white men residents of the Confederate States, between the ages of seventeen and fifty, shall be in the military service for the war.

The second section provides that all between eighteen and forty-five, now in service, shall be continued during the war in the same regiments, battalions, and companies to which they belong at the passage of this act, with the organization, officers, &c., provided that companies from one State organized against their consent, expressed at the time, with regrets, &c., from another State, shall have the privilege of being transferred to the same arm in a regiment from their own State, and men can be transferred to a company from their own State.

Section three gives a bounty eight months hence of $100 in rebel bonds.

Section four provides that no person shall be relieved from the operations of this act heretofore discharged for disability, *nor shall those who furnished substitutes be exempted, where no disability now exists;* but exempts religious persons who have paid an exemption tax.

Section five provides for the enrolling of all white male residents of the Confederate States between seventeen and eighteen, and forty-five and fifty, at such time and under such regulations as the President may prescribe; time allowed east of the Mississippi thirty, and west sixty days; any person failing to enroll without good excuse shall be placed in the field for the war as if he were between eighteen and forty-five. Persons mentioned in this section shall constitute a reserve for State defence and detail duty, and not required to perform service out of the State in which they reside.

Section seven provides that any person who shall fail to attend at the place of rendezvous appointed by the President, and not excused by him, shall be liable to be placed in the field service for the war.

Section eight declares that hereafter all positions as clerks, guards, agents, employees, or laborers on provost, hospital, or ordnance duty, or in the Quartermaster or Commissary Departments, and all similar duties, shall be filled by such persons between the ages of eighteen and forty-five as may be declared by a board of examining surgeons to be unfit for active field service, and when these are exhausted, then from those between seventeen and eighteen, and forty-five and fifty: provided that the President may detail artisans, mechanics, or persons of scientific skill to perform indispensable duties in the bureaux herein named.

The tenth section provides that no person shall be exempt except the following: ministers, superintendents of deaf, dumb, and blind, or insane asylums; one editor to each newspaper, and such employees as he may swear to be indispensable; the Confederate and State public printers, and the journeymen printers necessary to perform the public printing; one apothecary to each drug store, who was and has been continuously doing business as such since October 10, 1862; physicians over 30 years of age of seven years' practice, not including dentists; presidents and teachers of colleges, academies, and schools, who have not less than 30 pupils; superintendents of public hospitals established by law, and such physicians and nurses as may be indispensable for their efficient management.

One agriculturist on each farm where there is no white male adult not liable to duty employing fifteen able-bodied slaves, between 16 and 50 years of age, upon the following conditions:

The party exempted shall give bonds to deliver to the Government in the next twelve months, 100 pounds of bacon, or its equivalent in salt pork, at Government selection, and 100 pounds of beef for each such able-bodied slave employed on said farm, at commissioner's rates.

In certain cases this may be commuted in grain or other provisions.

The person shall further bind himself to sell all surplus provisons now on hand, or which he may raise, to the Government, or the families of soldiers, at commissioner's rates, the person to be allowed a credit of 25 per cent. on any amount he may deliver in three months from the passage of this act; Provided that no enrollment since Feb. 1, 1864, shall deprive the person enrolled from the benefit of this exemption.

In addition to the above, the Secretary of War is authorized to make such details as the public security requires.

The officers and employees of railroad companies engaged in military transportation, not beyond one for each mile used in such transportation, and under certain restrictions. Also, exempts mail contractors and carriers.

The eleventh section authorizes the President to detail either from between 45 and 50 or from the army in the field when necessity requires it, and may, when he thinks proper, revoke such details. Provided, that he shall not exempt or detail any contractor for furnishing supplies, &c., by reason of such contract, except the head of a department shall certify that such exemption is indispensable; the exemption to cease if the contractor fails to comply with his contract.

The twefth section declares that the Board of Surgeons shall not be appointed from the county or district in which they are required to make examinations.

The vote in the House of Respresentatives was—yeas, 41; nays, 31.

GUERRILLAS.

1862, April 21—The President was authorized to commission such officers as he may deem proper, with authority to form bands of partisan rangers, in companies, battalions or regiments, either as infantry or cavalry, to receive the same pay, rations, and quarters, and be subject to the same regulations as other soldiers. For any arms and munitions of war captured from the enemy by any body of partisan rangers, and delivered to any quartermaster at designated place, the rangers shall be paid their full value.*

The following resolution, in relation to partisan service, was adopted by the Virginia Legislature, May 17, 1862:

Whereas, this General Assembly places a high estimate upon the value of the ranger or partisan service in prosecuting the present war to a successful issue, and regards it as perfectly legitimate; and it being understood that a Federal commander on the northern border of Virginia has intimated his purpose, if such service is not discontinued, to lay waste by fire the portion of our territory at present under his power.

Resolved by the General Assembly, That in its opinion, the policy of employing such rangers and partisans ought to be carried out energetically, both by the authorities of this State and of the Confederate States, without the slightest regard to such threats.

By another act, the President was authorized, in addition to the volunteer force authorized under existing laws, to accept the services of volunteers who may offer them, without regard

* 1864, February 15—Repealed the above act, but provided for continuing organizations of partisan rangers acting as regular cavalry and so to continue; and authorizing the Secretary of War to provide for uniting all bands of partisan rangers with other organizations and bringing them under the general discipline of the provisional army. The act authorizes the Secretary of War, in his discretion, to exempt from its operation such companies as are serving within the lines of the enemy.

In a late cavalry raid by Col. Lowell, towards Upperville, Va., Lieut. Henry E. Alvord, of the Second Massachusetts Cavalry, captured Major Moseby's private papers, and found his commission as major of guerrillas, which is as follows:

Confederate States of America, War Department, Richmond, *March* 26, 1863.—You are hereby informed that the President has conferred upon you the rank of Major of Partisan Rangers, under the act approved April 21, 1862, in the Provisional Army of the Confederate States, to date as such from the 26th of March, 1863. Immediately on receipt thereof please communicate to this Department, to the Adjutant and Inspector General, announcing your acceptance of said appointment. With your letter of acceptance to the Adjutant and Inspector General, you will fill up properly the enclosed oath, and subscribe and swear to it; at the same time state your age, residence, and when appointed, and the State in which you were born. Should you accept, report for duty to General R. E. Lee.

JAMES A. SEDDON, *Secretary of War.*

Major John Mosby.

to the place of enlistment, to serve for and during the existing war.

1862, May 27—Maj. Gen. John B. Floyd was authorized by the Legislature of Virginia, to raise ten thousand men, not now in service or liable to draft, for twelve months.

1862, September 27—The President was authorized to call out and place in the military service for three years, all white men who are residents, between the ages of thirty-five and forty-five, at the time the call may be made, not legally exempt. And such authority shall exist in the President, during the present war, as to all persons who now are, or hereafter may become eighteen years of age, and all persons between eighteen and forty-five, once enrolled, shall serve their full time.

THE TWENTY-NEGRO EXEMPTION LAW.

1862, October 11—Exempted certain classes, described in the repealing law of the next session, as follows:

The dissatisfaction of the people with an act passed by the Confederate Congress, at its last session, by which persons owning a certain number of slaves were exempted from the operation of the conscription law, has led the members at the present session to reconsider their work, and already one branch has passed a bill for the repeal of the obnoxious law. This bill provides as follows:

"*The Congress of the Confederate States do enact*, That so much of the act approved October 11, 1862, as exempts from miltary service 'one person, either as agent, owner, or overseer, on each plantation on which one white person is required to be kept by the laws or ordinances of any State, and on which there is no white male adult not liable to military service, and in States having no such law, one person, as agent, owner, or overseer on such plantation of twenty negroes, and on which there is no white male adult not liable to military service;' and also the following clause in said act, to wit: 'and furthermore, for additional police of every twenty negroes, on two or more plantations, within five miles of each other, and each having less than twenty negroes, and on which there is no white male adult not liable to military duty, one person, being the oldest of the owners or overseers on such plantations,' be and the same are hereby repealed; and the persons so hitherto exempted by said clauses of said act are hereby made subject to military duty in the same manner that they would be had said clauses never been embraced in said act."

RESTRICTIONS UPON VOLUNTEERING.

From the Richmond *Examiner*, January 30, 1864:

General Orders have been issued in the Adjutant General's office, instructing the enrolling officers to proceed as rapidly as possible with the new conscription. The privilege of volunteering is restricted in these orders by two important conditions:

"1. The company selected must have been in service on the 16th of April, 1862.

"2. The company selected must be, at the time of volunteering, below the minimum number prescribed by regulations."

JUDICIAL RULINGS UPON CONSCRIPTION.

The Richmond papers of March, 1864, mention the following decision in reference to the conscription act:

"In the case of J. R. F. Borroughs *vs.* T. G. Peyton, and L. P. Abrahams *vs.* the same, the Court of Appeals of Virginia on yesterday rendered a decision. These cases came before the court on *habeas corpus*, the plaintiffs praying to be discharged from the custody of the conscript officer, on the ground that they had furnished substitutes—the one under the State law of February, 1862, the other the Confederate States law.

"The court unanimously rejected the petitions in both cases, and remanded the parties to the military officer. The opinion was delivered by Judge William J. Robertson, and is able and elaborate. It brought under review the constitutionality both of the conscript law and that repealing the exemptions of such conscripts as have furnished substitutes, and it fully sustained the action of Congress in both instances. The conscript law is a legitimate exercise of the power of Congress to raise armies, which is distinct from and additional to the power to employ the militia of the country. The privilege of putting in substitutes, until recently allowed, was an act of grace and favor to the citizen, and not a contract in any respect to which the Government was a party.

"Nor would the Government have had a right to make such contract as in this case is contended for. As an act of grace it was, of course, repealable at the will of Congress. Even if Congress had had the power to make such contract, and had exercised it, yet the conditions necessarily attaching would have rendered the contract repealable if, in the judgment of Congress, the exigencies of the country required it. Congress was the sole judge of a public necessity of this nature, and the preamble to the law repealir substitutions recogni¢ed this."

STATE RIGHTS AND PERSONAL LIBERTY.

The Macon (Georgia) *Telegraph* gives the points of the first legal decision made in the State of Georgia under the act of the Confederate Congress repealing the substitute law, and compelling those who had furnished substitutes to go into the army. It is the judgment of Judge Lochrane, of the Superior Court for Macon Circuit, and was delivered on the 11th of February, in the case of Dennis Daley and Philip Fitzgerald, and is interesting as showing what are held to be State-rights and personal liberty in the Confederate States. We quote:

"Judge Lochrane held it was not only the right, but the duty of a nation to prot ect itself, and that any contract or right flowing out of the operation of law which came in conflict with the preservation of the State, was an unconstitutional act—not obligatory on the law-making power, and within the constitutional power of the Government to repeal.

"That the act allowing substitutes was to be regarded as a contract discharging principals from being called into the service. It was then a contract that the principal should not fight in the defence of the country when it was endangered, and such contract was unauthorized by every principle of constitutional law. If our first Congress had agreed to exempt all men from taxation during the war who paid into the treasury $500, such exemption could have been set aside by any subsequent legislature, when the public safety and self-preservation of the Government demand it.

"He held that the interest of every citizen was the same as that of the Government of which he formed a part, and the military service rendered by the substitute was just as much rendered to the principal as a citizen of the Government itself—his life, his honor, his property, and his liberty were defended by the act, and the consideration enured to him as a member of the society which composed the Government.

"Contracts and vested rights must all bend to the exigencies of the Government, of which the legislature was the judge, and any act of the Legislature contravening the public interest may be repealed when the safety of the people becomes the supreme law.

"The vested rights of fathers may be annulled over their minor children, to make them soldiers when the public interests demand it, and the law-making power has so declared.

"All rights, all property, all persons who are citizens of a Government, may be used by the Government in time of war, and it was the duty of courts to sustain the Government in the appropriation of the means exercised rightfully by the Legislature to protect the whole people from subjugation and ruin."

1864, March 22—The Supreme Court of Georgia are reported as having, to-day, unanimously affirmed the constitutionality of the anti-substitute law.

IN NORTH CAROLINA.

[From Richmond Sentinel, March 8, 1864.]

Habeas Corpus Writs Refused.—The Raleigh *Confederate* states that Judge Battle has lately refused to issue writs of *habeas corpus* in a number of cases when applied for by persons who had placed substitutes in the army, on the ground that the writ was suspended in all such cases by the late act of Congress. It also learns that such is the opinion of Judge Manly. Judges Pearson, Battle, and Manly constitute the Supreme Court of North Carolina, and as two of the three judges sustain the Government in the suspension of the writ of *habeas corpus*, the final decision of the matter against the substitute men is only a question of time.

Judge Pearson is said to hold the contrary opinion.

MARTIAL LAW.

March 1, 1862—JEFFERSON DAVIS President, "by virtue of the power vested in him by law to declare the suspension of the privileges of the writ of *Habeas Corpus* in cities threatened with invasion," proclaimed that martial law was extended over Richmond and the adjoining country to the extent of ten miles. He prohibited all distillation of spirituous liquors, and directed that the distilleries be forthwith closed and the establishments for the sale thereof closed. Many Union men were arrested at once and imprisoned.

April 8, 1862, DAVIS issued a proclamation extending martial law over East Tennessee and suspending all civil jurisdiction and the writ of *Habeas Corpus*. Col. W. M. Churchwell was made provost marshal and was charged with the execution of the proclamation.

May 3, 1862, DAVIS issued a like proclamation with reference to the counties of Lee, Wise, Buchanan, McDowell, and Wyoming in Virginia, under the command of Brig. Gen. Humphrey Marshall.

August 14, 1861, DAVIS issued this

PROCLAMATION OF BANISHMENT:

Whereas, the Congress of the Confederate States of America did, by an act approved on the 8th day of August, 1861, entitled "An act respecting alien enemies," make provision that proclamation should be issued by the President in relation to alien enemies, and in conformity with the provisions of said act:

Now, therefore, I, Jefferson Davis, President of the Confederate States of America, do issue this my proclamation: and I do hereby warn and require every male citizen of the United States, of the age of fourteen years and upwards, now within the Confederate States, and adhering to the Government of the United States, and acknowledging the authority of the same, and not being a citizen of the Confederate States, to depart from the Confederate States within forty days from the date of this proclamation. And I do warn all persons above described, who shall remain within the Confederate States after the expiration of said period of forty days, that they will be treated as alien enemies.

Provided, however, That this proclamation shall not be considered as applicable, during the existing war, to citizens of the United States residing within the Confederate States with intent to become citizens thereof, and who shall make declaration of such intention in due form, acknowledging the authority of this Government; nor shall this proclamation be considered as extending to the States of Delaware, Maryland, Kentucky, Missouri, the District of Columbia, the Territories of Arizona and New Mexico, and the Indian Territory south of Kansas, who shall not be chargeable with actual hostility or other crime against the public safety, and who shall acknowledge the authority of the Government of the Confederate States.

And I do further proclaim and make known that I have established the rules and regulations hereto annexed in accordance with the provisions of said law.

Given under my hand and the seal of the Confederate States of America, at the city of Richmond, on the 14th day of August, A. D. 1861.

By the President: JEFFERSON DAVIS.
R. M. T. HUNTER, *Secretary of State.*

TO THE DISAFFECTED PEOPLE OF EAST TENNESSEE.

The undersigned, in executing martial law in this Department, assures those interested who have fled to the enemy's lines, and who are actually in their army, that he will welcome their return to their homes and families; they are offered annesty and protection if they come to lay down their arms and act as loyal citizens within the thirty days given them by Maj. Gen. E. KIRBY SMITH to do so.

At the end of that time, those failing to return to their homes and accept the amnesty thus offered, and provide for and protect their wives and children in East Tennessee, will have them sent to their care in Kentucky, or beyond the Confederate State lines, at their own expense.

All that leave after this date, with a knowledge of the above facts, will have their families sent immediately after them.

The women and children must be taken care of by husbands and fathers, either in East Tennessee or in the Lincoln Government.

W. M. CHURCHWELL,
Colonel and Provost Marshal.
KNOXVILLE, Tenn., *April* 23, 1862.

STRENGTH OF THE REBEL ARMY.

1864, Jan. 30.—In debating the bill to repeal the Substitute Exemption bill, Mr. Wm. N. H. Smith, of North Carolina, said, the "Confederates" had at this time four hundred thousand men on their muster roll "of whom probably one half were not there, and it was well known we were unable to feed the fractional part who were, in the field."

The Richmond *Whig* of Jan. 1, 1864, alluding to the passage of the above named bill, has these comments:

We wish at this time only to make some passing comments upon the tone manifested in Congress in the debates upon this measure. A Senator (Mr. Orr of S. C.,) among other objections to the passage of the bill gravely questioned its legality.

"If the pending bill becomes a law," said Mr. O., "there will be great difficulty in executing it, by reason of the decisions of the Courts in several of the States. We must acquiesce in the decisions of the Courts, or resort to measures which he was not prepared for." A Senator from Missouri (Mr. Clark,) representing a constituency wholly beyond the action and control of our laws, replied, in urging its passage, that "in regard to the action of the Courts, steps may and should be taken to remove the subject beyond their jurisdiction." The Senator from Mississippi, (Mr. Brown,) goes further: "We should not defer our legislation to consult the views of every State Judge—to ascertain whether he will overthrow it or not by his judicial decision. We have high duties to perform. Let us perform them without reference to State Judges. There was a remedy against the interference of the Courts, in the suspension of the writ of habeas corpus."

The vote of Congress upon this measure shows to what extent *the provisions of the Constitution are getting to be disregarded in the Legislative branch, and how far revolutionary sentiment already prevails in that body.* The strength of the popular respect for our Government, and the good sense of the quiet masses, may for the moment allow such declarations to pass without disturbance. The little respect in which substitute men are held may influence a temporary acquiesence in them. But the intelligent and ardent lover of his country cannot witness such proceedings *with indifference, nor will he, with submission.*

There is as much patriotism and intelligence out of the halls of Congress as in it, and the tendency of the legislative and executive declarations so far this session to a subversion of the liberties of the country and a military despotism is already sowing the seeds of a counter revolution. Our people claim it as their right, as the duty of the General Government to insure to them, as the basis of the compact by which they have associated together, *that the Confederacy is but a community of sovereign States.* They look to the Constitution as the supreme law of the Confederacy. They regard it as among the blessings for which they are indebted to their ancestry that they transmitted to us a written Constitution. It received the plighted faith of our fathers. It is the hope of our posterity. *To argue questions outside or above it is but to assail the cause of law, of right, and order.*

Meeting of the Thirty-Seventh Congress.

The first session began July 4, 1861, and closed August 6, 1861.

The second session began December 2, 1861, and closed July 17, 1862.

The third session began December 1, 1862, and closed March 4, 1863.

MEMBERS OF THE THIRTY-SEVENTH CONGRESS, MARCH 4, 1861, TO MARCH 4, 1863.

HANNIBAL HAMLIN, of Maine, *President.*
John W. Forney, of Pennsylvania, *Secretary.*

SENATORS.

MAINE—Lot M. Morrill, William P. Fessenden.

NEW HAMPSHIRE—John P. Hale, Daniel Clark.

Vermont—Solomon Foot, Jacob Collamer.
Massachusetts—Charles Sumner, Henry Wilson.
Rhode Island—James F. Simmons,* Henry B. Anthony.
Connecticut—James Dixon, Lafayette S. Foster.
New York—Preston King, Ira Harris.
New Jersey—John R. Thomson,* John C. Ten Eyck.
Pennsylvania—David Wilmot, Edgar Cowan.
Delaware—James A. Bayard, Willard Saulsbury.
Maryland—Anthony Kennedy, James A. Pearce.*
Virginia.*
Ohio—Benjamin F. Wade, John Sherman.
Kentucky—Lazarus W. Powell, John C. Breckinridge.*
Tennessee—Andrew Johnson.
Indiana—Jesse D. Bright,* Henry S. Lane.
Illinois—Orville H. Browning,* Lyman Trumbull.
Missouri—Trusten Polk,* Waldo P. Johnson.*
Michigan—Zachariah Chandler, Kinsley S. Bingham.*
Iowa—James W. Grimes, James Harlan.
Wisconsin—James R. Doolittle, Timothy O. Howe.
California—Milton S. Latham, James A. McDougall.
Minnesota—Henry M. Rice, Morton S. Wilkinson.
Oregon—Edward D. Baker,* James W. Nesmith.
Kansas—James H. Lane, Samuel C. Pomeroy.

REPRESENTATIVES.

Galusha A. Grow, of Pennsylvania, *Speaker*.
Emerson Etheridge, of Tennessee, *Clerk*.

Maine—John N. Goodwin, Charles W. Walton,* Samuel C. Fessenden, Anson P. Morrill, John H. Rice, Frederick A. Pike.
New Hampshire—Gilman Marston, Edward H. Rollins, Thomas M. Edwards.
Vermont—E. P. Walton, Jr., Justin S. Morrill, Portus Baxter.
Massachusetts—Thomas D. Eliot, James Buffinton, Benjamin F. Thomas, Alexander H. Rice, William Appleton,* John B. Alley, Daniel W. Gooch, Charles R. Train, Goldsmith F. Bailey,* Charles Delano, Henry L. Dawes.
Rhode Island—William P. Sheffield, George H. Browne.
Connecticut—Dwight Loomis, James E. English, Alfred A. Burnham,* George C. Woodruff.
New York—Edward H. Smith, Moses F. Odell, Benjamin Wood, James E. Kerrigan, William Wall, Frederick A. Conkling, Elijah Ward, Isaac C. Delaplaine, Edward Haight, Charles H. Van Wyck, John B. Steele, Stephen Baker, Abraham B. Olin, Erastus Corning, James B. McKean, William A. Wheeler, Socrates N. Sherman, Chauncey Vibbard, Richard Franchot, Roscoe Conkling, R. Holland Duell, William E. Lansing, Ambrose W. Clark, Charles B. Sedgwick, Theodore M. Pomeroy, Jacob P. Chamberlain, Alexander S. Diven, Robert B. Van Valkenburgh, Alfred Ely, Augustus Frank, Burt Van Horn, Elbridge G. Spaulding, Reuben E. Fenton.
New Jersey—John T. Nixon, John L. N. Stratton, William G. Steele, George T. Cobb, Nehemiah Perry.
Pennsylvania—William E. Lehman, Charles J. Biddle,* John P. Verree, William D. Kelley, William Morris Davis, John Hickman, Thomas B. Cooper,* Sydenham E. Ancona, Thaddeus Stevens, John W. Killinger, James H. Campbell, Hendrick B. Wright, Philip Johnson, Galusha A. Grow, James T. Hale, Joseph Baily, Edward McPherson, Samuel S. Blair, John Covode, Jesse Lazear, James K. Moorhead, Robert McKnight, John W. Wallace, John Patton, Elijah Babbitt.
Delaware—George P. Fisher.
Maryland—John W. Crisfield, Edwin H. Webster, Cornelius L. L. Leary, Henry May, Francis Thomas, Charles B. Calvert.
Virginia—Charles H. Upton,* William G. Brown, John S. Carlile,* Kellian V. Whaley, Joseph Segar.*
Ohio—George H. Pendleton, John A. Gurley, Clement L. Vallandigham, William Allen, Jas. M. Ashley, Chilton A. White, Richard A. Harrison, Samuel Shellabarger, Warren P. Noble, Carey A. Trimble, Valentine B. Horton, Samuel S. Cox, Samuel T. Worcester, Harrison G. Blake, Robert H. Nugen, William P. Cutler, James R. Morris, Sidney Edgerton, Albert G. Riddle, John Hutchins, John A. Bingham.
Kentucky—Henry C. Burnett,* James S. Jackson,* Henry Grider, Aaron Harding, Chas. A. Wickliffe, George W. Dunlap, Robert Mallory, John J. Crittenden, William H. Wadsworth, John W. Menzies.
Tennessee—Horace Maynard,* Andrew J. Clements,* George W. Bridges.*
Indiana—John Law, James A. Cravens, W. McKee Dunn, William S. Holman, George W. Julian, Albert G. Porter, Daniel W. Voorhees, Albert S. White, Schuyler Colfax, William Mitchell, John P. C. Shanks.
Illinois—Ellihu B. Washburne, Isaac N. Arnold, Owen Lovejoy, William Kellogg, William A. Richardson,* John A. McClernand,* James C. Robinson, Philip B. Fouke, John A. Logan.*
Missouri—Francis P. Blair, Jr., James S. Rollins, John B. Clark,* Elijah H. Norton, John W. Reid,* John S. Phelps,* John W. Noell.
Michigan—Bradley F. Granger, Fernando C. Beaman, Francis W. Kellogg, Rowland E. Trowbridge.
Iowa—Samuel R. Curtis,* William Vandever.
Wisconsin—John F. Potter, Luther Hanchett,* A. Scott Sloan.
California—Timothy G. Phelps and Aaron A. Sargent, qualified Dec. 2, 1861; and Frederick F. Low, (now Governor,) June 3, 1862.
Minnesota—Cyrus Aldrich, William Windom.
Oregon—Andrew J. Thayer.*
Kansas—Martin F. Conway.

* See memorandum at end of list.

* See memorandum at end of list.

MEMORANDUM OF CHANGES.

The following changes took place during the Congress:

IN SENATE.

RHODE ISLAND—1862, Dec. 1, Samuel G. Arnold succeeded James F. Simmons, resigned.

NEW JERSEY—1862, Dec. 1, Richard S. Field succeeded, by appointment, John R. Thomson, deceased Sept. 12, 1862. 1863, Jan. 21, James W. Wall succeeded, by election, Richard S. Field.

MARYLAND—1863, Jan. 14, Thomas H. Hicks, first by appointment and then by election, succeeded James A. Pearce, deceased Dec. 20, 1862.

VIRGINIA—1861, July 13, John S. Carlile and Waitman T. Willey, sworn in place of Robert M. T. Hunter and James M. Mason, withdrawn and abdicated.

KENTUCKY—1861, Dec. 23, Garrett Davis succeeded John C. Breckinridge, expelled December 4.

INDIANA—1862, March 3, Joseph A. Wright succeeded Jesse D. Bright, expelled Feb. 5. 1863, Jan. 22, David Turpie superseded, by election, Joseph A. Wright.

ILLINOIS—1863, Jan. 30, William A. Richardson superseded, by election, O. H. Browning.

MISSOURI—1862, Jan. 24, R. Wilson succeeded Waldo P. Johnson, expelled Jan. 10. 1862, Jan. 29, John B. Henderson succeeded Trusten Polk, expelled Jan. 10.

MICHIGAN—1862, Jan. 17, Jacob M. Howard succeeded K. S. Bingham, deceased Oct. 5, 1862.

OREGON—1862, Dec. 1, Benjamin F. Harding succeeded Edward D. Baker, deceased Oct. 21, 1862.

IN HOUSE OF REPRESENTATIVES.

MAINE—1862, December 1, Thomas A. D. Fessenden succeeded Charles W. Walton, resigned May 26, 1862.

MASSACHUSETTS—1862, December 1, Amasa Walker succeeded Goldsmith F. Bailey, deceased May 8, 1862; 1861, December 2, Samuel Hooper succeeded William Appleton, resigned.

CONNECTICUT—1861, December 2, Alfred A. Burnham qualified.

PENNSYLVANIA—1861, December 2, Charles J. Biddle qualified; 1862, June 3, John D. Stiles succeeded T. B. Cooper, deceased April 4, 1862.

VIRGINIA—1861, July 13, John S. Carlile resigned to take a seat in the Senate; 1861, December 2, Jacob B. Blair succeeded John S. Carlile, resigned; 1862, February 28, Charles H. Upton unseated by a vote of the House; 1862, May 6, Joseph Segar qualified.

KENTUCKY—1862, December 1, George H. Yeaman succeeded James S. Jackson, deceased; 1862, March 10, Samuel L. Casey succeeded Henry C. Burnett, expelled December 3, 1861.

TENNESSEE—1861, December 2, Horace Maynard qualified; 1862, January 13, Andrew J. Clements qualified; 1863, February 25, George W. Bridges qualified.

ILLINOIS—1861, December 12, A. L. Knapp qualified, in place of J. A. McClernand, resigned; 1862, June 2, William J. Allen qualified, in place of John A. Logan, resigned; 1863, January 30, William A. Richardson withdrew to take a seat in the Senate.

MISSOURI—1862, January 21, Thomas L. Price succeeded John W. Reid, expelled December 2, 1861; 1862, January 20, William A. Hall succeeded John B. Clark, expelled July 13, 1861; 1862, May 9, John S. Phelps qualified.

IOWA—1861, December 2, James F. Wilson succeeded Samuel R. Curtis, resigned August 4, 1861.

WISCONSIN—1863, January 26, Walter D. McIndoe succeeded Luther Hanchett, deceased November 24, 1862.

OREGON—1861, July 30, George K. Shiel succeeded Andrew J. Thayer, unseated.

LOUISIANA—1863, February 17, Michael Hahn qualified; 1863, February 23, Benjamin F. Flanders qualified.

President Lincoln's First Message, July 4, 1861.

Fellow-Citizens of the Senate and House of Representatives:

Having been convened on an extraordinary occasion, as authorized by the Constitution, your attention is not called to any ordinary subject of legislation.

At the beginning of the present Presidential term, four months ago, the functions of the Federal Government were found to be generally suspended within the several States of South Carolina, Georgia, Alabama, Mississippi, Louisiana, and Florida, excepting only those of the Post Office Department.

Within these States, all the forts, arsenals, dock-yards, custom-houses, and the like, including the movable and stationary property in and about them, had been seized, and were held in open hostility to this Government, excepting only Forts Pickens, Taylor, and Jefferson, on and near the Florida coast, and Fort Sumter, in Charleston harbor, South Carolina. The forts thus seized had been put in improved condition; new ones had been built, and armed forces had been organized, and were organizing, all avowedly with the same hostile purpose.

The forts remaining in the possession of the Federal Government in and near these States were either besieged or menaced by warlike preparations, and especially Fort Sumter was nearly surrounded by well-protected hostile batteries, with guns equal in quality to the best of its own, and outnumbering the latter as perhaps ten to one. A disproportionate share of the Federal muskets and rifles had somehow found their way into these States, and had been seized to be used against the Government. Accumulations of the public revenue, lying within them, had been seized for the same object. The navy was scattered in distant seas, leaving but a very small part of it within the immediate reach of the Government Officers of the Federal army and navy had resigned in great numbers; and of those resigning a large proportion had taken up arms against the Government. Simultaneously, and in connection with all this, the purpose to sever the Federal Union was openly avowed. In accordance with this purpose an ordinance had been adopted in each of these States, declaring the States, respectively, to be separated from the National Union.

A formula for instituting a combined government of these States had been promulgated; and this illegal organization, in the character of Confederate States, was already invoking recognition, aid, and intervention from foreign Powers.

Finding this condition of things, and believing it to be an imperative duty upon the incoming Executive to prevent, if possible, the consummation of such attempt to destroy the Federal Union, a choice of means to that end became indispensable. This choice was made, and was declared in the inaugural address. The policy chosen looked to the exhaustion of all peaceful measures before a resort to any stronger ones. It sought only to hold the public places and property not already wrested from the Government, and to collect the revenue; relying for the rest on time, discussion, and the ballot-box. It promised a continuance of the mails, at Government expense, to the very people who were resisting the Government; and it gave repeated pledges against any disturbance to any of the people, or any of their rights. Of all that which a President might constitutionally and justifiably do in such a case, everything was forborne without which it was believed possible to keep the Government on foot.

On the 5th of March (the present incumbent's first full day in office) a letter of Major Anderson, commanding at Fort Sumter, written on the 28th of February, and received at the War Department on the 4th of March, was, by that Department, placed in his hands. This letter expressed the professional opinion of the writer that reinforcements could not be thrown into that fort within the time for his relief, rendered necessary by the limited supply of provisions, and with a view of holding possession of the same, with a force of less than twenty thousand good and well-disciplined men. This opinion was concurred in by all the officers of his command, and their *memoranda* on the subject were made enclosures of Major Anderson's letter. The whole was immediately laid before Lieut. General Scott, who at once concurred with Major Anderson in opinion. On reflection, however, he took full time, consulting with other officers, both of the army and the navy, and, at the end of four days, came reluctantly, but decidedly, to the same conclusion as before. He also stated at the same time that no such sufficient force was then at the control of the Government, or could be raised and brought to the ground within the time when the provisions in the fort would be exhausted. In a purely military point of view this reduced the duty of the Administration in the case to mere matter of getting the garrison safely out of the fort.

It was believed, however, that to so abandon that position, under the circumstances, would be utterly ruinous; that the *necessity* under which it was to be done would not be fully understood; that by many it would be construed as a part of a *voluntary* policy; that at home it would discourage the friends of the Union, embolden its adversaries, and go far to insure to the latter a recognition abroad; that in fact it would be our national destruction consummated. This could not be allowed. Starvation was not yet upon the garrison; and ere it would be reached *Fort Pickens* might be re-inforced. This last would be a clear indication of *policy*, and would better enable the country to accept the evacuation of Fort Sumter as a military *necessity*. An order was at once directed to be sent for the landing of the troops from the steamship Brooklyn into Fort Pickens. This order could not go by land, but must take the longer and slower route by sea. The first return news from the order was received just one week before the fall of Fort Sumter. The news itself was that the officer commanding the Sabine, to which vessel the troops had been transferred from the Brooklyn, acting upon some *quasi* armistice of the late Administration, (and of the existence of which the present Administration, up to the time the order was dispatched, had only too vague and uncertain rumors to fix attention,) had refused to land the troops. To now reinforce Fort Pickens, before a crisis would be reached at Fort Sumter, was impossible—rendered so by the near exhaustion of provisions in the latter named fort. In precaution against such a conjuncture the Government had, a few days before, commenced preparing an expedition, as well adapted as might be, to relieve Fort Sumter, which expedition was intended to be ultimately used, or not, according to circumstances. The strongest anticipated case for using it was now presented; and it was resolved to send it forward. As had been intended in this contingency, it was resolved to notify the Governor of South Carolina that he might expect an attempt would be made to provision the fort;* and that if the attempt should not be resisted there would be no effort to throw in men, arms, or ammunition, without further notice, or in case of an attack upon the fort. This notice was accordingly given; whereupon the fort was attacked and bombarded to its fall, without even awaiting the arrival of the provisioning expedition.

It is thus seen that the assault upon and reduction of Fort Sumter was, in no sense a matter of self-defence on the part of the assailants. They well knew that the garrison in the fort could, by no possibility, commit aggression upon them. They knew—they were expressly notified—that the giving of bread to the few brave and hungry men of the garrison was all which would on that occasion be attempted, unless themselves, by resisting so much, should provoke more. They knew that this Government desired to keep the garrison in the fort, not to assail them, but merely to maintain in visible possession, and thus to preserve the Union from actual and immediate dissolution—trusting, as hereinbefore stated, to time, discussion, and the ballot-box for final adjustment; and they assailed and reduced the fort for precisely the reverse object—to drive out the visible authority of the Federal Union, and thus force it to immediate dissolution. That this was their object the Executive well understood; and having said to them, in the Inaugural Address, "you can have no conflict without being

* See page 113.

yourselves the aggressors," he took pains not only to keep this declaration good, but also to keep the case so free from the power of ingenious sophistry as that the world should not be able to misunderstand it. By the affair at Fort Sumter, with its surrounding circumstances, that point was reached. Then and thereby the assailants of the Government began the conflict of arms, without a gun in sight or in expectancy to return their fire, save only the few in the fort sent to that harbor years before for their own protection, and still ready to give that protection in whatever was lawful. In this act, discarding all else, they have forced upon the country, the distinct issue: "Immediate dissolution or blood."

And this issue embraces more than the fate of these United States. It presents to the whole family of man the question whether a Constitutional Republic or Democracy—a government of the people by the same people—can or cannot maintain its territorial integrity against its own domestic foes. It presents the question whether discontented individuals, too few in numbers to control administration according to organic law in any case, can always, upon the pretences made in this case, or on any other pretences, or arbitrarily without any pretence, break up their Government, and thus practically put an end to free government upon the earth. It forces us to ask: "Is there, in all republics, this inherent and fatal weakness?" "Must a Government of necessity be too *strong* for the liberties of its own people, or too *weak* to maintain its own existence?"

So viewing the issue, no choice was left but to call out the war power of the Government; and so to resist force, employed for its destruction, by force, for its preservation.

The call was made, and the response of the country was most gratifying, surpassing in unamimity and spirit the most sanguine expectations. Yet none of the States commonly called slave States, except Delaware, gave a regiment through regular State organization. A few regiments have been organized within some others of those States by individual enterprise, and received into the Government service. Of course, the seceded States, so called, (and to which Texas had been joined about the time of the inauguration,) gave no troops to the cause of the Union. The border States, so called, were not uniform in their action; some of them being almost for the Union, while in others—as Virginia, North Carolina, Tennessee, and Arkansas—the Union sentiment was nearly repressed and silenced. The course taken in Virginia was the most remarkable, perhaps the most important. A Convention, elected by the people of that State to consider this very question of disrupting the Federal Union, was in session at the capital of Virginia when Fort Sumter fell. To this body the people had chosen a large majority of *professed* Union men. Almost immediately after the fall of Sumter, many members of that majority went over to the original disunion minority, and, with them, adopted an ordinance for withdrawing the State from the Union. Whether this change was wrought by their great approval of the assault upon Sumter, or their great resentment at the Government's resistance to that assault, is not definitely known. Although they submitted the ordinance, for ratification, to a vote of the people, to be taken on a day then somewhat more than a month distant, the Convention, and the Legislature, (which was also in session at the same time and place,) with leading men of the State, not members of either, immediately commenced acting as if the State were already out of the Union. They pushed military preparations vigorously forward all over the State. They seized the United States armory at Harper's Ferry, and the navy-yard at Gosport, near Norfolk. They received—perhaps invited—into their State large bodies of troops, with their warlike appointments, from the so-called seceded States. They formally entered into a treaty of temporary alliance and co-operation with the so-called "Confederate States," and sent members to their Congress at Montgomery. And, finally, they permitted the insurrectionary Government to be transferred to their capital at Richmond

The people of Virginia have thus allowed this giant insurrection to make its nest within her borders; and this Government has no choice left but to deal with it *where* it finds it. And it has the less regret, as the loyal citizens have, in due form, claimed its protection. Those loyal citizens this Government is bound to recognize, and protect, as being Virginia.

In the Border States, so-called—in fact, the Middle States—there are those who favor a policy which they call "armed neutrality;" that is, an arming of those States to prevent the Union forces passing one way, or the disunion the other, over their soil. This would be disunion completed. Figuratively speaking, it would be the building of an impassable wall along the line of separation; and yet not quite an impassable one; for, under the guise of neutrality, it would tie the hands of the Union men, and freely pass supplies from among them to the insurrectionists, which it could not do as an open enemy. At a stroke it would take all the trouble off the hands of secession, except only what proceeds from the external blockade. It would do for the disunionists that which, of all things, they most desire—feed them well, and give them disunion without a struggle of their own. It recognizes no fidelity to the Constitution, no obligation to maintain the Union; and while very many who have favored it are doubtless loyal citizens, it is, nevertheless, very injurious in effect.

Recurring to the action of the Government, it may be stated that, at first, a call was made for seventy-five thousand militia; and rapidly following this, a proclamation was issued for closing the ports of the insurrectionary districts by proceedings in the nature of blockade. So far all was believed to be strictly legal. At this point the insurrectionists announced their purpose to enter upon the practice of privateering.

Other calls were made for volunteers to serve three years, unless sooner discharged, and also for large additions to the regular army and navy. These measures, whether strictly legal or not, were ventured upon, under what appeared to be a popular demand and a public necessity; trusting then, as now, that Congress would readily ratify them. It is believed that nothing has been done beyond the constitutional competency of Congress.

Soon after the first call for militia it was considered a duty to authorize the Commanding General, in proper cases, according to his discretion, to suspend the privilege of the writ of habeas corpus, or, in other words, to arrest and detain, without resort to the ordinary processes and forms of law, such individuals as he might deem dangerous to the public safety. This authority has purposely been exercised but very sparingly. Nevertheless the legality and propriety of what has been done under it are questioned, and the attention of the country has been called to the proposition that one who is sworn to "take care that the laws be faithfully executed" should not himself violate them. Of course some consideration was given to the questions of power and propriety before this matter was acted upon. The whole of the laws which were required to be faithfully executed were being resisted and failing of execution in nearly one third of the States. Must they be allowed to finally fail of execution, even had it been perfectly clear that, by the use of the means necessary to their execution, some single law, made in such extreme tenderness of the citizen's liberty that practically it relieves more of the guilty than of the innocent, should to a very limited extent be violated? To state the question more directly, are all the laws *but one* to go unexecuted and the Government itself go to pieces lest that one be violated? Even in such a case would not the official oath be broken, if the Government should be overthrown, when it was believed that disregarding the single law would tend to preserve it? But it was not believed that this question was presented. It was not believed that any law was violated. The provision of the Constitution that "the privilege of the writ of habeas corpus shall not be suspended unless when, in cases of rebellion or invasion, the public safety may require it," is equivalent to a provision, is a provision, that such privilege may be suspended when, in cases of rebellion or invasion, the public safety *does* require it. It was decided that we have a case of rebellion, and that the public safety does require the qualified suspension of the privilege of the writ which was authorized to be made. Now it is insisted that Congress, and not the Executive, is vested with this power. But the Constitution itself is silent as to which or who is to exercise the power; and as the provision was plainly made for a dangerous emergency, it cannot be believed the framers of the instrument intended that in every case the danger should run its course until Congress could be called together, the very assembling of which might be prevented, as was intended in this case, by the rebellion.

No more extended argument is now offered, as an opinion at some length will probably be presented by the Attorney General. Whether there shall be any legislation upon the subject, and if any, what, is submitted entirely to the better judgment of Congress.

The forbearance of this Government had been so extraordinary, and so long continued as to lead some foreign nations to shape their action as if they supposed the early destruction of our National Union was probable. While this, on discovery, gave the Executive some concern, he is now happy to say that the sovereignty and rights of the United States are now everywhere practically respected by foreign Powers, and a general sympathy with the country is manifested throughout the world.

The reports of the Secretaries of the Treasury, War, and the Navy will give the information in detail deemed necessary and convenient for your deliberation and action; while the Executive, and all the departments, will stand ready to supply omissions, or to communicate new facts considered important for you to know.

It is now recommended that you give the legal means for making this contest a short and a decisive one; that you place at the control of the Government, for the work, at least four hundred thousand men and four hundred millions of dollars. That number of men is about one tenth of those of proper ages within the regions where, apparently, *all* are willing to engage; and the sum is less than a twenty-third part of the money value owned by the men who seem ready to devote the whole. A debt of six hundred millions of dollars *now*, is a less sum per head than was the debt of our Revolution when we came out of that struggle; and the money value in the country now bears even a greater proportion to what it was *then* than does the population. Surely, each man has as strong a motive *now* to *preserve* our liberties as each had *then* to *establish* them.

A right result, at this time, will be worth more to the world than ten times the men and ten times the money. The evidence reaching us from the country leaves no doubt that the material for the work is abundant; and that it needs only the hand of legislation to give it legal sanction, and the hand of the Executive to give it practical shape and efficiency. One of the greatest perplexities of the Government is to avoid receiving troops faster than it can provide for them. In a word, the people will save their Government if the Government itself will do its part only indifferently well.

It might seem, at first thought, to be of little difference whether the present movement at the South be called "secession" or "rebellion." The movers, however, well understand the difference. At the beginning they knew they could never raise their treason to any respectable magnitude by any name which implies *violation* of law. They knew their people possessed as much of moral sense, as much of devotion to law and order, and as much pride in and reverence for the history and Government of their common country as any other civilized and patriotic people. They knew they could make no advancement directly in the teeth of these strong and noble sentiments. Accordingly they commenced by an insidious debauching of the public mind. They invented an ingenious sophism, which, if conceded, was followed by perfectly logical steps, through all the incidents, to the complete destruction of the Union. The sophism itself is, that any State of the Union may, *consistently* with the national Constitution, and therefore *lawfully* and *peacefully*, withdraw from the Union without the consent of the Union or of any other State. The little disguise that the supposed right is to be exercised only for just cause, themselves to be the sole judge of its justice, is too thin to merit any notice.

With rebellion thus sugar-coated, they have been drugging the public mind of their section for more than thirty years; and until at length they have brought many good men to a willingness to take up arms against the Government the day *after* some assemblage of men have enacted the farcical pretence of taking their State out of the Union who could have been brought to no such thing the day *before*.

This sophism derives much, perhaps the whole, of its currency from the assumption that there is some omnipotent and sacred supremacy pertaining to a *State*—to each State of our Federal Union. Our States have neither more nor less power than that reserved to them, in the Union, by the Constitution—no one of them ever having been a State *out* of the Union. The original ones passed into the Union even *before* they cast off their British colonial dependence; and the new ones each came into the Union directly from a condition of dependence, excepting Texas. And even Texas, in its temporary independence, was never designated a State. The new ones only took the designation of States on coming into the Union, while that name was first adopted for the old ones in and by the Declaration of Independence. Therein the "United Colonies" were declared to be "free and independent States;" but, even then, the object plainly was not to declare their independence of *one another*, or of the *Union*, but directly the contrary, as their mutual pledge and their mutual action, before, at the time, and afterwards, abundantly show. The express plighting of faith, by each and all of the original thirteen, in the Articles of Confederation, two years later, that the Union shall be perpetual, is most conclusive. Having never been States, either in substance or in name, *outside* of the Union, whence this magical omnipotence of "State rights," asserting a claim of power to lawfully destroy the Union itself? Much is said about the "sovereignty" of the States; but the word even is not in the National Constitution; nor, as is believed, in any of the State constitutions. What is a "sovereignty," in the political sense of the term? Would it be far wrong to define it "a political community without a political superior?" Tested by this, no one of our States, except Texas, ever was a sovereignty. And even Texas gave up the character on coming into the Union; by which act she acknowledged the Constitution of the United States, and the laws and treaties of the United States made in pursuance of the Constitution, to be, for her, the supreme law of the land. The States have their *status* IN the Union, and they have no other legal *status*. If they break from this, they can only do so against law and by revolution. The Union, and not themselves separately, procured their independence and their liberty. By conquest, or purchase, the Union gave each of them whatever of independence and liberty it has. The Union is older than any of the States, and, in fact, it created them as States. Originally some dependent colonies made the Union, and, in turn, the Union threw off their old dependence for them, and made them States, such as they are. Not one of them ever had a State constitution independent of the Union. Of course it is not forgotten that all the new States framed their constitutions before they entered the Union; nevertheless, dependent upon and preparatory to coming into the Union.

Unquestionably the States have the powers and rights reserved to them in and by the National Constitution; but among them surely are not included all conceivable powers, however mischievous or destructive, but, at most, such only as were known in the world at the time as governmental powers; and certainly a power to destroy the Government itself had never been known as a governmental, as a merely administrative power. This relative matter of national power and State rights, as a principle, is no other than the principle of *generality* and *locality*. Whatever concerns the whole should be confided to the whole—to the General Government; while whatever concerns *only* the State should be left exclusively to the State. This is all there is of original principle about it. Whether the National Constitution, in defining boundaries between the two, has applied the principle with exact accuracy, is not to be questioned. We are all bound by that defining, without question.

What is now combatted is the position that secession is *consistent* with the Constitution—is *lawful* and *peaceful*. It is not contended that there is any express law for it; and nothing should ever be implied as law which leads to unjust or absurd consequences. The nation purchased with money the countries out of which several of these States were formed. Is it just that they shall go off without leave, and without refunding? The nation paid very large sums (in the aggregate, I believe, nearly a hundred millions) to relieve Florida of the aboriginal tribes. Is it just that they shall now be off without consent, or without making any return? The nation is now in debt for money applied to the benefit of these so-called seceding States, in common with the rest. Is it just either that creditors shall go unpaid or the remaining States pay the whole? A part of the present national debt was contracted to pay the old debts of Texas. Is it just that she shall leave and pay no part of this herself?

Again, if one State may secede, so may another; and when all shall have seceded, none is left to pay the debts. Is this quite just to creditors? Did we notify them of this sage view of ours when we borrowed their money? If we now recognize this doctrine by allowing the seceders to go in peace, it is difficult to see what we can do if others choose to go, or to extort terms upon which they will promise to remain.

The seceders insist that our Constitution admits of secession. They have assumed to make a national constitution of their own, in which, of necessity, they have either *discarded* or *retained* the right of secession as, they insist, it exists in ours. If they have discarded it they thereby admit that, on principle, it ought not to be in ours. If they have retained it by their own construction of ours, they show that to be consistent they must secede from one another whenever they shall find it the easiest way of settling their debts, or effecting any other selfish or unjust object. The principle itself is one of disintegration, and upon which no Government can possibly endure.

If all the States save one should assert the power to *drive* that one out of the Union, it is presumed the whole class of seceder politicians would at once deny the power and denounce the act as the greatest outrage upon State rights. But suppose that precisely the same act, instead of being called "driving the one out," should be called "the seceding of all the others from that one," it would be exactly what the seceders claim to do; unless, indeed, they make the point that the one, because it is a minority, may rightfully do what the others, because they are a majority, may not rightfully do. These politicians are subtle and profound on the rights of minorities. They are not partial to that power which made the Constitution, and speaks from the preamble, calling itself "We, the People."

It may well be questioned whether there is to-day a majority of the legally qualified voters of any State, except perhaps South Carolina, in favor of disunion. There is much reason to believe that the Union men are the majority in many, if not in every other one, of the so-called Seceded States. The contrary has not been demonstrated in any one of them. It is ventured to affirm this, even of Virginia and Tennessee; for the results of an election, held in military camps, where the bayonets are all on one side of the question voted upon, can scarcely be considered as demonstrating popular sentiment. At such an election all the large class who are, at once, *for* the Union, and *against* coercion, would be coerced to vote against the Union.

It may be affirmed, without extravagance, that the free institutions we enjoy have developed the powers and improved the condition of our whole people beyond any example in the world. Of this we now have a striking and an impressive illustration. So large an army as the Government has now on foot was never before known, without a soldier in it but who had taken his place there of his own free choice. But more than this: there are many single regiments whose members, one and another, possess full practical knowledge of all the arts, sciences, professions, and whatever else, whether useful or elegant, is known in the world; and there is scarcely one from which there could not be selected a President, a Cabinet. a Congress, and perhaps a Court, abundantly competent to administer the Government itself. Nor do I say this is not true also in the army of our late friends, now adversaries, in this contest; but if it is, so much better the reason why the Government, which has conferred such benefits on both them and us, should not be broken up. Whoever, in any section, proposes to abandon such a Government would do well to consider in deference to what principle it is that he does it, what better he is likely to get in its stead, whether the substitute will give or be intended to give so much of good to the people. There are some foreshadowings on this subject. Our adversaries have adopted some declaration of independence, in which, unlike the good old one penned by Jefferson, they omit the words "all men are created equal." Why? They have adopted a temporary National Constitution, in the preamble of which, unlike our good old one signed by Washington, they omit "We, the people," and substitute, "We, the deputies of the sovereign and independent States." Why? Why this deliberate pressing out of view the rights of men and the authority of the people?

This is essentially a People's contest. On the side of the Union it is a struggle for maintaining in the world that form and substance of government whose leading object is to elevate the condition of men, to lift artificial weights from all shoulders, to clear the paths of laudable pursuit for all, to afford all an unfettered start and a fair chance in the race of life. Yielding to partial and temporary departures from necessity, this is the leading object of the Government for whose existence we contend.

I am most happy to believe that the plain people understand and appreciate this. It is worthy of note that, while in this the Government's hour of trial, large numbers of those in the Army and Navy who have been favored with the offices have resigned, and proved false to the hand which had pampered them, not one common soldier or common sailor is known to have deserted his flag.

Great honor is due to those officers who remained true, despite the example of their treacherous associates; but the greatest honor and most important fact of all is the unanimous firmness of the common soldiers and common sailors. To the last man, so far as known, they have successfully resisted the traitorous efforts of those whose commands but an hour before they obeyed as absolute law. This is the patriotic instinct of plain people. They understand, without an argument, that the destroying the Government which was made by Washington means no good to them.

Our popular Government has often been called an experiment. Two points in it our people have already settled—the successful *establishing* and the successful *administering* of it. One still remains—its successful *maintenance* against a formidable internal attempt to overthrow it. It is now for them to demonstrate to the world that those who can fairly carry an election can also suppress a rebellion; that ballots are the rightful and peaceful successors of bullets; and that when ballots have fairly and constitutionally decided, there can be no successful appeal back to bullets; that there can be no successful appeal except to ballots themselves at succeeding elections. Such will be a great lesson of peace, teaching men that what they cannot take by an election, neither can they take it by a war; teaching all the folly of being the beginners of a war.

Lest there be some uneasiness in the minds of candid men as to what is to be the course of the Government towards the Southern States after the rebellion shall have been suppressed, the Executive deems it proper to say, it will be his purpose then, as ever, to be guided by the Constitution and the laws; and that he probably will have no different understanding of the powers and duties of the Federal Government relatively to the rights of the States and the people, under the Constitution, than that expressed in the inaugural address.

He desires to preserve the Government, that it may be administered for all, as it was administered by the men who made it. Loyal citizens everywhere have the right to claim this of their Government, and the Government has no right to withhold or neglect it. It is not perceived that, in giving it, there is any coercion, any conquest, or any subjugation, in any just sense of those terms.

The Constitution provides, and all the States have accepted the provision, that "the United States shall guaranty to every State in this Union a republican form of government." But, if a State may lawfully go out of the Union, having done so, it may also discard the republican form of government; so that to prevent its going out is an indispensable *means* to the *end* of maintaining the guarantee mentioned; and when an end is lawful and obligatory, the indispensable means to it are also lawful and obligatory.

It was with the deepest regret that the Executive found the duty of employing the war power, in defence of the Government, forced upon him. He could but perform this duty or surrender the existence of the Government. No compromise by public servants could in this case be a cure; not that compromises are not often proper, but that no popular government can long survive a marked precedent, that those who carry an election can only save the Government from immediate destruction by giving up the main point upon which the people gave the election. The people themselves, and not their servants, can safely reverse their own deliberate decisions.

As a private citizen the Executive could not have consented that these institutions shall perish; much less could he in betrayal of so vast and so sacred a trust as these free people had confided to him. He felt that he had no moral right to shrink, nor even to count the chances of his own life, in what might follow. In full view of his great responsibility he has, so far, done what he has deemed his duty. You will now, according to your own judgment, perform yours. He sincerely hopes that your views and your action may so accord with his as to assure all faithful citizens, who have been disturbed in their rights, of a certain and speedy restoration to them under the Constitution and the laws.

And having thus chosen our course, without guile and with pure purpose, let us renew our trust in God, and go forward without fear and with manly hearts.

ABRAHAM LINCOLN.

July 4, 1861.

President Lincoln's First Annual Message, Dec. 3, 1861.

Fellow-Citizens of the Senate and House of Representatives:

In the midst of unprecedented political troubles, we have cause of great gratitude to God for unusual good health, and most abundant harvests.

You will not be surprised to learn that in the peculiar exigencies of the times, our intercourse with foreign nations has been attended with profound solicitude, chiefly turning upon our own domestic affairs.

A disloyal portion of the American people have, during the whole year, been engaged in an attempt to divide and destroy the Union. A nation which endures factious domestic division, is exposed to disrespect abroad; and one party, if not both, is sure, sooner or later, to invoke foreign intervention.

Nations thus tempted to interfere, are not always able to resist the counsels of seeming expediency and ungenerous ambition, although measures adopted under such influences seldom fail to be unfortunate and injurious to those adopting them.

The disloyal citizens of the United States who have offered the ruin of our country, in return for the aid and comfort which they have invoked abroad, have received less patronage and encouragement than they probably expected. If it were just to suppose, as the insurgents have seemed to assume, that foreign nations, in this case, discarding all moral, social, and treaty obligations, would act solely, and selfishly, for the speedy restoration of commerce, including, especially, the acquisition of cotton, those nations appear, as yet, not to have seen their way to their object more directly or clearly through the destruction, than through the preservation, of the Union. If we could dare to believe that foreign nations are actuated by no higher principle than this, I am quite sure a sound argument could be made to show them that they can reach their aim more readily and easily by aiding to crush this rebellion than by giving encouragement to it.

The principal lever relied on by these insurgents for exciting foreign nations to hostility against us, as already intimated, is the embarrassment of commerce. Those nations, however, not improbably, saw from the first that it was the Union which made as well our foreign as our domestic commerce. They can scarcely have failed to perceive that the effort for disunion produces the existing difficulty; and that one strong nation promises more durable peace, and a more extensive, valuable, and reliable commerce, than can the same nation broken into hostile fragments.

It is not my purpose to review our discussions with foreign States; because whatever might be their wishes or dispositions, the integrity of our country, and the stability of our Government, mainly depend, not upon them, but on the loyalty, virtue, patriotism, and intelligence of the American people. The correspondence itself, with the usual reservations, is herewith submitted.

I venture to hope it will appear that we have practiced prudence and liberality toward foreign Powers, averting causes of irritation, and, with firmness, maintaining our own rights and honor.

Since, however, it is apparent that here, as in every other State, foreign dangers necessarily attend domestic difficulties, I recommend that adequate and ample measures be adopted for maintaining the public defenses on every side. While, under this general recommendation, provision for defending our sea-coast line readily occurs to the mind, I also, in the same connection, ask the attention of Congress to our great lakes and rivers. It is believed that some fortifications and depots of arms and munitions, with harbor and navigation improvements, all at well selected points upon these, would be of great importance to the national defense and preservation. I ask attention to the views of the Secretary of War, expressed in his report, upon the same general subject.

I deem it of importance that the loyal regions of East Tennessee and Western North Carolina should be connected with Kentucky, and other faithful parts of the Union, by railroad. I therefore recommend, as a military measure, that Congress provide for the construction of such road, as speedily as possible. Kentucky, no doubt, will co-operate, and, through her Legislature, make the most judicious selection of a line. The northern terminus must connect with some existing railroad; and whether the route shall be from Lexington, or Nicholasville, to the Cumberland Gap; or from Lebanon to the Tennessee line, in the direction of Knoxville; or on some still different line, can easily be determined. Kentucky and the General Government co-operating, the work can be completed in a very short time; and when done, it will be not only of vast present usefulness, but also a valuable permanent improvement, worth its cost in all the future.

Some treaties, designed chiefly for the interests of commerce, and having no grave political importance, have been negotiated, and will be submitted to the Senate for their consideration.

Although we have failed to induce some of the commercial Powers to adopt a desirable melioration of the rigor of maritime war, we have removed all obstructions from the way of this humane reform, except such as are merely of temporary and accidental occurrence.

I invite your attention to the correspondence between her Britannic Majesty's minister accredited to this Government and the Secretary of State, relative to the detention of the British ship Perthshire, in June last, by the United States steamer Massachusetts, for a supposed breach of the blockade. As this detention was occasioned by an obvious misapprehension of the facts, and as justice requires that we should commit no belligerent act not founded in strict right, as sanctioned by public law, I recommend that an appropriation be made to satisfy the reasonable demand of the owners of the vessel for her detention.

I repeat the recommendation of my predecessor, in his annual message to Congress in December last, in regard to the disposition of the surplus which will probably remain after satisfying the claims of American citizens against China, pursuant to the awards of the commissioners under the act of the 3d of March, 1859. If, however, it should not be deemed advisable to carry that recommendation into effect, I would suggest that authority be given for investing the principal, over the proceeds of the surplus referred to, in good securities, with a view to the satisfaction of such other just claims of our citizens against China as are not unlikely to arise hereafter in the course of our extensive trade with that empire.

By the act of the 5th of August last, Congress authorized the President to instruct the commanders of suitable vessels to defend themselves against, and to capture pirates. This authority has been exercised in single instances only. For the more effectual protection of our extensive and valuable commerce, in the eastern seas especially, it seems to me that it would also be advisable to authorize the commanders of sailing vessels to recapture any prizes which pirates may make of United States vessels and their cargoes, and the consular courts, now established by law in eastern countries, to adjudicate the case, in the event that this should not be objected to by the local authorities.

If any good reason exists why we should persevere longer in withholding our recognition of the independence and sovereignty of Hayti and Liberia, I am unable to discern it. Unwilling, however, to inaugurate a novel policy in regard to them without the approbation of Congress, I submit for your consideration the expediency of an appropriation for maintaining a chargé d'affaires near each of those new States. It does not admit of doubt that important commercial advantages might be secured by favorable treaties with them.

The operations of the Treasury during the period which has elapsed since your adjournment have been conducted with signal success. The patriotism of the people has placed at the disposal of the Government the large means demanded by the public exigencies. Much of the national loan has been taken by citizens of the industrial classes, whose confidence in their country's faith, and zeal for their country's deliverance from present peril, have induced them to contribute to the support of the Government the whole of their limited acquisitions. This fact imposes peculiar obligations to economy in disbursement and energy in action.

The revenue from all sources, including loans, for the financial year ending on the 30th June, 1861, was $86,835,900 27, and the expenditures for the same period, including payments on account of the public debt, were $84,578,834 47; leaving a balance in the Treasury, on the 1st July, of $2,257,065 80. For the first quarter of the financial year, ending on the 30th September, 1861, the receipts from all sources, including the balance of 1st of July, were $102,532,509 27, and the expenses $98,239,733 09; leaving a balance on the 1st of October, 1861, of $4,292,776 18.

Estimates for the remaining three quarters of the year, and for the financial year 1863, together with his views of ways and means for meeting the demands contemplated by them, will be submitted to Congress by the Secretary of the Treasury. It is gratifying to know that the expenditures made necessary by the rebellion are not beyond the resources of the loyal people, and to believe that the same patriotism which has thus far sustained the Government will continue to sustain it till peace and union shall again bless the land.

I respectfully refer to the report of the Secretary of War for information respecting the numerical strength of the Army, and for recommendations having in view an increase of its efficiency and the well-being of the various branches of the service intrusted to his care. It is gratifying to know that the patriotism of the people has proved equal to the occasion, and that the number of troops tendered greatly exceeds the force which Congress authorized me to call into the field.

I refer with pleasure to those portions of his report which make allusion to the creditable degree of discipline already attained by our troops, and to the excellent sanitary condition of the entire army.

The recommendation of the Secretary for an organization of the militia upon a uniform basis, is a subject of vital importance to the future safety of the country, and is commended to the serious attention of Congress.

The large addition to the regular army, in connection with the defection that has so considerably diminished the number of its officers, gives peculiar importance to his recommendation for increasing the corps of cadets to the greatest capacity of the Military Academy.

By mere omission, I presume, Congress has failed to provide chaplains for hospitals occupied by volunteers. This subject was brought to my notice, and I was induced to draw up the form of a letter, one copy of which, properly addressed, has been delivered to each of the persons, and at the dates respectively named and stated, in a schedule, containing also the form of the letter, marked A, and herewith transmitted.

These gentlemen, I understand, entered upon the duties designated, at the times respectively stated in the schedule, and have labored faithfully therein ever since. I therefore recommend that they be compensated at the same rate as chaplains in the army. I further suggest that general provision be made for chaplains to serve in hospitals, as well as with regiments.

The report of the Secretary of the Navy presents in detail the operations of that branch of the service, the activity and energy which have characterized its administration, and the results of measures to increase its efficiency and power. Such have been the additions, by construction and purchase, that it may almost be said a navy has been created and brought into service since our difficulties commenced.

Besides blockading our extensive coast, squadrons larger than ever before assembled under our flag have been put afloat and performed deeds which have increased our naval renown.

I would invite special attention to the recommendation of the Secretary for a more perfect organization of the navy by introducing additional grades in the service.

The present organization is defective and unsatisfactory, and the suggestions submitted by the Department will, it is believed, if adopted, obviate the difficulties alluded to, promote harmony, and increase the efficiency of the Navy.

There are three vacancies on the bench of the Supreme Court—two by the decease of Justices Daniel and McLean, and one by the resignation of Justice Campbell. I have so far forborne making nominations to fill these vacancies for reasons which I will now state. Two of the outgoing judges resided within the State now overrun by revolt; so that if successors were appointed in the same localities, they could not now serve upon their circuits; and many of the most competent men there probably would not take the personal hazard of accepting to serve, even here, upon the supreme bench. I have been unwilling to throw all the appointments northward, thus disabling myself from doing justice to the South on the return of peace; although I may remark that to transfer to the North one which has heretofore been in the South, would not, with reference to territory and population, be unjust.

During the long and brilliant judicial career of Judge McLean his circuit grew into an empire—altogether too large for any one judge to give the courts therein more than a nominal attendance—rising in population from one million four hundred and seventy thousand and eighteen, in 1830, to six million one hundred and fifty-one thousand four hundred and five in 1860.

Besides this, the country generally has outgrown our present judicial system. If uniformity was at all intended, the system requires that all the States shall be accommodated with circuit courts attended by supreme judges, while, in fact, Wisconsin, Minnesota, Iowa, Kansas, Florida, Texas, California, and Oregon, have never had any such courts. Nor can this well be remedied without a change of the system; because the adding of judges to the Supreme Court, enough for the accommodation of all parts of the country, with circuit courts, would create a court altogether too numerous for a judicial body of any sort. And the evil, if it be one, will increase as new States come into the Union. Circuit courts are useful, or they are not useful. If useful, no State should be denied them; if not useful, no State should have them. Let them be provided for all, or abolished as to all.

Three modifications occur to me, either of which, I think, would be an improvement upon our present system. Let the Supreme Court be of convenient number in every event. Then, first, let the whole country be divided into circuits of convenient size, the supreme judges to serve in a number of them corresponding to their own number, and independent circuit judges be provided for all the rest. Or, secondly, let the supreme judges be relieved from circuit duties, and circuit judges be provided for all the circuits. Or, thirdly, dispense with circuit judges altogether, leaving the judicial functions wholly to the district courts and an independent Supreme Court.

I respectfully recommend to the consideration of Congress the present condition of the statute laws, with the hope that Congress will be able to find an easy remedy for many of the inconveniences and evils which constantly embarrass those engaged in the practical administration of them. Since the organization of the Government, Congress has enacted some five thousand acts and joint resolutions, which fill more than six thousand closely printed pages, and are scattered through many volumes. Many of these acts have been drawn in haste, and without sufficient caution, so that their provisions are often obscure in themselves, or in conflict with each other, or at least so doubtful as to render it very difficult for even the best informed persons to ascertain precisely what the statute law really is.

It seems to me very important that the statute laws should be made as plain and intelligible as possible, and be reduced to as small a compass as may consist with the fullness and precision of the will of the legislature, and the perspicuity of its language. This, well done, would, I think, greatly facilitate the labors of those whose duty it is to assist in the administration of the laws, and would be a lasting benefit to the people, by placing before them, in a more accessible and intelligible form the laws which so deeply concern their interest and their duties.

I am informed by some whose opinions I respect that all the acts of Congress now in force, and of a permanent and general nature, might be revised and rewritten, so as to be embraced in one volume (or at most two volumes) of ordinary and convenient size. And I respectfully recommend to Congress to consider of the subject, and, if my suggestion be approved, to devise such plan as to their wisdom shall seem most proper for the attainment of the end proposed.

One of the unavoidable consequences of the present insurrection is the entire suppression, in many places, of all the ordinary means of administering civil justice by the officers, and in the forms of existing law. This is the case, in whole or in part, in all the insurgent States; and as our armies advance upon and take possession of parts of those States, the practical evil becomes more apparent. There are no courts nor officers to whom the citizens of other States may apply for the enforcement of their lawful claims against citizens of the insurgent States; and there is a vast amount of debt constituting such claims. Some have estimated it as high as $200,000,000, due, in large part, from insurgents, in open rebellion, to loyal citizens, who are, even now, making great sacrifices in the discharge of their patriotic duty to support the Government.

Under these circumstances, I have been urgently solicited to establish, by military power, courts to administer summary justice in such cases. I have thus far declined to do it, not because I had any doubt that the end proposed —the collection of the debts—was just and right in itself, but because I have been unwilling to go beyond the pressure of necessity in the unusual exercise of power. But the powers of Congress I suppose are equal to the anomalous occasion, and therefore I refer the whole matter to Congress, with the hope that a plan may be devised for the administration of justice in all such parts of the insurgent States and Territories as may be under the control of this Government, whether by a voluntary return to allegiance and order, or by the power of our arms. This, however, not to be a permanent institution, but a temporary substitute, and to cease as soon as the ordinary courts can be re-established in peace.

It is important that some more convenient means should be provided, if possible, for the adjustment of claims against the Government, especially in view of their increased number by reason of the war. It is as much the duty of Government to render prompt justice against itself, in favor of citizens, as it is to administer the same between private individuals. The investigation and adjudication of claims, in their nature belong to the judicial department; besides, it is apparent that the attention of Congress will be more than usually engaged, for some time to come, with great national questions. It was intended by the organization of the Court of Claims mainly to remove this branch of business from the Halls of Congress; but while the court has proved to be an effective and valuable means of investigation, it in a great degree fails to effect the object of its creation, for want of power to make its judgments final.

Fully aware of the delicacy, not to say the danger, of the subject, I commend to your careful consideration whether this power of making judgments final may not properly be given to the court, reserving the right of appeal on questions of law to the Supreme Court, with such other provisions as experience may have shown to be necessary.

I ask attention to the report of the Postmaster General, the following being a summary statement of the condition of the Department:

The revenue from all sources during the fiscal year ending June 30, 1861, including the annual permanent appropriation of $700,000 for the transportation of free mail matter, was $9,049,296 40, being about two per cent. less than the revenue for 1860.

The expenditures were $13,606,750 11, showing a decrease of more than eight per cent. as compared with those of the previous year, and leaving an excess of expenditure over the revenue for the last fiscal year of $4,557,462 71.

The gross revenue for the year ending June 30, 1863, is estimated at an increase of four per cent on that of 1861, making $8,683,000, to which should be added the earnings of the Department in carrying free matter, viz: $700,000, making $9,383,000.

The total expenditures for 1863 are estimated at $12,528,000, leaving an estimated deficiency of $3,145,000, to be supplied from the Treasury, in addition to the permanent appropriation.

The present insurrection shows, I think, that the extension of this District across the Potomac river, at the time of establishing the capital here, was eminently wise, and consequently that the relinquishment of that portion of it which lies within the State of Virginia was unwise and dangerous. I submit for your consideration the expediency of regaining that part of the District, and the restoration of the original boundaries thereof, through negotiations with the State of Virginia.

The report of the Secretary of the Interior, with the accompanying documents, exhibits the condition of the several branches of the public business pertaining to that Department. The depressing influences of the insurrection have been especially felt in the operations of the Patent and General Land Offices. The cash receipts from the sales of public lands during the past year have exceeded the expenses of our land system only about two hundred thousand dollars. The sales have been entirely suspended in the southern States, while the interruptions to the business of the country, and the diversion of large numbers of men from labor to military service, have obstructed settlements in the new States and Territories of the Northwest.

The receipts of the Patent Office have declined in nine months about one hundred thousand dollars, rendering a large reduction of the force employed necessary to make it self-sustaining.

The demands upon the Pension Office will be largely increased by the insurrection. Numerous applications for pensions, based upon the casualties of the existing war, have already been made. There is reason to believe that many who are now upon the pension rolls, and in receipt of the bounty of the Government, are in the ranks of the insurgent army, or giving them aid and comfort. The Secretary of the Interior has directed a suspension of the payment of the pensions of such persons upon proof of their disloyalty. I recommend that Congress authorize that officer to cause the names of such persons to be stricken from the pension rolls.

The relations of the Government with the Indian tribes have been greatly disturbed by the insurrection, especially in the southern superintendency and in that of New Mexico. The Indian country south of Kansas is in the possession of insurgents from Texas and Arkansas. The agents of the United States, appointed since the 4th of March, for this superintendency have been unable to reach their posts, while the most of those who were in office before that time have espoused the insurrectionary cause, and assume to exercise the powers of agents by virtue of commissions from the insurrectionists. It has been stated in the public press that a portion of those Indians have been organized as a military force, and are attached to the army of the insurgents. Although the Government has no official information upon this subject, letters have been written to the Commissioner of Indian Affairs by several prominent chiefs, giving assurance of their loyalty to the United States, and expressing a wish for the presence of Federal troops to protect them. It is believed that upon the repossession of the country by the Federal forces the Indians will readily cease all hostile demonstrations, and resume their former relations to the Government.

Agriculture, confessedly the largest interest of the nation, has, not a department, nor a bureau, but a clerkship only, assigned to it in the Government. While it is fortunate that this great interest is so independent in its nature as to not have demanded or extorted more from the Government, I respectfully ask Congress to consider whether something more cannot be given voluntarily, with general advantage.

Annual reports, exhibiting the condition of our agriculture, commerce, and manufactures would present a fund of information of great practical value to the country. While I make no suggestions as to details, I venture the opinion that an agricultural and statistical bureau might profitably be organized.

The execution of the laws for the suppression of the African slave trade has been confided to the Department of the Interior. It is a subject of gratulation that the efforts which have been made for the suppression of this inhuman traffic have been recently attended with unusual success. Five vessels being fitted out for the slave trade have been seized and condemned. Two mates of vessels engaged in the trade, and one person in equipping a vessel as a slaver, have been convicted and subjected to the penalty of fine and imprisonment, and one captain, taken with a cargo of Africans on board his vessel, has been convicted of the highest grade of offence under our laws, the punishment of which is death.

The Territories of Colorado, Dakotah, and Nevada, created by the last Congress, have been organized, and civil administration has been inaugurated therein under auspices especially gratifying, when it is considered that the leaven of treason was found existing in some of these new countries when the Federal officers arrived there.

The abundant natural resources of these Territories, with the security and protection afforded by organized government, will doubtless invite to them a large immigration when peace shall restore the business of the country to its accustomed channels. I submit the resolutions of the Legislature of Colorado, which evidence the patriotic spirit of the people of the Territory. So far the authority of the United States has been upheld in all the Territories, as it is hoped it will be in the future. I commend their interests and defence to the enlightened and generous care of Congress.

I recommend to the favorable consideration of Congress the interests of the District of Columbia. The insurrection has been the cause of much suffering and sacrifice to its inhabitants, and as they have no representative in Congress, that body should not overlook their just claims upon the Government.

At your late session a joint resolution was adopted authorizing the President to take measures for facilitating a proper representation of the industrial interests of the United States at the exhibition of the industry of all nations to be holden at London in the year 1862. I regret to say I have been unable to give personal attention to this subject—a subject at once so interesting in itself, and so extensively and intimately connected with the material prosperity of the world. Through the Secretaries of State and of the Interior a plan, or system, has been devised, and partly matured, and which will be laid before you.

Under and by virtue of the act of Congress entitled "An act to confiscate property used for insurrectionary purposes," approved August 6, 1861, the legal claims of certain persons to the labor and service of certain other persons have become forfeited; and numbers of the latter, thus liberated, are already dependent on the United States, and must be provided for in some way. Besides this, it is not impossible that some of the States will pass similar enactments for their own benefit respectively, and by operation of which, persons of the same class will be thrown upon them for disposal. In such case, I recommend that Congress provide for accepting such persons from such States, according to some mode of valuation, in lieu, *pro tanto* of direct taxes, or upon some other plan to be agreed on with such States respectively; that such persons, on such acceptance by the General Government, be at once deemed free; and that, in any event, steps be taken for colonizing both classes (or the one first mentioned, if the other shall not be brought into existence,) at some place, or places, in a climate congenial to them. It might be well to consider, too, whether the free colored people already in the United States could not, so far as individuals may desire, be included in such colonization.

To carry out the plan of colonization may involve the acquiring of territory, and also the appropriation of money beyond that to be expended in the territorial acquisition. Having practiced the acquisition of territory for nearly sixty years, the question of constitutional power to do so is no longer an open one with us. The power was questioned at first by Mr. Jefferson, who, however, in the purchase of Louisiana, yielded his scruples on the plea of great expediency. If it be said that the only legitimate object of acquiring territory is to furnish homes for white men, this measure effects that object; for the emigration of colored men leaves additional room for white men remaining or coming here. Mr. Jefferson, however, placed the importance of procuring Louisiana more on political and commercial grounds than on providing room for population.

On this whole proposition, including the appropriation of money with the acquisition of territory, does not the expediency amount to absolute necessity—that, without which the Government itself cannot be perpetuated?

The war continues. In considering the policy to be adopted for suppressing the insurrection, I have been anxious and careful that the inevitable conflict for this purpose shall not degenerate into a violent and remorseless revolutionary struggle. I have, therefore, in every case, thought it proper to keep the integrity of the Union prominent as the primary object of the contest on our part, leaving all questions which are not of vital military importance to the more deliberate action of the Legislature.

In the exercise of my best discretion I have adhered to the blockade of the ports held by the insurgents, instead of putting in force, by proclamation, the law of Congress enacted at the late session for closing those ports.

So, also, obeying the dictates of prudence, as well as the obligations of law, instead of transcending, I have adhered to the act of Congress to confiscate property used for insurrectionary purposes. If a new law upon the same subject shall be proposed, its propriety will be duly considered. The Union must be preserved; and hence, all indispensable means must be employed. We should not be in haste to determine that radical and extreme measures, which may reach the loyal as well as the disloyal, are indispensable.

The inaugural address at the beginning of the Administration, and the message to Congress at the late special session, were both mainly devoted to the domestic controversy out of which the insurrection and consequent war have sprung. Nothing now occurs to add or subtract, to or from, the principles, or general purposes, stated and expressed, in those documents.

The last ray of hope for preserving the Union peaceably expired at the assault upon Fort Sumter; and a general review of what has occurred since may not be unprofitable. What was painfully uncertain then, is much better defined and more distinct now; and the progress of events is plainly in the right direction. The insurgents confidently claimed a strong support from North of Mason and Dixon's line, and the friends of the Union were not free from apprehension on the point. This, however, was soon settled definitely, and on the right side. South of the line, noble little Delaware led off right from the first. Maryland was made to *seem* against the Union. Our soldiers were assaulted, bridges were burned, and railroads torn up within her limits, and we were many days, at one time, without the ability to bring a single regiment over her soil to the capital. Now her bridges and railroads are repaired and open to the Government; she already gives seven regiments to the cause of the Union, and none to the enemy; and her people, at a regular election, have sustained the Union, by a larger majority, and a larger aggregate vote than they ever before gave to any candidate or any question. Kentucky, too, for some time in doubt, is now decidedly, and, I think, unchangeably, ranged on the side of the Union. Missouri is comparatively quiet, and I believe cannot again be overrun by the insurrectionists. These three States of Maryland, Kentucky, and Missouri, neither of which would promise a single soldier at first, have now an aggregate of not less than forty thousand in the field for the Union; while, of their citizens, certainly not more than a third of that number, and they of doubtful whereabouts, and doubtful existence, are in arms against it. After a somewhat bloody struggle of months, winter closes on the Union people of Western Virginia, leaving them masters of their own country.

An insurgent force of about fifteen hundred, for months dominating the narrow peninsula region, constituting the counties of Accomac and Northampton, and known as eastern shore of Virginia, together with some contiguous parts of Maryland, have laid down their arms; and the people there have renewed their allegiance to, and accepted the protection of, the old flag. This leaves no armed insurrectionist north of the Potomac, or east of the Chesapeake.

Also we have obtained a footing at each of the isolated points, on the southern coast, of Hatteras, Port Royal, Tybee Island, near Savannah, and Ship Island; and we likewise have some general accounts of popular movements, in behalf of the Union, in North Carolina and Tennessee.

These things demonstrate that the cause of the Union is advancing steadily and certainly southward.

Since your last adjournment, Lieutenant General Scott has retired from the head of the Army. During his long life, the nation has not been unmindful of his merit; yet, on calling to mind how faithfully, ably, and brilliantly he has served the country, from a time far back in our history, when few of the now living had been born, and thenceforward continually, I cannot but think we are still his debtors. I submit, therefore, for your consideration, what further mark of recognition is due to him and to ourselves, as a grateful people.

With the retirement of General Scott came the executive duty of appointing, in his stead, a General-in-Chief of the Army. It is a fortunate circumstance that neither in council nor country was there, so far as I know, any difference of opinion as to the proper person to be selected. The retiring chief repeatedly expressed his judgment in favor of General McClellan for the position; and in this the nation seemed to give a unanimous concurrence. The designation of General McClellan is, therefore, in considerable degree, the selection of the country as well as of the Executive; and hence there is better reason to hope there will be given him the confidence and cordial support thus, by fair implication, promised, and without which, he cannot, with so full efficiency, serve the country.

It has been said that one bad general is better than two good ones; and the saying is true, if taken to mean no more than that an army is better directed by a single mind, though inferior, than by two superior ones at variance, and cross-purposes with each other.

And the same is true, in all joint operations wherein those engaged, can have none but a common end in view, and *can* differ only as to the choice of means. In a storm at sea, no one on board *can* wish the ship to sink; and yet, not unfrequently, all go down together, because too many will direct, and no single mind can be allowed to control.

It continues to develop that the insurrection is largely, if not exclusively, a war upon the first principle of popular government—the rights of the people. Conclusive evidence of this is found in the most grave and maturely considered public documents, as well as in the general tone of the insurgents. In those documents we find the abridgment of the existing right of suffrage, and the denial to the people of all right to participate in the selection of public officers, except the legislative, boldly advocated, with labored arguments to prove that large control of the people in government is the source of all political evil. Monarchy itself is sometimes hinted at as a possible refuge from the power of the people.

In my present position, I could scarcely be justified were I to omit raising a warning voice against this approach of returning despotism.

It is not needed, nor fitting here, that a general argument should be made in favor of popular institutions; but there is one point, with its connections, not so hackneyed as most others, to which I ask brief attention. It is the effort to place *capital* on an equal footing with, if not above, *labor*, in the structure of government. It is assumed that labor is available only in connection with capital; that nobody labors unless somebody else, owning capital, somehow by the use of it, induces him to labor. This assumed, it is next considered whether it is best that capital shall *hire* laborers, and thus induce them to work by their own consent, or *buy* them, and drive them to it without their consent. Having proceeded so far, it is naturally concluded that all laborers are either *hired* laborers, or what we call slaves. And further, it is assumed that whoever is once a hired laborer is fixed in that condition for life.

Now, there is no such relation between capital and labor as assumed; nor is there any such thing as a free man being fixed for life, in the condition of a hired laborer. Both these assumptions are false, and all inferences from them are groundless.

Labor is prior to, and independent of, capital. Capital is only the fruit of labor, and could never have existed if labor had not first existed. Labor is the superior of capital, and deserves much the higher consideration. Capital has its rights, which are as worthy of protection as any other rights. Nor is it denied that there is, and probably always will be, a relation between labor and capital, producing mutual benefits. The error is in assuming that the whole labor of community exists within that relation. A few men own capital, and that few avoid labor themselves, and with their capital hire or buy another few to labor for them. A large majority belong to neither class—neither work for others, nor have others working for them. In most of the southern States, a majority of the whole people of all colors are neither slaves nor masters; while in the northern, a large majority are neither hirers nor hired. Men with their families—wives, sons, and daughters—work for themselves, on their farms, in their houses, and in their shops, taking the whole product to themselves, and asking no favors of capital on the one hand, nor of hired laborers or slaves on the other. It is not forgotten that a considerable number of persons mingle their own labor with capital—that is they labor with their own hands, and also buy or hire others to labor for them; but this is only a mixed, and not a distinct class. No principle stated is disturbed by the existence of this mixed class.

Again, as has already been said, there is not, of necessity, any such thing as the free hired laborer being fixed to that condition for life. Many independent men everywhere in these States, a few years back in their lives, were hired laborers. The prudent, penniless beginner in the world labors for wages awhile, saves a surplus for which to buy tools or land for himself, then labors on his own account another while, and at length hires another new beginner to help him. This is the just and generous and prosperous system, which opens the way to all, gives hope to all, and consequent energy and progress, and improvement of condition to all. No men living are more worthy to be trusted than those who toil up from poverty—none less inclined to take or touch aught which they have not honestly earned. Let them beware of surrendering a political power which they already possess, and which, if surrendered, will surely be used to close the door of advancement against such as they, and to fix new disabilities and burdens upon them, till all of liberty shall be lost.

From the first taking of our national census to the last are seventy years; and we find our population at the end of the period eight times as great as it was at the beginning. The increase of those other things which men deem desirable has been even greater. We thus have, at one view, what the popular principle applied to government, through the machinery of the States and the Union, has produced in a given time, and also what, if firmly maintained, it promises for the future. There are already among us those who, if the Union be preserved, will live to see it contain two hundred and fifty millions. The struggle *of* to-day is not altogether *for* to-day—it is for a vast future also. With a reliance on Providence, all the more firm and earnest, let us proceed in the great task which events have devolved upon us.

ABRAHAM LINCOLN.

WASHINGTON, *December* 3, 1861.

President Lincoln's Second Annual Message, December 1, 1862.

Fellow-citizens of the Senate
and House of Representatives:

Since your last annual assembling another year of health and bountiful harvests has passed. And while it has not pleased the Almighty to bless us with a return of peace, we can but press on, guided by the best light He gives us, trusting that in His own good time, and wise way, all will yet be well.

The correspondence touching foreign affairs which has taken place during the last year is herewith submitted, in virtual compliance with a request to that effect made by the House of Representatives near the close of the last session of Congress.

If the condition of our relations with other nations is less gratifying than it has usually been at former periods, it is certainly more satisfactory than a nation so unhappily distracted as we are, might reasonably have apprehended. In the month of June last there were some grounds to expect that the maritime powers which, at the beginning of our domestic difficulties, so unwisely and unnecessarily, as we think, recognized the insurgents as a belligerent, would soon recede from that position, which has proved only less injurious to themselves than to our own country. But the temporary reverses which afterwards befell the national arms, and which were exaggerated by our own disloyal citizens abroad, have hitherto delayed that act of simple justice.

The civil war, which has so radically changed, for the moment, the occupations and habits of the American people, has necessarily disturbed the social condition, and affected very deeply the prosperity of the nations with which we have carried on a commerce that has been steadily increasing throughout a period of half a century. It has, at the same time, excited political ambitions and apprehensions which have produced a profound agitation throughout the civilized world. In this unusual agitation we have forborne from taking part in any controversy between foreign States, and between parties or factions in such States. We have attempted no propagandism, and acknowledged no revolution. But we have left to every nation the exclusive conduct and management of its own affairs. Our struggle has been, of course, contemplated by foreign nations with reference less to its own merits than to its supposed and often exaggerated effects and consequences resulting to those nations themselves. Nevertheless, complaint on the part of this Government, even if it were just, would certainly be unwise.

The treaty with Great Britain for the suppression of the slave trade has been put into operation with a good prospect of complete success. It is an occasion of special pleasure to acknowledge that the execution of it, on the part of her Majesty's Government, has been marked with a jealous respect for the authority of the United States, and the rights of their moral and loyal citizens.

The convention with Hanover for the abolition of the stade dues has been carried into full effect, under the act of Congress for that purpose.

A blockade of three thousand miles of seacoast could not be established, and vigorously enforced, in a season of great commercial activity like the present, without committing occasional mistakes and inflicting unintentional injuries upon foreign nations and their subjects.

A civil war occurring in a country where foreigners reside and carry on trade under treaty stipulations, is necessarily fruitful of complaints of the violation of neutral rights. All such collisions tend to excite misapprehensions, and possibly to produce mutual reclamations between nations which have a common interest in preserving peace and friendship. In clear cases of these kinds I have, so far as possible, heard and redressed complaints which have been presented by friendly Powers. There is still, however, a large and an augmenting number of doubtful cases upon which the Government is unable to agree with the Governments whose protection is demanded by the claimants. There are, moreover, many cases in which the United States, or their citizens, suffer wrongs from the naval or military authorities of foreign nations, which the Governments of those States are not at once prepared to redress. I have proposed to some of the foreign States, thus interested, mutual conventions to examine and adjust such complaints. This proposition has been made especially to Great Britain, to France, to Spain, and to Prussia. In each case it has been kindly received, but has not yet been formally adopted.

I deem it my duty to recommend an appropriation in behalf of the owners of the Norwegian bark Admiral P. Tordenskiold, which vessel was, in May, 1861, prevented by the commander of the blockading force off Charleston from leaving that port with cargo, notwithstanding a similar privilege had, shortly before, been granted to an English vessel. I have directed the Secretary of State to cause the papers in the case to be communicated to the proper committees.

Applications have been made to me by many free Americans of African descent to favor their emigration, with a view to such colonization as was contemplated in recent acts of Congress. Other parties, at home and abroad—some from interested motives, others upon patriotic considerations, and still others influenced by philanthropic sentiments—have suggested similiar measures; while, on the other hand, several of the Spanish-American republics have protested against the sending of such colonies to their respective territories. Under these circumstances, I have declined to move any such colony to any State, without first obtaining the consent of its government, with an agreement on its part to receive and protect such emigrants in all the rights of freemen; and I have, at the same time, offered to the several States situated within the tropics, or having colonies there, to negotiate with them, subject to the advice and consent of the Senate, to favor the voluntary emigration of persons of that class to their respective territories, upon conditions which shall be equal, just, and humane. Liberia and Hayti are, as yet, the only countries to which colonists of African descent from here, could go with certainty of being received and adopted as citizens; and I regret to say such persons, contemplating colonization, do not seem so willing to migrate to those countries, as to some others, nor so willing as I think their interest demands. I believe, however, opinion among them in this respect, is improving; and that, ere long, there will be an augmented, and considerable migration to both these countries, from the United States.

The new commercial treaty between the United States and the Sultan of Turkey has been carried into execution.

A commercial and consular treaty has been negotiated, subject to the Senate's consent, with Liberia; and a similar negotiation is now pending with the republic of Hayti. A considerable improvement of the national commerce is expected to result from these measures.

Our relations with Great Britain, France, Spain, Portugal, Russia, Prussia, Denmark, Sweden, Austria, the Netherlands, Italy, Rome, and the other European States, remain undisturbed. Very favorable relations also continue to be maintained with Turkey, Morocco, China, and Japan.

During the last year there has not only been no change of our previous relations with the independent States of our own continent, but more friendly sentiments than have heretofore existed, are believed to be entertained by these neighbors, whose safety and progress are so intimately connected with our own. This statement especially applies to Mexico, Nicaragua, Costa Rica, Honduras, Peru, and Chile.

The commission under the convention with the republic of New Granada closed its session without having audited and passed upon all the claims which were submitted to it. A proposition is pending to revive the convention, that it may be able to do more complete justice. The joint commission between the United States and the republic of Costa Rica has completed its labors and submitted its report.

I have favored the project for connecting the United States with Europe by an Atlantic telegraph, and a similar project to exend the telegraph from San Francisco, to connect by a Pacific telegraph with the line which is being extended across the Russian empire.

The Territories of the United States, with unimportant exceptions, have remained undisturbed by the civil war; and they are exhibiting such evidence of prosperity as justifies an expectation that some of them will soon be in a condition to be organized as States, and be constitutionally admitted into the Federal Union.

The immense mineral resources of some of those Territories ought to be developed as rapidly as possible. Every step in that direction would have a tendency to improve the revenues of the Government, and diminish the burdens of the people. It is worthy of your serious consideration whether some extraordinary measures to promote that end cannot be adopted. The means which suggests itself as most likely to be effective, is a scientific exploration of the mineral regions in those Territories, with a view to the publication of its results at home and in foreign countries—results which cannot fail to be auspicious.

The condition of the finances will claim your most diligent consideration. The vast expenditures incident to the military and naval operations required for the suppression of the rebellion, have hitherto been met with a promptitude and certainty unusual in similar circumstances; and the public credit has been fully maintained. The continuance of the war, however, and the increased disbursements made necessary by the augmented forces now in the field, demand your best reflections as to the best modes of providing the necessary revenue, without injury to business, and with the least possible burdens upon labor.

The suspension of specie payments by the banks, soon after the commencement of your last session, made large issues of United States notes unavoidable. In no other way could the payment of the troops, and the satisfaction of other just demands, be so economically or so well provided for. The judicious legislation of Congress, securing the receivability of these notes for loans and internal duties, and making them a legal tender for other debts, has made them an universal currency; and has satisfied, partially, at least, and for the time, the long felt want of an uniform circulating medium, saving thereby to the people immense sums in discounts and exchanges.

A return to specie payments, however, at the earliest period compatible with due regard to all interests concerned, should ever be kept in view. Fluctuations in the value of currency are always injurious, and to reduce these fluctuations to the lowest possible point will always be a leading purpose in wise legislation. Convertibility, prompt and certain convertibility into coin, is generally acknowledged to be the best and surest safeguard against them; and it is extremely doubtful whether a circulation of United States notes, payable in coin, and sufficiently large for the wants of the people, can be permanently, usefully, and safely maintained.

Is there, then, any other mode in which the necessary provision for the public wants can be made, and the great advantages of a safe and uniform currency secured?

I know of none which promises so certain results, and is, at the same time, so unobjectionable, as the organization of banking associations, under a general act of Congress, well guarded in its provisions. To such associations the Government might furnish circulating notes, on the security of United States bonds deposited in the Treasury. These notes, prepared under the supervision of proper officers, being uniform in appearance and security, and convertible always into coin, would at once protect labor against the evils of a vicious currency, and facilitate commerce by cheap and safe exchanges.

A moderate reservation from the interest on the bonds would compensate the United States for the preparation and distribution of the notes, and a general supervision of the system, and would lighten the burden of that part of the public debt employed as securities. The public credit, moreover, would be greatly improved, and the negotiation of new loans greatly facilitated by the steady market demand for Government bonds which the adoption of the proposed system would create.

It is an additional recommendation of the measure, of considerable weight, in my judgment, that it would reconcile, as far as possible, all existing interests, by the opportunity offered to existing institutions to reorganize under the act, substituting only the secured uniform national circulation for the local and various circulation, secured and unsecured, now issued by them.

The receipts into the Treasury from all sources, including loans, and balance from the preceding year, for the fiscal year ending on the 30th June, 1862, were $583,885,247 06, of which sum $49,056,397 62 were derived from customs; $1,795,331 73 from the direct tax; from public lands, $152,203 77; from miscellaneous sources, $931,787 64; from loans in all forms, $529,692,460 50. The remainder, $2.257,065 80, was the balance from last year.

The disbursements during the same period were for congressional, executive, and judicial purposes, $5,939,009 29; for foreign intercourse, $1,339,710 35; for miscellaneous expenses, including the mints, loans, post office deficiencies, collection of revenue, and other like charges, $14,129,771 50; for expenses under the Interior Department, $3,102,985 52; under the War Department, $394,368,407 36; under the Navy Department, $42,674,569 69; for interest on public debt, $13,190,324 45; and for payment of public debt, including reimbursement of temporary loan, and redemptions, $96,096,922 09; making an aggregate of $570,841,700 25, and leaving a balance in the Treasury on the first day of July, 1862, of $13,043,546 81.

It should be observed that the sum of $96,096,922 09, expended for reimbursements and redemption of public debt, being included also in the loans made, may be properly deducted, both from receipts and expenditures, leaving the actual receipts for the year, $487,788,324 97; and the expenditures, $474,744,778 16.

Other information on the subject of the finances will be found in the report of the Secretary of the Treasury, to whose statements and views I invite your most candid and considerate attention.

The reports of the Secretaries of War, and of the Navy, are herewith transmitted. These reports, though lengthy, are scarcely more than brief abstracts of the very numerous and extensive transactions and operations conducted through those departments. Nor could I give a summary of them here, upon any principle, which would admit of its being much shorter than the reports themselves. I therefore content myself with laying the reports before you, and asking your attention to them.

It gives me pleasure to report a decided improvement in the financial condition of the Post Office Department, as compared with several preceding years. The receipts for the fiscal year 1861 amounted to $8,349,296 40, which embraced the revenue from all the States of the Union for three quarters of that year. Notwithstanding the cessation of revenue from the so-called Seceded States during the last fiscal year, the increase of the correspondence of the loyal States has been sufficient to produce a revenue during the same year of $8,299,820 90, being only $50,000 less than was derived from all the States of the Union during the previous year. The expenditures show a still more favorable result. The amount expended in 1861 was $13,606,759 11. For the last year the amount has been reduced to $11,125,364 13, showing a decrease of about $2,481,000 in the expenditures as compared with the preceding year, and about $3,750,000 as compared with the fiscal year 1860. The deficiency in the Department for the previous year was $4,551,-

966 98. For the last fiscal year it was reduced to $2,112,814 57. These favorable results are in part owing to the cessation of mail service in the insurrectionary States, and in part to a careful review of all expenditures in that Department in the interest of economy. The efficiency of the postal service, it is believed, has also been much improved. The Postmaster General has also opened a correspondence, through the Department of State, with foreign Governments, proposing a convention of postal representatives for the purpose of simplifying the rates of foreign postage, and to expedite the foreign mails. This proposition, equally important to our adopted citizens, and to the commercial interests of this country, has been favorably entertained, and agreed to, by all the Governments from whom replies have been received.

I ask the attention of Congress to the suggestions of the Postmaster General in his report respecting the further legislation required in his opinion, for the benefit of the postal service.

The Secretary of the Interior reports as follows in regard to the public lands:

"The public lands have ceased to be a source of revenue. From the 1st of July, 1861, to the 30th September, 1862, the entire cash receipts from the sale of lands were $137,476 26—a sum much less than the expenses of our land system during the same period. The homestead law, which will take effect on the 1st of January next, offers such inducements to settlers, that sales for cash cannot be expected, to an extent sufficient to meet the expenses of the General Land Office, and the cost of surveying and bringing the land into market."

The discrepancy between the sum here stated as arising from the sales of the public lands, and the sum derived from the same source as reported from the Treasury Department arises, as I understand, from the fact that the periods of time, though apparently, were not really, coincident at the beginning point—the Treasury report including a considerable sum now, which had previously been reported from the Interior—sufficiently large to greatly overreach the sum derived from the three months now reported by the Interior, and not by the Treasury.

The Indian tribes upon our frontiers have, during the past year, manifested a spirit of insubordination, and, at several points, have engaged in open hostilities against the white settlements in their vicinity. The tribes occupying the Indian country south of Kansas, renounced their allegiance to the United States, and entered into treaties with the insurgents. Those who remained loyal to the United States were driven from the country. The chief of the Cherokees has visited this city for the purpose of restoring the former relations of the tribe with the United States. He alleges that they were constrained, by superior force, to enter into treaties with the insurgents, and that the United States neglected to furnish the protection which their treaty stipulations required.

In the month of August last the Sioux Indians, in Minnesota, attacked the settlements in their vicinity with extreme ferocity, killing, indiscriminately, men, women. and children. This attack was wholly unexpected, and, therefore, no means of defence had been provided. It is estimated that no less than eight hundred persons were killed by the Indians, and a large amount of property was destroyed. How this outbreak was induced is not definitely known, and suspicions, which may be unjust, need not be stated. Information was received by the Indian bureau, from different sources, about the time hostilities were commenced, that a simultaneous attack was about to be made upon the white settlements by all the tribes between the Mississippi river and the Rocky Mountains. The State of Minnesota has suffered great injury from this Indian war. A large portion of her territory has been depopulated, and a severe loss has been sustained by the destruction of property. The people of that State manifest much anxiety for the removal of the tribes beyond the limits of the State as a guarantee against future hostilities. The Commissioner of Indian Affairs will furnish full details. I submit for your special consideration whether our Indian system shall not be remodelled. Many wise and good men have impressed me with the belief that this can be profitably done.

I submit a statement of the proceedings of commissioners, which shows the progress that has been made in the enterprise of constructing the Pacific railroad. And this suggests the earliest completion of this road, and also the favorable action of Congress upon the projects now pending before them for enlarging the capacities of the great canals in New York and Illinois, as being of vital, and rapidly increasing importance to the whole nation, and especially to the vast interior region hereinafter to be noticed at some greater length. I propose having prepared and laid before you at an early day some interesting and valuable statistical information upon this subject. The military and commercial importance of enlarging the Illinois and Michigan canal, and improving the Illinois river, is presented in the report of Colonel Webster to the Secretary of War, and now transmitted to Congress. I respectfully ask attention to it.

To carry out the provisions of the act of Congress of the 15th of May last, I have caused the Department of Agriculture of the United States to be organized.

The Commissioner informs me that, within the period of a few months this department has established an extensive system of correspondence and exchanges, both at home and abroad, which promises to effect highly beneficial results in the development of a correct knowledge of recent improvements in agriculture, in the introduction of new products, and in the collection of the agricultural statistics of the different States.

Also that it will soon be prepared to distribute largely seeds, cereals, plants and cuttings, and has already published, and liberally diffused, much valuable information in anticipation of a more elaborate report, which will in due time be furnished, embracing some valuable tests in chemical science now in progress in the laboratory.

The creation of this department was for the more immediate benefit of a large class of our most valuable citizens; and I trust that the liberal basis upon which it has been organized will not only meet your approbation, but that it will realize, at no distant day, all the fondest anticipations of its most sanguine friends, and become the fruitful source of advantage to all our people.

For the residue of the Message, see chapter on "Confiscation and Emancipation." p. 220

Members of the 38th Congress, 1st Session, Dec. 7, 1863–July 4, 1864.

SENATE.

The following are the changes from the list as it stood at the close of the 37th Congress:

Rhode Island—Wm. Sprague, in place of Samuel G. Arnold.

New York—Edwin D. Morgan, in place of Preston King.

New Jersey—Wm. Wright, in place of James W. Wall.

Pennsylvania — Charles R. Buckalew, in place of David Wilmot.

Delaware—1864, Feb. 2, George Read Riddle, in place of James A. Bayard resigned Jan. 29, 1864.

Maryland—Reverdy Johnson, in place of Anthony Kennedy.

Virginia—Lemuel J. Bowden, in place of Waitman T. Willey, term expired. Mr. B. died Jan. 2, 1864. His vacancy not filled.

West Virginia—(New Senators) Waitman T. Willey, term to expire March 3, 1865, Peter G. Van Winkle, term to expire March 3, 1869.

Indiana—Thomas A. Hendricks, in place of David Turpie.

Missouri—1863, Dec. 14, B. Gratz Brown, elected for the unexpired term of Waldo P. Johnson, expelled, and in place of R. Wilson, appointed.

California—John Conness, in place of Milton S. Latham.

Minnesota—Alexander Ramsey, in place of Henry M. Rice.

Tennessee—Unrepresented.

Memorandum — Messrs. Elisha Baxter and Wm. M. Fishback, claiming to represent the State of Arkansas, were not admitted.

HOUSE OF REPRESENTATIVES.

Schuyler Colfax, of Indiana, *Speaker*.

Edward McPherson, of Pennsylvania, *Clerk*.

Maine—Lorenzo D. M. Sweat, Sidney Perham, James G. Blaine, John H. Rice, Frederick A. Pike.

New Hampshire—Daniel Marcy, Edward H. Rollins, James W. Patterson.

Vermont—Frederick E. Woodbridge, Justin S. Morrill, Portus Baxter.

Massachusetts—Thomas D. Eliot, Oakes Ames, Alexander H. Rice, Samuel Hooper, John B. Alley, Daniel W. Gooch, George S. Boutwell, John D. Baldwin, William B. Washburn, Henry L. Dawes.

Rhode Island—Thomas A. Jenckes, Nathan F. Dixon.

Connecticut—Henry C. Deming, James E. English, Augustus Brandegee, John H. Hubbard.

New York — Henry G. Stebbins, Martin Kalbfleisch, Moses F. Odell, Benjamin Wood, Fernando Wood, Elijah Ward, John W. Chanler, James Brooks, Anson Herrick, William Radford, Charles H. Winfield, Homer A. Nelson, John B. Steele, John V. L. Pruyn, John A. Griswold, Orlando Kellogg, Calvin T. Hulburd, James M. Marvin, Samuel F. Miller, Ambrose W. Clark, Francis Kernan, De Witt C. Littlejohn, Thomas T. Davis, Theodore M. Pomeroy, Daniel Morris, Giles W. Hotchkiss, Robert B. Van Valkenburgh, Freeman Clarke, Augustus Frank, John Ganson, Reuben E. Fenton.

New Jersey—John F. Starr, George Middleton, William G. Steele, Andrew J. Rogers, Nehemiah Perry,

Pennsylvania—Samuel J. Randall, Charles O'Neill, Leonard Myers, William D. Kelley, M. Russell Thayer, John D. Stiles, John M. Broomall, Sydenham E. Ancona, Thaddeus Stevens, Myer Strouse, Philip Johnson, Charles Denison, Henry W. Tracy, William H. Miller, Joseph Baily, Alexander H. Coffroth, Archibald McAllister, James T. Hale, Glenni W. Scofield, Amos Myers, John L. Dawson, James K. Moorhead, Thomas Williams, Jesse Lazear.

Delaware—Nathaniel B. Smithers.

Maryland—John A. J. Creswell, Edwin H. Webster, Henry Winter Davis, Francis Thomas, Benjamin G. Harris.

Ohio—Geo. H. Pendleton, Alexander Long, Robert C. Schenck, John F. McKinney, Francis C. LeBlond, Chilton A. White, Samuel S. Cox, William Johnson, Warren P. Noble, James M. Ashley, Wells A. Hutchins, William E. Finck, John O'Neill, George Bliss, James R. Morris, Joseph W. White, Ephraim R. Eckley, Rufus P. Spalding, James A. Garfield.

Kentucky—Lucien Anderson, George H. Yeaman, Henry Grider, Aaron Harding, Robert Mallory, Green Clay Smith, Brutus J. Clay, William H. Randall, William H. Wadsworth.

Indiana—John Law, James A. Cravens, Henry W. Harrington, William S. Holman, George W. Julian, Ebenezer Dumont, Daniel W. Voorhees, Godlove S. Orth, Schuyler Colfax, Joseph K. Edgerton, James F. McDowell.

Illinois—Isaac N. Arnold, John F. Farnsworth, Ellihu B. Washburne, Charles M. Harris, Owen Lovejoy,* Jesse O. Norton, John R. Eden, John T. Stuart, Lewis W. Ross, Anthony L. Knapp, James C. Robinson, William R. Morrison, William J. Allen, James C. Allen.

Missouri—Francis P. Blair, jr.,* Henry T. Blow, John G. Scott, Joseph W. McClurg, Sempronius H. Boyd, Austin A. King, Benjamin F. Loan, William A. Hall, James S. Rollins.

Michigan—Fernando C. Beaman, Charles Upson, John W. Longyear, Francis W. Kellogg, Augustus C. Baldwin, John F. Driggs.

Iowa—James F. Wilson, Hiram Price, Wm. B. Allison, Josiah B. Grinnell, John A. Kasson, Asahel W. Hubbard.

Wisconsin —James S. Brown, Ithamar C.

* See memorandum at close of list.

Sloan, Amasa Cobb, Charles A. Eldridge, Ezra Wheeler, Walter D. McIndoe.

CALIFORNIA—Thomas B. Shannon, William Higby, Cornelius Cole.

MINNESOTA.—Wm. Windom, Ignatius Donnelly.

OREGON—John R. McBride.

KANSAS—A. Carter Wilder.

WEST VIRGINIA—Jacob B. Blair, William G. Brown, Kellian V. Whaley.

MEMORANDUM OF CHANGES.

These changes occurred during the session:

1864, Jan. 12, Francis P. Blair, jr., took his seat, and June 11th was unseated by vote of the House—yeas 81, nays 33. Same day, the House—yeas 70, nays 53—voted that Samuel Knox, the contestant, was entitled to the seat, and June 15th he was qualified.

1864, March 25, Owen Lovejoy died. May 20, Ebon C. Ingersoll qualified as his successor.

The names of A. P. Fields and Thomas Cottman, claiming seats from Louisiana, were placed upon the roll by the Clerk of the 37th Congress, and voted for Speaker, but their credentials were referred to the Committee on Elections—yeas 100, nays 71—and, Feb. 10, they were voted not entitled to seats, without a division. The names of the Maryland delegation; of Messrs. Blair, Blow, McClurg, Boyd, Loan and Hall, of the Missouri delegation; of Mr. McBride, of Oregon; of Mr. Wilder, of Kansas; and of the West Virginia delegation, omitted by the Clerk, were ordered by the House, to be placed upon the roll. The claims of Messrs. Chandler, Segar, and Kitchen, of Virginia, were referred to the Committee on Elections, and subsequently reported against—the House concurring in the report. Messrs. A. A. C. Rogers, James M. Johnson, and T. M. Jacks, claiming seats from Arkansas, were not admitted.

President Lincoln's Third Annual Message, December 8, 1863.

Fellow-citizens of the Senate
and House of Representatives:

Another year of health, and of sufficiently abundant harvests, has passed. For these, and especially for the improved condition of our national affairs, our renewed and profoundest gratitude to God is due.

We remain in peace and friendship with foreign Powers.

The efforts of disloyal citizens of the United States to involve us in foreign wars, to aid an inexcusable insurrection, have been unavailing. Her Britannic Majesty's Government, as was justly expected, have exercised their authority to prevent the departure of new hostile expeditions from British ports. The Emperor of France has, by a like proceeding, promptly vindicated the neutrality which he proclaimed at the beginning of the contest. Questions of great intricacy and importance have arisen out of the blockade and other belligerent operations, between the Government and several of the maritime Powers, but they have been discussed, and, as far as was possible, accommodated in a spirit of frankness, justice, and mutual good will. It is especially gratifying that our prize courts, by the impartiality of their adjudications, have commanded the respect and confidence of maritime Powers.

The supplemental treaty between the United States and Great Britain for the suppression of the African slave trade, made on the 17th day of February last, has been duly ratified and carried into execution. It is believed that, so far as American ports and American citizens are concerned, that inhuman and odious traffic has been brought to an end.

I shall submit, for the consideration of the Senate, a convention for the adjustment of possessory claims in Washington Territory, arising out of the treaty of the 15th June, 1846, between the United States and Great Britain, and which have been the source of some disquiet among the citizens of that now rapidly improving part of the country.

A novel and important question, involving the extent of the maritime jurisdiction of Spain in the waters which surround the island of Cuba, has been debated without reaching an agreement, and it is proposed, in an amicable spirit, to refer it to the arbitrament of a friendly Power. A convention for that purpose will be submitted to the Senate.

I have thought it proper, subject to the approval of the Senate, to concur with the interested commercial Powers in an arrangement for the liquidation of the Scheldt dues upon the principles which have been heretofore adopted in regard to the imposts upon navigation in the waters of Denmark.

The long pending controversy between this Government and that of Chili, touching the seizure of Sitana, in Peru, by Chilian officers, of a large amount in treasure belonging to citizens of the United States, has been brought to a close by the award of his Majesty the King of the Belgians, to whose arbitration the question was referred by the parties. The subject was thoroughly and patiently examined by that justly respected magistrate, and although the sum awarded to the claimants may not have been as large as they expected, there is no reason to distrust the wisdom of his Majesty's decision. That decision was promptly complied with by Chili, when intelligence in regard to it reached that country.

The joint commission, under the act of the last session, for carrying into effect the convention with Peru on the subject of claims, has been organized at Lima, and is engaged in the business intrusted to it.

Difficulties concerning inter-oceanic transit through Nicaragua are in course of amicable adjustment.

In conformity with principles set forth in my last annual message, I have received a representative from the United States of Colombia, and have accredited a minister to that republic.

Incidents occurring in the progress of our civil war have forced upon my attention the uncertain state of international questions touching the rights of foreigners in this country and of United States citizens abroad. In regard to some Governments these rights are at least partially defined by treaties. In no instance, however, is it expressly stipulated that, in the event of civil war, a foreigner residing in this country, within the lines of the insurgents, is to be exempted from the rule which classes him as a belligerent, in whose behalf the Government of his country cannot expect any privileges or immunities distinct from that character. I regret to say, however, that such claims have been put forward, and, in some instances, in behalf of foreigners who have lived in the United States the greater part of their lives.

There is reason to believe that many persons born in foreign countries, who have declared their intentions to become citizens, or who have been fully naturalized, have evaded the military duty required of them by denying the fact, and thereby throwing upon the Government the burden of proof. It has been found difficult or impracticable to obtain this proof, from the want of guides to the proper sources of information. These might be supplied by requiring clerks of courts, where declarations of intentions may be made or naturalizations effected, to send, periodically, lists of the names of the persons naturalized, or declaring their intention to become citizens, to the Secretary of the Interior, in whose department those names might be arranged and printed for general information.

There is also reason to believe that foreigners frequently become citizens of the United States for the sole purpose of evading duties imposed by the laws of their native countries, to which, on becoming naturalized here, they at once repair, and, though never returning to the United States, they still claim the interposition of this Government as citizens. Many altercations and great prejudices have heretofore arisen out of this abuse. It is, therefore, submitted to your serious consideration. It might be advisable to fix a limit, beyond which no citizen of the United States residing abroad may claim the interposition of his Government.

The right of suffrage has often been assumed and exercised by aliens, under pretences of naturalization, which they have disavowed when drafted into the military service. I submit the expediency of such an amendment of the law as will make the fact of voting an estoppel against any plea of exemption from military service, or other civil obligation, on the ground of alienage.

In common with other western Powers, our relations with Japan have been brought into serious jeopardy, through the perverse opposition of the hereditary aristocracy of the empire to the enlightened and liberal policy of the Tycoon, designed to bring the country into the society of nations. It is hoped, although not with entire confidence, that these difficulties may be peacefully overcome. I ask your attention to the claim of the minister residing there for the damages he sustained in the destruction by fire of the residence of the legation at Yedo.

Satisfactory arrangements have been made with the Emperor of Russia, which, it is believed, will result in effecting a continuous line of telegraph through that empire from our Pacific coast.

I recommend to your favorable consideration the subject of an international telegraph across the Atlantic ocean; and also of a telegraph between this capital and the national forts along the Atlantic sea-board and the Gulf of Mexico. Such communications, established with any reasonable outlay, would be economical as well as effective aids to the diplomatic, military, and naval service.

The consular system of the United States, under the enactments of the last Congress, begins to be self-sustaining; and there is reason to hope that it may become entirely so, with the increase of trade which will ensue whenever peace is restored. Our ministers abroad have been faithful in defending American rights. In protecting commercial interests, our consuls have necessarily had to encounter increased labors and responsibilities, growing out of the war. These they have, for the most part, met and discharged with zeal and efficiency. This acknowledgment justly includes those consuls who, residing in Morocco, Egypt, Turkey, Japan, China, and other Oriental countries, are charged with complex functions and extraordinary powers.

The condition of the several organized Territories is generally satisfactory, although Indian disturbances in New Mexico have not been entirely suppressed. The mineral resources of Colorado, Nevada, Idaho, New Mexico, and Arizona, are proving far richer than has been heretofore understood. I lay before you a communication on this subject from the Governor of New Mexico. I again submit to your consideration the expediency of establishing a system for the encouragement of immigration. Although this source of national wealth and strength is again flowing with greater freedom than for several years before the insurrection occurred, there is still a great deficiency of laborers in every field of industry, especially in agriculture and in our mines, as well of iron and coal as of the precious metals. While the demand for labor is much increased here, tens of thousands of persons, destitute of remunerative occupation, are thronging our foreign consulates, and offering to emigrate to the United States if essential, but very cheap, assistance can be afforded them. It is easy to see that, under the sharp discipline of civil war, the nation is beginning a new life. This noble effort demands the aid, and ought to receive the attention and support of the Government.

Injuries, unforeseen by the Government and unintended, may, in some cases, have been inflicted on the subjects or citizens of foreign countries, both at sea and on land, by persons in the service of the United States. As this Government expects redress from other Powers when similar injuries are inflicted by persons in their service upon citizens of the United States, we must be prepared to do justice to foreigners. If the existing judicial tribunals are inadequate to this purpose, a special court may be authorized, with power to hear and decide such claims of the character referred to as may have arisen under treaties and the public law. Conventions for adjusting the claims by joint commission have been proposed to some Governments, but no definite answer to the proposition has yet been received from any.

In the course of the session I shall probably have occasion to request you to provide indemnification to claimants where decrees of restitution have been rendered, and damages awarded by admiralty courts; and in other cases, where this Government may be acknowledged to be liable in principle, and where the amount of that liability has been ascertained by an informal arbitration.

The proper officers of the Treasury have deemed themselves required by the law of the United States upon the subject, to demand a tax upon the incomes of foreign consuls in this country. While such a demand may not, in strictness, be in derogation of public law, or perhaps of any existing treaty between the United States and a foreign country, the expediency of so far modifying the act as to exempt from tax the income of such consuls as are not citizens of the United States, derived from the emoluments of their office, or from property not situated in the United States, is submitted to your serious consideration. I make this suggestion upon the ground that a comity which ought to be reciprocated exempts our consuls, in all other countries, from taxation to the extent thus indicated. The United States, I think, ought not to be exceptionably illiberal to international trade and commerce.

The operations of the Treasury during the last year have been successfully conducted. The enactment by Congress of a national banking law has proved a valuable support of the public credit; and the general legislation in relation to loans has fully answered the expectations of its favorers. Some amendments may be required to perfect existing laws, but no change in their principles or general scope is believed to be needed.

Since these measures have been in operation, all demands on the Treasury, including the pay of the Army and Navy, have been promptly met and fully satisfied. No considerable body of troops, it is believed, were ever more amply provided, and more liberally and punctually paid; and it may be added, that by no people were the burdens incident to a great war ever more cheerfully borne.

The receipts during the year from all sources, including loans and balance in the Treasury at its commencement, were $901,125,674 86, and the aggregate disbursements $895,796,630 65, leaving a balance on the 1st of July, 1863, of $5,329,044 21. Of the receipts there were derived from customs $69 059,642 40; from internal revenue, $37,640,787 95; from direct tax, $1,485,103 61; from lands, $167,617 17; from miscellaneous sources, $3,046,615 35; and from loans, $776,682,361 57; making the aggregate, $901,125,674 86. Of the disbursements there were for the civil service, $23,253,922 08; for pensions and Indians, $4,216,520 79; for interest on public debt, $24,729,846 51; for the War Department, $599,298,600 83; for the Navy Department, $63,211,105 27; for payment of funded and temporary debt, $181,086,635 07; making the aggregate, $895,796,630 65, and leaving the balance of $5,329,044 21. But the payment of funded and temporary debt, having been made from moneys borrowed during the year, must be regarded as merely nominal payments, and the moneys borrowed to make them as merely nominal receipts; and their amount, $181 086,635 07, should therefore be deducted both from receipts and disbursements. This being done, there remains as actual receipts $720,039,039 79, and the actual disbursements $714,709,995 58, leaving the balance as already stated.

The actual receipts and disbursements for the first quarter, and the estimated receipts and disbursements for the remaining three quarters of the current fiscal year, 1864, will be shown in detail by the report of the Secretary of the Treasury, to which I invite your attention. It is sufficient to say here that it is not believed that actual results will exhibit a state of the finances less favorable to the country than the estimates of that officer heretofore submitted; while it is confidently expected that at the close of the year both disbursements and debt will be found very considerably less than has been anticipated.

The report of the Secretary of War is a document of great interest. It consists of—

1. The military operations of the year, detailed in the report of the General-in-Chief.

2. The organization of colored persons into the war service.

3. The exchange of prisoners, fully set forth in the letter of Gen. Hitchcock.

4. The operations under the act for enrolling and calling out the national forces, detailed in the report of the Provost Marshal General.

5. The organization of the invalid corps; and

6. The operation of the several departments of the Quartermaster General, Commissary General, Paymaster General, Chief of Engineers, Chief of Ordnance, and Surgeon General.

It has appeared impossible to make a valuable summary of this report except such as would be too extended for this place, and hence I content myself by asking your careful attention to the report itself.

The duties devolving on the naval branch of the service during the year, and throughout the whole of this unhappy contest, have been discharged with fidelity and eminent success. The extensive blockade has been constantly increasing in efficiency, as the navy has expanded; yet on so long a line it has so far been impossible to entirely suppress illicit trade. From returns received at the Navy Department it appears that more than one thousand vessels have been captured since the blockade was instituted, and that the value of prizes already sent in for adjudication amounts to over thirteen millions of dollars.

The naval force of the United States consists at this time of five hundred and eighty-eight vessels, completed and in the course of completion, and of these seventy-five are iron-clad or armored steamers. The events of the war give an increased interest and importance to the Navy which will probably extend beyond the war itself.

The armored vessels in our Navy, completed and in service, or which are under contract and approaching completion, are believed to exceed in number those of any other Power. But while these may be relied upon for harbor defence and coast service, others of greater strength and capacity will be necessary for cruising purposes, and to maintain our rightful position on the ocean.

The change that has taken place in naval vessels and naval warfare since the introduction of steam as a motive power for ships of war demands either a corresponding change in some of our existing navy-yards, or the establishment of new ones, for the construction and necessary repair of modern naval vessels. No inconsiderable embarrassment, delay, and public injury have been experienced from the want of such governmental establishments. The necessity of such a navy yard, so furnished, at some suitable place upon the Atlantic seaboard, has on repeated occasions been brought to the attention of Congress by the Navy Department, and is again presented in the report of the Secretary which accompanies this communication. I think it my duty to invite your special attention to this subject, and also to that of establishing a yard and depot for naval purposes upon one of the western rivers. A naval force has been created on those interior waters, and under many disadvantages, within little more than two years, exceeding in numbers the whole naval force of the country at the commencement of the present administration. Satisfactory and important as have been the performances of the heroic men of the Navy at this interesting period, they are scarcely more wonderful than the success of our mechanics and artisans in the production of war vessels which has created a new form of naval power.

Our country has advantages superior to any other nation in its resources of iron and timber, with inexhaustible quantities of fuel in the immediate vicinity of both, all available and in close proximity to navigable waters. Without the advantage of public works the resources of the nation have been developed and its power displayed in the construction of a navy of such magnitude which has, at the very period of its creation, rendered signal service to the Union.

The increase of the number of seamen in the public service, from seven thousand five hundred men, in the spring of 1861, to about thirty-four thousand at the present time, has been accomplished without special legislation, or extraordinary bounties to promote that increase. It has been found, however, that the operation of the draft, with the high bounties paid for army recruits, is beginning to affect injuriously the naval service, and will, if not corrected, be likely to impair its efficiency, by detaching seamen from their proper vocation and inducing them to enter the army. I therefore respectfully suggest that Congress might aid both the army and naval service by a definite provision on this subject, which would at the same time be equitable to the communities more especially interested.

I commend to your consideration the suggestions of the Secretary of the Navy in regard to the policy of fostering and training seamen, and also the education of officers and engineers for the naval service. The Naval Academy is rendering signal service in preparing midshipmen for the highly responsible duties which in after life they will be required to perform. In order that the country should not be deprived of the proper quota of educated officers, for which legal provision has been made at the Naval School, the vacancies caused by the neglect or omission to make nominations from the States in insurrection have been filled by the Secretary of the Navy. The school is now more full and complete than at any former period, and in every respect entitled to the favorable consideration of Congress.

During the past fiscal year the financial condition of the Post Office Department has been one of increasing prosperity, and I am gratified in being able to state that the actual postal revenue has nearly equalled the entire expenditures; the latter amounting to $11,314,206 84, and the former to $11,163,789 59, leaving a deficiency of but $160,417 25. In 1860, the year immediately preceding the rebellion, the deficiency amounted to $5,656,705 49, the postal receipts of that year being $2,645,722-19 less than those of 1863. The decrease since 1860 in the annual amount of transportation has been only about 25 per cent., but the annual expenditure on account of the same has been reduced 35 per cent. It is manifest, therefore, that the Post Office Department may become self-sustaining in a few years, even with the restoration of the whole service.

The international conference of postal delegates from the principal countries of Europe and America, which was called at the suggestion of the Postmaster General, met at Paris on the 11th of May last, and concluded its deliberations on the 8th of June. The principles established by the conference as best adapted to facilitate postal intercourse between nations, and as the basis of future postal conventions, inaugurate a general system of uniform international charges, at reduced rates of postage, and cannot fail to produce beneficial results.

I refer you to the report of the Secretary of the Interior, which is herewith laid before you, for useful and varied information in relation to the public lands, Indian affairs, patents, pensions, and other matters of public concern pertaining to this department.

The quantity of land disposed of during the last and the first quarter of the present fiscal years was three million eight hundred and forty-one thousand five hundred and forty-nine acres, of which one hundred and sixty-one thousand nine hundred and eleven acres were sold for cash, one million four hundred and fifty-six thousand five hundred and fourteen acres were taken up under the homestead law, and the residue disposed of under laws granting lands for military bounties, for railroad and other purposes. It also appears that the sale of the public lands is largely on the increase.

It has long been a cherished opinion of some of our wisest statesmen that the people of the United States had a higher and more enduring interest in the early settlement and substantial cultivation of the public lands than in the amount of direct revenue to be derived from the sale of them. This opinion has had a controlling influence in shaping legislation upon the subject of our national domain. I may cite, as evidence of this, the liberal measures adopted in reference to actual settlers; the grant to the States of the overflowed lands within their limits in order to their being reclaimed and rendered fit for cultivation; the grants to railway companies of alternate sections of land upon the contemplated lines of their roads which, when completed, will so largely multiply the facilities for reaching our distant possessions. This policy has received its most signal and beneficent illustration in the recent enactment granting homesteads to actual settlers. Since the first day of January last the beforementioned quantity of one million four hundred and fifty-six thousand five hundred and fourteen acres of land have been taken up under its provisions. This fact and the amount of sales, furnish gratifying evidence of increasing settlement upon the public lands, notwithstanding the great struggle in which the energies of the nation have been engaged, and which has required so large a withdrawal of our citizens from their accustomed pursuits. I cordially concur in the recommendation of the Secretary of the Interior, suggesting a modification of the act in favor of those engaged in the military and naval service of the United States. I doubt not that Congress will cheerfully adopt such measures as will, without essentially changing the general features of the system, secure, to the greatest practicable extent, its benefits to those who have left their homes in the defence of the country in this arduous crisis.

I invite your attention to the views of the Secretary as to the propriety of raising, by appropriate legislation, a revenue from the mineral lands of the United States.

The measures provided at your last session for the removal of certain Indian tribes have been carried into effect. Sundry treaties have been negotiated, which will, in due time, be submitted for the constitutional action of the Senate. They contain stipulations for extinguishing the possessory rights of the Indians to large and valuable tracts of land. It is hoped that the effect of these treaties will result in the establishment of permanent friendly relations with such of these tribes as have been brought into frequent and bloody collision with our outlying settlements and emigrants. Sound policy and our imperative duty to these wards of the Government demand our anxious and constant attention to their material well-being, to their progress in the arts of civilization, and above all, to that moral training which, under the blessing of Divine Providence, will confer upon them the elevated and sanctifying influences, the hopes and consolations of the Christian faith.

I suggested in my last annual message the propriety of remodelling our Indian system. Subsequent events have satisfied me of its necessity. The details set forth in the report of the Secretary evince the urgent need for immediate legislative action.

I commend the benevolent institutions established or patronized by the Government in this District to your generous and fostering care.

The attention of Congress, during the last session, was engaged to some extent with a proposition for enlarging the water communication between the Mississippi river and the northeastern seaboard, which proposition, however, failed for the time. Since then, upon a call of the greatest respectability, a convention has been held at Chicago upon the same subject, a summary of whose views is contained in a memorial addressed to the President and Congress, and which I now have the honor to lay before you. That this interest is one which, ere long, will force its own way, I do not entertain a doubt, while it is submitted entirely to your wisdom as to what can be done now. Augmented interest is given to this subject by the actual commencement of the work on the Pacific railroad, under auspices so favorable to rapid progress and completion. The enlarged navigation becomes a palpable need to the great road.

I transmit the second annual report of the Commissioner of the Department of Agriculture, asking your attention to the developments in that vital interest of the nation.

When Congress assembled a year ago the war had already lasted nearly twenty months, and there had been many conflicts on both land and sea with varying results. The rebellion had been pressed back into reduced limits; yet the tone of public feeling and opinion, at home and abroad, was not satisfactory. With other signs, the popular elections, then just past, indicated uneasiness among ourselves, while amid much that was cold and menacing, the kindest words coming from Europe were uttered in accents of pity, that we were too blind to surrender a hopeless cause. Our commerce was suffering greatly by a few armed vessels built upon and furnished from foreign shores, and we were threatened with such additions from the same quarter as would sweep our trade from the sea and raise our blockade. We had failed to elicit from European Governments anything hopeful upon this subject. The preliminary emancipation proclamation, issued in September, was running its assigned period to the beginning of the new year. A month later the final proclamation came, including the announcement that colored men of suitable condition would be received into the war service. The policy of emancipation, and of employing black soldiers, gave to the future a new aspect, about which hope, and fear, and doubt contended in uncertain conflict. According to our political system, as a matter of civil administration, the General Government had no lawful power to effect emancipation in any State, and for a long time it had been hoped that the rebellion could be suppressed without resorting to it as a military measure. It was all the while deemed possible that the necessity for it might come, and that if it should, the crisis of the contest would then be presented. It came, and, as was anticipated, it was followed by dark and doubtful days.

Eleven months having now passed, we are permitted to take another view. The rebel borders are pressed still further back, and by the complete opening of the Mississippi the country dominated by the rebellion is divided into distinct parts, with no practical communication between them. Tennessee and Arkansas have been substantially cleared of insurgent control, and influential citizens in each, owners of slaves and advocates of slavery at the beginning of the rebellion, now declare openly for emancipation in their respective States. Of those States not included in the emancipation proclamation, Maryland and Missouri, neither of which three years ago would tolerate any restraint upon the extension of slavery into new territories, only dispute now as to the best mode of removing it within their own limits.

Of those who were slaves at the beginning of the rebellion, full one hundred thousand are now in the United States military service, about one half of which number actually bear arms in the ranks; thus giving the double advantage of taking so much labor from the insurgent cause, and supplying the places which otherwise must be filled with so many white men. So far as tested, it is difficult to say they are not as good soldiers as any. No servile insurrection, or tendency to violence or cruelty, has marked the measures of emancipation and arming the blacks. These measures have been much discussed in foreign countries, and contemporary with such discussion the tone of public sentiment there is much improved. At home the same measures have been fully discussed, supported, criticised, and denounced, and the annual elections following are highly encouraging to those whose official duty it is to bear the country through this great trial. Thus we have the new reckoning. The crisis which threatened to divide the friends of the Union is past.

Looking now to the present and future, and with reference to a resumption of the national authority within the States wherein that authority has been suspended, I have thought fit to issue a proclamation, a copy of which is herewith transmitted. On examination of this proclamation it will appear, as is believed, that nothing will be attempted beyond what is amply justified by the Constitution. True, the form of an oath is given, but no man is coerced to take it. The man is only promised a pardon in case he voluntarily takes the oath. The Constitution authorizes the Executive to grant or withhold the pardon at his own absolute discretion; and this includes the power to grant on terms, as is fully established by judicial and other authorities.

It is also proffered that if, in any of the States named, a State government shall be, in the mode prescribed, set up, such government shall be recognized and guarantied by the United States, and that under it the State shall, on constitutional conditions, be protected against invasion and domestic violence. The constitutional obligation of the United States to guaranty to every State in the Union a republican form of government, and to protect the State, in the cases stated, is explicit and full. But why tender the benefits of this provision only to a State government set up in this particular way? This section of the Constitution contemplates a case wherein the element within a State, favorable to republican government, in the Union, may be too feeble for an opposite and hostile element external to or even within the State; and such are precisely the cases with which we are now dealing.

An attempt to guaranty and protect a revived State government, constructed in whole, or in preponderating part, from the very element against whose hostility and violence it is to be protected, is simply absurd. There must be a test by which to separate the opposing elements so as to build only from the sound; and that test is a sufficiently liberal one which accepts as sound whoever will make a sworn recantation of his former unsoundness.

But if it be proper to require, as a test of admission to the political body, an oath of allegiance to the Constitution of the United States, and to the Union under it, why also to the laws and proclamations in regard to slavery? Those laws and proclamations were enacted and put forth for the purpose of aiding in the suppression of the rebellion. To give them their fullest effect, there had to be a pledge for their maintenance. In my judgment they have aided, and will further aid, the cause for which they were intended. To now abandon them would be not only to relinquish a lever of power, but would also be a cruel and an astounding breach of faith. I may add at this point, that while I remain in my present position I shall not attempt to retract or modify the emancipation proclamation; nor shall I return to slavery any person who is free by the terms of that proclamation, or by any of the acts of Congress. For these and other reasons it is thought best that support of these measures shall be included in the oath; and it is believed the Executive may lawfully claim it in return for pardon and restoration of forfeited rights, which he has clear constitutional power to withhold altogether, or grant upon the terms which he shall deem wisest for the public interest It should be observed, also, that this part of the oath is subject to the modifying and abrogating power of legislation and supreme judicial decision.

The proposed acquiescence of the national Executive in any reasonable temporary State arrangement for the freed people is made with the view of possibly modifying the confusion and destitution which must at best, attend all classes by a total revolution of labor throughout whole States. It is hoped that the already deeply afflicted people in those States may be somewhat more ready to give up the cause of their affliction, if, to this extent, this vital matter be left to themselves; while no power of the national Executive to prevent an abuse is abridged by the proposition.

The suggestion in the proclamation as to maintaining the political frame-work of the States on what is called reconstruction, is made in the hope that it may do good without danger of harm. It will save labor, and avoid great confusion.

But why any proclamation now upon the subject? This question is beset with the conflicting views that the step might be delayed too long or be taken too soon. In some States the elements for resumption seem ready for action, but remain inactive, apparently for want of a rallying point—a plan of action. Why shall A adopt the plan of B, rather than B that of A? And if A and B should agree, how can they know but that the General Government here will reject their plan? By the proclamation a plan is presented which may be accepted by them as a rallying point, and which they are assured in advance will not be rejected here. This may bring them to act sooner than they otherwise would.

The objection to a premature presentation of a plan by the national Executive consists in the danger of committals on points which could be more safely left to further developments. Care has been taken to so shape the document as to avoid embarrassments from this source. Saying that, on certain terms, certain classes will be pardoned, with rights restored, it is not said that other classes, or other terms, will never be included. Saying that reconstruction will be accepted if presented in a specified way, it is not said it will never be accepted in any other way.

The movements, by State action, for emancipation in several of the States, not included in the emancipation proclamation, are matters of profound gratulation. And while I do not repeat in detail what I have heretofore so earnestly urged upon this subject, my general views and feelings remain unchanged; and I trust that Congress will omit no fair opportunity of aiding these important steps to a great consummation.

In the midst of other cares, however important, we must not lose sight of the fact that the war power is still our main reliance. To that power alone we can look, yet for a time, to give confidence to the people in the contested regions, that the insurgent power will not again overrun them. Until that confidence shall be established, little can be done anywhere for what is called reconstruction. Hence our chiefest care must still be directed to the army and navy, who have thus far borne their harder part so nobly and well. And it may be esteemed fortunate that in giving the greatest efficiency to these indispensable arms, we do also honorably recognize the gallant men, from commander to sentinel, who compose them, and to whom, more than to others, the world must stand indebted for the home of freedom disenthralled, regenerated, enlarged, and perpetuated.

ABRAHAM LINCOLN.

December 8, 1863.

PROCLAMATION OF AMNESTY.

Whereas, in and by the Constitution of the United States, it is provided that the President "shall have power to grant reprieves and pardons for offenses against the United States, except in cases of impeachment;" and whereas a rebellion now exists whereby the loyal State governments of several States have for a long time been subverted, and many persons have committed and are now guilty of treason against the United States; and whereas, with reference to said rebellion and treason, laws have been enacted by Congress declaring forfeitures and confiscation of property and liberation of slaves, all upon terms and conditions therein stated, and also declaring that the President was thereby authorized at any time thereafter, by proclamation, to extend to persons who may have participated in the existing rebellion, in any State or part thereof, pardon and amnesty, with such exceptions and at such times and on such conditions as he may deem expedient for the public welfare; and whereas the congressional declaration for limited and conditional pardon accords with well established judicial exposition of the pardoning power; and whereas, with reference to said rebellion, the President of the United States has issued several proclamations, with provisions in regard to the liberation of slaves; and whereas it is now desired by some persons heretofore engaged in said rebellion to resume their allegiance to the United States, and to reinaugurate loyal State governments within and for their respective States:

Therefore, I, ABRAHAM LINCOLN, President of the United States, do proclaim, declare, and make known to all persons who have directly, or by implication, participated in the existing rebellion, except as hereinafter excepted, that a full pardon is hereby granted to them and each of them, with restoration of all rights of property, except as to slaves, and in property cases where rights of third parties shall have intervened, and upon the condition that every such person shall take and subscribe an oath, and thenceforward keep and maintain said oath inviolate; and which oath shall be registered for permanent preservation, and shall be of the tenor and effect following, to wit:

"I, ——— ———, do solemnly swear, in presence of Almighty God, that I will henceforth faithfully support, protect, and defend the Constitution of the United States, and the union of the States thereunder; and that I will, in like manner, abide by and faithfully support all acts of Congress passed during the existing rebellion with reference to slaves, so long and so far as not repealed, modified, or held void by Congress, or by decision of the Supreme Court; and that I will, in like manner, abide by and faithfully support all proclamations of the President made during the existing rebellion having reference to slaves, so long and so far as not modified or declared void by decision of the Supreme Court. So help me God."

The persons excepted from the benefits of the foregoing provisions are all who are, or shall have been, civil or diplomatic officers or agents of the so-called Confederate Government; all who have left judicial stations under the United States to aid the rebellion; all who are, or shall have been, military or naval officers of said so-called Confederate Government above the rank of colonel in the Army, or of lieutenant in the Navy; all who left seats in the United States Congress to aid the rebellion; all who resigned commissions in the Army or Navy of the United States, and afterwards aided the rebellion; and all who have engaged in any way in treating colored persons, or white persons in charge of such, otherwise than lawfully as prisoners of war, and which persons may have been found in the United States service as soldiers, seamen, or in any other capacity.

And I do further proclaim, declare, and make known that whenever in any of the States of Arkansas, Texas, Louisiana, Mississippi, Tennessee, Alabama, Georgia, Virginia, Florida, South Carolina, and North Carolina, a number of persons, not less than one tenth in number of the votes cast in such State at the presidential election of the year of our Lord one thousand eight hundred and sixty, each having taken the oath aforesaid and not having since violated it, and being a qualified voter by the election law of the State existing immediately before the so-called act of secession, and excluding all others, shall re-establish a State government which shall be republican, and in nowise contravening said oath, such shall be recognized as the true government of the State, and the State shall receive thereunder the benefits of the constitutional provision which declares that "the United States shall guaranty to every State in this Union a republican form of government, and shall protect each of them against invasion; and, on application of the Legislature, or the Executive, (when the Legislature cannot be convened,) against domestic violence."

And I do further proclaim, declare, and make known that any provision which may be adopted by such State government in relation to the freed people of such State, which shall recognize and declare their permanent freedom, provide for their education, and which may yet be consistent, as a temporary arrangement, with their present condition as a laboring, landless, and homeless class, will not be objected to by the national Executive. And it is suggested as not improper, that, in constructing a loyal State government in any State, the name of the State, the boundary, the subdivisions, the constitution, and the general code of laws, as before the rebellion, be maintained, subject only to the modifications made necessary by the conditions hereinbefore stated, and such others, if any, not contravening said conditions, and which may be deemed expedient by those framing the new State government.

To avoid misunderstanding, it may be proper to say that this proclamation, so far as it relates to State governments, has no reference to States wherein loyal State governments have all the while been maintained. And for the same reason, it may be proper to further say, that whether members sent to Congress from any State shall be admitted to seats constitutionally, rests exclusively with the respective Houses, and not to any extent with the Executive. And still further, that this proclamation is intended to present the people of the States wherein the national authority has been suspended, and loyal State governments have been subverted, a mode in and by which the national and loyal State governments may be re-established within said States, or in any of them; and, while the mode presented is the best the Executive can suggest, with his present impressions, it must not be understood that no other possible mode would be acceptable.

Given under my hand, at the City of Washington, the eighth day of December, A. D. one thousand eight hundred and sixty-three, and of the independence of the United States of America the eighty-eighth.

ABRAHAM LINCOLN.

By the President:

WILLIAM H. SEWARD, *Secretary of State.*

AMNESTY DEFINED.

By the President of the United States—A Proclamation.

Whereas it has become necessary to define the cases in which insurgent enemies are entitled to the benefits of the Proclamation of the President of the United States, which was made on the 8th day of December, 1863, and the manner in which they shall proceed to avail themselves of those benefits: and whereas the objects of that proclamation were to suppress the insurrection, and to restore the authority of the United States: and whereas the amnesty therein provided by the President was offered with reference to these objects alone:

Now, therefore, I, ABRAHAM LINCOLN, President of the United States, do hereby proclaim and declare that the said proclamation does not apply to the cases of persons who, at the time when they seek to obtain the benefits thereof by taking the oath thereby prescribed, are in military, naval, or civil confinement or custody, or under bonds or on parole of the civil, military, or naval authorities, or agents of the United States as prisoners of war, or persons detained for offences of any kind, either before or after conviction; and that, on the contrary, it does apply only to persons who, being yet at large and free from any arrest, confinement, or duress, shall voluntarily come forward and take the said oath with the purpose of restoring peace and establishing the national authority.

Prisoners excluded from the amnesty offered in the said proclamation may apply to the President for clemency, like all other offenders, and their application will receive due consideration.

I do further declare and proclaim that the oath prescribed in the aforesaid proclamation of the 8th of December, 1863, may be taken and subscribed to before any commissioned officer, civil, military, or naval, in the service of the United States, or any civil or military officer of a State or Territory, not in insurrection, who by the law thereof may be qualified for administering oaths.

All officers who receive such oaths are hereby authorized to give certificates thereon to the persons respectively by whom they are made. And such officers are hereby required to transmit the original records of such oaths at as early a day as may be convenient to the Department of State, where they will be deposited and remain in the archives of the Government.

The Secretary of State will keep a register thereof, and will, on application in proper cases, issue certificates of such records in the customary form of such certificates.

In testimony whereof I have hereunto set my hand, and caused the seal of the United States to be affixed.

Done at the city of Washington, the 26th day of March, in the year of our Lord one thousand eight hundred and sixty-four, and of the independence of the United States the eighty-eighth.

ABRAHAM LINCOLN.

By the President:

WILLIAM H. SEWARD, *Secretary of State.*

CIRCULAR OF THE ATTORNEY GENERAL.

WASHINGTON, *February* 19, 1864—The following important circular letter has been addressed to United States District Attorneys:

SIR: Many persons, against whom criminal indictments, or against whose property proceedings under the confiscation laws are pending in the courts of the United States, growing out of the participation of such persons in the existing rebellion, have, in good faith, taken the oath prescribed by the proclamation of the President of 8th December, 1863, and have therefore entitled themselves to the full pardon and restoration of all rights of property, except as to slaves and where rights of third parties have intervened, which that proclamation offers and secures.

The President's pardon of a person guilty of acts of rebellion will of course relieve that person from the penalties incurred by his crime, and, where an indictment is pending against him therefor, the production of the pardon signed by the President, or of satisfactory evidence that he has complied with the conditions on which the pardon is offered, (if he be not of the class excepted from the benefits of the proclamation,) will be a sufficient reason for discontinuing such criminal proceedings, and discharging him from custody therein.

Nor is it less doubtful that a *bona fide* acceptance of the terms of the President's Proclamation, by persons guilty of acts of rebellion, and not of the excepted class, will secure to such persons a restoration of all the rights of property, except as to slaves and where the rights of third parties shall have intervened, notwithstanding such property may, by reason of those acts of rebellion, have been subject to confiscation under the provisions of the Confiscation act of of 6th August, 1861, chap. 60, and 17th July, 1862, chap. 195. For, without adverting to any other source of power in the President to restore or protect their rights of property, the 13th section of the act of 17th of July, 1862, authorizes the President at any time thereafter, by proclamation, to extend to persons who may have participated in the existing rebellion in any State or part thereof, pardon and amnesty, with such exceptions, and at such time and on such conditions, as he may deem expedient for the public welfare. It will hardly be questioned, I suppose, that the purpose of this section, inserted in a law mainly intended to reach the property of persons engaged in rebellion, was to vest the President with power to relieve such persons, on such conditions as he should prescribe, from the penalty of loss of their property by confiscation. Although the proceedings for confiscation under the acts of Aug. 6, 1861, and July 17, 1862, are *in rem*, against the property seized, yet, under both acts, the ground of condemnation is the personal guilt of the owner in aiding the rebellion. By the pardon and amnesty, not only is the punishment of that personal guilt remitted, but the offence itself is effaced, that being the special effect of an act of amnesty by the Government. Of course it arrests and puts an end to all penal proceedings founded thereon, whether they touch the persons or the property of the offender.

There is, therefore, no case of judicial proceedings to enforce the penalties of acts of rebellion which cannot be reached and cured by the constitutional or statutory power of the President to grant pardon and amnesty, whether those proceedings be against the person of the offender by criminal indictment or against his property under the confiscation acts referred to.

The President has accordingly directed me to instruct you that, in any case where proceedings have been commenced and are pending and undetermined in the District or Circuit Court of the United States for your district against a person charged with acts of rebellion, and not of the excepted class, whether they be by indictment or by seizure and libel of his property for confiscation, (the rights of other parties not having intervened,) you will discontinue and put an end to those proceedings, whenever the person so charged shall produce evidence satisfactory to you that he has, in good faith, taken the oath and complied with the conditions prescribed by the President's proclamation of the 8th December, 1863. Nor is it necessary that the evidence which he produces should be a deed of pardon signed by the President.

It would be quite impossible for the President to furnish the multitudes who are now availing themselves of the benefits of the Proclamation, and who are likely to do so hereafter, with his formal evidence of pardon. It will be sufficient to justify your action if the party seeking to be relieved from further proceedings shall prove to your full satisfaction that he has, in good faith, taken the oath and brought himself within the conditions of pardon and amnesty set forth in the Proclamation.

If, in any case, you have good reason to believe that the oath has been taken for the mere purpose of obtaining the possession of personal property seized under the Confiscation acts, with intent to remove it from the subsequent reach of the officers of the law, you will make report of the facts and reasons for your belief to this office before discontinuing the proceedings or restoring such property to the possession of the owner. Forfeitures under the fifth section of the act of 13th July, 1861, chapter 3, are not of the class reached by the President's Proclamation, for, under that act, the question whether the property seized is subject to forfeiture depends upon the predicament of the property itself, and not upon the general guilt or innocence of its owner. In this respect, forfeitures under that act have more resemblance to cases of prize of war, captured at sea as enemy's property than to proceedings under the acts of August, 1861, and July, 1862. Such forfeitures are enforced not so much to punish the owner for disloyal acts as to prohibit commercial intercourse, and to weaken the public enemy, which are always efficient instruments and legitimate effects of public war.

But although the remission of forfeitures under the act of July, 1861, are thus not within the scope of the Proclamation of pardon, still ample power is conferred on the Secretary of the Treasury by the eighth section of that act to mitigate or remit all forfeitures and penalties incurred under the act. And it is not to be doubted that in all proper cases under that act, where the owner of the property, residing in the territory in rebellion, complies with the conditions of the Proclamation, the Secretary of the Treasury will exercise the power of remission of such forfeitures in the same spirit of generous forbearance and liberality which inspired and characterizes the Proclamation.

Very respectfully, &c., TITIAN J. COFFEY, *Acting Attorney General.*

To ——, United States District Attorney at ——.

Other Proclamations of the President.

THE BLOCKADE.

Whereas an insurrection against the Government of the United States has broken out in the States of South Carolina, Georgia, Alabama, Florida, Mississippi, Louisiana, and Texas, and the laws of the United States for the collection of the revenue cannot be effectually executed therein conformably to that provision of the Constitution which requires duties to be uniform throughout the United States:

And whereas a combination of persons engaged in such insurrection have threatened to grant pretended letters of marque to authorize the bearers thereof to commit assaults on the lives, vessels, and property of good citizens of the country lawfully engaged in commerce on the high seas, and in waters of the United States:

And whereas an executive proclamation has been already issued, requiring the persons engaged in these disorderly proceedings to desist therefrom, calling out a militia force for the purpose of repressing the same, and convening Congress in extraordinary session to deliberate and determine thereon:

Now, therefore, I, Abraham Lincoln, President of the United States, with a view to the same purposes before mentioned, and to the protection of the public peace, and the lives and property of quiet and orderly citizens pursuing their lawful occupations, until Congress shall have assembled and deliberated on the said unlawful proceedings, or until the same shall have ceased, have further deemed it advisable to set on foot a blockade of the ports within the States aforesaid, in pursuance of the laws of the United States and of the law of nations in such case provided. For this purpose a competent force will be posted so as to prevent entrance and exit of vessels from the ports aforesaid. If, therefore, with a view to violate such blockade, a vessel shall approach, or shall attempt to leave either of the said ports, she will be duly warned by the commander of one of the blockading vessels, who will indorse on her register the fact and date of such warning; and if the same vessel shall again attempt to enter or leave the blockaded port, she will be captured and sent to the nearest convenient port, for such proceedings against her and her cargo as prize as may be deemed advisable.

And I hereby proclaim and declare that if any person, under the pretended authority of the said States, or under any other pretence, shall molest a vessel of the United States, or the persons or cargo on board of her, such person will be held amenable to the laws of the United States for the prevention and punishment of piracy. ABRAHAM LINCOLN.

By the President:
William H. Seward, *Secretary of State.*
Washington, *April* 19, 1861.

OF VIRGINIA AND NORTH CAROLINA.

On the 27th of April, the following additional proclamation, extending the blockade, was issued:

Whereas, for the reasons assigned in my proclamation of the 19th instant, a blockade of the ports of the States of South Carolina, Georgia, Florida, Alabama, Louisiana, Mississippi, and Texas, was ordered to be established: and whereas, since that date, public property of the United States has been seized, the collection of the revenue obstructed, and duly commissioned officers of the United States, while engaged in executing the orders of their superiors, have been arrested and held in custody as prisoners, or have been impeded in the discharge of their official duties, without due legal process, by persons claiming to act under authority of the States of Virginia and North Carolina: An efficient blockade of the ports of those States will also be established.

In witness whereof, I have hereunto set my hand, and caused the seal of the United States to be affixed.

Done at the city of Washington, this 27th day of April, in the year of our Lord 1861, and of the independence of the United States the eighty-fifth.

ABRAHAM LINCOLN.

By the President:
William H. Seward, *Secretary of State.*

1862, May 12—The President issued a proclamation opening the ports of Beaufort, Port Royal, and New Orleans.

1863, September 24—The President issued a proclamation opening the port of Alexandria, Virginia.

1864, February 18—The President issued a proclamation opening the port of Brownsville, Texas.

1864, November 19—Norfolk, Fernandina, and Pensacola opened after December 1.

COMMERCIAL INTERCOURSE WITH THE REBELLIOUS STATES PROHIBITED.

Whereas, on the 15th day of April, 1861, the President of the United States, in view of an insurrection against the laws, Constitution, and Government of the United States, which had broken out within the States of South Carolina, Georgia, Alabama, Florida, Mississippi, Louisiana, and Texas, and in pursuance of the provisions of the act entitled "An act to provide for calling forth the militia to execute the laws of the Union, suppress insurrections, and repel invasions, and to repeal the act now in force for that purpose," approved February 28, 1795, did call forth the militia to suppress said insurrection and to cause the laws of the Union to be duly executed, and the insurgents have failed to disperse by the time directed by the President; and whereas such insurrection has since broken out and yet exists within the States of Virginia, North Carolina, Tennessee, and Arkansas; and whereas the insurgents in all the said States claim to act under the authority thereof, and such claim is not disclaimed or repudiated by the persons exercising the functions of government in such State or States, or in the part or parts thereof, in which such combinations exist, nor has such insurrection been suppressed by said States:

Now, therefore, I, Abraham Lincoln, President of the United States, in pursuance of the act of Congress approved July 13, 1861, do hereby declare that the inhabitants of the said States of Georgia, South Carolina, Virginia, North Carolina, Tennessee, Alabama, Louisiana, Texas, Arkansas, Mississippi, and Florida, (except the inhabitants of that part of the State of Virginia lying west of the Alleghany Mountains, and of such other parts of that State and the other States hereinbefore named as may maintain a loyal adhesion to the Union and the Constitution, or may be from time to time occupied and controlled by the forces of the United States engaged in the dispersion of said insurgents) are in a state of insurrection against the United States, and that all commercial intercourse between the same and the inhabitants thereof, with the exceptions aforesaid, and the citizens of other States and other parts of the United States, is unlawful and will remain unlawful until such insurrection shall cease or has been suppressed; that all goods and chattels, wares and merchandise, coming from any of said States, with the exceptions aforesaid, into other parts of the United States, without the special license and permission of the President, through the Secretary of the Treasury, or proceeding to any of said States, with the exceptions aforesaid, by land or water, together with the vessel or vehicle conveying the same or conveying persons to or from the said States, with said exceptions, will be forfeited to the United States; and that, from and after fifteen days from the issuing of this proclamation, all ships and vessels belonging, in whole or in part, to any citizen or inhabitant of any of said States, with said exceptions, found at sea or in any port of the United States, will be forfeited to the United States; and I hereby enjoin upon all district attorneys, marshals, and officers of the revenue and of the military and naval forces of the United States, to be vigilant in the execution of said act, and in the enforcement of the penalties and forfeitures imposed or declared by it; leaving any party who may think himself aggrieved thereby to his application to the Secretary of the Treasury for the remission of any penalty or forfeiture, which the said Secretary is authorized by law to grant, if, in his judgment, the special circumstances of any case shall require such remission.

In witness whereof I have hereunto set my hand, and caused the seal of the United States to be affixed.

Done at the city of Washington, this sixteenth day of August, in the year of our Lord one thousand eight hundred and sixty-one, and of the independence of the United States of America the eighty-sixth. ABRAHAM LINCOLN.

By the President:
William H. Seward, *Secretary of State.*

1863, April 2—The President issued a proc-

lamation modifying the above, and reciting his reasons therefor:

And whereas experience has shown that the exceptions made in and by said proclamation embarrass the due enforcement of said act of July 13, 1861, and the proper regulation of the commercial intercourse authorized by said act with the loyal citizens of said States:

Now, therefore, I, ABRAHAM LINCOLN, President of the United States, do hereby revoke the said exceptions, and declare that the inhabitants of the States of Georgia, South Carolina, North Carolina, Tennessee, Alabama, Louisiana, Texas, Arkansas, Mississippi, Florida, and Virginia, (except the forty-eight counties of Virginia designated as West Virginia, and except, also, the ports of New Orleans, Key West, Port Royal, and Beaufort, in North Carolina,) are in a state of insurrection against the United States, and that all commercial intercourse, not licensed and conducted as provided in said act, between the said States and the inhabitants thereof, with the exceptions aforesaid, and the citizens of other States and other parts of the United States, is unlawful, and will remain unlawful until such insurrection shall cease or has been suppressed, and notice thereof has been duly given by proclamation; and all cotton, tobacco, and other products, and all other goods and chattels, wares, and merchandise coming from any of said States, with the exceptions aforesaid, into other parts of the United States, or proceeding to any of said States, with the exceptions aforesaid, without the license and permission of the President, through the Secretary of the Treasury, will, together with the vessel or vehicle conveying the same, be forfeited to the United States.

DECLARING BOUNDARIES OF THE INSURRECTION.

Whereas, in and by the second section of an act of Congress passed on the 7th day of June, A. D. 1862, entitled "An act for the collection of direct taxes in insurrectionary districts within the United States, and for other purposes," it is made the duty of the President to declare, on or before the 1st day of July then next following, by his proclamation, in what States and parts of States insurrection exists:

Now, therefore, be it known that I, ABRAHAM LINCOLN, President of the United States of America, do hereby declare and proclaim that the States of South Carolina, Florida, Georgia, Alabama, Louisiana, Texas, Mississippi, Arkansas, Tennessee, North Carolina, and the State of Virginia, except the following counties: Hancock, Brooke, Ohio, Marshall, Wetzel, Marion, Monongalia, Preston, Taylor, Pleasants, Tyler, Ritchie, Doddridge, Harrison, Wood, Jackson, Wirt, Roane, Calhoun, Gilmer, Barbour, Tucker, Lewis, Braxton, Upshur, Randolph, Mason, Putnam, Kanawha, Clay, Nicholas, Cabell, Wayne, Boone, Logan, Wyoming, Webster, Fayette, and Raleigh, are now in insurrection and rebellion, and by reason thereof the civil authority of the United States is obstructed so that the provisions of the "Act to provide increased revenue from imports, to pay the interest on the public debt, and for other purposes," approved August 5, 1861, cannot be peaceably executed, and that the taxes legally chargeable upon real estate under the act last aforesaid, lying within the States and parts of States as aforesaid, together with a penalty of fifty per centum of said taxes, shall be a lien upon the tracts or lots of the same, severally charged, till paid.

In witness whereof, I have hereunto set my hand, and caused the seal of the United States to be affixed.

Done at the city of Washington, this 1st day of July, in the year of our Lord one thousand eight hundred and sixty-two, and of the independence of the United States of America the eighty-sixth. ABRAHAM LINCOLN.

By the President:

F. W. SEWARD, *Acting Secretary of State.*

PROCEEDINGS OF CONGRESS.

ACTS OF THE PRESIDENT APPROVED—FIRST SESSION, THIRTY-SEVENTH CONGRESS.

1861, August 5—Congress passed a bill, the third section of which was as follows:

That all the acts, proclamations, and orders of the President of the United States after the 4th of March, 1861, respecting the army and navy of the United States, and calling out or relating to the militia or volunteers from the States, are hereby approved and in all respects legalized and made valid, to the same intent and with the same effect, as if they had been issued and done under the previous express authority and direction of the Congress of the United States.

In SENATE, the bill passed—yeas 33, nays 5, as follows:

YEAS—Messrs. Anthony, Baker, Browning, *Carlile*, Chandler, Collamer, Cowan, Dixon, Doolittle, Fessenden, Foot, Foster, Grimes, Hale, Harlan, Harris, Howe, Johnson of Tennessee, King, Lane of Indiana, Lane of Kansas, *Latham*, *McDougall*, Morrill, *Rice*, Sherman, Simmons, Sumner, Ten Eyck, Trumbull, Wade, Wilkinson, Wilson—33.

NAYS—Messrs. *Breckinridge*, *Kennedy*, *Polk*, *Powell*, *Saulsbury*—5.

In HOUSE, the motion to strike from the bill the ratifying section, was lost—yeas 19, nays 74; as follows;

YEAS—Messrs. *Allen*, *Ancona*, *George H. Browne*, *Calvert*, *Cox*, *Crisfield*, Jackson, *Johnson*, *May*, *Noble*, *Pendleton*, *James S. Rollins*, *Shiel*, *Smith*, *Vallandigham*, *Voorhees*, *Wadsworth*, *Ward*, Webster—19.

NAYS—Messrs. Aldrich, Alley, Arnold, Ashley, Goldsmith F. Bailey, Baxter, Beaman, Francis P. Blair, Samuel S. Blair, Blake, Buffinton, *Cobb*, Colfax, Frederick A. Conkling, Conway, Covode, Diven, Duell, Dunn, Edwards, Eliot, Fenton, Fessenden, Frank, Goodwin, Granger, Gurley, Haight, Hale, Hanchett, Harrison, Horton, Hutchins, Julian, Kelley, Francis W. Kellogg, William Kellogg, Lansing, Leary, Loomis, Lovejoy, McKean, McKnight, McPherson, Mitchell, Moorhead, Anson P. Morrill, Justin S. Morrill, Olin, Pike, Porter, Alexander H. Rice, John H. Rice, Riddle, Edward H. Rollins, Sedgwick, Shanks, *Sheffield*, Shellabarger, Sherman, Stevens, Benjamin F. Thomas, Francis Thomas, Train, Trowbridge, Van Horn, Verree, Wall, Charles W. Walton, E. P. Walton, Albert S. White, Windom, Worcester—74.

The bill then passed without a division.

African Slave Trade.

1862, April 7—A treaty was made between William H. Seward and Lord Lyons for the suppression of the African Slave Trade, which was ratified by the Senate, and announced by proclamation of the President, June 7, 1862, Article 1 of which is as follows:

The two high contracting parties mutually consent that those ships of their respective navies which shall be provided with special instructions for that purpose, as hereinafter mentioned, may visit such merchant vessels of the two nations as may, upon reasonable grounds, be suspected of being engaged in the African slave trade, or of having been fitted out for that purpose; or of having, during the voyage on which they are met by the said cruisers, been engaged in the African slave trade, contrary to the provision of this treaty; and that such cruisers may detain, and send or carry away, such vessels, in order that they may be brought to trial in the manner hereinafter agreed upon.

In order to fix the reciprocal right of search in such a manner as shall be adapted to the attainment of the object of this treaty, and at the same time avoid doubts, disputes, and complaints, the said right of search shall be understood in the manner and according to the rules following:

First. It shall never be exercised except by vessels of war, authorized expressly for that object, according to the stipulations of this treaty.

Secondly. The right of search shall in no case be exercised with respect to a vessel of the navy of either of the two Powers, but shall be exercised only as regards merchant vessels; and it shall not be exercised by a vessel of war of either contracting party within the limits of a settlement or port, nor within the territorial waters of the other party.

Thirdly. Whenever a merchant vessel is searched by a ship of war, the commander of the said ship shall, in the act of so doing, exhibit to the commander of the merchant vessel the special instructions by which he is duly authorized to search; and shall deliver to such commander a certificate, signed by himself, stating his rank in the naval service of his country, and the name of the vessel he commands, and also declaring that the only object of the search is to ascertain whether the vessel is employed in the African slave trade, or is fitted up for the said trade. When the search is made by an officer of the cruiser who is not the commander, such officer shall exhibit to the captain of the merchant vessel a copy of the before-mentioned special instructions, signed by the commander of the cruiser; and he shall in like manner deliver a certificate signed by himself, stating his rank in the navy, the name of the commander by whose orders he proceeds to make the search, that of the cruiser in which he sails, and the object of the search, as above described. If it appears from the search that the papers of the vessel are in regular order, and that it is employed on lawful objects, the officer shall enter in the log-book of the vessel that the search has been made in pursuance of the aforesaid special instructions; and the vessel shall be left at liberty to pursue its voyage. The rank of the officer who makes the search must not be less than that of lieutenant in the navy, unless the command, either by reason of death or other cause, is at the time held by an officer of inferior rank.

Fourthly. The reciprocal right of search and detention shall be exercised only within the distance of two hundred miles from the coast of Africa, and to the southward of the thirty-second parallel of north latitude, and within thirty leagues from the coast of the Island of Cuba.

1862, June 26—In Senate, the bill to carry into effect this treaty, by providing for the officials, &c., passed—yeas 34, nays 4, (Messrs. *Carlile, Kennedy, Powell, Saulsbury.*)

July 7—The bill passed the House without a division.

1863, February 17—The treaty was modified by the addition of an article authorizing the exercise of the reciprocal right of visit and detention within thirty leagues of the island of Madagascar, within thirty leagues of the island of Puerto Rico, and within thirty leagues of the island of San Domingo.

THE "CONFEDERATE" RECORD.

Soon after the adoption of their Constitution in 1861, the rebel Congress passed a bill in relation to the slave trade, which JEFFERSON DAVIS returned, with his objections, as follows:

EXECUTIVE DEPARTMENT,
February 28, 1861.

GENTLEMEN OF CONGRESS: With sincere deference to the judgment of Congress, I have carefully considered the bill in relation to the slave trade, and to punish persons offending therein, but have not been able to approve it, and, therefore, do return it with a statement of my objections.

The Constitution—section seven, article one—provides that the importation of African negroes from any foreign country other than slaveholding States of the United States is hereby forbidden, and Congress is required to pass such laws as shall effectually prevent the same. The rule herein given is emphatic, and distinctly directs the legislation which shall effectually prevent the importation of African negroes. The bill before me denounces as high misdemeanor the importation of African negroes, or other persons of color, either to be sold as slaves or to be held to service or labor, affixing heavy, degrading penalties on the act if done with such intent. To that extent it accords with the requirements of the Constitution, but in the sixth section of the bill provision is made for the transfer of persons who may have been illegally imported into the Confederate States to the custody of foreign States or societies, upon condition of deportation and future freedom, and, if the proposition thus to surrender them shall not be accepted, it is then made the duty of the President to cause said negroes to be sold at public outcry to the highest bidder in any one of the States where such sale shall not be inconsistent with the laws thereof. This provision seems to me to be in opposition to the policy declared in the Constitution—the prohibition of the importation of African negroes—and in derogation of its mandate to legislate for the effectuation of that object. Wherefore the bill is returned to you for your further consideration, and, together with the objections, most respectfully submitted.

JEFFERSON DAVIS.

This veto was sustained by the following vote—the question being, "Shall the bill pass notwithstanding the President's objections?"

YEAS—Messrs. Curry and Chilton, of Alabama; Morton and Owens, of Florida; Toombs, H. Cobb, T. R. R. Cobb, Bartow, Nisbet, and Kenan, of Georgia; Rhett, Barnwell, Keitt, and Miles, of South Carolina; Ochiltree, of Texas—15.

NAYS—Messrs. Smith, Hale, Shorter, and Fearn of Alabama; Wright and Stephens, of Georgia; DeClouet, Conrad, Kenner, Sparrow, and Marshall, of Louisiana; Harris, Brooke, Wilson, Clayton, Barry, and Harrison, of Mississippi; Chesnut, Withers, and Boyce, of South Carolina; Reagan, Waul, Gregg, and Oldham, of Texas—24.

INTERCEPTED "CONFEDERATE" DESPATCH UPON THE AFRICAN SLAVE TRADE.

As showing the temper of the "Confederate" Government upon the revival of the African slave trade, it is instructive to read the letter of J. P. Benjamin, Secretary of State of the "Confederate" Government, to L. Q. C. Lamar, "Confederate" Commissioner at St. Petersburg, which was intercepted and transmitted from St. Petersburg, March 3, 1863, by Bayard Taylor, Chargé d' Affaires:

CONFEDERATE STATES OF AMERICA,
DEPARTMENT OF STATE, RICHMOND, *January* 15, 1863.

SIR: It has been suggested to this Government, from a source of unquestioned authenticity, that after the recognition of our independence by the European Powers, an expectation is generally entertained by them, that in our treaties of amity and commerce a clause will be introduced making stipulations against the African slave trade. It is even thought that neutral Powers may be inclined to insist upon the insertion of such a clause as a *sine qua non.*

You are well aware how firmly fixed in our constitution is the policy of this Confederacy against the opening of that trade; but we are informed that false and insidious suggestions have been made by the agents of the United States at European courts of an intention to change our constitution as soon as peace is restored, and of authorizing the importation of slaves from Africa. If, therefore, you should find in your intercourse with the Cabinet to which you are accredited that any such impressions are entertained, you will use every proper effort to remove them; and if an attempt is made to introduce into any treaty which you may be charged with negotiating stipulations on the subject just mentioned, you will assume in behalf of your Government the position which, under the direction of the President, I now proceed to develop.

The constitution of the Confederate States is an agreement made between independent States. By its terms all the powers of government are separated into classes as follows, viz:

1. Such powers as the States delegate to the General Government.

2. Such powers as the States agree to refrain from exercising, although they do not delegate them to the General Government.

3. Such powers as the States, without delegating them to the General Government, thought proper to exercise, by direct agreement between themselves contained in the constitution.

4. All remaining powers of sovereignty which, not being delegated to the Confederate States by the constitution, nor prohibited by it to the States, are reserved to the States, respectively, or to the people thereof.

On the formation of the constitution, the States thought proper to prevent all possible future discussions on the subject of slavery, by the direct exercise of their own power, and delegated no authority to the Confederate Government, save immaterial exceptions, presently to be noticed.

Especially in relation to the importation of African negroes was it deemed important by the States that no power to permit it should exist in the Confederate Government. The States, by the Constitution, (which is a treaty between themselves of the most solemn character that States can make,) unanimously stipulated "that the importation of negroes of the African race, from any foreign country other than the slaveholding States or Territories of the United States of America, is hereby forbidden; and Congress is required to pass such laws as shall effectually prevent the same." (Art. 1, sec. 9, par. 1.)

It will thus be seen that no power is delegated to the Confederate Government over this subject, but that it is included in the third class above referred to, of power exercised directly by the States.

It is true that the *duty* is imposed on Congress to pass laws to render effectual the prohibition above quoted. But this very imposition of a duty on Congress is the strongest proof of the absence of power in the President and Senate alone, who are vested with authority to make treaties. In a word, as the only provision on the subject directs the two branches of the legislative department, in connection with the President, to pass *laws* on this subject, it is out of the power of the President, aided by one branch of the legislative department, to control the same subject by treaties; for there is not only an absence of express delegation of authority to the treaty-making power, which alone would suffice to prevent the exercise of such authority, but there is the implied prohibition resulting from the fact that all duty on the subject is imposed on a different branch of the Government.

I need scarcely enlarge upon the familiar principle, that authority expressly delegated to Congress cannot be assumed in our Government by the treaty-making power. The authority to levy and collect taxes, to coin money, to declare war, &c., &c., are ready examples, and you can be at no loss for argument or illustration in support of so well recognized a principle.

The view above expressed is further enforced by the clause in the Constitution which follows immediately that which has already been quoted. The second paragraph of the same section provides that "Congress shall also have power to prohibit the introduction of slaves from any State not a member of, or territory not belonging to, this Confederacy." Here there is no direct exercise of power by the States which formed our Constitution, but an express delegation to Congress. It is thus seen that while the States were willing to trust Congress with the power to prohibit the introduction of African slaves from the United States, they were not willing to trust it with the power of prohibiting their introduction from any other quarter, but determined to insure the execution of their will by a direct interposition of their own power.

Moreover, any attempt on the part of the treaty-making power of this Government to prohibit the African slave trade, in addition to the insuperable objections above suggested, would leave open the implication that the same power has authority to permit such introduction. No such implication can be sanctioned by us. This Government unequivocally and absolutely denies its possession of any power whatever over the subject, and cannot entertain any proposition in relation to it.

While it is totally beneath the dignity of this Government to give assurances for the purpose of vindicating itself from any unworthy suspicions of its good faith on this subject, that may be disseminated by the agents of the United States, it may not be improper that you should point out the superior efficacy of our constitutional provision to any treaty stipulations we could make. The constitution is itself a treaty between the States, of such binding force, that it cannot be changed or abrogated without the deliberate and concurrent action of nine out of the thirteen States that compose the Confederacy. A treaty might be abrogated by a party temporarily in power in our country, at the sole risk of disturbing amicable relations with a foreign Power. The Constitution, unless by approach to unanimity, could not be changed without the destruction of this Government itself; and even should it be possible hereafter to procure the consent of the number of States necessary to change it, the forms and delays, designedly interposed by the framers to check rash innovations, would give ample time for the most mature deliberation, and for strenuous resistance on the part of those opposed to such a change.

After all, it is scarcely the part of wisdom to attempt to impose restraint on the actions and conduct of men for all future time. The policy of the Confederacy is as fixed and immutable on this subject as the imperfection of human nature permits human resolve to be. No additional agreements, treaties, or stipulations can commit these States to the prohibition of the African slave trade with more binding efficacy than those they have themselves devised. A just and generous confidence in their good faith on this subject, exhibited by friendly Powers, will be far more efficacious than persistent efforts to induce this Government to assume the exercise of powers which it does not possess, and to bind the Confederacy by ties which would have no constitutional validity. We trust, therefore, that no unnecessary discussion on this matter will be introduced into your negotiations. If, unfortunately, this reliance should prove ill-founded, you will decline continuing negotiations on your side, and transfer them to us at home, where, in such event, they could be conducted with greater facility and advantage, under the direct supervision of the President.

With great respect, your obedient servant,

J. P. BENJAMIN, *Secretary of State.*

HON. L. Q. C. LAMAR,
Commissioner, &c., &c., St. Petersburg, Russia.

Arrests of Citizens, and the writ of Habeas Corpus.

June 27, 1861, Major General N. P. BANKS, commanding the Department of Annapolis, had George P. Kane, Chief of Police of Baltimore, arrested for being, in contravention of his duty and in violation of law, by direction or indirection, both witness and protector to transactions hostile to the authority of the Government, and to conspirators avowedly its enemies.

Same day, Charles Howard, Wm. H. Gatchell, Charles D. Hinks, John W. Davis, and George Wm. Brown, Mayor and ex-officio member of Board of Police of Baltimore, protested against the arrest of Marshal Kane, and the suspension of the Board of Police, by a military provost marshal.

July 1, General Banks, in pursuance of orders from the Headquarters of the Army at Washington, arrested the four first-named members, for these reasons:

The incidents of the past week afforded full justification for this order. The headquarters, under the charge of the board, when abandoned by the officers, resembled in some respects, a concealed arsenal. After public recognition and protest against the "suspension of their functions," they continued their sessions daily. Upon a forced and unwarrantable construction of my proclamation of the 27th ultimo, they declared that the police law was suspended, and the police officers and men put off duty for the present, intending to leave the city without any police protection whatever. They refused to recognize the officers or men necessarily selected by the provost marshal for its protection, and hold subject to their orders, now and hereafter, the old police force, a large body of armed men, for some purpose not known to the Government, and inconsistent with its peace or security. To anticipate any intentions or orders on their part, I have placed temporarily a portion of the force under my command within the city. I disclaim on the part of the Government I represent, all desire, intention, and purpose to interfere, in any manner whatever, with the ordinary municipal affairs of the city of Baltimore. Whenever a loyal citizen can be named who will execute its police laws with impartiality and in good faith to the United States, the military force will be withdrawn from the central parts of the municipality at once. No soldier will be permitted in the city, except under regulations satisfactory to the marshal; and if any so admitted violate the municipal law, they shall be punished according to the civil law, by the civil tribunals.

They were transferred to Fort Lafayette, and on the 6th of August, Judge Garrison of Brooklyn, issued a writ directing Col. Burke to produce the persons in court. Col. Burke declined on the authority of an order from Lieut. Gen. Scott. Col. Burke was then cited to answer for contempt of court, but he did not appear, and August 22, Judge Garrison, "submiting to inevitable necessity," dismissed the proceedings. They were subsequently released. See President's Orders, p. 154.

ARREST OF MEMBERS OF THE LEGISLATURE OF MARYLAND.

NEWSPAPER ACCOUNT.

By Telegraph to the Associated Press.

BALTIMORE, *Sept.* 13.—The Provost Marshal, George P. Dodge, this morning, before day, arrested the Mayor of Baltimore, Mr. Brown, and Messrs. Chas. S. Pitts, Lawrence Sangston, S. Teackle Wallis, T. Parkin Scott, and Ross Winans, members of the Maryland Legislature of Baltimore city, and F. K. Howard, the editor of the *Exchange* newspaper. They were taken to Fort McHenry.

BALTIMORE, *Sept.* 13.—The following additional arrests have been made: Messrs. Dennison, Quinlan, and Dr. Lynch, members of the Legislature from Baltimore county; and Messrs. Henry M. Warfield, Dr. J. Hanson Thomas, John C. Brune, city members; also, Thomas W. Hall, editor of the *South* newspaper.

The day of the meeting of the Legislature is Tuesday next, when, it is suspected, further legislation hostile to the Government was to be attempted. All the arrests made were under orders direct from the War Department.

BALTIMORE, *Sept.* 13.—I just hear of the arrest of Henry May, member of Congress; also, Henry M. Morfit and W. G. Harrison, members of the Legislature from this city. These, with the names previously sent, complete the ten city delegates. Upon the arrest of Gordon, (member of the Maryland Legislature,) some days ago, papers were found in his baggage reading like amendments to be offered to a proposed secession ordinance to be brought up at the coming meeting of the Legislature.

BALTIMORE, *Sept.* 18.—The police are arresting secession members of the Legislature as fast as they reach this city, on their way to Frederick. To-morrow is the day set apart for the meeting of the Legislature, but there can be no quorum present, as nearly three fourths of both Houses are secessionists, all of whom it is presumed, will be arrested. This evening Messrs. Dennis and Heckart, of the Senate, and Messrs. Landing and Raisin, of the House of Delegates, were arrested. There are now fifteen members of the House and three of the Senate under arrest. Many of the members cannot be found, and have, it is said, fled from the State.

[From the Baltimore American.]

We are not advised of the specific charges against those members of the Legislature and others prominent as public functionaries who have been arrested in the State by order of the General Government; but, from what has already occurred, the inference seems safe enough that the reasons were such as were fully justified in the needful preservation of the peace of the State. One thing is certain—that the majority of the distinguished body thus interfered with was thoroughly disloyal; and judging from what they already have done, and their persistant waiting for something to happen to give them a chance to do something more in the direction of "State sovereignty," we believe they thought the time might come when they might follow other illustrious examples, and treat the State to that outrage upon the people, the Constitution, and the Union, a "secession ordinance." They are effectually estopped from such a purpose now, and will have a chance to reflect at their leisure on their utter disregard of the wishes of the people in their doings.

The astounding disregard of popular sentiment, definitely shown, has been the chief feature in the secession movement, and Maryland has only escaped the worst consequences of it by the firm action of the Governor in the first instance, and now by the interposition of the strong hand of the General Government.

COPELAND'S REPORT.

FREDERICK, Md., *September* 18, 1861.

To Major General BANKS, *Darnestown:*

SIR: I have just telegraphed to General Dix that we have seized seven members of the house of a very bitter character, and four officers, clerks, &c., who are intensely bitter, and are said to have been very forward and to have kept some of the weaker men up to the work. Several arrests were made of violent or resisting persons, whom I shall let go after the others are gone. I shall send four men at least to General Dix, at Baltimore, who are very bad men. I have advised Colonel Ruger to send to Sharpsburg Landing to seize 500 sacks of salt, which are waiting for the Southerners to come and take them. They have tried twice to do it. We have also heard of some arms which the colonel will look up. There is a very bitter man here, a Mr. Sinn, who is currently reported by General Shriver and others to be the medium of communication with the Southern Confederacy. The names of the members are: B. S. Salmon, R. C. McCubbin, J. H. Gordon, C. J. Durant, Thomas Cleggett, Andrew Kessler, and Bernard Mills. We shall get T. Lawrence Jones. The officers of the Legislature: J. N. Brewer, Chief Clerk Senate; Thomas Moore, reading do; Samuel Penrose, jr., Assistant; N. Kilgore, reading do.; Milton Kidd, Chief of the House. Mr. Jones is taken; Edward Houser, citizen; Riley, (very bad,) Printer to the House; John Hogan, (very bad,) citizen; Joseph Elkins, do.; Mr. Mason, Folder to the House. We shall leave here for headquarters this afternoon. The arrested were nearly all seized by the policemen.

I am, yours respectfully,

R. MORRIS COPELAND,
Aid-de-Camp.

Mr. McCubbin is a person whom I should recommend you to set at large if he takes the oath, which I have no doubt he will. He is brother-in-law to General Hammond, and a man much respected; also a man of rather timid nature, and greatly troubled by his arrest. General Shriver has been very active for us, and is very earnest that we should let him go on these terms. If you can do it, it will be well to telegraph to Annapolis to have the oath tendered, and release him. I should do it under my instructions, only that Colonel Ruger thinks he has no authority to allow any man on the list any liberty. R. M. C.

OTHER ARRESTS.

PHILADELPHIA, *August* 19.

Pierce Butler was arrested this afternoon by the United States Marshal by order of Secretary Cameron. He was taken to New York this evening, en route to Fort Hamilton.

LOUISVILLE, *September* 19.

Early this morning the United States Marshal seized the office of the *Louisville Courier*, arrested ex-Governor Morehead, Reuben T. Murrett, one of the proprietors of the *Courier*, and Martin W. Barr, telegraphic news reporter for the New Orleans press, on charges of treason or complicity with treason. The prisoners were all carried to Jeffersonville, and will be transferred to the custody of the Marshal of Indiana district.

CINCINNATI, *September* 26.

Yesterday afternoon Lieutenant Colonel Letcher, with a detachment of Colonel Woodward's regiment, captured James B. Clay, with sixteen of his men, while on the way to join Zollicoffer. They were taken to Camp Dick Robinson. John C. Breckinridge was with their party in this city, but escaped.

Ex-Mayor James G. Berret, of Washington, was arrested in August, but released September 12, 1861, on taking the oath of allegiance, and resigning the office of mayor.

Ellis B. Schnable, of Pennsylvania, was also arrested late in August.

James W. Wall, of Burlington, N. J., was arrested, and others.

ORDERS ON WHICH CERTAIN ARRESTS WERE MADE.

Secretary of War to General Banks.

WAR DEPARTMENT, *Sept.* 11, 1861.

GENERAL: The passage of any act of secession by the Legislature of Maryland must be prevented. If necessary all, or any part, of the members must be arrested. Exercise your own judgment as to the time and manner, but do the work effectually.

Very respectfully, your obedient servant,

SIMON CAMERON,
Secretary of War.

—

Gen. McClellan to Gen. Banks.

[CONFIDENTIAL.]

HEADQUARTERS ARMY OF THE POTOMAC,
WASHINGTON, *Sept.* 12, 1861.

GENERAL: After full consultation with the President, Secretaries of State, War, &c., it has been decided to effect the operation proposed for the 17th. Arrangements have been made to have a Government steamer at Annapolis to receive the prisoners and carry them to their destination.

Some four or five of the chief men in the affair are to be arrested to-day. When they meet on the 17th, you will please have everything prepared to arrest the whole party, and be sure that none escape.

It is understood that you arranged with Gen. Dix and Gov. Seward the *modus operandi.* It has been intimated to me that the meeting might take place on the 14th; please be prepared. I would be glad to have you advise me frequently of your arrangements in regard to this very important matter.

If it is successfully carried out it will go far toward breaking the backbone of the rebellion. It would probably be well to have a special train quietly prepared to take prisoners to Annapolis.

I leave this exceedingly important affair to your tact and discretion—and have but one thing to impress upon you—the absolute necessity of secrecy and success. With the highest regard, I am, my dear General, your sincere friend,

GEO. B. McCLELLAN,
Maj. Gen. U. S. A.

—

Copy of Gen. Banks's instructions concerning the Legislature.

[IMPORTANT AND CONFIDENTIAL.]

HEADQUARTERS, CAMP NEAR DARNESTOWN,
September 16, 1863.

Lieut. Col. RUGER, *Commanding Third Wisconsin regiment, on special service at Frederick:*

SIR: The Legislature of Maryland is appointed to meet in special session to-morrow, Tuesday, Sept. 16. It is not impossible that the members, or a portion of them may be deterred from meeting there on account of certain arrests recently made in Baltimore. It is also quite possible that on the first day of meeting the attendance may be small. Of the facts, as to this matter, I shall see that you are well informed, as they transpire. It becomes necessary that any meeting of this Legislature, at any place or time, shall be prevented.

You will hold yourself and your command in readiness to arrest the members of both Houses; a list of such as you are to detain will be enclosed to you, herewith, among whom are to be specially included the presiding officers of the two houses, secretaries, clerks, and all subordinate officials. Let the arrests be certain, and allow no chance of failure. The arrests should be made while they are in session, I think.

You will, upon the receipt of this, quietly examine the premises. I am informed that escape will be impossible, if the entrance to the building be held by you, of that you will judge upon examination. If no session is to be held, you will arrest such members as can be found in Frederick. The process of arrest should be to enter both Houses at the same time, announcing that they were arrested by orders of the Government, command them to remain as they are, subject to your orders.

Any resistance will be forcibly suppressed, whatever the consequences. Upon these arrests being effected, the members that are to be detained will be placed on board a special train for Annapolis where a steamer will await them.

Everything in the execution of these orders is confided to your secrecy, discretion, and promptness.

The Case of Algernon S. Sullivan.

DEPARTMENT OF STATE,
WASHINGTON, *September* 10, 1861.

To DANIEL LORD, Esq., New York:

SIR: I have received your letter of yesterday relating to Algernon S. Sullivan, a political prisoner now in custody at Fort Lafayette. This Department is possessed of treasonable correspondence of that person which no right or privilege of a lawyer or counsel can justify or excuse. The public safety will not admit of his being discharged.

In view of the many representations made to me in this case, I pray your excuse for giving this letter to the public.

With great respect, sir, your obedient servant,
WILLIAM H. SEWARD.

The Case of Robert Elliot.

DEPARTMENT OF STATE,
WASHINGTON, *October* 4, 1861.

To his Excellency ISRAEL WASHBURN, Augusta, Me.:

GOVERNOR: Application has been made to the President for the release of Robert Elliot, a political prisoner held in custody at Fort Lafayette.

The evidence taken in his case shows that he had not only conceived the purpose of treasonable co-operation in the State of Maine with the insurrectionary citizens arrayed in arms, in other States, for the overthrow of the Government and the Union, but that he had even gone to the extreme length of getting up an unlawful armed force to operate in Maine against the lawful action of the State and of the Federal Government. His associates in that treasonable enterprise, since his arrest, have taken an oath of allegiance to the United States. This proceeding is very proper in itself. But the representations they make, that they and he were loyal to the Union at the time when they were combining in arms against it, cannot be accepted, at least in his behalf. It appears that he is too intelligent to misunderstand the legitimate tendency of his criminal acts. He cannot be released. On the contrary, your vigilance in ferreting out the conspiracy and in arresting it, by denouncing it to the Government and the country, is deemed worthy of especial commendation.

If any of the other offenders are still persisting in their treasonable course, you will, I am sure, not fail to give information to this Department.

I have the honor to be, very respectfully, your obedient servant, WILLIAM H. SEWARD.

THE PRESIDENT'S ORDERS.

1862, February 14—The PRESIDENT issued an order reciting the circumstances of the country, the defection of officials in every department, the treason which pervaded and paralyzed every branch of the service, in justification of the resort to extraordinary measures, and adds:

Meantime a favorable change of public opinion has occurred. The line between loyalty and disloyalty is plainly defined; the whole structure of the Government is firm and stable; apprehensions of public danger and facilities for treasonable practices have diminished with the passions which prompted heedless persons to adopt them. The insurrection is believed to have culminated and to be declining.

The President, in view of these facts, and anxious to favor a return to the normal course of the Administration, as far as regard for the public welfare will allow, directs that all political prisoners or State prisoners now held in military custody, be released on their subscribing to a parole engaging them to render no aid or comfort to the enemies in hostility to the United States.

The Secretary of War will, however, at his discretion, except from the effect of this order any persons detained as spies in the service of the insurgents, or others whose release at the present moment may be deemed incompatible with the public safety.

To all persons who shall be so released, and who shall keep their parole, the President grants an amnesty for any past offences of treason or disloyalty which they may have committed.

Extraordinary arrests will hereafter be made under the direction of the military authorities alone.

By order of the President:

EDWIN M. STANTON,
Secretary of War.

1862, February 27—The PRESIDENT issued this order:

Executive Order No. 2—In Relation to State Prisoners.

WAR DEPARTMENT, WASHINGTON CITY, *Feb.* 27, 1862.

It is ordered:

First. That a special commission of two persons, one of military rank and the other in civil life, be appointed to examine the cases of the State prisoners remaining in the military custody of the United States, and to determine whether in view of the public safety and the existing rebellion, they should be discharged, or remain in military custody, or be remitted to the civil tribunals for trial.

Second. That Major General John A. Dix, commanding in Baltimore, and the Hon. Edwards Pierrepont, of New York, be and they are hereby appointed Commissioners for the purposes above mentioned, and they are authorized to examine, hear, and determine the cases aforesaid *ex parte* and in a summary manner, at such times and places as in their discretion they may appoint, and make full report to the War Department.

By order of the President:

EDWIN M. STANTON,
Secretary of War.

ORDER OF THE SECRETARY OF WAR.

WAR DEPARTMENT,
WASHINGTON, *November* 22, 1862.

Ordered—1. That all persons now in military custody, who have been arrested for discouraging volunteer enlistments, opposing the draft, or for otherwise giving aid and comfort to the enemy, in States where the draft has been made, or the quota of volunteers and militia has been furnished, shall be discharged from further military restraint.

2. The persons who, by the authority of the military commander or governor in rebel States, have been arrested and sent from such State for disloyalty or hostility to the Government of the United States, and are now in military custody, may also be discharged upon giving their parole to do no act of hostility against the Government of the United States, nor render aid to its enemies. But all such persons shall remain subject to military surveillance and liable to arrest on breach of their parole. And if any such persons shall prefer to leave the loyal States on condition of their not returning again during the war, or until special leave for that purpose be obtained from the President, then such person shall, at his option, be released and depart from the United States, or be conveyed beyond the military lines of the United States forces.

3. This order shall not operate to discharge any person who has been in arms against the Government, or by force and arms has resisted or attempted to resist the draft, nor relieve any person from liability to trial and punishment by civil tribunals, or by court-martial or military commission, who may be amenable to such tribunals for offences committed.

By order of the Secretary of War:

E. D. TOWNSEND,
Assistant Adjutant General.

ARREST OF JOHN MERRYMAN AND PROCEEDINGS THEREON.

1861, May 25—John Merryman, of Baltimore county, Md., was arrested, charged with holding a commission as lieutenant in a company avowing its purpose of armed hostility against the Government; with being in communication with the rebels, and with various acts of treason. He was lodged in Fort McHenry, in command of Gen. Geo. Cadwalader. Merryman at once forwarded a petition to Chief Justice Roger B. Taney, reciting his arrest, and praying for a writ of *habeas corpus* and a hearing. The writ was issued for the 27th, to which General Cadwalader declined to respond, alleging, among other things, that he was duly authorized by the President of the United States to suspend the writ of *habeas corpus* for the public safety. May 27, the Chief Justice issued a writ of attachment, directing United States Marshal Bonifant to produce the body of General Cadwalader on Tuesday, May 28th, "to answer for his contempt in refusing to produce the body of John Merryman." May 28th, the Marshal replied that he proceeded to the fort to serve the writ, that he was not permitted to enter the gate, and that he was informed "there was no answer to his writ."

CHIEF JUSTICE TANEY'S REMARKS.

I ordered the attachment yesterday, because upon the face of the return the detention of the prisoner was unlawful upon two grounds.

1. The President, under the Constitution and laws of the United States, cannot suspend the privilege of the writ of *habeas corpus*, nor authorize any military officer to do so.

2. A military officer has no right to arrest and detain a person, not subject to the rules and articles of war, for an offence against the laws of the United States, except in and of the judicial authority and subject to its control; and if the party is arrested by the military, it is the duty of the officer to deliver him over immediately to the civil authority, to be dealt with according to law.

I forbore yesterday to state orally the provisions of the Constitution of the United States which make these principles the fundamental law of the Union, because an oral statement might be misunderstood in some portions of it, and I shall therefore put my opinion in writing and file it in the office of the Clerk of the Circuit Court, in the course of this week.

After reading the above, the Chief Justice orally remarked:

In relation to the present return, I propose to say that the marshal has legally the power to summon out the *posse comitatus* to seize and bring into court the party named in the attachment; but it is apparent he will be resisted in the discharge of that duty by a force notoriously superior to the *posse comitatus*, and such being the case, the Court has no power under the law to order the necessary force to compel the appearance of the party. If, however, he was before the Court, it would then impose the only punishment it is empowered to inflict—that by fine and imprisonment.

Under these circumstances the Court can barely say, to-day, I shall reduce to writing the reasons under which I have acted and which have led me to the conclusions expressed in my opinion, and shall report them with these proceedings to the President of the United States, and call upon him to perform his constitutional duty to enforce the laws; in other words, to enforce the process of this Court. This is all this Court has now the power to do.

Subjoined is the opinion of the Chief Justice:*

Ex parte JOHN MERRYMAN.

Before the Chief Justice of the Supreme Court of the United States, at Chambers.

The application in this case for a writ of *habeas corpus* is made to me under the 14th section of the judiciary act of 1789, which renders effectual for the citizen the constitutional privilege of the writ of *habeas corpus* That act gives to the courts of the United States, as well as to each Justice of the Supreme Court, and to every District Judge, power to grant writs of *habeas corpus*, for the purpose of an inquiry into the cause of commitment. The petition was presented to me at Washington, under the impression that I would order the prisoner to be brought before me there, but as he was confined in Fort McHenry, at the city of Baltimore, which is in my circuit, I resolved to hear it in the latter city, as obedience to the writ, under such circumstances, would not withdraw Gen. Cadwalader, who had him in charge, from the limits of his military command.

The petition presents the following case: The petitioner resides in Maryland, in Baltimore county. While peaceably in his own house, with his family, it was at two o'clock, on the morning of the 25th of May, 1861, entered by an armed force, professing to act under military orders. He was then compelled to rise from his bed, taken into custody, and conveyed to Fort McHenry, where he is imprisoned by the commanding officer, without warrant from any lawful authority.

The commander of the fort, Gen. George Cadwalader, by whom he is detained in confinement, in his return to the writ, does not deny any of the facts alleged in the petition. He states that the prisoner was arrested by order of Gen. Keim, of Pennsylvania, and conducted as a prisoner to Fort McHenry by his order, and placed in his (Gen. Cadwalader's) custody, to be there detained by him as a prisoner.

A copy of the warrant, or order, under which the prisoner was arrested, was demanded by his counsel, and refused. And it is not alleged in the return that any specific act, constituting an offence against the laws of the United States, has been charged against him upon oath; but he appears to have been arrested upon general charges of treason and rebellion, without proof, and without giving the names of the witnesses, or specifying the acts, which, in the judgment of the military officer, constituted these crimes. And having the prisoner thus in custody upon these vague and unsupported accusations, he refuses to obey the writ of *habeas corpus*, upon the ground that he is duly authorized by the President to suspend it.

The case, then, is simply this: A military officer residing in Pennsylvania issues an order to arrest a citizen of Maryland, upon vague and indefinite charges, without any proof, so far as appears. Under this order his house is entered in the night; he is seized as a prisoner, and conveyed to Fort McHenry, and there kept in close confinement. And when a *habeas corpus* is served on the commanding officer, requiring him to produce the prisoner before a Justice of the Supreme Court, in order that he may examine into the legality of the imprisonment, the answer of the officer is that he is authorized by the President to suspend the writ of *habeas corpus* at his discretion, and, in the exercise of that discretion, suspends it in this case, and on that ground refuses obedience to the writ.

As the case comes before me, therefore, I understand that the President not only claims the right to suspend the writ of *habeas corpus* himself, at his discretion, but to delegate that discretionary power to a military officer, and to leave it to him to determine whether he will or will not obey judicial process that may be served upon him.

No official notice has been given to the courts of justice, or to the public, by proclamation or otherwise, that the President claimed this power, and had exercised it in the manner stated in the return. And I certainly listened to it with some surprise, for I had supposed it to be one of those points of constitutional law upon which there was no difference of opinion, and that it was admitted on all hands that the privilege of the writ could not be suspended except by act of Congress.

When the conspiracy of which Aaron Burr was the head became so formidable, and was so extensively ramified as to justify, in Mr. Jefferson's opinion, the suspension of the writ, he claimed, on his part, no power to suspend it, but communicated his opinion to Congress, with all the proofs in his possession, in order that Congress might exercise its discretion upon the subject, and determine whether the public safety required it. And in the debate which took place upon the subject no one suggested that Mr. Jefferson might exercise the power himself, if, in his opinion, the public safety demanded it.

Having, therefore, regarded the question as too plain and too well settled to be open to dispute, if the commanding officer had stated that upon his own responsibility, and in the exercise of his own discretion, he refused obedience to the writ, I should have contented myself with referring to the clause in the Constitution, and to the construction it received from every jurist and statesman of that day, when the case of Burr was before them. But being thus officially notified that the privilege of the writ has been suspended under the orders and by the authority of the President, and believing as I do that the President has exercised a power which he does not possess under the Constitution, a proper respect for the high office he fills requires me to state plainly and fully the grounds of my opinion, in order to show that I have not ventured to question the legality of his act without a careful and deliberate examination of the whole subject.

The clause in the Constitution which authorizes the suspension of the privilege of the writ of *habeas corpus* is in the ninth section of the first article.

This article is devoted to the Legislative Department of the United States, and has not the slightest reference to the Executive Department. It begins by providing "that all legislative powers therein granted shall be vested in a Congress of the United States, which shall consist of a Senate and House of Representatives." And after prescribing the manner in which these two branches of the legislative department shall be chosen, it proceeds to enumerate specifically the legislative powers which it thereby grants, and legislative powers which it expressly prohibits, and, at the conclusion of this specification, a clause is inserted giving Congress "the power to make all laws which may be necessary and proper for carrying into execution the foregoing powers, and all other powers vested by this Constitution in the Government of the United States or in any department or office thereof."

The power of legislation granted by this latter clause is by its word carefully confined to the specific objects before enumerated. But as this limitation was unavoidably somewhat indefinite, it was deemed necessary to guard more effectually certain great cardinal principles essential to the liberty of the citizen and to the rights and equality of the States by denying to Congress, in express terms, any power of legislation over them. It was apprehended, it seems, that such legislation might be attempted under the pretext that it was necessary and proper to carry into execution the powers granted; and it was determined that there should be no room to doubt, where rights of such vital importance were concerned, and accordingly this clause is immediately followed by an enumeration of certain subjects to which the powers of legislation shall not

* For a reply by Hon. Reverdy Johnson, see Moore's Rebellion Record, vol. 2, p. 185.

extend; and the great importance which the framers of the Constitution attached to the privilege of the writ of *habeas corpus*, to protect the liberty of the citizen, is proved by the fact that its suspension, except in cases of invasion and rebellion, is first in the list of prohibited powers; and even in these cases the power is denied and its exercise prohibited unless the public safety shall require it. It is true that in the cases mentioned Congress is of necessity the judge of whether the public safety does or does not require it; and its judgment is conclusive. But the introduction of these words is a standing admonition to the legislative body of the danger of suspending it and of the extreme caution they should exercise before they give the Government of the United States such power over the liberty of a citizen.

It is the second article of the Constitution that provides for the organization of the Executive Department, and enumerates the powers conferred on it, and prescribes its duties. And if the high power over the liberty of the citizens now claimed was intended to be conferred on the President, it would undoubtedly be found in plain words in this article. But there is not a word in it that can furnish the slightest ground to justify the exercise of the power.

The article begins by declaring that the Executive power shall be vested in a President of the United States of America, to hold his office during the term of four years, and then proceeds to describe the mode of election, and to specify in precise and plain words the powers delegated to him and the duties imposed upon him. And the short term for which he is elected, and the narrow limits to which his power is confined, show the jealousy and apprehensions of future danger which the framers of the Constitution felt in relation to that department of the Government, and how carefully they withheld from it many of the powers belonging to the executive branch of the English Government which were considered as dangerous to the liberty of the subject, and conferred (and that in clear and specific terms) those powers only which were deemed essential to secure the successful operation of the Government.

He is elected, as I have already said, for the brief term of four years, and is made personally responsible, by impeachment, for malfeasance in office. He is, from necessity, and the nature of his duties, the Commander-in-Chief of the army and navy, and of the militia, when called into actual service. But no appropriation for the support of the army can be made by Congress for a longer term than two years, so that it is in the power of the succeeding House of Representatives to withhold the appropriation for its support, and thus disband it, if, in their judgment, the President used or designed to use it for improper purposes. And although the militia, when in actual service, are under his command, yet the appointment of the officers is reserved to the States, as a security against the use of the military power for purposes dangerous to the liberties of the people or the rights of the States.

So, too, his powers in relation to the civil duties and authority necessarily conferred on him are carefully restricted, as well as those belonging to his military character. He cannot appoint the ordinary officers of Government, nor make a treaty with a foreign nation or Indian tribe without the advice and consent of the Senate, and cannot appoint even inferior officers unless he is authorized by an act of Congress to do so. He is not empowered to arrest any one charged with an offence against the United States, and whom he may, from the evidence before him, believe to be guilty; nor can he authorize any officer, civil or military, to exercise this power, for the fifth article of the amendments to the Constitution expressly provides that no person "shall be deprived of life, liberty, or property without due process of law;" that is, judicial process. And even if the privilege of the writ of *habeas corpus* was suspended by act of Congress, and a party not subject to the rules and articles of war was afterwards arrested and imprisoned by regular judicial process, he could not be detained in prison or brought to trial before a military tribunal, for the article in the Amendments to the Constitution immediately following the one above referred to—that is, the sixth article—provides that, "in all criminal prosecutions, the accused shall enjoy the right to a speedy and public trial by an impartial jury of the State and district wherein the crime shall have been committed, which district shall have been previously ascertained by law, and to be informed of the nature and cause of the accusation; to be confronted with the witnesses against him; to have compulsory process for obtaining witnesses in his favor, and to have the assistance of counsel for his defence."

And the only power, therefore, which the President possesses, where the "life, liberty, or property" of a private citizen is concerned, is the power and duty prescribed in the third section of the second article, which requires "that he shall take care that the laws be faithfully executed." He is not authorized to execute them himself, or through agents or officers, civil or military, appointed by himself, but he is to take care that they be faithfully carried into execution as they are expounded and adjudged by the coördinate branch of the Government to which that duty is assigned by the Constitution. It is thus made his duty to come in aid of the judicial authority, if it shall be resisted by a force too strong to be overcome without the assistance of the Executive arm. But in exercising this power, he acts in subordination to judicial authority, assisting it to execute its process and enforce its judgments.

With such provisions in the Constitution, expressed in language too clear to be misunderstood by any one, I can see no ground whatever for supposing that the President, in any emergency or in any state of things, can authorize the suspension of the privilege of the writ of *habeas corpus*, or arrest a citizen, except in aid of the judicial power. He certainly does not faithfully execute the laws if he takes upon himself legislative power by suspending the writ of *habeas corpus*—and the judicial power, also, by arresting and imprisoning a person without due process of law. Nor can any argument be drawn from the nature of sovereignty, or the necessities of government for self-defense, in times of tumult and danger. The Government of the United States is one of delegated and limited powers. It derives its existence and authority altogether from the Constitution, and neither of its branches—executive, legislative, or judicial—can exercise any of the powers of government beyond those specified and granted. For the tenth article of the amendments to the Constitution, in express terms, provides that "the powers not delegated to the United States by the Constitution, nor prohibited by it to the States, are reserved to the States, respectively, or to the people."

Indeed, the security against imprisonment by Executive authority, provided for in the fifth article of the Amendments of the Constitution, which I have before quoted, is nothing more than a copy of a like provision in the English constitution, which had been firmly established before the Declaration of Independence.

Blackstone, in his Commentaries, (1st vol., 137,) states it in the following words:

"To make imprisonment lawful, it must be either by process from the courts of judicature or by warrant from some legal officer having authority to commit to prison."

And the people of the United Colonies, who had themselves lived under its protection while they were British subjects, were well aware of the necessity of this safeguard for their personal liberty. And no one can believe that in framing the Government intended to guard still more efficiently the rights and the liberties of the citizens against executive encroachment and oppression, they would have conferred on the President a power which the history of England had proved to be dangerous and oppressive in the hands of the Crown, and which the people of England had compelled it to surrender after a long and obstinate struggle on the part of the English Executive to usurp and retain it.

The right of the subject to the benefit of the writ of *habeas corpus*, it must be recollected, was one of the great points in controversy during the long struggle in England between arbitrary government and free institutions, and must therefore have strongly attracted the attention of statesmen engaged in framing a new and, as they supposed, a freer government than the one which they had thrown off by the Revolution. For, from the earliest history of the common law, if a person was imprisoned—no matter by what authority—he had a right to the writ of *habeas corpus* to bring his case before the King's Bench, and, if no specific offence was charged against him in the warrant of commitment, he was entitled to be forthwith discharged; and if an offence was charged which was bailable in its character the court was bound to set him at liberty on bail. And the most exciting contests between the Crown and the people of England from the time of Magna Charta were in relation to the privilege of this writ, and they continued until the passage of the statute of 31st Charles 2d, commonly known as the great *habeas corpus* act. This statute put an end to the struggle, and finally and firmly secured the liberty of the subject from the usurpation and oppression of the executive branch of the Government. It nevertheless conferred no new right upon the subject, but only secured a right already existing; for, although the right could not justly be denied, there was often no effectual remedy against its violation. Until the statute of the 13th of William III the judges held their offices at the pleasure of the King, and the influence which he exercised over timid, time-serving, and partisan judges often induced them, upon some pretext or other, to refuse to discharge the party although he was entitled to it by law, or delayed their decisions from time to time, so as to prolong the imprisonment of persons who were obnoxious to the King for their political opinions, or had incurred his resentment in any other way.

The great and inestimable value of the *habeas corpus* act of the 31st Charles II is that it contains provisions which compel courts and judges, and all parties concerned, to perform their duties promptly, in the manner specified in the statute.

A passage in Blackstone's Commentaries, showing the ancient state of the law upon this subject, and the abuses which were practiced through the power and influence of the Crown, and a short extract from Hallam's Constitutional History, stating the circumstances which gave rise to the passage of this statute, explain briefly, but fully, all that is material to this subject.

Blackstone, in his Commentaries on the laws of England, (3d vol., 133, 134,) says:

"To assert an absolute exemption from imprisonment in all cases is inconsistent with every idea of law and political society, and in the end would destroy all civil liberty, by rendering its protection impossible.

"But the glory of the English law consists in clearly defining the times, the causes, and the extent, when, wherefore, and to what degree the imprisonment of the subject may be lawful. This it is which induces the absolute necessity of expressing upon every commitment the reason for which it is made, that the court upon a *habeas corpus* may examine into its validity, and, according to the circumstances of the case, may discharge, admit to bail, or remand the prisoner.

"And yet early in the reign of Charles I the Court of King's Bench, relying on some arbitrary precedents, (and those perhaps misunderstood,) determined that they would not, upon a *habeas corpus* either bail or deliver a prisoner, though committed without any cause assigned, in case he was committed by the special command of the King or by the Lords of the Privy Council. This drew on a Parliamentary inquiry, and produced the Petition of Rights—3 Chas. I—which recites this illegal judgment, and enacts that no freeman hereafter shall be so imprisoned or detained. But when in the following year Mr. Selden and others were committed by the Lords of the Council in pursuance of his Majesty's special command, under a general charge of 'notable contempts, and stirring up sedition against the King and the Government,' the judges delayed for two terms (including also the long vacation) to deliver an opinion how far such a charge was bailable. And when at length they agreed that it was, they however annexed a condition of finding sureties for their good behavior, which still protracted their imprisonment; the Chief Justice, Sir Nicholas Hyde, at the same time declaring that 'if they were again remanded for that cause perhaps the court would not afterward grant a *habeas corpus* being already acquainted with the cause of the imprisonment.' But this was heard with indignation and astonishment by every lawyer present, according to Mr. Selden's own account of the matter, whose resentment was not cooled at the distance of four and twenty years."

It is worthy of remark that the offences charged against the prisoner in this case, and relied on as a justification for his arrest and imprisonment, in their nature and character, and in the loose and vague manner in which they are stated, bear a striking resemblance to those assigned in the warrant for the arrest of Mr. Selden. And yet, even at that day, the warrant was regarded as such a flagrant violation of the rights of the subject that the delay of the time-serving judges to set him at liberty upon the *habeas corpus* issued in his behalf excited universal indignation at the bar. The extract from Hallam's Constitutional History is equally impressive end equally in point. It is in vol. 4, p. 14:

"It is a very common mistake, and not only among foreigners, but many from whom some knowledge of our constitutional laws might be expected, to suppose that this statute of Charles II enlarged in a great degree our liberties, and forms a sort of epoch in their history. But though a very beneficial enactment, and eminently remedial in many cases of illegal imprisonment, it introduced no new principle, nor conferred any right upon the subject. From the earliest records of the English law, no freeman could be detained in prison, except upon a criminal charge or conviction, or for a civil debt. In the former case it was always in his power to demand of the Court of King's Bench a writ of *habeas corpus ad subjiciendum* directed to the person detaining him in custody, by which he was enjoined to bring up the body of the prisoner with the warrant of commitment, that the court might judge of its sufficiency, and remand the party, admit him to bail, or discharge him, according to the nature of the charge. This writ issued of right, and could not be refused by the court. It was not to bestow an immunity from arbitrary imprisonment, which is abundantly provided for in *Magna Charta*, (if indeed it was not more ancient,) that the statute of Charles II was enacted, but to cut off the abuses by which the Government's lust of power and servile subtlety of Crown lawyers had impaired so fundamental a privilege."

While the value set upon this writ in England has been so great that the removal of the abuses which embarrassed its enjoyment have been looked upon as almost a new grant of liberty to the subject, it is not to be wondered at that the continuance of the writ thus made effective should have been the object of the most jealous care. Accordingly, no power in England short of that of Parliament, can suspend or authorize the suspension of the writ of *habeas corpus*. I quote again from Blackstone (1 Comm., 136:) "But the happiness of our Constitution is, that it is not left to the executive power to determine when the danger of the State is so great as to render this measure expedient. It is the Parliament only or legislative power that, whenever it sees proper, can authorize the Crown, by suspending the *habeas corpus* for a short and limited time, to imprison suspected persons without giving any reason for so doing." And if the President of the United States may suspend the writ, then the Constitution of the United States has conferred upon him more regal and absolute power over the liberty of the citizen than the people of England have thought it safe to entrust to the Crown—a power which the Queen of England cannot exercise at this day, and which could not have been lawfully exercised by the sovereign even in the reign of Charles the First.

But I am not left to form my judgment upon this great question from analogies between the English Government and our own, or the commentaries of English jurists, or the decisions of English courts, although upon this subject they are entitled to the highest respect, and are justly regarded and received as authoritative by our courts of justice. To guide me to a right conclusion, I have the Commentaries on the Constitution of the United States of the late Mr. Justice Story, not only one of the most eminent jurists of the age, but for a long time one of the brightest ornaments of the Supreme Court of the United States, and also the clear and authoritative decision of that Court itself, given more than half a century since, and conclusively establishing the principles I have above stated. Mr. Justice Story, speaking in his Commentaries of the *habeas corpus* clause in the Constitution, says:

"It is obvious that cases of a peculiar emergency may arise, which may justify, nay, even require, the temporary suspension of any right to the writ. But as it has frequently happened in foreign countries, and even in England, that the writ has, upon various pretexts and occasions, been suspended, whereby persons apprehended upon suspicion have suffered a long imprisonment, sometimes from design, and sometimes because they were forgotten, the right to suspend it is expressly confined to cases of rebellion or invasion, where the public safety may require it. A very just and wholesome restraint, which cuts down at a blow a fruitful means of oppression, capable of being abused in bad times to the worst of purposes. Hitherto no suspension of the writ has ever been authorized by Congress since the establishment of the Constitution. It would seem, as the power is given to Congress to suspend the writ of *habeas corpus* in cases of rebellion or invasion, that the right to judge whether the exigency had arisen must exclusively belong to that body."—3 Story's Com. on the Constitution, section 1,336.

And Chief Justice Marshall, in delivering the opinion of the Supreme Court in the case *ex parte* Bollman and Swartwout, uses this decisive language, in 4 Cranch, 95:

"It may be worthy of remark, that this act, (speaking of the one under which I am proceeding,) was passed by the First Congress of the United States, sitting under a Constitution which had declared 'that the privilege of the writ of *habeas corpus* should not be suspended unless when, in cases of rebellion or invasion, the public safety may require it.' Acting under the immediate influence of this injunction, they must have felt with peculiar force the obligation of providing efficient means by which this great constitutional privilege should receive life and activity; for if the means be not in existence, the privilege itself would be lost, although no law for its suspension should be enacted. Under the impression of this obligation they give to all the courts the power of awarding writs of *habeas corpus*."

And again, in page 101:

"If at any time the public safety should require the suspension of the powers vested by this act in the courts of the United States, it is for the Legislature to say so. That question depends on poltical considerations, on which the Legislature is to decide. Until the legislative will be expressed, this court can only see its duty, and must obey the laws."

I can add nothing to these clear and emphatic words of my great predecessor.

But the documents before me show that the military authority in this case has gone far beyond the mere suspension of the privilege of the writ of *habeas corpus*. It has, by force of arms, thrust aside the judicial authorities and officers to whom the Constitution has confided the power and duty of interpreting and administering the laws, and substituted a military government in its place, to be administered and executed by military officers. For at the time these proceedings were had against John Merryman, the District Judge of Maryland—the commissioner appointed under the act of Congress—the District Attorney and the Marshal, all resided in the city of Baltimore, a few miles only from the home of the prisoner. Up to that time there had never been the slightest resistance or obstruction to the process of any court or judicial officer of the United States in Maryland, except by the military authority. And if a military officer, or any other person, had reason to believe that the prisoner had committed any offense against the laws of the United States, it was his duty to give information of the fact and the evidence to support it to the District Attorney, and it would then have become the duty of that officer to bring the matter before the District Judge or Commissioner, and if there was sufficient legal evidence to justify his arrest, the Judge or Commissioner would have issued his warrant to the Marshal to arrest him, and, upon the hearing of the party, would have held him to bail, or committed him for trial, according to the character of the offense as it appeared in the testimony, or would have discharged him immediately if there was not sufficient evidence to support the accusation. There was no danger of any obstruction or resistance to the action of the civil authorities, and therefore no reason whatever for the interposition of the military. And yet, under these circumstances, a military officer, stationed in Pennsylvania, without giving any information to the District Attorney, and without any application to the judicial authorities, assumes to himself the judicial power in the district of Maryland; undertakes to decide what constitutes the crime of treason or rebellion; what evidence (if, indeed, he required any) is sufficient to support the accusation and justify the commitment; and commits the party, without having a hearing even before himself, to close custody in a strongly garrisoned fort, to be there held, it would seem, during the pleasure of those who committed him.

The Constitution provides, as I have before said, that "no person shall be deprived of life, liberty, or property, without due process of law." It declares that "the right of the people to be secure in their persons, houses, papers, and effects against unreasonable searches and seizures shall not be violated, and no warrant shall issue but upon probable cause, supported by oath or affirmation, and particularly describing the place to be searched and the persons or things to be seized." It provides that the party accused shall be entitled to a speedy trial in a court of justice.

And these great and fundamental laws, which Congress itself could not suspend, have been disregarded and suspended, like the writ of *habeas corpus*, by a military order, supported by force of arms. Such is the case now before me; and I can only say that if the authority which the Constitution has confided to the judiciary department and judicial officers may thus upon any pretext or under any circumstances be usurped by the military power at its discretion, the people of the United States are no longer living under a Government of laws, but every citizen holds life, liberty, and property at the will and pleasure of the army officer in whose military district he may happen to be found.

In such a case my duty was too plain to be mistaken. I have exercised all the power which the Constitution and laws confer on me, but that power has been resisted by a force too strong for me to overcome. It is possible that the officer who had incurred this grave responsibility may have misunderstood his instructions, and exceeded the authority intended to be given him. I shall, therefore, order all the proceedings in this case, with my opinion, to be filed and recorded in the Circuit Court of the United States for the District of Maryland, and direct the clerk to transmit a copy, under seal, to the President of the United States. It will then remain for that high officer, in fulfilment of his constitutional obligation to "take care that the laws be faithfully executed," to determine what measures he will take to cause the civil process of the United States to be respected and enforced.

R. B. TANEY,
Chief Justice of the Supreme Court of the United States.

OPINION OF ATTORNEY GENERAL BATES ON THE PRESIDENT'S POWER TO ARREST SUSPECTED PERSONS, AND SUSPEND THE WRIT OF HABEAS CORPUS.

ATTORNEY GENERAL'S OFFICE, *July* 5, 1861.

SIR: You have required my opinion in writing upon the following questions:

"I. In the present time of a great and dangerous insurrection, has the President the discretionary power to cause to be arrested and held in custody persons known to have criminal intercourse with the insurgents, or persons against whom there is probable cause for suspicion of such criminal complicity?

"II. In such cases of arrest is the President justified in refusing to obey a writ of *habeas corpus* issued by a court or a judge, requiring him or his agent to produce the body of the prisoner, and show the cause of his caption and detention, to be adjudged and disposed of by such court or judge?"

To make my answer to these questions at once consistent and plain, I find it convenient to advert to the great principle of government as recognized and acted upon in most, if not all, the countries in Europe, and to mark the difference between that principle and the great principle which lies at the bottom of our National Government.

Most European writers upon government assume, expressly or by implication, that every national Government is, and must be, the full expression and representation of the nation which it governs, armed with all its powers, and able to assert all its rights. In England, the form of whose Government more nearly approximates our own, and where the rights, interests, and powers of the people are more respected and cared for than in most of the nations of the European continent, it has grown into an axiom that "the Parliament is omnipotent," that is, that it can do anything that is possible to be done by legislation or by judgment. For all the ends of the Government the Parliament is the nation. Moreover, in Europe generally, the sovereignty is vested visibly in some designated man or set of men, so that the subject people can see their sovereign as well as feel the workings of his power. But in this country it has been carefully provided otherwise. In the formation of our national Government our fathers were surrounded with peculiar difficulties, arising out of their novel, I may say unexampled, condition. In resolving to break the ties which had bound them to the British Empire, their complaints were leveled chiefly at the King, not the Parliament nor the people. They seem to have been actuated by a special dread of the unity of power, and hence, in framing the Constitution, they preferred to take the risk of leaving some good undone, for lack of power in the agent, rather than arm any governmental officer with such great powers for evil as are implied in the dictatorial charge to "see that no damage comes to the commonwealth."

Hence, keeping the sovereignty always out of sight, they adopted the plan of "checks and balances," forming separate departments of government, and giving to each department separate and limited powers. These departments are co-ordinate and coequal; that is, neither being sovereign, each is independent in its sphere, and not subordinate to the others, either of them or both of them together. We have three of these co-ordinate departments. Now, if we allow one of the three to determine the extent of its own powers, and also the extent of the powers of the other two, that one can control the whole Government, and has in fact achieved the sovereignty.

We ought not to say that our system is perfect, for its defects (perhaps inevitable in all human things) are obvious. Our fathers having divided the Government into co-ordinate departments, did not even try (and if they had tried would probably have failed) to create an arbiter among them to adjudge their conflicts and keep them within their respective bounds. They were left, by design, I suppose, each independent and free to act out its own granted powers, without any ordained legal superior possessing the power to revise and reverse the action. And this with the hope that the three departments, mutually coequal and independent, would keep each other within their proper spheres by their mutual antagonism; that is, by the system of checks and balances to which our fathers were driven at the beginning by their fear of the unity of power.

In this view of the subject, it is quite possible for the same identical question (not case) to come up legitimately before each one of the three departments, and be determined in three different ways, and each decision stand irrevocable, binding upon the parties to each case; and that for the simple reason that the departments are co-ordinate, and there is no ordained legal superior with power to revise and reverse their decisions.

To say that the departments of our Government are co-ordinate is to say that the judgment of one of them is not binding upon the other two as to the arguments and principles involved in the judgment. It binds only the parties to the case decided. But if, admitting that the departments of Government are co-ordinate, it be still contended that the principles adopted by one department, in deciding a case properly before it, are binding upon another department, that obligation must of necessity be reciprocal; that is, if the President be bound by the principles laid down by the Judiciary, so also is the Judiciary bound by the principles laid down by the President. And thus we shall have a theory of constitutional government flatly contradicting itself. Departments co-ordinate and coequal, and yet reciprocally subordinate to each other! That cannot be. The several departments, though far from sovereign, are free and independent, in the exercise of the limited powers granted to them respectively by the Constitution. Our Government, indeed, as a whole, is not vested with the sovereignty and does not possess all the powers of the nation. It has no powers but such as are granted by the Constitution; and many powers are expressly withheld. The nation certainly is coequal with all other nations, and has equal powers, but it has not chosen to delegate all its powers to this Government, in any or all its departments.

The Government, as a whole, is limited; and limited in all its departments. It is the especial function of the judiciary to hear and determine cases, not to "establish principles," nor "settle questions," so as to conclude any person but the parties and privies to the cases adjudged. Its powers are specially granted and defined by the Constitution, article 3, section 2:

"The judicial power shall extend to all cases in law and equity arising under this Constitution, the laws of the United States, and treaties made and which shall be made under their authority; to all cases affecting ambassadors, other ministers, and consuls; to all cases of admiralty and maritime jurisdiction; to controversies to which the United States shall be a party; to controversies between two or more States; between States and citizens of other States; between citizens of different States; between citizens of the same State claiming lands under grants of different States, and between a State, or the citizens thereof, and foreign States, citizens, or subjects."

And that is the sum of its powers, ample, and efficient for all the purposes of distributive justice among individual parties, but powerless to impose rules of action and of judgment upon the other departments. Indeed, it is not itself bound by its own decisions, for it can, and often does, overrule and disregard them, as in common honesty it ought to do, whenever it finds, by its after and better lights, that its former judgments were wrong.

Of all the departments of the Government the President is the most active, and the most constant in action. He is called "the Executive;" and so in fact he is, and much more also, for the Constitution has imposed upon him many important duties, and granted to him great powers which are in their nature not executive—such as the veto power, the power to send and receive ambassadors, the power to make treaties, and the power to appoint officers. This last is not more an executive power when used by the President than it is when it is exercised by either House of Congress, by the courts of justice, or by the people at large.

The President is a department of the Government, and, although the only department which consists of a single man, he is charged with a greater range and variety of powers and duties than any other department. He is a civil magistrate, not a military chief; and in this regard we see a striking proof of the generality of the sentiment prevailing in this country at the time of the formation of our Government, to the effect that the military ought to be held in strict subordination to the civil power; for the Constitution, while it grants to Congress the unrestricted power to declare war, to raise and support armies, and to provide and maintain a navy, at the same time guards carefully against the abuse of that power, by withholding from Congress and from the army itself the authority to appoint the chief commander of a force so potent for good or evil to the State. The Constitution provides that "the President shall be Commander-in-Chief of the Army and Navy of the United States, and of the militia of the several States when called into the actual service of the United States." And why is this? Surely not because the President is supposed to be, or commonly is, in fact, a military man, a man skilled in the art of war, and qualified to marshal a host in the field of battle. No, it is for quite a different reason; it is, that whatever skillful soldier may lead our armies to victory against a foreign foe, or may quell a domestic insurrection, however high he may raise his professional renown, and whatever martial glory he may win, still he is subject to the orders of the civil magistrate, and he and his army are always "subordinate to the civil power."

And hence it follows that whenever the President, (the civil magistrate,) in the discharge of his constitutional duty to "take care that the laws be faithfully executed," has occasion to use the army to aid him in the performance of that duty, he does not thereby lose his civil character and become a soldier, subject to military law, and liable to be tried by a court-martial, any more than does a civil court lose its legal and pacific nature, and become military and belligerent by calling out the power of the country to enforce its decrees. The civil magistrates, whether judicial or executive, must of necessity employ physical power to aid them in enforcing the laws, whenever they have to deal with disobedient and refractory subjects, and their legal power and right to do so is unquestionable. The right of the courts to call out the whole power of the country to enforce their judgments is as old as the common law; and the right of the President to use force in the performance of his legal duties is not only inherent in his office, but has been frequently recognized and aided by Congress. One striking example of this is the act of Congress of March 3, 1807, (2 Stat., 445,) which empowered the President, without the intervention of any court, to use the marshal, and, if he be insufficient, to use the army, summarily to expel intruders and squatters upon the public lands. And that power has been frequently exercised, without, as far as I know, a question of its legality. To call as is sometimes done, the judiciary the civil power, and the President the military power, seems to me at once a mistake of fact and an abuse of language.

While the judiciary and the President, as departments of the General Government, are co-ordinate, equal in dignity and power, and equally trusted by the law in their respective spheres, there is, nevertheless, a marked diversity in the character of their functions and their modes of action. The judiciary is, for the most part, passive. It rarely, if ever, takes the initiative; it seldom or never begins an operation. Its great function is judgment, and, in the exercise of that function, it is confined almost exclusively to cases not selected by itself, but made and submitted by others. The President, on the contrary, by the very nature of his office, is active; he must often take the initiative; he must begin operations. His great function is execution, for he is required by the Constitution (and he is the only department that is so required) to "take care that the laws (all the laws) be faithfully executed;" and in the exercise of that function his duties are co-extensive with the laws of the land.

Often he comes to the aid of the judiciary in the execution of its judgments; and this is only a part, and a small part, of his constitutional duty, to take care that the laws be faithfully executed. I say it is a small part of his duty, because for every instance in which the President executes the judgment of a court there are a hundred instances in which he executes the law without the intervention of the judiciary, and without referring at all to its functions.

I have premised this much in order to show the separate and independent character of the several departments of our Government, and to indicate the inevitable differences in their modes of action and the characteristic diversity of the subjects upon which they operate; and all this as a foundation for the answers which I will now proceed to give to the particular questions propounded to me.

As to the first question, I am clearly of opinion that, in a time like the present, when the very existence of the nation is assailed by a great and dangerous insurrection, the President has the lawful discretionary power to arrest and hold in custody persons known to have criminal intercourse with the insurgents, or persons against whom there is probable cause for suspicion of such criminal complicity. And I think this position can be maintained, in view of the principles already laid down, by a very plain argument.

The Constitution requires the President, before he enters upon the execution of his office, to take an oath that he "will faithfully execute the office of President of the United States, and will, to the best of his ability, preserve, protect, and defend the Constitution of the United States."

The duties of the office comprehend all the executive power of the nation, which is expressly vested in the President by the Constitution, (article 2, section 1,) and also all the powers which are specially delegated to the President, and yet are not, in their nature, executive powers; for example, the veto power, the treaty-making power, the appointing power, the pardoning power. These belong to that class which in England are called prerogative powers, inherent in the Crown. And yet the framers of our Constitution thought proper to preserve them and to vest them in the President, as necessary to the good government of the country. The executive powers are granted generally and without specification; the powers not executive are granted specially, and for purposes obvious in the context of the Constitution. And all these are embraced within the duties of the President, and are clearly within that clause of his oath which requires him to "faithfully execute the office of President."

The last clause of the oath is peculiar to the President. All the other officers of Government are required to swear only "to support this Constitution;" while the President must swear to "preserve, protect, and defend" it, which implies the power to perform what he is required in so solemn a manner to undertake. And then follows the broad and compendious injunction to "take care that the laws be faithfully executed." And this injunction, embracing as it does all the laws—Constitution, treaties, statutes—is addressed to the President alone, and not to any other department or office of the Government. And this constitutes him, in a peculiar manner, and above all other officers, the guardian of the Constitution—its preserver, protector, and defender.

It is the plain duty of the President (and his peculiar duty, above and beyond all other departments of the Government) to preserve the Constitution and execute the laws all over the nation; and it is plainly impossible for him to perform this duty without putting down rebellion, insurrection, and all unlawful combinations to resist the General Government. The duty to suppress the insurrection being obvious and imperative, the two acts of Congress, of 1795 and 1807, come to his aid, and furnish the physical force which he needs to suppress the insurrection and execute the laws. Those two acts authorize the President to employ for that purpose the militia, the army, and the navy.

The argument may be briefly stated thus: It is the President's bounden duty to put down the insurrection, as, in the language of the act of 1795, the "combinations are too powerful to be suppressed by the ordinary course of judicial proceedings, or by the powers vested in the marshals." And this duty is imposed upon the President for the very reason that the courts and the marshals are too weak to perform it. The manner in which he shall perform that duty is not prescribed by any law, but the means of performing it are given in the plain language of the statutes, and they are all means of force—the militia, the Army, and the Navy. The end, the suppression of the insurrection, is required of him; the means and instruments to suppress it are lawfully in his hands; but the manner in which he shall use them is not prescribed, and could not be prescribed, without a foreknowledge of all the future changes and contingencies of the insurrection. He is therefore necessarily thrown upon his discretion as to the manner in which he will use his means to meet the varying exigencies as they arise. If the insurgents assail the nation with an army he may find it best to meet them with an army, and suppress the insurrection on the field of battle. If they seek to prolong the rebellion and gather strength by intercourse with foreign nations, he may choose to guard the coast and close the ports with a navy, as one of the most efficient means to suppress the insurrection. And if they employ spies and emissaries to gather information, to forward secret supplies, and to excite new insurrections in aid of the original rebellion, he may find it both prudent and humane to arrest and imprison them. And this may be done either for the purpose of bringing them to trial and condign punishment for their crimes, or they may be held in custody for the milder end of rendering them powerless for mischief until the exigency is past.

In such a state of things the President must, of necessity, be the sole judge, both of the exigency which requires him to act, and of the manner in which it is most prudent for him to employ the powers entrusted to him, to enable him to discharge his constitutional and legal duty; that is, to suppress the insurrection and execute the laws. And this discretionary power of the President is fully admitted by the Supreme Court in the case of Martin *vs.* Mott. (12 Wheaton's Reports, page 19; 7 Curtis, 10.)

This is a great power in the hands of the Chief Magistrate; and because it is great, and is capable of being perverted to evil ends, its existence has been doubted or denied. It is said to be dangerous in the hands of an ambitious and wicked President, because he may use it for the purposes of oppression and tyranny. Yes, certainly it is dangerous; all power is dangerous, and for the all-pervading reason that all power is liable to abuse; all the recipients of human power are men, not absolutely virtuous and wise. Still it is a power necessary to the piece and safety of the country, and undeniably belongs to the Government, and therefore must be exercised by some department or officer thereof.

Why should this power be denied to the President, on the ground of its liability to abuse, and not denied to the other departments on the same ground? Are they more exempt than he is from the frailties and vices of humanity? Or are they more trusted by the law than he is trusted, in their several spheres of action? If it be said that a President may be ambitious and unscrupulous, it may be said with equal truth that a legislature may be factious and unprincipled, and a court may be venal and corrupt. But these are crimes never to be presumed, even against a private man, and much less against any high and highly trusted public functionary. They are crimes, however, recognized as such, and made punishable by the Constitution; and whoever is guilty of them, whether a president, a senator, or a judge, is liable to impeachment and condemnation.

As to the second question: Having assumed, in answering the first question, that the President has the legal discretionary power to arrest and imprison persons who are guilty of holding criminal intercourse with men engaged in a great and dangerous insurrection, or persons suspected with "probable cause" of such criminal complicity, it might seem unnecessary to go into any prolonged argument to prove that in such a case the President is fully justified in refusing to obey a writ of *habeas corpus*, issued by a court or judge, commanding him to produce the body of his prisoner, and state when he took him, and by what authority, and for what cause he detains him in custody, and then yield himself to judgment, "to do, submit to, and receive whatsoever the judge or court, awarding the writ, shall consider in that behalf."

If it is true, as I have assumed, that the President and the Judiciary are co-ordinate departments of Government, and the one not subject to the other, I do not understand how it can be legally possible for a judge to issue a command to the President to come before him *ad subjiciendum*, that is to submit implicitly to his judgment, and, in case of disobedience, treat him as a criminal, in contempt of a superior authority, and punish him as for a misdemeanor, by fine and imprisonment. It is no answer to say, as has sometimes been said, that although the writ of *habeas corpus* cannot be issued and enforced against the President himself, yet that it can be against any of his subordinates; for that abandons the principle assumed, of giving relief in "all cases" of imprisonment, by color of authority of the United States, and attempts to take an untenable distinction between the person of the President and his office and legal power. The law takes no such distinction, for it is no respecter of persons. The President, in the arrest and imprisonment of men, must, almost always, act by subordinate agents; and yet the thing done is no less his act than if done by his own hand. But it is possible for the President to be in the actual custody of a prisoner, taken in civil war, or arrested on suspicion of being a secret agent and abettor of rebellion, and in that case the writ must be unavailing, unless it run against the President himself. Besides the whole subject-matter is political, and not judicial. The insurrection itself is purely political. Its object is to destroy the political government of this nation, and to establish another political government upon its ruins. And the President, as the chief civil magistrate of the nation, and the most active department of the Government, is eminently and exclusively political in all its principal functions. As the political chief of the nation, the Constitution charges him with its preservation, protection, and defense, and requires him to take care that the laws be faithfully executed And in that character, and by the aid of the acts of Congres of 1795 and 1807, he wages open war against armed rebellion, and arrests and holds in safe custody those whom, in the exercise of his political discretion, he believes to be friends of and accomplices in the armed insurrection, which it is his especial political duty to suppress. He has no judicial powers. And the Judiciary Department has no political powers, and claims none, and therefore (as well as for other reasons already assigned) no court or judge can take cognizance of the political acts of the President, or undertake to revise and reverse his political decisions.

The jurisdiction exercised under the writ of *habeas corpus* is, in the nature of an appeal, (4 Cr. 75,) for, as far as concerns the right of the prisoner, the whole object of the process is to re-examine and reverse or affirm the acts of the person who imprisoned him. And I think it will hardly be seriously affirmed that a judge, at chambers, can entertain an appeal, in any form, from a decision of the President of the United States, and especially in a case purely political.

There is but one sentence in the Constitution which mentions the writ of *habeas corpus*—art. 1. sec. 9, clause 2—which is in these words:

"The privileges of the writ of *habeas corpus* shall not be suspended unless when, in cases of rebellion or invasion, the public safety may require it."

Very learned persons have differed widely about the meaning of this short sentence, and I am by no means confident that I fully understand it myself. The sententious language of the Constitution, in this particular, must, I suppose, be interpreted with reference to the origin of our people, their historical relations to the mother country, and their inchoate political condition at the moment when our Constitution was formed. At that time the United States, as a nation, had no common law of its own, and no statutory provision for the writ of *habeas corpus*. Still the people, English by descent, even while in open rebellion against the English Crown, claimed a sort of historical right to the forms of English law and the guarantees of English freedom. They knew that the English Government had, more than once, assumed the power to imprison whom it would, and hold them, for an indefinite time, beyond the reach of judicial examination; and they desired, no doubt, to interpose a guard against the like abuses in this country; and hence the clause of the Constitution now under consideration. But we must try to construe the words, vague and indeterminate as they are, as we find them. "The privilege of the writ of *habeas corpus* shall not be suspended," &c. Does that mean that the writ itself shall not be issued, or that, being issued, the party shall derive no benefit from it? Suspended—does that mean delayed, hung up for a time, or altogether denied? The writ of *habeas corpus*—which writ? In England there were many writs called by that name, and used by the courts for the more convenient exercise of their various powers; and our own courts now, by acts of Congress—the Judiciary act of 1789, sec. 14, and the act of March 2, 1833, sec. 7—have, I believe, equivalent powers.

It has been decided by the Supreme Court, and I doubt not correctly—see Bollman Swartwout's case (4 Cr., 93)—that "for the meaning of the term *habeas corpus* resort must be had to the common law, but the power to award the writ by any of the courts of the United States must be given by written law." And the same high Court, judging, no doubt, by the history of our people and the circumstances of the times, has also decided that the writ of *habeas corpus* mentioned in the Constitution is the great writ *ad subjiciendum.*

That writ, in its nature, action, and objects, is tersely and accurately described by Sir William Blackstone. I adopt his language, as found in his Commentaries, Book 3, p. 131:

"But the great and efficacious writ, in all manner of illegal confinement, is that of *habeas corpus ad subjiciendum,* directed to the person detaining another and commanding him to produce the body of the prisoner, with the day and cause of his caption and detention, *ad faciendum, subjiciendum et recipiendum,* to do, submit to, and receive whatsoever the judge or court awarding such writ shall consider in that behalf. This is a high prerogative writ, and therefore by the common law, issuing out of the Court of King's Bench, not only in term time, but also during the vacation by a fiat from the Chief Justice or any other of the judges, and running into all parts of the King's dominions; for the King is at all times entitled to have an account why the liberty of any of his subjects is restrained, wherever that restraint may be inflicted."

Such is the writ of *habeas corpus,* of which the Constitution declares that the privilege thereof shall not be suspended except when, in cases of rebellion or invasion, the public safety may require it. But the Constitution is silent as to who may suspend it when the contingency happens. I am aware that it has been declared by the Supreme Court that "if, at any time, the public safety should require the suspension of the powers vested by this act (meaning the judiciary act of 1789, section 14) in the courts of the United States, it is for the Legislature to say so. That question depends upon political considerations, on which the Legislature is to decide." Upon this I remark only that the Constitution is older than the judiciary act, and yet it speaks of the privilege of the writ of *habeas corpus* as a thing in existence; it is in general terms, and does not speak with particular reference to powers which might or might not be granted by a future act of Congress. Besides, I take it for certain that, in the common course of legislation, Congress has power, at any time, to repeal the judiciary act of 1789 and the act of 1833 (which grants to the courts and to the judges the power to issue the writs) without waiting for a rebellion or invasion, and a consequent public necessity, to justify, under the Constitution, the suspension of the privilege of the writ of *habeas corpus.*

The court does not speak of suspending the privilege of the writ, but of suspending the powers vested in the court by the act. The power to issue a writ can hardly be called a privilege; yet the right of an individual to invoke the protection of his Government in that form may well be designated by that name. And I should infer, with a good deal of confidence, that the Court meant to speak only of its own powers, and not of the privilege of individuals, but for the fact that the court ascribe the power to suspend to the Legislature upon political grounds. It says "that question depends upon political considerations, on which the Legislature is to decide." Now, I had supposed that question did not belong exclusively to the Legislature, because they depend upon political considerations, inasmuch as the President, in his constitutional and official duties, is quite as political as is the Congress, and has daily occasion in the common routine of affairs to determine questions upon political considerations alone.

If by the phrase the suspension of the privilege of the writ of *habeas corpus,* we must understand a repeal of all power to issue the writ, then I freely admit that none but Congress can do it. But if we are at liberty to understand the phrase to mean, that in case of a great and dangerous rebellion like the present, the public safety requires the arrest and confinement of persons implicated in that rebellion, I as freely declare the opinion that the President has lawful power to suspend the privilege of persons arrested under such circumstances; for he is especially charged by the Constitution with the "public safety," and he is the sole judge of the emergency which requires his prompt action.

This power in the President is no part of his ordinary duty in time of peace; it is temporary and exceptional, and was intended only to meet a pressing emergency, when the judiciary is found to be too weak to insure the public safety—when (in the language of the act of Congress) there are "combinations too powerful to be suppressed by the ordinary course of judicial proceedings, or by the powers vested in the marshals." Then and not till then, has he the lawful authority to call to his aid the military power of the nation, and with that power perform his great legal and constitutional duty to suppress the insurrection. And shall it be said that when he has fought and captured the insurgent army, and has seized their secret spies and emissaries, he is bound to bring their bodies before any judge who may send him a writ of *habeas corpus,* "to do, submit to, and receive whatsoever the said judge shall consider in that behalf?"

I deny that he is under any obligation to obey such a writ, issued under such circumstances. And in making this denial I do but follow the highest judicial authority of the nation. In the case of Luther *vs.* Borden, (commonly called the Rhode Island case,) reported in 7 Howard, page 1, the Supreme Court discussed several of the most important topics treated of in this opinion, and among them the power of the President alone to decide whether the exigency exists authorizing him to call out the militia under the act of 1795. The court affirmed the power of the President in that respect, and denied the power of the court to examine and adjudge his proceedings. The opinion of the court, delivered by the learned Chief Justice Taney, declares that if the court had that power, "then it would become the duty of the court (provided that it came to the conclusion that the President had decided incorrectly) to discharge those who were arrested or detained by the troops in the service of the United States, or the Government which the President was endeavoring to maintain. If (says that learned court) the judicial power extends so far, the guarantee contained in the Constitution of the United States (meaning, of course, protection against insurrection) is a guarantee of anarchy and not of order."

Whatever I have said about the suspension of the privilege of the writ of *habeas corpus* has been said in deference to the opinions of others, and not because I myself thought it necessary to treat of that subject at all in reference to the present posture of our national affairs. For, not doubting the power of the President to capture and hold by force insurgents in open arms against the Government, and to arrest and imprison their suspected accomplices, I never thought of first suspending the writ of *habeas corpus* any more than I thought of first suspending the writ of replevin before seizing arms and munitions destined for the enemy.

The power to do these things is in the hand of the President, placed there by the Constitution and the statute law as a sacred trust, to be used by him in his best discretion in the performance of his great first duty—to preserve, protect, and defend the Constitution. And for any breach of that trust he is responsible before the high court of impeachment, and before no other human tribunal.

The powers of the President falling within this general class have been several times considered by the judiciary, and have, I believe, been uniformly sustained, without materially varying from the doctrines laid down in this opinion. I content myself with a simple reference to the cases, without encumbering this document, already too long, with copious extracts. (The Rhode Island case, 7 Howard, page 1; Fleming *vs.* Page, 9 Howard, page 615; Cross *vs.* Harrison, 16 Howard, page 189; the Santissima Trinidad, 7 Wheaton, page 305; Martin *vs.* Mott, 12 Wheaton, page 29.)

To my mind it is not very important whether we call a particular power exercised by the President a peace power or a war power, for undoubtedly he is armed with both. He is the chief civil magistrate of the nation, and, being such, and because he is such, he is the constitutional commander-in-chief of the army and navy; and thus, within the limits of the Constitution, he rules in peace and commands in war, and at this moment he is in the full exercise of all the functions belonging to both these characters. The civil administration is still going on in its peaceful course, and yet we are in the midst of war—a war in which the enemy is, for the present, dominant in many States, and has his secret allies and accomplices scattered through many other States which are still loyal and true; a war all the more dangerous, and more needing jealous vigilance and prompt action, because it is an internecine and not an international war.

This, sir, is my opinion, the result of my best reflections upon the questions propounded by you. Such as it is, it is submitted with all possible respect, by your obedient servant,

EDWARD BATES, *Attorney General.*

To the PRESIDENT.

VIEW OF HORACE BINNEY.

From his pamphlet entitled "The Privilege of the Writ of *Habeas Corpus* under the Constitution," pages 51, 52:

In this matter of suspension of the privilege of the Writ of *habeas corpus,* the Constitution of the United States stands in the place of the English act of Parliament. It ordains the suspension in the conditioned cases, by the act of the competent department—as Parliament does from time to time. Neither is mandatory in suspending, but only authoritative. Each leaves discretion to the executive power. The difference is, that Parliament limits a time and provides for the effect by technical terms. The Constitution connects the suspension with the time of rebellion, and provides for the effect, as it did for the privilege, by words that comprehend the right, and deny for a season the enjoyment of it.

It is further objected, that this is a most dangerous power. It is, fortunately, confined to most dangerous times.

In such times the people generally are willing, and are often compelled, to give up for a season, a portion of their freedom to preserve the rest; and fortunately again, it is that portion of the people, for the most part, who like to live on the margin of disobedience to the laws, whose freedom is most in danger. The rest are rarely in want of a *habeas corpus*.

VIEW OF PROFESSOR THEOPHILUS PARSONS.

The Boston Daily *Advertiser* of June 5, 1861, contained a summary of the lecture on the question raised respecting the right and power of the Executive branch of the Government to suspend the writ of *habeas corpus* in certain emergencies, of which this is a part:

The Constitution of the United States, art. 1, sec. 9, n. 2, provides that "the privilege of the writ of *habeas corpus* shall not be suspended unless when, in cases of rebellion or invasion, the public safety may require it." And many of the State constitutions have similar provisions. A fair inference from this is that the right to *habeas corpus* may be suspended, or, what is the same thing, martial law may be declared and exercised "in cases of rebellion or invasion, when the public safety may require it."

The first and most important question is, who may decide when the exigency occurs, and who may, if it occurs, declare martial law. On this point I have myself no doubt. The clause on this subject is contained in the first article of the Constitution, and this article relates principally to Congress. Nor can there be any doubt that Congress may, when the necessity occurs, suspend the right to the writ of *habeas corpus*, or, which is the same thing, declare or authorize martial law. The question is, has the President this power? The Constitution does not expressly give this power to any department of Government, nor does it expressly reserve it to Congress, although, in the same article, it does make this express reservation as to some of the provisions contained in the article. This may be a mere accidental omission, but it seems to me more reasonable and more consonant with the principles of legal interpretation to infer from it an absence of intention to confine it to Congress. And I am confirmed in this opinion by the nature of the case.

The very instances specified as those in which the right to *habeas corpus* may be suspended (invasion and rebellion) are precisely those in which the reasons for doing so may come suddenly, the necessity of determination be immediate, and a certainty exist that the suspension will be useless, and the whole mischief which the suspension might prevent take place if there be any delay. To guard against the suspension by limiting the cases, as is done, seems to me wise; to obstruct it by requiring the delay necessarily arising from legislative action would seem to be unreasonable. It is true that my construction gives to the President, in the two cases of rebellion and invasion, a vast power; but so is all military power. It is a vast power to send into a rebellious district 15,000 soldiers, as Washington did, whose duty it would be to meet the rebels, and, if necessary, kill as many as they could. But it was a power which belonged to him, of necessity, as President; and so, I think, did the power of martial law. If it did not, then, when his troops had captured the armed rebels whom they were sent to subdue, the nearest magistrate who could issue a writ of *habeas corpus* might have summoned the officer having them in charge to bring them before him, and might have liberated them at once to fight again, and this as often as they were captured, until a law could be passed by Congress.

If the power belongs to the President, he may exercise it at his discretion, when either invasion or rebellion occurs, subject, however, to two qualifications. One, a universal one, applicable to his exercise of every power. If he abuses it, or exercises it wrongfully, he is liable to impeachment. The other is more a matter of discretion or propriety. I suppose that he would of course report his doings in such a matter to Congress when he could, and be governed by their action.

My conclusion is, therefore, that in case of invasion from abroad or rebellion at home, the President may declare, or exercise or authorize, martial law at his discretion.

ARREST OF CLEMENT L. VALLANDIGHAM.

Major General BURNSIDE, commanding Department of the Ohio, issued on the 13th of April, 1863, General Order No. 38, announcing that hereafter "all persons found within our lines who commit acts for the benefit of the enemies of our country will be tried as spies or traitors, and, if convicted, will suffer death." It was added: "The habit of declaring sympathies for the enemy will not be allowed in this department. Persons committing such offences will be at once arrested, with a view to being tried, as above stated, or sent beyond our lines into the lines of their friends. It must be distinctly understood that treason, expressed or implied, will not be tolerated in this department."

1863, May 4—Mr. VALLANDIGHAM was arrested for violation of this order—charged with "publicly expressing sympathy for those in arms against the Government of the United States, and declaring disloyal sentiments and opinions, with the object and purpose of weakening the power of the Government in its efforts to suppress an unlawful rebellion." The specification alluded to his speech on or about May 1, 1863, at Mount Vernon, O.

May 16—The evidence having been heard, the Court—Brigadier General R. B. Potter presiding—found him guilty of the charge, and not guilty as to part, and guilty as to part, of the specification.

He was sentenced to be placed in close confinement in some fortress of the United States, to be designated by the commanding officer of this Department, there to be kept during the continuance of the war. General BURNSIDE designated Fort Warren, Boston harbor.

May 19—The PRESIDENT directed * that Mr. Vallandigham be taken, under secure guard, to the headquarters of General Rosecrans, to be put by him beyond our military lines; and that, in case of his return within our lines, he be arrested and kept in close custody for the term specified in his sentence.

This order was executed, but Mr. Vallandigham very soon ran the blockade at Wilmington, N. C., and went to Canada, remaining at Windsor.

On the 5th of May, 1863, Mr. Vallandigham applied through counsel to Judge Leavitt, of the Circuit Court of the United States at Cincinnati, for a writ of *habeas corpus*, to which Gen. Burnside responded with a letter detailing the case and justifying his action. The application was argued at length, and was refused by the judge, who said that the legality of the arrest depends upon the extent of the necessity for making it, and that was to be determined by the military commander. He added:

Men should know and lay the truth to heart, that there is a course of conduct not involving overt treason, and not therefore subject to punishment as such, which, nevertheless, implies moral guilt, and a gross offence against the country. Those who live under the protection and enjoy the blessings of our benignant Government, must learn that they cannot stab its vitals with impunity. If they cherish

* This is a copy of the order:

UNITED STATES MILITARY TELEGRAPH,
[Cipher.] *May* 19, 1863.
[*By telegraph from Washington*, 9.40 *p. m.*, 1863.]

To Maj. Gen. BURNSIDE,
Commanding Department of Ohio:

SIR: The President directs that, without delay, you send C. L. Vallandigham, under secure guard, to the headquarters of General Rosecrans, to be put by him beyond our military lines, and in case of his return within our lines he be arrested and kept in close custody for the term specified in his sentence.

By order of the President:

E. R. S. CANBY,
Brigadier General and A. A. G.

hatred and hostility to it, and desire its subversion, let them withdraw from its jurisdiction, and seek the fellowship and protection of those with whom they are in sympathy. If they remain with us, while they are not of us, they must be subject to such a course of dealing as the great law of self-preservation prescribes and will enforce. And let them not complain if the stringent doctrine of military necessity should find them to be the legitimate subjects of its action. I have no fear that the recognition of this doctrine will lead to an arbitrary invasion of the personal security or personal liberty of the citizen. It is rare indeed that a charge of disloyalty will be made on insufficient grounds. But if there should be an occasional mistake, such an occurrence is not to be put in competition with the preservation of the nation; and I confess I am but little moved by the eloquent appeals of those who, while they indignantly denounce violation of personal liberty, look with no horror upon a despotism as unmitigated as the world has ever witnessed.

CORRESPONDENCE BETWEEN NEW YORK DEMOCRATS AND PRESIDENT LINCOLN.

Letter of the Committee and Resolutions.

ALBANY, *May* 19, 1863.

To his Excellency the PRESIDENT OF THE UNITED STATES:

The undersigned, officers of a public meeting held at the city of Albany on the 16th day of May instant, herewith transmit to your Excellency a copy of the resolutions adopted at the said meeting, and respectfully request your earnest consideration of them. They deem it proper on their personal responsibility to state that the meeting was one of the most respectable as to numbers and character, and one of the most earnest in the support of the Union, ever held in this city.

Yours, with great regard,

ERASTUS CORNING, *President.*
ELI PERRY, *Vice President.*
PETER GANSEVOORT, *Vice President.*
PETER MONTEITH, *Vice President.*
SAMUEL W. GIBBS, *Vice President.*
JOHN NIBLACK, *Vice President.*
H. W. McCLELLAN, *Vice President.*
LEMUEL W. RODGERS, *Vice President.*
WILLIAM SEYMOUR, *Vice President.*
JEREMIAH OSBORN, *Vice President.*
WM. S. PADOCK, *Vice President.*
J. B. SANDERS, *Vice President.*
EDWARD MULCAHY, *Vice President.*
D. V. N. RADCLIFFE, *Vice President.*
WILLIAM A. RICE, *Secretary.*
EDWARD NEWCOMB, *Secretary.*
R. W. PECKHAM, JR., *Secretary.*
M. A. NOLAN, *Secretary.*
JOHN R. NESSEL, *Secretary.*
C. W. WEEKS, *Secretary.*

Resolutions adopted at the Meeting held in Albany, N. Y., on the 16th day of May, 1863.

Resolved, That the Democrats of New York point to their uniform course of action during the two years of civil war through which we have passed, to the alacrity which they have evinced in filling the ranks of the army, to their contributions and sacrifices; as the evidence of their patriotism and devotion to the cause of our imperilled country. Never in the history of civil wars has a government been sustained with such ample resources of means and men as the people have voluntarily placed in the hands of this Administration.

Resolved, That, as Democrats, we are determined to maintain this patriotic attitude, and despite of adverse and disheartening circumstances, to devote all our energies to sustain the cause of the Union; to secure peace through victory, and to bring back the restoration of all the States under the safeguard of the Constitution.

Resolved, That while we will not consent to be misapprehended upon these points, we are determined not to be misunderstood in regard to others not less essential. We demand that the Administration shall be true to the Constitution; shall recognize and maintain the rights of the States and the liberties of the citizen; shall everywhere, outside of the lines of necessary military occupation and the scenes of insurrection, exert all its powers to maintain the supremacy of the civil over military law.

Resolved, That, in view of these principles, we denounce the recent assumption of a military commander to seize and try a citizen of Ohio, Clement L. Vallandigham, for no other reason than words addressed to a public meeting, in criticism of the course of the Administration and in condemnation of the military orders of that general.

Resolved, That this assumption of power by a military tribunal, if successfully asserted, not only abrogates the right of the people to assemble and discuss the affairs of government, the liberty of speech and of the press, the right of trial by jury, the law of evidence, and the privilege of *habeas corpus*, but it strikes a fatal blow at the supremacy of law and the authority of the State and Federal Constitutions.

Resolved, That the Constitution of the United States—the supreme law of the land—has defined the crime of treason against the United States to consist "only in levying war against them, or adhering to their enemies, giving them aid and comfort," and has provided that "no person shall be convicted of treason, unless on the testimony of two witnesses to the same overt act, or on confession in open court." And it further provides that "no person shall be held to answer for a capital or otherwise infamous crime, unless on a presentment or indictment of a grand jury, except in cases arising in the land and naval forces, or in the militia, when in actual service in time of war or public danger;" and further, that "in all criminal prosecutions, the accused shall enjoy the right of a speedy and public trial by an impartial jury of the State and district wherein the crime was committed."

Resolved, That these safeguards of the rights of the citizen against the pretensions of arbitrary power were intended more especially for his protection in times of civil commotion. They were secured substantially to the English people, after years of protracted civil war, and were adopted into our Constitution at the close of the revolution. They have stood the test of seventy-six years of trial, under our republican system, under circumstances which show that, while they constitute the foundation of all free government, they are the elements of the enduring stability of the republic.

Resolved, That in adopting the language of Daniel Webster, we declare, "it is the ancient and undoubted prerogative of this people to canvass public measures and the merits of public men." It is a "homebred right," a fireside privilege. It had been enjoyed in every house, cottage, and cabin in the nation. It is as undoubted as the right of breathing the air or walking on the earth. Belonging to private life as a right, it belongs to public life as a duty, and it is the last duty which those whose representatives we are shall find us to abandon. Aiming at all times to be courteous and temperate in its use, except when the right itself is questioned, we shall place ourselves on the extreme boundary of our own right and bid defiance to any arm that would move us from our ground. "This high constitutional privilege we shall defend and exercise in all places—in time of peace, in time of war, and at all times. Living, we shall assert it; and should we leave no other inheritance to our children, by the blessing of God we will leave them the inheritance of free principles, and the example of a manly, independent, and constitutional defence of them."

Resolved, That in the election of Governor Seymour, the people of this State, by an emphatic majority, declared their condemnation of the system of arbitrary arrests and their determination to stand by the Constitution. That the revival of this lawless system can have but one result: to divide and distract the North, and destroy its confidence in the purposes of the Administration. That we deprecate it as an element of confusion at home, of weakness to our armies in the field, and as calculated to lower the estimate of American character and magnify the apparent peril of our cause abroad. And that, regarding the blow struck at a citizen of Ohio as aimed at the rights of every citizen of the North, we denounce it as against the spirit of our laws and Constitution, and most earnestly call upon the President of the United States to reverse the action of the military tribunal which has passed a "cruel and unusual punishment" upon the party arrested, prohibited in terms by the Constitution, and to restore him to the liberty of which he has beeen deprived.

Resolved, That the president, vice-presidents, and secretary of this meeting be requested to transmit a copy of these resolutions to his excellency the President of the United States, with the assurance of this meeting of their hearty and earnest desire to support the Government in every constitutional and lawful measure to suppress the existing rebellion.

—

PRESIDENT LINCOLN'S REPLY.

EXECUTIVE MANSION,
WASHINGTON, *June* 12, 1863.

Hon. ERASTUS CORNING, and others:

GENTLEMEN: Your letter of May 19, inclosing the resolutions of a public meeting held at

Albany, New York, on the 16th of the same month, was received several days ago.

The resolutions as I understand them are resolvable into two propositions—first, the expression of a purpose to sustain the cause of the Union, to secure peace through victory, and to support the Administration in every constitutional and lawful measure to suppress the rebellion; and secondly, a declaration of censure upon the Administration for supposed unconstitutional action, such as the making of military arrests. And, from the two propositions, a third is deduced, which is, that the gentlemen composing the meeting are resolved on doing their part to maintain our common Government and country, despite the folly or wickedness, as they may conceive, of any Administration. This position is eminently patriotic, and as such, I thank the meeting, and congratulate the nation for it. My own purpose is the same; so that the meeting and myself have a common object, and can have no difference, except in the choice of means or measures for effecting that object.

And here I ought to close this paper, and would close it, if there were no apprehension that more injurious consequences than any merely personal to myself might follow the censures systematically cast upon me for doing what, in my view of duty, I could not forbear. The resolutions promise to support me in every constitutional and lawful measure to suppress the rebellion; and I have not knowingly employed, nor shall knowingly employ, any other. But the meeting, by their resolutions, assert and argue that certain military arrests, and proceedings following them, for which I am ultimately responsible, are unconstitutional. I think they are not. The resolutions quote from the Constitution the definition of treason, and also the limiting safeguards and guarantees therein provided for the citizen on trials of treason, and on his being held to answer for capital or otherwise infamous crimes, and, in criminal prosecutions, his right to a speedy and public trial by an impartial jury. They proceed to resolve "that these safeguards of the rights of the citizen against the pretensions of arbitrary power were intended more *especially* for his protection in times of civil commotion." And, apparently to demonstrate the proposition, the resolutions proceed: "They were secured substantially to the English people *after* years of protracted civil war, and were adopted into our Constitution at the *close* of the revolution." Would not the demonstration have been better, if it could have been truly said that these safeguards had been adopted and applied *during* the civil wars and *during* our revolution, instead of *after* the one and at the *close* of the other? I, too, am devotedly for them *after* civil war, and *before* civil war, and at all times, "except when, in cases of rebellion or invasion, the public safety may require" their suspension. The resolutions proceed to tell us that these safeguards "have stood the test of seventy-six years of trial, under our republican system, under circumstances which show that while they constitute the foundation of all free government, they are the elements of the enduring stability of the republic." No one denies that they have so stood the test up to the beginning of the present rebellion, if we except a certain occurrence at New Orleans; nor does any one question that they will stand the same test much longer after the rebellion closes. But these provisions of the Constitution have no application to the case we have in hand, because the arrests complained of were not made for treason—that is, not for *the* treason defined in the Constitution, and upon the conviction of which the punishment is death—nor yet were they made to hold persons to answer for any capital or otherwise infamous crimes; nor were the proceedings following, in any constitutional or legal sense, "criminal prosecutions." The arrests were made on totally different grounds, and the proceedings following accorded with the grounds of the arrests. Let us consider the real case with which we are dealing, and apply to it the parts of the Constitution plainly made for such cases.

Prior to my installation here it had been inculcated that any State had a lawful right to secede from the national Union, and that it would be expedient to exercise the right whenever the devotees of the doctrine should fail to elect a President to their own liking. I was elected contrary to their liking; and, accordingly, so far as it was legally possible, they had taken seven States out of the Union, had seized many of the United States forts, and had fired upon the United States flag, all before I was inaugurated, and, of course, before I had done any official act whatever. The rebellion thus began soon ran into the present civil war; and, in certain respects, it began on very unequal terms between the parties. The insurgents had been preparing for it more than thirty years, while the Government had taken no steps to resist them. The former had carefully considered all the means which could be turned to their account. It undoubtedly was a well-pondered reliance with them that in their own unrestricted efforts to destroy Union, Constitution, and law, all together, the Government would, in great degree, be restrained by the same Constitution and law from arresting their progress. Their sympathizers pervaded all departments of the Government and nearly all communities of the people. From this material, under cover of "liberty of speech," "liberty of the press," and "*habeas corpus*," they hoped to keep on foot amongst us a most efficient corps of spies, informers, suppliers, and aiders and abettors of their cause in a thousand ways. They knew that in times such as they were inaugurating, by the Constitution itself, the "*habeas corpus*" might be suspended; but they also knew they had friends who would make a question as to who was to suspend it; meanwhile their spies and others might remain at large to help on their cause. Or if, as has happened, the Executive should suspend the writ, without ruinous waste of time, instances of arresting innocent persons might occur, as are always likely to occur in such cases; and then a clamor could be raised in regard to this, which might be, at least, of some service to the insurgent cause. It needed no very keen perception to discover this part of the enemy's programme, so soon as by open hostilities their machinery was fairly put in motion. Yet, thoroughly imbued with a reverence for the guaranteed rights of individuals, I was slow to adopt the strong measures which by degrees I have been forced to regard as being within the exceptions of the Constitution, and as indispensable to the public safety. Nothing is better known to history than that courts of justice are utterly incompetent to such cases. Civil courts are organized chiefly for trials of individuals, or, at most, a few individuals acting in concert; and this in quiet times, and on charges of crimes well defined in the law. Even in times of peace bands of horse-thieves and robbers frequently grow too numerous and powerful for ordinary courts of justice. But what comparison, in numbers, have such bands ever borne to the insurgent sympathizers even in many of the loyal States? Again, a jury too frequently has at least one member more ready to hang the panel than to hang the traitor. And yet, again, he who dissuades one man from volunteering, or induces one soldier to desert, weakens the Union cause as much as he who kills a Union soldier in battle. Yet this dissuasion or inducement may be so conducted as to be no defined crime of which any civil court would take cognizance.

Ours is a case of rebellion—so called by the resolutions before me—in fact, a clear, flagrant, and gigantic case of rebellion; and the provision of the Constitution that "the privilege of the writ of *habeas corpus* shall not be suspended, unless when in cases of rebellion or invasion, the public safety may require it," is *the* provision which specially applies to our present case. This provision plainly attests the understanding of those who made the Constitution, that ordinary courts of justice are inadequate to "cases of rebellion"—attests their purpose that, in such cases, men may be held in custody whom the courts, acting on ordinary rules, would discharge. *Habeas corpus* does not discharge men who are proved to be guilty of defined crime; and its suspension is allowed by the Constitution on purpose that men may be arrested and held who cannot be proved to be guilty of defined crime, "when, in cases of rebellion or invasion, the public safety may require it."

This is precisely our present case—a case of rebellion, wherein the public safety does require the suspension. Indeed, arrests by process of courts, and arrests in cases of rebellion do not proceed altogether upon the same basis. The former is directed at the small percentage of ordinary and continuous perpetration of crime, while the latter is directed at sudden and extensive uprisings against the Government, which, at most, will succeed or fail in no great length of time. In the latter case, arrests are made, not so much for what has been done, as for what probably would be done. The latter is more for the preventive and less for the vindictive than the former. In such cases the purposes of men are much more easily understood than in cases of ordinary crime. The man who stands by and says nothing when the peril of his Government is discussed, cannot be misunderstood. If not hindered, he is sure to help the enemy; much more, if he talks ambiguously—talks for his country with "buts" and "ifs" and "ands." Of how little value the constitutional provisions I have quoted will be rendered, if arrests shall never be made until defined crimes shall have been committed, may be illustrated by a few notable examples. General John C. Breckinridge, General Robert E. Lee, General Joseph E. Johnston, General John B. Magruder, General William B. Preston, General Simon B. Buckner, and Commodore Franklin Buchanan, now occupying the very highest places in the rebel war service, were all within the power of the Government since the rebellion began, and were nearly as well known to be traitors then as now. Unquestionably if we had seized and held them, the insurgent cause would be much weaker. But no one of them had then committed any crime defined in the law. Every one of them, if arrested, would have been discharged on *habeas corpus* were the writ allowed to operate. In view of these and similar cases, I think the time not unlikely to come when I shall be blamed for having made too few arrests rather than too many.

By the third resolution the meeting indicate their opinion that military arrests may be constitutional in localities where rebellion actually exists, but that such arrests are unconstitutional in localities where rebellion or insurrection does not actually exist. They insist that such arrests shall not be made "outside of the lines of necessary military occupation, and the scenes of insurrection." Inasmuch, however, as the Constitution itself makes no such distinction, I am unable to believe that there is any such constitutional distinction. I concede that the class of arrests complained of can be constitutional only when, in cases of rebellion or invasion, the public safety may require them; and I insist that in such cases they are constitutional *wherever* the public safety does require them; as well in places to which they may prevent the rebellion extending as in those where it may be already prevailing; as well where they may restrain mischievous interference with the raising and supplying of armies to suppress the rebellion, as where the rebellion may actually be; as well where they may restrain the enticing men out of the army, as where they would prevent mutiny in the army; equally constitutional at all places where they will conduce to the public safety, as against the dangers of rebellion or invasion. Take the peculiar case mentioned by the meeting. It is asserted, in substance, that Mr. Vallandigham was, by a military commander, seized and tried "for no other reason than words addressed to a public meeting, in criticism of the course of the Administration, and in condemnation of the military orders of the general." Now, if there be no mistake about this; if this assertion is the truth and the whole truth; if there was no other reason for the arrest, then I concede that the arrest was wrong. But the arrest, as I understand, was made for a very different reason. Mr. Vallandigham avows his hostility to the war on the part of the Union; and his arrest was made because he was laboring, with some effect, to prevent the raising of troops; to encourage desertions from the army; and to leave the rebellion without an adequate military force to suppress it. He was not arrested because he was damaging the political prospects of the Administration, or the personal interests of the commanding general, but because he was damaging the army, upon the existence and vigor of which the life of the nation depends. He was warring upon the military, and this gave the military constitutional jurisdiction to lay hands upon him. If Mr. Vallandigham was not damaging the military power of the country, then his arrest was made on mistake of fact, which I would be glad to correct on reasonably satisfactory evidence.

I understand the meeting, whose resolutions I am considering, to be in favor of suppressing the rebellion by military force—by armies. Long experience has shown that armies cannot be maintained unless desertion shall be punished by the severe penalty of death. The case requires, and the law and the Constitution sanction, this punishment. Must I shoot a simple-minded soldier boy who deserts, while I must not touch a hair of a wily agitator who induces him to desert? This is none the less injurious when effected by getting a father, or brother, or friend, into a public meeting, and there working upon his feelings till he is persuaded to write the soldier boy that he is fighting in a bad cause, for a wicked Administration of a contemptible Government, too weak to arrest and punish him if he shall desert. I think that, in such a case, to silence the agitator and save the boy is not only constitutional, but withal a great mercy.

If I be wrong on this question of constitutional power, my error lies in believing that certain proceedings are constitutional when, in cases of rebellion or invasion, the public safety requires them, which would not be constitutional when, in absence of rebellion or invasion, the public safety does not require them: in other words, that the Constitution is not, in its application, in all respects the same, in cases of rebellion or invasion involving the public safety, as it is in times of profound peace and public security. The Constitution itself makes the distinction; and I can no more be persuaded that the Government can constitutionally take no strong measures in time of rebellion, because it can be shown that the same could not be lawfully taken in time of peace, than I can be persuaded that a particular drug is not good medicine for a sick man because it can be shown to not be good food for a well one. Nor am I able to appreciate the danger apprehended by the meeting, that the American people will, by means of military arrests during the rebellion, lose the right of public discussion, the liberty of speech and the press, the law of evidence, trial by jury, and *habeas corpus*, throughout the indefinite peaceful future, which I trust lies before them, any more than I am able to believe that a man could contract so strong an appetite for emetics during temporary illness as to persist in feeding upon them during the remainder of his healthful life.

In giving the resolutions that earnest consideration which you request of me, I cannot overlook the fact that the meeting speak as "Democrats." Nor can I, with full respect for their known intelligence, and the fairly presumed deliberation with which they prepared their resolutions, be permitted to suppose that this occurred by accident, or in any way other than that they preferred to designate themselves "Democrats" rather than "American citizens." In this time of national peril I would have preferred to meet you on a level one step higher than any party platform; because I am sure that, from such more elevated position, we could do better battle for the country we all love than we possibly can from those lower ones where, from the force of habit, the prejudices of the past, and selfish hopes of the future, we are sure to expend much of our ingenuity and strength in finding fault with, and aming blows at, each other. But, since you have denied me this, I will yet be thankful, for the country's sake, that not all Democrats have done so. He on whose discretionary judgment Mr. Vallandigham was arrested and tried is a Democrat, having no old party affinity with me; and the judge who rejected the constitutional view expressed in these resolutions, by refusing to discharge Mr. Vallandigham on *habeas corpus*, is a Democrat of better days than these, having received his judicial mantle at the hands of President Jackson. And still more, of all those Democrats who are nobly exposing their lives and shedding their blood on the battle-field, I have learned that many approve the course taken with Mr. Vallandigham, while I have not heard of a single one condemning it. I cannot assert that there are none such. And the name of President Jackson recalls an instance of pertinent history. After the battle of New Orleans, and while the fact that the treaty of peace had been concluded was well known in the city, but before official knowledge of it had arrived, General Jackson still maintained martial or military law. Now, that it could be said the war was over, the clamor against martial law, which had existed from the first, grew more furious. Among other things a Mr. Louaillier published a denunciatory newspaper article. General Jackson arrested him. A lawyer by the name of Morel procured the U. S. Judge Hall to order a writ of *habeas corpus* to relieve Mr. Louaillier. General Jackson arrested both the lawyer and the judge. A Mr. Hollander ventured to say of some part of the matter that "it was a dirty trick." General Jackson arrested him. When the officer undertook to serve the writ of *habeas corpus*, General Jackson took it from him, and sent him away with a copy. Holding the judge in custody a few days, the general sent him beyond the limits of his encampment, and set him at liberty, with an order to remain till the ratification of peace should be regularly announced, or until the British should have left the southern coast. A day or two more elapsed, the ratification of the treaty of peace was regularly announced, and the judge and others were fully liberated. A few days more and the judge called General Jackson into court and fined him $1,000 for having arrested him and the others named. The General paid the fine, and there the matter rested for nearly thirty years, when Congress refunded principal and interest. The late Senator Douglas, then in the House of Representatives, took a leading part in the debates, in which the constitutional question was much discussed. I am not prepared to say whom the journals would show to have voted for the measure.

It may be remarked: First, that we had the same Constitution then as now; secondly, that we then had a case of invasion, and now we have a case of rebellion; and, thirdly, that the permanent right of the people to public discussion, the liberty of speech and of the press, the trial by jury, the law of evidence, and the *habeas corpus*, suffered no detriment whatever by that conduct of Gen. Jackson, or its subsequent approval by the American Congress.

And yet, let me say, that in my own discretion, I do not know whether I would have ordered the arrest of Mr. Vallandigham. While I cannot shift the responsibility from myself, I hold that, as a general rule, the commander in the field is the better judge of the necessity in any particular case. Of course, I must practice a general directory and revisory power in the matter.

One of the resolutions expresses the opinion of the meeting that arbitrary arrests will have the effect to divide and distract those who should be united in suppressing the rebellion, and I am specifically called on to discharge Mr. Vallandigham. I regard this as, at least, a fair appeal to me on the expediency of exercising a constitutional power which I think exists. In response to such appeal I have to say, it gave me pain when I learned that Mr. Vallandigham had been arrested—that is, I was pained that there should have seemed to be a necessity for arresting him—and that it will afford me great pleasure to discharge him so soon as I can, by any means, believe the public safety will not suffer by it.

I further say, that as the war progresses, it appears to me, opinion and action, which were in great confusion at first, take shape and fall into more regular channels, so that the necessity for strong dealing with them gradually decreases. I have every reason to desire that it should cease altogether, and far from the least is my regard for the opinions and wishes of those who like the meeting at Albany, declare their purpose to sustain the Government in every constitutional and lawful measure to suppress the rebellion. Still, I must continue to do so much as may seem to be required by the public safety. A. LINCOLN.

CORRESPONDENCE BETWEEN OHIO DEMOCRATS AND PRESIDENT LINCOLN.

The Letter to the President.

WASHINGTON, *June* 26, 1863.

To his Excellency the PRESIDENT OF THE UNITED STATES:

The undersigned, having been appointed a committee, under the authority of the resolutions of the State Convention held at the city of Columbus, Ohio, on the 11th instant, to communicate with you on the subject of the arrest and banishment of Clement L. Vallandigham, most respectfully submit the following as the resolutions of that Convention bearing upon the subject of this communication, and ask of your Excellency their earnest consideration. And they deem it proper to state that the Convention was one in which all parts of the State were represented, one of the most respectable as to numbers and character, and one the most earnest and sincere in support of the Constitution and the Union, ever held in that State:

Resolved, That the will of the people is the foundation of all free government; that, to give effect to this free will, free thought, free speech, and a free press are absolutely indispensable. Without free discussion there is no certainty of sound judgment: without sound judgment there can be no wise government.

2. That it is an inherent and constitutional right of the people to discuss all measures of their Government, and to approve or disapprove, as to their best judgment seems right. That they have a like right to propose and advocate that policy which in their judgment is best, and to argue and vote against whatever policy seems to them to violate the Constitution, to impair their liberties, or to be detrimental to their welfare.

3. That these and all other rights guarantied to them by their Constitutions are their rights in time of war as well as in time of peace, and of far more value and necessity in war than in peace, for in peace liberty, security, and property are seldom endangered; in war they are ever in peril.

4. That we now say to all whom it may concern, not by way of threat, but calmly and firmly, that we will not surrender these rights, nor submit to their forcible violation. We will obey the laws ourselves, and all others must obey them.

11. That Ohio will adhere to the Constitution and the Union as the best—it may be the last—hope of popular freedom, and for all wrongs which may have been committed, or evils which may exist, will seek redress, under the Constitution and within the Union, by the peaceful but powerful agency of the suffrages of a free people.

14. That we will earnestly support every constitutional measure tending to preserve the Union of the States. No men have a greater interest in its preservation than we have, none desire it more; there are none who will make greater sacrifices or endure more than we will to accomplish that end. We are, as we ever have been, the devoted friends of the Constitution and the Union, and we have no sympathy with the enemies of either.

15. That the arrest, imprisonment, pretended trial, and actual banishment of Clement L. Vallandigham, a citizen of the State of Ohio, not belonging to the land or naval forces of the United States, nor to the militia in actual service, by alleged military authority, for no other pretended crime than that of uttering words of legitimate criticism upon the conduct of the Administration in power, and of appealing to the ballot-box for a change of policy—said arrest and military trial taking place where the courts of law are open and unobstructed, and for no act done within the sphere of active military operations in carrying on the war—we regard as a palpable violation of the following provisions of the Constitution of the United States:

1. "Congress shall make no law abridging the freedom of speech or of the press, or the right of the people peaceably to assemble and to petition the Government for a redress of grievances."

2. "The right of the people to be secure in their persons, houses, papers, and effects, against unreasonable searches and seizures, shall not be violated; and no warrants shall issue but upon probable cause, supported by oath or affirmation, and particularly describing the place to be searched and the persons or things to be seized."

3. "No person shall be held to answer for a capital or otherwise infamous crime, unless on a presentment or indictment of a grand jury, except in cases arising in the land or naval forces, or in the militia, when in actual service in time of war or public danger."

4. "In all criminal prosecutions, the accused shall enjoy the right to a speedy and public trial, by an impartial jury of the State and district wherein the crime shall have been committed, which district shall have been previously ascertained by law."

And we furthermore denounce said arrest, trial, and banishment as a direct insult offered to the sovereignty of the people of Ohio, by whose organic law it is declared that no person shall be transported out of the State for any offence committed within the same.

16. That Clement L. Vallandigham was, at the time of

his arrest, a prominent candidate for nomination by the Democratic party of Ohio for the office of Governor of the State; that the Democratic party was fully competent to decide whether he is a fit man for that nomination, and that the attempt to deprive them of that right, by his arrest and banishment, was an unmerited imputation upon their intelligence and loyalty, as well as a violation of the Constitution.

17. That we respectfully, but most earnestly, call upon the President of the United States to restore Clement L. Vallandigham to his home in Ohio, and that a committee of one from each Congressional district of the State, to be selected by the presiding officer of this Convention, is hereby appointed to present this application to the President.

The undersigned, in the discharge of the duty assigned them, do not think it necessary to reiterate the facts connected with the arrest, trial, and banishment of Mr. Vallandigham—they are well known to the President, and are of public history—nor to enlarge upon the positions taken by the Convention, nor to recapitulate the constitutional provisions which it is believed have been contravened; they have been stated at length, and with clearness, in the resolutions which have been recited. The undersigned content themselves with brief reference to other suggestions pertinent to the subject.

They do not call upon your Excellency as suppliants, praying the revocation of the order banishing Mr. Vallandigham as a favor; but, by the authority of a Convention representing a majority of the citizens of the State of Ohio, they respectfully ask it as a right due to an American citizen, in whose personal injury the sovereignty and dignity of the people of Ohio, as a free State, have been offended. And this duty they perform the more cordially from the consideration that, at a time of great national emergency, pregnant with danger to our Federal Union, it is all important that the true friends of the Constitution and the Union, however they may differ as to *the mode* of administering the Government, and the measures most likely to be successful in the maintenance of the Constitution and the restoration of the Union, should not be thrown into conflict with each other.

The arrest, unusual trial, and banishment of Mr. Vallandigham have created wide-spread and alarming disaffection among the people of the State, not only endangering the harmony of the friends of the Constitution and the Union, and tending to disturb the peace and tranquillity of the State, but also impairing that confidence in the fidelity of your Administration to the great landmarks of free government essential to a peaceful and successful enforcement of the laws in Ohio.

You are reported to have used in a public communication on this subject, the following language:

"It gave me pain when I learned that Mr. Vallandigham had been arrested—that is, I was pained that there should have seemed to be a necessity for arresting him; and that it will afford me great pleasure to discharge him, so soon as I can by any means believe the public safety will not suffer by it."

The undersigned assure your Excellency, from our own personal knowledge of the feelings of the people of Ohio, that the public safety will be far more endangered by continuing Mr. Vallandigham in exile than by releasing him. It may be true that persons differing from him in political views may be found in Ohio, and elsewhere, who will express a different opinion. But they are certainly mistaken.

Mr. Vallandigham may differ with the President, and even with some of his own political party, as to the true and most effectual means of maintaining the Constitution and restoring the Union; but this difference of opinion does not prove him to be unfaithful to his duties as an American citizen. If a man, devotedly attached to the Constitution and the Union, conscientiously believes that, from the inherent nature of the Federal compact, the war, in the present condition of things in this country, cannot be used as a means of restoring the Union; or that a war to subjugate a part of the States, or a war to revolutionize the social system in a part of the States, could not restore, but would inevitably result in the final destruction of both the Constitution and the Union, is he not to be allowed the right of an American citizen to appeal to the judgment of the people for a change of policy by the constitutional remedy of the ballot-box?

During the war with Mexico many of the political opponents of the Administration then in power thought it their duty to oppose and denounce the war, and to urge before the people of the country that it was unjust and prosecuted for unholy purposes. With equal reason it might have been said of them that their discussions before the people were calculated to discourage enlistments, "to prevent the raising of troops," and to induce desertions from the army, and leave the Government without an adequate military force to carry on the war.

If the freedom of speech and of the press are to be suspended in time of war, then the essential element of popular government to effect a change of policy in the constitutional mode is at an end. The freedom of speech and of the press is indispensable, and necessarily incident to the nature of popular government itself. If any inconvenience or evils arise from its exercise, they are unavoidable.

On this subject you are reported to have said further:

"It is asserted, in substance, that Mr. Vallandigham was, by a military commander, seized and tried 'for no other reason than words addressed to a public meeting in criticism of the course of the Administration, and in condemnation of the military order of the general.' Now, if there be no mistake about this, if there was no other reason for the arrest, then I concede that the arrest was wrong. But the arrest, I understand, was made for a very different reason. Mr. Vallandigham avows his hostility to the war on the part of the Union, and his arrest was made because he was laboring, with some effect, to prevent the raising of troops, to encourage desertions from the army, and to leave the rebellion without an adequate military force to suppress it. He was not arrested because he was damaging the political prospects of the Administration or the personal interests of the commanding general, but because he was damaging the army, upon the existence and vigor of which the life of the nation depends. He was warring upon the military, and this gave the military constitutional jurisdiction to lay hands upon him. If Mr. Vallandigham was not damaging the military power of the country, then his arrest was made on mistake of facts, which I would be glad to correct on reasonable satisfactory evidence."

In answer to this permit us to say, first, that neither the charge nor the specifications in support of the charge on which Mr. Vallandigham was tried impute to him the act of either laboring to prevent the raising of troops or to encourage desertions from the army. Secondly, no evidence on the trial was offered with a view to support, or even tended to support, any such charge. In what instance, and by what act, did he either discourage enlistments or encourage desertion in the army? Who is the man who was discouraged from enlisting, and who encouraged to desert, by any act of Mr. Vallandigham? If it be assumed that perchance some person might have been discouraged from enlisting, or that some person might have been encouraged to desert, on account of hearing Mr. Vallandigham's views as to the policy of the war as a means of restoring the Union, would that have laid the foundation for his conviction and banishment? If so, upon the same grounds every political opponent of the Mexican war might have been convicted and banished from the country.

When gentlemen of high standing and extensive influence, including your Excellency, opposed, in the discussions before the people, the policy of the Mexican war, were they "warring upon the military," and did this "give the military constitutional jurisdiction to lay hands upon" them? And, finally, the charge in the specifications upon which Mr. Vallandigham was tried entitled him to a trial before the civil tribunals, according to the express provisions of the late acts of Congress, approved by yourself July 17, 1862, and March 3, 1863, which were manifestly designed to supersede all necessity or pretext for arbitrary military arrests.

The undersigned are unable to agree with you in the opinion you have expressed that the Constitution is different in time of insurrection or invasion from what it is in time of peace and public security. The Constitution provides for no limitation upon or exceptions to the guarantees of personal liberty, except as to the writ of *habeas corpus*. Has the President, at the time of invasion or insurrection, the right to engraft limitations or exceptions upon these constitutional guarantees whenever, in his judgment, the public safety requires it?

True it is, the article of the Constitution which defines the various powers delegated to Congress declares that "the privilege of the writ of *habeas corpus* shall not be suspended unless when, in cases of rebellion or invasion, the public safety may require it." But this qualification or limitation upon this restriction upon the powers of Congress has no reference to or connection with the other constitutional guarantees of personal liberty. Expunge from the Constitution this limitation upon the power of Congress to suspend the writ of *habeas corpus*, and yet the other guarantees of personal liberty would remain unchanged.

Although a man might not have a constitutional right to have an immediate investigation made as to the legality of his arrest upon *habeas corpus*, yet his "right to a speedy and public trial by an impartial jury of the State and district wherein the crime shall have been committed" will not be altered; neither will his right to the exemption from "cruel and unusual punishment;" nor his right to be secure in his person, houses, papers, and effects, against unreasonable seizures and searches; nor his right not to be deprived of life, liberty, or property, without due process of law; nor his right not to be held to answer for a capital or otherwise infamous offence, unless on presentment or indictment of a grand jury, be in anywise changed.

And certainly the restriction upon the power of Congress to suspend the writ of *habeas corpus*, in time of insurrection or invasion, could not affect the guaranty that the freedom of speech and of the press shall not be abridged. It is sometimes urged that the proceedings in the civil tribunals are too tardy and ineffective for cases arising in times of insurrection or invasion. It is a full reply to this to say that arrests by civil process may be equally as expeditious and effective as arrests by military orders.

True, a summary trial and punishment are not allowed in the civil courts. But if the offender be under arrest and imprisoned, and not entitled to a discharge on writ of *habeas corpus* before trial, what more can be required for the purposes of the Government? The idea that all the constitutional guarantees of personal liberty are suspended throughout the country at a time of insurrection or invasion in any part of it places us upon a sea of uncertainty, and subjects the life, liberty, and property of every citizen to the mere will of a military commander, or what he may say that he considers the public safety requires. Does your Excellency wish to have it understood that you hold that the rights of every man throughout this vast country are subject to be annulled whenever you may say that you consider the public safety requires it, in time of invasion or insurrection?

You are further reported as having said that the constitutional guarantees of personal liberty have "no application to the present case we have in hand, because the arrests complained of were not made for treason—that is, not for *the* treason defined in the Constitution, and upon the conviction of which the punishment is death—nor yet were they made to hold persons to answer for capital or otherwise infamous crimes; nor were the proceedings following in any constitutional or legal sense 'criminal prosecutions.' The arrests were made on totally different grounds, and the proceedings following accorded with the grounds of the arrests," &c.

The conclusion to be drawn from this position of your Excellency is, that where a man is liable to "a criminal prosecution," or is charged with a crime known to the laws of the land, he is clothed with all the constitutional guarantees for his safety and security from wrong and injustice; but that, where he is not liable to "a criminal prosecution," or charged with any crime known to the laws, if the President or any military commander shall say that he considers that the public safety requires it, this man may be put outside of the pale of the constitutional guarantees, and arrested without charge of crime, imprisoned without knowing what for, and any length of time, or be tried before a court-martial and sentenced to any kind of punishment, unknown to the laws of the land, which the President or the military commander may see proper to impose.

Did the Constitution intend to throw the shield of its securities around the man liable to be charged with treason as defined by it, and yet leave the man not liable to any such charge unprotected by the safeguards of personal liberty and personal security? Can a man not in the military or naval service, nor within the field of the operations of the army, be arrested and imprisoned without any law of the land to authorize it? Can a man thus, in civil life, be punished without any law defining the offence and describing the punishment? If the President or a court-martial may prescribe one kind of punishment unauthorized by law, why not any other kind? Banishment is an unusual punishment, and unknown to our laws. If the President has the right to prescribe the punishment of banishment, why not that of death and confiscation of property? If the President has the right to change the punishment prescribed by the court-martial from imprisonment to banishment, why not from imprisonment to torture upon the rack or execution upon the gibbet?

If an indefinable kind of constructive treason is to be introduced and engrafted upon the Constitution, unknown to the laws of the land and subject to the will of the President whenever an insurrection or invasion shall occur in any part of this vast country, what safety or security will be left for the liberties of the people?

The constructive treasons that gave the friends of freedom so many years of toil and trouble in England were inconsiderable compared to this. The precedents which you make will become a part of the Constitution for your successors, if sanctioned and acquiesced in by the people now.

The people of Ohio are willing to co-operate zealously with you in every effort warranted by the Constitution to restore the Union of the States, but they cannot consent to abandon those fundamental principles of civil liberty which are essential to their existence as a free people.

In their name we ask that, by a revocation of the order of his banishment, Mr. Vallandigham may be restored to the enjoyment of those rights of which they believe he has been unconstitutionally deprived.

We have the honor to be respectfully, yours, &c.,

M. BIRCHARD, *Chairman*, 19*th Dist.*
DAVID A. HOUK, *Secretary*, 3*d Dist.*
GEO. BLISS, 14*th Dist.*
T. W. BARTLEY, 8*th Dist.*
W. J. GORDON, 18*th Dist.*
JOHN O'NEILL, 13*th Dist.*
C. A. WHITE, 6*th Dist.*
W. E. FINCK, 12*th Dist.*
ALEXANDER LONG, 2*d Dist.*
J. W. WHITE, 16*th Dist.*
JAS. R. MORRIS, 15*th Dist.*
GEO. S. CONVERSE, 7*th Dist.*
WARREN P. NOBLE, 9*th Dist.*
GEO. H. PENDLETON, 1*st Dist.*
W. A. HUTCHINS, 11*th Dist.*
ABNER L. BACKUS, 10*th Dist.*
J. F. McKINNEY, 4*th Dist.*
F. C. LEBLOND, 5*th Dist.*
LOUIS SHAEFER, 17*th Dist.*

Letter from President Lincoln.

WASHINGTON, *June* 29, 1863.

Messrs. M. Birchard, David M. Houk, George Bliss, T. W Bartley, W. J. Gordon, John O'Niell, C. A. White, W. E. Finck, Alexander Long, J. W. White, George H. Pendleton, George S. Converse, Warren P. Noble, James R. Morris, W. A Hutchins, Abner L. Backus, J. F. McKinney, F. C. LeBlond, Louis Schaefer:

GENTLEMEN: The resolutions of the Ohio Democratic State Convention, which you present me, together with your introductory and closing remarks, being in position and argument mainly the same as the resolutions of the Democratic meeting at Albany, New York, I refer you to my response to the latter as meeting most of the points in the former.

This response you evidently used in preparing your remarks, and I desire no more than that it be used with accuracy. In a single reading of your remarks, I only discovered one inaccuracy in matter which I suppose you took from that paper. It is where you say, "The undersigned are unable to agree with you in the opinion you have expressed that the Constitution is different in time of insurrection or invasion from what it is in time of peace and public security."

A recurrence to the paper will show you that I have not expressed the opinion you suppose. I expressed the opinion that the Constitution is different *in its application* in cases of rebellion or invasion, involving the public safety, from what it is in times of profound peace and public security; and this opinion I adhere to, simply because by the Constitution itself things may be done in the one case which may not be done in the other.

I dislike to waste a word on a merely personal point, but I must respectfully assure you that you will find yourselves at fault should you ever seek for evidence to prove your assumption that I "opposed in discussions before the people the policy of the Mexican war."

You say: "Expunge from the Constitution this limitation upon the power of Congress to suspend the writ of *habeas corpus*, and yet the other guarantees of personal liberty would remain unchanged." Doubtless if this clause of the Constitution, improperly called, as I think, a limitation upon the power of Congress, were expunged, the other guarantees would remain the same; but the question is, not how those guarantees would stand with that clause *out* of the Constitution, but how they stand with that clause remaining in it, in case of rebellion or invasion, involving the public safety. If the liberty could be indulged in expunging that clause, letter and spirit, I really think the constitutional argument would be with you.

My general view on this question was stated in the Albany response, and hence I do not state it now. I only add that, as seems to me, the benefit of the writ of *habeas corpus* is the great means through which the guarantees of personal liberty are conserved and made available in the last resort; and corroborative of this view is the fact that Mr. Vallandigham, in the very case in question, under the advice of able lawyers, saw not where else to go but to the *habeas corpus*. But by the Constitution the benefit of the writ of *habeas corpus* itself may be suspended, when, in case of rebellion or invasion, the public safety may require it.

You ask, in substance, whether I really claim that I may override all the guarantied rights of individuals, on the plea of conserving the public safety—when I may choose to say the public safety requires it. This question, divested of the phraseology calculated to represent me as struggling for an arbitrary personal prerogative, is either simply a question *who* shall decide, or an affirmation that *nobody* shall decide, what the public safety does require in cases of rebellion or invasion. The Constitution contemplates the question as likely to occur for decision, but it does not expressly declare who is to decide it. By necessary implication, when rebellion or invasion comes, the decision is to be made, from time to time; and I think the man whom, for the time, the people have, under the Constitution, made the Commander-in-Chief of their Army and Navy, is the man who holds the power and bears the responsibility of making it. If he uses the power justly, the same people will probably justify him; if he abuses it, he is in their hands, to be dealt with by all the modes they have reserved to themselves in the Constitution.

The earnestness with which you insist that persons can only, in times of rebellion, be lawfully dealt with, in accordance with the rules for criminal trials and punishments in times of peace, induces me to add a word to what I said on that point in the Albany response. You claim that men may, if they choose, embarrass those whose duty it is to combat a giant rebellion and then be dealt with only in turn as if there were no rebellion. The Constitution itself rejects this view. The military arrests and detentions which have been made, including those of Mr. Vallandigham, which are not different in principle from the other, have been for *prevention*, and not for *punishment*—as injunctions to stay injury, as proceedings to keep the peace—and hence, like proceedings in such cases and for like reasons, they have not been accompanied with indictments, or trials by juries, nor in a single case by any punishment whatever beyond what is purely incidental to the prevention. The original sentence of imprisonment in Mr. Vallandigham's case was to prevent injury to the military service only, and the modification of it was made as a less disagreeable mode to him of securing the same prevention.

I am unable to perceive an insult to Ohio in the case of Mr. Vallandigham. Quite surely nothing of this sort was or is intended. I was wholly unaware that Mr. Vallandigham was, at the time of his arrest, a candidate for the Democratic nomination for Governor, until so informed by your reading to me the resolutions of the Convention. I am grateful to the State of Ohio for many things, especially for the brave soldiers and officers she has given in the present national trial to the armies of the Union.

You claim as I understand, that according to my own position in the Albany response, Mr. Vallandigham should be released; and this because, as you claim, he has not damaged the military service by discouraging enlistments, encouraging desertions, or otherwise; and that if he had, he should be turned over to the civil authorities under the recent acts of Congress. I certainly do not *know* that Mr. Vallandigham has specifically and by direct language advised against enlistments, and in favor of desertion and resistance to drafting. We all know that combinations, armed in some instances, to resist the arrest of deserters, began several months ago; that more recently the like has appeared in resistance to the enrollment preparatory to a draft; and that quite a number of assassinations have occurred from the same animus. These had to be met by military force, and this again has led to bloodshed and death. And now, under a sense of responsibility more weighty and enduring than any which is merely official, I solemnly declare my belief that this hindrance of the military, including maiming and murder, is due to the course in which Mr. Vallandigham has been engaged, in a greater degree than to any other cause; and it is due to him personally in a greater degree than to any other man.

These things have been notorious, known to all, and of course known to Mr. Vallandigham. Perhaps I would not be wrong to say they originated with his especial friends and adherents. With perfect knowledge of them he has frequently, if not constantly, made speeches in Congress and before popular assemblies; and if it can be shown that, with these things staring him in the face, he has ever uttered a word of rebuke or counsel against them, it will be a fact greatly in his favor with me, and one of which, as yet, I am totally ignorant. When it is known that the whole burden of his speeches has been to stir up men against the prosecution of the war, and that in the midst of resistance to it he has not been known in any instance to counsel against such resistance, it is next to impossible to repel the inference that he has counselled directly in favor of it.

With all this before their eyes, the Convention you represent have nominated Mr. Vallandigham for Governor of Ohio, and both they and you have declared the purpose to sustain the National Union by all constitutional means. But, of course, they and you, in common, reserve to yourselves to decide what are constitutional means, and, unlike the Albany meeting, you omit to state or intimate that, in your opinion, an army is a constitutional means of saving the Union against a rebellion, or even to intimate that you are conscious of an existing rebellion being in progress with the avowed object of destroying that very Union. At the same time, your nominee for Governor, in whose behalf you appeal, is known to you and to the world to declare against the use of an army to suppress the rebellion. Your own attitude, therefore, encourages desertion, resistance to the draft, and the like, because it teaches those who incline to desert and to escape the draft to believe it is your purpose to protect them and to hope that you will become strong enough to do so.

After a short personal intercourse with you, gentlemen of the committee, I cannot say I think you desire this effect to follow your attitude; but I assure you that both friends and enemies of the Union look upon it in this light. It is a substantial hope, and by consequence a real strength to the enemy. It is a false hope, and one which you would willingly dispel. I will make the way exceedingly easy. I send you duplicates of this letter, in order that you, or a majority, may, if you choose, endorse your names upon one of them, and return it thus endorsed to me, with the understanding that those signing are hereby committed to the following propositions, and to nothing else:

1. That there is now a rebellion in the United States, the object and tendency of which is to destroy the National Union; and that, in your opinion, an army and navy are constitutional means for suppressing that rebellion.

2. That no one of you will do anything which, in his own judgment, will tend to hinder the increase or favor the decrease or lessen the efficiency of the army and navy, while engaged in the effort to suppress that rebellion; and

3. That each of you will, in his sphere, do all he can to have the officers, soldiers, and seamen of the army and navy, while engaged in the effort to suppress the rebellion, paid, fed, clad, and otherwise well provided for and supported.

And with the further understanding that upon receiving the letter and names thus endorsed, I will cause them to be published, which publication shall be, within itself, a revocation of the order in relation to Mr. Vallandigham.

It will not escape observation that I consent to the release of Mr. Vallandigham upon terms not embracing any pledge from him or from others as to what he will or will not do. I do this because he is not present to speak for himself, or to authorize others to speak for him; and hence I shall expect that on returning he would not put himself practically in antagonism with his friends. But I do it chiefly because I thereby prevail on other influential gentlemen of Ohio to so define their position as to be of immense value to the army—thus more than compensating for the consequences of any mistake in allowing Mr. Vallandigham to return, so that, on the whole, the public safety will not have suffered by it. Still, in regard to Mr. Vallandigham and all others, I must hereafter, as heretofore, do so much as the public service may seem to require.

I have the honor to be, respectfully, yours, &c.

A. LINCOLN.

—

The Committee's Rejoinder.

NEW YORK, July 1, 1863.

To his Excellency the PRESIDENT OF THE UNITED STATES:

SIR: Your answer to the application of the undersigned for a revocation of the order of banishment of Clement L. Vallandigham requires a reply, which they proceed with as little delay as possible to make.

They are not able to appreciate the force of the distinction you make between *the Constitution* and *the application* of the Constitution, whereby you assume that powers are delegated to the President at the time of invasion or insurrection, in derogation of the plain language of the Constitution. The inherent provisions of the Constitution remaining the same in time of insurrection or invasion as in time of peace, the President can have no more right to disregard their positive and imperative requirements at the former time than at the latter. Because some things may be done by the terms of the Constitution at the time of invasion or insurrection which would not be required by the occasion in time of peace, you assume that *any thing whatever*, even though not expressed by the Constitution, may be done on the occasion of insurrection or invasion, which the President may choose to say is required by the public safety. In plainer terms, because the writ of *habeas corpus* may be suspended at time of invasion or insurrection, you infer that all other provisions of the Constitution having in view the protection of the life, liberty, and property of the citizen, may be in like manner suspended.

The provision relating to the writ of *habeas corpus* being contained in the first part of the Constitution, the purpose of which is to define the powers delegated to Congress, has no connection in language with the Declaration of Rights, as guarantees of personal liberty, contained in the additional and amendatory articles, and inasmuch as the provision relating to *habeas corpus* expressly provides for its suspension, and the other provisions alluded to do not provide for any such thing, the legal conclusion is that the suspension of the later is unauthorized. The provision for the writ of *habeas corpus* is merely intended to furnish a *summary* remedy, and not the means whereby personal security is conserved in the final resort; while the other provisions are guarantees of personal rights, the suspension of which puts an end to all pretence of free government. It is true Mr. Vallandigham applied for a writ of *habeas corpus* as a summary remedy against oppression. But the denial of this did not take away his right to a speedy public trial by an impartial jury, or deprive him of his other rights as an American citizen. Your assumption of the right to suspend all the constitutional guarantees of personal liberty, and even of the freedom of speech and of the press, because the summary remedy of *habeas corpus* may be suspended, is at once startling and alarming to all persons desirous of preserving free government in this country.

The inquiry of the undersigned, whether "you hold the rights of every man throughout this vast country, in time of invasion or insurrection, are subject to be *annulled* whenever *you may say* that *you* consider the public safety requires it?" was a plain question, undisguised by circumlocution, and intended simply to elicit information. Your affirmative answer to this question throws a shade upon the fondest anticipations of the framers of the Constitution, who flattered themselves that they had provided safeguards against the dangers which have ever beset and overthrown free government in other ages and countries. Your answer is not to be disguised by the phraseology that the question "is simply a question who shall decide, or an affirmation that nobody shall decide, what the public safety does require in case of rebellion or invasion." Our Government was designed to be a Government of *law, settled* and *defined*, and not of the arbitrary will of a single man. As a safeguard, the powers were delegated to the legislative, executive, and judicial branches of the Government, and each made co-ordinate with the others, and supreme within its sphere, and thus a mutual check upon each other in case of abuse of power.

It has been the boast of the American people that they had a *written Constitution*, not only expressly *defining*, but also *limiting* the powers of the Government, and providing effectual safeguards for personal liberty, security, and property. And, to make the matter more positive and explicit, it was provided by the amendatory articles nine and ten that "the *enumeration* in the Constitution of *certain rights* shall not be construed to *deny* or *disparage* others retained by the people," and that "the powers not delegated to the United States by the Constitution, nor prohibited by it to the States, are reserved to the States respectively or to the people." With this care and precaution on the part of our forefathers who framed our institutions, it was not to be expected that, at so early a day as this, a claim of the President to arbitrary power, limited only by his conception of the requirements of the public safety, would have been asserted. In derogation of the constitutional provisions making the President strictly an executive officer, and vesting all the delegated legislative powers in Congress, your position, as we understand it, would *make your will the rule of action*, and your declaration of the requirements of the public safety the law of the land. Our inquiry was not, therefore, "simply a question *who* shall decide, or the affirmation that *nobody* shall decide, what the public safety requires." Our Government is a Government of *law*, and it is the *law-making power* which ascertains what the public safety requires, and prescribes the rule of action; and the duty of the President is simply to execute the laws thus enacted, and not *to make or annul laws*. If any exigency shall arise, the President has the power to convene Congress at any time to provide for it; so that the plea of necessity furnishes no reasonable pretext for any assumption of legislative power.

For a moment contemplate the consequences of such a claim to power. Not only would the dominion of the President be absolute over the rights of individuals, but equally so over the other departments of the Government. If he should claim that the public safety required it, he could arrest and imprison a judge for the conscientious dischage of his duties, paralyze the judicial power, or supercede it by the substitution of courts-martial, subject to *his own will*, throughout the whole country. If any one of the States, even far removed from the rebellion, should not sustain his plan for prosecuting the war, he could, on the plea of public safety, annul and set at defiance the State laws and authorities, arrest and imprison the Governor of the State or the members of the Legislature, while in the faithful discharge of their duties, or he could absolutely control the action, either of Congress or of the Supreme Court, by arresting and imprisoning its members, and upon the same ground he could suspend the elective franchise, postpone the elections, and declare the perpetuity of his high prerogative. And neither the power of impeachment nor the elections of the people could be made available against such concentration of power.

Surely it is not necessary to subvert free government in this country in order to put down the rebellion; and it *cannot be done* under *the pretence* of putting down the rebellion. Indeed, it is plain that your Administration has been weakened, and greatly weakened, by the assumption of power not delegated in the Constitution.

In your answer you say to us: "You claim that men may, if they choose, embarras those whose duty it is to combat a giant rebellion and then be dealt with in terms as if there were no rebellion." You will find yourself in fault, if your will search our communication to you for any such idea. The undersigned believe that the Constitution and laws of the land, properly administered, furnish ample power to put down an insurrection without the assumption of powers not granted. And if existing legislation be inadequate, it is the duty of Congress to consider what further legislation is necessary, and to make suitable provision by law.

You claim that the military arrests made by your Administration are merely *preventive remedies*, "as injunctions to stay injury, or proceedings to keep the peace, and *not for punishment*." The *ordinary* preventive remedies alluded to are authorized by established law, but the preventive proceedings you institute have their authority merely in the will of the Executive or that of officers subordinate to his authority. And in this proceeding a discretion seems to be exercised as to whether the prisoner shall be allowed a trial or even be permitted to know the nature of the complaint alleged against him, or the name of his accuser. If the proceedings be merely preventive, why not allow the prisoner the benefit of a bond to keep the peace? But if no offence has been committed, why was Mr. Vallandigham tried, convicted, and sentenced by a court-martial? And why the actual punishment by imprisonment or banishment, without the opportunity of obtaining his liberty in the mode usual in preventive remedies, and yet say it is not for punishment?

You still place Mr. Vallandigham's conviction and banishment upon the ground that he had damaged the military service by discouraging enlistments and encouraging desertions, &c., and yet you have not even pretended to controvert our position that he was not charged with, tried, or convicted for any such offence before the court-martial.

In answer to our position that Mr. Vallandigham was entitled to a trial in the civil tribunals, by virtue of the late acts of Congress you say: "*I certainly do not know that Mr. Vallandigham has specifically and by direct language advised against enlistments and in favor of desertions and resistance to drafting,*" &c., and yet, in a subsequent part of your answer, after speaking of certain disturbances which are alleged to have occurred in resistance of the arrest of deserters and of the enrollment preparatory to the draft, and which you attribute mainly to the course Mr. Vallandigham has pursued, you say that he has made speeches against the war in the midst of resistance to it; that "he has never been known, in any instance, to counsel against such resistance;" and that "*it is next to impossible to repel the inference that he has counselled directly in favor of it.*" Permit us to say that your information is most grievously at fault.

The undersigned have been in the habit of hearing Mr. Vallandigham speak before popular assemblages, and they appeal with confidence to every truthful person who has ever heard him for the accuracy of the declaration, that he has never made a speech before the people of Ohio in which he has not counselled submission and obedience to the laws and the Constitution, and advised the peaceful remedies of the judicial tribunals and of the ballot-box for the redress of grievances and for the evils which afflict our bleeding and suffering country. And, were it not foreign to the purposes of this communication, we would undertake to establish to the satisfaction of any candid person that the disturbances among the people to which you allude, in opposition to the arrest of deserters and the draft, have been occasioned mainly by the measures, policy, and conduct of your Administration, and the course of its political friends. But if the circumstantial evidence exists, to which you allude, which makes "it next to impossible to repel the inference that Mr. Vallandigham has counselled directly in favor" of this resistance, and that the same has been mainly attributable to his conduct, why was he not turned over to the civil authorities to be tried under the late acts of Congress? If there be any foundation in fact for your statements implicating him in resistance to the constituted authorities, he is liable to such prosecution. And we now demand, as a mere act of justice to him, an investigation of this matter before a jury of his country; and respectfully insist that fairness requires either that you retract these charges which you make against him, or that you revoke your order of banishment and allow him the opportunity of an investigation before an impartial jury.

The committee do not deem it necessary to repel at length the imputation that the attitude of themselves or of the Democratic party in Ohio "encourage desertions, resistance to the draft, and the like." Suggestions of that kind are not unusual weapons in our ordinary political contests. They rise readily in the minds of politicians heated with the excitement of partisan strife. During the two years in which the Democratic party of Ohio has been constrained to oppose the policy of the Administration, and to stand up in defence of the Constitution and of personal rights, this charge has been repeatedly made. It has fallen harmless, however, at the feet of those whom it was intended to injure. The committee believe it will do so again. If it were proper to do so in this paper, they might suggest that the measures of the Administration, and its changes of policy in the prosecution of the war, have been the fruitful sources of discouraging enlistments and inducing desertions, and furnish a reason for the undeniable fact that the first call for volunteers was answered by very many more than were demanded, and that the next call for soldiers will probably be responded to by drafted men alone.

The observation of the President in this connection, that neither the Convention in its resolutions, nor the committee in its communication, intimate that they "are conscious of an existing rebellion being in progress with the avowed object of destroying the Union," needs, perhaps, no reply. The Democratic party of Ohio has felt so keenly the condition of the country, and been so stricken to the heart by the misfortunes and sorrows which have befallen it, that they hardly deemed it necessary by solemn resolution, when their very State exhibited everywhere the sad evidences of war, to remind the President that they were aware of its existence.

In the conclusion of your communication you propose that, if a majority of the committee shall affix their signatures to a duplicate copy of it, which you have furnished, they shall stand committed to three propositions, therein at length set forth, that he will publish the names thus signed, and that this publication shall operate as a revocation of the order of banishment. The committee cannot refrain from the expression of their surprise that the President should make the fate of Mr. Vallandigham depend upon the opinion of this committee upon these propositions. If the arrest and banishment were legal, and were deserved; if the President exercised a power clearly delegated, under circumstances which warranted its exercise, the order ought not to be revoked, merely because the committee hold, or express, opinions accordant with those of the President. If the arrest and banishment were not legal, or were not deserved by Mr. Vallandigham, then surely he is entitled to an immediate and unconditional discharge.

The people of Ohio were not so deeply moved by the action of the President merely because they were concerned for the personal safety and convenience of Mr. Vallandigham, but because they saw in his arrest and banishment an attack upon their own personal rights; and they attach value to his discharge chiefly as it will indicate an abandonment of the claim to the power of such arrest and banishment. However just the undersigned might regard the principles contained in the several propositions submitted by the President, or how much soever they might, under other circumstances, feel inclined to indorse the sentiments contained therein, yet they assure him that they have not been authorized to enter into any bargains, terms, contracts, or conditions with the President of the United States to procure the release of Mr. Vallandigham. The opinions of the undersigned touching the questions involved in these propositions are well known, have been many times publicly expressed, and are sufficiently manifested in the resolutions of the convention which they represent, and they cannot suppose that the President expects that they will seek the discharge of Mr. Vallandigham by a pledge implying not only an imputation upon their own *sincerity and fidelity* as citizens of the United States, and also carrying with it by implication a concession of *the legality* of his arrest, trial, and banishment, against which they and the convention they represent have solemnly protested. And, while they have asked the revocation of the order of banishment not as a favor, but as a *right* due to the people of Ohio, and with a view to avoid the possibility of conflict or disturbance of the public tranquillity, they do not do this, nor does Mr. Vallandigham desire it, at any sacrifice of their dignity and self-respect.

The idea that such a pledge as that asked from the undersigned would secure the public safety sufficiently to compensate for any mistake of the President in discharging Mr. Vallandigham is, in their opinion, a mere evasion of the grave questions involved in this discussion, and of a direct answer to their demand. And this is made especially apparent by the fact that this pledge is asked in a communication which concludes with an intimation of a disposition on the part of the President to repeat the acts complained of.

The undersigned, therefore, having fully discharged the duty enjoined upon them, leave the responsibility with the President.

M. BIRCHARD, 19*th Dist., Chairman.*
DAVID HOUK, *Sec'y*, 3*d Dist.*
GEO. BLISS, 14*th Dist.*
T. W. BARTLEY, 8*th Dist.*
W. J. GORDON, 18*th Dist.*
JOHN O'NEILL, 13*th Dist.*
C. A. WHITE, 6*th Dist.*
W. E. FINCK, 12*th Dist.*
ALEXANDER LONG, 2*d Dist.*
JAS. R. MORRIS, 15*th Dist.*
GEO. S. CONVERSE, 7*th Dist.*
GEO. H. PENDLETON, 1*st Dist.*
W. A. HUTCHINS, 11*th Dist.*
A. L. BACKUS, 10*th Dist.*
J. F. McKINNEY, 4*th Dist.*
J. W. WHITE, 16*th Dist.*
F. C. LEBLOND, 5*th Dist.*
LOUIS SCHÆFFER, 17*th Dist.*
WARREN P. NOBLE, 9*th Dist.*

The Case before the United States Supreme Court.

WASHINGTON, *February* 15, 1864.

The case of Mr. Vallandigham, *ex parte*, was decided in the Supreme Court of the United States to-day. The petitioner asked that the writ of *certiorari* be directed to the Judge Advocate General for a revision of the proceedings of the Military Commission which tried him, the jurisdiction of which was denied as extending to the case of a civilian, and the object being to have the sentence annulled, on the ground of illegality. The Judge Advocate, Col. Holt, had responded in a written argument that the Court might with as much propriety be called upon to restrain, by injunction, the proceedings of Congress, as to revise by *certiorari* and reverse the proceedings of the military authority in time of war in the punishment of all military offences, according to the usages of civilized nations and the power given by the Constitution and laws of the United States for the common defence and public safety.

Justice Wayne to-day delivered the opinion of the Court, refusing the writ, on the ground that even if the arrest, trial, and punishment of Vallandigham were illegal, there is no authority in the Court to grant relief in this mode, and that there is no law by which any appeal or proceedings in the nature of an appeal from a Military Commission to the Supreme Court can be taken.

His Letter on "Retaliation."

WINDSOR, C. W., *March* 7, 1864.

MESSRS. HUBBARD AND BROTHER, *Dayton, Ohio:*

GENTLEMEN: I read, several days ago, the telegraphic announcement of the "riddling" of the *Empire* office by "furloughed soldiers." I offer you no sympathy, for that will avail nothing now or hereafter. I do express to you my profound regret that you were not prepared to inflict on the spot, and in the midst of the assault, the complete punishment which the assailants deserved; but am gratified to learn that some of them did soon after receive their deserts. But these cowardly acts cannot always be guarded against. And they do not primarily come from the "soldiers." There is, therefore, but one remedy for past and preventive of future injuries; and that is, instant, summary, and ample reprisals upon the persons and property of the men at home who, by language and conduct, are always exciting these outrages.

No legal nor military punishment is ever inflicted upon the immediate instruments. Retaliation, therefore, is the only and rightful remedy in times like these. I speak advisedly, and recommend it in all cases hereafter. It is of no avail to announce the falsehood that "both parties condemn it," *after* the destruction has been consummated. The time has gone by for obedience without protection. I speak decided language; but the continual recurrence of these outrages—frequently attended with murder, and always without redress—demands it. They must be stopped, let the consequences be what they may. Reprisals in such cases are now the only way left for a return to law and order.

Very truly, C. L. VALLANDIGHAM.

Mr. Vallandigham's Return and Address.

1864, June 15—Mr. Vallandigham returned to Ohio, and that day addressed the Democratic Convention at Hamilton, Ohio, as follows:

MEN OF OHIO: To-day I am again in your midst and upon the soil of my native State. To-day I am once more within the district which for ten years extended to me the highest confidence, and three times honored me as its Representative in the Congress of the United States. I was accused of no crime against the Constitution or laws, and guilty of none. But whenever and wherever thus charged upon due process of law, I am now here ready to answer before any civil court of competent jurisdiction, to a jury of my countrymen, and in the meantime to give bail in any sum which any judge or court, State or Federal, may affix, and you, the 186,000 Democrats of Ohio, I offer as my sureties.

Never for one hour have I remained in exile because I recognized any obligation of obedience to the unconstitutional and arbitrary edict. Neither did personal fear ever restrain me. And to-day I return of my own act and pleasure, because it is my constitutional and legal right to return. Only by an exertion of arbitrary power, itself against the Constitution and law, and consummated by military force, I was abducted from my home and forced into banishment. The assertion or insinuation of the President that I was arrested "because laboring, with some effect, to prevent the raising of troops, and to encourage desertions from the army," and was responsible for numerous acts of resistance to the draft and to the arrest of deserters, causing "assassination, maiming, and murder," or that at any time, in any way, I had disobeyed or failed to counsel obedience to the lawful authority, or even to the semblance of law, is absolutely false.

I appeal for the proof to every speech I ever made upon those questions, and to the very record of the mock Military Commission by the trial and sentence of which I was outraged. No; the sole offence then laid to my charge was words of criticism of the public policy of the Administration, addressed to open and public political meetings of my fellow-citizens of Ohio, lawfully and peaceably assembled. And to-day, my only "crime" is, that in the way which they call treason, worship I the Constitution of my fathers. But for now more than one year, no public man has been arrested, and no newspaper suppressed within the States adhering still to the Union, for the expression of political opinion; while hundreds, in public assembly and through the press, have, with a license and violence in which I never indulged, criticised and condemned the acts and policies of the Administration, and denounced the war, maintaining even the propriety and necessity of the recognition of southern independence.

Indorsed by nearly two hundred thousand freemen of the Democratic party of my native State at the late elections, and still with the sympathy and support of millions more, I do not mean any longer to be the only man of that party who is to be the victim of arbitrary power. If Abraham Lincoln seeks my life, let him so declare; but he shall not again restrain me of my personal liberty except upon "due process of law." The unconstitutional and monstrous "Order 38," under which alone I was arrested thirteen months ago, was defied and spit upon at your State convention of 1863, by the gallant gentleman who bore the standard as your candidate for Lieutenant Governor, and by every Democratic press and public speaker ever since. It is dead. From the first it was against the Constitution and laws, and without validity; and all proceedings under it were and are utterly null and void and of no effect.

The indignant voice of condemnation long since went forth from the vast majority of the people and presses of America and from all free countries in Europe with entire unanimity. And more recently, too, the "platform" of an earnest, numerous, and most formidable Convention of the sincere Republicans, and still further, the emphatic letter of acceptance by the candidate of that Convention, Gen. John C. Fremont, the first candidate also of the Republican party for the Presidency eight years ago, upon the rallying cry of "Free speech and a free Press," give renenewed hope that at last the reign of arbitrary power is about to be brought to an end in the United States. It is neither just nor fit, therefore, that the wrongs inflicted under "Order 38," and the other edicts and acts of such power, should be any longer endured—certainly not by me alone.

But every ordinary means of redress has first been exhausted; yet either by the direct agency of the Administration and its subordinates, or through its influence or intimidation, or because of want of jurisdiction in the civil courts which no American in former times conceived to be possible here, all have failed. Counsel applied in my behalf to an unjust judge for the writ of *habeas corpus*. It was denied; and now the privilege of that writ is suspended by act of Congress and Executive order in every State. The Democratic Convention of Ohio, one year ago, by a resolution formally presented through a committee of your best and ablest men in person, at Washington, demanded of the President, in behalf of a very large minority of the people, a revocation of the edict of banishment.

Pretending that the public safety then required it, he refused; saying, at the same time, that "it would afford him pleasure to comply as soon as he could by any means be made to believe that the public safety would not suffer by it." One year has elapsed, yet this hollow pretence is still tacitly asserted, and to-day I am here to prove it unfounded in fact. I appealed to the Supreme Court of the United States; and because Congress had never conferred jurisdiction in behalf of a citizen tried by a tribunal unknown for such purpose, to the laws, and expressly forbidden by the Constitution, it was powerless to redress the wrong. The time has, therefore, arrived, when it becomes me as a citizen of Ohio and of the United States, to demand, and, by my own act, to vindicate the rights, liberties, and privileges which I never forfeited, but of which, for so many months, I have been deprived.

Wherefore, men of Ohio, I am again in your midst to-day. I owe duties to the State, and am here to discharge them. I have rights as a citizen, and am here to assert them; a wife, and child, and home, and would enjoy all the pleasures which are implied in those cheerful words. But I am here for peace, not disturbance; for quiet not convulsion; for order and law, not anarchy. Let no man of the Democratic party begin any act of violence or disorder; but let none shrink from any responsibility, however urgent, if forced upon him. Careful of the rights of others, let him see to it that he fully and fearlessly exacts his own. Subject to rightful authority in all things, let him submit to excess or usurpation in nothing. Obedient to the Constitution and law, let him demand and have the full measure of protection which law and Constitution secure to him.

Men of Ohio: You have already vindicated your right to *hear;* it is now my duty to assert my right to *speak.* Wherefore, as to the sole offence for which I was arrested, imprisoned, and banished—free speech in criticism and condemnation of the Administration—an Administration fitly described in a recent public paper by one of its early supporters, "marked at home by disregard of constitutional rights, by its violation of personal liberty and the liberty of the press, and, as its crowning shame, by its abandonment of the right of asylum, a right especially dear to all free nations abroad," I repeat it here to-day, and will again and yet again so long as I live, or the Constitution and our present form of Government shall survive.

The words then spoken and the appeal at that time made, and now enforced by one year more of taxation and debt, and of blood and disaster, entreating the people to change the public servants and their policy, not by force, but peaceably, through the ballot, I now and here reiterate in their utmost extent, and with all their significancy I repeat them, one and all, in no spirit of challenge or bravado, but as earnest, sober, solemn truth and warning to the people.

Upon another subject allow me here a word:

A powerful, widely-spread and very dangerous secret, oath-bound combination among the friends of the Administration, known as the "Loyal Union League," exists in every State, yet the very men who control it charge persistently upon the members of the Democratic party, that they have organized—especially in the North West—the "Order of Knights of the Golden Circle," or some other secret society, treasonable or "disloyal" in its character, affiliated with the South, and for the purpose of armed resistance to the Federal and State Governments. Whether any such ever existed I do not know; but the charge that organizations of that sort, or having any such purpose, do now exist among members of that party in Ohio or other non-slaveholding States, is totally and positively false.

That lawful political or party associations have been established, having, as their object, the organizing and strengthening of the Democratic party, and its success in the coming Presidential election, and designed as a counter-movement to the so-called "Union Leagues," and, therefore, secret in their proceedings, is very probable, and however objectionable hitherto, and in ordinary times, I recognize to the fullest extent, not the lawfulness only, but the propriety and necessity of such organizations—for "when bad men combine good men must associate." But they are no conspiracy against the Government, and their members are not conspirators, but patriots; men not leagued together for the overthrow of the Constitution or the laws, and still less, of liberty, but firmly united for the preservation and support of these great objects.

There is, indeed, a "conspiracy" very powerful, very ancient, and I trust that before long I may add, strongly consolidated also, upon sound principles, and destined yet to be triumphant—a conspiracy known as the Democratic party, the present object of which is the overthrow of the Administration in November next, not by force but through the ballot-box, the election of a President who shall be true to his oath, to Liberty and the Constitution. This is the sole conspiracy of which I know anything; and I am proud to be one of the conspirators. If any other exist, looking to unlawful armed resistance to the Federal State authorities anywhere, in the exercise of their legal and constitutional rights, I admonish all persons concerned, that the act is treason, and the penalty death.

But I warn also the men in power that there is a vast multitude, a host whom they cannot number, bound together by the strongest and holiest ties, to defend, by whatever means the exigencies of the times shall demand, their natural and constitutional rights as freemen, at all hazards and to the last extremity.

Three years have now passed, men of Ohio, and the great issue—constitutional liberty and free popular government—is still before you. To you I again commit it, confident that in this, the time of their greatest peril, you will be found worthy of the ancestors who for so many ages, in England and America, on the field, in prison, and upon the scaffold, defended them against tyrants and usurpers, whether in councils or in arms.

June 17—He is reported to have thus spoken in response to a serenade, in Dayton:

MY FRIENDS: I greet you to-night as you greet me, and I can truly say, that from this demonstration it is evident you are determined to support those principles which I have advocated and have suffered for. To me, this demonstration was unexpected, and I appear only to make my renewed acknowledgment to you for this continued expression of kindly feeling.

He would make no threats, but he did not come from a foreign country without a deliberate calculation of the cause and the consequences, *and a deliberate preparation to meet them.* He could be taken by any due civil process, by any crippled constable, but without that no force could do it. Three hundred men, armed to the teeth, would not again find him in his house after the door had been buttoned down, but they would *find him the next day and not far off,* [immense cheers,] and if any military commander of the President were to undertake such an arrest he warned them that in this town the persons and property of those instigating such a proceeding would be held as hostage. He should urge an eye for an eye, and a tooth for a tooth, so help him ever living Jehovah.

He appeared, not to speak upon questions of politics, he said, nor to add to what he had said the day before.

He had come, he said, for the purpose of living at home with the wife of his bosom and his child, to live in his own home from which he had been torn thirteen months before, and to receive in quiet the calls of his friends. He did not *expect* to be again molested unless by men in this city, and the former scenes revived. "If this be done," he said, "*I warn them that the result will be such as compared to it, the other was but dust in the scale.*"

He then reviewed his personal and political history, defying any person to show wherein he had merited the treatment he had received. He again repeated that he desired no disturbance, and believed there would be none. He did not believe there would be any attempt to arrest him again, but should there be, he repeated his warning, not, as he said, in a spirit of bravado, but to let his friends know that he and his friends were prepared for any emergency. This he several times repeated.

He then announced his intention of keeping his mouth closed until after the Democratic Convention at Chicago, when he would make his purpose known.

CINCINNATI, *June* 17.

A despatch from Dayton to the *Commercial* says: "There is but little doubt that Vallandigham's arrival was unexpected to his friends. His house was open yesterday and a large number of his friends called on him."

Vallandigham's Return.

A Washington dispatch to the *New York Herald* says: "A key to the policy of the President to be pursued toward Vallandigham has been recently given in a meeting between the Kentucky delegation in Congress and Mr. Lincoln relative to the case of Colonel Wolford. This officer, it will be remembered, was arrested by General Burbridge and sent to Washington, where he has since remained, reporting daily to the War Department. In answer to the request that the order of General Burbridge be rescinded, the President replied that he should not depart from the policy before pursued concerning Vallandigham. Mr. Mallory remarked that the Vallandigham order was inoperative, that individual having returned to Ohio. Mr. Lincoln replied, in substance, that he had no official knowledge of Vallandigham's return, and that when Mr. Vallandigham made his presence known by objectionable acts, the Executive would be prepared to act. The application in favor of Colonel Wolford was not granted."

SUSPENSION OF THE WRIT OF HABEAS CORPUS.

1861.

April 27—The PRESIDENT issued to Lieut. General Scott this order:

You are engaged in suppressing an insurrection against the laws of the United States. If at any point on or in the vicinity of any military line which is now or which shall be used between the city of Philadelphia and the city of Washington, you find resistance which renders it necessary to suspend the writ of *habeas corpus* for the public safety, you personally, or through the officer in command, at the point at which resistance occurs, are authorized to suspend that writ. ABRAHAM LINCOLN.

By the President:
WM. H. SEWARD, *Secretary of State.*

July 2—This order was extended to the military line between New York and Washington.

May 10—The PRESIDENT issued a proclamation authorizing the commander of the forces of the United States on the Florida coast, "if he shall find it necessary, to suspend there the writ of *habeas corpus*, and to remove from the vicinity of the United States fortresses all dangerous or suspected persons."

1862.

WASHINGTON, *September* 24.

Whereas, it has become necessary to call into service, not only volunteers, but also portions of the militia of the State by draft, in order to suppress the insurrection existing in the United States, and disloyal persons are not adequately restrained by the ordinary processes of law from hindering this measure, and from giving aid and comfort in various ways to the insurrection:

Now, therefore, be it ordered:

First. That during the existing insurrection, and as a necessary measure for suppressing the same, all rebels and insurgents, their aiders and abettors, within the United States, and all persons discouraging volunteer enlistments, resisting military drafts, or guilty of any disloyal practice affording aid and comfort to the rebels against the authority of the United States, shall be subject to martial law, and liable to trial and punishment by courts-martial or military commission.

Second. That the writ of *habeas corpus* is suspended in respect to all persons arrested, or who are now, or hereafter during the rebellion shall be, imprisoned in any fort, camp, arsenal, military prison, or other place of confinement, by any military authority, or by the sentence of any court-martial or military commission.

In witness whereof, I have hereunto set my hand and caused the seal of the United States to be affixed.

Done at the city of Washington, this twenty-fourth day of September, in the year of our Lord one thousand eight hundred and sixty-two, and of the independence of the United States the eighty-seventh.

ABRAHAM LINCOLN.

By the President:
WM. H. SEWARD, *Secretary of State.*

1863.

GENERAL SUSPENSION OF THE WRIT.

Whereas the Constitution of the United States has ordained that the privilege of the writ of *habeas corpus* shall not be suspended unless when in cases of rebellion or invasion the public safety may require it; and whereas, a rebellion was existing on the 3d day of March, 1863, which rebellion is still existing: and whereas by a statute which was approved on that day it was enacted by the Senate and House of Representatives of the United States in Congress assembled, that during the present insurrection the President of the United States, whenever in his judgment the public safety may require, is authorized to suspend the privilege of the writ of *habeas corpus* in any case throughout the United States, or any part thereof; and whereas in the judgment of the President the public safety does require that the privilege of the said writ shall now be suspended throughout the United States in the cases where, by the authority of the President of the United States, military, naval, and civil officers of the United States, or any of them, hold persons under their command or in their custody either as prisoners of war, spies, or aiders or abettors of the enemy, or officers, soldiers, or seamen enrolled or drafted or mustered or enlisted in or belonging to the land or naval forces of the United States, or as deserters therefrom, or otherwise amenable to the military law or the Rules and Articles of War, or the rules or regulations prescribed for the military or naval services by authority of the President of the United States, or for resisting a draft, or for any other offence against the military or naval service:

Now, therefore, I, ABRAHAM LINCOLN, President of the United States, do hereby proclaim and make known to all whom it may concern, that the privilege of the writ of *habeas corpus* is suspended throughout the United States in the several cases before mentioned, and that this suspension will continue throughout the duration of the said rebellion, or until this proclamation shall, by a subsequent one to be issued by the President of the United States, be modified or revoked. And I do hereby require all magistrates, attorneys, and other civil officers within the United States, and all officers and others in the military and naval services of the United States, to take distinct notice of this suspension, and to give it full effect, and all citizens of the United States to conduct and govern themselves accordingly and in conformity with the Constitution of the United States and the laws of Congress in such case made and provided.

In testimony whereof, I have hereunto set my hand and caused the seal of the United States to be affixed, this 15th day of September, 1863, and the independence of the United States of America the eighty-eighth.

ABRAHAM LINCOLN.

By the President:

WM. H. SEWARD, *Secretary of State.*

1864.

SUSPENSION OF THE WRIT IN KENTUCKY.

Whereas, by a proclamation which was issued on the 15th day of April, 1861, the President of the United States announced and declared that the laws of the United States had been for some time past, and then were, opposed and the execution thereof obstructed, in certain States therein mentioned, by combinations too powerful to be suppressed by the ordinary course of judicial proceedings, or by the powers vested in the marshals by law; and whereas, immediately after the issuing of the said proclamation, the land and naval forces of the United States were put into activity to suppress the said insurrection and rebellion; and whereas the Congress of the United States, by an act approved on the 3d day of March, 1863, did enact that during the said rebellion the President of the United States, whenever in his judgment the public safety may require it, is authorized to suspend the privilege of the writ of *habeas corpus* in any case throughout the United States, or in any part thereof; and whereas the said insurrection and rebellion still continue, endangering the existence of the Constitution and Government of the United States; and whereas the military forces of the United States are now actively engaged in suppressing the said insurrection and rebellion in various parts of the States where the said rebellion has been successful in obstructing the laws and public authorities, especially in the States of Virginia and Georgia;

And whereas, on the fifteenth day of September last, the President of the United States duly issued his proclamation, wherein he declared that the privilege of the writ of *habeas corpus* should be suspended throughout the United States in cases where, by the authority of the President of the United States, military, naval, and civil officers of the United States, or any of them, hold persons under their command or in their custody, either as prisoners of war, spies, or aiders or abettors of the enemy, or officers, soldiers, or seamen enrolled or drafted or mustered or enlisted in or belonging to the land or naval forces of the United States or as deserters therefrom, or otherwise amenable to military law or the rules and articles of war, or the rules or regulations prescribed for the military or naval service by authority of the President of the United States, or for resisting a draft, or for any other offence against the military or naval service;

And whereas many citizens of the State of Kentucky have joined the forces of the insurgents, and such insurgents have on several occasions entered the said State of Kentucky in large force, and, not without aid and comfort furnished by disaffected and disloyal citizens of the United States residing therein, have not only greatly disturbed the public peace, but have overborne the civil authorities and made flagrant civil war, destroying property and life in various parts of that State;

And whereas it has been made known to the President of the United States by the officers commanding the national armies that combinations have been formed in the said State of Kentucky with a purpose of inciting rebel forces to renew the said operations of civil war within the said State, and thereby to embarass the United States armies now operating in the said States of Virginia and Georgia, and even to endanger their safety:

Now, therefore, I, ABRAHAM LINCOLN, President of the United States, by virtue of the authority vested in me by the Constitution and laws, do hereby declare that, in my judgment, the public safety especially requires that the suspension of the privilege of the writ of *habeas corpus*, so proclaimed in the said proclamation of the 15th of September, 1863, be made effectual and be duly enforced in and throughout the said State of Kentucky, and that martial law be for the present established therein. I do, therefore, hereby require of the military officers in the said State that the privileges of the writ of *habeas corpus* be effectually suspended within the said State, according to the aforesaid proclamation, and that martial law be established therein, to take effect from the date of this proclamation, the said suspension and establishment of martial law to continue until this proclamation shall be revoked or modified, but not beyond the period when the said rebellion shall have been suppressed or come to an end. And I do hereby require and command, as well all military officers as all civil officers and authorities existing or found within the said State of Kentucky, to take notice of this proclamation and to give full effect to the same.

The martial law herein proclaimed, and the things in that respect herein ordered, will not be deemed or taken to interfere with the holding of lawful elections, or with the proceedings of the constitutional Legislature of Kentucky, or with the administration of justice in the courts of law existing therein between citizens of the United States in suits or proceedings which do not affect the military operations or the constituted authorities of the Government of the United States.

In testimony whereof I have hereunto set my hand and caused the seal of the United States to be affixed.

Done at the city of Washington, this 5th day of July, in the year of our Lord, 1864, and of the independence of the United States the eighty-ninth.

ABRAHAM LINCOLN.

By the President:

WILLIAM H. SEWARD, *Secretary of State.*

The Military Governors, appointed by the

President, were clothed with like power. This is the letter of appointment:

WAR DEPARTMENT,
WASHINGTON CITY, D. C., *May* 19, 1862.

SIR: You are hereby appointed military governor of the State of North Carolina, with authority to exercise and perform within the limits of that State all and singular the powers, duties, and functions pertaining to the office of military governor, (including the power to establish all necessary offices and tribunals, and suspend the writ of *habeas corpus*,) during the pleasure of the President, or until the loyal inhabitants of that State shall organize a civil government in conformity with the Constitution of the United States. EDWIN M. STANTON,
Secretary of War.

NOTE.—Major General McCLELLAN authorized General BANKS to suspend the writ of *habeas corpus*, if necessary in carrying out the instructions of the former for the arrest of certain members of the Maryland Legislature in October, 1861. (See "Military Orders respecting Elections.")

ACTION OF CONGRESS.

First Session, Thirty-Seventh Congress.

IN SENATE.

1861, July 29—Mr. TRUMBULL, from the Committee on the Judiciary, reported back the memorial of Charles Howard and others, Police Commissioners of Baltimore, arrested and confined as prisoners in Fort McHenry, and asked to be discharged from the subject, the Committee being of opinion that no legislation by Congress is practicable with reference to the matter set forth in the memorial.*

Mr. BAYARD proposed to amend the report by substituting:

Resolved, That the members of the police board of the city of Baltimore ought to be either surrendered to the civil authorities on some charge sufficient in law for their arrest and detention, or be discharged from confinement at Fort McHenry, and suffered to resume their official functions.

Resolved, That the control of the municipal police of Baltimore ought to be restored to those civil officers to whom, by the laws of Maryland, it is intrusted.

Resolved, That George P. Kane, marshal of police in the city of Baltimore, ought either to be delivered up to the civil authorities on some charge sufficient in law to hold him in custody, or be discharged from confinement in Fort McHenry.

The subject was postponed.

Aug. 6—Mr. POWELL proposed in the Senate a resolution similar to Mr. May's in the House, but the motion to take it up was lost—yeas 7, nays 33. The seven were Messrs. *Breckinridge*, *Bright*, *Johnson* of Missouri, *Latham*, *Polk*, *Powell*, *Saulsbury*.

IN HOUSE.

1861, July 31—Mr. MAY offered this resolution:

Whereas the Constitution of the United States declares that no warrant shall issue but upon probable cause, supported by oath or affirmation; that no citizen shall be deprived of his liberty without due process of law; and that the accused shall enjoy the right of a speedy trial by a jury of the district where the offence was committed: and whereas Charles Howard, William H. Gatchell, and John W. Davis, citizens of Baltimore, in the State of Maryland, were, on the 1st day of July, 1861, seized without warrant, and without any process of law whatever, by a body of soldiers from the Army of the United States, by order of Major General Banks, alleged to have been made in pursuance of orders issued from the headquarters of the Army at Washington, and were removed by force and against their will from their homes to Fort McHenry, where they have ever since been, and now are, confined as prisoners; and whereas the said military officer, without warrant or authority of law, superceded and suspended the official functions of the said Charles Howard and others, members of the board of police of Baltimore: and whereas, since their said arrest, a grand jury attending the United States district court in Baltimore, and selected and summoned by a marshal appointed by the present Executive of the United States, having jurisdiction in the premises, and having fully investigated all cases of alleged violation of law, has finally adjourned its session without finding any presentment or indictment or other proceeding against them, or either of them; and the President of the United States, being requested by a resolution of the House of Representatives to communicate the grounds, reasons and evidence for their arrest and imprisonment, has declined so to do, because he is advised that it is incompatible with the public interests: and whereas, since these proceedings, the said citizens, with others, have been, by force and against their wills, transferred by the authority of the Government of the United States beyond the State of Maryland and the jurisdiction of that court which it is their constitutional right to claim, and are to be subjected to an indefinite, a hopeless, and cruel imprisonment in some fort or military place, unfit for the confinement of the citizen, at a remote distance from their families and friends, and this without any accusation, investigation, or trial whatever: and whereas the constitutional privilege of the writ of *habeas corpus* has been treated with contempt, and a military officer (the predecessor of General Banks) has taken upon himself the responsibility of wilful disobedience to the writ, and the privilege of the same now continues suspended, thereby subordinating the civil to the military power, thus violating and overthrowing the Constitution of the United States, and setting up in its stead a military despotism: and whereas the Congress of the United States regards the acts aforesaid as clear and palpable violations of the Constitution of the United states, and destructive to the liberties of a free people: Therefore,

Resolved, That the arrest and imprisonment of Charles Howard, William H. Gatchell, and John W. Davis, and others, without warrant and process of law, is flagrantly unconstitutional and illegal; and they should, without delay, be released, or their case remitted to the proper judicial tribunals, to be lawfully heard and determined.

Ruled out of order under the rule regulating the business of the session.

Second Session, Thirty-Seventh Congress.

IN SENATE.

1861, Dec. 16—Mr. TRUMBULL offered the following resolution:

Resolved, That the Secretary of State be directed to inform the Senate whether, in the loyal States of the Union, any person or persons have been arrested and imprisoned, and are now held in confinement by orders from him or his Department; and if so, under what law said arrests have been made, and said persons imprisoned.

Which was referred to the Judiciary Committee—yeas 25, nays 17, as follows:

YEAS—Messrs. Anthony, Browning, Chandler, Clark, Collamer, Cowan, Dixon, Doolittle, Fessenden, Foot, Foster, Harris, Howe, *Johnson* of Tennessee, King, Lane of Indiana, Morrill, Pomeroy, *Rice*, Sherman, Simmons, Sumner, Ten Eyck, Wade, Wilson—25.

NAYS—Messrs. *Bayard*, *Bright*, *Carlile*, Grimes, Hale, Harlan, *Kennedy*, *Latham*, *McDougall*, *Nesmith*, *Pearce*, *Powell*, *Saulsbury*, *Thomson*, Trumbull, Wilkinson, Willey—17.

1861, December 23—Mr. KING offered this resolution, which was referred to the Committee on the Judiciary:

Resolved, That the President be requested to cause proceedings to be instituted in the courts of law against persons who have been arrested by executive authority or order since the breaking out of the present insurrection, and who are now detained in custody, so that a judicial examination may be had in each case to ascertain who, if any of them, may be allowed to take the oath of allegiance to the United States, and be discharged, and who shall be detained for a further examination or be prosecuted for treason or other crime; and to communicate the names of all persons that have been so arrested, and the date of arrest, to the Senate.

CASE OF GENERAL CHARLES P. STONE.

1862, April 11—Mr. McDOUGALL offered this resolution:

Resolved, That the Secretary of War be requested to inform the Senate at once on the following points, namely: 1. Whether or not Brigadier General Charles P. Stone has been arrested by any person in authority in the War Department or in the Army of the United States; and if he has been so arrested, from whom the order for General Stone's

* For further facts, see "The Conspiracy of Disunion."

arrest originally proceeded—whether the Secretary himself or the general then commanding the army of the Potomac. 2. Also, whether at the time of such arrest General Stone was not subject to the Articles of War, and entitled to the benefit of them; and if he was so subject and entitled, whether or not he was arrested for a violation of any and which of those articles; and on whose complaint General Stone was arrested, and by whom, if by any persons, charges have been preferred against him; and that the Secretary of War be requested to communicate to the Senate the specifications under such charges as fully as his present information will enable him to state them. 3. Also, whether any, and if any, what, steps have been taken toward the preparation of such charges and specifications; and if any such steps have been so taken, whether or not the prosecution of the matter has been intrusted to the judge advocate general of the Army, or of the army of the Potomac, or to some other, and what other, special judge advocate; and if not to either of said judges advocate general, why the case of General Stone did not take the customary course when a general officer is arrested, and whether or not either of the judges advocate above specially named has been, and when first, consulted in this matter. 4. Also, whether or not General Stone has at any time, and when, and how often, in person or by counsel, applied for an immediate trial; and whether he has not represented to the Secretary of War the injustice which he supposed would result to him from deferring his trial by reason of the death of important witnesses in any manner connected with the administration of his late command upon the Potomac; and what answer, if any, has been made to such representation by or on behalf of General Stone. 5. Also, whether or not the substance of said charges, more or less, has been in any, and what way, and upon whose application, communicated to General Stone; and if not, why not; and if not, whether or not General Stone has applied directly or indirectly for such charges. 6. Also, whether any, and what, privileges have inured to General Stone under the Articles of War Nos. 74, 79, 80, and 82, and Nos. 221 and 223 of the Revised Regulations of the Army, and what degree of confinement was originally ordered in reference to General Stone, and whether any and what change has been made, and when, from its original severity. 7. Also, if General Stone was not arrested for some alleged violation of the Articles of War, upon what pretence is he kept in close custody.

April 22—On motion of Mr. WILSON, the resolution was amended so as to read thus, and passed:

That the President of the United States be requested to communicate to the Senate any information touching the arrest and imprisonment of Brigadier General Stone, not deemed incompatible with the public interest.

May 2—The PRESIDENT transmitted this message in reply:

EXECUTIVE MANSION,
WASHINGTON, *May* 1, 1862.

To the SENATE OF THE UNITED STATES:

In answer to the resolution of the Senate in relation to Brigadier General Stone, I have the honor to state that he was arrested and imprisoned under my general authority, and upon evidence which, whether he be guilty or innocent, required, as appears to me, such proceedings to be had against him for the public safety. I deem it incompatible with the public interest, as also, perhaps, unjust to General Stone, to make a more particular statement of the evidence.

He has not been tried because, in the state of military operations at the time of his arrest and since, the officers to constitute a court-martial and for witnesses could not be withdrawn from duty without serious injury to the service. He will be allowed a trial without any unnecessary delay; the charges and specifications will be furnished him in due season, and every facility for his defence will be afforded him by the War Department.

ABRAHAM LINCOLN.

1862, May 14—Mr. POWELL offered the following:

Resolved, That the Secretary of State be directed to inform the Senate, how many citizens of Kentucky have been arrested and confined outside the limits of the State by his order since 1st September last, and state the names of such citizens, places where imprisoned, and how long confined, and also the number and names of persons released and where imprisoned.

Mr. SUMNER offered the following as a substitute:

Resolved, That the President of the United States be requested to communicate to the Senate, if not incompatible with the public interests, any information in his possession touching the arrest of persons in Kentucky since the 1st of September, 1861, and their imprisonment beyond the limits of that State.

Which was adopted—yeas 30, nays 7, as follows:

YEAS—Messrs. Anthony, Browning, Chandler, Clark, Collamer, Dixon, Doolittle, Fessenden, Foot, Foster, Grimes, Harlan, Harris, Howard, Howe, King, Lane of Indiana, Lane of Kansas, Morrill, Pomeroy, Sherman, Simmons, Sumner, Ten Eyck, Trumbull, Wade, Wilkinson, Wilmot, Wilson of Massachusetts, *Wright*—30.

NAYS—Messrs. *Davis, McDougall, Nesmith, Powell, Saulsbury*, Willey, *Wilson* of Missouri—7.

IN HOUSE.

1861, December 10—Mr. BINGHAM, from the Judiciary Committee, asked to be discharged from the further consideration of the memorial of Messrs. Howard, Gatchell, and Davis, Police Commissioners of Baltimore.

Mr. PENDLETON moved to recommit the report, with these instructions:

Resolved, That the Congress alone has the power, under the Constitution of the United States, to suspend the privilege of the writ of *habeas corpus*; that the exercise of that power by any other department of the Government is a usurpation, and therefore dangerous to the liberties of the people; that it is the duty of the President to deliver Charles Howard, William H. Gatchell, and John W. Davis to the custody of the marshal of the proper district, if they are charged with any offence against the laws of the United States, to the end that they may be indicted, and "enjoy the right of a speedy and public trial by an impartial jury of the State and district wherein the crime" is alleged to have been committed.

Mr. BINGHAM moved to lay the whole subject on the table, which was agreed to—yeas 108, nays 26, as follows:

YEAS—Messrs. Aldrich, Alley, Arnold, Babbitt, Goldsmith F. Bailey, Baker, Baxter, Beaman, Bingham, Francis P. Blair, Jacob B. Blair, Samuel S. Blair, Blake, Buffinton, Burnham, *Calvert*, Campbell, Chamberlain, Clark, *Cobb*, Colfax, Frederick A. Conkling, Roscoe Conkling, *Cravens*, Davis, Dawes, Delano, Diven, Duell, *Dunlap*, Dunn, Edgerton, Edwards, Eliot, *English*, Fenton, Fessenden, Franchot, Frank, Goodwin, Granger, *Grider, Haight*, Hale, Hanchett, Harrison, *Holman*, Hooper, Horton, Hutchins, Julian, Kelley, Francis W. Kellogg, William Kellogg, Killinger, Lansing, *Law*, Loomis, Lovejoy, McPherson, *Mallory*, Maynard, *Menzies*, Moorhead, Anson P. Morrill, Justin S. Morrill, Nixon, *Noell*, Olin, Patton, T. G. Phelps, Pike, Pomeroy, Porter, Potter, Alexander H. Rice, Riddle, Edward H. Rollins, Sargent, Sedgwick, Shanks, *Sheffield*, Shellabarger, Sherman, Sloan. *Smith*, Stevens, Stratton, Benjamin F. Thomas, Francis Thomas, Train, Trimble, Trowbridge, Upton, Van Horn, Van Wyck, Verree, Wall, Wallace, Charles W. Walton, E. P. Walton, Washburne, Wheeler, Albert S. White, Wilson, *Woodruff*, Worcester, *Wright*—108.

NAYS—Messrs. *Allen, Ancona, Joseph Baily, Biddle, George H. Browne*, William G. Brown, *Cooper, Fouke, Harding, Johnson, Lazear, May, Morris, Noble, Norton, Pendleton, Perry, Robinson, Shiel, John B. Steele, William G. Steele, Vallandigham, Wadsworth, Ward, Chilton A. White, Wickliffe*—26.

Third Session, Thirty-Seventh Congress.

IN SENATE.

1862, December 2—Mr. POWELL, offered the following resolution:

Resolved, That the President be requested to inform the Senate the number and the names of citizens of Kentucky who have been, and who are now confined in the military prisons and camps of the United States, outside the limits of said State; what are the charges against them, by whom made, and by whose order the arrests were made.

December 5—Mr. CLARK offered an amendment: to insert the words "if not incompatible with the public service;" which was agreed to, and the resolution as amended was adopted.

December 16—Mr. SAULSBURY offered the following resolution:

Resolved, That the Secretary of War be and is hereby directed to inform the Senate whether Dr. John Law and Whiteley Meredith, or either of them, citizens of the State of Delaware, have been arrested and imprisoned in Fort Delaware; when they were arrested and so imprisoned; the charges against them; by whom made; by what orders they were arrested and imprisoned; and that he communicate to the Senate all papers relating to their arrest and imprisonment.

Which was laid upon the table—yeas 29, nays 13, as follows:

YEAS—Messrs. Anthony, Arnold, Browning, Chandler, Clark, Collamer, Dixon, Doolittle, Fessenden, Field, Foot, Foster, Grimes, Hale, Harlan, Harris, Howard, Howe, King, Lane of Kansas, Morrill, Sumner, Ten Eyck, Trumbull, Wade, Wilkinson, Wilmot, Wilson of Massachusetts, *Wright*—29.

NAYS—Messrs. *Bayard*, *Carlile*, Cowan, *Davis*, *Harding*, Henderson, *Kennedy*, *Nesmith*, *Powell*, *Rice*, *Saulsbury*, Willey, *Wilson* of Missouri—13.

December 3—Mr. POWELL offered the following joint resolution:

Whereas, many citizens of the United States have been seized by persons acting, or pretending to be acting, under the authority of the United States, and have been carried out of the jurisdiction of the States of their residence and imprisoned in the military prisons and camps of the United States without any public charge being preferred against them, and without any opportunity being allowed to learn or disprove the charges made or alleged to be made against them; and whereas, it is the sacred right of every citizen that he shall not be deprived of liberty without due process of law, and when arrested shall have a speedy and public trial by an impartial jury: Therefore

Be it resolved by the Senate and House of Representatives of the United States of America in Congress assembled, That all such arrests are unwarranted by the Constitution and laws of the United States, and a usurpation of power never given by the people to the President or any other official. All such arrests are hereby condemned and declared palpable violations of the Constitution of the United States; and it is hereby demanded that all such arrests shall hereafter cease, and that all persons so arrested and yet held should have a prompt and speedy public trial according to the provisions of the Constitution, or should be immediately released.

Laid on the table and printed.

1863, February 26—Mr. POWELL offered the following resolution:

Resolved, That a committee of three be appointed to investigate the conduct of Colonel Gilbert, who, in command of a regiment of United States soldiers, dispersed a Democratic Convention of peaceable citizens of the State of Kentucky, assembled at the capital of that State, on the 18th of February, 1863, for the purpose of nominating candidates for Governor and Lieutenant Governor and other State officers. That said committee investigate all the facts connected with the aforesaid action of Colonel Gilbert and the officers and soldiers under his command; and the said committee are hereby authorized to send for persons and papers, to examine witnesses, and that they be authorized to administer oaths to witnesses; and that said committee be authorized to hold sessions in the State of Kentucky or elsewhere, and to employ a reporter to take down testimony; and that they report, &c.

March 3—The Senate refused to take up the resolution—yeas 10, nays 25, as follows:

YEAS—Messrs. *Carlile*, Cowan, *Davis*, Lane of Kansas, *Latham*, *Nesmith*, *Powell*, *Saulsbury*, *Wall*, *Wilson* of Missouri—10.

NAYS—Messrs. Anthony, Arnold, Clark, Collamer, Dixon, Fessenden, Foot, Foster, Grimes, Harding, Harlan, Harris, Henderson, Hicks, Howe, Morrill, Pomeroy, *Rice*, Sumner, Ten Eyck, Wade, Wilkinson, Willey, Wilmot, Wilson of Massachusetts—25.

THE CASE OF MADISON Y. JOHNSON.

Feb. 2—Mr. RICHARDSON offered this resolution:

Resolved, That a committee of three be appointed to investigate the facts in reference to the arrest and imprisonment of Madison Y. Johnson, and that said committee have the power to send for persons and papers, to examine witnesses under oath, and administer oaths to said witnesses.

The memorial of Madison Y. Johnson was read when Mr. HOWE, of Wisconsin, moved to lay the whole subject on the table; which was agreed to—yeas 22, nays 16, as follows:

YEAS—Messrs. Anthony, Arnold, Chandler, Clark, Fessenden, Foot, Foster, Grimes, Hale, Harlan, Harris, Hicks, Howard, Howe, King, Lane of Kansas, Morrill, Pomeroy, Sumner, Wade, Wilkinson, Wilson of Massachusetts—22.

NAYS—Messrs. *Bayard*, *Carlile*, *Davis*, *Harding*, Henderson, *Kennedy*, *Latham*, *McDougall*, *Powell*, *Rice*, *Richardson*, *Saulsbury*, *Turpie*, *Wall*, Willey, *Wilson* of Missouri—16.

IN HOUSE.

1862, Dec. 1—Mr. COX offered the following preamble and resolution:

Whereas, many citizens of the United States have been seized by persons acting, or pretending to be acting, under the authority of the United States, and have been carried out of the jurisdiction of the States of their residence, and imprisoned in the military prisons and camps of the United States, without any public charge being preferred against them, and without any opportunity being allowed to learn or disprove the charges made, or alleged to be made, against them: and whereas, such arrests have been made in States where there was no insurrection or rebellion, or pretence thereof, or any other obstruction against the authority of the Government: and whereas, it is the sacred right of every citizen of the United States, that he shall not be deprived of liberty without due process of law, and when arrested, that he shall have a speedy and public trial by an impartial jury of his countrymen: Therefore,

Resolved, That the House of Representatives do hereby condemn all such arrests as unwarranted by the Constitution and laws of the United States, and as a usurpation of power never given up by the people to their rulers, and do hereby demand that all such arrests shall hereafter cease, and that all persons so arrested and yet held should have a prompt and public trial, according to the provisions of the Constitution.

Which was laid on the table—yeas 80, nays 40. The NAYS were:

Messrs. *Ancona*, *Baily*, *Biddle*, Jacob B. Blair, *Calvert*, *Corning*, *Cox*, *Crittenden*, *English*, *Fouke*, Granger, *Grider*, *Haight*, *Hall*, *Harding*, *Holman*, *Knapp*, *Law*, *Lazear*, *Menzies*, *Morris*, *Noble*, *Norton*, *Nugen*, *Odell*, *Price*, *Richardson*, *Sheffield*, *Shiel*, *John B. Steele*, *William G. Steele*, *Stiles*, Benjamin F. Thomas, Francis Thomas, *Vallandigham*, *Ward*, *Chilton A. White*, *Wickliffe*, *Wright*, *Yeaman*—40.

December 1—Mr. RICHARDSON offered the following resolution:

Resolved, That the President of the United States be requested to inform this House what citizens of Illinois are now confined in the Forts Warren, Lafayette, and Delaware, or the Old Capitol prison, and any other forts or places of confinement; what the charges are against said persons; also the places where they were arrested. That the President be further requested to inform this House of the names of the persons that have been arrested in Illinois and taken to and confined in prisons outside of the limits of said State, and who have been released, what were the charges against each of them, by whom the charges were made, also by whose order said arrests were made, and the authority of law for such arrests.

Which was laid upon the table—yeas 74, nays 40. The NAYS were—

Messrs. *Ancona*, *Baily*, *Biddle*, *Calvert*, Roscoe Conkling, Conway, *Corning*, *Cox*, *Crittenden*, Dunn, *English*, *Fouke*, Granger, *Grider*, *Hall*, *Harding*, *Holman*, William Kellogg, *Knapp*, *Law*, *Lazear*, Leary, *Menzies*, *Morris*, *Noble*, *Norton*, *Nugen*, *Odell*, Porter, *Price*, *Richardson*, *Shiel*, *John B. Steele*, *William G. Steele*, *Stiles*, Benjamin F. Thomas, *Vallandigham*, *Ward*, *Chilton A. White*, *Wright*—40.

Dec. 22—Mr. MAY offered the following resolution:

Resolved, That the Secretary of State be requested to communicate to this House a copy of an order which, on or about the 28th of November, 1861, he caused to be read to State prisoners confined in Fort Warren, whereby they were forbidden to employ counsel in their behalf, and informed that such employment of counsel would be regarded by the Government and by the State Department as a reason for prolonging the term of their imprisonment.

Which was laid upon the table—yeas 63, nays 48. The NAYS were—

Messrs. *William Allen*, *William J. Allen*, *Ancona*, *Biddle*,

Burnham, *Calvert*, Clements, *Cobb*, *Cox*, *Cravens*, *Crittenden*, Dunn, *English*, Granger, *Grider*, Hale, *Harding*, *Johnson*, William Kellogg, *Kerrigan*, *Knapp*, *Law*, *Lazear*, Leary, *May*, *Morris*, *Noble*, *Norton*, *Nugen*, *Pendleton*, *Price*, *Robinson*, *James S. Rollins*, *Shiel*, *Smith*, Benjamin F. Thomas, Francis Thomas, *Vallandigham*, *Vibbard*, *Voorhees*, *Wadsworth*, *Ward*, *Chilton A. White*, *Wickliffe*, *Woodruff*, *Worcester*, *Wright*, *Yeaman*—48.

December 15—Mr. PENDLETON offered the following resolution:

Resolved, That the President be requested to inform this House, if in his opinion not inconsistent with the public interest, whether in any oath of allegiance or parole required to be taken by any prisoner held in custody as a so-called political prisoner, there has been inserted a clause to the effect that he should not bring suit for the recovery of damages for such imprisonment, or that he should not oppose, by speech or otherwise, the war measures of the Administration.

Which was laid on the table by the following vote—yeas 77, nays 43.

March 3—Mr. MAY offered the following resolution:

Whereas it is represented that Major General Schenck, commanding the forces of the United States stationed in Baltimore, Maryland, has ordered, as a condition to be annexed to the worship of Almighty God by certain religious societies or congregations of the Methodist Church of that city, that the flag of the United States shall be conspicuously displayed at the time and place of such worship: and whereas the said order is a plain violation of the inalienable right to worship God according to the dictates of every one's conscience, as it is asserted by the said congregations, and also by our declarations of fundamental rights and secured by our State and Federal Constitutions: and whereas a minister of the said congregation, the Rev. John H. Dashiell, having, on Monday, the 15th ultimo, removed the said flag from his own premises, which was also the place of worship of one of said congregations, where the said flag had been placed surreptitiously by some evil-minded person, and for so doing was arrested by order of the said General Schenck and held as a prisoner: Therefore,

Be it resolved, That the Judiciary Committee be, and hereby is, instructed to inquire into the allegations aforesaid, and ascertain by what authority the said General Schenck exercises a power to regulate or interfere with the privileges of divine worship, and also to arrest and detain as a prisoner the said minister of the Gospel, as aforesaid; and, further, that said committee be instructed to report upon the same at an early day.

The House refused to suspend the rules to get the resolution before the House—ayes 28, noes 79, (yeas and nays not called.)

First Session, Thirty-Eighth Congress.

1863, December 17—Mr. HARRINGTON offered this resolution:

Whereas the Constitution of the United States (article one, section nine) provides: "The privilege of the writ of *habeas corpus* shall not be suspended, unless when, in cases of rebellion or invasion, the public safety may require it:" and whereas such provision is contained in the portion of the Constitution defining legislative powers, and not in the provisions defining executive power; and whereas the Constitution (article four of Amendments) further provides: "The right of the people to be secure in their persons, houses, papers, and effects, against unreasonable searches and seizures, shall not be violated," &c.; and whereas the Thirty-Seventh Congress did, by act, claim to confer upon the President of the United States the power, at his will and pleasure, to suspend the privilege of the writ of *habeas corpus* throughout the United States, without limitations or conditions; and whereas the President of the United States, by proclamation, has assumed to suspend such privileges of the citizen in the loyal States; and whereas the people of such States have been subjected to arbitrary arrests without process of law, and to unreasonable search and seizures, and have been denied the right to a speedy trial and investigation, and have languished in prisons at the arbitrary pleasure of the Chief Executive and his military subordinates: Now, therefore,

Resolved by the House of Representatives of the United States, That no power is delegated by the Constitution of the United States, either to the legislative or executive power, to suspend the privileges of the writ of *habeas corpus* in any State loyal to the Constitution and Government not invaded, and in which the civil and judicial powers are in full operation.

2. *Resolved*, That Congress has no power under the Constitution to delegate to the President of the United States the authority to suspend the privilege of the writ of *habeas corpus*, and imprison at his pleasure, without process of law or trial, the citizens of the loyal States.

3. *Resolved*, That the assumption of the right by the Executive of the United States to deprive the citizens of such loyal States of the benefits of the writ of *habeas corpus*, and to imprison them at his pleasure, without process of law, is unworthy the progress of the age, is consistent only with a despotic power unlimited by constitutional obligations, and is wholly subversive of the elementary principles of freedom, upon which the Government of the United States and of the several States is based.

4. *Resolved*, That the Judiciary Committee be instructed to prepare and report a bill to this House protecting the rights of the citizens in the loyal States, in strict accordance with the foregoing provisions of the Constitution of the United States.

Which was negatived—yeas 67, nays 90, as follows:

YEAS—Messrs. *James C. Allen*, *William J. Allen*, *Ancona*, *Augustus C. Baldwin*, *Bliss*, *Brooks*, *Brown*, *Chanler*, *Coffroth*, *Cox*, *Cravens*, *Dawson*, *Denison*, *Eden*, *Edgerton*, *Eldridge*, *English*, *Finck*, *Ganson*, *Grider*, *Hall*, *Harding*, *Harrington*, *Benjamin G. Harris*, *Herrick*, *Holman*, *William Johnson*, *Kernan*, *King*, *Knapp*, *Law*, *Le Blond*, *Long*, *Mallory*, *Marcy*, *McAllister*, *McDowell*, *McKinney*, *Middleton*, *William H. Miller*, *James R. Morris*, *Morrison*, *Nelson*, *Noble*, *Odell*, *John O'Neill*, *Pendleton*, *Perry*, *Radford*, *Samuel J. Randall*, *Robinson*, *Rogers*, *Ross*, *Scott*, *John B. Steele*, *William G. Steele*, *Stiles*, *Strouse*, *Sweat*, *Voorhees*, *Wadsworth*, *Ward*, *Wheeler*, *Chilton A. White*, *Joseph W. White*, *Winfield*, *Wood*—67.

NAYS—Messrs. Alley, Allison, Ames, Arnold, Ashley, John D. Baldwin, Beaman, Blaine, Blow, Boutwell, Brandegee, Broomall, William G. Brown, Ambrose W. Clark, Freeman Clarke, *Clay*, Cobb, Cole, Creswell, Henry Winter Davis, Thomas T. Davis, Dawes, Dixon, Donnelly, Driggs, Dumont, Eckley, Eliot, Farnsworth, Fenton, Frank, Garfield, Gooch, Grinnell, Hale, Higby, Hooper, Hotchkiss, Asahel W. Hubbard, John H. Hubbard, Hulburd, Jenckes, Julian, Kasson, Kelley, Francis W. Kellogg, Orlando Kellogg, Loan, Longyear, Lovejoy, Marvin, McBride, McClurg, McIndoe, Samuel F. Miller, Moorhead, Morrill, Daniel Morris, Amos Myers, Leonard Myers, Norton, Charles O'Neill, Orth, Perham, Pike, Pomeroy, Price, William H. Randall, Alexander H. Rice, John H. Rice, Edward H. Rollins, Schenck, Scofield, Shannon, Sloan, Smithers, Spalding, Stevens, Thayer, Tracy, Van Valkenburgh, Ellihu B. Washburne, William B. Washburn, Whaley, Williams, Wilder, Wilson, Windom, Woodbridge—90.

1864, February 29—Mr. PENDLETON offered the following resolution:

Resolved, (as the sense of this House,) That the military arrest, without civil warrant, and trial by military commission without jury, of Clement L. Vallandigham, a citizen of Ohio, not in the land or naval forces of the United States or the militia in actual service, by order of Major General Burnside, and his subsequent banishment by order of the President, executed by military force, were acts of mere arbitrary power, in palpable violation of the Constitution and laws of the United States.

Which the House refused to table—yeas 33, nays 84, and then rejected—yeas 47, nays 77, as follows:

YEAS—Messrs. *James C. Allen*, *Ancona*, *Augustus C. Baldwin*, *Brooks*, *Chanler*, *Coffroth*, *Cox*, *Dawson*, *Denison*, *Eden*, *Eldridge*, *Finck*, *Ganson*, *Harding*, *Harrington*, *Herrick*, *Holman*, *Hutchins*, *Kernan*, *Knapp*, *Law*, *Long*, *Marcy*, *McDowell*, *McKinney*, *William H. Miller*, *Morrison*, *Nelson*, *Noble*, *John O'Neill*, *Pendleton*, *Radford*, *Samuel J. Randall*, *Rogers*, *Ross*, *Scott*, *Stebbins*, *John B. Steele*, *William G. Steele*, *Stiles*, *Strouse*, *Stuart*, *Sweat*, *Voorhees*, *William H. Wadsworth*, *Chilton A. White*, *Winfield*—47.

NAYS—Messrs. Alley, Allison, Anderson, Arnold, *Baily*, John D. Baldwin, Baxter, Francis P. Blair, jr., Blow, Boutwell, Boyd, Brandegee, Ambrose W. Clark, Freeman Clarke, *Clay*, Cobb, Cole, Creswell, Henry Winter Davis, Dawes, Deming, Dixon, Donnelly, Driggs, Dumont, Eckley, Eliot, Farnsworth, Frank, Grinnell, Hale, Higby, Hooper, Hotchkiss, Asahel W. Hubbard, John H. Hubbard, Jenckes, Julian, Kelley, Francis W. Kellogg, Orlando Kellogg, Loan, Marvin, McBride, McClurg, Moorhead, Morrill, Daniel Morris, Amos Myers, Leonard Myers, Norton, Charles O'Neill, Patterson, Perham, Pomeroy, Price, William H. Randall, John H. Rice, Schenck, Scofield, Shannon, Sloan, Smithers,

Starr, Stevens, Thayer, Thomas, Upson, Van Valkenburgh, Ellihu B. Washburne, William B. Washburn, Whaley, Williams, Wilder, Wilson, Windom, Woodbridge—77.

January 25—Mr. McDowell offered the following resolutions, which were laid over under the rule:

Resolved, 1. That the House fully recognizes the great fundamental provision of the Constitution of the United States which guarantees the freedom of speech to every American citizen; and that neither the President, nor any person acting in a subordinate capacity to him, has the rightful authority to arrest and imprison a citizen of the loyal States for the utterance of sentiments distasteful to the men in power.

2. That we recognize in the freedom of the press the great bulwark of civil liberty; and that those persons temporarily intrusted with power have not the rightful authority, in those States not in rebellion, to subvert this great constitutional guarantee by issuing military orders, or by a resort to any other means unknown to the laws of the country.

3. That the right to security of person from arrest in the loyal States, when no crime is charged, is a sacred right guaranteed to every citizen; and that neither the President, nor any one acting by his authority, has the legal right to arrest, imprison, or transport our people without "due *process of law*," requiring affidavit, warrant, arrest, and trial by a jury of the country, impartially selected.

4. That the privilege of the writ of *habeas corpus* is a fundamental and inherent right belonging to the American people, solemnly guaranteed by express provision of the Constitution, that cannot be denied to the citizens of the loyal States, where the courts are open and the administration of justice is unobstructed, and "invasion and rebellion" do not exist.

5. That the Constitution of the United States is one of expressed and limited powers, and that neither Congress nor the Executive have the "lawful right" to interfere with the established rights and domestic institutions of the several States.

6. That we reaffirm our unalterable devotion to the Constitution of the United States, and to each and every provision thereof, as framed by the fathers, including those provisions relating to the rights of property and the inviolability of contracts, as understood and interpreted by the Supreme Court of the United States.

March 21—Mr. Eldridge offered this resolution, which was laid over under the rule:

Resolved, That the President of the United States be respectfully requested, and that the Secretary of State and the Secretary of War be directed, to report and furnish to this House the names of all persons, if any there are, arrested and held in prison or confinement in any prison, fort, or other place whatsoever, for political offences, or any other alleged offence against the Government or authority of the United States, by the order, command, consent, or knowledge of them or either of them, respectively, and who have not been charged, tried, or convicted before any civil or criminal (not military) court of the land, together with the charge against such person, or cause for such arrest and imprisonment, if there be any, and the name of the prison, fort, or place where they are severally kept or confined. Also, whether any person or persons, for any alleged like offence, have been banished or sent from the United States, or from the States not in rebellion to the rebellious States; and the names, times, alleged offence or cause thereof; and whether with or without trial; and if tried, before what court.

April 4—The resolution, on motion of Mr. Edward H. Rollins, was laid upon the table—yeas 62, nays 40. The Nays were—

Messrs. *James C. Allen, Ancona, A. C. Baldwin, Bliss, J. S. Brown, Chanler, Cox, Cravens, Dawson, Denison, Eden, Eldridge, English, Finck, Grider, Griswold, Harrington, Herrick, Holman, P. Johnson, Kalbfleisch, Law, Lazear, Long, Mallory, Marcy, McKinney, Middleton, J. R. Morris, Morrison, J. O'Neill, Pruyn, S. J. Randall, Robinson, Rogers, J. B. Steele, Wheeler, C. A. White, Winfield, Yeaman*—40.

June 20—Mr. Ross offered the following resolution, which went over under the rule:

Resolved, That all persons not in the military or naval service of the United States who have been arrested and imprisoned by the agents of the Government without process of law, and released without trial or examination, are entitled to the same pay and mileage for the time they were deprived of their liberties as members of Congress; and the Committee of Claims are hereby instructed to report a bill at an early day for that purpose.

Same day, in Senate—Mr. Morrill offered this bill, which was referred to the Committee on the Judiciary:

Be it enacted, &c., That upon all arrests under section 6, of chapter 200, of an act approved the 17th of July, 1862, bail shall be admitted, and such bail, on the demand of the party so arrested, may be taken before any judge of the United States, any chancellor, judge of a supreme or superior court, or chief or first judge of court of common pleas of any State, who shall exercise their discretion therein, regarding the nature and circumstances of the offence, and of the evidence and the usages of the law.

Third Session, Thirty-Seventh Congress.

THE ACT OF INDEMNITY OF MARCH 3, 1863.

Section 1 provides: That, during the present rebellion, the President of the United States, whenever, in his judgment, the public safety may require it, is authorized to suspend the privilege of the writ of *habeas corpus* in any case throughout the United States, or any part thereof. And whenever and wherever the said privilege shall be suspended, as aforesaid, no military or other officer shall be compelled, in answer to any writ of *habeas corpus*, to return the body of any person or persons detained by him by authority of the President; but upon the certificate, under oath, of the officer having charge of any one so detained that such person is detained by him as a prisoner under authority of the President, further proceedings under the writ of *habeas corpus* shall be suspended by the judge or court having issued the said writ, so long as said suspension by the President shall remain in force, and said rebellion continue.

Section 2 directs the Secretary of State and the Secretary of War to furnish to the judges of the circuit and district courts of the United States and of the District of Columbia, a list of the names of all persons, citizens of loyal States, held as State or political prisoners of the United States, in any fort, arsenal, or other place; and provides that where a grand jury has adjourned without finding an indictment against any such person, the judge shall forthwith make an order that any such prisoner desiring a discharge be brought before him to be discharged, and every officer of the United States is directed immediately to obey this order, under penalty of fine and imprisonment—the party first to take a prescribed oath of allegiance. Another section provides: That any order of the President, or under his authority, made at any time during the existence of the present rebellion, shall be a defence in all courts to any action or prosecution, civil or criminal, pending, or to be commenced, for any search, seizure, arrest, or imprisonment, made, done, or committed, or acts omitted to be done, under and by virtue of such order, or under color of any law of Congress, and such defence may be made by special plea, or under the general issue.

Suits begun in State courts may be transferred to United States Courts under circumstances described. Any suit described in this act may be carried on writ of error to the Supreme Court of the United States, and all suits or prosecutions for any arrest or imprisonment or other trespasses or wrongs, shall be commenced within two years.

This bill passed the House of Representatives, March 2, 1863—yeas 99, nays 45, as follows:

YEAS—Messrs. Aldrich, Arnold, Ashley, Babbitt, Baker, Baxter, Beaman, Bingham, Jacob B. Blair, Samuel S. Blair, Blake, William G. Brown, Buffinton, Campbell, Casey, Chamberlain, Clark, Colfax, Frederick A. Conkling, Roscoe Conkling, Conway, Cutler, Davis, Dawes, Delano, Dunn, Edgerton, Eliot, Ely, Fenton, Samuel C. Fessenden, Thomas A. D. Fessenden, Fisher, Flanders, Franchot, Frank, Goodwin, Gurley, Hahn, Hale, Harrison, Hooper, Horton, Hutchins, Julian, Kelley, Francis W. Kellogg, William Kellogg, Killinger, Lansing, Leary, *Lehman*, Loomis, Low, McIndoe, McKean, McKnight, McPherson, Marston, Maynard, Mitchell, Moorhead, Anson P. Morrill, Nixon, Olin, Patton, Timothy G. Phelps, Pike, Pomeroy, Porter, John H. Rice, Riddle, Edward H. Rollins, Sargent, Sedgwick, Segar, Shanks, Shellabarger, Sherman, Sloan, Spaulding, Stevens, Stratton, Francis Thomas, Trimble, Trowbridge, Van Horn, Van Valkenburgh, Van Wyck, Verree, Walker, Wall, Wallace, Washburne, Wheeler, Albert S. White, Wilson, Windom, Worcester—99.

NAYS—Messrs. *William Allen*, *William J. Allen*, *Ancona*, *Biddle*, *Calvert*, *Cravens*, *Crisfield*, *Delaplaine*, *Dunlap*, *English*, Granger, *Grider*, *Hall*, *Harding*, *Holman*, *Johnson*, *Kerrigan*, *Knapp*, *Law*, *Mallory*, *May*, *Menzies*, *Morris*, *Noble*, *Norton*, *Nugen*, *Pendleton*, *Perry*, *Price*, *Robinson*, *Shiel*, *Smith*, *John B. Steele*, *William G. Steele*, *Stiles*, Benjamin F. Thomas, *Vallandigham*, *Voorhees*, *Wadsworth*, *Ward*, *Chilton A. White*, *Wickliffe*, *Wood*, *Woodruff*, *Yeaman*—45.

Same day, the bill passed the SENATE, without a record of yeas and nays, owing to a misunderstanding respecting the putting of the vote.

March 3—Mr. BAYARD moved that the Secretary of the Senate be directed to request the House of Representatives, to return to the Senate the above report of the Committee of Conference; which was rejected—yeas 13, nays 25, as follows:

YEAS—Messrs. *Bayard*, *Carlile*, *Davis*, Henderson, *Latham*, *Nesmith*, *Powell*, *Rice*, *Richardson*, *Saulsbury*, *Turpie*, Willey, *Wilson*, of Missouri—13.

NAYS—Messrs. Anthony, Chandler, Clark, Dixon, Doolittle, Foster, Grimes, Harlan, Harris, Hicks, Howard, Howe, King, Lane of Indiana, Lane of Kansas, Morrill, Pomeroy, Sherman, Sumner, Ten Eyck, Trumbull, Wade, Wilkinson, Wilmot, Wilson of Massachusetts—25.

While this subject was pending before Congress, the House, December 8, 1862, passed an indemnity bill—yeas 90, nays 45, against which, on the 22d of December, thirty-six members of the House moved to enter on the journal this protest:

Resolved, That the following protest of thirty-six members of this House against the passage of the House bill No. 591 be entered upon the Journal:

On the 8th day of December, A. D. 1862, and during the present session of Congress, Mr. STEVENS, of Pennsylvania, introduced the bill No. 591, entitled "An act to indemnify the President, and other persons, for suspending the privilege of the writ of *habeas corpus*, and acts done in pursuance thereof," and after its second reading moved that its consideration be made the special order for the Thursday then next ensuing, which motion being objected to, he moved the previous question, and this being sustained, under the operation thereof the bill was read a third time, and passed.

This bill involves questions of the gravest importance. It provides that all suspensions of the privilege of the writ of *habeas corpus*, all arrests and imprisonments upon whatever pretexts or by whomsoever made, under the authority of the President, however arbitrary or tyrannical or unjust, are confirmed and made valid; and that all persons who advised or executed or assisted in the execution of any such acts are discharged from all liability, whether to the State or to individuals "in respect thereof;" and that all proceedings against them of any nature, whether for the recovery of damages or for the infliction of punishment "commenced or to be commenced," are discharged and made void. It also provides that the President may, during the existence of this rebellion, at any time and anywhere throughout any of the United States, and as to any person, suspend the privilege of the writ of *habeas corpus*.

The bill is framed upon the idea that the acts recited were illegal, and without just cause or excuse; that they were violations of the rights of the persons arrested and imprisoned; and that for them redress might be had in the courts of the United States, by resort to the peaceful, regular, and ordinary administration of the law. It is framed upon the idea that the citizen was arrested without the existence of crime on his part, or even probable cause to suspect it, and that in making such arrests, the substance, as well as the form, of those provisions of law intended to secure personal *liberty* were entirely disregarded. It makes no exception of those cases in which the arrests have been made with malice, and the imprisonments have been inflicted with circumstances of brutality and cruelty, in which the "public good" has been made the cloak wherewith to cover the gratification of political animosity or private hatred. It distinguishes in nothing between the cases in which an honest mistake has been followed by its immediate correction, and cases in which malignity has been enabled, by false pretences, to procure the arrest and to prolong the imprisonment, to the loss of property, the destruction of health, and, in some instances, the insanity, suicide, or lingering death of the unhappy victim. It distinguishes in nothing between the active officer, zealous in the full discharge of his official duties, and the base miscreant who volunteers to assume the degrading character of spy and informer, that he may, with more effect and security, use the falsehood which the venom of his heart prompted him to invent. It proposes to condone all offences, to protect all offenders, and to take away all redress for injuries, however great, or with whatever circumstances of aggravation or bad motive inflicted.

If these acts had been done in all cases from the purest motives, with an eye single to the public good, with as little aggression as possible on private rights, with all circumspection and care that only those who were really guilty should suffer such confinement as would prevent the commission of an unlawful act—if the public good were in fact subserved by them—it might be proper to protect the President, and those acting under his authority, from criminal prosecution and penal sentence; it might be proper to protect them from pecuniary loss, by the payment, from the public Treasury, of the damages assessed against them. Even then, whilst admitting that circumstances like these would in seasons of great public dangers negative all wrongful intent in the commission of these illegal acts, it would be the duty of the Representatives of the people to affirm that at all times the President of the United States, before all other men, should adhere most strictly to the forms of legal procedure when directing his powers against the personal liberty of the citizen. It could never be proper to indemnify the President, and those acting under his authority, at the expense of the citizen whom they had injured, or to add to their security by the destruction of his remedies.

The Constitution of the United States guards most carefully the rights of the citizen; it was ordained "to establish justice, insure domestic tranquillity," and to "secure the blessings of liberty;" and so steadily was this object kept in view, that in addition to the reservation of all powers not granted, there are special prohibitions of seizures without warrant, detentions without indictment, imprisonment without a speedy and public trial, and deprivation of life, liberty, or property without due process of law; and there are clauses which extend the judicial power of the United States to all controversies between citizens of different States, and secure a trial by jury in all cases in which the value in controversy exceeds twenty dollars. Congress has hitherto uniformly maintained, and, as far as was necessary, has perfected by its legislation these guarantees of personal liberty, and the courts have enforced them by the assessment of damages for their infraction. This bill proposes to deprive the courts of the power to afford such protection. It will, if carried out into practical and general operation, release the people from the duty of appealing to such peaceful and legal means of redress, and will provoke more summary and less constitutional measures. Yet this bill, without precedent in our history, suggesting such grave questions of constitutionality and expediency, believed by many members to be utterly subversive of the rights of the citizen and of the express provisions of the Constitution, by the force of mere numbers and against the remonstrance of the minority, was passed within one hour of its first introduction, without having been printed, without having been referred to any committee, select or standing, and without any opportunity for consideration or discussion.

The undersigned, members of the House of Representatives, do therefore most solemnly remonstrate against this action of the House, and respectfully ask that this their protest may be entered upon the Journal.

They protest against the refusal of the House to permit consideration and discussion of the bill as an arbitrary exercise of power by the majority, unjust to the members, unjust to their constituents, and derogatory to its character as a deliberative legislative body.

They protest against the passage of the bill—

1. Because it purports to deprive the citizen of all existing, peaceful, legal modes of redress for admitted wrongs,

and thus constrains him tamely to submit to the injury inflicted or to seek illegal and forcible remedies.

2. Because it purports to indemnify the President and all acting under his authority for acts admitted to be wrongful, at the expense of the citizen upon whom the wrongful acts have been perpetrated, in violation of the plainest principles of justice, and the most familiar precepts of constitutional law.

3. Because it purports to confirm and make valid, by act of Congress, arrests and imprisonments which were not only not warranted by the Constitution of the United States, but were in palpable violation of its express prohibitions.

4. Because it purports to authorize the President, during this rebellion, at any time, as to any person, and everywhere throughout the limits of the United States, to suspend the privilege of the writ of *habeas corpus*, whereas by the Constitution the power to suspend the privilege of that writ is confided to the discretion of Congress alone, and is limited to the places threatened by the dangers of invasion or insurrection.

5. Because, for these and other reasons, it is unjust and unwise, an invasion of private rights, an encouragement to lawless violence, and a precedent full of hope to all who would usurp despotic power and perpetuate it by the arbitrary arrest and imprisonment of those who oppose them.

6. And finally, because in both its sections it is "a deliberate, palpable, and dangerous" violation of the Constitution, "according to the plain sense and intention of that instrument," and is therefore utterly null and void.

George H. Pendleton,	C. A. Wickliffe,
W. A. Richardson,	Charles J. Biddle,
J. C. Robinson,	J. A. Cravens,
P. B. Fouke,	Elijah Ward,
James R. Morris,	Philip Johnson,
A. L. Knapp,	John D. Stiles,
C. L. Vallandigham,	D. W. Voorhees,
C. A. White,	G. W. Dunlap,
Warren P. Noble,	Hendrick B. Wright,
W. Allen,	H. Grider,
William J. Allen,	W. H. Wadsworth,
S. S. Cox,	A. Harding,
E. H. Norton,	Charles B. Calvert,
George K. Shiel,	James E. Kerrigan,
S. E. Ancona,	Henry May,
J. Lazear,	R. H. Nugen,
Nehemiah Perry,	George H. Yeaman,
C. Vibbard,	B. F. Granger.
John Law,	

The motion to enter this protest was tabled—yeas 75, nays 41.

The above bill of Mr. Stevens was amended in the Senate, and finally passed that body—yeas 33, nays 7, as follows, January 28:

Yeas—Messrs. Anthony, Arnold, Browning, Chandler, Clark, Collamer, Cowan, Dixon, Doolittle, Fessenden, Foot, Foster, Grimes, Hale, Harlan, Harris, Henderson, Hicks, Howard, King, Lane of Indiana, Lane of Kansas, Morrill, Pomeroy, Sherman, Sumner, Ten Eyck, Trumbull, Wade, Wilkinson, Willey, Wilmot, Wilson of Massachusetts—33.

Nays—Messrs. *Bayard, Carlile, McDougall, Powell, Turpie, Wall, Wilson* of Missouri—7.

The House non-concurred in the amendments, and a Committee of Conference having met, agreed upon a report, which was agreed to in both Houses as stated before, p. 184.

VOTE ON SUSPENSION OF HABEAS CORPUS.

Pending the consideration of the original House bill in the Senate,

1863, Feb. 19—Mr. Powell moved to strike out the third section authorizing the President to suspend, by proclamation, the writ of *habeas corpus* in certain contingencies; which was rejected—yeas 13, nays 27, as follows:

Yeas—Messrs. *Bayard, Carlile,* Cowan, *Kennedy, Latham, Nesmith, Powell, Rice, Richardson, Saulsbury, Turpie,* Willey, *Wilson* of Missouri—13.

Nays—Messrs. Anthony, Arnold, Chandler, Clark, *Davis,* Dixon, Doolittle, Fessenden, Foot, Grimes, Harris, Henderson, Hicks, Howard, Howe, King, Lane of Indiana, Lane of Kansas, Morrill, Pomeroy, Sherman, Sumner, Ten Eyck, Trumbull, Wilkinson, Wilmot, Wilson of Massachusetts—27.

VOTE ON ARRESTS.

Feb 23—Mr. Carlile moved this substitute for the bill:

From and after the passage of this act, and during the present rebellion, it shall not be lawful for any officer or servant of the United States to arrest or detain any citizen of the United States who may be supposed or alleged to be disloyal thereto, or for any other cause, except upon oath or affirmation of some person or persons well known to be loyal to the United States, and particularly describing in said oath or affirmation the act of disloyalty or other cause for which the said citizen should be arrested and detained.

Sec. 2. That any and every officer or servant of the United States who shall arrest or detain any citizen of the United States in contravention of the provisions of the first section of this act shall, on conviction thereof in any court having jurisdiction in the case, suffer a fine of not less than $10,000, or imprisonment in the penitentiary for a term not less than five years.

Sec. 3. That all persons arrested under the provisions of this act upon the charge of disloyalty to the Government of the United States, or for any other cause, shall have the privilege of the writ of *habeas corpus;* and the said writ shall not be suspended at any time so far as the same may relate to persons arrested as aforesaid.

Sec. 4. That nothing in this act shall be so construed as to prevent the arrest of any person, a citizen of any or either of the States now in rebellion against the Government of the United States, who may be charged with treason or disloyalty thereto: *Provided,* That all arrests of such persons shall be made as provided in the first section of this act, or upon the precept of the President of the United States.

Which was rejected—yeas 7, (Messrs. *Carlile, Kennedy, Powell, Richardson, Saulsbury, Turpie, Wall,*) nays 29.

THE ACT SUSTAINED BY THE COURTS.

The important case of George W. Jones, ex-Minister to Bogota, *vs.* William H. Seward, has been decided in New York by the Supreme Court. Mr. Jones was arrested on a telegraphic dispatch from Secretary Seward, and imprisoned at Fort Lafayette. When released he brought a suit for $5,000 damages for false imprisonment. Mr. Seward, by counsel, moved to transfer the case to the United States Circuit Court, under the act of March, 1863. The motion was denied, and the General Term decided an appeal which was taken to it. The majority of the judges affirm the act; one, Clerke, dissented.

George W. Jones *vs.* William H. Seward.

Leonard, J.—The question is not whether the 4th section of the act of Congress passed March 3, 1863, affords a valid defence to the action. The true question is this: Is it in the power of Congress to give the circuit court jurisdiction of the case?

The Constitution extends the judicial power of the Union to all cases in law and equity arising under the Constitution, laws, and treaties of the United States.

The defence in this case arises under the act of Congress, and the validity of that act, considered in the light afforded by the Constitution, will be one of the principal subjects to be determined at the trial. It has been decided that a case arises within the meaning of the Constitution as well when the defendant seeks protection under a law of Congress, as when a plaintiff comes into court to demand some right conferred by law.

It has been objected that the original jurisdiction of all actions may be drawn into the Federal courts, by similar enactments of Congress, and that the case arises within the meaning of the Constitution only after a trial and judgment in this court, when the action can be referred by a writ of error or appeal, and brought before the Federal courts for review.

The power of transferring causes to the United States Circuit in a similar manner, where the question involved was of an appellate and not original jurisdiction, has long been sustained.

Chief Justice Marshall says, in the case of Osborn *vs.* The Bank of the United States (9 Wheaton, 821): "We perceive no ground on which the proposition can be maintained, that Congress is incapable of giving the circuit courts original jurisdiction, in any case to which the appellate jurisdiction extends."

Congress has enacted that the defendant may interpose in his defence the orders, &c., of the President, and has directed the transfer of cases involving such a defence, in the manner prescribed, into the circuit conrt.

According to the statements of the defendant such a case

has arisen. We have nothing to do with the validity of the law as a defence to the action. It is sufficient for the State court that the defence involves the construction and effect of a law of Congress. The case has then arisen when the courts of the United States may have jurisdiction, if Congress so directs. If the law does not afford a constitutional or valid defence, it cannot now be doubted that the learned justices of the United States Courts will so declare it, when the jurisdiction of such cases will remain in the State courts, as before the enactment of the law. It is not our duty to assert the independence of our State sovereignty and jurisdiction; for the final construction and effects of all acts of Congress may be brought before the United States Courts by the express provision of the Constitution.

The manner of taking the cause to those courts is of consequence. The Supreme Court of the Union must be relied on to prevent its jurisdiction from being unlawfully extended by Congress. I am of the opinion, therefore, that Congress has the power to direct the transfer of such cases.

In my opinion this application was necessary in order to vest the U. S. Circuit Court with the possession of the action, but the discussion has not been lost, inasmuch as it will be now settled that this Court will not, in this judicial district, take further cognizance of cases which have been transferred under this act of Congress. It is very proper that an order be entered transferring the cause to the U. S. Circuit, as it affords the evidence in the Court of the disposition made of it.

In arriving at my conclusions I have consulted Story's Com. on the Constitution, chap. 38, §§ 903, 906, &c.; 1 Wheat., Martin *vs.* Hunter; 6 Wheat., Cohen *vs.* The State of Virginia; 9 Wheat., Osborn *vs.* The Bank of United States.

As a rule of practice I think the Court should not approve any sureties unless the amount of the bond is equal to the sum in which the defendant in the action has been held to bail, if bail has been required in the State Court. This fact should be made to appear to the satisfaction of the judge to whom the bond is presented for approval.

The decision in this case will also embrace the case of Gudeman *vs.* Wool, argued at the same general term as the present case.

The order appealed from should be reversed, and the motion below should be granted without costs.

SUTHERLAND, J.—The question is not as to the constitutionality of the fourth section of the act declaring that the order or authority of the President, during the rebellion, shall be a defence in all Courts, to any order for any arrest, imprisonment, or act done, or omitted to be done, under or by color of the President's order, or of any law of Congress; but the question is as to the constitutionality of the fifth section of the act, authorizing the defendant in any such action, to remove the same from the State Court to the Circuit of the United States for the district where the suit is brought for trial, on complying with certain requirements specified in the section; that is, on entering his appearance, filing his petition stating the facts, offering good and sufficient surety, &c.

The question presented by this appeal is not as to the constitutional power of the President to order the arrest, imprisonment, &c., or as to the constitutional power of Congress to authorize the President to order the arrest, imprisonment, &c.; but the question presented by the appeal is as to the constitutional power of Congress to give the Circuit Courts of the United States, primary or original, and (as to the State Courts) exclusive jurisdiction, of the trial of actions for such arrests, imprisonments, &c.

In determining the question as to the constitutionality of the sixth section of the act, we must assume, I think, that the trial of this action will involve the determination of the question as the constitutionality of the fourth section; that Congress, in passing the act, considered that the trials of the actions to be removed to the Circuit Courts of the United States under it would involve the determination of the question as to the constitutionality of the fourth section, whether tried in the State or United States Courts; and that Congress intended by the fifth section to take from the State Courts, and give it to the Circuit Courts of the United States, the right and power to determine that question.

Had Congress the constitutional power to do this? That is the question.

If Congress had the power, then the order appealed from denying the defendant's motion to remove the action and all proceedings therein to the Circuit Court of the United States for the Southern District of New York should be reversed, and I think an order made directing such removal. If Congress had not the power, then the order appealed from should be affirmed.

If no steps had been taken for the removal of the action from this Court, and the action should be tried in this Court, and the question as the constitutionality of the fourth section of the act should be decided adversely to the defendant by the Court of Appeals of this State, the Supreme Court of the United States would have final and conclusive appellate jurisdiction of the question. (Const. U. S. Art. 3; sec 25 of the Judiciary Act; 1 Stat. at Large, 85: Cohen *vs.* Virginia, 6 Wheaton, 264; Miller *vs.* Nicholls, 4 Wheaton, 311.)

Cannot Congress give the Circuit Court of the United States original jurisdiction in any case to which this appellate jurisdiction extends?

In Osborn *vs.* United States Bank, 9 Wheaton, cited by Judge Leonard, Chief Justice Marshall said he could perceive no ground for saying that Congress could not.

In that case one of the questions was whether Congress could constitutionally confer on the Bank the right to sue and be sued "in every Circuit Court of the United States."

It was held that such a suit was a case arising under a law of the United States, consequently that it was within the judicial power of the United States, and Congress could confer upon the Circuit Court jurisdiction over it.

See, also, Curtiss's Com. on the Jurisdiction, &c., of the Courts of the United States, sections 12 and 13; the latter section, containing a quotation from another portion (p. 865) of the opinion of Chief Justice Marshall in Osborn *vs.* the Bank of the United States, apparently quite pertinent to the question in this case.

I concur, then, in the conclusion of Judge Leonard, that Congress had the power to direct the transfer to the Circuit Court of the United States.

Probably an order of this Court directing such transfer is not absolutely necessary, but to make one would be in accordance with usage in like cases; and besides, such an order would be the best evidence of the determination of this Court, that it no longer had jurisdiction of this action.

It appearing that the defendant has complied with the requirements of the act for such transfer, the order appealed from should be reversed, and an order made by this Court for the removal of the action and all proceedings therein to the Circuit Court of the United States.

Dissenting Opinion.

CLERKE, J.—I see nothing whatever in the arguments of my brethren, or in those of other judges on the same subject, to induce me to recede from the position which I have attempted to maintain at Special Term. They have all alike, in my very humble judgment, unaccountably overlooked the only point claiming consideration on this great constitutional subject.

According to the doctrine upheld by my brethren, we can scarcely conceive of any act committed by any officer of the General Government, under color of any authority derived from or under the President, which may not constitute a genuine, veritable case arising under the Constitution of the United States, and which, therefore, may not rightly come within the cognizance of their judicial power. It is only necessary to claim that it was committed under color of that authority, and was, therefore, justified by the Constitution, however monstrous and appalling the act may be, to make it, according to this doctrine, a case arising under that Constitution. For, of course, according to the terms of that claim, the claimant appeals through this remarkable statute, to the Constitution for his justification, and, however palpably frivolous such a claim may be—however palpably manifest may be the conviction that the Constitution no more sanctions such an act than it sanctions the burning of the Capitol, the dispersion of Congress, and the shooting, imprisonment or exile of the men of whom it is composed, yet it is claimed to present a question, and, therefore, a case arising under the Great Charter of Constitutional Liberty in America—the perpetrator of the outrage making that a question which is unquestionably no question; and the judicial power of the State is ousted of its legitimate jurisdiction. Thus, this extraordinary statute prescribes not only that the character, but the mere assertion of the wrong-doer shall determine jurisdiction, and that the subject-matter, which has been always held, except in cases affecting Embassadors, other diplomatic Ministers and Consuls, as alone the criterion of jurisdiction, shall be excluded from consideration. Surely, if this can be done by Congress, the Government of the United States of America, is not as all men have heretofore supposed, incontestably a Government of limited powers and duties, and is, if not one of unlimited powers and duties, nevertheless, of very accommodating expansibility. This is a novel and strange theory of development in America.

But, it is asserted as the appellate power of the Supreme Court of the United States extends in certain cases to State tribunals, that this case would, after judgment, reach the Federal jurisdiction, and that, therefore, it may as well be transferred to the United States Circuit Court before judgment. Even if the Supreme Court of the United States would entertain such a case on appeal this is no controlling reason why it should, necessarily, be transferred to the United States Circuit for adjudication in the first instance. For, the only question to be determined by us on this motion, is whether Congress has the power to transfer cases of this description to the Circuit Court of the United States, not whether, ultimately, it may reach the appellate jurisdiction of the United States Supreme Court.

The act of Congress, passed in 1789, "to establish the judicial courts of the United States," no doubt provides that a final judgment or decree in any suit in the highest court of law or equity of a State, where is drawn in question the validity of a statute of the United States, and the decision is against its validity, may be re-examined and revised or affirmed in the Supreme Court of the United States. But, if it is too clear for controversy that the statute is an outrage on the Constitution, if it is palpably usurpation, if it is plain to the most unlettered citizen, that the statute is an attempt to subvert all the securities which the founders of the Government have provided for the preservation of personal liberty, and to invest one man with unlimited dictatorial power, and, therefore, that the appeal was palpably frivolous, I presume the court would hear no argument on such an appeal, and would, forthwith, affirm the judgment or dismiss the writ.

Would they, for instance, hearken to an appeal involving the validity of an act of Congress giving the President or any other member of the Government power, by a *coup d'etat*, to extinguish the legislative branch, as Cromwell did the Long Parliament, and substitute a Barebones Legislature in its place? Surely not; if they, too, were not struck down, and were not (if said debasement can be imagined) by force, by fear, or by corrupt appliances or selfish aspirations, robbed of independence. So that the consideration whether the act is not palpably void must present itself on appeal as it now presents itself to us on this motion; and, if it is palpably void, I repeat it would not be treated on appeal as worthy of being for a moment entertained.

I still consider the defence in this case just as destitute of color as the case which I have imagined. Whether, under the pretext of authority from the President of the United States, any one citizen, at his mere will and pleasure, without any intervention of the judicial tribunals, can incarcerate another citizen not subject to military law in a loathsome dungeon, for many months, or for a day or an hour, cannot, under any circumstances in which the nation may be placed, be treated as a question constituting a case arising under the Constitution; and any statute which declares the contrary is palpably void. The order at Special Term should be affirmed with costs.

MILITARY ARRESTS.

The following order has been issued by General Augur:

HEADQUARTERS DEPARTMENT OF WASHINGTON,
22D ARMY CORPS, *June* 20, 1864.

GENERAL ORDER No. 51.—*First:* Hereafter no citizen, commissioned officer, or enlisted man, will be arrested on the report of a detective employed by any officer subject to the jurisdiction of this department, except in extreme cases where there is no doubt of guilt, and immediate action is needed, until the report has first been forwarded for action at these headquarters.

Second: All officers serving in this department employing detectives will send with as little delay as possible a list of those employed to these headquarters, specifying the authority by whom employed; and they are notified that they will be held responsible for improper action or abuse of authority on the part of their employees.

By command of Major General C. C. AUGUR:
J. H. TAYLOR,
Chief of Staff, A. A. G.

"Confederate" Legislation.

[From the Richmond Sentinel, Feb. 17, 1864.]

SUSPENSION OF THE WRIT OF HABEAS CORPUS.

The following bill passed both Houses of Congress:

A Bill to suspend the privilege of the writ of *habeas corpus* in certain cases.

Whereas, the Constitution of the Confederate States of America provides, in article 1, section 9, paragraph 3, that "the privilege of the writ of *habeas corpus* shall not be suspended, unless when, in cases of rebellion or invasion, the public safety may require it;" and whereas the power of suspending the privilege of said writ, as recognized in said article 1, is vested solely in the Congress, which is the exclusive judge of the necessity of such suspension; and whereas, in the opinion of the Congress, the public safety requires the suspension of said writ in the existing case of the invasion of these States by the armies of the United States; and whereas, the President has asked for the suspension of the writ of *habeas corpus*, and informed Congress of conditions of public danger which render the suspension of the writ a measure proper for the public defence against invasion and insurrection: Now, therefore,

I. That during the present invasion of the Confederate States, the privilege of the writ of *habeas corpus* be and the same is hereby suspended; but such suspension shall apply only to the cases of persons arrested or detained by order of the President, Secretary of War, or the general officer commanding the Trans-Mississippi Military Department, by the authority and under the control of the President. It is hereby declared that the purpose of Congress in the passage of this act is to provide more effectually for the public safety by suspending the writ of *habeas corpus* in the following cases, and no other:

1. Of treason, or treasonable efforts or combinations, to subvert the Government of the Confederate States.

2. Of conspiracies to overthrow the Government, or conspiracies to resist the lawful authority of the Confederate States.

3. Of combining to assist the enemy, or of communicating intelligence to the enemy, or giving him aid and comfort.

4. Of conspiracies, preparations and attempts to incite servile insurrection.

5. Of desertions or encouraging desertions, or harboring deserters, and of attempts to avoid military service: *Provided*, That in cases of palpable wrong and oppression by any subordinate officer, upon any party who does not legally owe military service, his superior officer shall grant prompt relief to the oppressed party, and the subordinate shall be dismissed from office.

6. Of spies and other emissaries of the enemy.

7. Of holding correspondence or intercourse with the enemy, without necessity, and without the permission of the Confederate States.

8. Of unlawful trading with the enemy and other offences against the laws of the Confederate States, enacted to promote their success in the war.

9. Of conspiracies, or attempts to liberate prisoners of war held by the Confederate States.

10. Of conspiracies, or attempts or preparations to aid the enemy.

11. Of persons aiding or inciting others to abandon the Confederate cause, or to resist the Confederate States, or to adhere to the enemy.

12. Of unlawful burning, destroying or injuring, or attempting to burn, destroy or injure any bridge or railroad, or telegraph line of communication, or other property with the intent of aiding the enemy.*

13. Of treasonable designs to impair the military power of the Government by destroying or attempting to destroy the vessels or arms, or munitions of war, or arsenals, foundries, workshops, or other property of the Confederate States.

The remaining sections are unimportant. The act to continue in force 90 days after meeting of next Congress.

EXTENT OF POWER CLAIMED BY THE GOVERNMENT.

The instructions of the War Department with respect to proceedings under the law making a limited or *quasi* suspension of the *habeas corpus*, remove many grounds of clamor, and propose what may be considered as a very moderate execution of the law. Parties arrested, in the cases specified in the law, will not be denied a trial, but their cases will be investigated by commissioners, who will

---

* Respecting this offence, this order was issued in 1861:

WAR DEPARTMENT,
RICHMOND, *November* 25, 1861.

SIR: Your report of the 20th instant is received, and I now proceed to give you the desired instructions in relation to the prisoners taken by you among the traitors of East Tennessee.

First. All such as can be identified in having been engaged in bridge burning are to be tried summarily by drum-head court-martial, and, if found guilty, executed on the spot by hanging. It would be well to leave their bodies hanging in the vicinity of the burnt bridges.

Second. All such as have not been so engaged are to be treated as prisoners of war, and sent with an armed guard to Tuscaloosa, Alabama, there to be kept imprisoned at the depot selected by the Government for prisoners of war.

Whenever you can discover that arms are concentrated by these traitors, you will send out detachments, search for and seize the arms. In no case is one of the men known to have been up in arms against the Government to be released on any pledge or oath of allegiance. The time for such measures is past. They are to be held as prisoners of war, and held in jail till the end of the war. Such as come in voluntarily, take the oath of allegiance, and surrender their arms, are alone to be treated with leniency.

Your vigilant execution of these orders is earnestly urged by the Government.

Your obedient servant,
J. P. BENJAMIN, *Secretary of War.*

Col. W. B. WOOD, *Knoxville, Tenn.*

P. S.—Judge Patterson, Col. Pickens, and other ringleaders of the same class, must be sent at once to Tuscaloosa to jail as prisoners of war.

be appointed for these duties in the different military departments.

Information of all arrests under the law will be given by the department commander as soon as practicable after they are made, and the commissioner will proceed to investigate the same. If, upon examination, a reasonable and probable cause for detention does not appear, he will certify the fact to the general or other officer in command, who will immediately discharge the prisoner from arrest. But if a reasonable and probable cause does appear, the commissioner will forthwith transmit to the War Department a copy of the evidence taken in the case, with his opinion thereon, for instructions, and meanwhile the prisoner will remain in custody.

In cases where persons not belonging to the military service shall apply to any court or officer in the Confederate States for a writ of *habeas corpus*, it will be the duty of the officer having the command or custody of such person forthwith to report the case, with all the relevant facts, to the War Department, for instructions as to the proper answer to be made to such writ.

Newspaper Exclusion and Suppression.

August 16, 1861—In the United States Circuit Court of New York the grand jury presented the *Journal of Commerce*, the *Daily News*, the *Freeman's Journal*, and the *Brooklyn Eagle* as aiders and abettors of treason, in terms following:

To the Circuit Court of the United States for the Southern District of New York:

The Grand Inquest of the United States of America for the Southern District of New York beg leave to present the following facts to the Court and ask its advice thereon:

There are certain newspapers within this district which are in the frequent practice of encouraging the rebels now in arms against the Federal Government by expressing sympathy and agreement with them, the duty of acceding to their demands, and dissatisfaction with the employment of force to overcome them. These papers are the New York daily and weekly *Journal of Commerce*, the daily and weekly *News*, the daily and weekly *Day-Book*, the *Freeman's Journal*, all published in the city of New York, and the daily and weekly *Eagle*, published in the city of Brooklyn. The first named of these has just published a list of newspapers in the free States opposed to what it calls "*the present unholy war*"—a war in the defence of our country and its institutions, and our most sacred rights, and carried on solely for the restoration of the authority of the Government.

The Grand Jury are aware that free Governments allow liberty of speech and of the press to their utmost limit, but there is nevertheless a limit. If a person in a fortress or an army were to preach to the soldiers submission to the enemy he would be treated as an offender. Would he be more culpable than the citizen who, in the midst of the most formidable conspiracy and rebellion, tells the conspirators and rebels that they are right, encourages them to persevere in resistance, and condemns the effort of loyal citizens to overcome and punish them as an "unholy war?" If the utterance of such language in the streets or through the press is not a crime, then there is a great defect in our laws, or they were not made for such an emergency.

The conduct of these disloyal presses is of course condemned and abhorred by all loyal men; but the Grand Jury will be glad to learn from the Court that it is also subject to indictment and condign punishment.

All which is respectfully presented.

CHARLES GOULD, *Foreman.*

NEW YORK, *August* 16, 1861.

[Signed by all the Grand Jurors.]

ORDER OF THE POSTMASTER GENERAL.

POST OFFICE DEPARTMENT, *August* 22, 1861.

SIR: The Postmaster General directs that from and after your receipt of this letter none of the newspapers published in New York city which were lately presented by the grand jury as dangerous, from their disloyalty, shall be forwarded in the mails.

I am, respectfully, your obedient servant,

T. B. TROTT, *Chief Clerk.*

To the POSTMASTER, *New York City.*

SEIZURES OF NEWSPAPERS.

PHILADELPHIA, *August* 22—On the arrival of the New York train this morning Marshal Millward, and his officers, examined all the bundles of papers and seized every copy of the New York Daily News. The sale of this paper is totally suppressed in this city. Marshal Millward also seized all the bundles of the Daily News at the Express offices for the West and South, including over one thousand copies for Louisville, and nearly five hundred copies for Baltimore, Washington, Alexandria, and Annapolis. The Marshal also took possession of the office of the Christian Observer in consequence of a late violent article on the "unholy war."

Other newspapers were similarly excluded from the mails, and in due time, the subject engaged the attention of Congress; resolutions of inquiry having been offered in the Senate, January 14, 1863, by Mr. CARLILE, and in the House, December 1, 1862, by Mr. VALLANDIGHAM.

1863, January 20—The Committee on Judiciary of the House of Representatives made a report, which embodied the following letter of the Postmaster General:

POST OFFICE DEPARTMENT, *January* 5, 1863.

SIR: I have the honor to acknowledge the receipt of the communication signed by you in behalf of the Judiciary Committee, embracing a copy of the resolution of the House of Representatives, in the following words:

"*Resolved*, That the Committee on the Judiciary be instructed to inquire and report to the House at an early day by what authority of Constitution and law, if any, the Postmaster General undertakes to decide what newspapers may and what shall not be transmitted through the mails of the United States."

On the first day of the last session of Congress, being the earliest opportunity after the action to which the resolution relates, I submitted to Congress a statement of my action, and of the general reasons and authority for the same, in the following language:

"Various newspapers, having more or less influence within the sphere of their circulation, were represented to be, and were, in fact, devoting their columns to the furtherance of the schemes of our national enemies. These efforts were persistently directed to the advancement of hostile interests, to thwart the efforts made to preserve the integrity of the Union, and to accomplish the results of open treason without incurring its judicial penalties. To await the results of slow judicial prosecution was to allow crime to be consummated, with the expectation of subsequent punishment, instead of preventing its accomplishment by prompt and direct interference.

"The freedom of the press is secured by a high constitutional sanction. But it is freedom and not license that is guaranteed. It is to be used only for lawful purposes. It cannot aim blows at the existence of the Government, the Constitution, and the Union, and at the same time claim its protection. As well could the assassin strike his blow at human life, at the same time claiming that his victim should not commit a breach of the peace by a counter blow. While, therefore, this department neither enjoyed nor claimed the power to suppress such treasonable publications, but left them free to publish what they pleased, it could not be called upon to give them circulation. It could not and would not interfere with the freedom secured by law, but it could and did obstruct the dissemination of that license which was without the pale of the Constitution and law. The mails established by the United States Government could not, upon any known principle of law or public right, be used for its destruction. As well could the common carrier be legally required to transport a machine designed for the destruction of the vehicle conveying it, or an innkeeper be compelled to entertain a traveller whom he knew to be intending to commit a robbery in his house.

"I find these views supported by the high authority of the late Justice Story, of the Supreme Court of the United States. He says, in commenting on that clause of the Constitution securing the freedom of the press:

"'That this amendment was intended to secure to every citizen an absolute right to speak, or write, or print whatsoever he might please, without any responsibility, public or private, therefor, is a supposition too wild to be indulged in by any rational man. This would be to allow to every citizen the right to destroy at his pleasure the reputation, the peace, the property, and even the personal safety of every other citizen. A man might, out of mere malice or revenge, accuse another of the most infamous crimes; might excite against him the indignation of all his fellow-citizens by the most atrocious calumnies; might disturb, nay, overturn all his domestic peace and embitter his parental affections; might inflict the most distressing punishment upon the weak, the timid, and the innocent; might prejudice all a man's civil and political and private rights; and might stir up sedition, rebellion, and treason, even against the Government itself, in the wantonness of his passions, or the corruption of his heart. Civil society could not go on under such circumstances. Men would then be obliged to resort to private vengeance to make up the deficiency of the law; and assassinations and savage cruelties would be perpetrated with all the frequency belonging to barbarous and cruel communities. It is plain, then, that the language of this amendment imports no more than that every man has a right to speak, write, and print his opinions upon any subject whatever, without any prior restraint, so always that he does not injure any other person in his rights, person, property, or reputation; *and so always that he does not thereby disturb the public peace, or attempt to subvert the Government.*'"

"Of the cases presented for my action, upon the principles above named, I have by order excluded from the mails twelve of these treasonable publications, of which several had been previously presented by the grand jury as incendiary and hostile to constitutional authority."

I am not aware that at any time, nor from any quarter, during that long session, any inquiry or complaint was made, or objection taken touching that action, or the considerations then presented in support of it. From this it was fairly inferred that Congress then unanimously recognized the action as not only in harmony with, but in direct aid of, the Constitution of the United States, then shaken by the assaults of its avowed enemies.

The immediate occasion of the orders excluding certain newspapers from the mails was a communication to this department of the action of a grand jury of the United States circuit court for the Southern District of New York. Their presentment was in the following words. [See *ante* for presentment.]

This authoritative exhibition of the character of these papers, as disseminators of treason and instigators of the highest crime known to our laws, could not be disregarded, accompanied, as it was, by representations of their dangerous effect upon the military operations of the country. Entertaining the highest possible regard for the liberty of the press, distinguished from its uncontrolled and criminal license, I would not, except in time of war, have adopted the arguments of my predecessors in office, in justification of the non-delivery of printed matter sent through the mails. The question has been repeatedly presented to my predecessors in time of peace in relation to printed matter styled "incendiary," or "abolition in its character," and in respect to the States now in insurrection. While justifying postmasters in their refusal to receive or forward mail matter described by the general terms of the postal laws as "mailable matter," an eminent Postmaster General of the administration of General Jackson, under date of August 22, 1835, addressed a letter to the postmaster at New York giving his views upon the question under discussion. The New York postmaster had assumed to decide that certain newspapers, placed in that post office for conveyance in the mails, were incendiary in their character, and calculated to promote insurrection. He refused to forward them. The Postmaster General, declining himself to decide upon the character of the publications in question, and refusing to make the orders thereon, justified his deputy postmaster in the decision made by him, and supported him by the following arguments, extracted from his letter of that date, to which the attention of Congress was subsequently called. That Congress, however, by its inaction, seemed to concur in the right and the policy of excluding such alleged treasonable and insurrectionary publications from the mails.

POST OFFICE DEPARTMENT, *August* 22, 1835.

* "Postmasters may lawfully know, in all cases, the contents of newspapers, because the law expressly provides that they shall be so put up that they may be readily examined; and if they know those contents to be calculated and designed to produce, and, if delivered, will certainly produce, the commission of the most aggravated crimes upon the property and persons of their fellow citizens, it cannot be doubted that it is their duty to detain them, if not even to hand them over to the civil authorities. *

* "If it be justifiable to detain papers passing through the mail, for the purpose of preventing or punishing isolated crimes against individuals, how much more important is it that this responsibility should be assumed to prevent insurrections and save communities? If, in time of war, a postmaster should detect a letter of an enemy or spy passing through the mail, which, if it reached its destination, would expose his country to invasion and her armies to destruction, ought he not to arrest it? Yet, where is the legal power to do so?

"*As a measure of great public necessity, therefore, you and the other postmasters who have assumed the responsibility of stopping these inflammatory papers will, I have no doubt, stand justified in that step before your country and all mankind.*

* * "Are the officers of the United States compelled by the Constitution and laws to become the instruments and accomplices of those who design to baffle and make nugatory the constitutional laws of the States; to fill them with sedition and murder and insurrection; to overthrow those institutions which are recognized and guarantied by the Constitution itself? * * In these considerations there is reason to doubt whether the abolitionists have a right to make use of the mails of the United States to convey their publications into States where their circulation is forbidden by law, and it is by no means certain that mail-carriers and postmasters are secure from the penalties of that law, if they knowingly carry, distribute, or hand them out. * * As well may the counterfeiter and robber demand the use of the mails for consummating their crimes, and complain of a violation of their rights when it is denied.

"Upon these grounds a postmaster may well hesitate to be the agent of the abolitionists in sending their incendiary publications into States where their circulation is prohibited by law; and much more may postmasters residing in those States refuse to distribute them. * * I do not desire to be understood as affirming that the suggestions here thrown out ought, without the action of higher authority, to be considered as the settled construction of the law, or regarded by postmasters as the rule of their future action. It is only intended to say that in a sudden emergency, involving principles so grave and consequences so serious, the safest course for postmasters and the best for the country is that which you have adopted. * * * You prevent your Government from being the unwilling agent and abettor of crimes against the States which strike at their very existence, and give time for the proper authorities to discuss the principles involved and digest a safe rule for the future guidance of the department.

"While persisting in a course which philanthropy recommends and patriotism approves, I doubt not that you and the other postmasters who have assumed the responsibility of stopping these inflammatory papers in their passage to the South will perceive the necessity of performing your duty in transmitting and delivering ordinary newspapers, magazines, and pamphlets, with perfect punctuality. Occasion must not be given to charge the postmasters with carrying their precautions beyond the necessities of the case, or capriciously applying them to other cases in which there is no necessity; and it would be the duty, as well as the inclination, of the department to punish such assumption with unwonted severity. This suggestion I do not make because I have any apprehension that it is needed for your restraint, but because I wish this paper to bear upon its face a complete explanation of the views which I take of my own duty in the existing emergency."

The question was afterwards repeatedly presented in this department. In February, 1857, it was brought before Postmaster General Campbell, in connection with the exclusion of the Cincinnati *Gazette* from postal privileges in Mississippi. A certain postmaster at Yazoo had denied it the privilege of his post office. Mr. Campbell referred the question to the Attorney General of President Pierce's administration. Under date of March 2, 1857, the Attorney General, as the law officer of the Government, replied officially to the Postmaster General, justifying such action on the part of postmasters, and asserting, among others, the following arguments and conclusions:

"ATTORNEY GENERAL'S OFFICE,
"*March* 2, 1857.

* * "With these premises we have the main question very much simplified. It is this: Has a citizen of one of the United States plenary indisputable right to employ the functions and the officers of the Union as the means of enabling him to produce insurrection in another of the United States? Can the officers of the Union lawfully lend its functions to the citizens of one of the States for the purpose of promoting insurrection in another State?

"Taking the last of these questions first, it is obvious to say that, inasmuch as it is the constitutional obligation of the United States to protect each of the States against 'domestic violence,' and to make provision to 'suppress insurrections,' it cannot be the right of the United States, or of any of its officers, and, of course, it cannot be their duty to promote, or be the instrument of promoting, insurrection in any part of the United States.

"As to the first question, likewise, it seems obvious to say, that, as insurrection in any one of the States is violation of law, not only so far as regards that State itself, but also as regards the United States, therefore no citizen of the Union can lawfully incite insurrection in any one of the States. * * * It would be preposterous to suppose that any citizen of the United States has lawful right to do that which he is bound by law to prevent when attempted by any and all others; and monstrous to pretend that a citizen of one of the States has a moral right to promote or commit insurrection or domestic violence, that is, robbery, burglary, arson, rape, and murder, by wholesale, in another of the States.

"These considerations, it seems to me, are decisive of the question of the true construction of the act of Congress. Of that it is impossible for me to doubt. Its enactment is, that 'if any postmaster shall unlawfully detain,' he shall be subject to fine, imprisonment, and disqualification.

Then, if the thing be of lawful delivery, it cannot be lawfully detained; while, on the other hand, it cannot be unlawful to detain that which it is unlawful to deliver. Such is the plain language and the manifest import of the act of Congress.

"I do not mean to be understood that the word 'unlawfully' of the act determines the case: on the contrary, my conclusion would be the same, though that word had not been here inserted. By employing it, indeed, the act expressly admits that there may be lawful cause of detention. But such lawful cause would not the less exist, although its existence were not thus expressly recognized. And, of all conceivable causes of detention, there can be none more operative than treasonableness of character, for in every society the public safety is the supremest of laws.

"Nay, if, instead of expressly admitting lawful causes of detention, the act had undertaken to exclude them—if, for instance, it had in terms required the postmasters to circulate papers, which, in tendency and purpose, are of character to incite insurrection in any of the States—still my conclusion would be the same. I should say of such a provision of law it is a nullity, it is unconstitutional; not so by reason of conflict with any State law, but because inconsistent with the Constitution of the United States.

"The Constitution forbids insurrection; it imposes on Congress and the President the duty of suppressing insurrection; this obligation descends through Congress and the President to all the subordinate functionaries of the Union, civil and military; and any provision of an act of Congress requiring a Federal functionary to be the agent or minister of insurrection in either of the States would violate palpably the positive letter, and defeat one of the primary objects, of the Constitution.

"These, my conclusions, apply only to newspapers, pamphlets, or other printed matter, the character of which is of public notoriety, or is necessarily brought to the knowledge of the postmaster by publicity of transmission through the mails unsealed, and as to the nature of which he cannot plead ignorance.

* * "It is intimated in one of the documents before me that to permit a deputy postmaster to detain a newspaper because of its imputed unlawfulness would be to erect him into a censor of the press. These are but words of rhetorical exaggeration. Public journals are a necessary part of our social life, just as much as the steamboat, the railway train, or the telegraph. There is not the least reason to apprehend that we shall suffer ourselves to be deprived of them by the interposition of unlawful impediments to their circulation.

* * "We shall appreciate the true legal relation of the whole question if we consider a supposition which has more than once heretofore been actual fact, and may be such again. Suppose that some European Government—whether in the prosecution of war, or induced by hostility of purpose not yet become war, but tending towards it, or in the spirit of misdirected propagandism of its own particular social or political opinions—should undertake to produce revolution or insurrection in the United States. Would it, in that case, be the duty, would it be the right, of the Government or officers of the Union to aid the foreign Government in its inimical machinations? To this general inquiry, of course, there can be but one possible answer. It would be the manifest duty of every officer of the United States—nay, of every officer of each State—nay, of every citizen of the United States, to resist, and to do everything in his power to defeat all such machinations; for every citizen of the United States is under engagement, express or implied, to uphold and maintain the Constitution.

"In the general contingency supposed it is quite immaterial whether foreign attempts to produce revolution consist of exhortations to insurrection by word of mouth—that is, the introduction of emissaries of sedition into the country—or of exhortations to insurrection in the form of handbills, newspapers, or pamphlets. In whatever manner attempted, the thing itself would be an act of wrongful or hostile attack on our sovereignty and on our national and private peace; defensible as an act of war on the part of an enemy Government, but otherwise against natural law, against public law, against municipal law; and therefore, on all these accounts, requiring to be manfully withstood and counteracted by every sound-hearted and true-minded citizen of the United States, and more especially by all officers, civil and military, of the Federal Government, from the President down to the humblest village postmaster in the land.

"The general supposition includes printed, equally with oral, exhortations to insurrection. Take now, by itself, the case of printed matter of that description. Is it the legal duty of the Post Office Department knowingly to circulate such matter? Is it the legal duty of deputy postmasters? Or reducing the general supposition down to its narrowest expression in the limited exigencies of the present case, is a deputy postmaster required knowingly to circulate such matter under penalty of indictment, removal from office, and disqualification? Is the inconvenience which the foreign Government or its emissary may suffer, in not being able to effect the free circulation of such treasonable matter—or the inconvenience which the disaffected person to whom it was addressed suffers, in his not being able to receive and to circulate further such treasonable matter—are these inconveniences to outweigh the inconvenience to the whole country, as well as to individuals, of insurrection, and of civil or servile war? Is that the true construction of the act of Congress? I think no legal expositor could hesitate to say, no.

"Now in what does the general case supposed, with its all but self-evident conclusions, differ from the specific case under consideration? Simply, that any European Government possesses the sovereign right, as an act of war, to attack us with attempts to excite insurrection as well as with cannon—subject to be repelled by the sovereign power of the Union—but no citizen of the United States possesses legal right to promote rebellious acts in any part of the country, whether as against the authority of the United States or of the particular State in which he is, or of any other of the States.

* * "In fine, the proposition may be made universal to the effect that no person in the United States, whether he be citizen, subject, or alien, has the legal right to promote rebellion. * * In the foregoing series of suppositions we have reasoned out a conclusion from the premises of the attempt of a foreign Government, by the use of our mails and post offices, to promote insurrection in the United States. * * And shall not the citizens of one of the States of the Union be held entitled to the same security from attempts to promote insurrection among them, on the part of their fellow-citizens of other States? * * On the whole, then, it seems clear to me that a deputy postmaster, or other officer of the United States, is not required by law to become knowingly the enforced agent or instrument of enemies of the public peace, to disseminate, in their behalf, within the limits of any one of the States of the Union printed matter, the design and tendency of which are to promote insurrection in such State."*

Again, in 1859, Mr. Holt, then at the head of this department, in a letter dated the 5th of December of that year, addressed to a postmaster in Virginia, adhered to the precedents, and said:

"One of the most solemn constitutional obligations imposed on the Federal Government is that of protecting the States against 'insurrection' and 'domestic violence;' of course none of its instrumentalities can be lawfully employed in inciting, even in the remotest degree, to the very crime which involves in its train all others, and with the suppression of which it is especially charged."

These citations show that a course of precedents has existed in this department for twenty-five years—known to Congress, not annulled or restrained by act of Congress—in accordance with which newspapers and other printed matter, decided by postal officers to be insurrectionary, or treasonable, or in any degree inciting to treason or insurrection, have been excluded from the mails and post offices of the United States solely by authority of the executive administration. This, under the rules settled by the Supreme Court of the United States, as applicable to executive construction of laws with whose execution the departments are specially

---

* JEFFERSON DAVIS thus expressed himself on this opinion of Attorney General CUSHING a few months after its publication:

WASHINGTON, *January* 4, 1858.

GENTLEMEN: When I last addressed you in answer to your letter communicating the views and feelings of the citizens of Yazoo City, in relation to the circulation of incendiary matter through the mails of the United States, I promised that you should hear from me further, and gave you assurance of such action by the last Administration as would be satisfactory to you.

I have thus long delayed the promised communication in expectation of receiving the opinion of the Attorney General upon the legal merits of the case, the question having been referred to him by the Postmaster General, the Hon. James Campbell.

The Attorney General, in the opinion enclosed, sustains the conclusion of the President and the Postmaster General, and so satisfactorily disposes of the question at issue that I hope that we shall be saved from any further agitation of it.

Concurring fully with you in your opinion of the powers of a State, the duty of its citizens, and the obligation of our community in such contingency as that presented by the case reported in your letter, I trust we shall also agree that the matter has been concluded in a manner worthy of the State-Rights Administration under which it arose.

With great regard, I am your friend and fellow-citizen,

JEFFERSON DAVIS.

To Messrs. Robert Bowman, George B. Wilkinson, and A. M. Harlow, committee, Yazoo City.

charged, would establish my action as within the legal construction of the postal acts authorizing the transportation of printed matter in the United States mails. It would settle the right of this department and its various officers to resist all efforts to make them *particeps criminis* of treason and rebellion, by compelling them to circulate and distribute with their own hands the moral weapons which are to bring civil war to their firesides, with its horrible train of barbarities in the destruction of life and property.

Upon the like considerations I have, at different times, excluded from the mails obscene and scandalous printed matter on exhibition of its criminal immorality. If an unsealed printed publication were offered to the mails, instigating murder, arson, destruction of railroads, or other crimes, and advocating an organization for such purposes, I should, upon the same principles, without hesitation, exclude it from the mails as unlawful matter, in the absence of a contravening act of Congress.

I do not wish to be understood, however, as indorsing, but rather as distinctly dissenting from, some of the arguments and conclusions, and from the extent to which preceding Administrations have gone, as indicated by some of the foregoing citations. The precedents and arguments go far beyond any action which I have taken, or would be willing to take, under the like circumstances.

1st. I reject that portion of the precedents which allows twenty-eight thousand postmasters of the country to judge, each for himself, what newspapers are lawful and what unlawful; what may go in the mails and what shall be excluded. I have refused to allow postmasters to sit in final judgment upon all the interests involved, subject as they are to conflicting local prejudices. The Postmaster General, who is more directly responsible to Congress, and more accessible to their inquiries, should alone exercise such authority, in whatever degree it exists, and should not devolve it on subordinates. Whatever control can be lawfully exercised over the mails by a postmaster may always be exercised or ordered by the chief, under whose direction the law expressly subordinates the postmaster. This is a self-evident proposition. It has, however, been sustained by the official opinion of the Attorney General of the United States, dated March 2, 1857.

2d. I dissent from the extent to which the doctrine has been carried by late administrations, that in time of peace, and in the absence of all hostile or criminal organizations, operating against Constitution or law, either a Postmaster General, or any postmaster, can at will exclude from the mails newspapers and other printed matter which contain discussions obnoxious to some special interest, but not aimed against Government, law, or the public safety. It is too dangerous a discretion to be exercised or desired by any executive officer attached to the constitutional freedom of the press. Such has been, in some cases, the action of this department in late years, and I take this occasion to break the too great uniformity of its decisions in this respect. Even in time of war, the power so long conceded should be used with great care and delicacy. I say in time of war, because the executive department has powers then which do not attach to it in time of peace. The Constitution provides that no person shall "be deprived of life, liberty, or property without due process of law; nor shall private property be taken for public use without just compensation." Yet, in time of war, the life, liberty, and property of persons in the United States, being also insurrectionary enemies of the United States, are necessarily taken without any process except that of powder and the bayonet. And no man denies the right as an incident of war. Yet, in peace, it could not be done. These acts are as thoroughly constitutional in war as they are unconstitutional in peace. In harmony with this principle, I would give far greater latitude to alleged wrongful and obnoxious printed matter in a period of peace than would be justifiable in a time of war.

This reply to the inquiry transmitted to me by the committee embraces the following conclusions:

First. That the exercise of the authority inquired of rests upon the Constitution of the United States, and the definition of mailable matter given in the postal law, as construed by past administrations of this department, enforced by the official opinion of a late Attorney General of the United States, and known to and recognized by former Congresses of the United States.

Second. That a power and a duty to prevent hostile printed matter from reaching the enemy, and to prevent such matter from instigating others to co-operate with the enemy, by the aid of the United States mails, exist in time of war, and in the presence of treasonable and armed enemies of the United States, which do not exist in time of peace, and in the absence of criminal organizations.

Third. That the present Postmaster General has restricted the exercise of the power during this war far within the scope claimed and allowed by former Administrations in periods of national peace.

I have the honor to be, very respectfully, your obedient servant, M. BLAIR, *Postmaster General.*

The committee review the case, and conclude as follows:

Your committee are not unmindful of the fact that too great caution cannot be exercised in arriving at a conclusion as to what is and what is not lawful mailable matter; or, in other words, what papers, publications, or messages are treasonable in their character, or for other reasons unlawful, and should, therefore, be excluded from the mails.

In the case now before the committee the grand jury of one of the federal courts in the State of New York concurred in opinion with the head of the Post Office Department in the construction of the character of the publications, and the purposes of the publishers, it being, too, in a time when extreme vigilance was demanded in the executive department of the Government to preserve the integrity of the Union. And the object being to secure that noble and patriotic object, your committee believe the act of the Postmaster General was not only within the scope of his powers, but induced solely by considerations of the public good.

Mr. Geo. H. Pendleton, of Ohio, (of the Judiciary Committee,) in his speech, March 3, 1863, in the House, quoted these two additional paragraphs from Amos Kendall's opinion of 1835:

"After mature consideration of the subject, and seeking the best advice within my reach, I am confirmed in the opinion that the Postmaster General has no legal authority, by any order or regulation of the Department, to exclude from the mails any species of magazines, newspapers, or pamphlets. Such a power vested in the head of this Department would be fearfully dangerous, and has therefore been withheld. Any order or letter of mine directing or officially sanctioning the step you have taken would, therefore, be utterly powerless and void, and would not in the slightest degree relieve you from its responsibility. * *

"The Postmaster General has no legal power to prescribe any rules for the government of postmasters in such cases; nor has he ever attempted to do so. They act in each case on their own responsibility; and if they improperly detain or use papers sent to their offices for transmission or delivery it is at their peril, and on their heads falls the punishment. If in time of war a postmaster should detect the letter of an enemy or a spy passing through the mail, which, if it reached its destination, would expose his country to invasion and her armies to destruction, ought he not to arrest it? Yet where is his legal power to do so?"

He added:

In 1836, Mr. Calhoun, as chairman of a special committee of the Senate, reported a bill making it a penal offence for any postmaster to receive into the mails for transmission to any person within a State, or to deliver out of the mails to any such person, any publication the circulation of which was forbidden by that State. Subsequently the first clause of the bill was stricken out, and the latter, relating to the delivery of such matter, was retained. It gave rise to much discussion, and elicited an extremely able debate from the most eminent members of that then very able body. Mr. Calhoun, the zealous advocate of the bill, contended that a bill of this nature was the only one which Congress had the power to pass; that Congress could not discriminate in reference to character what publications shall or shall not be transmitted through the mail, without abridging the liberty of the press, and subjecting it to the control of congressional legislation; but that no such restriction applied to the States; they might forbid such publications as they thought dangerous, and that Congress had the power, and ought to exercise it, of co-operating with the States in repressing the circulation of publications thus prohibited.

The circulation of anti-slavery documents, tending to excite servile insurrection, had become a great evil. It had awakened fears of trouble among the slaves, and had therefore exasperated the people. Most of the slaveholding States had passed laws forbidding their circulation under severe penalties. They were still carried through the mails, and it began to be questioned whether the postmasters were not relieved from the penalties of the State law because they were acting under the sanction of Federal law. Great anxiety existed to relieve the apprehensions of the southern people. The President, General Jackson, recommended the subject most earnestly to Congress. He did not pretend that there existed any power of relief in any of the Executive Departments. Senators, almost without exception, expressed a determination to go as far as they could to apply a remedy. But the bill was most strenuously opposed. It was said to curtail the freedom of the press. * * * * *

The bill was lost by a majority of seven; Messrs. Benton, Clay, Crittenden, Southard, Wall, Leigh, Goldsborough, among others from the slaveholding States; and Messrs.

Webster, Niles, Ewing, and Davis, with others from the non-slaveholding States voting against it. And yet it is in reference to this discussion and this action that the Postmaster General in his letter to the committee says "that Congress by its inaction seemed to concur in the right and the policy of excluding such alleged treasonable and insurrectionary publications from the mails." On the contrary, Congress expressly refused to sanction the idea that it had the power; and certainly no other department of the Government has.

Generals commanding departments frequently prohibit the circulation of certain newspapers within the limits of their commands. Major General Wallace, May 18, 1864, suppressed the Baltimore *Evening Transcript*. Major General Rosecrans, May 26, 1864, prohibited the circulation of the *Metropolitan Record* in the department of Missouri. The circulation of the Cincinnati *Enquirer* has recently been prohibited, by the General commanding, in Kentucky.

A REMINISCENCE.

VIRGINIA AND THE TRIBUNE.

POST OFFICE, LYNCHBURG, VIRGINIA,
December 2, 1859.

MR. HORACE GREELEY:

SIR: I hereby inform you that I shall not, in future, deliver from this office the copies of the *Tribune* which come here, because I believe them to be of that incendiary character which are forbidden circulation alike by the laws of the land, and a proper regard for the safety of society. You will, therefore, discontinue them.

Respectfully, R. H. GLASS, *Postmaster*.

—

Reply.

NEW YORK, *December* 9, 1859.

MR. POSTMASTER OF LYNCHBURG, VIRGINIA:

SIR: I take leave to assure you that I shall do nothing of the sort. The subscribers to the *Tribune* in Lynchburg have paid for their papers; we have taken their money, and shall fairly and fully earn it, according to contract. If *they* direct us to send their papers to some other post office, we shall obey the request; otherwise, we shall send them as originally ordered. If you or your masters choose to steal and destroy them, that is your affair—at all events, not ours; and if there is no law in Virginia to punish the larceny, so much the worse for her and our plundered subscribers. If the Federal Administration, whereof you are the tool, after monopolizing the business of mail-carrying, sees fit to become the accomplice and patron of mail-robbery, I suppose the outrage must be borne until more honest and less servile rulers can be put into high places at Washington, or till the people can recover their natural right to carry each other's letters and printed matter, asking no odds of the Government. Go ahead in your own base way. I shall stand steadfast for human liberty and the protection of all natural rights.

Yours, stiffly, HORACE GREELEY.

THE RECENT SUPPRESSION IN NEW YORK.

1864, May 19—By order of the Secretary of War, the offices of the *Journal of Commerce* and the *World*—in which papers had appeared a forged proclamation of the President for 400,000 troops—were seized by the military authorities and held for several days. This led to these proceedings:

Gov. Seymour's Letter to the District Attorney.

STATE OF NEW YORK, EXECUTIVE DEPARTMENT,
ALBANY, *May* 23, 1864.

To A. OAKEY HALL, Esq.,
District Attorney of the County of New York:

SIR: I am advised that on the 19th inst., the office of *The Journal of Commerce* and that of *The New York World* were entered by armed men, the property of the owners seized, and the premises held by force for several days. It is charged that these acts of violence were done without due legal process, and without the sanction of State or national laws.

If this be true the offenders must be punished.

In the month of July last, when New York was a scene of violence, I gave warning that "the laws of the State must be enforced, its peace and order maintained, and the property of its citizens protected at every hazard." The laws were enforced at a fearful cost of blood and life.

The declaration I then made was not intended merely for that occasion or against any class of men. It is one of an enduring character, to be asserted at all times and against all condition of citizens, without favor or distinction. Unless all are made to bow to the law, it will be respected by none.

Unless all are made secure in their rights of person and property, none can be protected. If the owners of the above-named journals have violated State or national laws, they must be proceeded against and punished by those laws. Any action against them outside of legal procedures is criminal. At this time of civil war and disorder, the majesty of the law must be upheld or society will sink into anarchy. Our soldiers in the field will battle in vain for constitutional liberty if persons or property, or opinions, are trampled upon at home. We must not give up home freedom, and thus disgrace the American character while our citizens in the army are pouring out their blood to maintain the national honor. They must not find when they come back that their personal and fireside rights have been despoiled.

In addition to the general obligation to enforce the laws of the land, there are local reasons why they must be upheld in the city of New York. If they are not, its commerce and greatness will be broken down. If this great center of wealth, business, and enterprise is thrown into disorder and bankruptcy, the National Government will be paralyzed. What makes New York the heart of our country? Why are its pulsations felt at the extremities of our land? Not through its position alone, but because of the world-wide belief that property is safe within its limits from waste by mobs and from spoliation by Government.

The laborers in the workshop, the mine, and in the field, on this continent and in every other part of the globe, send to its merchants, for sale or exchange, the products of their toil. These merchants are made the trustees of the wealth of millions living in every land, because it is believed that in their hands property is safe under the shield of laws administered upon principle and according to known usages. This great confidence has grown up in the course of many years by virtue of a painstaking, honest performance of duty by the business men of your city. In this they have been aided by the enforcement of laws based upon the solemnly-recorded pledges that "the right of the people to be secure in their persons, houses, papers, and effects against unreasonable searches and seizures shall not be violated, and that no one shall be deprived of liberty or property without due process of law."

For more than eighty years have we as a people been building up this universal faith in the sanctity of our jurisprudence. It is this which carries our commerce upon every ocean and brings back to our merchants the wealth of every clime. It is now charged that, in utter disregard of the sensitiveness of that faith, at a moment when the national credit is undergoing a fearful trial, the organs of commerce are seized and held, in violation of constitutional pledges, that this act was done in a public mart of your great city, and was thus forced upon the notice of the commercial agents of the world, and they were shown in an offensive way that property is seized by military force and arbitrary orders.

These things are more hurtful to the national honor and strength than the loss of battles. The world will confound such acts with the principles of our Government, and the folly and crimes of officials will be looked upon as the natural results of the spirit of our institutions. Our State and local authorities must repel this ruinous inference. If the merchants of New York are not willing to have their harbor sealed up and their commerce paralyzed, they must unite in this demand for the security of persons and property. If this is not done, the world will withdraw from their keeping its treasures and its commerce.

History has taught all that official violation of law in times of civil war and disorder goes before acts of spoilation and other measures which destroy the safeguards of commerce.

I call upon you to look into the facts connected with the seizure of *The Journal of Commerce* and of *The New York World*. If these acts were illegal, the offenders must be punished. In making your inquiries and in prosecuting the parties implicated, you will call upon the Sheriff of the county and the heads of the Police Department for any needed force or assistance. The failure to give this by any official under my control will be deemed a sufficient cause for his removal.

Very respectfully yours, &c.,
HORATIO SEYMOUR.

CHARGE OF JUDGE RUSSELL,

Of the New York Court of General Sessions, June 13, to the grand jury, composed as follows:

Cyrus Mason, Foreman, John E. Anderson, Nathaniel W. Carter, Martin L. Delafield, Mathew Hettrick, John J. Hayer, David C. Newell, James H. Pinckney, Wm. Palen, Wm.

R... won, J. Austin Stevens, jr., Amos H. Trowbridge, Samuel L. Beekman, Seabury Brewster, Jacob D. T. Hersey, Benedict Lewis, jr., Willard Phelps, Wm. T. Skeff, W. M. Thurman, John P. Worstell, John Townsend, John D. Welsh, Chris. Zabriskie, jr.

The grand jury having taken the usual oath, Judge Russell delivered a charge in which he thus alluded to the order for the arrest of the proprietors, and for the suppression of their journals:

The first part of the order was never fully executed. The latter part was, and the forcible possession maintained for several days. The author of the fraud, it is said, has been discovered, and the newspapers in question have been exonerated from all suspicion of guilt or blame. If this be so, this is an instance of innocent men being summarily interfered with, or trespassed upon, in the sanctity of their persons and property. As such, it is a violation of both the Federal and State Constitutions, and it is your duty to examine into it. This is not a self-imposed or self-assumed duty by this court. The facts were communicated to the Executive of this State, and he addressed to the district attorney of this county the communication I now read to you.

[The Judge then read Governor Seymour's letter.]

Acting upon the duty this Court owes to the laws of this State, which is repeated in the official document I have just read to you, I beg to submit the matter to your calmest and most careful consideration. The Court is convinced that you will deal with it in such a manner as becomes the dutiful and loyal citizens of a dutiful and loyal State. Anything like political bias should be discarded. The question is simply thus: Have the laws of the State, in reference to the protection of person and property, been violated, and if so, who are the parties who have been concerned in it? No matter what their station may be, they must answer for the wrong, if there be one. If the President of the United States, or other officer who assumed to issue the order, had no such power or authority, those who obeyed and enforced it are clearly responsible.

For the purposes of this occasion, the Court instructs you that such an order as has been referred to would not, under the circumstances stated, be any protection to those concerned in its execution. This will raise the question at issue between the State and General Government in a legal way. Any attempt to interfere with freedom of speech or liberty of the press has been regarded and watched with the greatest jealousy by the constituents of our Federal and State Governments. These invaluable privileges are protected in both the Federal and State Constitutions. Neither Congress nor our State Legislature can make a law abridging either right. In the year 1798, the famous "Sedition law" was passed by Congress, giving the Government extraordinary power in reference to publications calculated to weaken its authority. So unpalatable was this law that it was finally repealed. Two of the State Legislatures expressly declared against its constitutionality. At the time it was passed, the Government being in a state of comparative infancy, it ought probably to have been more favorably regarded; but it involved rights too dear to be trenched upon or surrendered. In reference to the alleged author of the spurious proclamation, you will receive evidence of the fact establishing his guilt, and if you are satisfied of it, you will present him for such an offence as, under the advice of the district attorney, (to whom you are entitled to appeal for advice,) may be proper. At common law, the "spreading false news to make discord between the king and nobility, or concerning any great man of the realm," was an offence against the public peace, punishable with fine and imprisonment.

It may be that the elements of the common law will be invoked by the district attorney in reference to this offender. In reference to the parties engaged in taking and maintaining forcible possession of the newspaper establishments, the court instructs you that if there were three or more of them, they would be liable as for riot, which has been defined to be "where three or more actually do an unlawful act of violence, either with or without a common cause or quarrel, or even do a lawful act, as removing a nuisance, in a violent or tumultuous manner."

RESPONSE OF THE GRAND JURY.

Resolved, That the grand inquest respectfully represent to the honorable court that, in their judgment, it is inexpedient to examine into the subject referred to in the communication of the Executive of the State and the charge of the court, namely: the action of the General Government as to certain newspapers in this city.

CYRUS MASON, *Foreman*.

JOHN AUSTIN STEVENS, Jr., *Secretary*.

13

THE LAWS TO BE ENFORCED.

Letter from Governor Seymour to District Attorney Hall, of New York.

EXECUTIVE CHAMBER,
ALBANY, *June* 25.

A. OAKEY HALL, Esq.,
District Attorney of the City and County of New York:

SIR: In the matter of the seizure of the offices of *The World* and *Journal of Commerce*, the grand jury, in disregard of their oaths, "to diligently inquire into and true presentment make of all such matters and things as should be given them in charge," have refused to make such inquiries, and declare that "it is inexpedient to examine into the subject referred to in the charge of the court" with respect to such seizures. It becomes my duty, under the express requirements of the constitution, "to take care that the laws of the State are faithfully executed." If the grand jury, in pursuance of the demands of the law and the obligations of their oaths, had inquired into the matter given them in charge by the court and the public prosecutor, their decision, whatever it might have been, would have been entitled to respect. As they have refused to do their duty, the subject of the seizure of these journals should at once be brought before some proper magistrate. If you wish any assistance in the prosecution of these investigations, it will be given to you.

As it is a matter of public interest that violations of the laws of the State be punished, the views or wishes of the parties immediately affected must not be suffered to influence the action of public officers. If through fear or other motives they are unwilling to aid you in getting at facts, it will be your duty to compel their attendance as witnesses in behalf of the people.

Respectfully yours,

HORATIO SEYMOUR.

The newspapers give this account of further proceedings:

THE ARREST OF GENERAL DIX.

The arrest of General Dix and several other officers on Friday, July 1, was made upon warrants issued by City Judge Russell. Several persons appeared before the city judge, in answer to subpœnas allowed by him, at the instance of District Attorney Hall, and had testified to facts relating to the seizure of *The World* and *Journal of Commerce* newspapers. The letter of Governor Seymour to the district attorney, condemning the grand jury for its return in the case of those newspapers, and saying that "the subject should be brought before some proper magistrate," is said to have induced the district attorney to procure the affidavits to be made before Russell. The district attorney first made an affidavit in the form of a complaint, dated 28th June, in which he declared that he had been informed and believed that "Hon. A. Lincoln" directed "John A. Dix" to do several acts against *The World* and *Journal of Commerce*, and the editors of those journals, enumerated in the complaint of the district attorney, and charging that the said Dix "feloniously ordered one William Barstow" (Captain Barstow) to arrest the editors of the newspapers named, and "mischievously ordered one William Hays" (Acting Assistant Provost Marshal General Hays) to procure the closing up of the newspaper offices; that the arrest of Mr. Hallock was procured, and that gentleman kept for the space of about three hours; that "the said Hays instructed Major Powers, who caused one Fundy" (Captain Fundy) and some commissioned officers and privates, whom the district attorney names, to "go armed and equipped" to take possession of the *Journal of Commerce* office; and that the said Hays caused similar acts to be done to *The World*, through Lieutenant Gabriel Tuthill and several other soldiers. The district attorney then charges that John A. Dix and William Barstow are guilty of kidnapping, and the others, with John A. Dix, of inciting to a riot and forcibly detaining property; and the district attorney prays that action be taken to sustain the dignity of the State.

Judge Russell then issued subpœnas, directed to Messrs. William H. Hallock, of the *Journal of Commerce*; David G. Croly, of *The World*; William W. Jacobus, John S. Betts, auctioneer, Daniel R. Kirwan, and Washington Hills, Jr., clerk in *The World* office, who appeared before the judge and made their several affidavits, the district attorney examining the witnesses.

ARREST OF GENERAL DIX BY THE SHERIFF.

In accordance with the letter of Governor Seymour, directing the matter of the suppressed newspapers to be brought before a magistrate, Mr. A. Oakey Hall commenced taking evidence and submitting testimony before Judge Russell on Tuesday. After examining the witnesses, Judge Russell came to the conclusion that it was a proper case for him to issue his warrant. Accordingly warrants were placed in the hands of the sheriff, who arrested Major General Dix, Major Barstow, Captain Fundy, Major Powers. and other officers on guard at the offices of *The World* and *Journal of Commerce.*

The military gentlemen very courteously submitted to the arrest, and their counsel, E. Delafield Smith, appeared before Judge Russell. Mr. Smith asked for time to examine into the papers and consult with his associate, ex-Judge Pierrepont, as to the future course to be pursued by them. The matter was then adjourned, the defendants in the meantime being released on their own verbal recognizances.

—

First Session, Thirty-Eighth Congress.

IN SENATE.

1864, May 26—Mr. POWELL offered this resolution, which went over:

Resolved, That the conduct of the executive authority of this Government, in recently closing the offices and suppressing the publication of *The World* and *Journal of Commerce*, newspapers in the city of New York, under circumstances which have been placed before the public, was an act unwarranted in itself, dangerous to the cause of the Union, in violation of the Constitution, and subversive of the principles of civil liberty, and as such is hereby censured by the Senate.

—

IN HOUSE.

May 23—Mr. GRINNELL asked consent to offer this resolution, but it was objected to:

Resolved, That the President be requested to communicate to this House whether, by any order of the Government, or by any officer thereof, *The World* and *Journal of Commerce*, newspapers in the city of New York, were suspended from being published; and if so, that said order be communicated to this House, and the proceedings in the execution of that order.

May 23—Mr. PRUYN asked consent, on behalf of a portion of the New York delegation, to offer this resolution:

Resolved, That the conduct of the executive authority of the Government in recently closing the offices and suppressing the publication of *The World and Journal of Commerce*, newspapers in the city of New York, under circumstances which have been placed before the public, was an act unwarranted in itself, dangerous to the cause of the Union, in violation of the Constitution, and subversive of the principles of civil liberty, and as such is hereby censured by this House.

Several members objected. At a later hour he moved a suspension of the rules for the purpose of offering it, but this motion was rejected—yeas 54, nays 79, as follows:

YEAS—Messrs. *James C. Allen, Augustus C. Baldwin, Bliss, Brooks, James S. Brown, Chanler, Coffroth, Cox, Dawson, Denison, Eden, Edgerton, Eldridge, Finck, Grider, Harding, Charles M. Harris, Herrick, Holman, Hutchins, Philip Johnson, William Johnson, Kalbfleisch, Kernan, King, Knapp, Law, Lazear, Mallory, Marcy, McAllister, McDowell, William H. Miller, Morrison, Nelson, Noble, John O'Neill, Pendleton, Pruyn, Radford, Samuel J. Randall, Robinson, James S. Rollins, Ross, Scott, John B. Steele, William G. Steele, Strouse, Voorhees, Wadsworth, Ward, Wheeler, Joseph W. White, Fernando Wood*—54.

NAYS—Messrs. Alley, Ames, Arnold, John D. Baldwin, Baxter, Beaman, Jacob B. Blair, Blow, Boutwell, Boyd, Broomall, William G. Brown, Ambrose W. Clark, Freeman Clarke, Cobb, Cole, Creswell, Henry Winter Davis, Thomas T. Davis, Dawes, Deming, Dixon, Donnelly, Driggs, Eckley, Eliot, Farnsworth, Garfield, Gooch, Grinnell, Higby, Hooper, Hotchkiss, Asahel W. Hubbard, Ingersoll, Jenckes, Julian, Kelley, Francis W. Kellogg, Loan, Longyear, Marvin, McBride, McClurg, Samuel F. Miller, Moorhead, Morrill, Amos Myers, Leonard Myers, Charles O'Neill, Orth, Patterson, Perham, Pike, Pomeroy, Price, William H. Randall, John H. Rice, Edward H. Rollins, Schenck, Scofield, Shannon, Sloan, Smith, Smithers, Spalding, Stevens, Thayer, Thomas, Upson, Elihu B. Washburne, William B. Washburn, Webster, Whaley, Williams, Wilder, Wilson, Windom, Woodbridge—79.

Same day, Mr. ARNOLD offered this resolution, which was adopted:

Resolved, That the Committee on the Judiciary be instructed to inquire and report what, if any, additional legislation may be necessary to punish the forgery and publication of official documents, and what legislation is necessary to punish those who through the press or otherwise give information, aid, or comfort to the rebels.

CONFISCATION AND EMANCIPATION.

CONFISCATION.

First Session, Thirty-Seventh Congress.

1861, August 6 —A bill was approved, of which these are the first and fourth sections:

That if, during the present or any future insurrection against the Government of the United States, after the President of the United States shall have declared, by proclamation, that the laws of the United States are opposed, and the execution thereof obstructed, by combinations too powerful to be suppressed by the ordinary course of judicial proceedings, or by the power vested in the marshals by law, any person or persons, his, her, or their agent, attorney, or employee, shall purchase or acquire, sell or give, any property of whatsoever kind or description, with intent to use or employ the same, or suffer the same to be used or employed, in aiding, abetting, or promoting such insurrection or resistance to the laws, or any persons engaged therein; or if any person or persons, being the owner or owners of any such property, shall knowingly use or employ, or consent to the use or employment of the same as aforesaid, all such property is hereby declared to be lawful subject of prize and capture wherever found; and it shall be the duty of the President of the United States to cause the same to be seized, confiscated, and condemned.

SEC. 4. That whenever hereafter, during the present insurrection against the Government of the United States, any person claimed to be held to labor or service under the law of any State shall be required or permitted by the person to whom such labor or service is claimed to be due, or by the lawful agent of such person, to take up arms against the United States; or shall be required or permitted by the person to whom such labor or service is claimed to be due, or his lawful agent, to work or to be employed in or upon any fort, navy-yard, dock, armory, ship, entrenchment, or in any military or naval service whatsoever, against the Government and lawful authority of the United States, then, and in every such case, the person to whom such labor or service is claimed to be due shall forfeit his claim to such labor, any law of the State or of the United States to the contrary notwithstanding. And whenever thereafter the person claiming such labor or service shall seek to enforce his claim, it shall be a full and sufficient answer to such claim that the person whose service or labor is claimed had been employed in hostile service against the Government of the United States, contrary to the provisions of this act.

This bill, as reported from the Judiciary Committee of the Senate, did not contain the fourth section, and while it was pending in the Senate Mr. TRUMBULL moved to add this as a new section July 22:

That whenever any person claiming to be entitled to the service or labor of any other person under the laws of any State, shall employ such person in aiding or promoting any insurrection, or in resisting the laws of the United States, or shall permit him to be so employed, he shall forfeit all right to such service or labor, and the person whose labor or service is thus claimed shall be thenceforth discharged therefrom, any law to the contrary notwithstanding.

Which was agreed to—yeas 33, nays 6, as follows:

YEAS—Messrs. Anthony, Bingham, Browning, Chandler, Clark, Collamer, Cowan, Dixon, Doolittle, Fessenden, Foot, Foster, Grimes, Hale, Harlan, Harris, Howe, *Johnson* of Tennessee, King, Lane of Kansas, *McDougall*, Morrill, *Nesmith*, Pomeroy, Sherman, Simmons, Sumner, Ten Eyck, Trumbull, Wade, Wilkinson, Wilmot, Wilson—33.

NAYS—Messrs. *Breckinridge*, *Johnson* of Missouri, *Kennedy*, *Pearce*, *Polk*, *Powell*—6.

The bill then passed without a division.

IN HOUSE.

August 2—The House Committee on the Judiciary reported a substitute for the bill, which provides that whenever hereafter, during the existence of the present insurrection against the Government of the United States, any person held to labor or service under the laws of any State shall be required or permitted, by the person to whom such labor or service is due, or his legal agent, to take up arms against the United States, or to work, or be employed in or about any fort, navy-yard, armory, dock-yard, ship, or in any military or naval service, against the Government of the United States, or as the servant of any person engaged in active hostilities against the United States, then the person to whom such labor is due shall forfeit all claim to such service or labor, any law of any State, or of the United States, to the contrary notwithstanding; and, in case of a claim for such labor, such facts shall be a full and sufficient answer.

Which was rejected without a division; when, after debate, the bill was recommitted to the committee.

August 3—The committee reported the Senate bill with a substitute for section four, adopted above in the Senate, being the fourth section of the act as approved.

A motion to table the bill was lost—yeas 47, nays 66; and the amendment was agreed to, and the bill passed—yeas 61, nays 48, as follows:

YEAS—Messrs. Aldrich, Alley, Arnold, Ashley, Babbitt, Baxter, Beaman, Bingham, Francis P. Blair, Samuel S. Blair, Blake, Buffinton, Chamberlain, Clark, Colfax, Frederick A. Conkling, Covode, Duell, Edwards, Eliot, Fenton, Fessenden, Franchot, Frank, Granger, Gurley, Hanchett, Harrison, Hutchins, Julian, Kelley, Francis W. Kellogg, William Kellogg, Lansing, Loomis, Lovejoy, McKean, Mitchell, Justin S. Morrill, Olin, Potter, Alexander H. Rice, Edward H. Rollins, Sedgwick, *Sheffield*, Shellaberger, Sherman, Sloan, Spaulding, *W. G. Steele*, Stevens, Benjamin F. Thomas, Train, Van Horn, Verree, Wallace, Charles W. Walton, E. P. Walton, Wheeler, Albert S. White, Windom—61.

NAYS—Messrs. *Allen*, *Ancona*, *Joseph Baily*, *George H. Browne*, *Burnett*, *Calvert*, *Cox*, *Cravens*, *Crisfield*, *Crittenden*, Diven, *Dunlap*, Dunn, *English*, *Fouke*, *Grider*, *Haight*, Hale, *Harding*, *Holman*, Horton, *Jackson*, *Johnson*, *Law*,

May, McClernand, McPherson, *Mallory, Menzies, Morris, Noble, Norton, Odell, Pendleton*, Porter, *Reid, Robinson, James S. Rollins, Shiel, Smith, John B. Steele*, Stratton, Francis Thomas, *Vallandigham, Voorhees, Wadsworth*, Webster, *Wickliffe*—48.

August 5—The Senate concurred in the amendment of the House—yeas 24, nays 11, as follows:

YEAS—Messrs. Anthony, Bingham, Browning, Clark, Collamer, Dixon, Doolittle, Fessenden, Foot, Foster, Grimes, Hale, Harris, King, Lane of Indiana, Lane of Kansas, *McDougall*, Sherman, Simmons, Sumner, Ten Eyck, Trumbull, Wade, Wilson—24.

NAYS—Messrs. *Breckinridge, Bright, Carlile*, Cowan, *Johnson* of Missouri, *Latham, Pearce, Polk, Powell, Rice, Saulsbury*—11.

Second Session, Thirty-Seventh Congress.

1862, July 17—A bill was approved to "suppress insurrection, to punish treason and rebellion, to seize and confiscate the property of rebels, and for other purposes," which contains these provisions:

That every person who shall hereafter commit the crime of treason against the United States, and shall be adjudged guilty, shall suffer death, or be imprisoned not less than five years and fined not less than $10,000, (the fine to be levied on all property excluding slaves,) and all his slaves, if any, shall be declared and made free.

That if any person shall hereafter incite, set on foot, assist, or engage in any rebellion or insurrection against the authority of the United States, or the laws thereof, or shall give aid or comfort thereto, or shall engage in, or give aid and comfort to, any such existing rebellion or insurrection, and be convicted thereof, such person shall be punished by imprisonment for a period not exceeding ten years, or by a fine not exceeding ten thousand dollars, and by the liberation of all his slaves, if any he have; or by both of said punishments, at the discretion of the court.

That every person guilty of either of the offences described in this act shall be forever incapable and disqualified to hold any office under the United States.

That this act shall not be construed in any way to affect or alter the prosecution, conviction, or punishment of any person or persons guilty of treason against the United States before the passage of this act, unless such person is convicted under this act.

That, to insure the speedy termination of the present rebellion, it shall be the duty of the President of the United States to cause the seizure of all the estate and property, money, stocks, credits, and effects of the persons hereinafter named in this section, and to apply and use the same and the proceeds thereof for the support of the army of the United States, that is to say:

First. Of any person hereafter acting as an officer of the army or navy of the rebels in arms against the Government of the United States.

Secondly. Of any person hereafter acting as President, Vice President, member of Congress, judge of any court, cabinet officer, foreign minister, commissioner or consul of the so-called Confederate States of America.

Thirdly. Of any person acting as Governor of a State, member of a convention or legislature, or judge of any court of any of the so-called Confederate States of America.

Fourthly. Of any person who, having held an office of honor, trust, or profit in the United States, shall hereafter hold an office in the so-called Confederate States of America.

Fifthly. Of any person hereafter holding any office or agency under the Government of the so-called Confederate States of America, or under any of the several States of the said Confederacy, or the laws thereof, whether such office or agency be national, State, or municipal in its name or character: *Provided*, That the persons, thirdly, fourthly, and fifthly above described, shall have accepted their appointment or election since the date of the pretended ordinance of secession of the State, or shall have taken an oath of allegiance to, or to support the Constitution of the so-called Confederate States.

Sixthly. Of any person who, owning property in any loyal State or Territory of the United States, or in the District of Columbia, shall hereafter assist and give aid and comfort to such rebellion; and all sales, transfers, or conveyances of any such property shall be null and void; and it shall be a sufficient bar to any suit brought by such person for the possession or the use of such property, or any of it, to allege and prove that he is one of the persons described in this section.

That if any other persons in armed rebellion, or abetting it, shall not, within sixty days after proclamation to be made, return to their allegiance, all their estate and property shall be liable to seizure, and it shall be the duty of the President to seize and use them as aforesaid.

To secure condemnation and sale of such property, proceedings *in rem* shall be instituted in the name of the United States in any district or territorial court thereof within which the property may be found, &c.

That all slaves of persons who shall hereafter be engaged in rebellion against the Government of the United States, or who shall in any way give aid or comfort thereto, escaping from such persons and taking refuge within the lines of the army; and all slaves captured from such persons or deserted by them and coming under the control of the Government of the United States; and all slaves of such persons found *on* [or] being within any place occupied by rebel forces and afterwards occupied by the forces of the United States, shall be deemed captives of war, and shall be forever free of their servitude and not again held as slaves.

That no slave escaping into any State, Territory, or the District of Columbia, from any other State, shall be delivered up, or in any way impeded or hindered of his liberty, except for crime or some offence against the laws, unless the person claiming said fugitive shall first make oath that the person to whom the labor or service of such fugitive is alleged to be due is his lawful owner, and has not borne arms against the United States in the present rebellion, nor in any way given aid and comfort thereto; and no person engaged in the military or naval service of the United States shall, under any pretence whatever, assume to decide on the validity of the claim of any person to the service or labor of any other person, or surrender up any such person to the claimant, on pain of being dismissed from the service.

That the President of the United States is authorized to employ as many persons of African descent as he may deem necessary and proper for the suppression of this rebellion, and for this purpose he may organize and use them in such manner as he may judge best for the public welfare.

That the President of the United States is hereby authorized to make provision for the transportation, colonization, and settlement, in some tropical country beyond the limits of the United States, of such persons of the African race made free by the provisions of this act as may be willing to emigrate, having first obtained the consent of the Government of said country to their protection and settlement within the same, with all the rights and privileges of freemen.

That the President is hereby authorized, at any time hereafter, by proclamation, to extend to persons who may have participated in the existing rebellion in any State or part thereof, pardon and amnesty, with such exceptions and at such time and on such conditions as he may deem expedient for the public welfare.

Same day—This joint resolution was approved:

That the provisions of the third clause of the fifth section of "An act to suppress insurrection, to punish treason and rebellion, to seize and confiscate the property of rebels, and for other purposes," shall be so construed as not to apply to any act or acts done prior to the passage thereof; nor to include any member of a State Legislature, or judge of any State court, who has not in accepting or entering upon his office, taken an oath to support the Constitution of the so-called Confederate States of America; nor shall any punishment or proceedings under said act be so construed as to work a forfeiture of the real estate of the offender beyond his natural life.

VOTE ON THE BILL.

July 11—The bill, being the report of a committee of conference, passed the House—yeas 82, nays 42, as follows:

YEAS—Messrs. Aldrich, Alley, Arnold, Ashley, Babbitt, Baxter, Beaman, Bingham, Jacob B. Blair, Samuel S. Blair, Blake, Buffinton, Campbell, Casey, Clark, Colfax, Frederick A. Conkling, Roscoe Conkling, Covode, Cutler, Davis, Dawes, Duell, Dunn, Edwards, Eliot, Ely, Fenton, Fessenden, Fisher, Frank, Gooch, Goodwin, Gurley, Hale, Hooper, Hutchins, Julian, Kelley, Francis W. Kellogg, William Kellogg, Lansing, Loomis, Lovejoy, Low, McKnight, McPherson, Maynard, Mitchell, Moorhead, Anson P. Morrill, Justin S. Morrill, Nixon, Patton, Timothy G. Phelps, Pike, Porter, Potter, Alexander H. Rice, John H. Rice, Riddle, Edward H. Rollins, Sargent, Sedgwick, Shanks, Shellabarger, Sherman, Stevens, Stratton, Trimble, Trowbridge, Van Horn, Verree, Wall, Wallace, Walton, Washburne, Wheeler, Albert S. White, Wilson, Windom, Worcester—82.

NAYS—Messrs. *William Allen*, *William J. Allen*, *Ancona*, *Baily*, *Biddle*, *George H. Browne*, Clements, *Cobb*, *Cox*, *Crisfield*, *Crittenden*, *Dunlap*, *Fouke*, Granger, *Grider*, *Haight*, *Hall*, *Harding*, *Holman*, *Kerrigan*, *Knapp*, *Law*, *Lazear*, *Lehman*, *Mallory*, *Menzies*, *Morris*, *Nugen*, *Odell*, *Pendleton*, *James S. Rollins*, Segar, *Shiel*, *John B. Steele*, *William G. Steele*, *Stiles*, Benjamin F. Thomas, Francis Thomas, *Ward*, Webster, *Wickliffe*, *Wood*—42.

July 12—The bill passed the Senate—yeas 28, nays 13, as follows:

YEAS—Messrs. Anthony, Chandler, Clark, Doolittle, Fessenden, Foot, Foster, Grimes, Hale, Harlan, Harris, Howard, Howe, King, Lane of Indiana, Lane of Kansas, Morrill, Pomeroy, Sherman, Simmons, Sumner, Ten Eyck, Trumbull, Wade, Wilkinson, Wilmot, Wilson of Massachusetts, *Wright*—28.

NAYS—Messrs. *Bayard*, Browning, *Carlile*, Cowan, *Davis*, Henderson, *Kennedy*, *McDougall*, *Powell*, *Saulsbury*, *Stark*, Willey, *Wilson* of Missouri—13.

THE JOINT RESOLUTION.

July 15—Mr. MAYNARD, on a suspension of the rules, (yeas 68, nays 33,) introduced the joint resolution, which is the same as the above, omitting the last clause, and which passed the House without a division.

July 16—In SENATE,

Mr. CLARK moved to add the last clause.

Mr. POWELL moved to strike out the word "real"; which was rejected—yeas 6, nays 31, as follows:

YEAS—Messrs. *Davis*, Henderson, *Powell*, *Saulsbury*, *Stark*, *Wilson* of Missouri—6.

NAYS—Messrs. Anthony, Browning, Chandler, Clark, Cowan, Doolittle, Fessenden, Foot, Foster, Grimes, Hale, Harlan, Harris, Howard, Howe, King, Lane of Indiana, Lane of Kansas, *McDougall*, Morrill, Pomeroy, Sherman, Simmons, Sumner, Ten Eyck, Trumbull, Wade, Wilkinson, Wilmot, Wilson of Massachusetts, *Wright*—31.

The amendment of Mr. CLARK was agreed to—yeas 25, nays 15, as follows:

YEAS—Messrs. Anthony, Browning, Chandler, Clark, Collamer, Cowan, Doolittle, Fessenden, Foot, Foster, Hale, Harris, Henderson, Howard, Howe, Lane of Kansas, Morrill, Pomeroy, Sherman, Simmons, Sumner, Ten Eyck, Willey, Wilson of Massachusetts, *Wright*—25.

NAYS—Messrs. *Carlile*, *Davis*, Grimes, Harlan, *Kennedy*, King, Lane of Indiana, *Powell*, *Saulsbury*, *Stark*, Trumbull, Wade, Wilkinson, Wilmot, *Wilson* of Missouri—15.

July 17—The PRESIDENT sent this message to Congress:

Fellow-Citizens of the Senate and
House of Representatives:

Considering the bill for "An act to suppress insurrection, to punish treason and rebellion, to seize and confiscate the property of rebels, and for other purposes," and the joint resolution explanatory of said act, as being substantially one, I have approved and signed both.

Before I was informed of the resolution, I had prepared the draft of a message, stating objections to the bill becoming a law, a copy of which draft is herewith submitted.

ABRAHAM LINCOLN.

July 12, 1862.

[Copy.]

Fellow-Citizens of the House of Representatives:

I herewith return to your honorable body, in which it originated, the bill for an act entitled "An act to suppress treason and rebellion, to seize and confiscate the property of rebels, and for other purposes," together with my objections to its becoming a law.

There is much in the bill to which I perceive no objection. It is wholly prospective; and it touches neither person or property of any loyal citizen, in which particular it is just and proper.

The first and second sections provide for the conviction and punishment of persons who shall be guilty of treason, and persons who shall "incite, set on foot, assist, or engage in any rebellion or insurrection against the authority of the United States, or the laws thereof, or shall give aid or comfort thereto, or shall engage in or give aid and comfort to any such existing rebellion or insurrection." By fair construction, persons within those sections are not punished without regular trials in duly constituted courts under the forms and all the substantial provisions of law and the Constitution applicable to their several cases. To this I perceive no objection; especially as such persons would be within the general pardoning power, and also the special provision for pardon and amnesty contained in this act.

It is also provided that the slaves of persons convicted under these sections shall be free. I think there is an unfortunate form of expression, rather than a substantial objection, in this. It is startling to say that Congress can free a slave within a State, and yet if it were said the ownership of the slave had first been transferred to the nation, and Congress had then liberated him, the difficulty would at once vanish. And this is the real case. The traitor against the General Government forfeits his slave at least as justly as he does any other property; and he forfeits both to the Government against which he offends. The Government, so far as there can be ownership, thus owns the forfeited slaves, and the question for Congress in regard to them is, "shall they be made free or sold to new masters?" I perceive no objection to Congress deciding in advance that they shall be free. To the high honor of Kentucky, as I am informed, she is the owner of some slaves by *escheat*, and has sold none, but liberated all. I hope the same is true of some other States. Indeed, I do not believe it will be physically possible for the General Government to return persons so circumstanced to actual slavery. I believe there would be physical resistance to it, which could neither be turned aside by argument nor driven away by force. In this view I have no objection to this feature of the bill. Another matter involved in these two sections and running through other parts of the act will be noticed hereafter.

I perceive no objections to the third and fourth sections.

So far as I wish to notice the fifth and sixth sections, they may be considered together. That the enforcement of these sections would do no injustice to the persons embraced within them is clear. That those who make a causeless war should be compelled to pay the cost of it is too obviously just to be called in question. To give governmental protection to the property of persons who have abandoned it and gone on a crusade to overthrow that same Government is absurd, if considered in the mere light of justice. The severest justice may not always be the best policy. The principle of seizing and appropriating the property of the person embraced within these sections is certainly not very objectionable, but a justly discriminating application of it would be very difficult, and, to a great extent impossible. And would it not be wise to place a power of remission somewhere, so that these persons may know they have something to lose by persisting and something to gain by desisting? I am not sure whether such power of remission is or is not within section thirteen. Without any special act of Congress, I think our military commanders, when, in military phrase, "they are within the enemy's country," should, in an orderly manner, seize and use whatever of real or personal property may be necessary or convenient for their commands; at the same time preserving, in some way, the evidence of what they do.

What I have said in regard to slaves while commenting on the first and second sections is appplicable to the ninth, with the difference that no provision is made in the whole act for determining whether a particular individual slave does or does not fall within the classes defined in that section. He is to be free upon certain conditions; but whether those conditions do or do not pertain to him, no mode of ascertaining is provided. This could be easily supplied.

To the tenth section I make no objection. The oath therein required seems to be proper, and the remainder of the section is substantially identical with a law already existing.

The eleventh section simply assumes to confer discretionary power upon the Executive. Without the law, I have no hesitation to go as far in the direction indicated as I may at any time deem expedient. And I am ready to say now, I think it is proper for our military commanders to employ, as laborers, as many persons of African descent as can be used to advantage.

The twelfth and thirteenth sections are something better than objectionable; and the fourteenth is entirely proper, if all other parts of the act shall stand.

That to which I chiefly object pervades most part of the act, but more distinctly appears in the first, second, seventh, and eighth sections. It is the sum of those provisions which results in the divesting of title forever.

For the causes of treason and ingredients of treason, not amounting to the full crime, it declares forfeiture extending beyond the lives of the guilty parties; whereas the Constitution of the United States declares that "no attainder of treason shall work corruption of blood, or forfeiture except during the life of the person attainted." True, there is to be no formal attainder in this case; still, I think the greater punishment cannot be constitutionally inflicted, in a different form, for the same offence.

With great respect I am constrained to say I think this feature of the act is unconstitutional. It would not be difficult to modify it.

I may remark that the provision of the Constitution, put in language borrowed from Great Britain, applies only in this country, as I understand, to real or landed estate.

Again, this act, *in rem*, forfeits property for the ingredients of treason without a conviction of the supposed criminal, or a personal hearing given him in any proceeding. That we may not touch property lying within our reach because we cannot give personal notice to an owner who is absent endeavoring to destroy the Government is certainly satisfactory. Still, the owner may not be thus engaged; and I think a reasonable time should be provided for such parties to appear and have personal hearings. Similar provisions are not uncommon in connection with proceedings *in rem*.

For the reasons stated, I return the bill to the House in which it originated.

—

Other Proceedings.

IN HOUSE.

1862, May 14—The Select Committee consisting of Messrs. Eliot of Mass., Sedgwick of New York, Noell of Missouri, Hutchins of Ohio, Mallory of Kentucky, Beaman of Michigan, and Cobb of New Jersey, reported two bills—one "to confiscate the property of rebels for the payment of the expenses of the present rebellion, and for other purposes;" and the other "to free from servitude the slaves of rebels engaged in or abetting the existing rebellion against the Government of the United States."

The former bill was first considered. It provided "that all the estate and property, money, stocks, credits, and effects of the persons hereafter named in this section, are hereby forfeited to the Government of the United States, and are declared lawful subjects of seizure and of prize and capture wherever found, for the indemnity of the United States against the expenses of suppressing the present rebellion."

The classes are substantially as stated in the act, and the provisions of the bill are, in large part, those of the act.

Pending its consideration,

May 26—Mr. Roscoe Conkling moved the addition of the proviso to the fifth clause of the fifth section, which was agreed to—yeas 100, nays 50—as follows:

Yeas—Messrs. Aldrich, Alley, Arnold, Ashley, Babbitt, Baker, Baxter, Beaman, Francis P. Blair, Jacob B. Blair, Samuel S. Blair, Blake, William G. Brown, Buffinton, Campbell, Chamberlain, Clark, Clements, Colfax, Frederick A. Conkling, Roscoe Conkling, Cutler, Davis, Dawes, Delano, Duell, Dunn, Edgerton, Edwards, Eliot, Ely, Fenton, Fessenden, Fisher, Frank, Gooch, Goodwin, Granger, Gurley, Hanchett, Harrison, Hickman, Hooper, Horton, Hutchins, Julian, Kelley, Francis W. Kellogg, William Kellogg, Killinger, Lansing, Loomis, Lovejoy, McKnight, McPherson, Mitchell, Moorhead, Anson P. Morrill, Justin S. Morrill, Nixon, *Noell*, Olin, Patton, Timothy G. Phelps, Pike, Pomeroy, Porter, Potter, *Price*, Alexander H. Rice, John H. Rice, Riddle, Edward H. Rollins, Sargent, Sedgwick, Shanks, *Sheffield*, Sloan, *Smith*, Spaulding, Stevens, Stratton, Benjamin F. Thomas, Francis Thomas, Train, Trimble, Trowbridge, Van Horn, Van Valkenburgh, Verree, Wall, Wallace, E. P. Walton, Washburne, Wheeler, Whaley, Albert S. White, Wilson, Windom, Worcester—100.

Nays—Messrs. *Allen, Ancona, Baily, Biddle, George H. Browne, Calvert, Cobb, Corning, Cox, Cravens, Crisfield, Crittenden, Dunlap, English, Grider, Haight, Hall, Harding, Holman, Johnson, Kerrigan, Knapp, Law, Lazear*, Leary, *Lehman, Mallory*, Maynard, *Menzies, Noble, Norton, Nugen, Odell, Pendleton, Perry, John S. Phelps, Richardson, Robinson, James S. Rollins, Shiel, John B. Steele, William G. Steele, Vallandigham, Voorhees, Wadsworth, Ward*, Webster, *Wickliffe, Wood, Woodruff*—50.

Mr. Maynard submitted a substitute, defining the offence of treason and affixing the penalty of death by hanging; "and if the offender shall theretofore have held any office under the Government of the United States, of honor or profit, whether military, naval, or civil, he shall be adjudged in a fine at least equal to the proven value of his entire estate." It also defines misprision of treason, and affixes the punishment of confinement at hard labor for not less than five years and a fine equal to his or her entire estate. It makes other offences, described, high misdemeanors, punishable, on conviction, with fine not less than $100, a...

imprisonment not less than fifty days. It provides for trying persons charged with the described offences upon the presentment or the indictment of a grand jury in any of the circuit or district courts within the judicial district in which the crimes shall be alleged to have been committed, or authorizes a writ of *capias* to the marshals of the districts, to be furnished, on application to the President, with sufficient military force to execute the writ. An oath is prescribed for all officials, jurors, &c., and the President is authorized to grant an amnesty to all offenders within the act, except those who, having held office under the United States, have at any time engaged in rebellion and held office.

This was rejected—yeas 9, (Messrs. J. B. Blair, Clements, Diven, Fisher, Harrison, Horton, *Lazear*, Maynard, Mitchell,) nays 140.

Mr MORRILL, of Vermont, offered a substistute whose principal difference was the omission of this the second section of the reported bill:

That if any person within any State or Territory of the United States, other than those named as the aforesaid, after the passage of this act, being engaged in armed rebellion against the Government of the United States, or aiding or abetting such rebellion, shall not, within sixty days after public warning and proclamation duly given and made by the President of the United States, cease to aid, countenance, and abet such rebellion, and return to his allegiance to the United States, all the estate and property, moneys, stocks, and credits of such person are hereby forfeited thereafterwards to the Government of the United States, and the same are declared lawful subjects of seizure and of prize and capture wherever found; and the President of the United States shall cause the same to be seized, to the end that they may be confiscated and condemned, as hereinafter provided, to the use of the United States; and all sales, transfers, or conveyances, of any such property after the expiration of the said sixty days from the date of such warning and proclamation shall be null and void; and it shall be a sufficient bar to any suit brought by such person for the possession or the use of such property, or any of it, to allege and prove that he is one of the persons described in this section.

And this addition:

That every person guilty of the acts described in the first section shall, in addition to the forfeitures, be incapable of voting for President or Vice President, and not be an elector of the United States, and disqualified from holding the office of President or Vice President, or holding any office by appointment from the President.

The substitute was rejected—yeas 25, nays 122. The YEAS were:

Messrs. Baxter, Jacob B. Blair, W. G. Brown, Roscoe Conkling, Diven, Dunn, Fisher, Goodwin, *Haight*, William Kellogg, Killinger, McKnight, McPherson, Maynard, Mitchell, Moorhead, Justin S. Morrill, Nixon, Timothy G. Phelps, Porter, *Sheffield*, Stratton, Trimble, E. P. Walton, Worcester—25.

The bill reported by the committee was then passed—yeas 82, nays 68, as follows:

YEAS—Messrs. Aldrich, Alley, Arnold, Ashley, Babbitt, Baker, Baxter, Beaman, Francis P. Blair, Samuel S. Blair, Blake, William G. Brown, Buffinton, Campbell, Chamberlain, Clark, Colfax, Frederick A. Conkling, Roscoe Conkling, Cutler, Davis, Duell, Dunn, Edgerton, Edwards, Eliot, Ely, Fenton, Fessenden, Frank, Gooch, Goodwin, Gurley, Hickman, Hooper, Hutchins, Julian, Kelley, Francis W. Kellogg, William Kellogg, Killinger, Lansing, Loomis, Lovejoy, McKnight, McPherson, Mitchell, Moorhead, Anson P. Morrill, Justin S. Morrill, *Noell*, Olin, Patton, Pike, Pomeroy, Porter, Potter, John H. Rice, Riddle, Edward H. Rollins, Sargent, Sedgwick, Shanks, Sloan, Spaulding, Stevens, Stratton, Trimble, Trowbridge, Van Horn, Van Valkenburgh, Verree, Wall, Wallace, E. P. Walton, Washburne, Wheeler, Whaley, Albert S. White, Wilson, Windom, Worcester—82.

NAYS—Messrs. *Allen*, *Ancona*, *Baily*, *Biddle*, Jacob B. Blair, *George H. Browne*, *Calvert*, Clements, *Cobb*, *Corning*, *Cox*, *Cravens*, *Crisfield*, *Crittenden*, Dawes, Delano, Diven, *Dunlap*, *English*, Fisher, Granger, *Grider*, *Haight*, *Hall*, *Harding*, Harrison, *Holman*, Horton, *Johnson*, *Kerrigan*, *Knapp*, *Law*, *Lazear*, Leary, *Lehman*, *Mallory*, *Maynard*, *Menzies*, Nixon, *Noble*, *Norton*, *Nugen*, *Odell*, *Pendleton*, *Perry*, *John S. Phelps*, *Price*, Alexander H. Rice, *Richardson*, *Robinson*, *James S. Rollins*, Segar, *Sheffield*, *Shiel*, *Smith*, *John B. Steele*, *William G. Steele*, Benjamin F. Thomas, Francis Thomas, Train, *Vallandigham*, *Voorhees*, Wadsworth, *Ward*, Webster, *Wickliffe*, *Wood*, *Woodruff*—68.

AN EMANCIPATION BILL.

May 14—The Select Committee reported this bill:

That if any person within any State or Territory of the United States shall, after the passage of this act, wilfully engage in armed rebellion against the Government of the United States, or shall wilfully aid or abet such rebellion, or adhere to those engaged in such rebellion, giving them aid and comfort, every such person shall thereby forfeit all claim to the service or labor of any persons, commonly known as slaves; and all such slaves are hereby declared free and forever discharged from such servitude, anything in the laws of the United States or of any State to the contrary notwithstanding. And whenever thereafter any person claiming the labor or service of any such slave shall seek to enforce his claim, it shall be a sufficient defence thereto that the claimant was engaged in the said rebellion, or aided or abetted the same, contrary to the provisions of this act.

That whenever any person claiming to be entitled to the service or labor of any other person shall seek to enforce such claim, he shall, in the first instance, and before any order shall be made for the surrender of the person whose service or labor is claimed, establish not only his claim to such service or labor, but also that such claimant has not in any way aided, assisted, or countenanced the existing rebellion against the Government of the United States.

May 26, pending its consideration,

Mr. FRANCIS P. BLAIR Jr., offered an amendment, to add to the bill sections providing for the appointment by the President of commissioners for each slave States, to make lists of the names of slaves held by persons described in the first section, to be reported to the district court of the United States, of the proper district. If the slaves are not claimed by any one, they will be declared free by the court; if they are claimed, the claimant must prove that he has not been engaged in, nor aided and abetted the rebellion, nor given aid and comfort to those engaged; or if engaged under compulsion this must be proved. In failure of proof, the slaves shall be declared free, and be given a certificate of freedom, and to be employed under the direction of the commissioners, in cultivating lands belonging to the United States, or other useful labor, and may be employed by the commanding officers of the army, with the consent of the commissioners, as may be agreed upon. Commissioners authorized to bind them as apprentices to loyal proprietors of lands or mechanics, for not over five years where the slaves are over twenty-one, and if under, not to extend beyond their twenty-fifth year. The President was authorized to purchase lands in Mexico, Central or South America, or islands in the Gulf of Mexico, to be removed with their own consent, they to receive not exceeding fifty acres to an individual, or eighty to the head of a family, and be guaranteed the civil and political rights secured to all other citizens in said countries—the proceeds of confiscation and the earnings of those liberated persons to be applied to the payment of those expenses.

This was rejected—yeas 52, nays 95, as follows:

YEAS—Messrs. Aldrich, Arnold, Baker, Baxter, Francis P. Blair, Campbell, Clements, Colfax, Roscoe Conkling, Dawes, Delano, Diven, Dunn, Edgerton, Edwards, Fenton, Fisher, Frank, Gooch, Goodwin, Gurley, Kelley, Killinger, Mc-

Knight, McPherson, Maynard, Moorhead, Anson P. Morrill, Justin S. Morrill, Nixon, Olin, Patton, Timothy G. Phelps, Pike, Pomeroy, Porter, Alexander H. Rice, Riddle, Edward H. Rollins, *James S. Rollins*, Shanks, Stratton, Train, Trimble, Verree, Wallace, E. P. Walton, Washburne, Wheeler, Whaley, Albert S. White, Worcester—52.

NAYS—Messrs. *Allen*, Alley, *Ancona*, Ashley, Babbitt, *Baily*, Beaman, *Biddle*, Jacob B. Blair, Samuel S. Blair, Blake, *George H. Browne*, William G. Brown, Buffinton, *Calvert*, Chamberlain, Clark, *Cobb*, Frederick A. Conkling, *Corning*, *Cox*, *Cravens*, *Crisfield*, *Crittenden*, Cutler, Davis, Duell, *Dunlap*, Eliot, *English*, Fessenden, Granger, *Grider*, *Haight*, *Hall*, Hanchett, *Harding*, Harrison, Hickman, *Holman*, Hooper, *Horton*, Hutchins, *Johnson*, Julian, Francis W. Kellogg, William Kellogg, *Kerrigan*, *Knapp*, Lansing, *Law*, *Lazear*, Leary, *Lehman*, Lovejoy, *Mallory*, *Noble*, *Noell*, *Norton*, *Nugen*, *Odell*, *Pendleton*, *Perry*, *John S. Phelps*, Potter, *Price*, John H. Rice, *Richardson*, *Robinson*, Sargent, Sedgwick, Segar, *Sheffield*, *Shiel*, Sloan, Spaulding, *John B. Steele*, *William G. Steele*, Stevens, Benjamin F. Thomas, Francis Thomas, Trowbridge, *Vallandigham*, Van Horn, Van Valkenburgh, *Voorhees*, *Wadsworth*, Wall, *Ward*, Webster, *Wickliffe*, Wilson, Windom, *Wood*, *Woodruff*—95.

Mr. SEDGWICK's substitute, as follows:

And whereas the several States of Virginia, North Carolina, South Carolina, Georgia, Tennessee, Alabama, Mississippi, Louisiana, Florida, Texas, and Arkansas, wickedly and unlawfully combining under the title of the Confederate States of America, have, together, made war upon and rebelled against the Government of the United States, and continue in such state of war and rebellion: Therefore,

SEC. 3. *Be it further enacted*, That every commanding military or naval officer whose military district shall embrace any portion of the above-named States may, and it shall be his duty, by proclamation or otherwise, to invite all loyal persons to come within his lines and be enrolled in the service of the United States; and it shall be his duty to enroll every such loyal person and to employ such of them as may be necessary in the service of the United States, and no person so enrolled and declaring his loyalty to the United States shall ever thereafter be held to involuntary service or labor, (excepting as a punishment for crime,) any law or regulation of any State to the contrary notwithstanding: *Provided*, That if the slaves of any person or persons who have been and continued loyal to the Government of the United States shall be made free by the operation of this section, such loyal citizen or citizens shall be entitled to just and reasonable compensation for his claim to the service or labor of such slave: *And provided further*, That if the slaves of any person or persons who are minors or married women shall be made free by the operation of this section, they shall also be entitled to just and reasonable compensation for their claim to the service or labor of such slaves.

Was rejected—yeas 33, nays 116 as follows:

YEAS—Messrs. Aldrich, Babbitt, Baker, Beaman, Samuel S. Blair, Blake, Buffinton, Clark, Davis, Duell, Edgerton, Eliot, Fessenden, Frank, Hickman, Hutchins, Julian, Francis W. Kellogg, Lansing, Lovejoy, Anson P. Morrill, Pike, Potter, John H. Rice, Riddle, Edward H. Rollins, Sedgwick, Sloan, Trowbridge, Van Valkenburgh, E. P. Walton, Wilson, Windom—33.

NAYS—Messrs. *Allen*, *Ancona*, Arnold, Ashley, *Baily*, Baxter, *Biddle*, Francis P. Blair, Jacob B. Blair, *George H. Browne*, William G. Brown, *Calvert*, Campbell, Chamberlain, Clements, *Cobb*, Colfax, Frederick A. Conkling, Roscoe Conkling, *Corning*, *Cox*, *Cravens*, *Crisfield*, *Crittenden*, Cutler, Dawes, Delano, Diven, *Dunlap*, Dunn, Edwards, Ely, *English*, Fenton, Fisher, Gooch, Goodwin, Granger, *Grider*, Gurley, *Haight*, *Hall*, Hanchett, *Harding*, Harrison, *Holman*, Horton, *Johnson*, Kelley, William Kellogg, *Kerrigan*, Killinger, *Knapp*, *Law*, *Lazear*, Leary, *Lehman*, McKnight, McPherson, *Mallory*, Maynard, *Menzies*, Mitchell, Moorhead, Justin S. Morrill, Nixon, *Noble*, *Noell*, *Norton*, *Nugen*, *Odell*, Olin, Patton, *Pendleton*, *Perry*, *John S. Phelps*, Timothy G. Phelps, Pomeroy, Porter, *Price*, Alexander H. Rice, *Richardson*, *Robinson*, *James S. Rollins*, Sargent, Segar, Shanks, *Sheffield*, *Shiel*, *Smith*, Spaulding, *John B. Steele*, *William G. Steele*, Stevens, Stratton, Benjamin F. Thomas, Francis Thomas, Train, Trimble, *Vallandigham*, Van Horn, Verree, *Voorhees*, *Wadsworth*, Wall, Wallace, *Ward*, Washburne, Webster, Wheeler, Whaley, Albert S. White, *Wickliffe*, *Wood*, *Woodruff*, Worcester—116.

Mr. E. P. WALTON's substitute provides:

SEC. 1. That every person who shall hereafter commit treason, shall suffer death, and all his slaves made free; or be imprisoned not less than five years, and fined not less than $10,000, and all his slaves made free; said fine shall be levied on property excluding slaves.

SEC. 2. That if any person shall engage in rebellion against the United States, or give aid and comfort thereto, shall be punished by the forfeiture of his personal property, including choses in action, and his life estate in any real property within the United States, and by the liberation of his slaves.

SEC. 3. That every such person described disqualified to hold any office under the Government.

SEC. 4. This act shall not be construed as to affect prosecution or conviction of persons guilty of treason before the passage of this act, unless convicted under it.

SEC. 5. The duty of the President, by his marshals or other officers, to seize and sequester property of every kind, of persons engaged in rebellion and especially of officers of the rebel army and navy, and of the President and other officers, military, naval, or civil, of persons formerly holding office under the United States and taking up arms, or give aid and comfort to the rebellion, or persons owning property in loyal portions of the country hereafter engaged in the rebellion; to hold and possess such property until appearance and trial of the offender. No slave to be seized under this act, but the United States to have a lien on all slaves of the persons described to answer such order as may be made touching their liberation, and no sale of any force made after the commission of the offence.

SEC. 6. That the property so seized and sequestered shall be held or rented until the owners can be proceeded against, and if convicted, said property shall be forfeited and all perishable property may be sold and proceeds paid into the Treasury, and if owner discharged on trial shall be returned to said owner.

SEC. 7. That if the owner of any property seized shall flee from justice, and cannot be brought to trial, an order shall be made by the court requiring such person to appear at a certain time, and if he do not, all his estate shall be forfeited, and the liberation of his slaves, and himself and heirs forever barred from recovery thereof.

SEC. 8. That the President of the United States, when he deems it necessary that any personal property seized by the army and navy, and belonging to a person hereafter engaged in the rebellion or given aid and comfort thereto should be confiscated, may cause proceedings *in rem* against such property, and if found to belong to a person engaged in the rebellion, said property shall be forfeited.

SEC. 9. President may by proclamation command insurgents to lay down their arms within sixty days, and if they do not, their property shall be confiscated and slaves freed.

SEC. 10. That no person discharged from labor under this act, nor the descendants of any one, shall ever be reduced to involuntary servitude, (except as a punishment for crime,) and entitled to be discharged on *habeas corpus*.

SEC. 11. That whenever any person shall be discharged from service or labor owing to another, the court shall give such person a certificate of discharge, under seal of the court, and conclusive evidence of his freedom, and if thereafter seized, shall be discharged on *habeas corpus*, and if the person so holding the freed man shall be convicted, he shall be punished with imprisonment for not less than one year or more than five years.

SEC. 12. That no slave escaping from one State or territory to another shall be delivered up, (except for crime,) unless the owner make oath that he has not been engaged in the rebellion or aided and abetted it; and no person in the military or naval service of the country shall assume to pass on the validity of any claim of one person to the services of another.

SEC. 13. That the President is authorized to employ negroes for the suppression of rebellion and treason, and organize and use them as he may deem proper.

SEC. 14. And is also authorized to make provision for the colonization of negroes made free by this act as may be willing to emigrate, and obtain the consent of the Government of the said country to their protection and settlement within the same, with all the rights and privileges of freemen.

SEC. 15. And is also authorized to extend pardon and amnesty to those engaged in the rebellion.

SEC. 16. That the courts shall have full power to carry this act into effect.

Which was rejected—yeas 29, nays 121. The YEAS were

Messrs. Baxter, Francis P. Blair, Dawes, Delano, Dunn, Fisher, Frank, Gooch, Goodwin, Granger, Killinger, McKnight, Maynard, Mitchell, Moorhead, Justin S. Morrill, Nixon, Olin, Patton, Timothy G. Phelps, Porter, Alexander H. Rice, *Sheffield*, Stratton, Train, Trimble, Verree, E. P. Walton, Worcester.

Mr. MORRILL, of Vermont, offered a substitute providing

SEC. 2. That the President shall appoint commissioners for each State by whose laws persons are held to service, who shall make a list of the names of slaves and their owners and return it to the district where the slave resides; which list shall be published, requiring all persons to appear and show cause why certain persons held to labor should not be discharged; and on failure of such persons to appear, their slaves shall be declared free, and on appearance the claimant shall file an affidavit that he has not been engaged in rebellion, or aided and abetted it, or if engaged under compulsion must show it, and if proved that he was not engaged in rebellion his slaves shall be returned to him; but on failure of such proof, or on the failure or refusal to take the foregoing affidavit to prove the compulsion when alleged as an excuse, the court shall declare the person so claimed as free, and grant him a certificate of the same under seal, and shall be conclusive evidence of his freedom. And all persons so declared free, if seized, shall be forthwith discharged on *habeas corpus;* and the court, acting on said writ, shall commit for trial for kidnapping the person so holding the freed man, and on conviction imprisoned for not less than one or more than five years, and any one swearing falsely shall be guilty of perjury.

SEC. 3. That if any person held to labor by one engaged in rebellion, if omitted from the commissioner's list may, on summary application to the district court, be placed on the list, and to be treated in every way the same as if his name had been placed on the list by the commissioner.

Commissioners shall have ample time to complete their lists.

SEC. 4. That no such person or his descendants shall ever again be reduced to involuntary servitude, and every such person shall be entitled to discharge from such service on *habeas corpus.*

Which was rejected—yeas 16, nays 126. The YEAS were—

Messrs. Roscoe Conkling, Dunn, Frank, Goodwin, Killinger, Loomis, McKnight, Justin S. Morrill, Nixon, Olin, Patton, Timothy G. Phelps, Porter, Stratton, E. P. Walton, Worcester—16.

The original bill reported from the committee was then negatived—yeas 74, nays 78; as follows:

YEAS—Messrs. Aldrich, Alley, Arnold, Ashley, Babbitt, Baker, Baxter, Beaman, Francis P. Blair, Samuel S. Blair, Blake, Buffinton, Campbell, Chamberlain, Clark, Colfax, Frederick A. Conkling, Roscoe Conkling, Cutler, Davis, Duell, Edgerton, Edwards, Eliot, Ely, Fenton, Fessenden, Frank, Gooch, Goodwin, Gurley, Hanchett, Hickman, Hooper, Hutchins, Julian, Kelley, Francis W. Kellogg, Lansing, Loomis, Lovejoy, McKnight, McPherson, Moorhead, Anson P. Morrill, Justin S. Morrill, Olin, Patton, Timothy G. Phelps, Pike, Pomeroy, Potter, John H. Rice, Riddle, Edward H. Rollins, Sargent, Sedgwick, Shanks, Sloan, Spaulding, Stevens, Trowbridge, Van Horn, Van Valkenburgh, Verree, Wall, Wallace, E. P. Walton, Washburne, Wheeler, Albert S. White, Wilson, Windom, Worcester—74.

NAYS—Messrs. *Allen, Ancona, Baily, Biddle,* Jacob B. Blair, *George H. Browne,* William G. Brown, *Calvert,* Clements, *Cobb, Corning, Cox, Cravens, Crisfield, Crittenden,* Dawes, Delano, Diven, *Dunlap,* Dunn, *English,* Fisher, Granger, *Grider, Haight, Hall, Harding,* Harrison, *Holman,* Horton, *Johnson,* William Kellogg, *Kerrigan,* Killinger, *Knapp, Law, Lazear,* Leary, *Lehman, Mallory,* Maynard, *Menzies,* Mitchell, Nixon, *Noble, Noell, Norton, Nugen, Odell, Pendleton, Perry, John S. Phelps,* Porter, *Price,* Alexander H. Rice, *Richardson, Robinson, James S. Rollins,* Segar, *Sheffield, Shiel, Smith, John B. Steele, William G. Steele,* Stratton, Benjamin F. Thomas, Francis Thomas, Train, Trimble, *Vallandigham, Voorhees, Wadsworth, Ward,* Webster, Whaley, *Wickliffe, Wood, Woodruff*—78.

May 27—Mr. PORTER moved to reconsider this vote. A motion to table the motion to reconsider was lost—yeas 69, nays 73.

June 4—The motion to reconsider was agreed to—yeas 84, nays 65; and

Mr. PORTER moved that the bill be recommitted to the Committee with instructions to prepare a substitute, providing that the slaves of the persons included in the classification in the confiscation law, are declared forever discharged from service or labor, and providing for an enrolment of them by commissioners, and the action of United States judges, as indicated in other amendments, for colonization of them in Mexico, Central or South America, or the Gulf Islands, with homesteads, and declaring every person embraced in the classification incapable of holding or exercising any office of honor, trust, or profit under the Government of the United States; which was agreed to—yeas 84, nays 66, as follows:

YEAS—Messrs. Aldrich, Alley, Arnold, Ashley, Babbitt, Baker, Baxter, Beaman, Bingham, Francis P. Blair, Blake, Buffinton, Burnham, Chamberlain, Clark, Colfax, Federick A. Conkling, Roscoe Conkling, Covode, Davis, Dawes, Duell, Dunn, Edgerton, Edwards, Ely, Fessenden, Fisher, Franchot, Frank, Gooch, Goodwin, Gurley, Hale, Hanchett, Hickman, Hooper, Hutchins, Julian, Kelley, Francis W. Kellogg, Killinger, Lansing, Loomis, Lovejoy, Low, McKnight, McPherson, Mitchell, Moorhead, Anson P. Morrill Justin S. Morrill, Nixon, Timothy G. Phelps, Pike, Pomeroy, Porter, Potter, Alexander H. Rice, John H. Rice, Riddle, Edward H. Rollins, Sargent, Sedgwick, Shanks, Shellabarger, Sloan, Spaulding, Stevens, Stratton, Train, Trimble, Trowbridge, Van Horn, Van Valkenburgh, Verree, Wall Wallace, E. P. Walton, Washburne, Albert S. White, Wilson Windom, Worcester—84.

NAYS—Messrs. *W. J. Allen, Ancona, Baily, Biddle,* J. B. Blair, *George H. Browne,* William G. Brown, *Calvert,* Clements, *Cobb, Corning, Cox, Cravens, Crittenden,* Delano, *Delaplaine, Dunlap, English, Fouke,* Granger, *Grider, Haight, Harding,* Harrison, *Holman,* Horton, *Johnson,* William Kellogg, *Kerrigan, Knapp, Law, Lazear,* Leary, *Lehman, Mallory, May,* Maynard, *Menzies, Noble, Noell, Norton, Nugen, Pendleton, John S. Phelps, Price, Robinson, James S. Rollins,* Segar, *Sheffield, Shiel, Smith, John B. Steele, William G. Steele, Stiles,* Benjamin F. Thomas, Francis Thomas, *Vallandigham, Vibbard, Voorhees, Wadsworth, Ward,* Webster, *Chilton A. White, Wickliffe, Woodruff, Wright*—66.

June 18—The House passed a bill reported in pursuance of these instructions—yeas 82, nays 34. It was not considered in the Senate; but emancipation clauses were inserted in the confiscation bill, and agreed to by both Houses.

During the pendency of another bill (107) to forfeit the property and slaves of persons who shall engage in, or aid and abet, armed rebellion against the United States,

1862, April 22—Mr. BINGHAM offered a substitute—

That if any person or persons, within any State or Territory of the United States, shall, after the taking effect of this act, engage in armed rebellion against the Government of the United States, or shall aid or abet such rebellion, all the property, moneys, stocks, credits, and effects of such person or persons are hereby declared lawful subjects of prize and capture, wherever found, for the indemnity of the United States against the expenses of suppressing such rebellion; and it is hereby made the duty of the President of the United States to cause all such property, wherever found, to be seized, to the end that the same may be confiscated and condemned as hereinafter provided for the use of the United States.

SEC. 2. That all property so captured or seized shall be condemned in the district courts of the United States, and that the proceedings of condemnation shall be *in rem,* and shall be instituted and prosecuted in the name of the United States in any district court of the United States within any district in which the same may be seized or situate, or into which the same may be taken and proceedings first instituted, and which proceedings shall conform as nearly as may be to proceedings in prize cases, or to cases of forfeiture arising under the revenue laws; and in all cases the property so seized and condemned, whether real or personal, shall be sold pursuant to such rules as the Secretary of the Treasury may prescribe, and the proceeds deposited in the Treasury of the United States for the sole use of the United States.

SEC. 3. That the Attorney General or any district attorney of the United States of any district in which the said property or effects may at the time be, or into which the same may be taken, shall institute the proceedings of condemnation as hereinbefore provided.

Which was agreed to—yeas 62, nays 48; as follows:

YEAS—Messrs. Aldrich, Arnold, Ashley, Babbitt, Baker, Beaman, Bingham, Samuel S. Blair, Blake, Buffinton, Burnham, Chamberlain, Colfax, Frederick A. Conkling, Roscoe Conkling, Covode, Cutler, Davis, Duell, Edwards, Eliot, Ely, Fenton, Franchot, Frank, Gooch, Granger, Gurley, Hooper, Julian, Kelley, Francis W. Kellogg, Lansing, Loomis, Lovejoy, McKnight, McPherson, Mitchell, Moorhead, Nixon, *Noell,* Patton, Timothy G. Phelps, Pike, Porter, Potter, John H. Rice, Riddle, Edward H. Rollins, Sargent, Shanks, Shellabarger, Stevens, Stratton, Trimble, Trowbridge, Van Horn, Van Valkenburgh, Albert S. White, Wilson, Windom, Worcester—62.

NAYS—Messrs. *Allen*, *Joseph Baily*, Baxter, *Biddle*, Francis P. Blair, Jacob B. Blair, *George H. Browne*, William G. Brown, *Calvert*, Casey, Clements, *Cox*, *Crisfield*, *Crittenden*, Diven, *Dunlap*, *Grider*, *Hall*, *Harding*, Harrison, Hickman, *Kerrigan*, *Knapp*, *Law*, *Lehman*, *Mallory*, *May*, *Menzies*, Justin S. Morrill, *Morris*, *Noble*, *Norton*, *Odell*, Olin, *James S. Rollins*, *Sheffield*, *Smith*, *John B. Steele*, Benjamin F. Thomas, Francis Thomas, *Vallandigham*, *Vibbard*, *Voorhees*, E. P. Walton, *Ward*, *Chilton A. White*, *Woodruff*, *Wright*—48.

Mr. E. P. WALTON offered a substitute, defining the crime of treason, and affixing a penalty of death, or imprisonment and fine, on conviction or confession, and his slaves shall be free. The President is authorized to appoint commissioners to sequester and seize the property, real and personal, of persons bearing arms against the United States, or giving them aid and comfort, and is also authorized to grant pardon and amnesty. These are the concluding sections:

SEC. 6. *And be it further enacted*, That if any State, or part thereof, in which the inhabitants have by the President been declared in a state of insurrection, the said insurrection shall have continued for a period of six months, then and in that case the President is hereby authorized, if in his opinion it shall be necessary to the successful suppression of said insurrection, by proclamation to fix and appoint a day when all persons holden to service or labor in any such State, or part thereof as he shall declare, whose service or labor is by the law or custom of said State due to any person or persons, who, after the day so fixed by said proclamation, shall levy war or participate in insurrection against the United States, or give aid to the same, shall be free and discharged from all such claim to labor or service; and thereupon said person shall be forever free and discharged from said labor and service, any law or custom of said State to the contrary notwithstanding.

SEC. 7. That whenever any person claiming to be entitled to the service of any other person as a slave shall seek to enforce such claim, he shall, in the first instance, and as preliminary to the trial of such claim, show satisfactorily that he and the person to whom said service was claimed to be due during the period of insurrection or rebellion was loyal to the United States.

Which was rejected—yeas 33, nays 70, as follows:

YEAS—Messrs. Baxter, Francis P. Blair, William G. Brown, *Calvert*, Casey, Clements, Roscoe Conkling, *Crittenden*, *Dunlap*, Dunn, Fisher, Goodwin, Granger, *Grider*, Gurley, *Harding*, Harrison, McKnight, McPherson, *Mallory*, Menzies, Mitchell, Moorhead, Justin S. Morrill, Nixon, Olin, Edward H. Rollins, *James S. Rollins*, *Sheffield*, Shellabarger, Stratton, E. P. Walton, Worcester—33.

NAYS—Messrs. Aldrich, *Allen*, Arnold, Ashley, Babbitt, *Joseph Baily*, Baker, Beaman, *Biddle*, Bingham, Jacob B. Blair, Samuel S. Blair, Blake, *George H. Browne*, Buffinton, Chamberlain, Colfax, Frederick A. Conkling, Covode, *Cox*, Cutler, Davis, Duell, Eliot, Ely, Fenton, Franchot, Frank, Gooch, Hickman, Julian, Kelley, Francis W. Kellogg, *Kerrigan*, *Knapp*, Lansing, *Law*, Loomis, Lovejoy, *May*, *Morris*, *Noble*, *Noell*, *Odell*, Patton, Timothy G. Phelps, Pike, Potter, John H. Rice, Riddle, Sargent, Shanks, *Smith*, *John B. Steele*, Benjamin F. Thomas, Francis Thomas, Trimble, Trowbridge, *Vallandigham*, Van Horn, Van Valkenburgh, *Voorhees*, Wall, *Ward*, Albert S. White, *Chilton A. White*, Wilson, Windom, *Woodruff*, *Wright*—70.

Mr. PORTER also proposed a substitute, which was rejected—yeas 30, nays 72.

April 23—The bill was tabled—yeas 59, nays 52.

Subsequently a new bill was prepared by the Select Committee, to whom, April 24, the whole subject was referred.

IN SENATE.

Pending the consideration of a bill to confiscate the property and free the slaves of rebels,

1862, April 24—Mr. SHERMAN moved to strike from the first section the words:

Belonging to any person or persons beyond the jurisdiction of the same, or to any person or persons in any State or district within the United States, now in a State of insurrection and rebellion against the authority thereof, so that in either case the ordinary process of law cannot be served upon them, who shall during the present rebellion be found in arms against the United States, or giving aid and comfort to said rebellion.

And to insert in lieu thereof the following:

First. Persons hereafter acting as officers of the army or navy of the rebels now or hereafter in arms against the United States. Second. Persons hereafter acting as President, Vice President, member of Congress, judge, foreign minister, consul, or commissioner of the so-called Confederate States. Third. Persons hereafter acting as an officer, whether civil, military, or naval, of any State or Territory who by the Constitution of the so-called Confederate States is required to take an oath to support said Constitution. Fourth. Persons who having held an office of honor, trust, or profit under the United States, shall hereafter take up arms against the United States. Fifth. Persons who, owning property in the loyal States or Territories, or the loyal portions of disloyal States, shall hereafter assist or give aid and comfort to the present rebellion.

Mr. KING moved to amend by adding:

Sixth. Persons in the present insurrection levying war against the United States or adhering to their enemies, giving them aid and comfort.

Which was rejected—yeas 7, nays 32, as follows:

YEAS—Messrs. Chandler, Grimes, King, Pomeroy, Trumbull, Wade, Wilkinson—7.

NAYS—Messrs. Anthony, Browning, *Carlile*, Clark, Cowan, *Davis*, Dixon, Doolittle, Fessenden, Foot, Foster, Hale, Henderson, Howard, Howe, Lane of Indiana, Lane of Kansas, *Latham*, Morrill, *Nesmith*, *Powell*, *Saulsbury*, Sherman, Simmons, *Stark*, Sumner, Ten Eyck, *Thomson*, Willey, Wilson of Massachusetts, *Wilson* of Missouri, *Wright*—32.

The amendment of Mr. SHERMAN was then agreed to—yeas 26, nays 11, as follows:

YEAS—Messrs. Anthony, Browning, Chandler, Clark, Cowan, *Davis*, Dixon, Doolittle, Fessenden, Foot, Foster, Grimes, Hale, Henderson, Howard, Howe, Lane of Indiana, *Nesmith*, Sherman, Simmons, Sumner, Ten Eyck, *Thomson*, Willey, of Wilson Massacuhsetts, *Wright*—26.

NAYS—Messrs. *Carlile*, King, Lane of Kansas, Morrill, Pomeroy, *Saulsbury*, *Stark*, Trumbull, Wade, Wilkinson, *Wilson* of Missouri—11.

The bill was referred to a select committee, and was not reported; but this classification was introduced into the confiscation act.

SECOND AMENDATORY JOINT RESOLUTION.

First Session, Thirty-Eighth Congress.

IN HOUSE.

1864, February 5—The House passed this joint resolution:

That the last clause of a "joint resolution explanatory of 'An act to suppress insurrection, to punish treason and rebellion, to seize and confiscate the property of rebels, and for other purposes,'" approved July 17, 1862, be, and the same hereby is, so amended as to read: "nor shall any punishment or proceeding under said act be so construed as to work a forfeiture of the estate of the offender contrary to the Constitution of the United States: *Provided*, That no other public warning or proclamation under the act of July 17, 1862, chapter ninety-five, section six, is or shall be required than the proclamation of the President, made and published by him on the 25th day of July, 1862, which proclamation so made shall be received and held sufficient in all cases now pending, or which may hereafter arise under said act."

By a vote of yeas 83 to nays 76, as follows:

YEAS—Messrs. Alley, Allison, Ames, Anderson, Arnold, Ashley, John D. Baldwin, Baxter, Beaman, Blow, Boutwell, Boyd, Brandegee, Broomall, Ambrose W. Clark, Freeman Clarke, Cobb, Cole, Creswell, Henry Winter Davis, Thomas T. Davis, Dawes, Deming, Donnelly, Driggs, Eliot, Farnsworth, Fenton, Frank, Garfield, Gooch, Grinnell, Higby, Hooper, Hotchkiss, Asahel W. Hubbard, John H. Hubbard, Hulburd, Jenckes, Julian, Kasson, Kelley, Francis W. Kellogg, Orlando Kellogg, Loan, Longyear, Marvin, McBride, McClurg, McIndoe, Samuel F. Miller, Moorhead, Morrill, Daniel Morris, Amos Myers, Leonard Myers, Norton, Charles O'Neill, Orth, Patterson, Perham, Pike, Pomeroy, Alexander

H. Rice, John H. Rice, Edward H. Rollins, Schenck, Scofield, Shannon, Sloan, Smithers, Spalding, Stevens, Thayer, Tracy, Upson, Van Valkenburgh, Ellihu B. Washburne, William B. Washburn, Williams, Wilson, Windom, Woodbridge—83.

NAYS—Messrs. *James C. Allen, Ancona, Baily, Augustus C. Baldwin*, Jacob B. Blair, *Bliss, Brooks, James S. Brown*, William G. Brown, *Chanler, Clay, Coffroth, Cox, Cravens, Dawson, Denison, Eden, Edgerton, Eldridge, Finck, Ganson, Grider, Harding, Harrington, Benjamin G. Harris, Herrick, Holman, Hutchins, William Johnson, Kalbfleisch, Kernan, King, Knapp, Law, Lazear, LeBlond, Long, Mallory, Marcy, McDowell, McKinney, Middleton, Wm. H. Miller, James R. Morris, Morrison, Nelson, Noble, Odell, John O'Neill, Pendleton, Pruyn, Radford, Samuel J. Randall*, William H. Randall, *Robinson, Rogers, James S. Rollins, Ross, Scott, John B. Steele, William G. Steele, Stiles, Strouse, Stuart, Sweat*, Thomas, *Voorhees, Wadsworth*, Webster, Whaley, *Wheeler, Chilton A. White, Joseph W. White, Winfield, Fernando Wood, Yeaman*—76.

IN SENATE.

February 17—Mr. REVERDY JOHNSON, from the Committee on the Judiciary, reported back this joint resolution, without amendment, and with a recommendation that it do not pass.

June 27—Pending the consideration of the bill to establish a bureau of Freedmen's Affairs.

Mr. TRUMBULL offered this as a new section:

And be it further enacted, That the last clause of a joint resolution explanatory of an act to suppress insurrection, to punish treason and rebellion, to seize and confiscate the property of rebels, and for other purposes, approved July 17, 1862, be, and the same is hereby, repealed.

The words proposed to be repealed are, "nor shall any punishment or proceedings under said act be so construed as to work a forfeiture of the real estate of the offender beyond his natural life."

June 28—This was agreed to—yeas 23, nays 15, as follows:

YEAS—Messrs. Anthony, Brown, Chandler, Conness, Foot, Grimes, Hale, Harlan, Harris, Howe, Lane of Indiana, Lane of Kansas, Morgan, Morrill, Pomeroy, Sherman, Sprague, Sumner, Trumbull, Van Winkle, Wade, Wilkinson, Wilson—23.

NAYS—Messrs. *Carlile*, Clark, Collamer, Cowan, *Davis*, Doolittle, Henderson, *Hendricks*, Hicks, *McDougall, Powell, Riddle, Saulsbury*, Ten Eyck, Willey—15.

Same day, Mr. HENDRICKS moved to strike out this section; which was disagreed to—yeas 13, nays 16, as follows:

YEAS—Messrs. *Buckalew, Carlile*, Clark, Cowan, *Davis*, Doolittle, *Hendricks, McDougall, Powell, Riddle*, Ten Eyck, Van Winkle, Willey—13.

NAYS—Messrs. Anthony, Chandler, Conness, Foot, Harlan, Howe, Lane of Indiana, Morgan, Morrill, Pomeroy, Ramsey, Sprague, Sumner, Trumbull, Wilkinson, Wilson—16. (see page 260.)

"Rebel" Sequestration.

861, August 6—The "Confederate" Congress passed a bill "for the sequestration of the estates, property, and effects of alien enemies, and for the indemnity of citizens of the Confederate States, and persons aiding the same in the existing war against the United States," of which the Richmond *Examiner* of the following Monday gave an abstract.

The following is the principal legislative clause:

Be it enacted by the Congress of the Confederate States, That all and every the lands, tenements, and hereditaments, goods and chattels, rights and credits within these Confederate States, and every right and interest therein held, owned, possessed, or enjoyed by or for any alien enemy since the twenty-first day of May, 1861, except such debts due to an alien enemy as may have been paid into the Treasury of any one of the Confederate States prior to the passage of this law, be and the same are hereby sequestrated by the Confederate States of America, and shall be held for the full indemnity of any true and loyal citizen, a resident of these Confederate States, or other person aiding said Confederate States in the prosecution of the present war between said Confederate States and the United States of America, and for which he may suffer any loss or injury under the act of the United States, or of any State thereof, authorizing the seizure or confiscation of the property of citizens or residents of the Confederate States, or other persons aiding said Confederate States, and the same shall be seized and disposed of as provided for in this act: *Provided, however*, When the estate, property, or rights to be effected by this act were or are within some State of this Confederacy, which has become such since said twenty-first day of May, then the act shall operate upon and as to such estate, property, or rights, and all persons claiming the same from and after the day such State became a member of this Confederacy, and not before: *Provided further*, That the provisions of this act shall not extend to the stocks or other public securities of this Confederate Government, or of any of the States of this Confederacy, held or owned by an alien enemy, or to any debt, obligation, or sum due from the Confederate Government, or any of the States to such alien enemy. *And provided, also*, That the provisions of this act shall not embrace the property of citizens or residents of either of the States of Delaware, Maryland, Kentucky, Missouri, or the District of Columbia, or the Territories of New Mexico, Arizona, or the Indian Territory south of Kansas, except such of said citizens or residents as shall commit actual hostilities against the Confederate States, or aid or abet the United States in the existing war against the Confederate States.

Sections 2 to 13 provide for the appointment of receivers in each county, and impose a penalty of $2,000 on all who may endeavor to conceal the ownership of property belonging to alien enemies. Section 14 provides for the appointment of three commissioners to take charge of the sequestration fund, and to hear and decide on all claims against it.

For its enforcement, the then Attorney General, J. P. Benjamin, issued this circular:

DEPARTMENT OF JUSTICE,
RICHMOND, *September* 12, 1861.

Instructions to receivers under the act entitled "An act for the sequestration of the estates, property, and effects of alien enemies, and for the indemnity of citizens of the Confederate States and persons aiding the same in the existing war against the United States," approved August 8th, 1861.

The following persons are subject to the operation of the law as alien enemies:

All citizens of the United States, except citizens or residents of Delaware, Maryland, Kentucky, or Missouri, or the District of Columbia, or the Territories of New Mexico, Arizona, or the Indian territory south of Kansas.

All persons who have a *domicil* within the States with which this Government is at war, no matter whether they be *citizens* or not: thus the subjects of Great Britain, France, or other neutral nations, who have a domicil, or are carrying on business or traffic within the States at war with this Confederacy, are alien enemies under the law.

All such citizens or residents of the States of Delaware, Maryland, Kentucky, or Missouri, and of the Territories of New Mexico, Arizona, and the Indian territory south of Kansas, and of the District of Columbia, as shall commit actual hostilities against the Confederate States, or aid or assist the United States in the existing war against the Confederate States.

Immediately after taking your oath of office, you will take possession of all the property of every nature and kind whatsoever within your district belonging to alien enemies as above defined.

You will forthwith apply to the clerk of the court for writs of garnishment under the 8th section of the law, and will propound to the garnishees the interrogatories of which a form is annexed. These interrogatories you will propound to the following persons, viz:

1st. All attorneys and counsellors practicing law within your district.

2d. The presidents and cashiers of all banks, and principal administrative officers of all railroad and other corporations within your district.

All agents of foreign corporations, insurance agents, commission merchants engaged in foreign trade, agents of foreign mercantile houses, dealers in bills of exchange, executors and administrators of estates, assignees and syndics of insolvent estates, trustees, and generally all persons who are known to do business as agents for others.

In the first week of each month you will exhibit to the judge a statement showing the whole amount of money in your hands as receiver, and deposit the same for safe keeping in such bank or other depository as may be selected for that purpose by the judge—reserving only such amount as may be required for immediate necessary expenditure in the discharge of your duties as receivers.

Whenever, in the discharge of your duties, you discover that any attorney, agent, former partner, trustee, or other person holding or controlling any property, rights, or credits of an alien enemy, has wilfully failed to give you information of the same, you will immediately report the fact to the district attorney for your district, to the end that the guilty party may be subjected to the pains and penalties prescribed by the third section of the law.

J. P. BENJAMIN, *Attorney General.*

The following interrogatories to garnishees have been prepared for your use, together with a note annexed for the information of the garnishee:

1. Have you now, or have you had in your possession or under your control, since the twenty-first day of May last, (1861,) and if yea, at what time, any land or lands, tenement or tenements, hereditament or hereditaments, chattel or chattels, right or rights, credit or credits, within the Confederate States of America, held, owned, possessed, or enjoyed for or by an alien enemy, or in or to which any alien enemy had, and when, since that time, any right, title, or interest, either directly or indirectly?

2. If you answer any part of the foregoing interrogatory in the affirmative, then set forth, specifically and particularly, a description of such property, right, title, credit, or interest, and if you have disposed of it in whole or in part, or of the profit, or rent, or interest accruing therefrom, then state when you made such disposition, and to whom, and where such property now is, and by whom held?

3. Were you, since the twenty-first day of May, 1861, and if yea, at what time, indebted, either directly or indirectly, to any alien enemy or alien enemies? If yea, state the amount of such indebtedness, if one, and of each indebtedness if more than one; give the name or names of the creditor or creditors, and the place or places of residence, and state whether and to what extent such debt or debts have been discharged, and also the time and manner of the discharge.

4. Do you know of any land or lands, tenement or tenements, hereditament or hereditaments, chattel or chattels, right or rights, credit or credits, within the Confederate States of America, or any right or interest held, owned, possessed, or enjoyed, directly or indirectly, by or for one or more alien enemies since the twenty-first day of May, 1861, or in or to which any one or more alien enemies had since that time any claim, title, or interest, direct or indirect? If yea, set forth specially and particularly what and where the property is, and the name and residence of the holder, debtor, trustee, or agent.

5. State all else that you know which may aid in carrying into full effect the sequestration act of the 30th of August, 1861, and state the same as fully and particularly as if thereunto specially interrogated. A. B., Receiver.

NOTE—The garnishee in the foregoing interrogatories is specially warned that the sequestration act makes it the duty of each and every citizen to give the information asked in said interrogatories.—[Act 30th August, 1861, sec. 2.] And if any attorney, agent, former partner, trustee, or other person holding or controlling any property or interest therein of or for any alien enemy shall fail speedily to inform the receiver of the same, and to render him an account of such property or interest, he shall be guilty of a high misdemeanor and, upon conviction, shall be fined in a sum not exceeding five thousand dollars, and imprisoned not longer than six months, and be liable to pay besides to the Confederate States double the value of the property or interest of the alien enemies so held or subject to his control.— Sec. 3.]

This act was rigidly enforced. Subjoined are two notices, preserved from the newspapers of the day:

Thomas T. Giles, who has been appointed receiver for the eastern district of Virginia, has issued a notice addressed "to all whom it may concern," in the following words:

"I hereby notify every attorney, agent, former partner, trustee, or other person holding or controlling any lands, tenements, or hereditaments, goods or chattels, rights or credits, or any interest therein, within the eastern district of Virginia, of or for any alien enemy of the Confederate States of America, speedily to inform me, appointed receiver for the said district, of the same; and to render to me an account thereof, and, so far as is practicable, to place the same in my hands. Any such person wilfully failing to do so will be guilty of a high misdemeanor, and liable to be indicted, convicted, fined, and imprisoned, as provided by law.

"I also notify each and every citizen of the Confederate States speedily to give information to me (as he is required by law to do) of any and every lands, tenements, and hereditaments, goods and chattels, rights and credits, within the said eastern district of Virginia, and of every right and interest therein held, owned, possessed, or enjoyed by or for any such alien enemy.

"My office is on the northern side of Main street, in the city of Richmond, between Tenth and Eleventh streets."

SEQUESTRATION NOTICE.

Merchants and all other persons residing in Nansemond, Norfolk city, city of Portsmouth, Princess Anne, and Isle of Wight who owe debts to alien enemies, or have property of any kind in their possession, or under their control, belonging to any such alien enemies, and who have failed and neglected to make report thereof, are hereby notified that unless a report of the said debts and information of said property is rendered by them to the undersigned, receiver of this district, on or before Saturday, the 30th instant, they will be reported as delinquents and subject to the fine of five thousand dollars imposed by law.

JOHN T. FRANCIS,
Receiver.

This is a copy of the writ served upon the wife of Hon. Horace Maynard, of Tennessee, while he was in Washington, in attendance upon Congress, quoted in his speech of May 23, 1862:

To Hon. WEST H. HUMPHREYS, *Judge of the District Court of the Confederate States of America for the District of Tennessee:*

The Confederate States of America, through Landon C. Haynes, the receiver for the eastern district of Tennessee, respectfully represents unto your honor that within the jurisdiction of this court there are [various items of property specifically enumerated.] The said States, by said receiver, show that said property, real, and personal, and mixed, belongs to one Horace Maynard, who has his domicil and who resides in Kentucky, or some one of the States or districts of the United States, and who is in actual hostility to the Government of the Confederate States of America, and who adheres to the enemy of said States by speeches, words, and acts, giving them aid and comfort in Kentucky and other places in the United States, and is an alien enemy to said Confederate States. All of which are situate and being in the counties of Knox and Campbell, in the State and within the district of said receiver. And the said Confederate States further represent that the said property, debts, claims, choses in action, are, as said States have been informed by said receiver, under the control and supervision of Mrs. Maynard, wife of said Horace Maynard, and the said W. P. Washburn, who resides in Knox county, in this State, which property is liable to be seized, under the act of the Confederate Congress for the sequestration of the estates, property, and effects of alien enemies. The said Mrs. Maynard and Washburn are required to set forth, on oath, and specifically to describe said property, and debts, and choses in action, as they have full knowledge of the same, and answer the interrogatories herewith filed, on oath, and marked exhibit A, as a part of this petition.

The Confederate States of America, through said receiver, therefore pray that the said persons having supervision and control over said property, as aforesaid, who reside in the county of Knox, be made parties to this petition, and that a copy thereof, together with notice, be issued by the clerk of this court to the marshal or his deputy, to be served on said persons. Said Confederate States further pray that your honor direct said property to be seized and sequestrated, and placed in the hands of said receiver, and by him sold or disposed of upon such terms and conditions as your honor may direct. And on final hearing, the Confederate States pray for all such other, further, and different relief in the premises as may be consistent with the act of the Confederate Congress.

LANDON C. HAYNES,
Receiver for the Eastern District of Tennessee.

A true copy of the original.
WILLIAM G. MCADOO, *Clerk, &c.*

Proceedings were also taken against Judge Catron and Andrew Johnson.

SUNDRY ITEMS.

The Southern Commercial Convention which met at Macon, Oct. 16, 1861, passed a series of resolutions in relation to the sequestration act, and recommending that the payment of debts sequestered be not required during the war; that claims for indemnity and indebtedness due the North be allowed as a set-off; that the courts be empowered in certain cases to modify the retroactive effect of the bill; and that the property of northern residents laboring under the disabilities of coverture of infancy be exempted.

The Richmond *Enquirer* of Oct 14th says:

"It was understood at Richmond by a gentleman who is connected with the Department of the Interior, that the returns were being made of debts due to the alien enemies with the utmost promptitude, and that from the city of Petersburg there would be realized a sum not less than six hundred thousand dollars. As for Richmond, it was difficult to estimate the aggregate, but the lowest estimate placed it at two millions of dollars."

The Confederate States Court in Richmond have confiscated $15,000 in the hand of the bankers Purcell, in that city, the property of Ashmead *et als.*, of Philadelphia.

In April, 1863, the "Confederate" Senate considered a bill to confiscate the leasehold interest and shares of stock owned by the American Telegraph Company and other alien enemies in the lines of telegraph in the Confederate States. Mr. Oldham and Mr. Hill favored the bill, and Mr. Johnson, of Arkansas, and Mr. Johnson, of Georgia, opposed it—the former, because many of the stockholders whose property it was proposed to confiscate were not enemies, but friends living in Washington city and Maryland—the latter because he considered confiscation "an act of legal plunder unworthy of the age." The bill was postponed until the next day, and its fate is not known.

A movement was made about the same time in the Legislature of Virginia, appropriating so much of the public debt of the State and other securities held by resident citizens of the United States and the District of Columbia as may be necessary to indemnify the citizens of Virginia who are loyal to the State for losses sustained by them in consequence of any confiscation act of the Congress of the United States, or any other act growing out of the war.

Up to September 30, 1863, the rebel treasury had received from sequestration $1,862,550 27, as reported by the Secretary of the Treasury.

THE "SEQUESTRATION" ACT DECLARED CONSTITUTIONAL.

In the fall of 1861, in the first session of the Confederate States Court, in Charleston, after Judge Magrath charged the Jury, the following proceedings are reported to have taken place:

Mr. Petigru read a writ of garnishment, served upon him, and interrogatories attached, in reference to alien enemy's property.

Mr. Petigru said the objection he had to these interrogatories was, that no human authority has the right to put these questions to him or any one in the same circumstances. He might recognize the authority of South Carolina to do as proposed by the act, *because in a State like South Carolina a sufferer has no security or remedy against those in power*, unless from some guarantee in the constitution of the State; *for a State may do whatever it is not forbidden to do by the fundamental law of the State.* But the Confederate States have no such claim to generality. Their authority is confined to the constitution which confers it and the powers delegated to them, and whereas, in the case of a sovereign, we must show a guarantee *against* the power, in the case of the Confederacy they must show a warrant *for* their power.

There is no article in the Constitution of the Confederate States which authorizes them to set up an *inquisition*, or to proceed otherwise than according to the laws of the land. In fact, the best authority for this proceeding is Hudson's treatise on the Star Chamber, in *Second Collutanea Juridicia.* It will be found that the method prescribed in this confiscation act is precisely that of the Star Chamber. They call this a writ of garnishment; Mr. Hudson calls it a subpœna. This calls upon me to disclose all the cases in my knowledge of property held by an alien enemy. Mr. Hudson requires the party to appear before the Star Chamber, and answer all questions which may be put to him. These are alike in being general. There is no plaintiff. It is an *inquisition.* * * If no such power has been granted, how can such a thing be legal? * * What is incident to cases of the war power, the grant of the war power covers; but does the war power require the creation of a Star Chamber to wrong and harass our people? * * Where is the authority given? Where is the power to call upon the citizen in a new and unheard-of manner to answer questions upon oath for the purpose of enforcing the confiscation law? Shall it be said that it is to furnish the means to carry on the war? How can that be said to be necessary, which is *absolutely never known to have been done before?* Was there anybody that ever fought before Gen. Beauregard? War unfortunately is not a now thing. Its history is found on every page. Was there ever a law like this endured, practiced, or heard of? It certainly was not found among the people from whom we derive the common law. No English monarch or Parliament has ever sanctioned or undertaken such a thing. It is utterly inconsistent with the common law to require an inquisitorial examination of the subjects of the laws of war. It is no more a part of the law of war than it is a part of the law of peace. * * *

All that can be said in favor of the end and object proposed can be said in favor of the Star Chamber and the Spanish Inquisition. Torquemada set out on the latter institution with the best of motives. It was to save men's souls. He labored most earnestly, in season and out of season; and when high necessity commanded, he burnt their bodies to save their souls. * * * We do not consider that the end justifies the means in these days, but Torquemada *might have burnt Jews and Protestants, without calling upon their best friends to inform against them, and making it penal not to do so.* * * *

The war power includes as an incident, everything which is necessary or usual. It cannot be pretended that this is necessary or usual, since it never was done before. This is not the first war that ever was waged; and the laws of war are not the subject of wild speculation. Now, the means granted to attain this end are based upon the supposition that the end deserves all commendation; *that nothing in the world is more calculated to advance the repute of the country than to be keen in searching out the property of enemies, and proceeding against them when they have no opportunity of being heard, and to impoverish them by taking away the earnings of their industry and applying it to other uses.* * * It would be the most intolerable hardship for me, for a citizen, at every quarter section to be obliged to tell all he knows or suspects against his neighbor. It is pretended that it is an innocent proceeding. How can that be innocent which calls upon one to commit a breach of trust? *

The law protects every man in keeping silence when a question is asked that involves professional confidence. There can be no greater oppression than to compel a person to violate a moral or legal duty.

Something should be said about the objects of this law, for there is a very common error in supposing that it applies to the estates of native citizens who are living abroad in an enemy's country. The term alien enemy is the only one used in the act. It is a definite, technical construction An alien enemy must be born out of the legiance of the sovereign. There can be no dispute about it. He is not an alien enemy if he was born within the domains of the sovereign. A sovereign has a right to require his return. He may call on him to come home. What is it in the sovereign's power to do, and what he *may* do with his subject when he refuses to return, is another matter. But until he has been called on by his sovereign to return, a man commits no breach of duty in living in an enemy's country, according to law. It is impossible that the makers of the law should not be aware of this, and they seem to have purposely left this open for the interposition of humanity.

Mr. Petigru denied that there was any precedent for this law; and a freeman could not be compelled to aid this confiscating law, by informing against both his friends and enemies. It was this which moved those brave men, who not only shook the pillars of monarchy to its base, and abolished the Star Chamber, but did it with the declaration that no such thing should be tolerated again. Are we going, in the hey-day of our youth, to set an example which has been repudiated by every lover of freedom from the beginning of time to this day, which has never found an advocate, shocks the conscience, and invades the rights of the private citizen.

It is an extraordinary stretch of power, in an extraordinary time, when we are endeavoring to make good before the world our right to its respect as an enlightened people, a people capable of self-government, and of governing themselves in a manner worthy of the civilization and light of the age; and this act, *borrowed from the darkest period of tyranny, is dug up from the very quarters of despotism*, and put forward as our sentiments. *They are not my sentiments;* and sorry will I be if in this sentiment I am solitary and alone. * * With regard to that which requires the violation of professional confidence, he must be better instructed before making up his mind to the order of responsibility or not. There are cases when it is dishonor or death

—and death will certainly be chosen by every man who deserves the name.

Mr. Miles, the District Attorney, moved that Mr. Petigru make a return to the court of garnishment, in which the question stated by him should be raised, that if the first duty which devolved upon his honor since he had put on his robes, and opened the first term of the Confederate court in South Carolina, was to listen to an invective against the Government whose commission he bore, at least so much respect might be paid to the mandate of the court, which issued, with the sanction of his honor's name, that a formal return might be made to it, so that the points made by the respondent, in which not only the constitutionality of the law passed by the Congress of the Confederate States, *but the very authority of that Congress itself, and the validity of the Government which it represents, are drawn in question,* may be at least set down for argument, and not be allowed to be treated only with invective. * * *

He might be pardoned, however, if, in passing, he called the attention of the audience *for whose benefit the remarks of the respondent seem to have been made,* to the singular position which the succinct respondent to-day for the first time occupied. It was not strange that one who had so often distinguished himself by the undaunted boldness with which he threw himself in opposition to the weight of public opinion, should be the one who now invoked the aid of the Court to protect those whom the law of Congress designates as alien enemies, *but whom he still prides himself on calling "fellow-countrymen," from the tyranny of a Government which attempts to make their property subject to the rules of war.* This was consistent with his past position. But it was certainly a remarkable metamorphosis, that the eminent jurist who fearlessly, and almost alone, in his opposition to the political sentiments of the State, should now invoke the strictest and sternest construction of State rights that had ever been contended for even in South Carolina, in opposition to the power of the Confederate Government to pass a law in relation to a subject-matter expressly intrusted to Congress by the Constitution.

It is true that the profession of submission to the authority of the State in this matter was accompanied by the explanation, that such submission would be given only because *there could be no successful resistance to the tyranny.* But even with this qualification, the acknowledgment of the authority of the State was remarkable from such a quarter.

Subsequently Judge Magrath, refusing to sustain the demurrer of Messrs. Petigru, Mitchell and Whaley, sustained the constitutionality of the act.

JUDICIAL ACTION UNDER THE CONFISCATION LAW.

The law has been enforced. The life estate of Joseph R. Anderson, an officer in the rebel army, in about 50,000 acres of land in Allegany county, Maryland, has been condemned. Also, that of Hunter, Ould, Aiken, Magoffin, Boyce, McQueen, Corcoran, and Flournoy, in lands in Wisconsin. Also of rebel owners, various properties in Washington city, New York, Alexandria, &c.

In Alexandria, Judge John C. Underwood of the United States District Court for the eastern district of Virginia, has condemned "all the right, title, and interest" of parties under his view of the law, which he thus argues:

United States vs. *the Right, Title, and Interest of Hugh Latham, &c.*

The decree in this and similar cases must depend upon the construction given to article third, section third, of the Constitution of the United States, and the legislation of the last Congress for the confiscation of rebel property.

As the Supreme Court of the United States has never decided the questions involved in this case, and this court feels constrained to differ from the opinion of the supreme court of the neighboring district in some recent cases, a brief statement of the reasons of such dissent from the able jurists of that court may not be inappropriate.

This Court cannot limit a decree to a condemnation of a traitor's right, title, and interest in the property forfeited for the term of his own life, with a reversion to his heirs, for the reason that it does not consider such limitation warranted by the section and acts of Congress above referred to. The language of the Constitution is as follows:

"The Congress shall have power to declare the punishment of treason, but no attainder of treason shall work corruption of the blood or forfeiture, except during the life of the person so attainted."

The general power to punish treason is expressly granted in the first part of the above constitutional provision. The consequences of attainder of treason mentioned in the latter part of the provision would not require notice, as this is not a case of attainder of treason, were it not for the reference made to the limitations of this provision in the joint explanatory resolution passed by Congress July 17, 1862. But that reference and the quotation of the limitations made it necessary to inquire what was the "forfeiture" to be worked, and when the "work" was to be effected.

The authors of the constitutional provision were doubtless profound lawyers, and used the term "forfeiture," in its strict technical and well settled legal meaning. Blackstone gives us a whole chapter on this important word, which he begins thus:

"Forfeiture is a punishment annexed by law to some illegal act or negligence in the owner of lands, tenements, and hereditaments, whereby he loses all his interest therein, and they go to the party injured as a recompense for the wrong sustained."

Again, he enumerates "forfeiture," deed, device, &c., as the modes of absolute conveyance of real estate; and it seems clearly that this was the sense in which it was used in the constitutional provision. Besides being good lawyers, the authors were evidently thorough scholars, familiar with King James's translation of the Bible and the old English classics, and employed the word "except," in the phrase—"Except during the life of the person attainted," in a sense now nearly obsolete, though common a hundred years ago, and at the date of the Constitution making it synonymous with the word "unless," as in the Bible declarations—"Except ye repent ye shall all likewise perish." "Except a man be born again he cannot see the Kingdom of God." "Except these abide in the ship ye cannot be saved." Shakspeare and other English classics abound in examples of the use of this word as a conditional conjunction, but one will suffice:

The Bishop of Winchester, when accused of sedition in King Henry VI, act III, scene 1, indignantly exclaims—

> "And for dissension, who preferreth peace,
> More than I do—except I be provoked?"

We find a similar definition of the term in Webster's Dictionary.

If we use the word "except" in the above sense in the the constitutional provision, or make it read "unless during the life of the person attainted," we shall at once come to the true intent and meaning of the provision, to wit: That the forfeiture was to be perfected *during*, and not *after*, the lifetime of the party attainted.

Bills of attainder were common in the British Parliament. Several of the Colonial Legislatures passed similar acts during the war of the Revolution. They were summary and sweeping in their character, requiring no process or any action of courts of law, but included in a single bill many persons, and in a single section confiscated all their property, both real and personal. In some cases the dead as well as the living were included in these bills, so transcendingly wicked did the crime of treason appear to our ancestors. The Government thus convicted men of this crime without trial, and after they were dead and buried, taking as a punishment estates which had already descended to their heirs or passed to innocent purchasers in good faith. This mode of proceeding was manifestly in violation of the general spirit and principles of English and American criminal laws, by which crimes, trespasses, and torts of every description, from the highest to the lowest, are alone punishable during the life of the wrong-doer, whose death before final judgment is a perpetual stay of all proceedings and all legal consequences. According to the maxim: *"Actio personalis, cum persona moritor."* The Constitutional provision was therefore inserted to correct this harsh anomaly, and to bring the punishment of treason into harmony with that of all other crimes and misdemeanors.

It also abolished entirely the cruel doctrine of "corruption of the blood," which prevented the children of a traitor who had been attainted from ever inheriting *from* or *through* the father either title or estate. Its limitation was as to time of working forfeiture and not as to the definition of the term or character of the estate forfeited, and it made no distinction between personal and real estate.

Nor is there anything in the act of Congress of July 17, 1862, limiting the forfeiture within more narrow bounds than those of the Constitution. On the contrary, the only fear ever expressed in relation to that act was that it transcended the Constitution.

The only ground for restricting the forfeiture then must be found in the joint resolution of the two Houses of Congress of the same date of the act aforesaid.

The first branch of this resolution was evidently intended to explain the act and to prevent its application in such a way as to give it an unconstitutional and *ex post facto* operation. And a careful consideration of its last clause affords the strongest internal evidence that it also was intended simply to prevent an infringement of the Constitution. Its language is copied almost verbatim from the Constitution. Even the very unusual legal phrase, "work a forfeiture," is borrowed from the same source, and means finish, perfect and complete, the necessary legal proceedings for a forfeiture or conveyance of estate, as we work out or perfect a problem. The only variance is the substitution of the preposition "beyond" for the conjunction "except" in the phrase "beyond the life," instead of "except during the life." But the similarity of language is so great as to force a conviction that the last part of the resolution, like the first part, was intended to restrain the courts within the bounds of the Constitution. It cannot be supposed that Congress intended to repeal its own act by the resolution, or so to emasculate it as to make it worse than a nullity.

It seems also but reasonable that we should give such a construction to the resolution as will, if possible, bring it into harmony with those more weighty and formal instruments, the act and the Constitution. The variation of a single word in quoting the Constitution is not surprising when we consider the probable hurry and pressure which attended the passage of this resolution among many others on the last day of a long session of Congress. We could hardly expect the same precision of language under such circumstances as in an act passed with mature consideration in committees, and after three separate readings in each house of Congress. And though the construction given by the court of the District of Columbia would seem very natural, taking the clause without its connections, yet when we consider those connections, it will appear that our construction will not only best secure the objects of the law, but entirely harmonizes with the act and Constitution, without the least violence to the language of the resolution. By quoting the language of the Constitution, the conclusion is inevitable that the constitutional authority and power was referred to the action of the courts.

If the construction that only a life estate is to be confiscated shall be established, the bill passed by Congress on the 17th of July, 1862, instead of being true to its title, "An Act to suppress insurrection, to punish treason and rebellion, to seize and confiscate the property of rebels," would in its effects become an act to prevent the re-settlement and improvement of the country; an act to promote jealousy, envy, and hatred between the holders of life estates and reversionary interests, and to continue the desolations caused by the rebellion for a whole generation without any benefit to the National Treasury, to the parties interested, or to anybody else except the lovers of discord and officers of law; an act to defeat the leading objects of its own friends in and out of Congress, which objects are well known to be, 1st—by the sale of rebel estates to reimburse in some degree the immense expenditures incurred in suppressing the rebellion, and 2d—to supply the places of departed rebels with loyal men and bring again into cultivation and improvement those deserted and wasted estates. But if only a life interest is to be acquired, no purchaser could afford to take on so uncertain a tenure, at even a nominal price, the wasted plantations, and restore the destroyed houses and fences by building valuable and permanent structures.

Those of us who remember the condition of the country between the Potomac and the Rappahannock from twenty to forty years ago, the desolation and heart-burning, the agony and despair, the ejectments and expulsions attending the expiration of the anti-republican life leases of the old proprietor, Lord Fairfax, will certainly pray to be delivered from a repetition of the scenes which this construction would inevitably produce. The life state theory also involves the absurdity that in proportion to the enormity and certainty of the guilt of any person, should be the shortness of the forfeiture of his estate, for in the most flagrant cases the time between conviction and execution is usually very brief, and forfeiture for that brief period would be both puerile and preposterous. Applying, then, the well settled rule of interpretation, that where two constructions can be given to a written instrument, that must be presumed which is most just and beneficial to the public in its operation, we can have no doubt of the meaning of this resolution.

Judging from the many wise enactments of the last Congress, we should be forced to the belief that its intentions were uniformly beneficent, and therefore it could not have intended to open the door to such absurdities and calamities. We must conclude from its words and connections that the resolution had its origin in an abundant caution against a violation of the Constitution, but was never intended to confine the action of the courts within any limits less extended than the Constitution, nor to give a construction to the Constitution. It was not meant to prevent the full and just action of all the proper and legitimate powers of the Government for the punishment of treason. Nor has our construction any color of undue harshness and severity toward the great criminals who have brought upon the country this terrible civil war. In all Christian or civilized nations on the earth, the punishment of treason has been a total forfeiture both of estate and life, and justly so, for it is not in its consequences simply murder, but wholesale murder with all the other crimes of the decalogue added thereto.

And how absurd is the idea that we may take the life of a traitor but may not take that which is less valuable than life, to wit: his property? Does not the greater always include the less?

By this court, then, looking for light and guidance to the tribunal of Eternal Justice, it must be held that enough loyal blood, and widows' and orphans' tears, have been poured out and mingled with the soil of Virginia to extinguish all rebel rights and establish a perfect title in the Government, for the benefit of the heirs of those who have fallen defending the republican institutions received from our patriot fathers—institutions which we are bound to preserve and to transmit unimpaired and, if possible, improved and purified to our posterity.

The point raised by the respondent's counsel against the constitutionality of the law under which this suit is brought, because it does not provide a jury trial in any case, is one of very grave import. In the judgment of this court it would be much more in the spirit, not only of the Constitution, but of the great charter ratified at Runnymede, if a respondent, on putting in his answer and taking the oath of allegiance to the Government, was permitted to demand a trial by jury.

But the decisions of the Supreme Court of the United States in the Dred Scott case, and other cases under the fugitive slave laws of Congress, deprived men of liberty, which is dearer than property, without trial by jury, will not permit this court, especially where no oath of allegiance is offered by the respondent, to declare the law unconstitutional on this ground.

It is to be hoped, however, that all uncertainty arising from different constructions of the courts may be speedily removed by the action of the Supreme Court of the United States, or by the explanatory legislation of Congress now about to be assembled.

The decree of the court in this case is, that all right, title, interest and estate of the said Hugh Latham, in and to the property mentioned in the libel in this case, be forfeited and confiscated to the United States, and that the marshal of the court proceed to sell said right, title, interest and estate at public auction for cash to the highest bidder, after having given ten days' notice of the time, place, and terms of sale of the personal property, and at least twenty days' notice of the time, place, and terms of sale of the real estate, by advertisement in one or more newspapers printed and published in the cities of Alexandria and Washington. That said marshal deliver the personal property to the purchaser, and also make and deliver a deed of the real estate to the purchaser on the payment of the purchase money therefor, and that the marshal bring the proceeds of said sale into this court to await the further order thereof.

MILITARY ORDERS.*

CONFISCATION OF PROPERTY.

The following important military order has been issued by Major General Wallace:

HEADQUARTERS MIDDLE DEPARTMENT, 8TH ARMY CORPS,
BALTIMORE, MD., *April* 26, 1864.

[General Orders No. 30.]

Many citizens of this department have gone voluntarily into the States in rebellion against the United States, some to join the rebel army, others to aid and encourage the rebellion by their presence and otherwise, who have left property in real estate, slaves, stocks of various descriptions, and other securities for money in this department. And many citizens of the States in rebellion, who have participated in and encouraged that movement, have similar property within this department. It is deemed important that such property should not be under the control of such persons, and liable to be used in whole or in part in the support of the rebellion, and against the interests of the United States.

It is therefore hereby ordered that the proceeds of all real estate, the hire of all slaves, the interest on all debts due from persons in this department, the current interest on all private debts, the dividends and interest on all stocks and bonds of railroad companies, banks, turnpike road companies, manufacturing companies, and public corporations, howsoever declared and payable, which are the property of the persons above described, and are within this department, shall be withheld by the persons authorized, and whose duty it is to pay the same, from such persons, their representatives, agents, and attorneys, howso-

* The President has suspended the execution of these orders. Moneys paid under them are ordered repaid.

ever constituted; and that the same shall be paid over to Lieutenant Colonel Alexander Bliss, Quartermaster of this department, or such other agent as the general commanding may authorize and appoint from time to time. All persons having authority over such property will be held responsible for such sums as may be paid in violation of this order, and be otherwise punished by military commission.

The hire and the proceeds of the labor of such slaves as are in the counties of Maryland in this department, and belonging to the persons above described, will in due proportion be set apart and reserved for the use of such slaves when they shall have been freed by the constitutional law of Maryland, as it is hoped they soon will be.

By command of Major General Wallace:

SAMUEL B. LAWRENCE, *Asst. Adj. Gen.*

Official: JAS. R. ROSS, *A. D. C.*

HEADQUARTERS MIDDLE DEPARTMENT, 8TH ARMY CORPS, BALTIMORE, MD., *May* 1, 1864.

[General Orders No. 33.]

In order more effectually to carry out the provisions of General Orders No. 30, from these headquarters, it is ordered:

1st—That the President and directors, or other authorized agents and representatives of all banks, insurance companies, railroad, turnpike, ferry, and manufacturing companies, and all other monied corporations, institutions, and joint stock companies whatsoever within this military department, shall, with the least possible delay, and not later than the 15th day of June next, forward to the office of Lieut. Col. Alexander Bliss, Quartermaster of this department, a written statement verified under oath by the president, and by the secretary or treasury of such corporation or company, &c., setting forth the names and address of all the proprietors or stockholders, or others having now or within the past year, any interest whatsoever in the capital stock, the bonds or other debt, funded or otherwise of such corporation or company, or in the dividends, interest, premiums or other profits whatsoever arising therefrom or from its business, who are, or who since April 19th, 1861, have been residents of, or have lived within any of the States now in rebellion, or who now are, or who have been in the rebel army, or in the employment of the rebel government, to the best knowledge and belief of the deponents—the exact amount and nature of the share or other interest of every such person, the date of the commencement of such interest, or of any increase thereof; also, the dates and amounts of all payments of dividends, interest, premiums or other profits by said company since May 1st, 1863, to any such person, or to any one whatsoever on account of any such persons, and the names of those to whom paid. Also the name of any of the said persons to whom any interests or profits are now payable, and the amounts and dates when due.

2d.—It is ordered that all corporations, joint stock companies, and all individuals within this department, who now owe, or who since May 1st, 1863, have owed any interest upon any mortgage, bond or note, or other security, or who since May 1st, 1863, have paid any interest upon any mortgage, bond, note, or other security, or any other interest, or profit whatsoever to any person of any of the classes enumerated in the preceding paragraph, (or to any agent, attorney, or representative of any of the said persons,) shall, with the least possible delay, and not later than the 15th day of June, 1864, forward to the office of Lieutenant Colonel Alexander Bliss, Quartermaster of the Middle department, a written statement verified under oath setting forth the names and address of all persons to whom any such interest has been or is due, or to whom paid, the amount thereof, the amount of the principal upon which it is due or has been paid, the nature of the debt, whether bond, (secured or not by mortgage,) or note, or other security or evidence of debt whatsoever, and the date of its maturity.

3d. It is ordered that all corporations and joint stock companies, and all individuals within this department who now occupy or enjoy the use of, or since May 1st, 1863, have occupied or enjoyed the use of any lands, tenements, buildings, or other real estate whatsoever owned either in whole or in part by, or of which the rent or other proceeds in any manner accrue to, any of the persons of any of the classes above enumerated in paragraph 1 of this Order, shall, with the least possible delay, and not later than the 15th day of June next, forward to the office of Lieutenant Colonel Alexander Bliss, Quartermaster of the Middle department, a written statement, verified under oath, setting forth their names and address, the location and description of any such lands, buildings, or other real estate, the names of the owners, lessees, &c., thereof, the rate of the rent or hire thereof, and any amount now due on account of the rent or hire thereof, or which have since May 1st, 1863, been due, or which have since that date been paid to any person whatsoever, and the names and address of all persons to whom said amounts are or have been due or paid, and the date when due or paid.

4th. It is ordered that all persons in the counties of Maryland within this department now hiring, or who since January 1st, 1864, have hired slaves, belonging wholly or in part, now or within the past year, to any of the persons of the class enumerated in paragraph 1 of this Order, shall furnish to Lieutenant Colonel Alexander Bliss, Quartermaster of the Middle department, a written statement, verified under oath, of their names and address, of the number of such slaves hired by them, the rate of hire, the names of the owners of each, the name of each slave, and the names of the persons to whom any payments have been since January 1st, 1864, made, or are now due on account of such hire, the amounts of such payments, and the amounts now due.

And all slaves are required to furnish themselves such of the above information as is in their power, by appearing personally at the above place for that purpose, or otherwise, as they may be able.

By command of Major General Wallace:

SAMUEL B. LAWRENCE, *Asst. Adj. Gen.*

Official: MAX WOODHULL, *A. D. C.*

THE PRESIDENT'S PROCLAMATION UNDER THE CONFISCATION LAW.

In pursuance of the sixth section of the act of Congress entitled "An act to suppress insurrection, to punish treason and rebellion, to seize and confiscate the property of rebels, and for other purposes," approved July 17, 1862, and which act, and the joint resolution explanatory thereof, are herewith published, I, ABRAHAM LINCOLN, President of the United States, do hereby proclaim to and warn all persons within the contemplation of said sixth section to cease participating in, aiding, countenancing, or abetting the existing rebellion, or any rebellion, against the Government of the United States, and to return to their proper allegiance to the United States, on pain of the forfeitures and seizures as within and by said sixth section provided.

In testimony whereof, I have hereunto set my hand and caused the seal of the United States to be affixed.

Done at the city of Washington, this twenty-fifth day of July, in the year of our Lord one thousand eight hundred and sixty-two, and of the Independence of the United States the eighty-seventh.

ABRAHAM LINCOLN.

By the President:

WM. H. SEWARD, *Secretary of State.*

EMANCIPATION.

Compensated Emancipation.

Second Session, Thirty-Sixth Congress.

IN HOUSE.

Feb. 11, 1861—Mr. JAMES B. McKEAN, of New York, introduced into the House the following resolution, which—Mr. BURNETT, of Kentucky, indicating a desire to discuss it—was laid on the table under the rule, and was not again considered:

Whereas the "Gulf States" have assumed to secede from the Union, and it is deemed important to prevent the "border slave States" from following their example; and whereas it is believed that those who are inflexibly opposed to any measure of compromise or concession that involves, or may involve, a sacrifice of principle or the extension of slavery, would nevertheless cheerfully concur in any lawful measure for the emancipation of the slaves: Therefore,

Resolved, That the select committee of five be instructed to inquire whether, by the consent of the people, or of the State governments, or by compensating the slaveholders, it be practicable for the General Government to procure the emancipation of the slaves in some, or all, of the "border States;" and if so, to report a bill for that purpose.

—

Second Session, Thirty-Seventh Congress.

THE PRESIDENT'S RECOMMENDATION TO CONGRESS.

March 6, 1862—The PRESIDENT sent the following message to Congress:

Fellow-Citizens of the Senate and House of Representatives:

I recommend the adoption of a joint resolution by your honorable bodies, which shall be substantially as follows:

Resolved, That the United States ought to co-operate with any State which may adopt gradual abolishment of slavery, giving to such State pecuniary aid, to be used by such State in its discretion, to compensate for the inconveniences, public and private, produced by such change of system.

If the proposition contained in the resolution does not meet the approval of Congress and the country, there is the end; but if it does command such approval, I deem it of importance that the States and people immediately interested should be at once distinctly notified of the fact, so that they may begin to consider whether to accept or reject it. The Federal Government would find its highest interest in such a measure, as one of the most efficient means of self-preservation. The leaders of the existing insurrection entertain the hope that this Government will ultimately be forced to acknowledge the independence of some part of the disaffected region, and that all the slave States north of such part will then say, "the Union for which we have struggled being already gone, we now choose to go with the southern section." To deprive them of this hope, substantially ends the rebellion; and the initiation of emancipation completely deprives them of it as to all the States initiating it. The point is not that *all* the States tolerating slavery would very soon, if at all, initiate emancipation; but that, while the offer is equally made to all, the more northern shall, by such initiation, make it certain to the more southern that in no event will the former ever join the latter in their proposed confederacy. I say "initiation," because, in my judgment, gradual, and not sudden emancipation, is better for all. In the mere financial or pecuniary view, any member of Congress, with the census tables and Treasury reports before him, can readily see for himself how very soon the current expenditures of this war would purchase, at fair valuation, all the slaves in any named State. Such a proposition on the part of the General Government sets up no claim of a right by Federal authority to interfere with slavery within State limits, referring, as it does the absolute control of the subject in each case to the State and its people immediately interested. It is proposed as a matter of perfectly free choice with them.

In the annual message last December, I thought fit to say, "the Union must be preserved; and hence all indispensable means must be employed." I said this not hastily, but deliberately. War has been made, and continues to be an indispensable means to this end. A practical reacknowledgment of the national authority would render the war unnecessary, and it would at once cease. If, however, resistance continues, the war must also continue; and it is impossible to foresee all the incidents which may attend, and all the ruin which may follow it. Such as may seem indispensable, or may obviously promise great efficiency toward ending the struggle, must and will come.

The proposition now made, though an offer only, I hope it may be esteemed no offence to ask whether the pecuniary consideration tendered would not be of more value to the States and private persons concerned, than are the institution, and property in it, in the present aspect of affairs?

While it is true that the adoption of the proposed resolution would be merely initiatory, and not within itself a practical measure, it is recommended in the hope that it would soon lead to important practical results. In full view of my great responsibility to my God and to my country, I earnestly beg the attention of Congress and the people to the subject.

ABRAHAM LINCOLN.

March 6, 1862.

IN HOUSE.

March 10—Mr. ROSCOE CONKLING, of New York, introduced under a suspension of the rules, which was carried—yeas 86, nays 35, this joint resolution:

Resolved, &c., That the United States ought to co-operate with any State which may adopt gradual abolishment of slavery, giving to such State pecuniary aid, to be used by such State in its discretion, to compensate for the inconveniences, public and private, produced by such change of system.

March 11—The resolution passed the House of Representatives—yeas 97, nays 36, as follows:

YEAS—Messrs. Aldrich, Arnold, Ashley, Babbitt, Baker,

Baxter, Beaman, Bingham, Francis P. Blair, Jacob B. Blair, Samuel S. Blair, Blake, William G. Brown, Buffinton, Campbell, Chamberlain, Clark, Clements, *Cobb*, Colfax, Frederick A. Conkling, Roscoe Conkling, Conway, Covode, Cutler, Davis, Delano, Diven, Duell, Dunn, Edgerton, Edwards, Eliot, Ely, Fessenden, Fisher, Franchot, Frank, Gooch, Goodwin, Granger, Gurley, *Haight*, Hale, Harrison, Hickman, Hooper, Horton, Hutchins, Julian, Kelley, Francis W. Kellogg, William Kellogg, Killinger, Lansing, *Lehman*, Loomis, Lovejoy, McKnight, McPherson, Mitchell, Moorhead, Anson P. Morrill, Justin S. Morrill, Nixon, Olin, Patton, Timothy G. Phelps, Pike, Pomeroy, Porter, Alexander H. Rice, John H. Rice, Riddle, Edward H. Rollins, Sargent, Shanks, *Sheffield*, Shellabarger, Sloan, Stratton, B. F. Thomas, Trimble, Trowbridge, Van Valkenburgh, Verree, Wall, Wallace, Charles W. Walton, E. P. Walton, Whaley, Wheeler, Albert S. White, Wilson, Windom, Worcester—97.

NAYS—Messrs. *Ancona*, *Joseph Baily*, *Biddle*, *Calvert*, *Corning*, *Cox*, *Cravens*, *Crisfield*, *Crittenden*, *Dunlap*, *English*, *Grider*, *Harding*, *Johnson*, *Knapp*, *Law*, Leary, *Mallory*, *Menzies*, *Morris*, *Noble*, *Norton*, *Pendleton*, *Perry*, *Richardson*, *Robinson*, *Shiel*, *John B. Steele*, Francis Thomas, *Voorhees*, *Wadsworth*, *Ward*, *Chilton A. White*, *Wickliffe*, *Wood*, *Woodruff*—36.

April 2—The resolution passed the Senate—yeas 32, nays 10, as follows

YEAS—Messrs. Anthony, Browning, Chandler, Clark, Collamer, *Davis*, Dixon, Doolittle, Fessenden, Foot, Foster, Grimes, Hale, Harlan, Henderson, Howard, Howe, King, Lane of Indiana, Lane of Kansas, Morrill, Pomeroy, Sherman, Sumner, Ten Eyck, *Thomson*, Trumbull, Wade, Wilkinson, Willey, Wilmot, Wilson of Massachusetts—32.

NAYS—Messrs. *Bayard*, *Carlile*, *Kennedy*, *Latham*, *Nesmith*, *Powell*, *Saulsbury*, *Stark*, *Wilson*, of Missouri, *Wright*—10.

MEMORANDUM OF AN INTERVIEW BETWEEN THE PRESIDENT AND SOME BORDER SLAVE STATE REPRESENTATIVES, MARCH 10, 1862, BY HON. J. W. CRISFIELD.

"DEAR SIR: I called, at the request of the President, to ask you to come to the White House to-morrow morning, at nine o'clock, and bring such of your colleagues as are in town."

WASHINGTON, *March* 10, 1862.

Yesterday on my return from church I found Mr. Postmaster General Blair in my room, writing the above note, which he immediately suspended, and verbally communicated the President's invitation; and stated that the President's purpose was to have some conversation with the delegations of Kentucky, Missouri, Maryland, Virginia, and Delaware, in explanation of his message of the 6th inst.

This morning these delegations, or such of them as were in town, assembled at the White House at the appointed time, and after some little delay were admitted to an audience. Mr. Leary and myself were the only members from Maryland present, and, I think, were the only members of the delegation at that time in the city. I know that Mr. Pearce, of the Senate, and Messrs. Webster and Calvert, of the House, were absent.

After the usual salutations and we were seated, the President said, in substance, that he had invited us to meet him to have some conversation with us in explanation of his message of the 6th; that since he had sent it in several of the gentlemen then present had visited him, but had avoided any allusion to the message, and he therefore inferred that the import of the message had been misunderstood, and was regarded as inimical to the interests we represented; and he had resolved he would talk with us, and disabuse our minds of that erroneous opinion.

The President then disclaimed any intent to injure the interests or wound the sensibilities of the slave States. On the contrary, his purpose was to protect the one and respect the other; that we were engaged in a terrible, wasting, and tedious war; immense armies were in the field, and must continue in the field as long as the war lasts; that these armies must, of necessity, be brought into contact with slaves in the States we represented and in other States as they advanced; that slaves would come to the camps and continual irritation was kept up; that he was constantly annoyed by conflicting and antagonistic complaints; on the one side, a certain class complained if the slave was not protected by the army; persons were frequently found who, participating in these views, acted in a way unfriendly to the slaveholder; on the other hand, slaveholders complained that their rights were interfered with, their slaves induced to abscond and protected within the lines; these complaints were numerous, loud, and deep; were a serious annoyance to him and embarrassing to the progress of the war; that it kept alive a spirit hostile to the Government in the States we represented; strengthened the hopes of the confederates that at some day the border States would unite with them, and thus tend to prolong the war; and he was of opinion, if this resolution should be adopted by Congress and accepted by our States, these causes of irritation and these hopes would be removed, and more would be accomplished towards shortening the war than could be hoped from the greatest victory achieved by Union armies; that he made this proposition in good faith, and desired it to be accepted, if at all, voluntarily, and in the same patriotic spirit in which it was made; that emancipation was a subject exclusively under the control of the States, and must be adopted or rejected by each for itself; that he did not claim nor had this Government any right to coerce them for that purpose; that such was no part of his purpose in making this proposition, and he wished it to be clearly understood; that he did not expect us there to be prepared to give him an answer, but he hoped we would take the subject into serious consideration; confer with one another, and then take such course as we felt our duty and the interests of our constituents required of us.

Mr. NOELL, of Missouri, said that in his State slavery was not considered a permanent institution; that natural causes were there in operation which would, at no distant day, extinguish it, and he did not think that this proposition was necessary for that; and, besides that, he and his friends felt solicitous as to the message on account of the different constructions which the resolution and message had received. The *New York Tribune* was for it, and understood it to mean that we must accept gradual emancipation according to the plan suggested, or get something worse.

The PRESIDENT replied, he must not be expected to quarrel with the *New York Tribune* before the right time; he hoped never to have to do it; he would not anticipate events. In respect to emancipation in Missouri, he said that what had been observed by Mr. Noell was probably true, but the operation of these natural causes had not prevented the irritating conduct to which he had referred, or destroyed the hopes of the Confederates that Missouri would at some time range herself alongside of them, which, in his judgment, the passage of this resolution by Congress and its acceptance by Missouri would accomplish.

Mr. CRISFIELD, of Maryland, asked what would be the effect of the refusal of the State to accept this proposal, and desired to know if the President looked to any policy beyond the acceptance or rejection of this scheme.

The PRESIDENT replied that he had no designs beyond the action of the States on this particular subject. He should lament their refusal to accept it, but he had no designs beyond their refusal of it.

Mr. MENZIES, of Kentucky, inquired if the President thought there was any power except in the States themselves to carry out his scheme of emancipation.

The PRESIDENT replied, he thought there could not be. He then went off into a course of remark not qualifying the foregoing declaration nor material to be repeated to a just understanding of his meaning.

Mr. CRISFIELD said he did not think the people of Maryland looked upon slavery as a permanent institution; and he did not know that they would be very reluctant to give it up if provision was made to meet the loss, and they could be rid of the race; but they did not like to be coerced into emancipation, either by the direct action of the Government or by indirection, as through the emancipation of slaves in this District, or the confiscation of southern property as now threatened; and he thought before they would consent to consider this proposition they would require to be informed on these points.

The PRESIDENT replied that, "unless he was expelled by the act of God or the Confederate armies, he should occupy that house for three years, and as long as he remained there Maryland had nothing to fear, either for her institutions or her interests, on the points referred to."

Mr. CRISFIELD immediately added: "Mr. President, if what you now say could be heard by the people of Maryland they would consider your proposition with a much better feeling than I fear without it they will be inclined to do."

The PRESIDENT. "That (meaning a publication of what he said) will not do; it would force me into a quarrel before the proper time;" and, again intimating, as he had before done, that a quarrel with the "Greeley faction" was impending, he said "he did not wish to encounter it before the proper time, nor at all if it could be avoided."

Governor WICKLIFFE, of Ky., then asked him respecting the constitutionality of his scheme.

The PRESIDENT replied: "As you may suppose, I have considered that; and the proposition now submitted does not encounter any constitutional difficulty. It proposes simply to co-operate with any State by giving such State pecuniary aid; and he thought that the resolution, as proposed by him, would be considered rather as the expression of a sentiment than as involving any constitutional question."

Mr. HALL, of Mo., thought that if this proposition was adopted at all it should be by the votes of the free States, and come as a proposition from them to the slave States, affording them an inducement to put aside this subject of discord; that it ought not to be expected that members representing slaveholding constituencies should declare at once, and in advance of any proposition to them, for the emancipation of slavery.

The PRESIDENT said he saw and felt the force of the objection; it was a fearful responsibility, and every gentleman must do as he thought best; that he did not know how this scheme was received by the members from the free States; some of them had spoken to him and received it kindly; but for the most part they were as reserved and chary as we had been, and he could not tell how they would vote. And in reply to some expression of Mr. Hall as to his own opinion regarding slavery, he said he did not pretend to disguise his anti-slavery feeling; that he thought it was wrong and should continue to think so; but that was not the question we had to deal with now. Slavery existed, and that, too, as well by the act of the North as of the South; and in any scheme to get rid of it, the North, as well as the South, was morally bound to do its full and equal share. He thought the institution wrong, and ought never to have existed; but yet he recognized the rights of property which had grown out of it, and would respect those rights as fully as similar rights in any other property; that property can exist, and does legally exist. He thought such a law wrong, but the rights of property resulting must be respected; he would get rid of the odious law, not by violating the right, but by encouraging the proposition and offering inducements to give it up.

Here the interview, so far as this subject is concerned, terminated by Mr. Crittenden's assuring the President that, whatever might be our final action, we all thought him solely moved by a high patriotism and sincere devotion to the happiness and glory of his country; and with that conviction we should consider respectfully the important suggestions he had made.

After some conversation on the current war news, we retired, and I immediately proceeded to my room and wrote out this paper.

J. W. CRISFIELD.

We were present at the interview described in the foregoing paper of Mr. CRISFIELD, and we certify that the substance of what passed on the occasion is in this paper faithfully and fully given.

J. W. MENZIES,
J. J. CRITTENDEN,
R. MALLORY.

March 10, 1862.

COMPENSATED EMANCIPATION IN THE DISTRICT OF COLUMBIA.

April 16—A bill was passed liberating all persons of African descent held to service or labor within the District of Columbia, and prohibiting slavery or involuntary servitude in the

District except as a punishment for crime. It provided for a commission to appraise the valuation of the slaves liberated, but limited their allowance in the aggregate to an amount equal to $300 per slave; and appropriated $1,000,000 to pay loyal owners, and $100,000 to colonize such of the slaves as desired to emigrate to Hayti or Liberia, this expenditure not to exceed $100 for each person emigrating.*

* Pending the civil appropriation bill in the Senate and House, June 25 and 29, 1864, a section was adopted without a division, repealing this section, and also that part of the first section of the civil appropriation bill of July 16, 1862, which appropriated $500,000 to colonize emancipated slaves of the District of Columbia, to be repaid to the Treasury out of the proceeds of confiscated property.

This report from the Secretary of the Interior, March 7, 1864, to the President, gives a statement of the results of the experiment:

DEPARTMENT OF THE INTERIOR,
WASHINGTON, D. C., *March* 7, 1864.

SIR: I have the honor to return herewith the letter of Hon. Benjamin F. Wade, chairman of the Committee on Territories in the Senate, requesting to be informed how much of the fund appropriated by the Thirty-Seventh Congress for colonization purposes has been paid out, for what purpose, and to whom, which you referred to this Department for report, and to state that as the accounts of all the persons to whom money was advanced for colonization purposes have not yet been finally settled at the Treasury, I am not able, at the present time, to state the exact amount actually expended. The total amount drawn from the Treasury up to the present time, however, is $33,226 97.

It was paid or advanced to the following named persons, and for the objects herein stated:

Amount paid to John D. Defrees, Superintendent of Public Printing, for binding in paper 5,000 copies "White and African Races"	$127 50
Amount paid Green & Williams for six cane-seat chairs	12 00
Amount advanced Hon. S. C. Pomeroy, special agent for colonization in Central America	25,000 00
Amount paid Watt J. Smith for traveling expenses to New York and back	52 40
Amount paid John P. Usher for traveling expenses to New York and back, and for advance made to agent sent to the East to obtain information in relation to colonization	152 40
Amount paid James Mitchel, for clerical services of W. B. Smith and Thomas R. Smith; for services of Rev. A. Bemar, (colored minister;) and for advance to J. E. Williams, (colored,) agent of A. W. Thompson	112 00
Amount advanced Rev. R. R. Gurley, corresponding secretary of the American Colonization Society, to aid the Rev. Chancey Leonard, pastor of the First Baptist Church in Washington city, in visiting Liberia, with reference to the establishment of a colony on the St. John's river	200 00
Amount paid Augustus A. Smith, as clerk	18 33
Amount paid J. Mitchell, for office furniture, and for services of J. W. Menard, in emigration office	60 00
Amount paid J. W. Menard, for services as clerk in emigration office	50 00
Amount paid Aug. A. Smith, for services as clerk	100 00
Amount paid J. W. Fitzhugh, for furniture for emigration office	326 15
Amount paid James Mitchell to 31st December, 1863, as agent of emigration	2,838 46
Amount advanced to D. C. Donnohue, to defray his expenses as special agent to Ile à Vache	300 00
Amount paid Cronin, Hurxthal & Sears, for clothing purchased and sent to colonists at Ile à Vache	900 00
Amount paid to Hurxthal & Barnum, for clothing purchased and sent to colonists at Ile à Vache.	1,786 33
Amount paid American Colonization Society, for passage engaged for J. W. Menard to Liberia	95 00
Amount paid American Colonization Society, for passage, &c., to Liberia of three colored emigrants from the District of Columbia	285 00
Amount paid Wilson & Cammann, for draft of D. C. Donnohue, special agent	750 00
Amount paid Hallet Kilbourn, for traveling expenses to New York as special agent to purchase clothing for the relief of the colonists at Ile à Vache	61 40
Making in all	33,226 97

April 3—The bill passed the Senate—yeas 29, nays 14; as follows:

YEAS—Messrs. Anthony, Browning, Chandler, Clark, Collamer, Dixon, Doolittle, Fessenden, Foot, Foster, Grimes, Hale, Harlan, Harris, Howard, Howe, King, Lane of Indiana, Lane of Kansas, Morrill, Pomeroy, Sherman, Sumner, Ten Eyck, Trumbull, Wade, Wilkinson, Wilmot, Wilson of Massachusetts—29.

NAYS—Messrs. *Bayard, Carlile, Davis,* Henderson, *Kennedy, Latham, McDougall, Nesmith, Powell, Saulsbury, Stark,* Willey, *Wilson* of Missouri, *Wright*—14.

April 11—It passed the House—yeas 92, nays 39, as follows:

YEAS—Messrs. Aldrich, Alley, Arnold, Ashley, Babbitt, Baker, Baxter, Beaman, Bingham, Francis P. Blair, Samuel S. Blair, Blake, *George H. Browne*, Buffinton, Campbell, Chamberlain, Clark, Colfax, Frederick A. Conkling, Roscoe Conkling, Covode, Davis, Dawes, Delano, Diven, Duell, Dunn, Edgerton, Edwards, Eliot, *English*, Fenton, Fessenden, Fisher, Franchot, Frank, Gooch, Goodwin, Granger, *Haight*, Hale, Hanchett, Harrison, Hickman, Hooper, Hutchins, Julian, Kelley, Francis W. Kellogg, Killinger, Lansing, Loomis, Lovejoy, McKnight, McPherson, Mitchell, Moorhead, Anson P. Morrill, Justin S. Morrill, Nixon, *Odell*, Olin, Patton, Pike, Porter, Potter, Alexander H. Rice, John H. Rice, Riddle, Edward H. Rollins, Sargent, Sedgwick, Shanks, *Sheffield*, Shellabarger, Sloan, Spaulding, Stevens, Stratton, Benjamin F. Thomas, Train, Trowbridge, Van Horn, Van Valkenburgh, Verree, Wallace, E. P. Walton, Washburne, Wheeler, Albert S. White, Wilson, Windom—92.

NAYS—Messrs. *Allen, Joseph Baily, Biddle*, Jacob B. Blair, William G. Brown, Casey, *Crittenden, Delaplaine, Dunlap, Grider, Hall, Harding, Holman, Johnson, Knapp, Law, Lazear, Mallory, Menzies, Morris, Noble, Norton, Nugen, Pendleton, Perry, Price, James S. Rollins, Shiel, John B. Steele, William G. Steele*, Francis Thomas, *Vallandigham, Voorhees, Wadsworth, Ward, Chilton A. White, Wickliffe, Wright*—39.

April 16—The PRESIDENT sent to Congress this message:

Fellow-Citizens of the Senate and House of Representatives:

The act entitled "An act for the release of certain persons held to service or labor in the District of Columbia," has this day been approved and signed.

I have never doubted the constitutional authority of Congress to abolish slavery in this District; and I have ever desired to see the national capital freed from the institution in some satisfactory way. Hence there has never been in my mind any question upon the subject except the one of expediency, arising in view of all the circumstances. If there be matters within and about this act which might have taken a course or shape more satisfactory to my judgment, I do not attempt to specify them. I am gratified that the two principles of compensation and colonization are both recognized and practically applied in the act. In the matter of compensation, it is provided that claims may be presented within ninety days from the passage of the act, "but not thereafter;" and there

It is proper that I should state that the claim of Messrs. Forbes & Tuckerman, for transporting a number of emigrants to Ile à Vache, is not yet liquidated, and that the colonization fund is also liable for the expenses which have been incurred by the special agent sent by the Government to Ile à Vache to look into and report upon the condition of the colonists there. The agent has not yet returned, and consequently the expenses incurred by him cannot now be ascertained. It is also liable for the expenses of the vessel sent out to return the colonists to the United States.

IN HOUSE.

April 5, 1864—Mr. Cox asked leave to offer this resolution, but it was objected to:

Resolved, That the Secretary of State communicate to this House all correspondence between our consul at Aux Cayes and the State Department in regard to our colony of blacks at the Isle à Vache.

is no saving for minors, *femmes covert*, insane, or absent persons. I presume this is an omission by mere oversight, and I recommend that it be supplied by an amendatory or supplemental act.

ABRAHAM LINCOLN.

An amendatory bill, meeting the President's suggestions, was passed in the House—yeas 69, nays 36; and in the Senate—yeas 28, nays 6, and approved by him.

COMPENSATED EMANCIPATION IN THE BORDER STATES.

IN HOUSE.

1862, April 7—Mr. ALBERT S. WHITE, of Indiana, offered a resolution for the appointment of a select committee of nine members, to report whether any plan can be proposed and recommended for the gradual emancipation of all the African slaves, and the extinction of slavery in Delaware, Maryland, Virginia, Kentucky, Tennessee, and Missouri, by the people or local authorities thereof, and how far and in what way the Government of the United States can and ought equitably to aid in facilitating either of the above objects.

Mr. MALLORY moved to lay the resolution on the table, which was disagreed to—yeas 51, nays 68; and the resolution was adopted—yeas 67, nays 52, as follows:

YEAS—Messrs. Alley, Arnold, Ashley, Babbitt, Baker, Baxter, Beaman, Bingham, Francis P. Blair, Blake, Buffinton, Campbell, Chamberlain, Clark, Colfax, Frederick A. Conkling, Davis, Dawes, Duell, Edgerton, Eliot, Fenton, Fessenden, Gurley, Hanchett, Hickman, Hutchins, Julian, Kelley, Francis W. Kellogg, Lansing, Loomis, Lovejoy, McKnight, McPherson, Moorhead, Anson P. Morrill, Justin S. Morrill, Nixon, Olin, Pike, Pomeroy, Potter, Alexander H. Rice, John H. Rice, Riddle, Edward H. Rollins, Sargent, Shanks, *Sheffield*, Shellabarger, Sherman, Sloan, Stevens, Stratton, Train, Van Horn, Van Valkenburgh, Verree, Wallace, Charles W. Walton, E. P. Walton, Washburne, Wheeler, Albert S. White, Wilson, Windom—67.

NAYS—Messrs. *Allen*, *Biddle*, Jacob B. Blair, *George H. Browne*, William G. Brown, *Calvert*, Casey, *Cobb*, *Corning*, *Cox*, *Cravens*, *Crittenden*, Delano, *Delaplaine*, Diven, *Dunlap*, *English*, Fisher, *Grider*, *Haight*, *Harding*, Harrison, Horton, *Kerrigan*, *Knapp*, *Law*, *Lazear*, Leary, *Lehman*, *Mallory*, *Menzies*, Mitchell, *Noble*, *Noell*, *Norton*, *Nugen*, *Pendleton*, *Perry*, Timothy G. Phelps, *Price*, *Richardson*, *Shiel*, *Smith*, *John B. Steele*, *William G. Steele*, *Vallandigham*, *Voorhees*, *Wadsworth*, *Ward*, Webster, *Chilton A. White*, *Wickliffe*—52.

April 14—The SPEAKER appointed the committee as follows: Albert S. White of Indiana, Francis P. Blair of Missouri, George P. Fisher of Delaware, *William E. Lehman* of Pennsylvania, C. L. L. Leary of Maryland, K. V. Whaley of Virginia, James F. Wilson of Iowa, Samuel L. Casey of Kentucky, and Andrew J. Clements of Tennessee.

In July, 1862, the President requested and obtained an interview with the border State Congressmen, the result of which is contained in this statement:

THE PRESIDENT'S APPEAL TO THE BORDER STATES.

The Representatives and Senators of the border slaveholding States having, by special invitation of the President, been convened at the Executive Mansion, on Saturday morning last, (July 12,) Mr. Lincoln addressed them as follows from a written paper held in his hand:

"GENTLEMEN: After the adjournment of Congress, now near, I shall have no opportunity of seeing you for several months. Believing that you of the border States hold more power for good than any other equal number of members, I feel it a duty which I cannot justifiably waive, to make this appeal to you.

"I intend no reproach or complaint when I assure you that, in my opinion, if you all had voted for the resolution in the gradual emancipation message of last March, the war would now be substantially ended. And the plan therein proposed is yet one of the most potent and swift means of ending it. Let the States which are in rebellion see definitely and certainly that in no event will the States you represent ever join their proposed Confederacy, and they cannot much longer maintain the contest. But you cannot divest them of their hope to ultimately have you with them so long as you show a determination to perpetuate the institution within your own States. Beat them at elections, as you have overwhelmingly done, and, nothing daunted, they still claim you as their own. You and I know what the lever of their power is. Break that lever before their faces, and they can shake you no more forever.

"Most of you have treated me with kindness and consideration, and I trust you will not now think I improperly touch what is exclusively your own, when, for the sake of the whole country, I ask, 'Can you, for your States, do better than to take the course I urge?' Discarding *punctilio* and maxims adapted to more manageable times, and looking only to the unprecedentedly stern facts of our case, can you do better in any possible event? You prefer that the constitutional relations of the States to the nation shall be practically restored without disturbance of the institution; and, if this were done, my whole duty, in this respect, under the Constitution and my oath of office, would be performed. But it is not done, and we are trying to accomplish it by war. The incidents of the war cannot be avoided. If the war continues long, as it must, if the object be not sooner attained, the institution in your States will be extinguished by mere friction and abrasion—by the mere incidents of the war. It will be gone, and you will have nothing valuable in lieu of it. Much of its value is gone already. How much better for you and for your people to take the step which at once shortens the war and secures substantial compensation for that which is sure to be wholly lost in any other event! How much better to thus save the money which else we sink forever in the war! How much better to do it while we can, lest the war ere long render us pecuniarily unable to do it! How much better for you, as seller, and the nation, as buyer, to sell out and buy out that without which the war could never have been, than to sink both the thing to be sold and the price of it in cutting one another's throats!

"I do not speak of emancipation *at once*, but of a *decision* at once to emancipate *gradually*. Room in South America for colonization can be obtained cheaply and in abundance, and when numbers shall be large enough to be company and encouragement for one another, the freed people will not be so reluctant to go.

"I am pressed with a difficulty not yet mentioned, one which threatens division among those who, united, are none too strong. An instance of it is known to you. General Hunter is an honest man. He was, and I hope still is, my friend. I valued him none the less for his agreeing with me in the general wish that all men everywhere could be freed. He proclaimed all men free within certain States, and I repudiated the proclamation. He expected more good and less harm from the measure than I could believe would follow. Yet, in repudiating it, I gave dissatisfaction, if not offence, to many whose support the country cannot afford to lose. And this is not the end of it. The pressure in this direction is still upon me, and is increasing. By conceding what I now ask you can relieve me, and, much more, can relieve the country in this important point.

"Upon these considerations I have again begged your attention to the message of March last. Before leaving the Capitol, consider and discuss it among yourselves. You are patriots and statesmen, and as such I pray you consider this proposition; and at the least commend it to the consideration of your States and people. As you would perpetuate popular government for the best people in the world, I beseech you that you do in nowise omit this. Our common country is in great peril, demanding the loftiest views and boldest action to bring a speedy relief. Once relieved, its form of government is saved to the world, its beloved history and cherished memories are vindicated, and its happy future fully assured and rendered inconceivably grand. To you, more than to any others, the privilege is given to assure that happiness and swell that grandeur, and to link your own names therewith forever."

At the conclusion of these remarks some conversation was had between the President and several members of the delegations from the border States, in which it was represented that these States could not be expected to move in so great a matter as that brought to their notice in the foregoing address while as yet the Congress had taken no step beyond the passage of a resolution, expressive rather of a sentiment than presenting a substantial and reliable basis of action.

The President acknowledged the force of this view, and admitted that the border States were entitled to expect a substantial pledge of pecuniary aid as the condition of taking into consideration a proposition so important in its relations to their social system.

It was further represented, in the conference, that the people of the border States were interested in knowing the great importance which the President attached to the policy in question, while it was equally due to the country, to the President, and to themselves, that the representatives of the border slaveholding States should publicly announce the motives under which they were called to act, and the considerations of public policy urged upon them and their constituents by the President.

With a view to such a statement of their position, the members thus addressed met in council to deliberate on the reply they should make to the President, and, as the result of a comparison of opinions among themselves, they determined upon the adoption of a majority and minority answer.

REPLY OF THE MAJORITY.

The following paper was yesterday sent to the President, signed by the majority of the Representatives from the border slaveholding States:—

WASHINGTON, *July* 14, 1862.

To the PRESIDENT:

The undersigned, Representatives of Kentucky, Virginia, Missouri, and Maryland, in the two Houses of Congress, have listened to your address with the profound sensibility naturally inspired by the high source from which it emanates, the earnestness which marked its delivery, and the overwhelming importance of the subject of which it treats. We have given it a most respectful consideration, and now lay before you our response. We regret that want of time has not permitted us to make it more perfect.

We have not been wanting, Mr. President, in respect to you, and in devotion to the Constitution and the Union. We have not been indifferent to the great difficulties surrounding you, compared with which all former national troubles have been but as the summer cloud; and we have freely given you our sympathy and support. Repudiating the dangerous heresies of the secessionists, we believed, with you, that the war on their part is agressive and wicked, and the objects for which it was to be prosecuted on ours, defined by your message at the opening of the present Congress, to be such as all good men should approve. We have not hesitated to vote all supplies necessary to carry it on vigorously. We have voted all the men and money you have asked for, and even more; we have imposed onerous taxes on our people, and they are paying them with cheerfulness and alacrity; we have encouraged enlistments and sent to the field many of our best men; and some of our number have offered their persons to the enemy as pledges of their sincerity and devotion to the country.

We have done all this under the most discouraging circumstances, and in the face of measures most distasteful to us and injurious to the interests we represent, and in the hearing of doctrines avowed by those who claim to be your friends, must be abhorrent to us and our constituents. But, for all this, we have never faltered, nor shall we as long as we have a Constitution to defend and a Government which protects us. And we are ready for renewed efforts, and even greater sacrifices, yea, any sacrifice, when we are satisfied it is required to preserve our admirable form of government and the priceless blessings of constitutional liberty.

A few of our number voted for the resolution recommended by your message of the 6th of March last, the greater portion of us did not, and we will briefly state the prominent reasons which influenced our action.

In the first place, it proposed a radical change of our social system, and was hurried through both Houses with undue haste, without reasonable time for consideration and debate, and with no time at all for consultation with our constituents, whose interests it deeply involved. It seemed like an interference by this Government with a question which peculiarly and exclusively belonged to our respective States, on which they had not sought advice or solicited aid. Many of us doubted the constitutional power of this Government to make appropriations of money for the object designated, and all of us thought our finances were in no condition to bear the immense outlay which its adoption and faithful execution would impose upon the national Treasury. If we pause but a moment to think of the debt its acceptance would have entailed, we are appalled by its magnitude. The proposition was addressed to all the States, and embraced the whole number of slaves.

According to the census of 1860 there were then nearly four million slaves in the country; from natural increase they exceed that number now. At even the low average of $300, the price fixed by the emancipation act for the slaves of this District, and greatly below their real worth, their value runs up to the enormous sum of $1,200,000,000; and if to that we add the cost of deportation and colonization, at $100 each, which is but a fraction more than is actually paid by the Maryland Colonization Society, we have $400,000,000 more. We were not willing to impose a tax on our people sufficient to pay the interest on that sum, in addition to the vast and daily increasing debt already fixed upon them by the exigencies of the war, and if we had been willing, the country could not bear it. Stated in this form the proposition is nothing less than the deportation from the country of $1,600,000,000 worth of producing labor, and the substitution in its place of an interest-bearing debt of the same amount.

But, if we are told that it was expected that only the States we represent would accept the proposition, we respectfully submit that even then it involves a sum too great for the financial ability of this Government at this time. According to the census of 1860—

	Slaves.
Kentucky had	225,490
Maryland	87,188
Virginia	490,887
Delaware	1,798
Missouri	114,965
Tennessee	275,784
Making in the whole	1,196,112
At the same rate of valuation these would amount to	$358,933,500
Add for deportation and colonization $100 each	118,244,533
And we have the enormous sum of	$478,038,133

We did not feel that we should be justified in voting for a measure which, if carried out, would add this vast amount to our public debt at a moment when the Treasury was reeling under the enormous expenditure of the war.

Again, it seemed to us that this resolution was but the annunciation of a sentiment which could not or was not likely to be reduced to an actual tangible proposition. No movement was then made to provide and appropriate the funds required to carry it into effect; and we were not encouraged to believe that funds would be provided. And our belief has been fully justified by subsequent events. Not to mention other circumstances, it is quite sufficient for our purpose to bring to your notice the fact that, while this resolution was under consideration in the Senate, our colleague, the Senator from Kentucky, moved an amendment appropriating $500,000 to the object therein designated, and it was voted down with great unanimity. What confidence, then, could we reasonably feel that if we committed ourselves to the policy it proposed, our constituents would reap the fruits of the promise held out; and on what ground could we, as fair men, approach them and challenge their support?

The right to hold slaves is a right appertaining to all the States of this Union. They have the right to cherish or abolish the institution, as their tastes or their interests may prompt, and no one is authorized to question the right or limit the enjoyment. And no one has more clearly affirmed that right than you have. Your inaugural address does you great honor in this respect, and inspired the country with confidence in your fairness and respect for the law. Our States are in the enjoyment of that right. We do not feel called on to defend the institution or to affirm it is one which ought to be cherished; perhaps, if we were to make the attempt, we might find that we differ even among ourselves. It is enough for our purpose to know that it is a right; and, so knowing, we did not see why we should now be expected to yield it. We had contributed our full share to relieve the country at this terrible crisis; we had done as much as had been required of others in like circumstances; and we did not see why sacrifices should be expected of us from which others, no more loyal, were exempt. Nor could we see what good the nation would derive from it.

Such a sacrifice submitted to by us would not have strengthened the arm of this Government or weakened that of the enemy. It was not necessary as a pledge of our loyalty, for that had been manifested beyond a reasonable doubt, in every form, and at every place possible. There was not the remotest probability that the States we represent would join in the rebellion, nor is there now, or of their electing to go with the southern section in the event of a recognition of the independence of any part of the disaffected region. Our States are fixed unalterably in their resolution to adhere to and support the Union. They see no safety for themselves, and no hope for constitutional liberty but by its preservation. They will, under no circumstances, consent to its dissolution; and we do them no more than justice when we assure you that, while the war is conducted to prevent that deplorable catastrophe, they will sustain it as long as they can muster a man or command a dollar. Nor will they ever consent, in any event, to unite with the Southern Confederacy. The bitter fruits of the peculiar doctrines of that region will forever prevent them from placing their security and happiness in the custody of an association which has incorporated in its organic law the seeds of its own destruction.

We cannot admit, Mr. President, that, if we had voted for the resolution in the emancipation message of March last, the war would now be substantially ended. We are unable to see how our action in this particular has given, or could give, encouragement to the rebellion. The resolution has passed; and, if there be virtue in it, it will be quite as efficacious as if we had voted for it. We have no power to bind our States in this respect by our votes here; and, whether we had voted the one way or the other, they are in the same condition of freedom to accept or reject its provisions. No, sir, the war has not been prolonged or hindered by our action on this or any other measure. We must look for other causes for that lamented fact. We think there is not much difficulty, not much uncertainty, in pointing out others far more probable and potent in their agencies to that end.

The rebellion derives its strength from the union of all classes in the insurgent States; and while that union lasts the war will never end until they are utterly exhausted. We know that at the inception of these troubles southern society was divided, and that a large portion, perhaps a majority, were opposed to secession. Now the great mass of southern people are united. To discover why they are so we must glance at southern society, and notice the classes into which it has been divided, and which still distinguish it. They are in arms, but not for the same objects; they are moved to a common end, but by different and even inconsistent reasons. The leaders, which comprehends what was previously known as the State-rights party, and is much the lesser class, seek to break down national independence and set up State domination. With them it is a war against nationality. The other class is fighting, as it supposes, to maintain and preserve its rights of property and domestic safety, which it has been made to believe are assailed by this Government. This latter class are not disunionists *per se;* they are so only because they have been made to believe that this Administration is inimical to their rights, and is making war on their domestic institution. As long as these two classes act together they will never assent to a peace.

The policy, then, to be pursued, is obvious. The former class will never be reconciled, but the latter may be. Remove their apprehensions; satisfy them that no harm is intended to them and their institutions; that this Government is not making war on their rights of property, but is simply defending its legitimate authority, and they will gladly return to their allegiance as soon as the pressure of military dominion imposed by the Confederate authority is removed from them.

Twelve months ago both Houses of Congress, adopting the spirit of your message, then but recently sent in, declared with singular unanimity the objects of the war, and the country instantly bounded to your side to assist you in carrying it on. If the spirit of that resolution had been adhered to, we are confident that we should before now have seen the end of this deplorable conflict. But what have we seen?

In both Houses of Congress we have heard doctrines subversive of the principles of the Constitution, and seen measure after measure founded in substance on those doctrines proposed and carried through which can have no other effect than to distract and divide loyal men, and exasperate and drive still further from us and their duty the people of the rebellious States. Military officers, following these bad examples, have stepped beyond the just limits of their authority in the same direction, until in several instances you have felt the necessity of interfering to arrest them. And even the passage of the resolution to which you refer has been ostentatiously proclaimed as the triumph of a principle which the people of the southern States regard as ruinous to them. The effect of these measures was foretold, and may now be seen in the indurated state of southern feeling.

To these causes, Mr. President, and not to our omission to vote for the resolution recommended by you, we solemnly believe we are to attribute the terrible earnestness of those in arms against the Government and the continuance of the war. Nor do we (permit us to say, Mr. President, with all respect to you) agree that the institution of slavery is "the lever of their power," but we are of the opinion that "the lever of their power" is the apprehension that the powers of a common Government, created for common and equal protection to the interests of all, will be wielded against the institutions of the southern States.

There is one other idea in your address we feel called on to notice. After stating the fact of your repudiation of General Hunter's proclamation, you add:

"Yet, in repudiating it, I gave dissatisfaction, if not offence, to many whose support the country cannot afford to lose. And this is not the end of it. The pressure in this direction is still upon me and is increasing. By conceding what I now ask, you can relieve me, and, much more, can relieve the country, in this important point."

We have anxiously looked into this passage to discover its true import, but we are yet in painful uncertainty. How can we, by conceding what you now ask, relieve you and the country from the increasing pressure to which you refer? We will not allow ourselves to think that the proposition is, that we consent to give up slavery, to the end that the Hunter proclamation may be let loose on the southern people, for it is too well known that we would not be parties to any such measure, and we have too much respect for you to imagine you would propose it. Can it mean that by sacrificing our interest in slavery we appease the spirit that controls that pressure, cause it to be withdrawn, and rid the country of the pestilent agitation of the slavery question? We are forbidden so to think, for that spirit would not be satisfied with the liberation of 700,000 slaves, and cease its agitation while 3,000,000 remain in bondage. Can it mean that by abandoning slavery in our States we are removing the pressure from you and the country, by preparing for a separation on the line of the cotton States?

We are forbidden so to think, because it is known that we are, and we believe that you are, unalterably opposed to any division at all. We would prefer to think that you desire this concession as a pledge of our support, and thus enable you to withstand a pressure which weighs heavily on you and the country. Mr. President, no such sacrifice is necessary to secure our support. Confine yourself to your constitutional authority; confine your subordinates within the same limits; conduct this war solely for the purpose of restoring the Constitution to its legitimate authority; concede to each State and its loyal citizens their just rights, and we are wedded to you by indissoluble ties. Do this, Mr. President, and you touch the American heart and invigorate it with new hope. You will, as we solemnly believe, in due time restore peace to your country, lift it from despondency to a future of glory, and preserve to your countrymen, their posterity, and man, the inestimable treasure of a constitutional government.

Mr. President, we have stated with frankness and candor the reasons on which we forbore to vote for the resolution you have mentioned; but you have again presented this proposition, and appealed to us with an earnestness and eloquence which have not failed to impress us, to "consider it, and at the least to commend it to the consideration of our States and people." Thus appealed to by the Chief Magistrate of our beloved country, in the hour of its greatest peril, we cannot wholly decline. We are willing to trust every question relating to their interest and happiness to the consideration and ultimate judgment of our own people. While differing from you as to the necessity of emancipating the slaves of our States as a means of putting down the rebellion, and while protesting against the propriety of any extra-territorial interference to induce the people of our States to adopt any particular line of policy on a subject which peculiarly and exclusively belongs to them, yet, when you and our brethren of the loyal States sincerely believe that the retention of slavery by us is an obstacle to peace and national harmony, and are willing to contribute pecuniary aid to compensate our States and people for the inconveniences produced by such a change of system, we are not unwilling that our people shall consider the propriety of putting it aside.

But we have already said that we regarded this resolution as the utterance of a sentiment, and we had no confidence that it would assume the shape of a tangible, practical proposition, which would yield the fruits of the sacrifice it required. Our people are influenced by the same want of confidence, and will not consider the proposition in its present impalpable form. The interest they are asked to give up is to them of immense importance, and they ought not to be expected even to entertain the proposal until they are assured that when they accept it their just expectations will not be frustrated. We regard your plan as a proposition from the Nation to the States to exercise an admitted constitutional right in a particular manner and yield up a valuable interest. Before they ought to consider the proposition, it should be presented in such a tangible, practical, efficient shape as to command their confidence that its fruits are contingent only upon their acceptance. We cannot trust anything to the contingencies of future legislation.

If Congress, by proper and necessary legislation, shall provide sufficient funds and place them at your disposal, to be applied by you to the payment of any of our States or the citizens thereof who shall adopt the abolishment of slavery, either gradual or immediate, as they may determine, and the expense of deportation and colonization of the liberated slaves, then will our State and people take this proposition into careful consideration, for such decision as in their judgment is demanded by their interest, their honor, and their duty to the whole country. We have the honor to be, with great respect,

C. A. WICKLIFFE, *Ch'n.*,	CHAS. B. CALVERT,
GARRETT DAVIS,	C. L. L. LEARY,
R. WILSON,	EDWIN H. WEBSTER,
J. J. CRITTENDEN,	R. MALLORY,
JOHN S. CARLILE,	AARON HARDING,
J. W. CRISFIELD,	JAMES S ROLLINS,
J. S. JACKSON,	J. W. MENZIES,
H. GRIDER,	THOMAS L. PRICE,
JOHN S. PHELPS,	G. W. DUNLAP,
FRANCIS THOMAS,	WM. A. HALL.

REPLY OF THE MINORITY.

WASHINGTON, *July* 15, 1862.

MR. PRESIDENT: The undersigned, members of Congress from the border States, in response to your address of Saturday last, beg leave to say that they attended a meeting on the same day the address was delivered, for the purpose of considering the same. The meeting appointed a committee to report a response to your address. That report was made on yesterday, and the action of the majority indicated clearly that the response, or one in substance the same, would be adopted and presented to you.

Inasmuch as we cannot, consistently with our own sense of duty to the country, under the existing perils which surround us, concur in that response, we feel it to be due to you and to ourselves to make to you a brief and candid answer over our own signatures.

We believe that the whole power of the Government, upheld and sustained by all the influences and means of all loyal men in all sections, and of all parties, is essentially necessary to put down the rebellion and preserve the Union and the Constitution. We understand your appeal to us to have been made for the purpose of securing this result. A very large portion of the people in the northern States believe that slavery is the "lever-power of the rebellion." It matters not whether this belief be well founded or not. The belief does exist, and we have to deal with things as they are, and not as we would have them be. In consequence of the existence of this belief, we understand that an immense pressure is brought to bear for the purpose of striking down this institution through the exercise of military authority. The Government cannot maintain this great struggle if the support and influence of the men who entertain these opinions be withdrawn. Neither can the Government hope for early success if the support of that element called "conservative" be withdrawn.

Such being the condition of things, the President appeals to the border State men to step forward and prove their patriotism by making the first sacrifice. No doubt, like appeals have been made to extreme men in the North to meet us half way, in order that the whole moral, political, pecuniary, and physical force of the nation may be firmly and earnestly united in one grand effort to save the Union and the Constitution.

Believing that such were the motives that prompted your address, and such the results to which it looked, we cannot reconcile it to our sense of duty, in this trying hour, to respond in a spirit of fault-finding or querulousness over the things that are past. We are not disposed to seek for the cause of present misfortunes in the errors and wrongs of others who now propose to unite with us in a common purpose. But, on the other hand, we meet your address in the spirit in which it was made, and, as loyal Americans, declare to you and to the world that there is no sacrifice that we are not ready to make to save the Government and institutions of our fathers.

That we, few of us though there may be, will permit no

man, from the North or from the South, to go further than we in the accomplishment of the great work before us. That, in order to carry out these views, we will, so far as may be in our power, ask the people of the border States calmly, deliberately, and fairly to consider your recommendations. We are the more emboldened to assume this position from the fact, now become history, that the leaders of the southern rebellion have offered to abolish slavery among them as a condition to foreign intervention in favor of their independence as a nation.

If they can give up slavery to destroy the Union, we can surely ask our people to consider the question of emancipation to save the Union.

With great respect, your obedient servants,

JOHN W. NOELL,
SAMUEL L. CASEY,
GEORGE P. FISHER,
A. J. CLEMENTS,
WILLIAM G. BROWN,
JACOB B. BLAIR,
W. T. WILLEY.

REPLY OF MR. MAYNARD.

HOUSE OF REPRESENTATIVES, *July* 16, 1862.

SIR: The magnitude and gravity of the proposition submitted by you to Representatives from the slave States would naturally occasion diversity, if not contrariety, of opinion. You will not, therefore, be surprised that I have not been able to concur in view with the majority of them. This is attributable, possibly, to the fact that my State is not a border State, properly so called, and that my immediate constituents are not yet disenthralled from the hostile arms of the rebellion. This fact is a physical obstacle in the way of my now submitting to their consideration this or any other proposition looking to political action, especially such as, in this case, would require a change in the organic law of the State.

But do not infer that I am insensible to your appeal. I am not. You are surrounded with difficulties far greater than have embarrassed any of your predecessors. You need the support of every American citizen, and you ought to have it—active, zealous, and honest. The union of every Union man to aid you in preserving the Union is the duty of the time. Differences as to policy and methods must be subordinated to the common purpose.

In looking for the cause of this rebellion, it is natural that each section and each party should ascribe as little blame as possible to itself, and as much as possible to its opponent section and party. Possibly you and I might not agree on a comparison of our views. That there should be differences of opinion as to the best mode of conducting our military operations, and the best men to lead our armies, is equally natural. Contests on such questions weaken ourselves and strengthen our enemies. They are unprofitable, and possibly unpatriotic. Somebody must yield, or we waste our strength in a contemptible struggle among ourselves.

You appeal to the loyal men of the slave States to sacrifice something of feeling and a great deal of interest. The sacrifices they have already made and the sufferings they have endured give the best assurance that the appeal will not have been made in vain. He who is not ready to yield all his material interests, and to forego his most cherished sentiments and opinions for the preservation of his country, although he may have periled his life on the battle-field in her defence, is but half a patriot. Among the loyal people that I represent there are no half patriots.

Already the rebellion has cost us much, even to our undoing; we are content, if need be, to give up the rest to suppress it. We have stood by you from the beginning of this struggle, and we mean to stand by you, God willing, till the end of it.

I did not vote for the resolution to which you allude, solely for the reason that at the time I was absent at the capital of my own State. It is right.

Should any of the slave States think proper to terminate that institution, as several of them, I understand, or at least some of their citizens propose, justice and a generous comity require that the country should interpose to aid it in lessening the burden, public and private, occasioned by so radical a change in its social and industrial relations.

I will not now speculate upon the effect, at home or abroad, of the adoption of your policy, nor inquire what action of the rebel leaders has rendered something of the kind important. Your whole administration gives the highest assurance that you are moved, not so much from a desire to see all men everywhere made free, as from a higher desire to preserve free institutions for the benefit of men already free; not to make slaves freemen, but to prevent freemen from being made slaves; not to destroy an institution, which a portion of us only consider bad, but to save institutions which we all alike consider good. I am satisfied you would not ask from any of your fellow-citizens a sacrifice not, in your judgment, imperatively required by the safety of the country.

This is the spirit of your appeal, and I respond to it in the same spirit.

I am, very respectfully, your obedient servant,

HORACE MAYNARD.

To the PRESIDENT.

SENATOR HENDERSON'S REPLY TO THE PRESIDENT.

WASHINGTON CITY, *July* 21, 1862.

MR. PRESIDENT: The pressure of business in the Senate during the last few days of the session prevented my attendance at the meeting of the border State members, called to consider your proposition in reference to gradual emancipation in our States.

It is for this reason only, and not because I fail to appreciate their importance or properly respect your suggestions, that my name does not appear to any of the several papers submitted in response. I may also add that it was my intention, when the subject came up practically for consideration in the Senate, to express fully my views in regard to it. This of course would have rendered any other response unnecessary. But the want of time to consider the matter deprived me of that opportunity, and, lest now my silence be misconstrued, I deem it proper to say to you that I am by no means indifferent to the great questions so earnestly, and as I believe so honestly, urged by you upon our consideration.

The border States, so far, are the chief sufferers by this war, and the true Union men of those States have made the greatest sacrifices for the preservation of the Government. This fact does not proceed from mismanagement on the part of the Union authorities, or a want of regard for our people, but it is the necessary result of the war that is upon us. Our States are the battle-fields. Our people, divided among themselves, maddened by the struggle and blinded by the smoke of battle, invited upon our soil contending armies—the one to destroy the Government, the other to maintain it. The consequence to us is plain. The shock of the contest upturns society and desolates the land. We have made sacrifices, but at last they were only the sacrifices demanded by duty, and unless we are willing to make others, indeed any that the good of the country, involved in the overthrow of treason, may exact at our hands, our title to patriotism is not complete.

When you submitted your proposition to Congress, in March last, "that the United States ought to co-operate with any State which may adopt a gradual abolishment of slavery, giving to such State pecuniary aid, to be used by such State in its discretion, to compensate for the inconveniences, public and private, produced by such change of system," I gave it a most cheerful support, and I am satisfied it would have received the approbation of a large majority of the border States delegations in both branches of Congress, if, in the first place, they had believed the war, with its continued evils—the most prominent of which, in a material point of view, is its injurious effect on the institution of slavery in our States—could possibly have been protracted for another twelve months; and if, in the second place, they had felt assured that the party having the majority in Congress would, like yourself, be equally prompt in practical action as in the expression of a sentiment. While scarcely any one doubted your own sincerity in the premises, and your earnest wish speedily to terminate the war, you can readily conceive the grounds for difference of opinion where conclusions could only be based upon conjecture.

Believing, as I did, that the war was not so near its termination as some supposed, and feeling disposed to accord to others the same sincerity of purpose that I should claim for myself under similar circumstances, I voted for the proposition. I will suppose that others were actuated by no sinister motives.

In doing so, Mr. President, I desire to be distinctly understood by you and by my constituents. I did not suppose at the time that I was personally making any sacrifice by supporting the resolution, nor that the people of my State were called upon to make any sacrifice, either in considering or accepting the proposition, if they saw fit. I agreed with you in the remarks contained in the message accompanying the resolution, that "the Union must be preserved, and hence all indispensable means must be employed. * * * War has been and continues to be an indispensable means to this end. A practical reacknowledgment of the national authority would render the war unnecessary, and it would at once cease. If, however, resistance continues, the war must also continue; and it is impossible to foresee all the incidents which may attend and all the ruin which may follow it." It is truly "impossible" to foresee all the evils resulting from a war so stupendous as the present. I shall be much rejoiced if something more dreadful than the sale of freedom to a few slaves in the border States shall not result from it. If it closes with the Government of our fathers secure, and constitutional liberty in all its purity guarantied to the white man, the result will be better than that having a place in the fears of many good men at present, and much better than the past history of such revolutions can justify us in expecting.

In this period of the nation's distress, I know of no human institution too sacred for discussion; no material interest belonging to the citizen that he should not willingly place upon the altar of his country, if demanded by the public good. The man who cannot now sacrifice party and put aside selfish considerations is more than half disloyal. Such a man does not deserve the blessings of good government. Pride of opinion, based upon sectional jealousies, should not be permitted to control the decision of any political question. These remarks are general, but apply with peculiar force to the people of the border States at present.

Let us look at our condition. A desolating war is upon us. We cannot escape it if we would. If the Union armies were to-day withdrawn from the border States without first crushing the rebellion in the South, no rational man can doubt for a moment that the adherents of the Union cause in those States would soon be driven in exile from their homes by the exultant rebels, who have so long hoped to return and take vengeance upon us.

The people of the border States understand very well the unfriendly and selfish spirit exercised toward them by the leaders of this cotton State rebellion; beginning some time previous to its outbreak. They will not fail to remember their insolent refusal to counsel with us, and their haughty assumption of responsibility upon themselves for their misguided action. Our people will not soon forget that, while declaiming against coercion, they closed their doors against the exportation of slaves from the border States into the South, with the avowed purpose of forcing us into rebellion through fears of losing that species of property. They knew very well the effect to be produced on slavery by a civil war, especially in those States into which hostile armies might penetrate, and upon the soil of which the great contests for the success of republican government were to be decided. They wanted some intermediate ground for the conflict of arms—territory where the population would be divided. They knew, also, that by keeping slavery in the border States the mere "friction and abrasion," to which you so appropriately allude, would keep up a constant irritation, resulting necessarily from the frequent losses to which the owners would be subjected. They also calculated largely, and not without reason, upon the repugnance of non-slaveholders in those States to a free negro population. In the meantime they intended persistently to charge the overthrow of slavery to be the object of the Government, and hostility to this institution the origin of the war. By this means the unavoidable incidents of the strife might easily be charged as the settled purposes of the Government. Again, it was well understood by these men that exemplary conduct on the part of every officer and soldier employed by the Government could not in the nature of things be expected, and the hope was entertained, upon the most reasonable grounds, that every commission of wrong and every omission of duty would produce a new cause for excitement and a new incentive to rebellion.

By these means the war was to be kept in the border States, regardless of our interests, until an exhausted treasury should render it necessary to send the tax-gatherer among our people, to take the little that might be left them from the devastations of war. They then expected a clamor for peace by us, resulting in the interference of France and England, whose operatives in the meantime would be driven to want, and whose aristocracy have ever been ready to welcome a dissolution of the American Union.

This cunningly-devised plan for securing a Gulf-Confederacy, commanding the mouths of the great western rivers, the Gulf of Mexico, and the southern Atlantic ocean, with their own territory unscathed by the horrors of war, and surrounded by the border States, half of whose population would be left in sympathy with them for many years to come, owing to the irritations to which I have alluded, has so far succeeded too well.

In Missouri they have already caused us to lose a third or more of the slaves owned at the time of the last census. In addition to this, I can make no estimate of the vast amount of property of every character that has been destroyed by military operations in the State. The loss from general depreciation of values, and the utter prostration of every business interest of our people, is wholly beyond calculation. The experience of Missouri is but the experience of other sections of the country similarly situated. The question is therefore forced upon us, "How long is this war to continue; and, if continued, as it has been, on our soil, aided by the treason and folly of our own citizens, acting in concert with the Confederates, how long can slavery, or, if you please, any other property interest, survive in our States?"

As things now are, the people of the border States yet divided, we cannot expect an immediate termination of the struggle, except upon condition of southern independence, losing thereby control of the lower Mississippi. For this we in Missouri are not prepared, nor are we prepared to become one of the Confederate States, should the terrible calamity of dissolution occur. This, I presume, the Union men of Missouri would resist to the death. And whether they should do so or not, I will not suppose for an instant that the Government of the United States would upon any condition submit to the loss of territory so essential to its future commercial greatness as is the State of Missouri. But should all other reasons fail to prevent such a misfortune to our people of Missouri, there is one that cannot fail. The Confederates never wanted us, and would not have us. I assume, therefore, that the war will not cease, but will be continued until the rebellion shall be overcome. It cannot and will not cease, so far as the people of Missouri are concerned, except upon condition of our remaining in the Union, and the whole West will demand the entire control of the Mississippi river to the Gulf. Our interest is therefore bound up with the interests of those States maintaining the Union, and especially with the great States of the West, that must be consulted in regard to the terms of any peace that may be suggested, even by the nations of Europe, should they at any time unfortunately depart from their former pacific policy and determine to intervene in our affairs.

The war, then, will have to be continued until the Union shall be practically restored. In this alone consists the future safety of the border States themselves. A separation of the Union is ruinous to them. The preservation of the Union can only be secured by a continuation of the war. The consequences of that continuation may be judged of by the experience of the last twelve months. The people of my State are as competent to pass judgment in the premises as I am. I have every confidence in their intelligence, their honesty, and their patriotism.

In your own language, the proposition you make "sets up no claim of a right by Federal authority to interfere with slavery within State limits, referring, as it does, the absolute control of the subject in each case to the State and its people immediately interested. It is proposed as a matter of perfectly free choice with them."

In this view of the subject I can frankly say to you that, personally, I never could appreciate the objections so frequently urged against the proposition. If I understood you properly, it was your opinion, not that slavery should be removed in order to secure our loyalty to the Government, for every personal act of your administration precludes such as inference, but you believe that the peculiar species of property was in imminent danger from the war in which we were engaged, and that common justice demanded remuneration for the loss of it. You then believed, and again express the opinion, that the peculiar nature of the contest is such that its loss is almost inevitable, and lest any pretext for a charge of injustice against the Government be given to its enemies, you propose to extend to the people of those States standing by the Union the choice of payment for their slaves or the responsibility of loss, should it occur, without complaint against the Government.

Placing the matter in this light, (a mere remuneration for losses rendered inevitable by the casualties of war,) the objection of a constitutional character may be rendered much less formidable in the minds of northern Representatives whose constituents will have to share in the payment of the money ; and, so far as the border States are concerned, this objection should be most sparingly urged, for it being a matter entirely of their "own free choice," in case of a desire to accept, no serious argument will likely be urged against the receipt of the money, or a fund for colonization. But, aside from the power derived from the operations of war, there may be found numerous precedents in the legislation of the past, such as grants of land and money to the several States for specified objects deemed worthy by the Federal Congress. And in addition to this may be cited a deliberate opinion of Mr. Webster upon this very subject, in one of the ablest arguments of his life.

I allude to this question of power merely in vindication of the position assumed by me in my vote for the resolution of March last. In your last communication to us, you beg of us "to commend this subject to the consideration of our States and people." While I entirely differ with you in the opinion expressed, that had the members from the border States approved of your resolution of March last "the war would now be substantially ended," and while I do not regard the suggestion "as one of the most potent and swift means of ending" the war, I am yet free to say that I have the most unbounded confidence in your sincerity of purpose in calling our attention to the dangers surrounding us. I am satisfied that you appreciate the troubles of the border States, and that your suggestions are intended for our good. I feel the force of your urgent appeal, and the logic of surrounding circumstances brings conviction even to an unwilling believer. Having said that, in my judgment, you attached too much importance to this measure as a means for suppressing the rebellion, it is due to you that I shall explain.

Whatever may be the status of the border States in this respect, the war cannot be ended until the power of the Government is made manifest in the seceded States. They appealed to the sword; give them the sword. They asked for war; let them see its evils on their own soil. They have erected a Government and they force obedience to its behests. This structure must be destroyed; this image, before which an unwilling people have been compelled to bow, must be broken. The authority of the Federal Government must be felt in the heart of the rebellious district. To do this let armies be marched upon them at once, and let them feel what they have inflicted on us in the border. Do not fear our States; we will stand by the Government in this work.

I ought not to disguise from you or the people of my State that personally I have fixed and unalterable opinions on the subject of your communication. Those opinions I shall communicate to the people in that spirit of frankness that should characterize the intercourse of the representative with his constituents. If I were to-day the owner of the lands and slaves of Missouri, your proposition, so far as that State is concerned, would be immediately accepted. Not a day would be lost. Aside from public considerations, which you suppose to be involved in the proposition, and which no patriot, I agree, should disregard at present, my own personal interest would prompt favorable and immediate action.

But having said this, it is proper that I say something more. The representative is the servant and not the master of the people. He has no authority to bind them to any course of action, or even to indicate what they will or will not do when the subject is exclusively theirs and not his. I shall take occasion, I hope honestly, to give my views of existing troubles and impending dangers, and shall leave the rest to them, disposed, as I am, rather to trust their judgment upon the case stated than my own, and at the same time most cheerfully to acquiesce in their decision.

For you, personally, Mr. President, I think I can pledge the kindest considerations of the people of Missouri, and I shall not hesitate to express the belief that your recommendation will be considered by them in the same spirit of kindness manifested by you in its presentation to us, and that their decision will be such as is demanded "by their interests, their honor, and their duty to the whole country."

I am, very respectfully, your obedient servant,

J. B. HENDERSON.

To his Excellency A. LINCOLN, *President.*

December 1, 1862 — The President, in his second annual message, recurs to the subject:

EXTRACT FROM PRESIDENT LINCOLN'S SECOND ANNUAL MESSAGE.

On the 22d day of September last, a proclamation was issued by the Executive, a copy of which is herewith submitted.

In accordance with the purpose expressed in the second paragraph of that paper, I now respectfully recall your attention to what may be called "compensated emancipation."

A nation may be said to consist of its territory, its people, and its laws. The territory is the only part which is of certain durability. "One generation passeth away, and another generation cometh, but the earth abideth forever." It is of the first importance to duly consider and estimate this ever-enduring part. That portion of the earth's surface which is owned and inhabited by the people of the United States, is well adapted to be the home of one national family; and it is not well adapted for two, or more. Its vast extent, and its variety of climate and productions, are of advantage, in this age, for one people, whatever they might have been in former ages. Steam, telegraphs, and intelligence, have brought these to be an advantageous combination for one united people.

In the inaugural address I briefly pointed out the total inadequacy of disunion, as a remedy for the differences between the people of the two sections. I did so in language which I cannot improve, and which, therefore, I beg to repeat:

"One section of our country believes slavery is *right*, and ought to be extended, while the other believes it is *wrong*, and ought not to be extended. This is the only substantial dispute. The fugitive slave clause of the Constitution, and the law for the suppression of the foreign slave trade, are each as well enforced, perhaps, as any law can ever be in a community where the moral sense of the people imperfectly supports the law itself. The great body of the people abide by the dry legal obligation in both cases, and a few break over in each. This, I think, cannot be perfectly cured; and it would be worse in both cases *after* the separation of the sections, than before. The foreign slave trade, now imperfectly suppressed, would be ultimately revived without restriction in one section; while fugitive slaves, now only partially surrendered, would not be surrendered at all by the other.

"Physically speaking, we cannot separate. We cannot remove our respective sections from each other, nor build an impassable wall between them. A husband and wife may be divorced, and each go out of the presence and beyond the reach of each other; but the different parts of our country cannot do this. They cannot but remain face to face; and intercourse, either amicable or hostile, must continue between them. Is it possible, then, to make that intercourse more advantageous or more satisfactory *after* separation than *before?* Can aliens make treaties easier than friends can make laws? Can treaties be more faithfully enforced between aliens than laws can among friends? Suppose you go to war, you cannot fight always; and when, after much loss on both sides, and no gain on either, you cease fighting, the indentical old questions as to terms of intercourse are again upon you."

There is no line, straight or crooked, suitable for a national boundary upon which to divide. Trace through, from East to West, upon the line between the free and slave country, and we shall find a little more than one third of its length are rivers, easy to be crossed, and populated, or soon to be populated, thickly upon both sides; while nearly all its remaining length are merely surveyor's lines, over which people may walk back and forth without any consciousness of their presence. No part of this line can be made any more difficult to pass by writing it down on paper or parchment as a national boundary. The fact of separation, if it comes, gives up on the part of the seceding section the fugitive slave clause, along with all other constitutional obligations upon the section seceded from, while I should expect no treaty stipulation would ever be made to take its place.

But there is another difficulty. The great interior region, bounded east by the Alleghanies, north by the British dominions, west by the Rocky mountains, and south by the line along which the culture of corn and cotton meets, and which includes part of Virginia, part of Tennessee, all of Kentucky, Ohio, Indiana, Michigan, Wisconsin, Illinois, Missouri, Kansas, Iowa, Minnesota, and the Territories of Dakota, Nebraska, and part of Colorado, already has above ten million people, and will have fifty millions within fifty years, if not prevented by any political folly or mistake. It contains more than one third of the country owned by the United States—certainly more than one million square miles. Once half as populous as Massachusetts already is, it would have more than seventy-five million people. A glance at the map shows that, territorially speaking, it is the great body of the Republic. The other parts are but marginal borders to it, the magnificent region sloping west from the Rocky Mountains to the Pacific, being the deepest and also the richest in undeveloped resources. In the production of provisions, grains, grasses, and all which proceed from them, this great interior region is naturally one of the most important in the world. Ascertain from the statistics the small proportion of the region which has, as yet, been brought into cultivation, and also the large and rapidly increasing amount of its products, and we shall be overwhelmed with the magnitude of the prospect presented. And yet this region has no seacoast, touches no ocean anywhere. As part of one nation, its people now find, and may forever find, their way to Europe by New York, to South America and Africa by New Orleans, and to Asia by San Francisco. But separate our common country into two nations, as designed by the present rebellion, and every man of this great interior region is thereby cut off from some one or more of these outlets, not, perhaps, by a physical barrier, but by embarrassing and onerous trade regulations.

And this is true, *wherever* a dividing or boundary line may be fixed. Place it between the now free and slave country, or place it south of Kentucky, or north of Ohio, and still the truth remains, that none south of it can trade to any port or place north of it, and none north of it can trade to any port or place south of it except upon terms dictated by a Government foreign to them. These outlets, east, west, and south, are indispensable to the well-being of the people inhabiting, and to inhabit, this vast interior region. *Which* of the three may be the best is no proper question. All are better than either; and all of right belong to that people, and to their successors forever. True to themselves, they will not ask *where* a line of separation shall be, but will vow rather that there shall be no such line. Nor are the marginal regions less interested in these communications to and through them, to the great outside world. They, too, and each of them, must have access to this Egypt of the West without paying toll at the crossing of any national boundary.

Our national strife springs not from our permanent part; not from the land we inhabit; not from our national homestead. There is no possible severing of this, but would multiply and not mitigate evils among us. In all its adaptations and aptitudes it demands union and abhors separation. In fact it would, ere long, force reunion, however much of blood and treasure the separation might have cost.

Our strife pertains to ourselves—to the passing generations of men; and it can, without convulsion, be hushed forever with the passing of one generation.

In this view, I recommend the adoption of the following resolution and articles amendatory to the Constitution of the United States:

"*Resolved by the Senate and House of Representatives of the United States of America in Congress assembled*, (two thirds of both Houses concurring,) That the following articles be proposed to the Legislatures (or conventions) of the several States as amendments to the Constitution of the United States, all or any of which articles when ratified by three fourths of the said Legislatures (or conventions) to be valid as part or parts of the said Constitution, namely:

"ARTICLE —. Every State, wherein slavery now exists, which shall abolish the same therein, at any time, or times, before the first day of January, in the year of our Lord one thousand nine hundred, shall receive compensation from the United States, as follows, to wit:

"The President of the United States shall deliver to every such State bonds of the United States, bearing interest at the rate of —— per cent. per annum, to an amount equal to the aggregate sum of —— for each slave shown to have been therein by the eighth census of the United States, said bonds to be delivered to such States by instalments, or in one parcel, at the completion of the abolishment, accordingly as the same shall have been gradual, or at one time, within such State; and interest shall begin to run upon any such bond only from the proper time of its delivery as aforesaid. Any State having received bonds as aforesaid, and afterwards reintroducing or tolerating slavery therein, shall refund to the United States the bonds so received, or the value thereof, and all interest paid thereon.

"ARTICLE —. All slaves who shall have enjoyed actual freedom by the chances of the war at any time before the end of the rebellion, shall be forever free; but all owners of such, who shall not have been disloyal, shall be compensated for them, at the same rates as is provided for States adopting abolishment of slavery, but in such way that no slave shall be twice accounted for.

"ARTICLE —. Congress may appropriate money and otherwise provide for colonizing free colored persons, with their own consent, at any place or places without the United States."

I beg indulgence to discuss these proposed articles at some length. Without slavery the rebellion could never have existed; without slavery it could not continue.

Among the friends of the Union there is great diversity of sentiment and of policy in regard to slavery, and the African race among us. Some would perpetuate slavery; some would abolish it suddenly, and without compensation; some would abolish it gradually, and with compensation; some would remove the freed people from us, and some would retain them with us; and there are yet other minor diversities. Because of these diversities, we waste much strength in struggles among ourselves. By mutual concession we should harmonize and act together. This would be compromise; but it would be compromise among the friends, and not with the enemies of the Union. These articles are intended to embody a plan of such mutual concessions. If the plan shall be adopted, it is assumed that emancipation will follow, at least, in several of the States.

As to the first article, the main points are: first, the emancipation; secondly, the length of time for consummating it—thirty-seven years; and, thirdly, the compensation.

The emancipation will be unsatisfactory to the advocates of perpetual slavery; but the length of time should greatly mitigate their dissatisfaction. The time spares both races from the evils of sudden derangement—in fact, from the necessity of any derangement—while most of those whose habitual course of thought will be disturbed by the measure will have passed away before its consummation. They will never see it. Another class will hail the prospect of emancipation, but will deprecate the length of time They will feel that it gives too little to the now living slaves. But it really gives them much. It saves them from the vagrant destitution which must largely attend immediate emancipation in localities where their numbers are very great; and it gives the inspiring assurance that their posterity shall be free forever. The plan leaves to each State, choosing to act under it, to abolish slavery now or at the end of the century or at any intermediate time or by degrees, extending over the whole or any part of the period; and it obliges no two States to proceed alike. It also provides for compensation, and generally, the mode of making it. This, it would seem, must further mitigate the dissatisfaction of those who favor perpetual slavery, and especially of those who are to receive the compensation. Doubtless some of those who are to pay, and not to receive, will object. Yet the measure is both just and economical. In a certain sense, the liberation of slaves is the destruction of property—property acquired by descent, or by purchase, the same as any other property. It is no less true for having been often said, that the people of the South are not more responsible for the original introduction of this property than are the people of the North; and when it is remembered how unhesitatingly we all use cotton and sugar, and share the profits of dealing in them, it may not be quite safe to say that the South has been more responsible than the North for its continuance. If, then, for a common object, this property is to be sacrificed, is it not just that it be done at a common charge?

And if, with less money, or money more easily paid, we can preserve the benefits of the Union by this means than we can by the war alone, is it not also economical to do it? Let us consider it then. Let us ascertain the sum we have expended in the war since compensated emancipation was proposed last March, and consider whether, if that measure had been promptly accepted, by even some of the slave States, the same sum would not have done more to close the war than has been otherwise done. If so, the measure would save money, and, in that view, would be a prudent and economical measure. Certainly it is not so easy to pay *something* as it is to pay *nothing;* but it is easier to pay a *large* sum than it is to pay a *larger* one. And it is easier to pay any sum *when* we are able, than it is to pay it *before* we are able. The war requires large sums, and requires them at once. The aggregate sum necessary for compensated emancipation of course would be large. But it would require no ready cash, nor the bonds, even, any faster than the emancipation progresses. This might not, and probably would not, close before the end of the thirty-seven years. At that time we shall probably have a hundred million people to share the burden, instead of thirty-one millions, as now. And not only so, but the increase of our population may be expected to continue for a long time after that period as rapidly as before; because our territory will not have become full. I do not state this inconsiderately. At the same ratio of increase which we have maintained, on an average, from our first national census in 1790, until that of 1860, we should, in 1900, have a population of 103,208,415. And why may we not continue that ratio far beyond that period? Our abundant room—our broad national homestead—is our ample resource. Were our territory as limited as are the British Isles, very certainly our population could not expand as stated. Instead of receiving the foreign born, as now, we should be compelled to send part of the native born away.

But such is not our condition. We have two million nine hundred and sixty-three thousand square miles. Europe has three million and eight hundred thousand, with a population averaging seventy-three and one third persons to the square mile. Why may not our country, at some time, average as many? Is it less fertile? Has it more waste surface, by mountains, rivers, lakes, deserts, or other causes? Is it inferior to Europe in any natural advantage? If, then, we are at some time to be as populous as Europe, how soon? As to when this *may* be, we can judge by the past and the present; as to when it *will* be, if ever, depends much on whether we maintain the Union. Several of our States are already above the average of Europe—seventy-three and a third to the square mile. Massachusetts has 157; Rhode Island, 133; Connecticut, 99; New York and New Jersey, each, 80. Also two other great States, Pennsylvania and Ohio, are not far below, the former having 63 and the latter 59. The States already above the European average, except New York, have increased in as rapid a ratio, since passing that point, as ever before; while no one of them is equal to some other parts of our country in natural capacity for sustaining a dense population.

Taking the nation in the aggregate, and we find its population and ratio of increase, for the several decennial periods, to be as follows:

1790	3,929,827			
1800	5,305,937	35.02	per cent.	ratio of increase.
1810	7,239,814	36.45	"	"
1820	9,638,131	33.13	"	"
1830	12,866,020	33.49	"	"
1840	17,069,453	32.67	"	"
1850	23,191,876	35.87	"	"
1860	31,443,790	35.58	"	"

This shows an average decennial increase of 34.69 per cent. in population through the seventy years from our first to our last census yet taken. It is seen that the ratio of increase, at no one of these seven periods, is either two per cent. below or two per cent. above the average; thus showing how inflexible, and, consequently, how reliable, the law of increase, in our case, is. Assuming that it will continue, gives the following results:

1870	42,323,341
1880	56,967,216
1890	76,677,872
1900	103,208,415
1910	138,918,526
1920	186,984,335
1930	251,680,914

These figures show that our country *may* be as populous as Europe now is at some point between 1920 and 1930—say about 1925—our territory, at seventy-three and a third persons to the square mile, being of capacity to contain 217,186,000.

And we *will* reach this, too, if we do not ourselves relinquish the chance by the folly and evils of disunion, or by long and exhausting war springing from the only great element of national discord among us. While it cannot be foreseen exactly how much one huge example of secession, breeding lesser ones indefinitely, would retard population, civilization, and prosperity, no one can doubt that the extent of it would be very great and injurious.

The proposed emancipation would shorten

the war, perpetuate peace, insure this increase of population, and proportionately the wealth of the country. With these, we should pay all the emancipation would cost, together with our other debt, easier than we should pay our other debt without it. If we had allowed our old national debt to run at six per cent. per annum, simple interest, from the end of our revolutionary struggle until to-day, without paying anything on either principal or interest, each man of us would owe less upon that debt now than each man owed upon it then; and this because our increase of men through the whole period has been greater than six per cent.; has run faster than the interest upon the debt. Thus, time alone relieves a debtor nation, so long as its population increases faster than unpaid interest accumulates on its debt.

This fact would be no excuse for delaying payment of what is justly due; but it shows the great importance of time in this connection—the great advantage of a policy by which we shall not have to pay until we number a hundred millions, what, by a different policy, we would have to pay now, when we number but thirty-one millions. In a word, it shows that a dollar will be much harder to pay for the war than will be a dollar for emancipation on the proposed plan. And then the latter will cost no blood, no precious life. It will be a saving of both.

As to the second article, I think it would be impracticable to return to bondage the class of persons therein contemplated. Some of them, doubtless, in the property sense, belong to loyal owners, and hence provision is made in this article for compensating such.

The third article relates to the future of the freed people. It does not oblige, but merely authorizes, Congress to aid in colonizing such as may consent. This ought not to be regarded as objectionable on the one hand or on the other, insomuch as it comes to nothing, unless by the mutual consent of the people to be deported, and the American voters, through their representatives in Congress.

I cannot make it better known than it already is, that I strongly favor colonization. And yet I wish to say there is an objection urged against free colored persons remaining in the country which is largely imaginary, if not sometimes malicious.

It is insisted that their presence would injure and displace white labor and white laborers. If there ever could be a proper time for mere catch arguments, that time surely is not now. In times like the present men should utter nothing for which they would not willingly be responsible through time and in eternity. Is it true, then, that colored people can displace any more white labor by being free than by remaining slaves? If they stay in their old places, they jostle no white laborers; if they leave their old places, they leave them open to white laborers. Logically, there is neither more nor less of it. Emancipation, even without deportation, would probably enhance the wages of white labor, and, very surely would not reduce them. Thus, the customary amount of labor would still have to be performed; the freed people would surely not do more than their old proportion of it, and, very probably, for a time would do less, leaving an increased part to white laborers, bring their labor into greater demand, and consequently enhancing the wages of it. With deportation, even to a limited extent, enhanced wages to white labor is mathematically certain. Labor is like any other commodity in the market—increase the demand for it and you increase the price of it. Reduce the supply of black labor by colonizing the black laborer out of the country, and by precisely so much you increase the demand for and wages of white labor.

But it is dreaded that the freed people will swarm forth, and cover the whole land? Are they not already in the land? Will liberation make them any more numerous? Equally distributed among the whites of the whole country, and there would be but one colored to seven whites. Could the one, in any way, greatly disturb the seven? There are many communities now, having more than one free colored person to seven whites; and this, without any apparent consciousness of evil from it. The District of Columbia, and the States of Maryland and Delaware, are all in this condition. The District has more than one free colored to six whites; and yet, in its frequent petitions to Congress, I believe it has never presented the presence of free colored persons as one of its grievances. But why should emancipation south, send the freed people north? People, of any color, seldom run, unless there be something to run from. *Heretofore* colored people, to some extent, have fled north from bondage, and now, perhaps, from both bondage and destitution. But if gradual emancipation and deportation be adopted, they will have neither to flee from. Their old masters will give them wages at least until new laborers can be procured; and the freed men, in turn, will gladly give their labor for the wages, till new homes can be found for them, in congenial climes, and with people of their own blood and race. This proposition can be trusted on the mutual interests involved. And, in any event, cannot the North decide for itself, whether to receive them?

Again, as practice proves more than theory, in any case, has there been any irruption of colored people northward because of the abolishment of slavery in this District last spring?

What I have said of the proportion of free colored persons to the whites in the District is from the census of 1860, having no reference to persons called contrabands, nor to those made free by the act of Congress abolishing slavery here.

The plan consisting of these articles is recommended, not but that a restoration of the national authority would be accepted without its adoption.

Nor will the war, nor proceedings under the proclamation of September 22, 1862, be stayed because of the *recommendation* of this plan. Its timely *adoption*, I doubt not, would bring restoration, and thereby stay both.

And, notwithstanding this plan, the recommendation that Congress provide by law for compensating any State which may adopt emancipation before this plan shall have been acted upon is hereby earnestly renewed. Such would be only an advance part of the plan, and the same arguments apply to both.

This plan is recommended as a means, not in exclusion of but additional to all others for restoring and preserving the national authority throughout the Union. The subject is presented exclusively in its economical aspect. The plan would, I am confident, secure peace more speedily, and maintain it more permanently, than can be done by force alone; while all it would cost, considering amounts, and manner of payment, and times of payment, would be easier paid than will be the additional cost of the war, if we rely solely upon force. It is much, very much, that it would cost no blood at all.

The plan is proposed as permanent constitutional law. It cannot become such without the concurrence of, first, two thirds of Congress, and afterwards, three fourths of the States. The requisite three fourths of the States will necessarily include seven of the slave States. Their concurrence, if obtained, will give assurance of their severally adopting emancipation at no very distant day upon the the new constitutional terms. This assurance would end the struggle now, and save the Union forever.

I do not forget the gravity which should characterize a paper addressed to the Congress of the nation by the Chief Magistrate of the nation. Nor do I forget that some of you are my seniors, nor that many of you have more experience than I in the conduct of public affairs. Yet I trust that in view of the great responsibility resting upon me, you will perceive no want of respect to yourselves in any undue earnestness I may seem to display.

Is it doubted, then, that the plan I propose, if adopted, would shorten the war, and thus lessen its expenditure of money and of blood? Is it doubted that it would restore the national authority and national prosperity, and perpetuate both indefinitely? Is it doubted that we here—Congress and Executive—can secure its adoption? Will not the good people respond to a united and earnest appeal from us? Can we, can they, by any other means so certainly or so speedily assure these vital objects? We can succeed only by concert. It is not "can *any* of us *imagine* better?" but "can we *all* do better?" Object whatsoever is possible, still the question recurs "can we do better?" The dogmas of the quiet past are inadequate to the stormy present. The occasion is piled high with difficulty, and we must rise with the occasion. As our case is new, so we must think anew and act anew. We must disenthrall ourselves, and then we shall save our country.

Fellow-citizens, *we* cannot escape history. We, of this Congress and this Administration, will be remembered in spite of ourselves. No personal significance, or insignificance, can spare one or another of us. The fiery trial through which we pass will light us down, in honor or dishonor, to the latest generation. We *say* we are for the Union. The world will not forget that we say this. We know how to save the Union. The world knows we do know how to save it. We—even *we here*—hold the power and bear the responsibility. In *giving* freedom to the *slave* we *assure* freedom to the *free*—honorable alike in what we give and what we preserve. We shall nobly save, or meanly lose, the last, best hope of earth. Other means may succeed; this could not fail. The way is plain, peaceful, generous, just—a way which, if followed, the world will forever applaud, and God must forever bless.

ABRAHAM LINCOLN.

COMPENSATED EMANCIPATION IN MISSOURI.*

Third Session, Thirty-Seventh Congress.

IN HOUSE.

1863, Jan. 6—Mr. NOELL, of Missouri, from the Select Committee, reported a bill, providing that the following propositions be submitted to the State of Missouri to be accepted or rejected by the Legislature or people thereof:

1. The Government of the United States will, upon the passage by said State of a good and valid act of emancipation of all the slaves therein, to take effect within the period hereinafter named, and to be irrepealable unless by the consent of the United States, apply the sum of $10,000,000, in United States bonds, redeemable in thirty years from their date, and bearing interest, payable semi-annually, at the rate of five per cent. per annum, for the purpose of paying to the loyal owners of such slaves in said State a just compensation for the loss of the services of such slaves; the said bonds to be prepared and issued by the Secretary of the Treasury, under such rules and regulations as he may prescribe to make effective the provisions of this act.

2. That in the event of the adoption by the said State of abolishment of slavery therein, as hereinbefore provided, the Government of the United States will employ all reasonable means for the deportation of such of said emancipated slaves, and for their settlement or colonization in some place outside of the United States, as may consent thereto, so soon as and whenever proper negotiations can be made with any country for such settlement or colonization in a congenial climate, or within a reasonable time thereafter.

The semi-annual interest to be payable, and the bonds redeemable out of moneys to be hereafter appropriated by Congress, and to be reimbursed to the United States Treasury from the property of rebels confiscated, and no part of the money to be paid to persons who have, at any time engaged in or in any manner aided in the rebellion, or held office under the Confederate States, &c. The bonds to be delivered to the Governor of Missouri when the President shall be satisfied that a valid act of immediate emancipation shall have been passed by the Legislature, irrepealable without the consent of the United States, and within one year from Jan. 1, 1863.

Mr. HOLMAN moved to lay the bill on the table; which was lost—yeas 42, nays 73.

An unimportant amendment was made, when Mr. PENDLETON moved to lay the bill on the table; which was lost—yeas 44, nays 72.

Mr. CRAVENS then moved that the House adjourn; which was lost—yeas 19, nays 82.

When the bill passed—yeas 83, nays 50, as follows:

YEAS—Messrs. Aldrich, Alley, Ashley, Babbitt, Baker, Baxter, Bingham, Jacob B. Blair, Blake, Buffinton, Burnham, Campbell, Chamberlain, Clark, Colfax, Frederick A. Conkling, Roscoe Conkling, Covode, Duell, Edgerton, Edwards, Eliot, Ely, Fenton, Samuel C. Fessenden, Thomas A. D. Fessenden, Fisher, Franchot, Gooch, Goodwin, Hale, Harrison, Hickman, Hooper, Horton, Hutchins, Julian, Kelley, Francis W. Kellogg, Lansing, *Lehman*, Loomis, Lovejoy, Low, McKean, McKnight, McPherson, Maynard, Moorhead, Anson P. Morrill, Justin S. Morrill, *Noell*, Olin, Patton, Timothy G. Phelps, Pike, Pomeroy, Alexander H. Rice, John H. Rice, Riddle, Edward H. Rollins, *James S. Rollins*, Sargent, Sedgwick, Shanks, *Sheffield*, Shellabarger, Sherman, Spaulding, Stevens, Benjamin F. Thomas, Train, Trowbridge, Van Horn,

* See resolutions of Convention, *supra*.

Van Valkenburgh, Verree, Walker, Wall, Wallace, Wheeler, Albert S. White, Windom, Worcester—83.

NAYS—Messrs. *William Allen, Ancona, Baily, Biddle, Calvert*, Clements, *Cobb, Corning, Cox, Cravens, Crittenden*, Davis, *Dunlap*, Dunn, Granger, *Grider, Haight, Hall, Harding, Holman, Johnson*, William Kellogg, *Kerrigan, Knapp, Law, Mallory, Menzies, Morris, Norton, Odell, Pendleton, Perry*, Porter, *Price, Shiel, Smith, John B. Steele, William G. Steele, Stiles*, Stratton, Trimble, *Vallandigham, Voorhees, Wadsworth, Ward*, Webster, *Wickliffe*, Wilson, *Wood, Woodruff*—50.

—

IN SENATE.

January 14—Mr. TRUMBULL, from the Committee on the Judiciary, reported a substitute as follows:

That whenever satisfactory evidence shall be presented to the President of the United States that the State of Missouri has adopted a valid and constitutional law, ordinance, or other provision for the gradual or immediate emancipation of all the slaves therein, and the exclusion of slavery forever thereafter from said State, it shall be his duty to prepare and deliver to the Governor of said State, as hereinafter provided, to be used by said State to compensate for the inconveniences produced by such change of system, bonds of the United States to the amount of $20,000,000, the same to bear interest at the rate of five per cent. per annum, and payable thirty years after the date thereof: *Provided*, That the said bonds shall not be delivered as herein directed unless the act of emancipation shall be adopted by said State within twelve months after the passage of this act, nor unless said act shall provide that slavery or involuntary servitude within said State, except in punishment of crime, shall forever cease and determine on some day not later than the 4th day of July, 1876, and never afterwards be introduced therein: *And provided further*, That said bonds in their aggregate amount shall not exceed the sum of $300 for each slave emancipated under the provisions of this act and the act of emancipation to be passed in the State of Missouri in pursuance thereof, not including any slave who shall be introduced into said State subsequently to the passage of this act, or has been emancipated or shall become free under the provisions of an act entitled "An act to suppress insurrection, to punish treason and rebellion, to seize and confiscate the property of rebels, and for other purposes," approved July 17, 1862.

SEC. 2. *And be it further enacted*, That in the event of the adoption by said State of an act or ordinance for the abolition of slavery therein, as hereinbefore provided, the President shall, from time to time, as they may be required, cause bonds to be prepared and delivered, as aforesaid, in such amounts as may be necessary to pay for each slave made free under the provisions of this act, and the act to be passed by the State of Missouri in pursuance thereof, not to exceed an average of $300; said bonds to be delivered only as said slaves are made free, and in the aggregate not to exceed $20,000,000; and not to exceed $10,000,000, unless the law or act of emancipation to be adopted by said State shall provide for the full and perfect manumission of all the slaves therein on or before the 4th day of July, A. D. 1865, and the future exclusion of the system of slavery from the State forever thereafter.

SEC. 3. *And be it further enacted*, That upon the enactment of a law by said State referring to this act, accepting its provisions and adopting laws for the ultimate extinction of slavery therein, the faith of the United States and of the said State will be pledged to carry out the terms of the compact thus created: *Provided*, That nothing herein contained shall prevent the State from making at any time such alterations or amendments in its emancipation laws as do not conflict with this act, or such as shall only decrease the time during which slavery may exist in the said State.

Feb. 7—Mr. WILSON, of Missouri, offered the following amendment:

That the said bonds shall not be delivered as herein directed unless the act of emancipation shall be adopted by said State within three years after the passage of this act.

Striking out "twelve months" and inserting "three years;" which was disagreed to—yeas 8, nays 27, as follows:

YEAS—Messrs. *Carlile, Davis, Kennedy, Nesmith, Powell, Richardson, Wall, Wilson* of Missouri—8.

NAYS—Messrs. Anthony, Arnold, Chandler, Clark, Collamer, Dixon, Doolittle, Fessenden, Foot, Foster, Grimes, *Harding*, Harlan, Harris, Henderson, Hicks, King, Lane of Indiana, Lane of Kansas, Morrill, Pomeroy, Sumner, Ten Eyck, Trumbull, Willey, Wilmot, Wilson of Massachusetts—27.

Mr. WILSON, of Missouri, moved to strike out the provision limiting the amount to be paid for each slave, as follows:

And provided further, That said bonds in their aggregate amount shall not exceed the sum of $300 for each slave emancipated under the provisions of this act and the act of emancipation to be passed by the State of Missouri in pursuance thereof.

Which was disagreed to—yeas 9, nays 27, as follows:

YEAS—Messrs. *Davis, Kennedy, Latham, Nesmith, Powell, Rice, Wall*, Willey, *Wilson* of Missouri—9.

NAYS—Messrs. Anthony, Arnold, Chandler, Clark, Collamer, Dixon, Doolittle, Fessenden, Foot, Foster, Grimes, *Harding*, Harlan, Harris, Henderson, Hicks, King, Lane of Indiana, Lane of Kansas, Morrill, Pomeroy, Sherman, Sumner, Ten Eyck, Trumbull, Wilmot, Wilson of Massachusetts—27.

Mr. POWELL moved to strike out of the first section the words "not to exceed $20,000,000," and insert "$11,000,000;" which was disagreed to—yeas 13, nays 22, as follows:

YEAS—Messrs. *Carlile*, Clark, Collamer, *Davis*, Fessenden, Grimes, *Harding*, Harlan, Lane of Indiana, *Nesmith, Powell, Rice, Wall*—13.

NAYS—Messrs. Anthony, Arnold, Chandler, Dixon, Doolittle, Foot, Foster, Harris, Henderson, Howard, King, Lane of Kansas, Morrill, Pomeroy, Sumner, Ten Eyck, Trumbull, Wade, Willey, Wilmot, Wilson of Massachusetts, *Wilson* of Missouri—22.

Mr. WILSON, of Missouri, offered the following amendment:

And be it further enacted, That no part of the bonds herein specified shall be delivered until the act of the Legislature or the Constitutional Convention of the State of Missouri providing for the emancipation of the slaves in said State shall be submitted to a vote of the people and approved by a majority of the legal voters of said State.

Which was disagreed to—yeas 13, nays 27, as follows:

YEAS—Messrs. *Carlile, Davis, Harding, Kennedy, Nesmith, Powell, Rice, Richardson, Saulsbury, Turpie, Wall*, Willey, *Wilson* of Missouri—13.

NAYS—Messrs. Anthony, Arnold, Chandler, Clark, Collamer, Dixon, Doolittle, Fessenden, Foot, Foster, Grimes, Harlan, Harris, Henderson, Howard, Howe, King, Lane of Indiana, Lane of Kansas, Morrill, Pomeroy, Sumner, Ten Eyck, Trumbull, Wade, Wilmot, Wilson of Massachusetts—27.

Mr. SUMNER offered an amendment to strike out "seventy-six," in the first section, and insert "sixty-four," making the act to take effect on the 4th of July, 1864; which was disagreed to—yeas 11, nays 26, as follows:

YEAS—Messrs. Fessenden, Grimes, Harlan, Lane of Indiana, Lane of Kansas, Pomeroy, *Rice*, Sumner, Wade, Wilmot, Wilson of Massachusetts—11.

NAYS—Messrs. Anthony, Arnold, Chandler, Clark, Cowan, *Davis*, Dixon, Doolittle, Foot, Foster, *Harding*, Harris, Henderson, Howard, Howe, King, *Latham*, Morrill, *Nesmith, Powell*, Sherman, Ten Eyck, Trumbull, *Wall*, Willey, *Wilson* of Missouri—26.

February 12—Mr. SUMNER offered the following amendment:

That said bonds, in their aggregate amount, shall not exceed the sum of $200 for each slave emancipated.

Which was agreed to—yeas 19, nays 17, as follows:

YEAS—Messrs. *Carlile*, Clark, Collamer, Fessenden, Grimes, Harlan, Howe, King, Lane of Indiana, Lane of Kansas, Pomeroy, *Rice*, Sherman, Sumner, Trumbull, Wade, Wilkinson, Wilmot, Wilson of Massachusetts—19.

NAYS—Messrs. Anthony, Arnold, Cowan, Dixon, Doolittle, Foster, Harris, Henderson, Hicks, Howard, *Latham, McDougall*, Morrill, *Richardson*, Ten Eyck, *Wall, Wilson* of Missouri—17.

Mr. SUMNER offered an amendment to strike out of the first section the word "gradual," making the operation of emancipation immediate; which was disagreed to—yeas 11, nays 27, as follows:

YEAS—Messrs. *Carlile*, Collamer, Cowan, Fessenden, Grimes, Harlan, Lane of Kansas, Pomeroy, Sumner, Wade, Wilson of Massachusetts—11.

NAYS—Messrs. Anthony, Arnold, Chandler, Clark, *Davis*, Dixon, Doolittle, Foster, Harris, Henderson, Hicks, Howard, Howe, King, *Latham*, *McDougall*, Morrill, *Nesmith*, *Powell*, *Rice*, *Richardson*, Sherman, Ten Eyck, Trumbull, Wilkinson, Wilmot, *Wilson* of Missouri—27.

The bill, as amended, then passed the Senate —yeas 23, nays 18, as follows:

YEAS—Messrs. Anthony, Arnold, Chandler, Clark, Collamer, Doolittle, Foot, Foster, Harlan, Harris, Henderson, Howard, Howe, King, Lane of Kansas, Morrill, Pomeroy, Sumner, Trumbull, Wade, Wilkinson, Wilmot, Wilson of Massachusetts—23.

NAYS—Messrs. *Carlile*, Cowan, *Davis*, Fessenden, Grimes, *Harding*, *Kennedy*, Lane of Indiana, *Latham*, *McDougall*, *Nesmith*, *Powell*, *Richardson*, *Saulsbury*, Ten Eyck, *Turpie*, *Wall*, *Wilson* of Missouri—18.

February 18—The bill was considered in the House of Representatives, and recommitted to the Select Committee—yeas 81, nays 51.

February 25—The committee reported back the bill, but it was not again considered by the House.

March 3—Mr. WHITE, of Indiana, moved to suspend the rules to take it up, but the motion was lost—yeas 62, nays 57, (two thirds being required.)

COMPENSATED EMANCIPATION IN MARYLAND.

1863, January 12—Mr. FRANCIS THOMAS offered the following resolution, which was agreed to:

Resolved, That the Committee on Emancipation and Colonization be instructed to inquire into the expediency of making an appropriation to aid the State of Maryland in a system of emancipation and colonization of persons of color, inhabitants of said State.

January 19—Mr. BINGHAM, of Ohio, introduced a bill giving aid to the State of Maryland, for the purpose of securing the abolishment of slavery in said State.

February 25—Mr. WHITE, of Indiana, reported back the bill with amendments. The bill appropriated $10,000,000, upon the passage of an emancipation bill, to take effect within two years from Jan. 1, 1863, upon substantially the terms set forth in the Missouri bill, as passed by the House.

After some debate, the bill was re-committed to the Select Committee by a vote of—yeas 75, nays 55, as follows:

YEAS—Messrs. Aldrich, Alley, Arnold, Ashley, Babbitt, Baker, Beaman, Bingham, Jacob B. Blair, Samuel S. Blair, Blake, William G. Brown, Buffinton, Campbell, Casey, Chamberlain, Clark, Clements, Colfax, Frederick A. Conkling, Roscoe Conkling, Cutler, Davis, Dawes, Diven, Edgerton, Edwards, Eliot, Ely, Fenton, Samuel C. Fessenden, Thomas A. D. Fessenden, Fisher, Flanders, Frank, Gooch, Gurley, Hahn, Hutchins, Kelley, Lansing, Leary, *Lehman*, Loomis, Lovejoy, Low, McIndoe, McKean, McKnight, Maynard, Mitchell, Moorhead, Justin S. Morrill, Nixon, *Pendleton*, Timothy G. Phelps, Pomeroy, Alexander H. Rice, John H. Rice, Riddle, Edward H. Rollins, Sargent, Sedgwick, *Sheffield*, Shellabarger, Sherman, Stevens, Francis Thomas, Trowbridge, Verree, Walker, Wallace, Albert S. White, Wilson, Windom—75.

NAYS—Messrs. *William Allen*, *William J. Allen*, *Ancona*, *Biddle*, *Calvert*, Conway, *Cox*, *Cravens*, *Crisfield*, Delano, *Dunlap*, Dunn, *Fouke*, Granger, *Haight*, Hale, *Hall*, *Harding*, Harrison, *Holman*, *Johnson*, *Kerrigan*, *Knapp*, *Law*, *Lazear*, McPherson, *Mallory*, *May*, *Menzies*, *Morris*, *Noble*, *Norton*, *Nugen*, *Perry*, Porter, *Price*, *Robinson*, *James S. Rollins*, Segar, *Smith*, *John B. Steele*, *William G. Steele*, *Stiles*, Benjamin F. Thomas, Train, Trimble, *Vallandigham*, *Wadsworth*, *Ward*, Webster, *Wickliffe*, *Wood*, *Woodruff*, Worcester, *Yeaman*—55.

It was not again reached.

EMANCIPATION IN MARYLAND—ITS DAWNING.

At the meeting of the Union Convention of Baltimore city, May 28, 1862, Mr. P. G. Sauerwein, from the Business Committee, reported these resolutions, which were adopted, *seriatim*, unanimously:

Whereas, the Union men of the city of Baltimore have recently, by large meetings in their respective wards, chosen this City Convention to represent their political interest for the ensuing year, and it is proper that amid the rapid progress of events, and in these times of emergency and peril, we should more definitely settle and define our position and principles in the face of the country: Therefore,

Resolved, By the Union City Convention of Baltimore, that we reaffirm our unconditional adhesion to the Constitution and Government of the United States.

2. That the National Government ought not to lay down its arms until its authority shall be acknowledged and obeyed in every portion of the national territory.

3. That the attempt to revive a political organization under the leadership of men who have, by their votes and speeches, encouraged the rebellion, or carped at the necessary measures of the Government in its hour of trial, or failed to sympathize in the great uprising of the people to defend the Union, ought to be discouraged by every true patriot as a selfish and disloyal effort to obtain power in the future by conciliating those who are now in flagrant rebellion.

4. That we cordially approve the firm and vigorous efforts of the Administration to maintain the integrity and honor of our country, to crush rebellion, and to anticipate and defeat the acts of traitors; and we are fully persuaded that, so long as the insurrection is raging, leniency is wasted alike upon the rebels in arms, and upon their malignant sympathizers at home; and that all efforts at conciliation will prove unavailing till the Government shall have fully demonstrated its power.

5. That we approve the wise and conservative policy proposed by the President in his message of the 6th March, 1862, and sanctioned by Congress, tendering pecuniary aid to such States as may choose to adopt a system of gradual emancipation; and that it is not only the *duty* of the loyal people of Maryland to meet the Government in this endeavor to relieve them, in the only practical way, from the evils which armed insurrection has brought upon the land, thus sustaining the Government as well against the treason of secession as against the radical and violent projects of fanatical abolitionists, but that it is likewise for the *interest* of all the people of this State, more especially of the slave-owners, promptly to accept the aid thus tendered, and remove from our midst an institution which has ceased to be profitable, and is now injurious to our political and material interests, and dangerous to our peace and safety, by inaugurating such a plan of emancipation and colonization as will be equitable to those interested, and as will tend to secure the industry of the State to the white labor of the State.

6. That the Legislature, at its late session, in failing to adopt stringent measures for the suppression of treason; in failing to make adequate provision for the families of our volunteers; in failing to organize the military of the State; in putting forth unnecessary protests calculated to embarrass the action of the Government and throw doubt upon the position of the State; and, in neglecting to comply with its constitutional duty, to provide for a vote on the question of a Constitutional Convention, did not meet the demands of the crisis, or answer the just expectations of the loyal people of Maryland.

Whereas, the principle of equal rights underlies the foundation of republican institutions; and whereas notwithstanding the eight counties (this city included) lying north of the Sassafras and Patapsco rivers contain about three fourths of the white population and wealth of this State, and pay more than three fourths of the taxes, yet, according to the basis of representation under the present constitution, the southern counties, containing one fourth of the population and wealth, and paying less than one fourth of the taxes, possess the virtual control of the whole State, sending thirty-four out of the seventy four delegates, and fourteen out of twenty-two senators, to the Legislature, being an average of one delegate to 3,831 white persons in the southern counties, against one delegate to 9,641 in the northern, and one senator to 9,205 in the former against one senator to 48,205 free white persons in the latter; and whereas, in the present arrangement of representation, according to which Baltimore city has no more voice in the Senate than counties containing hardly more voters than one of her wards, and was deprived of fifteen delegates to which she was entitled, which were distributed among the southern counties exclusively, the object was to secure the power of the State to the slave-owners, constituting less than sixteen thousand individuals, as is apparent from the fact that the number of slaves in the city is less than one per cent. of the whole population, and that the proportion of slaves to the whites throughout the northern part of the State is less than four of the former to one hundred of the latter, whilst the proportion in the favored counties is fifty-six slaves to one hundred white people; and whereas, the Governor, the judges of the court of appeals, and the United States Senators are elected according to a similar unjust arrangement, for the same purpose of confirming and perpetuating this domination of the slaveholding counties; and whereas, in pursuance of the same partial and iniquitous scheme, the owners of slave property are exempted from equal taxation, while they are compensated to its full value in the case of convict slaves—all of which is an intolerable burden to the majority of our people, who are, nevertheless, without a remedy under the present constitution; Therefore

Resolved, That the State constitution ought to be changed, so as to correct the present unequal representation of the people in the Legislature, and to secure the right of representation in proportion to white population to all parts of the State. ARCHIBALD STIRLING, Jr., *Pres't.*

JOHN H. LLOYD, *Secretary.*

IN CONSTITUTIONAL CONVENTION.

1864, June 24—The question recurred on the twenty-third article of the Bill of Rights:

Hereafter, in this State, there shall be neither slavery nor involuntary servitude, except in punishment of crime, whereof the party shall have been duly convicted, and all persons held to labor as slaves are hereby declared free.

An amendment was pending, offered by Mr. Brown, of Queen Anne's, as follows:

And the Legislature shall make provision from the treasury of the State for the comfortable support and maintenance of the helpless and paupers hereby emancipated.

The amendment was rejected—yeas 27, nays 53:

YEAS—Messrs. Berry of Baltimore county, Berry of Prince George's, Billingsley, Blackiston, Briscoe, Brown, Chambers, Clarke, Crawford, Dail, Dennis, Duvall, Edelen, Gale, Harwood, Hollyday, Horsey, Johnson, Lansdale, Lee, Marbury, Mitchell, Miller, Parran, Peter, Smith of Dorchester, Turner—27.

NAYS—Messrs. President (H. H. Goldsborough), Abbott, Annan, Audoun, Baker, Barron, Carter, Cunningham, Cushing, Daniel, Davis of Charles, Davis of Washington, Earle, Ecker, Farrow, Galloway, Greene, Hatch, Hebb, Hoffman, Hopkins, Hopper, Jones of Cecil, Keefer, Kennard, King, Larsh, Mace, Markey, McComas, Mullikin, Murray, Negley, Nyman, Parker, Purnell, Ridgely, Robinette, Russell, Sands, Schley, Schlosser, Scott, Smith of Carroll, Sneary, Stirling, Stockbridge, Sykes, Thomas, Thruston, Valliant, Wickard, Wooden—53.

The article was then adopted—yeas 53, nays 27:

YEAS—Messrs. H. H. Goldsborough, E. A. Abbott, A. Annan, J. H. Audoun, H. Baker, J. Barron, J. S. Berry, Jas. D. Carter, B. A. Cunningham, Jos. M. Cushing, Wm. Daniel, J. F. Davis, G. Earle, J. Ecker, W. H. W. Farrow, W. Galloway, A. C. Greene, S. T. Hatch, H. Hebb, W. H. Hoffman, Joel Hopkins, J. A. Hopper, T. P. Jones, S. Keefer, B. H. Kennard, D. King, S. Larsh, W. H. Mace, D. J. Markey, G. M. McComas, J. F. Mullikin, F. T. Murray, P. Negley, L. B. Nyman, E. L. Parker, W. T. Purnell, J. L. Ridgely, J. Robinette, T. Russell, G. W. Sands, F. Schley, P. G. Schlosser, D. Scott, J. E. Smith, J. R. Sneary, A. Stirling, H. Stockbridge, J. Sykes, J. L. Thomas, Jr., G. A. Thruston, J. Valliant, J. Wickard, W. S. Wooden—53.

NAYS—Messrs. S. H. Berry, C. Billingsley, D. G. Blackiston, J. T. Briscoe, J. Brown, E. F. Chambers, D. Clarke, A. J. Crawford, T. I. Dail, Peregrine Davis, J. U. Dennis, E. P. Duvall, R. H. Edelen, W. H. Gale, S. Harwood, G. S. Hollyday, C. Horsey, A. Johnson, Thomas Lansdale, J. Lee, F. Marbury, J. W. Mitchell, O. Miller, C. S. Parran, G. Peter, W. A. Smith, J. Turner—27.

Emancipation.

PROCLAMATIONS OF THE PRESIDENT.

September 22, 1862.*

I, ABRAHAM LINCOLN, President of the United States of America, and Commander-in-Chief of the army and navy thereof, do hereby proclaim and declare that hereafter, as heretofore, the war will be prosecuted for the object of practically restoring the constitutional relation between the United States and each of the States and the people thereof, in which States that relation is or may be suspended or disturbed.

That it is my purpose, upon the next meeting of Congress, to again recommend the adoption of a practical measure tendering pecuniary aid to the free acceptance or rejection of all slave States, so called, the people whereof may not then be in rebellion against the United States, and which States may then have voluntarily adopted, or thereafter may voluntarily adopt, immediate or gradual abolishment of slavery within their respective limits; and that the effort to colonize persons of African descent with their consent upon this continent or elsewhere, with the previously obtained consent of the Governments existing there, will be continued.

That on the first day of January, in the year of our Lord one thousand eight hundred and sixty-three, all persons held as slaves within any State or designated part of a State, the people whereof shall then be in rebellion against the United States, shall be then, thenceforward, and forever free; and the Executive Government of the United States, including the military and

---

* Major General McClellan's Order respecting it:

HEADQUARTERS ARMY OF THE POTOMAC,
[General Order No. 163.] *October* 7, 1862.

The attention of the officers and soldiers of the army of the Potomac is called to General Order No. 139, War Department, September 24th, 1862, publishing to the army the President's proclamation of September 22d.

A proclamation of such grave moment to the nation, officially communicated to the army, affords to the General Commanding an opportunity of defining specifically to the officers and soldiers under his command the relation borne by all persons in the military service of the United States towards the civil authorities of the Government.

The Constitution confides to the civil authorities—legislative, judicial, and executive—the power and duty of making, expounding, and executing the Federal laws. Armed forces are raised and supported simply to sustain the civil authorities, and are to be held in strict subordination thereto in all respects. This fundamental law of our political system is essential to the security of our republican institutions, and should be thoroughly understood and observed by every soldier.

The principle upon which and the objects for which armies shall be employed in suppressing rebellion must be determined and declared by the authorities, and the Chief Executive, who is charged with the administration of the national affairs, is the proper and only source through which the views and orders of the Government can be made known to the armies of the nation.

Discussion by officers and soldiers concerning public measures determined upon and declared by the Government, when carried beyond the ordinary, temperate, and respectful expression of opinion, tend greatly to impair and destroy the discipline and efficiency of the troops, by substituting the spirit of political faction for the firm, steady, and earnest support of the authority of the Government, which is the highest duty of the American soldier. The remedy for political errors, if any are committed, is to be found only in the action of the people at the polls.

In thus calling the attention of this army to the true relation between the soldiers and the Government, the General Commanding merely adverts to an evil against which it has been thought advisable during our whole history to guard the armies of the Republic, and in so doing he will not be considered, by any right minded person, as casting any reflection upon that loyalty and good conduct which has been so fully illustrated upon so many battle-fields.

In carrying out all measures of public policy this army will, of course, be guided by the same rules of mercy and Christianity that have ever controlled its conduct towards the defenceless.

By command of Maj. Gen. McClellan:

JAMES A. HARDIE, *Lieut. Col.*
Aid-de-Camp and Act'g Ass't Adjt. General.

naval authority thereof, will recognize and maintain the freedom of such persons, and will do no act or acts to repress such persons, or any of them, in any efforts they may make for their actual freedom.

That the Executive will, on the first day of January aforesaid, by proclamation, designate the States and parts of States, if any, in which the people thereof respectively, shall then be in rebellion against the United States; and the fact that any State, or the people thereof, shall on that day be, in good faith, represented in the Congress of the United States by members chosen thereto at elections wherein a majority of the qualified voters of such State shall have participated, shall, in the absence of strong countervailing testimony, be deemed conclusive evidence that such State, and the people thereof, are not in rebellion against the United States.

That attention is hereby called to an act of Congress entitled "An act to make an additional article of war," approved March 3, 1862, and which act is in the words and figures following:

"*Be it enacted by the Senate and House of Representatives of the United States of America in Congress assembled*, That hereafter the following shall be promulgated as an additional article of war, for the government of the army of the United States, and shall be obeyed and observed as such.

"Article —. All officers or persons in the military or naval service of the United States are prohibited from employing any of the forces under their respective commands for the purpose of returning fugitives from service or labor who may have escaped from any persons to whom such service or labor is claimed to be due, and any officer who shall be found guilty by a court-martial of violating this article shall be dismissed from the service.

"Sec. 2. *And be it further enacted*, That this act shall take effect from and after its passage."

Also to the ninth and tenth sections of an act entitled "An act to suppress insurrection, to punish treason and rebellion, to seize and confiscate property of rebels, and for other purposes," approved July 17, 1862, and which sections are in the words and figures following:

"Sec. 9. *And be it further enacted*, That all slaves of persons who shall hereafter be engaged in rebellion against the Government of the United States or who shall in any way give aid or comfort thereto, escaping from such persons and taking refuge within the lines of the army; and all slaves captured from such persons or deserted by them, and coming under the control of the Government of the United States; and all slaves of such persons found *on* [or] being within any place occupied by rebel forces and afterwards occupied by the forces of the United States, shall be deemed captives of war, and shall be forever free of their servitude, and not again held as slaves.

"Sec. 10. *And be it further enacted*, That no slave escaping into any State, Territory, or the District of Columbia, from any other State, shall be delivered up, or in any way impeded or hindered of his liberty, except for crime, or some offence against the laws, unless the person claiming said fugitive shall first make oath that the person to whom the labor or service of such fugitive is alleged to be due is his lawful owner, and has not borne arms against the United States in the present rebellion, nor in any way given aid and comfort thereto; and no person engaged in the military or naval service of the United States shall, under any pretence whatever, assume to decide on the validity of the claim of any person to the service or labor of any other person, or surrender up any such person to the claimant, on pain of being dismissed from the service."

And I do hereby enjoin upon and order all persons engaged in the military and naval service of the United States to observe, obey, and enforce, within their respective spheres of service, the act and sections above recited.

And the Executive will in due time recommend that all citizens of the United States who shall have remained loyal thereto throughout the rebellion shall (upon the restoration of the constitutional relation between the United States and their respective States and people, if that relation shall have been suspended or disturbed) be compensated for all losses by acts of the United States, including the loss of slaves.

In witness whereof, I have hereunto set my hand, and caused the seal of the United States to be affixed.

Done at the city of Washington this twenty-second day of September, in the year of our Lord one thousand eight hundred and sixty-two, and of the Independence of the United States the eighty-seventh.

ABRAHAM LINCOLN.

By the President:

William H. Seward, *Secretary of State.*

—

January 1, 1863.

Whereas, on the twenty-second day of September, in the year of our Lord one thousand eight hundred and sixty-two, a proclamation was issued by the President of the United States, containing, among other things, the following, to wit:

"That on the first day of January, in the year of our Lord one thousand eight hundred and sixty-three, all persons held as slaves within any State or designated part of a State, the people whereof shall then be in rebellion against the United States, shall be then, thenceforward, and forever, free; and the Executive Government of the United States, including the military and naval authority thereof, will recognize and maintain the freedom of such persons, and will do no act or acts to repress such persons, or any of them, in any efforts they may make for their actual freedom.

"That the Executive will, on the first day of January aforesaid, by proclamation, designate the States and parts of States, if any, in which the people thereof, respectively, shall then be in rebellion against the United States; and the fact that any State, or the people thereof, shall on that day be in good faith represented in the Congress of the United States, by members chosen thereto at elections wherein a majority of the qualified voters of such States shall have participated, shall, in the absence of strong countervailing testimony, be deemed conclusive evidence that such State, and the people thereof, are not then in rebellion against the United States."

Now, therefore, I, Abraham Lincoln, President of the United States, by virtue of the power in me vested as Commander-in-Chief of the Army and Navy of the United States, in time of actual armed rebellion against the authority and Government of the United States, and as a fit and necessary war measure for suppressing said rebellion, do, on this first day of January, in the year of our Lord one thousand eight hundred and sixty-three, and in accordance with my purpose so to do, publicly proclaimed for the full period of one hundred days from the day first above mentioned, order and designate as the States and parts of States wherein the people thereof, respectively, are this day in rebellion against the United States, the following, to wit:

Arkansas, Texas, Louisiana, (except the parishes of St. Bernard, Plaquemines, Jefferson, St. John, St. Charles, St. James, Ascension, Assumption, Terre Bonne, Lafourche, St. Mary, St. Martin, and Orleans, including the city of New Orleans,) Mississippi, Alabama, Florida, Georgia, South Carolina, North Carolina, and Virginia, (except the forty-eight counties designated as West Virginia, and also the counties of Berkeley, Accomac, Northampton, Elizabeth City, York, Princess Ann, and Norfolk, including the cities of Norfolk and Portsmouth,) and which excepted parts are for the present left precisely as if this proclamation were not issued.

And by virtue of the power and for the purpose aforesaid, I do order and declare that all persons held as slaves within said designated States and parts of States are, and henceforward shall be, free; and that the Executive Government of the United States, including the military and naval authorities thereof, will recognize and maintain the freedom of said persons.

And I hereby enjoin upon the people so declared to be free to abstain from all violence, unless in necessary self-defence; and I recommend to them that, in all cases when allowed, they labor faithfully for reasonable wages.

And I further declare and make known that such persons, of suitable condition, will be received into the armed service of the United States to garrison forts, positions, stations, and other places, and to man vessels of all sorts in said service.

And upon this act, sincerely believed to be an act of justice, warranted by the Constitution upon military necessity, I invoke the considerate judgment of mankind and the gracious favor of Almighty God.

In witness whereof, I have hereunto set my hand and caused the seal of the United States to be affixed.

Done at the city of Washington this first day of January, in the year of our Lord one thousand eight hundred and sixty-three, and of the independence of the United States of America the eighty-seventh.

ABRAHAM LINCOLN.

By the President:

WILLIAM H. SEWARD, *Secretary of State.*

—

VOTE ON THE EMANCIPATION PROCLAMATION.

Third Session, Thirty-Seventh Congress.

IN HOUSE.

1862, December 11—Mr. YEAMAN, of Ky., offered the following resolutions:

Resolved by the House of Representatives, (the Senate concurring,) That the proclamation of the President of the United States, of date the 22d of September, 1862, is not warranted by the Constitution.

Resolved, That the policy of emancipation, as indicated in that proclamation, is not calculated to hasten the restoration of peace, was not well chosen as a war measure, and is an assumption of power dangerous to the rights of citizens and to the perpetuity of a free people.

Which were laid on the table—yeas 95, nays 47, as follows:

YEAS—Messrs. Aldrich, Alley, Arnold, Ashley, Babbitt, Baker, Baxter, Beaman, Bingham, Samuel S. Blair, Blake, Buffinton, Burnham, Campbell, Casey, Chamberlain, Clark, Colfax, Frederick A. Conkling, Roscoe Conkling, Conway, Covode, Cutler, Davis, Dawes, Duell, Dunn, Edgerton, Edwards, Eliot, Ely, Fenton, S. C. Fessenden, Thomas A. D. Fessenden, Franchot, Frank, Gooch, Goodwin, Gurley, *Haight*, Hale, Hickman, Horton, Hutchins, Julian, Kelley, Francis W. Kellogg, William Kellogg, Killinger, Lansing, Leary, *Lehman*, Loomis, Lovejoy, Low, McKnight, McPherson, Mitchell, Moorhead, Anson P. Morrill, Justin S. Morrill, *Noell*, Olin, Patton, Timothy G. Phelps, Pike, Pomeroy, Porter, Potter, Alexander H. Rice, John H. Rice, Riddle, Edward H. Rollins, Sargent, Sedgwick, Shanks, Shellabarger, Sloan, Spaulding, Stevens, Stratton, Train, Trimble, Trowbridge, Vandever, Van Horn, Verree, Walker, Wall, Wallace, Washburne, Albert S. White, Wilson, Windom, Worcester—95.

NAYS—Messrs. *William J. Allen, Ancona, Baily, Biddle*, Clements, *Cobb, Cox, Crisfield, Crittenden, Delaplaine, Dunlap, English, Fouke*, Granger, *Grider, Hall, Harding*, Harrison, *Holman, Knapp, Law, Lazear, Mallory, May*, Maynard, *Menzies, Morris, Noble, Norton, Odell, Pendleton, Price, Robinson, Sheffield, Shiel, Smith, John B. Steele, William G. Steele, Stiles*, Benjamin F. Thomas, *Vallandigham, Voorhees, Wadsworth, Chilton A. White, Wickliffe, Woodruff, Yeaman*—47.

1862, December 15—Mr. S. C. FESSENDEN, of Maine, offered the following resolutions:

Resolved, That the proclamation of the President of the United States, of the date of 22d September, 1862, is warranted by the Constitution.

Resolved, That the policy of emancipation, as indicated in that proclamation, is well adapted to hasten the restoration of peace, was well chosen as a war measure, and is an exercise of power with proper regard for the rights of the States, and the perpetuity of free government.

Which were adopted—yeas 78, nays 52, as follows:

YEAS—Messrs. Aldrich, Alley, Arnold, Babbitt, Baker, Beaman, Bingham, Samuel S. Blair, Blake, Buffinton, Burnham, Chamberlain, Clark, Colfax, Frederick A. Conkling, Roscoe Conkling, Cutler, Dawes, Delano, Duell, Edgerton, Edwards, Eliot, Ely, Fenton, Samuel C. Fessenden, Thomas A. D. Fessenden, Fisher, Franchot, Frank, Gooch, Goodwin, Gurley, *Haight*, Hickman, Hooper, Hutchins, Julian, Kelley, Francis W. Kellogg, William Kellogg, Killinger, Lansing, Loomis, Lovejoy, Low, McPherson, Mitchell, Moorhead, Anson P. Morrill, Justin S. Morrill, *Noell*, Patton, Pike, Pomeroy, Porter, Potter, Alexander H. Rice, John H. Rice, Riddle, Edward H. Rollins, Sargent, Sedgwick, Shellabarger, Sloan, Spaulding, Train, Trowbridge, Van Valkenburgh, Van Wyck, Verree, Walker, Wall, Washburne, Albert S. White, Wilson, Windom, Worcester—78.

NAYS—Messrs. *W. J. Allen, Ancona, Baily, Biddle, Calvert, Cobb, Cox, Cravens, Crisfield, Crittenden, Delaplaine, Dunlap, English, Fouke*, Granger, *Grider, Hall, Harding*, Harrison, *Holman, Kerrigan, Knapp*, Leary, *Mallory*, Maynard, *Menzies, Morris, Noble, Norton, Odell, Pendleton, Perry, Price, Richardson, Robinson, James S. Rollins, Sheffield, Shiel, Smith, John B. Steele, Stiles*, Benjamin F. Thomas, Francis Thomas, *Vallandigham, Wadsworth, Ward*, Whaley, *Chilton A. White, Wickliffe, Woodruff, Wright, Yeaman*—52.

—

First Session, Thirty-Eighth Congress.

IN SENATE.

1864, Feb. 10—Mr. CLARK introduced to the Senate a bill ratifying the emancipation proclamation and giving it the force of statute; which was referred to the Committee on Slavery and Freedmen. (See Reconstruction bill for a vote of the Senate. page 318.)

—

IN HOUSE.

1863, Dec. 14—Mr. ARNOLD introduced this bill:

A bill to aid the President of the United States in carrying into more immediate execution the proclamation of emancipation issued by him on the first day of January, A. D. 1863, prohibiting the holding of certain persons as slaves in all that portion of the United States designated therein.

Whereas the President of the United States, by his proclamation issued on the 1st day of January, in the year 1863, as Commander-in-Chief of the Army thereof, did, as a fit and lawful means of suppressing the rebellion, in accordance with the laws of war and with the dictates of justice and humanity, order, proclaim, and declare that all persons held as slaves within the limits of certain States and parts of States therein designated were, and should thereafter and forever be, free; and that the executive, military, and naval authorities would and should thenceforward recognize and maintain the freedom of all such persons; and whereas by said proclamation and order the President has guarantied to all such persons their freedom, and has pledged the faith and honor of the country that their freedom shall be recognized and *forever maintained*; and whereas it is the right and the duty of Congress to make all laws which may be necessary and proper for carrying into execution all the powers, whether civil or military, vested by the Constitution in the President as Commander-in-Chief of the Army and Navy; and among such military powers is that of making and executing the proclamation aforesaid; and whereas all persons heretofore held as slaves, as aforesaid, within said designated States or parts of States are now of right free, and ought to be hereafter forever unmolested in the enjoyment of that freedom which the Government of the United States is bound to "recognize *and maintain*:"

Now, therefore, for the purpose of carrying into more complete and immediate execution the aforesaid proclamation, and to secure forever the recognition and maintenance of the freedom of all persons designated therein, and thereby to provide more effectually for the suppression of the rebellion, the securing of domestic tranquillity, the maintaining of the common defence, and the preservation of the liberties of the people:

Be it enacted by the Senate and House of Representatives of the United States of America in Congress assembled, That in all States and parts of States designated in said proclamation as in rebellion, the re-enslaving or holding, or attempting to hold, in slavery or in involuntary servitude of any person who shall have been made or declared to be free by said proclamation, or any of their descendants, from and after the date of said proclamation, otherwise than in punishment of crime whereof the accused shall have been duly convicted, is and shall be forever prohibited, any law or regulation of either of such States to the contrary notwithstanding.

Which was referred to the Committee on the Judiciary.

RESOLUTIONS OFFERED.

Second Session, Thirty-Seventh Congress.

IN HOUSE.

1861, December 3—Mr. Shellabarger offered these resolutions:

Whereas the Constitution has wisely withdrawn from Congress the command of the armies of the United States; and, after they have been called forth, organized, and disciplined, under the rules which it is competent for Congress to make, and which it has made for the government of the land and naval forces, has placed that supreme command exclusively in the President of the United States: Therefore,

Resolved, That it is neither within the province of this House, nor would it be wise, to lay down any rules whatever regulating or attempting to control any part of that chief command of our armies in the field, either in the matter as to what "military necessities" do or do not exist as to the treatment or use of slaves within any of the States, nor in any other matter whatever affecting the supreme command of the President.

Resolved, That whilst this House refrains from all attempts to assume any of the functions of the Commander-in-Chief of the Army, and hereby expresses its confidence in the wisdom, prudence, and patriotism of the President, as indicated in the discharge of the most responsible and arduous duties of the present Executive term, and its willingness to continue to him the untrammelled exercise of his powers as the Commander-in-Chief of the Army and Navy, yet the House deems it appropriate to express its earnest sense and conviction that in the prosecution of this war no resort, on the one hand, should be had to a plea of "military necessity" as a cover for any violation of any constitutional right of any citizen of the United States, either in slaves or any other right of the citizen; nor, on the other hand, should any privileges or protections whatever be extended by our armies either to the title in slaves or in any property whatever which is incompatible with the safety of the Government itself or with the success of our arms in suppressing the rebellion; but all individual rights of property, when necessary, should, in the prosecution of the war, be made to yield to the paramount right of the Government to re-establish the authority of the Constitution over all the people and States of the Union.

Which were postponed, and not voted upon.

December 4—Mr. Conway, on leave, introduced the following joint resolution:

Joint resolution in relation to persons claimed as slaves in the States now in rebellion.

Whereas the belligerent character acquired by the States now in rebellion confers upon them a recognized status among nations, in contravention of their Federal status, and arising from incompatible relations, which, though not implying nationality, is, nevertheless, one from which they derive important advantage in making war upon the United States; and whereas the Federal Government is by this fact fully exonerated from respecting, in any manner whatsoever, the constitutional obligations it would otherwise be under to said States: Therefore—

Be it resolved by the Senate and House of Representatives of the United States of America in Congress assembled, That the President be requested not to permit the enforcement of any law or usage under which persons may be claimed as slaves within any of said States into which the authority of the United States may be extended, and that he be requested to declare, by proclamation, all persons so claimed to be free, and to employ them in the service of the United States in any capacity to which they may be suited, and in such numbers as the public service may require.

Resolved, further, That the faith of the nation be pledged to all persons sustaining loss through the operation of this measure who are now and shall remain loyal to the United States.

The resolutions were postponed.

Third Session, Thirty-Seventh Congress.

1863, January 12—Mr. Wilson introduced a joint resolution to approve, ratify, and confirm the proclamation issued by the President, as Commander-in-Chief of the Army and Navy of the United States, dated January 1, 1863.

Mr. Cox moved that it be tabled; which was lost—yeas 50, nays 85. It was then referred to the Committee on the Judiciary.

First Session, Thirty-Eighth Congress.

1863, December 17—Mr. Edgerton offered this resolution:

Whereas the proclamations of the President of January 1, 1863, and December 8, 1863, in relation to emancipation, impose conditions of pardon and amnesty to the persons who have participated in the existing rebellion, as well as conditions precedent to the establishment and recognition of State government in the States to which said proclamations apply, which, in the judgment of a large number of faithful citizens, have a tendency to give to the rebellion "the advantage of a changed issue," and "to reinvigorate the otherwise declining insurrection in the South," and to prolong the war: and whereas this House cannot but regard with anxiety the unprecedented and extraordinary claims and assumption of high prerogative by the President in said proclamations, especially in view of the fact that the President, in his inaugural address of the 4th day of March, 1861, declared, "I have no purpose directly or indirectly to interfere with the institution of slavery in the States where it exists; I believe I have no right to do so, and I have no inclination to do so:" Therefore,

Resolved, As the judgment of this House, that the maintenance inviolate of the constitutional powers of Congress, and the rights of the States, and especially the right of each State to order and control its own domestic institutions according to its own judgment exclusively, is essential to the balance of power on which the perfection and endurance of our political fabric of federal union depends; and we denounce, as among the gravest of crimes, the invasion or occupation, by armed force, of any State, under the pretext or for the purpose of coercing the people thereof to modify or abrogate any of their laws or domestic institutions that are consistent with the Constitution of the United States; and we affirm the principle declared in this resolution to be a law, alike to the President and the people of the United States.

Mr. Grinnell moved to table the resolution; which was agreed to—yeas 90, nays 66, as follows:

Yeas—Messrs. Alley, Allison, Ames, Anderson, Arnold, Ashley, John D. Baldwin, Beaman, Blaine, Blow, Boutwell, Boyd, Brandegee, Broomall, William G. Brown, Ambrose W. Clark, Freeman Clarke, Cobb, Cole, Creswell, Henry Winter Davis, Thomas T. Davis, Dawes, Deming, Dixon, Driggs, Dumont, Eliot, Farnsworth, Fenton, Frank, Garfield, Gooch, Grinnell, Hale, Higby, Hooper, Hotchkiss, Asahel W. Hubbard, John H. Hubbard, Hulburd, Julian, Kasson, Kelley, Francis W. Kellogg, Orlando Kellogg, Loan, Longyear, Lovejoy, Marvin, McBride, McClurg, McIndoe, S. F. Miller, Moorhead, Morrill, Daniel Morris, Amos Myers, Leonard Myers, Norton, Charles O'Neill, Orth, Patterson, Perham, Pike, Pomeroy, Price, William H. Randall, Alexander H. Rice, John H. Rice, Edward H. Rollins, Schenck, Scofield, Shannon, Sloan, Smith, Smithers, Spalding, Stevens, Thayer, Tracy, Van Valkenburgh, Ellihu B. Washburne, William B. Washburn, Whaley, Williams, Wilder, Wilson, Windom, Woodbridge—90.

NAYS—Messrs. *James C. Allen, Ancona, Augustus C. Baldwin, Bliss, Brooks, James S. Brown, Cox, Cravens, Dawson, Denison, Eden, Edgerton, Eldridge, Finck, Ganson, Grider, Griswold, Hall, Harding, Harrington, C. M. Harris, Herrick, Holman, William Johnson, Kernan, King, Knapp, Law, Lazear, LeBlond, Long, Mallory, Marcy, McDowell, McKinney, Middleton, Wm. H. Miller, James R. Morris, Morrison, Nelson, Noble, John O'Neill, Pendleton, Perry, Radford, Samuel J. Randall, Robinson, Rogers, James S. Rollins, Ross, Scott, John B. Steele, Wm. G. Steele, Stiles, Strouse, Stuart, Sweat, Voorhees, Wadsworth, Ward, Wheeler, Chilton A. White, Joseph W. White, Winfield, Fernando Wood, Yeaman*—66.

1864, Jan. 25—Mr. EDGERTON offered the following preamble and resolutions, which were laid over under the rule:

Whereas this House on the 17th day of December last adopted, with but one dissentient vote, the following resolution, to wit: "*Resolved*, That we hold it to be the duty of Congress to pass all necessary bills to supply men and money, and the duty of the people to render every aid in their power to the constituted authorities of the Government in the crushing out of the rebellion, and in bringing the leaders thereof to condign punishment;"

Therefore in explanation of the foregoing resolution, and in further expression of the opinion and purpose of this House,

Resolved, That the aid hitherto liberally supplied in men and money by the people of the United States, to enable the Federal Executive to prosecute the existing civil war, has been so supplied by all citizens truly faithful to the Federal Union and Constitution, for the purpose, and no other, expressed in the resolution adopted by Congress in July, 1861, declarative of the object of the war, and commonly known as "the Crittenden resolution;" and public faith, true Christian humanity, and wise statesmanship alike demand strict adherence by the "constituted authorities of the Government" to the purpose or object of the war, as thus declared by Congress and accepted by the people.

2. That the demand of the President, in his proclamation of December 8, 1863, that the people of the States wherein rebellion exists shall swear to abide by and support his proclamation of emancipation (in other words, change, or submit to the change, at his dictation, of their State constitutions, local laws, and domestic institutions, not inconsistent with the Constitution of the United States) before such States or their people will by him be considered to have ceased to be in rebellion, and entitled to pardon or amnesty, and entitled to their constitutional rights of State government, in harmony with the Government of the United States, is, in the judgment of this House, an oppressive and unconstitutional demand, the tendency and effect of which, if persisted in and enforced by war, will be to substantially change the object and character of the war on the part of the Federal Government, from one to preserve, protect, and defend the Constitution of the United States as the supreme law of the land, to a revolutionary war against the constitutional rights and sovereignty of Federal States, and virtually subversive of the constitutional Government of the United States; and of such a war we now record our disapproval.

3. That in view of the immense power of war demanded by the President and supplied to him by a patriotic people, and hitherto wielded by him according to his own will, with little deference or regard to the opinions and convictions of the very large number, if not majority, of faithful Union citizens in the United States who have doubted or disapproved his policy in the conduct of the war and his extraordinary assumptions of executive power, and in view of the dangers to constitutional liberty and the manifold evils that ever attend civil war, we desire peace, and the replacement under its healthful and benign influence, with the least possible further waste of blood and treasure of the people, of all the relations and functions of constitutional government, State and Federal, now disturbed and endangered; and we therefore deprecate all vindictive and revolutionary measures and policy, military or civil, as tending to divide the Union men of the country, to aggravate the evils and to intensify the animosity of the war and prolong its duration; and we advise, and do cordially invite and pledge our co-operation in negotiations, proposals, and efforts for peace upon the basis of a restoration of the Federal Union under the Constitution as it is, leaving to the free constitutional action of the people the questions of amendments of the Federal Constitution, and leaving also to the people of each State, as their unquestionable right, the right, and its free exercise, to form, regulate, and control their State constitutions, laws, and domestic institutions in their own way, subject only to the Constitution of the United States.

Respecting the Issue of the Proclamation.

THE PRESIDENT AND THE CHICAGO DEPUTATION.

1862, September 13—The President gave an audience to a deputation from all the religious denominations of Chicago, presenting a memorial for the immediate issue of an emancipation proclamation, which was enforced by some remarks by the chairman. The President replied:

The subject presented in the memorial is one upon which I have thought much for weeks past, and I may even say for months. I am approached with the most opposite opinions and advice, and that by religious men, who are equally certain that they represent the Divine will. I am sure that either the one or the other class is mistaken in that belief, and perhaps, in some respect, both. I hope it will not be irreverent for me to say that if it is probable that God would reveal his will to others, on a point so connected with my duty, it might be supposed he would reveal it directly to me; for, unless I am more deceived in myself than I often am, it is my earnest desire to know the will of Providence in this matter. And if I can learn what it is I will do it! These are not, however, the days of miracles, and I suppose it will be granted that I am not to expect a direct revelation. I must study the plain physical facts of the case, as certain what is possible, and learn what appears to be wise and right.

The subject is difficult, and good men do not agree. For instance, the other day four gentlemen of standing and intelligence from New York called as a delegation on business connected with the war; but before leaving two of them earnestly besought me to proclaim general emancipation, upon which the other two at once attacked them. You know also that the last session of Congress had a decided majority of anti-slavery men, yet they could not unite on this policy. And the same is true of the religious people. Why, the rebel soldiers are praying with a great deal more earnestness, I fear, than our own troops, and expecting God to favor their side; for one of our soldiers who had been taken prisoner told Senator Wilson a few days since that he met nothing so discouraging as the evident sincerity of those he was among in their prayers. But we will talk over the merits of the case.

What good would a proclamation of emancipation from me do, especially as we are now situated? I do not want to issue a document that the whole world will see must necessarily be inoperative, like the Pope's bull against the comet! Would my word free the slaves, when I cannot even enforce the Constitution in the rebel States? Is there a single court, or magistrate, or individual that would be influenced by it there? And what reason is there to think it would have any greater effect upon the slaves than the late law of Congress, which I approved, and which offers protection and freedom to the slaves of rebel masters who come within our lines? Yet I cannot learn that that law has caused a single slave to come over to us. And suppose they could be induced by a proclamation of freedom from me to throw themselves upon us, what should we do with them? How can we feed and care for such a multitude? General Butler wrote me a few days since that he was issuing more rations to the slaves who have rushed to him than to all the white troops under his command. They eat, and that is all; though it is true General Butler is feeding the whites also by the thousand; for it nearly amounts to a famine there. If, now, the pressure of the war should call off our forces from New Orleans to defend some other point, what is to prevent the masters from reducing the blacks to slavery again; for I am told that whenever the rebels take any black prisoners, free or slave, they immediately auction them off! They did so with those they took from a boat that was aground in the Tennessee river a few days ago. And then I am very ungenerously attacked for it! For instance, when, after the late battles at and near Bull Run, an expedition went out from Washington under a flag of truce to bury the dead and bring in the wounded, and the rebels seized the blacks who went along to help, and sent them into slavery, Horace Greeley said in his paper that the Government would probably do nothing about it. What could I do?

Now, then, tell me, if you please, what possible result of good would follow the issuing of such a proclamation as you desire? Understand, I raise no objections against it on legal or constitutional grounds, for, as Commander-in-Chief of the Army and Navy, in time of war I suppose I have a right to take any measure which may best subdue the enemy, nor do I urge objections of a moral nature, in view of possible consequences of insurrection and massacre at the South. I view this matter as a practical war measure, to be decided on according to the advantages or disadvantages it may offer to the suppression of the rebellion.

The committee replied to these remarks, and the President responded:

I admit that slavery is at the root of the rebellion, or at least its *sine qua non*. The ambition of politicians may have instigated them to act, but they would have been impotent without slavery as their instrument. I will also concede that emancipation would help us in Europe, and convince them that we are incited by something more than ambition. I grant, further, that it would help somewhat at the North, though not so much, I fear, as you and those you represent imagine. Still, some additional strength would be added in that way to the war, and then, unquestionably, it would weaken the rebels by drawing off their laborers, which is of great importance; but I am not so sure we could do much with the blacks. If we were to arm them, I fear that in a few weeks the arms would be in the hands of the rebels; and, indeed, thus far, we have not had arms enough to equip our white troops. I will mention another thing, though it meet only your scorn and contempt. There are 50,000 bayonets in the Union Army from the border slave States. It would be a serious matter if, in consequence of a proclamation such as you desire, they should go over to the rebels. I do not think they all would—not so many, indeed, as a year ago, or as six months ago—not so many today as yesterday. Every day increases their Union feeling. They are also getting their pride enlisted, and want to beat the rebels. Let me say one thing more: I think you should admit that we already have an important principle to rally and unite the people, in the fact that constitutional government is at stake. This is a fundamental idea going down about as deep as anything.

After further remarks from the committee, the President said:

Do not misunderstand me because I have mentioned these objections. They indicate the difficulties that have thus far prevented my action in some such way as you desire. I have not decided against a proclamation of liberty to the slaves, but hold the matter under advisement. And I can assure you that the subject is on my mind, by day and night, more than any other. Whatever shall appear to be God's will I will do. I trust that in the freedom with which I have canvassed your views I have not in any respect injured your feelings.

REMARKS IN THE HOUSE.

First Session, Thirty-Eighth Congress.

1864, June 25—Mr. BOUTWELL, of Massachusetts: The gentleman from Kentucky [Mr. Mallory] said this morning that the whole policy of the country was changed by the proclamation of the President, and he attributed that proclamation to the meeting of the Governors of certain States at Altoona. I am not here to be put upon the witness stand, but it so happens that I have the means of knowing that the proclamation of September, 1862, was entirely independent of and antecedent to the meeting of the Governors at Altoona. The meeting of the Governors had no connection with the proclamation. The gentleman from Kentucky should remember that prior to the issuing of that proclamation we had met with but few successes, and that we had endured many, many reverses. Lee had battled for four days under the fortifications of the capital, and had finally crossed the Potomac into Maryland. It was not until the country put itself on the side of justice that it had a right to expect the favor of Divine Providence, or any of those successes which have rendered this war glorious in the cause of freedom, truth, and justice.

Mr. MALLORY. Will the gentleman state when that convention of Governors assembled at Altoona?

Mr. BOUTWELL. I think it assembled at Altoona previous to the 22d of September, but I assert as within my own knowledge that the issuing of the proclamation was determined upon previous to the meeting at Altoona.

Mr. MALLORY. Can the gentleman inform me when the issuing of that proclamation was determined upon?

Mr. BOUTWELL. I cannot go far in this matter. I assert distinctly the fact which is within my own knowledge that the President, previous to the meeting of the Governors at Altoona, had decided in a certain contingency, which happened upon the Wednesday preceding the 22d of September, to issue the proclamation, and therefore the inference I draw is in contravention of the declaration of the gentleman from Kentucky that that proclamation was the result of the meeting of the Governors at Altoona.

Mr. MALLORY. Will the gentleman tell us the contingency on the happening of which that proclamation was to be issued?

Mr. BOUTWELL. I said, Mr. Speaker, when I mentioned this fact, that I was not to be put upon the stand as a witness. I have made a statement as of a fact within my own knowledge, and history will confirm the statement.

Mr. MALLORY. If the gentleman from Massachusetts does not wish to answer the question or to state the fact, I will not insist.

ADDRESS OF LOYAL GOVERNORS TO THE PRESIDENT,

Adopted at a meeting of Governors of loyal States, held to take measures for the more active support of the Government, at Altoona, Pennsylvania, on the 22d day of September, 1862.

After nearly one year and a half spent in contest with an armed and gigantic rebellion against the national Government of the United States, the duty and purpose of the loyal States and people continue, and must always remain as they were at its origin—namely, to restore and perpetuate the authority of this Government and the life of the nation. No matter what consequences are involved in our fidelity, this work of restoring the Republic, preserving the institutions of democratic liberty, and justifying the hopes and toils of our fathers shall not fail to be performed.

And we pledge without hesitation, to the President of the United States, the most loyal and cordial support, hereafter as heretofore, in the exercise of the functions of his great office. We recognize in him the Chief Executive Magistrate of the nation, the Commander-in-Chief of the Army and Navy of the United States, their responsible and constitutional head, whose rightful authority and power, as well as the constitutional powers of Congress, must be rigorously and religiously guarded and preserved, as the condition on which alone our form of Government and the constitutional rights and liberties of the people themselves can be saved from the wreck of anarchy or from the gulf of despotism.

In submission to the laws which may have been or which may be duly enacted, and to the lawful orders of the President, co-operating always in our own spheres with the national Government, we mean to continue in the most vigorous exercise of all our lawful and proper powers, contending against treason, rebellion, and the public enemies, and, whether in public life or in private station, supporting the arms of the Union, until its cause shall conquer, until final victory shall perch upon its standard, or the rebel foe shall yield a dutiful, rightful, and unconditional submission.

And, impressed with the conviction that an army of reserve ought, until the war shall end, to be constantly kept on foot, to be raised, armed, equipped, and trained at home, and ready for emergencies, we respectfully ask the President to call for such a force of volunteers for one year's service, of not less than one hundred thousand in the aggregate, the quota of each State to be raised after it shall have filled its quota of the requisitions already made, both for volunteers and militia. We believe that this would be a measure of military prudence, while it would greatly promote the military education of the people.

We hail with heartfelt gratitude and encouraged hope the proclamation of the President, issued on the 22d instant, declaring emancipated from their bondage all persons held to service or labor as slaves in the rebel States, whose rebellion shall last until the first day of January now next ensuing. The right of any person to retain authority to compel any portion of the subjects of the national Government to rebel against it, or to maintain its enemies, implies in those who are allowed possession of such authority the right to rebel themselves; and therefore the right to establish martial law or military government in a State or Territory in rebellion implies the right and the duty of the Government to liberate the minds of all men living therein by appropriate proclamations and assurances of protection, in order that all who are capable, intellectually and morally, of loyalty and obedience, may not be forced into treason as the unwilling tools of rebellious traitors. To have continued indefinitely the most efficient cause, support, and stay of the rebellion, would have been, in our judgment, unjust to the loyal people whose treasure and lives are made a willing sacrifice on the altar of patriotism—would have discriminated against the wife who is compelled to surrender her husband, against the parent who is to surrender his child to the hardships of the camp and the perils of battle, in favor of rebel masters permitted to retain their slaves. It would have been a final decision alike against humanity, justice, the rights and dignity of the Government, and against sound and wise national policy. The decision of the President to strike at the root of the rebellion will lend new vigor to the efforts and new life and hope to the hearts of the people. Cordially tendering to the President our respectful assurances of personal and official confidence, we trust and believe that the policy now inaugurated will be crowned with success, will give speedy and triumphant victories over our enemies, and secure to this nation and this people the blessing and favor of Almighty God. We believe that the blood of the heroes who have already fallen, and those who may yet give their lives to their country, will not have been shed in vain.

The splendid valor of our soldiers, their patient endurance, their manly patriotism, and their devotion to duty, demand from us and from all their countrymen the homage of the sincerest gratitude and the pledge of our constant reinforcement and support. A just regard for these brave men, whom we have contributed to place in the field, and for the importance of the duties which may lawfully pertain to us hereafter, has called us into friendly conference. And now, presenting to our national Chief Magistrate this conclusion of our deliberations, we devote ourselves to our country's service, and we will surround the President with our constant support, trusting that the fidelity and zeal of the loyal States and people will always assure him that he will be constantly maintained in pursuing with the utmost vigor this war for the preservation of the national life and the hope of humanity.

A. G. CURTIN,
JOHN A. ANDREW,
RICHARD YATES,
ISRAEL WASHBURNE, Jr.,
EDWARD SOLOMON,
SAMUEL J. KIRKWOOD,
O. P. MORTON,
By D. G. Rose, his representative,
WM. SPRAGUE.
F. H. PEIRPOINT,
DAVID TOD,
N. S. BERRY,
AUSTIN BLAIR.

—

LETTER FROM CHARLES SUMNER.

Senate Chamber, *June* 5, 1862.

My Dear Sir: Your criticism of the President is hasty. I am confident that, if you knew him as I do, you would not make it.

Of course, the President cannot be held responsible for the misfeasances of subordinates, unless adopted or at least tolerated by him. And I am sure that nothing unjust or ungenerous will be tolerated, much less adopted, by him.

I am happy to let you know that he has no sympathy with Stanly in his absurd wickedness, closing the schools, nor again in his other act of turning our camp into a hunting ground for slaves. He repudiates both—positively. The latter point has occupied much of his thought; and the newspapers have not gone too far in recording his repeated declarations, which I have often heard from his own lips, that slaves finding their way into the national lines are never to be re-enslaved. This is his conviction, expressed without reserve.

Could you have seen the President—as it was my privilege often—while he was considering the great questions on which he has already acted—the invitation to emancipation in the States, emancipation in the District of Columbia, and the acknowledgment of the independence of Hayti and Liberia—even your zeal would have been satisfied, for you would have felt the sincerity of his purpose to do what he could to carry forward the principles of the Declaration of Independence. His whole soul was occupied, especially by the first proposition, which was peculiarly his own. In familiar intercourse with him, I remember nothing more touching than the earnestness and completeness with which he embraced this idea. To his mind, it was just and beneficent while it promised the sure end of slavery. Of course, to me who had already proposed a bridge of gold for the retreating fiend, it was most welcome. Proceeding from the President, it must take its place among the great events of history.

If you are disposed to be impatient at any seeming short-comings, think, I pray you, of what has been done in a brief period, and from the past discern the sure promise of the future. Knowing something of my convictions and of the ardor with which I maintain them, you may, perhaps, derive some assurance from my confidence. I may say to you, therefore, stand by the Administration. If need be, help it by word and act, but stand by it and have faith in it.

I wish that you really knew the President, and had heard the artless expression of his convictions on those questions which concern you so deeply. You might, perhaps, wish that he were less cautious, but you would be grateful that he is so true to all that you have at heart. Believe me, therefore, you are wrong, and I regret it the more because of my desire to see all our friends stand firmly together.

If I write strongly it is because I feel strongly; for my constant and intimate intercourse with the President, beginning with the 4th of March, not only binds me peculiarly to his Administration, but gives me a personal as well as a political interest in seeing that justice is done him.

Believe me, my dear sir, with much regard, ever faithfully yours, CHARLES SUMNER.

—

LETTER FROM OWEN LOVEJOY.

The *Boston Liberator* publishes a letter from the late Owen Lovejoy, addressed to William Lloyd Garrison, under the date of Washington, February 22, 1864. In this letter Mr. Lovejoy says:

"I write you, although ill-health compels me to do it by the hand of another, to express to you my gratification at the position you have taken in reference to Mr. Lincoln. I am satisfied, as the old theologians used to say in regard to the world, that if he is not the best conceivable President, he is the best possible. I have known something of the facts inside during his Administration, and I know that he has been just as radical as any of his Cabinet. And although he does not do everything that you or I would like, the question recurs, whether it is likely we can elect a man who would. It is evident that the great mass of Unionists prefer him for re-election; and it seems to me certain that the providence of God, during another term, will grind slavery to powder. I believe now that the President is up with the average of the House.

"Recurring to the President, there are a great many reports concerning him which seem to be reliable and authentic, which, after all, are not so. It was currently reported among the anti-slavery men of Illinois that the emancipation proclamation was extorted from him by the outward pressure, and particularly by the delegation from the Christian Convention that met at Chicago. Now, the fact is this, as I had it from his own lips: He had written the proclamation in the summer, as early as June, I think—but will not be certain as to the precise time—and called his Cabinet together, and informed them he had written it, and meant to make it, but wanted to read it to them for any criticism or remarks as to its features or details. After having done so, Mr. Seward suggested whether it would not be well for him to withhold its publication until after we had gained some substantial advantage in the field, as at that time we had met with many reverses, and it might be considered a cry of despair. He told me he thought the suggestion a wise one, and so held on the proclamation until after the battle of Antietam.

"I mention this as a sample of a great many others."

REPEAL OF THE FUGITIVE SLAVE LAWS,

"CONTRABANDS," AND KINDRED SUBJECTS.

The act of 1793 was passed by the following vote:

IN SENATE.

January 18, 1793—Without a call of the yeas and nays.

IN HOUSE.

February 5, 1793—Yeas 48, nays 7, as follows:

YEAS—Messrs. Fisher Ames, John Baptist Ashe, Abraham Baldwin, Robert Barnwell, Egbert Benson, Elias Boudinot, Shearjashub Bourne, Benjamin Bourne, Abraham Clark, Jonathan Dayton, William Findley, Thomas Fitzsimons, Elbridge Gerry, Nicholas Gilman, Benjamin Goodhue, James Gordon, Christopher Greenup, Andrew Gregg, Samuel Griffin, William Barry Grove, Thomas Hartley, James Hillhouse, William Hindman, Daniel Huger, Israel Jacobs, Philip Key, Aaron Kitchell, Amasa Learned, Richard Bland Lee, George Leonard, Nathaniel Macon, Andrew Moore, Frederick Augustus Muhlenberg, William Vans Murray, Alexander D. Orr, John Page, Cornelius C. Schoonmaker, Theodore Sedgwick, Peter Silvester, Israel Smith, William Smith, John Steele, Thomas Sumpter, Thomas Tudor Tucker, Jeremiah Wadsworth, Alexander White, Hugh Williamson, Francis Willis—48.

NAYS—Samuel Livermore, John Francis Mercer, Nathaniel Niles, Josiah Parker, Jonathan Sturges, George Thatcher, Thomas Tredwell—7.

GEORGE WASHINGTON, President, approved it February 12, 1793.

The act of 1850 was passed by the following vote:

IN SENATE.

August 23, 1850—yeas 27, nays 12, as follows:

YEAS—Messrs. Atchison, Badger, Barnwell, Bell, Berrien, Butler, Davis of Mississippi, Dawson, Dodge of Iowa, Downs, Foote, Houston, Hunter, Jones, King, Mangum, Mason, Pearce, Rusk, Sebastian, Soulé, Spruance, Sturgeon, Turney, Underwood, Wales, Yulee—27.

NAYS—Messrs. Baldwin, Bradbury, Chase, Cooper, Davis of Massachusetts, Dayton, Dodge of Wisconsin, Greene, Smith, Upham, Walker, Winthrop—12.

IN HOUSE.

September 12, 1850—yeas 109, nays 76, as follows:

YEAS—Messrs. Nathaniel Albertson, William J. Alston, Josiah M. Anderson, William S. Ashe, Thomas H. Averett, William V. N. Bay, Thomas H. Bayly, James M. H. Beale, William H. Bissell, Franklin W. Bowdon, Richard I. Bowie, James B. Bowlin, Lynn Boyd, Daniel Breck, Albert G. Brown, William J. Brown, Alexander W. Buel, Armistead Burt, George Alfred Caldwell, Joseph P. Caldwell, Thomas L. Clingman, Williamson R. W. Cobb, William F. Colcock, John R. J. Daniel, Edmund Deberry, Milo M. Dimmick, Cyrus L. Dunham, Henry A. Edmundson, Samuel A. Eliot, Andrew Ewing, Winfield S. Featherston, Thomas J. D. Fuller, Meredith P. Gentry, Elbridge Gerry, Edward Gilbert, Willis A. Gorman, James S. Green, Willard P. Hall, William T. Hamilton, Hugh A. Haralson, Isham G. Harris, S. W. Harris, Thomas L. Harris, Thomas S. Haymond, Harry Hibbard, Henry W. Hilliard, Moses Hoagland, Alexander R. Holladay, Isaac E. Holmes, John W. Houston, Volney E. Howard, David Hubbard, Samuel W. Inge, Joseph W. Jackson, Andrew Johnson, James L. Johnson, Robert W. Johnson, George W. Jones, David S. Kaufman, John B. Kerr, Emile LaSère, Shepperd Leffler, Nathaniel S. Littlefield, Job Mann, Humphrey Marshall, John C. Mason, John A. McClernand, Joseph E. McDonald, Edward W. McGaughey, James X. McLanahan, Finis E. McLean, Fayette McMullen, John McQueen, William McWillie, Richard K. Meade, John K. Miller, John S. Millson, Jeremiah Morton, James L. Orr, David Outlaw, Allen F. Owen, Richard Parker, Charles H. Peaslee, John S. Phelps, Paulus Powell, William A. Richardson, John Robbins, jr., Thomas Ross, John H. Savage, James A. Seddon, Augustine H. Shepperd, Edward Stanly, Frederick P. Stanton, Richard H. Stanton, John L. Taylor, James H. Thomas, Jacob Thompson, James Thompson, John B. Thompson, Robert Toombs, Abraham W. Venable, Hiram Walden, Daniel Wallace, Albert G. Watkins, Marshall J. Wellborn, Isaac Wildrick, Christopher H. Williams, Joseph A. Woodward, Timothy R. Young—109.

NAYS—Henry P. Alexander, Charles Allen, Edward D. Baker, Henry Bennett, Kinsley S. Bingham, Walter Booth, George Briggs, Lorenzo Burrows, Thomas B. Butler, Joseph Cable, Samuel Calvin, Lewis D. Campbell, David K. Cartter, Joseph R. Chandler, Charles E. Clarke, Orsamus Cole, Moses B. Corwin, John Crowell, Jesse C. Dickey, David T. Disney, Nathan F. Dixon, James Duane Doty, James H. Duncan, Charles Durkee, Nathan Evans, Graham N. Fitch, Orin Fowler, John Freedly, Joshua R. Giddings, Daniel Gott, Herman D. Gould, Ransom Halloway, Moses Hampton, Andrew J. Harlan, Andrew K. Hay, William Hebard, William Henry, John W. Howe, William F. Hunter, William T. Jackson, George W. Julian, George G. King, James G. King, John A. King, Preston King, Horace Mann, Orsamus B. Matteson, Thomas McKissock, James Meacham, Henry D. Moore, Jonathan D. Morris, William Nelson, John Otis, Charles W. Pitman, Harvey Putnam, Robert R. Reed, John L. Robinson, Joseph M. Root, David Rumsey, jr., William A. Sackett, Cullen Sawtelle, Ab'm M. Schermerhorn, John L. Schoolcraft, Peter H. Silvester, William Sprague, Thaddeus Stevens, Charles Stetson, John R. Thurman, Amos Tuck, Walter Underhill, Samuel F. Vinton, Loren P. Waldo, John Wentworth, William A. Whittlesey, Amos E. Wood, George W. Wright—76.

MILLARD FILLMORE, *President*, approved it, September 18, 1850.

—

MOVEMENTS FOR ITS REPEAL.

First Session, Thirty-Second Congress.

IN SENATE.

1852, Aug 26—The civil and diplomatic bill pending,

Mr. SUMNER offered an amendment to add to a section appropriating money to pay ministerial officers of the United States extraordinary expenses incurred, this proviso:

That no such allowance shall be authorized for any expenses incurred in executing the act of September 18, 1850, for the surrender of fugitives from service or labor; which said act is hereby repealed.

Which was rejected—yeas 4, nays 47, as follows:

YEAS—Messrs. Chase of Ohio, Hale of N. H., Sumner of Mass., Wade of Ohio—4.

NAYS—Messrs. Adams of Miss., Badger of N. C., Bayard of Del., Bell of Tenn., Borland of Ark., Bradbury of Maine, Bright of Ind., Brodhead of Penn., Brooke of Miss., Butler of S. C., Cass of Mich., Charlton of Geo., Clark of R. I., Clemens of Ala., Cooper of Penn., Dawson of Geo., DeSaussure of S. C., Dodge of Iowa, Douglass of Ill., Fitch of Mich., Fish of N. Y., Geyer of Mo., Gwin of Cal., Hamlin of Maine, Houston of Texas, Hunter of Va., James of R. I., Jones of Iowa, King of Ala., Mallory of Florida, Mangum of N. C., Mason of Va., Meriwether of Ky., Miller of N. J., Morton of Fla., Pearce of Md., Pratt of Md., Rusk of Texas, Shields of Ill., Smith of Conn., Soule of La., Spruance of Del., Toucey of Conn., Underwood of Ky., Upham of Vt., Walker of Wis., Weller of Cal.—47.

—

First Session, Thirty-Third Congress.

IN HOUSE.

1854, July 28—Mr. THOMAS D. ELIOT, of Massachusetts, asked leave to introduce a bill to repeal the fugitive slave law. Mr. BRIDGES, of Pennsylvania, objected.

Mr. ELIOT moved to suspend the rules for that purpose; which was rejected—yeas 45, nays 120, as follows:

YEAS—Messrs. Edward Ball, Henry Burnett, Samuel P. Benson, L. D. Campbell, David Carpenter, Moses B. Corwin, Samuel L. Crocker, Thomas Davis, Alexander DeWitt, John Dick, Edward Dickinson, Ben. C. Eastman, J. Wiley Edmands, Thomas D. Eliot, William Everhart, Joshua R. Giddings, John Z. Goodrich, Aaron Harlan, Thomas M. Howe, Daniel T. Jones, James Knox, O. B. Matteson, Samuel Mayall, Edwin B. Morgan, Jesse O. Norton, Samuel W. Parker, Alexander C. M. Pennington, Benjamin Pringle, David Ritchie, Samuel L. Russell, Alvah Sabin, Russell Sage, William R. Sapp, George A. Simmons, Gerrit Smith, Andrew Stuart, Benjamin B. Thruston, M. C. Trout, C. W. Upham, Edward Wade, Samuel H. Walley, Ellihu B. Washburne, Israel Washburn, jr., Daniel Wells, jr., Tappan Wentworth—45.

NAYS—William Aiken, James C. Allen, Willis Allen, William S. Ashe, D. J. Bailey, W. S. Barry, T. H. Benton, T. S. Bocock, W. W. Boyce, J. C. Breckinridge, S. A. Bridges, P. S. Brooks, S. Caruthers, E. M. Chamberlain, E. S. Chastain, J. S. Chrisman, W. M. Churchwell, S. Clark, T. L. Clingman, W. R. W. Cobb, J. P. Cook, L. M. Cox, B. Craige, C. B. Curtis, J. G. Davis, J. L. Dawson, D. T. Disney, J. F. Dowdell, A. Drum, W. Dunbar, N. Eddy, A. P. Edgerton, H. A. Edmundson, J. M. Elliott, A. Ellison, W. H. English, E. W. Farley, C. J. Faulkner, T. B. Florence, T. J. D. Fuller, W. O. Goode, A. B. Greenwood, G. A. Grow, S. W. Harris, W. P. Harris, J. S. Harrison, S. G. Haven, T. A. Hendricks, B. Henn, H. Hibbard, C. S. Hill, G. S. Houston, T. G. Hunt, H. H. Johnson, G. W. Jones, R. Jones, L. M. Keitt, J. Kerr, Z. Kidwell, G. W. Kettridge, W. H. Kurtz, A. W. Lamb, M. S. Latham, J. Letcher, J. J. Lindley, F. McMullen, J. McNair, J. McQueen, J. B. Macy, J. Maurice, A. E. Maxwell, J. G. Miller, S. Miller, J. S. Millson, G. W. Morrison, W. Murray, M. H. Nichols, D. A. Noble, E. B. Olds, A. Oliver, J. L. Orr, R. W. Peckham, J. S. Phelps, P. Phillips, J. T. Pratt, W. Preston, R. C. Puryear, D. A. Reese, G. R. Riddle, J. Robbins, jr., S. H. Rogers, T. Ruffin, J. L. Seward, W. Shannon, H. M. Shaw, J. Shower, C. Skelton, S. A. Smith, W. R. Smith, G. W. Smyth, A. R. Sollers, F. P. Stanton, R. H. Stanton, A. H. Stephens, H. L. Stevens, N. T. Stratton, C. M. Straub, D. Stuart, F. J. Taylor, J. L. Taylor, N. G. Taylor, G. Vail, J. Vansant, H. Walbridge, W. A. Walker, J. Wheeler, W. H. Witte, D. B. Wright, H. B. Wright, F. K. Zollicoffer—120.

—

Second Session, Thirty-Seventh Congress.*

IN SENATE.

1861, December 26—Mr. HOWE, of Wisconsin, introduced a bill to repeal the fugitive slave law; which was referred to the Committee on the Judiciary.

1862, May 24—Mr. WILSON, of Massachusetts, introduced a bill to amend the fugitive slave law; which was ordered to be printed and lie on the table.

June 10—Mr. WILSON moved to take up the bill; which was agreed to—yeas 25, nays 10, as follows:

YEAS—Messrs. Anthony, Browning, Chandler, Clark, Cowan, Dixon, Doolittle, Fessenden, Foot, Grimes, Hale, Harlan, Harris, Howard, Howe, King, Lane of Kansas, Morrill, Pomeroy, Simmons, Sumner, Ten Eyck, Trumbull, Wade, Wilson of Massachusetts—25.

NAYS—Messrs. *Carlile, Davis, Latham, McDougall, Nesmith, Powell, Saulsbury, Stark,* Willey, *Wright*—10.

The bill was to secure to claimed fugitives a right to a jury trial in the district court for the United States for the district in which they may be, and to require the claimant to prove his loyalty. The bill repeals sections 6, 7, 8, 9, and 10 of the act of 1850, and that part of section 5, which authorizes the summoning of the *posse comitatus*. When a warrant of return is made either on jury trial or confession of the party in the presence of counsel, having been warned of his rights, the fugitive is to be surrendered to the claimant, or the marshal where necessary, who shall remove him to the boundary line of the district, and there deliver him to the claimant. The bill was not further considered.

IN HOUSE.

1861, December 20—Mr. JULIAN offered this resolution:

Resolved, That the Judiciary Committee be instructed to report a bill, so amending the fugitive slave law enacted in 1850 as to forbid the recapture or return of any fugitive from labor without satisfactory proof first made that the claimant of such fugitive is loyal to the Government.

Mr. HOLMAN moved to table the resolution, which was disagreed to—yeas 39, nays 78, as follows:

YEAS—Messrs. *Ancona, Joseph Baily, Biddle, George H. Browne, Cobb, Cooper, Cox, Cravens, Crittenden, Dunlap, English, Fouke, Grider, Harding, Holman, Johnson, Law, Lazear,* Leary, *Lehman, Mallory, Morris, Noble, Noell, Norton, Nugen, Odell, Pendleton, Robinson, Shiel, John B. Steele, William G. Steele, Vallandigham, Wadsworth,* Webster, *Chilton A. White, Wickliffe, Woodruff, Wright*—39.

NAYS—Messrs. Aldrich, Alley, Arnold, Babbitt, Baker, Baxter, Beaman, Bingham, Francis P. Blair, Samuel S. Blair, Blake, Buffinton, Burnhan, Chamberlain, Clark, Colfax, Frederick A. Conkling, Roscoe Conkling, Cutler, Davis, Dawes, Delano, Duell, Edwards, Eliot, Fessenden, Franchot, Frank, Gooch, Goodwin, Gurley, Hale, Hanchett, Harrison, Hooper, Hutchins, Julian, William Kellogg, Lansing, Loomis, Lovejoy, McKnight, McPherson, Marston, Mitchell, Moorhead, Anson P. Morrill, Justin S. Morrill, Olin, Patton, Pike, Pomeroy, Porter, Potter, John H. Rice, Riddle, Edward H. Rollins, Sargent, Sedgwick, Shanks, Shellabarger, Sherman, Sloan, Spaulding, Stevens, Benjamin F. Thomas, Train, Vandever, Wall, Wallace, E. P. Walton, Washburne, Wheeler, Whaley, Albert S. White, Wilson, Windom, Worcester—78.

---

* On the 23d of July, 1861, the Attorney General, in answer to a letter from the United States marshal of Kansas, inquiring whether he should assist in the execution of the fugitive slave law, wrote:

ATTORNEY GENERAL'S OFFICE, *July* 23, 1861.

J L. MCDOWELL, *U. S. Marshal, Kansas*:

Your letter of the 11th of July, received 19th, (under frank of Senator Lane, of Kansas,) asks advice whether you should give your official services in the execution of the fugitive slave law.

It is the President's constitutional duty to "take care that the laws be faithfully executed." That means all the laws. He has no right to discriminate, no right to execute the laws he likes, and leave unexecuted those he dislikes And of course you and I, his subordinates, can have no wider latitude of discretion than he has. Missouri is a State in the Union. The insurrectionary disorders in Missouri are but individual crimes, and do not change the legal status of the State, nor change its rights and obligations as a member of the Union

A refusal by a ministerial officer to execute any law which properly belongs to his office, is an official misdemeanor, of which I have no doubt the President would take notice.

Very respectfully, EDWARD BATES.

The resolution was then adopted—yeas 78, nays 39.

1862, June 9—Mr. Julian, of Indiana, introduced into the House a resolution instructing the Judiciary Committee to report a bill for the purpose of repealing the fugitive slave law; which was tabled—yeas 66, nays 51, as follows:

Yeas—Messrs. *William J. Allen*, *Ancona*, *Baily*, *Biddle*, Francis P. Blair, Jacob B. Blair, *George H. Browne*, William G. Brown, Burnham, *Calvert*, Casey, Clements, *Cobb*, *Corning*, *Crittenden*, Delano, Diven, Granger, *Grider*, *Haight*, Hale, *Harding*, *Holman*, *Johnson*, William Kellogg, *Kerrigan*, *Knapp*, *Lazear*, Low, Maynard, *Menzies*, Moorhead, *Morris*, *Noble*, *Noell*, *Norton*, *Odell*, *Pendleton*, *John S. Phelps*, Timothy G. Phelps, Porter, *Richardson*, *Robinson*, *James S. Rollins*, Sargent, Segar, *Sheffield*, *Shiel*, *Smith*, *John B. Steele*, *William G. Steele*, Benjamin F. Thomas, Francis Thomas, Trimble, *Vallandigham*, Verree, *Vibbard*, *Voorhees*, *Wadsworth*, Webster, *Chilton A. White*, *Wickliffe*, *Wood*, *Woodruff*, Worcester, *Wright*—66.

Nays—Messrs. Aldrich, Alley, Baker, Baxter, Beaman, Bingham, Blake, Buffinton, Chamberlain, Colfax, Frederick A. Conkling, Davis, Dawes, Edgerton, Edwards, Eliot, Ely, Franchot, Gooch, Goodwin, Hanchett, Hutchins, Julian, Kelley, Francis W. Kellogg, Lansing, Lovejoy, McKnight, McPherson, Mitchell, Anson P. Morrill, Pike, Pomeroy, Potter, Alexander H. Rice, John H. Rice, Riddle, Edward H. Rollins, Shellabarger, Sloan, Spaulding, Stevens, Train, Trowbridge, Van Horn, Van Valkenburgh, Wall, Wallace, Washburne, Albert S. White, Windom—51.

Same day—Mr. Colfax, of Indiana, offered this resolution:

Resolved, That the Committee on the Judiciary be instructed to report a bill modifying the fugitive slave law so as to require a jury trial in all cases where the person claimed denies under oath that he is a slave, and also requiring any claimant under such act to prove that he has been loyal to the Government during the present rebellion.

Which was agreed to—yeas 77, nays 43, as follows:

Yeas—Messrs. Aldrich, Alley, Arnold, Ashley, Babbitt, Baker, Baxter, Beaman, Bingham, Francis P. Blair, Blake, Buffinton, Burnham, Chamberlain, Colfax, Frederick A. Conkling, Davis, Dawes, Delano, Diven, Edgerton, Edwards, Eliot, Ely, Franchot, Gooch, Goodwin, Granger, Gurley, *Haight*, Hale, Hanchett, Hutchins, Julian, Kelley, Francis W. Kellogg, William Kellogg, Lansing, Loomis, Lovejoy, Low, McKnight, McPherson, Mitchell, Anson P. Morrill, Justin S. Morrill, Nixon, Timothy G. Phelps, Pike, Pomeroy, Porter, Potter, Alexander H. Rice, John H. Rice, Riddle, Edward H. Rollins, Sargent, Shanks, *Sheffield*, Shellabarger, Sloan, Spaulding, Stevens, Stratton, Benjamin F. Thomas, Train, Trimble, Trowbridge, Van Valkenburgh, Verree, Wall, Wallace, Washburne, Albert S. White, Wilson, Windom, Worcester—77.

Nays—Messrs. *William J. Allen*, *Ancona*, *Baily*, *Biddle*, Jacob B. Blair, William G. Brown, *Calvert*, Casey, Clements, *Cobb*, *Corning*, *Crittenden*, *Fouke*, *Grider*, *Harding*, *Holman*, *Johnson*, *Knapp*, Maynard, *Menzies*, *Noble*, *Noell*, *Norton*, *Pendleton*, *John S. Phelps*, *Richardson*, *Robinson*, *James S. Rollins*, Segar, *Shiel*, *Smith*, *John B. Steele*, *William G. Steele*, Francis Thomas, *Vallandigham*, *Vibbard*, *Voorhees*, *Wadsworth*, Webster, *Chilton A. White*, *Wickliffe*, *Wood*, *Wright*—43.

—

Third Session, Thirty-Seventh Congress.

IN SENATE.

1863, February 11—Mr. Ten Eyck, from the Committee on the Judiciary, to whom was referred a bill, introduced by Senator Howe, in second session, December 26, 1861, to repeal the fugitive slave act of 1850, reported it back without amendment, and with a recommendation that it do not pass.

—

First Session, Thirty-Eighth Congress.

IN HOUSE.

1863, Dec. 14—Mr. Julian, of Indiana, offered this resolution:

Resolved, That the Committee on the Judiciary be instructed to report a bill for the repeal of the third and fourth sections of the "act respecting fugitives from justice and persons escaping from the service of their masters," approved February 12, 1793, and the act to amend and supplementary to the aforesaid act, approved September 18, 1850.

Mr. Holman moved that the resolution lie upon the table, which was agreed to—yeas 81, nays 73, as follows:

Yeas—Messrs. *James C. Allen*, *William J. Allen*, *Ancona*, Anderson, *Baily*, *Augustus C. Baldwin*, Jacob B. Blair, *Bliss*, *Brooks*, *James S. Brown*, William G. Brown, *Clay*, Cobb, *Coffroth*, *Cox*, *Cravens*, Creswell, *Dawson*, Deming, *Denison*, *Eden*, *Edgerton*, *Eldridge*, *English*, *Finck*, *Ganson*, *Grider*, *Griswold*, *Hall*, *Harding*, *Harrington*, *Benjamin G. Harris*, *Charles M. Harris*, Higby, *Holman*, *Hutchins*, *William Johnson*, *Kernan*, *King*, *Knapp*, *Law*, *Lazear*, *Le Blond*, *Long*, *Mallory*, *Marcy*, Marvin, McBride, *McDowell*, *McKinney*, *William H. Miller*, *James R. Morris*, *Morrison*, *Nelson*, *Noble*, *Odell*, *John O'Neill*, *Pendleton*, William H. Randall, *Robinson*, *Rogers*, *James S. Rollins*, *Ross*, *Scott*, Smith, Smithers, *Stebbins*, *John B. Steele*, *Stuart*, *Sweat*, Thomas, *Voorhees*, *Wadsworth*, *Ward*, *Wheeler*, *Chilton A. White*, *Joseph W. White*, Williams, *Winfield*, *Fernando Wood*, *Yeaman*—81.

Nays—Messrs. Alley, Allison, Ames, Arnold, Ashley, John D. Baldwin, Baxter, Beaman, Blaine, Blow, Boutwell, Boyd, Brandegee, Broomall, Ambrose W. Clark, Freeman Clarke, Cole, Henry Winter Davis, Dawes, Dixon, Donnelly, Driggs, Dumont, Eckley, Eliot, Farnsworth, Fenton, Frank, Garfield, Gooch, Grinnell, Hooper, Hotchkiss, Asahel W. Hubbard, John H. Hubbard, Hulburd, Jenckes, Julian, Francis W. Kellogg, Orlando Kellogg, Loan, Longyear, Lovejoy, McClurg, McIndoe, Samuel F. Miller, Moorhead, Morrill, Amos Myers, Leonard Myers, Norton, Charles O'Neill, Orth, Patterson, Pike, Pomeroy, Price, Alexander H. Rice, John H. Rice, Edward H. Rollins, Schenck, Scofield, Shannon, Spalding, Thayer, Van Valkenburgh, Ellihu B. Washburne, William B. Washburn, Whaley, Wilder, Wilson, Windom, Woodbridge—73.

1864, June 6—Mr. Hubbard, of Connecticut, offered this resolution:

Resolved, That the Committee on the Judiciary be instructed to report to this House a bill for the repeal of all acts and parts of acts which provide for the rendition of fugitive slaves, and that they have leave to make such report at any time.

Which went over under the rule. May 30, he had made an ineffectual effort to offer it, Mr. Holman objecting.

REPEALING BILLS.

1864, April 19—The Senate considered the bill to repeal all acts for the rendition of fugitives from service or labor. The bill was taken up—yeas 26, nays 10.

Mr. Sherman moved to amend by inserting these words at the end of the bill:

Except the act approved February 12, 1793, entitled "An act respecting fugitives from justice, and persons escaping from the service of their masters."

Which was agreed to—yeas 24, nays 17, as follows:

Yeas—Messrs. *Buckalew*, *Carlile*, Collamer, Cowan, *Davis*, Dixon, Doolittle, Foster, Harris, Henderson, *Hendricks*, Howe, Johnson, Lane of Indiana, *McDougall*, *Nesmith*, *Powell*, *Riddle*, *Saulsbury*, Sherman, Ten Eyck, Trumbull, Van Winkle, Willey—24.

Nays—Messrs. Anthony, Brown, Clark, Conness, Fessenden, Grimes, Hale, Howard, Lane of Kansas, Morgan, Morrill, Pomeroy, Ramsey, Sprague, Sumner, Wilkinson, Wilson—17.

Mr. Saulsbury moved to add these sections:

And be it further enacted, That no white inhabitant of the United States shall be arrested, or imprisoned, or held to answer for a capital or otherwise infamous crime, except in cases arising in the land or naval forces, or in the militia when in actual service in time of war or public danger, without due process of law.

And be it further enacted, That no person engaged in the executive, legislative, or judicial departments of the Government of the United States, or holding any office or trust recognized in the Constitution of the United States, and no person in military or naval service of the United States, shall, without due process of law, arrest or imprison any white inhabitant of the United States who is not, or has not been, or shall not at the time of such arrest or imprisonment be, engaged in levying war against the United States, or in adhering to the enemies of the United States, giving them aid and comfort, nor aid, abet, procure, or advise the same, except in cases arising in the land or naval forces, or in the militia when in actual service in time of war or public danger. And any person as aforesaid so arresting, or imprisoning, or holding, as aforesaid, as in this and the second section of this act mentioned, or aiding, abetting, or procuring, or advising the same, shall be deemed guilty of felony, and, upon conviction thereof in any court of competent jurisdiction, shall be imprisoned for a term of not less than one nor more than five years, shall pay a fine of not less than $1,000 nor more than $5,000, and shall be forever incapable of holding any office or public trust under the Government of the United States.

Mr. HALE moved to strike out the word "white" wherever it occurs; which was agreed to.

The amendment of Mr. SAULSBURY, as amended, was then disagreed to—yeas 9, nays 27, as follows:

YEAS—Messrs. *Buckalew*, *Carlile*, Cowan, *Davis*, *Hendricks*, *McDougall*, *Powell*, *Riddle*, *Saulsbury*—9.

NAYS—Messrs. Anthony, Clark, Collamer, Conness, Doolittle, Fessenden, Foster, Grimes, Hale, Harris, Howard, Howe, Lane of Indiana, Lane of Kansas, Morgan, Morrill, Pomeroy, Ramsey, Sherman, Sprague, Sumner, Ten Eyck, Trumbull, Van Winkle, Wilkinson, Willey, Wilson—27.

Mr. CONNESS moved to table the bill; which was disagreed to—yeas 9, (Messrs. *Buckalew*, *Carlile*, Conness, *Davis*, *Hendricks*, *Nesmith*, *Powell*, *Riddle*, *Saulsbury*,) nays 31.

It was not again acted upon.

1864, June 13—The House passed this bill, reported from the Committee on the Judiciary by Mr. MORRIS, of New York, as follows:

Be it enacted, &c., That sections three and four of an act entitled "An act respecting fugitives from justice and persons escaping from the service of their masters," passed February 12, 1793, and an act entitled "An act to amend, and supplementary to, the act entitled 'An act respecting fugitives from justice, and persons escaping from their masters,' passed February 12, 1793," passed September 18, 1850, be, and the same are hereby, repealed.

Yeas 90, nays 62, as follows:

YEAS—Messrs. Alley, Allison, Ames, Arnold, Ashley John D. Baldwin, Baxter, Beaman, Blaine, Blair, Blow Boutwell, Boyd, Brandegee, Broomall, Ambrose W. Clark, Freeman Clarke, Cobb, Cole, Creswell, Henry Winter Davis, Thomas T. Davis, Dawes, Deming, Dixon, Donnelly, Driggs, Eckley, Eliot, Farnsworth, Fenton, Frank, Garfield, Gooch, *Griswold*, Higby, Hooper, Hotchkiss, Asahel W. Hubbard, John H. Hubbard, Hulburd, Ingersoll, Jenckes, Julian, Kelley, Francis W. Kellogg, Orlando Kellogg, Littlejohn, Loan, Longyear, Marvin, McBride, McClurg, McIndoe, Samuel F. Miller, Moorhead, Morrill, Daniel Morris. Amos Myers, Leonard Myers, Norton, Chas. O'Neill, Orth, Patterson, Perham, Pike, Price, Alexander H. Rice, John H. Rice, Edward H. Rollins, Schenck, Scofield, Shannon, Sloan, Spalding, Starr, Stevens, Thayer, Thomas, Tracy, Upson, Van Valkenburgh, Wm. B. Washburn, Webster, Whaley, Williams, Wilder, Wilson, Windom, Woodbridge—90.

NAYS—Messrs. *James C. Allen*, *William J. Allen*, *Ancona*, *Augustus C. Baldwin*, *Bliss*, *Brooks*, *James S. Brown*, *Chanler*, *Coffroth*, *Cox*, *Cravens*, *Dawson*, *Denison*, *Eden*, *Edgerton*, *Eldridge*, *English*, *Finck*, *Ganson*, *Grider*, *Harding*, *Harrington*, *Charles M. Harris*, *Herrick*, *Holman*, *Hutchins*, *Philip Johnson*, *Kalbfleisch*, *Kernan*, *King*, *Knapp*, *Law*, *Lazear*, *Le Blond*, *Mallory*, *Marcy*, *McDowell*, *McKinney*, *William H. Miller*, *James R. Morris*, *Morrison*, *Odell*, *Pendleton*, *Pruyn*, *Radford*, *Samuel J. Randall*, *Robinson*, *James S. Rollins*, *Ross*, Smithers, *John B. Steele*, *William G. Steele*, *Stiles*, *Strouse*, *Stuart*, *Sweat*, *Wadsworth*, *Ward*, *Wheeler*, *Chilton A. White*, *Joseph W. White*, *Fernando Wood*—62.

June 22—This bill was taken up in the Senate, when Mr. SAULSBURY moved this substitute:

That no person held to service or labor in one State, under the laws thereof, escaping into another, shall, in consequence of any law or regulation therein, be discharged from such service or labor, but shall be delivered up on claim of the party to whom such service or labor may be due; and Congress shall pass all necessary and proper laws for the rendition of all such persons who shall so, as aforesaid, escape.

Which was rejected—yeas 9, nays 29, as follows:

YEAS—Messrs. *Buckalew*, *Carlile*, Cowan, *Davis*, *McDougall*, *Powell*, *Richardson*, *Riddle*, *Saulsbury*—9.

NAYS—Messrs. Anthony, Brown, Chandler, Clark, Conness, Dixon, Foot, Grimes, Hale, Harlan, Harris, Hicks, Howard, Howe, Johnson, Lane of Indiana, Lane of Kansas, Morgan, Morrill, Pomeroy, Ramsey, Sprague, Sumner, Ten Eyck, Trumbull, Van Winkle, Wade, Willey—29.

Mr. JOHNSON, of Maryland, moved an amendment to substitute a clause repealing the act of 1850; which was rejected—yeas 17, nays 22, as follows:

YEAS—Messrs. *Buckalew*, *Carlile*, Cowan, *Davis*, Harris, Hicks, Johnson, Lane of Indiana, *McDougall*, *Powell*, *Richardson*, *Riddle*, *Saulsbury*, Ten Eyck, Trumbull, Van Winkle, Willey—17.

NAYS—Messrs. Anthony, Brown, Chandler, Clark, Conness, Dixon, Fessenden, Foot, Grimes, Hale, Harlan, Howard, Howe, Lane of Kansas, Morgan, Morrill, Pomeroy, Ramsey, Sprague, Sumner, Wade, Wilson—22.

The bill then passed—yeas 27, nays 12, as follows:

YEAS—Messrs. Anthony, Brown, Chandler, Clark, Conness, Dixon, Fessenden, Foot, Grimes, Hale, Harlan, Harris, Hicks, Howard, Howe, Lane of Indiana, Lane of Kansas, Morgan, Morrill, Pomeroy, Ramsey, Sprague, Sumner, Ten Eyck, Trumbull, Wade, Wilson—27.

NAYS—Messrs. *Buckalew*, *Carlile*, Cowan, *Davis*, Johnson, *McDougall*, *Powell*, *Richardson*, *Riddle*, *Saulsbury*, Van Winkle, Willey—12.

ABRAHAM LINCOLN, *President*, approved it, June 28, 1864.

ESCAPE OF FUGITIVE SLAVES, FROM 1850 TO 1860.

The census report shows that notwithstanding all the controversies upon the subject of the fugitive slave law and its enforcement, from 1850 down to 1860, there were less per cent. escapes of fugitive slaves than at any former period of the Government. The report states:

"The number of slaves who escaped from their masters in 1860 is not only much less in proportion than in 1850, but greatly reduced numerically. The greatest increase of escapes appears to have occurred in Mississippi, Missouri, and Virginia, while the decrease is most marked in Delaware, Georgia, Louisiana, Maryland, and Tennessee.

"That the complaint of insecurity to slave property by the escape of this class of persons into the free States, and their recovery impeded, whereby its value has been lessened, is the result of misapprehension, is evident not only from the small number who have been lost to their owners, but from the fact that up to the present time the number of escapes has been gradually diminishing to such an extent that the whole annual loss to the southern States from this cause bears less proportion to the amount of capital involved than the daily variations which in ordinary times occur in the fluctuations of State or Government securities in the city of New York alone.

"From the tables annexed it appears that while there escaped from their masters 1,011 slaves in 1850, or 1 in each 3,165 held in bondage, (being about one thirtieth of one per cent.) during the census year ending June 1, 1860, out of 3,949.557 slaves, there escaped only 803, being 1 to about 5,000, or at the rate of one fiftieth of one per cent.

THE NEW ARTICLE OF WAR—MARCH 13, 1862.

Second Session, Thirty-Seventh Congress.

IN HOUSE.

ART. 102. All officers or persons in the military or naval service of the United States are prohibited from employing any of the forces under their respective commands for the purpose of returning fugitives from service or labor who may have escaped from any persons to whom such service or labor is claimed to be due, and any officer who shall be found guilty by a court-martial of violating this article shall be dismissed from the service.

SEC. 2. That this act shall take effect from and after its passage.

1862, February 25—The article passed the House—yeas 95, nays 51, as follows:

YEAS—Messrs. Aldrich, Alley, Arnold, Ashley, Babbitt, Baker, Baxter, Beaman, Bingham, Francis P. Blair, Samuel S. Blair, Blake, Buffinton, Campbell, Chamberlain, Clark, Colfax, Frederick A. Conkling, Roscoe Conkling, Conway, Covode, Cutler, Davis, Dawes, Diven, Duell, Edgerton, Edwards, Eliot, Ely, Fessenden, Franchot, Frank, Gooch, Goodwin, Granger, Gurley, Hale, Hanchett, Harrison, Hickman, Hooper, Hutchins, Julian, Kelley, Francis W. Kellogg, William Kellogg, Lansing, Loomis, Lovejoy, McKnight, McPherson, Mitchell, Moorhead, Anson P. Morrill, Justin S. Morrill, Nixon, Olin, Patton, Timothy G. Phelps, Pike, Pomeroy, Porter, Potter, Alexander H. Rice, John H. Rice, Riddle, Edward H. Rollins, Sargent, Sedgwick, Shanks, *Sheffield*, Shellabarger, Sherman, Sloan, Spaulding, Stevens, Stratton, Benjamin F. Thomas, Train, Trimble, Trowbridge, Van Horn, Van Valkenburgh, Van Wyck, Wall, Wallace, Charles W. Walton, E. P. Walton, Washburne, Wheeler, Albert S. White, Wilson, Windom, Worcester—95.

NAYS—Messrs. *Ancona*, *Joseph Baily*, *Biddle*, Jacob B. Blair, *Calvert*, Clements, *Cobb*, *Corning*, *Cox*, *Cravens*, *Crisfield*, *Crittenden*, *Dunlap*, *English*, *Grider*, *Hall*, *Harding*, *Holman*, *Johnson*, *Knapp*, *Law*, *Lazear*, Leary, *Lehman*, *Mallory*, *May*, *Maynard*, *Menzies*, *Morris*, *Noell*, *Norton*, *Nugen*, *Pendleton*, *Perry*, *Price*, *Robinson*, *James S. Rollins*, *Shiel*, *Smith*, *John B. Steele*, *William G. Steele*, Francis Thomas, *Vallandigham*, *Vibbard*, *Voorhees*, *Ward*, Webster, *Wickliffe*, *Wood*, *Woodruff*, *Wright*—51.

IN SENATE.

March 10—The article was considered.

Mr. DAVIS, of Kentucky, moved to amend by inserting after the word "due" the words "and also from detaining, harboring, or concealing any such fugitives;" which was disagreed to—yeas 10, nays 29, as follows:

YEAS—Messrs. *Bayard*, *Carlile*, *Davis*, Henderson, *Latham*, *McDougall*, *Powell*, *Rice*, *Saulsbury*, *Wilson* of Missouri—10.

NAYS—Messrs. Anthony, Browning, Chandler, Clark, Collamer, Cowan, Dixon, Doolittle, Fessenden, Foot, Foster, Grimes, Hale, Harlan, Harris, Howard, Howe, King, Lane of Indiana, Lane of Kansas, Morrill, Pomeroy, Sherman, Sumner, Ten Eyck, Trumbull, Wade, Wilson of Massachusetts, Wright—29.

Mr. SAULSBURY moved to exempt from the operation of the article, Delaware, Maryland, Missouri, and Kentucky, and elsewhere where the Federal authority is recognized or can be enforced; which was lost—yeas 7, (*Bayard*, *Carlile*, *Latham*, *McDougall*, *Powell*, *Saulsbury*, *Wilson* of Missouri,) nays 30.

Mr. SAULSBURY moved to add after the word "due" the words "or for the purpose of enticing or decoying any person held to service or labor from the service of their loyal masters;" which was lost—yeas 10, nays 29, (same as above.)

The article then passed—yeas 29, nays 9. The affirmative vote was the same as above, except that Mr. Cowan did not vote, and Mr. *McDougall* voted aye. The negative vote was:

Messrs. *Bayard*, *Carlile*, *Davis*, Henderson, *Latham*, *Powell*, *Rice*, *Saulsbury*, *Wilson* of Missouri—9.

The following action had previously been taken in the House:

First Session, Thirty-Seventh Congress.

1861, July 9—Mr. LOVEJOY offered the following resolution:

Resolved, That, in the judgment of this House, it is no part of the duty of the soldiers of the United States to capture and return fugitive slaves.

Which was agreed to—yeas 92, nays 55, as follows:

YEAS—Messrs. Aldrich, Alley, Arnold, Ashley, Babbitt, Goldsmith F. Bailey, Baker, Baxter, Beaman, Bingham, Francis P. Blair, Samuel S. Blair, Blake, Buffinton, Campbell, Chamberlain, Ambrose W. Clark, Colfax, Frederick A. Conkling, Roscoe Conkling, Conway, Covode, Cutler, Davis, Dawes, Delano, Diven, Duell, Dunn, Edgerton, Edwards, Eliot, Ely, Fessenden, Franchot, Frank, Gooch, Granger, Gurley, Hale, Hickman, Hutchins, Julian, Kelley, Francis W. Kellogg, Killinger, Lansing, Loomis, Lovejoy, McKean, McPherson, Mitchell, Moorhead, Anson P. Morrill, Justin S. Morrill, Olin, Patton, Pike, Pomeroy, Porter, Potter, Alexander H. Rice, John H. Rice, Riddle, Edward H. Rollins, Sedgwick, Shanks, Shellabarger, Sherman, Sloan, Spaulding, Stevens, Stratton, Benjamin F. Thomas, Thayer, Train, Trimble, Trowbridge, Vandever, Van Horn, Van Valkenburgh, Van Wyck, Verree, Wall, Wallace, Charles W. Walton, E. P. Walton, Washburne, Wheeler, Albert S. White, Windom, Worcester—92.

NAYS—Messrs. *Allen*, *Ancona*, *Joseph Baily*, *Burnett*, *Calvert*, *Carlile*, *Cobb*, *Cooper*, *Cox*, *Cravens*, *Crisfield*, *Crittenden*, *Dunlap*, *English*, Fenton, Fisher, *Fouke*, *Grider*, *Haight*, *Harding*, *Holman*, Horton, *Jackson*, *Johnson*, William Kellogg, *Law*, *Lazear*, *Logan*, *McClernand*, *Mallory*, *Menzies*, *Morris*, Nixon, *Noble*, *Noell*, *Nugen*, *George H. Pendleton*, *Richardson*, *Robinson*, *Sheffield*, *Smith*, *John B. Steele*, *Wm. G. Steele*, Francis Thomas, Upton, *Vallandigham*, *Wadsworth*, *Ward*, Webster, Whaley, *Chilton A. White*, *Wickliffe*, *Wood*, *Woodruff*, *Wright*—55.

Dec. 20—Mr. SHANKS offered this resolution, which was referred, Dec. 23, to the Committee on the Judiciary:

Resolved, That the constitutional power to return fugitive slaves to their masters rests solely with the civil departments of the Government; and that the order of the Secretary of War, under date of December 6, 1861, to General Wool, for the delivery of a slave to Mr. Jessup, of Maryland, as well as all other military orders for the return of slaves, are assumptions of the military power over the civil law and the rights of the slave.

Second Session, Thirty-Seventh Congress.

1861, December 23—Mr. WILSON, of Iowa, offered this resolution:

Resolved, That the Committee on Military Affairs be instructed to report to this House a bill for the enactment of an additional article of war for the government of the army, whereby the officers in the military service of the United States shall be prohibited from using any portion of the forces under their respective commands for the purpose of returning fugitives from service or labor; and providing for the punishment of such officers as may violate said article by dismissal from the service.

Which Mr. NOELL moved to lay on the table; lost—yeas 33, nays 70. The YEAS were:

YEAS—Messrs. *Joseph Baily*, *Biddle*, Jacob B. Blair, *George H. Browne*, *Calvert*, *Cobb*, *Cravens*, *Dunlap*, Dunn, *Fouke*, *Grider*, *Haight*, *Harding*, *Knapp*, *Law*, Leary, *Logan*, Maynard, *Menzies*, *Noble*, *Noell*, *Norton*, *Nugen*, *Odell*, *Perry*, *Robinson*, *Shiel*, *Smith*, *John B. Steele*, Francis Thomas, Upton, *Vallandigham*, *Webster*—33.

The resolution was then adopted.

ON EMPLOYMENT OF SLAVES IN DOCK-YARDS, ETC.

Second Session, Thirty-Seventh Congress.

IN SENATE.

1862, June 14—Mr. WILSON, of Massachusetts, offered this additional section to the naval appropriation bill:

That persons held to service or labor, commonly called slaves, shall not be employed in any capacity whatever in any navy-yard, dock-yard, arsenal, magazine, fort, or in the Naval Academy.

Which was agreed to in Committee of the Whole.

June 16—It was rejected in open Senate—yeas 17, nays 18, as follows:

YEAS—Messrs. Clark, Collamer, Dixon, Foot, Grimes, Hale, Harlan, King, Lane of Indiana, Lane of Kansas, Morrill, Pomeroy, Sumner, Trumbull, Wilmot, Wilson of Massachusetts, *Wright*—17.

NAYS—Messrs. Anthony, Browning, Chandler, *Davis*, Doolittle, Fessenden, Foster, Henderson, Howard, Howe, *Latham*, *McDougall*, *Powell*, *Saulsbury*, *Stark*, Ten Eyck, Willey, *Wilson* of Missouri—18.

RECOGNITION OF HAYTI AND LIBERIA.

Second Session, Thirty-Seventh Congress.

The bill to authorize the President to appoint diplomatic representatives to the republics of Hayti and Liberia, respectively, each representative to be accredited as commissioner and consul general, and to receive the pay of commissioners, that at Liberia not to exceed $4,000 per annum—

1862, April 24—Passed the Senate—yeas 32, nays 7, as follows:

YEAS—Messrs. Anthony, Browning, Chandler, Clark, Collamer, Cowan, Dixon, Doolittle, Fessenden, Foot, Foster, Grimes, Hale, Henderson, Howard, Howe, King, Lane of Indiana, Lane of Kansas, *Latham*, *McDougall*, Morrill, Pomeroy, Sherman, Simmons, Sumner, Ten Eyck, Trumbull, Wade, Wilkinson, Wilson of Massachusetts, *Wright*—32.

NAYS—Messrs. *Bayard*, *Carlile*, *Davis*, *Powell*, *Saulsbury*, *Stark*, *Thomson*—7.

Previously, an amendment like that offered in the House by Mr. Cox was lost—yeas 8, nays 30.

June 3—It was taken up in the House.

Mr. Cox, of Ohio, offered an amendment providing for the appointment of a consul general to each, with authority to negotiate any treaties of commerce between Hayti and Liberia and this country, and with the compensation of consuls general; which was lost—yeas 40, nays 82.

The bill then passed—yeas 86, nays 37, as follows:

YEAS—Messrs. Aldrich, Alley, Ashley, Babbitt, Baker, Baxter, Beaman, Bingham, Francis P. Blair, Blake, Buffinton, Casey, Chamberlain, Clark, Clements, Colfax, Frederick A. Conkling, Roscoe Conkling, Covode, Davis, Dawes, Delano, Duell, Dunn, Edgerton, Ely, Fessenden, Fisher, Frank, Gooch, Goodwin, Granger, Gurley, Hale, Hickman, Hooper, Horton, Hutchins, Julian, Kelley, William Kellogg, Lansing, *Lehman*, Loomis, Lovejoy, Low, McKnight, McPherson, Maynard, Mitchell, Moorhead, Anson P. Morrill, Justin S. Morrill, Nixon, Timothy G. Phelps, Pike, Pomeroy, Porter, Alexander H. Rice, John H. Rice, Riddle, Edward H. Rollins, Sargent, Sedgwick, Shanks, *Sheffield*, Shellabarger, Sloan, Spaulding, Stevens, Stratton, Benjamin F. Thomas, Francis Thomas, Train, Trimble, Trowbridge, Van Horn, Van Valkenburgh, Verree, Wallace, Walton, Washburne, Albert S. White, Wilson, Windom, Worcester—86.

NAYS—Messrs. *W. J. Allen*, *Ancona*, *Baily*, *Biddle*, Jacob B. Blair, *George H. Browne*, *Calvert*, *Cobb*, *Corning*, *Cox*, *Dunlap*, *Grider*, *Harding*, *Holman*, *Knapp*, *Law*, *Lazear*, *Mallory*, *May*, *Menzies*, *Noell*, *Norton*, *Nugen*, *John S. Phelps*, *Price*, Segar, *Smith*, *John B. Steele*, *William G. Steele*, *Stiles*, *Vibbard*, *Voorhees*, *Wadsworth*, *Ward*, Webster, *Wickliffe*, *Wright*—37.

ROBERT SMALL.

Second Session, Thirty-Seventh Congress.

IN SENATE.

May 19—Mr. GRIMES brought in a bill for the relief of Robert Small, which passed without a division.

It authorizes the Secretary of the Navy to cause the steam transport boat Planter, recently in the rebel service in the harbor of Charleston, and all the arms, munitions, tackle, and other property on board of her at the time of her delivery to the Federal authorities, to be appraised by a board of competent officers, and, when the value shall be thus ascertained, to cause an equitable apportionment of one half of such value, so ascertained, to be made between Robert Small and his associates who assisted in rescuing her from the enemies of the Government. The Secretary of the Navy may, if he deems it expedient, cause the sum of money allotted to each individual under this bill to be invested in United States securities for his benefit, the interest to be paid to him or to his heirs annually until such time as the Secretary of the Navy may deem it expedient to pay to him or his heirs the principal sum.

IN HOUSE.

May 26—It passed—yeas 121, nays 9.—(Messrs. *Calvert*, *Dunlap*, *Harding*, *Johnson*, *Kerrigan*, *Norton*, *Shiel*, *Vallandigham*, *Voorhees*.)

TO REMOVE DISQUALIFICATION OF COLOR IN CARRYING THE MAILS.

Second Session, Thirty-Seventh Congress.

IN SENATE.

1862, April 11—The Senate considered a bill "to remove all disqualification of color in carrying the mails of the United States." It directed that after the passage of the act no person, by reason of color, shall be disqualified from employment in carrying the mails, and all acts and parts of acts establishing such disqualification, including especially the seventh section of the act of March 3, 1825,* are hereby repealed.

The vote in the Senate was, yeas 24, nays 11, as follows:

YEAS—Messrs. Anthony, Browning, Chandler, Clark, Collamer, Dixon, Doolittle, Fessenden, Foot, Foster, Grimes, Hale, Howard, Howe, King, Lane of Kansas, Morrill, Pomeroy, Sherman, Simmons, Sumner, Wade, Wilkinson, and Wilson of Massachusetts—24.

NAYS—Messrs. *Davis*, Henderson, *Kennedy*, Lane of Indiana, *Latham*, *Nesmith*, *Powell*, *Stark*, Willey, *Wilson* of Missouri, Wright—11.

---

* The section referred to is in these words:

That no other than a free white person shall be employed in conveying the mail, and any contractor who shall employ or permit any other than a free white person to convey the mail shall, for every such offence, incur a penalty of twenty dollars.

The act of 1825 passed the Senate March 1, and the House March 2, without a division. The suggestion of this measure appears to have been first made in 1802 by Gideon Granger, Postmaster General under President Jefferson, in the following letter:

GENERAL POST OFFICE, *March* 23, 1802.

SIR: An objection exists against employing negroes, or people of color, in transporting the public mails, of a nature too delicate to ingraft into a report which may become public, yet too important to be omitted or passed over without full consideration. I therefore take the liberty of making to the committee, through you, a private representation on that subject. After the scenes which St. Domingo has exhibited to the world, we cannot be too cautious in attempting to prevent similar evils in the four southern States, where there are, particularly in the eastern and old settled parts of them, so great a proportion of blacks as to hazard the tranquillity and happiness of the free citizens. Indeed, in Virginia and South Carolina (as I have been informed) plans and conspiracies have already been concerted by them, more than once, to rise in arms, and subjugate their masters.

Everything which tends to increase their knowledge of natural rights, of men and things, or that affords them an opportunity of associating, acquiring, and communicating sentiments, and of establishing a chain or line of intelligence, must increase your hazard, because it increases their means of effecting their object.

The most active and intelligent are employed as post-riders. These are the most ready to learn, and the most able to execute. By traveling from day to day, and hourly mixing with people, they must, they will acquire information. *They will learn that a man's rights do not depend on his color. They will, in time, become teachers to their brethren.* They become acquainted with each other on the line. Whenever the body, or a portion of them, wish to act, they are an organized corps, circulating our intelligence openly, their own privately.

Their traveling creates no suspicion, excites no alarm. One able man among them, perceiving the value of this machine, might lay a plan which would be communicated by your post-riders from town to town, and produce a general and united operation against you. It is easier to prevent the evil than to cure it. The hazard may be small and the prospect remote, but it does not follow that at some day the event would not be certain.

With respect and esteem, GIDEON GRANGER.

Hon. JAMES JACKSON, *Senator from Georgia*.

IN HOUSE.

May 21—It was considered in the House and laid on the table—yeas 82, nays 45, as follows:

YEAS—Messrs. *Allen, Ancona*, Babbitt, *Baily, Biddle*, Francis P. Blair, Jacob B. Blair, William G. Brown, *Calvert*, Casey, Clements, Colfax, Roscoe Conkling, *Corning, Cox, Cravens, Crisfield, Crittenden*, Diven, *Dunlap*, Dunn, Ely, *English*, Franchot, Granger, *Grider, Haight*, Hale, *Hall*, Hanchett, *Harding*, Harrison, *Holman*, Horton, *Johnson*, Kelley, William Kellogg, *Kerrigan*, Killinger, *Law, Lazear*, Leary, *Lehman*, McKnight, McPherson, *Mallory*, Maynard, *Menzies*, Nixon, *Noell, Nugen, Odell*, Patton, *Pendleton, Perry, John S. Phelps*, Timothy G. Phelps, Porter, *Price, Richardson, Robinson*, Sargent, *Shiel, Smith, William G. Steele*, Stratton, Francis Thomas, Trowbridge, Van Valkenburgh, Verree, *Vibbard, Voorhees, Wadsworth*, Wall, *Ward*, Webster, Whaley, Albert S. White, *Chilton A. White, Wickliffe, Woodruff*, Worcester—82.

NAYS—Messrs. Aldrich, Alley, Beaman, Bingham, Samuel S. Blair, Blake, Buffinton, Chamberlain, Frederick A. Conkling, Cutler, Davis, Dawes, Delano, Duell, Edgerton, Edwards, Eliot, Fenton, Fessenden, Frank, Gooch, Goodwin, Hooper, Hutchins, Julian, Lansing, Loomis, Pike, Pomeroy, Potter, Alexander H. Rice, Riddle, Edward H. Rollins, Sedgwick, *Sheffield*, Sloan, Spaulding, Benjamin F. Thomas, Train, Van Horn, Wallace, Charles W. Walton, E. P. Walton, Wilson, Windom—45.

—

First Session, Thirty-Eighth Congress.

1864, February 26—The Senate considered the bill—the question being on agreeing to a new section proposed by the Committee on Post Offices and Post Roads—as follows:

SEC. 2. That in the courts of the United States there shall be no exclusion of any witness on account of color.

Mr. POWELL moved to amend by inserting after the word "States" the words: "in all cases for robbing or violating the mails of the United States."

No further progress was made on the bill.

NEGRO SUFFRAGE IN MONTANA TERRITORY.

1864, March 18—The House passed, without a division, a bill in the usual form, to provide a temporary government for the Territory of Montana.

March 31—The Senate considered it, when Mr. WILKINSON moved to strike from the second line of the fifth section, (defining the qualifications of voters,) the words "white male inhabitant" and insert the words: "male citizen of the United States, and those who have declared their intention to become such;" which was agreed to—yeas 22, nays 17, as follows:

YEAS—Messrs. Brown, Chandler, Clark, Collamer, Conness, Dixon, Fessenden, Foot, Foster, Grimes, Hale, Harlan, Harris, Howard, Howe, Morgan, Morrill, Pomeroy, Sumner, Wade, Wilkinson, Wilson—22.

NAYS—Messrs, *Buckalew, Carlile*, Cowan, *Davis, Harding*, Henderson, Johnson, Lane of Indiana, *Nesmith, Powell, Riddle, Saulsbury*, Sherman, Ten Eyck, Trumbull, Van Winkle, Willey—17.

The bill was then passed—yeas 29, nays 8, (Messrs. *Buckalew, Davis*, Johnson, *Powell, Riddle, Saulsbury*, Van Winkle, Willey.)

April 15—The Senate adopted the report of the Committee of Conference on the Montana bill, which recommended the Senate to recede from their second amendment, and the House to agree to the first and third amendments of the Senate, (including the above.)

April 15—Mr. BEAMAN presented the report of the Committee of Conference on the Montana bill, a feature of which was that the House should recede from its disagreement to the Senate amendment striking out the word "white" in the description of those authorized to vote.

Mr. HOLMAN moved that the report be tabled; which was lost by the casting vote of the Speaker—yeas 66, nays 66.

Upon agreeing to the report the yeas were 54, nays 85, as follows:

YEAS—Messrs. Alley, Allison, Ames, Anderson, Ashley, John D. Baldwin, Baxter, Beaman, Blaine, Boyd, Ambrose W. Clark, Cole, Dawes, Driggs, Dumont, Eckley, Farnsworth, Frank, Garfield, Gooch, Higby, Hooper, Hotchkiss, John H. Hubbard, Jenckes, Julian, Kelley, Orlando Kellogg, Loan, Longyear, Marvin, McClurg, McIndoe, Morrill, Daniel Morris, Amos Myers, Leonard Myers, Charles O'Neill, Patterson, Perham, Pike, Price, Alexander H. Rice, John H. Rice, Edward H. Rollins, Shannon, Sloan, Stevens, Upson, Van Valkenburgh, William B. Washburn, Williams, Windom, Woodbridge—54.

NAYS—Messrs. *James C. Allen, William J. Allen, Baily, Augustus C. Baldwin*, Francis P. Blair, *Bliss, Brooks, James S. Brown, Chanler, Clay, Coffroth, Cox, Cravens*, Creswell, Henry Winter Davis, *Dawson*, Deming, *Denison, Eden, Eldridge, Finck, Ganson, Grider, Hall, Harding, Benjamin G. Harris, Herrick, Holman*, Asahel W. Hubbard, *Hutchins, William Johnson, Kalbfleisch*, Kasson, Francis W. Kellogg, *Kernan, Knapp, Law, Lazear, Long, Mallory, Marcy*, McBride, *McDowell, McKinney, William H. Miller, James R. Morris, Morrison, Nelson, Noble, Odell*, Orth, *Pendleton*, Pomeroy, *Pruyn, Radford, Samuel J. Randall*, William H. Randall, *Robinson, Rogers, James S. Rollins, Ross*, Schenck, *Scott*, Smith, Smithers, *Stebbins, John B. Steele, William G. Steele, Strouse, Stuart, Sweat*, Thayer, Thomas, Tracy, *Voorhees*, Ellihu B. Washburne, Webster, Whaley, *Wheeler, Chilton A. White, Joseph W. White*, Wilson, *Winfield, Fernando Wood, Yeaman*—85.

On a motion to adhere to its amendments, and ask another Committee of Conference, Mr. WEBSTER moved instructions:

And that said committee be instructed to agree to no report that authorizes any other than free white male citizens, and those who have declared their intention to become such, to vote.

Which was agreed to—yeas 75, nays 67, as follows:

YEAS—Messrs. *James C. Allen, Wm. J. Allen, Baily, Augustus C. Baldwin*, Francis P. Blair, *Bliss, Brooks, James S. Brown*, Wm. G. Brown, *Chanler, Clay, Coffroth, Cox, Cravens*, Creswell, Henry Winter Davis, *Dawson, Denison, Eden, Eldridge, Finck, Ganson, Grider, Hall, Harding, Benjamin G. Harris, Herrick, Holman, Hutchins, William Johnson, Kalbfleisch, Kernan, Knapp, Law, Lazear, Long, Mallory, Marcy*, McBride, *McDowell, McKinney, Wm. H. Miller, James R. Morris, Morrison, Nelson, Noble, Odell, Pendleton, Radford, Samuel J. Randall*, Wm. H. Randall, *Robinson, Rogers, James S. Rollins, Ross, Scott*, Smith, Smithers, *Stebbins, John B. Steele, Wm. G. Steele, Strouse, Stuart, Sweat*, Thomas, Tracy, *Voorhees*, Webster, Whaley, *Wheeler, Chilton A. White, Joseph W. White, Winfield, Fernando Wood, Yeaman*—75.

NAYS—Messrs. Alley, Allison, Ames, Anderson, Ashley, John D. Baldwin, Baxter, Beaman, Blaine, Boutwell, Boyd, Broomall, Ambrose W. Clark, Cobb, Cole, Dawes, Deming, Driggs, Dumont, Farnsworth, Frank, Gooch, Grinnell, Higby, Hooper, Hotchkiss, Asahel W. Hubbard, John H. Hubbard, Jenckes, Julian, Kelley, Francis W. Kellogg, Orlando Kellogg, Loan, Longyear, Marvin, McClurg, McIndoe, Samuel F. Miller, Morrill, Daniel Morris, Leonard Myers, Norton, Charles O'Neill, Orth, Patterson, Perham, Pike, Pomeroy, Price, Alexander H. Rice, John H. Rice, Edward H. Rollins, Schenck, Shannon, Sloan, Stevens, Thayer, Upson, Van Valkenburgh, Ellihu B. Washburne, William B. Washburn, Williams, Wilder, Wilson, Windom, Woodbridge—67.

April 15—The Senate declined the conference upon the terms proposed by the House resolution of that day.

April 18—The House proposed a further free conference, to which, April 25, the Senate acceded.

May 17—In Senate, Mr. MORRILL submitted a report from the Conference Committee who recommend that qualified voters shall be:

All citizens of the United States, and those who have declared their intention to become such, and who are otherwise described and qualified under the fifth section of the act of Congress providing for a temporary government for the Territory of Idaho approved March 3, 1863.*

The report was concurred in—yeas 26, nays 13, as follows:

YEAS—Messrs. *Buckalew*, *Carlile*, Collamer, Cowan, *Davis*, Doolittle, Foot, Foster, *Harding*, Harris, Henderson, *Hendricks*, Howard, Johnson, Lane of Indiana, Morrill, *Nesmith*, *Powell*, Ramsey, *Saulsbury*, Ten Eyck, Trumbull, Van Winkle, Wade, Wilkinson, Willey—26.

NAYS—Messrs. Anthony, Chandler, Clark, Dixon, Grimes, Hale, Harlan, Lane of Kansas, Morgan, Pomeroy, Sprague, Sumner, Wilson—13.

May 20—The above report was made by Mr. WEBSTER in the House, and agreed to—yeas 102, nays 26, as follows:

YEAS—Messrs. *James C. Allen*, *Baily*, Beaman, Blaine, Jacob B. Blair, *Bliss*, *Brooks*, William G. Brown, *Chanler*, *Coffroth*, *Cox*, *Cravens*, Creswell, Thomas T. Davis, *Dawson*, Donnelly, Driggs, *Eden*, *Edgerton*, *Eldridge*, Farnsworth, *Finck*, *Grider*, Hale, *Hall*, *Harding*, *Harrington*, *Charles M. Harris*, *Herrick*, *Holman*, Hooper, Hotchkiss, Ashahel W. Hubbard, *Hutchins*, Ingersoll, *Wm. Johnson*, *Kalbfleisch*, Kasson, Francis W. Kellogg, *Kernan*, *King*, *Law*, *Lazear*, *Long*, Longyear, *Mallory*, *Marcy*, *McAllister*, McBride, *McDowell*, McIndoe, *McKinney*, Samuel F. Miller, *James R. Morris*, *Morrison*, Amos Myers, *Nelson*, *Noble*, Norton, Charles O'Neill, *John O'Neill*, Orth, *Pendleton*, Perham, Pike, Pomeroy, *Pruyn*, *Radford*, *S. J. Randall*, Wm. H. Randall, Alexander H. Rice, John H. Rice, *Robinson*, *James S. Rollins*, *Ross*, Scofield, *Scott*, Shannon, Sloan, Smith, Smithers, *John B. Steele*, *Wm. G. Steele*, *Stiles*, *Strouse*, *Stuart*, *Sweat*, Thayer, Tracy, Upson, Van Valkenburgh, *Voorhees*, Ellihu B. Washburne, William B. Washburn, Webster, Whaley, *Wheeler*, Wilson, Windom, *Fernando Wood*, Woodbridge, *Yeaman*—102.

NAYS—Messrs. Alley, Allison, Ames, John D. Baldwin, Boutwell, Ambrose W. Clark, Cobb, Cole, Dawes, Dixon, Eliot, Gooch, Grinnell, Higby, John H. Hubbard, Julian, Kelley, Orlando Kellogg, Loan, Moorhead, Morrill, Price, Edward H. Rollins, Spalding, Stevens, Wilder—26.

IN WASHINGTON CITY.†

1864, May 6—The Senate considered the bill for the registration of voters in the city of Washington, when

Mr. COWAN moved to insert the word "white" in the first section, so as to confine the right of voting to white male citizens.

May 12—Mr. MORRILL moved to amend the amendment by striking out the words—

And shall have paid all school taxes and all taxes on personal property properly assessed against him, shall be entitled to vote for mayor, collector, register, members of the board of aldermen and board of common council, and assessor, and for every officer authorized to be elected at any election under any act or acts to which this is amendatory or supplementary.

and inserting the words—

And shall within the year next preceding the election have paid a tax, or been assessed with a part of the revenue of the District, county, or cities therein, or been exempt from taxation having taxable estate, and who can read and write with facility, shall enjoy the privileges of an elector.

May 26—Mr. SUMNER moved to amend the bill by adding this proviso:

Provided, That there shall be no exclusion of any person from the registry on account of color.

May 27—Mr. HARLAN moved to amend the amendment by making the word "person" read "persons," and adding the words—

Who have borne arms in the military service of the United States, and have been honorably discharged therefrom.

Which was agreed to—yeas 26, nays 12, as follows:

YEAS—Messrs. Anthony, Chandler, Clark, Collamer, Conness, Dixon, Fessenden, Foot, Foster, Grimes, Hale, Harlan, Harris, Johnson, Lane of Indiana, Lane of Kansas, Morgan, Morrill, Pomeroy, Ramsey, Sherman, Ten Eyck, Trumbull, Wade, Willey, Wilson—26.

NAYS—Messrs. *Buckalew*, *Carlile*, Cowan, *Davis*, *Hendricks*, *McDougall*, *Powell*, *Richardson*, *Saulsbury*, Sumner, Van Winkle, Wilkinson—12.

May 28—Mr. SUMNER moved to add these words to the last proviso:

And provided further, That all persons, without distinction of color, who shall, within the year next preceding the election, have paid a tax on any estate, or been assessed with a part of the revenue of said District, or been exempt from taxation having taxable estate, and who can read and write with facility, shall enjoy the privilege of an elector. But no person now entitled to vote in the said District, continuing to reside therein, shall be disfranchised hereby.

Which was rejected—yeas 8, nays 27, as follows:

YEAS—Messrs. Anthony, Clark, Lane of Kansas, Morgan, Pomeroy, Ramsey, Sumner, Wilkinson—8.

NAYS—Messrs. *Buckalew*, *Carlile*, Collamer, Cowan, *Davis*, Dixon, Fessenden, Foot, Foster, Grimes, Hale, Harlan, Harris, *Hendricks*, Hicks, Johnson, Lane of Indiana, *McDougall*, Morrill, *Powell*, *Saulsbury*, Sherman, Ten Eyck, Trumbull, Van Winkle, Willey, Wilson—27.

The other proposition of Mr. SUMNER, amended on motion of Mr. HARLAN, was then rejected—yeas 18, nays 20, as follows:

YEAS—Messrs. Anthony, Chandler, Clark, Dixon, Foot, Foster, Hale, Harlan, Howard, Howe, Lane of Kansas, Morgan, Pomeroy, Ramsey, Sherman, Sumner, Wilkinson, Wilson—18.

NAYS—Messrs. *Buckalew*, *Carlile*, Cowan, *Davis*, Grimes, Harris, *Hendricks*, Hicks, Johnson, Lane of Indiana, *McDougall*, Morrill, *Nesmith*, *Powell*, *Richardson*, *Saulsbury*, Ten Eyck, Trumbull, Van Winkle, Willey—20.

The bill then passed the Senate, and afterward the House, without amendment.

EXCLUDING COLORED PERSONS FROM CARS.

Third Session, Thirty-Seventh Congress.

IN SENATE.

1863, February 27—Pending a supplement to the charter of the Washington and Alexandria Railroad Company,

Mr. SUMNER offered this proviso to the first section:

That no person shall be excluded from the cars on account of color.

Which was agreed to—yeas 19, nays 18, as follows:

YEAS—Messrs. Arnold, Chandler, Clark, Fessenden, Foot, Grimes, Harris, Howard, King, Lane of Kansas, Morrill, Pomeroy, Sumner, Ten Eyck, Trumbull, Wade, Wilkinson, Wilmot, Wilson of Massachusetts—19.

NAYS—Messrs. Anthony, *Bayard*, *Carlile*, Cowan, *Davis*,

---

* This section is as follows:

SEC. 5. *And be it further enacted*, That every free white male inhabitant above the age of twenty-one years, who shall have been an actual resident of said Territory at the time of the passage of this act, shall be entitled to vote at the first election, and shall be eligible to any office within the said Territory; but the qualifications of voters, and of holding office, at all subsequent elections, shall be such as shall be prescribed by the Legislative Assembly.

† In 1860 a vote was had in the State of New York on a proposition to permit negro suffrage without a property qualification. The result in the city was—yeas 1,640, nays 37,471. In the State—yeas 197,503, nays 337,984. In 1864 a like proposition was defeated—yeas 85,406, nays 224,336.

In 1862, in August, a vote was had in the State of Illinois, on several propositions relating to negroes and mulattoes, with this result:

For excluding them from the State	171,893	
Against	71,306	
		100,587
Against granting them suffrage or right to office	211,920	
For	35,649	
		176,271
For the enactment of laws to prohibit them from going to, or voting in, the State	198,938	
Against	44,414	
		154,524

Henderson, Hicks, Howe, *Kennedy*, Lane of Indiana, *Latham, McDougall, Powell, Richardson, Saulsbury, Turpie*, Willey, *Wilson* of Missouri—18.

March 2—The House concurred in the amendment without debate, under the previous question.

—

First Session, Thirty-Eighth Congress.

IN SENATE.

1864, February 10—Mr. SUMNER offered the following:

Resolved, That the Committee on the District of Columbia be directed to consider the expediency of further providing by law against the exclusion of colored persons from the equal enjoyment of all railroad privileges in the District of Columbia.

Which was agreed to—yeas 30, nays 10, as follows:

YEAS—Messrs. Anthony, Brown, Chandler, Clark, Collamer, Conness, Cowan, Dixon, Fessenden, Foot, Foster, Grimes, Hale, Harlan, Harris, Howard, Howe, Lane of Kansas, Morgan, Morrill, Pomeroy, Ramsey, Sherman, Sprague, Sumner, Ten Eyck, Trumbull, Wade, Wilkinson, Wilson—30.

NAYS—Messrs. *Buckalew, Davis, Harding, Hendricks, Nesmith, Powell, Richardson, Riddle, Saulsbury*, Van Winkle—10.

February 24—Mr. WILLEY, from the Committee on the District of Columbia, made this report, and the committee were discharged:

The Committee on the District of Columbia, who were required by resolution of the Senate, passed February 8, 1864, "to consider the expediency of further providing by law against the exclusion of colored persons from the equal enjoyment of all railroad privileges in the District of Columbia," have had the matter thus referred to them under consideration, and beg leave to report:

The act entitled "An act to incorporate the Washington and Georgetown Railroad Company," approved May 17, 1862, makes no distinction as to passengers over said road on account of the color of the passenger, and that in the opinion of the committee colored persons are entitled to all the privileges of said road which other persons have, and to all the remedies for any denial or breach of such privileges which belong to any person.

The committee therefore ask to be discharged from the further consideration of the premises.

March 17—The Senate considered the bill to incorporate the Metropolitan Railroad Company, in the District of Columbia, the pending question being an amendment, offered by Mr. SUMNER, to add to the fourteenth section the words:

Provided, That there shall be no regulation excluding any person from any car on account of color.

Which was agreed to—yeas 19, nays 17, as follows:

YEAS—Messrs. Anthony, Brown, Clark, Conness, Fessenden, Foot, Foster, Grimes, Harlan, Howe, Lane of Kansas, Morgan, Morrill, Pomeroy, Ramsey, Sumner, Wade, Wilkinson, Wilson—19.

NAYS—Messrs. *Buckalew, Carlile, Davis*, Doolittle, Harding, Harris, *Hendricks*, Johnson, Lane of Indiana, *Powell, Riddle, Saulsbury*, Sherman, Ten Eyck, Trumbull, Van Winkle, Willey—17.

The bill then passed the Senate.

June 19—The House refused to strike out the proviso last adopted in the Senate—yeas 62, nays 76, as follows:

YEAS—Messrs. *James C. Allen, William J. Allen, Ancona, Baily, Augustus C. Baldwin*, Blair, *Bliss, Brooks, James S. Brown*, William G. Brown, *Chanler, Coffroth, Cravens, Dawson, Denison, Eden, Edgerton, Eldridge, Finck, Ganson, Grider, Griswold, Harding, Charles M. Harris, Holman, Hutchins, Philip Johnson, William Johnson, Kernan, Knapp, Law, Lazear, Le Blond, Long, Mallory, Marcy, McDowell, McKinney, Middleton, Wm. H. Miller, James R. Morris, Morrison, Nelson, Noble, Pendleton, Perry, Pruyn, Radford, Samuel J. Randall, J. S. Rollins, Ross, Scott, John B. Steele, Stiles, Stuart*, Thomas, *Wadsworth, Ward*, Whaley, *Wheeler, Joseph W. White Winfield*—62.

NAYS—Messrs. Alley, Ames, Anderson, Arnold, Ashley, John D. Baldwin, Baxter, Beaman, Blaine, Boutwell, Boyd, Brandegee, Broomall, Ambrose W. Clark, Freeman Clarke, Cobb, Cole, Dawes, Deming, Dixon, Driggs, Eckley, Eliot, Farnsworth, Fenton, Frank, Garfield, Gooch, Higby, Hooper, Hotchkiss, Asahel W. Hubbard, John H. Hubbard, Hulburd, Ingersoll, Julian, Kelley, Orlando Kellogg, Knox, Loan, Longyear, Marvin, McClurg, McIndoe, Samuel F. Miller, Moorhead, Morrill, Daniel Morris, Amos Myers, Leonard Myers, Norton, Charles O'Neill, Orth, Patterson, Perham, Pike, Pomeroy, Price, Alexander H. Rice, John H. Rice, Edward H. Rollins, Schenck, Scofield, Shannon, Sloan, Smithers, Stevens, Thayer, Upson, Ellihu B. Washburne, William B. Washburn, Williams, Wilder, Wilson, Windom, Woodbridge—76.

And the bill passed the House and was approved by the President.

IN SENATE.

June 21—On a supplement to the charter of the Washington and Georgetown Railroad Company, in Committee of the Whole, Mr. SUMNER moved to insert:

Provided, That there shall be no exclusion of any person from any car on account of color.

Which was rejected—yeas 14, nays 16, as follows:

YEAS—Messrs. Anthony, Brown, Chandler, Clark, Collamer, Conness, Dixon, Foot, Howard, Morgan, Pomeroy, Sumner, Wade, Wilson—14.

NAYS—Messrs. *Buckalew, Carlile*, Cowan, *Davis*, Foster, Grimes, *Hendricks*, Johnson, Lane of Indiana, *Powell, Riddle, Saulsbury*, Sherman, Ten Eyck, Trumbull, Willey—16.

Same day, in the Senate, Mr. SUMNER renewed the amendment, which was agreed to—yeas 17, nays 16:

YEAS—Messrs. Brown, Clark, Conness, Dixon, Foot, Hale, Harlan, Howe, Lane of Kansas, Morgan, Morrill, Pomeroy, Ramsey, Sprague, Sumner, Wade, Wilson—17.

NAYS—Messrs. *Buckalew, Carlile*, Cowan, Doolittle, Foster, Grimes, Johnson, Lane of Indiana, *Powell, Riddle, Saulsbury*, Sherman, Ten Eyck, Trumbull, Van Winkle, Willey—16.

The bill then passed the Senate—yeas 23, nays 8, (Messrs. *Buckalew, Carlile*, Cowan, Hale, Lane of Indiana, *Powell, Riddle, Saulsbury*.)

June 29—The bill fell, the House having tabled the report of the Committee of Conference on the disagreeing votes of the two Houses on it.

COLORED PERSONS AS WITNESSES. (See App.)

Second Session, Thirty-Seventh Congress.

IN SENATE.

Pending the confiscation bill, June 28, 1862, Mr. SUMNER moved these words as an addition to the 14th section:

And in all proceedings under this act there shall be no exclusion of any witness on account of color.

Which was rejected—yeas 14, nays 25, as follows:

YEAS—Messrs. Chandler, Grimes, Harlan, Howard, King, Lane of Kansas, Morrill, Pomeroy, Sumner, Trumbull, Wade, Wilkinson, Wilmot—14.

NAYS—Messrs. Anthony, Browning, *Carlile*, Clark, Collamer, Cowan, *Davis*, Dixon, Doolittle, Fessenden, Foot, Foster, Harris, Henderson, Lane of Indiana, *Nesmith, Pearce, Powell*, Sherman, Simmons, *Stark*, Ten Eyck, Willey, *Wilson* of Missouri, *Wright*—25.

Pending the consideration of the supplement to the emancipation bill for the District of Columbia,

1862, July 7—Mr. SUMNER moved a new section:

That in all the judicial proceedings in the District of Columbia there shall be no exclusion of any witness on account of color.

Which was adopted—yeas 25, nays 11, as follows:

YEAS—Messrs. Anthony, Chandler, Clark, Collamer, Doolittle, Fessenden, Foot, Foster, Grimes, Hale, Harlan, Harris, Howe, King, Lane of Kansas, Morrill, Sherman, Simmons, Sumner, Ten Eyck, Trumbull, Wade, Wilkinson, Wilmot, Wilson of Massachusetts—25.

NAYS—Messrs. Browning, *Carlile*, Cowan, *Davis*, Henderson, *Kennedy*, *McDougall*, *Powell*, *Rice*, Willey, *Wright*—11.

The bill then passed—yeas 29, nays 6, (Messrs. *Carlile*, *Davis*, *Kennedy*, *Powell*, *Wilson*, of Missouri, *Wright*.)

July 9—The bill passed the House—yeas 69, nays 36. There was no separate vote on the above proposition. The NAYS were:

NAYS—Messrs. *William Allen*, *Ancona*, *Baily*, *Biddle*, Jacob B. Blair, Clements, *Cobb*, *Corning*, *Cox*, *Crisfield*, *Dunlap*, *English*, *Fouke*, *Grider*, *Harding*, *Knapp*, *Law*, *Lazear*, *Mallory*, Maynard, *Menzies*, *Morris*, *Nugen*, *Pendleton*, *Perry*, *Richardson*, *James S. Rollins*, *Shiel*, *John B. Steele*, *William G. Steele*, *Stiles*, Francis Thomas, *Voorhees*, *Ward*, Webster, *Wood*—36.

Pending the consideration in the Senate of the House bill in relation to the competency of witnesses in trials of equity and admiralty,

1862, July 15—Mr SUMNER offered this proviso to the first section:

Provided, That there shall be no exclusion of any witness on account of color.

Which was rejected—yeas 14, nays 23, as follows:

YEAS—Messrs. Chandler, Grimes, Harlan, Howard, Howe, King, Lane of Kansas, Pomeroy, *Rice*, Sumner, Wade, Wilkinson, Wilmot, Wilson of Massachusetts—14.

NAYS—Messrs. Anthony, *Bayard*, Browning, Clark, Cowan, *Davis*, Doolittle, Foster, Hale, Harris, Henderson, *Kennedy*, Lane of Indiana, *Powell*, *Saulsbury*, Sherman, Simmons, *Stark*, Ten Eyck, Trumbull, Willey, *Wilson* of Missouri, *Wright*—23.

—

First Session, Thirty-Eighth Congress.

1864, June 25—Pending the civil appropriation bill, in Committee of the Whole, Mr. SUMNER offered this proviso:

Provided, That in the courts of the United States there shall be no exclusion of any witness on account of color.

Mr BUCKALEW moved to add:

Nor in civil actions because he is a party to or interested in the issue tried.

Which was agreed to; and the amendment as amended was agreed to—yeas 22, nays 16, as follows:

YEAS—Messrs. Anthony, Brown, Chandler, Clark, Collamer, Conness, Foot, Foster, Grimes, Hale, Harlan, Howard, Howe, Lane of Kansas, Morgan, Morrill, Pomeroy, Sprague, Sumner, Wade, Wilkinson, Wilson—22.

NAYS—Messrs. *Buckalew*, *Carlile*, Cowan, *Davis*, Harris, *Hendricks*, Hicks, Johnson, *Nesmith*, *Powell*, *Richardson*, *Saulsbury*, Sherman, Trumbull, Van Winkle, Willey—16.

The Senate subsequently concurred in this amendment—yeas 29, nays 10, as follows:

YEAS—Messrs. Anthony, Brown, Chandler, Clark, Conness, Dixon, Doolittle, Fessenden, Foot, Foster, Grimes, Hale, Harlan, Harris, Howard, Howe, Lane of Indiana, Lane of Kansas, Morgan, Morrill, Pomeroy, Ramsey, Sherman,* Sprague, Sumner, Ten Eyck, Wade, Wilkinson, Wilson—29.

NAYS—Messrs. *Buckalew*, *Carlile*, *Hendricks*, Hicks, *Nesmith*, *Powell*, *Saulsbury*, Trumbull, Van Winkle, Willey—10.

IN HOUSE.

June 29—The question being on agreeing to the amendment,

Mr. MALLORY moved to add this proviso to the section amended in the Senate:

Provided, That negro testimony shall only be taken in the United States courts in those States the laws of which authorize such testimony.

Which was rejected—yeas 47, nays 66.

The amendment of the Senate was then agreed to—yeas 68, nays 48, as follows:

YEAS—Messrs. Allison, Ames, Arnold, Ashley, *Baily*, John D. Baldwin, Beaman, Boutwell, Boyd, Broomall, Cobb, Cole, Thomas T. Davis, Dawes, Deming, Dixon, Donnelly, Driggs, Eckley, Eliot, Farnsworth, Fenton, Frank, Garfield, Gooch, Higby, Hooper, Hotchkiss, Hulburd, Ingersoll, Jenckes, Julian, F. W. Kellogg, Orlando Kellogg, Knox, Littlejohn, Loan, Longyear, McBride, McClurg, Moorhead, Morrill, Daniel Morris, Amos Myers, Leonard Myers, Norton, Charles O'Neill, Patterson, Perham, Alexander H. Rice, John H. Rice, Edward H. Rollins, Schenck, Scofield, Shannon, Sloan, Smithers, Spalding, Stevens, Thayer, Upson, Van Valkenburgh, Ellihu B. Washburne, William B. Washburn, Williams, Wilder, Wilson, Windom—68.

NAYS—Messrs. *William J. Allen*, *Ancona*, *Augustus C. Baldwin*, Blair, *Bliss*, *Brooks*, William G. Brown, *Chanler*, *Coffroth*, *Dawson*, *Denison*, *Eden*, *Edgerton*, *Eldridge*, *Finck*, *Harding*, *Benjamin G. Harris*, *Charles M. Harris*, *Herrick*, *Holman*, *William Johnson*, *Knapp*, *Le Blond*, *Mallory*, *Marcy*, *James R. Morris*, *Morrison*, *Noble*, *John O'Neill*, *Pendleton*, *Perry*, *Samuel J. Randall*, *Robinson*, *Ross*, *John B. Steele*, *William G. Steele*, *Stiles*, *Strouse*, *Stuart*, Thomas, Tracy, *Wadsworth*, *Ward*, Webster, Whaley, *Wheeler*, *Chilton A. White*, *Joseph W. White*—48.

REPEAL OF LAWS REGULATING THE COASTWISE SLAVE TRADE.

First Session, Thirty-Eighth Congress.

1864, June 25—Mr. SUMNER offered this additional section, the Senate sitting as in Committee of the Whole, pending the consideration of the civil bill:

And be it further enacted, That sections eight and nine of the act entitled "An act to prohibit the importation of slaves into any port or place within the jurisdiction of the United States from and after the 1st day of January, in the year of our Lord 1808," which sections undertake to regulate the coastwise slave trade, are hereby repealed, and the coastwise slave trade prohibited forever.

Which was rejected—yeas 13, nays 20, as follows:

YEAS—Messrs. Conness, Grimes, Harlan, Howard, Lane of Kansas, Morgan, Morrill, Pomeroy, Ramsey, Sprague, Sumner, Wade, Wilson—13.

NAYS—Messrs. *Buckalew*, *Carlile*, Clark, Collamer, Cowan, *Davis*, Harris, *Hendricks*, Hicks, Howe, Johnson, *McDougall*, *Nesmith*, *Powell*, *Richardson*, *Riddle*, *Saulsbury*, Sherman, Trumbull, Van Winkle—20.

Same day, in open Senate,

Mr. SUMNER renewed the amendment, which was agreed to—yeas 23, nays 14, as follows:

YEAS—Messrs. Anthony, Brown, Chandler, Conness, Dixon, Doolittle,* Fessenden, Foot, Harlan, Harris, Howard, Howe, Lane of Kansas, Morgan, Morrill, Pomeroy, Sprague, Sumner, Ten Eyck, Wade, Wilkinson, Wilson—23.

NAYS—Messrs. *Buckalew*, *Carlile*, Clark, *Hendricks*, Hicks, Johnson, Lane of Indiana, *Nesmith*, *Powell*, *Richardson*, *Saulsbury*, Sherman, Trumbull, Van Winkle, Willey—14.

The bill passed the Senate—yeas 32, nays 4, (Messrs. *Carlile*, *Hendricks*, *Powell*, *Saulsbury*.)

June 29—The House agreed to the amendment without a division, after a brief debate.

---

* Before this vote was taken, Mr. SHERMAN said:

"It is due to myself to say in explanation that I voted against and opposed this amendment for the sole ground, as I stated, that it ought not to be put upon this bill. That is my deliberate conviction yet; but as the Senate have by a majority vote decided to put the amendment on the bill in spite of my remonstrances and resistance, I feel bound now to vote according to my conviction on the merits of the proposition."

* Before the vote was taken, Mr. DOOLITTLE said:

"I voted against this amendment before on the ground that I did not like to vote for such measures on appropriation bills; but two or three others have been put on, and if this is to be legislated upon, as I am in favor of the abolition of the coastwise slave trade, I shall vote in the affirmative."

T. W. HIGGINSON'S PARTICIPATION IN THE BURNS CASE.

1864, March 14—Mr. DAVIS offered this resolution:

Whereas in the history of the attempt to rescue Anthony Burns, a fugitive slave from the State of Virginia, from the custody of the United States officers in Boston, in 1854, it is represented, and it is also generally reported, that T. W. Higginson, now the colonel of a regiment of negro troops in the service of the United States, led, or was engaged in, an assault made by a body of men, with force and arms, upon the court-house in Boston, where the said Anthony Burns was held in the custody of the law and officers of the United States, with the intent and purpose of forcibly rescuing him from such custody; and whereas it is represented and generally reported that a citizen of the United States, then having the custody of said Burns, was killed and murdered by said assailants: Therefore, be it

Resolved, That the president of the Senate appoint a committee of three members of the Senate to investigate whether the said T. W. Higginson had any connection, and if any, what, with the said attempt to rescue the said Burns, and with the killing and murdering of any person having his custody, and that said committee have power to send for persons and papers.

March 17—Mr. TRUMBULL moved to table it; which was agreed to—yeas 29, nays 10, as follows:

YEAS—Messrs. Anthony, Brown, Chandler, Collamer, Dixon, Doolittle, Fessenden, Foot, Foster, Grimes, *Harding*, Harlan, Howard, Howe, Lane of Indiana, Lane of Kansas, Morgan, Morrill, Pomeroy, Ramsey, Sherman, Sprague, Sumner, Ten Eyck, Trumbull, Van Winkle, Wilkinson, Willey, Wilson—29.

NAYS—Messrs. *Buckalew*, *Carlile*, Conness, *Davis*, *Hendricks*, Johnson, *McDougall*, *Powell*, *Riddle*, *Saulsbury*—10.

COLORED SCHOOLS.

June 8—The House passed a bill to provide for the public instruction of youth in Washington city, with an amendment providing for separate schools for the colored children, by setting apart such a proportion of the entire school fund as the number of colored children between the ages of six and seventeen bear to the whole number of children in the District. The bill, with amendments, passed both Houses without a division.

Military Reports, Orders, and Proclamations.

MAJOR GENERAL M'CLELLAN'S PROCLAMATION IN WESTERN VIRGINIA.

HEADQUARTERS DEPARTMENT OF OHIO,
CINCINNATI, *May* 26, 1861.

To the Union men of Western Virginia:

VIRGINIANS: The General Government has long enough endured the machinations of a few factious rebels in your midst. Armed traitors have in vain endeavored to deter you from expressing your loyalty at the polls. Having failed in this infamous attempt to deprive you of the exercise of your dearest rights, they now seek to inaugurate a reign of terror, and thus force you to yield to their schemes and submit to the yoke of the traitorous conspiracy dignified by the name of the Southern Confederacy. They are destroying the property of citizens of your State and ruining your magnificent railways.

The General Government has heretofore carefully abstained from sending troops across the Ohio, or even from posting them along its banks, although frequently urged by many of your prominent citizens to do so. It determined to wait the result of the State election, desirous that no one might be able to say that the slightest effort had been made from this side to influence the free expression of your opinions, although the many agencies brought to bear upon you by the rebels were well known. You have now shown, under the most adverse circumstances, that the great mass of the people of Western Virginia are true and loyal to that beneficent Government under which we and our fathers lived so long.

As soon as the result of the election was known the traitors commenced their work of destruction. The General Government cannot close its ears to the demand you have made for assistance. I have ordered troops to cross the river. They come as your friends and brothers—as enemies only to armed rebels, who are preying upon you; your homes, your families, and your property are safe under our protection. All your rights shall be religiously respected, notwithstanding all that has been said by the traitors to induce you to believe our advent among you will be signalized by an interference with your slaves. Understand one thing clearly: not only will we abstain from all such interference, but we will, on the contrary, *with an iron hand crush any attempt at insurrection on their part.* Now that we are in your midst, I call upon you to fly to arms and support the General Government; sever the connection that binds you to traitors; proclaim to the world that the faith and loyalty so long boasted by the Old Dominion are still preserved in Western Virginia, and that you remain true to the stars and stripes.

G. B. McCLELLAN,
Major General Commanding.

MAJOR GENERAL ROBERT PATTERSON'S PROCLAMATION.

HEADQUARTERS DEPARTMENT OF PENNSYLVANIA.
CHAMBERSBURG, PA., *June* 3, 1861.

To the United States Troops of this Department:

The restraint which has necessarily been imposed upon you, impatient to overcome those who have raised their parricidal hands against our country, is about to be removed. You will soon meet the insurgents.

You are not the aggressors. A turbulent faction, misled by ambitious rulers, in times of profound peace and national prosperity, have occupied your forts and turned the guns against you; have seized your arsenals and armories, and appropriated to themselves Government supplies; have arrested and held as prisoners your companions marching to their homes under State pledge of security, and have captured vessels and provisions voluntarily assured by State legislation from molestation, and now seek to perpetuate a reign of terror over loyal citizens.

They have invaded a loyal State, and entrenched themselves within its boundaries in defiance of its constituted authorities.

You are going on American soil to sustain the civil power, to relieve the oppressed, and to retake that which is unlawfully held.

You must bear in mind you are going for the good of the whole country, and that, while it is your duty to punish sedition, you must protect the loyal, *and, should the occasion offer, at once suppress servile insurrection.*

Success will crown your efforts; a grateful country and a happy people will reward you.

By order of MAJOR GENERAL PATTERSON:

F. J. PORTER, *Asst. Adj. General.*

SECRETARY CAMERON'S LETTER TO GEN. BUTLER.

WASHINGTON, *May* 30, 1861.

SIR: Your action in respect to the negroes who came within your lines from the service of the rebels is approved. The Department is sensible of the embarrassments which must surround officers conducting military operations in a State by the laws of which slavery is sanctioned. The Government cannot recognize the rejection by any State of the Federal obligations, nor can it refuse the performance of the Federal obligations resting upon itself. Among these Federal obligations, however, none can be more important than that of suppressing and dispersing armed combinations formed for the purpose of overthrowing its whole constitutional authority. While, therefore, you will permit no interference by the persons under your command with the relations of persons held to service under the laws of any State, you will, on the other hand, so long as any State within which your military operations are conducted is under the control of such armed combinations, refrain from surrendering to alleged masters any persons who may come within your lines. You will employ such persons in the services to which they may be best adapted, keeping an account of the labor by them performed, of the value of it, and the expenses of their maintenance. The question of their final disposition will be reserved for future determination.

SIMON CAMERON,
Secretary of War.

To Major General BUTLER.

MAJOR GENERAL BUTLER TO LIEUTENANT GENERAL SCOTT.

HEADQUARTERS DEPARTMENT OF VIRGINIA,
May 27, 1861.

* * Since I wrote my last despatch the question in regard to slave property is becoming one of very serious magnitude. The inhabitants of Virginia are using their

negroes in the batteries, and are preparing to send the women and children south. The escapes from them are very numerous, and a squad has come in this morning to my pickets bringing their women and children. Of course these cannot be dealt with upon the theory on which I designed to treat the services of able-bodied men and women who might come within my lines, and of which I gave you a detailed account in my last despatch. I am in the utmost doubt what to do with this species of property. Up to this time I have had come within my lines men and women with their children, entire families, each family belonging to the same owner. I have, therefore, determined to employ, as I can do very profitably, the able-bodied persons in the party, issuing proper food for the support of all, and charging against their services the expense of care and sustenance of the non-laborers, keeping a strict and accurate account as well of the services as of the expenditure, having the worth of the services and the cost of the expenditure determined by a board of survey, to be hereafter detailed. I know of no other manner in which to dispose of this subject and the questions connected therewith. As a matter of property to the insurgents, it will be of very great moment, the number that I now have amounting. as I am informed, to what, in good times, would be of the value of sixty thousand dollars. Twelve of these negroes, I am informed, have escaped from the batteries on Sewall's Point, which, this morning, fired upon my expedition as it passed by out of range. As a means of offence therefore in the enemy's hands, these negroes, when able-bodied, are of the last importance Without them the batteries could not have been erected, at least for many weeks. As a military question, it would seem to be a measure of necessity to deprive their masters of their services. How can this be done? As a political question and a question of humanity, can I receive the services of a father and mother, and not take the children? Of the humanitarian aspect I have no doubt. Of the political one I have no right to judge. I therefore submit all this to your better judgment, and as the questions have a political aspect, I have ventured, and I trust I am not wrong in so doing, to duplicate the parts of my despatch relating to this subject, and forward them to the Secretary of War. * * * * * * *

Very respectfully, your obedient servant,

B. F. BUTLER.

Lieutenant General SCOTT.

—

SECRETARY CAMERON'S REPLY TO GEN. BUTLER.

WASHINGTON, *August* 8, 1861.

GENERAL: The important question of the proper disposition to be made of fugitives from service in States in insurrection against the Federal Government, to which you have again directed my attention in your letter of July 30, has received my most attentive consideration.

It is the desire of the President that all existing rights, in all the States, be fully respected and maintained. The war now prosecuted on the part of the Federal Government is a war for the Union, and for the preservation of all constitutional rights of States, and the citizens of the States, in the Union. Hence no question can arise as to fugitives from service within the States and Territories in which the authority of the Union is fully acknowledged. The ordinary forms of judicial proceeding, which must be respected by military and civil authorities alike, will suffice for the enforcement of all legal claims. But in States wholly or partially under insurrectionary control, where the laws of the United States are so far opposed and resisted that they cannot be effectually enforced, it is obvious that rights dependent on the execution of those laws must, temporarily, fail; and it is equally obvious that rights dependent on the laws of the States within which military operations are conducted must be necessarily subordinated to the military exigencies created by the insurrection, if not wholly forfeited by the treasonable conduct of parties claiming them. To this general rule rights to services can form no exception.

The act of Congress approved August 6, 1861, declares that if persons held to service shall be employed in hostility to the United States, the right to their services shall be forfeited, and such persons shall be discharged therefrom. It follows of necessity that no claim can be recognized by the military authorities of the Union to the services of such persons when fugitives.

A more difficult question is presented in respect to persons escaping from the service of loyal masters. It is quite apparent that the laws of the State, under which only the services of such fugitiues can be claimed, must needs be wholly, or almost wholly, suspended, as to remedies, by the insurrection and the military measures necessitated by it. And it is equally apparent that the substitution of military for judicial measures for the enforcement of such claims must be attended by great inconveniences, embarrassments, and injuries.

Under these circumstances it seems quite clear that the substantial rights of loyal masters will be best protected by receiving such fugitives, as well as fugitives from disloyal masters, into the service of the United States, and employing them under such organizations and in such occupations as circumstances may suggest or require. Of course a record should be kept showing the name and description of the fugitives, the name and the character, as loyal or disloyal, of the master, and such facts as may be necessary to a correct understanding of the circumstances of each case after tranquillity shall have been restored. Upon the return of peace, Congress will, doubtless, properly provide for all the persons thus received into the service of the Union, and for just compensation to loyal masters. In this way only, it would seem, can the duty and safety of the Government and the just rights of all be fully reconciled and harmonized.

You will therefore consider yourself as instructed to govern your future action, in respect to fugitives from service, by the principles herein stated, and will report from time to time, and at least twice in each month, your action in the premises to this Department. You will, however, neither authorize nor permit any interference, by the troops under your command, with the servants of peaceful citizens in house or field; nor will you, in any way, encourage such servants to leave the lawful service of their masters; nor will you, except in cases where the public safety may seem to require, prevent the voluntary return of any fugitive, to the service from which he may have escaped.

I am, General, very respectfully, your obedient servant,

SIMON CAMERON, *Secretary of War.*

Maj. Gen. B. F. BUTLER, *Commanding Department of Virginia, Fortress Monroe.*

—

CONCERNING FUGITIVE SLAVES.

HEADQUARTERS DEPARTMENT OF WASHINGTON,
WASHINGTON, *July* 17, 1861.

[General Orders No 33.]

Fugitive slaves will, under no pretext whatever, be permitted to reside or be in any way harbored in the quarters and camps of the troops serving in this Department. Neither will such slaves be allowed to accompany troops on the march.

Commanders of troops will be held responsible for a strict observance of this order.

By command of Brigadier General Mansfield:

THEO. TALBOT,
Assistant Adjutant General.

Complaint having been made that slaves were abducted by soldiers going North on the cars, the following order was issued:

HEADQUARTERS CITY GUARD,
WASHINGTON, *August* 10, 1861.

To Captain H. DAVIDSON,
Commanding Guard at Railroad Depot:

SIR: It is directed by the Provost Marshal that you permit no soldiers to leave this city by the railroad who are unable to show that they have been properly discharged from the service of the United States; also, that no negroes, without sufficient evidence of their being free or of their right to travel, are permitted to leave the city upon the cars.

I am, Captain, very respectfully, your obedient servant,

W. W. AVERELL, *A. A. A. G.*

EMANCIPATION PROCLAMATION OF GEN. FREMONT.*

HEADQUARTERS OF THE WESTERN DEPARTMENT,
ST. LOUIS, *August* 31, 1861.

Circumstances in my judgment, of sufficient urgency, render it necessary that the commanding general of this

* This Retaliatory Proclamation was issued by a rebel officer:

HEADQUARTERS FIRST MILITARY DISTRICT M. S. G.
CAMP HUNTER, *September* 2, 1861.

To all whom it may concern:

Whereas Major General John C. Fremont, commanding the minions of Abraham Lincoln in the State of Missouri, has seen fit to declare martial law throughout the whole State, and has threatened to shoot any citizen soldier found in arms within certain limits; also, to confiscate the property and free the negroes belonging to the members of the Missouri State Guard:

Therefore, know ye that I, M. Jeff. Thompson, Brigadier General of the first military district of Missouri, having not only the military authority of Brigadier General, but certain police powers granted by Acting Governor Thomas C. Reynolds, and confirmed afterwards by Governor Jackson, do most solemnly promise that for every member of the Missouri State Guard or soldier of our allies, the armies of the Confederate States, who shall be put to death in pursu-

Department should assume the administrative powers of the State. Its disorganized condition, the helplessness of the civil authority, the total insecurity of life, and the devastation of property by bands of murderers and marauders, who infest nearly every county of the State, and avail themselves of the public misfortunes and the vicinity of a hostile force to gratify private and neighborhood vengeance, and who find an enemy wherever they find plunder, finally demand the severest measures to repress the daily increasing crimes and outrages which are driving off the inhabitants and ruining the State.

In this condition the public safety and the success of our arms require unity of purpose, without let or hindrance, to the prompt administration of affairs.

In order, therefore, to suppress disorder, to maintain as far as now practicable the public peace, and to give security and protection to the persons and property of loyal citizens, I do hereby extend and declare established martial law throughout the State of Missouri.

The lines of the army of occupation in this State are for the present declared to extend from Leavenworth by way of the posts of Jefferson City, Rolla, and Ironton, to Cape Girardeau, on the Mississippi river.

All persons who shall be taken with arms in their hands within these lines shall be tried by court-martial, and if found guilty will be shot.

The property, real and personal, of all persons, in the State of Missouri, who shall take up arms against the United States, or who shall be directly proven to have taken an active part with their enemies in the field, is declared to be confiscated to the public use, and their slaves, if any they have, are hereby declared free men.

All persons who shall be proven to have destroyed, after the publication of this order, railroad tracks, bridges, or telegraphs, shall suffer the extreme penalty of the law.

All persons engaged in treasonable correspondence, in giving or procuring aid to the enemies of the United States, in fomenting tumults, in disturbing the public tranquillity by creating and circulating false reports or incendiary documents, are in their own interests warned that they are exposing themselves to sudden and severe punishment.

All persons who have been led away from their allegiance are required to return to their homes forthwith; any such absence, without sufficient cause, will be held to be presumptive evidence against them.

The object of this declaration is to place in the hands of the military authorities the power to give instantaneous effect to existing laws, and to supply such deficiencies as the conditions of war demand. But this is not intended to suspend the ordinary tribunals of the country, where the law will be administered by the civil officers in the usual manner, and with their customary authority, while the same can be peaceably exercised.

The commanding general will labor vigilantly for the public welfare, and in his efforts for their safety hopes to obtain not only the acquiescence, but the active support of the loyal people of the country.

J. C. FREMONT,
Major General Commanding.

[SPECIAL MILITARY ORDER.]

HEADQUARTERS WESTERN DEPARTMENT,
ST. LOUIS, *August* 30, 1861.

The commanding general sincerely regrets that he finds it necessary to make any reproach to the patriotic army under his command. He had hoped that the rigid enforcement of discipline and the good example of the mass of the enlightened soldiery which he has the honor to lead, would have been sufficient to correct in good time the irregularities and licence of the few who have reflected discredit upon our cause and ourselves

But the extension of martial law to all the State of Missouri, rendered suddenly necessary by its unhappy condition, renders it equally imperative to call the army to good order and rigorous discipline. They are reminded that the power to inflict the extraordinary severities of the now governing law is rigidly confined to few, who are to be held strictly accountable for its exercise. They are also reminded that the same necessity which requires the establishment of martial law demands also the enforcement of the military law, which governs themselves with the same sudden severity.

The commanding general therefore strictly prohibits all vexatious proceedings calculated unnecessarily to harass the citizens, and also unauthorized searches, seizures, and destruction of property, except in cases of military necessity, and for which the officer authorizing or permitting it will be held strictly and personally responsible.

All officers commanding districts, posts, or detachments are enjoined to use the utmost prudence and circumspection in the discharge of their duties. Under the circumstances a strict obedience to orders, close attention to duties, and an earnest effort to protect and to avoid harassing innocent persons, is requested and expected everywhere from officers and men.

The commanding general trusts that he will find few occasions to reproach the troops. He hopes and believes that he will find many to admire and commend them.

J. C. FREMONT,
Major General Commanding.

PRESIDENT LINCOLN'S FIRST LETTER TO GENERAL FREMONT.

[Private.]

WASHINGTON, D. C., *Sept.* 2, 1861.

MY DEAR SIR: Two points in your proclamation of August 30th give me some anxiety:

First. Should you shoot a man according to the proclamation, the Confederates would very certainly shoot our best men in their hands, in retaliation; and so, man for man, indefinitely. It is, therefore, my order that you allow no man to be shot under the proclamation without first having my approbation or consent.

Second. I think there is great danger that the closing paragraph, in relation to the confiscation of property, and the liberating slaves of traitorous owners, will alarm our Southern Union friends and turn them against us; perhaps ruin our rather fair prospect for Kentucky.

Allow me, therefore, to ask that you will, as of your own motion, modify that paragraph so as to conform to the *first* and fourth sections of the act of Congress entitled, "An act to confiscate property used for insurrectionary purposes," approved August 6, 1861, and a copy of which act I herewith send you.

This letter is written in a spirit of caution, and not of censure.

I send it by a special messenger, in that it may certainly and speedily reach you.

Yours, very truly, A. LINCOLN.
Major General FREMONT.

GEN. FREMONT'S REPLY.

HEADQUARTERS WESTERN DEPARTMENT,
ST. LOUIS, *September* 8, 1861.

MY DEAR SIR: Your letter of the second, by special messenger, I know to have been written before you had received my letter, and before my telegraphic dispatches and the rapid development of critical conditions here had informed you of affairs in this quarter. I had not written to you fully and frequently; first, because in the incessant change of affairs I would be exposed to give you contradictory accounts; and, secondly, because the amount of the subjects to be laid before you would demand too much of your time.

Trusting to have your confidence, I have

---

ance of the said order of Gen. Fremont, I will *hang, draw, and quarter* a minion of said Abraham Lincoln.

While I am anxious that this unfortunate war shall be conducted, if possible, upon the most liberal principles of civilized warfare—and every order that I have issued has been with that object—yet, if this rule is to be adopted, (and it must first be done by our enemies,) I intend to exceed Gen. Fremont in his excesses, and will make all tories that come within my reach rue the day that a different policy was adopted by their leaders. Already mills, barns, warehouses, and other private property have been wastefully and wantonly destroyed by the enemy in this district, while we have taken nothing except articles strictly contraband or absolutely necessary. Should these things be repeated, I will retaliate ten-fold, so help me God!

M. JEFF. THOMPSON,
Brig. Gen. Commanding.

been leaving it to events themselves to show you whether or not I was shaping affairs here according to your ideas. The shortest communication between Washington and St. Louis generally involves two days, and the employment of two days in time of war goes largely toward success or disaster. I therefore went along according to my own judgment, leaving the result of my movement to justify me with you. And so in regard to my proclamation of the thirtieth. Between the rebel armies, the provisional government, and home traitors, I felt the position bad, and saw danger. In the night I decided upon the proclamation and the form of it—I wrote it the next morning and printed it the same day. I did it without consultation or advice with any one, acting solely with my best judgment to serve the country and yourself, and perfectly willing to receive the amount of censure which should be thought due, if I had made a false movement. This is as much a movement in the war as a battle, and in going into these I shall have to act according to my judgment of the ground before me, as I did on this occasion. If, upon reflection, your better judgment still decides that I am wrong in the article respecting the liberation of slaves, I have to ask that you will openly direct me to make the correction. The implied censure will be received as a soldier always should the reprimand of his chief. If I were to retract of my own accord, it would imply that I myself thought it wrong, and that I had acted without the reflection which the gravity of the point demanded. But I did not. I acted with full deliberation, and upon the certain conviction that it was a measure right and necessary, and I think so still.

In regard to the other point of the proclamation to which you refer, I desire to say that I do not think the enemy can either misconstrue or urge anything against it, or undertake to make unusual retaliation. The shooting of men who shall rise in arms against an army in the military occupation of a country is merely a necessary measure of defence, and entirely according to the usages of civilized warfare. The article does not at all refer to prisoners of war, and certainly our enemies have no grounds for requiring that we should waive in their benefit any of the ordinary advantages which the usages of war allow to us.

As promptitude is itself an advantage in war, I have also to ask that you will permit me to carry out upon the spot the provisions of the proclamation in this respect.

Looking at affairs from this point of view, I am satisfied that strong and vigorous measures have now become necessary to the success of our arms; and hoping that my views may have the honor to meet your approval,

I am, with respect and regard, very truly yours.

The PRESIDENT. J. C. FREMONT.

—

THE PRESIDENT'S REJOINDER ORDERING A MODIFICATION OF THE PROCLAMATION.

WASHINGTON, *September* 11, 1861.

SIR: Yours of the 8th, in answer to mine of the 2d instant, is just received. Assuming that you, upon the ground, could better judge of the necessities of your position than I could at this distance, on seeing your proclamation of August 30th, I perceived no general objection to it. The particular clause, however, in relation to the confiscation of property and the liberation of slaves, appeared to me to be objectionable in its non-conformity to the act of Congress passed the 6th of last August upon the same subjects; and hence I wrote you expressing my wish that that clause should be modified accordingly. Your answer, just received, expresses the preference, on your part, that I should make an open order for the modification, which I very cheerfully do. It is therefore ordered that the said clause of said proclamation be so modified, held, and construed as to conform to and not to transcend the provisions on the same subject contained in the act of Congress entitled "An act to confiscate property used for insurrectionary purposes," approved August 6, 1861, and that said act be published at length with this order.

Your obedient servant,

A. LINCOLN.

Maj. Gen. JOHN C. FREMONT.

—

GENERAL FREMONT'S LETTER TO REBEL COLONEL TAYLOR, EXPLAINING HIS PROCLAMATION.

HEADQUARTERS WESTERN DEPARTMENT, *September* 14, 1861.

Col. T. T. TAYLOR, *Commanding at Springfield, Mo.:*

SIR: Yours of the 8th instant, containing an erroneous construction of my proclamation of the 30th ultimo, has had my attention.

I understand the object of your note to be to enquire whether it was my intention to shoot the wounded who might be made prisoners by the forces under my command. The following paragraph, extracted from the proclamation, will be strictly enforced within the lines prescribed against the class of offenders for whom it was intended, viz:

"All persons who shall be taken with arms in their hands within these lines shall be tried by a court martial, and if found guilty will be shot."

The lines are expressly declared to be those of the army in the military occupation of this State.

You have wholly misapprehended the meaning of the proclamation. Without undertaking to determine the condition of any man engaged in this rebellion, I desire it to be clearly understood that the proclamation is intended distinctly to recognize the usual rights of an open enemy in the field, and to be in all respects strictly conformable with the usages of war. It is hardly necessary for me to say that it was not prepared with any purpose to ignore the ordinary rights of humanity with respect to the wounded men, or those who are humanely engaged in alleviating their sufferings.

J. C. FREMONT,
Major General Commanding.

—

GENERAL INSTRUCTIONS OF THE WAR OFFICE.

WAR DEPARTMENT, *October* 14, 1861.

SIR: In conducting military operations within States declared by the proclamation of the President to be in a state of insurrection, you will govern yourself, so far as persons held to service under the laws of such States are concerned, by the principles of the letters addressed by me to Major General Butler on the 30th of May and the 8th of August, copies of which are herewith furnished to you. As special directions, adapted to special circumstances, cannot be given, much must be referred to your own discretion as commanding general of the expedition. You will, however, in general avail yourself of the services of any persons, whether fugitives from labor or not, who may offer them to the national Government; you will employ such persons in such services as they may be fitted for, either as ordinary employés, or, if special circumstances seem to require it, in any other capacity with such organization, in squads, companies, or otherwise, as you deem most beneficial to the service. This, however, not to mean a general arming of them for military service. You will assure all loyal masters that Congress will provide just compensation to them for the loss of the services of the persons so employed. It is believed that the course thus indicated will best secure the substantial rights of loyal masters, and the benefits to the United States of the services of all disposed to support the Government, while it avoids all interference with the social systems or local institutions of every State, beyond that which insurrection makes unavoidable, and which a restoration of peaceful relations to the Union, under the Constitution, will immediately remove.

Respectfully, SIMON CAMERON,
Secretary of War.

Brigadier General T. W. SHERMAN,
Commanding Expedition to the Southern Coast.

In pursuance of these instructions, a proclamation was issued by General Sherman to the people of South Carolina, saying that—

In obedience to the orders of the President of these United States of America, I have landed on your shores with a small force of national troops. The dictates of a duty which, under these circumstances, I owe to a great sovereign State, and to a proud and hospitable people, among whom I have passed some of the pleasantest days of my life, prompt me to proclaim that we have come amongst you with no feelings of personal animosity, no desire to harm your citizens, destroy your property, or interfere with any of your lawful rights or your social or local institutions, beyond what the causes herein alluded to may render unavoidable.

Major General Dix also issued a proclamation to the people of Accomac and Northampton counties, Virginia, dated November 13, 1861, beginni g as follows:

The military forces of the United States are about to enter your counties as a part of the Union. They will go among you as friends, and with the earnest hope that they may not, by your own acts, be forced to become your enemies. They will invade no rights of person or property. On the contrary, your laws, your institutions, your usages, will be scrupulously respected. There need be no fear that the quietude of any fireside will be disturbed, unless the disturbance is caused by yourselves.

Special directions have been given not to interfere with the condition of any person held to domestic service; and, in order that there may be no ground for mistake or pretext for misrepresentation, commanders of regiments and corps have been instructed not to permit any such persons to come within their lines.

The same day, Major General Wool issued this order:

HEADQUARTERS DEPARTMENT OF VIRGINIA,
FORT MONROE, *October* 14, 1861.

[Special Orders No. 72.]

All colored persons called contrabands, employed as servants by officers and others residing within Fort Monroe, or outside of the Fort at Camp Hamilton and Camp Butler will be furnished with their subsistence and at least eight dollars per month for males, and four dollars per month for females, by the officers or others thus employing them.

So much of the above named sums, as may be necessary to furnish clothing, to be decided by the Chief Quartermaster of the department, will be applied to that purpose, and the remainder will be paid into his hands to create a fund for the support of those contrabands who are unable to work for their own support.

All able-bodied colored persons who are under the protection of the troops of this department, and who are not employed as servants, will be immediately put to work in either the Engineer's or Quartermaster's Department.

By command of Major General Wool:
(Signed) WM. D. WHIPPLE,
Assistant Adjutant General.

Again, November 1, 1861

HEADQUARTERS DEPARTMENT OF VIRGINIA,
FORT MONROE, *November* 1, 1861.

[General Orders No. 34.]

The following pay and allowances will constitute the valuation of the labor of the contrabands at work in the Engineer, Ordnance, Quartermaster, Commissary, and Medical Departments at this post, to be paid as hereinafter mentioned:

Class 1st.—Negro men over eighteen years of age, and able-bodied, ten dollars per month, one ration and the necessary amount of clothing.

Class 2d.—Negro boys from 12 to 18 years of age, and sickly and infirm negro men, five dollars per month, one ration, and the necessary amount of clothing.

The quartermaster will furnish all the clothing. The department employing these men will furnish the subsistence specified above, and as an incentive to good behavior (to be withheld at the direction of the chiefs of the departments respectively) each individual of the first class will receive $2 per month, and each individual of the second class $1 per month, for their own use. The remainder of the money valuation of their labor will be turned over to the quartermaster, who will deduct from it the cost of the clothing issued to them; the balance will constitute a fund to be expended by the quartermaster under the direction of the commanding officer of the department of Virginia for the support of the women and children and those that are unable to work.

For any unusual amount of labor performed they may receive extra pay, varying in amount from fifty cents to one dollar, this to be paid by the departments employing them, to the men themselves, and to be for their own use.

Should any man be prevented from working, on account of sickness, for six consecutive days, or ten days in any one month, one half of the money value will be paid. For being prevented from laboring for a longer period than ten days in any one month all pay and allowances cease.

By command of Major General Wool:
(Signed) WM. D. WHIPPLE,
Assistant Adjutant General.

GENERAL HALLECK'S ORDER OF NOVEMBER 20, 1861.*

HEADQUARTERS DEPARTMENT OF MISSOURI,
ST. LOUIS, *November* 20, 1861.

[General Orders No. 3.]

I. It has been represented that important information, respecting the number and condition of our forces, is conveyed to the enemy by means of fugitive slaves who are admitted within our lines. In order to remedy this evil, it is directed that no such persons be hereafter permitted to enter the lines of any camp, or of any forces on the march; and that any now within such lines be immediately excluded therefrom.

CONTRABANDS IN THE DISTRICT.

DEPARTMENT OF STATE,
WASHINGTON, *December* 4, 1861.

To Major General GEO. B. MCCLELLAN, *Washington.*

GENERAL: I am directed by the President to call your attention to the following subject:

Persons claimed to be held to service or labor under the laws of the State of Virginia, and actually employed in hostile service against the Government of the United States, frequently escape from the lines of the enemy's forces and are received within the lines of the army of the Potomac.

This Department understands that such persons afterwards coming into the city of Washington are liable to be arrested by the city police, upon the presumption, arising from color, that they are fugitives from service or labor.

By the 4th section of the act of Congress approved August 6th, 1861, entitled "An act to confiscate property used for insurrectionary purposes," such hostile employment is made a full and sufficient answer to any further claim to service or labor. Persons thus employed and escaping are received into the military protection of the United States, and their arrest as fugitives from service or labor should be immediately followed by the military arrest of the parties making the seizure.

Copies of this communication will be sent to the Mayor of the city of Washington and to the Marshal of the Dis-

* General Halleck, in a letter, thus explained the order:

HEADQUARTERS DEPARTMENT OF THE MISSOURI,
ST. LOUIS, *December* 8, 1861.

MY DEAR COLONEL: Yours of the 4th instant is just received. Order No. 3 was, in my mind, clearly a military necessity. Unauthorized persons, black or white, free or slaves, must be kept out of our camps, unless we are willing to publish to the enemy everything we do or intend to do. It was a *military* and not a *political* order.

I am ready to carry out any lawful instructions in regard to fugitive slaves which my superiors may give me, and to enforce any law which Congress may pass. But I cannot make law, and will not violate it. You know my private opinion on the policy of confiscating the slave property of rebels in arms. If Congress shall pass it, you may be certain that I shall enforce it. Perhaps my policy as to the treatment of rebels and their property is as well set out in Order No. 13, issued the day your letter was written, as I could now describe it.

Hon. F. P. BLAIR, *Washington.*

trict of Columbia, that any collision between the civil and military authorities may be avoided.

I am, General, your very obedient,

WILLIAM H. SEWARD.

FROM THE REPORT OF THE SECRETARY OF WAR, DEC. 1, 1861.

It is already a grave question what shall be done with those slaves who were abandoned by their owners on the advance of our troops into southern territory, as at Beaufort district, in South Carolina. The number left within our control at that point is very considerable, and similar cases will probably occur. What shall be done with them? Can we afford to send them forward to their masters, to be by them armed against us, or used in producing supplies to sustain the rebellion? Their labor may be useful to us; withheld from the enemy it lessens his military resources, and withholding them has no tendency to induce the horrors of insurrection, even in the rebel communities. They constitute a military resource, and, being such, that they should not be turned over to the enemy is too plain to discuss. Why deprive him of supplies by a blockade, and voluntarily give him men to produce them?

The disposition to be made of the slaves of rebels, after the close of the war, can be safely left to the wisdom and patriotism of Congress. The Representatives of the people will unquestionably secure to the loyal slaveholders every right to which they are entitled under the Constitution of the country.

SIMON CAMERON,
Secretary of War.

It is understood that the Report of the Secretary of War, as originally prepared was as follows, and that it was modified at the request of the PRESIDENT:

It has become a grave question for determination what shall be done with the slaves abandoned by their owners on the advance of our troops into southern territory, as in the Beaufort district of South Carolina. The whole white population therein is six thousand, while the number of negroes exceeds thirty-two thousand. The panic which drove their masters in wild confusion from their homes, leaves them in undisputed possession of the soil. Shall they, armed by their masters, be placed in the field to fight against us, or shall their labor be continually employed in reproducing the means for supporting the armies of rebellion?

The war into which this Government has been forced by rebellious traitors is carried on for the purpose of repossessing the property violently and treacherously seized upon by the enemies of the Government, and to re-establish the authority and laws of the United States in the places where it is opposed or overthrown by armed insurrection and rebellion. Its purpose is to recover and defend what is justly its own.

War, even between independent nations, is made to subdue the enemy, and all that belongs to that enemy, by occupying the hostile country, and exercising dominion over all the men and things within its territory. This being true in respect to independent nations at war with each other, it follows that rebels who are laboring by force of arms to overthrow a Government, justly bring upon themselves all the consequences of war, and provoke the destruction merited by the worst of crimes. That Government would be false to national trust, and would justly excite the ridicule of the civilized world, that would abstain from the use of any efficient means to preserve its own existence, or to overcome a rebellious and traitorous enemy, by sparing or protecting the property of those who are waging war against it.

The principal wealth and power of the rebel States is a peculiar species of property, consisting of the service or labor of African slaves, or the descendants of Africans. This property has been variously estimated at the value of from seven hundred million to one thousand million dollars.

Why should this property be exempt from the hazards and consequences of a rebellious war?

It was the boast of the leader of the rebellion, while he yet had a seat in the Senate of the United States, that the southern States would be comparatively safe and free from the burdens of war, if it should be brought on by the contemplated rebellion, and that boast was accompanied by the savage threat that "northern towns and cities would become the victims of rapine and military spoil," and that "northern men should smell southern gunpowder and feel southern steel." No one doubts the disposition of the rebels to carry that threat into execution. The wealth of northern towns and cities, the produce of northern farms, northern workshops and manufactories would certainly be seized, destroyed, or appropriated as military spoil. No property in the North would be spared from the hands of the rebels, and their rapine would be defended under the laws of war. While the loyal States thus have all their property and possessions at stake, are the insurgent rebels to carry on warfare against the Government in peace and security to their own property?

Reason and justice and self-preservation forbid that such should be the policy of this Government, but demand, on the contrary, that, being forced by traitors and rebels to the extremity of war, all the rights and powers of war should be exercised to bring it to a speedy end.

Those who war against the Government justly forfeit all rights of property, privilege, or security, derived from the Constitution and laws, against which they are in armed rebellion; and as the labor and service of their slaves constitute the chief property of the rebels, such property should share the common fate of war to which they have devoted the property of loyal citizens.

While it is plain that the slave property of the South is justly subjected to all the consequences of this rebellious war, and that the Government would be untrue to its trust in not employing all the rights and powers of war to bring it to a speedy close, the details of the plan for doing so, like all other military measures, must, in a great degree, be left to be determined by particular exigencies. The disposition of other property belonging to the rebels that becomes subject to our arms is governed by the circumstances of the case. The Government has no power to hold slaves, none to restrain a slave of his liberty, or to exact his service. It has a right, however, to use the voluntary service of slaves liberated by war from their rebel masters, like any other property of the rebels, in whatever mode may be most efficient for the defence of the Government, the prosecution of the war, and the suppression of rebellion. It is clearly a right of the Government to arm slaves when it may become necessary as it is to take gunpowder from the enemy. Whether it is expedient to do so is purely a military question. The right is unquestionable by the laws of war. The expediency must be determined by circumstances, keeping in view the great object of overcoming the the rebels, re-establishing the laws, and restoring peace to the nation.

It is vain and idle for the Government to carry on this war, or hope to maintain its existence against rebellious force, without employing all the rights and powers of war. As has been said, the right to deprive the rebels of their property in slaves and slave labor is as clear and absolute as the right to take forage from the field, or cotton from the warehouse, or powder and arms from the magazine. To leave the enemy in the possession of such property as forage and cotton and military stores, and the means of constantly reproducing them, would be madness. It is, therefore, equal madness to leave them in peaceful and secure possession of slave property, more valuable and efficient to them for war than forage, cotton, and military stores. Such policy would be national suicide. What to do with that species of property is a question that time and circumstances will solve, and need not be anticipated further than to repeat that they cannot be held by the Government as slaves. It would be useless to keep them as prisoners of war; and self-preservation, the highest duty of a Government, or of individuals, demands that they should be disposed of or employed in the most effective manner that will tend most speedily to suppress the insurrection and restore the authority of the Government. If it shall be found that the men who have been held by the rebels as slaves are capable of bearing arms and performing efficient military service, it is the right, and may become the duty, of this Government to arm and equip them, and employ their services against the rebels, under proper military regulations, discipline, and command.

But in whatever manner they may be used by the Government, it is plain that, once liberated by the rebellious act of their masters, they should never again be restored to bondage. By the master's treason and rebellion he forfeits all right to the labor and service of his slave; and the slave of the rebellious master, by his service to the Government, becomes justly entitled to freedom and protection.

The disposition to be made of the slaves of rebels, after the close of the war, can be safely left to the wisdom and patriotism of Congress. The representatives of the people will unquestionably secure to the loyal slaveholders every right to which they are entitled under the Constitution of the country.

GENERAL BURNSIDE'S PROCLAMATION.

ROANOKE ISLAND, N. C., *February* 18, 1862.

TO THE PEOPLE OF NORTH CAROLINA:

The mission of our joint expedition is not to invade any of your rights, but to assert the authority of the United States, and to close with you the desolating war brought upon your State by comparatively a few bad men in your midst. * * * * *

The Government asks only that its authority may be recognized; and we repeat, in no manner or way does it desire to interfere with your laws, constitutionally established, your institutions of any kind whatever, your property of any sort, or your usages in any respect.

L. M. GOLDSBOROUGH, *Flag Officer, Commanding North Carolina Blockading Squadron.*
A. E. BURNSIDE, *Brigadier General, Commanding Department of North Carolina.*

GENERAL HALLECK'S PROCLAMATION.

HEADQUARTERS DEPARTMENT OF MISSOURI,
ST. LOUIS, *February* 23, 1862.

The major general commanding the department desires to impress upon all officers the importance of preserving good order and discipline among their troops as the armies of the West advance into Tennessee and the southern States. * * *

Soldiers! let no excess on your part tarnish the glory of our arms!

The order heretofore issued in this department, in regard to pillaging and marauding, the destruction of private property, and the stealing or concealment of slaves, must be strictly enforced. It does not belong to the military to decide upon the relation of master and slave. Such questions must be settled by the civil courts. No fugitive slave will therefore be admitted within our lines or camps, except when specially ordered by the general commanding. *

Military stores and the public property of the enemy must be surrendered, and any attempt to conceal such property, by fraudulent transfer or otherwise, will be punished, but no private property will be touched unless by order of the general commanding. Wherever it becomes necessary to obtain forced contributions for the supply and subsistence of our troops, such levies will be made as light as possible, and be so distributed as to produce no distress among the people. All property so taken must be receipted and fully accounted for, as heretofore directed.

These orders will be read at the head of every regiment, and all officers are commanded to strictly enforce them.

By command of Major General Halleck:

N. H. McLEAN, *Adjutant General.*

GENERAL BUELL'S LETTER.

HEADQUARTERS DEPARTMENT OF THE OHIO,
Nashville, March 6, 1862.

DEAR SIR: I have had the honor to receive your communication of the 1st instant on the subject of fugitive slaves in the camps of the army.

It has come to my knowledge that slaves sometimes make their way improperly into our lines, and in some instances they may be enticed there, but I think the number has been magnified by report. Several applications have been made to me by persons whose servants have been found in our camps, and in every instance that I know of the master has recovered his servant and taken him away.

I need hardly remind you that there will always be found some lawless and mischievous persons in every army; but I assure you that the mass of this army is law-abiding, and that it is neither its disposition nor its policy to violate law or the rights of individuals in any particular.

With great respect, your obedient servant,

D. C. BUELL,
Brig. Gen. Commanding Department.

Hon. J. R. UNDERWOOD,
Chairman Military Committee, Frankfort, Ky.

GENERAL HOOKER'S ORDER IN A FUGITIVE SLAVE CASE.

HEADQUARTERS, HOOKER'S DIVISION, CAMP BAKER,
LOWER POTOMAC, *March* 26, 1862.

TO BRIGADE AND REGIMENTAL COMMANDERS OF THIS DIVISION:

Messrs. Nally, Gray, Dummington, Dent, Adams, Speake, Price, Posey, and Cobey, citizens of Maryland, have negroes supposed to be with some of the regiments of this division; the brigadier general commanding directs that they be permitted to visit all the camps of his command, in search of their property, and if found, that they be allowed to take possession of the same, without any interference whatever. Should any obstacle be thrown in their way by any officer or soldier in the division, they will be at once reported by the regimental commanders to these headquarters.

By command of Brigadier General Hooker:

JOSEPH DICKINSON,
Assistant Adjutant General.

The following report was made in relation to said order by direction of General Sickles:

HEADQUARTERS SECOND REGIMENT, EXCELSIOR BRIGADE,
CAMP HALL, *March* 27, 1862.

LIEUTENANT: In compliance with verbal directions from Brigadier General D. E. Sickles, to report as to the occurrence at this camp on the afternoon of the 26th instant, I beg leave to submit the following:

At about 3.30 o'clock p. m., March 26, 1862, admission within our lines was demanded by a party of horsemen, (civilians,) numbering, perhaps, fifteen. They presented the lieutenant commanding the guard with an order of entrance from Brigadier General Joseph Hooker, commanding division, (copy appended,) the order stating that nine men should be admitted. I ordered that the balance of the party should remain without the lines; which was done. Upon the appearance of the others, there was visible dissatisfaction and considerable murmuring among the soldiers, to so great an extent that I almost feared for the safety of the slave-owners. At this time General Sickles opportunely arrived, and instructed me to order them outside the camp, which I did, amidst the loud cheers of our soldiers. It is proper to add, that before entering our lines, and within about seventy-five or one hundred yards of our camp, one of their number discharged two pistol shots at a negro, who was running past them, with an evident intention of taking his life. This justly enraged our men.

All of which is respectfully submitted.

Your obedient servant, JOHN TOLEN,
Major Commanding Second Regiment, E. B.

To Lieutenant J. L. PALMER, Jr.,
A. D. C. and A. A. A. General.

GENERAL DOUBLEDAY'S ORDER.

HEADQUARTERS MILITARY DEFENSES
NORTH OF THE POTOMAC,
WASHINGTON, *April* 6, 1862.

SIR: I am directed by General Doubleday to say, in answer to your letter of the 2d instant, that all negroes coming into the lines of any of the camps or forts under his command, are to be treated as persons, and not as chattels.

Under no circumstances has the commander of a fort or camp the power of surrendering persons claimed as fugitive slaves, as it cannot be done without determining their character.

The additional article of war recently passed by Congress positively prohibits this.

The question has been asked, whether it would not be better to exclude negroes altogether from the lines. The general is of the opinion that they bring much valuable information, which cannot be obtained from any other source. They are acquainted with all the roads, paths, fords, and other natural features of the country, and they make excellent guides. They also know and frequently have exposed the haunts of secession spies and traitors and the existence of rebel organizations. They will not, therefore, be excluded.

The general also directs me to say that civil process cannot be served directly in the camps or forts of his command, without full authority be obtained from the commanding officer for that purpose.

I am, very respectfully, your obedient servant,

E. P. HALSTED,
Assistant Adjutant General.

Lieut. Col. JOHN D. SHAUL,
Commanding 76th Reg. N. Y. Vols.

PRESIDENT'S PROCLAMATION RESCINDING GENERAL HUNTER'S PROCLAMATION—MAY 19, 1862.

Whereas there appears in the public prints what purports to be a proclamation of Major General Hunter, in the words and figures following, to wit:

HEADQUARTERS DEPARTMENT OF THE SOUTH,
HILTON HEAD, S. C., *May* 9, 1862.

[General Orders No. 11.]

The three States of Georgia, Florida, and South Carolina, comprising the military department of the South, having deliberately declared themselves no longer under the protection of the United States of America, and having taken up arms against the said United States, it becomes a military necessity to declare them under martial law. This was accordingly done on the 25th day of April, 1862. Slavery and martial law in a free country are altogether incompatible; the persons in these three States—Georgia, Florida, and South Carolina—heretofore held as slaves, are therefore declared forever free.

DAVID HUNTER,
Major General Commanding.

Official:
ED. W. SMITH, *Acting Assistant Adjutant General.*

And whereas the same is producing some excitement and misunderstanding,

Therefore, I, ABRAHAM LINCOLN, President of the United States, proclaim and declare, that the Government of the United States had no knowledge, information, or belief, of an intention on the part of General Hunter to issue such a proclamation; nor has it yet any authentic information that the document is genuine. And further, that neither General Hunter, nor any other commander, or person, has been authorized by the Government of the United States to make proclamations declaring the slaves of any State free; and that the supposed proclamation, now in question, whether genuine or false, is altogether void, so far as respects such declaration.

I further make known that whether it be competent for me, as Commander-in-Chief of the Army and Navy, to declare the slaves of any State or States free, and whether, at any time, in any case, it shall have become a necessity indispensable to the maintenance of the Government, to exercise such supposed power, are questions which, under my responsibility, I reserve to myself, and which I cannot feel justified in leaving to the decision of commanders in the field. These are totally different questions from those of police regulations in armies and camps.

On the sixth day of March last, by a special message, I recommended to Congress the adoption of a joint resolution to be substantially as follows:

Resolved, That the United States ought to co-operate with any State which may adopt a gradual abolishment of slavery, giving to such State pecuniary aid, to be used by such State, in its discretion, to compensate for the inconveniences, public and private, produced by such change of system.

The resolution, in the language above quoted, was adopted by large majorities in both branches of Congress, and now stands an authentic, definite, and solemn proposal of the nation to the States and people most immediately interested in the subject matter. To the people of those States I now earnestly appeal—I do not argue—I beseech you to make the argument for yourselves—you cannot, if you would, be blind to the signs of the times—I beg of you a calm and enlarged consideration of them, ranging, if it may be, far above personal and partisan politics. This proposal makes common cause for a common object, casting no reproaches upon any. It acts not the Pharisee. The changes it contemplates would come gently as the dews of Heaven, not rending or wrecking anything. Will you not embrace it? So much good has not been done, by one effort, in all past time, as, in the Providence of God, it is now your high privilege to do. May the vast future not have to lament that you have neglected it.

In witness whereof, I have hereunto set my hand and caused the seal of the United States to be affixed.

Done at the City of Washington this nineteenth day of May, in the year of our Lord one thousand eight hundred and sixty-two, and of the Independence of the United States the eighty-sixth.

ABRAHAM LINCOLN.

By the President:

WILLIAM H. SEWARD, *Secretary of State.*

AN ORDER OF MAJOR GENERAL M'DOWELL.

HEADQUARTERS DEPARTMENT OF THE RAPPAHANNOCK,
OPPOSITE FREDERICKSBURG, VA., *May* 26, 1862.

[Special Order No. 68.]

Colonel Meredith, commanding the fifty-sixth Pennsylvania volunteers will furnish from his regiment a guard for the house and property of Mr. L. J. Huffman, who lives near Belle Plain. Colonel Meredith will see that no more corn is taken from Mr. Huffman, and that no more fencing is disturbed. The guard will be so placed as to make this sure, even if it should be necessary to place a sentinel over every panel of fence.

By command of Major General McDowell:

SAMUEL BRECK, *A. A. G.*

COL. S. A. MEREDITH,
Commanding fifty-sixth Pennsylvania Volunteers.

Sent by Mr. Huffman.

I certify that the above is a true copy,

E. P. HALSTED, *Capt., A. A. G.*

AN ORDER OF GENERAL T. WILLIAMS.

HEADQUARTERS SECOND BRIGADE,
BATON ROUGE, *June* 5, 1862.

[General Orders No. 46.]

In consequence of the demoralizing and disorganizing tendencies to the troops of harboring runaway negroes, it is hereby ordered that the respective commanders of the camps and garrisons of the several regiments, second brigade, turn all such fugitives in their camps or garrisons out beyond the limits of their respective guards and sentinels.

By order of Brigadier General T. Williams:

WICKHAM HOFFMAN,
Assistant Adjutant General.

Colonel H. E. Paine, Fourth Wisconsin, declined to have his regiment employed "in violation of law for the purpose of returning fugitives to rebels," and reported that he could not obey the order. He was then placed under arrest, his command devolving on the next ranking officer.

Lieutenant Colonel D. R. Anthony, Seventh Kansas, issued this order:

HEADQUARTERS MITCHELL'S BRIGADE,
ADVANCE COLUMN, FIRST BRIGADE, FIRST DIVISION,
GENERAL ARMY OF THE MISSISSIPPI,
CAMP ETHERIDGE, TENNESSEE, *June* 18, 1862.

[General Orders No. 26.]

1. The impudence and impertinence of the open and armed rebels, traitors, secessionists, and southern-rights men of this section of the State of Tennessee, in arrogantly demanding the right to search our camp for fugitive slaves, has become a nuisance, and will no longer be tolerated.

Officers will see that this class of men, who visit our camp for this purpose, are excluded from our lines.

2. Should any such person be found within our lines, they will be arrested and sent to headquarters.

3. Any officer or soldier of this command who shall arrest and deliver to his master a fugitive slave shall be summarily and severely punished, according to the laws relative to such crimes.

4. The strong Union sentiment in this section is most gratifying, and all officers and soldiers, in their intercourse with the loyal and those favorably disposed, are requested to act in their usual kind and courteous manner and protect them to the fullest extent.

By order of D. R. Anthony, Lieutenant Colonel Seventh Kansas volunteers, commanding:

W. W. H. LAWRENCE,
Captain and Assistant Adjutant General.

And was put under arrest.

SECRETARY OF WAR TO GENERAL SAXTON.

WAR DEPARTMENT,
WASHINGTON CITY, *D. C.*, *June* 16, 1862.

SIR: You are hereby assigned to duty in the department of the South, to act under orders of the Secretary of War. You are directed to take possession of all the plantations heretofore occupied by the rebels, and take charge of the inhabitants remaining thereon within the department, or which the fortunes of war may hereafter bring into it, with authority to take such measures, make such rules and regulations for the cultivation of the land, and for the protection, employment, and government of the inhabitants as circumstances may seem to require.

You are authorized to exercise all sanitary and police

powers that may be necessary for the health and security of the persons under your charge, and may imprison or exclude all disorderly, disobedient, or dangerous persons from the limits of your operations.

The major general commanding the department of the South will be instructed to give you all the military aid and protection necessary to enable you to carry out the views of the Government. You will have the power to act upon the decisions of courts-martial which are called for the trial of persons not in the military service to the same extent that a commander of a department has over courts-martial called for the trial of soldiers in his department; and, so far as the persons above described are concerned, you will also have a general control over the action of the provost marshals.

It is expressly understood that, so far as the persons and purposes herein specified are concerned, your action will be independent of that of the other military authorities of the department, and in all other cases subordinate only to the major general commanding.

In cases of need or destitution of the inhabitants, you are directed to issue such portions of the army rations and such articles of clothing as may be suitable to the habits and wants of the persons supplied, which articles will be furnished by the quartermaster and commissary of the department of the South upon requisitions approved by yourself. It is expected that by encouraging industry, skill in the cultivation of the necessaries of life, and general self-improvement, you will, as far as possible, promote the real well being of all people under your supervision.

Medical and ordnance supplies will be furnished by the proper officers, which you will distribute and use according to your instructions.

You will account regularly with the proper bureaus of this department and report frequently—once a week, at least. Yours, truly,

EDWIN M. STANTON,
Secretary of War.

GENERAL INSTRUCTIONS FROM THE PRESIDENT THROUGH THE WAR OFFICE.*

WAR DEPARTMENT,
WASHINGTON, *July* 22, 1862.

First. Ordered that military commanders within the States of Virginia, North Carolina, Georgia, Florida, Alabama, Mississippi, Louisiana, Texas, and Arkansas, in an orderly manner seize and use any property, real or personal, which may be necessary or convenient for their several commands, for supplies, or for other military purposes; and that while property may be destroyed for proper military objects, none shall be destroyed in wantonness or malice.

Second. That military and naval commanders shall employ as laborers, within and from said States, so many persons of African descent as can be advantageously used for military or naval purposes, giving them reasonable wages for their labor.

Third. That, as to both property, and persons of African descent, acccounts shall be kept sufficiently accurate and in detail to show quantities and amounts, and from whom both property and such persons shall have come, as a basis upon which compensation can be made in proper cases; and the several departments of this Government shall attend to and perform their appropriate parts towards the execution of these orders.

By order of the President:

EDWIN M. STANTON,
Secretary of War.

GEN. M'CLELLAN'S PROMULGATION OF IT.

August 9, 1862—Major General McClellan, from his headquarters at Harrison's Landing, promulgated this order, with directions for its observance. We quote several pertinent paragraphs:

Inhabitants, especially women and children, remaining peaceably at their homes, must not be molested; and wherever commanding officers find families peculiarly exposed in their persons or property to marauding from this army, they will, as heretofore, so far as they can do with safety and without detriment to the service, post guards for their protection.

In protecting private property, no reference is intended to persons held to service or labor by reason of African descent. Such persons will be regarded by this army, as they heretofore have been, as occupying simply a peculiar legal status under State laws, which condition the military authorities of the United States are not required to regard at all in districts where military operations are made necessary by the rebellious action of the State governments.

Persons subject to suspicion of hostile purposes, residing or being near our forces, will be, as heretofore, subject to arrest and detention, until the cause or necessity is removed. All such arrested parties will be sent, as usual, to the Provost Marshal General, with a statement of the facts in each case.

The general commanding takes this occasion to remind the officers and soldiers of this army that we are engaged in supporting the Constitution and the laws of the United States and suppressing rebellion against their authority; that we are not engaged in a war of rapine, revenge, or subjugation; that this is not a contest against populations, but against armed forces and political organizations; that it is a struggle carried on with the United States, and should be conducted by us upon the highest principles known to Christian civilization.

Since this army commenced active operations, persons of African descent, including those held to service or labor under State laws, have always been received, protected, and employed as laborers at wages. Hereafter it shall be the duty of the Provost Marshal General to cause lists to be made of all persons of African descent employed in this army as laborers for military purposes—such lists being made sufficiently accurate and in detail to show from whom such persons shall have come.

Persons so subject and so employed have always understood that after being received into the military service of the United States, in any capacity, they could never be reclaimed by their former holders. Except upon such understanding on their part the order of the President, as to this class of persons, would be inoperative. The general commanding therefore feels authorized to declare to all such employees, that they will receive permanent military protection against any compulsory return to a condition of servitude.

By command of Major General McClellan:

S. WILLIAMS,
Assistant Adjutant General.

MAJOR GENERAL BUTLER AND BRIGADIER GENERAL PHELPS.

August 2, 1862—Major General Benjamin F. Butler, commanding Department of the Gulf, declined to approve of the conduct of Brigadier General J. W. Phelps, in organizing five companies of negroes, whom he proposed to arm and equip, upon the ground that the President alone had the authority to employ Africans in arms, and that he had not indicated this purpose. General Phelps resigned his commission in consequence.

REPLY OF THE WAR DEPARTMENT ON THE CASE.

WAR DEPARTMENT,
WASHINGTON CITY, *July* 3, 1862.

GENERAL: I wrote you last under date of the 29th ultimo, and have now to say that your dispatch of the 18th ultimo, with the accompanying report of General Phelps, concerning certain fugitive negroes that have come to his pickets, has been considered by the President.

He is of opinion that under the law of Congress they cannot be sent back to their master; that in common humanity they must not be permitted to suffer for want of food, shelter, or other necessaries of life; that to this end they should be provided for by the quartermaster's and commissary's departments, and that those who are capable of labor should be set to work and paid reasonable wages.

In directing this to be done, the President does not mean, at present, to settle any general rule in respect to slaves or slavery, but simply to provide for the particular case under the circumstances in which it is now presented.

I am, General, very respectfully, your obedient servant,

EDWIN M. STANTON,
Secretary of War.

Major General B. F. BUTLER,
Commanding, &c., New Orleans, Louisiana.

THE PRESIDENT'S ORDER TO GEN. SCHOFIELD.

OCT. 1, 1863.

* * Under your recent order, which I have approved, you will only arrest individuals, and suppress assemblies or newspapers,

* The issue of this Order is one of the reasons given by JEFFERSON DAVIS for his Order of August 1, 1862, directing that the commissioned officers of Pope's and Steinwehr's commands be not entitled, when captured, to be treated as soldiers, and entitled to the benefit of the cartel of exchange.

when they may be working *palpable* injury to the military in your charge; and in no other case will you interfere with the expression of opinion in any form, or allow it to be interfered with violently by others. In this you have a discretion to exercise with great caution, calmness, and forbearance. * * *

I think proper, however, to enjoin upon you the following: Allow no part of the military under your command to be engaged in either returning fugitive slaves, or in forcing or enticing slaves from their homes; and, so far as practicable, enforce the same forbearance upon the people.

Report to me your opinion upon the availability for good of the enrolled militia of the State. Allow no one to enlist colored troops, except upon orders from you, or from here through you.

Allow no one to assume the functions of confiscating property, under the law of Congress, or otherwise, except upon orders from here.

At elections see that those and only those, are allowed to vote, who are entitled to do so by the laws of Missouri, including as of those laws the restrictions laid by the Missouri Convention upon those who may have participated in the rebellion.

GENERAL TUTTLE'S ORDERS AT NATCHEZ, MISS., MARCH 19, 1864.

NATCHEZ, MISS., *February* 16, 1864.

[General Order No. 2.]

* * From henceforward, all contraband negroes of Natchez are forbidden from the renting of houses, and living to themselves, but are required to secure legitimate employment with responsible respectable persons, or otherwise be sent to the contraband encampment. Those hiring them are expected to aid in the enforcement of the foregoing regulations by the proper employment of them in their families or messes.

The congregation of so many negroes in one house, with their filthy and lazy habits, (as the undersigned has found to be the case,) if continued, will eventually prove fatal to the health of the city.

All owners or renters of houses are forbidden the renting or sub-renting of the same to contraband negroes under a penalty for so doing. Otherwise it will be impossible for the undersigned to carry out a system of sanitary regulations essential to the well being of the city.

By order of A. W. Kelley, Surgeon and Health Officer:

T. A. RALSTON,
A. A. Gen. Post.

NATCHEZ, (MISS.,) *March* 19, 1864.

To preserve the general health of the troops stationed in the city of Natchez and of the inhabitants, and to guard against the origination here, and the introduction of pestilential diseases the ensuing summer and autumn, it imperatively requires the prompt, vigorous, and steady enforcement of the sanitary regulations heretofore prescribed in this city.

It is of the first and greatest importance and necessity that all causes tending to the engendering and dissemination of pestilential diseases here, so soon as their existence is known, shall be at once abated or removed, so far as practicable. It is to be apprehended that serious danger to the health of this city will result from the congregation within its limits of the large number of idle negroes which now throng the streets, lanes, and alleys, and overcrowd every hovel. Lazy and profligate, unused to caring for themselves; thriftless for the present, and recklessly improvident of the future, the most of them loaf idly about the streets and alleys, prowling in secret places, and lounge lazily in crowded hovels, which soon become dens of noisome filth, the hot-beds fit to engender and rapidly disseminate the most loathsome and malignant diseases.

To prevent these evil effects, it is hereby ordered that after the first day of April, 1864, no contraband shall be allowed to remain in the city of Natchez, who is not employed by some responsible white person in some legitimate business, and who does not reside at the domicil of his or her employer; and no contraband will be allowed to hire any premises in the city for any purpose whatever, and no other person will be allowed to hire such premises for the purpose of evading this order, nor allowed to hire or harbor any contraband who cannot satisfy the health officer that he or she needs the services of said contraband in some legitimate employment. All contrabands remaining in the city in contravention of this order after April 1st will be removed to the contraband encampment.

The word contraband is hereby defined to mean all persons formerly slaves who are not now in the employ of their former owners.

Persons drawing rations from the United States Government are not supposed to need any hired servants. The number allowed to each family will be determined by the undersigned.

By order of A. W. Kelly, Surgeon and Health Officer.

Approved:

J. M. TUTTLE, *Brig. Gen. Com'g District.*

HEADQUARTERS OF DEFENCES,
NEW ORLEANS, *March* 24, 1864.

Citizens having colored people in their employ, who are superfluous or insubordinate, will be promptly relieved of them by reporting the fact to Col. Hanks, Superintendent of Negro Labor.

OFFICE PROVOST MARSHAL,
PARISHES OF JEFFERSON AND ST. CHARLES, LA.
CARROLLTON, *March* 28, 1864.

* * The Provost Marshal of the Parish of Jefferson is also charged with the execution of General Order No. 12, Headquarters of Defences of New Orleans, March 24, 1864, so far as it relates to its execution within this district. All persons within this district are requested to report at once to his office the names of their colored servants of either sex, in order that he may give them an employment certificate, and all colored people of either sex who shall not on the first of April have such certificate in their possession will be considered unemployed, the males organized into squads and companies for labor on the parapet, and the females turned over to Col. Hanks.

By command of Brig. Gen. Roberts:

R. SKINNER, *First Lieut.,*
10th U. S. Infantry, A. D. C. and A. A. A. G.
R. B. BROWN,
Colonel and Provost Marshal.

RESOLUTION OF INQUIRY.

First Session, Thirty-Eighth Congress.

IN HOUSE.

1864, May 16—Mr. GRINNELL offered this resolution which was adopted:

Resolved, That the committee on the conduct of the war be instructed to inquire as to the occasion of the military order of Brigadier General J. M. Tuttle for the government of the city of Natchez, Mississippi, which forbids any contraband remaining in the city of Natchez who is not employed by some responsible white person; and also forbids any contraband from hiring any house in said city; whereby hundreds of children have been taken from the schools and many of the families of soldiers have been delivered to slavery.

PROPOSED CENSURE OF GEN. HALLECK'S ORDER.

Second Session, Thirty-Seventh Congress.

1861, Dec. 9—Mr. LOVEJOY offered a resolution requiring the Secretary of War to revoke the first section of General Halleck's order, No. 3, Nov. 20, 1861.

A motion to table the resolution was lost—yeas 63, nays 68, as follows:

YEAS — Messrs. *Allen, Ancona, Joseph Baily, Biddle,* Jacob B. Blair, *George H. Browne,* William G. Brown, Burnham, *Cobb, Cox, Cravens, Crisfield, Crittenden,* Dawes, Delano, *Dunlap,* Dunn, *English, Fouke, Grider, Harding,* Harrison, *Holman,* Horton, *Johnson,* William Kellogg, Killinger, *Law, Lazear,* Leary, *Lehman,* McKnight, McPherson, *Mallory,* Maynard, *Menzies,* Nixon, *Noble, Noell, Norton, Odell,* Olin, *Pendleton, Richardson, Robinson, Sheffield,* Shellabarger, *Shiel, Smith, John B. Steele, William G. Steele,* Stratton, Benjamin F. Thomas, Francis Thomas, Upton, *Vallandigham, Wadsworth,* Webster, *Chilton A. White, Wickliffe, Wood, Woodruff, Wright*—63.

NAYS—Messrs. Aldrich, Alley, Ashley, Babbitt, Goldsmith F. Bailey, Baker, Baxter, Bingham, Francis P. Blair, Samuel S. Blair, Blake, Buffinton, Chamberlain, Clark, Colfax, Frederick A. Conkling, Roscoe Conkling, Conway, Davis, Diven, Duell, Edgerton, Edwards, Eliot, Fenton, Fessenden, Franchot, Frank, Gooch, Granger, Gurley, Hutchins, Julian, Kelley, Lansing, Loomis, Lovejoy, Moorhead, Anson P. Morrill, Justin S. Morrill, T. G. Phelps, Pomeroy, Porter, Potter, Alexander H. Rice, Riddle, Edward H. Rollins, Sargent, Sedgwick, Shanks, Sherman, Sloan, Spaulding, Stevens, Train, Trimble, Trowbridge, Vandever, Van Horn, Van Wyck, Wall, Wallace, Charles W. Walton, E. P. Walton, Washburne, Wheeler, Wilson, Worcester—68.

Mr. LOVEJOY then modified this resolution so as to "request" (instead of "requiring") the Sécretary of War to revoke it,

When Mr. LANSING, of New York, offered the following as a substitute, which Mr. LOVEJOY ac epted:

Whereas Major General Halleck, of the western department, has issued an order prohibiting negroes from coming within the lines of our army, and excluding those already under the protection of our troops, and whereas a different policy and practice prevails in other departments, by the direct sanction of the Administration; and whereas said order is cruel and inhuman, and in the judgment of this House based upon no military necessity: Therefore,

Resolved, That the President be respectfully requested to direct General Halleck to recall said order, or cause it to conform with the practice of the other departments of the army.

Dec 11—The whole subject was then laid on the table—yeas 78, nays 64, as follows:

YEAS—Messrs. *Allen, Ancona, Joseph Baily, Biddle*, Francis P. Blair, Jacob B. Blair, *George H. Browne*, William G. Brown, Burnham, *Calvert, Cobb, Cooper, Cox, Cravens, Crisfield, Crittenden*, Delano, *Delaplaine*, Diven, *Dunlap*, Dunn, *English*, Fisher, *Fouke*, Granger, *Grider, Haight*, Hanchett, *Harding*, Harrison, *Holman*, Horton, *Johnson*, William Kellogg, Killinger, *Law, Lazear*, Leary, *Lehman*, McPherson, *Mallory*, Maynard, *Menzies, Morris*, Nixon, *Noble, Noell, Norton, Odell*, Olin, *Pendleton, Perry*, T. G. Phelps, Porter, Alexander H. Rice, *Richardson*, Riddle, *Robinson, Sheffield*, Shellabarger, *Shiel, Smith, John B. Steele, William G. Steele*, Stratton, Benjamin F. Thomas, Trimble, Upton, *Vallandigham, Voorhees, Wadsworth, Ward*, Webster, Whaley, *Chilton A. White, Wickliffe, Woodruff, Wright*—78.

NAYS—Messrs. Alley, Arnold, Ashley, Babbitt, Goldsmith F. Bailey, Baker, Baxter, Bingham, Blake, Buffinton, Campbell, Chamberlain, Clark, Colfax, Frederick A. Conkling, Roscoe Conkling, Conway, Covode, Davis, Dawes, Duell, Edgerton, Edwards, Eliot, Fenton, Fessenden, Franchot, Frank, Gooch, Goodwin, Hooper, Hutchins, Julian, Kelley, Francis W. Kellogg, Lansing, Loomis, Lovejoy, Moorhead, Anson P. Morrill, Justin S. Morrill, Patton, Pike, Potter, Edward H. Rollins, Sedgwick, Shanks, Sherman, Sloan, Spaulding, Stevens, Train, Trowbridge, Van Horn, Van Wyck, Wall, Wallace, Charles W. Walton, E. P. Walton, Washburne, Wheeler, Albert S. White, Wilson, Worcester—64.

LEGISLATION PROHIBITING THE EXISTENCE OF SLAVERY IN TERRITORIES, ETC.

Second Session, Thirty-Seventh Congress.

IN HOUSE.

1862, May 12—Mr. LOVEJOY proposed this bill, being a substitute for one previously reported by him, and introduced by Mr. ISAAC N. ARNOLD:

To the end that freedom may be and remain forever the fundamental law of the land in all places whatsoever, so far as it lies within the powers or depends upon the action of the Government of the United States to make it so; Therefore,

***Be it enacted by the Senate and House of Representatives of the United States of America in Congress assembled*, That slavery or involuntary servitude, in all cases whatsoever, (other than in the punishment of crime, whereof the party shall have been duly convicted,) shall henceforth cease, and be prohibited forever in all the Territories of the United States, now existing, or hereafter to be formed or acquired in any way.**

Mr. Cox moved that it be tabled; which was rejected—yeas 49, nays 81; and the bill was then passed—yeas 85, nays 50, as follows:

YEAS—Messrs. Aldrich, Alley, Arnold, Ashley, Babbitt, Baker, Baxter, Beaman, Bingham, Francis P. Blair, Samuel S. Blair, Blake, Buffinton, Campbell, Chamberlain, Clark, Colfax, Frederick A. Conkling, Roscoe Conkling, Cutler, Davis, Dawes, Delano, Diven, Duell, Dunn, Edgerton, Edwards, Eliot, Ely, Fenton, Fessenden, Franchot, Frank, Gooch, Granger, Hale, Harrison, Hickman, Hooper, Horton, Hutchins, Julian, Kelley, William Kellogg, Lansing, Loomis, Lovejoy, McKnight, McPherson, Mitchell, Moorhead, Anson P. Morrill, Justin S. Morrill, Olin, Pike, Porter, Potter, Alexander H. Rice, John H. Rice, Riddle, Edward H. Rollins, Sargent, Sedgwick, Shanks, *Sheffield*, Shellabarger, Stevens, Stratton, Benjamin F. Thomas, Train, Trimble, Trowbridge, Van Horn, Verree, Wall, Wallace, Charles W. Walton, E. P. Walton, Washburne, Wheeler, Albert S. White, Wilson, Windom, Worcester 85.

NAYS—Messrs. *Allen, Ancona, Joseph Baily, Biddle*. Jacob B. Blair, *George H. Browne*, Wm. G. Brown, *Calvert*, Casey, Clements, *Cobb, Cox, Cravens, Crisfield, Crittenden, Dunlap, English, Grider, Haight, Hall, Harding, Holman, Johnson, Kerrigan, Knapp, Law, Lazear*, Leary, *Lehman, Mallory*, Maynard, *Menzies, Morris, Noell, Odell, Perry, John S. Phelps, Richardson, Robinson*, Segar, *John B. Steele, Wm. G. Steele*, Francis Thomas, *Vibbard, Voorhees, Wadsworth, Ward*, Webster, *Wickliffe, Woodruff*—50.

As originally reported the bill proposed that slavery should cease in all the Territories; the forts, arsenals, dock-yards, &c., of the United States; in all vessels on the high seas, and "in all places where the national Government is supreme, or has exclusive jurisdiction or power."

A motion to table it was rejected—yeas 50, nays 64.

May 9—Mr. LOVEJOY offered a substitute, containing the other proposition and this addition:

SEC. 2. That any person now held or attempted to be held hereafter as a slave in any of the places above named is hereby declared to be free, and the right to freedom hereby declared may be asserted in any of the courts of the United States or of the several States, in behalf of the party, or his or her posterity, after any lapse of time.

A motion to table the bill was rejected—yeas 50, nays 65.

May 12—Modified and passed without the preamble.

IN SENATE.

June 9—The bill was reported amended by inserting this substitute:

That from and after the passage of this act there shall be neither slavery nor involuntary servitude in any of the Territories of the United States now existing, or which may at any time hereafter be formed or acquired by the United States, otherwise than in punishment of crimes whereof the party shall have been duly convicted.

And was passed—yeas 28, nays 10, as follows:

YEAS—Messrs. Anthony, Browning, Chandler, Clark, Collamer, Cowan, Dixon, Fessenden, Foot, Foster, Grimes, Hale, Harlan, Harris, Howard, Howe, King, Lane of Indiana, Pomeroy, *Rice*, Simmons, Sumner, Ten Eyck, Trumbull, Wade, Wilkinson, Wilmot, Wilson of Massachusetts—28.

NAYS—Messrs. *Carlile, Davis, Kennedy, Latham, McDougall, Nesmith, Powell, Saulsbury, Stark, Wright*—10.

June 17—The House concurred in the amendment of the Senate—yeas 72, nays 38.

IN THE TERRITORY OF MONTANA.

Third Session, Thirty-Seventh Congress.

IN HOUSE.

1863, February 12—Mr. ASHLEY, from the Committee on Territories, reported a bill to provide a temporary government for the Territory of Montana.

Mr. Cox moved to strike out the proviso to the sixth section, as follows:

Provided, That whereas slavery is prohibited in said Territory by act of Congress of June 19, 1862, nothing herein contained shall be construed to authorize or permit its existence therein.

Which was disagreed to—yeas 39, nays 96, as follows:

YEAS—Messrs. *William Allen, Ancona, Baily, Biddle, Cal-*

vert, Cobb, Cox, Crisfield, Grider, Hall, Harding, Holman, Kerrigan, Knapp, Law, Mallory, Menzies, Morris, Noble, Norton, Nugen, Pendleton, Price, Robinson, Segar, *Shiel, Smith, John B. Steele, Wm. G. Steele, Stiles, Vallandigham, Voorhees, Wadsworth,* Webster, *Chilton A. White, Wickliffe, Woodruff, Wright, Yeaman*—38.

NAYS—Messrs. Aldrich, Alley, Arnold, Ashley, Babbitt, Baxter, Beaman, Bingham, Jacob B. Blair, Samuel S. Blair, Blake, William G. Brown, Buffinton, Chamberlain, Clark, Clements, Colfax, Frederick A. Conkling, Conway, Covode, Cutler, Davis, Dawes, Delano, Dunn, Edgerton, Eliot, Ely, Fenton, Samuel C. Fessenden, Thomas A. D. Fessenden, Fisher, Franchot, Frank, Gooch, Goodwin, Granger, Gurley, *Haight,* Harrison, Hickman, Horton, Julian, Kelley, Francis W. Kellogg, William Kellogg, Lansing, *Lehman,* Loomis, Lovejoy, Low, McIndoe, McKean, McKnight, Maynard, Moorhead, Anson P. Morrill, Justin S. Morrill, Nixon, *Noell,* Olin, Patton, Timothy G. Phelps, Pike, Pomeroy, Porter, Potter, Alexander H. Rice, John H. Rice, Riddle, Edward H. Rollins, Sargent, Shanks, *Sheffield,* Shellabarger, Sherman, Sloan, Spaulding, Stevens, Benjamin F. Thomas, Francis Thomas, Train, Trimble, Trowbridge, Van Horn, Van Valkenburgh, Van Wyck, Verree, Walker, Wallace, Walton, Washburne, Wheeler, Albert S. White, Wilson, Windom—96.

—

First Session, Thirty-Eighth Congress.

1864, March 17—The House considered the bill to enable the people of Colorado to form a Constitution and State Government, when

Mr. MALLORY moved to strike from the fourth section this clause:

First. That there shall be neither slavery nor involuntary servitude in the said State otherwise than in the punishment of crimes, whereof the party shall have been duly convicted.

Which was disagreed to—yeas 18, nays 87, as follows:

YEAS—Messrs. *James C. Allen, Ancona, Chanler, Cox, Dawson, Denison, Eldridge, Hall, Harding, Knapp, Long, Mallory, William H. Miller, Morrison, John O'Neill, Rogers, Ross, Stiles*—18.

NAYS—Messrs. Allison, Ames, Anderson, Arnold, Ashley, *Baily, Augustus C. Baldwin,* John D. Baldwin, Baxter, Beaman, Francis P. Blair, jr., Jacob B. Blair, Blow, Boutwell, Boyd, Broomall, *James S. Brown,* Ambrose W. Clark, Cobb, Cole, Henry Winter Davis, Thomas T. Davis, Dawes, Donnelly, Driggs, Dumont, Eckley, Eliot, Farnsworth, Fenton, Frank, Garfield, Gooch, *Griswold,* Higby, Hotchkiss, John H. Hubbard, *Hutchins,* Jenckes, Julian, Kasson, Kelley, Francis W. Kellogg, *Kernan,* Longyear, Marvin, *McAllister,* McBride, McClurg, McIndoe, S. F. Miller, Moorhead, Daniel Morris, Amos Myers, Leonard Myers, Norton, *Odell,* Charles O'Neill, Orth, Perham, Pike, Price, Alexander H. Rice, John H. Rice, *James S. Rollins,* Scofield, Shannon, Smith, Smithers, Spalding, Starr, Stevens, *Sweat,* Thayer, Thomas, Tracy, Upson, Van Valkenburgh, Ellihu B. Washburne, William B. Washburn, Webster, Whaley, Williams, Wilder, Wilson, Windom, Woodbridge—87.

—

Proposed Amendment of the Constitution.

IN SENATE.

1864, January 11—Mr. HENDERSON offered this joint resolution, which was referred to the Committee on the Judiciary, proposing amendments to the Constitution:

Be it resolved, &c., That the following articles be proposed as amendments to the Constitution of the United States, which, when adopted by the Legislatures of three-fourths of the several States, shall be valid, to all intents and purposes, as a part of the said Constitution, to wit:

ARTICLE 1. Slavery or involuntary servitude, except as a punishment for crime, shall not exist in the United States.

ARTICLE 2. The Congress, whenever a majority of the members elected to each house shall deem it necessary, may propose amendments to the Constitution, or, on the application of the Legislatures of a majority of the several States, shall call a convention for proposing amendments, which in either case shall be valid, to all intents and purposes, as part of the Constitution, when ratified by the Legislatures of two-thirds of the several States, or by conventions in two-thirds thereof, as the one or the other mode of ratification may be proposed by Congress.

1864, Feb. 8—Mr SUMNER introduced this joint resolution, which was similarly referred:

Be it resolved, &c., That the following article be proposed to the Legislatures of the several States as an amendment to the Constitution of the United States, which, when ratified by three fourths of such Legislatures, shall become a part of the Constitution, to wit:

ARTICLE —. Everywhere within the limits of the United States, and of each State or Territory thereof, all persons are equal before the law, so that no person can hold another as a slave.

Mr. SAULSBURY moved to postpone it indefinitely; which was disagreed to—yeas 8, nays 31, as follows:

YEAS—Messrs. *Buckalew, Carlile, Davis, Harding, Hendricks, Powell, Saulsbury, Wright*—8.

NAYS—Messrs. Anthony, Chandler, Clark, Collamer, Conness, Cowan, Dixon, Doolittle, Fessenden, Foot, Foster, Grimes, Hale, Harlan, Harris, Howard, Howe, Johnson, Lane of Indiana, Lane of Kansas, Morgan, Morrill, Nesmith, Pomeroy, Ramsey, Sherman, Sprague, Sumner, Trumbull, Van Winkle, Wilson—31.

Feb. 9—Mr. POWELL introduced the following joint resolution, (embodying, as he stated, the view of Judge Nicholas, of Kentucky,) which was referred to the Committee on the Judiciary:

Resolved by the Senate and House of Representatives of the United States of America in Congress assembled, That the Constitution of the United States be amended as follows:

ARTICLE No. —.

SEC. 1. Congress shall at its first session after the adoption of this amendment, and from time to time thereafter, apportion among the several States the electors of President and Vice President according to the following ratio of population in Federal numbers: One elector to each State having less than a million; two to each State having one but less than two million; three to each having two but less than three million; four to each having three but less than four million; five to each having four but less than six million; six to each having six but less than eight million; and seven to each having eight million of population. Each State having but one elector shall be an electoral district, and each of the other States shall be divided by Congress into districts equal to the number of its electors, to be composed of coterminous territory, and as near as may be the districts to have equality of population.

SEC. 2. The voters of each district, qualified to vote for members of the most numerous branch of its Legislature, shall elect an elector.

The election for electors shall be held during the month of October next preceeding the commencement of any presidential term.

The several State Legislatures shall prescribe the time and manner for holding those elections and making returns thereof; also, for deciding them when contested, and making new elections therein; but Congress may discharge this duty, in whole or in part, when deemed necessary.

SEC. 3. The electors shall convene in the Senate Chamber at the seat of Government, at noon of the first Monday in February next preceding the commencement of the ensuing presidential term, and form an electoral college.

Two thirds of all the electors elected shall be a quorum of the college.

The Chief Justice of the United States, or in his absence the President of the Senate, or in the absence of both, the Speaker of the House of Representatives shall be the presiding officer of the college.

The presiding officer shall cause all the electors elected, whether present or not, to be listed in the alphabetical order of their names, and in that order divide them into six classes of equal numbers, distributing by lot separately among the several classes such electors at the bottom of the list, if any, as are left out in the division.

He shall by lot, under the supervision of one from each class, designate the several classes by numbers from one to six.

When a quorum is present he shall announce that the college is formed, and note the time at which the enunciation is made; but, when necessary, the enunciation shall be postponed until after the verification, by a majority of the electors present, of the returns and qualifications of members.

SEC. 4. After the college is formed the electors present of each class shall choose an elector from the class next succeeding it in number, except class six, which shall choose from class one.

In open session of the college the presiding officer, under the supervision and control of the six so chosen, or a majority of them, shall cause two of those six to be designated by lot.

From those two the college shall choose one, who shall be President for the next ensuing term of four years, and the other shall be the Vice President for that term.

The voting by class or college shall be *viva voce* in open session of the college.

In cases of tie, the casting vote shall be given by the presiding officer, who, if he be also an elector, shall not vote except in cases of tie.

The college may adopt rules for expediting a decision by the several classes, and to prevent more than two persons from receiving an equality of votes on the final vote of a class.

If there be a failure to choose one of the six from any class within the time prescribed by the college, the members of that class shall themselves make the choice.

There shall be no reconsideration of a vote given.

SEC. 5. If the college fail, except from exterior violence or intimidation, to make an election of President and Vice President within twenty-four hours from the time when the college was formed, it shall be dissolved, and the offices of its electors vacated.

Thereupon the presiding officer shall order a new election of electors on any day, not less than thirty from the date of his proclamation, and at least thirty before the next month of June, which election shall be held, and the electors chosen shall convene at the time and place designated by the proclamation, and proceed to the election of a President and Vice President as before directed, within twenty-four hours from the time of their formation into a college, and under like penalty for their failure.

Should the failure to elect be caused by exterior violence or intimidation, the functions of the college shall not cease, but it shall reconvene when and where a majority of its members shall by proclamation direct, and make or complete an election as before directed, within the time specified, under like penalty.

SEC. 6. Should no election of President and Vice President be made by an electoral college before the 1st day of June next ensuing the commencement of a presidential term, the Senate of the United States shall convene in its Chamber at noon of the first Monday in July next thereafter, constitute all its elected members, whether present or not, into an electoral college, as though each Senator had been elected an elector, and proceed in all respects as before directed, within twenty-four hours, to choose a President and Vice President to fill the vacancy.

Should the Senate fail to elect, the discharge of the duties of President and Vice President for the residue of that term shall devolve upon such officers of the Government as Congress shall have theretofore directed.

SEC. 7. No office shall be incompatible with that of an elector except the office of Chief Justice of the United States.

SEC. 8. An act or resolution passed by Congress, which shall be returned by the President with his objections, shall be valid without his signature, if repassed by each House of Congress by a vote equal to a majority of all the members elected thereto.

SEC. 9. It shall not be deemed compatible with the duty of a President habitually to use the patronage of his office for the special advantage of any particular political party, or to suffer the patronage of any subordinate office so to be used.

SEC. 10. Should a vacancy occur in both the office of President and in that of Vice President while there are two years remaining of the then presidential term, the Chief Justice of the United States, or in his absence the Secretary of State, shall convene the electoral college after thirty days' notice by proclamation, who shall fill the vacancies for the remainder of the term in all respects as if it were an original election.

SEC. 11. Every elector, before entering on the duties of his office, shall, by oath or affirmation, promise to support the Constitution of the United States, and declare that he has not, and will not, pledge his vote as an elector in favor of any person or toward aiding any political party.

AMENDMENT FOR THE EXTINCTION OF SLAVERY.

1864, February 10—Mr. TRUMBULL, from the Committee on the Judiciary reported a joint resolution:

Be it resolved, &c., That the following article be proposed to the legislatures of the several States as an amendment to the Constitution of the United States, which, when ratified by three fourths of said legislatures, shall be valid, to all intents and purposes, as a part of the said Constitution, namely:

ARTICLE XIII.

SECTION 1. Neither slavery nor involuntary servitude, except as a punishment for crime, whereof the party shall have been duly convicted, shall exist within the United States, or any place subject to their jurisdiction.

SEC. 2. Congress shall have power to enforce this article by appropriate legislation.

April 5—Mr. DAVIS moved to strike out the above and insert—

No negro, or person whose mother or grandmother is or was a negro, shall be a citizen of the United States, or be eligible to any civil or military office, or to any place of trust or profit under the United States.

Which was disagreed to—yeas 5, nays 32, as follows:

YEAS—Messrs. *Buckalew*, *Davis*, *Powell*, *Riddle*, *Saulsbury*—5.

NAYS—Messrs. Anthony, Chandler, Clark, Collamer, Conness, Dixon, Doolittle, Fessenden, Foot, Grimes, Hale, *Harding*, Harlan, Harris, Howard, Howe, Johnson, Lane of Indiana, Lane of Kansas, Morgan, Morrill, Pomeroy, Ramsey, Sherman, Sprague, Sumner, Ten Eyck, Trumbull, Van Winkle, Wade, Willey, Wilson—32.

Mr. POWELL moved to amend by adding to section 1, the words—

No slave shall be emancipated by this article, unless the owner thereof shall be first paid the value of the slave or slaves so emancipated.

Which was disagreed to—yeas 2, (Messrs. *Davis*, and *Powell*,) nays 34:

NAYS—Messrs. Anthony, *Buckalew*, *Carlile*, Chandler, Clark, Collamer, Conness, Dixon, Doolittle, Fessenden, Foot, Grimes, Hale, *Harding*, Harlan, Harris, Howard, Howe, Johnson, Lane of Indiana, Lane of Kansas, Morgan, Morrill, Pomeroy, Ramsey, Sherman, Sprague, Sumner, Ten Eyck, Trumbull, Van Winkle, Wade, Willey, Wilson—34.

April 6—Mr. POWELL moved to add a new article to the Constitution, as follows:

ARTICLE XIV.

The President and Vice President shall hold their offices for the term of six years. A person who has filled the office of President shall not be re-eligible.

Which was disagreed to—yeas 12, nays 32:

YEAS—Messrs. Brown, *Davis*, Foster, Grimes, *Hendricks*, *Nesmith*, Pomeroy, *Powell*, *Riddle*, *Saulsbury*, Wade, Wilkinson—12.

NAYS—Messrs. Anthony, Chandler, Clark, Collamer, Conness, Cowan, Dixon, Doolittle, Fessenden, Foot, Hale, *Harding*, Harlan, Harris, Henderson, Howard, Howe, Johnson, Lane of Indiana, Lane of Kansas, *McDougall*, Morgan, Morrill, Ramsey, Sherman, Sprague, Sumner, Ten Eyck, Trumbull, Van Winkle, Willey, Wilson—32.

Mr. POWELL moved to add an article, as follows:

ARTICLE XV.

The principal officer in each of the Executive Departments, and all persons connected with the diplomatic service, may be removed from office at the pleasure of the President. All other civil officers of the Executive Departments may be removed at any time by the President, or other appointing power, when their services are unnecessary, or for dishonesty, incapacity, inefficiency, misconduct, or neglect of duty; and when so removed the removal shall be reported to the Senate, together with the reasons therefor.

Which was disagreed to—yeas 6, nays 38, as follows:

YEAS—Messrs. *Davis*, *Hendricks*, *Powell*, *Riddle*, *Saulsbury*, Wade—6.

NAYS—Messrs. Anthony, Brown, Chandler, Clark, Collamer, Conness, Cowan, Dixon, Doolittle, Fessenden, Foot, Foster, Grimes, Hale, *Harding*, Harlan, Harris, Henderson, Howard, Howe, Johnson, Lane of Indiana, Lane of Kansas, *McDougall*, Morgan, Morrill, *Nesmith*, Pomeroy, Ramsey, Sherman, Sprague, Sumner, Ten Eyck, Trumbull, Van Winkle, Wilkinson, Willey, Wilson—38.

Mr. POWELL offered a new article, as follows:

ARTICLE XVI.

Every law, or resolution having the force of law, shall relate to but one subject, and that shall be expressed in the title.

Which was disagreed to—yeas 6, nays 37, as follows:

YEAS—Messrs. Cowan, *Davis*, *Hendricks*, *Powell*, *Riddle*, *Saulsbury*—6.

NAYS—Messrs. Anthony, Brown, Chandler, Clark, Conness, Dixon, Doolittle, Fessenden, Foot, Foster, Grimes,

Hale, *Harding*, Harlan, Harris, Henderson, Howard, Howe, Johnson, Lane of Indiana, Lane of Kansas, *McDougall*, Morgan, Morrill, *Nesmith*, Pomeroy, Ramsey, Sherman, Sprague, Sumner, Ten Eyck, Trumbull, Van Winkle, Wade, Wilkinson, Willey, Wilson—37.

April 8—Mr. SAULSBURY moved to strike out all after the word "Article xiii," and insert the following:

SECTION 1. All persons shall have the right peaceably to assemble and worship God according to the dictates of their own conscience.

SEC. 2. The use of the public press shall not be obstructed; but criminal publications made in one State against the lawful institutions of another State shall not be allowed.

SEC. 3. The right of citizens to free and lawful speech in public assemblies shall not be denied. Access of citizens to the ballot-box shall not be obstructed either by civil or military power. The military shall always be subordinate to the existing judicial authority over citizens. The privilege of the writ of *habeas corpus* shall never be suspended in the presence of the judicial authority.

SEC. 4. The militia of a State or of the United States shall not be employed to invade the lawful rights of the people of any of the several States; but the United States shall not be hereby deprived of the right and power to defend and protect its property and rights within the limits of any of the States.

SEC. 5. Persons held to service or labor for life, in any State under the laws thereof, may be taken into any Territory of the United States south of north latitude 36° 30′, and the right to such service or labor shall not be impaired thereby, and the Territorial Legislature thereof shall have the exclusive right to make and shall make all needful rules and regulations for the protection of such right, and also for the protection of such persons: but Congress or any Territorial Legislature shall not have power to impair or abolish such right of service in the said Territory while in a territorial condition without the consent of all the States south of said latitude which maintain such service.

SEC. 6. Involuntary servitude, except for crime, shall not be permanently established within the district set apart for the seat of government of the United States: but the right of sojourn in such district with persons held to service or labor for life shall not be denied.

SEC. 7. When any Territory of the United States south of north latitude 36° 30′ shall have a population equal to the ratio of representation for one member of Congress, and the people thereof shall have formed a constitution for a republican form of government, it shall be admitted as a State into the Union, on an equal footing with the other States; and the people may in such constitution either prohibit or sustain the right to involuntary labor or service, and alter or amend the constitution at their will.

SEC. 8. The present right of representation in section two, article one, of this Constitution shall not be altered without the consent of all the States maintaining the right to involuntary service or labor south of latitude 36° 30′, but nothing in this Constitution or its amendments shall be construed to deprive any State south of said latitude 36° 30′ of the right of abolishing involuntary servitude at its will

SEC. 9. The regulation and control of the right to labor or service in any of the States south of latitude 36° 30′ is hereby recognized to be exclusively the right of each State within its own limits; and this Constitution shall not be altered or amended to impair this right of each State without its consent: *Provided*, This article shall not be construed to absolve the United States from rendering assistance to suppress insurrections or domestic violence, when called upon by any State, as provided for in section four, article four, of this Constitution.

SEC. 10. No State shall pass any law in any way interfering with or obstructing the recovery of fugitives from justice, or from labor or service, or any law of Congress made under article four, section two, of this Constitution; and all laws in violation of this section may, on complaint made by any person or State, be declared void by the Supreme Court of the United States.

SEC. 11. As a right of comity between the several States south of latitude 36° 30′ the right of transit with persons held to involuntary labor or service from one State to another shall not be obstructed, but such persons shall not be brought into the States north of said latitude.

SEC. 12. The traffic in slaves with Africa is hereby forever prohibited on pain of death and the forfeiture of all the rights and property of persons engaged therein; and the descendants of Africans shall not be citizens.

SEC. 13. Alleged fugitives from labor or service, on request, shall have a trial by jury before being returned.

SEC 14. All alleged fugitives charged with crime committed in violation of the laws of a State shall have the right of trial by jury, and if such person claims to be a citizen of another State, shall have a right to appeal or of a writ of error to the Supreme Court of the United States.

SEC. 15. All acts of any inhabitant of the United States tending to incite persons held to service or labor to insurrection or acts of domestic violence, or to abscond, are hereby prohibited and declared to be a penal offence, and all the courts of the United States shall be open to suppress and punish such offences at the suit of any citizen of the United States or the suit of any State.

SEC. 16. All conspiracies in any State to interfere with lawful rights in any other State or against the United States shall be suppressed; and no State or the people thereof shall withdraw from this Union without the consent of three fourths of all the States, expressed by an amendment proposed and ratified in the manner provided in article five of the Constitution.

SEC. 17. Whenever any State wherein involuntary servitude is recognized or allowed shall propose to abolish such servitude, and shall apply for pecuniary assistance therein, the Congress may in its discretion grant such relief, not exceeding one hundred dollars, for each person liberated; but Congress shall not propose such abolishment or relief to any State. Congress may assist free persons of African descent to emigrate and civilize Africa.

SEC. 18. Duties on imports may be imposed for revenue, but shall not be excessive or prohibitory in amount.

SEC. 19. When all of the several States shall have abolished slavery, then and thereafter slavery or involuntary servitude, except as a punishment for crime, shall never be established or tolerated in any of the States or Territories of the United States, and they shall be forever free.

SEC. 20. The provisions of this article relating to involuntary labor or servitude shall not be altered without the consent of all the States maintaining such servitude.

Which was rejected, without a division.

The joint resolution proposing the amendment, as reported from the Committee on the Judiciary, was then passed—yeas 38, nays 6, as follows:

YEAS—Messrs. Anthony, Brown, Chandler, Clark, Collamer, Conness, Cowan, Dixon, Doolittle, Fessenden, Foot, Foster, Grimes, Hale, *Harding*, Harlan, Harris, Fessenden, Howard, Howe, Johnson, Lane of Indiana, Lane of Kansas, Morgan, Morrill, *Nesmith*, Pomeroy, Ramsey, Sherman, Sprague, Sumner, Ten Eyck, Trumbull, Van Winkle, Wade, Wilkinson, Willey, Wilson—38.

NAYS—Messrs. *Davis, Hendricks, McDougall, Powell, Riddle, Saulsbury*—6.

VOTE IN THE HOUSE OF REPRESENTATINES.

May 31—This joint resolution coming up, Mr. HOLMAN objecting to its second reading, the vote on rejecting the bill was yeas 55, nays 76, as follows:

YEAS—Messrs. *James C. Allen, Ancona, Bliss, Brooks, James S. Brown, Chanler, Coffroth, Cox, Cravens, Dawson, Denison, Eden, Edgerton, Eldridge, Finck, Ganson, Grider, Hall, Harrington, Herrick, Holman, Philip Johnson, William Johnson, Kalbfleisch, Kernan, King, Knapp, Law, Long, Mallory, Marcy, McAllister, McDowell, James R. Morris, Morrison, Nelson, Noble, Odell, Pendleton, Pruyn, Radford*, William H. Randall, *Ross, John B. Steele, William G. Steele, Stiles, Sweat, Voorhees, Wadsworth, Ward, Wheeler, Chilton A. White, Joseph W. White, Winfield, Fernando Wood*—55.

NAYS—Messrs. Alley, Allison, Ames, Anderson, John D. Baldwin, Baxter, Beaman, Blaine, Jacob B. Blair, Boyd, Broomall, Ambrose W. Clark, Cobb, Cole, Creswell, Henry Winter Davis, Thomas T. Davis, Dawes, Donnelly, Driggs, Eckley, Eliot, Fenton, Frank, Garfield, Gooch, Grinnell, *Griswold*, Hale, Higby, Hooper, Hotchkiss, Asahel W. Hubbard, John H. Hubbard, Hulburd, Ingersoll, Jenckes, Kelley, Francis W. Kellogg, Orlando Kellogg, Littlejohn, Loan, Longyear, Marvin, McClurg, Morrill, Daniel Morris, Amos Myers, Leonard Myers, Charles O'Neill, Orth, Patterson, Perham, Pike, Pomeroy, Price, Alexander H. Rice, John H. Rice, Edward H. Rollins, Schenck, Scofield, Shannon, Sloan, Spalding, Stevens, Thomas, Tracy, Upson, Elihu B. Washburne, William B. Washburn, Webster, Whaley, Williams, Wilder, Wilson, Windom—76.

June 14—Mr. WHEELER offered an amendment, to add this proviso:

That this article shall not apply to the States of Kentucky, Missouri, Delaware, and Maryland until after the expiration of ten years from the time the same shall be ratified.

June 15—The amendment offered by Mr. WHEELER was disagreed to. Also the amendment of Mr. PENDLETON, that the proposed amendments to the Constitution be submitted to conventions instead of the Legislatures of the States, so that the ratification, if at all, shall be by conventions of three fourths of the States.

The joint resolution of the Senate was then rejected—yeas 95, nays 66, (two-thirds being necessary,) as follows:

YEAS—Messrs. Alley, Allison, Ames, Anderson, Arnold, *Baily*, J. D. Baldwin, Baxter, Beaman, Blaine, J. B. Blair, Blow, Boutwell, Boyd, Brandegee, Broomall, Ambrose W. Clark, Freeman Clarke, Cobb, Cole, Creswell, Dawes, Deming, Dixon, Donnelly, Driggs, Eckley, Eliot, Farnsworth, Fenton, Frank, Garfield, Gooch, Griswold, Hale, Higby, Hooper, Hotchkiss, Asahel W. Hubbard, John H. Hubbard, Hulburd, Ingersoll, Jenckes, Julian, Kasson, Kelley, Francis W. Kellogg, Orlando Kellogg, Littlejohn, Loan, Longyear, Marvin, McClurg, McIndoe, Samuel F. Miller, Moorhead, Morrill, Daniel Morris, Amos Myers, Leonard Myers, Norton, *Odell*, Charles O'Neill, Orth, Patterson, Perham, Pike, Price, Alexander H. Rice, John H. Rice, Edward H. Rollins, Schenck, Scofield, Shannon, Sloan, Smith, Smithers, Spalding, Starr, Stevens, Thayer, Thomas, Tracy, Upson, Van Valkenburgh, Ellihu B. Washburne, Wm. B. Washburn, Webster, Whaley, *Wheeler*, Williams, Wilder, Wilson, Windom, Woodbridge—95.

NAYS—Messrs. *James C. Allen*, *Wm. J. Allen*, *Ancona*, Ashley, *Augustus C. Baldwin*, *Bliss*, *Brooks*, *James S. Brown*, *Chanler*, *Coffroth*, *Cox*, *Cravens*, *Dawson*, *Denison*, *Eden*, *Edgerton*, *Eldridge*, *English*, *Finck*, *Ganson*, *Grider*, *Harding*, *Harrington*, *Herrick*, *Holman*, *Hutchins*, *Philip Johnson*, *William Johnson*, *Kalbfleisch*, *Kernan*, *King*, *Law*, *Lazear*, *Le Blond*, *Long*, *Mallory*, *Marcy*, *McAllister*, *McDowell*, *McKinney*, *Wm. H. Miller*, *James R. Morris*, *Morrison*, *Noble*, *J. O'Neill*, *Pendleton*, *Perry*, *Pruyn*, *Radford*, *S. J. Randall*, *Robinson*, *Rogers*, *James S. Rollins*, *Ross*, *Scott*, *John B. Steele*, *Wm. G. Steele*, *Stiles*, *Strouse*, *Stuart*, *Sweat*, *Wadsworth*, *Ward*, *Chilton A. White*, *Joseph W. White*, *Fernando Wood*—66.

NOT VOTING—Messrs. William G. Brown, *Clay*, Henry Winter Davis, Thomas T. Davis, Dumont, Grinnell, *Hall*, *Benjamin G. Harris*, *Charles M. Harris*, *Knapp*, McBride, *Middleton*, *Nelson*, Pomeroy, Wm. H. Randall, *Stebbins*, *Voorhees*, *Winfield*, *Benjamin Wood*, *Yeaman*—20.

Same day, Mr. ASHLEY entered a motion to reconsider the above vote.

OTHER PROPOSITIONS.

IN HOUSE.

1864, February 15—Mr. ARNOLD offered this resolution:

Resolved, That the Constitution should be so amended as to abolish slavery in the United States wherever it now exists, and to prohibit its existence in every part thereof forever.

The House refused to table it—yeas 58, nays 79; and passed it—yeas 78, nays 62, as follows:

YEAS—Messrs. Allison, Anderson, Arnold, Ashley, *Baily*, John D. Baldwin, Baxter, Beaman, Jacob B. Blair, Blow, Boutwell, Boyd, Brandegee, Broomall, Cobb, Cole, Creswell, Henry Winter Davis, Thomas T. Davis, Dawes, Dixon, Donnelly, Driggs, Dumont, Eckley, Eliot, Farnsworth, Frank, Garfield, Gooch, Grinnell, Higby, Hooper, Asahel W. Hubbard, John H. Hubbard, Hulburd, Jenckes, Julian, Kelley, Francis W. Kellogg, Loan, Longyear, Marvin, McClurg, Samuel F. Miller, Moorhead, Morrill, Daniel Morris, Amos Myers, Leonard Myers, Norton, Charles O'Neill, Orth, Patterson, Perham, Pike, Pomeroy, Price, Alexander H. Rice, John H. Rice, Edward H. Rollins, Schenck, Scofield, Shannon, Smithers, Spalding, Stevens, Thayer, Thomas, Upson, Van Valkenburgh, Ellihu B. Washburne, William B. Washburn, Whaley, Williams, Wilder, Wilson, Windom—78.

NAYS—Messrs. *James C. Allen*, *William J. Allen*, *Ancona*, *Augustus C. Baldwin*, *Bliss*, *Brooks*, *James S. Brown*, *Clay*, *Coffroth*, *Cox*, *Cravens*, *Dawson*, *Denison*, *Eden*, *Edgerton*, *Eldridge*, *Finck*, *Ganson*, *Grider*, *Hall*, *Harding*, *Harrington*, *Benjamin G. Harris*, *Herrick*, *Holman*, *William Johnson*, Orlando Kellogg, *Kernan*, *King*, *Knapp*, *Law*, *Lazear*, *Long*, *Mallory*, *McAllister*, McBride, *McDowell*, *McKinney*, *Wm. H. Miller*, *James R. Morris*, *Morrison*, *Nelson*, *Noble*, *Odell*, *John O'Neill*, *Pendleton*, *Perry*, *Samuel J. Randall*, William H. Randall, *Robinson*, *James S. Rollins*, *Ross*, *Scott*, *John B. Steele*, *Stiles*, *Strouse*, *Stuart*, *Sweat*, *Chilton A. White*, *Joseph W. White*, *Winfield*, *Fernando Wood*—62.

February 15—Mr. WINDOM offered this resolution, which was referred to the Committee on the Judiciary:

Resolved by the Senate and House of Representatives, &c., That (two thirds of both Houses concurring) the following article be proposed to the Legislatures of the several States as an amendment to the Constitution of the United States, which, when ratified by three fourths of said Legislatures, shall be valid, to all intents and purposes, as part of said Constitution, namely:

ARTICLE 13.

SEC. 1. Neither slavery nor involuntary servitude, except as a punishment for crime whereof the party shall have been duly convicted, shall exist within the United States or any place subject to their jurisdiction.

SEC. 2. Congress shall have power to enforce this article by appropriate legislation.

1864, March 28—Mr. STEVENS offered the following joint resolution:

Resolved by the Senate and House of Representatives of the United States of America in Congress assembled, That the following articles be proposed to the several States as amendments to the Constitution of the United States:

ARTICLE 1. Slavery and involuntary servitude, except for the punishment of crimes whereof the party shall have been duly convicted, is forever prohibited in the United States and all its Territories.

ART. 2. So much of article four, section two, as refers to the delivery up of persons held to service or labor escaping into another State is annulled.

On a motion to reject the resolution, the yeas were 45, nays 75, as follows:

YEAS—Messrs. *James C. Allen*, *William J. Allen*, *Ancona*, *Augustus C. Baldwin*, *Bliss*, *Brooks*, *James S. Brown*, *Chanler*, *Clay*, *Cravens*, *Dawson*, *Denison*, *Eldridge*, *English*, *Finck*, *Ganson*, *Grider*, *Hall*, *Harding*, *Harrington*, *Benjamin G. Harris*, *Herrick*, *Holman*, *Philip Johnson*, *Knapp*, *Law*, *Mallory*, *Marcy*, *James R. Morris*, *Morrison*, *Noble*, *John O'Neill*, *Pendleton*, *Perry*, *Pruyn*, *Samuel J. Randall*, *Rogers*, *James S. Rollins*, *Ross*, *Scott*, *John B. Steele*, *William G. Steele*, *Sweat*, *Winfield*, *Yeaman*—45.

NAYS—Messrs. Alley, Allison, Ames, Anderson, Ashley, *Baily*, John D. Baldwin, Baxter, Beaman, Blaine, Francis P. Blair, jr., Blow, Boutwell, Boyd, Brandegee, Broomall, Ambrose W. Clark, Cobb, Cole, Henry Winter Davis, Thomas T. Davis, Deming, Dixon, Driggs, Dumont, Eckley, Eliot, Frank, Garfield, Grinnell, Hale, Higby, Hooper, Hotchkiss, Asahel W. Hubbard, John H. Hubbard, Hulburd, Jenckes, Julian, Kasson, Kelley, Francis W. Kellogg, Longyear, McBride, McClurg, Samuel F. Miller, Moorhead, Morrill, Leonard Myers, Norton, Charles O'Neill, Orth, Perham, Pike, Pomeroy, Price, Alexander H. Rice, John H. Rice, Edward H. Rollins, Schenck, Scofield, Shannon, Smithers, Spalding, Stevens, Thomas, Tracy, Upson, Van Valkenburgh, Ellihu B. Washburne, William B. Washburn, Webster, Whaley, Wilson, Windom—75.

It was then laid over.

On motion of Mr. STEVENS the second article was stricken out.

IN SENATE.

1864, Feb. 8—Mr. ANTHONY offered a joint resolution to repeal the joint resolution to amend the Constitution of the United States, approved March 2, 1861, which was as follows:

Resolved, &c., That the following article be proposed to the Legislatures of the several States as an amendment to the Constitution of the United States, which, when ratified by three fourths of said Legislatures, shall be valid to all intents and purposes as part of the said Constitution, namely:

ART. XIII. No amendment shall be made to the Constitution which will authorize or give to Congress the power to abolish or interfere within any State with the domestic institutions thereof, including that of persons held to labor or service by the laws of said State.

May 11—On motion of Mr. TRUMBULL, the Committee on the Judiciary were discharged from its further consideration.

OTHER PROPOSED AMENDMENTS.

A convention held in Alleghany City, Penn., January 27, 1864, adopted the following resolutions:

Resolved, First, That we deem it a matter of paramount

importance to the life and prosperity and permanency of our nation that the Constitution be so amended as fully to express the Christian national character.

Resolved, Second, That we are encouraged by the success attending the labors of the friends of this movement to persevere in the hope that, with the blessing of God, it will speedily result in the consummation of its great object.

Resolved, Third, That the late proclamation of his Excellency the President of the United States, recommending the observance of days of national fasting, humiliation, and prayer, as suggested by the Senate, for the purpose of confessing our national sins, which have provoked the divine displeasure, and of imploring forgiveness through Jesus Christ; and also days of national thanksgiving for the purpose of making grateful acknowledgments of God's mercies; we have pleasing evidence that God is graciously inclining the hearts of those who are in authority over us to recognize His hand in national affairs, and to cherish a sense of our dependence as a nation upon Him.

Which was subsequently presented to the President by a committee of the convention, with an address. The President made this reply:

GENTLEMEN: The general aspect of your movement I cordially approve. In regard to particulars I must ask time to deliberate, as the work of amending the Constitution should not be done hastily. I will carefully examine your paper in order more fully to comprehend its contents than is possible from merely hearing it read, and will take such action upon it as my responsibility to our Maker and our country demands.

Numerously signed petitions were presented to Congress during the late session.

1864, April 11—Mr. CRAVENS offered these resolutions, which went over, under the rule:

Resolved, That in the present condition of the country, when the passions of the people are inflamed and their prejudices are excited, it is unwise and dangerous to attempt to alter or amend the Constitution of the United States; that ample power is contained within its limits as it now exists to protect and defend the national life, and the exercise of power not warranted by its provisions would be to enter the field of revolution, and dangerous to the liberties of the people, tending to the establishment of military despotism and the final overthrow of free government in America.

Resolved, That any attempt by Congress to reduce States to the condition of Territories is as odious and as revolutionary in its character and tendency as secession itself.

Resolved, That it is the duty of the Government to listen to and consider any proposition for reconciliation that may be offered by the insurgents which does not involve the question of separation.

Resolved, That the thanks of the nation are due, and are hereby tendered, to the officers, soldiers, and seamen who have so gallantly borne our flag in this hour of peril to our country.

March 24—Mr. BLAINE offered this resolution, which was adopted:

Resolved, That the Judiciary Committee be directed to inquire into the expediency of proposing an amendment to the Constitution of the United States, by striking out the fifth clause of section nine, article one, which forbids the levying of a tax on articles exported from any State.

IN SENATE.

March 3—Mr. DAVIS presented, for printing, an amendment he proposed to offer to the amendment of the Constitution reported by the Judiciary Committee:

First. That no negro or person whose mother or grandmother is or was a negro shall be a citizen of the United States, or be eligible to any civil or military office, or to any place of trust or profit under the United States.

Second. That the States of Maine and Massachusetts shall form and constitute one State of the United States, to be called East New England, and the States of New Hampshire, Rhode Island, Connecticut, and Vermont shall form and constitute one State of the United States, to be called West New England.

Resolutions on Slavery.

First Session Thirty-Eighth Congress.

1864, Jan. 18—Mr. HARDING offered this resolution:

Resolved, That the maintenance inviolate of the rights of the States, and especially the right of each State to order and control its own domestic institutions according to its own judgment exclusively, is essential to that balance of power on which the perfection and endurance of our political fabric depend.

Mr. STEVENS moved to lay it on the table; which was lost—yeas 73, nays 75, as follows:

YEAS—Messrs. Alley, Allison, Ames, Ashley, John D. Baldwin, Baxter, Beaman, Jacob B. Blair, Boutwell, Boyd, Brandegee, Broomall, Ambrose W. Clark, Freeman Clarke, Cole, Creswell, Thomas T. Davis, Deming, Dixon, Donnelly, Driggs, Eckley, Eliot, Farnsworth, Frank, Garfield, Gooch, Grinnell, Higby, Hooper, Hotchkiss, Asahel W. Hubbard, Hulburd, Jenckes, Julian, Kelley, Francis W. Kellogg, Orlando Kellogg, Loan, Longyear, Marvin, McBride, McClurg, McIndoe, Samuel F. Miller, Moorhead, Morrill, Daniel Morris, Leonard Myers, Charles O'Neill, Patterson, Perham, Pike, Pomeroy, Price, John H. Rice, Edward H. Rollins, Schenck, Smithers, Spalding, Stevens, Thayer, Thomas, Upson, Ellihu B. Washburne, William B. Washburn, Whaley, Williams, Wilder, Wilson, Windom, Woodbridge—73.

NAYS—Messrs. *James C. Allen, William J. Allen, Ancona, Augustus C. Baldwin*, Francis P. Blair, jr., *Bliss, Brooks, James S. Brown*, W. G. Brown, *Chanler, Clay, Coffroth, Cox, Cravens, Dawson, Denison, Eden, Edgerton, Eldridge, English, Finck, Ganson, Grider, Griswold*, Hale. *Hall, Harding, Harrington, Benjamin G. Harris, Herrick, Holman, Hutchins, William Johnson, Kernan, King, Knapp, Lazear, Le Blond, Long, Marcy, McAllister, McDowell, McKinney, Middleton, Wm. H. Miller, James R. Morris, Morrison*, Amos Myers, *Nelson, Noble, John O'Neill*, Orth, *Pendleton*, Wm. H. Randall, *Robinson, James S. Rollins, Ross*, Scofield, *John G Scott*, Smith, *John B. Steele, Stiles, Strouse, Stuart, Sweat*, Tracy, *Voorhees, Wadsworth, Webster, Wheeler, Chilton A. White, Joseph W. White, Winfield, Fernando Wood, Yeaman*—75.

It was then referred to the Committee on the Rebellious States—yeas 83, nays 68, as follows:

YEAS—Messrs. Alley, Allison, Ames, Arnold, Ashley, John D. Baldwin, Baxter, Beaman, Blaine, Jacob B. Blair, Boutwell, Boyd, Broomall, Ambrose W. Clark, Freeman Clarke, *Clay*, Cole, Creswell, Thomas T. Davis, Dawes, Deming, Dixon, Donnelly, Driggs, Eckley, Eliot, Farnsworth, Fenton, Frank, Garfield, Gooch, Grinnell, Higby, Hotchkiss, John H. Hubbard, Hulburd, Jenckes, Julian, Kasson, Kelley, Orlando Kellogg, Loan, Longyear, Lovejoy, Marvin, McBride, McClurg, McIndoe, Samuel F. Miller, Moorhead, Morrill, Daniel Morris, Amos Myers, Leonard Myers, Charles O'Neill, Orth, Patterson, Perham, Pike, Pomeroy, Price, Alexander H. Rice, John H. Rice, Edward H. Rollins, Schenck, Scofield, Shannon, Smithers, Spalding, Stevens, Thayer, Thomas, Upson, Van Valkenburgh, Ellihu B. Washburne, William B. Washburn, Webster, Whaley, Williams, Wilder, Wilson, Windom, Woodbridge—83.

NAYS—Messrs. *James C. Allen, William J. Allen, Ancona, Augustus C. Baldwin*, Francis P. Blair, jr., *Brooks, James S. Brown*, William G. Brown, *John W. Chanler, Cox, Cravens, Dawson, Denison, Eden, Edgerton, Eldridge, English, Finck, Ganson, Grider, Griswold*, Hale, *Hall, Harding, Harrington, Benjamin G. Harris, Herrick, Holman, Hutchins, William Johnson, Kernan, King, Knapp, Le Blond, Long, Marcy, McAllister, McDowell, McKinney, Middleton, William H. Miller, James R. Morris, Morrison, Nelson, Noble, John O'Neill, Pendleton, Radford, Samuel J. Randall, Robinson, James S. Rollins, Ross, Scott*, Smith, *John B. Steele, Stiles, Strouse, Stuart, Sweat*, Tracy, *Voorhees, Wadsworth, Wheeler, Chilton A. White, Joseph W. White, Winfield, Fernando Wood, Yeaman*—68.

1864, February 29—Mr. MORRISON offered the following resolution; which was laid over under the rule:

Resolved, That slavery legally exists in some of the States of the Union by virtue of the Constitution and laws of such States, and that neither the Government of the United States nor the people, as such, are responsible therefor, nor have they any legal duty to perform in relation thereto except such as is enjoined by section two, article four, of the Federal Constitution, in these words: "No person held to service or labor in one State, under the laws thereof, escaping into another, shall in consequence of any law or regulation therein, be discharged from such service or labor, but shall be delivered up on claim of the party to whom such service or labor may be due."

Bureau of Freedmen's Affairs.

IN HOUSE.

1864, March 1—The House passed a bill to

establish a Bureau of Freedmen's Affairs—yeas 69, nays 67, as follows:

YEAS—Messrs. Alley, Allison, Ames, Anderson, Arnold, John D. Baldwin, Baxter, Beaman, Blow, Boutwell, Boyd, Brandegee, Ambrose W. Clark, Cobb, Cole, Creswell, Dawes, Dixon, Donnelly, Driggs, Dumont, Eckley, Eliot, Farnsworth, Fenton, Frank, Garfield, Grinnell, Higby, Hooper, Hotchkiss, Asahel W. Hubbard, John H. Hubbard, Jenckes, Julian, Kasson, Kelley, Francis W. Kellogg, Orlando Kellogg, Longyear, Lovejoy, Marvin, McClurg, McIndoe, Samuel F. Miller, Moorhead, Morrill, Daniel Morris, Amos Myers, Norton, Charles O'Neill, Perham, Pike, Pomeroy, Price, Alexander H. Rice, John H. Rice, Schenck, Shannon, Sloan, Smithers, Stevens, Thayer, Van Valkenburgh, William B. Washburn, Wilder, Wilson, Windom, Woodbridge—69.

NAYS—Messrs. *Ancona, Baily, Augustus C. Baldwin*, Francis P. Blair, jr., Jacob B. Blair, *Brooks, James S. Brown*, William G. Brown, *Chanler, Clay, Coffroth, Cox, Dawson, Denison, Eden, Eldridge, Finck, Ganson, Grider, Griswold*, Hale, *Hall, Harding, Harrington, Harris, Herrick, Holman, Hutchins, Kalbfleisch, Kernan, King, Knapp, Law, Long, Mallory, McAllister*, McBride, *McDowell, McKinney, Middleton, William H. Miller, Morrison, Nelson, Noble, Pendleton, Radford, Samuel J. Randall, Rogers, Ross, Scott, Stebbins, John B. Steele, William G. Steele, Stiles, Strouse, Stuart, Sweat*, Thomas, Tracy, *Voorhees, Wadsworth*, Webster, Whaley, *Chilton A. White, Joseph W. White*, Williams, *Winfield*—67.

[The bill created in the War Department a Bureau of Freedmen's Affairs, with a Commissioner, (at a compensation of $4,000 per annum,) to whom shall be referred the adjustment and determination of all questions concerning persons of African descent, and persons who are or shall become free by virtue of any proclamation, law, or military order issued during the present rebellion, or by virtue of any State act of Emancipation, or who shall be otherwise entitled to their freedom. The Commissioner is authorized to make all needful rules and regulations for the general superintendence, direction, and management of all such persons, and to appoint a chief and other clerks. All military and civil officers charged with the execution of any law or order liberating slaves, are required to make returns of their proceedings to the Commissioner, who is authorized to establish regulations for the treatment and disposition of all freedmen, that their rights and those of the Government may be duly determined and maintained. Assistant Commissioners of Freedmen are to be appointed in the rebellious States when brought under military authority, (each with an annual salary of $2,500,) with power to permit freedmen to cultivate lands in those districts which have been, or may be, abandoned by their former owners, and all real estate within such districts to which the United States shall have acquired title and not previously appropriated to other uses, to adjust wages, receive returns, &c.]

IN SENATE.

1864, April 12—Mr. SUMNER reported from the Committee on Slavery and Freedmen a bill to establish a Bureau of Freedmen, which was read and passed to a second reading.

May 25—Mr. SUMNER reported back the House bill with an amendment in the nature of a substitute.

June 8—It was considered in the Senate.

June 15—Mr. CARLILE moved to postpone the bill until the first Monday of December next; which was rejected—yeas 13, nays 23, as follows:

YEAS—Messrs. *Buckalew, Carlile, Davis*, Grimes, *Hendricks*, Hicks, Johnson, *Powell, Richardson, Riddle, Saulsbury*, Van Winkle, Willey—13.

NAYS—Messrs. Anthony, Brown, Clark, Conness, Dixon, Doolittle, Fessenden, Foot, Hale, Harlan, Harris, Howe, Lane of Indiana, Lane of Kansas, Morgan, Morrill, Ramsey, Sherman, Sumner, Ten Eyck, Trumbull, Wade, Wilson—23.

The amendment of Mr. SAULSBURY (offered on the 13th) to add this new section:

That all white persons in the States not in revolt shall be protected, in their constitutional rights, and that no such person shall be deprived of life, liberty, or property, without due process of law; nor shall any such person be held to answer for a capital or otherwise infamous crime unless on a presentment or indictment of a grand jury except in cases arising in the land or naval forces, or in the militia when in actual service in time of war or public danger; nor shall any such person, except as aforesaid, be tried for any crime or offence whatever by court-martial or military commission.

Was rejected—yeas 8, nays 29, as follows:

YEAS—Messrs. *Buckalew, Carlile, Davis, Hendricks, Powell, Richardson, Riddle, Saulsbury*—8.

NAYS—Messrs. Anthony, Brown, Clark, Conness, Dixon, Doolittle, Fessenden, Foot, Foster, Grimes, Hale, Harlan, Harris, Hicks, Howe, Johnson, Lane of Indiana, Morgan, Morrill, Pomeroy, Ramsey, Sherman, Sumner, Ten Eyck, Trumbull, Van Winkle, Wade, Willey, Wilson—29.

June 28—The bill passed—yeas 21, nays 9, as follows:

YEAS—Messrs. Anthony, Chandler, Clark, Conness, Doolittle, Foot, Foster, Harlan, Howe, Lane of Indiana, Morgan, Morrill, Pomeroy, Ramsey, Sprague, Sumner, Trumbull, Van Winkle, Wade, Wilkinson, Wilson—21.

NAYS—Messrs. *Buckalew, Carlile*, Cowan, *Davis, Hendricks, McDougall, Powell, Riddle*, Willey—9.

During the pendency of the bill in the Senate as in Committee of the Whole, Mr. WILLEY offered this as a new section:

That whenever the said Commissioner cannot find abandoned real estate on which to employ all of the freedmen who may come under his care and control by virtue of this act, it shall be his duty, so far as may be practical, to provide for them homes and employment with humane and suitable persons at fair and just compensation for their services; and that in order the more effectually to accomplish this purpose the said Commissioner shall open a correspondence with the Governors and the various municipal authorities of the different States requesting their co-operation in this behalf.

Which was agreed to—yeas 19, nays 15, as follows:

YEAS—Messrs. Anthony, Brown, Clark, *Davis*, Doolittle, Foot, Grimes, Harlan, Harris, Henderson, Hicks, Howe, Lane of Indiana, Ramsey, *Riddle, Saulsbury*, Sprague, Van Winkle, Willey—19.

NAYS—Messrs. *Buckalew*, Conness, Cowan, Foster, *Hendricks*, Lane of Kansas, Morgan, Morrill, *Powell*, Sumner, Ten Eyck, Trumbull, Wade, Wilkinson, Wilson—15.

In open Senate—

Mr. WILSON moved to strike out these words; which was rejected—yeas 14, nays 14, as follows:

YEAS—Messrs. *Buckalew*, Chandler, Clark, Conness, *Hendricks*, Morgan, Morrill, Pomeroy, Sumner, Ten Eyck, Trumbull, Wade, Wilkinson, Wilson—14.

NAYS—Messrs. Brown, *Davis*, Foot, Grimes, Harlan, Harris, Hicks, Johnson, Lane of Indiana, *Powell*, Ramsey, *Saulsbury*, Van Winkle, Willey—14.

The last clause, "and that," &c., was afterwards stricken out as unnecessary, the Commissioner having full discretion over the subject-matter, and being accessible to all persons interested.

June 30—The bill as amended by the Senate, was referred to the Select Committee in the House, who recommended a non-concurence in the Senate amendments; when the bill was postponed to December 20th next.

The postponement of the bill leaves unsettled the proposition to repeal the joint resolution amendatory of the confiscation act. Each House passed a repealing section, but neither passed the other's. (See p. 203.)

LEGISLATION, ORDERS, PROCLAMATIONS,

AND

PROPOSITIONS RELATIVE TO THE WAR AND TO "PEACE."

The Enrollment Acts.

ACT OF MARCH 3, 1863.—p. 115.

Third Session, Thirty-Seventh Congress.

The bill passed the Senate without a call of the yeas and nays.

IN HOUSE.

February 25—Mr. Cox moved to insert the word "white" so as to limit the enrolment to "white" able-bodied males.

Mr. LOVEJOY called the yeas and nays, but they were not ordered. And the amendment was disagreed to—yeas 53, nays 85.

Mr. WICKLIFFE, of Kentucky, moved to add the following to the thirteenth section:

Provided, That the men thus called into the service shall be by the Governor of the State organized into companies and regiments, and officers to command them shall be appointed and commissioned by authority of the State according to the provisions of the constitution and laws thereof, and in obedience to the Constitution of the United States.

Which was negatived—yeas 55, nays 104. The YEAS were:

YEAS—Messrs. *William Allen*, *William J. Allen*, *Ancona*, *Baily*, *Biddle*, Clements, Conway, *Corning*, *Cox*, *Cravens*, *Crittenden*, *English*, Fisher, *Fouke*, Granger, *Grider*, Hale, *Hall*, *Harding*, *Holman*, *Johnson*, *Kerrigan*, Killinger, *Knapp*, *Law*, *Lazear*, *Mallory*, *May*, *Menzies*, *Morris*, *Noble*, *Norton*, *Nugen*, *Pendleton*, *Perry*, *Price*, *Robinson*, *James S. Rollins*, *Shiel*, *Smith*, *John B. Steele*, *William G. Steele*, *Stiles*, *Vallandigham*, *Voorhees*, *Wadsworth*, *Ward*, Webster, Whaley, *Chilton A. White*, *Wickliffe*, *Wood*, *Woodruff*, *Wright*, *Yeaman*—55.

THE $300 COMMUTATION CLAUSE.*

Mr. HOLMAN moved to strike out the thirteenth section, which provides for a commutation, not exceeding $300, where parties are drafted; which was disagreed to—yeas 67, nays 87, as follows:

YEAS—Messrs. *William Allen*, *William J. Allen*, Alley, *Ancona*, Beaman, Samuel S. Blair, Blake, Clements, Colfax, Roscoe Conkling, Conway, *Corning*, *Cox*, *Cravens*, Davis, Dawes, *Delaplaine*, Diven, Eliot, *Fouke*, Franchot, Granger, *Hall*, *Holman*, Hutchins, *Johnson*, Julian, Francis W. Kellogg, William Kellogg, *Kerrigan*, *Knapp*, *Law*, McPherson, *May*, *Morris*, *Noble*, *Norton*, *Nugen*, *Pendleton*, *Perry*, Porter, *Price*, Riddle, *Robinson*, Edward H. Rollins, *James S. Rollins*, Shanks, Sherman, *Shiel*, *John B. Steele*, *William G. Steele*, *Stiles*, *Vallandigham*, Van Wyck, *Voorhees*, *Wadsworth*, Wall, *Ward*, Washburne, Albert S. White, *Chilton A. White*, *Wickliffe*, Wilson, Windom, *Wood*, Worcester, *Yeaman*—67.

YEAS—Messrs. Aldrich, Arnold, Ashley, Babbitt, *Baily*, Baker, Baxter, *Biddle*, Bingham, Jacob B. Blair, William G. Brown, Buffinton, *Calvert*, Campbell, Casey, Chamberlain, Clark, Frederick A. Conkling, *Crisfield*, Cutler, Delano, Dunn, Edgerton, Edwards, Ely, *English*, Fenton, Samuel C. Fessenden, Thomas A. D. Fessenden, Fisher, Flanders, Frank, Gooch, Goodwin, Gurley, Hahn, Harrison, Hickman, Hooper, Horton, Kelley, Killinger, Lansing, *Lazear*, Leary, *Lehman*, Loomis, Lovejoy, Low, McIndoe, McKean, McKnight, Marston, Maynard, Moorhead, Anson P. Morrill, Nixon, Olin, Patton, Timothy G. Phelps, Pike, Pomeroy, Alexander H. Rice, John H. Rice, Sargent, Sedgwick, Segar, *Sheffield*, Shellabarger, Sloan, *Smith*, Spaulding, Stratton, Benjamin F. Thomas, Francis Thomas, Train, Trimble, Trowbridge, Van Horn, Verree, Walker, Wallace, Walton, Webster, Wheeler, *Woodruff*, *Wright*—87.

Mr. HOLMAN moved a substitute, the leading features of which are embodied in these sections:

That such militia of the several States shall be enrolled under the authority of the respective States, and when any number thereof shall be called out by the President of the United States as authorized by law, the same shall be organized into companies and regiments by the Governor of such State, subject to the regulations established by the President of the United States in pursuance with existing law, and the company, field, and staff officers of the forces so organized shall be commissioned by such Governor as now provided by law for commissioning officers for the volunteer forces: *Provided*, That such militia shall not be called out for a period of more than one year: *And provided further*, That the President of the United States in calling out the militia shall apportion the number from each State according to population, having regard to the number of volunteers or militia already furnished by the States respectively.

That the pay of the privates in the regular army and volunteers and militia in the service of the United States shall be $15 per month, from and after the 1st day of March, 1863, until otherwise provided by law.

Which was negatived—yeas 44, nays 108. The YEAS were:

YEAS—Messrs. *William Allen*, *Ancona*, *Biddle*, Conway, *Corning*, *Cox*, *Cravens*, *Crittenden*, *Delaplaine*, *English*, *Fouke*, Granger, *Hall*, *Harding*, *Holman*, *Johnson*, *Kerrigan*, Killinger, *Knapp*, *Law*, *Mallory*, *May*, *Menzies*, *Morris*, *Noble*, *Norton*, *Nugen*, *Pendleton*, *Price*, *James S. Rollins*, *Shiel*, *Smith*, *John B. Steele*, *William G. Steele*, *Stiles*, *Voorhees*, *Wadsworth*, *Ward*, Whaley, *Chilton A. White*, *Wood*, *Woodruff*, *Wright*, *Yeaman*—44.

The bill then passed—yeas 115, nays 49, as follows:

YEAS—Messrs. Aldrich, Alley, Arnold, Ashley, Babbitt, *Baily*, Baker, Baxter, Beaman, Bingham, Jacob B. Blair, Samuel S. Blair, Blake, William G. Brown, Buffinton, *Calvert*, Campbell, Casey, Chamberlain, Clark, Colfax, Frederick A. Conkling, Roscoe Conkling, *Crisfield*, Cutler,

---

* Pending the engineer bill in Senate,

March 2—Mr. TRUMBULL offered a section repealing the commutation clause; which was rejected—yeas 10, nays 25, as follows:

YEAS—Messrs. Grimes, Harlan, Howe, Lane of Indiana, *Powell*, *Saulsbury*, Ten Eyck, Trumbull, Wilkinson, *Wilson* of Missouri—10.

NAYS—Messrs. Arnold, Chandler, Clark, Collamer, Cowan, *Davis*, Dixon, Fessenden, Foot, Foster, Harris, Henderson, Hicks, Howard, *Kennedy*, King, Lane of Kansas, Morrill, *Nesmith*, Pomeroy, Sherman, Sumner, *Turpie*, Willey, Wilson of Massachusetts—25.

Davis, Dawes, Delano, Diven, Dunn, Edgerton, Edwards, Eliot, Ely, Fenton, Samuel C. Fessenden, Thomas A. D. Fessenden, Fisher, Flanders, Franchot, Frank, Gooch, Goodwin, Granger, Gurley, Hahn, *Haight*, Hale, Harrison, Hickman, Hooper, Horton, Hutchins, Julian, Kelley, Francis W. Kellogg, William Kellogg, Killinger, Lansing, Leary, *Lehman*, Loomis, Lovejoy, Low, McIndoe, McKean, McKnight, McPherson, Marston, Maynard, Mitchell, Moorhead, Anson P. Morrill, Justin S. Morrill, Nixon, Olin, Patton, Timothy G. Phelps, Pike, Pomeroy, Porter, Alexander H. Rice, John H. Rice, Riddle, Edward H. Rollins, Sargent, Sedgwick, Segar, Shanks, *Sheffield*, Shellabarger, Sherman, Sloan, Spaulding, Stevens, Stratton, Benjamin F. Thomas, Francis Thomas, Train, Trimble, Trowbridge, Vandever, Van Horn, Verree, Walker, Wall, Wallace, Walton, Washburne, Webster, Wheeler, Albert S. White, Wilson, Windom, Worcester—115.

NAYS—Messrs. *William Allen*, *William J. Allen*, *Ancona*, *Biddle*, Clements, Conway, *Corning*, *Cox*, *Cravens*, *Crittenden*, *Delaplaine*, *Dunlap*, *English*, *Fouke*, *Grider*, *Hall*, *Harding*, *Holman*, *Johnson*, *Kerrigan*, *Knapp*, *Law*, *Lazear*, *Mallory*, *May*, *Menzies*, *Morris*, *Noble*, *Norton*, *Nugen*, *Pendleton*, *Perry*, *Price*, *Robinson*, *James S. Rollins*, *Shiel*, *John B. Steele*, *William G. Steele*, *Stiles*, *Vallandigham*, *Voorhees*, *Wadsworth*, *Ward*, Whaley, *Chilton A. White*, *Wickliffe*, *Wood*, *Woodruff*, *Yeaman*—49.

IN SENATE.

February 28—The Senate resumed the consideration of the amendments made by the House, as recommended by the Military Committee, when, after debate,

Mr. BAYARD moved to postpone the bill indefinitely, which was negatived—yeas 11, nays 35, as follows:

YEAS—Messrs. *Bayard*, *Carlile*, *Davis*, *Kennedy*, *Latham*, *Powell*, *Rice*, *Richardson*, *Saulsbury*, *Wall*, *Wilson* of Missouri—11.

NAYS—Messrs. Anthony, Arnold, Chandler, Clark, Collamer, Cowan, Dixon, Doolittle, Fessenden, Foot, Foster, Grimes, *Harding*, Harlan, Harris, Henderson, Hicks, Howard, Howe, King, Lane of Indiana, Lane of Kansas, *McDougall*, Morrill, *Nesmith*, Pomeroy, Sherman, Sumner, Ten Eyck, Trumbull, Wade, Wilkinson, Willey, Wilmot, Wilson of Massachusetts—35.

The amendments of the House were then concurred in, and the bill was declared passed.

THE SUPPLEMENT TO THE ENROLLMENT ACT, FEBRUARY 24, 1864—p. 116.

First Session, Thirty-Eighth Congress.

1864, January 18—The bill passed the Senate—yeas 30, nays 10, as follows:

YEAS—Messrs. Anthony, Clark, Collamer, Conness, Cowan, *Davis*, Dixon, Doolittle, Fessenden, Foot, Foster, Hale, *Harding*, Harlan, Harris, Howard, Johnson, Lane of Kansas, Morgan, Morrill, *Nesmith*, Pomeroy, Ramsey, Sprague, Sumner, Ten Eyck, Van Winkle, Wade, Willey, Wilson—30.

NAYS—Messrs. *Buckalew*, *Carlile*, Grimes, *Hendricks*, Howe, Lane of Indiana, *Powell*, *Saulsbury*, Wilkinson, *Wright*—10.

The bill contained a provision that colored troops enlisted and mustered into the service of the United States in any State shall not be credited upon the quota of any other State; which was adopted—yeas 27, nays 11, as follows:

YEAS—Messrs. Brown, *Buckalew*, Conness, Cowan, *Davis*, Doolittle, Foot, Grimes, Hale, *Harding*, Harlan, Henderson, *Hendricks*, Howe, Johnson, Lane of Indiana, Lane of Kansas, Morgan, Morrill, *Nesmith*, Pomeroy, Ramsey, *Saulsbury*, Sherman, Ten Eyck, Trumbull, *Wright*—27.

NAYS—Messrs. Anthony, Clark, Dixon, Fessenden, Foster, Harris, Howard, Sprague, Sumner, Wilkinson, Wilson—11.

February 1—The House considered, in Committee of the Whole, the substitute for the Senate bill reported by the House Committee on Military Affairs.

February 12—The House agreed to the amendments made by the Committee of the Whole, reserving a few for special vote; among these was the following substitute for the 27th section, as reported:

ENROLLMENT OF COLORED PERSONS.

SEC. 27. That nothing contained in this act shall be so construed as to prevent or prohibit the enlistment of men in the States in rebellion under the orders of the War Department.

And in lieu thereof insert:

All able-bodied male persons of African descent, between the ages of twenty and forty-five years of age, whether citizens or not, resident in the United States, shall be enrolled according to the provisions of the act to which this is a supplement, and form part of the national forces; and when a slave of a loyal citizen shall be drafted and mustered into the service of the United States his master shall have a certificate thereof. The bounty of $100, now payable by law for each drafted man, shall be paid to the person to whom such drafted person owes service or labor at the time of his muster into the service of the United States, on freeing the person. The Secretary of War shall appoint a commission in each of the slave States represented in Congress charged to award a just compensation, not exceeding $300, to each loyal person to whom the colored volunteer may owe service, who may volunteer into the service of the United States, payable out of the commutation money upon the master freeing the slave.

Which was agreed to—yeas 84, nays 71, as follows:

YEAS—Messrs. Alley, Allison, Anderson, Arnold, Ashley, John D. Baldwin, Baxter, Beaman, Jacob B. Blair, Boutwell, Boyd, Brandegee, Broomall, William G. Brown, Cobb, Creswell, Henry Winter Davis, Thomas T. Davis, Dawes, Deming, Dixon, Driggs, Eckley, Eliot, Frank, Garfield, Gooch, Grinnell, Hale, Hooper, Hotchkiss, Asahel W. Hubbard, John H. Hubbard, Hulburd, Julian, Kasson, Kelley, Francis W. Kellogg, Orlando Kellogg, Loan, Longyear, Marvin, McBride, McClurg, McIndoe, Samuel F. Miller, Moorhead, Morrill, Daniel Morris, Amos Myers, Leonard Myers, Norton, Charles O'Neill, Orth, Patterson, Perham, Pike, Pomeroy, Alexander H. Rice, John H. Rice, Edward H. Rollins, Schenck, Scofield, Shannon, Sloan, Smith, Smithers, Spalding, Starr, Stevens, Thayer, Thomas, Tracy, Upson, Van Valkenburgh, Elihu B. Washburne, William B. Washburn, Webster, Whaley, Williams, Wilder, Wilson, Windom, Woodbridge—84.

NAYS—Messrs. *James C. Allen*, *William J. Allen*, *Ancona*, *Baily*, *Augustus C. Baldwin*, *Bliss*, *Brooks*, *James S. Brown*, *Chanler*, *Coffroth*, Cole, *Cox*, *Cravens*, *Dawson*, *Denison*, *Eden*, *Edgerton*, *Eldridge*, *Finck*, *Ganson*, *Grider*, *Griswold*, *Hall*, *Harding*, *Harrington*, *Benjamin G. Harris*, *Herrick*, Higby, *Holman*, *Hutchins*, *William Johnson*, *Kalbfleisch*, *Kernan*, *King*, *Knapp*, *Law*, *Lazear*, *LeBlond*, *Long*, *Mallory*, *Marcy*, *McDowell*, *McKinney*, *James R. Morris*, *Morrison*, *Nelson*, *Noble*, *Odell*, *John O'Neill*, *Pendleton*, *Radford*, *Samuel J. Randall*, William H. Randall, *Robinson*, *Rogers*, *James S. Rollins*, *Ross*, *Scott*, *John B. Steele*, *Wm. G. Steele*, *Stiles*, *Strouse*, *Stuart*, *Sweat*, *Voorhees*, *Wadsworth*, *Wheeler*, *Chilton A. White*, *Joseph W. White*, *Winfield*, *Fernando Wood*—71.

The bill passed—yeas 94, nays 65, as follows:

YEAS—Messrs. Alley, Allison, Anderson, Arnold, Ashley, *Baily*, John D. Baldwin, Baxter, Beaman, Jacob B. Blair, Boutwell, Boyd, Brandegee, Broomall, William G. Brown, Cobb, Cole, Creswell, Henry Winter Davis, Thomas T. Davis, Dawes, Deming, Dixon, Driggs, Eckley, Eliot, Farnsworth, Frank, Garfield, Gooch, Grinnell, *Griswold*, Hale, Higby, Hooper, Hotchkiss, Asahel W. Hubbard, John H. Hubbard, Hulburd, Jenckes, Julian, Kasson, Kelley, Francis W. Kellogg, Orlando Kellogg, Loan, Longyear, Marvin, *McAllister*, McBride, McClurg, McIndoe, Samuel F. Miller, Moorhead, Morrill, Daniel Morris, Amos Myers, Leonard Myers, Norton, *Odell*, Charles O'Neil, Orth, Patterson, Perham, Pike, Pomeroy, William H. Randall, Alexander H. Rice, John H. Rice, Edward H. Rollins, Schenck, Scofield, Shannon, Sloan, Smith, Smithers, Spalding, Starr, Stevens, Thayer, Thomas, Tracy, Upson, Van Valkenburgh, Ellihu B. Washburne, William B. Washburn, Webster, Whaley, *Wheeler*, Williams, Wilder, Wilson, Windom, Woodbridge—94.

NAYS—Messrs. *James C. Allen*, *William J. Allen*, *Ancona*, *Augustus C. Baldwin*, *Bliss*, *Brooks*, *James S. Brown*, *Chanler*, *Coffroth*, *Cox*, *Cravens*, *Dawson*, *Denison*, *Eden*, *Edgerton*, *Eldridge*, *Finck*, *Ganson*, *Grider*, *Hall*, *Harding*, *Harrington*, *Benjamin G. Harris*, *Herrick*, *Holman*, *Hutchins*, *William Johnson*, *Kalbfleisch*, *Kernan*, *King*, *Knapp*, *Law*, *Lazear*, *Le Blond*, *Long*, *Mallory*, *Marcy*, *McDowell*, *McKinney*, *Wm. H. Miller*, *Jas. R. Morris*, *Morrison*, *Nelson*, *Noble*, *John O'Neill*, *Pendleton*, *Radford*, *Samuel J. Randall*, *Robinson*, *Rogers*, *J. S. Rollins*, *Ross*, *Scott*, *John B. Steele*, *W. G. Steele*, *Stiles*, *Strouse*, *Stuart*, *Sweat*, *Voorhees*, *Wads-*

worth, C. A. White, Joseph W. White, Winfield, Fernando Wood—65.

February 15—The Senate non-concurred in the amendments of the House.

February 16—The House insisted on its amendments, and asked a Committee of Conference.

February 19—The Senate concurred in the report of the Committee of Conference—being the law as it now is—yeas 26, nays 16, as follows:

YEAS—Messrs. Anthony, Clark, Dixon, Doolittle, Fessenden, Foot, Foster, Grimes, Hale, *Harding*, Harris, Henderson, Johnson, Lane of Kansas, Morgan, Morrill, *Nesmith*, Ramsey, Sherman, Sprague, Sumner, Ten Eyck, Van Winkle, Wade, Willey, Wilson—26.

NAYS—Messrs. *Buckalew, Carlile*, Chandler, Conness, *Davis*, Harlan, *Hendricks*, Howard, Howe, Lane of Indiana, *Powell, Riddle, Saulsbury*, Trumbull, Wilkinson, *Wright*, —16.

February 19—The House concurred in the report of the Committee of Conference—yeas 71, nays 23, as follows:

YEAS—Messrs. Alley, Allison, Anderson, Arnold, John D. Baldwin, Baxter, Beaman, Francis P. Blair, Blow, Boutwell, Brandegee, Broomall, Ambrose W. Clark, Cobb, Cole, Henry Winter Davis, Dawes, Deming, Dixon, Dumont, Eckley, Eliot, Farnsworth, Fenton, Frank, Gooch, Grinnell, Hale, Higby, Hooper, Asahel W. Hubbard, Jenckes, Julian, Kasson, Kelley, Orlando Kellogg, Loan, Longyear, Marvin, McBride, McClurg, Samuel F. Miller, Moorhead, Amos Myers, Leonard Myers, *Odell*, Charles O'Neill, Orth, Patterson, Perham, Pike, Pomeroy, Price, William H. Randall, Alexander H. Rice, John H. Rice, Edward H. Rollins, Schenck, Scofield, Shannon, Smithers, Spalding, Starr, *Stebbins*, Upson, Van Valkenburgh, Elihu B. Washburne, Williams, Wilder, Wilson, Windom—71.

NAYS—Messrs. *Augustus C. Baldwin, Brooks, Chanler, Cox, Dawson, Edgerton, Eldridge, Benjamin G. Harris, Le Blond, Long, McDowell, McKinney, James R. Morris, Morrison, Noble, John O'Neill, Pendleton, Samuel J. Randall, James S. Rollins, Ross, Ward, Chilton A. White, Joseph W. White*—23.

SUPPLEMENT OF JULY 4, 1864*—p 117.

IN SENATE.

1864, June 8—The Senate took up this bill reported from the Military Committee:

That so much of the act entitled "An act for enrolling and calling out the national forces, and for other purposes," approved March 3, 1863, and the acts amendatory thereof, as authorizes the discharge of any drafted person from liability to military service by reason of the payment of $300 for the procuration of a substitute, or otherwise, be, and the same is hereby, repealed: *Provided*, That nothing contained in this act shall be construed to alter the provisions of existing laws relative to persons actually furnishing substitutes.

SEC. 2. That nothing in the act approved February 24, 1864, amending the act approved March 3, 1863, for enrolling and calling out the national forces, shall be construed to repeal that part of the said act approved March 3, 1863, which requires that the board of enrollment, in making drafts, shall "make a draft of the required number and fifty per centum in addition."

SEC. 3. That section twelve of the act for enrolling and calling out the national forces, and for other purposes, approved March 3, 1863, be, and is hereby, so amended that the notice to be served on drafted men may be served within ten days after such draft or at any time within six months therefrom.

June 9—Mr. COLLAMER moved the following additional sections:

That all calls for drafts hereafter made under the act entitled "An act for enrolling and calling out the national forces, and for other purposes," approved March 3, 1863, and of any act in addition to or amendment thereof, shall be for a term not exceeding one year.

That this act shall not extend to or include drafts to be made in any district or subdivision thereof, to fill its quota on calls already made, but the same shall be completed under the laws in force before the passage hereof.

That no person drafted on future calls shall be liable to be again drafted until the present enrollment shall be exhausted.

That the number of men furnished from any district for the service of the United States beyond and above its quota on calls heretobefore made, and the term of service of such men, shall be considered and allowed to said district in calls hereafter made.

The first section of the amendments was agreed to—yeas 22, nays 17, as follows:

YEAS—Messrs. Anthony, *Buckalew*, Clark, Collamer,

---

* Additional legislation is asked by the President, Secretary of War, and Provost Marshal General, whose communications are appended:

To the Senate and
House of Representatives:

I have the honor to submit for the consideration of Congress a letter and inclosure from the Secretary of War, with my concurrence in the recommendation therein made.

ABRAHAM LINCOLN.

WASHINGTON, D. C., *June* 8, 1864.

WAR DEPARTMENT,
WASHINGTON CITY, *June* 7, 1864.

SIR: I beg leave to submit to you a report made to me by the Provost Marshal General, showing the result of the draft now going on to fill the deficiency in the quotas of certain States, and recommending a repeal of the clause in the enrollment act commonly known as the $300 clause. The recommendation of the Provost Marshal General is approved by this Department, and I trust that it will be recommended by you to Congress.

The recent successes that have attended our arms lead to the hope that by maintaining our military strength and giving it such an increase as the extended field of operations may require, an early termination of the war may be attained. But to accomplish this it is absolutely necessary that efficient means be taken, with vigor and promptness, to keep the Army up to its strength and supply deficiencies occasioned by the losses sustained by casualties in the field. To that end resort must be had to a draft, but ample experience has now shown that the pecuniary exemption from service frustrates the object of the enrollment law by furnishing money instead of men.

An additional reason for repealing the $300 clause is that it is contemplated to make the draft for a comparatively short term. The burden of military service will therefore be lightened, but its certainty of furnishing troops is an absolute essential to success.

I have the honor to be, your obedient servant,

EDWIN M. STANTON,
Secretary of War.

To the PRESIDENT.

WAR DEPARTMENT,
PROVOST MARSHAL GENERAL'S OFFICE,
WASHINGTON, D. C., *June* 6, 1864.

SIR: In accordance with the amended enrollment act approved February 24, 1864, and your orders on the subject, I am now conducting a draft in various sub-districts for their respective deficiencies on quotas of troops heretofore assigned. The results of this draft, so far as shown by reports of this date, are worthy of attention. They are, briefly, as follows:

Number of drafted men examined		14,741
Number exempted for physical disability	4,374	
Number exempted for all other causes	2,632	
Total exempted		7,016
Number paid commutation money	5,050	
Number who have furnished substitutes	1,416	
Number held for personal service	1,259	
(This last includes some who may yet pay commutation money.)		
Total not exempted		7,725

These reports come from sub-districts in eight different States. I invite your attention to the small proportion of soldiers being obtained under the existing law. I see no reason to believe that the army can be materially strengthened by draft so long as the $300 clause is in force, nor do I think it safe to assume that the commutation paid by a drafted man will enable the Government to procure a volunteer or substitute in his place. I do not think that large bounties by the United States should be again resorted to for raising troops. I recommend that the $300 clause, as it is known, be repealed.

I am, sir, very respectfully, your obedient servant,

JAMES B. FRY,
Provost Marshal General.

Hon. E. M. STANTON, *Secretary of War.*

Davis, Doolittle, Fessenden, Foot, Foster, Harris, Howard, Howe, Lane of Kansas, Morrill, *Powell*, *Richardson*, Sumner, Van Winkle, Wade, Wilkinson, Willey, Wilson—22.

NAYS—Messrs. Brown, *Carlile*, Chandler, Conness, Grimes, Harlan, Henderson, Johnson, *McDougall*, Morgan, *Nesmith*, Pomeroy, Ramsey, Sherman, Sprague, Ten Eyck, Trumbull—17.

The remaining sections were agreed to.

ENLISTMENT OF INDIANS.

June 20—Mr. BROWN moved this new section:

That in any draft which may hereafter take place, all Indian tribes with whom treaties have been made by the United States and who are receiving annuities from the Government shall be required to furnish their respective quota cf men; and that the duties of enrollment, or ascertaining the approximate numbers of said tribes, shall, whenever the same is necessary, be performed by the Indian agents as part of their appropriate duty, without further compensation, under instructions from the Provost Marshal General. And in the event that any tribe receiving annuities as aforesaid shall refuse or fail to furnish its required quota, then and in that event the whole or such part of their said annuities as the Secretary of the Interior shall deem adequate to provide substitutes shall be withheld from the annual payment, and shall be placed in the Treasury along with the commutation fund heretofore paid for a like purpose: *And provided further*, That the force thus raised may be employed by the Government for the purpose of maintaining peace and protecting from hostile incursion the Indian and other Territories, and of relieving such troops as are now engaged in that duty.

Mr. DOOLITTLE moved this substitute for the above:

That the Secretary of War is authorized to receive into the military service of the United States Indians of tribes in treaty with the United States, to be employed as a part of the military force of the United States for the purpose of maintaining peace and protecting from hostile incursion the Indian Territory and other Territories where the hostile or invading force is in whole or in part composed of hostile Indians.

Which was agreed to—yeas 24, nays 12, as follows:

YEAS—Messrs. Chandler, Clark, Collamer, Conness, Dixon, Doolittle, Foot, Foster, Harlan, Harris, Howard, Lane of Indiana, Lane of Kansas, *McDougall*, Morgan, Pomeroy, Sherman, Sprague, Sumner, Ten Eyck, Van Winkle, Wade, Willey, Wilson—24.

NAYS—Messrs. Brown, *Buckalew*, *Carlile*, *Davis*, Grimes, *Hendricks*, Johnson, *Powell*, Ramsey, *Richardson*, *Saulsbury*, Wilkinson—12.

The amendment, as amended, was then rejected—yeas 10, nays 29, as follows:

YEAS—Messrs. Brown, Doolittle, Grimes, Harlan, Lane of Indiana, Lane of Kansas, *McDougall*, Pomeroy, Ramsey, Sprague—10.

NAYS—Messrs. Anthony, *Buckalew*, *Carlile*, Chandler, Clark, Collamer, Cowan, *Davis*, Dixon, Foot, Foster, Harris, *Hendricks*, Howard, Johnson, Morgan, *Powell*, *Richardson*, *Riddle*, *Saulsbury*, Sherman, Sumner, Ten Eyck, Trumbull, Van Winkle, Wade, Wilkinson, Willey, Wilson—29.

NO SUBSTITUTION.

Mr. McDOUGALL moved to insert this provision:

And from and after ten days from the passage of this act substitutes shall not be allowed in place of persons subject to draft and regularly drafted into the service of the United States.

Which was rejected—yeas 6, nays 35, as follows:

YEAS—Messrs. Chandler, Doolittle, Grimes, *McDougall*, Ramsey, Wilkinson—6.

NAYS—Messrs. Brown, *Buckalew*, *Carlile*, Clark, Collamer, Conness, Cowan, *Davis*, Dixon, Foot, Foster, Harlan, Harris, *Hendricks*, Howard, Howe, Johnson, Lane of Indiana, Lane of Kansas, Morgan, Morrill, *Nesmith*, Pomeroy, *Powell*, *Richardson*, *Riddle*, Sherman, Sprague, Sumner, Ten Eyck, Trumbull, Van Winkle, Wade, Willey, Wilson—35.

Mr. HENDRICKS moved to strike out the first section; which was agreed to—yeas 21, nays 18, as follows:

YEAS—Messrs. *Buckalew*, *Carlile*, Clark, Collamer, Cowan, *Davis*, Dixon, Foot, Foster, Harris, *Hendricks*, Johnson, *McDougall*, Morrill, *Powell*, *Richardson*, *Riddle*, *Saulsbury*, Van Winkle, Willey, Wilson—21.

NAYS—Messrs. Anthony, Brown, Chandler, Conness, Fessenden, Grimes, Harlan, Howe, Lane of Indiana, Lane of Kansas, Morgan, *Nesmith*, Ramsey, Sherman, Sprague, Sumner, Ten Eyck, Trumbull—18.

Pending other propositions, the bill was recommitted to the Committee on Military Affairs, and all the amendments fell by the recommitment.

June 23—The Senate considered the bill, which was reported back in the shape in which it was originally reported.

Mr. MORGAN moved to amend by adding this section:

That in the calls for drafts hereafter made under the act "for enrolling and calling out the national forces," and the acts in addition to or amendatory thereof, the same may be made for such term of time as the President shall direct, not exceeding one year.

Mr. WILSON moved to amend the amendment by making it read "shall be made for one year;" which was rejected—yeas 12, nays 18, as follows:

YEAS—Messrs. Clark, Collamer, *Davis*, Dixon, Foot, Harris, *Hendricks*, Howe, Johnson, Sumner, Willey, Wilson—12.

NAYS—Messrs. Brown, Chandler, Foster, Grimes, Harlan, Howard, Lane of Kansas, Morgan, Pomeroy, *Powell*, Ramsey, *Riddle*, *Saulsbury*, Sherman, Sprague, Ten Eyck, Trumbull, Wade—18.

Mr. CHANDLER moved to amend the amendment by striking out "not exceeding one year," and inserting "not less than one nor more than three years;" which was rejected—yeas 16, nays 23, as follows:

YEAS—Messrs. Anthony, Brown, Chandler, Conness, Grimes, Harlan, Howard, Howe, Lane of Kansas, Pomeroy, Ramsey, Sherman, Sprague, Ten Eyck, Trumbull, Wilkinson—16.

NAYS—Messrs. *Buckalew*, *Carlile*, Clark, Collamer, *Davis*, Dixon, Doolittle, Foot, Foster, Hale, Harris, *Hendricks*, Johnson, Morgan, Morrill, *Powell*, *Riddle*, *Saulsbury*, Sumner, Van Winkle, Wade, Willey, Wilson—23.

The amendment offered by Mr. MORGAN was then agreed to—yeas 25, nays 14, as follows:

YEAS—Messrs. *Buckalew*, Clark, Collamer, Cowan, *Davis*, Dixon, Doolittle, Foot, Hale, Harris, *Hendricks*, Howe, Johnson, Lane of Kansas, Morgan, Morrill, Pomeroy, *Powell*, *Richardson*, Sumner, Ten Eyck, Van Winkle, Wade, Willey, Wilson—25.

NAYS—Messrs. Brown, *Carlile*, Chandler, Conness, Foster, Grimes, Howard, *McDougall*, Ramsey, *Riddle*, Sherman, Sprague, Trumbull, Wilkinson—14.

Mr. COLLAMER moved to strike out the first section and insert this:

That the thirteenth section of the act entitled "An act for enrolling and calling out the national forces, and for other purposes," approved March 3, 1863, is hereby so amended that the sum to be paid by a drafted man to the Government for the procuration of a substitute shall not exceed $500, instead of $300.

Which was rejected without a division.

Mr GRIMES moved a new section, which was agreed to:

That the number of men furnished from any district for the service of the United States beyond and above its quota on calls heretofore made, and the term of service of such men, shall be considered and allowed to said district in calls hereafter made.

Mr. WILSON offered this new section, which he afterwards withdrew, decided opposition to it being manifested:

That any persons resident in the States of Virginia, North Carolina, South Carolina, Georgia, Florida, Alabama, Mississippi, Louisiana, Texas, or Arkansas, who may voluntarily enlist in the military service of the United States for the term of three years or during the war, shall be entitled to the benefits and privileges of existing laws, and such persons shall be mustered into the regiments or other organizations of whatsoever State they may elect, or, in the case of colored troops, shall be assigned as now provided by law. And the States or subdivisions of States procuring such enlistments shall receive credit for such persons, in accordance with the laws in other cases; but such enlistments as are authorized in any State, under the provisions of this act, shall only continue until such State shall have been made subject to a call for troops.

Mr. GRIMES offered the following new section, which was agreed to:

That no person drafted on future calls or who shall volunteer to fill the same shall be liable to be again drafted, until the existing enrollment shall be exhausted.

The bill, as amended, passed—yeas 24, nays 7, as follows:

YEAS—Messrs. Anthony, Brown, Chandler, Clark, Doolittle, Foot, Foster, Grimes, Harlan, Howard, Howe, Lane of Kansas, Morgan, Pomeroy, Ramsey, Sherman, Sprague, Ten Eyck, Trumbull, Van Winkle, Wade, Wilkinson, Willey, Wilson—24.

NAYS—Messrs. *Buckalew*, *Carlile*, *McDougall*, *Powell*, *Richardson*, *Riddle*, *Saulsbury*—7.

June 29—The House having returned a new bill, it was considered in the Senate and amended by substituting the former Senate bill, with an additional section or two.

Mr. SHERMAN offered this new section:

That for the purpose of paying the bounties and of enforcing the draft provided for in this act, there be levied and collected in addition to the duties imposed by law, a special duty of five per cent. on all incomes exceeding $600, accruing during the year 1864, which duty shall be assessed and collected in the mode and according to the provisions, penalties, and restrictions provided in the act approved ——, entitled "An act to provide internal revenue to support the Government, to pay interest on the public debt, and for other purposes." And this duty shall be payable on the 1st day of October next, and the Secretary of the Treasury is authorized to prescribe such rules and regulations as to the time and mode of assessment as will secure the collection of this special tax.

Which was agreed to—yeas 25, nays 7, as follows:

YEAS—Messrs. Anthony, Brown, Chandler, Clark, Conness, Doolittle, Foot, Foster, Grimes, Hale, Harlan, Howe, Lane of Indiana, Lane of Kansas, Morgan, Pomeroy, Ramsey, Sherman, Sprague, Sumner, Ten Eyck, Wade, Wilkinson, Willey, Wilson—25.

NAYS—Messrs. *Buckalew*, *Davis*, Harris, *Hendricks*, *McDougall*, *Powell*, *Riddle*—7.

Mr. POWELL offered this, which was agreed to:

That no officers or persons engaged in the military service of the United States shall enlist, recruit, or muster into the military service of the United States any person in any State of the United States to fill the quota of any State in which the person so enlisted, recruited, or mustered into the service of the United States does not reside. Any recruiting or military officer who shall violate this section shall be dismissed the service of the United States with forfeiture of all pay and allowances, and shall be subject to such further punishment as a court-martial may direct.

The bill then passed the Senate.

June 30—The Senate, after receiving the message from the House stated in House proceedings of this date, reconsidered their action, and struck out the tax section.

The bill went to a Committee of Conference, whose report being the law as passed (page 116) the Senate, June 2, first rejected —yeas 16, nays 18, as follows:

YEAS—Messrs. Anthony, Clark, Foot, Foster, Hale, Johnson, Lane of Indiana, Lane of Kansas, Morgan, Morrill, Pomeroy, Ramsey, Sumner, Wade, Wilkinson, Wilson—16.

NAYS—Messrs. *Buckalew*, *Carlile*, Conness, Cowan, *Davis*, Henderson, *Hendricks*, Hicks, *McDougall*, *Powell*, *Riddle*, *Saulsbury*, Sherman, Sprague, Ten Eyck, Trumbull, Van Winkle, Willey—18.

Afterward the vote was reconsidered, and the report adopted—yeas 18, nays 17, as follows:

YEAS—Messrs. Anthony, Chandler, Clark, Conness, Fessenden, Foot, Foster, Hale, Lane of Kansas, Morgan, Morrill, Pomeroy, Ramsey, Sumner, Van Winkle, Wade, Wilkinson, Wilson—18.

NAYS—Messrs. *Buckalew*, *Carlile*, *Davis*, Doolittle, Harlan, Harris, Henderson, *Hendricks*, Howe, Lane of Indiana, *McDougall*, *Powell*, *Riddle*, *Saulsbury*, Sherman, Trumbull, Willey—17.

IN HOUSE.

1864, June 13—Mr. SCHENCK introduced this bill amendatory of the conscription act:

SEC. 1. That so much of the act entitled "An act for enrolling and calling out the national forces, and for other purposes," approved March three, eighteen hundred and sixty-three, and of the several acts amendatory thereof, as provides for a commutation in money, to be paid by persons enrolled or drafted for military service, in lieu of actually rendering such military service, be, and the same is hereby, repealed; and hereafter no payment of money shall be accepted or received by the Government to release any enrolled or drafted man from obligation to perform military duty.

SEC. 2. That hereafter no person shall be received or accepted to serve in the army of the United States, as a substitute for any other person liable to military duty and who may have been enrolled or drafted for that purpose, unless such substitute be the father, brother, or son of the person so enrolled or drafted, and for whom he proposes to become such substitute.

SEC. 3. That the President of the United States may, at his discretion, at any time hereafter, order a draft under the provisions of the "Act for enrolling and calling out the national forces, and for other purposes," approved March third, eighteen hundred and sixty-three, and of the several acts amendatory thereto, for soldiers to serve for a less period than three years: *Provided, however*, That no such draft shall be for a less term of service than one year.

SEC. 4. That the President shall accompany any order for a draft of men for military service with a notice that he will accept volunteers in lieu of such drafted men prior to the day appointed for the draft, to fill the quota or any part thereof of any town, township, precinct, or election district; and every person so volunteering, in lieu of a man to be drafted, shall be credited to such town, township, precinct, or election district; and if he volunteers and is accepted and mustered into the service for a term of one year, unless sooner discharged, shall receive and be paid by the United States a bounty of one hundred dollars, and if for a term of two years, unless sooner discharged, a bounty of two hundred dollars, and if for a term of three years, unless sooner discharged, a bounty of three hundred dollars, one half of which said bounty shall be paid to the soldier at the time of his being mustered into the service, one fourth at the expiration of one half his term of service, and one fourth at the end of his term of service; and the President in any call or order for a draft shall specify the exact time of service for which such draft is to be made, and the volunteers accepted in lieu of the whole or any part of the quotas to be provided under that draft shall be for not less than the term of service for which that draft is ordered.

SEC. 5. That section three of an act entitled "An act to amend an act entitled an act for enrolling and calling out the national forces, and for other purposes," approved February 24th, 1864, be, and the same is hereby, amended so as to authorize and direct district provost marshals, under the direction of the Provost Marshal General, to make a draft for fifty per centum in addition to the number required to fill the quota of any district, as provided by said section.

SEC. 6. That, instead of travelling pay, all drafted persons reporting at the place of rendezvous shall be allowed transportation from their places of residence; and persons discharged at the place of rendezvous shall be allowed transportation to their places of residence.

Mr. SCHENCK demanded the previous question; but the House refused to second it—yeas 45, nays 60. The bill was laid over.

June 21—The subject was resumed. On a motion to reject the bill, the yeas were 75, nays 75—the SPEAKER voting nay.

VOTE ON SECTION REPEALING THE $300 COMMUTATION CLAUSE.

The first section was then stricken out—yeas 100, nays 50, as follows:

YEAS—Messrs. *James C. Allen*, *William J. Allen*, Alley, Ames, *Ancona*, *Baily*, *Augustus C. Baldwin*, John D. Baldwin, Blaine, *Bliss*, Boutwell, *Brooks*, Broomall, *James S. Brown*, William G. Brown, *Chanler*, Freeman Clarke, *Coffroth*, *Cravens*, Thomas T. Davis, Dawes, *Dawson*, Deming,

Denison, Eden, Edgerton, Eldridge, Eliot, *English,* Fenton, *Finck,* Frank, *Ganson,* Gooch, *Grider, Griswold,* Hale, *Harding, Harrington, Benjamin G. Harris, Herrick, Holman,* Hooper, Hotchkiss, *Hutchins, Philip Johnson, Wm. Johnson, Kalbfleisch, Knapp, Law, Lazear, LeBlond, Mallory, Marcy, McDowell, McKinney, Middleton,* Samuel F. Miller, *Wm. H. Miller,* Daniel Morris, *James R. Morris, Morrison,* Amos Myers, Leonard Myers, *Nelson, Noble, Odell, John O'Neill,* Patterson, *Pendleton,* Perham, *Perry, Pruyn, Radford, Samuel J. Randall,* Alexander H. Rice, *Robinson, Rogers,* Edward H. Rollins, Scofield, *Scott, John B. Steele, Wm. G. Steele,* Stevens, *Stiles, Strouse, Stuart, Sweat,* Thomas, Upson, *Wadsworth, Ward,* William B. Washburn, Webster, Whaley, *Wheeler, Chilton A. White, Joseph W. White,* Williams, *Winfield*—100.

NAYS—Messrs. Arnold, Ashley, Baxter, Beaman, Blair, Blow, Boyd, Ambrose W. Clark, Cobb, Cole, Dixon, Donnelly, Driggs, Eckley, Farnsworth, Garfield, Higby, Asahel W. Hubbard, John H. Hubbard, Hulburd, Ingersoll, Julian, Kelley, Francis W. Kellogg, Knox, Loan, Longyear, Marvin, McClurg, Moorhead, Morrill, Norton, Charles O'Neill, Orth, Pike, Pomeroy, Price, John H. Rice, *Ross,* Schenck, Shannon, Sloan, Smithers, Thayer, Tracy, Van Valkenburgh, Ellihu B. Washburne, Wilder, Wilson, Windom—50.

The second section was stricken out without a division.

Several substitutes were offered, but no votes were taken on them.

June 25—Mr. SCHENCK offered a substitute for the bill, the first sections of which were:

That so much of the act entitled "An act for enrolling and calling out the national forces, and for other purposes," approved March 3, 1863, and of the several acts amendatory thereof, as provides for a commutation in money, to be paid by persons enrolled or drafted for military service, in lieu of actually rendering such military service, be, and the same is hereby, repealed; and hereafter no payment of money shall be accepted or received by the Government to release any enrolled or drafted man from obligation to perform military duty.

SEC. 2. *And be it further enacted,* That the President of the United States may, at his discretion, at any time hereafter, order a draft for soldiers to serve for a less period than three years: *Provided, however,* That no such draft shall be for a less term of service than one year.

The third section provided for the acceptance of volunteers before the draft, with $100 bounty for a one year volunteer, $200 for a two year, and $300 for a three year. Drafted men, substitutes, and volunteers to be organized together according to States, and, as far as possible, to select their own regiments. Recruiting of persons under sixteen prohibited, and the Secretary of War authorized to discharge persons under eighteen.

After debate,

Mr. Cox moved that the bill be tabled, which was rejected—yeas 57, nays 78, as follows:

YEAS—Messrs. *William J. Allen, Ancona, Augustus C. Baldwin, James S. Brown, Chanler, Coffroth, Cox, Cravens, Dawson, Eden, Edgerton, Eldridge, English, Finck, Grider, Harding, Harrington, Benjamin G. Harris, Charles M. Harris, Herrick, Holman, Hutchins, Philip Johnson, William Johnson, Kernan, Law, Lazear, Le Blond, Mallory, Marcy, McDowell, McKinney, William H. Miller, James R. Morris, Morrison, Nelson, Noble, John O'Neill, Pendleton, Pruyn, Radford, Samuel J. Randall, Robinson, Rogers, James S. Rollins, Ross, John B. Steele, William G. Steele, Stiles, Strouse, Stuart, Sweat, Chilton A. White, Joseph W. White, Winfield, Benjamin Wood, Fernando Wood*—57.

NAYS—Messrs. Alley, Allison, Ames, Anderson, Arnold, Ashley, John D. Baldwin, Baxter, Beaman, Blaine, Blair, Blow, Boutwell, Boyd, William G. Brown, Ambrose W. Clark, Cobb, Cole, Creswell, Thomas T. Davis, Dawes, Deming, Dixon, Donnelly, Driggs, Eliot, Farnsworth, Fenton, Garfield, Gooch, *Griswold,* Hale, Higby, Hooper, Asahel W. Hubbard, John H. Hubbard, Hulburd, Jenckes, Julian, Kelley, Francis W. Kellogg, Orlando Kellogg, Knox, Littlejohn, Loan, Longyear, Marvin, McClurg, Moorhead, Morrill, Daniel Morris, Amos Myers, Leonard Myers, Norton, *Odell,* Charles O'Neill, Orth, Patterson, Perham, Pike, Pomeroy, Price, John H. Rice, Edward H. Rollins, Schenck, Sloan, Smithers, Stevens, Thayer, Thomas, Tracy, Van Valkenburgh, Ellihu B. Washburne, William B. Washburn, Webster, Whaley, Wilson, Windom—78.

June 27—The substitute of Mr. SCHENCK, as above, with the addition of a section authorizing persons resident in Virginia, North Carolina, South Carolina, Georgia, Florida, Mississippi, Louisiana, Texas, and Arkansas, enlisting for the war, or not less than one year, to have the benefit of existing laws, credit for them to go to the States procuring the enlistments; provided, that such enlistments as are authorized in any State, under the provisions of this act, shall only continue until such State shall have been made subject to a call for troops; and provided further, that no enlistments shall be made of any soldiers, either in or out of any State, except those enumerated herein, unless full credit is given to the State to which the enlisted soldier belongs, was rejected—yeas 62, nays 92, as follows:

YEAS—Messrs. Allison, Anderson, Arnold, Ashley, Baxter, Beaman, Blair, Blow, Boyd, William G. Brown, Ambrose W. Clark, Cobb, Cole, Creswell, Henry Winter Davis, Dixon, Donnelly, Driggs, Garfield, Higby, Hotchkiss, Asahel W. Hubbard, Jno. H. Hubbard, Hulburd, Ingersoll, Jenckes, Julian, Kelley, Knox, Littlejohn, Loan, Marvin, McBride, McClurg, McIndoe, Samuel F. Miller, Moorhead, Morrill, Daniel Morris, Amos Myers, Leonard Myers, Norton, Charles O'Neill, Orth, Pike, Pomeroy, William H. Randall, John H. Rice, Schenck, Shannon, Sloan, Smith, Smithers, Spalding, Thayer, Tracy, Upson, Van Valkenburgh, Ellihu B. Washburne, Wilder, Wilson, Windom—62.

NAYS—Messrs. *William J. Allen,* Alley, Ames, *Ancona, Baily, Augustus C. Baldwin,* John D. Baldwin, Blaine, *Bliss,* Boutwell, *Brooks,* Broomall, *James S. Brown, Chanler, Coffroth, Cox, Cravens,* Dawes, *Dawson,* Deming, *Denison, Eden, Edgerton, Eldridge,* Eliot, *English, Finck,* Frank, *Ganson,* Gooch, *Grider, Griswold,* Hale, *Harding, Harrington, Benjamin G. Harris, Charles M. Harris, Herrick, Holman, Hutchins, Philip Johnson, William Johnson, Kalbfleisch,* Orlando Kellogg, *Kernan, Knapp, Law, Lazear, LeBlond, Long, Mallory, Marcy, McAllister, McDowell, McKinney, Wm. H. Miller, James R. Morris, Morrison, Nelson, Noble, Odell, John O'Neill,* Patterson, *Pendleton,* Perham, *Pruyn, Radford, Samuel J. Randall,* Alexander H. Rice, *Robinson, Rogers,* Edward H. Rollins, *James S. Rollins, Ross, John B. Steele, Wm. G. Steele,* Stevens, *Stiles, Strouse, Stuart, Sweat,* Thomas, *Wadsworth,* William B. Washburn, Webster, Whaley, *Wheeler, Chilton A. White, Joseph W. White,* Williams, *Winfield, Fernando Wood*—92.

Mr. BROOMALL's substitute was rejected without a division:

That hereafter no person shall be received or accepted to serve in the army of the United States as a substitute for any other person liable to military duty and who may have been enrolled or drafted for that purpose.

SEC. 2. That the term of service of all soldiers hereafter volunteering or being drafted shall be one year unless sooner discharged, and that, in lieu of all bounties, their pay shall be thirty dollars per month.

SEC. 3. That all persons hereafter volunteering shall be credited to the city or county in which they are liable to draft, if so liable, and if not, then to the city or county which they shall elect.

SEC. 4. That the payment of commutation money under existing laws shall exempt the person paying it from draft for one year, unless within that period all persons liable to draft in his city or county shall be drafted and mustered into service, or shall pay commutation money, in which case he shall be again liable to draft.

SEC. 5. That section three of an act entitled "An act to amend an act entitled 'An act for enrolling and calling out the national forces, and for other purposes,'" approved February 24, 1864, be, and the same is hereby, amended so as to authorize and direct district provost marshals, under the direction of the Provost Marshal General, to make a draft for fifty per cent. in addition to the number required to fill the quota of any district, as provided by said section.

SEC. 6. That, instead of travelling pay, all drafted persons reporting at the place of rendezvous shall be allowed transportation from their places of residence; and persons discharged at the place of rendezvous shall be allowed transportation to their places of residence.

Mr. STEVENS proposed this substitute:

Be it enacted, &c., That the President of the United States is authorized to call into military service not exceeding 500,000 men, in addition to those already called for, to serve for two years, unless sooner discharged, and that if not otherwise obtained a draft may be ordered to take place within forty days, or at such time thereafter as the President may direct.

SEC. 2. That any person who is liable to draft and has been regularly enrolled, may purchase exemption from draft for the term of two years or until the roll is exhausted, by paying $300 at any time not less than ten days before the time fixed for such draft. Any person who may be drafted may purchase the like exemption by paying $500 at any time not less than ten days after he shall be duly notified that he is drafted. The commutation money thus paid shall go into the Treasury for the purpose of paying the bounties herein provided for.

SEC. 3. That to enable the several States to raise the number of troops allotted to them respectively, the Governors of said States may appoint such number of recruiting officers as they may deem proper, and when companies and regiments shall be enlisted, shall commission such company and regimental officers as shall be deemed competent.

SEC. 4. That when, in the judgment of the President, the regiments of the Army are so reduced as to require consolidation, they may be consolidated, and the supernumerary officers may be detailed for the purpose of raising new companies and regiments.

SEC. 5. That if the requisite number of soldiers shall not be raised at the first draft, a second draft may be ordered to take place within ten days, or any longer period which the President may deem proper, of the men remaining unexempted and undrawn, and may be repeated from time to time until the full number shall be obtained.

SEC. 6. That every person who shall volunteer as a soldier and be regularly enlisted, shall receive a bounty of $500, one half thereof to be paid to him when mustered into the service of the United States, and the other half at the end of his term of service, or if honorably discharged; or if he shall be killed or die in the service before the expiration of his term of enlistment, it shall go to his widow, if there be one, and in case there be no widow, then to his children, and in case there be no widow or children, then to his personal representatives.

SEC. 7. That it shall be lawful for any of the States to send recruiting agents into any of the rebel States to enlist soldiers, who shall be credited to the State that may procure their enlistment; and it shall be the duty of the Secretary of War to approve the appointment of agents by the Governors of the respective States.

SEC. 8. That enrolled men may furnish substitutes either before or after they may be drafted according to the present law, who shall be accepted without regard to color, if otherwise competent.

SEC. 9. That the law with regard to persons conscientiously opposed to bearing arms shall not be altered or affected by this act, except so far as it regards the amount of money to be paid for exemptions.

SEC. 10. That it shall be lawful for the President, if he shall deem it expedient, to accept the services of any number not exceeding fifty thousand volunteers, between the ages of forty-five and fifty-five, to be used for post or garrison duty, who shall be called the "Old Guard." Such soldiers, when enlisted for two years, unless sooner discharged, shall be entitled to receive $100 bounty, one half to be paid when mustered into service, the other half at the expiration of their term, if honorably discharged; and if they should be killed or die in the service of the United States, it shall be paid to their respective widows, children, or personal representatives, in the same manner as is provided in section six of this act; and they and their heirs shall be entitled to such pensions as are now provided by law for other soldiers. When a drafted man shall claim exemption on account of physical disability, the surgeon shall examine into the degree of disability. If found unfit for active field service, and fit for garrison or post service, he shall be certified accordingly and placed into the "Old Guard."

Section eleven is the same as the fifth section of the law.

Mr. BLAIR, of Virginia, offered this substitute:

That so much of the act entitled "An act for enrolling and calling out the national forces, and for other purposes," approved March 3, 1863, and of the several acts amendatory thereof, as provides for a commutation in money, to be paid by persons enrolled or drafted for military service, in lieu of actually rendering such military service, be, and the same is hereby, repealed; and hereafter no payment of money shall be accepted or received by the Government to release an enrolled or drafted man from obligation to perform military duty: *Provided*, That hereafter no person shall be received or accepted to serve in the army of the United States as a substitute for any other person liable to military duty and who may have been enrolled or drafted for that purpose.

Which was rejected, on a count—yeas 25, nays 93.

Mr. SCHENCK then offered this substitute:

Be it enacted, &c., That so much of the act entitled "An act for enrolling and calling out the national forces, and for other purposes," approved March 3, 1863, and the acts amendatory thereof, as authorizes the discharge of any drafted person from liability to military service by reason of the payment of $300 for the procuration of a substitute or otherwise, be, and the same is hereby, repealed: *Provided*, That nothing contained in this act shall be construed to alter the provisions of existing laws relative to persons actually furnishing substitutes.

SEC. 2. That in calls for drafts hereafter made under the act for enrolling and calling out the national forces, and the acts in addition to or amendatory thereof, the same may be made for such term of time as the President shall direct, not exceeding one year.

SEC. 3. That the number of men furnished from any district for the service of the United States beyond and above its quota on calls heretofore made, and the term of service of such men, shall be considered and allowed to said district in calls hereafter made.

SEC. 4 That no person drafted on future calls, or who shall volunteer to fill the same, shall be liable to be again drafted until the existing enrollment shall be exhausted.

Which was rejected—yeas 58, nays 93, as follows:

YEAS—Messrs. Allison, Anderson, Arnold, Ashley, Baxter, Beaman, Blair, Blow, Boyd, Ambrose W. Clark, Cole, Creswell, Dixon, Donnelly, Driggs, Eckley, Garfield, Higby, Hotchkiss, Asahel W. Hubbard, John H. Hubbard, Hulburd, Ingersoll, Jenckes, Julian, Kelley, Knox, Littlejohn, Loan, Marvin, McBride, McClurg, McIndoe, Samuel F. Miller, Moorhead, Morrill, Daniel Morris, Amos Myers, Leonard Myers, Norton, Charles O'Neill, Orth, Pike, Pomeroy, William H. Randall, John H. Rice, Schenck, Shannon, Sloan, Smithers, Spalding, Thayer, Thomas, Tracy, Upson, Ellihu B. Washburne, Wilson, Windom—58.

NAYS—Messrs. *William J. Allen*, Alley, Ames, *Ancona*, *Baily*, *Augustus C. Baldwin*, John D. Baldwin, Blaine, *Bliss*, Broomall, Boutwell, *Brooks*, *James S. Brown*, William G. Brown, *Chanler*, *Coffroth*, *Cox*, *Cravens*, Dawes, *Dawson*, *Denison*, *Eden*, *Edgerton*, *Eldridge*, Eliot, *English*, Fenton, *Finck*, Frank, *Ganson*, Gooch, *Grider*, *Griswold*, *Harding*, *Harrington*, *Benjamin G Harris*, *Charles M. Harris*, *Herrick*, *Holman*, *Hutchins*, *Philip Johnson*, *William Johnson*, *Kalbfleisch*, Francis W. Kellogg, Orlando Kellogg, *Kernan*, *Knapp*, *Law*, *Lazear*, *LeBlond*, *Long*, Mallory, *Marcy*, *McAllister*, *McDowell*, *McKinney*, *Middleton*, *William H. Miller*, *James R. Morris*, *Morrison*, *Nelson*, *Noble*, *Odell*, *John O'Neill*, Patterson, *Pendleton*, Perham, *Pruyn*, *Radford*, *Samuel J. Randall*, Alexander H. Rice, *Robinson*, *Rogers*, Edward H. Rollins, *James S. Rollins*, *Ross*, Scofield, *John B. Steele*, *William G. Steele*, Stevens, *Stiles*, *Strouse*, *Stuart*, *Sweat*, *Wadsworth*, *Ward*, William B. Washburn, Webster, Whaley, *Wheeler*, *Chilton A. White*, *Joseph W. White*, *Winfield*—93.

Mr. STEVENS's substitute was then rejected—yeas 24, nays 120, as follows:

YEAS—Messrs. Alley, Ames, *Baily*, Boutwell, Broomall, William G. Brown, Eliot, *English*, *Ganson*, *Griswold*, Hale, Hotchkiss, *Kernan*, *Lazear*, Loan, Orth, Alexander H. Rice, Edward H. Rollins, *Ross*, Scofield, *William G. Steele*, Stevens, Webster, Wilder—24.

NAYS—Messrs. *William J. Allen*, Allison, *Ancona*, Anderson, Arnold, Ashley, *Augustus C. Baldwin*, John D. Baldwin, Baxter, Beaman, Blair, *Bliss*, Blow, Boyd, *Brooks*, *Chanler*, Ambrose W. Clark, *Coffroth*, Cole, *Cox*, *Cravens*, Creswell, Dawes, *Dawson*, *Denison*, Dixon, Donnelly, Driggs, Eckley, *Eden*, *Edgerton*, *Eldridge*, Fenton, *Finck*, Frank, Garfield, Gooch, *Grider*, *Harding*, *Harrington*, *Benjamin G. Harris*, *Charles M. Harris*, *Herrick*, Higby, *Holman*, Hulburd, *Hutchins*, Ingersoll, Jenckes, *Philip Johnson*, *William Johnson*, Julian, *Kalbfleisch*, Kelley, Francis W. Kellogg, Orlando Kellogg, Knox, *Le Blond*, Littlejohn, *Long*, *Mallory*, *Marcy*, Marvin, McBride, McClurg, *McDowell*, McIndoe, *McKinney*, *Middleton*, Samuel F. Miller, *William H. Miller*, Moorhead, Morrill, Daniel Morris, *James R. Morris*, *Morrison*, *Nelson*, *Noble*, Norton, *Odell*, Charles O'Neill, *John O'Neill*, *Pendleton*, Perham, Pike, Pomeroy, *Pruyn*, *Radford*, *Samuel J. Randall*, William H. Randall, John H. Rice, *Rogers*, *James S. Rollins*, Schenck, Shannon, Sloan, Smithers, Spalding, *John B. Steele*, *Stiles*, *Strouse*, *Stuart*, *Sweat*, Thayer, Thomas, Tracy, Upson, Van Valkenburgh, *Wadsworth*, *Ward*, Ellihu B. Washburne, William B. Washburn, Whaley, *Wheeler*, *Chilton A. White*, *Joseph W. White*, Williams, Wilson, Windom, *Winfield*—120.

Mr. SMITHERS then offered a subs'itute:

The first section became the law, except that in the substitute the bounty was fixed at $200, $300, and $400, payable one half at muster, one fourth at expiration of half the term of service, and one fourth at expiration, and in case of death while in service the residue unpaid to be paid to the widow, or children, or legal representatives. If honorably discharged by reason of wounds or sickness incurred in the service, to receive full bounty.

Second section became law, except that "fifty" days was substituted for "sixty."

Third section became third section of the law.

Fourth section became fourth section of the law.

Fifth section became nfth section of the law.

Section six is the sixth section of the law, except that "fifty" *per centum* reads "one hundred."

Section seven was unchanged.

Section eight is substantially the eighth section of the law.

Section nine is the ninth section of the law.

Which was rejected—yeas 76, nays 77, as follows:

YEAS—Messrs. Alley, Allison, Ames, Anderson, Arnold, Ashley, John D. Baldwin, Baxter, Beaman, Blow, Boutwell, Boyd, Broomall, Ambrose W. Clark, Cobb, Cole, Creswell, Dawes, Dixon, Donnelly, Driggs, Eckley, Eliot, Fenton, Garfield, Gooch, Higby, Hooper, Hotchkiss, Asahel W. Hubbard, John H. Hubbard, Hulburd, Ingersoll, Jenckes, Julian, Kelley, Francis W. Kellogg, Orlando Kellogg, Knox, Littlejohn, Loan, Marvin, McBride, McClurg, McIndoe, Samuel F. Miller, Moorhead, Morrill, Daniel Morris, Amos Myers, Leonard Myers, Norton, Charles O'Neill, Orth, Patterson, Perham, Pomeroy, William H. Randall, Alexander H. Rice, John H. Rice, Edward H. Rollins, Schenck, Scofield, Shannon, Sloan, Smithers, Spalding, Thayer, Tracy, Upson, Ellihu B. Washburne, William B. Washburn, Williams, Wilder, Wilson, Windom—76.

NAYS—Messrs. *William J. Allen*, *Ancona*, *Baily*, *Augustus C. Baldwin*, Blair, *Bliss*, *Brooks*, *James S. Brown*, William G. Brown, *Chanler*, *Coffroth*, *Cox*, *Cravens*, *Dawson*, *Denison*, *Eden*, *Edgerton*, *Eldridge*, *English*, *Finck*, *Ganson*, *Grider*, *Griswold*, Hale, *Harding*, *Harrington*, *Benjamin G. Harris*, *Charles M. Harris*, *Herrick*, *Holman*, *Hutchins*, *Philip Johnson*, *Wm. Johnson*, *Kalbfleisch*, *Kernan*, *Knapp*, *Law*, *Lazear*, *Le Blond*, *Long*, *Mallory*, *Marcy*, *McAllister*, *McDowell*, *McKinney*, *Middleton*, *Wm. H. Miller*, *James R. Morris*, *Morrison*, *Nelson*, *Noble*, *Odell*, *John O'Neill*, *Pendleton*, *Pruyn*, *Radford*, *Samuel J. Randall*, *Robinson*, *Rogers*, *Jas. S. Rollins*, *Ross*, *John B. Steele*, *Wm. G. Steele*, Stevens, *Stiles*, *Strouse*, *Stuart*, *Sweat*, Thomas, *Wadsworth*, *Ward*, Webster, Whaley, *Wheeler*, *Chilton A. White*, *Joseph W. White*, *Winfield*—77.

June 28—Mr. BLAIR moved to reconsider this vote.

Mr. HOLMAN moved to table the motion, which was lost—yeas 73, nays 85. The motion to reconsider was then agreed to—yeas 83, nays 71, as follows:

YEAS—Messrs. Alley, Allison, Ames, Anderson, Arnold, Ashley, John D. Baldwin, Baxter, Beaman, Blair, Blow, Boutwell, Boyd, Broomall, Freeman Clarke, Cobb, Cole, Creswell, Henry Winter Davis, Thomas T. Davis, Dawes, Deming, Dixon, Donnelly, Driggs, Eckley, Eliot, Garfield, Gooch, Higby, Hooper, Hotchkiss, Asahel W. Hubbard, John H. Hubbard, Hulburd, Ingersoll, Jenckes, Julian, Kelley, Francis W. Kellogg, Orlando Kellogg, Knox, Littlejohn, Loan, Longyear, Marvin, McBride, McClurg, McIndoe, Samuel F. Miller, Moorhead, Daniel Morris, Amos Myers, Leonard Myers, Norton, Charles O'Neill, Orth, Patterson, Perham, Pike, Pomeroy, William H. Randall, Alexander H. Rice, John H. Rice, Edward H. Rollins, Schenck, Scofield, Shannon, Sloan, Smith, Smithers, Spalding, Thayer, Thomas, Tracy, Upson, Van Valkenburgh, Ellihu B. Washburne, William B. Washburn, Williams, Wilder, Wilson, Windom—83.

NAYS—Messrs. *William J. Allen*, *Ancona*, *Baily*, *Augustus C. Baldwin*, Blaine, *Bliss*, *James S. Brown*, Wm. G. Brown, *Chanler*, *Coffroth*, *Cravens*, *Dawson*, *Denison*, *Eden*, *Edgerton*, *Eldridge*, *English*, *Finck*, *Ganson*, *Grider*, Hale, *Harding*, *Harrington*, *Benjamin G. Harris*, *Charles M. Harris*, *Herrick*, *Holman*, *Hutchins*, *Philip Johnson*, *Wm. Johnson*, *Kalbfleisch*, *Knapp*, *Law*, *Lazear*, *Le Blond*, *Long*, *Mallory*, *Marcy*, *McAllister*, *McDowell*, *McKinney*, *Middleton*, *Wm. H. Miller*, *Morrison*, *Nelson*, *Noble*, *Odell*, *John O'Neill*, *Pendleton*, *Perry*, *Pruyn*, *Radford*, *Samuel J. Randall*, *Robinson*, *James S. Rollins*, *Ross*, *John B. Steele*, *Wm. G. Steele*, Stevens, *Stiles*, *Strouse*, *Stuart*, *Sweat*, *Wadsworth*, *Ward*, Webster, Whaley, *Wheeler*, *Chilton A. White*, *Joseph W. White*, *Winfield*—71.

The substitute was modified by adding after "service" in the last line of the first section, the words: "in the line of his duty;" and was then agreed to—yeas 81, nays 75, as follows:

YEAS—Messrs. Alley, Allison, Ames, Anderson, Arnold, Ashley, John D. Baldwin, Baxter, Beaman, Blair, Blow, Boutwell, Boyd, Broomall, Cobb, Cole, Creswell, Henry Winter Davis, Thomas T. Davis, Dawes, Deming, Dixon, Donnelly, Driggs, Eckley, Eliot, Garfield, Gooch, Higby, Hooper, Hotchkiss, Asahel W. Hubbard, John H. Hubbard, Hulburd, Ingersoll, Jenckes, Julian, Kelley, Francis W. Kellogg, Orlando Kellogg, Knox, Littlejohn, Loan, Longyear, Marvin, McBride, McClurg, McIndoe, Samuel F. Miller, Moorhead, Daniel Morris, Amos Myers, Leonard Myers, Norton, Charles O'Neill, Orth, Patterson, Perham, Pike, Pomeroy, William H. Randall, Alexander H. Rice, John H. Rice, Edward H. Rollins, Schenck, Scofield, Shannon, Sloan, Smith, Smithers, Spalding, Thayer, Tracy, Upson, Van Valkenburgh, Ellihu B. Washburne, William B. Washburn, Williams, Wilder, Wilson, Windom—81.

NAYS—Messrs. *William J. Allen*, *Ancona*, *Baily*, *Augustus C. Baldwin*, Blaine, *Bliss*, *James S. Brown*, William G. Brown, *Chanler*, *Coffroth*, *Cravens*, *Dawson*, *Denison*, *Eden*, *Edgerton*, *Eldridge*, *English*, *Finck*, Frank, *Ganson*, *Grider*, *Griswold*, Hale, *Harding*, *Harrington*, *Benjamin G. Harris*, *Charles M. Harris*, *Herrick*, *Holman*, *Hutchins*, *Philip Johnson*, *William Johnson*, *Kalbfleisch*, *Kernan*, *Knapp*, *Law*, *Lazear*, *Le Blond*, *Long*, *Mallory*, *Marcy*, *McAllister*, *McDowell*, *McKinney*, *Middleton*, *William H. Miller*, *James R. Morris*, *Morrison*, *Nelson*, *Noble*, *John O'Neill*, *Pendleton*, *Perry*, *Pruyn*, *Radford*, *Samuel J. Randall*, *Robinson*, *James S. Rollins*, *Ross*, *John B. Steele*, *William G. Steele*, Stevens, *Stiles*, *Strouse*, *Stuart*, *Sweat*, Thomas, *Wadsworth*, *Ward*, Webster, Whaley, *Wheeler*, *Chilton A. White*, *Joseph W. White*, *Winfield*—75.

Mr. STEVENS moved to add this new section:

That nothing contained in this act shall be construed to alter or in any way affect the law relative to those conscientiously opposed to bearing arms.

Mr. PIKE moved to amend the amendment by adding:

That hereafter, persons between the ages of forty-five and fifty years shall be enrolled and subject to draft in the same manner as persons between the ages of twenty and forty-five.

Which was rejected—yeas 47, nays 102. The YEAS were:

Messrs. Alley, Allison, Ames, Arnold, Ashley, *Augustus C. Baldwin*, Baxter, Blow, Broomall, *James S. Brown*, *Chanler*, Freeman Clarke, *Coffroth*, Creswell, Henry Winter Davis, Dawes, Deming, Donnelly, Garfield, Gooch, *Griswold*, Hale, Asahel W. Hubbard, John H. Hubbard, Ingersoll, Julian, Littlejohn, Marvin, McBride, McClurg, Moorhead, Daniel Morris, *Nelson*, Orth, Patterson, *Pendleton*, Pike, Pomeroy, Alexander H. Rice, John H. Rice, Smith, Stevens, Tracy, Van Valkenburgh, *Wadsworth*, Ellihu B. Washburne, *Chilton A. White*—47.

The amendment of Mr. STEVENS was then agreed to—yeas 77, nays 64, as follows:

YEAS—Messrs. Alley, Ames, Ashley, *Baily*, John D. Baldwin, Baxter, Beaman, Blaine, Blow, Boutwell, Broomall, *Chanler*, Creswell, Thomas T. Davis, Dawes, *Dawson*, Deming, Dixon, Donnelly, Driggs, Eckley, *Edgerton*, Eliot, Frank, *Ganson*, Gooch, *Grider*, *Griswold*, Hale, *Charles M. Harris*, Higby, Hooper, Hotchkiss, Asahel W. Hubbard, John H. Hubbard, *Hutchins*, Ingersoll, Jenckes, Julian, Kelley, Francis W. Kellogg, Orlando Kellogg, *Kernan*, Knox, Loan, *McAllister*, McClurg, *Middleton*, Moorhead, Daniel Morris, Amos Myers, Leonard Myers, Norton, Charles O'Neill, Perham, *Perry*, Pike, *Radford*, Alexander H. Rice, John H. Rice, Edward H. Rollins, Sloan, Smithers, Spalding, Stevens, *Stuart*, *Sweat*, Thayer, Thomas, Upson, Van Valkenburgh, Ellihu B. Washburne, Webster, *Wheeler*, Wilder, Wilson, Windom—77.

NAYS—Messrs. *William J. Allen*, Allison, *Ancona*, *Augustus C. Baldwin*, *Bliss*, *James S. Brown*, Wm. G. Brown, Freeman Clarke, *Cobb*, *Coffroth*, Cole, *Cravens*, *Denison*, *Eden*, *Eldridge*, *English*, *Finck*, Garfield, *Harding*, *Harrington*, *Benjamin G. Harris*, *Herrick*, *Holman*, Hulburd, *Philip Johnson*, *Kalbfleisch*, *Knapp*, *Law*, *Le Blond*, Littlejohn, *Long*, Longyear, *Marcy*, Marvin, *McDowell*, McIndoe, *McKinney*, Samuel F. Miller, *William H. Miller*, *James R. Morris*, *Morrison*, *Noble*, *John O'Neill*, Orth, *Pendleton*, Pomeroy, *Samuel J. Randall*, *Robinson*, *James S. Rollins*, *Ross*, Schenck, Shannon, Smith, *William G. Steele*, *Stiles*, *Strouse*, Tracy, *Wadsworth*, *Ward*, William B. Washburn, Whaley, *Chilton A. White*, *Joseph W. White*, Williams—64.

The bill then passed—yeas 82, nays 77, as follows:

YEAS—Messrs. Alley, Allison, Ames, Anderson, Arnold, Ashley, John D. Baldwin, Baxter, Beaman, Blair, Blow, Boutwell, Boyd, Broomall, Freeman Clarke, Cobb, Cole, Creswell, Thomas T. Davis, Dawes, Deming, Dixon, Donnelly, Driggs, Eckley, Eliot, Farnsworth, Fenton, Garfield, Gooch, Higby, Hooper, Hotchkiss, Asahel W. Hubbard, John H. Hubbard, Hulburd, Ingersoll, Jenckes, Julian, Kelley, Francis W. Kellogg, Orlando Kellogg, Knox, Littlejohn, Loan, Longyear, Marvin, McBride, McClurg, McIndoe, S. F. Miller, Moorhead, Morrill, Daniel Morris, Amos Myers, Leonard Myers, Norton, Charles O'Neill, Orth, Patterson, Perham, Pike, Pomeroy, Alexander H. Rice, John H. Rice, Edward H. Rollins, Schenck, Shannon, Sloan, Smith, Smithers, Spalding, Thayer, Tracy, Upson, Van Valkenburgh, Ellihu B. Washburne, William B. Washburn, Williams, Wilder, Wilson, Windom—82.

NAYS—Messrs. *William J. Allen, Ancona, Baily, Augustus C. Baldwin*, Blaine, *Bliss, Brooks, James S. Brown*, William G. Brown, *Chanler, Coffroth, Cox, Cravens, Dawson, Denison, Eden, Edgerton, Eldridge, English, Finck*, Frank, *Ganson, Grider, Griswold*, Hale, *Harding, Benjamin G. Harris, Charles M. Harris, Herrick, Holman, Hutchins, Philip Johnson, William Johnson, Kalbfleisch, Kernan, Knapp, Law, Lazear, Le Blond, Long, Mallory, Marcy, McAllister, McDowell, McKinney, Middleton, William H. Miller, James R. Morris, Morrison, Nelson, Noble, Odell, John O'Neill, Pendleton, Perry, Pruyn, Radford, Samuel J. Randall, James S. Rollins, Ross*, Scofield, *John B. Steele, William G. Steele*, Stevens, *Stiles, Strouse, Stuart, Sweat*, Thomas, *Wadsworth, Ward*, Webster, Whaley, *Wheeler, Chilton A. White, Joseph W. White, Winfield*—77.

June 30—The bill having been returned from the Senate with sundry amendments, one of which imposed a five per cent. income duty, the House unanimously directed the return of the bill to the Senate as contravening the first clause of the seventh section of the first article of the Constitution, and as an infringement of the privileges of the House.

July 1—The House considered the Senate substitute for its bill, when several amendments were proposed.

Mr. INGERSOLL moved to add, after the word "soldiers," at the end of the fourth line, "except such States or Territories or parts thereof declared in rebellion."

Which was rejected on a count—yeas 28.

Mr. THOMAS offered this as a new section:

That it shall not be lawful for any of the States to send recruiting agents into other States and Territories to enlist soldiers to be credited to the States that may procure their enlistment; and no State shall be credited with soldiers recruited who are not citizens of the State claiming the credit, or foreigners who do not owe allegiance to the United States.

Which was rejected—yeas 63, nays 63, (the Speaker voting in the negative,) as follows:

YEAS—Messrs. *Wm. J. Allen, Ancona, Baily*, Blair, *Brooks, James S. Brown, Chanler, Coffroth*, Creswell, Henry Winter Davis, *Dawson, Denison, Eden, Edgerton, Eldridge, English*, Farnsworth, *Finck, Ganson*, Hale, *Harding, Benjamin G. Harris, Charles M. Harris, Holman, Hutchins, Philip Johnson*, Julian, *Kalbfleisch, Kernan, Knapp, Law, Lazear, Le Blond, Long, Mallory, McAllister, Middleton, William H. Miller, James R. Morris, Morrison, Nelson, Noble, Odell, John O'Neill, Pendleton, Pruyn, Radford, Robinson, James S. Rollins, Ross*, Shannon, *John B. Steele, Stiles, Strouse, Stuart*, Thomas, Tracy, *Wadsworth*, Webster, Whaley, *Wheeler, Chilton A. White, Winfield*—63.

NAYS—Messrs. Alley, Allison, Ames, Ashley, John D. Baldwin, Baxter, Beaman, Boutwell, Boyd, Broomall, Cobb, Dawes, Deming, Dixon, Driggs, Eckley, Eliot, Fenton, Frank, Garfield, Gooch, Higby, Hooper, Hotchkiss, Asahel W. Hubbard, John H. Hubbard, Hulburd, Ingersoll, Jenckes, Kelley, Littlejohn, Loan, *Marcy*, McBride, Samuel F. Miller, Moorhead, Morrill, Amos Myers, Leonard Myers, Norton, Charles O'Neill, Orth, Patterson, Perham, John H. Rice, Edward H. Rollins, Schenck, Scofield, Sloan, Smithers, Spalding, *William G. Steele*, Thayer, Upson, Van Valkenburgh, Ellihu B. Washburne, William B. Washburn, Williams, Wilder, Wilson, Windom, Woodbridge—62.

Mr. WILLIAM G. STEELE moved to reconsider this vote.

Mr. E. B. WASHBURNE moved to lay that motion on the table; which was disagreed to—yeas 61, nays 62.

The motion to reconsider was then agreed to—yeas 65, nays 62.

The proposition of Mr. THOMAS was then again rejected—yeas 63, nays 65, as follows:

YEAS—Messrs. *William J. Allen, Ancona, Baily*, Blair, *Brooks, James S. Brown, Coffroth*, Creswell, Henry Winter Davis, *Dawson, Denison, Eden, Edgerton, Eldridge, English*, Farnsworth, *Finck, Ganson*, Hale, *Harding, Benjamin G. Harris, Charles M. Harris, Holman, Hutchins, Philip Johnson, Kalbfleisch, Kernan, Knapp, Law, Lazear, Le Blond, Long, Mallory, McAllister, Middleton, William H. Miller, James R. Morris, Morrison, Nelson, Noble, Odell, John O'Neill, Pendleton, Pruyn, Radford*, William H. Randall, *Robinson, James S. Rollins, Ross*, Smith, *John B. Steele, William G. Steele, Stiles, Strouse, Stuart*, Thomas, Tracy, *Wadsworth*, Webster, Whaley, *Wheeler, Chilton A. White, Winfield*—63.

NAYS—Messrs. Alley, Allison, Ames, Arnold, Ashley, John D. Baldwin, Baxter, Beaman, Boutwell, Boyd, Broomall, Cobb, Cole, Dawes, Deming, Dixon, Donnelly, Driggs, Eliot, Fenton, Frank, Garfield, Gooch, Higby, Hooper, Hotchkiss, Asahel W. Hubbard, John H. Hubbard, Hulburd, Julian, Kelley, Littlejohn, Loan, McBride, McClurg, Samuel F. Miller, Moorhead, Morrill, Daniel Morris, Amos Myers, Leonard Myers, Norton, Charles O'Neill, Orth, Patterson, Perham, Alexander H. Rice, John H. Rice, Edward H. Rollins, Schenck, Scofield, Shannon, Sloan, Smithers, Spalding, Thayer, Upson, Van Valkenburgh, Ellihu B. Washburne, William B. Washburn, Williams, Wilder, Wilson, Windom, Woodbridge—65.

Mr. ORTH offered the following amendment; which was agreed to:

That the number of men heretofore furnished by any of the States shall be credited to said State on her quota in any future draft in proportion to the length of time for which said men were furnished.

Mr. GARFIELD offered four new sections, the second, third, and fourth of which are the same as the fifth, sixth, and seventh sections of the act, and the first is as follows:

That any persons resident in Virginia, North Carolina, South Carolina, Georgia, Florida, Alabama, Mississippi, Louisiana, Texas, or Arkansas, who may voluntarily enlist in the military service of the United States for a term of not more than three years, or during the war, or not less than one year, shall be entitled to the benefits and privileges of existing laws; and such persons shall be mustered into the regiments or other organizations of whatsoever State they may elect, or, in the case of colored troops, shall be assigned as now provided by law. And the States or subdivisions of States procuring such enlistments shall receive credit for such persons in accordance with the laws in other cases: *Provided*, That such enlistments as are authorized in any State, under the provisions of this act, shall only continue until such State shall have been made subject to a call for troops: *And provided further*, That no enlistments shall be made of any soldier, either in or out of any State, except those enumerated herein, unless full credit is given to the State to which the enlisted soldier belongs.

Which was agreed to—yeas 69, nays 53, as follows:

YEAS—Messrs. Alley, Allison, Ames, Arnold, Ashley, John D. Baldwin, Baxter, Beaman, Boyd, Broomall, Cobb, Cole, Creswell, Henry Winter Davis, Dawes, Deming, Dixon, Donnelly, Driggs, Eckley, Eliot, English, Farnsworth, Fenton, Frank, Garfield, Gooch, Higby, Hotchkiss, Asahel W. Hubbard, John H. Hubbard, Hulburd, Ingersoll, Julian, Kelley, Littlejohn, Loan, McBride, McClurg, Samuel F. Miller, Moorhead, Morrill, Daniel Morris, Amos Myers, Leonard Myers, Norton, Charles O'Neill, Orth, Patterson, Perham, Alexander H. Rice, John H. Rice, Edward H. Rollins, Schenck, Scofield, Shannon, Sloan, Smithers, Spalding, Thayer, Upson, Van Valkenburgh, Ellihu B. Washburne, William B. Washburn, Williams, Wilder, Wilson, Windom, Woodbridge—69.

NAYS—Messrs. *William J. Allen, Ancona*, Blair, *Brooks, James S. Brown, Chanler, Coffroth, Denison, Eden, Edgerton, Eldridge, Finck, Ganson, Harding, Benjamin G. Harris, Charles M. Harris, Holman, Hutchins, Philip Johnson, Kalbfleisch, Kernan, Knapp, Law, LeBlond, Long, Mallory, Marcy, McAllister, Middleton, William H. Miller, James R. Morris, Morrison, Nelson, John O'Neill, Pendleton, Pruyn,*

Radford, William H. Randall, *Robinson*, *James S. Rollins*, *Ross*, *John B. Steele*, *Wm. G. Steele*, *Stiles*, *Strouse*, *Sweat*, Thomas, *Wadsworth*, Webster, Whaley, *Wheeler*, *Chilton A. White*, *Winfield*—53.

The other sections were agreed to without a division.

Mr. HENRY WINTER DAVIS moved that the House concur in the Senate amendments with this amendment:

That no person drafted shall be entitled to be exempted from personal service on payment of commutation money.

That all enrolled persons shall be divided into two classes, one comprising those between eighteen and twenty-five years of age, and the other those over twenty-five and under forty years of age.

That every year during the continuance of the rebellion the President shall cause 250,000 men to be drafted from the first class, who shall be organized, drilled, and either sent into the field or held as a reserve to meet the exigencies of the service.

That in the event of the service requiring a levy of more than 250,000 men in any year, the residue beyond that number shall be drafted from the second class.

That prior to any draft, and during the execution of the same, till the requisition is filled, the President shall call for volunteers to fill the same, and is authorized to offer and pay every volunteer $300 who shall volunteer for three years, and proportionably for any shorter period designated by the President, one half at the time of mustering in and the other half on his discharge.

That every drafted man not appearing by the assessment for the internal revenue to have an income of $300 on whom wife, parent, child, brother, or sister is dependent for support shall be allowed ten dollars a month for the support of every such dependent, payable directly to such dependent or the person charged with the guardianship of any of them: *Provided*, That not more than twenty dollars shall be paid for this purpose in any month on account of any drafted man.

That it shall be the duty of the President to order and execute a draft in each of the States heretofore declared in rebellion, so far as the territory of said State shall be under the military occupation of the United States; and any State may procure volunteers from any of the States declared in rebellion except Tennessee and have them credited to the quotas of the State procuring the same; but all persons residents of any loyal State volunteering in any other loyal State shall be credited to the State of his residence.

Which was rejected—yeas 26, nays 101. The YEAS were:

Messrs. Allison, Arnold, Ashley, Baxter, Broomall, Freeman Clarke, Creswell, Henry Winter Davis, Donnelly, Eckley, Garfield, Hooper, Asahel W. Hubbard, John H. Hubbard, Hulburd, Julian, Longyear, McBride, McClurg, Moorhead, Morrill, Orth, Scofield, Sloan, Stevens, Woodbridge—26.

VOTE ON FINAL PASSAGE OF THE ACT OF JULY 4, 1864.

The House then non-concurred in the Senate amendment, and asked a Committee of Conference on the disagreeing votes of the two Houses, whose report, being the law as it stands, was adopted, July 2—yeas 66, nays 55, as follows:

YEAS—Messrs. Allison, Ames, Arnold, Ashley, John D. Baldwin, Baxter, Beaman, Blair, Boutwell, Boyd, Cobb, Cole, Creswell, Henry Winter Davis, Dawes, Deming, Dixon, Driggs, Eckley, Eliot, Farnsworth, Fenton, Garfield, Gooch, Higby, Hooper, Hotchkiss, A. W. Hubbard, John H. Hubbard, Ingersoll, Jenckes, Julian, Kelley, Littlejohn, Loan, Longyear, McBride, McClurg, Samuel F. Miller, Moorhead, Morrill, Daniel Morris, Amos Myers, Leonard Myers, Norton, Charles O'Neill, Orth, William H. Randall, John H. Rice, Schenck, Shannon, Sloan, Smith, Smithers, Spalding, Tracy, Upson, Van Valkenburgh, Elihu B. Washburne, William B. Washburn, Whaley, Williams, Wilder, Wilson, Windom, Woodbridge—66.

NAYS—Messrs. *William J. Allen*, Alley, *Ancona*, *Baily*, Blaine, *Bliss*, *Chanler*, *Coffroth*, *Cox*, *Dawson*, *Denison*, *Eden*, *Edgerton*, *Eldridge*, *English*, Frank, *Ganson*, *Griswold*, *Benjamin G. Harris*, *Charles M. Harris*, *Hutchins*, *Kernan*, *Knapp*, *Law*, *Lazear*, *Le Blond*, *Long*, *Mallory*, *Marcy*, *Middleton*, *William H. Miller*, *James R. Morris*, *Morrison*, *Noble*, *Odell*, Patterson, *Pendleton*, Perham, *Pruyn*, *Samuel J. Randall*, Alexander H. Rice, *Robinson*, Edward H. Rollins, *J. S. Rollins*, *Ross*, Scofield, *John B. Steele*, *W. G. Steele*, Stevens, *Stiles*, Thomas, *Wadsworth*, Webster, *Wheeler*, *Winfield*—55.

A CALL FOR 500,000 MEN UNDER THE ACT.

1864, July 18—The PRESIDENT issued a call for 500,000 men for one year, to be drafted for after September 5, if not furnished before.

RESOLUTIONS CONCERNING ENROLLMENT.

1863, December 22—Mr. PHILIP JOHNSON offered this preamble and resolution:

Whereas the supreme judicial tribunal of the State of Pennsylvania has solemnly decided that the act of Congress approved March 3, 1863, commonly called the conscription act, is in its provisions contrary to and in violation of the Constitution of the United States, and therefore null and void: Therefore,

Resolved, That it is the sworn duty of the executive department of the Government to either acquiesce in that decision within that State, or to bring the questions involved before the Supreme Court of the United States for final adjudication, to the end that if Congress shall deem such legislation necessary, another bill may be prepared which shall not be subject to constitutional objections.

Which was tabled—yeas 81, nays 43. The NAYS were:

Messrs. *Ancona*, *Augustus C. Baldwin*, *Bliss*, *Brooks*, *Coffroth*, *Cox*, *Dawson*, *Denison*, *Eden*, *Edgerton*, *Eldridge*, *Finck*, *Grider*, *Hall*, *Harding*, *Benjamin G. Harris*, *Charles M. Harris*, *Holman*, *Philip Johnson*, *William Johnson*, *Le Blond*, *Long*, *McDowell*, *McKinney*, *Middleton*, *Morrison*, *Nelson*, *Noble*, *John O'Neill*, *Pendleton*, *Perry*, *Rogers*, *Ross*, *Scott*, *John B. Steele*, *William G. Steele*, *Stiles*, *Strouse*, *Sweat*, *Wheeler*, *Chilton A. White*, *Joseph W. White*, *Fernando Wood*—43.

1864, January 11—Mr. BROOMALL offered the following preamble and resolution:

Whereas the burden of government should be made to fall as nearly equally as possible upon all parts of the country; and whereas the southern portion of the country has for several years contributed little, either in men or money, towards the support of the Government; and whereas almost the only way to get men from that portion is to take black men; and whereas for every black man enlisted in the South some man in the overburdened North may be exempted from draft:

It is therefore hereby declared to be the sense of this House that the Government should use its most strenuous efforts to procure the voluntary enlistment of persons claimed as slaves in the rebel territory, by giving them the full bounty and pay of other soldiers, and by guaranteeing their freedom, at once, upon enlistment.

Mr. Cox moved to lay them upon the table; which was disagreed to—yeas 61, nays 74; and they were then referred to the Military Committee.

1864, January 15—Mr. ANCONA offered this resolution, which was laid over under the rule:

Whereas the act of Congress approved March 3, 1863, commonly called the conscription law, is oppressive, unjust, and unconstitutional; because, 1st, it takes from the States the control of their own militia; 2d, it subjects the rights of the States and the liberties of the people to the unlimited power of the Federal Government; 3d, it is calculated to create and build up a central military despotism which may be used for the worst and most dangerous purposes; 4th, it falsely imputes the crime of desertion to every man whose name is drawn in the "lottery of death" and who fails to join the army, and subjects him to trial, condemnation, and capital punishment, without a jury of his peers, contrary to the fundamental law of the land: Therefore,

Be it resolved, That the Committee on Military Affairs be instructed to bring in a bill for the unconditional repeal of said act of Congress, and substitute in its place some constitutional and just mode of raising armies for the service of the United States.

1864, Feb. 1—Mr. ELDRIDGE offered the following preamble and resolution:

Whereas all conscription or other forced service of the citizen to the State is contrary to the genius and principles of republican government and opposed to the principles of self-government, which is the true basis of the American republic; and whereas the laws for conscripting or drafting citizens into the military service of the United States have thus far proved, if not an entire failure, at least ineffectual for the supplying to the Government the necessary number of men requisite for the military service in putting down the rebellion; and whereas the principles of equity and justice require in a government like ours, founded on the will of the majority, that the burdens of maintaining and preserving it should fall alike and equally upon all and every of the citizens, the rich as well as the poor, in proportion to their ability to bear the same; and whereas the military is a profession to which men are called as well from the inducements of personal gain and family advantage as from motives of patriotism and hopes of future fame: Therefore,

Resolved, That the Committee on Military Affairs be, and they are hereby, instructed to examine and inquire immediately into the propriety and expediency of repealing or suspending, so far as any future or further draft is concerned, all acts and parts of acts authorizing or empowering the conscripting or drafting of, or in any way forcing, the citizen into the military service of the country, either in putting down rebellion or otherwise; and in lieu thereof providing by law for, and authorizing the President of the United States from time to time, and as he may deem it expedient and necessary, to offer the payment of such sum or sums of money for volunteers in bounties or monthly payments, or otherwise, as may be best to induce enlistments and secure such moneys to the soldier and his family, and as will secure just so many and just such men as may be requisite or necessary to put down the rebellion and restore the supremacy of the Constitution; and that said committee do report by bill.

Which were laid upon the table, on Mr. STEVENS's motion — yeas 84, nays 42. The NAYS were:

Messrs. *James C. Allen, William J. Allen, Ancona, Augustus C. Baldwin, Bliss, Coffroth, Dawson, Denison, Eden, Edgerton, Eldridge, Finck, Hall, Harrington, Knapp, Law, Lazear, Long, Marcy, McDowell, McKinney, Middleton, Wm. H. Miller, James R. Morris, Morrison, Noble, John O'Neill, Pendleton, Perry, Pruyn, Samuel J. Randall, Robinson, Rogers, Ross, Scott, John B. Steele, Stiles, Strouse, Stuart, Sweat, Chilton A. White, Joseph W. White*—42.

Of the Democrats, Messrs. *Grider, Hutchins*, and *Yeaman* voted aye.

1864, February 8—Mr. ELDRIDGE offered this resolution, which was laid over under the rule:

Resolved, That the Secretary of War be, and he is hereby, required to furnish to this House information as to the amount of moneys received up to this time for commutation by drafted men; also what disposition has been made of said moneys. If substitutes have been purchased for drafted men, how many; where and who have been procured as such substitutes; what sum has been paid for each, and whether for white or black, and how much for each.

April 4—The House considered the resolution, when Mr. STEVENS moved that it lie upon the table; which was agreed to—yeas 60, nays 46. The NAYS were:

Messrs. *James C. Allen, Ancona, Augustus C. Baldwin, Bliss, Brooks, James S. Brown, Chanler, Clay, Cox, Cravens, Dawson, Denison, Eden, Eldridge, English, Finck, Grider, Griswold, Harrington, Benjamin G. Harris, Herrick, Holman, Philip Johnson, Kalbfleisch, King, Law, Lazear, Long, Mallory, Marcy, McKinney, Middleton, James R. Morris, Morrison, Nelson, Odell, John O'Neill, Price, Pruyn, Robinson, John B. Steele, Strouse, Wheeler, Chilton A. White, Winfield, Yeaman*—46.

1864, Feb. 1—Mr. GRINNELL offered the following preamble and resolution:

Whereas the war policy of the Government having brought into the military service as soldiers and laborers free colored men and persons claimed to be held by rebels, who have rendered invaluable service to the army; and whereas the more extended employment and enlistment of colored persons will be a relief to our northern soldiers, unacclimated and unused to manual labor, and lessen the number to be taken from their homes and from the industrial pursuits in the United States, where there is now an unusual demand for labor: Therefore,

Resolved, That a more vigorous policy to enlist, at an early day and in larger numbers, in our army persons of African descent would meet the approbation of this House.

Mr. STILES moved to lay them on the table, but the House refused—yeas 49, nays 76; and the resolution was then passed — yeas 80, nays 46.

BILL FOR THE PUNISHMENT OF GUERRILLAS.

June 6—The Committee on Military Affairs reported this bill to punish guerrillas:

Be it enacted, &c., That the provisions of the twenty-first section of an act entitled "An act for enrolling and calling out the national forces, and for other purposes," approved March 3, 1863, shall apply as well to the sentences of military commissions as to those of courts-martial; and hereafter the commanding general in the field, or the commander of the department, as the case may be, shall have power to carry into execution all sentences against guerrillas, for robbery, arson, burglary, rape, assault with intent to commit rape, and for violation of the laws and customs of war, as well as sentences against spies, mutineers, deserters, and murderers.

SEC. 2. That every officer authorized to order a general court-martial shall have power to pardon or mitigate any punishment ordered by such court, including that of confinement in the penitentiary, except the sentence of death or of cashiering or dismissing an officer, which sentences it shall be competent during the continuance of the present rebellion for the general commanding the army in the field, or the department commander, as the case may be, to remit or mitigate; and the fifth section of the act approved July 17, 1862, chapter 201, be, and the same is hereby, repealed, so far as it relates to sentences of imprisonment in the penitentiary.

Mr. LONG moved that the bill be tabled; which was disagreed to.

After further proceedings,

Mr. ELDRIDGE moved that it be tabled; which was disagreed to—yeas 35, nays 67.

And the bill passed—yeas 72, nays 37. The NAYS were:

Messrs. *James C. Allen, Ancona, Augustus C. Baldwin, Bliss, Coffroth, Cravens,* Henry Winter Davis, *Dawson, Denison, Eden, Edgerton, Eldridge, Finck, Grider, Harding, Harrington, Charles M. Harris, Hutchins, King, Knapp, Le Blond, Long, Mallory, Marcy, McDowell, Morrison, Noble, Pendleton, Perry, Robinson, Rogers, Ross, Strouse, Voorhees, Wadsworth, Chilton A. White, Joseph W. White*—37.

Of the Democrats, Messrs. *Baily* and *Griswold* voted aye.

IN SENATE.

June 14—The Military Committee reported the House bill for the more speedy punishment of guerrillas; which was debated.

June 30—Mr. HENDRICKS offered this proviso to the first section:

Provided, That the term "guerrillas" herein contained shall not be held to include persons employed in the authorized military service of the enemy.

Which was agreed to, and the bill passed.

The House concurred, and the bill became a law.

INCREASED PAY OF SOLDIERS.

First Session, Thirty-Seventh Congress.

1861, August 6—This section was passed by both Houses:

Be it enacted, &c., That the pay of the privates in the regular army and volunteers in the service of the United States be thirteen dollars per month for three years from and after the passage of this act, and until otherwise ordered.

First Session, Thirty-Eighth Congress.

IN HOUSE.

May 3—The Senate bill to increase the pay of soldiers was reported from the Committee on Military Affairs, making the pay, from May 1, of "all soldiers in the military service sixteen dollars per month;" corporals, eighteen dollars; sergeants, twenty dollars.

Mr. HOLMAN sought the floor to move an amendment that white soldiers should have twenty dollars per month, and colored eighteen dollars.

Mr. COX sought to move an amendment to

increase the pay of soldiers and non-commissioned officers two dollars per month.

Mr. DAWSON, to move to make it twenty dollars in the present currency.

But Mr. SCHENCK declined to yield the floor.

After a brief explanation the bill passed—yeas 135, nays none.

IN SENATE.

May 11—The Senate Military Committee reported the bill with amendments, the principal one of which fixed the rates as now existing and stated in the summary of "our Military Legislation," which was agreed to, without division in either House. While the bill was pending in the Senate,

May 17—Mr. RICHARDSON offered the following:

That from and after the first day of May, 1864, the officers, non-commissioned officers, musicians, and privates in the regular army and volunteers and drafted forces in the service of the United States shall be paid in gold: *Provided*, That said officers, non-commissioned officers, musicians, and privates may be paid in Treasury notes or paper money when the Government cannot pay in gold. If not paid in gold, they shall be paid in paper an amount equal to the value of gold at the time of payment.

Which was rejected—yeas 6, nays 23, as follows:

YEAS—Messrs. *Buckalew, Davis, Hendricks*, Lane of Indiana, *Powell, Richardson*—6.

NAYS—Messrs. Anthony, Chandler, Clark, Collamer, Conness, Dixon, Doolittle, Foot, Foster, Grimes, Harlan, Harris, Henderson, Howe, Johnson, Lane of Kansas, Morgan, Morrill, Ramsey, Sumner, Ten Eyck, Van Winkle, Wilson—23.

Mr. POWELL offered this amendment:

Provided, That the provisions of this act shall not apply to colored soldiers.

Which was rejected—yeas 5, nays 26, as follows:

YEAS—Messrs. *Buckalew, Davis, Hendricks, Powell, Richardson*—5.

NAYS—Messrs. Anthony, Chandler, Clark, Collamer, Conness, Dixon, Doolittle, Foot, Foster, Grimes, Harlan, Harris, Henderson, Howard, Howe, Johnson, Lane of Indiana, Lane of Kansas, Morgan, Morrill, Pomeroy, Ramsey, Sumner, Ten Eyck, Van Winkle, Wilson—26.

ORDERS ISSUED BY THE SECRETARY OF WAR IN ENFORCING THE DRAFT.

The Secretary of War, in executing the draft of 1862, issued these orders:

WAR DEPARTMENT, WASHINGTON CITY, D. C., *August* 8, 1862.

Orders to prevent the evasion of military duty and for the suppression of disloyal practices.

First. By direction of the President of the United States, it is hereby ordered that, until further order, no citizen liable to be drafted into the militia shall be allowed to go to a foreign country, and all marshals, deputy marshals, and military officers of the United States, are directed, and all police authorities, especially at the ports of the United States on the seaboard and on the frontier, are requested to see that this order is faithfully carried into effect. And they are hereby authorized and directed to arrest and detain any person or persons about to depart from the United States in violation of this order, and report to Major L. C. Turner, Judge Advocate, at Washington city, for further instruction respecting the person or persons so arrested and detained.

Second. Any person liable to draft who shall absent himself from his county or State before such draft is made, will be arrested by any provost marshal, or other United States or State officer, wherever he may be found within the jurisdiction of the United States, and conveyed to the nearest military post or depot, and placed on military duty for the term of the draft; and the expenses of his own arrest and conveyance to such post or depot, and also the sum of five dollars as a reward to the officer who shall make such arrest, shall be deducted from his pay.

Third. The writ of *habeas corpus* is hereby suspended in respect to all persons arrested and detained, and in respect to all persons arrested for disloyal practices.

(Signed) EDWIN M. STANTON, *Secretary of War.*

WAR DEPARTMENT, *Washington City, Aug.* 8.

Ordered—First. That all United States Marshals, and superintendents, and chiefs of police of any town, city or district, be and they are hereby authorized and directed to arrest and imprison any person or persons who may be engaged, by any act of speech or writing, in discouraging volunteer enlistments, or in any way giving aid and comfort to the enemy, or in any other disloyal practice against the United States.

Second. That immediate report be made to Major L. C. Turner, Judge Advocate, in order that such persons may be tried before a military commission.

Third. The expenses of such arrest and imprisonment will be certified to the chief clerk of the War Department for settlement and payment.

EDWIN M. STANTON, *Secretary of War.*

WASHINGTON, *August* 14.

The following was issued to-day from the War Department:

ADDITIONAL REGULATIONS FOR THE ENROLLMENT AND DRAFT OF THE MILITIA.

Ordered—Eighth—That in filling all requisitions for militia the quotas of the several States will be apportioned by the Governors among the several counties, and where practicable among the subdivisions of counties, so that allowance shall be made to such counties and subdivisions for all volunteers heretofore furnished by them and mustered into the service of the United States, and whose stipulated terms of service shall not have expired.

(Signed) E. M. STANTON, *Secretary of War.*

WAR DEPARTMENT, WASHINGTON, *September* 7, 1862.

INSTRUCTIONS TO UNITED STATES MARSHALS, MILITARY COMMANDANTS, PROVOST MARSHALS, POLICE OFFICERS, SHERIFFS, ETC.

The quota of volunteers and enrollment of militia having been completed in the several States, the necessity for a stringent enforcement of the orders of the War Department in respect to volunteering and drafting no longer exists. Arrests for violation of these orders and for disloyal practices will hereafter be made only upon express warrant, or by direction of the military commanders or Governor of the State in which such arrests may be made. And restrictions upon travel imposed by these orders are rescinded.

L. C. TURNER, *Judge Advocate.*

THE PRESIDENT'S PROCLAMATION RELATIVE TO ALIENS.

1863, May 8—The PRESIDENT issued a proclamation relative to an exemption from the draft on the plea of alienage, in which he declares:

Now, therefore, to avoid all misapprehensions concerning the liability of persons concerned to perform the service required by such enactment, and to give it full effect, I do hereby order and proclaim that no plea of alienage will be received, or allowed to exempt from the obligations imposed by the aforesaid act of Congress any person of foreign birth who shall have declared on oath his intention to become a citizen of the United States, under the laws thereof, and who shall be found within the United States at any time during the continuance of the present insurrection and rebellion, at or after the expiration of the period of sixty-five days from the date of this proclamation; nor shall any such plea of alienage be allowed in favor of any such person who has so, as aforesaid, declared his intention to become a citizen of the United States, and shall have exercised at any time the right of suffrage, or any other political franchise within the United States, under the laws thereof, or under the laws of any of the several States.

JUDICIAL DECISIONS UPON THE CONSTITUTIONALITY OF THE CONSCRIPTION ACT.

In the Circuit Court of the United States for the eastern district of Pennsylvania, Judge Cadwalader delivered an opinion in September, 1863, a condensation of which is subjoined from the New York *Tribune* of September 11, 1863:

The powers conferred by the Constitution upon Congress, to raise and support armies and make rules for their government, are distinct from the powers which are conferred on it as to the militia of the respective States. Until the act in question, the national armies had been raised by voluntary enlistment. The system of enrollment and draft had long been matured as to the militia of the States. But until the summer of 1862 the utmost penalty for not serving when drafted from such militia for the service of the United States had been pecuniary, with limited imprisonment for non-payment. The act of Congress of 17th July, 1862, authorized impressment into the military service of the United States of those persons drafted from the militia under that act, who, when ordered to attend at the place of muster, disobeyed.

The specific power of impressment had not been previously conferred. But, under the former system, though the fine for not serving had, when received, been considered an equivalent for service, the payment had nevertheless been enforced, or the penalty of imprisonment inflicted by courts-martial when the money was not otherwise collected. The constitutionality of this former jurisdiction of courts-martial may be considered as established, (5 Wheaton 1.) It would not have been constitutional if disobedience to attend at a place of muster had not been a military offence. Congress, unless it had the power of absolutely subjecting a drafted person to military rule from the time of the draft, could not have thus made his disobedience before he was mustered into service a military offence.

The act of Congress of 1795, which fixed the time of arrival at the place of rendezvous as the period of the commencement of the military service, might constitutionally, in the opinion of the Supreme Court, have made the time of draft the period. (5 Wheaton, 17, 18, 30, and see pp. 36, 37, 56, 64, 65.) The constitutionality of the act of 17th July, 1862, when the question was considered here in March last, in McCall's case, appeared therefore to be established by authority. If the question had been thought an open one, the same view of the effect of the Constitution would have been taken.

The act of 3d of March, 1863, has adopted a like system on an extended scale, for the purpose of raising national armies independently of the militia of the States. Under the former laws which have been mentioned, a question such as that now under consideration could not arise. The question under those laws could only have been that of a military court's exercise of jurisdiction over a person who having been lawfully drafted already owed military service. There could not have been any dispute that the primary question whether he had been lawfully drafted or was liable to serve, was open to decision by the ordinary tribunals under a writ of *habeas corpus*. Here, however, the question is whether a military commission can so decide the original question of liability to serve as absolutely as to deprive all other tribunals of cognizance of it.

The enactments of the law in question are not so arranged that its provisions for the preparatory enrollment, and those for the draft, are always separated. They must however, be kept distinct when they are considered with reference to the Constitution. The most unlimited system of mere enrollment could not be constitutionally objectionable.

But a system of drafting might be arbitrary and latitudinarian to such an extent as to encroach upon constitutional rights. * * * * * The constitutional authority to enact the law which is under consideration was derived exclusively from the power to raise armies. It cannot be enlarged under the authority which the Constitution also confers to make all laws necessary and proper for carrying the powers delegated, this one included, into execution.

After citing the provision of the act, the judge says:

This review of the principal enactment of the law suffices to indicate its general purposes. The organization of armies under it is to cease on the termination of the civil war, for whose exigencies it provides; and the term of service of those drafted under it cannot exceed three years, though the war should continue longer. Such limitations of the time would have prevented the compulsory requirement of military service from being unconstitutional, though it had included every able-bodied male inhabitant.

[From the Illinois State Journal of June 17, 1864.]

THE CONSTITUTIONALITY OF THE ENROLLMENT ACT AFFIRMED.

In the United States Circuit Court, Judges David Davis and S. H. Treat upon the bench, an important decision was rendered on the 15th instant. It was on a motion to quash the indictment in the case of "The United States agt. John Graham and others," for resistance to the enrollment in Fulton county last summer. The case was ably argued for the prosecution by Messrs. Lawrence Weldon and W. H. Herndon, and by Messrs. Judd and James for the defence. The court rendered a decision affirming the constitutionality of the enrollment act, based upon the provision of the Constitution empowering Congress to raise and equip armies. This is the first decision under the enrollment act rendered in this State, and is therefore important. The motion to quash the indictment was granted, on the ground that the punishment of the particular class of offenders charged was not specifically provided for in the act of July, 1863. It was admitted, however, that the act as amended by the act of February, 1864, covers the whole point, and that, as the law now stands, resistance to the enrollment is liable to the severest penalties. The decision was rendered by Judge Treat, Judge Davis concurring.

THE TWO DECISIONS OF THE SUPREME COURT OF PENNSYLVANIA.

A majority of the judges of the Supreme Court of Pennsylvania, as constituted in November, 1863, pronounced the enrollment law unconstitutional. Chief Justice Lowrie and Justices George W. Woodward and James Thompson concurred in this judgment, and Justices William Strong and John M. Read dissented. These points are covered by the decision:

1. The Constitution of the United States recognizes only two sorts of military land forces, viz., "the militia," and the "regular or standing army."

2. The conscription act of March 3, 1863, is not founded on that clause of the Constitution which provides for calling forth the militia, because the persons drafted under the act are not to be armed, organized, and disciplined under the militia law, nor are they called forth under State officers, as required by the Constitution.

3. There is no power given to recruit the regular Army by forced levies. This can only be done by voluntary enlistments.

4. The mode of "raising armies" by forced recruiting for the suppression of rebellion or insurrection is not authorized by the Constitution, because such cases are expressly provided for by the power therein given for calling out the dormant forces, or militia.

5. The Constitution authorizes levies of the "militia of the States" in its organized form in cases of rebellion and invasion, but in no other case or mode than is therein provided.

6. The mode of coercion provided for this purpose by the act of March 3, 1862, is unconstitutional, because

(1.) It is incompatible with the provisions of the Constitution relative to the militia.

(2.) It exhausts the militia force of the several States, which existed as an institution before the formation of the Federal Government, and was not only not granted away but expressly reserved at the formation of the Constitution; annuls the remedy for insurrection expressly provided by the Constitution, and substitutes a new one not therein provided for; and converts into national forces as part of the regular army of the General Government the whole militia force of the States, not on the contingency therein provided for nor in the form therein prescribed, but entirely irrespective thereof.

(3.) It incorporates into this new national force every civil officer of the State except the Governor, and every officer of its social institutions and military organization within the prescribed age, thus subjecting the civil, social, and military organizations of the States to the Federal power to "raise armies."

(4.) It provides for a thorough fusion of the army and the militia, two forces which are kept distinct by the Constitution, by investing the President with power to assign the soldiers obtained by the draft to any corps, regiment, or branch of service at his pleasure.

(5.) It subjects the citizen to the rules and articles of war before he is in "actual service," and proposes to effect this purpose by merely drawing his name from a wheel and serving notice of that fact upon him.

The key-note of Judge Woodward's opinion is this paragraph:

"The great vice of the conscript law is, that it is founded on an assumption that Congress may take away, not the State rights of the citizen, but the security and foundation of his State rights. And how long is civil liberty expected to last, after the securities of civil liberty are destroyed? The Constitution of the United States committed the liberties of the citizen in part to the Federal Government, but expressly reserved to the States, and the people of the States, all it did not delegate. It gave the General Government a standing army, but left to the States their militia. Its purposes in all this balancing of powers were wise and good, but this legislation disregards these distinctions and upturns the whole system of government when it converts the State militia into "National forces," and claims to use and govern them as such.

Chief Justice Lowrie and Justice Thompson elaborate the same point.

1864, Jan. 16—The same court, then differently constituted by the defeat of Chief Justice Lowrie at the October election and the choice of Daniel Agnew, directed the orders granted in the cases heard in November to be vacated, and affirming the constitutionality of the enrollment act, overruled the motions for injunctions to restrain certain provost marshals from proceeding with the enrollment and draft. Messrs. Strong, Read and Agnew constituted the majority, and Woodward and Thompson the minority.

Justice Agnew closed his opinion with stating these conclusions:

The constitutional authority to use the national forces creates a corresponding duty to provide a number adequate to the necessity. The duty is vital and essential, falling back on the fundamental right of self-preservation, and the powers expressed to declare war, raise armies, maintain navies, and provide for the common defence. Power and duty now go hand in hand with the extremity until every available man in the nation is called into service, if the emergency requires it, and of this there can be no judge but Congress.

They may proceed, therefore, to the exhaustion of the whole element from which the State draws its militia, for the people, under the two powers, are the same; while the supremacy of the national power, provided in section 2 of article 6, necessarily draws to itself the whole number, if required by the exigency, to the exclusion of the State power.

And in reason why should a major power be restricted by a minor? The power to raise armies comprehends for its purposes the whole scope of the purposes of armies, while the authority to call out the militia is confined to the enumerated three.

But it is a mistake in fact to say this case exhausts the militia. It enrolls probably all; for how can any be drafted without all be known? But the draft is confined to so many as are needed for the emergency, while the others remain in the militia. And if you deny the power to repeat the draft, what is that but to say your force shall not increase with the necessity?

Nor is it true that the enrollment under this law exhausts the militia. Neither the law of Congress, nor the laws of the States, so far as we know them, have enrolled all able bodied men capable of militia duty. A wide margin yet exists in the law of the nation; but we do hear of this margin being written all over in the seceded States.

As to the objection to the 13th section, providing the punishment of desertion for those who fail to appear, it is only necessary to say, we cannot presume the complainant will be guilty of failing to perform his legal duty subsequent to the draft, when he finds the law valid which drafts him. He asks us to relieve him from the draft, not from a military trial for misconduct. Whenever he chooses to incur the proposed penalty for disobeying a valid law, it will be in time for the proper tribunal to arrest an illegal mode of punishment.

The question of jurisdiction is unnecessary to a decision. The point is too important, the cases too numerous, and the labor too great. It should therefore be left for a decision when it shall have to be met.

For all these reasons I concur in rescinding the order for a preliminary injunction.

GOVERNOR SEYMOUR AND THE DRAFT.

The result of the repeated conferences between the State authorities of New York and the War Department, was to ascertain that the State had been called to furnish 12,533 men more than her quota; and the House of Representatives of that State, during its late session, passed this resolution:

Resolved, That the thanks of this House be and are hereby tendered to his Excellency Governor Seymour for calling the attention of the General Government at Washington to the errors in the apportionment of the quota of this State under the enrollment act of 3d March, 1863, and for his prompt and efficient efforts in procuring a correction of the same.

GENERAL M'CLELLAN URGED A DRAFT IN 1861.

Soon after General McClellan assumed command of the army, succeeding General Scott, he wrote this letter to the President:

WASHINGTON, *August* 20, 1861.

SIR: I have just received the inclosed dispatch in cipher Colonel Marcy knows what he says, and is of the coolest judgment. I recommend that the Secretary of War ascertain at once by telegram how the enrollment proceeds in New York and elsewhere, and that, if it is not proceeding with great rapidity, drafts to be made at once. We must have men without delay.

Respectfully your obedient servant,
GEORGE B. McCLELLAN, *Maj. Gen. U. S. A.*

DISPATCH FROM COL. R. B. MARCY TO GENERAL MCCLELLAN.

NEW YORK, *August* 20, 1861.

I urge upon you to make a positive and unconditional demand for an immediate draft of the additional troops you require. Men will not volunteer now, and drafting is the only successful plan. The people will applaud such a course, rely upon it. I will be in Washington to-morrow.

R. B. MARCY.

Colored Soldiers.

Second Session, Thirty-Seventh Congress.

1862, July 17—These provisions became law:

That the President be, and he is hereby, authorized to receive into the service of the United States, for the purpose of constructing intrenchments, or performing camp service, or any other labor, or any military or naval service for which they may be found competent, persons of African descent; and such persons shall be enrolled and organized under such regulations, not inconsistent with the Constitution and laws, as the President may prescribe.

That when any man or boy of African descent, who by the laws of any State shall owe service or labor to any person who, during the present rebellion, has levied war or has borne arms against the United States, or adhered to their enemies by giving them aid and comfort, shall render any such service as is provided for in this act, he, his mother, and his wife and children shall forever thereafter be free, any law, usage, or custom whatsoever to the contrary notwithstanding: *Provided*, That the mother, wife and children of such man or boy of African descent shall not be made free by the operation of this act except where such mother, wife or children owe service or labor to some person who, during the present rebellion, has borne arms against the United States or adhered to their enemies by giving them aid and comfort.

That the expenses incurred to carry this act into effect shall be paid out of the general appropriation for the army and volunteers.

That all persons who have been or shall be hereafter enrolled in the service of the United States under this act shall receive the pay and rations now allowed by law to soldiers, according to their respective grades: *Provided*, That persons of African descent, who under this law shall be employed, shall receive ten dollars per month and one ration, three dollars of which monthly pay may be in clothing.

1863, May 3—Section 10 of the *Engineer bill* provides that the President of the United States be, and he is hereby, authorized to cause to be enlisted, for each cook, two under-cooks, of African descent, who shall receive for their full compensation ten dollars per month, and one ration per day—three dollars of said monthly pay may be in clothing.

1863, March 3—Includes all able-bodied males.

1864, Feb. 24—(Section 24) directs that all able-bodied male colored persons between twenty and forty-five, resident in the United States, shall be enrolled and form part of the national forces. When a slave of a loyal master shall be drafted, his master shall have a certificate and the bounty of $100 and the slave shall be free. [For whole section, and for other votes on colored soldiers, see other pages.]

IN SENATE.

Pending the consideration of the bill of 1862,

1862, July 10—Mr. DAVIS, of Kentucky, moved to strike out the words "or any military or naval service for which they may be found competent;" which was rejected—yeas 11, nays 27, as follows:

YEAS—Messrs. *Carlile*, Cowan, *Davis*, Henderson, *Kennedy*, *Powell*, *Saulsbury*, *Stark*, Willey, *Wilson* of Missouri, *Wright*—11.

NAYS—Messrs. Anthony, Browning, Chandler, Clark, Collamer, Doolittle, Fessenden, Foot, Grimes, Hale, Harlan, Harris, Howard, King, Lane of Indiana, Lane of Kansas, Morrill, Pomeroy, *Rice*, Sherman, Simmons, Sumner, Ten Eyck, Trumbull, Wade, Wilkinson, Wilson of Massachusetts—27.

Mr. HENDERSON moved to limit the section to "free" persons of African descent, and to "such persons of African descent as may owe service or labor to persons engaged in the rebellion;" which was negatived—yeas 13, nays 22, as follows:

YEAS—Messrs. Anthony, Browning, Cowan, *Davis*, Henderson, Lane of Indiana, *McDougall*, *Powell*, *Rice*, *Stark*, Willey, *Wilson* of Missouri, *Wright*—13.

NAYS—Messrs. Chandler, Clark, Collamer, Doolittle, Fessenden, Foot, Grimes, Hale, Harlan, Harris, Howard, King, Lane of Kansas, Morrill, Pomeroy, Sherman, Simmons, Sumner, Trumbull, Wilkinson, Wilmot, Wilson of Massachusetts—22.

Mr. HENDERSON moved to add the following:

Provided, That all loyal persons entitled to the service or labor of such persons, according to the laws of the State in which the owner of such slave may reside, employed under the provisions of this act, shall be compensated for the loss of such service.

Which was agreed to—yeas 20, nays 17, as follows:

YEAS—Messrs. Anthony, Browning, Collamer, Cowan, *Davis*, Doolittle, Foot, Foster, Harlan, Henderson, Howe, Lane of Indiana, *McDougall*, *Powell*, Simmons, *Stark*, Ten Eyck, Willey, *Wilson* of Missouri, *Wright*—20.

NAYS—Messrs. Chandler, Clark, Fessenden, Grimes, Hale, Harris, Howard, King, Lane of Kansas, Morrill, Pomeroy, Sherman, Sumner, Trumbull, Wilkinson, Wilmot, Wilson of Massachusetts—17.

Mr. LANE, of Kansas, moved to amend the section by "directing" as well as "authorizing" the President to receive into the service, &c., which was rejected.

Mr. SHERMAN moved to amend by making the section read—

That when any man or boy of African descent, who by the laws of any State shall owe service or labor to any person who, during the present rebellion, has levied war or borne arms against the United States, or adhered to their enemies by giving them aid and comfort, shall render any such service as is provided for in the first section of this act, he, his mother, and his wife and children shall forever thereafter be free, any law, usage, or custom whatsoever to the contrary notwithstanding.

Which was agreed to—yeas 22, nays 16, as follows:

YEAS—Messrs. Anthony, Browning, Collamer, Cowan, *Davis*, Doolittle, Foster, Harris, Henderson, Howard, Howe, *Kennedy*, Lane of Indiana, *McDougall*, *Rice*, Sherman, Simmons, *Stark*, Ten Eyck, Willey, *Wilson* of Missouri, *Wright*—22.

NAYS—Messrs. Chandler, Clark, Foot, Grimes, Hale, Harlan, King, Lane of Kansas, Morrill, Pomeroy, Sumner, Trumbull, Wade, Wilkinson, Wilmot, Wilson of Mass—16.

The bill was then dropped, and, July 14,

Mr. WILSON reported a bill to amend the act calling forth the militia, containing the provisions which were finally passed, and providing that when any man or boy of African descent shall render any such service, he, his mother, and his wife and children are forever thereafter to be free. July 15,

Mr. BROWNING moved to strike out the clause liberating the mother, wife, and children; which was negatived—yeas 17, nays 20:

YEAS—Messrs. Browning, Collamer, Cowan, *Davis*, Doolittle, Foster, Harris, Henderson, Lane of Indiana, *Powell*, *Rice* *Saulsbury*, Sherman, *Stark*, Ten Eyck, *Wilson* of Missouri, *Wright*—17.

NAYS—Messrs. Chandler, Clark, Fessenden, Foot, Grimes, Hale, Harlan, Howard, Howe, King, Lane of Kansas, Morrill, Pomeroy, Simmons, Sumner, Trumbull, Wade, Wilkinson, Wilmot, Wilson of Massachuetts—20.

Mr. BROWNING moved to limit the liberation of the mother, wife, and children to cases in which the owner has borne arms against the United States or adhered to their enemies, by giving them aid and comfort; which was agreed to—yeas 21, nays 16, as follows:

YEAS—Messrs. Browning, Collamer, Cowan, *Davis*, Doolittle, Fessenden, Foster, Harris, Henderson, *Kennedy*, Lane of Indiana, *Powell*, *Rice*, *Saulsbury*, Sherman, Simmons, *Stark*, Ten Eyck, Willey, *Wilson* of Missouri, *Wright*—21.

NAYS—Messrs. Chandler, Clark, Foot, Grimes, Hale, Harlan, Howard, Howe, King, Lane of Kansas, Sumner, Trumbull, Wade, Wilkinson, Wilmot, Wilson of Massachusetts—16.

The bill was passed—yeas 28, nays 9, (*Bayard*, *Carlile*, *Davis*, *Kennedy*, *Powell*, *Saulsbury*, *Stark*, Willey, *Wilson* of Missouri.)

1862, May 16—Pending the consideration of a bill to suppress insurrection and to punish treason and rebellion,

Mr. DAVIS moved to strike from the first section the words "and all his slaves, if any, shall be declared and made free," and make the imprisonment not less than five nor more than twenty years; which was rejected—yeas 7, nays 31, as follows:

YEAS—Messrs. *Davis*, *McDougall*, *Pearce*, *Powell*, *Saulsbury*, *Stark*, *Wilson* of Missouri—7.

NAYS—Messrs. Anthony, Browning, Chandler, Clark, Collamer, Cowan, Dixon, Doolittle, Fessenden, Foot, Foster, Grimes, Harris, Henderson, Howard, Howe, King, Lane of Indiana, Lane of Kansas, Morrill, Pomeroy, Sherman, Simmons, Sumner, Ten Eyck, Trumbull, Wade, Willey, Wilmot, Wilson of Massachusetts, *Wright*—31.

May 19—Mr. POWELL moved to strike out the eleventh section:

That the President of the United States is authorized to employ as many persons of African descent as he may deem necessary and proper for the suppression of this rebellion, and for this purpose he may organize and use them in such manner as he may judge best for the public welfare.

Which was rejected—yeas 11, nays 25, as follows:

YEAS—Messrs. *Carlile*, *Davis*, Henderson, *Latham*, *Pearce*, *Powell*, *Saulsbury*, *Stark*, Willey, *Wilson* of Missouri, *Wright*—11.

NAYS — Messrs. Anthony, Browning, Clark, Collamer, Cowan, Dixon, Doolittle, Fessenden, Foot, Foster, Grimes, Harlan, Harris, Howard, Howe, Lane of Kansas, Pomeroy, Sherman, Sumner, Ten Eyck, Trumbull, Wade, Wilkinson, Wilmot, Wilson of Massachusetts—25.

The bill did not get to a final vote.

IN HOUSE.

July 16—The Senate bill quoted above was taken up, when

Mr. HOLMAN moved that it do lie upon the table, which was negatived—yeas 30, nays 77, as follows:

YEAS—Messrs. *William Allen*, *William J. Allen*, *Biddle*, *Calvert*, *Clements*, *Cobb*, *Cox*, *Crisfield*, *Dunlap*, *Fouke*, *Grider*, *Hall*, *Harding*, *Holman*, *Kerrigan*, *Knapp*, *Law*, *Lazear*, *Mallory*, *May*, Maynard, *Menzies*, *Pendleton*, *John S. Phelps*,

Shiel, John B. Steele, William G. Steele, Stiles, Webster, *Wickliffe*—30.

NAYS—Messrs. Aldrich, Alley, Arnold, Ashley, Babbitt, Baxter, Beaman, Bingham, Samuel S. Blair, Blake, Buffinton, Campbell, Colfax, Roscoe Conkling, Cutler, Davis, Dawes, Duell, Dunn, Edwards, Ely, Fenton, Fessenden, Frank, Goodwin, Granger, *Haight,* Hale, Hanchett, Hooper, Julian, Kelley, Francis W. Kellogg, William Kellogg, Leary, Loomis, Lovejoy, Low, McKnight, McPherson, Moorhead, Anson P. Morrill, Justin S. Morrill, Nixon, *Noell,* Olin, Patton, Timothy G. Phelps, Pike, Porter, Potter, Alexander H. Rice, John H. Rice, Riddle, Edward H. Rollins, Sargent, Sedgwick, Shanks, Shellabarger, Sherman, *Smith,* Spaulding, Stevens, Stratton, Benjamin F. Thomas, Train, Trimble, Trowbridge, Van Horn, Verree, Wall, Wallace, Walton, *Ward,* Wilson, Windom, Worcester—77.

The bill then passed.

OTHER PROCEEDINGS ON THIS SUBJECT.

Third Session, Thirty-Seventh Congress.

IN HOUSE.

1863, January 27—Mr, STEVENS offered a bill for the enlistment of 150,000 soldiers, persons of color or of African descent, to serve for five years, and to receive a bounty of $5, and pay at the rate of $10 per month, recruiting stations to be established in free or slave States, regimental officers to be white, company officers white or colored as the President may direct. Slaves and freemen may be enlisted; such persons shall never again be slaves but the United States shall pay for such of them as belong to persons not dlsloyal.

Mr. HICKMAN offered a substitute authorizing the organization of three hundred colored regiments to be uniformed in a special and marked manner, to serve for seven years, at a monthly pay of $6 50, one half to be retained till discharged—their officers to be of collegiate education and receive twice the pay of other officers. The bill contained a colonization feature, and appropriated the proceeds of confiscation to be applied to educational purposes in the States in which the property confiscated, lies.

The bill was repeatedly before the House, was severely "filibustered," and was finally modified by Mr. STEVENS to read as follows:

Be it enacted by the Senate and House of Representatives of the United States of America in Congress assembled, That the President be, and he is hereby, authorized to enroll, arm, equip, and receive into the land and naval service of the United States, such number of volunteers of African descent as he may deem useful to suppress the present rebellion, for such term of service as he may prescribe, not exceeding five years. The said volunteers to be organized according to the regulations of the branch of service in which they may be enlisted, to receive the same rations, clothing, and equipments as other volunteers, and a monthly pay not to exceed that of other volunteers; to be officered by persons appointed and commissioned by the President, and to be governed by the rules and articles of war and such other rules and regulations as may be prescribed by the President: *Provided,* That nothing herein contained, or in the rules and articles of war, shall be so construed as to authorize or permit any officer of African descent to be appointed to rank, or to exercise military or naval authority over white officers, soldiers, or men in the military or naval service of the United States; nor shall any greater pay than ten dollars per month, with the usual allowance of clothing and rations, be allowed or paid to privates or laborers of African descent which are, or may be, in the military or naval service of the United States: *Provided further,* That the slaves of loyal citizens in the States exempt by the President's proclamation of January 1, 1863, shall not be received into the armed service of the United States, nor shall there be recruiting offices opened in either of the States of Delaware, Maryland, West Virginia, Kentucky, Tennessee, or Missouri, without the consent of the Governor of said State having been first obtained.

February 2—It passed the House—yeas 85, nays 57. The NAYS were—

NAYS—Messrs. *William Allen, William J. Allen, Ancona, Baily, Biddle,* Jacob B. Blair, *Calvert,* Clements, *Cobb, Cox, Cravens, Crisfield, Crittenden, Delaplaine,* Granger, *Grider, Haight,* Hale, *Hall, Harding, Harrison, Holman,* Horton, *Johnson,* William Kellogg, *Kerrigan, Law, Lazear,* Leary, *Mallory, May,* Maynard, *Menzies, Morris, Noble, Norton, Odell, Pendleton, Perry, Price, Robinson, James S. Rollins, Shiel, Stiles,* Benjamin F. Thomas, Francis Thomas, *Vallandigham, Vibbard, Wadsworth,* Webster, Whaley, *Chilton A. White, Wickliffe, Wood, Woodruff, Wright, Yeaman*—57.

February 13—The Senate Committee reported adversely to its passage.

IN SENATE.

Pending the engineer bill,

March 2—Mr. DAVIS offered this new section:

That no negro, free or slave, shall be enrolled in the military, marine, or naval service of the United States.

Which was not agreed to—yeas 12, nays 23, as follows:

YEAS—Messrs. *Davis,* Henderson, Hicks, *Kennedy, Nesmith, Powell, Richardson, Saulsbury, Turpie, Wall,* Willey, *Wilson* of Missouri—12.

NAYS—Messrs. Chandler, Clark, Collamer, Cowan, Doolittle, Fessenden, Foot, Foster, Grimes, *Harding,* Harlan, Harris, Howard, Howe, Lane of Indiana, Lane of Kansas, Morrill, Pomeroy, Sumner, Ten Eyck, Trumbull, Wilkinson, Wilson of Massachusetts—23.

Mr. POWELL offered to amend the eighth section by adding this proviso:

Provided, That no person of African descent shall be commissioned or hold an office in the army of the United States.

Which was agreed to—yeas 18, nays 17, as follows:

YEAS—Cowan, *Davis, Harding,* Harris, Henderson. Hicks, Howe, *Kennedy,* Lane of Indiana, *Nesmith. Powell, Richardson, Saulsbury,* Ten Eyck, *Turpie, Wall,* Willey, *Wilson* of Missouri—18.

NAYS—Messrs. Chandler, Clark, Doolittle, Fessenden, Foot, Foster, Grimes, Harlan, Howard, King, Lane of Kansas, Morrill, Pomeroy, Sumner, Trumbull, Wilkinson, Wilson of Massachusetts—17.

Mr. LANE, of Kansas, moved to add to the above proviso the following words:

Except company officers in companies composed exclusively of persons of African descent.

Which was agreed to—yeas 19, nays 17, as follows:

YEAS—Messrs. Chandler, Clark, Collamer, Doolittle, Fessenden, Foot, Foster, Grimes, Harlan, Howe, King, Lane of Kansas, Morrill, Pomeroy, Sumner, Trumbull, Wilkinson, Wilmot, Wilson of Massachusetts—19.

NAYS—Messrs. Cowan, *Davis, Harding,* Harris, Henderson, Hicks, Howard, Lane of Indiana, *Nesmith, Powell, Richardson, Saulsbury,* Sherman, Ten Eyck, *Wall,* Willey, *Wilson* of Missouri—17.

The eighth section was then stricken out without a division.

PAY OF COLORED SOLDIERS.

First Session, Thirty-Eighth Congress.

IN SENATE.

1864, February 23—The Senate considered the joint resolution to equalize the pay of soldiers.

Mr. COWAN moved to strike out all after the enacting clause, and insert:

That from and after the passage of this joint resolution the soldiers of the United States of America, of the same grade and service, shall be entitled to the same pay, rations, and pensions.

Mr. DAVIS moved to insert the following as a substitute:

All negroes and mulattoes, by whatever term designated, in the military service of the United States, be, and the same are hereby declared to be, discharged from such service, and shall be disarmed as soon as practicable; but the President of the United States may retain such of said negroes and mulattoes as he shall deem proper in the military service as teamsters and [illegible]rs; and the commandants of the respective regiments to which said slaves may be attached shall issue to their owner or owners a certificate of their employment in the service of the Government.

That every loyal owner of any slave that has been heretofore, or that may hereafter be taken into the service, or for the use of the United States, shall be entitled to a fair and reasonable compensation for the service of such slave for the time such slave may have been, or may be, in such service, to be paid quarterly; and where any slave may have been killed or died from exposure, or may have been disabled in such service, the owner or owners of all such slave or slaves shall be entitled to such compensation as will reasonably satisfy them for all damages that he, she, or they may have sustained by reason of the death or disability of any such slave or slaves. And where any such slave or slaves may become a fugitive, and be not returned to the owner, the United States shall pay to such owner or owners the reasonable value of the service of said slave or slaves.

That the owner or owners of any slave, entitled to pay and compensation, as hereinbefore provided for, may make out his, her, or their account therefor against the United States, and upon filing the same at the Treasury Department, sustained by vouchers and proofs as are required ordinarily to support accounts against the United States, the same shall be audited and paid by the proper officers out of any money in the Treasury not otherwise appropriated.

Which was disagreed to—yeas 7, nays 30, as follows:

YEAS—Messrs. *Buckalew*, *Carlile*, *Davis*, *Powell*, *Riddle*, *Saulsbury*, *Wright*—7.

NAYS—Messrs. Chandler, Clark, Collamer, Conness, Dixon, Fessenden, Foot, Foster, Grimes, Hale, Harding, Harlan, Harris, Henderson, Howard, Howe, Johnson, Lane of Indiana, Lane of Kansas, Morgan, Morrill, *Nesmith*, Ramsey, Sherman, Sumner, Ten Eyck, Van Winkle, Wade, Willey, Wilson—30.

February 25—Mr. COLLAMER moved to amend by adding to the resolution the following:

All persons enlisted or mustered into service as volunteers under the call dated October 17, 1863, for three hundred thousand volunteers, who were at the time of enlistment actually, and for six months previous had been, resident inhabitants of the State in which they volunteered, shall receive from the United States the same amount of bounty without regard to color: *Provided, however*, That the foregoing provision shall not extend to any State which the President by proclamation has declared in a state of insurrection.

Mr. SUMNER moved to amend the amendment by adding the words:

And provided also, That all persons whose papers of enlistment show that they were enlisted under the act of Congress of July, 1861, shall receive from the time of their enlistment the pay promised by that statute.

Which was agreed to—yeas 19, nays 18, as follows:

YEAS—Messrs. Clark, Collamer, Conness, Dixon, Doolittle, Foot, Foster, Hale, Harding, Howard, Lane of Kansas, Morgan, Morrill, Pomeroy, Sprague, Sumner, Ten Eyck, Van Winkle, Wilson—19.

NAYS—Messrs. *Buckalew*, Chandler, *Davis*, Grimes, Harlan, Harris, Henderson, *Hendricks*, Howe, Johnson, Lane of Indiana, *Nesmith*, *Powell*, Ramsey, *Saulsbury*, Wilkinson, Willey, *Wright*—18.

Feb. 29—The bill was recommitted to the Committee on Military Affairs, and again reported amended.

March 10—Mr. DAVIS offered a new section:

That for every slave or slaves that may have been heretofore, or may hereafter, be taken into the service of the United States, the loyal owner or owners of such slave or slaves shall be entitled to their fair and reasonable value, to be ascertained by three commissioners to be appointed by the United States district court for the district from which such slave or slaves may have been taken. And said commissioners shall take evidence and report on the points of the loyalty and ownership of the claimants, and the value of such slave or slaves; and when said report is confirmed by the district court aforesaid, it shall be conclusive on the points embraced by it; and on the presentation of an authoritative copy of said report to the Treasury Department, any sum or sums therein appearing to be due any loyal owner or owners shall be paid out of any money in the Treasury not otherwise appropriated.

Which was disagreed to—yeas 6, nays 31, as follows:

YEAS—Messrs. *Davis*, Johnson, *Nesmith*, *Powell*, *Riddle*, *Wright*—6.

NAYS—Messrs. Anthony, Brown, *Buckalew*, Chandler, Clark, Collamer, Conness, Dixon, Doolittle, Fessenden, Foot, Foster, Grimes, *Harding*, Harlan, Harris, Howard, Lane of Indiana, Lane of Kansas, Morgan, Morrill, Pomeroy, Ramsey, Sherman, Sumner, Ten Eyck, Van Winkle, Wade, Wilkinson, Willey, Wilson—31.

Mr. DAVIS offered an additional section:

That in every case where heretofore any person has agreed to join, and has in fact joined, or hereafter may join, the military service of the United States, and has been received into the said service by any military officer thereof, the person so joining and received into such service shall, for all purposes whatever, be deemed to have been regularly mustered into said service in the position of officer, non-commissioned officer, or private, in which he may have served, notwithstanding he may not have been mustered in according to law and the regulations of the War Department.

Which was lost—yeas 7, nays 29, as follows:

YEAS—Messrs. *Davis*, *Hendricks*, Johnson, *Nesmith*, *Powell*, Wade, *Wright*—7.

NAYS—Messrs. Anthony, Brown, *Buckalew*, Chandler, Clark, Collamer, Conness, Dixon, Doolittle, Fessenden, Foot, Foster, Grimes, *Harding*, Harlan, Harris, Howard, Lane of Indiana, Lane of Kansas, Morgan, Morrill, Pomeroy, Ramsey, Sherman, Sumner, Ten Eyck, Van Winkle, Willey, Wilson—29.

The bill then passed—yeas 31, nays 6, as follows:

YEAS—Messrs. Anthony, Brown, Chandler, Clark, Conness, Cowan, Dixon, Doolittle, Fessenden, Foot, Foster, Grimes, Harlan, Harris, Howard, Howe, Johnson, Lane of Indiana, Lane of Kansas, Morgan, Morrill, *Nesmith*, Pomeroy, Ramsey, Sherman, Sumner, Ten Eyck, Van Winkle, Wade, Willey, Wilson—31.

NAYS—Messrs. *Buckalew*, *Davis*, *Hendricks*, *Powell*, *Riddle*, *Wright*—6.

IN HOUSE.

It was referred to the Committee on Military Affairs, and not reported upon, when the Senate added propositions respecting the subject to the army appropriation bill, as follows:

IN SENATE.

Pending the army appropriation bill,

1864, April 22—Mr. WILSON offered these resolutions:

That all persons of color who have been or may be mustered into the service of the United States shall receive the same uniform, clothing, arms, equipments, camp equipage, rations, medical and hospital attendance, pay and emoluments, other than bounty, as other soldiers of the regular or volunteer forces of the United States of like arm of the service, from and after the 1st day of January, 1864, and that every person of color who shall hereafter be mustered into the service shall receive such sums in bounty as the President shall order in the different States and parts of the United States, not exceeding one hundred dollars.

That all persons enlisted and mustered into service as volunteers under the call dated October 17, 1864, for 300,000 volunteers, who were at the time of enlistment actually enrolled and subject to draft in the State in which they volunteered, shall receive from the United States the same amount of bounty, without regard to color.

That all persons of color, who have been enlisted and mustered into the service of the United States shall be entitled to receive the pay and clothing allowed by law to other volunteers in the service from the date of their muster into the service: *Provided*, That the same shall have been pledged or promised to them by any officer or person who, in making such pledge or promise, acted by authority of the War Department; and the Secretary of War is hereby authorized to determine any question of fact arising under this provision.

That the same premium shall be allowed for each colored recruit now mustered, or hereafter to be mustered, into the service of the United States, as is or shall be allowed for white recruits: *Provided*, That the Secretary of War shall previously give his assent to the same.

Which were agreed to—yeas 31, nays 5, as follows:

YEAS—Messrs. Anthony, Brown, Clark, Collamer, Conness,

Cowan, Dixon, Doolittle, Fessenden, Foster, Grimes, Hale, *Harding*, Henderson, Howard, Howe, Johnson, Lane of Indiana, *McDougall*, Morgan, Morrill, Pomeroy, Ramsey, Sherman, Sprague, Sumner, Ten Eyck, Trumbull, Van Winkle, Willey, Wilson—31.

NAYS—Messrs. *Buckalew, Davis, Hendricks, Powell, Saulsbury*—5.

Mr. DAVIS moved to add these words as a new section:

That when the existing insurrection and rebellion shall have been suppressed, and the authority and laws of the United States shall have been re-established in the States where the people are in rebellion, all negroes then in the military service of the United States shall thereupon be discharged from such service.

Which was disagreed to—yeas 10, (Messrs. *Buckalew, Carlile*, Cowan, *Davis*, Henderson, *Hendricks*, Johnson, *McDougall, Powell, Saulsbury*,) nays 27.

Mr. HENDRICKS offered a new section:

That the pay of the soldiers and non-commissioned officers of the army of the United States shall hereafter be fifty per cent. greater than is now allowed by law: *Provided*, That the pay of non-commissioned officers shall not exceed twenty-two dollars per month.

Which was disagreed to—yeas 6, nays 30, as follows:

YEAS—Messrs. *Buckalew, Carlile, Davis, Hendricks*, Lane of Indiana, *Powell*—6.

NAYS—Messrs. Anthony, Brown, Chandler, Clark, Collamer, Conness, Cowan, Dixon, Doolittle, Fessenden, Foot, Foster, Grimes, Hale, *Harding*, Henderson, Howard, Howe, *McDougall*, Morgan, Morrill, Pomeroy, Ramsey, Sherman, Sumner, Ten Eyck, Trumbull, Wilkinson, Willey, Wilson —30.

The army appropriation bill was then passed —yeas 36, nay 1, (Mr. *Powell*.)

IN HOUSE.

April 30—The House Committee on Military Affairs proposed to amend by substituting a bill, making these changes. May 1st was fixed as the date of increased pay; the bounty to be given to those colored soldiers enlisted under the call of Oct. 17, 1863, is limited to $100; and these two sections are substituted for the Senate's last two:

That in every case where it shall be made to appear to the satisfaction of the Secretary of War, that any regiment, or any battery, or any company of cavalry, of colored troops, has been enlisted and mustered into the service of the United States, under any authorized assurance given by any officer or agent of the United States, or by any Governor of any State, authorized thereto by the President or the Secretary of War, that the non-commissioned officers and privates of such regiment, battery, or company, should be paid the same as other troops of the same arm of the service, then they shall be so paid for the period of time counting from the date of their being respectively mustered into the service to the 1st day of May, A. D. 1864.

That there may be reserved at the discretion of the Secretary of War, and under such regulation as he may prescribe, a portion of the pay of any colored soldier, not exceeding in any case more than one-third thereof, to be applied to the support of the family of such soldier, or of other near relatives dependent on him for support.

Mr. HOLMAN moved to strike from the section the word "pay," which was lost—yeas 53, nays 85.

A division of the question was called; the first amendment of the House was disagreed to; and that of the Senate—being the first paragraph of bill passed, April 22, above—was agreed to—yeas 80, nays 51, as follows:

YEAS—Messrs. Alley, Allison, Ames, Anderson, Arnold, John D. Baldwin, Baxter, Beaman, Blaine, John B. Blair, Blow, Boutwell, Boyd, Brandegee, Broomall, Cobb, Cole, Creswell, Henry Winter Davis, Dawes, Deming, Dixon, Donnelly, Driggs, Eckley, Eliot, Farnsworth, Fenton, Frank, Garfield, Grinnell, *Griswold*, Higby, Hooper, Hotchkiss, Asahel W. Hubbard, John H. Hubbard, Hulburd, Jenckes, Julian, Kelley, Francis W. Kellogg, Orlando Kellogg, Loan, Longyear, Marvin, McBride, McClurg, McIndoe, Samuel F. Miller, Moorhead, Morrill, Daniel Morris, Amos Myers, Leonard Myers, Norton, *Odell*, Charles O'Neill, Orth, Patterson, Perham, Pomeroy, Price, Alexander H. Rice, John H. Rice, Edward H. Rollins, Schenck, Scofield, Shannon, Sloan, Spalding, Stevens, Thayer, Upson, Elihu B. Washburne, William B. Washburn, Williams, Wilder, Wilson, Windom—80.

NAYS—Messrs. *James C. Allen, Ancona, Brooks*, William G. Brown, *Chanler, Clay, Cox, Dawson, Denison, Eden, Eldridge, Finck, Grider, Hall, Harding, Harrington, Charles M. Harris, Herrick, Holman, Kernan, King, Knapp, Law, Lazear, Le Blond, Long, Marcy, McDowell, McKinney, William H. Miller, James R. Morris, Morrison, Noble, John O'Neill, Perry, Samuel J. Randall, Robinson, James S. Rollins, Ross, Scott*, Smith, *John B. Steele, Stiles, Strouse, Voorhees*, Whaley, *Wheeler, Chilton A. White, Joseph W. White, Fernando Wood, Yeaman*—51.

The second amendment of the Committee (with regard to bounty) was agreed to, and the Senate amendment, as amended, was agreed to—yeas 79, nays 52.

The third and fourth House amendments were disagreed to. The following amendment was then adopted as a substitute for the third proposition of the Senate:

That all free persons of color who have been or may be mustered into the military service of the United States shall from the date of their enlistment receive the same uniform, clothing, arms, equipments, camp equipage, rations, medical and hospital attendance, pay and emoluments, and bounty, as other soldiers of the regular or volunteer forces of the United States of like arm of the service.

Yeas 73, nays 55. The NAYS were—

Messrs. *James C. Allen, Ancona*, Anderson, *Augustus C. Baldwin*, Jacob B. Blair, *Brooks*, William G. Brown, *Chanler, Clay, Cox, Cravens, Dawson, Eden, Eldridge, Finck, Ganson, Grider, Griswold, Hall, Harding, Harrington, Benjamin G. Harris, Charles M. Harris, Herrick, Holman, Philip Johnson, Kernan, King, Knapp, Law, Le Blond, Long, Marcy, William H. Miller, James R. Morris, Morrison, Noble, John O'Neill, Perry, Radford, Robinson, James S. Rollins, Ross, Scott*, Smith, *John B. Steele, Stiles, Strouse, Voorhees*, Whaley, *Wheeler, Chilton A. White, Joseph W. White, Fernando Wood, Yeaman*—55.

The fourth amendment of the Senate was non-concurred in, being in another bill.

May 3—The Senate insisted on its amendments, and appointed a Committee of Conference, which,

May 25—Reported, and recommended the adoption of this section as a substitute for those adopted by the two Houses:

That in every case where it shall be made to appear to the satisfaction of the Secretary of War that any regiment of infantry, or any battery, or any company of cavalry, of colored troops has been enlisted and mustered into the service of the United States, under any authorized assurance given by any officer or agent of the United States, or by any Governor of any State authorized thereto by the President or the Secretary of War, the non-commissioned officers and privates of such regiment, battery, or company shall be paid the same as other troops of the same arm of the service, then they shall be so paid for the period of time counting from the date of their being respectively mustered into the service to the 1st day of January, 1864: *Provided, however*, That this section shall not be construed to prevent like payment to other colored troops from the time of their being mustered into the service, if such shall be held by the proper authority to be their right under the law.

Which was rejected—yeas 25, nays 121. The YEAS were:

Messrs. *Baily*, Boyd, William G. Brown, Ambrose W Clark, Thomas T. Davis, Farnsworth, Garfield, *Griswold*, Hooper, Kasson, *McAllister*, McBride, McIndoe, Morrill, Amos Myers, Perham, Price, Schenck, Shannon, Smith, Smithers, Thomas, Tracy, Whaley, Woodbridge—25.

ANOTHER CONFERENCE REPORT.

June 10—The second Committee of Conference on the army appropriation bill recommended the following section relating to the pay of colored troops, as a substitute:

That all persons of color who were free on the 19th day of

April, 1861, and who have been enlisted and mustered into the military service of the United States, shall from the time of their enlistment be entitled to receive the pay, bounty, and clothing allowed to such persons by the laws existing at the time of their enlistment. And the Attorney General of the United States is hereby authorized to determine any question of law arising under this provision. And if the Attorney General aforesaid shall determine that any such enlisted persons are entitled to receive any pay, bounty, or clothing in addition to what they have already received, the Secretary of War shall make all necessary regulations to enable the pay department to make payment in accordance with such determination.

June 11—It was concurred in, without division in the Senate.

June 13—The report was adopted in the House—yeas 72, nays 58, as follows:

YEAS—Messrs. Allison, Ames, Anderson, Arnold, Ashley, *Baily*, Baxter, Beaman, Blaine, Blair, Blow, Boyd, Brandegee, Ambrose W. Clark, Cobb, Cole, Thomas T. Davis, Dixon, Donnelly, Driggs, Eckley, Fenton, Frank, Garfield, Higby, Hooper, Hotchkiss, Asahel W. Hubbard, John H. Hubbard, Ingersoll, Jenckes, Julian, Kelley, Francis W. Kellogg, Littlejohn, Loan, Longyear, Marvin, McClurg, McIndoe, Samuel F. Miller, Moorhead, Morrill, Daniel Morris, Amos Myers, Leonard Myers, Norton, Charles O'Neill, Orth, Patterson, Perham, Pike, Price, John H. Rice, Scofield, Shannon, Smith, Smithers, Spalding, Starr, Stevens, Thayer, Thomas, Tracy, Upson, Van Valkenburgh, Webster, Williams, Wilder, Wilson, Windom, Woodbridge—72.

NAYS—Messrs. *James C. Allen*, *William J. Allen*, Alley, *Augustus C. Baldwin*, John D. Baldwin, *Bliss*, Boutwell, *James S. Brown*, *Chanler*, *Cox*, *Cravens*, Henry Winter Davis, Dawes, *Dawson*, *Denison*, *Eden*, *Edgerton*, *Eldridge*, Eliot, *Finck*, *Ganson*, Gooch, *Grider*, *Harding*, *Harrington*, *Charles M. Harris*, *Herrick*, *Holman*, *Hutchins*, *Kalbfleisch*, *Kernan*, *King*, *Law*, *Le Blond*, *Marcy*, *McDowell*, *McKinney*, *Wm. H. Miller*, *James R. Morris*, *Morrison*, *John O'Neill*, *Pendleton*, *Radford*, Alexander H. Rice, *Robinson*, *James S. Rollins*, *Ross*, *John B. Steele*, *Wm. G. Steele*, *Stiles*, *Strouse*, *Stuart*, *Sweat*, *Wadsworth*, *Wheeler*, *Chilton A. White*, *Joseph W. White*, *Fernando Wood*—58.

1863, Dec. 14—Mr. LOVEJOY moved that the Committee on Military Affairs be instructed to inquire into the expediency of placing, in any bill or bills they may report on the subject, all regular enlisted soldiers on the same footing as to pay without distinction of color.

Mr. Cox moved to table the motion; which was disagreed to—yeas 68, nays 87.

The resolution was then adopted.

1864, May 16—Mr. RICE, of Maine, introduced a bill for the enrollment, organization, and service of certain persons of African descent in the militia of the several States; which was referred to the Committee on the Militia.

OPINION OF ATTORNEY GENERAL BATES ON PAYING A COLORED CHAPLAIN.

ATTORNEY GENERAL'S OFFICE,
April 23, 1864.

SIR: You have done me the honor to refer to me a communication to yourself from his excellency John A. Andrew, Governor of Massachusetts, with accompanying papers, relative to the claim of Rev. Samuel Harrison for pay as chaplain of the 54th regiment of Massachusetts volunteers.

It appears by Governor Andrew's letter and the other papers that Mr. Harrison, who is a colored man, was duly elected, and on the 8th day of September, 1863, commissioned by Governor Andrew as a chaplain of the 54th regiment of Massachusetts volunteers in the service of the United States; that on the 12th of November, 1862, he was mustered and accepted into the service of the United States at Morris island, South Carolina, by the proper mustering officer, and actually performed the duties of chaplain of that regiment then and since serving in South Carolina. On demanding his pay as chaplain, he was met by the following refusal in writing, signed by the paymaster at Hilton Head:

"Samuel Harrison, chaplain of the 54th regiment Massachusetts volunteers, (colored troops,) asks pay at the usual rate, $100 per month and two rations, which, he being of African descent, I decline paying, under act of Congress passed July 17, 1862, employing persons of African descent in military service of the United States. The chaplain declines to receive anything less."

You have requested my opinion whether the paymaster should have paid as demanded, and, if he should, whether it is your duty to order him to do so.

The 54th regiment of Massachusetts volunteers was organized in the same manner as were other regiments of State volunteers under the following order of the War Department, dated January 26, 1863, viz:

"*Ordered*, That Governor Andrew, of Massachusetts, is authorized, until further orders, to raise such number of volunteer companies of artillery for duty in the forts of Massachusetts and elsewhere, and such corps of infantry for the volunteer military service, as he may find convenient, such volunteers to be enlisted for three years or until sooner discharged, and may include persons of African descent, organized into separate corps. He will make the usual needful requisitions on the appropriate staff bureaus and officers for the proper transportation, organization, supplies, subsistence, arms, and equipments of such volunteers."

"EDWIN M. STANTON,
"*Secretary of War.*"

I do not know that any rule of law, constitutional or statutory, even prohibited the acceptance, organization, and muster of "persons of African descent" into the military service of the United States as enlisted men or volunteers. But whatever doubt might have existed on the subject had been fully resolved before this order was issued, by the eleventh section of the act of 17th July, 1862, chapter 195, which authorized the President to employ as many persons of African descent as he might deem necessary and proper for the suppression of the rebellion, and for that purpose to organize and use them in such manner as he may judge best for the public welfare, and the twelfth section of the act of same date, chapter 201, which authorized the President to receive into the service of the United States for the purpose of constructing entrenchments, or performing camp service, or any other labor, or any military or naval service for which they might be found competent, persons of African descent, such persons to be enrolled and organized under such regulations, not inconsistent with the Constitution and laws, as the President might prescribe.

The 54th Massachusetts regiment was therefore organized and mustered into the service of the United States under clear authority of law.

But the fifteenth section of the act of 17th July, 1862, chapter 201, after directing that all persons who have been or shall be enrolled in the service of the United States under that act shall receive the pay and rations then allowed by law to soldiers, according to their respective grades, contains this *proviso:* "That persons of African descent who under this law shall be employed shall receive ten dollars per month and one ration, three dollars of which monthly pay may be in clothing."

Whether persons of African descent "enrolled in the service of the United States" as private soldiers are included within the words "persons of African descent who under this law shall be employed," thereby limiting their pay as soldiers to ten dollars a month, is not the question you have submitted to me; for Mr. Harrison was not a private soldier, but an officer, serving under the commission of the Governor of Massachusetts, the authenticity and validity of which were recognized and admitted by the United States when he was mustered into its service. But the question is, can a person of African descent lawfully hold the office and receive the pay of chaplain of a volunteer regiment in the service of the United States?

I have already said that I knew of no provision of law, constitutional or statutory, which prohibited the acceptance of persons of African descent into the military service of the United States; and if they could be lawfully accepted as private soldiers, so also might they be accepted as commissioned officers, if otherwise qualified therefor. But the express power conferred on the President by the eleventh section of the act of 17th July, 1862, chapter 195, before cited, to employ this class of persons for the suppression of the rebellion as he may judge best for the public welfare, furnishes all needful sanction of law to the employment of a colored chaplain for a volunteer regiment of his own race. Nor is any prohibition of the employment of such person found in the statutes which declare the qualifications of chaplains. The ninth section of the act to authorize the employment of volunteers, &c., of 22d July, 1861, chapter 9, provides that there shall be allowed to each regiment one chaplain, who shall be appointed by the regimental commander on the vote of the field officers and company commanders on duty with the regiment at the time the appointment shall be made. The chaplain so appointed must be a regularly ordained minister of a Christian denomination, &c. The seventh section of the act of 3d August, 1861, chapter 42, for the better organization of the military establishment, declares that one chaplain shall be allowed to each regiment of the army, to be selected and appointed as the President may direct, provided that none but regularly ordained ministers of some Christian denomination shall be eligible to selection or appointment. The eighth section of the act of 17th July, 1862, chapter 200, declares that the two sections last cited shall be construed to read as follows:

"That no person shall be appointed a chaplain in the United States army who is not a regular ordained minister of some religious denomination, and who does not present testimonials of his present good standing as such minister, with a recommendation for his appointment as an army chaplain from some authorized ecclesiastical body, or not less than five accredited ministers belonging to said religious denomination."

The closest inspection of these provisions will discover nothing that precludes the appointment of a Christian minister to the office of chaplain because he is a person of African descent. I therefore conclude that Mr. Harrison was the lawfully appointed and qualified chaplain of the 54th Massachusetts regiment.

The ninth section of the act of the 17th July, 1862, chapter 200, provides that thereafter, the compensation of all chaplains in the regular or volunteer service or army hospitals shall be one hundred dollars per month and two rations a day when on duty. Was Mr. Harrison entitled to this rate of compensation, or was he limited to the pay of ten dollars a month and one ration, fixed by the *proviso* to the fifteenth section of the act of 17th July, 1862, chapter 201?

It will be observed that this *proviso* declares that ten dollars a month and one ration shall be received by persons of African descent employed under the law of which it is a part, viz., the act of 17th July, 1862, chapter 201. Now, we have seen that it is not necessary to resort to that law to find authority for the appointment of Mr. Harrison as chaplain, for, apart from the authority which might be presumed to exist prior to the enactment of any of these statutes, the eleventh section of the act of 17th July, 1862, chapter 195, sufficiently warranted it. To bring him, then, within the sweep of this proviso, and thus withdraw him from the reach of the act which specifically fixes the pay of the class of officers to which by clear law he belongs, would violate the plainest principles of construction. The act, of which the *proviso* is a part, was not intended, in my opinion, either to authorize the employment or fix the pay of any persons of African descent, except those who might be needed to perform the humble offices of labor and service for which they might be found competent. The twelfth section authorizes them to be received into service for the purpose of constructing entrenchments, or performing camp service, or any other labor, or any military or naval service for which they might be found competent. The thirteenth section declares that when any man or boy of African descent, who, by the laws of any State, shall owe service or labor to any person aiding the rebellion, shall render such service as this act provides for, he, his mother, wife and children shall be free thereafter, with certain exceptions. And the fifteenth section fixes their pay as before stated.

While it is true that the words of the twelfth section are broad enough to embrace all persons of African descent who may be received into the military or naval service of the United States, it is yet quite evident from the terms of the whole section, as well as from the promise of freedom held out to such persons who were slaves, in the thirteenth section, that in limiting their pay to ten dollars a month and one ration, Congress had in view the class who were fitted only for the humbler kinds of service referred to, and not persons who, under the authority of other laws, might be appointed to positions requiring higher qualifications, and entitled to a higher rate of pay. To assume that because Mr. Harrison is a person of African descent he shall draw only the pay which this law establishes for the class it obviously refers to, and be deprived of the pay which another law specifically affixes to the office he lawfully held, would be, in my opinion, a distortion of both laws, not only unjust to him, but in plain violation of the purpose of Congress.

I therefore think that the paymaster should have paid Mr. Harrison his full pay as chaplain of a volunteer regiment.

Your attention having been specially called to the wrong done in this case, I am also of opinion that your constitutional obligation to take care that the laws be faithfully executed makes it your duty to direct the Secretary of War to inform the officers of the pay department of the army that such is your view of the law, and I do not doubt that it will be accepted by them as furnishing the correct rule for their action.

I am, sir, very respectfully, your obedient servant,

EDWARD BATES,
Attorney General.

The PRESIDENT.

PROTECTION OF COLORED SOLDIERS.

THE PRESIDENT'S ORDER.

[General Orders No. 252.]

WAR DEPARTMENT, ADJUTANT GENERAL'S OFFICE,
WASHINGTON, *July* 31, 1863.

The following order of the President is published for the information and government of all concerned:

EXECUTIVE MANSION,
WASHINGTON, *July* 30, 1863.

It is the duty of every Government to give protection to its citizens, of whatever class, color, or condition, and especially to those who are duly organized as soldiers in the public service. The law of nations, and the usages and customs of war, as carried on by civilized powers, permit no distinction as to color in the treatment of prisoners of war as public enemies. To sell or enslave any captured person, on account of his color, and for no offence against the laws of war, is a relapse into barbarism, and a crime against the civilization of the age.

The Government of the United States will give the same protection to all its soldiers; and if the enemy shall sell or enslave any one because of his color, the offence shall be punished by retaliation upon the enemy's prisoners in our possession.

It is therefore ordered that for every soldier of the United States killed in violation of the laws of war, a rebel soldier shall be executed; and for every one enslaved by the enemy, or sold into slavery, a rebel soldier shall be placed at hard labor on public works, and continued at such labor until the other shall be released and receive the treatment due to a prisoner of war. ABRAHAM LINCOLN.

By order of Secretary of War.

E. D. TOWNSEND, *Assistant Adjutant General.*

FROM THE RULES OF WAR ADOPTED BY THE GOVERNMENT.

57. So soon as a man is armed by a sovereign Government, and takes the soldier's oath of fidelity, he is a belligerent; his killing, wounding, or other warlike acts are no individual crimes or offences. No belligerent has a right to declare that enemies of a certain class, color, or condition, when properly organized as soldiers, will not be treated by him as public enemies.

58. The law of nations knows of no distinction of color, and if an enemy of the United States should enslave and sell any captured persons of their army, it would be a case for the severest retaliation, if not redressed upon complaint. The United States cannot retaliate by enslavement; therefore death must be the retaliation for this crime against the law of nations.

THE PRESIDENT'S SPEECH AT THE BALTIMORE FAIR, APRIL 18, 1864.

LADIES AND GENTLEMEN: Calling it to mind that we are in Baltimore, we cannot fail to note that the world moves. [Applause.] Looking upon the many people I see assembled here to serve as they best may the soldiers of the Union, it occurs to me that three years ago those soldiers could not pass through Baltimore. I would say, blessings upon the men who have wrought these changes, and the ladies who have assisted them. [Applause.] This change which has taken place in Baltimore is part only of a far wider change that is taking place all over the country.

When the war commenced three years ago, no one expected that it would last this long, and no one supposed that the institution of slavery would be materially affected by it. But here we are. [Applause.] The war is not yet ended, and slavery has been very materially affected or interfered with. [Loud applause.] So true is it that man proposes and God disposes.

The world is in want of a good definition of the word liberty. We all declare ourselves to be for liberty, but we do not all mean the same thing. Some mean that a man can do as he pleases with himself and his property. [Applause.] With others it means that some men can do as they please with other men and other men's labor. Each of these things are called liberty, although they are entirely different. To give an illustration: A shepherd drives the wolf from the throat of his sheep when attacked by him, and the sheep of course thanks the shepherd for the preservation of his life; but the wolf denounces him as despoiling the sheep of his liberty, especially if it be a black sheep. [Applause.]

This same difference of opinion prevails among some of the people of the North. But the people of Maryland have recently been doing something to properly define the meaning of the word, and I thank them from the bottom of my heart for what they have done and are doing. [Applause.]

It is not very becoming for a President to make a speech at great length, but there is a painful rumor afloat in the country in reference to which a few words shall be said. It is reported that there has been a wanton massacre of some hundreds of colored soldiers at Fort Pillow, Tennessee, during a recent engagement there, and he thought it fit to explain some facts in relation to the affair. It is said by some persons that the Government is not in this matter doing its duty. At the commencement of the war it was doubtful whether black men would be used as soldiers or not. The matter was examined into very carefully, and after mature deliberation, the whole matter resting as it were with himself, he in his judgment decided that they should. [Applause.] He was responsible for the act to the American people, to a Christian nation, to the future historian, and, above all, to his God, to whom he would have one day to render an account of his stewardship. [Applause.] He would now say that in his opinion the black soldier should have the same protection as the white soldier, and he would have it. [Applause.] It was an error to say that the Government was not acting in the matter. The Government has no direct evidence to confirm the reports in existence relative to this massacre, but he himself believed the facts in relation to it to be as stated. When the Government does know the facts from official sources, and they prove to substantiate the reports, retribution will be surely given. [Applause.] What is reported, he thought, would make a clear case. If it is not true, then all such stories are to be considered as false. If proved true, when the matter is thoroughly examined, what shape is to be given to the retribution? Can we take the man who was captured at Vicksburg and shoot him for the victim of this massacre? If it should happen that it was the act of only one man, what course is to be pursued then? It was a matter requiring careful examination and deliberation, and if it should be substantiated by sufficient evidence all might rest assured that retribution would be had. [Applause.]

Confederate Use of Colored Persons.

1861.

A dispatch from Charleston, dated January 1, 1861, from R. R. Riordan to Hon. Perry Walker, at Mobile, describes the preparations for war, and contains this closing paragraph:

Large gangs of negroes from plantations are at work on the redoubts, which are substantially made of sand-bags and coated with sheet-iron.

A Washington dispatch to the *Evening Post* says:

A gentleman from Charleston says that everything there betokens active preparations for fight. The thousand negroes busy in building batteries, so far from inclining to insurrection, were grinning from ear to ear at the prospect of shooting the Yankees.

The Charleston *Mercury* of January 3, 1861, announced:

We learn that one hundred and fifty able-bodied free colored men, of Charleston, yesterday offered their services gratuitously to the Governor to hasten forward the important work of throwing up redoubts wherever needed along our coast.

In April, the Lynchburg (Va.) *Republican* announced:

We learn that about seventy of the most respectable free negroes in this city have enrolled themselves and design tendering their services to the Governor, to act in whatever capacity may be assigned them in defence of the State. Three cheers for the patriotic free negroes of Lynchburg.

A letter in the Petersburg (Va.) *Express*, dated at Norfolk on the 23d April, says:

The negroes in all this section of the country, slave and free, are as loyal as could be desired. They freely proffer their services to the State, and zealously contend for the privilege of being allowed to work on the batteries. Yesterday Gen. Gwynn declined the services of three hundred from Hampton who solicited employment on the batteries, and twice and thrice that number could be obtained in this city and vicinity in a single day, if it was thought advisable to accept them. Indeed, the entire fortifications of this harbor might be constructed by the voluntary labor of negroes, who would claim no higher reward than the privilege of being allowed to contribute their share toward the defence of the State, and the protection of their masters and mistresses, who had always extended a sheltering hand over them.

In June, the rebel Legislature of Tennessee passed this enlistment bill, which became a law:

SEC. 1. *Be it enacted by the General Assembly of the State of Tennessee*, That from and after the passage of this act the Governor shall be, and he is hereby, authorized, at his discretion, to receive into the military service of the State all male free persons of color between the ages of fifteen and fifty, or such numbers as may be necessary, who may be sound in mind and body, and capable of actual service.

2. That such free persons of color shall receive, each, eight dollars per month, as pay, and such persons shall be entitled to draw, each, one ration per day, and shall be entitled to a yearly allowance each for clothing.

3. That, in order to carry out the provisions of this act, it shall be the duty of the sheriffs of the several counties in this State to collect accurate information as to the number and condition, with the names of free persons of color, subject to the provisions of this act, and shall, as it is practicable, report the same in writing to the Governor.

4. That a failure or refusal of the sheriffs, or any one or more of them, to perform the duties required, shall be deemed an offence, and on conviction thereof shall be punished as a misdemeanor.

5. That in the event a sufficient number of free persons of color to meet the wants of the State shall not tender their services, the Governor is empowered, through the sheriffs of the different counties, to press such persons until the requisite number is obtained.

6. That when any mess of volunteers shall keep a servant to wait on the members of the mess, each servant shall be allowed one ration.

This act to take effect from and after its passage.

W. C. WHITTHORNE,
Speaker of the House of Representatives.
B. L. STOVALL,
Passed June 28, 1861. *Speaker of the Senate.*

HOW SLAVES ARE EMPLOYED BY THE "CONFEDERATES."

The following paragraph appears in the Memphis (Tennessee) *Avalanche* of the 3d of September:

A procession of several hundred stout negro men, members of the "domestic institution," marched through our streets yesterday in military order, under command of Confederate officers. They were all armed and equipped with shovels, axes, blankets, &c. A merrier set were never seen. They were brimfull of patriotism, shouting for Jeff. Davis and singing war songs.

The *Avalanche* of the 7th September said:

Upwards of one thousand negroes, armed with spades and pickaxes, have passed through the city within the past few days. Their destination is unknown, but it is supposed that they are on their way to the "other side of Jordan."

NEW ORLEANS, *November* 23.

Over twenty-eight thousand troops were reviewed to-day by Governor Moore, Major General Lovell, and Brigadier General Ruggles. The line was over seven miles long. One regiment comprised 1,400 free colored men.

1862.

THE ENROLLMENT OF FREE NEGROES IN REBELDOM.

In the Virginia House of Delegates, on the 4th of February, on the subject of enrolling free negroes for the rebel army, the following debate took place. We copy the official report of the proceedings from the Richmond *Examiner*:

The bill amending the convention act for the enrollment of free negroes was, on motion of Mr. Prince, taken up. Among the amendments in this bill Mr. Prince called attention to the one allowing ten cents for each negro so enrolled to the sheriff or officer so enrolling them. He proposed to strike out this amendment and insert in lieu of the proposed compensation that if the said officers fail to comply with the requisitions of this law, they be subjected to a penalty of not less than fifty nor more than one hundred dollars. As these officers were exempt from military duty, he said, it was about as little as they could do to perform the service of enrolling the free negroes of their respective counties as a part of their official duties. His amendment was adopted.

Mr. RIVES proposed that the amendment in the bill respecting the term of the enlistment of negroes be amended to make the term ninety days, instead of a hundred and eighty. His reason for this was the fact that the families of many of the free negroes so enlisted, having no other means of support, would, as had been the case in his own county, suffer very much from want.

Mr. PRINCE agreed to compromise with the gentleman on one hundred and twenty days.

Mr. ANDERSON, of Botetourt, hoped that the amendment would not pass. One hundred and eighty days were only six months; and if white men could be drafted for two years, he saw no reason why free negroes should be entitled to such charitable discrimination.

Mr. RIVES replied that he made the proposition from no particular friendship to free negroes; *if it were in his power, he would convert them all into slaves to-morrow.* But it was simply to call the attention of the House to the fact that, in his own county, many severe cases of suffering had occurred among the families of free negroes from this cause, and he thought that possibly some alleviation might be brought about by the amendment proposed.

The amendment was rejected, and the bill was then ordered to its engrossment.

In the debate in the Rebel Congress, March 10, Mr. FOOTE of Tennessee, alluding to the fall of Nashville, said:

Gen. Johnston had called for 1,000 or 1,500 slaves to work on the fortifications, and that the *call had been fully answered*, when Nashville was surrendered.

DRAFT OF NEGROES FOR MILITARY SERVICE.

[From the Richmond Examiner, October 18, 1862.]

We notice that in Texas, and in some portions of the Mississippi valley, the proposition is urged to make a conscription or forced levy of slaves, where their labor is necessary for the army. Since the invasion of the South the Yankees have stolen tens of thousands of negroes, and made them useful as teamsters, laborers in camp, &c. It appears that slaveholders are averse, for some reasons, to hire their negroes in the Confederate army. The prejudice is certainly an ignorant and mean one. As the war originated and is carried on in great part for the defence of the slaveholder in his property, rights, and the perpetuation of the institution, it is reasonable to suppose that he ought to be first and foremost in aiding and assisting, by every means in his power, the triumph and success of our arms. Good wages are offered, and proper care and attention will be given every negro hired to the army, and the slaveholder ought to remember that for every negro he thus furnishes he puts a soldier in the ranks.

November 2—Governor Joseph E. Brown, of Georgia, issued a call announcing that if a sufficient supply of negroes be not tendered within ten days, General Mercer will, in pursuance of authority given him, proceed to impress, and asking of every planter of Georgia a tender of one fifth of his negroes to complete the fortifications around Savannah. This one fifth is estimated at 15,000.

1863.

This paragraph was published in the *New York Times*, July 15, 1862:

The Adjutant General of the Confederate States publishes a general order from the Rebel War Department, directing recruiting officers, duly accredited, to draft every white or mulatto male found throughout the South who is able to bear arms, and who is between the ages of twenty and fifty-five years, whether such persons may have obtained substitutes for themselves or not; and willful evasion of this order is to be severely punished.

The Governor of South Carolina in July, issued a proclamation for 3,000 negroes to work on the fortifications, "the need for them being pressing."

GEORGIA, ALABAMA, AND MISSISSIPPI SENTIMENT.

[From the Savannah, (Ga.) News, Sept 2.]

EMPLOYMENT OF NEGROES IN THE REBEL ARMY.

A joint committee of the Alabama Legislature, just adjourned, reported a resolution in favor of the proposition to employ slaves in the military service of the Confederate States, which proposition, we see, is favored by many of the presses of Mississippi and Alabama. After discussion in the Alabama House, the resolution was adopted by a vote of sixty-eight yeas to twelve nays, after striking out the words "military" before service, and "soldiers" at the end of the resolution. The resolution was amended and read as follows:

That it is the duty of Congress to provide by law for the employment in the service of the Confederate States of America, in such situations and in such numbers as may be found absolutely necessary, the able-bodied slaves of the country, whether as pioneers, sappers and miners, cooks, nurses and teamsters.

In this form we can see no objection to the resolution.

THE CHANGING SENTIMENT OF CONGRESS.

In the Rebel House of Representatives, December 29th, Mr. DARGAN, of Alabama, introduced a bill to receive into the military service all that portion of population in Alabama, Mississippi, Louisiana, and Florida, known as "Creoles."

Mr. Dargan supported the bill in some remarks. He said the Creoles were a mixed-blooded race. Under the treaty of Paris in 1803, and the treaty of Spain in 1810, they were recognized as freemen. Many of them owned large estates, and were intelligent men. They were as much devoted to our cause as any class of men in the South, and were even anxious to go into service. They had applied to him to be received into service, and he had applied to Mr. Randolph, then Secretary of War. Mr. Randolph decided against the application, on the ground that it might furnish to the enemy a pretext of arming our slaves against us. Some time after this he was again applied to by them, and he went to the present Secretary of War, Mr. Seddon, and laid the matter before him. Mr. Seddon refused to entertain the proposition, on the ground that it did not come up before him through the military authorities. To obviate this objection, Gen. Maury, at Mobile, soon afterwards represented their wishes to the War Department. Mr. Seddon refused the offer of their services, on the ground that it would be incompatible with the position we occupied before the world; that it could not be done.

Mr. Dargan said he differed with the Secretary of War. He cared not for "the world." He cared no more for their opinions than they did for ours. He was anxious to bring into service every free man, be he who he may, willing to strike for our cause. He saw no objection to employing Creoles; they would form a potent element in our army. In his district alone a brigade of them could be raised. The crisis had been brought upon us by the enemy, and he believed the time would yet come when the question would not be the Union or no Union, but whether Southern men should be permitted to live at all. In resisting subjugation by such a barbarous foe he was for employing all our available force. *He would go further and say that he was for arming and putting the slaves into the military service. He was in favor even of employing them as a military arm in the defence of the country.*

1864.

[From the Charleston Courier of January 27.]

NEGRO LABOR UPON FORTIFICATIONS.

The Mayor of Charleston, Charles Macbeth, summons all slaveholders within the city to furnish to the military authorities forthwith, one-fourth of all their male slaves between the ages of fifteen and fifty, to labor upon the fortifications. The penalty announced, in case of failure to comply with this requisition is a fine of $200 for every slave not forthcoming. Compensation is allowed at the rate of $400 a year.

All free male persons of color between the ages of fifteen and fifty are required to give themselves up for the same purpose. Those not complying will be imprisoned, and set to work upon the fortifications along the coast. To free negroes no other compensation than rations is allowed.

NEGROES IN THE ARMY.

The Richmond press publish the official copy of "An act to increase the efficiency of the army by the employment of free negroes and slaves in certain capacities," passed Feb. 17, by the

Rebel Congress. The negroes are to perform "such duties as the Secretary of War or Commanding General may prescribe." The first section is as follows:

The Congress of the Confederate States of America do enact, That all male free negroes, and other free persons of color, not including those who are free under the treaty of Paris, of 1803, or under the treaty of Spain, of 1819, resident in the Confederate States, between the ages of eighteen and fifty years, shall be held liable to perform such duties with the army, or in connection with the military defences of the country, in the way of work upon the fortifications, or in government works for the production or preparation of materials of war, or in military hospitals, as the Secretary of War or the Commanding General of the Trans-Mississippi Department may, from time to time, prescribe; and while engaged in the performances of such duties shall receive rations and clothing and compensation at the rate of eleven dollars a month, under such rules and regulations as the said Secretary may establish: *Provided,* That the Secretary of War or the Commanding General of the Trans-Mississippi Department, with the approval of the President, may exempt from the operations of this act such free negroes as the interests of the country may require should be exempted, or such as he may think proper to exempt on the ground of justice, equity or necessity.

The third section provides that when the Secretary of War shall be unable to procure the services of slaves in any military department, then he is authorized to impress the services of as many male slaves, not to exceed twenty thousand, as may be required, from time to time, to discharge the duties indicated in the first section of the act.

The owner of the slave is to be paid for his services; or, if he be killed or "escape to the enemy," the owner shall receive his full value.

Governor Smith, of Virginia, has made a call for five thousand male slaves to work on the batteries, to be drawn from fifty counties. The call for this force has been made by the President under a resolution of Congress.

General Magruder's proclamation to Texans, March 4, thus closes:

The slaveholding gentlemen of each county are respectfully requested to meet together at their respective county seats, or some convenient point, and appoint one or more of their number to accompany their negroes to Houston, and see that they are made comfortable. One-fourth of all the male hands between the ages of seventeen and fifty years in each county, without regard at this time to the numbers which have been previously furnished, will accomplish the purpose of fortifying Houston within a short time; and planters and all others are assured that the necessity of this course is manifest to the Major General commanding, and could be made so to them, but that his plans would thus be made known to the enemy.

By command of Maj. Gen. J. Bankhead Magruder:
EDMUND P. TURNER, *A. A. Gen.*
HOUSTON, *March* 4, 1864.

"CONFEDERATE" LEGISLATION UPON NEGRO PRISONERS AND THEIR WHITE OFFICERS WHEN CAPTURED.*

1863, May 1—An act was approved declaring that the commissioned officers of the enemy ought not to be delivered to the authorities of the respective States, (as suggested in Davis's message;) but all captives taken by the Confederate forces ought to be dealt with and disposed of by the Confederate Government.

President Lincoln's emancipation proclamations of September 22, 1862, and January 1, 1863, were resolved to be inconsistent with the usages of war among civilized nations, and should be repressed by retaliation; and the President is authorized to cause full and complete retaliation for every such violation, in such manner and to such extent as he may think proper.

Every white commissioned officer commanding negroes or mulattoes in arms against the Confederate States shall be deemed as inciting servile insurrection, and shall, if captured, be put to death, or be otherwise punished, at the discretion of the court.

Every person charged with an offence made punishable under the act shall be tried by the military court of the army or corps of troops capturing him; and, *after conviction, the President may commute the punishment in such manner and on such terms as he may deem proper.*

All negroes and mulattoes who shall be engaged in war or taken in arms against the Confederate States, or shall give aid or comfort to the enemies of the Confederate States, shall, when captured in the Confederate States, be delivered to the authorities of the State or States in which they shall be captured, to be dealt with according to the present or future laws of such State or States. (See Appendix.)

PROPOSED PROHIBITION OF PAYMENT TO COLORED SOLDIERS.

First Session, Thirty-Seventh Congress.

IN HOUSE.

Pending the army appropriation bill in the House,

1861, July 11—Mr. VALLANDIGHAM offered this proviso to come in at the end of the bill:

Provided, That no part of the money hereby appropriated shall be employed in subjugating, or holding as a conquered province, any sovereign State now or lately one of the United States; nor in abolishing or interfering with African slavery in any of the States.

Which was rejected, without a call of the yeas and nays.

Second Session, Thirty-Seventh Congress.

IN SENATE.

1862, June 2—Mr. SAULSBURY offered this additional section:

That no part of the money arising from the taxes, imposts, and excises in this bill provided for, shall be applied to or expended for the support or maintenance of fugitive slaves or free negroes.

Which was rejected—yeas 5, nays 34, as follows:

YEAS—Messrs. *Davis, Nesmith, Powell, Saulsbury, Stark*—5.

NAYS—Messrs. Anthony, Browning, Chandler, Clark, Cowan, Dixon, Doolittle, Fessenden, Foot, Foster, Grimes, Hale, Harlan, Harris, Howard, Howe, King, Lane of Indiana, Lane of Kansas, *Latham, McDougall,* Morrill, Pomeroy, Sherman, Simmons, Sumner, *Thomson,* Trumbull, Wade, Wilkinson, Willey, Wilmot, Wilson of Massachusetts, *Wright*—34.

June 6—Pending the internal revenue bill, Mr. DAVIS offered this as a new section:

That no money raised under this act shall ever be applied to pay or subsist any armed negroes in the service of the United States for any period of time after it goes into operation and effect.

Which was rejected without a division.

Third Session, Thirty-Seventh Congress.

IN SENATE.

Pending the army appropriation bill,

---

* December 23, 1862—Jefferson Davis issued a proclamation of outlawry against Major General B. F. Butler, the last two clauses of which are:

Third. That all negro slaves captured in arms be at once delivered over to the executive authorities of the respective States to which they belong, to be dealt with according to the laws of said States.

Fourth. That the like orders be executed in all cases with respect to all commissioned officers of the United States when found serving in company with said slaves in insurrection against the authorities of the different States of this Confederacy.

1863, Jan. 28—Mr. DAVIS moved to add this proviso to the bill:

Provided, That no part of the sums appropriated by this act shall be disbursed for the pay, subsistence, or any other supplies of any negro, free or slave, in the armed military service of the United States.

Which was rejected—yeas 8, nays 28, as follows:

YEAS—Messrs. *Carlile, Davis, Kennedy, Latham, Nesmith, Powell, Turpie, Wall*—8.

NAYS—Messrs. Anthony, Browning, Chandler, Clark, Collamer, Cowan, Dixon, Doolittle, Fessenden, Foot, Foster, Grimes, Hale, Harlan, Harris, Howe, King, Lane of Indiana, Lane of Kansas, Morrill, Pomeroy, Sherman, Sumner, Ten Eyck, Trumbull, Wilkinson, Willey, Wilson of Massachusetts—28.

—

First Session, Thirty-Eighth Congress.

IN HOUSE.

1863, December 21—Pending the deficiency bill, Mr. HARDING offered an amendment:

Provided, That no part of the moneys aforesaid shall be applied to the raising, arming, equipping, or paying of negro soldiers.

Which was disagreed to—yeas 41, nays 105. The YEAS were:

Messrs. *Ancona, Bliss, James S. Brown, Coffroth, Cox, Dawson, Denison, Eden, Edgerton, Eldridge, Finck, Grider, Hall, Harding, Harrington, Benjamin G. Harris, Charles M. Harris, Philip Johnson, William Johnson, King, Knapp, Law, Long, Marcy, McKinney, William H. Miller, James R. Morris, Morrison, Noble, John O'Neill, Pendleton, Samuel J. Randall, Rogers, Ross, Scott, Stiles, Strouse, Stuart, Chilton A. White, Joseph W. White, Yeaman*—41.

1864, March 21—Pending the army appropriation bill—On concurring in the amendment made in Committee of the Whole, viz., to add to the end of the bill the words:

Provided, That no part of the money herein appropriated shall be applied or used for the purpose of raising, arming, equipping, or paying negro soldiers.

The yeas were 18, nays 81. The YEAS were:

Messrs. *Ancona, Dawson, Denison, Eldridge, Harding, Harrington, Benjamin G. Harris, Long, Mallory, Marcy, Wm. H. Miller, Morrison, Samuel J. Randall, James S. Rollins, Ross, Stiles, Stuart, Wadsworth*—18.

Of the Democrats, Messrs. *Baily, Augustus C. Baldwin, Kernan, Odell, Radford, Stebbins, Wheeler*, and *Winfield* voted nay.

—

Homesteads For Soldiers.

First Session, Thirty-Eighth Congress.

IN HOUSE.

1863, December 17—Mr. WILSON offered the following; which was agreed to:

Resolved, That the Committee on Public Lands be instructed to inquire what legislation is necessary to enable persons in the military and naval service of the United States to avail themselves, while engaged in said service, of the benefits of the homestead act, and to report by bill or otherwise.

1864, May 11—The House considered the bill to secure to persons in the military or naval service of the United States, homesteads from confiscated estates in insurrectionary districts; and

May 12—Passed it—yeas 76, nays 65, as follows:

YEAS—Messrs. Alley, Allison, Ames, Anderson, Ashley, John D. Baldwin, Baxter, Beaman, Boutwell, Boyd, Brandegee, Broomall, Ambrose W. Clark, Freeman Clarke, Cole, Creswell, Henry Winter Davis, Dawes, Deming, Driggs, Farnsworth, Fenton, Garfield, Gooch, Grinnell, Hale, Higby, Hooper, Hotchkiss, Asahel W. Hubbard, John H. Hubbard, Hulburd, Jenckes, Julian, Kelley, Francis W. Kellogg, Orlando Kellogg, Littlejohn, Loan, Longyear, McBride, McClurg, McIndoe, Samuel F. Miller, Moorhead, Morrill, Daniel Morris, Amos Myers, Leonard Myers, Norton, Charles O'Neill, Orth, Patterson, Perham, Pike, Pomeroy, Price, Alexander H. Rice, John H. Rice, Edward H. Rollins, Schenck, Scofield, Shannon, Sloan, Smithers, Spalding, Stevens, Tracy, Upson, Van Valkenburgh, Ellihu B. Washburne, William B. Washburn, Wilder, Wilson, Windom, Woodbridge—76.

NAYS—Messrs. *William J. Allen, Ancona, Baily, Augustus C. Baldwin*, Jacob B. Blair, *Bliss, Brooks, James S. Brown*, W. G. Brown, *Chanler, Coffroth, Cox, Cravens, Dawson, Eden, Edgerton, Eldridge, English, Finck, Grider, Griswold, Hall, Harding, Harrington, Benjamin G. Harris, Herrick, Hutchins, Philip Johnson, William Johnson, Kalbfleisch, Kernan, King, Law, Lazear, Long, Mallory, Marcy, McAllister, McDowell, McKinney, Middleton, William H. Miller, James R. Morris, Morrison, Nelson, Noble, Odell, John O'Neill, Pendleton, Pruyn, Robinson, James S. Rollins, Ross, Scott, John B. Steele, Stiles, Strouse, Stuart*, Thomas, *Voorhees, Wadsworth*, Whaley, *Wheeler, Fernando Wood, Yeaman*—65.

The bill provides that all persons who have served, or may honorably serve in the army or navy of the United States for two years during the present rebellion, or have been or shall be discharged by reason of wounds or disease, shall be entitled to enter eighty acres, or less; and all who have rendered or shall render honorable service as soldiers or sailors in the army or navy, or as laborers therein, shall be entitled to forty acres, of all lands condemned under the confiscation act of July 17, 1862, and its amendments, and of all lands sold under the internal revenue law, and the direct tax law for insurrectionary districts. No distinction of color or race shall be made. In case of the death of the person entering lands, the required proof and payments may be made by his legal representatives.

This bill was not taken up in the Senate.

PREVIOUS ACTION ON THE SUBJECT.

1864, March 18—The House considered Senate bill amendatory of the homestead law and for other purposes, when

Mr. HOLMAN offered the following amendment:

Provided, however, That no non-commissioned officer or private soldier or seaman who shall be at the time of such entry in the military or naval service of the United States, or who shall have been in such service for a period not less than three months and honorably discharged therefrom, shall be required to pay the ten dollars fee or the commissions mentioned in this act and the act to which this is an amendment: *And provided further*, That any such non-commissioned officer, private soldier, or seaman, being a citizen of the United States, or having declared his intention to become a citizen thereof in conformity with law, and having served in the military or naval service of the United States for a period of not less than two years and been honorably discharged, having made an entry of land in conformity with this act and the act to which this is amendatory, shall be entitled to the patent therefor at any time after having resided on and cultivated such land for a period of one year, and the widow, if unmarried, or if no widow, the children of such non-commissioned officer, private soldier, or seaman, shall be entitled to such patent on like condition.

Which was disagreed to—yeas 54, nays 58, as follows:

YEAS—Messrs. *James C. Allen, Ancona*, Anderson, *Augustus C. Baldwin*, Jacob B. Blair, *Bliss, James S. Brown, Chanler, Clay, Coffroth*, Creswell, *Dawson, Denison*, Dumont, *Eldridge, Hall, Harding, Harrington, Charles M. Harris, Herrick, Holman, Kalbfleisch, Kernan, Law, Long, Mallory, Marcy, Middleton*, Daniel Morris, *Morrison*, Amos Myers, *Noble, Odell, John O'Neill*, Orth, *Pendleton, Perry, Pruyn, Radford, Samuel J. Randall, James S. Rollins, Ross*, Smith, *Stebbins, John B. Steele, Stiles, Strouse, Stuart, Wadsworth, Ward*, Webster, Whaley, *Wheeler, Yeaman*—54.

NAYS—Messrs. Alley, Allison, Ames, Ashley, John D. Baldwin, Baxter, Beaman, Boutwell, Brandegee, Broomall, Ambrose W. Clark, Cobb, Cole, Henry Winter Davis, Thomas T. Davis, Dawes, Deming, Donnelly, Driggs, Eckley, Eliot, Fenton, Frank, Gooch, Higby, Hotchkiss, John H. Hubbard,

Julian, Kasson, Kelley, Francis W. Kellogg, Loan, Longyear, Marvin, McBride, McClurg, Samuel F. Miller, Moorhead, Leonard Myers, Norton, Perham, Pike, Price, Alexander H. Rice, John H. Rice, Schenck, Scofield, Shannon, Smithers, Spalding, Starr, Stevens, Thayer, Upson, Ellihu B. Washburne, Wilder, Wilson, Windom—58.

The bill then passed.

Unemployed Generals.

1863, December 13—Mr. FARNSWORTH offered this resolution, which was agreed to:

Resolved, That the Secretary of War be directed to inform this House of the names, number, pay, and emoluments of major generals and brigadier generals of volunteers, and of the regular army, and their staffs respectively, not on duty, and the length of time which has elapsed since each of them has been relieved from duty, and which of them, and how many, are not now on duty in consequence of wounds or disability incurred in the service.

The Secretary of War replied, substantially, that twenty-five general officers—fourteen major generals and eleven brigadier generals—were entirely unemployed, and that certain officers of their personal staffs were also unemployed with them, numbering twenty-five. At the same time another list was furnished of general officers on duty who were not actually commanding or serving with troops, amounting in number to thirty-nine, making an aggregate of eighty-nine officers reported as being either unemployed altogether or not employed in the command of troops.

A similar resolution was adopted in the Senate, on motion of Mr. TRUMBULL:

Resolved, That the Secretary of War be directed to furnish the Senate with the names of all the major and brigadier generals who are without commands equal to a brigade, stating how long each has been without such command, and whether each has a staff; and if so, how numerous, and of what rank, and what amount of pay, including commutations and rations, each, including those of his staff, has been receiving while so without a command; and also that he inform the Senate how many major and brigadier generals are in command of departments, districts, and posts in the loyal States; and whether any necessity exists that requires that these departments, districts, and posts should be commanded by officers of such high rank, with their numerous and expensive staffs.

1864, January 18—Mr. HOLMAN offered this preamble and resolution; which were agreed to:

Whereas this House has been officially informed that a large number of officers of the army, including a number of major and brigadier generals, have been for a long period of time, relieved from active service, while still receiving the full pay pertaining to their rank; and whereas such policy, while embarrassing to the officers so relieved, is manifestly unjust to the country, and interferes with just and proper promotions in the army: Therefore,

Resolved, That, in the judgment of this House, the policy of retaining in the pay of the Government officers who have been indefinitely relieved from active service, not physically disabled by wounds, and who have not been placed on the retired list, ought to be discontinued; and that the Committee on Military Affairs be instructed to inquire what legislation, if any, is necessary to effect a remedy in the premises, and reduce the number of general officers not employed in active service, and report by bill or otherwise.

May 12—The House resumed consideration of the joint resolution providing that all major and brigadier generals, who, on the 1st of July, 1864, shall not be in the performance of duty or service corresponding to their respective grades and rank, and who shall not have been engaged in such duty or service for three months continuously next prior to that date, shall then be dropped from the rolls of the army—no officer to be included whose absence from duty shall have been occasioned by wounds received, or disease contracted in the line of his duty while in the military service or while a prisoner. This to vacate volunteer commissions only.

Mr. Cox moved to add this proviso:

Provided, That when any officer comprehended in this act shall demand a board of inquiry according to the rules and regulations in such cases, and who shall be willing to serve, that such board shall be forthwith convened; and if said board shall find him competent to command in the rank to which he is entitled, he shall be at once restored to active service with full pay: *And provided further*, That all officers who have received the thanks of Congress during the present war shall be exempted from the provisions of this act.

Which was disagreed to—yeas 46, nays 69.

Mr. KERNAN offered a substitute providing for a board to examine into the competency, fitness, and efficiency of major and brigadier generals, as described in the joint resolution; and each officer found by the board to be incapable of properly and efficiently following his duties shall be dropped, &c.; which was disagreed to—yeas 50, nays 69.

The joint resolution was then passed—yeas 72, nays 45, as follows:

YEAS—Messrs. Alley, Allison, Ames, Anderson, Arnold, Ashley, John D. Baldwin, Baxter, Beaman, Jacob B. Blair, Boutwell, Boyd, Ambrose W. Clark, Freeman Clarke, Cole, Creswell, Henry Winter Davis, Deming, Driggs, Eliot, Farnsworth, Garfield, Gooch, Grinnell, Higby, Hotchkiss, Jenckes, Julian, Kasson, Kelley, Francis W. Kellogg, Littlejohn, Loan, Longyear, McBride, McClurg, McIndoe, Moorhead, Morrill, Daniel Morris, Amos Myers, Leonard Myers, Norton, Charles O'Neill, Orth, Patterson, Perham, Pike, Pomeroy, Price, William H. Randall, Alexander H. Rice, John H. Rice, Edward H. Rollins, Schenck, Scofield, Shannon, Sloan, Smithers, Spalding, Thomas, Tracy, Upson, Van Valkenburgh, William B. Washburn, Webster, Whaley, Wilder, Wilson, Windom, Woodbridge, *Yeaman*—72.

NAYS—Messrs. *Ancona, Baily, Augustus C. Baldwin, Brooks, James S. Brown*, William G. Brown, *Chanler, Cravens, Eden, Edgerton, Eldridge, English, Finck, Grider, Hall, Harrington, Herrick, Hutchins, Philip Johnson, Kalbfleisch, Kernan, King, Long, Mallory, Marcy, McKinney, Middleton, William H. Miller, James R. Morris, Morrison, Noble, Odell, John O'Neill, Pendleton, Pruyn, Robinson, Ross, Scott, John B. Steele*, Stevens, *Stiles, Stuart, Wadsworth, Wheeler, Fernando Wood*—45.

The Senate did not consider the bill.

Resolutions relating to the War.

ITS OBJECT.

First Session, Thirty-Seventh Congress.

IN HOUSE.

1861, July 13—Mr. HOLMAN asked leave to offer these resolutions:

Resolved, That the sole object of the Government in its present and future military operations, resulting from the armed resistance to its authority, is, and ought to be, to maintain the integrity of the Union, as established by the Constitution, the enforcement of the laws, and the protection of the constitutional rights of the loyal citizens of every State; and such operations ought not to be suspended until the authority of the Federal Government shall have been firmly established throughout its territorial limits.

Resolved, That the Union must be preserved, and that no adjustment of pending difficulties can ever be sanctioned by the Government that is not based on the acknowledged integrity of the Union, and the supremacy of the Constitution of the United States.

Leave was not obtained.

1861, July 15—Mr. ALLEN, of Ohio, offered the following resolutions:

Resolved, That whenever the States now in rebellion against the General Government shall cease their rebellion and become loyal to the Union, it is the duty of the Government to suspend the further prosecution of the present war.

Resolved, That it is no part of the object of the present war against the rebellious States to interfere with the institution of slavery therein.

Which were ruled out of order by the Speaker.

August 5—Mr. ALLEN moved to suspend the rules, that he might offer a similar resolution, but it was disagreed to.

1861, July 22—Mr. NOBLE, of Ohio, offered this resolution:

Resolved, That the contest now existing between the Government of the United States and the disloyal organizations now existing in certain States which are now waging an unjustifiable war upon the constitutional authority of the Government, should be treated and regarded by all loyal citizens not as a sectional war, nor an anti-slavery war, nor a war of conquest or subjugation, but simply as a war for the maintenance of the Government, the suppression of rebellion, and the preservation of all the rights of all the States full and undiminished, as they were purchased by the blood of the Revolution of 1776, and secured by all the provisions and compromises of the Federal Constitution, and for no other purpose whatever.

The resolution went over, Mr. BURNETT indicating a desire to debate it. It was not again reached.

1861, July 22—Mr. CRITTENDEN offered the following resolution:

Resolved, That the present deplorable civil war has been forced upon the country by the disunionists of the southern States now in revolt against the constitutional Government and in arms around the capital; that in this national emergency Congress, banishing all feeling of mere passion or resentment, will recollect only its duty to the whole country; that this war is not waged upon our part in any spirit of oppression, nor for any purpose of conquest or subjugation, nor purpose of overthrowing or interfering with the rights or established institutions of those States; but to defend and maintain the supremacy of the Constitution and to preserve the Union with all the dignity, equality, and rights of the several States unimpaired; that as soon as these objects are accomplished the war ought to cease.

The question being divided,

The House adopted the first clause of the resolution:

Resolved, That the present deplorable civil war has been forced upon the country by the disunionists of the southern States now in revolt against the constitutional Government, and in arms around the capital.

Yeas 122, nays 2, as follows:

YEAS—Messrs. Aldrich, *Allen*, Alley, Ashley, Babbitt, Goldsmith F. Bailey, *Joseph Baily*, Baker, Baxter, Beaman, Bingham, Francis P. Blair, jr., Samuel S. Blair, Blake, Buffinton, *Calvert*, Campbell, Chamberlain, Clark, *Cobb*, Colfax, Frederick A. Conkling, Roscoe Conkling, Conway, *Cox*, *Crittenden*, Curtis, Cutler, Davis, Dawes, Delano, *Delaplaine*, Diven, Duell, *Dunlap*, Dunn, Edgerton, Edwards, *English*, Fenton, Fessenden, Franchot, Frank, Gooch, Granger, *Grider*, Gurley, *Haight*, Hale, *Harding*, Harrison, *Holman*, Horton, Hutchins, Jackson, Julian, Kelley, Wm. Kellogg, Killinger, Lansing, *Law*, Leary, *Lehman*, Loomis, Lovejoy, *McClernand*, McKean, *Mallory*, *Menzies*, Moorhead, Anson P. Morrill, Justin S. Morrill, *Morris*, Nixon, *Noble*, *Nugen*, *Odell*, Olin, Patton, *Pendleton*, *Perry*, Pike, Pomeroy, Porter, Potter, Alexander H. Rice, John H. Rice, Riddle, Edward H. Rollins, *James S. Rollins*, *Sheffield*, Shellabarger, Sherman, Sloan, *Smith*, Spaulding, *John B. Steele*, *William G. Steele*, Stratton, Francis Thomas, Train, Trowbridge, Upton, Vandever, Van Valkenburgh, Van Wyck, Verree, *Vibbard*, *Wadsworth*, Charles W. Walton, E. P. Walton, *Ward*, Webster, Wheeler, Whaley, Albert S. White, *Chilton A. White*, *Wickliffe*, Windom, *Woodruff*, Worcester, *Wright*—122.

NAYS—Messrs. *Burnett*, *Reid*—2.

The second clause of the resolution:

That in this national emergency Congress, banishing all feeling of mere passion or resentment, will recollect only its duty to the whole country; that this war is not waged upon our part in any spirit of oppression, or for any purpose of conquest or subjugation, or purpose of overthrowing or interfering with the rights or established institutions of those States, but to defend and maintain the supremacy of the Constitution and to preserve the Union with all the dignity, equality, and rights of the several States unimpaired; and that as soon as these objects are accomplished the war ought to cease.

Was adopted—yeas 119, nays 2, as follows:

YEAS—Messrs. Aldrich, *Allen*, Alley, Babbitt, Goldsmith F. Bailey, *Joseph Baily*, Baxter, Beaman, Francis P. Blair, Samuel S. Blair, Blake, *George H. Browne*, Buffinton *Calvert*, Campbell, Chamberlain, Clark, *Cobb*, Colfax, F. A. Conkling, Roscoe Conkling, *Cooper*, *Corning*, *Cox*, *Crittenden*, Curtis, Cutler, Dawes, Delano, Diven, Duell, *Dunlap*, Dunn, Edwards, *English*, Fenton, Fessenden, *Fouke*, Franchot, Frank, Gooch, Granger, *Grider*, Gurley, *Haight*, Hale, *Harding*, Harrison, *Holman*, Horton, Jackson, *Johnson*, Kelley, William Kellogg, Killinger, *Law*, *Lazear*, Leary, *Lehman*, *Logan*, Loomis, *McClernand*, *Mallory*, *Menzies*, Mitchell, Moorhead, Anson P. Morrill, Justin S. Morrill, *Morris*, Nixon, *Noble*, *Nugen*, *Odell*, Olin, Patton, *Pendleton*, *Perry*, Pike, Pomeroy, Porter, *Reid*, Alexander H. Rice, John H. Rice, *Richardson*, *Robinson*, Edward H. Rollins, *James S. Rollins*, *Sheffield*, Shellabarger, Sherman, *Smith*, Spaulding, *John B. Steele*, *William G. Steele*, Stratton, Francis Thomas, Train, Trowbridge, Upton, *Vallandigham*, Van Horn, Van Valkenburgh, Van Wyck, Verree, *Vibbard*, *Wadsworth*, Charles W. Walton, E. P. Walton, *Ward*, Webster, Wheeler, Whaley, Albert S. White, *Chilton A. White*, *Wickliffe*, Windom, *Woodruff*, Worcester, *Wright*—119.

NAYS—Messrs. Potter, Riddle—2.

1861, July 24—Mr. JOHNSON, of Tennessee, offered substantially the same resolution in the Senate, which was ordered to be printed.

July 25—Mr. POLK, of Missouri, moved to strike out and insert so as to make the first clause close thus: by "the disunionists of the Southern *and the Northern States*;" which was disagreed to—yeas 4, nays 33, as follows:

YEAS—Messrs. *Johnson* of Missouri, *Kennedy*, *Polk*, *Saulsbury*—4.

NAYS—Messrs. Anthony, Bingham, Browning, Clark, Collamer, Cowan, Dixon, Doolittle, Fessenden, Foster, Grimes, Hale, Harlan, Harris, Howe, *Johnson* of Tennessee, King, Lane of Indiana, Lane of Kansas, *Latham*, Morrill, *Nesmith*, Pomeroy, Sherman, Simmons, Sumner, Ten Eyck, Trumbull, Wade, Wilkinson, Willey, Wilmot, Wilson—33.

Mr. TRUMBULL moved to strike out the words, "and in arms around the capital," and the word "subjugation," which was rejected.

The resolution was then passed—yeas 30, nays 5, as follows:

YEAS—Messrs. Anthony, Browning, Chandler, Clark, Cowan, Dixon, Doolittle, Fessenden, Foot, Foster, Grimes, Harlan, Harris, Howe, *Johnson* of Tennessee, *Kennedy*, King, Lane of Indiana, Lane of Kansas, *Latham*, Morrill, *Nesmith*, Pomeroy, *Saulsbury*, Sherman, Ten Eyck, Wade, Wilkinson, Willey, Wilson—30.

NAYS—Messrs. *Breckinridge*, *Johnson* of Missouri, *Polk*, *Powell*, Trumbull—5.

1861, July 31—Mr. PENDLETON, of Ohio, offered this joint resolution:

Resolved, That, under the Constitution, the rights, powers, and duties of all the States of the Union are equal; that the Union is founded in this equality; that in order to maintain the Constitution and the Union, this equality must be preserved; that every honest effort to perpetuate the Union must be made in accordance with the Constitution, and with a purpose to maintain this equality; that an attempt on the part of the Federal Government to subjugate any of the States, and hold them as territories or provinces, or in any position inferior to that of every other State, or to interfere with their State governments, or with their domestic institutions, or to abolish or interfere with slavery within their limits, would be an attempt to destroy this equality, and would, if successful, subvert the Constitution and the Union.

Resolved, therefore, &c., That Congress does hereby solemnly declare that hostilities against the so-called confederate States shall be so prosecuted as to enforce obedience to the obligations of the Constitution, and the laws passed in accordance therewith; and that they shall not be so prosecuted as to reduce to a position of inferiority any of the States, or to interfere with their State governments, or to abolish slavery within their limits.

Ruled out of order by the Speaker.

—

Second Session, Thirty-Seventh Congress.

1861, December 2—Mr. ELIOT offered this joint resolution:

Resolved, &c, 1. That in behalf of the people of these States, we do again solemnly declare that the war in which we are engaged against the insurgent bodies now in arms against the Government has for its object the suppression of such rebellion and the re-establishment of the rightful authority of the National Constitution and laws over the entire extent of our common country. 2. That while we disclaim all power under the Constitution to interfere, by ordinary legislation, with the institutions of the several States, yet the war now existing must be conducted according to the usages and rights of military service, and that during its continuance the recognized authority of the maxim that the safety of the State is the highest law, subordinates rights of property and dominates over civil relations. 3. That therefore we do hereby declare that, in our judgment, the President of the United States, as the commander-in-chief of our army, and the officers in command under him, have the right to emancipate all persons held as slaves in any military district in a state of insurrection against the National Government, and that we respectfully advise that such order of emancipation be issued whenever the same will avail to weaken the power of the rebels in arms, or to strengthen the military power of the loyal forces.

Mr. DUNN moved that it be tabled, which was disagreed to—yeas 56, nays 70, as follows:

YEAS—Messrs. *Allen, Ancona, Joseph Baily, Biddle,* Francis P. Blair, Jacob B. Blair, Burnham, *Calvert,* Campbell, *Cobb,* Conway, *Corning, Cox, Cravens,* Delano, *Dunlap,* Dunn, *Fouke, Haight, Harding,* Harrison, *Holman,* Horton, Wm. Kellogg, *Law, Lazear,* Leary, *Lehman,* McPherson, Maynard, *May, Menzies, Morris, Noble, Noell, Norton, Odell, Pendleton, Perry,* Alexander H. Rice, *Richardson, Robinson, Sheffield, Shiel,* Smith, *John B. Steele, William G. Steele,* Benjamin F. Thomas, Train, Trimble, Upton, *Vallandigham,* Verree, *Ward, Chilton A. White, Woodruff*—56.

NAYS—Messrs. Aldrich, Alley, Arnold, Ashley, Babbitt, Goldsmith F. Bailey, Baker, Baxter, Beaman, Bingham, S. S. Blair, Blake, Buffinton, Clark, Colfax, F. A. Conkling, Roscoe Conkling, Davis, Dawes, Duell, Edgerton, Edwards, Eliot, Fessenden, Franchot, Frank, Goodwin, Granger, Gurley, Hickman, Hooper, Hutchins, Julian, Kelley, Lansing, Loomis, Lovejoy, McKean, Mitchell, Anson P. Morrill, Justin S. Morrill, Patton, T. G. Phelps, Pike, Pomeroy, Porter, Potter, John H. Rice, Riddle, Edward H. Rollins, Sargent, Sedgwick, Shanks, Shellabarger, Sherman, Sloan, Spaulding, Stevens, Trowbridge, Van Horn, Van Valkenburgh, Van Wyck, Wall, Wallace, Chas. W. Walton, E. P. Walton, Washburne, Wheeler, Wilson, Worcester—70.

Mr. ROSCOE CONKLING moved to insert in the third resolution, after the word "slaves," the words, "held by rebels;" which was agreed to.

It was then postponed; and December 17th, was referred to the Committee on the Judiciary—yeas 77, nays 57.

Same day, Mr. CAMPBELL offered this resolution:

Resolved, That in legislating to meet the exigencies of the present rebellion, Congress should confiscate the property, slaves included, of all rebels, and protect the property and rights, under the Constitution and laws, of all loyal citizens.

Which was postponed for the present.

Same day, Mr. STEVENS offered this preamble and resolution:

Whereas slavery has caused the present rebellion in the United States; and whereas there can be no solid and permanent peace and union in this Republic so long as that institution exists within it; and whereas slaves are now used by the rebels as an essential means of supporting and protracting the war; and whereas by the law of nations it is right to liberate the slaves of an enemy to weaken his power: Therefore,

Be it resolved by the Senate and House of Representatives of the United States of America in Congress assembled, That the President be requested to declare free, and to direct all of our generals and officers in command to order freedom to all slaves who shall leave their masters, or who shall aid in quelling this rebellion.

SEC. 2. *And be it further resolved,* That the United States pledge the faith of the Union to make full and fair compensation to all loyal citizens who are and shall remain active in supporting the Union for all the loss they may sustain by virtue of this act.

Which, also, was postponed for the present.

Dec. 4—Mr. HOLMAN offered the following resolution:

Whereas this House, on the 22d day of July last, by an almost unanimous vote, adopted the following resolution submitted to the House by Hon. J. J. CRITTENDEN, of Kentucky:

Resolved by the House of Representives of the Congress of the United States, That the present deplorable civil war, has been forced upon the country by the disunionists of the southern States now in revolt against the constitutional Government and in arms around the capital; that in this national emergency Congress, banishing all feelings of mere passion or resentment, will recollect only its duty to the whole country; that this war is not waged upon our part in any spirit of oppression nor for any purpose of conquest or subjugation, nor for the purpose of overthrowing or interfering with the rights or established institutions of the States, but to defend and maintain the supremacy of the Constitution and to preserve the Union with its dignities, equality, and the rights of the several States unimpaired, and that as soon as these objects are accomplished the war ought to cease.

And whereas since that time no event has occurred to change the policy of the Government: Therefore,

Resolved, That the principles above expressed are solemnly reaffirmed by this House.

Which was laid upon the table—yeas 71, nays 65, as follows:

YEAS—Messrs. Aldrich, Alley, Arnold, Ashley, Goldsmith F. Bailey, Baker, Baxter, Beaman, Bingham, Francis P. Blair, Samuel S. Blair, Blake, Buffinton, Burnham, Chamberlain, Clark, Colfax, Frederick A. Conkling, Conway, Davis, *Delaplaine,* Duell, Edgerton, Edwards, Eliot, Fenton, Fessenden, Franchot, Gooch, Gurley, Hooper, Hutchins, Julian, Kelley, Lansing, Loomis, Lovejoy, McPherson, Moorhead, Anson P. Morrill, Justin S. Morrill, Olin, Patton, T. G. Phelps, Pike, Pomeroy, Potter, John H. Rice, Riddle, Edward H. Rollins, Sargent, Sedgwick, Shanks, Sherman, Sloan, Spaulding, Stevens, Train, Trimble, Trowbridge, Van Horn, Verree, Wall, Wallace, Charles W. Walton, E. P. Walton, Washburne, Wheeler, Albert S. White, Wilson, Worcester—71.

NAYS—Messrs. *Allen, Ancona, Joseph Baily, Biddle,* Jacob B. Blair, *Calvert,* Campbell, *Cobb, Corning, Cox, Cravens, Crisfield,* Dawes, Delano, Diven, *Dunlap,* Dunn, *English, Fouke,* Frank, Goodwin, Granger, *Grider,* Hanchett, *Harding,* Harrison, *Holman,* Horton, William Kellogg, *Law, Lazear,* Leary, *Lehman,* McKnight, Maynard, *Menzies,* Mitchell, *Morris,* Nixon, *Noble, Noell, Norton, Odell, Pendleton, Perry,* Porter, *Richardson, Sheffield,* Shellabarger, *Shiel, Smith, John B. Steele, William G. Steele,* Stratton, Benjamin F. Thomas, Francis Thomas, Upton, Van Valkenburgh, *Wadsworth, Ward,* Webster, *Chilton A. White, Wickliffe, Woodruff, Wright*—65.

1862, January 20—Mr. ALLEN, of Ohio, offered the following resolution:

Resolved, That, in the judgment of this House, no part of the appropriation now made or hereafter made, nor of the taxes now or hereafter laid by Congress should be used in or applied to the prosecution of a war for the purpose of the emancipation of slaves in the slaveholding States of the Union.

Which was laid upon the table—yeas 90, nays 36, as follows:

YEAS—Messrs. Aldrich, Alley, Arnold, Babbitt, Goldsmith F. Bailey, Baker, Baxter, Beaman, Bingham, Francis P. Blair, Blake, Buffinton, Burnham, Campbell, Chamberlain, Clark, Clements, Colfax, Frederick A. Conkling, Roscoe Conkling, Conway, Cutler, Davis, Dawes, Delano, Duell, Dunn, Edgerton, Edwards, Eliot, Fenton, Fessenden, Frank, Granger, Gurley, Hale, Hanchett, Hooper, Horton, Hutchins, Kelley, Francis W. Kellogg, William Kellogg, Killinger, Lansing, Loomis, Lovejoy, McKean, McKnight, McPherson, Marston, Mitchell, Moorhead, Anson P. Morrill, Justin S. Morrill, Nixon, Olin, Patton, Timothy G. Phelps, Pomeroy, Porter, Alexander H. Rice, Riddle, Edward H. Rollins, Sargent, Shanks, *Sheffield,* Sherman, Sloan, Spaulding, Stevens, Stratton, Benjamin F. Thomas, Train, Trimble, Trowbridge, Van Horn, Van Valkenburgh, Van Wyck, Verree, Wall, Wallace, Charles W. Walton, E. P. Walton, Washburne, Wheeler, Albert S. White, Wilson, Windom, Worcester—90.

NAYS—Messrs. *Allen, Ancona, Joseph Baily,* Jacob B. Blair, William G. Brown, *Calvert, Cobb, Corning, Cravens, Crisfield, English, Fouke, Haight,* Harrison, *Holman, Johnson, Knapp, Law, Lazear,* Leary, *Morris, Noble, Norton, Nugen, Robinson, James S. Rollins, Shiel, John B. Steele, William G. Steele, Vallandigham, Vibbard, Voorhees, Chilton A. White, Wickliffe, Woodruff, Wright*—36.

1862, March 3—Mr. HOLMAN offered the following resolution:

Resolved, That in the judgment of this House, the unfortunate civil war into which the Government of the United States has been forced by the treasonable attempt of the southern secessionists to destroy the Union, should not be prosecuted for any other purpose than the restoration of the authority of the Constitution, and that the welfare of the whole people of the United States is permanently involved in maintaining the present form of Government under the Constitution, without modification or change.

Which was laid on the table—yeas 59, nays 59, as follows:

YEAS—Messrs. Aldrich, Alley, Arnold, Ashley, Babbitt, Baker, Baxter, Beaman, Bingham, Samuel S. Blair, Blake, Buffinton, Burnham, Campbell, Chamberlain, Clark, Colfax, Frederick A. Conkling, Roscoe Conkling, Conway, Cutler, Davis, Delano, Duell, Ely, Fessenden, Franchot, Frank, Hooper, Hutchins, Francis W. Kellogg, Lansing, Loomis, Lovejoy, McKnight, McPherson, Mitchell, Moorhead, Anson P. Morrill, Justin S. Morrill, Patton, Pike, Pomeroy, John H. Rice, Riddle, Sargent, Sedgwick, Shanks, Stevens, Trowbridge, Van Wyck, Verree, Wallace, Charles W. Walton, Wheeler, Albert S. White, Wilson, Windom, Worcester —59.

NAYS—Messrs. *Joseph Baily*, *Biddle*, Jacob B. Blair, *George H. Browne*, Wm. G. Brown, *Calvert*, Clements, *Cobb*, *Corning*, *Cox*, *Cravens*, *Crisfield*, *Crittenden*, Diven, *Dunlap*, Dunn, Goodwin, Granger, Hale, *Hall*, *Harding*, Harrison, *Holman*, Horton, *Johnson*, William Kellogg, *Knapp*, *Law*, *Lazear*, Leary, *Mallory*, Maynard, *Menzies*, Nixon, *Noble*, *Noell*, *Norton*, *Nugen*, *Odell*, *Pendleton*, *Perry*, *Richardson*, *Robinson*, *James S. Rollins*, *Sheffield*, Shellabarger, *Smith*, *John B. Steele*, Stratton, Benjamin F. Thomas, Francis Thomas, Trimble, *Vibbard*, *Wadsworth*, Webster, Whaley, *Wickliffe*, *Woodruff*, *Wright*—59.

The Speaker, (Mr. GROW,) voted aye, and the resolution was tabled.

IN SENATE.

1861, December 20—Mr. WILLEY introduced the following, which was not acted upon:

Resolved, That the existing war, forced upon the country by the instigators of the rebellion without justifiable cause or provocation, was, and is, designed by them to destroy the Union and the Constitution; and their purpose, moreover, was at first, and is now, to disavow and repudiate the fundamental principles of republican government on which our fathers established the Union and the Constitution.

1861, December 16—Mr. TEN EYCK offered this resolution:

Resolved, That the present war is for the Union, according to the Constitution; that its object is to save the former and enforce the latter—was so in the beginning, is now as carried on, and should be, to the last; that measures, extreme and radical, disruptive in themselves, involving in a common fate as well the loyal as disloyal, should not be resorted to; and that in crushing treason—wide-spread and hateful as it is—the Government itself cannot prove traitor to organic law.

Third Session, Thirty-Seventh Congress.

IN HOUSE.

1862, Dec. 4—Mr. STEVENS offered the following resolutions:

Resolved, That this Union must be, and remain, one and indivisible forever.

2. That if any person in the employment of the United States, in either the legislative or executive branch, should propose to make peace, or should accept, or advise the acceptance, of any such proposition on any other basis than the integrity and entire unity of the United States and their Territories as they existed at the time of the rebellion, he will be guilty of a high crime.

3. That this Government can never accept the mediation or permit the intervention of any foreign nation, during this rebellion, in our domestic affairs.

4. That no two Governments can ever be permitted to exist within the territory now belonging to the United States, and which acknowledged their jurisdiction at the time of the insurrection.

Which were read, and postponed for the present.

Same day, Mr. WICKLIFFE offered this amendment, which, being out of order, was not entertained:

That any officer of the United States, either executive, legislative, or judicial, who is opposed to close the present war upon preserving the Constitution as it is, with all its guarantees and privileges, and the union of the States as established by said Constitution, is unworthy to hold such office, and should be dismissed or removed from the same.

1862, December 5—Mr. VALLANDIGHAM offered the following resolutions:

1. *Resolved*, That the Union as it was must be restored and maintained one and indivisible forever under the Constitution as it is—the fifth article, providing for amendments, included.

2. That if any person in the civil or military service of the United States shall propose terms of peace, or accept or advise the acceptance of any such terms, on any other basis than the integrity and entirety of the Federal Union, and of the several States composing the same, and the Territories of the Union, as at the beginning of the civil war, he will be guilty of a high crime.

3. That this Government can never permit the intervention of any foreign nation in regard to the present civil war.

4. That the unhappy civil war in which we are engaged was waged in the beginning, professedly, not in any spirit of oppression or for any purpose of conquest or subjugation, or purpose of overthrowing or interfering with the rights or established institutions of those States, but to defend and maintain the supremacy of the Constitution and to preserve the Union with all the dignity, equality, and rights of the several States unimpaired, and was so understood and accepted by the people, and especially by the army and navy of the United States; and that, therefore, whoever shall pervert, or attempt to pervert, the same to a war of conquest and subjugation, or for the overthrowing or interfering with the rights or established institutions of any of the States, and to abolish slavery therein, or for the purpose of destroying or impairing the dignity, equality, or rights of any of the States, will be guilty of a flagrant breach of public faith and of a high crime against the Constitution and the Union.

5. That whoever shall propose by Federal authority to extinguish any of the States of this Union, or to declare any of them extinguished, and to establish territorial governments within the same, will be guilty of a high crime against the Constitution and the Union.

6. That whoever shall affirm that it is competent for this House or any other authority to establish a dictatorship in the United States, thereby superseding or suspending the constitutional authorities of the Union, and shall proceed to make any move toward the declaring of a dictator, will be guilty of a high crime against the Constitution and the Union and public liberty.

Which were laid upon the table—yeas 79, nays 50, as follows:

YEAS—Messrs. Aldrich, Arnold, Ashley, Babbitt, Baker, Baxter, Beaman, Bingham, Samuel S. Blair, Blake, Buffinton, Chamberlain, Clark, Colfax, Frederick A. Conkling, Roscoe Conkling, Covode, Cutler, Davis, Dawes, Delano, Duell, Edgerton, Eliot, Ely, Fenton, Samuel C. Fessenden, Thomas A. D. Fessenden, Fisher, Franchot, Frank, Goodwin, Gurley, Hale, Harrison, Hickman, Hooper, Horton, Hutchins, Julian, Kelley, Francis W. Kellogg, Loomis, Lovejoy, Low, McPherson, Mitchell, Moorhead, Justin S. Morrill, Nixon, Pike, Pomeroy, Porter, Potter, John H. Rice, Riddle, Edward H. Rollins, Sargent, Sedgwick, Shanks, Shellabarger, Sherman, Sloan, Spaulding, Stevens, Stratton, Benjamin F. Thomas, Train, Trowbridge, Van Horn, Van Valkenburgh, Van Wyck, Walker, Wall, Wallace, Washburne, Wilson, Windom, Worcester—79.

NAYS—Messrs. *William J. Allen*, *Ancona*, *Bailey*, *Biddle*, William G. Brown, Clements, *Cobb*, Conway, *Corning*, *Cox*, *Cravens*, *Crisfield*, *Dunlap*, *English*, *Fouke*, Granger, *Grider*, *Hall*, *Harding*, *Holman*, *Johnson*, *Knapp*, *Law*, *Lazear*, Leary, *Mallory*, Maynard, *Menzies*, *Noble*, *Norton*, *Nugen*, *Pendleton*, *Perry*, *Price*, *Richardson*, *Robinson*, *Sheffield*, *Shiel*, *Smith*, *John B. Steele*, *William G. Steele*, *Stiles*, *Vallandigham*, *Vibbard*, *Voorhees*, *Chilton A. White*, *Wickliffe*, *Woodruff*, *Wright*, *Yeaman*—50.

1862, December 8—Mr. WRIGHT offered the following joint resolutions:

Resolved, &c., That the rebellion, on the part of the seceding States, against the Government and laws of this Union, was deliberately wicked, and without reasonable cause; the compact of the Union being perpetual, no State has the constitutional power to forcibly secede, and that there was no grievance, real or imaginary, upon the part of the seceding States, for the redress of which the Constitution does not furnish ample remedies.

2. That the rebellion being in contravention of the Constitution and laws, it is the duty of the Government to put it down, without regard to cost, or the consequences that may befall those engaged in it, and all necessary constitutional means for this purpose, and this alone, should be furnished by the people. That inasmuch as the great and wicked crime invoked the power of the sword, the war should be prosecuted with all the vigor and strength and

means of the Federal Government till rebellion be subdued, and no longer.

3. That an honorable peace is desirable; but no peace while armed opposition menaces the Capital and threatens the overthrow of the Union; nor that peace which would be established upon the dismembered fragments of a mighty and prosperous nation; and that man who would entertain peace upon these conditions is a traitor to his country, and unworthy the protection of its laws.

4. That the war was inaugurated *solely* for the suppression of the rebellion, and the restoration of the Union as it was; that any and all attempts to change or divert this line of policy is a fraud upon the nation, a fraud upon the memory of the gallant men who have sacrificed their lives, and a fraud upon the living soldiers who now stand up as a wall between their loved country and its wicked invaders.

5. That the value of dollars and cents does not enter into the momentous question of the maintenance of popular liberty, or the preservation of a free Government, any more than the lives and comfort of the traitors who have conspired or leagued together for their destruction.

6. That the Union restored the war should cease, and the seceding States be received back into the Union with all the privileges and immunities to which they were originally entitled.

Mr. LOVEJOY moved to table them, which was rejected—yeas 43, nays 68, as follows:

YEAS—Messrs. Aldrich, Alley, Baxter, Beaman, Bingham, Samuel S. Blair, Buffinton, Chamberlain, Frederick A. Conkling, Cutler, Davis, Dawes, Edgerton, Eliot, Ely, Samuel C. Fessenden, Thomas A. D. Fessenden, Gooch, Goodwin, Gurley, Hooper, Horton, Hutchins, Julian, Francis W. Kellogg, Lovejoy, Anson P. Morrill, Justin S. Morrill, Pike, Potter, John H. Rice, Sargent, Sedgwick, Sloan, Spaulding, Stevens, Train, Van Horn, Walker, Wall, Albert S. White, Wilson, Windom—43

NAYS—Messrs. *Ancona*, Babbitt, *Baily*, Jacob B. Blair, Blake, William G. Brown, Burnham, Campbell, Clark, Clements, *Cobb*, Conway, *Cox*, *Cravens*, *Crisfield*, *Crittenden*, Duell, *Dunlap*, Dunn, Edwards, Frank, Granger, *Grider*, Hale, *Hall*, *Harding*, *Holman*, *Johnson*, William Kellogg, *Knapp*, *Law*, *Lazear*, Loomis, Low, McKnight, *Mallory*, *Menzies*, Moorhead, *Morris*, Nixon, *Noble*, Olin, Patton, *Pendleton*, *Price*, Alexander H. Rice, Edward H. Rollins, *Sheffield*, Shellabarger, Sherman, *Smith*, *John B. Steele*, *Wm. G. Steele*. *Stiles*, Stratton, Benjamin F. Thomas, Francis Thomas, Trimble, Trowbridge, Wallace, Washburne, Whaley, *Chilton A. White*, *Wickliffe*, *Woodruff*, Worcester, *Wright*, *Yeaman*—68.

They were then postponed.

First Session, Thirty-Eighth Congress.

IN HOUSE.

1863, December 14—Mr. FINCK offered this resolution, which was laid over under the rule:

Whereas, in the opinion of this House, the Federal Government is invested by the Constitution of the United States with all necessary power and authority to suppress any resistance to the due execution of the laws thereof, and to employ the army and navy in aid of the civil authority to disperse all armed resistance to the rightful power and jurisdiction of the United States; and whereas, in the judgment of this House, the army and navy cannot be rightfully used to subjugate and hold as conquered territory any of the States of this Union: Therefore,

Be it resolved, That in this national emergency Congress will forego all feeling of mere passion or resentment, and will recollect only its duty to the country; that this war should not be waged on our part in any spirit of oppression, nor in any spirit of conquest or subjugation, or for the purpose of overthrowing or interfering with the rights or established institutions of the States, but to defend and maintain the supremacy of the Constitution and preserve the Union, with all the dignity, equality, and rights of the several States unimpared; and as soon as these objects are attained the war ought to cease.

April 11—The resolution was laid on the table—yeas 81, nays 64, as follows:

YEAS—Messrs. Alley, Allison, Ames, Anderson, Arnold, Ashley, John D. Baldwin, Baxter, Beaman, Blaine, Boutwell, Boyd, Broomall, Wm. G. Brown, Ambrose W. Clark, Freeman Clarke, Cobb, Cole, Henry Winter Davis, Thomas T. Davis, Deming, Driggs, Dumont, Eckley, Eliot, Farnsworth, Frank, Garfield, Gooch, Grinnell, Higby, Hooper, Hotchkiss, Asahel W. Hubbard, John H. Hubbard, Jenckes, Julian, Kasson, Kelley, Francis W. Kellogg, Orlando Kellogg, Loan, Marvin, McBride, McClurg, Samuel F. Miller, Morrill, Daniel Morris, Amos Myers, Leonard Myers, Norton, Charles O'Neill, Orth, Patterson, Pike, Pomeroy, Price, William H. Randall, Alexander H. Rice, Edward H. Rollins, Schenck, Scofield, Shannon, Sloan, Smith, Smithers, Spalding, Starr, Stevens, Thayer, Thomas, Upson, Van Valkenburgh, Ellihu B. Washburne, William B. Washburn, Whaley, Williams, Wilder, Wilson, Windom, Woodbridge—81.

NAYS—Messrs. *James C. Allen*, *William J. Allen*, *Ancona*, *Augustus C. Baldwin*, Francis P. Blair, jr., *Bliss*, *James S. Brown*, *Chanler*, *Clay*, *Coffroth*, *Cox*, *Cravens*, *Dawson*, *Denison*, *Eden*, *Eldridge*, *English*, *Finck*, *Ganson*, *Grider*, Hale, *Harding*, *Harrington*, *Benjamin G. Harris*, *Herrick*, *Holman*, *Philip Johnson*, *Wm. Johnson*, *Kernan*, *King*, *Knapp*, *Law*, *Lazear*, *Long*, *Marcy*, *McAllister*, *McDowell*, *McKinney*, *Middleton*, *James R. Morris*, *Morrison*, *Nelson*, *Odell*, *Pendleton*, *Perry*, *Pruyn*, *Samuel J. Randall*, *Robinson*, *Rogers*, *James S. Rollins*, *Ross*, *Scott*, *John B. Steele*, *Wm. G. Steele*, *Strouse*, *Stuart*, *Sweat*, *Voorhees*, Webster, *Wheeler*, *Chilton A. White*, *Joseph W. White*, *Winfield*, *Fernando Wood*—64.

1863, Dec. 14—Mr. HOLMAN offered these resolutions:

Resolved, that the doctrine, recently announced, that the States in which an armed insurrection has existed against the Federal Government have ceased to be States of the Union, and shall be held, on the ultimate defeat of that insurrection, as Territories or subjugated provinces, and governed as such by the absolute will of Congress and the Federal Executive, or restored to the Union on conditions unknown to the Constitution of the United States, ought to be rebuked and condemned as manifestly unjust to the loyal citizens of those States, tending to prolong the war and to confirm the treasonable theory of secession, and if carried into effect must greatly endanger the public liberty and the constitutional powers and rights of all of the States, by centralizing and consolidating the powers of the government, State and national, in the Federal Executive.

2. That the only object of the war ought to be to subjugate the armed insurrection which for the time being suspends the proper relations of certain States with the Federal Government, and to re-establish the supremacy of the Constitution; and the loyal citizens of those States, and the masses of the people thereof, submitting to the authority of the Constitution, ought not to be hindered from restoring the proper relations of their respective States with the Federal Government, so far as the same is dependent on the voluntary act of the people, by any condition except unconditional submission to the Constitution and laws of the United States. In the language heretofore solemnly adopted by Congress, the war ought not to be waged on our part for any purpose of conquest or subjugation, or purpose of overthrowing or interfering with the rights or established institutions of those States, but to defend and maintain the supremacy of the Constitution and to preserve the Union, with all the dignity, equality, and rights of the several States unimpaired; and as soon as those objects are accomplished the war ought to cease.

3. That all necessary and proper appropriations of money ought to be promptly made by this Congress for the support of the military and naval forces of the Government, and all measures of legislation necessary to increase and promote the efficiency of the army and navy and to maintain the public credit ought to be adopted; that through a vigorous prosecution of the war, peace, on the basis of the union of the States and the supremacy of the Constitution, may be the most speedily obtained.

Which were laid upon the table—yeas 88, nays 66, as follows:

YEAS—Messrs. Alley, Arnold, Ashley, John D. Baldwin, Baxter, Beaman, Blaine, Blow, Boutwell, Boyd, Brandegee, Broomall, Ambrose W. Clark, Freeman Clarke, *Clay*, Cobb, Cole, Creswell, Henry Winter Davis, Dawes, Dixon, Donnelly, Driggs, Dumont, Eckley, Eliot, Farnsworth, Fenton, Frank, Garfield, Gooch, Grinnell, Higby, Hooper, Hotchkiss, Asahel W. Hubbard, John H. Hubbard, Hulburd, Jenckes, Julian, Kasson, Francis W. Kellogg, Orlando Kellogg, Loan, Longyear, Lovejoy, Marvin, McBride, McClurg, McIndoe, Samuel F. Miller, Moorhead, Morrill, Daniel Morris, Amos Myers, Leonard Myers, Norton, Charles O'Neill, Orth, Patterson, Perham, Pike, Pomeroy, Price, William H. Randall, Alexander H. Rice, John H. Rice, Edward H. Rollins, *James S. Rollins*, Schenck, Scofield, Shannon, Sloan, Smithers, Spalding, Stevens, Thayer, Thomas, Upson, Van Valkenburgh, Ellihu B. Washburne, William B. Washburn, Whaley, Williams, Wilder, Wilson, Windom, Woodbridge—88.

NAYS—Messrs. *James C. Allen*, *William J. Allen*, *Ancona*, *Baily*, *Augustus C. Baldwin*, Jacob B. Blair, *Bliss*, *Brooks*, William G. Brown, *Chanler*, *Coffroth*, *Cox*, *Cravens*, *Dawson*, *Denison*, *Eden*, *Edgerton*, *Eldridge*, *English*, *Finck*, *Ganson*, *Grider*, *Griswold*, *Hall*, *Harding*, *Harrington*, *Benjamin G. Harris*, *Charles M. Harris*, *Herrick*, *Holman*,

William Johnson, Kernan, King, Knapp, Law, Lazear, Le Blond, Long, Mallory, Marcy, McDowell, McKinney, William H. Miller, James R. Morris, Morrison, Nelson, Noble, Odell, John O'Neill, Pendleton, Robinson, Rogers, Ross, Scott, Smith, *John B. Steele, Stuart, Voorhees, Wadsworth, Ward, Wheeler, Chilton A. White, Joseph W. White, Winfield, Fernando Wood, Yeaman*—66.

Feb. 3—Mr. COFFROTH asked consent to offer this preamble and resolution:

Whereas this once happy and prosperous nation has been for nearly three years attempting to crush a cruel, unjust, and unrighteous rebellion; and whereas Congress did on the 22d of July, 1861, with unparalleled unanimity declare "that in this national emergency, Congress, banishing all feelings of mere passion or resentment, will recollect only its duty to the whole country; that this war is not waged on their part in any spirit of oppression, or for any purpose of conquest, or subjugation, or purpose of overthrowing or interfering with the rights or established institutions of these States, but to defend and maintain the *supremacy* of the Constitution, and to preserve the Union with all the dignity, equality, and rights of the several States unimpaired; and that as soon as these objects are accomplished the war ought to cease;" and whereas the President of the United States did, on the 22d of September, A. D. 1862, and on the 1st of January, A. D. 1863, and on the 8th of December, A. D. 1863, issue proclamations in direct violation of this resolution; and whereas said proclamations have divided the Union people of the North, who at one time were united in their efforts to crush the rebellion: Therefore, in order to unite all the Union-loving people, and to carry out the spirit of said resolution and restore the "Union as it was" under the "Constitution as it is."

Be it resolved, That the President of the United States be respectfully requested to withdraw said proclamations, so that all the Union-loving people may again unite to mantain the supremacy of the Constitution, and to preserve the Union with all the dignity, equality, and rights of the several States unimpaired.

To which Mr. GRINNELL objected.

1863, December 16—Mr. JAMES S. ROLLINS offered this resolution:

Resolved, That, prompted by a just patriotism, we are in favor of an earnest and successful prosecution of the war, and that we will give a warm and hearty support to all those measures which will be most effective in speedily overcoming the rebellion and in securing a restoration of peace, and which may not substantially infringe the Constitution and tend to subvert the true theory and character of the Government; and we hereby reiterate that the present deplorable civil war has been forced upon the country by the disunionists now in revolt against the constitutional government; that in the progress of this war, Congress, banishing all feeling of mere passion or resentment, will recollect only its duty to the whole country; that this war is not waged on our part in any spirit of oppression, nor for any purpose of conquest or subjugation, nor purpose of overthrowing or interfering with the rights or established institutions of those States, but to defend and maintain the supremacy of the Constitution, and to preserve the Union with all the dignity, equality, and rights of the several States unimpaired; that as soon as these objects are accomplished, the war ought to cease.

A motion that the resolution be tabled was disagreed to—yeas 52, nays 115, as follows:

YEAS—Messrs. Alley, Allison, Ames, Anderson, Ashley, Baxter, Beaman, Blow, Boutwell, Boyd, Brandegee, Broomall, Cole, Thomas T. Davis, Dixon, Donnelly, Driggs, Dumont, Eckley, Eliot, Garfield, Gooch, Grinnell, Hooper, Hotchkiss, Hulburd, Julian, Kelley, Francis W. Kellogg, Loan, Longyear, Lovejoy, McClurg, McIndoe, Moorhead, Amos Myers, Leonard Myers, Norton, Charles O'Neill, Orth, Perham, Pomeroy, Price, Schenck, Sloan, Spalding, Stevens, Upson, Van Valkenburgh, William B. Washburn, Whaley, Wilder—52.

NAYS—Messrs. *James C. Allen, William J. Allen, Ancona, Baily, Augustus C. Baldwin*, John D. Baldwin, Blaine, Jacob B. Blair, *Bliss, Brooks, James S. Brown, Chanler*, Ambrose W. Clark, *Clay*, Cobb, *Coffroth, Cox, Cravens*, Creswell, Henry Winter Davis, Dawes, *Dawson*, Deming, *Denison, Eden, Edgerton, Eldridge, English*, Farnsworth, Fenton, *Finck*, Frank, *Ganson, Grider, Griswold*, Hale, *Hall, Harding, Harrington, Benjamin G. Harris, Charles M. Harris, Herrick*, Higby, *Holman*, Asahel W. Hubbard, *Hutchins, Philip Johnson, Wm. Johnson*, Kasson, Orlando Kellogg, *Kernan, King, Knapp, Law, Lazear, Le Blond, Long, Mallory, Marcy*, Marvin, *McAllister*, McBride, *McDowell, McKinney, Middleton*, Samuel F. Miller, *Wm. H. Miller*, Morrill, Daniel Morris, *James R. Morris, Morrison, Nelson, Noble, Odell, John O'Neill*, Patterson, *Pendleton, Perry, Pike, Radford, Samuel J. Randall*, William H. Randall, Alexander H. Rice, *Robinson, Rogers*, Edward H. Rollins, *Jas. S. Rollins, Ross*, Scofield, *Scott*, Shannon, Smith, Smithers, *Stebbins, John B. Steele, Wm. G. Steele, Stiles, Strouse, Stuart, Sweat*, Thayer, Tracy, *Voorhees, Wadsworth, Ward*, Ellihu B. Washburne, Webster, *Wheeler, Chilton A. White, Joseph W. White*, Wilson, *Winfield, Fernando Wood*, Woodbridge, *Yeaman*—115.

It then went over under the rule; and

May 30—Mr. FERNANDO WOOD moved that it be laid on the table, which was rejected—yeas 27, nays 114, as follows:

YEAS—Messrs. Allison, Ames, Anderson, Arnold, John D. Baldwin, Brandegee, Creswell, Thomas T. Davis, Dawes, Donnelly, Eliot, Farnsworth, Garfield, Grinnell, Asahel W. Hubbard, John H. Hubbard, Hulburd, Littlejohn, Schenck, Sloan, Spalding, Stevens, Ellihu B. Washburne, Wilder, Wilson, Windom, *Fernando Wood*—27.

NAYS—Messrs. *James C. Allen*, Alley, *Ancona, Baily, Augustus C. Baldwin*, Baxter, Beaman, Blaine, Jacob B. Blair, *Bliss*, Boyd, *Brooks, James S. Brown, Chanler*, Ambrose W. Clark, Freeman Clarke, Cobb, *Coffroth*, Cole, *Cox, Cravens, Dawson*, Eckley, *Eden, Edgerton, Eldridge, English*, Fenton, *Finck*, Frank, *Ganson*, Gooch, *Griswold, Harding, Harrington, Charles M. Harris, Herrick*, Higby, *Holman*, Hooper, Hotchkiss, *Hutchins*, Ingersoll, Jenckes, *Philip Johnson, William Johnson*, Kasson, Kelley, Orlando Kellogg, *Kernan, King, Knapp, Le Blond*, Loan, *Long*, Longyear, *Mallory, Marcy*, Marvin, *McAllister*, McBride, McClurg, *McDowell*, Samuel F. Miller, Morrill, *James R. Morris, Morrison*, Amos Myers, Leonard Myers, *Nelson, Noble, Odell*, Charles O'Neill, *John O'Neill*, Orth, Patterson, *Pendleton*, Perham, Pike, Pomeroy, Price, *Pruyn, Radford, Samuel J. Randall*, Wm. H. Randall, Alexander H. Rice, John H. Rice, *Rogers*, Edward H. Rollins, *James S. Rollins, Ross*, Scofield, *Scott*, Shannon, Smith, Smithers, *John B. Steele, William G. Steele, Stiles, Sweat*, Thayer, Thomas, Upson, Van Valkenburgh, *Voorhees, Wadsworth*, William B. Washburn, Webster, Whaley, *Wheeler, Joseph W. White*, Williams, Woodbridge, *Yeaman*—114.

On motion of Mr. MORRILL, it was then referred to the Committee on the Rebellious States—yeas 81, nays 66.

First Session, Thirty-Eighth Congress.

IN SENATE.

1864, February 23—Mr. CARLILE introduced this joint resolution, which was ordered to be printed:

Resolved, &c., 1. That the military power of the Government can only be rightfully exerted against individuals in arms opposing its authority. That the prosecution of hostilities against the citizens of the States in rebellion ought to be for the sole purpose of maintaining the constitutional Union, and for the restoration of the Union upon the basis of the Constitution, leaving to each State the regulation of its own domestic policy, and protecting each and all in the enjoyment of the right of self-government as recognized by the Constitution of the United States.

2. That the President be requested to declare by proclamation, whenever the people of any of the States now resisting the authority of the United States shall reorganize their State government by repudiating the ordinances of secession adopted in their name and shall recognize their obligations to the Union under the Constitution, full pardon and amnesty to the people of such State, assuring the citizens thereof that all their rights of person and of property under the Constitution shall be restored to and enjoyed by them; excepting, however, from such pardon and amnesty such persons as shall be designated by the Legislatures of the several States as fit persons to be held for trial before the judicial tribunals of the United States under the laws thereof.

ITS PROSECUTION.

Special Session of Senate—1861.

1861, March 26—Mr. BRECKINRIDGE offered this resolution:

Resolved, That the Senate recommend and advise the removal of the United States troops from the limits of the Confederate States.

Mr. CLINGMAN offered this substitute:

Resolved, That, in the opinion of the Senate, it is expedient that the President should withdraw all the troops of the United States from the States of South Carolina, Georgia,

Florida, Alabama, Mississippi, Louisiana, and Texas, and abstain from all attempts to collect revenues in the said States.

March 27—Mr. TRUMBULL offered this resolution:

Resolved, That, in the opinion of the Senate, the true way to preserve the Union is to enforce the laws of the Union; that resistance to their enforcement, whether under the name of anti-coercion or any other name, is encouragement to disunion; and that it is the duty of the President to use all the means in his power to hold and protect the public property of the United States, and enforce the laws thereof, as well in the States of South Carolina, Georgia, Florida, Mississippi, Alabama, Louisiana, and Texas, as within the other States of the Union.

No vote was taken upon either of these propositions.

First Session, Thirty-Seventh Congress.

IN SENATE.

1861, July 26—The Senate passed the following resolution, offered by Mr. CLARK:

Be it resolved, &c., That we, as representatives of the people and States, respectively, do hereby declare our fixed determination to maintain the supremacy of the Government and the integrity of the Union of all these United States; and to this end, as far as we may do so, we pledge the entire resources of the Government and people, until all rebels shall submit to the one and cease their efforts to destroy the other.

The vote was—yeas 34, nays 1, as follows:

YEAS—Messrs. Anthony, Bingham, Browning, Chandler, Clark, Collamer, Cowan, Dixon, Doolittle, Fessenden, Foot, Foster, Grimes, Hale, Harris, Howe, *Johnson* of Tennessee, King, Lane of Indiana, Lane of Kansas, *Latham*, *McDougall*, Morrill, *Nesmith*, Pomeroy, *Saulsbury*, Sherman, Simmons, Sumner, Ten Eyck, *Thomson*, Trumbull, Wade, Willey—34.
NAYS—Mr. *Breckinridge*—1.

IN HOUSE.

July 15—Mr. MCCLERNAND offered the following resolution:

Whereas a portion of the people of the United States, in violation of their constitutional obligations, have taken up arms against the National Government, and are now striving, by aggressive and iniquitous war, to overthrow it and break up the Union of these States: Therefore,

Resolved, That this House hereby pledges itself to vote for any amount of money and any number of men which may be necessary to insure a speedy and effectual suppression of such rebellion and the permanent restoration of the Federal authority everywhere within the limits and jurisdiction of the United States.

The resolution was agreed to—yeas 121, nays 5, (*Burnett*, *Grider*, *Norton*, *Reid*, and *Benjamin Wood*.)

July 22—Mr. VANDEVER asked consent to offer this resolution:

Resolved, That the maintenance of the Constitution, the preservation of the Union, and the enforcement of the laws, are sacred trusts which must be executed; that no disaster shall discourage us from the most ample performance of this high duty; and we pledge to the country and the world the employment of every resource, national and individual, for the suppression, overthrow, and punishment of rebels in arms.

Consent was first refused, but it was afterwards offered, and by unanimous consent, considered and agreed to.

July 22—Mr. WRIGHT, of Pennsylvania, offered this resolution:

Resolved, That the reverses of the army of the United States yesterday, the 21st instant, at Bull's Run, caused by the rebel army, have in no manner impaired the ultimate success of our arms, but that the cause of human liberty, the preservation of the Union, and the maintenance of the laws pervading the hearts and affections of more than twenty millions of people, are a sure and certain guarantee that the flag of our country shall be upheld, and the Union preserved to the people; that we call on all loyal people of the Union to respond manfully to the demand of the Government in furnishing men and money, and to stand together in its support with their lives and fortunes.

The resolution was laid on the table, with a call of the yeas and nays.

Second Session, Thirty-Seventh Congress.

IN SENATE.

1862, May 26—Mr. SUMNER offered this resolution:

Resolved, That in the prosecution of the present war for the suppression of a wicked rebellion, the time has come for the Government of the United States to appeal to the loyalty of the whole people everywhere, but especially in the rebel districts, and to invite all, without distinction of color or class, to make their loyalty manifest by ceasing to fight or labor for the rebels, and also by rendering every assistance in their power to the cause of the Constitution and the Union, according to their ability, whether by arms, or labor, or information, or in any other way; and, since protection and allegiance are reciprocal duties, dependent upon each other, it is the further duty of the Government of the United States to maintain all such loyal people, without distinction of color or class, in their rights as *men*, according to the principles of the Declaration of Independence.

June 18—Mr. GRIMES offered this resolution:

Resolved, (as the opinion of the Senate,) That it is the right and duty of the Government to call all loyal persons within the rebellious States to its armed defence against the traitors who are seeking its overthrow.

Third Session, Thirty-Seventh Congress.

IN HOUSE.

1862, December 5—Mr. MORRILL offered the following resolution:

Resolved, That at no time since the commencement of the existing rebellion, have the forces and materials in the hands of the executive department of the Government been so ample and abundant for the speedy and triumphant termination of the war as at the present moment; and it is the duty of all loyal American citizens, regardless of minor differences of opinion, and especially the duty of every officer and soldier in the field, as well as the duty of every department of the Government—the legislative branch included—as a unit, to cordially and unitedly strike down the assassins, at once and forever, who have conspired to destroy our Constitution, our nationality, and that prosperity and freedom of which we are justly proud at home and abroad, and which we stand pledged to perpetuate forever.

Which was agreed to—yeas 105, nays 1, as follows:

YEAS—Messrs. Aldrich, Arnold, Ashley, Babbitt, *Baily*, Baker, Baxter, Beaman, Bingham, Blake, William G. Brown, Buffinton, Chamberlain, Clark, Clements, *Cobb*, Colfax, Frederick A. Conkling, Roscoe Conkling, *Corning*, *Cox*, *Cravens*, Cutler, Davis, Dawes, Delano, Duell, *Dunlap*, Dunn, Edgerton, Eliot, Ely, Fenton, Samuel C. Fessenden, Thomas A. D. Fessenden, Fisher, Franchot, Frank, Gooch, Goodwin, Granger, *Grider*, Gurley, Hale, *Hall*, Harrison, Hickman, *Holman*, Hooper, Horton, Hutchins, Julian, Kelley, Francis W. Kellogg, Wm. Kellogg, Leary, Loomis, Lovejoy, Low, McPherson, Maynard, Mitchell, Moorhead, Justin S. Morrill, Nixon, *Noble*, *Nugen*, *Odell*, Olin, Patton, *Perry*, Pike, Pomeroy, Porter, *Price*, John H. Rice, Riddle, E. H. Rollins, Sargent, Sedgwick, Segar, Shanks, *Sheffield*, Shellabarger, *Smith*, Spaulding, *John B. Steele*, *Wm. G. Steele*, Stevens, Stratton, Benjamin F. Thomas, Francis Thomas, Train, Trowbridge, Van Horn, Van Valkenburgh, Van Wyck, Walker, Wallace, Whaley, Wilson, Windom, *Woodruff*, Worcester, *Wright*—105.
NAY—Mr. *William J. Allen*—1.

Mr. Cox offered the following resolution:

Resolved, That the word "assassins," used in the resolution this day offered by the member from Vermont, [Mr. MORRILL,] is intended by this House to include all men, whether from the North or the South, who have been instrumental in producing the present war, and especially those in and out of Congress who have been guilty of flagrant breaches of the Constitution, and who are not in favor of the establishment of the Union as it was and the Constitution as it is.

Which was laid upon the table—yeas 85, nays 41, as follows:

YEAS—Messrs. Aldrich, Arnold, Ashley, Babbitt, *Baily*, Baker, Baxter, Beaman, Bingham, Jacob B. Blair, Samuel S. Blair, Blake, Buffinton, Chamberlain, Clark, Colfax, Frederick A. Conkling, Roscoe Conkling, Conway, Covode, Cutler, Davis, Dawes, Duell, Dunn, Edgerton, Eliot, Ely,

Fenton, Samuel C. Fessenden, Thomas A. D. Fessenden, Fisher, Franchot, Frank, Goodwin, Hale, Harrison, Hickman, Hooper, Horton, Hutchins, Julian, Kelley, Leary, Loomis, Lovejoy, Low, McPherson, Maynard, Mitchell, Moorhead, Justin S. Morrill, Olin, Patton, Pike, Pomeroy, Porter, Potter, John H. Rice, Riddle, Edward H. Rollins, Sargent, Sedgwick, Segar, Shanks, *Sheffield*, Shellabarger, Sherman, Sloan, Spaulding, Stevens, Stratton, Benjamin F. Thomas, Francis Thomas, Train, Trowbridge, Van Horn, Van Valkenburgh, Van Wyck, Walker, Wallace, Washburne, Wilson, Windom, Worcester—85.

NAYS—Messrs. *William J. Allen*, *Ancona*, William G. Brown, Clements, *Cobb*, *Corning*, *Cox*, *Dunlap*, *English*, Granger, *Grider*, *Hall*, *Harding*, *Holman*, *Johnson*, *Lazear*, *Mallory*, *Menzies*, *Noble*, *Norton*, *Nugen*, *Pendleton*, *Perry*, *Price*, *Richardson*, *Robinson*, *Shiel*, *Smith*, *John B. Steele*, *Wm. G. Steele*, *Stiles*, *Vallandigham*, *Vibbard*, *Voorhees*, *Ward*, Whaley, *Chilton A. White*, *Wickliffe*, *Woodruff*, *Wright*, *Yeaman*—41.

1862, December 15—Mr. CONWAY offered the following resolutions:

Resolved, That freedom and slavery cannot co-exist in the same Government without producing endless strife and civil war; that "a house divided against itself cannot stand;" and that "this nation must be all free or all slave."

2. That the American Union consists of those States which are now loyal to the Federal Constitution.

3. That a restoration of the Union, as it existed prior to the rebellion, would be a greater calamity than the rebellion itself, since it would give new life to the "irrepressible conflict," and entail upon the nation another cycle of bitter contention and civil war.

4. That the seceded States can only be put down, if at all, by being regarded as out of constitutional relations with the Union, and by being assailed upon principles of ordinary warfare as between separate nations.

5. That if any person in the employment of the United States, in either the legislative or executive branches, should propose to make peace, or should accept or advise the acceptance of any such proposition on any basis which would restore the slave power to its former supremacy in the Government, or by any new compromise or amendment of the Constitution recognize slavery as an element of power, such person will be guilty of a high crime.

6. That the superior resources and military prowess of the North in the struggle are beyond dispute, and that the question of its success turns not upon its relative ability, but on the fitness of its chief Executive Magistrate to give effect to its power.

7. That it is unsafe to intrust the execution of any system of administration to persons who are not in cordial sympathy therewith, and that no change of policy in the conduct of the war is more than nominal which is not accompanied by a complete change in the *personnel* of the executive department.

8. That it is a matter for serious reflection whether another election for President must not supervene before the rightful authority of the nation can be established, and whether, in the mean time, it is not a flagrant waste of our energies to continue the war.

9. That unless the army of the West shall have swept through the valley of the Mississippi to its mouth, and the army of the Potomac annihilated the legions of Lee and Jackson, thus subverting the military power of the rebellion, within a reasonable time, the best interests of the country and humanity will require a cessation of hostilities.

10. That the States of the North, composing the American nation and wielding its power, must ever remain one and indivisible on the basis of freedom for all, without distinction of race, color, or condition; that their mission must ever be to extend their own civilization over the entire continent; and that whatever derangements, difficulties, checks, or defeats they may encounter, they must forever cherish and pursue the inspiring idea of nationality and continental dominion.

Which were laid upon the table—yeas 132, nay 1, as follows:

YEAS—Messrs. Aldrich, *William J. Allen*, Alley, *Ancona*, Babbitt, *Baily*, Baker, Beaman, *Biddle*, Bingham, Samuel S. Blair, Blake, William G. Brown, Buffinton, *Calvert*, Chamberlain, Clark, Clements, *Cobb*, Colfax, Frederick A. Conkling, Roscoe Conkling, *Cox*, *Crisfield*, *Crittenden*, Cutler, Dawes, Delano, *Delaplaine*, Duell, *Dunlap*, Dunn, Edgerton, Edwards, Eliot, *English*, Fenton, Samuel C. Fessenden, Thomas A. D. Fessenden, Fisher, *Fouke*, Franchot, Frank, Gooch, Goodwin, Granger, *Grider*, Gurley, *Haight*, Hall, *Harding*, Harrison, Hickman, *Holman*, Hooper, *Hutchins*, Julian, Kelley, William Kellogg, *Kerrigan*, Killinger, Lansing, Leary, Loomis, Lovejoy, Low, McKnight, McPherson, *Mallory*, Maynard, *Menzies*, Mitchell, Moorhead, Anson P. Morrill, Justin S. Morrill, *Morris*, Nixon, *Noble*, *Noell*, *Norton*, *Odell*, Patton, *Pendleton*, Pike, Pomeroy, Porter, Potter, Price, Alexander H. Rice, John H. Rice, *Richardson*, Riddle, *Robinson*, Edward H. Rollins, Sargent, Sedgwick, Segar, Shanks, *Sheffield*, Shellabarger, *Shiel*, Sloan, *Smith*, Spaulding, *John B. Steele*, *Stiles*, Stratton, Benjamin F. Thomas, Francis Thomas, Train, Trimble, Trowbridge, *Vallandigham*, Van Horn, Van Valkenburgh, Verree, *Wadsworth*, Walker, Wall, Wallace, *Ward*, Washburne, Whaley, Albert S. White, *Chilton A. White*, *Wickliffe*, Wilson, Windom, *Woodruff*, Worcester, *Wright*, *Yeaman*—132.

NAY—Mr. Conway—1.

1863, January 5—Mr. BLAKE offered the following resolution:

Resolved, That this House earnestly desires the most speedy and effectual measures taken to put down the rebellion; that any propositions for peace or cessation of hostilities at this time on any terms other than an unconditional submission of the rebels now in arms against the Government to the requirements of the Constitution and laws, would be pusillanimous and traitorous; that the members of this House do hereby give the most earnest assurances to the people of the United States that they will cheerfully co-operate with the President as Commander-in-Chief of the Army and Navy in any measures he may deem proper, sanctioned by the Constitution and the laws of civilized warfare, to strengthen the military power of our gallant soldiers in the field defending the Government, and to weaken that of the enemy laboring to destroy it.

2. That the only alternative Government can or ought at this time to offer to rebels, is, submit or be conquered.

Which was considered, but no action taken thereon.

January 8—Mr. HOLMAN offered the following resolution:

Resolved, That the duty of maintaining the integrity of the Union of the States under the present form of government, with the limitations of the Constitution unimpaired, is most sacred and obligatory, and no proposition tending to destroy the Union, or violate the obligations of the Constitution, can rightfully be entertained or considered by the representatives of the people in any of the departments of the Government.

2. That the free and unrestricted navigation of the Mississippi river must be restored and maintained as the common and absolute right of the people of all of the States, and the duty to vindicate the same against every effort to impair it, is imperative, and cannot, under any circumstances, be abandoned by the Government of the United States.

The consideration of which was postponed until the 14th instant, but not again called up.

First Session, Thirty-Eighth Congress.

IN HOUSE.

1864, January 7—Mr. AMOS MYERS offered the following, which were referred to the Select Committee on the Rebellious States:

Whereas, in the opinion of this House, the Federal Government is invested by the Constitution of the United States with all necessary power and authority to suppress any resistance, whether armed or unarmed, to the rightful power and jurisdiction of the United States: Therefore,

Be it resolved, That in this national emergency Congress will forego all feeling of mere passion, except that which loyalty dictates, all resentment except such as is due to treason; and that this war of national self-defence against armed rebels, insurrectionary traitors, and sympathizing abettors, should be waged on our part until such rebels and traitors are conquered into love for the Union, and made obedient to the Constitution and laws of the United States, and take the oath of allegiance to the country, and of submission to the emancipation proclamation, and the proclamation of December 8, 1863; and when those objects are accomplished, the leading rebels and chief traitors should be hung, and the war cease.

1864, January 18—Mr. GREEN CLAY SMITH offered this preamble and resolution:

Whereas a most desperate, wicked, and bloody rebellion exists within the jurisdiction of the United States, and the safety and security of personal and national liberty depend upon its utter and absolute extinction: Therefore,

Resolved, That it is the political, civil, moral, and sacred duty of the people to meet it, fight it, crush it, and forever destroy it.

Mr. James C. Allen moved to lay them on the table; which was disagreed to—yeas 26, nays 102.

The Yeas were:

Messrs. *James C. Allen, Ancona, Brooks, Chanler,* Deming, *Denison, Eden, Edgerton, Eldridge, Herrick, William Johnson, Knapp, Long, Marcy, McDowell, McKinney, Wm. H. Miller, Pendleton, Robinson, Ross, Stiles, Strouse, Voorhees, Chilton A. White, Fernando Wood, Yeaman*—26.

The resolution was then agreed to—yeas 112, nays 16, as follows:

Yeas—Messrs. Alley, Allison, Ames, Arnold, Ashley, *Baily, Augustus C. Baldwin,* John D. Baldwin, Baxter, Blaine, Francis P. Blair, jr., Jacob B. Blair, Boutwell, Boyd, Brandegee, Broomall, *James S. Brown,* William G. Brown, Ambrose W. Clark, Freeman Clarke, Cole, *Cravens,* Cresswell, Dawes, Deming, Dixon, Donnelly, Driggs, Eckley, *Eldridge,* Eliot, *English,* Farnsworth, Fenton, Frank, *Ganson,* Garfield, Gooch, Grinnell, *Griswold,* Hale, *Harding,* Higby, *Holman,* Hooper, Hotchkiss, Asahel W. Hubbard, *Hutchins,* Jenckes, Julian, Kasson, Kelley, Francis W. Kellogg, Orlando Kellogg, *Kernan,* Loan, Longyear, Lovejoy, Marvin, McBride, McClurg, McIndoe, *Middleton,* Samuel F. Miller, Moorhead, Morrill, Daniel Morris, Amos Myers, Leonard Myers, *Nelson, Odell,* Charles O'Neill, Orth, Patterson, Pike, Pomeroy, Price, *Radford,* William H. Randall, Alexander H. Rice, John H. Rice, *Rogers,* Edward H. Rollins, *James S. Rollins,* Schenck, Scofield, Shannon, Smith, Smithers, Spalding, *Stebbins,* Stevens, *Strouse, Stuart, Sweat,* Thayer, Thomas, Tracy, Upson, Van Valkenburgh, *Wadsworth,* Ellihu B. Washburne, William B. Washburn, Webster, Whaley, *Wheeler,* Williams, Wilder, Wilson, Windom, *Winfield,* Woodbridge—112.

Nays—Messrs. *J. C. Allen, Ancona, Denison, Benjamin G. Harris, Long, Marcy, McDowell, William H. Miller, Morrison, John O'Neill, Pendleton, Robinson, Stiles, Voorhees, Chilton A. White, Fernando Wood*—16.

1864, Feb. 8—Mr. Wm. G. Brown offered the following resolutions, which were laid over under the rule:

Whereas our beloved country, our highly cherished institutions, Constitution, and Union of the States, are all imperilled by a causeless and wicked rebellion: Be it therefore,

Resolved, That it is the duty of every loyal citizen to give to the Government, and to the agents in its employ, both in the cabinet and in the field, all the legitimate aid and comfort in his power in their efforts to put down such rebellion.

2. That, as the rebels began the war, we will prosecute it until the last insurgent is disarmed and the authority of the United States acknowledged over every foot of ground belonging to the Republic.

3. That in the prosecution of the war we will use all the military power of the Government, but will combine with it all the means of conciliation calculated to give to the Government and country an honorable and lasting peace.

4. That it is the duty of the Government, so far as it is in its power to give equal protection to all loyal citizens without reference to their locality, whether residing within the seceded or loyal States; and one of the strong incentives to a vigorous prosecution of the war is to rescue our loyal brethren of the rebellious States from the domination of a military despotism.

1864, Feb. 8—Mr. Jacob B. Blair offered the following preamble and resolutions, which were laid over under the rule:

Whereas the present deplorable civil war was inaugurated and is still carried on by a few desperate but daring men who, without any cause whatever, have not only filled the land with widows and orphans and caused almost untold millions of treasure to be spent, but have put in peril the very life of that Government which never deprived them of one solitary right, but which was so mild and beneficent it was only known by the blessings it conferred. And whereas Jefferson Davis, the chief of rebels, is reported to have said in a speech delivered in Jackson, Mississippi, in December, 1862: "My only wonder is that we consented to live so long a time in association with such miscreants (referring to the people of the North) and have loved a Government rotten to the core. Were it ever to be proposed again to enter into a union with such a people I could no more consent to do it than to trust myself in a den of thieves." And whereas this same high official in the great synagogue of rebeldom has repeatedly since, in his messages to the Rebel Congress, utterly repudiated the idea of ever ceasing his wicked designs and returning to his allegiance to the Government, whose Constitution and laws he has trampled under foot; and has also declared that no compromise would be entertained by him, or those he represents, that did not secure to the States in rebellion their independence and final separation from the United States. And whereas Alexander H. Stephens, the Vice President of the so-called Southern Confederacy, is reported to have said in a speech delivered in the month of July, 1863, at Charlotte, North Carolina, "As for reconstruction, such a thing was impossible; such an idea must not be tolerated for an instant. Reconstruction would not end the war, but would produce a more horrible war than that in which we are now engaged. The only terms on which we can obtain permanent peace is final and complete separation from the North. Rather than submit to anything short of that, let us all resolve to die like men worthy of freedom." And whereas John Letcher, in one of his messages to the rebel legislature of the State of Virginia, declared: "The alliance between us is dissolved, (meaning between the United States and the southern States,) never, I trust, to be renewed, at any time, under any conceivable state of circumstances." And whereas the *Richmond Enquirer,* one of the organs and advocates of this imaginary Southern Confederacy, in its issue of January 9, 1863, says: "Separation is inevitable. War has failed to prevent it. Peace cannot stop it. An armistice with propositions for reconstruction by constitutional amendments of conventions of States would very soon reveal the fact that separation was final; and so far as one generation can speak for its successors, it is eternal." And whereas the *Richmond Dispatch* of January 10, 1863, another organ of the leaders of this wanton and unprovoked rebellion, said in response to a peace and reunion speech, delivered in New York by the editor of the *Express,* "That we assure him that the people of the Confederate States would infinitely prefer being the vassals of France or England; nay, they would prefer to be serfs of Russia, to becoming in any manner whatever associated politically or otherwise with the Yankee States." And further, "that President Davis expressed the sentiment of the entire Confederacy in his speech the other night, (in Richmond,) when he said 'the people would sooner unite with a nation of hyenas than with the detestable Yankee nation. Anything but that. English colonization, French vassalage, Russian serfdom—all, all are preferable to any association with the Yankees.'" And whereas the *Richmond Sentinel,* still another advocate of this new-fledged Confederacy, in its comments on the proceedings of what is known as the Frank Pierce meeting, held at Concord, New Hampshire, on the 4th of July, 1863, says, "Do the New Hampshire Democrats suppose for one moment that we could so much as *think* of a reunion with such a people? Rather tell one to be wedded to a corpse; rather join hands with the fiend from the pit. The blood of many thousands of martyrs is between us. A thousand feelings of horror repel the idea of a renewal of affection." And whereas the *Richmond Whig,* another mouth-piece of treason and of crime, in its issue of the 10th of January, 1863, speaking of those who are opposed to breaking up the Union bequeathed to them by their fathers, says, "They are by nature menials, and fitted only for menial duties. They are in open and flagrant insurrection against their natural lords and masters, the gentlemen of the South. In the exercise of their assumed privileges they deport themselves with all the extravagant airs, the insolence, the cruelty, the cowardice and love of rapine, which have ever characterized the revolt of slaves. The former leniency of their masters only serves to aggravate the ferocity of their nature. When they are again reduced to subjection, and taught to know their place, we must take care to put such trammels about them that they will never have an opportunity to play their tricks again." It is, therefore,

1. *Resolved,* That any attempt on the part of the Government of the United States to conciliate the leaders of the present rebellion, or compromise the questions involved, would be but an attempt on the one hand to rob the gallows of its own, and on the other to humiliate and bring into utter contempt this Government in the estimation of the civilized world.

2. That every State which has ever been is still a State in the Union, and that when this rebellion shall have been put down each of the so-called seceding States will have the same rights, privileges, and immunities under the Constitution as any of the loyal States, except so far as the holding of African slaves in bondage is affected by the President's proclamation of the 1st of January, 1863, the action of Congress on the subject, or the events of the war.

3. That this House utterly repudiate the doctrine advanced by some, that the so-called seceding States have ceased to be States of and in the Union, and have become Territories thereof, or stand in the relation of foreign powers at war therewith.

1864, Feb. 29—Mr. SCHENCK offered these resolutions:

Resolved, That the present war which this Government is carrying on against armed insurrectionists and others, banded together under the name of "Southern Confederacy," was brought on by a wicked and wholly unjustifiable rebellion, and all those engaged in or aiding or encouraging it are public enemies, and should be treated as such.

2. That this rebellion shall be effectually put down; and that, to prevent the recurrence of such rebellion, in future, the causes which led to this one must be permanently removed.

3. That in this struggle which is going on for the saving of our country and free government, there is no middle ground on which any good citizen or true patriot can stand; neutrality, or indifference, or anything short of a hearty support of the Government, being a crime where the question is between loyalty and treason.

A division of the question having been called, The first resolution and the first branch of the second were agreed to. The second branch of the second resolution, "And that, to prevent the recurrence of such rebellions in future, the causes which led to this one must be permanently removed," was agreed to—yeas 124, nays none, as follows:

YEAS—Messrs. *James C. Allen*, Alley, Allison, Ames, *Ancona*, Anderson, Arnold, *Baily*, *Augustus C. Baldwin*, John D. Baldwin, Baxter, Francis P. Blair, jr., Jacob B. Blair, *Bliss*, Blow, Boutwell, Boyd, Brandegee, *Brooks*, Ambrose W. Clark, Freeman Clarke, *Clay*, Cobb, *Coffroth*, Cole, *Cox*, Creswell, Henry Winter Davis, Dawes, *Dawson*, Deming, *Denison*, Dixon, Donnelly, Driggs, Dumont, Eckley, *Eden*, *Eldridge*, Eliot, Farnsworth, Fenton, *Finck*, Frank, *Ganson*, *Grider*, *Griswold*, Hale, *Herrick*, Higby, *Holman*, Hooper, Hotchkiss, Asahel W. Hubbard, John H. Hubbard, *Hutchins*, Jenckes, Julian, Kelley, Orlando Kellogg, *Kernan*, *King*, *Knapp*, *Law*, Loan, *Long*, Lovejoy, *Marcy*, Marvin, McBride, McClurg, McIndoe, Samuel F. Miller, *Wm. H. Miller*, Moorhead, Morrill, Daniel Morris, *Morrison*, Amos Myers, Leonard Myers, *Nelson*, *Noble*, Norton, Charles O'Neill, *John O'Neill*, Patterson, Perham, Pomeroy, Price, *Radford*, *Samuel J. Randall*, William H. Randall, John H. Rice, *Ross*, Schenck, Scofield, *Scott*, Shannon, Sloan, Smithers, Spalding, Starr, *Stebbins*, *John B. Steele*, *Wm. G. Steele*, Stevens, *Stiles*, *Strouse*, *Stuart*, *Sweat*, Thayer, Thomas, Tracy, Upson, Van Valkenburgh, *Voorhees*, William B. Washburn, Whaley, Williams, Wilder, Wilson, Windom, *Winfield*, Woodbridge—124.

NAYS—None.

The third resolution was agreed to—yeas 109, nays none, as follows:

YEAS—Messrs. *James C. Allen*, Alley, Allison, Ames, Anderson, Arnold, *Baily*, *Augustus C. Baldwin*, John D. Baldwin, Baxter, Jacob B. Blair, Boutwell, Boyd, Brandegee, *Brooks*, Ambrose W. Clark, Freeman Clarke, Cobb, Cole, *Cox*, Creswell, Henry Winter Davis, Dawes, Deming, *Denison*, Dixon, Donnelly, Driggs, Dumont, Eckley, *Eldridge*, Eliot, Fenton, *Finck* Frank, *Ganson*, Garfield, Grinnell, *Griswold*, Hale, *Harrington*, Higby, *Holman*, Hotchkiss, Asahel W. Hubbard John H. Hubbard, *Hutchins*, Jenckes, Julian, Kelley, Francis W. Kellogg, Orlando Kellogg, *Kernan*, *King*, *Knapp*, Loan, Lovejoy, Marvin, McBride, McClurg, McIndoe, *McKinney*, *William H. Miller*, Moorhead, Morrill, Daniel Morris, *Morrison*, Amos Myers, Leonard Myers, *Nelson*, *Noble*, Norton, Charles O'Neill, *John O'Neill*, Patterson, Perham, Pomeroy, Price, *Radford*, *Samuel J. Randall*, William H. Randall, John H. Rice, *Rogers*, *Ross*, Schenck, Scofield, Shannon, Sloan, Smithers, Spalding, Starr, *Stebbins*, *John B. Steele*, *William G. Steele*, *Strouse*, *Stuart*, Thayer, Thomas, Upson, Van Valkenburgh, Ellihu B. Washburne, William B. Washburn, Whaley, Williams, Wilder, Wilson, Windom, *Winfield*, Woodbridge—109.

NAYS—None.

1864, March 14—Mr. JOHN H. RICE offered the following resolutions, which were laid over under the rule:

Whereas the vital principle of our national life emanated from and survives in the grand and Heaven-inspired declaration "that all men are created equal; that they are endowed by their Creator with certain inalienable rights; that among these are life, liberty, and the pursuit of happiness;" and whereas the Government of the United States was established and the Constitution adopted in the earnest desire and confident expectation that both would speedily and finally operate in harmony with said "declaration," and thereby secure to all native and naturalized citizens equal civil rights and privileges, regardless of all conditions of birth, race, descent, worldly possessions, or religious faith; and whereas the system of American slavery has been and is utterly subversive and destructive of the aforesaid principles, desires, and expectations, and has been the fruitful progenitor of all manner of evils—social, moral, and political—producing cruelty and oppression to the slave, demoralization and degradation to the free laborer, and brutalization and arrogance in the slave-driver and the slave-master, and has finally culminated in robbery and murder, rebellion and civil war, and has thus conclusively demonstrated that it cannot be longer tolerated with safety to the Government and peace to the Union, and that justice, sound morality, and national unity, each and all, demand its entire extinction; and whereas our people of African descent have in the present war been more unanimous in their loyalty to the Government and their devotedness to the Union than any other class, and have, at the call of Congress and the Executive, sprung to arms to protect the one and maintain the other, and have bravely and nobly vindicated their courage and their manhood upon the land and upon the water—on the battle-field and on the gun-deck; and whereas the freedmen in the District of Columbia and elsewhere in the United States have, by their obedience to the laws, their willingness to labor, their desire for improvement, and their ability to perform military service, evinced their capabilities as citizens and soldiers, and thus practically reversed and annihilated the monstrous judicial dictum and heartless party dogma that "they have no rights which white men are bound to respect:" Therefore,

Resolved, That the Congress of the United States should, by positive and effective legislation, and in accordance with the true theory of our republican form of government, guaranty and secure equality of civil rights and privileges to all classes of persons residing within the District of Columbia and the Territories, and whatever else the Government of the United States possesses sole and exclusive jurisdiction, who are required and made liable, under the Constitution and the laws, to contribute to the support and maintenance of the Government by taxation and military service, and in like manner to protect, secure, and defend all persons in life, liberty, and lawful pursuits, throughout the length and breadth of the Republic.

2. That American slavery, having engendered the rebellion and sustained and prolonged the war, by which un counted thousands of the best citizens of the Republic have been made to suffer and bleed and die, and being subversive of natural right and justice, contrary to the spirit of our institutions, destructive of the best interests of society, disgraceful to our civilization, dangerous to the Republic, and accursed of God and all good men, should not be longer tolerated, but should, by force of law in the adhering States and the power of arms in the rebellious States, be forever abolished and exterminated.

3. That all statutes, legislative acts, and city ordinances, having the force of law, in the District of Columbia and the organized Territories of the United States, whereby persons of African descent residing therein are deprived of their civil rights and restrained of their just privileges, ought in justice to be repealed and declared void.

May 23—Mr. KINNEY, of Utah Territory, offered this resolution; which was adopted:

Resolved, (as the sense of this House,) That the present crisis in the history of this causeless and unjustifiable rebellion calls loudly upon Congress for united patriotic legislation; that while our gallant and self-sacrificing soldiers are, with a courage unexampled either in ancient or modern warfare, sustaining the honor of the nation in the field, they are entitled to the thanks of the country and the hearty support of Congress; and, forgetting for the present all differences upon old party issues, it is the duty of Congress to sustain the constituted authorities of the country in their efforts to suppress the rebellion.

Propositions for "Peace."

First Session, Thirty-Seventh Congress.

IN HOUSE. (See Appendix.)

1861, July 15—Mr. BENJAMIN WOOD offered this resolution:

Resolved, That this Congress recommend the Governors of the several States, to convene their Legislatures for the purpose of calling an election to select two delegates from each Congressional District, to meet in general Convention at Louisville, in Kentucky, on the first Monday in September next, the purpose of the said Convention to be to devise measures for the restoration of peace to our country.

The resolution was laid on the table—yeas 93, nays 51, as follows:

Yeas—Messrs. Aldrich, Alley, Appleton, Arnold, Ashley, Babbitt, Baker, Baxter, Beaman, Bingham, Francis P. Blair, Samuel S. Blair, Blake, Buffinton, Chamberlain, Clark, Colfax, Frederick A. Conkling, Roscoe Conkling, Conway, Curtis, Cutler, Davis, Dawes, Delano, Diven, Duell, Dunn, Edgerton, Edwards, Eliot, Ely, Fenton, Fessenden, Franchot, Gooch, Goodwin, Granger, Gurley, Hale, Hanchett, Harrison, Hickman, Horton, Hutchins, Julian, Kelley, Francis W. Kellogg, William Kellogg, Lansing, Loomis, Lovejoy, McKean, McKnight, McPherson, Mitchell, Moorhead, Justin S. Morrill, Nixon, Olin, Patton, Pike, Porter, Potter, John H. Rice, Riddle, Edward H. Rollins, Sedgwick, Shanks, Sheffield, Shellabarger, Sherman, *Shiel*, Sloan, Spaulding, Stevens, Stratton, Benjamin F. Thomas, Trowbridge, Upton, Vandever, Van Horn, Van Valkenburgh, Van Wyck, Verree, Wall, Wallace, Charles W. Walton, E. P. Walton, Washburne, Wheeler, Albert S. White, Windom—93.

Nays—Messrs. *Allen, Ancona, Joseph Baily, George H. Browne, Burnett, Calvert, Cobb, Cooper, Corning, Cox, Cravens, Crittenden, Delaplaine, Dunlap, English*, Fisher, *Fouke, Grider, Haight, Harding, Holman*, Jackson, *Johnson, Law, Lazear, Logan, McClernand, Mallory, Morris, Noble, Noell, Norton, Nugen, Odell, Pendleton, Reid, Richardson, Robinson, James S. Rollins, Smith, John B. Steele, William G. Steele, Vallandigham, Vibbard, Voorhees, Wadsworth, Ward, Chilton A. White, Wickliffe, Wood, Woodruff*—51.

July 29—Mr. Cox asked leave to offer this resolution:

Whereas it is the part of rational beings to terminate their differences by rational methods, and inasmuch as the differences between the United States authorities and the seceding States have resulted in a civil war, characterized by bitter hostility and extreme atrocity; and although the party in the seceded States are guilty of breaking the national unity and resisting the national authority: Yet,

Be it resolved, First. That while we make undiminished and increased exertions by our navy and army to maintain the integrity and stability of this Government, the common laws of war, consisting of those maxims of humanity, moderation, and honor, which are a part of the international code, ought to be observed by both parties, and for a stronger reason than exists between two alien nations, inasmuch as the two parties have a common ancestry, history, prosperity, glory, Government, and Union, and are now unhappily engaged in lacerating their common country. Second. That, resulting from these premises, while there ought to be left open, as between two alien nations, the same means for preventing the war being carried to outrageous extremities, there ought also to be left open some means for the restoration of peace and union. Third. That to this end—the restoration of peace and union on the basis of the Constitution—there be appointed a committee of one member from each State, who shall report to this House, at its next session, such amendments to the Constitution of the United States, as shall assuage all grievances, and bring about a reconstruction of the national unity; and that for the preparation of such adjustment and the conference requisite for that purpose, there be appointed a commission of seven citizens of the United States, consisting of Edward Everett of Massachusetts, Franklin Pierce of New Hampshire, Millard Fillmore of New York, Reverdy Johnson of Maryland, Martin Van Buren of New York, Thomas Ewing of Ohio, and James Guthrie of Kentucky, who shall request from the so-called Confederate States the appointment of a similar commission, and who shall meet and confer on the subject in the city of Louisville on the first Monday of September next. And that the committee appointed from this House notify said commissioners of their appointment and function, and report their action to the next session as an amendment of the Constitution of the United States to be proposed by Congress to the States for their ratification, according to the fifth article of said Constitution.

The motion to suspend the rules and allow its introduction was lost—yeas 41, nays 85, as follows:

Yeas—Messrs. *Allen, Ancona, Joseph Baily, Burnett, Calvert, Cox, Cravens, Crisfield, Crittenden, Dunlap, Grider, Haight, Harding, Holman*, Jackson, *Johnson, Law*, Leary, *Logan, Mallory, May, Menzies, Morris, Noble, Norton, Nugen, Pendleton, Perry, Reid, Richardson, Robinson, Smith, William G. Steele, Vallandigham, Voorhees, Wadsworth*, Webster, *Chilton A. White, Wickliffe, Wood, Woodruff*—41.

Nays—Messrs. Aldrich, Alley, Arnold, Ashley, Babbitt, Baker, Baxter, Beaman, Bingham, Francis P. Blair, Samuel S. Blair, Blake, Buffinton, Campbell, Chamberlain, Clark, Colfax, Frederick A. Conkling, Roscoe Conkling, Conway, Covode, Cutler, Davis, Dawes, Delano, Diven, Duell, Edgerton, Edwards, Eliot, Fessenden, Franchot, Frank, Gooch, Goodwin, Granger, Gurley, Hale, Harrison, Horton, Hutchins, Julian, Kelley, Francis W. Kellogg, William Kellogg, Lansing, Loomis, Lovejoy, McKean, McKnight, McPherson, Moorhead, Anson P. Morrill, Justin S. Morrill, Olin, Pike, Pomeroy, Porter, Potter, Alexander H. Rice, John H. Rice, Riddle, Edward H. Rollins, Sedgwick, Shanks, *Sheffield*, Shellabarger, Sherman, Spaulding, Stevens, Benjamin F. Thomas, Train, Trowbridge, Upton, Vandever, Van Wyck, Wall, Wallace, Charles W. Walton, E. P. Walton, Washburne, Albert S. White, Windom, Worcester, *Wright*—85.

August 5—Mr. Calvert offered the following resolution:

That whilst it is the duty of Congress, by appropriate legislation, to strengthen the hands of Government in its efforts to maintain the Union and enforce the supremacy of the laws, it is no less our duty to examine into the original causes of our dissensions, and to apply such remedies as are best calculated to restore peace and Union to the country: Therefore, it is

Resolved, (The Senate concurring herein,) That a joint committee, to consist of nine members of this House and four members of the Senate, be appointed to consider and report to Congress such amendments to the Constitution and laws as may be necessary to restore mutual confidence and insure a more perfect and durable Union amongst these States.

Which was laid on the table—yeas 72, nays 39, as follows:

Yeas—Messrs. Aldrich, Alley, Arnold, Ashley, Babbitt, Goldsmith F. Bailey, Baker, Baxter, Bingham, Francis P. Blair, Samuel S. Blair, Blake, Buffinton, Clark, Colfax, Frederick A. Conkling, Roscoe Conkling, Conway, Dunn, Edwards, Eliot, Fenton, Fessenden, Frank, Goodwin, Granger, Gurley, Hale, Harrison, Hutchins, Julian, Kelley, Francis W. Kellogg, William Kellogg, Lansing, Loomis, Lovejoy, McKean, McKnight, McPherson, Moorhead, Anson P. Morrill, Justin S. Morrill, Olin, Pike, Porter, Potter, Alexander H. Rice, John H. Rice, Riddle, Edward H. Rollins, Sedgwick, Shanks, *Sheffield*, Shellabarger, Sherman, Sloan, Spaulding, Stevens, Benjamin F. Thomas, Train, Trimble, Trowbridge, Van Horn, Verree, Wall, Wallace, Charles W. Walton, E. P. Walton, Albert S. White, Windom, Worcester—72.

Nays—Messrs. *Allen, Ancona, Joseph Baily, George H. Browne, Calvert, Cox, Cravens, Crisfield, Dunlap, English*, Fisher, *Fouke, Grider, Haight, Harding*, Horton, *Johnson, Law*, Leary, *Logan, May, McClernand, Morris, Noble, Odell, Pendleton, Phelps, Richardson, Robinson, James S. Rollins, Shiel, Smith, William G. Steele*, Francis Thomas, *Vallandigham, Wadsworth, Ward*, Webster, *Wickliffe*—39.

August 5—Mr. May offered the following:

Whereas the Government of the United States of America was created by its written Constitution, and derived its first powers alone from the consent of the people, as contained in that instrument, and it has no other powers, and force and arms can neither preserve nor rightfully be permitted to violate it under any authority whatsoever: and whereas Washington and other great sages and patriots, who founded our General Government, solemnly warning their countrymen, predicted its destruction from the establishment of a sectional political party; and they also entreated a spirit of compromise whenever necessary to preserve the Union; and whereas a civil war now exists among the States which have been united, and which, having already prostrated the peace, prosperity, and happiness of the people, and destroyed many valuable citizens, now threatens their destruction in countless numbers, and by its inevitable tendency, if not necessity, the final overthrow of free constitutional government: Therefore,

Be it resolved, That the success of the Republican party, founded, as it is, on a sectional, social, and political question, is justly responsible for the origin of our present national misfortunes.

2. That the uncompromising spirit hitherto manifested by the representatives of that party has prevented a peaceful compromise and adjustment of our unhappy difficulties when the same was practicable.

3. That if the present war continues, the only safety and refuge of constitutional government and civil liberty will be found in the constitutions and sovereignty of the several States, and afterwards, through them, the only hope of a future and more harmonious reconstruction of the Union.

4. That it is impossible by arms to subjugate the people of the seceded States, united as they are in such numbers, so fully prepared and resolved, and actuated by motives which represent the just pride and dignity of equals, of trained freemen, of American citizens; and also believing, as they do to a man, that State, home, wife, children, property, all and every security and benefit of Government is at stake, and that the most cruel and merciless means, forced

by the necessities of an exhausting and desolating war, are to be employed against them.

5. That in view of all these public calamities, and to avoid them, recognizing the necessities which control human affairs, as our fathers of the revolution did, it becomes the duty of Congress, before it closes its present session, to provide for the appointment of commissioners to procure an armistice between the contending armies, and restore peace at all events; and who shall be empowered to arrange a compromise to preserve the Union, if possible; but if not, then a peaceful separation of the respective States of the Union, as well such as now claim to have seceded, as others which may by the sovereign will of their citizens also hereafter ordain to secede; and that the said commissioners be solemnly enjoined so to conduct their negotiations as to obtain, if possible, in the future, a happy, harmonious, and perpetual reconstruction of our Union of States.

Mr. May moved to suspend the rules so as to consider it at once; which was lost—yeas and nays not ordered.

Second Session, Thirty-Seventh Congress.

IN SENATE.

1861, December 4—Mr. Saulsbury offered this joint resolution:

Whereas the people of the States of Virginia, North Carolina, South Carolina, Georgia, Florida, Alabama, Mississippi, Louisiana, Texas, Arkansas, and Tennessee are in revolt against the constitutional Government and authority of the United States, and have assumed to secede from the Federal Union, and to form an independent government under the name of the Confederate States of America: and whereas the Congress of the United States approving the sentiment expressed by the President, in his annual message, "that the Union must be preserved, and hence all indispensable means must be employed," and believing that kind and fraternal feeling between the people of all the States is indispensable to the maintenance of a happy and prosperous Union, and being willing to manifest such feeling on their part, to the end that peace may be restored to a distracted country, and the Union and Constitution be preserved and maintained, and inviting the co-operation of the people of the aforesaid States in the accomplishment of objects so beneficial to each and all, do resolve as follows:

Resolved, &c., That Millard Fillmore, Franklin Pierce, Roger B. Taney, Edward Everett, George M. Dallas, Thomas Ewing, Horace Binney, Reverdy Johnson, John J. Crittenden, George E. Pugh, and Richard W. Thompson be, and they are hereby, appointed commissioners on the part of Congress, to confer with a like number of commissioners, to be appointed by the States aforesaid, for the preservation of the Union and the maintenance of the Constitution, and that they report the result of their said conference to Congress for approval or rejection.

2. That upon the appointment of commissioners, as hereby invited, by said States, and upon the meeting of the joint commission for the purpose of conference as aforesaid, active hostilities shall cease, and be suspended, and shall not be renewed unless said commission shall be unable to agree, or in case of an agreement by them, said agreement shall be rejected either by Congress or by the aforesaid States.

It was laid on the table.

Third Session, Thirty-Seventh Congress.

IN SENATE.

1862, December 3—Mr. Davis offered the following joint resolution:

Resolved, &c., That it be, and is hereby, recommended to all the States to choose as many delegates, severally, as they are entitled to Senators and Representatives in Congress, to meet in convention in Louisville, Kentucky, on the first Monday in April next, to take into consideration the condition of the United States, and the proper means for the restoration of the Union; and that the Legislatures of the several States take such action on this proposition as they may deem fit at the earliest practicable day.

Which was ordered to lie on the table, and be printed.

IN HOUSE.

Mr. Vallandigham offered the following resolution:

Resolved, That this House does earnestly desire that the most speedy and effectual measures be taken for restoring peace in America; and that no time may be lost in proposing an immediate cessation of hostilities, in order to the speedy final settlement of the unhappy controversies which brought about this unnecessary and injurious civil war, by just and adequate security against the return of the like calamities in times to come; and this House desires to offer the most earnest assurances to the country that they will, in due time, cheerfully co-operate with the Executive and the States for the restoration of the Union, by such explicit and most solemn amendments and provisions of the Constitution as may be found necessary for securing the rights of the several States and sections within the Union under the Constitution.

The resolution giving rise to debate, was laid over.

CORRESPONDENCE BETWEEN PRESIDENT LINCOLN AND HON. FERNANDO WOOD.

MR. WOOD TO PRESIDENT LINCOLN.

New York, *December* 8, 1862.

Hon. Abraham Lincoln, *President of the United States:*

Dear Sir: On the 25th of November last I was advised by an authority, which I deemed likely to be well informed as well as reliable and truthful, that the Southern States would send Representatives to the next Congress, provided that a full and general amnesty should permit them to do so. No guarantee or terms were asked for other than the amnesty referred to. Deeming this information of great value, if well founded, I communicated it in substance to the Hon. George Opdyke, the mayor of this city, whom I knew to hold confidential relations to members of your Administration, and proposing, through him, that if the Government would permit the correspondence, under its own inspection, I would undertake to procure something definite and positive from persons connected with the so-called Confederate authorities. Mr. Opdyke stated in reply that several Senators from New England States were then in this city on their way to Washington, to whom he would at once communicate the proposition, and advise me of the answer. Knowing that these gentlemen were your friends, and supposing that they would immediately confer with you on their arrival at the capital, and supposing that I should be speedily informed of the result, I have delayed until now making a communication direct to you.

I now learn, however, from Mr. Opdyke this day, that he failed to see these Senators when in New York, and that he had not made the proposition, and that therefore you are not in possession of it as coming from myself.

As an humble but loyal citizen, deeply impressed with the great necessity of restoring the Union of these States, I ask your immediate attention to this subject. The magnitude of the interests at stake warrant some executive action predicated upon this information, if it be only to ascertain if it be grounded upon even probable foundation. If it shall prove groundless no harm shall have been done, provided the inquiry be made, as it can be, without compromising the Government or injury to the cause in which it is now engaged. If, however, it shall prove well founded, there is no estimate too high to place upon its national value.

Now, therefore, Mr. President, I suggest that gentlemen whose former political and social relations with the leaders of the Southern revolt may be allowed to hold unofficial correspondence with them on this subject—the correspondence to be submitted to you. It may be thus ascertained what, if any, credence may be given to these statements, and also whether a peaceful solution of the present struggle may not be attainable. I am sure nothing that I can say can add to your own well known desire to produce this result. Your exalted position, the embarrassments and responsibilities which surround you upon all sides, the bleeding condition of the country, becoming exhausted, not only in the impoverishment of its best life blood, of industrial production, but in the deterioration and consequent destruction of our political institutions—all call upon you, as our chief ruler, to take one step upon the road of peaceful effort, by which to ascertain whether the time has not arrived when other methods than brute fighting may not accomplish what military force has failed to do.

In the origin of this struggle, you foresaw, that such a time would come. Your inaugural address delivered near two years ago, pointed with prophetic vision the certain results of the impending conflict of arms. Your language then was, "Suppose you go to war, you cannot fight always, and when, after much loss on both sides, and no gain on either, you cease fighting, the identical questions as to terms of intercourse are again upon you." You saw that after a bloody and terrible struggle "the still small voice of reason" would intervene and settle the controversy. You know that since the establishment of Christian civilization negotiation and compromise have, sooner or later, determined every military conquest. It cannot be otherwise here. Has not the time arrived when, to quote your own language, we should "cease fighting," at least long enough to ascertain whether "the identical questions" about which we began the fight may not be amicably and honorably adjusted, and the "terms of intercourse" be once more peaceably established? It is to this end that I now address you—with confidence in your patriotism, and with no desire to interfere with your legitimate constitutional prerogatives.

I am, with high respect, yours very truly,

FERNANDO WOOD.

—

PRESIDENT LINCOLN TO MR. WOOD.

EXECUTIVE MANSION,
WASHINGTON, *December* 12, 1862.

HON. FERNANDO WOOD:

MY DEAR SIR: Your letter of the 8th, with the accompanying note of same date, was received yesterday.

The most important paragraph in the letter, as I consider, is in these words: "On the 26th of November last I was advised by an authority which I deemed likely to be well informed as well as reliable and truthful, that the Southern States would send representatives to the next Congress, provided that a full and general amnesty should permit them to do so. No guarantee or terms were asked for other than the amnesty referred to."

I strongly suspect your information will prove to be groundless; nevertheless, I thank you for communicating it to me. Understanding the phrase in the paragraph above quoted—"the Southern States would send representatives to the next Congress"—to be substantially the same as that "the people of the Southern States would cease resistance, and would reinaugurate, submit to, and maintain the national authority within the limits of such States, under the Constitution of the United States," I say that in such case the war would cease on the part of the United States; and that if within a reasonable time "a full and general amnesty" were necessary to such end, it would not be withheld.

I do not think it would be proper now to communicate this, formally or informally, to the people of the Southern States. My belief is that they already know it; and when they choose, if ever, they can communicate with me unequivocally. Nor do I think it proper now to suspend military operations to try any experiment of negotiation.

I should nevertheless receive, with great pleasure, the exact information you now have, and also such other as you may in any way obtain. Such information might be more valuable before the 1st of January than afterward.

While there is nothing in this letter which I shall dread to see in history, it is, perhaps, better for the present that its existence should not become public. I therefore have to request that you will regard it as confidential.

Your obedient servant,

ABRAHAM LINCOLN.

—

MR. WOOD TO PRESIDENT LINCOLN.

NEW YORK, *December* 17, 1862.

His Excellency ABRAHAM LINCOLN:

MY DEAR SIR: Your letter of the 12th instant was handed to me on the afternoon of the 15th instant by Mr. Wakeman, the postmaster of this city.

Pardon me, Mr. President, when I say that your reply has filled me with profound regret. It declines what I had conceived to be an innocent effort to ascertain the foundation for information in my possession of a desire in the South to return to the Union. It thus appears to be an indication on your part to continue a policy which, in my judgment, is not only unwise, but, in the opinion of many, is in conflict with the constitutional authority vested in the Federal Government.

I think, however, that my proposition is in keeping with your own expressed conditions upon which the war shall cease. You say that "when the people of the southern States would cease resistance, and would reinaugurate, submit to, and maintain the national authority within the limits of such States under the Constitution of the United States, that in such case the war would cease on the part of the United States."

Admitting this position as correct, you will see that as a condition precedent to such submission the opportunity to do so must be afforded. It cannot be expected that the southern people will cease resistance, so long as we proclaim our intention to destroy their local institutions, their property, and their lives, and accompany the declaration with corresponding legislative, executive, social, and political action. They cannot cease resistance, and reinaugurate, submit to, and maintain the Federal authority, if we will not let them alone long enough to do so. If they really desire acquiescence, and are willing to send delegates to the next Congress, as I am advised, how can they do so without the opportunity, and without some intimations or guarantees as to the reception of their representatives at Washington? The act of sending representatives to Congress is within itself a full compliance with your own conditions. If thus represented by their own selected agents, chosen under the forms and in pursuance of their own local State laws governing such elections, they will compose an integral portion of the Government, and thus give the assurance of an "acquiescence and submission" of the very highest and most satisfactory character.

My respectful suggestion was that you should put it in their power to take this course. It would require a simple proclamation of general amnesty, to be qualified, if you please, by such conditions as to render it void in case of non-compliance within a limited period. You have established a precedent for this mode of speaking to those people. Your Emancipation Proclamation told of punishment. Let another be issued, speaking the language of mercy and breathing the spirit of conciliation.

The painful events which have occured since my communication of the 8th instant but embolden me to renew its suggestions. I hope you will now no longer refuse "to suspend military operations to try an experiment of negotiation." I feel that military operations so bloody and exhausting as ours must sooner or later be suspended. The day of suspension must come. The only question is, whether it shall be before the whole American people, North and South, shall be involved in general ruin, or whether it shall be whilst there is remaining sufficient of the recuperative element of life by which to restore our once happy, prosperous, and peaceful American Union.

In compliance with your request that your letter shall not for the present become public, I shall withhold its publication at this time.

With high regard, yours, &c.,

FERNANDO WOOD.

—

First Session, Thirty-Eighth Congress.

IN SENATE.

1864, June 9—Mr. DAVIS, of Kentucky, sought to introduce this joint resolution, but objection was made:

A joint resolution to restore peace among the people of the United States.

Resolved, &c., That three years of civil war in which the enormous expenditure of blood and treasure has no parallel in the world's history, and whose wide-spread rapine and diabolical cruelties have shocked Christendom, and which, from alternating success, has produced no essential results, prove that war was not the proper remedy for our national troubles.

2. That if the people of America would save and restore their shattered Constitution and avert from themselves and their posterity the slavery of a military despotism and of a public debt, the interest upon which all the avails of their labor and economy will never meet, they must bring this war to a speedy close.

3. That the President of the United States be, and he is hereby, authorized to propose a cessation of arms and an amnesty to the authorities of the Confederate States of America, with a view to a convention of the people of all the States to reconstruct their Union; and if that cannot be effected, then that said convention agree upon the terms of a separation of the States without the further effusion of blood, and of a lasting peace among them.

IN HOUSE.

1863, Dec. 14—Mr. FERNANDO WOOD offered this resolution:

Whereas the President, in his message delivered to this House on the 9th instant, and in his recommendation to the people to assemble at their places of worship and give thanks to God for recent victories, claims that the Union cause has gained important and substantial advantages; and whereas, in view of these triumphs, it is no longer beneath our dignity nor dangerous to our safety to evince a generous magnanimity becoming a great and powerful people, by offering to the insurgents an opportunity to return to the Union without imposing upon them degrading or destructive conditions: Therefore,

Resolved, That the President be requested to appoint three commissioners, who shall be empowered to open negotiations with the authorities at Richmond, to the end that this bloody, destructive, and inhuman war shall cease, and the Union be restored upon terms of equity, fraternity, and equality, under the Constitution.

Mr. ELLIHU B. WASHBURNE moved that the

resolution lie on the table, which was agreed to—yeas 98, nays 59, as follows:

YEAS—Messrs. Alley, Allison, Anderson, Arnold, Ashley, *Baily*, J. D. Baldwin, Baxter, Beaman, Blaine, J. B. Blair, Blow, Boutwell, Boyd, Brandegee, Broomall, William G. Brown, Ambrose W. Clark, Freeman Clarke, Cobb, Cole, Creswell, Henry Winter Davis, Dawes, Deming, Dixon, Donnelly, Driggs, Dumont, Eckley, Eliot, Farnsworth, Fenton, *Ganson*, Garfield, Gooch, Grinnell, *Griswold*, Higby, Hooper, Hotchkiss, Asahel W. Hubbard, J. H. Hubbard, Hulburd, Jenckes, Julian, Kasson, Francis W. Kellogg, Orlando Kellogg, Loan, Longyear, Lovejoy, Marvin, McBride, McClurg, McIndoe, Samuel F. Miller, Moorhead, Morrill, Daniel Morris, Amos Myers, Leonard Myers, Norton, Charles O'Neill, Orth, Patterson, Perham, Pike, Pomery, Price, William H. Randall, Alexander H. Rice, John H. Rice, Edward H. Rollins, Schenck, Scofield, Shannon, Sloan, Smith, Smithers, Spalding, Stevens, Thayer, Thomas, Tracy, Upson, Van Valkenburgh, *Ward*, Ellihu B. Washburne, Wm. B. Washburn, Whaley, *Wheeler*, Williams, Wilder, Wilson, Windom, Woodbridge, *Yeaman*—98.

NAYS—Messrs. *James C. Allen*, *Wm. J. Allen*, *Ancona*, *Augustus C. Baldwin*, *Bliss*, *Brooks*, *Chanler*, *Clay*, *Coffroth*, *Cox*, *Cravens*, *Dawson*, *Denison*, *Eden*, *Edgerton*, *Eldridge*, *English*, *Finck*, *Grider*, *Harding*, *Harrington*, *Benjamin G. Harris*, *Charles M. Harris*, *Herrick*, *Holman*, *William Johnson*, *Kernan*, *King*, *Knapp*, *Law*, *Lazear*, *Le Blond*, *Long*, *Mallory*, *Marcy*, *McDowell*, *McKinney*, *William H. Miller*, *James R. Morris*, *Morrison*, *Nelson*, *Noble*, *Odell*, *John O'Neill*, *Pendleton*, *Robinson*, *James S. Rollins*, *Ross*, *Scott*, *Stebbins*, *John B. Steele*, *Stuart*, *Sweat*, *Voorhees*, *Wadsworth*, *Chilton A. White*, *Joseph W. White*, *Winfield*, *Wood*—59.

Dec. 17—Mr. GREEN CLAY SMITH offered these resolutions:

1. *Resolved*, That as our country, and the very existence of the best government ever instituted by man, are imperilled by the most causeless and wicked rebellion that the world has seen, and believing, as we do, that the only hope of saving this country and preserving this Government is by the power of the sword, we are for the most vigorous prosecution of the war until the Constitution and laws shall be enforced and obeyed in all parts of the United States; and to that end we oppose any armistice, or intervention, or mediation, or proposition for peace from any quarter, so long as there shall be found a rebel in arms against the Government; and we ignore all party names, lines, and issues, and recognize but two parties in this war—patriots and traitors.

2. That we hold it to be the duty of Congress to pass all necessary bills to supply men and money, and the duty of the people to render every aid in their power to the constituted authorities of the Government in the crushing out of the rebellion, and in bringing the leaders thereof to condign punishment.

3. That our thanks are tendered to our soldiers in the field for their gallantry in defending and upholding the flag of the Union, and defending the great principles dear to every American patriot.

A division of the question having been called, and the question being on the first resolution:

Mr. ANCONA moved that it be laid on the table; which was disagreed to—yeas 60, nays 100, as follows:

YEAS—Messrs. *James C. Allen*, *William J. Allen*, *Ancona*, *Bliss*, *Brooks*, *Chanler*, *Clay*, *Coffroth*, *Cox*, *Cravens*, *Dawson*, *Denison*, *Eden*, *Edgerton*, *Eldridge*, *English*, *Finck*, *Grider*, *Hall*, *Harding*, *Harrington*, *Benjamin G. Harris*, *Charles M. Harris*, *Herrick*, *William Johnson*, *Kernan*, *King*, *Knapp*, *Law*, *Le Blond*, *Long*, *Mallory*, *McDowell*, *McKinney*, *Middleton*, *William H. Miller*, *James R. Morris*, *Morrison*, *Nelson*, *Noble*, *John O'Neill*, *Pendleton*, *Radford*, *Samuel J. Randall*, *Robinson*, *Rogers*, *James S. Rollins*, *Ross*, *John B. Steele*, *Stiles*, *Strouse*, *Stuart*, *Sweat*, *Voorhees*, *Wadsworth*, *Wheeler*, *Chilton A. White*, *Joseph W. White*, *Winfield*, *Wood*—60.

NAYS—Messrs. Allison, Ames, Arnold, Ashley, *Baily*, *Augustus C. Baldwin*, John D. Baldwin, Beaman, Blaine, Blow, Boutwell, Boyd, Brandegee, Broomall, *James S. Brown*, William G. Brown, Ambrose W. Clark, Freeman Clarke, Cobb, Cole, Creswell, Henry Winter Davis, Thomas T. Davis, Dawes, Deming, Dixon, Donnelly, Driggs, Dumont, Eckley, Eliot, Farnsworth, Fenton, Frank, *Ganson*, Garfield, Gooch, Grinnell, *Griswold*, Hale, Higby, Hooper, Hotchkiss, Asahel W. Hubbard, Jno. H. Hubbard, Hulburd, *Hutchins*, Jenckes, Julian, Kasson, Kelley, Francis W. Kellogg, Orlando Kellogg, Loan, Lovejoy, Marvin, *McAllister*, McBride, McClurg, McIndoe, Samuel F. Miller, Moorhead, Morrill, Daniel Morris, Amos Myers, Leonard Myers, Norton, *Odell*, Charles O'Neill, Orth, Patterson, Perham, Pike, Pomeroy, Price, William H. Randall, Alexander H. Rice, John H. Rice, Edward H. Rollins, Schenck, Scofield, Shannon, Sloan, Smith, Smithers, Spalding, *Stebbins*, Stevens, Thayer, Tracy, Van Valkenburgh, *Ward*, Ellihu B. Washburne, William B. Washburn, Whaley, Williams, Wilder, Wilson, Windom, Woodbridge—100.

The resolution was then agreed to—yeas 94, nays 65, as follows:

YEAS—Messrs. Alley, Allison, Ames, Anderson, Arnold, Ashley, *Baily*, John D. Baldwin, Beaman, Blaine, Blow, Boutwell, Boyd, Brandegee, Broomall, Ambrose W. Clark, Cobb, Cole, Creswell, Henry Winter Davis, Thos. T. Davis, Dawes, Deming, Dixon, Donnelly, Driggs, Dumont, Eckley, Eliot, Farnsworth, Fenton, Frank, Garfield, Gooch, Grinnell, Hale, Higby, Hooper, Hotchkiss, Asahel W. Hubbard, John H. Hubbard, Hulburd, Jenckes, Kasson, Kelley, Francis W. Kellogg, Orlando Kellogg, Loan, Longyear, Lovejoy, Marvin, *McAllister*, McBride, McClurg, McIndoe, Samuel F. Miller, Moorhead, Morrill, Daniel Morris, Amos Myers, Leonard Myers, Norton, *Odell*, Charles O'Neill, Orth, Patterson, Perham, Pike, Pomeroy, Price, William H. Randall, Alexander H. Rice, John H. Rice, Edward H. Rollins, Schenck, Scofield, Shannon, Sloan, Smith, Smithers, Spalding, Stevens, Thayer, Tracy, Van Valkenburgh, Ellihu B. Washburne, Wm. B. Washburn, Whaley, Williams, Wilder, Wilson, Windom, Woodbridge, *Yeaman*—94.

NAYS—Messrs. *James C. Allen*, *William J. Allen*, *Ancona*, *Augustus C. Baldwin*, *Bliss*, *Brooks*, *Chanler*, *Coffroth*, *Cox*, *Cravens*, *Dawson*, *Denison*, *Eden*, *Edgerton*, *Eldridge*, *English*, *Finck*, *Ganson*, *Grider*, *Griswold*, *Hall*, *Harding*, *Benjamin G. Harris*, *Charles M. Harris*, *Herrick*, *Hutchins*, *William Johnson*, *Kernan*, *Knapp*, *Law*, *Le Blond*, *Long*, *Mallory*, *Marcy*, *McDowell*, *McKinney*, *Middleton*, *Wm. H. Miller*, *James R. Morris*, *Morrison*, *Nelson*, *Noble*, *John O'Neill*, *Pendleton*, *Perry*, *Radford*, *Samuel J. Randall*, *Robinson*, *Rogers*, *James S. Rollins*, *Ross*, *Scott*, *John B. Steele*, *William G. Steele*, *Stiles*, *Strouse*, *Stuart*, *Voorhees*, *Wadsworth*, *Ward*, *Wheeler*, *Chilton A. White*, *Joseph W. White*, *Winfield*, *Fernando Wood*—65.

The second resolution was agreed to—yeas 153, nays 1, as follows:

YEAS—Messrs. Alley, Allison, Ames, Anderson, Arnold, Ashley, *Baily*, *Augustus C. Baldwin*, John D. Baldwin, Beaman, Blaine, *Bliss*, Blow, Boutwell, Boyd, Brandegee, *Brooks*, Broomall, *James S. Brown*, William G. Brown, *Chanler*, Ambrose W. Clark, Freeman Clarke, *Clay*, Cobb, *Coffroth*, Cole, *Cox*, *Cravens*, Creswell, Henry Winter Davis, Thomas T. Davis, Dawes, *Dawson*, Deming, *Denison*, Dixon, Donnelly, Driggs, Dumont, Eckley, *Edgerton*, *Eldridge*, Eliot, *English*, Farnsworth, Fenton, *Finck*, Frank, *Ganson*, Garfield, Gooch, *Grider*, Grinnell, *Griswold*, Hale, *Hall*, *Harding*, *Charles M. Harris*, *Herrick*, Higby, *Holman*, Hooper, Hotchkiss, Asahel W. Hubbard, John H. Hubbard, Hulburd, *Hutchins*, Jenckes, *Wm. Johnson*, Julian, Kasson, Kelley, Francis W. Kellogg, Orlando Kellogg, *Kernan*, *King*, *Law*, *Lazear*, *Le Blond*, Loan, Lovejoy, *Mallory*, Marvin, *McAllister*, McBride, McClurg, McIndoe, *McKinney*, *Middleton*, Samuel F. Miller, *William H. Miller*, Moorhead, Morrill, Daniel Morris, *James R. Morris*, *Morrison*, Amos Myers, Leonard Myers, *Nelson*, *Noble*, Norton, *Odell*, Charles O'Neill, *John O'Neill*, Orth, Patterson, Perham, *Perry*, Pike, Pomeroy, Price, *Radford*, *Samuel J. Randall*, William H. Randall, Alexander H. Rice, John H. Rice, *Rogers*, Edward H. Rollins, *James S. Rollins*, Schenck, Scofield, *Scott*, Shannon, Sloan, Smith, Smithers, Spalding, *Stebbins*, *John B. Steele*, *William G. Steele*, Stevens, *Strouse*, *Stuart*, *Sweat*, Thayer, Thomas, Tracy, Van Valkenburgh, *Wadsworth*, *Ward*, Ellihu B. Washburne, William B. Washburn, Whaley, *Wheeler*, *Joseph W. White*, Williams, Wilder, Wilson, Windom, *Winfield*, Woodbridge, *Yeaman*—153.

NAY—Mr. *Benjamin G. Harris*—1.

The third resolution was agreed to—yeas 168, nays 1, (Mr. *B. G. Harris*.)

On this vote, Messrs. *James C. Allen*, *Wm. J. Allen*, *Ancona*, *Eden*, *Harrington*, *Knapp*, *Long*, Longyear, *McDowell*, *Pendleton*, *Robinson*, *Stiles*, *Voorhees*, Webster, *Chilton A. White* and *Fernando Wood*—16, who are *not* recorded before, voted *aye;* and Mr. Hooper, who *is* recorded before, did not vote.

1864, Jan. 7—Mr. JOHN D. BALDWIN offered this preamble and resolution:

Whereas the organized treason having its headquarters at Richmond exists in defiant violation of the national Constitution and has no claim to be treated otherwise than as an outlaw; and whereas this Richmond combination of conspirators and traitors can have no rightful authority over the people of any portion of the national Union, and no warrant for assuming control of the political destiny of the people of any State or section of this Union, and no apology but that of conspiracy and treason for any assumption of authority whatever: Therefore,

Resolved, That any proposition to negotiate with the rebel leaders at Richmond (sometimes called "the authorities at Richmond") for a restoration of loyalty and order in those portions of the Republic which have been disorganized by the rebellion is, in effect, a proposition to recognize the ringleaders of the rebellion as entitled to represent and bind the loyal citizens of the United States whom they oppress, and to give countenance and support to the pretensions of conspiracy and treason; and therefore every such proposition should be rejected without hesitation and delay.

Mr. Cox moved to lay the resolution on the table, which was disagreed to; and it was then passed—yeas 88, nays 24, as follows:

YEAS—Messrs. Alley, Allison, Ames, Anderson, Arnold, *Baily*, *Augustus C. Baldwin*, John D. Baldwin, Baxter, Beaman, Blaine, Jacob B. Blair, Blow, Boutwell, Boyd, Brandegee, Broomall, *James S. Brown*, William G. Brown, Cobb, Cole, Creswell, Henry Winter Davis, Dawes, Deming, Dixon, Donnelly, Eckley, Eliot, Farnsworth, Fenton, Garfield, Gooch, Grinnell, *Griswold*, Hale, Higby, *Holman*, Hooper, John H. Hubbard, Hulburd, Julian, Kasson, Kelley, Francis W. Kellogg, *Kernan*, *King*, Loan, Longyear, Lovejoy, Marvin, McBride, McClurg, *Middleton*, Morrill, Daniel Morris, Amos Myers, Leonard Myers, *Moses F. Odell*, Charles O'Neill, Orth, Perham, Pike, Pomeroy, Price, William H. Randall, John H. Rice, Scofield, Shannon, Sloan, Smith, Smithers, Spalding, *Stebbins*, Stevens, *Sweat*, Thayer, Tracy, Upson, Van Valkenburgh, Ellihu B. Washburne, William B. Washburn, Webster, Williams, Wilson, Windom, Woodbridge, *Yeaman*—88.

NAYS—Messrs. *Ancona*, *Bliss*, *Brooks*, *Cox*, *Denison*, *Edgerton*, *Finck*, *Harrington*, *Charles M. Harris*, *Herrick*, *Knapp*, *Long*, *Marcy*, *William H. Miller*, *Morrison*, *Noble*, *Pendleton*, *Perry*, *Pruyn*, *Samuel J. Randall*, *Rogers*, *Ross*, *Strouse*, *Fernando Wood*—24.

The preamble was then agreed to—yeas 102, nays none, as follows:

YEAS—Messrs. Alley, Allison, Ames, Anderson, Arnold, *Baily*, *Augustus C. Baldwin*, John D. Baldwin, Baxter, Blaine, Jacob B. Blair, Blow, Boutwell, Brandegee, *Brooks*, Broomall, *James S. Brown*, Wm. G. Brown, Cobb, *Coffroth*, Cole, *Cox*, *Cravens*, Creswell, Thomas T. Davis, Dawes, Deming, *Denison*, Dixon, Eliot, Fenton, *Finck*, Frank, Garfield, Gooch, *Grider*, Grinnell, *Griswold*, Hale, *Harrington*, *Herrick*, Higby, *Holman*, Hooper, John H. Hubbard, Hulburd, Julian, Kasson, Kelley, Francis W. Kellogg, *Kernan*, *King*, *Lazear*, Loan, Longyear, Lovejoy, Marvin, McBride, McClurg, *Middleton*, *Wm. H. Miller*, Morrill, Daniel Morris, Amos Myers, Leonard Myers, *Noble*, Norton, *Odell*, Charles O'Neill, Orth, Pike, Pomeroy, Price, *Pruyn*, *Samuel J. Randall*, William H. Randall, John H. Rice, *Rogers*, Scofield, Sloan, Smith, Smithers, Spalding, *Stebbins*, *John B. Steele*, *Wm. G. Steele*, Stevens, *Strouse*, *Sweat*, Thayer, Tracy, Upson, Van Valkenburgh, Ellihu B. Washburne, William B. Washburn, Webster, *Joseph W. White*, Williams, Wilson, Windom, Woodbridge, *Yeaman*—102.

NAYS—None.

January 7—Mr. ROGERS offered these resolutions:

Resolved, That as our country and the existence of the old Union are imperilled by a rebellion against the wisest and best government ever devised by man, we are for the most united, determined, and vigorous prosecution of the war for the purpose of enforcing the Constitution of the United States and the laws made in pursuance thereof in all parts of the United States; but at the same time we are for adding to force the power of conciliation and compromise so far as is consistent with an honorable and lasting peace, and founded solely upon a restoration of the Union under the Constitution, and in no event to agree to or countenance a dissolution of the Union; and that we believe the appointment of commissioners upon the part of the Federal Government, to meet commissioners similarly appointed by the insurgent States, to convene in some suitable place for the purpose of considering whether any, and if any, what plan may be adopted consistent with the honor and dignity of the nation, and based upon a restoration of the whole Union, by which the present war may be brought to a close, and the lives, limbs, and health of the gallant officers and soldiers of the Union preserved, and the liberties of the people maintained, is not inconsistent with the honor and dignity of the Federal Government, but, as an indication of the spirit which animates the adhering States, would, in any event, tend to strengthen us in the opinion of other nations and the loyal people of the insurgent States; and hoping, as we sincerely do, that the people of the southern States would reciprocate the peaceful indications thus evinced, and believing, as we do, that under the blessings of God great benefits would arise from such conference, we most earnestly recommend such conference to the consideration of the President and Senate of the United States, and request their co-operation therein, and hope that the President will appoint commissioners for that purpose.

2. That the people of the several States now in rebellion against the Government of the United States, whenever they shall desire to return to the Union and obey the Constitution of the United States, and laws made in pursuance thereof, have a right under and by virtue of the said Constitution to reorganize their respective State governments with all their domestic institutions as they were before the war, and to elect representatives to the Congres of the United States, and to be represented in the Union with all the rights of the people of the several States, and without any conditions precedent except that of being liable to be punished according to the Constitution and laws made in pursuance thereof, as their laws and acts of secession are unconstitutional and void.

On motion of Mr. STEVENS they were laid upon the table—yeas 78, nays 42, as follows:

YEAS—Messrs. Alley, Allison, Ames, Anderson, Arnold, *Baily*, John D. Baldwin, Baxter, Beaman, Blaine, Jacob B. Blair, Blow, Boutwell, Boyd, Brandegee, Broomall, William G. Brown, Cobb, Cole, Creswell, Thomas T. Davis, Dawes, Deming, Dixon, Donnelly, Eckley, Eliot, Farnsworth, Fenton, Frank, Garfield, Gooch, Grinnell, Hale, Higby, Hooper, Hulburd, Julian, Kasson, Kelley, Francis W. Kellogg, Orlando Kellogg, Loan, Lovejoy, Marvin, McBride, McClurg, Morrill, Daniel Morris, Amos Myers, Leonard Myers, *Moses F. Odell*, Charles O'Neill, Orth, Perham, Pomeroy, Price, William H. Randall, Scofield, Shannon, Sloan, Smith, Smithers, Spalding, *Stebbins*, Stevens, Thayer, Thomas, Tracy, Upson, Van Valkenburgh, Ellihu B. Washburne, William B. Washburn, Webster, Williams, Wilson, Windom, Woodbridge—78.

NAYS—Messrs. *William J. Allen*, *Ancona*, *Augustus C. Baldwin*, *Brooks*, *James S. Brown*, *Chanler*, *Cox*, *Cravens*, *Dawson*, *Denison*, *Eden*, *Edgerton*, *Finck*, *Grider*, *Griswold*, *Harrington*, *Charles M. Harris*, *Herrick*, *Holman*, *Kernan*, *Knapp*, *Lazear*, *Long*, *Marcy*, *William H. Miller*, *Morrison*, *Noble*, *Pendleton*, *Perry*, *Pruyn*, *Samuel J. Randall*, *Robinson*, *Rogers*, *James S. Rollins*, *Ross*, *John B. Steele*, *William G. Steele*, *Strouse*, *Sweat*, *Joseph W. White*, *Fernando Wood*, *Yeaman*—42.

Jan. 18—Mr. DAWSON, of Pennsylvania, offered the following preamble and resolution:

Whereas a great civil war like that which now afflicts the United States is the most grievous of all national calamities, producing as it does, spoliation, bloodshed, anarchy, public debt, official corruption, and private immorality, the American Government cannot rightfully wage such a war upon any portion of its people, except for the sole purpose of vindicating the Constitution and laws and restoring both to their just supremacy; and whereas this House, on the 22d day of July, 1861, speaking in the name of the American people and in the face of the world, solemnly and truly declared that it was waged for no purpose of conquest or oppression, but solely to restore the Union, with all the rights of the people aud the State unimpaired; and whereas in every war, especially in every war of invasion, and most particularly if it be a civil war between portions of the same country, the object of it ought to be clearly defined and the terms distinctly stated upon which hostilities will cease; and the advancing armies of the Government should carry the Constitution in one hand, while they hold the sword in the other, so that the invaded party may have its choice between the two: Therefore,

Resolved, That the President be requested to make known by public proclamation or otherwise, to all the country, that whenever any State now in insurrection shall submit herself to the authority of the Federal Government, as defined in the Constitution, all hostilities against her shall cease, and such State shall be protected from all external interference with the local laws and institutions, and her people shall be guarantied in the full enjoyment of all those rights which the Federal Constitution gave them.

Mr. STEVENS moved that they be laid upon the table, which was agreed to—yeas 79, nays 56, as follows:

YEAS—Messrs. Allison, Ames, Arnold, Ashley, John D.

Baldwin, Baxter, Beaman, Blaine, Francis P. Blair, jr., Jacob B. Blair, Boutwell, Brandegee, Broomall, Ambrose W. Clark, Freeman Clarke, Cole, Creswell, Henry Winter Davis, Thomas T. Davis, Dawes, Deming, Dixon, Driggs, Eckley, Eliot, Farnsworth, Fenton, Frank, Garfield, Gooch, Higby, Hooper, Hotchkiss, Asahel W. Hubbard, Hulburd, Jenckes, Julian, Kasson, Kelley, Francis W. Kellogg, Longyear, Lovejoy, Marvin, McBride, McClurg, McIndoe, Samuel F. Miller, Moorhead, Morrill, Daniel Morris, Amos Myers, Leonard Myers, Charles O'Neill, Orth, Patterson, Pike, Price, William H. Randall, Alexander H. Rice, John H. Rice, Edward H. Rollins, Schenck, Scofield, Shannon, Smith, Smithers, Spalding, Stevens, Thayer, Thomas, Upson, Van Valkenburgh, Ellihu B. Washburne, William B. Washburn, Whaley, Williams, Wilson, Windom, Woodbridge—79.

NAYS—Messrs. *James C. Allen, Ancona, Augustus C. Baldwin, Bliss, Brooks, James S. Brown,* William G. Brown, *Chanler, Coffroth, Cox, Dawson, Denison, Eden, Edgerton, Eldridge, English, Finck, Ganson, Grider, Griswold,* Hale, *Hall, Harding, Harrington, Benjamin G. Harris, Herrick, Holman, Hutchins, William Johnson, Kernan, Lazear, Le Blond, Long, Marcy, McAllister, McDowell, McKinney, Middleton, William H. Miller, James R. Morris, Morrison, Nelson, Pendleton, Robinson, Ross, John B. Steele, Stiles, Stuart, Sweat, Voorhees, Wm. H. Wadsworth, Wheeler, Chilton A. White, Joseph W. White, Fernando Wood, Yeaman*—56.

February 29—Mr. LONG, of Ohio, offered this preamble and resolution:

Whereas history teaches that there never has been a civil war that was not settled in the end by compromise, and inasmuch as no possible harm can result either to the character or dignity of the United States from an honest effort to stop the effusion of fraternal blood, and restore the Union by the return of the States in rebellion to their allegiance under the Constitution; and whereas the President, with a full knowledge of the lessons taught by history in relation to all civil wars, in his inaugural address said, "suppose you go to war, you cannot fight always; and when, after much loss on both sides, and no gain on either, you cease fighting, the identical old questions as to terms of intercourse are again upon you;" and whereas we now have an armistice, decreed by the Almighty, and executed for the past two months by the snows and ice of winter, thereby affording time and opportunity for reflection upon the past three years of horrible, relentless, and destructive civil war with all its calamities, and a prospective view of increased horrors in the approaching conflicts; and whereas a preamble and resolutions were, on the 7th of February, instant, introduced in the House of Representatives of the Confederate Congress at Richmond denying the statement of the President of the United States "that no propositions for peace had been made to the United States by the Confederate States," and affirming that such propositions were prevented from being made by the President of the United States, in that he had refused to hear, or even to receive, two commissioners appointed to treat expressly for peace: Therefore, be it

Resolved, That the President be, and he is hereby, most earnestly, but respectfully, requested to appoint Franklin Pierce, of New Hampshire; Millard Fillmore, of New York; Thomas Ewing, of Ohio, and such other persons as the President may see proper to select, as commissioners on behalf of the United States, who shall be empowered to meet a commission of like number when appointed for the same object on behalf of the Confederate States, at such time and place as may be agreed upon, for the purpose of ascertaining, before the renewal of hostilities shall have again commenced, whether the war shall not now cease, and the Union be restored by the return of all the States to the allegiance and their rights under the Constitution.

Which was disagreed to—yeas 22, nays 96, as follows:

YEAS—Messrs. *James C. Allen, Ancona, Brooks, Coffroth, Denison, Eden, Eldridge, Finck, Knapp, Long, McDowell, Wm. H. Miller, Morrison, John O'Neill, Pendleton, Samuel J. Randall, Rogers, Ross, Stiles, Strouse, Voorhees, Chilton A. White*—22.

NAYS—Messrs. Alley, Allison, Ames, Anderson, Arnold, Ashley, *Augustus C. Baldwin*, John D. Baldwin, Baxter, Jacob B. Blair, Blow, Boutwell, Boyd, Brandegee, William G. Brown, Ambrose W. Clark, Freeman Clarke, Cobb, Cole, Creswell, Henry Winter Davis, Dawes, Deming, Dixon, Donnelly, Driggs, Dumont, Eckley, Eliot, Farnsworth, Fenton, Frank, *Ganson*, Garfield, Grinnell, *Griswold*, Hale, Higby, *Holman*, Hooper, Hotchkiss, John H. Hubbard, *Hutchins*, Jenckes, Julian, Kelley, Orlando Kellogg, *Kernan, King*, Loan, Lovejoy, Marvin, McBride, McClurg, McIndoe, Samuel F. Miller, Moorhead, Morrill, Daniel Morris, Amos Myers, Leonard Myers, *Nelson*, Norton, Charles O'Neill, Perham, Pike, Pomeroy, Price, *Radford*, William H. Randall, John H. Rice, Schenck, Scofield, Shannon, Sloan, Smithers, Spalding, Starr, *Stebbins, John B. Steele*, Stevens, Thayer, Thomas, Tracy, Upson, Van Valkenburgh, *Wadsworth*, Ellihu B. Washburne, William B. Washburn, Whaley, Williams, Wilder, Wilson, Windom, *Winfield*, Woodbridge—96.

May 30—Mr. LAZEAR asked consent to offer this resolution:

Whereas the fratricidal war which has for the last three years filled every neighborhood of our once united and happy country with mourning, and has drenched a hundred battle-fields with the blood of our fellow-citizens, and laid waste many of the fairest portions of the land, and yet has failed to restore the authority of the Federal Government in the seceded States; and whereas we believe a misapprehension exists in the minds of a large portion of the people of the South as to the feelings which actuate a large portion of the people of the free States, and which misapprehension we are called upon by every consideration of humanity and a sense of justice to correct and if possible remove, whether we regard in making this effort what we owe to ourselves, to our fellow-countrymen of the South, or to the world: Therefore,

Resolved, That no truly loyal citizen of the United States desires the application of any rule or law in determining the rights and privileges and the measure of responsibility of the people of any of the States but such as shall have been determined by the Supreme Court to be in accordance with and sanctioned by the Constitution and well-established usages of the country.

2. That the President, in his capacity of Commander-in-Chief of the Army and Navy of the United States, be, and he is hereby, required to adopt such measures as he may think best, with a view to a suspension of hostilities between the armies of the North and the South for a period not exceeding —— days; and that he be also authorized to adopt or agree upon some plan by which the decision of the great body of the people North and South may be secured upon the question of calling a convention composed of delegates from all the States, to which shall be referred the settlement of all questions now dividing the southern States from the rest of the Union, with a view to the restoration of the several States to the places they were intended to occupy in the Union, and the privileges intended to be granted to them by the framers of our national Constitution, who were in our opinion the most enlightened statesmen and purest patriots that ever lived, and than whom we cannot hope to find wiser or better counsellors in the present exigency in our national affairs.

Objection was made.

June 30—Pending the consideration of the Enrollment Bill, the following amendment was offered by Mr. LE BLOND, of Ohio:

Provided, That no levy of troops shall be made under the provisions of this act, except by volunteering, till such time as the President of the United States shall have made a request for an armistice; and shall have made such efforts as are consistent with honor to restore harmony among the States, by the appointment of commissioners empowered to negotiate for peace upon the terms of a restoration of the Union under the Constitution, and until such offer shall have been rejected by the so-called Confederate government.

Which was rejected—yeas 13, nays 91, as follows:

YEAS—Messrs. *Ancona, Bliss, Edgerton, Eldridge, Finck, William Johnson, Long, James R. Morris, Noble, John O'Neill, Pendleton, Ross, Chilton A. White*—13

NAYS—Messrs. Alley, Allison, Ames, Ashley, *Baily*, John D. Baldwin, Baxter, Beaman, Jacob B. Blair, Boutwell, Broomall, *J. S. Brown*, W. G. Brown, Cobb, Cole, Creswell, Dawes, Dixon, Donnelly, Driggs, Eckley, Eliot, *English*, Farnsworth, Fenton, Frank, *Ganson*, Garfield, Gooch, *Griswold*, Hale, *Harding*, Higby, Hooper, Hotchkiss, A. W. Hubbard, Hulburd, Ingersoll, Jenckes, Julian, *Kalbfleisch*, Kelley, *Kernan*, Littlejohn, Loan, Longyear, *Mallory, McAllister*, McBride, McClurg, Samuel F. Miller, Moorhead, Morrill, Amos Myers, Leonard Myers, Norton, *Odell*, Charles O'Neill, Orth, Patterson, *Radford*, Randall, Alexander H. Rice, John H. Rice, Edward H. Rollins, Schenck, Scofield, Shannon, Sloan, Smithers, Spalding, Stevens, *Stuart, Sweat*, Thayer, Thomas, Tracy, Upson, Van Valkenburgh, *Wadsworth*, Ellihu B. Washburne, William B. Washburn, Webster, Whaley, *Wheeler*, Williams, Wilder, Wilson, Windom, *Winfield*, Woodbridge—91.

THE LATE PEACE NEGOTIATION AT NIAGARA FALLS.

The following correspondence explains itself:

[Private and confidential.]

CLIFTON HOUSE, NIAGARA FALLS,
CANADA WEST, *July* 12, 1864.

DEAR SIR: I am authorized to say that the Hon. Clement C. Clay, of Alabama, Prof. James P. Holcombe, of Virginia, and George N. Sanders, of Dixie, are ready and willing to go at once to Washington, upon complete and unqualified protection being given either by the President or Secretary of War. Let the permission include the three names and one other. Very respectfully,

GEORGE N. SANDERS.

To the Hon. HORACE GREELEY.

—

NIAGARA FALLS, N. Y., *July* 17, 1864.

GENTLEMEN: I am informed that you are duly accredited from Richmond as the bearer of propositions looking to the establishment of peace; that you desire to visit Washington in the fulfillment of your mission, and that you further desire that Mr. George N. Sanders shall accompany you. If my information be thus far substantially correct, I am authorized by the President of the United States to tender you his safe conduct on the journey proposed, and to accompany you at the earliest time that will be agreeable to you.

I have the honor to be, gentlemen, yours,

HORACE GREELEY.

Messrs. CLEMENT C. CLAY, JACOB THOMPSON, JAMES P. HOLCOMBE, *Clifton House, C. W.*

CLIFTON HOUSE, NIAGARA FALLS,
July 18, 1864.

SIR: We have the honor to acknowledge your favor of the 17th instant, which would have been answered on yesterday but for the absence of Mr. Clay.

The safe conduct of the President of the United States has been tendered us, we regret to state, under some misapprehension of facts. We have not been accredited to him from Richmond as the bearers of propositions looking to the establishment of peace.

We are, however, in the confidential employment of our Government, and are entirely familiar with its wishes and opinions on that subject; and we feel authorized to declare that, if the circumstances disclosed in this correspondence were communicated to Richmond we would be at once invested with the authority to which your letter refers, or other gentlemen clothed with full powers would be immediately sent to Washington with the view of hastening a consummation so much to be desired, and terminating at the earliest possible moment the calamities of the war.

We respectfully solicit through your intervention a safe conduct to Washington, and thence by any route which may be designated through your lines to Richmond. We would be gratified if Mr. George N. Sanders was embraced in this privilege.

Permit us in conclusion to acknowledge our obligations to you for the interest you have manifested in the furtherance of our wishes, and to express the hope that, in any event, you will afford us the opportunity of tendering them in person before you leave the Falls.

We remain, very respectfully, &c.,

C. C. CLAY, JR.,
J. P. HOLCOMBE.

P. S. It is proper to add that Mr. Thompson is not here, and has not been staying with us since our sojourn in Canada.

—

INTERNATIONAL HOTEL,
NIAGARA, N. Y., *July* 18, 1864.

GENTLEMEN: I have the honor to acknowledge the receipt of yours of this date by the hand of Mr. W. C. Jewett. The state of facts therein presented being materially different from that which was understood to exist by the President when he entrusted me with the safe conduct required, it seems to me on every account advisable that I should communicate with him by telegraph and solicit fresh instructions, which I shall at once proceed to do. I hope to be able to transmit the result this afternoon; and, at all events, I shall do so at the earliest moment.

Yours, truly, HORACE GREELEY.

Messrs. CLEMENT C. CLAY and JAMES P. HOLCOMBE,
Clifton House, C. W.

—

CLIFTON HOUSE, NIAGARA FALLS, *July* 18, 1864.

To the Hon. H. GREELEY, *Niagara Falls, N. Y.*

SIR: We have the honor to acknowledge the receipt of your note of this date by the hands of Col. Jewett, and will await the further answer which you propose to send us.

We are, very respectfully, &c.

C. C. CLAY, jr.
JAMES P. HOLCOMBE.

INTERNATIONAL HOTEL,
NIAGARA FALLS, N. Y., *July* 19, 1864.

GENTLEMEN: At a late hour last evening (too late for communication with you) I received a dispatch informing me that further instructions left Washington last evening, which must reach me, if there be no interruption, at noon to-morrow. Should you decide to await their arrival, I feel confident that they will enable me to answer definitely your note of yesterday morning. Regretting a delay which I am sure you will regard as unavoidable on my part,

I remain, yours, truly,

HORACE GREELEY.

The Hon. Messrs. C. C. CLAY, jr., and J. P. HOLCOMBE,
Clifton House, Niagara, C. W.

—

CLIFTON HOUSE, NIAGARA FALLS, C. W.,
July 19, 1864.

SIR: Colonel Jewett has just handed us your note of this date, in which you state that further instructions from Washington will reach you by noon to-morrow, if there be no interruption. One, or possibly both of us, will be obliged to leave the Falls to-day, but will return in time to receive the communication which you promise to-morrow.

We remain, truly yours, &c.,

JAMES P. HOLCOMBE,
C. C. CLAY, Jr.

The Hon. HORACE GREELEY,
Now at the International Hotel.

—

EXECUTIVE MANSION,
WASHINGTON, *July* 18, 1864.

To whom it may concern:

Any proposition which embraces the restoration of peace, the integrity of the whole Union, and the abandonment of slavery, and which comes by and with an authority that can control the armies now at war against the United States, will be received and considered by the Executive Government of the United States, and will be met by liberal terms on other substantial and collateral points, and the bearer or bearers thereof shall have safe conduct both ways.

ABRAHAM LINCOLN.

—

INTERNATIONAL HOTEL, *Wednesday*.

Major Hay would respectfully inquire whether Professor Holcombe and the gentlemen associated with him desire to send to Washington by Major Hay any messages in reference to the communication delivered to him on yesterday, and in that case when he may expect to be favored with such messages.

—

Mr. Holcombe presents his compliments to Major Hay, and greatly regrets if his return to Washington has been delayed by any expectation of an answer to the communication which Mr. Holcombe received from him on yesterday, to be delivered to the President of the United States. That communication was accepted as the response to a letter of Messrs. Clay and Holcombe to the Hon. H. Greeley, and to that gentleman an answer has been transmitted.

—

CLIFTON HOUSE, NIAGARA FALLS, *July* 21.

[Copy of original letter held by me to deliver to the Hon. Horace Greeley, and which duplicate I now furnish the Associated Press. WM. CORNELL JEWETT.]

NIAGARA FALLS, CLIFTON HOUSE, *July* 21, 1864.

To the Hon. HORACE GREELEY.

SIR: The paper handed to Mr. Holcombe, on yesterday, in your presence, by Major Hay, A. A. G., as an answer to the application in our note of the 18th instant, is couched in the following terms:

"EXECUTIVE MANSION,
"WASHINGTON, *July* 18, 1864.

"*To whom it may concern:*

"Any proposition which embraces the restoration of peace, the integrity of the whole Union, and the abandonment of slavery, which comes by and with an authority that can control the armies now at war against the United States, will be received and considered by the Executive Government of the United States, and will be met by liberal terms, on other substantial and collateral points, and the bearer or bearers thereof shall have safe conduct both ways.

"ABRAHAM LINCOLN."

The application to which we refer was elicited by your letter of the 17th instant, in which you inform Mr. Jacob Thompson and ourselves that you were authorized by the President of the United States to tender us his safe conduct, on the hypothesis that we were "duly accredited from Richmond as bearers of propositions looking to the establishment of peace," and desire a visit to Washington in the fulfilment of this mission. This assertion, to which we then gave, and still do, entire credence, was accepted by us as the evidence of an unexpected but most gratifying change in the policy of the President—a change which we felt authorized to hope might terminate in the conclusion of a peace mutually just, honorable, and advantageous to the North and to the South, exacting no condition but that we should be "duly accredited from Richmond as bearers of propositions looking to the establishment of peace."

Thus proffering a basis for conference as comprehensive as we could desire, it seemed to us that the President opened a door which had previously been closed against the Confederate States for a full interchange of sentiment, free discussion of conflicting opinions, and untrammeled effort to remove all causes of controversy by liberal negotiations. We indeed could not claim the benefit of a safe-conduct which had been extended to us in a character we had no right to assume and had never affected to possess; but the uniform declarations of our Executive and Congress, and their thrice-repeated and as often repulsed attempts to open negotiations, furnish a sufficient pledge to us that this conciliatory manifestation on the part of the President of the United States would be met by them in a temper of equal magnanimity. We had, therefore, no hesitation in declaring that if this correspondence was communicated to the President of the Confederate States, he would promptly embrace the opportunity presented for seeking a peaceful solution of this unhappy strife.

We feel confident that you must share our profound regret that the spirit which dictated the first step toward peace had not continued to animate the councils of your President. Had the representatives of the two Governments met to consider this question, the most momentous ever submitted to human statesmanship, in a temper of becoming moderation and equity, followed, as their deliberations would have been, by the prayers and benedictions of every patriot and Christian on the habitable globe, who is there so bold as to pronounce that the frightful waste of individual happiness and public prosperity which is daily saddening the universal heart might not have been terminated, or if the desolation and carnage of war must still be endured through weary years of blood and suffering, that there might not at least have been infused into its conduct something more of the spirit which softens and partially redeems its brutalities?

Instead of the safe conduct which we solicited, and which your first letter gave us every reason to suppose would be extended for the purpose of initiating a negotiation in which neither Government would compromise its rights or its dignity, a document has been presented which provokes as much indignation as surprise. It bears no feature of resemblance to that which was originally offered, and is unlike any paper which ever before emanated from the constitutional executive of a free people. Addressed "to whom it may concern," it precludes negotiation, and prescribes in advance the terms and conditions of peace. It returns to the original policy of "no bargaining, no negotiations, no truce with rebels except to bury their dead, until every man shall have laid down his arms, submitted to the Government, and sued for mercy."

Whatever may be the explanation of this sudden and entire change in the views of the President, of this rude withdrawal of a courteous overture for negotiation at the moment it was likely to be accepted, of this emphatic recall of words of peace just uttered, and fresh blasts of war to the bitter end, we leave for the speculation of those who have the means or inclination to penetrate the mysteries of his Cabinet or fathom the caprice of his imperial will. It is enough for us to say that we have no use whatever for the paper which has been placed in our hands.

We could not transmit it to the President of the Confederate States without offering him an indignity, dishonoring ourselves, and incurring the well-merited scorn of our countrymen. While an ardent desire for peace pervades the people of the Confederate States, we rejoice to believe that there are few, if any, among them who would purchase it at the expense of liberty, honor, and self-respect. If it can be secured only by their submission to terms of conquest, the generation is yet unborn which will witness its restitution.

If there be any military autocrat in the North who is entitled to proffer the conditions of this manifesto, there is none in the South authorized to entertain them. Those who control our armies are the servants of the people—not their masters; and they have no more inclination than they have the right to subvert the social institutions of the sovereign States, to overthrow their established constitutions, and to barter away their priceless heritage of self-government.

This correspondence will not, however, we trust, prove wholly barren of good result. If there is any citizen of the Confederate States who has clung to a hope that peace was possible with this administration of the Federal Government it will strip from his eyes the last film of such delusion; or if there be any whose hearts have grown faint under the suffering and agony of this bloody struggle, it will inspire them with fresh energy to endure and brave whatever may yet be requisite to preserve to themselves and their children all that gives dignity and value to life or hope and consolation to death. And if there be any patriots or Christians in your land who shrink appalled from the illimitable vista of private misery and public calamity which stretches before them, we pray that in their bosoms a resolution may be quickened to recall the abused authority and vindicate the outraged civilization of the country. For the solicitude you have manifested to inaugurate a movement which contemplates results the most noble and humane, we return our sincere thanks, and are, most respectfully and truly, your obedient servants,

C. C. CLAY, jr.
JAMES P. HOLCOMBE.

CLIFTON HOUSE, NIAGARA FALLS,
WEDNESDAY, *July* 20, 1864.

COL. W. C. JEWETT, *Cataract House, Niagara Falls:*

SIR: We are in receipt of your note, admonishing us of the departure of the Hon. Horace Greeley from the Falls; that he regrets the sad termination of the initiatory steps taken for peace, in consequence of the change made by the President in his instructions to convey commissioners to Washington for negotiations unconditionally, and that Mr. Greeley will be pleased to receive any answer we may have to make through you.

We avail ouselves of this offer to enclose a letter to Mr. Greeley, which you will oblige us by delivering. We cannot take leave of you without expressing our thanks for your courtesy and kind offices as the intermediary through whom our correspondence with Mr. Greeley has been conducted, and assuring you that we are, very respectfully, your obedient servants,

C. C. CLAY, Jr.
JAMES P. HOLCOMBE.

MR. GREELEY TO MR. JEWETT.

NIAGARA FALLS, (N. Y.,) *July* 20, 1864.

DEAR SIR: In leaving the Falls, I feel bound to state that I have had no intercourse with the Confederate gentlemen at the Clifton House *but such as I was fully authorized to hold by the President of the United States, and that I have done nothing in the premises but in fulfillment of his injunctions.* The notes, therefore, which you have kindly interchanged between those gentlemen and myself can in no case subject you to the imputation of unauthorized dealing with public enemies.

Yours, HORACE GREELEY.

W. C. JEWETT, Esq.

MR. JEWETT TO MR. CLAY AND OTHERS.

NIAGARA FALLS, *July* 20, 1864.

Hon. C. C. CLAY, Hon. JACOB THOMPSON, Hon. GEO. N. SANDERS, Hon. BEVERLY TUCKER, and the other Hon. Representatives of the Southern Confederacy.

GENTLEMEN: I am directed by Mr. Greeley to acknowledge the receipt of the following telegram from Mr. Clay:

"ST. CATHERINE'S, *July* 20, 1864.

"To GEO. N SANDERS:

"Will be with you at five o'clock. Detain Greeley until I see him. C. C. CLAY."

And to state that, in view of his mission being ended, through the rejection of the terms of negotiation in the letter of the President of the United States, delivered to you by Major Hay, he does not feel himself authorized to take any further steps in the matter. He regrets the sad termination of the steps taken for peace, from the change made by the President in his instructions given him to convey commissioners to Washington for negotiations unconditionally. He will be pleased to receive any answer you may have to make in writing through me or any mode you may desire.

I enclose you a copy of a note from Mr. Greeley addressed to me justifying the intercourse I have had with you during this short negotiation for peace.

In conclusion, I tender to you my heartfelt thanks for the kind and generous manner in which you have received me personally, and for the noble and magnanimous sentiments you have advanced in a desire to end the bloody conflict between the two sections. I can only regret that our Government should not have seen the policy, duty, and justice of meeting your generous offer to meet in council unconditionally—terms of a peace to depend upon circumstances transpiring during negotiations. My efforts shall be as ever unceasing for peace that shall secure to the section you represent that justice that shall meet with the approval of the civilized world, of the coming International Congress proposed by the wise and noble Napoleon.

Very truly, WM. CORNELL JEWETT.

MAJOR HAY TO MR. HOLCOMBE.

INTERNATIONAL HOTEL, *July* 21, 1864.

Major Hay has just received Mr. Holcombe's note of this

date, and thanking him for his prompt response, will start at once for Washington. Both Mr. Greeley and Major Hay understood Mr. Holcombe to say, yesterday, that he would send to Major Hay any communication he might wish to transmit to-day, and on that supposition Mr. Greeley set out for New York yesterday, and Major Hay remained. It is a matter of no special importance. Major Hay only wishes to explain his note of to-day.

—

[From the New York Tribune of July 22.]

The telegraphic stories concerning peace conferences at Niagara Falls have a slender foundation in fact, but most of the details are very wide of the truth. The Editor of this paper has taken part in and been privy to no further or other negotiations than were fully authorized, and more than authorized; but these related solely to bringing the antagonists face to face in amicable rather than belligerent attitude, with a view to the initiation of an earnest effort for peace, to be prosecuted at Washington. The movement has had no immediate success.

Of course all reports that the writer has been engaged in proposing, or receiving, or discussing hypothetical terms or basis of peace, whether with accredited agents of the Richmond authorities or others, are utterly mistaken. He has never had the slightest authorization to do anything of the sort; and he is quite aware of those provisions of law which relate to volunteer negotiators with public enemies. Those provisions he heartily approves, and is nowise inclined to violate.

More than this he does not at yet feel at liberty to state, though he soon may be. All that he can now add is his general inference that the pacification of our country is neither so difficult nor so distant as seems to be generally supposed.

Rebel Views of "Peace."

1862.

In September, 1862, these proceedings are published as having taken place in the Rebel Congress:

In the House of Representatives Mr. Foote, of Tennessee, offered the following joint resolution proposing to send a commissioner to Washington, empowered to propose terms of just and honorable peace:

Be it enacted by the Congress of the Confederate States of America, That the signal success with which Divine Providence has so continually blessed our arms for several months past would fully justify the Confederate Government in dispatching a commissioner or commissioners to the Government at Washington city, empowered to propose the terms of a just an honorable peace.

Mr. Holt, of Georgia, asked the consent of the House to offer the following substitute for the resolution:

The people of the Confederate States are, and have been from the beginning, anxious that the war with the United States should be conducted with the sense established by the rule of civilized and Christian nations, and have, on their part, so conducted it, and the said people ardently desire that said war should cease and peace be restored, and have so announced from the beginning: Therefore,

Resolved, That, whenever the United States Government shall manifest a like anxiety and a like desire, it shall be the duty of the President of the Confederate States to appoint ——— commissioners to treat and negotiate with the said United States Government upon said subjects, or either of them.

On motion of Mr. Kenan, of Georgia, the resolution and substitute were laid upon the table—yeas 59, nays 26.

1863.

In January, Mr. Crockett, of Kentucky, introduced into the House a resolution with reference to the conditions on which peace should be negotiated; which was debated.

Mr Foote, of Tennessee,* also introduced these, which were referred to the Committee on Foreign Affairs:

The people of the Confederate States of America having, in the progress of the pending war, most clearly demonstrated their ability to maintain by arms the claim to separate independence, which they have heretofore asserted before the world, and being inflexibly resolved never to relinquish the struggle in which they are engaged until the great object for which they are contending shall have been finally accomplished; in view of the fact that a great political reaction in opposition to the bloody and unnatural war now in course of prosecution, has displayed itself in several of the most populous and influential States of what was once honorably known as "The United States of America;" and, in view of the additional fact that, even among the avowed opponents of despotism, and the recognized friends of peace in the North, a grave and deplorable misapprehension has of late arisen in regard to the true condition of public sentiment in the South touching the question of reconstructing that political Union once existing under the protection of what is known as the Federal Constitution. Now, in order that no further misunderstanding of the kind referred to may hereafter prevail, and in order that the unchangeable determination of our Government and people, in reference to the terms upon which alone they would bring the sanguinary struggle to a close, may be made known, the Congress of the Confederate States of America do resolve as follows:

1. There is no plan of reconstructing what was formerly known as the Federal Union to which the people of the Confederate States will ever consent. Wrongs too grievous and multiplied have been committed upon us and upon our most cherished rights by a united North, since this unprovoked and most wicked war commenced; a majority of the people of the northern States have too evidently shown themselves to be utterly incapable of self-government and unmindful of all the fundamental principles upon which alone republican institutions can be maintained. They have too long submitted patiently to the iron rule of the basest and most degraded despotism that the world has yet known; for too long a period of time they have openly and unblushingly sympathized with the lawless and ferocious miscreants who have been sent into the bosom of the unoffending South to spill the precious blood of our most valued citizens; to pollute and desecrate all that we hold in especial veneration; to rob us of our property; to expel us from our homes and wantonly to devastate our country, to allow even of the possibility of our ever again consenting to hold the least political connection with those who have so cruelly outraged our sensibilities and so profoundly dishonored themselves, and in association with whom we feel that we could not expect that freedom which we love, that self-respect which we are determined ever to cultivate, and the esteem and sympathy of civilized and Christian nations.

2. While the Confederate States of America are not at all responsible for the existing war, and have been at all times ready to participate in such arrangements as would be best suited to bring it to a close, in a manner consistent with their own safety and honor, they could not yield their consent to an *armistice* of a single day or hour, so long as the incendiary proclamation of the atrocious monster, now bearing rule in Washington city, shall remain unrevoked; nor could the government of said Confederate States agree to negotiate at all in regard to a suspension of hostilities, except upon the basis of a formal and unconditional recognition of their independence.

3. Whenever the friends of peace in the North shall grow strong enough to constrain Abraham Lincoln and his flagitious Cabinet to withdraw said proclamation, and propose an armistice upon the basis aforesaid, the Government of the Confederate States will be ready to accede to said proposition of armistice with a view to the settlement of all existing difficulties.

4. Should peace be at any time brought about, the Confederate States of America would freely consent to the formation of a just and mutually advantageous commercial

* The Atlanta (Georgia) *Intelligencer* of the 20th of January has the following:

"The resolution introduced by Mr. Foote in Congress bearing upon a reconstruction of our Government with the Northwestern States, we desire now solemnly to protest against, and we trust that they will be tabled by the Confederate Congress, whenever they are taken up to be considered. We are fighting this war for Southern independence and for a Government of Southern States, recognizing African slavery as an institution ordained of God, beneficial to mankind, a necessity in our social and political relations as States, and in our intercourse with all other nations or States. Hence the admission of any free State into our Union is not only repugnant to us, but it will be only a continuance of that evil which has brought on the war, and which to get rid of we are now fighting. If the Northwestern States should shake off the North and East, and set up for themselves a new Government, and desire to be at peace with the South, no barrier will be placed in their way by our Government, and we shall be willing to treat with them as an independent Government—in peace, as friends; in war, as foes."

treaty with all the States now constituting the United States, except New England, with whose people, and in whose ignoble love of gold and brutifying fanaticism this disgraceful war has mainly originated; in consideration of which fact the people of the Confederate States of America are firmly and deliberately resolved to have no intercourse whatever hereafter, either direct or indirect, political, commercial, or social, under any circumstances which could be possibly imagined to exist, with said States of New England, or the people therein resident.

5. The Government of the Confederate States, in consideration of the change in public sentiment which has occurred in several of the Northern States, wherein political elections have been recently held—sympathizing most kindly with those by whose manly exertions that change has been brought about—would be willing to conclude a just and honorable peace with any one or more of said States who, renouncing all political connection with New England, may be found willing to stipulate for desisting at once from the further prosecution of the war against the South, and in such case the Government of the Confederate States would be willing to enter into a league, offensive and defensive, with the States thus desisting, of a permanent and enduring character.

6. The Government of the Confederate States is now willing, as it has heretofore repeatedly avowed itself to be, whenever the States bordering upon the Mississippi river, or any of them, shall have declared their inclination to withdraw from the further prosecution of the war upon the South, (which, could it be successful, would only have the effect of destroying their own best market,) to guaranty to them in the most effectual and satisfactory manner the peaceful and uninterrupted navigation of the said Mississippi river and its tributaries, and to open to them at once the markets of the South, greatly enhanced in value to them as they would be by the permanent exclusion of all articles of New England growth or manufacture.

7. The course of practical neutrality in regard to the pending war heretofore pursued by the States and Territories west of the Rocky Mountains has afforded the highest gratification to the people of the Confederate States of America; and it is hoped that the day is not far distant when said States and Territories, consulting their own obvious safety and future welfare, will withdraw from all political connection with a Government which has heretofore been a source of continual oppression to them; and when said States and Territories, asserting their separate independence, shall appropriate to themselves the manifold advantages sure to result from such a movement, among which may be reckoned: 1st. Relief from grievous and exhausting tariff regulations, now being rigidly enforced. 2d. Relief from all the discredit resulting inevitably from the prosecution of the present unjust and unauthorized war. 3d. Relief from the pressure of a despotism the most heartless and atrocious ever yet established. 4th. Relief from the crushing weight of taxation unavoidably growing out of the war. 5th. The exclusive use and enjoyment of all the rich mineral lands stretching along the slope of the Pacific. 6th. Free trade with all the nations of the earth, and a future maritime growth and power that has no parallel; and lastly, a monopoly of the trade of the Pacific ocean.

8. *Resolved*, That the President be respectfully requested, if he shall approve these resolutions, to cause them to be promulgated and transmitted to the States of the North by such means as he shall deem most judicious; and that he accompany them, if he think it advisable, with such an address or proclamation, expository of the matters embodied therein, as he shall judge most suitable and proper.

Jan. 21—Mr. FOOTE remarked in relation to proposed retaliation by Mr. Clopton:

He (Mr. Foote) did not certainly intend to call into question the motives or acts of the President in reference to this matter; but the gentleman from Virginia must be aware that the judiciaries of most of the States were most familiar with their own laws on the subject under consideration, and know what would be most satisfactory to their own people better than the Confederate Government could possibly know. But one point he desired especially to notice. It could not but be apparent to every one how these measures of retaliation would result—the amount of bloodshed and terrible atrocities to which it would lead. Therefore he desired that a messenger or messengers should be sent to the Northern Government, to propose terms of honorable peace—to let them know what was to be expected by a continuance of the war under present auspices. This would give heart to that great Peace party which is now springing up at the North and daily increasing in strength, especially in the Northwestern States, where the people are already clamorous for peace. And if the Lincoln Government still persisted in their atrocious course, our action would show the world that upon that Government rested all the future responsibility. It would show that if they persisted in this demoniacal and hellish warfare, we are not to blame. He was sure, however, that these political uprisings in the States of Illinois, Indiana, and Ohio, were of no little moment, and the results would presently appear.

In September, certain "peace resolutions" were introduced into the Senate of Virginia, which proposed in substance that three commissioners should be appointed by each of the Confederate States, to repair to each of the States remaining in the old Union, and make known to the Governors of each of them that the Confederate States demand that they will, by the ballot-box, consent that the Confederate States be allowed thenceforth to be separated from them in peace.

These resolutions were discussed at some length, and then indefinitely postponed by a unanimous vote. When they were first offered and read—

Mr. ARMSTRONG moved that the rules be suspended for the purpose of acting on the resolutions forthwith.

Mr. COLLIER appealed to the Senate to allow the resolutions to lay on the table, in order that Senators might have full time to reflect on their importance.

Mr. SEDDON was unwilling to allow the silent sanction of the Senate to endorse for an hour these resolutions. He was in favor of disposing of them without delay.

The rules were then suspended.

Mr. NASH moved the indefinite postponement of the resolutions. He regretted painfully to see such resolutions offered. He objected to them *toto cœlo*. He was as much opposed to sending commissioners to Gov. Morgan, or any other northern Governor, as to Mr. Lincoln. In their views and public policy they were all alike.

Mr. COLLIER thought the action of the Senate was hasty and inconsiderate. The scheme he proposed never had been attempted. There was no clause in the Constitution that provided for a peaceful dissolution of the Union. A sort of dread filled the public mind in regard to propositions of peace, because they might do harm. If there was any expression in the preamble or resolutions which inculcates the idea that we are to desist from the struggle till the independence of this Confederacy was achieved he would like to know it. He was willing to fight on, to fight on till we should obtain our independence; but while fighting with one hand he would hold out the olive-branch of peace with the other. He hoped, if the resolutions were to be buried, they would be allowed the decent respect shown to all corpses, of remaining twenty-four hours before interment.

The roll was called, and the vote stood—ayes 38, noes 1, (Mr. Collier.) So the preamble and resolutions were indefinitely postponed.

In the Legislature of Georgia, the same subject was considered, on which the Savannah *Republican* remarked:

We hope the Georgia Legislature will let this question alone, and turn their attention to war. The peace talk is designed to help the Northern Democrats, but it is a great mistake. It helps Lincoln, as we shall see to our sorrow.

In the Legislature of North Carolina,* some

* March 4, 1864, Wm. W. Holden issued this card:

To the People of North Carolina: In compliance with the wishes of many friends, I announce myself a candidate for the office of Governor of North Carolina, at the election to be held on the first Tuesday in August next.

My principles and views, as a conservative, "after the strictest sect," are well known to the people of the State. These principles and views are what they have been. They will not be changed.

I am not disposed, at a time like this, to invite the people from their employments, and add to the excitement which prevails in the public mind by haranguing them for their votes. We need all our energies to meet the common enemy, and to provide means of subsistence for our troops in the field and the people at home. Let the people go calmly and firmly to the polls and vote for the man of their choice. I will cheerfully abide their decision, whatever it may be.

If elected I will do everything in my power to promote the interests, the honor, and the glory of North Carolina, and to secure an honorable peace.

resolutions were submitted, which are thus described by a Richmond paper:

They assert the right of the people to meet and consult for the good of the country; denounce mob violence and military aggression upon the freedom of the press; pledge the State to a firm maintenance of the decisions of its legal tribunals, and applaud Gov. Vance for his manly defence of the State judiciary. They further compliment the army for its gallantry and heroism, and urge a faithful discharge of duty in vigorously prosecuting the war for national independence. They further declare that formal negotiations for peace, on the basis of separation from the United States, should be instituted by the treaty-making power, and urge our Representatives in Congress to exert themselves to bring about such negotiations. They further recommend proposals from the Confederate authorities to the Federal Congress looking to the holding of a peace convention for the adjustment of difficulties, whose action shall be subject to the ratification of the people.

TERMS OF PEACE INDICATED BY THE RICHMOND ENQUIRER.

[From the Richmond Enquirer, Oct. 16.]

Notwithstanding the cheering rumors of an early recognition by France, notwithstanding the fact that the Cabinet at Washington has been considering "proposals for peace" —proposals of its own, for it has none of ours to consider—notwithstanding the White Flag that was seen in the heavens by a respectable woman, and the march of ærial troops northwards, witnessed by a man of good character, in the clouds—in spite of all this, there is not the slightest prospect of speedy peace visible to us. There will be no peace until the military power of the Yankee nation is entirely broken, and its people so thoroughly sickened of the war that we can exact our own terms.

Save on our own terms, we can accept no peace whatever, and must fight till doomsday rather than yield an iota of them; and our terms are:

Recognition by the enemy of the independence of the Confederate States.

Withdrawal of Yankee forces from every foot of Confederate ground, including Kentucky and Missouri.

Withdrawal of Yankee soldiers from Maryland until that State shall decide, by a free vote, whether she shall remain in the old Union or ask admission into the Confederacy.

Consent, on the part of the Federal Government to give up to the Confederacy its proportion of the navy as it stood at the time of secession, or to pay for the same.

Yielding up of all pretension, on the part of the Federal Government, to that portion of the old Territories which lies west of the Confederate States.

An equitable settlement—on the basis of our absolute independence and equal rights—of all accounts of the public debts and public lands, and of the advantages accruing from foreign treaties.

These provisions, we apprehend, comprise the *minimum* of what we must require before we lay down our arms. That is to say, the North must yield all; we nothing. The whole pretension of that country to prevent by force the separation of the States must be abandoned, which will be an equivalent to an avowal that our enemies were wrong from the first; and, of course, as they waged a causeless and wicked war upon us, they ought, in strict justice, to be required, according to usages in such cases, to reimburse to us the whole of our expenses and losses in the course of that war.

Whether this last proviso is to be insisted upon or not, certain we are that we cannot have any peace at all until we shall be in a position, not only to demand and exact, but also to enforce and collect, the treasure for our own reimbursement out of the wealthy cities in the enemy's country. In other words, unless we can destroy or scatter their armies and break up their Government, we can have *no* peace; and if we can do that, then we can, and ought not only to extort from them our own full terms, and ample acknowledgment of their wrong, but also a handsome indemnity for the trouble and expense caused to us by their crime.

Now, we are not yet in a position to dictate those terms to our enemies, with Rosecrans's army still in the heart of our country, and Meade still on Virginia soil; but though it is too soon to propose such conditions to them, yet it is important that we should keep them plainly before our own eyes as the only admissible basis of any conceivable peace. This well fixed in the Confederate mind, there will be no more fearful looking for of news from Europe, as if that blessed peace were to come to us over the sea, and not to be conquered on our own ground; no more gaping for hints of recognition, "filling the belly with the east wind;" no more distraction or diversion from the single momentous business of bracing up every nerve and sinew of the country for battle.

It is especially now, at a moment when great and perhaps decisive battles are impending at two or three points, that we think it most essential to insist upon the grand entire magnificence of the stake and of the cause. Once more we say, it is all or nothing. This Confederacy or the Yankee nation, one or the other, goes down, down to perdition; that is to say, one or the other must forfeit its national existence, and lie at the mercy of its mortal enemy. We all know by this time the fate in store for us if we succumb. The other party has no smaller stake. As surely as we completely ruin their armies—and without that is no peace nor truce at all—so surely shall we make them pay our war debt, though we wring it out of their hearts. And they know it well; and therefore they cannot make peace except through utter exhaustion and absolute inability to strike another blow.

The stake they have to forfeit, then, if they lose this dreadful game, is as vital as ours. So is the stake to be won if they win anything. It is no less than entire possession of our whole country, with us in it, and everything that is ours, from the Ohio to the Rio Grande, to have and to hold to them and their heirs forever. But, on the other hand, what we mean to win is utter separation from them for all time. We do not want to govern their country; but after levying upon it what seemeth good to us, by way of indemnity, we leave it to commence its political life again from the beginning, hoping that the lesson may have made them sadder and wiser Yankees. We shut them out forever, with all their unclean and scoundrelly ways, intending to lead our lives here in our own Confederate way within our own well-guarded bounds; and without, as St. John says, "without are dogs."

And let no Confederate of feeble knees and tremulous backbone say to us, this complete triumph is impossible; say that we must be content with some kind of compromise, and give and take. On the contrary, we must gain all or lose all; and that the Confederates will indeed win the giant game, we take to be as certain as any future event in this uncertain world. Meade's army and Rosecrans's once scattered, Lincoln can get no more armies. The draft turns out manifestly fruitless. Both the German and the Irish elements are now for peace! The Yankees have to bear the brunt of the war themselves; but, in the mean time, their inevitable bankruptcy is advancing like an armed man; "hungry ruin has them in the wind." It cannot be long before the Cabinet at Washington will have indeed to consider seriously "proposals of peace," under auspices and circumstances very different from the present.

For the present the war rolls and thunders on—and may God defend the right!

1864.

[From the Richmond Examiner, February 8.]

The following extraordinary resolutions were yesterday introduced in the House of Representatives, by Mr. Wright, of Georgia. The House went into secret session before taking any action upon them:

Whereas the President of the United States, in a late public communication, did declare that no propositions for peace had yet been made to that Government by the Confederate States, when, in truth, such propositions were prevented from being made by the President of the United States, in that he refused to hear, or to receive, two commissioners appointed to treat expressly of the preservation of amicable relations between the two Governments.

Nevertheless that the Confederate States may stand justified in the sight of the conservative men of the North of all parties, and that the world may know which of the two Governments it is that urges on a war unparalleled for the fierceness of the conflict, and intensifying into a sectional hatred unsurpassed in the annals of mankind: Therefore,

Resolved, That the Confederate States invite the United States, through their Government at Washington, to meet them by Representatives equal to their Representatives and Senators in their respective Congress, at ——, on the —— day of —— next, to consider,

First. Whether they cannot agree upon the recognition of the Confederate States of America.

Second. *In the event of such recognition, whether they cannot agree upon the formation of a new government, founded upon the equality and sovereignty of the States*; but if this cannot be done, to consider—

Third. Whether they cannot agree upon treaties, offensive, defensive, and commercial.

Resolved, In the event of the passage of these resolutions, the President be requested to communicate the same to the Government at Washington in such manner as he shall deem most in accordance with the usages of nations; and in the event of their acceptance by that Government, he do issue his proclamation of election of delegates, under such regulations as he may deem expedient.

In the House of Representatives, May 23, Mr. J. T. LEACH, of North Carolina, submitted the

following preamble and resolutions, which were read by the clerk, creating quite a sensation on the floor, among the privileged seats, and in the galleries:

Whereas, The unconstitutional enactment of laws by the Congress of the United States, upon subjects of vital importance to the harmony and independence of the States, the happiness and prosperity of the people, the preservation and perpetuation of the Union, against the demands of justice, the appeals and admonitions of her best and wisest statesmen, made it our painful duty to fall back upon the rights for which the colonies maintained the war of the Revolution, and which our forefathers asserted and maintained to be clear and inalienable:

Resolved, by the Congress of the Confederate States, That the delegates from each State, acting in sovereign and independent character, for the purpose of adding moral to our physical force, and placing ourselves properly before the civilized world, do most earnestly appeal to the President, by and with the advice and consent of the Senate, to appoint commissioners whose duty it shall be to propose an armistice of ninety days to the proper authorities of the Federal Government, preliminary to negotiation upon State sovereignty and independence; and the said commissioners shall report in writing to the President the answer received from the Federal Government upon the subject.

Resolved, That should the peace-making power of the Federal Government accede to the proposition for an armistice of ninety days, the President be requested to convene the Congress of the Confederate States for the purpose of appointing commissioners, by and with the advice and consent of the Senate; and that he be also requested to notify the executive of the several States of the fact, and ask their co-operation by appointing commissioners, either by the Legislature or by convention, to co-operate with the commissioners appointed by the President, and to negotiate with the commissioners appointed by the Federal Government upon such terms of peace as will be consistent with the honor, dignity, and independence of the States, and compatible with the safety of our social and political rights.

Resolved, That in maintaining the rights guaranteed to us by the blood and treasure of our revolutionary fathers, and dear at all times to freemen, we desire to be let alone. We take no man's property; we fight not for conquest, but for our rights, the independence of the States, our equality, our civil and religious liberties.

Resolved, That such terms of peace as agreed to by the commissioners ought to be endorsed by the President and Senate, and submitted to the people for their ratification or rejection.

Mr. FOOTE, of Tennessee, moved the reference of the preamble and resolutions to the Committee on Foreign Affairs.

Mr. MCMULLEN inquired whether the subject of the resolutions was not a proper one for the secret session.

Mr. LEACH said he desired it to be discussed in open session.

Mr. CONRAD rose to a point of order. A rule was adopted at the last session, which is still force, requiring that all such resolutions be received and discussed in secret session.

The SPEAKER said that such a rule had been adopted, but it had special reference to the last session.

Mr. LEACH insisted that the importance of the question involved in the resolutions should commend them to the gravest considerations of the body. They were not his views only, but the views of his constituents, and a good portion of the people of North Carolina.

Mr. A. H. GARLAND, of Arkansas, hoped the gentleman would not proceed until the Chair had settled the point of order that had been raised.

Mr. FOOTE renewed his motion to refer the resolutions to the Committee on Foreign Affairs.

Mr. MCMULLEN moved to lay the resolutions upon the table.

Mr. MARSHALL, of Kentucky, rose to a point of order. The gentleman from North Carolina [Mr. Leach] had the floor, and he had not yielded it. The gentleman from Virginia [Mr. McMullen] was usurping the floor.

Mr. FOOTE didn't want to cut off any remarks the gentleman from North Carolina might have to make in support of his resolutions.

Mr. LEACH said the presentment of the resolutions was a duty he owed to himself and his constituents. If the House didn't like the resolutions, it can dispose of them in any manner that it sees proper. All he asked was a full and impartial hearing; that accorded him and his resolutions, he would be satisfied.

Mr. MCMULLEN withdrew his motion, and Mr. HEISKELL, of Tennessee, renewed his—the call for the ayes and noes upon laying the resolutions upon the table.

The ayes and noes were taken and the resolutions tabled.

After a short interval, Mr. CONRAD, of Louisiana, rose to a personal explanation. He had read over the peace resolutions submitted by the gentleman from North Carolina, [Mr. Leach,] and he found that they look to separate State action in the prosecution of peace. Taking that view of them, he could not give them his countenance or support. He asked leave to change his vote on the motion to lay them upon the table. He had voted "aye;" he would now vote "no."

Mr. J. T. LEACH said he held in his hand the address of the last Congress to the people of the Confederate States. The principles there enunciated were embodied almost wholly in these resolutions.

Mr. SWAN, of Tennessee, asked and obtained leave to change his vote on the motion to lay the resolutions on the table.

Mr. READ, of Kentucky, moved to reconsider the vote by which the resolutions were disposed of, so that all the members might exercise their discretion in voting.

Mr. MARSHALL, of Kentucky, was for treating the resolutions of the gentleman from North Carolina with becoming respect. They did not represent his own views more than the views of his congressional district. He thinks they are proper and right, and so think his constituents.

The debate soon began to be somewhat stormy and personal, and, after much wrangling, the resolutions were tabled by 62 ayes to 22 nays.

CORRESPONDENCE BETWEEN JEFF. DAVIS AND GOV. VANCE, OF NORTH CAROLINA.

[From the Petersburg Express, May 24.]

STATE OF NORTH CAROLINA, EXECUTIVE DEPARTMENT,
RALEIGH, *December* 30, 1863.

His Excellency President DAVIS:

MY DEAR SIR: After a careful consideration of all the sources of discontent in North Carolina, I have concluded that it will be impossible to remove it, except by making some effort at negotiation with the enemy.

The recent action of the Federal House of Representatives, though meaning very little, has greatly excited the public hope that the northern mind is looking toward peace. I am promised by all men who advocate this course that if fair terms are rejected it will tend greatly to strengthen and intensify the war feeling, and will rally all classes to a more cordial support of the Government.

And although our position is well known as demanding only to be let alone, yet it seems to me that for the sake of humanity, without having any weak or improper motives attributed to us, we might, with propriety, *constantly tender negotiations*. In doing so we would keep conspicuously before the world a disclaimer of our responsibility for the great slaughter of our race, and convince the humblest of our citizens—who sometimes forget the actual situation—that the Government is tender of their lives and happiness, and would not prolong their sufferings unnecessarily one moment.

Though statesmen might regard this as useless, the people will not, and I think our cause will be strengthened thereby. I have not suggested the method of these negotiations or their terms. The effort to obtain peace is the principal matter.

Allow me to beg your earnest consideration of this suggestion.

Very respectfully yours, Z. B. VANCE.

DAVIS'S REPLY.

EXECUTIVE OFFICE,
RICHMOND, *January* 8, 1864.

DEAR SIR: I have received your letter of the 30th ult., containing suggestions of the measures to be adopted for the purpose of removing "the sources of discontent" in North Carolina. The contents of the letter are substantially the same as those of the letter addressed by you to Senator Dortch, extracts of which were by him read to me.

I remarked to Mr. Dortch that you were probably not aware of the obstacles to the course you indicated, and, without expressing an opinion on the merits of the proposed policy, desired him in answering your letter to write for suggestions as to the method of opening negotiations, and as to the terms which you thought should be offered to the enemy.

I felt persuaded you would appreciate the difficulties as soon as your attention was called to the necessity of considering the subject in detail. As you have made no suggestions touching the manner of overcoming the obstacles, I infer that you were not apprised by Mr. Dortch of my remarks to him.

Apart from insuperable objections to the line of policy you propose (and to which I will presently advert) I cannot see how the more material obstacles are to be surmounted. We have made three distinct efforts to communicate with the authorities at Washington, and have been invariably unsuccessful. Commissioners were sent before hostilities were begun, and the Washington Government refused to receive them or hear what they had to say.

A second time I sent a military officer, with a communication addressed by myself to President Lincoln. The letter was received by General Scott, who did not permit the officer to see Mr. Lincoln; but promised that an answer would be sent. No answer has ever been received. The third time, a few months ago, a gentleman was sent, whose position, character, and reputation were such as to insure his reception, if the enemy were not determined to receive no proposals whatever from the Government. Vice President Stephens made a patriotic tender of his services in the hope of being able to promote the cause of humanity, and although little belief was entertained of his success, I cheerfully yielded to his suggestion, that the experiment should be tried.

The enemy refused to let him pass through their lines, or to hold any conference with them. He was stopped before he ever reached Fortress Monroe on his way to Washington.* To attempt again in the face of these repeated rejections of all conference with us, to send commissioners or agents to propose peace, is to invite insult and contumely, and to subject ourselves to indignity without the slightest chance of being listened to.

No true citizen, no man who has our cause at heart, can desire this; and the good people of North Carolina would be the last to approve of such an attempt, if aware of all the facts. So far from removing sources of discontent, such a course would receive, as it would merit, the condemnation of those true patriots who have given their blood and their treasure to maintain the freedom, equality, and independence which descended to them from the immortal heroes of King's Mountain and other battle-fields of the Revolution. If, then, these proposals cannot be made through envoys, because the enemy would not receive them, how is it possible to communicate our desire for peace otherwise than by the public announcements contained in almost every message I ever sent to Congress?

I cannot recall at this time one instance in which I have failed to announce that our only desire was peace, and the only terms which formed a *sine qua non*, were precisely those that you suggested, namely "a demand only to be let alone." But suppose it were practicable to obtain a conference through commissioners with the Government of President Lincoln, is it at this moment that we are to consider it desirable or even at all admissible?

Have we not just been apprised by that despot that we can only expect his gracious pardon by emancipating all our slaves, swearing allegiance and obedience to him and his proclamation, and becoming, in point of fact, the slaves of our own negroes? Can there be in North Carolina one citizen so fallen beneath the dignity of his ancestors as to accept, or to enter conference on the basis of these terms?

That there are a few traitors in the State who would be willing to betray their fellow-citizens to such a degraded condition, in hope of being rewarded for treachery by an escape from the common doom, may be true. But I do not believe that the vilest wretch would accept such terms for himself. I cannot conceive how the people of your State, than which none has sent nobler or more gallant soldiers to the field of battle, (one of whom it is your honor to be,) can have been deceived by anything to which you refer in "the recent action of the Federal House of Representatives." I have seen no action of that House that does not indicate, by a very decided majority, the purpose of the enemy to refuse all terms of the South, except absolute, unconditional subjugation or extermination. But if it were otherwise, how are we to treat with the House of Representatives?

It is with Lincoln alone that we ever could confer, and his own partisans at the North avow unequivocally that his purpose in his message and proclamation was to shut out all hope that he could ever treat with us on any terms. If we will break up our Government, dissolve the Confederacy, disband our armies, emancipate our slaves, take an oath of allegiance binding ourselves to obedience to him and of disloyalty to our own States, he proposes to pardon us and not to plunder us of anything more than the property already stolen from us, and such slaves as still remain. In order to render his proposals so insulting as to secure their rejection, he joins to them a promise to support with his army one-tenth of the people of any State who will attempt to set up a government over the other nine-tenths, thus seeking to sow discord and suspicion among the people of the several States, and excite them to civil war in furtherance of his ends.

I know well it would be impossible to get your people, if they possessed full knowledge of these facts, to consent that proposals should now be made by us to those who control the Government at Washington. Your own well-known devotion to the great cause of liberty and independence, to which we have all committed whatever we have of earthly possessions, would induce you to take the lead in repelling the bare thought of abject submission to the enemy.

Yet peace on other terms is now impossible. To obtain the sole terms to which you or I could listen, this struggle must continue until the enemy is beaten out of his vain confidence of our subjugation. Then, and not till then, will it be possible to treat for peace. Till then, all tender of terms to the enemy will be received as proof that we are ready for submission, and will encourage him in the atrocious warfare which he is waging.

I fear much from the tenor of the news I receive from North Carolina, that an attempt will be made by some bad men to inaugurate movements which must be considered as equivalent to aid and comfort to the enemy, and which all patriots should combine to put down at any cost.

You may count on my aid in every effort to spare your State the scenes of civil warfare, which will devastate its homes if the designs of these traitors be suffered to make headway. I know that you will place yourself in your legitimate position in the lead of those who will not suffer the name of the Old North State to be blackened by such a stain.

Will you pardon me for suggesting that my only source of disquietude on the subject arises from the fear that you will delay too long the action which now appears inevitable, and that by an overearnest desire to reclaim by conciliation men whom you believe to be sound at heart, but whose loyalty is more than suspected elsewhere, you will permit them to gather such strength as to require more violent measures than are now needed?

With your influence and position, the promoters of the unfounded discontent now prevalent in your State would be put down without the use of physical force if you would abandon a policy of conciliation and set them at defiance. In this course, frankly and firmly pursued, you could rally around you all that is best and noblest in your State, and your triumph would be bloodless.

If the contrary policy be adopted, I much fear you will be driven to the use of force to repress treason. In either event, however, be assured that you will have my cordial concurrence and assistance in maintaining with you the honor, dignity, and fair fame of your State, and in your efforts to crush treason, whether incipient, as I believe it now to be, or more matured, as I believe, if not firmly met, it will in our future inevitably become.

I have the honor to be, very respectfully, yours,

JEFFERSON DAVIS.

His Excellency Z. B. VANCE,

Governor of North Carolina, Raleigh, N. C.

*This is the correspondence:

CONFEDERATE STATES STEAMER TORPEDO,
IN JAMES RIVER, *July* 4, 1863.

SIR: As military commissioner, I am the bearer of a communication in writing from Jefferson Davis, Commander-in-Chief of the land and naval forces of the Confederate States, to Abraham Lincoln, Commander-in-Chief of the land and naval forces of the United States. The Hon. Robert Ould, Confederate States agent of exchange, accompanies me as secretary, for the purpose of delivering the communication in person and conferring upon the subject to which it relates. I desire to proceed to Washington in the steamer Torpedo, commanded by Lieut. Hunter Davidson, of the Confederate States Navy, no person being on board but the Hon. Mr. Ould, myself, and the boat's officers and crew.

Yours, most respectfully,

ALEX. H. STEPHENS.

To S. H. LEE, *Admiral.*

—

Acting Rear Admiral S. H. LEE, *Hampton Roads:*

The request of Alex. H. Stephens is inadmissible. The customary agents and channels are adequate for all needful military communications and conference between the United States forces and the insurgents.

GIDEON WELLES,
Sec. of the Navy.

THE LATEST FROM JEFF. DAVIS.

James R. Gilmore—otherwise known as "Edmund Kirke"—who recently visited Richmond with Col. Jacques, writes an explanatory note respecting his visit to the Boston *Transcript* of July 22, 1864, in which he says of their "mission":

It will result in nothing. Jefferson Davis said to me last Sunday, (and with all his faults I believe him to be a man of truth): "This war must go on till the last of this generation falls in his tracks, and his children seize his musket and fight our battle, unless you acknowledge our right to self-government. We are not fighting for slavery; we are fighting for independence, and that or extermination we will have."

MILITARY ORDERS RESPECTING ELECTIONS.

Maryland.

EXTRACT FROM AN ACT OF ASSEMBLY OF 1860.

No commissioned or non-commissioned officer, having command of any soldier or soldiers quartered or posted in any district of any county in this State, shall muster or embody any of the said troops, or march any recruiting party within the view of any place of election, during the time of holding said election, under the penalty of one hundred dollars. This section not to apply to the city of Baltimore.

ELECTION OF 1861.

1861, Oct. 29—General Marcy, Chief of McClellan's Staff, issued this order:

HEADQUARTERS ARMY OF THE POTOMAC,
WASHINGTON, *October* 29, 1861.

GENERAL: There is an apprehension among Union citizens in many parts of Maryland of an attempt at interference with their rights of suffrage by disunion citizens on the occasion of the election to take place on the 6th of November next.

In order to prevent this, the major general commanding directs that you send detachments of a sufficient number of men to the different points in your vicinity where the elections are to be held to protect the Union voters, and to see that no disunionists are allowed to intimidate them, or in any way to interfere with their rights.

He also desires you to arrest and hold in confinement till after the election all disunionists who are known to have returned from Virginia recently and who show themselves at the polls, and to guard effectually against any invasion of the peace and order of the election. For the purpose of carrying out these instructions you are authorized to suspend the *habeas corpus*. General Stone has received similar instructions to these. You will please confer with him as to the particular points that each shall take the control of.

I am, sir, very respectfully, your obedient servant,

R. B. MARCY,
Chief of Staff.

Major General N. P. BANKS,
Commanding Division, Muddy Branch, Md.

Nov. 1—Gen. John A. Dix issued this order:

HEADQUARTERS, BALTIMORE, *November* 1, 1861.

To the United States Marshal of Maryland, and the Provost Marshal of the city of Baltimore.

Information has come to my knowledge that certain individuals who formerly resided in this State, and who are known to have been recently in Virginia bearing arms against the authority and the forces of the United States, have returned to their former homes with the intention of taking part in the election of the 6th of November instant, thus carrying out at the polls the treason they have committed in the field. There is reason also to believe that other individuals lately residents in Maryland, who have been engaged in similar acts of hostility to the United States, or in actively aiding and abetting those in arms against the United States, are about to participate in the election for the same treacherous purpose, with the hope of carrying over the State by disloyal votes to the cause of rebellion and treason. I, therefore, by virtue of the authority vested in me to arrest all persons in rebellion against the United States, require you to take into custody all such persons in any of the election districts or precincts in which they may appear at the polls to effect their criminal attempt to convert the elective franchise into an engine for the subversion of the Government, and for the encouragement and support of its enemies.

In furtherance of this object, I request the judges of election of the several precincts of the State, in case any such person shall present himself and offer his vote, to commit him until he can be taken into custody by the authority of the United States; and I call on all good and loyal citizens to support the judges of election, the United States marshal, and his deputies, and the provost marshal of Baltimore and police, in their efforts to secure a free and fair expression of the voice of the people of Maryland, and at the same time to prevent the ballot-box from being polluted by treasonable votes.

JOHN A. DIX,
Major General Commanding.

Same day, he addressed this letter to the inspectors of the election at New Windsor, Carroll county:

HEADQUARTERS DEPARTMENT OF PENNSYLVANIA,
BALTIMORE, MD., *November* 1, 1861.

GENTLEMEN: I have received your letter of the 29th ultimo, asking me to issue a proclamation authorizing you to administer to all persons of doubtful loyalty, who offer their votes at the approaching election, an oath to support the Constitution of the United States. If I had the power I would most cheerfully do so, for no one who is false to the Government ought to be allowed to vote. But the constitution and laws of Maryland provide for the exercise of the elective franchise by regulations with which I have no right to interfere. I have this day issued an order, of which I enclose a copy, to the United States marshal and the provost marshal of Baltimore to arrest any persons who have been in arms in Virginia if they appear at the polls and attempt to vote, as we are told some such persons intend, and to take into custody all who aid and abet them in their treasonable designs; and I have requested the judges of election, in case any such person presents himself at the polls and attempts to vote, to commit him until he can be taken into custody by the authority of the United States.

I consider it of the utmost importance that the election should be a fair one, and that there should be no obstruction to the free and full expression of the voice of the people of the State, believing, as I do, that it will be decidedly in favor of the Union. But it is in the power of the judges of election, under the authority given them, to satisfy themselves as to the qualifications of the voters, to put to those who offer to poll such searching questions in regard to residence and citizenship as to detect traitors, and, without any violation of the constitution or laws of Maryland, to prevent the pollution of the ballot-boxes by their votes.

I am, very respectfully, yours,

JOHN A. DIX,
Major General Commanding.

DANIEL ENGEL and WILLIAM ECKER, *Inspectors of Election, New Windsor.*

MAJOR GENERAL DIX'S ORDER TO PROVOST MARSHAL DODGE BEFORE THE MARYLAND ELECTION OF 1861.*

BALTIMORE, *November* 5, 1861.

To Provost Marshal DODGE:

Use all your power to-morrow to have the polls unobstructed. We have shown that we can control Maryland

* The above, General Dix says, is in all essential particulars accurate, and is given by him from memory. The original of the order has been mislaid.

by force. We now wish to show that we can control it by the power of opinion, and we shall lose the whole moral influence of our victory if the right of suffrage is not free, and maintained.

JOHN A. DIX,
Major General Commanding.

FURLOUGHING OF SOLDIERS TO VOTE IN MARYLAND.

SECRETARY OF WAR TO GEN. M'CLELLAN.

WAR DEPARTMENT,
WASHINGTON, *October* 28, 1841.

Major Gen. McCLELLAN, *Commanding:*

SIR: In order to have a full vote in Maryland at the coming election, Wednesday, November 6, so that the legal voters may decide by their ballots all public questions, you are hereby directed to grant three days' furlough to the soldiers of the 1st, 2d, and 3d regiments of Maryland volunteers, all to return to duty on Thursday, Nov. 7.

Very respectfully,

SIMON CAMERON,
Secretary of War.

GEN. M'CLELLAN'S ORDER TO GEN. BANKS.

HEADQUARTERS ARMY OF THE POTOMAC,
WASHINGTON, *October* 29, 1861.

Major Gen. N. P. BANKS, *Commanding, &c.:*

GENERAL: Pursuant to directions from the Secretary of War, of the 28th inst., of which I inclose you a copy, the Major General commanding directs that such soldiers of the 1st, 2d, and 3d regiments of Maryland volunteers as may be within the limits of your command receive furloughs for such a length of time as will enable them to reach the place wherein they may be entitled to vote by the 6th of November. Wherever it may be necessary, in order to facilitate the presence of these men at their places of voting, to furnish them transportation, it may be furnished. It is desired that the most liberal and prompt circulation may be given to these instructions, in order to secure with certainty the carrying into effect the design proposed.

Sufficient time is to be allowed the soldiers thus furloughed to enable them to return after voting, without exceeding the term fixed for their furlough; but a prompt return is desired.

Whenever it may be necessary, the absent soldier should be replaced for the time by other troops.

The General Commanding desires that the receipt of this communication be acknowledged at once.

I have the honor to be, General, very respectfully, your obedient servant,

S. WILLIAMS,
Asst. Adj. Gen.

ELECTION OF 1863.

1863, October 27—General Schenck issued this order:

[General Orders No. 53.]

HEADQUARTERS, MIDDLE DEPARTMENT,
EIGHTH ARMY CORPS,
BALTIMORE, MARYLAND, *October* 27, 1863.

It is known that there are many evil disposed persons, now at large in the State of Maryland, who have been engaged in rebellion against the lawful Government, or have given aid and comfort or encouragement to others so engaged, or who do not recognize their allegiance to the United States, and who may avail themselves of the indulgence of the authority which tolerates their presence to embarrass the approaching election, or, through it, to foist enemies of the United States into power. It is therefore ordered,

1. That all provost marshals and other military officers do arrest all such persons found at, or hanging about, or approaching any poll or place of election on the 4th of November, 1863, and report such arrest to these headquarters.

2. That all provost marshals and other military officers commanding in Maryland shall support the judges of election on the 4th of November, 1863, in requiring an oath of allegiance to the United States, as the test of citizenship of any one whose vote may be challenged on the ground that he is not loyal, or does not admit his allegiance to the United States, which oath shall be in the following form and terms:

I do solemnly swear that I will support, protect, and defend the Constitution and Government of the United States against all enemies, whether domestic or foreign; that I hereby pledge my allegiance, faith, and loyalty to the same, any ordinance, resolution, or law of any State convention, or State Legislature, to the contrary notwithstanding; that I will at all times yield a hearty and willing obedience to the said Constitution and Government, and will not, either directly or indirectly, do any act in hostility to the same, either by taking up arms against them, or aiding, abetting, or countenancing those in arms against them; that, without permission from the lawful authority, I will have no communication, direct or indirect, with the States in insurrection against the United States, or with either of them, or with any person or persons within said insurrectionary States; and that I will in all things deport myself as a good and loyal citizen of the United States. This I do in good faith, with full determination, pledge, and purpose to keep this, my sworn obligation, and without any mental reservation or evasion whatsoever.

3. Provost marshals and other military officers are directed to report to these headquarters any judge of an election who shall refuse his aid in carrying out this order, or who, on challenge of a vote being made on the ground of disloyalty or hostility to the Government, shall refuse to require the oath of allegiance from such voter.

By order of Major General Schenck:

W. H. CHESEBROUGH,
Lieutenant Colonel and Assistant Adjutant General.

PROVOST MARSHAL GENERAL'S ORDER.

WAR DEPARTMENT,
PROVOST MARSHAL GENERAL'S OFFICE,
WASHINGTON, D. C., *October* 31, 1863.

Direct your provost marshals to give their aid in carrying out General Schenck's orders for preserving the purity of elections at the polls in Maryland.

JAMES B. FRY,
Provost Marshal General.

Major JEFFRIES, *Acting Assistant Provost Marshal General, Baltimore, Maryland.*

November 2—Governor BRADFORD issued this proclamation:

To the citizens of the State, and more especially the judges of election:

A military order, issued from the headquarters of the "Middle Department," bearing date the 27th ult., printed and circulated, as it is said, through the State, though never yet published here, and designed to operate on the approaching election, has just been brought to my attention, and is of such a character and issued under such circumstances as to demand notice at my hands.

This order reciting, "that there are many evil disposed persons now at large in the State of Maryland, who have been engaged in rebellion against the lawful Government, or have given aid and comfort, or encouragement to others so engaged, or who do not recognize their allegiance to the United States, and who may avail themselves of the indulgence of the authority which tolerates their presence, to embarrass the approaching election, or through it to foist enemies of the United States into power," proceeds, among other things, to direct "all provost marshals and other military officers, to arrest all such persons found at or hanging about, or approaching any poll or place of election, on the 4th of November, 1863, and report such arrest to these headquarters."

This extraordinary notice has not only been issued without any notice to, or consultation with the constituted authorities of the State, but at a time and under circumstances when the condition of the State, and the character of the candidates are such as to preclude the idea that the result of that election can in any way endanger either the safety of the Government, or the peace of the community.

It is a well known fact that, with perhaps one single exception, there is not a congressional candidate in the State whose loyalty is even of a questionable character, and in not a county of the State outside of the same congressional district is there, I believe, a candidate for the Legislature or any State office, whose loyalty is not equally undoubted. In the face of this well known condition of things, the several classes of persons above enumerated are not only to be arrested *at* but "*approaching any poll or place of election.*" And who is to judge whether voters thus on their way to the place of voting have given "aid, comfort, *or encouragement*" to persons engaged in the rebellion, or that they "do not recognize their allegiance to the United States," and may avail themselves of their presence at the polls "to foist enemies of the United States into power?" As I have already said, in a very large majority of the counties of the State there are not to be found among the candidates any such "enemies of the United States," but the provost marshals—created for a very different purpose—and the other military officials who are thus ordered to arrest approaching voters are necessarily made by the order the sole and exclusive judges of who fall within the proscribed category; an extent of arbitrary discretion, under any circumstances the most odious and more especially offensive and dangerous in view of the known fact that two at least of the five provost marshals of the State are themselves candidates for important offices, and sundry of their deputies for others.

This military order, therefore, is not only without justification when looking to the character of the candidates before the people, and rendered still more obnoxious by the means appointed for its execution, but is equally offensive to the sensibilities of the people themselves and the authorities of the State, looking to the repeated proofs they have furnished of an unalterable devotion to the Government. For more than two years past there has never been a time when, if every traitor and every treasonable sympathizer in the State had voted, they could have controlled, whoever might have been their candidates, a single department of the State or jeopardized the success of the General Government. No State in the Union has been or is now actuated by more heartfelt or unwavering loyalty than Maryland—a loyalty intensified and purified by the ordeal through which it has passed; and yet looking to what has lately transpired elsewhere and to the terms and character of this military order, one would think that in Maryland and nowhere else is the Government endangered by the "many evil disposed persons that are now at large."

Within less than a month the most important elections have taken place in two of the largest States in the Union; in each of them candidates were before the people, charged by the particular friends of the Government, with being hostile to its interests, and whose election was deprecated as fraught with the most dangerous consequences to its success. One of the most prominent of these candidates was considered so dangerously inimical to the triumph of the national cause, that he has been for months past banished from the country, and yet hundreds of thousands of voters were allowed to approach the polls, and to attempt "to foist" such men into power, and no provost marshals or other military officers were order to arrest them on the way, or, so far as we have ever heard, even test their allegiance by an oath.

With these facts before us, it is difficult to believe that the suggestion that the enemies of the United States may be foisted into power at our coming election, was the consideration that prompted this order; but whatever may have been that motive, I feel it to be my duty to solemnly protest against such an intervention with the privileges of the ballot-box, and so offensive a discrimination against the rights of a loyal State.

I avail myself of the occasion to call to the particular attention of the judges of election the fact that they are on the day of election clothed with all the authority of conservators of the peace, and may summon to their aid any of the executive officers of the county, and the whole power of the county itself to preserve order at the polls and secure the constitutional rights to voters.

It is also made their "special duty" to give information to the State's attorney for the county of all infractions of the State laws on the subject of elections, and by these laws it is forbidden to any "commissioned or non-commissioned officers, having command of any soldier or soldiers quartered or posted in any district of any county of the State, to muster or embody any of said troops, or march any recruiting party within the view of any place of election during the time of holding said election."

I need not, I am sure, remind them of the terms of the oath they are required to take before entering upon their duties, and according to which they swear "to permit all persons to vote who shall offer to poll at the election, &c., who in *their judgment, shall, according to the directions contained in the Constitution and laws, be entitled to poll at the same election*, and not permit any person to poll at the same election who is not in their judgment qualified to vote as aforesaid."

It is the *judgment of the judges of election* alone, founded upon the provisions of the constitution and the laws of the State, that must determine the right to vote of any person offering himself for that purpose. I trust and believe that they will form that judgment, and discharge their duty, as their conscientious convictions of its requirements, under the solemn obligations they assume shall dictate, undeterred by an order to provost marshals to report them to "headquarters."

Whatever power the State possesses shall be exerted to protect them for anything done in the proper execution of its laws.

Since writing the above, I have seen a copy of the President's letter to the chairman of the Union State Central Committee, bearing the same date with the order, and evidently showing that the order was unknown to him, that it would not have been approved by him if he had known it, and that it is therefore all the more reprehensible.

A. W. BRADFORD.

By the Governor:

Wm. B. Hill, *Secretary of State.*

After the above was in print, at three o'clock this afternoon, I received from the President the following dispatch:

"I revoke the first of the three propositions in General Schenck's General Order No. 53, not that it is wrong in principle, but because the military, being of necessity exclusive judges as to who shall be arrested, the provision is liable to abuse; for the revoked part I substitute the following:

"That all provost marshals and other military officers do prevent all disturbance and violence at or about the polls, whether offered by such persons as above described, or by any other person or persons whomsoever; the other two propositions I allow to stand; my letter at length will reach you to-night. "A. LINCOLN."

Whilst this modification revokes the authority of the provost marshals and military officers to arrest the classes of persons enumerated in the preamble to the order, "found at or hanging about, or approaching any poll or place of election," it directs them to prevent all violence or disturbance about the polls, &c.

To meet such disturbances, the judges of election, as I have already stated, are clothed with ample powers, and I had received no previous intimation that there was any reason to apprehend a disturbance of any kind at the polls on the day of election. In the absence of any military display, there would certainly seem to be as little cause for such apprehensions as ever before existed. A preparation by the Government, by military means, to provide for such a contingency, will be quite as likely to provoke as to subdue such a disposition. Not only so, but the military thus required to prevent violence or disturbance about the polls must necessarily be empowered to arrest the parties they may charge with such disorder, and they are still left in effect "exclusive judges as to who shall be arrested"—a power they may as readily abuse as any other.

I regret, therefore, that I can perceive no such change in the general principles of the order as to induce me to change the aforegoing proclamation. A. W. BRADFORD.

Baltimore, *Monday evening, Nov. 2*, 1863.

Nov. 2—The President wrote this letter to Governor Bradford:

War Department
Washington, *November* 2, 1862.

Sir: Yours of the 31st ultimo was received yesterday about noon, and since then I have been giving most earnest attention to the subject-matter of it. At my call General Schenck has attended, and he assures me it is almost certain that violence will be used at some of the voting places on election day, unless prevented by his provost guards. He says that in some of those places the Union voters will not attend at all, or run a ticket, unless they have assurance of protection. This makes the Missouri case of my action, in regard to which you express your approval.

The remaining point of your letter is a protest against any person offering to vote being put to any test not found in the laws of Maryland. This brings us to a difference between Missouri and Maryland. With the same reason in both States, Missouri has, by law, provided a test for the voter with reference to the present rebellion, while Maryland has not. For example, General Trimble, captured fighting us at Gettysburg, is, without recanting his treason, a legal voter by the laws of Maryland. Even General Schenck's order admits him to vote, if he recants upon oath. I think that is cheap enough. My order in Missouri, which you approve, and General Schenck's order here, reach precisely the same end. Each assures the right of voting to all loyal men, and whether that man is loyal, each allows that man to fix by his own oath. Your suggestion that nearly all the candidates are loyal I do not think quite meets the case. In this struggle for the nation's life, I cannot so confidently rely on those whose election may have depended upon disloyal votes. Such men, when elected, may prove true, but such votes are given them in expectation that they will prove false. Nor do I think that to keep the peace at the polls, and to prevent the persistently disloyal from voting, constitutes just cause of offence to Maryland. I think she has her own example for it. If I mistake not, it is precisely what General Dix did when your excellency was elected Governor. I revoke the first of the three propositions in General Schenck's General Order No. 53, not that it is wrong in principle, but because the military being, of necessity, exclusive judges as to who shall be arrested, the provision is liable to abuse. For the revoked part I substitute the following:

That all provost marshals and other military officers do prevent all disturbance and violence at or about the polls, whether offered by such persons as above described, or by any other person or persons whatsoever.

The other two propositions of the order I allow to stand. General Schenck is fully determined, and has my strict order besides, that all loyal men may vote, and vote for whom they please.

Your obedient servant, A. LINCOLN,
President of the United States.

His Excellency A. W. Bradford,
Governor of Maryland.

GENERAL SCHENCK'S MODIFICATION OF THE ORDER.

[General Orders No. 55.]

HEADQUARTERS, MIDDLE DEPARTMENT,
EIGHTH ARMY CORPS,
BALTIMORE, MARYLAND, *November* 2, 1863.

Paragraph I, of General Orders No. 53, from these headquarters, is modified so as to read as follows:

I. That all provost marshals and other military officers do prevent all disturbance and violence at or about the polls, whether offered by such persons as above described, or by any other person, or persons, whomsoever.

By command of Major General Schenck:

WILLIAM H. CHESEBROUGH,
Lieutenant Colonel and Assistant Adjutant General.

November 3—General Schenck issued this address, in reply to the proclamation of Governor Bradford:

HEADQUARTERS MIDDLE DEPARTMENT, 8TH ARMY CORPS,
BALTIMORE, MD., *November* 3, 1863.

A very extraordinary proclamation was issued last evening by his Excellency A. W. Bradford, Governor of Maryland, in relation to General Order No. 53, from these headquarters. I will not presume, with my knowledge of Governor Bradford, that that proclamation was designed to produce collision between the military power and the citizens who may be assembled at the polls to vote at the election to-morrow; but I cannot doubt that its obvious tendency is to invite and suggest such disturbance. When that proclamation came to my knowledge, late last night, I felt it my duty to take measures for restricting, as far as possible, its circulation in those parts of the State to be most affected by it, until there could go out with it the letter of the President of the United States on the subject, written yesterday to Governor Bradford, a copy of which I have now obtained.

I will make, for myself, but one or two comments on the proclamation.

The intimation of the Governor that my order might have been prompted by some other consideration than patriotic purpose or official duty, is unworthy of reply, and unworthy of him. He knows, and the people of Maryland and of this military department know, how single and earnest and constant has been my aim to avoid all side influences, and to keep in view, and act steadily upon, the idea of maintaining the just authority of the national Government against disloyalty in all its forms, and for the general good only.

It was in this spirit that I issued the general order in question. Its principal purpose is to prevent traitorous persons from controling, in any degree, by their votes, or taking part in the coming election. The order is not aimed at candidates, either individually or as a class, as the Governor would presume. Neither is it aimed at, nor can it by any proper interpretation in any way interfere with the rights of loyal voters. It is only framed and intended to exclude from a voice in the election of those who are to administer the affairs either of the national Government or of this loyal State such individuals as are hostile to that Government of which Maryland is a part. Will any good citizen pretend that the exclusion of such persons is not a wise and wholesome protection, due to those who adhere to and sustain the Constitution and lawful authority? And it is clearly not a hardship, to be complained of by the individual challenged for such disqualification, when he is permitted to purge himself by his own oath of allegiance to the Government, in the management of which he claims a share.

Governor Bradford himself cannot appreciate more highly than I do, the sterling loyalty of the great majority of the people of Maryland, but he must know, as I do, that there still remains at large, from forbearance of the Government authorities, a very considerable number who are more or less actively engaged in aiding and encouraging rebels in arms. Even in his proclamation he admits the existence of such prevailing disloyalty in the counties of at least one of the congressional districts.

But my general order was only put forth after the receipt, through all the last month, of a great number of letters, petitions, and appeals in person, from respectable and loyal citizens, throughout the southern part of the State particularly, on both sides of the bay, imploring the issue of such an order. I have only failed in complying with this request by making its provisions less stringent than justice and fairness to loyal citizens seemed to them to demand.

I will add only, to show with what anxiety I have sought, on this occasion, to secure peace and good order at the polls, that officers intrusted with this duty have, in every instance, been furnished with written or printed instructions, of which the following is one clause:

"The officers and men are to be cautioned not to commit or permit any unlawful violence. They must not enter into political discussions, and are to remember, that while protecting the polls from rebel sympathizers, they are conservators of the peace, and are there to support the judges of election." Even Governor Bradford could scarcely object to this. I now repeat to the provost guards that instruction, and enjoin upon them, that while they enforce the observance of the general order firmly and faithfully, as directed, they do it in every respect discreetly and temperately.

I append copies of the President's letter, and of the general order, as modified.

ROBERT C. SCHENCK,
Major General Commanding.

LIEUTENANT COLONEL TEVIS'S ORDER AT CHESTERTOWN.

HEADQUARTERS THIRD MARYLAND CAVALRY,
CHESTERTOWN, *November* 3, 1863.

Whereas the President of the United States, in reply to a letter addressed to him by Hon. Thomas Swann, of Baltimore city, has stated that all loyal qualified voters should have a right to vote, it therefore becomes every truly loyal citizen to avail himself of the present opportunity offered to place himself honorably upon the record or poll-book at the approaching election, by giving a full and ardent support to the whole Government ticket, upon the platform adopted by the Union League convention. None other is recognized by the Federal authorities as loyal or worthy of the support of any one who desires the peace and restoration of this Union.

CHARLES CARROLL TEVIS,
Lieutenant Colonel Commanding.

This order was at once suppressed by General Schenck, and Colonel Tevis ordered under arrest. November 6, he made a statement of his action, and requested to be released from arrest and restored to his command, which was granted November 9, as stated in the subjoined order:

HEADQUARTERS MIDDLE DEPARTMENT, 8TH ARMY CORPS,
BALTIMORE, MARYLAND, *November* 9, 1863.

The within explanation and report having been submitted with permission by Colonel Tevis, under arrest and restored to duty—

The general commanding remarks that Colonel Tevis appears to have acted himself in good faith and from a sense of duty, but to have been misled by the bad course and instructions of Captain Frazier, provost marshal of the first congressional district of Maryland, who framed the order issued by him, and perhaps also by the mistaken advice of other over-zealous persons. But Colonel Tevis should have understood that the whole scope and purpose of the General Orders 53 and 55, and of accompanying instructions, was to prevent disloyal persons from voting and to suppress disturbances at the polls. The only test of loyalty prescribed was the oath of allegiance embodied in General Order No. 53. No directions were given to interfere with candidates, as such, nor with the voters because of their supporting any particular ticket, nor was any such interference contemplated or intended to be sanctioned by the general commanding. The idea of a "Government ticket" was only with Colonel Tevis or the provost marshal, Frazier, and other indiscreet or bad advisers, and was not put forth from these headquarters. Colonel Tevis's printed order was therefore wholly unauthorized and wrong.

The general commanding directs that a copy of this indorsement be furnished to Colonel Tevis, and also that a copy of the same be sent, duly certified, to Major H. L. Jeffries, assistant provost marshal general for the States of Maryland and Delaware.

By command of Major General Schenck:

W. H. CHESEBROUGH,
Lieut. Col. and Assistant Adjutant General.

ELECTION OF 1864.

Pending the constitutional convention election in Maryland, April 6, 1864, Major General Lewis Wallace and Gov. Bradford had a correspondence as to the oath prescribed by law to to be administered to the delegates chosen, and the power possessed by the judges of election to investigate and decide upon a charge of disloyalty as affecting the right to vote. The Governor recited the law, and the duties of the judges, and the penalties for non-performance, and expressed the opinion that the laws, if faithfully executed, as he hoped they would be, would be found "entirely sufficient to exclude disloyal voters from the polls."

Delaware.

An act to secure the freedom of elections in this State.

Whereas the Constitution of this State declares that "all elections shall be free and equal," and whereas the freedom of elections and the free enjoyment of the right of suffrage according to the Constitution and laws of the State are essential to the enjoyment of public liberty; and whereas, evil disposed persons did cause armed soldiers to be brought into this State and to be present at different voting places in the State on the day of the last general election, and a free election was thereby prevented; and whereas, it is proper that a repetition of so grave an offence against the peace and dignity of the State shall be prevented: Therefore—

SECTION 1. *Be it enacted, &c.*, That if any person, being a citizen or inhabitant of this State, shall send or cause to be sent, bring or cause to be brought, into this State, or shall aid, abet, procure, advise, counsel, or in any manner assist in sending or bringing into this State any armed soldier or soldiers, to be present at any voting place in this State, or within five miles thereof, on the day of any general, special, or other election hereafter to be holden in this State, or shall aid, abet, procure, advise, counsel, or in any manner assist the presence or attendance of any armed soldier or soldiers at any such voting place, or within five miles thereof, on any such election day, every person so offending shall be guilty of felony, and upon conviction thereof by indictment, shall forfeit and pay to the State a fine not less than one thousand dollars and not more than ten thousand dollars, and shall be imprisoned for a term not less than one nor more than five years, and shall forever thereafter be incapable of exercising the right of suffrage in this State.

SEC. 2. That if any person, being a citizen or inhabitant of this State, shall aid, abet, procure, advise, counsel, or in any manner assist or be guilty of military interference in any manner with the freedom of any election in this State, every person so offending shall be guilty of felony, and upon conviction thereof by indictment shall forfeit and pay to the State a fine of not less than one thousand dollars nor more than ten thousand dollars, and shall be imprisoned for a term not less than one nor more than five years, and shall forever thereafter be incapable of exercising the right of suffrage in this State.

SEC. 3. That if any inspector, presiding officer, or judge of any election in this State, or any other person, shall administer or cause to be administered to any legal voter in this State, any oath or affirmation not authorized by the Constitution and laws of this State for that purpose, as a pre-requisite or condition of voting at any election in this State, except when such oath or affirmation shall be administered in order to satisfy such inspector, presiding officer, or judge, that such vote is a legal vote according to the Constitution and laws of this State, such inspector, presiding officer, judge, or other person so offending, shall be guilty of a misdemeanor, and upon conviction thereof by indictment shall, for every such offence forfeit and pay to the State a fine of not less than five hundred dollars and not more than one thousand dollars, and shall be imprisoned for a term of ten days.

Passed at Dover, *March* 25, 1863.

GENERAL SCHENCK'S ORDER.

HEADQUARTERS MIDDLE DEPARTMENT, 8TH ARMY CORPS,
BALTIMORE, MD., *November* 13, 1863.

[General Orders No. 59.]

It is known that there are many evil disposed persons now at large in the State of Delaware, who have been engaged in rebellion against the lawful Government, or have given aid or comfort or encouragement to others so engaged, or who do not recognize their allegiance to the United States, and who may avail themselves of the indulgence of the authority which tolerates their presence to attempt to take part in or embarrass the approaching special election in that State. It is therefore ordered:

I. That all provost marshals and other military officers do prevent all disturbance and violence at or about the polls, whether offered by such persons as above described, or by any other person or persons whomsoever.

II. That all provost marshals and other military officers commanding in Delaware, shall support the judges of election on the 19th of November, 1863, in requiring an oath of allegiance to the United States, as a test of citizenship of any one whose vote may be challenged on the ground that he is not loyal or does not admit his allegiance to the United States, which oath shall be in the following form and terms:

I do solemnly swear that I will support, protect, and defend the Constitution and Government of the United States against all enemies, whether domestic or foreign; that I hereby pledge my allegiance, faith, and loyalty to the same any ordinance, resolution, or law of any State convention or State legislature to the contrary notwithstanding; that I will at all times yield a hearty and willing obedience to the said Constitution and Government, and will not, directly or indirectly, do any act in hostility to the same, either by taking up arms against them, or aiding, abetting, or countenancing those in arms against them; that, without permission from the lawful authority, I will have no communication, direct or indirect, with the States in insurrection against the United States, or with either of them, or with any person or persons within said insurrectionary States; and that I will in all things report myself as a good and loyal citizen of the United States. This I do in good faith, with full determination, pledge, and purpose to keep this, my sworn obligation, and without any mental reservation or evasion whatsoever.

III. Provost marshals and other military officers are directed to report to these headquarters any judge of election who shall refuse his aid in carrying out this order, or who, on challenge of a vote being made on the ground of disloyalty or hostility to the Government, shall refuse to require the oath of allegiance from such voter.

By command of Major General Schenck:

W. H. CHESEBROUGH,
Lieut. Col. and Asst. Adj. Gen.

GOVERNOR CANNON'S PROCLAMATION ON THE FOREGOING ORDER.

STATE OF DELAWARE, EXECUTIVE DEPARTMENT,
DOVER, *November* 13, 1863.

All civil officers and good citizens of this State are enjoined to obey the above military order, issued by the commanding general of the Middle department, and to give all needful aid for the proper enforcement of the same.

WILLIAM CANNON,
Governor of Delaware.

GENERAL TYLER'S ORDER.

HEADQUARTERS DISTRICT OF DELAWARE,
MIDDLE DEPARTMENT,
WILMINGTON, DELAWARE, *Nov.* 15, 1863.

The following instructions have been received from the General Commanding, and will be strictly and carefully observed by all detachments of officers and soldiers within the "District of Delaware," while carrying out the provisions of Department General Orders No. 59, during the election to be held on the 19th instant:

Every officer or non-commissioned officer in command of a detachment will be held strictly accountable for the good conduct and obedience of the men in his charge.

Officers and soldiers must be strictly sober, and, while preventing disturbance by others, must avoid all disturbance themselves, and are required not to hang around the polls, or engage in political discussions.

It will be borne in mind that the whole object of the order of the Commanding General is to preserve peace at the places of voting, to sustain the judges or inspectors of election, to protect loyal voters, and to prevent from voting disloyal and traitorously disposed persons, who refuse to take the oath of allegiance.

In enforcing Paragraph I, of the General Order, to prevent violence and disturbance at the polls, care will be taken that disloyal citizens of other States do not, as it is apprehended they will attempt to do, intrude themselves at the places of voting, and endeavor to intimidate the lawful and loyal voters of Delaware.

DANIEL TYLER,
Brigadier General Commanding.

Kentucky.

1863, March 11—The Legislature passed this bill by a two-thirds vote over the veto of Governor Magoffin:

An act to amend chapter 15 of the Revised Statutes, entitled "Citizens, expatriation, and aliens."

SEC. 1. *Be it enacted, &c.*, That any citizen of this State who shall enter into the service of the so-called Confederate States, in either a civil or military capacity, or enter into the service of the so-called provisional government of Kentucky in either a civil or military capacity, or, having heretofore entered such service of either the Confederate States or provisional government, shall continue in such service after this act takes effect, or shall take up and continue in arms against the military forces of the United States or the State of Kentucky, or shall give voluntary aid and assistance to those in arms against said forces, shall be deemed to have expatriated himself, and shall no longer be a citizen of Kentucky, nor shall he again be a citizen, except by permission of the Legislature by a general or special statute.

SEC. 2. That whenever a person attempts or is called on to exercise any of the constitutional or legal rights and privileges belonging only to citizens of Kentucky, he may be required to negative on oath the expatriation provided in the first section of this act, and upon his failure or refusal to do so, shall not be permitted to exercise any such right or privilege.

SEC. 3. This act to be of force in thirty days from and after its passage.

1863, July 10—Governor J. F. Robinson issued this proclamation:

COMMONWEALTH OF KENTUCKY,
Executive Department.

For the information and guidance of all officers at the approaching election, I have caused to be herewith published an act of the Legislature of Kentucky entitled "An act to amend chapter 15 of the Revised Statutes, entitled 'Citizens, expatriation, and aliens.'" The strict observance and enforcement of this and all other laws of this State regulating elections are earnestly enjoined and required as being alike due to a faithful discharge of duty, to the purity of the elective franchise, and to the sovereign will of the people of Kentucky expressed through their Legislature.

Given under my hand, as Governor of Kentucky, at Frankfort, this 10th day of July, 1863, and in the seventy-second year of the Commonwealth.

J. F. ROBINSON.

By the Governor:
D. C. WICKLIFFE, *Secretary of State.*

July 31—General Burnside issued this order:

HEADQUARTERS DEPARTMENT OF THE OHIO,
CINCINNATI, OHIO, *July* 31, 1863.

[General Orders No. 120.]

Whereas the State of Kentucky is invaded by a rebel force with the avowed intention of overawing the judges of elections, of intimidating the loyal voters, keeping them from the polls, and forcing the election of disloyal candidates at the election on the 3d of August; and whereas the military power of the Government is the only force that can defeat this attempt, the State of Kentucky is hereby declared under martial law, and all military officers are commanded to aid the constituted authorities of the State in support of the laws and of the purity of suffrage as defined in the late proclamation of his Excellency Governor Robinson.

As it is not the intention of the commanding general to interfere with the proper expression of public opinion, all discretion in the conduct of the election will be, as usual, in the hands of the legally appointed judges at the polls, *who will be held strictly responsible that no disloyal person be allowed to vote, and to this end the military power is ordered to give them its utmost support.*

The civil authority, civil courts, and business, will not be suspended by this order. It is for the purpose only of protecting, if necessary, the rights of loyal citizens and the freedom of election.

By command of Major General Burnside:

LEWIS RICHMOND,
Assistant Adjutant General.

LIEUT. COLONEL THOS. JOHNSON'S ORDER.

HEADQUARTERS UNITED STATES FORCES,
SMITHLAND, KY., *July* 16, 1863.

The county court judges of the counties of Trigg, Caldwell, Lyon, Crittenden, and Livingston, are hereby directed, in appointing judges and clerks for conducting the State elections in August next, to observe strictly the laws of Kentucky, which require that such judges and clerks shall be *unconditional Union men.*

Judges and clerks so appointed are hereby directed not to place the name of any person on the poll-books to be voted for at the said election who is not a Union man, or who may be opposed to *furnishing men and money for a vigorous prosecution of the war* against the rebellion against the United States Government. The judges and clerks are further directed to permit no person to vote at said election without taking the oath required by the laws of Kentucky, unless said person so presenting himself to vote is personally known to the judges to be a Union man.

Any person violating this order will be regarded as an enemy to the Government of the United States, and will be arrested and punished accordingly.

By order of THOMAS JOHNSON,
Lieutenant Colonel Commanding.

The oath prescribed by Lieutenant Colonel Johnson, to be taken by the voters, is in substance similar to the oath attached to the proclamation of General Shackleford.

MAJOR GENERAL HURLBUT'S ORDER.

HEADQUARTERS SIXTEENTH ARMY CORPS,
MEMPHIS, TENN., *July*, 1863.

I. In so much of the State of Kentucky as is within the district of Columbus, it is ordered—

1. That no person be permitted to be a candidate for office who is not avowedly and unconditionally for the Union and the suppression of the rebellion.

2. That no person shall exercise the privilege of an elector and vote at the said elections who is not avowedly and unconditionally for the Union and the suppression of the rebellion.

3. The military authorities in said district of Columbus will see to it that this order be carried out. Judges of election will be governed by the principles herein set forth, and will demand evidence upon oaths in such cases as may be in doubt, and allow no person to exercise the franchise of voting who does not take the oath required.

By order of Major General S. A. Hurlbut:

HENRY DINMORE,
Assistant Adjutant General.

BRIGADIER GENERAL ASBOTH'S ORDER.

HEADQUARTERS DISTRICT OF COLUMBUS,
SIXTH DIVISION, SIXTEENTH ARMY CORPS,
COLUMBUS, KENTUCKY, *July* 15, 1863.

The above orders of the general commanding corps are communicated to the civil and military authorities for their information. Military officers making arrests for violation of these orders will be governed by the circular from office of Commissary General of Prisoners, dated Washington, May 11, 1863.

By order of Brigadier General Asboth:

T. H. HARRIS,
Assistant Adjutant General.

BRIGADIER GENERAL ASBOTH'S ORDER.

DISTRICT OF COLUMBUS,
HEADQUARTERS SIXTH DIVISION, SIXTEENTH ARMY CORPS,
COLUMBUS, KY., *July* 29, 1863.

That no further doubt may exist as to the intent and meaning of Special Orders No. 159, dated Headquarters Sixteenth Army Corps, July 14, 1863, it is ordered that no person shall be permitted to be voted for, or be a candidate for office, who has been or is now under arrest or bonds, by proper authority, for uttering disloyal language or sentiments.

County judges within this district are hereby ordered to appoint, as judges and clerks of the ensuing August election, only such persons as are avowedly and unconditionally for the Union and the suppression of the rebellion, and are further ordered to revoke and recall any appointment of judges and clerks already made who are not such loyal persons.

Judges and clerks of elections are hereby ordered not to place the name of any person upon the poll-books, to be voted for at said election, who is not avowedly and unconditionally for the Union and the suppression of the rebellion, or who may be opposed to furnishing men and money for the suppression of the rebellion.

The following oath is prescribed and will be administered by judges of elections to voters and to such candidates as reside within the district:

"I do solemnly swear that I have never entered the service of the so-called Confederate States; that I have not been engaged in the service of the so-called 'provisional government of Kentucky,' either in a civil or military capacity; that I have never, either directly or indirectly, aided the rebellion against the Government of the United States or the State of Kentucky; that I am unconditionally for the Union and the suppression of the rebellion, and am willing to furnish men and money for the vigorous prosecution of the war against the rebellious league known as the 'Confederate States;' so help me God."

Any voter, judge, or clerk of elections, or other person, who may evade, neglect, or refuse compliance with the provisions of this order will be arrested and sent before a military commission as soon as the facts are substantiated.

By order of Brigadier General Asboth:

T. H. HARRIS,
Assistant Adjutant General.

BRIGADIER GENERAL SHACKLEFORD'S ORDER.

HEADQUARTERS FIRST BRIGADE,
SECOND DIVISION, TWENTY-THIRD ARMY CORPS,
RUSSELLVILLE, KY., *July* 30, 1863.

In order that the proclamation of the Governor and the laws of the State of Kentucky may be observed and enforced, post commandants and officers of this command will see that the following regulations are strictly complied with at the approaching State election:

None but loyal citizens will act as officers of the election. No one will be allowed to offer himself as a candidate for office, or be voted for at said election, who is not in all things loyal to the State and Federal Government, and in favor of a vigorous prosecution of the war for the suppression of the rebellion.

The judges of election will allow no one to vote at said election unless he is known to them to be an undoubtedly loyal citizen, or unless he shall first take the oath required by the laws of the State of Kentucky.

No disloyal man will offer himself as a candidate, or attempt to vote, except for treasonable purposes; and all such efforts will be summarily suppressed by the military authorities.

All necessary protection will be supplied and guaranteed at the polls to Union men by all the military force within this command.

By order of Brigadier General J. M. Shackleford, commanding: J. E. HUFFMAN,
Assistant Adjutant General.

Colonel John W. Foster, of the sixty-fifth Indiania regiment, commanding post at Henderson, Kentucky, issued an order similar to the above order of General Shackleford.

COLONEL MUNDY'S ORDER.

All loyal citizens, who have not forfeited their citizenship, can safely and quietly cast their votes for the candidates of their choice; but all who have forfeited their right of citizenship, under the provisions of the act of Assembly, who shall present themselves at the polls and fraudulently attempt to vote, will be immediately arrested by the guard detailed for that purpose at such precinct, and confined in the military prison.

Missouri.

1862, June 12—The convention of Missouri adopted this ordinance:

SEC. 1. No person shall vote at any election to be hereafter held in this State, under or in pursuance of the constitution and laws thereof, whether State, county, township, or municipal, who shall not, in addition to possessing the qualifications already prescribed for electors, previously take an oath in form as follows, namely: "I, ———, do solemnly swear (or affirm, as the case may be) that I will support, protect, and defend the Constitution of the United States and the constitution of the State of Missouri against all enemies and opposers whether domestic or foreign; that I will bear true faith, loyalty, and allegiance to the United States, and will not, directly or indirectly, give aid and comfort, or countenance, to the enemies or opposers thereof, or of the provisional government of the State of Missouri, any ordinance, law, or resolution of any State convention or Legislature, or of any order or organization, secret or otherwise, to the contrary notwithstanding; and that I do this with a full and honest determination, pledge, and purpose, faithfully to keep and perform the same, without any mental reservation or evasion whatever. And I do further solemnly swear (or affirm) that I have not, since the 17th day of December, A. D. 1861, wilfully taken up arms or levied war against the United States, or against the provisional government of the State of Missouri: So help me God."

CONGRESSIONAL ELECTION OF 1862.

[General Orders No. 45.]

HEADQUARTERS STATE OF MISSOURI,
ADJUTANT GENERAL'S OFFICE,
ST. LOUIS, *October* 23, 1862.

I. A general election is to take place throughout the State the first Tuesday in November next.

This is the first attempt of the people to choose their officers since the war of the rebellion commenced. It will be an occasion when angry passions, excited by this war, might produce strife, and prevent the full expression of the popular will in the selection of officers.

The convention has provided by ordinance that every voter shall, before voting, take a prescribed oath, and that no vote shall be counted in favor of any candidate for a State or county office, unless he shall have taken an oath prescribed for candidates. The ordinance of the convention fixes heavy penalties upon those who take the oath falsely. These are the safeguards which the convention has judged necessary to keep unfaithful and disloyal persons from exercising power in the State. They are sufficient. No person must be allowed to interfere with the freedom of those qualified to vote under this ordinance.

The enrolled militia being citizens of the State, and very nearly all entitled by age to vote, will doubtless be generally at places of voting. They are a body organized for the purpose of preventing violations of the law of the State, and they all know that it is essential to the maintenance of our Government that all qualified voters shall be allowed, without molestation of any kind, to cast their votes as they please.

II. It is required of all officers and men of the enrolled militia that they keep perfect order at the polls on the day of election, and that they see that no person is either kept from the polls by intimidation or in any way interfered with in voting at the polls for whatever candidate he may choose.

III. If any officer or private shall either interfere with the rights of voters, or countenance such interference by others, it will be treated as a high military offence, and punished with the utmost rigor.

IV. Whenever there is any reason to apprehend any interference with the election on the part of bands of guerrillas, the commanding officer of the nearest regiment will detail a sufficient force to prevent any such interference, and station it where there is apprehended danger.

V. In case of disturbance arising which cannot be arrested by the civil authorities, any commissioned officer present is hereby ordered, at the request of any judge, sheriff, or justice of the peace, to use the necessary military force to suppress it.

VI. Commanding officers of the enrolled Missouri militia are hereby directed to see that the foregoing orders are strictly obeyed.

By order of the commander-in-chief:
WILLIAM D. WOOD,
Acting Adjutant General Missouri.

BRIGADIER GENERAL HALL'S ORDER.

HEADQUARTERS SEVENTH MILITARY DISTRICT,
ST. JOSEPH, MISSOURI, *November* 1, 1862.

[General Orders, No. 33.]

The attention of all officers and soldiers of the militia of this district is called to General Order No. 45, dated "Headquarters State of Missouri, Adjutant General's office, St. Louis, October 23, 1862," with reference to the election on Tuesday next. The military should bear in mind that they are not the judges of the qualifications of voters. That duty is devolved by law on the judge of the election. If those officers either admit improper persons to vote, or exclude proper persons from voting, the statutes of this State provide an ample remedy. The militia will carefully abstain from all acts calculated to interfere with the freedom of election. All officers who interfere with the rights of voters will be reported to the commander-in-chief, to be dealt with as he may decide. All soldiers guilty of the same offence will be punished as a court-martial shall determine.

By order of Brigadier General Willard P. Hall:
ELWOOD KIRBY,
Assistant Adjutant General.

MAJOR GENERAL SCHOFIELD'S ORDERS OF 1863.

HEADQUARTERS DEPARTMENT OF THE MISSOURI,
ST. LOUIS, MISSOURI, *September* 28, 1863.

[General Orders No. 101.]

The right of the people to peaceably assemble for all lawful purposes, and the right to freely express their will at the polls according to law, are essential to civil liberty.

No interference with these rights, either by violence, threats, intimidation, or otherwise, will be tolerated.

Any commissioned officer who shall incite or encourage any interference with any lawful assemblage of the people, or who shall fail to do his utmost to prevent such interference, shall be dismissed the service; and any officer, soldier, or civilian, who shall, by violence, threats, or otherwise, actually interfere with any such lawful assemblage of the people, shall be punished by imprisonment or otherwise, at the discretion of a court-martial or military commission.

Any officer, soldier, or civilian, who shall attempt to intimidate any qualified voter in the exercise of his right to vote, or who shall attempt to prevent any qualified voter from going to the polls or voting, shall be punished by imprisonment or otherwise, at the discretion of a court-martial or military commission.

Special attention is called to the fifth article of war, which will be applied to commissioned officers of Missouri militia not in active service, as well as to officers and soldiers in active service.

By command of Major General Schofield:
C. W. MARSH,
Assistant Adjutant General.

HEADQUARTERS DEPARTMENT OF THE MISSOURI,
ST. LOUIS, *October* 20, 1863.

[General Orders No. 120.]

Judges of elections of the various precincts in Missouri are notified that they will be held responsible that at the election on the 3d of November next, those persons, and only those, be permitted to vote who are entitled to do so by the laws of the State; and especially that the ordinance of the State convention, adopted June 10, 1862, and published herewith, be enforced in every case.

It is the duty of judges of election at each precinct in the State to see that every person qualified by the constitution and laws of the State shall be permitted to exercise the elective franchise without let or hindrance; and it is equaly their duty to see that those who are not qualified under the constitution and laws, or who refuse to qualify according to the terms of the annexed ordinance, shall not be allowed to vote; and any action on their part excluding qualified voters from the polls, or admitting those who are not qualified as stated, will be punished as a military offence.

Any person who has borne arms against the Government of the United States, or voluntarily given aid and comfort to its enemies during the present rebellion, and who shall presume to act as judge or clerk at said election, and any county judge who shall knowingly appoint any such person as above described to act as judge at said election, will be deemed guilty of violation of military orders, and upon conviction thereof, will be punished accordingly.

In those parts of the State where there is danger of interference by guerrilla bands, or by combinations of persons intended to overawe or intimidate legal voters, district commanders will so dispose their troops as will most certainly prevent such interference.

Where no such protection may be deemed necessary, all troops will absent themselves from the polls entirely; and in all cases when ordered by the district commanders to be present, their action will be strictly confined to the suppression of violence and removing the interference above named, to the end that the laws may be enforced and the purity of the ballot-box maintained. Under the pretext of guarding against violence at the polls, no officer or soldier will be permitted to interfere with the peaceful and legal expression of public sentiment, and no officer will be excused for a willful failure to remove any interference intended to prevent such expression.

District commanders will designate, on the day previous to the election, those counties in their respective districts in which such protection may be deemed necessary, and cause their troops to be disposed accordingly.

Any willful violation of this order will be promptly punished as a military offence.

Missouri troops will vote at the company polls, opened for that purpose at the headquarters of their posts, camps, or detachments, in accordance with the ordinance of the State convention, passed June 12, 1862, and at no other place.

Special attention is directed to General Orders No. 101 from these headquarters, dated September 28, 1863, and its observance strictly enjoined upon all in Missouri.

By command of Major General Schofield:

O. D. GREENE,
Assistant Adjutant General.

Orders Respecting Impressments of Property.

MAJOR GENERAL HARTSUFF'S ORDER.

HEADQUARTERS TWENTY-THIRD ARMY CORPS,
LEXINGTON, KENTUCKY, *July* 24, 1863.

For the information and guidance of officers in impressing property, it is hereby directed that, whenever its impressment may become necessary for the troops of the twenty-third army corps, it will be taken exclusively from rebels and rebel sympathizers; and so long as the property needed is to be found belonging or pertaining to either of the above-named classes, no man of undoubted loyalty will be molested.

Among rebel sympathizers will be classed those persons in Kentucky, nominally Union men, but opposed to the Government and to the prosecution of the war, whose acts and words alike hinder the speedy and proper termination of the rebellion.

Property will only be taken by the proper staff officers, who will in every case give receipts for it. Appropriate blank receipts will be furnished by the chief commissary and chief quartermaster at these headquarters.

By command of Major General Hartsuff:

GEORGE B. DRAKE, *A. A. G.*

BRIGADIER GENERAL BOYLE'S ORDER.

HEADQUARTERS DISTRICT OF KENTUCKY,
LOUISVILLE, *July* 25, 1863.

By authority of the general commanding the department, the following general order is made:

1. It is ordered that no forage or other property belonging to loyal citizens in the State of Kentucky be seized or impressed except in cases of absolute necessity, and then only on the written authority from the headquarters of the twenty-third army corps or from these headquarters.

2. Whenever it becomes necessary to seize or impress private property for military purposes, the property of sympathizers with the rebellion and of those opposed to furnishing any more men or any more money to maintain the Federal Government and suppress the rebellion will be first seized and impressed.

3. The negroes of loyal citizens will not be impressed on the public works and military roads unless absolutely necessary. The negroes of citizens who are for no more men and no more money to suppress the rebellion, and the supporters, aiders, and abettors of such, will be first impressed, and officers detailed for this purpose are required strictly to observe this order in the execution of their duties.

4. All horses of the enemy captured or subject to capture will be taken possession of by quartermasters and reported to Captain Jenkins, chief quartermaster, Louisville, who is ordered to allow loyal citizens to retain horses to supply the places of those stolen by the enemy; but disloyal persons mentioned in paragraphs two and three, who encourage raids by the enemy, will not in any case be allowed to retain captured horses or horses justly subject to capture.

5. For all property seized or impressed proper and regular vouchers will be given, with indorsement as to the loyalty or disloyalty of the owners of the property.

By order of Brigadier General Boyle:

A. C. SEMPLE, *A. A. G.*

Action of Congress.

First Session, Thirty-Eighth Congress.

TO PREVENT OFFICERS OF THE ARMY AND NAVY FROM INTERFERING IN ELECTIONS.

IN SENATE.

1864, January 5—Mr. POWELL brought in a bill to prevent officers of the army and navy, and other persons engaged in the military service, from interfering in elections in the States; which was ordered to be printed.

January 6—Mr. POWELL moved it be referred to the Committee on the Judiciary; which was lost—yeas 16, (Messrs. *Buckalew*, *Carlile*, Cowan, *Davis*, *Harding*, *Hendricks*, Hicks, Johnson, Lane of Indiana, *Nesmith*, *Powell*, *Saulsbury*, Sherman, Sprague, Van Winkle, Willey,) nays 21. It was then referred to the Military Committee.

January 16—The Senate adopted this resolution:

Resolved, That the Secretary of War be directed to transmit to the Senate all orders or proclamations, in his department, concerning elections issued by military authority in the States of Kentucky, Missouri, Maryland, and Delaware.

February 12—Mr. HOWARD, of Michigan, made an adverse report upon the bill.

June 22—The bill was amended so as to read as follows:

Be it enacted, &c., That it shall not be lawful for any military officer of the United States, or any person engaged in the civil, military, or naval service of the United States, to order, bring, keep, or have under his authority or control, any troops or armed men within one mile of the place where any general or special election is held in any State of the United States of America, unless it shall be necessary to repel the armed enemies of the United States or to keep the peace at the polls. And that it shall not be lawful for any officer of the army or navy of the United States to prescribe or fix, or attempt to prescribe or fix, by proclamation, order, or otherwise, the qualifications of voters in any State of the United States of America, or in any manner to interfere with the freedom of any election in any State, or with the exercise of the free right of suffrage in any State of the United States. Any officer of the army or navy of the United States, or other person engaged in the civil, military, or naval service of the United States, who violates this section of this act, shall, for every such offence, be liable to indictment as for a misdemeanor, in any court of the United States having jurisdiction to hear, try, and determine cases of misdemeanor, and on conviction thereof shall pay a fine not exceeding $5,000, and suffer imprisonment in the penitentiary not less than three months nor more than five years, at the discretion of the court trying the same; and any person convicted as aforesaid shall, moreover, be disqualified from holding any office of honor, profit, or trust under the Government of the United States: *Provided*, That nothing herein contained shall be so construed as to prevent any officer, soldier, sailor, or marine from exercising the right of suffrage in any election district to which he may belong, if otherwise qualified, according to the laws of the State in which he shall offer to vote.

SEC. 2. That any officer or person in the military or naval service of the United States who shall order or advise, or who shall directly or indirectly, by force, threat, menace, intimidation, or otherwise, prevent or attempt to prevent any qualified voter of any State of the United States of America from freely exercising the right of suffrage at any general or special election in any State of the United States, or who shall in like manner compel, or attempt to compel, any officer of an election in any such State to receive a vote from a person not legally qualified to vote, or who shall impose or attempt to impose any rules or regulations for conducting such election different from those prescribed by law, or interfere in any manner with any officer of said election in the discharge of his duties, shall for every such offense be liable to indictment as for a misdemeanor, in any court of the United States having jurisdiction to hear, try, and determine cases of misdemeanor, and on conviction thereof shall pay a fine not exceeding $5,000, and suffer imprisonment in the penitentiary not exceeding five years, at the discretion of the court trying the same, and any person convicted as aforesaid shall, moreover, be disqualified from holding any office of honor, profit, or trust under the Government of the United States.

And passed—yeas 19, nays 13, as follows:

YEAS—Messrs. *Buckalew*, *Carlile*, *Davis*, Grimes, Hale, Harlan, *Hendricks*, Hicks, Johnson, Lane of Kansas, *McDougall*, Pomeroy, *Powell*, *Richardson*, *Riddle*, *Saulsbury*, Trumbull, Wade, Willey—19.

NAYS—Messrs. Anthony, Chandler, Clark, Collamer, Dixon, Foot, Foster, Harris, Howard, Morgan, Sumner, Ten Eyck, Wilson—13.

Mr. HARLAN entered a motion to reconsider.

June 28—The Senate refused to reconsider it—yeas 19, nays 23, as follows:

YEAS—Messrs. Anthony, Chandler, Clark, Collamer, Conness, Doolittle, Foot, Foster, Howard, Lane of Indiana, Lane of Kansas, Morgan, Morrill, Ramsey, Sprague, Sumner, Ten Eyck, Wilkinson, Wilson—19.

NAYS—Messrs. Brown, *Buckalew*, *Carlile*, Cowan, *Davis*, Grimes, Hale, Harlan, Harris, Henderson, *Hendricks*, Hicks, *McDougall*, *Nesmith*, Pomeroy, *Powell*, *Riddle*, *Saulsbury*, Sherman, Trumbull, Van Winkle, Wade, Willey—23.

The bill was not acted upon in the House.

RECONSTRUCTION OF STATES.

Bill for Reconstruction.

First Session, Thirty-Eighth Congress.

IN HOUSE.

1863, December 15—Mr. HENRY WINTER DAVIS moved that so much of the President's message as relates to the duty of the United States to guarantee a republican form of government to the States in which the governments recognized by the United States have been abrogated or overthrown, be referred to a select committee of nine to report the bills necessary and proper for carrying into execution the foregoing guarantee; which was agreed to—yeas 89, nays 80.

May 4—The House passed the bill reported from the committee—yeas 74, nays 66, as follows:

YEAS—Messrs. Alley, Allison, Ames, Anderson, Arnold, Ashley, John D. Baldwin, Baxter, Beaman, Blow, Boutwell, Brandegee, Broomall, Cole, Creswell, Henry Winter Davis, Dawes, Deming, Dixon, Donnelly, Driggs, Eliot, Farnsworth, Fenton, Frank, Garfield, Higby, Hooper, Hotchkiss, A. W. Hubbard, J. H. Hubbard, Hulburd, Julian, Kelley, Francis W. Kellogg, Orlando Kellogg, Littlejohn, Loan, Longyear, Marvin, McBride, McClurg, McIndoe, Samuel F. Miller, Moorhead, Morrill, Daniel Morris, Amos Myers, Leonard Myers, Norton, Charles O'Neill, Orth, Patterson, Perham, Pike, Pomeroy, Price, Alexander H. Rice, John H. Rice, Edward H. Rollins, Schenck, Scofield, Shannon, Sloan, Smithers, Spalding, Thayer, Upson, William B. Washburn, Williams, Wilder, Wilson, Windom, Woodbridge—74.

NAYS—Messrs. *William J. Allen, Ancona, Augustus C. Baldwin*, J. B. Blair, *Brooks, J. S. Brown*, W. G. Brown, *Chanler, Clay, Cox, Cravens, Dawson, Denison, Eden, Eldridge, English, Finck, Ganson, Grider*, Hale, *Hall, Harding, Benjamin G. Harris, Charles M. Harris, Herrick, Holman, Philip Johnson, William Johnson, Kernan, King, Knapp, Law, Lazear, LeBlond, Long, Marcy, McAllister, McDowell, McKinney, Middleton, Morris, Morrison, Noble, Odell, John O'Neill, Pendleton, Perry, Radford, Samuel J. Randall, William H. Randall, Robinson, James S. Rollins, Ross, Scott*, Smith, *John B. Steele, William G. Steele, Stiles, Strouse, Stuart, Ward*, Webster, Whaley, *Wheeler, Chilton A. White, Yeaman*—66.

The preamble to the bill, which was in these words—

Whereas the so-called Confederate States are a public enemy, waging an unjust war, whose injustice is so glaring that they have no right to claim the mitigation of the extreme rights of war which are accorded by modern usage to an enemy who has a right to consider the war a just one; and whereas none of the States which, by a regularly recorded majority of its citizens, have joined the so-called Southern Confederacy, can be considered and treated as entitled to be represented in Congress, or to take any part in the political government of the Union: Therefore—

was rejected—yeas 57, nays 75, as follows:

YEAS—Messrs. Alley, Allison, Ames, Anderson, Ashley, John D. Baldwin, Baxter, Beaman, Boutwell, Boyd, Broomall, Cole, Henry Winter Davis, Donnelly, Driggs, Eckley, Eliot, Frank, Garfield, Grinnell, Higby, Hooper, Hotchkiss, Asahel W. Hubbard, John H. Hubbard, Julian, Kasson, Kelley, Francis W. Kellogg, Littlejohn, Loan, Longyear, McBride, McClurg, Moorhead, Daniel Morris, Amos Myers, Leonard Myers, Norton, Charles O'Neill, Orth, Patterson, Perham, Pike, Price, John H. Rice, Edward H. Rollins, Schenck, Shannon, Sloan, Spalding, Stevens, Upson, William B. Washburn, Williams, Wilder, Woodbridge—57.

NAYS—Messrs. *Wm. J. Allen, Ancona*, Arnold, *Augustus C. Baldwin*, Jacob B. Blair, Blow, *Brooks, James S. Brown*, William G. Brown, *Chanler, Clay, Cox*, Creswell, *Dawson, Denison, Eden, Eldridge*, Farnsworth, Fenton, *Finck, Ganson, Grider*, Hale, *Hall, Harding, Benjamin G. Harris, Chas. M. Harris, Herrick, Holman*, Hulburd, *Philip Johnson*, Orlando Kellogg, *Kernan, Knapp, Law, Lazear, Le Blond, Long, Marcy*, Marvin, *McAllister*, McIndoe, *Middleton*, Morrill, *Noble, Moses F. Odell, John O'Neill, Pendleton, Perry*, Pomeroy, *Radford, Samuel J. Randall*, William H. Randall, Alexander H. Rice, *James S. Rollins, Ross*, Scofield, *Scott*, Smith, Smithers, *John B. Steele, Wm. G. Steele, Stiles, Strouse, Stuart*, Thayer, *Ward*, Webster, Whaley, *Wheeler, Chilton A. White, Joseph W. White*, Wilson, Windom, *Yeaman*—75.

The bill authorizes the President to appoint in each of the States declared in rebellion, a Provisional Governor, with the pay and emoluments of a brigadier; to be charged with the civil administration until a State government therein shall be recognized. As soon as the military resistance to the United States shall have been suppressed, and the people sufficiently returned to their obedience to the Constitution and laws, the Governor shall direct the marshal of the United States to enroll all the white male citizens of the United States, resident in the State in their respective counties, and whenever a majority of them take the oath of allegiance, the loyal people of the State shall be entitled to elect delegates to a convention to act upon the re-establishment of a State government—the proclamation to contain details prescribed. Qualified voters in the army may vote in their camps. No person who has held or exercised any civil, military, State, or Confederate office, under the rebel occupation, and who has voluntarily borne arms against the United States, shall vote or be eligible as a delegate. The convention is required to insert in the constitution provisions—

1st. No person who has held or exercised any civil or military office, (except offices merely ministerial and military offices below a colonel,) State or Confederate, under the usurping power, shall vote for, or be a member of the legislature or governor.

2d. Involuntary servitude is forever prohibited, and the freedom of all persons is guaranteed in said State.

3d. No debt, State or Confederate, created by or under the sanction of the usurping power, shall be recognized or paid by the State.

Upon the adoption of the constitution by the convention, and its ratification by the electors of the State, the Provisional Governor shall so certify to the President, who, after obtaining the assent of Congress, shall, by proclamation, recognize the government as established, and none other, as the constitutional government of the State; and from the date of such recognition, and not before, senators and representatives and electors for President and Vice President may be elected in such State. Until reorganization the Provisional Governor shall enforce the laws of the Union and of the State before the rebellion.

The remaining sections are as follows:

SEC. 12. That all persons held to involuntary servitude or labor in the States aforesaid are hereby emancipated and discharged therefrom, and they and their posterity shall be forever free. And if any such persons or their posterity shall be restrained of liberty, under pretence of any claim to such service or labor, the courts of the United States shall, on *habeas corpus*, discharge them.

SEC. 13. That if any person declared free by this act, or any law of the United States, or any proclamation of the President, be restrained of liberty, with intent to be held in or reduced to involuntary servitude or labor, the person convicted before a court of competent jurisdiction of such act shall be punished by fine of not less than $1,500, and be imprisoned not less than five, nor more than twenty years.

SEC. 14. That every person who shall hereafter hold or exercise any office, civil, or military, except offices merely ministerial and military offices below the grade of colonel, in the rebel service, State or confederate, is hereby declared not to be a citizen of the United States.

IN SENATE.

May 27—Mr. WADE, from the Committee on Territories, reported the bill with two amendments; one fixing the compensation of the provisional Governor at $3,000 a year, and the other striking out the word "white" wherever it occurs.

The Senate as in Committee of the Whole,

July 1—Mr. BROWN offered this as a substitute for the bill:

That when the inhabitants of any State have been declared in a state of insurrection against the United States by proclamation of the President, by force and virtue of the act entitled "An act to provide for the collection of duties on imports, and for other purposes," approved July 13, 1861, they shall be, and are hereby declared to be, incapable of casting any vote for electors of President or Vice President of the United States, or of electing Senators or Representatives in Congress, until said insurrection in said State is suppressed or abandoned and said inhabitants have returned to their obedience to the Government of the United States, nor until such return to obedience shall be declared by proclamation of the President issued by virtue of an act of Congress, hereafter to be passed authorizing the same.

Which was agreed to—yeas 17, nays 16, as follows:

YEAS—Messrs. Brown, *Carlile*, Cowan, *Davis*, Doolittle, Grimes, Henderson, *Hendricks*, Johnson, Lane of Indiana, *McDougall*, *Powell*, *Richardson*, *Riddle*, *Saulsbury*, Trumbull, Van Winkle—17.

NAYS—Messrs. Chandler, Clark, Conness, Hale, Harlan, Lane of Kansas, Morgan, Morrill, Pomeroy, Ramsey, Sherman, Sprague, Sumner, Wade, Wilkinson, Wilson—16.

Mr. SUMNER proposed the following new section:

TO MAKE THE EMANCIPATION PROCLAMATION A STATUTE.

That the proclamation of emancipation issued by the President of the United States on the first day of January, 1863, so far as the same declares that the slaves in certain designated States and parts of States thenceforward should be free, is hereby adopted and enacted as a statute of the United States, and as a rule and article for the government of the military and naval forces thereof.

Which was rejected—yeas 11, nays 21, as follows:

YEAS—Messrs. Chandler, Conness, Lane of Kansas, Morgan, Morrill, Pomeroy, Ramsey, Sumner, Wade, Wilkinson, Wilson—11.

NAYS—Messrs. Brown, *Carlile*, *Davis*, Doolittle, Grimes, Hale, Harris, Henderson, *Hendricks*, Johnson, Lane of Indiana, *McDougall*, *Powell*, *Richardson*, *Riddle*, *Saulsbury*, Sherman, Sprague, Ten Eyck, Trumbull, Van Winkle—21.

The Senate adopted the amendment made in Committee of the Whole—yeas 20, nays 13, as follows:

YEAS—Messrs. Brown, *Carlile*, *Davis*, Doolittle, Grimes, Harlan, Harris, Henderson, *Hendricks*, Johnson, Lane of Indiana, *McDougall*, Pomeroy, *Powell*, *Richardson*, *Riddle*, *Saulsbury*, Sprague, Trumbull, Van Winkle—20.

NAYS—Messrs. Clark, Conness, Hale, Lane of Kansas, Morgan, Morrill, Ramsey, Sherman, Sumner, Ten Eyck, Wade, Wilkinson, Wilson—13.

And the bill passed—yeas 26, nays 3, as follows:

YEAS—Messrs. Brown, Chandler, Conness, Doolittle, Grimes, Harlan, Harris, Henderson, Johnson, Lane of Indiana, Lane of Kansas, *McDougall*, Morgan, Pomeroy, Ramsey, *Riddle*, Sherman, Sprague, Sumner, Ten Eyck, Trumbull, Van Winkle, Wade, Wilkinson, Wilson—26.

NAYS—Messrs. *Davis*, *Powell*, *Saulsbury*—3.

July 2—The House non concurred in the amendment of the Senate, and asked a Committee of Conference; but the Senate, on motion, receded from its amendments—(thus passing the House bill)—yeas 18, nays 14, as follows:

YEAS—Messrs. Anthony, Chandler, Clark, Conness, Foot, Harlan, Harris, Howe, Lane of Kansas, Morgan, Pomeroy, Ramsey, Sherman, Sprague, Sumner, Wade, Wilkinson, Wilson—18.

NAYS—Messrs. *Buckalew*, *Carlile*, *Davis*, Doolittle, Henderson, *Hendricks*, Lane of Indiana, *McDougall*, *Powell*, *Riddle*, *Saulsbury*, Ten Eyck, Trumbull, Van Winkle—14.

THE PRESIDENT'S PROCLAMATION RESPECTING IT.

The PRESIDENT failed to approve this bill; and, July 8, 1864, issued this proclamation respecting it:

Whereas, at the late session, Congress passed a bill "to guarantee to certain States, whose governments have been usurped or overthrown, a republican form of government," a copy of which is hereunto annexed;

And whereas the said bill was presented to the President of the United States for his approval less than one hour before the *sine die* adjournment of said session, and was not signed by him;

And whereas the said bill contains, among other things, a plan for restoring the States in rebellion to their proper practical relation in the Union, which plan expresses the sense of Congress upon that subject, and which plan it is now thought fit to lay before the people for their consideration:

Now, therefore, I, ABRAHAM LINCOLN, President of the United States, do proclaim, declare, and make known, that, while I am (as I was in December last, when by proclamation I propounded a plan for restoration) unprepared, by a formal approval of this bill, to be inflexibly committed to any single plan of restoration; and, while I am also unprepared to declare that the free State constitutions and governments already adopted and installed in Arkansas and Louisiana shall be set aside and held for nought, thereby repelling and discouraging the loyal citizens who have set up the same as to further effort, or to declare a constitutional competency in Congress to abolish slavery in States, but am at the same time sincerely hoping and expecting that a constitutional amendment abolishing slavery throughout the nation may be adopted, nevertheless I am fully satisfied with the system for restoration contained in the bill as one very proper plan for the loyal people of any State choosing to adopt it, and that I am, and at all times shall be, prepared to give the Executive aid and assistance to any such people, so soon as the military resistance to the United States shall have been suppressed in any such State, and the people thereof shall have sufficiently returned to their obedience to the Constitution and laws of the United States, in which cases Military Governors will be appointed, with directions to proceed according to the bill.

ELECTORAL VOTE OF REBEL STATES.

June 13—Mr. Garfield introduced a joint resolution resolving that no State declared to be in rebellion by proclamation of the President is entitled to appoint electors of President and Vice President, and that no electoral vote from any such State shall be received or counted until both Houses of Congress, by concurrent action, shall have recognized a State government in such State.

It was read a first and second time; was ordered to be engrossed, and read the third time, under the operation of the previous question, when the following proceedings took place:

Mr. McKinney. Is it in order to inquire whether Mr. Johnson could be a candidate for the Vice Presidency under that rule?

The Speaker. It is not in order to make the inquiry.

Mr. Blaine. Is it too late now to raise a point of order?

The Speaker. It is entirely too late. The joint resolution has received its third reading, and the main question has been ordered on its passage.

Mr. Blaine. Has the morning hour expired?

The Speaker. It has; but the House has ordered the main question to be now put.

Mr. Blaine. I move to lay the joint resolution on the table.

Which was agreed to—yeas 104, nays 33, as follows:

Yeas—Messrs. *James C. Allen*, *William J. Allen*, Allison, Ames, Anderson, *Baily*, *Augustus C. Baldwin*, John D. Baldwin, Blaine, Blair, *Bliss*, Boutwell, *Brooks*, *James S. Brown*, *Chanler*, Ambrose W. Clark, Freeman Clarke, Cobb, *Coffroth*, *Cox*, *Cravens*, Dawes, *Denison*, Dixon, Driggs, *Eden*, *Edgerton*, *Eldridge*, Eliot, *English*, Farnsworth, Fenton, *Finck*, Frank, *Ganson*, Gooch, *Grider*, *Griswold*, *Harding*, *Harrington*, *Charles M. Harris*, *Herrick*, *Holman*, Hotchkiss, Asahel W. Hubbard, *Hutchins*, Ingersoll, Jenckes, *William Johnson*, *Kalbfleisch*, Francis W. Kellogg, Orlando Kellogg, *Kernan*, *King*, *Knapp*, *Law*, *Le Blond*, Littlejohn, *Marcy*, Marvin, *McDowell*, McIndoe, McKinney, Samuel F. Miller, *William H. Miller*, Moorhead, *James R. Morris*, Amos Myers, Leonard Myers, *Odell*, Charles O'Neill, *John O'Neill*, Orth, *Pendleton*, Perham, Pike, Price, *Pruyn*, *Radford*, Alexander H. Rice, John H. Rice, *Robinson*, *James S. Rollins*, *Ross*, Scofield, Sloan, Smith, *John B. Steele*, *William G. Steele*, *Stiles*, *Strouse*, *Stuart*, *Sweat*, Thayer, Thomas, *Wadsworth*, Webster, Whaley, *Wheeler*, *Chilton A. White*, *Joseph W. White*, Wilson, Windom, *Fernando Wood*—104.

Nays—Messrs. Alley, Ashley, Baxter, Beaman, Blow, Brandegee, Cole, Creswell, Henry Winter Davis, Thomas T. Davis, Donnelly, Eckley, Garfield, Higby, Hooper, John H. Hubbard, Julian, Kelley, *Lazear*, Longyear, McClurg, Morrill, Daniel Morris, Norton, Shannon, Smithers, Spalding, Starr, Stevens, Upson, Van Valkenburgh, Williams, Woodbridge—33.

June 20—Mr. Ashley asked leave to offer this joint resolution, but it was objected to:

Resolved, &c., That when the inhabitants of any State have been declared in a state of insurrection against the United States by proclamation of the President, by force and virtue of the act entitled "An act further to provide for the collection of duties on imports, and for other purposes," approved July 13, 1861, they shall be and are hereby declared to be incapable of casting any vote for electors of President or Vice President of the United States, or of electing Senators or Representatives in Congress, until said insurrection in said State is suppressed or abandoned, and said inhabitants have returned to their obedience to the Constitution and Government of the United States, nor until such return to obedience shall be declared by proclamation of the President, issued by virtue of an act of Congress authorizing the same.

PROPOSED APPOINTMENT OF COMMISSION OF INQUIRY.

June 22—Mr. Dawes, from the Committee on Elections, in the application of certain persons to be received as Representatives from Arkansas, made a report, which closes with this joint resolution:

Resolved, &c., That there be appointed by the President, by and with the consent of the Senate, a commission consisting of three persons, residents of States not involved in the present rebellion, whose duty it shall be during the recess of the present Congress to visit those States declared by the proclamation of the President to have been in rebellion, and which have already taken or may before the next session of the present Congress take measures to establish or reorganize State governments, and after careful examination and hearing testimony report to the President for the information of Congress at as early day in the next session as possible all such evidence as they may be able to obtain upon the question, whether the loyal people in any such States have succeeded in re-establishing a State government, to what extent such State government represents and has the support of the loyal people in such State, and what is the ability of such people therein to maintain the same against domestic violence.

Resolved further, That until Congress shall be satisfied upon evidence submitted to them that the rebellion has so far been suppressed in any such State that there has been established therein a State government, republican in form, and prohibiting the existence of slavery in the same, and so firmly established as to be able to maintain itself against domestic violence, representation from any such State ought not to be admitted into either branch of Congress.

Mr. James S. Brown, from the Minority Committee, presented these resolutions:

Whereas by article six of the Constitution of the United States it and the laws made in pursuance thereof are declared to be the supreme law of the land, and every act of secession by any State is in direct violation of such supreme laws: Therefore,

Resolved, That the acts of secession by the Legislatures of the several States whose people are now in rebellion are mere nullities, having no force or effect to change the relation either of States themselves or of the people thereof toward the General Government; and that by such acts the people neither freed themselves from the penalties attaching by law to treason nor lost any rights as citizens of the States and United States, except such as may follow upon conviction of crime; that the duty of the people of such States to send true and loyal men to Congress, and the right so to do as consequent upon the duty, still remain by force of the Constitution, requiring no act of the President or Congress to confirm them; that no State can under the Constitution assent to the presence of armed rebels from other States within its borders, and that any act of the authorities of a State giving such assent is a nullity; that the entrance of such armed rebels of one State upon Territories of another is an invasion from which by article four of the Constitution the United States are bound to protect the invaded State; that this obligation of protection on the part of the United States is due to each citizen individually as a consequence of his duty of allegiance, and continues so long as there is a single loyal citizen in a State oppressed by such invasion; that so long as the Constitution and laws of the United States cannot be enforced in any congressional district on account of the presence of armed rebels there can be no free election, and a person claiming a seat through an election under such circumstances should be rejected.

Be it further resolved, That the Constitution, in article two, determines the qualifications of electors for Representatives, and that any order of the President or act of Congress changing such qualifications would be a usurpation and a nullity.

Be it further resolved, That whenever by pestilence, foreign invasion, or domestic conspiracy, the officers of a State required by its laws to conduct an election have been destroyed or carried off, the State does not thereby cease to exist, nor do its people forfeit their rights as citizens of the States or of the United States, but, from the very necessity of the case, and by virtue of the power impliedly reserved to the people, they may, in a practicable and reasonable manner, supply the deficiency, and hold an election, conducting it, however, as far as possible, in conformity with the existing laws and Constitution of the State; and the duty of Congress in passing upon such an election claimed to be held under such circumstances is limited to ascertaining whether it was a fair expression of a majority of the people, and in the mode of conducting it departed from the general laws of the State only so far as was necessary to supply the deficiency of officers required to conduct the election.

Be it further resolved, That the right of the claimants from Arkansas should be determined by the principles here enunciated; and if they shall satisfy the House that the Constitution and laws of the United States and of the State held peaceful sway over their respective districts, that in their elections they departed in nothing from the Constitution and existing laws of that State, save in supplying requisite officers, and that they received a vote of a majority in their respective districts, then they are entitled to seats, but not otherwise.

A motion to table the whole subject was lost—yeas 43, nays 63.

A motion to postpone until next session, was lost—yeas 50, nays 78.

June 29—The report was further debated, when, on motion of Mr. DAVIS, the whole subject was laid on the table—yeas 80, nays 47, as follows:

YEAS—Messrs. *William J. Allen*, Allison, *Ancona*, *Augustus C. Baldwin*, Beaman, Blair, *Bliss*, Blow, Boyd, *Brooks*, Broomall, *James S. Brown*, Cole, *Cox*, Henry Winter Davis, Thomas T. Davis, *Dawson*, Deming, *Denison*, Dixon, Driggs, *Eden*, *Edgerton*, *English*, *Finck*, *Griswold*, Hale, *Herrick*, Higby, *Holman*, Asahel W. Hubbard, John H. Hubbard, Hulburd, Jenckes, *William Johnson*, *Kalbfleisch*, Kelley, Francis W. Kellogg, *Kernan*, *Knapp*, *Law*, *Lazear*, Loan, Longyear, *McAllister*, *McDowell*, McIndoe, *McKinney*, Samuel F. Miller, Moorhead, *James R. Morris*, *Morrison*, Amos Myers, Leonard Myers, Norton, Charles O'Neill, Orth, *Pendleton*, Perham, *Perry*, *Radford*, *Samuel J. Randall*, *Robinson*, *Ross*, Schenck, Shannon, Sloan, Smith, Smithers, *William G. Steele*, Stevens, *Stiles*, *Strouse*, *Stuart*, Thayer, Webster, *Chilton A. White*, *Joseph W. White*, Williams, Windom—80.

NAYS—Messrs. Alley, Ames, Anderson, Ashley, *Baily*, John D. Baldwin, Blaine, Boutwell, William G. Brown, *Chanler*, Cobb, Dawes, Donnelly, Eckley, Eliot, Farnsworth, *Ganson*, Gooch, *Harding*, *Benjamin G. Harris*, *Charles M. Harris*, Hooper, *Hutchins*, Julian, Knox, Littlejohn, *Long*, *Mallory*, *Marcy*, McClurg, Morrill, *Odell*, *John O'Neill*, Pike, Pomeroy, John H. Rice, Edward H. Rollins, *James S. Rollins*, Scofield, Thomas, Upson, Van Valkenburgh, Ellihu B. Washburne, William B. Washburn, Whaley, *Winfield*—47.

FREE STATE GOVERNMENT IN ARKANSAS.

June 10—Mr. LANE of Kansas, introduced this joint resolution:

For the recognition of the free State government of the State of Arkansas.

Whereas the President of the United States, by proclamation of the 1st of January, A. D. 1863, did, among other things, proclaim and declare that the "people" of Arkansas "are this day in rebellion" against the United States; and whereas the loyal people of the State of Arkansas have, since that time, by a free and untrammelled vote, organized and have in operation a State government upon a free basis and republican in form; and whereas, pending the organization of said government, the President of the United States did, by proclamation of the 8th day of December, A. D. 1863, invite, among others, the people of Arkansas to organize a loyal State government upon a free basis; and whereas the President of the United States approved said organization in the State of Arkansas and officially recognized the same: Therefore,

Be it resolved, &c., That so much of the proclamation or proclamations of the President of the United States, and so much of all laws of Congress, as declares the people or State of Arkansas in rebellion, be, and is hereby, declared inoperative and void.

SEC. 2. That the present organized government in the State of Arkansas be, and it is hereby, recognized, upon the condition that slavery and involuntary servitude shall never exist in said State, except as a punishment for crime.

June 11—Mr. LANE of Kansas, offered this additional resolution:

SEC. 3. That this joint resolution shall be in force from and after the acceptance of its provisions by the people of the said State and proclamation of the same by the President of the United States.

He also offered this resolution, which was adopted:

That the President of the United States be requested to furnish to the Senate copies of all correspondence, orders, and documents on file in the Departments in relation to the organization by the loyal people of Arkansas of the free State government of that State.

June 13—The Senate considered the joint resolution; refused—yeas 5, (Messrs. Chandler, Howard, *Richardson*, Sumner, Wade,) nays 32, to lay the subject on the table, and then referred it to the Committee on the Judiciary, and with it the resolution of Mr. SUMNER, offered May 27, as follows:

That a State pretending to secede from the Union and battling against the national Government to maintain this pretension must be regarded as a rebel State, subject to military occupation, and without title to representation on this floor until it has been readmitted by a vote of both Houses of Congress; and the Senate will decline to entertain any application from any such rebel State until after such vote of both Houses of Congress.

ADMISSION OF SENATORS FROM ARKANSAS.

IN SENATE.

First Session, Thirty-Eighth Congress.

1864, June 27—Mr. TRUMBULL made this report:

The Committee on the Judiciary, to whom were referred the credentials of William M. Fishback and Elisha Baxter, claiming seats from the State of Arkansas, report:

That the credentials are presented in due form, purporting to be under the seal of the State of Arkansas, and to be signed by Isaac Murphy, Governor thereof; and if the right to seats were to be determined by an inspection of the credentials, Messrs. Fishback and Baxter would be entitled to be sworn as members of this body. It is, however, admitted by the persons claiming seats, and known to the country, that in the spring of 1861, the State of Arkansas, through its constituted authorities, undertook to secede from the Union, set up a government in hostility to the United States, and maintain the same by force of arms. Congress, in view of the condition of affairs in Arkansas and some other States similarly situated passed an act, July 13, 1861, authorizing the President, in case of an insurrection in any State against the laws of the United States, and when the insurgents claimed to act under authority of the State, and such claim was not repudiated, nor the insurrection suppressed by the persons exercising the functions of government in such State, to declare the inhabitants of such State or part thereof where such insurrection existed, to be in a state of insurrection against the United States; and that, thereupon, all commercial intercourse by and between the same and the citizens of the United States, except under license and upon certain conditions, should cease and be unlawful so long as such condition of hostility should continue.

In pursuance of this act, the President, August 16, 1861, issued his proclamation declaring the inhabitants of the State of Arkansas, except the inhabitants of such parts thereof as should maintain a loyal adhesion to the Union and the Constitution, or might be from time to time occupied and controlled by forces of the United States engaged in the dispersion of said insurgents, to be in a state of insurrection against the United States, and that all commercial intercourse between them and citizens of other States was and would be unlawful, except when carried on under special license, until such insurrection should cease. At the date of this proclamation no part of the State of Arkansas was occupied and controlled by the forces of the United States, nor did the inhabitants of any part of the State, at that time, publicly maintain a loyal adhesion to the Union and the Constitution. Hence, upon the issuing of said proclamation, a state of hostility or civil war existed between the inhabitants of the State of Arkansas and the United States, and there was not at that time any organized authority in Arkansas, loyal to the Constitution, competent to choose or appoint Senators of the United States. It is claimed, however, that since that period the State, or the greater portion of it, has been occupied and controlled by the forces of the United States, engaged in the dispersion of the insurgents, and that the inhabitants of said State, loyal to the Union and the Constitution, have reorganized their

State government, and have the right, through the Legislature they have instituted, to choose two Senators for said State.

The Constitution declares that "the Senate of the United States shall be composed of two Senators from each State, chosen by the Legislature thereof, for six years," and makes each House "the judge of the election, returns, and qualifications of its own members." In the investigation of the claimants' right to seats, the first question to be determined is, was the body by whom they were elected clothed with authority to elect Senators; in other words, was it, in a constitutional sense, "the Legislature of Arkansas?"

A question similar to this arose some years since between Robbins and Potter, each claiming to have been elected Senator by the Legislature of Rhode Island, though by different bodies. In that case the Senate was called upon to decide, and did decide, which of the two bodies, each claiming to be legitimate, was the Legislature contemplated by the Constitution. The Supreme Court of the United States, in the case of Luther *vs.* Borden, growing out of the political difficulties in Rhode Island in 1841 and 1842, held that "when the Senators and Representatives of a State are admitted into the councils of the Union, the authority of the government under which they are appointed, as well as its republican character, is recognized by the proper constitutional authority. And its decision is binding on every other department of the Government."

The claimants laid before the committee a statement of the circumstances attending the assembling of the body by which they were elected, in which, after detailing the condition of the State while under rebel control, and prior to September, 1863, they say: "Upon the advent of the Union army the rebels in the State, guerrillas and all, for the most part left with their armies, leaving about two-thirds of the State comparatively free from guerrilla depredation.

"The Union men came flocking from the mountains, where they had lain for two years, to the Federal standard, and nearly every man whom the medical examiners would receive joined the Federal army.

"Those who were rejected, (and their number was enormous, their constitutions having been broken by exposure and their hardships,) and those whom circumstances prevented from joining the army, found themselves, so far as law was concerned, in a state of chaos. Many of them, living remote from military posts, had not even the protection of military law.

"Immediately they began to agitate the question of a reorganization of their State government. They first moved in primary meetings, and on the 30th of October, 1863, they held a mass meeting in the city of Fort Smith, in which some twenty counties are said to have been represented, and at which they called upon all counties in the State to elect delegates (after having elected commissioners of election) to a State convention, to be held in the city of Little Rock on the 8th day of January, 1864, for the purpose of so amending the constitution as to abolish slavery. Simultaneously with this meeting, meetings were held in a number of other counties. In every single one (in ignorance of the action of others in many instances) they declared for a convention and the abolition of slavery.

"Commissioners of election were first elected, and they held the election for the delegates.

"All this was prior to the President's amnesty proclamation.

"When the convention met, forty-five delegates were present, representing about one-half of the State. (Several of the delegates failed to attend.) They repudiated the rebel debt, State and Confederate, abolished slavery, and submitted the constitution to the people for their ratification. They also provided for taking the vote for State and county officers, and members of the legislature at the same time with the vote for the ratification of the constitution.

"The result of those elections was 12,177 for the constitution and 226 against it, an election of State and county officers, an election of delegates to the lower house of Congress, and a representation in the State legislature from forty-six of the fifty-four counties of the State."

The number of persons in Arkansas who voted for President in 1860 was 54,053, less than one-fourth of whom as appears from the statement of the claimants, took part in the reorganization of the State government. This, however, would not be fatal to the reorganization, if all who were loyal to the Union had an opportunity to participate, and the State was free from military control. Such, however, is understood not to have been the case. The President had not then, nor has he up to this time, recalled his proclamation, which declared the inhabitants of Arkansas in a state of insurrection against the United States, nor was there any evidence before the committee that said insurrection had ceased or been suppressed. At the time when the body which chose the claimants was elected, when it assembled, and at this time, the State of Arkansas is occupied by hostile armies, which exercise supreme authority within the districts subject to their control. While a portion of Arkansas is at this very time, as the committee are informed, in the actual possession and subject to the control of the enemies of the United States, other parts of the State are only held in subordination to the laws of the Union by the strong arm of military power. While this state of things continues, and the right to exercise armed authority over a large part of the State is claimed and exerted by the military power, it cannot be said that a civil government, set up and continued only by the sufferance of the military, is that republican form of government which the Constitution requires the United States to guarantee to every State in the Union.

When the rebellion in Arkansas shall have been so far suppressed that the loyal inhabitants thereof shall be free to re-establish their State government upon a republican foundation, or to recognize the one already set up, and by the aid and not in subordination to the military to maintain the same, they will then, and not before, in the opinion of your committee, be entitled to a representation in Congress, and to participate in the administration of the Federal Government. Believing that such a state of things did not at the time the claimants were elected, and does not now, exist in the State of Arkansas, the committee recommend for adoption the following resolution:

Resolved, That William M. Fishback and Elisha Baxter are not entitled to seats as Senators from the State of Arkansas.

1864, June 29—The resolution of the Committee on the Judiciary was adopted—yeas 27, nays 6, as follows:

YEAS—Messrs. Anthony, Brown, *Buckalew*, *Carlile*, Chandler, Clark, Cowan, *Davis*, Fessenden, Foot, Foster, Hale, Harlan, Harris, *McDougall*, Morgan, Morrill, *Powell*, Ramsey, *Riddle*, *Saulsbury*, Sherman, Sumner, Ten Eyck, Trumbull, Wade, Wilkinson—27.

NAYS—Messrs. Doolittle, Hicks, Howe, Lane of Kansas, *Nesmith*, Pomeroy—6.

Process of Reconstruction.

In ARKANSAS, a new State government is organized with Isaac Murphy, Governor, who was reported to have received nearly 16,000 votes at a called election. The other State officers are.

Lieutenant Governor, C. C. Bliss; Secretary of State, R. J. T. White; Auditor, J. B. Berry; Treasurer, E. D. Ayers; Attorney General, C. T. Jordan; Judges of the Supreme Court, T. D. W. Yowley, C. A. Harper, E. Baker.

The legislature also elected Senators, but neither Senators nor Representatives obtained their seats.

In LOUISIANA, a free State government has also been organized—Michael Hahn, Governor. The clause in the constitution abolishing slavery was adopted in convention—yeas 72, nays 13. The legislature is prohibited from passing any law recognizing the right of property in slaves. At the election for Governor, 10,725 votes were polled; one parish, (Terrebonne,) 630 votes, not in the official count. J. Madison Wells is Lieutenant Governor; Stanislaus Wrotnowski, Secretary of Sate; J. G. Belden, Treasurer; B. L. Lynch, Attorney General; A. P. Dostie, Auditor; John McNair, School Superintendent.

In VIRGINIA, the constitutional convention, recently in session in Alexandria, abolished slavery—yeas 13, nays 1, as follows:

YEAS—Messrs. Beach, Boush, Downey, Dix, Edwards, Gover, Henshaw, Hawxhurst, Penn, Thomas, Tennis, Wood, Watkins 13.

NAYS—Mr. Moore.

IN LOUISIANA.

1863, June 19—The President wrote this letter:

EXECUTIVE MANSION,
WASHINGTON, *June* 19, 1863.

GENTLEMEN: Since receiving your letter, reliable information has reached me that a respectable portion of the Louisiana people desire to amend their State constitution, and contemplate holding a convention for that object. This fact alone, it seems to me, is a sufficient reason why the General Government should not give the committee the authority you seek, to act under the existing State constitution. I may add, that while I do not perceive how such a committee could facilitate our military operations in Louisiana, I really apprehend it might be so used as to embarrass them.

As to an election to be held in November, there is abundant time without any order or proclamation from me just now. The people of Louisiana shall not lack an opportunity for a fair election for both Federal and State officers by want of anything within my power to give them.

Your obedient servant, A. LINCOLN.

IN ARKANSAS.

EXECUTIVE MANSION,
WASHINGTON, *January* 20, 1864.

Major General STEELE: Sundry citizens of the State of Arkansas petition me that an election may be held in that State, at which to elect a Governor; that it be assumed at that election, and thenceforward, that the constitution and laws of the State, as before the rebellion, are in full force, except that the constitution is so modified as to declare that there shall be neither slavery nor involuntary servitude, except in the punishment of crimes, whereof the party shall have been duly convicted; that the General Assembly may make such provisions for the freed people as shall recognize and declare their permanent freedom, and provide for their education, and which may yet be construed as a temporary arrangement, suitable to their present condition as a laboring, landless, and homeless class; that said election shall be held on the 28th March, 1864, at all the usual places of the State, for all such voters as may attend for that purpose; that the voters attending at each place at eight o'clock in the morning of said day may choose judges and clerks of election for that purpose; that all persons qualified by said constitution and laws, and taking the oath presented in the President's proclamation of December 8, 1863, either before or at the election, and none others, may be voters; that each set of judges and clerks may make returns directly to you on or before the ——— day of ——— next; that in all other respects said election may be conducted according to said modified constitution and laws; that, on receipt of said returns, when 5,406 votes shall have been cast, you can receive said votes and ascertain all who shall thereby appear to have been elected; that, on the ——— day of ——— next, all persons so appearing to have been elected, who shall appear before you at Little Rock and take the oath, to be by you severally administered, to support the Constitution of the United States and the modified constitution of the State of Arkansas, shall be declared by you qualified and empowered to immediately enter upon the duties of the offices to which they shall have been respectively elected.

You will please order an election to take place on the 28th of March, 1864, and returns to be made in fifteen days thereafter.

A. LINCOLN.

—

WASHINGTON, *February* 18, 1864.

TO WILLIAM M. FISHBACK:

When I formed a plan for an election in Arkansas, I did it in ignorance that your convention was at the same work. Since I learned the latter fact, I have been constantly trying to yield my plan to them. I have sent two letters to General Steele, and three or four dispatches to you and others, saying that he (General Steele) must be master, but that it will probably be best for him to keep the convention on its own plan. Some single mind must be master, else there will be no agreement on anything, and General Steele, commanding the military and being on the ground, is the best man to be that master. Even now citizens are telegraphing me to postpone the election to a later day than either affixed by the convention or me. This discord must be silenced.

A. LINCOLN.

RELATIONS OF THE REBELLIOUS STATES TO THE GOVERNMENT.

IN SENATE.

Second Session, Thirty-Seventh Congress.

1862, Feb. 11—Mr. SUMNER offered the following resolutions:

Resolutions declaratory of the relations between the United States and the territory once occupied by certain States, and now usurped by pretended governments, without constitutional or legal right.

Whereas certain States, rightfully belonging to the Union of the United States, have through their respective governments wickedly undertaken to abjure all those duties by which their connection with the Union was maintained; to renounce all allegiance to the Constitution; to levy war upon the national Government; and, for the consummation of this treason, have unconstitutionally and unlawfully confederated together, with the declared purpose of putting an end by force to the supremacy of the Constitution within their respective limits; and whereas this condition of insurrection, organized by pretended governments, openly exists in South Carolina, Georgia, Florida, Alabama, Mississippi, Louisiana, Texas, Arkansas, Tennessee, and Virginia, except in Eastern Tennessee and Western Virginia, and has been declared by the President of the United States, in a proclamation duly made in conformity with an act of Congress, to exist throughout this territory, with the exceptions already named; and whereas the extensive territory thus usurped by these pretended governments and organized into a hostile confederation, belongs to the United States, as an inseparable part thereof, under the sanctions of the Constitution, to be held in trust for the inhabitants in the present and future generations, and is so completely interlinked with the Union that it is forever dependent thereupon; and whereas the Constitution, which is the supreme law of the land, cannot be displaced in its rightful operation within this territory, but must ever continue the supreme law thereof, notwithstanding the doings of any pretended governments acting singly or in confederation, in order to put an end to its supremacy: Therefore—

1. *Resolved*, That any vote of secession or other act by which any State may undertake to put an end to the supremacy of the Constitution within its territory is inoperative and void against the Constitution, and when sustained by force it becomes a practical *abdication* by the State of all rights under the Constitution, while the treason which it involves still further works an instant *forfeiture* of all those functions and powers essential to the continued existence of the State as a body politic, so that from that time forward the territory falls under the exclusive jurisdiction of Congress as other territory, and the State being, according to the language of the law, *felo-de-se*, ceases to exist.

2. That any combination of men assuming to act in the place of such State, attempting to insnare or coerce the in-

habitants thereof into a confederation hostile to the Union is rebellious, treasonable, and destitute of all moral authority; and that such combination is a usurpation incapable of any constitutional existence and utterly lawless, so that everything dependent upon it is without constitutional or legal support.

3. That the termination of a State under the Constitution necessarily causes the termination of those peculiar local institutions which, having no origin in the Constitution or in those natural rights which exist independent of the Constitution, are upheld by the sole and exclusive authority of the State.

4. That slavery, being a peculiar local institution, derived from local laws, without any origin in the Constitution or in natural rights, is upheld by the sole and exclusive authority of the State, and must therefore cease to exist legally or constitutionally when the State on which it depends no longer exists; for the incident cannot survive the principal.

5. That in the exercise of its exclusive jurisdiction over the territory once occupied by the States, it is the duty of Congress to see that the supremacy of the Constitution is maintained in its essential principles, so that everywhere in this extensive territory slavery shall cease to exist practically, as it has already ceased to exist constitutionally or legally.

6. That any recognition of slavery in such territory, or any surrender of slaves under the pretended laws of the extinct States by any officer of the United States, civil or military, is a recognition of the pretended governments, to the exclusion of the jurisdiction of Congress under the Constitution, and is in the nature of aid and comfort to the rebellion that has been organized.

7. That any such recognition of slavery or surrender of pretended slaves, besides being a recognition of the pretended governments, giving them aid and comfort, is a denial of the rights of persons who, by the extinction of the States have become free, so that under the Constitution, they cannot again be enslaved.

8. That allegiance from the inhabitant and protection from the Government are corresponding obligations, dependent upon each other, so that while the allegiance of every inhabitant of this territory, without distinction of color or class, is due to the United States, and cannot in any way be defeated by the action of any pretended Government, or by any pretence of property or claim to service, the corresponding obligation of protection is at the same time due by the United States to every such inhabitant, without distinction of color or class; and it follows that inhabitants held as slaves, whose paramount allegiance is due to the United States, may justly look to the national Government for protection.

9. That the duty directly cast upon Congress by the extinction of the States is reinforced by the positive prohibition of the Constitution that "no State shall enter into any confederation," or "without the consent of Congress keep troops or ships-of-war in time of peace, or enter into any agreement or compact with another State," or "grant letters of marque and reprisal," or "coin money," or "emit bills of credit," or "without the consent of Congress lay any duties on imports or exports," all of which have been done by these pretended governments, and also by the positive injunction of the Constitution, addressed to the nation, that "the United States shall guaranty to every State in this Union a republican form of government;" and that in pursuance of this duty cast upon Congress, and further enjoined by the Constitution, Congress will assume complete jurisdiction of such vacated territory where such unconstitutional and illegal things have been attempted, and will proceed to establish therein republican forms of government under the Constitution; and in the execution of this trust will provide carefully for the protection of all the inhabitants thereof, for the security of families, the organization of labor, the encouragement of industry, and the welfare of society, and will in every way discharge the duties of a just, merciful, and paternal Government.

Feb. 13—Mr. Garrett Davis offered these resolutions:

1. *Resolved*, That the Constitution of the United States is the fundamental law of the Government, and the powers established and granted, and as parted out and vested by it, the limitations and restrictions which it imposes upon the legislative, executive, and judicial departments, and the States, and the rights, privileges, and liberties which it assures to the people of the United States, and the States respectively, are fixed, permanent, and immutable through all the phases of peace and war, until changed by the power and in the mode prescribed by the Constitution itself; and they cannot be abrogated, restricted, enlarged, or differently apportioned, or vested, by any other power, or in any other mode.

2. That between the Government and the citizen the obligation of protection and obedience form mutual rights and obligations; and to enable every citizen to perform his obligations of obedience and loyalty to the Government it should give him reasonable protection and security in such performance; and when the Government fails in that respect, for it to hold the citizen to be criminal in not performing his duties of loyalty and obedience would be unjust, inhuman, and an outrage upon this age of Christian civilization.

3. That if any powers of the Constitution or Government of the United States, or of the States, or any rights, privileges, immunities, and liberties of the people of the United States, or the States, are, or may hereafter be, suspended by the existence of this war, or by any promulgation of martial law, or by the suspension of the writ of *habeas corpus*, immediately upon the termination of the war such powers, rights, privileges, immunities, and liberties would be resumed, and would have force and effect as though they had not been suspended.

4. That the duty of Congress to guarantee to every State a republican form of government, to protect each of them against invasion, and, on the application of the legislature or executive thereof, against domestic violence, and to enforce the authority, Constitution, and laws of the United States in all the States, are constitutional obligations which abide all times and circumstances.

5. That no State can, by any vote of secession, or by rebellion against the authority, Constitution, and laws of the United States, or by any other act, abdicate her rights or obligations under that Constitution or those laws, or absolve her people from their obedience to them, or the United States from their obligation to guarantee to such State a republican form of government, and to protect her people by causing the due enforcement within her territories of the authority, Constitution, and laws of the United States.

6. That there cannot be any forfeiture or confiscation of the rights of person or property of any citizen of the United States who is loyal and obedient to the authority, Constitution and the laws thereof, or of any person whatsoever, unless for acts which the law has previously declared to be criminal, and for the punishment of which it has provided such forfeiture or confiscation.

7. That it is the duty of the United States to subdue and punish the existing rebellion by force of arms and civil trials in the shortest practicable time, and with the least cost to the people, but so decisively and thoroughly as to impress upon the present and future generations as a great truth that rebellion, except for grievous oppression of government, will bring upon the rebels incomparably more of evil than obedience to the Constitution and the laws.

8. That the United States Government should march their armies into all the insurgent States, and promptly put down the military power which they have arrayed against it, and give protection and security to the loyal men thereof, to enable them to reconstruct their legitimate State governments, and bring them and the people back to the Union and to obedience and duty under the Constitution and the laws of the United States, bearing the sword in one hand and the olive branch in the other, and whilst inflicting on the guilty leaders condign and exemplary punishment, granting amnesty and oblivion to the comparatively innocent masses; and if the people of any State cannot, or will not, reconstruct their State government and return to loyalty and duty, Congress should provide a government for such State as a territory of the United States, securing to the people thereof their appropriate constitutional rights.

1862, June 11—Mr. Dixon offered this resolution:

Resolved, That all acts or ordinances of secession, alleged to have been adopted by any legislature or convention of the people of any State, are, as to the Federal Union, absolutely null and void; and that while such acts may and do subject the individual actors therein to forfeitures and penalties, they do not, in any degree, affect the relations of the State wherein they purport to have been adopted to the Government of the United States, but are as to such Government acts of rebellion, insurrection, and hostility, on the part of the individuals engaged therein, or giving assent thereto; and that such States are, notwithstanding such acts or ordinances, members of the Federal Union, and as such are subject to all the obligations and duties imposed upon them by the Constitution of the United States; and the loyal citizens of such States are entitled to all the rights and privileges thereby guarantied or conferred.

IN HOUSE.

1862, May 26—Mr. Wickliffe presented these resolutions:

Resolved, That the Constitution, and the laws of the United States made in pursuance thereof, and all treaties made under the authority of the United States, are the supreme law of the land in time of war or rebellion, as well as intime of peace, anything in the constitution or laws of any State to the contrary notwithstanding.

2. The right to disregard and violate the Constitution, or any part thereof, by either of the departments of the Government, does not exist any more in time of war or rebellion than in time of peace.

3. That the powers vested in Congress by the Constitution of the United States are not enlarged by a state of war, but are ample and full to enable the Government to suppress a rebellion, or to prosecute a war, without the exercise of powers not granted therein.

4. A disregard of the provisions of the Constitution, under the plea of *necessity*, by Congress, is dangerous to free government, and ultimately will make it a despotism if controlled by an unprincipled majority, dangerous to private rights and destructive of public liberty.

5. That no State has the right, by any act, ordinance, or law, to absolve itself or any citizens from their obligations and duties imposed by the Constitution of the United States.

6. A rebellion and open resistance to the Constitution and the laws of the United States made in pursuance thereof, cannot abrogate the same; but during such rebellion and resistance the rights and powers of the Constitution do extend to the citizen in every portion of the United States, and the right and power of the Government, though obstructed, are not destroyed. And when that obstruction shall be overcome, the State governments and the citizens thereof are restored to all the rights and privileges secured by the Constitution.

7. That open and forcible resistance, by arms, by the citizens of any portion of the United States is treason, to be punished as such by the power of the Government under the provisions and limitations of the Constitution.

8. That a citizen not engaged in actual war, but who resides within the territory of a *de facto* Government, which is in rebellion and at war with the United States, is not guilty of treason by obeying the orders of such *de facto* Government, or by contributing to its support.

9. That neither the Executive nor military has the right to seize the property of a non-combatant in any of the seceded States, and confiscate the same, even under the authority of an act of Congress. "No person shall be deprived of life, liberty, or property, without due process of law," is the language of the Constitution. Therefore, all wholesale bills confiscating estates, or property of any kind, whether lands, slaves, or chattels, are in violation of the laws of Christian warfare, and forbidden by the Constitution of the United States.

Third Session, Thirty-Seventh Congress.

1863, January 8—Mr. Clements offered this resolution, which went over:

Resolved, That the acts of secession claiming to have been passed by a part of the people of a part of the States of this Government were null and void, and of no effect; and that the State Constitutions and laws of the States so claiming to have seceded are the same as they were previous to said acts; they have not committed State suicide, for their Constitutions and laws still exist in the loyal people.

IN SENATE.

First Session, Thirty-Eighth Congress.

1864, Jan. 5—Mr. Garrett Davis offered these resolutions:

1. *Resolved*, That the Government of the United States was established by the people of States which before had been separate, sovereign, and independent; and they formed their common national Government by a written Constitution, and delegated to it so much of their sovereign political power as they adjudged to be necessary and proper to enable it to manage all their affairs with foreign nations and among the several States; and, both by its leading principle and express provision, they reserved "to the States, respectively, or to the people," "all powers not delegated to the United States, nor prohibited by it to the States."

2. That our system consists of a limited national Government for the whole United States, of supreme authority as to all the powers with which the Constitution has invested it, and State governments for each State, formed by the people thereof, and holding the entire residuum of political sovereignty within their respective States—each government, within its sphere, being alike supreme; and as the governors, and all other civil and military officers of the States, as other individuals, may commit treason against the United States, "by levying war against them, or in adhering to their enemies, giving them aid and comfort," so the President of the United States, and the civil and military officers thereof, may commit treason against any State whose government is in the performance of its duties under the Federal Constitution, by levying war against it, or in adhering to its enemies, giving them aid and comfort, as resisting with an armed force the execution of its laws, or adhering to such armed force, giving it aid and comfort.

3. That in all the States, and parts of States, where the laws of the United States and the States can be executed, the military authorities should not be brought into conflict with the civil power, but should be strictly held to be, as they rightfully are, in subordination to it.

4. That all elections to civil offices, Federal or State, should be in strict accordance with the Constitution and laws of the United States and of the States, respectively, and be understood by officers appointed by the proper authorities for that purpose; and where from the presence or apprehension of force, violence, or other cause, any election cannot be so conducted, it ought not to be held at all; and every election at which any military force may interfere by imposing additional oaths or qualifications for the electors, or regulations for conducting the said election, or by changing or modifying the oaths and qualifications of the electors, or regulations to govern it, provided as by law, or to constrain, control, or direct the officers of such election in conducting it, should be held to be void and of no effect.

5. That the experience of the world proves that there can be neither security nor liberty in any country without wise and just laws, firmly sustained and uniformly executed; that this is the life, the spirit, the soul of the nation; and all neglect and departures from law, and particularly from constitutional law, by agents appointed to administer it, although sometimes attended with seeming advantage, are sure to produce always, sooner or later, much greater and more enduring mischief: wherefore, disregard of law by such agents is never tolerated by a wise and free people.

6. That the powers of the Government of the United States are derived wholly from, and limited by the Constitution, and by it are divided into legislative, executive, and judicial; and each class of those powers is vested in a separate department; that the President is the chief of the executive department, and has no legislative or judicial power whatever, and only such executive powers as are enumerated in the second and third sections of the second article of the Constitution, and such other powers as may be, from time to time, conferred upon him by Congress in virtue of this provision: "Congress shall have power to make *all laws* which shall be necessary and proper for carrying into execution the foregoing powers, and *all other powers* vested by this Constitution in the *Government* of the United States, or any *department* or officer thereof."

7. That the President cannot be divested of any powers with which he is directly invested by the Constitution, nor controlled or interfered with in their execution, but all powers conferred on him by law of Congress he holds in subordination to that department, which may supervise, modify, and correct his execution of them, or resume them, by repealing the laws intrusting their execution to him.

8. That the power of the President to recognize the existence of a state of case amounting to "an invasion, or imminent danger of an invasion, of the United States," or "insurrection in any State against the government thereof," or "obstruction to the execution of the laws of the United States by combinations too powerful to be suppressed by the ordinary course of judicial proceedings," and to call forth the military power to meet such conditions, is conferred on him by the laws of Congress; and the repeal of those laws would withdraw from the President all that power.

9. That Congress is invested with the power "to lay and collect taxes, duties, imposts, and excises, to pay the debts and provide for the common defence and general welfare of the United States," "to declare war, grant letters of marque and reprisal, and make rules concerning captures on land and water," "to raise and support armies," "to provide and maintain a navy," "to provide for calling forth the militia to execute the laws of the Union, suppress insurrections, and repel invasions," "to provide for arming, organizing, and disciplining the militia, and governing such part of them as may be employed in the service of the United States," "to guarantee to every State in the Union a republican form of government, and to protect each of them against invasion;" and thus the entire *war* power and *quasi war power, external and internal*, of the Government, is vested by the Constitution in Congress, and no part of it whatever in the President.

10. That whenever there is an insurrection in the United States, Congress is vested with the power to *suppress* it, and with no other power whatever over the insurrection; and when it is suppressed, either by the arms of the United States or by the submission of the insurgents to the Constitution, laws, and authorities thereof, thereupon the power of Congress over the whole subject is exhausted, and the insurgents are immediately remitted to all the rights, privileges, liberties, and duties of citizens, subject to such forfeiture thereof as may have been declared by law, after it shall have been adjudged by the civil courts in the mode

prescribed by the Constitution; and Congress, much less the President, has no power to impose upon them any other terms or conditions.

11. That the whole power and duty of the President, in the existing insurrection, is to grant pardons to those engaged in it, and, as Commander-in-Chief of the Army and Navy, to direct their operations for its suppression; and as such, his powers are strictly military, and are not different or greater than would be those of the senior general in the service, if the Constitution had designated *him* to be the *Commander-in-Chief:* the power to devise a policy or measures for its suppression is legislative, to which the President is incompetent, whether as the first executive officer of the Government, or Commander-in-Chief of the Army and Navy.

12. That the *law of military necessity* is not established, but only tolerated, in the United States. It does not, nor cannot, in peace or war abrogate or suspend the Constitution in whole or in part. It cannot authorize arbitrary arrests and imprisonment, or in any way interfere with the person of the citizen, but only with his property. It does not appertain to the *President*, or to the *Commander-in-Chief*, unless he be in the actual command of a military force, and then only under particular circumstances. It results from a present and urgent need of an army or military corps, which is so pressing that it cannot await other modes, but must be supplied anywhere within its reach by its own power and action. It is not an *expediency*, but a *necessity* of a military body, and creates a law and confers a power, for the *occasion only*, on its commander, of whatever grade he may be, to supply that necessity by taking property with summary military force, without depriving the owner of his right to be compensated for it by the United States. Each case of military necessity makes its own law, adapted to its own peculiar circumstances, and expiring with that particular necessity. There is not, and cannot be, any uniform, permanent, or even continuing law of military necessity. The idea that a law always accidental, evanescent, and, in truth, so inconsiderable, should have the magic force to enable Abraham Lincoln to bound over the Constitution and all its limitations and restrictions, and clutch the vast powers which he claims under it, is a *gigantic* absurdity.

13. That at the beginning of the war, under the panic of the defeat of Bull Run, the party in power professed to carry it on for the Constitution, and to put down the rebellion, and vindicate the laws and authority of the United States in the insurgent States, and when that was effected it was to cease. But more than a year ago another, and a paramount and unconstitutional one, the total subversion of slavery was inaugurated by them; and at length, to carry on the war in this augmented and perverted form, the annual expenditure, on the part of the United States, has swollen to one hundred thousand lives, a much larger amount of personal disability, and a thousand millions of money, and yet the wisest cannot see the end of the war; verily, the people north, and people south, ought to revolt against their war-leaders, and take this great matter into their own hands; and elect members to a national convention of all the States, to terminate a war that is enriching hundreds of thousands of officers, plunderers, and spoilsmen in the loyal States, and threatens the masses of both sections with irretrievable bankruptcy and indefinite slaughter; and to restore their Union and common government upon the great principles of liberty and compromise, devised by Washington and his associates.

14. That the present Executive Government of the United States has subverted, for the time, in large portions of the loyal States, the freedom of speech, the freedom of the press, and free suffrage, the Constitutions and laws of the United States, the civil courts and trial by jury; it has ordered, *ad libitum*, arbitrary arrests by military officers, not only without warrant, but without any charge or imputation of crime or offence; and has hurried the persons so arrested from home and vicinage to distant prisons, and kept them incarcerated there for an indefinite time; some of whom it discharged without trial, and in utter ignorance of the cause of their arrest and imprisonment; and others it caused to be brought before courts, created by itself, and to be tried and punished without law, in violation of the constitutional guarantee to the citizen of his right to keep and bear arms, and of his rights of property; it has forcibly deprived as well the loyal as the disloyal of both; it has usurped the power to suspend the writ of *habeas corpus*, and to proclaim martial law, and establish military tribunals in States and parts of States where there was no obstruction to the due administration of the laws of the United States and the States by the civil courts and authorities; and ordered many citizens, who were not connected with the army or navy, to be dragged before its drum-head courts, and to be tried by them for new and strange offences, declared by itself, and by undefined and indefinable law, being but the arbitrary will of the court; it has ordained at pleasure a military despotism in the loyal States, by means of courts-martial, provost marshals, and military forces, governed neither by law, principles, nor rules, from whose tyranny and oppressions no man can claim immunity; all of which must be repudiated and swept away by the sovereign people.

15. That a free press, free speech, and free elections are the great and peaceful forces by which the mal-administration of our Government, whether in the legislative or executive departments, is prevented, reformed, and reversed, and its authors brought to public condemnation and punishment; and these bulwarks of constitutional Government and popular liberty are formidable to malversators, usurpers, and tyrants only, and they must be held by the people at all hazards.

16. That as the Constitution and laws afford no means to exclude from the office of President a man appointed to it by military power, or who is declared to be chosen to it by reason of the suppression of the freedom of election, or by the exclusion of legal voters from the polls, or by any other means, the people of the United States would be incompetent to defend, and unworthy to have received the rich heritage of freedom bequeathed to them by their fathers, if they permit that great office so to be filled, or in any other mode than by their own free suffrages.

17. That the scheme of the President to bring back the insurgent States is open to many and insuperable objections. The pardon and amnesty offered by him is upon the condition that those who accept it shall renounce their right to their slave property, and swear to support his unconstitutional proclamation, and unconstitutional acts of Congress, which attempted to take it from them. He must have intended to put this condition in a form so obnoxious as to secure its rejection by most of those to whom it was offered. He affects the position that ten of the insurgent States have forfeited or dissolved their State governments, and requires that they be reconstructed on a condition prescribed by himself, and this against the true principle which he and the legislative department of the Government had previously recognized: that all the acts of the insurgent States and people, tending to their secession, separation, and independence, were void, and when the inundation with which their insurrection covered over the authority of the Constitution and laws of the United States in them passed away, it would leave the constitutions, laws, property, and institutions of those States in every respect the same that they were previously, excepting only the changes that were produced by the mere shock of arms, the principle *status ante bellum* being applicable. He ignores the constitutions of Tennessee and Arkansas, and others that have not been altered in any particular, but are the same that they were before their revolt; and he requires those States to repudiate their constitutions that governed them many years peacefully in the Union, and to form new ones. He has no right to take cognizance, in any way, of the governments and constitutions of those States or of any other States; to the extent that such a power is vested in the Government of the United States, it is congressional, not presidential. He has no authority whatever to impose any conditions on the insurgents, and they are subject to none but what are prescribed by the Constitution and laws of the United States, to be determined by their courts. What right has the President to proclaim that one-tenth of as many of the voters of those States as voted at the last presidential election may pull down and revolutionize their State governments, and erect new ones for the other nine-tenths, which he will recognize and uphold with the armies and navies of the United States? His project is to continue the war upon slavery by his further usurpations of power, and to get together and buy up a desperate faction of mendicants and adventurers in the rebel States, give them possession of the polls by interposing the bayonet, as in Maryland, Delaware, and portions of Missouri, and Kentucky, and to keep off loyal pro-slavery voters, and thus to form bastard constitutions to abolitionize those States.

18. That the impending destiny of our country can no longer be blinked. The people of the loyal States are resolved into two great parties, *the destructives* and *the conservatives*. The first consists of Abraham Lincoln, his office-holders, contractors, and other followers; the second of all men who are for ejecting Lincoln and his party from office and power. The *professed objects* of the first are, to *preserve the Union* and to *abolish slavery* in all the States; they have about ceased to make a *pretence* of supporting the Constitution and the laws. Their real objects are to perpetuate their party power, and to hold possession of the Government to continue the aggrandizement of their leaders, great and small, by almost countless offices and employments, by myriads of plundering contracts, and by putting up to sale the largest amount of spoils that were ever offered to market by any Government on earth. Their object is not to eradicate slavery, but only to abolish its form and the mastery; to subjugate wholly the rebel States, and utterly to revolutionize their political and social organization; to destroy or banish, and strip of their property, all the pro-slavery

people, secessionists and anti-secessionists, loyal and disloyal, combatants and non-combatants, old men, women, and children, the decrepit, and the *non compos mentis*, all whom they cannot abolitionize, and to distribute the lands of the subjugated people among their followers, as was done by the Roman conquerors of their own countrymen; to proclaim a mock freedom to the slaves, but by military power to take possession of the freedmen, and work them for their own profit; to do all this, and also to enslave the white man, by trampling under foot the Constitution and laws of the United States and the States, by the power of a subsidized army, and, lest it should falter, by hundreds of thousands of negro janizaries, organized for that purpose by the Secretary of War and the Adjutant General. The first and paramount object of the conservatives is to preserve their own liberties by saving the Union, the Constitution, and the laws from utter and final overthrow by the destructives, not themselves to be enslaved under the pretext of giving a fictitious freedom to the negro, and to restore and perpetuate the Union, and to bring back the people in revolt by renewed and sufficient guarantees of all their constitutional rights. There is no choice left to any man but to be a destructive or a conservative.

January 7—Mr. Carlile offered these resolutions:

Resolved, That the Government of the United States, in the language of Mr. Webster, is "the result of compact between the States," each State for itself adopting for its government the Constitution of the United States.

2. That the people of each State adopted for their government the Constitution of the United States, in the same way as they adopted their State constitution.

3. That the Constitution of the United States was not binding, nor had it force or effect in any State until it was ratified and adopted by the people thereof, as is evidenced by the fact that the people of North Carolina were not bound by it, nor was North Carolina a member of the Union created by it, for some time after the Government had been organized under it, and after it had been ratified by eleven other States.

4. That the Government created by the Constitution of the United States is "neither wholly *national* nor wholly *federal*. Were it wholly national, the supreme and ultimate authority would reside in the *majority* of the people of the Union, and this authority would be competent at all times, like that of a majority of every national society, to alter or abolish its established government. Were it wholly federal, on the other hand, the concurrence of each State in the Union would be essential to every alteration that would be binding on all." The mode provided by the Constitution for its amendment "is not founded on either of these principles" "In requiring more than a majority, and particularly in computing the proportion by *States*, not by *citizens*, it departs from the *national* and advances towards the *federal* character. In rendering the concurrence of less than the whole number of States sufficient, it loses again the *federal* and partakes of the *national* character." The Government created by the Constitution of the United States, therefore, is neither a national nor a federal government, "but a composition of both." "In its foundation it is federal, not national; in the sources from which the ordinary powers of the Government are drawn, it is partly federal and partly national; in the operation of these powers it is national, not federal; in the extent of them it is federal, not national."

5. That it is essential to the preservation of the Government created by the Constitution that the military should be subordinate to the civil power, and that such was the intention of the founders of the Government is evidenced by the fact that the President was made Commander-in-Chief of the Army and Navy.

6. That Congress alone can declare what are crimes against the United States, and can alone legislate for the punishment thereof. That it is not competent for the President, in any character, or for any military commander, to restrict the right of suffrage in any State, or to impose conditions precedent to the exercise thereof; nor can the will or judgment of the President enlarge his powers beyond what are conferred by the Constitution.

7. That all the powers of the General Government are derived from the Constitution; that the Constitution of the United States confers power, and the Constitutions of the several States limit power; that the General Government can only exercise such powers as are conferred by the Constitution of the United States; that but for the State Constitutions each State, within its own jurisdiction, could exercise all governmental power.

8. That Governments are instituted for the protection of minorities, the chief objects being to secure to the citizen his right to personal liberty, and to protect him in the possession and enjoyment of his private property.

9. That there is no such power as "the war power" known to the Government of the United States, outside of the powers conferred by and enumerated in the Constitution of the United States.

10. That the Government of the United States enforces obedience to the Constitution and laws, as do the State Governments, by acting directly upon the citizens; that it cannot create a State Government or a State Constitution, or alter one; that it has no right to interfere, directly or indirectly, to alter, abolish, or procure a change in the Constitution of any State, but is bound to protect existing Constitutions in each and every State from any attempt to substitute for them a Government not republican in form, and cannot act against States or political communities as such, but is confined in its action to the punishment of persons, there being no right of eminent domain in the Government of the United States, the soil of each State belonging to it and the people thereof.

11. That any attempt on the part of the Government of the United States, or any department thereof, to destroy the State Governments, and substitute for them Territorial or any other form of Government, would be an exercise of arbitrary and usurped power, destructive to the liberties of the people, violative of the Constitution, and an overthrow of the Government created by it.

12. That it is the duty of the servants of the people to whom the administration of the Government is intrusted, and to whom its powers have been confided, to put down rebellion against its authority whenever organized, to the end that the law-abiding citizen may be protected in the enjoyment of the blessings the Government was designed to confer; that, if necessary to this end, the whole military and naval power of the Government can and should be used, not against the States as such, nor in a war against populations and homes, but against the citizens and persons so resisting the authority of the Government and defying its power.

13. That the whole millitary power of the Government should be directed against the armies of the Confederates, and that, until they are broken and dispersed, there can be no peace upon the basis of a re-union of the States.

Feb. 8—Mr. Sumner offered these resolutions:

Resolved, That, in order to determine the duties of the national Government at the present moment, it is of the first importance that we should see and understand the real character of the contest which has been forced upon the United States, for a failure truly to appreciate this contest must end disastrously in a failure of those proper efforts which are essential to the re-establishment of unity and concord; that, recognizing the contest in its real character, as it must be recorded by history, it will be apparent beyond controversy, that this is not an ordinary rebellion, or an ordinary war, but, that it is absolutely without precedent, differing clearly from every other rebellion and every other war, inasmuch as it is an audacious attempt, for the first time in history, to found a wicked power on the corner-stone of slavery; and that such an attempt having this single object—whether regarded as rebellion or as war—is so completely penetrated and absorbed, so entirely filled and possessed by slavery, that it can be justly regarded as nothing else than the huge impersonation of this crime, at once rebel and belligerent, or in other words, as slavery in arms.

2. That, recognizing the unquestionable identity of the rebellion and of slavery, so that each is to the other as another self, it becomes plain that the rebellion cannot be crushed without crushing slavery, as slavery cannot be crushed without crushing the rebellion; that every forbearance to the one is a forbearance to the other, and every blow at the one is a blow at the other; that all who tolerate slavery tolerate the rebellion, and all who strike at slavery strike at the rebellion; and that, therefore, it is our supremest duty, in which all other present duties are contained, to take care that the barbarism of slavery, in which alone the rebellion has its origin and life, is so utterly trampled out that it can never spring up again anywhere in the rebel and belligerent region; for leaving this duty undone nothing is done, and all our blood and treasure have been lavished in vain.

3. That in dealing with the rebel war the National Government is invested with two classes of rights—one the *rights of sovereignty*, inherent and indefeasible everywhere within the limits of the United States, and the other the *rights of war*, or belligerent rights, which have been superinduced by the nature and extent of the contest; that, by virtue of the rights of sovereignty, the rebel and belligerent region is now subject to the National Government as its only rightful Government, bound under the Constitution to all the duties of sovereignty, and by special mandate bound also "to guarantee to every State a republican form of government, and to protect it against invasion;" that, by virtue of the rights of war, this same region is subject to all

the conditions and incidents of war, according to the established usages of Christian nations, out of which is derived the familiar maxim of public duty, "Indemnity for the past and security for the future."

4. That, in seeking the restoration of the States to their proper places as members of the Republic, so that every State shall enjoy again its constitutional functions, and every star on our national flag shall represent a State, in reality as well as in name, care must be taken that the rebellion is not allowed, through any negligence or mistaken concession, to retain the least foothold for future activity, or the least germ of future life; that, whether proceeding by the exercise of sovereign rights or of belligerent rights, the same precautions must be exacted against future peril; that, therefore, any system of "reconstruction" must be rejected, which does not provide by irreversible guarantees against the continued existence or possible revival of slavery, and that such guarantees can be primarily obtained only through the agency of the national Government, which to this end must assert a temporary supremacy, military or civil, throughout the rebel and belligerent region, of sufficient duration, to stamp upon this region the character of freedom.

5. That, in the exercise of this essential supremacy of the national Government, a solemn duty is cast upon Congress to see that no rebel State is prematurely restored to its constitutional functions until, within its borders, all proper safeguards are established, so that loyal citizens, including the new-made freedmen, cannot at any time be molested by evil-disposed persons, and especially that no man there may be made a slave; that this solemn duty belongs to Congress under the Constitution, whether in the exercise of rights of sovereignty or rights of war, and that in its performance that system of "reconstruction" will be found the best, howsoever it may be named, which promises most surely to accomplish the desired end, so that slavery, which is the synonym of the rebellion, shall absolutely cease throughout the whole rebel and belligerent region, and the land which it has maddened, impoverished, and degraded, shall become safe, fertile, and glorious, from assured emancipation.

6. That, in the process of "reconstruction," it is not enough to secure the death of slavery throughout the rebel and belligerent region only; that experience testifies against slavery wherever it exists, not only as a crime against humanity, but as a disturber of the public peace and the spoiler of the public liberties, including the liberty of the press, the liberty of speech, and the liberty of travel and transit; that obviously, in the progress of civilization, it has become incompatible with good government, and especially with that "republican form of government" which the United States are bound to guarantee to every State; that from the outbreak of this rebel war, even in States professing loyalty, it has been an open check upon patriotic duty and an open accessory to the rebellion, so as to be a source of unquestionable weakness to the national cause; that the defiant pretensions of the master, claiming the control of his slave, are in direct conflict with the paramount rights of the national Government; and that, therefore, it is the further duty of Congress, in the exercise of its double powers, under the Constitution, as guardian of the national safety, to take all needful steps to secure the extinction of slavery, even in States professing loyalty, so that this crime against humanity, this disturber of the public peace, and this spoiler of the public liberties shall no longer exist anywhere to menace the general harmony; that civilization may be no longer shocked; that the constitutional guaranty of a republican form of government to every State may be fulfilled; that the rebellion may be deprived of the traitorous aid and comfort which slavery has instinctively volunteered; and that the master claiming an unnatural property in human flesh, may no longer defy the national Government.

7. That in addition to the guaranties stipulated by Congress, and as the cap-stone to its work of restoration and reconciliation, the Constitution itself must be so amended as to prohibit slavery everywhere within the limits of the Republic; that such a prohibition, leaving all personal claims, whether of slave or master, to the legislation of Congress and of the States, will be in itself a sacred and inviolable guaranty, representing the collective will of the people of the United States, and placing universal emancipation under the sanction of the Constitution, so that freedom shall be engraved on every foot of the national soil, and be woven into every star of the national flag, while it elevates and inspires our whole national existence, and the Constitution, so often invoked for slavery, but at last in harmony with the Declaration of Independence, will become, according to the holy aspirations of its founders, the sublime guardian of the inalienable right of every human being to life, liberty, and the pursuit of happiness; all of which must be done in the name of the Union, in duty to humanity, and for the sake of permanent peace.

IN HOUSE.

1863, Dec. 14—Mr. HARDING offered this resolution which was laid over under the rule:

Resolved, That the Union has not been dissolved, and that whenever the rebellion in any of the seceded States shall be put down and subdued, either by force of the Federal arms or by the voluntary submission of the people of such State to the authority of the Constitution, then such State will be thereby restored to all its rights and privileges as a State of the Union, under the constitution of such State and the Constitution of the United States, including the right to regulate, order and control its own domestic institutions according to the constitutution and laws of such State, free from all congressional or executive control or dictation.

May 2—The resolution was laid on the table —yeas 67, nays 56, as follows:

YEAS—Messrs. Alley, Allison, Ames, Anderson, Arnold, Ashley, John D. Baldwin, Baxter, Beaman, Blow, Boutwell, Boyd, Brandegee, Broomall, Cole, Henry Winter Davis, Deming, Donnelly, Driggs, Eckley, Eliot, Farnsworth, Fenton, Frank, Garfield, Grinnell, Hooper, Hotchkiss, A. W. Hubbard, J. H. Hubbard, John H. Hubbard, Hulburd, Julian, Kelley, Francis W. Kellogg, Loan, Longyear, McClurg, McIndoe, S. F. Miller, Moorhead, Morrill, Daniel Morris, Amos Myers, Leonard Myers, Norton, Charles O'Neill, Orth, Perham, Pike, Pomeroy, Price, Alexander H. Rice, John H. Rice, Edward H. Rollins, Schenck, Scofield, Shannon, Sloan, Spalding, Stevens, Thayer, Upson, William B. Washburn, Williams, Wilder, Wilson, Windom—67.

NAYS—Messrs. *Ancona, Baily, Augustus C. Baldwin*, Jacob B. Blair, *Brooks*, William G. Brown, *Chanler, Clay, Cox, Dawson, Denison, Eden, Eldridge, Finck, Ganson, Grider, Griswold, Hall, Harding, Harrington, Charles M. Harris, Herrick, Holman, Hutchins, Philip Johnson, William Johnson, Kernan, King, Knapp, Law, Lazear, Le Blond, Long, Mallory, Marcy, McDowell, McKinney, Morrison, Noble, Perry, Radford, Robinson, James S. Rollins, Ross, Scott*, Smith, *John B. Steele, Stiles, Strouse, Stuart*, Whaley, *Wheeler, Chilton A. White, Joseph W. White, Fernando Wood, Yeaman*—56.

December 14—Mr. WADSWORTH offered this resolution, which was laid over under the rule:

Resolved, That the powers not delegated to the United States by the Constitution nor prohibited by it to the States are reserved to the States respectively, or to the people, and the Federal Executive can, neither directly nor indirectly, exercise any of the powers thus reserved or lawfully restrict or obstruct the exercise thereof by the people.

May 2—The resolution was referred to the Committee on the Rebellious States—yeas 69, nays 50, as follows:

YEAS—Messrs. Alley, Allison, Ames, Anderson, Arnold, Ashley, John D. Baldwin, Baxter, Beaman, Blaine, Blow, Boutwell, Boyd, Brandegee, Broomall, Cobb, Cole, Dawes, Deming, Dixon, Donnelly, Driggs, Eliot, Farnsworth, Fenton, Frank, Garfield, Grinnell, Higby, Hotchkiss, A. W. Hubbard, J. H. Hubbard, Hulburd, Julian, Kelley, O. Kellogg, Loan, Longyear, McBride, McClurg, McIndoe, Sam'l F. Miller, Moorhead, Amos Myers, Leonard Myers, Norton, Charles O'Neill, Orth, Perham, Pike, Price, Alexander H. Rice, John H. Rice, Edward H. Rollins, Schenck, Scofield, Shannon, Smith, Spalding, Stevens, Thayer, Thomas, Upson, William B. Washburn, Whaley, Williams, Wilder, Wilson, Windom—69.

NAYS—Messrs. *William J. Allen, Ancona, Baily, Augustus C. Baldwin, Brooks*, William G. Brown, *Chanler, Cox, Denison, Eden, Eldridge, Finck, Ganson, Grider, Griswold, Hall, Harding, Benjamin G. Harris, Charles M. Harris, Herrick, Holman, Hutchins, Philip Johnson, Wm. Johnson, Kernan, King, Knapp, Law, Le Blond, Long, Marcy, McDowell, McKinney, Morrison, Noble, Perry, Radford, Robinson, James S. Rollins, Ross, Scott, John B. Steele, Stiles, Strouse, Stuart, Wheeler, Chilton A. White, Joseph W. White, Fernando Wood, Yeaman*—50.

1863, December—Mr. YEAMAN offered these resolutions; which were refered to the Judiciary Committee:

Joint resolutions concerning the restoration of the civil authority of the United States and of certain States within regions once or now under the control of the existing rebellion.

Be it resolved, &c., 1. That a combination of persons, in the name of a State, or an assumed confederation of States, for levying war against the United States, or for withdrawing such States from the Union, does not alter the legal character of the act done, nor excuse those engaged in it, nor does any such combination, levying of war, or attempted withdrawal amount to any destruction, forfeiture, or abdication of the right of those who at any time acknowledge allegiance and render obedience to the United States to administer, amend, or establish a State government.

2. That a formal return or readmission of any State to the Union is not necessary. It is sufficient that the people, or those who are loyal in any State, and qualified by the election laws thereof in force before the rebellion, shall at any time resume the functions of a State government compatible with the Union and with the Constitution and laws of the United States, and doing this is sufficient evidence of loyalty for the purpose of doing it.

3. That all questions touching property-rights and interests arising out of confiscation and emancipation, and the effect of any law, proclamation, military order, or emergency of war, or act of rebellion, upon the title to any property, or upon the status of any persons heretofore held to service or labor in any State, are left for the judicial determination of the courts of the United States.

4. That the whole power of the nation is pledged for the suppression of the rebellion, the execution of the laws, the defense of loyal citizens in any State, the territorial integrity of the Republic, and the nationality of the Constitution.

5. That nothing herein contained shall be construed to abridge or lessen any valid defense, or as waiving the right of the Government to inflict punishment; the purpose being to declare the nullity of secession as a State ordinance, to define the objects of the war, and to express the sense of Congress as to the proper mode of restoring harmonious relations between the Government and certain of the States and the disaffected people thereof.

Subsequently, December 21, he offered these resolutions, being, in part, a modification of the others, upon which he addressed the House, January 12, 1864:

Resolved, That a conspiracy of persons combined together, and assuming the name of a State, or a confederation of States, for levying war upon the United States, or for withdrawing such States from the Union, does not extinguish the political franchises of the loyal citizens of such States: and such loyal citizens have the right, at any time, to administer, amend, or establish a State government without other condition than that it shall be republican in form.

2. That a formal return or readmission of any State into the Union is not necessary. It is sufficient that the people, or those who are loyal in any State, and qualified by the election laws thereof in force before the rebellion, shall, at any time, resume the functions of a State government compatible with the Union, and with the Constitution and laws of the United States; and doing this is sufficient evidence of loyalty for the purpose of doing it.

3. That all questions touching property-rights and interests, arising out of confiscation and emancipation, and the effect and validity of any law, proclamation, military order, emergency of war, or act of rebellion, upon the title to any property, or upon the status of any persons heretofore held to service or labor in any State under the laws thereof, are left for the judicial determination of the courts of the United States.

The House refusing to second the demand for the previous question on their passage, they were, on motion of Mr. LOVEJOY, referred to the Select Committee on the Rebellious States.

Feb. 16—Mr. BOUTWELL proposed these resolutions:

Resolved, That the Committee on the rebellious States be instructed to consider and report upon the expediency of recommending to this House the adoption of the following

Declaration of Opinions:

In view of the present condition of the country, and especially in view of the recent signal successes of the national arms, promising a speedy overthrow of the rebellion, this House makes the following declaration of opinions concerning the institution of slavery in the States and parts of States engaged in the rebellion, and embraced in the proclamation of emancipation issued by the President on the 1st day of January, A. D. 1863; and also concerning the relations now subsisting between the people of such States and parts of States on the one side and the American Union on the other.

It is therefore declared, (as the opinion of the House of Representatives,) That the institution of slavery was the cause of the present rebellion, and that the destruction of slavery in the rebellious States is an efficient means of weakening the power of the rebels; that the President's proclamation, whereby all persons heretofore held as slaves in such States and parts of States have been declared free, has had the effect to increase the power of the Union and to diminish the power of its enemies; that the freedom of such persons was desirable and just in itself, and an efficient means by which the Government was to be maintained and its authority re-established in all the territory and over all the people within the legal jurisdiction of the United States; that it is the duty of the Government and of loyal men everywhere to do what may be practicable for the enforcement of the proclamation, in order to secure in fact as well as by the forms of law the extinction of slavery in such States and parts of States; and finally, that it is the paramount duty of the Government and of all loyal men to labor for the restoration of the American Union on the basis of freedom.

And this House does further declare, That a State can exist or cease to exist only by the will of the people within its limits, and that it cannot be created or destroyed by the external force or opinion of other States, or even by the judgment or action of the nation itself; that a State when created by the will of its people can become a member of the American Union only by its own organized action and the concurrent action of the existing National Government; that when a State has been admitted to the Union, no vote, resolution, ordinance, or proceeding, on its part, however formal in character or vigorously sustained, can deprive the National Government of the legal jurisdiction and sovereignty over the territory and people of such State which existed previous to the act of admission, or which were acquired thereby; that the effect of the so-called acts, resolutions, and ordinances of secession adopted by the eleven States engaged in the present rebellion is, and can only be, to destroy those political organizations as States, while the legal and constitutional jurisdiction and authoriy of the National Government over the people and territory remain unimpaired; that these several communities can be organized into States only by the will of the loyal people expressed freely and in the absence of all coercion; that States so organized can become States of the American Union only when they shall have applied for admission and their admission shall have been authorized by the existing National Government; that when a people have organized a State upon the basis of allegiance to the Union, and applied for admission, the character of the institutions of such proposed State may constitute a sufficient justification for granting or rejecting such application; and inasmuch as experience has shown that the existence of human slavery is incompatible with a republican form of Government in the several States or in the United States, and inconsistent with the peace, prosperity, and unity of the nation, it is the duty of the people and of all men in authority to resist the admission of slave States wherever organized within the jurisdiction of the National Government.

1864, March 14—Mr. WILLIAMS offered these resolutions, which were laid over under the rule:

Resolved, That the existing relation between the Union and the rebel States constitutes a condition of public war, with all the consequences attaching thereto under the law of nature and of nations.

2. That the appeal of the rebel States from the jurisdiction of the ordinary tribunals established by the Constitution to the arbitrament of the sword has not, however, withdrawn the case beyond the purview of the Constitution, which, in conferring the war power on the General Government, has made the law of war the rule of conduct in the prosecution and adjustment of the pending controversy.

3. That while the rebel States are, by that law and by the solemn recognition thereof in the proclamation made by the President of the United States on the 16th of August, A. D. 1861, under and in pursuance of the authority conferred on him by the act of Congress of the 13th of July of the same year, interdicting all commercial intercourse between their citizens and those of the loyal States, in the attitude of belligerents, and outside of the Union as States, by construction of law as well as in point of fact, and have thereby either abdicated or forfeited their rights to membership therein, the jurisdiction and powers of the Government over their territory and citizens continue unimpaired, and the latter are still amenable to the law and the judicial tribunals of the United States for their treason and other crimes against the same

4. That so long as those States continue under the armed occupation of the forces of the United States employed in suppressing the rebellion against its authority, the local laws are necessarily subordinated, and the functions of the civil authorities so far suspended therein as to prevent the exercise of all the rights arising out of their relations to this Government, and to disable them from electing members of either branch of Congress, or electors for the choice of a President of the United States.

5. That the occupation of these States by the armed forces of the United States, either under military commanders or provisional Governors appointed by the Executive, resting for its lawfulness upon the condition of insurrection existing therein, is a purely military one, and ought to determine with the necessity which produced it.

6. That as soon as the rebellion is suppressed in any of the revolted States, by the reconquest and occupation thereof by the armies of the United States, and the same are so tranquilized as to furnish adequate assurance against the recurrence of disturbance therein, it will become the duty of the President to communicate the fact to Congress in order that it may take the proper measures for the reorganization of the civil governments and the re-establishment of the civil functionaries therein, and prescribe such terms as it may deem wise and proper and consistent with the public safety for the readmission of those districts as States of this Union.

7. That it is the exclusive right of the legislative power of the Government to say upon what terms those Territories shall be allowed to return to the Union; and that in the adjustment of the existing controversy in the Government *ad interim* of the reconquered territory, and in the arrangement of the terms of reorganization and readmission, it will be entirely within their competency to punish the treason of individuals and provide indemnity for the expenses of the war and security against any future outbreak of the like kind by removing its causes and confiscating absolutely the property and estate of the guilty authors and abettors thereof.

Rebel Views of "Reconstruction."

1861.

By Jefferson Davis, February 16, 1861, at Montgomery:

The time for compromise has now passed, and the South is determined to maintain her position, and make all who oppose her smell southern powder and feel southern steel if coercion is persisted in. He had no doubts as to the result. He said we will maintain our rights and Government at all hazards. We ask nothing, we want nothing; we will have no complications. If the other States join our confederation they can freely come in on our terms. Our separation from the old Union is now complete. No compromise, no reconstruction is now to be entertained.

By Walter Brooke, of Mississippi, in "Confederate" Provisional Congress, March 5, 1861, quoting Davis and Stephens:

These men have long since given up all hope of receiving satisfaction from the General Government, and the entire people of Mississippi stand to-day upon the same platform. I am authorized, I think, to speak their sentiments on this floor, from the information I am daily receiving. I do not believe that there is a man in Mississippi who desires a reconstruction of this Government, or who will not fully indorse the sentiments uttered by you, Mr. President, that "the separation is perfect, complete, and perpetual," and likewise the sentiments of our distinguished President of the Confederate States, when he declared that "a reconstruction is neither practicable nor desirable."

T. R. R. Cobb, of Georgia, a member of the Provisional Congress, spoke at Atlanta on reconstruction:

I am against it now and forever. What have we worked for? Simply a new Constitution? No! we sought to be relieved of the North because they were fleecing us; giving fishing bounties and otherwise squandering the public treasure, and filling their pockets from our labors. I would not unite with them if they were to bind themselves in amounts more than they were worth, and give me a distress warrant to sell them out. I wish the people of Georgia to say—this shall be a slaveholding confederacy, and nothing else.

Jeff. Davis, in his message of November, 1861, says:

If, instead of being a dissolution of a league, it were indeed a rebellion in which we are engaged, we might find ample vindication in the course we have adopted in the scenes which are now being enacted in the United States. Our people now look with contemptuous astonishment on those with whom they have been so recently associated. They shrink with aversion from the bare idea of renewing such a connection.

JOINT RESOLUTIONS OF GEORGIA,

December 11, 1861.

Resolved, by the Senate and House of Representatives of Georgia, in General Assembly met, That it is the sense of this General Assembly that the separation of those States now forming the Confederate States of America from the United States is, and ought to be, final and irrevocable; and that Georgia will, under no circumstances, entertain any proposition from any quarter which may have for its object a restoration or reconstruction of the late Union, on any terms or conditions whatever.

Resolved, That the war which the United States is waging upon the Confederate States should be met on our part with the utmost vigor and energy, until our independence and nationality are unconditionally acknowledged by the United States.

Resolved, That Georgia pledges herself to her sister States of the Confederacy that she will stand by them throughout the struggle; she will contribute all the means which her resources will supply, so far as the same may be necessary to the support of the common cause, and will not consent to lay down arms until peace is established on the basis of the foregoing resolutions.

WARREN AIKEN,
Speaker of the House of Representatives.

L. Carrington, *Clerk of the House of Representatives.*

JOHN BILLUPS,
President of the Senate.

James M. Morley, *Secretary of the Senate.*

Approved *December* 11, 1861.

JOSEPH E. BROWN, *Governor.*

See Roger A. Pryor's declaration at Charleston, page 112.

1862.

Feb. 3—The Congress adopted this preamble and resolution unanimously:

Whereas, the United States are waging war against the Confederate States, with the avowed purpose of compelling the latter to re-unite with them under the same constitution and government; and whereas, the waging of war with such an object is in direct opposition to the sound republican maxim, that "all government rests upon the consent of the governed," and can only tend to consolidation in the General Government, and the consequent destruction of the rights of the States; and whereas, this result being attained, the two sections can only exist together in the relation of the oppressor and the oppressed, because of the great preponderance of power in the Northern section, coupled with dissimilarity of interests; and whereas, we, the representatives of the people of the Confederate States, in Congress assembled, may be presumed to know the sentiments of said people, having just been elected by them: Therefore be it

Resolved, That this Congress do solemnly declare and publish to the world that it is the unalterable determination of the people of the Confederate States (in humble reliance upon Almighty God) to suffer all the calamities of the most protracted war, but that they will *never*, on any terms, politically affiliate with a people who are guilty of an invasion of their soil and the butchery of their citizens.

John C. Breckinridge, announcing himself a candidate in the Eleventh District of Kentucky for the permanent "Confederate" Congress, at the election held Jan. 22, said:

I am utterly opposed to a reconstruction of the old Government, or any measure which in the remotest degree tends in that direction. For one, I shall never consent that peace shall be made until the very last of all the enemies of our liberty shall be driven, not only from our hallowed soil, but from every foot of territory which, by its geographical position, naturally belongs to the South. God grant that the day may not be far distant when Kentucky will arise, free and disenthralled, and assume her true position as one, the fairest, among the sisters of the South.

Alexander R. Boteler, of Virginia, about the same time said the same thing:

In regard to the canvass for Congress, I have been studiously silent, as I have a special repugnance to whatever may seem like thrusting myself on the public; but you can say for me that I have consented to become a candidate, which I suppose will be sufficient. In doing so, however, it is but proper that I should say that, having done all that I could, consistent with self-respect, to preserve the Union upon its original basis of constitutional equality, I am equally resolute in my determination to resist all attempts, should any be made, for its restoration; being unalterably opposed to reconstruction, at any time or on any terms. This much is due to the people that I should make known before the election, so that they may be aware of the course I shall pursue, if elected.

In the winter of 1862, George N. Sanders, in his letter to "Governor Seymour, Dean Richmond, John Van Buren, Charles O'Connor, Washington Hunt, Fernando Wood, and James Brooks, representative men of the triumphant revolutionary party of New York," under date of December 24, said:

Not only do you owe it to yourselves to *repudiate every dollar* of this unconstitutional debt, but you owe it equally to your posterity to *pay the half, if not all the debt the people of the South have had to incur* to maintain the rights of citizens and of States, in the establishment of free trade.

* * * * * * * *

Let heart and brain into the revolution; accelerate and direct the movement; get rid of the Baboon, (or What is it!) Abraham Lincoln, pacifically if you can, but by the blood of his followers if necessary. Withdraw your support, material and moral, from the invading armies, and the South will make quick work with the Abolitionists that remain on her soil. Suffer no degenerate son of the South, upon however plausible pretext, to idly embarrass your action by throwing into your way *rotten planks of reconstruction. Unity is no longer possible.* The very word Union, once so dear, has been made the cover for so many atrocious acts that the mere mention of it is *odious in the ears of Southern people.* The State Legislature will be called upon to obliterate the hated name from counties and towns.

In the fall of 1862, after the Democratic successes in the election, the Richmond papers took occasion to assure the North that there could be no peace except by recognizing the independence of the Southern Confederacy.

The *Examiner* said of the North:

They do not yet understand that we are resolute to be rid of them forever, and determined rather to die than to live with them in the same political community again.

The *Dispatch* anticipating Democratic ascendency in the Union Congress, said:

It is probable, therefore, that they might propose a reconstruction of the Union, with certain pledges, guaranties, &c. To this the South will never consent. They will never exist in the same political association, be its name what it may, be its terms what they will, and be the guaranties whatever the good will of the Democrats may make them. They want nothing more to do with the Yankees, and they are determined to have nothing more to do with them. Let them pay off their own debt with their own resources, we have as much as we can do to pay off ours. We cannot consent to return to the state of vassalage from which we have emerged. We cannot consent to sit in a Congress in which nothing is debated but the *nigger* from the beginning of the longest session to the end of it. We can never again affiliate with people who made a martyr of the cold-blooded assassin, John Brown, and thought he was doing a glorious deed when he was dying his hands in the blood of our people. We of the Confederate States have made up our minds to endure the worst extremity to which war can reduce a people. We are prepared for it. The Government that should propose to reunite us with the Yankees could not exist a day. It would sink so deep beneath the deluge of popular indignation that even history would not be able to fish up the wreck.

Again, October 18, the *Dispatch* said:

Nor, after the sacrifices which the South has suffered at Northern hands, could she ever consent, of her own free will, to live under the same Government with that people. The blood of our murdered children would cry from the ground against their fathers if they could ever be guilty of such unnatural and monstrous ingratitude. If the South has given her blood without a murmur to this contest, it is not because she does not value that blood but because she values freedom more than life or any earthly possession. Precious, more than aught else save her honor, are the jewels she has laid upon the altar of liberty, and never can she consent to shake hands again under one Government with men who have made so many vacant places in southern households, and whose steel is dripping with the blood of our brethren and children.

Henceforth we are two people.

December 2—The Legislature of North Carolina adopted these, among other, resolutions:

Resolved, That the Confederate States have the means and the will to sustain and perpetuate the Government they have established, and to that end North Carolina is determined to contribute all of her power and resources.

Resolved, That the separation between the Confederate States and the United States is final, and that the people of North Carolina will never consent to reunion at any time or upon any terms.

December 8—Governor Letcher, of Virginia, wrote:

It cannot be that the people of the Confederate States can again entertain a feeling of affection and respect for the Government of the United States. We have, therefore, separated from them; and now let it be understood that the separation is and ought to be final and irrevocable; that Virginia "will under no circumstances entertain any proposition from any quarter which may have for its object a restoration or reconstruction of the late Union, on any terms or conditions whatever."

Jeff. Davis addressed the Mississippi Legislature, December 26, 1862, and is reported in the Jackson *Mississipian* to have said:

He alluded to it, however, as a matter of regret that the best affections of his heart should have been bestowed upon an object so unworthy—that he should have loved so long a Government which was rotten to its very core. He had predicted from the beginning a fierce war, though it had assumed more gigantic proportions than he had calculated upon. He had predicted war not because our right to secede was not an undoubted one, and defined in the spirit of that declaration which rests the right to govern upon the consent of the governed: but the wickedness of the North would entail war upon the country.

The present war, waged against the rights of a free people, was unjust, and the fruit of the evil passions of the North. In the progress of the war those evil passions have been brought out and developed; and so far from reuniting with such a people—a people whose descendants Cromwell had gathered from the bogs and fens of Ireland and Scotland—a people whose intolerance produced discord and trouble wherever they went—who persecuted Catholics, Episcopalians, and every other sect that did not subscribe to their bigoted and contracted notions—who hung witches, and did a thousand other things calculated to make them forever infamous.

The President was emphatic in his declaration that under no circumstances would he consent to reunion. He drew a glowing picture of the horrors of war, and the ravages of the enemy, and while his tears flowed for those who suffered, yet all these would be endured cheerfully before our manhood and our liberties would be surrendered."

1863.

From the speech of Jeff. Davis, delivered in Richmond, as reported in the Richmond *Enquirer* of January 7:

You have shown yourselves in no respect to be degenerate sons of your fathers. You have fought mighty battles, and your deeds of valor will live among the richest spoils of Time's ample page. It is true, you have a cause which binds you together more firmly than your fathers were. They fought to be free from the usurpation of the British crown, but they fought against a manly foe. *You fight the offscourings of the earth.* [Applause.] * * *

They have come to disturb your social organizations on the plea that it is a military necessity. For what are they waging war? They say to preserve the Union. Can they preserve the Union by destroying the social existence of a portion of the South? Do they hope to reconstruct the Union by striking at everything which is dear to men? By showing themselves so utterly disgraced that if the question was proposed to you whether you would combine with Hyenas or Yankees, I trust every Virginian would say, give me the Hyenas. [Cries of "Good! good!" and applause.]

[From the Richmond Dispatch of January 11.]

Reconstruction! Can they reconstruct the family circles which they have broken—can they reconstruct the fortunes which they have scattered—can they reconstruct the bodies of our dead kindred, which by tens of thousands they have destroyed? When they can do this they can reconstruct the old Union. When they can do this—when they can breathe the breath of life into the pallid faces of our sons and brothers, and restore them once more, living and happy, to our desolate firesides, they may dream of bringing back that Union whose only principle of cohesion was the mutual love and confidence of its people.

* * * * * * *

We warn the Democrats and conservatives of the North to dismiss from their minds at once the miserable delusion that the South can ever consent to enter again, upon any terms, the old Union. If the North will allow us to write the Constitution ourselves, and give us every guarantee we would ask, we would sooner be under the Government of England or France than under a Union with men who have shown that they cannot keep good faith, and are the most barbarous and inhuman, as well as treacherous of mankind.

If the reconstructionists want peace, they can easily have it upon the terms on which they could have always had it—letting us alone. We ask neither more nor less. We are making no war on them. We are not invadng their territory, nor giving their homes to the flames, their populations to prison and the sword, their women to a fate worse than death. Let us alone! That is all we ask. Let us alone, and peace will return once more to bless a distracted land! *But do not expect us to degrade ourselves and cast dishonor upon the graves of our kindred by ever returning to the embrace of those whose hands are dripping with the tears and blood of our people.*

The Richmond *Sentinel* refers to the address of the Democrats of New Hampshire declaring that if the South will "come back into the Union, the Democracy of the North will do all in their power to gain for them (the Southern States) such guarantees as will secure their safety," and remarks that the proposition is frank and courteous, but inadmissible. It adds:

"They (the Democrats) are powerless to secure for us those guarantees of which they admit the necessity. Less than three years ago the States which now form the Confederacy, sought, in the spirit of conservatism and forbearance, to avoid disruption, with an importunity that now appears to us amazing. When we look back at it now it makes us tremble to think that we offered to take the Crittenden compromise. But conciliation on our part was met only by contumely and defiance by the Republican majority. From that time the men who willfully destroyed the Union have been assailing us with all the engines of destruction. They have evinced towards us a malignity which has seldom been paralleled in human history.

"Do the New Hampshire Democrats suppose for one moment that we could so much as think of reunion with such a people? Rather tell one to be wedded to a corpse! Rather join hands with a fiend from the pit. Since that time the only greeting of kind words which has come to us from the North, the New Hampshire men have sent. All, or nearly all beside, has been conflagration, sword, demoniac denunciation, and brutal menace of destruction. When those in the United States who are disposed to deal fairly with us shall gain the rule, we may in time begin to bury the many bitter memories which now add energy to our resentment, and may make with them treaties that shall be mutually advantageous. Perhaps, hereafter, good will may be revived again. But Union—never let it be mentioned! It is impossible."

FROM ALEXANDER H. STEPHENS.

The Richmond *Dispatch* of July 23, gives a sketch of ALEX. H. STEPHENS's speech at Charlotte, N. C., on his way to Richmond, in which after alluding to Lee's invasion of Maryland and Pennsylvania, and the loss of Vicksburg, and exhorting the people to give the government a cordial support, he said:

As for reconstruction, such a thing was impossible—such an idea must not be tolerated for an instant. Reconstruction would not end the war, but would produce a more horrible war than that in which we are now engaged. The only terms on which we can obtain permanent peace is final and complete separation from the North. Rather than submit to anything short of that, let us all resolve to die like men worthy of freedom.

FROM ROBERT TOOMBS.

WASHINGTON, GA., *August* 17, 1863.

MY DEAR SIR: Your letter of the 15th instant, asking my authority to contradict the report that "I am in favor of reconstruction," was received this evening. I can conceive of no extremity to which my country could be reduced in which I would for a single moment entertain any proposition for any union with the North on any terms whatever. When all else is lost, I prefer to unite with the thousands of our own countrymen who have found honorable deaths, if not graves, on the battle-field. Use this letter as you please.

Very truly, your friend, &c. R. TOOMBS.

Dr. A. BEES, Americus, Ga.

WM. SMITH, then recently elected Governor of Virginia, made a speech in Richmond in September, published in the Richmond *Examiner*, in which he "denounced, in bitter terms, as an utter impossibility, any thought of reconstruction on any conditions."

THE QUESTION ABOUT NORTHERN "TONE AND TEMPER."

[From the Richmond Sentinel, September 29.]

The House of Delegates yesterday, in the most summary manner, disposed of a resolution for inquiring into the tone and temper of the people of the United States on the subject of peace, with a view to responding, if favorable. The House knew what everybody knows—that such resolutions are both idle and mischievous, for they will only be taken by our enemies as evincing more or less readiness on our part for reconstruction. The House, by a unanimous vote, put its foot on the resolution, without a word of discussion or a moment of delay. In this they but fairly represented the manliness and the unanimity of our people.

1864.

GOV. ZEBULON B. VANCE of North Carolina, in his elaborate speech at Wilkesboro', used this language:

RECONSTRUCTION.

It is a favorite idea with a great many, that possibly the old order of things could be restored; that our rights under that Constitution could be guaranteed to us, and everything move on peacefully as before the war. My friends, there are a great many desirable things; but the question, not what may be wished, but what may be obtained, is the one reasonable men may consider. It is desirable to have a lovely wife and plenty of pretty children: but every man can't have them. I tell you now, candidly, there is no more possibility of reconstructing the old Union and reinstating things as they were four years ago, than exists for you to gather up the scattered bones of your sons who have fallen in this struggle, from one end of the country to the other, re-clothe them with flesh, fill their veins with the blood they have so generously shed, and their lungs with the same breath with which they breathed out their last prayer for their country's triumph and independence. [Immense applause.]

The new rebel Governor of Louisiana, HENRY W. ALLEN, in his inaugural, says:

Peace is not so sweet as to be purchased at the cost of reconstruction. Reconstruction means subjugation, ruin, death. Lose negroes, lose lands, lose everything, lose life itself, but never think of reconstruction. He says: "I speak to-day by authority, I speak as the Governor of Louisiana, and I wish it known at Washington and elsewhere that rather than reconstruct this Government and go back to the Union, on any terms whatever, the people of Louisiana will, in convention assembled, without a dissenting voice, cede the State to any European Power. * * * I speak to-day not only for the loyal citizens of Louisiana, who have stood by her in all trials, but in behalf of the misguided individuals who have been compelled to take the oath of allegiance to the Federal Government. In their hearts they are true to us, and are daily praying for the triumph of our arms. They have felt the iron in their souls, and know full well the curse of reconstruction. I speak by authority, for they write to me daily that they would rather, by 'ten thousand times, be the subjects of the Emperor of France than the slaves of Lincoln.'"

The Richmond *Dispatch*, in March, discussed President Lincoln's amnesty proclamation, and adds:

No one, however, knows better than Abraham Lincoln that any terms he might offer the southern people which contemplate their restoration to his bloody and brutal Government, would be rejected with scorn and execration. *If, instead of devoting to death our President and military and civil officers, he had proposed to make Jeff. Davis his successor, Lee Commander-in-Chief of the Yankee armies, and our domestic institutions not only recognized at home but readopted in the free States, provided the South would once more enter the Yankee Union, there is not a man, woman, or child in the Confederacy who would not spit upon the proposition. We desire no companionship upon any terms with a nation of robbers and murderers.* The miscreants, whose atrocities in this war have caused the whole civilized world to shudder, must keep henceforth their distance. They shall not be our masters, and we would not have them for our slaves.

JOINT RESOLUTION OF THE REBEL LEGISLATURE OF LOUISIANA.

Be it resolved, &c., That the barbarous manner in which our enemies have waged war against us deserves the execration of all men, and has confirmed and strengthened us in the determination to oppose to the last extremity a re-union with them, and that the spirit of our people is unabated in the resolution to resist every attempt at their subjugation.

1864, August 5—Messrs. BENJAMIN F. WADE and HENRY WINTER DAVIS published in the New York *Tribune* a paper arraigning President LINCOLN for his course on the Reconstruction bill. A few extracts are subjoined:

The President, by preventing this bill from becoming a law, holds the electoral votes of the rebel States at the dictation of his personal ambition. If those votes turn the balance in his favor, is it to be supposed that his competitor, defeated by such means, will acquiesce? If the rebel majority assert their supremacy in those States, and send votes which elect an enemy of the Government, will we not repel his claims? And is not that civil war for the Presidency inaugurated by the votes of rebel States?

Seriously impressed with these dangers, Congress, "*the proper constitutional authority*," formally declared that there are no State governments in the rebel States, and provided for their erection at a proper time; and both the Senate and the House of Representatives rejected the Senators and Representatives chosen under the authority of what the President calls the free constitution and government of Arkansas. The President's proclamation "*holds for naught*" this judgment, and discards the authority of the Supreme Court, and strides headlong toward the anarchy his proclamation of the 8th of December inaugurated. If electors for President be allowed to be chosen in either of those States, a sinister light will be cast on the motives which induced the President to "hold for naught" the will of Congress rather than his government in Louisiana and Arkansas. That judgment of Congress which the President defies was the exercise of an authority exclusively vested in Congress by the Constitution to determine what is the established government in a State, and in its own nature and by the highest judicial authority binding on all other departments of the Government. * * A more studied outrage on the legislative authority of the people has never been perpetrated. Congress passed a bill; the President refused to approve it, and then by proclamation puts as much of it in force as he sees fit, and proposes to execute those parts by officers unknown to the laws of the United States and not subject to the confirmation of the Senate! The bill directed the appointment of Provisional Governors by and with the advice and consent of the Senate. The President, after defeating the law, proposes to appoint without law, and without the advice and consent of the Senate, *Military* Governors for the rebel States! He has already exercised this dictatorial usurpation in Louisiana, and he defeated the bill to prevent its limitation. * * The President has greatly presumed on the forbearance which the supporters of his Administration have so long practiced, in view of the arduous conflict in which we are engaged, and the reckless ferocity of our political opponents. But he must understand that our support is of a cause and not of a man; that the authority of Congress is paramount and must be respected; that the whole body of the Union men of Congress will not submit to be impeached by him of rash and unconstitutional legislation; and if he wishes our support, he must confine himself to his executive duties—to obey and execute, not make the laws—to suppress by arms armed rebellion, and leave political reorganization to Congress. If the supporters of the Government fail to insist on this, they become responsible for the usurpations which they fail to rebuke, and are justly liable to the indignation of the people whose rights and security, committed to their keeping, they sacrifice. Let them consider the remedy for these usurpations, and, having found it, fearlessly execute it.

ABOLITION OF SLAVERY IN LOUISIANA.

1864, May 11—The vote in Convention was—yeas 72, nays 13:

YEAS—Messrs. M. R. Ariail, O. W. Austin, John T. Barrett, Raphael Beauvais, J. V. Bofill, Robert Bradshaw Bell, Robert W. Bennie, M. F. Bonzano, J. B. Bromley, Young Burke, Emile Collin, J. K. Cook, Terence Cook, F. M. Crozat, R. King Cutler, John L. Davies, James Duane, Joseph Dupaty, H. C. Edwards, W. R. Fish, G. H. Flagg, Edmond Flood, John Foley, G. A. Fosdick, James Fuller, George Geier, E. Goldman, Joseph Gorlinski, Jeremiah J. Healy, Patrick Harnan, Edward Hart, John Henderson, Jr., Alfred C. Hills, William H. Hire, George Howes, P. A. Kugler, H. Maas, William Davis Mann, H. Millspaugh, John P. Montamat, Robert Morris, Edward Murphy, M. W. Murphy, J. A. Newell, Lucien P. Normand, P. K. O'Conner, Thomas Ong, Benjamin H. Orr, John Payne, J. T. Paine, Eudaldo G. Pintado, O. H. Poynot, John Purcell, Samuel Pursell, J. B. Schroeder, Martin Schnurr, John Sullivan, Alfred Shaw, Charles Smith, John A. Spellicy, William Tompkins Stocker, John Stumpf, J. H. Stiner, C. W. Stauffer, Robert W. Taliaferro, J. Randall Terry, T. B. Thorpe, John W. Thomas, Ernest J. Wenck, Thomas M. Wells, Joseph Hamilton Wilson, and E. H. Durell, *President*—72.

NAYS—Messrs. Edmund Abell, John Buckley, Jr., Benj. Campbell, Thomas J. Decker, ——— Dufresne, of Iberville, Robert J. Duke, Louis Gastinel, C. H. L. Gruneberg, H. J. Heard, Xavier Maurer, John A. Mayer, A. Mendiverri, H. W. Waters—13.

A. Cazabat and James Ennis voted aye the next day, having been absent when the vote was taken.

May 9—Mr. JOSEPH H. WILSON moved to provide: "And that loyal owners shall be compensated."

Mr. GOLDMAN moved to lay the motion on the table; which was agreed to—yeas 45, nays 30, as follows:

YEAS—Messrs. Ariail, Austin, Bailey, Bonzano, Burke, Collin, Cazabat, J, K. Cook, Cutler, Davies, Duane, Dupaty, Edwards, James Ennis, Fish, Flagg, Flood, Foley, Fosdick, Goldman, Gorlinski, Healy, Harnan, Hills, Hire, Howes, Maas, Mann, Millspaugh, E. Murphy, Newell, Normand, J. Payne, Pintado, S. Pursell, Schroeder, Schnurr, Shaw, Smith, Spellicy, Stauffer, Taliaferro, Terry, Thorpe, Wells—45

NAYS—Messrs. Abell, Barrett, Bell, Bofill, George F. Brott, Buckley, T. Cook, Crozat, Dufresne, Duke, Fuller, Gruneberg, Hart, Heard, Henderson, E. H. Knobloch, Maurer, Mayer, Mendiverri, Montamat, M. W. Murphy, O'Conner, Ong, W. H. Seymour, Stocker, Stumpf, Stiner, Sullivan, Waters, Wilson—30.

ABOLITION OF SLAVERY IN ARKANSAS.

The Free State Convention met January 11, 1864, and adopted a Constitution, which was submitted to a vote of the people, March 14th, 15th, and 16th, and received 12,177 votes, 226 being polled against it.

The Emancipation clause was adopted unanimously. The following named persons constituted the Convention:

John McCoy, President of Convention, Luther C. White, C. A. Harper, John Austin, Josiah Harrell, Harmon L. Holleman, John R. Smoot, Randolph D. Swindell, G. W. Seamans, James T. Swafford, W. Holleman, John M. Demint, Enoch H. Vance, Miles L. Langly, J. M. Stapp, C. D. Jordan, John Burton, John C. Pridy, Reuben Lamb, E. D. Ayres, T. D. W. Yonley, E. L. Maynard, William Stout, Burk Johnson, Elias Cook, L. D. Cantrell, Willis Jones, James A. Butler, T. M. Jacks, Horace B. Allis, John Box, Calvin C. Bliss, A. B. Fryrear, Lemuel Helms, R. L. Turner, Thomas J. Young, James Huey, Andrew G. Evans, R. H. Stanfield, William Cox, L. Dunscomb.

ABOLITION OF SLAVERY IN MISSOURI.

1865, January 11—The vote in Convention was—yeas 59, nays 4, as follows:

YEAS—W. B. Adams, A. M. Bedford, David Bonham, Geo. K. Budd, Harvey Bunce, Isador Bush, R. L. Childress, Henry A. Clover, R. C. Cowden, Samuel T. Davis, John H. Davis, Isham B. Dodson, Wm. D. D'Oench, Charles D. Drake, John H. Ellis, John Esther, Ellis J. Evans, Chauncey I. Filley, J. W. Fletcher, Wm. H. Folmsbee, F. M. Fulkerson, John W. Gamble, Archibald Gilbert, Abner L. Gilstrap, Moses P. Green, J. M. Grammer, David Henderson, E. A. Holcomb, John H. Holdsworth, Wm. S. Holland, B. F. Hughes, Jos. F. Hume, Geo. Husmann, Wyllis King, R. Leonard, M. L. Linton, J. F. McKernan, A. M. McPherson, John A. Mack, A. H. Martin, Ferdinand Meyer, James P. Mitchell, A. G. Newgent, A. P. Nixdorf, James W. Owens, Dorastus Peck, J. T. Rankin, Phillip Rohrer, Gustavus St. Gemme, K. G. Smith, Eli Smith, Geo. P. Strong, James T. Sutton, John R. Swearinger, G. C. Thilenius, S. W. Weatherby, Jeremiah Williams, Eugene Williams, Arnold Krekel, *President*—59.

NAYS—Samuel A. Gilbert, Thomas B. Harris, William A. Martin, William F. Switzler—4.

ABSENT—A. J. Barr, Emory S. Foster, J. Roger. The last named had not attended the Convention up to the day of voting.

ABOLITION OF SLAVERY IN TENNESSEE.

1865, January 10—A convention of Unionists met in Nashville, and adopted a series of propositions to be submitted to the people February 22d, the first of which decrees the abolition of slavery. Over five hundred delegates attended, representing nearly every county. March 4, a Governor and Legislature are to be chosen. William G. Brownlow is the Convention's nominee for Governor.

The latest returns published comprise 8 counties in East Tennessee, 21 in Middle, 1 in West, and 10 hospitals, regiments, &c., giving an aggregate of 21,104 for, and 40 against the Constitution. March 4, the Union State ticket was chosen.

REMAINING PAPERS OF PRESIDENT LINCOLN.

EXPLANATORY OF GOVERNMENT PURCHASES IN MAY, 1861.

1862, May 29—The PRESIDENT sent this message* to Congress:

To the Senate and
House of Representatives:

The insurrection which is yet existing in the United States, and aims at the overthrow of the Federal Constitution and the Union, was clandestinely prepared during the winter of 1860 and 1861, and assumed an open organization in the form of a treasonable provisional government at Montgomery, in Alabama, on the 18th day of February, 1861. On the 12th day of April, 1861, the insurgents committed the flagrant act of civil war by the bombardment and capture of Fort Sumter, which cut off the hope of immediate conciliation. Immediately afterwards all the roads and avenues to this city were obstructed, and the capital was put into the condition of a siege. The mails in every direction were stopped, and the lines of telegraph cut off by the insurgents, and military and naval forces, which had been called out by the Government for the defence of Washington, were prevented from reaching the city by organized and combined treasonable resistance in the State of Maryland. There was no adequate and effective organization for the public defence. Congress had indefinitely adjourned. There was no time to convene them. It became necessary for me to choose whether, using only the existing means, agencies, and processes which Congress had provided, I should let the Government fall at once into ruin, or whether, availing myself of the broader powers conferred by the Constitution in cases of insurrection, I would make an effort to save it with all its blessings for the present age and for posterity.

I thereupon summoned my constitutional advisers, the heads of all the Departments, to meet on Sunday, the 20th day of April, 1861, at the office of the Navy Department, and then and there, with their unanimous concurrence, I directed that an armed revenue cutter should proceed to sea, to afford protection to the commercial marine, and especially the California treasure ships then on their way to this coast. I also directed the commandant of the navy-yard at Boston to purchase or charter, and arm as quickly as possible, five steamships, for purposes of public defence. I directed the commandant of the navy-yard at Philadelphia to purchase, or charter and arm, an equal number for the same purpose. I directed the commandant at New York to purchase, or charter and arm, an equal number. I directed Commander Gillis to purchase, or charter and arm, and put to sea two other vessels. Similar directions were given to Commodore Du Pont, with a view to the opening of passages by water to and from the capital. I directed the several officers to take the advice and obtain the aid and efficient services in the matter of his Excellency Edwin D. Morgan, the Governor of New York, or, in his absence, George D. Morgan, William M. Evarts, R. M. Blatchford, and Moses H. Grinnell, who were, by my directions, especially empowered by the Secretary of the Navy to act for his Department in that crisis, in matters pertaining to the forwarding of troops and supplies for the public defence.

On the same occasion I directed that Governor Morgan and Alexander Cummings, of the city of New York, should be authorized by the Secretary of War, Simon Cameron, to make all necessary arrangements for the transportation of troops and munitions of war, in aid and assistance of the officers of the Army of the United States, until communication by mails and telegraph should be completely re-established between the cities of Washington and New York. No security was required to be given by them, and either of them was authorized to act in case of inability to consult with the other.

On the same occasion I authorized and directed the Secretary of the Treasury to advance, without requiring security, two millions of dollars of public money to John A. Dix, George Opdyke, and Richard M. Blatchford, of New York, to be used by them in meeting such requisitions as should be directly consequent upon the military and naval measures necessary for the defence and support of the Government, requiring them only to act without compensation, and to report their transactions when duly called upon.

The several departments of the Government at that time contained so large a number of disloyal persons that it would have been impos-

* Called forth by the passage of a resolution, April 30, in the House—yeas 79, nays 45—censuring Secretary Cameron for a supposed responsibility for, and connection with, the circumstances detailed.

sible to provide safely, through official agents only, for the performance of the duties thus confided to citizens favorably known for their ability, loyalty, and patriotism.

The several orders issued upon these occurrences were transmitted by private messengers, who pursued a circuitous way to the seaboard cities, inland, across the States of Pennsylvania and Ohio and the Northern Lakes. I believe that by these and other similar measures taken in that crisis, some of which were without any authority of law, the Government was saved from overthrow. I am not aware that a dollar of the public funds thus confided without authority of law to unofficial persons was either lost or wasted, although apprehensions of such misdirection occurred to me as objections to those extraordinary proceedings, and were necessarily overruled.

I recall these transactions now because my attention has been directed to a resolution which was passed by the House of Representatives on the 30th day of last month, which is in these words:

Resolved, That Simon Cameron, late Secretary of War, by investing Alexander Cummings with the control of large sums of the public money, and authority to purchase military supplies without restriction, without requiring from him any guarantee for the faithful performance of his duties, when the services of competent public officers were available, and by involving the Government in a vast number of contracts with persons not legitimately engaged in the business pertaining to the subject-matter of such contracts, especially in the purchase of arms for future delivery, has adopted a policy highly injurious to the public service, and deserves the censure of the House.

Congress will see that I should be wanting equally in candor and in justice if I should leave the censure expressed in this resolution to rest exclusively or chiefly upon Mr. Cameron. The same sentiment is unanimously entertained by the heads of Departments, who participated in the proceedings which the House of Representatives has censured. It is due to Mr. Cameron to say that, although he fully approved the proceedings, they were not moved nor suggested by himself, and that not only the President but all the other heads of Departments were at least equally responsible with him for whatever error, wrong, or fault was committed in the premises.

ABRAHAM LINCOLN.

WASHINGTON, *May* 26, 1862.

THE PRESIDENT'S REMARKS AT A UNION MEETING IN WASHINGTON, AUGUST 6, 1862.

FELLOW-CITIZENS: I believe there is no precedent for my appearing before you on this occasion, but it is also true that there is no precedent for your being here yourselves, and I offer, in justification of myself and of you, that, upon examination, I have found nothing in the Constitution against it. I, however, have an impression that there are younger gentlemen who will entertain you better, and better address your understanding than I will or could, and therefore I propose but to detain you a moment longer.

I am very little inclined on any occasion to say anything unless I hope to produce some good by it. The only thing I think of just now not likely to be better said by some one else, is a matter in which we have heard some other persons blamed for what I did myself. There has been a very widespread attempt to have a quarrel between Gen. McClellan and the Secretary of War. Now, I occupy a position that enables me to observe, that these two gentlemen are not nearly so deep in the quarrel as some pretending to be their friends. General McClellan's attitude is such that, in the very selfishness of his nature, he cannot but wish to be successful, and I hope he will—and the Secretary of War is in precisely the same situation. If the military commanders in the field cannot be successful, not only the Secretary of War, but myself, for the time being the master of them both, cannot but be failures. I know General McClellan wishes to be successful, and I know he does not wish it any more than the Secretary of War for him, and both of them together no more than I wish it. Sometimes we have a dispute about how many men General McClellan has had, and those who would disparage him say that he has had a very large number, and those who would disparage the Secretary of War insist that General McClellan has had a very small number. The basis for this is, there is always a wide difference, and on this occasion, perhaps a wider one than usual, between the grand total on McClellan's rolls and the men actually fit for duty; and those who would disparage him talk of the grand total on paper, and those who would disparage the Secretary of War talk of those at present fit for duty. General McClellan has sometimes asked for things that the Secretary of War did not give him. General McClellan is not to blame for asking for what he wanted and needed, and the Secretary of War is not to blame for not giving when he had none to give. And I say here, as far as I know, the Secretary of War has withheld no one thing at any time in my power to give him. I have no accusation against him. I believe he is a brave and able man, and I stand here, as justice requires me to do, to take upon myself what has been charged on the Secretary of War, as withholding from him.

I have talked longer than I expected to do, and now I avail myself of my privilege of saying no more.

The President's Letters on Politics.

TO HORACE GREELEY.

EXECUTIVE MANSION,
WASHINGTON, *Friday*, *Aug.* 22, 1862.

HON. HORACE GREELEY:

DEAR SIR: I have just read yours of the 19th instant, addressed to myself through the New York *Tribune*.

If there be in it any statements or assumptions of fact which I may know to be erroneous, I do not now and here controvert them.

If there be any inferences which I may believe to be falsely drawn, I do not now and here argue against them.

If there be perceptible in it an impatient and dictatorial tone, I waive it in deference to an old friend whose heart I have always supposed to be right.

As to the policy I "seem to be pursuing," as you say, I have not meant to leave any one in doubt. I would save the Union. I would save it in the shortest way under the Constitution.

The sooner the national authority can be restored, the nearer the Union will be—the Union as it was.

If there be those who would not save the Union unless they could at the same time save slavery, I do not agree with them.

If there be those who would not save the Union unless they could at the same time destroy slavery, I do not agree with them.

My paramount object is to save the Union and not either to save or destroy slavery.

If I could save the Union without freeing any slave, I would do it—and if I could save it by freeing all the slaves, I would do it—and if I could save it by freeing some and leaving others alone, I would also do that.

What I do about slavery and the colored race, I do because I believe it helps to save the Union, and what I forbear, I forbear because I do not believe it would help to save the Union.

I shall do less whenever I shall believe what I am doing hurts the cause, and shall do more whenever I believe doing more will help the cause.

I shall try to correct errors when shown to be errors, and I shall adopt new views so fast as they shall appear to be true views.

I have here stated my purpose according to my view of official duty, and I intend no modification of my oft-expressed personal wish that all men everywhere could be free.

Yours, A. LINCOLN.

THE PRESIDENT'S RESPONSE TO A SERENADE.

JULY, 1863.

FELLOW-CITIZENS: I am very glad indeed to see you to night, and yet I will not say I thank you, for this call; but I do most sincerely thank Almighty God for the occasion on which you have called. How long ago is it,—eighty odd years since on the Fourth of July, for the first time, in the history of the world, a nation, by its representatives, assembled and declared as a self-evident truth, "that all men are created equal." That was the birthday of the United States of America. Since then the Fourth of July has had several very peculiar recognitions. The two men most distinguished in the framing and support of the Declaration were Thomas Jefferson and John Adams—the one having penned it, and the other sustained it the most forcibly in debate—the only two of the fifty-five who signed it, and were elected Presidents of the United States. Precisely fifty years after they put their hands to the paper, it pleased Almighty God to take both from this stage of action. This was indeed an extraordinary and remarkable event in our history. Another President, five years after, was called from this stage of existence on the same day and month of the year; and now on this last Fourth of July, just passed, when we have a gigantic rebellion, at the bottom of which is an effort to overthrow the principle that all men were created equal, we have the surrender of a most powerful position and army on that very day. And not only so, but in a succession of battles in Pennsylvania, near to us, through three days, so rapidly fought that they might be called one great battle, on the first, second, and third of the month of July; and on the fourth the cohorts of those who opposed the Declaration that all men are created equal, "turned tail" and run. [Long continued cheers.] Gentlemen, this is a glorious theme, and the occasion for a speech, but I am not prepared to make one worthy of the occasion. I would like to speak in terms of praise due to the many brave officers and soldiers who have fought in the cause of the Union and liberties of their country from the beginning of the war. These are trying occasions, not only in success, but for the want of success. I dislike to mention the name of one single officer, lest I might do wrong to those I might forget. Recent events bring up glorious names, and particularly prominent ones; but these I will not mention. Having said this much, I will now take the music.

THE PRESIDENT'S LETTER TO THE ILLINOIS CONVENTION.

EXECUTIVE MANSION,
WASHINGTON, *August* 26, 1863.

HON. JAMES C. CONKLING:

MY DEAR SIR: Your letter inviting me to attend a mass meeting of unconditional Union men, to be held at the capital of Illinois, on the 3d day of September, has been received. It would be very agreeable for me thus to meet my old friends at my own home: but I cannot just now be absent from here so long as a visit there would require.

The meeting is to be of all those who maintain unconditional devotion to the Union; and I am sure that my old political friends will thank me for tendering, as I do, the nation's gratitude to those other noble men whom no partisan malice or partisan hope can make false to the nation's life.

There are those who are dissatisfied with me. To such I would say: you desire peace, and you blame me that we do not have it. But how can we attain it? There are but three conceivable ways: First—to suppress the Rebellion by force of arms. This I am trying to do. Are you for it? If you are, so far we are agreed. If you are not for it, a *second* way is to give up the Union. I am against this. Are you for it? If you are, you should say so plainly. If you are not for *force*, nor yet for *dissolution*, there only remains some imaginable *compromise*.

I do not believe that any compromise embracing the maintenance of the Union is now possible. All that I learn leads to a directly opposite belief. The strength of the Rebellion is its military, its army. That army dominates all the country, and all the people within its range. Any offer of terms made by any man or men within that range, in opposition to that army, is simply nothing for the present; because such man or men have no power whatever to enforce their side of a compromise, if one were made with them.

To illustrate: Suppose refugees from the South and peace men of the North get together in convention, and frame and proclaim a compromise embracing a restoration of the Union. In what way can that compromise be used to keep Lee's army out of Pennsylvania? Meade's army can keep Lee's army out of Pennsylvania, and, I think, can ultimately drive it out of existence. But no paper compromise to which the controllers of Lee's army are not agreed can at all affect that army. In an effort at such compromise we would waste time, which the enemy would improve to our disadvantage; and that would be all.

A compromise, to be effective, must be made either with those who control the rebel army, or with the people, first liberated from the domination of that army by the success of our own army. Now, allow me to assure you that no word or intimation from that rebel army, or from any of the men controlling it, in relation to any peace compromise, has ever come to my knowledge or belief. All charges and insinuations to the contrary are deceptive and groundless. And I promise you that if any such proposition shall hereafter come, it shall not be rejected and kept a secret from you. I freely acknowledge myself to be the servant of the people, according to the bond of service, the United States Constitution; and that, as such, I am responsible to them.

But, to be plain. You are dissatisfied with me about the negro. Quite likely there is a difference of opinion between you and myself upon that subject. I certainly wish that all men could be free, while you, I suppose, do not. Yet, I have neither adopted nor proposed any measure which is not consistent with even your view, provided that you are for the Union. I suggested compensated emancipation; to which you replied you wished not to be taxed to buy negroes. But I had not asked you to be taxed to buy negroes, except in such a way as to save you from greater taxation to save the Union exclusively by other means.

You dislike the Emancipation Proclamation, and perhaps would have it retracted. You say it is unconstitutional. I think differently. I think the Constitution invests its Commander-in-Chief with the law of war in time of war. The most that can be said, if so much, is, that slaves are property. Is there, has there ever been, any question that by the law of war, property, both of enemies and friends, may be taken when needed? And is it not needed whenever it helps us and hurts the enemy? Armies, the world over, destroy enemies' property when they cannot use it; and even destroy their own to keep it from the enemy. Civilized belligerents do all in their power to help themselves or hurt the enemy, except a few things regarded as barbarous or cruel. Among the exceptions are the massacre of vanquished foes and non-combatants, male and female.

But the Proclamation, as law, either is valid or is not valid. If it is not valid it needs no retraction. If it is valid it cannot be retracted, any more than the dead can be brought to life. Some of you profess to think its retraction would operate favorably for the Union. Why better *after* the retraction than *before* the issue? There was more than a year and a half of trial to suppress the rebellion before the Proclamation was issued, the last one hundred days of which passed under an explicit notice that it was coming, unless averted by those in revolt returning to their allegiance. The war has certainly progressed as favorably for us since the issue of the Proclamation as before.

I know as fully as one can know the opinion of others that some of the commanders of our armies in the field, who have given us our most important victories, believe the emancipation policy and the use of colored troops constitute the heaviest blows yet dealt to the rebellion, and that at least one of those important successes could not have been achieved when it was but for the aid of black soldiers.

Among the commanders who hold these views are some who have never had an affinity with what is called "abolitionism," or with "Republican party politics," but who hold them purely as military opinions. I submit their opinions as entitled to some weight against the objections often urged that emancipation and arming the blacks are unwise as military measures, and were not adopted as such in good faith.

You say that you will not fight to free negroes. Some of them seem willing to fight for you; but no matter. Fight you, then, exclusively, to save the Union. I issued the proclamation on purpose to aid you in saving the Union. Whenever you shall have conquered all resistance to the Union, if I shall urge you to continue fighting, it will be an apt time then for you to declare you will not fight to free negroes. I thought that in your struggle for the Union, to whatever extent the negroes should cease helping the enemy, to that extent it weakened the enemy in his resistance to you. Do you think differently? I thought whatever negroes can be got to do as soldiers, leaves just so much less for white soldiers to do in saving the Union. Does it appear otherwise to you? But negroes, like other people, act upon motives. Why should they do anything for us if we will do nothing for them? If they stake their lives for us they must be prompted by the strongest motives, even the promise of freedom. And the promise, being made, must be kept.

The signs look better. The Father of Waters again goes unvexed to the sea. Thanks to the great Northwest for it; nor yet wholly to them. Three hundred miles up they met New England, Empire, Keystone, and Jersey, hewing their way right and left. The sunny South, too, in more colors than one, also lent a helping hand. On the spot, their part of the history was jotted down in black and white. The job was a great national one, and let none be slighted who bore an honorable part in it. And while those who have cleared the great river may well be proud, even that is not all. It is hard to say that anything has been more bravely and well done than at Antietam, Murfreesboro, Gettysburg, and on many fields of less note. Nor must Uncle Sam's web feet be forgotten. At all the watery margins they have been present, not only on the deep sea, the broad bay, and the rapid river, but also up the narrow, muddy bayou, and wherever the ground was a little damp they have been and made their tracks. Thanks to all. For the great Republic—for the principle it lives by and keeps alive—for man's vast future—thanks to all.

Peace does not appear so distant as it did. I hope it will come soon and come to stay; and so come as to be worth the keeping in all future time. It will then have been proved that among freemen there can be no successful appeal from the ballot to the bullet, and that they who take such appeal are sure to lose their case and pay the cost. And there will be some black men who can remember that with silent tongue, and clinched teeth, and steady eye, and well-poised bayonet, they have helped mankind on to this great consummation, while I fear there will be some white ones unable to forget that with malignant heart and deceitful speech they have striven to hinder it.

Still, let us not be over-sanguine of a speedy, final triumph. Let us be quite sober. Let us diligently apply the means, never doubting that a just God, in his own good time, will give us the rightful result.

Yours, very truly, A. LINCOLN.

THE PRESIDENT'S LETTER TO THE NORTH AMERICAN REVIEW.

EXECUTIVE MANSION,
WASHINGTON, *January* 16, 1864.

Messrs. CROSBY & NICHOLS:

GENTLEMEN: The number for this month and year of the *North American Review* was duly received, and for which please accept my thanks. Of course, I am not the most impartial judge, yet, with due allowance for this, I venture to hope that the article entitled "The President's Policy," will be of value to the country. I fear I am not quite worthy of all which is therein kindly said of me personally.

The sentence of twelve lines, commencing at the top of page 252, I could wish to be not exactly as it is. In what is there expressed the writer has not correctly understood me. I have never had a theory that secession could absolve States or people from their obligations. Precisely the contrary is asserted in the inaugural address; and it was because of my belief in the continuation of these obligations that I was puzzled, for a time, as to denying the legal rights of those citizens who remained individually innocent of treason or rebellion. But I mean no more now than to merely call attention to this point.

Yours respectfully, A. LINCOLN.

The sentence in the January number, refered to by Mr. Lincoln, is as follows:

Even so long ago as when Mr. Lincoln, not yet convinced of the danger and magnitude of the crisis, was endeavoring to persuade himself of Union majorities at the South, and to carry on a war that was half peace in hope of a peace that would have been all war, while he was still enforcing the fugitive slave law, under some theory that secession, however it might absolve States from their obligations, could not escheat them of their claims under the Constitution, and that slaveholders in rebellion had alone, among mortals, the privilege of having their cake and eating it at the same time—the enemies of free government were striving to persuade the people that the war was an abolition crusade. To rebel without reason was proclaimed as one of the rights of man, while it was carefully kept out of sight that to suppress rebellion is the first duty of the Government.

To this the editors of the *Review* append a note, as follows:

Nothing could have been further from the intention of the editors than to misrepresent the opinions of the President. They merely meant that, in their judgment, the policy of the administration was at first such as practically to concede to any rebel who might choose to profess loyalty, rights under the Constitution whose corresponding obligations he repudiated.

THE PRESIDENT'S LETTER TO COLONEL HODGES OF KENTUCKY.

EXECUTIVE MANSION,
WASHINGTON, *April* 4, 1864.

A. G. HODGES, Esq., *Frankfort, Ky:*

MY DEAR SIR: You ask me to put in writing the substance of what I verbally said the other day, in your presence, to Governor Bramlette and Senator Dixon. It was about as follows:

"I am naturally anti-slavery. If slavery is not wrong, nothing is wrong. I cannot remember when I did not so think and feel, and yet I have never understood that the Presidency conferred upon me an unrestricted right to act officially upon this judgment and feeling. It was in the oath I took that I would to the best of my ability preserve, protect, and defend the Constitution of the United States. I could not take the office without taking the oath. Nor was it my view that I might take an oath to get power, and break the oath in using the power. I understood, too, that in ordinary and civil administration this oath even forbade me to practically indulge my primary abstract judgment on the moral question of slavery. I had publicly declared this many times, and in many ways. And I aver that, to this day, I have done no official act in mere deference to my abstract judgment and feeling on slavery. I did understand, however, that my oath to preserve the Constitution to the best of my ability, imposed upon me the duty of preserving, by every indispensable means, that Government—that nation, of which that Constitution was the organic law. Was it possible to lose the nation and yet preserve the Contution? By general law, life *and* limb must be protected; yet often a limb must be amputated to save a life; but a life is never wisely given to save a limb. I felt that measures, otherwise unconstitutional, might become lawful, by becoming indispensable to the preservation of the Constitution, through the preservation of the nation. Right or wrong, I assumed this ground, and now avow it. I could not feel that, to the best of my ability I had even tried to preserve the Constitution, if, to save slavery, or any minor matter, I should permit the wreck of Government, country, and Constitution, altogether. When early in the war, General Fremont attempted military emancipation, I forbade it, because I did not then think it an indispensable necessity. When a little later, General Cameron, then Secretary of War, suggested the arming of the blacks, I objected, because I did not yet think it an indispensable necessity. When, still later, General Hunter attempted military emancipation, I again forbade it, because I did not yet think the indispensable necessity had come. When in March and May, and July, 1862, I made earnest and successive appeals to the border States to favor compensated emancipation, I believed the indispensable necessity for military emancipation and arming the blacks would come, unless averted by that measure. They declined the proposition, and I was, in my best judgment, driven to the alternative of either surrendering the Union, and with it, the Constitution, or of laying strong hand upon the colored element. I chose the latter. In choosing it, I hoped for greater gain than loss, but of this I was not entirely confident. More than a year of trial now shows no loss by it in our foreign relations, none in our home popular sentiment, none in our white military force, no loss by it any how, or anywhere. On the contrary, it shows a gain of quite a hundred and thirty thousand soldiers, seamen, and laborers. These are palpable facts, about which, as facts, there can be no cavilling. We have the men; and we could not have had them without the measure.

"And now let any Union man who complains of this measure, test himself by writing down in one line, that he is for subduing the rebellion by force of arms; and in the next, that he is for taking three hundred and thirty thousand men from the Union side, and placing them where they would be best for the measure he condemns. If he cannot face his case so stated, it is only because he cannot face the truth."

I add a word which was not in the verbal conversation. In telling this tale, I attempt no compliment to my own sagacity. I claim not to have controlled events, but confess plainly that events have controlled me. Now at the end of three years' struggle, the nation's condition is not what either party, or any man devised, or expected. God alone can claim it. Whither it is tending seems plain. If God now wills the removal of a great wrong, and wills also that we of the North, as well as you of the South, shall pay fairly for our complicity in that wrong, impartial history will find therein new causes to attest and revere the justice and goodness of God. Yours, truly,

A. LINCOLN.

TO A NEW YORK MEETING.

EXECUTIVE MANSION,
WASHINGTON, *June* 3, 1864.

Hon. F. A. CONKLING, and others:

GENTLEMEN: Your letter, inviting me to be present at a mass meeting of loyal citizens to be held at New York, on the 4th inst., for the purpose of expressing gratitude to Lieutenant General Grant for his signal services, was received yesterday. It is impossible for me to attend. I approve, nevertheless, whatever may tend to strengthen and sustain General Grant and the noble armies now under his direction.

My previous high estimate of General Grant has been maintained and heightened by what has occurred in the remarkable campaign he is now conducting. While the magnitude and difficulty of the task before him do not prove less than I expected, he and his brave soldiers are now in the midst of their great trial, and I trust at your meeting you will so shape your good words that they may turn to men and guns, moving to his and their support.

Yours, truly, A. LINCOLN.

SPEECH OF MR. LINCOLN AT THE PHILADELPHIA FAIR, JUNE 16, 1864.

I suppose that this toast was intended to open the way for me to say something.

War, at the best, is terrible, and this war of ours, in its magnitude and in its duration, is one of the most terrible. It has deranged business, totally in many localities, and partially in all localities. It has destroyed property and ruined homes; it has produced a national debt and taxation unprecedented, at least in this country; it has carried mourning to almost every home, until it can almost be said that the "heavens are hung in black."

Yet the war continues, and several relieving coincidents have accompanied it from the very beginning which have not been known, as I understand, or have any knowledge of, in any former wars in the history of the world. The Sanitary Commission, with all its benevolent labors; the Christian Commission, with all its Christian and benevolent labors; and the various places, arrangements, so to speak, and institutions, have contributed to the comfort and relief of the soldiers. You have two of these places in this city—the Cooper Shop and Union Volunteer Refreshment Saloons. And, lastly, these Fairs, which, I believe, began only in last August, if I mistake not, in Chicago, then at Boston, at Cincinnati, Brooklyn, New York, at Baltimore, and those at present held at St. Louis, Pittsburgh, and Philadelphia. The motive and object that lie at the bottom of all these are most worthy; for, say what you will, after all, the most is due to the soldier, who takes his life in his hands and goes to fight the battles of his country. In what is contributed to his comfort when he passes to and fro, and in what is contributed to him when he is sick and wounded, in whatever shape it comes, whether from the fair and tender hand of woman, or from any other source, it is much, very much. But I think that there is still that which is of as much value to him in the continual reminders he sees in the newspapers that while he is absent he is yet remembered by the loved ones at home. Another view of these various institutions, if I may so call them, is worthy of consideration, I think. They are voluntary contributions, given zealously and earnestly, on top of all the disturbances of business, of all the disorders, of all the taxation, and of all the burdens that the war has imposed upon us, giving proof that the national resources are not at all exhausted, and that the national spirit of patriotism is even firmer and stronger than at the commencement of the war.

It is a pertinent question, often asked in the mind privately, and from one to the other, when is the war to end? Surely I feel as deep an interest in this question as any other can, but I do not wish to name a day, a month, or a year when it is to end. I do not wish to run any risk of seeing the time come, without our being ready for the end, for fear of disappointment, because the time had come and not the end. We accepted this war for an object, a worthy object, and the war will end when that object is attained. Under God, I hope it never will end until that time. Speaking of the present campaign, General Grant is reported to have said, I am going through on this line if it takes all summer. This war has taken three years; it was begun or accepted upon the line of restoring the national authority over the whole national domain, and for the American people, as far as my knowledge enables me to speak, I say we are going through on this line if it takes three years more.

My friends, I did not know but that I might be called upon to say a few words before I got away from here, but I did not know it was coming just here. I have never been in the habit of making predictions in regard to the war, but I am almost tempted to make one. If I were to hazard it, it is this: That Grant is this evening, with General Meade and General Hancock, and the brave officers and soldiers with him, in a position from whence he will never be dislodged until Richmond is taken, and I have but one single proposition to put now, and, perhaps, I can best put it in the form of an interrogative. If I shall discover that General Grant and the noble officers and men under him can be greatly facilitated in their work by a sudden pouring forward of men and assistance, will you give them to me? Are you ready to march? [Cries of "yes."] Then, I say, stand ready, for I am watching for the chance. I thank you, gentlemen. [Laughter and cheers.]

This speech was repeatedly interrupted by applause, and at its close three cheers were given for the army of the Potomac, and successive cheers for Grant and Meade and Hancock, and their brave soldiers. In the mean time the President retired from the room.

OUR FOREIGN RELATIONS.

The Trent Affair.

SECRETARY SEWARD TO MR. ADAMS.

NOVEMBER 30, 1861.

* * * Since that conversation was held Captain Wilkes, in the steamer San Jacinto, has boarded a British colonial steamer and taken from her deck two insurgents who were proceeding to Europe on an errand of treason against their own country. This is a new incident, unknown to and unforeseen, at least in its circumstances, by Lord Palmerston. It is to be met and disposed of by the two Governments, if possible, in the spirit to which I have adverted. Lord Lyons has prudently refrained from opening the subject to me, as, I presume, waiting instructions from home. We have done nothing on the subject to anticipate the discussion, and we have not furnished you with any explanations. We adhere to that course now, because we think it more prudent that the ground taken by the British Government should be first made known to us here, and that the discussion, if there must be one, shall be had here. It is proper, however, that you should know one fact in the case, without indicating that we attach much importance to it, namely, that, in the capture of Messrs. Mason and Slidell on board a British vessel, Captain Wilkes having acted without any instructions from the Government, the subject is therefore free from the embarrassment which might have resulted if the act had been specially directed by us.

I trust that the British Government will consider the subject in a friendly temper, and it may expect the best disposition on the part of this Government.

EARL RUSSELL TO LORD LYONS.

NOVEMBER 30, 1861.

MY LORD: Intelligence of a very grave nature has reached her Majesty's Government.

This intelligence was conveyed officially to the knowledge of the Admiralty by Commander Williams, agent for mails on board the contract steamer Trent.

It appears from the letter of Commander Williams, dated "Royal Mail Contract Packet Trent, at sea, November 9," that the Trent left Havana on the 7th instant, with her Majesty's mails for England, having on board numerous passengers. Commander Williams states that shortly after noon, on the 8th, a steamer having the appearance of a man-of-war, but not showing colors, was observed ahead. On nearing her, at 1.15 p. m., she fired a round shot from her pivot-gun across the bows of the Trent and showed American colors. While the Trent was approaching her slowly, the American vessel discharged a shell across the bows of the Trent, exploding half a cable's length ahead of her. The Trent then stopped, and an officer with a large armed guard of marines boarded her. The officer demanded a list of the passengers; and, compliance with this demand being refused, the officer said he had orders to arrest Messrs. Mason, Slidell, McFarland, and Eustis, and that he had sure information of their being passengers in the Trent. While some parley was going on upon this matter, Mr. Slidell stepped forward and told the American officer that the four persons he had named were then standing before him. The commander of the Trent and Commander Williams protested against the act of taking by force out of the Trent these four passengers, then under the protection of the British flag. But the San Jacinto was at that time only two hundred yards from the Trent, her ship's company at quarters, her ports open, and tompions out. Resistance was therefore out of the question, and the four gentlemen before named were forcibly taken out of the ship. A further demand was made that the commander of the Trent should proceed on board the San Jacinto, but he said he would not go unless forcibly compelled likewise, and this demand was not insisted upon.

It thus appears that certain individuals have been forcibly taken from on board a British vessel, the ship of a neutral Power, while such vessel was pursuing a lawful and innocent voyage—an act of violence which was an affront to the British flag and a violation of international law.

Her Majesty's Government, bearing in mind the friendly relations which have long subsisted between Great Britain and the United States, are willing to believe that the United States naval officer who committed the aggression was not acting in compliance with any authority from his Government, or that if he conceived himself to be so authorized he greatly misunderstood the instructions which he had received. For the Government of the United States must be fully aware that the British Government could not allow such an affront to the national honor to pass without full reparation, and her Majesty's Government are unwilling to believe that it could be the deliberate intention of the Government of the United States unnecessarily to force into discussion between the two Governments a question of so grave a character, and with regard to which the whole British nation would be sure to entertain such unanimity of feeling.

Her Majesty's Government, therefore, trust that when this matter shall have been brought under the consideration of the Government of the United States that Government will, of its own accord, offer to the British Government such redress as alone could satisfy the British nation, namely, the liberation of the four gentlemen and their delivery to your lordship, in order that they may again be placed under British protection, and a suitable apology for the aggression which has been committed.

Should these terms not be offered by Mr. Seward, you will propose them to him.

You are at liberty to read this dispatch to the Secretary of State, and, if he shall desire it, you will give him a copy of it.

SECRETARY SEWARD TO LORD LYONS.

DECEMBER 26, 1861.

MY LORD: Earl Russell's despatch of November the 30th, a copy of which you have left with me at my request, is of the following effect, namely:

That a letter of Commander Williams, dated Royal Mail Contract Packetboat Trent, at sea, November 9th, states that that vessel left Havana on the 7th of November, with her Majesty's mails for England, having on board numerous passengers. Shortly after noon, on the 8th of November, the United States war steamer San Jacinto, Capt. Wilkes, not showing colors, was observed ahead. That steamer, on being neared by the Trent, at one o'clock fifteen minutes in the afternoon, fired a round shot from a pivot-gun across her bows, and showed American colors. While the Trent was approaching slowly towards the San Jacinto, she discharged a shell across the Trent's bows, which exploded at half a cable's length before her. The Trent then stopped, and an officer with a large armed guard of marines boarded her. The officer said he had orders to arrest Messrs. Mason, Slidell, McFarland, and Eustis, and had sure information that they were passengers in the Trent. While some parley was going on upon this matter, Mr. Slidell stepped forward and said to the American officer that the four persons he had named were standing before him. The commander of the Trent and Commander Williams protested against the act of taking those four passengers out of the Trent, they then being under the protection of the British flag. But the San Jacinto was at this time only two hundred yards distant, her ship's company at quarters, her ports open and tompions out, and so resistance was out of the question. The four persons before named were then forcibly taken out of the ship. A further demand was made that the commander of the Trent should proceed on board the San Jacinto, but he said he would not go unless forcibly compelled likewise, and this demand was not insisted upon.

Upon this statement Earl Russell remarks that it thus appears that certain individuals have been forcibly taken from on board a British vessel, the ship of a neutral power, while that vessel was pursuing a lawful and innocent voyage—an act of violence which was an affront to the British flag and a violation of international law.

Earl Russell next says that her Majesty's Government, bearing in mind the friendly relations which have long subsisted between Great Britian and the United States, are willing to believe that the naval officer who committed this aggression was not acting in compliance with any authority from his Government, or that, if he conceived himself to be so authorized, he greatly misunderstood the instructions which he had received.

Earl Russell argues that the United States must be fully aware that the British Government could not allow such an affront to the national honor to pass without full reparation, and they are willing to believe that it could not be the deliberate intention of the Government of the United States unnecessarily to force into discussion between the two Governments a question of so grave a character, and with regard to which the whole British nation would be sure to entertain such unanimity of feeling.

Earl Russell, resting upon the statement and the argument which I have thus recited, closes with saying that her Majesty's government trust that when this matter shall have been brought under the consideration of the Government of the United States, it will, of its own accord, offer to the British Government such redress as alone could satisfy the British nation, namely, the liberation of the four prisoners taken from the Trent, and their delivery to your lordship, in order that they may again be placed under British protection, and a suitable apology for the aggression which has been committed. Earl Russell finally instructs you to propose those terms to me, if I should not first offer them on the part of the Government.

This despatch has been submitted to the President.

The British government has rightly conjectured, what it is now my duty to state, that Captain Wilkes, in conceiving and executing the proceeding in question, acted upon his own suggestions of duty, without any direction or instruction, or even foreknowledge of it, on the part of this Government. No directions had been given to him, or any other naval officer, to arrest the four persons named, or any of them, on the Trent or any other British vessel, or on any other neutral vessel, at the place where it occurred or elsewhere. The British government will justly infer from these facts that the United States not only have had no purpose, but even no thought, of forcing into discussion the question which has arisen, or any other which could affect in any way the sensibilities of the British nation.

It is true that a round shot was fired by the San Jacinto from her pivot-gun when the Trent was distantly approaching. But, as the facts have been reported to this government, the shot was nevertheless intentionally fired in a direction so obviously divergent from the course of the Trent as to be quite as harmless as a blank shot, while it should be regarded as a signal.

So also we learn that the Trent was not approaching the San Jacinto slowly when the shell was fired across her bows, but, on the contrary, the Trent was, or seemed to be, moving under a full head of steam, as if with a purpose to pass the San Jacinto.

We are informed also that the boarding officer, (Lieutenant Fairfax,) did not board the Trent with a large armed guard, but he left his marines in his boat when he entered the Trent. He stated his instructions from Captain Wilkes to search for the four persons named, in a respectful and courteous, though decided manner, and he asked the captain of the Trent to show his passenger list, which was refused. The lieutenant, as we are informed, did not employ absolute force in transferring the passengers, but he used just so much as was necessary to satisfy the parties concerned that refusal or resistance would be unavailing.

So, also, we are informed that the captain of the Trent was not at any time or in any way required to go on board the San Jacinto.

These modifications of the case, as presented by Commander Williams, are based upon our official reports.

I have now to remind your lordship of some facts which doubtlessly were omitted by Earl Russell, with the very proper and becoming motive of allowing them to be brought into the case, on the part of the United States, in the way most satisfactory to this Government. These facts are, that at the time the transaction occurred an insurrection was existing in the United States which this Government was engaged in suppressing by the employment of land and naval forces; that in regard to this domestic strife the United States considered Great Britain as a friendly power, while she had assumed for herself the attitude of a neutral; and that Spain was considered in the same light, and had assumed the same attitude as Great Britain.

It had been settled by correspondence that the United States and Great Britain mutually recognized as applicable to this local strife these two articles of the declaration made by the Congress of Paris in 1856, namely, that the neutral or friendly flag should cover enemy's goods not contraband of war, and that neutral goods not contraband of war are not liable to capture under an enemy's flag. These exceptions of contraband from favor were a negative acceptance by the parties of the rule hitherto everywhere recognized as a part of the law of nations, that whatever is contraband is liable to capture and confiscation in all cases.

James M. Mason and E. J. McFarland are citizens of the United States and residents of Virginia. John Slidell and George Eustis are citizens of the United States and residents of Louisiana. It was well known at Havana when these parties embarked in the Trent that James M. Mason was proceeding to England in the affected character of a minister plenipotentiary to the Court of St. James, under a pretended commission from Jefferson Davis, who had assumed to be president of the insurrectionary party in the United States, and E. J. McFarland was going with him in a like unreal character of secretary of legation to the pretended mission. John Slidell, in similar circumstances, was going to Paris as a pretended minister to the Emperor of the French, and George Eustis was the chosen secretary of legation for that simulated mission. The fact that these persons had assumed such characters has been since avowed by the same Jefferson Davis in a pretended message to an unlawful and insurrectionary Congress. It was, we think, rightly presumed that these ministers bore pretended credentials and instructions, and such papers are in the law known as despatches. We are informed by our consul at Paris that these despatches, having escaped the search of the Trent, were actually conveyed and delivered to emissaries of the insurrection in England. Although it is not essential, yet it is proper to state, as I do also upon information and belief, that the owner and agent, and all the officers of the Trent, including Commander Williams, had knowledge of the assumed characters and purposes of the persons before named when they embarked on that vessel.

Your lordship will now perceive that the case before us, instead of presenting a merely flagrant act of violence on the part of Captain Wilkes, as might well be inferred from the incomplete statement of it that went up to the British government, was undertaken as a simple legal and customary belligerent proceeding by Captain Wilkes to arrest and capture a neutral vessel engaged in carrying contraband of war for the use and benefit of the insurgents.

The question before us is, whether this proceeding was authorized by and conducted according to the law of nations. It involves the following inquiries:

1st. Were the persons named and their supposed despatches contraband of war?

2d. Might Captain Wilkes lawfully stop and search the Trent for these contraband persons and despatches?

3d. Did he exercise that right in a lawful and proper manner?

4th. Having found the contraband persons on board and in presumed possession of the contraband dispatches, had he a right to capture the persons?

5th. Did he exercise that right of capture in the manner allowed and recognized by the laws of nations?

If all these inquires shall be resolved in the affirmative the British government will have no claim for reparation.

I address myself to the first inquiry, namely, were the four persons mentioned, and their supposed despatches, contraband?

Maritime law so generally deals, as its professors say, *in rem*, that is with property, and so seldom with persons, that it seems a straining of the term contraband to apply it to them. But persons, as well as property, may become contraband, since the word means broadly "contrary to proclamation, prohibited, illegal, unlawful."

All writers and judges pronounce naval or military persons in the service of the enemy contraband. Vattel says war allows us to cut off from an enemy all his resources, and to hinder him from sending ministers to solicit assistance. And Sir William Scott says you may stop the ambassador of your enemy on his passage. Despatches are not less clearly contraband, and the bearers or couriers who undertake to carry them fall under the same condemnation.

A subtlety might be raised whether pretended ministers of a usurping power, not recognized as legal by either the belligerent or the neutral, could be held to be contraband. But it would disappear on being subjected to what is the true test in all cases—namely, the spirit of the law. Sir

William Scott, speaking of civil magistrates who are arrested and detained as contraband, says:

"It appears to me on principle to be but reasonable that when it is of sufficient importance to the enemy that such persons shall be sent out on the public service at the public expense, it should afford equal ground of forfeiture against the vessel that may be let out for a purpose so intimately connected with the hostile operations."

I trust that I have shown that the four persons who were taken from the Trent by Captain Wilkes, and their despatches, were contraband of war.

The second inquiry is, whether Captain Wilkes had a right by the law of nations to detain and search the Trent.

The Trent, though she carried mails, was a contract or merchant vessel—a common carrier for hire. Maritime law knows only three classes of vessels—vessels of war, revenue vessels, and merchant vessels. The Trent falls within the latter class. Whatever disputes have existed concerning a right of visitation or search in time of peace, none, it is supposed, has existed in modern times about the right of a belligerent in time of war to capture contraband in neutral and even friendly merchant vessels, and of the right of visitation and search, in order to determine whether they are neutral, and are documented as such according to the law of nations.

I assume in the present case what, as I read British authorities, is regarded by Great Britain herself as true maritime law: That the circumstances that the Trent was proceeding from a neutral port to another neutral port does not modify the right of the belligerent captor.

The third question is whether Captain Wilkes exercised the right of search in a lawful and proper manner.

If any doubt hung over this point, as the case was presented in the statement of it adopted by the British Government, I think it must have already passed away before the modifications of that statement which I have already submitted.

I proceed to the fourth inquiry, namely: Having found the suspected contraband of war on board the Trent, had Captain Wilkes a right to capture the same?

Such a capture is the chief, if not the only recognized, object of the permitted visitation and search. The principle of the law is, that the belligerent exposed to danger may prevent the contraband persons or things from applying themselves or being applied to the hostile uses or purposes designed. The law is so very liberal in this respect that when contraband is found on board a neutral vessel not only is the contraband forfeited, but the vessel which is the vehicle of its passage or transportation, being tainted, also becomes contraband, and is subjected to capture and confiscation.

Only the fifth question remains, namely: Did Captain Wilkes exercise the right of capturing the contraband in conformity with the law of nations?

It is just here that the difficulties of the case begin. What is the manner which the law of nations prescribes for disposing of the contraband when you have found and seized it on board of the neutral vessel? The answer would be easily found if the question were what you shall do with the contraband vessel. You must take or send her into a convenient port, and subject her to a judicial prosecution there in admiralty, which will try and decide the questions of belligerency, neutrality, contraband, and capture. So, again, you would promptly find the same answer if the question were, What is the manner of proceeding prescribed by the law of nations in regard to the contraband, if it be property or things of material or pecuniary value?

But the question here concerns the mode of procedure in regard, not to the vessel that was carrying the contraband, nor yet to contraband things which worked the forfeiture of the vessel, but to contraband persons.

The books of law are dumb. Yet the question is as important as it is difficult. First, the belligerent captor has a right to prevent the contraband officer, soldier, sailor, minister, messenger, or courier from proceeding in his unlawful voyage and reaching the destined scene of his injurious service. But, on the other hand, the person captured may be innocent—that is, he may not be contraband. He, therefore, has a right to a fair trial of the accusation against him. The neutral State that has taken him under its flag is bound to protect him if he is not contraband, and is therefore entitled to be satisfied upon that important question. The faith of that State is pledged to his safety, if innocent, as its justice is pledged for his surrender if he is really contraband. Here are conflicting claims, involving personal liberty, life, honor, and duty. Here are conflicting national claims, involving welfare, safety, honor, and empire. They require a tribunal and a trial. The captors and the captured are equals; the neutral and the belligerent State are equals.

While the law authorities were found silent, it was suggested at an early day by this Government that you should take the captured persons into a convenient port, and institute judicial proceedings there to try the controversy. But only courts of admiralty have jurisdiction in maritime cases, and these courts have formulas to try only claims to contraband chattels, but none to try claims concerning contraband persons. The courts can entertain no proceedings and render no judgment in favor of or against the alleged contraband men.

It was replied all this was true; but you can reach in those courts a decision which will have the moral weight of a judicial one by a circuitous proceeding. Convey the suspected men, together with the suspected vessel, into port, and try there the question whether the vessel is contraband. You can prove it to be so by proving the suspected men to be contraband, and the court must then determine the vessel to be contraband. If the men are not contraband the vessel will escape condemnation. Still, there is no judgment for or against the captured persons. But it was assumed that there would result from the determination of the court concerning the vessel a legal certainty concerning the character of the men.

This course of proceeding seemed open to many objections. It elevates the incidental inferior private interest into the proper place of the main paramount public one, and possibly it may make the fortunes, the safety, or the existence of a nation depend on the accidents of a merely personal and pecuniary litigation. Moreover, when the judgment of the prize court upon the lawfulness of the capture of the vessel is rendered, it really concludes nothing, and binds neither the belligerent State nor the neutral upon the great question of the disposition to be made of the captured contraband persons. That question is still to be really determined, if at all, by diplomatic arrangement or by war.

One may well express his surprise when told that the law of nations has furnished no more reasonable, practical, and perfect mode than this of determining questions of such grave import between sovereign powers. The regret we may feel on the occasion is nevertheless modified by the reflection that the difficulty is not altogether anomalous. Similar and equal deficiencies are found in every system of municipal law, especially in the system which exists in the greater portions of Great Britain and the United States. The title to personal property can hardly ever be resolved by a court without resorting to the fiction that the claimant has lost and the possessor has found it, and the title to real estate is disputed by real litigants under the names of imaginary persons. It must be confessed, however, that while all aggrieved nations demand, and all impartial ones concede, the need of some form of judicial process in determining the characters of contraband persons, no other form than the illogical and circuitous one thus described exists, nor has any other yet been suggested. Practically, therefore, the choice is between that judicial remedy or no judicial remedy whatever.

If there be no judicial remedy, the result is that the question must be determined by the captor himself, on the deck of the prize vessel. Very grave objections arise against such a course. The captor is armed, the neutral is unarmed. The captor is interested, prejudiced, and perhaps violent; the neutral, if truly neutral, is disinterested, subdued, and helpless. The tribunal is irresponsible, while its judgment is carried into instant execution. The captured party is compelled to submit, though bound by no legal, moral, or treaty obligation to acquiesce. Reparation is distant and problematical, and depends at last on the justice, magnanimity, or weakness of the State in whose behalf and by whose authority the capture was made. Out of these disputes reprisals and wars necessarily arise, and these are so frequent and destructive that it may well be doubted whether this form of remedy is not a greater social evil than all that could follow if the belligerent right of search were universally renounced and abolished forever. But carry the case one step further. What if the State that has made the capture unreasonably refuse to hear the complaint of the neutral or to redress it? In that case, the very act of capture would be an act of war—of war begun without notice, and possibly entirely without provocation.

I think all unprejudiced minds will agree that, imperfect as the existing judicial remedy may be supposed to be, it would be, as a general practice, better to follow it than to adopt the summary one of leaving the decision with the captor, and relying upon diplomatic debates to review his decision. Practically, it is a question of choice between law, with its imperfections and delays, and war, with its evils and desolations. Nor is it ever to be forgotten that neutrality, honestly and justly preserved, is always the harbinger of peace, and therefore is the common interest of nations, which is only saying that it is the interest of humanity itself.

At the same time it is not to be denied that it may sometimes happen that the judicial remedy will become impossible, as by the shipwreck of the prize vessel, or other circumstances which excuse the captor from sending or taking her into port for confiscation. In such a case the right of the captor to the custody of the captured persons, and to dispose of them, if they are really contraband, so as to defeat their unlawful purposes, cannot reasonably be denied. What rule shall be applied in such a case? Clearly, the captor ought to be required to show that the failure of the judicial remedy results from circumstances beyond his control, and without his fault. Otherwise, he would be allowed to derive advantage from a wrongful act of his own.

In the present case, Captain Wilkes, after capturing the contraband persons and making prize of the Trent in what seems to be a perfectly lawful manner, instead of sending her into port, released her from the capture, and permitted her to proceed with her whole cargo upon her voyage. He thus effectually prevented the judicial examination which might otherwise have occurred.

If, now, the capture of the contraband persons and the capture of the contraband vessel are to be regarded, not as two separate or distinct transactions under the law of nations, but as one transaction, one capture only, then it follows that the capture in this case was left unfinished, or was abandoned. Whether the United States have a right to retain the chief public benefits of it, namely, the custody of the captured persons on proving them to be contraband, will depend upon the preliminary question whether the leaving of the transaction unfinished was necessary, or whether it was unnecessary, and therefore voluntary. If it was necessary, Great Britain, as we suppose, must, of course, waive the defect, and the consequent failure of the judicial remedy. On the other hand, it is not seen how the United States can insist upon her waiver of that judicial remedy, if the defect of the capture resulted from an act of Captain Wilkes, which would be a fault on their own side.

Captain Wilkes has presented to this Government his reasons for releasing the Trent. "I forebore to seize her," he says, "in consequence of my being so reduced in officers and crew, and the derangement it would cause innocent persons, there being a large number of passengers who would have been put to great loss and inconvenience, as well as disappointment, from the interruption it would have caused them in not being able to join the steamer from St. Thomas to Europe. I therefore concluded to sacrifice the interest of my officers and crew in the prize, and suffered her to proceed after the detention necessary to effect the transfer of those commissioners, considering I had obtained the important end I had in view, and which affected the interest of our country and interrupted the action of that of the confederates."

I shall consider, first, how these reasons ought to affect the action of this Government; and secondly, how they ought to be expected to affect the action of Great Britain.

The reasons are satisfactory to this Government, so far as Captain Wilkes is concerned. It could not desire that the San Jacinto, her officers and crew, should be exposed to danger and loss by weakening their number to detach a prize crew to go on board the Trent. Still less could it disavow the humane motive of preventing inconveniences, losses, and perhaps disasters, to the several hundred innocent passengers found on board the prize vessel. Nor could this Government perceive any ground for questioning the fact that these reasons, though apparently incongruous, did operate in the mind of Captain Wilkes and determine him to release the Trent. Human actions generally proceed upon mingled, and sometimes conflicting motives. He measured the sacrifices which this decision would cost. It manifestly, however, did not occur to him that beyond the sacrifice of the private interests (as he calls them) of his officers and crew, there might also possibly be a sacrifice even of the chief and public object of his capture, namely, the right of his Government to the custody and disposition of the captured persons. This Government cannot censure him for this oversight. It confessess that the whole subject came unforeseen upon the Government, as doubtless it did upon him. Its present convictions on the point in question are the result of deliberate examination and deduction now made, and not of any impressions previously formed.

Nevertheless, the question now is, not whether Captain Wilkes is justified to his Government in what he did, but what is the present view of the Government as to the effect of what he has done. Assuming now, for argument's sake only, that the release of the Trent, if voluntary, involved a waiver of the claim of the Government to hold the captured persons, the United States could in that case have no hesitation in saying that the act which has thus already been approved by the Government must be allowed to draw its legal consequence after it. It is of the very nature of a gift or a charity that the giver cannot, after the exercise of his benevolence is past, recall or modify its benefits.

We are thus brought directly to the question whether we are entitled to regard the release of the Trent as involuntary, or whether we are obliged to consider that it was voluntary. Clearly the release would have been involuntary had it been made solely upon the first ground assigned for it by Captain Wilkes, namely, a want of a sufficient force to send the prize vessel into port for adjudication. It is not the duty of a captor to hazard his own vessel in order to secure a judicial examination to the captured party. No large prize crew, however is legally necessary, for it is the duty of the captured party to acquiesce, and go willingly before the tribunal to whose jurisdiction it appeals. If the captured party indicate purposes to employ means of resistance which the captor cannot with probable safety to himself overcome, he may properly leave the vessel to go forward; and neither she nor the State she represents can ever afterwards justly object that the captor deprived her of the judicial remedy to which she was entitled.

But the second reason assigned by Captain Wilkes for releasing the Trent differs from the first. At best, therefore, it must be held that Captain Wilkes, as he explains himself, acted from combined sentiments of prudence and generosity, and so that the release of the prize vessel was not strictly necessary or involuntary.

Secondly. How ought we to expect these explanations by Captain Wilkes of his reasons for leaving the capture incomplete to affect the action of the British government?

The observation upon this point which first occurs is, that Captain Wilkes's explanations were not made to the authorities of the captured vessel. If made known to them, they might have approved and taken the release upon the condition of waiving a judicial investigation of the whole transaction, or they might have refused to accept the release upon that condition.

But the case is one not with them, but with the British government. If we claim that Great Britain ought not to insist that a judicial trial has been lost because we voluntarily released the offending vessel out of consideration for her innocent passengers, I do not see how she is to be bound to acquiesce in the decision which was thus made by us without necessity on our part, and without knowledge of conditions or consent on her own. The question between Great Britain and ourselves thus stated would be a question not of right and of law, but of favor to be conceded by her to us in return for favors shown by us to her, of the value of which favors on both sides we ourselves shall be the judge. Of course the United States could have no thought of raising such a question in any case.

I trust that I have shown to the satisfaction of the British Government, by a very simple and natural statement of the facts, and analysis of the law applicable to them, that this Government has neither meditated, nor practiced, nor approved any deliberate wrong in the transaction to which they have called its attention; and, on the contrary, that what has happened has been simply an inadvertency, consisting in a departure, by the naval officer, free from any wrongful motive, from a rule uncertainly established, and probably by the several parties concerned either imperfectly understood or entirely unknown. For this error the British Government has a right to expect the same reparation that we, as an independent State, should expect from Great Britain or from any other friendly nation in a similar case.

I have not been unaware that, in examining this question, I have fallen into an argument for what seems to be the British side of it against my own country. But I am relieved from all embarrassment on that subject. I had hardly fallen into that line of argument when I discovered that I was really defending and maintaining, not an exclusively British interest, but an old, honored, and cherished American cause, not upon British authorities, but upon principles that constitute a large portion of the distinctive policy by which the United States have developed the resources of a continent, and thus becoming a considerable maritime power, have won the respect and confidence of many nations. These principles were laid down for us in 1804, by James Madison, when Secretary of State, in the administration of Thomas Jefferson, in instructions given to James Monroe, our Minister to England. Although the case before him concerned a description of persons different from those who are incidentally the subjects of the present discussion, the ground he assumed then was the same I now occupy, and the arguments by which he sustained himself upon it have been an inspiration to me in preparing this reply.

"Whenever," he says, "property found in a neutral vessel is supposed to be liable on any ground to capture and condemnation, the rule in all cases is, that the question shall not be decided by the captor, but be carried before a legal tribunal, where a regular trial may be had, and where the captor himself is liable to damages for an abuse of his power. Can it be reasonable, then, or just, that a belligerent commander who is thus restricted, and thus responsible in a case of mere property of trivial amount, should be permitted, without recurring to any tribunal whatever, to examine the crew of a neutral vessel, to decide the important question of their respective allegiances, and to carry that decision into execution by forcing every individual he may choose into a service abhorrent to his feelings, cutting him off from his most tender connexions, exposing his mind and his person to the most humiliating discipline, and his life itself to the greatest danger. Reason, justice, and humanity unite in protesting against so extravagant a proceeding."

If I decide this case in favor of my own Government, I must disavow its most cherished principles, and reverse and forever abandon its essential policy. The country cannot afford the sacrifice. If I maintain those principles, and adhere to that policy, I must surrender the case itself. It will be seen, therefore, that this Government could not deny the justice of the claim presented to us in this respect upon its merits. We are asked to do the British nation just what we have always insisted all nations ought to do to us.

The claim of the British government is not made in a discourteous manner. This Government, since its first organization, has never used more guarded language in a similar case.

In coming to my conclusion I have not forgotten that, if the safety of this Union required the detention of the captured persons, it would be the right and duty of this Government to detain them. But the effectual check and waning proportions of the existing insurrection, as well as the comparative unimportance of the captured persons themselves, when dispassionately weighed, happily forbid me from resorting to that defence.

Nor am I unaware that American citizens are not in any case to be unnecessarily surrendered for any purpose into the keeping of a foreign State. Only the captured persons, however, or others who are interested in them, could justly raise a question on that ground.

Nor have I been tempted at all by the suggestions that cases might be found in history where Great Britian refused to yield to other nations, and even to ourselves, claims like that which is now before us. Those cases occurred when Great Britain, as well as the United States, was the home of generations, which, with all their peculiar interests and passions, have passed away. She could in no other way so effectually disavow any such injury as we think she does by assuming now as her own the ground upon which we then stood. It would tell little for our own claims to the character of a just and magnanimous people if we should so far consent to be guided by the law of retaliation as to lift up buried injuries from their graves to oppose against what national consistency and the national conscience compel us to regard as a claim intrinsically right.

Putting behind me all suggestions of this kind, I prefer to express my satisfaction that, by the adjustment of the present case upon principles confessedly American, and yet, as I trust, mutually satisfactory to both of the nations concerned, a question is finally and rightly settled between them, which, heretofore exhausting not only all forms of peaceful discussion, but also the arbitrament of war itself, for more than a half a century alienated the two countries from each other, and perplexed with fears and apprehensions all other nations.

The four persons in question are now held in military custody at Fort Warren, in the State of Massachusetts. They will be cheerfully liberated. Your lordship will please indicate a time and place for receiving them.

EARL RUSSELL TO LORD LYONS.

JANUARY 10, 1862.

MY LORD: In my despatch to you of the 30th of November, after informing you of the circumstances which had occurred in relation to the capture of the four persons taken from on board the Trent, I stated to you that it thus appeared that certain individuals had been forcibly taken from on board a British vessel, the ship of a neutral power, while such vessel was pursuing a lawful and innocent voyage; an act of violence which was an affront to the British flag, and a violation of international law. I concluded by directing you, in case the reparation which her Majesty's government expected to receive should not be offered by Mr. Seward, to propose to that minister to make such redress as alone would satisfy the British nation, namely: first, the liberation of the four gentlemen taken from on board the Trent, and their delivery to your lordship, in order that they might again be placed under British protection; and, secondly, a suitable apology for the aggression which had been committed.

I received yesterday your lordship's despatch of the 27th ultimo, enclosing a note to you from Mr. Seward, which is in substance the answer to my despatch of the 30th of November.

Proceeding at once to the main points in discussion between us, her Majesty's government have carefully examined how far Mr. Seward's note, and the conduct it announces, comply substantially with the two proposals I have recited.

With regard to the first, viz: the liberation of the prisoners with a view to their being again placed under British protection, I find that the note concludes by stating that the prisoners will be cheerfully liberated, and by calling upon your lordship to indicate a time and place for receiving them. No condition of any kind is coupled with the liberation of the prisoners.

With regard to the suitable apology which the British government had a right to expect, I find that the Government of the United States distinctly and unequivocally declares that no directions had been given to Captain Wilkes, or to any other naval officer, to arrest the four persons named or any of them, on the Trent, or on any other British vessel, or on any other neutral vessel, at the place where it occurred or elsewhere.

I find further that the Secretary of State expressly forbears to justify the particular act of which her Majesty's government complained. If the United States Government had alleged that, although Captain Wilkes had no previous instructions for that purpose, he was right in capturing the persons of the four prisoners, and in removing them from the Trent on board his own vessel, to be afterwards carried into a port of the United States, the Government which had thus sanctioned the proceeding of Captain Wilkes would have become responsible for the original violence and insults of the act. But Mr. Seward contents himself with stating that what has happened has been simply an inadvertency, consisting in a departure by a naval officer, free from any wrongful motive, from a rule uncertainly established, and probably by the several parties concerned either imperfectly understood or entirely unknown. The Secretary of State goes on to affirm that for this error the British government has a right to expect the same reparation which the United States as an independent State should expect from Great Britain or from any other friendly nation in a similar case.

Her Majesty's government having carefully taken into their consideration the liberation of the prisoners, the delivery of them into your hands, and the explanations to which I have just referred, have arrived at the conclusion that they constitute the reparation which her Majesty and the British nation has a right to expect.

It gives her Majesty's government great satisfaction to be enabled to arrive at a conclusion favorable to the maintenance of the most friendly relations between the two nations. I need not discuss the modifications in my statement of facts which Mr. Seward says he has derived from the reports of officers of his Government. I cannot conclude, however, without adverting shortly to the discussions which Mr. Seward has raised upon points not prominently brought into question in my despatch of the 30th of November. I there objected, on the part of her Majesty's government, to that which Captain Wilkes had done. Mr. Seward, in his answer, points out what he conceives Captain Wilkes might have done without violating the law of nations.

It is not necessary that I should here discuss in detail the five questions ably argued by the Secretary of State. But it is necessary that I should say that her Majesty's government differ from Mr. Seward in some of the conclusions at which he has arrived; and it may lead to a better understanding between the two nations on several points of international law which may, during the present contest, or at some future time be brought into question, that I should state to you, for communication to the Secretary of State, wherein those differences consist. I hope to do so in a few days.

In the meantime, it will be desirable that the commanders of the United States cruisers should be instructed not to repeat acts for which the British government will have to ask for redress, and which the United States Government cannot undertake to justify.

You will read and give a copy of this despatch to the Secretary of State.

COMMENT OF THE LONDON TIMES.

The London *Times* of January 11, 1863, commenting on the proper reception to be given these visitors, remarked:

So we do sincerely hope that our countrymen will not give these fellows anything in the shape of an ovation. The civility that is due to a foe in distress is all that they can claim. We have returned them good for evil, and, sooth to say, we should be exceedingly sorry that they should ever be in a situation to choose what return they will make for the good we have now done them. They are here for their own interest, in order, if possible, to drag us into their own quarrel, and, but for the unpleasant contingencies of a prison, rather disappointed perhaps that their detention has not provoked a new war. When they stepped on board the Trent they did not trouble themselves with the thought of the mischief they might be doing an unoffending neutral; and if now, by any less perilous device, they could entangle us in the war, no doubt they would be only too happy. We trust there is no chance of their doing this, for, impartial as the British public is in the matter, it certainly has no prejudice in favor of slavery, which, if anything, these gentlemen represent. What they and their secretaries are to do here passes our conjecture. They are personally nothing to us. They must not suppose, because we have gone to the very verge of a great war to rescue them, that therefore they are precious in our eyes. We should have done just as much to rescue two of their own negroes; and, had that been the object of the rescue, the swarthy Pompey and Cæsar would have had just the same right to triumphal arches and municipal addresses as Messrs. Mason and Slidell. So, please, British public, let's have none of these things. Let the commissioners come up quietly to town, and have their say with anybody who may have time to listen to them. For our part, we cannot see how anything they have to tell can turn the scale of British duty and deliberation. There have been so many cases of peoples and nations establishing an actual independence, and compelling the recognition of the world, that all we have to do is what we have done before, up to the very last year. This is now a simple matter of precedent. Our statesmen and lawyers know quite as much on the subject as Messrs. Mason and Slidell, and are in no need of their information or advice.

ACTION OF CONGRESS.
Second Session, Thirty-Seventh Congress.
IN HOUSE.

1861, December 2—Mr. LOVEJOY, by unanimous consent, offered this joint resolution:

That the thanks of Congess are due, and are hereby tendered, to Captain Wilkes of the United States Navy, for his brave, adroit, and patriotic conduct in the arrest and detention of the traitors James M. Mason and John Slidell.

Mr. EDGERTON moved this as a substitute:

That the President of the United States be requested to present to Captain Charles Wilkes a gold medal, with suitable emblems and devices, in testimony of the high sense entertained by Congress of his good conduct in promptly arresting the rebel ambassadors James M. Mason and John Slidell.

Which was agreed to; and the resolution passed.

1862, February 19—The Senate indefinitely postponed it.

1861, December 16—Mr. VALLANDIGHAM offered this resolution:

Whereas the Secretary of the Navy has reported to this House that Captain Charles Wilkes, in command of the San Jacinto, an armed public vessel of the United States, did, on the 8th of November, 1861, on the high seas, intercept the Trent, a British mail steamer, and forcibly remove therefrom James M. Mason and John Slidell—"disloyal citizens, leading conspirators, rebel enemies, and dangerous men"—who, with their suite, were on their way to Europe "to promote the cause of the insurrection," claiming to be ambassadors from the so-called Confederate States; and whereas the Secretary of the Navy has further reported to this House, that "the prompt and decisive action of Captain Wilkes on this occasion merited and received the emphatic approval of the Department," and moreover, in a public letter has thanked Captain Wilkes for the act; and whereas this House, on the first day of the session, did propose to tender the thanks of Congress to Captain Wilkes, for his "brave, adroit, and patriotic conduct in the arrest and detention of the traitors James M. Mason and John Slidell;" and whereas further, on the same day, this House did request the President to confine the said James M. Mason and John Slidell in the cells of convicted felons until certain military officers of the United States, captured and held by the so-called Confederate States, should be treated as prisoners of war: Therefore,

Be it resolved, (as the sense of this House,) That it is the duty of the President to now firmly maintain the stand thus taken, approving and adopting the act of Captain Wilkes, in spite of any menace or demand of the British government; and that this House pledges its full support to him in upholding now the honor and vindicating the courage of the Government and people of the United States against a foreign power.

Which, on motion of Mr. FENTON, was referred to the Committee on Foreign Affairs—yeas 109, nays 16, as follows:

YEAS—Messrs. Aldrich, Alley, Arnold, Babbitt, *Joseph Baily*. Baker, Baxter, Beaman, *Biddle*, Bingham, Francis P. Blair, Jacob B. Blair, Samuel S. Blair, Blake, William G. Brown, Buffinton, Burnham, *Calvert*, Chamberlain, Clark, *Cobb*, Colfax, Roscoe Conkling, *Cooper*, Covode, Davis, Delano, Diven, Duell, *Dunlap*, Dunn, Edwards, Eliot, *English*, Fenton, Fessenden, Franchot, Frank, Gooch, Granger, *Grider*, Gurley, Hale, *Harding*, Harrison, Hickman, Hutchins, Julian, Francis W. Kellogg, William Kellogg, *Knapp*, *Law*, *Lazear*, Leary, *Lehman*, Loomis, Lovejoy, McKnight, McPherson, *Mallory*, Maynard, *Menzies*, Mitchell, Moorhead, Justin S. Morrill, *Noell*, *Odell*, Olin, Patton, *Perry*, T. G. Phelps, Pike, Pomeroy, Porter, Alexander H. Rice, John H. Rice, *Richardson*, Edward H. Rollins, Sargent, Sedgwick, Shanks, *Sheffield*, Shellabarger, Sherman, *Smith*, Spaulding, *William G. Steele*, Stevens, Benjamin F. Thomas, Francis Thomas, Train, Trimble, Trowbridge, Van Horn, Verree, *Wadsworth*, Wall, E. P. Walton, *Ward*, Washburne, Wheeler, Whaley, Albert S. White, *Wickliffe*, Wilson, Windom, *Woodruff*, Worcester, *Wright*—109.

NAYS—Messrs. *Allen*, *George H. Browne*, Frederick A. Conkling, *Cox*, *Cravens*, *Haight*, *Holman*, *Morris*, *Noble*, *Nugen*, *Pendleton*, *Shiel*, *John B. Steele*, *Vallandigham*, Vandever, *Chilton A. White*—16.

Monarchical Intrigues in Central and South America.

1864, March 15—Mr. McDOUGALL offered this resolution, which was adopted:

Resolved, That the President be requested to communicate to the Senate, if not incompatible with the public interest, any correspondence or other information in possession of the Government, relating to any plan or plans now projected or being projected with a view to the establishment of monarchical governments in Central and South America.

March 24—The PRESIDENT transmitted this paper from the Secretary of State, in reply:

The Secretary of State, to whom has been referred the resolution of the Senate of the 15th instant, requesting the President "to communicate to the Senate, if not incompatible with the public interest, any correspondence or other information in possession of the Government relating to any plan or plans now projected, or being projected, with a view to the establishment of monarchical governments in Central and South America," has the honor to report, that surmises and jealousies are constantly arising on the subject to which the resolution refers, which are brought to the notice of the Department by our representatives abroad. But there is no correspondence or other form of information which furnishes any reliable facts showing the existence of "plans" for the accomplishment of the object mentioned.

Any correspondence which might be regarded as embraced in the resolution, besides being very vague, is, in its nature, confidential, and its publication at the present time would be incompatible with the public interest.

Alleged Foreign Enlistments.

1864, June 28—The PRESIDENT transmitted, in reply to a Senate resolution of 24th, these reports:

FROM THE SECRETARY OF STATE.

WASHINGTON, *June* 25, 1864.

The Secretary of State, to whom has been referred the resolution of the Senate of the 24th instant, requesting the President to inform that body "if any authority has been given any one, either in this country or elsewhere, to obtain recruits in Ireland or Canada for our army and navy; and whether any such recruits have been obtained, or whether, to the knowledge of the Government, Irishmen or Canadians have been induced to emigrate to this country in order to be recruited; and if so, what measures, if any, have been adopted in order to arrest such conduct," has the honor, in reply to the inquiries thus submitted, to report, that no authority has been given by the Executive of this Government, or by any executive department, to any one, either in this country or elsewhere, to obtain recruits either in Ireland, or in Canada, or in any foreign country, for either the army or the navy of the United States; and on the contrary, that whenever application for such authority has been made, it has been refused and absolutely withheld.

If any such recruits have been obtained, either in the provinces named in the resolution, or in any foreign country, they have been obtained by persons who are not even citizens of the United States, but subjects or citizens of the country where the recruits were obtained. The persons who obtained such recruits, if any were so obtained, were answerable to the laws of the foreign province or country where their offences were committed, and at the same time they were not within the reach of our own laws and tribunals; and such persons acted without any authority or consent, and even without the knowledge of this Government. This Government has no knowledge that any such recruits have been obtained in the provinces named, or in any foreign country. In two or three instances it has been reported to this department that recruiting agents crossed the Canadian frontier, without authority, with a view to engage recruits or reclaim deserters. The complaints thus made were immediately investigated, the proceedings of such recruiting agents were promptly disavowed and condemned, the recruits or deserters, if any had been brought into the United States, were at once returned, and the offending agents were dismissed from the public service.

In the land and naval forces of the United States there are found not only some Canadians, some Englishmen, and some Irishmen, but also many subjects of continental European powers. All of these persons were voluntary immigrants into the United States. They enlisted after their arrival on our shores, of their own free accord, within our own limits and jurisdiction, and not in any foreign country. The executive government has no knowledge of the nature of the special inducements which led these volunteers to emigrate from their native countries, or of the purposes for which they emigrated. It has, however, neither directly nor indirectly invited their immigration by any offers of employment in the military or naval service. When such persons were found within the United States, exactly the same inducements to military service were open to them which by authority of law were offered at the same time to citizens of the United States.

Having thus answered the inquiries contained in the resolution of the Senate, the Secretary of State might here without impropriety close this report. Nevertheless, the occasion is a proper one for noticing complaints on the subject of recruitment in our army and navy which have recently found utterance in the British House of Lords. The Secretary of State has, therefore, further to report that the Government of the United States has practiced the most scrupulous care in preventing and avoiding in Great Britain, and in all other foreign countries, any violation of international or municipal laws in regard to the enlistment of soldiers and seamen.

Moreover, when the British government, or any other foreign government, has complained of any alleged violation of the rights of its subjects within the United States, this Government has listened to the complaints patiently, investigated them promptly, and where redress was found due, and was practicable, has cheerfully accorded it. This Government, on the other hand, has been obliged to submit, in the ordinary way, grave complaints of the enlistment, equipment, and periodical payment in British ports of seamen and mariners employed in making unauthorized war from such ports against the United States.

It is a notorious fact, manifest to all the world, that a vigorous and continual tide of emigration is flowing from Europe, and especially from portions of the British empire, and from Germany and Sweden, into the United States. This immigration, like the immigration which preceded it, results from the reciprocal conditions of industrial and social life in Europe and America. Of the mass of immigrants who arrive on our shores, far the largest number go immediately into the occupations of peaceful industry. Those, on the contrary, who are susceptible to the attractions of military life, voluntarily enter the national service with a similar class of our own native citizens, upon the same equal inducements, and with the same patriotic motives. There is no law of nations, and no principles of international comity, which requires us to refuse their aid in the cause of the country and of humanity.

This Government does not repudiate or discourage immigration. The Government frankly avows that it encourages immigration from all countries, but only by open, lawful, and honorable agencies and means. However statesmen in other countries may have at the beginning misunderstood the nature and direction of the present civil war, that nature and that direction were not misunderstood by the Government of the United States. It was foreseen here that the seditious attempt to divide the American Union, if not discouraged by other commercial and maritime powers, would not merely produce great commercial and social embarrassment in the United States, but that, if it should be persisted in and protracted, it must seriously disturb the commerce and industry of other nations. Upon this ground, among others, the Government of the United States earnestly remonstrated with foreign States against their award of unusual commercial and belligerent privileges to the insurgents, in derogation of the sovereignty of the United States. When, however, it was fully disclosed that the insurrection aimed at nothing less than to separate fifteen of these States from the rest, and to re-establish them within our own lawful territory as one single independent nation upon the foundation of African slavery, this Government did not hesitate, so far as authorized by law, to draw upon all the resources of the country, and to call into activity all the energies of the American people to prevent so great a crime. It further resolved to devote its best efforts within the limits of international law and the Constitution of the United States, first to bring African slavery to an end throughout the world, and secondly to strengthen the interest of free labor upon the American continent. It recognized and entered into commercial relations with free States founded on African colonization. It refused a market for slaves, and it pursues the slave trader on the high seas, and denies to him an asylum on our own shores. On the contrary, it invites honest and industrious freemen hither from all parts of the world, and gives them free homes and ample fields, while it opens to them virgin mines and busy workshops, with all the privileges of perfect civil and religious liberty. So far as increase of immigration has resulted from the action of the Government during the present civil war, it is due exclusively to what has thus lawfully been done with those two ends of extinguishing slavery and fortifying freedom always in view. Nor has this Government any reason to be disappointed with the results. The country has sustained a very destructive war for the period of three years. Yet it is not here that national resources or credit fails. It is not here that patriots are wanting to defend the country of their birth or their choice, nor is it here that miners, farmers, merchants, artisans, and laborers lack either subsistence or employment, with abundant rewards. The number of slaves is rapidly diminishing, and the number of freemen continues to augment, even during the convulsions of domestic war, more rapidly than ever a free population advanced in any other country, or even in our own.

Respectfully submitted,

WILLIAM H. SEWARD.

The PRESIDENT.

—

FROM THE SECRETARY OF WAR.

WAR DEPARTMENT,
WASHINGTON CITY, *June* 27, 1864.

SIR: In answer to the Senate resolution of inquiry, passed June 24, 1864, and referred by you to this department, I have the honor to reply:

First. That no authority has been given by this department to any one, either in this country or elsewhere, to obtain recruits in Ireland or Canada for the army of the United States.

Second. That no recruits have been obtained in Ireland or in Canada for the army of the United States with my knowledge or consent, and, to the best of my information and belief none have been obtained, nor any effort made to obtain them.

Third. That neither Irishmen nor Canadians have, with my knowledge, approbation, or consent, or with the knowledge, approbation, or consent of any one in this department, been induced to emigrate to this country in order to enlist into the army.

Fourth. That no measures have been adopted by this department to arrest any such conduct, because no information of any such conduct has reached the department, and I do not believe that it has been practiced in any instance.

I will add that no encouragement or inducement whatever has been extended by this department to any person or persons to obtain recruits for the army anywhere beyond the limits of the United States.

I have the honor to be, very respectfully, your obedient servant,

EDWIN M. STANTON,
Secretary of War.

—

FROM THE SECRETARY OF THE NAVY.

NAVY DEPARTMENT, *June* 27, 1864.

SIR: I have the honor to acknowledge the reference to this Department of a resolution passed in the Senate of the United States on the 24th instant, requesting the President of the United States "to inform the Senate if any authority has been given to any one, either in this country or elsewhere, to obtain recruits in Ireland or in Canada for our army or navy; and whether any such recruits have been obtained, or whether, to the knowledge of the Government, Irishmen or Canadians have been induced to emigrate to this country in order to be so recruited; and if so, what measures, if any, have been adopted to arrest such conduct;" and to state, in reply, that no such order as that indicated in the resolution has been given by the Navy Department to any one, either in this country or elsewhere, nor is the Navy Department aware that any such recruits have been obtained, or that inducements have been offered to Irishmen or Canadians to emigrate to this country in order to be so recruited.

On the occasion of a visit of the United States steamer Kearsarge to Queenstown, Ireland, in November last, several Irishmen secreted themselves on board the vessel, were carried off in her, and when discovered were returned to that port and put ashore. This circumstance gave rise to a charge that the Kearsarge had violated the foreign enlistment act of Great Britain. Captain Winslow, commanding the Kearsarge, disavowed having violated this act or any intention of permitting others under his command to do so. Explanations have been made to the British government, and it is presumed the matter has been satisfactorily settled.

I am, sir, with very great respect, your obedient servant,
GIDEON WELLES,
Secretary of the Navy.

Foreign Mediation.

SECRETARY SEWARD'S LETTER TO GOV. HICKS.

DEPARTMENT OF STATE, *April* 22, 1861.

His Excellency THOS. H. HICKS, *Governor of Maryland:*

SIR: I have had the honor to receive your communication this morning, in which you inform me that you have felt it to be your duty to advise the President of the United States to order elsewhere the troops then off Annapolis, and also that no more may be sent through Maryland; and that you have further suggested that Lord Lyons be requested to act as mediator between the contending parties in our country to prevent the effusion of blood. * * *

If eighty years could have obliterated all the other noble sentiments of that age in Maryland, the President would be hopeful, nevertheless, that there is one that would forever remain there and everywhere. That sentiment is that no domestic contention whatever, that may arise among the parties of this Republic, ought in any case to be referred to any foreign arbitrament, least of all to the arbitrament of an European monarchy.

I have the honor to be, with distinguished consideration, your Excellency's most obedient servant.
WILLIAM H. SEWARD.

FRENCH MEDIATION.

During 1862, the French Government proposed to the Russian and English governments to join it in trying to bring about an armistice for six months between "the Federal Government and the Confederates of the South;" which they declined.

Jan. 9, 1863—M. Drouyn de l'Huys, Minister of Foreign Affairs, addressed M. Mercier, the French Minister at Washington, on this subject.

We add a few paragraphs:

SIR: In forming the purpose of assisting, by the proffer of our good offices, to shorten the period of those hostilities which are desolating the American continent, had we not been guided, beyond all, by the friendship which actuates the government of the Emperor in regard to the United States, the little success of our overtures might chill the interests with which we follow the fluctuations of this contest; but the sentiment to which we have yielded is too sincere for indifference to find a place in our thoughts, and that we should cease to be painfully affected, whilst the war continues to rage.

We cannot regard without profound regret this war, worse than civil, comparable to the most terrible distractions of the ancient republics, and whose disasters multiply in proportion to the resources and the valor which each of the belligerent parties develop.

The government of his Majesty have therefore seriously examined the objections which have been made to us. Where we have suggested the idea of a friendly mediation, and we have asked ourselves whether they are truly of a nature to set aside as premature every tentative to a reconciliation, on one part has been opposed to us the repugnance of the United States to admit the intervention of foreign influence in the dispute, on the other, the hope, which the Federal Government has not abandoned, of attaining its solution by force of arms.

Assuredly, sir, recourse to the good offices of one or several neutral powers contains nothing incompatible with the pride so legitimate amidst a great nation, and wars purely international are not those alone which furnish examples of the useful character of mediation.

SECRETARY SEWARD'S LETTER TO MR. DAYTON.

DEPARTMENT OF STATE,
WASHINGTON, *6th Feb.*, 1863.

SIR: The intimation given in your dispatch of January 15th, No. 255, that I might expect a special visit from M Mercier, has been realized. He called on the 3d instant, and gave me a copy of a dispatch which he had just then received from M. Drouyn de l'Huys under the date of the 21st of January. I have taken the President's instructions, and I now proceed to give you his views upon the subject in question.

It has been considered with seriousness resulting from the reflection that the people of France are known to be faultless sharers with the American nation in the misfortunes and calamities of our unhappy civil war; nor do we on this, any more than on other occasions, forget the traditional friendship of the two countries, which we unhesitatingly believe has inspired the counsels that M. Drouyn de l'Huys has imparted.

He says, "the Federal Government does not despair, we know, of giving more active impulse to hostilities;" and again he remarks, "the protraction of the struggle, in a word, has not shaken the confidence (of the Federal Government) in the definite success of its efforts." These passages seem to me to do unintentional injustice to the language, whether confidential or public, in which this Government has constantly spoken on the subject of the war. It certainly has had and avowed only one purpose—a determination to preserve the integrity of the country. So far from admitting any laxity of effort, or betraying any despondency, the Government, has on the contrary, borne itself cheerfully in all vicissitudes with unwavering confidence in an early and complete triumph of the national cause. Now, when we are, in a manner, invited by a friendly power to review the twenty-one months' history of the conflict, we find no occasion to abate that confidence. Through such an alternation of victories and defeats as is the appointed incident of every war, the land and naval forces of the United States have steadily advanced, reclaiming from the insurgents the ports, forts, and posts, which they had treacherously seized before the strife actually began, and even before it was seriously apprehended. So many of the States and districts which the insurgents included in the field of their projected exclusive slaveholding dominions, have already been re-established under the flag of the Union, that they now retain only the States of Georgia, Alabama, and Texas, with half of Virginia, half of North Carolina, two thirds of South Carolina, half of Mississippi, and one third respectively of Arkansas and Louisiana. The national forces hold even this small territory in close blockade and siege.

This Government, if required, does not hesitate to submit its achievements to the test of comparison; and it maintains that in no part of the world, and in no times, ancient or modern, has a nation, when rendered all unready for combat by the enjoyment of eighty years of almost unbroken peace, so quickly awakened at the alarm of sedition, put forth energies so vigorous, and achieved successes so signal and effective, as those which have marked the progress of this contest on the part of the Union.

M. Drouyn de l'Huys, I fear, has taken other light than the correspondence of this Government for his guidance, in ascertaining its temper and firmness. He has probably read of divisions of sentiment among those who hold themselves forth as organs of public opinion here, and has given to them an undue importance. It is to be remembered that this is a nation of thirty millions, civilly divided into forty-one States and Territories, which cover an expanse hardly less than Europe; that the people are a pure democracy, exercising everywhere the utmost freedom of speech and suffrage; that a great crisis necessarily produces vehement as well as profound debate, with sharp collisions of individual, local, and sectional interests, sentiments and ambitions, and that this heat of controversy is increased by the intervention of speculations, interests, prejudices, and passions from every other part of the civilized world. It is, however, through such debates that the agreement of the nation upon any subject is habitually attained, its resolution formed, and its policy established. While there has been much difference of popular opinion and favor concerning the agents who shall carry on the war, the principles on which it shall be waged, and the means with which it shall be prosecuted, M. Drouyn de l'Huys has only to refer to the statute book of Congress and the Executive ordinances, to learn that the national activity has hitherto been, and yet is, as efficient as that of any other nation—whatever its form of government—ever was, under circumstances of equally grave import to its peace, safety and welfare. Not one voice has been raised anywhere, out of the immediate field of the insurrection, in favor of foreign intervention, of mediation, of arbitration, or of compromise, with the relinquishment of one acre of the national domain, or the surrender of even one constitutional franchise. At the same time, it is manifest to the world that our resources are yet abundant, and our credit adequate to the existing emergency.

What M. Drouyn de l'Huys suggests is that this Government shall appoint commissioners to meet, on neutral ground, commissioners of the insurgents. He supposes that in the conferences to be thus held reciprocal complaints could be discussed, and in place of the accusations which the North and the South now mutually cast upon each other, the conferees would be engaged with discussions of the interests which divide them. He assumes, further, that the commissioners would seek, by means of well-ordered and profound deliberation, whether these interests are definitively irreconcilable, whether separation is an extreme that can no longer be avoided, or whether the memories of a common existence, the ties of every kind which have made of the North and the South one whole Federative State, and have borne them on to so high a degree of prosperity, are not more powerful than the causes which have placed arms in the hands of the two populations.

The suggestion is not an extraordinary one, and it may well have been thought by the Emperor of the French, in the earnestness of his benevolent desire for the restoration of peace, a feasible one. But when M. Drouyn de l'Huys shall come to review it in the light in which it must necessarily be examined in this country, I think he can hardly fail to perceive that it amounts to nothing less than a proposition that, while this Government is engaged in suppressing an armed insurrection, with the purpose of maintaining the constitutional national authority, and preserving the integrity of the country, it shall enter into diplomatic discussion with the insurgents upon the questions whether that authority shall not be renounced, and whether the country shall not be delivered over to disunion, to be quickly followed by ever increasing anarchy.

If it were possible for the Government of the United States to compromise the National authority so far as to enter into such debates, is it not easy to perceive what good results could be obtained by them.

The commissioners must agree in recommending either that the Union shall stand, or that it shall be voluntarily dissolved; or else they must leave the vital question unsettled, to abide at last the fortunes of the war. The Government has not shut out knowledge of the present temper, any more than of the past purposes of the insurgents. There is not the least ground to suppose that the controling actors would be persuaded at this moment, by any arguments which national commissioners could offer, to forego the ambition that has impelled them to the disloyal position they are occupying. Any commissioners who should be appointed by these actors, or through their dictation or influence, must enter the conference imbued with the spirit, and pledged to the personal fortunes of the insurgent chiefs. The loyal people in the insurrectionary States would be unheard, and any offer for peace by this Government, on the condition of the maintenance of the Union must necessarily be rejected.

On the other hand, as I have already intimated, this Government has not the least thought of relinquishing the trust which has been confided to it by the nation, under the most solemn of all political sanctions; and if it had any such thought, it would still have abundant reason to know that peace proposed at the cost of dissolution would be immediately, unreservedly, and indignantly rejected by the American people. It is a great mistake that European statesmen make, if they suppose this people are demoralized. Whatever, in the case of an insurrection, the people of France, or of Great Britain, or of Switzerland, or the Netherlands would do to save their national existences, no matter how the strife might be regarded by or affect foreign nations, just so much, and certainly no less, the people of the United States will do, if necessary to save for the common benefit the region which is bounded by the Pacific and Atlantic coasts, and by the shores of the Gulfs of St. Lawrence and Mexico, together with the free and common navigation of the Rio Grande, Missouri, Arkansas, Mississippi, Ohio, St. Lawrence, Hudson, Delaware, Potomac, and other natural highways by which this land, which to them is at once a land of inheritance and a land of promise, is opened and watered. Even if the agents of the American people now exercising their power, should, through fear or faction, fall below this height of the national virtue, they would be speedily, yet constitutionally, replaced by others of sterner character and patriotism.

I must be allowed to say, also, that M. Drouyn de l'Huys errs in his description of the parties to the present conflict. We have here, in a political sense, no North and South, no southern and northern States. We have an insurrectionary party, which is located chiefly upon and adjacent to the shore of the Gulf of Mexico; and we have, on the other hand, a loyal people, who constitute not only northern States, but also eastern, middle, western, and southern States.

I have on many occasions heretofore submitted to the French Government the President's views of the interests and the ideas more effective for the time than even interests which lie at the bottom of the American Government and people to sustain the Federal Union. The President has done the same thing in his messages and other public declarations. I refrain, therefore, from reviewing that argument in connection with the existing question.

M. Drouyn de l'Huys draws to his aid the conferences which took place between the colonies and Great Britain, in our Revolutionary war. He will allow us to assume, that action in the crisis of a nation must accord with its necessities, and therefore can seldom be conformed to precedents. Great Britain, when entering on the negotiations had manifestly come to entertain doubts of her ultimate success; and it is certain that the councils of the colonies could not fail to take new courage, if not to gain other advantage, when the parent State compromised so far as to treat of peace on the terms of conceding their independence.

It is true, indeed, that peace must come at some time, and that conferences must attend, if they are not allowed to precede the pacification. There is, however, a better form for such conferences than the one which M. Drouyn de l'Huys suggests. The latter would be palpably in derogation of the Constitution of the United States, and would carry no weight because destitute of the sanction necessary to bind either the disloyal or the loyal portions of the people. On the other hand, the Congress of the United States furnishes a constitutional forum for debates between the alienated parties. Senators and Representatives from the loyal portion of the people are there already, freely empowered to confer; and seats also are vacant, and inviting Senators and Representatives of the discontented party who may be constitutionally sent there from the States involved in the insurrection. Moreover, the conferences which can thus be held in Congress have this great advantage over any that could be organized upon the plan of M. Drouyn de l'Huys, namely: that the Congress, if it were thought wise, could call a national convention to adopt its recommendations, and give them all the solemnity and binding force of organic law. Such conferences between the alienated parties may be said to have already begun. Maryland, Virginia, Kentucky, Tennessee, and Missouri—States which are claimed by the insurgents—are already represented in Congress, and submitting with perfect freedom, and in a proper spirit, their advice upon the course best calculated to bring about, in the shortest time, a firm, lasting, and honorable peace. Representatives have been sent, also, from Louisiana, and others are understood to be coming from Arkansas.

There is a preponderating argument in favor of the congressional form of conference over that which is suggested by M. Drouyn de l'Huys, namely: that while an accession to the latter would bring this Government into a concurrence with the insurgents in disregarding and setting aside an important part of the Constitution of the United States, and so would be of pernicious example, the congressional conference, on the contrary, preserves and gives new strength to that sacred writing which must continue through future ages the sheet anchor of the Republic.

You will be at liberty to read this dispatch to M. Drouyn de l'Huys, and to give him a copy, if he shall desire it.

To the end that you may be informed of the whole case, I transmit a copy of M. Drouyn de l'Huys's dispatch.

I am, sir, your obedient servant,

WILLIAM H. SEWARD.

RESOLUTIONS OF CONGRESS UPON FOREIGN MEDIATION.

Third Session, Thirty-Seventh Congress.

Whereas it appears from the diplomatic correspondence submitted to Congress that a proposition, friendly in form, looking to pacification through foreign mediation, has been made to the United States by the Emperor of the French and promptly declined by the President; and whereas the idea of mediation or intervention in some shape may be regarded by foreign governments as practicable, and such governments, through this misunderstanding, may be led to proceedings tending to embarrass the friendly relations which now exist between them and the United States; and whereas, in order to remove for the future all chance of misunderstanding on this subject, and to secure, for the United States the full enjoyment of that freedom from foreign interference which is one of the highest rights of independent States, it seems fit that Congress should declare its convictions thereon: Therefore,

Resolved, (the House of Representatives concurring,) That while, in times past, the United States have sought and accepted the friendly mediation or arbitration of foreign powers for the pacific adjustment of international questions, where the United States were the party of the one part and some other sovereign power the party of the other part; and while they are not disposed to misconstrue the natural and humane desire of foreign powers to aid in arresting domestic troubles, which, widening in their influence, have afflicted other countries, especially in view of the circumstance, deeply regretted by the American people, that the blow aimed by the rebellion at the national life has fallen heavily upon the laboring population of Europe; yet, notwithstanding these things, Congress cannot hesitate to regard every proposition of foreign interference in the present contest as so far unreasonable and inadmissible that its only explanation will be found in a misunderstanding of the true state of the question, and of the real character of the war in which the Republic is engaged.

2. That the United States are now grappling with an unprovoked and wicked rebellion, which is seeking the destruction of the Republic that it may build a new power, whose corner-stone, according to the confession of its chiefs, shall be slavery; that for the suppression of this rebellion, and thus to save the Republic and to prevent the establishment of such a power, the national Government is now employing armies and fleets in full faith that through these efforts all the purpose of conspirators and rebels will be crushed; that while engaged in this struggle, on which so much depends, any proposition from a foreign power, whatever form it may take, having for its object the arrest of these efforts, is, just in proportion to its influence, an encouragement to the rebellion and to its declared principles, and on this account, is calculated to prolong and imbitter the conflict, to cause increased expenditure of blood and treasure, and to postpone the much desired day of peace; that, with these convictions, and not doubting that every such proposition, although made with good intent, is injurious to the national interests, Congress will be obliged to look upon any further attempt in the same direction as an unfriendly act, which it earnestly deprecates, to the end that nothing may occur abroad to strengthen the rebellion or to weaken those relations of good will with foreign powers which the United States are happy to cultivate.

3. That the rebellion from its beginning, and far back even in the conspiracy which preceded its outbreak, was encouraged by the hope of support from foreign powers; that its chiefs frequently boasted that the people of Europe were so far dependent upon regular supplies of the great southern staple that sooner or later their governments would be constrained to take side with the rebellion in some effective form, even to the extent of forcible intervention, if the milder form did not prevail; that the rebellion is now sustained by this hope, which every proposition of foreign interference quickens anew, and that without this life-giving support it must soon yield to the just and paternal authority of the national Government; that, considering these things, which are aggravated by the motive of the resistance thus encouraged, the United States regret that foreign powers have not frankly told the chiefs of the rebellion that the work in which they are engaged is hateful, and that a new government, such as they seek to found, with slavery as its acknowledged corner-stone, and with no other declared object of separate existence, is so far shocking to civilization and the moral sense of mankind that it must not expect welcome or recognition in the commonwealth of nations.

4. That the United States, confident in the justice of their cause, which is the cause also of good government and of human rights everywhere among men; anxious for the speedy restoration of peace, which shall secure tranquillity at home and remove all occasion of complaint abroad; and awaiting with well-assured trust the final suppression of the rebellion, through which all these things, rescued from present danger, will be secured forever, and the Republic, one and indivisible, triumphant over its enemies, will continue to stand an example to mankind, hereby announce, as their unalterable purpose, that the war will be vigorously prosecuted, according to the humane principles of Christian States, until the rebellion shall be suppressed; and they reverently invoke upon their cause the blessings of Almighty God.

5. That the President be requested to transmit a copy of these resolutions, through the Secretary of State, to the ministers of the United States in foreign countries, that the declaration and protest herein set forth may be communicated by them to the government to which they are accredited.

1863, March 3—The resolutions were passed by the Senate—yeas 31, nays 5, as follows:

YEAS—Messrs. Anthony, Arnold, Chandler, Clark, Collamer, *Davis*, Dixon, Doolittle, Fessenden, Foot, Foster, Grimes, *Harding*, Harlan, Harris, Henderson, Hicks, Howard, Howe, King, Lane of Indiana, Morrill, *Nesmith*, Pomeroy, Sumner, Ten Eyck, Trumbull, Wade, Willey, Wilmot, Wilson of Massachusetts—31.

NAYS—Messrs. *Carlile*, *Latham*, *Powell*, *Saulsbury*, *Wall*—5.

1863, March 3—The above resolutions were considered in the House.

Mr. VALLANDIGHAM moved to lay them on the table; which was negatived—yeas 29, nays 92.

They were then passed—yeas 103, nays 28, as follows:

YEAS—Messrs. Aldrich, Alley, Arnold, Ashley, Babbitt, *Baily*, Baker, Baxter, Bingham, Jacob B. Blair, Samuel S. Blair, Blake, Bridges, William G. Brown, Buffinton, Campbell, Casey, Chamberlain, Clark, Clements, Colfax, Frederick A. Conkling, Roscoe Conkling, Conway, Covode, Cutler, Dawes, Dunn, Edgerton, Eliot, Ely, Fenton, Samuel C. Fessenden, Thomas A. D. Fessenden, Fisher, Flanders, Franchot, Frank, Gooch, Goodwin, Granger, Gurley, *Haight*, Hale, Harrison, Horton, Hutchins, Julian, Kelley, Francis W. Kellogg, William Kellogg, Leary, *Lehman*, Loomis, Low, McIndoe, McKean, McKnight, McPherson, Marston, Maynard, Mitchell, Moorhead, Anson P. Morrill, Justin S. Morrill, Nixon, Olin, Patton, Timothy G. Phelps, Pike, Pomeroy, Porter, Alexander H. Rice, John H. Rice, Edward H. Rollins, Sargent, Sedgwick, Shanks, *Sheffield*, Shellabarger, Sloan, *Smith*, Spaulding, Stevens, Stratton, Benjamin F. Thomas, Francis Thomas, Train, Trimble, Trowbridge, Van Valkenburgh, Van Wyck, Verree, Walker, Wallace, Washburne, Webster, Wheeler, Albert S. White, Wilson, Windom, Worcester, *Wright*—103.

NAYS—Messrs. *William Allen*, *Ancona*, *Calvert*, *Crittenden*, *Dunlap*, *Grider*, *Johnson*, *Kerrigan*, *Knapp*, *Lazear*, *Mallory*, *May*, *Noble*, *Norton*, *Nugen*, *Pendleton*, *Perry*, *Price*, *Robinson*, *Shiel*, *Stiles*, *Vallandigham*, *Voorhees*, *Wadsworth*, *Ward*, *Chilton A. White*, *Wickliffe*, *Yeaman*—28.

LETTER OF LORD LYONS TO EARL RUSSELL RESPECTING MEDIATION.

WASHINGTON, *November* 17, 1862.

In his dispatches of the 17th and of the 24th ultimo, and of the 7th instant, Mr. Stuart reported to your lordship the result of the elections for members of Congress and State officers, which have recently taken place in several of the most important States of the Union. Without repeating the details, it will be sufficient for me to observe that the success of the Democratic, or (as it now styles itself) the Conservative Party, has been so great as to manifest a change in public feeling, among the most rapid and the most complete that has ever been witnessed, even in this country.

On my arrival at New York on the 8th instant I found the Conservative leaders exulting in the crowning success achieved by the party in that State. They appeared to rejoice, above all, in the conviction that personal liberty and freedom of speech had been secured for the principal State of the Union. They believed that the Government must at once desist from exercising in the State of New York the extraordinary (and as they regarded them) illegal and unconstitutional powers which it had assumed. They were confident that at all events after the 1st of January next, on which day the newly elected Governor would come into office, the suspension of the writ of *habeas corpus* could not be practically maintained. They seemed to be persuaded that the result of the elections would be accepted by the President as a declaration of the will of the people; that he would increase the moderate and conservative element in the Cabinet; that he would seek to terminate the war, not to push it to extremity; that he would endeavor to effect a reconciliation with the people of the South, and renounce the idea of subjugating or exterminating them.

On the following morning, however, intelligence arrived from Washington which dashed the rising hopes of the Conservatives. It was announced that General McClellan had been dismissed from the command of the army of the Potomac, and ordered to repair to his home; that he had, in fact, been removed altogether from active service. The general had been regarded as the representative of Conservative principles in the army. Support of him had been made one of the articles of the Conservative electoral programme. His dismissal was taken as a sign that the President had thrown himself entirely into the arms of the extreme radical party, and that the attempt to carry out the policy of that party would be persisted in. The irritation of the Conservatives at New York was certainly very great; it seemed, however, to be not unmixed with consternation and despondency.

Several of the leaders of the Democratic party sought interviews me, both before and after the arrival of the intelligence of General McClellan's dismissal. The subject uppermost in their minds while they were speaking to me, was naturally that of foreign mediation between the North and South. Many of them seemed to think that this mediation must come at last, but they appeared to be very much afraid of its coming too soon. It was evident that they apprehended that a premature proposal of foreign intervention would afford the Radical party a means of reviving the violent war spirit, and of thus defeating the peaceful plans of the Conservatives. They appeared to regard the present moment as peculiarly unfavorable for such an offer, and indeed, to hold that it would be essential to the success of any proposal from abroad that it should be deferred until the control of the Executive Government should be in the hands of the Conservative party.

I gave no opinion on the subject. I did not say whether or no I myself thought foreign intervention probable or advisable, but I listened with attention to the accounts given me of the plans and hopes of the Conservative party. At the bottom I thought I perceived a desire to put an end to the war, even at the risk of losing the southern States altogether; but it was plain that it was not thought prudent to avow this desire. Indeed some hints of it, dropped before the elections, were so ill received that a strong declaration in the contrary sense was deemed necessary by the Democratic leaders.

At the present moment, therefore, the chiefs of the Conservative party call loudly for a more vigorous prosecution of the war, and reproach the Government with slackness as well as with want of success in its military measures. But they repudiate all idea of interfering with the institutions of the southern people, or of waging a war of subjugation or extermination. They maintain that the object of the military operations should be to place the North in a position to demand an armistice with honor and effect. The armistice should (they hold) be followed by a convention, in which such changes of the Constitution should be proposed as would give the South ample security on the subject of its slave property, and would enable the North and the South to reunite and to live together in peace and harmony. The Conservatives profess to think that the South might be induced to take part in such a convention, and that a restoration of the Union would be the result.

The more sagacious members of the party must, however, look upon the proposal of a convention merely as a last experiment to test the possibility of reunion. They are no doubt well aware that the more probable consequence of an armistice would be the establishment of Southern independence, but they perceive that if the South is so utterly alienated that no possible concessions will induce it to return voluntarily to the Union, it is wiser to agree to separation than to prosecute a cruel and hopeless war.

It is with reference to such an armistice as they desire to attain, that the leaders of the Conservative party regard the question of foreign mediation. They think that the offer of mediation, if made to a radical administration, would be rejected; that, if made at an unpropitious moment, it might increase the virulence with which the war is prosecuted. If their own party were in power, or virtually controlled the administration, they would rather, if possible, obtain an armistice without the aid of foreign governments, but they would be disposed to accept an offer of mediation if it appeared to be the only means of putting a stop to hostilities. They would desire that the offer should come from the great powers of Europe conjointly, and in particular that as little prominence as possible should be given to Great Britain.

At Washington I have had fewer opportunities than I had at New York of ascertaining the present views of the chiefs of the political parties. At the interview which I had with Mr. Seward the day after my arrival he showed no disposition to enter upon political matters. He did not appear to expect or to desire to receive from me any special communication from her Majesty's government. The President, when I waited upon him, talked to me only on ordinary topics. I, for my part, gladly shunned all allusion to foreign intervention, my principal object being to avoid saying anything which might embarrass me in carrying out any instructions on the subject which I may receive from your lordship.

All things considered, my own opinion certainly is that the present moment is not a favorable one for making an offer of mediation. It might embarrass the peace party, and even oblige them, in order to maintain their popularity, to make some declaration against it, and this might make it difficult for them to accept a similar offer at a more propitious time. It would in all probability be rejected by the President, who appears to have thrown himself into the arms of the extreme radical party.

The views of that party are clear and definite. They declare that there is no hope of reconciliation with the Southern people; that the war must be pursued, *per fas et nefas*, until the disloyal men of the South are ruined and subjugated, if not exterminated; that not an inch of the old territory of the Republic must be given up; that foreign intervention, in any shape, must be rejected and resented. This party would desire to turn an offer of mediation to account, for the purpose of inflaming the war spirit and producing a reaction against the Conservatives.

Is is probable, too, that the Government would urge, in answer to an offer of mediation, that it has by no means abandoned the hope of putting down the rebellion within a reasonable time; that at all events, this is not a moment at which it can reasonably be called upon to put a stop to hostilities. It would observe that the armies of the United States are everywhere advancing, and that expeditions are prepared against Texas, as well as against Charleston, Mobile, and other points on the coast. It would point out that it had equipped a considerable number of war-vessels, iron-clad as well as others, at a vast expense; that the season had just arrived when the autumn rains would render the rivers navigable by armed vessels, and when the Southern coast would be free from epidemic disease.

It might even represent an advance of the Army of the Potomac to Richmond as a probable event. The experience of the past is certainly not calculated to inspire any great confidence in the results of these warlike preparations, but the political interests of the party now in power render a continuance of the war a necessity to it. Its only chance of regaining its lost popularity lies in successful military operations. Unless it can obtain a much higher place in public estimation than it now occupies, not only will its tenure of power become extremely precarious, but some of its leading members may be called to a severe account for their extra-legal proceedings. During the session of Congress which begins next month, the present Administration has indeed reason to expect an uncompromising support from a majority of both Houses of Congress. But on the 4th of March next, the existing House of Representatives is dissolved by the terms of the Constitution, and at the same time several of the present Senators go out of office. The majority of the members chosen at the recent elections for the new House of Representatives are of the Democratic or Conservative party, and in some States, Senators of that party will be returned in the room of those whose term of office expires next March. The new Congress is likely to be hostile to the Administration and to the Radical party; and although it will not, in the ordinary course of things, assemble until the last month of next year, the President will hardly be able to persist in his present policy and in his assumption of extraordinary powers, unless he can, in virtue of military successes, obtain a reputation with the people which will sustain him in a contest with the Legislature.

It would seem, then, to be vain to make an offer of mediation to the present Government, in their present mood, with any notion that it would be accepted. A change of mood may, however, take place after the 4th of March, if no great military successes occur in the interval. Such a change may possibly be produced sooner by military reverses. A proposal, however, to mediate, made even under the present circumstances, by three or more of the great powers of Europe conjointly might not produce any great inconvenience.

It is, indeed, urged by some people that mediation should be offered, not so much with a view to its being accepted as to its clearing the way for a recognition of the Southern Confederacy. And, indeed, if it were determined that the time had come for recognizing that Confederacy, no doubt an offer of mediation would be a suitable preliminary. But I do not clearly understand what advantage is expected to result from a simple recognition of the southern government; and I presume that the European powers do not contemplate breaking up the blockade by force of arms, or engaging in hostilities with the United States in support of the independence of the South.

I have, indeed, heard it maintained that Great Britain should recognize the independence of the South as soon as possible, with a view to impede the success of the efforts o[f] the conservative party to reconstruct the Union. The advocates of this opinion consider a re-union as a probabl[e] event, and apprehend that the first result of it would be that the combined forces of the North and the South woul[d] be let loose upon Canada. I certainly do not at present share these apprehensions. All hope of the reconstruction of the Union appears to be fading away, even from th[e] minds of those who most ardently desire it. But if the reconstruction be still possible, I do not think we need conclude that it would lead to an invasion of Canada, or to an[y] consequences injurious to Great Britain. At any rate danger[s] of this kind are remote. The immediate and obvious interest of Great Britain, as well as of the rest of Europe, i[s] that peace and prosperity should be restored to this countr[y] as soon as possible. The point chiefly worthy of consider[ation] appears to be whether separation or reunion be th[e] more likely to effect this object.

The French in Mexico.

Third Session, Thirty-Seventh Congress.

IN SENATE.

1863, January 19—Mr. McDougall offere[d] the following concurrent resolutions:

Resolved by the Senate, (the House of Representative[s] concurring,) That the present attempt by the governmen[t] of France to subject the Republic of Mexico to her autho[r]ity by armed force is a violation of the established an[d] known rules of international law, and that it is, moreover, [a] violation of the faith of France, pledged by the treaty ma[de] at London on the 31st day of October, 1861, between th[e] allied governments of Spain, France, and England, commu[]nicated to this Government over the signatures of the r presentatives of the allies by letter of the 30th day of November, 1861, and particularly and repeatedly assured to this Government through its ministers resident at the Court of France.

Resolved further, That the attempt to subject the Republic of Mexico to the French authority is an act not merely unfriendly to this Republic, but to free institutions everywhere, and that it is regarded by this Republic as not only unfriendly, but as hostile.

Resolved further, That it is the duty of this Republic to require of the government of France that her armed forces be withdrawn from the territories of Mexico.

Resolved further, That it is the duty and proper office of this Republic now, and at all times, to lend such aid to the Republic of Mexico as is or may be required to prevent the forcible interposition of any of the States of Europe in the political affairs of that Republic.

Resolved further, That the President of the United States be requested to cause to be communicated to the government of Mexico the views now expressed by the two Houses of Congress, and be further requested to cause to be negotiated such treaty or treaties between the two Republics as will best tend to make these views effective.

1863, February 4—The resolutions were, on motion of Mr. SUMNER, laid on the table—yeas 34, nays 10, as follows:

YEAS—Messrs. Anthony, Arnold, *Carlile*, Chandler, Clark, Collamer, Cowan, *Davis*, Dixon, Doolittle, Fessenden, Foot, Foster, Grimes, Hale, *Harding*, Harlan, Harris, Henderson, Howard, Howe, King, Lane of Indiana, Lane of Kansas, Morrill, Pomeroy, Sherman, Sumner, Ten Eyck, Wade, Wilkinson, Wilmot, Wilson of Massachusetts—34.

NAYS Messrs. *Kennedy*, *Latham*, *McDougall*, *Powell*, *Rice*, *Richardson*, *Saulsbury*, Trumbull, *Turpie*, *Wilson* of Missouri—10.

First Session, Thirty-Eighth Congress.

IN SENATE.

1864, Jan. 11—Mr. McDOUGALL offered this joint resolution, which was referred to the Committee on Foreign Relations:

IN RELATION TO THE OCCUPATION OF MEXICO.

Resolved, &c., That the occupation of a portion of the territory of the Republic of Mexico by the armed forces of the government of France, with the purposes avowed by the government of France, is an act unfriendly to the Republic of the United States of America.

SEC. 2. *And be it further resolved*, That it is the duty of the proper department of this Government to demand of the government of France the withdrawal of her armed forces from the Mexican territory within a reasonable time.

SEC. 3. *And be it further resolved*, That in the event the government of France shall decline or refuse to so withdraw her armed forces, or shall fail to take measures to that effect, on or before the fifteenth day of March next, then it will become the duty of the Congress of the United States of America to declare war against the government of France.

June 14—Mr. McDOUGALL sought to introduce this resolution, but objection was made:

Resolved, That the people of the United States can never regard with indifference the attempt of any foreign power to overthrow by force or to supplant by fraud the institutions of any republican government on the western continent, and that they will view with extreme jealousy, as menacing to the peace and independence of their own country, the efforts of any such power to obtain any footholds for monarchical Governments sustained by foreign military force in near proximity to the United States.

IN HOUSE.

1864, April 4—Mr. H. WINTER DAVIS, from the Committee on Foreign Affairs, reported to the House of Representatives the following joint resolution, which was passed—yeas 109, nays none, as follows:

YEAS—Messrs. *James C. Allen*, *William J. Allen*, Alley, Allison, Ames, *Ancona*, Anderson, Arnold, Ashley, *Baily*, *Augustus C. Baldwin*, John D. Baldwin, Baxter, Beaman, Blaine, Francis P. Blair, jr., *Bliss*, Blow, Boutwell, Boyd, *Brooks*, Broomall, *James S. Brown*, William G. Brown, *Chanler*, Ambrose W. Clark, *Clay*, Cobb, Cole, *Cox*, *Cravens*, Creswell, Henry Winter Davis, Thomas T. Davis, *Dawson*, *Denison*, Dixon, Driggs, Dumont, Eckley, *Eden*, *Eldridge*, Eliot, *English*, Fenton, *Finck*, Frank, *Ganson*, Garfield, Gooch, *Grider*, Grinnell, *Griswold*, Hale, *Harding*, *Harrington*, *Herrick*, Higby, *Holman*, Hooper, Hotchkiss, Asahel W. Hubbard, Jenckes, *Philip Johnson*, Julian, *Kalbfleisch*, Kasson, Kelley, Francis W. Kellogg, Orlando Kellogg, *Kernan*, *King*, *Law*, *Lazear*, *Long*, Longyear, *Mallory*, *Marcy*, Marvin, McBride, McClurg, *McKinney*, *Middleton*, Samuel F. Miller, Moorhead, Morrill, Daniel Morris, *James R. Morris*, *Morrison*, Amos Myers, Leonard Myers, *Nelson*, Norton, *Odell*, Charles O'Neill, *John O'Neill*, Orth, Patterson, *Pendleton*, Perham, Pike, Pomeroy, Price, *Pruyn*, *Samuel J. Randall*, William H. Randall, Alexander H. Rice, John H. Rice, *Rogers*, Edward H. Rollins, *James S. Rollins*, Schenck, Scofield, *Scott*, Shannon, Sloan, Smithers, Spalding, Starr, *John B. Steele*, Stevens, *Strouse*, *Stuart*, *Sweat*, Thayer, Tracy, Upson, Van Valkenburgh, *Voorhees*, *Ward*, Ellihu B. Washburne, William B. Washburn, Webster, Whaley, *Wheeler*, *Chilton A. White*, *Joseph W. White*, Williams, Wilder, Wilson, Windom, *Winfield*, *Benjamin Wood*, Woodbridge, *Yeaman*—109.

NAYS—None.

The resolution is as follows:

Relative to the substitution of monarchial for republican Government in Mexico, under European auspices.

Resolved, &c., That the Congress of the United States are unwilling, by silence, to leave the nations of the world under the impression that they are indifferent spectators of the deplorable events now transpiring in the Republic of Mexico; and they therefore think fit to declare that it does not accord with the policy of the United States to acknowledge a monarchical government, erected on the ruins of any republican government in America, under the auspices of any European power.

IN SENATE.

1864, April 5—The resolution was referred to the Committee on Foreign Relations, and it remained unreported at the close of the session.

April 27—Mr. McDOUGALL offered a resolution that the Committee on Foreign Relations be instructed to report to the Senate the joint resolution printed above.

May 28—Mr. McDOUGALL offered a resolution that the committee be discharged from the subject, both of which went over.

IN HOUSE.

May 23—Mr. H. W. DAVIS offered this resolution, which was agreed to without a division:

Whereas the following announcement appeared in the *Moniteur*, the official journal of the French Government:

"Le gouvernement de l'Empereur a reçu du gouvernement des Etats-Unis des explications satisfaisantes sur le sens et la portée de la résolution prise par l'assemblée des représentans à Washington, au sujet des affairs du Mexico.	"The Emperor's Government has received from that of the United States satisfactory explanations as to the sense and bearing of the resolution come to by the House of Representatives at Washington relative to Mexico.
"On sait, d'ailleurs, que le Sénat avait déjà ajourné indéfinement l'examen de cette résolution, à laquelle, dans tous les cas, le pouvoir exécutif n'eût point accordé sa sanction."—*Moniteur*.	"It is known, besides, that the Senate had indefinitely postponed the examination of that question, to which in any case the executive power would not have given its sanction."

Therefore,

Resolved, That the President be requested to communicate to this House, if not inconsistent with the public interest, any explanations given by the Government of the United States to the Government of France respecting the sense and bearing of the joint resolution relative to Mexico, which passed the House of Representatives unanimously on the 4th of April, 1864.

May 24—The PRESIDENT transmitted the following correspondence, communicated by the Secretary of State, in response to the resolution of the House:

MR. SEWARD'S LETTER TO MR. DAYTON, DATED DEPARTMENT OF STATE, WASHINGTON, APRIL 7, 1864.

I send you a copy of a resolution which passed the House of Representatives on the 4th instant, by a unanimous vote, and which declares the opposition of that body to a recognition of a monarchy in Mexico. M. Geofrey has lost no time in asking for an explanation of this proceeding.

It is hardly necessary, after what I have heretofore written with perfect candor for the information of France, to say that this resolution truly interprets the unanimous sentiment of the people of the United States in regard to Mexico. It is, however, another and distinct question whether the United States would think it necessary or proper to express themselves in the form adopted by the House of Representatives at this time. This is a practical and purely Executive question, and the decision of its constitutionality belongs not to the House of Representatives, nor even to Congress, but to the President of the United States. You will, of course, take notice that the declaration made by the House of Representatives is in the form of a joint resolution, which, before it can acquire the character of a legislative act, must receive, first, the concurrence of the Senate, and, secondly, the approval of the President of the United States; or, in case of his dissent, the renewed assent of both houses of Congress, to be expressed by a majority of two-thirds of each body. While the President receives the declaration of the House of Representatives with the profound respect to which it is entitled, as an exposition of its sentiments upon a grave and important subject, he directs that you inform the Government of France that he does not at present contemplate any departure from the policy which this Government has hitherto pursued in regard to the war which exists between France and Mexico. It is hardly necessary to say that the proceeding of the House of Representatives was adopted upon suggestions arising within itself, and not upon any communication of the Executive department; and that the French Government would be seasonably apprised of any change of policy upon this subject which the President might at any future time think it proper to adopt.

—

Mr. Dayton's Letter, dated Paris, April 22, 1864.

Sir: I visited M. Drouyn de l'Huys yesterday at the department of foreign affairs. The first words he addressed to me, on entering the room, were: "Do you bring us peace, or bring us war?" I asked him to what he referred, and he said he referred more immediately to those resolutions recently passed by Congress in reference to the invasion of Mexico by the French, and the establishment of Maximilian upon the throne of that country. I said to him, in reply, that I did not think France had a right to infer that we were about to make war against her on account of anything contained in those resolutions; that they embodied nothing more than had been constantly held out to the French government from the beginning; that I had always represented to the government here that any action upon their part interfering with the form of government in Mexico would be looked upon with dissatisfaction in our country, and they could not expect us to be in haste to acknowledge a monarchical government, built upon the foundations of a republic which was our next neighbor; that I had reason to believe you held the same language to the French Minister in the United States. This allegation he did not seem to deny, but obviously viewed the resolutions in question as a serious step upon our part; and I am told that the leading secessionists here build largely upon these resolutions as a means of fomenting ill-feeling between this country and some others and ourselves. Mr. Mason and his secretary have gone to Brussels to confer with Mr. Dudley Mann, who is their commissioner at that place. Mr. Slidell, it is said, was to have gone to Austria, although he has not yet got off.

Second Letter from Mr. Dayton, Paris, May 2, 1864, being in reply to Mr. Seward's of April 7.

Sir: Immediately upon the receipt of your dispatch No. 525, I applied to M. Drouyn de l'Huys for a special interview, which was granted for Saturday last. I then said that I knew that the French government had felt some anxiety in respect to the resolution which had recently been passed by the House of Representatives, in reference to Mexico; and inasmuch as I had just received a copy of that resolution, together with the views of the President of the United States, I begged, if agreeable, to read to him your dispatch in reference to the latter. To this he assented, and as the shortest and most satisfactory mode, following out my instructions, I read to him that entire portion of your dispatch which applies to this subject, stating, at the same time, that I thought it was a remarkable illustration of the frankness and straightforwardness of the President. When the reading was closed, M. Drouyn de l'Huys expressed his gratification, and after asking some questions in regard to the effect of laying a resolution upon the table in the Senate, the conversation terminated.

The extreme sensitiveness which was manifested by this government when the resolution of the House of Representatives was first brought to its knowledge has, to a considerable extent, at least, subsided.

Mr. Seward's responses of May 9 and May 21:

Sir: Your dispatch of April 22 (No. 454) has been received. What you have said to M. Drouyn de l'Huys on the subject of the resolution of the House of Representatives concerning Mexico, as you have reported it, is entirely approved. The resolution yet remains unacted upon in the Senate.

Mr. Corwin was to leave Vera Cruz on the 3d instant under the leave of absence granted to him by this department on the 8th of August last.

Sir: I have the honor to acknowledge the receipt of your dispatch of May 2, (No. 461,) and to approve of your proceedings therein mentioned. We learn that Mr. Corwin, our minister plenipotentiary to Mexico, is at Havana, on his return to the United States, under leave of absence.

June 4—Mr. Davis, of Maryland, asked unanimous consent to make a written report from the Committee on Foreign Affairs, in response to the above message of the President. Mr. Broomall objected.

June 6—He asked consent, and Mr. Arnold objected. He then moved to suspend the rules, which was rejected—yeas 43, nays 55, (two thirds being required,) as follows:

Yeas—Messrs. Allison, *Ancona*, *Augustus C. Baldwin*, *Cox*, Henry Winter Davis, *Dawson*, *Eden*, *Edgerton*, *Eldridge*, *Finck*, *Ganson*, Garfield, *Grider*, *Griswold*, *Harding*, *Harrington*, *Charles M. Harris*, *Herrick*, *Holman*, Jenckes, *King*, *Knapp*, *Lazear*, *Le Blond*, *Long*, *Mallory*, *Marcy*, *James R. Morris*, *Morrison*, *Noble*, *Odell*, Orth, *Pendleton*, *Perry*, *Robinson*, *Ross*, *Scott*, Spalding, *Strouse*, *Sweat*, *Wadsworth*, *Chilton A. White*, *Joseph W. White*—43.

Nays—Messrs. Alley, Ames, Arnold, *Baily*, John D. Baldwin, Beaman, Blaine, Jacob B. Blair, Broomall, Ambrose W. Clark, Freeman Clarke, Cobb, *Coffroth*, Cole, Thomas T. Davis, Dawes, Dixon, Donnelly, Driggs, Eliot, Farnsworth, Fenton, Frank, Gooch, Grinnell, Hale, Hotchkiss, John H. Hubbard, Ingersoll, Kelley, Orlando Kellogg, Littlejohn, Longyear, Marvin, Samuel F. Miller, Moorhead, Daniel Morris, Amos Myers, Charles O'Neill, Patterson, Perham, Price, Alexander H. Rice, John H. Rice, Edward H. Rollins, Shannon, Smithers, Thayer, Tracy, Upson, Ellihu B. Washburne, William B. Washburn, Whaley, Wilson, Windom—55.

June 27—Mr. Davis made this report, which was ordered to be printed:

The Committee on Foreign Affairs have examined the correspondence submitted by the President relative to the joint resolution on Mexican affairs with the profound respect to which it is entitled, because of the gravity of its subject and the distinguished source from which it emanated.

They regret that the President should have so widely departed from the usage of constitutional governments as to make a pending resolution of so grave and delicate a character the subject of diplomatic explanations. They regret still more that the President should have thought proper to inform a foreign government of a radical and serious conflict of opinion and jurisdiction between the depositories of the legislative and executive power of the United States.

No expression of deference can make the denial of the right of Congress constitutionally to do what the House did with absolute unanimity, other than derogatory to their dignity.

They learn with surprise that, in the opinion of the President, the form and term of expressing the judgment of the United States on recognizing a monarchical government imposed on a neighboring republic is a "purely executive question, and the decision of it constitutionally belongs not to the House of Representatives, nor even to Congress, but to the President of the United States."

This assumption is equally novel and inadmissible. No President has ever claimed such an exclusive authority. No Congress can ever permit its expression to pass without dissent.

It is certain that the Constitution nowhere confers such authority on the President.

The precedents of recognition, sufficiently numerous in this revolutionary era, do not countenance this view; and if there be one not inconsistent with it, the committee have not found it.

All questions of recognition have heretofore been debated and considered as grave questions of national policy, on which the will of the people should be expressed in Congress assembled; and the President, as the proper medium of foreign intercourse, has executed that will. If he has ever anticipated its expression, we have not found the case.

The declaration and establishment of the independence of the Spanish American colonies first brought the question of recognition of new governments or nations before the Government of the United States; and the precedents then set have been followed ever since, even by the present Administration.

The correspondence now before us is the first attempt to

depart from that usage, and deny the nation a controlling deliberative voice in regulating its foreign policy.

The following are the chief precedents on recognition of new governments, and the policy of the United States Government on that topic:

On the 9th of February, 1821, Henry Clay moved in the House of Representatives to amend the appropriation bill by the following clause:

"For an outfit, and one year's salary, to such minister as the President, by and with the consent of the Senate, may send to any government of South America, which has established and is maintaining its independency on Spain, a sum not exceeding $18,000." It failed.

On the 10th of February, he moved that the House of Representatives participates with the people of the United States in the deep interest which they feel for the success of the Spanish provinces of South America, which are struggling for their liberty and independence, and that it will give its constitutional support to the President of the United States whenever he may deem it expedient to recognize the sovereignty and independence of any of the said provinces.

A motion to amend by the proviso "that this resolution shall not be construed to interfere with the independent exercise of the treaty-making power," and another, "that the House approves of the course heretofore pursued by the President of the United States with regard to the said provinces," were negatived.

The resolution was adopted, and a committee appointed to lay it before President Monroe.

The committee, on the 17th February, reported—

"That the President assured the committee that, in common with the people of the United States and the House of Representatives, he felt great interest in the success of the provinces of Spanish America, which are struggling to establish their freedom and independence, and that he would take the resolution into deliberate consideration, with the most perfect respect for the distinguished body from which it had emanated."

So the House of Representatives took the initiative towards recognizing the new republics. The amendment to the appropriation bill would have been a legislative recognition. The resolution was a formal statement of the opinion of the House to the President, which he did not think beyond their constitutional authority.

At the first session of the next Congress the House of Representatives, on motion of Mr. Nelson, of Virginia, resolved—

"That the President of the United States be requested to lay before this House such communications as may be in the possession of the Executive, from the agents of the United States with the governments south of the United States, which have declared their independence, and the communications from the agents of such governments in the United States with the Secretary of State, as tend to show the political condition of those governments, and the state of the war between them and Spain, as it may be consistent with the public interest to communicate."

President Monroe answered the application on the 8th of March in an elaborate message, of which the following extracts sufficiently show that he did not think recognition "a purely executive question," and that the decision of it constitutionally belongs, "not to the House of Representatives, nor even to Congress, but to the President of the United States:"

"In transmitting to the House of Representatives the documents called for by the resolution of that House of January, I consider it *my duty* to *invite* the attention of *Congress* to a very important subject, and to communicate the sentiments of the Executive on it; that should *Congress* entertain similar sentiments, there may be such co-operation between the two departments of the Government as their respective rights and duties may require."

"This contest has now reached such a stage, and been attended with such decisive success on the part of the provinces, that it merits the most profound consideration, whether their right to the rank of independent nations, with all the advantage incident to it in their intercourse with the United States, is not complete."

After narrating the events, he proceeds:

"When the result of such a contest is manifestly settled, the new governments have a claim to recognition by other powers which ought not to be resisted."

"When we regard, then, the great length of time which the war has been prosecuted, the complete success which has attended it in favor of the provinces, the present condition of the parties, and the utter inability of Spain to produce any change in it, we are compelled to conclude that its fate is settled, and that the provinces which have declared their independence, and are in the enjoyment of it, ought to be recognized."

"*In proposing this measure*, it is not contemplated to change thereby in the slightest manner our friendly relations with either of the parties."

"*The measure is proposed* under a thorough conviction that it is in strict accord with the law of nations, and that the United States owe it to their position and character in the world, as well as to their essential interests, to adopt it."

"Should Congress concur *in the view herein presented*, they will doubtless see the propriety of making the necessary appropriations for carrying it into effect."

It is quite apparent that President Monroe was far from countenancing the opinion that the form and time in which the United States would think it necessary to express themselves on the policy of the recognition is a purely *executive question*, and that he did not think the decision of it *constitutionally* belongs not to the House of Representatives, nor even to Congress, but to the President of the United States, to the exclusion of Congress. Had he so thought, he would have refused the production of the papers, as President Washington did the diplomatic instructions relative to the English treaty.

He would have announced his purpose to recognize the republics, and left it to Congress to provide for diplomatic intercourse with them.

Far from that, he proposes for their consideration the policy of recognition; and, if they concur in *that*, asks them to make the necessary appropriations to carry *it* into effect.

He consulted the *will* of the nation at the mouth of Congress, and proposed to concur in its execution.

So Congress understood him, for the papers and message were referred to the Committee on Foreign Affairs. That committee considered, in an elaborate report, the question of independence of the republics, the policy and principles involved in their recognition, and on the 19th of March, 1822, they submitted it to the House. It concluded as follows:

"Your committee having thus considered the subject referred to them in all its aspects, are *unanimously* of opinion that it is *just* and *expedient* to acknowledge the *independence of the several nations of Spanish America* without any reference to the diversity in the form of their governments; and in accordance with this opinion they respectfully submit the following resolutions:

"*Resolved*, That the House of Representatives concur in the opinion expressed by the President in his message of the 8th of March, 1822, that the American provinces of Spain which have declared their independence, and are in the enjoyment of it, *ought to be recognized by the United States* as independent nations.

"*Resolved*, That the Committee of Ways and Means be instructed to report a bill appropriating a sum not exceeding $100,000 *to enable the President to give due effect to such recognition.*"

It is, therefore, equally apparent that the House of Representatives of the 17th Congress was clearly of opinion with President Monroe that the question of recognition was not purely executive, but that it constitutionally belongs to Congress as well as to the President; that the Legislature declares the will of the United States, which the Executive gives effect to—each concurring in the act of recognition according to their respective constitutional functions.

In obedience to that resolution the following bill, recognizing the new nation, was reported and passed and approved on the 4th of May, 1862:

"That for such missions to the *independent nations on the American continent* as the President may deem proper, there be, and hereby is, appropriated a sum not exceeding $100,000, to be paid out of any money in the Treasury not otherwise appropriated."

The approval of that law completed the recognition of the new nations. The sending ministers to some or all of them was a matter of executive discretion, not at all essential to or connected with the fact of recognition. Ministers were appointed to Mexico, Colombia, Buenos Ayres, and Chili, on the 27th of January, 1823. None was appointed to Peru till May, 1826; yet it is certain Peru was as much recognized by the United States as the other governments from the 4th of May, 1822.

This great precedent has governed all that follow it.

The acknowledgment of the independence of Texas stands next in our history. It is a most instructive precedent, strictly following the forms observed respecting the governments of Spanish America.

On the 18th of June, 1836, on the motion of Henry Clay, the Senate adopted the resolution—

"That the independence of Texas ought to be acknowledged by the United States whenever satisfactory information shall be received that it has in successful operation a civil government capable of performing the duties and fulfilling the obligations of an independent power."

The House of Representatives, on the 4th of July, 1836, adopted a resolution in the same words; and added a second:

"That the House of Representatives perceive with satisfaction that the President of the United States has adopted measures to ascertain the political, military, and civil condition of Texas."—(Congressional Globe, 1st session 24th Congress, pp. 453, 486.)

Those resolutions were not formal acknowledgments of a government of Texas; the report of the Senate Committee showed the circumstances were not sufficiently known; and both Senate and House awaited further information at the hands of the President.

On the 2d December, while communicating the information, President Jackson accepted the occasion to express to Congress his opinion on the subject. The following passages are very instructive, touching the authority to recognize new States:

"Nor has any deliberative inquiry ever been instituted in Congress, or in any of our legislative bodies, as to whom belonged the power of recognizing a new State; a power, the exercise of which is equivalent, under some circumstances, to a declaration of *war;* a power nowhere expressly delegated, and only granted in the Constitution, as it is necessarily involved in some of the great powers given to *Congress*, in that given to the President and Senate to form treaties and to appoint ambassadors and other public ministers, and in that conferred on the President to receive ministers from foreign nations."

"In the preamble to the resolution of the House of Representatives, it is distinctly intimated that the expediency of recognizing the independence of Texas should be *left to the decision of Congress.* In this view, on the ground of expediency, I am disposed to concur; and do not, therefore, think it necessary to express any opinion as to the strict constitutional right of the Executive, either apart from, or in conjunction with, the Senate over the subject. *It is to be presumed that on no future occasion will a dispute arise, as none has heretofore occurred, between the Executive and Legislature in the exercise of the power of recognition.* It will always be considered *consistent with the spirit of the Constitution and most safe* that it should be exercised, when probably leading to war, with a previous understanding with that body by whom war can alone be declared, and by whom all the provisions for sustaining its perils must be furnished. Its submission to Congress, which represents in one of its branches the States of this Union, and in the other the people of the United States, where there may be reasonable ground to apprehend so grave a consequence, would certainly afford the fullest satisfaction to our own country, and a perfect guarantee to all other countries, of the justice and prudence of the measures which ought to be adopted."

After forcibly stating why he thought "we should still stand aloof," he closed with the following declaration:

"Having thus discharged my duty, by presenting with simplicity and directness the views which, after much reflection, I have been led to take of this important subject, I have only to add the expression of my confidence that if Congress should differ with me upon it, their judgment will be the result of dispassionate, prudent, and wise deliberation; with the assurance that, during the short time which I shall continue connected with the Government, I shall promptly and cordially unite with you in such measures as may be deemed best fitted to increase the prosperity and perpetuate the peace of our favored country."

The concurrent resolutions of the Senate and House of Representatives, and that message of President Jackson, leave no doubt that the views which presided over the recognition of the South American Governments still prevailed, and that the President was as far from asserting as Congress from admitting that the recognition of new nations and the foreign policy of the United States is a purely Executive question.

The independence of Texas was finally recognized in pursuance of the following enactment in the appropriation bill of the second session of the Twenty-Fourth Congress which appropriates money—

"For the outfit and salary of a diplomatic agent to be sent to the *republic of Texas*, whenever the President of the United States may receive satisfactory evidence that Texas is an independent power, and shall deem it expedient to appoint such minister."

That law was approved by President Jackson.

Not only is this exclusive assumption without countenance in the early history of the Republic, but it is irreconcilable with the most solemn acts of the present Administration. The independence of Hayti is nearly as old as that of the United States; it antedated that of the South American republics, and the republic of Liberia has long been recognized by European nations. Both were first recognized by act of Congress, approved by President Lincoln on the 5th of July, 1862, which enacted—

"That the President of the United States be, and he is hereby, *authorized*, by and with the advice and consent of the Senate, to appoint diplomatic representatives of the United States to the *republics of Hayti and Liberia* respectively. Each of the representatives so appointed shall be accredited as commissioner and consul general, and shall receive the compensation of commissioners," &c., &c.

That was a formal recognition of those republics by *law*, whether the President sent diplomatic representatives or not.

Quite in the spirit of these precedents is the well-considered language of the Supreme Court:

"Those questions which respect the rights of a part of a foreign empire which asserts and is contending for its independence, belong more properly to those who can declare what the law shall be, who can place the nation in such a position with respect to foreign powers as to their own judgment shall appear wise, to whom are entrusted its foreign relations, than to that tribunal whose power as well as duty is confined to the application of the rule which the legislature may prescribe for it."

But the joint resolution of the 4th of April does more than declare the refusal of the United States to recognize a monarchical usurpation in Mexico. It declares a general rule of policy, which can be authentically and authoritatively expressed only by the body charged with the legislative power of the United States.

"*Resolved, &c.*, That the Congress of the United States are unwilling, by silence, to leave the nations of the world under the impression that they are indifferent spectators of the deplorable events now transpiring in the republic of Mexico; and they, therefore, think fit to declare that it does not accord with the policy of the United States to acknowledge a monarchical government erected on the ruins of any republican government in America, under the auspices of any European power."

The committee are of opinion that this authority, to speak in the name of the United States, has never, before the correspondence in question, been considered a purely executive function.

The most remarkable declaration of this kind in our history, which events seem now likely to make of as grave practical interest as when it was uttered, is President Monroe's declaration in his message of the 2d December, 1823:

"With the governments which have declared their independence and maintained it, and whose independence we have, after great consideration and on just principles acknowledged, we could not view any interposition, for the purpose of oppressing them or controlling in any other manner their destiny by any European power, in any other light than as the manifestation of an unfriendly disposition toward the United States."

But though always the accurate expression of the feelings of the American people, it was not regarded as the settled policy of the nation, because not formally declared by Congress. By the administration of President John Quincy Adams, which followed, it was treated as merely an executive expression on behalf of the people, which Congress alone could elevate to the dignity of a national policy by its formal adoption.

In 1826, Mr. Poinsett, the minister to Mexico, having used language supposed to commit the United States to that policy in behalf of Mexico, a resolution was promptly introduced into the House of Representatives and adopted on the 27th of March, 1826—

"That the Committee on Foreign Affairs inquire and report to this House upon what authority, if any, the minister of the United States to the Mexican republic, in his official character, declared to the plenipotentiary of that government that the United States have pledged themselves not to permit any other power than Spain to interfere either with their (the South American republics) independence, or form of government," &c., &c.—2 Cong. Deb., 19th Con., 1st sess., p. 1820.)

Mr. Poinsett hastened to explain by his letter of the 6th of May, 1826, to Henry Clay, then Secretary of State:

"I cannot rest satisfied without stating explicitly that, in the observations I made during my conference with the Mexican plenipotentiaries, I alluded only to the message of the President of the United States to Congress in 1823.

"That message, dictated, in my opinion, by the soundes policy, has been regarded both in Europe and America as a solemn declaration of the views and intentions of the *Executive* of the United States, and I have always considered that declaration as a pledge, so far forth as the language of the *President* can pledge the *nation*, to defend the new American republics from the attacks of any of the powers of Europe other than Spain. That *the people of the United States are not bound by any declarations of the Executive is known and understood as well in Mexico, where the government is modelled on our own political institutions, as in the United States themselves.* But in order to correct any erroneous impressions these words might have made on the minds of the Mexican plenipotentiaries, I explained to them in the course of our conference this morning their precise meaning: that the declaration of Mr. Monroe in his message of 1823, to which I had alluded, indicated only the course of policy the Executive of the United States was disposed to pursue towards these countries, *but was not binding on the nation unless sanctioned by the Congress of the United States;* and when I spoke of the United States having pledged themselves not to permit any other power than Spain to interfere with the independence or form of government of the American republics, I meant only to allude to the above-cited declaration of the President of the United States in his message of 1823, and to nothing more."

This explanation is the more significant from the fact that Mr. Clay's instructions to Mr. Poinsett directed him to bring to the notice of the Mexican government the message of the late President of the United States to their Congress on the 2d of December, 1823, asserting certain important principles of intercontinental law in the relations of Europe and America; and, after stating and enlarging on them, Mr. Clay proceeds: "Both principles were laid down after much and anxious deliberation on the part of the late administration. *The President, who then formed a part of it, continues entirely to coincide in both*, and you will urge upon the government of Mexico the propriety and expediency of asserting the same principles on all proper occasions."

And in reply to the resolution of inquiry of the 27th of March, Mr. Clay accompanied his instructions with the declaration—entirely in the spirit of Mr. Poinsett's letter—"that the United States have contracted no engagement, *nor made any pledge* to the governments of Mexico and South America, or either of them, that the United States would not permit the interference of any foreign power with the independence or form of government of those nations. * * * * * * * * * *

"If, indeed, an attempt by force had been made by allied Europe to subvert the liberties of the southern nations on this continent, and to erect *upon the ruins of their free institutions monarchical systems*, the people of the United States would have stood pledged, *in the opinion of the Executive*, not to any foreign State, but to themselves and their posterity, by their dearest interests and highest duties, to resist to the utmost such attempt; and it is to a pledge of that character that Mr. Poinsett above refers."—(2 Cong. Debates, 19th Congress, 1st session, App. 83, 84.)

Such were the views of the administration of President John Quincy Adams, whose Secretary of State was Henry Clay, and whose minister to Mexico was Mr. Poinsett, upon the supremacy of the legislature in declaring the foreign policy of the United States, the diplomatic execution and conduct of which is confided to the President.

It is impossible to condense the elaborate message of President Adams of the 15th of March, 1826, dedicated to persuading Congress to concur in and sanction the Panama mission; but that message and the great debate which consumed the session in both Houses are unmeaning on the assumptions of this correspondence with the French government; and the consideration and approval of its recommendations elevate President Monroe's declaration to the dignity and authority of the policy of the nation solemnly and legally proclaimed by Congress.

That message was in reply to a resolution requesting the President to inform the House of Representatives "in regard to what objects the agents of the United States are expected to take part in the deliberations of that congress"—of Panama.

Among the subjects of deliberation, the President enumerated the declaration of President Monroe above quoted and on that topic said:

"Most of the new American republics have declared their entire assent to them; and they now propose, among the subjects of consideration at Panama, to take into consideration the means of *making effectual* the assertion of that principle as well as the *means of resisting interference from abroad* with the domestic concerns of the American governments.

"In alluding to these means, it would obviously be premature at this time to anticipate that which is offered merely as matter for consultation, or to pronounce upon those measures which have been or may be suggested. The purpose of this government is to concur in none which would import hostility to Europe, or justly excite resentment in any of her States. Should it be deemed advisable to contract any conventional engagement on this topic, our views would extend no further than to a mutual pledge of the parties to the compact, to maintain the principle in application to its own territory, and to permit no colonial lodgments or establishments of European jurisdiction upon its own soil; and with respect to the obtrusive interference from abroad, if the future character may be inferred from that which has been, and perhaps still is, exercised in more than one of the new States, a joint declaration of its character and exposure of it to the world would be probably all that the occasion would require.

"Whether the United States should or should not be parties to such a declaration may justly form a part of the deliberation. That there is an evil to be remedied needs little insight into the secret history of late years to know, and that this remedy may best be considered at the Panama meeting deserves at least the experiment of consideration."

Upon this message, after elaborate debates, Congress passed in May an appropriation "for carrying into effect the appointment of a mission to the congress of Panama;" and the President, by and with the advice and consent of the Senate, appointed ministers to that congress, and furnished them with instructions in conformity with the message, and in execution of the policy approved by Congress.

Accident and delays prevented the arrival of our mission before the dissolution of the congress; but President Adams thought the gravity of the precedent justified him in communicating to Congress, in 1829, Mr. Clay's instructions to the ministers for our information; and the precedent remains, forever to vindicate the authority of Congress to declare and present the foreign policy of the United States.

The great name of Daniel Webster is justly considered authoritative on any question of constitutional power; and in that debate, when the enemies of the Administration strove to insert *particular instructions* to the diplomatic agents sent to *that congress*, he clearly defined the limits of executive and congressional authority, in declaring the policy and conducting the negotiations to effectuate it.

On the 4th of April, 1826, he is reported to have said in the House of Representatives:

"He would ask two questions: First, Does not the Constitution vest the power of the Executive in the President? Second, Is not the giving of instructions to ministers abroad an exercise of Executive power? Why should we take this responsibility on ourselves? He denied that the President had devolved, or could devolve, his own constitutional responsibility, or any part of it, on this House. The President had sent this subject to the House for its concurrence, by voting the necessary appropriation. Beyond this the House was not called on to act. We might refuse the appropriation if we saw fit, but we had not the power to make our vote conditional, and to attach instructions to it.

"There was a way, indeed, in which this House might express its opinion in regard to foreign politics. That is by resolution. He agreed entirely with the gentleman that, if the House were of opinion that a wrong course was given to our foreign relations, it ought to say so, and say so by some measure that should affect the whole, and not a part, of our diplomatic intercourse. It ought to control all missions, and not one only.

"There was no reason why the ministers to Panama should act under these restrictions that did not equally apply to other diplomatic agents—for example, to our minister at Colombia, Mexico, or other new States. A resolution expressive of the sense of the House would, on the contrary, lead to instructions to be given to them all. *A resolution was, therefore, the regular mode of proceeding.* We saw, for instance, looking at these documents, that our government had declared to some of the governments of Europe, perhaps it has declared to all the principal powers, that we could not consent to the transfer of Cuba to any European power. No doubt the executive government can maintain that ground only so long as it receives the approbation and support of Congress. If Congress be of opinion that this course of policy is wrong, then he agreed it was in the power, and, he thought, indeed, the duty of *Congress* to interfere and to express dissent. If the amendment now offered prevailed, the declarations so distinctly made on this point could not be reported, under any circumstances, at Panama; but they might, nevertheless, be reported anywhere and everywhere else. Therefore, if we dissent from this opinion, that dissent should be declared by resolution, and that would change the whole course of our diplomatic correspondence on that subject in all places. If any gentleman thinks, therefore, that we ought to take no measure, under any circumstances, to prevent the transfer of Cuba into the hands of any government, European or American, let him bring forward his resolution to that effect. If it should pass, it will effectually prevent the repetition of such declarations as have been made."—(2 Cong. Debates, 19th Congress, 1st session, pp, 2021, 2022.)

This view is, in the opinion of the committee, at once the just view and the traditional practice of the government; the will of the people expressed in the legislative form by the legislative power can declare authoritatively the foreign policy of the nation; to the President is committed the diplomatic measures for effecting it.

The constitutional authority of Congress over the foreign relations of the United States can hardly be considered an open question, after the concurrent resolutions of Mr. Senator Sumner, adopted in the last Congress, it is believed, at the suggestion, certainly with the approval of the President, and by him officially notified to foreign governments, as the most authentic and authoritative expression of the national will respecting intervention, mediation, and every other form of foreign intrusion into the domestic struggle in the United States.

The committee are not inclined to discuss theoretically questions of relative power. The Constitution is a practical, and not a theoretical instrument. It has been administered and construed by men of practical sagacity, and in their hands the voice of the people has been heard authoritatively in the executive chamber, on the conduct of foreign affairs.

But this correspondence requires us to say, that in view of the historic precedents, it is not a purely executive question whether the United States would think it necessary to express themselves in the form adopted by the House of Representatives at this time; it does belong to Congress to declare and decide on the foreign policy of the United States, and it is the duty of the President to give effect to that policy by means of the diplomatic negotiations, or military power if it be authorized.

The President is not less bound to execute the national will expressed by law in its foreign than in its domestic concerns.

The President appoints all officers of the United States, but their duties are regulated, not by his will, but by law. He is the commander of the army and navy, but he has no power to use it except when the law points out the occasion and the object. He appoints foreign ministers, but neither in this case are they, by reason of their appointment, anything but the ministers of the law. If it be true that the appointment of an ambassador to a nation implies the recognition of the nation, it is just as sound logic to argue that none can be appointed to a nation that does not exist by the recognition of Congress, as that the President can recognize alone, because he can appoint.

But we prefer to waive the question. We are anxious not to depart from the approved precedents of our history. Our desire is to preserve, not to change. We will not inquire what would be the effect of a recognition of a new nation by the President against the will of Congress. We prefer to indulge the hope so wisely expressed by President Jackson, that "it is to be presumed that on no future occasion will a dispute arise, as none has heretofore occurred, between the Executive and Legislature in the exercise of the power of recognition."

Hitherto new nations, new powers, have always been recognized upon consultation and concurrence of the executive and legislative departments, and on the most important occasions by and in pursuance of law in the particular cases.

Changes of the person or dynasty of rulers of recognized powers, which created no new power, have not been treated always with the same formality; but usually the general law providing for diplomatic intercourse with the power whose internal administration had changed remained on the statute book and conferred a plenary discretion on the President, under the sanction of which he has accredited ministers to the new possessors of power. It is not known that hitherto the President has ever undertaken to recognize a new nation or a new power not before known to the history of the world, and not before acknowledged by the United States, without the previous authority of Congress.

It is peculiarly unfortunate that the new view of the executive authority should have been announced to a foreign government, the tendency of which was to diminish the force and effect of the legislative expression of what is admitted to be the unanimous sentiment of the people of the United States, by denying the authority of Congress to pronounce it.

Of the prudence of that expression at this time Congress is the best and only judge under the forms of the Constitution, and the President has no right to influence it otherwise than in the constitutional expression of his assent or his dissent when presented to him for his consideration.

It is vain to suppose that such a declaration increases the danger of war with France. The Emperor of the French will make war on the United States when it suits his convenience, and it can be done without danger to his dynastic interests. Till then, in the absence of wrong or insult on our part, there will be no war. When that time arrives we shall have war, no matter how meek, inoffensive, or pusillanimous our conduct may be, for our sin is our freedom and our power, and the only safety of monarchical, imperial, aristocratic, or despotic *rule*, lies in our failure or our overthrow.

It postpones the inevitable day to be ready and powerful at home, and to express our resolution not to recognize acts of violence to republican neighbors on our borders perpetrated to our injury. That declaration will encourage the republicans of America, to resist and endure, and not to submit. It is not perceived how an attack on the United States can promote the establishment of a monarch in Mexico. It might seriously injure us, but it would be an additional obstacle to the accomplishment of that enterprise. It is fortunate that events in Europe, in great measure, embarrass any further warlike enterprise on this continent, and the ruler who has not thought fit to mingle in the strife of Poland or Schleswig-Holstein will hardly venture to provoke a war with the United States.

The committee are content to bide their time, confident in the fortune and fortitude of the American people, but resolved not to encourage by a weak silence complications with foreign powers inimical to our greatness and safety, which, in the words of Mr. Webster, "a firm and timely assertion of what we hold to be our own rights and our own interests would strongly tend to avert."

The committee recommend the adoption of the following resolution:

Resolved, That Congress has a constitutional right to an authoritative voice in declaring and prescribing the foreign policy of the United States, as well in the recognition of new powers as in other matters; and it is the constitutional duty of the President to respect that policy, not less in diplomatic negotiations than in the use of the national force when authorized by law; and the propriety of any declaration of foreign policy by Congress is sufficiently proved by the vote which pronounces it; and such proposition while pending and undetermined is not a fit topic of diplomatic explanation with any foreign power.

FRANCE, MEXICO, AND THE UNITED STATES.

The *Courier du Dimanche*, of Paris, publishes a circular letter addressed by M. Drouyn de l'Huys, the French Minister of Foreign Affairs, to the agents of the Empire abroad, respecting the relation of France to the American Government. This letter is a sequel to the correspondence between Mr. Seward and Mr. Dayton with regard to the Mexican question, and is as follows:—

PARIS, *May* 7, 1864.—Mr. Dayton has called on me to read to me a despatch addressed to him by the Secretary of State of the Union, in order to define the responsibility of the Government of Washington, and to show that a vote of the House of Representatives, or of the Senate, or even of the two Houses, while it naturally recommends itself to the attention of the Government, did not oblige it to modify its policy and take from it its liberty of action.

Mr. Seward sees no reason to follow in the Mexican question a line of conduct other than that which he had adopted heretofore; and if his disposition should happen to be modified, we should be directly and in good time informed of this resolution and its motives.

I have replied to Mr. Dayton that in the opinion of the Government of the Emperor, nothing could justify this change; that our confidence in the wisdom and enlightenment of the American Cabinet was too great to permit us to suppose it to have any idea of compromising, by thoughtless action, the true interests of the United States.

While expressing to Mr. Dayton the entire satisfaction which the assurances he was charged with giving to us caused to the government of the Emperor, I added that I thought, in effect, that, even from the point of view of the United States, the choice would not be doubtful between the establishment in Mexico of a stable and regular government, and the perpetuation of an anarchy of which they had been the first to suffer and to point out the great inconvenience.

The reorganization of a vast country which, after the restoration of order and security, is expected to play an important economical part in the world, would be for the United States especially a real source of advantage, since it would open a new market to them from which they, because of their proximity, would profit more than others.

The prosperity of Mexico would therefore agree with their rightly understood interests, and I certainly do not believe that the Government of Washington could misunderstand this truth.

DROUYN DE L'HUYS.

The Arguelles Case.

1864, May 28—In the SENATE, Mr. JOHNSON offered this resolution, which was agreed to:

Resolved, That the President be requested to inform the Senate, if he shall not deem it incompatible with the public interest, whether he has, and when, authorized a person alleged to have committed a crime against Spain or any of its dependencies, to be delivered up to officers of that government; and whether such delivery was had; and if so, under what authority of law or treaty it was done.

May 31—The PRESIDENT transmitted a reply covering a report from the Secretary of State and other documents, by which it appears that Don Josè Augustin Arguelles, an officer in the Spanish army in Cuba, had captured a slave expedition, while he was acting as Lieutenant Governor of the district of Colon, in Cuba. It was subsequently discovered that he had, with the connivance of the curate of Colon, made representations to the Spanish Government that one hundred and forty-one of the recaptured negroes had died of small-pox, though, in fact, he had sold them into slavery, and succeeded in escaping to the United States, where he was arrested by the officers of the United States and surrendered to the Cuban authorities.

In explanation of this act on the part of the Government of the United States, the Secretary of State reports as follows:

DEPARTMENT OF STATE,
WASHINGTON, *May* 30, 1864.

The Secretary of State, to whom was referred the resolution of the Senate of the 28th instant, requesting the President to inform that body, "if he shall not deem it incompatible with the public interest, whether he has, and when, authorized a person, alleged to have committed a crime against Spain, or any of its dependencies, to be delivered up to officers of that government; and whether such delivery was had; and if so, under what authority of law or of treaty it was done," has the honor to submit to the President a copy of the papers which are on file or on record in this department relative to the subject of the resolution.

By the act of Congress of the 15th of May, 1820, the African slave trade is declared to be piracy.

By the ninth article of the treaty of 1842 with Great Britain, it is stipulated that, "Whereas, notwithstanding all efforts which may be made on the coast of Africa for suppressing the slave trade, the facilities for carrying on that traffic, and avoiding the vigilance of cruisers, by the fraudulent use of flags and other means, are so great, and the temptations for pursuing it, while a market can be found for slaves, so strong, as that the desired result may be long delayed, unless all markets be shut against the purchase of African negroes, the parties to this treaty agree that they will unite in all becoming representations and remonstrances with any and all powers within whose dominions such markets are allowed to exist, and that they will urge upon all such powers the propriety and duty of closing such markets effectually at once and forever."

There being no treaty of extradition between the United States and Spain, nor any act of Congress directing how fugitives from justice in Spanish dominions shall be delivered up, the extradition in the case referred to in the resolution of the Senate is understood by this department to have been made in virtue of the law of nations and the Constitution of the United States.

Although there is a conflict of authorities concerning the expediency of exercising comity towards a foreign government by surrendering, at its request, one of its own subjects charged with the commission of crime within its territory, and although it may be conceded that there is no national obligation to make such a surrender upon a demand therefor, unless it is acknowledged by treaty or by statute law, yet a nation is never bound to furnish asylum to dangerous criminals who are offenders against the human race; and it is believed that if in any case the comity could with propriety be practiced, the one which is understood to have called forth the resolution furnished a just occasion for its exercise.

Respectfully submitted. WILLIAM H. SEWARD.

To the PRESIDENT.

Upon the arrival at Havana of the fugitive Arguelles, General Dulce, the Captain-General of Cuba, addressed to the Spanish minister at Washington the following note:

MOST EXCELLENT SIR: My aide-de-camp, with the person expected, arrived in the steamer Eagle.

I request your excellency to render thanks in my name to Mr. Seward for the service which he has rendered to humanity by furnishing the medium through which a great number of human beings will obtain their freedom, whom the desertion of the person referred to would have reduced to slavery. His presence alone in this island a very few hours has given liberty to eighty-six.

I also render thanks to your excellence for the efficiency of your action.

God preserve your excellency many years.

DOMINGO DULCE.

HAVANA, *May* 19, 1864.

Murray, United States Marshal for the Southern District of New York, was indicted by the grand jury for the arrest of Arguelles, on a charge of kidnapping, and the matter came up before the General Sessions in New York, upon a petition of the counsel for defendant to transfer the case to the United States District Court, on the ground that under the act of Congress passed March 3, 1863, relating to *habeas corpus*, &c., any officer of the Federal Government, exposed to criminal prosecution, might remove the case in the Federal courts by filing a petition setting forth that the offence charged was done by the authority of the President or the Congress of the United States.

July 6—Judge Russell and Recorder Hoffmann concurring, decided that the petition to remove the case to the United States courts must be denied, the State courts having jurisdiction thereof. The counsel for the defence then made a motion to quash the indictment.

IN HOUSE.

June 6—Mr. Cox offered this resolution:

Resolved, That the recent extradition of a Spanish subject, by the action of the Chief Executive of the United States, in the absence of a law or treaty on the subject, was a violation of the Constitution of the United States and of the law of nations, and in derogation of the right of asylum, which has ever been a distinguishing feature of our political system.

The House refused to second the demand for the previous question—yeas 38, nays 57.

It was then referred to the Committee on the Judiciary—yeas 72, nays 43. The NAYS were—

Messrs. *James C. Allen, Ancona, Augustus C. Baldwin, Bliss, James S. Brown, Coffroth, Cox, Cravens, Dawson, Denison, Eden, Edgerton, Eldridge, Finck, Ganson, Harding, Harrington, Charles M. Harris, Holman, Hutchins, William Johnson, King, Knapp, Law, Lazear, Le Blond, Long, Mallory, Marcy, McDowell, James R. Morris, Morrison, Pendleton, Perry, Robinson, Rogers, Ross, Scott, Strouse, Wadsworth, Wheeler, Chilton A. White, Joseph W. White*—43.

THE FINANCES.

Our Financial Legislation.

The financial legislation has been as follows:

1860, December 17—Authorized an issue of $10,000,000 in TREASURY NOTES, to be redeemed after the expiration of one year from the date of issue, and bearing such a rate of interest as may be offered by the lowest bidders. Authority was given to issue these notes in payment of warrants in favor of public creditors at their par value, bearing six per cent. interest per annum.

1861, February 8—Authorized a LOAN of $25,000,000, bearing interest at a rate not exceeding six per cent. per annum, and reimbursable within a period not beyond twenty years nor less than ten years. This loan was made for the payment of the current expenses, and was to be awarded to the most favorable bidders.

March 2—Authorized a LOAN of $10,000,000, bearing interest at a rate not exceeding six per cent. per annum, and reimbursable after the expiration of ten years from July 1, 1861. In case proposals for the loan were not acceptable, authority was given to issue the whole amount in TREASURY NOTES, bearing interest at a rate not exceeding six per cent. per annum. Authority was also given to substitute TREASURY NOTES for the whole or any part of the loans for which the Secretary was by law authorized to contract and issue bonds, at the time of the passage of this act, and such treasury notes were to be made receivable in payment of all public dues, and redeemable at any time within two years from March 2, 1861.

March 2—Authorized an issue, should the Secretary of the Treasury deem it expedient, of $2,800,000 in coupon BONDS, bearing interest at the rate of six per cent. per annum, and redeemable in twenty years, for the payment of expenses incurred by the Territories of Washington and Oregon in the suppression of Indian hostilities during the years 1855–'56.

July 17—Authorized a loan of $250,000,000, for which could be issued BONDS bearing interest at a rate not exceeding 7 per cent. per annum, irredeemable for twenty years, and after that redeemable at the pleasure of the United States.

TREASURY NOTES bearing interest at the rate of 7.30 per cent. per annum, payable three years after date; and

United States NOTES without interest, payable on demand, to the extent of $50,000,000. (Increased by act of February 12, 1862, to $60,000,000.)

The bonds and treasury NOTES to be issued in such proportions of each as the Secretary may deem advisable.

August 5—Authorized an issue of BONDS bearing 6 per cent. interest per annum, and payable at the pleasure of the United States after twenty years from date, which may be issued in exchange for 7.30 treasury notes; but no such bonds to be issued for a less sum than $500, and the whole amount of such bonds not to exceed the whole amount of 7.30 treasury notes issued.

1862, February 25—Authorized the issue of $150,000,000 in *legal tender United States* NOTES, $50,000,000 of which to be in lieu of demand notes issued under act of July 17, 1861, $500,000,000 in 6 per cent. bonds, redeemable after five years, and payable twenty years from date, which may be exchanged for United States notes, and a temporary loan of $25,000,000 in United States notes for not less than thirty days, payable after ten days' notice at 5 per cent. interest per annum.

March 17—Authorized an increase of TEMPORARY LOANS of $25,000,000, bearing interest at a rate not exceeding 5 per cent. per annum.

July 11—Authorized a further increase of TEMPORARY LOANS of $50,000,000, making the whole amount authoı $100,000,000.

March 1—Authorized an issue of CERTIFICATES OF INDEBTEDNESS, payable one year from date, in settlement of audited claims against the Government. Interest 6 per cent. per annum, payable in gold on those issued prior to March 4, 1863, and in lawful currency on those issued on and after that date. Amount of issue not specified.

1862, July 11—Authorized an additional issue of $150,000,000 *legal tender* NOTES, $35,000,000 of which might be in denominations less than five dollars. Fifty million dollars of this issue to be reserved to pay temporary loans promptly in case of emergency.

July 17—Authorized an issue of NOTES of the fractional part of one dollar, receivable in payment of all dues, except customs, less than five dollars, and exchangeable for United States notes in sums not less than five dollars. Amount of issue not specified.

1863, January 17—Authorized the issue of $100,000,000 in United States NOTES for the immediate payment of the army and navy; such notes to be a part of the amount provided for in any bill that may hereafter be passed by this Congress. The amount in this resolution is included in act of March 3, 1863.

March 3—Authorized a LOAN of $300,000,000 for this and $600,000,000 for the next fiscal year, for which could be issued bonds running not less than ten nor more than forty years, principal and interest payable in coin, bearing interest at a rate not exceeding 6 per cent. per annum, payable on bonds not exceeding $100, annually, and on all others semi-annually. And TREASURY NOTES (to the amount of $400,000,000) not exceeding three years to run, with interest at not over 6 per cent. per annum, principal and interest payable in lawful money, which may be made a legal tender for their face value, excluding interest, or convertible into United States notes. And a further issue of $150,000,000 in United States NOTES for the purpose of converting the treasury notes which may be issued under this act, and for no other purpose. And a further issue, if necessary, for the payment of the army and navy, and other creditors of the Government, of $150,000,000 in United States NOTES, which amount includes the $100,000,000 authorized by the joint resolution of Congress, January 17, 1863. The whole amount of bonds, treasury notes, and United States notes issued under this act not to exceed the sum of $900,000,000.

March 3—Authorized an issue not exceeding $50,000,000 in FRACTIONAL CURRENCY, (in lieu of postage or other stamps,) exchangeable for United States notes in sums not less than three dollars, and receivable for any dues to the United States less than five dollars, except duties on imports. The whole amount issued, including postage and other stamps issued as currency, not to exceed $50,000,000. Authority was given to prepare it in the Treasury Department, under the supervision of the Secretary.

1864, March 3—Authorized, in lieu of so much of the loan of March 3, 1863, a LOAN of $200,000,000 for the current fiscal year, for which may be issued bonds redeemable after five and within forty years, principal and interest payable in coin, bearing interest at a rate not exceeding 6 per cent. per annum, payable annually on bonds not over $100, and on all others semi-annually. These bonds to be exempt from taxation by or under State or municipal authority.

1864, June 30—Authorized a LOAN of $400,000,000, for which may be issued bonds, redeemable after five nor more than thirty years, or if deemed expedient, made payable at any period not more than forty years from date—interest not exceeding six per cent. semi-annually, in coin. Secretary of the Treasury is authorized to dispose of these bonds, or any part, and of the remainder of the five-twenties, in the United States or in Europe, on such terms as he may deem most advisable, for lawful money of the United States, or, at his discretion, for Treasury notes, certificates of indebtedness, or certificates of deposit issued under any act of Congress. And all bonds, Treasury notes, and other obligations of the United States shall be exempt from taxation by or under State or municipal authority. In lieu of an equal amount of bonds, not exceeding $200,000,000, the Secretary is authorized to issue Treasury notes of not less than $10, payable at any time not exceeding three years, or, if thought expedient, redeemable at any time after three years, at an interest not exceeding seven and three tenths per cent., payable in lawful money at maturity, or, at the discretion of the Secretary, semi-annually. And the said Treasury notes may be disposed of by the Secretary of the Treasury, on the best terms that can be obtained, for lawful money; and such of them as shall be made payable, principal and interest, at maturity, shall be a legal tender to the same extent as United States notes for their face value, excluding interest, and may be paid to any creditor of the United States at their face value, excluding interest, or to any creditor willing to receive them at par, including interest; and any Treasury notes issued under the authority of this act may be made convertible, at the discretion of the Secretary of the Treasury, into any bonds issued under the authority of this act. And the Secretary of the Treasury may redeem and cause to be cancelled and destroyed any Treasury notes or United States notes heretofore issued under authority of previous acts of Congress, and substitute, in lieu thereof, an equal amount of Treasury notes such as are authorized by this act, or of other United States notes: *Provided*, That the total amount of bonds and Treasury notes authorized by the first and second sections of this act shall not exceed $400,000,000 in addition to the amounts heretofore issued; nor shall the total amount of United States notes, issued or to be issued, ever exceed $400,000,000, and such additional sum, not exceeding $50,000,000, as may be temporarily required for the redemption of temporary loan; nor shall any Treasury note bearing interest, issued under this act, be a legal tender in payment or redemption of any notes issued by any bank, banking association, or banker, calculated or intended to circulate as money.

SEC. 3. That the interest on all bonds heretofore issued, payable annually, may be paid semi-annually; and in lieu of such bonds authorized to be issued, the Secretary of the Treasury may issue bonds bearing interest payable semi-annually. And he may also issue in exchange for Treasury notes heretofore issued bearing seven and three-tenths per centum interest, besides the six per cent bonds heretofore authorized, like bonds of all the denominations in which said Treasury notes have been issued; and the interest on such Treasury notes after maturity shall be paid in lawful money, and they may be exchanged for such bonds at any time within three months from the date of notice of redemption by the Secretary of the Treasury, after which the interest on such Treasury notes shall cease. And so much of the law approved March 3, 1864, as limits the loan authorized therein to the current fiscal year, is hereby repealed; and the authority of the Secretary of the Treasury to borrow money and issue therefor bonds or notes conferred by the first section of the act of March 3, 1863, entitled "An act to provide ways and means for the support of the Government," shall cease on and after the passage of this act, except so far as it may effect [affect] $75,000,000 of bonds already advertised.

SPECIAL WAR INCOME TAX.

Resolved, &c., That, in addition to the income duty already imposed by law, there shall be levied, assessed, and collected on the first day of October eighteen hundred and sixty-four, a special income duty upon the gains, profits, or income for the year ending the thirty-first day of December next preceding the time herein named, by levying, assessing, and collecting said duty of all persons residing within the United States, or of citizens of the United States residing abroad, at the rate of five per centum on all sums exceeding six hundred dollars, and the same shall be levied, assessed, estimated, and collected, except as to the rates, according to the provisions of existing laws for the collection of an income duty, annually, where not inapplicable hereto; and the Secretary of the Treasury is hereby authorized to make such rules and regulations as to time and mode, or other matters, to enforce the collection of the special income duty herein provided for, as may be necessary: *Provided*, That in estimating the annual gains, profits, or income, as aforesaid, for the foregoing special income duty, no deductions shall be made for dividends or interest received from any association, corporation, or company, nor shall any deduction be made for any salary or pay received.

This resolution passed the House, July 4—yeas 53, nays 49, as follows:

YEAS—Messrs. Alley, Allison, Ames, Isaac N. Arnold, Baxter, Boutwell, Boyd, Cobb, Cole, Creswell, Dawes, Deming, Dixon, Driggs, Eckley, Eliot, Garfield, Gooch, Higby, Hooper, Hotchkiss, J. H. Hubbard, Ingersoll, Jenckes, Julian, Kelley, Longyear, McClurg, Moorhead, Morrill, D. Morris, Leonard Myers, Norton, Charles O'Neill, Perham, Alexander H. Rice, John H. Rice, Edward H. Rollins, Schenck, Shannon, Sloan, Smith, Smithers, Francis Thomas, Tracy, Upson, Ellihu B. Washburne, William B. Washburn, Webster, Wilder, Wilson, Windom, Woodbridge—53.

NAYS—Messrs. *Ancona, Baily, Bliss, Brooks, Chanler, Coffroth, Cox, Dawson, Denison, Eden, Edgerton, Eldridge, English, Ganson, Harding, Benjamin G. Harris, Charles M. Harris, Hutchins, William Johnson, Kernan, Knapp, Law, Lazear, Le Blond*, Littlejohn, *Long, Marcy, Middleton, Wm. H. Miller, James R. Morris, Morrison, Noble, Odell, John O'Neill, Pendleton, Pruyn, Samuel J. Randall, Robinson, James S. Rollins, Ross*, Scofield, *John B. Steele, William G. Steele*, Stevens, *Stiles, Sweat, Ward*, Williams, *Winfield*—49.

Seventy-eight absentees.

It passed the Senate same day—yeas 28, nay 7, as follows:

YEAS—Messrs. Anthony, Clark, Conness, Cowan, Doolittle, Foot, Foster, Hale, Harlan, Harris, Hicks, Howe, Johnson, Lane of Indiana, Lane of Kansas, *McDougall*, Morgan, Morrill, Pomeroy, Ramsey, Sherman, Sumner, Ten Eyck, Trumbull, Van Winkle, Wilkinson, Willey, Wilson—28.

NAYS—Messrs. *Buckalew, Carlile, Davis, Powell, Richardson, Riddle, Saulsbury*—7.

"Legal Tenders."

Second Session, Thirty-Seventh Congress.

1862, Feb. 6—The House came to a vote on two propositions for the issue of $150,000,000 in Treasury notes.

The one, for notes without interest, and denomination not below $5—of which $50,000,000 should be in lieu of so many of the "Demand notes"—to be receivable for all duties, imposts, excises, debts, and demands of every kind due to the United States, and all salaries, &c., from the United States, "*and shall also be lawful money, and a legal tender in payment of all debts, public and private, within the United States*," to be exchangeable for twenty year six per cent. bonds, interest payable semi-annually, or five year seven per cent. bonds with interest payable semi-annually in coin. Such United States notes to be received the same as coin in payment for loans. Five hundred millions of bonds authorized, payable after twenty years, at six per cent. interest payable semi-annually.

The other, offered as an amendment, authorized $100,000 of Treasury notes at 3.65 per cent. per annum, payable in two years, to be receivable for all public dues except duties on imports, and for all salaries, debts, and demands owing by the United States to individuals, corporations, and associations within the United States, at the option of such individuals, corporations, and associations, exchangeable for 7.30 bonds with interest payable semi-annually in coin, and receivable the same as coin in payment of loans. $500,000,000 of bonds authorized—$200,000,000 at 7:30 interest payable semi-annually in coin, and redeemable after ten years, and $300,000,000, redeemable after twenty-four years, at 6 per cent., payable semi-annually in coin.

The latter was rejected—yeas 55, nays 95, as follows:

YEAS—Messrs. *Ancona*, Baxter, *Biddle, George H. Browne*, William G. Brown, *Cobb*, Frederick A. Conkling, Roscoe Conkling, Conway, *Corning, Cox, Cravens Crisfield, Crittenden*, Diven, Eliot, *English*, Goodwin, *Grider, Harding, Holman*, Horton, *Johnson, Law, Lazear*, Lovejoy, *May*,

Menzies, Justin S. Morrill, *Morris*, Nixon, *Noble*, *Norton*, *Nugen*, *Odell*, *Pendleton*, *Perry*, Pomeroy, Porter, Edward H. Rollins, Sedgwick, *Sheffield*, *Shiel*, *William G. Steele*, Stratton, Benjamin F. Thomas, Francis Thomas, Train, *Vallandigham*, *Wadsworth*, E. P. Walton, *Ward*, Webster, *Chilton A. White*, *Wright*—55.

NAYS—Messrs. Aldrich, Alley, Arnold, Ashley, Babbitt, Goldsmith F. Bailey, *Joseph Baily*, Baker, Beaman, Bingham, Francis P. Blair, Jacob B. Blair, Samuel S. Blair, Blake, Buffinton, Burnham, Campbell, Chamberlain, Clark, Colfax, Cutler, Davis, Delano, *Delaplaine*, Duell, *Dunlap*, Dunn, Edgerton, Edwards, Ely, Fenton, Fessenden, Fisher, Franchot, Frank, Gooch, Granger, Gurley, *Haight*, Hale, Hanchett, Harrison, Hickman, Hooper, Hutchins, Julian, Kelley, Francis W. Kellogg, William Kellogg, Killinger, *Knapp*, Lansing, Leary, Loomis, McKean, McKnight, McPherson, Marston, Maynard, Mitchell, Moorhead, Anson P. Morrill, Olin, Patton, Timothy G. Phelps, Pike, *Price*, Alexander H. Rice, John H. Rice, *Richardson*, *James S. Rollins*, Sargent, Shanks, Shellabarger, Sherman, Sloan, Spaulding, *John B. Steele*, Stevens, Trimble, Trowbridge, Upton, Van Horn, Van Valkenburgh, Van Wyck, Verree, Wall, Wallace, Charles W. Walton, Whaley, Albert S. White, *Wickliffe*, Wilson, Windom, Worcester—95.

The affirmative vote on the passage of the former was the same as the negative on the amendment except that Messrs. W. G. Brown and *Crittenden*, who voted aye on the amendment, did not vote on the passage of the bill; Messrs. *Dunlap*, *Knapp*, *Richardson*, and *Wickliffe*, who voted *nay* on the amendment, voted *nay* on the passage; Messrs. *Mallory*, *Robinson*, and *Voorhees*, who did not vote on the amendment, voted *nay* on the passage; Mr. *Nugen*, who voted *aye* on the amendment, voted *aye* on the passage; and Messrs. Dunn and Riddle, who did not vote on the amendment, voted *aye* on the passage.

IN SENATE.

February 12—The Committee of Finance recommended instead of making these notes receivable for all demands due to, and all demands owing by, the United States, this substitute:

> And such notes herein authorized shall be receivable in payment of all public dues and demands of every description, and of all claims and demands against the United States of every kind whatsoever, except for interest upon bonds and notes, which shall be paid in coin.

Mr. SHERMAN moved to include with these notes, "the notes authorized by the act of July 17, 1861;" which was agreed to.

The amendment as amended was agreed to.

Feb. 13—Mr. COLLAMER moved to strike out these words:

> And such notes herein authorized and the notes authorized by the act of July 17, 1861, shall be receivable in payment of all public dues and demands of every description, and of all claims and demands against the United States of every kind whatsoever, except for interest upon bonds and notes, which shall be paid in coin, and shall also be lawful money and a legal tender in payment of all debts, public and private, within the United States, except interest as aforesaid.

Which was rejected—yeas 17, nays 22, as follows:

YEAS—Messrs. Anthony, *Bayard*, Collamer, Cowan, Fessenden, Foot, Foster, *Kennedy*, King, *Latham*, *Nesmith*, *Pearce*, *Powell*, *Saulsbury*, Simmons, *Thomson*, Willey—17.

NAYS—Messrs. Chandler, Clark, *Davis*, Dixon, Doolittle, Harlan, Harris, Henderson, Howard, Howe, Lane of Indiana, *McDougall*, Morrill, Pomeroy, *Rice*, Sherman, Sumner, Ten Eyck, Wade, Wilkinson, Wilson of Massachusetts, *Wilson* of Missouri—22.

Mr. DOOLITTLE moved to amend the bill so as to make the notes a legal tender "in payment of all public debts, and all private debts hereafter contracted within the United States;" which was rejected without a division.

Mr. KING offered an amendment, proposing, among other things, to strike out the legal tender clause; but it was rejected without a division.

The bill was then passed—yeas 30, nays 7, as follows:

YEAS—Messrs. Anthony, Chandler, Clark, *Davis*, Dixon, Doolittle, Fessenden, Foot, Foster, Grimes, Hale, Harlan, Harris, Henderson, Howard, Howe, Lane of Indiana, *Latham*, *McDougall*, Morrill, Pomeroy, *Rice*, Sherman, Sumner, Ten Eyck, Trumbull, Wade, Wilkinson, Wilson of Massachusetts, *Wilson* of Missouri—30.

NAYS—Messrs. Collamer, Cowan, *Kennedy*, King, *Pearce*, *Powell*, *Saulsbury*—7.

Feb. 20—In the House, the question being on concurring in the amendment of the Senate making the interest upon bonds and notes payable in coin,

Mr. STEVENS moved to include also "payments to officers, soldiers, and sailors, in the Army and Navy of the United States, and for all supplies purchased for the said Government;" which was rejected—yeas 67, nays 72.

The amendment of the Senate, making interest payable in coin was then concurred in—yeas 88, nays 55, as follows:

YEAS—Messrs. *Ancona*, Arnold, Ashley, Baxter, Beaman, *Biddle*, Jacob B. Blair, *George H. Browne*, William G. Brown, Burnham, *Calvert*, Clements, *Cobb*, Frederick A. Conkling, Roscoe Conkling, Conway, Covode, *Cox*, *Cravens*, *Crittenden*, Diven, *Dunlap*, Dunn, Eliot, *English*, Goodwin, *Grider*, Gurley, *Haight*, *Hall*, *Harding*, *Holman*, Horton, *Johnson*, Kelley, *Knapp*, *Law*, Leary, *Lehman*, Loomis, Lovejoy, McKnight, *Mallory*, *May*, *Menzies*, Justin S. Morrill, Nixon, *Noble*, *Norton*, *Nugen*, *Odell*, Patton, *Pendleton*, *Perry*, Timothy G. Phelps, Pike, Pomeroy, Alexander H. Rice, Riddle, *Robinson*, Edward H. Rollins, *James S. Rollins*, Sargent, Sedgwick, *Sheffield*, Sherman, *Shiel*, *Smith*, *John B. Steele*, *William G. Steele*, Stratton, Benjamin F. Thomas, Francis Thomas, Train, Trimble, *Vallandigham*, *Vibbard*, *Voorhees*, Charles W. Walton, E. P. Walton, *Ward*, Washburne, Webster, Whaley, Wheeler, *Wickliffe*, *Woodruff*, *Wright*—88.

NAYS—Messrs. Aldrich, Alley, Babbit, *Joseph Baily*, Baker, Bingham, Francis P. Blair, Samuel S. Blair, Blake, Buffinton, Campbell, Chamberlain, Clark, Davis, Dawes, Duell, Edwards, Ely, Fenton, Fessenden, Fisher, Franchot, Frank, Granger, Hale, Hanchett, Harrison, Hickman, Hooper, Julian, William Kellogg, Killinger, Lansing, McPherson, Marston, Maynard, Moorhead, Anson P. Morrill, *Noell*, Olin, John H. Rice, Shanks, Sloan, Spaulding, Stevens, Trowbridge, Van Horn, Van Valkenburgh, Verree, Wall, Wallace, Albert S. White, Wilson, Windom, Worcester—55.

Other amendments were non-concurred in, and a Committee of Conference agreed upon the bill as it became a law.

One feature of this report was to provide that the Treasury notes issued under the bill should not be a legal tender in payment of duties, and the duties on imports, made payable in coin, should be pledged for the payment of interest on the bonds.

The report was agreed to in the House—yeas 98, nays 22. The NAYS were—

Messrs. Baker, *Biddle*, Buffinton, *Cox*, Edwards, *English*, *Haight*, Hooper, *Johnson*, Justin S. Morrill, *Odell*, *Pendleton*, *Perry*, Pike, *Robinson*, *Sheffield*, *William G. Steele*, Van Wyck, *Voorhees*, *Wickliffe*, *Wood*, *Woodruff*—22.

The Senate concurred without a division.

While this question was pending before the Committee of Ways and Means, the Secretary of the Treasury, Mr. CHASE, addressed them a letter, from which this is an extract:

> TREASURY DEPARTMENT, *January* 29, 1862.
>
> SIR: I have the honor to acknowledge the receipt of a resolution of the Committee of Ways and Means, referring me to House bill No. 240, and requesting my opinion as to the propriety and necessity of its immediate passage by Congress.
>
> The condition of the Treasury certainly renders immediate action on the subject of affording provision for the e...

penditures of the Government, both expedient and necessary. The general provisions of the bill submitted to me, seem to me well adapted to the end proposed. There are, however, some points which may, perhaps, be usefully amended.

The provision making United States notes a legal tender has doubtless been well considered by the committee, and their conclusion needs no support from any observation of mine. I think it my duty, however, to say, that in respect to this provision my reflections have conducted me to the same conclusions they have reached. It is not unknown to them that I have felt, nor do I wish to conceal that I now feel, a great aversion to making anything but coin a legal tender in payment of debts. It has been my anxious wish to avoid the necessity of such legislation. It is, however, at present impossible, in consequence of the large expenditures entailed by the war, and the suspension of the banks, to procure sufficient coin for disbursements; and it has, therefore, become indispensably necessary that we should resort to the issue of United States notes. The making them a legal tender might, however, still be avoided if the willingness manifested by the people generally, by railroad companies, and by many of the banking institutions, to receive and pay them as money in all transactions were absolutely or practically universal; but, unfortunately, there are some persons and some institutions which refuse to receive and pay them, and whose action tends not merely to the unnecessary depreciation of the notes, but to establish discrimination in business against those who, in this matter, give a cordial support to the Government, and in favor of those who do not. Such discriminations should, if possible, be prevented; and the provision making the notes a legal tender, in a great measure at least, prevents it, by putting all citizens, in this respect, on the same level both of rights and duties.

The committee, doubtless, feel the necessity of accompanying this measure by legislation necessary to secure the highest credit as well as the largest currency of these notes. This security can be found, in my judgment, by proper provisions for funding them in interest bearing bonds, by well-guarded legislation authorizing banking associations with circulation based on the bonds in which the notes are funded, and by a judicious system of adequate taxation, which will not only create a demand for the notes, but—by securing the prompt payment of interest—raise and sustain the credit of the bonds. Such legislation, it may be hoped, will divest the legal lender clause of the bill of injurious tendencies, and secure the earliest possible return to a sound currency of coin and promptly convertible notes.

I beg leave to add that vigorous military operations and the unsparing retrenchment of all necessary expenses will also contribute essentially to this desirable end.

* * * * * * * *

I have the honor to be, with very great respect, yours truly, S. P. CHASE.

Hon. THADDEUS STEVENS, *Chairman.*

During the pendency of this question,

1862, January 15—Mr. CORNING offered this joint resolution:

Resolved, &c., That in order to pay the ordinary expenses of the Government, the interest on the national loans, and have an ample sinking fund for the ultimate liquidation of the public debt, a tax shall be imposed, which shall, with the tariff on imports, secure an annual revenue of not less than $150,000,000.

Which was adopted—yeas 133, nays 6. The NAYS were:

Messrs. *Allen, Norton, Robinson, Shiel, Voorhees, Wood*—6.

The following Democrats voted aye:

Messrs. *Ancona, Joseph Baily, Charles J. Biddle, G. H. Browne, C. B. Calvert, G. T. Cobb, E. Corning, S. S. Cox, J. W. Crisfield, Crittenden, Dunlap, J. E. English, Grider, E. Haight, A. Harding, W. S. Holman, P. Johnson, J. Lazear, W. E. Lehman, R. Mallory, J. W. Menzies, J. R. Morris, W. P. Noble, J. W. Noell, R. H. Nugen, Odell, G. H. Pendleton, N. Perry, J. S. Rollins, W. P. Sheffield, J. B. Steele, W. G. Steele, C. L. Vallandigham, C. Vibbard, Wadsworth, E. Ward, C. A. Wickliffe, G. C. Woodruff, H. B. Wright*—38.

January 17—The Senate passed the resolution—yeas 30, nays 1, (Mr. *Powell.*)

SMALL BANK NOTES—VETO MESSAGE.

To the Senate of the United States:

The bill which has passed the House of Representatives and the Senate, entitled "An act to repeal that part of an act of Congress which prohibits the circulation of bank notes of a less denomination than five dollars in the District of Columbia," has received my attentive consideration, and I now return it to the Senate, in which it originated, with the following objections:

1. The bill proposes to repeal the existing legislation, prohibiting the circulation of bank notes of a less denomination than five dollars within the District of Columbia, without permitting the issuing of such bills by banks not now legally authorized to issue them. In my judgment, it will be found impracticable, in the present condition of the currency, to make such a discrimination. The banks have generally suspended specie payments; and a legal sanction given to the circulation of the irredeemable notes of one class of them, will almost certainly be so extended, in practical operation, as to include those of all classes, whether authorized or unauthorized. If this view be correct, the currency of the District, should this act become a law, will certainly and greatly deteriorate to the serious injury of honest trade and honest labor.

2. This bill seems to contemplate no end which cannot be otherwise more certainly and beneficially attained. During the existing war, it is peculiarly the duty of the National Government to secure to the people a sound circulating medium. This duty has been, under existing circumstances, satisfactorily performed, in part at least, by authorizing the issue of United States notes, receivable for all Government dues except customs, and made a legal tender for all debts public and private, except interest on the public debt. The object of the bill submitted to me, namely, that of providing a small note currency during the present suspension, can be fully accomplished by authorizing the issue—as part of any new emission of United States notes made necessary by the circumstances of the country—of notes of a similar character, but of less denomination than five dollars. Such an issue would answer all the beneficial purposes of the bill; would save a considerable amount to the treasury, in interest; would greatly facilitate payments to soldiers and other creditors of small sums; and would furnish to the people a currency as safe as their own Government.

Entertaining these objections to the bill, I feel myself constrained to withhold from it my approval, and return it for the further consideration and action of Congress.

ABRAHAM LINCOLN.

June 23, 1862.

State Taxation.

First Session, Thirty-Eighth Congress.

June 22—The loan bill before the House in Committee of the Whole, and the question being on the first section, authorizing a loan of $400,000,000, closing with this clause:

And all bonds, Treasury notes, and other obligations of the United States shall be exempt from taxation by or under State or municipal authority.

Mr. HOLMAN moved to strike out the clause, which was agreed to—yeas 61, nays 44.

Mr. HOLMAN moved to insert at the end of the first section these words:

And that the bonds and other obligations issued under this act shall be subject to State and municipal taxation.

Mr. NOBLE moved to amend the amendment by substituting the following:

And all bonds, Treasury notes, and other obligations of the United States, shall be subject to State and municipal taxation, on equal terms, the same as other property.

Which was rejected.

Mr. KERNAN moved this substitute for Mr. HOLMAN's amendment:

And that the owners of the bonds and obligations issued under and by virtue of the provisions of this act shall be liable to State and municipal taxation upon the value thereof to the same extent as they are liable to such taxation upon any other securities or similar personal estate owned by them.

Mr. HOLMAN accepted the amendment, which was rejected—yeas 56, nays 59.

June 23—Pending the consideration of the loan bill in the House, being in Committee of the Whole,

Mr. STEVENS offered this substitute for the bill:

That the Secretary of the Treasury be, and he is hereby, authorized to borrow, from time to time, on the credit of the United States, $400,000,000, for the service of the fiscal year ending June 30, 1865, and to issue therefor, coupon or registered bonds of the United States, redeemable, at the pleasure of the Government, after any period not less than five nor more than thirty years, and, if deemed expedient, made payable at any period not more than forty years from date, payable in coin. And said bonds shall be of such denominations as the Secretary of the Treasury shall direct, not less than fifty dollars, and bear an annual interest not exceeding eight per cent., payable semi-annually, and the interest on all bonds heretofore issued, payable annually, may be paid semi-annually; and in lieu of such bond, authorized to be issued, the Secretary of the Treasury may issue bonds, bearing interest, payable semi-annually. And he may also issue in exchange for Treasury notes heretofore issued bearing seven and three tenths per cent. interest, besides the six per cent. bonds heretofore authorized, like bonds of the denomination of $100 and of $50. And all bonds, Treasury notes, and other obligations of the United States shall be exempt from taxation by or under State or municipal authority.

Mr. HOLMAN moved to strike out the last sentence; which was rejected, on division—yeas 58, nays 73.

The amendment was agreed to in Committee, yeas 72, nays 51; but immediately after was rejected in the House—yeas 59, nays 81, as follows:

YEAS—Messrs. *William J. Allen*, Anderson, *Baily*, *Augustus C. Baldwin*, Baxter, Blair, Blow, Boyd, *Brooks*, Broomall, William G. Brown, Cole, *Dawson*, *Denison*, Donnelly, *Eden*, *Eldridge*, Farnsworth, *Grider*, *Harding*, *Benjamin G. Harris*, Higby, *Holman*, Hotchkiss, Asahel W. Hubbard, Ingersoll, *Philip Johnson*, *William Johnson*, *Kalbfleisch*, *Knapp*, *Law*, Loan, *Long*, *Marcy*, *McAllister*, McClurg, *McDowell*, *William H. Miller*, Moorhead, *James R. Morris*, *Morrison*, Amos Myers, *John O'Neill*, Orth, *Robinson*, *Ross*, *Scott*, Shannon, *John B. Steele*, Stevens, *Sweat*, Thayer, Van Valkenburgh, Whaley, *Wheeler*, *Chilton A. White*, *Joseph W. White*, Wilson, *Winfield*—59.

NAYS—Messrs. Alley, Allison, Ames, *Ancona*, Arnold, Ashley, John D. Baldwin, Beaman, Blaine, Boutwell, Ambrose W. Clark, Freeman Clarke, Cobb, Creswell, Thomas T. Davis, Dawes, Dixon, Driggs, Eckley, *Edgerton*, Eliot, *English*, Fenton, *Finck*, Frank, *Ganson*, Garfield, Gooch, *Griswold*, Hale, *Herrick*, Hooper, John H. Hubbard, Hulburd, Jenckes, Julian, Kelley, Francis W. Kellogg, Orlando Kellogg, *Kernan*, Knox, Longyear, Marvin, McBride, Samuel F. Miller, Morrill, Daniel Morris, Leonard Myers, *Noble*, Norton, *Odell*, Charles O'Neill, Patterson, *Pendleton*, Perham, Pike, Pomeroy, Price, Pruyn, *Radford*, *Samuel J. Randall*, John H. Rice, Edward H. Rollins, *James S. Rollins*, Schenck, Scofield, Sloan, Smithers, Spalding, *William G. Steele*, *Stiles*, *Strouse*, *Stuart*, Upson, *Ward*, Ellihu B. Washburne, William B. Washburn, Webster, Williams, *Benjamin Wood*, *Fernando Wood*—81.

Mr. POMEROY moved this substitute for the second section of the bill:

SEC. 2. *And be it further enacted*, That the Secretary of the Treasury may issue, upon the credit of the United States, bonds of any denomination not less than $100, payable in lawful money, three years from the date thereof, and bearing interest not exceeding eight per cent. per annum, payable semi-annually in lawful money, and may receive at par therefor the lawful money of the United States, Treasury notes, certificates of indebtedness, or certificates of deposit issued under any act of Congress. And the Secretary of the Treasury, in addition to the total amounts of bonds authorized by the first and second sections of this act, shall issue at par, in redemption of any outstanding notes, certificates of deposit, certificates of indebtedness of the United States, bonds similar to those hereinbefore in this second section authorized, in denominations of not less than $100, or of like denominations similar to those authorized by the first section, and payable five years from date, with interest at six per cent., payable semi-annually. And the Secretary of the Treasury is further authorized to issue, in lieu of any bonds heretofore authorized by law, and not now issued in pursuance thereof, bonds similar to and in the denominations hereby authorized. All outstanding notes, other than United States notes, shall cease to be a legal tender in payment of public or private indebtedness on and after the 1st day of October, 1864. And no notes, other than United States notes, shall hereafter be issued or reissued. Nor shall the total amount of United States notes issued or to be issued ever exceed $400,000,000, and such additional sum, not exceeding $50,000,000, as may be temporarily required for the redemption of temporary loan.

Which was rejected—yeas 44, nays 81, as follows:

YEAS—Messrs. *Ancona*, *Augustus C. Baldwin*, *Brooks*, William G. Brown, Freeman Clarke, *Coffroth*, Cole, *Cravens*, Creswell, Dawes, *Dawson*, *Edgerton*, *English*, Farnsworth, *Ganson*, *Griswold*, *Harrington*, *Herrick*, *Holman*, Hotchkiss, Jenckes, *Kalbfleisch*, *Kernan*, *Law*, *Marcy*, Samuel F. Miller, *James R. Morris*, *Morrison*, *Nelson*, *Odell*, Pike, Pomeroy, Price, *Pruyn*, *James S. Rollins*, *Ross*, Scofield, *John B. Steele*, Thayer, Van Valkenburgh, William B. Washburn, Whaley, *Wheeler*, Wilson—44.

NAYS—Messrs. *William J. Allen*, Alley, Allison, Ames, Arnold, Ashley, *Baily*, John D. Baldwin, Baxter, Beaman, Blair, Blow, Boutwell, Boyd, Broomall, *James S. Brown*, Ambrose W. Clark, Cobb, Thomas T. Davis, *Denison*, Dixon, Donnelly, Driggs, *Eden*, *Eldridge*, Eliot, Frank, Gooch, Hale, *Harding*, *Benjamin G. Harris*, Hooper, Asahel W. Hubbard, John H. Hubbard, Hulburd, *Philip Johnson*, Julian, Kelley, Francis W. Kellogg, Orlando Kellogg, *Knapp*, Knox, Loan, *Long*, Longyear, *McAllister*, McBride, McClurg, *Wm. H. Miller*, Moorhead, Morrill, Daniel Morris, Amos Myers, Leonard Myers, *Noble*, Norton, Charles O'Neill, *John O'Neill*, Orth, Perham, John H. Rice, E. H. Rollins, Schenck, Shannon, Sloan, Smithers, Spalding, *Wm. G. Steele*, Stevens, *Stiles*, *Strouse*, *Stuart*, Tracy, Upson, Ellihu B. Washburne, Webster, Williams, Windom, *Winfield*, *Benjamin Wood*, *Fernando Wood*—81.

The bill then passed without the yeas and nays being ordered.

June 27—The bill was slightly amended in the Senate, and passed without a division.

STATE TAXATION—AGAIN.

June 28—On concurring in Senate amendments, Mr. HOLMAN moved to add this proviso to one of them:

Provided, That nothing in this act shall impair the right of the States to tax the bonds, notes, and other obligations issued under this act.

Which was rejected—yeas 71, nays 77, as follows:

YEAS—Messrs. *William J. Allen*, *Ancona*, *Bliss*, *Brooks*, *James S. Brown*, *Chanler*, *Coffroth*, *Cox*, *Cravens*, Dawes, *Dawson*, *Denison*, *Eden*, *Edgerton*, *Eldridge*, *English*, *Finck*, *Ganson*, *Grider*, *Griswold*, *Harding*, *Harrington*, *Charles M. Harris*, *Herrick*, *Holman*, Hotchkiss, *Hutchins*, *Philip Johnson*, *William Johnson*, *Kalbfleisch*, *Kernan*, *Knapp*, *Law*, *Lazear*, *Le Blond*, *Long*, *Mallory*, *Marcy*, *McDowell*, *McKinney*, *Middleton*, Samuel F. Miller, *William H. Miller*, *James R. Morris*, *Morrison*, *Noble*, *John O'Neill*, *Pendleton*, *Perry*, Pomeroy, *Pruyn*, *Radford*, *Samuel J. Randall*, *Robinson*, *Ross*, *John B. Steele*, *William G. Steele*, *Stiles*, *Strouse*, *Stuart*, *Sweat*, Thomas, Tracy, Van Valkenburgh, *Wadsworth*, *Ward*, Whaley, *Wheeler*, *Chilton A. White*, *Joseph W. White*, *Winfield*—71.

NAYS—Messrs. Alley, Allison, Ames, Anderson, Arnold, John D. Baldwin, Baxter, Beaman, Blaine, Blair, Blow, Boutwell, Boyd, Broomall, William G. Brown, Cobb, Cole, Creswell, Henry Winter Davis, Thomas T. Davis, Deming, Dixon, Donnelly, Driggs, Eckley, Eliot, Fenton, Garfield, Gooch, Hale, Higby, Hooper, Asahel W. Hubbard, John H. Hubbard, Hulburd, Ingersoll, Jenckes, Julian, Kelley, Francis W. Kellogg, Orlando Kellogg, Littlejohn, Loan, Longyear, Marvin, McBride, McClurg, McIndoe, Moorhead, Daniel Morris, Amos Myers, Leonard Myers, Norton, Chas. O'Neill, Orth, Perham, Pike, Alexander H. Rice, John H. Rice, Edward H. Rollins, Schenck, Scofield, Shannon, Sloan, Smith, Smithers, Spalding, Stevens, Thayer, Upson, Ellihu B. Washburne, Wm. B. Washburn, Webster, Williams, Wilder, Wilson, Windom—77.

Taxation.

THE INTERNAL REVENUE AND TARIFF ACT OF 1861.

First Session, Thirty-Seventh Congress.

The bill to provide increased revenue from imports, &c., passed the House August 2, 1861—yeas 89, nays 39. The NAYS were:

Messrs. *Allen*, *Ancona*, Beaman, *Burnett*, *Cox*, *Cravens*, *Crittenden*, *Dunlap*, *English*, *Grider*, *Haight*, *Harding*, *Holman*, Jackson, *Johnson*, *Law*, *Logan*, *Mallory*, *May*, *Menzies*, *Morris*, *Noble*, *Norton*, *Odell*, *Pendleton*, *Reid*, *James S. Rollins*, *Shiel*, *Smith*, Trowbridge, *Vallandigham*, *Vibbard*, *Voorhees*, *Wadsworth*, *Ward*, Webster, *Chilton A. White*, *Woodruff*, *Wright*—39.

Same day, it passed the Senate—yeas 34, nays 8, (Messrs. *Breckinridge*, *Bright*, *Johnson* of Missouri, *Kennedy*, *Latham*, *Polk*, *Powell*, *Saulsbury*.)

THE INTERNAL REVENUE ACT OF 1862.

Second Session, Thirty-Seventh Congress.

1862, April 8—The House passed the bill to provide internal revenue, support the Government, and pay interest on the public debt—yeas 126, nays 15. The NAYS were—

Messrs. *William Allen*, *George H. Browne*, Buffinton, *Cox*, *Kerrigan*, *Knapp*, *Law*, *Norton*, *Pendleton*, *Richardson*, *Shiel*, *Vallandigham*, *Voorhees*, *Chilton A. White*, *Wickliffe*—15.

June 6—The bill passed in the Senate—yeas 37, nay 1, (Mr. *Powell*.)

TAX ON SLAVES.

While this bill was pending in the House, April 8—Mr. BLAIR, of Missouri, offered this as a new section:

SEC. —. That any person who shall claim to own the service or labor for life of any person under the laws of any State, shall pay on account of the service of each person so held the sum of two dollars.

Which was rejected—yeas 51, nays 76, as follows:

YEAS—Messrs. Aldrich, Arnold, Babbitt, Baxter, Beaman, Francis P. Blair, Samuel S. Blair, Blake, Campbell, Clark, Clements, Colfax, Frederick A. Conkling, Roscoe Conkling, Covode, Davis, Dawes, Duell, Edgerton, Eliot, Fessenden, Gurley, Hanchett, Hickman, Kelley, Francis W. Kellogg, Killinger, Lansing, Loomis, McPherson, Mitchell, Moorhead, Anson P. Morrill, Justin S. Morrill, Olin, Patton, Pike, John H. Rice, Edward H. Rollins, Shanks, Sherman, Sloan, Spaulding, Stevens, Van Valkenburgh, Verree, Wallace, E. P. Walton, Wheeler, Wilson, Windom—51.

NAYS—Messrs. *Allen*, Alley, Baker, *Biddle*, Bingham, Jacob B. Blair, William G. Brown, Buffinton, *Calvert*, Chamberlain, *Cobb*, *Corning*, *Cox*, *Cravens*, *Crittenden*, *Delaplaine*, Diven, *Dunlap*, Dunn, Edwards, *English*, Fisher, Frank, Granger, *Grider*, *Haight*, Hale, *Hall*, *Harding*, Harrison, Hooper, Horton, Hutchins, Julian, *Kerrigan*, *Knapp*, *Law*, *Lazear*, Leary, *Lehman*, Lovejoy, *Mallory*, *Menzies*, *Noble*, *Noell*, *Norton*, *Nugen*, *Pendleton*, *Perry*, Timothy G. Phelps, Pomeroy, Porter, Potter, *Price*, Alexander H. Rice, Riddle, *James S. Rollins*, Sargent, *Sheffield*, Sheilabarger, *Shiel*, *Smith*, *John B. Steele*, *William G. Steele*, Stratton, Benjamin F. Thomas, Francis Thomas, Trowbridge, *Vallandigham*, Van Horn, *Wadsworth*, Webster, Albert S. White, *Chilton A. White*, *Wickliffe*, *Wright*—76.

IN SENATE.

May 29—Mr. SUMNER offered this new section:

That an annual tax of five dollars shall be paid by every person or persons, corporation, or society, for and on account of the service or labor of every other person between the ages of ten and sixty-five years, whose service or labor, for a term of years or for life, is claimed to be owned by such first mentioned person or persons, corporation, or society, whether in a fiduciary capacity, or otherwise, under and by virtue of the laws or customs of any State; and said annual tax shall be levied and collected of the person or persons, corporation, or society, making such claim, and of their goods, chattels, or lands, as is hereinbefore provided; but in no case shall the person or persons whose service or labor is so claimed, or their service or labor, be sold for the purpose of collecting said tax: *Provided*, That this tax shall not apply to service due to parents.

Mr. HENDERSON moved to add this proviso:

That the tax herein prescribed shall not be levied or collected in any State where a system of gradual emancipation may have been adopted at the time of the collection.

Which was rejected—yeas 15, nays 20, as follows:

YEAS—Messrs. Browning, Dixon, Doolittle, Grimes, Hale, Harlan, Harris, Howe, Lane of Indiana, Pomeroy, Sherman, Ten Eyck, Wiley, Wilson of Massachusetts, *Wright*—15.

NAYS—Messrs. Anthony, *Carlile*, Chandler, Clark, Collamer, Cowan, *Davis*, Fessenden, Foster, Howard, *Kennedy*, King, Lane of Kansas, Morrill, *Powell*, *Saulsbury*, Sumner, Trumbull, Wilkinson, Wilmot—20.

Mr. FESSENDEN moved to amend Mr. SUMNER'S, by reducing the tax from *five* to *two* dollars, which was agreed to:

YEAS—Messrs. Anthony, Browning, Chandler, Clark, Collamer, Cowan, *Davis*, Dixon, Doolittle, Fessenden, Foster, Grimes, Hale, Harlan, Harris, Howard, Howe, *Kennedy*, Lane of Indiana, Lane of Kansas, Morrill, *Powell*, Sherman, Simmons, Ten Eyck, Wade, Willey, *Wright*—28.

NAYS—Messrs. *Carlile*, King, *Latham*, *McDougall*, Pomeroy, *Saulsbury*, Sumner, Trumbull, Wilmot, Wilson of Massachusetts—10.

Mr. SUMNER'S amendment was then rejected—yeas 14, nays 22, as follows:

YEAS—Messrs. Anthony, Clark, Fessenden, Grimes, Harlan, Howard, Howe, King, Lane of Kansas, Morrill, Simmons, Sumner, Trumbull, Wade—14.

NAYS—Messrs. *Bayard*, Browning, *Carlile*, Cowan, *Davis*, Dixon, Doolittle, Foster, Hale, Harris, *Kennedy*, Lane of Indiana, *Latham*, *McDougall*, Pomeroy, *Powell*, *Saulsbury*, Sherman, Ten Eyck, Willey, Wilson of Massachusetts, *Wright*—22.

June 5—Mr. SUMNER offered this as a new section:

That every person claiming the service or labor of any other person as a slave, shall pay a tax of two dollars on account of every person so claimed. But in no case shall any person so claimed be sold for the purpose of collecting the tax.

Which was agreed to—yeas 19, nays 16, as follows:

YEAS—Messrs. Anthony, Chandler, Clark, Collamer, Fessenden, Foot, Grimes, Harlan, Howard, Howe, King, Morrill, Pomeroy, *Rice*, Simmons, Sumner, Wilkinson, Wilmot—19.

NAYS—Messrs. Browning, *Carlile*, Cowan, *Davis*, Dixon, Doolittle, Foster, Hale, Lane of Indiana, *Latham*, *Nesmith*, *Powell*, Willey, Wilson of Massachusetts, *Wright*—16.

June 6—Mr. ANTHONY moved to reconsider this vote; which was agreed to—yeas 22, nays 18, as follows:

YEAS—Messrs. *Bayard*, Browning, *Carlile*, Cowan, *Davis*, Dixon, Doolittle, Foster, Hale, Harris, *Kennedy*, Lane of Indiana, *Latham*, *McDougall*, *Nesmith*, *Powell*, *Rice*, *Saulsbury*, *Stark*, Ten Eyck, Willey, *Wright*—22.

NAYS—Messrs. Anthony, Chandler, Clark, Fessenden, Foot, Grimes, Harlan, Howard, Howe, King, Morrill, Pomeroy, Simmons, Sumner, Trumbull, Wade, Wilkinson, Wilmot—18.

Mr. HOWE moved to amend the amendment by inserting after the word "claimed" the words, "except those under ten and over sixty years of age," which was agreed to, and the amendment, as amended, was then rejected—yeas 17, nays 23, as follows:

YEAS — Messrs. Anthony, Chandler, Clark, Fessenden, Foot, Grimes, Harlan, Howard, Howe, King, Morrill, Simmons, Sumner, Trumbull, Wade, Wilkinson, Wilmot—17.

NAYS—Messrs. *Bayard*, Browning, *Carlile*, Cowan, *Davis*, Dixon, Doolittle, Foster, Hale, Harris, *Kennedy*, Lane of Indiana, *Latham*, *McDougall*, *Nesmith*, *Powell*, *Rice*, *Saulsbury*, *Stark*, Ten Eyck, Willey, Wilson of Mass., *Wright*—23.

First Session, Thirty-Eighth Congress.

INTERNAL REVENUE ACT OF 1864.

April 28—The House passed the act of 1864—yeas 110, nays 39. The NAYS were:

Messrs. *James C. Allen*, *William J. Allen*, *Ancona*, *Brooks*, *Chanler*, *Cox*, *Dawson*, *Denison*, *Eden*, *Eldridge*, *Finck*, *Harrington*, *Benjamin G. Harris*, *Herrick*, *Philip Johnson*, *William Johnson*, *Knapp*, *Law*, *Le Blond*, *Long*, *Marcy*, *McDowell*, *McKinney*, *James R. Morris*, *Morrison*, *Noble*, *John O'Neill*, *Pendleton*, *Perry*, *Robinson*, *Ross*, *Stiles*, *Strouse*, *Stuart*, *Voorhees*, *Ward*, *Chilton A. White*, *Joseph W. White*, *Fernando Wood*—39.

June 6—The Senate amended and passed the bill—yeas 22, nays 3, (Messrs. *Davis*, *Hendricks*, *Powell*.)

The bill, as finally agreed upon by a Committee of Conference, passed without a division.

TARIFF ACT OF 1862.

Second Session, Thirty-Seventh Congress.

IN HOUSE.

1862, July 1—The House passed, without a division, a bill increasing temporarily the duties on imports, and for other purposes.

July 8—The Senate passed it without a division.

THE TARIFF ACT OF 1864.

June 4—The House passed the bill—yeas 81, nays 28. The NAYS were:

Messrs. *James C. Allen*, *Bliss*, *James S. Brown*, *Cox*, *Edgerton*, *Eldridge*, *Finck*, *Grider*, *Harding*, *Harrington*, *Chas. M. Harris*, *Herrick*, *Holman*, *Hutchins*, *Le Blond*, *Long*, *Mallory*, *Marcy*, *McDowell*, *Morrison*, *Noble*, *Pendleton*, *Perry*, *Pruyn*, *Ross*, *Wadsworth*, *Chilton A. White*, *Joseph W. White*—28.

June 17—The Senate passed the bill—yeas 22, nays 5, (Messrs. *Buckalew*, *Hendricks*, *McDougall*, *Powell*, *Richardson*.)

TAXES IN INSURRECTIONARY DISTRICTS, 1862.

Second Session, Thirty-Seventh Congress.

1862, May 12—The bill for the collection of taxes in the insurrectionary districts passed the Senate—yeas 32, nays 3, as follows:

YEAS—Messrs. Anthony, Browning, Chandler, Clark, *Davis*, Dixon, Doolittle, Fessenden, Foot, Foster, Harlan, Harris, Henderson, Howe, King, Lane of Indiana, Lane of Kansas, *Latham*, *McDougall*, Morrill, *Nesmith*, Pomeroy, *Rice*, Sherman, Sumner, Ten Eyck, Trumbull, Wade, Wilkinson, Willey, Wilson of Massachusetts, *Wright*—32.

NAYS—Messrs. Howard, *Powell*, *Saulsbury*—3.

May 28—The bill passed House—yeas 98, nays 17. The NAYS were:

Messrs. *Biddle*, *Calvert*, *Cravens*, *Johnson*, *Kerrigan*, *Law*, *Mallory*, *Menzies*, *Noble*, *Norton*, *Pendleton*, *Perry*, Francis Thomas, *Vallandigham*, *Ward*, *Wickliffe*, *Wood*—17.

The Democrats who voted AYE were:

Messrs. *Ancona*, *Baily*, *Cobb*, *English*, *Haight*, *Holman*, *Lehman*, *Odell*, *Phelps*, *Richardson*, *James S. Rollins*, *Sheffield*, *Smith*, *John B. Steele*, *Wm. G. Steele*—14.

TAXES IN INSURRECTIONARY DISTRICTS, 1864.

IN SENATE.

June 27—The bill passed the Senate without a division.

July 2—It passed the House without a division.

The National Currency Act* of 1863.

Third Session, Thirty-Seventh Congress.

IN SENATE.

1863, February 12—The bill passed—yeas 23, nays 21, as follows:

YEAS—Messrs. Anthony, Arnold, Chandler, Clark, Doolittle, Fessenden, Foster, *Harding*, Harlan, Harris, Howard, Howe, Lane of Kansas, Morrill, *Nesmith*, Pomeroy, Sherman, Sumner, Ten Eyck, Wade, Wilkinson, Wilmot, Wilson of Massachusetts—23.

---

* January 17—The President sent this message to Congress:

To the Senate and House of Representatives:

I have signed the joint resolution to provide for the immediate payment of the army and navy of the United States, passed by the House of Representatives on the 14th and by the Senate on the 15th instant.

The joint resolution is a simple authority, amounting, however, under existing circumstances, to a direction to the Secretary of the Treasury to make an additional issue of $100,000,000 in United States notes, if so much money is needed, for the payment of the army and navy.

My approval is given in order that every possible facility may be afforded for the prompt discharge of all arrears of pay due to our soldiers and our sailors.

While giving this approval, however, I think it my duty to express my sincere regret that it has been found necessary to authorize so large an additional issue of United States notes when this circulation, and that of the suspended banks together, have become already so redundant as to increase prices beyond real values, thereby augmenting the cost of living to the injury of labor, and the cost of supplies to the injury of the whole country.

It seems very plain that the continued issues of United States notes, without any check to the issues of suspended banks and without adequate provision for the raising of money by loans, and for funding the issues so as to keep them within due limits, must soon produce disastrous consequences. And this matter appears to me so important that I feel bound to avail myself of this occasion to ask the especial attention of Congress to it.

That Congress has power to regulate the currency of the country can hardly admit of a doubt; and that a judicious measure to prevent the deterioration of this currency, by a reasonable taxation of bank circulation or otherwise, is needed, seems equally clear. Independently of this general consideration, it would be unjust to the people at large to exempt banks enjoying the special privilege of circulation from their just proportion of the public burdens.

In order to raise money by way of loans most easily and cheaply, it is clearly necessary to give every possible support to the public credit. To that end, a uniform currency, in which taxes, subscriptions to loans, and all other ordinary public dues, as well as all private dues, may be paid, is almost if not quite indispensable. Such a currency can be furnished by banking associations, organized under a general act of Congress, as suggested in my message at the beginning of the present session. The securing of this circulation by the pledge of United States bonds, as therein suggested, would still further facilitate loans, by increasing the present and causing a future demand for such bonds.

In view of the actual financial embarrassments of the Government, and of the greater embarrassments sure to come if the necessary means of relief be not afforded, I feel that I should not perform my duty by a simple announcement of my approval of the joint resolution which proposes relief only by increasing circulation, without expressing my earnest desire that measures, such in substance as those I have just referred to, may receive the early sanction of Congress.

By such measures, in my opinion, will payment be most certainly secured, not only to the army and navy, but to all honest creditors of the Government, and satisfactory provision made for future demands on the Treasury.

ABRAHAM LINCOLN.

January 17, 1863.

NAYS—Messrs. *Carlile*, Collamer, Cowan, *Davis*, Dixon, Foot, Grimes, Henderson, Hicks, *Kennedy*, King, *Latham*, *McDougall*, *Powell*, *Rice*, *Richardson*, *Saulsbury*, Trumbull, *Turpie*, *Wall*, *Wilson* of Missouri—21.

IN HOUSE.

February 20—The bill passed—yeas 78, nays 64, as follows:

YEAS—Messrs. Aldrich, Alley, Ashley, Babbitt, Beaman, Bingham, Jacob B. Blair, Blake, Buffinton, *Calvert*, Campbell, Casey, Chamberlain, Clements, Colfax, Conway, Covode, Cutler, Davis, Delano, Dunn, Edgerton, Eliot, Ely, Fenton, Samuel C. Fessenden, Thomas A. D. Fessenden, Fisher, Frank, Goodwin, Granger, Hahn, *Haight*, Hickman, Hooper, Hutchins, Julian, Kelley, Francis W. Kellogg, William Kellogg, Lansing, Leary, Lovejoy, Low, McIndoe, McKean, McPherson, Marston, Maynard, Moorhead, Anson P. Morrill, *Noell*, Olin, Patton, Timothy G. Phelps, Potter, Alexander H. Rice, John H. Rice, Sargent, Sedgwick, Segar, Shanks, Shellabarger, Sherman, Sloan, Spaulding, Stevens, Trimble, Trowbridge, Van Horn, Van Wyck, Verree, Wall, Wallace, Washburne, Albert S. White, Windom, Worcester—78.

NAYS—Messrs. *William Allen*, *Ancona*, *Baily*, Baker, Baxter, *Biddle*, *Cobb*, Frederick A. Conkling, Roscoe Conkling, *Cox*, *Cravens*, *Crittenden*, Dawes, Edwards, *English*, Gooch, *Grider*, Gurley, *Hall*, *Harding*, Harrison, *Holman*, Horton, *Johnson*, *Kerrigan*, *Knapp*, *Law*, *Lazear*, Loomis, *Mallory*, *May*, *Menzies*, Justin S. Morrill, *Morris*, Nixon, *Noble*, *Norton*, *Nugen*, *Odell*, *Pendleton*, *Perry*, Pike, Pomeroy, Porter, *Price*, *Robinson*, *James S. Rollins*, *Sheffield*, *Shiel*, *John B. Steele*, *William G. Steele*, *Stiles*, Stratton, Benjamin F. Thomas, F. Thomas, *Vallandigham*, *Wadsworth*, Wheeler, Whaley, *Chilton A. White*, *Wickliffe*, Wilson, *Woodruff*, *Wright*—64.

THE ACT OF 1864.

April 18—The bill passed the House—yeas 80, nays 66, as follows:

YEAS—Messrs. Alley, Allison, Ames, Anderson, Arnold, Ashley, John D. Baldwin, Baxter, Beaman, Blaine, Jacob B. Blair, Boutwell, Boyd, Broomall, W. G. Brown, A. W. Clark, Freeman Clarke, Cobb, Cole, Creswell, Dawes, Deming, T. T. Davis, Donnelly, Driggs, Dumont, Eckley, Farnsworth, Fenton, Frank, Garfield, Gooch, Grinnell, Higby, Hooper, Hotchkiss, Asahel W. Hubbard, John H. Hubbard, Jenckes, Julian, Kasson, Kelley, Francis W. Kellogg, Orlando Kellogg, Loan, Longyear, Marvin, McBride, McClurg, McIndoe, Samuel F. Miller, Moorhead, Morrill, Daniel Morris, Amos Myers, Norton, Charles O'Neill, Orth, Patterson, Perham, Price, William H. Randall, John H. Rice, Edward H. Rollins, Shannon, Sloan, Smith, Stevens, Thayer, Tracy, Upson, Van Valkenburgh, Ellihu B. Washburne, William B. Washburn, Webster, Williams, Wilder, Wilson, Windom, Woodbridge—80.

NAYS—Messrs. *J. C. Allen*, *W. J. Allen*, *Ancona*, *Baily*, *A. C. Baldwin*, Francis P. Blair, *Bliss*, *Brooks*, *Chanler*, *Clay*, *Coffroth*, *Cravens*, *Dawson*, *Denison*, *Eden*, *Eldridge*, *Finck*, *Ganson*, *Grider*, *Griswold*, *Hall*, *Harding*, *Harrington*, *Benjamin G. Harris*, *Charles M. Harris*, *Herrick*, *Holman*, *Hutchins*, *William Johnson*, *Kernan*, *King*, *Knapp*, *Law*, *Lazear*, *Long*, *Mallory*, *Marcy*, *McDowell*, *McKinney*, *Middleton*, *William H. Miller*, *James R. Morris*, *Morrison*, *Nelson*, *Noble*, *Odell*, *Pendleton*, *Pruyn*, *Radford*, *Samuel J. Randall*, *Robinson*, *Rogers*, *Ross*, *Scott*, *John B. Steele*, *W. G. Steele*, *Stiles*, *Strouse*, *Stuart*, Thomas, *Wheeler*, *Chilton A. White*, *Joseph W. White*, *Winfield*, *Fernando Wood*, *Yeaman*—66.

May 10—The Senate passed it—yeas 30, nays 9, as follows:

YEAS—Messrs. Anthony, Chandler, Clark, Collamer, Conness, Dixon, Doolittle, Fessenden, Foot, Foster, Hale, Harlan, Howard, Howe, Johnson, Lane of Indiana, Lane of Kansas, Morgan, Morrill, Pomeroy, Ramsey, Sherman, Sprague, Sumner, Ten Eyck, Trumbull, Van Winkle, Wilkinson, Willey, Wilson—30.

NAYS—Messrs. *Buckalew*, Cowan, *Davis*, Grimes, Henderson, *Powell*, *Richardson*, *Riddle*, *Saulsbury*—9.

IN HOUSE.

SMALL NOTES.

Pending the consideration of this bill,

April 6—A section was adopted, authorizing the issue to those banks of notes of the denominations of one, two, three, five, ten, twenty, fifty, one hundred, five hundred, and one thousand dollars—yeas 76, nays 54, as follows:

YEAS—Messrs. Alley, Allison, Ames, Anderson, Ashley, John D. Baldwin, Baxter, Beaman, Blaine, Blow, Boutwell, Boyd, Broomall, Ambrose W. Clark, Cobb, Cole, Dixon, Donnelly, Driggs, Eckley, Eliot, Frank, *Ganson*, Gooch, Grinnell, *Griswold*, Hale, Hotchkiss, Asahel W. Hubbard, John H. Hubbard, Jenckes, Julian, Kasson, Kelley, Francis W. Kellogg, Orlando Kellogg, Loan, Longyear, Marvin, McBride, McClurg, Samuel F. Miller, Moorhead, Morrill, Daniel Morris, Amos Myers, Leonard Myers, Charles O'Neill, Orth, Patterson, Perham, Pomeroy, Price, *Pruyn*, *Radford*, William H. Randall, Alexander H. Rice, John H. Rice, Edward H. Rollins, Schenck, Scofield, Shannon, Spalding, Starr, Stevens, Thayer, Upson, Van Valkenburgh, Ellihu B. Washburne, William B. Washburn, Whaley, Williams, Wilder, Wilson, Windom, Woodbridge—76.

NAYS—Messrs. *James C. Allen*, *William J. Allen*, *Ancona*, *Baily*, *Augustus C. Baldwin*, *Bliss*, *Brooks*, *James S. Brown*, William G. Brown, *Chanler*, *Cox*, *Dawson*, *Denison*, *Eden*, *Eldridge*, *English*, *Finck*, *Grider*, *Harrington*, *Herrick*, *Holman*, *Philip Johnson*, *William Johnson*, *Kalbfleisch*, *Kernan*, *Law*, *Long*, *Mallory*, *Marcy*, *McKinney*, *Middleton*, *William H. Miller*, *James R. Morris*, *Morrison*, *Nelson*, *John O'Neill*, *Pendleton*, *Samuel J. Randall*, *Robinson*, *Rogers*, *James S. Rollins*, *Scott*, *John B. Steele*, *William G. Steele*, *Strouse*, *Sweat*, Thomas, *Voorhees*, *Wheeler*, *Chilton A. White*, *Joseph W. White*, *Winfield*, *Benjamin Wood*, *Yeaman*—54.

INTEREST.

The section enacting that seven per cent, interest shall be deemed the lawful interest in all States where no rate is established, but each bank shall be bound by the State law regulating interest in the State where it is located, was agreed to—yeas 89, nays 45.

STATE TAXATION.

This section:

That nothing in this act shall be construed to prevent the taxation by States of the capital stock of banks organized under this act, the same as the property of other moneyed corporations, for State or municipal purposes; but no State shall impose any tax upon such associations or their capital, circulation, dividends, or business, at a higher rate of taxation than shall be imposed by such State upon the same amount of moneyed capital in the hands of individual citizens of such State.

Was adopted—yeas 78, nays 56, as follows:

YEAS—Messrs. *James C. Allen*, *William J. Allen*, *Ancona*, *Baily*, *Augustus C. Baldwin*, *Bliss*, *Brooks*, Broomall, *James S. Brown*, William G. Brown, *Chanler*, *Clay*, *Cox*, *Cravens*, *Dawson*, *Denison*, *Eden*, *Eldridge*, *English*, *Finck*, *Ganson*, *Grider*, *Griswold*, *Hall*, *Harrington*, *Benjamin G. Harris*, *Herrick*, *Holman*, Hotchkiss, *Philip Johnson*, *William Johnson*, *Kalbfleisch*, Orlando Kellogg, *Kernan*, *Law*, *Lazear*, *Long*, *Mallory*, *Marcy*, *McKinney*, *Middleton*, Samuel F. Miller, *William H. Miller*, *James R. Morris*, *Morrison*, Amos Myers, *Nelson*, *Odell*, *John O'Neill*, Orth, *Pendleton*, Pike, Pomeroy, *Pruyn*, *Radford*, *Samuel J. Randall*, William H. Randall, John H. Rice, *Robinson*, *Rogers*, Scofield, *Scott*, Starr, *John B. Steele*, *William G. Steele*, *Strouse*, *Sweat*, Tracy, Van Valkenburgh, *Ward*, Whaley, *Wheeler*, *Chilton A. White*, *Joseph W. White*, Windom, *Winfield*, *Benjamin Wood*, *Yeaman*—78.

NAYS—Messrs. Alley, Allison, Ames, Anderson, Ashley, John D. Baldwin, Baxter, Beaman, Blaine, Blow, Boutwell, Boyd, Ambrose W. Clark, Cobb, Cole, Thomas T. Davis, Dixon, Donnelly, Driggs, Eckley, Eliot, Frank, Gooch, Grinnell, Hale, Hooper, Asahel W. Hubbard, John H. Hubbard, Jenckes, Julian, Kasson, Kelley, Francis W. Kellogg, Loan, Longyear, Marvin, McBride, McClurg, Morrill, Daniel Morris, Leonard Myers, Charles O'Neill, Perham, Price, Alexander H. Rice, Edward H. Rollins, Schenck, Shannon, Smithers, Spalding, Stevens, Thayer, Upson, Ellihu B. Washburne, William B. Washburn, Wilder—56.

MR. STEVENS'S SUBSTITUTE.

Upon these and other amendments being adopted, Mr. STEVENS offered a substitute for the whole bill, which he explained as differing from the amended bill in these respects only:

The substitute provides for a uniform rate of interest at seven per cent., and withdraws these national banks from State taxation and leaves them to be taxed by the national Government.

Which was rejected—yeas 59, nays 78, as follows:

YEAS—Messrs. Alley, Allison, Ames, Anderson, Ashley, John D. Baldwin, Baxter, Beaman, Blow, Boutwell, Boyd, Broomall, Ambrose W. Clark, Cobb, Cole, Thomas T. Davis, Dixon, Donnelly, Driggs, Eckley, Eliot, Frank, Garfield, Gooch, Grinnell, Hale, Hooper, John H. Hubbard, Jenckes, Julian, Kasson, Kelley, Francis W. Kellogg, Loan, Longyear, Marvin, McBride, McClurg, Morrill, Daniel Morris, Leonard Myers, Charles O'Neill, Patterson, Perham, Alexander H. Rice, Edward H. Rollins, Schenck, Scofield, Shannon, Spalding, Starr, Stevens, Thayer, Thomas, Upson, William B. Washburn, Wilder, Windom, Woodbridge—59.

NAYS—Messrs. *James C. Allen*, *William J. Allen*, *Ancona*, *Baily*, *Augustus C. Baldwin*, Blaine, *Bliss*, *Brooks*, *James S. Brown*, William G. Brown, *Chanler*, *Clay*, *Cox*, *Cravens*, *Dawson*, *Denison*, *Eden*, *Eldridge*, *English*, *Finck*, *Ganson*, *Grider*, *Griswold*, *Hall*, *Harrington*, *Benjamin G. Harris*, *Herrick*, *Holman*, Hotchkiss, Asahel W. Hubbard, *Philip Johnson*, *William Johnson*, *Kalbfleisch*, Orlando Kellogg, *Kernan*, *Law*, *Long*, *Mallory*, *Marcy*, *McKinney*, *Middleton*, *William H. Miller*, *James R. Morris*, *Morrison*, Amos Myers, *Nelson*, *Odell*, *John O'Neill*, Orth, *Pendleton*, Pike, Pomeroy, Price, *Pruyn*, *Radford*, *Samuel J. Randall*, William H. Randall, John H. Rice, *Robinson*, *Rogers*, *James S. Rollins*, *Scott*, Smithers, *John B. Steele*, *W. G. Steele*, *Strouse*, *Sweat*, Tracy, Van Valkenburgh, *Ward*, Ellihu B. Washburne, *Wheeler*, *Chilton A. White*, *Joseph W. White*, Wilson, *Winfield*, *Benjamin Wood*, *Yeaman*—78.

On Mr. STEVENS's motion, the bill was then tabled--yeas 91, nays 44.

STATE TAXATION.

April 16—A new bill, previously introduced, was considered, containing (among others) this provision:

"Every organization under this act shall pay to the Treasurer of the United States a duty of one per cent. each half year, from and after the 1st day of April, in the year 1864, upon the maximum amount of their circulating notes during the six months; and in default of such payment the Treasurer of the United States is hereby authorized to retain one per cent. of the amount of bonds required to be deposited as security for such circulation at each semi-annual payment of the interest thereon; and such duty and the taxes or duties imposed by Congress from time to time shall be in lieu of all other taxes on such associations: *Provided*, That nothing in this act shall be construed to prevent the market value of the shares in any of the said banking associations, held by any person or body-corporate created by State law, being included in the valuation of the aggregate personal property of such person or State corporation in assessing any tax imposed by any State or municipal authority on the aggregate personal estate of all persons subject to the authority of such State or municipality."

Mr. FENTON moved to substitute this:

And that nothing in this act shall be construed to prevent the taxation by States of the capital stock of banks organized under this act, the same as the property of other moneyed corporations for State or municipal purposes; but no State shall impose any tax upon such associations or their capital, circulation, dividends, or business, at a higher rate of taxation than shall be imposed by such State upon the same amount of moneyed capital in the hands of individual citizens of such State: *Provided*, That no State tax shall be imposed on any part of the capital stock of such association invested in the bonds of the United States, deposited as security for its circulation.

Which was agreed to—yeas 70, nays 60, as follows:

YEAS—Messrs. Alley, Allison, Ames, Arnold, Ashley, *Baily*, John D. Baldwin, Baxter, Beaman, Blaine, Boutwell, Broomall, William G. Brown, Ambrose W. Clark, Freeman Clarke, *Clay*, Cobb, Cole, Dawes, Driggs, Dumont, Eckley, Farnsworth, Fenton, Frank, Gooch, Grinnell, Higby, Hooper, Hotchkiss, John H. Hubbard, Jenckes, Julian, Kasson, Francis W. Kellogg, Orlando Kellogg, Loan, Longyear, Marvin, McClurg, McIndoe, Samuel F. Miller, Moorhead, Morrill, Daniel Morris, Amos Myers, Charles O'Neill, Orth, Patterson, Perham, Pike, Pomeroy, Price, William H. Randall, Alexander H. Rice, John H. Rice, Edward H. Rollins, Shannon, Sloan, Smith, Tracy, Upson, Van Valkenburgh, Ellihu B. Washburne, William B. Washburn, Webster, Wilder, Wilson, Windom, Woodbridge—70.

NAYS—Messrs. *James C. Allen*, *William J. Allen*, *Augustus C. Baldwin*, *Brooks*, *James S. Brown*, *Chanler*, *Cravens*, Creswell, Henry Winter Davis, *Dawson*, *Eden*, *Eldridge*, *Finck*, *Ganson*, *Hall*, *Harding*, *Harrington*, *Benjamin G. Harris*, *Herrick*, *Holman*, Asahel W. Hubbard, *Hutchins*, *William Johnson*, *Kalbfleisch*, Kelley, *Kernan*, *King*, *Knapp*, *Law*, *Lazear*, *Long*, *Marcy*, McBride, *McDowell*, *McKinney*, *William H. Miller*, *James R. Morris*, *Morrison*, *Nelson*, *Noble*, *Odell*, *Pendleton*, *Pruyn*, *Radford*, *Samuel J. Randall*, *Robinson*, *James S. Rollins*, *Ross*, *Scott*, *John B. Steele*, *Strouse*, *Stuart*, Thayer, Thomas, *Wheeler*, *Chilton A. White*, *Joseph W. White*, Williams, *Winfield*, *Fernando Wood*—60.

The bill was then passed.

IN SENATE.

ON TAXATION.

April 29—The Senate committee reported a substitute for Mr. FENTON's amendment adopted by the House, which proposed that—

In lieu of all other taxes every association shall pay to the Treasurer of the United States, in the months of January and July, a duty of one half of one per cent. each half year from and after the 1st day of January, 1864, upon the average amount of its notes in circulation, and a duty of one quarter of one per cent. each half year upon the average amount of its deposits, and a duty of one quarter of one per cent. each half year, as aforesaid, on the average amount of its capital stock beyond the amount invested in United States bonds. * * * *Provided*, That nothing in this act shall be construed to prevent the market value of the shares in any of the said associations, held by any person or body-corporate, from being included in the valuation of the personal property of such person or corporation in the assessment of all taxes imposed by or under State authority for State, county, or municipal purposes; but not at a greater rate than is assessed upon all other moneyed capital in the hands of individual citizens of such State. And all the remedies provided by State laws for the collection of such taxes shall be applicable thereto: *Provided, also*, That nothing in this act shall exempt the real estate of associations from either State, county, or municipal taxes to the same extent, according to its value, as other real estate is taxed.

Mr. POMEROY moved to strike out the first proviso, and insert:

Provided, That nothing in this act shall be construed as exempting the capital stock of an association, beyond the amount invested in United States bonds and deposited with the Treasurer of the United States as part of its capital or as security for its circulating notes, from being subject to the same rate of State and municipal taxation as is imposed upon other personal property in the State, city, or town in which the association is located.

Which was rejected—yeas 11, nays 28, as follows:

YEAS—Messrs. Chandler, Conness, *Harding*, Howard, Lane of Indiana, Pomeroy, Ramsey, Sherman, Sprague, Sumner, Wilkinson—11.

NAYS—Messrs. *Buckalew*, *Carlile*, Clark, Collamer, Cowan, *Davis*, Dixon, Fessenden, Foot, Foster, Grimes, Hale, Harlan, Henderson, *Hendricks*, Howe, Johnson, Lane of Kansas, *McDougall*, Morgan, Morrill, *Nesmith*, *Powell*, *Riddle*, Ten Eyck, Van Winkle, Willey, Wilson—28.

Mr. HOWARD moved to amend the proviso so as to make it read:

Provided, That nothing in this act shall be construed to prevent the market value of the shares in any of the said associations, held by any person or body-corporate, from being included in the valuation of the personal property of such person or corporation in the assessment of all taxes imposed by or under State authority for State, county, or municipal purposes in the State where the bank is situated; &c.

Which was rejected—yeas 11, nays 27, as follows:

YEAS—Messrs. Chandler, Conness, Harlan, *Hendricks*, Howard, Morrill, Pomeroy, Ramsey, Sherman, Sumner, Wilkinson—11.

NAYS—Messrs. Anthony, *Buckalew*, Clark, Collamer, Cowan, *Davis*, Dixon, Doolittle, Fessenden, Foot, Foster, Grimes, Hale, Henderson, Howe, Johnson, Lane of Indiana, Lane of Kansas, Morgan, *Nesmith*, *Powell*, *Riddle*, Sprague, Ten Eyck, Van Winkle, Willey, Wilson—27.

May 6—Mr. SUMNER's substitute:*

And in lieu of all other taxes on the capital, circulation, deposits, shares, and other property, every association shall pay to the Treasurer of the United States, in the months of January and July, a duty of one per cent. each half year from and after the 1st day of January, 1864, upon the average amount of its notes in circulation, and the duty of one half of one per cent. each half year upon the average amount of its deposits, and a duty of one half of one per cent. each half year, as aforesaid, on the average amount of its capital stock beyond the amount invested in United States bonds: * * *Provided*, That nothing in this act shall exempt the real estate of associations from either State, county, or municipal taxes to the same extent, according to its value, as other real estate is taxed: *Provided also*, That all taxes imposed by this or any future act on banking associations organized under national legislation shall be applied exclusively to the payment of the interest and principal of the national debt of the United States.

Which was rejected—yeas 11, nays 24, as follows:

YEAS—Messrs. Chandler, Conness, Howard, Lane of Indiana, Pomeroy, Ramsey, Sherman, Sprague, Sumner, Wilkinson, Wilson—11.

NAYS—Messrs. Anthony, *Buckalew*, *Carlile*, Clark, Collamer, Cowan, *Davis*, Dixon, Doolittle, Fessenden, Foot, Foster, Grimes, Hale, Henderson, Howe, Johnson, Morgan, *Powell*, *Richardson*, *Riddle*, Ten Eyck, Trumbull, Van Winkle—24.

ON SMALL NOTES.

May 10—Mr. BUCKALEW moved to strike out of the twenty-second section the words allowing one, two, and three dollar bills; which was rejected—yeas 8, nays 27, as follows:

YEAS—Messrs. *Buckalew*, Cowan, Doolittle, Henderson, *Powell*, *Richardson*, *Riddle*, *Saulsbury*—8.

NAYS—Messrs. Anthony, Clark, Collamer, Conness, Dixon, Foot, Foster, Grimes, Hale, Harlan, Howe, Johnson, Lane of Indiana, Lane of Kansas, Morgan, Morrill, Ramsey, Sherman, Sprague, Sumner, Ten Eyck, Trumbull, Van Winkle, Wade, Wilkinson, Willey, Wilson—27.

ON REPEALING THE BANKING SYSTEM.

Mr. POWELL moved to substitute for the whole bill, a section repealing the banking act of February 25, 1863; which was rejected—yeas 6, (Messrs. *Buckalew*, Henderson, *Powell*, *Richardson*, *Riddle*, *Saulsbury*,) nays 31.

The bill then passed.

The House non-concurred in the Senate's amendments, when a Committee of Conference was appointed, who reported, June 1. The tax question was settled by adding these words to the thirty-second section:

And nothing in this act shall be construed to prevent all the shares in any of the said associations, held by any person or body corporate, from being included in the valuation of personal property of such person or corporation, in the assessment of taxes imposed by or under State authority, at the place where such bank is located, and not elsewhere; but not at a greater rate than is assessed on other moneyed capital in the hands of individual citizens of said States: *Provided further*, That the tax so imposed under the law of any State upon the shares of any of the associations authorized by this act shall not exceed the rate imposed on shares in any of the bank organizations under the authority of the State where such association is located.

The bill provides for a tax of one per cent. on the circulation of national banks, one half of one per cent. on their deposits, and one per cent. on their capital above the amount invested in United States bonds.

The report was concurred in, without a division in either house.

The Public Debt.

THE PUBLIC CREDIT UNDER BUCHANAN.

December 28, 1860—Bids for $5,000,000 in six per cent. Treasury notes, authorized by act of December 17, 1860, were opened by Philip F. Thomas, Secretary of the Treasury, when it was found that only $2,500,000 were bid for, and this at a rate of discount from seven to thirty-six per cent. Eight thousand five hundred were bid for at seven per cent.; $151,600 at from seven to ten per cent; $1,087,000 at twelve per cent.; $140,000 at from twelve to twenty per cent.; $325,000 at from twenty to thirty-six per cent.

January 19, 1861—The balance of this loan was taken, the bids being for nearly triple the amount and ranging from eight and a half to fifteen per cent. discount. One bid

---

* Mr. SUMNER read this letter from Secretary Chase:

TREASURY DEPARTMENT,
May 5, 1864.

SIR: Nothing but my deep sense of the importance of sustaining by every possible means the public credit, upon which the sole dependence of the Government to suppress the insurrection must rest, would induce me to address you this letter upon a subject which has already received so much consideration.

The bill in relation to the national banking system now under debate is in the nature of an amendment to the act of the last session. Though a complete bill in itself, it contains few provisions not substantially embraced in that act, among which that in relation to the measure and distribution of taxation may be regarded perhaps as the most important. Under ordinary circumstances there might be no insuperable objection to leaving the property organized under the national banking law, subject as are almost all descriptions of property to general taxation, State, national, and municipal. But in the present condition of the country, I respectfully submit that this particular description of property should be placed in the same category with imported goods before their entry into general consumption, and be subjected to exclusive national taxation.

At the present moment the duties on imports form the sole reliance of the Government for means to pay the interest on the public debt. If to these means the taxes to be paid by the national banks shall be added a most important addition will be made to these measures. The mere fact that these taxes are made payable to the national Government and so rendered available for the payment of interest on the public debt, and for the reduction of its principal, will strengthen the public credit and facilitate the negotiation of the necessary loans at moderate rates of interest. I have no doubt that such a disposition of these taxes would be worth more to the Government during the present struggle in practical results than three times the actual value of the taxes themselves.

I do not at all suggest that this description of property should not be taxed as heavily as any other description. On the contrary, I think it just that it should bear its full proportion of the public burdens. I am only anxious that the taxation upon it shall be made to contribute as largely as possible to the general welfare, and it is the conviction deeply impressed on my mind that it will contribute more when aggregated in one mass, and made to tell upon the general public credit, than when distributed between the nation and the States and numerous municipal corporations, that prompts me to address these views to you.

Under any plan of partition that may be adopted the amount of taxation distributable to the several States and municipalities will be comparatively small and unimportant, and it is quite possible that the total taxation of banking property for all purposes, will be less than it will if taxed exclusively for national purposes. The advantages of partition to States and municipalities will therefore be small, and the banks may not lose by it. The nation alone will be injured. It will not be understood, of course, that the foregoing suggestions are intended to apply to real estate held by any banking institutions; that description of property must necessarily be held by titles under State laws, and should properly be subjected exclusively to State taxation, except in the event of a direct tax by Congress.

The case is otherwise with the personal property and credits of the banking associations. These receive their organization from national law and for great national purposes, and may therefore be with great propriety, and—as I have endeavored to show at the present time—with great public advantage be subjected to exclusive national taxation.

Respectfully yours, S. P. CHASE.

The Hon. WILLIAM PITT FESSENDEN,
Chairman of the Committee on Finance, Senate Chamber.

of $10,000 was made at twenty per cent. discount.

February 23, 1861—John A. Dix, Secretary of the Treasury, opened the bids for $8,000,000 of six per cent. twenty years' stock of the United States. Over $14,000,000 were offered; the lowest accepted bid was $90 15 for $100; the highest bid over ninety-six dollars. The whole loan was taken at an average of about 90½. Over $4,000,000 were bid for at $90 15.

Debt of the United States, from June 30, 1860, to May 14, 1864.

June 30, 1860, the public debt was $64,769,703 08
Of which $45,079,203 08 were in bonds, and $19,690,500 in Treasury notes.
June 30, 1861, the public debt was 90,867,823 68
May 29, 1862, the public debt was 491,445,984 11
as follows:

Under what act.	Rate of interest.	Amount.	Total.
Loan of 1842	6 per cent	$2,833,364 11	
Do 1847	do	9,415,250 00	
Do 1848	do	8,908,341 80	
Do 1858	5 per cent	20,000,000 00	
Do 1860	do	7,022,000 00	
Do 1861	6 per cent	18,415,000 00	
Texan indemnity	5 per cent	3,461,000 00	
			$70,104,955 91
Treasury notes issued prior to 1857	Interest stopped	105,111 64	
Treasury notes under act of December 23, 1857	do	175,900 00	
Treasury notes under act of December 17, 1860	do	221,650 00	
Treasury notes under acts of June 22, 1860, and February and March, 1861	6 per cent	2,767,900 00	
Treasury notes under acts of March 2, July 17, and August 5, 1861	do	111,600 00	
			3,382,161 64
Three years' 7.30 bonds	7.30 per cent	120,523,450 00	
Twenty years' bonds	6 per cent	50,000,000 00	
			170,523,450 00
Oregon war debt	do		878,450 00
United States notes	No interest		145,880,000 00
Certificates of indebtedness	6 per cent	47,199,000 00	
5-20 years' bonds	do	2,699,400 00	
			49,898,400 00
Four per cent. temporary loan	4 per cent	5,913,042 21	
Five per cent. temporary loan	5 per cent	44,865,524 35	
			50,778,566 56
			$491,445,984 11

Average rate of interest paid on the entire debt is 4 354.1000 per cent. per annum.

Of this, these items belonged to the old debt:

Funded	$70,104,955 91
Treasury notes	3,270,561 64
Oregon war debt	878,450 00
	74,253,967 55
Leaving due to the war	417,195,016 56

June 30, 1862, the debt was		$517,372,802 93
June 30, 1863—The public debt was		$1,098,793,181 37
As follows:		
Loan of 1842, 6 per cent		$302,620 75
" 1847, 6 per cent		9,415,250 00
" 1848, 6 per cent		8,908,341 80
" 1858, 5 per cent		20,000,000 00
" 1860, 5 per cent		7,022,000 00
" 1861, (Feb. 8,) 6 per cent		18,415,000 00
" 1861, (March 2,) 6 per cent		776,750 00
Old funded and unfunded debt (1800 and 1812,) 3 and 6 per cent		114,115 48
Texan indemnity, 5 per cent		3,461,000 00
Treasury notes issued prior to 1857, (int. stopped,)	$104,561 64	
Treasury notes issued under act of Dec. 23, 1857	13,000 00	
Treasury notes issued under act of Dec, 17, 1860	1,000 00	
Demand notes July 17, and Aug. 5, 1861	3,351,019 75	
U. S. notes, Feb. 25, 1862	147,767,114 00	
U. S. notes, July 11, 1862	150,000,000 00	
Postal currency, July 17, 1862	20,192,456 00	
U. S. notes, (new issues,) March 3, 1863	89,879,475 00	
		411,308,626 39
Three years' 7.30 bonds, 7.30 per cent (two issues,)		139,970,500 00
Twenty years' bonds, 6 per cent. (two issues,)		50,028,500 00
Oregon war debt, 6 per cent		1,021,300 00
Certificates of indebtedness, 6 per cent		156,784,241 65
5-20 years' bonds, 6 per cent		168,880,250 00
Temporary loan, 4 and 5 per cent		102,384,085 30
		$1,098,793,181 37
Feb. 2, 1864, the debt was		1,473,225,714 00
May 10, 1864, the public debt was		1,726,248,411 65
May 14, 1864, the debt was		1,730,870,9[illegible]6 00

Statement of the Public Debt of the United States, June 30, 1864.

DEBT BEARING INTEREST IN COIN.

RATE OF INTEREST.	CHARACTER OF ISSUE.	AMOUNT OUTSTANDING.	INTEREST.
6 per cent	Bonds	$9,415,250 00	$564,915 00
6 per cent	Bonds	8,908,341 80	534,500 50
5 per cent	Bonds	20,000,000 00	1,000,000 00
5 per cent	Bonds	7,022,000 00	351,100 00
6 per cent	Bonds	18,415,000 00	1,104,900 00
6 per cent	Bonds	50,000,000 00	3,000,000 00
6 per cent	Bonds exchanged for 7 3.10	30,923,600 00	1,855,416 00
6 per cent	Bonds, 5-20's*	510,756,900 00	30,645,414 00
5 per cent	Bonds, 10-40's	72,963,850 00	3,648,192 50
5 per cent	Bonds, Texan Indemnity	2,159,000 00	107,950 00
6 per cent	Bonds, Oregon War	1,016,000 00	60,960 00
7 3.10 per cent	Notes, Three years*	109,075,750 00	7,962,529 75
6 per cent	Bonds	19,816,096 65	1,188,965 79
Aggregate of debt bearing Coin Interest		$860,471,788 45	$52,024,843 54

DEBT BEARING INTEREST IN LAWFUL MONEY.

RATE OF INTEREST.	CHARACTER OF ISSUE.		AMOUNT OUTSTANDING.	INTEREST.
4 per cent	Temporary Loan		$662,474 49	$26,496 97
5 per cent	Temporary Loan		7,414,622 47	370,731 12
6 per cent	Temporary Loan		67,080,718 24	4,024,843 09
6 per cent	Certificates of Indebtedness		159,570,000 00	9,574,200 00
5 per cent	One Year Notes		44,520,000 00	2,226,000 00
5 per cent	Two Years Notes		16,480,000 00	824,000 00
5 per cent	Two Years Notes, with Coupons,	$150,000,000 00		
	Less withdrawn and destroyed or ready to be destroyed	57,279,150 00		
			92,720,850 00	4,636,042 50
6 per cent	3 years Compound Interest Notes		3,880,000 00	
Aggregate of debt bearing Lawful Money interest			$392,328,665 20	$21,682,315 68

DEBT ON WHICH INTEREST HAS CEASED.

CHARACTER OF ISSUE.	AMOUNT OUTSTANDING.
Bonds	$203,808 45
Treasury Notes	104,511 64
Treasury Notes	9,900 00
Treasury Notes	600 00
Treasury Notes	47,150 00
Temporary Loan Coin	4,200 00
Aggregate of debt on which Interest has ceased	$370,170 09
Aggregate of debt not bearing Interest†	486,866,065 70

RECAPITULATION.

DEBT—	AMOUNT OUTSTANDING.	INTEREST.
Bearing interest in coin	$860,471,788 45	$52,024,843 54
Bearing interest in lawful money	392,328,665 20	21,682,315 68
On which interest has ceased	370,170 09	
Bearing no interest	486,866,065 79	
	$1,740,036,689 53	$73,707,159 22

* TREASURY DEPARTMENT, *May* 18, 1864.

SIR: Your letter of the 13th instant, making inquiries in regard to the kind of currency with which the five-twenty years six per cent. and the three years seven-thirty per cent. notes are to be redeemed, has been received.

It has been the constant usage of the Department to redeem all coupon and registered bonds forming part of the funded or permanent debt of the United States in coin, and this usage has not been deviated from during my administration of its affairs.

All the treasury notes and other obligations forming part of the temporary loan are payable and will be redeemed in lawful money: that is to say, in United States notes until after the resumption of specie payments, when they also will doubtless be redeemed in coin, or equivalent notes.

The five-twenty sixes being payable twenty years from date, though redeemable after five years, are considered as belonging to the funded or permanent debt, and so also are the twenty years sixes into which the three years seven-thirty notes are convertible. These bonds, therefore, according to the usage of the Government, are payable in coin.

The three years seven-thirty treasury notes are part of the temporary loan, and will be paid in United States notes, unless holders prefer conversion to payment.

Very respectfully,

S. P. CHASE,
Secretary of the Treasury.

† This item is thus composed:

United States Notes, July 17, August 5, 1861, and February 12, 1862		$781,073 00
" " February 25, July 11, 1862, and July 17, 1863		399,218,927 00
" " in redemption of temporary loan		26,160,569 00
Fractional Currency, July 17, 1862, and March 3, 1863		22,210,483 10
		448,371,052 10
Unpaid requisitions	$50,262,000 00	
Amount in Treasury	11,766,986 40	
		38,495,013 60
		$486,866,065 70

The increase of debt between periods has been as follows:

	Days.	Increase of Debt per day.	Amount out.
June 30, 1863	...	....	$1,098,793.181
Sept. 30, 1863	92	$1,340,000	1.222,113,559
Feb. 2, 1864	123	2,041.000	1,473,2[illegible]5,714
March 2, 1864	29	1,395,000	1,513.702,837
" 15, 1864	13	5,550,000	1,596,999,4[illegible]9
May 10, 1864	55	2,330,000	1,726,248,411
" 14, 1864	4	1,130,629	1,730,870,926

The Rebel Debt.

December 31, 1862, the receipts of the Treasury from the commencement of the "Permanent Government," (February 18, 1862,) were as follows:

RECEIPTS.	
Patent fund	$13,920 00
Customs	668,566 00
Miscellaneous	2,291,812 00
Repayments of disbursing officers	3,839,263 00
Interest on loans	26,583 00
Call loan certificates	59,742,796 00
One hundred million loan	41,398,286 00
Treasury notes	215,554,885 00
Interest bearing notes	113,740,000 00
War tax	16,664,513 00
Loan 28th of February, 1861	1,375,476 00
Coin received from Bank of Louisiana	2,539,799 00
Total	$457,855,704 00
Total debt up to December 31, 1862	556,105,100 00
Estimated amount at that date necessary to support the Government to July, 1863, was	357,929,229 00

Up to December 31, 1862, the issues of the Treasury were:

Notes	$440,678,510 00
Redeemed	30,193,479 50
Outstanding	$410,485,030 50

From January 1, 1863, to September 30, 1863, the receipts of the Treasury were:

For 8 per cent. stock	$107,292,900 70
For 7 per cent. stock	38,757,650 70
For 6 per cent. stock	6,810,050 00
For 5 per cent. stock	22,992,900 00
For 4 per cent. stock	482,200 00
Cotton certificates	2,000,000 00
Interest on loans	140,210 00
War tax	4,128,988 97
Treasury notes	391,623,530 00
Sequestration	1,862,550 27
Customs	934,798 68
Export duty on cotton	8,101 78
Patent fund	10,794 04
Miscellaneous, including repayments by disbursing officers	24,498,217 93
Total	$601,522,893 12

EXPENDITURES DURING THAT TIME.	
War Department	$377,988,244 00
Navy Department	38,437,661 00
Civil, miscellaneous, &c	11,629,278 00
Customs	56,636 00
Public debt	32,212,290 00
Notes canceled and redeemed	59,044,449 00
Total expenditures	$519,368,559 00
Total receipts	601,522,893 00
Balance in treasury	$82,154,334 00

But from this amount is to be deducted the amount of all Treasury notes that have been funded, but which have not yet received a true estimation, $65,000,000; total remaining, $17,154,334.

CONDITION OF THE TREASURY, JANUARY 1, 1864.

Jan. 25—The Secretary of the Treasury (C. G. Memminger) laid before the Senate a statement in reply to a resolution of the 20th, asking information relative to the funded debt, to call certificates, to non-interest and interest-bearing Treasury notes, and other financial matters. From this it appears that, January 1864, the funded debt was as follows:

Act Feb. 28, 1861, 8 ₩ cent.,	$15,000,000 00	
Act May 16, 1861, 8 ₩ cent.,	8,774,900 00	
Act Aug. 19, 1861, 8 ₩ cent.,	100,000,000 00	
Act April 12, 1862, 8 ₩ cent.,	3,612,300 00	
Act Feb. 20, 1863, 8 ₩ cent.,	95,785,000 00	
Act Feb. 20, 1863, 7 ₩ cent.,	63,615,750 00	
Act March 23, 1863, 6 ₩ cent.,	2,831,700 00	
Act April 30, 1863 (cotton interest coupons)	8,252,000 00	
		$297,871,650 00
Call certificates		89,206,770 00
Non-interest bearing Treasury notes outstanding:		
Act May 16, 1861—payable two years after date	8,320,875 00	
Act Aug. 19, 1861—General currency	189,719,251 00	
Act Oct. 13, 1861—All denominations	131,028,366 50	
Act March 23—All denominations	391,829,702 50	
		720,898,095 00
Interest-bearing Treasury notes outstanding		102,465,450 00
Amount of Treasury notes under $5, outstanding Jan. 1, 1864, viz:		
Act April 17, 1862, denomination of $1 and $2	4,860,277 50	
Act Oct. 13, 1862, $1 and $2	2,344,800 00	
Act March 23, 1863, 50 cents,	3,419,000 00	
Total under $5		10,424,077 50
Total debt, Jan. 1, 1864		$1,220,866,042 50

ITS CONDITION, MARCH 31, 1864.

The Register of the Treasury, Robert Tyler, gave a statement, which appeared in the Richmond *Sentinel* after the passage of the funding law, which gives the amount of outstanding non-interest-bearing Treasury notes, March 31, 1864, as $796,264,403, as follows:

Act May 16, 1861—Ten-year notes	$7,201,375 00
Act Aug. 19, 1861—General currency	154,356,631 00
Act April 19, 1862—Ones and twos	4,516,509 00
Act Oct. 18, 1862—General currency	118,997,321 50
Act March 23, 1863—General currency	511,182,566 50
Total	$796,264,403 00

He also publishes this statement of the issue of non-interest-bearing Treasury notes since the organization of the "Confederate" Government:

Fifty cents	$911,258 50
Ones	4,882,000 00
Twos	6,086,320 00
Fives	79,090,315 00
Tens	157,982,750 00
Twenties	217,425,120 00
Fifties	188,088,200 00
Total	$973,277,363 50

Rebel Financial Legislation.

The following is the funding act:

[From the Richmond Sentinel, Feb. 17, 1864.]

SEC. 1. *The Congress of the Confederate States of America do enact,* That the holders of all Treasury notes above the denomination of five dollars not bearing interest, shall be allowed until the first day of April, 1864, east of the Mississippi River, and until the first day of July, 1864, west of the Mississippi River, to fund the same, and until the periods and at the places stated, the holders of all such Treasury notes shall be allowed to fund the same in registered bonds payable twenty years after, they bearing interest at the rate of four per cent. per annum payable on the first day of January and July of each year.

SEC. 2. The Secretary of the Treasury is hereby authorized to issue the bonds required for the funding provided for in the preceding section; and until the bonds can be provided, he may issue certificates to answer the purpose. Such bonds and certificates shall be receivable without interest, in payment of all Government dues payable in the year 1864, except export and import duties.

SEC. 3. That all Treasury notes of all denominations of one hundred dollars, not bearing interest, which shall not be presented for funding under the provisions of the first section of this act, shall, from and after the first day of April, 1864, east of the Mississippi River, and the first day of July, 1864, west of the Mississippi, cease to be receivable in payment of public dues, and said notes, if not so presented at the time, shall, in addition to the tax of thirty-three and one-third cents imposed in the fourth section of this act, be subject to a tax of ten per cent. per month until so presented; which taxes shall attach to said notes wherever circulated, and shall be deducted from the face of said notes wherever presented for payment or for funding, and such notes shall not be exchangeable for the new issue of Treasury notes provided for in this act.

SEC. 4. That on all the said Treasury notes not funded or used in payment of taxes at the dates and places prescribed in the first section of this act, there shall be levied at said dates and places a tax of 33⅓ cents for every dollar funded on the face of said notes. Said tax shall attach to said notes wherever circulated, and shall be collected by deducting the same at the Treasury, its depositories and by the collectors, and by all Government officers receiving the same, wherever presented for payment, or for funding, or in payment of Government dues, or for postage or in exchange for new notes as hereinafter provided, and said Treasury notes shall be fundable in bonds as provided in the first section of this act, until the first day of January, 1865, at the rate of sixty-six cents and two thirds on the dollar, and it shall be the duty of the Secretary of the Treasury at any time between the first of April east and the first of July, 1864, west of the Mississippi river, and the first of January, 1865, to substitute and exchange new Treasury notes for same, at the rate of sixty-six and two thirds cents on the dollar: *Provided*, That notes of the denomination of $100 shall not be entitled to the privilege of said exchange: *Provided, further*, That on the right to fund all such Treasury notes which may remain outstanding on the first day of January, 1865, and which may not be exchanged for new Treasury notes, as herein provided, a tax of one hundred per cent is hereby imposed.

SEC. 5. That after the 1st day of April next, all authority heretofore given to the Secretary of the Treasury to issue Treasury notes shall be, and is hereby, revoked, provided the Secretary of the Treasury may after that time issue new Treasury notes in such forms as he may prescribe, payable two years after the ratification of a treaty of peace with the United States, said new issue to be receivable in payment of all public dues except export and import duties, and to be issued in exchange for old notes at the rate of $2 of the new issue for $3 of the old issues, whether said old notes be surrendered for exchange by the holders thereof or be received into the Treasury under the provisions of this act; and the holders of the new notes or of the old notes, except those of the denomination of $100, after they are reduced to 66⅔ cents on the dollar by the tax aforesaid, may convert them into call certificates bearing interest at the rate of four per cent per annum, and payable two years after a ratification of a treaty of peace with the United States, unless sooner converted into new notes.

SEC. 6. That to pay the expenses of the Government, not otherwise provided for, the Secretary of the Treasury is hereby authorized to issue six per cent bonds to an amount not exceeding $500,000,000, the principal and interest whereof shall be free from taxation, and for the payment of the interest thereon, the entire net receipts of any export duty hereinafter laid on the value of all cotton, tobacco, and naval stores, which shall be exported from the Confederate States, and the net proceeds of the import duties now laid, or so much thereof as may be necessary to pay the interest are hereby specially pledged: *Provided*, That the duties now laid upon imports, and hereby pledged, shall hereafter be paid in specie or in sterling exchange, or in the coupons of said bonds.

SEC. 12. That any State holding Treasury notes received before the times herein fixed for taxing said notes shall be allowed until the 1st day of January, 1865, to fund the same in six per cent. bonds of the Confederate States, payable twenty years after date, and the interest payable semi-annually. But all Treasury notes received by any State after the time fixed for taxing the same, as aforesaid, shall be held to have been received, diminished by the amount of said tax. The discrimination between the notes subject to the tax and those not so subject shall be left to the good faith of each State, and the certificate of the Governor thereof shall in each case be conclusive.

SEC. 13. That Treasury notes heretofore issued, bearing interest at the rate of seven dollars and thirty cents on the hundred dollars per annum, shall no longer be received in payment of public dues, but shall be deemed and considered bonds of the Confederate States, payable two years after the ratification of a treaty of peace with the United States, bearing the rate of interest specified on their face, payable the 1st of January in each and every year.

SPECULATIONS ON THE FUNDING.

The Richmond *Examiner* of the 11th of April, 1864, gives the following statistics of the rebel currency, from which it will be seen that a desperate attempt is making to retrieve the financial disasters of the South:

The depletion of the Confederate currency under the recent legislation is much greater than is generally supposed; and in this connection it will be interesting to refer to well established figures. The entire issue of the old circulation we may take at $800,000,000. The number of one hundred dollar bills in circulation has been about $250,000,000. Of lesser denominations that will be funded, there are, at least, say $50,000,000. Deduct now the $300,000,000 funded, and we have $500,000,000. This, reduced by the discount of thirty-three and one-third per cent., will, in round numbers, leave us $330,000,000.

The tax levied for 1864 is estimated considerably above $400,000,000. There being only $330,000,000 funded in four per cents., it follows that $100,000,000 of currency must be used in addition to the above for the payment of taxes for 1864, which will still further reduce the circulating medium to $230,000,000. From the last named sum there must be substracted the amount required to pay the additional taxes imposed by the late Congress on the income tax of 1863, as well as some portion of the old taxes that will not be paid on the first of April, 1864. The circulation would thus be reduced to $200,000,000, without reference to the manufacture and emission of more paper money.

But here comes up the important question of the new issue, which involves the vitality of the whole scheme. The first interpretation of the currency act was that it denied power to the Secretary of the Treasury to issue one dollar notes except in exchange for the present currency at the rate of two dollars of the new for three dollars of the old, which may remain unfunded on the first of April. Others construe the act to empower the Secretary of the Treasury to issue two dollars of the new issue for three dollars of the old, whether funded or unfunded—whether exchanged or paid in for taxes.

The latter construction is said to be favored by Mr. Memminger, namely, that he is authorized to issue new notes to the amount of two-thirds of the whole of the old issue. In other words, supposing the old notes in circulation amounted to $800,000,000 the first of April, the Secretary of the Treasury is empowered to issue two-thirds of this amount, that is, $533,333,333, affording a supply to the Treasury for about eight months, irrespective of the sum that may be raised by the sale of six per cent. bonds.

[From the Richmond Sentinel.]

There is but little doubt that the funding, east and west of the Mississippi, will amount to $300,000,000. The total issue outstanding March 31 is thereby reduced say to $485,000,000. Of this, a considerable portion, probably $100,000,000, is in $100 notes. Excluding these, we have $385,000,000 left, of which the issues of $5 and under amount to $90,969,898 50. Suppose $85,000,000 of these are now in circulation, and we have for all others $300,000,000, which the tax of one third has reduced to $200,000,000. The total circulation at the present time, irrespective of the new issue, is therefore, largely less than $300,000,000, and of this a considerable amount is always to be found in the hands of the disbursing officers and depositaries.

We have not included in the above any estimates of the amount of circulation lost or destroyed, and thereby gained to the Government. It is doubtless considerable.

The amount of currency which has been canceled and destroyed (irrespective of the operations of the present currency law) is nearly twenty per cent. of the whole issue. If this reduction be applied to the five dollar notes, the amount of these in circulation would appear to be $63,272,252.

[From The Examiner of the 21st March, 1864.]

Only ten days now intervene before the currency remaining in circulation is taxed *one-third*, and, consequently, during the week commencing Monday, the holders of Treasury notes *must* decide whether they will keep them until the 1st of April and submit to the Government shave, fund the amount in four per cent. bonds, or exchange it for bonds or personal property. The necessity of coming to a conclusion is "sharpening the wits" of the people, though it is not improbable that some who esteem themselves "wondrous wise" in financial matters will commit a blunder in disposing of their surplus cash. The ability to penetrate the future is a power which few, if any, possess, and hence the views expressed in regard to the effect of the financial legislation of Congress, after the currency is reduced, are diverse and vaguely theoretical.

Everybody knows that a $10 note, after 1st April, will only represent a net value of $6 66⅔, and accordingly the universal desire is to dispose of the currency in hand at this time, so as to avoid this apparent loss, very few being willing to hold it with the expectation that $66 of the new currency will, in a few weeks, buy more of any article than $100 will purchase now. They must see the fact before they will believe it, but then it will be too late to profit by the development.

In the meantime, all kinds of "cornering" processes are in vogue, and it must be admitted that some of them are plausible enough. For instance, it is argued that certain bonds and stocks may be bought now, and sold in the new currency at a decline not exceeding fifteen to twenty-five per cent.—thereby saving ten to fifteen in the *transmutory* tax.

On the last day of the session, June 15, President Davis vetoed the bill allowing further time to persons within the enemy's lines to fund their Treasury notes. The consideration of the subject was postponed until the next session.

RICHMOND, *April* 22, 1864.

The outstanding amount of Treasury notes, of the denomination of five dollars and under, is about seventy-five millions.

The funding returns sum up an aggregate of two hundred and thirty-seven million dollars. Twenty small depositories yet to hear from. The only State from which complete returns have been received is Georgia, where the amount funded is seventy-two millions one hundred and eighty-four thousand dollars.

TAXATION.

THE TAX ACT OF JULY, 1861.

The Richmond *Enquirer* gives the following summary of the act authorizing the issue of Treasury notes and bonds, and providing a war tax for their redemption:

Section one authorizes the issue of Treasury notes, payable to bearer at the expiration of six months after the ratification of a treaty of peace between the Confederate States and the United States. The notes are not to be of a less denomination than five dollars, to be re-issued at pleasure, to be received in payment of all public dues, except the export duty on cotton, and the whole issue outstanding at one time, including the amount issued under former acts, are not to exceed one hundred millions of dollars.

Section two provides that, for the purpose of funding the said notes, or for the purpose of purchasing specie or military stores, &c., bonds may be issued, payable not more than twenty years after date, to the amount of one hundred millions of dollars, and bearing an interest of eight per cent. per annum. This amount includes the thirty millions already authorized to be issued. The bonds are not to be issued in less amounts than $100, except when the subscription is for a less amount, when they may be issued as low as $50.

Section three provides that holders of Treasury notes may at any time exchange them for bonds.

Section four provides that, for the special purpose of paying the principal and interest of the public debt, and of supporting the Government, a war tax shall be assessed and levied of fifty cents upon each one hundred dollars in value of the following property in the Confederate States, namely: Real estate of all kinds; slaves; merchandise; bank stocks; railroad and other corporation stocks; money at interest or invested by individuals in the purchase of bills, notes, and other securities for money, except the bonds of the Confederate States of America, and cash on hand or on deposit in bank or elsewhere; cattle, horses, and mules; gold watches, gold and silver plate; pianos and pleasure carriages: *Provided, however*, That when the taxable property, herein above enumerated, of any head of a family is of value less than five hundred dollars, such taxable property shall be exempt from taxation under this act. It provides further that the property of colleges, schools, and religious associations shall be exempt.

The remaining sections provide for the collection of the tax.

THE TAX ACT OF DECEMBER 19, 1861

An act supplementary to an act to authorize the issue of Treasury notes, and to provide a war tax for their redemption.

SEC. 1. *The Congress of the Confederate States of America do enact*, That the Secretary of the Treasury is hereby authorized to pay over to the several banks, which have made advances to the Government, in anticipation of the issue of Treasury notes, a sufficient amount, not exceeding $10,000,000, for the principal and interest due upon the said advance, according to the engagements made with them.

SEC. 2. The time fixed by the said act for making assignments is hereby extended to the 1st day of January next, and the time for the completion and delivery of the lists is extended to the 1st day of March next, and the time for the report of the said lists to the chief collector is extended to the 1st day of May next; and in cases where the time thus fixed shall be found insufficient, the Secretary of the Treasury shall have power to make further extension, as circumstances may require.

SEC. 3. The cash on hand, or on deposit in the bank, or elsewhere, mentioned in the fourth section of said act, is hereby declared to be subject to assessment and taxation, and the money at interest, or invested by individuals in the purchase of bills, notes, and other securities for money, shall be deemed to include securities for money belonging to non-residents, and such securities shall be returned, and the tax thereon paid by any agent or trustee having the same in possession or under his control. The term merchandise shall be construed to include merchandise belonging to any non-resident, and the property shall be returned, and the tax paid by any person having the same in possession as agent, attorney, or consignee: *Provided*, That the words "money at interest," as used in the act to which this act is an amendment, shall be so construed as to include all notes, or other evidences of debt, bearing interest, without reference to the consideration of the same. The exception allowed by the twentieth section for agricultural products shall be construed to embrace such products only when in the hands of the producers, or held for his account. But no tax shall be assessed or levied on any money at interest when the notes, bond, bill, or other security taken for its payment, shall be worthless from the insolvency and total inability to pay of the payor or obligor, or person liable to make such payment; and all securities for money payable under this act shall be assessed according to their value, and the assessor shall have the same power to ascertain the value of such securities as the law confers upon him with respect to other property.

SEC. 4. That an amount of money, not exceeding $25,000, shall be and the same is hereby appropriated, out of any money in the treasury not otherwise appropriated, to be disbursed under the authority of the Secretary of the Treasury, to the chief State tax collectors, for such expenses as shall be actually incurred for salaries of clerks, office hire, stationary, and incidental charges; but the books and printing required shall be at the expense of the department, and subject to its approval.

SEC. 5. The lien for the tax shall attach from the date of the assessment, and shall follow the same into every State in the Confederacy; and in case any person shall attempt to remove any property which may be liable to tax, beyond the jurisdiction of the State in which the tax is payable, without payment of the tax, the collector of the district may distrain upon and sell the same, in the same manner as is provided in cases where default is made in the payment of the tax.

SEC. 6. On the report of any chief collector, that any county, town or district, or any part thereof, is occupied by the public enemy, or has been so occupied as to occasion destruction of crops or property, the Secretary of the Treasury may suspend the collection of tax in such region until the same can be reported to Congress, and its action had thereon.

SEC. 7. In case any of the Confederate States shall undertake to pay the tax to be collected within its limits before the time at which the district collectors shall enter upon the discharge of their duties, the Secretary of the Treasury may suspend the appointment of such collectors, and may direct the chief collector to appoint assessors, and to take proper measures for the making and perfecting the returns, assessments and lists required by law; and the returns, assessments and and lists so made, shall have the same legal validity, to all intents and purposes, as if made according to the provisions of the act to which this act is supplementary.

SEC. 8. That tax lists already given, varying from the provisions of this act, shall be corrected so as to conform thereto.

THE TAX ACT OF APRIL 24, 1863.

[From the Richmond Whig, April 21.]

We present below a synopsis of the bill to lay taxes for

the common defence and to carry on the government of the Confederate States, which has passed both branches of Congress. It is substantially the bill proposed by the committee on conference:

1. The first section imposes a tax of eight per cent. upon the value of all naval stores, salt, wines and spirituous liquors, tobacco, manufactured or unmanufactured, cotton, wool, flour, sugar, molasses, syrup, rice, and other agricultural products, held or owned on the 1st day of July next, and not necessary for family consumption for the unexpired portion of the year 1863, and of the growth or production of any year preceding the year 1863; and a tax of one per cent. upon all moneys, bank notes or other currency on hand or on deposit on the 1st day of July next, and on the value of all credits on which the interest has not been paid, and not employed in a business, the income derived from which is taxed under the provisions of this act: *Provided*, That all moneys owned, held or deposited beyond the limits of the Confederate States shall be valued at the current rate of exchange in Confederate treasury notes. The tax to be assessed on the 1st day of July and collected on the 1st day of October next, or as soon thereafter as may be practicable.

2. Every person engaged, or intending to engage, in any business named in the fifth section, shall, within sixty days after the passage of the act, or at the time of beginning business, and on the 1st of January in each year thereafter, register with the district collector a true account of the name and residence of each person, firm, or corporation engaged or interested in the business, with a statement of the time for which, and the place and manner in which the same is to be conducted, &c. At the time of the registry there shall be paid the specific tax for the year ending on the next 31st of December, and such other tax as may be due upon sales or receipts in such business.

3. Any person failing to make such registry and pay such tax, shall, in addition to all other taxes upon his business imposed by the act, pay double the amount of the specific tax on such business, and a like sum for every thirty days of such failure.

4. Requires a separate registry and tax for each business mentioned in the fifth section, and for each place of conducting the same; but no tax for mere storage of goods at a place other than the registered place of business. A new registry required upon every change in the place of conducting a registered business, upon the death of any person conducting the same, or upon the transfer of the business to another, but no additional tax.

5. Imposing the following taxes for the year ending 31st of December, 1863, and for each year thereafter:

Bankers shall pay $500.

Auctioneers, retail dealers, tobacconists, pedlers, cattle brokers, apothecaries, photographers, and confectioners, $50, and two and a half per centum on the gross amount of sales made.

Wholesale dealers in liquors, $200, and five per centum on gross amount of sales. Retail dealers in liquors, $100, and ten per centum on gross amount of sales.

Wholesale dealers in groceries, goods, wares, merchandise, &c., $200, and two and a half per centum.

Pawnbrokers, money and exchange brokers, $200.

Distillers, $200, and twenty per centum. Brewers, $100, and two and a half per centum.

Hotels, inns, taverns, and eating-houses, first class, $500; second class, $300; third class, $200; fourth class, $100; fifth class, $30. Every house where food or refreshments are sold, and every boarding house where there shall be six boarders or more, shall be deemed an eating house under this act.

Commercial brokers or commission merchants, $200, and two and a half per centum.

Theatres, $500, and five per centum on all receipts. Each circus, $100, and $10 for each exhibition. Jugglers and other persons exhibiting shows, $50.

Bowling alleys and billiard rooms, $40 for each alley or table registered.

Livery stable keepers, lawyers, physicians, surgeons, and dentists, $50.

Butchers and bakers, $50, and one per centum.

6. Every person registered and taxed is required to make returns of the gross amount of sales from the passage of the act to the 30th June, and every three months thereafter.

7. A tax upon all salaries, except of persons in the military or naval service, of one per cent. when not exceeding $1,500, and two per cent. upon an excess over that amount: *Provided*, That no taxes shall be imposed by virtue of this act on the salary of any person receiving a salary not exceeding $1,000 per annum, or at a like rate for another period of time, longer or shorter.

8. Provides that the tax on annual incomes, between $500 and $1,500, shall be five per cent.; between $1,500 and $3,000, five per cent. on the first $1,500 and ten per cent. on the excess; between $3,000 and $5,000, ten per cent.; between $5,000 and $10,000, twelve and a half per cent.; over $10,000, fifteen per cent., subject to the following deductions: On incomes derived from rents of real estate, manufacturing, and mining establishments, &c., a sum sufficient for necessary annual repairs; on incomes from any mining or manufacturing business, the rent, (if rented,) cost of labor actually hired, and raw material; on incomes from navigating enterprizes, the hire of the vessel, or allowance for wear and tear of the same, not exceeding ten per cent.; on incomes derived from the sale of merchandise or any other property, the prime cost, cost of transportation, salaries of clerks, and rent of buildings; on incomes from any other occupation, the salaries of clerks, rent, cost of labor, material, &c.; and in case of mutual insurance companies, the amount of losses paid by them during the year. Incomes derived from other sources are subject to no deductions whatever.

All joint stock companies and corporations shall pay one tenth of the dividend and reserved fund annually. If the annual earnings shall give a profit of more than ten and less than twenty per cent. on capital stock, one eighth to be paid; if more than twenty per cent, one sixth. The tax to be collected on the 1st of January next, and of each year thereafter.

9. Relates to estimates and deductions, investigations, referees, &c.

10. A tax of ten per cent. on all profits in 1862 by the purchase and sale of flour, corn, bacon, pork, oats, hay, rice, salt, iron or the manufactures of iron, sugar, molasses made of cane, butter, woolen cloths, shoes, boots, blankets, and cotton cloths. Does not apply to regular retail business.

11. Each farmer, after reserving for his own use fifty bushels sweet and fifty bushels Irish potatoes, one hundred bushels corn or fifty bushels wheat produced this year, shall pay and deliver to the Confederate Government one tenth of the grain, potatoes, forage, sugar, molasses, cotton, wool, and tobacco produced. After reserving twenty bushels peas or beans he shall deliver one tenth thereof.

12. Every farmer, planter, or grazier, one tenth of the hogs slaughtered by him, in cured bacon, at the rate of sixty pounds of bacon to one hundred pounds of pork; one per cent. upon the value of all neat cattle, horses, mules, not used in cultivation, and asses, to be paid by the owners of the same; beeves sold to be taxed as income.

13. Gives in detail the duties of post quartermasters under the act.

14. Relates to the duties of assessors and collectors.

15. Makes trustees, guardians, &c., responsible for taxes due from estates, &c., under their control.

16. Exempts the income and moneys of hospitals, asylums, churches, schools, and colleges from taxation under the act.

17. Authorizes the Secretary of the Treasury to make all rules and regulations necessary to the operation of the act.

18. Provides that the act shall be in force for two years from the expiration of the present year, unless sooner repealed; that the tax on naval stores, flour, wool, cotton, tobacco, and other agricultural products of the growth of any year preceding 1863, imposed in the first section, shall be levied and collected only for the present year.

The tax act of February 17, 1864, levies, in addition to the above rates, the following, as stated in the Richmond *Sentinel* of February, 1864:

SEC. 1. Upon the value of real, personal, and mixed property, of every kind and description, except the exemptions hereafter to be named, five per cent.; the tax levied on property employed in agriculture to be credited by the value of property in kind.*

---

* This is the section in full:

That on the 1st day of January, 1863, there shall be levied and assessed on each person residing in the Confederate States, for the support of the Government and the defence of the country, the following tax, to wit: One fifth the value of all the wheat, corn, rice, rye, oats, potatoes, hemp, flax, peas, beans, barley, hay, wool, rosin, tar, pitch, turpentine, cotton, sugar, molasses, and tobacco produced by him in these States during the previous calendar year; also, one fifth of the value of the increase for the preceding calendar year of the horses, asses, cattle, sheep, and swine; and also, one fifth of the profits made in the preceding calendar year of the feeding of swine, sheep, cattle, or mules; also, one fifth of each person's yearly income for the preceding calendar year, from all sources whatsoever, except from the sources hereinafter described, and except from the interest on Confederate bonds, certificates, or treasury notes; *Provided*, That said tax so levied and assessed shall be due and payable on the 1st day of April, 1863. *Provided further*,

On gold and silver ware, plate, jewels, and watches, ten per cent.

The tax to be levied on the value of property in 1860, except in the case of land, slaves, cotton, and tobacco, purchased since January 1st, 1862, upon which the tax shall be levied on the price paid.

SEC. 2. A tax of five per cent on the value of all shares in joint stock companies of any kind, whether incorporated or not. The shares to be valued at their market value at the time of assessment.

SEC. 3. Upon the market value of gold and silver coin or bullion, five per cent.; also the same upon moneys held abroad, or all bills of exchange drawn therefor.

A tax of five per cent. on all solvent credits, and on all bank bills and papers used as currency, except non-interest bearing Confederate Treasury notes, and not employed in a registered business taxed twenty-five per cent.

SEC. 4. Profits in trade and business taxed as follows:

On the purchase and sale of agricultural products and mercantile wares generally, from January 1, 1863, to January 1, 1865, ten per cent in addition to the tax under the act of April 24, 1863.

The same on the purchase and sale of coin, exchange, stocks, notes, and credits of any kind, and any property not included in the foregoing.

On the amount of profits exceeding twenty-five per cent. of any bank, banking company, or joint stock company of any description, incorporated or not, twenty-five per cent. on such excess.

SEC. 5. The following are exempted from taxation:

Five hundred dollars' worth of property for each head of a family, and a hundred dollars additional for each minor child; and for each son in the army or navy, or who has fallen in the service, and a member of the family when he enlisted, the further sum of $500.

One thousand dollars of the property of the widow or minor children of any officer, soldier, sailor, or marine, who has died in the service.

A like amount of property of any officer, soldier, sailor, or marine, engaged in the service, or who has been disabled therein, provided said property, exclusive of furniture, does not exceed in value $1,000.

When property has been injured or destroyed by the enemy, or the owner unable temporarily to use or occupy it by reason of the presence or proximity of the enemy, the assessment may be reduced in proportion to the damage sustained by the owner, and the tax in the same ratio by the district collector.

SEC. 6. The taxes on property for 1864 to be assessed as on the day of the passage of this act, and collected the 1st of June next, with ninety days extension west of the Mississippi. The additional tax on incomes or profits for 1863, to be paid forthwith; the tax on incomes, &c., for 1864, to be collected according to the acts of 1863.

SEC. 7. Exempts from tax on income for 1864, all property herein taxed *ad valorem*. The tax on Confederate bonds in no case to exceed the interest payable on the same; and said bonds exempt from tax when held by minors or lunatics, if the interest do not exceed one thousand dollars.

THE TAX LAW.

We learn that, according to the construction of the recent tax law in the Treasury Department, tax payers will be required to state the articles and objects subjected to a specific or *ad valorem* tax, held, owned, or possessed by them on the 17th day of February, 1864, the date of the act.

The daily wages of detailed soldiers and other employés of the Government are not liable to taxation as income, although they may amount, in the aggregate, to the sum of $1,000 per annum.

A tax additional to both the above was imposed as follows, June 1, 1864:

A bill to provide supplies for the army, and to prescribe the mode of making impressments.*

SEC. 1. *The Congress of the Confederate States of America do enact*, Every person required to pay a tax in kind, under the provisions of the "Act to lay taxes for the common defense and carry on the Government of the Confederate States," approved April 24, 1863, and the act amendatory thereof, approved February 17, 1864, shall, in addition to the one tenth required by said acts to be paid as a tax in kind, deliver to the Confederate Government, of the products of the present year and of the year 1865, one other tenth of the several products taxed in kind by the acts aforesaid, which additional one tenth shall be ascertained, assessed and collected, in all respects, as is provided by law for the said tax in kind, and shall be paid for, on delivery, by the Post Quartermasters in the several districts at the assessed value thereof, except that payment for cotton and tobacco shall be made by the agents of the Treasury Department appointed to receive the same.

SEC. 2. The supplies necessary to the support of the producer and his family, and to carry on his ordinary business, shall be exempted from the contribution required by the preceding section, and from the additional impressments authorized by the act: *Provided, however*, That nothing herein contained shall be construed to repeal or affect the provisions of an act entitled "An act to authorize the impressment of meat for the use of the army, under certain circumstances," approved Feb. 17, 1864, and if the amount of any article or product so necessary cannot be agreed upon between the assessor and the producer, it shall be ascertained and determined by disinterested freeholders of the vicinage, as is provided in cases of disagreement as to the estimates and assessments of tax in kind. If required by the assessor, such freeholder shall ascertain whether a producer, who is found unable to furnish the additional one tenth of any one product, cannot supply the deficiency by the delivery of an equivalent in other products, and upon what terms such commutation shall be made Any commutation thus awarded shall be enforced and collected, in all respects, as is provided for any other contribution required by this act.

SEC. 3. The Secretary of War may, at his discretion, decline to assess, or, after assessment, may decline to collect the whole or any part of the additional one tenth herein provided for, in any district or locality; and it shall be his duty promptly to give notice of any such determination, specifying, with reasonable certainty, the district or locality and the product, or the proportion thereof, as to which he so declines.

SEC. 4. The products received for the contribution herein required, shall be disposed of and accounted for in the same manner as those received for the tax in kind; and the Secretary of War may, whenever the exigencies of the public service will allow, authorize the sale of products received from either source, to public officers or agents charged in any State with the duty of providing for the families of soldiers. Such sale shall be at the prices paid or assessed for the products sold, including the actual cost of collections.

SEC. 5. If, in addition to the tax in kind and the contribution herein required, the necessities of the army or the good of the service shall require other supplies of food or forage, or any other private property, and the same cannot be procured by contract, then impressments may be made of such supplies or other property, either for absolute ownership or for temporary use, as the public necessities may require. Such impressments shall be made in accordance with the provisions, and subject to the restrictions of the existing impressment laws, except so far as is herein otherwise provided.

SEC. 6. The right and the duty of making impressments is hereby confided exclusively to the officers and agents charged in the several districts with the assessment and collection of the tax in kind and of the contribution herein required; and all officers and soldiers in any department of the army are hereby expressly prohibited from undertaking in any manner to interfere with these officers and agents in any part of their duties in respect to the tax in kind, the contribution, or the impressment herein provided for: *Provided*, That this prohibition shall not be applicable to any district, county, or parish in which there shall be no officer or agent charged with the appointment and collection of the tax in kind.

SEC. 7. Supplies or other property taken by impressment shall be paid for by the post quartermasters in the several districts, and shall be disposed of and accounted for by them as is required in respect to the tax in kind and the contribution herein required: and it shall be the duty of the post quartermasters to equalize and apportion the impressments within their districts, as far as practicable, so as to avoid oppressing any portion of the community.

That foreigners resident within the Confederate States shall not be required to pay, except from the aforesaid articles produced by or for them, or from income or profits derived from business conducted by them within those States; nor shall any tax be levied upon the produce of residents where the total value of such products during said years is less than $500; nor shall any tax be levied on the income of residents where the total value of such income is less than $500.

*The Georgia Supreme Court has made an important decision in the case of impressment of sugar in the hands of a merchant. One of the points was that "the Congress of the Confederate States have the constitutional power to authorize, by statute, the accumulation of supplies for future use of the army by impressment, where holders refuse to sell at fair prices: *Provided*, 'Just compensation' be made or tendered to the owner."

SEC 8. If any one not authorized by law to collect the tax in kind or the contribution herein required, or to make impressments, shall undertake, on any pretence of such authority, to seize or impress, or to collect or receive any such property, or shall, on any such pretence, actually obtain such property, he shall, upon conviction thereof, be punished by fine not exceeding five times the value of such property, and be imprisoned not exceeding five years, at the discretion of the court having jurisdiction. And it shall be the duty of all officers and agents charged with the assessment and collection of the tax in kind and of the contribution herein required, promptly to report, through the post quartermasters in the several districts, any violation or disregard of the provisions of this act by any officer or soldier in the service of the Confederate States.

SEC. 9. That it shall not be lawful to impress any sheep, milch cows, brood mares, stud horses, jacks, bulls, or other stock kept or necessary for raising horses, mules, or cattle.

The following is the vote by which the bill passed the Senate:

YEAS Messrs. Caperton, Graham, Haynes, Jemison, Johnson (Ark.), Johnson (Mo.), Mitchel, Orr, Walker, Watson—10.

NAYS—Messrs. Baker, Burnett, Henry, Hunter, Maxwell, Semmes, Sparrow—7.

MISCELLANEOUS.

The President on Colonization, in August, 1862.

1862, August 14—The President received a deputation of colored persons relative to emigration. The interview is thus reported:

WASHINGTON, THURSDAY, *August* 14, 1862.

This afternoon the President of the United States gave an audience to a committee of colored men at the White House. They were introduced by Rev. J. Mitchell, Commissioner of Emigration. E. M. Thomas, the chairman, remarked that they were there by invitation to hear what the Executive had to say to them.

Having all been seated, the President, after a few preliminary observations, informed them that a sum of money had been appropriated by Congress, and placed at his disposition, for the purpose of aiding the colonization in some country of the people, or a portion of them, of African descent, thereby making it his duty, as it had for a long time been his inclination, to favor that cause; and why, he asked, should the people of your race be colonized, and where? Why should they leave this country? This is, perhaps, the first question for proper consideration. You and we are different races. We have between us a broader difference than exists between almost any other two races. Whether it is right or wrong I need not discuss; but this physical difference is a great disadvantage to us both, as I think. Your race suffer very greatly, many of them by living among us, while ours suffer from your presence. In a word we suffer on each side. If this is admitted, it affords a reason, at least, why we should be separated. You here are freemen, I suppose.

A VOICE—Yes, sir.

The PRESIDENT—Perhaps you have long been free, or all your lives. Your race are suffering, in my judgment, the greatest wrong inflicted on any people. But even when you cease to be slaves, you are yet far removed from being placed on an equality with the white race. You are cut off from many of the advantages which the other race enjoys. The aspiration of men is to enjoy equality with the best when free, but on this broad continent not a single man of your race is made the equal of a single man of ours. Go where you are treated the best, and the ban is still upon you. I do not propose to discuss this, but to present it as a fact, with which we have to deal. I cannot alter it if I would. It is a fact about which we all think and feel alike, I and you. We look to our condition. Owing to the existence of the two races on this continent, I need not recount to you the effects upon white men, growing out of the institution of slavery. I believe in its general evil effects on the white race. See our present condition—the country engaged in war! our white men cutting one another's throats—none knowing how far it will extend—and then consider what we know to be the truth. But for your race among us there could not be war, although many men engaged on either side do not care for you one way or the other. Nevertheless, I repeat, without the institution of slavery, and the colored race as a basis, the war could not have an existence. It is better for us both, therefore, to be separated. I know that there are free men among you who, even if they could better their condition, are not as much inclined to go out of the country as those who, being slaves, could obtain their freedom on this condition. I suppose one of the principal difficulties in the way of colonization is that the free colored man cannot see that his comfort would be advanced by it. You may believe that you can live in Washington, or elsewhere in the United States, the remainder of your life; perhaps more so than you can in any foreign country, and hence you may come to the conclusion that you have nothing to do with the idea of going to a foreign country. This is (I speak in no unkind sense) an extremely selfish view of the case. But you ought to do something to help those who are not so fortunate as yourselves. There is an unwillingness on the part of our people, harsh as it may be, for you free colored people to remain with us. Now if you could give a start to the white people you would open a wide door for many to be made free. If we deal with those who are not free at the beginning, and whose intellects are clouded by slavery, we have very poor material to start with. If intelligent colored men, such as are before me, would move in this matter, much might be accomplished. It is exceedingly important that we have men at the beginning capable of thinking as white men, and not those who have been systematically oppressed. There is much to encourage you. For the sake of your race you should sacrifice something of your present comfort for the purpose of being as grand in that respect as the white people. It is a cheering thought throughout life, that something can be done to ameliorate the condition of those who have been subject to the hard usages of the world. It is difficult to make a man miserable while he feels he is worthy of himself and claims kindred to the great God who made him. In the American Revolutionary war sacrifices were made by men engaged in it, but they were cheered by the future. General Washington himself endured greater physical hardships than if he had remained a British subject, yet he was a happy man, because he was engaged in benefiting his race, in doing something for the children of his neighbors, having none of his own.

The colony of Liberia has been in existence a long time. In a certain sense it is a success. The old President of Liberia, Roberts, has just been with me the first time I ever saw him. He says they have within the bounds of that colony between three and four hundred thousand people, or more than in some of our old States, such as Rhode Island or Delaware, or in some of our newer States, and less than in some of our larger ones. They are not all American colonists or their descendants. Something less than 12,000 have been sent thither from this country. Many of the original settlers have died, yet, like people elsewhere, their offspring outnumber those deceased. The question is, if the colored people are persuaded to go anywhere, why not there? One reason for unwillingness to do so is, that some of you would rather remain within reach of the country of your nativity. I do not know how much attachment you may have toward our race. It does not strike me that you have the greatest reason to love them. But still you are attached to them at all events. The place I am thinking about having for a colony is in Central America. It is nearer to us than Liberia—not much more than one fourth as far as Liberia, and within seven days' run by steamers. Unlike Liberia, it is a great line of travel—it is a highway. The country is a very excellent one for any people, and with great natural resources and advantages, and especially because of the similarity of climate with your native soil, thus being suited to your physical condition. The particular place I have in view is to be a great highway from the Atlantic or Caribbean Sea to the Pacific Ocean, and this particular place has all the advantages for a colony. On both sides there are harbors among the finest in the world. Again, there is evidence of very rich coal mines. A certain amount of coal is valuable in any country. Why I attach so much importance to coal is, it will afford an opportunity to the inhabitants for immediate employment till they get ready to settle permanently in their homes. If you take colonists where there is no good landing, there is a bad show; and so where there is nothing to cultivate, and of which to make a farm. But if something is started so that you can get your daily bread as soon as you reach there, it is a great advantage. Coal land is the best thing I know of with which to commence an enterprise. To return—you have been talked to upon this subject, and told that a speculation is intended by gentlemen who have an interest in the country, including the coal mines. We have been mistaken all our lives if we do not know whites, as well as blacks, look to their self-interest. Unless among those deficient of intellect, everybody you trade with makes something. You meet with these things here and everywhere. If such persons have what will be an advantage to them, the question is, whether it cannot be made of advantage to you? You are intelligent and know that success does not as much depend on external help as on self-reliance. Much, therefore, depends upon yourselves. As to the coal mines, I think I see the means available for your self-reliance. I shall, if I get a sufficient number of you engaged, have provision made that you shall not be wronged. If you will engage in the enterprise, I will spend some of the money intrusted to me. I am not sure you will succeed. The Government may lose the money, but we cannot succeed unless we try; but we think with care we can succeed. The political affairs in Central America are not in quite as satisfactory condition as I wish. There are contending factions in that quarter; but it is true, all the factions are agreed alike on the subject of colonization, and want it, and are more generous than we are here. To your colored race they have no objection. Besides, I would endeavor to have you made equals, and have the best assurance that you should be the equals of the best. The practical thing I want to ascertain is, whether I can get a number of able-bodied men, with their wives and children, who are willing to go, when I present evidence of encouragement and protection. Could I get a hundred tolerably intelligent men, with their wives and children, and able to "cut their own fodder," so to speak? Can I have fifty? If I could find twenty-five able-bodied men, with a mixture of women and children—good things in the family relation, I think—I could make a successful commencement. I want you to let me know whether this can be done or not. This is the practical part of my wish to see you. These are subjects of very great importance—worthy of a month's study, of a speech delivered in an hour. I ask you, then, to consider seriously, not pertaining to yourselves merely, nor for your race and ours for the present time, but as one of the things, if successfully managed, for the good of mankind—not confined to the present generation, but as

"From age to age descends the lay
To millions yet to be,
Till far its echoes roll away
Into eternity."

The above is merely given as the substance of the President's remarks.

The chairman of the delegation briefly replied, that "they would hold a consultation, and in a short time give an answer." The President said, "Take your full time—no hurry at all."

The delegation then withdrew.

It was proposed to settle these persons on a tract of country in New Grenada, but that Government objected, and no further attempt has been made in that direction. (For further particulars see page 212.)

Incompatibility of Civil and Military Office.

ROBERT C. SCHENCK and FRANCIS P. BLAIR, Jr., were elected in the fall of 1862 members of the Thirty-Eighth Congress, the first named then being a Major General. The latter was commissioned a Brigadier, and then a Major General, subsequently to the election. The former resigned his commission November 13, 1863, to take his seat in Congress, the resignation to have effect December 5, 1863; the President accepted it November 21. The latter resigned January 1, 1864, which the President accepted January 12, giving it effect that day. He took the oath of office as Representative in Congress, January 12. April 23, he requested to withdraw his resignation as Major General of Volunteers; and, same day, the President assigned him to the command of the Seventeenth Army Corps.

IN SENATE.

June 15—The Judiciary Committee reported this resolution:

Resolved, That an officer of the United States whose resignation has been duly accepted and taken effect, or who, having been elected a member of either House of Congress, qualifies and enters on the discharge of the duties of a member, is thereby, in either case, out of the office previously held, and cannot be restored to it without a new appointment, in the manner prescribed by the Constitution.

June 30—This resolution passed without division.

IN HOUSE.

June 13—The Committee on Elections made a report, and submitted these resolutions:

Resolved, That ROBERT C. SCHENCK, having resigned the office of Major General of Volunteers which he then held on the 13th day of November, 1863, which resignation was accepted November 21, 1863, to take effect December 5, 1863, was not, by reason of having held such office, disqualified from holding a seat as a Representative in the Thirty-Eighth Congress, whose first session commenced on the 7th day of December, 1863.

Resolved, That FRANCIS P. BLAIR, Jr., by continuing to hold the office of Major General of Volunteers to which he was appointed November 29, 1862, and to discharge the duties thereof till January 1, 1864, the date of his resignation, did thereby decline and disqualify himself to hold the office of Representative in the Thirty-Eighth Congress, the first session of which commenced on the first Monday in December, 1863.

June 29—They were adopted without a division.

Repeal of the Fishing Bounties.

First Session, Thirty-Seventh Congress.

Pending the consideration of a tax bill in the Senate,

July 29, 1861, Mr. SAULSBURY moved to add this section:

That from and after the 6th day of October, 1861, all acts and parts of acts granting allowances or bounties on the tonnage of vessels employed in the bank or other cod fisheries, be, and the same are hereby, repealed.

Which was rejected—yeas 15, nays 19, as follows:

YEAS—Messrs. Browning, *Carlile*, Chandler, Doolittle, Grimes, Harlan, *Johnson* of Missouri, *Polk*, *Powell*, *Rice*, *Saulsbury*, Sherman, Trumbull, Wilkinson, Willey—15.

NAYS—Messrs. Anthony, Clark, Collamer, Dixon, Fessenden, Foot, Foster, Harris, King, Lane of Indiana, Lane of Kansas, *McDougall*, Morrill, Pomeroy, Simmons, Sumner, Ten Eyck, Wade, Wilson—19.

Third Session, Thirty-Seventh Congress.

IN SENATE.

1863, Feb. 2—Pending the legislative bill, Mr. POWELL offered this new section:

That all laws or parts of laws allowing or giving bounties on the tonnage of vessels engaged in the cod or other bank fisheries, be, and the same are hereby, repealed.

Which was rejected—yeas 8, nays 35, as follows:

YEAS—Messrs. *Carlile*, *Kennedy*, *Powell*, *Richardson*, Sherman, *Turpie*, *Wall*, *Wilson* of Missouri—8.

NAYS—Messrs. Anthony, Arnold, Chandler, Clark, Collamer, Cowan, *Davis*, Dixon, Doolittle, Fessenden, Foot, Foster, Grimes, Hale, *Harding*, Harlan, Harris, Hicks, Howard, Howe, King, Lane of Indiana, Lane of Kansas, *Latham*, *McDougall*, Morrill, Pomeroy, *Rice*, Sumner, Trumbull, Wade, Wilkinson, Willey, Wilmot, Wilson of Mass—35.

First Session, Thirty-Eighth Congress.

1864, April 12—The Naval appropriation bill being under consideration in the Senate,

Mr. POWELL offered the following as a new section:

That from and after the first day of July, 1864, all acts and parts of acts granting allowances or bounties on the tonnage of vessels engaged in the Bank or other cod fisheries be, and the same are hereby, repealed.

Which was rejected—yeas 18, nays 20, as follows:

YEAS—Messrs. *Buckalew*, Cowan, *Davis*, *Harding*, Harlan, Henderson, *Hendricks*, Lane of Indiana, Lane of Kansas, *McDougall*, *Nesmith*, Pomeroy, *Powell*, *Saulsbury*, Trumbull, Wilkinson, Willey, *Wright*—18.

NAYS—Messrs. Anthony, Chandler, Conness, Doolittle, Fessenden, Foot, Foster, Grimes, Hale, Harris, Howe, Johnson, Morgan, Ramsey, Sherman, Sprague, Sumner, Ten Eyck, Wade, Wilson—20.

May 31—Pending the Internal Revenue bill, Mr. POWELL offered the same section, which was rejected—yeas 11, nays 24, as follows:

YEAS—Messrs. *Buckalew*, Conness, *Davis*, Grimes, *Hendricks*, *Nesmith*, *Powell*, *Richardson*, *Saulsbury*, Sherman, Trumbull—11.

NAYS—Messrs. Anthony, Chandler, Clark, Dixon, Doolittle, Fessenden, Foot, Foster, Hale, Howard, Howe, Johnson, Lane of Kansas, Morgan, Morrill, Pomeroy, Ramsey, Sumner, Ten Eyck, Van Winkle, Wade, Wilkinson, Willey, Wilson—24.

To prohibit Polygamy in Utah.

Second Session, Thirty-Seventh Congress.

IN HOUSE.

1862, April 28—The House passed, without a division, a bill to punish and prevent the practice of polygamy in the Territories of the United States and other places, and disapproving and annulling certain acts of the territorial legislature of Utah. (It is the identical bill passed at the first session of the Thirty-Sixth Congress, with the difference that this bill strikes out the exception of the District of Columbia from its provisions, which was contained in the other.)

June 3—The bill, amended, passed the Senate—yeas 37, nays 2, (Messrs. *Latham* and *McDougall.*)

Declaring Certain Persons Ineligible to Office.

Second Session, Thirty-Seventh Congress.

IN HOUSE.

1861, December 23—Mr. MOORHEAD offered this resolution, which was adopted:

Resolved, That the Judiciary Committee be instructed to inquire into the expediency of reporting a bill providing that any person or persons engaged or implicated in the present rebellion against the Constitution of the United States be forever hereafter rendered ineligible to hold any office under the Constitution and laws of the United States.

1862, March 13—Mr. WILSON gave notice of a bill declaring certain persons ineligible to office.

June 4—The House passed a bill declaring certain persons ineligible to office.

It provides that any person elected or appointed to any office of honor or profit under the Government of the United States, either in the civil, military, or naval department, shall, before entering on the duties of such office, and before being entitled to any of the salary or other emoluments thereof, take and subscribe an oath that he had never voluntarily borne arms against the Government of the United States since he had been a citizen thereof; had voluntarily given no aid, countenance, counsel, or encouragement to persons engaged in armed hostility thereto; had never sought or accepted or attempted to exercise the functions of any office whatever under any authority or pretended authority in hostility to the Government of the United States; that he had neither voluntarily renounced his allegiance to the Government of the United States nor yielded a voluntary support to any pretended government, authority, power, or constitution, hostile or inimical thereto; that he will support and defend the Constitution and Government of the United States and all laws made in pursuance thereof, against all enemies, foreign or domestic; bear true faith and allegiance to the same; that he takes the obligation without any mental reservation or evasion; and that he will well and faithfully discharge the duties of the office on which he is about to enter. This oath is to be preserved among the files of the court, House of Congress, or department to which such office may appertain; and any person falsely taking such oath shall be guilty of perjury, and on conviction thereof, shall, in addition to the penalties now prescribed, be deprived of his office, and rendered incapable forever thereafter of holding any office under the Government of the United States.

Yeas 78, nays 47. The NAYS were:

Messrs. *William J. Allen*, *Ancona*, Jacob B. Blair, *George H. Browne*, *Calvert*, Casey, *Cobb*, *Corning*, *Cox*, *Dunlap*, *English*, *Grider*, *Haight*, *Harding*, *Holman*, *Johnson*, *Kerrigan*, *Knapp*, *Law*, *May*, *Menzies*, *Noble*, *Noell*, *Norton*, *Nugen*, *Pendleton*, *John S. Phelps*, *Richardson*, *Robinson*, *James S. Rollins*, Segar, *Shiel*, *Smith*, *John B. Steele*, *William G. Steele*, *Stiles*, Benjamin F. Thomas, Francis Thomas, *Vallandigham*, *Vibbard*, *Voorhees*, *Wadsworth*, *Ward*, *Chilton A. White*, *Wickliffe*, *Woodruff*, *Wright*—47.

June 23—The bill was amended and passed in the Senate—yeas 23, nays 5, (Messrs. *Bayard*, *Carlile*, *Kennedy*, *Powell*, *Saulsbury.*)

June 24—The House non-concurred in the amendments of the Senate. A Committee of Conference arranged the differences, and their report, being the existing law, was adopted in the House without a division, and in the Senate—yeas 27, nays 8, (Messrs. *Bayard*, *Carlile*, *Davis*, Henderson, *Nesmith*, *Powell*, *Saulsbury*, *Stark.*)

Bill to Punish Conspiracies.

The bill to define and punish conspiracies provides that if two or more persons within any State or Territory of the United States shall conspire together to overthrow, or to put down, or to destroy by force, the Government of the United States, or to levy war against the United States, or to oppose by force the authority of the Government of the United States; or by force to prevent, hinder, or delay the execution of any law of the United States; or by force to seize, take, or possess any property of the United States against the will, or contrary to the authority of the United States; or by force, or intimidation, or threat, to prevent any person from accepting or holding any office, or trust, or place of confidence, under the United States; each and every person so offending shall be guilty of a high crime, and upon conviction in any district or circuit court of the United States having jurisdiction, or district or supreme court of any Territory of the United States having jurisdiction, shall be punished by a fine not less than $500 and not more than $5,000, or by imprisonment, solitary or social, and with or without hard labor, as the court shall determine, for a period not less than six months nor greater than six years; or by both such fine and imprisonment.

1861, July 15—It passed the House—yeas 123, nays 7, (Messrs. Ashley, *Burnett*, Diven, Edgerton, Goodwin, Pomeroy, *Wood.*)

July 26—The bill passed the Senate without a division.

Same day—Mr. POWELL presented this protest against its passage:

Protest of the minority of the Senate of the United States against the passage of the House bill No. 45, entitled "An act to define and punish certain conspirators."

The undersigned, members of the Senate, dissent from the passage of the bill on the following grounds:

The government of the United States is a Government of specially delegated powers; and though treason is one of the highest crimes known to the law, it is a political offence.

To guard against the abuses which in times of high excitement had, in the history of England previous to the revolution of 1688, too often sacrificed able, virtuous, and innocent men on charges of treason and kindred offences, unaccompanied by acts, the Constitution of the United

States expressly defines the crime of treason in the following terms:

ART. 3, SEC. 3. "Treason against the United States shall consist only in levying war against them, or in adhering to their enemies, giving them aid and comfort."

It further provides that "no person shall be convicted of treason unless on the testimony of two witnesses to the same overt act, or on confession in open court."

The intent to restrict Congress in the creation of crimes of the nature created by this bill seems obvious; for in treason all are principals, and in any conspiracy of the kind stated in the bill, an overt act in pursuance of it, proved by two witnesses, would be treason against the United States.

Thus the creation of an offence, resting in intention alone, without overt act, would render nugatory the provision last quoted, and the door would be opened for those similar oppressions and cruelties which, under the excitement of political struggles, have so often disgraced the past history of the world. The undersigned can conceive no possible object in defining the crime of treason by our ancestors, and requiring proof by two witnesses to the same overt act to justify the conviction of the accused, unless it be to restrict the power of Congress in the creation of a political crime kindred to treason, and charged as resting in intent alone, which would, if accompanied by an overt act, be treason.

It matters not that the punishment prescribed in the law is not death, but imprisonment; for the passage of the bill, though it might not affect the life of an innocent man, would give, from the uncertainty of the offence charged, and the proof requisite to sustain it, the utmost latitude to prosecutions founded on personal enmity and political animosity and the suspicions as to intention which they inevitably engender.

JAMES A. BAYARD,
L. W. POWELL,
J. D. BRIGHT,
W. SAULSBURY,
TRUSTEN POLK,
J. A. PEARCE,
A. KENNEDY,
JOHN C. BRECKINRIDGE,
WALDO P. JOHNSON.

Letters of Marque.

Second Session, Thirty-Seventh Congress.

Be it enacted, &c., That in all domestic and foreign wars the President of the United States is authorized to issue to private armed vessels of the United States commissions, or letters of marque and general reprisal, in such form as he shall think proper, and under the seal of the United States, and make all needful rules and regulations for the government and conduct thereof, and for the adjudication and disposal of the prizes and salvages made by such vessels: *Provided*, That the authority conferred by this act shall cease and terminate at the end of three years from the passage of this act.

IN SENATE.

February 17, 1863—Mr. SUMNER offered the following amendment:

That, to aid in putting down the present rebellion, the President of the United States is authorized to issue to private armed vessels of the United States, &c.

Which was rejected—yeas 13, nays 22.

The bill passed the Senate—yeas 27, nays 9, as follows:

YEAS—Messrs. Anthony, Arnold, Chandler, Clark, Collamer, Cowan, Doolittle, Fessenden, Foot, Foster, Grimes, *Harding*, Harlan, Harris, Hicks, Howe, King, Lane of Kansas, *Latham*, *McDougall*, Morrill, *Nesmith*, *Rice*, Sherman, *Turpie*, Wade, Wilson of Massachusetts—27.

NAYS—Messrs. *Davis*, Dixon, Henderson, Howard, Lane of Indiana, Pomeroy, Sumner, Trumbull, *Wilson* of Missouri—9.

March 2—The bill passed the House without division.

Enabling Act for Nebraska.

1864, March 17—The House considered the bill to enable the people of Nebraska to form a constitution and State government, when Mr. Cox moved to add a proviso:

That the said Territory shall not be admitted as a State until Congress shall be satisfied, by a census taken under authority of law, that its population shall be equal to that required as a ratio for one member of Congress under the apportionment.

Which was disagreed to—yeas 43, nays 72. The YEAS were:

Messrs. *James C Allen*, *Ancona*, *Augustus C. Baldwin*, *James S. Brown*. *Chanler*, *Cox*. *Dawson*, *Denison*, *Eldridge*, *Hall*, *Harding*, *Harrington*, *Herrick*, *Holman*, *Kalbfleisch*, *Kernan*, *Law*, *Long*, *Mallory*. *Marcy*, *McAllister*, *McDowell*, *Middleton*, *James R. Morris*. *Noble*, *Odell*, *John O'Neill*, *Pendleton*. *Perry*, *Pruyn*, *Rogers*. *James S. Rollins*, *Ross*, *John B. Steele*, *William G. Steele*, *Stiles*. *Strouse*, *Sweat*, *Voorhees*, *Wadsworth*, Webster, *Wheeler*, *Yeaman*—43.

April 14—The Senate passed the bill without a division.

State of West Virginia.

Second Session, Thirty-Seventh Congress.

IN SENATE.

1862, July 14—The bill providing for the admission of the State of West Virginia into the Union, passed—yeas 23, nays 17, as follows:

YEAS—Messrs. Anthony, Clark, Collamer, Fessenden, Foot, Foster, Grimes, Hale, Harlan, Harris, Howe, Lane of Indiana, Lane of Kansas, Morrill, Pomeroy, *Rice*, Sherman, Simmons, Ten Eyck, Wade, Wilkinson, Willey, Wilson of Massachusetts—23.

NAYS—Messrs. *Bayard*, Browning, *Carlile*, Chandler, Cowan, *Davis*, Howard, *Kennedy*, King, *McDougall*, *Powell*, *Saulsbury*, *Stark*, Sumner, Trumbull, *Wilson* of Missouri, *Wright*—17.

During the pendency of this bill, July 14, 1862, Mr. SUMNER moved to strike from the first section of the second article the words: "the children of all slaves born within the limits of said State shall be free," and insert:

Within the limits of the said State there shall be neither slavery nor involuntary servitude, otherwise than in punishment of crimes whereof the party shall be duly convicted.

Which was rejected—yeas 11, nays 24, as follows:

YEAS—Messrs. Chandler, Clark, Grimes, King, Lane of Kansas, Pomeroy, Sumner, Trumbull, Wilkinson, Wilmot, Wilson of Massachusetts—11.

NAYS—Messrs. Anthony, *Bayard*, Browning, *Carlile*, Collamer, Doolittle, Foot, Foster, Harris, Henderson, Howe, *Kennedy*, Lane of Indiana, *Powell*, *Rice*, *Saulsbury*, Sherman, Simmons, *Stark*, Ten Eyck, Wade, Willey, *Wilson* of Missouri, *Wright*—24.

Mr. WILLEY proposed to strike out all after the word "That" in the first section, and insert:

That the State of West Virginia be, and is hereby, declared to be one of the United States of America, and admitted into the Union on an equal footing with the original States in all respects whatever, and until the next general census shall be entitled to three members in the House of Representatives of the United States: *Provided always*, That this act shall not take effect until after the proclamation of the President of the United States hereinafter provided for.

SEC. 2. It being represented to Congress that since the convention of the 26th of November, 1861, that framed and proposed the constitution for the said State of West Virginia, the people thereof have expressed a wish to change the seventh section of the eleventh article of said constitution by striking out the same, and inserting the following in its place, namely, "The children of slaves born within the limits of this State after the 4th day of July, 1863, shall be free and no slave shall be permitted to come into the State for permanent residence therein:" Therefore,

Be it further enacted, That whenever the people of West Virginia shall, through their said convention, and by a vote to be taken at an election to be held within the limits of the State at such time as the convention may provide, make and ratify the change aforesaid and properly certify the same under the hand of the president of the convention, it shall be lawful for the President of the United States to issue his proclamation stating the fact, and thereupon this act shall take effect and be in force from and after sixty days from the date of said proclamation.

Mr. LANE, of Kansas, moved to amend the

amendment by inserting after the word "therein" and before the word "Therefore" the words—

And that all slaves within the said State who shall at the time aforesaid be under the age of ten years shall be free when they arrive at the age of twenty-one years; and all slaves over ten and under twenty-one years shall be free when they arrive at the age of twenty-five years.

Which was agreed to—yeas 25, nays 12, as follows:

YEAS—Messrs. Anthony, Clark, Collamer, Doolittle, Foot, Foster, Grimes, Harlan, Harris, Howard, Howe, King, Lane of Indiana, Lane of Kansas, Morrill, Pomeroy, Sherman, Simmons, Sumner, Ten Eyck, Trumbull, Wade, Wilkinson, Wilmot, Wilson of Massachusetts—25.

NAYS—Messrs. Browning, *Carlile*, *Davis*, Henderson, *Kennedy*, *McDougall*, *Powell*, *Saulsbury*, *Stark*, Willey, *Wilson* of Missouri, *Wright*—12.

The amendment as amended was then agreed to.

A motion to postpone the bill to the first Monday of the next December was lost—yeas 17, nays 23.

IN HOUSE.

July 16—The bill was postponed until the second Tuesday of the next December—yeas 63, nays 33.

Third Session, Thirty-Seventh Congress.

1862, Dec. 10—The House passed the bill*—yeas 96, nays 57, as follows:

YEAS—Messrs. Aldrich, Arnold, Babbitt, Baker, Baxter, Beaman, Bingham, Jacob B. Blair, Samuel S. Blair, Blake, William G. Brown, Buffinton, Burnham, Campbell, Casey, Chamberlain, Clark, Clements, Colfax, Frederick A. Conkling, Covode, Cutler, Davis, Duell, Dunn, Edgerton, Edwards, Eliot, Ely, Fenton, Samuel C. Fessenden, Thomas A. D. Fessenden, Franchot, Frank, Goodwin, Gurley, *Haight*, Hale, Harrison, Hickman, Hooper, Horton, Hutchins, Julian, Kelley, Francis W. Kellogg, William Kellogg, Killinger, Lansing, *Lehman*, Loomis, Lovejoy, Low, McKnight, McPherson, Maynard, Mitchell, Moorhead, Anson P. Morrill, Justin S. Morrill, Nixon, *Noell*, Olin, Patton, Timothy G. Phelps, Pike, Pomeroy, Porter, Potter, John H. Rice, Riddle, Edward H. Rollins, Sargent, Sedgwick, Shanks, *Sheffield*, Shellabarger, Sherman, Sloan, Spaulding, Stevens, Stratton, Trimble, Trowbridge, Van Horn, Van Valkenburgh, Van Wyck, Verree, Walker, Wall, Washburne, Whaley, Albert S. White, Wilson, Windom, Worcester—96.

NAYS—Messrs. *William J. Allen*, Alley, *Ancona*, Ashley, *Baily*, *Biddle*, *Cobb*, Roscoe Conkling, Conway, *Cox*, *Cravens*, *Crisfield*, *Crittenden*, Delano, *Delaplaine*, Diven, *Dunlap*, *English*, Gooch, Granger, *Grider*, *Hall*, *Harding*, *Holman*, *Johnson*, *Kerrigan*, *Knapp*, *Law*, *Mallory*, *Menzies*, *Morris*, *Noble*, *Norton*, *Odell*, *Pendleton*, *Price*, Alexander H. Rice, *Richardson*, *Robinson*, *James S. Rollins*, Segar, *Shiel*, *Smith*, *John B. Steele*, *William G. Steele*, *Stiles*, Benjamin F. Thomas, Francis Thomas, Train, *Vallandigham*, *Voorhees*, *Wadsworth*, *Ward*, *Chilton A. White*, *Wickliffe*, *Wright*, *Yeaman*—57.

1863, April 20—The President issued a proclamation announcing the compliance, by West Virginia, of the conditions of admission.

Colored Men as Citizens.

OPINION OF ATTORNEY GENERAL BATES.

ATTORNEY GENERAL'S OFFICE,
November 29, 1862.

HON. S. P. CHASE, *Secretary of the Treasury:*

SIR: Some time ago I had the honor to receive your letter submitting, for my opinion, the question whether or not *colored men* can be citizens of the United States. The urgency of other unavoidable engagements, and the great importance of the question itself, have caused me to delay the answer until now.

Your letter states that "the schooner Elizabeth and Margaret, of New Brunswick, is detained by the revenue cutter Tiger, at South Amboy, New Jersey, because commanded by a 'colored man,' and so by a person not a citizen of the United States. As colored masters are numerous in our coasting trade, I submit, for your opinion, the question suggested by Captain Martin, of the Tiger: *Are colored men citizens* of the United States, and therefore competent to command American vessels?"

The question would have been more clearly stated if, instead of saying *are colored men citizens,* it had been said, *can colored men be citizens of the United States;* for within our borders and upon our ships, both of war and commerce, there may be *colored* men, and *white* men, also, who are not citizens of the United States. In treating the subject, I shall endeavor to answer your question as if it imported only this: Is a man legally incapacitated to be a citizen of the United States by the sole fact that he is a *colored*, and not a white man?

Who is a citizen? What constitutes a citizen of the United States? I have been often pained by the fruitless search in our law books and the records of our courts, for a clear and satisfactory definition of the phrase *citizen of the United States.* I find no such definition, no authoritative establishment of the meaning of the phrase, neither by a course of judicial decisions in our courts, nor by the continued and consentaneous action of the different branches of our political government. For aught I see to the contrary, the subject is now as little understood in its details and elements, and the question as open to argument and to speculative criticism, as it was at the beginning of the government. Eighty years of practical enjoyment of citizenship, under the Constitution, have not sufficed to teach us either the exact meaning of the word, or the constituent elements of the thing we prize so highly.

In most instances, within my knowledge, in which the matter of citizenship has been discussed, the argument has not turned upon the existence and the intrinsic qualities of citizenship itself, but upon the claim of some right or privilege as belonging to and inhering in the character of citizen. In this way we are easily led into errors both of fact and principle. We see individuals, who are known to be citizens, in the actual enjoyment of certain rights and privileges, and in the actual exercise of certain powers, social and political, and we, inconsiderately, and without any regard to legal and logical consequences, attribute to those individuals, and to all of their class, the enjoyment of those rights and privileges and the exercise of those powers as incidents to their citizenship, and belonging to them only in their quality of citizens.

In such cases it often happens that the rights enjoyed and the powers exercised have no relation whatever to the quality of citizen, and might be as perfectly enjoyed and exercised by known aliens. For instance, General Bernard, a distinguished soldier and devoted citizen of France, for a long time filled the office of general of engineers in the service of the United States, all the time avowing his French allegiance, and, in fact, closing his relations with the United States by resigning his commission and returning to the service of his own native country. This, and all such instances, (and they are many,) go to prove that in this country the legal capacity to hold office is not confined to citizens, and therefore that the fact of holding any office for which citizenship is not specially prescribed by law as a qualification, is no proof that the incumbent is an American citizen.

Again, with regard to the right of suffrage, that is, the right to choose officers of government, there is a very common error to the effect that the right to vote for public officers is one of the constituent elements of American citizenship, the leading faculty indeed of the citizen, the test at once of his legal right, and the sufficient proof of his membership of the body politic. No error can be greater than this, and few more injurious to the right understanding of our constitutions and the actual working of our political governments. It is not only not true in law or in fact, in principle or in practice, but the reverse is conspicuously true; for I make bold to affirm that, viewing the nation as a whole, or viewing the States separately, there is no district in the nation in which a majority of the known and recognized citizens are not excluded by law from the right of suffrage. Besides those who are excluded specially on account of some personal defect, such as paupers, idiots, lunatics, and men convicted of infamous crimes, and, in some States, soldiers, all females and all minor males are also excluded. And these, in every community, make the majority; and yet, I think, no one will venture to deny that women and children, and lunatics, and even convict felons, may be citizens of the United States.

Our code (unlike the codes of France, and perhaps some other nations) makes no provision for loss or legal deprivation of citizenship. Once a citizen (whether *natus* or *datus*

---

* It includes these counties: Hancock, Brooke, Ohio, Marshall, Wetzel, Marion, Monongalia, Preston, Taylor, Tyler, Pleasants, Ritchie, Doddridge, Harrison, Wood, Jackson, Wirt, Roane, Calhoun, Gilmer, Barbour, Tucker, Lewis, Braxton, Upshur, Randolph, Mason, Putnam, Kanawha, Clay, Nicholas, Cabell, Wayne, Boone, Logan, Wyoming, Mercer, McDowell, Webster, Pocahontas, Fayette, Raleigh, Greenbrier, Monroe, Pendleton, Hardy, Hampshire, and Morgan.

as Sir Edward Coke expresses it,) always a citizen, unless changed by the volition and act of the individual. Neither infancy nor madness nor crime can take away from the subject the quality of citizen. And our laws do, in express terms, declare women and children to be citizens. See, for one instance, the act of Congress of February 10, 1855, 10 Stat., 604.

The Constitution of the United States does not declare who are and who are not citizens, nor does it attempt to describe the constituent elements of citizenship. It leaves that quality where it found it, resting upon the fact of home-birth, and upon the laws of the several States. Even in the important matter of electing members of Congress, it does no more than provide that "the House of Representatives shall be composed of members chosen every second year *by the people* of the several States; and the *electors* in the several States shall have the qualifications requisite for the electors of the most numerous branch of the State legislature." Here the word *citizen* is not mentioned, and it is a legal fact, known of course to all lawyers and publicists, that the constitutions of several of the States, in specifying the qualifications of electors, do altogether omit and exclude the word *citizen* and *citizenship*. I will refer, in proof, to but three instances:

1. The constitution of Massachusetts, adopted in 1779-'80, in article 4 of section 3, chapter 1, provides as follows: "Every *male person* (being twenty-one years of age, and *resident* of a particular town in this Commonwealth for the space of one year next preceding) having a freehold estate within the same town of the annual income of three pounds, or any estate of the value of sixty pounds, shall have the right to vote in the choice of representative or representatives for said town."

2. The constitution of North Carolina, adopted in 1776, after a bill of rights, and after reciting that "whereas allegiance and protection are, in their nature, reciprocal, and the one should of right be refused when the other is withdrawn," declares, in section eight, "that all *freemen* at the age of twenty-one years, who have been *inhabitants* of any one county within the State twelve months immediately preceding the day of any election, and shall have paid public taxes, shall be entitled to vote for members of the House of Commons for the county in which he resides."

3. The constitution of Illinois, adopted in 1818, in article two, section twenty-seven, declares that "in all elections all *white male inhabitants* above the age of twenty-one years, having resided in the State six months next preceding the election, shall enjoy the right of an elector; but no person shall be entitled to vote except in the county or district in which he shall actually reside at the time of the election."

These three constitutions belong to States widely separated in geographical position, varying greatly from each other in habits, manners, and pursuits, having different climates, soils, productions, and domestic institutions; and yet not one of the three has made *citizenship* a necessary qualification for a voter; all three of them exclude all females, but only one of them (Illinois) has excluded the black man from the right of suffrage. And it is historically true that the practice has conformed to the theory of those constitutions, respectively; for, without regard to citizenship, the colored man has not voted in Illinois, and freemen of all colors have voted in North Carolina and Massachusetts.

From all this it is manifest that American citizenship does not necessarily depend upon nor coexist with the legal capacity to hold office and the right of suffrage, either or both of them. The Constitution of the United States, as I have said, does not define citizenship; neither does it declare who may vote, nor who may hold office, except in regard to a few of the highest national functionaries. And the several States, as far as I know, in exercising that power, act independently and without any controlling authority over them, and hence it follows that there is no limit to their power in that particular but their own prudence and discretion; and therefore we are not surprised to find that those faculties of voting and holding office are not uniform in the different States, but are made to depend upon a variety of facts, purely discretionary, such as age, sex, race, color, property, residence in a particular place, and length of residence there.

On this point, then, I conclude that no person in the United States did ever exercise the right of suffrage in virtue of the naked, unassisted fact of citizenship. In every instance the right depends upon some additional fact and cumulative qualification, which may as perfectly exist without as with citizenship.

I am aware that some of our most learned lawyers and able writers have allowed themselves to speak upon this subject in loose and indeterminate language. They speak of "all the rights, privileges, and immunities guarantied by the Constitution to the citizen" without telling us what they are. They speak of a man's citizenship as defective and imperfect, because he is supposed not to have "all the civil rights," (all the *jura civitatis*, as expressed by one of my predecessors,) without telling what particular rights they are nor what relation they have, if any, with citizenship. And they suggest, without affirming, that there may be different grades of citizenship of higher and lower degree in point of legal virtue and efficacy; one grade "in the sense of the Constitution," and another inferior grade made by a State and not recognized by the Constitution.

In my opinion the Constitution uses the word citizen only to express the political quality of the individual in his relations to the nation; to declare that he is a member of the body politic, and bound to it by the reciprocal obligation of allegiance on the one side and protection on the other. And I have no knowledge of any other kind of political citizenship, higher or lower, statal or national; or of any other sense in which the word has been used in the Constitution, or can be used properly in the laws of the United States. The phrase "a citizen of the United States," without addition or qualification, means neither more nor less than a member of the nation. And all such are, politically and legally, equal—the child in the cradle and its father in the Senate are equally citizens of the United States. And it needs no argument to prove that every citizen of a State is, necessarily, a citizen of the United States; and to me it is equally clear that every citizen of the United States is a citizen of the particular State in which he is domiciled.

And as to voting and holding office, as that privilege is not essential to citizenship, so the deprivation of it by law is not a deprivation of citizenship. No more so in the case of a negro than in case of a white woman or child.

In common speech the word citizen, with more or less of truth and pertinency, has a variety of meanings. Sometimes it is used in contrast with *soldier;* sometimes with *farmer* or *countryman;* sometimes with *alien* or *foreigner*. Speaking of a particular man we ask, is he a citizen or a soldier? meaning, is he engaged in civil or military pursuits? Is he a citizen or a countryman? meaning, does he live in the city or in the country? Is he a citizen or an alien? meaning, is he a member of our body-politic or of some other nation. The first two predicates relate only to the pursuits and to the place of abode of the person. The last is always and wholly political, and concerns only the political and governmental relations of the individual. And it is only in this last sense, the political, that the word is ever used in the Constitution and statutes of the United States.

We have *natural-born* citizens, (Constitution, article 2, sec. 5,) not made by law or otherwise, but *born*. And this class is the large majority; in fact, the mass of our citizens; for all others are exceptions specially provided for by law. As they became citizens in the natural way, *by birth*, so they remain citizens during their natural lives, unless, by their own voluntary act, they expatriate themselves and become citizens or subjects of another nation. For we have no law (as the French have) to *decitizenize* a citizen, who has become such either by the natural process of birth, or by the legal process of adoption. And in this connection the Constitution says not one word, and furnishes not one hint, in relation to the color or to the ancestral race of the "natural-born citizen." Whatever may have been said, in the opinion of judges and lawyers, and in State statutes, about negroes, mulattoes, and persons of color, the Constitution is wholly silent upon that subject. The Constitution itself does not *make* the citizens, (it is, in fact, made by them.) It only intends and recognizes such of them as are natural—home-born—and provides for the *naturalization* of such of them as were alien—foreign-born—making the latter, as far as nature will allow, like the former.

And I am not aware of any provision in our laws to warrant us in presuming the existence in this country of a class of persons intermediate between citizens and aliens. In England there is such a class, clearly defined by law, and called *denizens*. "A denizen (says Sir William Blackstone) is an *alien born*, but who has obtained, *ex donatione regis*, letters patent to make him an English subject; a high and incommunicable branch of the *royal prerogative*. A denizen is in a kind of middle state between an alien and a natural-born subject, and partakes of both of them." (1 *Sharswood's Bl. Com.*, 374.) In this country I know of but one legal authority tending to show the existence of such a class among us. One of my learned predecessors, Mr. Legaré, (4 *Opin.*, 147,) supposes that there may be such a class, and that free colored persons may be ranked in it. Yet, in that same opinion, he declares that a "free man of color, a *native* of this country, may be admitted to the privileges of a pre-emptioner under the 10th section of the act of the 4th September, 1841." And that act declares that a pre-emptioner must be either a citizen of the United States or a person who had declared his intention to become a citizen, as required by the naturalization laws. Of course, the "colored man" must have been a *citizen* or he could not have entered the land under that act of Congress. If not a citizen *then*, by virtue of his native birth, he never could become one by force of law. For our laws extend the privileges of naturalization to such persons only as are "*aliens*, being free *white* persons," and he was neither; not alien, because natural-born in the country, and not a free *white* person, because, though free, confessedly "a man of color."

It occurs to me that the discussion of this great subject of national citizenship has been much embarrassed and obscured by the fact that it is beset with artificial difficulties, extrinsic to its nature, and having little or no relation to its great political and national characteristics. And these difficulties, it seems to me, flow mainly from two sources: First, the existence among us of a large class of people whose physical qualities visibly distinguish them from the mass of our people, and mark a different race, and who, for the most part, are held in bondage. This visible difference and servile connection present difficulties hard to be conquered; for they unavoidably lead to a more complicated system of government, both legislative and administrative, than would be required if all our people were of one race, and undistinguishable by outward signs. And this, without counting the effect upon the opinions, passions, and prejudices of men. Second, the common habit of many of our best and most learned men (the wise aptitude of which I have not been able to perceive) of testing the political status and governmental relation of our people by standards drawn from the laws and history of ancient Greece and Rome, without, as I think, taking sufficient account of the organic differences between their governments and ours.

A very learned writer upon the Politics of Greece (Heeren, Bancroft's translation, p. 105) informs us "that the essential character of the new political form assumed by Greece consisted in the circumstance that the free States which were formed were *nothing but cities* with their districts; and their constitutions were, consequently, only *forms of city governments.* This point of view (the learned author warns us) must never be lost sight of."

And the wise observation of the author applies to Italy as well; for the earliest free cities of Italy were but Grecian colonies, which (bringing along with them the higher civilization of their parent country, and its better notions of civil polity) by degrees diffused the light of knowledge, and consequently the love of liberty among the then barbarous people of the Italian peninsula. The Italians, profiting by the good example, founded cities of their own upon the Grecian models, and each new Italian city became an independent State. How long this condition of thing continued I know not; but it continued until Rome outgrew all the neighboring communities, and subdued them all (the Grecian colonies included) under its power. Still *the city* ruled, and from time to time granted to such as it would (and withheld from such as it would) the title of *Roman*, and the rights of Roman citizens.

In the process of time, when the dominant power of Rome had expanded over Greece and western Asia, the same civil polity was still continued. As it had been in Italy, so it was in Greece and Asia. In the countries and kingdoms subdued by the Roman arms and transformed into Roman provinces, the same system of government still prevailed.

Rome, by her pro-consuls and other governors, ruled the conquered nations with absolute sway. And the ruling power at Rome, whether republican or imperial, granted, from time to time, to communities and to individuals in the conquered east the title of *Roman* and the rights of Roman citizens.

A striking example of this Roman naturalization, of its controlling authority as a political law, and of its beneficent power to protect a persecuted citizen, may be found in the case of St. Paul, as it is graphically reported in the Acts of the Apostles. Paul, being at Jerusalem, was in great peril of his life from his own countrymen, the Jews, who accused him of crimes against their own law and faith, and were about to put him to death by mob violence, when he was rescued by the commander of the Roman troops and taken into a fort for security. He first explained, both to the Roman officer and to his own countrymen, who were clamoring against him, his local status and municipal relations, that he was a Jew of Tarsus, a *natural-born citizen* of no mean city, and that he had been brought up in Jerusalem in the strictest manner according to the law and faith of the fathers. But this did not appease the angry crowd, who were proceeding with great violence to kill him. And then "the chief captain commanded that he be brought into the castle, and bade that he should be *examined by scourging,*" (that is, tortured to enforce confession.) "And as they bound him with thongs, Paul said unto the centurion that stood by, Is it lawful for you to scourge a man that is *a Roman and uncondemned?* When the centurion heard *that* he went out and told the chief captain, saying, Take heed what thou doest, *for this man is a Roman.* Then the chief captain came and said, Tell me, art thou a *Roman?* He said yea, and the chief captain said, With a great sum obtained I *this freedom.* And Paul said, But I was *free born.* Then straightway *they* departed from him which should have *examined* him. And the chief captain also was *afraid*, after he knew he was a *Roman*, and because he had *bound him.*"

Thus Paul, under circumstances of great danger and obloquy, asserted his immunity, as "a Roman uncondemned," from ignominious constraint and cruel punishment, a constraint and punishment against which, as a mere provincial subject of Rome, he had no legal protection. And thus the Roman officers instantly, and with fear, obeyed the law of their country and respected the sacred franchise of the Roman citizen.

Paul, as we know by this record, was a natural-born citizen of Tarsus, and as such, no doubt, had the municipal freedom of that city; but that would not have protected him against the thongs and the lash. How he became a *Roman* we learn from other historical sources. Cæsar granted to the people of Tarsus (for some good service done, probably for taking his side in the war which resulted in the establishment of the empire) the title of *Roman*, and the freedom of Roman citizens. And, considering the chronology of events, this grant must have been older than Paul; and therefore he truly said *I was free born*—a free citizen of Rome, and as such exempt by law from degrading punishment.

And this immunity did not fill the measure of his rights as a citizen. As a Roman, it was his right to be tried by the supreme authority, at the capital of the empire. And when he claimed that right, and appealed from the jurisdiction of the provincial governor to the Emperor at Rome, his appeal was instantly allowed, and he was remitted to "Cæsar's judgment."

I have dwelt the longer upon this case of Paul, because it is a *leading case* in Roman jurisprudence in the matter of the "*jus Romanum.*" And in so far as there is any analogy between Roman and American citizenship, it is strictly applicable to us. Its authenticity is unquestionable, and by its lucid statement of facts in minute detail leaves no room to doubt the legal merits of the case. It establishes the great *protective rights* of the citizen, but, like our own national constitution, it is silent about his *powers.* It protected Paul against oppression and outrage, but said nothing about his right of suffrage or his eligibility to office.

As far as I know, Mr. Secretary, you and I have no better title to the citizenship which we enjoy than the "accident of birth"—the fact that we happened to be born in the United States. And our Constitution, in speaking of *natural-born citizens*, uses no affirmative language to make them such, but only recognizes and reaffirms the universal principle, common to all nations, and as old as political society, that the people born in a country do constitute the nation, and, as individuals, are *natural* members of the body politic.

If this be a true principle, and I do not doubt it, it follows that every person born in the country is, at the moment of birth, *prima facie* a citizen; and he who would deny it must take upon himself the burden of proving some great disfranchisement strong enough to override the "*natural-born*" right as recognized by the Constitution in terms the most simple and comprehensive, and without any reference to race or color, or any other accidental circumstance.

That *nativity* furnishes the rule, both of duty and of right as between the individual and the government, is a historical and political truth so old and so universally accepted that it is needless to prove it by authority. Nevertheless, for the satisfaction of those who may have doubts upon the subject, I note a few books, which, I think, cannot fail to remove all such doubts—Kent's Com., vol. 2, part 4, sec. 25; Bl. Com., book 1, ch. 10, p. 365; 7 Co. Rep., Calvin's case; 4 Term Rep., p. 300, Doe *vs.* Jones; 3 Pet. Rep., p. 246, Shanks *vs.* Dupont; and see a very learned treatise, attributed to Mr. Binney, in 2 Am. Law Reporter, 193.

In every civilized country the individual is *born* to dutie[s] and rights—the duty of allegiance and the right to protec[-]tion; and these are correlative obligations, the one the pric[e] of the other, and they constitute the all-sufficient bond o[f] union between the individual and his country; and the coun[-]try he is born in *is, prima facie, his* country. In most coun[-]tries the old law was broadly laid down that this natural con[-]nection between the individual and his native country wa[s] perpetual; at least, that the tie was indissoluble by the ac[t] of the subject alone.—(See Bl. Com. *supra;* 3 Pet. Rep[.] *supra.*)

But that law of the perpetuity of allegiance is no[w] changed, both in Europe and America. In some countrie[s] by silent acquiescence, in others by affirmative legislatio[n.] In England, while asserting the perpetuity of natural alle[-]giance, the King, for centuries past, has exercised the powe[r] to grant letters of denization to foreigners, making the[m] English subjects, and the Parliament has exercised at plea[s-]ure the power of naturalization.

In France the whole subject is regulated by written la[w] which plainly declares who are citizens (*citoyens Françai[s]*) and who are only *the French*, (*Français,*) meaning the who[le] body of the French people. (See *Les Codes Français, tit[re] premier.*) And the same law distinctly sets forth by wha[t] means citizenship and the quality of *French* may be lo[st] and regained; and maintains fully the right of expatriatio[n] in the subject, and the power of naturalization in the nation to which he goes.

In the United States it is too late now to deny the political rights and obligations conferred and imposed by nativity; for our laws do not pretend to create or enact them, but do assume and recognize them as things known to all men, because pre-existent and natural; and therefore things of which the laws must take cognizance. Acting out this guiding thought, our Constitution does no more than grant to Congress (rather than to any other department) the power "to establish a *uniform rule* of naturalization." And our laws made in pursuance thereof indue the *made* citizen with all the rights and obligations of the *natural* citizen. And so strongly was Congress impressed with the great legal fact that the child takes its political status in the nation where it is born, that it was found necessary to pass a law to prevent the *alienage* of children of our known fellow-citizens who happen to be born in foreign countries. The act of February 10, 1852, 10 Statutes, 604, provides that "persons," (not *white* persons) "persons heretofore born, or hereafter to be born, out of the limits and jurisdiction of the United States, whose fathers were or shall be, at the time of their birth, citizens of the United States, shall be deemed and considered, and are hereby declared to be, citizens of the United States: *Provided, however*, That the rights of citizenship shall not descend to persons whose fathers never resided in the United States.

"SEC. 2. *And be it further enacted*, That any woman who might lawfully be naturalized under the existing laws, married, or who shall be married to a citizen of the United States, shall be deemed and taken to be a citizen."

But for that act, children of our citizens who happen to be born at London, Paris, or Rome, while their parents are there on a private visit of pleasure or business, might be brought to the native home of their parents, only to find that they themselves were aliens in their father's country, incapable of inheriting their father's land, and with no right to demand the protection of their father's Government.

That is the law of birth at the common law of England, clear and unqualified; and now, both in England and America, modified only by statutes, made from time to time, to meet emergencies as they arise.

I have said that, *prima facie*, every person in this country is born a citizen; and that he who denies it in individual cases assumes the burden of stating the exception to the general rule, and proving the fact which works the disfranchisement. There are but a few exceptions commonly made and urged as disqualifying facts. I lay no stress upon the small and admitted class of the *natural-born* composed of the children of foreign ministers and the like; and

1. *Slavery*, and whether or no it is legally possible for a slave to be a citizen. On that point I make no question, because it is not within the scope of your inquiry, and does not concern the person to whom your inquiry relates.

2. *Color*.—It is strenuously insisted by some that "persons of color," though born in the country, are not capable of being citizens of the United States. As far as the Constitution is concerned, this is a naked assumption; for the Constitution contains not one word upon the subject. The exclusion, if it exist, must then rest upon some fundamental fact which, in the reason and nature of things, is so inconsistent with citizenship that the two cannot coexist in the same person. Is mere *color* such a fact? Let those who assert it prove that it is so. It has never been so understood nor put into practice in the nation from which we derive our language, laws, and institutions, and our very morals and modes of thought; and, as far as I know, there is not a single nation in Christendom which does not regard the new-found idea with incredulity, if not disgust. What can there be in the mere *color* of a man (we are speaking now not of *race*, but of *color* only) to disqualify him for bearing true and faithful allegiance to his native country, and for demanding the protection of that country? And these two, allegiance and protection, constitute the sum of the duties and rights of a "natural-born citizen of the United States."

3. *Race*.—There are some who, abandoning the untenable objection of *color*, still contend that no person descended from *negroes of the African race* can be a citizen of the United States. Here the objection is not *color* but *race* only. The individual objected to may be of very long descent from African negroes, and may be as white as leprosy, or as the intermixture for many generations with the Caucasian race can make him; still, if he can be traced back to *negroes of the African race*, he cannot, they say, be a citizen of the United States! And why not? The Constitution certainly does not forbid it, but is silent about the *race* as it is about *color*.

Our nationality was created and our political Government exists by written law, and inasmuch as that law does not exclude persons of that descent, and as its terms are manifestly broad enough to include them, it follows inevitably that such persons, born in the country, must be citizens, unless the fact of African descent be so incompatible with the fact of citizenship that the two cannot exist together. If they can coexist, in nature and reason, then they do coexist in persons of the indicated class, for there is no law to the contrary. I am not able to perceive any antagonism, legal or natural, between the two facts.

But it is said that African negroes are a degraded race, and that all who are tainted with that degradation are forever disqualified for the functions of citizenship. I can hardly comprehend the thought of the absolute incompatibility of degradation and citizenship. I thought that they often went together. But if it be true with regard to races, it seems to me more cogently true with regard to individuals. And if I be right in this, there are many sorrowful examples in the legislation and practice of various States in the Union to show how low the citizen may be degraded by the combined wisdom and justice of his fellow-citizens. In the early legislation of a number of States the most humiliating punishments were denounced against persons guilty of certain crimes and misdemeanors—the lash, the pillory, the cropping of the ears, and the branding of the face with an indelible mark of infamy. And yet a lower depth: in several of the States the common punishment of the crime of *vagrancy* was *sale into bondage at public auction!* And yet I have not read that such unfortunates thereby lost their natural-born citizenship, nor that their descendants are doomed to perpetual exclusion and degradation.

I am inclined to think that these objections, as to color and ancestral race, arise entirely from a wrong conception of the nature and qualities of citizenship, and from the loose and unguarded phraseology too often used in the discussion of the subject. I have already given, at some length, my own views of the word and the thing—citizenship. And now I will add only a few observations before drawing your attention to certain authorities upon the subject mostly relied upon by those who support the objections.

In my opinion it is a great error, and the fruitful parent of errors, to suppose that *citizens* belong exclusively to republican forms of government. English subjects are as truly citizens as we are, and we are as truly subjects as they are. Imperial France (following imperial Rome) in the text of her laws calls her people citizens.—(*Les Codes Français*, book 1, tit. 1, ch. 1, and notes.) And we have a treaty with the present Emperor of the French, stipulating for reciprocal rights in favor of the *citizens* of the two countries respectively. (10 Stat., p. 996, art. 7.)

It is an error to suppose that citizenship is ever hereditary. It never "passes by descent." It is as original in the child as it was in the parents. It is always either born with him or given to him directly by law.

In discussing this subject it is a misleading error to fail to mark the natural and characteristic distinction between political *rights* and political *powers*. The former belong to all citizens alike, and cohere in the very name and nature of citizenship. The latter (participation in the powers of government by voting and exercising office) does not belong to all citizens alike, nor to any citizen, merely in virtue of citizenship. His *power* always depends upon extraneous facts and superadded qualifications; which facts and qualifications are common to both citizens and aliens.

In referring to the authorities commonly adduced by those who deny the citizenship of colored people, I do not pretend to cite them all, but a few only of such as I believe to be most usually relied upon. And I will not trouble you with a detailed examination of the reasoning employed in each case, for I have already stated my own views of the principles and laws involved in the question; and where they conflict with the arguments upon which the contrary opinion is founded, I still adhere to my own.

The first of these authorities of which I will treat is the opinion of my predecessor, Mr. Wirt, upon a case precisely like the present, except that in that case the "free person of color" was a Virginian, and the objections to his competency were founded mainly, if not entirely, upon Virginia law.—(See Opinions of Attorneys General, vol. 1, p. 506, date November 7, 1821.) I have examined this opinion with the greater care, because of the writer's reputation for learning and his known and varied excellencies as a man.

In that case the precise question was, "whether free persons of color are, *in Virginia*, citizens of the United States, within the intent and meaning of the acts regulating foreign and coasting trade, so as to be qualified to command vessels." And thus Mr. Wirt was in a manner invited to consider the question rather in a statal than a national point of view; and hence we ought not to be surprised to find the whole argument for the exclusion based upon local institutions and statal laws.

As a general answer to all such arguments, I have this to say: Every citizen of the United States is a component member of the nation, with rights and duties, under the Constitution and laws of the United States, which cannot be destroyed or abridged by the laws of any particular State. The laws of the State, if they conflict with the laws of the nation, are of no force. The Constitution is plain beyond cavil upon this point. Article 6: "This Constitution, and the laws of the United States which shall be made in pursuance thereof, and all treaties, &c., shall be the supreme law of the land, and the judges in *every State* shall be bound thereby, anything in the constitution or laws of *any State* to the contrary notwithstanding." And from this I assume that every person who is a citizen of the United States, whether by birth or naturalization, holds his great franchise by the laws of the United States, and above the control of any particular State. Citizenship of the United States is an integral thing, incapable of legal existence in fractional parts Whoever, then, has that franchise is a whole citizen and a citizen of the whole nation, and cannot be (as the argument of my learned predecessor seems to suppose) such citizen in one State and not in another.

I fully concur in the statement that "the description, *citizen of the United States*, used in the Constitution, has the same meaning that it has in the several acts of Congress passed under the authority of the Constitution." And I freely declare my inability to conceive of any second or subordinate meaning of the phrase as used in all those instruments. It means in them all the simple expression of the political status of the person in connection with the nation—that he is a member of the body politic. And that is all it means, for it does not specify his rights and duties as a citizen, nor in any way refer to such "rights, privileges, and immunities" as he may happen to have, by State laws or otherwise, over and beyond what legally and naturally belong to him in his quality of citizen of the United States. State laws may and do, nay must, vest in individuals great privileges, powers, and duties which do not belong to the mass of their fellow-citizens, and in doing so they consult discretion and convenience only. One citizen, who happens to be a judge, may, under proper circumstances, sentence another to be hanged, and a third, who happens to be a governor, may grant a pardon to the condemned man, who, *as a citizen*, is the undoubted peer of both the judge and the governor.

As to the objection (not in law, but sentiment only) that if a negro can be a citizen of the United States, he might, possibly, become President, the legal inference is true. There would be such a legal possibility. But those who make that objection are not arguing upon the Constitution as it is, but upon what, in their own minds and feelings, they think it ought to be. Moreover, they seem to forget that all limitations upon eligibility to office are less restrictions upon the rights of aspirants than upon the powers of electors. Even the legislature of the State, however unanimous, have no power to send to the Senate of the United States their wisest and best man unless he be thirty years old. And all the people of the nation, speaking with one united voice, cannot, constitutionally, make any man President who happens to be under thirty-five. This is, obviously, a restriction upon the appointing power—that is, in our popular government, a restriction upon the people themselves. As individuals, we may like it or dislike it, and flatter ourselves into the belief that *we* could make a wiser and better frame of government than our fathers made. Still it is our Constitution, binding upon us and upon every citizen from the moment of birth or naturalization.

The Constitution, I suppose, says what it means, and does not mean what it does not say. It says nothing about "the high characteristic privileges of a citizen of the State" (of Virginia or any other.) I do not know what they were, but certainly in Virginia, for the first half of the existence of the commonwealth, the right of suffrage was not one of them. For during that period no man ever voted there *because* he was a free white adult male citizen. He voted on his freehold, in land; and no candidate, in soliciting his election, appealed to the people or the citizens, but to the *freeholders* only, for they alone could vote.

I shall not trouble you with any argument touching the list of disabilities declared by the laws of Virginia against free negroes and mulattoes, as stated in the opinion, because they are such only as the Legislature, if so minded, might have denounced as well against a portion of its own acknowledged citizens, whose weakness might necessitate submission.

It is said in the opinion that "the allegiance which the free man of color owes to the State of Virginia is no evidence of citizenship, for he owes it not in consequence of an oath of allegiance." This proposition surprises me; perhaps I do not understand it. I did verily believe that the oath of allegiance was not the cause but the sequence of citizenship, given only as a solemn guarantee for the performance of duties already incurred. But if it be true that the oath of allegiance must either create or precede citizenship, then it follows, of necessity, that there can be no *natural-born citizen*, as the Constitution affirms, because the child must needs be born before it can take the oath.

The opinion, supported by the arguments upon which I have commented, is in these words:

"Upon the whole, I am of the opinion that free persons of color *in Virginia* are not citizens of the United States, within the intent and meaning of the acts regulating foreign and coasting trade, so as to be qualified to command vessels."

As an authority this opinion is rebutted by the opinion of Attorney General Legaré, above cited.—(4 Op. A. G., 147, date March 15, 1843.) Under an act of Congress which limited the pre-emption of public land to citizens of the United States and aliens who had declared intention to become citizens, according to the naturalization laws, Mr Legaré was of opinion that a free colored man was competent to pre-empt the land.

In that same opinion Mr. Legaré makes a just distinction between political and civil rights, which, I believe, is common to most nations. The French code expresses it very plainly, thus: "L'exercice des droits civils est ind pendant de la qualité de *citoyen*, laquelle ne s'acquiert et ne se conserve que conformément à la loi constitutionelle."

The next authority I shall consider is a decision of the Department of State made in Mr. Marcy's time, November 4, 1856, and evidenced by a letter of that date from Mr. Thomas, Assistant Secretary, to Mr. Rice, of New York.* That decision is entitled to great consideration, because upon such political questions the Secretary of State is of high authority. The case was an application for passports to travel in foreign parts, in favor of certain free blacks of some of the northern States, and the time was a few months after the passage of the act of August 18, 1856, (the first act directing the issuing of passports to individuals and restricting the issue to *citizens* of the United States, though the practice is much older.)

The letter, after stating the case, declares emphatically that "if this be so (*i. e.*, if they be negroes) there can be no doubt that they are not citizens of the United States." If this stood alone there could be no doubt of the opinion of the department at that time. But it does not stand alone. The letter, after citing several authorities, and among them one from Tennessee, to which I will have occasion to refer by name, concludes with this qualifying paragraph, which leaves some doubt as to what was the real practical opinion of Mr. Secretary Marcy at that time. The letter, assuming that a passport is a certificate of citizenship, proceeds to say:

"Such being the construction of the Constitution in regard to free persons of color, it is conceived that they cannot be regarded, *when beyond the jurisdiction of this government*, as entitled to the *full rights* of citizens, but the Secretary directs me to say that though the department could not certify that such persons are citizens of the United States, yet, if satisfied of the truth of the facts, it would

---

* This is the letter alluded to:

DEPARTMENT OF STATE,
WASHINGTON, *November* 4, 1856.

SIR: Your letters of the 29th ultimo and 3d instant, requesting passports for eleven colored persons, have been received, and I am directed by the Secretary to inform you that the papers transmitted by you do not warrant the department in complying with your request. The question whether free negroes are citizens is not now presented for the first time, but has repeatedly arisen in the administration of both the national and State governments. In 1821 a controversy arose as to whether free persons of color were citizens of the United States, within the intent and meaning of the acts of Congress regulating foreign and coasting trade, so as to be qualified to command vessels, and Wirt, Attorney General, decided that they were not, and he moreover held that the words "citizens of the United States" were used in the acts of Congress in the same sense as in the Constitution. This view is also fully sustained in a recent opinion of the present Attorney General.

The judicial decisions of the country are to the same effect.

In Kent's Commentaries, volume 2, page 277, it is stated that in 1833, Chief Justice Daggett of Connecticut, held that free blacks are not "citizens," within the meaning of the term, as used in the Constitution of the United States; and the Supreme Court of Tennessee, in the case of the State against Clairbone, held the same doctrine.

Such being the construction of the Constitution in regard to free persons of color, it is conceived that they cannot be regarded, when beyond the jurisdiction of this Government as entitled to the full rights of citizens; but the Secretary directs me to say that, though the department could not certify that such persons are citizens of the United States yet, if satisfied of the truth of the facts, it would give a certificate that they were born in the United States, are free, and that the Government thereof would regard it to be its duty to protect them if wronged by a foreign government while within its jurisdiction for a legal and proper purpose.

I am, sir, respectfully, your obedient servant,

J. A. THOMAS, *Assistant Secretary.*

H. H. RICE, Esq., *New York City.*

give a certificate that they were *born in the United States*, are free, and that *the government thereof would regard it to be its duty* to protect them, if wronged by a foreign government, while within its jurisdiction for a legal and proper purpose."

It seems to me that the certificate proposed to be given would be, in substance and fact, a good passport, for the act of Congress prescribes no form for the passport, and requires no particular fact to appear upon its face. And I confidently believe that there is not a government in Europe which, in view of our laws of citizenship, would question the validity of a passport which declares upon its face that the bearer is *a free natural-born inhabitant of the United States*.

I turn now to the consideration of the Tennessee case, referred to and relied upon in the letter from the State Department—the State of Tennessee *vs.* Ambrose, (1 Meigs' R., 331,) adjudged in 1838. Ambrose, being a free negro emancipated in Kentucky, moved to and settled in Tennessee. He was indicted for that crime against the Tennessee statute, made to prevent the ingress of that sort of people. He demurred to the indictment upon the ground that he was a citizen of Kentucky, and as such had a right under the Constitution of the United States (art. 4, sec. 2,) to go to and abide in Tennessee in spite of the State statute. The court in which the indictment was found sustained the demurrer. The public prosecutor took the case up to the supreme court, where the judgment below was reversed, and it was held by the court that Ambrose, under the circumstances, could not be a citizen of Kentucky, and therefore could not claim the protection of the national constitution as against the Tennessee statute.

I must trouble you with a few remarks upon certain passages in the opinion of the court, which constitute the foundation of the judgment, and without which the judgment itself, having no legal basis to rest upon, ought not to have any authority as a precedent.

The court, after stating the case and citing from the Constitution, (art. 4, sec. 2,) "the citizens *of* each State shall be entitled to all the privileges and immunities of citizens *in* the several States," proceeds: "the citizens here spoken of (says the supreme court of Tennessee) are those who are entitled to '*all* the privileges and immunities of citizens.' But free negroes, by whatever appellation we call them, were never *in any of the States* entitled to *all* the privileges and immunities of citizens, and consequently were not intended to be included when this word was used in the Constitution.

"In this country," (continues the court,) "under the free government created by the Constitution, whose language we are expounding, the humblest *white* citizen is entitled to *all* 'the privileges and immunities' which the *most exalted one enjoys*. Hence, in speaking of the rights which a citizen of one State shall enjoy in every other State, as applicable to *white men*, it is very properly said that he should be entitled to *all* the privileges and immunities of citizens in each other State. The meaning of the language is that no privilege enjoyed by, or immunity allowed to, the most favored class of citizens in said State shall be withheld from a citizen of any other State. How can it be said that he enjoys *all* the *privileges*, when he is scarcely allowed a *single right* in common with the mass of the citizens of the State?

"It cannot be; and therefore either the free negro is not a citizen, in the sense of the Constitution, or, if a citizen, ht is entitled to 'all the privileges and immunities' of the *mose favored class of citizens*. But this latter consequence will be contended by no one. It must then follow that they are not citizens."

These are the foundations of the judgment in the case of Ambrose, and not only in that but in almost every similar case which I have had occasion to examine. A good deal of what I have already said is strictly applicable here, and in trying to show the fallacy of the reasoning of the court in Tennessee, I must take the risk of some needless repetition.

The leading thought, that indeed which seems to have compelled the judgment against Ambrose, is, in my opinion, a naked assumption, not supported by any word of written law, nor maintainable by logical argument. It is assumed that a person to be a citizen at all *must* have *all* the rights, privileges, and immunities which the *favored one* enjoys; all of the most *favored class* of citizens. Now, if there be grades and classes of citizens, (which I am not exactly willing to admit,) it would seem that there must be something to distinguish the grades; some difference in the rights, privileges, and immunities of the different classes. And yet the court, while asserting the existence of different classes of citizens, asserts also their equality, by declaring that "*the humblest* white citizen is entitled to *all* the 'privileges and immunities' which the *most exalted* one enjoys." Then what marks the difference of classes? By what line can we separate humility from exaltation, as applied to a citizen?

In fact, it seems to me that the difficulties which surround the subject are artificial, created by the habitual confounding of things different in their nature and origin, and by the persistent abuse of language. No distinction is drawn between the rights and duties as a member of society, without regard to his citizenship. The first are political merely—the last civil and social only. And the words *rights, privileges, immunities* are abusively used, as if they were synonymous. The word *rights* is generic, common, embracing whatever may be lawfully claimed. *Privileges* are special rights belonging to the individual or class, and not to the mass. *Immunities* are rights of exemption only—freedom from what otherwise would be a duty, obligation, or burden. For instance, the constitution of Tennessee (art. 4, sec. 1) declares that "all free men of color shall be exempt from military duty, *in time of peace*, and also from paying a free poll-tax." This is immunity.

But whether there be or be not grades and classes of citizens, higher or lower, more or less favored, is wholly immaterial to this question. For the Constitution speaks of *citizens* only, without any reference to their rank, grade, or class, or to the number or magnitude of their rights, privileges, and immunities—*citizens* simply, without an adjective to qualify, enlarge, or diminish their rights and capacities. Therefore, if there be grades and classes of citizens, still the lowest individual of the lowest possible class is a citizen, and as such fills the requirement of the Constitution.

If we must have grades and classes of citizens, higher and lower, more and less favored, it seems to me impossible to sustain the proposition of the court that the humblest and most exalted are entitled to equal privileges and immunities A free, white, natural-born female infant is certainly a citizen, and I suppose it would be but reasonable to place her in the lowest class. And I assume that it would not be deemed unreasonable to call that class the highest, out of which the President must be chosen. If eligibility to the presidency be a *privilege* in the lawful candidate—a peculiar right belonging to him, and not to the mass of citizens, then there *is* some difference; *she* is not entitled to *all* his privileges.

Those who most indulge in the assumption that to constitute a citizen at all the person must have all the privileges and immunities which any citizen can enjoy, rarely venture to specify precisely what they mean. Generally, I think, the inference is plain that they mean suffrage and eligibility; and, in that connection, I think I have already shown that suffrage and eligibility have no necessary connection with citizenship, and that the one may, and often does, exist without the other.

Again, "immunities" are enjoyed to a very large extent by free negroes in all the slaveholding States. They are generally exempted by law from the onerous duties of jurors in the courts, and militia men in the field; and these are immunities eagerly desired by many white men in all the States.

In another part of that opinion, the court declares that the word "freemen," as used in the constitution of Tennessee, is equivalent to *citizen;* and yet the court denies that the phrase "freemen of color," used in the same constitution, is a proper designation of citizens! I close my remarks upon that case with an extract from the constitution of Tennessee, (which was originally made in 1795, and amended in 1835,) reminding you only that, until 1790, Tennessee was a part of North Carolina, and subject to its constitution and laws, and hence the peculiar phraseology of the extract:

"Article 4, section 1. Every free white man, of the age of twenty-one years, being a citizen of the *United States* and a citizen of the *county* wherein he may offer his vote six months next preceding the day of election, shall be entitled to vote for members of the general assembly and other civil officers for the county or district in which he resides: *Provided*, That no person shall be disqualified for voting, in any election, *on account of color*, who is now, by the laws of this State, a competent witness in a court of justice against a white man. All freemen of color shall be exempt from military duty in time of peace, and also from paying a free poll-tax."

Finally, the celebrated case of Scott *vs.* Sandford, 19 Howard's Reports, 393, is sometimes cited as a direct authority against the capacity of free persons of color to be citizens of the United States. That is an entire mistake. The case, as it stands of record, does not determine, nor purport to determine, that question. It was an ordinary suit for freedom, very common in our jurisprudence, and especially provided for in the legislation of most of the slaveholding States, as it is in Missouri, For convenience the form of the action usually is (and is in this case) *trespass*, alleging an assault and battery and false imprisonment, so as to enable the defendant, (the master,) if he choose, to make a direct issue upon the freedom or slavery of the plaintiff, which is the real point and object of the action, by pleading, in justification of the alleged trespass, that the plaintiff is a slave—his own or another man's.

Such an action Dred Scott, if entitled to freedom, might have brought in the State court, without any allegation of citizenship, and without being, in fact, a citizen. But it seems he desired to bring his action in the circuit court of the United States in Missouri; and, to enable him to do that he had to allege citizenship, because Mr. Sandford, the defendant, was a citizen of New York, and unless the plaintiff were a citizen of Missouri (or some other State) the national court had no jurisdiction of the case.

The plaintiff having made his election to sue in the United States court, the defendant might, if he would, have pleaded *in bar* to the merits of the action, but he exercised his election to plead *in abatement* to the jurisdiction of the court; thus, that the action, if any, "accrued to the said Dred Scott out of the jurisdiction of this court, and exclusively within the jurisdiction of the courts of the State of Missouri, for that, to wit, the said plaintiff, Dred Scott, is not a citizen of the State of Missouri, as alleged in his declaration, [not because he was not born there, and born free, but] *because he is a negro* of African descent; his ancestors were of pure African blood, and were brought into this country and sold as negro slaves, and this the said Sandford is ready to verify. Wherefore he prays judgment whether this court can or will take further cognizance of the action aforesaid." To this plea the plaintiff demurred, and the circuit court sustained the demurrer, thereby declaring that the facts stated in the plea, and confessed by the demurrer, did not disqualify Scott for being a citizen of Missouri, and so that the United States circuit court had jurisdiction of the cause.

The circuit court having taken jurisdiction, the defendant had, of course, to *plead over* to the merits of the action. He did so, and issues were joined, and there was an elaborate trial of the facts, which resulted in a verdict and judgment in favor of the defendant. And thereupon the plaintiff brought the case up to the Supreme Court by writ of error.

The power of the Supreme Court over the proceedings and judgments of the circuit court is appellate only, and this for the sole purpose of enabling the court above to affirm what has been rightly done, and reverse what has been wrongly done in the court below. If the error of the court below consist in the illegal assumption of power to hear and determine the merits of a case not within its jurisdiction, of course the court above will correct that error, by setting aside whatever may have been done by that usurped authority. And in doing this the court above has no more power than the court below had to hear and determine the merits of the case. And to assume the power to determine a case not within the jurisdiction is as great an error in the court above as in the court below; for it is equally true, in all courts, that the jurisdiction must first be ascertained before proceeding to judgment.

In this particular case the Supreme Court did first examine and consider the plea in abatement, and did adjudge that it was a good plea, sufficient to oust the jurisdiction of the circuit court. And hence it follows, as a necessary legal consequence, that whatever was done in the circuit court after the plea in abatement, and touching the merits of the case, was simply void, because done *coram non judice*.

Pleas in abatement were never favorites with the courts in England or America. Lord Coke tells us that they must be "certain to a certain intent, in every particular," and in practice they are always dealt with very strictly. When, therefore, the Supreme Court affirmed the plea in abatement in this case, I assume that it is affirmed, in manner and form, as written, and not otherwise. And this not merely because pleas in abatement are always considered *stricti legis*, but also, and chiefly, because the decision tends to abridge the valuable rights of persons natural-born in the country, which rights ought not to be impaired, except upon the clearest evidence of fact and law.

Taking the plea, then, strictly as it is written, the persons who are excluded by this judgment from being citizens of Missouri must be negroes, not mulatoes, nor mestizos, nor quadroons. They must be of *African* descent, not Asiatic, even though they come of the blackest Malays in south-eastern Asia. They must have had *ancestors*, (yet that may be doubtful, if born in slavery, of putative parents, who were slaves, and being slaves, incapable of contracting matrimony, and therefore every child must needs be a bastard, and so, by the common law, *nullius filius*, and incapable of ancestors.) His ancestors, if he had any, must have been of *pure* African blood, not mixed with the tawny Moor of Morocco or the dusky Arab of the desert, both of whom had their origin in Asia. They must have been *brought* to this country, not come voluntarily; and *sold*, not kept by the importer for his own use, nor given to his friends.

In this argument I raise no question upon the legal validity of the judgment in Scott *vs.* Sandford. I only insist that the judgment in that case is limited in law, as it is, in fact, limited on the face of the record, to the plea in abatement; and, consequently, that whatever was said in the long course of the case, as reported, (240 pages.) respecting the legal merits of the case, and respecting any supposed legal disability resulting from the mere fact of color, though entitled to all the respect which is due to the learned and upright sources from which the opinions come, was "*dehors the record*," and of no authority as a judicial decision.

To show that, notwithstanding all that was *said* upon other subjects, the *action* of the court was strictly confined to the plea in abatement, I copy the judgment:

"Upon the whole, therefore, it is the judgment of this court that it appears by the record before us that the plaintiff in error is not a citizen of Missouri, *in the sense in which that word is used in the Constitution*, and that the circuit court of the United States, for that reason, *had no jurisdiction in the case, and could give no judgment in it*. Its judgment for the defendant must, consequently, be reversed, and a mandate issued, directing the suit to be *dismissed for want of jurisdiction*."

And now, upon the whole matter, I give it as my opinion that the *free man of color*, mentioned in your letter, if born in the United States, is a citizen of the United States, and, if otherwise qualified, is competent, according to the acts of Congress, to be master of a vessel engaged in the coasting trade.

All of which is respectfully submitted by your obedient servant,

EDWARD BATES,
Attorney General.

Pay of Colored Soldiers.

Attorney General Bates has decided that persons of color who were free on the 19th of April, 1861, and who were enlisted and mustered into the military service of the United States between December, 1862, and 16th of June. 1864, are entitled by law to receive the same amounts of pay, bounty and clothing, as are, by the law existing at the times of their enlistment, allowed to other soldiers in the volunteer forces of the United States of like arms of the service.

THE OPINION IN FULL.

ATTORNEY GENERAL'S OFFICE,
July 14, 1864.

TO THE PRESIDENT:

SIR: By your communication of the 24th ultimo, you require my opinion in writing, as to what amounts of pay, bounty and clothing are allowed by law to persons of color who were free on the 19th day of April, 1861, and who have been enlisted and mustered into the military service of the United States between the month of December, 1862, and the 16th of June, 1864.

I suppose that whatever doubt or difficulty may exist with regard to the amount of pay and allowances to which the soldiers to whom you refer are entitled, has mainly its origin in the several provisions of the act of July 17th, 1862, chap. 201, (12 Stat. 599,) relative to the employment and enrollment of persons of *African descent* in the service of the United States. The 12th section of that statute provides, "That the President be and he is hereby authorized to receive into the service of the United States, for the purpose of constructing intrenchments or performing camp service, or any other labor, or any military or naval service for which they may be found competent, persons of African descent, and such persons shall be enrolled and organized under such regulations, not inconsistent with the Constitution and laws, as the President may prescribe." The 15th section of the same statute enacts, that "persons of *African descent* who under this law shall be employed shall receive ten dollars per month and one ration, three dollars of which monthly pay may be in clothnig."

The first and main question, therefore, is, whether the persons of color referred to in your letter, who were mustered into the military service of the United States during the period of time which you indicate, are "persons of African descent," employed UNDER the statute of July 17th, 1862, chap. 201. If they are not thus employed, their compensation should not be governed and is not regulated by the words of the 15th section of the statute, which I have just quoted.

Now I think that it is clear—too clear indeed to admit of doubt or discussion—that those persons of color who have voluntarily enlisted and have been mustered into our military service—who have been organized with appropriate officers into companies, regiments, and brigades of soldiers—and who have done and are doing in the field and in garrison the duty and service of soldiers of the United States—are not persons of African descent employed *under* the statute to which I have referred.

I do not find, indeed, in the act any authority to enlist

persons of *African descent* into the service, as *soldiers.* It will be observed that the said *twelfth* section enumerates two kinds of employment for which those persons are authorized to be enrolled, namely, *constructing intrenchments* and *performing camp service.* The section then contains a more general authority—authority to receive such persons into the service for the purpose of performing "any *other labor* or any military or naval service for which they may be found competent." I am bound, however, by every rule of law, respecting the construction of statutes, to construe these words of more general authority with reference to the character, nature and quality of the particular kinds of labor and service which are, in the first instance, specifically enumerated in the statute, as those for the performance of which persons of *African descent* are authorized to be received into the service, and, therefore, I must suppose that Congress, when it conferred authority upon the President to receive into the service of the United States persons of *African descent* for the purpose of performing any *other labor* or any military service for which they may be found competent, meant and intended that that *other labor* and military service should be of the same general character, nature and quality as that which it had previously in the statute, specially named and designated. "Always in statutes," says Coke, "relation shall be made according to the matter precedent." Dwarris says: "sometimes words and sections are governed and explained by conjoined words and clauses: *noscitur a socis.*" (Dwarris on stat. 604.)

Applying these rules of construction then to the act before me, I am constrained to hold, that if the authority to enlist and muster into the military service soldiers of African descent depended upon this statute, (as it does not,) it would furnish no foundation for such authority. It is manifest that the labor and service that United States soldiers are enlisted to perform, are of an essentially different character from, and are essentially of a higher nature, order and quality than those kinds of labor and service specifically named in the statute, and for the performance of which the President is specially authorized to employ "persons of African descent." In my late opinion in the case of the claim of Rev. Samuel Harrison for full pay as Chaplain of the 54th Regiment of Massachusetts Volunteers, I expressed the same view when I said that the act of July 17, 1862, chap. 201, "was not intended either to authorize the employment or to fix the pay of any persons of African descent, except those who might be needed to perform the humbler offices of labor and service for which they might be found competent."

This view finds confirmation in a statute that received the approval of the President on the same day as the act before me—the statute of July 17, 1862, chap. 195 (12 Stat., 592)—which conferred upon the President the authority to employ as many persons of African descent as he might deem necessary and proper for the suppression of the rebellion, and gave him power to organize and use them in such manner as he might judge best for the public welfare. In these words we may find clear and ample authority for the enlistment of persons of African descent as United States soldiers. It is *under* this act, if under either of the acts of July 17, 1862, that colored volunteer soldiers may be said to have been employed. There is no need to resort, therefore, to the statute of July 17, 1862, chap. 201, for any authority with respect to their employment, or for any rule in regard to their compensation. Persons of *African descent* employed as soldiers are not embraced at all, as I have shown, by the act of July 17, 1862, chap. 201, as objects or subjects of legislation; and we must therefore look to some other law for the measure of their compensation.

I find the law for the compensation of the *persons of color* referred to in your letter to me in the acts of Congress in force at the dates of the enlistments of those persons, respecting the amount of pay and bounty to be given and the amount and kind of clothing to be allowed to soldiers in the volunteer service of the United States. For, after a careful and critical examination, I believe, of every statute enacted since the foundation of the present Government relative to the enlistment of soldiers in the regular and volunteer forces of the United States, I have found no law which at any time prohibited the enlistment of free colored men into either branch of the national military service. The words of Congress descriptive of the recruits competent to enter the service were, in the act of April 30, 1790, "able-bodied men not under five feet six inches in height without shoes, not under the age of eighteen nor above the age of forty-five;" in the act of March 3, 1795, "able-bodied, of at least five feet six inches in height, and not under the age of eighteen nor above the age of forty-six years;" in the act of March 3, 1799, "able-bodied and of a size and age suitable for the public service according to the directions which the President of the United States shall and may establish;" in the act of March 16, 1802, "effective able-bodied citizens of the United States, of at least five feet six inches high and between the ages of eighteen and forty-five years;" in the acts of December 24, 1811, January 11, 1812, January 20, 1813, and January 27, 1814, "effective able-bodied men;" in the act of December 10, 1814, "free, effective able-bodied men between the ages of eighteen and fifty years;" and in the act of January 12, 1847, "able-bodied men." Some of the foregoing statutes are obsolete; others of them are still in force, and furnished, before the suspension of the writ of *habeas corpus*, the rule by which the validity of the enlistments of persons alleged to have been minors was every day tried in the State and Federal courts. They organized the military establishments of the United States in time of peace and in time of war. They embrace the periods of all the wars, previously to the present, in which the United States has been engaged. By no one of them was or is the enlistment of free colored men into the military service of the United States, whether as volunteers or as regulars, prohibited. After the war of 1812 claims for bounty land preferred by persons of color who had enlisted and served in the army under the statutes of 24th December, 1811, January 11, 1812, and December 10, 1814, were sustained as valid by the then Attorney General, William Wirt. (1 Opin., 603.) And when I turn to more recent statutes—those which authorized the raising and regulate the organization of the whole body of the volunteer forces now in the field, and provided for the maintenance and increase of the regular forces in the service—I discover throughout them no other statutory qualifications for recruits than those established by the earliest legislation to which I have referred.

It is not needed that I should specially recite the words of those acts of Congress that provide for the pay, bounty, and clothing to be allowed to soldiers in the volunteer military service of the United States. It is enough to say that under the statutes relative to those subjects, and in force during the period of time mentioned in your communication, all volunteers competent and qualified to be members of the national forces, are entitled respectively to receive like amounts of pay, bounty, and clothing from the Government.

In view, therefore, of the foregoing considerations, I give it to you unhesitatingly, as my opinion, that the same pay, bounty, and clothing are allowed by law to the persons of color referred to in your communication, and who were enlisted and mustered into the military service of the United States between the months of December, 1862, and the 16th of June, 1864, as are by the laws existing at the times of the enlistments of said persons, authorized and provided for, and allowed to, *other* soldiers in the volunteer forces of the United States of like arms of the service.

I have the honor to be, very respectfully, your obedient servant, EDWARD BATES.

Gen. McClellan's Letters.

ON POLITICAL ADMINISTRATION, JULY 7, 1862.

HEADQUARTERS ARMY OF THE POTOMAC,
CAMP NEAR HARRISON'S LANDING, VA., *July* 7, 1862.

MR. PRESIDENT: You have been fully informed that the rebel army is in the front, with the purpose of overwhelming us by attacking our positions or reducing us by blocking our river communications. I cannot but regard our condition as critical, and I earnestly desire, in view of possible contingencies, to lay before your excellency, for your private consideration, my general views concerning the existing state of the rebellion, although they do not strictly relate to the situation of this army, or strictly come within the scope of my official duties. These views amount to convictions, and are deeply impressed upon my mind and heart. Our cause must never be abandoned; it is the cause of free institutions and self-government. The Constitution and the Union must be preserved, whatever may be the cost in time, treasure, and blood. If secession is successful, other dissolutions are clearly to be seen in the future. Let neither military disaster, political faction, nor foreign war shake your settled purpose to enforce the equal operation of the laws of the United States upon the people of every State.

The time has come when the government must determine upon a civil and military policy, covering the whole ground of our national trouble.

The responsibility of determining, declaring, and supporting such civil and military policy, and of directing the whole course of national affairs in regard to the rebellion, must now be assumed and exercised by you, or our cause will be lost. The Constitution gives you power, even for the present terrible exigency.

This rebellion has assumed the character of a war; as such it should be regarded, and it should be conducted upon the highest principles known to Christian civilization. It should not be a war looking to the subjugation of the people of any State, in any event. It should not be at all a war upon population, but against armed forces and political organizations. Neither confiscation of property, political executions of persons, territorial organization of States, or forcible abolition of slavery, should be contemplated for a moment.

In prosecuting the war, all private property and unarmed persons should be strictly protected, subject only to the necessity of military operations; all private property taken for military use should be paid or receipted for; pillage and waste should be treated as high crimes; all unnecessary trespass sternly prohibited, and offensive demeanor by the military towards citizens promptly rebuked. Military arrests should not be tolerated, except in places where active hostilities exist; and oaths, not required by enactments, constitutionally made, should be neither demanded nor received.

Military government should be confined to the preservation of public order and the protection of political right. Military power should not be allowed to interfere with the relations of servitude, either by supporting or impairing the authority of the master, except for repressing disorder, as in other cases. Slaves, contraband under the act of Congress, seeking military protection, should receive it. The right of the government to appropriate permanently to its own service claims to slave labor should be asserted, and the right of the owner to compensation therefor should be recognized. This principle might be extended, upon grounds of military necessity and security, to all the slaves of a particular State, thus working manumission in such State; and in Missouri, perhaps in Western Virginia also, and possibly even in Maryland, the expediency of such a measure is only a question of time. A system of policy thus constitutional, and pervaded by the influences of Christianity and freedom, would receive the support of almost all truly loyal men, would deeply impress the rebel masses and all foreign nations, and it might be humbly hoped that it would commend itself to the favor of the Almighty.

Unless the principles governing the future conduct of our struggle shall be made known and approved, the effort to obtain requisite forces will be almost hopeless. A declaration of radical views, especially upon slavery, will rapidly disintegrate our present armies. The policy of the government must be supported by concentrations of military power. The national forces should not be dispersed in expeditions, posts of occupation, and numerous armies, but should be mainly collected into masses, and brought to bear upon the armies of the Confederate States. Those armies thoroughly defeated, the political structure which they support would soon cease to exist.

In carrying out any system of policy which you may form, you will require a commander-in-chief of the army, one who possesses your confidence, understands your views, and who is competent to execute your orders, by directing the military forces of the nation to the accomplishment of the objects by you proposed. I do not ask that place for myself. I am willing to serve you in such position as you may assign me, and I will do so as faithfully as ever subordinate served superior.

I may be on the brink of eternity; and as I hope forgiveness from my Maker, I have written this letter with sincerity towards you and from love for my country.

Very respectfully, your obedient servant,

GEORGE B. McCLELLAN,
Major General Commanding.

His Excellency A. LINCOLN, *President.*

—

IN FAVOR OF THE ELECTION OF GEORGE W. WOODWARD AS GOVERNOR OF PENNSYLVANIA.

ORANGE, NEW JERSEY, *October* 12, 1863.

DEAR SIR: My attention has been called to an article in the Philadelphia *Press*, asserting that I had written to the managers of a Democratic meeting at Allentown, disapproving the objects of the meeting, and that if I voted or spoke it would be in favor of Governor Curtin, and I am informed that similar assertions have been made throughout the State.

It has been my earnest endeavor heretofore to avoid participation in party politics. I had determined to adhere to this course, but it is obvious that I cannot longer maintain silence under such misrepresentations. I therefore request you to deny that I have written any such letter, or entertained any such views as those attributed to me in the Philadelphia *Press*, and I desire to state clearly and distinctly, that having some days ago had a full conversation with Judge Woodward, I find that our views agree, and I regard his election as Governor of Pennsylvania called for by the interests of the nation.

I understand Judge Woodward to be in favor of the prosecution of the war with all the means at the command of the loyal States, until the military power of the rebellion is destroyed. I understand him to be of the opinion that while the war is urged with all possible decision and energy, the policy directing it should be in consonance with the principles of humanity and civilization, working no injury to private rights and property not demanded by military necessity and recognized by military law among civilized nations.

And, finally, I understand him to agree with me in the opinion that the sole great objects of this war are the restoration of the unity of the nation, the preservation of the Constitution, and the supremacy of the laws of the country. Believing our opinions entirely agree upon these points, I would, were it in my power, give to Judge Woodward my voice and vote.

I am, very respectfully, yours,

GEORGE B. McCLELLAN.

Hon. CHARLES J. BIDDLE.

—

Proposed Censures of Officials.

OF PRESIDENT LINCOLN.

First Session, Thirty-Seventh Congress.

IN HOUSE.

July 15—Mr. VALLANDIGHAM offered the following:

Resolved, That the Constitution of the United States confers upon Congress alone the power to "raise and support armies," and to "provide and maintain a navy;" and therefore the President, in the proclamation of May 3, 1861, and the orders and action, by his authority, of the War and Navy Departments, increasing the Army and Navy, and calling for and accepting the services of volunteers for three years without warrant of law, usurped powers belonging solely to Congress, and so violated the Constitution.

2. That the right to declare a blockade as against an independent power, is a belligerent right, depending upon the existence of a state of war; and that as Congress, and Congress alone, have the power to declare or recognize the existence of war, the President has no right to order a blockade until after Congress shall have declared or recognized war with the power whose ports are to be blockaded; and further, that Congress alone can abolish or shut up the ports of entry of any State within the Union; and that, therefore, the President, in blockading and shutting up the ports of entry in certain of the States of the Union, without the authority of Congress, violated the Constitution.

3. That Congress alone have the constitutional power to suspend the writ of *habeas corpus;* and that until the writ has been suspended by act of Congress, it is the duty of the President, and all other officers, civil and military, to obey it; and that, therefore, the President, in suspending said writ himself, or attempting to authorize certain military officers to suspend it, or to disobey it, or in sustaining them in disobedience to it, violated the Constitution.

4. That by the Constitution "no money shall be drawn from the Treasury but in consequence of appropriations made by law;" and that in ordering the drawing from the Treasury of money unappropriated or appropriated for one purpose, and applying the same to purposes for which no appropriations had been made by law, the President violated the Constitution.

5. That the search of certain telegraph offices in the month of May last, by several officers and agents of the Executive, without search warrant upon probable cause, supported by oath or affirmation, and particularly describing the place to be searched, and the things to be seized; and the seizure of papers and despatches in said offices was a violation of the constitutional "right of the people to be secure in their persons, houses, papers, and effects against unreasonable searches and seizures;" and that the President, in ordering such search and seizures, violated the Constitution.

6. That neither Congress, nor the President, nor the judiciary, have any constitutional power to abridge the freedom of speech or of the press; and that the suspension of newspaper presses by military authority and force, and the arrest of citizens by military or civil authority, for the expression by speech, or through the press, of opinions upon political subjects, or subjects of any kind, is a violation of the Constitution.

7. That the arrest without civil process of persons not subject to the rules and articles of war, nor in cases arising in the land or naval forces or in the militia, when in actual service, by soldiers in the service of the United States, is a breach of the Constitution, and a violation of the constitutional liberty of the person.

On motion of Mr. LOVEJOY, these resolutions were at once laid upon the table—the House refusing to order the yeas and nays.

OF EX-PRESIDENT BUCHANAN.

Third Session, Thirty-Seventh Congress.

IN SENATE.

1862, Dec. 15—Mr. DAVIS, of Kentucky, offered this resolution:

Resolved, That after it had become manifest that an insurrection against the United States was about to break out in several of the southern States, James Buchanan, then President, from sympathy with the conspirators and their treasonable project, failed to take necessary and proper measures to prevent it; wherefore he should receive the censure and condemnation of the Senate and the American people.

Dec 16—Mr. SAULSBURY offered this amendment:

Resolved further, That a copy of the foregoing resolution be served upon the said James Buchanan, and that he be notified that he has liberty to defend himself before the Senate against the charges in said resolution contained, if he shall choose so to do.

Same day—The resolution and proposed amendment were laid upon the table—yeas 38, nays 3, as follows:

YEAS—Messrs. Anthony, Arnold, Browning, *Carlile*, Clark, Collamer, Cowan, Dixon, Doolittle, Fessenden, Field, Foot, Foster, Grimes, Hale, *Harding*, Harlan, Harris, Henderson, *Kennedy*, King, Lane of Indiana, Lane of Kansas, *Latham*, Morrill, *Nesmith*, Pomeroy, *Powell*, *Rice*, *Saulsbury*, Sherman, Ten Eyck, Trumbull, Wade, Willey, Wilson of Massachusetts, *Wilson* of Missouri, *Wright*—38.

NAYS—Messrs. *Davis*, Howe, Wilkinson—3.

—

OF MESSRS. LONG AND HARRIS.

First Session, Thirty-Eighth Congress.

IN HOUSE.

1864, April 9—Mr. COLFAX, the Speaker, (Mr. ROLLINS, of New Hampshire, in the Chair,) offered this preamble and resolution:

Whereas on the 8th of April, 1864, when the House of Representatives was in Committee of the Whole on the state of the Union, ALEXANDER LONG, a Representative from the second district of Ohio, declared himself in favor of recognizing the independence and nationality of the so-called confederacy now in arms against the Union; and whereas, the said so-called confederacy, thus sought to be recognized and established on the ruins of a dissolved or destroyed Union, has as its chief officers, civil and military, those who have added perjury to their treason, and who seek to obtain success for their parricidal efforts by the killing of the loyal soldiers of the nation who are seeking to save it from destruction; and whereas the oath required of all members, and taken by the said ALEXANDER LONG on the first day of the present Congress, declares "that I have voluntarily given no aid, countenance, counsel, or encouragement to persons engaged in armed hostility to the United States," thereby declaring that such conduct is regarded as inconsistent with membership in the Congress of the United States: Therefore,

Resolved, That ALEXANDER LONG, a Representative from the second district of Ohio, having, on the 8th of April, 1864, declared himself in favor of recognizing the independence and nationality of the so-called confederacy now in arms against the Union, and thereby "given aid, countenance, and encouragement to persons engaged in armed hostility to the United States," is hereby expelled.

Pending which, April 9, Mr. WASHBURNE, of Illinois, offered this resolution:

Whereas Hon. BENJAMIN G. HARRIS, a member of the House of Representatives of the United States from the State of Maryland has on this day used the following language, to wit: "The South asked you to let them go in peace. But, no; you said you would bring them into subjection. That is not done yet, and God Almighty grant that it never may be. I hope that you will never subjugate the South." And whereas such language is treasonable, and is a gross disrespect of this House: Therefore,

Be it resolved, That the said BENJAMIN G. HARRIS be expelled from this House.

Which was rejected—yeas 84, nays 58, (two thirds being required:)

YEAS—Messrs. Alley, Allison, Ames, Anderson, Arnold, Ashley, *Baily*, John D. Baldwin, Baxter, Beaman, Blaine, Francis P. Blair, Boutwell, Boyd, Broomall, William G. Brown, Ambrose W. Clark, Freeman Clarke, Cobb, Cole, Creswell, Henry Winter Davis, Thomas T. Davis, Dixon, Donnelly, Driggs, Dumont, Eckley, Eliot, Frank, Garfield, Gooch, Grinnell, Hale, Higby, Hooper, Hotchkiss, Asahel W. Hubbard, John H. Hubbard, Jenckes, Julian, Kasson, Kelley, Francis W. Kellogg, Orlando Kellogg, Loan, Marvin, McBride, McClurg, McIndoe, Samuel F. Miller, Morrill, Daniel Morris, Amos Myers, Leonard Myers, Norton, Orth, Patterson, Pike, Pomeroy, Price, William H. Randall, Edward H. Rollins, Schenck, Scofield, Shannon, Smith, Smithers, Spalding, Starr, Thayer, Thomas, Tracy, Upson, Van Valkenburgh, Ellihu B. Washburne, William B. Washburn, Webster, Whaley, Williams, Wilder, Wilson, Windom, Woodbridge—84.

NAYS—Messrs. *James C. Allen*, *Ancona*, *Augustus C. Baldwin*, *Bliss*, *James S. Brown*, *Chanler*, *Clay*, *Cox*, *Cravens*, *Dawson*, *Denison*, *Eden*, *Eldridge*, *English*, *Finck*, *Ganson*, *Grider*, *Harding*, *Harrington*, *Herrick*, *Holman*, *Hutchins*, *Philip Johnson*, *William Johnson*, *Kernan*, *Law*, *Lazear*, *Le Blond*, *Long*, *Mallory*, *Marcy*, *McAllister*, *McDowell*, *McKinney*, *Middleton*, *William H. Miller*, *James R. Morris*, *Morrison*, *Nelson*, *Odell*, *Pendleton*, *Pruyn*, *Samuel J. Randall*, *Robinson*, *Rogers*, *James S. Rollins*, *Ross*, *Scott*, *John B. Steele*, *William G. Steele*, *Strouse*, *Sweat*, *Voorhees*, *Ward*, *Chilton A. White*, *Joseph W. White*, *Winfield*, *Fernando Wood*—58.

Mr. SCHENCK then offered this resolution:

Resolved, That BENJAMIN G. HARRIS, a Representative from the fifth district of the State of Maryland, having spoken words this day in debate, manifestly tending and designed to encourage the existing rebellion and the enemies of this Union, is declared to be an unworthy member of this House, and is hereby severely censured.

A motion to table the resolution was lost—yeas 23, nays 80; two motions to adjourn were made and voted down; and the resolution was then adopted—yeas 98, nays 20, as follows:

YEAS—Messrs. Alley, Allison, Ames, Anderson, Arnold, Ashley, *Baily*, *Augustus C. Baldwin*, John D. Baldwin, Baxter, Beaman, Blaine, F. P. Blair, Boutwell, Boyd, Broomall, *James S. Brown*, Ambrose W. Clark, Freeman Clarke, Cobb, Cole, Creswell, *Cox*, Henry Winter Davis, Thomas T. Davis, Dixon, Donnelly, Driggs, Dumont, Eckley, Eliot, *English*, Frank, *Ganson*, Garfield, Gooch, Grinnell, Hale, *Harrington*, Higby, *Holman*, Hotchkiss, Asahel W. Hubbard, John H. Hubbard, Jenckes, Julian, Kasson, Kelley, Francis W. Kellogg, Orlando Kellogg, *Kernan*, Loan, Marvin, *McAllister*, McBride, McClurg, McIndoe, *Middleton*, Samuel F. Miller, Morrill, Daniel Morris, Amos Myers, Leonard Myers, *Nelson*, Norton, *Odell*, Orth, Patterson, Pike, Pomeroy, Price, William H. Randall, Edward H. Rollins, Schenck, Scofield, Shannon, Sloan, Smith, Smithers, Spalding, Starr, *John B. Steele*, *William G. Steele*, Thayer, Thomas, Tracy, Upson, Van Valkenburgh, Ellihu B. Washburne, William B. Washburn, Webster, Whaley, Williams, Wilder, Wilson, Windom, *Winfield*, *Yeaman*—98.

NAYS—Messrs. *James C. Allen*, *Ancona*, *Bliss*, *Chanler*, *Denison*, *Eden*, *Eldridge*, *Law*, *Le Blond*, *Long*, *Wm. H. Miller*, *Morrison*, *Pendleton*, *Pruyn*, *Samuel J. Randall*, *Ross*, *Strouse*, *Voorhees*, *Chilton A. White*, *Fernando Wood*—20.

The question recurring upon the resolution offered by Mr. COLFAX—

April 14—Mr. BROOMALL offered this amendment, as a substitute, which Mr. COLFAX accepted:

Whereas ALEXANDER LONG, a Representative from the second district of Ohio, by his open declarations in the national Capitol and publications in the city of New York, has shown himself to be in favor of a recognition of the so-called confederacy now trying to establish itself upon the ruins of our country, thereby giving aid and comfort to the enemy in that destructive purpose—aid to avowed traitors in creating an illegal government within our borders—comfort to them by assurances of their success, and affirmations of the justice of their cause; and whereas such conduct is at the same time evidence of disloyalty and inconsistent with his oath of office and his duty as a member of this body: Therefore,

Resolved, That the said ALEXANDER LONG, a Representative from the second district of Ohio, be, and he is hereby, declared to be an unworthy member of the House of Representatives.

Resolved, That the Speaker shall read these resolutions to the said ALEXANDER LONG during the session of the House.

Mr. Cox moved to lay the preamble and resolution on the table; which was disagreed to—yeas 70, nays 80. A division of the question was called, when

The first resolution was agreed to—yeas 80, nays 70, as follows:

YEAS—Messrs. Alley, Allison, Ames, Anderson, Arnold, Ashley, *Baily*, John D. Baldwin, Baxter, Beaman, Blaine, Boutwell, Boyd, Broomall, Ambrose W. Clark, Cobb, Cole, Creswell, Dawes, Deming, Driggs, Dumont, Eckley, Farnsworth, Frank, Garfield, Gooch, Grinnell, Higby, Hooper, Hotchkiss, John H. Hubbard, Jenckes, Julian, Kasson, Kelley, Francis W. Kellogg, Orlando Kellogg, Loan, Longyear, Marvin, McBride, McClurg, McIndoe, Samuel F. Miller, Morrill, Daniel Morris, Amos Myers, Leonard Myers, Norton, Charles O'Neill, Orth, Patterson, Perham, Pike, Pomeroy, Price, William H. Randall, Alexander H. Rice, John H. Rice, Edward H. Rollins, Schenck, Shannon, Sloan, Smith, Smithers, Starr, Stevens, Thayer, Thomas, Upson, Van Valkenburg, Ellihu B. Washburne, William B. Washburn, Webster, Whaley, Wilder, Wilson, Windom, Woodbridge—80.

NAYS—Messrs. *James C. Allen*, *William J. Allen*, *Ancona*, *Augustus C. Baldwin*, Francis P. Blair, *Bliss*, *James S. Brown*, William G. Brown, *Chanler*, *Clay*, *Coffroth*, *Cox*, *Cravens*, *Dawson*, *Denison*, *Eden*, *Eldridge*, *Finck*, *Ganson*, *Grider*, *Hall*, *Harding*, *Harrington*, *B. G. Harris*, *Herrick*, *Holman*, *Hutchins*, *P. Johnson*, *Wm. Johnson*, *Kalbfleisch*, *Kernan*, *King*, *Knapp*, *Law*, *Lazear*, *Mallory*, *Marcy*, *McDowell*, *McKinney*, *William H. Miller*, *James R. Morris*, *Morrison*, *Nelson*, *Noble*, *Odell*, *John O'Neill*, *Pendleton*, *Perry*, *Pruyn*, *Radford*, *Samuel J. Randall*, *Robinson*, *Rodgers*, *James S. Rollins*, *Ross*, *Scott*, *Stebbins*, *John B. Steele*, *William G. Steele*, *Strouse*, *Stuart*, *Sweat*, *Voorhees*, *Ward*, *Wheeler*, *Chilton A. White*, *Joseph W. White*, *Winfield*, *Fernando Wood*, *Yeaman*—70.

The second resolution was laid on the table—yeas 71, nays 70, as follows:

YEAS—Messrs. *James C. Allen*, *William J. Allen*, *Ancona*, *Baily*, *Augustus C. Baldwin*, *Bliss*, *James S. Brown*, Wm. G. Brown, *Chanler*, *Clay*, *Coffroth*, *Cox*, *Dawson*, *Denison*, *Eden*, *Eldridge*, *Finck*, *Ganson*, *Grider*, *Hall*, *Harding*, *Harrington*, *Benjamin G. Harris*, *Herrick*, *Holman*, *Hutchins*, *William Johnson*, *Kalbfleisch*, *Kernan*, *King*, *Knapp*, *Law*, *Lazear*, *Mallory*, *Marcy*, *McDowell*, *McKinney*, *William H. Miller*, *James R. Morris*, *Morrison*, *Nelson*, *Noble*, *Odell*, *John O'Neill*, *Pendleton*, *Perry*, *Pruyn*, *Radford*, *Samuel J. Randall*, William H. Randall, *Robinson*, *Rogers*, *James S. Rollins*, *Ross*, *Scott*, Smith, *Stebbins*, *John B. Steele*, *William G. Steele*, *Strouse*, *Stuart*, *Sweat*, *Voorhees*, *Ward*, Webster, *Wheeler*, *Chilton A. White*, *Joseph W. White*, *Winfield*, *Fernando Wood*, *Yeaman*—71.

NAYS—Messrs. Alley, Allison, Ames, Anderson, Arnold, Ashley, John D. Baldwin, Baxter, Beaman, Blaine, Boutwell, Boyd, A. W. Clark, Cobb, Cole, Creswell, Dawes, Deming, Driggs, Dumont, Eckley, Farnsworth, Frank, Garfield, Gooch, Grinnell, Higby, Hooper, Hotchkiss, J. H. Hubbard, Jenckes, Julian, Kasson, Kelly, Francis W. Kellogg, Orlando Kellogg, Loan, Longyear, Marvin, McBride, McClurg, McIndoe, Morrill, Daniel Morris, Amos Myers, Norton, Charles O'Neill, Orth, Patterson, Perham, Pike, Pomeroy, Price, Alexander H. Rice, John H. Rice, Schenck, Shannon, Sloan, Smithers, Starr, Stevens, Thayer, Upson, Van Valkenburg, Ellihu B. Washburne, William B. Washburn, Wilder, Wilson, Windom, Woodbridge—70.

The preamble was then agreed to—yeas 78, nays 63, as follows:

YEAS—Messrs. Alley, Allison, Ames, Anderson, Arnold, Ashley, *Baily*, John D. Baldwin, Baxter, Beaman, Blaine, Boutwell, Boyd, Broomall, Ambrose W. Clark, Cobb, Cole, Creswell, Dawes, Driggs, Dumont, Eckley, Frank, Garfield, Gooch, Grinnell, Higby, Hooper, Hotchkiss, John H. Hubbard, Jenckes, Julian, Kasson, Kelley, Francis W. Kellogg, Orlando Kellogg, Loan, Longyear, Marvin, McBride, McClurg, McIndoe, Samuel F. Miller, Morrill, Daniel Morris, Amos Myers, Leonard Myers, Norton, Charles O'Neill, Orth, Patterson, Perham, Pike, Pomeroy, Price, William H. Randall, Alexander H. Rice, John H. Rice, Edward H. Rollins, Schenck, Shannon, Sloan, Smith, Smithers, Starr, Stevens, Thayer, Thomas, Upson, Van Valkenburgh, Ellihu B. Washburne, William B. Washburn, Webster, Whaley, Wilder, Wilson, Windom, Woodbridge—78.

NAYS—Messrs. *James C. Allen*, *William J. Allen*, *Ancona*, *Augustus C. Baldwin*, *Bliss*, *James S. Brown*, William G. Brown, *Chanler*, *Clay*, *Coffroth*, *Cox*, *Dawson*, *Denison*, *Eden*, *Eldridge*, *Finck*, *Ganson*, *Grider*, *Hall*, *Harding*, *Benjamin G. Harris*, *Herrick*, *Holman*, *Hutchins*, *William Johnson*, *Kalbfleisch*, *Kernan*, *Knapp*, *Law*, *Lazear*, *Marcy*, *McDowell*, *McKinney*, *William H. Miller*, *James R. Morris*, *Morrison*, *Nelson*, *Noble*, *Odell*, *John O'Neill*, *Pendleton*, *Perry*, *Pruyn*, *Radford*, *Samuel J. Randall*, *Robinson*, *Rodgers*, *James S. Rollins*, *Ross*, *Scott*, *Stebbins*, *John B. Steele*, *William G. Steele*, *Strous*, *Stuart*, *Voorhees*, *Ward*, *Wheeler*, *Chilton A. White*, *Joseph W. White*, *Winfield*, *Fernando Wood*, *Yeaman*—63.

THE CONSPIRACY OF DISUNION.

In the slaveholding States, a considerable body of men have always been disaffected to the Union. They resisted the adoption of the National Constitution, then sought to refine away the rights and powers of the General Government, and by artful expedients, in a series of years, using the excitements growing out of passing questions, finally perverted the sentiments of large masses of men, and prepared them for revolution.

I had prepared an extensive collection of statements and facts bearing upon this point, but am obliged to omit them for want of space. The well-read in our politics can readily recur to a multitude of proofs. I append a few conspicuous points, the first of which is less well known, being from an unpublished journal by Hon. William Maclay, United States Senator from Pennsylvania, from March 4, 1789, to March 3, 1791, being the First Congress under the Constitution. This journal is the property of his relative, George W. Harris, Esq., of Harrisburg, Pa.

An early Threat of Dissolution.

FROM SENATOR MACLAY'S JOURNAL.

1789, June 9—In relation to the tariff bill, the affair of confining the East India Trade to the citizens of America had been *negatived*, and a committee had been appointed to report on this business. The report came in with very high duties, amounting to a prohibition. But a new phenomenon had made its appearance in the House (meaning the Senate) since Friday.

Pierce Butler, from South Carolina, had taken his seat, and flamed like a meteor. He arraigned the whole Impost law, and then charged (indirectly) the whole Congress with a design of oppressing South Carolina. He cried out for encouraging the Danes and Swedes, and foreigners of every kind, to come and take away our produce. In fact, he was for a navigation act reversed.

June 11—Attended at the hall as usual.

Mr. *Izard** and Mr. *Butler* opposed the whole of the drawbacks in every shape whatever.

Mr. *Grayson*,† of Virginia, warm on this subject, said we were not ripe for such a thing. We were a *new nation*, and had no business for any such regulations—a nation *sui generis*.

Mr. *Lee*‡ said drawbacks were right, but would be so much abused, he could not think of admitting them.

Mr. *Ellsworth*‖ said *New England* rum would be exported, instead of *West India*, to obtain the drawback.

I thought it best to say a few words in reply to each. We were a new *nation*, it was true, but we were not a new *people*. We were composed of individuals of like manners, habits, and customs with the European nations. What, therefore, had been found useful among them, came well recommended by experience to us. *Drawbacks* stand as an example in this point of view to us. If the thing was right in itself, there could be no just argument drawn against the use of a thing from the abuse of it. It would be the duty of Government to guard against abuses, by prudent appointments and watchful attention to officers. That as to changing the kind of rum, I thought the collection bill would provide for this, by limiting the exportation to the *original* casks and packages. I said a great deal more, but really did not feel much interest either way. But the debates were very lengthy.

Butler flamed away, and THREATENED A DISSOLUTION OF THE UNION, with regard to his State, *as sure as God was in the firmament*. He scattered his remarks over the whole impost bill, calling it partial, oppressive, &c., and solely calculated to oppress South Carolina, and yet ever and anon declaring how clear of local views and how candid and dispassionate he was. He degenerates into mere declamation. His State would live free, or die glorious.

* Ralph. † William. ‡ Richard Henry, from Virginia. ‖ Oliver, of Connecticut.

Opinions of Jackson, Benton, Clay, and others.

Referring to the *modus operandi* of southern disunionists, General JACKSON'S recently-discovered letter to Rev. A. J. Crawford is curious for the keenness of its perceptions, and the accuracy of its prediction:

["Private."]

WASHINGTON, *May* 1, 1833.

"MY DEAR SIR: * * * I have had a laborious task here, but nullification is dead; and its actors and courtiers will only be remembered by the people to be execrated for their wicked designs to sever and destroy the only good Government on the globe, and that prosperity and happiness we enjoy over every other portion of the world. Haman's gallows ought to be the fate of all such ambitious men who would involve their country in civil war, and all the evils in its train, that they might reign and ride on its whirlwinds and direct the storm. The free people of these United States have spoken, and consigned these wicked demagogues to their proper doom. Take care of your nullifiers; you have them among you; let them meet with the indignant frowns of every man who loves his country. The tariff, it is *now* known, was a mere pretext—its burden was on your coarse woolens. By the law of July, 1832, coarse woolen was reduced to five per cent. for the benefit of the South. Mr. Clay's bill takes it up and classes it with woolens at fifty per cent., reduces it gradually down to twenty per cent., and there it is to remain, and Mr. Calhoun and all the nullifiers agree to the principle. The cash duties and home valuation will be equal to fifteen per cent. more, and after the year 1842, you pay on coarse woolens thirty-five per cent. If this is not protection, I cannot understand; therefore the tariff was only the pretext, and disunion and a southern confederacy the real object. *The next pretext will be the negro or slavery question.*

"My health is not good, but is improving a little. Present me kindly to your lady and family, and believe me to be your friend. I will always be happy to hear from you.

"ANDREW JACKSON."

BENTON in his Thirty Years' View, says:

The regular inauguration of this slavery agitation dates from the year 1835; but it had commenced two years before, and in this way: nullification and disunion had commenced in 1830, upon complaint against protective tariff. That, being put down in 1833 under President Jackson's proclamation and energetic measures, was immediately substituted by the slavery agitation. Mr. Calhoun, when he went home from Congress in the spring of that year, told his friends that "the South could never be united against the North on the tariff question—that the sugar interest of Louisiana would keep her out—and that the basis of southern union must be shifted to the slave question." Then all the papers in his interest, and especially the one at Washington, published by Mr. Duff Green, dropped tariff agitation, and commenced upon slavery, and in two years had the agitation ripe for inauguration on the slavery question. And in tracing this agitation to its present stage, and to comprehend its *rationale*, it is not to be forgotten that it is a mere continuation of old tariff disunion, and preferred because more available.—*Thirty Years in the Senate*, vol. 2.

Mr. CLAY, in a letter to an Alabamian in 1844, (see his private correspondence, p. 490,) said:

From the developments now being made in South Carolina, it is perfectly manifest that a party exists in that State seeking a dissolution of the Union, and for that purpose employ the pretext of the rejection of Mr. Tyler's abominable treaty. South Carolina being surrounded by slave States, would, in the event of a dissolution of the Union, suffer only comparative evils; but it is otherwise with Kentucky. She has the boundary of the Ohio extending four hundred miles on three free States. What would our condition be in the event of the greatest calamity that could befall this nation?

Hon. Nathan Appleton, of Boston, member of Congress in 1832–3, in a letter dated December 15, 1860, said that when in Congress he "made up his mind that Messrs. Calhoun, Hayne, McDuffie, &c., were desirous of a separation of the slave States into a separate confederacy, as more favorable to the security of slave property."

About 1835, some South Carolinians attempted a disunion demonstration. It is thus described by Ex-Governor Francis Thomas of Maryland, in his speech in Baltimore, October 29, 1861:

Full twenty years ago, when occupying my seat in the House of Representatives, I was surprised one morning, after the assembling of the House, to observe that all the members from the slaveholding States were absent. Whilst reflecting on this strange occurrence, I was asked why I was not in attendance on the Southern caucus assembled in the room of the Committee on Claims. I replied that I had received no invitation.

I then proposed to go to the committee room, to see what was being done. When I entered I found that little cock-sparrow, Governor Pickens of South Carolina, addressing the meeting, and strutting about like a rooster around a barn-yard coop, discussing the following resolution, which he was urging on the favorable consideration of the meeting:

"*Resolved*, That no member of Congress representing a Southern constituency shall again take his seat until a resolution is passed satisfactory to the South on the subject of slavery."

I listened to his language, and when he had finished, I obtained the floor, asking to be permitted to take part in the discussion. I determined at once to kill the treasonable plot hatched by John C. Calhoun, the Cataline of America, by asking questions. I said to Mr. Pickens, "What next do you propose we shall do? Are we to tell the people that Republicanism is a failure? If you are for that I am not. I came here to sustain and uphold American institutions; to defend the rights of the North as well as the South; to secure harmony and good fellowship between all sections of our common country." They dared not answer these questions. The southern temper had not then been gotten up. As my questions were not answered, I moved an adjournment of the caucus *sine die*. Mr. Craig, of Virginia, seconded the motion, and the company was broken up. We returned to the House, and Mr. Ingersoll, of Pennsylvania, a glorious patriot then as now, introduced a resolution which temporarily calmed the excitement.

Respecting this event, the *National Intelligencer* of November 4, 1861, makes these remarks:

However busy Mr. Pickens may have been in the caucus after it met, the most active man in getting it up and pressing the southern members to go into it was Mr. R. B. Rhett, also a member from South Carolina. The occasion, or alleged cause of this withdrawal from the House into secret deliberation was an anti-slavery speech of Mr. Slade, of Vermont, which Mr. Rhett violently denounced, and proposed to the southern members to leave the House and go into conclave in one of the committee rooms, which they generally did, if not all of them. We are able to state, however, what may not have been known to Governor Thomas, that at least three besides himself of those who did attend it went there with a purpose very different from an intention to consent to any treasonable measure. These three men were Henry A. Wise, Balie Peyton, and Wm. Cost Johnson. Neither of them opened his lips in the caucus; they went to observe; and we can assure Governor Thomas that if Mr. Pickens or Mr. Calhoun (whom he names) or any one else had presented a distinct proposition looking to disunion, or revolt, or secession, he would have witnessed a scene not soon to be forgotten. The three whom we have mentioned were as brave as they were determined. Fortunately, perhaps, the man whom they went particularly to watch remained silent and passive.

EARLY HOPES OF THE REBELS.*

Mr. LAWRENCE M. KEITT, when declaiming in Charleston in November, 1860, in favor of the separate secession of that State, used this language, as reported in the Charleston *Mercury:*

But we have been threatened. Mr. Amos Kendall wrote a letter, in which he said to Col. Orr, that if the State went out, three hundred thousand volunteers were ready to march against her. I know little about Kendall—and the less the better. He was under General Jackson; but for him the Federal treasury seemed to have a magnetic attraction. Jackson was a pure man, but he had too many around him who made fortunes far transcending their salaries. [Applause.] And this Amos Kendall had the same good fortune under Van Buren. He (Kendall) threatened us on the one side, and John Hickman on the other. John Hickman said, defiantly, that if we went out of the Union, eighteen millions of Northern men would bring us back. Let me tell you, *there are a million of Democrats in the North, who, when the Black Republicans attempt to march upon the South, will be found a wall of fire in the front.* [Cries of "that's so!" and applause.]

Recently-found letters in Fredericksburg, Virginia, noticed editorially in *Harpers' Weekly* of May 28, 1864, show that the South calculated confidently upon the defection of large masses of men at the North. The *Weekly*, commenting on M. F. Maury's letters, says:

How far Maury and his fellow-conspirators were justified in their hopes of seducing New Jersey into the rebellion, may be gathered from the correspondence that took place in the spring of 1861 between Ex-Governor Price, of New Jersey, who was one of the representatives from that State in the Peace Congress, and L. W. Burnet, Esq., of Newark. Mr. Price, in answering the question what ought New Jersey to do, says: "I believe the Southern Confederation permanent. The proceeding has been taken with forethought and deliberation—it is no hurried impulse, but an irrevocable act, based upon the sacred, as was supposed, 'equality of the States;' and in my opinion every slave State will in a short period of time be found united in one confederacy. * * Before that event happens we cannot act, however much we may suffer in our material interests. It is in that contingency, then, that I answer the second part of your question—'what position for New Jersey will best accord with her interests, honor, and the patriotic instincts of her people?' I say emphatically *she would go with the South from every wise, prudential, and patriotic reason.*" Ex-Governor Price proceeds to say that he is confident the States of Pennsylvania† and New York will "choose also to cast their lot with the South," and after them the western and northwestern States.

---

* See page 20.

† January 16, 1861—A meeting of Democrats was held in National Hall, Philadelphia, Charles Macalester presiding, at which Robert P. Kane offered this, among other resolutions which were put to the meeting, and declared adopted, and which, read in the light of this revelation, appear to

LETTER OF EX-PRESIDENT FRANKLIN PIERCE TO JEFFERSON DAVIS, OF JANUARY 6, 1860, FOUND IN DAVIS'S MISSISSIPPI HOME, WHEN TAKEN BY OUR TROOPS:

CLARENDON HOTEL, *January* 6, 1860.

MY DEAR FRIEND: I wrote you an unsatisfactory note a day or two since. I have just had a pleasant interview with Mr. Shepley, whose courage and fidelity are equal to his learning and talents. He says he would rather fight the battle with you as the standard-bearer in 1860 than under the auspices of any other leader. The feeling and judgment of Mr. S. in this relation is, I am confident, rapidly gaining ground in New England. Our people are looking for "the coming man," one who is raised by all the elements of his character above the atmosphere ordinarily breathed by politicians, a man really fitted for this exigency by his ability, courage, broad statesmanship, and patriotism. Colonel Seymour (Thos. H.) arrived here this morning, and expressed his views in this relation in almost the identical language used by Mr. Shepley. It is true that, in the present state of things at Washington and throughout the country, no man can predict what changes two or three months may bring forth. Let me suggest that, in the running debates in Congress, full justice seems to me not to have been done to the Democracy of the North. I do not believe that our friends at the South have any just idea of the state of feeling, hurrying at this moment to the pitch of intense exasperation, between those who respect their political obligations and those who have apparently no impelling power but that which fanatical passion on the subject of domestic slavery imparts. Without discussing the question of right, of abstract power to secede, I have never believed that actual disruption of the Union can occur without blood; and if, through the madness of northern abolitionism, that dire calamity must come, the fighting will not be along Mason's and Dixon's line merely. It [will] be within our own borders, in our own streets, between the two classes of citizens to whom I have referred. Those who defy law and scout constitutional obligations will, if we ever reach the arbitrament of arms, find occupation enough at home. Nothing but the state of Mrs. Pierce's health would induce me to leave the country now, although it is quite likely that my presence at home would be of little service. I have tried to impress upon our people, especially in New Hampshire and Connecticut, where the only elections are to take place during the coming spring, that while our Union meetings are all in the right direction, and well enough for the present, they will not be worth the paper upon which their resolutions are written unless we can overthrow political abolitionism at the polls and repeal the unconstitutional and obnoxious laws which, in the cause of "personal liberty," have been placed upon our statute-books. I shall look with deep interest, and not without hope, for a decided change in this relation.

Ever and truly, your friend,

FRANKLIN PIERCE.

HON. JEFF. DAVIS,
Washington, D. C.

The Disunion Programme.

From the *National Intelligencer* of Friday, January 11, 1861:

The subjoined communication, disclosing the designs of those who have undertaken to lead the movement now threatening a permanent dissolution of the Union, comes to us from a distinguished citizen of the South,* who formerly represented his State with great distinction in the popular branch of Congress. Temporarily sojourning in this city he has become authentically informed of the facts recited in the subjoined letter, which he communicates to us under a sense of duty, and for the accuracy of which he makes himself responsible. Nothing but assurances coming from such an intelligent, reliable source could induce us to accept the authenticity of these startling statements, which so deeply concern not only the welfare but the honor of the Southern people. To them we submit, without present comment, the programme to which they are expected to yield their implicit adhesion, without any scruples of conscience as without any regard to their own safety.

WASHINGTON, *January* 9, 1861.

I charge that on last Saturday night a caucus was held in this city by the Southern Secession Senators from Florida, Georgia, Alabama, Mississippi, Louisiana, Arkansas, and Texas. It was then and there resolved in effect to assume to themselves the political power of the South, and, to control all political and military operations for the present, they telegraphed to complete the plan of seizing forts, arsenals, and custom-houses, and advised the conventions now in session, and soon to assemble, to pass ordinances for immediate secession; but, in order to thwart any operations of the Government here, the Conventions of the seceding States are to retain their representations in the Senate and the House.

They also advised, ordered, or directed the assembling of a Convention of delegates from the seceding States at Montgomery on the 13th of February. This can of course only be done by the revolutionary Conventions usurping the powers of the people and sending delegates over whom they will lose all control in the establishment of a Provional Government, which is the plan of the dictators.

This caucus also resolved to take the most effectual means to dragoon the Legislatures of Tennessee, Kentucky, Missouri, Arkansas, Texas, and Virginia into following the seceding States. Maryland is also to be influenced by such appeals to popular passion as have led to the revolutionary steps which promise a conflict with the State and Federal Governments in Texas.

They have possessed themselves of all the avenues of information in the South—the telegraph, the press, and the general control of the postmasters. They also confidently rely upon defections in the army and navy.

The spectacle here presented is startling to contemplate. Senators entrusted with the representative sovereignty of the States, and sworn to support the Constitution of the United States, while yet acting as the privy councillors of the President, and anxiously looked to by their constituents to effect some practical plan of adjustment, deliberately conceive a conspiracy for the overthrow of the Government through the military organizations, the dangerous secret order, the Knights of the Golden Circle, "Committees of Safety," Southern leagues, and other agencies at their command; they have instituted as thorough a military and civil despotism as ever cursed a maddened country.

It is not difficult to foresee the form of government which a convention thus hurriedly thrown together at Montgomery will irrevocably fasten upon a deluded and unsuspecting people. It must essentially be "a monarchy founded upon military principles," or it cannot endure. Those who usurp power never fail to forge strong chains.

It may be too late to sound the alarm. Nothing may be able to arrest the action of revolutionary tribunals whose decrees are principally in "secret sessions." But I call upon the people to pause and reflect before they are forced to surrender every principle of liberty, or to fight those who are becoming their masters rather than their servants.

EATON.

As confirming the intelligence furnished by our informant we may cite the following extract from the Washington correspondence of yesterday's Baltimore *Sun:*

"The leaders of the Southern movement are consulting as to the best mode of consolidating their interests into a Confederacy under a *Provisional Government*. The plan is to make Senator Hunter, of Virginia, Provisional President, and Jefferson Davis Commander-in-Chief of the army of defence. Mr. Hunter possesses in a more eminent degree the philosophical characteristics of Jefferson than any other statesman now living. Colonel Davis is a graduate of West Point, was distinguished for gallantry at Buena Vista, and served as Secretary of War under President Pierce, and is not second to General Scott in military science or courage."

The Charleston *Mercury* of January 7, 1860, published the following telegraphic dispatch:

[From our own Correspondent.]

WASHINGTON, *Jan.* 6.—The Senators from those of the Southern States which have called Conventions of their

disclose a plan of which ex-Governor Price was likely aware:

Twelfth, That in the deliberate judgment of the Democracy of Philadelphia, and, so far as we know it, of Pennsylvania, the dissolution of the Union by the separation of the whole South, a result we shall most sincerely lament, may release this Commonwealth to a large extent from the bonds which now connect her with the Confederacy, except so far as for temporary convenience she chooses to submit to them, and would authorize and require her citizens, through a convention, to be assembled for that purpose, to determine with whom her lot should be cast, whether with the North and the East, whose fanaticism has precipitated this misery upon us, or with our brethren of the South, whose wrongs we feel as our own; or whether Pennsylvania should stand by herself, as a distinct community, ready when occasion offers to bind together the broken Union, and resume her place of loyalty and devotion.

* Understood to be Hon. Lemuel D. Evans, Representative from Texas in the 34th Congress, from March 4, 1855, to March 3, 1857.

people met in caucus last night, and adopted the following resolutions:

"*Resolved*, That we recommend to our respective States immediate secession.

"*Resolved*, That we recommend the holding of a General Convention of the said States, to be holden in the city of Montgomery, Alabama, at some period not later than the 15th day of February, 1861."

These resolutions were telegraphed this evening to the Conventions of Alabama, Mississippi, and Florida. A third resolution is also known to have been adopted, but it is of a confidential character, *not to be divulged at present*. There was a good deal of discussion in the caucus on the question of whether the seceding States ought to continue their delegations in Congress till the 4th of March, to prevent unfriendly legislation, or whether the Representatives of the seceding States should all resign together, and leave a clear field to the Opposition to pass such bills, looking to coercion, as they may see fit. It is believed that the opinion that they should remain prevailed.

CERTAIN "SECRET" DOCUMENTS.

LETTER FROM U. S. SENATOR YULEE OF FLORIDA.

WASHINGTON, *Jan.* 7, 1861.

MY DEAR SIR: On the other side is a copy of resolutions adopted at a consultation of the Senators from the seceding States—in which Georgia, Alabama, Louisiana, Arkansas, Texas, Mississippi, and Florida were present.

The idea of the meeting was that the States should go out at once, and provide for the early organization of a Confederate Government, not later than 15th February. This time is allowed to enable Louisiana and Texas to participate. It seemed to be the opinion that if we left here, force, loan, and volunteer bills might be passed, which would put Mr. LINCOLN in immediate condition for hostilities; whereas, by remaining in our places until the 4th of March, *it is thought we can keep the hands of Mr. Buchanan tied, and disable the Republicans from effecting any legislation which will strengthen the hands of the incoming Administration.*

The resolutions will be sent by the delegation to the President of the Convention. I have not been able to find Mr. Mallory this morning. Hawkins* is in Connecticut. I have therefore thought it best to send you this copy of the resolutions.

In haste, yours truly, D. L. YULEE.

JOSEPH FINEGAN, Esq.,

"*Sovereignty Convention*," *Tallahasee, Fla.*

The following were the resolutions referred to:

Resolved 1. That in our opinion each of the Southern States should, as soon as may be, secede from the Union.

Resolved 2. That provision should be made for a convention to organize a Confederacy of the seceding States, the convention to meet not later than the 15th of February, at the city of Montgomery, in the State of Alabama.

Resolved, That in view of the hostile legislation that is threatened against the seceding States, and which may be consummated before the 4th of March, we ask instructions whether the delegations are to remain in Congress until that date for the purpose of defeating such legislation.

Resolved, That a committee be and are hereby appointed, consisting of Messrs. Davis, Slidell, and Mallory, to carry out the objects of this meeting.

The preceding letter was found in Fernandina, Florida, upon the capture of that city in the winter of 1862, and the orginal letter was forwarded to the editor of the N. Y. *Times* by its correspondent who accompanied the expedition. The *Times* of Saturday, March 15, 1862, comments on this development:

The telegraphic columns of the *Times* of January 7, 1861, contained the following Washington despatch: "The Southern Senators last night (Jan. 5) held a conference, and telegraphed to the conventions of their respective States to advise immediate secession." Now, the present letter is a report by Mr. Yulee, who was present at this "consultation," as he calls it, of the resolutions adopted on this occasion, transmitted to the said Finegan, who, by the way, was a member of the "Sovereign Convention" of Florida, then sitting in the town of Tallahassee.

It will thus be seen that this remarkable letter, which breathes throughout the spirit of the conspirator, in reality lets us into one of the most important of the numerous secret conclaves which the plotters of treason then held in the capital. It was then, as it appears, that they determined to strike the blow and precipitate their States into secession. But at the same time they resolved that it would be imprudent for them openly to withdraw, as in that case Congress might pass "force, loan, and volunteer bills, which would put Mr. Lincoln in immediate condition for hostilities." No, no! that would not do. (So much patriotic virtue they half suspected, half feared was left in the country.) On the contrary, "by remaining in our places until the 4th of March it is thought we can keep the hands of Mr. Buchanan tied, and disable the Republicans from effecting any legislation which will strengthen the hands of the incoming Administration." Ah! what a tragic background, full of things unutterable, is there there!

It appears, however, that events were faster than they, and instead of being able to retain their seats up to the 4th of March, they were able to remain but a very few weeks. Mr. Davis withdrew on the 21st of January—just a fortnight after this "consultation." But for the rest, mark how faithfully the programme here drawn up by this knot of traitors in secret session was realized. Each of the named States represented by this cabal did, "as soon as may be, secede from the Union"—the Mississippi Convention passing its ordinance on the heels of the receipt of these resolutions, on the 9th of January; Florida and Alabama on the 11th; Louisiana on the 26th, and Texas on the 1st of February; while the "organization of the Confederate Government" took place at the very time appointed, Davis being inaugurated on the 18th of February.

And here is another plot of the traitors brought to light. These very men, on withdrawing from the Senate, urged that they were doing so in obedience to the command of their respective States. As Mr. Davis put it, in his parting speech, "the ordinance of secession having passed the Convention of his State, he felt obliged to obey the summons, and retire from all official connection with the Federal Government." This letter of Mr. Yulee's clearly reveals that they had themselves pushed their State Conventions to the adoption of the very measure which they had the hardihood to put forward as an imperious "summons" which they could not disobey. It is thus that treason did its work.

Mr. James L. Pugh, member of Congress from Alabama, in a letter, Nov. 24, 1860—"made public his reasons for going to Washington," and taking his seat in Congress. He says: "The sole object of my visit is to promote the cause of secession."

Douglas's Farewell Words.

IN CHICAGO May 1, 1861.

The election of Mr. Lincoln is a mere pretext. The present secession movement is the result of an enormous conspiracy formed more than a year since—formed by leaders in the Southern Confederacy more than twelve months ago. They use the slavery question as a means to aid the accomplishment of their ends. They desired the election of a northern candidate by a sectional vote, in order to show that the two sections cannot live together. When the history of the two years from the Lecompton question down to the Presidential election shall be written, it will be shown that the scheme was deliberately made to break up this Union.

They desired a northern Republican to be elected by a purely northern vote, and then assign this fact as a reason why the sections cannot live together. If the disunion candidate in the late Presidential contest had carried the united South, their scheme was, the northern candidate successful, to seize the Capital last spring, and by a united South and divided North, hold it. Their scheme was defeated, in the defeat of the disunion candidates in several of the southern States.

But this is no time for a detail of causes. The conspiracy is now known; armies have been raised, war is levied to accomplish it. There are only two sides to the question. Every man must be for the United States or against it. There can be no neutrals in this war; *only patriots or traitors!* (Cheer after cheer.)

The Conspiracy in Maryland.

On page 152, the arrest of Marshal Kane*

---

* The Representative from Florida.

* Marshal Kane, on his way to burn the bridges on the railroads to Philadelphia and to Harrisburg, sent this telegram for troops:

MARSHAL KANE'S DESPATCH TO BRADLEY T. JOHNSON, OF FREDERICK.

BALTIMORE, *April* 19, 1861.

Thank you for your offer; bring your men in by the first train, and we will arrange with the railroad afterwards.

and the Board of Police of Baltimore in June, 1861, by General Banks, is noticed. After their arrest, the minutes of their proceedings during the "reign of terror" in Baltimore were found, from which these interesting extracts are taken:

EXTRACTS FROM THE "MINUTES" OF THE POLICE COMMISSIONERS OF BALTIMORE, AND FROM THEIR LETTER BOOK; FOUND IN THEIR OFFICE AFTER THEIR ARREST BY GENERAL BANKS.

1861, April 19th, 20th, and 21st—No entry.

April 22d—After debate, *Resolved*, That notice be immediately given of election for Legislature on Wednesday 24th April, and the sheriff be requested to unite in giving the necessary call therefor.

The Board declared itself to be in permanence. D. J. Foley & Bros.' powder purchased, and the disposition of the same and all other powder to be purchased committed to Col. Isaac Trimble.* Henry Thompson, Esq., appointed Quartermaster General, to act under the Mayor.†

Order passed to prevent the transportation of provisions without special permission. Colonel Trimble appointed to enforce the order.

Charles Pitts ‡ appeared and offered 200 to 300 negroes to perform any service which the authorities may call on them to do. The Mayor returns thanks, and assures them they shall be called on when any occasion arises when their services can be availed of.

Coleman Yellott § authorized to charter a steamer to summon the members of the State Legislature.

Unnecessary parades forbidden in the streets.

Extract from a note from Col. Trimble to Howard, President of the Board, found among the papers:

"The display of military will be a sorry one as to the strength of the military of the city, and calculated to dishearten our own citizens, and if represented abroad will rather invite and encourage attempts from the north to defy us and pass through the city, whereas without this display many will think that the military force of the city is much stronger than it really is."

Order passed authorizing Col. Trimble to permit steamboats to leave for the eastern shore, to and below the Sassafras river, upon condition that in going and returning they shall not stop at Annapolis.

April 23. U. S. SHIP ALLEGHANY,
BALTIMORE, *April* 23, 1861.

CHARLES HOWARD, Esq., *President of the Board of Police*.

SIR: Having occasion to employ a steamtug in the service of the United States, I have to request that you will authorize me to use one this day in the harbor of Baltimore and the adjacent waters.

I am, respectfully,
WM. W. HUNTER, *Com. U. S. N.*

Respectfully declined.

Communication from Col. Trimble in regard to the removal of the Alleghany. Answer given through Charles Wethered, that the matter was attended to, and *the removal forbidden*.

Mr. Zenas Barnum called in regard to repairing the telegraph wires on the road to Philadelphia; no action determined on. Mr. Barnum was informed that *no communications can pass over the wires for Washington, whether for the War Department or citizens, without being subjected to the inspection of the police board*.

Commissary Lee applied for permission to convey provisions into Fort McHenry. He was informed of the impossibility of ensuring him protection in carrying provisions to the fort during the present excitement of public feeling.

Application received from Mr. Clarke, Superintendent of the Northern Central Railroad, for permission to rebuild the bridges [which had been destroyed by Kane on the night of the 19th] at Melville and the Relay House. *This was refused*.

Application by Messrs. Tucker [British subjects] to complete the loading of the Queen Victoria, [British.] In reply were informed that instructions would be given to Col. Trimble to permit the Queen Victoria to depart with her present loading, but that no other articles prohibited to be removed from the city can be permitted to be shipped on board the vessel. *American* vessels partly laden shall not depart without further and distinct action being taken by the board.

The following were loose papers accompanying the "minutes" but not recorded:

1. Despatch by Morse's line, dated
"HARPER'S FERRY, 1861.

Received Baltimore 22, 1861."

TO POLICE COMMISSIONERS:

I want to communicate. What have you to say?
KENTON HARPER,
[Rebel] *Commanding*.

2. Baltimore and Ohio Railroad Telegram, dated
HARPER'S FERRY, *April* 22, 1861.

Received 11 o'clock, 8 min., A. M.

To W. H. GATCHELL, *Police Commissioner*:

Very satisfactory interview here with General Harper.
C. J. M. GWINN.

3. Memorandum in pencil—omited in the "minutes:"
APRIL 23, 1861.

"Telegraphed General Harper, Harper's Ferry, to the effect, that the town is quiet, expressing thanks for his communication, and promising to let him know when any exigency requiring it shall arise; mentioning that Gwinn had been seen by us."

Gwinn reported "six thousand men ready to come down."

4. Another memorandum:

"Gwinn asserts that six thousand troops are at Harper's Ferry."

APRIL 25.*

"All police officers and others in the employ of the Board, and all other parties whatsoever, are requested to offer no obstruction to the running of the trains." (*i. e.*, to Washington.)

In a letter to John Garrett, Esq., Col. Trimble directed to allow and grant facility for the transportation of 40 kegs of powder to be used by the Baltimore and Ohio Railroad Company in Virginia.

Restrictions on the export of provisions, breadstuffs, and bituminous coal, removed.

Propositions to repair the telegraphic lines to Cockeysville, and also to Havre de Grace and Belair, *were declined*.

Appointment made with Col. Trimble and Gen. Thompson by the Mayor and Board, for 6 p. m., to consider and determine certain matters in reference to the disbursement of moneys under the ordinance, appropriating $500,000.

Col. Huger furnished plans and specifications for a bombproof.

Letter from General Stewart † found among the papers:
April 22, 1861.

"MY DEAR HOWARD: I will endeavor to put on duty the *same company of cavalry that was ordered out last night*. ‡ I know not what to think of the rumors from Annapolis; but if the Massachusetts troops are on the march from that place to Washington, I shall be in motion very early tomorrow morning to pay my respects to them, of course making arrangements for an adequate force being here in my absence."

LETTER FROM THE SECRETARY OF THE MAYOR TO THE PRESIDENT OF POLICE BOARD.

MAYOR'S OFFICE, *April* 23, 1861.

CHARLES HOWARD, Esq.:

DEAR SIR: A messenger from Virginia called to inform the Mayor that Senator Mason will be in the city either on to-morrow evening or the next day, and wishes an interview with Governor Pratt, Hon. Robert McLean, and J. Mason Campbell. Respectfully,
D. H. BLANCHARD,
Secretary.

April 26—Colonel Kane reports that the powder purchased by Colonel Trimble's orders, and stored in a church in the west end, has been ordered to be transferred to Vicker's house.

Negroes said to be offering *northern notes* (!) General

Streets red with Maryland blood! Send expresses over the mountains and valleys of Maryland and Virginia for the riflemen to come without delay. Fresh hordes will be down on us to-morrow, (the 20th.) We will fight them or die.
GEO. P. KANE.

This was posted in Frederick, with a placard as follows, signed by Bradley T. Johnson:

All men who will go with me will report themselves as soon as possible; providing themselves with such arms and accoutrements as they can. Double-barrelled shot guns and buck-shot are efficient. They will assemble after reporting themselves at 10½ o'clock, so as to go down in the 11½ train.

---

* Now Major General in rebel service, and a prisoner in our hands, captured at Gettysburg.

† The Mayor was one of the Board.

‡ Elected to the Legislature at the election of 24th April.

§ Member of the State Senate.

* The day after the election for members of House of Delegates, when but 9,000 votes were cast, of the 30,000 in Baltimore.

† Stewart was Major General of the 5th Division Maryland militia; is now in the rebel service and our prisoner, having been captured in one of the battles of the Wilderness.

‡ To take Fort McHenry.

Ing reports a revolving cannon* in William Wilkens & Co's. warehouse. But Colonel Huger and Ross Winans do not approve of such batteries.

Application made for permission to repair telegraph lines to Havre de Grace. Granted; it being understood that the board shall have cognizance of all communications made by the American Telegraph Company. (Letter Book, *folio* 97.)

Certain directors of the Philadelphia, Wilmington, and Baltimore railroad [O'Donnell, Pratt, Cohen, and T. Donelson] ask for the privilege of reconstructing the bridges and repairing the rails upon their road, [destroyed by Marshal Kane.] They assumed that a promise could be had by them from the General Government not to ask for the passage of troops over the road. Answer given that they should first learn what time would be required for repairing the road, and what assurance they could get from the Government that troops shall not seek that means of transportation, and *then that the application for permission to rebuild the road shall be renewed to the board.*

Prohibition to remove flour and breadstuffs re-enacted.†

April 27 1861—*Full Board and Mayor.*

Resignation of David Daneker and William T. Butler, of the police force, received.

DANEKER'S LETTER.

To the Board of Police:

Gents: I hereby tender my resignation as a member of the police force of Baltimore. As an American citizen I cannot condescend to pull down the American flag.

DAVID DANEKER,‡ *26th April.*

Colonel Trimble instructed to allow shipments of breadstuffs, &c., in limited quantities, within the State; must use his discretion: "Keep a list of parties shipping the articles, and quantities, and make daily reports."

General Stewart appeared and stated that he had information of 2,000 stand of arms having arrived at Camden Station, (Baltimore and Ohio railroad,) which he claimed as officer of the State.

Reply, (Letter Book, page 111:)

"A gentleman representing the house of W. T. Walters & Co., has just called. Their house has bill of lading for the arms, and desires to hand them over to the police depot solely for safe-keeping."

April 28th—General Stewart notifies the Board that 2,000 guns were yesterday morning at Harper's Ferry, awaiting his orders, and that he had given directions for them to be forwarded to his orders.

LETTER FROM GENERAL STEWART TO THE BOARD.

Headquarters, 1st Light Division, M. V.
Baltimore, *2d May*, 1861.

To the Board of Police of the City of Baltimore:

Gents: I have the pleasure to lay before you the official dispatches of Governor Letcher, of 24th April, addressed to me, and several other communications between myself and Major General Kenton Harper, commanding at Harper's Ferry, as well as Brigadier General Cocke, commanding at Alexandria, all showing that the 5,000 flint-lock guns furnished by the State of Virginia are for the use of Maryland, and are destined to be delivered to my order.

Understanding that 2,000 of these arms, which arrived two or three days ago from Harper's Ferry, consigned to Mr. W. T. Walters, (but contrary to the instructions of Major General Harper, as he assures me in a dispatch,) are now in a warehouse at the corner of Second and Gay streets, occupied by your Board or by the city authorities, I, as the officer of the State of Maryland, commanding here, and agent of the State, to whom the arms were destined, require that the whole be delivered to my order, it being understood that I assume the responsibility of receiving those arms on account of the State of Maryland. You are aware that upon special application to me on behalf of the companies of Calvert county, I agreed to delivery of 120 of those arms."

Extract from the reply of the Commissioners (C. Howard) to General Stewart—same date.

"And you having also understood that a gentleman now in Frederick has full power to control or alter the destination of them, we were unwilling to exercise any authority over them. I showed you a copy of my letter to that gentleman from whom I have yet no reply."

Letter referred to, Letter Book, page 116, to Senator Mason, dated April 30, 1861.

My Dear Sir: Since I had the pleasure of seeing you I have had a good deal of annoyance in consequence of the irregular manner in which some of our townsmen obtained in your State some arms. I do not question their motives, but it was unfortunate that we had no information of what had been done by them until we learned it from you. Can you inform me whether these arms mentioned by General Harper are a part of the original quantity mentioned by you, and of which I understand you have full power to control the destination?

If so, do you desire General Stewart, as a military officer of the State, to receive them for its use?

(Signed) CHARLES HOWARD.

GOVERNOR LETCHER'S LETTER TO GENERAL STEWART.

Dear Sir: I called this morning to see you, having received a dispatch from J. S. Barbour, Esq., Alexandria, giving information respecting matters in Baltimore. I have issued an order to General Harper to send 1,000 stand of arms to General Stewart. Stirring times in your State.

Truly, JOHN LETCHER.

THE ORDINANCE APPROPRIATING $500,000.

This ordinance (No. 22) was approved April 20, 1861, and a portion of the money expended. The following report, made April 4th, 1862, shows how:

The Joint Select Committee, to whom was referred the resolution for the appointment of a committee "to examine and dispose of all papers and vouchers relating to the expenditure of money under the provisions of the ordinance for the preservation of the peace of the city, approved April 20th, 1861, to inquire and report what has become of the articles then purchased and in whose possession they now are, and also what disposition shall be made of the balance of the funds now in the city treasury," have discharged the duty imposed upon them, and submit to the Councils the following report, with accompanying resolutions:

The duties imposed upon the committee were three-fold; first, to examine and dispose of all papers and vouchers relating to the expenditure of money, under the provisions of the ordinance specified; secondly, to inquire and report what has become of the articles thus purchased, and in whose possession they now are; and thirdly, to decide what disposition shall be made of the balance of the funds now in the city treasury.

On the first head, your committee have to report that no "papers" have come under their cognizance, except a note addressed by Col. Henry A. Thompson to the Mayor, which accompanied a statement of his agency, in the capacity of Quartermaster General, in the disbursement of $38,000 of the money in question, and in which he claims to have saved a considerable sum for the city treasury, by efforts to prevent lavish expenditure, and by annulling numerous contracts and returning many articles already delivered.

Your committee regard it as a cause of profound regret, that such an agency had not been earlier in action; but it is due to the gentleman referred to, to say, that he appears to have performed the difficult duties confided to him, with fidelity and discretion. Acknowledgments are also due to Col. Thompson, for a courteous note, tendering any assistance in his power, in the examination of the "vouchers," so far as his agency was concerned; but no occasion has arisen for making use of the proffered aid.

The "vouchers," as placed in the hands of your committee by the city Register, have been carefully examined, and found to be in due form, authenticated by the parties having control of affairs at that period, and accounting for the expenditure of the gross amount reported, allowing for interest and the balance on hand. Each account has been singly inspected, the objects of expenditure have been classified, and present the results stated below.

Having served the purposes of your committee in affording the points of information it was necessary to obtain, no other disposition of them seems necessary than to restore them to the custody of the city officer, in whose charge they properly belong, as vouchers for disbursements under the ordinance.

The labors of your committee under the second head of instructions, "to inquire and report what has become of the articles then purchased, and in whose possession they now are," have resulted in the following classified summary of expenditures for different objects:

SUMMARY.

Arms, ammunition, &c.	$24,174 74
Blankets, mattresses, &c.	2,825 57
Surgical instruments and medicines	99 37
Marine and navy (embracing hire and alterations of steamers, and wages of men)	5,461 31

* This was afterwards captured *en route* for Harper's Ferry.

† The argument of the rebels then was that otherwise Government would suddenly buy up and remove all the supplies.

‡ It had been determined to suppress the American flag, and the military had been put in array to put this through; vide letters from Stewart to Howard, 26th April, and the replies of the Board in Letter Book.

Carpenters, bricklayers, materials, &c	$2,568 05
Rations	9,914 39
Pay of officers and men	7,736 30
Horse and hack hire, and hauling arms	3,472 86
Advertising, stationery, &c	234 78
Rent of armories and repairs	1,748 02
Workmen on parks, by resolution, approved June 11, 1861	8,508 19
Poor Association, for use of indigent widows, sewing women, &c	2,000 00
Interest	5,775 56
Cash in Bank	24,576 86
Total	$99,096 00

From the above summary it will be seen that the expenditures for "Arms and ammunition" reached the large amount of nearly $25,000. The articles purchased include fixtures for cannon, carbines, rifles, muskets, pistols, swords, spears, drums, canister and grape shot, bullets, lead, powder, cartridges, caps and other kindred materials, the precise number and quantities of which, as nearly as could be ascertained, are given in the two following schedules:

1,217 carbines, from F. W. Bennett.
407 Hall's patent rifles, from Denson & Buck.
80 carbines, from Denson & Buck.
6 cutlasses, from Denson & Buck.
12 gun carriages, from A. & W. Denmead & Son.
3,285 iron spears, from A. & W. Denmead & Son.
2 muskets, from Levi Cromwell.
16 pistols, from Wm. Harris.
302 pikes, from Hayward, Bartlett & Co.
23 guns, from T. Foy.
9 pistols, from Merrill, Thomas & Co.
12 flasks, from Merrill, Thomas & Co.
4 ship pistols, from Levi Cromwell.
1 sword, from Canfield, Bro. & Co.
414 pikes, from George Page & Co.
7 revolvers, from C. Schumaker.
3 drums, from — Eisenbrandt.

AMMUNITION.

—— lbs. powder, (value $4,526) from Foley & Bro.
8,194 lbs. canister shot, from A. W. Denmead & Son.
119 " musket balls, " Levi Cromwell.
21,000 caps, from Cugle & Co.
1 keg rifle powder, from F. Devlin.
2 bags balls, from F. Devlin.
2,000 caps, from F. Devlin.
4,958 lbs. lead, from Baltimore Water Board.
200 blank cartridges, from Green & Yoe.
2 boxes caps, from Green & Yoe.
1 bag shot, from Green & Yoe.
113 yards flannel, for cartridges, from —— ——
10,000 ball cartridges, from Wm. Harris.
10,860 do do do
800 do do Hoffman.
—— do do Poultney & Trimble.
429 cylinders for 6-pound guns, from O. H. Cromwell.
86 lbs. antimony, for balls, from Regester & Webb.
102 lbs. tin, for balls, do do
102,000 caps, from Merrill, Thomas & Co.
13 bags and 14 lbs. balls, from Merchants' Shot Tower.
3,031 cartridges, from Merrill, Thomas & Co.
8 boxes cartridges, from Merrill, Thomas & Co.
30,000 caps, do do
349 lbs. of lead, from John Rodgers.
7,740 lbs. cannon balls, from Denson & Buck.
473 cylinders, do do
54 lbs. match rope do do

The expenditures for "Blankets, Mattresses, &c.," were $2,825 57; and the articles purchased were as follows:

BLANKETS, MATTRESSES, ETC.

445 blankets, from Whitely, Stone & Co., and others.
540 straps, do do do do
425 flannel shirts, from John H. Rea, and others.
225 mattresses, from C. S. Frey & Co., A. Pollack, and others.
240 pillows, do do do do
400 caps, from White & Rosenberg.
1 desk, 10 chairs, 1 washstand, by S. S. Lee.

For "Surgical Instruments, &c.," the expenditures, considering the formidable nature of the preparations, offensive and defensive, were moderate, reaching only the sum of $99 37; and of this amount a portion is for damage to instruments returned. The list of these articles is here given:

SURGICAL INSTRUMENTS AND MEDICINES.

3 tourniquets, ordered by Dr. Robinson.
6 ternaculums, do do
2 bullet forceps, do
Sponges, Wadding, Muslin, Spirits, &c.

Having thus ascertained what articles had been purchased, your committee proceeded "to inquire what has become of them, and in whose possession they now are." This investigation was attended with considerable difficulty, owing to the various changes which have taken place since the period of the purchases; the abdication of the former Police Commissioners, the absence of the Mayor, the substitution of the United States Provost Marshal and his police force, and the seizure, by way of precaution, by the United States, of arms and military materials stored in different parts of the city. Many articles and equipments have undoubtedly disappeared; but your committee are enabled to present the following list of arms and other articles, furnished by Mr. James L. McPhail, Deputy Provost Marshal, which will account for a portion of the articles. Identification of those purchased was, of course, impossible:

38 rifles, found at the old City Hall.
3 single barrel shot guns.
1 double do do
27 single do do
2 double do do
2 rifles.
49 Hall's carbines.
7 U. S. do
2 Hall's rifles.
1 percussion musket.
1 ship gun.
2 six pound field pieces, mounted.
2 field pieces, complete.
20 rounds of canister shot.
26 do grape do
1½ tons do do
1 lot of 24 and 32 lb. shot.
10 mattresses.
33 pillows.
37 blankets.
6 sheets.
25 pillow-cases.
5 beds.
9 doz. boxes Hicks's hat caps.

Of the above articles, (your committee are informed by Mr. McPhail,) the beds and bedding were distributed to the several station-houses, they having been found, on taking possession, to be generally destitute of such articles, and those found being in bad repair and very dirty. Besides the bedding thus appropriated, a considerable number of mattresses, some tin ware, &c., were transferred, with the approbation of the mayor, to the warden of the jail, for use at that institution, where they were much needed. A portion of the arms purchased by the parties who had control of affairs during the period of the "crisis" are still at Fort McHenry, where they were placed after seizure by the United States authorities. According to a return made to the mayor on the 12th of August, 1861, by Samuel W. Bowen, Captain of the Middle District Station, the following arms, taken by order of General Butler from the corner of Gay and Second streets, were then at Fort McHenry:

58 boxes, marked "Va. muskets," 20 in each box	1,160
15 " " " Armory, do.	300
40 Hall's carbines, 20 in each box and 141 loose	941
13 Hall's rifles, " 74 "	334
46 Minie muskets, percussion locks	46
38 old muskets, flint locks	38
23 " " percussion	23
27 new " flint	27
50 Yager rifles	50
	2,919

1 box accoutrements.
115 boxes pikes.

Of the above, issues to a considerable extent have been made by the United States authorities, and some have been returned to Denson & Buck. Your committee are obliged to Deputy Marshal McPail for the following statement of arms at present to be found at Fort McHenry:

60 boxes of pikes, containing 60 each.
11 " carbines.
300 carbines.
5 guns, 7 carriages, 13 rammers.

It is understood that these articles, and such others belonging to the city as may be found in possession, will be restored by the Government of the United States as soon as their restoration is deemed compatible with a proper regard for its own protection.

A few words more are necessary, in explanation of the remaining items of the summary.

Of the amount charged to the "Marine and Navy," the principal portion is made up of sums expended on the hire and alterations of steam-tugs Hercules and Tiger, charges for use of the Potomac, George's Creek, and other steamers, amounting to $1,500 53, and $55 paid for the purchase of a boat and oars. The balance was principally expended in the payment of officers and "harbor police." The only articles known to be remaining from this department are a boat and oars, said to have been left in the care of John Henderson, Esq., and two spy-glasses in the possession of the city register.

In the charges for "carpenters, bricklayers, materials," &c., is included a considerable sum, say about $1,250, for reconstruction of the bridge at Canton. Considerable quantities of bricks and lumber are also included, mostly used in the erection or repair of a "powder-house," of the locality of which your Committee are not informed. Wherever situated, if not retained in use, the second-hand materials may be of some value to the city.

The payments for "rations," "pay-rolls," "horse and hack hire," "hauling," "armories," "advertising," &c., amounting in the aggregate to $23,106 35, represent so much outlay, from which the city reaps no tangible return.

The amounts of $8,518 19 for "workmen on parks," and $2,000 for "indigent widows, sewing-women," &c., were withdrawn from the fund by special resolutions of the council and expended for the benevolent purposes designated.

The charge for "interest," is a necessary result of the loan, authorized by the ordinance of April 20th, 1861.

The remaining item is the "cash in bank"—and this brings your committee to the third and last clause of the duties assigned them, viz: "to decide what disposition shall be made of the remaining funds now in the City Treasury."

On this point your committee are unanimously of the opinion that the balance should be returned, *pro rata*, to the several banks from which the whole amount was borrowed, thus canceling so much of the city's indebtedness, and stopping the payment or accumulation of interest.

In accordance with which statements and views, your committee respectfully recommend the adoption of the following resolutions:

S. F. STREETER,
WM. SULLIVAN,
JOHN DUKEHART,
First Branch.
JOSEPH ROBB,
WM. SWINDELL,
ASA HIGGINS,
Second Branch.

Resolved, By both Branches of the City Council of Baltimore, that the papers and vouchers relating to expenditures under Ordinance No. 22, approved April 20th, 1861, be restored to the custody of the City Register.

Resolved furthermore, That the Mayor be and is hereby authorized and requested to have collected, at the earliest possible moment, the arms and military materials belonging to the city, in the custody of the U. S. Marshal, or elsewhere, and, reserving such as, in his judgment, may be necessary for public use, to dispose of the balance, and place the proceeds in the City Treasury.

Resolved, By the Mayor and City Council of Baltimore, that the Register be and he is hereby authorized and directed to repay, *pro rata*, to the several banks, the balance remaining on hand from the sum borrowed of them, under authority of ordinance No. 22, approved April 20th, 1861, "to appropriate $500,000, or so much thereof as may be necessary for the defence of the city against any danger that may arise out of the present crisis."

These resolutions passed both branches.

THE LEGISLATURE CONFIRMED THE LOAN.

The Legislature of Maryland passed the bill, reported by Mr. Wallis from the Special Committee consisting of the Baltimore city delegation, "to ratify an ordinance of the Mayor and City Council of Baltimore appropriating $500,000 for the use of the city."

April 27, 1861, (the second day of the session,) this bill, under a suspension of the rules, passed the House of Delegates—yeas 58, nay 1, as follows:

YEAS—Messrs. E. G. Kilbourn, *Speaker*, Clarke J. Durant, George H. Morgan, Philip F. Rasin, Albert Medders, James T. Briscoe, Benjamin Parran, Bernard Compton, F. B. F. Burgess, Thos. C. Worthington, Robt. M. Denison, Leonard J. Quinlan, T. W. Renshaw, J. Laurence Jones, Alex. Chaplain, James U. Dennis, Edward Long, John R. Keene, Wm. Holland, John R. Brown, James W. Maxwell, E. P. Bryan, Richard Wooten, Ethan A. Jones, Wm. H. Legg, William L. Starkey, Curtis W. Jacobs, George W. Landing, Stephen P. Dennis, Andrew Kessler, jr., Thomas J. Claggett, John A. Johnson, William E. Salmon, Henry Straughn, G. W. Goldsborough, John C. Brune, Henry M. Warfield, Charles H. Pitts, William G. Harrison, J. Hanson Thomas, S. Teakle Wallis, T. Parkin Scott, Ross Winans, H. M. Morfit, Laurence Sangston, Joshua Wilson, William F. Bayless, Richard M'Coy, James Coudy, Martin Eakle, John C. Brining, Howard Griffith, Josiah H. Gordon, W. R. Barnard, David Roop of A., John W. Gorsuch, Bernard Mills, William Turner—58.

NAYS—Mr. William T. Lawson—1.

Same day, the bill passed the Senate—yeas 16, nays none, as follows:

YEAS—Messrs. John B. Brooke, Thomas J. M'Kaig, John E. Smith, Coleman Yellott, John S. Watkins, Teagle Townsend, Stephen J. Bradley, James F. Dashiell, H. H. Goldsborough, Charles F. Goldsborough, Daniel C. Blackistone, Franklin Whitaker, Tilghman Nuttle, Anthony Kimmel, Oscar Miles, Washington Duvall—16.

$500,000 MORE.

IN HOUSE OF DELEGATES.

May 9—The House passed—yeas 56, nays none, a bill giving authority to the Mayor and City Council of Baltimore, to issue certificates of debt to any amount not exceeding $500,000, in addition to the amount authorized to be issued by section 939 of the fourth article of the code of public laws.

May 10—It passed the Senate—yeas 16, nays none.

INDEFINITE AUTHORITY TO RAISE MONEY.

April 27—Mr. Wallis, from the Special Committee of the Baltimore city delegation, reported a bill "to add to the fourth article of the code of public local laws the following sections, empowering the Mayor and City Council of Baltimore to raise and appropriate money for the defence of the said city;" which was passed—yeas 58, nays none.

Same day, it passed the Senate—yeas 16, nays none, as on the previous bill.

ACTS OF INDEMNITY.

IN THE HOUSE OF DELEGATES.

May 4—Mr. Pitts, from Special Committee, reported a bill, entitled "an act to relieve the Mayor and Board of Police of the city of Baltimore, and all persons who acted under the orders of the Mayor or of the Board of Police of Baltimore city, in their efforts to maintain peace and good order and prevent further strife, on and after the occurrences of the 19th April, 1861, in said city from prosecution in consequence of their acts of obedience to said order."

Pending the bill—

May 5—Mr. Pitts offered these amendments; which were adopted:

That no prosecuting attorney nor any officer in any court in this State, shall be entitled to charge or receive any compensation or cost in any prosecution which has been or may be instituted against any person for whose relief the act is intended.

That this act may be given as evidence under the general issue.

And the bill passed—yeas 43, nays none, as follows:

YEAS—Messrs. Kilbourn, Sp'r, Durant, Morgan, Rasin, Medders, Briscoe, Parran, Burgess, Ford, Denison, Renshaw, Chaplain, Long, Lawson, Maxwell, Wotten, Landing, Dennis of Wor., Routzahn, Johnson, Naill, Straughn, Goldsborough, Warfield, Brune, Winans, Pitts, Harrison, Thomas, Wallis, Sangston, Morfit, Scott, Wilson of Har., Bayless, Coudy, Eakle, Brining, Stake, Barnard, Roop, Mills, Brown,—43.

May 8—Under the suspension of the rules, the bill passed—yeas 17, nays 2, (Kimmel and Stone.)

June 20—Mr. MILLS, from the Military Committee, reported a bill entitled an act to repeal sections 41, 42, 43, 46, 47, 48, and 112, of article LXIII, of the Code of Public General Laws, and sections 741, 742, 745, of article IV, of the Code of Local Laws of this State, in relation to the uniformed and ununiformed militia and volunteer force in the several counties of this State, and in the city of Baltimore and the reclamation, custody, control, and redelivery of arms heretofore delivered to the officers and men under them; and to add to the said article LXV of the Code of Public General Laws a section providing for the prevention and suspension of proceedings upon bonds heretofore given under the laws of this State for the return of such arms; which was agreed to—yeas 40; nays 12.

The nays were Messrs. Medders, Keene, McIntire, Routzahn, Naill, Wilson, M'Coy, Fiery, Stake, McCleary, Roop, Gorsuch—12.

IN SENATE.

June 22—The bill passed—yeas 12, nays none.

PROTEST AGAINST THE WAR, AND RECOGNITION OF REBEL INDEPENDENCE DEMANDED.

IN HOUSE OF DELEGATES.

May 9—Mr. Wallis, from the Committee on Federal Relations, reported these resolutions:

Whereas, in the judgment of the General Assembly of Maryland, the war now waged by the Government of the United States upon the people of the Confederate States is unconstitutional in its origin, purposes and conduct; repugnant to civilization and sound policy; subversive of the free principles upon which the Federal Union was founded, and certain to result in the hopeless and bloody overthrow of our existing institutions; and whereas, the people of Maryland, while recognizing the obligations of their State, as a member of the Union, to submit in good faith to the exercise of all the legal and constitutional powers of the General Government, and join as one man in fighting its authorized battles, do reverence nevertheless, the great American principle of self-government and sympathize deeply with their Southern brethren in the noble and manly determination to uphold and defend the same; and whereas not merely on their own account, turn away from their own soil the calamities of civil war, but for the blessed sake of humanity, and to arrest the wanton shedding of fraternal blood, in a miserable contest which can bring nothing with it but sorrow, shame, and desolation, the people of Maryland are enlisted with their whole hearts, upon the side of reconciliation and peace; Now therefore, it is hereby

Resolved by the General Assembly of Maryland, That the State of Maryland owes it to her own self-respect and her respect for the Constitution, not less than to her deepest and most honorable sympathies, to register this, her solemn protest, against the war which the Federal Government has declared upon the Confederate States of the South, and our sister and neighbor Virginia, and to announce her resolute determination to have no part or lot, directly or indirectly, in its prosecution.

2. That the State of Maryland earnestly and anxiously desires the restoration of peace between the belligerent sections of the country; and the President, authorities and people of the Confederate States having over and over officially and unofficially, declared, that they seek only peace and self-defence and to be let alone, and that they are willing to throw down the sword, the instant the sword now drawn against them shall be sheathed, the Senators and Delegates of Maryland do fervently beseech and implore the President of the United States, to accept the olive branch which is thus held out to him, and in the name of God and of humanity, to cease this unholy and most wretched and unprofitable strife, at least until the assembling of the Congress at Washington shall have given time for the prevalence of cooler and better counsels.

3. That the State of Maryland desires the peaceful and immediate recognition of the independence of the Confederate States, and hereby gives her cordial consent thereunto as a member of the Union—entertaining the profound conviction that the willing return of the Southern people to their former federal relations is a thing beyond hope, and that the attempt to coerce them will only add slaughter and hate to impossibility.

4. That the present military occupation of Maryland, being for purposes which, in the opinion of this Legislature, are in flagrant violation of the Constitution, the General Assembly of the State, in the name of her people, does hereby protest against the same, against the arbitrary restrictions and illegalities with which it is attended, calling upon all good citizens at the same time, in the most earnest and authoritative manner, to abstain from all violent and unlawful interference of every sort, with the troops in transit through our territory or quartered among us, and patiently and peacefully to leave to time and reason the ultimate and certain re-establishment and vindication of the right.

5. That under existing circumstances it is inexpedient to call a Sovereign Convention of the State at this time, or to take any measures for the immediate organization for arming of the militia.

6. That when the Legislature adjourn, it adjourn to meet at ——, on the —— day of —— next.

The report was accepted, and 10,000 copies ordered to be printed—yeas 50, nays 11

May 10—They were considered, and Mr. McCleary moved these as a substitute:

Whereas, it is right and proper, that the General Assembly of Maryland should give such expression of opinion as will call forth the united voice of the whole people of Maryland in the present emergency; and the border States, with the exception of Maryland, have already, through their legislatures or conventions, defined their positions and course of action: Therefore be it

Resolved by the General Assembly of Maryland, The present position of Maryland in the Union, is that of strict neutrality, and will remain unchanged so long as Washington continues the seat of Government: *Provided*, the United States affords ample protection to slaves and other property.

Resolved, That when the seat of the United States Government ceases to be at Washington, and a division of the country takes place, the people shall have the free right and choice of deciding which section they will be attached to, by a free expression and decision of the popular will at the ballot-box.

Which were rejected—yeas 13, nays 43, as follows:

Yeas—Messrs. Medders, Lawson, Keene, Miller, Jonathan Routzahn, Salmon, Naill, Joshua Wilson of Har'd, Bayless, McCoy, Stake, David W. McCleary, Gorsuch—13.

Nays—Messrs. Kilbourn, Sp'r., Morgan, Rasin, Briscoe, Compton, Ford, Jacobs, Landing, Dennis of Wor'r, Kessler, Claggett, Johnson, Sangston, Morfit, Scott, Coudy, Eakle, Brining, Denison, Quinlan, Renshaw, Chaplain, Holland, Bryan, Jones of P. G's, Legg, Starkey, Goldsborough, Warfield, Brune, Winans, Pitts, Harrison, Thomas, Wallis, Fiery, Griffith, Harding, Gordon, Barnard, Mills, Turner, Brown—43.

The blank in the resolutions reported, was then filled by "Frederick," and "Tuesday, the 4th day of June, at one o'clock, p. m."

And the resolutions were then adopted—yeas 45, nays 12, as follows:

Yeas—Messrs. Kilbourn, *Speaker*, Morgan, Rasin, Briscoe, Compton, Ford, Worthington, Denison, Quinlan, Renshaw, Jones of Talbot, Chaplain, Holland, Bryan, Wootten, Legg, Jones of Prince Georges, Starkey, Jacobs, Landing, Dennis of Worcester, Kessler, Johnson, Salmon, Goldsborough, Warfield, Brune, Winans, Pitts, Harrison, Thomas, Wallis, Sangston, Morfit, Scott, Coudy, Eakle, Brining, Griffith, Harding, Gordon, Barnard, Mills, Turner, Brown—45.

Nays—Messrs. Medders, Lawson, Keene, Routzahn, Nail, Wilson of Harford, Bayless, McCoy, Fiery, Stake, McCleary, Gorsuch—12.

IN SENATE.

May 14—The committee recommended certain amendments; when these votes were taken:

The first resolution was adopted—yeas 11, nays 3, as follows:

Yeas—Messrs. John B. Brooke, *President*, Wash. Duvall, Thos. Franklin, J. F. Gardiner, John J. Heckart, Andrew A. Lynch, Thomas J. McKaig, Teagle Townsend, John S. Watkins, Franklin Whitaker, Coleman Yellott—11.

Nays—Messrs. H. H. Goldsborough, Anthony Kimmel, John G. Stone—3.

The *second* resolution was adopted—yeas 14, (being all the above-named.)

The *fifth* resolution received all the above votes, and the *third* and *fourth* passed—yeas 11, nays 3, as the *first*.

The amendment of the committee, substituting the following for the sixth:

That a committee be appointed to consist of four members of the Senate and four members of the House of Delegates, four of which committee, (to be selected of themselves,) shall as ea.ly as possible, wait on the President of the United States at Washington, and the other four of said committee shall wait on the President of the Southern Confederacy, for the purpose of laying the foregoing resolutions before them, and that said committee be and is hereby especially instructed to obtain, if possible, a general cessation of hostilities, now impending, until the meeting of Congress in July next, in order that said body may, if possible, arrange for an adjustment of existing troubles by means of negotiation, rather than the sword.

Resolved, That said committee consist of Messrs. Brooke, Yellott, McKaig, and Lynch, of the Senate, and Messrs. ——, ——, —— and ——, of the House of Delegates.

Resolved, That said committee be requested to report, if practicable, to the General Assembly, on the 5th day of June next.

Passed—yeas 11, nays 3, as before; and the resolutions, as amended, were then adopted by the same vote.

May 14—The House filled the blanks with the names of Harding, Morgan, Compton, and Goldsborough, and passed the resolution—yeas 24, nays 18, as follows:

YEAS—Messrs. Kilbourn, (Speaker,) Morgan, Ford, Quinlan, Renshaw, Jones of Talbot, Chaplain, Jones of P. G., Starkey, Kessler, Straughn, Goldsborough, Warfield, Brune, Winans, Pitts, Harrison, Thomas, Wallis, Sangston, Scott, Griffith, Harding, Turner—24.

NAYS—Messrs. Welch, Worthington, Denison, Keene, Holland, Maxwell, Landing, Claggett, Routzahn, Johnson, Salmon, Morfit, Fiery, Barnard, McCleary, Roop, Mills, Brown—18.

RECOGNITION AGAIN DEMANDED.

June 10—The House passed resolutions previously offered by Mr. Chaplain, after having amended them to read as follows:

Resolved by the General Assembly of Maryland, That the Representatives of the State of Maryland in the Congress of the United States at the approaching extra session of that legislative body be, and they are hereby, earnestly desired and requested to urge and vote for an immediate recognition of the independence of the government of the Confederate States of America.

Resolved, That the Speaker of the House of Delegates and the President of the Senate, together, forward to Hon. James Alfred Pearce and Hon. Anthony Kennedy, the Representatives of the sovereign State of Maryland in the Senate of the United States, a copy of the report of the Committee on Federal Relations and the accompanying resolutions, together with these resolutions.

Yeas 31, nays 22, as follows:

YEAS—Messrs. Kilbourn, *Speaker*, Durant, Morgan, Rasin, Welch, Briscoe, Parran, Compton, Jones of Talbot, Chaplain, Holland, Maxwell, Bryan, Wootten, Legg, Starkey, Landing, Kessler, Goldsborough, Warfield, Brune, Winans, Harrison, Thomas, Wallis, Sangston, Morfit, Scott, Griffith, Gordon, Mills—31.

NAYS—Messrs. Medders, Ford, Denison, Quinlan, Renshaw, Dennis of Somerset, Stanford, Lawson, McIntire, Miller, Routzahn, Johnson, Salmon, Naill, Straughn, Wilson, Bayless, McCoy, Fiery, Brining, McCleary, Gorsuch—22.

IN SENATE.

June 22—The Senate passed these resolutions—yeas 9, nays 3, as follows:

YEAS—Messrs. Brooke, President, Blakistone, Dashiell, Franklin, Gardiner, McKaig, Townsend, Watkins, Whitaker—9.

NAYS—Messrs. Duvall, Heckart, Lynch—3.

THE "PUBLIC SAFETY" BILL.

IN SENATE.

May 2—It was taken up—yeas 14, nays 8, as follows:

YEAS—Messrs. Brooke, President; Blackistone, Duvall, Dashiell, Franklin, Grahame, Gardiner, Heckart, Lynch, McKaig, Townsend, Watkins, Whitaker, Yellott—14.

NAYS—Messrs. Bradley, Goldsborough of Talbot, Goldsborough of Dorchester, Kimmel, Miles, Nuttle, Smith, Stone—8.

Mr. Goldsborough of Talbot moved to amend so as to give the power of appointment of the commissioners provided for to the Governor, one from each of the gubernatorial districts; rejected—yeas 6, nays 12.

A motion to recommit was lost—yeas 10, nays 12.

Motions to adjourn, recommit, change the names of the commissioners, were made and lost.

May 3—Mr. Goldsborough of Talbot moved to give the people, on the 13th of June, the election of three commissioners, one from each gubernatorial district, which was lost—yeas 8, nays 13, as follows:

YEAS—Messrs. Bradley, Grahame, Goldsborough of Talbot, Goldsborough of Dorchester, Kimmel, Nuttle, Smith, Stone—8.

NAYS—Messrs. Brooke, President; Blackistone, Duvall, Dashiell, Franklin, Gardiner, Heckart, Lynch, Miles, Townsend, Watkins, Whitaker, Yellott—13.

A like motion, for six commissioners, was lost—yeas 8, nays 12.

On the section respecting disbursements of money, Mr. Goldsborough of Talbot moved this proviso:

Provided, That the same shall not extend to the exercise of any powers for the disbursement of any moneys that may be hereafter appropriated for the arming of the military forces of this State and for the formation of any alliance offensive or defensive, with any other State in this Confederacy.

Which was rejected—yeas 8, nays 12, as follows:

YEAS—Messrs. Bradley, Grahame, Goldsborough of Talbot Kimmel, Miles, Nuttle, Smith, Stone—8.

NAYS—Messrs. Brooke, President; Blackistone, Duvall, Dashiell, Franklin, Gardiner, Heckart, Lynch, Townsend, Watkins, Whitaker, Yellott—12.

Mr. STONE offered an additional section:

That no member of the board shall act as such, until he has taken the same oath as is now administered to the members of the Legislature.

Which was rejected—yeas 7, nays 12, as follows:

YEAS—Messrs. Bradley, Grahame, Goldsborough of Talbot, Kimmel, Yuttle, Smith, Stone—7.

NAYS—Messrs. Brooke, President; Blackistone, Duvall, Dashiell, Franklin, Gardiner, Heckart, Lynch, Townsend, Watkins, Whitaker, Yellott—12.

At this stage, and after a most obstinate contest, the bill was abandoned by its friends, and Maryland was spared a bloody baptism.

Votes on Secession Ordinances* in South Carolina, Florida, and Arkansas.

In South Carolina, it passed unanimously:

YEAS—Messrs. James H. Adams, Robert T. Allison, David C. Appleby, Samuel Taylor Atkinson, Lewis Malone Ayer, Jr., R. W. Barnwell, A. I. Barron, Donald Rowe Barton, Thomas W. Beaty, A. W Bethea, E. St. P. Bellinger, Simpson Bobo, Peter P. Bonneau, J. J. Brabham, Alexander H. Brown, C. P. Brown, Jno. Buchanan, A. W. Burnett, William Cain, John Alfred Calhoun, Joseph Caldwell, W. H. Campbell, Meyrick E. Carn, James H. Carlisle, James Parsons Carroll, H. I. Caughman, W. C. Cauthen, Edgar W. Charles, James Chesnut, Jr., Langdon Cheves, Ephraim M. Clark, H. W. Conner, R. L. Crawford, William Curtis, A. T. Darby, Julius A. Dargan, R. J. Davant, Henry Campbell Davis, W. F. DeSaussure, Richard De Treville, Anthony W. Dozier, Perry E. Duncan, Benjamin Faneuil Dunkin, A. Q. Dunovant, R. G. M. Dunovant, Daniel DuPre, W. K. Easley,

* For Vote on Virginia Ordinance, see *note*, page 7; and on Tennessee League, *note*, page 5.

William J. Ellis, Thomas Reese English, Sr., Chesley D. Evans, Simeon Fair, W. Peronneau Finley, Daniel Flud, Alexander M. Forster, B. B. Foster, John E. Frampton, James C. Furman, Jas. M. Gadberry, H. W. Garlington, John C. Geiger, Wm. H. Gist, Thos Worth Glover, E. W. Goodwin, Robert N. Gourdin, T. L. Gourdin, H. D. Green, Maxcy Gregg, William Gregg, William S. Grisham, Andrew J. Hammond, Thomas M. Hanckel, William W. Harlee, James Harrison, Isaac W. Hayne, E. R. Henderson, John H. Honour, William Hopkins, William Hunter, W. Ferguson Hutson, John A. Inglis, John J. Ingram, Stephen Jackson, James Jefferies, John Jenkins, Joseph E. Jenkins, William D. Johnson, Lawrence M. Keitt, Joseph Brevard Kershaw, Benjamin F. Kilgore, John P. Kinnard, John H. Kinsler, John G. Landrum, Benjamin W. Lawton, Andrew F. Lewis, R. C. Logan, William Strother Lyles, Edward McCrady, Henry McIver, John McKee, Alexander McLeod, A. G. Magrath, Gabriel Manigault, John L. Manning, Benjamin Franklin Mauldin, John Maxwell, Alexander Mazyck, John Hugh Means, C. G. Memminger, John Izard Middleton, William Middleton, William Porcher Miles, Thomas W. Moore, Robert Moorman, Matthew P. Moyes, Edward Noble, John N. Nowell, John S. O'Hear, James L. Orr, John S. Palmer, Francis S. Parker, Thomas Chiles Perrin, Joseph Daniel Pope, Francis J. Porcher, John G. Pressley, Paul Quattlebaum, Samuel Rainey, J. P. Reed, R. Barnwell Rhett, George Rhodes, F. D. Richardson, John P. Richardson, D. P. Robinson, W. B. Rowell, B. H. Rutledge, Elias B. Scott, E. M. Seabrook, George W. Seabrook, Benj. E. Sessions, Jno. M. Shingler, W. Pinkney Shingler, Thos Y. Simons, R. F. Simpson, J. S. Sims, Jas. C. Smiley, John Julius Pringle Smith, P. G. Snowden, Albertus Chambers Spain, L. W. Spratt, A. Baxter Springs, Peter Stokes, Robert A. Thompson, Thomas Thomson, John M. Timmons, James Tompkins, John Townsend, Theodore D. Wagner, John J. Wannamaker, David Lewis Wardlaw, Francis Hugh Wardlaw, W. D. Watts, Thomas Weir, J. N. Whitner, John D. Williams, Isaac D. Wilson, J. H. Wilson, William Blackburn Wilson, T. J. Withers, Richard Woods, Henry C. Young, David F. Jamison, *President*—170.

NAYS—None.

In Florida, this was the vote:

YEAS—Mr. President, Judge John C. McGehee, Messrs. Alderman, Allison, Anderson, Baker of Calhoun, Barrington, Beard, Bethel, Chanler, Collier, Coon, Cooper, Daniel, Davis, Dawkins, Devall, Dilworth, Finegan, Folsom, Gary, Gettis, Glazier, Golden, Helvenston, Henry, Hunter, Irwin, Kirksey, Ladd, Lamar, Lamb, Lea of Madison, Leigh of Sumter, Lewis, Love, McGahagin, McLean, McIntosh, McNealy, Mays, Morton, Newmans, Nicholson, Owens, Palmer, Parkhill, Pelot, Pinckney, Sanderson, Saxon, Sever, Spencer, Simpson, Solana, Stephens, Thomas, Tift, Turman, Ward, Wright of Escambia, Wright of Columbia, Yates—62.

NAYS—Messrs. Baker of Jackson, Gregory, Hendricks, McCaskill, Morrison, Rutland, Woodruff—7.

In Arkansas, the Convention adjourned March 21st, until the 19th of August, 1861, (see page 4,) but its President, David Walker, as authorized in an exigency in his opinion requiring it, on the 20th of April issued a Proclamation convening it on the 6th of May—the reason given being that "preparations are being made for a war between the citizens of the free and the slave States."

1861, May 6—The question being on an ordinance of secession, Mr. A. W. Dinsmore offered this amendment:

And that the above ordinance be submitted to the citizens of the State of Arkansas, for their acceptance or rejection, by a writ of election, issued by the president of this Convention, to be held on the 1st Monday of June next.

On motion of J. Henry Patterson, this amendment was tabled—yeas 55, nays 15, as follows:

YEAS—Messrs. Alexander Adams, Charles W. Adams, Thomas F. Austin, Milton D. Baber, Felix I. Batson, Thomas H. Bradley, James W. Bush, H. Bussey, A. H. Carrigan, Alexander M. Clingman, James W. Crenshaw, Wiley P. Cryer, Jesse N. Cypert, Samuel W. Cochran, James S. Dollarhide, Philip H. Echols, H. Flanagin, William W. Floyd, Urban E. Fort, Robert T. Fuller, R. K. Garland, A. H. Garland, Josiah Gould, W. P. Grace, Thomas B. Hanly, Marcus L. Hawkins, Benjamin F. Hawkins, L. D. Hill, Isaac Hilliard, Burr H. Hobbs, A. W. Hobson, J. P. Johnson, M. Shelby Kennard, Felix R. Lanier, G. W. Laughinghouse, W. W. Mansfield, William M. Mayo, J. Henry Patterson, Archibald Ray, J. A. Rhodes, Samuel Robinson, J. N. Shelton, W. F. Slemons, J. M. Smith, George P. Smoote, W. H. Spivey, J. Stillwell, William Stout, William V. Tatum, James L. Totten, Benjamin C. Totten, E. T. Walke, I. C. Wallace, W. W. Watkins, James Yell—55.

NAYS—H. H. Bolinger, John Campbell, F. W. Desha, A. W. Dinsmore, Isaiah Dodson, W. M. Fishback, Samuel L. Griffith, T. M. Gunter, Samuel Kelley, I. Murphy, John P. A. Parks, S. J. Stallings, Hugh F. Thomason, Jesse Turner, David Walker, *President*—15.

The Ordinance of Secession then passed—yeas 65, nays 5, as follows:

YEAS—Messrs. Alexander Adams, Charles W. Adams, Austin, Baber, Batson, Bradley, Bush, Bussey, Carrigan, Clingman, Crenshaw, Cryer, Cypert, Cochran, Desha, Dinsmore, Dodson, Dollarhide, Echols, Fishback, Flanagin, Floyd, Fort, Fuller, R. K. Garland, A. H. Garland, Gould, Grace, Griffith, Hanly, Marcus L. Hawkins, Benjamin F. Hawkins, Hill, Hilliard, Hobbs, Hobson, Johnson, Kennard, Lanier, Laughinghouse, Mansfield, Mayo, Parks, J. Henry Patterson, Ray, Rhodes, Robinson, Shelton, Slemons, Smith, Smoote, Spivey, Stallings, Stillwell, Stout, Tatum, Thomason, James L. Totten, Benjamin C. Totten, Turner, E. T. Walker, Wallace, Watkins, Yell, and David Walker, *President*—65.

NAYS—Messrs. Bolinger, Campbell, Gunter, Kelley, Murphy—5.

On the President urging unanimity, Messrs. Bolinger and Campbell changed their votes to aye, with the explanation "that they voted against the ordinance as pledged to the people, but to secure unanimity changed, at the same time denying the right of secession;" Messrs. Kelley and Gunter changed to aye, with the explanation that they "were in favor of revolution, but ignored the right of secession." Mr. Fishback explained his vote. As declared, the yeas were 69, nay 1—Mr. Isaac Murphy, now Governor of the free State, who also refused to sign the ordinance after its passage. The names of H. Jackson, Joseph Jester, and H. W. Williams are not appended, though they are among the yeas. Craighead county was not represented. J. H. Stirman was permitted to affix his name, May 14.

Elias C. Boudinot was Secretary of the Convention, with John P. Jones as assistant. Benjamin F. Arthur was clerk of the South Carolina Convention, and Albert R. Lamar secretary of the Georgia.

REBEL ITEMS.

The Legislature of Georgia and Mississippi have passed resolutions disapproving, as unconstitutional, the bill suspending the privilege of the writ of *habeas corpus*, and demanding its repeal.

Alabama is reported to have furnished 40,000 men to the army; Florida, 4,000; Georgia, 54,000; Louisiana, 36,000; Mississippi, 40,000; North Carolina, 25,000; South Carolina, 25,000; Texas, 29,000; Tennessee, 34,000; Virginia, 103,000; Arkansas, 28,000; Kentucky, 20,000; Maryland, 20,000; Missouri, 35,000; total, 501,000. The estimate of Maryland must be excessive.

THE REBEL ADMINISTRATION.

The "Provisional."

February 18, 1861, to February 18, 1862.

Those formerly members of the Congress of the United States are *italicized.*

President—Jefferson Davis, of Mississippi.
Vice President—Alexander H. Stephens, of Georgia.

THE CABINET.

Secretary of State—Robert Toombs, of Georgia, from February 21 to July 30; resigned, and succeeded by *Robert M. T. Hunter*, of Virginia.
Secretary of the Treasury—Charles G. Memminger, of South Carolina, from February 21.
Secretary of War—Leroy Pope Walker, of Alabama, from February 21 to September 10; resigned, and succeeded by *Judah P. Benjamin*, of Louisiana.
Secretary of the Navy—Stephen R. Mallory, of Florida, from March 4.
Attorney General—Judah P. Benjamin, of Louisiana, from February 21 to September; resigned, and succeeded by Thomas H. Watts, of Alabama.
Postmaster General—John H. Reagan, of Texas, from March 6, Henry J. Ellet, of Mississippi, first appointed, having declined.

—

MEMORANDUM.

Secretary of War—It was reported that the position was offered to General Braxton Bragg, of Louisiana, but declined, after Mr. Walker's resignation.
Secretary of the Navy—Also, that John Perkins, Jr., of Louisiana, was first appointed, but declined.
Mr. Toombs was appointed a brigadier general in July, 1861, and Mr. Walker August 20, 1861.
The President and Vice President were elected by the Congress, February 9, 1861, receiving the unanimous vote of the six States then composing the Confederacy.

THE CONGRESS.

The Deputies who organized the Confederacy at Montgomery remained in office one year, the "permanent" Government having been instituted in February, 1862.

There were four sessions of that body:

The *first* at Montgomery, from February 4 to March 16, 1861.
The *second* at Montgomery, from May 6 to May 21, 1861.
The *third* at Richmond, from July 20 to September 2, 1861.
The *fourth* at Richmond, from November 18, 1861, to February 17, 1862.

—

The following are the names of members:

President—Howell Cobb, of Georgia.
*Alabama**—Robert H. Smith, Richard Wilde Walker, Colin J. McRae, John Gill Shorter, William P. Chilton, Stephen F. Hale, David P. Lewis, Thomas Fearn, *Jabez L. M. Curry.*
Arkansas—Robert W. Johnson, Albert Rust*, Augustus H. Garland, William W. Watkins, Hugh F. Thomasson.
Florida—Jackson Morton, J. Patton Anderson*, James B. Owens.
Georgia—Robert Toombs, Howell Cobb*, Francis S. Bartow, *Martin J. Crawford, Eugenius A. Nisbet*, Benjamin H. Hill, *Augustus R. Wright*, Thomas R. R. Cobb, Augustus H. Kenan, *Alexander H. Stephens.*
Kentucky—Henry C. Burnett*, John Thomas, Theo. L. Burnett, S. H. Ford, Thos. B. Johnson, Geo. W. Ewing, D. V. White, *J. M. Elliott*, M. S. B. Munroe, G. B. Hodges.
Louisiana—John Perkins, Jr., A. de Clouet, *Charles M. Conrad*, Duncan F. Kenner, Edward Sparrow, Henry Marshal.
Mississippi—Wiley P. Harris, Walter Brooke, W. S. Wilson, A. M. Clayton, *William S. Barry*, James T. Harrison, J. A. P. Campbell.
*Missouri**—William H. Cook, Thomas A. Harris, Caspar W. Bell, A. H. Conrow, George G. Vest, Thomas W. Freeman, Samuel Hyer.
*North Carolina**—George Davis, William W. Avery, *William N. H. Smith, Thomas Ruffin*, Thomas D. McDowell, *Abram W. Venable*, John M. Morehead, *Robert C. Puryear, Burton Craige*, Andrew J. Davidson.
South Carolina—R. Barnwell Rhett, Sr.*, Robert W. Barnwell, *Lawrence M. Keitt, James Chesnut, Jr.*, Charles G. Memminger, *William Porcher Miles*, Thomas J. Withers, *William W. Boyce.*
*Tennessee**—W. H. DeWitt, Robert L. Caruthers, *James H. Thomas*, Thomas M. Jones, John F. House, *John D. C. Atkins*, David M. Currin.
Texas—Louis T. Wigfall, John H Reagan, John Hemphill*, T. N. Waul, William B. Ochiltree, W. S. Oldham, John Gregg.
Virginia—James A. Seddon, William Ballard Preston, Robert M. T. Hunter, John Tyler, Sr.*, William H. Macfarland, *Roger A. Pryor, Thomas S. Bocock, William C. Rives*, Robert E. Scott, *James M. Mason*, J. W. Brockenbrough, Charles W. Russell, Robert Johnson, Waller R. Staples, Walter Preston.

—

MEMORANDUM.

J. Johnson Hooper, of Alabama, was Secretary of the Congress.
Alabama—David P. Lewis and Thomas Fearn, elected Deputies, were succeeded during the year by H. C. Jones and Nicholas Davis, Jr. Mr. Shorter was elected Governor in November, 1861. Mr. McRae was afterwards appointed a brigadier general, and is now the cotton loan agent in Paris. Mr. Yancey was nominated for, but declined election to, the Provisional Congress, and was sent to Europe to negotiate for "Confederate" recognition.
Arkansas—Admitted, at second session, in May, 1861.
Florida—J. Patton Anderson resigned early in the term, and was succeeded by G. T. Ward.
Georgia—Mr. Toombs resigned, February 21, to become Provisional Secretary of State; in July was appointed a brigadier general. Mr. Howell Cobb subsequently became brigadier general, and now is a major general. Mr. Crawford subsequently became a cavalry colonel in the army, and was once a prisoner. Mr. Thomas R. R. Cobb became colonel of the Georgia Legion late in 1861 or early in 1862, and was killed at the first Fredericksburg battle, December 13, 1862. Mr. Stephens accepted the Vice Presidency, February 11, 1861.
Kentucky—Admitted, at fourth session, in December, 1861.
Missouri—Admitted, at fourth session, in December, 1861;

* See memorandum at the close of the list.

the Delegates were self-elected, and held over the first Congress. Mr. Hyer is reported to have taken the oath of allegiance to the Government of the United States.

North Carolina—These Delegates were elected by the Convention, June 18, 1861. Mr. Ruffin afterwards became a cavalry colonel, and died in the spring of 1864, a prisoner in Alexandria, Va., of wounds received in battle.

South Carolina—Mr. Memminger became Secretary of the Treasury, February 21, 1861. Mr. Keitt died in Richmond, June 2, 1864, of wounds received May 31 in battle, colonel of the 20th South Carolina regiment. Mr. Chesnut served as aid to Beauregard at the bombardment of Sumter; and Mr. Miles as an aid at the battle of Bull Run.

Tennessee—Admitted, at second session, in May, 1861; members took their seats at the third session.

Texas—Admitted, at first session, March 2, 1861. Mr. Reagan resigned to become Postmaster General, March 6, 1861. Mr. Wigfall was appointed a brigadier general, October 29, 1861, but did not yield his seat in the "Provisional" or the "Permanent" Congress. Mr. Hemphill died January 4, 1862.

Virginia—Admitted, at second session, May 7, 1861, when Messrs. Brockenbrough and Staples took their seats; the others were sworn at the third session, at Richmond, July 20, 1861. Mr. Hunter became Secretary of State, July 30, and resigned. Mr. Mason resigned in the fall of 1861 to go to England, and November 19 the State Convention elected *Alexander R. Boteler* to succeed him.

The "Permanent" Administration.

FROM FEBRUARY 19, 1862.

President—Jefferson Davis, of Mississippi.
Vice President—Alexander H. Stephens, of Georgia.

THE CABINET.

CONFIRMED, MARCH 23, 1862.

Secretary of State—Judah P. Benjamin, of Louisiana.
Secretary of the Treasury—Charles G. Memminger, of South Carolina; resigned, in June, 1864, and succeeded by George A. Trenholm, of South Carolina.
Secretary of War—George W. Randolph, of Virginia; resigned, and succeeded by *James A. Seddon*, of Virginia.
Secretary of the Navy—Stephen R. Mallory, of Florida.
Attorney General—Thomas H. Watts, of Alabama; resigned on election as Governor of Alabama, in November, 1863, and succeeded by George Davis, of North Carolina.
Postmaster General—John H. Reagan, of Texas.

MEMORANDUM.

Mr. Randolph was appointed a colonel of Virginia troops by Governor Letcher, in the fall of 1861; tendered his resignation but withdrew it, and in November of that year appointed a brigadier general, and assigned to the command of the district between Suffolk, in Nansemond, and Weldon, on the Roanoke; he was a candidate for Congress in November, 1861, but withdrew on the morning of the election.

Mr. Memminger was born in Wirtemberg, Germany, January 7, 1803; was brought to this country when nine years old; was early left an orphan; adopted by Governor Thomas Bennett, and educated in South Carolina college, graduating in 1820; began the practice of law in 1825; in 1832–33 he was against nullification; for nearly twenty years he was at the head of the Finance Committee of the lower house of the Legislature of South Carolina, retiring in 1852; he filled other State offices.

THE FIRST CONGRESS.

FEBRUARY, 1862, TO FEBRUARY, 1864.

It held four sessions:

The *first* from February 18 to April 21, 1862.
The *second* from August 12 to October 13, 1862.
The *third* from January 12, 1863, to May —, 1863.
The *fourth* from December 7, 1863, to February 18, 1864.

SENATORS.

Alabama—William L. Yancey, Clement C. Clay, Jr.*
Arkansas—Robert W. Johnson*, Charles B. Mitchel.
Florida—James M. Baker, *Augustus E. Maxwell.*
*Georgia**—Benjamin H. Hill, *Robert Toombs.*
Kentucky—Henry C. Burnett, William E. Simms.
Louisiana—Edward Sparrow, Thomas J. Semmes.
Mississippi—Albert G. Brown*, James Phelan.
Missouri—John B. Clark, Robert L. Y. Peyton.
*North Carolina**—George Davis, William T. Dortch.
South Carolina—Robert W. Barnwell, *James L. Orr.*
*Tennessee**—Landon C. Haynes, Gustavus A. Henry.
Virginia—Robert M. T. Hunter, William Ballard Preston.*
Texas—Louis T. Wigfall, William S. Oldham.

* See memorandum at the end of the list.

MEMORANDUM.

Jefferson Davis was inaugurated as "Permanent" President of the "Confederate" States, February 22, 1862, in Richmond.

On the first day of the session, Vice President Stephens presiding, Robert M. T. Hunter, of Virginia, was elected President *pro tempore;* James H. Nash, of South Carolina, Secretary; and James Page, of North Carolina, Doorkeeper.

Alabama—Mr. Yancey died, and Robert Jemison was elected, August 22, 1863, to the vacancy.

Arkansas—Mr. Mitchel had been elected, shortly before secession, to the United States Senate for six years, from March 4, 1861.

Georgia—Mr. Toombs having accepted a brigadier's commission did not take his seat, and he was succeeded, March, 1862, by Dr. John W. Lewis, appointed by Governor Brown, and, December, 1862, by *Herschel V. Johnson*, elected by the Legislature.

Mississippi—Mr. Brown, when elected, was captain of a company in the 17th Mississippi volunteers. Mr. Walter Brooke was at first announced elected over Mr. Phelan, but the latter appeared and was qualified at the first session.

North Carolina—Mr. Davis, when he resigned to become Attorney General, was succeeded by *William A. Graham.*

Tennessee—Mr. Henry, early in 1862, was A. A. G. on General Pillow's staff.

Virginia—Mr. Preston was succeeded, January 28, 1863, by Allen T. Caperton.

REPRESENTATIVES.

Speaker—Thomas S. Bocock, of Virginia.
Alabama—Thomas J. Foster, *William R. Smith*, John P. Ralls, *Jabez L. M. Curry, Francis S. Lyon*, William P. Chilton, *David Clopton, James L. Pugh*, Edward S. Dargan—9.
*Arkansas**—Felix I. Batson, Grandison D. Royston, Augustus H. Garland, Thomas B. Hanley—4.
Florida—James B. Dawkins, Robert B. Hilton—2.
Georgia—Julien Hartridge, C. J. Munnerlyn, Hines Holt, Augustus H. Kenan, Daniel W. Lewis, William W. Clark, *Robert P. Trippe, Lucius J. Gartrell*, Hardy Strickland, *Augustus R. Wright*—10.
Kentucky†*—Willie B. Machen, John W. Crockett, Henry E. Read, George W. Ewing, *James S. Chrisman*, Theodore L. Burnett, H. W. Bruce, G. B. Hodge, Ely M. Bruce, James W. Moore, Robert J. Breckinridge, Jr., *John M. Elliott*—12.
Louisiana—Charles J. Villere, *Charles M. Conrad*, Duncan F. Kenner, Lucius J. Dupre, Henry Marshall, *John Perkins, Jr.*—6.
*Mississippi**—J. W. Clapp, *Reuben Davis*, Israel Welsh,

* See memorandum at the end of the list.

† Members sworn August 18, 1862. The Provisional Legislature of Kentucky thus districted the State:

First District—Fulton, Hickman, McCracken, Graves, Calloway, Marshall, Livingston, Lyon, Caldwell, Trigg, Ballard.
Second District—Union, Webster, Hopkins, Christian, Todd, Henderson, Daviess, Muhlenburgh, Crittenden.
Third District—Hancock, Ohio, Grayson, Breckinridge, Meade, Hardin, Larue, Butler, Hart.
Fourth District—Logan, Simpson, Allen, Monroe, Barren, Edmondson, Warren, Metcalfe.
Fifth District—Cumberland, Clinton, Wayne, Pulaski, Casey, Lincoln, Taylor, Green, Adair, Russell.
Sixth District—Spencer, Bullitt, Nelson, Washington, Marion, Mercer, Boyle, Garrard, Anderson.
Seventh District—Jefferson, Shelby, Oldham.
Eighth District—Henry, Trimble, Carroll, Boone, Gallatin, Grant, Kenton, Campbell.
Ninth District—Pendleton, Bracken, Nicholas, Harrison, Bourbon, Fleming, Mason.
Tenth District—Bath, Lewis, Greenup, Boyd, Carter, Lawrence, Montgomery, Powell, Morgan, Rowan, Wolfe, Estill, Magoffin.
Eleventh District—Franklin, Woodford, Jessamine, Fayette, Madison, Clarke, Owen, Scott.
Twelfth District—Rockcastle, Knox, Harlan, Laurel, Whitley, Clay, Perry, Owsley, Letcher, Breathitt, Floyd, Pike, Johnson, Jackson.

Henry C. Chambers, *Otho R. Singleton*, Ethelbert Barksdale, *John J. McRae*—7.

Missouri—Thomas A. Harris, Casper W. Bell, A. H. Conrow, George G. Vest, Thomas W. Freeman, William H. Cook—6.

North Carolina—*W. N. H. Smith*, Robert R. Bridgers, Owen R. Kenan, Thomas D. McDowell, A. H. Arrington, J. B. McLean, *Thomas S. Ashe*, William Lander, Burgess S. Gaither, A. J. Davidson—10.

*South Carolina**—*John McQueen*, *William Porcher Miles*, *Milledge L. Benham*, William D. Simpson, James Farrow, *William W. Boyce*—6.

*Tennessee**—Joseph B. Heiskell, William G. Swan, William B. Tibbs, E. L. Gardenhire, *Henry S. Foote*, *Meredith P. Gentry*, *George W. Jones*, Thomas Menees, *John D. C. Atkins*, *John V. Wright*, David M. Currin—11.

*Texas**—*John A. Wilcox*, Clark C. Herbert, Peter W. Gray, Frank B. Sexton, Malcolm D. Graham, William B. Wright—6.

*Virginia**—*Muscoe R. H. Garnett*, John R. Chambliss, James Lyons, *Roger A. Pryor*, *Thomas S. Bocock*, John Goode, Jr., James P. Holcombe, *Dan'l C. De Jarnette*, *William Smith*, *Alexander R. Boteler*, John B. Baldwin, Waller R. Staples, Walter Preston, *Albert G. Jenkins*, Robert Johnston, Charles W. Russell—16.

October 9, 1862, at the second session, Elias C. Boudinot was admitted a delegate from the Cherokee nation.

MEMORANDUM.

Emmet Dixon, of Georgia, was elected Clerk of the House, and R. H. Wynn, of Alabama, Doorkeeper.

Arkansas—Mr. Garland's seat was contested by Jilson P. Johnson.

Kentucky—Mr. Hodges was not sworn until August 16, 1862.

Mississippi—Mr. Davis resigned, and was succeeded by William D. Holder.

South Carolina—Mr. Bonham was elected Governor in January, 1863, and was succeeded by Lewis M. Ayer.

Tennessee—Mr. Currin died during the Congress, after his election to the second Congress.

Texas—Mr. Wilcox died during the Congress, after his election to the second Congress.

Virginia—Mr. Garnett died, January 12, 1864. Mr. Pryor was appointed a brigadier general in the fall of 1862, and was succeeded by Charles F. Collier. Mr. Smith accepted a colonel's commission, was succeeded by David Funsten, and was elected Governor in 1863. Mr. Baldwin was appointed a colonel of Virginia troops in the fall of 1861, by Governor Letcher. Mr. Jenkins was appointed brigadier general, and resigned in June or July, 1862; was succeeded by Samuel A. Miller; and died in the summer of 1864, in Southwestern Virginia, of wounds received in battle.

THE SECOND CONGRESS.

FEBRUARY 19, 1864, TO FEBRUARY 18, 1866.

The first session closed June 15; the second began Nov. 7.

SENATORS.

The following are the changes from the first Congress:

Alabama—Richard Wilde Walker, in place of Clement C. Clay, Jr.

Mississippi—J. W. C. Watson, in place of James Phelan.

*Arkansas**—Augustus H. Garland, in place of Dr. Charles B. Mitchel, deceased.

*Missouri**—*Waldo P. Johnson*, in place of Mr. Peyton; and L. M. Louis, in place of Mr. Clark.

MEMORANDUM.

Arkansas—Mr. Garland was elected September 27, receiving, according to the Washington (Ark.) *Telegraph*, on the first ballot, 28 votes, Albert Pike receiving 14, and Alfred B. Greenwood 1. Mr. Garland's vacancy in the House has not yet been filled.

Missouri—L. M. Louis was elected Senator, in the recess between the first and second sessions.

The officers of the Senate are: J. H. Nash, of South Carolina, secretary; E. H. Stevens, of South Carolina, assistant secretary; C. T. Bruen, of Virginia, journal clerk; J. W. Anderson, recording clerk; Lafayette H. Fitzhugh, of Kentucky, sergeant-at-arms; James Page, of North Carolina, doorkeeper.

REPRESENTATIVES.

Speaker—*Thomas S. Bocock*, of Virginia.

Alabama—Thomas J. Foster,* *William R. Smith*,* *Williamson R. W Cobb*,† Marcus H. Cruikshank, *Francis S. Lyon*,* William P. Chilton,* *David Clopton*,* *James L. Pugh*,* J. S. Dickinson—9.

*Arkansas**—Felix I. Batson,* Rufus K. Garland, Augustus H. Garland,* Thomas B. Hanley*—4.

Florida—St. George Rogers, Robert B. Hilton*—2.

Georgia—Julien Hartridge,* William E. Smith, Mark H. Blanford, Clifford Anderson, J. T. Shewmake, J. H. Echols, James M. Smith, H. P. Bell, George N. Lester, Warren Aiken—10.

Kentucky—Willie B. Machen,* George W. Triplett, Henry E. Read,* George W. Ewing,* *James S. Chrisman*,* Theodore L. Burnett,* H. W. Bruce,* *Humphrey Marshall*, Ely M. Bruce,* James W. Moore,* Benjamin F. Bradley, *John M. Elliott**—12.

*Louisiana**—Charles J. Villere,* *Charles M. Conrad*,* Duncan F. Kenner,* Lucius J. Dupre,* B. L. Hodge, *John Perkins, Jr**—6.

Mississippi—John A. Orr, William D. Holder,* Israel Welsh,* Henry C. Chambers,* *Otho R. Singleton*,* Ethelbert Barksdale,* J. T. Lumpkin—7.

*Missouri**—Thomas L. Snead, N. L. Norton, *John B. Clark*, A. H. Conrow,* George G. Vest,* Peter S. Wilkes, R. A. Hatcher—7.

North Carolina—*William N. H. Smith*,* Robert R. Bridgers,* J. T. Leach, Thomas C. Fuller, Josiah Turner, Jr., *John A. Gilmer*, *James M. Leach*, James G. Ramsay, Burgess S. Gaither,* George W. Logan—10.

South Carolina—James M. Witherspoon, *William Porcher Miles*,* Lewis M. Ayer,* William D. Simpson,* James Farrow,* *William W. Boyce**—6.

*Tennessee**—Joseph B. Heiskell,* William G. Swan,* A. S. Colyer, John P. Murray, *Henry S. Foote*,* F. A. Keeble, James McCallum, Thomas Menees,* *John D. C. Atkins*,* *John V. Wright*,* Michael W. Cluskey—11.

*Texas**—Stephen H. Darden, Claiborne C. Herbert,* A. M. Branch, Frank B. Sexton,* J. R. Baylor, S. H. Morgan—6.

Virginia—Robert L. Montague, Robt. H. Whitfield, Williams C. Wickham, Thomas S. Gholson, *Thomas S. Bocock*,* John Goode, Jr.,* *William C. Rives*, *Daniel C. De Jarnette*,* David Funsten,* F. W. M. Holladay, John B. Baldwin,* Waller R. Staples,* *Fayette McMullen*, Samuel A. Miller,* Robert Johnston,* Charles W. Russell*—16.

DELEGATES.

Arizona—M. H. Macwillie.

Cherokee Nation—E. C. Boudinot.

Choctaw Nation—R. M. Jones.

Creek and Seminole Nations—S. B. Callahan.

MEMORANDUM.

Arkansas—Augustus H. Garland between the two sessions was elected a Senator in place of Mr. Mitchel, deceased. His vacancy in the House has not yet been filled.

Louisiana—B. L. Hodge, sitting at the first session, was not a member at the second, and the vacancy has not been filled.

Missouri—Messrs. Snead, Norton and Wilkes were elected during the recess between the two sessions.

Tennessee—Michael W. Cluskey was elected during the recess to Mr. Currin's vacancy.

Texas—Stephen H. Darden was chosen between the two sessions to the vacancy caused by the death of Mr. Wilcox.

The officers of the House are: Albert R. Lamar, of Georgia, clerk; James McDonald, De Louis Dalton, Henry C. Lowring, assistant clerks; R. H. Wynn, of Alabama, doorkeeper.

Those marked thus * were members of the last House.

*** States marked thus * see memorandum at the end of each list.**

†1864, May 3—Mr. Chilton offered this resolution, which was adopted—yeas 60, nays 6:

Whereas, the report is in circulation and has found its way into the public prints impugning the loyalty of the Hon. Williamson R. W. Cobb, member elect of this House from the State of Alabama, and tending to show that he is in complicity with and giving aid and comfort to the enemies of the Confederate States, and therefore unfit to be a representative of a loyal constituency; Therefore,

Resolved, That a committee of five members be appointed by the Speaker to inquire into such reports, and to collect and report upon the testimony bearing upon the loyalty or disloyalty of said member, and report the same to this House, with such recommendation as to its further action in the premises as to said committee shall seem proper; and that Mr. Cobb be notified by the committee, if practicable, of the sitting of the committee, and that said committee have power to send for persons and papers.

Mr. Cobb has since come within our lines, and, at the present session, November 17, was expelled from the House.

NATIONAL POLITICAL CONVENTIONS.

Union National Convention.

This body met at 12 o'clock, noon, on Tuesday, June 7, at Baltimore, in accordance with the call of the National Executive Committee:

The undersigned, who by original appointment, or subsequent designation to fill vacancies, constitute the Executive Committee created by the National Convention held at Chicago on the 16th day of May, 1860, do hereby call upon all qualified voters who desire the unconditional maintenance of the Union, the supremacy of the Constitution, and the complete suppression of the existing rebellion, with the cause thereof, by vigorous war, and all apt and efficient means, to send delegates to a convention to assemble at Baltimore on Tuesday, the 7th day of June, 1864, at 12 o'clock, noon, for the purpose of presenting candidates for the offices of President and Vice President of the United States. Each State having a representation in Congress will be entitled to as many delegates as shall be equal to twice the number of electors to which such State is entitled in the Electoral College of the United States.

EDWIN D. MORGAN, New York, *Chairman.*
CHARLES J. GILMAN, Maine.
E. H. ROLLINS, New Hampshire.
L. BRAINERD, Vermont.
J. Z. GOODRICH, Massachusetts.
THOMAS G. TURNER, Rhode Island.
GIDEON WELLES, Connecticut.
DENNING DUER, New Jersey.
EDWARD McPHERSON, Pennsylvania.
N. B. SMITHERS, Delaware.
J. F. WAGNER, Maryland.
THOMAS SPOONER, Ohio.
H. S. LANE, Indiana.
SAMUEL L. CASEY, Kentucky.
E. PECK, Illinois.
HERBERT M. HOXIE, Iowa.
AUSTIN BLAIR, Michigan.
CARL SHURZ, Wisconsin.
W D. WASHBURN, Minnesota.
CORNELIUS COLE, California.
WM. A. PHILLIPS, Kansas.
O. H. IRISH, Nebraska.
JOS. GERHARDT, District of Columbia.

WASHINGTON, *February* 22, 1864.

The Convention was called to order by the Chairman of the Executive Committee, Senator Morgan, of New York, who said:

MEMBERS OF THE CONVENTION: It is a little more than eight years since it was resolved to form a national party to be conducted upon the principles and policy which had been established and maintained by those illustrious statesmen, George Washington and Thomas Jefferson. A Convention was held in Philadelphia, under the shade of the trees that surrounded the Hall of Independence, and candidates—Fremont and Dayton—were chosen to uphold our cause. But the State of Pennsylvania gave its electoral vote to James Buchanan, and the election of 1856 was lost.

Nothing daunted by defeat, it was immediately determined "to fight on this line," not only "all summer," [applause,] but four summers and four winters; and in 1860 the party banner was again unfurled, with the names of Abraham Lincoln [applause] and Hannibal Hamlin inscribed thereon. This time it was successful, but with success came rebellion; and with rebellion of course came war; and war, terrible civil war, has continued with varying success up to nearly the period when it is necessary, under our Constitution, to prepare for another Presidential election. It is for this highly responsible purpose that you are to-day assembled. It is not my duty nor my purpose to indicate any general course of action for this Convention; but I trust I may be permitted to say that, in view of the dread realities of the past, and of what is passing at this moment—and of the fact that the bones of our soldiers lie bleaching in every State of this Union, and with the knowledge of the further fact that this has all been caused by slavery, the party of which you, gentlemen, are the delegated and honored representatives, will fall short of accomplishing its great mission, unless, among its other resolves, it shall declare for such an amendment of the Constitution as will positively prohibit African slavery in the United States. [Prolonged applause, followed by three cheers.]

In behalf of the National Committee, I now propose for temporary President of this Convention, Robert J. Breckinridge, of Kentucky [applause,] and appoint Governor Randall, of Wisconsin, and Governor King, of New York, as a committee to conduct the President *pro tem.* to the chair.

On being introduced, Dr. Breckinridge, who was most enthusiastically received, said:

GENTLEMEN OF THE CONVENTION: You cannot be more sensible than I am that the part which I have to perform here to-day is merely a matter of form; and acting upon the principles of my whole life, I was inclined, when the suggestion was made to me from various quarters, that it was in the mind of many members of the Convention to confer this distinction upon me, to earnestly decline to accept; because I have never sought honors—I have never sought distinction. I have been a working man, and nothing else. But certain considerations led me to change my mind. [Applause.]

There is a class of men in the country, far too small for the good of the country—those men who merely by their example, by their pen, by their voice, try to do good—and all the more in perilous times—without regard to the reward that may come. It was given to many such men to understand, by the distinction conferred upon one of the humblest of their class, that they were men whom the country would cherish, and who would not be forgotten.

There is another motive relative to yourselves and to the country at large. It is good for you, it is good for every nation and every people, every State and every party, to cherish all generous impulses, to follow all noble instincts; and there are none more noble, none more generous than to purge yourselves of all self-seekers and betrayers, and to confer official distinctions, if it be only in mere forms, upon those who are worthy to be trusted, and ask nothing more. [Applause.]

Now according to my convictions of propriety, having said this, I should say nothing more. [Cries of "go on."]

But it has been intimated to me from many quarters, and in a way which I cannot disregard, that I should disappoint the wishes of my friends, and perhaps the just expectations of the Convention, if I did not as briefly, and yet as precisely as I could, say somewhat upon the great matters which have brought us here. Therefore, in a very few words, and as plainly as I can, I will endeavor to draw your attention to one and another of these great matters in which we are all engaged.

In the first place, nothing can be more plain than the fact that you are here as the representatives of a great nation—voluntary representatives chosen without forms of law, but as really representing the feelings, the principles, and if you choose, the prejudices of the American people, as if it were written in laws and already passed by votes—for the man that you will nominate here for the Presidency of the United States, and ruler of a great people in a great cricis, is just as certain I suppose to become that ruler as anything under heaven is certain before it is done. [Prolonged cheering.] And, moreover, you will allow me to say, though perhaps it is hardly strictly proper that I should—but as far as I know your opinions I suppose it is just as certain now before you utter it whose name you will utter, and which will be responded to from one end to the other of this nation, as it will be after it has been uttered and recorded by your secretary. Does any man doubt that this Convention intends to say that Abraham Lincoln shall be the nominee? [Great applause.] What I wish, however, to call your attention to is the grandeur of the mission upon which you are met, and therefore the dignity and solemnity, earnestness and conscientiousness with which, representing one of the greatest and certainly one of the first people of the world, you ought to discharge these duties. [Applause.]

Now, besides the nomination of President and Vice President, in regard to which second office I will say nothing, because I know there is more or less difference of opinion among you; but besides these nominations, you have other most solemn duties to perform. You have to organize this party thoroughly throughout the United States. You have to put it in whatever form your wisdom will suggest that will unite all your wisdom, energy, and determination to gain the victory which I have already said was in our power. More than that, you have to lay down with clearness and precision the principles on which you intend to carry on this great political contest and prosecute the war which is underneath them, and the glory of the country which lies before us if we succeed. Plainly—not in a double sense—briefly—not in a treatise—with the dignity and precision of a great people to utter, by its representatives, the political principles by which they intend to live, and for the sake of which they are willing to die. So that all men everywhere may understand precisely what we mean, and lay that furrow so deeply and clearly that while every man who is worthy to associate with freemen may see it and pass over it, every man who is unworthy may be either unable to pass it or may be driven far from us. We want none but those who are like us to be with us [Applause.]

Now, among these principles, if you will allow me to say it, the first and most distinct is, that we do not intend to permit this nation to be destroyed. [Applause.] We are a nation—no doubt a peculiar one—a nation formed of States, and no nation except as these States form it. And these States are no States except as they are States in that nation. They had no more right to repudiate the nation than the nation has to repudiate them. None of them had even the shadow of a right to do this, and God helping us, we will vindicate that truth so that it shall never be disputed any more in this world. [Applause.] It is a fearful alternative that is set before us, but there are great compensations for it. Those of you who have attended to this subject know, or ought to know, that from the foundation of the present Government, before and since our present Constitution was formed, there have always been parties that had no faith in our Government. The men that formed it were doubtful of its success, and the men that opposed its formation did not desire its success. And I am bold to say, without detaining you on this subject, that with all the outcry about our violations of the Constitution, this present living generation and this present Union party are more thoroughly devoted to that Constitution than any generation that has ever lived under it. [Applause.] While I say that, and solemnly believe it, and believe it is capable of the strongest proof, I may also add that it is a great error which is being propagated in our land, to say that our national life depends merely upon the sustaining of that Constitution. Our fathers made it, and we love it.

But if it suits us to change it we can do so. [Applause.] And when it suits us to change it we will change it. [Applause.] If it were torn into ten thousand pieces the nation would be as much a nation as it was before the Constitution was made—a nation always that declared its independence as a united people, and lived as a united people until now—a nation independent of all particular institutions under which they lived, and capable of modelling them precisely as their interests require. We ought to have it distinctly understood by friends and enemies that while we love that instrument we will maintain it, and will, with undoubted certainty, put to death friend or foe who undertakes to trample it under foot; yet, beyond a doubt, we will reserve the right to alter it to suit ourselves from time to time and from generation to generation. [Applause.] One more idea on that subject. We have incorporated in that instrument the right of revolution, which gives us, without a doubt, the right to change it. It never existed before the American States, and by the right to change there is no need of rebellion, insurrection, or civil war, except upon a denial of the fundamental principles of all free governments—that the major part must rule; and there is no other method of carrying on society, except that the will of the majority shall be the will of the whole—or that the will of the minority shall be the will of the whole. So that, in one word, to deny the principles I have tried to state is to make a dogmatic assertion that the only form of government that is possible with perfect liberty and acknowledged by God is a pure and absolute despotism. The principles therefore which I am trying to state before you are principles which, if they be not true, freedom is impossible, and no government but one of pure force can exist or ought to endure among men. But the idea which I wished to carry out, as the remedy for these troubles and sorrows, is this: Dreadful as they are, this fearful truth runs through the whole history of mankind, that whatever else may be done to give stability to authority, whatever else may be done to give perpetuity to institutions—however wise, however glorious, practicable, and just may be the philosophy of it—it has been found that the only enduring, the only imperishable cement of all free institutions, has been the blood of traitors. No Government has ever been built upon imperishable foundations which foundations were not laid in the blood of traitors. It is a fearful truth, but we had as well avow it at once, and every blow you strike, and every rebel you kill, every battle you win, dreadful as it is to do it, you are adding, it may be, a year—it may be ten years—it may be a century—it may be ten centuries to the life of the Government and the freedom of your children. [Great applause.]

Now, passing over that idea—passing over many other things which it would be right for me to say, did the time serve and were this the occasion, let me add—you are a Union party. [Applause.] Your origin has been referred to as having occurred eight years ago. In one sense it is true. But you are far older than that. I see before me not only primitive Republicans and primitive Abolitionists, but I see also primitive Democrats and primitive Whigs—primitive Americans, and, if you will allow me to say so, I myself am here, who all my life have been in a party to myself. [Laughter and applause.] As a Union party I will follow you to the ends of the earth and to the gates of death. [Applause.] But as an Abolition party—as a Republican party—as a Whig party—as a Democratic party—as an American party, I will not follow you one foot. [Applause.] But it is true of the mass of the American people, however you may divide and scatter while this war lasts, while the country is in peril, while you call yourselves as you do in the call of the Convention, the Union party—you are for the preservation of the Union and the destruction of this rebellion, root and branch. And in my judgment, one of the greatest errors that has been committed by our administration of the Federal Government, the Chief of which we are about to nominate for another term of office—one of the errors has been to believe that we have succeeded where we have not succeeded, and to act in a manner which is precisely as if we had succeeded, You will not, you cannot, succeed until you have utterly broken up the military power of these people. [Applause.]

I will not detain you upon these incidental points, one of which has been made prominent in the remarks of the excellent Chairman of the National Committee. I do not know that I would be willing to go so far as probably he would. But I cordially agree with him in this—I think, considering what has been done about slavery, taking the thing as it now stands, overlooking altogether, either in the way of condemnation or in the way of approval, any act that has brought us to the point where we are, but believing in my conscience and with all my heart, that what has brought us where we are in the matter of slavery, is the original sin and folly of treason and secession, because you remember that the Chicago Convention itself was understood to say, and I believe it virtually did explicitly say, that they would not touch slavery in the States, leaving it therefore altogether out of the question how we came where we are, on that particular point, we are prepared to go further than the original Republicans themselves were prepared to go. We are prepared to demand not only that the whole territory of the United States shall not be made slave, but that the General Government of the American people shall do one of two things—and it appears to me that there is nothing else that can be done—either to use the whole power of the Government, both the war power and the peace power, to put slavery as nearly as possible back where it was—for, although that would be a fearful state of society, it is better than anarchy; or else to use the whole power of the Government, both of war and peace, and all the practical power that the people of the United States will give them to exterminate and extinguish slavery. [Prolonged applause.]

I have no hesitation in saying for myself that if I were a pro-slavery man, if I believed this institution was an ordinance of God, and was given to man, I would unhesitatingly join those who demand that the Government should be put back where it was. But I am not a pro-slavery man—I never was; I unite myself with those who believe it is contrary to the brightest interests of all men and of all governments, contrary to the spirit of the Christian religion, and incompatible with the natural rights of man. I join myself with those who say away with it forever; [applause;] and I fervently pray God that the day may come when throughout the whole land every man may be as free as you are, and as capable of enjoying regulated liberty. [Prolonged applause.]

I will not detain you any longer. One single word you will allow me to say in behalf of the State from which I come, one of the smallest of the thousands of Israel. We know very well that our eleven votes are of no consequence in the Presidential election. We know very well that in our present unhappy condition, it is by no means certain that we are here to-day representing the party that will cast the majority of the votes in that unhappy State. I know very well that the sentiments which I am uttering will cause me great odium in the State in which I was born, which I love, where the bones of two generations of my ancestors and some of my children are, and where very soon I shall lay my own. I know very well that my colleagues will incur odium if they indorse what I say, and they, too, know it. But we have put our faces toward the way in which we intend to go, and we will go in it to the end. If we are to perish, we will perish in that way. All I have to say to you is, help us if you can; if you cannot, believe in your hearts that we have died like men.

Rev. J. McKendree Reiley, of the Methodist Episcopal church, offered a prayer, when those States which are represented in Congress were called for lists of delegates.

At the *evening session* of Tuesday the permanent organization was made, with Hon. William Dennison, of Ohio, as President. On taking the chair, he said:

I thank you for the honor you have conferred upon me, and while I shall bring to the discharge of the duties of the chair little experience in parliamentary rules, it will be my pleasure, as my duty, to spare no effort in contributing, to the extent of my ability, to the facilitating of the business of the Convention, and securing such results from your deliberations as will meet the loyal expectations of the country.

We meet here as representatives of the true friends of the Government and of impartial liberty—of that large portion of the people who gratefully appreciate the unmatched blessings which flow from our institutions well administered, and reject any form of human enslavement, not in punishment of crime, as no less incompatible with the rights of humanity than with the genius and the peaceful workings of republican government. [Prolonged applause.]

In no sense do we meet as members or representatives of either of the old political parties which bound the people, or as the champions of any principle or doctrine peculiar to either. The extraordinary condition of the country since the outbreak of the rebellion has, from necessity, taken from the issues of these parties their practical significance, and compelled the formation of substantially new political organizations; hence the origin of the Union party—if party it can be called—of which this Convention is for the purpose of its assembling, the accredited representative, and the only test of membership in which is an unreserved, unconditional loyalty to the Government and the Union.

Let me congratulate you upon the favorable auspices of your meeting. While the deepest anxiety is felt by all patriotic men as to the result of the war unjustifiably forced upon the Government by the bad, ambitious men and their deceived followers in the rebellious States, and the country is filled with distress and mourning over the loss of so many of our brave men who have fallen in battle, or died in hospitals from wounds received in defence of the constitutional authorities of the Government, we yet have, in what has been accomplished towards the suppression of the rebellion and the extinguishment of its cause—in the heroic deeds of our noble armies and gallant navy—in the renewal of the patriotism of the country that almost seemed to be paralyzed under the influence of our national prosperity—in the unprecedented generosity of the people, awakened by the wants of the Government and the necessities of its defenders—much, very much of the highest felicitation, and for which the country is grateful to Almighty God. [Applause.]

And may I not add to these causes of congratulation the formation of the political organization of which this Convention is a representative, which has so nobly sustained the Government in its efforts to put down the rebellion, and to the complete accomplishment of which its energies are consecrated; the patriotic harmony that has marked our assembling and will characterize all our proceedings, and presenting that harmony which will display itself in the unanimous nomination for the Presidency of the United States of the wise and good man whose unselfish devotion to the country, in the administration of the Government, has secured to him not only the admiration, but the warmest affection of every friend of constitutional liberty? [Applause.]

I need not remind you of the very grave responsibilities that devolve upon you as members of this convention. The loyal people of the country have authorized and expect you to renew on their part the pledge of their faith to support the Government, in the most vigorous prosecution of the war, to the complete suppression of the rebellion, regardless of the time or the resources required to that end, and they equally expect and call upon you to declare the cause and the support of the rebellion to be slavery, which, as well for its treasonable offences against the Government as for its incompatibility with the rights of humanity and the permanent peace of the country, must, with the termination of the war, and as much speedier as possible, be made to cease forever in every State and Territory of the Union. But I must not refer to other subjects of interest that will challenge your attention.

Let me repeat my thanks for your expressions of confidence in me in having selected me to preside over your deliberations. [Applause.]

REPORT OF COMMITTEE ON CREDENTIALS.

Mr. Preston King, of New York, submitted the report of the majority committee; which was substantially as follows:

1st. That the delegations from the States of Maine, New Hampshire, Massachusetts, Connecticut, Vermont, Rhode Island, New York, New Jersey, Pennsylvania, Delaware, Maryland, Ohio, Kentucky, Indiana, Illinois, Iowa, Minnesota, Oregon, California, Kansas, and West Virginia were all regular, and are admitted to seats with all the rights and privileges of members, except one district of Pennsylvania, which had elected four instead of two members. The committee admit the two who received the largest number of votes as delegates, and the other two as alternates.

2d. That there being two delegations from the State of Missouri, claiming seats, the committee recommend that those styling themselves the Radical Union Delegation be awarded the seats. [Applause and cheering.]

3d. That the delegates from Virginia, Tennessee, Louisiana, and Arkansas be admitted to all the privileges of the floor, except that of voting.

4th. That the delegations from the Territories and the District of Columbia be admitted to seats and all the privileges except that of voting.

5th. That the persons presenting themselves as delegates from the State of South Carolina are not entitled to the rights of delegates on the floor.

Mr. W. E. Stevenson, of Virginia, and Mr. Hiram Smith, of Oregon, made a minority report, and recommended that the delegates from the States of Virginia, Louisiana, Arkansas, Kansas, Tennessee, and Florida, and from all the Territories, be admitted, with the right to vote.

Mr. A. H. Insley, of Kansas, made a report arguing that, especially in the cases of the Territories of Nebraska, Colorado, and Nevada, the delegates be admitted with the right to vote.

That part of the report of the majority relating to the uncontested seats was then adopted.

Mr. King, of New York, offered a substitute covering three points in report of the majority:

1st. He proposed to admit both of the Missouri delegations, and that where they agree they cast the vote to which the State is entitled; where they disagree, the vote of the State shall not be cast.

2d. He proposed to give all the delegates admitted all the rights and privileges of delegates, without exception; but that the District of Columbia and the Territories should have but two votes each, and that no State, District, or Territory should cast more votes than it has delegates present in the Convention.

A division of the question was called,

When Mr. King's amendment relative to Missouri was lost; and the report of the committee, on that point, was adopted, by States, and as follows:

	Ayes.	Nays.
Maine	14	0
New Hampshire	10	0
Vermont	10	0
Massachusetts	24	0
Rhode Island	8	0
Connecticut	12	0
New York	66	0
New Jersey	14	0
Pennsylvania	49	3
Delaware	6	0
Maryland	14	0
Kentucky	21	1
Ohio	42	0
Indiana	26	0
Illinois	32	0
Michigan	16	0
Wisconsin	16	0
Iowa	16	0
Minnesota	8	0
California	10	0
Oregon	6	0
West Virginia	10	0
Kansas	6	0
	440	4

The question was still further divided, and a vote then taken upon admitting the fifteen delegates from Tennessee, with the right to vote; which was agreed to, by States, as follows:

	For.	Against.
Maine	3	11
New Hampshire	0	10
Vermont	2	8
Massachusetts	0	24
Rhode Island	2	6
Connecticut	10	2
New York	66	0
New Jersey	14	0
Pennsylvania	31	21
Delaware	1	4
Maryland	1	13
Missouri	19	3
Kentucky	4	18
Ohio	42	0
Indiana	24	2
Illinois	32	0
Michigan	2	14
Wisconsin	15	1
Iowa	9	7
Minnesota	1	7
California	10	0
Oregon	6	0
West Virginia	10	0
Kansas	6	0
Total	310	151

The delegates from Louisiana and Arkansas were then admitted, by States, as follows:

	For.	Against.
Maine	3	11
New Hampshire	0	10
Vermont	5	5
Massachusetts	0	24
Rhode Island	1	7
Connecticut	10	2
New York	61	3
New Jersey	14	0
Pennsylvania	5	46
Delaware	0	5
Maryland	1	13
Missouri	17	5
Tennessee	15	0
Kentucky	12	10
Ohio	42	0
Indiana	22	4
Illinois	32	0
Michigan	10	6
Wisconsin	15	1
Iowa	14	2
Minnesota	0	8
California	6	4
Oregon	6	0
West Virginia	10	0
Kansas	6	0
Total	307	167

The portions of the majority report, as thus amended, were then agreed to.

The Delegates from Nebraska, Colorado, and Nevada, were then admitted with the right to vote.

And the balance of the report—admitting the Delegates from Virginia and Florida, without the right to vote, rejecting the Delegates from South Carolina, and admitting the Delegates from the remaining Territories without the right to vote, was adopted.

This PLATFORM was then adopted unanimously, as reported by Mr. Raymond, of New York, Chairman of the Committee:

1. *Resolved*, That it is the highest duty of every American citizen to maintain against all their enemies the integrity of the Union and the paramount authority of the Constitution and laws of the United States; and that, laying aside all differences of political opinion, we pledge ourselves, as Union men, animated by a common sentiment and aiming at a common object, to do everything in our power to aid the Government in quelling by force of arms the Rebellion now raging against its authority, and in bringing to the punishment due to their crimes the Rebels and traitors arrayed against it. [Prolonged applause.]

2. *Resolved*, That we approve the determination of the Government of the United States not to compromise with Rebels, or to offer them any terms of peace, except such as may be based upon an unconditional surrender of their hostility and a return to their just allegiance to the Constitution and laws of the United States, and that we call upon the Government to maintain this position, and to prosecute the war with the utmost possible vigor to the complete suppression of the Rebellion, in full reliance upon the self-sacrificing patriotism, the heroic valor and the undying devotion of the American people to their country and its free institutions. [Applause.]

3. *Resolved*, That as Slavery was the cause, and now constitutes the strength, of this Rebellion, and as it must be, always and everywhere, hostile to the principles of Republican Government, justice and the national safety demand its utter and complete extirpation from the soil of the Republic [applause;]—and that while we uphold and maintain the acts and proclamations by which the Government, in its own defence, has aimed a death-blow at this gigantic evil, we are in favor, furthermore, of such an amendment to the Constitution, to be made by the people in conformity with its provisions, as shall terminate and forever prohibit the existence of Slavery within the limits or the jurisdiction of the United States. [Tremendous applause, the delegates rising and waving their hats.]

4. *Resolved*, That the thanks of the American people are due to the soldiers and sailors of the Army and Navy [applause,] who have periled their lives in defence of their country and in vindication of the honor of its flag; that the nation owes to them some permanent recognition of their patriotism and their valor, and ample and permanent provision for those of their survivors who have received disabling and honorable wounds in the service of the country; and that the memories of those who have fallen in its defence shall be held in grateful and everlasting remembrance. [Loud applause and cheers.]

5. *Resolved*, That we approve and applaud the practical wisdom, the unselfish patriotism and the unswerving fidelity to the Constitution and the principles of American liberty, with which Abraham Lincoln has discharged, under circumstances of unparalleled difficulty, the great duties and responsibilities of the Presidential office; that we approve and endorse, as demanded by the emergency and essential to the preservation of the nation and as within the provisions of the Constitution, the measures and acts which he has adopted to defend the nation against its open and secret foes; that we approve, especially, the Proclamation of Emancipation, and the employment as Union soldiers of men heretofore held in slavery, [applause;] and that we have full confidence in his determination to carry these and all other Constitutional measures essential to the salvation of the country into full and complete effect. [Vociferous applause.]

6. *Resolved*, That we deem it essential to the general welfare that harmony should prevail in the National Councils, and we regard as worthy of public confidence and official trust those only who cordially endorse the principles proclaimed in these resolutions, and which should characterize the administration of the Government. [Applause.]

7. *Resolved*, That the Government owes to all men employed in its armies, without regard to distinction of color, the full protection of the laws of war, [applause,] and that any violation of these laws, or of the usages of civilized nations in time of war, by the Rebels now in arms, should

be made the subject of prompt and full redress. [Prolonged applause.]

8. *Resolved*, That foreign immigration, which in the past has added so much to the wealth, development of resources and increase of power to this nation, the asylum of the oppressed of all nations, should be fostered and encouraged by a liberal and just policy. [Applause.]

9. *Resolved*, That we are in favor of a speedy construction of the Railroad to the Pacific coast. [Applause.]

10. *Resolved*, That the National faith, pledged for the redemption of the public debt, must be kept inviolate, and that for this purpose we recommend economy and rigid responsibility in the public expenditures, and a vigorous and just system of taxation; and that it is the duty of every loyal State to sustain the credit and promote the use of the National currency. [Applause.]

11. *Resolved*, That we approve the position taken by the Government that the people of the United States can never regard with indifference the attempt of any European Power to overthrow by force or to supplant by fraud the institutions of any Republican Government on the Western Continent—[prolonged applause]—and that they will view with extreme jealousy, as menacing to the peace and independence of their own country, tie efforts of any such power to obtain new footholds for Monarchial Governments, sustained by foreign military force, in near proximity to the United States. [Long-continued applause.]

RE-NOMINATION OF PRESIDENT LINCOLN.

The vote was taken by States, when all were found to have voted for Mr. LINCOLN, except Missouri—for General Grant.

Before the announcement of the result, Mr. HUME, of Missouri, moved that the nomination of ABRAHAM LINCOLN be declared unanimous. His delegation had been instructed to vote for General Grant, but he was now in favor of declaring the nomination already made to be unanimous.

The motion was agreed to amidst a *furore* of applause.

The president then announced the result, stating that ABRAHAM LINCOLN, of Illinois, was the unanimous choice of the Union National party of the country for the next Presidency.

VOTE FOR VICE-PRESIDENT.

STATES AND TERRITORIES.	Johnson.	Dickinson.	Hamlin.	Butler.	Rosseau.	Burnside.	Colfax.	Holt.	Tod.	King.
Maine	......	......	14							
New Hampshire	1	3	4	2						
Vermont	5	1	2	2						
Massachusetts	......	17	3	2	...	..	...	2		
Rhode Island	......	1	3	2	...	2				
Connecticut	12									
New York	32	28	6							
New Jersey	2	12								
Pennsylvania	......	......	52							
Delaware	......	6								
Maryland	2	11	1							
Louisiana	7	7								
Arkansas	10									
Missouri	2	......	......	20						
Tennessee	15									
Kentucky	......	......	......	...	21	...	..	...	1	
Ohio	42									
Indiana	26									
Illinois	......	......	32							
Michigan	......	......	16							
Wisconsin	2	10	4							
Iowa	16									
Minnesota	....	3	5							
California	5		5							
Oregon	......	......	.....	...	...	...	6			
West Virginia	10									
Kansas	2	2	2							
Nebraska	3	1	1	...	...	...	...	..	...	1
Colorada	......	6								
Nevada	6									
	200	108	150	28	21	2	6	2	1	1

Several of the States changed their votes to JOHNSON, and the final result reached was as follows:

	Johnson.	Dickinson.	Hamlin.
Maine	14	0	0
New Hampshire	10	0	0
Vermont	10	0	0
Massachusetts	21	3	0
Rhode Island	7	1	0
Connecticut	12	0	0
New York	66	0	0
New Jersey	14	0	0
Pennsylvania	52	0	0
Delaware	6	0	0
Maryland	14	0	0
Louisiana	14	0	0
Arkansas	10	0	0
Missouri	22	0	0
Tennessee	15	0	0
Kentucky	21	0	0
Ohio	42	0	0
Indiana	26	0	0
Illinois	32	0	0
Michigan	16	0	0
Wisconsin	2	10	4
Iowa	16	0	0
Minnesota	0	3	5
California	10	0	0
Oregon	6	0	0
West Virginia	10	0	0
Kansas	6	0	0
Nebraska	6	0	0
Colorado	6	0	0
Nevada	6	0	0
Total	494	17	9

The PRESIDENT. Andrew Johnson, having received a majority of all the votes, is declared duly nominated as the candidate of the National Union Party for Vice President of the United States.

On motion of Mr. TREMAIN, of New York, the nomination of Andrew Johnson was declared unanimous.

After the transaction of some routine business, the convention adjourned.

THE PRESIDENT'S RECEPTION OF THE NOMINATION.

Thursday, June 9—The committee to ratify the nominees called upon the President, when the following proceedings took place:

Governor Dennison, president of the convention and chairman of said committee, addressed the President as follows:

MR. PRESIDENT: The National Union Convention, which closed its sittings at Baltimore yesterday, appointed a committee consisting of one from each State, with myself as its chairman, to inform you of your unanimous nomination by that convention for election to the office of President of the United States. That committee, I have the honor of now informing you, is present. On its behalf, I have also the honor of presenting you with a copy of the resolutions or platform which were adopted by that convention, as expressive of its sense, and of the sense of the loyal people of the country which it represents; of the principles and the policy that should characterize the administration of the Government in the present condition of the country. I need not say to you, sir, that the convention, in thus unanimously nominating you for re-election, but gave utterance to the almost universal voice of the loyal people of the country. To doubt of your triumphant election would be little short of abandoning the hope of the final suppression of the rebellion, and the restoration of the authority of the Government over the insurgent States.

Neither the convention nor those represented by that body entertained any doubt as to the final result. Under your administration, sustained by that loyal people and by our noble army and gallant navy, neither did the convention nor do this committee doubt the speedy suppression of this most wicked and unprovoked rebellion. [A copy of the resolutions were here handed to the President.]

I should add, Mr. President, it would be the pleasure of the committee to communicate to you, within a few days, through one of its most accomplished members, Mr. Curtis, of New York, by letter, more at length the circumstances under which you have been placed in nomination for the Presidency.

THE PRESIDENT'S RESPONSE.

The President, taking the resolutions from his pocket where he had placed them, and unfolding the same, said:

MR. CHAIRMAN AND GENTLEMEN OF THE COMMITTEE: I will neither conceal my gratification nor restrain the expression of my gratitude that the Union people through their convention, in the continued effort to save and advance the nation, have deemed me not unworthy to remain in my present position.

I know no reason to doubt that I shall accept the nomination tendered; and yet, perhaps, I should not declare definitely before reading and considering what is called the platform.

I will say now, however, I approve the declaration in favor of so amending the Constitution as to prohibit slavery throughout the nation. When the people in revolt, with a hundred days of explicit notice that they could within those days resume their allegiance without the overthrow of their institutions, and that they could not resume it afterwards, elected to stand out, such amendment to the C nstitution as is now proposed became a fitting and necessary conclusion to the final success of the Union cause. Such alone can meet and cover all cavils. Now, the unconditional Union men, North and South, preceive its importance, and embrace it. In the joint names of Liberty and Union, let us labor to give it legal form and practical effect.

Same day, a delegation of the National Union League called upon the President, to congratulate him upon his re-nomination, to whom he made this reply:

GENTLEMEN: I can only say in response to the kind remarks of your chairman, as I suppose, that I am very grateful for the renewed confidence which has been accorded to me both by the Convention and by the National League. I am not insensible at all to the personal compliment there is in this, and yet I do not allow myself to believe that any but a small portion of it is to be appropriated as a personal compliment. That really the Convention and the Union League assembled with a higher view—that of taking care of the interests of the country for the present and the great future—and that the part I am entitled to appropriate as a compliment is only that part which I may lay hold of as being the opinion of the Convention and of the League, that I am not entirely unworthy to be entrusted with the place which I have occupied for the last three years. But I do not allow myself to suppose that either the Convention or the League have concluded to decide that I am either the greatest or best man in America, but rather they have concluded that it is not best to swap horses while crossing the river, and have further concluded that I am not so poor a horse that they might not make a botch of it in trying to swap. [Laughter and applause.]

To a delegation from Ohio he said:

SPEECH OF PRESIDENT LINCOLN.

GENTLEMEN: I am very much obliged to you for this compliment. I have just been saying, and as I have just said it, I will repeat it: The hardest of all speeches which I have to answer is a serenade. I never know what to say on such occasions. I suppose that you have done me this kindness in connection with the action of the Baltimore Convention, which has recently taken place, and with which, of course, I am very well satisfied. [Laughter and applause.] What we want still more than Baltimore Conventions or Presidential elections is success under General Grant. [Cries of "Good," and applause.] I propose that you constantly bear in mind that the support you owe to the brave officers and soldiers in the field is of the very first importance, and we should therefore bend all our energies to that point. Now, without detaining you any longer, I propose that you help me to close up what I am now saying with three rousing cheers for General Grant and the officers and soldiers under his command.

PRESIDENT LINCOLN'S ACCEPTANCE.

NEW YORK, *June* 14, 1864.

Hon. ABRAHAM LINCOLN:

SIR: The National Union Convention, which assembled in Baltimore on June 7, 1864, has instructed us to inform you that you were nominated with enthusiastic unanimity for the Presidency of the United States for four years from the 4th of March next.

The resolutions of the Convention, which we have already had the honor of placing in your hands, are a full and clear statement of the principles which inspired its action, and which, as we believe, the great body of Union men in the country heartily approve. Whether those resolutions express the national gratitude to our soldiers and sailors; or the national scorn of compromise with Rebels, and consequent dishonor; or the patriotic duty of union and success; whether they approve the Proclamation of Emancipation, the constitutional amendment, the employment of former slaves as Union soldiers, or the solemn obligation of the Government promptly to redress the wrongs of every soldier of the Union, of whatever color or race; whether they declare the inviolability of the pledged faith of the nation, or offer the national hospitality to the oppressed of every land, or urge the union by railroad of the Atlantic and Pacific oceans; whether they recommend public economy and vigorous taxation, or assert the fixed popular opposition to the establishment by armed force of foreign monarchies in the immediate neighborhood of the United States, or declare that those only are worthy of official trust who approve unreservedly the views and policy indicated in the resolutions—they were equally hailed with the heartiness of profound conviction.

Believing with you, sir, that this is the people's war for the maintenance of a Government which you have justly described as "of the people, by the people, for the people," we are very sure that you will be glad to know, not only from the resolutions themselves, but from the singular harmony and enthusiasm with which they were adopted, how warm is the popular welcome of every measure in the prosecution of the war, which is as vigorous, unmistakable, and unfaltering as the national purpose itself. No right, for instance, is so precious and sacred to the American heart as that of personal liberty. Its violation is regarded with just, instant, and universal jealousy. Yet in this hour of peril every faithful citizen concedes that, for the sake of national existence and the common welfare, individual liberty may, as the Constitution provides in the case of rebellion, be sometimes summarily constrained, asking only with painful anxiety that in every instance, and to the least detail, that absolutely necessary power shall not be hastily or unwisely exercised.

We believe, sir, that the honest will of the Union men of the country was never more truly represented than in this Convention. Their purpose we believe to be the overthrow of armed rebels in the field, and the security of permanent peace and union by liberty and justice under the Constitution. That these results are to be achieved amid cruel perplexities, they are fully aware. That they are to be reached only by cordial unanimity of counsel, is undeniable. That good men may sometimes differ as to the means and the time, they know. That in the conduct of all human affairs the highest duty is to determine, in the angry conflict of passion, how much good may be practically accomplished, is their sincere persuasion. They have watched your official course, therefore, with unflagging attention; and amid the bitter taunts of eager friends and the fierce denunciation of enemies, now moving too fast for some, now too slowly for others, they have seen you throughout this tremendous contest patient, sagacious, faithful, just; leaning upon the heart of the great mass of the people, and satisfied to be moved by its mighty pulsations.

It is for this reason that, long before the Convention met, the popular instinct had plainly indicated you as its candidate; and the Convention, therefore, merely recorded the popular will. Your character and career prove your unswerving fidelity to the cardinal principles of American Liberty and of the American Constitution. In the name of that Liberty and Constitution, sir, we earnestly request your acceptance of this nomination. Reverently commending our beloved country, and you, its Chief Magistrate, with all its brave sons who, on sea and land, are faithfully defending the good old American cause of equal rights, to the blessing of Almighty God,

We are, sir, very respectfully, your friends and fellow-citizens,

WILLIAM DENNISON, Ohio, Chairman.
JOSIAH H. DRUMMOND. Maine.
THOMAS E. SAWYER, New Hampshire.
BRADLEY BARLOW, Vermont.
A. H. BULLOCK, Massachusetts.
A. M. CAMPBELL, Rhode Island.
C. S. BUSHNELL, Connecticut.
G. W. CURTIS, New York.
W. A. NEWELL, New Jersey.
HENRY JOHNSON, Pennsylvania.
N. B. SMITHERS, Delaware.
W. L. W. SEABROOK, Maryland.
JOHN F. HUME, Missouri.
G. W. HAIGHT, Kentucky.
E. P. PYFFE, Ohio.
CYRUS M. ALLEN, Indiana.
W. BUSHNELL, Illinois.
L. P. ALEXANDER, Michigan.
A. W. RANDALL, Wisconsin.
PETER VALINDA, Iowa.
THOMAS SIMPSON, Minnesota.
JOHN BIDWELL, California.
THOMAS H. PEARNE, Oregon.
LEROY KRAMER, West Virginia.

A. C. WILDER, Kansas.
M. M. BRYAN, Tennessee.
T. WINTER, Nevada.
A. A. ATOCHA, Louisiana.
A. S. PADDOCK, Nebraska.
VALENTINE DELL, Arkansas.
JOHN A. NYE, Colorado.
A. B. SLOANAKER, Utah.

EXECUTIVE MANSION, WASHINGTON, *June* 27, 1864.

Hon. WILLIAM DENNISON *and others, a Committee of the National Union Convention:*

GENTLEMEN: Your letter of the 14th instant formally notifying me that I have been nominated by the convention you represent for the Presidency of the United States for four years from the 4th of March next, has been received. The nomination is gratefully accepted, as the resolutions of the convention, called the platform, are heartily approved.

While the resolution in regard to the supplanting of republican government upon the western continent is fully concurred in, there might be misunderstanding were I not to say that the position of the Government in relation to the action of France in Mexico as assumed through the State department and indorsed by the Convention, among the measures and acts of the Executive, will be faithfully maintained so long as the state of facts shall leave that position pertinent and applicable.

I am especially gratified that the soldier and the seaman were not forgotten by the Convention, as they forever must and will be remembered by the grateful country for whose salvation they devote their lives.

Thanking you for the kind and complimentary terms in which you have communicated the nomination and other proceedings of the convention, I subscribe myself,

Your obedient servant,

ABRAHAM LINCOLN.

HON. ANDREW JOHNSON'S LETTER OF ACCEPTANCE.

NASHVILLE, TENN., *July* 2, 1864.

Hon. WM. DENNISON, *Chairman, and others, Committee of the National Union Convention:*

GENTLEMEN: Your communication of the 9th ult., informing me of my nomination for the Vice Presidency of the United States, by the National Union Convention, held at Baltimore, and enclosing a copy of the resolutions adopted by that body, was not received until the 25th ult.

A reply on my part had been previously made to the action of the Convention in presenting my name, in a speech delivered in this city, on the evening succeeding the day of the adjournment of the Convention, in which I indicated my acceptance of the distinguished honor conferred by that body, and defined the grounds upon which that acceptance was based, substantially saying what I now have to say. From the comments made upon that speech by the various presses of the country to which my attention has been directed, I considered it to be regarded as a full acceptance.

In view, however, of the desire expressed in your communication, I will more fully allude to a few points that have been heretofore presented. My opinions on the leading questions at present agitating and distracting the public mind, and especially in reference to the rebellion now being waged against the Government and authority of the United States, I presume, are generally understood. Before the southern people assumed a belligerent attitude, (and frequently since,) I took occasion most frankly to declare the views I then entertained in relation to the wicked purposes of the southern politicians. They have since undergone but little, if any change. Time and subsequent events have rather confirmed than diminished my confidence in their correctness.

At the beginning of this great struggle I entertained the same opinion of it I do now, and in my place in the Senate I denounced it as treason, worthy the punishment of death, and warned the Government and people of the impending danger. But my voice was not heard or counsel heeded until it was too late to avert the storm. It still continued to gather over us without molestation from the authorities at Washington, until at length it broke with all its fury upon the country. And now, if we would save the government from being overwhelmed by it, we must meet it in the true spirit of patriotism, and bring traitors to the punishment due their crime, and *by force of arms* crush out and subdue the last vestige of rebel authority in every State. I felt then as now that the destruction of the government was deliberately determined upon by wicked and designing conspirators, whose lives and fortunes were pledged to carry it out, and that no compromise, short of an unconditional recognition of the independence of the southern States, could have been or could now be proposed which they would accept. The clamor for "southern rights," as the rebel journals were pleased to designate their rallying cry, was not to secure their assumed rights *in the Union and under the Constitution*, but to disrupt the government and establish an independent organization based upon slavery, which they could at all times control.

The separation of the Government has for years been the cherished purpose of the southern leaders. Baffled, in 1832, by the stern, patriotic heroism of Andrew Jackson, they sullenly acquiesced, only to mature their diabolical schemes, and await the recurrence of a more favorable opportunity to execute them. Then the pretext was the tariff, and Jackson, after foiling their schemes of nullification and disunion, with prophetic perspicacity, warned the country against the renewal of their efforts to dismember the Government.

In a letter dated May 1, 1833, to the Rev. A. J. Crawford, after demonstrating the heartless insincerity of the southern nullifiers, he said:

"Therefore the tariff was only a pretext, and disunion and a southern confederacy the real object. The next pretext will be the negro, or slavery question."

Time has fully verified this prediction, and we have now not only "the negro, or slavery question," as the pretext, but the real cause of the rebellion, and both must go down together. It is vain to attempt to reconstruct the Union with the distracting element of slavery in it. Experience has demonstrated its incompatibility with free and republican governments, and it would be unwise and unjust longer to continue it as one of the institutions of the country. While it remained subordinate to the Constitution and laws of the United States I yielded to it my support, but when it became rebellious and attempted to rise above the Government, and control its action, I threw my humble influence against it.

The authority of the Government is supreme, and will admit of no rivalry. No institution can rise above it, whether it be slavery or any other organized power. In our happy form of government all must be subordinate to the will of the people, when reflected through the Constitution and laws made pursuant thereto—State or Federal. This great principle lies at the foundation of every government, and cannot be disregarded without the destruction of the government itself. In the support and practice of correct principles we can never reach wrong results, and by rigorously adhering to this great fundamental truth the end will be the preservation of the Union and the overthrow of an institution which has made war upon and attempted the destruction of the government itself.

The mode by which this great change—the emancipation of the slave—can be effected, is properly found in the power to amend the Constitution of the United States. This plan is effectual, and of no doubtful authority; and while it does not contravene the timely exercise of the war power by the President in his emancipation proclamation, it comes stamped with the authority of the people themselves, acting in accordance with the written rule of the supreme law of the land, and must, therefore, give more general satisfaction and quietude to the distracted public mind.

By recurring to the principles contained in the resolutions so unanimously adopted by the Convention, I find that they substantially accord with my public acts and opinions heretofore made known and expressed, and are, therefore, most cordially indorsed and approved; and the nomination, having been conferred without any solicitation on my part, it is with the greater pleasure accepted.

In accepting the nomination I might here close, but I cannot forego the opportunity of saying to my old friends of the Democratic party *proper*, with whom I have so long and pleasantly been associated, that the hour has now come when that great party can justly vindicate its devotion to true democratic policy and measures of expediency. The war is a war of great principles. It involves the supremacy and life of the Government itself. If the rebellion triumphs free government North and South fails. If, on the other hand, the Government is successful, as I do not doubt, its destiny is fixed, its basis permanent and enduring, and its career of honor and glory just begun. In a great contest like this for the existence of free government the path of duty is patriotism and principle. Minor considerations and questions of administrative policy should give way to the higher duty of first preserving the Government, and then there will be time enough to wrangle over the men and measures pertaining to its administration.

This is not the hour for strife and division among ourselves. Such differences of opinion only encourage the enemy, prolong the war, and waste the country. Unity of action and concentration of power should be our watchword and rallying cry. This accomplished, the time will rapidly approach when their armies in the field—the great power of the rebellion—will be broken and crushed by our gallant officers and brave soldiers, and ere long they will return to their homes and firesides to resume again the avocations of peace, with the proud consciousness that they have aided in the noble work of re-establishing upon a surer and more permanent basis the great temple of American freedom.

I am, gentlemen, with sentiments of high regard, yours truly,

ANDREW JOHNSON.

The National Union League—The Platform Adopted.

BALTIMORE, *June* 8, 1864.

The following are the resolutions passed by the Grand National Council of the Union League of America, assembled at the New Assembly Rooms in this city. The injunction of secrecy has been removed:

1. *Resolved*, That we will support the Administration in the vigorous prosecution of the war to the complete and final suppression of the rebellion, and to this we pledge all our energies and efforts.

2. *Resolved*, That slavery, being the cause of the rebellion and the bond of union among traitors, ought to be abolished without delay, and it is the sense of this organization that slavery, in all its forms, should be prohibited by an amend- to the Federal Constitution.

3. *Resolved*, That we hereby approve of the principles involved in the policy known as the Monroe doctrine.

4. *Resolved*, That the confiscation acts of Congress should be promptly and vigorously enforced, and that homesteads on the lands confiscated under it should be granted to our soldiers and others who have been made indigent by the acts of traitors and rebels.

5. *Resolved*, That every person who bears arms in defence of the national flag, is entitled, without distinction of color or nationality, to the protection of the government he defends, to the full extent of that government's power.

6. *Resolved*, That we hereby tender our thanks to the soldiers of the army and the sailors of the navy.

The Cleveland Convention.

May 31—A convention of about three hundred and fifty persons, as reported, met in Cleveland, pursuant to sundry calls:

A CALL TO THE RADICAL MEN OF THE NATION.

Whereas a Convention has been called by certain parties favorable to changing the present Administration, and for the purpose of "counseling concerning the approaching Presidential election," to meet in the city of Cleveland, Ohio, on Tuesday, the 31st of the present month; and whereas we are glad to learn that such a convention is to assemble, and having confidence that the objects of those issuing the call are in unison with those of the radical men of the country;

Therefore, the undersigned, having been appointed by the "Central Fremont Club" of the city of New York, for that purpose, do hereby invite their radical fellow-citizens in every State, county, and town throughout the country to meet them in the above-named Convention, on the said Tuesday, the 31st of this month, in order, then and there, to recommend the nomination of John C. Fremont for the Presidency of the United States, and to assist in organizing for his election.

The imbecile and vacillating policy of the present Administration in the conduct of the war, being just weak enough to waste its men and means to provoke the enemy, but not strong enough to conquer the rebellion—and its treachery to justice, freedom, and genuine democratic principles in its plan of reconstruction, whereby the honor and dignity of the nation have been sacrificed to conciliate the still existing and arrogant slave power, and to further the ends of an unscrupulous partisan ambition—call in thunder tones upon the lovers of justice and their country to come to the rescue of the imperiled nationality and the cause of impartial and universal freedom, threatened with betrayal and overthrow.

The way to victory and salvation is plain. Justice must be throned in the seats of national legislation, and guide the executive will. The things demanded, and which we ask you to join us to render sure, are, *the immediate extinction of slavery throughout the whole United States by Congressional action, the absolute equality of all men before the law, without regard to race or color*, and such a plan of reconstruction as shall *conform entirely to the policy of freedom for all*, placing the political power *alone in the hands of the loyal*, and *executing with vigor the law for confiscating the property of the rebels.*

Come, then, in formidable numbers, and let us take counsel together, in this crisis of the nation's calamity, and, with one united effort, endeavor to redeem the country from slavery and war, that it may be consecrated to FREEDOM and PEACE FOREVER MORE. Men of God! Men of humanity! Lovers of justice! Patriots and freemen! One and all, rally!!

Most respectfully, your fellow-citizens,

DAVID PLUMB,
EDWARD GILBERT,
FREDERICK KAPP,
ERNEST KRACKOWIZER,
WILLIAM J. DEMAREST,
Committee.

NEW YORK, *May* 6, 1864.

The undersigned join in the foregoing call:

Geo. B. Cheever, N. Y.	Pantaleon Candidus, N. Y.
Henry T. Cheever, Mass.	R. F. Hibbard, N. Y.
J. W. Alden, N. J.	Edmund Tuttle, Conn.
F. O. Irish, N. Y.	Peter G. Tuttle, Conn.
William Goodell, N. Y.	F. N. Bixby, Conn.
S. S. Jocelyn, N. Y.	James R. Surtliff, Conn.
E. Cady Stanton, N. Y.	James Tuttle, Conn.
Wm. F. Knowles, N. Y.	E. B. Hall, Conn.
W. H. Woodruff, N. J.	Edward H. Tuttle, Conn.
C. Fromont, N. Y.	S. B. Hall, Conn.
Ira H. Cobb, N. Y.	George H. Sears, N. Y.
Doct. H. Joslyn, N. Y.	Nathaniel R. Harris, N. Y.
H. L. Green, N. Y.	C. E. Hawley, Conn.
T. O. Warner, N. Y.	C. B. Smith, N. Y.
J. Henry Warner, N. Y.	J. G. Livingston, N. Y.
T. O. Warner, jr., N. Y.	Edwin Ferris, N. Y.
E. M. Mason, Mich.	Joel Greeley, N. Y.
Chas. A. Lane, N. Y.	Wm. Gilbert, N. Y.
David C. Harrington, N. Y.	Henry B. Harrington, N. Y.
A. S. Betts, N. Y.	Stephen Betts, N. Y.
David Downs, N. Y.	Wm. H. H. Downs, N. Y.
W. H. Hathaway, N. Y.	C. S. Middlebrook, Conn.
T. C. Harrison, N. J.	A. B. Pratt, Mich.
J. R. Johnson, Va.	Wm. Cumming, Mich.
James W. Vail, Wis.	Ira Chase, Mich.
Elisha Galpin, Mich.	C. C. Foote, Mich.
B. A. Fay, Mich.	Elisha Hill, Mich.
A. J. Fay, Mich.	Robert Garner, Mich.
Thomas C. Post, N. Y.	

TO THE PEOPLE OF THE UNITED STATES.

After having labored ineffectually to defer as far as was in our power the critical moment when the attention of the people must inevitably be fixed upon the selection of a candidate for the Chief Magistracy of the country; after having interrogated our conscience and consulted our duty as citizens, obeying at once the sentiment of a mature conviction and a profound affection for the common country, we feel ourselves impelled, on our own responsibility, to declare to the people that the time has come for all independent men, jealous of their liberties and of the national greatness, to confer together and unite to resist the swelling invasion of an open, shameless, and unrestrained patronage which threatens to engulf under its destructive wave the rights of the people, the liberty and dignity of the nation.

Deeply impressed with the conviction that, in a time of revolution, when the public attention is turned exclusively to the success of armies, and is consequently less vigilant of the public liberties, the patronage derived from the organization of an army of a million of men, and an administration of affairs which seeks to control the remotest parts of the country in favor of its supreme chief, constitute a danger seriously threatening to the stability of republican institutions, we declare that the principle of one term, which has now acquired nearly the force of law by the consecration of time, ought to be inflexibly adhered to in the approaching election.

We further declare that we do not recognize in the Baltimore Convention the essential conditions of a truly National Convention. Its proximity to the centre of all the interested influences of administration, its distance from the centre of the country, its mode of convocation, the corrupting practices to which it has been and inevitably will be subjected, do not permit the people to assemble there with any expectation of being able to deliberate at full liberty. Convinced, as we are, that in presence of the critical circumstances in which the nation is placed, it is only in the energy and good sense of the people that the general safety can be found, satisfied that the only way to consult it is to indicate a central position to which every one may go without too much expenditure of means and time, and where the assembled people, far from all administrative influence, may consult freely and deliberate peaceably with the presence of the greatest possible number of men whose known principles guarantee their sincere and enlightened devotion to the rights of the people and to the preservation of the true basis of republican government—we earnestly invite our fellow-citizens to unite at Cleveland, Ohio, on Tuesday, the 31st of May next, for consultation and concert of action in respect to the approaching Presidential election.

B. Gratz Brown, Mo.	Frederick Kapp, N. Y.
Stephen S. Foster, Mass.	Charles E. Moss, Mo.
A. Van Antwerp, N. Y.	E. G. Parker, Me.
Bird B. Chapman, Ohio.	Ernest Pruessing, Ill.
Ezra C. Andrews, Me.	Wm. D. Robinsin, Me.
Henry A. Clover, Miss.	John S. Savery, N. Y.
Peter Engleman, Wis.	E. Cluseret.

Caspar Butz, Ill. — Emil Pretorius, Mo.
George Field, N. Y. — Nath. P. Sawyer, Pa.
Edward Gilbert, N. Y. — Ernest Schmidt, Ill.
Peter Gillen, N. Y. — James Redpath, Mass.
Isaac W. Haff, N. Y. — Walter H. Shupe, Ohio.
Wm. Herries, N. Y. — Wm. H. Smith, Me.
James Hill, Me. — P. W. Kenyon, N. Y.
K. Heinzen, Mass. — James Taussig, Mo.
S. P. Dinsmore, D. C. — Ph. Stoppelrein, N. Y.
And. Humbert, Pa. — Wm. H. Dwinelle, N. Y.
J. W. Alden, N. J. — Samuel Taylor.
L. Sieboldt, Iowa. — Jas. S. Thomas, Mo.
Wm. Morris Davis, Pa. — F. Munch, Mo.
E. M. Davis, Pa. — J. Q. Westbrook, Me.
Wm. F. Johnston, Pa. — J. F. Whipple, N. Y.

THEO. OLSHAUSEN, Missouri,
of the People's Committee.

TO THE PEOPLE.

Citizens of the United States who mean to uphold the Union, who believe that the rebellion can be suppressed without infringing the rights of individuals or of States, who regard the extinction of slavery as among the practical effects of the war for the Union, and favor an amendment of the Federal Constitution for the exclusion of slavery, and who demand integrity and economy in the administration of government, are respectfully invited to meet in Mass Convention, at Cleveland, on Tuesday, the 31st day of May inst., for consultation and concert of action in respect to the approaching Presidential election.

Lucius Robinson. — Charles F. French, Ky.
John Cochrane. — Rob. Kraus, Mo.
Andrew J. Colvin. — Hanson Brent, Mo.
Thomas B. Carroll. — J. B. Clairbour, Mo.
Edward Wade. — Wm Freel, Mo.
George W. Demers. — Charles H. Frost, Mo.
Ira Porter. — Thomas J. Riddle, Mo.
Brace Millerd. — Wm. L. Bookstaver, Mo.
Howard Holdridge. — Fred. L. Braden, Ill.
Francis G. Fine. — Caspar O. Fitch, Ill.
Lemon Thomson. — Wallace Furman.
Charles Requa. — Frederick Smith.
Smith Requa. — Peter B. Lent, Ind.
Thomas P. White, Ky. — Andrew F. Butler.
Edward Cole, Ky. — Thomas Willks.
Francis F. Williams, Ky. — O. Whaley, Mass.
Smith Thompson, Ky. — Johnson Stemmer.
Leroy McArdle, Ky. — Alfred Moses.
William Bentley, Ky. — Leonard J. Timon.
John F. Smithers, Ky. — John F. Pendleton, N. J.
David S. Whiteley, Ky. — Patrick Clare.
Peter McCall, Ky. — Simon Munson.

LETTER FROM MRS. STANTON.

MAY 14, 1864.

TO THE CENTRAL FREMONT CLUB:

GENTLEMEN: To your call "to the radical men of the nation," taking it for granted you use "men" in its largest sense, I desire to append my name, and for the following reasons:

1. This is the only call ever issued for a political convention, demanding the right of suffrage for the black man—that safeguard of civil liberty, without which emancipation is a mockery.

2. When a body of men thus consecrate themselves to "freedom and peace," and declare their high resolve to found a republic on the eternal principles of justice, they have lifted politics into the sphere of morals and religion, and made it the duty of all true men and women to unite with them in building up the *New Nation.*

Yours respectfully,
E. CADY STANTON.

LETTER FROM WENDELL PHILLIPS.

BOSTON, *April* 21.

JUDGE STALLO:

DEAR SIR: Since you asked my judgment as to the course to be taken in nominating a candidate for the Presidency, I have been requested to sign a call for a convention for that purpose, to meet at Cleveland, in May next. Let me tell you the national policy I advocate:

Subdue the South as rapidly as possible. The moment territory comes under our flag reconstruct States thus: Confiscate and divide the lands of rebels; extend the right of suffrage broadly as possible to whites and blacks; let the Federal Constitution prohibit slavery throughout the Union, and forbid the States to make any distinction among their citizens on account of color or race.

I shall make every effort to have this policy pursued. Believing that the present Administration repudiates it and is carrying us to a point where we shall be obliged either to acknowledge the Southern Confederacy or to reconstruct the Union on terms grossly unjust, intolerable to the masses, and sure soon to result in another war, I earnestly advise an unpledged and independent convention, like that proposed, to consider public affairs and nominate for the Presidency a statesman and a patriot.

Yours, faithfully, WENDELL PHILLIPS.

The Convention was called to order by Edward Gilbert, of New York, on whose motion Ex-Governor William F. Johnston, of Pennsylvania, was chosen temporary Chairman. Mr. B. H. Brooks, of California, and Mr. Walfe, of the District of Columbia, were chosen Secretaries. A Committee on Credentials was proposed but not created. It was subsequently reported that the following States were repsented:

Ohio, Illinois, Massachusetts, New York, Iowa, Missouri, Michigan, Pennsylvania, Maryland, Wisconsin, Tennessee, Maine, Indiana, New Hampshire, New Jersey, and the District of Columbia.

The Committee on Permanent Organization reported officers, with General John Cochrane, of New York, as President.

Gen. Cochrane, on returning his thanks to the Convention, said:

GENTLEMEN OF THE CONVENTION: The formal routine of duty for the presiding officer, prescribes that he return set thanks for the honor conferred upon him. I am not disposed to follow in this path. The formality is too heartless for the solemnity and importance of the occasion. I assume my duties with cheerfulness and I trust that in this grand army of freedom I may well perform my humble part, and that that duty may be so performed that we may command the universal applause of all men. [Cheers.] I see before me representatives of the West, on which depends so much of the interests and destinies of the country—of the great central region of the country—its support and sustenance. I look further to the East and see before me the companions of my early life, assembled now by a common motive from the devious paths in which the exigencies of politics had lead them—the War Democrats of the State of New York. [Applause.] For them party possesses no claims when it is not identified with principle. There are also those here, who while they wait anxiously the tidings from the shattered cohorts under the banner of freedom, still turn affectionately to a Fatherland on the other side of the raging sea. [Applause.] We meet with such emotions suggested by the melancholy vista of the past—such reflections upon the scenes of the present. We have come together regarding party as nothing—country as everything.

Our national existence is at issue. Three years ago the question of national life fell like a thunderbolt at the feet of the people and they sprang to arms, with a wild shout in which all faction, all party, went down. Everywhere was heard the steady tramp of armed men and the patriotism and power of the North has swept on until the hour is almost striking when time shall proclaim the rebels defeated and the Union triumphant. [Applause.] In this hour men should review the past and speculate as to the dangers and vicissitudes of the future. For this purpose you assemble here—intending to support the army in the field, and at the same time to organize a great civil army, to fight for prinples, and to save for all generations the precious legacy obtained for us by the sacrifices of the soldiers of the Union. [Applause.] The rebellion, it must be suppressed—The Union, it must be preserved. [Great applause.] But we shall allow no criticism of the Government which represents us all, shall cast no impediment in the way of our Union soldiers, shall entertain no thought unworthy of American citizens.

The speaker then referred to the various discussions of the past. Since 1787 slavery has been the root of every political party of the country. The convention had assembled from all positions on this question, and now occupied one common ground. All are now united in demanding that slavery be destroyed and its last vestige wiped out. [Cheers.]

In this connection the speaker referred to the War Democrats of New York—virtual and virtuous—denying that the convention at Syracuse represented them, and denouncing that convention as a medley party of trading, scurvy politicians. He solemnly declared before high heaven that, since the war broke out, he had never belonged to party, that his feet had not been soiled by its touch, that he never crossed its lines, that he would never till the war was over consent to be "cabined, cribbed, confined" by party influences. As he had gone up and down the Hudson, he had indeed heard echoes from these "convocations of most political worms," and they had all been tuned to the key of "roast beef and cabbage on a trencher."

But he had been betrayed into prolixity by the interest of the occasion. Before closing he wished to speak of one other thing. All men on this continent are free and equal, and our Government must regard the private rights of civilians. If private rights are not respected, public liberty dies. We contend for individual rights, and whoever attacks them wounds the vital parts of the Republic. Not even the plea of necessity allows any one to trample upon them. To be sure these rights depend on circumstances, and may be superceded by martial law. Till that is proclaimed they must not be infringed. Law is the reflex of order, which is the principle of the universe and God himself. When it is stricken down all things fall with it.

Most sacred is the grand, noble old liberty of the press. Over that, in far Europe the struggle for freedom has been most sternly and pertinaciously waged. Let a free people guard with jealous care the liberty of the press, and declare the administration who would strike at it as guilty of incivism and little less than traitors. [Applause.]

Gen. Cochrane referred to his early belief that America was the light-house of the world—the asylum of the oppressed. He had heard that the light had been extinguished. He demanded that America should remain the sanctuary of freedom, the asylum of the oppressed throughout the world. The refugee from other lands must be held innocent until, in accordance with law, you pronounce him guilty. [Applause.]

The speaker closed with a brief reference to the Monroe doctrine, and an enthusiastic assertion of his belief in the speedy triumph of our arms, which was rapturously applauded.

After the adoption of the platform, nominations were made.

JOHN C. FREMONT was nominated for President by acclamation.

Gen. JOHN COCHRANE was nominated for Vice President, with but few voices in the negative.

The following letters were addressed to the Convention: that of Wendell Phillips, read in Convention, is reported to have been warmly applauded:

FROM WENDELL PHILLIPS.

BOSTON, *May* 27, 1864.

DEAR SIR: I deeply regret that it is out of my power to attend the Cleveland Convention. Allow me to suggest one or two things which I hoped to urge on its attention.

Without denying what the friends of the Administration claim—that it has done something toward crushing the rebellion—my charge against it is that it has not done half that it should and could have done toward that end, had it used the means in its hands with an earnest and single purpose to close the strife thoroughly and forever. It has thought more of conciliating rebels than of subduing them. It has avowedly forborne the use of lawful and efficient means (to wit, the abolition of slavery) until it was thought indispensable, and even then has used it in a half-hearted, halting way, wishing to save the feelings of rebels.

We have three tools with which to crush the rebellion—men, money, and the emancipation of the negro. We were warned to be quick and sharp in the use of these, because every year the war lasted hardened the South from a rebellion into a nation, and doubled the danger of foreign interference. Slavery has been our great trouble in the past, and, as every man saw, was our great danger in the future. Statesmanship, said, therefore, seize at once the God-given opportunity to end it, at the same time that you, in the quickest, shortest, and cheapest manner, annihilate the rebellion.

For three years the Administration has lavished money without stint, and drenched the land in blood, and it has not yet thoroughly and heartily struck at the slave system. Confessing that the use of this means is indispensable, the Administration has used it just enough to irritate the rebels and not enough to save the State. In sixty days after the rebellion broke out the Administration suspended *habeas corpus* on the plea of military necessity—justly. For three years it has poured out the treasure and blood of the country like water. Meanwhile slavery was too sacred to be used; that was saved lest the feelings of the rebels should be hurt. The Administration weighed treasure, blood, and civil liberty against slavery, and, up to the present moment, has decided to exhaust them all before it uses freedom, heartily, as a means of battle.

Mr. Lincoln's friends tell us that if he is re-elected he is re-elected to pursue the same policy and obey the same Cabinet. What will be the result of another four years of such policy? Unless the South is recognized the war will continue; the taxation needed to sustain our immense debt, doubled by that time, will grind the laboring man of the North down to the level of the pauper labor of Europe; and we shall have a Government accustomed to despotic power for eight years—a fearful peril to democratic institutions.

Mr. Lincoln's model of reconstruction is the experiment in Louisiana, which puts all power into the hands of the unchanged white race, soured by defeat, hating the laboring classes, plotting constantly for aristocratic institutions. To reconstruct the rebel States on that model is only continuing the war in the Senate Chamber after we have closed it in the field. Such reconstruction, leaving the South with its labor and capital at war, puts the whole payment of the debt on the industrious North, and in that way it will hang on us for a century. Such reconstruction makes the freedom of the negro a sham, and perpetuates slavery under a softer name. Such reconstruction, leaving the seeds of discontent and division in the South in the places of power, tempts and facilitates another rebellion, at the instigation or with the aid of French-Mexico. Such reconstruction dooms us to a second or third-rate place among nations, and provokes foreign insult and aggression.

There is no plan of reconstruction possible within twenty years, unless we admit the black to citizenship and the ballot, and use him, with the white, as the basis of States. There is not in the rebel States sufficient white basis to build on. If we refuse this method we must subdue the South and hold it as territory until this generation of white men have passed away, and their sons, with other feelings, have taken their places, and northern capital, energy, and immigration have forced their way into the South. Should we adopt that plan, and wait for those changes, twenty years must elapse before we can venture to rebuild States. Meanwhile a large and expensive army, and the use of despotic power by a Government holding half its territory and citizens as subjects, make every thoughtful man tremble for the fate of free government.

A quick and thorough reorganization of States on a democratic basis—every man and race equal before the law—is the only sure way to save the Union. I urge it not for the black man's sake alone, but for ours—for the nation's sake. Against such recognition of the blacks Mr. Lincoln stands pledged by prejudice and avowal. Men say, if we elect him he may change his views. Possibly. But three years have been a long time for a man's education in such hours as these. The nation cannot afford more. At any rate, the Constitution gives this summer an opportunity to make President a man fully educated. I prefer that course.

The Administration, therefore, I regard as a civil and military failure, and its avowed policy ruinous to the North in every point of view. Mr. Lincoln may wish the end—peace and freedom—but he is wholly unwilling to use the means which can secure that end. If Mr. Lincoln is re-elected I do not expect to see the Union reconstructed in my day, unless on terms more disastrous to liberty than even disunion would be. If I turn to General Fremont, I see a man whose first act was to use the freedom of the negro as his weapon, I see one whose thorough loyalty to democratic institutions, without regard to race, whose earnest and decisive character, whose clear-sighted statesmanship and rare military ability justify my confidence that in his hands all will be done to save the State that foresight, skill, decision, and statesmanship can do.

I think the Convention should incorporate in its platform the demand for an amendment to the Constitution prohibiting slavery everywhere within the Republic, and forbidding the States to make any distinction among their citizens on account of color or race. I think it should demand a reconstruction of States as speedily as possible on the basis of every loyal man, white or black, sharing the land and the ballot. But if some of these points are not covered I shall still support its action with all my heart if it puts the name of Fremont or Butler on its flag. Fremont is my first choice, but I can support either of them; and this is an hour of such peril to the Republic that I think men should surrender all party and personal partiality, and support any man able and willing to save the State.

If the Baltimore Convention shall nominate Mr. Lincoln then I hope we shall fling our candidate's name, the long honored one of J. C. Fremont, to the breeze, and appeal to the patriotism and common sense of the people to save us from another such three years as we have seen. If, on the contrary, the Baltimore convention shall give us the name of any man whom the Radicals of the Loyal States can trust, I hope we shall be able to arrange some plan which will unite all on a common basis and carry our principles into the Government.

Wishing you all success, and prepared to second your effort to remove the Administration, I am, yours &c.,

WENDELL PHILLIPS.

EDWARD GILBERT, Esq., *New York*.

FROM LUCIUS ROBINSON.

STATE OF NEW YORK,
COMPTROLLER'S OFFICE, ALBANY, *May* 28.

To Hon. A. J. COLVIN:

My official duties and the illness of my deputy will prevent me from attending the meeting called for consultation at Cleveland, the 31st instant. I trust that you will be there with your judicious advice.

There was never a time when the safety and welfare of the country more imperatively demanded careful deliberation, with wise and resolute action. We have lived through three years of war, and have survived many bad mistakes, simply because the popular mind has been intensely fixed upon the single purpose of suppressing the rebellion at all hazards and at every cost. This one idea has had such controlling power, and the masses have followed so steadily, that it has served as a substitute for proper governmental leadership. But it is evident that the time is near at hand when the re-establishment of order, the removal of the cause of the rebellion and the repairing of the terrible desolation it has produced, will require at the head of the Government the very highest qualities of leadership. How can we hope to live as a nation through the crisis before us with a weak Executive and Cabinet in a state of discord and anarchy? Will not the country be in imminent danger of falling into the same condition when it ceases to be held together by the pressure of war? It appears to me that a firm assertion of sound principles and the election of the greatest men, regardless of former party organizations, are essential to the safety of the nation.

Whether a nomination should be made at Cleveland or not can best be determined after meeting and consulting with those who will assemble there; but if it shall be decided to nominate I have no hesitation in saying that I believe the hopes of the people throughout the country are resting upon General Grant as the candidate. He has displayed the qualities which give all men confidence. He has shown himself possessed of great ability and skill, the most indomitable courage and most unselfish devotion to the cause of his country. Victory has attended him wherever he has gone. One year ago all confidence in the Administration was lost. The brilliant victories which have since been won by Gen. Grant have so far restored it as to encourage the Administration to attempt to re-elect itself on the strength of his achievements. But in my judgment we should let him who has won the honors wear them, and should entrust power to one who has shown that he knows how to wield it; we shall then have a leader at the head of affairs in whom all loyal men will have confidence, against whom there will be no prejudices, and whom all will aid with alacrity.

Yours,
LUCIUS ROBINSON.

FROM FREDERICK DOUGLASS.

ROCHESTER, *May* 23, 1864.

SIR: I mean the complete abolition of every vestige, form, modification of slavery in every part of the United States, perfect equality for the black man in every State before the law, in the jury-box, at the ballot-box, and on the battle-field; ample and salutary retaliation for every instance of enslavement or slaughter of prisoners of any color. I mean that in the distribution of offices and honors under this Government no discrimination shall be made in favor of or against any class of citizens, whether black or white, of native or foreign birth. And supposing that the Convention which is to meet at Cleveland means the same thing, I cheerfully give my name as one of the signers of the call.

Yours, respectfully, FREDERICK DOUGLASS.

E. GILBERT, Esq.

THE PLATFORM.

Mr. Carroll, Chairman of the Committee on Resolutions,* reported the following resolutions:

First. That the Federal Union shall be preserved.

Second. That the Constitution and laws of the United States must be observed and obeyed.

Third. That the rebellion must be suppressed by force of arms, and without compromise.

Fourth. That the rights of free speech, free press, and the *habeas corpus* be held inviolate, save in districts where martial law has been proclaimed.

Fifth. That the rebellion has destroyed slavery, and the Federal Constitution should be amended to prohibit its re-establishment, and to secure to all men absolute equality before the law.

Sixth. That integrity and economy are demanded at all times in the administration of the Government; and that in time of war the want of them is criminal.

Seventh. That the right of asylum, except for crime and subject to law, is a recognized principle of American liberty; that any violation of it cannot be overlooked, and must not go unrebuked.

Eighth That the national policy known as the "Monroe doctrine" has become a recognized principle, and that the establishment of an anti-republican Government on this continent by any foreign power cannot be tolerated.

Ninth. That the gratitude and support of the nation are due to the faithful soldiers and the earnest leaders of the Union army and navy for their heroic achievements and deathless valor in defence of our imperiled country and of civil liberty.

Tenth. That the one-term policy for the Presidency, adopted by the people, is strengthened by the force of the existing crisis, and should be maintained by constitutional amendments.

Eleventh. That the Constitution should be so amended that the President and Vice President shall be elected by a direct vote of the people.

Twelfth. That the question of the reconstruction of the rebellious States belongs to the people, through their representatives in Congress, and not to the Executive.

Thirteenth. That the confiscation of the lands of the rebels, and their distribution among the soldiers and actual settlers, is a measure of justice.

Mr. Carroll stated that the committee were unanimous on all the resolutions, save one—the last. As a matter of expediency it was thought not advisable to recommend it, but the majority of the committee had instructed him to report it for the consideration of the Convention.

At this juncture, Mr. Gilbert announced the receipt of a letter from Wendell Phillips, which was warmly applauded while being read by the secretary.

Mr. Ransom of New Jersey, moved that the question on the resolutions be taken separately.

It was then decided to take up the resolutions separately. The first, second, third, and fourth were adopted without dissent.

Mr. Goodell moved to amend the fifth by declaring that slavery shall die, instead of saying that it is dead; for, said the mover, although it is legally dead, the fact is that there are over three millions of people now enslaved in the southern States. He moved to substitute these words:

"That the rebellion must be suppressed by the destruction of its motive cause, slavery."

This was lost after a debate, and the resolution was adopted.

The remainder were then adopted.

LETTERS OF ACCEPTANCE.

FROM GENERAL FREMONT.

NEW YORK, *June* 4, 1864.

GENTLEMEN: In answer to the letter which I have had the honor to receive from you, on the part of the representatives of the people assembled at Cleveland, the 31st of May, I desire to express my thanks for the confidence which led them to offer me the honorable and difficult position of their candidate in the approaching Presidential election.

Very honorable, because in offering it to me you act in the name of a great number of citizens who seek above all things the good of their country, and who have no sort of selfish interest in view. Very difficult, because in accepting the candidacy you propose to me, I am exposed to the

* During the Convention, Mr. Langer, of Iowa, offered these resolutions, which, on the suggestion of the Chair, were referred to the committee:

"*Resolved,* That the members of this Convention, or of any Convention arising from this, to nominate or participate in the nomination of a candidate for the next Presidential term, and the Presidential electors of this party, pledge themselves upon their honor not to accept offices of trust, honor, or profit from the Administration in power during the next Presidential term, and not to be connected directly or indirectly with any contract or business transaction in the power of the Administration.

"*Resolved,* To make it obligatory on the Presidential candidate of this party, if successful, to act accordingly.

"*Resolved,* That this is not to be construed to prevent any member from becoming an active combatant in the Navy and Army of the United States, in such capacity as his respective State may elect to employ him."

reproach of creating a schism in the party with which I have been identified.

Had Mr. Lincoln remained faithful to the principles he was elected to defend, no schism could have been created, and no contest could have been possible. This is not an ordinary election. It is a contest for the right even to have candidates, and not merely, as usual, for the choice among them. Now, for the first time since '76, the question of constitutional liberty has been brought directly before the people for their serious consideration and vote. The ordinary rights secured under the Constitution and the laws of the country have been violated and extraordinary powers have been usurped by the Executive. It is directly before the people now to say whether or not the principles established by the Revolution are worth maintaining.

If, as we have been taught to believe, those guarantees for liberty which made the distinctive name and glory of our country, are in truth inviolably sacred, then here must be a protest against the arbitrary violation which had not even the excuse of a necessity. The schism is made by those who force the choice between a shameful silence or a protest against wrong. In such considerations originated the Cleveland Convention. It was among its objects to arouse the attention of the people to such facts, and to bring them to realize that, while we are saturating Southern soil with the best blood of the country in the name of liberty, we have really parted with it at home.

To-day we have in the country the abuses of a military dictation without its unity of action and vigor of execution—an Administration marked at home by disregard of constitutional rights, by its violation of personal liberty and the liberty of the press, and as a crowning shame, by its abandonment of the right of asylum, a right especially dear to all free nations abroad. Its course has been characterized by a feebleness and want of principle which has misled European powers and driven them to a belief that only commercial interests and personal aims are concerned, and that no great principles are involved in the issue. The admirable conduct of the people, their readiness to make every sacrifice demanded of them, their forbearance and silence under the suspension of everything that could be suspended, their many acts of heroism and sacrifices, were all rendered fruitless by the incapacity, or to speak more exactly, by the personal ends for which the war was managed. This incapacity and selfishness naturally produced such results as led the European powers, and logically enough, to the conviction that the North, with its greatly superior population, its immense resources, and its credit, will never be able to recover the South. Sympathies which would have been with us from the outset of this war were turned against us, and in this way the Administration has done the country a double wrong abroad. It created hostility, or at best indifference, among those who would have been its friends if the real intentions of the people could have been better known, while, at the same time, it neglected no occasion for making the most humiliating concessions.

Against this disastrous condition of affairs the Cleveland Convention was a protest.

The principles which form the basis of its platform have my unqualified and cordial approbation, but I cannot so heartily concur in all the measures which you propose. *I do not believe that confiscation extended to the property of all rebels, is practicable*, and if it were so, I do not think it a measure of sound policy. It is, in fact, a question belonging to the people themselves to decide, and is a proper occasion for the exercise of their original and sovereign authority. As a war measure, in the beginning of a revolt which might be quelled by prompt severity, I understand the policy of confiscation, but not as a final measure of reconstruction after the suppression of an insurrection.

In the adjustments which are to follow peace no considerations of vengeance can consistently be admitted.

The object of the war is to make permanently secure the peace and happiness of the whole country, and there was but a single element in the way of its attainment. This element of *slavery may be considered practically destroyed* in the country, and it needs only your proposed amendment of the Constitution, to make its extinction complete.

With this extinction of slavery the party divisions created by it have also disappeared. And if in the history of the country there has ever been a time when the American people, without regard to one or another of the political divisions, were called upon to give solemnly their voice in a matter which involved the safety of the United States, it is assuredly the present time.

If the Convention at Baltimore will nominate any man whose past life justifies a well-grounded confidence in his fidelity to our cardinal principles, there is no reason why there should be any division among the really patriotic men of the country. To any such I shall be most happy to give a cordial and active support.

My own decided preference is to aid in this way, and not to be myself a candidate. But *if Mr. Lincoln should be nominated*—as I believe *it would be fatal to the country* to indorse a policy and renew a power which has cost us the lives of thousands of men, and needlessly put the country on the road to bankruptcy—there will remain no other alternative but to organize against him every element of conscientious opposition with the view to prevent the misfortune of his re-election.

In this contingency, I accept the nomination at Cleveland, and, as a preliminary step, *I have resigned my commission in the army*. This was a sacrifice it gave me pain to make. But I had for a long time fruitlessly endeavored to obtain service. I make this sacrifice now only to regain liberty of speech, and to leave nothing in the way of discharging to my utmost ability the task you have set for me.

With my earnest and sincere thanks for your expressions of confidence and regard, and for the many honorable terms in which you acquaint me with the actions of the Convention, I am, gentlemen,

Very respectfully and truly yours,

J. C. FREMONT.

To Worthington G. Snethen of Maryland, Edward Gilbert of New York, Casper Butz of Illinois, Charles E. Moss of Missouri, N. P. Sawyer of Pennsylvania, a Committee, &c.

FROM GENERAL COCHRANE.

NEW YORK, *June* 4, 1864.

GENTLEMEN: I have received your note informing me officially of my nomination by the Radical Democracy at Cleveland, on the 31st ultimo, as their candidate for Vice President of the United States, on the ticket with John C. Fremont as their candidate for President.

I have been accustomed to regard simply as a duty performed what you are pleased to represent as personally meritorious, and to regret the physical disability which alone withdrew me from the immediate scene of war.

I concur in the action and agree with the principles of the Convention. Where by its twelfth resolution the question of reconstruction is referred to the constitutional action of the people, it wisely committed to them an issue peculiarly within the province of the future, and not yet sufficiently emerged from war, to warrant positive opinion.

While I have ever supposed confiscation and use of the property of an enemy in arms to be a laudable exercise of an established and essential rule of civilized war, I am pleased to observe that the Convention, when asserting the justice of the principle, intended to remit its exercise to the discretion of the people, hereafter manifested through their representatives in Congress, when considering the paramount question of reconstruction This was judicious; for, indeed, so blended must be the various methods—sequestration, confiscation, military absorption and occupation—that shall hereafter co-operate to evolve order from confusion, and to restore the Government, that it is difficult, if not impossible, now, when affirming the principle, to provide for its application.

I have the honor, gentlemen, to accept the nomination for the Vice President of the United States, which you have tendered to me under the direction of the Convention.

I am, very respectfully, yours,

JOHN COCHRANE.

To the COMMITTEE.

Speech of Colonel Cochrane.

DELIVERED TO HIS REGIMENT, FIRST UNITED STATES CHASSEURS, NOVEMBER 13, 1861.

It having been announced that Colonel John Cochrane would speak to his regiment, at their camp, on the occasion of their first appearance in new uniforms, on the afternoon of Friday, the 13th of November, instant, a large assemblage of ladies and gentlemen was congregated to hear him. A staging had been improvised beneath a spreading oak, where, conspicuous among the audience, sat the Secretary of War, dignified and composed. In front, in enclosing lines, stood the imposing regiment—the first United States Chasseurs, steady, exact, and attentive. Within the square a regimental band uttered harmonious music, while the reddening rays of the descending sun enveloped the audience, soldiers, Secretary, and orator, in rosy rays, that imparted a soft beauty to the scene, and conveyed the pleasing illusion attendant upon dramatic effect. The Colonel then advanced and notified his hearers that one of the companies of the regiment had selected this as a fitting opportunity to present to one of their lieutenants (Morton) a small token of their admiration and esteem. The preliminary ceremony was agreeably and satisfactory finished. It was then that Colonel Cochrane arose, and, justly inspired by the scene and the circumstances which produced it, spoke as follows:

Soldiers of the First United States Chasseurs:

[Bravo Colonel.] I have a word to say to you to-day. You have engaged in an arduous struggle. You have prosecuted it; you intend to prosecute it; you have stood unflinchingly before the enemy; you have proved yourselves patriotic, able, and tried soldiers, and you are entitled to the meed of praise. I, your commander, this day feel that it is a proud duty to extend to you the hand of approbation, and to declare that you are worthy of your country.

Soldiers, you have undergone labor; you have faced the enemy; you have stood without retreating before their fire; you have borne the inclemencies of the season, and you are ready to advance with that grand army of which you are a part. Your country opens its arms, and receives you to its bosom. It will always praise and applaud you. Its commanders stand at the head of the column, and, with you behind them, they are not to be deterred. But the command is forthcoming—forward, march! toward the enemy. Take his possessions, for they are yours; they are yours to occupy; they are yours to enjoy; you are no marauders, you are no plunderers of property not your own, but you are the avengers of the law; you are the right arm of the Constitution; under your flag march patriotism and order, and republican institutions; in your train follow peace, prosperity and liberty; you are the servants of these high potentates, and the arm through which they strike is the arm of the worthy public servant who stands behind me on this occasion, the Secretary of War.

Soldiers, you have been called to the field, not as marauders and mercenaries, but as the defenders of our high faith, defenders of our glorious reputation, defenders of our honor and renown, around which cluster the memories of the past, and whose feats and performances will yet distinguish the future. You are led forward by a commander under whom to serve it is a pride for the highest among us. He enjoys the confidence of the people, and his reputation already renders powerless the arms of your enemies. By him we have won victories in the South, and by these victories we have assurances of triumph yet to come. Beaufort is ours—Charleston may be ours—the whole country now disintegrated may shortly be united by the force of those arms of which you are a part, and the Union once more signify to the world the intent of that glorious motto, *E Pluribus Unum*. Then no longer shall be heard that fell doctrine of secession, which would tear us asunder, and distract, part from part, this glorious Union; but we shall all be as we have been, one and inseparable, under the flag of our glorious nationality, won by our fathers, and preserved by you. [Applause.] Here is assembled upon the banks of the Potomac an army the like of which the world has never seen. The motive which has gathered that army together never before was presented to the eye of history. It was congregated by no despotic order; it was the voluntary wish, the motive power, of every man composing it—the power of men rushing, as with one purpose, to reinstate the flag of our Union and save the Republic. That, soldiers, is your mission; and you have a commander who with lightning speed will lead you to conquest, and with equal speed will transmit the glory of your labors to the remotest corners of our country. And now permit me, though the shades of night are falling upon us, to indulge in a few words as to the cause of the war, and the means by which it is to be brought to a successful termination. The material aid I have already averted to; the motive power remains to be commented upon. On the one side you have the Confederate army; on the other side you have the grand Union—the Federal army. Now, the difference between these two words, in their common acceptation, is the cause for which these two armies are fighting. It is Secession against Federation, Federation against Secession. Nationality against disunion; confusion against order; anarchy against a good, free, and liberal Government—a Government made equally by the Fathers of the South and the Fathers of the North. We are in a revolutionary period. The South contends for the right of revolution. We admit the right; but, while we admit it, we invoke the sole umpire which may be invoked on such occasions—the umpire of the sword, the umpire of force, the *ultima ratio*, that last effort to which men appeal when they have differences otherwise irreconcileable.

They—the South—have resorted to arms, and they have compelled us to the same resort; and if they claim that it is a war of self-preservation on their part, it is equally a war of self-preservation on ours; and if we are in controversy for very existence, then I contend that all the resources, all the means within ourselves, individually, collectively, and nationally, must be resorted to and adopted. [Applause.] But some friend—a doubter—exclaims: "Would you disrupt and tear asunder the Constitution?" Where is the Constitution? Would you tread and trample upon that sacred instrument, and no longer acknowldge its binding force, no longer be bound by its compromises and decrees? I answer, no. The Constitution, by the necessity of the controversy, is cast behind the arena of the strife. May it rest there safe, until the present strife being over it shall be restored to its original purity and force. Like the sibyl leaves when lost, the remainder become more valuable in our eyes, and in the midst of the carnage we will clasp to our bosoms that instrument whose worth has never been transcended by human efforts. Soldiers, to what means shall we resort for our existence? This war is devoted not merely to victory and its mighty honors, not merely to the triumph which moves in glorious procession along our streets. But it is a war which moves towards the protection of our homes, the safety of our families, the continuation of our domestic altars, and the protection of our firesides. In such a war we are justified, are bound to resort to every force within our power. Having opened the port of Beaufort, we shall be able to export millions of cotton bales, and from these we may supply the sinews of war. Do you say that we should not seize the cotton? No; you are clear upon that point. Suppose the munitions of war are within our reach, would we not be guilty of shameful neglect, if we availed not ourselves of the opportunity to use them? Suppose the enemy's slaves were arrayed against you, would you, from any squeamishness, refrain from pointing against them the hostile gun, and prostrating them in death? No; that is your object and purport; and if you would seize their property, open their ports, and even destroy their lives, I ask you whether you would not use their slaves? Whether you would not *arm their slaves* [great applause,] *and carry them in battalions against their masters?* [Renewed and tumultuous applause.] *If necessary to save this Government, I would plunge their whole country black and white, into one indiscriminate sea of blood*, so that we should in the end have a Government which would be the vicegerent of God. Let us have no more of this *dilletante* system, but let us work with a will and a purpose that cannot be mistaken. Let us not put aside from too great a delicacy of motives. Soldiers, you know no such reasoning as this. You have arms in your hands, and those arms are placed there for the purpose of exterminating an enemy unless he submits to law, order, and the Constitution. *If he will not submit, explode every thing that comes in your way. Set fire to the cotton. Explode the cotton. Take property wherever you may find it. Take the slave and bestow him upon the non-slaveholder if you please.* [Great applause.] *Do to them as they would do to us. Raise up a party of interest against the absent slaveholder, distract their counsels, and if this should not be sufficient, take the slave by the hand, place a musket in it, and in God's name bid him strike for the liberty of the human race.* [Immense applause.] Now, is this emancipation? Is this abolitionism? I do not regard it as either. It no more partakes of Abolitionism than a spaniel partakes of the nature of the lion. Abolitionism is to free the slaves. It is to make war upon the South for that purpose. It is to place them above their masters in the social scale. It is to assert the great abstract principles of equality among men. But to take the slave and make him an implement of war in overcoming your enemy, that is a military scheme. It is a military necessity, and the commander who does not this, or something equivalent to it, is unworthy of the position he holds, and equally unworthy of your confidence. Emancipation! Are we engaged in a war of emancipation? If so, who commenced the war? Not we. And if we did not commence the war, we cannot be charged with its consequences. Where had it its origin? It had its origin in the South. It was and has been a war of the South against the free institutions of the North. Let me illustrate. Are we to free their slaves? We do not intend it. Do you recollect the resolution which was passed the last session of Congress, which distinctly declares that it never was intended by anybody in this wide land to free the slave. "Compromise," too, has been talked of this matter. Why did they not compromise? Because it was not their object. I say this fearlessly, for I infer it from scenes in which I was an actor.

At Charleston, I remember, that when satisfied that Mr. Douglas could not, while they remained in the convention, be nominated for the Presidency, they nevertheless withdrew. It was, if my remembrance is not at fault, near the midnight hour, at the prominent headquarters of the southern array, that Messrs. Yancey and Percy Walker entered the room. Those present had previously concluded, upon careful calculations, that the South abiding by the convention, Judge Douglas could not receive two thirds of the vote of the convention. This conclusion was communicated to these gentlemen, who, as I understand, having reviewed the calculations, and expressed their reliance upon them, declared, when leaving, their determination to remain in the convention. It was at the opening of the convention on the very next morning, that Mr. Walker sent to the chair the act of secession of Alabama therefrom. The morning deed declared marvelously, when contrasted with the midnight profession, that the act of secession was but a foregone conclusion, necessary to precipitate the only issue to which they desired to be a party.

Nothing could be satisfactory to these, except that arms should be resorted to, and the fate of revolution abided by. I declare, therefore, that the war is not of our originating, but it has been forced upon us by a crafty enemy—an enemy resolved to do or die; to destroy our free Government, or perish in the attempt. And what is their object? Why, their object is to tear down this proud, noble, and beneficent Government, to establish a reign of terror, anarchy, and confiscation, in the land; to implant upon this our soil the hideous doctrine of the right of secession, so that when one State secedes another may secede, and still another, and still another, so that within forty-eight hours, by the light of their reason and the exactness of their judgment, you may establish on this continent thirty-four independent governments. Thirty-four, did I say? Why, no, not thirty-four merely, but every county and every city, and every village and hamlet; nay, every person who suffers from indigestion at the dinner table may claim the same right; and thus, soldiers, we shall have the confusion and disorder which will plunge into dismay and ruin the best and most benevolent government in the world. Now, what is our object? It is simply to arrest the sway of this fell spirit of secession. It is to maintain our Government, to establish and vindicate law and order, without which neither happiness nor prosperity can exist. You are engaged, too, by the strength of your arms, to protect our commerce with other nations, and when victory crowns your devotion to your country's cause—as it assuredly will—you will be proudly pointed at as the champions of American rights, as men who have maintained their dearest principles, and as those who, from this time forward, shall live in the most grateful remembrance of the living, and whose names shall descend with marks of imperishable honor to the remotest posterity. But, soldiers, to accomplish all this, not merely arms are necessary, not merely men to carry them, but that powerful and overwhelming spirit which constitutes and makes us men, that spirit which lifts us above the creeping things of the earth, and brings near the Deity, in accomplishing his work on earth. Oh, then, let us not think that the "battle is to the strong"—let us not merely depend on discipline and order, but with that fervidness of soul which inspired our fathers at Bunker Hill, and Saratoga, and Yorktown, come forward and give effect to all that is valuable in the name of patriotism, and honor, and religion.

Never, no never, will you succeed until that spirit is once more manifested and developed which actuated the soldiers of Cromwell, who, on the field, invoked the Lord their God to arise. So let it be with us. We must be at least one with Him in spirit. Let us, like Cromwell, invoke the Almighty blessing, and, clothed with the panoply of patriotism and religion, strike for our homes and our country. [Immense cheering.] Let us—oh, let us—without reference to any differences of the past, keep our eyes steadfastly on the great object to be achieved, the nationality and independence of this country, the salvation of civilization from the insults and assaults of barbarism; and then, but not till then, will you be worthy to be recognized as a distinguished portion of our great American army. [Long continued cheering from the whole regiment.]

Upon the conclusion of Colonel Cochrane's speech, loud and repeated calls being made for the Secretary of War, Mr. Cameron came before the regiment, and said:

Soldiers: It is too late for me to make you a speech to-night, but I will say that I heartily approve every sentiment uttered by your noble commander. The doctrines which he has laid down I approve of as if they were my own words. They are my sentiments—sentiments which will not only lead you to victory, but which will in the end reconstruct this our glorious Federal Constitution. It is idle to talk about treating with these rebels upon their own terms. We must meet them as our enemies, treat them as enemies, and punish them as enemies, until they shall learn to behave themselves. *Every means which God has placed in our hands it is our duty to use for the purpose of protecting ourselves.* I am glad of the opportunity to say here, what I have already said elsewhere, in these few words, that *I approve the doctrines this evening enunciated by Colonel Cochrane.* [Loud and prolonged cheering.]

APPENDIX.

Democratic National Convention.

1864, August 29—The body met at 12 o'clock, in Chicago, Ill., and was called to order by the Chairman of the Democratic National Committee, August Belmont, who said:

Gentlemen of the Convention: We are assembled here to-day, at the National Democratic Convention, for the purpose of nominating candidates for the Presidency and Vice Presidency of the United States. This task, at all times a most important and arduous one, has, by the sad events of our civil war, assumed an importance and responsibility of the most fearful nature. Never, since the formation of our government, has there been an assemblage, the proceedings of which were fraught with more momentous and vital results, than those which must flow from your action. Towards you, gentlemen, are directed at this moment the anxious fears and doubts, not only of millions of American citizens, but also of every lover of civil liberty throughout the world. [Cheers.] In your hands rests, under the ruling of an all-wise Providence, the future of this Republic. Four years of misrule by a sectional, fanatical and corrupt party, have brought our country to the very verge of ruin. The past and present are sufficient warnings of the disastrous consequences which would befall us if Mr. Lincoln's re-election should be made possible by our want of patriotism and unity. The inevitable results of such a calamity must be the utter disintegration of our whole political and social system amidst bloodshed and anarchy, with the great problems of liberal progress and self-government jeopardized for generations to come.

The American people have at last awakened to the conviction that a change of policy and administration can alone stay our downward course; and they will rush to the support of your candidate and platform, provided you will offer to their suffrage a tried patriot, who has proved his devotion to the Union and the Constitution, and provided that you pledge him and yourselves to maintain that hallowed inheritance by every effort and sacrifice in your power. [Loud applause.] Let us, at the very outset of our proceedings, bear in mind that the dissensions of the last democratic convention were one of the principal causes which gave the reins of government into the hands of our opponents; and let us beware not to fall again into the same fatal error. We must bring at the altar of our country the sacrifice of our prejudices, opinions and convictions—however dear and long cherished they may be—from the moment they threaten the harmony and unity of action so indispensable to our success. We are here not as war democrats, nor as peace democrats, but as citizens of the great Republic, which we will strive to bring back to its former greatness and prosperity, without one single star taken from the brilliant constellation that once encircled its youthful brow. [Cheers.] Let peace and disinterested patriotism, tempered by moderation and forbearance, preside over our deliberations; and, under the blessings of the Almighty, the sacred cause of the Union, the constitution and the laws, must prevail against fanaticism and treason. [Loud cheering.]

Mr. Belmont named as temporary chairman Ex-Governor William Bigler, of Pennsylvania, who said:

Gentlemen of the Convention: I am greatly honored in your selection of me to preside over the preliminary deliberations of this body. My acknowledgments for this high compliment, and for the kind greetings just extended to me by this vast concourse of my fellow citizens, will be best manifested by a proper discharge of the duties of the position to which you have called me.

It is not expected, nor would it be befitting in one assuming the temporary Presidency of the convention, that he should enter upon any general discussion of the many interesting topics suggested by the unhappy condition of our country. A brief allusion to the occasion and purposes of our assembling is all that will be necessary. No similar body ever assembled in America with mightier objects before it, or to which such a vast proportion of the American people looked with such profound solicitude for measures to promote the welfare of the country and advance their individual happiness.

The termination of democratic rule in this country was the end of peaceful relations between the States and the people. The elevation of a sectional party to authority at Washington, the culmination of a long indulged and acrimonious war of crimination and re-crimination between extreme men of the North and South, was promptly followed by dissolution and civil war. And in the progress of that war the very bulwarks of civil liberty have been imperiled and the whole fabric brought to the very verge of destruction. And now, at the end of more than three years of a war unparalleled in modern times, for its magnitude and for its barbarous desolations—after more than two millions of men have been called into the field, on our side alone, after the land has been literally drenched in fraternal blood, and wailings and lamentations are heard in every corner of our common country, the hopes of the Union, our cherished object, are in nowise improved. The men now in authority, because of the feud which they have so long maintained with violent and unwise men of the South, and because of a blind fanaticism about an institution of some of the States, in relation to which they have no duties to perform and no responsibilities to bear, are rendered incapable of adopting the proper means to rescue our country—our whole country—from its present lamentable condition. Then, gentlemen, it is apparent that the first indispensable step to the accomplishment of this great work is the overthrow, by the ballot, of the present administration, and the inauguration of another in its stead, which shall directly and zealously, but temperately and justly, wield all the influence and power of the government to bring about a speedy settlement of the national troubles on the principles of the constitution and on terms honorable and just to all sections, North and South, East and West; one which shall stand unfalteringly by civil and religious liberty; one which, instead of relying solely on its own peculiar dogmas and doctrines and the ravages of the sword, shall refer the national troubles to the people, the fountain of political authority, and to the States under the forms of the constitution; one which shall have no conditions precedent to the restoration of the Union, but which shall diligently seek that result as the consummation of permanent peace amongst the States and renewed fraternity amongst the people.

Gentlemen, we have been commissioned by the people to come here and initiate steps to accomplish these great objects; to select an agent and the agencies in this good work. That the task will be well performed I have unfaltering faith; and that the people may sanction and God may bless these means to the desired end, is my sincere prayer.

Rev. Dr. Robert H. Clarkson, of the Episcopal Church, offered a prayer, after which the names of delegates were called, and Committees appointed on Credentials, Organization, and Resolutions. The latter was thus composed:

Committee on Resolutions—Maine, John W. Dana; New Hampshire, Edwin Pease; Massachusetts, George Lunt; Connecticut, Charles R. Ingersoll; Vermont, T. P. Redfield; Rhode Island, Charles S. Bradley; New York, Samuel J. Tilden; New Jersey, Abraham Browning; Pennsylvania, William A. Wallace; Delaware, Charles Brown; Maryland, Thomas G. Pratt; Kentucky, Thomas N. Lindsey and James Guthrie; Ohio, Clement L. Vallandigham; Indiana, James M. Hanna; Illinois, S. S. Marshall; Michigan, Augustus C. Baldwin; Missouri, William A. Hall; Minnesota, E. O. Hamlin; Wisconsin, George B. Smith; Iowa,

James F. Bates; California, John B. Weller; Kansas, Wm. C. McDowell; Oregon, Benjamin Stark.

And to it were referred the resolutions offered in open convention, as follows:

By Washington Hunt, of New York:

Resolved, That in the future, as in the past, we will adhere with unswerving fidelity to the Union and the Constitution, and insist on maintaining our national unity as the only solid foundation of our strength, security and happiness as a people, and as a framework of government, equally conducive to the welfare and prosperity of all the States both Northern and Southern; and, with a view to terminate the pending conflict and restore the blessings of peace, we are in favor of an armistice, and of earnest, honorable efforts to adjust the terms of settlement and Union on the basis of the constitution of the United States; and, for the final solution of all differences, we would recommend a convention of the States to review the constitution, and adopt such amendments and modifications as may seem necessary, more fully to insure to each State the enjoyment of all its rights and the undisturbed control of its domestic concerns, according to the original intent and purpose of the Federal compact.

By Thomas L. Price, of Missouri:

Resolved, That, in this great crisis of our national history, the freedom and purity of the elective franchise—that sacred right of freemen secured to us by the blood of our fathers, and the guaranties of the constitution, must be maintained against all assaults, intimidation, or interference; and we hereby pledge, each to the other, and all of us to our common country, our lives, our fortunes, and our sacred honors, to make common cause with the people of any and every State where the same may be assailed or trampled upon; to the end that the constitutional expression of the popular will and the inestimable right of self-government may be secured for ourselves and our posterity.

By Alexander Long, of Ohio:

Resolved, That a committee, to be composed of one member from each State represented in this Convention, to be selected by the respective delegations thereof, be appointed for the purpose of proceeding forthwith to the city of Washington, and, on behalf of this Convention and the people, to ask Mr. Lincoln to suspend the operation of the pending draft for 500,000 more men until the people shall have an opportunity through the ballot box in a free election—uninfluenced in any manner by military orders or military interference—of deciding the question, now fairly presented to them, of war or peace, at the approaching election in November; and that said committee be and they are hereby instructed to urge upon Mr. Lincoln, by whatever argument they can employ, to stay the flow of fraternal blood, at least so far as the pending draft will continue to augment it, until the people, the source of all power, shall have an opportunity of expressing their will for or against the further prosecution of the war in the choice of candidates for the Presidency.

By Hamilton Alricks, of Pennsylvania:

We, the representatives of the democratic party of the United States of America, in National Convention assembled, for the purpose of nominating candidates for the high offices of President and Vice President, to be voted for at the ensuing election, point with pride and satisfaction to the past history of our common country, her great and marvelous prosperity, under democratic administration. Therefore, in order to restore and preserve the integrity of our once happy Union, re-establish justice and domestic tranquility throughout our borders, promote the general welfare, and secure the return of the blessings of liberty vouchsafed to us by our forefathers, we here renew and declare our unalterable attachment to the Union, and that it must be preserved in its integrity. Believing that the desirable object can be obtained if we profit by the wisdom of our forefathers, we here adopt as our sure and broad platform the constitution of the United States in its length and breadth, and pledge our candidates to maintain, preserve, protect, and defend the same.

Resolved, That we cannot view with indifference the open repudiation and violation of the Monroe doctrine, the establishment of an empire on the ruins of a neighboring republic; and that we view with greater alarm and distrust the fearful strides of the general administration at our national capital towards despotism, in their repeated interference with State rights, with the liberty of speech, of the press, and the right of private property; wherefore, we call on all true and incorruptible patriots to lay aside their partisan prejudices, to look our bleeding country's troubles in the face, calmly to consider the fearful waste of blood and treasure through the unwise acts and misguided policy of the present national administration, and assist in changing our rulers, that we may rescue our beloved country and the liberties of the people from certain ruin.

Resolved, That we will use all honorable means known to civilized nations to bring to a speedy termination the unhappy difficulties that disturb our country.

August 30—The permanent organization was made, with Governor Horatio Seymour, of New York, as President. On taking the chair, he said:

GENTLEMEN OF THE CONVENTION: I thank you for the high honor you have conferred upon me in making me President of this body. The importance of the occasion has already been expressed in fitting words by your temporary chairman. I have not language to tell with what anxious solicitude the people of this country watch our proceedings. The prayers of men and women in ten thousand homes go up to heaven that we may be so guided in our deliberations that our action may conduce to the restoration of our Union, to the return of peace, and the maintenance of liberty in this land. [Cheers.]

It is not for me to forecast your action—it is not for me to say what methods may be adopted to relieve this afflicted country of ours. But while I may not speak on that subject, I can, with propriety, allude to the sentiments which animate you all. There is no man here who does not love the Union. [Cheers.] There is no man here who does not desire peace. [Cheers.] There is no man here who is not resolved to uphold the great principles of constitutional freedom. [Applause.]

I know that the utmost importance attaches to all your proceedings. I know it is of vital consequence that you should select such men, as your candidates, as enjoy the confidence of the American people. But beyond platforms and beyond candidates, there are other considerations of still greater significance and importance. When you wish to know what the policy of party will be, you must strive to learn the passions and sentiments which animate that party. Four years ago, in this city, there was an assemblage of citizens from the different parts of our country, who met here for the purpose of placing in nomination a candidate for the Presidency. They put forth declarations that they would not interfere with the rights of the States of this Union. They did not intend to destroy our country—they did not mean to break down its institutions. But unhappily they were influenced by sectional prejudices, by fanaticism, by bigotry, and by intolerance; and we have found in the course of the last four years that their animating sentiments have overruled their declarations and their promises, and swept them on, step by step, until they have been carried on to actions from which at the outset they would have shrunk away with horror. Even now, when war has desolated our land, has laid its heavy burthens upon labor, when bankruptcy and ruin overhang us, they will not have Union except upon conditions unknown to our constitution; they will not let the shedding of blood cease, even for a little time, to see if Christian charity, or the wisdom of statesmanship may not work out a method to save our country. Nay, more than this, they will not listen to a proposal for peace which does not offer that which this government has no right to ask.

This administration cannot now save this Union if it would. It has, by its proclamations, by vindictive legislation, by displays of hate and passion, placed obstacles in its own pathway which it cannot overcome, and has hampered its own freedom of action by unconstitutional acts. It cannot be said that the failure of its policy is due to the want of courage and devotion on the part of our armies. [Cheers.] Never in the world's history have soldiers given up their lives more freely than have those of the armies which have battled for the flag of our Union in the Southern States. The world will hold that they have done all that arms can do; and had wise statesmanship secured the fruits of their victories, to-day there would have been peace in our land. [Much applause.] But while our soldiers have desperately struggled to carry our banner southward to the Gulf of Mexico, even now the government declares that rebellious discontent has worked northward to the shores of the great lakes. The guaranteed right of the people to bear arms has been suspended by the edict of a General up to the very borders of Canada; so that American servitude is put in bold contrast with British liberty.* This

---

* Supposed to refer to this order:

HEADQUARTERS NORTHERN DEPARTMENT,
COLUMBUS, OHIO, *August* 27, 1864.

[SPECIAL ORDER NO. 53.]

During the ensuing sixty days no fire arms, powder, or ammunition of any kind will be received, transported, or delivered by any railroad, express, or other forwarding company within the States comprised within the limits of this department—viz: Ohio, Indiana, Illinois, and Michigan

administration thus declares to the world it has now no faith in the people of States whose votes placed it in power; and it also admits by such edict that these people have no faith in this administration. While those in power, without remorse, sacrifice the blood and treasure of our people, they will not give up their own passions for the public good. This Union is not held asunder by military ambition. If our political troubles could be referred to the peaceful arbitrament of the contending armies in the field, our Union would be restored, the rights of States would be guaranteed, the sacredness of homes and persons again respected, and an insulted judiciary would again administer the laws of the land. Let not the ruin of our country be charged to our soldiers. It is not due to their teachings or their fanaticism. In my constant official intercourse with them, I have never heard uttered one sentiment of hatred towards the people of the South. Beyond all men they value the blessings of peace and the virtues of mercy, of gentleness and of charity; while many who stay at home cry havoc, and demand that no mercy shall be shown. The bigotry of fanatics and the intrigues of placemen have made the bloody pages of the history of the past three years.

But if the administration cannot save this Union, we can. [Loud applause.] Mr. Lincoln values many things above the Union; we put it first of all. [Continued cheering.] He thinks a proclamation worth more than peace; we think the blood of our people more precious than the edicts of the President. [Cheers.] There are no hindrances in our pathways to Union and to peace. We demand no conditions for the restoration of our Union; we are shackled with no hates, no prejudices, no passions. We wish for fraternal relationship with the people of the South. [Applause.] We demand for them what we demand for ourselves—the full recognition of the rights of States. We mean that every star on our nation's banner shall shine with an equal lustre.

In the coming election men must decide with which of the two parties, into which our people are divided, they will act. If they wish for the Union they will act with that party which does now and always did love and reverence that Union. If they wish for peace, they will act with those who sought to avert this war, and who now seek to restore good will and harmony among all sections of our country. If they care for their rights as persons and the sacredness of their homes, they will act with those who have stood up to resist arbitrary arrests, despotic legislation, and the overthrow of the judiciary. [Loud and continued applause.] If, upon the other hand, they are willing to continue the present policy of government and condition of affairs, let them act with that organization which made the present condition of our country. And there are many good men who will be led to do this by their passions and prejudices; and our land swarms with placemen who will hold upon power and plunder with a deadly grasp. But as for us, we are resolved that the party who have made the history of our country, since their advent to power, seem like some unnatural and terrible dream shall be overthrown. [Applause.] Four years ago it had its birth upon this spot. Let us see, by our action, that it shall die here where it was born. [Loud and continued cheering.]

In the political contest in which we are now engaged, we do not seek partisan advantages. We are battling for the rights of those who belong to all political organizations. We mean that their rights of speech shall be unimpaired, although that right may be used to denounce us. We intend that rights of conscience shall be protected, although mistaken views of duty may turn the temples of religion into theatres for partisan denunciation. We mean that home rights and the sacredness of the fireside shall be respected by those in authority, no matter what political views may be held by those who sit beneath their roof-trees. When the democratic party shall have gained power, we shall not be less, but more tenacious upon these subjects. We have forborne much because those who are now charged with the conduct of public affairs knew but little about the principles of our government. We were unwilling to present an appearance of factious opposition. But when we shall have gained power, that official who shall violate one principle of law, one single right of the humblest man in our land, shall be punished by the full rigor of the law; it matters not if he sits in the Presidential chair or holds a humbler office under our government. [Cheers.]

We have had upon this floor a touching and significant proof of the folly of this administration, who have driven from its support those upon whom it chiefly leaned at the outset of this rebellion; when their hopes, even for their own personal safety, hung upon the noble men of the border States, [loud and continued cheering,] who, under circumstances most trying, severed family relations and ancient associations, to uphold the flag of our Union. Many of these men are members of this convention. They bear impressed upon their countenances and manifest in their persons the high and generous purposes which animate them; and yet it is true—great God, that it should be true!—that they are stung with a sense of the injustice and ingratitude of low and unworthy men, who have insulted and wronged them, their families and their rights, by vindictive legislation or through the agency of miserable dishonored subordinates. [Cheers.]

Gentlemen, I trust that our proceedings will be marked by harmony. I believe we shall all be animated by the greatness of this occasion. It may be—in all probability it is true—that the future destinies of our country hang upon our action. Let this consideration inspire us with a spirit of harmony. God of our fathers bless us now; lift us above all personal consideration; fill us with a just sense of the great responsibilities which rest upon us, and give again to our land its Union, its peace, and its liberty.

[Enthusiastic and long continued cheering followed the conclusion of Gov. Seymour's remarks. The entire assemblage participated, and thousands of voices united in pouring forth round after round of tumultuous applause. When the enthusiasm had only partially subsided,]

The President came forward, and addressing the assemblage, said: I wish to say one word to the audience here assembled. The delegates who compose this convention have come up from different parts of the Union for the purpose of acting upon your most important interests. We are most happy that you should be the witnesses of our proceedings, but one thing you must bear in mind: That you are not members of this body, and, while our hearts will be cheered to find that patriotic sentiments are received as patriotic sentiments should be by the American people, you must not undertake to attempt to influence the deliberations of the Convention, or allow your feelings to take such form of expression as are unbecoming in the presence of those upon whom rest the responsibilities of the occasion. [Cheers, followed by loud calls for Vallandigham, mingled with applause and hisses.]

THE PLATFORM

was then adopted, as reported by Mr. Guthrie, Chairman of the Committee:

Resolved, That in the future, as in the past, we will adhere with unswerving fidelity to the Union under the Constitution as the only solid foundation of our strength, security and happiness as a people, and as a framework of government equally conducive to the welfare and prosperity of all the States, both northern and southern.

Resolved, That this convention does explicitly declare, as the sense of the American people, that after four years of failure to restore the Union by the experiment of war, during which, under the pretense of a military necessity, or war power higher than the Constitution, the Constitution itself has been disregarded in every part, and public liberty and private right alike trodden down and the material prosperity of the country essentially impaired—justice, humanity, liberty and the public welfare demand that immediate efforts be made for a cessation of hostilities, with a view to an ultimate convention of the States, or other peaceable means, to the end that at the earliest practicable moment peace may be restored on the basis of the Federal Union of the States.

Resolved, That the direct interference of the military authorities of the United States in the recent elections held in Kentucky, Maryland, Missouri and Delaware, was a shameful violation of the Constitution; and a repetition of such acts in the approaching election will be held as revolutionary, and resisted with all the means and power under our control.

Resolved, That the aim and object of the Democratic party is to preserve the Federal Union and the rights of the States unimpaired; and they hereby declare that they con-

---

—without a permit from these headquarters; from Gen. A. P. Hovey, Indianapolis, Indiana; Gen. H. E. Paine, Springfield, Illinois; or Lieut. Col. B. H. Hill, Detroit, Michigan, unless shipped by or delivered to an authorized officer of the United States Government.

Dealers in these articles, or others having them in their possession, will in no event be permitted to sell or deliver them during that time.

It is the duty of all military commanders and all provost marshals and their assistants to see that this order is enforced, and to seize all such articles as may be clandestinely sold, shipped, or delivered in evasion of it. Such property will at once be reported to these headquarters for the decision of the commander as to its disposition.

Forwarding, selling, or delivering such articles during this time, if now in transitu, excepting that they may be forwarded by such railroads as now have them in possession for safe keeping, will be considered an evasion of this order. The facts of such forwarding will be reported to these headquarters.

By command of Major-General Heintzelman:

C. H. POTTER, *A. A. General.*

sider that the administrative usurpation of extraordinary and dangerous powers not granted by the constitution; the subversion of the civil by military law in States not in insurrection; the arbitrary military arrest, imprisonment, trial and sentence of American citizens in States where civil law exists in full force; the suppression of freedom of speech and of the press; the denial of the right of asylum; the open and avowed disregard of State rights; the employment of unusual test-oaths, and the interference with and denial of the right of the people to bear arms in their defence, is calculated to prevent a restoration of the Union and the perpetuation of a government deriving its just powers from the consent of the governed.

Resolved, That the shameful disregard of the administration to its duty in respect to our fellow-citizens who now are, and long have been, prisoners of war in a suffering condition, deserves the severest reprobation, on the score alike of public policy and common humanity.

Resolved, That the sympathy of the Democratic party is heartily and earnestly extended to the soldiery of our army and sailors of our navy, who are, and have been in the field and on the sea, under the flag of their country; and, in the event of its attaining power, they will receive all the care, protection, and regard that the brave soldiers and sailors of the Republic have so nobly earned.

NOMINATIONS OF GEO B. M'CLELLAN AND GEORGE H. PENDLETON.

Mr. John P. Stockton, of New Jersey, in behalf of the delegation of that State, nominated General George B. McClellan.

Mr. S. S. Cox, of Ohio, seconded the nomination.

Mr. Saulsbury, of Delaware, nominated Governor Powell, of Kentucky. Mr. Powell returned his thanks to the gentleman, but he firmly believed the crisis demanded the candidate of the party should come from a non-slaveholding State. Believing so, he begged the gentleman and his colleague from the gallant State of Delaware to withdraw his name.

Mr. Stuart, on behalf of a portion of the Ohio delegation, nominated Thomas H. Seymour.

Mr. Wickliffe, on behalf of a portion of the delegation from Kentucky, nominated Franklin Pierce, but subsequently withdrew it.

The day was spent in debate upon the merits of the candidates.

August 31—The vote for President was taken. The first ballot, as taken, stood: McClellan, 174; Thomas H. Seymour, 38; Horatio Seymour, 12; Charles O'Conor, ½; Blank, 1½. As revised and finally declared, it was: McClellan, 202½, Thos. H. Seymour, 28½, as follows:

Maine—seven for McClellan.
New Hampshire—five for McClellan.
Vermont—five for McClellan.
Massachusetts—twelve for McClellan.
Rhode Island—four for McClellan.
Connecticut—nine for McClellan.
New York—thirty-three for McClellan.
New Jersey—seven for McClellan.
Pennsylvania—twenty-six for McClellan.
Delaware—two for Thomas H. Seymour.
Maryland—seven for Thomas H. Seymour.
Kentucky—eleven for McClellan.
Ohio—fifteen for McClellan, six for Thomas H. Seymour.
Indiana—nine and a half for McClellan, and three and a half for Thomas H. Seymour.
Illinois—sixteen for McClellan.
Michigan—eight for McClellan.
Missouri—seven for McClellan, four for Thomas H. Seymour.
Minnesota—four for McClellan.
Wisconsin—eight for McClellan.
Iowa—eight for McClellan.
Kansas—three for McClellan.
California—five for McClellan.
Oregon—three for McClellan.

Mr. Vallandigham moved that the nomination of George B. McClellan be made the unanimous sense of the Convention, which was seconded by Mr. McKeon.

Governor Powell briefly addressed the Convention, pledging his most earnest efforts for the success of the ticket.

Judge Allen, of Ohio, and others, made brief speeches, and the question was then taken on making the nomination unanimous, which was declared carried amid deafening applause.

Mr. Wickliffe offered a resolution to the effect that Kentucky expects the first act of McClellan, when inaugurated in March next, will be to open Abraham Lincoln's prison doors and let the captives free.

The Convention then proceeded to vote for Vice President.

The first ballot resulted as follows:

James Guthrie, 65½; George H. Pendleton, 55½; Daniel W. Voorhees, 13; George W. Cass, 26; Augustus C. Dodge, 9; J. H. Caton, 16; L. W. Powell, 32½; John S. Phelps, 8; blank, ½.

On the second ballot New York threw its whole vote for Mr. Pendleton, its chairman stating that its former vote for Guthrie was against his wishes. The other candidates were then withdrawn, and Mr. Pendleton, of Ohio, was unanimously nominated, who then took the stand, and said:

MR. PRESIDENT, AND GENTLEMEN OF THE CONVENTION: I have received with profound sensibility this mark of the confidence and kindness of the Democracy of the United States. I can say no more than this now. You will consider said all that is proper for me to say upon an occasion of this kind. I can only promise, in future, to endeavor, with the same fidelity that I have tried to exercise in the past—in entire devotion to those principles which lie at the very foundation of our government, and which are the basis of the Federal Constitution and of the rights of the States and of the liberties of the individual citizens—[immense applause]—shall endeavor to be faithful to those principles which lie at the very bottom of the organization of the democratic party. And I hope, aye, my friends, animated with the fervent hope that if, by the selection of proper men, we can give a true and faithful application to those principles, we will again build up the shattered fabric of our government and hand it to the next generation as we received it from the past—the most beautiful structure of government which the world has ever seen. I again tender to you, gentlemen, my grateful acknowledgments for the compliment you have done me, and leave the floor. [Loud and long-continued cheers.]

After a vote of thanks to the officers of the Convention, with nine cheers for the ticket, the Convention adjourned, subject to the call of the National Committee, in pursuance of this action, taken early in the session:

Mr. Wickliffe said the delegates from the West were of the opinion that circumstances may occur between now and the 4th of March next which will make it proper for the Democracy of the country to meet in convention again, and he therefore moved the following resolution, which was unanimously adopted:

Resolved, That the Convention shall not be dissolved by adjournment at the close of its business, but shall remain as organized, subject to be called at any time and place that the Executive National Committee shall designate.

Gen. McClellan's Acceptance.

LETTER ANNOUNCING THE NOMINATION.

NEW YORK, *Sept.* 8, 1864.

Maj. Gen. GEORGE B. MCCLELLAN:

SIR: The undersigned were appointed a Committee by the National Democratic Convention, which met at Chicago on the 29th of August, to advise you of your unanimous nomination by that body as the candidate of the Democratic party for President of the United States, and also to present to you a copy of the proceedings and resolutions of the Convention.

It gives us great pleasure to perform this duty, and to act as the representatives of that Convention whose deliberations were witnessed by a vast assemblage of citizens, who attended and watched its proceedings with intense interest. Be assured that those for whom we speak were animated with the most earnest, devoted and prayerful desire for the salvation of the American Union, and preservation of the Constitution of the United States; and that the accomplishment of these objects was the guiding and impelling motive in every mind.

And we may be permitted to add, that their purpose to maintain the Union is manifested in their selection, as their candidate, of one whose life has been devoted to its cause; while it is their earnest hope and confident belief that your election will restore to our country *Union, Peace, and Constitutional Liberty*.

We have the honor to be your obedient servants,
Horatio Seymour, *Chairman.*
John Bigler, of California.
Alfred P. Edgerton, of Indiana.
Isaac Lawrence, of Rhode Island.
John Merritt, of Delaware.
Hugh McCurdy, of Michigan.
Joseph E. Smith, of Maine.
John Cain, of Vermont.
Benjamin Stark, of Oregon.
John M. Douglas, of Illinois.
Charles Negus, of Iowa.
John D. Stiles, of Pennsylvania.
Wilson Shannon, of Kansas.

George H. Carman, of Maryland.
J. G. Abbott, of Massachusetts.
C. H. Berry, of Minnesota.
James Guthrie, of Kentucky.
Charles A. Wickliffe, of Kentucky.
C. G. W. Harrington, of New Hampshire.
Geo. W. Morgan, of Ohio.
Alfred E. Burr, of Connecticut.
Theodore Runyon, of New Jersey.
Weston F. Birch, of Missouri.
John A. Green, Jr., of New York.
W. T. Galloway, of Wisconsin.

LETTER ACCEPTING THE NOMINATION.

ORANGE, N. J., *September* 8, 1864.

GENTLEMEN: I have the honor to acknowledge the receipt of your letter informing me of my nomination, by the Democratic National Convention recently assembled at Chicago, as their candidate at the next election for President of the United States.

It is unnecessary for me to say to you that this nomination comes to me unsought. I am happy to know that when the nomination was made, the record of my public life was kept in view.

The effect of long and varied service in the army during war and peace, has been to strengthen and make indelible in my mind and heart the love and reverence for the Union, Constitution, laws, and flag of our country impressed upon me in early youth. These feelings have thus far guided the course of my life, and must continue to do so to its end.

The existence of more than one government over the region which once owned our flag is incompatible with the peace, the power, and the happiness of the people.

The preservation of our Union was the sole avowed object for which the war was commenced. It should have been conducted for that object only, and in accordance with those principles which I took occasion to declare when in active service.

Thus conducted, the work of reconciliation would have been easy, and we might have reaped the benefits of our many victories on land and sea.

The Union was originally formed by the exercise of a spirit of conciliation and compromise. To restore and preserve it the same spirit must prevail in our councils and in the hearts of the people. The re-establishment of the Union in all its integrity is and must continue to be the indispensable condition in any settlement. So soon as it is clear, or even probable, that our present adversaries are ready for peace, upon the basis of the Union, we should exhaust all the resources of statesmanship practiced by civilized nations and taught by the traditions of the American people, consistent with the honor and interests of the country, to secure such peace, re-establish the Union, and guarantee for the future the constitutional rights of every State. The Union is the one condition of peace—we ask no more.

Let me add, what I doubt not was, although unexpressed, the sentiment of the Convention, as it is of the people they represent, that when any one State is willing to return to the Union, it should be received at once, with a full guaranty of all its constitutional rights.

If a frank, earnest, and persistent effort to obtain these objects should fail, the responsibility for ulterior consequences will fall upon those who remain in arms against the Union. But the Union must be preserved at all hazards.

I could not look in the face of my gallant comrades of the army and navy, who have survived so many bloody battles, and tell them that their labors and the sacrifice of so many of our slain and wounded brethren had been in vain; that we had abandoned that Union for which we have so often periled our lives. A vast majority of our people, whether in the army and navy or at home, would, as I would, hail with unbounded joy the permanent restoration of peace, on the basis of the Union under the Constitution, without the effusion of another drop of blood. But no peace can be permanent without Union.

As to the other subjects presented in the resolutions of the Convention, I need only say that I should seek in the Constitution of the United States, and the laws framed in accordance therewith, the rule of my duty and the limitations of executive power; endeavor to restore economy in public expenditure, re-establish the supremacy of law, and, by the operation of a more vigorous nationality, resume our commanding position among the nations of the earth.

The condition of our finances, the depreciation of the paper money, and the burdens thereby imposed on labor and capital, show the necessity of a return to a sound financial system; whilst the rights of citizens and the rights of States, and the binding authority of law over President, army, and people, are subjects of not less vital importance in war than in peace. Believing that the views here expressed are those of the Convention and the people you represent, I accept the nomination.*

I realize the weight of the responsibility to be borne, should the people ratify your choice. Conscious of my own weakness, I can only seek fervently the guidance of the Ruler of the Universe, and relying on His all-powerful aid, do my best to restore union and peace to a suffering people, and to establish and guard their liberties and rights.

I am, gentlemen, very respectfully, your obedient servant,
GEORGE B. McCLELLAN.

Hon. HORATIO SEYMOUR and others, *Committee.*

LETTER OF GENERAL M'CLELLAN.

ORANGE, *October* 13, 1864.

MY DEAR SIR: In consequence of an absence of several days from home, your letter of the 8th did not meet my eye until to-day.

I accept with pride the honorary membership of the Legion you have done me the honor to call by my name. No greater compliment could have been paid to me than this association of my name with a society composed of my comrades in the present war. My love and gratitude for them have remained unchanged during our long separation, and I have watched with the most intense interest their noble and persistent gallantry in the many battles they have fought under the commanders who have succeeded me in the Army of the Potomac. You and they may rest satisfied that I remain the same man that I was when I had the honor to command the Army of the Potomac, and that I shall never willingly disappoint their confidence.

With my sincere thanks for the compliment you have paid me, and my earnest wishes for the prosperity of my former comrades, and of our country, I am, very respectfully and truly, your friend, GEORGE B. McCLELLAN.

Speeches and Letters of Mr. Pendleton.

HIS SPEECH AT DAYTON.

[*From the Dayton* (*Ohio*) *Empire, Sept.* 17.]

We had last night another of those magnificent demonstrations, now so common everywhere, showing conclusively with what force the tide of public sentiment is moving against Abraham Lincoln and in favor of the Democracy. Mr. Pendleton came to the city yesterday evening after the *Empire* had gone to press, and consequently too late to make any notice of his arrival. Nevertheless, the news spread rapidly, a band was engaged, and a serenade appointed at eight o'clock. As Mr. Pendleton was the guest of Mr. Vallandigham, a crowd soon began to assemble in front of Mr. Vallandigham's residence, which was augmented to thousands by the arrival of an immense procession, headed by the band.

Mr. Pendleton being loudly called, came forward and spoke as follows:

"LADIES AND GENTLEMEN: I thank you for this very flattering compliment; I thank you for this manifestation of the hospitality of Dayton, which has become proverbial throughout the United States.

"At four o'clock this afternoon I did not expect to be here this evening. I came unexpectedly, on purely personal business, disconnected with public affairs. I had no idea of seeing any number of my fellow-citizens or discussing political questions.

"This immense concourse thus suddenly convened fills me with renewed hope—it gives me confidence that soon again you will be called together, not as now to commence a vigorous contest, but to rejoice over its result, to rejoice that the powers of the Government will again be in the possession of the Democratic party, whose beneficent principles, recently solemnly announced in national convention, will bring us peace, maintain the rights of the States, reinvigorate the Union, and, with peace and union, will secure us the blessings of personal liberty, material prosperity, and national power. But I will not repay your kindness by detaining you with a speech; I intended only to thank you for the honor you have done me, and now I beg leave to wish you good night."

Mr. Vallandigham was next called, and responded in a

* Mr. Vallandigham, in a public speech at Sidney, Ohio, September 24, thus alludes to the Chicago platform:

"I claim, as the member from Ohio of the Committee on Resolutions in that Convention, to have official personal knowledge that he (Gen. McClellan) is mistaken. The two principal points in that letter of acceptance to which I object were brought before the committee. The one containing the threat of future war was unanimously rejected. The other to the effect that, until the States and people of the South had returned to the Union, we would not exhaust these 'arts of statesmanship,' as they are called, received but three votes in that committee, though presented almost in the very words of the letter itself."

masterly speech of half an hour, which was repeatedly interrupted by cheers. He spoke in defence of the Democratic party and of State rights and peace, and in support of the Chicago platform. The Democratic party was a State rights party—a constitutional party—a Union party—and just now a peace party. It was his party, and its candidates were his candidates. It bore the Ark of the Covenant; it carried the fortunes of the Republic, and in its success lay the only hope of the Republic. The Chicago platform enunciated its policy and principles by authority, and was binding upon every Democrat, and by them the democratic administration must and should be governed. It was the only authorized exposition of the Democratic creed, and he repudiated all others. The unity and harmony of the party were essential to success, and without success in November the country was lost. In conclusion, he declared his purpose to vote for the nominees of the Chicago Convention as the only hope of securing the defeat of Lincoln, and the rescue of the republic.

HIS SPEECH IN NEW YORK.

Mr. Pendleton was serenaded on Monday night, October 24, at the New York Hotel, by the McClellan Legion, an association composed of former soldiers of the Army of the Potomac. An audience of several thousand persons having assembled, Mr. Pendleton was introduced by Hon. John Van Buren, when he said:

I thank you for this manifestation of your kind feeling toward myself. I am the more grateful for it as it comes from men who have stood in the forefront of danger, and periled their lives for their country. [Loud cheers] I accept it as an evidence of your confidence in and of your sympathy with my devotion to the Union and the Constitution. ["Three cheers for George H. Pendleton."]

I have rarely found it necessary to reply to any personal attack. A friend has just handed me a pamphlet, which he tells me has extensive circulation both here and in the army. It professes to be a record of my speeches and votes in Congress, and to prove from them my hostility to the Republic. It professes to be published by the "Union Congressional Committee," and to be compiled from the *Congressional Globe*, to which it appeals for its entire accuracy. On the seventh page of that pamphlet I am charged with having voted against certain resolutions on the 7th July, 1864. Now, if any of you gentlemen will examine the *Globe*, or the file of any daily newspaper of your city, or will even tax his recollection, he will find that Congress adjourned on the 4th day of July, 1864. [Great laughter.] From this specimen of fraud and forgery I leave you to judge of the credibility of the whole fabrication.

I was born in Ohio; I have lived all my life in the North-west; I know the sentiment of the people; I sympathize entirely with it. They are attached by every tie of affection and interest to this Union. [Loud cheering.]

Unlike New York, they have never known another Government. They never existed as a political community before this Government was formed, and their hearts cling to this Government with indescribable tenacity. [Great applause.] Unlike you, they are inland people, chiefly devoted to agriculture. As an integral and controlling portion of the Union, they have prestige and power; they fear from disunion isolation from the world and the loss of that prestige and power. [Cheers.] Their interest requires that they should have speedy and easy communication with the ocean, and this they intend to have both by the Gulf of Mexico and the city of New York, by conciliation and in peace if they can, by all the force and power which a teeming population and a fruitful soil give them if they must. [Loud cheers.] They believe that the first step towards maintaining the Union is the election of General McClellan. [Great cheering.] They believe that the restoration of the Democratic party to power will produce Union. [Cheers.] They believe the policy of this Administration toward both the Southern and Northern States is fatal to the Union. ["That's so."] General McClellan, in his Harrison-Landing letter, said: "Neither confiscation of property, nor political executions of persons, nor territorial organization of States, nor forcible abolition of slavery, should be for one moment thought of." [Cheers.]

In his letter of acceptance he said: "The Union was originally formed by the exercise of a spirit of conciliation and compromise. To restore and preserve it, a like spirit must prevail in the councils of the country and in the hearts of the people." [Cheers.]

The Democratic party is pledged to an unswerving fidelity to the Union under the Constitution. [Cheers.] It is pledged to "the restoration of peace on the basis of the Federal Union of the States." [Loud applause.]

We believe, nay, we know, that if this party shall be restored to power, if this policy shall prevail, the Union shall be restored, State after State will return to us, and the echoes of our rejoicing will come down to us from the vaults of Heaven itself, in token that Deity approves that statesmanship which tempers all its policy with moderation and justice and conciliation. [Cheers.]

When next I meet you I hope we may have already entered on that work. Again, gentlemen, I thank you for your attention, and wish you good night. [Loud and long cheers followed the speech.]

HIS LETTERS.

The following was written to a Democratic meeting in Missouri:

CINCINNATI, *September* 28, 1864.

GENTLEMEN: I regret much that it will be out of my power to attend the mass meeting which you propose to hold on the 6th proximo. The cordial terms of your invitation, the evidences of kindness which I have received at the hands of those whom you represent, and my own desire to catch an inspiration of your faith and courage and zeal for the interests of our country, combine to make me regret the necessity to decline your invitation.

I promised to be with you, but when I made the promise I expected to be zealous and active, in season and out of season, urging, by every consideration which appeals to patriots, the utmost exertion to secure the success of the nominees at Chicago.

Your kindness has put me in a position where delicacy forbids such efforts. I could only say—what I have often before said—that if success crowns the work of the Democratic party, every aspiration of my heart would be gratified by, as every effort of my life would be directed to, the preservation of the Union, the maintenance of the Constitution, and the securing of all their rights to the States, and of all their liberties to the people. Very truly, yours,

GEO. H. PENDLETON.

CINCINNATI, *October* 17, 1864.

MY DEAR SIR: I have received your friendly letter. Malignant misrepresentations and falsehoods are so frequent in our political struggles, that I have rarely undertaken to correct or refute them.

I make no professions of a new faith, and only repeat my reiterated professions of an old one, when I say that there is no one who cherishes a greater regard for the Union, who has a higher sense of its inestimable benefits, who would more earnestly labor for its restoration by all means which will effect that end than myself.

The Union is the guarantee of the peace, the power, the prosperity of this people, and no man would deprecate more heartily, or oppose more persistently, the establishment of another Government over any portion of the territory within its limits.

I am in favor of exacting no conditions, insisting upon no terms not prescribed in the Constitution, and I am opposed to any course of policy which will defeat the re-establishment of the Government upon its old foundation, and in its territorial integrity.

I am, very truly, yours, &c.,

GEORGE H. PENDLETON.

Hon. JOHN B. HASKIN, New York.

CINCINNATI, *October* 18, 1864.

MY DEAR SIR: I have received your letter. In the very beginning of this war, in the first days of the extra session of 1861, I said, in my place in Congress, that I would vote for all measures necessary to enable the Government to maintain its honor and dignity, and prevent disaster to its flag. I have done so. I thought that by the adoption of such measures the faith of the Government was pledged to the troops in the field, and must not be forfeited by inadequate supplies. I never gave a vote which was incompatible with this sentiment.

All appropriations, pure and simple, for the support and efficiency of the army and navy, had my cordial concurrence. It was only when they were connected with other and improper appropriations; when by reason of their popularity they were loaded down with fraudulent items for the benefit of contractors or speculators, and every attempt to separate them failed; when they were made a stalking-horse for some Abolition scheme, that I was constrained reluctantly to vote against the whole bill.

But I repeat, that I voted against no bill which was confined simply to the object of supplies for the army and the navy.

I am, very truly, yours,

GEO. H. PENDLETON.

Hon. C. L. WARD, Philadelphia.

MR. VALLANDIGHAM'S LETTER ON THE CHICAGO PLATFORM, &C.

SHERMAN HOUSE, CHICAGO, *October* 22.

To the Editor of the New York News:

In the *World* of the 20th I observed an article copied from the Albany *Argus*, relating to Judge Advocate Holt's "Great Copperhead Conspiracy," and which contains the following:

"Mr. Vallandigham was in a miserable minority in the Chicago Convention. He sought to be Chairman of the Committee on Resolutions, and was beaten two to one. He led the opposition to McClellan, and after his letter of acceptance threw up his engagements to speak."

Now I have refrained in every speech, except the first—and I have made many in support of the Democratic candidates for President and Vice President—from any allusion to the private history of the Chicago Convention, and did not propose to refer to it further till after the election. But I do not choose to suffer the foregoing to pass unnoticed even now. It would be difficult to compress more misrepresentation, in a small way, within the same compass.

1. Mr. Vallandigham was *not* "in a miserable minority at the Chicago Convention," and no one knows it better than the man Cassidy, who wrote, and Marble who endorses the statement. The latter I hand over to ex-Mayor Opdyke for judgment.

2. Mr. Vallandigham was not "beaten two to one" for the Chairmanship of the Committee on Resolutions. Through the artifices of Cassidy, Tilden, and other New York politicians, Mr. Guthrie, of Kentucky, received twelve votes to his eight for that post; but Mr. Guthrie was himself afterwards emphatically repudiated by the Convention when presented by "the ring" as their candidate for the Vice Presidency. Mr. Vallandigham wrote the second, the material resolution of the Chicago platform, and carried it through the sub-Committee and the General Committee, in spite of the most desperate, persistent opposition on the part of Cassidy and his friends, Mr. Cassidy himself in an adjoining room laboring to defeat it. But the various substitutes never at any time received more than three votes.

3. Mr. Vallandigham did *not* "*lead* the opposition to McClellan," but confined his efforts almost exclusively to the question of platform. He did, indeed, vote against General McClellan on the first, but for him on the revised ballot, and moved that the nomination be made unanimous; whereupon Cassidy threw up his hat and shouted, and he and all his fellows proclaimed Vallandigham a very proper man.

4. As to engagements to speak in support of the Democratic candidates, Mr. Vallandigham has fulfilled as many as any Democratic speaker in any State, and is now here, in Illinois, on the same errand; and, without immodesty, he may say that he has accomplished quite as much of good for the cause as Cassidy and his *Argus*. The people lack "confidence" in Cassidy.

5. The secret of this and similar assaults on the part of a certain class of New York politicians is, that they cannot "use" Mr. Vallandigham. Of one thing further let them be assured—*neither can they kill him.*

6. As to the charge of "conspiracy" set forth in Judge Advocate Holt's pamphlet, and the eleven specifications summed up by Mr. Horace Greeley, I have only to say that, so far as I am concerned, they are absolute falsehoods and fabrications from beginning to end. They are false in the aggregate and false in detail. More than that, they are as preposterous and ridiculous as they are without foundation; and all this Mr. Judge Advocate Holt, Mary Ann Pitman, and Mr. Horace Greeley very well know.

C. L. VALLANDIGHAM.

Mass Convention of Conservative National Union Men.

CHICAGO, *August* 27, Midnight.—A mass Convention of the conservative National Union men was held this afternoon, and was largely attended. The Convention met in Bryan Hall.

Hon. Amos Kendall was elected President, and a list of Vice Presidents was adopted, among whom were representatives from all the States, North and South, with the exception of three or four.

Resolutions were adopted denouncing the policy of the Administration as calculated to impel both sections of the country to interminable warfare; proclaiming a determination to maintain the Union and the Constitution; declaring that the only solution of the existing troubles is in the unrestrained exercise of the elective franchise and displacement of the present Administration; declaring that the declaration of the Southern leaders as well as Mr. Lincoln's ultimatum are alike impracticable, and favoring the earliest peace attainable on the basis of the Constitution and Union.

Among the speakers were Coombs, of Kentucky; Perrin, of New York; Governor Wells, of California, and Reed, of Kentucky.

Additional Addresses and Papers from President Lincoln.

HIS SPEECH TO THE 148TH OHIO REGIMENT.

SOLDIERS OF THE 148TH OHIO: I am most happy to meet you on this occasion. I understand that it has been your honorable privilege to stand, for a brief period, in the defence of your country, and that now you are on your way to your homes. I congratulate you, and those who are waiting to bid you welcome home from the war; and permit me in the name of the people to thank you for the part you have taken in this struggle for the life of the nation. You are soldiers of the Republic, everywhere honored and respected. Whenever I appear before a body of soldiers, I feel tempted to talk to them of the nature of the struggle in which we are engaged. I look upon it as an attempt on the one hand to overwhelm and destroy the national existence, while on our part we are striving to maintain the Government and institutions of our fathers, to enjoy them ourselves, and transmit them to our children and our children's children forever.

To do this the Constitutional Administration of our Government must be sustained, and I beg of you not to allow your minds or your hearts to be diverted from the support of all necessary measures for that purpose, by any miserable picayune arguments addressed to your pockets, or inflammatory appeal made to your passions and your prejudices.

It is vain and foolish to arraign this man or that for the part he has taken or has not taken, and to hold the Government responsible for his acts. In no Administration can there be perfect equality of action and uniform satisfaction rendered by all.

But this Government must be preserved in spite of the acts of any man or set of men. It is worthy your every effort. Nowhere in the world is presented a Government of so much liberty and equality. To the humblest and poorest amongst us are held out the highest privileges and positions. The present moment finds me at the White House, yet there is as good a chance for your children as there was for my father's.

Again I admonish you not to be turned from your stern purpose of defending our beloved country and its free institutions by any arguments urged by ambitious and designing men, but stand fast to the Union and the old flag.

Soldiers, I bid you God-speed to your homes.

TO THE 164TH OHIO.

SOLDIERS: You are about to return to your homes and your friends, after having, as I learn, performed in camp a comparatively short term of duty in this great contest. I am greatly obliged to you and to all who have come forward at the call of the country.

I wish it might be more generally and universally understood what the country is now engaged in. We have, as all will agree, a free Government, where every man has a right to be equal with every other man. In this great struggle, this form of Government, and every form of human rights, is endangered if our enemies succeed. There is more involved in this contest than is realized by every one. There is involved in this struggle the question whether your children and my children shall enjoy the privileges we have enjoyed.

I say this in order to impress upon you, if you are not already so impressed, that no small matter should divert you from our great purpose. There may be some inequalities in the practical application of our system. It is fair that each man shall pay taxes in exact proportion to the value of his property, but if we should wait before collecting a tax to adjust the taxes upon each man in exact proportion with every other man, we should never collect any tax at all. There may be mistakes made. Sometimes things may be done wrong, while the officers of the Government do all they can to prevent mistakes; but I beg of you as citizens of this great republic, not to let your minds be carried off from the great work we have before us.

The struggle is too large for you to be diverted from it by any small matter. When you return to your homes, rise up to the dignity of a generation of men worthy of a free Government, and we will carry out the work we have commenced.

I return you my sincere thanks, soldiers, for the honor you have done me this afternoon.

HIS LETTER ON THE ADOPTION OF THE NEW CONSTITUTION OF MARYLAND.

EXECUTIVE MANSION, WASHINGTON, *Oct.* 10.

HON. H. W. HOFFMAN:

MY DEAR SIR: A convention of Maryland has formed a new Constitution for the State. A public meeting is called for this evening, at Baltimore, to aid in securing its ratification by the people, and you ask a word from me on the occasion. I presume the only feature of the instrument about which there is serious controversy is that which provides for the extinction of slavery.

It needs not to be a secret, and I presume it is no secret, that I wish success to this provision. I desire it on every consideration. I wish all men to be free. I wish the material prosperity of the already free, which I feel secure the extinction of slavery would bring. I wish to see in process of disappearing that only thing which could bring this nation to civil war.

I attempt no argument. Argument upon the question is already exhausted by the abler, better informed and more immediately interested sons of Maryland herself. I only add that I shall be gratified exceedingly if the good people of the State shall by their votes ratify the new Constitution. Yours truly,

A. LINCOLN.

Oct. 19—The President was serenaded at the White House to-night, and, on appearing at an upper window, spoke as follows:

I am notified that this is a compliment paid me by the loyal Marylanders resident in this District. I infer that the adoption of the new Constitution for the State furnishes the occasion, and that, in your view, the extirpation of slavery constitutes the chief merit of the new Constitution.

Most heartily do I congratulate you and Maryland, and the nation, and the world upon the event. I regret that it did not occur two years sooner, which, I am sure, would have saved to the nation more money than would have met all the private loss incident to the measure. But it has come at last, and I sincerely hope its friends may fully realize all their anticipations of good from it, and that its opponents may, by its effects, be agreeably and profitably disappointed.

A word upon another subject. Something said by the Secretary of State, in his recent speech at Auburn, has been construed by some into a threat that, if I shall be beaten at the election, I will, between then and the end of my constitutional term, do what I may be able to ruin the Government. Others regard the fact that the Chicago Convention adjourned not *sine die*, but to meet again, if called to do so by a particular individual, as the intimation of a purpose that if their nominee shall be elected he will at once seize the control of the Government. I hope the good people will permit themselves to suffer no uneasiness on this point.

I am struggling to maintain the Government, not to overthrow it. I am struggling especially to prevent others from overthrowing it. I therefore say that, if I shall live, I shall remain President until the fourth of next March, and that whoever shall be constitutionally elected therefor, in November, shall be duly installed as President on the fourth of March, and that, in the interval, I shall do my utmost that whoever is to hold the helm for the next voyage shall start with the best possible chance to save the ship.

This is due to the people both on principle and under the Constitution. Their will, constitutionally expressed, is the ultimate law for all. If they should deliberately resolve to have immediate peace, even at the loss of their country and their liberties, I have not the power or the right to resist them. It is their own business, and they must do as they please with their own. I believe, however, they are still resolved to preserve their country and their liberty; and, in this office or out, I am resolved to stand by them.

I may add, that in this purpose to save the country and its liberties no classes of people seem so nearly unanimous as the soldiers in the field and seamen afloat. Do they not have the hardest of it? Who should quail while they do not? God bless the soldiers and seamen, with all their brave commanders.

PRESIDENT LINCOLN'S INTERVIEW WITH HON. JOHN T. MILLS, OF WISCONSIN.

In August, the President had an interview with Judge Mills, of the the fifth judicial circuit, Wisconsin, the political features of which Judge M. thus reports in a letter to the Grant county (Wis.) *Herald:*

"Mr. President," said Governor Randall, "why can't you seek seclusion, and play hermit for a fortnight? It would reinvigorate you."

"Ah," said the President, "two or three weeks would do me no good. I cannot fly from my thoughts—my solicitude for this great country follows me wherever I go. I do not think it is personal vanity or ambition, though I am not free from these infirmities, but I cannot but feel that the weal or woe of this great nation will be decided in November. There is no programme offered by any wing of the Democratic party but that must result in the permanent destruction of the Union."

"But, Mr. President, General McClellan is in favor of crushing out this rebellion by force. He will be the Chicago candidate."

"Sir, the slightest knowledge of arithmetic will prove to any man that the Rebel armies cannot be destroyed by Democratic strategy. It would sacrifice all the white men of the North to do it. There are now in the service of the United States nearly 200,000 able-bodied colored men, most of them under arms, defending and acquiring Union territory. The Democratic strategy demands that these forces be disbanded, and that the masters be conciliated by restoring them to slavery. The black men who now assist Union prisoners to escape are to be converted into our enemies, in the vain hope of gaining the good will of their masters. We shall have to fight two nations instead of one.

"You cannot conciliate the South if you guarantee to them ultimate success; and the experience of the present war proves their success is inevitable if you fling the compulsory labor of millions of black men into their side of the scale. Will you give our enemies such military advantages as insure success, and then depend on coaxing, flattery and concession to get them back into the Union? Abandon all the posts now garrisoned by black men, take 200,000 men from our side and put them in the battle-field or corn-field against us, and we would be compelled to abandon the war in three weeks.

"We have to hold territory in inclement and sickly places; where are the Democrats to do this? It was a free fight, and the field was open to the War Democrats to put down this Rebellion by fighting against both master and slave, long before the present policy was inaugurated.

"There have been men base enough to propose to me to return to slavery the black warriors of Port Hudson and Olustee, and thus win the respect of the masters they fought. Should I do so, I should deserve to be damned in time and eternity. Come what will, I will keep my faith with friend and foe. My enemies pretend I am now carrying on this war for the sole purpose of abolition. So long as I am President, it shall be carried on for the sole purpose of restoring the Union. But no human power can subdue this rebellion without the use of the emancipation policy, and every other policy calculated to weaken the moral and physical forces of the rebellion.

"Freedom has given us 200,000 men, raised on Southern soil. It will give us more yet. Just so much it has substracted from the enemy, and, instead of alienating the South, there are now evidences of a fraternal feeling growing up between our men and the rank and file of the rebel soldiers. Let my enemies prove to the country that the destruction of slavery is not necessary to a restoration of the Union. I will abide the issue."

PRESENTATION TO THE PRESIDENT.

Recently, a committee of loyal colored people of Baltimore formally presented to the President an imperial quarto Bible, splendidly bound, costing $580, as a token of their respect and gratitude to him for his active part in the cause of emancipation. They say that since they have been incorporated in the American family they have been true and loyal, and now stand ready to defend the country, and that they are prepared to be armed and trained to protect and defend the star-spangled banner.

The President replied: "I can only say now, as I have often said before, that it has always been a sentiment with me that all mankind should be free. So far as I have been able, or so far as came within my sphere, I have always acted as I believed was right and just, and have done all I could for the good of mankind. I have in letters and documents sent forth from this office expressed myself better than I can now. In regard to the Great Book, I have only to say that it is the best gift which God has given man. All the good from the Saviour of the world is communicated to us through this book. But for this book we could not know right from wrong. All those things desirable to man are contained in it.

"I return you my sincere thanks for this very elegant copy of the great Book of God which you present."

THE PROTEST OF TENNESSEE—REPLY OF THE PRESIDENT.

EXECUTIVE MANSION, WASHINGTON, D. C.,
October 22, 1864.

Messrs. WM. B. CAMPBELL, THOMAS A. R. NELSON, JAMES T. P. CARTER, JOHN WILLIAMS, A. BLIZZARD, HENRY COOPER, BAILIE PEYTON, JOHN LELLYETT, E. ETHERIDGE, JOHN D. PERRYMANS:

GENTLEMEN: On the 15th day of this month, as I remember, a printed paper, with a few manuscript interlineations, called a protest, with your names appended thereto, and accompanied by another printed paper purporting to be a proclamation by Andrew Johnson, Military Governor of Tennessee, and also a manuscript paper purporting to be extracts from the Code of Tennessee, was laid before me. The protest, proclamation and extracts are respectively as follows:

[The protest is here recited, and also the proclamation of Governor Johnson, dated September 30, to which it refers, together with a list of the counties in East, Middle, and West Tennessee; also, an extract from the Code of Tennessee, in relation to electors of President and Vice President of the United States, the qualifications of voters for members of the General Assembly, and the places of holding elections of officers of popular elections.]

The PRESIDENT then says:

At the time these papers were presented, as before stated, I had never seen either of them, nor heard of the subject to which they relate, except in a general way, only one day previously. Up to the present moment nothing whatever has passed between Governor Johnson, or any one else connected with the proclamation, and myself. Since receiving the papers, as stated, I have given the subject such brief consideration as I have been able to do in the midst of so many pressing public duties.

My conclusion is that I have nothing to do with the matter, either to sustain the plan as the Convention and Governor Johnson have initiated it, or to revoke or modify it as you demand. By the Constitution and laws, the President is charged with no duty in the conduct of a Presidential election in any State; nor do I, in this case, perceive any military reason for his interference in the matter.

The movement set on foot by the Convention and Governor Johnson does not, as seems to be assumed by you, emanate from the National Executive. In no proper sense can it be considered other than as an independent movement of at least a portion of the loyal people of Tennessee.

I do not perceive in the plan any menace of violence or coercion towards any one. Governor Johnson, like any other loyal citizen of Tennessee, has the right to favor any political plan he chooses, and, as Military Governor, it is his duty to keep the peace among and for the loyal people of the State. I cannot discern that by this plan he purposes any more.

But you object to the plan. Leaving it alone will be your perfect security against it. Do as you please on your own account, peacefully and loyally, and Governor Johnson will not molest you, but will protect you against violence so far as in his power.

I presume that the conducting of a Presidential election in Tennessee, in strict accordance with the old Code of the State, is not now a possibility.

It is scarcely necessary to add that if any election shall be held, and any votes shall be cast in the State of Tennessee for President and Vice President of the United States, it will belong, not to the military agents, nor yet to the Executive department, but exclusively to another department of the Government, to determine whether they are entitled to be counted, in conformity with the Constitution and laws of the United States.

Except it be to give protection against violence, I decline to interfere in any way with any Presidential election.

ABRAHAM LINCOLN.

REMARKS TO THE 189TH NEW YORK REGIMENT.

On Monday, October 24, this regiment, organized under the late call for 500,000 men, Col. Wm. W. Hoyt commanding, passed through Washington, on their way to the front. Previous to their departure by transport, the regiment was paraded in front of the White House, and presented to the President of the United States by the Colonel, in a few appropriate remarks. Mr. Lincoln was received with the utmost enthusiasm, and replied to the greeting which met him as follows:

SOLDIERS: I am exceedingly obliged to you for this mark of respect. It is said that we have the best Government the world ever knew, and I am glad to meet you, the supporters of that Government. To you who render the hardest work in its support should be given the greatest credit. Others who are connected with it, and who occupy higher positions, their duties can be dispensed with, but we cannot get along without your aid. While others differ with the Administration, and, perhaps, honestly, the soldiers generally have sustained it; they have not only fought right, but, so far as could be judged from their actions, they have voted right, and I for one thank you for it. I know you are *en route* for the front, and therefore do not expect me to detain you long, and will therefore bid you good morning.

The President retired, and the regiment gave him three cheers, heartily and enthusiastically. Col. Hoyt is an old soldier, having served since the commencement of the existing rebellion in the army. His regiment is raised chiefly in Steuben and Allegany counties, and will, with its gallant Colonel, be heard from in the coming campaign.

CORRESPONDENCE BETWEEN PRESIDENT LINCOLN AND GEN. GRANT.

EXECUTIVE MANSION,
WASHINGTON, *April* 30, 1864.

LIEUTENANT GENERAL GRANT:

Not expecting to see you before the Spring campaign opens, I wish to express, in this way, my entire satisfaction with what you have done up to this time, so far as I understand it. The particulars of your plans I neither know nor seek to know.

You are vigilant and self-reliant, and, pleased with this, I wish not to obtrude any restraints or constraints upon you. While I am very anxious that any great disaster or capture of any of our men in any great numbers shall be avoided, I know that these points are less likely to escape your attention than they would be mine. If there be anything wanting which is within my power to give, do not fail to let me know it. And now, with a brave army and a just cause, may God sustain you.

Yours, very truly, A. LINCOLN.

—

HEADQUARTERS ARMIES UNITED STATES,
CULPEPER C. H., VA., *May* 1, 1864.

THE PRESIDENT:

Your very kind letter of yesterday is just received. The confidence you express for the future and satisfaction for the past, in my military administration, is acknowledged with pride. It shall be my earnest endeavor that you and the country shall not be disappointed.

From my first entrance into the volunteer service of the country to the present day I have never had cause of complaint, have never expressed or implied a complaint against the Administration or the Secretary of War for throwing any embarrassment in the way of my vigorously prosecuting what appeared to be my duty. Indeed, since the promotion which placed me in command of all the armies, and in view of the great responsibility and importance of success, I have been astonished at the readiness which everything asked for has been yielded, without even an explanation being asked.

Should my success be less than I desire and expect, the least I can say is, the fault is not with you.

Very truly, your obedient servant,
U. S. GRANT,
Lieutenant General.

Withdrawal of Generals Fremont and Cochrane.

BOSTON, *August* 20.

General FREMONT:

SIR: You must be aware of the wide and growing dissatisfaction in the Republican ranks with the Presidential nomination at Baltimore, and you may have seen notices of a movement just commenced to unite the thorough and earnest friends of a vigorous prosecution of the war in a new Convention which shall represent the patriotism of all parties.

To facilitate the movement, it is emphatically advisable that the candidates nominated at Cleveland and Baltimore should withdraw, and leave the field entirely free for such a united effort. Permit us, sir, to ask whether, in case Mr. Lincoln will withdraw, you will do so, and join your fellow-citizens in this attempt to place the Administration on a basis broad as the patriotism of the country and as its needs?

GEORGE L. STEARNS,
S. R. URBINO,
JAMES M. STONE,
ELIZUR WRIGHT,
EDWARD HABICH,
SAMUEL G. HOWE.

—

NAHANT, *August* 25.

GENTLEMEN: I have to acknowledge the receipt of your letter of the 20th, addressed to me in New York.

If your letter were in effect an appeal only to my own sentiments in favor of a re-union of parties, I should not hesitate to renounce my personal views, but would be entirely ready to defer to the public opinion which your names represent.

But the conditions are no longer the same as when I expressed my readiness to retire in the event of a contingency which might have occurred at Baltimore. Having now definitely accepted the Cleveland nomination, I have not the right to act independently of the truly patriotic and earnest party who conferred that honor upon me. In any event it would be necessary first to consult with them. It might, besides, have only the effect still further to unsettle the public mind, and defeat the object you have in view, if we should disorganize before first proceeding to organize something better.

To this end I suggest that a direct effort be made to obtain an immediate understanding between the supporters of the Baltimore and Cleveland nominations, in order that the friends of both may coalesce, and unite upon an early day for holding such a convention as you propose. I am satisfied that I do not assume too much in saying that my friends will unite heartily in such a movement.

A really popular convention, upon a broad and liberal basis, so that it could be regarded as a convocation in mass of the people, and not the work of politicians, would command public confidence. Such a convention, acting in the large and liberal spirit in which it was called, without considerations of persons or political cliques, and without reference to bygone situations, rising to the level of the occasion and taking the conditions of the country as they present themselves to-day, could safely be trusted to propose such a policy and name such a man as should, and undoubtedly would, receive the cordial and united support of the patriotic masses of the people. To the great body of these, so far as my information allows me to form any opinion, I think that the following propositions would be acceptable:

1. Respect for the practical liberty and the constitutional rights and dignity of the citizen.

2. The maintenance of the dignity of the United States in their relations to foreign Powers.

3. The re-establishment of the Union; by peace if it is possible; by war, if the employment of peaceful measures cannot be made to succeed.

Much has been said of late about peace, and you will therefore excuse me if I say here what I understand by it. For me, peace signifies the integral re-establishment of the Union without slavery; because slavery is the source of all our political dissensions, and because the institution itself is condemned by the enlightened and liberal spirit of the age. These are to me the essential conditions of peace. If it is practicable to attain this result, it would not be paying too dearly for it—taking also into consideration the material strength which the South has been permitted to acquire by the conduct of the war—to make concessions upon some points of secondary importance, such as that of paying an indemnity for their slaves to those who have remained in a sort of neutral condition during the unhappy war which has convulsed the country. To terminate this we are now expending life and money; it would certainly be a gain to reduce it simply to a question of money.

If, in spite of all these efforts to spare the South humiliation, or losses of capital likely to be too severely felt, the political chiefs who direct the South persist in war, then the policy of the Convention should be to pronounce in that case for war with all the force and energy of the nation. For peace upon any terms, and merely because it is peace—a peace recognizing a North and a South—would not bring about a stable equilibrium. It would only prepare the way for new struggles, and for a condition of disastrous anarchy.

The paramount question is the Union. By peace, if it can be had on honorable and right terms—by war, if the political leaders who are directing the South insist upon war.

The situation of our country is unquestionably critical. It demands the devotion and patriotism of all men who really love their country, and it is one of those moments when all personal aspirations should vanish in the face of the great questions of principle and national existence which are at stake.

Thanking you, gentlemen, for the evidence which your letter gives me of your confidence in my disposition to do everything in my power for the interests of the country,

I am, very truly yours,

J. C. FREMONT.

This is General Fremont's letter of withdrawal:

NAHANT, *Sept.* 17.

GENTLEMEN: I enclose you my letter of reply to an invitation of some of my Republican friends to meet me at Faneuil Hall.

In declining their invitation, I have informed them of my intention to stand aside from the Presidential canvass, and assigned my reasons for doing so. To avoid repetition, I enclose you the letter in communicating to you now officially my desire to withdraw my name from the Presidential candidates.

In this decision I have the approval of such of our friends as I have been able to consult. I have thought it not prudent to incur the longer delay of consulting others, but I have reason to believe that they will unite with me fully upon the propriety of the step I have taken.

But in withdrawing from the post of candidate, I do not in any way intend to withdraw from my share in the labor, which we jointly undertook, to secure the triumph of the ideas represented by the radical Democracy.

Whatever the next Administration may be, we owe it to ourselves to form a phalanx compact and capable, by its thorough unity, of exercising a pressure strong enough to secure the eventual success of the principles for which we have been contending—the re-establishment of the Union, the abolition of slavery, and practical respect for liberty.

In the present composition of parties, it is indispensable that earnest men should devote themselves to watching the progress and insuring the success of these issues, regardless of men or parties.

Mr. Lincoln says he does not lead, but follows the will of the people. It remains, then, for the people, in the event of his re-election, vigilantly to require the following at his hands, and, further, to require that, in the execution of his duties, he keeps scrupulously within the Constitution and the laws; to make him recognize that he holds his place and his power, not as belonging to himself, but as a really faithful servant of the people.

This is the important duty which we have now to perform.

Although, as representatives of the Cleveland movement, we surrender our functions, the duty of watching party politics, the Constitution remains. What steps are necessary in the performance of that duty must be the subject for future consideration.

I am, gentlemen, respectfully and truly yours, &c.,

JOHN C. FREMONT.

To Messrs. WORTHINGTON G. SNETHEN and others, a committee, &c.

This letter is upon the same subject:

BOSTON, *September* 21.

GENTLEMEN: I feel it my duty to make one step more in the direction indicated by my letter of the 25th of August, and withdraw my name from the list of candidates.

The Presidential question has, in effect, been entered upon in such a way that the union of the Republican party has become a paramount necessity. The policy of the Democratic party signifies either separation or re-establishment with slavery. The Chicago platform is simply separation. General McClellan's letter of acceptance is re-establishment with slavery.

The Republican candidate, on the contrary, is pledged to the re-establishment of the Union without slavery; and, however hesitating his policy may be, the pressure of his party will, we may hope, force him to it.

Between these issues, I think, no man of the liberal party can remain in doubt, and I believe I am consistent with my antecedents in withdrawing—not to aid in the triumph of Mr. Lincoln, but to do my part towards preventing the election of the Democratic candidate.

In respect to Mr. Lincoln, I continue to hold exactly the sentiments contained in my letter of acceptance. I consider that his administration has been politically, militarily, and financially a failure, and that its necessary continuance is a cause of regret for the country.

There never was a greater unanimity in a country than was exhibited here at the fall of Sumter, and the South was powerless in the face of it; but Mr. Lincoln completely paralyzed this generous feeling. He destroyed the strength of the position and divided the North, when he declared to the South that slavery should be protected. He has built up for the South a strength which otherwise they could have never attained, and this has given them an advocate on the Chicago platform.

The Cleveland Convention was to have been an open avowal of that condemnation which men had been freely expressing to each other for the past two years, and which had been made fully known to the President; but in the uncertain condition of affairs, leading men were not found willing to make public a dissatisfaction and condemnation which could have rendered Mr. Lincoln's nomination impossible, and their continued silence and support established for him a character among the people which leaves now no choice.

United, the Republican party is reasonably sure of success; divided, the result of the Presidential election is at least doubtful.

I am, gentlemen, very truly, yours,

J. C. FREMONT.

To Messrs. GEORGE L. STEARNS and others, a committee, &c.

GEN. COCHRANE'S WITHDRAWAL.

To the War Democrats of the United States:

A convention of men of various political tenets assembled at Cleveland on the 31st day of May last, for the purpose of discharging from the suppression of the rebellion the infraction of the rights of both individuals and States which attended it. The presence of a large number of War Democrats unexpectedly contributed to my nomination by the convention for the Vice Presidency, preceded by that of John C. Fremont for President.

The principles which dictated my acceptance of the nomination approved themselves at the time to very general regard, and have since, in my opinion, lost none of their original virtue or vigor. Their practical assertion was required, it was thought, by the success with which personal liberty had been assailed, and the extremities to which constitutional freedom had been reduced. Not the least inducement, however, was the consideration that the redress of grievances, in the manner proposed, could not interrupt, but would entirely consort with a vigorous prosecution of the war. It certainly was not contemplated that the success of the candidates should, in any degree, impair or endanger that most important part of the platform which resolved "that the rebellion must be suppressed by force of arms, and without compromise."

Instead of the Democratic party, as was then hoped and expected, co-operating at this point, they flouted the war at Chicago, and pronounced for unconditional peace. When, "to exhaust the resources of statesmanship," and to allow "the spirit of conciliation and compromise to prevail," General McClellan virtually asserts that there should be a "cessation of hostilities," he is in agreement with the convention which nominated him. When, however, he proposes, in the alternative of the war, that the rebellious States shall be restored to precisely their former condition in the Union, with precisely the same political representation as when they departed from it, he rejects a convention of States, on which, as the peaceable means, the Chicago Convention evidently relied for reconstructing the Union out of States physically debilitated and politically shorn. While, therefore, General McClellan resolves upon an impossible Union as it was, through war, the convention resolves upon an impossible Union as it should be, through peace. That the candidate does not stand erect upon his platform, though admitting a question whether, if elected, he would negotiate a peace, permits none that, if elected, he could not effectively prosecute the war.

The success of the Chicago nominees would therefore, at the best, but place in power a party of divided councils, of uncertain policy, and of indecisive action. Clearly, such an event would be at the farthest from "a suppression of the rebellion by force of arms, and without compromise."

The Baltimore platform, however objectionable at other points, is unimpeachable at this; and while it fails to vindicate personal rights, and the rights of free speech and the press, it does not fail to refer the re-establishment of constitutional liberty and the restoration of the Union to the arbitrament of arms, in which, and in which alone, the national safety is to be found. We stand within view of a rebellion suppressed; within hail of a country reunited and saved. War lifts the curtain and discloses the prospect. War has given to us Atlanta, and war offers to us Richmond.

Shall we exchange the proffered victory for a "cessation of hostilities?" No! As we fought at the beginning, we should fight at the end; and when rebellion shall have laid down its arms, may we peacefully reconstruct whatever the war for the Union shall be found to have spared. "Lay down your arms," then; as it was at the commencement, so it is now, all that is demanded by loyal Americans of their rebellious brothers.

I would certainly prefer that the American people could be brought to a vote on the several propositions peculiar to the Cleveland platform. The right of asylum, the one-term policy, the direct vote of the people for their national Chief Magistrate, the Monroe doctrine, the confining exclusively to the representatives of the people in Congress the reconstruction of States, and the amendment of the Federal Constitution to prohibit slavery, are principles of primary magnitude and importance. But before all these is our country. It is menaced by rebellion. Loyal armies alone protect it. Should those armies retreat, and our protection be withdrawn; or should they advance, and our safety be established? Shall there be peace through the concessions of politicians, or peace through the actions of war? That is the question.

Peace and division, or war and the Union. Other alternative there is none. And, as I am still of the mind that once led me to the field with the soldiers of the Republic, I cannot now hold a position which, by dividing, hazards the success of all those who, whatever their differences at other points, agree, as upon the question of the first consequence, that the restoration of the Union cannot be effected without the uninterrupted continuation of the war.

I, therefore, withdraw my name from the Cleveland ticket. Very truly yours,

JOHN COCHRANE.

NEW YORK, *September* 21, 1864.

Rebel Items.

AN IMPORTANT AND SIGNIFICANT CIRCULAR.

The Richmond *Examiner* of Sept. 17 alludes to an "important circular," issued to the people of Richmond recently. We quote the substance of the circular:

Captain Coke, enrolling officer for this district, will proceed to-day with the enforcement of a circular issued from the War Department, providing for a registry of all white males between the ages of seventeen and fifty years, not actually in service in the field; with the grounds of their exemption or detail; also a registry of all boys who will arrive at the age of seventeen years within the next twelve months, with the month at which they will attain that age. To obviate the possibility of any alarm that the enforcement of the order, unexplained, might tend to create, we will state that it is not intended to enroll the citizens falling within this category. The registry is simply intended as a basis upon which the Government may hereafter act in the matter of conscription and enrollment, as the emergencies of the service may require. We trust that every man and boy within the jurisdiction of the circular will respond with alacrity to the call, and that they will give the enrolling officers as little trouble as possible in obtaining the desired registry.

THE ENROLLMENT IN RICHMOND.

The military registry, ordered by the Bureau of Conscription, of all males between the ages of seventeen and fifty years not actually in the army in the field or with the reserves, commenced yesterday morning in Monroe ward, at No. 306 Broad street, nearly opposite Lacey's shop, and will be continued to-day. The order is very emphatic and must be executed, and the present mode has been adopted as most agreeable to the citizens. The exemptions in Richmond embrace only those with the army in the field and those in the reserves attached to the regiments of Colonels Evans and Danforth. It may as well be understood that this is not an enrollment, but a military census. Citizens failing to report lay themselves liable to arrest by the enrolling officers. Time, temper and trouble will therefore be saved by reporting promptly to the advisory board in the respective wards.—*Richmond Examiner, Sept.* 21.

ENROLLMENT OF NEGROES.*

Hake's *Weekly Bulletin*, of the 14th, 18th and

---

*This Order from General Canby contains an additional indication of purpose:

HEADQ'RS MIL. DIV. WEST MISSISSIPPI,
NEW ORLEANS, LA., *Oct.* 11, 1864.

General Orders No. 58.

The subjoined extract from a despatch from Henry W. Allen, styling himself Governor of Louisiana, to the rebel Secretary of War, is published for general information:

EXECUTIVE OFFICE,
SHREVEPORT, LA., *Sept.* 26, 1864.

To Hon. JAMES A. SEDDON, *Secretary of War, Richmond, Va.:*

MY DEAR SIR: The time has come for us to put into the army every able-bodied negro man as a soldier. This should be done immediately. Congress should, at the coming session, take action on this most important question. The negro knows that he cannot escape conscription if he goes

21st August, published at Galveston, contains the following intelligence:

NEGROES IN THE SERVICE OF THE CONFEDERACY.

HEADQ'RS DEPARTMENT TRANS-MISSISSIPPI,
SHREVEPORT, LA., *July* 20, 1864.

General Orders No. 45.

I. In accordance with an act of Congress, entitled "An Act to Increase the Efficiency of the Army by Employment of Free Negroes and Slaves in certain Capacities," approved February 17, 1864, all male free negroes and other persons of color, not including those who are free under the treaty of Paris of 1803, or under the treaty of Spain of 1819, resident in the Confederate States, between the ages of eighteen and fifty years, will be immediately enrolled under the direction of the Bureau of Conscription.

II. The Bureau of Conscription will take the necessary steps, through the enrolling officers, to enroll immediately one fifth of all the male slaves in this department between the ages of eighteen and forty-five years.

III. All free negroes and slaves so enrolled will be sent to rendezvous designated by the commandants of negro labor for the several States, accompanied by descriptive rolls.

IV. Requisitions for negro labor must be made upon the commandants of negro labor of the several States.

V. All officers and agents of the Government, in charge of slaves, will furnish monthly, to the commandants of negro labor of the several States to which the slaves belong, correct and certified muster rolls of those in their charge.

By command of General E. Kirby Smith:

S. S. ANDERSON,
Assistant Adjutant General.

REVOCATION OF DETAILS.*

[OFFICIAL.]

ADJUTANT AND INSPECTOR GENERAL'S OFFICE,
RICHMOND, *October* 5, 1864.

GENERAL ORDERS, No. 76.—1. All details heretofore granted, under authority of the War Department, to persons between the ages of eighteen and forty-five years, are revoked, and all such detailed men, together with those within the said ages who hold furloughs or temporary exemptions by reason of pending applications for details, will be promptly assembled at the camps of instruction, and appropriately assigned among the armies for service; except that men detailed and now actually employed in manufacturing, providing, collecting and forwarding munitions and other indispensable supplies for the army and navy, or in work indispensable to military operations, will be continued in their present employments until their details shall be revised.

2. The heads of departments and chiefs of bureaus will, within the next twenty days, forward to the Generals of Reserves lists of all detailed men in their employment, in the several States, specially distinguishing and certifying those who are experts and those absolutely indispensable for the performance of the above-mentioned Government work and business; and all detailed employés not so certified within the prescribed period will, upon the expiration thereof, be forthwith assigned to the army.

3. All persons called out by this order, who claim exemption on acount of physical disability, will be examined by select medical boards, after their arrival at the camps of instructions.

4. All men found for light duty, who are unassigned, will at once report to the camps of instruction, under the penalty of being forthwith assigned to the active forces. By order.

S. COOPER,
Adjutant and Inspector General.

NEGROES AS REBEL SOLDIERS.

[*From the Richmond Enquirer, Oct.* 6.]

The general order for the revocation of details will be found in this issue of the *Enquirer*. This step has been taken by the Government to fill up the army. It is necessary and proper, and if this order is promptly enforced the increase of the army will be speedy and rapid. We should like to see steps taken to promptly enforce the law of Congress for the employment of negroes in the army, as teamsters, &c. The law of Congress on this subject is plain, and though it does not go far enough, yet by promptly enforcing its provisions, many soldiers will be returned to their command and the army very greatly strengthened. The details should come forward promptly; their services are greatly needed; and if they are speedily collected and sent to the front there will be no danger at Richmond, and the condition of the country present the most encouraging aspect. It is useless to seek to conceal that more men are greatly wanted. The President has emphatically announced the startling fact that two thirds of the army are absent from the ranks. There would be no need of reinforcements but for this most disgraceful straggling and deserting. But as the fact exists, and the evil must be repaired, the details are called upon to do service. How long their service will be required cannot now be said, but sixty to ninety days will terminate the active operations of the campaign, and then details may be resumed. But, at present, all are needed, and all must come forward. Those that delay or shirk will be hunted down, and permanently sent to the army.

The law of Congress authorizing the employment of negroes, if fully carried out, would give ten thousand men to the Army of Northern Virginia. The slaves and free negroes can be impressed just as any other property, and the law provides for their support and clothing, and pays the owner soldier's wages.

The law of February 17 makes all "male free negroes, (with certain exceptions,) between the ages of eighteen and fifty" liable to perform such duties in the army, or in connection with the military defences of the country, in the way of work upon fortifications, or in Government works, &c., as the Secretary of War may from time to time prescribe, and provides rations, clothing and compensation. The Secretary of War is also authorized to employ for similar duty twenty thousand male negro slaves, and their owners are guaranteed against escape or death. The Secretary is authorized to impress the slaves when he cannot hire them; and General Orders No. 32, March 11, 1861, directed the enrolment of the free negroes, and their assignment to the performance of the duties mentioned in the act. Also the employment and impressment of slaves was ordered by the same general orders, and the provisions of General Orders No. 138, of the 24th October, 1863, pointed out as governing in this matter. Has this law and general order been enforced?

The General Orders No. 138, Oct. 24, 1863, says: "No impressments shall be made of slaves employed in domestic and family service exclusively, nor upon farms or plantations where there are not more than three slaves of the age specified, and not more than five per cent. of the population of slaves shall be impressed in any county at the same time, unless the necessity is very great, and after consultation with this department or the Governor of the State in which the impressment is to be made." Here is the law and the general order. Have they been enforced? If they have not been executed, no longer delay should be allowed. We call upon the authorities to enforce this law immediately.

The question of making soldiers of negroes, of regularly enlisting them and fighting them for their safety, as well as our own, must have presented itself to every reflecting mind. Because the Yankees have not been able to make soldiers out of their drafted negroes, it does not follow that we cannot train our slaves to make very efficient soldiers. *We believe that they can be, by drill and discipline, moulded into steady and reliable soldiers. The propriety of employing negroes as soldiers we shall not at present discuss; but whenever the subjugation of Virginia or the employment of her slaves as soldiers are alternative positions, then certainly we are for making them soldiers, and giving freedom to those negroes that escape the casualties of battle.*

---

to the enemy. He must play an important part in the war. He caused the fight, and he will have his portion of the burthen to bear. We have learned from dear-bought experience that negroes can be taught to fight, and that all who leave us are made to fight against us. I would free all able to bear arms, and put them in the field at once. They will make much better soldiers with us than against us, and swell the now depleted ranks of our armies.

I beg you to give this your earnest attention.

With assurances of my friendly regards and very high esteem, I remain, very respectfully, your obedient servant,

HENRY W. ALLEN,
Governor of Louisiana.

The class of persons to whom it refers will not be conscripted into the armies of the United States if they come within our lines. All will be freed, and they will be received and treated as refugees. They will be accepted as volunteers, or will be employed in the public service, and their families will be cared for until they are in a condition to care for themselves. If a draft should become necessary, no discrimination against them will be made on the enrollment or draft.

By order of Major General E. R. S. Canby:

C. T. CHRISTENSEN,
Lieutenant Colonel and A. A. G.

* The Richmond *Dispatch* of September 12, 1864, makes the authoritative statement that "there are 114,000 men detailed as farmers, and some 32,000 exempt as necessary in some form to the Government and public institutions of the States."

We should be glad to see the Confederate Congress provide for the purchase of two hundred and fifty thousand negroes, present them with their freedom and privilege of remaining in the States, and arm, equip, drill and fight them. We believe that the negroes, identified with us by interest, and fighting for their freedom here, would be faithful and reliable soldiers, and, under officers who would drill them, could be depended on for much of the ordinary service, and even for the hardest fighting. It is not necessary now to discuss this matter, and may never become so, but neither negroes nor slavery will be permitted to stand in the way of the success of our cause. The war is for national independence on our side, and for the subjugation of white and the emancipation of negroes on the side of the enemy. If we fail, the negroes are nominally free and their masters really slaves. We must, therefore, succeed. Other States may decide for themselves, but Virginia, after exhausting her whites, will fight her blacks through to the last man. She will be free at all costs.

USING THE SLAVES.

[*From the Enquirer of October* 18.]

The proposition to extend the Conscript Law to the slaves of the States was first formerly advanced by the *Enquirer* in the issue of the 6th instant. Since that time, we have received many assurances of its popular favor, and none whatever of opposition to it. We learn that the planters in the extreme Southern States favor the proposition, and some have signified their readiness to free five, ten, or fifteen of their slaves, if they will enter the army. The near approach of the time when the Congress meets again requires that expression be given to the sentiments of the country upon this important measure. We therefore earnestly invite its discussion, and open our columns to opponents as well as friends of the proposition.

The result of the late elections is still in doubt, and whether Lincoln or McClellan will be elected it is yet impossible to determine; but there is no uncertainty as to the question of carrying on the war. Whether Lincoln or McClellan be the next President, the voice, and the almost unanimous voice, of that people is for a vigorous prosecution of the war. The duty of preparing to meet that issue will be before the approaching session of the Confederate Congress; that body will have before it, for consideration, the ways and means, as well of men as of money, for carrying on the war on our part.

The war-cry of the enemy—"No parley with rebellion in the field; no compromise with slavery in the readjustment"—fully informs our people that, in plain vernacular, the whites of these States are to be subjugated to slavery, and their slaves reduced to the miserable condition of Yankee free negroes. This is the view of the people among our enemies, and this will be the result of the war, whether ended by Lincoln or McClellan, if the people of these States permit themselves to be conquered.

The conscription of negroes should be accompanied with freedom and the privilege of remaining in the States; this is no part of abolitionism; it is the exercise by the master of the unquestionable right of manumission; it is remunerating those who defend our cause with the privilege of freedom. Nor should this important subject be prejudiced with questions about putting the negro on an equality with our friends, brothers, and fathers. Many of the soldiers in their childhood were fondled and nursed by faithful negro nurses, and yet no question of equality was ever raised. Many a man has manumitted slaves without ever being subjected to the suspicion of being an abolitionist.

The issues involved in this war are too exalted in their importance and character for us to permit them to be compromised by being degraded to a question of property. The liberty and freedom of ourselves and of our children, the nationality of our country, the right of enjoying any kind of property, the houses over our heads, and the very graves of our children and friends, are involved in this struggle. Failure makes slaves of all, white and black; robs all of property, real and personal; divides our lands among our conquerors, who will plough up the very graves of our dead as fertilized ground for making money. We have in our midst a half million of fighting material which is property—shall we use that property for the common cause?

Justice and sound policy demand that we make freemen of those who fight for freedom. We conscript the master and we impress his horses, cattle, wheat, and every other property except slaves. This very exception is an imputation that this war is for slavery and not for freedom. By conscripting the negroes we show to the world the earnestness that is in our people; we prove to our enemies that at the moment of our supposed exhaustion, in the fifth year of the war, we shall meet them with larger armies than we have before raised; and we explode the false accusation that we are fighting for slavery, or a slaveholders' Confederacy.

There are those who doubt whether sound policy would trust negroes with arms. We are not of those who entertain any fears upon that subject. Drill and discipline make valuable soldiers of Russian serfs, and no negroes in these States are so ignorant and brutal as those serfs. Between service with the Confederacy and with the Yankees, between living among us with all their strong local attachments, and going among strangers, who are now openly buying and selling them to recruiting officers, our slaves will find no difficulty in choosing. And, when once it is understood that freedom and a home in the South are the privileges offered by the Confederate authorities, while the enemy extend the beggarly hospitalities of Yankee philanthropy, not only will desertion from our ranks be unfrequent, but the drafted negroes of the Yankee armies will exchange services.

This subject addresses itself to the consideration of our people, at this particular time, with great force. The prospect of four more years of war are before our people; the enemy will not even "parley" with us without unconditional surrender, the fruits of which would be the confiscation of all property, the deportation of whole communities, the degradation of the people, and the domination and tyranny of Yankee masters. There can be no reconstruction which does not embrace a surrender first, which will not permit confiscation afterwards, which does not insure enslaving the white, without freeing the blacks.

If there are any weak-kneed people who imagine they can save their property by reconstruction, let them study the Shibboleth of all parties in the United States—"No parley with rebellion in the field; no compromise with slavery in the adjustment." Unconditional surrender is first demanded before even a parley. We are to lay down our arms and submit to the kindness of the Butlers, Grants, Shermans, and Sheridans; to the fate of New Orleans, the condition of the Valley, the misery of Atlanta, and, after all that degradation, to give up all our slaves in the adjustment. If there are any reasons against extending the conscription to slaves, we should like to have them stated; but we are decidedly of opinion that the whole country will agree to the proposition, and that at an early day the next Congress will be called upon to provide for it by law.

CONFERENCE OF THE GOVERNORS.

[*From the Richmond Sentinel, October* 24.]

In another column we publish the resolutions adopted at a conference of the Governors of a number of the Confederate States. The united resolve of the Governors to use every effort to increase the effective force of the army; to strengthen the Confederate authorities in the discharge of their duties; to consider the interests of all the States as identical, and to favor the sending of State troops beyond the State limits when their services are needed; to favor stringent laws for the arrest by the State authorities of stragglers and deserters, will be greeted with the popular acclamation. The determined resolve which they declare for themselves and their constituencies, "to maintain our right of self-government, to establish our independence, and to uphold the rights and sovereignty of the States, or to perish in the attempt," is an exhibition of the spirit proper to their high positions, and shared by our people throughout the country.

The Governors also recommend to the Confederate Government to send all able-bodied civil employees into the field, and to dispense in a great measure with provost and post guards. They further propose a course of action in reference to slaves near the enemy's lines, and the employment of slaves in the Confederate service, which is eminently proper, and in accordance with a growing sentiment among the people.

On the whole, we trust the conference of the Governors will be productive of much good.

THE CONFERENCE.

At a meeting of the Governors of the States of Virginia, North Carolina, South Carolina, Georgia, Alabama, and Mississippi, held in Augusta, Ga., on the 17th inst., Governor William Smith presiding, after a full, free, and harmonious consultation and interchange of counsel, the following, among other views, were expressed:

Resolved, That there is nothing in the present aspect of public affairs to cause any abatement of our zeal in the prosecution of the war, to the accomplishment of a peace based on the independence of the Confederate States. And to give encouragement to our brave soldiers in the field, and to strengthen the Confederate authorities in the pursuit of this desirable end, we will use our best exertions to increase the effective force of our armies.

Resolved, That the interests of each of our States are identical in the present struggle for self-government, and wisdom and true patriotism dictate that the military forces of each should aid the others against invasion and subjugation, and for this purpose we shall recommend to our several Legislatures to repeal all such laws as prohibit the Executives from sending their forces beyond their respective limits, in order that they may render temporary service wherever most urgently required.

Resolved, That, whilst it is our purpose to use every exertion to increase the strength and efficiency of our State and Confederate forces, we respectfully and earnestly request that the Confederate authorities will send to the field every able-bodied man, without exception, in any of its various departments, whose place can be filled by either disabled officers and soldiers, senior reserves, or negroes, and dispense with the use of all provost and post guards, except in important cities and localities where the presence of large bodies of troops make them necessary, and with all passport agents upon railroads not in the immediate vicinity of the armies, as we consider these agents an unnecessary annoyance to good citizens, and of no possible benefit to the country.

Resolved, That we recommend our respective Legislatures to pass stringent laws for the arrest and return to their commands of all deserters and stragglers from the Confederate armies or State troops, and that it be made the special duty, under appropriate penalties, of all civil and military officers to arrest and deliver to the proper authorities all such delinquents.

And whereas the public enemy, having proclaimed the freedom of our slaves, are forcing into their armies the able-bodied portion thereof, the more effectually to wage their cruel and bloody war against us; therefore, be it

Resolved, That it is the true policy and obvious duty of all slave owners timely to remove their slaves from the line of the enemy's approach, and especially those able to bear arms; and when they shall fail to do so, that it should be made the duty of the proper authorities to enforce the performance of this duty, and to give to such owners all necessary assistance as far as practicable.

Resolved, That the course of the enemy, in appropriating our slaves who happen to fall into their hands to purposes of war, seems to justify a change of policy on our part; and whilst owners of slaves, under the circumstances, should freely yield them to their country, we recommend to our authorities, under proper regulations, to appropriate such part of them to the public service as may be required.

Resolved, That the States have a right to export such productions and to import such supplies as may be necessary for State use, or for the comfort or support of their troops in service, upon any vessel or vessels owned or chartered by them; and that we request Congress at its next session to pass laws removing all restrictions which have been imposed by Confederate authority upon such exports or imports by the States.

And, lastly, we deem it not inappropriate to declare our firm and unalterable purpose, as we believe it to be that of our fellow-citizens, to maintain our right of self-government, to establish our independence, and to uphold the rights and sovereignty of the States, or to perish in the attempt.

Resolved, That the chairman be requested to send a copy of these resolutions to his Excellency President Davis, one each to the President of the Senate and Speaker of the House of Representatives, to be laid before their respective bodies, and one to the Governor of each State in the Confederacy.

The Richmond *Whig*, of the 24th, thus comments upon the above:

THE GOVERNORS IN COUNCIL.

The Governors of several of our States have been in consultation in Georgia, and have agreed in making a number of recommendations to Congress, the Confederate Executive, and the Legislatures of the several States, the adoption of which, it is thought, will promote the cause in which each of these States have so vital an interest. There does not appear to have been any discord or diversity of opinion in this conference; and, indeed, it may be said there is no difference among our people, except in some matters, as to the wisdom with which the means placed at the disposal of the authorities are employed.

The paramount question with all—the one question—is, how can the power of the Confederacy be most efficiently and successfully employed for the defence and deliverance of the Confederacy? All agree that its entire military resources, to the last man and the last dollar if needed, must be thrown into the struggle. No one thinks of turning back, or so much as looking back, till the work is finished. No one dreams of any adjustment that would compromise our independence. Liberty or death is the language and purpose of all. With such a resolve animating the whole body of our people, armies, authorities, and citizens, subjugation is impossible.

LETTER OF ALEXANDER H. STEPHENS ON PEACE.

CRAWFORDSVILLE, GA., *September* 22, 1864.

GENTLEMEN: You will please excuse me for not answering your letter of the 14th instant sooner. I have been absent nearly a week on a visit to my brother in Sparta, who has been quite out of health for some time. Your letter I found here on my return home yesterday. The delay of my reply thus occasioned I regret.

Without further explanation or apology allow me now to say to you that no person living can possibly feel a more ardent desire for an end to be put to this unnatural and merciless war upon honorable and just terms than I do. But I really do not see that it is in my power or yours, or that of any number of persons in our position, to inaugurate any movement that will even tend to aid in bringing about a result that we and so many more desire.

The movement by our Legislature at its last session, at the suggestion of the Executive, on this subject, was by authority properly constituted for such a purpose. That movement, in my judgment, was timely, judicious, and in the right direction. Nor has it been without results. The organization of that party at the North to which you refer may justly be claimed as a part of the fruits of it. These, it is to be hoped, will be followed by others of a more marked character, if all in both sections who sincerely desire peace upon correct terms will give that movement thus inaugurated all the aid in their power.

The resolutions of the Georgia Legislature, at its last session, upon the subject of peace, in my judgment, embodied and set forth very clearly those principles upon which alone there can be permanent peace between the different sections of this extensive, once happy and prosperous, but now distracted country.

Easy and perfect solution to all present troubles, and those far more grievous ones which loom in prospect, and portentously threaten in the coming future, is nothing more than the simple recognition of the fundamental principle and truth upon which all American constitutional liberty is founded, and upon the maintenance of which alone it can be preserved—that is, the sovereignty, the ultimate, absolute sovereignty, of the States. This doctrine our Legislature announced to the people of the North and to the world. It is the only key-note to peace—permanent, lasting peace—consistent with the security of the public liberty.

The old Confederation was formed upon this principle. The old Union was afterwards formed upon this principle. No league can ever be formed or maintained between any State, North or South, securing public liberty, upon any other principle. The whole framework of American institutions, which in so short a time had won the admiration of the world, and to which we were indebted for such an unparalleled career of prosperity and happiness, was formed upon this principle. All our present troubles sprung from a departure from this principle, from a violation of this essential law of our political organization.

In 1776 our ancestors, and the ancestors of those who are waging this unholy crusade against us, together proclaimed the great and eternal truth for the maintenance of which they jointly pledged their lives, their fortunes, and their sacred honor, that governments are instituted amongst men, deriving their just powers from the consent of the governed, and that whenever any form of government becomes destructive of those ends for which it was formed, it is the right of the people to alter or abolish it and institute a new Government, laying its foundations on such principles, and organizing its powers in such a form as to them may seem most likely to effect their safety and happiness.

It is needless here to state that by "people" and "governed," in this annunciation, is meant communities and bodies of men capable of organizing and maintaining a government, not individual members of society. The consent of the governed refers to the will of the mass of the community or State in its organized form, and expressed through its legitimate and properly constituted organs. It was upon this principle the Colonists stood justified before the world in effecting their separation from the mother country. It was upon this principle that the original thirteen co-equal and co-sovereign States formed the Federal compact of the old Union in 1787. It is upon the same principle that the present co-equal and co-sovereign States of our Confederacy formed their new compact of Union.

The idea that the old Union or any Union between sovereign States, consistently with this fundamental truth, can be maintained by force is preposterous. This war springs from an attempt to do this preposterous thing. Superior power may compel a Union of some sort, but it would not be the Union of the old Constitution or of our new. It would be that sort of Union that results from despotism.

The subjugation of the people of the South by the people of the North would necessarily involve the destruction of the Constitution, and the overthrow of their liberties as well as ours. The men or party at the North, to whom you refer, who favor peace, must be brought to a full realization of this truth in all its bearings before their efforts will result in much practical good. Any peace growing out of a union of States established by force will be as ruinous to them as to us.

The action of the Chicago Convention, so far as its platform of principles goes, presents, as I have said on another occasion, a ray of light, which, under Providence, may prove the dawn of day to this long and cheerless night, the first ray of light I have seen from the North since the war began. This cheers the heart, and towards it I could almost exclaim, "Hail! holy light, offspring of Heaven, first born of the eternal co-eternal beam. May I express thee unblamed, since God is light." Indeed, I could have quite so exclaimed, but for the sad reflection that whether it shall bring healing in its beams or be lost in a dark and ominous eclipse ere its good work be done, depends so much upon the action of others who may not regard it and view it as I do. So at best it is but a ray, a small and tremulous ray, enough only to gladden the heart and quicken the hope.

The prominent and leading idea of that Convention seems to have been a desire to reach a peaceful adjustment of our present difficulties and strife through the medium of a convocation of the States. They propose to suspend hostilities, to see what can be done, if anything, by negotiations of some sort. This is one step in the right direction. To such a convention of the States I should have no objection, as a peaceful conference and interchange of views between equal and sovereign Powers, just as the Convention of 1787 was called and assembled. The proper constituted authorities at Washington and Richmond, the duly authorized representatives of the two confederacies of States now at war with each other, might give their assent to such a proposition. Good might result from it. It would be an appeal on both sides from the sword to reason and justice. All wars which do not result in the extinction and extermination on one side or the other must be ended sooner or later by some sort of negotiation.

From the discussion or interchange of views in such a Convention, the history as well as the true nature of our institutions, and the relation of the States towards each other and towards the Federal head, would doubtless be much better understood generally than they now are; but I should favor such a proposition only as a peaceful conference, as the Convention of 1787 was. I should be opposed to leaving the question at issue to the absolute decision of such a body. Delegates might be clothed with powers to consult and agree, if they could, upon some plan of adjustment, to be submitted for subsequent ratification by the sovereign States whom it affected, before it should be obligatory or binding, and then binding only on such as should so ratify it. It becomes the people of the South as well as the people of the North to be quite as watchful and jealous of their rights as their common ancestors were. The maintenance of liberty in all ages, times, and countries, when and where it has existed, has required not only constant vigilance and jealousy, but it has often required the greatest privations and sufferings and sacrifices that people of States are ever subjected to. Through such an ordeal we are now passing. Through a like and even a severer ordeal our ancestors passed in their struggle for the principles which it has devolved upon us thus to defend and maintain.

But, great as our sufferings and sacrifices have been and are, to which you allude, they are as yet far short of the like sufferings and sacrifices which our fathers bore with patience, courage and fortitude in the crisis that tried men's souls in their day. These are the virtues that sustained them in their hour of need. Their illustrious and glorious example bids us not to under-estimate the priceless inheritance they achieved for us at such a cost of treasure and blood. Great as are the odds we are struggling against, they are not greater than those against which they successfully struggled. In point of reverses our condition is not to be compared with theirs. Should Mobile, Savannah, Charleston, Augusta, Macon, Montgomery, and even Petersburg and Richmond fall, our condition would not then be worse or less hopeful than theirs was in the darkest hour that rested on their fortunes. With wisdom on the part of those who control our destiny in the Cabinet and in the field, in husbanding and properly wielding our resources at their command, and in securing the hearts and affections of the people in the great cause of right and liberty for which we are struggling, we could suffer all their losses and calamities, and greater even, and still triumph in the end.

At present, however, I do not see, as I stated in the outset, that you or I, or any number of persons in our position, can do anything towards inaugurating any new movement looking to a peaceful solution of the present strife. The war on our part is fairly and entirely defensive in its character. How long it will continue to be thus wickedly and mercilessly waged against us depends upon the people of the North. Georgia, our own State, to whom we owe allegiance, has with great unanimity proclaimed the principles upon which a just and permanent peace ought to be sought and obtained. The Congress of the Confederate States has followed with an endorsement of these principles. All you and I, and others in our position, therefore, can do on that line at this time is to sustain the movement already inaugurated, and, to the utmost of our ability, to hold up these principles as the surest hope of restoring soundness to the public mind of the North, as the brazen serpent was held up for the healing of Israel in the wilderness. The chief aid and encouragement we can give the peace party at the North is to keep before them these great fundamental principles and truths, which alone will lead them and us to permanent and lasting peace, with possession and enjoyment of constitutional liberty. With these principles once recognized, the future would take care of itself, and there would be no more war so long as they should be adhered to. All questions of boundaries, confederacies, and union or unions would naturally and easily adjust themselves, according to the interests of parties and the exigencies of the times. Here lies the true law of the balance of power and the harmony of States.

Yours, respectfully,

ALEXANDER H. STEPHENS.

LETTER FROM WILLIAM W. BOYCE ON PEACE.

WINSBORO, S. C., *Sept.* 29, 1864.

His Excellency JEFFERSON DAVIS:

SIR: The Democratic party of the United States, in their recent convention at Chicago, resolved that if they attained power they would agree to an armistice and a convention of all the States, to consider the subject of peace. I think that action demands a favorable response from our Government. You are the only person who can make that response, because our Congress does not meet until after the time appointed for the Presidential election. If our Congress met in time I should propose the action I desire taken to that body, and submit to its judgment my argument; but as that opportunity does not occur, I have no alternative but to remain silent, or address myself to you. I cannot, consistently with my ideas of duty, remain silent. I therefore address myself to you. We are waging war to obtain a satisfactory peace. By a satisfactory peace, I mean a peace consistent with the preservation of our free institutions. By a satisfactory peace, I do not mean that cessation of hostilities which might, after a protracted contest, result from the exhaustion of the belligerents, whereby the sword would fall from their nerveless hands, their hearts a prey to the furies. Such a peace as that would be but a hollow truce, in which each party would be incessantly preparing for a new, final and decisive struggle. The peace which I mean is a peace which reconciles the interests and the feelings of the belligerents; a peace, in short, which restores harmony. Unless we can obtain such a peace as this, our republican institutions totter to their fall, and we become the subjects of a military despotism. Every government must exist; that is the law of its being. If it is attacked by a great force it must bring a proportionately great force to its defence. If its form is such as not to furnish military strength to the full extent of its means, it must disregard that form. The republican form, especially the form of a Confederacy of free States, is not the best adapted for war. In fact, it is a peace establishment. The form best adapted for war is a national military despotism. The Republic at war is gradually passing into military despotism. As the war continues and the pressure of its enemies increases, this transition is accelerated. A Republic forced to the wall by a powerful enemy must end in despotism. If we turn our eyes to Europe we find only two nations with free institutions, Great Britain and Switzerland. Why is this? The reason is obvious. The necessity of being constantly in the highest state of preparation for war compels every country to the utmost development of its military strength. Absolute government is a part of that state of preparation, and therefore absolute government is the ordinary condition. If there were no other obstacle to France being a republic, the immense standing armies she is compelled to keep constantly under arms would be conclusive. France is compelled to keep six hundred thousand men always in arms. France is obliged, therefore, to be what she is, a military despotism. Take the case of Prussia in the celebrated seven years' war. Suppose her institutions had been liberal, what would have been the result? Frederick the Great would either have had to abandon the struggle, or seize all power. Nothing but absolute power in the hands of Frederick enabled him to come forth victorious from the contest. He sacrificed everything else in Prussia to the one idea of military strength. As Prussia had no natural defences, and was greatly inferior in strength to the other great powers, it was necessary to give exclusive development to the military idea; this Frederick did. As Macaulay said, he made Prussia "all sting." This was logical in Frederick. To save Prussia it was necessary to give her the maximum of military strength; he did this. Prussia still has a place on the map, but he made no effort to save liberty. Frederick found Prussia an absolute monarchy; he left it an entrenched camp. Liberty was never thought of. It is impossible in her condition. If Prussia, with her excellent population, were at a vast distance from where she is, and protected by oceans and mountains, she might be a republic; but where she is, it is impossible. On the continent of Europe no State can exist with free institutions, because the form of government must be such as furnishes the greatest amount of military strength. Perhaps it may be said that Switzerland contradicts my theory. I reply that Switzerland is an exceptional case—a few nests of poor people buried in remote valleys, surrounded by inaccessible mountains; they are not worth conquering. Besides, the mutual jealousy of the great powers is their real safeguard. England is the only free and great power in Europe. This is owing to her insular position. The ocean is the divine charter of her freedom. If nothing but a surveyor's line separated England from France, England would be a military despotism as France is. No country can be free which has to sleep with her hand on her sword.

But why resort to general reasoning and the condition of European nations to prove what I have asserted, when the proof stares us in the face in the example of our own country. We see it in every sight; we feel it in every emotion; we hear it in every sound. When our present Government was established, everything possible was done in the interest of State rights, every conceivable guarantee was taken for individual freedom—as little as possible was conceded to the Federal Government. The Federal Government was "cabined, cribbed, confined," "hedged in by saucy doubts and fears." The school of extreme State rights were at work framing a Constitution for a Federal Government, with the accumulated suspicions of seventy years. They did their work well. The problem to be solved was the framing of a Federal Government, with the minimum of power to function. I thought at the time it was useless labor, because I conceived, in the humility of my judgment, that the constitution of a country was that which its necessities pointed out, and that you could not in advance say what would be the necessities of a Confederacy exposed to perpetual war with a neighboring power of superior force. But the framers of our Constitution were not deterred by any such considerations as these from their work. They established their Confederacy, guarded and limited in the interests of the rights of the separate States as much as possible. Well, we have been at war not quite four years, and what is the result? Is not our Federal Government in the exercise of every possible power of a national central military despotism? Suppose there were no States, only provinces, and unlimited power was conferred upon you and Congress—what greater powers would you exercise than you do now? Have we not carried conscription to its last limits? Is not every man in the country between 17 and 50 subject to military authority? None are exempt except upon considerations of public interest. Have we not been compelled to lay direct taxes in the very teeth of the theory of the Constitution? Have we not issued such vast amounts of paper money as to unsettle all value? Have we not compelled the holders of our paper money to fund it, or lose one-third? Have we not seized all the railroads? Have we not destroyed railroads and built others? Have we not established a universal system of impressment of property, at our own prices, in our own money? Have we not established a Government monopoly of the exportations of the great staples of the country? Have we not forbidden the importation of luxuries? Have we not compelled those whom we permit to remain at home to execute bonds to furnish their products to us at our prices? Have we not suspended the writ of *habeas corpus?* Have we not introduced the passport system, which we used to think belonged to the iron despotism of Europe? In short, has not our Federal Government done everything that a centralized military despotism could do? Indeed, if you were appointed Military Dictator, what greater powers could you exercise than you now do? I allude to these things not to complain of them, but to lament them. If you tell me they are necessary, I reply that is precisely my argument. My argument assumes and requires that necessity. It is plain that our Government exercises the powers of a central despotism. I blame no one for it. I am sure those who are at the head of the Government would gladly have it otherwise; but necessity compels the course they have taken. But I shall be told, perhaps, this necessity is limited to the war, and when peace returns we will go back to our old state of liberty. That depends upon the kind of peace. A peace without reconciliation carries in his bosom the seeds of new wars. This armed peace and its offspring, war, would fasten upon us permanently a central military despotism. It is common to hear it said that the United States have gone into despotism. If so, then it is a very sad truth for us, for that would develop their maximum military power, and would, of course, necessitate the same thing in the same way on our part. The truth is, we are vitally interested in the preservation of free institutions in the Northern States, because the people of the United States will not only make their institutions, but they will make ours. If they acquire their maximum military strength by going into despotism, we must do the same, just as if they were to originate new and overpoweringly destructive modes of warfare, we would have to resort to the same or be overwhelmed. Some persons of intelligence concede that the Northern people have gone into despotism, but ridicule the idea of such a calamity befalling us. To such I would reply, we are but human beings, not gods, and we are acted upon by necessity as other people. The truth is, that the Government at Washington has not dared to exercise power on the grand scale that our Government has. The Lincoln Government has not ventured to resort to an effective conscription; it has not resorted to taxation as we have; it has no tax in kind; it does not prohibit imports; it does not monopolize the exports; it does not rely on impressments. It plays the tyrant, but it hesitates to seize the sceptre.

I think I have established my proposition, that our Republican institutions are lost unless we have a peace accompanied by harmony with the North. The great question for us then is, how are we to obtain such a peace?

Before I consider this question, I would call your attention to this fact, that the peace we are to make with the North is to be made by us and the North alone. There is no probability of any foreign intervention; by that I mean any armed interference in our behalf. The peace between the North and the South, when it comes, must come, then, by the action of these parties alone. Foreign Powers will not interfere. The question then is, how are these belligerent States, now so fiercely engaged, to obtain this peace with reconciliation, which I have said is necessary to preserve their Republican form of government? It is a great question. I now approach it.

I admit in the first place that a successful military defence is indispensable. Without that nothing can be anticipated but utter ruin. But is this all? I think not. There is something over and above success in war. That is political policy. If Mr. Lincoln remains in power, there is no hope of accomplishing anything by political policy. Mr. Lincoln is the exponent of the fanaticism and hatred of the North. He holds power because he is the exponent of these sentiments of his party; in order to be master of others he has to be their slave. He cannot be rational upon the subject of slavery, because he represents madmen; he cannot exercise what Burke calls the truest political wisdom, magnanimity, because he represents malignants. Besides, Mr. Lincoln is committed by his past career to the most violent course. If he had been a statesman when he became President, he could, by a wise policy, have restored harmony. But in that great crisis, when statesmanship could have accomplished so much, he used no efforts to harmonize, but yielded himself up a mere instrument of the foolish mob, as if statesmanship came from below upwards. Mr. Wm. H. Seward, by his speeches made in the winter of '60, showed that he comprehended the policy of conciliation, but just at the moment when it became necessary to put in force his fine maxims, he found no use for them. Mr. Lincoln's mode of carrying on the war, his emancipation policy, the license he gave his armies to commit the greatest outrages, shows that he relies on nothing but force. I confess, therefore, I have no hope of Mr. Lincoln as a pacificator. I should as soon have selected Charles IX to pacify the Huguenots after the massacre of St. Bartholomew. But fortunately Mr. Lincoln and those he represents are not all of the North. There is a powerful party there which condemns his policy. That party is rational on the subject of slavery. It represents whatever of amity or conservatism is left at the North. This party proposes that the war shall cease, at least temporarily, and that all the States should meet in amicable council, to make peace if possible. This is the most imposing demonstration in favor of peace made at the North since the war broke out. I think our only hope of a satisfactory peace, one consistent with the preservation of free institutions, is in the supremacy of this party at some time or other. Our policy, therefore, is to give this party all the capital we can. You should, therefore, at once, in my opinion, give this party all the encouragement possible, by declaring your willingness to an armistice, and a convention of all the States in their sovereign capacity, to enter upon the subject of peace. The theory upon which this party goes is, that we are willing to cease hostilities, at least temporarily, and meet in council to attain peace if possible. The theory upon which Mr. Lincoln goes is, that there is no use to attempt any negotiation with us; that the sword is the only possible arbiter. Our policy is to show that the theory of the Chicago platform is the true one. To put this matter in another light, let us ask the question, what is the policy that Mr. Lincoln wishes us to pursue? Of course he wishes us to verify his theory and falsify the opposite theory. He wishes us to treat the advances of the Chicago Convention with contempt. He wishes to be able to say to the Northern people, "see, the Government of Richmond tramples upon your tenders of peaceful negotiation; McClellan could accomplish nothing by negotiation; war is all that is left; don't remove me, I am carrying that on with especial zeal." When we know what Mr. Lincoln wants us to do, then we know very certainly what he ought to do.

It may be said, the proposed convocation of the States is unconstitutional. To this I reply, we can amend the Constitution. It may be further objected that to meet the Northern States in convention is to abandon our present form of Government. But this no more follows than that their meeting us implies an abandonment of their form of Government. A Congress of the States in their sovereign capacity is the highest acknowledgment of the principles of State rights. This imposing assemblage is, in my opinion, the best, while it is the most august tribunal to which the great question of peace could possibly be referred. Imagine this grand council of States in the act of convening, after the people, everywhere in peaceful possession of the right to elect their ambassadors, had done so. What a sublime spectacle it would present! There would be nothing to compare with it in moral grandeur, in ancient or modern times. The friends of humanity and progress and civilization, and all Christians in every land, would rejoice at the spectacle, and millions in every clime, the good everywhere, would mingle their prayers in all tongues for an auspicious issue to these great deliberations. The question rests with you; the responsibility is with you; the consequences will be with your country. You and Mr. Lincoln can never make peace. You may traverse indefinitely the same bloody circles you have been moving in for the last four years, but you will never approach any nearer than you now are. Your only hope of peace is in the ascendancy of the conservative party North. Fortify that party if you can by victories, but do not neglect diplomacy. It was the boast of Philip, the great king, that he gained more cities by his policy than by his arms. A weak power, engaged with a stronger, must make up in sagacity for what it lacks in physical force, otherwise the monuments of its glory become the tomb of its nationality.

With sentiments of the highest respect, I remain your fellow-citizen,

WILLIAM W. BOYCE.

LETTER FROM HERSCHEL V. JOHNSON ON PEACE.

SANDY GROVE, NEAR BARTOW P. O., GA., *Sept.* 25, 1864.

GENTLEMEN: Your letter of the 14th inst. was received several days ago. I have taken time to consider the object which it proposes—"the inauguration of a peace movement at the South." I long for peace as ardently as "the hart pants for the cooling water brook." I agree with you, that "this unnatural strife cannot be terminated by arms."

To this end, we should lose no occasion, nor omit any proper means to convince the North that we are still, as we always have been, willing to adjust the difficulties between us, upon honorable terms. We have avowed our desire for peace and readiness for negotiation from the very beginning of the war, in every form in which organized communities can give expression to their will. We have avowed it in executive messages, in legislative resolves and congressional manifestoes.

What more can we do, in view of our situation? Gladly would I do more, if it were possible. But I do not believe that it is. We can inaugurate no movement that would lead to the result so earnestly desired by every friend of humanity, and so urgently demanded by the interests of both sections. Our military situation would seem to forbid even the attempt. The capture of Atlanta and Richmond is regarded by the authorities of the United States as all that is necessary for our ultimate subjugation. They have captured Atlanta, and General Grant says the early capture of Richmond is certain, beyond a doubt.

What, under the circumstances, would be the probable effect of any peace movement at the South? Would it conciliate the North? Would it inspire the Government of the United States with a sense of justice, or forbearance, or magnanimity? So far from this, it would be construed into intimidation on our part, and it would stimulate and intensify the war spirit of the North. It would be regarded as our confession of overthrow, and the premonitory symptom of our readiness to sue for mercy on the bended knees of unconditional surrender.

In view of the avowed object of the war on the part of the Northern Government, it is very certain that there can be no peace, upon any honorable terms, so long as its present rulers are in power. The President of the United States has proclaimed emancipation, and his determination to enforce it by the sword. He has announced, in advance of any formal offer of negotiation on our part, that he will not treat with rebels, (as he is pleased to call the people of the Confederate States,) except upon the condition that we lay down our arms, abandon slavery, and return to the Union. He will then grant such terms as may be compatible with his sense of justice, liberality, and magnanimity. So long, therefore, as its present rulers are in power, and this policy shall be adhered to, there can be no peace between us and the Government of the United States which will not bring upon us confiscation, social disorganization, poverty, degradation, and intolerable dishonor. What worse would be our doom if subjugated by military power? Subjugation is no worse than the submission offered to us as the only condition of peace. It would at least save to us our honor.

We must have negotiations which will not compromise our status in any way; which will not affect our national honor, or the rights of States. Peace upon any other terms involves the loss of liberty, because it will be the result of force—not of choice and compact between co-equal and sovereign States. Peace upon any other terms means despotism enthroned in empire—not Republicanism founded upon "the consent of the governed," and organized "in such forms as to them shall seem most likely to effect their safety and happiness." This is the kind of peace which the United States now propose to enforce upon the people of the Confederate States—the peace of death to constitutional liberty—the stagnant peace of despotism—the peace which chains and prison bars impose.

I look with anxiety to the approaching Presidential election in the United States. For, although the Chicago platform falls below the great occasion, and the nominee still lower, yet the triumph of the Democratic party of the North will certainly secure a temporary suspension of hostilities and an effort to make peace by an appeal to reason. They confess that four years of bloody war, as a means of restoring the Union, has proven a failure. They declare that the true principles of American Government have been disregarded and trampled under foot by the present Executive of the United States. Their success will bring a change of Administration, and, with that, a change of policy. It will do more, and what is of infinitely greater importance, it will bring the two contending parties face to face, in the arena of reason and consultation. Then and there can be discussed the history of all our difficulties, the principles involved in the bloody issue, and the respective interests of both Governments. Such is my conviction of the omnipotence of truth and right, that I feel an abiding confidence that an honorable peace would ultimately spring from such deliberations.

In their long-cherished devotion to the Union of the States—a sentiment which challenges my respect—the people of the North, it seems to me, have fallen into two grave and capital errors. On the one hand, they attach an undue importance to the mere fact or form of Union, ignoring the principles and objects of the Union, and forgetting that it ceases to be valuable when it fails to secure that object and maintain those principles. On the other hand, they think that the States of the Confederacy have separated from the United States in contempt of that Union, in a wanton disposition to insult its flag and to destroy the Government of which it is the emblem. Both opinions are wrong. The old Union was an organization of States. But it was more: it was such an organization, founded upon great principles, in order to give the most efficient security for the maintenance of those very same principles.

These principles are the sovereignty of the States—the right of the people to govern themselves; the right of each State to regulate its own domestic affairs, to establish its own municipal institutions, to organize its own system of labor, and to pursue its own career of enterprise, subject to no restrictions except such as are expressed in the Federal Constitution. On these the Union was based, and constituted the solemn guarantee of all, that each State should be protected in their undisturbed enjoyment. When it failed to do this, or, what is worse, when its Government passed into the administration of those whose avowed policy and measures must lead to the overthrow of those principles, it was virtually at an end, and, in their opinion, ceased to be valuable to the people of the Confederate States. Hence, secession was not resorted to merely to throw off the Union.

Our people loved the Union and honored its once glorious flag for the rich memories that clustered around it. They left it with a reluctance and regret to which history will scarcely do justice. They were, as they are now, wedded to the principles on which the Union was founded; they separated from it but to vindicate and maintain them. Whether they acted wisely or unwisely must be left to the imperial arbitrament of time and coming events. But no people were ever prompted to so momentous a step by loftier devotion to constitutional liberty. For this we are denounced as rebels against the Government of the United States, and threatened with the bloody doom of traitors; our country is invaded, our homes desolated, and our people slain by hostile armies.

This is the naked truth. When thus viewed, how cruel and unnatural is this war! Why should the North fight us?

Especially why should the thousands of professed constitutional men at the North lend their countenance and aid to our subjugation? We are struggling for principles which should be as dear to them as they are to us. Do they not see that our overthrow will be the downfall of constitutional liberty—fatal to their freedom as well as ours—the inauguration of an irresponsible and unlimited despotism? Correct ideas are slow in the progress of leavening the mass of mind; truth is ever trampled upon when passion gains sway. But the ultimate prevalence of the one and the ascendancy of the other is only a question of time, and their end, peace.

The light already begins to break in upon the thinking and better portion of the Northern people. They begin to see that this war is not waged to restore the Union in good faith—the Union of the Constitution; but either to secure disunion, by avowing impossible and degrading terms of peace, or to convert it into a despotism by subjugating the South. Hence the Chicago movement. Hence the note of discontent that is being sounded by a portion of the press and statesmen of the North. God opened the light, that the people of the North may understand the position which we occupy, and discern the volcano that threatens to engulph their liberty. Then they will consider negotiation not only politically but absolutely necessary. Then peace will come, predicated upon those principles so essential to both Governments, and all our strifes and difficulties solved in conformity to the best interests of the parties.

In view of our position, permit me to repeat, I do not see how we can inaugurate any movement likely to lead to an honorable peace. We are the party assailed. Peace movements must come from the assailing party. I would not be understood, however, as standing on any point of etiquette as to who should take the initiative—I have no such feeling. All I mean to say is, that in view of the avowed policy of the United States Government, any advance on our part is already rejected before made, and that we cannot make any upon the conditions announced by its President. I would not hesitate to take the initiative if there was the least hope of a favorable response or an honorable result. But if the Government of the United States should pass into other hands, repudiate the policy of subjugation, and indicate a desire for negotiation, I would, if need be, have our Government propose it—certainly accept the offer of it, if tendered by the Federal authorities.

Such I believe to be the spirit and temper of our people. Such I am satisfied is the sentiment of the President of the Confederate States. He has avowed it on every occasion which required him to allude to the subject. The North can have peace at any moment. All that they need to do is to let us alone—cease to fight us; or, if they prefer, agree to negotiate a peace on terms honorable to both parties. We are willing, always have been willing, and shall continue to be willing. But as long as they fight us the war must continue. For what can we do but defend? We have no power to stop their fighting short of unconditional submission to the terms announced by the President of the United States.

Are our people prepared for peace upon those terms? It is an insult to ask the question, unless, indeed, we suppose, contrary to the whole history of our struggle, that they did not count the cost in the beginning, and have no just appreciation of the mighty principles involved. The President of the Confederate States never uttered anything more true than when he said to the unofficial messenger of President Lincoln that "we are not fighting for slavery, but for the right of self-government."

So long as the people will keep this great truth in view and obey the inspiration which it should kindle in the breasts of freemen, they cannot be conquered. They may have their land desolated, their property destroyed, their towns and cities burned and sacked, but subjugated they never can be. We cannot have peace so long as the present rulers of the United States are in power. We may not even if the Chicago movement should be successful. But let us wait and hope for the change and for peace. If it come not, then we must rely upon the omnipotence of truth and right, and the judicious economy and use of the means which God has given us. Patience, fortitude, courage, hope, and faith are as much elements of heroic patriotism as they are of Christian perfection.

It is indispensable to cherish them with untiring devotion, and as the only condition on which liberty can be gained or preserved. Her christening, from the beginning, was the baptism of blood. She requires her votaries to lock arms and shields around her altar, resolved to die freemen rather than live slaves. If this be the spirit of the people, ultimate success will be the reward for their sufferings and sacrifices. For their encouragement history is replete with examples, of which none is more striking or more inspiring than that of the revolution of 1776. Then let there be no despondency, no relaxation of effort and energy, no abatement of courage and heroic resolve.

I am, very respectfully, your obedient servant,

HERSCHEL V. JOHNSON.

Letters from Lieut. Gen. Grant.

MEMPHIS, TENN., *August* 26, 1863.

GENTLEMEN: I received a copy of the resolutions passed by the "loyal citizens of Memphis, at a meeting held at the rooms of the Chamber of Commerce, August 25, 1863," tendering me a public reception.

In accepting this testimonial, which I do at a great sacrifice of my personal feelings, I simply desire to pay a tribute to the first public exhibition in Memphis of loyalty to the Government which I represent in the Department of the Tennessee. I should dislike to refuse, for considerations of personal convenience, to acknowledge, anywhere or in any form, the existence of sentiments which I have so long and so ardently desired to see manifested in this Department. The stability of this Government and the unity of this nation depend solely on the cordial support and the earnest loyalty of the people. While, therefore, I thank you sincerely for the kind expressions you have used toward myself, I am profoundly gratified at this public recognition, in the city of Memphis, of the power and authority of the Government of the United States.

I thank you, too, in the name of the noble army which I have the honor to command. It is composed of men whose loyalty is proved by their deeds of heroism and their willing sacrifices of life and health. They will rejoice with me that the miserable adherents of the rebellion, whom their bayonets have driven from this fair land, are being replaced by men who acknowledge human liberty as the only true foundation of human government. May your efforts to restore your city to the cause of the Union be as successful as has been theirs to reclaim it from the despotic rule of the leaders of the rebellion.

I have the honor to be, gentlemen, your very obedient servant,

U. S. GRANT,
Major General.

To Messrs. R. HOUGH, and others, Committee, Memphis.

The following is an extract of a letter from Lieut. Gen. Grant, dated,

HEADQUARTERS ARMIES OF THE UNITED STATES,
CITY POINT, VA., *Aug.* 16, 1864.

Hon. E. B. WASHBURNE:

DEAR SIR: I state to all citizens who visit me that all we want now to ensure an early restoration of the Union is a determined unity of sentiment North. The Rebels have now in their ranks their last man. The little boys and old men are guarding prisoners, guarding railroad bridges, and forming a good part of their garrisons for entrenched positions.

A man lost by them cannot be replaced. They have robbed alike the cradle and the grave to get their present force. Besides what they lose in frequent skirmishes and battles, they are now losing, from desertions and other causes, at least one regiment per day. With this drain upon them the end is not far distant if we will only be true to ourselves. Their only hope now is in a divided North. This might give them re-enforcements from Tennessee, Kentucky, Maryland and Missouri, while it would weaken us. With the draft quietly enforced, the enemy would become despondent and would make but little resistance.

I have no doubt but the enemy are exceedingly anxious to hold out until after the Presidential election. They have many hopes from its effects. They hope a counter revolution; they hope the election of a Peace candidate; in fact, like Micawber, they hope for something to turn up.

Our peace friends, if they expect peace from separation, are much mistaken. It would be but the beginning of war, with thousands of Northern men joining the South because of our disgrace in allowing separation. To have "peace on any terms," the South would demand the restoration of their slaves already freed. They would demand indemnity for losses sustained, and they would demand a treaty which would make the North slave hunters for the South. They would demand pay or the restoration of every slave escaping to the North.

Yours truly, U. S. GRANT.

Grant and Sherman on the Draft.

CITY POINT, *September* 13, 10.30 A. M.

Hon. EDWIN M. STANTON, *Secretary of War:*

We ought to have the whole number of men called for by the President in the shortest possible time. Prompt action in filling our armies will have more effect upon the enemy than a victory over them. They profess to believe, and make their men believe, there is such a party North in favor of recognizing Southern independence that the draft cannot be enforced. Let them be undeceived. Deserters come into our lines daily, who tell us that the men are nearly universally tired of the war, and that desertions would be much more frequent, but that they believe peace will be negotiated after the fall election.

The enforcement of the draft and prompt filling up of our armies will save the shedding of blood to an immense degree. U. S. GRANT, *Lieutenant General.*

—

ATLANTA, GA., *September* 13, 6.30 A. M.

Hon. EDWIN M. STANTON, *Secretary of War:*

I am very glad to hear the draft will be enforced. First we need the men; and secondly, they come as privates to fill up our old and tried regiments, with their experienced officers already on hand; and thirdly, because the enforcement of the law will manifest a power resident in our Government equal to the occasion.

Our Government, though a democracy, should, in times of trouble and danger, be able to wield the power of a great nation.

All is well here. W. T. SHERMAN, *Major General.*

Unpublished Letters from General Jackson.

The following letters of President Andrew Jackson, which have never before been published, have been handed to us by the gentleman to whom they were written. They contain sentiments and advice which we recommend to all who love the Union now.—*N. Y. Post.*

WASHINGTON, *November* 2, 1832.

MY DEAR SIR: I have just received your letter of the 31st ultimo, with the enclosure, for which I thank you.

I am well advised of the views and proceedings of the great leading nullifiers of the South in my native State, (S. C.,) and weep for its fate, and over the delusion into which the people are led by the wickedness, ambition, and folly of their leaders. I have no doubt of the intention of their leaders, first to alarm the other States to submit to their views rather than a dissolution of the Union should take place. If they fail in this, to cover their own disgrace and wickedness, to nullify the tariff, and secede from the Union.

We are wide awake here. *The Union will be preserved, rest assured of this.* There has been too much blood and treasure shed to obtain it, to let it be surrendered without a struggle. Our liberty and that of the whole world rests upon it, as well as the peace, prosperity, and happiness of these United States. *It must be perpetuated.* I have no time to say more. My health is good, improved by the travel. With a tender of my kind salutations to you and your amiable family, I am, sincerely your friend,

ANDREW JACKSON.

Col. J. A. HAMILTON.

—

WASHINGTON, *December* 6, 1832.

MY DEAR SIR: Yours of the 3d instant is just received. I accord with you fully in the propriety of the people giving fully and freely their sentiment and opinions on nullification, and the course pursued by South Carolina in her late proceedings.

The ordinance passed, when taken in connection with the Governor's Message, is rebellion and war against the Union. The raising of troops under them to resist the laws of the United States is absolute treason The crisis must be, and as far as my constitutional and legal powers go will be, met with energy and firmness. Therefore the propriety of the public voice being heard, and it ought now to be spoken in a voice of thunder that will make the leaders of the nullifiers tremble, and which will cause the good citizens of South Carolina to retrace their steps and adhere to that Constitution of perpetual Union they have sworn to support. This treasonable procedure against the Union is a blow against not only our liberties, but the liberties of the world.

This nullifying movement in the South has done us great injury abroad, and must not only be promptly met and put down, but frowned down by public opinion. It is therefore highly proper for the people to speak all over the Union.

I am preparing a proclamation to the people of the South, and as soon as officially advised of these rebellious proceedings, will make a communication to Congress. I can say no more, as I am surrounded at present, and bid you, for the present, adieu. ANDREW JACKSON.

Col. J. A. HAMILTON.

Constitutional Convention.

To complete the record on pages 62, 64, 69, 70, and 294, these proceedings should be inserted:

FIRST SESSION THIRTY-SEVENTH CONGRESS.

1861, August 5—Pending the Engineer bill in the Senate,

Mr. JOHNSON, of Missouri, offered this section:

That this Congress recommend to the Governors of the several States to convene their Legislatures, for the purpose of calling an election to select two delegates from each Congressional District, to meet in general convention, in Louisville, in Kentucky, on the first Monday in September next; the purpose of the said convention to be to devise measures for the restoration of peace to our country.

Which was rejected—yeas 9, nays 29, as follows:

YEAS—Messrs. *Bayard, Breckinridge, Bright, Johnson* of Missouri, *Latham, Pearce, Polk, Powell, Saulsbury*—9.

NAYS—Messrs. Baker, Browning, *Carlile*, Chandler, Clark, Collamer, Cowan, Dixon, Doolittle, Fessenden, Foot, Foster, Grimes, Harris, Howe, King, Lane of Indiana, Lane of Kansas, *McDougall*, Morrill, Rice, Sherman, Sumner, Ten Eyck, Trumbull, Wade, Wilkinson, Wilmot, Wilson—29.

The Reconstruction of States.

LOUISIANA.

MESSAGE OF GOVERNOR HAHN.

The newly-elected Legislature of Louisiana met October 3, 1864, and the Senate was organized by the election of John E. Neellis as Secretary, and John T. Wood as Sergeant-at-Arms.

The House of Representatives elected the following officers: Speaker, S. Belden; Secretary, H. C. Westerfield; Sergeant-at-Arms, M. DeCoursey.

On the 6th, Governor Hahn delivered his message, from which we make the following extracts:

The unsettled condition of the country, the absence or destruction of most of the public archives and various other causes, have conspired to throw much difficulty in the way of a full organization of a State Government. The want of a Legislature, and the sudden uprooting of many important, yet unwise and illiberal laws and institutions, by military orders, rendered it extremely difficult, if not impossible, for the Executive of the State to perform his duties satisfactorily and understandingly to the public, or to properly reconcile and harmonize the various conflicting rules of government and interests of the State. I was somewhat aided in this dilemma by the President of the United States, who, shortly after my inauguration, invested me, without any solicitation or suggestion on my part, "with the powers exercised hitherto by the Military Governor of Louisiana." Fortunately, the harmony which has characterized the intercourse of the military and civil authorities of this State has rendered the exercise of any such powers by me almost unnecessary. The principal subject upon which I have used these powers are, the appointment of public officers, the payment of money from the State Treasury for just and pressing purposes, and after recommendation from proper officers, and the exercise of executive clemency. As I said in my inaugural address, "for the moment civil government must necessarily harmonize with military administration;" and, while we recognize the paramount authority of the military power, we should not forget that it desires to surrender as speedily as possible the power to the people. The very object of the army of the United States in remaining here is to maintain Louisiana and the neighboring States in the Union; and the only way of doing this is to disperse and overthrow those who pretend to set up a rebel government, and to guarantee to the loyal a republican form of State government.

The great duty of the Legislature will be to provide a system of laws applicable to the new condition of things consequent upon the attempt to overthrow the Government. The obliteration of an interest so extended as that of slavery necessarily makes great changes in the events, opinions and business of the people; and the highest possible wisdom is required to adapt the State to its new condition. The change from servile to compensated labor requires careful, liberal and humane legislation, in order to secure the rights of those people who have not been accustomed to provide for and protect themselves. Inasmuch as Louisiana is the first State that makes this change upon an extended scale, so it ought to be the first to establish a form of government which shall meet all the exigencies of the case, securing to the public the products upon which the wealth of the State and people depend, and to laborers their full rights. * * * * * Counsel should be taken and suggestions invited from intelligent people of all parts of the world upon this subject, and such system established as will, while it will meet our wants, furnish a model for the legislation of other States. It need not be executed in a hurry; the subject is of the highest possible importance, and should be dealt with in a spirit of enlightened liberality and humanity. The assistance of the military authorities furnishes an immediate government, but another system must be established ultimately, and the people cannot begin too soon to prepare.

* * * * * * * *

According to law, the election of Presidential electors is to take place in November. I know of no reason why Louisiana should not participate in that election on a footing with the other States. She has forfeited her rights under no Constitutional provision or Congressional statute. She has instituted civil rule, and has a loyal State Government, embracing executive, legislative, and judicial branches; all of which are in effective operation. In the attributes of State government, she stands the peer of the loyal States whose soil has never been trodden by the foot of rebellion, has suffered by the rebellion, and the temporary rule of the rebel Confederacy is her misfortune; but so far as the laws at present stand, it is no abridgement of the rights of her loyal citizens. * * * *

Although the new Constitution has fixed the term of the State officers at four years, it has wisely provided that the term of those now in office (who were elected at a time when many parishes could not participate in the election) shall expire at an early day, in case of the restoration of peace in the whole State; and it is made my duty, as soon as an election can be held "in every parish of the State," to declare the fact and order a new election. I need hardly tell you that I shall have real pleasure when this event shall be at hand. While I have the best reasons for believing that the rebellion is now almost extinct in every portion of the State, and that only scattered fragments smoulder in insignificant proportions at different points, the time so anxiously desired by me to deliver my trust has not yet come. Let us hope that it may not be delayed many months. We have good grounds for believing that circumstances will soon have completely changed, so that every parish will have returned to its duty, assisted and protected by the national power, and the whole people will exercise their right to elect State officers.

LOUISIANA UNITED STATES SENATORS.

The free State Legislature of Louisiana has chosen Charles Smith, of the parish of St. Mary's, a United States Senator, vice Judah P. Benjamin, whose time expires with the ensuing session, and R. K. Cutler, to fill, for the three ensuing years, the seat which was left vacant by John Slidell. Mr. Smith is a carpenter by trade. He has been Sheriff of, and is now the State Senator from, his own parish. Mr. Cutler is a leading lawyer of New Orleans, and has filled several important posts in the parish of Jefferson. He was a prominent member of the Constitutional Convention.

TENNESSEE.

1862, March 3—Andrew Johnson was appointed Military Governor of Tennessee. For form of appointment, see page 179.

1863, September 19—The President gave him this further direction:

Hon. Andrew Johnson, *Military Governor of Tennessee*:

You are hereby authorized to exercise such powers as may be necessary and proper to enable the loyal people of Tennessee to present such a republican form of State government as will entitle the State to the guarantee of the United States therefor, and to be protected, under such State government, by the United States, against invasion and domestic violence. All according to the 4th section of the 4th article of the Constitution of the United States.

ABRAHAM LINCOLN.

1864, September 30—Gov. Johnson issued a proclamation, ordering an election in Tennessee for electors for President and Vice President, under certain regulations and restrictions, as follows:

PROCLAMATION BY THE GOVERNOR.

State of Tennessee, Executive Department,
Nashville, Tenn, *Sept.* 30, 1864.

Whereas, a respectable portion of the loyal people of Tennessee, representing a large number of the counties of the State, and supposed to reflect the will of the Union men in their respective counties, recently held a convention in the city of Nashville, in which, among other things touching the reorganization of the State, they with great unanimity adopted the following resolutions;

2. *Resolved*, That the people of Tennessee who are now and have been attached to the National Union do hold an election for President and Vice President in the ensuing election in November.

3. *Resolved*, That the electors shall be the following and no others; the same being free white men, twenty-one years of age, citizens of the United States, and for six months previous to the election citizens of the State of Tennessee:

1st. All who have voluntarily borne arms in the service of the United States during the present war, and who are either in the service or have been honorably discharged.

2. All the known active friends of the Government of the United States in each county.

4. *Resolved*, That the citizen electors designated in the foregoing resolutions shall, at least fifteen days before the election, register their names with an agent to be appointed for that purpose, and no citizen not thus registered shall be allowed to vote. Such registration shall be open to the public for inspection, and to be executed according to such regulations as may hereafter be prescribed: *Provided*, that the officers of election, in the discharge of their duty, may reject any party so registered on proof of disloyalty.

5. *Resolved*, That, as means for ascertaining the qualifications of the voters, the registrars and officers holding the election may examine the parties on oath touching any matter of fact. And each voter, before depositing his vote shall be required to take and subscribe the following oath, viz:

I solemnly swear that I will henceforth support the Constitution of the United States, and defend it against the assaults of all enemies; that I am an active friend of the Government of the United States, and the enemy of the so-called Confederate States; that I ardently desire the suppression of the present rebellion against the Government of the United States; that I sincerely rejoice in the triumph of the armies and navies of the United States, and in the defeat and overthrow of the armies, navies, and of all armed combinations in the interest of the so-called Confederate States; that I will cordially oppose all armistices or negotiations for peace with rebels in arms, until the Constitution of the United States, and all laws and proclamations made in pursuance thereof, shall be established over all the people of every State and Territory embraced within the National Union, and that I will heartily aid and assist the loyal people in whatever measures may be adopted for the attainment of these ends; and further, that I take this oath freely and voluntarily, and without mental reservation. So help me God.

Said oath being *prima facie* evidence, subject to be disapproved by other testimony.

6. *Resolved*, That the polls be opened at the county seat, or some other suitable place in each county, and the ballot-box be so guarded and protected as to secure to electors a free, fair, and impartial election, and that polls also be opened for the convenience of the soldiers, at such places as may be accessible to them.

And whereas, it further appears from the proceedings of said Convention, "That the Military Governor of the State of Tennessee is requested to execute the foregoing resolutions in such manner as he may think best subserves the interests of the Government:"

And whereas, I, Andrew Johnson, Military Governor of the State of Tennessee, being anxious to co-operate with the loyal people of the State, and to encourage them in all laudable efforts to restore the State to law and order again, and to secure the ballot-box against the contamination of treason by every reasonable restraint that can be thrown around it, I do therefore order and direct that an election for President and Vice President of the United States of America be opened and held at the county seat, or other suitable place, in every county in the State of Tennessee, upon the first Tuesday after the first Monday in the month of November next, at which all citizens and soldiers, being free white men, twenty-one years of age, citizens of the United States, and for six months prior to the election citizens of the State of Tennessee, who have qualified themselves by registration, and who take the oath prescribed in the foregoing resolutions, shall be entitled to vote, unless said oath shall be disapproved by other testimony, for the candidates for President and Vice President of the United States.

And to the end that the foregoing resolutions, which are made part of this proclamation, may be faithfully executed, and the loyal citizens of the State, and none others, be permitted to exercise the right of suffrage, I do hereby appoint the several gentlemen whose names are affixed to this proclamation to aid in said election, and superintend the registration of the loyal voters in their respective counties, as provided by the fourth resolution above quoted.

But as the day of election is near at hand, and there may be a difficulty in completing the registration within the time limited, it is not intended that the registration be an indispensable prerequisite to the qualification of the voter; and in such cases, where it is impracticable, and where the voter is of known and established loyalty, he shall be entitled to vote, notwithstanding he may not have registered his name as required by the foregoing resolution.

The election shall be opened, conducted, returns made, &c., in all respects as provided by the 4th chapter of the "Code of Tennessee," except so far as the same is modified by this proclamation.

But in cases where the County Court fail or neglect to appoint inspectors or judges of election, and there is no sheriff or other civil officer in the county qualified by law to open and hold said election, the registrating agents hereto appended may act in his stead, and in all respects discharge the duties imposed in such cases upon sheriffs.

In like manner it is declared the duty of the military officers commanding Tennessee regiments, battalions, or detached squads, and surgeons in charge of the hospitals of Tennessee soldiers, to open and hold elections on the day aforesaid, under the same rules and regulations hereinbefore prescribed, and at such suitable places as will be convenient to the soldiers, who are hereby declared entitled to vote without oath or registration.

In testimony whereof, I, Andrew Johnson, Military Governor of the State of Tennessee, do hereunto set my hand, and have caused the Great Seal of the State to be affixed at this Department, on the 30th day of September, A. D. 1864.

By the Governor: ANDREW JOHNSON. [L. S.]

Attest: EDWARD H. EAST, *Secretary of State.*

EAST TENNESSEE COUNTIES.

Anderson—John Leinart, Henry Holloway, John Baker.
Bledsoe—William Foster, Frank Bridgeman.
Blount—Horace Foster, Stephen Mathis, James Henry, Jr.
Bradley—K. Clingam, W. R. Davis, John McPherson, A. J. McCaullie.
Campbell—John Preston, Reuben Rogers, Pryor Perkins.
Carter—Pleasant Williams, (of Stony Creek,) Elijah Simerly, Jones Smith.
Claiborne—Canady Rodgers, William D. Eppes, Ferney Jones.
Cocke—Jacob Reagan, Andrew Huff, Lt. Worthington, Sheriff Smith.
Cumberland—James Hamby, Thomas B. Swan, James H. Hamby.
Fentress—Henry Williams, Dr. J. D. Hale, David Baty, Rufus Dowdy.
Granger—John F. Nov, Anderson Acuff, M. Goldman.
Greene—R. C. Carter, Calvin Smith, Anderson W. Walker, James H. Reeves.
Hancock—William Gilbert, Elbert Campbell, Isaac Campbell, Capt. Lewis Jarvis.
Hamilton—Col. C. C. McCaleb, Abe Pearson, Wash Evans.
Hawkins—William D. Kanner, B. G. Wetherland, W. W. Willis.
Jefferson—J. Duffell Rankin, Press Swann, Wm. Harris, Duff G. Thornburgh.
Johnson—Col. R. R. Butler, Col. Sam Howard, Col. James Grayson.
Knox—Capt. Thos. Stephens, Andrew L. Knott, William Hofner, Samuel McCammon.
Marion—Alexander Kelley, Robert Ralston, Pleasant Pryor, Wm. Pryor, Esq.
McMinn—James M. Henderson, John Mc——, G. W. Ross, F. B. McElwee.
Meigs—Wm. Adams, F. J. Mathis, Col. A. Cox, Robert Allen, James Gettys.
Monroe—Joseph Divine, Henry Duggan, Daniel Heiskell.
Morgan—James Langley, Sr., James Langley, Jr., S. C. Hunuycutt.
Overton—Robert Smith, Anderson Winham, George W. Bowman, Ellison Gussett.
Polk—Gen. James Gamble, Col. John Elliot, Charles McClary.
Rhea—Capt. J. B. Walker, William H. Lowe, Samuel Lowe.
Roane—Joe D. Turner, Wm. Lowery, Wm. M. Alexander, J. Christopher Ables, Allen Robb, Sam. L. Childress.
Scott—Balie Putram, Craven Duncan, James Lay.
Sevier—Colonel Wm. Pickens, Reuben Hines, David McCroskey, Lemuel Duggan.
Sullivan—E. A. Millard, Wm. Mullenox, Esq., Enoch Shipley.
Union—James W. Turner, John Bayless, Calvin Monroe.
Washington—Calvin Hoss, John Muhoney, B. F. Swingle.
Sequatchie—Washington Hurd, Daniel McWilliams, B. F. Smith.

MIDDLE TENNESSEE COUNTIES.

Bedford—Joseph Thompson, Richard Phillips, William T. Tune, Robert T. Cannon.
Cannon—Hiram Morris, William Barten.
Cheatham—Warr[illegible] Jordan.
Coffee—John F. Tho[illegible]s.
Davidson—John Carpet, Charles Sayers, General J. Stubblefield, James Warren, T. J. Yarbrough, L. D. Wheeler, P. T. Phillips, J. B. Canfield, James Davis, W. W. Garrett.
DeKalb—William Hathaway, William Blackburn, Andrew J. Garrison.
Dickson—Marsh Binkley.
Franklin—
Giles—J. C. Walker, Edward W. Rose, J. W. Alley, R. J. Gorden.
Grundy—William McCran, John Myes.
Hickman—
Humphreys—William McKimmons, Wilkins Waggoner, David R. Owen, J. S. Spane, T. J. Winfrey, Mr. Thomas.
Jackson—James McKinney, John Gillem, Allen Davis.
Lawrence—
Lewis—
Lincoln—J. H. Fulgham, James J. Kirkpatrick.
Macon—Pleasant Chitwood, L. S. Clements, George W. Clements.
Marshall—A. A. Steele.
Maury—W. W. Jones, John D. Moore, John H. Campbell.
Montgomery—O. M. Blackman, Caleb Jones, D. S. Nye, Isah Barbee, Thomas F. Betters, George Hampton.
Berry—W. O. Britt, F. M. Brasher, Jackson Taylor, J. S. Webb, A. H. Eathers.
Putman—Joseph Rhea McColet.
Robertson—B. F. Aurt, Wiley Woodward, Joseph Starks.
Rutherford—Edward Jordan, William Spence, William C. Burt, James H. Carlton.
Smith—John W. Bowen, Asberry Griffin, Francis M. McKee.
Sumner—
Stewart—
Van Buren—
Warren—Samuel Henderson, Dr. J. B. Armstrong, Samuel L. Colville, Miles Bonner.
White—Edward D. Pennington, Alexander Payne, James Cotey.
Williamson—A. W. Moss, William P. Campbell, Franklin Hardeman, William S. Campbell.
Wilson—William Waters, William J. Waters.
Wayne—Theodore H. Gibbs, James Dougherty, F. Hall, Jasper Lypert, John Stamps.

WEST TENNESSEE COUNTIES.

Benton—David Brewer, Allen Bearsons, David Little, Abraham Gussett, Samuel Tippett.
Carroll—Young W. Allen, John Wood, John Norman, Lucian Hawkins, Isaac Bouch.
Dyer—William Wesson.
Decatur—John Stegall, Simon Bonman, G. Menzies, James Roberts, W. H. Johnson.
Fayette—
Gibson—
Haywood—
Henderson—Robert Kizer, James Hart, James Smith.
Hardeman—
Henry—Anderson ———, Dr. J. W. Mathewson, Charles White, Temple Cowan.
Hardin—Thomas Maxwell, Michell Hood, Balley Hinkell.
Lauderdale—
Madison—T. Skurlock.
McNairy—William Suayne, John Barnes, ——— Gregg.
Obion—Dr. S. R. Chapin.
Shelby—J. B. Bingham, G. B. Ware, A. Gregg.
Tipton—
Weakley—J. W. Hays, William Bell.

EXTRACTS FROM THE CODE OF TENNESSEE.

CHAPTER 4.

Of the Electors of President and Vice President.

913. Each congressional district shall be an electoral district, and one Elector shall reside in each of said districts.

914. There shall be two Electors for the State who may reside in any part of the State.

915. Any citizen qualified by law to vote for members of the General Assembly may vote for the whole number of Electors.

916. Said qualified voters shall meet at the places appointed by law for holding elections in every county, on the

first Tuesday next after the first Monday in the month of November, in the years in which the President and Vice President are to be elected, and to vote for a number of Electors equal to the whole number of Senators and Representatives to which the State is entitled in Congress.

917. The officer or person holding the election shall advertise at the court-house in every county, and in every civil district of the county, the day on which said election shall take place, at least sixty days before the time of holding it.

918. The county court of every county shall appoint judges for every place of voting in the county, all of whom shall be sworn to conduct said election in the manner prescribed for electing members of the General Assembly.

919. If the county court neglect to appoint judges of the said elections, or those appointed refuse to act, the officer holding the election shall appoint judges out of the by-standers to hold the same.

920. [Of clerks and their qualifications.]

921. The election shall be conducted in the manner prescribed for electing members of the General Assembly.

[The other sections of this chapter prescribe rules concerning the comparison of polls, statements of same, returns, comparisons of returns, proceedings of Electors, vacancy, time of meeting to vote, certificate of voting, messenger, certificate by mail, list of electors, and penalties on officers.]

Qualification of Voters for Members of the General Assembly referred to in Sec. 915 *above.*

"Every free white man of the age of twenty-one years, being a citizen of the United States, and a citizen of the county where he may offer his vote, six months next preceding the day of election, shall be entitled to vote for members of the General Assembly."—*Code, Sec.* 833, *and Const. of Tenn., Art.* 4, *Sec.* 1.

Places of Holding elections, referred to in Sec. 916 *above.*

"The places of holding elections shall be in each civil district, at some convenient locality, to be designated by the county court at least six months before the election, and entered on record."—*Code* 837.

EXTRACTS FROM CODE.—ART VI.

Officers of Popular Elections, referred to in Sec. 917 *above.*

839. The sheriff, or, if he is a candidate, the coroner, or if there be no coroner, some person appointed by the county court, shall hold all popular elections; and said officer or person shall appoint a sufficient number of deputies to hold said elections.

841. The county court, at the session next preceding the day of election, shall appoint three inspectors or judges for each voting place, to superintend the election.

842. If the county court fail to make the appointment, or any person appointed refuse to serve, the sheriff, with the advice of three justices, or, if none be present, three respectable freeholders, shall, before the beginning of the election, appoint said inspectors or judges.

843. If the sheriff or other officer whose duty it is to attend at a particular place of voting under the foregoing provisions fail to attend, any justice of the peace present, or, if no justice of the peace be present, any three freeholders, may perform the duties prescribed by the preceding sections, or in case of necessity may act as officers or inspectors.

PROTEST AGAINST THE PROCLAMATION.

1864, October 15—JOHN LELLYETT, Esq., of Nashville, presented to the PRESIDENT this protest:

To his Excellency Abraham Lincoln,
President of the United States:

SIR: The undersigned, loyal citizens of the United States and of the State of Tennessee, on our own behalf and on behalf of the loyal people of our State, ask leave to submit this protest against the proclamation of his Excellency, Andrew Johnson, Military Governor, ordering an election to be held for President and Vice President, under certain regulations and restrictions therein set forth. A printed copy of said proclamation is herewith enclosed.

The Constitution of the United States provides that "each State shall appoint, *in such manner as the Legislature thereof may direct*, a number of electors," &c. Under this provision of the Federal Constitution, the Legislature of Tennessee, years before the present rebellion, prescribed the mode of election to be observed, which will be found to differ essentially from the mode prescribed by the Military Governor. We herewith enclose a copy of the law of Tennessee governing the holding of said election.

The Military Governor expressly assumes, by virtue of authority derived from the President, so to alter and amend the election law of Tennessee, (enacted under authority of the Constitution of the United States, as above set forth,) as to make the same conform to his own edict as set forth in the proclamation aforesaid. He assumes so to modify our law as to admit persons to vote at the said election who are not entitled to vote under the law and the constitution of Tennessee. Instance this: our constitution and law require that each voter shall be "a citizen of the *county* wherein he may offer his vote for six months next preceding the day of election;" while the Governor's order only requires that he shall (with other qualifications named) be a citizen of Tennessee for six months, &c. This provision would admit to vote many persons not entitled by law.

We will, for the sake of brevity, pass over some less important points of conflict betwwen the proclamation and the law, but will instance in this place another. By our law it is provided that the polls shall be opened in every civil district in each county in the State; but the proclamation provides only for their being opened at one place in each county. This provision would put it out of the power of many legal voters to exercise the elective franchise.

We solemnly protest against these infringements of our law, conflicting as they do with the very letter of the Federal Constitution, because they are without authority, and because they will prevent a free, fair, and true expression of the will of the loyal people of Tennessee.

But we protest still more emphatically against the most unusual and impracticable test oath which it is proposed to require of all citizen voters in Tennessee.

[The oath is as follows: "I solemnly swear that I will henceforth support the Constitution of the United States, and defend it against the assaults of all enemies; that I am an active friend of the Government of the United States, and the enemy of the so-called Confederate States; that I ardently desire the suppression of the present rebellion against the Government of the United States; that I sincerely rejoice in the triumph of the armies of the United States, and in the defeat and overthrow of the armies, navies, and of all armed combinations in the interest of the so-called Confederate States; *that I will cordially oppose all armistices or negotiations for peace with rebels in arms, until the Constitution of the United States, and all laws and proclamations made in pursuance thereof, shall be established over all the people of every State and Territory embraced within the national Union*, and that I will heartily aid and assist the loyal people *in whatever measures may be adopted* for the attainment of these ends; and further, that I take this oath freely and voluntarily and without mental reservation. So help me God."]

A citizen, qualified to vote, and whose loyalty cannot be "disproved by other testimony," is to be required to swear, first, that he "will henceforth support the Constitution of the United States, and defend it against all enemies." This obligation we are willing to renew daily. But this is not yet deemed a sufficient test of loyalty. He is required to make oath and subscribe to a mass of vain repetitions concerning his activity as a friend of the Union and the enemy of its enemies—concerning his desires, his hopes, and fears—and that he finds it in his heart to rejoice over the scenes of blood and of wounds, of anguish and death, wherein his friends, his kindred, his loved ones are slain, or maimed, or made prisoners of war—whereby the land of his birth or adoption is made desolate, and lamentation and mourning are spread over the whole nation. While all the civilized world stands aghast in contemplation of the unequalled horrors of our tremendous strife, the citizen of Tennessee is called upon by her Military Governor, under your authority, to swear that in these things he finds occasion to *rejoice!* As if this were still not enough, the citizen is further required to swear to the indefinite prolongation of this war, as follows: "That I will cordially oppose all armistices or *negotiations for peace with rebels in arms* until the Constitution of the United States, and all laws and proclamations made in pursuance thereof, shall be established over all the people of every State and Territory embraced within the National Union;" until (in brief) the war shall be at an end. Now, we freely avow to your Excellency, and to the world, that we earnestly desire the return of peace and good will to our now unhappy country; that we seek neither pleasure, profit, nor honor in the perpetuation of war; that we should feel bound as Christians, as patriots, and as civilized men—that we are bound by the oaths we have taken—to countenance and encourage any negotiations which may be entered into by the proper authorities with the intent to restore peace and union under the Constitution we have sworn to support and defend. We should be traitors to our country, false to our oaths—false, indeed, to the primary clause of the oath we are now discussing, to oppose such negotiations. We cannot consent to swear at the ballot-box a war of extermination against our countrymen and kindred, or to prolong by our opposition, for a single day after it can be brought to an honorable and lawful conclusion, a contest the most sanguinary and ruinous that has scourged mankind.

You will not have forgotten that in the month of July last you issued the following proclamation:

EXECUTIVE MANSION,
WASHINGTON, *July* 18, 1864.

To whom it may concern:

Any proposition which embraces the restoration of peace, the integrity of the whole Union, and the abandonment of slavery, and which comes by and with an authority that can control the armies now at war against the United States, will be received and considered by the Executive Government of the United States, and will be met by liberal terms on other substantial and collateral points, and the bearer or bearers thereof shall have safe conduct both ways. ABRAHAM LINCOLN.

This is certainly a proposition to treat with rebels in arms—with their chiefs. Are we now to understand by this proclamation of one acting under your authority, and himself a candidate with you for the second office, that even the above proposition is withdrawn—that you will henceforth have no negotiations upon any terms but unrelenting war to the bitter end? Or are we to understand that while you hold this proposition open, or yourself free to act as your judgment may dictate, we, the citizens of Tennessee, shall *swear* to OPPOSE your negotiations?

In the next breath, the voter who has already been thus far *qualified* is required to swear that he will "heartily aid and assist the loyal people *in whatever measures may be adopted* for the attainment of these ends." Adopted by whom? The oath does not say. We cannot tell what measures may be adopted. We cannot comment upon the absurdity of the obligation here imposed without danger of departing from that respectful propriety of language which we desire to observe in addressing the Chief Magistrate of the American people. But this is the clause of an oath which the candidate for the Vice Presidency requires at the lips of the loyal and qualified voters of Tennessee, before these citizens shall be allowed to vote for or against you and himself at the coming election!

For these reasons, and others which, for the sake of brevity, we omit, we solemnly protest against the interference of the Military Governor with the freedom of the elective franchise in Tennessee. We deny his authority and yours to alter, amend, or annul any law of Tennessee. We demand that Tennessee be allowed to appoint her electors as expressly provided by the Federal Constitution, which you have sworn to support, protect, and defend, in the manner which the Legislature thereof has prescribed. And to that end we respectfully demand of you, as the principal under whose authority this order has been issued, that the same shall be revoked. We ask that all military interference shall be withdrawn so far as to allow to the loyal men of Tennessee a full and free election. By the loyal men of Tennessee we mean those who have not participated in the rebellion, or given it aid and comfort; or who may have complied with such terms of amnesty as have been offered them under your authority.

On the 8th day of December, 1863, you, as President, issued a proclamation declaring that "a full pardon is hereby granted," "with restoration of all rights of property," &c., to each of our citizens having participated, directly or by implication, in the existing rebellion, (with certain exceptions,) "upon the condition that every such person shall take and subscribe an oath, and thenceforward keep and maintain said oath inviolate." And it is further provided in the proclamation aforesaid that in the contingency of the reorganization of a State Government in Tennessee, or certain other States named, the persons having taken the oath referred to, being otherwise qualified by the election law of the State, shall be entitled to vote. The undersigned would state that many of our citizens have complied in good faith with the terms of amnesty proposed in your proclamation aforesaid, and are, therefore, by reason of the full pardon granted them, fully entitled to vote and exercise all other rights belonging to loyal citizens, without let or hindrance; and we respectfully appeal to you, as President of the United States, to make good your promise of pardon to these citizens by the removal of all other and further hindrance to their exercise of the elective franchise.

But if it be claimed upon the plea of military necessity that guards and restrictions shall be thrown around the ballot-box in Tennessee, we still ask the withdrawal of the proclamation of the Military Governor, because the conditions thereby imposed upon the loyal men of Tennessee as a qualification for voters are irrelevant, unreasonable, and not in any sense a test of loyalty. But they pledge the citizen to oppose the lawful authorities in the discharge of their duty. The oath required is only calculated to keep legal and rightful voters from the polls. We suggest that no oath be required but such as is prescribed by law. Our people will not hesitate, however, to take the usual oath of loyalty—for example, in the language of the primary clause of the oath in question: "That I will henceforth support the Constitution of the United States, and defend it against the assaults of its enemies." Denying your right to make any departure from the law in the case, we shall, however, feel no hardship in this.

The Convention to which Gov. Johnson refers was a mere partisan meeting, having no authority, and not representing the loyal men of Tennessee in any sense.

The names of the signers of this protest have been placed before the people of Tennessee as candidates for electors, who, if chosen, are expected to cast the electoral voice of Tennessee for George B. McClellan for President and George H. Pendleton for Vice-President. By virtue of such position it becomes our province especially to appear before you in the attitude we do. We are aware that grave questions may arise, in any event, with regard to the regularity of the vote of Tennessee, in consequence of the partially disorganized condition of the State. The friends of your re-election, however, announced an electoral ticket, and the public became aware that preparations were being made for the holding of the election, leaving that matter no longer a question. Some time thereafter our electoral ticket was placed before the public, and within a few days followed the proclamation complained of. We, for ourselves and those we represent, are willing to leave all questions involving the right of Tennessee to participate in the election to the decision of competent authority.

WM. B. CAMPBELL, of Wilson county.
THOS. A. R. NELSON, of Washington co.
For the State at large.
JAS. T. P. CARTER, of Carter county.
JOHN WILLIAMS, of Knox county.
A. BLIZARD, of McMinn county.
HENRY COOPER, of Bedford county.
BAILIE PEYTON, of Sumner county.
JOHN LELLYETT, of Davidson county.
EM. ETHERIDGE, of Weakly county.
JOHN D. PERRYMAN, of Shelby county.
For the Districts.

After the foregoing paper had been read, a brief colloquy ensued between the President and Mr. Lellyett, as described in the following communication:

WASHINGTON, *October* 15, 1864.

To the Editors of the National Intelligencer:

I called upon the President to-day, and presented and read to him the above protest. Having concluded, Mr. Lincoln responded: "May I inquire how long it took you and the New York politicians to concoct that paper?"

I replied: "It was concocted in Nashville, without communication with any but Tennesseans. We communicated with citizens of Tennessee outside of Nashville, but not with New York politicians."

"I will answer," said Mr. Lincoln, emphatically, "that I expect to let the friends of George B. McClellan manage their side of this contest in their own way, and I will manage my side of it in my way."

"May we ask an answer in writing?" I suggested.

"Not now. Lay those papers down here. I will give no other answer now. I may or may not write something about this hereafter. I understand this. I know you intend to make a point of this. But go ahead. You have my answer."

"Your answer then, is, that you expect to let General McClellan's friends manage their side of this contest in their own way, and you will manage your side of it in your way?"

"Yes."

I then thanked the President for his courtesy in giving us a hearing at all, and took my leave.

Judge Mason of this city was present at the interview, to whom I refer in regard to the correctness of this report. On stepping outside the door of the Executive Mansion I immediately wrote down the President's emphatic response, and submitted it to Judge Mason and another gentleman who happened to be present, and they both pronounced it accurate.

And now I have a word to say to the people of the United States, who are or ought to be the masters of Abraham Lincoln. The paper which I had the honor to present to the President is not the "concoction of New York politicians," however that might affect its merits. It is the solemn voice of a once free and proud people, protesting against their own disfranchisement by the agent of Abraham Lincoln. It is the voice of those loyal men in Tennessee who have borne the reproach of a people they still loved, supporting the President in all lawful efforts to preserve the Union. The reward of our loyalty is disfranchisement. The cup of perjury is commended to our lips because it is known that we wil not touch its contents. Judge ye between the people of Tennessee and Abraham Lincoln. It may be meet that our solemn and respectful appeal should be thrown aside with a contemptuous sneer. Look to it. If you, the people of the Northern States, shall sustain this act of tyranny, your own time will soon come. If the President of the United States may "manage his side of this contest" by setting aside the very letter of the Constitution and altering the elective laws of the States, so as to disfranchise his opponents, liberty is already dead. JOHN LELLYETT.

The Hon. Charles Mason, having accompanied Mr. Lellyett in his visit to the President, and having been present at the interview accorded to Mr. Lellyett, has been called by the latter in the following note to authenticate his report of the conversation had with the President. The reply of Mr. Mason is also appended:

WASHINGTON, *Oct.* 15, 1864.

Hon. CHAS. MASON:

DEAR SIR: I submit to your inspection what I have written in reference to my interview with the President to-day, and will ask you to state if you regard the same as an accurate report. Respectfully,

JOHN LELLYETT.

—

WASHINGTON, *Oct.* 15, 1864.

JOHN LELLYETT, Esq.:

DEAR SIR: In compliance with the request in your note of this day, I have only to say that I was present at the interview referred to. You statement of what took place is substantially correct; and on all material points I believe it literally so. Yours, truly,

CHAS. MASON.

[For President LINCOLN's reply see page 425.]

REPLY OF THE PROTESTANTS.

To ABRAHAM LINCOLN, *President of the United States:*

SIR: Your letter in reply to the Tennessee Protest has reached us, and has no doubt been read by the people. The argument on this subject is nearly exhausted, but we have some additional and most important *facts* to submit to the people, in further elucidation of the subject.

Our wonder is not excited to learn that you had not seen the proclamation of Governor Johnson, and scarcely heard of it until presented by us. It is an evil of no small magnitude, connected with your Administration, that military subordinates assume despotic powers without asking the sanction of their superiors—even presuming to give law to the people by proclamation and to repeal and modify our laws at will. The idea that the President himself can make, or repeal, or modify a law of the land, State or national, constitutional or statutory, though freely practiced upon by yourself, is a doctrine of despotism in "irrepressible conflict" with the principles of public liberty. And when these things are done by *subordinates*, the evil becomes intolerably oppressive, and calls for the firmest and most active lawful resistance which a people deserving to be free can offer.

You tell us that "the movement set on foot by the convention and Governor Johnson does not, as seems to be assumed by you, emanate from the National Executive." What we did assume is, that the plan was promulgated by proclamation of the Military Governor, who has no authority but that derived directly from you, and it was given the force of law by his edict. It thus became indirectly your act; and now that you decline to order the edict to be recalled or modified, it becomes your own as fully as if it had *emanated* from you. "In no proper sense," you say, "can it be considered other than an independent movement of at least a portion of the loyal people of Tennessee." Independent of what? Manifestly independent of all lawful authority—independent of and at war with the Federal Constitution, which you have both sworn to support, protect, and defend. What right has a citizen or officer to favor an "independent movement" at variance with the Constitution, and support the same by force of arms? What less is this than waging war against the Constitution of the United States and the Government established thereby? "An *independent movement*" against the Constitution, supported by a Military Governor by force of arms! recommended by an assembly calling itself a convention!

Such in principle were the "independent movements" of governors and "portions of the people" which set at first in motion the great rebellion in the South with which we are contending. The "convention" calls upon a Military Governor to order an "independent movement" to help your re-election, and to support it by force of arms, placing "guards" around the ballot-box. And their recommendation is adopted by the Military Governor and "made" by him "part of this proclamation." And yet you say, "I do not perceive in the plan any menace of coercion or violence toward any one." Just so with the earlier "independent movement" of Governor Harris in this State, which we opposed as we oppose this. There was no menace of coercion or violence toward any who should consent to see the Constitution violated and the "political plan" carried out without opposition. But the bayonet was kept in view, as it is in this case. Public meetings were menaced, and perhaps broken up by armed force. And so it is now. Those opposed to the "independent movement" were denounced as traitors, and so they are now. Troops from our own and from other States were used to overawe the people, and so they are now. We had vigilance committees and mob violence then. We have now secret leagues, and are liable at any time to arbitrary arrest, as well as to mob violence, which is now used in our midst.

These are general facts, in support of which we add the following specifications:

We have held a number of peaceable and loyal public meetings in this city, more than one of which has been "menaced" by your partisans. On the 21st instant such a meeting was held at the court-house in this city. It was held "peacefully" and conducted "loyally," the assembly consisting chiefly of the "friends of George B. McClellan." A number of provost guards were present, by request of those who conducted the meeting, to preserve order. The meeting had been addressed by a gentleman who is an exile from his home because of his loyalty, and who has spent much time in the military service of the Government during the war. One of the undersigned, a McClellan Elector, [Hon. Bailie Peyton,] had taken the stand to address the meeting, when the hall was suddenly entered by a large party of soldiers, and the meeting violently broken up. These men rushed in with guns and drawn pistols, crying "Disperse you d—d rebels and traitors," extinguishing the lights and driving the people from the hall.

We specify further that on the 25th instant, the rioters, thirty in number, published a card in the "Nashville *Times*," the organ in this city of Governor Johnson, to which they appended their names, as "all members of Company D, 1st Tennessee Light Artillery." This company was raised and its officers appointed (as we understand) under the superintendence of Governor Johnson. The rioters speak thus in their card: "Neither Governor Johnson, nor any other individual *outside of the men who were active participants, knew anything of our intentions till the affair was over. Some colored men may have followed us, but we knew nothing of them.*" "*We do not fear a court-martial,*" they defiantly add, "and therefore cheerfully give our names as loyal and Union-loving soldiers."

We specify further that on the evening of the 24th inst., only three days after the McClellan meeting was broken up, our streets were paraded by an immense procession of negroes bearing torches and transparencies, with such inscriptions on the latter as "Lincoln and Johnson," "Liberty or Death." Some disorders occurred in connection with this demonstration, and shots were freely fired by the negroes—some at a window where white persons were standing, and some at persons on the streets. One of the latter (an employé of the Government) was dangerously if not mortally wounded, and it was thought others were hit. In the course of these orgies the procession waited on Governor Andrew Johnson, at the Capitol, and he delivered to the negro assembly an address. A report of his speech was published and re-published in his organ, the "*Times*," and from that report we take the following extract. Governor Johnson says:

"I speak to-night as a citizen of Tennessee. I am here on my own soil and mean to remain here, and fight this great battle of freedom through to the end. *Loyal men from this day forward are to be the controllers of Tennessee's grand and* SUBLIME *destiny*, and REBELS MUST BE DUMB. We will not listen to their counsels. NASHVILLE IS NO LONGER THE PLACE FOR THEM TO HOLD THEIR MEETINGS. LET THEM GATHER THEIR TREASONABLE CONCLAVES ELSEWHERE—AMONG THEIR FRIENDS IN THE CONFEDERACY. THEY SHALL NOT HOLD THEIR CONSPIRACIES IN NASHVILLE."

The language of the rioters, "Disperse REBELS and TRAITORS," and the common application of such terms of abuse and terror to the friends of General McClellan here, do not admit of our ignoring the meaning of Governor Johnson in the language quoted. The allusion is evidently to the riotous dispersion of our meeting three evenings previous. He also seems to adopt your idea, that as a citizen of Tennessee he "has the right to favor any political plan he chooses." And he unmistakably evinces his determination to "*manage*" *his* "*side of his contest in his own way.*"

"Governor Johnson," you say, "like any other loyal citizen, has a right to favor any political plan he chooses." We do not so read the duty of the citizen. Some of the political plans of our day are devised to overturn the Constitution and Government of the United States—*and this is one of them.* The Southern rebellion is another. Neither the citizen nor Governor Johnson has a right to favor such plans, unless it be upon the principle advanced by you as a member of Congress, that "any people, any where, being inclined, and having the power, have the right" to revolutionize their Government; that "this is a most valuable, a most *sacred* right." We shall despair of the republic if these principles of anarchy, as embodied in you, shall be adopted by the people in your re-election.

In the face of the reign of terror which has been established in Tennessee under the eyes of Governor Johnson, you say to us: "Do as you please on your own account, peacefully and loyally, and Governor Johnson will not molest you, but will protect you against violence as far as is in his power." If you mean that Governor Johnson will allow us to stay away from the polls without molestation, we trust there is some truth in your assurance. But if you mean to suggest that we hold separate elections "on our own account," and to assure us that we shall not be molested but protected in such a "movement," we know by experience, and by the facts above set forth, that your assurance is a cruel mockery. We will not advise our citizens to put in jeopardy their lives in going through the farce you propose, of holding an election under the laws at one ballot-box, while Governor Johnson holds an election under his "plan" at another. Too many unoffending citizens have already been murdered in our streets by negro soldiers—too many reputable women have been insulted by them. We do not wish to provoke further outrage. There will be no election for President in Tennessee in 1864. You and Governor Johnson may "manage your side of it in your own way," but it will be no *election*.

After consultation with our friends, therefore, in different parts of the State, and having communicated with nearly all of our colleagues, we respectfully announce to the people of Tennessee that in view of what is set forth above—in view of the fact that our people are overawed by military power, the laws set aside and violated with impunity—and in view of the fact that we have appealed in vain to the President whose duty it is "to see that the laws be faithfully executed," and that those who act by his authority shall hold sacred the liberties of the people; in view of these things we announce that the McClellan Electoral Ticket in Tennessee is withdrawn.

W. B. CAMPBELL, *of Wilson Co.*
BAILIE PEYTON, *of Sumner Co.*
JOHN LELLYETT, *of Davidson Co.*

NASHVILLE, *October* 29, 1864.

Suppression of Newspapers—(See pp. 188, 194.)

Below is a newspaper report of a trial in October, 1864, growing out of the suppression of a newspaper in Pennsylvania:

UNITED STATES CIRCUIT COURT—*Judges Grier and Cadwalader.*—Wm. H. Hodgson *vs.* Wm. Millward, United States Marshal. This is an action to recover damages alleged to have been sustained by the plaintiff by reason of the seizure of the presses, type, paper, and other printing material used in the publication of the newspaper known as the *Jeffersonian*, published at West Chester, in this State. The seizure was made on the 23d of August, 1861, by the marshal's deputies, Messrs. Jenkins and Schuyler. The office was closed, and plaintiff alleges that he was deprived of the use of his property, and thereby compelled to suspend the issue of his paper until the 14th of October, 1861, to his great loss and damage, and for which he now seeks to recover. The authority for the seizure, and upon which the defendant relies as his defence, was the following warrant issued by the then United States District Attorney, Geo. A. Coffey, Esq., who claimed to have issued the same by direction of the Secretary of War at Washington:

EASTERN DISTRICT OF PENNSYLVANIA,
OFFICE U. S. ATTORNEY.

TO WM. MILLWARD, Marshal:

According to the provisions of the act of 6th of August, 1861, I hereby request you to seize upon all copies of the *Jeffersonian* newspaper, published in the borough of West Chester, Chester County, Pennsylvania, as well as all property of every kind whatsoever used in and about the publication of said newspaper that may be found in your bailiwick, for condemnation and confiscation according to law, I being authorized by the President of the United States.

GEORGE A. COFFEY, *United States Attorney.*

PHILADELPHIA, 23*d August*, 1861.

The case was tried before Chief Justice Lowrie, in the Supreme Court at Nisi Prius, in February last, and was prosecuted to judgment, but subsequently, under the provisions of the act of Congress of March 3d, 1863, entitled "an act relating to *habeas corpus* cases, and for other purposes," the record of the proceedings in the *nisi prius* was removed into this court, where yesterday it came up for trial *de novo.*

The evidence offered to the court and jury was mainly that adduced upon the former trial, and at that time reduced to writing. The defence set up that the order of District Attorney Coffey to seize the property was a justification, and as the act of Congress authorized the President to direct such seizure, the jury, if they found that Mr. Coffey did receive such instructions, and in turn issued his order to Mr. Millward, the verdict should be for the defendants.

Defendant's points, on which the court was requested to charge, were as follows:

1. That by the third section of the act of Congress of August 6, 1861, the District Attorney of the Eastern District of the United States is authorized to institute proceedings for the confiscation and condemnation of any property within the said district, of the character described in the first section of the act, and that for this purpose the said District Attorney had authority to direct the seizure of such property so found, preparatory to filing an information in and issuing an attachment from the proper court, and that his order to the marshal of the district to seize the *Jeffersonian* printing-press, and other materials, followed up as it was by the proceedings in the courts of the United States, is a legal justification of the marshal and his deputies for such seizure.

If the court should decline to affirm the foregoing proposition, then it is respectfully requested to charge:

I. That if the jury find from the evidence that the order from the District Attorney to the marshal was issued under the authority of the President of the United States, then the said order is a justification to the marshal and his deputies for the seizure complained of in this suit.

II. That after the information was filed in the District Court of the United States, and the attachment was issued therefrom and the property attached, it was in the custody of the law, and the marshal was in nowise liable for damages for its detention, and that the plaintiff can only recover for the taking and detention of the property from the 23d of August to the 12th of September, a period of twenty days.

III. That the measure of damages in this case is the actual pecuniary loss which the plaintiff sustained by reason of the possession of his printing establishment having been taken by the marshal and continued for the period of twenty days, and that there is no evidence in the cause which would justify the jury in giving vindictive damages.

JUDGE GRIER'S CHARGE.

GENTLEMEN OF THE JURY: After the elaborate arguments of counsel, it is not necessary to say much about the facts of this case. It is your province to deal with the facts. You are the sole judges of them, and are to apply to them the principles of law that will be laid down by the court. You are not to decide the law. That is for the court. You must take care not to let party feeling or passion influence you. You must hear the small as well as the great. While you may recollect that this was done in times of great excitement, yet that a trespass, and a gross one, has been committed, it is not denied. It is a fact, to be sure, for you, but it is not denied that property of the plaintiff was taken. If so, have the defendants made out a justification?

The court instruct you, they have not. The marshal cannot plead the order of the Attorney General or his deputy. This is not a justification. If a marshal arrests A when told to arrest B, it is no defence that he had a right to arrest B.

The marshal would have had a right to seize for condemnation the kind of property specified in the act of Congress of the 6th of August, 1861, without the order of the District Attorney. But this act had nothing to do with the liberty of the press. It never gave authority for such a seizure as the present one.

The order of the District Attorney that has been shown here was no more of a justification to the marshal than if issued by any one now in the court-house.

The District Attorney had no right to make such an order. You may arrest a man for murder without warrant, but you show the man committed the felony; otherwise it is no defence to an action of trespass.

If the property, then, was within the meaning of the act of Congress, the seizure was justifiable; if not, the marshal is liable in damages. Certain points, or prayers for instruction on the law, have been submitted to me by the defendants, which I will now proceed to answer:

I. The first point, to a certain extent, is true. The District Attorney might advise the issuing of an attachment, and seize property that was liable under the act of Congress. But it is not the law that this order of the District Attorney was a justification of the marshal in this case. The marshal could act, if the property was liable to seizure, as well without the order of the District Attorney as with it. If the court had decided that the property was liable, the marshal would have been justified. But if the court had decided the property was not properly seized, then the seizure was unlawful and it was trespass, and the marshal was liable. There is not even a certificate as to probable cause for seizure. But I say nothing on this head, for it does not appear that it was asked, or that it was a case for it. No attempt, however, was made at the hearing of the information in the circuit court to show any cause. It was clear that the act of Congress did not apply. There was no law forbidding this man, the plaintiff, to write against the war. I doubt whether any act of Congress could have prevented a man giving his opinions candidly against the war. He had a right to write and to print. The order of the District Attorney makes the case no better. He had no right to issue the order. The marshal had no right to obey it. It was no warrant. If the marshal had consulted counsel, counsel would have told him he was not to obey such an order. I doubt any counsel could have been found who would have advised obedience to such an order.

II. In answer to the second point, I say there is no competent evidence of any authority from the President or any of his Cabinet, and if there had been it would make the case no better. If there had been a proceeding in court, and a seizure under protest, it would have protected the officer. But the marshal or sheriff cannot justify under an order like this.

III. As to the third point, I instruct you on the question of damages that the jury should give full compensatory damages for all the loss that has accrued to the plaintiff. But the damages should not be vindictive or punitive. There is no evidence that the marshal acted from malice, or was influenced by political feeling, or committed any excess. There is some evidence that the District Attorney did this to gratify some people out of doors. He is not, however, here to answer, and this is not imputable to the marshal. But, for the purpose of vindicating public justice when an officer of the law commits an act almost without a pretence of authority, the damages should be exemplary to vindicate the outraged law, that men in authority may be careful how they trespass on the rights of citizens. There is a difference in this respect between the case of a public officer and a private person, no matter how high the public officer—even the President or one of his Secretaries. The marshal is here liable for the whole time the property was detained. He is liable for all the damages from the beginning to the end. The decree of this court was conclusive against him. I have thus laid down the principles of law which are to guide you, and it will be for you to apply them to the facts of the cause.

The jury was out about twenty hours, and returned a verdict for the plaintiff for $504 23. George W. Biddle and Wm. B. Reed for plaintiff; John C. Knox and David Webster for defendant.

Colored Persons as Witnesses.

To complete the record on pages 242, 243, it should be stated that these proceedings were prior to those there recorded:

Pending the emancipation bill for the District of Columbia, Second Session of Thirty-Seventh Congress, in Senate, 1862, April 3—MR. SUMNER, moved to amend Section 7, by adding the words: "without the exclusion of any witness on account of color;" which was agreed to, yeas 26, nays 9, as follows:

YEAS—Messrs. Anthony, Browning, Chandler, Clark, Collamer, Dixon, Doolittle, Fessenden, Foster, Grimes, Harris, Howard, Howe, King, Lane of Indiana, Lane of Kansas, Morrill, Pomeroy, Sumner, Ten Eyck, Trumbull, Wade, Wilkinson, Wilmot, Wilson of Mass.—26.

NAYS—Messrs. *Bayard, Carlile, Davis, Kennedy, Nesmith, Powell, Saulsbury*, Willey, *Wilson* of Missouri, *Wright*.—9.

There was no separate vote in the House on this proposition.

Connected with this subject, as stated on page 243, is the following opinion of Judge John C. Underwood, of the United States District Court for the Eastern District of Virginia, delivered at the late term:

[*From the Alexandria, Va., State Journal.*]

United States District Court, District of Virginia, in the matter of the petition of Israel Dorsey, a citizen of Massachusetts.

The use of the courts of the country, and the right to give testimony in them are privileges so fundamental and important to the security of personal and domestic peace, as to make their denial one of the greatest wrongs, next to slavery itself, which can be inflicted on a human being.

If the denial is permitted the victim may be robbed upon the highway, his house burned over his head, his wife or child ravished or murdered before his eyes without remedy or redress. We see, therefore, that the right to testify in courts of justice is not only essential to personal dignity and safety, but it is the very bulwark of defence of all other individual, domestic, and social rights, and that nothing but a conviction of a high crime can possibly justify its invasion. The clause of the United States Constitution on which the petitioner relies is the first of the second section of Article 4, and is in these words:

"The citizens of each State shall be entitled to all the privileges and immunities of citizens in the several States."

Alexander Hamilton, in commenting upon this clause in the 80th number of the *Federalist*, says:

"It may be esteemed the basis of the Union. And if it be a just principle that every government ought to possess the means of executing its own provisions, by its own authority, it will follow that in order to the inviolable maintenance of that equality of privileges and immunities to which the citizens of the Union will be entitled, the national judiciary ought to preside in all cases in which one State or its citizens are opposed to another State or its citizens. To secure the full effect of so fundamental a provision against all evasion and subterfuge, it is necessary that its construction should be committed to that tribunal, which, having no local attachments, will be likely to be impartial between the different States and their citizens, and which, owing its official existence to the Union, will never be likely to feel any bias inauspicious to the principles on which it is founded."

In the same paper he says: "There ought always to be a constitutional method to give efficacy to constitutional provisions." It will be remembered that, to give effect to this very provision, and to secure the invaded rights of her citizens, the Legislature of Mssachusetts many years ago sent an eminent jurist, Judge Hoar, to the State of South Carolina, with an appeal to the courts of justice. His appeal was rudely rejected, and himself and daughter by mob violence driven from that State of lawless madmen, who were then just beginning their wild rush from the crime of slavery to the kindred crimes of treason and rebellion against the best Government that ever blessed the world. Nor is it too much to assert that the neglect to give practical effect to this constitutional provision has been an efficient cause of the war now desolating the country.

In support of these views the case of Corfield *vs.* Coryell, 4th volume Washington Circuit Court Reports, pages 380 and 381, is directly in point and would seem conclusive. Mr. Justice Washington in his opinion says of the clause in question:

"The inquiry is, what are the privileges and immunities of citizens in the several States? We find no hesitation in confining these expressions to those privileges and immunities which are in their nature fundamental. They may be all comprehended under the following general heads: Protection by the Government; the enjoyment of life and liberty, with the right to acquire and possess property of every kind, and to pursue and obtain happiness and safety. The right of a citizen of one State to pass through or to reside in any other State, for purposes of trade, agriculture, professional pursuits or otherwise, to claim the benefit of the writ of *habeas corpus*, to institute and maintain actions of any kind in the courts of the State, to take, hold, and dispose of property, real and personal, and an exemption from higher taxes or impositions than are paid by the other citizens of the State. These and many others which might be mentioned are strictly privileges and immunities, and the enjoyment of them by the citizens of each State in every other State are manifestly calculated (to use the expressions of the preamble of the corresponding provision in the old articles of confederation) the better to secure and perpetuate mutual frienship and intercourse among the people of the different States of the Union."

The right to testify must be included in the foregoing enumeration as a part of the right to use the courts, and several of the rights enumerated are certainly less vital and fundamental than the right in question.

No one who has read the able opinion of Attorney General Bates, utterly demolishing the unfortunate *obiter dicta* in the Dred Scott case, can doubt that colored men may be citizens of the United States and of the several States; and indeed, all the counsel in this case seem to admit that the petitioner is a citizen of Massachusetts.

This court has no doubt that a citizen of Massachusetts has a right to demand the protection of his oath, and the use of the courts of Virginia, or any other State of this Union, in virtue of the above-quoted constitutional provision, which, like a treaty stipulation between independent States, abrogates every State law which may attempt to defeat its wise and benevolent and truly national operation.

Massachusetts may with perfect propriety say to Virginia—no matter with what wrongs, for the sake of sustaining a bloody and barbarous system, you outrage humanity in the persons of colored men born and reared upon your own soil, I demand of you, by the sacred guaranty of your constitutional obligations, that the humblest of my citizens, when a sojourner in your territory, shall be secure in all the great fundamental rights of human nature.

On the 22d day of June, 1772, the court of the King's Bench decided in the case of James Somerset, claimed as a slave by a Virginia planter named Charles Stewart, that "the state of slavery is of such a nature that it is incapable of being introduced on any reasons, moral or political, but only by positive law. It is so odious that nothing can be suffered to support it but positive law, and therefore the black must be discharged." Such in that celebrated case was the language of Lord Mansfield, the most brilliant light in that constellation of British judges who made their land immortal and raised themselves to the most sublime moral elevation by stooping to lift the lowly and crushed of their fellow-citizens, and to place them upon the great table-land of British security and protection. It was on the argument of the same case that Counselor Davy made the never-to-be-forgotten declaration that the air of England was "too pure for a slave to breathe in."

It is time for us to say the soil of Virginia, soaked by the blood of so many martyrs of freedom, is too sacred to be ever again pressed by the footstep of a slave.

The Senator from Virginia, who in 1850 excited the indignation of all christendom by demanding of Congress additional enactments to facilitate man and woman hunting through the length and breadth of the country, freely admitted that there was no positive law in Virginia establishing slavery, and that the system rested alone upon custom. He might well have added,

> "It is a custom
> More honored in the breach than the observance."

How then can any one who respects the humane principles declared in Lord Mansfield's time-honored opinion, for one moment regard slavery or any of its incidents as of any legal force in this State?

This court will always be ready to apply Lord Mansfield's principles to slavery and its supports and incidents, and the law in question is nothing more, and it has also the strongest conviction that the State law excluding the testimony of colored men from the courts of justice is utterly null and void, because it is utterly repugnant to her glorious Declaration of Rights, which, following the decision of Lord Mansfield, was adopted in June, 1776, as part of the constitution of the State. Never has that Declaration been repealed, but it has been repeatedly reaffirmed and continued as the basis of every State constitution of Virginia up to and including that of 1864.

Among the provisions of that Declaration are the following:

1. That all men are by nature equally free and independent, and have certain inherent rights, of which, when they enter into a state of society, they cannot, by any compact, deprive or divest their posterity; namely, the enjoyment of life and liberty, with the means of acquiring and possessing property, and pursuing and obtaining happiness and safety.

4. That no man or set of men are entitled to exclusive or separate emoluments or privileges from the community, but in consideration of public services.

15. That no free government or the blessing of liberty can be preserved to any people but by a firm adherence to justice, moderation, temperance, frugality and virtue, and by a frequent recurrence to fundamental principles.

In the light of such guaranties the enactment excluding the testimony of any man unconvicted of an infamous crime could not be executed or tolerated for a moment by a civilized and christian people, but for the debasing and demoralizing influence of the great abomination of slavery; which, invading every department of society, ascending even the pulpit and the halls of justice, has too successfully labored to poison and paralyze the public conscience, pronouncing itself, with all the blazen impudence of the bottomless pit, a divine institution, and asserting the cruel doctrine that the dearest human rights are only skin deep, and that dusky men have none which paler men are bound to respect.

Never should the courts of Virginia deny this fundamental privilege of manhood to any innocent human being, and least of all to a citizen of Massachusetts—the cradle of the American Revolution of 1776—the first State to abolish slavery, the first to scatter the seeds of knowledge and science throughout her bounds, to bless all the people who dwell within the influence of her generous and beneficent institutions.

Had Congress clearly conferred upon this court the necessary power, the relief prayed for by the petitioner would be cheerfully and speedily granted. But the method of proceeding in order to secure the benefit of a right fully guaranteed by the Constitution has been left in great doubt and obscurity from some cause, probably from an influence which in the future will neither be felt nor feared. With a view, therefore, of obtaining the aid of Congress at the approaching session, and with the hope also that the Legislature of this State, soon to assemble, may do itself and our old Commonwealth the honor of wiping the wicked enactment, excluding the testimony of colored men in any of our courts, from our code of laws, burying it in the same grave with its barbarous twin brother, slavery, thus obviating the necessity of further action by this court, the case is put over for final action, and, if desired, for further argument, to the next term.

Gen. Grant's Orders Respecting Fugitive Slaves.

As an addenda to the military reports, orders, and proclamations, respecting "contrabands," on pages 244, 253, the following, issued at different times by Gen. Grant, and not before published as a whole, are inserted:

HEADQUARTERS DISTRICT OF WEST TENNESSEE,
FORT DONELSON, *February* 26, 1862.

GENERAL ORDERS No. 14.

I. General Orders No. 3, series 1861, from Headquarters Department of the Missouri, is still in force, and must be observed. The necessity of its strict enforcement is made apparent by the numerous applications from citizens for permission to pass through the camps to look for fugitive slaves. In no case whatever will permission be granted to citizens for this purpose.

II. All slaves at Fort Donelson at the time of its capture, and all slaves within the line of military occupation that have been used by the enemy in building fortifications, or in any manner hostile to the Government, will be employed by the Quartermaster's Department for the benefit of the Government, and will under no circumstance be permitted to return to their masters.

III. It is made the duty of all officers of this command to see that all slaves above indicated are promptly delivered to the Chief Quartermaster of the district.

By order of Brig. Gen. U. S. GRANT:

JNO. A. RAWLINS, *A. A. G.*

HEADQUARTERS DISTRICT OF WEST TENNESSEE,
CORINTH, MISS., *August* 11, 1862.

GENERAL ORDERS No. 72.

Recent acts of Congress prohibit the army from returning fugitives from labor to their claimants, and authorizing the employment of such persons in the service of the Government. The following orders are therefore published for the guidance of the army in this military district in this matter:

I. All fugitives thus employed must be registered, the names of the fugitives and claimants given, and must be borne upon morning reports of the command in which they are kept, showing how they are employed.

II. Fugitive slaves may be employed as laborers in the Quartermaster's, Subsistence, and Engineer Departments, and wherever by such employment a soldier may be saved to the ranks. They may be employed as teamsters, as company cooks, (not exceeding four to a company,) or as hospital attendants or nurses. Officers may employ them as private servants, in which latter case the fugitive will not be paid or rationed by the Government. Negroes, not thus employed, will be deemed unauthorized persons, and must be excluded from the camps.

III. Officers and soldiers are prohibited from enticing slaves to leave their masters. When it becomes necessary to employ this kind of labor, commanding officers of posts or troops must send details (always under the charge of a suitable non-commissioned officer) to press into service the slaves of disloyal persons to the number required.

IV. Citizens within the reach of any military station, known to be disloyal and dangerous, may be ordered away or arrested, and their crops and stocks taken for the benefit of the Government or the use of the army.

V. All property taken from rebel owners must be duly reported and used for the benefit of Government, and be issued to troops through the proper departments, and when practicable the act of taking should be avowed by the written certificate of the officer taking, to the owner or agent of such property.

It is enjoined on all commanding officers to see that this order is strictly executed. The demoralization of troops consequent on being left to execute laws in their own way, without a proper head, must be avoided.

By order of Maj. Gen. U. S. GRANT:

JNO. A. RAWLINS, *A. A. G.*

HEADQUARTERS DEPARTMENT OF THE TENNESSEE,
MILLIKEN'S BEND, LA., *April* 22, 1863.

GENERAL ORDERS No. 25. [Extract.]

I. Corps, division, and post commanders will afford all facilities for the completion of the negro regiments now organizing in this department. Commissaries will issue supplies, and Quartermasters will furnish stores on the same requisitions and returns as are required from other troops.

It is expected that all commanders will especially exert themselves in carrying out the policy of the Administration, not only in organizing colored regiments and rendering them efficient, but also in removing prejudice against them.

* * * * * * *

By order of Maj. Gen. U. S. Grant:
(Signed) JNO. A. RAWLINS,
Asst. Adjt. Gen.

Headquarters Department of the Tennessee,
Vicksburg, Miss., *August* 10, 1863.

General Orders No. 51.

I. At all military posts in States within the Department, where slavery has been abolished by the proclamation of the President of the United States, camps will be established for such freed people of color as are out of employment.

II. Commanders of posts or districts will detail suitable officers from the army as superintendents of such camps. It will be the duty of such superintendents to see that suitable rations are drawn from the Subsistence Department for such people as are confided to their care.

III. All such persons supported by the Government will be employed in every practicable way, so as to avoid, as far as possible, their becoming a burden upon the Government. They may be hired to planters or other citizens, on proper assurances that the negroes so hired will not be run off beyond the military jurisdiction of the United States; they may be employed on any public works; in gathering crops from abandoned plantations; and generally, in any manner local commanders may deem for the best interests of the Government, in compliance with law and the policy of the Administration.

IV. It will be the duty of the Provost Marshal at every military post to see that every negro within the jurisdiction of the military authority is employed by some white person or is sent to the camps provided for freed people.

V. Citizens may make contracts with freed persons of color for their labor, giving wages per month in money, or employ families of them by the year on plantations, &c., feeding, clothing, and supporting the infirm as well as the able-bodied, and giving a portion—not less than one-twentieth—of the commercial part of their crops, in payment for such service.

VI. Where negroes are employed under this authority, the parties employing will register with the Provost Marshal their names, occupation, and residence, and the number of negroes employed. They will enter into such bonds as the Provost Marshal, with the approval of the local commander, may require, for the kind treatment and proper care of those employed, and as security against their being carried beyond the employer's jurisdiction.

VII. Nothing in this order is to be construed to embarrass the employment of such colored persons as may be required by the Government.

By order of Major General U. S. Grant:
(Signed) T. S. BOWERS,
Acting Asst. Adj't Gen'l.

Headquarters Department of the Tennessee,
Vicksburg, Miss., *August* 23, 1863.

General Orders No. 53.

I. Hereafter, negroes will not be allowed in or about the camps of white troops, except such as are properly employed and controlled.

II. They may be employed in the Quartermaster's Department, Subsistence Department, Medical Department, as hospital nurses and laundresses, in the Engineer Department as pioneers. As far as practicable, such as have been or may be rejected as recruits for colored regiments by the examining surgeon will be employed about hospitals and in pioneer corps.

III. In regiments and companies they may be employed as follows: One cook to each fifteen men, and one teamster to each wagon. Officers may employ them as servants, but not in greater numbers than they are entitled to commutation for.

IV. Commanders of regiments and detachments will see that all negroes in or about their respective camps, not employed as provided in this order, are collected and turned over to the Provost Marshal of the division, post, or army corps to which their regiment or detachment belongs.

V. Provost Marshals will keep all negroes thus coming into their hands from straggling and wandering about, until they can be put in charge of the superintendent of the camp for colored people nearest them; and all negroes unemployed in accordance with this or previous orders, not in and about camps of regiments and detachments, will be required to go into the camps established for negroes, and it is enjoined upon Provost Marshals to see that they do so.

VI. Recruiting for colored regiments in negro camps will be prohibited, except when special authority to do so is given.

VII. All able-bodied negro men who are found, ten days after publication of this order, without a certificate of the officer or person employing them, will be regarded as unemployed, and may be pressed into service. Certificates given to negroes must show how, when, and by whom they are employed, and if as officers' servants, that the officer employing them has not a greater number than by law he is entitled to commutation for.

By order of Major General U. S. Grant:
JNO. A. RAWLINS,
Assistant Adjutant General.

Protection to Colored Soldiers.

On page 280 is the President's order on this subject, which has been the occasion of more or less correspondence between the Union and Rebel authorities. The latest and most satisfactory statement is included in the subjoined correspondence:

Headquarters Army Northern Virginia,
October 19, 1864.

Lieut. Gen. U. S. Grant, *Commanding U. S. Armies:*

General: In accordance with instructions from the Honorable Secretary of the Confederate States, I have the honor to call your attention to the subject of two communications recently addressed by Major General B. F. Butler, an officer under your command, to the Hon. Robert Ould, commissioner for the exchange of prisoners. For the better understanding of the matter, I enclose copies of the communications.

You will perceive by one of them that the writer has placed a number of officers and men belonging to the Confederate service, prisoners of war captured by the United States forces, at labor in the canal at Dutch Gap, in retaliation, as is alleged, for a like number of Federal colored soldiers, prisoners of war in our hands, who are said to have been put to work on our fortifications. The evidence of this fact is found in the affidavits of two deserters from our service.

The other letter refers to a copy of a notice issued by a Confederate officer commanding a camp near Richmond, calling upon the owners to come forward and establish their claims to certain negroes in the custody of that officer. The writer of the letter proceeds to state that some of the negroes mentioned in the notice are believed to be soldiers of the United States army, captured in arms, and that, upon that belief, he has ordered to such manual labor as he deems most fitting to meet the exigency an equivalent number of prisoners of war held by the United States, and announces that he will continue to order to labor captives in war to a number equal to that of all the United States soldiers whom he has reason to believe are held to service or labor by the Confederate forces, until he shall be notified that the alleged practice on the part of the Confederate authorities has ceased.

Before stating the facts with reference to the particular negroes alluded to, I beg to explain the policy pursued by the Confederate Government towards this class of persons when captured by our forces.

All negroes in the military or naval service of the United States taken by us, who are not identified as the property of citizens or residents of any of the Confederate States are regarded as prisoners of war, being held to be proper subjects of exchange, as I recently had the honor to inform you. No labor is exacted from such prisoners by the Confederate authorities.

Negroes who owe service or labor to citizens or residents of the Confederate States, and who, through compulsion, persuasion, or their own accord, leave their owners and are placed in the military or naval service of the United States occupy a different position.

The rights to the service or labor of negro slaves in the Confederate States is the same now as when the States were members of the Federal Union. The constitutional relations and obligations of the Confederate States to the owners of this species of property are the same as those so frequently and so long recognized as those appertaining to the Government of the United States with reference to the same class of persons by virtue of its organic law.

From the earliest period of the independence of the American States it has been held that one of the duties incumbent upon the several common governments under which they have from time to time been associated was the return to their lawful owners of slaves recaptured from the publi enemy. It has been uniformly held that the capture or abduction of a slave does not impair the right of the owner to such a slave, but that the right attaches to him immediately on recapture.

Such was the practice of the American States during their struggle for independence. The Government under which they were then associated restored to the owners slaves abducted by the British forces and subsequently recaptured by the American armies.

In the war of 1812 with Great Britain the course pursued by the United States Government was the same, and it recognized the right of the owner to the slaves recaptured from the enemy. Both the Continental and United States Governments, in fact, denied that the abduction of slaves was a belligerent right; and the latter Power insisted upon, and ultimately secured by treaty, pecuniary indemnity from the British Government for slaves taken by its forces during the war of 1812.

And it is supposed that if a slave belonging to a citizen of a State in which slavery is recognized, and which is regarded as one of the United States, were to escape into the Confederate States, or be captured or abducted by their armies, the legal right of the owner to reclaim him would be as clear now as in 1812, the Constitution of the United States being unchanged in this particular, and that instrument having been interpreted in the judicial decisions, legislative and diplomatic acts, and correspondence of the United States, as imposing upon that Government the duty of protecting, in all cases coming within the scope of its authority, the owners of slaves, as well as of any other kind of property recognized as such by the several States.

The Confederate Government, bound by the same constitutional obligations, considers, as that of the United did, that the capture or abduction of a negro slave does not preclude the lawful owner from reclaiming him when captured, and I an instructed to say that all such slaves, when properly identified as belonging to citizens of any of the Confederate States, or to persons enjoying the protection of their laws, will be restored, like other recaptured private property, to those entitled to them.

Having endeavored to explain the general policy of the Confederate Government with regard to this subject, I beg leave to state the facts concerning the particular transactions referred to in the enclosed communications.

The negroes recently captured by our forces were sent to Richmond with other Federal prisoners. After their arrival it was discovered that a number of them were slaves belonging to citizens or residents of some of the Confederate States; and of this class, fifty-nine, as I learn, were sent, with other negroes, to work on the fortifications around Richmond until their owners should appear and claim them. As soon as I was informed of the fact, less than two days afterwards, not wishing to employ them here, I ordered them to be sent to the rear. By a misapprehension of the engineer officer in charge, they were transferred to our lines south of the James river, but when apprized of the error, I repeated the order for their removal. If any negroes were included among this number who were not identified as the slaves of citizens, or residents of some of the Confederate States, they were so included without the knowledge or authority of the War Department, as already explained, and the mistake, when discovered, would have been corrected.

It only remains for me to say that negroes employed upon our fortifications are not allowed to be placed where they will be exposed to fire, and there is no foundation for any statement to the contrary. The author of the communications referred to has considered himself justified by the reports of two deserters, who do not allege that the negroes in question were exposed to any danger, in placing our prisoners under the fire of our batteries.

In view of the explanations of the practice of the Confederate Government above given, and of the statement of facts I have made, I have now, in accordance with my instructions, respectfully to inquire whether the course pursued toward our prisoners, as set forth in the accompanying letters, has your sanction, and whether it will be maintained?

Very respectfully, your obedient servant,

R. E. LEE, *General.*

HEADQUARTERS ARMIES OF THE UNITED STATES,
October 29, 1864.

Gen. R. E. LEE, C. S. A.,
Commanding Army Northern Virginia:

GENERAL: Understanding from your letter of the 19th that the colored prisoners who are employed at work in the trenches near Fort Gilmer have been withdrawn, I have directed the withdrawal of the Confederate prisoners employed in the Dutch Gap canal.

I shall always regret the necessity of retaliating for wrongs done our soldiers; but regard it my duty to protect all persons received into the army of the United States, regardless of color or nationality. When acknowledged soldiers of the Government are captured they must be treated as prisoners of war, or such treatment as they receive will be inflicted upon an equal number of prisoners held by us.

I have nothing to do with the discussion of the slavery question; therefore decline answering the arguments adduced to show the right to return to former owners such negroes as are captured from our army.

In answer to the question at the conclusion of your letter, I have to state that all prisoners of war falling into my hands shall receive the kindest treatment possible, consistent with securing them, unless I have good authority for believing any number of our men are being treated otherwise. Then, painful as it may be to me, I shall inflict like treatment on an equal number of Confederate prisoners.

Hoping that it may never become my duty to order retaliation upon any man held as a prisoner of war, I have the honor to be, very respectfully, your obedient servant,

U. S. GRANT,
Lieutenant General.

Military Order Respecting the Election in Missouri—(See p. 314.)

1864, October 12—Maj. Gen. Rosecrans issued an order establishing the regulations for the election in Missouri. The following are passages from the order:

The General commanding expects the united assistance of the true men of all parties in his efforts to secure a full and fair opportunity for all who are entitled to vote at the approaching elections in the State of Missouri, and in excluding from the polls those who, by alienage, treason, guerillaism, and other crimes and disabilities, have no just right to vote.

I. Those, and only those, who have the qualifications, and who take the oath prescribed by the laws of the State, copies of which are hereto annexed, shall vote.

Voting, or attempting to vote, in contravention of law or orders, is declared a military offence, subjecting the offender to arrest, trial, and punishment, if convicted.

II. No one who has borne arms against the Government of the United States, or voluntarily given aid and comfort to its enemies during the present rebellion, shall act as judge or clerk at election; nor shall any county judge knowingly appoint any such person to act as judge at election. Violation of this will be promptly noticed, and the offenders brought to trial by the local military authorities.

III. Outrages upon the freedom of election by violence or intimidation; attempting to hinder legal or to procure or encourage illegal voting; interfering with the legal challenge of voters; acting as officers of election in contravention of law or orders; wilful neglect to perform their duties, under the laws and these orders, by officers of elections, and especially taking the voters' or officers' oath falsely; and all other acts and words interfering with the purity and freedom of elections, are crimes against the liberties of the people, and are declared military offences, and will be rigorously punished.

The oath is as provided in the ordinance of the Convention of Missouri, and printed on page 314.

Report of Hon. J. Holt, Judge Advocate General, on certain "Secret Associations."

WAR DEPARTMENT, BUREAU OF MILITARY JUSTICE,
WASHINGTON, D. C., *October* 8, 1864.

Hon. E. M. STANTON, *Secretary of War:*

SIR: Having been instructed by you to prepare a detailed report upon the mass of testimony furnished me from different sources in regard to the *Secret Associations and Conspiracies against the Government*, formed, principally in the Western States, by traitors and disloyal persons, I have now the honor to submit as follows:

During more than a year past it has been generally known to our military authorities that a secret treasonable organization, affiliated with the Southern rebellion, and chiefly military in its character, has been rapidly extending itself throughout the West. A variety of agencies, which will be specified herein, have been employed, and successfully, to ascertain its nature and extent, as well as its aims and its results; and, as this investigation has led to the arrest, in several States, of a number of its prominent members as dangerous public enemies, it has been deemed proper to set forth in full the acts and purposes of this organization, and thus to make known to the country at large its intensely treasonable and revolutionary spirit.

The subject will be presented under the following heads:

I. The origin, history, names, &c., of the Order.
II. Its organization and officers.
III. Its extent and numbers.
IV. Its armed force.
V. Its ritual, oaths, and interior forms.
VI. Its written principles.
VII. Its specific purposes and operations.
VIII. The witnesses and their testimony.

I.—THE ORIGIN, HISTORY, NAMES, ETC., OF THE ORDER.

This secret association first developed itself in the West in the year 1862, about the period of the first conscription of troops, which it aimed to obstruct and resist. Originally known in certain localities as the "Mutual Protection Society," the "Circle of Honor," or the "Circle," or "Knights of the Mighty Host," but more widely as the "Knights of the Golden Circle," it was simply an inspiration of the rebellion, being little other than an extension among the disloyal and disaffected at the North of the association of the latter name, which had existed for some years at the South, and from which it derived all the chief features of its organization.

During the summer and fall of 1863, the Order, both at the North and South, underwent some modifications as well as a change of name. In consequence of a partial exposure which had been made of the signs and ritual of the "Knights of the Golden Circle," Sterling Price had instituted as its successor in Missouri a secret political association, which he called the "Corps de Belgique," or "Southern League;" his principal coadjutor being Charles L. Hunt, of St. Louis, then Belgian Consul at that city, but whose *exequatur* was subsequently revoked by the President on account of his disloyal practices. The special object of the Corps de Belgique appears to have been to unite the rebel sympathizers of Missouri, with a view to their taking up arms and joining Price upon his proposed grand invasion of that State, and to their recruiting for his army in the interim.

Meanwhile, also, there had been instituted at the North, in the autumn of 1863, by sundry disloyal persons, prominent among whom were Vallandigham and P. C. Wright, of New York, a secret Order, intended to be general throughout the country, and aiming at an extended influence and power, and at more positive results than its predecessor, and which was termed, and has since been widely known as the O. A. K., or "*Order of American Knights.*"

The opinion is expressed by Col. Sanderson, Provost Marshal General of the Department of Missouri, in his official report upon the progress of this Order, that it was founded by Vallandigham during his banishment, and upon consultation at Richmond with Davis and other prominent traitors. It is, indeed, the boast of the Order in Indiana and elsewhere, that its "ritual" came direct from Davis himself; and Mary Ann Pitman, formerly attached to the command of the rebel Forrest, and a most intelligent witness, whose testimony will be hereafter referred to, states positively that Davis is a member of the Order.

Upon the institution of the principal organization, it is represented that the "Corps de Belgique" was modified by Price, and became a southern section of the O. A. K., and that the new name was generally adopted for the Order, both at the North and South.

The secret signs and character of the Order having become known to our military authorities, further modifications in the ritual and forms were introduced, and its name was finally changed to that of the O. S. L., or "Order of the *Sons of Liberty*," or the "Knights of the Order of the Sons of Liberty." These later changes are represented to have been first instituted, and the new ritual compiled, in the State of Indiana, in May last, but the new name was at once generally adopted throughout the West, though in some localities the association is still better known as the "Order of American Knights."

Meanwhile, also, the Order has received certain local designations. In parts of Illinois it has been called at times the "Peace Organization," in Kentucky the "Star Organization," and in Missouri the "American Organization;" these, however, being apparently names used outside of the lodges of the Order. Its members have also been familiarly designated as "Butternuts" by the country people of Illinois, Indiana, and Ohio, and its separate lodges have also frequently received titles intended for the public ear; that in Chicago, for instance, being termed by its members the "Democratic Invincible Club;" that in Louisville, the "Democratic Reading Room," &c.

It is to be added that in the State of New York and other parts of the North, the secret political association known as the "*McClellan Minute Guard*" would seem to be a branch of the O. A. K., having substantially the same objects, to be accomplished, however, by means expressly suited to the localities in which it is established. For, as the Chief Secretary of this association, Dr. R. F. Stevens, stated in June last to a reliable witness, whose testimon has been furnished, "those who represent the McClella interest are compelled to preach a vigorous prosecution (the war, in order to secure the popular sentiment an allure voters."

II.—ITS ORGANIZATION AND OFFICERS.

From printed copies, heretofore seized by the Governmen of the constitutions of the Supreme Council, Grand Cou cil, and County Parent Temples, respectively, of the Orde of Sons of Liberty, in connection with other and abundan testimony, the organization of the Order, in its latest forn is ascertained to be as follows:

1. The government of the Order throughout the Unite States is vested in a Supreme Council, of which the officer are a Supreme Commander, Secretary of State, and Treas urer. These officers are elected for one year, at the annu meeting of the Supreme Council, which is made up of th Grand Commanders of the several States *ex officio*, and tw delegates elected from each State in which the Order is es tablished.

2. The government of the Order in a State is vested in Grand Council, the officers of which are a Grand Con mander, Deputy Grand Commander, Grand Secretary Grand Treasurer, and a certain number of Major Generals or one for each Military District. These officers also ar elected annually by "representatives" from the Count Temples, each Temple being entitled to two representatives and one additional for each thousand members. This bod of representatives is also invested with certain legislativ functions.

3. The Parent Temple is the organization of the Orde for a county, each Temple being formally instituted b authority of the Supreme Council, or of the Grand Counc or Grand Commander of the State. By the same authorit or by that of the officers of the Parent Temple, branch o subordinate Temples may be established for townships i the county.

But the strength and significance of this organization li in its *military* character. The secret constitution of th Supreme Council provides that the Supreme Comman "*shall be commander-in-chief of all military forces belongin to the Order in the various States when called into actual se*

---

* LETTER OF R. F. STEVENS.

NEW YORK, *Oct.* 17.

To the Editor of the World:

DEAR SIR: In Judge Holt's report to the Secretary War, just published, statements are made, to the effect th the Minute Guard Association is a secret organizatio Second, That its objects are identical with the traitorou objects of an alleged Northwestern association. Thir That it is a branch of the O. A. K. Fourth, That I said i June, that "those who represent the McClellan interest ar compelled to preach a vigorous prosecution of the war, i order to secure the popular sentiment, and allure voters. None of the members of the association ever held a secr meeting, and nothing of a secret or traitorous nature wa ever connected with it. It was never connected with th O. A. K., or any other association. Its members were neve compelled to "preach," as alleged, and all the above stat ments of Judge Holt are absolute and entire falsehood Mr. Greeley, in his editorial of the 15th instant, makes like statement, to the effect that the Minute Guard is co nected with the alleged Northwestern conspiracy, and pa rades my name with the evident intent of fixing upon m the character of a traitor. The whole of which are bas insinuations and fabrications, and worthy of the man wh wrote of our national flag, "Tear down the flaunting lie,"- and of the slave States, that they had a clear right to s cede, and he would oppose all coercive attempts to kee them in.

The Minute Guard is an association for ordinary politic campaign work. It has no secrets like the oath-boun Loyal (?) League. On public occasions, each member ca ries, or wears, the American flag. On election days the work for votes; and the results of their work will be se all over the Union, as it has been seen in the recent ele tion in Pennsylvania.

In these fabrications of Judge Holt and Mr. Greeley; in t low buffoonery contained in the answer to the recent com munication from the Union men of Tennessee; in the u paralleled election frauds in Indiana; in the open boasts a company of Massachusetts soldiers that they voted at se eral of the polls in Philadelphia; in the discharge of wor men at the navy-yard for being in favor of McClellan; the thousands of arbitrary arrests, and the hundreds suppressions of a hitherto free press, all men may see th the re-election of Mr. Lincoln, and the continuance in po er of such men as support him, will be the most unmitig ted curse ever inflicted upon a free people.

Yours, &c., R. F. STEVENS

vice;" and further, that the Grand Commanders "*shall be commanders-in-chief of the military forces of their respective States.*" Subordinate to the Grand Commander in the State are the "*Major Generals,*" each of whom commands his separate district and army. In Indiana the Major Generals are four in number. In Illinois, where the organization of the order is considered most perfect, the members in each Congressional District compose a "*brigade,*" which is commanded by a "*Brigadier General.*" The members of each county constitute a "*regiment,*" with a "*colonel,*" in command, and those of each township form a "*company.*" A somewhat similar system prevails in Indiana, where also each company is divided into "*squads,*" each with its chief —an arrangement intended to facilitate the *guerilla* mode of warfare in case of a general outbreak or local disorder.

The "McClellan Minute Guard," as appears from a circular issued by the Chief Secretary in New York in March last, is organized upon a military basis similar to that of the Order proper. It is composed of companies, one for each election district, ten of which constitute a "brigade," with a "brigadier general" at its head. The whole is placed under the authority of a "Commander-in-chief." A strict obedience on the part of members to the orders of their superiors is enjoined.

The first "Supreme Commander" of the Order was P. C. Wright, of New York, editor of the New York *News*, who was in May last placed in arrest and confined in Fort Lafayette. His successor in office was Vallandigham,* who was elected at the annual meeting of the Supreme Council in February last. Robert Holloway, of Illinois, is represented to have acted as Lieutenant General, or Deputy Supreme Commander, during the absence of Vallandigham from the country. The Secretary of State chosen at the last election was Dr. Massey, of Ohio.

In Missouri the principal officers were Charles L. Hunt, Grand Commander, Charles E. Dunn, Deputy Grand Commander, and Green B. Smith, Grand Secretary. Since the arrest of these three persons (all of whom have made confessions which will be presently alluded to) James A. Barrett has, as it is understood, officiated as Grand Commander. He is stated to occupy also the position of chief of staff to the Supreme Commander.

The Grand Commander in Indiana, H. H. Dodd, is now on trial at Indianapolis by a military commission for "conspiracy against the Government," "violation of the laws of war," and other charges. The Deputy Grand Commander in that State is Horace Heffren, and the Grand Secretary, W. M. Harrison. The Major Generals are W. A. Bowles, John C. Walker, L. P. Milligan, and Andrew Humphreys. Among the other leading men of the Order in that State are Dr. Athon, State Secretary, and Joseph Ristine, State Auditor.

The Grand Commander in Illinois is —— Judd, of Lewistown; and B. B. Piper, of Springfield, who is entitled "Grand Missionary" of the State, and designated also as a member of Vallandigham's staff, is one of the most active members, having been busily engaged throughout the summer in establishing Temples and initiating members.

In Kentucky, Judge Bullit, of the Court of Appeals, is Grand Commander, and, with Dr. U. F. Kalfus and W. R. Thomas, jailor in Louisville, two other of the most prominent members, has been arrested and confined by the military authorities. In New York, Dr. R. F. Stevens, the chief secretary of the McClellan Minute Guard, is the most active ostensible representative of the Order.

The greater part of the chief and subordinate officers of the Order and its branches, as well as the principal members thereof, are known to the Government, and, where not already arrested, may regard themselves as under a constant military surveillance. So complete has been the exposure of this secret league, that however frequently the conspirators may change its names, forms, passwords, and signals, its true purposes and operations cannot longer be concealed from the military authorities.

It is to be remarked that the Supreme Council of the Order, which annually meets on February 22, convened this year at New York city, and a special meeting was then appointed to be held at Chicago on July 1, or just prior to the day then fixed for the convention of the Democratic party. This convention having been postponed to August 29, the special meeting of the Supreme Council was also postponed to August 27, at the same place, and was duly convened accordingly. It will be remembered that a leading member of the convention, in the course of a speech made before that body, alluded approvingly to the session of the Sons of Liberty at Chicago at the same time, as that of an organization in harmony with the sentiment and projects of the convention.

It may be observed, in conclusion, that one not fully acquainted with the true character and intentions of the Order might well suppose that, in designating its officers by high military titles, and in imitating in its organization that established in our armies, it was designed merely to render itself more popular and attractive with the masses, and to invest its chiefs with a certain sham dignity; but when it is understood that the Order comprises within itself a large army of well-armed men, constantly drilled and exercised as soldiers, and that this army is held ready at any time for such forcible resistance to our military authorities, and such active co-operation with the public enemy, as it may be called upon to engage in by its commanders, it will be perceived that the titles of the latter are not assumed for a mere purpose of display, but they are the chiefs of an actual and formidable force of conspirators against the life of the Government, and that their military system is, as it has been remarked by Colonel Sanderson, "the grand lever used by the rebel Government for its army operations."

* Mr. Vallandigham's notice of this report, see page 423.

III.—ITS EXTENT AND NUMBERS.

The "Temples" or "Lodges" of the Order are numerously scattered through the States of Indiana, Illinois, Ohio, Missouri, and Kentucky. They are also officially reported as established, to a less extent, in Michigan and the other Western States, as well as in New York, Pennsylvania, New Hampshire, Rhode Island, Connecticut, New Jersey, Maryland, Delaware, and Tennessee. Dodd, the Grand Commander of Indiana, in an address to the members in that State of February last, claims that at the next annual meeting of the Supreme Council (in February, 1865) every State in the Union will be represented, and adds, "this is the first and only true national organization the Democratic and Conservative men of the country have ever attempted." A provision made in the constitution of the Council for a representation from the *Territories*, shows, indeed, that the widest extension of the Order is contemplated.

In the States first mentioned the Order is most strongly centred at the following places, where are situated its principal "Temples." In Indiana, at Indianapolis and Vincennes; in Illinois, at Chicago, Springfield, and Quincy, (a large proportion of the lodges in and about the latter place having been founded by the notorious guerilla chief, Jackman;) in Ohio, at Cincinnati, Dayton, and in Hamilton county, (which is proudly termed by members "the South Carolina of the North;") in Missouri, at St. Louis; in Kentucky, at Louisville; and in Michigan, at Detroit, (whence communication was freely had by the leaders of the Order with Vallandigham during his banishment, either by letters addressed to him through two prominent citizens and members of the Order, or by personal interviews at Windsor, C. W.) It is to be added that the regular places of meeting, as also the principal rendezvous and haunts of the members in these and less important places, are generally well known to the Government.

The actual *numbers* of the Order have, it is believed, never been officially reported, and cannot, therefore, be accurately ascertained. Various estimates have been made by leading members, some of which are no doubt considerably exaggerated. It has been asserted by delegates to the Supreme Council of February last, that the number was there represented to be from 800,000 to 1,000,000; but Vallandigham, in his speech last summer at Dayton, Ohio, placed it at 500,000, which is probably much nearer the true total. The number of its members in the several States has been differently estimated in the reports and statements of its officers. Thus, the force of the Order in Indiana is stated to be from 75,000 to 125,000; in Illinois, from 100,000 to 140,000; in Ohio, from 80,000 to 108,000; in Kentucky, from 40,000 to 70,000; in Missouri, from 20,000 to 40,000; and in Michigan and New York, about 20,000 each. Its representation in the other States above mentioned does not specifically appear from the testimony; but, allowing for every exaggeration in the figures reported, they may be deemed to present a tolerably faithful view of what, at least, is regarded by the Order as its true force in the States designated.

It is to be noted that the Order, or its counterpart, is probably much more widely extended at the South even than at the North, and that a large proportion of the officers of the rebel army are represented by credible witnesses to be members. In Kentucky and Missouri the Order has not hesitated to admit as members, not only officers of that army, but also a considerable number of guerillas, a class who might be supposed to appreciate most readily its spirit and purposes. It is fully shown that as lately as in July last several of these ruffians were initiated into the first degree by Dr. Kalfus, in Kentucky.

IV.—ITS ARMED FORCE.

A review of the testimony in regard to the *armed* force of the Order will materially aid in determining its real strength and numbers.

Although the Order has from the outset partaken of the military character, it was not till the summer or fall of 1863 that it began to be generally organized as an armed body. Since that date its officers and leaders have been busily engaged in placing it upon a military basis, and in preparing it for a revolutionary movement. A general system of drilling has been instituted and secretly carried out. Members have been instructed to be constantly provided with weapons, and in some localities it has been absolutely required that each member should keep at his residence, at all times, certain arms and a specified quantity of ammunition.

In March last the entire armed force of the Order, capable of being mobilized for effective service, was represented to be 340,000 men. As the details upon which this statement was based are imperfectly set forth in the testimony, it is not known how far this number may be exaggerated. It is abundantly shown, however, that the Order, by means of a tax levied upon its members, has accumulated considerable funds for the purchase of arms and ammunition, and that these have been procured in large quantities for its use. The witness Clayton, on the trial of Dodd, estimated that *two-thirds* of the Order are furnished with arms.

Green B. Smith, Grand Secretary of the Order in Missouri, states in his confession of July last: "I know that arms, mostly revolvers, and ammunition have been purchased by members in St. Louis to send to members in the country where they could not be had;" and he subsequently adds that he himself alone clandestinely purchased and forwarded, between April 15th and 19th last, about 200 revolvers, with 5,000 percussion caps and other ammunition. A muster-roll of one of the country lodges of that State is exhibited, in which, opposite the name of each member, are noted certain numbers, under the heads of "Missouri Republican," "St. Louis Union," "Anzeiger," "Miscellaneous Periodicals," "Books," "Speeches," and "Reports;" titles which, when interpreted, severally signify *single-barrelled guns, double-barrelled guns, revolvers, private ammunition, private lead, company powder, company lead*—the roll thus actually setting forth the amount of arms and ammunition in the possession of the lodge and its members.

In the States of Ohio and Illinois the Order is claimed by its members to be unusually well armed with revolvers, carbines, &c.; but it is in regard to the arming of the Order in Indiana that the principal statistics have been presented, and these may serve to illustrate the system which has probably been pursued in most of the States. One intelligent witness, who has been a member, estimates that in March last there were in possession of the Order in that State 6,000 muskets and 60,000 revolvers, besides private arms. Another member testifies that at a single lodge meeting of two hundred and fifty-two persons, which he attended early in the present year, the sum of $4,000 was subscribed for arms. Other members present statements in reference to the number of arms in their respective counties, and all agree in representing that these have been constantly forwarded from Indianapolis into the interior. Beck & Brothers are designated as the firm in that city to which most of the arms were consigned. These were shipped principally from the East; some packages, however, were sent from Cincinnati, and some from Kentucky, and the boxes were generally marked "pick-axes," "hardware," "nails," "household goods," &c.

General Carrington estimates that in February and March last, nearly 30,000 guns and revolvers entered the State, and this estimate is based upon actual inspection of invoices. The true number introduced was therefore probably considerably greater. That officer adds that on the day in which the sale of arms was stopped by his order, in Indianapolis, nearly 1,000 additional revolvers had been contracted for, and that the trade could not supply the demand. He further reports that after the introduction of arms into the Department of the North had been prohibited in General Orders of March last, a seizure was made by the Government of a large quantity of revolvers and 135,000 rounds of ammunition, which had been shipped to the firm in Indianapolis, of which H. H. Dodd, Grand Commander, was a member; that other arms about to be shipped to the same destination were seized in New York city; and that all these were claimed as the private property of John C. Walker, one of the Major Generals of the Order in Indiana, and were represented to have been "*purchased for a few friends.*" It should also be stated that at the office of Hon. D. W. Voorhees, M. C., at Terre Haute, were discovered letters which disclosed a correspondence between him and ex-Senator Wall, of New Jersey, in regard to the purchase of 20,000 Garibaldi rifles, to be forwarded to the West.

It appears in the course of the testimony that a considerable quantity of arms and ammunition were brought into the State of Illinois from Burlington, Iowa, and that ammunition was sent from New Albany, Indiana, into Kentucky; it is also represented that, had Vallandigham been arrested on his return to Ohio, it was contemplated furnishing the Order with arms from a point in Canada, near Windsor, where they were stored and ready for use.

There remains further to be noticed, in this connexion, the testimony of Clayton upon the trial of Dodd, to the effect that arms were to be furnished the Order from Nassau, N. P., by way of Canada; that, to defray the expense of these arms or their transportation, a formal assessment was levied upon the lodges, but that the transportation into Canada was actually to be furnished by the Confederate authorities.

A statement was made by Hunt, Grand Commander of Missouri, before his arrest, to a fellow member, that shells and all kinds of munitions of war, as well as infernal machines, were manufactured by the Order at Indianapolis; and the late discovery in Cincinnati of samples of hand-grenades, conical shells, and rockets, of which one thousand were about to be manufactured, under a special contract, for the O. S. L., goes directly to verify such a statement.

These details will convey some idea of the attempts which have been made to place the Order upon a war footing and prepare it for aggressive movements. But, notwithstanding all the efforts that have been put forth, and with considerable success, to arm and equip its members as fighting men, the leaders have felt themselves still very deficient in their armament, and numerous schemes for increasing their armed strength have been devised. Thus, at the time of the issuing of the general order in Missouri requiring the enrollment of all citizens, it was proposed in the lodges of the O. A. K., at St. Louis, that certain members should raise companies in the militia, in their respective wards, and thus get command of as many Government arms and equipments as possible, for the future use of the Order. Again it was proposed that *all* the members should enroll themselves in the militia, instead of paying commutation, in this way obtaining possession of United States arms, and having the advantage of the drill and military instruction. In the councils of the Order in Kentucky, in June last, a scheme was devised for disarming all the negro troops, which it was thought could be done without much difficulty, and appropriating their arms for military purposes.

The despicable treachery of these proposed plans, as evincing the *animus* of the conspiracy, need not be commented upon.

It is to be observed that the Order in the State of Missouri has counted greatly upon support from the enrolled militia, in case of an invasion by Price, as containing many members and friends of the O. A. K.; and that the "Paw-Paw militia," a military organization of Buchanan county, as well as the militia of Platte and Clay counties, known as "Flat Foots," have been relied upon, almost to a man, to join the revolutionary movement.

V.—ITS RITUAL, OATHS, AND INTERIOR FORMS.

The ritual of the Order, as well as its secret signs, passwords, &c., has been fully made known to the military authorities. In August last one hundred and twelve copies of the ritual of the O. A. K. were seized in the office of Hon. D. W. Voorhees, M. C., at Terre Haute, and a large number of rituals of the O. S. L., together with copies of the Constitutions of the councils, &c., already referred to, were found in the building at Indianapolis, occupied by Dodd, the Grand Commander of Indiana, as had been indicated by the Government witness and detective, Stidger. Copies were likewise discovered at Louisville, at the residence of Dr. Kalfus, concealed within the mattress of his bed, where Stidger had ascertained that they were kept.

The ritual of the O. A. K. has also been furnished by the authorities at St. Louis. From the ritual, that of the O. S. L. does not materially differ. Both are termed "progressive," in that they provide for *five* separate *degrees* of membership, and contemplate the admission of a member of a lower degree into a higher one only upon certain vouchers and proofs of fitness, which, with each ascending degree, are required to be stronger and more imposing.

Each degree has its commander or head; the Fourth or "Grand" is the highest in a State; the Fifth or "Supreme" the highest in the United States; but to the first or lower degree only do the great majority of members attain. A large proportion of these enter the Order, supposing it to be a "Democratic" and political association merely; and the history of the Order furnishes a most striking illustration of the gross and criminal deception which may be practiced upon the ignorant masses by unscrupulous and unprincipled leaders. The members of the lower degree are often for a considerable period kept quite unaware of the true purposes of their chiefs. But to the latter they are bound, in the language of their obligation, "*to yield prompt and implicit obedience to the utmost of their ability, without remonstrance, hesitation, or delay,*" and meanwhile their minds, under the discipline and teachings to which they are subjected, become educated and accustomed to contemplate with comparative unconcern the treason for which they are preparing.

The oaths, "invocations," "charges," &c., of the ritual, expressed as they are in bombastic and extravagant phraseology, would excite in the mind of an educated person only ridicule and contempt, but upon the illiterate they are calculated to make a deep impression, the effect and importance of which were doubtless fully studied by the framers of the instrument.

The *oath* which is administered upon the introduction of a member into any degree is especially imposing in its language; it prescribes as a penalty for a violation of the obligation assumed "a shameful death," and further, that the body of the person guilty of such violation shall be divided into four parts and cast out at the four "gates" of the Temple. Not only, as has been said, does it enjoin a blind obedience to the commands of the superiors of the Order, but it is required to be held of *paramount obligation* to any oath which may be administered to a member in a court of justice or elsewhere. Thus, in cases where members have been sworn by officers empowered to administer oaths to speak the whole truth in answer to questions that may be put to them, and have then been examined in reference to the Order, and their connection therewith, they have not only refused to give any information in regard to its character, but have denied that they were members, or even that they knew of its existence. A conspicuous instance of this is presented in the cases of Hunt, Dunn, and Smith, the chief officers of the Order in Missouri, who, upon their first examination under oath, after their arrest, denied all connection with the Order, but confessed, also under oath, at a subsequent period, that this denial was wholly false, although in accordance with their obligations as members. Indeed, a deliberate system of deception in regard to the details of the conspiracy is inculcated upon the members, and studiously pursued; and it may be mentioned, as a similarly despicable feature of the organization, that it is held bound to injure the Administration and officers of the Government, in every possible manner, by misrepresentation and falsehood.

Members are also instructed that their oath of membership is to be held paramount to an oath of allegiance, or any other oath which may impose obligations inconsistent with those which are assumed upon entering the Order. Thus, if a member, when in danger, or for the purpose of facilitating some traitorous design, has taken the oath of allegiance to the United States, he is held at liberty to violate it on the first occasion, his obligation to the Order being deemed superior to any consideration of duty or loyalty prompted by such oath.

It is to be added that where members are threatened with the penalties of perjury, in case of their answering falsely to questions propounded to them in regard to the Order before a court or grand jury, they are instructed to refuse to answer such questions, alleging, as a ground for their refusal, that their answers may *criminate* themselves. The testimony shows that this course has habitually been pursued by members, especially in Indiana, when placed in such a situation.

Besides the oaths and other forms and ceremonies which have been alluded to, the ritual contains what are termed "Declarations of Principles." These declarations, which are most important as exhibiting the creed and character of the Order, as inspired by the principles of the rebellion, will be fully presented under the next branch of the subject.

The *signs, signals, passwords*, &c., of the Order are set forth at length in the testimony, but need only be briefly alluded to. It is a significant fact, as showing the intimate relations between the Northern and Southern sections of the secret conspiracy, that a member from a Northern State is enabled to pass without risk through the South by the use of the signs of recognition which have been established throughout the Order, and by means of which members from distant points, though meeting as strangers, are at once made known to each other as "brothers." Mary Ann Pitman expressly states in her testimony that whenever important despatches are required to be sent by rebel generals beyond their lines, members of the Order are always selected to convey them. Certain passwords are also used in common in both sections, and of these, none appears to be more familiar than the word "Nu-oh-lac," or the name "Calhoun" spelt backward, and which is employed upon entering a Temple of the first degree of the O. A. K.—certainly a fitting password to such dens of treason.

Beside the signs of recognition, there are *signs of warning and danger*, for use at night as well as by day; as, for instance, signs to warn members of the approach of United States officials seeking to make arrests. The Order has also established what are called *battle-signals*, by means of which, as it is asserted, a member serving in the army may communicate with the enemy in the field, and thus escape personal harm in case of attack or capture. The most recent of these signals represented to have been adopted is a five-pointed copper star, worn under the coat, which is to be disclosed upon meeting an enemy, who will thus recognize in the wearer a sympathizer and an ally. A similar star of German silver, hung in a frame, is said to be numerously displayed by members or their families in private *houses* in Indiana, for the purpose of insuring protection to their property in case of a raid or other attack; and it is stated that in many dwellings in that State a portrait of John Morgan is exhibited for a similar purpose.

Other signs are used by members, and especially the officers of the Order in their *correspondence*. Their letters, when of an official character, are generally conveyed by special messengers, but when transmitted through the mail are usually in cipher. When written in the ordinary manner, a character at the foot of the letter, consisting of a circle with a line drawn across the centre, signifies to the member who receives it that the statements as written are to be understood in a sense directly the opposite to that which would ordinarily be conveyed.

It is to be added that the meetings of the Order, especially in the country, are generally held at night and in secluded places, and that the approach to them is carefully guarded by a line of sentinels, who are passed only by means of a special *countersign*, which is termed the "picket."

VI.—ITS WRITTEN PRINCIPLES.

The "*Declaration of Principles*," which is set forth in the ritual of the Order, has already been alluded to. This declaration, which is specially framed for the instruction of the great mass of members, commences with the following proposition:

"All men are endowed by the Creator with certain rights, equal as far as there is equality in the capacity for the appreciation, enjoyment, and exercise of those rights." And subsequently there is added: "In the Divine economy no individual of the human race must be permitted to encumber the earth, to mar its aspects of transcendent beauty, nor to impede the progress of the physical or intellectual man, neither in himself nor in the race to which he belongs. Hence, a people, upon whatever plane they may be found in the ascending scale of humanity, whom neither the divinity within them nor the inspirations of divine and beautiful nature around them can impel to virtuous action and progress onward and upward, should be subjected to a just and humane servitude and tutelage to the superior race until they shall be able to appreciate the benefits and advantages of civilization."

Here, expressed in studied terms of hypocrisy, is the whole theory of human bondage—the right of the strong, because they are strong, to despoil and enslave the weak, because they are weak! The languages of earth can add nothing to the cowardly and loathsome baseness of the doctrine, as thus announced. It is the robber's creed, sought to be nationalized, and would push back the hand on the dial plate of our civilization to the darkest periods of human history. It must be admitted, however, that it furnishes a fitting "corner-stone" for the government of a rebellion, every fibre of whose body and every throb of whose soul is born of the traitorous ambition and slave-pen inspirations of the South.

To these detestable tenets is added that other pernicious political theory of State sovereignty, with its necessary fruit, the monstrous doctrine of secession—a doctrine which, in asserting that in our federative system a part is greater than the whole, would compel the General Government, like a Japanese slave, to commit hari-kari whenever a faithless or insolent State should command it to do so.

Thus, the ritual, after reciting that the States of the Union are "free, independent, and sovereign," proceeds as follows:

"The government designated 'The United States of America' has no *sovereignty*, because that is an attribute with which the people, in their several and distinct political organizations, are endowed and is inalienable. It was constituted by the terms of the *compact*, by all the States, through the express will of the people thereof, respectively—a common agent, to use and exercise certain named, specified, defined, and limited powers which are inherent of the sovereignties within those States. It is permitted, so far as regards its status and relations, as common agent in the exercise of the powers carefully and jealously delegated to it, to call itself 'supreme,' but not '*sovereign*.' In accordance with the principles upon which is founded the *American theory*, government can exercise only delegated power; hence, if those who shall have been chosen to administer the government shall assume to exercise powers not delegated, they should be regarded and treated as *usurpers*. The reference to 'inherent power,' 'war power,' or 'military necessity,' on the part of the functionary for the sanction of an arbitrary exercise of power by him, we will not accept in palliation or excuse."

To this is added, as a corollary, "it is incompatible with the history and nature of our system of government that Federal authority should coerce by arms a sovereign State."

The declaration of principles, however, does not stop here, but proceeds one step further, as follows:

"Whenever the chosen officers or delegates shall fail or

refuse to administer the Government in strict accordance with the letter of the accepted Constitution, it is the inherent right and the solemn and imperative duty of the people to *resist* the functionaries, and, if need be, to *expel them by force of arms!* Such resistance is not revolution, but is solely the assertion of right—the exercise of all the noble attributes which impart honor and dignity to manhood."

To the same effect, though in a milder tone, is the platform of the order in Indiana, put forth by the Grand Council at their meeting in February last, which declares that "the right to alter or *abolish* their government, whenever it fails to secure the blessings of liberty, is one of the inalienable rights of the people that can never be surrendered."

Such, then, are the principles which the new member swears to observe and abide by in his obligation, set forth in the ritual, where he says: "I do solemnly promise that I will ever cherish in my heart of hearts the sublime creed of the E. K., (Excellent Knights,) and will, so far as in me lies, illustrate the same in my intercourse with men, and will defend the principles thereof, if need be, with my life, whensoever assailed, in my own country first of all. I do further solemnly declare that I will never take up arms in behalf of any government which does not acknowledge the sole authority or power to be the will of the governed."

The following extracts from the ritual may also be quoted as illustrating the principle of the right of revolution and resistance to constituted authority insisted upon by the Order:

"Our swords shall be unsheathed whenever the great principles which we aim to inculcate and have sworn to maintain and defend are assailed."

Again: "I do solemnly promise, that whensoever the principles which our Order inculcates shall be assailed in my own State or country, I will defend these principles with my sword and my life, in whatsoever capacity may be assigned me by the competent authority of our Order."

And further: "I do promise that I will, at all times, if need be, take up arms in the cause of the oppressed—in my own country first of all—against any power or government usurped, which may be found in arms and waging war against a people or peoples who are endeavoring to establish, or have inaugurated, a government for themselves of their own free choice."

Moreover, it is to be noted that all the addresses and speeches of its leaders breathe the same principle, of the right of forcible resistance to the Government, as one of the tenets of the Order.

Thus P. C. Wright, Supreme Commander, in his general address of December, 1863, after urging that "the spirit of the fathers may animate the free minds, the brave hearts, and still unshackled limbs of the *true democracy*," (meaning the members of the Order,) adds as follows: "To be prepared for the crisis now approaching, we must catch from afar the earliest and faintest breathings of the spirit of the storm; to be successful when the storm comes, we must be watchful, patient, brave, confident, organized, *armed*."

Thus, too, Dodd, Grand Commander of the Order in Indiana, quoting, in his address of February last, the views of his chief, Vallandigham, and adopting them as his own, says:

"He (Vallandigham) judges that the Washington power will not yield up its power until it is taken from them by an indignant people *by force of arms*."

Such, then, are the written principles of the Order in which the neophyte is instructed, and which he is sworn to cherish and observe as his rule of action, when, with arms placed in his hands, he is called upon to engage in the overthrow of his Government. This declaration—first, of the absolute right of slavery; second, of State sovereignty and the right of secession; third, of the right of armed resistance to constituted authority on the part of the disaffected and the disloyal, whenever their ambition may prompt them to revolution—is but an assertion of that abominable theory which, from its first enunciation, served as a pretext for conspiracy after conspiracy against the Government on the part of Southern traitors, until their detestable plotting culminated in open rebellion and bloody civil war. What more appropriate password, therefore, to be communicated to the new member upon his first admission to the secrets of the Order could have been conceived than that which was actually adopted—"Calhoun!"—a man who, baffled in his lust for power, with gnashing teeth turned upon the Government that had lifted him to its highest honors, and upon the country that had borne him, and down to the very close of his fevered life labored incessantly to scatter far and wide the seeds of that poison of death now upon our lips. The thorns which now pierce and tear us are of the tree he planted.

VII.—ITS SPECIFIC PURPOSES AND OPERATIONS.

From the principles of the Order, as thus set forth, its general purpose of co-operating with the rebellion may readily be inferred, and, in fact, those principles could logically lead to no other result. This general purpose, indeed, is distinctly set forth in the personal statements and confessions of its members, and particularly of its prominent officers, who have been induced to make disclosures to the Government. Among the most significant of these confessions are those already alluded to, of Hunt, Dunn, and Smith, the heads of the order in Missouri. The latter, whose statement is full and explicit, says: "At the time I joined the Order I understood that its object was to aid and assist the Confederate Government, and endeavor to restore the Union as it was prior to this rebellion." He adds: "The Order is hostile in every respect to the General Government, and friendly to the so-called Confederate Government. It is exclusively made up of disloyal persons—of all Democrats who are desirous of securing the independence of the Confederate States with a view of restoring the Union as it was."

It would be idle to comment on such gibberish as the statement that "the independence of the Confederate States" was to be used as the means of restoring "the Union as it was;" and yet, under the manipulations of these traitorous jugglers, doubtless the brains of many have been so far muddled as to accept this shameless declaration as true.

But proceeding to the *specific* purposes of the Order, which its leaders have had in view from the beginning, and which, as will be seen, it has been able, in many cases, to carry out with very considerable success, the following are found to be most pointedly presented by the testimony:

1. *Aiding Soldiers to Desert and Harboring and Protecting Deserters.*—Early in its history the Order essayed to undermine such portions of the army as were exposed to its insidious approaches. Agents were sent by the K. G. C. into the camps to introduce the Order among the soldiers, and those who became members were instructed to induce as many of their companions as possible to desert, and for this purpose the latter were furnished by the Order with money and citizens' clothing. Soldiers who hesitated at desertion, but desired to leave the army, were introduced to lawyers who engaged to furnish them some *quasi* legal pretext for so doing, and a certain attorney of Indianapolis, named Walpole, who was particularly conspicuous in furnishing facilities of this character to soldiers who applied to him, has boasted that he has thus aided five hundred enlisted men to escape from their contracts. Through the schemes of the Order in Indiana whole companies were broken up—a large detachment or a battery company, for instance, deserting on one occasion to the enemy with two of its guns—and the camps were imbued with a spirit of discontent and dissatisfaction with the service. Some estimate of the success of these efforts may be derived from the report of the Adjutant General of Indiana, of January, in 1863, setting forth that the number of deserters and absentees returned to the army through the post of Indianapolis alone, during the month of December, 1862, was nearly two thousand six hundred.

As soon as arrests of these deserters began to be generally made, writs of *habeas corpus* were issued in their cases by disloyal judges, and a considerable number were discharged thereon. In one instance in Indiana, where an officer in charge of a deserter properly refused to obey the writ, after it had been suspended in such cases by the President, his attachment for contempt was ordered by the chief justice of the State, who declared that "the streets of Indianapolis might run with blood, but that he would enforce his authority against the President's order." On another occasion certain United States officers who had made the arrests of deserters in Illinois were themselves arrested for kidnapping, and held to trial by a disloyal judge, who at the same time discharged the deserters, though acknowledging them to be such.

Soldiers, upon deserting, were assured of immunity from punishment and protection on the part of the Order, and were instructed to bring away with them their arms, and, if mounted, their horses. Details sent to arrest them by the military authorities were in several cases forcibly resisted, and, where not unusually strong in numbers, were driven back by large bodies of men, subsequently generally ascertained to be members of the Order. Where arrests were effected, our troops were openly attacked and fired upon on their return. Instances of such attacks occurring in Morgan and Rush counties, Indiana, are especially noticed by General Carrington. In the case of the outbreak in Morgan county, J. S. Bingham, editor of the Indianapolis *Sentinel*, a member or friend of the Order, sought to forward to the disloyal newspapers of the West false and inflammatory telegraphic dispatches in regard to the affair, to the effect that cavalry had been sent to arrest all the Democrats in the county, that they had committed gross outrages, and that several citizens had been shot; and adding "ten thousand soldiers cannot hold the men arrested this night. Civil war and bloodshed are inevitable." The assertions in this despatch were entirely false, and may serve to illustrate the fact heretofore noted, that a studious misrepresentation of the acts of the Government and its officers is a part of the prescribed duty of members of the Order. It is proper to mention that seven of the party in Morgan county who made the attack upon our troops were convicted of their offence by a State court. Upon their trial it was proved that the party was composed of members of the K. G. C.

One of the most pointed instances of protection afforded to deserters occurred in a case in Indiana, where seventeen intrenched themselves in a log cabin with a ditch and palisade, and were furnished with provisions and sustained in their defence against our military authorities for a considerable period by the Order or its friends.

2. *Discouraging Enlistments and Resisting the Draft.*—It is especially inculcated by the Order to oppose the re-enforcement of our armies, either by volunteers or drafted men. In 1862 the Knights of the Golden Circle organized generally to resist the draft in the Western States, and were strong enough in certain localities to greatly embarrass the Government. In this year and early in 1863 a number of enrolling officers were shot in Indiana and Illinois. In Blackford county, Indiana, an attack was made upon the court-house, and the books connected with the draft were destroyed. In several counties of the State a considerable military force was required for the protection of the United States officials, and a large number of arrests were made, including that of one Reynolds, an ex-Senator of the Legislature, for publicly urging upon the populace to resist the conscription—an offence of the same character, in fact, as that upon which Vallandigham was apprehended in Ohio. These outbreaks were no doubt, in most cases, incited by the Order and engaged in by its members. In Indiana nearly 200 persons were indicted for conspiracy against the Government, resisting the draft, &c., and about sixty of these were convicted.

Where members of the Order were forced into the army by the draft, they were instructed, in case they were prevented from presently escaping, and were obliged to go to the field, to use their arms against their fellow-soldiers rather than the enemy, or if possible to desert to the enemy, by whom, through the signs of the Order, they would be recognized and received as friends. Whenever a member volunteered in the army he was at once expelled from the Order.

3. *Circulation of Disloyal and Treasonable Publications.*—The Order, especially in Missouri, has secretly circulated throughout the country a great quantity of treasonable publications, as a means of extending its own power and influence, as well as of giving encouragement to the disloyal and inciting them to treason. Of these, some of the principal are the following: "Pollard's Southern History of the War," "Official Reports of the Confederate Government," "Life of Stonewall Jackson," Pamphlets containing articles from the "Metropolitan Record," "Abraham Africanus, or Mysteries of the White House," "The Lincoln Catechism, or a Guide to the Presidential Election of 1864," "Indestructible Organics," by Tirga. These publications have generally been procured by formal requisitions drawn upon the grand commander by leading members in the interior of a State. One of these requisitions, dated June 10th last, and drawn by a local secretary of the Order at Gentryville, Missouri, is exhibited in the testimony. It contains a column of the initials of subscribers, opposite whose names are entered the number of disloyal publications to be furnished, the particular book or books, &c., required being indicated by fictitious titles.

4. *Communicating with, and Giving Intelligence to, the Enemy.*—Smith, Grand Secretary of the Order in Missouri, says, in his confession: "Rebel spies, mail-carriers, and emissaries have been carfully protected by this Order ever since I have been a member." It is shown in the testimony to be customary in the rebel service to employ members of the Order as spies, under the guise of soldiers furnished with furloughs to visit their homes within our lines. On coming within the territory occupied by our forces, they are harbored and supplied with information by the Order. Another class of spies claim to be deserters from the enemy, and at once seek an opportunity to take the oath of allegiance, which, however, though voluntarily taken, they claim to be administered while they are under a species of duress, and, therefore, not to be binding. Upon swearing allegiance to the Government, the pretended deserter engages, with the assistance of the Order, in collecting contraband goods or procuring intelligence to be conveyed to the enemy, or in some other treasonable enterprise. In his official report of June 12th last, Colonel Sanderson remarks: "This department is filled with rebel spies, all of whom belong to the Order."

In Missouri regular mail communication was for a long period maintained through the agency of the Order from St. Louis to Price's army, by means of which private letters, as well as official despatches between him and the Grand Commander of Missouri were regularly transmitted. The mail-carriers started from a point on the Pacific railroad, near Kirkwood Station, about fourteen miles from St. Louis, and, travelling only by night, proceeded (to quote from Colonel Sanderson's report) to "Mattox Mills, on the Maramee river, thence past Mineral Point to Webster, thence to a point fifteen miles below Van Buren, where they crossed the Black river, and thence to the rebel lines." It is, probably, also by this route that the secret correspondence, stated by the witness Pitman to have been constantly kept up between Price and Vallandigham, the heads of the Order at the North and South, respectively, was successfully maintained.

A similar communication has been continuously held with the enemy from Louisville, Kentucky. A considerable number of women in that State, many of them of high position in rebel society, and some of them outwardly professing to be loyal, were discovered to have been actively engaged in receiving and forwarding mails, with the assistance of the Order and as its instruments. Two of the most notorious and successful of these, Mrs. Woods and Miss Cassell, have been apprehended and imprisoned.

By means of this correspondence with the enemy the members of the Order were promptly apprized of all raids to be made by the forces of the former, and were able to hold themselves prepared to render aid and comfort to the raiders. To show how efficient for this purpose was the system thus established, it is to be added that our military authorities have, in a number of cases, been informed through members of the Order employed in the interest of the Government, of impending raids and important army movements of the rebels, not only days, but sometimes weeks, sooner than the same intelligence could have reached them through the ordinary channels.

On the other hand, the system of *espionage* kept up by the Order, for the purpose of obtaining information of the movements of our own forces, &c., to be imparted to the enemy, seems to have been as perfect as it was secret. The Grand Secretary of the Order in Missouri states, in his confession: "One of the especial objects of this Order was to place members in steamboats, ferry-boats, telegraph offices, express offices, department headquarters, provost marshal's office, and, in fact, in every position where they could do valuable service:" and he proceeds to specify certain members who, at the date of his confession, (August 2d last,) were employed at the express and telegraph offices in St Louis.

5. *Aiding the Enemy, by recruiting for them, or assisting them to recruit, within our lines.*—This has also been extensively carried on by members of the Order, particularly in Kentucky and Missouri. It is estimated that 2,000 men were sent South from Louisville alone during a few weeks in April and May, 1864. The Order and its friends at that city have a permanent fund, to which there are many subscribers, for the purpose of fitting out with pistols, clothing, money, &c., men desiring to join the Southern service; and, in the lodges of the Order in St. Louis and Northern Missouri, money has often been raised to purchase horses, arms, and equipments for soldiers about to be forwarded to the Southern army. In the latter State, parties empowered by Price, or by Grand Commander Hunt as his representative, to recruit for the rebel service, were nominally authorized to "*locate lands*," as it was expressed, and in their reports, which were formally made, the number of acres, &c., located represented the number of men recruited. At Louisville, those desiring to join the Southern forces were kept hidden, and supplied with food and lodging until a convenient occasion was presented for their transportation South. They were then collected, and conducted at night to a safe rendezvous of the Order, whence they were forwarded to their destination, in some cases stealing horses from the United States corrals on their way. While awaiting an occasion to be sent South, the men, to avoid the suspicion which might be excited by their being seen together in any considerable number, were often employed on farms in the vicinity of Louisville, and the farm of one Grant, in that neighborhood, (at whose house, also, meetings of the Order were held,) is indicated in the testimony as one of the localities where such recruits were rendezvoused and employed.

The same facilities which were afforded to recruits for the Southern army were also furnished by the Order to persons desiring to proceed beyond our lines for any illegal purpose. By these Louisville was generally preferred as a point of departure, and, on the Mississippi river, a particular steamer, the Graham, was selected as the safest conveyance.

6. *Furnishing the Rebels with Arms, Ammunition, &c.*—In this, too, the Order, and especially its female members and allies, has been sedulously engaged. The rebel women of Louisville and Kentucky are represented as having rendered the most valuable aid to the Southern army, by transporting large quantities of percussion caps, powder, &c., concealed upon their persons, to some convenient locality near the lines, whence they could be readily conveyed to those for whom they were intended. It is estimated

that at Louisville, up to May 1st last, the sum of $17,000 had been invested by the Order in ammunition and arms, to be forwarded principally in this manner to the rebels. In St. Louis several firms, who are well known to the Government, the principal of which is Beauvais & Co., have been engaged in supplying arms and ammunition to members of the Order, to be conveyed to their Southern allies. Mary Ann Pitman, a reliable witness, and a member of the O. A. K., who will hereafter be specially alluded to, states in her testimony that she visited Beauvais & Co. three times, and procured from them on each occasion about $80 worth of caps, besides a number of pistols and cartridges, which she carried in person to Forrest's command, as well as a much larger quantity of similar articles which she caused to be forwarded by other agents. The guerillas in Missouri also received arms from St. Louis, and one Douglas, one of the most active conspirators of the O. A. K. in Missouri, and a special emissary of Price, was arrested while in the act of transporting a box of forty revolvers by railroad to a guerilla camp in the interior of the State. Medical stores in large quantities were likewise, by the aid of the Order, furnished to the enemy, and a "young doctor" named Moore, said to be now a medical inspector in the rebel army, is mentioned as having "made $75,000 by smuggling medicines"—principally from Louisville—through the lines of our army. Supplies were, in some cases, conveyed to the enemy through the medium of professed loyalists, who, having received permits for that purpose from the United States military authorities, would forward their goods, as if for ordinary purposes of trade, to a certain point near the rebel lines, where, by the connivance of the owners, the enemy would be enabled to seize them.

7. *Co-operating with the Enemy in Raids and Invasions.*—While it is clear that the Order has given aid, both directly and indirectly, to the forces of the rebels, and to guerilla bands, when engaged in making incursions into the border States, yet because, on the one hand, of the constant restraint upon its action exercised by our military authorities, and, on the other, of the general success of our armies in the field over those of the enemy, their allies at the North have never thus far been able to carry out their grand plan of a general armed rising of the Order, and its co-operation on an extended scale with the Southern forces. This plan has been two-fold, and consisted, first, of a rising of the Order in Missouri, aided by a strong detachment from Illinois, and a co-operation with a rebel army under Price; second, of a similar rising in Indiana, Ohio, and Kentucky, and a co-operation with a force under Breckinridge, Buckner, Morgan, or some other rebel commander, who was to invade the latter State. In *this* case the Order was first to cut the railroads and telegraph wires, so that intelligence of the movement might not be sent abroad and the transportation of Federal troops might be delayed, and then to seize upon the arsenals at Indianapolis, Columbus, Springfield, Louisville, and Frankfort, and, furnishing such of their number as were without arms, to kill or make prisoners of department, district, and post commanders, release the rebel prisoners at Rock Island, and at Camps Morton, Douglas, and Chase, and thereupon join the Southern army at Louisville or some other point in Kentucky, which State was to be permanently occupied by the combined force. At the period of the movement it was also proposed that an attack should be made upon Chicago by means of steam-tugs mounted with cannon. A similar course was to be taken in Missouri, and was to result in the permanent occupation of that State.

This scheme has long occupied the minds of members of the Order, and has been continually discussed by them in their lodges. A rising somewhat of the character described was intended to have taken place in the spring of this year, simultaneously with an expected advance of the army of Lee upon Washington; but the plans of the enemy having been anticipated by the movements of our own generals, the rising of the conspirators was necessarily postponed. Again, a general movement of the Southern forces was expected to occur about July 4, and with this the Order was to co-operate. A speech to be made by Vallandigham at the Chicago Convention was, it is said, to be the signal for the rising; but the postponement of the convention, as well as the failure of the rebel armies to engage in the anticipated movement, again operated to disturb the programme of the Order. During the summer, however, the grand plan of action above set forth has been more than ever discussed throughout the Order, and its success most confidently predicted, while at the same time an extensive organization and preparation for carrying the conspiracy into effect have been actively going on. But up to this time, notwithstanding the late raids of the enemy in Kentucky, and the invasion of Missouri by Price, no such general action on the part of the Order as was contemplated has taken place—a result, in great part, owing to the activity of our military authorities in strengthening the detachments at the prisons, arsenals, &c., and in causing the arrest of the leading conspirators in the several States, and especially in the seizure of large quantities of arms which had been shipped for the use of the Order in their intended outbreak. It was doubtless on account of these precautions that the day last appointed for the rising of the Order in Indiana and Kentucky (August 16) passed by with but slight disorder.

It is, however, the inability of the public enemy, in the now declining days of the rebellion, to initiate the desired movements which has prevented the Order from engaging in open warfare; and it has lately been seriously considered in their councils whether they should not proceed with their revolt, relying alone upon the guerilla bands of Syphert, Jesse, and others, for support and assistance.

With these guerillas the Order has always most readily acted along the border, and in cases of capture by the Union forces of Northern members of the Order engaged in co-operating with them, the guerillas have frequently retaliated by seizing prominent Union citizens and holding them as hostages for the release of their allies. At other times our Government has been officially notified by the rebel authorities that if the members of the Order captured were not treated by us as ordinary prisoners of war, retaliation would be resorted to.

An atrocious plan of concert between members of the Order in Indiana and certain guerilla bands in Kentucky, agreed upon last spring, may be here remarked upon. Some 2,500 or 3,000 guerillas were to be thrown around into the border counties, and were to assume the character of refugees seeking employment. Being armed, they were secretly to destroy Government property wherever practicable, and subsequently to control the elections by force, prevent enlistments, aid deserters, and stir up strife between the civil and military authorities.

A singular feature of the raids of the enemy remains only to be adverted to, viz: that the officers conducting these raids are furnished by the rebel Government with quantities of United States Treasury notes for use within our lines, and that these are probably most frequently procured through the agency of members of the Order.

Mary Ann Pitman states that Forrest, of the rebel army, at one time exhibited to her a letter to himself from a prominent rebel sympathizer and member of the Order in Washington, D. C., in which it was set forth that the sum of $25,000 in "greenbacks" had actually been forwarded by him to the rebel Government at Richmond.

8. *Destruction of Government Property.*—There is no doubt that large quantities of Government property have been burned or otherwise destroyed by the agency of the Order in different localities. At Louisville, in the case of the steamer Taylor, and on the Mississippi river, steamers belonging to the United States have been burned at the wharves, and generally when loaded with Government stores. Shortly before the arrest of Bowles, the senior of the major generals of the Order in Indiana, he had been engaged in the preparation of "Greek Fire," which it was supposed would be found serviceable in the destruction of public property. It was generally understood in the councils of the Order in the State of Kentucky, that they were to be compensated for such destruction by the rebel Government, by receiving a commission of ten per cent. of the value of the property so destroyed, and that this value was to be derived from the estimate of the loss made in each case by Northern newspapers.

9. *Destruction of Private Property and Persecution of Loyal Men.*—It is reported by General Carrington that the full development of the Order in Indiana was followed by "a state of terrorism" among the Union residents of "portions of Brown, Morgan, Johnson, Rush, Clay, Sullivan, Bartholomew, Hendricks, and other counties" in that State; that from some localities individuals were driven away altogether; that in others their barns, hay, and wheat-ricks were burned; and that many persons, under the general insecurity of life and property, sold their effects at a sacrifice and removed to other places. At one time in Brown county, the members of the Order openly threatened the lives of all "Abolitionists" who refused to sign a peace memorial which they had prepared and addressed to Congress. In Missouri, also, similar outrages committed upon the property of loyal citizens are attributable in a great degree to the secret Order.

Here the outbreak of the miners in the coal districts of eastern Pennsylvania, in the autumn of last year, may be appropriately referred to. It was fully shown in the testimony adduced, upon the trials of these insurgents, who were guilty of the destruction of property and numerous acts of violence, as well as murder, that they were generally members of a secret treasonable association, similar in all respects to the K. G. C., at the meetings of which they were incited to the commission of the crimes for which they were tried and convicted.

10. *Assassination and Murder.*—After what has been disclosed in regard to this infamous league of traitors and ruffians, it will not be a matter of surprise to learn that the cold-blooded assassination of Union citizens and soldiers

has been included in their devilish scheme of operations. Green B. Smith states in his confession that "the secret assassination of United States officers, soldiers, and Government employés has been discussed in the councils of the Order and recommended." It is also shown in the course of the testimony that at a large meeting of the Order in St. Louis, in May or June last, it was proposed to form a secret police of members for the purpose of patrolling the streets of that city at night and killing every detective and soldier that could be readily disposed of; that this proposition was coolly considered, and finally rejected, not because of its fiendish character—no voice being raised against its criminality—but because only it was deemed premature. At Louisville, in June last, a similar scheme was discussed among the Order for the waylaying and butchering of negro soldiers in the streets at night; and in the same month a party of its members in that city was actually organized for the purpose of throwing off the track of the Nashville railroad a train of colored troops, and seizing the opportunity to take the lives of as many as possible. Again, in July, the assassination of an obnoxious provost marshal, by betraying him into the hands of guerillas, was designed by members in the interior of Kentucky. Further, at a meeting of the Grand Council of Indiana at Indianapolis on June 14 last, the murder of one Coffin, a Government detective, who, as it was supposed, had betrayed the Order, was deliberately discussed and unanimously determined upon. This fact is stated by Stidger in his report to General Carrington of June 17 last, and is more fully set forth in his testimony upon the trial of Dodd. He deposes that at the meeting in question, Dodd himself volunteered to go to Hamilton, Ohio, where Coffin was expected to be found, and there "dispose of the latter." He adds that prior to the meeting, he himself conveyed from Judge Bullit, at Louisville, to Bowles and Dodd, at Indianapolis, special instructions to have Coffin "put out of the way"—"murdered"—"at all hazards."

The opinion is expressed by Colonel Sanderson, under date of June 12 last, that "the recent numerous cold-blooded assassinations of military officers and unconditional Union men throughout the military district of North Missouri, especially along the western border," is to be ascribed to the agency of the Order. The witness Pitman represents that it is "a part of the obligation or understanding of the Order" to kill officers and soldiers "*whenever it can be done by stealth*," as well as loyal citizens when considered important or influential persons; and she adds, that while at Memphis, during the past summer, she *knew* that men on picket were secretly killed by members of the Order approaching them in disguise.

In this connexion may be recalled the wholesale assassination of Union soldiers by members of the Order and their confederates at Charleston, Illinois, in March last, in regard to which, as a startling episode of the rebellion, a full report was addressed from this office to the President, under date of July 26 last. This concerted murderous assault upon a scattered body of men, mostly unarmed—apparently designed for the mere purpose of destroying as many lives of Union soldiers as possible—is a forcible illustration of the utter malignity and depravity which characterize the members of this Order in their zeal to commend themselves as allies to their fellow-conspirators at the South.

11. *Establishment of a Northwestern Confederacy.*—In concluding this review of some of the principal specific purposes of the Order, it remains only to remark upon a further design of many of its leading members, the accomplishment of which they are represented as having deeply at heart. Hating New England, and jealous of her influence and resources, and claiming that the interests of the West and South, naturally connected as they are through the Mississippi valley, are identical, and actuated further by an intensely revolutionary spirit as well as an unbridled and unprincipled ambition, these men have made the establishment of a Western or Northwestern Confederacy, in alliance with the South, the grand aim and end of all their plotting and conspiring. It is with this steadily in prospect that they are constantly seeking to produce discontent, disorganization, and civil disorder at the North. With this in view, they gloat over every reverse of the armies of the Union, and desire that the rebellion shall be protracted until the resources of the Government shall be exhausted, its strength paralyzed, its currency hopelessly depreciated, and confidence everywhere destroyed. Then, from the anarchy which, under their scheme, is to ensue, the new Confederacy is to arise, which is either to unite itself with that of the South, or to form therewith a close and permanent alliance. Futile and extravagant as this scheme may appear, it is yet the settled purpose of many leading spirits of the secret conspiracy, and is their favorite subject of thought and discussion. Not only is this scheme deliberated upon in the lodges of the Order, but it is openly proclaimed. Members of the Indiana Legislature, even, have publicly announced it, and avowed that they will take their own State out of the Union, and recognize the independence of the South. A citizen captured by a guerilla band in Kentucky last summer, records the fact that the establishment of a new confederacy as the deliberate purpose of the Western people was boastfully asserted by these outlaws, who also assured their prisoner that in the event of such establishment there would be "a greater rebellion than ever!"

Lastly, it is claimed that the new confederacy is already organized; that it has a "provisional government," officers, departments, bureaus, &c., in secret operation. No comment is necessary to be made upon this treason, not now contemplated for the first time in our history. Suggested by the present rebellion, it is the logical consequence of the ardent and utter sympathy therewith which is the life and inspiration of the secret Order.

VIII. THE WITNESSES AND THEIR TESTIMONY.

The facts detailed in the present report have been derived from a great variety of dissimilar sources, but all the witnesses, however different their situations, concur so pointedly in their testimony, that the evidence which has thus been furnished must be accepted as of an entirely satisfactory character.

The principal witnesses may be classified as follows:

1. Shrewd, intelligent men, employed as detectives, and with a peculiar talent for their calling, who have gradually gained the confidence of leading members of the Order, and in some cases have been admitted to its temples and been initiated into one or more of the degrees. The most remarkable of these is Stidger, formerly a private soldier in our army, who, by the use of an uncommon address, though at great personal risk, succeeded in establishing such intimate relations with Bowles, Builit, Dodd, and other leaders of the Order in Indiana and Kentucky, as to be appointed grand secretary for the latter State, a position the most favorable for obtaining information of the plans of these traitors and warning the Government of their intentions. It is to the rare fidelity of this man, who has also been the principal witness upon the trial of Dodd, that the Government has been chiefly indebted for the exposure of the designs of the conspirators in the two States named.

2. Rebel officers and soldiers voluntarily or involuntarily making disclosures to our military authorities. The most valuable witnesses of this class are prisoners of war, who, actuated by laudable motives, have of their own accord furnished a large amount of information in regard to the Order, especially as it exists in the South, and of the relations of its members with those of the Northern section. Among these, also, are soldiers at our prison camps, who, without designing it, have made known to our officials, by the use of the signs, &c., of the Order, that they were members.

3. Scouts employed to travel through the interior of the border States, and also within or in the neighborhood of the enemy's lines. The fact that some of these were left entirely ignorant of the existence of the Order, upon being so employed, attaches an increased value to their discoveries in regard to its operations.

4. Citizen prisoners, to whom, while in confinement, disclosures were made relative to the existence, extent, and character of the Order by fellow-prisoners who were leading members, and who in some instances, upon becoming intimate with the witness, initiated him into one of the degrees.

5. Members of the Order, who, upon a full acquaintance with its principles, have been appalled by its infamous designs, and have voluntarily abandoned it, freely making known their experience to our military authorities. In this class may be placed the female witness, Mary Ann Pitman, who, though in arrest at the period of her disclosures, was yet induced to make them for the reason that, as she says, "at the last meeting which I attended they passed an order which I consider as utterly atrocious and barbarous; so I told them I would have nothing more to do with them." This woman was attached to the command of the rebel Forrest, as an officer under the name of "Lieutenant Rawley;" but, because her sex afforded her unusual facilities for crossing our lines, she was often employed in the execution of important commissions within our territory, and, as a member of the Order, was made extensively acquainted with other members, both of the Northern and Southern sections. Her testimony is thus peculiarly valuable, and, being a person of unusual intelligence and force of character, her statements are succinct, pointed, and emphatic. They are also especially useful as fully corroborating those of other witnesses regarded as most trustworthy.

6. Officers of the Order of high rank, who have been prompted to present confessions, more or less detailed, in regard to the Order, and their connexion with it. The principals of these are Hunt, Dunn, and Smith, grand commander, deputy grand commander, and grand secretary of the Order in Missouri, to whose statements frequent reference has been made. These confessions, though in some

degree guarded and disingenuous, have furnished to the Government much important information as to the operations of the Order, especially in Missouri, the affiliation of its leaders with Price, &c. It is to be noted that Dunn makes the statement in common with other witnesses that, in entering the Order, he was quite ignorant of its ultimate purposes. He says: "I did not become a member understandingly; the initiatory step was taken in the dark, without reflection and without knowledge."

7. Deserters from our army, who, upon being apprehended, confessed that they had been induced and assisted to desert by members of the Order. It was, indeed, principally from these confessions that the existence of the secret treasonable organization of the K. G. C. was first discovered in Indiana, in the year 1862.

8. Writers of anonymous communications, addressed to heads of departments or provost marshals, disclosing facts corroborative of other more important statements.

9. The witnesses before the grand jury at Indianapolis, in 1863, when the Order was formally presented as a treasonable organization, and those whose testimony has been recently introduced upon the trial of Dodd.

It need only be added that a most satisfactory test of the credibility and weight of much of the evidence which has been furnished is afforded by the printed testimony in regard to the character and intention of the Order, which is found in its national and State constitutions and its ritual. Indeed, the statements of the various witnesses are but presentations of the logical and inevitable consequences and results of the principles therein set forth.

In concluding this review, it remains only to state that a constant reference has been made to the elaborate official reports, in regard to the Order, of Brigadier General Carrington, commanding District of Indiana, and of Colonel Sanderson, Provost Marshal General of the Department of Missouri. The great mass of the testimony upon the subject of this conspiracy has been furnished by these officers; the latter acting under the orders of Major General Rosecrans, and the former co-operating, under the instructions of the Secretary of War, with Major General Burbridge, commanding District of Kentucky, as well as with Governor Morton, of Indiana, who, though at one time greatly embarrassed, by a Legislature strongly tainted with disloyalty, in his efforts to repress this domestic enemy, has at last seen his State relieved from the danger of a civil war.

But, although the treason of the Order has been thoroughly exposed, and although its capacity for fatal mischief has, by means of the arrest of its leaders, the seizure of its arms, and the other vigorous means which have been pursued, been seriously impaired, it is still busied with its plottings against the Government, and with its perfidious designs in aid of the Southern rebellion. It is reported to have recently adopted new signs and pass-words, and its members assert that foul means will be used to prevent the success of the Administration at the coming election, and threaten an extended revolt in the event of the re-election of President Lincoln.

In the presence of the rebellion and of this secret Order—which is but its echo and faithful ally—we cannot but be amazed at the utter and wide-spread profligacy, personal and political, which these movements against the Government disclose. The guilty men engaged in them, after casting aside their allegiance, seem to have trodden under foot every sentiment of honor and every restraint of law, human and divine. Judea produced but one Judas Iscariot, and Rome, from the sinks of her demoralization, produced but one Cataline; and yet, as events prove, there has arisen together in our land an entire brood of such traitors, all animated by the same parricidal spirit, and all struggling with the same relentless malignity for the dismemberment of our Union. Of this extraordinary phenomenon—not paralleled, it is believed, in the world's history—there can be but one explanation, and all these blackened and fetid streams of crime may well be traced to the same common fountain. So fiercely intolerant and imperious was the temper engendered by Slavery, that when the Southern people, after having controlled the national councils for half a century, were beaten at an election, their leaders turned upon the Government with the insolent fury with which they would have drawn their revolvers on a rebellious slave in one of their negro quarters; and they have continued since to prosecute their warfare, amid all the barbarisms and atrocities naturally and necessarily inspired by the infernal institution in whose interests they are sacrificing alike themselves and their country. Many of these conspirators, as is well known, were fed, clothed, and educated at the expense of the nation, and were loaded with its honors, at the very moment they struck at its life with the horrible criminality of a son stabbing the bosom of his own mother while impressing kisses on his cheeks. The leaders of the traitors in the loyal States, who so completely fraternize with these conspirators, and whose machinations are now unmasked, it is as clearly the duty of the Administration to prosecute and punish as it is its duty to subjugate the rebels who are openly in arms against the Government. In the performance of this duty, it is entitled to expect, and will doubtless receive, the zealous co-operation of true men everywhere, who, in crushing the truculent foe ambushed in the haunts of this secret Order, should rival in courage and faithfulness the soldiers who are so nobly sustaining our flag on the battle-fields of the South.

Respectfully submitted.

J. HOLT, *Judge Advocate General.*

Opinions on the Legal Tender Act.

Subjoined is a statement made up from the Philadelphia *North American*, of a case recently decided by Judges Grier and Cadwallader. on the legal tender act, voted upon as recorded on pages 357, 358:

The Philadelphia and Reading Railroad Company *vs.* Charles Morrison *et al.*, executors, trustees, &c. This was a bill in equity, filed by the complainants to compel the defendants to accept the principal sum of certain ground rents and the arrears thereof in notes issued by the Government of the United States, and made lawful money and a "legal tender in payment of all debts," in payment and extinguishment of the said ground rents and all arrears thereof, and that it be decreed that cotemporaneously with said payment they shall execute a valid and sufficient deed of extinguishment, lawfully releasing, discharging and extinguishing the said rents. And further, that in the meantime the defendants be restrained from attempting the recovery of any alleged arrears of rent by suit at law, or by distress, and from entering upon the premises for non-payment.

The bill sets out the conveyance to the company of four certain lots of ground in this city, in fee, subject to the payment of yearly ground rents of $10,800, $1,200, $4,200, and $1,800 respectively, in "lawful money of the United States of America." That by certain other conveyances these ground rents became vested in James Morrison, of Berks county, England, who subsequently died, having first made his last will and testament, and thereby, among other things, appointed Charles Morrison, Alfred Morrison, John Dillon and Mary Ann Morrison his executors. The last three named were subsequently appointed trustees of all the ground rents secured upon lands in Pennsylvania, and have entered upon their duties.

The complainants aver that upon the 21st of December, 1863, they offered payment of the principal of said ground rents ($300,000) and all arrearages thereon, and tendered the money therefor in lawful money of the United States, viz: in notes issued by the Government of the United States, and declared to be lawful money and a legal tender in payment of all debts, (the covenants in said deeds provide for the extinguishment of the principal on the payment of lawful money in the United States,) to John Welsh and others, attorneys in fact for and substitutes in the place of William Smith, attorney in fact for the defendants, who denied for himself and others any authority to receive the same. That the defendants are aliens, and non-residents of the State of Pennsylvania, residing in England; and complainants are informed, and believe, that they deny their right to pay off and extinguish the said rents with the money aforesaid, and deny that they are bound to receive the same and execute the necessary deeds for the purpose of extinguishing the same, and are about to bring suit for the same, or to make distress upon the property on the premises for the collection of the rents as they become due and payable; which threatened proceedings the complainants, being ready and willing to pay, and having tendered payment as aforesaid, aver to be inequitable, and in respect thereto they need the interference of the Court. To that end this bill has been filed, praying as we have above set forth.

The case is one of great importance, not only on account of the large amount at stake, but also by reason of the great questions of constitutional law which are involved in it. It is the first time, too, we believe, that the question of the constitutionality of the act of Congress making these notes lawful money and a legal tender has been presented in a United States Court; and the great ability of the legal gentlemen conducting it will ensure a full and able discussion of it. Messrs. Charles Gibbons and St. Geo. T. Campbell appear for complainants, and Geo. M. Wharton and Geo. W. Biddle for the defendants.

Nov. 10—Judge Grier delivered this opinion:

Coined money, in modern times, forms but a very small portion of the current money used in commercial transactions. Paper money, representing credit, has long been used as current and lawful money. But no one could be compelled to accept the promise of a bank to pay money, instead of the coin itself. The notes of the Bank of the United States, issued under the authority of the Government, were current money and lawful money, because issued by such authority, but were never made a legal tender for the payment of debts.

A contract made in the United States for the payment of a certain number of dollars would be construed as meaning, not Prussian dollars or Spanish milled dollars, but lawful coin of the United States. The addition of the description "lawful money of the United States" is entirely superfluous, and does not change the nature of the obligation.

The statutes of Congress always take a distinction between lawful or current money and that which shall be a tender for payment of debts. Hence, we find when such is the intention, the language is, "and shall be a legal tender," &c.

Some coins of the Government are a legal tender below a certain amount, but not beyond. Thus, by act of 9th of February, 1793, after the expiration of three years all foreign coins except Spanish milled dollars shall cease to be a legal tender.

By act of April, 1806, "foreign gold and silver coins shall pass current as money, within the United States," and be a legal tender for the payment of all debts, &c., at the several respective rates following, &c.

Again, by act of 28th of June, 1834, "the following gold coins shall pass as current money, and be receivable in all payments by weight at the following rates," &c.

Hence we find that in all cases where other money than the coinage of the United States ordered to be received as current or lawful money, the statute carefully provides the rate and conditions under which they are made a legal tender for payment of debts. It is clear, therefore, that Congress has always observed the distinction between current and lawful money, which may be received in payment of debts, if the creditor sees fit to accept it, and that which he may be compelled to accept as a legal tender.

It is clear, also, that if Congress make any other thing than their own coin a legal tender, it may be used as such. Thus, in the act authorizing the National Banks, their notes are made a legal tender for certain debts due to the Government, for taxes, &c., but not for debts due from one citizen to another.

The treasury notes are made lawful or current money, "and a legal tender for debts," &c., as between individuals. As this is the first act in which this high prerogative of sovereignty has been exercised, it should be construed strictly. It is doubtful in policy and dangerous as a precedent.

The only question then is whether this case comes within the letter of the statute.

Is the money which *may be paid* to extinguish a ground rent within the category of the act?

Is it a debt? The owner of the land is not bound to pay it. The owner of the rent cannot compel him to pay it. There is no obligation as between the parties. It cannot be converted into an obligation by the election of one of the parties without the consent of the other. A man may execute his bond to me voluntarily, but unless I accept it he does not become my debtor.

These ground rents, in the nature of a rent service, are somewhat peculiar to Pennsylvania, and little known in other States. But the Supreme Court of the State has very clearly settled and determined their nature. The cases are too well known to the legal profession to need quotation. "A rent service (say the court in Bosler *vs.* Kuhn, 8 Watts & Sargeant, 186) is not a debt, and a covenant to pay it is not a covenant to pay *a debt*. The annual payments spring into existence and for the first time become debts when they are demandable."

I am of opinion, therefore, that the tender offered by the bill in this case is not authorized by the statute, and that the respondents cannot be compelled to extinguish their estate in the land by such a tender as that now made. The bill must, therefore, be dismissed.

The reporter of the *North American* adds:

Questions of a similar character have been discussed and variously decided in our State Courts.

In the case of Patterson *vs.* Blight, in the Common Pleas of this city, a bill similar to the above, to compel the extinguishment of ground rents payable in "lawful silver money of the United States," of a "peculiar fineness and weight," was dismissed by Judge Allison, who held that a ground rent was not a debt within the meaning of the act of Congress.

The case of Kroner *vs.* Colhoun, before the same court, was precisely similar to the Reading Railroad Company *vs.* Morrison, and the bill was also dismissed. The point was there discussed as to how far Congress had made their notes lawful money in all cases, and it was held that they were only made lawful money in payment of debts, and that therefore the condition precedent to the extinguishment by the payment in lawful money had not been performed by payment in these notes.

The case of Sailor *vs.* Martin, in the District Court, was an action to recover damages for the non-payment of certain ground rent arrears, payable in silver dollars, each dollar weighing seventeen penny weights and six grains, at the rate of the premium upon silver, and it was held that payment of such arrears in legal tender notes was sufficient.

In the case of Shollenberger *vs.* Brinton, before the Supreme Court at Nisi Prius, similar to Patterson *vs.* Blight, it was held by Judge Agnew that upon the tender by the ground tenant of the principal money of the ground rent, his election fixed it as a debt, and the prayer of the bill was granted.

It may be remarked here that Judge Grier, though the cases are not alike so far as the covenants in the ground rent deeds are concerned, arrives at the same conclusions, and in almost the same language as Judge Allison did in deciding the case of Patterson *vs.* Blight, the first that had then arisen under the act of Congress.

Relating to Peace.

MR. BENJAMIN TO MR. MASON.

On page 307 is found the closing statement made by Jefferson Davis to Col. Jacques and J. R. Gilmore, on the occasion of their visit to Richmond in August last.

August 25—Mr. Benjamin issued a circular from the State Department to James M. Mason, "Commissioner of the Continent, &c., &c., &c., Paris," giving the substance of the interview referred to, as understood by him. The important part is contained in the following summary of Mr. Davis's views:

The President came to my office at 9 o'clock in the evening, and Colonel Ould came a few moments later, with Messrs. Jacques and Gilmore. The President said to them that he had heard, from me, that they came as messengers of peace from Mr. Lincoln; that as such they were welcome; that the Confederacy had never concealed its desire for peace, and that he was ready to hear whatever they had to offer on that subject.

Mr. Gilmore then addressed the President, and in a few minutes had conveyed the information that these two gentlemen had come to Richmond impressed with the idea that this Government would accept a peace on a basis of a reconstruction of the Union, the abolition of slavery, and the grant of an amnesty to the people of the States as repentant criminals. In order to accomplish the abolition of slavery, it was proposed that there should be a general vote of all the people of both federations, in mass, and the majority of the vote thus taken was to determine that as well as all other disputed questions. These were stated to be Mr. Lincoln's views. The President answered, that as these proposals had been prefaced by the remark that the people of the North were a majority, and that a majority ought to govern, the offer was, in effect, a proposal that the Confederate States should surrender at discretion, admit that they had been wrong from the beginning of the contest, submit to the mercy of their enemies, and avow themselves to be in need of pardon for their crimes; that extermination was preferable to dishonor.

He stated that if they were themselves so unacquainted with the form of their own Government as to make such propositions, Mr. Lincoln ought to have known, when giving them his views, that it was out of the power of the Confederate Government to act on the subject of the domestic institutions of the several States, each State having exclusive jurisdiction on that point, still less to commit the decision of such a question to the vote of a foreign people; that the separation of the States was an accomplished fact; that he had no authority to receive proposals for negotiation except by virtue of his office as President of an independent Confederacy; and on this basis alone must proposals be made to him.

Nov. 7—President Davis thus closes his Annual Message, at the opening of the second session of the Second Rebel Congress:

The disposition of this Government for a peaceful solution of the issues which the enemy has referred to the arbitrament of arms has been too often manifested and is too well known to need new assurances. But while it is true that individuals and parties in the United States have indicated a desire to substitute reason for force, and by negotiation to stop the further sacrifice of human life, and to arrest the calamities which now afflict both countries, the authorities who control the Government of our enemies have too often and too clearly expressed their resolution to make no peace, except on terms of our unconditional submission and degradation, to leave us any hope of the cessation of hostilities until the delusion of their ability to conquer us is dispelled. Among those who are already disposed for peace, many are actuated by principle and by disapproval and abhorrence of the iniquitous warfare that their Government is waging, while others are moved by the conviction that it is no longer to the interest of the United States to continue a struggle in which success is unattainable.

Whenever this fast-growing conviction shall have taken firm root in the minds of a majority of the Northern people, there will be produced that willingness to negotiate for peace which is now confined to our side. Peace is manifestly impossible unless desired by both parties to this war, and the disposition for it among our enemies will be best and most certainly evoked by the demonstration on our part of ability and unshaken determination to defend our rights, and to hold no earthly price too dear for their purchase. Whenever there shall be on the part of our enemies a desire for peace, there will be no difficulty in finding means by which negotiation can be opened; but it is obvious that no agency can be called into action until this desire shall be mutual. When that contingency shall happen, the Government, to which is confided the treaty-making power, can be at no loss for means adapted to accomplish so desirable an end.

In the hope that the day will soon be reached when, under Divine favor, these States may be allowed to enter on their former peaceful pursuits, and to develop the abundant natural resources with which they are blessed, let us then resolutely continue to devote our united and unimpaired energies to the defence of our homes, our lives, and our liberties. This is the true path to peace. Let us tread it with confidence in the assured result.

RESOLUTIONS OF THE LEGISLATURE OF ALABAMA.

The Richmond *Enquirer* of the 14th October, 1864, publishes the annexed resolutions:

Whereas this General Assembly did, on the 20th August, 1863, adopt the two resolutions following, to wit:

Resolved, by the Senate and House of Representatives of the State of Alabama, in General Assembly convened, That the war now being waged against the people and property of the Confederate States, by the United States, is unprovoked and unjust, and is being conducted by our enemies in utter disregard of the principles which should control and regulate civilized warfare; that our oft-repeated purpose never to submit to Abolition rule remains unshaken; that our late reverses are not attributable to any want of courage or heroic self-sacrifice on the part of our brave armies, and should not discourage our people or produce doubts as to the final success; and that we hereby pledge to the cause of independence and perpetual separation from the United States all the resources of the State of Alabama.

Be it further resolved, That, in order to insure a speedy triumph of our cause and the firm establishment of our independence, it is the paramount duty of every citizen in the Confederate States to sustain, invigorate, and render effective our gallant armies to the full extent of his ability, by encouraging enlistments, by furnishing subsistence to the families of soldiers at prices corresponding with the means of such families, and by upholding the credit and currency of the Confederate Government; *and that to dishearten the people and the soldiers at a period like this, to enfeeble the springs of action and destroy the elasticity requisite to rise superior to the pressure of adverse circumstances, is to strike the most insidious, and yet the most fatal blow at the very life of the Confederacy.*

And whereas this General Assembly still entertains the opinions and cherishes the spirit herein expressed; therefore,

It is resolved by the Senate and House of Representatives of the State of Alabama, in General Assembly convened, 1, That the resolutions above copied be and the same are hereby re-asserted and re-adopted as expressive of the feelings, sentiments, wishes, and determination of this General Assembly at the present time and in the present exigency.

2. That in the military events of last year no cause for despondency is found, and that neither patriotism nor wisdom can tolerate any termination of the present war without the maintenance of the independence of the Confederate States.

VOTE IN THE REBEL HOUSE OF REPRESENTATIVES.

1864, Nov. 21—Mr. Russell, of Virginia, offered the following resolution:

Resolved, That this House deem it proper, in view of recent events, to repeat the views expressed in the resolution adopted by the last Congress, declaring the sense of Congress in reference to reuniting with the United States; that it is the unalterable determination of the Confederate States, who are suffering all the horrors and cruelties of a protracted war, that they will never, on any terms, politically affiliate with a people who are engaged in the invasion of their soil and the butchery of their citizens.

Mr. Clark, of Missouri, desired to submit a substitute for the resolution, embodying the same views, but in a more extended form.

Mr. Russell declined to withdraw the call for the question, but asked the yeas and nays, which were ordered, and resulted as follows:

YEAS—Messrs. Baldwin, Barksdale, Batson, Bell, Blandford, Boyce, Bradley, Branch, Bridgers, E. M. Bruce, H. W. Bruce, Burnett, Chambers, Chilton, Chrisman, Clark, Clopton, Cluskey, Colyar, Conrow, Cruikshank, Darden, De Jarnette, Dickinson, Dupre, Elliott, Farrow, Foote, Fuller, Gaither, Garland, Gohlson, Goode, Hanly, Hartridge, Hatcher, Herbert, Hilton, Holder, Halladay, Johnston, Keeble, Kenner, Lumpkin, Leach, J. M., Leach, J. T., Lester, Logan, Lyon, Machen, McMullen, Menees, Miles, Miller, Montague, Moore, Murray, Norton, Orr, Perkins, Ramsay, Read, Rives, Rogers, Russell, Sexton, Simpson, Smith, J. M., Smith, W. E., Smith of Ala., Smith of N. C., Snead, Staples, Swan, Triplett, Turner, Vest, Villers, Welsh, Wickham, Wilkes, Witherspoon, Mr. Speaker—83.

NAYS—None.

THE PEACE ADDRESS FROM GREAT BRITAIN.

WASHINGTON, D. C., *November* 26, 1864.

Hon. WILLIAM H. SEWARD, *Secretary of State, &c., &c.:*

HON. SIR: I beg to inform you that I have been deputed to convey to this country an address from the people of Great Britain and Ireland to the people of the United States of America. The address was presented to Governor Seymour for him to present through the proper channel. I was requested by him to convey it to the President of the United States, as the authorized channel of communication between the people of other nations and the people of the United States of America.

May I, therefore, ask the honor of an opportunity for so doing?

I am, Hon. sir, yours, most obediently,

JOSEPH PARKER.

—

DEPARTMENT OF STATE,
WASHINGTON, *November* 26, 1864.

To JOSEPH PARKER, Esq., *Washington, D. C.:*

SIR: Your letter of this date, stating that you are the bearer of an address from the people of Great Britain and Ireland to the people of the United States, has been received. Before answering the question which your letter contains, it is desirable to be further informed whether you have authority from the Government of Great Britain and Ireland for the purpose referred to, and whether your mission has been made known to the diplomatic agent of that Government accredited to the Government of the United States.

I am, sir, your very obedient servant,

WILLLIAM H. SEWARD.

—

METROPOLITAN HOTEL,
WASHINGTON, D. C., *November* 26, 1864.

Hon. W. H. SEWARD, *Secretary of State, &c., &c.:*

HON SIR: In reply to your letter of to-day, permit me to state that the address which I have had the honor of being deputed by the parties signing it to bring to this country, and containing the signatures of some three hundred and fifty thousand of my countrymen—from the peer to the artisan—is *not* from the Government of Great Britain nor from any political party. It is simply an expression of the earnest desire of the masses of the people of Great Britain to see peace again restored to this continent.

Waiting your favor, I am, Hon. sir,

Yours, most obediently,

JOSEPH PARKER.

—

DEPARTMENT OF STATE,
WASHINGTON, *November* 26, 1864.

To JOSEPH PARKER, Esq., *Metropolitan Hotel:*

SIR: The Government of the United States cannot receive the address which was mentioned in your notes of this morning. Your request for an interview with the President to present the address is therefore declined.

I am, sir, your obedient servant,

WILLIAM H. SEWARD.

"PEACE" IN THE REBEL CONGRESS.

1864, November 26—Mr. J. T. Leach, of North Carolina, offered the following resolutions:

Whereas the unfriendly, unjustifiable, and unpatriotic interference of citizens of the non-slaveholding States in their popular assemblies, from the pulpit, and by legislative enactments, with the reserved rights of the States, provided in the Constitution of the United States, and by the laws of Congress, has been the prolific cause of a cruel, bloody, and relentless war, that has no parallel in point of atrocity, in the annals of the world, between a people professing the Christian religion:

And whereas the citizens of the slave States, at an unguarded moment, under the influence of unwise counsel, without mature deliberation as to the fearful consequence, made the election of Abraham Lincoln to the Presidency of the United States the occasion for precipitating the Confederate States out of the Union, which has been followed by a train of fearful consequences not contemplated by those who advocated the measure:

And whereas, we, the representatives of the people of the Confederate States, desiring to place ourselves fairly before our constituents, our enemies, and the civil world, declare that it is our earnest desire that proper measures should be adopted by the respective Governments to secure an honorable, just, and permanent peace, not incompatible with the principles as laid down in the Constitution of the United States, nor with the inalienable rights of freemen;

Resolved, That the reserved rights of the States should be guarded with watchful and jealous vigilance, and that any attempt to infringe upon those rights should be resisted by all lawful and proper means.

Resolved, That whenever the Government of the United States shall signify its willingness to recognize the reserved rights of the States, and guarantee to the citizens of the States their rights of property, as provided in the Constitution of the United States, and the laws of Congress, to the end that peace may be restored, and our future happiness and prosperity perpetuated, we will agree to treat for peace; and that such terms of peace as may be agreed to by commissioners appointed by the respective Governments, or by the States acting in their sovereign and independent character, and ratified by a majority of the people, shall constitute the bond of peace between the North and the South.

Mr. Leach said: Mr. Speaker, the resolutions that I hold in my hand, and that I propose to read, by the permission of the Chair, are not intended as an apple of discord in our midst. I trust, sir, that they may not produce discord in our midst. All I ask is, that they may have a calm, careful, unprejudiced hearing.

I do not offer them unadvisedly. I have consulted my friends as to the propriety of introducing them, as well as the proper time and circumstances. There is a different opinion as to the propriety of time and circumstances.

I do not offer them for the purpose of strengthening the arm of the enemy. That has been effectually done by the President in his speech at Macon, Ga., and more effectually strengthened by the Governors of the Confederate States and the President when they recommended the use of negroes as soldiers in the Confederate army. I do not offer them for the purpose of discouraging our heroic soldiers, who have braved the leaden hail of death upon the bloody battle-field. I believe it will arouse them to know that they are fighting for something more dear to them than the negro.

I offer them because I believe there is something practical in them. I offer them because I am satisfied that my constituents, both citizens and soldiers, desire an honorable peace. I offer them because I am satisfied that the prayers of Christians, statesmen, and patriots have been poured out for peace, and that the great heart of the nation is pulsating for peace. I offer them because I know that war is a relentless, cruel, blind monster, killing where he cannot make alive, and reaping where he has not sown.

[Mr. Leach desires to be understood as not including the "Border States" in his resolutions, the ordinances of secession having been adopted in the "Cotton States" long before the "Border States" went out. The latter acted under the pressure of circumstances over which they had no control.]

Mr. Montague (Va.) said that he had not designed saying anything when he entered the hall to-day, but he was unwilling to let the resolutions of the gentleman from North Carolina pass without a protest. He reviewed them eloquently and earnestly, and moved that they be rejected.

Numerous gentlemen called the question.

Mr. Leach asked that the vote be taken by yeas and nays, and the House seemed to rise simultaneously to sustain the call.

The roll being called, all the members voted in the affirmative, except Messrs. Fuller, J. M. Leach, J. T. Leach, Logan, Ramsay, and Turner, all of North Carolina.

Messrs. Fuller, Ramsay, and J. M. Leach, after the vote was announced, asked leave to change their votes, as they had voted in the negative under the apprehension that it would be regarded as a discourtesy to an honorable colleague.

Their votes were, with the consent of the House, recorded in the affirmative.

Mr. J. M. Leach stated that he knew there was no member on the floor from North Carolina who desired peace upon any other terms than eternal separation from the North. [Applause in the galleries which was checked by the chair.]

A SECOND LETTER FROM HON. W. W. BOYCE.

WINNSBORO', S. C., *October* 20.

DEAR SIR: In reply to your note, I beg leave to say that I think the course I recommend the best possible course to attain the great object we are aiming at, the establishment of our independence. It proceeds upon two leading ideas:

1. To reconcile the North, or such portion as may be rational, to our independence, by harmonizing as much as possible our independence with their material interest.

2. To avail ourselves of the division of sentiment at the North.

It was to give potency to these two ideas at the South that I insisted so strenuously in my letter to the President on the danger to our republican institutions from the indefinite continuance of the war.

Let me call attention to this striking fact, that, of all the world, the only political organization which proposes to intervene between us and the war party North, is the party which adopted the Chicago platform. Now, should we pursue a policy to build up that party or not? I think most decidedly we should.

Let me call your attention to another fact. In the event of the assembling of a Congress of the States, it is manifest that, in that Congress, from the Northern States, would be represented two adverse systems of ideas—one having the animus of the Chicago platform, the other of the Lincoln programme.

The first of these would be in the ascendancy because the very convening of the Congress necessarily implies the defeat of Lincoln and his system, as it is well understood that Lincoln and the party he represents are utterly opposed to the assembling of this Congress.

Under this state of facts, an abrupt division of sentiment would be found in the Congress between the opponents and the supporters of Lincoln. From this there might result events of the vastest advantage to us, if our councils were guided by a masterly wisdom.

If, under that conjecture, we could dig up the head of Richelieu or Louis XI, or even the head of Elizabeth, the great Queen of England, and put it, full of its original brains, upon the shoulders of the man who would have the direction of our diplomacy in that Congress, the chances would be a thousand to one that our country would emerge from the clouds which now enshroud it, "redeemed, regenerated, disenthralled." War is but a blind giant, striking at random, unless the genius of diplomacy directs the blows. Ideas are the true divinities of this sublunary world. Let us consult these our oracles.

As regards the instructions to our delegates, I have no objection to their being of the character you indicate.

My great purpose is to break down the wall of fire which separates us from the influences of peace North. I have great faith that if Lincoln and his policy were once repudiated, and negotiations for peace entered upon, that every moment we would approach nearer and nearer to an auspicious result. With great respect, &c.,

WILLIAM W. BOYCE.

Mr. JAMES G. HOLMES.

SECOND LETTER FROM ALEXANDER H. STEPHENS.

Mr. Alexander H. Stephens, of Georgia, the Confederate Vice President, has published the following letter in further explanation of his views on the peace question. It originally appeared in the Augusta *Constitutionalist* of the 16th November, 1864, prefaced by a note from Mr. Stephens, by which it appears that this letter was not intended for the public eye, but that its publication has been induced by the strictures of the public press upon a prior letter of Mr. S. on the same subject. Some portions of the letter, as is indicated by asterisks, are omitted. Of these Mr. Stephens says that

some are omitted from public considerations, and others because they relate exclusively to individual affairs.

CRAWFORDSVILLE, (GA.,) *November* 5, 1864.

HON. THOMAS J. SEMMES, *C. S. Senate, Richmond.*

MY DEAR SIR: I have just read a report of your speech at Mobile. From that report I am persuaded you are greatly mistaken as to my views upon the subject of a Convention of the States, and I trust you will excuse and pardon me for this letter upon that subject.

I have by no means invited such a convention by any thing that I have said or written upon the subject. It is not at all a favorite idea with me as a mode of inaugurating negotiations for peace. I see many difficulties attending it. But as so respectable a body as the Chicago Convention, representing so large a portion of the enemy, had pledged themselves, if brought into power, to tender such a proposition, I did think, and do still think, that it was highly politic and wise on our part to respond favorably to that proposition, inasmuch as I saw no insuperable objection to it with the limitations and restrictions stated in my letter. Indeed, with those limitations I saw no objection at all, under present circumstances, to acceding to such a proposition (if it should be made) as the initiation of negotiations. It would be the first step, and in all such cases the first step is often the most difficult.

If the Federal Government should propose to ours a convention of the States, I do not see why it might not be accepted simply as an advisory body, as I suggested. I see no constitutional difficulties in the way. The treaty-making power in both Governments is ample to provide for it. The treaty-making power on both sides might agree to submit the questions at issue to the consideration of any set of men on earth, if they choose, and hear the report without any pledge in advance to be bound by that report. In personal quarrels, such submission is often made, and to the honor of humanity it may be said that, in most cases of this kind, the result is an amicable and honorable settlement. Whether such would be the result of a convention of the States in our case, is of course uncertain. The probabilities, I am free to say, in my judgment, are that it would be. At any rate there is a possibility that it might. When we look at the elements of such a body, if it should be tendered on the other side and accepted on ours, and the true nature of the controversy, I am not without strong hopes that it would so result.

There is no prospect of such proposition being tendered unless McClellan should be elected. He cannot be elected without carrying a sufficient number of the States, which, if united with those of the Confederacy, would make a majority of the States. In such a Convention then, so formed, have we not strong reasons to hope and expect that a resolution could be passed denying the constitutional power of the Government, under the compact of 1787, to coerce a State? The Chicago platform virtually does this already. Would not such a Convention most probably reaffirm the Kentucky and Virginia resolutions of 1798 and 1799? Are there not strong reasons, at least, to induce us to hope and believe that they might? If even that could be done it would end the war. It would recognize as the fundamental principle of American institutions the ultimate, absolute sovereignty of the several States. This fully covers our independence—as fully as I wish ever to see it covered. I wish no other kind of recognition, whenever it comes, than that of George III. of England, viz: the recognition of the sovereignty and independence of each State, separately and by name.

Our Confederation was formed by sovereign and independent States. It was formed for the defence and maintenance of the sovereignty of each. We have unity of name and unity of action, simply because the cause of each has become the cause of all. If, then, a majority of the States should, in solemn convention, settle this great principle, would it not virtually settle the controversy and end the war, covering everything for which we are contending? Would not the terms of a final treaty of peace be easily adjusted after the settlement of this great principle? And are there not sufficient reasons to hope that such might be the result, in case a convention should be proposed as I have stated, and accepted as a mode of inaugurating negotiations of peace, to justify our making a favorable response to the tender of the party at Chicago, in case they should be brought into power? To my mind it seems clear that they are.

You will also allow me to say, that I look upon the election of McClellan as a matter of vast importance to us in every view of the case, and hence I thought it judicious, patriotic, and wise to do everything that could be properly done to aid in his election. Whatever may be his individual opinions, he is the candidate of the State rights party at the North, in opposition to the Centralists and Consolidationists, whose hobby now is Abolitionism. I have thought from the beginning that our true policy was to build up and strengthen such a party at the North by all means in our power. Not only upon the wise maxim of Philip, of Macedon, to divide the enemy as a question of policy merely, but from a higher and much nobler motive. Not only an early peace, but our future safety, security, and happiness required it.

The people of the North are obliged to be our neighbors. It matters not how this war may terminate, they are alongside of us, and must, with the generations after them, there remain forever. It is of the utmost importance to us and our posterity that they should be good neighbors, whatever be the relations existing between them and us. To be good neighbors they must have a good Government. It is almost as vital to us that they have a good Government as that we have such ourselves. It is much better to govern, if it can be done, by ideas than the sword. If this war shall result in the establishment, permanently, of the fundamental principle lying at the foundation of American constitutional liberty, that is, the absolute, ultimate sovereignty of the States, it will more than compensate for all its sacrifices of blood and treasure, great as these have been, or may be. It will secure peace on the continent for ages to come. We therefore have a great interest in fostering, cherishing, and building up and raising to power at the North any party favoring these principles.

If the proper line of policy had been pursued by our authorities toward that element of popular sentiment at the North from the beginning, I believe the States rights party there would have been triumphant at the approaching election. I believe an out and out State rights man might and would have been nominated at Chicago and elected. But the policy of our authorities seems to me, as far as I can judge of it, to have been directed with a view to weaken, cripple, and annihilate that party. So far from acting even upon the policy of dividing the enemy, their object seems to have been to unite and inflame them. I do, moreover, verily believe that if President Davis, even after McClellan's nomination, had made a favorable response to the Chicago resolution looking to a Convention of the States, as a mode of inaugurating negotiations of peace, that it would greatly have aided his election. It might have secured it. All that he need have said in some public manner was, that if such proposition should be tendered by the Federal Government he would accede to it, with some such limitations and restrictions as stated by me in the letter before alluded to. The idea that this could not be constitutionally done is strange to me. In the most objectionable view of the subject, delegates, one or more from each State, would be but commissioners or plenipotentiaries from each Government respectively to initiate negotiations, &c. Their acts would be subject to the approval or disapproval of their Governments respectively. Why commissioners could not be appointed in this way as well as any other, without any violation of the Constitution, I do not see. The treaty-making power in both Governments is ample for this purpose. At least it seems so to me. Indeed, as I have said before, it seems to me that it is ample on both sides to submit the questions in issue to the consideration merely of any body on earth. But enough of this. * * * * *

I know that there are many persons among us, whose opinions are entitled to high consideration, who do not agree with me on the question of McClellan's election. They prefer Lincoln to McClellan. Perhaps the President belongs to that class. Judging from his acts, I should think that he did. Those of the class to whom I refer with whom I have met, think that if what they term a conservative man should be elected, or any on the Chicago platform even, that such terms for a restoration of the Union would be offered as our people would accept. The ghost of the Union haunts them. The spectre of reconstruction rears its ghastly head at every corner, to their imagination. These apprehensions, I doubt not, are sincere. But I entertain none such myself. I am no believer in ghosts of any kind. The old Union and the old Constitution are both dead—dead forever, except in so far as the Constitution has been preserved by us. There is, for the Union as it was, no resurrection by any power short of that which brought Lazarus from the tomb. There may be, and doubtless are, many at the North and some at the South who look forward to a restoration of the Union and the Constitution as it was; but such ideas are vain and illusory as the dreamy imaginings of the Indian warrior, who in death clings to his weapons in fond expectation that he will have use for them beyond the grave in other lands and new hunting grounds.

These fears of *voluntary* reconstruction are but chimeras of the brain. No one need entertain any such from McClellan's election. But, on the contrary, I think that peace, and peace upon the basis of a separation of the States and our independence, would be the almost certain ultimate result, if our authorities should act wisely, in the event of his election. My reasons for this opinion are briefly these: A proposition for an armistice and a Convention of the States might be expected from him soon after his induction into office. This, on our side, being acceded to, as it ought to be, some time would elapse before the conference could meet. The passion of the day on both sides would considerably subside in the interim. The Convention might adopt such a resolution as I have stated. Looking to its probable composition, as before stated, there is strong probability that it would. That, as before stated, would end the matter, and to our entire satisfaction. But, take the worst supposable view of it. Suppose that they should wrangle, do nothing, and adjourn, and that no other mode of settlement by negotiation should be proposed. How would matters then stand?

McClellan would doubtless, as his letter of acceptance indicates he would do, renew the war for the restoration of the Union and the old Constitution with all its guaranties. The moment he should do this, the whole abolition element at the North, now the life and the soul of the war, would turn against it. The old Union with the old Constitution is just what they do not want. They have always regarded it as no better than "a league with Satan and a covenant with Hell." The right arm of the war-spirit of the North will be paralyzed the moment the war is put upon that footing. Besides this at least two-thirds of McClellan's own party manfully hold and proclaim the doctrine that there is no power in the central Government constitutionally to coerce a State. These two elements would constitute an overwhelming majority at the North decidedly against the further prosecution of the war. Meanwhile financial embarrassments would be doing their work. The war would inevitably fail in consequence. When all efforts to persude our people to go back into the Union voluntarily failed, as they would, if our authorities shall so act as to secure the hearts and affections of the people as they ought, then McClellan would ultimately be compelled to give up the restoration of the Union as a forlorn hope. Peace would come slowly but surely upon our own terms and without any more fighting.

But this is not all. Other causes would operate to the same result, which, of themselves, even without considering those above stated, would effect the same thing. The moment McClellan should renew the war with the avowed object of restoring the Union with the old Constitution and all its guaranties, that moment, or as soon as possible, our recognition abroad would come. The silent sympathy of England, France, and other European Powers, at present with Lincoln, arises entirely from their mania upon the subject of negro slavery. * * * * * *

Lincoln had either to witness our recognition abroad, the moral power of which alone, he saw, would break down the war, or to make it an emancipation war. He chose the latter alternative, and the more readily because it chimed in so accordantly with the feelings and views of his own party. This, in my opinion, is the plain English of the whole matter; and just as soon as McClellan should renew the war with a view to restore the Union, the old Constitution, with slavery, &c., would England, France, and other European Powers throw all the moral power and influence of their recognition on our side. I am not certain that they would not go further, rather than see the Union thus restored, if it should become necessary. But it would not become necessary. The other causes alluded to would completely effect our deliverance without any material aid from them.

So, in any and every view I can take of the subject, I regard the election of McClellan and the success of the State rights party of the North, whose nominee he is, of the utmost importance to us. With these views, you readily perceive how I regarded the action of the Chicago Convention as "a ray of light, the first ray of *real* light I had seen from the North since this war began." You can also, from these views, more correctly appreciate my motives for giving what I considered a favorable response to that action. I bespeak your careful attention to the language of that response. From the report of your speech I am led to infer that you entertained the opinion that I was favoring and inviting a Convention of the States in some outside way, and not through the organized channels of the two Governments. No such idea was ever in my mind, and never can be until I am prepared for another revolution—if secession be a revolution; for the States could not go into such a Convention as you seem, from the report of your speech, to think I favored, without first seceding from their present alliance. This, to my mind, is as clear as it is to yours. Of course what I said had to be brief, covering only general points. I could not go into a full explanation of my reasons for what I said, because that would have done damage instead of good to the cause which I wished to aid.

I know that many of our people know that any allusion to peace on our side, or any public expression of a desire for peace, or the offer of terms upon which we ought to be willing to make peace, is injurious to our cause; that it has a bad effect upon our armies and encourages the enemy to fight on under the belief that such declaration indicates a disposition on our part to yield. Some go so far as to maintain that we cannot, consistently with our purpose to secure independence at all hazards, entertain any propositions unless they be based upon our independence, or unless this be promised and granted in the offer. I concur in none of this reasoning. Nothing would give us more strength at home or abroad, with our armies and the world, than to keep constantly before the public what we are fighting for and the terms upon which the contest forced upon us may be ended. The right is with us. The right always has of itself great moral power if properly used and wielded. This depends upon what may be styled diplomacy. Diplomacy does not necessarily involve interchange of views or intercourse between parties. It should not be neglected in wars, even though the enemy should refuse to receive any communications. The result of most wars depends as much upon diplomatic skill in its proper sense as it does upon arms. The real statesman knows when and how to use the pen as well as the sword. The constant proclamation to the world of what we are fighting for can never weaken our cause with those who are periling their lives in that cause, especially if all our acts toward them and all others show that our professions are true; nor is there the slightest inconsistency, in my opinion, between the most fixed determination on our part to end the war upon no terms short of independence, and, at the same time, entertaining, hearing, and accepting offers to negotiate upon any other basis whatever. The doors to treat, to negotiate, to confer, to reason, should always be kept widely open. Those who have the right on their side should never shun or avoid reason. They should never decline an encounter on that arena.

I have been led to these remarks more with a view to self-vindication than to the expression or utterance of any unrecognized truths. * * * * * * *

On the question of reconstruction, I stand now just where I did in October, 1861, when I wrote to a gentleman in answer to a letter from him, stating that I was charged with such sentiments, and desiring me to give a public denial of it. I told him, in reply, that I looked upon such "a charge as no less an imputation upon my intelligence than upon my integrity. The issue of this war, in my judgment, was subjugation or independence. I so understood it when the State of Georgia seceded, and it was with a full consciousness of this fact, with all its responsibilities, sacrifices, and perils, that I pledged myself, then and there, to stand by her and her fortunes, whatever they might be, in the course she had adopted." "As for making any public denial of such a charge, I felt too much self-respect to do it." * * *

Yours truly,

ALEXANDER H. STEPHENS.

P. S. It is but proper that I should add, even by postscript, to this letter, long as it is, that I was highly pleased with the general character and tone of your speech at Mobile, as reported. It was well calculated to do much good, and I doubt not it will. A. H. S.

Miscellaneous.

THE FREE CONSTITUTION OF MARYLAND.

The Free Constitution of Maryland, containing the provision for emancipation stated on page 227, was adopted at an election held on Wednesday and Thursday, October 9th and 10th, 1864. On the 29th of October, Governor A. W. Bradford issued a proclamation announcing the adoption of the Constitution, and that it would supersede the old Constitution on the 1st of November, 1864. The whole vote, as officially declared by him, was:

For the Constitution	30,174
Against the Constitution	29,799
Blank ballots	61
Ballots reported as against the Constitution, but not counted because the persons offering them refused to take the oath required by said Constitution	33
Total vote	60,067

The vote of the soldiers, counted by the Governor, was:

For the Constitution	2,633
Against the Constitution	263

Four returns from the army were rejected by

the Governor, for reasons stated by him in his published opinion, which gave:

For the Constitution..285
Against the Constitution.. 5

Application was made, before the issue of the Governor's proclamation, to the Court of Appeals, for a mandamus to prevent its issue; which the court refused, unanimously, to grant.

In addition to other features, the new Constitution of Maryland contains this article:

ARTICLE 5.—The Constitution of the United States, and the laws made in pursuance thereof, being the supreme law of the land, every citizen of this State owes paramount allegiance to the Constitution and Government of the United States, and is not bound by any law or ordinance of this State in contravention or subversion thereof.

In incorporating into her fundamemtal law this declaration of the duty of perpetual fidelity, and paramount allegiance to the United States, Maryland is in advance of all other States.

ADMISSION OF NEVADA.

1864, October 31—President LINCOLN issued a proclamation declaring that the people of NEVADA had complied with the act of Congress of March 21, 1864, to enable them "to form a constitution and State government, and for the admission of such State into the Union on an equal footing with the original States," and that the State of NEVADA is so admitted.

BRITISH AID TO THE REBELLION.

Mr. Adams to Mr. Seward.

No. 817.] LEGATION OF THE UNITED STATES, LONDON, *Nov.* 18, 1864.

SIR: I have received from Lord Wharncliffe, the chairman of the British association organized to give aid and comfort to the rebel cause, a note, a copy of which is transmitted herewith.

I append a copy of my reply.

I have the honor to be, sir, your obedient servant,
CHARLES FRANCIS ADAMS.

HON. WM. H. SEWARD,
Secretary of State, Washington, D. C.

—

Lord Wharncliffe to Mr. Adams.

WORTLEY HALL,
SHEFFIELD, *November* 12, 1864.

YOUR EXCELLENCY: A bazaar has been held in St. George's Hall, Liverpool, to provide a fund for the relief of Southern prisoners of war. It has produced a clear sum of about £17,000. In preference to any attempt to reach the intended object by circuitous means, a committee of English gentlemen has been formed to address you on the subject.

As chairman of this committee I venture to ask your excellency to request the permission of your government that an accredited agent may be sent out to visit the military prisons within the Northern States, and minister to the comfort of those for whom this fund is intended, under such supervision as your government may direct.

Permit me to state that no political end is aimed at by this movement. It has received support from many who were opposed to the political action of the South. Nor is it intended to impute that the Confederate prisoners are denied such attentions as the ordinary rules enjoin. But these rules are narrow and stern. Winter is at hand, and the clothing which may satisfy the rules of war will not protect the natives of a warm climate from the severe cold of the North.

Sir, the issue of this great contest will not be determined by individual suffering, be it greater or less; and you, whose family name is interwoven with American history, cannot view with indifference the suffering of American citizens, whatever their state or their opinions.

On more than one occasion aid has been proffered by the people of one country to special classes, under great affliction, in another. May it not be permitted to us to follow these examples, especially when those we desire to solace are beyond the reach of their immediate kinsmen? I trust these precedents, and the voice of humanity, may plead with your excellency, and induce you to prefer to the Government of the United States the request which I have the honor to submit.

I am, sir, your obedient, humble servant,
WHARNCLIFFE.

His Excellency HON. C. F. ADAMS.

—

Mr. Adams to Lord Wharncliffe.

LEGATION OF THE UNITED STATES,
LONDON, *Nov.* 18, 1864.

MY LORD: I have the honor to acknowledge the reception of your letter of the 12th instant, asking me to submit to the consideration of my government a request of certain English gentlemen, made through your lordship, to send out an accredited agent to visit the military prisoners held by the United States, and afford them such aid, additional to that extended by the ordinary rules of war, as may be provided by the fund which has been raised here for the purpose.

I am sure that it has never been the desire of my government to treat with unnecessary or vindictive severity any of the misguided individuals, parties in this deplorable rebellion, who have fallen into their hands in the regular course of war. I should greatly rejoice were the effects of your sympathy extended to the ministering to the mental ailment not less than the bodily sufferings of these unfortunate persons, thus contributing to put an end to a struggle which otherwise is too likely to be only procrastinated by your labors.

Be that as it may, I shall be happy to promote any humane endeavor to alleviate the horrors of this strife, and in that sense shall very cheerfully comply with your lordship's desire so far as to transmit, by the earliest opportunity, to my government a copy of the application which has been addressed to me.

I beg your lordship to receive the assurance of my distinguished consideration.
CHARLES FRANCIS ADAMS.

LORD WHARNCLIFFE, &c.

—

Mr. Seward to Mr. Adams.

No. 173.] DEPARTMENT OF STATE,
WASHINGTON, *December* 5, 1864.

SIR: I have received your dispatch of the 18th of November, No. 807, together with the papers therein mentioned, namely, a copy of a letter which was addressed to you on the 12th of November last by Lord Wharncliffe, and a copy of your answer to that letter.

Your proceeding in the matter is approved. You will now inform Lord Wharncliffe that permission for an agent of the committee described by him to visit the insurgents detained in military prisons of the United States, and to distribute among them seventeen thousand pounds of British gold, is disallowed. Here it is expected that your correspondence with Lord Wharncliffe will end.

That correspondence will necessarily become public. On reading it, the American people will be well aware that, while the United States have ample means for the support of prisoners, as well as for every other exigency of the war in which they are engaged, the insurgents, who have blindly rushed into that condition, are suffering no privations that appeal for relief to charity either at home or abroad.

The American people will be likely also to reflect that the sum thus insidiously tendered in the name of humanity constitutes no large portion of the profits which its contributors may be justly supposed to have derived from the insurgents by exchanging with them arms and munitions of war for the coveted productions of immoral and enervating slave labor. Nor will any portion of the American people be disposed to regard the sum thus ostentatiously offered for the relief of captured insurgents as a too generous equivalent for the devastation and desolation which a civil war, promoted and protracted by British subjects, has spread throughout States which before were eminently prosperous and happy.

Finally, in view of this last officious intervention in our domestic affairs, the American people can hardly fail to recall the warning of the father of our country, directed against two great and intimately connected public dangers, namely, sectional faction and foreign intrigue. I do not think that the insurgents have become debased, although they have sadly wandered from the ways of loyalty and patriotism. I think that, in common with all our countrymen, they will rejoice in being saved by their considerate and loyal government from the grave insult which Lord Wharncliffe, and his associates in their zeal for the overthrow of the United States, have prepared for the victims of this unnecessary, unnatural, and hopeless rebellion.

I am, sir, your obedient servant,
WILLIAM H. SEWARD.

CHARLES FRANCIS ADAMS, Esq., &c., &c., &c.

THE CHURCH AND THE REBELLION.

Testimony of the Churches.

PRESBYTERIAN.

GENERAL ASSEMBLY OF 1861, (OLD SCHOOL.)

May 16—The body met in Philadelphia.

May 18—Dr. Spring offered a resolution, that a Special Committee be appointed to inquire into the expediency of this Assembly making some expression of their devotion to the Union of these States, and their loyalty to the Government; and if in their judgment it is expedient so to do, they report what that expression shall be.

On motion of Mr. Hoyte, this resolution was laid on the table by a vote of 123 to 102.

A call for the yeas and nays, to be recorded, was made by Mr. Robertson, after the members had begun to vote by rising, which the Moderator declared to be out of order.

After the result of the vote had been announced, Mr. H. K. Clarke moved to take this resolution up from the table, and on this motion called for the yeas and nays. Points of order were discussed on this motion, until the Moderator called for the order of the day, to hear delegates from corresponding bodies.

May 22—Dr. Spring offered a paper with resolutions respecting the appointment of religious solemnities for the 4th of July next, and the duty of ministers and churches in relation to the present condition of our country.

May 24—Dr. Hodge proposed a substitute.

May 27—Dr. Hodge withdrew his substitute, and Dr. Wines moved one. A motion to table the whole subject was lost—yeas 87, (63 ministers, 24 elders,) nays 153, (76 ministers, 67 elders.

May 28—Drs. Musgrave, Hodge, Yeomans, Anderson, and Wines, ministers, and Messrs. Ryerson, Giles, White, and H. K. Clarke, ruling elders, were appointed a Special Committee on the subject. Same day, the Committee reported—Dr. Musgrave presenting the report of the majority (8 of the 9,) and Dr. Anderson the minority, being Dr. Spring's resolution, with a slight alteration.

THE MAJORITY REPORT.

Gratefully acknowledging the distinguished bounty and care of Almighty God towards this favored land, and also recognising our obligation to submit to every ordinance of man for the Lord's sake, this General Assembly adopts the following resolutions:

Resolved, 1. That in view of the present agitated and unhappy condition of this country, Monday, the first day of July next, be hereby set apart as a day of prayer throughout our bounds, and that on that day ministers and people are called upon humbly to confess and bewail our national sins, to offer our thanks to the Father of lights for his abundant and undeserved goodness to us as a nation, to seek His guidance and blessing upon our rulers and their counsels, as well as upon the Congress then about to assemble, and to implore Him, in the name of Jesus Christ, the Great High Priest of the Christian profession, to turn away His anger from us, and speedily restore to us the blessings of a safe and honorable peace.

Resolved, 2. That the members of this General Assembly, in the spirit of that Christian patriotism which the Scriptures enjoin, and which has always characterized this Church, do hereby acknowledge and declare their obligation, so far as in them lies, to maintain the Constitution of these United States in the full exercise of all its legitimate powers, to preserve our beloved Union unimpaired, and to restore its inestimable blessings to every portion of the land.

Resolved, 3. That in the present distracted state of the country, this Assembly, representing the whole Church, feel bound to abstain from any further declaration, in which all our ministers and members faithful to the Constitution and Standards of the Church might not be able conscientiously and safely to join, and therefore, out of regard as well to the interests of our beloved country, as to those of the Church, the Assembly adopts this Minute as its deliverance upon this subject.

Dr. Musgrave moved to amend by modifying the second resolution, after "the United States," so as to read: "and our constitutional rulers, in the full exercise of their legitimate powers;" which was lost.

The report was then rejected—yeas 84, nays 128, as follows:

YEAS—Messrs. Kennedy, J. T. Backus, L. Merrill Miller, Aitken, Lane, Hall, Westcott, Lindsley, Imbrie, Martin, Hornblower, Hodge, Hamill, Studdiford, Adams, Snowden, Schenck, Watts, Musgrave, Happersett, McPhail, Latta, Gayley, James Williamson, Lawrence, Yeomans, Dickson, Murray, Jos. Clark, Motzer, McMichael, Stockton, Alrich, Mahaffey, Lloyd, Hunt, Layman, Scott, Goodman, Bergen, Huckman, Lyon, Barnett, Taylor, Hamilton, Haines, Mutchmore, Wines, Mathes, Slagle, Matthews, Condit, Hawthorne, and Ogden, *Ministers*. Messrs. Church, Newland, Guest, Lockwood, Ballantyne, Rankin, Osborne, Scudder, Robert Barber of Burlington, Morris Patterson, Henry McKean, Macalester, Deal, Henry, Rea, R. Barber of Northumberland, Giles, Linn, Meredith, Sheets, William Semple, H. K. Clarke, Houston, Mercer, Young, Harbison, Warren, Tunstall, Hubbard, and White, *Ruling Elders*—84.

NAYS—Messrs. William Clark, Kellogg, Bullions, Cochran, Drake, Baldwin, Crane, Hubbard, Reeves, Barr, Kehoo, Edwards, Farquhar, Waller, Murphy, McPherson, Jacobus, Hastings, Donaldson, Coulter, Critchlow, S. J. M. Eaton, Annan, William Eaton, Maxwell, J. D. Smith, Kelly, Sackett, Semple, Pratt, Dubuar, William Campbell, Badeau, Eastman, Thomas, Monfort, Elliott, Long, Lee, T. M. Hopkins, Pelan, Irvin, Forbes, Fisk, John A. Campbell, Laird,

Newell, Stone, Price, Crozier, Vaill, Hanson, Coon, Lord, Swan, Mathers, Robertson, Thayer, Jones, Dodd, Conkey, McGuigan, Stryker, Reaser, Symington, Leighton, Rutherford, McInnis,* H. M. Smith, Gillespie, McNair, and Anderson, *Ministers.* Messrs. E. B. Miller, Wilkin, Lowrie, Beard, Hutchinson, Fithian, Gulick, William Wilson, Humphrey, Cunningham, Litle, Dungan, Martin, Kinkaid, Lawson, Ewing, John Johnston, Bailey, McConnell, Rodgers, Hamilton, Banks, Moore, Alexander, Lewis, Davy, Thomas Johnston, Samuel Price, Graham, L. H. Stewart, Hazeltine, Conn, Thomas, Frost, Neal, McChord, Kinnear, Fisher, J. L. Meredith, J. L. Williams, Seller, Neely, Waddel, Reynolds, Gregg, Rowland, Spring, Scates, Stirrat, Baldwin, Mason, Russell, Windsor, Wayland, Claypool, and Caldwell, *Ruling Elders*—128.

Messrs. Peden, Balch, and T. C. Stuart, *non liquet.*

Mr. Hoyte was excused from voting.

THE MINORITY REPORT.

Gratefully acknowledging the distinguished bounty and care of Almighty God towards this favored land, and also recognising our obligations to submit to every ordinance of man for the Lord's sake, this General Assembly adopt the following resolutions:

Resolved, 1. That in view of the present agitated and unhappy condition of this country, the first day of July next be hereby set apart as a day of prayer throughout our bounds; and that on this day ministers and people are called on humbly to confess and bewail our national sins; to offer our thanks to the Father of light for his abundant and underserved goodness towards us as a nation; to seek his guidance and blessing upon our rulers and their counsels, as well as on the Congress of the United States about to assemble; and to implore Him, in the name of Jesus Christ, the great High Priest of the Christian profession, to turn away His anger from us, and speedily restore to us the blessings of an honorable peace.

Resolved, 2. That this General Assembly, in the spirit of that Christian patriotism which the Scriptures enjoin, and which has always characterized this Church, do hereby acknowledge and declare our obligations to promote and perpetuate, so far as in us lies, the integrity of these United States, and to strengthen, uphold, and encourage the Federal Government in the exercise of all its functions under our noble Constitution; and to this Constitution, in all its provisions, requirements, and principles, we profess our unabated loyalty.

And, to avoid all misconception, the Assembly declare that by the term "Federal Government," as here used, is not meant any particular administration, or the peculiar opinions of any particular party, but that central administration which, being at any time appointed and inaugurated according to the forms prescribed in the Constitution of the United States, is the visible representative of our national existence.

Which was adopted—yeas 156, nays 66, as follows:

YEAS—Messrs. Wm. Clark, Kellogg, Bullions, Cochran, L. M. Miller, Westcott, Drake, Martin, Baldwin, Crane, Hubbard, Reeves, Studdiford, Barr, Snowden, Kehoo, Mackey, Schenck, Musgrave, Edwards, Latta, Farquhar, Jas. Williamson, Lawrence, Waller, Murray, Joseph Clark, McPherson, Jacobus, Hastings, Donaldson, Coulter, Critchlow, S. J. M. Eaton, Annan, Wm. Eaton, Maxwell, J. D. Smith, Kelly, Sackett, Semple, Pratt, Dubuar, Wm. Campbell, Badeau, Eastman, Thomas, Monfort, Elliott, Long, Lee, T. M. Hopkins, Pelan, Irwin, Goodman, Forbes, Fisk, John A. Campbell, Laird, Newell, Bergen, Stone, Price, Crozier, Vaill, Hanson, Coon, Lord, Swan, Mathers, Hickman, Robertson, Thayer, Lyon, Barnett, Jones, Dodd, Conkey, McGuigan, Taylor, Stryker, Hamilton, Haines, Reaser, Wines, Slagle, and Anderson, *Ministers.* Messrs. Newland, Guest, Miller, Wilkin, Lowrie, Rankin, Beard, Osborne, Litle, Hutchinson, Fithian, Ryerson, Gulick, Humphreys, Cunningham, Barber of Burlington, Patterson, Dungan, Macalester, Henry, Martin, Kinkaid, Rea, Barber of Northumberland, Lawson, Linn, Ewing, John Johnson, Bailey, McConnell, Rodgers, Hamilton, Banks, Moore, Alexander, Lewis, Davy, Thomas Johnston, Price, Sheets, Graham, Stewart, H. K. Clarke, Hazeltine, Conn, Thomas, Frost, Neal, McChord, Kinnear, Fisher, Houston, J. L. Meredith, J. L. Williams, Seller, Neely, Waddel, Reynolds, Gregg, Rowland, Spring, Scates, Stirrat, Baldwin, Mason, Russell, Young, Windsor, and Caldwell, *Ruling Elders*—156.

NAYS—Messrs. Kennedy, J. T. Backus, Aitken, Lane, Hall, Lindsley, Imbrie, Childs, Wells, Hornblower, Hodge, Hamill, Watts, Happersett, McPhail, Gayley, Yeomans, Dickson, Murphy, Motzer, McMichael, Stockton, Alrich, Mahaffey, Lloyd, Hunt, Layman, Scott, Mutchmore, Leighton, Mathes, H. H. Hopkins, Matthews, Frazer, Cheek, Condit, Hawthorne, Brown, Harrison, Ogden, Peden, Balch, Rutherford, McInnis,* H M. Smith, Gillespie, Stuart, McNair, and Baker, *Ministers.* Messrs. Church, Lockwood, Ballantyne, Wilson, Barber of Burlington, McKean, Deal, Giles, Geo. Meredith, Wm. Semple, Mercer, Wayland, Harbison, Warren, Tunstall, Hubbard, Claypool, and White, *Ruling Elders*—66.

Sundry protests were made.

GENERAL ASSEMBLY OF 1862, (OLD SCHOOL.)

May 15—The body met in Columbus, Ohio.

May 19—Dr. R. J. Breckinridge having previously submitted a paper on the state of the country, it, after being slightly amended on his own motion, was adopted, as follows:

The General Assembly of the Presbyterian Church in the United States of America, now in session at Columbus, in the State of Ohio:

Considering the unhappy condition of the country in the midst of a bloody civil war, and of the Church agitated everywhere, divided in sentiment in many places, and openly assailed by schism in a large section of it; considering, also, the duty which this chief tribunal, met in the name and by the authority of the glorified Saviour of sinners, who is also the Sovereign Ruler of all things, owes to Him, our Head and Lord, and to His flock committed to our charge, and to the people whom we are commissioned to evangelize, and to the civil authorities who exist by His appointment; do hereby, in this deliverance, give utterance to our solemn convictions and our deliberate judgment, touching the matters herein set forth, that they may serve for the guidance of all over whom the Lord Christ has given us any office of instruction, or any power of government.

I. Peace is amongst the very highest temporal blessings of the Church, as well as of all mankind; and public order is one of the first necessities of the spiritual as well as the civil commonwealth. Peace has been wickedly superseded by war, in its worst form, throughout the whole land; and public order has been wickedly superseded by rebellion, anarchy, and violence, in the whole Southern portion of the Union. All this has been brought to pass in a disloyal and traitorous attempt to overthrow the National Government by military force, and to divide the nation, contrary to the wishes of the immense majority of the people of the nation, and without satisfactory evidence that the majority of the people in whom the local sovereignty resided, even in the States which revolted, ever authorized any such proceeding, or ever approved the fraud and violence by which this horrible treason has achieved whatever success it has had. This whole treason, rebellion, anarchy, fraud, and violence, is utterly contrary to the dictates of natural religion and morality, and is plainly condemned by the revealed will of God. It is the clear and solemn duty of the National Government to preserve, at whatever cost, the national Union and Constitution, to maintain the laws in their supremacy, to crush force by force, and to restore the reign of public order and peace to the entire nation, by whatever lawful means that are necessary thereunto. And it is the bounden duty of the people who compose this great nation, each one in his several place and degree, to uphold the Federal Government, and every State Government, and all persons in authority, whether civil or military, in all their lawful and proper acts, unto the end herein before set forth.

II. The Church of Christ has no authority from him to make rebellion, or to counsel treason, or to favor anarchy in any case whatever. On the contrary, every follower of Christ has the personal liberty bestowed on him by Christ, to submit, for the sake of Christ, according to his own conscientious sense of duty, to whatever government, however bad, under which his lot may be cast. But while patient suffering for Christ's sake can never be sinful, treason, rebellion, and anarchy may be sinful—most generally, perhaps, are sinful; and, probably, are always and necessarily sinful, in all free countries, where the power to change the government by voting, in the place of force, which exists as a common right, is constitutionally secured to the people, who are sovereign. If, in any case, treason, rebellion, and anarchy can possibly be sinful, they are so in the case now desolating large portions of this nation, and laying waste great numbers of Christian congregations, and fatally obstructing every good word and work in those regions. To

* Then editor of the New Orleans *True Witness*, which contained, April 27, 1861, this paragraph, quoted in Rev. Dr. Stanton's Church and Rebellion:

"Maryland is kindling with Southern fire, while Baltimore has stood at the font of *baptismal blood, in solemn covenant* for the Confederate States; and Providence ordered that this thrilling deed, *this sealing* ordinance, should be on the anniversary of the battle of Lexington, Mass., the memorable 19th of April. Thus the same day beheld the first blood of '76 and of '61—fortunate omen of the result."

the Christian people scattered throughout those unfortunate regions, and who have been left of God to have any hand in bringing on these terrible calamities, we earnestly address words of exhortation and rebuke, as unto brethren who have sinned exceedingly, and whom God calls to repentance by fearful judgments. To those in like circumstances who are not chargeable with the sins which have brought such calamities upon the land, but who have chosen, in the exercise of their Christian liberty, to stand in their lot and suffer, we address words of affectionate sympathy, praying God to bring them off conquerors. To those in like circumstances, who have taken their lives in their hands, and risked all for their country and for conscience' sake, we say, we love such with all our heart, and bless God such witnesses were found in the time of thick darkness. We fear, and we record it with great grief, that the Church of God, and the Christian people, to a great extent, and throughout all the revolted States, have done many things that ought not to have been done, and have left undone much that ought to have been done, in this time of trial, rebuke, and blasphemy; but concerning the wide schism which is reported to have occurred in many Southern Synods, this Assembly will take no action at this time. It declares, however, its fixed purpose, under all possible circumstances, to labor for the extension and the permanent maintenance of the Church under its care, in every part of the United States. Schism, so far as it may exist, we hope to see healed. If that cannot be, it will be disregarded.

III. We record our gratitude to God for the prevailing unity of sentiment and general internal peace, which have characterized the Church in the States that have not revolted, embracing a great majority of the ministers, congregations, and people under our care. It may still be called, with emphasis, a loyal, orthodox, and pious Church; and all its acts and works indicate its right to a title so noble. Let it strive for divine grace to maintain that good report. In some respects, the interests of the Church of God are very different from those of all civil institutions. Whatever may befall this, or any other nation, the Church of Christ must abide on earth, triumphant even over the gates of hell. It is, therefore, of supreme importance that the Church should guard itself from internal alienations and divisions, founded upon questions and interests that are external as to her, and which ought not by their necessary workings to cause her fate to depend on the fate of things less important and less enduring than herself. Disturbers of the Church ought not to be allowed: especially disturbers of the Church in States that never revolted, or that have been cleared of armed rebels: disturbers who, under many false pretexts, may promote discontent, disloyalty, and general alienation, tending to the unsettling of ministers, to local schisms, and to manifold trouble. Let a spirit of quietness, of mutual forbearance, and of ready obedience to authority, both civil and ecclesiastical, illustrate the loyalty, the orthodoxy, and the piety of the Church. It is more especially to ministers of the gospel, and amongst them, particularly to any whose first impressions had been, on any account, favorable to the terrible military revolution which has been attempted, and which God's providence has hitherto so singularly rebuked, that these decisive considerations ought to be addressed. And in the name and by the authority of the Lord Jesus we earnestly exhort all who love God, or fear his wrath, to turn a deaf ear to all counsels and suggestions that tend towards a reaction favorable to disloyalty, schism, or disturbance either in the Church or in the country. There is hardly anything more inexcusable connected with the frightful conspiracy against which we testify than the conduct of those office-bearers and members of the Church who, although citizens of loyal States, and subject to the control of loyal Presbyteries and Synods, have been faithless to all authority, human and divine, to which they owed subjection. Nor should any to whom this deliverance may come fail to bear in mind that it is not only their outward conduct concerning which they ought to take heed; but it is also, and especially their heart, their temper, and their motives, in the sight of God, and towards the free and beneficent civil government which he has blessed us withal, and toward the spiritual commonwealth to which they are subject in the Lord. In all these respects, we must all give account to God in the great day. And it is in view of our own dread responsibility to the Judge of quick and dead that we now make this deliverance.

The vote was—yeas 206, nays 20, as follows:

Yeas—Messrs. Robertson, Crocker, Lane, S. M. Campbell, Gardiner, Jones, Remington, Patton, Maclise, Lowrey, Heroy, McCauley, Davidson, Stevenson, Lowrie, Stoddard, Stead, McDougall, Sheddan, Lockwood, Irving, Macdonald, Hale, Williamson, J. Y. Mitchell, Knighton, Van Wyck, Dewing, H. H. Welles, Chester, W. M. Wells, Junkin, Breed, Musgrave, Christian, Halsey, Belville, J. G. Ralston, Roberts, Smith, Zahnizer, Shaiffer, Doolittle, Grier, Brown, Niccolls, Tustin, Rosborough, Paxton, Marshall, Edgar, Cummins, Morgan, Coulter, R. Dickson, Dickey, McAboy, J. W. Scott, Sloan, Moffat, Dalzell, Hoge, Wolcott, M. R. Miller, W. M. Robinson, James Anderson, Beer, Kay, John McLean, Akey, Kost, Williams, Kemper, Reynolds, Cortelyou, McMillen, Telford, Matthews, Morton, Symmes, A. C. Allen, Abbott, Koutz, Killen, Donaldson, Palmer, Holliday, Wallace, McFarland, Dale, Marquis, Denny, R. Conover, Swan, Chase, Barr, Osmond, Thompson, Staples, Smiley, Monteith, S. Mitchell, J. A. McKee, Frothingham, Boggs, C. P. Taylor, Hughes, Caldwell, Bishop, Woodward, Coe, Mathes, James Cameron, R. A. Johnson, Hogue, Breckinridge, A. Scott, Boardman, *Ministers.* Messrs. Kinnicut, Pierce, Kelso, Cook, Curtis, McNair, Estabrook, Van Keuren, Joseph Banks, Huntting, Lord, Belknap, Belcher, McFarlane, Pierson, Woodruff, Demarest, Pruden, Hinchman, Easton, Hulshizer, Young, Van Gelder, Collier, Sargent, Combs, Piper, Weir, J. B. Mitchell, Ramsay, E. J. Dickey, Gwin, M. C. Grier, Linn, Gallaher, Blair, Reed, Allen, Burchfield, Hosack, Guthrie, S. G. Miller, Wilson, T. B. Wells, Culbertson, A. Cameron, Craig, Duncan, L. W. Ralston, S. Miller, D. Taylor, True, Burlingame, Shaw, Knowlton, Hays, Clark, Chapin, James Miller, J. Robinson, Leavitt, Joseph Anderson, Wade, Janvier, Karr, Inskeep, Pugh, Rainey, M. Wilson, Hills, Brooks, Patterson, Donnell, Rayburn, Bell, Wycoff, Crosby, Breeze, Candee, Chute, Waters, Irwin, Rodgers, Elliott, E. McLean, Garth, Welch, Waring, *Ruling Elders*—206.

Nays—B. R. Allen, Dumont, Backus, C. Dickson, McPheeters, Forman, S. Robinson, J. L. McKee, Caldwell, Tuck, *Ministers.* Messrs. Comfort, Canfield, Kirkpatrick, Poland, C. D. Campbell, Watt, Vredenburg, Gamble, Jacob Johnston, Tunstall, *Ruling Elders*—20.

Several protests were made.

GENERAL ASSEMBLY OF 1863, (OLD SCHOOL.)

May 21—The body met at Peoria, Illinois.

June 1—Dr. Beatty, from the Committee on Bills and Overtures, reported:

Overture No. 16, being a request from the Presbytery of Saline that the General Assembly solemnly re-affirm the testimony of 1818, in regard to slavery; the committee report:

The Assembly has, from the first, uttered its sentiments on the subject of slavery in substantially the same language. The action of 1818 was taken with more care, made more clear, full, and explict, and was adopted unanimously. It has since remained that true and scriptural deliverance on this important subject by which our church is determined to abide. It has never been repealed, amended, or modified, but has frequently been referred to, and reiterated in subsequent Assemblies. And when some persons fancied that the action of 1845 in some way interfered with it, the Assembly of 1846 declared with much unanimity, that the action of 1845 was not intended to deny or rescind the testimony on the subject, previously uttered by General Asssemblies; and by these deliverances we still abide.

Dr. Humphrey moved to insert the word "all" before the words, "these deliverances we still abide." Lost. His motion to table the report was lost; and it was then adopted without amendment.

May 27—Mr. T. H. Nevin moved for a committee of three to cause the national flag to be raised over the church edifice where the Assembly is met. A motion to table this was lost—yeas 93, nays 130, not voting, 1. Referred to a select committee: Drs. J. M. Lowrie, E. P. Humphrey, Loyal Young, and J. I. Brownson; and Messrs. H. H. Leavitt, H. K. Clarke, and R. Carter.

May 30—The committee reported.

June 1—Dr. Humphrey offered a substitute, which was read.

The report of the committee was adopted—yeas 180, nays 19, not voting 1, as follows:

Yeas—*Ministers*—R. A. DeLancey, H. F. Hickok, J. Wood, M. S. Goodall, J. Cleland, W. D. McKinley, A. T. Rankin, I. Faries, A. R. Macoubrey, J. Lillie, T. M. Gray, J. Cory, E. E. Rankin, E. C. Wines, W. Phraner, E. P. Benedict, G. F. Goodhue, J. J. A. Morgan, G. S. Plumley, S. S. Sheddan, A. D. White, R. S. Manning, E. P. Shields, G. S. Mott, W. H. Kirk, W. R. Glen, D. Cook, J. Osmond, M. J. Hickok, A. W. Sproull, W. Blackwood, A. Nevin, W. R. Work, J. Beggs, J. H. Life, J. Thomas, R. C. Galbraith, G.

P. Hays, W. C. Cattell, R. McCachren, J. T. Brown, R. J. Wilson, W. B. McIlvaine, S. McFarren, J. S. Elder, G. W. Mechlin, Loyal Young, J. W. Johnston, W. M. Blackburn, L. L. Conrad, J. I. Brownson, W. B. Keeling, C. C. Beatty, J. S. Marquis, W. R. Vincent, G. Carpenter, J. B. Blayney, S. Wilson, J. R. Duncan, J. Rowland, J. E. Carson, A. J. McMillan, J. F. Jennison, V. Noyes, D. S. Anderson, J. A. Meeks, J. Wiseman, E. B. Bower, T. E. Hughes, L. D. Potter, A. B. Gilliland, J. M. Cross, J. Crawford, E. S. Wilson, D. B. Reed, L. G. Hay, J. W. McClusky, J. L. Lower, J. M. Lowrie, T. Whallon, H. N. Corbett, J. Andrew, J. C. Hanna, J. Mack, G. W. Ash, J. Worrell, R. Frame, R. Beer, J. Fleming, H. B. Thayer, J. A. Pratt, G. Ainslie, W. Spear, A. S. Marshall, J. L. Wilson, W. E. Westervelt, J. A. Carothers, H. M Giltner, J. M. McElroy, W. Wilson, J. Leighton, A. Munson, A. Scott.

Ruling Elders—J. C. House, J. M. Lasher, A. W. Page, J. H. Millspaugh, J. S. Purdy, W. R. Post, J. Stuart, J. Darrach, R. Carter, W. L. Wood, J. Honeyman, H. Hedges, W. D. Sinclair, E. B. Fuller, J. Mackey, G. Fuller, G. H. Van Gelder, M. P. Rue, G. Junkin, Jr., S. H. Fulton, R. Graham, S. E. Weir, R. N. Brown, J. A. Christie, W. C. Lawson, J. N. Brown, A. Stirling, Jr., George Hench, R. M. Jones, J. P. Tustin, J. Giffen, J. Culbertson, J. Barnett, J. Cochran, J. McKee, J. Boyd, C. Byles, T. H. Nevin, J. Vance, T. McKennan, T. S. Milligan, G. B. Johnston, S. Sharp, W. Munro, J. Strine, A. G. Brown, H. K. Clarke, H. B. Myer, W. B. Franklin, C. A. Phelps, H. H. Leavitt, C. Williams, W. Mixer, W. McCulloch, J. W. Sprowle, H. T. Roseman, J. C. Burt, S. Vannuys, E. Wright, J. T. Eccles, W. Redick, W. Munro, T. Candor, Charles Crosby, S. Howe, T. Voorhees, R. S. Alexander, J. C. Walker, L. Hoadly, B. P. Baldwin, J. A. McAfee, A. M. McPherson, G. W. Lewis—Ayes, 180.

NOES—*Ministers*—J. P. Knox, L. C. Baker, F. Chandler, G. S. Inglis, J. A. Quarles, R. Valentine, H. D. V. Nevius, E. P. Humphrey, S. M. Bayless, H. M. Scudder, G. K. Perkins.

Ruling Elders—A. B. Conger, S. G. Malone, J. Tate, W. Risley, J. G. Barrett, R. Miller, E. W. Martin, C. Hubbard—Noes, 19.

NON LIQUET—*Minister*—J. P. McMillan—1.

Total—Ayes, 180; noes, 19; *non liquet*, 1.

So the report was adopted. It is as follows:

The Committee to whom was referred the resolution which proposed to raise the flag of the United States upon the building in which the Assembly is now convened, and to report in respect to the "State of the Country," respectfully present the following report:

Your Committee believe that the design of the mover of the original resolution, and of the large majority, who apparently are ready to vote for its adoption, is simply to call forth from the Assembly a significant token of our sympathy with this Government, in its earnest efforts to suppress a rebellion, that now for over two years has wickedly stood in armed resistance to lawful and beneficent authority. But as there are many among us who are undoubtedly patriotic; who are willing to express any righteous principle to which this Assembly should give utterance, touching the subjection and attachment of an American citizen to the Union and its institutions; who love the flag of our country, and rejoice in its successes by sea and by land; and who yet do not esteem this particular act a testimonial of loyalty entirely becoming to a church court,—and as many of these brethren, by the pressing of this vote, would be placed in a false position, as if they did not love the Union, of which that flag is the beloved symbol, your Committee deem themselves authorized, by the subsequent direction of the Assembly, to propose a different action to be adopted by this venerable court.

It is well known, on the one hand, that the General Assembly has ever been reluctant to repeat its testimonies upon important matters of public interest; but, having given utterance to carefully considered words, is content to abide calmly by its recorded deliverances. Nothing that this Assembly can say can more fully express the wickedness of the rebellion that has cost so much blood and treasure; can declare in plainer terms the guilt before God and man of those who have inaugurated, or maintained, or countenanced, for so little cause, this fratricidal strife; or can more impressively urge the solemn duty of the Government to the lawful exercise of its authority, and of the people, each in his several place, to uphold the civil authorities, to the end that law and order may again reign throughout this entire nation—than these things have already been done by previous Assemblies. Nor need this body declare its solemn rebukes towards those ministers and members of the church of Christ, who have aided in bringing on and sustaining these immense calamities; or tender our kind sympathies to those who are overtaken by troubles they could not avoid, and who mourn and weep in secret places, not unseen by the Father's eye; or reprove all wilful disturbers of the public peace; or exhort those that are subject to our care to the careful discharge of every duty tending to uphold the free and beneficent Government under which we are, and this specially for conscience' sake, and as in the sight of God—more than, in regard to all these things, the General Assembly has made its solemn deliverances, since these troubles began.

But, on the other hand, it may be well for this General Assembly to reaffirm, as it now solemnly does, the great principles to which utterance has already been given. We do this the more readily, because our beloved church may thus be understood to take her deliberate and well-chosen stand, free from all imputations of haste or excitement: because we recognise an entire harmony between the duties of the citizen, (especially in a land where the people frame their own laws, and choose their own rulers,) and the duties of the Christian to the great Head of the Church; because, indeed, least of all persons, should Christian citizens even seem to stand back from their duty, when bad men press forward for mischief; and because a true love for our country, in her times of peril, should forbid us to withhold an expression of our attachment, for the insufficient reason that we are not accustomed to repeat our utterances.

And because there are those among us who have scruples touching the propriety of any deliverance of a church-court respecting civil matters, this Assembly would add, that all strifes of party politics should indeed be banished from our ecclesiastical assemblies, and from our pulpits; that Christian people should earnestly guard against promoting partizan divisions; and that the difficulty of accurately deciding, in some cases, what are general and what party principles, should make us careful in our judgments; but that our duty is none the less imperative to uphold the constituted authorities, because minor delicate questions may possibly be involved. Rather, the sphere of the church is wider and more searching, touching matters of great public interest, than the sphere of the civil magistrate, *in this important respect*—that the civil authorities can take cognizance only of overt acts; while the law of which the church of God is the interpreter, searches the heart, makes every man subject to the civil authority, for conscience' sake, and declares that man truly guilty who allows himself to be alienated, in sympathy and feeling, from any lawful duty, or who does not conscientiously prefer the welfare, and especially the preservation of the Government, to any party or partizan ends. Officers may not always command a citizen's confidence; measures may by him be deemed unwise; earnest, lawful efforts may be made for changes he may think desirable; but no causes now exist to vindicate the disloyalty of American citizens towards the United States Government.

The General Assembly would not withhold from the Government of the United States, that expression of cordial sympathy which a loyal people should offer. We believe that God has afforded us ample resources to suppress this rebellion, and that, with his blessing, it will ere long be accomplished. We would animate those who are discouraged by the continuance and fluctuations of these costly strifes, to remember and rejoice in the supreme government of our God, who often leads through perplexity and darkness. We would exhort to penitence for all our national sins, to sobriety and humbleness of mind before the Great Ruler of all, and to constant prayerfulness for the divine blessing; and we would entreat our people to beware of all schemes implying resistance to the lawfully-constituted authorities, by any other means than are recognised as lawful to be openly prosecuted. And as this Assembly is ready to declare our unalterable attachment and adherence to the Union established by our fathers, and our unqualified condemnation of the rebellion; to proclaim to the world the United States, one and undivided, as our country; the lawfully chosen rulers of the land, our rulers; the Government of the United States, our civil government, and its honored flag, our flag; and to affirm that we are bound, in the truest and strictest fidelity, to the duties of Christian citizens under a government that has strown its blessings with a profuse hand, your Committee recommend that, as the trustees of this church, concurring in the desire of many members of this Assembly, have displayed from this edifice the American flag, the symbol of national protection, unity, and liberty, the particular action contemplated in the original resolution be no further urged upon the attention of this body.

Dr. Hickok moved now to adopt the paper of Dr. Humphrey.

On this question the ayes and noes were called, with the following result:

AYES—*Ministers*—R. A. De Lancey, H. F. Hickok, J. Wood, M. S. Goodale, J. Cleland, W. D. McKinley, A. T. Rankin, I. Faries, A. R. Macoubrey, J. Lillie, T. M. Gray, J. Cory, E. E. Rankin, E. C. Wines, W. Phraner, E. P. Benedict, G. F. Goodhue, J. P. Knox, G. S. Plumley, S. S. Sheddan, A. D. White, R. S. Manning, E. P. Shields, G. S. Mott, W. H. Kirk, W. R. Glen, D. Cook, J. Osmond, M. J.

Hickok, L. C. Baker, F. Chandler, A. W. Sproull, W. Blackwood, A. Nevin, W. R. Work, J. Beggs, J. H. M. Knox, J. C. Thompson, A. De Witt, C. W. Stewart, S M. Moore, D. H. Barron, W. Life, J. Thomas, R. C. Galbraith, G. P. Hays, W. C. Cattell, R. McCachren, F. T Brown, R. F. Wilson, W. B. McIlvaine, R. Lea, S. McFarren, J. S. Elder, G. W. Mechlin, L. Young, J. W. Johnston, W. M. Blackburn, L. L. Conrad, J. I Brownson, W. B. Keeling, C. C. Beatty, J. S. Marquis, W. R. Vincent, G. Carpenter, J. B. Blayney, S. Wilson, J. R. Duncan, J. E. Carson, A. J. McMillan, J. F. Jennison, V. Noyes, D. S. Anderson, J. A. Meeks, J. Wiseman, E. B. Bower, T. E. Hughes, L. D. Potter, A. B. Gilliland, J. M. Cross, J. Crawford, D. B. Reed, L. G. Hay, J. W. McCluskey, J. L. Lower, J. M. Lowrie, T. Whallon, H. M. Corbett, J. Andrew, J. C. Hanna, J. Mack, G. W. Ash, J. Worrell, G. S. Inglis, R. Frame, R. Beer, J. Fleming, H. B. Thayer, F. A. Pratt, G. Ainslie, W. Speer, A. S. Marshall, A. Caldwell, J. L Wilson, W. E. Westervelt, J. A. Carothers, H. M. Giltner, J. M. McElroy, J. A. Quarles, J. Leighton. A. Munson, J. P. McMillan, R. Valentine, H. V. D. Nevius, R. P. Humphrey, S M. Bayless, H. M. Scudder, G. K. Perkins, and A. Scott.

Ruling Elders—J. C. House, J. M. Lasher, A. W. Page, J. H. Millspaugh, J. S. Purdy, W. R. Post, J. Stuart, A. B. Conger, J. Darrach, R. Carter, W. L. Wood, J. Honeyman, H. Hedges, W. D. Sinclair, E. B. Fuller, J. Mackey, G. Fuller, G. H. Van Gelder, M. P. Rue, G. Junkin, Jr., S. H. Fulton, R. Graham, S. E. Weir, R. N. Brown, J. A. Christie, W. C. Lawson, J. N. Brown, A. Stirling, Jr., J. Clark, George Hench, R. M. Jones, J. P. Tustin, J. Giffen, J. Culbertson, J. Barnett, J. Cochran, J. McKee, J. Boyd, C. Byles, T. H. Nevin, J. Vance, T. McKennan, T. S. Milligan, G. B. Johnston, S. Sharp, J. W. Robinson, William Munro, M. Scott, R. Kerr, J. Strine, A. G. Brown, H. K. Clarke, H. B. Myer, W. B. Franklin, C. A. Phelps, H. H Leavitt, C. Williams, W. Mixer, W. McCulloch, J. W. Sprowle, H. T. Roseman, J. C. Burt, S. Vannuys, E. Wright, J. T. Eccles, W. Redick, S. G. Malone, W. Munro, T. Candor, C. Crosby, S. Howe, T. Voorhees, R. S. Alexander, J. C. Walker, L. Hoadley, B. P. Baldwin, J. Tate, W Risley, J. A. McAfee, A. M. McPherson, J. G. Barrett, R. Miller, G. W. Lewis, E. W. Martin, and C. Hubbard—Ayes, 206.

NOES—*Minister*—E. S. Wilson, 1.

NON LIQUET—*Minister*—J. Rowland, 1.

TOTAL—Ayes, 206; noes, 1; *non liquet*, 1.

The paper of Dr. Humphrey was therefore adopted. It is as follows:

The General Assembly of 1861 adopted a minute on the state of the church and the country. The Assembly of 1862 uttered a more formal and comprehensive deliverance. In the meantime, a certain number, perhaps the larger portion of the Presbyteries and Synods, have expressed their judgments on the same subject. This General Assembly is persuaded that the office-bearers and members of this church, within the Presbyteries represented here, are, in a remarkable degree, united in a strict and true allegiance to the Constitution and Government of the United States; and that they are, as a body, loyal both to the church and the civil government as ordinances of God.

This General Assembly contents itself, on that part of the subject, by enjoining upon all the people of God, who acknowledge this church as their church, to uphold, according as God shall give them strength, the authority of the Constitution and laws of the land, in this time of supreme national peril. But this Assembly would most distinctly and solemnly inculcate upon all its people the duty of humbly confessing before God the great unworthiness, and the many sins of the people of this land, and of acknowledging the holiness and justice of the Almighty in the present visitation. He is righteous in all His ways, and holy in all His works. We exhort our brethren to seek the gift of the Holy Ghost, by prayer and confession and repentance, so that the anger of the Lord may be turned away from us, and that the spirit of piety may become not less predominant and vital in the churches than the spirit of an awakened patriotism.

And this Assembly, connecting the experience of our present trials with the remembrance of those through which the church has passed, does now recall and adopt the sentiments of our fathers in the Church of Scotland, as these are expressed for substance in the Solemn League and Covenant of 1643: "And because the people of this land are guilty of many sins and provocations against God, and his Son Jesus Christ, as is manifest by our present distresses and dangers, the fruits thereof, we profess and declare before God and the world our unfeigned desire to be humbled for our own sins and the sins of the people, especially that we have not, as we ought, valued the inestimable benefit of the gospel, nor laboured for the purity and power thereof; and that we have not, as we ought, endeavoured to receive Christ in our hearts, nor to walk worthy of him in our lives, which are the cause of other sins and transgressions so much abounding among us; and our true and unfeigned purpose, desire, and endeavour for ourselves, and all others under our charge, both in public and private, in all duties we owe to God and man, to amend our lives, and each one to go before another in the example of a real reformation, that the Lord may turn away His wrath and heavy indignation, and establish the church and the land in truth and peace."

GENERAL ASSEMBLY OF 1864, (OLD SCHOOL.)

May 19—The body met at Newark, N. J.

May 20—Hon. Stanley Matthews, of Cincinnati, from the Committee on Bills and Overtures—which consisted of Drs. W. L. Breckinridge, J. M. Krebs, J. Greenleaf, J. Kirkpatrick, J. V. Reynolds, A. S. MacMaster, J. D. Paxton, and Rev. Messrs. J. J. Porter, J. A. Steele, and Ruling Elders R. Carter, T. Charlton Henry, A. G. McCandless, S. Matthews, and J. Y. Allison—made a report, which was amended in a few particulars and adopted with almost entire unanimity, as follows:

The Committee on Bills and Overtures report:

Overture No. 12, from the Presbytery of Newton, reciting the former deliverances of the General Assembly upon the subject of slavery in this country, and the duty of emancipation, and asking this General Assembly to take such action as in their wisdom seems proper to meet the present aspects of human bondage in our country, and recommend the adoption of the following:

In the opinion of the General Assembly, the solemn and momentous circumstances of our times, the state of our country, and the condition of our church, demand a plain declaration of its sentiments upon the question of slavery, in view of its present aspects in this country.

From the earliest period of our church, the General Assembly delivered unequivocal testimonies upon this subject, which it will be profitable now to re-affirm.

In the year 1787, the Synod of New York and Philadelphia, in view of movements then on foot looking to the abolition of slavery, and highly approving of them, declared that "inasmuch as men introduced from a servile state to a participation of all the privileges of civil society, without a proper education, and without previous habits of industry, may be, in many respects, dangerous to the community, therefore they earnestly recommend to all the members belonging to their communion to give these persons, who are at present held in servitude, such good education as to prepare them for the better enjoyment of freedom." * * * "And finally, they recommend it to all their people to use the most prudent measures consistent with the interest and the state of civil society in the countries where they live to procure eventually the final abolition of slavery in America."

In 1795, the General Assembly "assured all the churches under their care, that they view with the deepest concern any vestiges of slavery which may exist in our country."

In 1815 the following record was made:

"The General Assembly have repeatedly declared their cordial approbation of those principles of civil liberty which appear to be recognized by the Federal and State Governments in these United States. They have expressed their regret that the slavery of the Africans and of their descendants still continues in so many places, and even among those within the pale of the church, and have urged the Presbyteries under their care to adopt such measures as will secure, at least to the rising generation of slaves, within the bounds of the church, a religious education, that they may be prepared for the exercise and enjoyment of liberty when God in his providence may open a door for their emancipation."

The action of the General Assembly upon the subject of slavery in the year 1818 is unequivocal, and so well known that it need not be recited at length. The following extracts, however, we regard as applicable to our present circumstances, and proper now to be reiterated:

"We consider the voluntary enslaving of one portion of the human race by another as a gross violation of the most precious and sacred rights of human nature, as utterly inconsistent with the law of God, which requires us to love our neighbor as ourselves, and as totally irreconcilable with the spirit and principles of the gospel of Christ, which enjoins that 'all things whatsoever ye would that men should do to you, do ye even so to them.' Slavery creates a paradox in the moral system. It exhibits rational, moral, and accountable beings in such circumstances as scarcely to leave them the power of moral action. It exhibits them as dependent on the will of others, whether they shall receive religious instruction, whether they shall know and worship the true God, whether they shall enjoy the ordinances of the gospel, whether they shall perform the duties and cherish the endearments of husbands and wives, parents and children, neighbors and friends; whether they shall preserve their chastity and purity, or regard the dictates of justice and humanity. Such are some of the consequences of slavery—consequences not imaginary, but which connect themselves with its very existence.

"From this view of the consequences resulting from the practice, into which Christian people have most inconsistently fallen, of enslaving a portion of their brethren of mankind, it is manifestly the duty of all Christians, who enjoy the light of the present day, when the inconsistency of slavery, both with the dictates of humanity and of religion, has been demonstrated, and is generally seen and acknowledged, to use their honest, earnest, and unwearied endeavors to correct the errors of former times, and, as speedily as possible, to efface this blot on our holy religion, and to obtain the complete abolition of slavery throughout Christendom, and if possible throughout the world."

They earnestly exhorted those portions of the Church where the evil of slavery had been entailed upon them, "to continue, and, if possible, to increase their exertions to effect a total abolition of slavery, and to suffer no greater delay to take place in this most interesting concern than a regard to public welfare truly and indispensably demands;" and declare "that our country ought to be governed in this matter by no other consideration than an honest and impartial regard to the happiness of the injured party, uninfluenced by the expense or inconvenience which such a regard may involve;" warning "all who belong to our denomination of Christians against unduly extending this plea of necessity; against making it a cover for the love and practice of slavery, or a pretence for not using efforts that are lawful and practicable to extinguish this evil."

Such were the early and unequivocal instructions of our Church. It is not necessary too minutely to inquire how faithful and obedient to these lessons and warnings those to whom they were addressed have been. It ought to be acknowledged that we have all much to confess and lament as to our short-comings in this respect. Whether a strict and careful application of this advice would have rescued the country from the evil of its condition, and the dangers which have since threatened it, is known to the Omniscient alone. Whilst we do not believe that the present judgments of our Heavenly Father, and Almighty and Righteous Governor, have been inflicted solely in punishment for our continuance in this sin; yet it is our judgment that the recent events in our history, and the present condition of our Church and country furnish manifest tokens that *the time has at length come, in the providence of God, when it is His will that every vestige of human slavery among us should be effaced, and that every Christian man should address himself with industry and earnestness to his appropriate part in the performance of this great duty.*

Whatever excuses for its postponement may heretofore have existed, no longer avail. When the country was at peace within itself, and the Church was unbroken, many consciences were perplexed in the presence of this great evil, for the want of an adequate remedy. Slavery was so formidably intrenched behind the ramparts of personal interests and prejudices, that to attack it with a view to its speedy overthrow appeared to be attacking the very existence of the social order itself, and was characterized as the inevitable introduction of an anarchy, worse in its consequences than the evil for which it seemed to be the only cure. But the folly and weakness of men have been the illustrations of God's wisdom and power. Under the influence of the most incomprehensible infatuation of wickedness, those who were most deeply interested in the perpetuation of slavery *have taken away every motive for its further toleration.*

The spirit of American slavery, not content with its defences to be found in the laws of the States, the provisions of the Federal Constitution, the prejudices in favor of existing institutions, and the fear of change, has taken arms against law, organized a bloody rebellion against the national authority, made formidable war upon the Federal Union, and in order to found an empire upon the cornerstone of slavery, threatens not only our existence as a people, but the annihilation of the principles of free Christian government; and thus has rendered the continuance of negro slavery incompatible with the preservation of our own liberty and independence.

In the struggle of the nation for existence against this powerful and wicked treason, the highest executive authorities have proclaimed the abolition of slavery within most of the Rebel States, and decreed its extinction by military force. They have enlisted those formerly held as slaves to be soldiers in the national armies. They have taken measures to organize the labor of the freedmen, and instituted measures for their support and government in their new condition. It is the President's declared policy not to consent to the reorganization of civil government within the seceded States upon any other basis than that of emancipation. In the loyal States where slavery has not been abolished, measures of emancipation, in different stages of progress, have been set on foot, and are near their consummation; and propositions for an amendment to the Federal Constitution, prohibiting slavery in all the States and Territories, are now pending in the national Congress. So that, in our present situation, the interests of peace and of social order are identified with the success of the cause of emancipation. The difficulties which formerly seemed insurmountable, in the providence of God, appear now to be almost removed. The most formidable remaining obstacle, we think, will be found to be the unwillingness of the human heart to see and accept the truth against the prejudices of habit and of interest; and to act towards those who have been heretofore degraded as slaves, with the charity of Christian principle in the necessary efforts to improve and elevate them.

In view, therefore, of its former testimonies upon the subject, the General Assembly does hereby devoutly express its gratitude to Almighty God for having overruled the wickedness and calamities of the rebellion, so as to work out the deliverance of our country from the evil and guilt of slavery; its earnest desire for the extirpation of slavery, as the root of bitterness from which has sprung rebellion, war, and bloodshed, and the long list of horrors that follow in their train; its earnest trust that the thorough removal of this prolific source of evil and harm will be speedily followed by the blessings of our Heavenly Father, the return of peace, union and fraternity, and abounding prosperity to the whole land; and recommend to all in our communion to labor honestly, earnestly, and unweariedly in their respective spheres for this glorious consummation, to which human justice, Christian love, national peace and prosperity, every earthly and every religious interest, combine to pledge them.

ATTEMPTED CENSURE OF THE ASSEMBLY'S ACTION.

At the meeting of the Synod of New York in Jersey City, in October, the following preamble and resolutions were introduced by Rev. Henry J. Van Dyke, of Brooklyn, on the morning of the first day of the session. They refer to the recent action of the Old School General Assembly, held in the city of Newark, New Jersey, in May last:

Whereas, The General Assembly of 1864, in its action on the subject of slavery, has fully endorsed "the President's declared policy not to consent to the reorganization of civil government in the seceded States upon any other basis than that of emancipation;" affirming that the said policy is in accordance with the will of God, and that all in our communion are pledged by every earthly and every religious interest to labor unweariedly in their respective spheres for its consummation;

And whereas, The Assembly has virtually exerted its influence in support of that political party which has selected the President for its candidate, and adopted his declared policy as its platform in the approaching Presidential election;

And whereas, In the case of the Rev. Dr. McPheeters, the Assembly did apparently sanction the interference of the secular power with the spiritual affairs of our churches, the enforcement of political test oaths as a qualification for members sitting in our church courts, and the proscription of Christian ministers, against whom there is no charge of heresy or crime, upon the ground that they entertain, or are supposed to entertain, certain political opinions; therefore,

Resolved, That this Synod, while disavowing for itself all intention of entering, directly or indirectly, into the political contests of the day, does solemnly affirm and declare—

1. That according to the Word of God and the Constitution of the Presbyterian Church, the General Assembly has authority "to handle or conclude nothing but that which is ecclesiastical;" that it has no right "to intermeddle with civil affairs which concern the Commonwealth, unless by way of humble petition in cases extraordinary, or by way of advice for satisfaction of conscience, if thereunto required by the civil magistrate;" [Confession of Faith, ch. xxxi, sec. 4,] that its "power is wholly moral or spiritual, and *that* only ministerial and declarative;" that the limits within which this ministerial and declarative power may be lawfully exercised are clearly defined in ch. xii of our Form of Government; and that all acts and declarations of the Assembly which are contrary to, or aside from, these limits are null and void.

2. That all interference of civil magistrates or military commanders with the spiritual affairs of our churches—whether to destroy or restrict the right of the people to choose their own religious teachers, to define the qualifica-

tion of members of our church courts, or to prescribe to ministers the doctrine they shall preach or the prayers they shall offer to God—is a violation of the true principles of religious liberty, and an invasion of the prerogatives of Jesus Christ, who alone is head of the church. [See Confession of Faith, ch. xxiii, sec. 3.]

3. That the bond of union, the measure of obligation, and the charter of ecclesiastical rights for all the ministers and members of the Presbyterian Church, is the Word of God as expounded and summed up in our Confession of Faith, Form of Government, Book of Discipline, Catechisms, and Directory for Worship; and that no minister or church member can be lawfully impeached or proscribed, except upon conviction of heresy or crime according to the rules therein provided.

4. That the appropriate business of Christ's ambassadors is to preach the Gospel for the conversion of sinners and the edification of saints in their most holy faith, and that for our ministers to devote themselves unweariedly in their respective spheres to the consummation of the declared policy of any political party, would be unwise, unscriptural, injurious to the best interests of the church and of society, and a dereliction from their divine commission, in the discharge of which they are taught by inspired precept and example to "know nothing but Jesus Christ and him crucified."

After considerable debate the subject was referred to a Special Committee. The committee were Rev. Drs. Krebs, Imbrie, and Snodgrass; Rev. Mr. Knox and Elders Wilkin, Beard and Hubbell.

Two reports were made—the majority by Rev. Dr. Krebs, the minority by Rev. Mr. Knox, for himself.

THE MAJORITY REPORT.

The preamble of the paper submitted by Mr. Van Dyke not only invokes this Synod improperly to arraign the late General Assembly, and to hold it up to censure and reproach, but it is also an entire misrepresentation of the language, spirit, and intent, of the declarations of that body in regard to slavery, to the attitude and aspect of Divine Providence towards it, and to the relation and duty of the Church thereto at this time; and is also a misrepresentation of the Assembly's decision in the case of the Rev. Dr. McPheeters, and of the grounds thereof as set forth by the Assembly itself; because, in the judgment of this Synod, it was not the intention, and is not the legitimate effect of the General Assembly's action on slavery to determine what policy ought to be pursued by any Administration in the reorganization of civil government in the seceded States, nor to endorse any of the candidates for election to the office of Presidency of the United States, nor to express any approbation nor disapprobation of any of the political parties existing in these States, nor to give any intimation to ministers or church members that they should labor or vote for the success of one party rather than another.

And further, because in the case of Rev. Dr. McPheeters the Assembly, in the judgment of this Synod, gave no sanction whatever to the interference of the secular power with the spiritual affairs of our churches; neither did the Assembly sanction the proscription of Christian ministers against whom there is no charge of heresy or scandal, upon the ground that they entertain, or are supposed to entertain, any political opinions whatever. Furthermore—

Whereas the paper as a whole is calculated to make the impression that the Assembly has departed from the principles of our standards concerning the province of the Church and its courts, relative to civil affairs, to the question of religious liberty, and to the prerogatives of the Christian ministry, which principles are alluded to in the resolutions being proposed by the paper aforesaid; therefore,

Resolved, That while we steadfastly maintain the acknowledged principles of our standards referred to, in the resolutions of the paper, we see no necessity for expounding or re-affirming the same, and that the further consideration of the whole subject be and is hereby indefinitely postponed.

MINORITY REPORT.

Whereas, the preamble of the paper submitted by Mr. Van Dyke is calculated to make the impression that the Assembly has departed from the principle of our standards touching the subjects hereinafter mentioned,

Resolved, 1st. That in the judgment of this Synod it was not the intention and is not the legitimate effect of the General Assembly's action on slavery, to determine what policy ought to be pursued by any Administration in the reorganization of civil government in the seceded States, nor to endorse any of the candidates for election to the office of President of the United States, nor to express any approbation or disapprobation of any of the political parties existing in these States, nor to give any intimation to ministers or church members that they should labor or vote for the success of one party rather than the other.

Resolved, 2d. That in the case of the Rev. Dr. McPheeters, the Assembly, in the judgment of this Synod, gave no sanction whatever to the interference of the secular power with the spiritual affairs of our churches, neither did the Assembly sanction the prosecution of church ministers, against whom there is no charge of heresy or scandal, upon the ground that they entertain, or are supposed to entertain, any political opinions whatever.

Resolved, 3d. That in reference to the subjects embraced in the above resolutions, this Synod believes and does hereby solemnly affirm:

1st. That according to the Word of God, &c. (Here follow the four resolutions submitted by Rev. H. J. Van Dyke.)

After debate, the majority report was adopted.

YEAS—William D. Snodgrass, R. Bull, D. N. Freeland, D. McAlise, A. R. McCoubrey, W. S. Brown, S. H. Kellogg, Samuel J. Wilkin, James Van Keuren, William Wardell, Hiram Brink, H. Hall, J. Lillie, F. R. Masters, G. T. Woodhul, William Irvin, I. C. Tyson, J. H. Scofield, H. W. Couplin, H Hoyt, E. P. Benedict, A. L. Linsley, P. B. Heroy, C. W. Adams, H. W. Smuller, C. W. Baird, T. C. Perry, W. H. Hodge, J. O. Eggleston, E. Sours, S. Lyon, W. S. Van Renselaer, W. B. Reeve, E. Hopper, C. M. Oakley, T. M. Gray, E. F. Mundy, R. D. Gardner, C. W. Cooper, S. G. Law, R. Davidson, H. N. Wilson, S. Ireland, J. P. Foster, J. M. Huntting, J. E. Rockwell, B. F. Stead, P. D. Oakey, J. Hancock, N. West, H. Smith, J. S. Henderson, W. L. Wood, C. Roberts, A. Cruikshank, J. Dunbar, E. Beard, G. Spring, J. M Krebs, J. K. Campbell, J. Harkness, C. K. Imbrie, J Thompson, E. E. Rankin, M. Rowell, S. D. Alexander, Thomas J. Evan, A. P. Botsford, F. L. King, S. F. Farmer, A. D. L. Jewett, A. S. Stewart, C. C. Darling, C. G. Harmen, H. Day, W. H. Talcott, J. Aitken, E. C. Bridgman, R. W. Dickinson, D. M. Halliday, J. H. Leggett, C. A. Stoddard, S. T. Carter, A. R. Walsh, J. P. Cummings, W. Nelson, J. S. Tonnele, W. M. Pearson—88.

NAYS—D. Beattie, A. Harlow, F.T. Williams, S. L. Mershon, J. O. Hunting, J. P. Knox, H. J Van Dyke, J. C. Cook, A. McClelland, G. O. Woodhull, F. Steins, W. A. Scott, W. E. Lewis, D. C. Niven, D. Demarest—15.

EXCUSED FROM VOTING—T. S. Childs, J. Neander, J. D. Wells, W. B. Lee, J. H. Hopkins, N. L. Rice, A. McGlashan, G. Nixon—8.

The following additional proceedings took place:

PROTEST.

Against the action of this Synod in indefinitely postponing the whole subject of the action of the last General Assembly in regard to the political aspects of slavery and the mutual relations of Church and State as involved in the case of the Rev. Dr. McPheeters, the undersigned feel compelled to respectfully protest, and do so protest; because, first, the characterization of the preamble of Mr. Van Dyke's paper, passed by the report containing the above action, is unnecessarily denunciatory, unjust, and injurious; and, second, in the judgment of the protestants, in view of the sufferings of some of our churches and ministers from the encroachments of civil or military authorities, or both, upon the divine rights of the Church, it is high time for this Synod, without engaging in any way in the political strifes of the day, now to affirm and declare, I, that, &c., &c., (the resolution of Mr. Van Dyke's paper.)

Signed, A. McClelland, D. C. Niven, D. Beattie, A. Harlow, John C. Cook, John P. Knox, Henry J. Van Dyke, W. B. Lee, F. T. Williams, W. A. Scott.

ANSWER.

In answer to the above protest, the Synod deems it sufficient simply to record its judgment, that in view of the charges against the General Assembly made in the paper proposed to us by Mr. Van Dyke, and now recorded in our minutes and published to the world, it was our duty to *characterize* them, as in fact they are, a perversion and misrepresentation of the Assembly's action in the premises; and further, the Synod does regard itself as having virtually re-affirmed the general principles referred to, although the Synod did not deem it proper or needful at this time formally to recite and expound specifically and in the abstract those principles, in the form, and manner, and circumstances proposed by Mr. Van Dyke.

OTHER SYNODICAL, AND PRESBYTERIAL ACTION.

In 1861, the Synod of New York and New Jersey, sitting at Newark, appointed Rev.

Messrs. James P. Wilson, D. D., Wm. Adams, D. D., W. W. Newell, D. D., and Hon. Wm. Pennington, and Hon. Edw. A. Lambert, Elders, to prepare a minute on the condition of the country, which expressed the wantonness and wickedness of the rebellion of the Southern States, and the duty of all Christians and all patriots in the crisis. The report was unanimously adopted. and transmitted to the Secretary of State, who thus responded:

DEPARTMENT OF STATE,
WASHINGTON, *November* 27, 1861.

To the Synod of New York and New Jersey:

REVEREND GENTLEMEN: The minute containing your resolutions on the condition of the country, which you directed to be sent to me, has been submitted to the President of the United States.

I am instructed to express to you his great satisfaction with those proceedings, which are distinguished equally by their patriotic sentiments and a purely Christian spirit. It is a just tribute to our system of government that it has enabled the American people to enjoy unmolested more of the blessings of Divine Providence which affect the material conditions of human society than any other people ever enjoyed, together with a more absolute degree of religious liberty than, before the institution of that Government, had ever been hoped for among men. The overthrow of the Government might therefore justly be regarded as a calamity, not only to this nation, but a misfortune to mankind. The President is assured of the public virtue and of the public valor, but these are unavailing without the favor of God. The President thanks you for your invocations of that indispensable support, and he earnestly solicits the same invocations from all classes and conditions of men. Believing that those prayers will not be denied by the God of our Fathers, he trusts and expects that the result of the most unhappy attempt at revolution will confirm and strengthen the union of the Republic, and ultimately renew the fraternal affections among its members so essential to a restoration of the public welfare and happiness.

I am, very sincerely, your very humble servant,

WILLIAM H. SEWARD.

SYNOD OF MISSOURI, AND PRESBYTERY OF ST. LOUIS.

This Synod, at its meeting in November, 1861,

Resolved, That the action of the General Assembly in May last, in relation to the political condition of the country, was unscriptural, unconstitutional, unwise, and unjust; and we therefore solemnly protest against it, and declare it of no binding force whatever on this Synod or upon the members of the Presbyterian Church within our bounds.

But at its meeting in the city of St. Louis, October 13, 1864, this same Synod declared the above resolution to be rescinded, and that the Temporary Clerk be authorized and requested, in the presence of Synod, to write across the face of said resolution, where the same is recorded in the minutes, the words: "Rescinded by order of Synod, October 13, 1864," and sign his name thereto as clerk. Whereupon the Temporary Clerk did as authorized and requested, in the presence of Synod, and signed his name thereto.

The St. Louis Presbytery, at a recent session, adopted this resolution:

Resolved, That the Presbytery of St. Louis, acting from a sense of duty to the churches over which we rule, hereby earnestly entreat and warn all members of churches to abstain from all participation in the present rebellion, and from giving countenance or encouragement thereto by word or deed, as such participation by word or deed involves a sin against God, and exposes those engaged in it to the penalties of ecclesiastical discipline.

THE SYNOD OF KENTUCKY OF 1864, ON THE DELIVERANCE OF THE GENERAL ASSEMBLY.

The General Assembly, at different times, but especially in the years 1818 and 1845, set forth the opinions and views of the Presbyterian Church of the United States on the subject of slavery. By these deliverances this Synod was willing and is still willing to abide, and any further or different utterance on that subject, by the last General Assembly, was, in the judgment of this Synod, unnecessary, unwise, and untimely;—*unnecessary*, because the former deliverances were sufficiently expressive of the views of the Church, and had been acquiesced in, with great unanimity, for many years; *unwise*, because the whole country was excited upon the subject of slavery, and the means adopted by the President of the United States for its destruction, in regard to which there was great division of sentiment in the public mind;—and the Assembly could not take any action on the subject without at least seeming to cast its influence with the one or the other political parties which divided the country. Moreover, the minute of the Assembly was peculiarly liable to this interpretation, because in the latter part of it, some of its expressions may be misunderstood, and others may be taken in the sense of a political, if not partizan statement.

The action of the Assembly was untimely, because times of high political excitement are not proper occasions for ecclesiastical courts to express opinions upon the topics which constitute the party issues of the day. The mission of the Church of Christ is spiritual, and any interference with matters purely political is a departure from her duty, and without the pale of her authority, as conferred upon her by her Divine Head.

Whilst expressing these views, the Synod deems it timely again to declare, that it adheres with unbroken purpose to the Presbyterian Church of the United States of America, and hereby enjoins on all its members, and upon all under its control and care, to avoid all divisive and schismatical courses, to cultivate the peace of the Church, and to practice great mutual forbearance.

GENERAL ASSEMBLY OF 1861, (NEW SCHOOL.)

May 16—The body met at Syracuse, New York.

May 20—The report of the Committee on the State of the Country—Henry Kendall, D. D., Asa D. Smith, D. D., John Jenkins, D. D., Samuel M. Blatchford, and J. Mellen Smith—was adopted, as follows:

Whereas a portion of the people of the United States of America have risen up against the rightful authority of the Government; have instituted what they call the "Confederate States of America," in the name and defence of which they have made war against the United States; have seized the property of the Federal Government; have assailed and overpowered its troops in the discharge of their duty; and are now in armed rebellion against it; the General Assembly of the Presbyterian Church of the United States of America cannot forbear to express their amazement at the wickedness of such proceedings, and at the bold advocacy and defence thereof, not only in those States in which ordinances of "secession" have been passed, but in several others; and whereas the General Assembly—in the language of the Synod of New York and Philadelphia, on the occasion of the revolutionary war—"being met at a time when public affairs wore so threatening an aspect, and when (unless God in His own sovereign providence speedily prevent it) all the horrors of civil war are to be apprehended, are of opinion that they cannot discharge their duty to the numerous congregations under their care without addressing them at this important crisis; and as a firm belief and habitual recollection of the power and presence of the living God ought at all times to possess the minds of real Christians, so in seasons of public calamity, when the Lord is known by the judgments which He executeth, it would be an ignorance or indifference highly criminal not to look up to Him with reverence, to implore His mercy by humble and fervent prayer, and, if possible, to prevent His vengeance by unfeigned repentance;" therefore,

1. *Resolved*, That inasmuch as the Presbyterian Church, in her past history, has frequently lifted up her voice againt oppression, has shown herself a champion of constitutional liberty as against both despotism and anarchy, throughout the civilized world, we should be recreant to our high trust were we to withhold our earnest protest against all such unlawful and treasonable acts.

2. *Resolved*, That this assembly and the churches which it represents cherish an undiminished attachment to the great principles of civil and religious freedom on which our national Government is based, under the influence of which our fathers prayed and fought and bled; which issued in the establishment of our independence, and by the preservation of which we believe that the common interests of evangelical religion and civil liberty will be most effectually sustained.

3. *Resolved*, That inasmuch as we believe, according to our *form of government*, that "God, the Supreme Lord and King of all the world, hath ordained civil magistrates to be

under him over the people for his own glory and the public good, and to this end hath armed them with the power of the sword for the defence and encouragement of them that are good and for the punishment of evil-doers," there is, in the judgment of the Assembly, no blood or treasure too precious to be devoted to the defence and perpetuity of the Government in all its constitutional authority.

4. *Resolved*, That all those who are endeavoring to uphold the Constitution and maintain the Government of these United States in the exercise of its lawful prerogatives are entitled to the sympathy and support of all Christian and law-abiding citizens.

5. *Resolved*, That it be recommended to all our pastors and churches to be instant and fervent in prayer for the President of the United States and all in authority under him, that wisdom and strength may be given them in the discharge of their arduous duties; for the Congress of the United States; for the lieutenant-general commanding the army-in-chief, and all our soldiers, that God may shield them from danger in the hour of peril, and by the outpouring of the Holy Spirit upon the army and navy, renew and sanctify them, so that, whether living or dying, they may be the servants of the Most High.

6. *Resolved*, That in the countenance which many ministers of the gospel and other professing Christians are now giving to treason and rebellion against the Government we have great occasion to mourn for the injury thus done to the kingdom of the Redeemer; and that though we have nothing to add to our former significant and explicit testimonies on the subject of slavery, we yet recommend our people to pray more fervently than ever for the removal of this evil, and all others, both social and political, which lie at the foundation of our present national difficulties.

7. *Resolved*, That a copy of these resolutions, signed by the officers of the General Assembly, be forwarded to his Excellency Abraham Lincoln, President of the United States.

GENERAL ASSEMBLY OF 1862, (NEW SCHOOL.)

May 15—The body met at Cincinnati.

May 22—The report of the Committee on the State of the Country—Nathan S. S. Beman, D. D., LL. D., Rev. William Aikman, Rev. Horace Rood, and Mr. J. Culbertson Reynolds—was adopted, as follows:

Whereas this General Assembly is called, in the providence of God, to hold its deliberations at a time when a wicked and fearful rebellion is threatening to destroy the fair fabric of our Government, to lay waste our beloved country, and to blight and ruin, so far as the present life is concerned, all that is most dear to us as Christians; and whereas, as a branch of the Christian Church, (PRESBYTERIANS) have ever been found loyal and the friends of good order, believing, as they do, that civil government is "ordained of God," that "the magistrate is the minister of God for good," that "he beareth not the sword in vain," and they are therefore "subject" to this ordinance of God, "not only for wrath," or under the influence of fear, but also "for conscience' sake," or under the influence of moral and Christian principle; and, whereas the particular Church, whose representatives we are, and in whose behalf we are now and here called to act, have inscribed upon our banner, "THE CONSTITUTIONAL PRESBYTERIAN CHURCH"—having never favored secession, or nullification, either in Church or State, deem it quite becoming and proper in us to express ourselves, with great Christian sincerity and frankness, on those matters which now agitate our country; therefore,

Resolved, 1. That we deem the Government of these United States the most benign that has ever blessed our imperfect world; and, should it be destroyed after its brief career of good, another such in the ordinary course of human events, can hardly be anticipated for a long time to come; and for these reasons we revere and love it as one of the great sources of hope, under God, for a lost world; and it is doubly dear to our hearts because it was procured and established by the toil, and sacrifices, and blood of our fathers.

Resolved, 2. That rebellion against such a Government as ours, and especially by those who have ever enjoyed their full share of its protection, honor, and rich blessings of every name, can have no excuse or palliation, and can be inspired by no other motives than those of ambition and avarice, and can find no parallel, except in the first two great rebellions—that which assailed the throne of heaven directly, and that which peopled our world with miserable apostates.

Resolved, 3. That whatever diversity of sentiment may exist among us respecting international wars, or an appeal to the sword for the settlement of points of honor or interest between independent nations, we are all of one mind on the subject of rebellion, and especially against the best Government which God has yet given to the world; that our vast army now in the field is to be looked upon as one great police force, organized to carry into effect the Constitution and laws which the insurgents, in common with other citizens, have ordained by their own voluntary acts, and which they are bound by honor, and oath, and conscience, to respect and obey; so that the strictest advocates of peace may bear an active part in this deadly struggle for the life of the Government.

Resolved, 4. That while we have been utterly shocked at the deep depravity of the men who have planned and matured this rebellion, and who are now clad in arms, manifested in words and deeds, there is another class found in the loyal States who have excited a still deeper loathing—some in Congress, some high in civil life, and some in the ordinary walks of business—who never utter a manly thought or opinion in favor of the Government but they follow it, by way of comment, with two or three smooth apologies for Southern insurrectionists; presenting the difference between an open and avowed enemy in the field, and a secret and insidious foe in the bosom of our own family.

Resolved, 5. That, in our opinion, this whole insurrectionary movement can be traced to one primordial root, and to one only—AFRICAN SLAVERY, and the love of it, and a determination to make it perpetual; and, while we look upon this war as having one grand end in view—the restoration of the Union—by crushing out the last living and manifested fibre of rebellion, we hold that everything—the institution of slavery, if need be—must be made to bend to this one great purpose: and, while under the influence of humanity and Christian benevolence, we may commiserate the condition of the ruined rebels once in fraternity with ourselves, but now—should the case occur—despoiled of all that makes the world dear to them, we must be at the same time constrained to feel that the retribution has been self-inflicted, and must add, "*Fiat justitia ruat cœlum.*"

Resolved, 6. That we have great confidence in ABRAHAM LINCOLN, President of the United States, and in his Cabinet, and in the commanders of our armies and our navy, and the valiant men of this Republic prosecuting a holy warfare under their banners; and, while we bless God that He has stood by them, and cheered them on in what we trust will ever stand as the darkest days of our country's humiliation, and crowned them with many signal victories, and knowing that ultimate success is with God alone, we will ever pray that the last sad note of anarchy and misrule may soon die away, and the OLD FLAG OF OUR COUNTRY, radiant with stripes and brilliant with stars, may again wave over a great, and undivided, and happy people.

Resolved, 7. That we here, in deep humiliation for our sins and the sins of the nation, and in heartfelt devotion, lay ourselves, with all that we are and have, on the altar of God and our country; and we hesitate not to pledge the churches and Christian people under our care, as ready to join with us in the same fervent sympathies and united prayers, that our rulers in the Cabinet and our commanders in the field and on the waters, and the brave men under their leadership, may take courage under the assurance that "THE PRESBYTERIAN CHURCH IN THE UNITED STATES OF AMERICA" are with them in heart and hand, in life and effort, in this fearful exciting conflict.

Resolved, finally, That a copy of these resolutions, signed by the officers of the General Assembly, be forwarded to his Excellency, ABRAHAM LINCOLN, President of the United States, accompanied by the following respectful letter:

TO THE PRESIDENT OF THE UNITED STATES:

The General Assembly of the Presbyterian Church, holding its annual session in the city of Cincinnati, Ohio, in transmitting the accompanying resolutions, beg leave most respectfully to express to your Excellency, in a more personal manner, the sentiments of our church in reference to yourself and the great issues with which you are called to deal.

It is with no desire to bring a tribute of flattery, when we assure you, honored sir, of the affection and the confidence of our church. Since the day of your inauguration, the thousands of our membership have followed you with unceasing prayer, besieging the throne of Heaven in your behalf. In our great church courts, in our lesser judicatories, in our weekly assemblages in the house of God, at our family altars, in the inner place of prayer, you have been the burden of our hourly petitioning.

When we look at the history of your administration hitherto, and at the wonderful way in which this people have been led under your guidance, we glorify God in you. We give praise, not to man, but to God. In your firmness, your integrity, challenging the admiration of even our enemies, your moderation, your wisdom, the timeliness of your acts exhibited at critical junctures, your paternal words, so eminently fitting the chosen head of a great people, we recognize the hand and the power of God; we devoutly and humbly accept it as from Him, an answer to the innumerable prayers which have gone up from our hearts.

We desire, as a Church, to express to you our reverence, our love, our deep sympathy with you in the greatness of your trust, and in the depth of your personal bereavements; and to pledge you, as in the past, so in all the future, our perpetual remembrance of you before God, and all the support that loyal hearts can offer.

We have given our sons to the army and navy; some of our ministers and many of our church-members have died in hospital and field; we are glad that we gave them, and we exult in that they were true, even to death. We gladly pledge as many more as the cause of our country may demand.

We believe that there is but one path before this people: this gigantic and inexpressibly wicked rebellion must be destroyed; the interests of humanity, the cause of God and his church, demand it at our hands. May God give to you his great support, preserve you, impart to you more than human wisdom, and permit you, ere long, to rejoice in the deliverance of our beloved country in its peace and unity.

REPLY OF THE PRESIDENT.

DEPARTMENT OF STATE, WASHINGTON, *June* 9, 1862.

REVEREND GENTLEMEN: I have had the honor of receiving your address to the President of the United States, and the proceedings of your venerable body on the subject of the existing insurrection, by which that address was accompanied.

These papers have been submitted to the President. I am instructed to convey to you his most profound and grateful acknowledgements for the fervent assurances of support and sympathy which they contain. For many years hereafter, one of the greatest subjects of felicitation among good men will be the signal success of the Government of the United States in preserving our Federal Union, which is the ark of civil and religious liberty on this continent and throughout the world. All the events of our generation which preceded this attempt at revolution, and all that shall happen after it, will be deemed unimportant in consideration of that one indispensable and invaluable achievement. The men of our generation whose memory will be longest and the most honored will be they who thought the most earnestly, prayed the most fervently, hoped the most confidently, fought the most heroically, and suffered the most patiently in the sacred cause of freedom and humanity. The record of the action of the Presbyterian Church seems to the President worthy of its traditions and its aspirations as an important branch of the Church founded by the Saviour of men.

Commending our yet distracted country to the interposition and guardian care of the Ruler and Judge of Nations, the President will persevere steadily and hopefully in the great work committed to his hands, relying upon the virtue and intelligence of the people of the United States, and the candor and benevolence of all good men.

I have the honor to be, reverend gentlemen, your very obedient servant. WILLIAM H. SEWARD.

TO GEORGE DUFFIELD, D. D., *Moderator;* and EDWIN F. HATFIELD, *Stated Clerk.*

GENERAL ASSEMBLY OF 1863, (NEW SCHOOL.)

May 21—The body met in Philadelphia.

May 27—The report of the Committee on the State of the Country—Rev. Albert Barnes, Thomas H. Skinner, D. D., LL. D., Samuel T. Spear, D. D., Hon. Otis Allen, and Walter S. Griffith—was adopted, as follows:

Whereas a rebellion, most unjust and causeless in its origin, and unholy in its objects, now exists in this country, against the Government established by the wisdom and sacrifices of our fathers, rendering necessary the employment of the armed forces of the nation to suppress it, and involving the land in the horrors of civil war; and

Whereas the distinctly-avowed purpose of the leaders of this rebellion is the dissolution of our national Union, the dismemberment of the country, and the establishment of a new Confederacy within the present territorial limits of the United States, based on the system of human slavery as its chief corner-stone; and

Whereas from the relation of the General Assembly to the churches which they represent, and as citizens of the Republic, and in accordance with the uniform action of our church in times of great national peril, it is eminently proper that this General Assembly should give expression to its views, in a matter so vitally affecting the interests of good government, liberty, and religion; and

Whereas on two previous occasions, since the war commenced, the General Assembly has declared its sentiments in regard to this rebellion, and its determination to sustain the Government in this crisis of our national existence; and

Whereas unequivocal and decided as has been our testimony on all previous occasions, and true and devoted as has been the loyalty of our ministers, elders and people, this General Assembly deems it a duty to the church and the country, to utter its deliberate judgment on the same general subject; therefore,

Resolved, 1. That this General Assembly solemnly reaffirms the principles and repeats the declarations of previous General Assemblies of our church, so far as applicable to this subject, and to the present aspect of public affairs.

2. That in explanation of our views, and as a further and solemn expression of the sentiments of the General Assembly of the Presbyterian church in the United States of America, in regard to the duty of those whom we represent, and of all the American people at the present time, we now declare,

First, That civil government is ordained of God; and that submission to a lawful government, and to its acts in its proper sphere, is a duty binding on the conscience, and required by all the principles of our religion, as a part of our allegiance to God.

Second, That while there is, in certain respects, a ground of distinction between a *Government*, considered as referring to the Constitution of a country, and an *Administration*, considered as referring to the existing agencies through which the principles and provisions of the Constitution are administered; yet the government of a country, to which direct allegiance and loyalty are due at any time, is the administration duly placed in power. Such an administration is the government of a nation; having a right to execute the laws, and to demand the entire, unqualified, and prompt obedience of all who are under its authority; and resistance to such a government is rebellion and treason.

Third, That the present administration of the United States, duly elected under the Constitution, is the government in the land, to which alone, under God, all the citizens of this nation owe allegiance; who, as such, are to be honored and obeyed; whose efforts to defend the government against rebellion are to be sustained; and that all attempts to resist, or set aside, the action of the lawfully-constituted authorities of the government, in any way, by speech or action, to oppose, or embarrass, the measures which it may adopt to assert its lawful authority, except in accordance with the forms prescribed by the Constitution, are to be regarded as treason against the nation, as giving aid and comfort to its enemies, and as rebellion against God.

Fourth, That, in the execution of the laws, it is the religious duty of all good citizens, promptly and cheerfully to sustain the Government by every means in their power; to stand by it in its peril; and to afford all needful aid in suppressing insurrection and rebellion, and restoring obedience to lawful authority in every part of the land.

3. That, much as we lament the evils, the sorrows, the sufferings, the desolations, the sad moral influences of war, and its effect on the religion and churches of the land; much as we have suffered in our most tender relations; yet the war, in our view, is to be prosecuted with all the vigor and power of the nation, until peace shall be the result of victory, until rebellion is completely subdued, until the legitimate power and authority of the Government is fully re-established over every part of our territorial domain, and until the flag of the nation shall wave as the emblem of its undisputed sovereignty; and that, to the prosecution and attainment of this object, all the resources of the nation in men and wealth should be solemnly pledged.

4. That the Government of these United States, as provided for by the Constitution, is not only founded upon the great doctrine of human rights, as vested by God in the individual man, but is also expressly declared to be the supreme civil authority in the land, forever excluding the modern doctrine of secession as a civil or political right; that, since the existing rebellion finds no justification in the facts of the case, or the Constitution of the United States, in any law human or divine, the Assembly can regard it only as treason against the nation, and a most offensive sin in the sight of God, justly exposing its authors to the retributive vengeance of earth and Heaven; that this rebellion, in its origin, history, and measures, has been distinguished by those qualities which most sadly evince the depravity of our nature, especially in seeking to establish a new nationality on this continent, based on the perpetual enslavement and oppression of a weak and long-injured race; that the National forces are, in the view of the Assembly, called out, not to urge war against another Government, but to suppress insurrection, preserve the supremacy of law and order, and save the country from anarchy and ruin.

5. That, in such a contest, with such principles and interests at stake, not only affecting the peace, prosperity, and happiness of this our beloved country for all future time, but involving the cause of human liberty throughout the world, *loyalty*, unreserved and unconditional, to the

constitutionally-elected Government of the United States, not as the transient passion of the hour, but as the intelligent and permanent state of the public conscience, rising above all questions of party politics, rebuking and opposing the foul spirit of treason, whenever and in whatever form exhibited, speaking earnest words of truth and soberness alike through the pulpit, the press, and in all the walks of domestic and social life, making devout supplications to God, and giving the most cordial support to those who are providentially intrusted with the enactment and execution of the laws, is not only a sacred Christian obligation, but is indispensable, if we would save the nation, and perpetuate the glorious inheritance that we possess, to future generations.

6. That the system of human bondage, as existing in the slaveholding States, so palpably the root and cause of this whole insurrectionary movement, not only is a violation of the dearest rights of human nature, but is essentially hostile to the letter and spirit of the Christian religion; that the evil character and demoralizing tendencies of this system, so properly described, and justly condemned, by the General Assemblies of our Church, especially from 1818 to the present time, have been placed in the broad light of day by the history of this existing rebellion; that, in the sacrifices and desolations, the cost of treasure and blood caused thereby, the Assembly recognizes the chastening hand of God, applied to the punishment of national sins, especially the sin of slavery; that, in the Proclamation of Emancipation issued by the President as a war-measure, and submitted by him to the considerate judment of mankind, the Assembly recognizes with devout gratitude that wonder-working providence of God, by which military necessities become the instruments of justice, in breaking the yoke of oppression, and causing the oppressed to go free; and further, that the Assembly beseeches Almighty God in His own time to remove the last vestiges of slavery from this country, and give to the nation, preserved, disciplined, and purified, a peace that shall be based on the principles of eternal righteousness.

7. That this General Assembly commends the President of the United States, and the members of his Cabinet, to the care and guidance of the Great Ruler of Nations, praying that they may have that wisdom which is profitable to direct; and, also, that the patriotism and moral sense of the people may give to them all that support and co-operation, which the exigencies of their position and the perils of the nation so urgently demand.

8. That, in the ardor with which so many members of our Churches, and of the churches of all the religious denominations of our land, have gone forth to the defence of our country, placing themselves upon her altars in this struggle for national life, we see an illustration, not only of the principle of patriotism, but of the principles of our holy religion; that, in the readiness with which such vast numbers have, at the call of their country, devoted themselves to its service, we see a demonstration, which promises security to our institutions in all times of future danger; that we tender the expression of our admiration and hearty thanks to all the officers and men of our Army and Navy; that those who have nobly fallen, and those who survive, have secured an imperishable monument in the hearts of their countrymen; and that this Assembly regards all efforts for the physical comfort, or spiritual good, of our heroic defenders, as among the sweetest charities, which gratitude can impose, or grateful hearts can minister.

9. That this General Assembly exhorts all the churches and ministers connected with this branch of the Presbyterian church, and all our countrymen, to stand by their country; to pray for it; to discountenance all forms of complicity with treason; to sustain those who are placed in civil or military authority over them; and to adopt every means, and at any cost, which an enlightened, self-sacrificing patriotism may suggest, as appropriate to the wants of the hour; having on this subject one heart and one mind; waiting hopefully on Providence; patient amid delays; undaunted by reverses; persistent and untiring in effort, until, by the blessing of God, the glorious motto, "ONE COUNTRY, ONE CONSTITUTION, AND ONE DESTINY," shall be enthroned, as the sublime fact of the present, and the more sublime harbinger of the future.

10. That the General Assembly tenders its affectionate condolence and heartfelt sympathy, to the bereaved families of all the heroic men who have fallen in this contest for national life; and especially to the families of the officers and members of our churches, who have poured out their lives on the altar of their country, with the assurance that they will not be forgotten, in their bereavement, by us, or by a grateful people.

11 That a copy of this action, duly authenticated, be transmitted to the President of the United States, by the hands of those members of the Assembly, who are about to visit Washington city; and that this paper be read in all our pulpits.

REPLY OF THE PRESIDENT.

Upon the adjournment of the Assembly, about sixty-five of the members proceeded to Washington city, and presented the resolutions to the PRESIDENT, to whom they were introduced by John C. Smith, D. D., of that city. The Chairman, John A. Foote, of Cleveland, Ohio, read the resolution, when the PRESIDENT responded:

It has been my happiness to receive testimonies of a similar nature, from I believe, all denominations of Christians. They are all loyal, but perhaps not in the same degree, or in the same numbers; but I think they all claim to be loyal. This to me is most gratifying, because from the beginning I saw that the issues of our great struggle depended on the Divine interposition and favor. If we had that, all would be well. The proportions of this rebellion were not for a long time understood. I saw that it involved the greatest difficulties, and would call forth all the powers of the whole country. The end is not yet.

The point made in your paper is well taken as to "the Government" and the "administration" in whose hands are these interests. I fully appreciate its correctness and justice. In my administration I might have committed some errors. It would be, indeed, remarkable if I had not. I have acted according to my best judgment in every case. The views expressed by the Committee accord with my own; and on this principle "the Government" is to be supported though the administration may not in every case wisely act. As a pilot, I have used my best exertions to keep afloat our ship of State, and shall be glad to resign my trust at the appointed time to another pilot more skillful and successful than I may prove. In every case, and at all hazards, the Government must be perpetuated. Relying, as I do, upon the Almighty Power, and encouraged as I am by these resolutions which you have just read, with the support which I receive from Christian men, I shall not hesitate to use all the means at my control to secure the termination of this rebellion, and will hope for success.

I sincerely thank you for this interview, this pleasant mode of presentation, and the General Assembly for their patriotic support in these resolutions.

GENERAL ASSEMBLY OF 1864, (NEW SCHOOL.)

May 19—The body met in Dayton, Ohio.

May 23—The report of the Committee on the State of the Country—Howard Crosby, D. D., Daniel W. Poor, D. D., Robert W. Patterson, D. D., George W. Simons, and Edward D. Mansfield—was adopted, as follows:

1. *Resolved*, That this General Assembly heartily reaffirms the principles and renews the declarations of previous General Assemblies, so far as applicable to the present aspect of public affairs.

2. That we recognise clearly the good hand of our God in all the victories of the national arms, whereby the limits of the rebellion have been contracted, and its vitality impaired; and we look humbly and confidently to the same Divine source for further success until the nation shall be vindicated, and peace established on the grave of treason.

3. That we also recognise the same good hand of our God in the disappointments and delays of the war, by which He has made more sure the complete destruction of the vile system of human bondage, and rendered less self-confident and more religious the heart of the nation.

4. That in such recognition and hope we do by no means lose sight of our national and individual sins, which render us so utterly unworthy of the Divine favor, but confess them with penitent hearts, and trust to a covenant God in Christ Jesus, that this unworthiness will not hinder the might of God's grace in behalf of the cause of right and order.

5. That we exhort all our churches to renewed zeal and faithfulness in supplication to God for the deliverance of the land, and prosperity of Christ's kingdom, through the blessings of national peace and fraternity.

6. That we cordially uphold the government with our sympathies and prayers in its energetic efforts for the suppression of this most causeless and cruel rebellion, urge all Christians to refrain from weakening the authority of the Administration by ill-timed complaints and unnecessary criticism, fully believing that in such a crisis all speech and action which tend to difference should be sedulously avoided for the sake of the common weal.

7. That a copy of these resolutions, duly authenticated, be sent to the President of the United States by a special committee.

The pastors of the churches were requested to read the same to their congregations.

The special Committee provided for above, were Thomas Brainerd, D. D., Howard Crosby, D. D., Robert W. Patterson, D. D., Edwin F. Hatfield, D. D., Samuel H. Perkins, and Walter S. Griffith.

REFORMED PRESBYTERIAN CHURCH, (OLD SCHOOL,) 1862.

In December, a committee of this Church presented to President LINCOLN this address:

To His Excellency Abraham Lincoln,
President of the United States:

We visit you, Mr. President, as the representatives of the Reformed Presbyterian, or, as it is frequently termed, "Scotch Covenanter" Church—a Church whose sacrifices and sufferings in the cause of civil and religious liberty are a part of the world's history, and to which we are indebted, no less than to the Puritans, for those inestimable privileges so largely enjoyed in the free States of this Union, and which, true to its high lineage and ancient spirit, does not hold within its pale a single secessionist or sympathizer with rebellion in these United States.

Our church has unanimously declared, by the voice of her highest court, that the world has never seen a conflict in which right was more clearly wholly upon the one side, and wrong upon the other, than in the present struggle of this Government with the slaveholders' rebellion. She has also unanimously declared her determination to assist the Government, by all lawful means in her power, in its conflict with this atrocious conspiracy, until it be utterly overthrown and annihilated. Profoundly impressed with the immense importance of the issues involved in this contest, and with the solemn responsibilities which rest upon the Chief Magistrate in this time of the nation's peril, our brethren have commissioned us to come and address you words of sympathy and encouragement; also, to express to you views which, in their judgment, have an important bearing upon the present condition of affairs in our beloved country, to congratulate you on what has already been accomplished in crushing rebellion, and to exhort you to persevere in the work until it has been finally completed. Entertaining no shadow of doubt as to the entire justice of the cause in which the nation is embarked, we nevertheless consider the war a just judgment of Almighty God for the sin of rejecting his authority and enslaving our fellow-men, and are firmly persuaded that His wrath will not be appeased, and that no permanent peace will be attained, until His authority be recognized and the abomination that maketh desolate utterly extirpated. As an anti-slavery Church of the most radical school, believing slavery to be a heinous and aggravated sin both against God and man, and to be placed in the same category with piracy, murder, adultery, and theft, it is our solemn conviction that God, by His word and providence, is calling the nation to immediate, unconditional, and universal emancipation. We hear His voice in the thunders of war, saying to us, "Let my people go." Nevertheless, we have hailed with delighted satisfaction the several steps which you have taken in the direction of emancipation; especially do we rejoice in your late proclamation declaring your intention to free the slaves in the rebel States on the 1st day of January, 1863—an act which, when carried out, will give the death-blow to rebellion, strike the fetters from millions of bondmen, and secure for its author a place among the wisest of rulers and noblest benefactors of the race.

Permit us, then, Mr. President, most respectfully, yet most earnestly, to urge upon you the importance of enforcing that proclamation to the utmost extent of that power with which you are vested. Let it be placed on the highest grounds, Christian justice and philanthropy; let it be declared to be an act of national repentance for long complicity with the guilt of slavery; permit nothing to tarnish the glory of the act, or rob it of its sublime moral significance and grandeur, and it cannot fail to meet a hearty response in the conscience of the nation, and to secure infinite blessings to our distracted country. Let not the declaration of the immortal Burke be verified in this instance: "Good works are commonly left in a rude and imperfect state, through the lame circumspection with which a timid prudence so frequently enervates beneficence. In doing good we are cold, languid, and sluggish, and of all things afraid of being too much in the right." We urge you by every consideration drawn from the Word of God and the present condition of our bleeding country, not to be moved from the path of duty on which you have so auspiciously entered, either by the threats or blandishments of the enemies of human progress, nor to permit this great act to lose its power through fears of timid friends.

There is another point which we esteem of paramount importance, and to which we wish briefly to call your attention. The Constitution of the United States contains no acknowledgment of the authority of God, of His Christ, or of His law, as contained in the Holy Scriptures. This we deeply deplore as wholly inconsistent with all claims to be considered a Christian nation, or to enjoy the protection and favor of God. The Lord Jesus Christ is above all earthly rulers. He is King of Kings and Lord of Lords. He is the one mediator between God and man, through whom alone either nations or individuals can secure the favor of the Most High. God is saying to us in these judgments: "Be wise now, therefore, O ye kings; be instructed, ye judges of the earth. Serve the Lord with fear. Kiss the Son, lest he be angry, and ye perish from the way when His wrath is kindled but a little. Blessed are all they that trust in Him. For the nation and kingdom that will not serve Thee shall perish; yea, those nations shall be utterly wasted."

This time appears to us most opportune for calling the nation to a recognition of the name and authority of God; to the claims of Him who will overturn, overturn, and overturn, until the kingdoms of this world become the kingdoms of our Lord and of His Christ. We indulge the hope, Mr. President, that you have been called, with your ardent love of liberty, your profound moral convictions manifested in your Sabbath proclamations, and in your frequent declarations of dependence upon Divine Providence, to your present position of honor and influence, to free our beloved country from the curse of slavery, and secure for it the favor of the great Ruler of the universe. Shall we not now set the world an example of a Christian state, governed, not by the principles of mere political expediency, but acting under a sense of accountability to God and obedience to those laws of immutable morality which are binding alike upon nations and individuals.

Praying that you may be directed in your responsible position by Divine wisdom; that God may throw over you the shield of His protection; that we may soon see rebellion crushed, its cause removed, and our land become Immanuel's land, we subscribe ourselves, in behalf of the Reformed Presbyterian Church,

Yours, respectfully,

J. R. W. SLOANE,
A. M. MILLIGAN.

REFORMED PRESBYTERIAN (OLD SCHOOL) SYNOD, 1864.

At Philadelphia, June 1, the following resolutions offered by Mr. Sloane were unanimously adopted:

ON THE STATE OF THE COUNTRY.

Whereas the nation is now suffering from those inflictions of the Divine wrath which are the necessary result of its forgetfulness of God and oppression of man; and whereas, in our judgment, love to our country is best manifested not by flattery but by faithful warning and reproofs; and whereas Reformed Presbyterians have from the first existence of this nation predicted the present calamities, as the inevitable consequence of the course which it was pursuing; therefore,

Resolved, That we call this nation to an humble acknowledgment of its sins and a speedy national repentance as the only means of averting present and still greater judgments; to recognise in its Constitution the name and authority of God, the Scriptures as its fundamental law, and Christ as Ruler over the nations.

2. That we demand in the great name of that God, with whom there is no respect of persons, the immediate, unconditional emancipation of all persons held in slavery in the United States; the abolition of all laws making odious distinctions on account of color, and such amendment to the Constitution as will forever prevent involuntary servitude, except for crime, in the United States.

3. That while we cannot, until these demands be met, identify ourselves with the government by oaths of allegiance or any other acts which involve complicity in the guilt of the nation; that, nevertheless, in the present fearful conflict, our entire sympathies are with the North, and that we will exert our influence in all ways consistent with a faithful practical testimony, and with our well-considered and long-established principles, to secure the suppression of rebellion.

4. That we hold in utter abhorrence the present rebellion, as the most impious attempt to establish mischief by law that the world has ever seen; that we express our utter detestation of it, in all its purposes and principles, and will hold no fellowship—political or ecclesiastical—with its aiders and abettors, north or south.

5. That we deprecate the tardiness of the nation in meting out absolute justice to the colored race, as calculated to provoke Heaven, to protract the war, to intensify our present calamities, and to endanger our very existence as a nation.

6. That in the noble devotion of the colored race to the nation in this day of its calamity, their patient endurance of wrong, their sublime trust in Providence, their insatiable thirst for knowledge, their undaunted heroism and courage on the field of battle, and their forbearance under persecution, we find the refutation of the malignant slanders which have been heaped upon them—another illustration of the great truth, that God has "made of one blood all nations of men," and the signs of the approaching day in which "Ethiopia shall stretch out her hand to God."

7. That we have great cause to rejoice, thank God and take courage, that since our last meeting so many efforts have been made both among the people and in Congress, as well as by several ecclesiastical bodies, to effect amendments to the United States Constitution, and that such noble testimonies have been borne in favor of the rights of God and man, in which we clearly see how the testimony of the church has been leavening society, and how, under God, the present civil war is an educator of the people.

8. That we especially notice the late action of the General Conference of the Methodist Episcopal Church, one of the largest religious denominations in the United States, as particularly significant and encouraging; inasmuch as said Conference has not only resolved so to change the general rule of the discipline as to forbid slaveholding altogether, but has also unanimously passed the following resolutions, viz:

That we will use our efforts to make such a change in the Constitution of our country as shall recognise the being of God, our dependence upon Him for prosperity, and also His word as the foundation of civil law.

That we regard slavery as abhorrent to the principles of our holy religion, humanity and civilization; and that we are decidedly in favor of such an amendment to the Constitution, and such legislation on the part of the States, as shall prohibit slavery or involuntary servitude, except for crime throughout all the States and Territories of the country.

As friends of God and humanity, of Christ and the slave, we owe to them constant and untiring efforts to bring the nation into subjection to the Mediator and the enslaved to freedom; and therefore it is very desirable that the National Mass Convention for effecting amendments to the United States Constitution, to meet in Philadelphia on the 6th of July coming, be attended by all the friends of reformation possible, and that these should advocate in said convention nothing less than what Covenanters have always demanded—that the United States Constitution be unequivocally and fully Christian, scriptural and free.

GENERAL SYNOD OF THE REFORMED PRESBYTERIAN CHURCH, MAY, 1863.

Whereas there is a God revealed to man in Holy Scripture as the Creator, Preserver, Redeemer, and Moral Governor of the world; and

Whereas nations, as well as individuals, are the creatures of his power, the dependants of his providence, and the subjects of his authority; and

Whereas civil government is an ordinance of God, deriving its ultimate sanctions from his appointment and permission; and

Whereas it is the duty of all men to acknowledge the true God in all the relations they sustain; and

Whereas there is no specific mention of the authority of God in the Federal Constitution of the United States of America, the fundamental law of their existence as a nation; and

Whereas that Constitution and the Government which it organizes and defines are now undergoing the trial of a defensive civil war against a rebellion of a large portion of its own citizens and for its own national existence; and

Whereas the exigencies of the war have brought the authorities of the nation, civil and military, subordinate and supreme, to formal recognitions of the being, providence, and grace of God and of Jesus Christ his Son, to an extent and with a distinctness, such as the country has never witnessed before; therefore

Resolved, 1. That in the judgment of this Synod the time is come for the proposal of such amendments to the Federal Constitution, in the way provided by itself, as will supply the omissions above referred to, and secure a distinct recognition of the being and supremacy of the God of Divine revelation.

2. That in the judgment of Synod the amendments or additions to be made to the national Constitution should provide not only for a recognition of the existence and authority of God, but also of the mediatorial supremacy of Jesus Christ his Son, "the Prince of the kings of the earth and the Governor among the nations."

3. That, as several articles of the Federal Constitution have been and are construed in defence of slavery, Synod do earnestly ask the appropriate authorities to effect such change in them as will remove all ambiguity of phraseology on this subject, and make the Constitution, as its framers designed it to be, and as it really is in spirit, a document on the side of justice and liberty.

4. That Synod will petition the Congress of the United States, at its next meeting, to take measures for proposing and securing the amendments referred to according to the due order.

5. That Synod will transmit a copy of such action as they may themselves adopt, to the several religious bodies of the country, with the respectful request that they will take order on the subject.

6. That a Committee be appointed, composed of a member from each of the Presbyteries in Synod, to whom this matter shall be referred, and whose duty it shall be to correspond with such Christian statesmen and other individuals of influence as they may find disposed to further this dutiful and momentous object.

GENERAL SYNOD OF THE REFORMED PRESBYTERIAN CHURCH, 1864.

May 18—The body met in Philadelphia, and adopted these resolutions:

Resolved, 1. That it is the duty of the Church of Christ to encourage and sustain the Government of the country in all that they do for the honor of God, the freedom of the enslaved, the mitigation of the inevitable evils of war, and the preservation, at all hazards, of the national life, integrity, and power.

2. That, in the judgment of Synod, the present war is one of defence against a criminal rebellion, commenced and carried on under the auspices of a slaveholding aristocracy, whose success would eventuate in anarchy and the destruction of God's ordinance of civil government among us.

3. That the warmest sympathies of Synod are extended to the soldiers and sailors on the field and on the sea, in the camp and in the hospital, and that the prayer of Synod shall continue to be, that while they are periling and laying down their lives for their country, they may themselves be saved through Him who laid down his life for the world.

GENERAL ASSEMBLY OF THE CUMBERLAND PRESBYTERIAN CHURCH, MAY, 1863.

Whereas this General Assembly of the Cumberland Presbyterian Church in the United States of America cannot conceal from itself the lamentable truth that the very existence of our Church and nation is endangered by a gigantic rebellion against the rightful authority of the General Government of the United States, which rebellion has plunged the nation into the most dreadful civil war; and

Whereas the church is the light of the world, and cannot withhold her testimony upon great moral and religious questions, and upon measures so deeply affecting the great interests of Christian civilization, without becoming justly chargeable with the sin of hiding her light under a bushel; therefore

Resolved, That loyalty and obedience to the General Government, in the exercise of its legitimate authority, are the imperative Christian duties of every citizen, and that treason and rebellion are not mere political offenses of one section against another, but heinous sins against God and His authority.

2. That the interest of our common Christianity, and the cause of Christian civilization and national freedom throughout the world, impels us to hope and pray God (in whom is all our trust) that this unnatural rebellion may be put down, and the rightful authority of the General Government re-established and maintained.

3. That we deeply sympathize with our fellow-countrymen and brethren who, in the midst of great temptation and sufferings, have stood firm in their devotion to God and their country, and also with those who have been driven, contrary to their judgment and wishes, into the ranks of the rebellion.

4. That in this time of trial and darkness, we re-endorse the preamble and resolutions adopted by the General Assembly of the Presbyterian Church at Clarksville, Tennessee, on the 24th day of May, 1850, which are as follows:

Whereas, in the opinion of this General Assembly, the preservation of the Union of these States is essential to the civil and religious liberty of the people, and it is regarded as proper and commendable in the Church, and more particularly in the branch we represent (it having had its origin within the limits of the United States of America, and *that* soon after the blood of our Revolutionary fathers had ceased to flow, in that unequal contest through which they were successfully conducted by the strong arm of Jehovah), to express its devotion, on all suitable occasions, to the Government of their choice: therefore,

Resolved, That this General Assembly look with censure and disapprobation upon attempts, from any quarter, to dissolve the Union, and would regard the success of any such movement as exceedingly hazardous to the cause of religion as well as civil liberty. And this General Assembly would strongly recommend to all Christians to make it a subject of prayer to Almighty God to avert from our beloved country a catastrophe so direful and disastrous.

On the subject of American slavery, your committee submit that we should not view it as if it were about to be introduced, but as already in existence. We do not hesitate to declare that the introduction of slavery was an enormous crime, surpassed by few crimes that have disgraced the history of the world, and that there are at present great evils connected with it, and that we believe will more or less be connected with it while it exists. As to the remedy for these, the greatest and best minds of our country and the world have greatly differed and been much perplexed; therefore, we would recommend to those who, in the providence of God, have been placed in connection with this institution, to continue prayerfully to study the word of God, to determine their duty in regard to their slaves and slavery; and to those who are not thus situated, that they exercise forbearance towards their brethren who are connected with slavery, as the agitation of this subject at the present time in that part of the Church where slavery does not exist,* cannot result in any good either to the master or slave. Touching the subject of American slavery as set forth in the memorial before us, your committee are not prepared to make the simple holding of slaves a test of church-membership, as they understand the memorial before them to propose.

Resolved, That we disavow any connection with, or sympathy for, the extreme measures of ultra-abolitionists, whose efforts, as we believe, have been, and are now, aimed at the destruction of our civil government in order to abolish slavery. The committee would say, in conclusion, that the report herein submitted is agreed upon as a compromise measure, to unite the energies of our beloved Church, and harmonize all our interests in the future, and to bind the entire membership of our Church, if possible, in close bonds of Christianity and fellowship.

GENERAL ASSEMBLY OF THE UNITED PRESBYTERIAN CHURCH, 1861.

May 15—The body met at Monmouth, Illinois, and adopted a report and resolutions, from which the subjoined is extracted:

Slaveholding is the great and immediate cause of the present trouble, though seldom thought of as an evil by those who are directly concerned in it. Slavery must be exceedingly flagrant in the sight of the Great Parent and Ruler of men. If it is murder, the blackest of crimes, to violate the image of God enstamped on man, what is it to debase and trample on that image, and treat it as a brutal thing? To tear asunder the tender ties of nature and affection—what is it but horrible cruelty? To work a man, and give him no wages, or no sufficient wages, is nothing but robbery and oppression. To forbid the great God to speak to His own creatures, that they may be saved, is bidding defiance to the very heavens. To deprive a people of the ordinance and privileges of marriage, is to keep them in beastly concubinage. It should not be thought that we, in the Free States, have nothing to do with this monstrous iniquity. Have we not countenanced those who practised it? Have we not contributed to extend and establish and fortify it?

In view of these things, we doubt not but the Lord is calling us, in this day, to fasting and mourning and supplication; and we, therefore, recommend the adoption of the following resolutions:

Resolved, 1. That the General Assembly do advise and exhort all the people under her inspection to "search and try their ways, and turn to the Lord. Let them cease to do evil, and learn to do well."—Isaiah, i. 16.

2. That the clerk of the Assembly be directed, and hereby is directed, to forward to the President of the United States a letter in behalf of this Assembly, and assure him of our earnest sympathy, and the sympathy of our people, and our and their readiness to co-operate with him, in his endeavors to maintain the Constitution and the integrity of the nation.

GENERAL ASSEMBLY OF THE UNITED PRESBYTERIAN CHURCH, 1862.

May—The following preamble and resolutions were unanimously adopted:

Whereas, our country suffers under a desolating civil war, and calamities not often equaled in the history of the world are now endured by our fellow-countrymen; and whereas the ministers of the gospel, as witnesses for Christ and watchmen on the walls of Zion, are bound by their testimony to give the trumpet a certain and distinct sound in order to warn the people of their danger, and direct them in the way of duty: therefore,

Resolved, That we recognize in the defeats and disasters of our forces in the beginning of the conflict a deserved visitation of God's wrath upon us for our complicity in the sin of slavery; and while we have reason to fear further reverses to our arms, yet we feel and hereby express our gratitude to God for the recent victories and advantages obtained over the enemy, and cherish the hope and belief that God will continue his favor until rebellion shall be forever crushed and peace restored.

2. That, believing that, so long as slavery lives, no permanent peace can be enjoyed, we express our highest gratification at the emancipation policy indicated in the President's recent proposition, to aid the slave States in the "abolishment" of slavery. We thank God for the deliverance of the District of Columbia from the national curse and disgrace of slavery, and would hail with pleasure the proclamation of universal liberty; and we trust our worthy President and Congress will pursue the course of emancipation till liberty shall be proclaimed throughout all the land to all the inhabitants thereof.

3. That, believing compromise with wrong to be the rock on which our Union has been in danger of splitting, we warn our fellow-citizens, politicians, and statesmen, that a compromise with rebellion in behalf of slavery will be no less dangerous to the stability of our Government than to the cause of human freedom.

4. That, believing it to be a duty specially incumbent on the Church to let her light shine, and that her ministry are particularly bound in the present perilous crisis of our country's history to declare the counsel of God regarding the sin and crime of slavery, we trust that all the preachers of that gospel which proclaims liberty to the captive of every denomination, will hear and obey God's voice, now calling upon them louder than ever before, to open their mouth in behalf of the dumb. And we would especially urge upon our brethren under our care, to give a clear testimony on this subject, in order to instruct our people and the nation in the great truth that righteousness exalteth a nation, whilst sin is a reproach to any people.

5. That, as we can only succeed by depending entirely on Divine agency, we will call upon the Lord in our trouble, and ask Him to so overrule the present war, inaugurated for the purpose of extending and perpetuating slavery, that it shall issue in its final and complete overthrow; and that we will bear on our spirits continually, the Congress, the army and navy, and pray especially that God would preserve those who have enlisted in the cause of their country from the perils of the camps and the field, and restore them to their families and friends in peace and safety, and prepare those who may have to die in the conflict, for a victory over death and hell, and a triumphant entrance into heaven.

BAPTIST.

MEETING OF THE BAPTISTS AT BROOKLYN, N. Y., MAY 29, 1861.

A. B. Capwell, Esq., presided, and the following officers were apppointed:

Vice-Presidents—Hon. George N. Briggs, Rev. G S. Webb, D. D., Thomas Watson, Esq., A. Hubbell, Esq.

Secretaries—Rev. W. H. Shailer, D. D., Rev. J. B. Simmons.

Rev. George C. Baldwin, D. D., opened the proceedings with prayer, after which the Committee, appointed at a preliminary meeting—Rev. Dr. William R. Williams, N. Y., Rev. Dr. Rufus Babcock, N. J., Rev. Dr. E. E. Cummings, New Hampshire, Rev. Dr. Samuel Baker, Rev. J. Hyatt S. Smith, of Pa. Rev. Dr. W. H. Shailer, Maine, and Rev. Dr. S. B. Swain, Mass.—presented, through the Chairman, Rev. Dr. Williams, the following report, which was adopted:

The Assembly of Baptists gathered from the various Northern States of the Union would, in the present solemn crisis of our national history, put on record some expres sion of their judgment as Christians, loving their country, and seeking, in the fear and from the grace of God, its best interests. We are threatened to be rent as a people into two hostile camps; several States of the Union have claimed to release themselves by their own act from the national Constitution and Union, having formed what they designate as a Confederacy. They have seized the national forts, armaments, and ships. Such proceedings on the part of a neighboring community would be held actual war. Yet there has been no precedent such as in modern contests inaugurates ordinary hostilities. They have bombarded a national garrison. The General Government at Washington have refused to recognize the right of secession, and have proclaimed alike their own right and their own purpose to occupy the national property and defences now usurped. One of the foremost statesmen in the new movement, and himself the executive officer of the new assumed Confederacy, had declared African slavery the immediate cause of the revolution thus attempted. He has alleged that the old—and, as the North deems it, the only existing Constitution—regarded such slavery as wrong in principle, and that the founders of this Constitution expected the bondage, in some way, and at some time, to vanish. He declares of the new Confederate States that they assume, as their basis, the fundamental erroneousness of such original estimate and expectation on the part of the fathers of our land. Accepting not only the propriety, but the perpetuity of such servitude, he places the new government on the alleged inferiority of the negro race, as its corner-stone. He claims for the new Confederacy that it is the first government in all history thus inaugurated on this new truth, as he would call it. He invites the Northwestern States to enter the Confederacy. But he anticipated the disintegration of the older States; and he declares that in case of these last, admission to the new Confederacy must not be merely by reconstruction, but reorganization and assimilation. In other words, African bondage seems required as the mortar that is to agglutinate, and the rock that is to sustain the re-combined and re-built sovereignty that shall include even these last. Men in high position in the new organization of the South, have proclaimed their intent of seizing the national Capitol, and planting their flag on the seats of Northern State Government. The President of the United States has summoned a large, formidable force to the metropolis of the Union, rallying to the defence of the General Government. Remembering their own character, as the servants of the Prince of Peace this Assembly would speak fraternally, not heedlessly exasperating strife, but also with a frankness and decision as not indorsing injustice. The Church is a kingdom not of the world. But the men of the Church are not the less bound to recognize and loyally to uphold all rightful secular government.

The powers that be are ordained of God, and the magistracy is by His will to bear the sword not in vain. Christ, in His Messiahship, would not be made a judge or a divider as to the statutes and estates of this earth; but He did not, therefore, abrogate the tribunals of earthly judgment. To Cæsar He bade us render Cæsar's dues. He cherished and exemplified patriotism when answering to the appeal made to Him in the behalf of that Gentile ruler, as far as one who loved "our" (Jewish) nation. He showed it when weeping as He predicted the coming woes of His own people and of their chief city. The Gospel of Christ, then, sanctions and consecrates true patriotism. Shall the Christians of the North accept the revolution thus to be precipitated upon them, as warranted and necessary? or shall they acquiesce in it as inevitably dismissing the question of its origin in the irrecoverable past? Shall they wait hopefully the verdict of the nations and the sentence of Providence upon the new basis of this extemporized confederacy? Meanwhile shall they submit passively to the predicted disintegration of their own North, pondering wistfully upon the possibilities of their own reorganization to qualify them for admission on the novel platform, and for their initiation into the new principles of this most summary revolution? The memories of the past and the hopes of the future; history and Scripture; the fear of God and regard to the well-being of man; the best interests of their own estranged brethren at the South, and their own rights and duties, not to themselves and their children only, but as the stewards of constitutional liberty in behalf of all other nations, encouraged by our success, as such remotest nations are baffled and misled, as by our failure such nations would necessarily be,—all considerations unite in shutting up the Christians of the North to one course. The following resolutions present correspondingly what, in our judgment, is the due course of our churches and people:

Resolved, That the doctrine of secession is foreign to our Constitution, revolutionary, suicidal,—setting out in anarchy and finding its ultimate issue in despotism.

2. That the National Government deserves our loyal adhesion and unstinted support in its wise, forbearing, and yet firm maintenance of the national unity and life; and that, sore, long, and costly as the war may be, the North has not sought it, and the North does not shun it, if Southern aggressions press it; and that a surrender of the national Union and our ancestral principles would involve sorer evils and longer continuance, and vaster costliness.

3. That the wondrous uprising, in strongest harmony and largest self-sacrifice, of the whole North to assert and vindicate the national unity, is the cause of grateful amazement and devoutest acknowledgment to the God who sways all hearts and orders all events; and that this resurgent patriotism, wisely cherished and directed, may, in God's blessed discipline, correct evils that seemed chronic and irremediable in the national character.

4. That, fearful as is the scourge of war even in the justest cause, we need, as a nation, to humble ourselves before God for the vain-glory, self-confidence, greed, venality, and corruption of manners too manifest in our land; that in its waste of property and life, its invasion of the Sabbath, its demoralization, and its barbarism, we see the evils to which it strongly tends; but that, waged in a good cause and in the fear of God, it may be to a people, as it often in past times has been, a stern but salutary lesson for enduring good. In this struggle, the churches of the North should, by prayer for them, the distribution of Scripture and tract, and the encouragement of devout chaplains, seek the religious culture of their brave soldiers and mariners.

5. That the North seek not, in any sense, the subjugation of the South, or the horrors of a servile war, or the devastation of their homes by reckless and imbruted mercenaries, but believe most firmly the rejection, were it feasible, of the Constitution and Union, would annihilate the best safeguard of Southern peace.

6. That the churches of our denomination be urged to set apart the last Friday in June as a day of solemn humiliation and prayer for the interposition of God's gracious care to hinder or to limit the conflict, to stay the wrath, and to sanctify the trial; and that one hour also in the Friday evening of each week be observed as a season of intercession, privately, for our country during this period of her gloom and peril.

7. That, brought nearer as eternity and judgment are in such times of sharp trial and sudden change, it is the duty of all to redeem the fleeting hour,—the duty of all Christ's people to see that the walls of Zion be built in troublous times, and to hope only and ever in that wonder-working God who made British missions to India and the South Seas to grow amid the Napoleon wars; who trained, in Serampore missions, Havelock, the Christian warrior, as, two centuries before, He had prepared, in the wars of the Commonwealth, the warrior Baxter, who wrote, as army chaplain, the "Saint's Everlasting Rest," and the Bunyan, who described for all after time, the "Pilgrim's Progress," and "The Holy War."

8. That what was bought at Bunker Hill, Valley Forge, and Yorktown, was not, with our consent, sold at Montgomery; that we dispute the legality of the bargain, and, in the strength of the Lord God of our fathers, shall hope to contest, through this generation, if need be, the feasibility of the transfer.

WEST NEW JERSEY BAPTIST ASSOCIATION, 1861.

Sept. 10—The body met at Mount Holly.

Sept. 13—The report of the Committee on the State of the Country—Samuel Aaron, J. E. Wilson, E. M. Barker, J. M. Carpenter, L. G. Beck, J. H. Lambert, H. J. Mulford, Henry Samuel—was unanimously adopted:

Whereas, all genuine Baptists have ever contended for the principle of civil and religious liberty, (see Acts iv. 19, 20;) and whereas that *liberty* is most fully secured to a people under the form of a Democratic Republic; and whereas our Fathers, with the help of God, by the sacrifice of their fortunes and their lives, established such a Government for these "*United States*;" and whereas this Government is now assailed by armed traitors in the Slave States, and by their insidious accessories in the Free—the one set robbing and butchering the loyal—the other attempting to delude and divide them, and both co-operating to subvert the Government and annihilate the Union; Therefore,

Resolved, That it is our duty as citizens, as Baptists, and as Christians, to resist such *traitors, North and South*, by speech, with the pen and with the press; and, if need be, with the implements of death on the field of battle, pledging to the Government and the Constitution, as our fathers did, "*Our lives, our fortunes, and our sacred honor.*"

2. If the Rebels raise the issue between slavery and the Constitution, that we will support the Government in sweeping from the country that infamous outrage on the *Rights of man.*

3. That we approve of the President's appointment of a "national fast-day," and earnestly request the churches to observe the day by fasting, and by prayer, and by sermons or addresses, calculated to instruct the people and attach them to our noble institutions, the best ever enjoyed.

WEST NEW JERSEY BAPTIST ASSOCIATION OF 1862.

The President made the following reply to the resolutions of this body passed at its session of 1862:

DEPARTMENT OF STATE, *Sept* 29, 1862.

REVEREND GENTLEMEN: The resolutions concerning the state of public affairs, which you have transmitted to me, have been communicated to the President of the United States. I am instructed by him to reply that he accepts, with the most sincere and grateful emotions, the pledges they offer of all the magnanimous endeavors and all the vigorous efforts which the emergencies of the country demand. The President desires, also, that you may be well assured that, so far as it belongs to him, no vigor and no perseverance shall be wanting to suppress the existing insurrection, and to preserve and maintain the Union of the States and the integrity of the country. You may further rest assured that the President is looking for a restoration of peace on no other basis than that of the unconditional acquiescence by the people of all the States in the constitutional authority of the Federal Government. Whatever policy shall lead to that result will be pursued; whatever interest shall stand in the way of it, will be disregarded.

The President is, moreover, especially sensible of the wisdom of your counsels in recommending the cultivation by the Government and people of the United States, of a spirit of meekness, humiliation, and dependence on Almighty God, as an indispensable condition for obtaining that Divine aid and favor without which all human power, though directed to the wisest and most benevolent ends, is unavailing and worthless. In a time of public danger like this, a state, especially a republic, as you justly imply, ought to repress and expel all personal ambitions, jealousies, and asperities, and become one united, harmonious, loyal, and devotional people.

Your obedient servant,
WILLIAM H. SEWARD.

WEST NEW JERSEY BAPTIST ASSOCIATION, 1864.

September 13—The body met at Pemberton.

September 14—The report of the Committee on the State of the Country—Samuel Aaron, A. J. Hires, S. C. Dare, M. Jones, J. Hammett, T. G. Wright, and Joseph H. Kain—was adopted:

Resolved, That Civil Government, whether among Christian or Pagan nations, is an ordinance of God, intended to establish natural justice among men, and that our American Government is the nearest approach to right since the Institutions of Moses.

2. Therefore, that this Southern conspiracy against our nation's life is the greatest political atrocity since Israel rebelled against Jehovah.

3. That as the Lord appointed war, pestilence, and famine to humble and subjugate the Jews, so we believe this nation has His sanction for making the costliest sacrifice of treasure and blood that history records, in order to exterminate, even with fire and sword, those devoted agents of disunion and barbarism, who perseveringly swear that they will destroy the Union or themselves.

4. That the measures thus far employed by our public representatives and sanctioned by the people, have, for the most part, been right and expedient, and that their results do, just now, afford abundant promise and glorious hope of the triumph of liberty, justice and humanity.

5. That any terms of peace short of unqualified submission by the rebels, would be an act of unparalleled treason against the industrial, social, and moral interests of man; and a mockery of the Divine Providence, which has so eminently exalted us in the political heavens, to be the pole-star of liberty to the human race.

NEW JERSEY BAPTIST STATE CONVENTION, 1864.

November 10—The body met in Bordentown.

November 11—The report of the Committee on the State of the Country—Messrs. Wheelock H. Parmly, Henry C. Fish, Lewis Smith, J. Perry Hall, Robert F. Young—was accepted, "with remarkable unanimity," as follows:

Resolved, That we recognize, with deepest gratitude, the hand of God in the signal successes which have attended our gallant army and navy during the past year in their efforts to overthrow the present rebellion.

2. That we also recognize the same Divine hand in moving the hearts of the loyal masses of the country to rebuke, with unmistakable emphasis, through the agency of the ballot-box, the atrocious attempts of designing and corrupt men in the North to embarrass the General Government, and lend effectual aid and comfort to armed traitors.

3. That, since the war into which we have been forced is essentially a conflict between freedom and slavery, we see no method of terminating this conflict, and desire no other, than by the utter extinction of the system of slavery throughout all the national territory.

4. That God is calling us as Christians to put forth the most vigorous exertions for the religious welfare of the millions of oppressed people whom the fortunes of this war are bringing within the reach of our evangelical effort.

5. Inasmuch as success can come from God alone, we still feel the need of continued prayer for the further interposition of His power in our behalf, that this *cruel* conflict may be settled at last in such a manner as to heal all our differences, exalt us in righteousness, and bind all parties and sections into a firm and indissoluble Union.

6. That we heartily approve the President's Proclamation of Thanksgiving on the last Thursday of this month, and recommend that it be observed by all the churches represented in this body.

PHILADELPHIA BAPTIST ASSOCIATION, 1862.

On motion of Rev. J. Wheaton Smith, the following resolutions were adopted:

Resolved, That, as members of the Philadelphia Baptist Association, we reaffirm our unswerving loyalty to the Government of these United States.

2. That in the trials through which we are passing as a nation, we recognize the guidance of the Almighty, and see, not dimly, the purpose of his love to purify the fountains of our national life, and develop in righteousness the elements of our national prosperity.

3. That, as Christian citizens of this Republic, it is our bounden duty to renounce all sympathy with sin, to rebuke all complicity with evil, and cherish a simple, cheerful confidence in Him whose omnipotence flowed through a stripling's arm and sank into the forehead of the Philistine.

4. That, in pursuance of this spirit, we hail with joy the recent proclamation of our Chief Magistrate, declaring freedom on the first day of January next to the slaves in all the then disloyal States, and say to him, as the people said to Ezra, "Arise, for the matter belongeth unto thee; we, also, will be with thee; be of good courage and do it."

5. That, in the name of Liberty, which we love; in the name of Peace, which we would make enduring; in the name of humanity and of religion, whose kindred hopes are blended, we protest against any compromise with rebellion; and for the maintenance of the war on such a basis, whether for a longer or a shorter period, we pledge, in addition to our prayers, our "lives, our fortunes, and our sacred honor."

6. That a copy of these resolutions be forwarded to the President and his advisers, with assurances of the honor in which, as Christians, we hold them, and with our solemn entreaty that no one of them will, in the discharge of duties however faithful for his country, neglect the interests of his own personal salvation.

THE PRESIDENT'S REPLY.

WASHINGTON, *October* 18, 1862.

GENTLEMEN: I have the honor to acknowledge for the other heads of departments, as well as in my own behalf the reception of the resolutions which were adopted by your venerable association during the last week, and to assure you of our high appreciation of the personal kindness, patriotic fervor, and religious devotion which pervade their important proceedings. You seem, gentlemen, to have wisely borne in mind, what is too often forgotten that any government—especially a republican one—cannot be expected to rise above the virtue of the people over whom it presides. Government is always dependent on the support of the nation from whom it derives all its power and all its forces, and the inspiration which can give it courage, energy, and resolution, can come only from the innermost heart of the country which it is required to lead or to save. It is indeed possible for our Administration in this country to conceive and perfect policies which would be beneficent, but it oould not carry them into effect without the public consent; for the first instruction which the statesman derives from experience is, that he must do in every case, not what he wishes, but what he can.

In reviewing the history of our country, we find many instances in which it is apparent that grave errors have been committed by the Government; but candor will oblige us to own that heretofore the people have always had substantially the very kind of Administration which they at the time desired and preferred. Political, moral, and religious teachers exercise the greatest influence in forming and directing popular sentiments and resolutions. Do you, therefore, gentlemen, persevere in the inculcation of the principles and sentiments which you have expressed in your recent proceedings, and rest assured that, if the national magnanimity shall be found equal to the crisis through which the country is passing, no efforts on the part of the Administration will be spared to bring about a peace without a loss of any part of the national territories, or the sacrifice of any of the constitutional safeguards of civil or religious liberty. I need hardly say that the satisfaction which will attend that result will be immeasurably increased if it shall be found also, that in the operations which shall have produced it, humanity shall have gained new and important advantages. Commending ourselves to your prayers, and to the prayers of all who desire the welfare of our country and of mankind, I tender you the sincere thanks of my associates, with whom I have the honor to remain, gentlemen, your very obedient servant,

WILLIAM H. SEWARD.

PHILADELPHIA BAPTIST ASSOCIATION, 1864.

October 4—The Body met, and adjourned October 6. During the session, Rev. D. C. Eddy, D. D., presented the report of the Committee on the State of the Country, which was unanimously adopted, as follows:

Whereas, the gigantic rebellion which has, for more than three years been deluging the land with fratricidal blood, and sacrificing the lives of fathers, brothers and sons, remains unsubdued; therefore,

Resolved, That it becomes us, on this as on every proper occasion, to express our unswerving loyalty to the Government, our confidence in the perpetuity of the Union, and our steady adherence to the Constitution and the laws.

2. That while a single armed foe remains on our soil, or a single finger is lifted against the Government of our country, or a single element of treason menaces our national existence, it becomes the duty of all Christians to sink party considerations in a firm, hearty, united support of those whom God in his providence, and the people in the exercise of the elective franchise, have placed at the head of the Government, and who are striving to crush the rebellion and restore the unity of the States.

3. That whatever dire calamity may fall upon the States in rebellion, however severe may be the penalties of war, however bitter and heartrending the condition of besieged cities and desolated communities, they only are responsible who have lifted the sword of anarchy against a righteous Government; and, if they perish, their blood will be upon their own heads.

4. That American slavery (never to be justified by the mild, temporary, patriarchal servitude of the Old Testament), the enormity and brutality of which has few parallels in the history of ages, lies at the basis of the wicked attempt to overthrow the Government, is responsible for the bloodshed and crime of the past three years, and should be held accountable before God and man for every life sacrificed and every drop of blood shed.

5. That no permanent peace, no lasting Union, and no public safety can be expected while slavery exists; and as an outlaw upon civilization, a pirate on human rights, the foe of God and man, alike the enemy of the white and black, it should be utterly, immediately, unconditionally and eternally blotted out, as one of the foulest stains that ever rested upon any civilized land.

6. That the only road to peace, and the only hope of Union, lie in the subjugation of the rebellion, the extermination of its cause, and the overthrow of its supporters; and therefore, until the necessity ceases, we should welcome taxation, sacrifice, and if needful, universal conscription—our motto being "First Christ's, then our country's!"

7. That, in the successes which have crowned the Union army, we recognize the hand of God, who only can "organize victory;" that our most earnest thanksgiving be returned to Him, while we pray that in His infinite grace He will roll on the tide of success, and hasten the day when rebellion shall be conquered, slavery abolished, peace restored, the law vindicated, the national honor maintained, and the spirit of Christ shall unite North and South in one holy brotherhood.

8. That any compromise between the Government and the States in rebellion, which would revoke the proclamation of emancipation, and doom again to bondage a race, one hundred thousand of whose sons, clad in the uniform of the republic, have gone into the carnage of battle, displaying a heroism which has won the admiration of the nation which has never recognized their manhood, and to restore the flag which has never given them the protection of citizenship, would be so infamous as to provoke the scorn and merit the denunciation of the whole Christian world.

9. That in the constitutionally-elected President of the United States, we recognize the representative of Union, Liberty and Peace, and we cannot fail to pray that the Government may be sustained until the supremacy of the Constitution shall be established, and the flag of the Union shall wave in peaceful triumph over every inch of soil now polluted by war and cursed by treason.

10. That we appeal, away from every human aim, to the God of battles, and solemnly and unitedly invoke his gracious aid, praying "Let God arise, let his enemies be scattered; let them also that hate him flee before him. As smoke is driven away, so drive them away; as wax melteth before the fire, so let the wicked perish at the presence of God."

The Moderator and Clerk were instructed to convey a copy of the report to the Secretary of State of the United States, and also the Governor of Pennsylvania.

PENNSYLVANIA BAPTIST CONVENTION, 1862.

November 25—The body met at Harrisburg.

November 26—Rev. Dr. Loomis, Rev. S. G. Chace, and Rev. Dr. Jeffery were appointed a Committee on the State of the Country, and, same day, reported these resolutions, which were unanimously adopted:

Resolved, That this Convention, representing 40,000 of the citizens of Pennsylvania, mindful in the present national crisis of our solemn duties to our country and our God, hereby declare our profound conviction of the intimate relation there is between the cause of human liberty and the cause of pure religion, and also our set purpose as citizens, as Christians, and as Christian ministers, to employ our whole influence in supporting the supremacy of our National Constitution against all enemies whatsoever.

2. That as the institution of Slavery stands before the world as the confessed feeding source of the present mighty and wicked Rebellion against our National Constitution, we most heartily approve of the President's Proclamation of Emancipation, without modification in substance, and without change of time in its execution.

3. That a copy of these resolutions, duly authenticated, be forwarded to the President of the United States.

PENNSYLVANIA BAPTIST CONVENTION, 1863.

October 27—The body met at Salem, Westmoreland county Same day, Messrs. Mirick, Chace, McNeill, J. W. Smith, Wilder, and Cramer were appointed a Committee on the State of the Country.

October 28—They reported resolutions, which were amended so as to read as follows, and were adopted:

Whereas, The history of Baptists is interwoven with the history and triumphs of civil and religious liberty; and

Whereas, Our national Government grew out of Baptist polity, exemplified by men of whom Roger Williams was the type at the North, and a little Baptist church near the residence of Thomas Jefferson, from whom he declared he obtained his first ideas of Republican Government, was the type at the South:

Resolved, That we should be derelict to our principles as Baptists, and unworthy sons of worthy sires, if, in this crisis in our existence, we withheld our support, influence, and sympathy from our Government.

2. That it is our duty, both as citizens and Christians, to speak boldly our sentiments with regard to the causes of the existing rebellion, that ministers should speak boldly on the subject, and that those who take offence at such utterances are unworthy of a place in the Christian church.

3. That we, the members of this Convention, as patriots, as Baptists, and as Christians, do express our unqualified support of our National and State Governments, in their efforts to suppress the present rebellion.

4. That we have occasion for gratitude, that not only the full apostolic proportion of eleven-twelfths of the Christian ministry among us are truly loyal Government supporters, but that the mass of the piety of our churches and the intelligence of our country occupy the same position.

5. That the recent victories at the ballot-box should be accepted with thanksgiving to God, as exhibiting the loyalty of the people, and as an evidence of the continued blessing of God on us as a nation.

6. That in the President's Proclamation of Emancipation, made valid by the exigency which called it forth, and in his recent declaration to abide by it, we see the progress of Christ's kingdom, which will proclaim liberty to all the earth.

7. That we urge the churches throughout the Commonwealth to observe the last Thursday in November next,

according to the recommendation of the President, as a day of public Thanksgiving to God.

Same day—This resolution, offered by Rev. J. Wheaton Smith, was adopted:

Whereas, Rev. Joseph Smith, an enrolled delegate to this body, has declared, in our hearing, his belief that the Gospel has no balm for our beloved and bleeding country, and that, in his public ministrations, he finds no place for allusions to our national griefs; therefore,

Resolved, That we commend our brother to a better reading of his Master's message, and to broader views of pulpit ministration.

OHIO BAPTIST CONVENTION, 1862.

October—The body met, and passed these resolutions, prepared by Rev. Dr. M. Stone:

Whereas, The powers that be are ordained of God, and he that resisteth the power, resisteth the ordinance of God, and is threatened with damnation; therefore be it

Resolved, That it is our right and duty, as a body of Christian citizens, in these times of rebellion against our beneficent Government, to tender our hearty sympathy and support to those who are intrusted with it.

2. That we will accord a cheerful and earnest support to our rulers and our armies in their endeavors to crush the wicked rebellion, until that object shall be accomplished, and peace and order restored; and that we will offer up our prayers and supplications daily to the Sovereign Disposer of events for his interposition in this behalf.

3. That since the present terrible civil war was begun by our enemies without any just cause or provocation, for the purpose of *extending, strengthening, and perpetuating* the wicked institution of slavery, against the moral sense of the civilized world, and though in the beginning we had no intention of interfering with the institutions of the rebellious States, yet the progress of the war clearly indicates the purpose of God to be the summary extinction of slavery, therefore we approve the late proclamation of liberty of our President, and we will sustain him in carrying out that proclamation till our beloved country shall be purged of the accursed blot, both the cause of the war and the chief means in our enemy's hands of carrying it on, and will stand by our country in the adoption of such further measures as may be neccessary to put an end to this great rebellion.

NEW YORK BAPTIST CONVENTION, 1862.

October 7—The body met in Ithaca, and unanimously adopted the following:

Whereas, The civil war which was in progress in our country at our last annual meeting is still in existence, threatening the destruction of our Government, with all the precious interests it involves; therefore,

Resolved, That, as a religious body, we deem it our duty to cherish and manifest the deepest sympathy for the preservation and perpetuity of a Government which protects us in the great work of Christian civilization.

2. That, in our opinion, the history of civil governments furnishes no example of more audacious wickedness than is exhibited by the rebellion which has been inaugurated against the free government framed by our fathers, and so eminently in harmony with the conscious and obvious rights of man.

3. That while we see, with the profoundest sorrow, thousands of husbands, fathers, brothers, and sons falling on the battle-field, considering the interests to be preserved and transmitted to future generations, we cannot regard the sacrifice of treasure and of life too much for the object to be secured.

4. That as human slavery in the Southern portion of our country is, in our judgment, the procuring cause of the rebellion now raging among us, having been proclaimed as the corner-stone of the rebellion and as the institution for which they are fighting, as Christian men and citizens we fully and heartily endorse the recent proclamation of the President of the United States, declaring forever free all slaves in the rebel States on the 1st of January, 1863.

5. That the spirit of the age, the safety of the country, and the laws of God require that among the results of the present bloody war shall be found the *entire* removal of that relic of barbarism, *that bane and shame* of the nation, *American slavery*, and that the banner of freedom float triumphantly and *truthfully* over all the land.

6. That the foregoing preamble and resolutions be signed by the officers of the Convention, and transmitted to the President of the United States.

AMERICAN BAPTIST MISSIONARY UNION, 1863.

May—The body met in Cleveland, and adopted the following paper, reported from the Committee by Rev. Dr. Dowling:

Whereas, The officers and members of the American Baptist Missionary Union, at their last annual meeting in May, 1862, unanimously adopted a series of resolutions, characterizing "the war now waged by the national Government to put down the unprovoked and wicked rebellion that has risen against it, and to establish anew the reign of order and of law, as as a most righteous and holy one, sanctioned alike by God and all right-thinking men;" and also expressive of their conviction that "the principal cause and origin of this attempt to destroy the Government has been the institution of slavery; and that a safe, solid, and lasting peace cannot be expected short of its complete overthrow;" therefore,

Resolved, That the developments of the year since elapsed, in connection with this attempt to destroy the best Government on earth, have tended only to deepen our conviction of the truth of the sentiments which we then expressed, and which we now and here solemnly reiterate and reaffirm.

2. That the authors, aiders, and abettors of this slaveholders' rebellion, in their desperate efforts to nationalize the institution of slavery and to extend its despotic sway throughout the land, have themselves inflicted on that institution a series of most terrible, and fatal, and suicidal blows, from which, we believe, it can never recover, and they have themselves thus fixed its destiny and hastened its doom; and that for thus overruling what appeared at first to be a terrible national calamity, to the production of results so unexpected and glorious, our gratitude and adoration are due to that wonder-working God who still "maketh the wrath of man to praise Him, while the remainder of wrath He restrains."—Psalm lxxvi. 10.

3. That in the recent acts of Congress, abolishing slavery forever in the District of Columbia and the Territories, and in the noble proclamation of the President of the United States, declaring freedom to the slave in States in rebellion, we see cause for congratulation and joy, and we think we behold the dawn of that glorious day when, as in Israel's ancient jubilee, "liberty shall be proclaimed throughout all the land, unto all the inhabitants thereof."—Leviticus xxv. 10.

4. That as American Christians we rejoice in the growing sympathy of the enlightened portion of our Christian brethren in Great Britain and other European nations with the Government and people of the United States in this righteous war, and that while we cordially thank our friends across the water for all expressions of their confidence and approval, we embrace this opportunity of assuring them that, within our judgment, the United States possesses within herself the means, the men, and the courage necessary for the suppression of this rebellion, and that while we ask no assistance from other nations, we will brook no intervention or interference with our national affairs while engaged in this arduous struggle, which we believe will soon be completely successful in utterly suppressing and subduing this rebellion.

5. That we hereby pledge ourselves as ministers, and as Christians and patriots, to sustain the President of the United States and his associates in the administration by our prayers, our influence, and our personal sacrifices, till this rebellion shall be subdued, and peace, upon the basis of justice, freedom, and Union, shall be again restored.

LUTHERAN.

GENERAL SYNOD OF 1862.

May 1—This body met in Lancaster, Pa.

May 6—The Committee on the State of the Country, through the Chairman, submitted this Minute, which was taken up *seriatim*, discussed, and adopted. The Committee were: W. A Passavant, C. P. Krauth, H. H. Vandyke, E W. Hutter, G. F. Stelling, B. C. Suesserott, F A. Muhlenberg, B. Pope, D. Sell, H. Eggers, C Startzman, J. G. Morris, G. A. Lintner, S. Philson, W H. Harrison, A. R. Howbert, J. A Kunkelman, S. W. Harkey, W. G. Harter, H Wells, A. M. Geiger, A. Hiller:

Whereas our beloved country, after having long been favored with a degree of political and religious freedom security and prosperity, unexampled in the history of th world, now finds itself involved in a bloody war to suppres an armed rebellion against its lawfully constituted Goverr ment; and whereas the Word of God, which is the sole ru of our faith and practice, requires loyal subjection to "th powers that be," because they are ordained of God, t be a terror to evil-doers and a praise to those who do well, and at the same time declares, that they who "resist the power" shall receive to themselves condemnation; and whereas we, the representatives of the Evangelical Lutheran Synods of the United States, connected with the General Synod, assembled in Lancaster, Pennsylvania, recognize it as our duty to give public expression to our convictions of truth on this subject, and in every proper way to co-operate with our fellow-citizens in sustaining the great interests of law and authority, of liberty and righteousness; be it therefore

Resolved, That it is the deliberate judgment of this Synod, that the rebellion against the constitutional Government of this land is most wicked in its inception, unjustifiable in its cause, unnatural in its character, inhuman in its prosecution, oppressive in its aims, and destructive in its results to the highest interests of morality and religion.

2d. That, in the suppression of this rebellion and in the maintenance of the Constitution and the Union by the sword, we recognize an unavoidable necessity and a sacred duty, which the Government owes to the nation and to the world, and that, therefore, we call upon all our people to lift up holy hands in prayer to the God of battles, without personal wrath against the evil doers on the one hand, and without doubting the righteousness of our cause on the other, that He would give wisdom to the President and his counsellors, and success to the army and navy, that our beloved land may speedily be delivered from treason and anarchy.

3d. That while we regard this unhappy war as a righteous judgment of God, visited upon us because of the individual and national sins, of which we have been guilty, we nevertheless regard this rebellion as more immediately the natural result of the continuance and spread of domestic slavery in our land, and therefore hail with unmingled joy the proposition of our Chief Magistrate, which has received the sanction of Congress, to extend aid from the General Government to any State in which slavery exists, which shall deem fit to initiate a system of constitutional emancipation.

4th. That we deeply sympathize with all loyal citizens and Christian patriots in the rebellious portions of our country, and we cordially invite their co-operation in offering united supplications at a Throne of Grace, that God would restore peace to our distracted country, re-establish fraternal relations between all the States, and make our land in all time to come, the asylum of the oppressed, and the permanent abode of liberty and religion.

5th. That our devout thanks are due to Almighty God for the success which has crowned our arms, and while we praise and magnify His name for the help and succor He has graciously afforded our land and naval forces, in enabling them to overcome our enemies, we regard these tokens of His divine favor as cheering indications of the final triumph of our cause.

These resolutions were presented to President LINCOLN by a Committee, consisting of Drs. Sternberg, Lintner, Pohlman, and Stork, and H. H. Vandyke. The Chairman thus addressed him:

MR. PRESIDENT: We have the honor, as a committee of the General Synod of the Lutheran Church in the United States, to present to your Excellency a copy of the preamble and resolutions, in reference to the state of the country, adopted by that body at its late session in the city of Lancaster, Pennsylvania.

We are further charged to assure you that our fervent prayers shall ascend to the God of nations, that Divine guidance and support may be vouchsafed to you in the trying and responsible position to which a benignant Providence has called you.

With your permission the Rev. Dr. Pohlman, of Albany, New York, will briefly express to you the sentiments which animated the committee and the church they represent in view of the present crisis in our national affairs.

The Rev. Dr. Pohlman, of Albany, New York, in his speech, alluded to the fact that the late session of the General Synod of the Lutheran Church at Lancaster was the first that had been held since the troubles in our country commenced; that the General Synod represents twenty-six district synods, scattered over the Middle, Western, and Southern States, from twenty-one of which delegates were in attendance; that from the States in rebellion no delegates were present, except one from Tennessee, who had, in praying for the President, avoided arrest only in consequence of the fact that he conducted divine service in the German language, the vernacular of many in the Lutheran Church. He further expressed his deep conviction that we were greatly indebted for the degree of success that has crowned the efforts of the Government in quelling the rebellion to the prayers of Christians, and concluded by invoking the Divine benediction to rest on the President and on our beloved country.

REPLY OF THE PRESIDENT.

GENTLEMEN: I welcome here the representatives of the Evangelical Lutherans of the United States. I accept with gratitude their assurances of the sympathy and support of that enlightened, influential, and loyal class of my fellow-citizens in an important crisis, which involves, in my judgment, not only the civil and religious liberties of our own dear land, but in a large degree the civil and religious liberties of mankind in many countries and through many ages. You well know, gentleman, and the world knows how reluctantly I accepted this issue of battle forced upon me, on my advent to this place, by the internal enemies of our country. You all know, the world knows the forces and the resources the public agents have brought into employment to sustain a Government against which there has been brought not one complaint of real injury committed against society at home or abroad. You all may recollect that in taking up the sword thus forced into our hands, this Government appealed to the prayers of the pious and the good, and declared that it placed its whole dependence upon the favor of God. I now humbly and reverently, in your presence, reiterate the acknowledgment of that dependence, not doubting that, if it shall please the Divine Being who determines the destinies of nations, that this shall remain a united people, they will, humbly seeking the Divine guidance, make their prolonged national existence a source of new benefits to themselves and their successors, and to all classes and conditions of mankind.

The following resolutions were also adopted:

Resolved, That this Synod cannot but express its most decided disapprobation of the course of those Synods and ministers, heretofore connected with this body, in the open sympathy and active co-operation which they have given to the cause of treason and insurrection

Resolved, That we deeply sympathize with our people in the Southern States, who, maintaining their proper Christian loyalty, have in consequence been compelled to suffer persecution and wrong, and we hail with pleasure the near approach of their deliverance and restoration to our Christian and ecclesiastical fellowship.

LUTHERAN GENERAL SYNOD OF 1864.

May 5—The body met in York, Pennsylvania.

May 11—The Committee on the State of the Country—consisting of W. A. Passavant, M. L. Stoever, A. Wetzel, S. Sentman, S. Sechrist, N. W. Lilly, G. A. Wenzel, J. Getty, S. L. Endress, S. Yingling, F. Gebhart, D. Summers, S. Sayford, J. K. Bloom, J. Strayer, J. T. Williams. H. M. Brewer, D. J. Hauer, C. F. Heyer, T. W. Sargent, W. Waltman, G. Schmucker, J. I. Burrell, P. Wieting—presented this Minute, which was taken up *seriatim*, discussed, and unanimously adopted:

Resolved, That having assembled a second time, during the prevalence of civil war in our land, this Synod cannot separate, without solemnly re-affirming the declarations, adopted at our last Convention, in reference to the originating cause of the rebellion, the necessity of its forcible suppression, the righteousness of the war which is waged by the Government of the United States for the maintenance of the national life, and the consequent duty of every Christian to support it by the whole weight of his influence, his prayers and his efforts.

Resolved, That we acknowledge with profound gratitude to Almighty God, the various and important successes which have thus far crowned our arms; the merciful interposition of Providence in delivering us from the invasions of the enemy, and in protecting our homes, our churches, and our institutions from the desolations of war; and the cheering progress which has been made by the Government and the nation, in the recognition of the laws of God and the rights of man, in the measures which have been adopted for the suppression of the rebellion.

Resolved, That recognizing the sufferings and calamities of war, as the righteous judgment of a just God, visited upon us for our transgressions, we call upon our pastors and churches to unite with us in the confession of our many and grievous individual and national sins, and in fervent supplications for the Divine forgiveness, that as a people we may break off sins by righteousness, and do justly, love mercy, and walk humbly with God.

Resolved, That as persistent efforts are making among us, by professedly Christian writers, to prove from the Holy Scriptures the divine institution of American slavery—the principal cause of this wicked rebellion—we, the delegates of the General Synod of the Evangelical Lutheran Church in the United States, hereby express our unqualified condemnation of such a course, which claims the sanction of the merciful God and Father of us all for a system of human oppression, which exists only by violence, under cover of iniquitous laws.

On the last resolution the yeas and nays were called, and were:

AYES—*Clerical:* R. Adelberg, Peter Anstadt, A. Axline, C. Baird, J. B. Baltzly, Gottlieb Bassler, Henry L. Baugher, D. D., Wm. M. Baum, Peter Bergstresser, J. K. Bloom, V. F. Bolton, G. A. Bowers, H. M. Brewer, J. I. Burrell, J., Crouse, George Diehl, D. D., Michael Diehl, S. Domer, J. C. Duy, Daniel Garver, L. Gerhard, J. W. Goodlin, Simeon W. Harkey, D. D., William H. Harrison, D. D., C. F. Heyer, Reuben Hill, William Hull, Michael Jacobs, D. D., James R. Keiser, W. Kopp, J. A. Kunkelman, N. W. Lilly, A. H. Lochman, D. D., A. P. Ludden, G. Neff, R. Neumann, G. B. Ort, W. A. Passavant, D. D., John K. Plitt, H. N. Pohlman, D. D., Peter Raby, P. Rizer, P. Sahm, T. W. Sargent, S. Sayford, W. N. Scholl, E. Schwartz, S. Sechrist, J. Z. Senderling, S. Sentman, M. Sheeleigh, S. Sprecher, D. D., D. Steck, T. Stork, D. D., D. Summers, J. Swartz, J. W. Swick, S. H. Swingle, T. T. Titus, A. Uebelacker, N. Van Alstine, W. Waltman, A. C. Wedekind, H. Wells, A. Wetzel, P. Wieting, P. Willard, G. W. Wilson, S. Yingling, H. Ziegler, D. D.—72. *Lay:* J. Angstadt, P. Bishop, H. E. Breckbill, M. Buehler, P. Burket, J. J. Cochran, S. L. Endress, J. R. English, David Fahs, J. G. Fleck, F. Gebhart, J. Getty, M. Gillett, J. Haas, Wm. M. Kemp, D. Koons, D. Kraber, Hon. Chas. Kugler, G. W. Leisenring, J. P. Lilly, A. McFadden, J. A. Miller, J. G. Minnich, P. H. Moore, C. A. Morris, A. F. Ockershausen, W. Pepple, M. Plank, P. A. Shindler, G. Schmucker, A. Schock, J. G. Schultz, J. Shawber, J. Soliday, M. L. Stoever, J. Strayer, J. Teatsorth, D. J. Tritle—37. Total—109.

ABSENT—*Clerical:* J. Boetticher, William Caldwell, J. B. Crist, S. Curtis, D. H. Focht, D. J. Hauer, D. D., Wm. Hunt, L. D. Maier—8. *Lay:* P. S. Blackwelder, J. Comp, J. J. Culler, P. Emerick, J. Hamilton, J. B. Hileman, D. R. Hoxie, V. Hummel, Jr., J. Jordan, J. A. Lawrence, J. Loats, H. C. Peters, J. Plank, E. Roessler, J. G. L. Schindel, A. K. Seem, J. J. Sipperly, C. Yeager—18. Total—26.

There are several Synods not in connection with the General Synod. No one has taken action adverse to that of the General Synod.

CONGREGATIONAL.

GENERAL ASSOCIATION OF NEW YORK, NEW JERSEY, AND PENNSYLVANIA, 1864.

The General Association of the Congregational Ministers and Churches of New York has connected with it about twenty churches in New Jersey and Pennsylvania. At the meeting in September, Rev. Dr. Thompson, from the Committee on the State of the Country, reported a set of resolutions, which were adopted unanimously by a rising vote, given with much enthusiasm, and Drs. Thompson and Budington were appointed a committee to lay them before the President of the United States. Rev. H. G. Ludlow led in prayer of thanksgiving for the unanimity and spirit evinced. The resolutions are as follows:

RESOLUTIONS ON THE STATE OF THE COUNTRY.

1. That the signal victories which have crowned our arms, following so close upon a season of darkness and humiliation, call for present gratitude to Almighty God, who hath regarded the confessions and supplications of His people, and in the midst of righteous judgments hath remembered mercy.

2. That amid the rejoicings of victory which kindle our devotions and give tone to our praises, still having in remembrance the sins that have brought upon the nation the sufferings and sorrows of war, we will not cease to watch and to labor against the reviving of these iniquities with the prospect of peace, and will pray that this overflowing scourge may sweep them utterly away.

3. That, as the momentous issues of this long and eadlyd contest are approaching their solution in a combined struggle in the field and at the polls, we will sustain with our votes the brave and noble men who are defending our liberties with their lives, and will animate our fellow-citizens, by every consideration of religious hope and duty, of devotion to country and to liberty, to make the decision of the people on the 8th of November next final and fatal to the hopes of traitors in arms and conspirators in political council.

4. That our hopes for the preservation of our liberties a a nation, and for the complete emancipation of the African race in the South, depend, under God, upon sustaining the Government in upholding the integrity of the Union, through all the trials and doubts and disasters of the war, and in that policy which looks to "the abandonment of slavery" as the condition of permanent union and peace.

5. That, while we solemnly pledge ourselves before God to fill up, in our measure, that which is behind of suffering and of sacrifice for the redemption of the nation, and with unfaltering purpose to sustain the Government in subjugating the rebellion, we will pray day by day for the coming of peace, untarnished by concession to treason or by compromise with wrong and established injustice, in liberty and unity forever.

JOSEPH P. THOMPSON,
RAY PALMER,
RICHARD OSBORN,
DAVID HUESTIS,
THADDEUS S. HOYT,
L. SMITH HOBART,
H. M. DIXON,
Committee.

CONGREGATIONAL CONFERENCE OF MASSACHUSETTS, 1864.

September 13—The conference met at Fall River.

September 14—The report of the Committee on the State of the Country—Andrew L. Stone, D. D., Rev. Joshua W. Wellman, and Rev. James H. Merrill—was unanimously adopted as follows:

Resolved, That without one feeling either of despondency or of impatience, we watch the progress of the armies of the Union in putting down the most criminal rebellion the world ever saw; without despondency, for we believe God is on our side, and will give us in due time full and crowning success, and without impatience, for we have been instructed to interpret hopefully these divine delays, and have seen the issue ever widening and embracing more and more radical and precious revolutions and deliverances.

Resolved, That there can be no effectual re-establishment of the national authority by any negotiation which confesses the inability of the Government to subdue rebellion by force of arms, and proposes terms of peace to rebels still flying the flag of defiance.

Resolved, That the chief hope of rebellion is in the sympathy and distraction of a divided North, and that the surest and shortest way to peace is not to recall our armies and to relax our grasp upon the enemy, but to present a united loyal front, and an unconquerable determination to prosecute the war till the power of the Government meets no longer with armed resistance.

Resolved, That we rejoice in the recent victories won by our arms on the land and on the sea, as at once revealing the skill of our commanders, and the valor and endurance of our soldiers and sailors, and exhibiting evidence of God's gracious purpose to guide our marches and to give final victory to our cause.

Resolved, That the docility and industry, the discipline and heroism of the thousands of emancipated slaves, whether in scenes of peaceful labor or wearing the uniform of the national soldier, assert their claim to all the elements of a noble manhood, and the increased respect and confidence of all the friends of their race; and that we are moved to regard them with a more tender sympathy, to make them a subject of special prayer, and to do for them whatever is in our power.

Resolved, That we rejoice in the wide blossoming and harvesting of that public charity, by which such streams of treasure and so many products of industry have been contributed to the comfort and relief of our soldiers in the camp, the prison-house, the hospital, and the field; and in the personal labors of so many Christian men and women in bearing those material comforts to the beloved objects, and leading so many souls to Christ.

Resolved, That we believe it is the duty of Christian ministers to set forth by some appropriate public teaching the importance of the great principles at hazard in the impending and progressive political struggle, which is to issue in the choice of our national administration in such an eventful crisis of our national life.

CONFERENCE OF MAINE, 1864.

June 21—The body met in Searsport.

Same day—The Committee on the State of the Country—Rev. Wooster Parker, Rev. Alfred E. Ives, Rev. Henry F. Harding, Rev. Joseph Smith, and Bro. Eben. Steele—made this Report, which was unanimously adopted:

Resolved, That in the terrible visitation of domestic war, we recognize the rod of God's chastisement for our manifold sins; and in its fearful and prolonged evils, a solemn admonition to humble ourselves under his mighty hand—to seek His mercy, and to rely on Divine help for a happy issue of our national trouble.

2. That with devout gratitude we recognize God's hand in so ordering the course of events as to lead us to hope, with increasing confidence, that slavery will be utterly annihilated.

3. That we re-affirm our confidence in the general policy of the National Administration, and more than ever feel it our duty to give the government a cordial and earnest support in thoroughly suppressing the rebellion, and restoring the Union on the *basis of liberty*.

4. That as slavery has so deeply corrupted and dishonored our Christianity, and imperiled the life of the nation, the time has now fully come when Christian patriotism and fidelity to the gospel demand that it should be allowed no toleration, no shield or lurking place in any Christian church.

5. That in common with our noblest patriots and purest statesmen, we feel it our duty to lend our earnest and utmost influence to secure such a judgment of the people, and such an amendment of the Constitution, as shall *extinguish* and *prohibit slavery* in the land forever.

6. That the care of the Freedmen—a class so long and deeply wronged—so numerous, so poor, so ignorant, and yet so loyal; so anxious for education and elevation, and so capable of becoming good citizens and important colaborers in the kingdom of Christ, call for the benevolent action of Christians and philanthropists of this land with unsurpassed urgency and promise of good.

7. That we recognize with grateful admiration the patriotic self-sacrifice and heroic valor of our fellow-citizens and brethren who in the army and navy are struggling for our nationality, and for all the precious interests involved in it; that we deeply sympathize with them in their privations and sufferings, and with their often bereaved friends and kindred; that we bless God for the wonderful work of His grace among them, and for the succor and salvation the gospel has brought them; that we pledge ourselves to stand by them *for the war*, by our labors, and contributions, and prayers, doing what we can alike for their temporal and spiritual well-being.

Similar resolutions were passed by all the State Congregational Bodies. There is no Central Organization to represent the church.

REPLY OF PRESIDENT LINCOLN TO THE RESOLUTIONS OF THE GENERAL CONVENTION OF THE CONGREGATIONALISTS OF VERMONT.

DEPARTMENT OF STATE, WASHINGTON, *July* 11, 1862.

To Rev. CLARK E. FERRIN, *Moderator, &c.:*

SIR: I have the honor to acknowledge the reception of your note of the 23d of June, accompanied by a copy of resolutions which were unanimously adopted by the General Convention of Congregational ministers and churches recently assembled at Norwich. In compliance with your request, these resolutions have been submitted to the President of the United States.

I am instructed to express his cordial thanks for the assurance of confidence and support thus tendered to him by a body so deservedly respected and widely influential as the Congregational church of Vermont.

The President is deeply impressed by the fervent and hopeful patriotism and benevolence which pervade the resolutions. It is the Union and the Constitution of this country which are at stake in the present unhappy strife; but that Union is not a mere stringent political band; nor is that Constitution a lifeless or spiritless political body. The Union is a guarantee of perpetual peace and prosperity to the American people, and the Constitution is the ark of civil and religious liberty for all classes and conditions of men.

Who that carefully reads the history of the nations for the period that this republic has existed under this Constitution and this Union can fail to see and appreciate the influence it has exerted in ameliorating the condition of mankind? Who that justly appreciates that influence will undertake to foretell the misfortunes and despondency which must occur on every continent should this republic desist all at once from its auspicious career, and be resolved into a confused medley of small, discordant, and contentious States? The duty of the christian coincides with that of the patriot, and the duty of the priest with that of the soldier, in averting so sad and fearful a consummation.

Be pleased, sir, to express these sentiments of the President to the reverend gentlemen in whose behalf you have addressed me, together with assurances of profound respect, with which I have the honor to be their humble servant,

WILLIAM H. SEWARD.

REPLY OF THE PRESIDENT TO THE RESOLUTIONS OF THE CONGREGATIONAL WELSH ASSOCIATION OF PENNSYLVANIA.

DEPARTMENT OF STATE, WASHINGTON, *October* 6, 1862.

To the Congregational Welsh Association of Pennsylvania:

REVEREND GENTLEMEN: I have had the honor to receive the resolutions which you have adopted; and, in compliance with your request, I have submitted them to the consideration of the President of the United States.

The President entertains a lively gratitude for the assurances you have given him of your loyalty to the United States, and your solicitude for the safety of our free institutions, the confidence you have reposed in him, and your sympathy with him in the discharge of responsibilities which have devolved upon the Government. The President directs me to assure you that whenever the Constitution of the United States leads him in that path, he will move as steadily as shall be possible, rejoicing with yourselves whenever it opens the way to an amelioration of the condition of any portion of our fellow-men, while the country is escaping from the dangers of revolution.

The President is deeply touched by your sympathies with those of our fellow-citizens who suffer captivity or disease, and the grief with which you lament those who fall in defence of the country and humanity; and he invokes the prayers of all devotional men that these precious sufferings may not be altogether lost, but may be overruled by our heavenly Father to the advancement of peace on earth and good will to all men.

I have the honor to be, reverend gentlemen, your obedient servant,

WILLIAM H. SEWARD.

CONGREGATIONAL WELSH ASSOCIATION OF PENNSYLVANIA, 1864.

October—The Association met in Pittsburg and Brady's Bend, and passed these resolutions:

1. That we are highly grieved by the continuance of the Rebellion against our Government, and the inhuman treatment of our gallant soldiers by the enemy, into whose hands they unfortunately fell as prisoners of war—a treatment which is without any model for its cruelty in all history of war.

2. That we acknowledge the goodness of the Most High in the great success that has followed the arms of our army and navy in their contests with the enemy; we feel that the Lord hath invested them with unusual energy and courage, and that we shall look to Him for the same success in the future.

3. That we feel grateful to the Almighty for His patronage to the President of our country in protecting his person, and most of all for the wisdom and discretion with which he hath been pleased to invest him, and also for prospering his measures to such an extent.

4. That we humbly request his Excellency, the President, to use all the strength of the Government as the most efficient measure to subdue the rebels, and that no conciliation shall be offered by any gentle and tender means, for that would only continue the rebellion.

5. That we heartily rejoice in the bright light that radiates forth in the platform of the Baltimore Convention in

regard to the extension of liberty, and the entire abolition of human bondage.

6. That we congratulate all the friends of liberty on the great victory gained by freedom in Maryland, being a free constitution was adopted by the people of that State.

7. That we shall endeavor to secure the re-election of Abraham Lincoln to the Presidency of our country, as the representative of the great principles of human liberty and equality.

D. R. DAVIES, *President.*

JOHN E. JONES, *Secretary.*

GERMAN REFORMED.

PENNSYLVANIA GERMAN REFORMED SYNOD, 1863.

November—The body met at Pittsburg, and unanimously passed this resolution:

Resolved, That, in conformity with the admonition of the Holy Scriptures, and in imitation of the example of our ecclesiastical fathers during the period of the Revolution, this Synod admonish the pastors and members of the churches under its care, to remember that the powers that be are ordained of God, and that it is the solemn duty of all Christians, enjoying the protection of such civil rulers, to pray for them, and we should feel especially obligated to do so during a time of peril like that through which our beloved country is now passing.

PENNSYLVANIA GERMAN REFORMED SYNOD, 1864.

May—The body met in Reading, and passed these resolutions:

Resolved, That this Convention deems it right and proper to give expression to the unfaltering devotion with which the German Reformed Church in the United States has hitherto sustained the cause of our common country, and we earnestly urge upon our clergy and laity to continue to labor and pray for the success of the Government, in its efforts to suppress the existing rebellion, and to restore peace and union.

2. That we deeply sympathize with the brave soldiers and sailors who are enduring the dangers and privations of the military service, and we earnestly invoke the blessing of Almighty God upon them, and the patriotic endeavors to uphold the honor of the national flag and the integrity of the Government.

The resolution of 1863, above quoted, was reiterated by the Synod of the Church in the United States, at its Annual Session in Lancaster, October, 1864.

Like resolutions were passed by other State Synods.

REFORMED PROTESTANT DUTCH.

GENERAL SYNOD OF THE REFORMED PROTESTANT DUTCH CHURCH, 1863.

June—The Synod met in Newburgh, N. Y. The Report of the Committee on the State of the Country—Revs. Charles Wiley, J. H. Suydam, C. G. Vanderveer, and Elders C. Dusenberry, and E. Andrews—was adopted, as follows:

Whereas, It is the duty of the Church of Christ, and of all those who minister at her altars, agreeably to the teachings of the Scriptures, and the injunctions of our standards and formularies of doctrine and worship, to yield at all times a cordial support, both by precept and example, to the legitimate Government of the land; and whereas this duty is especially incumbent at a period when the Government is assailed by armed violence and insubordination, and its very existence and integrity are sought to be subverted by a powerful and persevering rebellion; therefore,

Resolved, 1. That we tender to the Government of the United States, and those who represent it, the renewed expression of our warmest and deepest sympathy in its present protracted struggle to maintain its lawful authority and to preserve unbroken the integrity and union of these States.

2. That we hold it to be our imperative duty as ministers of the Gospel and members of the Synod, while abstaining from all unseemly mixing up of ourselves with mere party politics, in our own appropriate sphere and by every possible means to strengthen the hands of the Government at the present imminent crisis, wherein are put at stake the national life and the noblest example and experiment of constitutional government the world has ever seen; and that we will yield a cordial support to all such measures, not incompatible with the great law of righteousness, as may be necessary to suppress the existing rebellion and to assert the complete authority of the Union over all proper territory and domain.

3. That we will hail with satisfaction the earliest practicable period for the introduction and establishment of a salutary peace—a peace founded on the full ascendancy of law and rightful authority, and guaranteed in its permanency by the removal or the sufficient coercion and restraint of whatever causes tend necessarily to imperil the existence of the nation and to endanger the preservation of the Union; and until such a peace can be obtained, we hold it to be a sacred duty to ourselves, our children, our country, the Church of God, and also to humanity at large, to prosecute to the last a war forced upon us by an imperative necessity, and waged on our part not in hatred or revenge, but in the great cause of constitutional liberty and rational self-government.

4. That we recognize devoutly our dependence upon God for a happy issue and termination to our present troubles; that we accept with profound humility and abasement the chastisements of His hand; that we make mention of our deep unworthiness and sin; and that we endeavor, by continual searching, repentance, and careful walking before God, to conciliate the Divine favor, so that ere long His heavy judgments in our national calamities may be removed, and a restoration may be accorded to us of the blessings of peace, fraternal harmony, fraternal union, and established government.

The Synod directed the following resolutions to be added to the Report of the Committee:

Resolved, That we view with admiration and gratitude those noble men, our sons, brothers and kindred, who have periled and sacrificed their lives in the present crisis in the cause of the country; that we follow them to the camp and to the fields with our warm sympathies and prayers; that we pledge to them our exertions to relieve their sufferings, and to smooth, as far as may be, the rough experience of war; that we honor them while they live, and cherish their names and memory when they die; and esteem these remembrances and respects the smallest return we can make for their personal sacrifices in the great cause of Constitutional liberty, and enlightened and national self-government.

Resolved, That a copy of the above resolutions be presented by the President of the Synod to the President of the United States.

GENERAL SYNOD OF THE REFORMED PROTESTANT DUTCH, 1864.

June—The body met in Schenectady; and the report of the Committee on the State of the Country—Rev. R. D. Van Kleek, J. Forsyth, O. E. Cobb, and Elders T. Jeremiah, and R. N. Perlee—was unanimously adopted, as follows:

In view of the duty to recognize the powers that be, as ordained of God, to render unto Cæsar the things that are Cæsar's; to pray for all men, for all that are in authority, that we may lead a quiet and peaceable life in all godliness and honesty, and to acknowledge and adore the providence of God, especially in trying and perilous times,

1. That the General Synod of the Reformed Dutch Church heartily sympathizes with the government of the United States in its efforts to crush rebellion against its rightful authority, and to restore to this now distressed people their once cherished integrity as a union of states.

2. This Synod gives thanks to God for all the successes which have attended the efforts to suppress this rebellion; and for all the encouragements to hope that peace may soon be restored. And we trust that our sense of gratitude to Him, the author of all good, may not be impaired by an acknowledgment of inexpressible and incalculable indebtedness to the tens of thousands of our fellow citizens, who have devoted their property and their labors, sacrificed their comforts and their lives, and given up their loved ones in our defence and for the salvation of their country. May God bless them with such rewards as He only can give. May He especially grant His grace, mercy, and peace to the sick, the wounded and the dying.

3. Inasmuch as all success depends on the favor of God, and can be hoped for only through His controlling influence upon the hearts and His blessing upon the efforts of the people of our land, our Synod will not cease to pray, and it earnestly urges the Churches under its care that they cease not to pray for repentance and forgiveness of all our sins, whether national or otherwise, for the gift of wisdom to our counselors and rulers, skill to our commanders, courage to our soldiers, and grace to all the peo-

ple, to the end that success may attend our arms, our government be maintained, and peace make its permanent abode in the land, if God please, never more to be disturbed.

4. In treating of the present state of our country, we cannot lose sight of the acknowledged principal cause of this deplorable rebellion. In time past, the General Synod has not deemed it necessary to give forth a judgment in regard to the system of American slavery, inasmuch as it existed in regions beyond the bounds of our Church; yet, as in the overruling Providence of that God who knows how to make the wrath of man to praise Him, there is a prospect opened for the ultimate and entire removal of that system which embodies so much of moral and social evil, and as by such removal there is opened a wide field of Christian labors to employ the energies of the Christian Church in this land, the Synod expresses its gratitude to God for this bright prospect, and would join in the prayer, that the day may be hastened when liberty shall be effectually and finally proclaimed throughout all the land, to all the inhabitants thereof.

MORAVIAN.

1861, May 30—The Synod of the Moravian Church adopted the following resolutions:

RESOLUTIONS UPON THE STATE OF THE COUNTRY.

Whereas, We, the Provincial Synod of the Moravian church of the Northern District of the United States, now assembled at Litiz, Lancaster county, Pennsylvania, feel it to be just and proper, that, in common with our brethren of other religious denominations, we should express our deep interest in the present unhappy and gloomy condition of our once happy and prosperous country; inasmuch as it is a duty enjoined upon us by the Head of our church, in the commandment "to render to Caesar, the things that are Caesar's, and to God, the things that are God's;"—therefore

Resolved, 1. That, while, as citizens of the United States, and as members of the Moravian church, we deeply deplore the calamity of civil war in our land, we acknowledge the chastening hand of God, and humbly bow to the decrees of Him, who holds the destinies of nations in his hands.

2. That, while we acknowledge, and submit to *that Power*, we also acknowledge "*the powers that are ordained of God*" *over us*, and therefore declare our continued, faithful, and unabated allegiance to the government and the constitution of the United States, and of the several States of which we are citizens.

3. That in acknowledging our constitutional government, and the liberty and blessings which we have been permitted to enjoy under it, we, as members of the Moravian church, deem it our duty to extend to it, our hearty support in its efforts and measures to uphold the constitution, to maintain the integrity of these United States, and to perpetuate to ourselves and to our children, the liberties and blessings of our republican institutions; so that we, as a church, "may continue to lead under them a quiet and peaceable life in all godliness and honesty."

4. That we will continue to unite in ardent prayer, that the Lord may grant unto the government of the United States, in these times of danger, His gracious counsel, and continue to be the gracious Protector of these United States, and of our national constitution; that He may defeat every evil design against us, and continue to show His tender mercies unto these United States as in days past; that He may in his tender mercy stop the effusion of human blood, and make discord and war to cease; and that to this end, He may put into the hearts of all citizens of these United States, thoughts of peace, that we may see it soon established, to the glory of his name.

5. That we will in our prayers, also remember those, who, in obedience to the call of their country, have left their families and homes, and are gone forth to protect our insulted flag, and in support of our constitution and laws—that the Lord of Hosts may strengthen and uphold them, and in the hour of distress, especially when in the arms of death, prove to them their only trust and consolation; and that He may comfort and dry the tears of parents, of brothers, of sisters and of friends, and protect the widows and fatherless children of those who, by His Divine dispensation, sacrifice their lives in the cause of our beloved country.

1864—June 3—In session at Bethlehem, Pennsylvania, it adopted the following on

THE STATE OF THE COUNTRY.

1. That this Synod is profoundly impressed with the peculiar character of the fearful and bloody war, now raging in and desolating large portions of our beloved country, as an awful and deserved judgment of Almighty God upon our people.

2. That this Synod regards it as clear and unquestionable, that African slavery as it now exists in the Southern States, and as formerly connived at by the nation at large, is the primary cause of this war, not only in having generally led to it, but in being a great moral wrong, on account of which, in connection with other heinous sins, such as covetousness, pride, intemperance, profanity, Sabbath-breaking, and the cruel and heartless conduct of our people in their treatment of the aborigines of our land, largely prevalent in our country, God is visiting the nation with His judgments.

3. That this Synod recommend to our churches and people a humble confession and hearty repentance of these and all other sins of which we are guilty, that the judgment which has overtaken the nation may be speedily removed, and peace and prosperity restored to our beloved country.

4. That this Synod emphatically deprecates that interpretation of the Word of God, almost universal in the South, and still largely prevalent in the North, by which the Scriptures of Truth are sought to be perverted into an instrument of oppression, and the pure, sweet wine of the Gospel changed into gall and wormwood.

5. That this Synod considers an earnest support of the Constitution and Laws, which, in God's providence, have come down to us from our forefathers, as well as an earnest support of the General and State Governments under them—a religious duty; and that we, of this Synod, hereby express our willingness to render the constituted authorities of our land all the aid in our power to subdue unrighteous rebellion, and extend the rightful authority of the Government over every portion of our country.

PROTESTANT EPISCOPAL.

GENERAL CONVENTION OF THE PROTESTANT EPISCOPAL CHURCH IN THE UNITED STATES, 1862.

October 1—The body met in New York.

October 4—Rev. William Cooper Mead, D. D., of Norwalk, Rev. Edward Y. Higbee, D. D., of New York, Rev. William D. Wilson, D. D., of Geneva, Rev. Silas Totten, D. D., of Iowa City, Rev. T. C. Thrall, of Burlington, N. J., and Messrs. Robert C. Winthrop, of Boston, Washington Hunt, of Lockport, John N. Conyngham, of Wilkesbarre, and Charles B. Goddard, of Zanesville, were appointed a Committee on the State of the Country and the Church; to whom were referred these propositions:

By Mr. F. R. Brunot, of Pennsylvania:

Whereas, It has pleased the Supreme Ruler of the universe to permit sedition and privy conspiracy in our midst to culminate in an extensive rebellion against the civil power ordained by Him, and for the just punishment of our sins there is war in our land, friend against friend, brother against brother, son against father; and whereas, a portion of our brethren of the Church have attempted to sever by ecclesiastical enactments the visible bonds of Christian sympathy heretofore existing between us and them, thereby grievously rending the body of Christ in His Church; and whereas, we acknowledge that there is no help but from God, and rejoice that we are permitted to fly to Him for succor in our sore distress; therefore be it

Resolved, That the House of Bishops is hereby requested to set forth for the use of this Convention during its present session a special form of prayer, confessing and bewailing our manifold transgressions, pleading for God's forgiveness, begging that it may please Him to be the defender and keeper of our national Government, giving it the victory over all its enemies; that He will abate their and our pride, assuage their malice and confound their devices, and, giving them better minds, forgive them for the evils they have wrought; that He will restore our national Union, bring back peace and prosperity to the State, and godly unity to the Church, and that He will keep us thereto by His perpetual mercy, to the honor and glory of His name.

This was laid on the table by this vote: Of the Clergy—ayes, 15; nays, 5; divided, 1. Of the Laity—ayes, 11; nays, 4; divided, 1. It was subsequently referred to the Committee.

By Thomas P. Carpenter, of Camden, N. J.:

Resolved, That in view of the danger of this country from civil war, the House of Bishops be respectfully requested to prepare a form of prayer to be used during the session of this Convention.

By Mr. Murray Hoffman, of New York:

Whereas, A number of the members of the Protestant Episcopal Church in the United States of America are in open resistance to the Government set over them, and others of such members are aiding in such unlawful rebellion; and whereas, the members of this Church in the several States did, through the agencies of parishes, assemblies, or conventions, appoint deputies to a General Convention, in which, in the year 1789, they adopted and declared a constitution for the government of the Church; and whereas, every one admitted to holy orders in such Church has, upon such admission, solemnly engaged "to conform to the doctrines and worship of the Protestant Episcopal Church in the United States," which doctrine and worship was set forth in the Book of Common Prayer, ratified in the year 1789, and declared to be the Liturgy of the Church, and required to be received as such by all the members of the same; and whereas, it is in such book directed that there shall be read "a prayer for the President of the United States, and all in civil authority," to which the people present are bidden to say Amen, and to which the members of this Church owe obedience; and whereas, the Convention of South Carolina did, in May, 1861, declare itself no longer under any obligation of obedience to the constitution of the Church, and permitted alterations in the Prayer Book to be made by the Bishop of the diocese, and recognized the power of bodies other than the General Convention to change such Book, and, in the month of June, 1861, the Convention of the diocese of Louisiana did resolve that it had ceased to be a diocese of the Protestant Episcopal Church in the United States, and, on the 3d of July, 1861, deputies from the Conventions of the dioceses of South Carolina, Georgia, Florida, Alabama, Louisiana, Arkansas, Mississippi, and Texas passed the following resolution:

"*Resolved*, That the secession of the States of Virginia, North Carolina, South Carolina, Georgia, Florida, Alabama, Mississippi, Louisiana, Texas, Arkansas, and Tennessee, from the United States, and the formation by them of a new Government, called the Confederate States of America, renders it necessary and expedient that the dioceses of the Protestant Episcopal Church within these States should form, within themselves, an independent organization;"

And did proceed to adopt and recommend for ratification a Constitution and form of Government independent of this Church; and in the month of July, 1862, the Convention of the diocese of Virginia did adopt such Constitution, and did assent to alterations of the Book of Common Prayer, and did substitute for the prayer for the President of the United States of America, a prayer for one designated as "President of the Confederate States of America," in open rebellion against such United States; therefore

Resolved, That the Protestant Episcopal Church in the United States of America is alone the particular or national Church for all who have acknowledged themselves its members, to which authority is given, as declared by the xxxivth Article, to ordain, change, and abolish rites and ceremonies.

That, in the opinion of this House, all ministers and other persons who have voluntarily united in the acts and proceedings before set forth, have fallen into the sins of rebellion, sedition and schism, and have greatly offended by their separation from this Church.

That the House of Bishops be requested, in their pastoral letter, to call upon the members of the church who have wandered into these offences to return to a better mind, and all others earnestly to pray that God in his mercy would bring them back, so that our Christian region may rest again in quiet and order, and being once more in godly concord, our Church, our land, our government and people may be continually saved and defended by his abounding goodness and almighty power.

And further Resolved, That the House of Bishops be requested to revise the first part of the Homily against "Disobedience and Wilful Rebellion," so that a portion thereof may be read in churches to the effect that "we all make continual prayer unto Almighty God, even from the bottom of our hearts, that he will give his grace, power, and strength unto the President of the United States, and all in authority over us, to vanquish and subdue as well rebels at home as foreign enemies, that all domestic rebellion being suppressed and pacified, and all outward invasions repulsed and abandoned, we may long continue in obedience to our lawful government, and in that peaceable and quiet of life which hitherto we have had; and may altogether in obedience unto God, the King of Kings, and unto his holy laws, lead our lives so in this world that in the world to come we may enjoy his everlasting kingdom."

Resolved, That these resolutions be sent to the House of Bishops.

By John W. Andrews, of Columbus:

Resolved, That loyalty to the government under which we live is a part of the law of the Protestant Episcopal Church of the United States, and that this convention pledges its constituents to stand by the government to the last in the work of putting down the existing rebellion.

By Rev. George Leeds, D.D., of Philadelphia:

Whereas, The absence from this convention of any and all representation from a large number of dioceses that have hitherto participated, under the Constitution of this Church, in its general council, has afflicted our hearts with grief and pain; and whereas, the cause of this absence is civil war and rebellion in that portion of the country in which these dioceses are planted, against the constituted authority of our beloved land; therefore

Resolved, That deeply as we deplore this unhappy strife, in which, also, we recognize the just judgment of God for our many sins, and earnestly as we lament and condemn the causes which have brought it upon us, so we also deprecate that grave error of judgment which has made it the occasion of severing the ties of visible communion and fellowship that have hitherto united us in our ecclesiastical Synod, and we will not abandon the hope that our absent brethren, guided by the grace of God, will retrace their steps for the honor of his name and the benefit of his holy church.

By Rev. Alexander Burgess, of Portland:

Resolved, That, in view of the afflictive state of our beloved nation, the House of Bishops be affectionately requested to prepare for the use of both Houses a form of prayer, invoking the interposition of God to restore us to peace and prosperity upon such a foundation as he shall approve.

By Mr. J. E. Warren, St. Paul, Minnesota:

Resolved, That the Protestant Episcopal Church throughout the world is one and a united Church, and that while there is no defection of faith, the unity of the Church is not violated or impaired by geographical lines, or national disintegrations, or civil or political disturbances.

Resolved, That this is a religious, and not a political body; that having met to legislate for the Church, and not for the State, that its deliberations be confined to this point, and that the introduction and discussion of all political subjects be deprecated and discouraged, as inimical to Christian unity.

October 9—The Committee made the following unanimous

REPORT.

The Committee have been deeply impressed with the importance and with the difficulty of the duty assigned to them. They have examined with care all the various resolutions which have been referred to them, and have not lost sight of the subsequent suggestions, which have been made in debate, by members of this body from many different parts of our country.

In framing the resolutions which they have at length, after much deliberation, agreed upon, they have had three leading objects in view. They have designed to leave no room for honest doubt, or even for invidious misconstruction, as to the hearty loyalty of this body to the government of the United States. They have desired to confirm and strengthen the unity of the Church, as represented in this convention. And they have attempted so to refer to the course of our brethren who are not represented here, as to shut no door of reconciliation which is still open, and to afford the best hope that they may still be induced to reconsider and retrace their steps, and to renew their relations, in Christian love and loyalty, to a common church and a common country.

The committee have felt that it was not fit for this convention to act or to speak as if they despaired, or in any degree doubted, of the ultimate restoration of the legitimate national authority over our whole land. They have felt, too, that the question before them was not so much as to what might be done, or what might be said, by this body, as a matter of stern justice, in vindication of the authority or the dignity of the Church, but as to what it was wise to do or say at this moment, consistently with our own convictions, and with a view to preserve, unbroken and undisturbed, every remaining link or tie of religious association and Christian sympathy, which might be of use hereafter in accomplishing the great end of restoring our National Union.

The committee are unwilling to conclude their report without one other suggestion. While there could have been no hesitation, under any circumstances, in expressing, now and always, our earnest and abiding loyalty and devotion to our country, its constitution and its laws, and to all its duly constituted authorities, they have felt that there yet rested upon this convention the most solemn obligation to abstain from entering upon any narrower questions, which peculiarly belong to the domain of secular politics. Our blessed Lord, in declaring that his kingdom is not of this world, and in directing us to render unto Cæsar the things that are Cæsar's, has clearly taught us, that, whether as Ministers or as Legislators and Councillors of his Church, we are to refrain from those matters which he has not committed to our care. There is, doubtless, a difficulty in the minds of many, in clearly discerning the precise boundary line between the subjects which come within our jurisdiction and the proper sphere of duty as Christian ministers and ecclesiastical councillors, and such as belong exclusively to secular politics. But the committee can hardly doubt that there will be a general concurrence in the opinion that, in this most critical period in the history of our Church and of our country, when words are things, and when rash utterances at one end of the Union may co-operate with rash acts at the other in extinguishing the best hopes which remain to us, it is wise for such a body as this to err on the safe side, if we must err at all; and to keep ourselves clearly within the limits which the Councils of our Church have hitherto so uniformly observed.

In accordance with these general views, the undersigned recommend the adoption of the following resolutions:

Resolved, By the House of Clerical and Lay Deputies of this stated Triennial Convention, That assembling, as we have been called to do, at a period of great national peril and deplorable civil convulsion, it is meet and proper that we should call to mind, distinctly and publicly, that the Protestant Episcopal Church in the United States hath ever held and taught, in the language of one of its Articles of Religion, that "it is the duty of all men who are professors of the Gospel to pay respectful obedience to the civil authority, regularly and legitimately constituted;" and hath accordingly incorporated into its Liturgy "a prayer for the President of the United States and all in civil authority," and a "prayer for the Congress of the United States, to be used during their session;" and hath bound all orders of its ministry to the faithful and constant observance, in letter and in spirit, of these and all other parts of its prescribed ritual.

2. That we cannot be wholly blind to the course which has been pursued, in their ecclesiastical as well as in their civil relations, since this Convention last met in perfect harmony and love, by great numbers of the ministers and members of this Church within certain States of our Union which have arrayed themselves in open and armed resistance to the regularly constituted Government of our country; and that while, in a spirit of Christian forbearance, we refrain from employing towards them any terms of condemnation and reproach, and would rather bow in humiliation before our common Father in Heaven for the sins which have brought His judgment on our land, we yet feel bound to declare our solemn sense of the deep and grievous wrong which they will have inflicted on the great Christian Communion which this Convention represents, as well as on the country within which it has been so happily and harmoniously established, should they persevere in striving to rend asunder those civil and religious bonds which have so long held us together in peace, unity, and concord.

3. That while, as individuals and citizens, we acknowledge our whole duty in sustaining and defending our country in the great struggle in which it is engaged, we are only at liberty, as Deputies to this Council of a Church which hath ever renounced all political association and action, to pledge to the national Government—as we now do—the earnest and devout prayers of all, that its efforts may be so guided by wisdom and replenished with strength, that they may be crowned with speedy and complete success, to the glory of God and the restoration of our beloved Union.

4. That if, in the judgment of the Bishops, any other forms of occasional prayer than those already set forth shall seem desirable and appropriate—whether for our Convention, our Church, or our country, for our rulers or our defenders, or for the sick and wounded and dying of our army and navy and volunteers—we shall gladly receive them and fervently use them.

5. That a certified copy of the foregoing report and resolutions be transmitted to the House of Bishops, in evidence of the views and feelings of this body in reference to the afflicting condition of our Church and of our country.

Mr. Hoffman moved his resolution as a substitute for the report.

Mr. William Welsh, of Philadelphia, moved to amend by striking from the second resolution the word "wholly," and inserting for the words "will have inflicted," the words "*are inflicting*," and by striking out the words "should they persevere."

October 15—Rev. Dr. Henry M. Mason, of Maryland, moved to table the whole subject, which was lost: of the Clergy, ayes 9, nays 11, divided 2; of the Laity, ayes 7, nays 10.

Mr. Welsh's amendments were lost: of the Clergy, yeas 9, nays 11, divided 2; of the Laity, yeas 7, nays 10.

Mr. Hoffman's substitute was lost: of the Clergy, yeas 7, nays 14, divided 1; of the Laity, yeas 2, nays 13, divided 1.

Rev. S. C. Thrall, D. D., then offered these resolutions, as a substitute:

Whereas this Church, in her thirty-seventh article, hath doctrinally taught the duty of loyalty to regularly constituted authority, and in her prayers for the President and Congress, hath practised that duty in such methods as becomes her as an ecclesiastical body, and any act of this House cannot add force to the solemn "ratification of the Book of Common Prayer;" and whereas the present affliction of our country arises from questions of civil polity, and as such is within the province of the State only, and any decision on such questions by the Church is a most disloyal assumption of the prerogative of the State; and whereas the alleged action of the members of the Church in the so-called seceded States in what has been done with reference to external order, administration or organization has been done under circumstances of the character and force of which it is impossible for this House to judge, until, by free and unrestrained intercourse and communication, we may hear from them the reasons of their action, and we have no knowledge of any action on their part affecting faith, ministry or sacraments; therefore,

Resolved, That there is no occasion for any action of this House, touching the declared and acknowledged loyalty of the Church.

2. That in the present affliction of this country by civil war, this House has no right, as a part of the Legislature of the Church, to take any action on the subject, as it is purely civil, and as such belongs to the constituted government only.

3. That in the matter of any action of the Church in the so-called seceded States, it is inexpedient for this House to express any opinion till it is in possession of more full and complete information than we can at present obtain.

4. That this preamble and resolutions be sent to the House of Bishops, to inform them of the action of this House.

Which was lost; of the Clergy, yeas 9, nays 12, divided 1; of the Laity, yeas 7, nays 10.

Rev. F. M. McAllister, of California, offered this, as a substitute:

Whereas the introduction of passing national events into this House, as a subject for its deliberation and action, has given pain and mortification to those many members of the Episcopal Church here and throughout the land who heartily believed that she was a kingdom not of this world; and that however as christian men her members might sympathize and suffer with the State in all its trials, triumphs, and adversities, this kingdom of God was one which should not be moved, attainted, or assailed by the heavings and distractions of secular dominion; and whereas the very introduction of this subject here has created expectations in the world around us, unacquainted with the nature and constitution of the Church of Christ, that this Convention must necessarily be as any one of the religious bodies of the land, reflecting the transient passions and emotions of the day, thus seriously and painfully embarrassing the action of many members of this body, who are required by the communities in which they respectively live to give some response to the resolutions upon the state of the country which have been introduced here; and whereas the preservation of this Church in its intact integrity as a part of the kingdom of Christ which is not of this world, is bound upon us as well by our loyalty to that Church and to its Divine Head as by the fact that the unshaken manifestation of such loyalty against all the pressure of the world's blandishments and terrorism in this fearful crisis, would exhibit a moral courage and a depth of religious principle that would make this Church of our God a praise and a glory in the land, and a true ark of refuge into which multitudes of the wise and good would gladly come for refuge from the storm and tempest of worldly interests; therefore, for the information of all,

Resolved, That as a legislative Council of the Church of Christ, all secular and national interests are foreign to the deliberations and decisions of this Convention, and that the true and divinely ordained relations of Christian men to the State are amply, constantly, and solemnly affirmed by this Church, in her daily teachings, and in her daily worship.

Which was lost: of the Clergy, yeas 7, nays 14, divided 1; of the Laity, yeas 5, nays 10, divided 2.

The report of the Committee was then adopted: of the Clergy, yeas 13, nays 6, divided 3; of the Laity, yeas 11, nays 5, divided 1, as follows:

AFFIRMATIVE DIOCESES.

CLERGY.

Delaware—Rev. Jacob Rambo, Rev. Samuel C. Brinckle—*Aye.*
Illinois—Rev. Alexander Capron, Robert H. Clarkson, D. D., Rev. Theodore N. Morrison, Rev. Warren H. Roberts—*Aye.*
Iowa—Edward W. Peet, D. D., Rev. George W. Watson, Rev. Charles B. Stout—*Aye.* Silas Totten, D. D.—*Nay.*
Maine—Rev. Alexander Burgess, Rev. Frederick Gardiner, Rev. William Stevens Perry—*Aye.*
Massachusetts—George M. Randall, D. D., Samuel P. Parker, D. D.—*Aye.* Theodore Edson, D. D.—*Nay.*
Michigan—Daniel T. Grinnell, D. D., Rev. Joseph F. Phillips, Rev. William E. Armitage—*Aye.*
Missouri—Montgomery Schuyler, D. D.—*Aye.*
New Hampshire—Rev. Henry A. Coit, Isaac G. Hubbard, D. D., Rev. Francis Chase—*Aye.* James H. Eames, D. D.—*Nay*
New York—J. H. Price, D. D., Edward Y. Higbee, D. D., Francis Vinton, D. D.—*Aye.*
Ohio—Erastus Burr, D. D.—*Aye,*
Pennsylvania—M. A. DeW. Howe, D. D., G. Emlen Hare, D. D., George Leeds, D. D., D. R. Goodwin, D. D.—*Aye.*
Rhode Island—Silas A. Crane, D. D.—*Aye.*
Western New York—Amos B. Beach, D. D., William D. Wilson, D. D., Rev. Andrew Hull—*Aye.*

LAITY.

Connecticut—Joseph E. Sheffield, Seth P. Beers—*Aye.*
Delaware—Franklin Fell—*Aye.*
Maine—Robert H. Gardiner—*Aye.*
Massachusetts—George C. Shattuck—*Aye.*
Michigan—Henry P. Baldwin—*Aye.*
New Hampshire—Simeon Ide—*Aye.*
New York—Murray Hoffman, Luther Bradish, Samuel B. Ruggles—*Aye.*
Ohio—John W. Andrew—*Aye.*
Pennsylvania—John N. Conyngham, Herman Cope, William Welsh, F. R. Brunot—*Aye.*
Rhode Island—Edward King—*Aye.*
Western New York—Joseph Juliand—*Aye.*

NEGATIVE DIOCESES.

CLERGY.

Kentucky—James Craik, D. D., Rev. Francis M. Whittle—*Nay.*
Maryland—W. E. Wyatt, D. D., William Pinkney, D. D., Henry M. Mason, D. D., Rev. Orlando Hutton—*Nay.*
Minnesota—Rev. Solon W. Manney, Rev. D. B. Knickerbacker, Rev. Timothy Wilcoxson—*Nay.* A. B. Patterson, D. D.—*Aye.*
New Jersey—Milo Mahan, D. D., Rev. W. Croswell Doane—*Nay.*
Vermont—Rev. David H. Buel, Rev. Andrew Oliver, Rev. Malcolm Douglass—*Nay.*
Wisconsin—William B. Ashley, D. D., Azel D. Cole, D. D—*Nay.* Rev. Lewis A. Kemper—*Aye.*

LAITY.

Illinois—S. Corning Judd—*Nay.*
Kentucky—A. H. Churchill, William Cornwall—*Nay.*
Maryland—Ezekiel F. Chambers—*Nay.*
New Jersey—J. C. Garthwaite, Henry Macfarlan—*Nay.* Thomas P. Carpenter—*Aye.*
Vermont—V. Atwood—*Nay.*

DIVIDED DIOCESES.

CLERGY.

California—S. C. Thrall, D. D—*Aye.* F. M. McAllister—*Nay.*
Connecticut—Jacob L. Clark, D. D., E. A. Washburn, D. D—*Aye.* W. Cooper Mead, D. D., Robert A. Hallam, D. D.—*Nay.*
Indiana—Rev. J. B. Wakefield—*Aye.* Rev. L. W. Russ—*Nay.*

LAITY.

Minnesota—E. T. Wilder—*Aye.* J. E. Warren—*Nay.*

PASTORAL LETTER OF THE BISHOPS OF THE PROTESTANT EPISCOPAL CHURCH, 1862.

October 1—The House of Bishops met in New York.

October 14—Two Pastoral Letters were reported from the committee, which consisted of the five senior Bishops present, viz: Bishops John H. Hopkins of Vermont, Benjamin Bosworth Smith of Kentucky, Charles Pettit McIlvaine of Ohio, Jackson Kemper of Wisconsin, Samuel Allen McCaskry of Michigan. The committee, "not being fully agreed as to the two letters read before them," presented both for the action of the House.

On motion of Bishop Whittingham, the subjoined was adopted as the Pastoral Letter, as follows:

BRETHREN: We have been assembled together in the Triennial Convention of our Church under most afflicting circumstances. Hitherto, whatever our Church had to contend with from the fallen nature of man, from the power of this evil world, or the enmity of that mighty adversary who is called by St. Paul "the god of this world," her Chief Council has been permitted to meet amidst the blessings of peace within our national boundaries, and as representing a household of faith at unity in itself. Our last meeting was in the metropolis of a State which has long held a high place and influence in the affairs of our Church and Country. Long shall we remember the affectionate hospitality which was then lavished upon us, and the delightful harmony and brotherly love which seemed to reign, almost without alloy, in a Convention composed of representatives of all our Dioceses! Never did the promise of a long continuance of brotherly union, among all parts and sections of our whole Church, appear more assuring. But, alas! what is man? How unstable our surest reliances, based on man's wisdom or will! How unsearchable the counsels of Him who "hath his way in the sea, and his path in the mighty waters, and whose footsteps are not known!" What is now the change? We look in vain for the occupants of seats in the Convention, belonging to the representatives of no less than ten of our Dioceses, and to ten of our Bishops. And whence such painful and injurious absence? The cause stands as a great cloud of darkness before us, of which, as we cannot help seeing it, and thinking of it, and that most sorrowfully, wherever we go and whatever we do, it is impossible not to speak when we address you in regard to the condition and wants of our Church. That cause is all concentrated in a stupendous rebellion against the organic law and the constituted Government of the Country, for the dismemberment of our national Union—under which, confessedly, all parts of the land have been signally prospered and blessed; a rebellion which is already too well known to you, brethren, in the vast armies it has compelled our Government to maintain, and in the fearful expense of life and treasure, of suffering and sorrow, which it has cost on both sides, to need any further description here.

We are deeply grieved to think how many of our brethren, clergy and laity, in the regions over which that dark tide has spread, have been carried away by its flood; not only yielding to it, so as to place themselves, as far as in them lay, in severance from our ecclesiastical Union, which has so long and so happily joined us together in one visible communion and fellowship; but, to a sad extent, sympathizing with the movement, and giving it their active co-operation.

In this part of our address, we do not attempt to estimate the moral character of such doings. At present we confine ourselves to the statement of notorious facts, except as to one matter, of which this is the convenient place to speak.

When the ordained Ministers of the Gospel of Christ, whose mission is so emphatically one of peace and good-will, of tenderness and consolation, do so depart from their sacred calling as to take the sword and engage in the fierce and bloody conflicts of war; when in so doing they are fighting against authorities which, as "*the powers that be,*" the Scriptures declare "are ordained of God," so that in resisting them they resist the ordinance of God; when especially one comes out from the exalted spiritual duties of an Overseer of the flock of Christ, to exercise high command in such awful work,—we cannot, as ourselves Overseers of the same flock, consistently with duty to Christ's Church, His Ministry and people, refrain from placing on such examples our strongest condemnation. We remember the words of our blessed Lord, uttered among His last words, and for the special admonition of His Ministers—"They that take the sword shall perish with the sword."

Returning to this great rebellion, with all its retinue of cost and sacrifice, of tribulation and anguish, of darkness and death, there are two aspects in which we must contemplate it, *namely:* as it comes *by the agency of man*, and as it comes *from the Providence of God.*

We desire, *first*, to call your attention to it as it proceeds from *the Providence of God.* So comprehensive is that Providence that it embraces all worlds and all nations; while so minute is it that not a sparrow falleth without the knowledge and will of our Father in Heaven. In its vast counsels, this deep affliction has its place. God's hand is in it. His power rules it. It is His visitation and chastening for the sins of this nation. Who can doubt it? Just as the personal affliction of any of you is God's visitation to turn him from the world and sin, unto Himself, so is this national calamity most certainly His judgment upon this nation for its good. And we trust, dear brethren, we are in no danger of seeming, by such interpretation of our distresses, to excuse, in any degree, such agency as men have had in bringing them upon us. God's Providence has no interference with man's responsibility. He works by man, but so that it is still man that wills and works. The captivities of God's chosen people were, as His Word declares, His judgments upon them for their sins; while the nations that carried them captive were visited of God for heinous guilt in so doing. St. Peter declares that our Lord was "delivered" unto death "by the determinate counsel and foreknowledge of God;" and that, nevertheless, it was "*by wicked hands*" that he was "crucified and slain." Thus we need be under no temptation to diminish our estimate of the present dispensation of sorrow, as coming from the hand of God, for the punishment of our sins, whatever the agency of men therein. It is our duty, as Christians and as patriots, so to consider it, that it may do us the good for which it is sent, and may the sooner be taken away.

It is not possible for us, in this address, to set before you, in detail, or in their true proportions, all the national and other sins which make us, as a people, deserve, and need, the chastisements of a holy God. It needs no Daniel, inspired from on high, to discover them. Surely you must all be painfully familiar with many of them, in the profaneness of speech with which God's name and majesty are assailed; in the neglect of public worship which so dishonors His holy day; in the ungodliness of life which erects its example so conspicuously; and especially in that one great sin for which Jerusalem was given over to be trodden down by the heathen, and the people of Israel have ever since been wanderers and a by-word among the nations, *namely*, the rejection, whether in positive infidelity, or only in practical unbelief of God's great gift of grace and mercy, His beloved Son, our Lord Jesus Christ, to be a sacrifice of propitiation for our sins, and an all-sufficient and all-glorious Saviour of our souls.

But there is a passage in the Scriptures which is of great use as a guide in this consideration of national sinfulness. It is a warning to the nation of Israel, and found in the eighth chapter of the book of Deuteronomy, as follows: "Beware that thou forget not the Lord thy God, in not keeping His commandments, and His judgments, and His statutes, which I command thee this day, lest when thou hast eaten and art full, and hast built goodly houses and hast dwelt therein, and when thy herds and thy flocks multiply, and thy silver and thy gold is multiplied, and all that thou hast is multiplied, then thy heart be lifted up, and thou forget the Lord thy God; for it is He that giveth thee power to get wealth. And it shall be, that if thou do at all forget the Lord thy God—as the nations which the Lord destroyeth before your face, so shall ye perish, because ye would not be obedient to the voice of the Lord your God."

Now it was because that nation was guilty of precisely such self-glorying, and such forgetfulness of its indebtedness to God and dependence on His favor, as this warning describes, that the grievous calamities which so fill its history, before the advent of Christ, were brought upon it. And it is because there is so much agreement between this description and the aspect which we, as a people, have presented before God, that we place the passage before you.

Marvellously have we been prospered in everything pertaining to national prosperity, riches, and strength. God has loaded us with benefits; and with our benefits have grown our ingratitude, our self-dependence, and self-sufficiency, our pride, our vain-glorying, and that sad deficiency, so much felt, in the representative acts and voices of the nation as to all adequate acknowledgment of God and of the Gospel of Christ. Let us mark the words of the prophet Jeremiah: "Let not the wise man glory in his wisdom, neither let the mighty man glory in his might; let not the rich man glory in his riches; but let him that glorieth, glory in this, that he understandeth and knoweth me that I am the Lord which exercise loving-kindness, judgment, and righteousness in the earth."—(Jer. ix.; 23, 24.) How remarkably do these words exhibit our sin as a nation! How seldom, in anything of a representative character, or anything that speaks for the nation, especially in the counsels of our chosen rulers, or in the enactments of our legislatures, do we see any such reference to God, as is here required as the basis on which He blesses a nation! How literally have we gloried in our wisdom, and power, and wealth; and said in our hearts, *Our power and our hand have gotten us all these things!*

Dear brethren, can we consider these things, so palpable to every eye, and not acknowledge that we deserve God's anger, and need, for our good, His chastening Providence? Is it wonderful that this tribulation hath come upon us? O, that when thus His judgments are upon the land, the inhabitants may learn righteousness! We exhort you, brethren, that, as citizens and as Christians, you will take these things seriously to heart. Search and try yourselves, that you may duly humble yourselves under God's mighty hand, and He may, in due time, exalt us out of the present distress. Such a spirit of humiliation, taking wide possession of the people, especially of those who, as members of the Church of Christ, profess to be His disciples—above all, such a spirit appearing among those whose official position makes their works and acts of eminent weight and responsibility in determining the nation's standing before God—would more encourage us concerning the prospect of a happy removal of our national afflictions, a happy future of stability in our civil institutions, and of peace in the whole land, than if many signal victories were given to our honored armies. Let us pray earnestly and constantly for that spirit, which, above all things, is a nation's wealth, and strength, and praise. "The Lord's hand is not shortened," that it cannot thus bless us. "His ear is not heavy, that it cannot hear" us when we seek so great a blessing. He is "able to do exceeding abundantly above all that we ask or think;" and prayer is the arm that places our wants on His mighty power.

Let us turn now to the other aspect of our great trial; namely, *as it comes from the agency of man.* We deeply feel, dear brethren, how momentous is this portion of our subject, and with what carefulness and charity, and at the same time with what decision and plainness of speech, with what faithfulness to Church and Country, and to those arrayed against us, as well as to ourselves, it becomes us to speak. Gladly would your Bishops avoid a subject so painful. But there is no possibility of avoiding it. Should we keep silence, we should not avoid it. Our silence would speak far and wide, and with a meaning by which we are not willing that our minds should be interpreted. At such an alarming crisis of our national and ecclesiastical union, as well as of our whole welfare, when a voice from such a body, occupying such intimate relations to a wide-spread communion, may be of such importance to the strength of the public counsels, through the guidance of the people of that communion,—should we address you on other topics of less prominence at the present time, and yet keep silence on that one which banishes almost every other from the thoughts of the nation, we should not only neglect an opportunity of usefulness which ought to be improved, and subject ourselves to imputations which we are not willing to bear, but we should inflict a serious injury upon a cause we are bound to aid.

It is the first time this Convention has met since these troubles began. God grant they may be ended long before it shall meet again! Ever since our Church had her Litany, we have been praying for deliverance "from sedition, privy conspiracy, and rebellion." And now that all the three are upon us, and in a depth of scheme, a force of action, a strength of purpose, and an extensiveness of sway such as the world never before saw united for the dismemberment of any government, shall we refuse to tell you in what light we regard that gigantic evil?

We are moved the more to speak, because we believe that you, brethren, desire it of us. You feel bound, by your views of duty, to take a position and manifest principles, too decided to be mistaken, in support of the national Constitution and Government in this day of their peril. Our communion is nobly represented wherever the nation's cause has dangers to brave, difficulties to be surmounted, sacrifices to be made, or sufferings to be borne. In the ranks, and through all the grades of command, our Church testifies her loyalty by the devotion of her sons. Many of them are her choice young men, whom it is hard to spare from works of Christian well-doing at home. Many of them are her Sunday-school teachers. They have gone to her armies, not in any bitterness of feeling towards those who have brought on us this war, but in a ready mind to love their enemies and to do good to those that hate them, as well as out of a well-considered and conscientious conviction of duty to their Country, to their Government, and to God. They look to us, their chief Pastors, especially as we are now gathered together here, to give them the support and comfort of our approbation, if we think they have rightly judged the great question of duty to the

Government in the present struggle. Amidst the perils of battle, in hospitals and prisons, under privations and wounds, they feel the preciousness of such comfort. Acknowledging the reasonableness of such desires, we have pleasure in complying with them; not apprehending that in touching on this subject it can with reason be objected that we enter amidst questions with which, as Ministers of Him whose "kingdom is not of this world," we have nothing to do. Whatever the Apostles of Christ were inspired by the Holy Ghost to teach the Church; the Ministers and Stewards of the Church are bound to illustrate and enforce, for instruction of her members. "All Scripture is profitable for doctrine, reproof, correction, and instruction in righteousness." Whatever is contained therein is part of what has thus been "written for our learning"—part of that spiritual provision which you, brethren, are to "read, mark, learn, and inwardly digest;" and which, therefore, God's Stewards must distribute, as varying circumstances shall make it "a word in season."

Then what say the Scriptures touching the subject before us? We have no need to go beyond the words of St. Paul, in the thirteenth chapter of the Epistle to the Romans—"Let every soul be subject to the higher powers. For there is no power but of God. The powers that be are ordained of God. Whosoever, therefore, resisteth the power, resisteth the ordinance of God; and they that resist shall receive to themselves damnation."

Now, it is the application of these words to our duties, under present circumstances, of which we have need to inquire, if we would use this portion of Scripture as "a light to our feet." Where, then, do we find those powers and ordinances to which, as "ordained of God," we, recognizing the great truth that "there is no power but of God," are bound, for His sake, to be subject? We answer, IN THE CONSTITUTION AND GOVERNMENT OF THE UNITED STATES. Under them, the people of all the States, now resisting them, were just as much bound to render obedience, when such resistance began, as we, whose allegiance is still unbroken. According to the Scriptures, that resistance, so far from making null and void those powers, is a resistance to ordinances of God still in force; and, therefore, brings His condemnation on those so engaged.

When St. Paul, in direct connection with the words just cited, exhorts us to "render to all their dues, tribute to whom tribute is due, custom to whom custom, fear to whom fear, honor to whom honor," and *that* "not only for wrath, but for conscience' sake;" we have no hesitation in teaching that the claim to all these duties and manifestations of allegiance and loyalty from us, and from all those States so recently united in rendering them, is rightfully in that Government which is now by force of arms maintaining such claim. The refusal of such allegiance we hold to be a *sin;* and when it stands forth in armed rebellion, it is a *great crime* before the laws of God, as well as man.

Thus, brethren, your Bishops teach, as official expositors of the Word of God. Less, they believe, they could not teach without unfaithfulness to the Scriptures.

If godly submission to the laws and constitutional rulers of the country should be regarded as a matter of less than the most religious obligation; if it shall be held a thing of indifference whether the Government, given us in the Providence of God, be obeyed "for conscience' sake," or be overthrown by conspiracy and armed rebellion, without the pretence of any existing and oppressive wrong, or of any wrong for which the remedy might not be found under, and by, provision of that very Government,—then all the horrors, of which such rebellion may be the prolific parent, may at any time be caused, and even intended, without guilt. But, let us hear what the Fathers of our Church, in one of those Homilies which our Articles declare to contain "a godly and wholesome doctrine," teaches on this head. We can well understand it now and appreciate it, as never before. In the Homily "Against Willful Rebellion" we have these wholesome words: "He that nameth rebellion, nameth not a singular, or one only sin, as is theft, robbery, murder, and such like; but he nameth the whole puddle and sink of all sins against God and man; against his country, his countrymen, his parents, his children, his kinsfolk, his friends, and against all men universally; all sins against God and all men heaped together, nameth he that nameth rebellion." In another passage, after speaking of the general miseries of all war, the Homily proceeds with a still darker description: "But when these mischiefs are wrought in rebellion by them that should be friends, by countrymen, by kinsmen, by those that should defend their country and countrymen from such miseries, the misery is nothing so great as are the mischief and wickedness where the subjects unnaturally do rebel * *; countrymen to disturb the public peace and quietness of their country, for defence of whose quietness they should spend their lives;" "and, universally, instead of all quietness, joy, and felicity, which so follow blessed peace and due obedience, to bring in all trouble, sorrow, disquietness of minds and bodies, and all mischief and calamities; to turn all good order upside down; to bring all good laws into contempt, and to tread them under foot; to oppress all virtue and honesty, and all virtuous and honest persons; and to set all vice and wickedness and all vicious and wicked men at liberty to work their wicked wills, which before were bridled by wholesome laws; to weaken, to overthrow, and to consume the strength of the realm, their natural country, which, by their mischief weakened, is thus ready to be a prey and spoil to all outward enemies."

Such is the testimony of our Homilies against "Willful Rebellion."

The reasons which make this so great a crime are the same which make the constituted authority so indispensable to the very existence of human society. God has invested the magistrate with power, and given him the sword to be borne, "not in vain," because he is His Minister "*for good;*" because, without him, all the floods of ungodliness would be set free; and the only remedy remaining for all social disorders would be that of force overcoming force, and of cunning overreaching cunning.

We have now, brethren, in strict confinement to the testimony of the Scriptures, ascertained a basis of principle and duty on which we may heartily rejoice in all the active and energetic loyalty with which the members of our Churches, in union with their fellow-citizens, of all classes and conditions, are sustaining the Government in its vast efforts to reinstate the rightful control of its laws, wherever they have been disowned. We bid them never to be weary of that well-doing; and particularly would we say to those who, out of love to their country, and not out of any vindictive exasperation towards her enemies, have gone in our armies, *be of good cheer!* Whatever the dangers you may have to meet, or sufferings to endure, let it be your consolation that you have gone to sustain the power, ordained of God, and which rightfully claims your most devoted loyalty.

And now, we can ask your further attention only to a few concluding words, touching great spiritual interests, which the absorbing claims and the strong excitements of these times endanger. No doubt, dear brethren, you have all been painfully conscious of the powerful tendency of the present anxieties and excitements to draw down your thoughts and affections from daily communion with God; to elevate earthly interests and duties into injurious rivalry with those of the soul and eternity; to carry your minds away on this powerful flood of feeling and active concern for our beloved country, till they become, in a great degree, separated from all earnest engagedness in God's service. With some minds, under divine grace, the tendency of these troubles is to lead them nearer to God; while with others it is to take them away from God, to make His Word less precious, His holy day less sacredly kept, secret prayer less faithfully observed, and less their refuge and consolation; Christian example less decided and exalted.

We desire affectionately to exhort you to increased watchfulness and prayer in consequence of such danger. Let not love of Country make your love to God and your gracious Saviour the less fervent. Immense as is this present earthly interest, it is only earthly. The infinitely greater interests of the soul and of the kingdom of God remain as paramount as ever. We counsel, not that you feel less concern for the former, but that you seek God's grace so to sanctify all its anxieties that it may constantly lead you to Him for refuge, and rest, and peace; making you only the more earnest to secure, in exchange for this sinful and troublesome world, that inheritance which is incorruptible, that better country where "sorrow and sighing flee away."

And we also charge you, brethren, that you watch and pray, lest during this unhappy strife you should allow any bitterness of spirit to dwell in you toward those who, from whatever cause, have brought on us this war, with its great injuries and calamities, or who are now waging it against us. To hate rebellion, so uncaused, is duty; but to hate those engaged therein, is the opposite of Christian duty. Nothing can release us from the charge of our blessed Lord to love even our greatest enemies; do good to them that hate us, and pray for such as despitefully use us and persecute us. In this temper of mind let us be followers of Him who, when *we* were enemies, died for us.

We are pained to learn, from the reports of committees of our General Missionary Society, to what extent the means of pursuing their great work have suffered by reason of these times. We are aware how much of the contributions of our people have gone to the relief and consolation of our brethren who, in exposing themselves to the dangers of battle for our defence, have fallen under wounds or sickness. We rejoice in all that is done for them; and it is a vast relief from the horrors of this war to see what a spirit of self-denying and devoted benevolence has appeared all over the land, in men and women of all conditions, banding them together in labors of love, or scattering them abroad over the field of suffering, on errands of compassion and tender ministration to our sick, wounded, dying soldiers. God be praised for all this! It goes far to comfort us in the great tribulation. But the claims of the kingdom of God are not diminished. The calls for the labors of men of God to preach the Gospel in destitute places are as loud as ever. And we believe that while the ability of many to contribute of their substance to the missionary work has been greatly impaired and almost taken away by our national troubles, that of many others is not so diminished or so drawn upon by objects peculiar to these circumstances that they may not enlarge their gifts to the work of missions, and greatly supply what is lacking by the disability of others. We pray them, and all our brethren, seriously to review their duty in this respect. The missions in Africa and China are afflicted at the prospect of being painfully reduced for want of means to sustain them as they are. In the domestic field, the absence in missionary stations of the labors of the Minister of the Word and Sacrament, is even a greater evil in such times than when no great national affliction carries its sorrows and clouds into every village of the land. Let us seek God's blessing upon our country's cause, by seeking to promote His kingdom and righteousness in all our borders.

But it is not merely for the support of our missionary work that we are concerned at this time. The ability of many a faithful parish Minister to continue his labor of love among a people beloved, is greatly endangered at this time for lack of the most slender pecuniary support; so that by the additional cause of Ministers feeling it their duty to see to the spiritual wants of our soldiers and taking service as chaplains in the army, we are increasing the number of vacant congregations to an alarming extent. We must therefore exhort our brethren to take heed and to do their utmost in their several parishes, that the blessing of a settled Minister be not lost for lack of the needed pecuniary support. If such privation, in ordinary circumstances, be of great detriment; much more is it so in days of affliction such as we have never known before. Never was it so important to all individual, domestic, and social interests, for the light of every household in a day of darkness, and the strengthening of every heart in a season of manifold burdens, that the lamp of the sanctuary should be trimmed and burning; that the precious "comfort of the Scriptures," through its appointed Messenger, should not be removed; that the soothing, purifying, governing, elevating influences of the public means of grace, under the hand of God's Minister, should be regularly enjoyed in the congregation. But if such cannot be the privilege, then we exhort vacant congregations that instead of forsaking the assembling of themselves together, as if, because they have no pastor, they could have no worship, one with another, they will take advantage of the great privilege of having our Book of Common Prayer, whereby a Church without a Pastor may still have its public worship and the Word of God, in purity, in fitness, and in power. Meet together regularly, brethren; have the Morning and Evening Prayer, and some approved published sermon, read by one of your number. You will thus have much to enjoy, though not all you need and desire. Lose it not, because you cannot have more.

And now, praying a merciful God and Father soon to restore to our beloved country the blessings of peace, under the banner of our honored national Union, and with our wholesome laws and righteous liberties more than ever strengthened, defended, and established; praying that those who have sought to depart from us may speedily and happily be reunited with us in the bonds of Christian, as well as national, fellowship; and that all bitterness, and wrath, and anger, and clamor, and evil speaking may be put away from us and them "with all malice;" that we may "be kind one to another, tender-hearted, forgiving one another even as we hope that God, for Christ's sake, hath forgiven us," we affectionately "commit you to God and the word of His grace." May the blessing of God so abide on you, beloved brethren, in all your families and congregations, that "your faith may grow exceedingly," "that your love may abound more and more," "that you may walk worthy of the Lord unto all pleasing, being fruitful in every good work and increasing in the knowledge of God;" "to whom be glory in the Church, throughout all ages, world without end."

CHARLES PETTIT McILVAINE, D. D., D. C. L.,
BISHOP OF OHIO,
Presiding in the House of Bishops, pro tem.

PROTEST OF BISHOP HOPKINS.

October 16—Bishop Hopkins read a protest against the Pastoral Letter adopted by the House, which he requested might be entered on the minutes. Bishop Kemper moved that the request be granted. On motion of Bishop Whittingham, it was received, and placed on file among the documents of this House.

The Protest of Bishop Hopkins, and his proposed Pastoral Letter, are subjoined:

PROTEST.

To the House of Bishops in General Convention assembled:—

RIGHT REVEREND BRETHREN,—It is with much regret that I find myself obliged to enter my solemn protest against the political aspect of the Pastoral Letter which your venerable Body has adopted, and to withdraw from the final act of its public delivery. On minor topics of opinion, during my Episcopate of thirty years, I have never departed from my obligation to preserve the unity of this House, to the utmost of my small ability. But this action, in my judgment, involves a fundamental principle in our ecclesiastical position. We stand opposed, in this country, to any Union between Church and State. In our individual capacity, as citizens, we are bound by the plain precepts of the inspired Apostles, to bear true allegiance to "the powers that be"—the earthly government under which the Providence of God has placed us. For *that*, our system sets forth an ample arrangement, in the Homily against rebellion, in the catechism appointed for the instruction of youth, in the Lessons of Scripture, in our Litany, and in the Prayers for the President and Congress, to say nothing of the special supplications set forth for the present national troubles, all uniting in the most positive testimony to the duty of Christian loyalty. But beyond this, I cannot allow that this House of Bishops, assembled in our official relations to the Church of God, has a right to go, by expressing any judgment on the measures of secular government. Under the American Constitution, the State has no right to declare its sentence on the legislation of the Church, so long as we do nothing to impair this duty of loyalty. And, under our Apostolic Constitution, the Church has no right to utter her sentence upon the legislation of the State, so long as it forbears to assail our Christian liberty. Their respective functions are distinct. The Almighty Ruler of the world has committed to the State the wide sphere of temporal interest, and He has committed to the Church the far higher sphere which embraces the interests of eternity. Each has its own allotted orbit, and I cannot comprehend how any reflecting and intelligent man in our Communion should desire that those orbits, in the present condition of mankind, should come together. I know, indeed, that this conjunction was attempted, though in different forms, by Popery and Puritanism. I know that it exists, to some extent, in the Establishment of England. But I also know that the primitive Church spread her triumphs throughout the earth, in total independence of the State, and that all our clergy have been educated to regard the union of Church and State as a mistake and a calamity.

Maintaining this as a fundamental principle of our ecclesiastical position, from which I cannot justify any departure, I proceed to show how the Church has acted with relation to the policy of war, along the main track of her history, even under the disadvantages of her secular connections.

From the period when Christianity became established in the old Roman empire, there were many insurrections, and intestine as well as foreign wars, but I can call to mind no instance, in all the councils, where the justice or the injustice of those wars was made a topic for ecclesiastical consideration. In the civil wars of England, which were numerous before the Reformation, I think it will not be found that the Church committed herself, by any formal and united action, either to the one side or to the other. In the great rebellion against Charles I., I am not aware that the Bishops were assembled to set forth any sentence on the political right or wrong involved in the conflict, although it threatened, and, for a season, accomplished, their own official downfall. And when the American Colonies revolted, and the Rev. William White became the first Chaplain to the Revolutionary Congress, I do not see the slightest movement in our Mother Church to condemn his course, or that of the ministers who acted with him. The Bishop of London was the Diocesan of all the clergy in the Colonies, and had the undoubted right to suspend or to depose them, if the act of secular rebellion had been a proper ground for ecclesiastical denunciation. But that, in every age, has been regarded as a subject for the action of the State, and I doubt whether an instance can be found in the whole range of the Church's history, where an ecclesiastical court has tried a man for secular rebellion. If the Church of England had held it to be her duty to adopt the principle which this House of Bishops has laid down in the Pastoral Address, the Rev. William White and his colleagues could hardly have been accepted as fit subjects for Episcopal consecration, and the whole character of our ministerial succession would most probably have passed away, forever.

It is due to the solemn responsibility under which I present this Protest, that I should enforce its positions by the citation of some high authorities.

Thus the general principle is set forth by the learned Palmer (London edition of 1839, vol. 2, p. 96):—

"In maintaining the right of the Church," saith he, "to judge in controversies, it is necessary to limit her authority to its proper object. It is not, then, supposed by any one, that the Church is authorized to determine questions relating to philosophy, science, legislation, or any other subjects beyond the doctrine of revelation. Her office relates entirely to the truth once revealed by Jesus Christ."

I need hardly remind my respected brethren of our XXth Article, in which it is declared that "the Church hath authority in controversies of faith:" excluding, by fair implication, controversies of secular policy.

The proper objects to be secured by the meetings of ecclesiastical Councils are thus set forth by Field, in his well known Treatise (p. 643):—

"The causes why General Councils assemble," saith he, "are three: 1st, the suppressing of heresies; 2d, a general and uniform reformation of abuses crept into the Church; and 3d, the taking away of schisms about the election of pastors and rejection of intruders. And the causes that were wont to be examined in the meetings of the Bishops of the Province (p. 514) were the ordinations of Bishops when any churches were void, and the depriving and rejecting all such as were found unworthy—and, in a word, any complaint or wrong done in any church was then to be heard."

To these I shall only add some interesting statements of the faithful and laborious Bingham (B. XVI., ch. 2, vol. 2, p. 880, of Bohn's London edition):

"The power of the Church originally," saith this author, "was a mere spiritual power, her sword only a spiritual sword, as Cyprian terms it, to affect the soul and not the body. Hence the ancient Bishops were accustomed to plead with the magistrates and the emperors, to save the lives of those who were condemned to death by law."

The writer proceeds to quote S. Augustine's language to an African judge, as follows:

"I know the Apostle says 'ye bear not the sword in vain, but are ministers of God to execute wrath upon them that do evil.' But the cause of the State is one thing, and the cause of the Church is another. The administration of the State is to be carried on by terror, but the meekness of the Church is to be commended by her clemency.

"These men, with the sword of unrighteousness, shed Christian blood: do you withhold even the lawful sword of judgment from being imbrued in their blood."

"It was also thought some cruelty," saith Bingham elsewhere (2 vol. p. 1055,) "or at least a very improper and unbecoming thing, for any clergyman to be concerned in judging or giving sentence in cases of blood. The laws allowed them to be chosen arbitrators of men's differences in civil causes, but they had no power at all in criminal causes except such as were purely ecclesiastical, and least of all in such criminal causes where life and death were concerned. Therefore there are many Canons forbidding this under the highest censure of deprivation. The Council of Tarragon universally forbids the clergy to sit as judges in any criminal causes. The Council of Auxerre more particularly enjoins presbyters not to sit in judgment when any man is to be condemned to die. The fourth Council of Toledo allows not priests to sit judges in cases of treason, even at the command of the prince, except the prince promised beforehand upon oath that he would pardon the offence, and remit the punishment. If they did otherwise, they were to be held guilty of bloodshed before Christ, and to lose their order and degree in the Church. And the eleventh Council of Toledo goes even further, refusing them lay-communion, until they were at the point of death."

These quotations might be greatly multiplied, but they must surely be sufficient to prove the broad distinction between the duty of the State and the office of the Church, at all times, but especially when wars and rebellions, which demand so large and awful an amount of bloodshed, are concerned. The great and glorious object of the divine Head of the Church was "not to destroy men's lives but to save them." And if the voice of His Church is to be lifted up at all, with reference to the avenging sword of earthly government, it would seem to be only when she is prepared to urge, for Christ's sake, the blessed work of peace and conciliation. If she may not, with propriety, do this, under the existing condition of our country, she is at least bound to abstain from any act which would make her a party in the mournful task of slaughter.

On the whole view, therefore, which I have been able to take of this deeply important question, I am constrained, however reluctantly, to stand entirely aloof from the novel movement, which pledges the Church to the State in its merely political administration. To that, as individual citizens, we owe all lawful obedience and support. But here, acting as Bishops in the Church of Christ, we have no right to pass beyond the circle of our spiritual functions, nor to express any opinion, direct or indirect, upon the measures of our secular government.

In the world, we are all ready to render unto Cæsar the things that are Cæsar's. In the Church, we must confine ourselves to our higher duty of rendering unto God the things that are God's.

The adoption of any other principle, in my humble judgment, can only lead to strife and confusion. For, if we claim the right to applaud the course of our secular government when it pleases us, we must also claim the right to condemn its measures when they may happen to be unacceptable. And the inevitable result must be that the clergy would have the warrant of our example to discuss every political movement in the House of God, and thus degrade our high and spiritual standing to the temporal uses of party and popular excitement.

In conclusion, I desire to say that I yield to no man in my loyalty as a citizen, in my attachment to the Federal Union of the States, or in my deep sorrow that any even should have occurred by which that Union could be endangered or destroyed. But my duty as a citizen is one thing, and my duty as a Bishop is another. By the first I hold a relation to the State, under the laws and the Constitution. By the second, I hold, however unworthy, a high office in the kingdom of Christ, which is not of this world. And while I maintain a just allegiance to the State, I am bound to maintain the infinitely more solemn and sublime allegiance to my omnipotent Lord and Master in such wise, that I may not confound the lines of demarcation which He has placed between them. I claim no influence, however, for my humble judgment over any other mind, and am perfectly aware that I am personally of too little importance to expect it. But I am compelled to act on my own conclusions of duty, knowing, as I do, that they have been formed on the widest examination in my power, against my personal sympathies and interest, and solely from my conviction of their truth. I deny not the same claim to conscientious sincerity, on the part of my respected brethren from whom I differ. I shall withdraw myself from any participation in the Pastoral Letter, with the kindliest feelings of fraternal affection towards all my colleagues, without exception. And I trust, by the mercy of God, that I shall be allowed to meet them at a future day, under happier circumstances, when we may assemble together again in a true union of sentiment and action.

JOHN H. HOPKINS,
Bishop of Vermont.

NEW YORK, HOUSE OF BISHOPS,
October 15, 1862.

THE PASTORAL LETTER REJECTED BY THE HOUSE OF BISHOPS.

For the first time, beloved brethren, since the separate organization of our American Church, your Bishops are called on to issue a Pastoral Address, under very mournful and depressing circumstances. Our country, so lately flourishing in prosperity and peace, lies bleeding under the terrible affliction of the bitterest national warfare. Thousands upon thousands have fallen upon the field of battle, and no one can estimate the desolated homes, the broken hearts, the misery of the widows and the orphans, the poverty and wretchedness, the woes and agonies, which have marked the awful conflict. The Church of God, in all our borders, mourns over the tremendous sacrifices of the deadly strife, and beholds in the sad spectacle of our diminished numbers, and the dark clouds which hang over our future progress, the dreadful results of disunion. The Lord of heaven and earth, whose chastening rod has been so sorely laid upon us, is the only power on whose favor we can depend for our deliverance, and we have sought, on our appointed day of fasting, humiliation, and prayer, to deprecate His wrath and implore His mercy. May our humble confession of sin be accepted at His throne of grace. May our penitent supplications be answered in the plenitude of His goodness, through the all-prevailing intercession of that divine Redeemer who atones for the transgressions and bears the sorrows of His people. And may He, in whose hand are all the hearts of men, turn away from us the bitter cup of our national calamities, and restore the land to unity and peace!

On the political questions which have been, in the eyes of the world, the instrumental causes of this mournful conflict, your Bishops have no wish to enter. As citizens, you have all formed your own conclusions on the secular aspect of the times, and with those conclusions it is not our province to interfere. We address you as the chief officers of the kingdom of Christ, which is not of this world. Our divine Master, when His enemies sought to entice Him into an avowal of His opinions on the right of the Romans to hold Judea in subjection, rejected the temptation, and gave them the admirable and comprehensive precept, "Render unto Cæsar the things that be Cæsar's, and unto God, the things that be God's." And the inspired S. Paul, faithfully following his Lord's example, declined all expressions involving the character or the measures of civil government, while he laid down, with clear precision, the rule of Christian duty: "Let every soul be subject to the higher powers. For there is no power but of God. The powers that be are ordained of God. Whosoever, therefore, resisteth the power, resisteth the ordinance of God: and they that resist, shall receive unto themselves damnation." Here then we have at once the warrant and the limitation of the doctrine, which the Church has always maintained. As followers of the blessed Apostles, we desire to tread in the same path, and presume not, in the exercise of our solemn office, to go one step beyond them. Leaving, therefore, the secular aspects of this awful war to statesmen and to politicians, to whom they properly belong, we confine ourselves to the religious character of our national afflictions, and proceed to place before you the primary cause to which, according to the principles of our sacred faith, we are compelled to ascribe the distracted condition of our country.

No truth is more plainly taught in the Bible than this: that the nations of the world depend on the government of heaven for all their peace, their honor and prosperity. Their rise, their progress, their wars, their victories, their decline, and their destruction, are all allotted to them by the judgment of God, in accordance with the measure of their loyalty to His government, or their rebellion against His sacred law. "Righteousness exalteth a nation, but sin is the reproach of any people:" not always in the judgment of the world, but in the judgment of Him who rules the world, that glorious and divine Redeemer, who has all power, both in heaven and on earth, the King of kings, the Lord of lords, the Almighty Master of the universe.

The government of earth is a divine institution, essential to the peace, good order, and civil rights of every organized community. A loyal submission to it is therefore enjoined by the Gospel as a branch of Christian duty, and rebellion against its lawful authority is a sin against the ordinance of God. But we know, from the history of Israel, that the government of earth may set itself against the government of heaven, to which it owes its own existence, and may thus incur the heavy chastisement of the Almighty. We know that the chosen nation which was distinguished above all others by the favor of the Lord—and amongst whom He had graciously established His peculiar dwelling place—fell away from their spiritual allegiance, and forfeited all their glorious privileges. We know that the revolt of the Ten Tribes against the lawful authority of Rehoboam was decreed by the express judgment of the Most High; in punishment of the idolatry introduced by the wise and famous Solomon, through a weak indulgence of his favorites. We know that this heavy punishment failed to reclaim them, and that wars and insurrections succeeded, through a long course of years, until at length the inhabitants of Samaria were led away into captivity, and the same destiny was afterwards appointed to rebellious Judah, while both of these events are recorded as the decrees of heaven on their iniquity. And we know that after the temporary restoration of Judah, their awful rejection of the Son of God was visited by their extinction as a nation, and that the posterity of Jacob have been for eighteen centuries scattered abroad, without a country or a government which they could call their own.

Nor is this the whole. The Bible declares that the fate of all nations depends on the same divine appointment. The Lord setteth up one, and putteth down another, according to His righteous will, and prophecy and history concur to prove the absolute power of His dominion. From the whole, therefore, of this sacred record, given for the instruction of the Church to the end of the world, we learn the solemn truth that rebellion against the government of heaven may be fearfully chastised by rebellion against the government of earth, and by every other form of human calamity, in just fulfilment of the judgment pronounced by the Almighty Himself on the sins of the nations.

No Christian man can doubt that such is still the principle on which the Lord administers His government, and such it must continue to the end, for God is the same, yesterday, to-day, and forever. If we look at the changes amongst the nations of Christendom in modern times, what do we behold but war after war, rebellion after rebellion, revolution after revolution, and no warrant for security or stability to any government under heaven, because there is no nation under heaven free from the plague of rebellion against the supreme government of their Creator and Redeemer—the King of kings.

On these manifest grounds of Scripture and history, it is easy to determine the religious aspect of our own national calamities, and therefore we are compelled to recognize the Divine judgment in the terrible scourge under which our once peaceful and united country now lies bleeding. Raised by the hand of Omnipotence to a state of marvellous prosperity; placed high amongst the powers of the earth by a career of advancement rapid and extraordinary beyond all example since the days of ancient Israel; the home of liberty and equal rights; the asylum of the exile, the persecuted, and the poor; the land of perfect Christian toleration: what region in the world had so many and such precious privileges conferred upon it by the favoring Providence of the Almighty? And if we have proved unthankful, proud, and faithless, towards our divine Benefactor; if we have given to our heroes and our statesmen the praise which was due to Him; if we have put our trust not in His favor but in our own enterprise, and strength, and courage, and sagacity; if we have made popularity and wealth the objects of our idolatry, and taken the voice of the people instead of the voice of God; if we have worshipped our political Constitution, while we despised and practically rejected the government of heaven; if even professing Christians themselves presumed to set up a higher law than the Bible, and established new terms for the communion, and made their modern notions of philanthropy the rule for their brethren, against the plain allowance of the inspired Apostles; if the great majority of our men stood aloof from the Gospel in contempt of the declaration of Christ when He said "He that is not with Me is against Me;" if the Lord's day was made a time for wordly amusement, and His churches were neglected as the houses of prayer, and only thronged when they were used for political denunciation or theatrical display; if infidelity and immorality were rewarded with public trusts and honors, and the mass of the people lived as if they had no God to obey, no souls to save, and no immortal happiness to secure; if all this and much more of bold and habitual rebellion against the government of heaven could be truly laid to our charge, why should not the judgment of the Lord fall on our nation, even as it had on others, and chasten us sorely for our sins?

And—painful as the acknowledgment must be—we cannot deny the truth of the accusation. On the contrary, beloved brethren, we are compelled to add yet more to the reproach which the Redeemer may most justly lay upon our people. Rebellion against Him has raised its front with brazen audacity, by direct assaults on Christianity in many quarters. "Oppositions of science, falsely so-called," have been received with general approbation. Infidel societies using the Lord's day for meetings to denounce and ridicule the Gospel, have become, in some cities, regular institutions. Necromancy, under the name of Spiritualism, has run like wild fire through the land, deluding multitudes to condemn the Church, in all its varieties, as the teacher of falsehood and superstition. The guardianship of the Bible over the oath of office has been openly and altogether disclaimed, and the delegates of polygamy, from the territory of Mormonism, are admitted side by side with the members of our Congress. The Chinese in San Francisco are even allowed to erect a pagan temple to their idol Buddha, thus publicly proclaiming to the world that our nation, once supposed to be Christian, is prepared to tolerate all the abominations of absolute heathenism. And how have the laws of morality been heeded in the oldest and best established portions of the land? Bribery in our elections, bribery in our legislatures, bribery in Congress itself; frauds in public contracts, falsehoods and deceits for party purposes, the rapidly increasing recklessness of human life, and the fearful growth of youthful licentiousness,—all concur to prove our mournful degeneracy. Alas! rebellion against the government of God has been at work for years in our once favored country, and we have no reason to wonder that it has at length brought down upon us the judgment of His righteous indignation.

We are far, however, from applying this statement to the whole. We are well aware that many wise and thoughtful men are scattered throughout the land who foresaw the approaching danger, and raised their warning voice in vain. We doubt not that there are thousands upon thousands who could not be justly accused of any share in the prevalent delinquency. But the character of nations, as such, is determined, in the sight of God, not by the comparative few, but by the immense majority. And linked together as we are by our social connections in this present life, it must needs be, to a large extent, that the innocent will suffer with the guilty.

The period in which we live, beloved brethren, is called in Scripture "the last days" preceding the second advent of the Lord to judge both the quick and the dead, and we confess, with sorrow, the application to ourselves of the description set forth by S. Paul when he saith that "in the last days perilous times shall come. For men shall be lovers of their own selves, covetous, boasters, proud, blasphemous, disobedient to parents, unthankful, unholy.

Without natural affections, truce-breakers, false accusers, incontinent, fierce, despisers of those that are good, traitors, heady, high-minded, lovers of pleasure more than lovers of God, having a form of godliness, but denying the power thereof." (2 Tim iii. 1–5.)

All this, sad as it is, has been mournfully exemplified in the growing degeneracy of Christendom, and we have traced it, to a large extent, in the condition of our own land. But while we confess, with humility and contrition, our share in the general declension of our age and country, we desire to render our fervent thanksgiving to God that the principles of the Church are the same as ever. Preserved to us, through the special blessing of His Providence, by that primitive and Scriptural Liturgy in which we never fail to hear the pure instructions of His Word, and in all of whose regular offices we have the constant recurrence of the primitive creeds to guard our faith, and the prayers of the ancient saints and martyrs to guide our devotions, we enjoy the inestimable privilege of a high and holy standard displayed continually before our eyes to keep us in the path of divine truth, and protect us against the errors of popular delusion.

As individuals, we deny not our liability to be affected by the spirit of the age. We deny not our personal defects. We seek not to extenuate or excuse our personal transgressions. We claim no superiority to ourselves over other Christian men. in wisdom, strength, or piety. But we acknowledge, with humble gratitude to our Almighty Lord and Master, the superior advantages which He has bestowed upon us, in the system of His Apostolic Church, and to that, through His blessing, we ascribe the precious peculiarity of our position, in relation to our present national calamities.

The doctrine of the Church proclaims complete and unswerving allegiance, first, to the divine Redeemer who has all power in heaven and in earth, and secondly, to the government under which His Providence has placed us. With respect to this we have already cited the language of the inspired Apostle: "Let every soul be subject to the higher powers, for there is no power but of God; the powers that be are ordained of God. Whosoever, therefore, resisteth the power, resisteth the ordinance of God, and they that resist shall receive to themselves damnation." No government on earth could frame so sure a guaranty of loyalty.

These principles, delivered to us from the Holy Spirit, have always been, and we trust will always be, the standard of the Church. They are the only unfailing warrant of that high Christian allegiance which rests obedience to the lawful authority of earth upon the paramount duty of obedience to the supreme authority of heaven. The Church knows nothing of that delusive "higher law," which presumes to set at naught the plain instructions of the Word of God, in subservience to a weak and visionary philanthropy. Faithful to the Constitution of His government, as contained in the holy Scriptures, faithful to the letter and the spirit of the Constitution of the land, faithful to the decisions of the Federal tribunals which that Constitution has established, the Church stands pre-eminent before the world, not in numbers, and far less in the work of party strife or political agitation, but pre-eminent nevertheless, as the Church of unity and peace, of law and order. We speak not of all its members. Exceptions there are, and must be, to every general rule. But we can confidently say—and we bless God for it—that as a whole, these are the principles which have guided our course. Our clergy have fulfilled their sacred office in preaching Christ and Him crucified, without falling into the dangerous error of mixing politics with religion. Our laity have desired no minister of God to entertain them with party diatribes instead of the Gospel. Our Conventions have adopted no resolution that was foreign to the proper duty of the Church. And no candid and intelligent mind can doubt that if every other religious body in the United States had been governed by the same principles, and had adhered with equal fidelity to the Word of God, we should at least have been saved from the miseries of this mournful war, and been allowed, for many years, to enjoy the temporal blessings of peaceful and fraternal union.

Your Bishops, beloved brethren, in compliance with your express desire, proceed, in conclusion, to address a few words of affectionate and pastoral counsel to all the clergy and the laity, who are placed, by the law of the Church, under their official supervision.

To the clergy we would strongly recommend the firm adherence to the same course, which we rejoice to say they have thus far generally pursued, and which is laid down, with such solemn plainness, in the office of Ordination. You cannot, reverend brethren, maintain your proper influence over your flocks, by descending from your high and sacred position as the ministers of Christ, in order to gratify the political feeling of the day, or by lowering the spiritual dignity of the sacred desk, under any pretext, to the level of a secular platform. As citizens of our great Republic, you are as free as all others to form and express your individual opinions. But take heed, we pray you, how you exercise even this liberty, to the prejudice of your sublime vocation. Remember that you are bound to be the ambassadors of Christ. And, in humble imitation of His example, let no earthly strife and no promise of earthly advantage draw you away from the great warfare against sin, the world, and the devil, or from the steadfast labor of making a rebellious generation lay to heart the supreme necessity of securing the kingdom of God and His righteousness, by the submission of their souls to their gracious Redeemer. In gentleness, in meekness, going in and out amongst your people, sympathising in their joys and especially in their sorrows, instructing the ignorant with patient kindness, guarding and teaching the young with solicitous affection, rebuking sin with mild firmness, preaching in public, with all authority, the terrors of the law, and the surpassing love and mercy of the Gospel, and showing, in all your deportment, that your own hearts are set upon the glorious inheritance of immortality, you will be enabled, by the blessing of God, to make full proof of your ministry, and in despite of all your difficulties and discouragements, the pleasure of the Lord will prosper in your hand.

To our beloved brethren of the laity we would say that the success of all ministerial work, and the pure consistency of all ministerial character, must depend, to a large extent, on your faithful co-operation. We are all men of like passions with yourselves, and you cannot expect us to be entirely exempt from the influence of social opposition, or social sympathy. O forget not that the Church is instituted for you and your children, that the clergy are ordained to be your servants for Jesus' sake, that it is for you they pray and study and labor and toil, in order rightly to divide the word of truth, and give to each his portion in due season. Tempt them not, we beseech you, to leave their sacred office, in the service of worldly strife, or political agitation. Sustain them in their proper work by a punctual and reverent attendance on their ministrations. Set to your families, and especially to your sons, the pure example which you know they ought to follow, and fall not into the too common error of supposing that a trifling contribution to the treasury of the Church is enough for the worship of God, while the whole practical influence of your life is openly given to the worship of Mammon.

We lament the sad decline of the Missions of the Church, both foreign and domestic, since the commencement of our national troubles. But is this consistent with Christian principle? Doubtless the burdens of public necessity are heavy, and your Bishops are ready to applaud the zeal and generous liberality with which you, our brethren of the laity, have so well sustained them. Yet, although the display of your patriotic feeling is worthy of commendation, and the universal effort to supply the wants and alleviate the sufferings of the army, is especially deserving of all praise, we would affectionately ask you whether these duties should be allowed to diminish the slender support of your ministers, or the missionary enterprises of the Church of God? Shall the soldiers of the Republic be tenderly supported, and shall the soldiers of Christ be neglected or forgotten? We do not see that the pressure of the times prevents the lavishing of a countless amount upon worldly pleasure and amusement, and shall that pressure be an apology for lessening the support of the everlasting Gospel? Surely, surely, these things ought not so to be. The salaries of the clergy should rather be increased in proportion to the increased price of the necessaries of life, and all the missions and institutions of the Church should be sustained more zealously than ever, for the very reason that the discipline of the Lord is resting on the land in punishment of our iniquities. For this proof of your devotion would go far to show your earnest desire to deprecate His wrath, and invoke His mercy, and would manifest your sincerity in the acknowledgment that the safety and prosperity of our government on earth depend on the blessing of that Saviour who is the Supreme Governor of earth and heaven.

We have only to add the expression of our humble and fervent hope that His goodness will be displayed in the speedy restoration of peace and unity, that our national distractions will cease, and that the terrible conflicts and sufferings of this tremendous warfare will prove to be, not a judgment sent to destroy our national Government, but a salutary chastisement from His fatherly hand, to purify us from corruption and impiety. We trust that it will impress upon the great body of our people the solemn truth, which so many profess while so few realize it, that the favor of God is essential to our earthly prosperity, and that rebellion against the authority of heaven is sure, sooner or later, to call down His righteous wrath and indignation. Happy shall we be if the inhabitants of our land, admonished by this severe discipline, submit themselves to the divine Redeemer, with deep repentance for their past transgressions of His laws, and with earnest resolutions of obedience, in faithful reliance on His grace for the time to come. Happy if we remember that fleets and armies can be no effectual substitute for the favor of the Lord of hosts. Happy if we truly learn that the hearts of men are in the hand of God, and that He alone can preserve our country in the enjoyment of peace and unity.

And now, beloved brethren, we bid you, one and all, an affectionate farewell. May the blessing of the Almighty accompany you to your homes, and protect you and yours from every danger. May you all—clergy and laity—the teachers and the taught—be guided by the sacred rules of living faith and grateful obedience, under the banner of that Saviour whose name is love. May every soul contribute by his personal example to make the Church of Christ a burning and a shining light, in the darkness of a sinful world. And may we all be united in the advancement of her sacred mission, proclaiming, with one heart and voice, "Glory to God in the highest, and on earth peace, good will to men!"

REPLY OF PRESIDENT LINCOLN TO THE PASTORAL LETTER.

RIGHT REVEREND AND DEAR SIR: The copy which you sent me of the "Pastoral Letter of the Bishops of the Protestant Episcopal Church in the United States of America," has been submitted to the President. He authorizes me to assure you that he receives with the most grateful satisfaction the evidences which that calm, candid, and earnest paper gives of the loyalty of the very extended religious communion over which you preside, to the Constitution and Government of the United States. I am further instructed to say that the exposition which the highest ecclesiastical authority of that communion has given in the Pastoral letter, of the intimate connection which exists between fervent patriotism and true Christianity, seems to the President equally seasonable and unanswerable. Earnestly invoking the Divine blessing equally upon our religious and civil institutions, that they may altogether safely resist the storm of faction, and continue hereafter, as heretofore, to sustain and invigorate each other, and so promote the common welfare of mankind, I have the honor to be, right reverend and dear sir, faithfully yours,

WILLIAM H. SEWARD.

To C. P. McILVAINE, D. D., D. C. L.

PROTESTANT EPISCOPAL CONVENTION OF THE DIOCESE OF PENNSYLVANIA.

At Pittsburg, May 26, 1864:

Resolved, That we hereby declare our unfaltering allegiance to the Government of the United States, and that we pledge it our willing devotion and service; and that, as a body of Christians, we will ever "pray that in God's own time and way this rebellion may be put down; that oppression and slavery in all its forms may be done away; that freedom of body and mind, political and religious, may everywhere prevail; that the emancipated negroes, whom God, in His providence, is committing to our care, may be the objects of our liberal and Christian regard and instruction; that war may soon cease throughout all our borders, and that our now lacerated country may again be so united that from the lakes on the North to the Gulf on the South, and from the Atlantic to the Pacific, there shall be but one Union, one Government, one flag, one Constitution, the whole culminating in that higher glory which shall make this nation Emanuel's land—a mountain of holiness and a dwelling place of righteousness."

This resolution was adopted as a substitute—yeas 125, nays 93—for these, (the latter offered by Rev. Dr. Goodwin, of Philadelphia; the former by Rev. Mr. Van Deusen, of Pittsburg :)

Whereas there exists in this country organized and armed rebellion, whose purpose is the destruction of our national Union and the perpetuation of negro slavery; and whereas this rebellion has more and more assumed a character of barbarous fanaticism and murderous ferocity, on the part of the enemies of the nation; therefore, in view of the cause and character of the struggle,

Resolved, That this convention of the Protestant Episcopal Church, in the diocese of Pennsylvania, as a body of Christian men, pledge the Government of our country our prayers, sympathy, and support in this war for existence, Union, liberty, and peace.

Resolved, That the authors and abettors of this rebellion, wherever they are found, are alone guilty of all the bloodshed and desolation on either side, entailed upon the North and South, now or hereafter.

Resolved, That, in the long delay of success in crushing this monstrous rebellion, we see wonderfully manifest the hand of God, training by His severest chastisements this reluctant people to do justice and show mercy to a long-oppressed and outraged race.

Resolved, That, under the present circumstances, the National Government, whether executive, legislative, or judicial, is, in our judgment, solemnly bound to use all its power and employ every authorized and constitutional means for the speedy and total abolition of slavery throughout the land, and that, as patriots, freemen and Christians, we shall hail with jubilant gladness and devout gratitude to God the day of its final extinction.

Subsequently, the preamble above recited was prefixed to the resolution adopted; and the resolution and preamble adopted with but one dissenting vote.

PROTEST OF PENNSYLVANIA EPISCOPALIANS AGAINST BISHOP HOPKINS'S DEFENCE OF SOUTHERN SLAVERY.

The subscribers deeply regret that the fact of the extensive circulation throughout this Diocese of a letter by "John Henry Hopkins, Bishop of the Diocese of Vermont," in defence of Southern slavery, compels them to make this public protest. It is not their province to mix in any political canvass. But as ministers of Christ, in the Protestant Episcopal Church, it becomes them to deny any complicity or sympathy with such a defence.

This attempt not only to apologize for slavery in the abstract, but to advocate it as it exists in the cotton States, and in States which sell men and women in the open market as their staple product, is, in their judgment, unworthy of any servant of Jesus Christ. As an effort to sustain, on Bible principles, the States in rebellion against the Government, in the wicked attempt to establish by force of arms a tyranny under the name of a republic, whose "corner-stone" shall be the perpetual bondage of the African, it challenges their indignant reprobation.

PHILADELPHIA, *September*, 1863.

Alonzo Potter,
John Rodney,
E. A. Washburne,
Peter Van Pelt,
H. W. Ducachet,
John S. Stone,
George Leeds,
Richard D. Hall,
Joseph D. Newlin,
B. Wistar Morris,
Daniel S. Miller,
Kingston Goddard,
Phillips Brooks,
Addison B. Atkins,
Herman Hooker,
Benjamin Watson,
Edward L. Lycett,
Lewis W. Gibson,
R. W. Oliver,
Henry Brown,
W. R. Stockton,
Edward A. Foggo,
Thomas S. Yocum,
Benjamin Dorr,
Jehu C. Clay,
William Suddards,
D. R. Goodwin,
M. A. DeW. Howe,
Henry S. Spackman,
James May,
John A. Childs,
Thomas C. Yarnall,
Edward Loundsbery,
Henry M. Stuart,
J. Gordon Maxwell,
John A. Vaughan,
Charles D. Cooper,
Wilbur F. Paddock,
Thomas Crumpton,
George D. Miles,
B. B. Killikelly,
Alexander McLeod,
Leighton Coleman,
Richard Smith,
J. Isador Mombert,
Joel Rudderow,
Archibald Beatty,
C. A. L. Richards,
George A. Strong,
Gustavus M. Murray,
George W. Shinn,
Samuel Hall,
George G. Field,
Reese C. Evans,
George A. Latimer,
R. Heber Newton,
John C. Furey,
Charles A. Maison,
Charles W. Quick,
H. T. Wells,
D. C. Millett,
J. W. Leadenham,
Jacob M. Douglass,
R. A. Carden,
R. C. Matlack,
L. Ward Smith,
Samuel E. Appleton,
William J. Alsten,
John Adams Jerome,
Joseph A. Stone,
Albra Wadleigh,
W. S. Perkins,
Francis E. Arnold,
George H. Jenks,
William S. Heaton,
Robert B. Peet,
John Reynolds,
William Hilton,
Washington B. Erben,
Benjamin J. Douglass,
John Ireland,
D. C. James,
E N. Potter,
W. H. D. Hatton,
Thomas W. Martin,
Frederick W. Beasley,
John P. Lundy,
George A. Crooke,
Richardson Graham,
E. S. Watson,
Samuel Edwards,
George A. Durborow,
Joseph R. Moore,
Thomas B. Barker,
S. Tweedale,
Marcus A. Tolman,
John H. Drumm,
S. Newton Spear,
Louis C. Newman,
Edward C. Jones,
E. W. Hening,
Samuel Durborow,
C. C. Parker,
Henry Purdon,
Benjamin H. Abbott,
John H. Marsden,
Samuel B. Dalrymple,
Alfred Elwyn,

Robert G. Chase,
Samuel Hazlehurst,
Edwin N. Lightner,
David C. Page,
John Cromlish,
William Preston,
George Slattery,
Francis J. Clerc,
Robert J. Parvin,
Richard Newton,
G. Emlen Hare,
W. W. Spear,
H. J. Morton,
Thomas H. Cullen,
J. McAlpin Harding,
William Ely,
Marison Byllesby,
J. Livingston Reese,
Augustus A. Marple,
B. T. Noakes,
D. Otis Kellogg,
Daniel Washburn,
Samuel E. Smith,
Treadwell Walden,
Herman L. Duhring,
Charles M. Dupuy,
John H. Babcock,
Anson B. Hard,
James W. Robins,
George Bringhurst,
Charles W. Duane,
George B. Allinson,
Joseph N. Mulford,
James DeW. Perry,
Thomas G. Clemson,
Francis D. Hoskins,
William P. Lewis,
J. L. Heysinger,
John Long,
Ormes B. Keith,
William N. Diehl,
William V. Feltwell,
John Leithead,
George C. Drake,
Peter Russell,
Roberts Paul,
George Kirke,
Henry B. Bartow,
John K. Murphy,
J. F. Ohl,
John Tetlow,
J. C. Laverty,
Charles Higbee,
William Wright,
S. T. Lord,
Charles R. Hall.

The names of Rowland Hill Brown, J. A. Harris and Edmund Leaf, were subsequently authorized to be affixed, making 167 in all.

METHODIST EPISCOPAL.

GENERAL CONFERENCE OF 1860.

May 1—The body met in Buffalo, N. Y.

May 2—The following Committee on Slavery was appointed: Calvin Kingsley, Daniel Wise, Joseph Brooks, Nicholas J. B. Morgan, Isaac S. Bingham, Edward Bannister, Michael Marlay, Hiram M. Shaffer, James S. Smart, George Hildt, John M. Reid, Ammi Prince, James M. Fuller, Peter Cartwright, Hayden Hays, Thomas E. Corkhill, Levin B. Dennis, William H. Black, Charles C. Cone, Resin Sapp, Benjamin F. Crary, Joseph H. Hopkins, John S. Porter, Erastus O. Haven, Lorenzo D. Barrows, Samuel Y. Monroe, Morris D'C. Crawford, Daniel Curry, John B. Birt, John P. Kellam, Richard Hargrave, James M. Jameson, Daniel W. Bristol, Alvin F. Waller, Andrew Magee, Pennel Coombe, Charles A. Holmes, Luke Hitchcock, Fernando C. Holliday, William Cliffe, Andrew Witherspoon, John C. Ayers, Andes T. Bullard, James Drummond, John L. Williams, Wessen G. Miller, John J. Pearce.

May 16—Mr. Kingsley, from the majority, made a report, concluding with these resolutions:

Resolved, 1. By the delegates of the several Annual Conferences in General Conference assembled, that we recommend the amendment of the General Rule on Slavery, so that it shall read: "The buying, selling, or holding of men, women, or children, with an intention to enslave them."

2. That we recommend the suspension of the 4th Restrictive Rule, for the purpose set forth in the foregoing resolution.

3. By the delegates of the several Annual Conferences in General Conference assembled, that the following be and hereby is substituted in the place of the seventh chapter on slavery:

Question. What shall be done for the extirpation of the evil of slavery?

Answer. We declare that we are as much as ever convinced of the great evil of slavery. We believe that the buying, selling, or holding of human beings as chattels is contrary to the laws of God and nature, inconsistent with the Golden Rule, and with that rule in our Discipline which requires all who desire to remain among us to "do no harm, and to avoid evil of every kind." We, therefore, affectionately admonish all our preachers and people to keep themselves pure from this great evil, and to seek its extirpation by all lawful and Christian means.

Mr. Porter, from the minority, made a report, concluding with these resolutions:

Resolved, 1. That the Methodist Episcopal Church has in good faith, in all the periods of its history proposed to itself the question, "What shall be done for the extirpation of the evil of slavery?" and it has never ceased openly before the world to bear its testimony against the sin, and to exercise its disciplinary powers to the end that its members might be kept unspotted from criminal connection with the system, and that the evil itself be removed from among us.

2. That any change of our Discipline upon the subject of slavery in the present highly excited condition of the country would accomplish no good whatever, but, on the contrary, would seriously disturb the peace of our Church, and would be especially disastrous to our ministers and members in the slave states.

3. That the Committee on the Pastoral Address be instructed to state our position in relation to slavery, and to give such counsel to our Churches as may be suited to the necessities of the case.

May 24—John P. Durbin, for himself, Henry W. Reed, John C. Ayers, and Philo E Brown, presented a substitute, concluding with this preamble and resolutions:

Seeing, then, that our uniform testimony, and our practice also, have been opposed to the traffic in slaves, and that the spirit of the provision in the Discipline is, and has been opposed to slaveholding for selfish or mercenary purposes, and that we have faithfully borne this testimony and applied these provisions in the administration of Discipline as far as a due regard to the laws of the several states have permitted in which the cases have arisen; therefore,

1. *Resolved*, That the administration of Discipline should be made faithfully to conform to the foregoing declaration of principles, so far as the laws of the several states will permit in which the cases may arise.

2. That in view of the clear declaration of principles and advice in regard to the administration of Discipline, as set forth in the preceding report and resolution, we judge that great moderation should be observed in the public discussion of this subject, constantly maintaining the true anti-slavery position of the Church.

On motion of Daniel Curry, the last named substitute was laid on the table—yeas, 135; nays, 85—as follows:

YEAS—Abbott, Armstrong, Ayers of Delaware, Baker of Black River, Baker of Erie, Barrows, Beach, Bennett, Bigelow, Bingham, Birt, Bixby, Blades, Blake, Bristol, Brooks of Arkansas, Brooks of Minnesota, Brown of New York, Brown of Providence, Bruce, Brunson, Bullard, Carpenter, Chapin of Erie, Chapin of New England, Clarke of Erie, Clark of New York, Coil, Colclazer of North Indiana, Cone, Connell, Cooke, Corkhill, Cowles, Crary, Crawford, Crews, Curry of New York East, Dean, Dempster, Dennis, Dunn of Troy, Dunning, Eddy, Erwin, Fillmore, Floy, Gavitt, Gillett, Golden, Goodwin, Goss, Griffin of Troy, Griswold, Haney, Hare, Hargrave, Harris, Harrower, Hatch, Hatfield, Haven, Hays, Helmershausen, Hibbard, Hill, Hitchcock, Hobart, Hodgson, Holliday, Howard, Hulburd, Jacokes, Jasper, Keeler, Kellam, Kingsley, Landon, Leihy, Leslie, Locke, Magee, Marlay, Mather, M'Kinstry, Merrick, Merrill, Miller, Mitchell of Cincinnati, Mitchell of Pittsburgh, Monson, Moody, Mulfinger, Munsell, Nash, Nast, Nuhfer, Nutt, Olin, Pearce, Penfield, Pike, Poe, Porter of New England, Prince, Raymond, Reddy, Reid of East Genesee, Russel, Sapp, Shaffer, Smart, Smith of Cincinnati, Smith of Indiana, Sprague, Stallard, Stanton, Starks, D., Starks, H. L., Stearns, Stoughton, Thomas of Wisconsin, Thomson of North Ohio, Thurston, Torsey, Townsend, Trimble, Twombly, Webster, Whedon, Whiteman, Williams, Wise, Witherspoon, Young—135.

NAYS—Ayers of Upper Iowa, Bannister, Barth, Battelle, Black, Briggs, Brown of East Baltimore, Brown of New Jersey, Brown of Upper Iowa, Cartwright, Castle, Clark of Pittsburgh, Cliffe, Colclazer of Philadelphia, Coombe, Cooper, Corrington, Cox, Crane of Illinois, Crane of Newark, Curry of Kentucky, Davidson, Day, Drummond, Durbin, Ellison, Ferris, Fuller, Goode, Griffen of New York, Griffith, Guyer, Hammond, Hildt, Holdich, Holmes, Hopkins, Hoyt, Hughes, Hunt, Hunter of Peoria, Hunter of Western Virginia, Jackson, Jameson, Johnson, Kiger, Kuhl, Martin, Mitchell of East Baltimore, Monroe, Morgan, Murphy, Nelson, Norris, Osbon, Parsons, Pearne, Peck, Petty, Porter of Newark, Power, Prentice, Reed of Cincinnati, Reed of Upper Iowa, Robinson, Rutledge, Sargent, Sewall, Shumate, Slicer, Smith of Genesee, Smith of Northwestern Indiana, Street, Thomas of California, Thompson of Philadelphia, Tippett, Travis, Tuttle of East

Genesee, Tuttle of Newark, Van Cleve, Veitch, Vincent, Waller, Wilson, Wood—85.

May 29—The Majority Report was voted on. The first resolution—requiring two-thirds—was lost—yeas 138, nays 74, as follows:

YEAS—Abbott, Armstrong, Ayers of Delaware, Bain, Baker of Black River, Baker of Erie, Barrows, Barth, Beach, Bennett, Bigelow, Bingham, Birt, Bixby, Blades, Blake, Bristol, Brooks of Minnesota, Brown of New York, Brown of Providence, Bruce, Brunson, Bullard, Carpenter, Chapin of Erie, Chapin of New England, Clarke of Erie, Clark of New York, Coil, Colclazer of North Indiana, Cone, Connell, Cooke, Corkhill, Cowles, Crary, Crawford, Crews, Curry of New York East, Dean, Dempster, Dennis, Dunn of Troy, Dunning, Eddy, Erwin, Ferris, Fillmore, Floy, Gavitt, Gillett, Golden, Goodwin, Goss, Griffin of Troy, Griswold, Haney, Hare, Harris, Harrower, Hatch, Hatfield, Haven, Hayes, Helmershausen, Hibbard, Hill, Hitchcock, Hobart, Holliday, Howard, Hulburd, Hunter of Peoria, Jacokes, Jasper, Johnson, Keeler, Kellam, Kiger, King, Kingsley, Landon, Leihy, Leslie, Locke, Magee, Marlay, Mather, M'Kinstry, Merrick, Merrill, Miller, Mitchell of Cincinnati, Mitchell of Pittsburgh, Monson, Moody, Mulfinger, Munsell, Nash, Nast, Nelson, Nuhfer, Nutt, Olin, Pearce, Penfield, Pike, Poe, Porter of New England, Prince, Raymond, Reddy, Reid of East Genesee, Russell, Sapp, Shaffer, Smart, Smith of Cincinnati, Smith of Indiana, Sprague, Stallard, Stanton, Starks, D., Starks, H. L., Stoughton, Thomas of Wisconsin, Thomson of North Ohio, Thurston, Townsend, Trimble, Tuttle of East Genesee, Twombly, Webster, Whedon, Whiteman, Williams, Wise, Witherspoon, Young—138.

NAYS—Ayers of Upper Iowa, Bannister, Battelle, Black, Briggs, Brown of East Baltimore, Brown of New Jersey, Brown of Upper Iowa, Carlton, Cartwright, Castle, Clark of Pittsburgh, Cliffe, Colclazer of Philadelphia, Coombe, Cooper, Corrington, Cox, Crane of Illinois, Crane of Newark, Curry of Kentucky, Davidson, Day, Drummond, Durbin, Ellison, Fuller, Goode, Griffen of New York, Griffith, Guyer, Hammond, Hildt, Hodgson, Holdich, Holmes, Hopkins, Hoyt, Hughes, Hunter of Western Virginia, Jackson, Jameson, Kuhl, Martin, Mitchell of East Baltimore, Monroe, Morgan, Murphy, Norris, Osbon, Parsons, Pearne, Peck, Petty, Porter of Newark, Power, Prentice, Reed of Cincinnati, Reed of Upper Iowa, Robinson, Rutledge, Sargent, Sewall, Shumate, Slicer, Smith of Genesee, Street, Thomas of California, Thompson of Philadelphia, Tippett, Travis, Tuttle of Newark, Van Cleve, Veitch, Waller, Wilson, Wood—74.

ABSENT—Brooks of Arkansas, Hargrave, Smith of Northwestern Indiana, and Torsey.

The second resolution fell with the first.

The third pending,

Mr. Kingsley moved to amend by inserting before the word "chattels," the words: "to be used."

May 31—Mr. George Hughes moved to amend the amendment by adding the words: "and treated," so as to make the clause read: "to be used and treated as chattels;" which was disagreed to.

The amendment was then agreed to.

Mr. Durbin moved to consider his substitute; but the motion was lost.

Mr. George Hughes moved the following substitute:

Whereas a change of such magnitude as is now proposed should not be made without the sanction of the laity as well as the ministry; therefore,

Resolved, That the chapter proposed shall be first submitted by the Bishops to the Annual Conferences, and by the Presiding Elders to the Quarterly Conferences in their respective districts, and if it receive the vote of three-fourths of the members of said Conferences it shall take effect.

Which was lost—yeas 61, nays 150. The YEAS were:

Messrs. Bannister, Battelle, Black, Briggs, Brown of East Baltimore, Brown of New Jersey, Brown of Upper Iowa, Carlton, Cartwright, Cliffe, Colclazer of Philadelphia, Coombe, Cooper, Corrington, Crane of Illinois, Crane of Newark, Curry of Kentucky, Day, Drummond, Ellison, Fuller, Goode, Griffen of New York, Guyer, Hildt, Hodgson, Holdich, Hopkins, Hoyt, Hughes, Hunter of Western Virginia, Jameson, Kuhl, Martin, Mitchell of East Baltimore, Monroe, Morgan, Murphy, Nast, Norris, Osbon, Porter of Newark, Prentice, Reed of Cincinnati, Robinson, Rutledge, Sargent, Sewall, Shumate, Slicer, Street, Thomas of California, Thompson of Philadelphia, Tippett, Travis, Tuttle of Newark, Van Cleve, Veitch, Waller, Wilson, Wood—61.

ABSENT, OR NOT VOTING—Bain, Cooke, Davidson, Hargrave, Holliday, Pearce, Shaffer, Smith of Northwestern Indiana, and Torsey—9.

Mr. Samuel Y. Monroe, for himself and nineteen others, offered this substitute:

Resolved, That we believe that the buying, selling, or holding of human beings, to be used as chattels, is contrary to the laws of God and nature, inconsistent with the Golden Rule, and with that Rule in our Discipline which requires all who desire to remain among us to "do no harm, and to avoid evil of every kind," we, therefore, affectionately admonish all our preachers and people to keep themselves pure from this great evil, and to seek its extirpation by all lawful and Christian means.

Which was lost—yeas 81, nays 132. The YEAS were:

Messrs. Ayers of Delaware, Ayers of Upper Iowa, Bannister, Battelle, Black, Brooks of Arkansas, Brown of East Baltimore, Brown of New Jersey, Brown of Upper Iowa, Carlton, Cartwright, Castle, Clark of Pittsburgh, Cliffe, Connell, Coombe, Cooper, Carrington, Cox, Crane of Illinois, Crane of Newark, Curry of Kentucky, Day, Drummond, Durbin, Ellison, Ferris, Fuller, Goode, Griffen of New York, Griffith, Guyer, Hildt, Hodgson, Holdich, Holmes, Hopkins, Hoyt, Hughes, Hunter of Peoria, Hunter of Western Virginia, Jameson, Kuhl, Mather, Mitchell of Cincinnati, Mitchell of East Baltimore, Monroe, Morgan, Mulfinger, Murphy, Nast, Nelson, Norris, Osbon, Pearne, Peck, Porter of Newark, Power, Prentice, Reed of Cincinnati, Reed of Upper Iowa, Robinson, Rutledge, Sargent, Sewall, Shumate, Slicer, Smith of Genesee, Street, Thomas of California, Thompson of Philadelphia, Tippett, Travis, Trimble, Tuttle of East Genesee, Tuttle of Newark, Van Cleve, Veitch, Waller, Wilson, Wood—81.

ABSENT, OR NOT VOTING—Davidson, Hargrave, Holliday, Pearce, Shaffer, Smith of Northwestern Indiana, Torsey—7.

Mr. Francis Hodgson moved to strike out the words, "to be used as chattels," and insert between the words "the" and "buying," the word "mercenary;" which was disagreed to.

Mr. Geo. Hildt moved to add the words: "*Provided*, that the section is understood to be only advisory;" which was lost—yeas 75, nays 137, absent 9.

The third resolution as amended was then agreed to—yeas 155, nays 58, as follows:

YEAS—Abbott, Armstrong, Ayers of Delaware, Ayers of Upper Iowa, Bain, Baker of Black River, Baker of Erie, Bannister, Barrows, Barth, Beach, Bennett, Bigelow, Bingham, Birt, Bixby, Blades, Blake, Briggs, Bristol, Brooks of Arkansas, Brooks of Minnesota, Brown of New York, Brown of Upper Iowa, Brown of Providence, Bruce, Brunson, Bullard, Carpenter, Chapin of Erie, Chapin of New England, Clark of Erie, Clark of New York, Clark of Pittsburgh, Coil, Colclazer of North Indiana, Cone, Cooke, Corkhill, Cowles, Cox, Crary, Crawford, Crews, Curry of New York East, Dean, Dempster, Dennis, Dunn of Troy, Dunning, Eddy, Erwin, Ferris, Fillmore, Floyd, Gavitt, Gillett, Golden, Goodwin, Goss, Griffin of Troy, Griswold, Hammond, Haney, Hare, Harris, Harrower, Hatch, Hatfield, Haven, Hays, Helmershausen, Hibbard, Hill, Hitchcock, Hobart, Holmes, Howard, Hoyt, Hulburd, Hunter of Peoria, Jacokes, Jackson, Jasper, Johnson, Keeler, Kellam, Kiger, King, Kingsley, Landon, Leihy, Leslie, Locke, Magee, Marlay, Mather, M'Kinstry, Merrick, Merrill, Miller, Mitchell of Cincinnati, Mitchell of Pittsburgh, Monson, Moody, Mulfinger, Munsell, Nash, Nast, Nelson, Norris, Nuhfer, Nutt, Olin, Parsons, Pearne, Peck, Penfield, Petty, Pike, Poe, Porter of New England, Prince, Raymond, Reddy, Reed of Cincinnati, Reid of East Genesee, Reed of Upper Iowa, Russell, Sap, Smart, Smith of Cincinnati, Smith of Genesee, Smith of Indiana, Sprague, Stallard, Stanton, Starks, D., Starks, H. L., Stoughton, Thomas of California, Thomas of Wisconsin, Thomson of North Ohio, Thurston, Townsend, Trimble, Tuttle of East Genesee, Twombly, Webster, Wheedon, Whiteman, Williams, Wise, Witherspoon, Young—155.

NAYS—Battelle, Black, Brown of East Baltimore, Brown of New Jersey, Carlton, Cartwright, Castle, Cliffe, Colclazer of Philadelphia, Connell, Coombe, Cooper, Corrington,

Crane of Illinois, Crane of Newark, Curry of Kentucky, Day, Drummond, Durbin, Ellison, Fuller, Goode, Griffen of New York, Griffith, Guyer, Hildt, Hodgson, Holdich, Hopkins, Hughes, Hunter of Western Virginia, Jameson, Kuhl, Martin, Mitchell of East Baltimore, Monroe, Morgan, Murphy, Osbon, Porter of Newark, Power, Prentice, Robinson, Rutledge, Sargent, Sewall, Shumate, Slicer, Street, Thompson of Philadelphia, Tippett, Travis, Tuttle of Newark, Van Cleve, Veitch, Waller, Wilson, Wood—58.

ABSENT, OR NOT VOTING—Davidson, Hargrave, Holliday, Pierce, Shaffer, Smith of North Western Indiana, and Torsey—7.

June 1—Francis A. Blades offered the following:

Whereas during the pendency of the Chapter on Slavery, the following amendment was offered as explanatory of the Chapter, "Provided that this section is understood to be only advisory,"

Resolved, That said amendment was rejected by this body because we regard the chapter in itself so clearly declarative and advisory as not to require any such explanation.

Which was adopted—yeas 175, nays 6. The NAYS were:

Messrs. Coil, Corkhill, Cowles, Hare, Hodgson, Olin—6.

ABSENT, OR PRESENT AND NOT VOTING—Abbott, Barrows, Brown of East Baltimore, Cartwright, Castle, Chapin of New England, Clarke of Erie, Cliffe, Colclazer of Philadelphia, Cooper, Davidson, Fuller, Goode, Guyer, Hargrave, Hildt, Holliday, Hopkins, Magee, Martin, Mitchell of East Baltimore, Morgan, Murphy, Pearce, Porter of New England, Raymond, Reed of Cincinnati, Robinson, Sewall, Shaffer, Shumate, Slicer, Smith of Cincinnati, Smith of Northwestern Indiana, Tippett, Torsey, Twombly, Veitch, Wilson—39.

THE BALTIMORE CONFERENCE, 1861.

The Baltimore Conference of the Methodist Episcopal Church, in session at Staunton, Virginia, adopted resolutions declaring the immediate separation of the Conference from the jurisdiction of the General Conference of the Methodist Episcopal Church, on account of the new chapter on slavery adopted last year. The vote stood for immediate separation eighty-two, declining to vote forty-four. Bishop Scott, the presiding officer of the Conference, refused to put the question on the adoption of the resolutions, and entered a protest against the action "as a violation of the order and discipline of the Methodist Episcopal Church." The resolutions were:

1st. *Be it resolved by the Baltimore Annual Conference in Conference assembled*, That we hereby declare that the General Conference of the M. E. Church, held at Buffalo, in May, 1860, by its unconstitutional action, has sundered the ecclesiastical relation which has hitherto bound us together as one Church, so far as any act of theirs could do so; that we will not longer submit to the jurisdiction of said General Conference, but hereby declare ourselves separate and independent of it, still claiming to be, notwithstanding, an integral part of the M. E. Church.

2d. That nevertheless, if, in accordance with the spirit of the foregoing preamble, three-fourths of the several Annual Conferences, to be held prior to the next session of the Annual Conference, seeing the great wrong and injury done to the Baltimore and other Border Conferences, shall disavow the act of their delegates and the action of the late General Conference on the subject of slavery, and shall unite in a demand that the most thorough and satisfactory redress shall be given, and shall instruct their delegates so to vote in any Convention that may be called for the purpose of a more perfect union—First, by abrogating the new chapter; second, by transferring the subject of slavery to the exclusive jurisdiction of the Annual Conferences, where it exists; third, that a fair proportion of the periodicals of the Church be placed under the charge and direction of said Conferences—then, and not until then, will we reunite with them in the organization of another General Conference.

3d. That this Conference has taken the action expressed in the above resolutions, after much long suffering and reproach, to give freedom to our preachers in the discharge of their duties in our territory, and cannot refrain from expressing the hope that the day may speedily come when agitation and strife shall have ceased among us, and the great Methodist family—East, West, North and South—be again united in the common effort which engaged the hearts and lives of our fathers, that of spreading Scriptural holiness all over the land

4th. That a committee of seven, consisting of S. Register, J. S. Martin, S. S. Roszel, E. R. Veitch, W. G. Eggleston, N. Wilson, and T. H. W. Munroe, be appointed to prepare a Pastoral Letter for our people, setting forth the grounds and aims of the action.

The following is the protest of the minority of the Conference:

We, the undersigned, members of the Baltimore Annual Conference, differing with a majority of our brethren in regard to the mode of obtaining relief from the evils which have been entailed upon us by the action of the late General Conference upon the subject of slavery, protest against the course which they have adopted—

1st. Because it is an appeal to revolution for redress, before the constitutional means have been tried, much less exhausted.

2d. Because it shapes our course without consultation with other non-concurring Conferences, all of whom have strong claim upon our fraternity, and some in slave territory will be materially affected, and probably prejudiced, in their interests thereby.

3d. Because the act is done, and announced, within the bosom of two States which are now the custodians of the Federal Union, and will strengthen the hands of political secessionists, and carry dismay to the hearts of all who would preserve our national inheritance.

But it is the mode of obtaining relief from our troubles alone in which we differ with our brethren.

We, too, protest against the "new chapter." We protest against the continuance of the subject of slavery as a question of legislation in the general councils of the church. And we ask a call of an extra session of the General Conference in 1862, and an expression by the Annual Conferences of their approval or disapproval of the terms of relief which our circumstances demand; and assure our people that, by the tone of that response and that of our sister sympathizing conferences, especially in slave territory, our course at our next session shall be controlled, whether it be further negotiation or immediate separation.

In Christian hope that these assurances will bring rest in the churches against the present year, we are, &c.

[*Signed by some thirty names.*]

The Western Virginia Methodist Episcopal Conference, at its annual session at Wheeling, in March, 1861, adopted the following preamble and resolutions:

Whereas the General Conference at its late session at Buffalo has inserted a new chapter in our Book of Discipline on the subject of slavery; and whereas there exists some difference of opinion as to its meaning, and whereas uniformity in administration and harmony among ourselves are very desirable: therefore

1. *Resolved*, That we deeply regret the action of the General Conference changing the chapter on slavery, we regarding such action as unnecessary.

2. *Resolved*, That, in our judgment as a Conference, the new chapter is not to be regarded as a law; that no administrative or judicial action can be had under it against any member or minister; and that we are left under it to be governed by the Scripture, amenable as individuals for our administration only to God and our annual Conference.

3. *Resolved*, That we utterly condemn any attempt, in any way whatever, to interfere with the legal relations of master and servant, and that we will seek to promote, as did our fathers, their best interests by preaching to them the unsearchable riches of Christ, and by teaching them their reciprocal duties as taught in the Holy Scriptures.

REPLY OF THE PRESIDENT TO THE RESOLUTIONS OF THE EAST BALTIMORE METHODIST CONFERENCE OF 1862.

Rev. I. A. GERE, A. A. REESE, D. D., G. D. CHENOWETH:—

GENTLEMEN:—Allow me to tender to you, and through you to the East Baltimore Conference of the Methodist Episcopal Church, my grateful thanks for the preamble and resolutions of that body, copies of which you did me the honor to present yesterday. These kind words of approval, coming from so numerous a body of intelligent Christian people, and so free from all suspicion of sinister motives, are indeed encouraging to me. By the help of an all-wise Providence, I shall endeavor to do my duty; and I shall expect the continuance of your prayers for a right solution of our national difficulties, and the restoration of our country to peace and prosperity.

Your obliged and humble servant,

A. LINCOLN.

GENERAL CONFERENCE OF 1864.

May 2—The body met in Philadelphia.

May 7—The Committee on Slavery were instructed to inquire into the expediency of so altering the General Rules as to prohibit the buying, selling, or holding persons as slaves.

ACTION ON SLAVERY.

May 17—The Committee on Slavery—consisting of B. F. Crary, E. P. Phelps, E. C Brace, H. C. Benson, A. Magee, A. Nelson, M. Dustin, J. S. Smart, J. S. M'Murray, F. G Hibbard, G. D. Strout, R. A. Caruthers, J. M. Fuller, J. P. Dimmitt, J. H. Noble, T. E. Corkhill, J. Denison, L. M. Reeves, J. Colby, H Penfield, N. Shumate, H. T. Davis, N. Vansant, J. H. Twombly, J Thurston, A. K. Street, P. R. Brown, R. M. Hatfield, J. V. R. Miller, G. W. Breckenridge, G. M. Boyd, T. C. Golden, B. N. Spahr, E. G. Andrews, T. H. Pearne, George Barton, D. L. Dempsey, D. Wise W. T. Harlow, W. Terrill, A. B. Nisbet, O. Gregg G. Clifford, W. D. Malcom, S. Haines, J. W. Reger, J. Lawson, C. D Pillsbury, H. R. Clark—made a majority and a minority report, as follows:

THE MAJORITY REPORT.

The long contest on the subject of slavery seems drawing to a close, and no doubtful tokens indicate the will of God, and point unerringly to the destruction of a system so inhuman.

The sufferings to be endured cannot be as great as those we have passed, and the heroism of the hour is adequate to bear the burdens which may be imposed upon us.

Patriotism and piety lead us to the conclusions to which we have arrived, and, aside from all questions of expediency, impel us to adopt the policy so strongly urged in the Episcopal Address.

We rejoice that we have from the beginning been foremost among American Churches in the contest against slavery. Slavery has nothing to commend it to our forbearance; on the other hand, it has inflicted upon us injuries we cannot forget. It has rent the Church in twain, and seeks to divide the nation.

It has kindled the fires of inextinguishable hatred along an extended border, and brought indescribable distress on our brethren who have labored there. These brethren we not only admire and love, but we pledge ourselves to share with them in all that is possible or necessary in the labors of the future.

The question has reached its present status not so much through our efforts in this behalf as through the guidings of the Divine hand, whose power we reverently behold in the grand movements of our times.

The proposed new rule is only an expression of a conviction long entertained by the majority of the Church, the utterance of an edict which conscience dictates, and the teaching of God's Word approves. Abhorrence of slavery has increased with the progress of the people in moral and religious knowledge, showing that morality and religion are against the system. The voices of our common humanity protest against its longer existence, and this judgment is God's decision, for nature is true to her Author.

Your Committee could not do otherwise than give expression to the truth which more than ever affects the Church and the nation, and array the moral forces of Methodism on the side of emancipation. The great families of Methodism throughout the world will rejoice that we have taken a step which wipes out the imputation of complicity with this evil, and gives up the decided advantage of leading still in the question which has so long perplexed the Church.

We feel that no answer is needed to the pleadings of expediency once so powerfully and eloquently urged. The grandeur of an overwhelming moral conviction uttered by the whole nation and Church, should not be impaired by answers to logic which the course of events has shown to be fallacious. So far as we are concerned, then, the question, "What shall be done for the extirpation of slavery?" shall be answered by a rule uprooting it and forbidding it forever. Local difficulties and special cases will adjust themselves, and we shall be untrammeled in our future operations in territory blighted by this departing curse. Relying on the promise and mercy of God, as far as we can we "proclaim liberty throughout all the land to all the inhabitants thereof."

Loyalty to the Government leads us to accept emancipation whenever and wherever the President proclaims it or the States decree it, and devotion to truth and to God impels us to bring the controversy to an end in the Church by adopting a rule which casuistry cannot distort into a license for slavery.

While reviewing the past, we gratefully acknowledge the goodness of God in guiding us so harmoniously to these conclusions, and with firm trust in Him, commit our work to the judgment of the Church and of mankind.

We recommend for adoption the following resolutions:

Resolved, 1. By the delegates of the several Annual Conferences in General Conference assembled, that we recommend the amendment of the General Rule on Slavery so that it shall read: *Slaveholding; buying or selling slaves.*

2. That we recommend the suspension of the 4th restrictive rule, for the purpose set forth in the foregoing resolution.

3. That the bishops be requested to submit the foregoing resolutions to the Annual Conferences at their next sessions, and if the requisite number of votes be obtained, to report to the Book Agents, who are hereby instructed to insert the new rule in all subsequent editions of the Discipline.

THE MINORITY REPORT,

Signed by E. P. Phelps, L. M. Reeves, and J. W. Reger, is as follows:

The minority of the Committee on Slavery beg leave to say that they have not been able to concur with the majority in the conclusions reached by them. For good and sufficient reasons, as they think, it would not be proper to change the general rule on slavery so as to exclude all persons sustaining the relation of master from the Church; they therefore respectfully submit the following as a substitute for the general rule on slavery reported by the majority, namely:

The selling of human beings, or the buying or holding them, except for reasons purely humane.

After debate, the majority report was adopted—yeas 207, nays 9, as follows:

YEAS—Elisha Adams, Augustine M. Alexander, Charles F. Allen, Ralph W. Allen, Edward G. Andrews, John W. Armstrong, Isaac N. Baird, Gardner Baker, Francis B. Bangs, Henry Bannister, John H. Barth, David W. Bartine, George Barton, Mathew Bennett, Henry C. Benson, William E. Bigelow, Isaac S. Bingham, Henry M. Blake, George M. Boyd, George W. Breckinridge, Alexander L. Brice, Daniel W. Bristol, Jabez Brooks, Paul R. Brown, Samuel C. Brown, Stephen D. Brown, Henry Brownscombe, Eli C. Bruce, Andes T. Bullard, Thomas Carlton, Richard A. Caruthers, Joseph Castle, George D. Chenowith, Albert Church, Ebenezer E. Chambers, Davis W. Clark, Horatio R. Clark, George Clifford, Daniel Cobb, Nelson E. Cobleigh, Joseph Colby, Sylvester L. Congdon, Thomas E. Corkhill, James B. Corrington, William F. Cowles, Townley W. Crane, Benjamin F. Crary, Morris D'C. Crawford, Joseph Cummings, James Cunningham, Daniel Curry, William A. Davidson, Henry T. Davis, Daniel L. Dempsey, Joseph Dennison, James P. Dimmitt, John P. Durbin, Mighill Dustin, Thomas M. Eddy, Charles Elliot, James Erwin, William H. Ferris, Henry Fiegenbaum, Hugh D. Fisher, John B. Foote, Randolph S. Foster, Thomas C. Gardner, Augustus C. George, Thomas C. Golden, William H. Goode, William H. Goodwin, Albert S. Graves, Oren Gregg, William Griffin, Edwin E. Griswold, Leonard B. Gurley, Robert E. Guthrie, Sanford Haines, Horace Hall, Benjamin B. Hamlin, Richard Haney, William L. Harris, William T. Harlow, Robert M. Hatfield, Bostwick Hawley, James Henderson, William McK. Hester, Freeborn G. Hibbard, Moses Hill, James Hill, Stacey W. Hilliard, Mathias Hinebaugh, Luke Hitchcock, Chauncy Hobart, Charles A. Homes, Horatio W. Houghton, Samuel Huffman, William H. Hunter, Russell H. Hurlburt, Kassimir P. Jervis, Samuel A. W. Jewett, Richard W. Keeler, Lucius H. King, Joseph E. King, Calvin Kingsley, Henry F. Koeneke, Philip Kuhl, Alpha J. Kynett, James Lawson, Orange V. Lemon, John W. Lindsay, James W. Lowe, Thomas H. Lynch, Lorenzo D. McCabe, William McCombs, Asahel S. McCoy, David P. McKenzie, Jacob S. McMurray, Andrew Magee, William D. Malcolm, Albert C. Manson, Joseph Mason, Frederick Merrick, John Miley, John G. Miller, John V. R. Miller, Samuel Y. Monroe, Granville Moody, William H. H. Moore, George L. Mulfinger, Oliver S. Munsell, William Nast, Alexander Nelson, Reuben Nelson, Samuel H. Nisbet, Alfred B. Nisbet, James H. Noble, Niram Norton, William H. Olin, Isaac Owen, David Patton, Thomas H. Pearne, George Peck, Jesse T. Peck, Henry Penfield, William E. Perry, Israel C. Pershing, James Pike,

Elijah H. Pilcher, Benjamin Pillsbury, Caleb D. Pillsbury, Adam Poe, James Porter, P. Putnam Ray, Miner Raymond, Seth Reed, Thomas M. Reese, John M. Reid, J. McKendree Reiley, William H. Richards, Reuben D. Robinson, Henry Roth, Jacob Rothweiler, David Sherman, Sampson Shinn, Nathan Shumate, Thomas H. Sinex, James S. Smart, David N. Smith, Giles C. Smith, John L. Smith, Moses Smith, Barzillai N. Spahr, Jacob M. Stallard, Desivignia Starks, William F. Stewart, Abraham K. Street, George D. Strout, Williamson Terrill, Samuel C. Thomas, Edward Thomson, James Thurston, Charles B. Tippett, Joseph M. Trimble, John H. Twombly, Nicholas Vansant, Joseph B. Wakeley, George W. Walker, Adam Wallace, Lorenzo D. Wardwell, George Webber, John B. Wentworth, Daniel A. Whedon, John W. White, Lafayette D. White, Charles H. Whitecar, Henry Whiteman, Albert D. Wilbor, James H. Wilbur, Isaac W. Wiley, Thomas H. Wilson, William F. Wilson, Daniel Wise, Aaron Wood, George W. Woodruff, John T. Wright, William Young—207.

NAYS—James L. Clark, James Drummond, William Harden, Isaac F. Harrison, John Lanahan, Nicholas J. B. Morgan, Elisha P. Phelps, Lemuel M. Reeves, John W. Reger —9.

INTERVIEW WITH THE PRESIDENT.

Bishop Edward R. Ames, Rev. Joseph Cummings, D. D., Rev. George Peck, D. D., Rev. Charles Elliott, D. D., and Rev. Granville Moody, were appointed a Committee to present to the President the action of the Conference, with this address, unanimously voted by the Conference:

To his Excellency Abraham Lincoln,
President of the United States:

The General Conference of the Methodist Episcopal Church, now in session in the city of Philadelphia, representing nearly seven thousand ministers and nearly a million of members, mindful of their duty as Christian citizens, takes the earliest opportunity to express to you the assurance of the loyalty of the Church, her earnest devotion to the interest of the country, and her sympathy with you in the great responsibilities of your high position in this trying hour.

With exultation we point to the record of our Church as having never been tarnished by disloyalty. She was the first of the Churches to express, by a deputation of her most distinguished ministers, the promise of support to the Government in the days of Washington. In her Articles of Religion she has enjoined loyalty as a duty, and has ever given to the government her most decided support.

In this present struggle for the nation's life, many thousands of her members, and a large number of her ministers, have rushed to arms to maintain the cause of God and humanity. They have sealed their devotion to their country with their blood on every battle-field of this terrible war.

We regard this dreadful scourge now desolating our land and wasting the nation's life as the result of a most unnatural, utterly unjustifiable rebellion, involving the crime of treason against the best of human governments and sin against God. It required our government to submit to its own dismemberment and destruction, leaving it no alternative but to preserve the national integrity by the use of the national resources. If the government had failed to use its power to preserve the unity of the nation and maintain its authority it would have been justly exposed to the wrath of heaven, and to the reproach and and scorn of the civilized world.

Our earnest and constant prayer is, that this cruel and wicked rebellion may be speedily suppressed; and we pledge you our hearty co-operation in all appropriate means to secure this object.

Loyal and hopeful in national adversity, in prosperity thankful, we most heartily congratulate you on the glorious victories recently gained, and rejoice in the belief that our complete triumph is near.

We believe that our national sorrows and calamities have resulted, in a great degree, from our forgetfulness of God and oppression of our fellow-men. Chastened by affliction, may the nation humbly repent of her sins, lay aside her haughty pride, honor God in all future legislation, and render justice to all who have been wronged.

We honor you for your proclamations of liberty, and rejoice in all the acts of the government designed to secure freedom to the enslaved.

We trust that when military usages and necessities shall justify interference with established institutions, and the removal of wrongs sanctioned by law, the occasion will be improved, not merely to injure our foes and increase the national resources, but also as an opportunity to recognize our obligations to God and to honor his law. We pray that the time may speedily come when this shall be truly a republican and free country, in no part of which, either state or territory, shall slavery be known.

The prayers of millions of Christians, with an earnestness never manifested for rulers before, daily ascend to heaven that you may be endued with all needed wisdom and power. Actuated by the sentiments of the loftiest and purest patriotism, our prayer shall be continually for the preservation of our country undivided, for the triumph of our cause, and for a permanent peace, gained by the sacrifice of no moral principles, but founded on the word of God, and securing in righteousness liberty and equal rights to all.

Signed in behalf of the General Conference of the Methodist Episcopal Church.

PHILADELPHIA, *May* 14, 1864.

PRESIDENT LINCOLN'S REPLY.

GENTLEMEN: In response to your address allow me to attest the accuracy of its historical statements, indorse the sentiments it expresses, and thank you in the nation's name for the sure promise it gives.

Nobly sustained as the government has been by all the Churches, I would utter nothing which might in the least appear invidious against any. Yet without this it may fairly be said that the Methodist Episcopal Church, not less devoted than the best, is, by its greater numbers, the most important of all. It is no fault in others that the Methodist Church sends more soldiers to the field, more nurses to the hospitals, and more prayers to heaven than any. God bless the Methodist church! bless all the churches! and blessed be God! who in this our great trial giveth us the Churches.

THE STATE OF THE COUNTRY.

May 27—The Committee on the State of the Country—consisting of Messrs. Joseph Cummings, J. Lanahan, I. S. Bingham, J. T. Peck, O. S. Munsell, L. B. Gurley, G. Moody, T. C. Gardner, T. M. Reese, A. C. George, G. D. Strout, J. W. Lowe, J. B Wentworth, A. S. McCoy, G. W. Walker, W. F. Cowles, H. D. Fisher, L. M. Reeves, J. Colby, T. H. Sinex, D. Cobb, S. Huffman, J. G. Miller, Nicholas Vansant, James Pike, Charles H. Whitecar, J. B. Wakeley, G. W. Woodruff, O. V. Lemon, E. Thomson, G. M. Boyd, C. Hobart, J. W. White, W. H. Olin, T. H. Pearne, W. M'Combs, J. Henderson, D. Patten, W. F. Stewart, G. C. Smith, N. E. Cobleigh, J. E. King, R. W. Keeler, W. D. Malcom, S. Haines, J. W. Reger, J. Lawson, C. O. Pillsbury, H. R. Clark—reported an address and these resolutions, which were unanimously adopted:

Resolved, 1. That in this hour of the nation's trial we will remember the President of the United States, all other officers of the government, and our army and navy, in never-ceasing prayer.

2 That it is the duty of the government to prosecute the war with all its resources of men and money till this wicked rebellion shall be subdued, the integrity of the nation shall be secured, and its legitimate authority shall be re-established, and that we pledge our hearty support and co-operation to secure this result.

3. That we regard our calamities as resulting from our forgetfulness of God, and from slavery, so long our nation's reproach, and that it becomes us to humble ourselves and forsake our sins as a people, and hereafter, in all our laws and acts, to honor God.

4. That we will use our efforts to secure such a change in the Constitution of our country as shall recognize the being of God, our dependence on Him for prosperity, and also his word as the foundation of civil law.

5. That we regard slavery as abhorrent to the principles of our holy religion, humanity, and civilization, and that we are decidedly in favor of such an amendment to the Constitution, and such legislation on the part of the states, as shall prohibit slavery or involuntary servitude, except for crime, throughout all the states and territories of the country.

6. That while we deplore the evils of war that has filled our land with mourning, we rejoice in the sublime manifestations of benevolence it has developed, as seen in the Sanitary and Christian Commissions, and in the associations formed to aid the vast multitudes who have recently become freemen, and that we pledge to these institutions our hearty co-operation and support.

THE PASTORAL ADDRESS.

May 27.—The report of the Committee on the Pastoral Address to the Members of the Church—Jesse T. Peck, D. D., Joseph Castle, D. D., L. B. Gurley, E. Adams, N. E. Cobleigh, W. H Ferris—was adopted. These extracts relate to public questions:

We have held our session in the midst of the fearful agitations and struggles of war. Our nation has reached a most eventful crisis. Ambitious and wicked men have led the people and States of the South into a most cruel and unprovoked rebellion. The Government has been compelled to resist this rebellion by force, and the delegates of all the Annual Conferences, in General Conference assembled, have solemnly recognized this stern necessity. Our reports, resolutions and acts, of which you have been already apprized, all sustained by unanimous votes, will show the Church and the world how heartily we are identified with the nation in her struggles, with our beloved army and navy in the deadly conflicts of this war, with the President and all other officers of the Government in the grave responsibilities of their present position, and with surviving sufferers, whether bond or free.

We call your attention to the fact that slavery is the evident and guilty cause of this terrible war, and express to you our deliberate opinion that there will be no peace or safety to the Republic till this vile usurpation is utterly destroyed. We have, therefore, resolved not only to sustain the Government most heartily in the struggle against treason, but in the high purpose to extirpate the guilty *cause* of the rebellion. And, in consistency with these resolutions, as well as under the highest sense of imperative duty, we have determined that the Methodist Episcopal Church shall, with the least possible delay, be delivered entirely from this enormous evil. We have, therefore, proposed to the Annual Conferences such a change in the general rules as will henceforth leave no occasion for misunderstanding or controversy. Providence has at length mysteriously led us through the struggles of ages to the highest unity in the assertion and vindication of the highest right. Let us give the glory to God alone.

The war is not yet over. We can have no adequate idea of the wrongs yet to be endured, of the valuable lives yet to be sacrificed, before the nation's new life shall be placed beyond the reach of the bloody hands which seek to destroy it; but we state to you calmly and solemnly, that, in our judgment, all true patriots ought to regard their lives and treasures, without reservation, as subject to the exigencies of this conflict, until it is honorably and triumphantly ended.

And especially do we urge you to obey, at all times, the great law of love; to pray for our unnatural enemies, as well as their surviving victims; extending your most active sympathy to our numerous families and friends who mourn the loss of brave husbands, fathers, brothers, sons, by this dreadful war. You will, we trust, on no account relax your efforts for the relief and Christian education of the multitudes of freedmen now appealing to your humanity. We do also most earnestly commend to your devoted attention our suffering soldiers, and urge you to enlarged liberality in the support of those humane institutions, the Christian and Sanitary Commissions.

METHODIST PROTESTANT.

GENERAL CONVENTION OF THE METHODIST PROTESTANT CHURCH, 1862.

November.—The body met in Cincinnati, and unanimously passed the following preamble and resolutions:

Whereas, Our country continues to be involved in all the horrors and dangers of a civil war unparalleled in the history of the world, alike in its gigantic proportions and in the vital interests which it shall affect for good or ill: and

Whereas, We cannot be cold spectators of the scenes occurring around us, because they appeal to our sympathies and our principles as patriots, as Christians, and as philanthropists: and

Whereas, We deem it our duty to our country, to the world at large, and to our God, to utter our sympathies and sentiments in this hour of danger to the country and to civil liberty: therefore

Resolved, 1. That we cling with fond affection to the institutions bequeathed to us by our Revolutionary sires, and that we infinitely prefer them to any other that ever have been, or that may be, proposed as a substitute for them.

2. That we therefore sanction, with all our hearts, the prosecution of the current war for their maintenance, and we recommend that this war be pushed with the utmost energy and to the last extremity: because in its successful prosecution alone we see the prevention of anarchy and misrule, of wide-spread dissensions, and mediæval tyranny and vassalage, of universal distraction, contentions, and bloodshed, more fearfully desolating and terrible than anything that can now result from the course that we thus recommend.

3. That we heartily endorse the Emancipation Proclamation of President Lincoln, because it strikes at that baleful cause of all our civil and ecclesiastical difficulties—American slavery—"the sum of all villanies," the darling idol of villains, the central power of villanous secessionism, but now, by the wisdom of the President, about to be made the agent of retributive justice in punishing that culmination of villanous enterprises, the attempt to overthrow the most glorious civil government that God's providence ever established upon earth.

4. That we earnestly deprecate all dissensions and divisions among those who profess loyalty to the Government and to our free institutions: and that we deem it suspicious, at least, if not strong evidence, of sympathy with our enemies, when men in our midst attempt to create such divisions or dissensions upon any pretext whatsoever.

5. That a committee be appointed to address the President of the United States, and express to him, in the name of the Methodist Protestant Church, the sentiments of loyalty contained in these resolutions, and to assure him that our people endorse his Proclamation, sustain the war, and are ready to do and suffer all things necessary for the maintenance of our glorious Government intact.

The Annual Conference at Pittsburg, September, 1864, unanimously adopted these resolutions:

Resolved, That this Conference does hereby declare its loyalty to the Government of the United States, and its approval of the Administration of Abraham Lincoln in his efforts to overthrow the rebellion and maintain the cause of the Union.

Resolved, That whatever may have been the design of the slaveholders of the South in bringing on this great rebellion, in our judgment, God is permitting this war in order to purify this nation from her sins—especially the great sin of slavery, which we hold to have been the main cause of the rebellion.

Resolved, That the Emancipation Proclamation is hereby endorsed by this Conference, and it is our prayer that the President, by judicious management, the power of his armies, and the help of the Almighty, may be able to carry it into practical effect in all the Rebel States.

Resolved, That party politics, in our judgment, should never be allowed to interfere with our allegiance to the Government of our country, and we hereby advise all our people to be faithful to the Administration in all its efforts to maintain the Union, constantly praying for the Government, and the success of our armies.

Resolved, That we desire a peace growing out of the salvation of our Government, based upon the principles of immutable righteousness, in order that the Christian religion may take a firmer hold than heretofore on the American mind.

The Maryland Annual Conference of the Methodist Protestant Church has not made any declaration since the opening of the war. The West Virginia Conference, which was in connection with it, undertook to ascertain its position in March last, with this result, as disclosed in these extracts from the report of the proceedings of the latter body at its meeting in September:

Dr. Laishley, our fraternal Messenger to the last Maryland Annual Conference, submitted his report, which states that owing to severe affliction in his family he was unable to attend said Conference in person, but that he addressed to them a fraternal letter, *in which he distinctly set forth the object of his mission, to wit: to ascertain the position occupied by the Maryland Conference in regard to its loyalty to the Government of the United States*,—to which he received the following reply:—

BALTIMORE, *Maryland*, March 21, 1864.

REV. DR. P. T. LAISHLEY—

DEAR BROTHER:—Your official communication as Messenger from the Western Virginia Annual Conference, was brought under the respectful consideration of the Maryland Annual Conference at its recent session in this city, and I was commissioned to answer it to the following effect:

We, as an Annual Conference, express our profound sympathy with Dr. Laishley in the sore affliction of his daughters, which, with some other uncontrollable circumstances, has deprived both him and the Conference of the desired and expected pleasure of fraternal greetings; and we hereby extend to Dr. Laishley and the Conference he represents our warm expression of Christian sympathy and affection and our prayers for their continued prosperity as an effectual agency in spreading spiritual holiness through our land. It was also determined to send a fraternal Messenger to the Western Virginia Conference at its Annual Session in September next.

I shall be happy to hear, my beloved brother, that your afflicted child is mercifully spared to you, and restored to the enjoyment of comfortable health.

With these sentiments, I am, most truly,

Yours in Christ,
F. WATERS.

The above letter was referred to a Committee, who submitted the following report, which was adopted:

We appreciate most cheerfully the expression of sympathy and affection set forth in said letter, but are grieved that the Conference did not think proper in its judgment to put us in possession of *the information we so earnestly desired*, to wit: *the position occupied by the Conference in regard to its loyalty to the Government of the United States*, and furthermore declare that we cannot affiliate or hold official connection with any Conference which is not outspoken on a subject of such vital importance, or which will not condescend to gratify us so far as to inform us whether it is for or against the Government, when treason threatens its destruction. Could we have been satisfied that the Maryland Conference as a body gave her sympathies and influence to the Government under which we live, it would have afforded us great pleasure to have continued in official connection with her; but for the want of such an expression on her part, we have to adopt the language of the Master and say, "*They who are not with us are against us.*"

The West Virginia Conference now holds connection with the Methodist Protestant Conferences of the Western, Northern, and Eastern States.

Of the proceedings of the Maryland Conference referred to, these have relation to the expected communication from the West Virginia Conference:

Rev. L. W. Bates offered this resolution, which was adopted:

Resolved, That in accordance with the suggestion of the President, (Rev. James K. Nichols,) in his executive paper, a committee of three ministers and delegates be appointed, whose duty it shall be to confer with all visitors having business with the Conference, and to decide whether and when those of them who wish to address the Conference shall be privileged to do so; and all communications not strictly belonging to the regular and annual business of the Conference, shall be referred to said committee.

Rev. Dr. F. Waters, Rev. L. W. Bates, Rev. T. D. Valiant, George Vickers, Esq., and L. J. Cox, Esq., were appointed on that Committee. On a subsequent day, it was announced to the Conference that a letter had been received from Rev. Dr. P. T. Laishley, appointed fraternal Messenger from the West Virginia Conference. *The letter was not read in open Conference*, but immediately referred to the committee aforesaid, and in relation to it the committee reported, on the same day, as follows:

A communication was received from Dr. P. T. Laishley, Messenger from West Virginia Conference, expressing his regret at not being able, owing to sickness in his family and other unfavorable circumstances, to visit our Conference.

The Committee recommend that the Conference express its sympathy for Dr. Laishley in the affliction of his daughter, which has deprived both him and the Conference of the pleasure of fraternal greetings, and that we extend to Dr. Laishley and the Conference he represents, our warm expression of Christian sympathy and affection, and our prayers for their continued prosperity as an efficient instrumentality in spreading scriptural holiness through our Land.

We further recommend, that the Conference elect a Messenger to visit the next session of West Virginia Conference, to be held in Fairmont, Va., in September, 1864.

And that a committee be appointed to address a letter to Bro. Laishley, expressing to him the above sentiments of our Conference.

F. WATERS,
GEO. VICKERS,
T. D. VALIANT,
L. W. BATES,
L. J. COX, JR.

On motion, Dr. F. Waters was appointed the committee named in the above report.

A number of the Ministers in this Conference are known to disapprove of the silence of the Conference, and to regret deeply the position it is thus made to occupy, and who, in their respective spheres of duty, urge the duty of maintaining the National authority and suppressing the Rebellion. Subjoined are the resolutions adopted in March, 1864, by the Ninth Street Methodist Protestant Church, Washington City:

Mr. Blackiston offered the following resolutions, and moved their adoption:

Whereas an opinion expressed that this church is virtually an organized society of religious sympathizers with rebellion has gained believers in the community; and whereas a strict adherence to the adopted silence on such matters, as a church, gives reasons for rebel sympathizers to hope that the assertion is true, and for loyal men to doubt the loyalty of the members of the church: Therefore be it

Resolved, That justice to ourselves and our brethren demands of us a full expression of our loyalty at this time.

Resolved, That in our opinion the rebellion, which has flooded the valleys and plains of the South and West with blood, is treasonable, wicked, and ought to be crushed, and the leaders punished as traitors.

Resolved, That we of Ninth street station have no sympathy with those engaged openly in the rebellion, and less with those who, while they are amassing fortunes from the Government, are secretly giving aid and comfort to its enemies.

Resolved, That though we may admire the talents and commend the zeal of every minister of the Conference, we consider no minister as acceptable to the Ninth street pulpit, against whose loyalty there is the slightest reason for doubt.

Resolved, That the Secretary is hereby ordered to prepare a copy of these resolutions and sign them; the chairman is hereby ordered to countersign them; and the delegate to the Maryland Annual Conference is hereby ordered to present them to the President of that body.

Rev. J. T. Ward is pastor, succeeding Rev. C. T. Cochel.

FREE METHODIST.

NEW YORK CONFERENCE OF THE FREE METHODIST CHURCH, 1864.

September—The body met at Akron, 29th and 30th, and October 1st, and adopted the following preamble and resolutions:

We are men of peace. Our Master, whom we supremely love and endeavor to serve, is the Prince of Peace. He has taught us to love our enemies and to do good as far as possible to all mankind. But he has also taught us that "the magistrate beareth not the sword in vain." He is to be a terror to evil doers; but how can this be if the laws against crime are not executed? And how can they be executed without the exercise of physical force? If force may be used to execute the laws against a single highwayman, may it not be against a band of criminals who set the laws at defiance? Does the magnitude of a conspiracy against just laws and the common rights of humanity, render the employment of whatever force, for whatever time may be necessary for its suppression, unchristian and wrong? Is it right to punish petit larceny, and wrong to punish murder? If not, then is the effort to suppress by force of arms this wicked rebellion, still existing in this country, entirely consistent with the Christian religion. Humanity demands that the rebellion be put down, no matter how great may be the expenditure of blood and treasure necessary to secure its overthrow. The fate of the ambitious, unscrupulous men who, because deprived, in a perfectly proper and legal manner, of the patronage of the Government which they had invariably used for the spread and perpetuation of human bondage, have conspired for the overthrow of the Nation, and who, in endeavoring to carry out their nefarious schemes, have deluged the land with blood and multiplied widows and orphans in all our borders, should stand upon the page of history as a warning to conspirators against the rights of men in all future ages.

In common with our fellow citizens we feel the burdens of this terrible struggle for national existence and the rights of humanity. We enjoy no immunity from the perils it involves. Some of the preachers of our denomination have bravely led their men upon the field of battle, and have nobly fallen in the sanguinary strife. Our brothers and our sons are still at the post of danger, or have laid down their lives for our beloved country. Should the war continue, we are liable to be called upon to follow their example. As Christians and as men we deprecate this great effusion of blood, and we devoutly and unitedly pray for the return of peace. But we would have a peace that promises to be permanent in its character and beneficial in its results: Therefore

Resolved, That as much as we deprecate the suffering caused by the civil war now raging in our land, we have no desire to have it stop until the rebellion is thoroughly subdued and Slavery, its guilty cause, is completely and forever extinguished in all our borders.

Resolved, That while we keep ourselves aloof from all party strife, we do most cordially sustain the Government in its efforts to subdue the rebellion, and especially in the emancipation policy; and we trust it will go on in the same direction until all their rights as men are restored to the colored race.

Resolved, That, while we do not believe in any unnecessary intermeddling with the political opinions of individuals, yet we do not see how any who sympathize with slaveholding and with the slave-holders' rebellion can consistently belong to the Free Methodist Church, or, indeed, to any religious body professing to be governed by the principles of the New Testament.

Resolved, That we render devout thanksgiving to God for the recent victories he has given our armies, and we will devoutly pray the Lord of Hosts to continue His interpositions in behalf of our nation, and give success to our arms, and restore peace and prosperity to our land, and establish our free institutions on the firm foundation of universal righteousness and justice.

B. T. ROBERTS,
Chairman of Committee.

EVANGELICAL ASSOCIATION.

GENERAL CONFERENCE OF THE EVANGELICAL ASSOCIATION, 1863.

October 1—The body met in Buffalo.

October 19—The Committee on the State of the Country made two reports, as follows:

MAJORITY REPORT.

Your Committee has the honor to lay the following report on the State of the Country before the Conference for consideration:

The great truth that God governs the world, and in his providence presides over the destinies of man, is not only founded on his Being and attributes, but it also stands legibly enstamped on every page of the History of the Human Race, and it cannot be misrepresented that the Supreme Ruler has, in all the alternations, in the struggle raging between the powers of light and darkness, ever since the Fall, so directed the course of events, that each of them brought man nearer the great end of his destination, viz: the emancipation from the dominion of evil, and the investiture of all with an equal title to the enjoyment of life, liberty and happiness.

The present inexcusable and unholy rebellion, that is now raging in our land, is nothing less than the expression and the outward appearance of the great world-wide struggle between the forever inalienable rights of mankind, on the one hand, and the unrighteousness of falsehood and tyranny on the other; in the status into which this world struggle, under the immediate righteous government of God, and the special elements of our national existence, has entered, and where both antagonistic powers are more fully expressed, and stand opposed to each other in a more rugged form, than has been the case heretofore of the theatre of history;—here, where for more than two hundred years, Liberty has found an asylum in the wilderness against the despotic oppression and papal persecutions of Europe—where the God-confiding Pilgrim Fathers, a company of persecuted Protestant Christians, laid the cornerstone of this republic, and its glorious institutions of "Liberty and Equality," according to the principles of the Holy Scriptures, for futurity—here, where in later years, the brave sons of these worthy ancestors, have laid this divinely selected foundation stone, reared on it the ideal of social, civil, and religious societies of all nations, (under a never before enjoyed measure of Heavenly favor,) and perfected, in a never before known greatness;—here, where, through the help of God with a strong arm, thus wrested from the grasp of Despotism, consecrated with their own blood, one of the best human governments that ever existed, and with it a country that should become a place of secure refuge for all the oppressed of the earth; but where Satan, the arch enemy of God and man, planted the upas of Slavery and man-brutalization, this excrescence of hell and sum total of all meanness and villainy, and through the poisonous curse to subvert this heritage of free men, to be made the stage of unheard-of abominations and sufferings, the burying-place of pure religion, liberty, and civilization, and, indeed the hopes of the world; and where further men who at the price of all higher motives and designs, driven by avarice and lust of power, for more than thirty years, worked according to a well laid plan for the subversion of the Constitution, the dissolution of the Union, and the overthrow of the Government, until at last, on the 12th day of April, 1861, by the first fire on the banner of the stars and stripes on Fort Sumter, made known that they were ready to carry out their treasonable design.

In view of these facts, be it, by us, the delegates of the several annual conferences of the Evangelical Association, in General Conference assembled, on the 19th day of October, A. D., 1863, solemnly

Resolved, 1. That notwithstanding our conviction that war and bloodshed is a terrible evil, and the extremely deplorable consequence of sin, in opposition to the spirit of Christianity, and its existence to be deeply deplored in our so-called Christian land; but inasmuch as the present terrible war raging in our land, was caused by the insurrection of a band of traitors and rebels, against the life and existence of the nation itself, whose chief object is the destruction of liberty, the exaltation of a comparatively small class over the larger—the laboring class, which constitutes the germ of the nation; the dishonoring of labor itself, and the extension and perpetuation of slavery;—in consideration of these undeniable facts it is the imperative duty of our Government, to use the sword entrusted to it of God, in defense of our rights, the execution of the laws, the protection of our free institutions, the maintenance of our forever indissoluble and inseparable Union, in accordance with the Constitution upon which it rests, and finally to punish the rebels against our Government, and it is the holiest duty of every citizen, faithfully to support the Government in the important duties devolving upon the same.

2. *Resolved*, That we cannot conceal the fact, that only the prevalent deep moral and religious corruption, in all the walks of life, made it possible to inaugurate its bloody struggle; therefore we acknowledge the same as a well-merited chastisement of God, and rebuking admonition to repentance and reformation, which applies particularly to the too worldly-minded church, and upon the heeding of which admonition depends the salvation of our country.

3. *Resolved*, That a republican form of Government can only exist where the principles of the Christian religion are deeply rooted in common life, and constitute the predominant element, where it is the mission, especially of the Christian ministry, to watch over the Christian religion, that it may not become the handmaid of unscrupulous demagogues or that the free discussion of such questions as relate to the temporal welfare of the people may not be prejudiced, but on the contrary, that the life of the whole nation be pervaded by the spirit and essence of Christianity.

4. *Resolved*, That we consider the fact, that the peaceable occupations in the Northern States have made undisturbed progress, and rejoice in an extraordinary advance, that the national prosperity and strength of our Government has attained a degree, which it did not reach in the long years of peace, as unmistakable evidences that it is God's gracious design and good will that our nation should come forth tried and purified, and that this Union of states, established on the principles of the Bible, shall be continued, with increased liberties.

5. *Resolved*, That in the midst of our national concussion, we behold the indubitable proofs of the favor of God in the fact, that He has given us rulers who, by their able statesmanship, have given their official acknowledgment of the higher Government of God over them, and by their well-tried probity and distinguished administration of the Government, have shown themselves worthy of the undivided confidence of the nation.

6. *Resolved*, That, as slavery is a social, moral, and civil evil, and the great cause of the present rebellion, we deem its continuance as incompatible with the exalted mission of our nation; and hence look upon the efforts of the present administration to inaugurate measures for its ultimate extinction, as righteous and patriotic; and therefore recognize also the so-called Emancipation Proclamation of the President, in his capacity of Commander-in-Chief of the Army and Navy of the United States, as well as the sus-

pension of the Writ of *Habeas Corpus*, as constitutional and in the highest degree proper measures for the suppression of the present insurrection.

7. *Resolved*, That we will not omit, as becoming our office and work, as preachers of the Gospel, to support the Government in every proper measure, which it may employ for the suppression of the rebellion, and the restoration of peace, and that we earnestly exhort all our members, according to the doctrine of the Bible, and profession of religion, to manifest toward the Government reverence, fidelity, and obedience, and not to neglect to pray for the same and the welfare of our country.

8. *Resolved*, That we consider the political partisanism,—where the interests of the country and religion are made of less importance than party interests, and are sacrificed inconsiderately—as entirely unworthy of a Christian citizen; and therefore urgently admonish our preachers and members to abstain from all such folly.

9. *Resolved*, That we appreciate the patriotism and bravery of our fellow-citizens, who have sacrificed the comforts of domestic life, and took up arms in defense of their country, and heartily sympathize with them and their families, and remember the sufferings and sacrifices which they have endured for the deliverance of the Union and preservation of the Republic, or may yet endure, that we will support them with word and deed, and will ever remember them in our prayers.

10. *Resolved*, That we will not omit to call upon God, to pour out His Spirit in an abundant measure upon the Church of our land, and upon the nation in general, that He will redeem our nation from its sin, eradicate its guilt, and speedily grant us a just and permanent peace.

J. J. ESHER,
R. DUBS,
H. HUELSTER,
M. LAUER,
J. STOLL,
A. STAHLY,
J. FUCHS,
S. G. RHOADS,
Committee.

MINORITY REPORT.

Whereas the majority report of the Committee on the state of the country contains expressions which we cannot conscientiously endorse; therefore we submit the following:

Whereas a wicked and causeless rebellion is still raging over a great part of our country, threatening our civil and religious liberties, imperiling the glorious Union of these states, and aiming, as we believe, at the overthrow of our glorious Republic; and

Whereas the Government of the United States, in its efforts to put down this wicked and gigantic insurrection, should have the undivided support of every citizen, who loves his country, and the heaven-born institutions of freedom, bequeathed unto us by our fathers; and

Whereas we recognize the hand of God, in the destinies of all the nations of the earth; therefore,

Resolved, That while we deeply deplore the existence of this fratricidal strife, and the necessity of bloodshed in the maintenance of the Union, nevertheless we believe it to be the duty of the Government to use every legitimate and constitutional means to suppress the abominable spirit of treason, exterminate rebellion, and, by the blessing of God, restore peace and union to our now distracted country.

Resolved, That we conceive it to be the duty of all, especially of every Christian, to sustain the Government in this hour of peril, by prayer, obedience, and every proper means, in its efforts to suppress this cruel rebellion, and to pray that God may grant wisdom to our rulers, and efficiency to our arms.

Resolved, That while we acknowledge God as the Supreme Ruler of the universe, and the Dispenser of the great events of nations, we, at the same time, acknowledge these calamities to be a just chastisement for our national sins, such as ingratitude, Sabbath-desecration, pride, revelry, profanity, infidelity, slavery, &c., and the present conflict, a struggle between the spirit of liberty and despotism; therefore we humbly bow to the chastening rod of the Almighty, confess our sins as a nation, praying that He may in His wrath remember mercy, mitigate the infliction of deserved punishment, and overrule this commotion, that the nation may come forth purified, His name glorified, and His purposes accomplished.

Whereas this terrible struggle has been, and still is fraught, with the loss of property, friends, health, life and limb, bringing distress, sorrow, and mourning into many families, while thousands of our brave fellow-citizens are still undergoing the privations of soldier's life, therefore,

Resolved, That we deeply sympathize with them in their losses and privations, especially with the sick and wounded, and assure then of our prayers, while the patriotic dead shall ever live fresh in our memories.

Whereas Slavery is a great moral, social, and political evil, one of the primary causes of this unreasonable rebellion; therefore,

Resolved, That we disapprove of the entire system of Slavery, and fully endorse the sentiments expressed in our Church Discipline.

Whereas much injury has been done in Christian communities by undue participation in political party strife; therefore,

Resolved, That we deeply regret that some permit themselves to be carried away by such party strife, and indulge in contemptuous epithets, and thereby ferment discord, and alienate brotherly feeling to such a degree that the interests of religion and the country become secondary matters and we hereby disapprove of such conduct as highly culpable and unworthy a Christian and especially a minister.

Whereas in God alone is our help and safety; therefore,

Resolved, That we call upon all Christians, everywhere, to unite with us in giving thanks to our great Benefactor for the many tokens of Good, which He in the midst of our calamities manifests unto us, at the same time confessing before God our many national sins, deprecating His wrath, and with us call upon God to give wisdom to our Rulers, and their legal advisers, discretion to our officers, and courage to our soldiers; that He may turn the hearts of the rebels from the errors of their ways; and upon the whole, to direct the course of events that victory may perch upon our banner, the tide of treason may flow backward, rebellion be crushed, and the balmy days of peace and prosperity may soon return and smile upon us again, and the *Star Spangled Banner* wave over the entire land of the free and *home* of the *brave*.

JACOB YOUNG.

VOTE OF THE CONFERENCE.

FOR THE MAJORITY REPORT—Messrs. J. J. Esher, R. Dubs, H. Huelster, M. Lauer, J. Stull, A. Stahly, J. Fuchs, S. G. Rhoads, S. Neitz, J. Yeakel, J. P. Leib, J. Schell, J. Koehl, G. T. Haines, L. Snyder, Fr. Hoffman, F. Krecker, H. Stetzel, E. Kohr, J. M. Young, C. F. Deininger, L. May, C. Lindeman, A. Niebel, J. Rank, J. G. Pfeuffer, J. L. W. Seibert, S. B. Kring, L. Jacoby, J. D. Jenni, M. Lehn, S. Weber, F. Herlan, G. F. Spreng, J. G. Zinser, John Dreisbach, C. M. Reinhold, John Walz, D. Strohman, G. Haley, L. Sheuerman, C. A. Munk, F. Frech, C. Cupp, S. A. Tobias, C. Hummel, C. Shæfle, Chr. Augenstein, E. Musselman, R. Rohland, Jos. Schneider, J. G. Esher, L. Buehler, C. A. Schnake, S. Dickover, I. Kuter, J. Keiper, M. W. Steffey, Joseph Weber, A. B. Shaefer, G. G. Platz, and M. Hoehn. 62.

FOR THE MINORITY REPORT—J. Young, P. Wagner, S. W. Seibert, and M. J. Carothers. 4.

CATHOLIC.

I have not been able to ascertain that any council or body of the Church has made a declaration on the subject. Several of the Bishops have, on sundry occasions. Bishop Hughes undertook a mission to Europe in the interest of the Government. His successor, Bishop McCloskey, at the late thanksgiving for victories, ordered a general observance of the day in his diocese, with appropriate services in the churches. Bishop Wood, of Philadelphia, issued this paper:

To the Clergy and Faithful of the Diocese of Philadelphia: Greeting:

We cheerfully call your attention to the invitation of his Excellency, the President of the United States, who, in announcing the recent successes of the Union arms, desires that all should unite in thanksgiving, supplications and prayers to the Great Ruler of the destinies of nations.

Let us, therefore, send up our thanksgivings to God for the merciful dispositions of His Divine Providence in our regard, and pour forth our earnest supplications that His Divine blessing may descend upon us, and procure for us the inestimable fruit of national harmony and fraternal union.

We request the Reverend Pastors to recite for this intention at the last Mass on Sunday, the Litany of the Saints, and to add such devotions as they may deem appropriate to the occasion.

Pax Domini sit semper vobiscum.

Given at Philadelphia this 9th day of September, A. D. 1864.

† JAMES F. WOOD,
Bishop of Philadelphia.

Archbishop Kenrick, of Baltimore, September 2, 1861, issued an address to the clergy of the diocese of Baltimore, directing the use "on all Sundays at the parochial Mass," of a prayer for the President of the United States, and for the authorities generally, being that framed by John Carroll and prescribed in 1791.

Archbishop John B. Purcell, of Cincinnati, published this Address on a like occasion:

The President of the United States and the Governor of the State of Ohio having, in conformity with a most proper and a time-honored practice, appointed the fourth Thursday of November as a day of devout thanksgiving to the Almighty God for His mercies; of humiliation for our sins; and of supplication for peace; we hereby ordain that the Catholic congregations of this diocese be earnestly exhorted by their pastors to meet in their respective churches on the day above specified, and assist in becoming sentiments of gratitude, penitence and prayer at the great Eucharistic, expiatory and impetratory Sacrifice of the New Law.

We, Catholics, have largely shared in the blessings of health, abundant harvests and exemption from the ravages of war which God has granted to the people of the North. Our sins have as largely merited the chastisement which has overtaken our erring brethren of the South, and which has cost the life-blood of so many thousands of our own brave soldiers who left their pleasant homes to check the advance of the foe and confine the deadly strife to the battle fields on which it madly originated. Our hopes of future happiness on earth are vain if the peace, the prosperity, the progress in arts, sciences and religion which have distinguished us among all the nations of the earth for fourscore and eight years, and which, under the Divine blessing, are mainly attributable to our Constitution and Union, be not continued by the maintenance of that Union and the elimination of those defects which Christian civilization and our own experience have shown us the Constitution contained. It therefore becomes our solemn duty to observe with no ordinary fervor the National holiday; and as we cannot enjoy, and should not desire, peace, happiness and independence except in the society of our fellow-citizens, we should pray for and promote, by every means in our power, their welfare as well as our own.

We confess that it has greatly pained us to hear that certain rash, irreverent and thoughtless men of our communion have denounced and abused the Government, the Administration, and their abettors. Now, God commands us to bless and curse not. And when bad men cursed the supporters of the Government, did they not reflect that they cursed the more than hundreds of thousands of Catholic voters, and Catholic soldiers of our army who defend that Government in the field? Did they not reflect that its downfall would be hailed with acclammation by our own hereditary oppressors, across the ocean? Did they reflect that if political salvation is ever to reach a far distant and beloved island, it must come to it from these United States which they would sever?

There is no justifying cause or reason to curse the Government or the Administration. They did not commence this war. They could scarcely bring themselves to believe that it was seriously commenced, even when forts had fallen and the blood of our people was shed by the hands of the South. And when force had to be repelled by force, when armies had to be raised and, therefore, troops to be drafted to raise the blockade of our rivers and stem the tide of aggression, what more did our Government do than was done in the South? Where in the North was the draft, the conscription, enforced as ruthlessly and as indiscriminately as in the South? Where was the citizens' property confiscated without compensation for the alleged uses of the Government, as it was in the South? We have conversed with Irish Catholic refugees from Georgia, from Arkansas, from Alabama and other Southern States, and we know how they were stripped of their money and their clothes, and cast into prison when they refused to go into the ranks of the Confederate army. Many an Irish laborer told us in the hospitals here and elsewhere, that when the war broke out in the South and the public works were suspended, they were either violently conscripted, or had to enlist or starve.

We do not adduce these facts to excite unkind feelings against the South, but to put to shame the journalists of the North, especially the *Freeman's Journal* and the *Metropolitan Record*, of New York, who instigated our too confiding people to evil words and deeds, and the people themselves who patronized such journalists and were duped and deceived by their malignity.

It is time, therefore, now that the election is past, that all should return to their sober second thought, and that we should rally round the constituted authorities, the "powers" which the Apostle commands us to obey, and thus presenting an undivided front to the enemy, re-establish the Union, without which there can be no panacea, present or prospective, for the ills they suffer. The South beholding us thus of one mind, will, we devoutly trust, hasten to make peace, and we, on our side, will show them that we are ready and willing to make greater sacrifices for peace and union with them than ever we made for war.

The Reverend Clergy will please recite the Litany of the Saints, in union with their beloved flock, before Mass, repeating three times the two prayers for peace, and the prayer: O God, who by sin art offended, and by repentance pacified, &c.

JOHN B. PURCELL,
Archbishop of Cincinnati.

CINCINNATI, 13th *Nov.*, 1864.

FRIEND OR QUAKER.

YEARLY MEETING FOR PENNSYLVANIA, NEW JERSEY, DELAWARE, AND EASTERN SHORE OF MARYLAND, 1862.

This Address was adopted:

To the President, Senate and House of Representatives of the United States of America:

At the yearly meeting of Friends, held in Philadelphia, for Pennsylvania, New Jersey, Delaware, and the Eastern Shore of Maryland, by adjournment from the twelfth day of the fifth month to the sixteenth of the same, inclusive, Anno Domini one thousand eight hundred and sixty-two,

The following minute was read, united with, directed to be signed by the clerks, and forwarded:

This meeting has been introduced into a deep concern relative to the present condition of our country. Our minds have been directed to those who preside over our National Government, and gratitude has been felt to the Great Ruler of Nations that he has so far moved the hearts of these that they have decreed the District of Columbia free from slavery. We earnestly desire that the Chief Magistrate of the Nation and our Congress may, in this season of deep trial, humbly seek Divine guidance, that under this influence they may act for the cause of justice and mercy, in that wisdom which is pure, peaceable and profitable to direct, and that the effusion of blood may be stayed.

Signed by direction and on behalf of the meeting aforesaid.

MARY S. LIPPINCOTT,
Clerk of the Women's Meeting.
WILLIAM GRISCOM,
Clerk of the Men's Meeting.

YEARLY MEETING, 1864.

The body adopted this address:

To the President, Senate and House of Representatives of the United States:

This Memorial of the Representative Committee, or Meeting for Sufferings of the Religious Society of Friends, of Pennsylvania, New Jersey, Delaware, and adjacent parts of Maryland, respectfully showeth, that

We respect, honor and love this Government, which we believe Divine Wisdom has placed over us, and because of this, we desire that it may, in no particular, be found striving against God, or persecuting His children, however humble in position or numbers they may be.

Under the present law of Congress, every able-bodied citizen within certain ages, in time of war, is liable to be called upon by the Government to bear arms in its defence.

We represent a people who cannot comply with this law without disobeying the command of God to them.

Neither can they furnish a substitute or pay any equivalent or fine imposed for exemption from military service, because in so doing, they feel that they would implicate themselves in a violation of their conscientious scruples in this respect.

We hold, that the doctrine that human governments are ordained of God, does not imply the infallibility of those who administer them, and gives them no right to require us to violate our allegiance to the Almighty, who is sovereign Lord of conscience, and whose right it is to rule and reign in the hearts of His children.

For more than two hundred years our Society has held the doctrine, that all wars and fightings were forbidden to them, as followers of Christ—differing in this respect from nearly all other associations of men claiming the Christian name.

For asserting and maintaining this, and other testimonies of the "Truth as it is in Jesus," they were brought under cruel persecution, enduring the despoiling of their estates, incarceration in prisons and loathsome dungeons, and death.

Through this long season of darkness, their dependence was upon Divine Power, under which, their patient suffering and earnest remonstrance obtained in some degree the favor of those in authority.

For the free enjoyment of civil and religious liberty, they came to this land, to seek amongst the so-called savages of the wilderness, immunities and privileges denied them at the hands of a professed Christian nation. Here William Penn and his friends planted their infant colony, and proved the efficacy of the principle of Peace. The conflict of arms was unknown, and history bears no record of strife between the Indian and the Friend.

We their descendants, now approach you, not alone with a view to shield ourselves from suffering, but under a sense of duty to God, to assert the sacred rights of conscience, to raise the standard of the Prince of Peace before the nation, and in His name to ask you to so modify the law, that it shall not require those who administer it, to bring under persecution innocent men for obeying His commands—"Ye are my friends if ye do whatsoever I command you."—"Whether it be right in the sight of God to hearken unto you more than unto God, judge ye."

In thus defining our position, we enter not into judgment or condemnation of those who differ from us. We appreciate the difficulties that surround those upon whom rests the responsibility of guiding the nation through the awful perils of civil war.

We appeal to you under a sense of suffering—afflictions and mourning surround us, and sorrow hath filled our hearts.

Many of our young men, overcome by the spirit of war, have rushed into the conflict, where some of them have found an early death; some have purchased their release from the draft by the payment of money; others have remained steadfast to their faith in the hour of trial, thereby subjecting themselves to the penalty for desertion. Trusting in the mercy of our Heavenly Father, we desire that He may so touch your hearts and understandings with His wisdom, that you may grant our petition.

Signed by the direction, and on behalf of the Committee.

SAMUEL PARRY, *Clerk.*

PHILADELPHIA, 1*st mo.* 22*d*, 1864.

UNITARIAN.

CONFERENCE OF THE WESTERN UNITARIAN ASSOCIATION, HELD AT TOLEDO, OHIO, JUNE, 1863.

June—The body met at Toledo, Ohio, and adopted the following resolutions:

Whereas our allegiance to the kingdom of God requires of us loyalty to every righteous authority on earth; therefore,

Resolved, That we give to the President of the United States, and to all who are charged with the guidance and defence of our nation in its present terrible struggle for the preservation of liberty, public order, and Christian civilization, against the powerful wickedness of treason and rebellion, the assurance of our cordial sympathy and steady support, and that we will cheerfully continue to share any and all needful burdens and sacrifices in the holy cause of our country.

2. That we hail with gratitude and hope the rapidly growing conviction among the loyal masses of our countrymen that the existence of human slavery is inconsistent with the national safety and honor, as it is inconsistent with natural right and justice, and that we ask the Government a thorough and vigorous enforcement of the policy of emancipation, as necessary alike to military success, to lasting peace, and to the just supremacy of the Constitution over all the land.

These resolutions are in harmony with the tone of Sermons, Addresses, and Discussions, at all the Annual and Semi-annual meetings of the Unitarians, since the war began. The central body—the "American Unitarian Association,"—by rule and established practice, abstain from organized ecclesiastical action. The general position of the denomination, however, is well known. With marked unanimity, its leading societies and ministers have given their earnest support to the policy of the National Government respecting Union, Emancipation, and Permanent Peace. The accredited organs of the denomination—the Christian Examiner, a bi-monthly, the Monthly Journal, the Religious Miscellany, the Christian Register, and the Christian Inquirer—have incessantly and uncompromisingly advocated the cause of Union and Freedom throughout the Republic. One of their ministers—Rev. William Henry Channing—is Chaplain of the present House of Representatives, 38th Congress. For the subjoined interesting facts I am indebted to Rev. A. Woodbury, of Providence, R. I.:

One minister of the Unitarian Church has been a colonel of a colored regiment; one a lieutenant colonel of the same; one a captain aide-de-camp; two lieutenants in the line, one of whom was killed in battle; one a corporal and two privates. The Church has furnished forty (40) chaplains, two of whom have been killed in action, and one died in the service. One minister is a secretary in the office of the New England Educational Commission. Three have been engaged in teaching the freedmen of South Carolina and Mississippi, one of whom contracted a fatal disease in the course of his labors. The Presidents of the United States Sanitary Commission and the Western Sanitary Commission are ministers of the Unitarian church. One is associate secretary of the United States Sanitary Commission; another is secretary of the Western Sanitary Commission, and a considerable number have been engaged in missionary and sanitary labors at different times during the progress of the war.

Since the commencement of the struggle nineteen tracts have been published, entitled as follows: The Soldier's Companion (a book of songs and tunes;) The Man and the Soldier; The Soldier of the Good Cross; The Home to the Camp; Liberty and Law, a poem for the hour; The Camp and the Field; The Home to the Hospital; a Letter to a Sick Soldier; An Enemy Within the Lines; Wounded and in the Hands of the Enemy; Traitors in Camp; A Change of Base; On Picket; The Rebel; To the Color; The Recruit; A Few Words with the Convalescent; The Reconnoissance, and The Reveille. Twelve of these were written by Rev. J. F. W. Ware, and the residue by Rev. Dr. Geo. Putnam, Rev. Messrs. Woodbury, Collyer and Winkley, and Messrs. Charles E. Norton and Elbridge J. Cutler. Of these no less than 496,000 copies had been distributed up to July, 1864, at an expense of about $8,000. The Association has also sent out one missionary to the Army of the Potomac, who was taken prisoner in the performance of his duty, and, after two months' confinement, was released on his parole. Other ministers have visited the camps and the hospitals at different times, and have done a faithful missionary work as opportunity and strength were given them. Arrangements have recently been made for the more extensive distribution of Unitarian publications among the armies of the Republic. To the amount of work performed by the ministers of the Unitarian Church are to be added the toils and sacrifices of the laymen. The members of the Church are to be found in all grades of the army, from the drummer-boy to the major general, and among the officers and sailors of the navy of the United States.

UNITED BRETHREN.

EAST PENNSYLVANIA CONFERENCE OF UNITED BRETHREN IN CHRIST, 1863.

March—The body adopted these resolutions:

Whereas our beloved and prosperous country, by the hellish intrigues of designing aspirants after power and gain, is now deluged by one of the most unholy and diabolical rebellions that ever cursed our world, thereby endangering the great, good principles of the Government, and threatening to overthrow our free institutions, and the destruction of our blood-purchased and heaven-sanctified liberties;

And whereas there appears no honorable or righteous element of power in our hands to put in force to subdue treason and crush rebellion but a resort to arms; and whereas an enlightened and christianized people may employ physical force, even to the destroying of human life, for the protection and preservation of its subjects and the perpetuation of its own existence, as we have in the following quotation from the Scripture of Truth: "For there is no power but of God; the powers that be are ordained of God.

"Whosoever, therefore, resisteth the powers resisteth the ordinance of God, and they that resist shall receive unto themselves damnation. For rulers are not a terror to good works but to the evil." * * * "For he is the minister of God to those for good. But if thou do that which is evil be afraid; for he beareth not the sword in vain, for he is the *minister of* GOD, *a revenger* to execute vengeance upon him that doeth evil." Therefore,

Resolved, 1. That we look upon the action of the so-named "Southern Confederacy," from first to last, as a record of the most hellish inhumanity, unrighteousness and barbarity ever known in the records of the nations.

2. That we look upon the efforts of Northern *Copperheads* to aid Southern miscreants in their nefarious work to overthrow our Government, as *beings* unworthy the protection of the Stars and Stripes, or the sympathy of any true, loyal man.

3. That we do most determinedly condemn the assertions of unholy, disloyal, foul-mouthed and designing politicians, that ministers of the Gospel are the cause of the present rebellion.

4. That our devout sympathies are with the thousands of our fellow-citizens who are enduring the privations, sufferings and dangers of the army, and also for their families and friends at home, and that we will continue our earnest petitions to God in their behalf.

5. That we believe God, in his divine providence, has put Abraham Lincoln, the proper man in the right place, the Presidential chair, and that we endorse his every effort to rid the country of the most heaven daring of all evils and sins—human slavery.

6. That we continue to offer to God our sincere prayers for our President, that he may be sustained in his great and arduous duties by divine power, and that every loyal heart may beat with warmest sympathies for him, and that heaven may mercifully hold his heart in his almighty hand.

7. That we believe that the deep-seated, unnatural, inhuman, unchristian, and *causeless* hatred to the colored race, should and must cease to render our nation acceptable to God.

8. That we will endeavor to make judicious and Christian efforts in our different fields of labor, publicly and privately, to collect funds to send missionaries and teachers among the now free, and yet to be freed, colored people.

9. That we approve heartily the course of Governor Curtin in his exertions to aid the General Government in subduing the present cursed rebellion, and in his efforts to save our State from the fierce, fiery tread of traitorous oppressors and cut-throats; and that we hurl back with contempt the assailing of his actions by Northern rebels in the press or private conversation.

10. That a copy of the foregoing preamble and resolutions be taken to President Lincoln, by Bishop Markwood, assuring him that there is unwavering and deeply-rooted loyalty glowing in the hearts of the members of this Conference, and the people whom they represent.

UNIVERSALIST.

GENERAL CONVENTION OF UNIVERSALISTS, 1861.

September 17—The body met in New York.

September 19—The Report of the Committee on the State of the Country—Revs. L. C. Browne, A. St. John Chambre, and Mr. Dean Clapp—after being amended to read as follows, was unanimously adopted:

Whereas, Our country is now unfortunately involved in a war occasioned by an unwarrantable and atrocious rebellion against its government constitutionally chosen, and the success of which would jeopardize the cause of civil and religious freedom throughout the world; therefore,

Resolved, That we hereby express our earnest sympathy with our rulers in this their hour of trial; with our countrymen in arms for the defence of our institutions, and with the ministers of our own and other Christian orders who are called, in the Providence of God, to administer Christian admonition and consolation in the camp and on the field.

2. That we, as a denomination, pledge our earnest labors, our pecuniary means, and our heartfelt prayers for the success of the Federal arms, the defeat of this unnatural rebellion, and the speedy return of an honorable peace, and the prosperity that has crowned us as a United Nation in the past.

A resolution offered by Rev. G. L. Demarest of Ohio—but not published in the Minutes—was discussed and tabled, and re-discussed and re-tabled.

GENERAL CONVENTION OF UNIVERSALISTS, 1862.

September 16—The body met at Chicago.—Rev. J. S. Dennis of Iowa, Rev. C. W. Biddle of New Jersey, and Rev. A. W. Bruce of Massachusetts, were appointed a Committee on Business.

September 17—Mr. Dennis reported the following preamble and resolutions:

Whereas our country is still afflicted by the bloody strife that has been precipitated upon us; and whereas we esteem it the duty of every loyal citizen, especially those representing the moral and Christian sentiment of the land, to declare fealty to the Government, in this hour of its peril, and to uphold the hands of those in authority over us; therefore,

Resolved, That while in our judgment, we must accept the existing strife as the natural and inevitable penalty of our national infidelity to our republican principles, and of our attempt to reconcile freedom and slavery (which are essentially irreconcilable,) we renewedly express our faith in the justice of our cause and in the certainty of our final triumph; and renewedly tender to the President and his Constitutional advisers, the assurance of our sympathies amidst the great responsibilities of their position; and of our hearty support in all proper and efficient efforts to suppress this atrocious rebellion.

Resolved, That we gratefully record our appreciation of the patriotism of our people, and of the valor and heroism of our soldiers; and that while we honor those who have relinquished the charms of home, and offered life as a sacrifice for our country, we invoke God's blessing upon them, amidst the exposures of war, and ask His comforting grace for the homes that have thus been darkened, and for the hearts that the casualties of battle have bereaved.

Resolved, That we have occasion, amidst the events through which we are passing, to be deeply impressed with the reality of God's moral rule, and to learn anew the lesson, that neither nations nor individuals can safely defy His law, nor hope to escape from the inexorable ordinance, that sinners must eat of the fruit of their doings.

Afternoon Session—Rev. T. T. Goodrich, of New York, moved to strike out the words, "and of our attempt to reconcile freedom and slavery, (which are essentially irreconcilable);"—which was lost.

On motion of Mr. L. J. Fletcher, the report was re-committed—yeas 17, nays 16.

September 18—Rev. C. W. Biddle, of New Jersey, offered the following:

Whereas our beloved country is still afflicted with a bloody civil war, and a determined foe is striving to usurp the authority of the Central Government in a portion of the land; and whereas, it is the duty of all loyal citizens and organizations to acknowledge the blessings of good Government, and to support the rulers of the nation; and whereas we are deeply interested in the present contest between our country and its foes; therefore,

Resolved, That we re-affirm our devotion to the cause of the nation, in this hour of its pain and peril; that we regard as second only to the cross of Christ the glorious banner of the country; that we look on it, in this strife, as the emblem of constitutional government and the symbol of our national unity and life.

Resolved, In the words of Washington, "That the unity of government that constitutes us one people, is the main pillar of our political independence and that the union of these States under one Constitution and Government, and the maintenance of our republic, is the hope of the oppressed of all nations;" that we find in dissolution, the seeds of future and indefinite conflict; and that the arm of the nation must be stretched forth till the rebellion is put down.

Resolved, That we tender to the President of the United States our sympathy in his efforts to maintain the integrity of the Government, and pray that by a vigorous exercise of all the energies of the nation, victory may perch upon our banner and peace be speedily restored to the land.

Resolved, That we implore the blessing of Almighty God on our Army and Navy, that they may be preserved in time of battle and triumph in every contest; and that we humbly pray, we may learn from these heavy chastisements under which we are passing, that there is a God that judgeth in the earth, and that only righteousness can exalt a nation.

Rev. J. T. Goodrich moved its adoption.

Rev. L. J. Fletcher moved as an amendment the adoption of the preamble and first resolution.

Hon. G. I. Parsons of Michigan moved to lay the report on the table; which was lost—yeas 9, nays 14. He then moved the substitution of the preamble and resolutions of yesterday's report; which was agreed to—yeas 26, nays 9, as follows:

YEAS—*Clerical:* A. W. Bruce of Massachusetts, C. H. Fay of Rhode Island, E. G. Brooks of New York, G. W. Montgomery of New York, D. Bacon of Pennsylvania, Marion Crosley of Ohio, W. J. Chaplin of Indiana, H. F. Miller of Indiana, A. G. Hibbard of Illinois, James Gorton of Michigan, J. S. Dennis of Iowa, G. W. Lawrence of Wisconsin—12. *Lay:* Dennis Britain of Vermont, J. W. Fairbanks of Massachusetts, J. A. Darling of Rhode Island, Isaac Tinkey of New York, Aaron D. Miller of Indiana, John Heuston of Indiana, Paul B. Ring of Illinois, Hon. Alfred Knowles of Illinois, A. G. Throop of Illinois, Hon. G. I. Parsons of Michigan, Hon. W. A. Robinson of Michigan, C. H. Wright of Iowa, H. M. Buttles of Wisconsin, N. H. Hemiup of Minnesota—14. Total, 26.

NAYS—*Clerical:* L. I. Fletcher of Massachusetts, C. W. Biddle of New Jersey, George Messenger of Ohio, J. P. Weston of Illinois, J. T. Goodrich of New York—5. *Lay:* Benjamin Kelley of Maine, Minot Tirrell of Massachusetts, John Osborn of Massachusetts, P. P. Demarest of New York—4. Total, 9.

The report of 17th made by Mr. Dennis, was then adopted, as substituted, yeas 28, nays 7. Same as before, except that Revs. Mr. Fletcher and Mr. Weston changed from nay to aye.

GENERAL CONVENTION OF UNIVERSALISTS, 1863.

September 15—The body met in Portland, Maine.

September 17—The Business Committee—Revs. J. G. Bartholomew, H. R. Walworth, and A. Battles—reported these resolutions:

Whereas the General Convention of Universalists in the United States of America, has ever been distinguished for its loyalty to Government and its devotion to the principles of freedom and humanity; therefore,

Resolved, That in this time of national peril, when the wicked hands of a blood-thirsty rebellion have been raised to strike a death-blow at the Constitution and the laws of the land, and overthrow the liberties of every citizen, we recognize the merciful hand of Providence in the constant and zealous loyalty of the great majority of our people, as well as in the victories which have recently crowned our arms; and while we still appeal to our rulers and the people not to abate their vigor in prosecuting the war until the rebellion is effectually subdued, we yet feel that our trust must be in God, who alone can give us permanent triumph.

2. That we renew our expressions of Christian fidelity and loyalty to the Government, and reaffirm our confidence in our Chief Magistrate, whose honesty of purpose stands unimpeached; and that we recognize in his Proclamation of January 1st, 1863, a carrying out of the injunction of Scripture to "break every yoke and let the oppressed go free."

3. That we recognize the wisdom which prompted our fathers in their struggle for National Independence to arm the negro in securing our freedom, and are sanguine in the belief that a similar policy adopted at this time, which shall call the blacks to share with the whites in the perils and sacrifices of our present struggle, and secure to them the blessings of a common freedom, will be equally effectual in re-establishing order among us, and striking at the root of this cruel rebellion, "*so that when peace comes, it will come so as to stay, and be a peace worth having.*"

4. That the President of this Council be instructed to forward to the President of the United States a copy of these resolutions.

The first resolution was adopted. On the second, the vote was:

YEAS—*Clerical:* A. Battles, F. A. Hodsdon, B. F. Bowles, Eli Ballou, T. R. Spencer, J. S. Barry, Benton Smith, A. M. Rhodes, Thomas Borden, H. Blanchard, C. W. Tomlinson, H. R. Walworth, Richard Eddy—13. *Lay:* Hon. Israel Washburn, E. F. Beal, W. A. Vaughn, Moses Humphrey, E. C. Starr, E. C. Fuller, J. M. Sargent, Benjamin Spinney, G. W. Hall, Willard Goldthwaite, H. J. Angell, Paschal Converse, James Cooper, N. Van Nostrand, G. W. Barnes, J. J. Van Zandt, David Tappen—17. Total, 30.

NAYS—*Clerical:* G. L. Demarest and George Messenger of Ohio—2. *Lay:* David Tichenor of New Jersey—1. Total, 3.

The remaining resolutions were adopted without division.

GENERAL CONVENTION OF UNIVERSALISTS, 1864.

September 20—The body met in Concord, N. H.

September 21—The report of the Committee on the State of the Country—J. V. Wilson of Conn., P. B. Ring of Ill., and Revs. M. Goodrich of R. I., Richard Eddy of Penn., L J. Fletcher of N. Y., and J. M. Usher of Mass.,—was unanimously adopted, as follows:

Whereas the fearful war with which our nation has been scourged for years still continues, and makes additional demands on our courage, energy, patience and faith; therefore

Resolved, That we recognize in it the punishment of our people for their persistent arrogance and oppression. We can not therefore hope for the return of peace through efforts to rivet anew the chains of the bondman, or to perpetuate the former glaring inconsistencies between our professions of love for liberty and the support of slavery.

2. That while we deplore the bloodshed, costliness and agonies of war, and earnestly pray for peace, we yet deem a cessation of hostilities which leaves it unsettled whether treason is to be rebuked or petted and fondled, a delusion and a snare. If followed by attempts to bribe traitors to return to a nominal allegiance by the promise of surrendering to their vengeance two hundred thousand colored men, who are now bravely battling in our armies for Union and order, it would show such dastardly perfidy in our Government, as would call down on our nation the stern displeasure of a righteous God, and condemnation from all good men; such attempts would sound the knell of our Union, the shipwreck of our country.

3. That while we gratefully accord the meed of praise to Grant, Sherman, and their brave associates in command on the land, and to Farragut, Stringham, Porter, and the other noble commanders on the sea, for their valor and skill, we desire to place on record our admiration for and gratitude to the common soldiers and sailors, who, with little hope of distinction and fame, have cheerfully periled their lives for country and humanity. While so many are found ready to serve, as well as to be served, to follow as well as to lead, we will not despair of the Republic.

4. That while we recollect that it was not alone by the sword of Joshua, but also by the uplifted arm of Moses, that Israel prevailed over Amalek of old, we recognize the power of earnest, trustful prayer. Most reverently, therefore, will we continue to supplicate the God of Sabbaoth, that justice and equity may be done in our land; that anarchy and misrule may be checked; that righteousness may triumph, and peace speedily return; and that the Lord God may lift his face upon us and bless us.

YOUNG MENS' CHRISTIAN ASSOCIATIONS.

NATIONAL CONVENTION OF YOUNG MEN'S CHRISTIAN ASSOCIATIONS OF THE UNITED STATES AND THE BRITISH PROVINCES, 1863.

May—The body met in Chicago. Delegates were present from most of the Northern States, the District of Columbia, Canada and England. The Association was presided over by George H. Stuart, of Philadelphia, and passed the following resolutions:

Resolved, That we hereby reaffirm our unconditional loyalty to the Government of the United States, and our determination to afford every required and Christian aid for the suppression of the infamous rebellion.

Resolved, That we are gratified by the steps already taken by the Administration for the removal of the great sin of slavery—"the sum of all villanies"—and must express our candid conviction that the war will last so long as its cause morally exists, and that when we as a nation do *fully* right, God will not delay to give success to our arms.

Resolved, That it is no time to confound liberty with lawlessness. We cherish the dearest boon of freedom with jealous vigilanee, but remember that true freedom can only continue under restraints, and exist at all as guarded by law.

Resolved, That neither is this a time for doubtful, timid measures. The counsels of time-serving, self-seeking, inconsistent politicians are not to be heeded; but the loud voice of the loyal people, the heroic demands of our teeming volunteers, and the vigorous measures of unselfish and uncompromising generals are to be respected by those who rule over us.

Resolved, That we remember with honest gratitude the noble and immense work accomplished by the Young Men's Christian Association of our land, and the sanitary and spiritual fields opened up by the providence of God for our willing hearts and hands, and pledge that we will continue to pray for our army and navy and to meet their wants in the future with greater fidelity, if possible.

THE AMERICAN BOARD OF FOREIGN MISSIONS.

October, 1864—At the recent meeting of the Board in Worcester, Massachusetts, Rev. Albert Barnes was, by unanimous vote, granted leave to present a series of important resolutions without the reference of the same to a special committee. The preamble and resolutions are as following:

Whereas this Board is called upon to conduct its operations at an important crisis of our country, the result of which must materially affect the missionary cause in time to come; and

Whereas this Board has on former occasions expressed its sense of the system of slavery in our country, which lies at the foundation of the present effort to overcome our civil institutions and to establish a separate government in our land; and

Whereas the missionaries of this Board have with entire unanimity expressed their interest in the cause of the country in its endeavors to maintain the Government, and have freely given their sons to the defence of the nation in its present crisis; therefore

Resolved, 1st. That this Board receives with affectionate sympathy these expressions of the interest thus manifested by those in its service, and the sacrifices thus made.

Resolved, 2d. That in connection with the purpose to spread the Gospel through the world, the results of the contest on the cause of missions, and in view of diffusing a religion that will be everywhere adapted to sustain just civil government and the principles of liberty, and that shall tend to deliver the world from the oppression of slavery, as well as in the relation of its members to the Government of this land, and their duty to sustain that Government,—this Board expresses its hearty sympathy in the efforts to suppress the rebellion, and gratefully acknowledges the divine interposition in the successes which have attended the arms of the nation, as an indication that we shall again be one people, united under one glorious Constitution, united in our efforts to spread the Gospel around the world.

The resolutions were seconded by Rev. Dr. Brainerd, of Philadelphia, and unanimously adopted, the audience rising *en masse* and spontaneously singing

My country, 'tis of thee,
Sweet land of liberty, &c.

UNITED PRESBYTERIAN.

The following arrived too late for insertion in their proper place, page 474:

GENERAL ASSEMBLY OF THE UNITED PRESBYTERIAN CHURCH, 1863.

May 27—The body met in Xenia, Ohio.

June 4—The report of the special Committee on the "freedmen of our Southern States"—Revs. G. C. Vincent, J. B. Johnston, John Van Eaton, and Elders William Walker and D. Mitchell—was adopted, as follows:

That in the interests of the United Presbyterian Church a Board be created for this special purpose, and that the following Constitution be adopted with a view to secure the objects contemplated:—

CONSTITUTION OF THE BOARD OF MISSIONS FOR THE FREEDMEN OF THE SOUTH.

I. There shall be a Board of Missions for the Freedmen, to be appointed by and amenable to the Assembly.

II. It shall consist of nine members, who shall hold their office three years, and five of whom shall constitute a quorum. Of those first chosen three shall go out of office annually in the order of their names; and thereafter three shall annually be elected by the Assembly.

III. The Board shall be located in the City of Allegheny.

IV. The Board shall meet quarterly, and as much oftener as necessary; and shall hold its first meeting on the 4th of July, 1863, at ten o'clock, A. M., in the Second Church.

V. The Board shall have power to fill any vacancies occurring therein during the year, and shall be styled, "The Board of Missions of the United Presbyterian Church of North America, for the Freedmen of our Southern States."

VI. To this Board shall be intrusted, with such directions and instructions as may from time to time be given by the Assembly, the superintendence of the Freedmen Missionary operations of the Church.

VII. The Board shall make to the Assembly an annual report of its proceedings, its condition, and its needs, and shall submit for approval such plans and measures as may be deemed necessary or useful.

VIII. To the board shall belong the duty, though not the exclusive right, of nominating and appointing Missionaries and Agents, and of designating fields of labor: to them shall belong the duty of receiving the reports of the Corresponding Secretary; of giving him needful directions in reference to all matters of business and correspondence intrusted to him; of preparing for the Assembly estimates of all appropriations and expenditures of money; and of taking the particular direction and oversight of the Freedmen's missionary work, subject to the revision and control of the Assembly.

IX. All property, houses, lands, tenements, and permanent funds belonging to the Board, shall be taken in the name of the Trustees of the Assembly, and held in trust by them for the use and benefit of "The Board of Missions of the United Presbyterian Church of North America for the Freedmen of the South."

X. The Board shall have power to enact its own By-Laws.

XI. This Constitution shall not be changed, unless by a vote of two-thirds of the General Assembly present at any of its sessions, of which notice shall be given at least one day previously.

XII. The Board shall submit an abstract of its condition, proceedings, wants, and plans, to the several Synods of the Church at their annual meetings.

As some Presbyteries have already taken action upon this subject, and have agencies on the field, your committee recommend the following resolutions:

Resolved, 1. That the doings of the Presbyteries of Wheeling, Muskingum, Chartiers, and 1st Presbytery of Ohio, be recognized and approved, and after the organization of this Board it shall be the duty of these agencies to report their doings and resources to said Board.

Resolved, 2. That such Presbyteries as may prefer it are hereby authorized to select their own mission field, procure their own laborers, and conduct their missions in their own way, provided that they report to the Board the location of their respective fields, the laborers employed and the amount of funds collected and disbursed.

Your committee would recommend the following persons as members of the Board of Missions to the Freedmen of the South:

Revs. J. B. Clark, Charles A. Dickey, J. W. Baine, J. G. Barnes, W. J. Reid, G. C. Vincent, and Messrs. John Dean, James Robb and James Mitchell, with power to fill vacancies.

GENERAL ASSEMBLY OF THE UNITED PRESBYTERIAN CHURCH, 1864.

May 25—The body met in Philadelphia.

June 2—The following report of the Committee on Bills and Overtures—Revs. S. Wilson, D. D., S. Wallace, William Davidson, Wm. M. McElwee, D. D., and Elders Jno. Dean, H. Warnock, Thomas McAlister—was adopted:

The Committee on Bills and Overtures beg leave to report on three papers submitted to them by the Assembly; the first from G. D. Henderson and S. Collins; the 2d from S. Wilson and A. M. Elliott; and the 3d from S. Livingston and W. M. McElwee, as follows:

I. The paper of G. D. Henderson and S. Collins asks for the appointment of a committee to prepare an address to President Lincoln, Secretary Stanton, and Lieut. General Grant, embodying the following items:—

1st. An assurance of the deep sympathy and earnest co-operation of this Assembly and of the people whom we represent, with the Government in its present trials and worthy efforts to maintain the principles on which it is based.

2d. The great satisfaction we have enjoyed in observing their recognition of the facts—"that God alone can organize victory," "that we need the Divine favor," and that we are warranted to expect this favor only in the way of a dutiful regard to His will as Governor among the nations.

3d. An assurance that we gladly recognize this favor in the successes which have attended the movements of our armies on the Potomac and in Georgia, and that it is only in the continuance of this favor that we can hope for final success.

That an address of the nature contemplated in the paper of these brethren should go forth from this Assembly, it appears to your Committee, is highly proper. We therefore recommend for adoption the following resolution, viz:

Resolved, That a Committee be appointed to prepare, at their earliest convenience, an address such as the paper of these brethren contemplates, and forward it to President Lincoln and his Cabinet.

II. The paper of S. Wilson and A. M. Elliott asks that a Committee be appointed to report whether any, and if so, what advice should be tendered by this Assembly to our National Executive, touching the *morality of retaliation* as a means of preventing the continuance of the cruelty and barbarity which has been practiced upon our soldiers by our rebel enemies. As this paper was presented under the impression that President Lincoln was *hesitating* on the question of retaliation, your Committee think no action is needed in the premises by this Assembly, as we have been informed that the President has already decided the course to be pursued by him, and that retaliation is being already practised to some extent by the Union army. We therefore recommend that this paper be dismissed.

III. The paper of S. Livingston and W. M. McElwee asks for the adoption of the following resolution:

That this Assembly hails the Emancipation Proclamation of President Lincoln as a measure of high military importance and necessity, and statesmanlike in striking at slavery, the root, cause, and strength of the rebellion, and that we recognize in it the voice of God speaking as he did to his ancient people Israel, saying by it to us, "Break every yoke and let the oppressed go free." The Committee present this resolution in another form, and recommend that in this amended form it be adopted, viz:

Resolved, That without expressing any judgment on the military importance and necessity, or the statesmanlike character of the Proclamation, we hail it as obedience to the voice of God, calling us, as he did his ancient people, Let the oppressed go free and break every yoke.

Action of Churches in the Insurrectionary States.

PRESBYTERIAN.

PRESBYTERIAN (OLD SCHOOL) SYNOD OF SOUTH CAROLINA, 1860.

December 3—Report of committee unanimously adopted, closing thus:

The Synod has no hesitation, therefore, in expressing the belief that the people of South Carolina are now solemnly called on to imitate their Revolutionary forefathers, and stand up for their rights. We have an humble and abiding confidence, that that God, whose truth we represent in this conflict, will be with us, and exhorting our churches and people to put their trust in God, and go forward in the solemn path of duty which his Providence opens before them, we, ministers and elders of the Presbyterian Church in South Carolina Synod assembled, would give them our benediction, and the assurance that we shall fervently and unceasingly implore for them the care and protection of Almighty God.

Several of the Presbyteries of the Old School Presbyterian Church in the Seceded States held their regular fall meetings in 1861, and, without exception, passed acts of separation from the General Assembly of the church, and appointed delegates to attend at Augusta, Georgia, on the 4th of December, for the purpose of forming a General Assembly of the Southern Confederacy portion of the denomination—which was done.

1861, July 24—The Presbytery of South Alabama met at Selma, and declared severed its ecclesiastical connection with the General Assembly of the United States, and recommended a meeting of a Confederate States Assembly at Memphis, on the 4th of the next December, suggesting, for a preliminary convention, if such be desired, Atlanta as the place and August 15th the time.

CHARLESTON (S. C.) PRESBYTERY, (OLD SCHOOL), 1861.

July 25—The body met in Columbia, when the following preamble and resolutions were unanimously adopted:

Whereas, The relations of the State of South Carolina, of ten other adjacent States, and of the people thereof, with the other States and people previously composing the United States of America, have been dissolved, and the former united in the separate and independent Government of the Confederate States of America, thereby making a separate and independent organization of the Church within the said Confederate States desirable and necessary, in order to the more faithful and successful fulfilment of its duty to its Divine Lord and Master; and whereas, the General Assembly of the Presbyterian Church in the United States of America, by the adoption of a paper known as Dr. Spring's Resolutions, ignoring the establishment of the Government of the Confederate States of America, and disregarding our rights, privileges, and duties as citizens thereof, enjoined our allegiance to, and support of, a Government foreign and hostile to our own, and required us not only to yield obedience to a political power which we, in common with our fellow-citizens of all classes and all churches, have disowned and rejected, but also to act as traitors and rebels against the rightful and legal authorities of the land in which we live; and whereas these resolutions of the General Assembly require us to continue united to a people who have violated the Constitution under which we were originally confederated, and broken the covenant entered into by their fathers and ours; and whereas, the said action of the General Assembly in the United States of America, demands of us and all members of the Presbyterian Church in the Confederate States, the approval and support of the wicked and cruel war now waged by the other States of the former United States of America against the States and people of the Confederate States, against our fellow-citizens, against our friends and neighbors, against our own households and ourselves; and whereas, we do most heartily, with the full approval of our consciences before our Lord God, unanimously approve the action of the States and people of the Confederate States of America; therefore,

Be it resolved by the Charleston Presbytery,

1. That the ecclesiastical relations heretofore subsisting between this Presbytery and the Presbyterian Church of the United States of America are dissolved; that we do not recognize the right or authority of the General Assembly to adopt the resolutions above referred to; and that we disown and repudiate those resolutions, both in their letter and their spirit, as having no authority over us, and as entitled to no respect or consideration from us.

2. That in the judgment of this Presbytery, it is expedient and necessary that the Presbyterian Churches in the Confederate States should formally separate themselves from the Presbyterian Church in the United States, and establish a separate and independent ecclesiastical organization.

3. That this Presbytery heartily approves of holding a Convention of all the Presbyteries in the Confederate States, for the purpose of considering this whole matter securing the united and harmonious action of the whole Church, and devising and recommending such measures as may be necessary fully to organize the Church in the Confederate States.

4. That this Presbytery will proceed to appoint two ministers and two ruling elders, with alternates, to attend such Convention, who shall be authorized to advise and act with similar delegates appointed by other Presbyteries in the Confederate States, as in their judgment may seem best; the action of said delegates and of the Convention to be submitted to this Presbytery for its action thereon.

5. That this Presbytery prefers Atlanta, Ga., as the place, and the 15th of August next as the time, for the meeting of the proposed Convention, but that our delegate be authorized and instructed to meet at any time or place that may be agreed on by the majority of the Presbyteries appointing similar delegates, previous to the next stated meeting of this Presbytery.

JOHN DOUGLAS,
Stated Clerk.

GENERAL ASSEMBLY OF THE PRESBYTERIAN CHURCH IN THE CONFEDERATE STATES, 1861.

December 4—The body met in Augusta, Georgia—35 ministers and 38 elders present.

Same day—A Committee consisting of James H. Thornwell, D. D., Theodoric Pryor, D. D., C. C. Jones, D. D., R. B. White, D. D., W. D.

Moore, D. D., J. H. Gillespie, J. I. Boozer, R. W. Bailey, D. D., and Frederick K. Nash, *Ministers;* J. D. Armstrong, Charles Phillips, Joseph A. Brooks, W. P. Finley, Samuel McCorkle, William P. Webb, William L. Black, T. L. Dunlap, and E. W. Wright, *Ruling Elders*—was appointed to prepare an Address "setting forth the causes of our separation from the churches in the United States, our attitude in relation to SLAVERY, and a general view of the policy, which, as a Church, we propose to pursue." Subsequently the Committee reported the following Address, which was unanimously adopted:

The General Assembly of the Presbyterian Church in the Confederate States of America, to all the Churches of Jesus Christ throughout the earth, greeting: Grace, mercy, and peace be multiplied unto you!

DEARLY BELOVED BRETHREN: It is probably known to you that the Presbyteries and Synods in the Confederate States, which were formerly in connection with the General Assembly of the Presbyterian Church in the United States of America, have renounced the jurisdiction of that body; and dissolved the ties which bound them ecclesiastically with their brethren of the North. This act of separation left them without any formal union among themselves. But as they were one in faith and order, and still adhered to their old standards, measures were promptly adopted for giving expression to their unity, by the organization of a Supreme Court, upon the model of the one whose authority they had just relinquished. Commissioners, duly appointed, from all the Presbyteries of these Confederate States, met accordingly, in the city of Augusta, on the fourth day of December, in the year of our Lord one thousand eight hundred and sixty-one, and then and there proceeded to constitute the General Assembly of the Presbyterian Church in the Confederate States of America. The Constitution of the Presbyterian Church in the United States—that is to say, the Westminster Confession of Faith, the Larger and Shorter Catechisms, the Form of Government, the Book of Discipline, and the Directory for Worship—were unanimously and solemnly declared to be the Constitution of the Church in the Confederate States, with no other change than the substitution of "Confederate" for "United" wherever the country is mentioned in the standards. The Church, therefore, in these seceded States, presents now the spectacle of a separate, and independent, and complete organization, under the style and title of the Presbyterian Church in the Confederate States of America. In thus taking its place among sister churches of this and other countries, it seems proper that it should set forth the causes which have impelled it to separate from the Church of the North, and to indicate a general view of the course which it feels it incumbent upon it to pursue in the new circumstances in which it is placed.

We should be sorry to be regarded by our brethren in any part of the world as guilty of schism. We are not conscious of any purpose to rend the body of Christ. On the contrary, our aim has been to promote the unity of the Spirit in the bonds of peace. If we know our own hearts, and can form any just estimate of the motives which have governed us, we have been prompted by a sincere desire to promote the glory of God, and the efficiency, energy, harmony, and zeal of his visible kingdom in the earth. We have separated from our brethren of the North as Abraham separated from Lot—because we are persuaded that the interests of true religion will be more effectually subserved by two independent Churches, under the circumstances in which the two countries are placed, than by one united body:

1. In the first place, the course of the last Assembly, at Philadelphia, conclusively shows that if we should remain together, the political questions which divide us as citizens, will be obtruded on our Church Courts, and discussed by Christian ministers and elders with all the acrimony, bitterness, and rancor, with which such questions are usually discussed by men of the world. Our Assembly would present a mournful spectacle of strife and debate. Commissioners from the Northern would meet with Commissioners from the Southern Confederacy, to wrangle over the questions which have split them into two confederacies, and involved them in furious and bloody war. They would denounce each other, on the one hand, as tyrants and oppressors, and on the other, as traitors and rebels. The Spirit of God would take his departure from these scenes of confusion, and leave the Church lifeless and powerless, an easy prey to the sectional divisions and angry passions of its members. Two nations, under any circumstances, except those of perfect homogeneousness, cannot be united in one Church, without the rigid exclusion of all civil and secular questions from its halls. Where the countries differ in their customs and institutions, and view each other with an eye of jealousy and rivalry, if national feelings are permitted to enter the Church Courts, there must be an end of harmony and peace. The prejudices of the man and the citizen will prove stronger than the charity of the Christian. When they have allowed themselves to denounce each other for their national peculiarities, it will be hard to join in cordial fellowship as members of the same spiritual family. Much more must this be the case where the nations are not simply rivals, but enemies—when they hate each other with a cruel hatred—when they are engaged in a ferocious and bloody war, and when the worst passions of human nature are stirred to their very depths. An Assembly composed of representatives from two such countries, could have no security for peace except in a steady, uncompromising adherence to the Scriptural principle, that it would know no man after the flesh; that it would abolish the distinctions of Barbarian, Scythian, bond and free, and recognize nothing but the new creature in Christ Jesus. The moment it permits itself to know the Confederate or the United States, the moment its members meet as citizens of these countries, our political differences will be transferred to the house of God, and the passions of the forum will expel the spirit of holy love and of Christian communion.

We cannot condemn a man, in one breath, as unfaithful to the most solemn earthly interests—his country and his race—and commend him in the next as a loyal and faithful servant of his God. If we distrust his patriotism, our confidence is apt to be very measured in his piety. The old adage will hold here as in other things, *falsus in uno, falsus in omnibus*.

The only conceivable condition, therefore, upon which the Church of the North and the South could remain together as one body, with any prospect of success, is the rigorous exclusion of the questions and passions of the forum from its halls of debate. This is what always ought to be done. The provinces of Church and State are perfectly distinct, and the one has no right to usurp the jurisdiction of the other. The State is a natural institute, founded in the constitution of man as moral and social, and designed to realize the idea of justice. It is the society of rights. The Church is a supernatural institute, founded in the facts of redemption, and is designed to realize the idea of grace. It is the society of the redeemed. The State aims at social order, the Church at spiritual holiness. The State looks to the visible and outward, the Church is concerned for the invisible and inward. The badge of the State's authority is the sword, by which it becomes a terror to evil doers, and a praise to them that do well. The badge of the Church's authority is the keys, by which it opens and shuts the Kingdom of Heaven, according as men are believing or impenitent. The power of the Church is exclusively spiritual, that of the State includes the exercise of force. The Constitution of the Church is a Divine revelation—the Constitution of the State must be determined by human reason and the course of Providential events. The Church has no right to construct or modify a government for the State, and the State has no right to frame a creed or polity for the Church. They are as planets moving in different orbits, and unless each is confined to its own track, the consequences may be as disastrous in the moral world as the collision of different spheres in the world of matter. It is true that there is a point at which their respective jurisdictions seem to meet—in the idea of duty. But even duty is viewed by each in very different lights. The Church enjoins it as obedience to God, and the State enforces it as the safeguard of order. But there can be no collision, unless one or the other blunders as to the things that are materially right. When the State makes wicked laws, contradicting the eternal principles of rectitude, the Church is at liberty to testify against them, and humbly to petition that they may be repealed. In like manner, if the Church becomes seditious and a disturber of the peace, the State has a right to abate the nuisance. In ordinary cases, however, there is not likely to be a collision. Among a Christian people, there is little difference of opinion as to the radical distinctions of right and wrong. The only serious danger is where moral duty is conditioned upon a political question. Under the pretext of inculcating duty, the Church may usurp the power to determine the question which conditions it, and that is precisely what she is debarred from doing. The condition must be given. She must accept it from the State, and then her own course is clear. If Cæsar is your master, then pay tribute to him; but whether the "if" holds, whether Cæsar is your master or not, whether he ever had any just authority, whether he now retains it, or has forfeited it, these are points which the Church has no commission to adjudicate.

Had these principles been steadily maintained by the

Assembly at Philadelphia, it is possible that the ecclesiastical separation of the North and the South might have been deferred for years to come. Our Presbyteries, many of them, clung with tenderness to the recollections of the past. Sacred memories gathered around that venerable Church which had breasted many a storm and trained our fathers for glory. It had always been distinguished for its conservative influence, and many fondly hoped that, even in the present emergency, it would raise its placid and serene head above the tumults of popular passion, and bid defiance to the angry billows which rolled at its feet. We expected it to bow in reverence only at the name of Jesus. Many dreamed that it would utterly refuse to know either Confederates or Federalists, and utterly refuse to give any authoritative degree without a "Thus saith the Lord." It was ardently desired that the sublime spectacle might be presented of one Church upon earth combining in cordial fellowship and in holy love—the disciples of Jesus in different and even hostile lands. But, alas! for the weakness of man, these golden visions were soon dispelled. The first thing which roused our Presbyteries to look the question of separation seriously in the face, was the course of the Assembly in venturing to determine, as a Court of Jesus Christ, which it did by necessary implication, the true interpretation of the Constitution of the United States as to the kind of government it intended to form. A political theory was, to all intents and purposes, propounded, which made secession a crime, the seceding States rebellious, and the citizens who obeyed them traitors. We say nothing here as to the righteousness or unrighteousness of these decrees. What we maintain is, that, whether right or wrong, the Church had no right to make them—she transcended her sphere, and usurped the duties of the State. The discussion of these questions, we are sorry to add, was in the spirit and temper of partizan declaimers. The Assembly, driven from its ancient moorings, was tossed to and fro by the waves of popular passion. Like Pilate, it obeyed the clamor of the multitude, and though acting in the name of Jesus, it kissed the sceptre and bowed the knee to the mandates of Northern phrenzy. The Church was converted into the forum, and the Assembly was henceforward to become the arena of sectional divisions and national animosities.

We frankly admit that the mere unconstitutionality of the proceedings of the last Assembly is not, in itself considered, a sufficient ground of separation. It is the consequences of these proceedings which make them so offensive. It is the door which they open for the introduction of the worst passions of human nature into the deliberations of Church Courts. The spirit of these proceedings, if allowed to prevail, would forever banish peace from the Church, and there is no reason to hope that the tide which has begun to flow can soon be arrested. The two Confederacies hate each more intensely now than they did in May, and if their citizens should come together upon the same floor, whatever might be the errand that brought them there, they could not be restrained from smiting each other with the fist of wickedness. For the sake of peace, therefore, for Christian charity, for the honor of the Church, and for the glory of God, we have been constrained, as much as in us lies, to remove all occasion of offence. We have quietly separated, and we are grateful to God that, while leaving for the sake of peace, we leave it with the humble consciousness that we, ourselves, have never given occasion to break the peace. We have never confounded Cæsar and Christ, and we have never mixed the issues of this world with the weighty matters that properly belong to us as citizens of the Kingdom of God.

2. Though the immediate occasion of separation was the course of the General Assembly at Philadelphia in relation to the Federal Government and the war, yet there is another ground on which the independent organization of the Southern Church can be amply and scripturally maintained. The unity of the Church does not require a formal bond of union among all the congregations of believers throughout the earth. It does not demand a vast imperial monarchy like that of Rome, nor a strictly universal council, like that to which the complete development of Presbyterianism would naturally give rise. The Church Catholic is one in Christ, but it is not necessarily one visible, all-absorbing organization upon earth. There is no schism where there is no breach of charity.

Churches may be perfectly at one in every principle of faith and order, and yet geographically distinct, and mutually independent. As the unity of the human race is not disturbed by its division into countries and nations, so the unity of the spiritual seed of Christ is neither broken nor impaired by separation and division into various Church constitutions. Accordingly, in the Protestant countries, Church organizations have followed national lines. The Calvinistic Churches of Switzerland are distinct from the Reformed Church of France. The Presbyterians of Ireland belong to a different Church from the Presbyterians of Scotland, and the Presbyterians of this country constitute a Church, in like manner, distinct from all other Churches on the globe. That the division into national Churches, that is, Churches bounded by national lines, is, in the present condition of human nature, a benefit, seems to us too obvious for proof. It realizes to the Church Catholic all the advantages of a division of labor. It makes a Church organization homogeneous and compact—it stimulates holy rivalry and zeal—it removes all grounds of suspicion and jealousy on the part of the State. What is lost in expansion is gained in energy. The Church Catholic, as thus divided, and yet spiritually one, divided, but not rent, is a beautiful illustration of the great philosophical principle which pervades all nature—the co-existence of the one with the many.

If it is desirable that each nation should contain a separate and an independent Church, the Presbyteries of these Confederate States need no apology for bowing to the decree of Providence, which, in withdrawing their country from the government of the United States, has, at the same time, determined that they should withdraw from the Church of their fathers. It is not that they have ceased to love it—not that they have abjured its ancient principles, or forgotten its glorious history. It is to give these same principles a richer, freer, fuller development among ourselves than they possibly could receive under foreign culture. It is precisely because we love that Church as it was, and that Church as it should be, that we have resolved, as far as in us lies, to realize its grand idea in the country, and under the Government where God has cast our lot. With the supreme control of ecclesiastical affairs in our hands, we may be able, in some competent measure, to consummate this result. In subjection to a foreign power, we could no more accomplish it than the Church in the United States could have been developed in dependence upon the Presbyterian Church of Scotland. The difficulty there would have been, not the distance of Edinburgh from New York, Philadelphia, or Charleston, but the difference in the manners, habits, customs, and ways of thinking, the social, civil, and political institutions of the people. These same difficulties exist in relation to the Confederate and United States, and render it eminently proper that the Church in each should be as separate and independent as the Governments.

In addition to this, there is one difference which so radically and fundamentally distinguishes the North and the South, that it is becoming every day more and more apparent that the religious, as well as the secular, interests of both will be more effectually promoted by a complete and lasting separation. The antagonism of Northern and Southern sentiment on the subject of slavery lies at the root of all the difficulties which have resulted in the dismemberment of the Federal Union, and involved us in the horrors of an unnatural war. The Presbyterian Church in the United States has been enabled by Divine grace to pursue, for the most part, an eminently conservative, because a thoroughly scriptural, policy in relation to this delicate question. It has planted itself upon the Word of God, and utterly refused to make slaveholding a sin, or non-slaveholding a term of communion. But though both sections are agreed as to this general principle, it is not to be disguised that the North exercises a deep and settled antipathy to slavery itself, while the South is equally zealous in its defence. Recent events can have no other effect than to confirm the antipathy on the one hand and strengthen the attachment on the other. The Northern section of the Church stands in the awkward predicament of maintaining, in one breath, that slavery is an evil which ought to be abolished, and of asserting in the next, that it is not a sin to be visited by exclusion from communion of the saints. The consequence is, that it plays partly into the hands of abolitionists and partly into the hands of slaveholders, and weakens its influence with both. It occupies the position of a prevaricating witness whom neither party will trust. It would be better, therefore, for the moral power of the Northern section of the Church to get entirely quit of the subject. At the same time, it is intuitively obvious that the Southern section of the Church, while even partially under the control of those who are hostile to slavery, can never have free and unimpeded access to the slave population. Its ministers and elders will always be liable to some degree of suspicion. In the present circumstances, Northern alliance would be absolutely fatal. It would utterly preclude the Church from a wide and commanding field of usefulness. This is too dear a price to be paid for a nominal union. We cannot afford to give up these millions of souls and consign them, so far as our efforts are concerned, to hopeless perdition, for the sake of preserving an outward unity which, after all, is an empty shadow. If we would gird ourselves heartily and in earnest, for the work which God has set before us, we must have the control of our ecclesiastical affairs, and declare ourselves separate and independent.

And here we may venture to lay before the Christian

world our views as a Church, upon the subject of slavery. We beg a candid hearing.

In the first place, we would have it distinctly understood that, in our ecclesiastical capacity, we are neither the friends nor the foes of slavery; that is to say, we have no commission either to propagate or abolish it. The policy of its existence or non-existence is a question which exclusively belongs to the State. We have no right, as a Church, to enjoin it as a duty, or to condemn it as a sin. Our business is with the duties which spring from the relation; the duties of the masters on the one hand, and of their slaves on the other. These duties we are to proclaim and enforce with spiritual sanctions. The social, civil, political problems connected with this great subject transcend our sphere, as God has not entrusted to His Church the organization of society, the construction of Government, nor the allotment of individuals to their various stations. The Church has as much right to preach to the monarchies of Europe, and the despotism of Asia, the doctrines of republican equality, as to preach to the Governments of the South the extirpation of slavery. This position is impregnable, unless it can be shown that slavery is a sin. Upon every other hypothesis, it is so clearly a question for the State, that the proposition would never for a moment have been doubted, had there not been a foregone conclusion in relation to its moral character. Is slavery, then, a sin?

In answering this question, as a Church, let it be distinctly borne in mind that the only rule of judgment is the written word of God. The Church knows nothing of the intuitions of reason or the deductions of philosophy, except those reproduced in the Sacred Canon. She has a positive constitution in the Holy Scriptures, and has no right to utter a single syllable upon any subject, except as the Lord puts words in her mouth. She is founded, in other words, upon express *revelation*. Her creed is an authoritative testimony of God, and not a speculation, and what she proclaims, she must proclaim with the infallible certitude of faith, and not with the hesitating assent of an opinion. The question, then, is brought within a narrow compass: Do the Scriptures directly or indirectly condemn slavery as a sin? If they do not, the dispute is ended, for the Church, without forfeiting her character, dares not go beyond them.

Now, we venture to assert that if men had drawn their conclusions upon this subject only from the Bible, it would no more have entered into any human head to denounce slavery as a sin, than to denounce monarchy, aristocracy, or poverty. The truth is, men have listened to what they falsely considered as primitive intuitions, or as necessary deductions from primitive cognitions, and then have gone to the Bible to confirm the crotchets of their vain philosophy. They have gone there determined to find a particular result, and the consequence is, that they leave with having made, instead of having interpreted, Scripture. Slavery is no new thing. It has not only existed for ages in the world, but it has existed, under every dispensation of the covenant of grace, in the Church of God. Indeed, the first organization of the Church as a visible society, separate and distinct from the unbelieving world, was inaugurated in the family of a slaveholder. Among the very first persons to whom the seal of circumcision was affixed, were the slaves of the father of the faithful, some born in his house, and others bought with his money. Slavery again re-appears under the Law. God sanctions it in the first table of the Decalogue, and Moses treats it as an institution to be regulated, not abolished; legitimated, and not condemned. We come down to the age of the New Testament, and we find it again in the Churches founded by the Apostles under the plenary inspiration of the Holy Ghost. These facts are utterly amazing, if slavery is the enormous sin which its enemies represent it to be. It will not do to say that the Scriptures have treated it only in a general, incidental way, without any clear implication as to its moral character. Moses surely made it the subject of express and positive legislation, and the Apostles are equally explicit in inculcating the duties which spring from both sides of the relation. They treat slaves as bound to obey and inculcate obedience as an office of religion—a thing wholly self-contradictory, if the authority exercised over them were unlawful and iniquitous.

But what puts this subject in a still clearer light is the manner in which it is sought to extort from the Scriptures a contrary testimony. The notion of direct and explicit condemnation is given up. The attempt is to show that the genius and spirit of Christianity are opposed to it—that its great cardinal principles of virtue are utterly against it. Much stress is laid upon the Golden Rule and upon the general denunciations of tyranny and oppression. To all this we reply, that no principle is clearer than that a case positively excepted cannot be included under a general rule. Let us concede, for a moment, that the laws of love, and the condemnation of tyranny and oppression, seem logically to involve, as a result, the condemnation of slavery; yet, if slavery is afterwards expressly mentioned and treated as a lawful relation, it obviously follows, unless Scripture is to be interpreted as inconsistent with itself, that slavery is, by necessary implication, excepted. The Jewish law forbade, as a general rule, the marriage of a man with his brother's wife. The same law expressly enjoined the same marriage in a given case. The given case was, therefore, an exception, and not to be treated as a violation of the general rule. The law of love has always been the law of God.* It was enunciated by Moses almost as clearly as it was enunciated by Jesus Christ Yet, notwithstanding this law, Moses and the Apostles alike sanctioned the relation of slavery. The conclusion is inevitable, either that the law is not opposed to it, or that slavery is an excepted case.

To say that the prohibition of tyranny and oppression includes slavery, is to beg the whole question. Tyranny and oppression involve either the unjust usurpation or the unlawful exercise of power. It is the unlawfulness, either in its principle or measure, which constitutes the core of the sin. Slavery must, therefore, be proved to be unlawful, before it can be referred to any such category. The master may, indeed, abuse his power, but he oppresses not simply as a master, but as a wicked master.

But, apart from all this, the law of love is simply the inculcation of universal equity. It implies nothing as to the existence of various ranks and gradations in society. The interpretation which makes it repudiate slavery would make it equally repudiate all social, civil, and political inequalities. Its meaning is, not that we should conform ourselves to the arbitrary expectations of others, but that we should render unto them precisely the same measure which, if we were in their circumstance, it would be reasonable and just in us to demand at their hands. It condemns slavery, therefore, only upon the supposition that slavery is a sinful relation—that is, he who extracts the prohibition of slavery from the Golden Rule, begs the very point in dispute.

We cannot prosecute the argument in detail, but we have said enough, we think, to vindicate the position of the Southern Church. We have assumed no new attitude We stand exactly where the Church of God has always stood—from Abraham to Moses, from Moses to Christ, from Christ to the Reformers, and from the Reformers to ourselves. We stand upon the foundation of the Prophets and Apostles, Jesus Christ himself being the chief cornerstone. Shall we be excluded from the fellowship of our brethren in other lands, because we dare not depart from the charter of our faith? Shall we be branded with the stigma of reproach, because we cannot consent to corrupt the word of God to suit the intuitions of an infidel philosophy? Shall our names be cast out as evil, and the finger of scorn pointed at us, because we utterly refuse to break our communion with Abraham, Isaac, and Jacob, with Moses, David, and Isaiah, with Apostles, Prophets, and Martyrs, with all the noble army of confessors who have gone to glory from slave-holding countries and from a slave-holding Church, without ever having dreamed that they were living in mortal sin, by conniving at slavery in the midst of them? If so, we shall take consolation in the cheering consciousness that the Master has accepted us. We may be denounced, despised, and cast out of the synagogues of our brethren. But while they are wrangling about the distinctions of men according to the flesh, we shall go forward in our Divine work, and confidently anticipate that, in the great day, as the consequence of our humble labors, we shall meet millions of glorified spirits, who have come up from the bondage of earth to a nobler freedom than human philosophy ever dreamed of. Others, if they please, may spend their time in declaiming on the tyranny of earthly masters; it will be our aim to resist the real tyrants which oppress the soul—Sin and Satan. These are the foes against whom we shall find it employment enough to wage a successful war. And to this holy war it is the purpose of our Church to devote itself with redoubled energy. We feel that the souls of our slaves are a solemn trust, and we shall strive to present them faultless and complete before the presence of God.

Indeed, as we contemplate their condition in the Southern States, and contrast it with that of their fathers before them, and that of their brethren in the present day in their native land, we cannot but accept it as a gracious Providence that they have been brought in such numbers to our shores, and redeemed from the bondage of barbarism and sin. Slavery to them has certainly been overruled for the greatest good. It has been a link in the wondrous chain of Providence, through which many sons and daughters have been made heirs of the heavenly inheritance. The Providential result is, of course, no justification, if the thing is intrinsically wrong; but it is certainly a matter of devout thanksgiving, and no obscure intimation of the will and purpose of God, and of the consequent duty of the Church. We cannot forbear to say, however, that the general operation of the system is kindly and benevolent;

it is a real and effective discipline, and without it, we are profoundly persuaded that the African race in the midst of us can never be elevated in the scale of being. As long as that race, in its comparative degradation, co-exists side by side, with the whites, bondage is its normal condition.

As to the endless declamation about human rights, we have only to say that human rights are not a fixed, but a fluctuating quantity. Their sum is not the same in any two nations on the globe. The rights of Englishmen are one thing, the rights of Frenchmen another. There is a minimum without which a man cannot be responsible; there is a maximum which expresses the highest degree of civilization and of Christian culture. The education of the species consists in its ascent along this line. As you go up, the number of rights increases, but the number of individuals who possess them diminishes. As you come down the line, rights are diminished, but the individuals are multiplied. It is just the opposite of the predicamental scale of the logicians. There comprehension diminishes as you ascend and extension increases, and comprehension increases as you descend and extension diminishes. Now, when it is said that slavery is inconsistent with human rights, we crave to understand what point in this line is the slave conceived to occupy. There are, no doubt, many rights which belong to other men—to Englishmen, to Frenchmen, to his master, for example—which are denied to him. But is he fit to possess them? Has God qualified him to meet the responsibilities which their possession necessarily implies? His place in the scale is determined by his competency to fulfil its duties. There are other rights which he certainly possesses, without which he could neither be human nor accountable. Before slavery can be charged with doing him injustice, it must be shown that the minimum which falls to his lot at the bottom of the line is out of proportion to his capacity and culture—a thing which can never be done by abstract speculation. The truth is, the education of the human race for liberty and virtue, is a vast Providential scheme, and God assigns to every man, by a wise and holy decree, the precise place he is to occupy in the great moral school of humanity. The scholars are distributed into classes, according to their competency and progress. For God is in history.

To avoid the suspicion of a conscious weakness of our cause, when contemplated from the side of pure speculation, we may advert for a moment to those pretended intuitions which stamp the reprobation of humanity upon this ancient and hoary institution. We admit that there are primitive principles in morals which lie at the root of human consciousness. But the question is, how are we to distinguish them? The subjective feeling of certainty is no adequate criterion, as that is equally felt in reference to crotchets and hereditary prejudices. The very point is to know when this certainty indicates a primitive cognition, and when it does not. There must, therefore, be some eternal test, and whatever cannot abide that test has no authority as a primary truth. That test is an inward necessity of thought, which, in all minds at the proper stage of maturity, is absolutely universal. Whatever is universal is natural. We are willing that slavery should be tried by this standard. We are willing to abide by the testimony of the race, and if man, as man, has everywhere condemned it—if all human laws have prohibited it as crime—if it stands in the same category with malice, murder, and theft; then we are willing, in the name of humanity, to renounce it, and to renounce it forever. But what if the overwhelming majority of mankind have approved it? what if philosophers and statesmen have justified it, and the laws of all nations acknowledged it? what then becomes of these luminous intuitions? They are an *ignis fatuus*, mistaken for a star.

We have now, brethren, in a brief compass, for the nature of this address admits only of an outline, opened to you our whole hearts upon this delicate and vexed subject. We have concealed nothing. We have sought to conciliate no sympathy by appeals to your charity. We have tried our cause by the word of God; and though protesting against its authority to judge in a question concerning the duty of the Church, we have not refused to appear at the tribunal of reason. Are we not right, in view of all the preceding considerations, in remitting the social, civil, and political problems connected with slavery to the State? Is it not a subject, save in the moral duties which spring from it, which lies beyond the province of the Church? Have we any right to make it an element in judging of Christian character? Are we not treading in the footsteps of the flock? Are we not acting as Christ and his Apostles have acted before us? Is it not enough for us to pray and labor, in our lot, that all men may be saved, without meddling as a Church with the technical distinction of their civil life. We leave the matter with you. We offer you the right hand of fellowship. It is for you to accept it or reject it. We have done our duty. We can do no more. Truth is more precious than union, and if you cast us out as sinners, the breach of charity is not with us, as long as we walk according to the light of the written word.

The ends which we propose to accomplish as a Church are the same as those which are proposed by every other Church. To proclaim God's truth as a witness to the nations; to gather his elect from the four corners of the earth, and through the Word, Ministers, and Ordinances, to train them for eternal life, is the great business of His people. The only thing that will be at all peculiar to us, is the manner in which we shall attempt to discharge our duty. In almost every department of labor, except the pastoral care of congregations, it has been usual for the Church to resort to societies more or less closely connected with itself, and yet, logically and really distinct. It is our purpose to rely upon the regular organs of our government, and executive agencies directly and immediately responsible to them. We wish to make the Church, not merely a superintendent, but an agent. We wish to develop the idea that the congregation of believers, as visibly organized, is the very society or corporation which is divinely called to do the work of the Lord. We shall, therefore, endeavor to do what has never yet been adequately done—bring out the energies of our Presbyterian system of government. From the Session to the Assembly we shall strive to enlist all our courts, as courts, in every department of Christian effort. We are not ashamed to confess that we are intensely Presbyterian. We embrace all other denominations in the arms of Christian fellowship and love, but our own scheme of government we humbly believe to be according to the pattern shown in the Mount, and, by God's grace, we propose to put its efficiency to the test.

Brethren, we have done. We have told you who we are, and what we are. We greet you in the ties of Christian brotherhood. We desire to cultivate peace and charity with all our fellow Christians throughout the world. We invite to ecclesiastical communion all who maintain our principles of faith and order. And now we commend you to God and the word of His grace. We devoutly pray that the whole Catholic Church may be afresh baptized with the Holy Ghost, and that she may speedily be stirred up to give the Lord no rest until he establish and make Jerusalem a praise in the earth.

[Signed,]
B. M. PALMER, *Moderator*,
JNO. N. WADDEL, *Stated Clerk*,
JOSEPH R. WILSON, *Permanent Clerk*,
D. McNEILL TURNER, *Temporary Clerk*.

Ministers.—John S. Wilson, Wm. Henry Foote, John H. Bocock, Samuel R. Houston, Francis McFarland, W. T. Richardson, Peyton Harrison, Theodoric Pryor, Samuel D. Stuart, James B. Ramsey, Drury Lacy, P. H. Dalton, Robert Hett Chapman, J. W. Elliott, R. B. McMullen, Shepard Wells, J. H. Lorance, John B. Adger, John S. Harris, J. Leighton Wilson, D. E. Frierson, J. H. Thornwell, A. W. Leland, J. E. Dubose, N. A. Pratt, G. W. Boggs, Robert B. White, A. B. McCorkle, John A. Smylie, James A. Lyon, J. Franklin Ford, W. C. Emerson, John Hunter, Richmond McInnis, W. D. Moore, J. H. Gillespie, W. N. Frierson, A. H. Caldwell, Thomas R. Welch, John I. Boozer, Cyrus Kingsbury, R. M. Loughridge, Rufus W. Bailey, Hillery Mosely, R. F. Bunting, Levi Tenney.

Ruling Elders.—James D. Armstrong, B. F. Renick, J. W. Gilkeson, J. L. Campbell, T. E. Perkinson, William F. C. Gregory, Samuel McCorkle, Jesse H. Lindsay, Charles Phillips, James H. Dickson, J. G. Shepherd, James G. Ramsey, William Murdock, Samuel B. McAdams, A. W. Putnam, Lewis B. Thornton, Thomas C. Perrin, Job Johnstone, R. S. Hope, J. S. Thompson, W. Perroneau Finley, John Bonner, William A. Forward, D. C. Houston, William P. Webb, James Montgomery, W. H. Simpson, William C. Black, David Hadden, H. H. Kimmons, J. T. Swayne, T. L. Dunlap, Edward W. Wright.

GENERAL ASSEMBLY OF 1862.

May 1—The body met in Montgomery, Alabama—31 ministers and 16 elders present.

The following is the Narrative on the State of Religion, reported by Rev. J. L. Girardeau, Chairman of the Committee:

It is but a few months since the first General Assembly of the Presbyterian Church in the Confederate States was organized, and our Zion was equipped for her great and distinctive work. We desire at this, our second meeting, to render devout thanksgiving to our Divine Lord and Head for the abundant favor which he has manifested to our Church in entering upon that new and solemn path of our duty to which his Providence has so clearly pointed her. Having, as she conceived, a Divine call to set up her banners as an independent organization, she has not been destitute of the Divine blessing in obeying it, and we trust will be yet more and more richly endowed for prosecuting as well the enterprises peculiarly entrusted to her as the general labors which are assigned to every church of the Redeemer.

We have to regret that in consequence of the distracted condition of the country, but few reports of our Presbyteries, touching the state of religion, have come up to us. All the Presbyteries which have reported, dwell upon the war in which we are now engaged, and its influence upon the religious interests of the Church. In the first place, we notice the relation of our congregations to the great struggle in which we are engaged. All the Presbyterial narratives, without exception, mention the fact that their congregations have evinced the most cordial sympathy with the people of the Confederate States in their efforts to maintain their cherished rights and institutions against the despotic power which is attempting to crush them. Deeply convinced that this struggle is not alone for civil rights, and property, and home, but also for religion, for the Church, for the gospel, and for existence itself, the churches in our connection have freely contributed to its prosecution of their substance, their prayers, and above all of their members and the beloved youth of their congregations. They have parted without a murmur with those who constitute the hope of the Church, and have bidden them go forth to the support of this great and sacred cause with their benedictions and with their supplications for their protection and success. The Assembly desire to record with its solemn approval this fact of the unanimity of our people in supporting a contest to which religion, as well as patriotism, now summons the citizens of this country, and to implore for them the blessing of God in the course which they are now pursuing. In this connection we would notice the fact that some of our ministers have entered the army as chaplains, and in the joint capacity of chaplains and soldiers, and are thus discharging a most important and useful office. One of these, a member of South Alabama Presbytery, is now a prisoner in the hands of the enemy; and another, Rev. Dabney Carr Harrison, a member of East Hanover Presbytery, a chaplain and an officer, fell mortally wounded at Fort Donelson, Tenn., while leading his men in one of the bloodiest battles fought in this war. His name will be embalmed in the hearts of his countrymen, and will be held in veneration by the Church of which he was an ornament. In the second place, the spiritual condition of the Church as affected by the war. In some Presbyteries a number of congregations have been disbanded, and their members driven from their homes as refugees, seeking an asylum among strangers. In other places prayer meetings are held, and in one or two Presbyteries, revivals of religion have been manifested. The different denominations of Christians have been drawn together by a common danger, and union prayer meetings have been abundant. In the third place, the efforts made to extend the kingdom of Christ have been preserved in some churches The collections for Foreign Missions and other objects of benevolence have been increased, and the Churches were about taking up the subject of Domestic Missions with vigor, when the assault of the enemy upon the city of New Orleans, and the consequent removal of the seat of operations of the Assembly's Committee, has delayed the prosecution of their plans. Nearly all the Presbyteries make special mention that religious instruction is faithfully imparted to the colored people. We cannot but rejoice in this intelligence. We have the motives to the discharge of a great missionary work, springing from the bosom of every family and the cabins of every plantation.

GENERAL ASSEMBLY OF 1864.

May 5—The body met in Charlotte, North Carolina—37 Ministers and 27 Elders present.

Reports made to the Assembly state that there are seven students at the Theological Seminary in Columbia, and one in Union Seminary, Virginia. Macon was fixed for the meeting of 1865.

UNION OF THE OLD AND NEW SCHOOL CHURCHES.

The Lynchburg *Virginian* of August, 1864. thus notices the meeting of the "United Synod of the Presbyterian Church:"

This body has been in session for several days in that city. But few ministers are present owing to the presence of the enemy in many portions of the South. The most important business executed by the body has been the consummation of the plan for uniting the two branches of the Church. The old and new schools are now one.

RELIGIOUS INSTRUCTION OF SLAVES.

In Harmony Presbytery, (S. C.,) October, 1863, a report of the Committee on the religious instruction of the colored people, written by Rev. J. Leighton Wilson, D. D., contains these recommendations:

1. That every Christian master should aim to have his negroes attend the same place of worship with himself. 2. That a small chapel should be erected on every plantation, where the black people might be assembled every Sabbath afternoon for religious worship, and where they may be taught hymns, portions of Scripture, and receive catechetical instruction. 3. That the servants of every plantation should be assembled at least once a day in the chapel for prayers. 4. That the household servants should be required to attend morning and evening prayers with the white family. 5. That some measures be adopted by Presbytery in regard to the baptism of children of believing colored parents. 6. That the Presbytery exert all the influence possible to render sacred and permanent the marriage relation between the colored people, and especially among the members of the Church.

AN EAST TENNESSEE CHURCH.

Rev. Dr. Vance's Church—Baker's Creek Church, Blount county, East Tennessee—never united with the Presbyterian Church South; and the session did not hold a regular meeting between September, 1861, and May 10, 1864. The Presbytery of Knoxville, at an adjourned meeting held at Pleasant Forrest Church, Knox county, on the Friday preceding the second Sabbath of September, 1861, passed resolutions announcing their withdrawal from the General Assembly in the United States, and recommended action for the immediate organization of a Southern Assembly. Rev. Dr. Vance and J. H. McConnell, the Ruling Elder of Baker's Creek Church, resisted this action; and declared their continued adherence to the old Assembly.

BAPTIST.

In November, 1860, the Alabama State Convention of Baptists unanimously passed a declaration, setting forth that the Union had "failed, in important particulars, to answer the purpose for which it was created." The declaration closed with the following announcement:

While, as yet, no particular mode of relief is before us on which to express an opinion, we are constrained, before separating to our several homes, to declare to our brethren and fellow-citizens, before mankind and before our God, that we hold ourselves subject to the call of proper authority in defence of the sovereignty and independence of the State of Alabama, and of her right, as a sovereignty, to withdraw from this Union, and to make any arrangement which her people, in constitutional assemblies, may deem best for securing their rights. And in this declaration *we heartily, deliberately, unanimously, and solemnly* UNITE.

GEORGIA BAPTIST CONVENTION, 1861.

April 29—The body met at Athens, and adopted, unanimously, these resolutions, which were transmitted to the "Confederate" Congress by Rev. H. M. Crawford:

Whereas the State Convention of Georgia, in the legitimate exercise of her sovereignty, has withdrawn from the Confederacy known as the United States of America, and, for the better maintenance of her rights, honor, and independence, has united with other States in a new Confederacy, under the title of the Confederate States of America; and whereas Abraham Lincoln is attempting, by force of arms, to subjugate these States, in violation of the fundamental principle of American liberty; therefore,

Resolved by the members of the Baptist Convention of the State of Georgia, That we consider it at once to be a pleasure and a duty to avow that both in feeling and principle, we approve, indorse, and support the Government of the Confederate States of America.

2. That while this Convention disclaims all authority, whether ecclesiastical or civil, yet as citizens we deem it a duty to urge the union of all the people of the South in defence of the Common Cause, and to express the confident belief that in whatever conflict the madness of Mr. Lincoln and his Government may force upon us, the Baptists of Georgia will not be behind any class of our fellow-citizens in maintaining the independence of the South by any sacrifice of treasure or of blood.

3. That we acknowledge with devout thanksgiving to Almighty God, the signal favor with which, up to this time, He has blessed our arms and our policy, and that the Baptist Churches of this State be requested to observe the first and second days of June next, as days of fasting and prayer, that God will deliver us from all the power of our enemies, and restore peace to our country.

4. That the Confederate Government be requested to invite the Churches of all denominations within the Confederacy to unite in observing said days of prayer and fasting.

5. That copies of these resolutions be sent to President Davis, the Confederate Congress, and the Governor of Georgia.

SOUTHERN BAPTIST CONVENTION, 1861.

May 13—The body met in Savannah; when the following report, said to have been drawn by Rev. Dr. R. Fuller, was unanimously adopted:

We hold this truth to be self-evident, that governments are established for the security, prosperity and happiness of the people. When, therefore, any government is perverted from its proper designs, becomes oppressive, and abuses its power, the people have a right to change it.

As to the States once combined upon this continent, it is now manifest that they can no longer live together as one confederacy.

The Union constituted by our forefathers was one of coequal sovereign States. The fanatical spirit of the North has long been seeking to deprive us of rights and franchises guaranteed by the Constitution; and after years of persistent aggression, they have at last accomplished their purpose.

In vindication of their sacred rights and honor, in self defence, and for the protection of all which is dear to man, the Southern States have practically asserted the right of seceding from a union so degenerated from that established by the Constitution, and they have formed for themselves a government based upon the principles of the original compact—adopting a charter which secures to each State its sovereign rights and privileges. This new government, in thus dissolving former political connections, seeks to cultivate relations of amity and good will, with its late confederates and with all the world; and they have thrice sent special commissioners to Washington with overtures of peace, and for a fair, amicable adjustment of all difficulties. The Government at Washington has insultingly repelled these proposals, and now insists upon letting loose hordes of armed soldiers to pillage and desolate the entire South, for the purpose of forcing the seceded States back into unnatural union, or of subjugating them and holding them as conquered provinces.

While the two sections of the land are thus arrayed against each other, it might naturally have been hoped that at least the churches of the North would interpose and protest against this appeal to the sword, this invoking of civil war, this deluging the country in fratricidal blood; but with astonishment and grief, we find churches and pastors of the North breathing out slaughter, and clamoring for sanguinary hostilities with a fierceness which we would have supposed impossible among the disciples of the Prince of Peace.

In view of such premises, this Convention cannot keep silence. Recognizing the necessity that the whole moral influence of the people, in whatever capacity or organization, should be enlisted in aid of the rulers who, by their suffrages, have been called to defend the endangered interests of person and property, of honor and liberty, it is bound to utter its voice distinctly, decidedly, emphatically; and your Committee recommend, therefore, the subjoined resolutions:

Resolved, That impartial history cannot charge upon the South the dissolution of the Union. She was foremost in advocating and cementing that Union. To that Union she clung through long years of calumny, injury, and insult. She has never ceased to raise her warning appeals against the fanaticism which has obstinately and incessantly warred against that Union.

2. That we most cordially approve of the formation of the government of the Confederate States of America, and admire and applaud the noble course of that government up to this present time.

3. That we shall assiduously invoke the Divine direction and favor in behalf of those who bear rule among us, that they may still exercise the same wise, prompt, elevated statesmanship which has hitherto characterized their measures; that their enterprises may be attended with success; and that they may attain a great reward, not only in seeing these Confederate States prosper under their administration, but in contributing to the progress of the transcendent kingdom of our Lord Jesus Christ.

4. That we most cordially tender to the President of the Confederate States, to his Cabinet, and the members of the Congress now convened at Montgomery, the assurances of our sympathy and entire confidence. With them are our hearts and our hearty co-operation.

5. That the lawless reign of terror at the North, the violence committed upon unoffending citizens, above all, the threats to wage upon the South a warfare of savage barbarity, to devastate our homes and hearths with hosts of ruffians and felons burning with lust and rapine, ought to excite the horror of all civilized people. God forbid that we should so far forget the spirit of Jesus as to suffer malice and vindictiveness to insinuate themselves into our hearts; but every principle of religion, of patriotism, and of humanity, calls upon us to pledge our fortunes and lives in the good work of repelling an invasion designed to destroy whatever is dear to our heroic traditions; whatever is sweet in our domestic hopes and enjoyments; whatever is essential to our institutions and our very manhood; whatever is worth living or dying for.

6. That we do now engage in prayer for our friends, brothers, fathers, sons, and citizen soldiers, who have left their homes to go forth for the defence of their families and friends and all which is dearest to the human heart; and we recommend to the churches represented in this body, that they constantly invoke a holy and merciful God to guard them from the temptations to which they are exposed, to cover their head in the day of battle, and to give victory to their arms.

7. That we will pray for our enemies in the spirit of that Divine Master, who "when He was reviled, He reviled not again," trusting that their pitiless purposes, may be frustrated, that God will grant to them a more politic, a more considerate, and a more Christian mind; that the fratricidal strife which they have decided upon, notwithstanding all our commissions and pleas for peace, may be arrested by the Supreme Power, who maketh the wrath of man to praise Him; and that thus, through a divine blessing, the prosperity of these sovereign and once allied States, may be restored under the two governments to which they now and henceforth respectively belong.

8. That we do recommend to the churches of the Baptist denomination in the Southern States to observe the 1st and 2d days of June as days of humiliation, fasting, and prayer to Almighty God, that he may avert any calamities due to our sins as a people, and may look with mercy and favor upon us.

9. That whatever calamities may come upon us, our firm trust and hope are in God, through the atonement of His Son, and we earnestly beseech the churches represented in this body, (a constituency of six or seven hundred thousand Christians,) that they be fervent and importunate in prayer, not only for the country, but for the enterprises of the Gospel which have been committed to our care. In the war of the Revolution, and in the war of 1812, the Baptist bated no jot of heart or hope for the Redeemer's cause. Their zeal and liberality abounded in their deepest afflictions. We beseech the churches to cherish the spirit and imitate the example of this noble army of saints and heroes; to be followers of them who, through faith and patience, inherit the promises; to be steadfast, unmoveable, always abounding in the work of the Lord, forasmuch as they know that their labor is not in vain in the Lord.

10. That these resolutions be communicated to the Congress of the "Confederate States" at Montgomery, with the signatures of the President and Secretaries of the Convention.

P. H. MELL, Ga.;	JAMES B. TAYLOR, Va.;
JAMES E. BROOME, Fla.;	R. B. C. HOWELL, Tenn.;
G. H. MARTIN, Miss.;	L. W. ALLEN, Ky.;
W. CAREY CRANE, La.;	J. L. PRICHARD, N. C.;
R. FULLER, Md.;	E. T. WINKLER, S. C.;

B. MANLEY, Sr., Ala.,

Committee.

BAPTIST CONVENTION OF SOUTH CAROLINA, 1861.

July 25—The body met at Spartanburg—Hon. J. B. O'Neall, President; Rev. Mr. Landrum, Vice-President; Rev. Mr. Breaker, Secretary; Prof Judson, Treasurer.

On the State of the Country, the following resolution, offered by Dr. W. Curtis, was unanimously adopted:

Resolved, That in the present peculiar condition of our

political affairs, it becomes us thus to assure our beloved country of our sympathies, prayers, and thanksgiving on her behalf; that so far as we can understand the remarkable openings and guidance of Divine Providence, we have but received, in almost every instance, the merciful blessings of our God as approbation upon the plans our State and the Southern Confederacy have deemed it best to adopt—that now especially, in the unprecedented, vindictive, and deadly strife against us, to which those who but recently spoke of us as brethren are urging one another, we can but rejoice in the oneness of our brethren of this State, in prayer and effort, to defend our homes, our liberties, and our churches; and encourage them to be assured, that, as hitherto, putting our faith in God, though each of us may have much to bear, yet the rod will not finally rest upon us, but that in this most wicked attack upon our otherwise peaceful homes, the wickedness of the wicked will return on their own heads.

MARRIAGE OF SLAVES.

The Baptist Association of Georgia, in its meeting of 1864, adopted this resolution:

Resolved, That it is the firm belief and conviction of this body that the institution of marriage was ordained by Almighty God for the benefit of the whole human race, without respect to color; that it ought to be maintained in its original purity among all classes of people, and in all countries, and in all ages until the end of time; and that, consequently, the law of Georgia, in its failure to recognize and protect this relation between our slaves, is essentially defective, and ought to be amended.

PROTESTANT EPISCOPAL.

DIOCESE OF ALABAMA, 1861.

May—The Protestant Episcopal Convention of Alabama adopted this ordinance:

Whereas the Constitution of the Diocese of Alabama was adopted when the said Diocese actually was, on the presumption of its continuing to be, a part of the "Protestant Episcopal Church in the United States;" and whereas the State of Alabama is no longer a part of the United States, therefore it is hereby declared by this Convention that the first article of the Constitution of the Diocese, with all those canons, or portions of canons, dependent upon it, are null and void. It is furthermore declared that all canons, or portions of canons, both Diocesan and general, not necessarily dependent upon the recognition of the authority of the Church in the United States, are hereby retained in force. This declaration is not to be construed as affecting faith, doctrine or communion.

The form of service in the seceded States passed through several transformations. First the Governor of every seceded State was substituted in the public prayer for the President of the United States. Then the Governors gave way to the President of the Southern Confederacy. An example of these variations is found in the following pastoral letter of the Bishop of the diocese of Louisiana:

To the Clergy of the Diocese of Louisiana:

The progress of affairs makes it expedient to direct further changes in the public service of the Church.

In the prayer for those in civil authority, for the words "the President of the United States," substitute the words "the President of the Confederate States."

In the special prayer set forth in my letter of the 30th ultimo, for the words "and the Convention of Southern States," substitute the words "and the Congress of the Confederate States."

The prayer for the Legislature, as already indicated, will be continued during its sessions.

I remain, very truly, your servant in Christ,

LEONIDAS POLK,
Bishop of the Diocese of Louisiana.

NEW ORLEANS, *Feb.* 20, 1861.

A pastoral letter from Bishop Polk, of that diocese, contains this passage:

"Our separation from our brethren of 'The Protestant Episcopal Church in the United States' has been effected, *because we must follow our nationality*. Not because there has been any difference of opinion as to Christian doctrine or catholic usage. Upon these points we are still one. With us it is a separation, not a division—certainly not alienation. And there is no reason why, if we should find the union of our dioceses under our national Church impracticable, we should cease to feel for each other the respect and regard with which purity of manners, high principle, and a manly devotion to truth never fail to inspire generous minds. Our relations to each other hereafter will be the relations we both now hold to the men of our mother Church of England."

"CONFEDERATE" EPISCOPAL CHURCH, 1861.

November—At a General Convention held in Columbia, S. C., the Constitution of the Protestant Episcopal Church in the Confederate States of America was adopted—all the bishops present except Bishop Polk,* with a full attendance of clerical and lay deputies; Bishop Meade presided. The Richmond *Examiner* of Nov. 14 says:

The general tone of its deliberations, though entirely free from asperity toward the Church of the North, gave evidence of a deep and settled conviction, on every hand, that the separation in church organization, like that in civil government, was, and ought to be, complete and perpetual.

PASTORAL LETTER OF THE BISHOPS, 1862.

Nov. 22—The session of the First General Council, held at Augusta, was closed by reading an Address, from which these extracts are made:

Seldom has any Council assembled in the Church of Christ under circumstances needing His presence more urgently than this which is now about to submit its conclusions to the judgment of the Universal Church. Forced by the Providence of God to separate ourselves from the Protestant Episcopal Church in the United States—a Church with whose doctrine, discipline, and worship we are in entire harmony, and with whose action, up to the time of that separation, we were abundantly satisfied—at a moment when civil strife had dipped its foot in blood, and cruel war was desolating our homes and firesides, we required a double measure of grace to preserve the accustomed moderation of the Church in the arrangement of organic law, in the adjustment of our code of canons, but above all, in the preservation, without change, of those rich treasures of doctrine and worship which have come to us enshrined in our Book of Common Prayer.

The Constitution of the Protestant Episcopal Church in the Confederate States, under which we have been exer-

* A correspondent of the New Orleans *Picayune*, writing from Richmond, gives these curious particulars of the way in which Right Rev. Dr. Polk, Bishop of the Episcopal Church for the Diocese of Louisiana, came to forsake the gown for the sword:

"The Right Rev. Leonidas Polk, of Louisiana, has been commissioned Major General in the army of the Confederate States. The appointment has been urged upon Bishop Polk for several weeks, but he has had some hesitation in accepting it. A few days since he paid a visit to the venerable Bishop Meade, at his home near Winchester, to consult with him about it. The result was that he has concluded to accept it.

"Bishop Meade told him truly that he already held a commission in a very different army, to which he held allegiance 'till life's journey ends.'

"'I know that very well,' replied Bishop Polk, 'and I do not intend to resign it. On the contrary, I shall only prove the more faithful to it by doing all that in me lies to bring this unhallowed and unnatural war to a speedy and happy close. We of the Confederate States are the last bulwarks of civil and religious liberty; we fight for our hearthstones and our altars; above all we fight for a race that has been by Divine Providence entrusted to our most sacred keeping. When I accept a commission in the Confederate army, therefore, I not only perform the duties of a good citizen, but contend for the principles which lie at the foundation of our social, political, and religious polity.'"

Bishop Burgess, of Maine, in addressing the Diocesan Convention of that State, thus alluded to this circumstance:

"It is probably stated, with every appearance of authenticity, that one of the Southern Bishops of our Church has accepted a high command in the army of the revolted States. The present remark will be withheld from the press, unless the statement should be confirmed. If it be true, it is an act of dishonor to the Episcopate, unparalleled except in the darkest periods and the most corrupt communions. The hands of the ministry were always held back from bloodshed, even though the cause were most just."

The Bishop-General was killed near Marietta, Georgia, June 14, 1864, by a shell fired from a gun belonging to the 4th Corps, General Sherman's army.

cising our legislative functions, is the same as that of the Church from which we have been providentially separated, save that we have introduced into it a germ of expansion which was wanting in the old constitution. This is found in the permission which is granted to existing Dioceses to form themselves by subdivision into Provinces, and by this process gradually to reduce our immense Dioceses into Episcopal Sees, more like those which in primitive times covered the territories of the Roman Empire. * *

The Prayer Book we have left untouched in every particular save where a change of our civil government and the formation of a new nation have made alteration essentially requisite. Three words comprise all the amendment which has been deemed necessary in the present emergency, for we have felt unwilling, in the existing confusion of affairs, to lay rash hands upon the Book, consecrated by the use of ages, and hallowed by associations the most sacred and precious.

Our next source of encouragement is that we enter upon our work with our Dioceses fully organized, and with the means which Christ has instituted in His Church well distributed throughout the Confederate States. When we remember the very different auspices under which the venerated Fathers of the American Church began their work, and mark how it has grown and prospered, we should indeed take courage and feel no fear for the future. In their case all their ecclesiastical arrangements had to be organized; in our case we find these arrangements all ready to our hand, and with the seal of a happy experience stamped upon them. In their case every prejudice of the land was strong against them. In our case we go forward with the leading minds of our new Republic cheering us on by their communion with us, and with no prejudications to overcome, save those which arise from a lack of acquaintance with our doctrine and worship. In their case they were indeed few and separated far from one another in their work upon the walls of Zion. In our case we are comparatively well compacted, extending in an unbroken chain of Dioceses from the Potomac to the confines of the Republic. Despite all these disadvantages, "the little one became a thousand and the small one a strong nation," and shall we despond? If we be watchful, and strengthen the things that remain, our God will not forsake us, but will "lengthen our cords and stretch forth the curtains of our habitations." In visible token of this fact, we have already, since our organization, added to the House of Bishops the Rt. Rev. Dr. Wilmer as Bishop of Alabama, and received into communion with the Church the Diocese of Arkansas.

Another source of encouragement is that there has been no division in the Church in the Confederate States. Believing, with a wonderful unanimity, that the providence of God had guided our footsteps, and for His own inscrutable purposes had forced us into a separate organization, there has been nothing to embarrass us in the preliminary movements which have conducted us to our present position. With one mind and with one heart we have entered upon this blessed work, and we stand together this day a band of brothers, one in faith, one in hope, one in charity. There may be among us, as there always must be, minute differences of opinion and feeling, but there is nothing to hinder our keeping the unity of the spirit in the bond of peace. We are all satisfied that we are walking in the path of duty, and that the light of God's countenance has been wonderfully lifted up upon us. He has comforted us in our darkest hours, and has not permitted our hearts to faint in the day of adversity. * * *

Many of the States of this Confederacy are Missionary ground. The population is sparse and scattered; the children of the Church are few and far between; the Priests of the Lord can reach them only after great labor and privation. Hitherto has their scanty subsistence been eked out from the common treasury of our united Church. Cut off from that recourse by our political action, in which they have heartily acquiesced, they turn to us and pray us to do at least as much for them, as we have been accustomed to do for the Church from which they have been separated by a civil necessity. We can do what they ask, and we ought cheerfully to do it. * * * *

The time has come when the Church should press more urgently than she has hitherto done upon her laity, the solemn fact, that the slaves of the South are not merely so much property, but are a sacred trust committed to us, as a people, to be prepared for the work which God may have for them to do in the future. While under this tutelage He freely gives to us their labor, but expects us to give back to them that religious and moral instruction which is to elevate them in the scale of Being. And while inculcating this truth, the Church must offer more freely her ministrations for their benefit and improvement. Her laity must set the example of readiness to fulfill their duty towards these people, and her clergy must strip themselves of pride and fastidiousness and indolence, and rush with the zeal of martyrs, to this labor of love. The teachings of the Church are those which best suit a people passing from ignorance to civilization, because while it represses all fanaticism, it fastens upon the memory the great facts of our religion, and through its objective worship attracts and enchains them. So far from relaxing, in their case, the forms of the Church, good will be permanently done to them just in proportion as we teach them through their senses and their affections. If subjected to the teachings of a bald spiritualism, they will find food for their senses and their child-like fancies in superstitious observances of their own, leading too often to crime and licentiousness.

It is likewise the duty of the Church to press upon the masters of the country their obligation, as Christian men, so to arrange this institution as not to necessitate the violation of those sacred relations which God has created, and which man cannot, consistently with Christian duty, annul. The systems of labor which prevail in Europe and which are, in many respects, more severe than ours, are so arranged as to prevent all necessity for the separation of parents and children, and of husbands and wives, and a very little care upon our part, would rid the system upon which we are about to plant our national life, of these unchristian features. It belongs, especially, to the Episcopal Church to urge a proper teaching upon this subject, for in her fold and in her congregations are found a very large proportion of the great slaveholders of the country. We rejoice to be enabled to say that the public sentiment is rapidly becoming sound upon this subject, and that the Legislatures of several of the Confederate States have already taken steps towards this consummation. Hitherto have we been hindered by the pressure of abolitionism; now that we have thrown off from us that hateful and infidel pestilence, we should prove to the world that we are faithful to our trust, and the Church should lead the hosts of the Lord in this work of justice and of mercy.

METHODIST EPISCOPAL.

It is difficult to get information respecting this Church. Its General Conference was to have been held in 1862, in New Orleans, but the city fell before that date; and there has been no meeting of the body since. Its book concern (in Nashville) came into our possession at an early day, and is under proceedings of confiscation. Few of the Annual Conferences have been held, and the organization of the Church appears to have been almost wrecked by the war. It separated in 1845, from the Methodist Church North, on the Slavery Question.

This item appeared in one of the Georgia newspapers:

AUGUSTA, *August* 1, 1864.—Bishop Pierce, of the Methodist Episcopal Church South, calls upon the Methodists of the State to meet on Wednesday, August 10, for special prayer for victory and the expulsion of the foe from our State.

CATHOLIC.

No Church body appears to have taken action.

Bishop Lynch of Charleston early espoused the "Confederate" cause, and early in 1861 had a correspondence with Archbishop Hughes on the rightfulness of secession. He has since been in Europe as Confederate agent.

In 1861, the *New Orleans Catholic Standard* published these editorial articles:

Let no Southern child be educated outside the limits of the Confederate States. We have excellent schools and colleges at Richmond and Norfolk in Virginia; at Charleston and Columbia in South Carolina; at Savannah and Augusta in Georgia; at St. Augustine in Florida; at Mobile in Alabama; at Bay St. Louis, Pass Christian, Sulphur Springs, Vicksburg, and Natchez, Mississippi; at Fort Smith, Helena and Little Rock in Arkansas; at Marksville and Memphis in Tennessee; at Galveston, New Braunfels, San Antonio, Brownsville, and Liberty in Texas; and at St. Michael's, Grand Coteau, Vermillionville, Thibodeaux, Donaldsonville, Natchitoches, Avoyelles, Alexandria, Shreveport, Iberville, Algiers, and New Orleans in Louisiana. The social bonds between us and the Catholics at the North have been severed by them. We acknowledge them no longer as our countrymen. They and their institutions have no claims upon us.

Our Charleston brother is not alone in the satisfaction he feels at the loyalty of the Catholic Celts to their adopted State. We are proud in being able to claim similar honors for our Hibernian friends. A very large majority of what is styled the Irish vote in this city, was cast for the Secession ticket. Precincts where the Irish formerly testified their devotion to the Union, by heavy majorities for the so-called Union ticket, gave in the recent elections either majorities for Secession or reduced the co-operation majority to a mere trifle. We are proud to say that this is not only true of the Celts, in particular, but of our entire Catholic population, a very large majority of whom voted the Secession ticket. Of practical Catholics, probably 19 out of every 20 who voted gave it their support. Religion, of course, was not directly involved in the question, but it is quite impossible to dissever patriotism from religion in the Catholic heart. That is a Union which cannot be dissolved. Even the wayward Catholic youth whose passions have led him astray from the house of his Father, and who has for years neglected his loving bounty, cannot have his patriotism aroused without at once burning with reawakened love and duty to his soul's true home. We cannot conceive such an impossibility as a Catholic heart in which Patriotism and Religion do not throb together. Like the Hibernians in Charleston, their countrymen in New Orleans, many of whom were partisans of Mr. Douglas, have organized military companies, not for mere pastime, but for work, and are ready for the struggle whenever the arrogant North shall presume to force it upon us.

THE POPE'S REPLY TO THE REBEL COMMISSIONERS.

Honorable Gentlemen: Mr. Soutter has handed me your letter of November 11, with which, in conformity to the instructions of your Government, you have sent me a copy of the manifesto issued by the Congress of the Confederate States and approved by the most honorable President, in order that the attention of the Government of the Holy See, to whom, as well as to the other Governments, you have addressed yourselves, might be called to it. The sentiments expressed in the manifesto, tending as they do to the cessation of the most bloody war which still rages in your countries, and the putting an end to the disasters which accompany it by proceeding to negotiations for peace, being entirely in accordance with the disposition and character of the august head of the Catholic Church, I did not hesitate a moment in bringing it to the notice of the Holy Father. His Holiness, who has been deeply afflicted by the accounts of the frightful carnage of this obstinate struggle, has heard with satisfaction the expression of the same sentiments. Being the vicar on earth of that God who is the author of peace, he yearns to see these wraths appeased and peace restored. In proof of this he wrote to the Archbishops of New York and New Orleans, as far back as October 18, 1862, inviting them to exert themselves in bringing about this holy object. You may then, honorable gentlemen, feel well assured that whenever a favorable occasion shall present itself, His Holiness will not fail to avail himself of it, to hasten so desirable a result, and that all nations may be united in the bonds of charity.

In acquainting you with this benignant disposition of the Holy Father, I am pleased to declare myself, with sentiments of the most distinguished esteem, truly your servant,

G. Card. ANTONELLI.

Rome, *December* 2, 1864.

Messrs. A. Dudley Mann, J. M. Mason, and John Slidell, *Commissioners of the Confederate States of America, Paris.*

CHRISTIAN ASSOCIATION, 1861.

The Young Men's Christian Association of New Orleans, under date of May 22, issued an "Address to the Young Men's Christian Associations of North America," in which they say:

We wish you to feel with us, that there is a terrible responsibility now resting upon us all as Christians, in this trying time of our country. * * * We in the South are satisfied in our judgments, AND IN OUR HEARTS, that the political severance of the Southern from the Northern States *is permanent,* and SHOULD BE SATISFACTORY. We believe that reason, history, and knowledge of human nature, will suggest the folly and futility of a war to re-establish a political union between the severed sections. * * * Has it not occurred to you, brethren, that the hand of God MAY BE in this political division, that both governments may more effectually work out His designs in the regeneration of the world? While such a possibility may exist, let His people be careful not to war against His will. It is not pretended that the war is to maintain religious freedom, or extend the kingdom of Christ. Then, God's people should beware how they wage or encourage it. In the name of Christ and His divine teachings, we protest against the war which the Government at Washington is waging against the territory and people of the Southern States; and we call upon all the Young Men's Christian Associations in the North to unite with us in this solemn protest.

ADDRESS OF THE "CONFEDERATE" CLERGY, 1863.

ADDRESS TO CHRISTIANS THROUGHOUT THE WORLD, BY THE CLERGY OF THE CONFEDERATE STATES OF AMERICA.

Christian Brethren,—In the name of our Holy Christianity, we address you in this form, respecting matters of great interest to us, which we believe deeply concern the cause of our Blessed Master, and to which we invoke your serious attention.

We speak not in the spirit of controversy, not by political inspiration, but as the servants of the Most High God, we speak the "truth in love," concerning things which make for peace.

In the midst of war—surrounded by scenes that pain the souls of all good men—deploring the evils which are inseparable from national contentions—we feel most deeply impressed by the conviction, that for our own sake, for the sake of our posterity, for the sake of humanity, for the sake of the truth, and, above all, for the sake of our Redeemer's Kingdom, it behoves us to testify of certain things in our beloved land, which seem to be neither understood nor appreciated by our enemies, nor yet clearly appreciated by Christians of other nations.

We put forth this address after much prayer, solemnly invoking the blessing of Almighty God, and committing what we say to that Providence by which we trust we are directed, and by whose authority and power the governments of the earth stand or fall.

If we were moved to make this address by any fears of the final issue of the war in which our country is now engaged, by any inclination to meddle with political questions, by any desire to resume controversy in respect to matters which have been referred to the arbitration of the sword; if indeed anything that compromised the simplicity, dignity, and purity of Christian duty moved us to issue this address, we should deserve to have it despised by you, and could hope for no blessing of God to rest upon it. But for all that we say in the following declarations, we are willing to be judged by succeeding generations, and to answer in that day when the secrets of all hearts shall be made known.

We do not propose to discuss the *causes* of the war. They are matters of recent history, easily known and read of all men. To discuss them would obviously involve much more than, as Christian ministers, we feel it our province to argue.

We submit for your consideration as the first point of our testimony and ground of protest,—

That the war waged against our people, in principle and in fact, proposes to achieve that which, in the nature of the case, it is impossible to accomplish by violence. The war proposes the restoration of the *Union.*

We can rationally suppose a war for conquest, or to expel an invader, or to compel respect for stipulations of peace and international intercourse which have been violated; but how measures of violence can reunite independent States, restore their broken fellowship, re-establish equality of representatives' rights, or coerce a people to brotherly kindness, unity, and devotion to each other, is utterly beyond our conception.

But if our enemies be disingenuous in their professions—if they fight not to *recover* seceded States, but to *subjugate* them, what promise do men find in the numbers, intelligence, courage, resources, and moral energies of the millions who inhabit the Confederate States, that such a people can ever become profitable or happy, as subordinate to mere military force? If subjugation, therefore, were possible, is it desirable? Would the United States gain anything? Would Christian civilization gain anything? Said a great British statesman in 1775, when arguing in favor of adopting conciliatory measures in respect to the revolted colonies of America—colonies, not seceding States—that were in actual rebellion against their sovereign: "The use of force is but *temporary.* It may subdue for a moment, but it does not remove the necessity for subduing again; and a nation is not governed which is perpetually to be conquered. My next objection is its uncertainty. Terror is not always the effect of force, and an armament is not a victory. * * * A further objection to force is that you *impair the object* by your very endeavors to preserve it. The thing you fought for is not the thing you recover."

Christian brethren, could the hand of violence win you to desire fellowship with a people while it destroyed your peace, polluted your sanctuaries, invaded the sacred precincts of your homes, robbed you of your property, slaughtered your noble sons, clothed your daughters in grief, filled your land with sorrow, and employed its utmost strength to reduce your country to the degradation of a subjugated province? Would it not rather animate you to prefer death—honorable death—the patriot's alternative, the Christian's martyrdom?

As an excuse for violence, our enemies charge that the Confederate States have attempted to overthrow the "*best Government on earth;*" and call us "traitors," "rebels." We deny the charge; and as to the epithets, if they defined our position, under the circumstances, we could glory in them, as do the people of God when persecuted for truth and conscience' sake. But we regard such terms as gratuitously assuming the very point at issue. If employed sincerely, we will not complain; but we are persuaded that many have uttered these expressions under the influence of resentful feelings, who would not otherwise assert the political doctrines they imply. We are not disposed to engage in an angry retort, and only mention these things to show that we appreciate them.

It will appear singular when men reflect upon it, that so many intelligent and Christian people should desire to withdraw from the "*the best Government on earth.*" And we need not discuss the kindness of those who so generously propose to confer on us by *force of arms* "*the best Government.*"

No attempt has been made to overthrow the Government of the United States, unless by the fanatical party which now administers its affairs. The South never entertained such an idea. If that Government fall for lack of Southern support, let men discriminate between the downfall of an oppression when the oppressed have escaped, and a wanton effort to break up good government. So Pharoah fell, but not by the hand of Israel. The dismemberment of the Union by secession was not a blow at the Government. It was for our own deliverance. It was an election of the people, only hastened and rendered in some cases imperative by the violent movements of the Executive of the United States. Virginia may be referred to as an illustration. That State was not willing to secede hastily; but the demand of President Lincoln, that she furnish troops to fight her sister States, ended all hesitation. At once she took position with the Confederacy, preferring to battle in defence of liberty, rather than, in opposition to all her principles, to invade or suffer the invasion of the South.

So far, therefore, from desiring to destroy the United States Government, the great object of those States which *first* seceded was to secure their own rights, and their tranquillity; while the *immediate* object of the States which *last* seceded was to place themselves as barriers in the way of a fanatical Administration, and, if possible, stay the bloody effort to coerce independent States to remain in the Union, when their constitutional rights would not be respected, and when the very purpose to coerce them showed a readiness to sacrifice the lives of citizens to the demands of sectional hostility. The South would never vote in favor of annexing or retaining a Northern State by force of arms. Instead, therefore, of waging war for the overthrow of the United States, the Confederate States simply defend themselves.

The war is forced upon us. We have always desired peace. After a conflict of opinions between the North and the South in Church and State, of more than thirty years, growing more bitter and painful daily, we withdraw from them to secure peace—they send troops to compel us into re-union! Our proposition was peaceable separation, saying, "We are *actually* divided, our *nominal* union is only a platform of strife." The answer is a call for *seventy-five thousand* troops, to force submission to a Government whose character, in the judgment of the South, had been sacrificed to sectionalism. From the speech of Mr. Burke, already referred to, the following language may be quoted as not inappropriate to our position in respect of peace,—

"THE PROPOSITION IS PEACE.—Not peace through the medium of war; not peace to be hunted through the labyrinth of intricate and endless negotiations; not peace to arise out of universal discord, fomented from principle, in all parts of the empire; not peace to depend on the judicial determination of perplexing questions, or the precise marking the shadowy boundaries of a complex government. It is simple peace, sought in the spirit of peace, and laid in principles purely pacific."

Such a proposition of peace was clearly the appropriate duty of a Christian people. The South can point out on the page of history the names, and refer to the earnest and repeated efforts of her commissioners of peace. But our foes preferred war—violence—and by violence the end they aimed at was unattainable, as the purpose was unworthy of a Christian nation. *Against this violence*, upon principle, and in the light of all the facts of the case, we, as the servants of God and the ministers of peace, testify and solemnly protest.

The second general point which we submit for your Christian consideration is,—

The separation of the Southern States is universally regarded by our people as final, and the formation of the Confederate States' Government as a fixed fact, promising in no respect, a restoration of the former Union.

Politically and ecclesiastically, the line has been drawn between North and South. It has been done distinctly, deliberately, finally, and in most solemn form. The Confederacy claims to possess all the conditions and essential characteristics of an independent Government. Our institutions, habits, tastes, pursuits, and religion, suggest no wish for reconstruction of the Union. We regard the Confederacy, in the wise providence of the Almighty, as the result of causes which render its independent existence a moral and political necessity, and its final and future independence of the United States not a matter that admits of the slightest doubt.

Among all the indefensible acts growing out of the inexcusable war waged against us, we will refer to one especially, in regard to which, for obvious reasons, we would speak, and as becometh us, plainly and earnestly:—*The recent proclamation of the President of the United States, seeking the emancipation of the slaves of the South, is, in our judgment, a suitable occasion for solemn protest on the part of the people of God throughout the world.*

First, upon the hypothesis that the proclamation could be carried out in its design, we have no language to describe the bloody tragedy that would appal humanity. Christian sensibilities recoil from the vision of a struggle that would inevitably lead to the slaughter of tens of thousands of poor deluded insurrectionists! Suppose their owners suffered; in the nature of things the slaves would suffer infinitely more. Make it absolutely necessary for the public safety that the slaves be slaughtered, and he who should write the history of that event would record the darkest chapter of human woe yet written.

But, *secondly*, suppose the proclamation—as indeed we esteem it in the South—a mere political document, devised to win favor among the most fanatical of the Northern people, uttering nothing that has not already been attempted, practically, but in vain, by the United States; suppose it to be worth no more than the paper upon which its bold iniquity is traced, nevertheless it is the avowal of a principle, the declaration of a wish, the deliberate attempt of the chief magistrate of a nation to do that which, as a measure of war, must be repugnant to civilisation, and which *we* calmly denounce as worthy of universal reprobation, and against which Christians in the name of humanity and religion ought to protest.

What shall sound Christianity say to that one-idea of philanthropy which, in the name of an *imaginary* good, in blind fury rushes upon a thousand *unquestionable* evils?

If it were the time for such argument, we should not fear the issue of a full discussion of this whole question of Slavery. We fear no investigation—we decline no debate; but we would not, at an hour like this, and in an address which is chiefly a protest, invoke the spirit of controversy. We content ourselves with what we regard as infinitely more solemn; we stand before the world, while war silences the voices of disputants, and men in deadly contention wrestle on fields of blood, *protesting* against the crimes that in the name of liberty and philanthropy are attempted! Let it go forth from our lips while we live; let it be recorded of us when we are dead, that we—ministers of our Lord Jesus Christ, and members of His holy Church, with our hands upon the Bible, at once the sacred charter of our liberties and the foundation of our faith—call heaven and earth to record, that in the name of Him whose we are, and whom we serve, *we protest!* No description we can give of this measure of the Executive of the United States, even though indignation alone inspired us to utter it, would exaggerate what we regard as an unholy infatuation, a ruthless persecution, a cruel and shameful device, adding severity and bitterness to a wicked and reckless war.

When it is remembered that, in the name of a "*military necessity*" this new measure was adopted, we may pass by the concession of weakness implied in this fact, and content ourselves with calling attention to the *immorality* of a necessity created by a needless war of invasion. "Military necessity!" an excuse, not for self-defence—not for self-preservation—but for violating the laws of civilized warfare, and attempting a barbarity. If "military necessity" be the inspiration to attempt emancipation, how shall men praise it as philanthropy? Are other nations uninterested in such conduct? Proclaim the right first to invade and subjugate independent States, exhaust all resources, and then avow the principle of "military necessity" as an excuse for adding severity to the wrong, as a plea upon which to project a scheme violating every manly, honorable, and

Christian sentiment! Suppose an invader happens to be too *weak* to conquer upon any other plan, has he therefore the right to proclaim that poison and the indiscriminate slaughter of women and children shall be his legal method? The common cause of humanity, and the common hopes of Christian civilization, as they appeal to every nation, cry out against this wretched subterfuge. If the "military necessity" of *weakness* may righteously adopt any measure that an invader's ingenuity can invent or his malice suggest, what laws, what principles of justice and equity, shall nations at war respect?

At one time the world is told "the rebellion is weak, and will be crushed out in sixty days;" at another, "Union men abound in the South, and will welcome United States' troops as deliverers;" and *now* the invader is so hopeless of his task, that it is a "military necessity" that he obtain help of slaves! May it not be pertinently asked, what, that is creditable to this invasion, ought men to believe, and to what end is this deceitful war waged? When this last resort, like all the enemy's preceding schemes, shall signally fail, as it certainly will, to achieve the ruin of the South, what is promised? Nothing, but war! cruel, relentless, desperate war! Because the President by his scheme violates the constitution, we *might* condemn him; though the constitutionality of his acts be less important to us than to the people over whom he presides; because he has violated his word, his *special promise*, and even his solemn oath of office, we *might* abhor his act; though that is a matter which may chiefly concern his conscientiousness, and illustrate the character of that officer whom Southerners refuse to salute as their President; because of the diabolical mischief *intended*, we might in the name of Heaven indignantly denounce his Proclamation, though no weapon formed against us be, practically, more harmless. But these are not the considerations which move us to protest: we solemnly protest *because, under the disguise of philanthropy, and the pretext of doing good, he would seek the approbation of mankind upon a war that promises to humanity only evil, and that continually.*

Let philanthropists observe, even according to its own terms, this measure is in no proper sense an act of mercy to the slave, but of malice toward the master. It provides for freeing *only the slaves of those who fight* against the United States. The effort is not to relieve that Government of slavery, where the philanthropy has full opportunity for displaying its generosity, and the power to exercise it in respect to slavery, if it exists at all, can be indulged; but the effort is simply to invoke slavery as an agent against the South, reckless of the consequences to the slaves themselves. Shall a pretext at once so weak and so base mislead intelligent men, and make them imagine Abraham Lincoln is a philanthropist? His position ought to be offensive to every sincere abolitionist, as well as disgusting to every sincere friend of the slave, of every shade of opinion on the question of slavery. How does it affect the cause of the Confederacy? If to awaken a deeper resentment than ever inflamed the people of the South before; if to quench the last sentiment of respect that lingered in their breasts for the United States' Government; if to unite them more resolutely than ever, and to make it to the individual interest of every person in the bounds of the Confederacy to sustain and strengthen it with every dollar and every arm, and every prayer, and every energy of manly virtue and Christian encouragement, be to advance the invader's interest, and give him hope of success, then has the proclamation furnished him opportunity of congratulating himself.

We submit further: *That the war against the Confederate States has achieved no good result, and we find nothing in the present state of the struggle that gives promise of the United States accomplishing any good by its continuance.* Though hundreds of thousands of lives have been lost, and many millions of treasure spent; though a vast amount of valuable property has been destroyed, and numbers of once happy homes made desolate; though cities and towns have been temporarily captured, and aged men and helpless women and children have suffered such things as it were even a shame to speak of plainly; though sanctuaries have been desecrated, and ministers of God been dragged from sacred altars to loathsome prisons; though slaves have been instigated to insurrection, and every measure has been adopted that the ingenuity of the enemy could devise, or his ample resources afford by sea and by land; yet we aver, without fear of contradiction, that the only possession which the United States hold in the Confederate States is the ground on which United States' troops pitch their tents; and that whenever those troops withdraw from a given locality in our territory, the people resident therein testify a warmer devotion to the Confederate cause than even before their soil was invaded. Nothing is therefore conquered—no part of the country is subdued; the civil jurisdiction of the United States, the real test of their success, *has not been established by any force of arms.* Where such civil jurisdiction exists at all along the border, it had existed all the while, was not obtained by force, and is not the fruit of conquest. The fact is admitted by our enemies themselves.

It is worthy of special notice, that, notwithstanding the gigantic exertions of the United States, they have not been able to secure the return of a single county, or section of a county, much less a single State, that has seceded. No civil order and peace spring up in the track of their armies. All in front of them is resolute resistance; and behind them, when they have entered our territory, is a deep, uncompromising opposition, over which only military force can for a moment be trusted. Thus the civilised world is called upon to observe an invasion which has lasted nearly two years, and achieved nothing but cruelty. Before it a people ready to die, but neither ready to submit, nor weak enough to be conquered; and for its gloomy prospect an interminable war, growing more bitter and unfeeling every day, because more hopeless to them that by it have sought things impossible as well as unrighteous. In the name of the great Prince of Peace, has Christianity, has civilisation, nothing to say to such an awful tragedy? Such is the war for the *Union!* Yet every day our foes are deepening and widening that river of blood which divides us from them for ever!

The only change of opinion among our people since the beginning of the war, that is of material importance to the final issue, has been the change from all lingering attachment to the former Union, to a more sacred and reliable devotion to the Confederate Government. The sentiments of the people are not alterable in any other respects by force of arms. If the whole country were occupied by United States' troops, it would merely exhibit a military despotism, against which the people would struggle in perpetual revolutionary effort, while any Southrons remained alive. Extermination of the inhabitants could alone realise civil possession of their soil. Subjugation is, therefore, clearly impossible. Is extermination desired by Christians?

The moral and religious interests of the South ought to be appreciated by Christians of all nations.

These interests have realised certainly no benefit from the war. We are aware that, in respect to the moral aspects of the question of slavery, we differ from those who conceive of emancipation as a measure of benevolence, and on that account we suffer much reproach which we are conscious of not deserving. With all the facts of the system of slavery in its practical operations before us, "as eye-witnesses and ministers of the Word, having had perfect understanding of all things" on this subject of which we speak, we may surely claim respect for our opinions and statements. Most of us have grown up from childhood among the slaves; all of us have preached to and taught them the word of life; have administered to them the ordinances of the Christian Church; sincerely love them as souls for whom Christ died; we go among them freely, and know them in health and sickness, in labor and rest, from infancy to old age. We are familiar with their physical and moral condition, and alive to all their interests; and we testify in the sight of God, that the relation of master and slave among us, however we may deplore abuses in this, as in other relations of mankind, is not incompatible with our holy Christianity, and that the presence of the Africans of our land is an occasion of gratitude on their behalf before God; seeing that thereby Divine Providence has brought them where missionaries of the Cross may freely proclaim to them the word of salvation, and the work is not interrupted by agitating fanaticism. The South has done more than any people on earth for the Christianization of the African race. The condition of slaves here is not wretched, as northern fictions would have men believe, but prosperous and happy, and would have been yet more so but for the mistaken zeal of the Abolitionists. Can emancipation obtain for them a better portion? The practicable plan for benefiting the African race must be the Providential plan—the Scriptural plan. We adopt that plan in the South; and while the State should seek by wholesome legislation to regard the interests of master and slave, we, as ministers, would preach the word to both as we are commanded of God. This war has not benefited the slaves. Those who have been encouraged or compelled to leave their masters have gone, and we aver can go, to no state of society that offers them any better things than they have at home, either in respect to their temporal or eternal welfare. We regard Abolitionism as an interference with the plans of Divine Providence. It has not the signs of the Lord's blessing. It is a fanaticism which puts forth no good fruit; instead of blessing, it has brought forth cursing; instead of love, hatred; instead of life, death—bitterness, and sorrow, and pain; and infidelity and moral degeneracy follow its labors. We remember how the apostle has taught the minister of Jesus upon this subject: "Let as many servants as are under the yoke count their own masters worthy of all honor, that the name of God and His doctrine be not blasphemed. And they that have believing masters, let them not despise them because they are brethren; but rather do them service because they are faithful and beloved, partakers of the benefit. *These things teach and exhort.* If any man teach otherwise, and consent not to wholesome words, even the words of our Lord Jesus Christ, and to the doctrine which is according to godliness, he is proud, knowing nothing, but doting about questions and strifes of words, whereof cometh envy, strife, railings, evil surmisings, perverse disputings of men of corrupt mind, and destitute of the truth, supposing that gain is godliness; from such withdraw thyself."

This is what we teach, and, obedient to the last verse of the text, from men that "teach otherwise"—hoping for peace—we "withdraw" ourselves.

The Christians of the South, we claim, are pious, intelligent, and liberal. Their pastoral and missionary works have points of peculiar interest. There are hundreds of thousands here, both white and colored, who are not strangers to the blood that bought them. We rejoice that the great Head of the Church has not despised us. We desire as much as in us lieth to live peaceably with all men, and though reviled, to revile not again.

Much harm has been done to the religious enterprises of the Church by the war; we will not tire you by enumerating particulars. We thank God for the patient faith and fortitude of our people during these days of trial.

Our soldiers were before the war our fellow-citizens, and many of them are of the household of faith, who have carried to the camp so much of the leaven of Christianity, that, amid all the demoralizing influences of army life, the good work of salvation has gone forward there.

Our President, some of our most influential statesmen, our commanding general, and an unusual proportion of the principal generals, as well as scores of other officers, are prominent, and we believe consistent members of the Church. Thousands of our soldiers are men of prayer. We regard our success in the war as due to Divine mercy, and our Government and people have recognized the hand of God in the formal and humble celebration of His goodness. We have no fear in regard to the future. If the war continue for years, we believe God's grace sufficient for us.

In conclusion, we ask for ourselves, our churches, our country, the devout prayers of all God's people,—"the will of the Lord be done!"

Christian brethren, think of these things; and let your answer to our address be the voice of an enlightened Christian sentiment going forth from you against war, against persecution for conscience' sake, against the ravaging of the Church of God by fanatical invasion. But if we speak to you in vain, nevertheless we have not spoken in vain in the sight of God; for we have proclaimed the truth —we have testified in behalf of Christian civilization—we have invoked charity—we have filed our solemn protest against a cruel and useless war. And our children shall read it, and honor our spirit, though in much feebleness we may have borne our testimony.

"Charity beareth all things, believeth all things, hopeth all things, endureth all things." We desire to "follow after charity;" and "as many as walk according to this rule, peace be on them, and mercy, and upon the Israel of God."

Signatures to the Address.

BAPTIST CHURCH.

Ro. Ryland, D.D., President of Richmond College, Richmond, Virginia.
L. W. Seeley, D.D., Richmond, Virginia.
J. B. Jeter, D.D., President of Foreign Missionary Board, Richmond, Virginia.
James B. Taylor, D.D., Secretary Foreign Missionary Board, Richmond, Virginia.
A. M. Poindexter, D.D., Secretary Foreign Missionary Board, Richmond, Virginia.
William F. Broaddus, D.D., Charlottesville, Virginia.
H. W. Dodge, Lynchburg, Virginia.
Cornelius Tyree, Powhatan Courthouse, Virginia.
A. D. Shaver, Editor of "Religious Herald," Richmond, Virginia.
C. George, Culpepper Courthouse, Virginia.
R. H. Bagby, Bruington Church, Virginia.
Thomas E. Skinner, Raleigh, North Carolina.
James P. Boyce, D.D., President Theological Seminary, Greenville, South Carolina.
John A. Broadus, D.D., Professor Theological Seminary, Greenville, South Carolina.
Basil Manly, jun., D.D., Professor Theological Seminary, Greenville, South Carolina.
William Williams, D.D., Professor Theological Seminary, Greenville, South Carolina.
J. M. C. Breaker, Editor "Confederate Baptist," Columbia, South Carolina.
J. L. Reynolds, D.D., Columbia, South Carolina.
N. M. Crawford, D.D., President of Mercer University, Georgia.
Joseph S. Baker, Quitman, Georgia.
H. C. Hornady, Atlanta, Georgia.
Samuel Henderson, Editor of "South West Baptist," Tuskegee, Alabama.
Thomas S. Savage, Livingston, Mississippi.
W. H. Meredith, Florida.

DISCIPLES.

W. J. Pettigrew, Richmond, Virginia.

METHODIST EPISCOPAL.

J. O. Andrew, D.D., Alabama, Bishop of Methodist Episcopal Church, South.
John Early, D.D., Virginia, Bishop of Methodist Episcopal Church, South.
G. F. Pierce, D.D., Georgia, Bishop of Methodist Episcopal Church, South.
A. M. Skipp, D.D., President of Wofford College, South Carolina.
Whiteford Smith, D.D., South Carolina.
J. T. Wightman, Charleston, South Carolina.
W. A. Gamewell, Marion, South Carolina.
Wm. A. Smith, D.D., President of Randolph Macon College, Virginia.
Leroy M. Lee, D.D., Virginia.
D. S. Doggett, Richmond, Virginia.
J. E. Edwards, Richmond, Virginia.
James A. Duncan, D.D., Editor "Richmond Christian Advocate," Virginia.
Braxton Craven, D.D., President of Trinity College, North Carolina.
Joseph Cross, D.D., Tennessee.
C. W. Chalton, Editor of "Holston Journal," Knoxville, Tennessee.
S. D. Huston, D.D., Editor of "Home Circle," Tennessee.
E. H. Myers, D.D., Editor of "Southern Christian Advocate."

METHODIST PROTESTANT.

W. A. Crocker, President of Virginia District.
R. B. Thompson, President of Lynchburg College, Virginia.
F. L. B. Shaver, President of Alabama District.

PROTESTANT EPISCOPAL.

Joshua Peterkin, D.D., Richmond, Virginia.
James A. Latane, Staunton, Virginia.
James Moore, Louisburg, North Carolina.
William N. Hawks, Columbus, Georgia.
K. J. Stewart, Alexandria.

PRESBYTERIAN.

Union Theological Seminary, Virginia.

Robert L. Dabney, D.D., Professor of Systematic Theology, &c.
Benjamin M. Smith, D.D., Professor of Oriental and Biblical Criticism.
Thomas E. Peck, Professor of Church History and Government.
John M. P. Atkinson, President of Hampden Sidney College, Virginia.
William S. White, D.D., Lexington, Virginia.
Francis McFarland, D.D., near Staunton, Virginia.
T. V. Moore, D.D., Richmond, Virginia.
William Brown, D.D., Editor, "Central Presbyterian," Richmond, Virginia.
Theodoric Pryor, D.D., Petersburg, Virginia.
A. W. Miller, Petersburg, Virginia.
Drury Lacy, D.D., North Carolina.
Robert H. Morrison, D.D., North Carolina.
Daniel A. Penick, North Carolina.
John L. Kirkpatrick, D.D., President Davidson College, North Carolina.
Moses D. Hoge, D.D., Second Presbyterian Church, Richmond, Virginia.

Theological Seminary, Columbia, South Carolina.

A. W. Leland, D.D., Professor of Pastoral Theology.
George Howe, D.D., Professor of Biblical Literature.
John B. Adger, D.D., Professor of Ecclesiastical History, &c.
James Woodrow Perkins, Professor of Natural Science, &c.
B. M. Palmer, D.D., Pastor of the First Presbyterian Church, New Orleans.
Thomas Smythe, D.D., Charleston, South Carolina.
W. C. Dana, Charleston, South Carolina.
Samuel K. Talmage, D.D., President of Oglethorpe University, Georgia.
John S. Wilson, D.D., Atlanta, Georgia.
Joseph R. Wilson, D.D., Augusta, Georgia.
Robert B. White, D.D., Tuscaloosa, Alabama.
George H. W. Petrie, D.D., Montgomery, Alabama.
Joseph Brown, Florida.
Archibald Baker, Madison, Florida.

UNITED SYNOD.

Charles H. Read. D.D., Richmond, Virginia.
A. Converse. D.D., Editor of "Christian Observer," Richmond, Virginia.
Thomas W. Hooper, Richmond, Virginia.
P. B. Price, Richmond, Virginia.
Jacob D. Mitchell, D.D., Lynchburg, Virginia.
Thomas D. Bell, Harrisonburg, Virginia.
J. H. C. Leach, D.D., Farmville, Virginia.
Mat. M. Marshall, Tennessee.
Joseph H. Martin, Knoxville, Tennessee.
Fred. A. Ross, D.D., Huntsville, Alabama.
J. M. M'Lean, Mobile, Alabama.
C. M. Atkinson, Canton, Mississippi.

ASSOCIATE REFORMED.

J. C. Pressly, D.D., South Carolina.
R. C. Grier, D.D., South Carolina.
E. L. Patton, President of Erskine College, South Carolina.
J. J. Bonner, Editor of the "Due West Telescope," South Carolina.

CUMBERLAND PRESBYTERIAN.

N. A. Davis, Texas.

LUTHERAN.

D. F. Bittle, D.D., President of Roanoke College, Virginia.

GERMAN REFORMED.

J. C. Hensell, Mt. Crawford, Virginia.

NOTES.

1. In publishing the foregoing Address, it is proper to declare explicitly, that its origin was from no political source whatever, but from a conference of ministers of the Gospel in the city of Richmond.

The signatures are confined to this class because it was believed that, on the points presented, the testimony of men holding this office might be received with less prejudice than that of any other. These signatures might have been indefinitely increased. Only a limited number of names—much less than at first intended—was solicited; and as they are still coming in, some will probably be received too late for insertion. Those appended represent more or less fully every accessible section of the Confederacy, and nearly every denomination of Christians. They are ample for the chief objects intended; namely, to bear witness to the Christian world that the representations here made concerning the public sentiment of the South are true, and to carry a solemn protest against the continuance of this fruitless and unrighteous war.

2. From the best sources of information it is ascertained that the whole number of communicants in the Christian churches in the Confederate States is about two millions and fifty thousand.

Of these the number of white communicants is about *one million five hundred and fifty thousand.* Supposing the total white population to be *eight millions*, and one-half that number to be over eighteen years of age, a little more than *one-third* of the adult population are members of the Church of Christ.

The number of *colored communicants* is about *five hundred thousand.* Assuming the colored population to be four millions, there would be, upon the same method of computation, *one-fourth* of the adult population in communion with the Church of Christ. Thus has God blessed us in gathering into His Church from the children of Africa more than twice as many as are reported from all the converts in the Protestant Missions throughout the heathen world.

In making this summary of facts, I have omitted mention of Sermons, Addresses, and Letters from Bishops and other clergymen, as chiefly of personal interest, and not indicative of organized Church action.

The Military Authorities and the Churches.

ORDERS OF THE SECRETARY OF WAR.

METHODIST EPISCOPAL CHURCH.

November 30, 1863—The following order in relation to the use of all houses of worship belonging to the Methodist Episcopal Church South was issued and delivered to Bishop Ames.

December 9, 1863—The same order was given concerning houses of worship of the same denomination in the Department of Virginia and North Carolina, and delivered to Bishop O. C. Baker, and those in the Department of the South, and delivered to Bishop Edmund S. Janes.

December 30, 1863—The same order was given concerning houses of worship of the same denomination in the States of Kentucky and Tennessee, and delivered to Bishop M. Simpson.

WAR DEPARTMENT, ADJUTANT GENERAL'S OFFICE,
WASHINGTON, *November* 30, 1863.

To the Generals commanding the Departments of the Missouri, the Tennessee, and the Gulf, and all Generals and officers commanding armies, detachments, and posts, and all officers in the service of the United States in the above mentioned Departments:

You are hereby directed to place at the disposal of Rev. Bishop Ames all houses of worship belonging to the Methodist Episcopal Church South in which a loyal minister, who has been appointed by a loyal Bishop of said church, does not now officiate.

It is a matter of great importance to the Government, in its efforts to restore tranquility to the community and peace to the nation, that Christian ministers should, by example and precept, support and foster the loyal sentiment of the people.

Bishop Ames enjoys the entire confidence of this Department, and no doubt is entertained that all ministers who may be appointed by him will be entirely loyal. You are expected to give him all the aid, countenance, and support practicable in the execution of his important mission.

You are also authorized and directed to furnish Bishop Ames and his clerk with transportation and subsistence when it can be done without prejudice to the service, and will afford them courtesy, assistance and protection.

By order of the Secretary of War:
E. D. TOWNSEND,
Assistant Adjutant General.

AMERICAN BAPTIST HOME MISSION SOCIETY.

WAR DEPARTMENT, ADJUTANT GENERAL'S OFFICE,
WASHINGTON, *January* 14, 1864.

To the Generals commanding the Military Division of the Mississippi, and the Departments of the Gulf, of the South, and of Virginia and North Carolina, and all Generals and officers commanding armies, detachments, and posts, and all officers in the service of the United States in the above mentioned departments:

You are hereby directed to place at the disposal of the American Baptist Home Mission Society all houses of worship belonging to the Baptist Church South in which a loyal minister of said church does not now officiate. It is a matter of great importance to the Government in its efforts to restore tranquility to the community, and peace to the nation, that Christian ministers should by example and precept support and foster the loyal sentiment of the people. The American Baptist Home Mission Society enjoys the entire confidence of this Department, and no doubt is entertained that all ministers who may be appointed by it will be entirely loyal. You are expected to give it all the aid, countenance, and support practicable in the execution of its important mission.

You are also authorized and directed to furnish their executive officer or agent and his clerk with transportation and subsistence when it can be done without prejudice to the service, and will afford them courtesy, assistance and protection.

By order of the Secretary of War:
E. D. TOWNSEND,
Assistant Adjutant General.

UNITED PRESBYTERIAN CHURCH.

WAR DEPARTMENT, ADJUTANT GENERAL'S OFFICE,
WASHINGTON, *February* 15, 1864.

To all Generals and officers commanding armies, detachments, and posts, and all officers in the service of the United States, in the States of Mississippi, Arkansas, Tennessee, Alabama, Georgia, Florida, and South and North Carolina:

You are hereby directed to place at the disposal of the authorized Agent of the "Board of Home Missions of the United Presbyterian Church" all houses of worship belonging to the Associate Reformed Presbyterian Church, in which a loyal minister who has been appointed by the Board of Home Missions of said church does not now officiate. It is a matter of great importance to the Government in its efforts to restore tranquility to the community, and peace to the nation, that Christian ministers should, by example and precept support and foster the loyal sentiment of the people. The Board of Home Missions of the United Presbyterian Church enjoys the entire confidence of this Department, and no doubt is entertained that all ministers who may be appointed by it will be entirely loyal. You are expected to give it all the aid, countenance, and support practicable in the execution of its important mission.

This authority is designed to apply only to such States as are by the President's Proclamation designated as being in rebellion, and is not designed to operate in loyal States, nor in cases where loyal congregations in rebel States shall be organized and worship upon the terms prescribed by the President's Amnesty.

You are also authorized and directed to furnish the authorized Agent of the Board of Home Missions of the United Presbyterian Church, and his clerk, with transportation and subsistence when it can be done without prejudice to the service, and will afford them courtesy, assistance, and protection.

By order of the Secretary of War:

E. D. TOWNSEND,
Assistant Adjutant General.

PRESBYTERIAN CHURCH, (O. S. AND N. S.)

WAR DEPARTMENT, ADJUTANT GENERAL'S OFFICE,
WASHINGTON, *March* 10, 1864.

To the Generals commanding the Military Division of the Mississippi, and the Department of the Gulf, of the South, and of Virginia and North Carolina, and all generals and officers commanding armies, detachments, and posts, and all officers in the service of the United States, in the above mentioned Departments:

The Board of Domestic Missions of the Presbyterian Church and the Presbyterian Committee of Home Missions enjoy the entire confidence of this Department, and no doubt is entertained that all ministers who may be appointed by them will be entirely loyal.

You are expected to permit such ministers of the Gospel bearing a commission of the "Board of Domestic Missions" or of the "Presbyterian Committee of Home Missions" of the Presbyterian Church, as may convince you that their commissions are genuine, to exercise the functions of their office within your command, and to give them all the aid, countenance, and support which may be practicable and in your judgment proper in the execution of their important mission.

By order of the Secretary of War:

E. D. TOWNSEND,
Assistant Adjutant General.

The above order was given at the solicitation of the Rev. Dr. Janeway, Mission Rooms, 910 Arch street, Philadelphia, Pennsylvania, and of Rev. Dr. Kendall, Presbyterian Rooms, 150 Nassau street, New York City, and copies sent to each of the commanding officers of the Military Division of the Mississippi, and the Departments of the Gulf, of the South, and of Virginia and North Carolina.*

UNITED BRETHREN IN CHRIST.

WAR DEPARTMENT, ADJUTANT GENERAL'S OFFICE,
WASHINGTON, *March* 23, 1864.

To the Generals commanding the Military Division of the Mississippi, the Departments of the Gulf, of the South, and of Virginia and North Carolina, and all Generals and officers commanding armies, detachments, and posts, and all officers in the service of the United States in the above mentioned Departments:

You are hereby directed to give to Teachers and Missionaries sent out by the "Church of the United Brethren in Christ," such privileges and facilities for their work within the limits of your command, as are usually given to others under similar circumstances and are not prejudicial to the service.

By order of the Secretary of War:

E. D. TOWNSEND,
Assistant Adjutant General.

The above was delivered to Rev. D. K. Flickinger, of Dayton, Ohio.

EXPLANATORY ORDER.*

WAR DEPARTMENT, ADJUTANT GENERAL'S OFFICE,
WASHINGTON, *February* 13, 1864.

MAJOR-GENERAL ROSECRANS, *U. S. Volunteers,*
Comdg. Department of the Missouri, St. Louis, Mo.:

SIR: I am directed by the Secretary of War to say that the orders from the Department placing at the disposal of the constituted Church authorities in the Northern States houses of worship in other States, is designed to apply only to such States as are by the President's Proclamation designated as being in rebellion and is not designed to operate in loyal States, nor in cases where loyal congregations in rebel States shall be organized and worship upon the terms prescribed by the President's Amnesty.

I am, Sir, very respectfully,
Your obedient servant,
E. D. TOWNSEND,
Assistant Adjutant General.

A copy of the above was sent to Bishop Ames.

ENFORCEMENT OF THESE ORDERS.

In pursuance of the above orders, Brigadier General Veatch issued this order at Memphis:

HEADQUARTERS DEPARTMENT OF MEMPHIS,
December 23, 1863.

Rev. Bishop AMES: In obedience to the orders of the

---

* The Presbytery of Louisville, O. S., at a late meeting, passed a series of resolutions, proposed by Dr. S. R. Wilson, in which the Presbytery enters a solemn protest against the action of the Board of Domestic Missions, in procuring an order from the Secretary of War, permitting ministers of the gospel bearing a commission from the Board, to exercise their ministry within the military departments in the Southern States. The Presbytery further calls upon the General Assembly "at once to disavow the said act, that so the Church may be saved from the sin, reproach, and ruin which this thing is calculated to bring upon her."

The following is the dissent of one of the members of the Presbytery:

The undersigned respectfully dissents from the action of Presbytery:

First—Because our commission is into all the world, and unto every creature; and there are some of them that we know not how to reach without a pass.

Secondly—Because the framers of our Confession of Faith, both by word and by deed, recognized the powers that be as "nursing fathers," bound "to protect the Church of our common Lord;" and we think it no disgrace, according to our ordination vows, still to adhere to this doctrine of our fathers.

Thirdly—Because the Apostle Paul asked leave to preach the gospel on various occasions, both of the civil and military authorities; and we are by no means convinced that he was guilty of "illicit alliances," of "spiritual whoredom," or that he was "demoralized" thereby.

Fourthly—Because that same great Apostle to the Gentiles rejoiced that the gospel was preached, even through envy and strife; and we have no infallible evidence that he went contrary, either to "the word of God," or to the "testimony of" any of "the fathers," except certain of the "sons of Issachar," who have recently risen up in the Presbytery of Louisville, "to tell the people what to do."

Fifthly—Because the General Assembly of "the Church in the wilderness" asked leave of the Ammonites to pass through their borders while journeying on ecclesiastical business; and we have never heard of any Presbytery protesting against their action as unconstitutional; nor have we ever heard of any individuals calling such right in question, except Pharoah and Sihon—both of them hardened monarchs—who did it to their own destruction; and the Presbytery of Louisville, "all honorable men," who, we fear, have done it to their own injury.

By dissenting only from this action of Presbytery, the undersigned does not wish to be understood, by any means, as endorsing every thing else that is now, or may hereafter become wrong in this wicked world of ours.

JAMES P. McMILLAN.

* This explanatory order was issued on the application of Loyal Methodists of Missouri, for whom Rev. John Hogan acted in bringing it to the attention of the President. This note to Mr. Hogan illustrates the President's views:

"As you see within, the Secretary modifies his order so as to exempt Missouri from it. Kentucky never was within it; nor, as I learn from the Secretary, was it ever intended for any more than a means of rallying the Methodist people in favor of the Union, in localities where the rebellion had disorganized and scattered them. Even in that view, I fear it is liable to some abuses, but it is not quite easy to withdraw it entirely and at once.

"A. LINCOLN.

"*February* 13, 1864."

Secretary of War, dated Washington, November 30th, 1863, a copy of which is here attached. I place at your disposal a "house of worship" known as "Wesley Chapel," in the city of Memphis, State of Tennessee, the said house being claimed as the property of the Methodist Episcopal Church South, and there being no loyal minister, appointed by a loyal Bishop, now officiating in said house of worship.

I am, very respectfully, your obedient servant.

JAMES C. VEATCH,
Brigadier General.

1864, March 23—Rev. J. P. Newman, D. D., Methodist Episcopal, delivered an address in New Orleans on an occasion described in the subjoined report from the *True Delta*, of March 28:

REV. DR. NEWMAN'S ADDRESS IN NEW ORLEANS.

[*From the True Delta, March* 28.]

In accordance with the Government plan concerning the churches of the South, the Board of Missions of the Methodist Episcopal Church have sent the Rev. J. P. Newman, D. D., to New Orleans, to take charge of all the churches of that powerful denomination there. A very large audience, composed of some of the most influential citizens, assembled on the evening of the 23d inst., at the Carondelet street Church, to extend to the reverend gentleman a cordial welcome.

On being introduced by the chairman, Dr. Newman said:

There were three reasons for sending a minister from New York to New Orleans:

1. It was in harmony with the theory of labor as held by the Methodist Church. There is no such Church as the Methodist Church North. Ours is the Methodist Episcopal Church. We are not sectional. We acknowledge no geographical limits less than the world itself. Every minister of our church may say with its founder, "The world is my parish and Heaven is my home." [Applause.] In the separation of 1844 our church relinquished no right to labor in the South, but since has claimed, as before, and still claims, to send her ministers to the equator and to the poles, and all latitudes between. We reject the sentiment that we are encroaching upon the rights of others. If the theory that we are sectional be true, what right have we to send ministers to Europe, to Scandinavia, Bulgaria and Constantinople? This movement, then, is in strict harmony with our system of labor.

2. It is required by the present state of the country. Thousands of our citizens have followed in the track of our victorious armies, "to build the old wastes, and raise up the former desolations and repair the waste cities," and the church had been recreant to her trust had she not provided them with the ministry of the Word. We have too long trusted our Northern men who have taken up their residence South to the exclusive influence of Southern teaching; but that day is past, and the Church now declares that she will not trust these thousands of her sons and daughters to—(the words of the speaker were here lost in a storm of applause.) Whatever mountains they may climb, into whatever valleys they may descend, on whatever plains they may spread themselves, or whatever seas they may cross, she claims the right to follow them with her ministers of truth and peace. [Applause.]

3. This movement was justified by the present disorganized and destitute condition of the Southern churches. Their former ministers had either fled or been silenced, or imprisoned, or banished, and it had become the solemn duty of the Mother Church to send shepherds to these deserted and scattered flocks. A shepherd should never leave his flock though all of Uncle Sam's guns were turned against him [Applause.]

Toward these, her children, has the Mother Church been "moved with compassion," seeing that they are as "sheep without a shepherd," and by her direction I came as a minister of Christ to supply the consolation of religion to her members. While I have much respect for balls and bayonets, my great hope for the salvation of the country is the Gospel. I expect to mingle with you in your prayer meetings, and by all ministerial and pastoral fidelity shall try to hold up the Cross, to preach a gospel which is "the power of God unto salvation to every one that believeth."

These are the reasons which influenced the Missionary Board to recommend to the Bishops to make this provision for the spiritual wants of this section of our country.

But we find ourselves met on the threshold by two embarrassments, of which I have heard since my arrival in New Orleans:

1. The question of property confronts us. We are denounced as church robbers; are charged with having robbed the people of the South of their church property.

My answer is: The right of church property has never been disturbed, as far as we are concerned.

The General Government has seen fit to seize these churches, but it has not conveyed their title to us. There has been no passing of deeds. We do not own an inch either of this or any other church in the South. The Secretary of War wrote to the General commanding this Department to place at the disposal of Bishop Ames the Methodist churches for the use of the loyal ministers. If there has been any robbery the accusation lies against the General Government. But the General Government has committed no robbery. It was aware that these churches were occupied (so far as they were occupied at all) by congregations united by disloyal sympathies and by teachers disposed to inculcate treason. It knew that if they were placed under the care of the Methodist Church they would be occupied by no ministers but would be loyal to the Government, and that they would be likely to gather around them loyal hearers. [Applause.] So much then for property. He did not want to hear another word about the robbery of church property while he was in New Orleans.

2. Another embarrassment is the charge that the Methodist Church is a political church, and, therefore, should not be tolerated in the South.

Let us analyze this charge. Does it mean that it is united to the State like the Church of England? Have we not recently heard the disclaimer of our President, that he does not "run the churches?"

Does it mean that it is a political party? that its ministers are stump orators? that its class meetings, prayer meetings, quarterly meetings, its annual and general conferences are so much political machinery, worked for political or partisan ends? It will not be pretended. Does it mean that our church is loyal to the General Government? If this be the meaning, I shall admit the charge. We hold and teach that loyalty is a religious duty, as truly obligatory as prayer itself. The twenty-third article of the Discipline is equally binding on the clergy and the laity, and constitutes us a confessedly loyal church. Nor is it optional with the minister whether he inculcates loyal sentiments or not, for how shall a man be saved unless he be loyal?

Does it mean that we are opposed to the doctrine of State sovereignty, Secession and Rebellion? I accept the definition. From the Sabbath-school scholar to the minister, from the exhorter to the bishop, our whole membership reprobate these doctrines.

Does it mean that our ministers denounce political corruptions? I accept the definition. If in this we go astray, we go astray with Moses, who confronted the greatest slaveholder that ever lived; with Paul, who reasoned before Felix "of righteousness, temperance, and judgment to come;" with John the Baptist, who said to Herod Antipas, "it is not lawful for thee to have thy brother Philip's wife;" with Luther, who attacked with the sword of truth the political abominations of Popery.

I have reproved sin in New York, and, God helping me, I shall reprove it in your Crescent city. I hate cowardice, and approbate the outspoken truthfulness of the ministers of the North; and on fidelity to the truth depends the salvation of our country. It is a truth verified by all history, as is the Church so is the State. With no war has the Church been more identified than with the present. With this war no Church has been more identified than the Methodist Church, both North and South.

The Methodist Church South has given no reluctant adhesion to the rebellion; has, perhaps, been foremost, *inter pares prima*, in the mad race of disunion.

The Methodist Church has not been less unanimous and zealous in the defence of the Union. Her bishops, her ministers and her laity have nobly responded to the call of their country in this the hour of her peril. The voice of Simpson has been heard pleading eloquently for the unity of his country. Ames, as patriotic as wise, has not hesitated to lend his aid to our unfortunate prisoners in Richmond, and to give his sons to the army. Janes has found no narrow field for his philanthropic heart in the labors of the Christian Commission. All our church papers and periodicals have given an uncompromising, zealous, persistent support to the Government, and have thrown the whole weight of their influence, intelligent as it was potent, on the side of the Union.

The speaker was glad that he was able to present these views and statements before an audience so large, intelligent and thoughtful. And now, in conclusion, what was the object he had in view?

The Board of Missions, which had been considered a conservative body, (a body of business men in a small room in the city of New York.) had requested that an appropriation should be made for the benefit of this work in the South, and that it should be applied without distinction of color.

Much had been said about equality. But he believed that all men were equal in religious privileges, and ought to be equal in law; and he admonished his audience that if the Caucasian should reject the Gospel and refuse to fill the churches, (casting his eyes toward the galleries, which were filled with faces of a darker hue,) we turn to the sons of Africa. [Applause.]

THE CHURCH QUESTION IN BALTIMORE.

THIRD SESSION, THIRTY-SEVENTH CONGRESS.

1863, March 3—Mr. May, of Maryland, moved that the rules be suspended, to enable him to submit the following:

Whereas, It is represented that Major General Schenck, commanding the forces of the United States stationed in Baltimore, Maryland, has ordered, as a condition to be annexed to the worship of Almighty God by certain religious societies or congregations of the Methodist Church of that city, that the flag of the United States shall be conspicuously displayed at the time and place of such worship; and

Whereas, The said order is a plain violation of the inalienable right to worship God according to the dictates of every one's conscience, as it is asserted by the said congregations, and also by our declarations of fundamental rights, and secured by our State and Federal Constitutions; and

Whereas, A minister of the said congregation, the reverend John H. Dashiell, having, on Sunday, the 15th ultimo, removed the said flag from his own premises, which was also the place of worship of one of said congregations, where the said flag had been placed surreptitiously by some evil-minded person, and for so doing was arrested by order of the said General Schenck, and held as a prisoner: Therefore

Resolved, That the Judiciary Committee be, and hereby is, instructed to inquire into the allegations aforesaid, and ascertain by what authority the said General Schenck exercises a power to regulate or interfere with the privileges of divine worship, and also to arrest and detain as a prisoner the said minister of the Gospel, as aforesaid; and further, that the said Committee be instructed to report upon the same at an early day.

Consent was not obtained, the subject being undetermined when the Speaker adjourned the House *sine die*.

The facts in the case were as follow:

FIRST ORDER OF GENERAL SCHENCK.

HEADQUARTERS MIDDLE DEPARTMENT, 8TH ARMY CORPS,
OFFICE PROVOST MARSHAL,
BALTIMORE, *Feb.* 9, 1863.

JOHN MCGEOCH, Esq., *Gen'l Sup'd't Assembly Rooms, Cor. Hanover and Lombard St.*:

SIR—I understand that considerable disgust is excited in the mind of a class of persons who assemble at your Rooms, in consequence of the American Flag having been displayed there.

You will hereafter cause constantly to be displayed in a conspicuous position at the head of the hall a large size American Flag until further orders.

By order Major General Schenck:

WM. S. FISH,
Major and Provost Marshal.

SECOND ORDER OF GENERAL SCHENCK.

HEADQUARTERS MIDDLE DEPARTMENT, 8TH ARMY CORPS,
OFFICE PROVOST MARSHAL,
BALTIMORE, *Feb.* 14, 1863.

JOHN M. BUCK, *Franklin Bank*, R. H. MILES, H. W. BROUGH, and others, *Trustees Central Methodist Church:*

GENTLEMEN—I understand that rather than to worship God under the shadow of the American Flag you have in consequence of the order for you to display in the building in which you hold your services, our glorious flag, concluded not to hold such worship at the place you have been accustomed to have it and have chosen some other place for no other purpose than evading this order. Therefore you will under these circumstances cause to be conspicuously displayed in the public building or buildings where you meet to-morrow (the 15th) the American Flag, as in accordance with first order to Mr. McGeoch. I understand the congregation of which you are the trustees are to meet in different places. The regulation mentioned above will have reference to each place.

By order Major General Schenck:

WM. S. FISH,
Major and Provost Marshal.

REPLY OF ONE OF THE TRUSTEES.

BALTIMORE, 14*th February*, 1863.

Major General SCHENCK:

GENERAL—A communication (without date) from the Provost Marshal, by your order, addressed to myself and others, as trustees of Central Methodist Church, was handed me at a late hour to-day.

Some of the other gentlemen named being absent from the city, I have deemed it my duty to reply individually. The communication referred to sets forth that "I understand that rather than to worship God under the shadow of the American flag you have in consequence of the order for you to display in the building in which you hold your services, our glorious flag, concluded not to hold such worship at the place you have been accustomed to have it, and have chosen some other place, for the no other purpose than evading this order. Therefore you will under these circumstances, cause to be conspicuously displayed in the public building or buildings, where you meet to-morrow (the 15th) the American flag as in accordance with first order to Mr. McGeoch. I understand the congregation of which you are the trustees are to meet in two different places. The regulation mentioned above will have reference to each place."

I beg to assure you, general, that from whatever source you may have derived your information, it is erroneous. The congregation worshipping at the Assembly Rooms have been doing so for nearly one year, and it may truthfully be said, a more respectable and well ordered congregation has nowhere assembled. Discarding all political associations, we have not only sought, but *insisted*, that we would only have the gospel preached unto us. With great profit and religious comfort, we have thus conducted our exercises for all the time referred to, and not one unpleasant circumstance, so far as we know, has ever occurred to interrupt such harmony. On last Sabbath, (8th) when the congregation assembled as usual, for the morning service, it was found that two large American flags were displayed immediately over and in rear of the preacher's stand. Of course so unusual an exhibition seemed strange, and may have been objected to by a few, but the voluntary explanations made by Mr. McGeoch, in effect, that the lateness of the hour at which the room was vacated on Saturday night, prevented him from arranging it as he had always heretofore done, was satisfactory; and especially so to the great body of the members. The congregation in the morning was very large; indeed, the room was crowded, and nothing was either said or done, so far, certainly, as the members were concerned, calculated to give offence, or in the smallest degree wound the feelings of the most sensitive—no indignity whatever, by look, or word, or gesture, was offered to the American flag.

The congregation at night was about the usual average night assembly. A few days thereafter the official members learned with deep regret, and no little surprise, that the agent (Mr. McGeoch) had received orders from you, that the American flag should always be displayed, as on last Sabbath, and as it was impossible for the official members to put any other construction upon such order than a denial to them of the right to worship God according to the dictates of their own consciences, and as such order was unusual, different from what they had all their lives been accustomed to, and not made applicable to other religious assemblies in this city, they felt impelled to vacate the Assembly Rooms.

Not, as you suppose, general, that they would not "worship God under the shadow of the American flag;" for this a very large congregation, including most of our members, had done on the previous Sabbath. But upon the ground, and for the reason, that they were denied the right to worship God, without the display of such ensign.

The undersigned begs to be pardoned for saying to so distinguished and so intelligent a gentleman as General Schenck, that the inalienable right to worship God, according to the dictates of every man's conscience, however much it may have been interfered with in other countries, has ever been accorded to all men in this land of liberty, as indeed it might well be to all the inhabitants living "under the best government the world ever saw."

So sacred has this right been esteemed that nearly, if not all the States of North America, have thrown around it the protection of legislative enactments; and for the maintenance of this great principle men have, in all ages, been willing "to count not only their own lives dear unto them"—have "taken joyfully the spoiling of their goods."

The difficulty, therefore, general, is not in the display of the American flag, abstractly considered, but it is as to whether this great principle of the free worship of God shall be surrendered.

Intimately associated with the congregation at the Assembly Rooms, we have two other appointments—one in Biddle street the other at Chatsworth. The latter has been a Mission school and place of worship for two years, and is the private property of Charles J. Baker, merchant of this city. The former is the private property of the Rev. John Dashiell, who occupies it for the instruction of youth during the week, and our association pays him rent for its use on the Sabbath and for week-night preaching. We have used it now for nearly one year. General Schenck, therefore, cannot fail to perceive that we have *not*, as the communication from the Provost Marshal states, "chosen some other place, for the no other purpose than evading this order"—meaning of course the order to display the flag at the Assembly Rooms.

At both of these appointments, large and highly respectable congregations assemble every Sabbath to hear the Gospel, a flourishing Sabbath school is also attached to each, and lately, under the influence of the Gracious Spirit, many have been added to the Church.

The undersigned, therefore, in view of all the circumstances, and with all that respect which the position of such a distinguished gentleman as General Schenck should ever command, begs leave to say that he (the undersigned) has neither the right nor the inclination to order the American flag or any other ensign to be displayed at either of the places referred to.

With very great respect,

JOHN M. BUCK,
Recording Steward.

CARD OF MR. DASHIELL.

"To prevent misrepresentation, it is deemed best to explain an incident that may be erroneously reported in the morning papers.

"Yesterday morning a small American flag was found nailed over the door of my school-building, 195 Biddle street, the large hall of which is rented for religious worship. I did not know by what hands or at what hour it had been done. Lest it should, by the oddness of the thing, attract around the door a crowd, and produce a difficulty, and because it was not done by constituted authority, but surreptitiously in the night, and furthermore, because it was my will, as the owner of the property, that no display of the kind should be made upon it, I removed it. Who put it there, and what were the motives or where was the policeman when it was done, I shall not now inquire.

"JOHN H. DASHIELL,
"287 *N. Howard Street.*
"*Monday Morning, Feb.* 16*th*, 1863."

ACTION OF THE OFFICIAL MEMBERS.

At an adjourned meeting of the official members of the several congregations worshipping at Chatsworth, Biddle street, and formerly at the New Assembly Rooms, held on Tuesday evening, February 17th, the following preamble and resolutions were unanimously adopted:—

Whereas, the inalienable right to worship God according to the dictates of every man's conscience has ever been accorded to all the inhabitants of this country, and is so sacred a privilege as not to be lightly esteemed or easily set aside, and has been guaranteed by the legislative action of nearly, if not quite all the States of this nation; and *whereas*, the congregation lately worshipping at the New Assembly Rooms have enjoyed this inestimable privilege, at said place, for nearly one year, with great religious comfort and edification, and free from any interruption whatever; and *whereas*, an order has now issued from Major-General Schenck, military commander of this district, directing the American flag to be constantly displayed in a conspicuous place in said building, and which in effect prohibits our worship without the display of such ensign; and *whereas*, such order is unusual, and not made applicable to other religious congregations of this city; and *whereas*, no other construction can be placed upon such order than a direct interference with the great principle of the free and untrammeled worship of Almighty God; therefore,

Resolved, That we respectfully but earnestly protest against the right of Major-General Schenck, or any other military or civil officer, to interfere with or interrupt us in our sacred and solemn duty of worshipping God.

Resolved, That by reason of such order and interference we decline any longer to occupy the New Assembly Rooms.

Resolved, That these proceedings be signed by the chairman and secretary, and published in the city papers.

JOHN M. BUCK, *Chairman.*
WILLIAM R. BARRY, *Secretary.*

ARREST AND RELEASE OF MR. DASHIELL.

Mr. Dashiell was arrested, but released on signing a parole, stated below:

HEADQUARTERS MIDDLE DEPARTMENT, 8TH ARMY CORPS,
OFFICE PROVOST MARSHAL,
BALTIMORE, *February* 17, 1863.

REV. JOHN H. DASHIELL:

DEAR SIR—I enclose another parole, which I sincerely hope you cannot take exceptions to sign; and indeed I cannot conceive how any citizen, or reasonable man, as I have abundant evidence you are, can hesitate to put his name to such a paper, no matter how ultra his private sentiments or views may be—which, as I assured you before, is none of my business. You said to me on Monday morning that you thought it would have been *better* for you first to have ascertained whether the flag in question was placed in your building by authority or not before taking the measures you did. And as to the remainder of the parole (or the parole proper), I think your feelings are exactly in consonance with what I ask you to give your parole to do. If you conclude to sign the accompanying parole, please do so, and send immediately back, and I will endeavor to procure your return to your family this evening.

I am, very respectfully,
Your most obedient,
WM. S. FISH,
Major and Provost Marshal.

HEADQUARTERS MIDDLE DEPARTMENT, 8TH ARMY CORPS,
OFFICE PROVOST MARSHAL,
BALTIMORE, *February* 17, 1863.

I, John H. Dashiell, frankly admit that it was my duty to have first inquired, or endeavored to learn from some reliable source, whether the national flag which was displayed at the window of the building in Biddle street, from which I took it on Sunday last, was placed there by authority, before I proceeded to take it down on my own responsibility; and I hereby give my parole of honor that I will in every respect demean myself as a true, loyal, law-abiding citizen of the United States should, neither doing myself, or aiding, abetting, or countenancing any act of others that is prejudicial to the good of my country, or the honor of its flag.

JOHN H. DASHIELL. [Seal.]

Witness—John K. Barbour, Capt. 9th Penna. Reserves, Provost Marshal, Fort McHenry, Md.

CORRESPONDENCE BETWEEN GOVERNOR BRADFORD AND THE STEWARDS OF THE CHURCH.

HEADQUARTERS MIDDLE DEPARTMENT,
EIGHTH ARMY CORPS,
BALTIMORE, MD., *March* 28, 1863.

His Excellency A. W. BRADFORD,
Governor of Maryland:

DEAR SIR—Certain parties here who took offence at the sight of the United States flag in their place of worship have, I understand, addressed a letter to you complaining of the orders issued from these headquarters in relation thereto.

One of these parties addressed to me, and afterwards published in the newspapers, a communication on the subject, which I did not deem it necessary in any way to answer.

But if not incompatible with the public interest I shall be glad to have you furnish me with a copy of your correspondence on the subject, with leave to make it public, as I think there might be corrected thereby some mistaken views and opinions of my action in the matter.

I am, very respectfully,
Your obedient servant,
ROBT. C. SCHENCK,
Major General Commanding.

STATE OF MARYLAND,
EXECUTIVE DEPARTMENT,
ANNAPOLIS, *April* 1, 1863.

Major General R. C. SCHENCK,
Commanding Middle Department:

DEAR SIR—I have received yours of 28th ultimo, in which, referring to a correspondence lately had between some gentlemen of Baltimore and myself, on the subject of your order directing the display of the United States flag in their place of worship, you request me to furnish you a copy of that correspondence, and to allow you to make it public, if not incompatible with the public interest.

The correspondence referred to took place some weeks since, and involving as it does an imputation upon your official conduct in this military department, you would seem to be entitled to a copy of it, as you request. I accordingly inclose it, and as the subject has been already repeatedly referred to through the press, can see no objection to its publication, especially if, as you suggest, it may be at all calculated to correct any mistaken views that may exist in reference to your course.

Very respectfully,
Your obedient servant,
A. W. BRADFORD.

LETTER OF TRUSTEES TO THE GOVERNOR.

BALTIMORE, *March* 3, 1863.

To His Excellency A. W. BRADFORD,
Governor of Maryland:

SIR—The undersigned, Stewards of the Central, Chatsworth, and Biddle Street Methodist Episcopal Churches in this city, having, by an extraordinary order from Major General Schenck, Military Commander for this district, been deprived of the right and privilege of holding public worship, except upon conditions prescribed by military authority, feel constrained to make application to your Excellency for that relief and protection which is guaranteed to them by the Constitution and laws of Maryland, and which we are well persuaded is entirely within the power of your Excellency to afford.

In bringing to the notice of your Excellency a statement of our grievances, we beg your indulgence for the reference we shall make to the commencement of our organization, it seeming to us to be essential in order to a correct understanding of the whole subject. The General Conference of the Methodist Episcopal Church which met at Buffalo, New York, in May, 1860, changed the Discipline of our Church, and unconstitutionally introduced a new dogma, or chapter, into the Discipline, very objectionable to a number of the Annual Conferences, and especially so to the Baltimore Conference; by reason of which a majority of the ministers and laymen determined that they would no longer hold affiliation with, or be subject to the jurisdiction of said General Conference.

In furtherance of this a Laymen's Convention, numerously attended by delegates from the various stations and circuits within the bounds of the Baltimore and East Baltimore Conferences, was held in the Eutaw Methodist Episcopal Church, in this city, in December, 1860. The Hon. J. Summerfield Berry was Chairman, and the Convention adopted resolutions declaring they would not submit to the new chapter, and in effect ignoring the jurisdiction of the Buffalo General Conference.

Another Laymen's Convention, convened under a call from the Presiding Elders and Lay Stewards, met at Staunton, Virginia, in March, 1861, (at the same time as the Baltimore Annual Conference,) and reaffirmed the position which had been taken at the Baltimore Eutaw Convention the preceding December, the most prominent supporters at this second Convention being Hon. J. Summerfield Berry and the Hon. Hugh L. Bond.

The Baltimore Conference, then in session at Staunton, received and acted upon the memorial from the Laymen's Convention—approved of, and agreed in sentiment with said Laymen's Convention, and resolved, "That we hereby declare that the General Conference of the Methodist Episcopal Church held at Buffalo in May, 1860, by its unconstitutional action, has sundered the ecclesiastical relation which has hitherto bound us together as one Church, so far as any act of theirs could do so. That we will not longer submit to the jurisdiction of said General Conference, but hereby declare ourselves separate and independent of it—still claiming to be, notwithstanding, an integral part of the Methodist Episcopal Church." This resolution was passed by the following vote: ayes 87, no 1, declining to vote 41. Soon after the adjournment of the Baltimore Conference at Staunton—in March, 1861—the unhappy civil war broke out, and was in existence in March, 1862, the time for the Baltimore Conference to meet again.

But the great body of the ministers were in Virginia, and unable to reach the place (Baltimore city) of its sitting. Most of the *minority*, however, (that is, the forty-one declining to vote,) were not so unfortunately situated, and hence this *minority*, notwithstanding the action had at Staunton, Virginia, did meet in the Light Street Church, under the jurisdiction of the General Conference, and under the Discipline of 1860, with the new chapter therein.

It followed, therefore, as a matter of course, that a large proportion of the membership in this city, and some of the preachers, in every self-respect, and in consonance with their doings at Staunton, were obliged to seek other places of worship, and to organize the Church for mutual benefit, until such time as the *genuine* Baltimore Conference could come together and take charge of us.

In the declaration which we adopted at our outset, a copy of which we inclose your Excellency, we distinctly and emphatically announced that we were influenced by "no political consideration whatever."

It occurs to us, therefore, that your Excellency will thus perceive that, as a Christian congregation, we were entitled to the great and inestimable privilege of worshipping God upon the same terms and conditions as all other religious assemblies of this city and State.

So believing, we secured in March, 1862, two places for public worship—the "New Assembly Rooms" and "Biddle Street." Chatsworth (another appointment) had been a preaching place, and under the Baltimore Conference since March, 1860, but joined our organization in March, 1862, for the reason that they would not submit to the new chapter.

We come to say to your Excellency that since March, 1862, up to the 15th February last, we have been conducting our public exercises to very large and highly respectable congregations, and free from any interruption whatever, and, as we fondly hope, and sincerely believe, exerting an influence creditable to society and the peace and welfare of this community. Nor did it ever, for one moment, occur to us that, without any cause whatever, military authority would be exercised to forbid us the right to worship our Maker. We were, however, disappointed, and, lamentable as it is for the age in which we live, such has actually taken place. We ask the attention of your Excellency to a copy of the order from Major Fish, Provost Marshal, to the agent of the New Assembly Rooms, and also to the order to the Trustees of the Central M. E. Church, and to the reply of our Recording Steward, and action of the official body, in which the subject is fully reviewed—all herewith inclosed.

We further beg to say to your Excellency that, being obliged to vacate the New Assembly Rooms, we rented from Mr. Edward Kearney a large public hall (Monumental Hall) and advertised, as was our custom, that we would have public preaching on Sunday, 22d of February, whereupon another order, issued by direction of Major General Schenck, a copy of which is herewith inclosed, arrested such contemplated public worship. To this last order we most respectfully ask a critical examination by your Excellency. You will perceive that it is directed to Mr. Kearney, the owner and proprietor of the Monumental Hall, a large public hall, in which several nights during the week there are public gatherings, parties, balls, soirees, &c., and yet this order to display the flag is only to be enforced "on every occasion when this congregation meets in your building."*

Sir, with the most distinguished consideration for your Excellency, we hold that it is not within the range of possibility that the Governor of Maryland can bring his mind to any other conclusion than that a more direct interference with the rights of public worship never was exercised in any country, and that such interference is in violation of the Bill of Rights of this State.

Coming, then, to your Excellency, as we now do, soliciting for our people that relief and protection which is guaranteed to us by the Constitution and laws of Maryland, we cannot and will not permit ourselves to doubt but that we shall have your sympathy and the sought-for relief, so entirely within your power to afford. Our people are scattered, our large and flourishing Sabbath school cannot meet, and by consequence the children go without that religious Sabbath training so beneficial and so important to the rising generation.

Pardon us, and we will ask of your Excellency what have we done that we are not permitted to meet as the other religious congregations in this city?

We appeal to this entire community to witness against us whether we be unworthy to enjoy the same rights and privileges as our fellow-citizens.

Finally, we say to your Excellency that as citizens of Maryland, law-abiding and order-loving, we have rights in common with our fellow-men. We ask for nothing more. Is it right to grant us less?

Will your Excellency consent that military authority shall, in violation of law, overturn and set at naught the

---

* The order is as follows:

HEADQUARTERS MIDDLE DEPARTMENT, 8TH ARMY CORPS,
OFFICE PROVOST MARSHAL,
BALTIMORE, *Feb.* 21, 1863.

MR. KEARNEY, *Owner and Proprietor of Central (Monumental) Hall, corner St. Paul's and Centre sreets, Baltimore City:*

SIR: The congregation and clergyman which intend worshipping at your hall to-morrow, Sunday, the 21st inst., have left the New Assembly Rooms, where they formerly held service, for the purpose of evading the order in regard to the display of National Flag. Therefore you are hereby ordered to display in a conspicuous place at the head of your hall, during the entire day, to-morrow, the 22d, a large size National Flag. This not only to-morrow, but on every occasion when this congregation meets in your building.

By order Major General SCHENCK:

WM. S. FISH,
Major and Provost Marshal.

dearest and most sacred right that any man can enjoy, that of worshipping God?

Who is it, sir, in God's name, who is it, of human composition, that shall assume to himself such high prerogative?

Begging your Excellency to excuse us for being tedious, and again imploring your aid in behalf of our afflicted congregation, whom we are anxious to bring together again by procuring a place for worship,

We are, with great respect,
Your Excellency's ob't servants,
JOHN M. BUCK,
CHARLES J. BAKER,
JOHN W. BRUFF,
J. B. BRINKLEY,
SAML. G. MILES,
CHARLES TOWSON,
JOSEPH P. SHIPLEY,
WM. R. BARRY,
LEONARD PASSANO,
Stewards M. E. Church.

REPLY OF GOVERNOR BRADFORD.

STATE OF MARYLAND,
EXECUTIVE DEPARTMENT,
ANNAPOLIS, *March* 10, 1863.

To Messrs. JOHN M. BUCK and others,
Stewards of Central M. E. Church, &c.:

GENTLEMEN—Your letter of the 3d instant has been received, and I avail myself of the first opportunity allowed by other engagements to reply to it.

You commence by saying that having been by an extraordinary order of Major General Schenck deprived of the right and privilege of holding public worship, except upon conditions prescribed by him, you feel constrained to make application to me for that relief and protection which is guaranteed by the Constitution and laws of Maryland, and which you say you are well persuaded is entirely within my power to afford.

I have looked through your letter with some interest and curiosity to ascertain, if I could, what is the particular relief and protection which you have in view, and which I, as you think, have clearly the power to afford. But there is nothing that indicates how or by what process you expect me to interfere to redress the grievance of which you complain. Under our system of government its various co-ordinate departments are carefully separated and distinguished, and it is distinctly declared by our Constitution that "no person exercising the functions of one of said departments shall assume or discharge the duties of any other." Such being the case, it rarely, if ever, happens that any personal wrong inflicted upon the citizen is, in the first instance, a proper subject of complaint to the Executive. That department of the Government is not adapted to the investigation always necessary to be made in determining the character and extent of all such wrongs. This is a duty confided to the judicial tribunals, which can ascertain the facts, apply the law, and provide the appropriate remedy.

If, therefore, you have been wrongfully ousted from your place of worship, or suffered any unlawful interruption in your religious exercises, the courts of the State are obviously the only tribunals where all the circumstances can be properly investigated, and your legal and constitutional rights lawfully determined.

This view of the case might, perhaps, relieve me of the necessity of a further reply to your communication; but as it would seem that the same considerations could scarcely have escaped your own notice, and as you have gone with such particularity into the full history of your religious association, and of the alleged outrage upon its rights, it would seem that you may have expected that, if I could do nothing more, I might express a sympathy in your complaints, and utter some protest against the proceedings which have led to them. It is due, therefore, to you, and to myself, as well as to that frankness I desire always to observe in all communications with my fellow-citizens, that I should take a more particular notice of the facts you have brought to my attention.

In making your statement you say that you deem it essential to a proper understanding of the subject to recur to the early history of your separate organization. Hence you advert to the proceedings of the General Conference of your Church at Buffalo, in May, 1860, and to an obnoxious addition which that body made to the Discipline of the Church, as the cause of your separate organization in 1862. You refer, also, to the proceedings of the lay members of the Church, repudiating the new article of Discipline—the one in Baltimore in December, 1860, and the other at Staunton in March, 1861—and you quote the action of the Baltimore Conference of Ministers, at the last mentioned date, as declaring that the action of the General Conference referred to "has sundered the ecclesiastical relation which has hitherto bound us together as one Church." Whilst these proceedings may no doubt be a matter of interest in your Church history, neither they nor the action of the highly respectable gentlemen whose names you quote in connection therewith, have, as it appears to me, any material bearing upon the subject of your complaint.

I cannot, however, forbear saying that I think it is greatly to be regretted that, continuing as you seem to have done in an unaltered membership of the Church, and in fellowship with the Baltimore Conference for nearly two years after the adoption of the Buffalo chapter, and fully one year after the proceedings of the two Conventions to which you refer, and of the Conference of 1861, you should in March, 1862, for the first time have practically sundered your Church connection, and abandoned the time-honored edifices and associations where you had previously worshipped. I say that I cannot but regret such a proceeding at such a time. We were then in the midst of a raging conflict of arms, brought upon us confessedly by this doctrine of the right of secession. It was a time for far more engrossing thoughts and important action than any connected with the stale proceedings of past conferences and conventions, and called for at least the temporary suspension of all religious disputes.

The question of ecclesiastical discipline in 1860 had been absorbed by that of a national existence in 1862. It was no longer a contest over the Church government of one denomination of Christians, but a contest to determine whether our country itself possessed a Government that deserved the name, or was to quietly acquiesce in its own dismemberment, and see State after State despoil it of its property and defy its authority at the bidding and for the benefit of aspiring traitors who desired to govern them. Hundreds, therefore, who, in the earlier stages of your Church difficulties might have cordially co-operated with you in protesting against the Buffalo Platform, now, that the whole aspect of public affairs had assumed so threatening a character, were necessarily prompted by every patriotic inducement to discountenance all secessional displays in the face of the calamities which political doctrines, apparently at least of a kindred kind, had already brought upon the nation.

With this passing remark upon the proceedings to which you refer as preliminary to the secession of your congregation, I proceed to the facts connected with the order of General Schenck, which you say has "set at naught the dearest and most sacred right that any man can enjoy, that of worshipping God."

This is, I agree with you, one of our most sacred rights, and he who sets it at naught merits the severest censure. But what are the facts, as I gather them from your communication and the orders and correspondence accompanying it?

It seems that in March, 1862, when you abandoned your former places of worship, you secured the "New Assembly Rooms," where, from that time to the 15th of February last, you continued your religious exercises "free from any interruption whatever."

In your letter to General Schenck, of 14th of February, (a copy of which you send me,) you say that when you assembled as usual for morning service, on the preceding Sunday (the 8th of February,) "it was found that two large American flags were displayed immediately over and in the rear of the preacher's stand." It is to this display, I presume, that the Provost Marshal, in his first order, refers. When addressing Mr. McGeoch, the agent of the rooms, he says: "I understand that considerable disgust is excited in the view of a class of persons who assemble at your rooms, in consequence of the American flag being displayed there," and then directs the said agent to cause that flag to be conspicuously displayed in the same place, until further orders.

It was, therefore, the *disgust* manifested by some of your congregation at the flag which confronted them on the morning of the 8th of February that occasioned the first order of the military authorities, directing its continuance there. It was not displayed on the morning of the 8th in consequence of any military order, but, as I understand to be conceded, was left there inadvertently, being one of many with which the room had been decorated on the previous night, on the occasion of some ball or concert.

Here the suggestion naturally arises, that whilst all religious congregations are equally entitled to the same privileges and protection, no matter where they may worship, yet any one that selects as its sanctuary a public ball and concert room should hardly manifest its surprise, much less its disgust, at any flag that may occasionally adorn its walls, and more especially the flag of the country that shelters it.

That such a disgust was exhibited by a portion at least of your congregation seems to be an admitted fact. It is expressly so stated, as we have seen, by Major Fish, in the first order which he issued, and although he states it as the very foundation of that order, yet the statement is not denied either in the proceedings of the official members of your Church, who met in consequence of said order, and "declined any longer to occupy the New Assembly Rooms," nor in your letter to General Schenck of 14th February, wherein you in effect admit the display of some such feeling when you say that the exhibition of the flag "may have been objected to by a few." Here, then, we have the *reason* for the first interference of the military authorities in ordering the display of the flag. It was not because the congregation had seceded from the Conference, or because they entertained, as some have supposed, sympathies with political Secession—for, although a similar military authority has existed in your city ever since your congregation was separately organized, you have more than once adverted to the fact that it has always heretofore enjoyed its religious services "free from any interruption whatever."

It was the disgust publicly manifested by some of its members at the sight of the national ensign, accidentally left in the room where they assembled, that obliged the authorities, charged especially with the duty of upholding that flag in a war now waged for its destruction, to notice, in some appropriate way, the insult it had thus received. And herein is the obvious answer to all the complaints of an unfair discrimination against your particular congregation in making it alone the subject of the order in question. It would have been obviously unjust and inappropriate to pass any order embracing all religious assemblages merely because of the conduct of one.

Is there anything in the order itself which warrants the construction you have put upon it as "setting at naught the dearest and most sacred right that man can enjoy—that of worshipping God;" or as being "a direct interference with the right of public worship greater than which was never exercised in any country?" How, I would most respectfully ask, does it prohibit or interfere with your worship of the Almighty, under any creed, or according to any form you may see fit to adopt? These are rights justly precious everywhere in the sight of our people, and nowhere more prized than here in Maryland.

But, in God's name, does the sight of our country's standard obstruct or impair the enjoyment of such rights? How is it, let me ask, that they have been so amply provided for? How is it that here, above all the earth besides, this religious liberty, this freedom of conscience and title to equal protection, which you seem to think have been so outraged by the presence of the American ensign, have all been so carefully secured to us? How, but under the auspices of the free Government symbolized by that very flag, and which those who have shared most abundantly in its blessings are now treacherously striving to destroy?

If the order for its display in the room where you assemble is an interference with the rights of conscience, and a violation of the Bill of Rights securing to every man his peculiar religious faith without molestation, then by a parity of reasoning to order the *removal* of any other emblem with which you might choose to adorn your place of meeting would be equally obnoxious to the same objection. You might, therefore, hoist the rebel ensign to-morrow, and defy the military authorities to pull it down, throwing yourself upon your rights of conscience and the guaranties of the Constitution.

I am aware that in your declaration, published simultaneously with your separation from the Conference, as also in your letter to General Schenck, you dwelt with some emphasis upon the determination of your congregation to exclude everything but the gospel; to repudiate "any interference with matters of State;" to meddle not "with questions of a political nature," and to hold "no connection with any ecclesiastical body that does."

So far as this evinces a purpose to banish politics, in the ordinary acceptation of that term, from the domain of the church—to exclude from the pulpit all such topics as usually divide political parties living under and recognizing the same Government—no resolution could be more commendable. And if this had been some party banner, used merely to garnish some partisan platform, I could well understand the disgust it might excite. But I am unable, I confess, to see how the two subjects or the two flags can be so confounded; and with the profoundest reverence for the teachings of religion in its most evangelical form, I have never been able to perceive how men of the purest religious faith, and devoted with the sincerest purpose to the solemn worship of God, can find, in such a purpose, anything inconsistent with the most ardent love of their country; how they can turn their back upon its flag, or refuse to offer up a prayer in its behalf, and call such an exhibition, or such offerings, *politics!*

Such was not the faith nor the practice of our fathers. In our revolutionary times, when making our first struggle for civil and religious freedom, patriotism and religion went hand in hand together. The men of those days clung to their country with an instinctive adoration, second only to that which they rendered to God himself; and the minister who would have refused or hesitated to worship under the flag of the one, would not long have been tolerated at the altars of the other.

Looking, therefore, to the conduct which provoked the first order of the military authorities, I can see no reason for the complaint that your congregation has been *causelessly* made an exception to all others; whilst in the requirements of the order itself there is certainly nothing to authorize the assumption that it is an interference with that constitutional provision which declares that no man, on account of his religious persuasion, ought "to be molested in his person or estate."

I take occasion here to suggest that if the order could be by any one regarded as trenching in any degree upon that religious liberty which it was the purpose of our Constitution to secure, there is nothing in that instrument which makes that right so absolutely sacred and paramount as the comments of yourselves, and occasionally of others, upon its inviolability, would lead us to suppose. On the contrary, the very clause which guarantees this right uses language which shows that those who framed it recognized other and higher obligations. The language employed is: "No person ought by any law to be molested in his person or estate on account of his religious persuasion or profession, or for his religious practice, *unless under color of religion any man shall disturb the good order, peace or safety of the State.*"

Here, then, as everywhere, and under all Governments, is the supreme law to which all others are subordinate—the public safety and the public peace.

I beg that you will not for a moment suppose that in quoting the above proviso I mean to impute to you or your congregation any design to do aught, under the color of religion, to disturb the good order, peace or safety of the State. I have no such thought. But however unobjectionable may have been your purpose, gentlemen of your intelligence must, on reflection, readily perceive that in such times as these, and in a loyal community like ours, with its sensibilities profoundly stirred by the sufferings and sacrifices, the mourning and death, daily being endured for that flag, and under it, nothing would be more likely to provoke a breach of the peace than to witness any demonstration towards it savoring even of indignity or insult, and its military guardians suffering it to pass without rebuke.

I regret, gentlemen, that for such reasons as you have indicated, or indeed, for any reasons, the condition of things to which you so feelingly refer should now exist in your church; that your "people are scattered," that your "large and flourishing Sabbath school cannot meet," and that your "children go without that religious Sabbath training so beneficial and so important to the rising generation." But who is responsible for this state of things? Surely General Schenck has issued no interdict calculated to scatter either your school or congregation. If when on the morning of the 8th of February some of your congregation manifested their disgust at the sight of the flag, or, as you have expressed it, "may have objected to it," and upon their conduct, taken as the expression of the congregation, Major Fish predicated his first order; if you, or the official members of your society representing the congregation, had rebuked the conduct of the few who manifested this contempt, and had disclaimed all intentions to offer insult or offence to our Government or the flag that represents it, I feel authorized to say that the order you deem so obnoxious would have been immediately revoked.

But instead of that, your official members, convened in consequence of the order, after reciting its purport, resolve, "That by reason of such order and interference, we decline any longer to occupy the New Assembly Rooms," thereby authorizing the inference that instead of repudiating the course of the few objecting members, you approved and adopted it as a congregational right and determined to abandon your church services and Sunday school at that place as long as the flag was there displayed.

As a matter of course, after this official action, when you selected another concert-room, the flag was ordered to follow you. To have done otherwise would have been but to suffer an easy evasion of the order and contempt of the authority that issued it.

Even now, I will venture to say, notwithstanding the past action of your official members, if they will still rebuke the expression of contempt referred to, and disclaim all hostility to the Government or the flag, your congregation and schools may again come together and enjoy all the advantages they ever did.

If you refuse this, and will not tolerate the presence of the flag, but, rather than either, choose to suffer your people to be scattered and your children to go without religious instruction, an intelligent community, especially jealous of all its religious rights, but still perfectly understanding the princples on which they rest, will be able to determine where lies the fault.

I am, very respectfully,
Your obedient servant,
A. W. BRADFORD.

BALTIMORE, *April 2d*, 1863.

To his Excellency A. W. BRADFORD,
Governor of Maryland:

SIR: The regard due to the rights and interests of the religious organization which we represent impels us to call your attention to the *misunderstanding* of the facts and principles embodied in our former communication, which pervades your reply of March 10th.

And we are sure that the interest of the question involved will be to your Excellency a sufficient apology for this second intrusion upon your time.

We do not claim to be thoroughly informed as to the technical distinctions between the various departments of Government, and there may have been wanting in the form of our address to you, as Governor of the State, the full sense of the distinctive rights and functions of each.

We had no intention to disregard these, nor would we, by any word or act, induce any one department to trench upon the prerogatives of the others.

But we did not suppose that the functions of the Governor were confined to any mere technical routine of performance. We were rather accustomed to look to the Governor as the guardian of the rights and honor of the State, sworn to see her Constitution and laws faithfully observed and enforced, and prepared, at least, to use his official influence to uphold and maintain the interests secured by law to the very least of her citizens whenever made cognizant of any assault thereupon.

The history of the past two years has quite satisfied us of the entire futility of any appeal to the judiciary, nor had we any disposition to bring about collision between these two. We preferred to employ means more congenial to the spirit of our religion, and sure, as we still are, that the official influence of the Governor of the State might be used with effect to relieve us of the embarrassments and disabilities under which we now labor as a Church.

In appealing to you to exercise that influence, we naturally endeavored to make it clear that we were not, in any sense or to any extent, an offending party; that we had not brought ourselves under the operation of that qualifying clause of the Constitution to which you refer, namely: "Unless under color of religion, any man shall disturb the good order, peace, and safety of society." For this purpose, we summed up the facts connected with the history of our organization, which all show that without the smallest reference to any State or political principles or measures, we were and are intent solely upon maintaining the truth and purity of Christian doctrine and practice.

We did not claim immunity from the pains and penalties attaching to crime against the State. We set up no "higher law" beneath which we might find shelter from the operation of the civil power. We were careful to set forth our recognition of, and obedience to, the "higher powers," and thought ourselves entitled, in all righteousness, to the protection in our worship guaranteed under these powers.

Thus, sir, your own references, besides the entire spirit of your communication, justify the recital of those facts and show their "bearing upon the subject of our complaint."

We regret to see the entire misconstruction of those facts in your reply to our statement.

Referring to the action of our body, you say: "I think it is greatly to be regretted that, continuing, as you seem to have done, in an unaltered membership of the Church, and in fellowship with the Baltimore Conference for nearly two years after the adoption of the Buffalo chapter, and fully one year after the proceedings of the two Conventions to which you refer, and of the Conference of 1861, you should in March, 1862, for the first time, have practically sundered your Church connection," &c.

Will your Excellency be pleased to revert to the acts in the case? The jurisdiction of the Buffalo General Conference was thrown off by the large majority of the Baltimore Conference immediately after the action referred to, or, more properly, that jurisdiction was never admitted. Its discipline was not received, that of 1856 being adhered to, and the membership by an overwhelming majority declaring their resolve no longer to accept the leadership of the Church in the North in matters of faith or practice.

The voice of the people was heard in the Convention of December, 1860, the earliest practicable moment, and again in March, 1861. In obedience to that voice and their own convictions, the session of the Baltimore Conference in March, 1861, being the first after the aforementioned action of the General Conference, declared its absolute independence of the jurisdiction of the General Conference, and its connection therewith dissolved. It was no prospective separation; it was an act accomplished, and so announced in the pastoral letter afterward issued by the authority of the Baltimore Conference.

At the instance, and for the sake of the minority, certain additional resolutions were passed, whose design was to prevent an immediate division in the Conference, and to give the minority opportunity to appeal to the annual conferences in the North for redress, they being pledged, in case of the failure of that appeal, to side with the majority.

Thus, sir, we did not remain in "unaltered connection with the Church" in the North.

By the authoritative action of the Conference, we were completely separated therefrom. We should otherwise have abandoned our connection with the Baltimore Conference. And it happened through the mere accident of the times that we were driven from "the time-honored edifices" in which we were wont to worship. The *minority*, taking advantage of the absence of the majority, an absence entirely unavoidable, declared *themselves* the Conference, and expelled their absent brethren, without trial or hearing, from their body. Of course, we, who adhered to the action of the Conference of Staunton, both ministers and laymen, shared the same fate.

Our present position, you may clearly see from all this, sir, is not owing to any want of promptness in recognizing and acting upon the principles which we now avow. That principle has been embodied in the action of our Conference ever since the session of the General Conference of 1860. We have had no connection with that body since the decisive action of the Baltimore Conference in March, 1861, and by our fellowship with the Baltimore Conference we meant then as we mean now—fellowship with the *majority* of that body; for we cannot recognize the right of some thirty-five or forty to declare more than twice their number to be no longer members of that body—a declaration beyond their power to make in the presence of the majority. Instead of measures so extreme, common courtesy should have suggested to these ministers that which was proposed by the few ministers of the majority, in connection with the laity, who happened to be within reach of the place appointed for the session of the Conference in 1862, namely: some measures of compromise by which the question at issue might be waived during these times of trouble, and the unity of the body preserved without committing any man to a final position. But we do not propose to judge those who differ from us. We only desire to show that we assert merely a Christian principle, having no connection with any principle or matter of State, and that, recognizing the extreme sensitiveness of the public mind, to which you make allusion, we exhausted all the means in our power to prevent any division at that time, and only took our action when we were driven to it by the relentless spirit of the minority, who by these unforeseen circumstances acquired the power in this section of our Conference.

We deem it almost entirely needless to reply to the charges alleged—if not in direct form, at least in the confusion of the terms applied to these movements in your communication—of endorsing and abetting the doctrine and practice of political secession by our action.

We distinctly disavow any connection in theory or practice with that or any other political or State doctrine. We simply affirm and have acted upon the right—never before questioned in a civilized land—of withdrawing from any religious organization so soon as we cease to put faith in its doctrine or endorse its ecclesiastical principles.

We do not think it possible that you should now question that right. Our faith as to the Government is embodied in the twenty-third article of religion—the same received by the whole M. E. Church North, and reads thus:

"*Of the Rulers of the United States of America.*

"The President, the Congress, the General Assemblies, the Governors, and the Councils of State, as the delegates of the people, are the rulers of the United States of America, according to the division of power made by the Constitution of the United States, and by the Constitutions of their respective States.

"And the said States are a sovereign and independent nation, and ought not to be subject to any foreign jurisdiction."

In a word, sir, we hold it to be our supreme duty and right as a Church to maintain and propagate all Christian truth, and to oppose, by purity of life, and by the pure preachings of the gospel, all error in doctrine or practice.

And in so far as the State is concerned, we declare ourselves "subject to the higher powers," believing that "the powers that be are ordained of God." And now, sir, bear with us, while, in as few words as may be, we restate, in entire conformity with all the foregoing principles and facts, the subject of our complaints.

It is *not* to the United States flag, abstractly considered, that we object. We live under that flag. We are governed by the Constitution and laws which that flag represents. We honor it as the symbol of those great principles which our fathers secured to us by sacrifices of which it is also the memorial. We mourn, sir, that that honored emblem should be tarnished by perversion to any uses at war with all the principles which it represents, and render to that extent utterly vain all the sacrifices which it brings to memory.

The order of Major Fish, grounded upon "disgust" said to have been excited by the display of the flag, certainly (we trust unintentionally) misrepresented our congregation. We said in our letter to General Schenck of February 14th, that a few "*may* have objected." Does that mean disgust? They may have objected to it as inappropriate to the worship of God, a service in which we lay aside for the time the relations of earth, and give expression only to our sense of our relation to the Most High. Or they may have objected, because such display was in violation of the contract with the janitor to *remove all worldly decorations*. Or they may have objected, as we do now, because they supposed it was done under an order which singled us out from all the worshippers of this land to be put, as such, under the control of the military power, and forbidden to engage in such worship except upon conditions and under circumstances ordained by that power.

Nor ought we be held responsible for the "few" who "*may* have objected," they not being members of our organization so far as we know. And when, by the explanation of the janitor of the building, it was made manifest that such was not the case, no word of complaint was heard. There was an hour of quiet worship, and then the throng of worshippers quietly returned to their homes, without one word or look of "disgust." This, too, was the case at the evening service.

We dare aver that less dissatisfaction or more entire respect for the flag could not nor would have been exhibited by any other congregation in the city. Nor was it "*in consequence* of the order" that our official body was convened on Tuesday night following: that was the regular weekly meeting of the body. And there—not by way of endorsing that "disgust" to which Major Fish's order, at that meeting first received, referred, for we knew then and know now of no such expressions of feeling; but solely because we held the simple worship of God too pure and sacred a thing to be brought under the dictation and control of any human power, so long as nothing therein conflicted with the good order, peace, and safety of the State—we declined any longer occupying the New Assembly Rooms.

Pardon us, sir, for insisting that the maintenance of this principle is essential to the very life of the Church of Christ. If we abandon it we lay open the Church to the whole tide of earthly influences, and all hope of accomplishing the mission of Christianity is lost.

From this your Excellency can see how entirely inapplicable is the very strange argument by which you would make it appear that we, "by throwing ourselves upon our rights of conscience and the guaranties of the Constitution, might hoist the rebel ensign and defy the authorities to pull it down." The guaranties of the Constitution, as you yourself show, and we admit, do not extend to the protection of any parties acting against the good order, peace and safety of society. We claim no rights of conscience beyond the limitations of the Constitution. To hoist an earthly ensign, more particularly one which to display is in direct violation of one of the laws of the State, and would so manifestly disturb the public peace, would sap the very life principle of our organization. No such inference as that, sir, can be drawn from this proceeding.

But we may infer that if Major General Schenck has the right to prescribe the terms under which alone we may worship God, then by parity of reasoning he may do the same for every other congregation in this city. He may suppress the Liturgy of the Protestant Episcopal Church, and take away the insignia of the Roman Catholic service. He may even go further, and upon the ground that there are some in each congregation unfriendly to the Administration, he may forbid entirely assemblages for worship.

Your Excellency, occupying a position of such influence and responsibility, should, above all others, consider to what these things tend. The parties may be few and the interests small concerned in this case,

"But the evil leaven will spread,"

and the time may come when it will be wished that occasion had been taken to stay this baneful principle while in its incipiency, its first birth, in this land. These inalienable rights of relation between God and man may yet be preserved in their integrity.

But, if this time pass and this cause be not sustained, the efforts and endurance of a generation will hardly suffice to restore to us our birthright of religious liberty.

For these reasons, and upon these grounds, we call upon your Excellency to exert your influence not only in our behalf, but in support of a great principle of our Government and of our common Christianity.

The community has decided upon this case and with great unanimity has condemned this infraction of religious right and privilege.

By endeavoring to do away with this evil you will but respond to the sentiment of this city and State, and of every community to which the whole facts are known.

If we fail to secure our rights, then we must suffer. We can only make our appeal to the Most High, the Great Head of the Church.

Very respectfully, your Excellency's obedient servants,

JOHN M. BUCK,
CHARLES J. BAKER,
JOHN W. BRUFF,
J. B. BRINKLEY,
S. G. MILES,
CHARLES TOWSON,
JOS. P. SHIPLEY,
WM. R. BARRY.
Stewards M. E. Church.

Leonard Passano, being absent from the city, could not sign it.

STATE OF MARYLAND, EXECUTIVE DEPARTMENT,
April 9, 1863.

TO JOHN M. BUCK, ESQ., and others,
Stewards, &c:

GENTLEMEN: I received, upon the 6th instant, your letter of the 2d, written, as you say, to call my attention to "the *misunderstanding* of the facts and principles" embodied in your former communication, and pervading my reply thereto of 10th March last.

Whatever may be my misunderstanding of the *principles* assumed in your former communication, it is not likely that anything I can add to what I have already said will tend to reconcile the different views we respectively take of the subject; nor have I the time to devote to such further discussions. I cannot perceive, however, wherein I have so misunderstood the *facts* of the case. You devote about one-half of your last letter to showing that when I said that "in March, 1862, you for the first time practically sundered your Church connection and abandoned the time-honored edifices," &c., I misapprehended the facts, and, to prove it, you recur again with great particularity to the proceedings of the Conferences and Conventions of 1861. But, though these have, as I before remarked, but little bearing on the subject, they were all fully recited in your former letter, and were repeated and quoted by me in my reply. And whilst allowing all that can be claimed for them, still I maintain that in making the declaration above quoted I stated the case strictly as it was.

The question was not what the Baltimore Conference of 1861 or the Laymen's Convention of 1860 had done or declared, but what was the origin and action of your particular congregation, and, if I am correctly informed, you never did until March, 1862, do any act or institute any proceeding to set on foot any separate congregational organization, but up to that time occupied the same churches, recognized the same appointments, listened to the same ministers, and were governed in all respects by the same laws and ordinances with all the other members of the Methodist Episcopal Church in the city of Baltimore. If this was the case, I certainly did not misapprehend the facts as I intended to state them when I said that you then, "for the first time, practically sundered your Church connections."

In referring to that part of my reply wherein I call your attention to the functions respectively pertaining to the different departments of the Government, and to the fact that such complaints as yours should come properly before the judicial tribunals, you say, "the history of the past two years has quite satisfied us of the entire futility of any appeal to the judiciary." And referring to the view you had been accustomed to take of the office of the Governor, as "the guardian of the rights and honor of the State," &c., evidently still assume that the case of your complaint was one that called for his interference or influence.

I do not understand how or why it is that you have such little faith in any appeal to the judiciary; it certainly does not accord with the views taken by other citizens who have thought themselves aggrieved by the action of military officers, and have, if I am rightly informed, instituted quite a number of appeals to that department on such account. As it regards your opinion of what ought to be the course of the Executive in interposing an influence against such aggressions, it may not be amiss to refer you to the example of other Governors. It is possible that the particular one I have in view, might with some have more weight than any argument I could offer.

On the 4th of March last, the day after the date of your

first letter to me, some gentlemen of Virginia, mill owners near the city of Richmond, addressed to the Governor of that State a communication very similar in its apparent object to your own.

They state to him that on the preceding day "the Commissary General of the Confederate States of America" had impressed all their flour in the mill, which cost them "considerably more than the price fixed by the Government." They further state that the Government had notified them that "it will forcibly take possession of the legitimate products of our mills, for which we pay, under the protection of the State of Virginia, heavy taxes, and also a special corporation tax." and they appeal to the Governor in these words: "We lay our grievances before you, and call upon you to protect us from the open and flagrant violation of our rights, and ask that an armed force may be furnished us to prevent our property from being carried off *vi et armis* not only at less than cost, but far less than its market value."

Here would seem to be, indeed, an open and flagrant violation of private rights that needed no straining to make it palpable. It was no technical or constructive wrong that required long arguments to elucidate, but a direct and most offensive invasion of the rights of property is obvious to every one.

Now let me call your attention to Governor Letcher's response to this appeal. It is contained in ten lines, and I give the pith and words of it:

"I regard the act of which you complain as oppressive and committed without lawful authority. The only remedy I know of is the institution of suits for damages against the officers committing these acts."

Whether "the history of the past two years" has or has not served to show that an appeal to the Virginia judiciary is less futile than to ours, is a question that you can as readily determine as I; but little as I am disposed to look to such places for precedents, yet considering the peculiar views of that Commonwealth and the particular pride it has heretofore taken in maintaining States rights against imaginary Federal encroachments—to say nothing of the confidence with which we have been advised to follow in its lead—when the Governor of such a State, in reference to such an outrage committed by "the Confederate Government," and, as he admits, without authority, "knows no other remedy" than suits against the officer committing it, I think the Governor of Maryland, sworn though he may be "to see her Constitution and laws faithfully observed and enforced," may be excused for referring you to similar tribunals, and from using his official influence to remove the National Flag from your meeting house.

I am glad to hear you say that you still reverence that flag as you do—that you "honor it as the symbol of those great principles which our fathers secured to us." Under the influence of such feelings I may still hope to hear you, as I suggested in my last letter, rebuke those who insulted it, and disavow all hostility to it or the Government it represents.

It is painful to remember how that "honored emblem" has been desecrated within the last two years by Southern mobs, as they dragged it at their horses' heels or trampled it under foot; but whilst the remembrance of these proceedings renders it all the more incumbent upon us to promptly screen it from even implied dishonor, I can hardly hope that these are the occurrences to which you refer when you say you mourn over the perversions which have tarnished it.

In endeavoring to show, as you do in your last letter, that there was no such expression of disgust on the part of any of your congregation as was imputed to them by Major Fish, you will pardon me for saying that I think you have hardly met the question with that frankness to be expected of you. You say "they may have objected to it as inappropriate to the worship of God, a service in which we lay aside, for the time, the relations of earth," &c., "or they may have objected to it because such display was in violation of the contract with the janitor to remove all worldly decorations." Now, let me ask you, as truthful and candid men, do you believe that they did object on any such grounds? Was it really, in your opinion, their pure and spiritual ideas of the proper adornments or appearance of the sanctuary that gave rise to their objections?

A portrait or a fancy painting, a kettle drum or a bass viol, are each and all of them about as much of a "worldly decoration," and have quite as much "relation to earth" and as little "relation to the Most High," as the American ensign, but do you really think that if the janitor had by chance left in view any such appliances of the assembly of the previous night that the men who left the room or refused to enter it whilst the flag was there would have manifested the same holy horror of such worldly mementoes, and refused to worship until they were removed? If such is your opinion, you are of course right in suggesting the possible explanations you do.

Equally imaginative, as it seems to me, are the monstrous evils you predict as likely to result from the unhallowed proceedings of General Schenck, and by reason of which you tell us that "the efforts and endurance of a generation will hardly suffice to restore to us our birthright of religious liberty." It seems almost impossible to conceive how the most exuberant fancy can, upon such a ground-work, conjure up so alarming a picture, and how it is that though the General had covered all the walls of the Assembly Rooms with the National ensign, that would lead us to expect him in the next place to "suppress the liturgy of the Protestant Episcopal Church, and take away the insignia of the Roman Catholic service."

That you should dwell, as you do, upon such unfounded and fanciful evils, and regard them with such engrossing and ominous forebodings in times like these, when the whole nation is groaning under the calamities which this unrighteous rebellion has brought upon us, is not among the least remarkable wonders which "the history of the past two years" has developed.

Fortunate, indeed, may you and your congregation be considered if this war imposes on them no burthen more serious than the one of which you complain, and that whilst "intent *solely* upon maintaining the truth and purity of Christian doctrine" you encounter no other interruption of that religious enjoyment, than the necessity of turning your eyes upon that flag, and witnessing the efforts of those intent upon maintaining its supremacy, and the truth and purity and very existence of all popular institutions.

Very respectfully your obedient servant,

A. W. BRADFORD.

The printing of these communications from the Baltimore *American* appears to be necessary to a full statement of the case:

THE METHODIST EPISCOPAL CHURCH AND THE DISLOYAL SEPARATORS.

To the Editors of the American:

The editor of the New York Journal of Commerce in a recent number of that paper prefaces a narrative of certain events in Baltimore with the following remarks:

"THE BALTIMORE CHURCH CASE.—Such cases as that of the arrest of the Rev. Mr. Dashiell, and the trouble in the Methodist Churches in Baltimore, are deeply to be regretted. They ought not to occur, and there is no need that they should occur. In every instance they weaken the hold of the Administration on the people, and shake confidence among the more quiet and non-demonstrative portion of the community.

"It appears that the division of the Methodist Church into North and South, which took place some time ago, and the adoption by the Church North of a special dogma on the subject of slaveholding, resulted in the establishment of two or three Methodist churches in Baltimore who were unwilling to accept the new items introduced into the creed. We do not profess to understand the differences, but the simple fact is that these Methodists in Baltimore issued a statement that they could not 'conscientiously submit to the jurisdiction of the Buffalo General Conference, nor become members of the church under the New Discipline of 1860.' It matters very little what the points were. In a question of religious worship, we suppose all American people agree that these people were free to follow their consciences, if their consciences did not impel them to a violation of law. There is a Chinese temple in full blast in San Francisco, and Jew and Gentile worship everywhere in this country according to their religious notions. There has, however, been a persecuting spirit among some of the Baltimore people against these worshippers of the Methodist persuasion. If they were a congregation of Rebels, which they are not, they ought not to be disturbed in the peaceful worship of God, so long as their worship was not treason. But some one wanted to get up a row. On Saturday night, in the dark, some one nailed a small cotton handkerchief flag over the door of one of their churches or places of worship. It was the notice, and doubtless intended to be the notice, of the collection of a crowd, and the disturbance of their morning service. What ensued is thus stated by Rev. Mr. Dashiell, who is a highly esteemed Methodist clergyman, and not at all liable to the charge of being a 'Secessionist.'"—[Here follows a history of the affair, with which the public is familiar.]

The history of the times demands an impartial and truthful statement concerning the relation of the Methodist Episcopal Church of this city with reference to the separation of a number of its members from the jurisdiction of its acknowledged Bishops and Conference, and the formation of the separatists into what they denominate the "Central M. E. Church." This Church, so called, which is composed of three distinct congregations, is presided over by several ministers formerly connected with the Baltimore Annual Conference.

The General Conference which met at Buffalo in 1860 introduced into the Discipline of the Church a new chapter on the subject of slavery. The adoption of this new rule excited the church in Maryland and Virginia as being unwise and offensive. Many of the ministers and laity solemnly protested against the objectionable canon, and declared their purpose to seek redress at the next General Conference in 1864, which body alone would have power to alter or change the offensive chapter.

Others, however, deemed the passage of the new chapter sufficient cause for a violent disintegration of the Church in Maryland and Virginia from the North and West, without awaiting or desiring any relief by the General Conference, and forthwith proceeded to institute disorganizing schemes leading to that result.

Much of this excitement doubtless arose from the sympathy which existed among the Church in Maryland for their brethren in Virginia, many of whom were connected with the Baltimore Conference.

Conventions of the laity were held during the year 1860 in this city and elsewhere, for the purpose of separating from the other portions of the Church that had adopted the obnoxious rule or chapter on slavery. In these conventions many highly respectable and loyal gentlemen participated; but as the political difficulties of the nation increased, and, to some extent, involved the Church, those persons sacrificed their personal preferences as to ecclesiastical organization for their country's good. Not so with others, who could see no connection between the disintegration of the Church and the proposed division of the nation—if indeed they did not desire it—although the subject of slavery was intimately connected with both.

On January 4th, 1861, a large and influential meeting of the Methodists of Baltimore was held in Light Street Church, designed to allay the excitement, to counsel moderation, and to prevent the evils of precipitate and improper action in reference to the new chapter. Among the reasons assigned in the proceedings is the following significant sentence: "It is regarded that the agitation of the subject of slavery in the councils of the Church is dangerous at this time, especially in view of the distracted condition of the country." This timely warning restrained many from further efforts in the cause of disruption, and strengthened the hands of those who were inclined to await the settlement of our national difficulties, which were daily becoming more and more intricate.

The Baltimore Annual Conference which met at Staunton, Virginia, in March 1861, consummated the plan of the *majority* of the preachers—and which was approved by the Laymen's Convention that assembled at the same time and place—for a prospective separation of the Conference from the other portions of the Church, and leaving the Bishops to decide before March, 1862, whether they would join their interests with the new organization under the old name, or otherwise.

Meanwhile our national troubles culminated, and the rebellious war was transferred from the farther South to the State of Virginia, and nearly all communication between the Church in that State and Maryland was cut off.

The Conference at Staunton adjourned to meet in Baltimore, March, 1862, at which time as many of the members as could or would attend its session convened; Bishop Janes presiding. The session held in Light Street Church was harmonious, and provision was made for the recognition of absent ministers who might report themselves at the next Conference—to be held in Georgetown in March next, 1863.

Up to the meeting of the Conference in March, 1862, no rupture had occurred in the Church in Baltimore. Revs. E. F. Busey, A. W. Wilson, T. E. Carson, W. J. Perry, and J. A. Williams, all of this city, refused to recognize the Conference which met at Light street, and were entered on the minutes as withdrawn.

In the Baltimore *American* of March 15, 1862, a notice appeared addressed "To the Methodist Community and Others," announcing that the Revs. E. F. Busey and A. W. Wilson would preach at the New Assembly Rooms on the following day, which was the Sabbath. On the 22d of March, the following week, an announcement was published for services in the "Central Methodist Episcopal Church," &c.

The new movement being now inaugurated, the separatists retired from the Church by certificate of membership, or otherwise, as best suited their own state of mind. It is believed that from all sources not more than five hundred persons have joined their organization; but their congregations, including their Sunday Schools, would perhaps number thrice as many.

The line has become distinctly drawn between the schismatics and the Church. The members of the Methodist Episcopal Church in Baltimore, if not almost to a man, at least very generally, are loyal to the General Government, and desire the perpetuity of the National Union; while none of the schismatics profess any sympathy for either. Naturally enough the new society was considered a disloyal association, while some of its adherents did not hesitate to call those who did not follow their leadership Abolitionists, Black Republicans, Lincolnites, &c. If there be any loyal citizens connected with the "Central Methodist Episcopal Church" they are certainly in such association as may well form the ground of reasonable doubt of their loyalty. In short, does not their every public act favor secession, point directly against the integrity of the United States, and treat with indignity our dearest national emblem? Our deliberate opinion is that there is not one truly loyal man, woman, or child, in connection with this so-called "Methodist" Church, and that it is composed entirely of the disloyal and discordant secession element of this city.

1. From the above statement it will be seen that there is *no* "trouble in the Methodist Episcopal Church in Baltimore," as erroneously stated by the *New York editor*. The number of white members and probationers in Baltimore is about ten thousand, of whom more than nine thousand adhere to the Church. The circumstance of Mr. Dashiell, who is a minister of the Methodist Episcopal Church, being connected with the "trouble" in this city, was altogether on his part voluntary, and a matter in which he, as a Methodist Episcopalian, was no more concerned than if he were a resident of New York. The whole thing, so far as he is concerned, grew out of the fact that he was the owner of the property where the flag was placed, which fact was probably unknown to the parties who placed it there. This, we think, sufficient on this point.

2. That it was neither "the division of the Methodist Church into North and South," which transpired nineteen years ago, in 1844, nor "the adoption by the Church North of a special dogma on the subject of slaveholding," which occurred in the spring of 1860, that "resulted in the establishment of two or three Methodist Churches in Baltimore," which did not occur until the spring of 1862, two years after the time the statement of the *New York editor* would lead its readers to believe the new organization took place; and so far from dating back nearly three years to the General Conference, it is not yet *one year old;* all this we think our narrative has made sufficiently apparent. These facts being established, all the conclusions of the *New York editor*, founded on the false premise of the loyalty of the "Central Methodist Episcopal Church," either to their mother church or the United States, are found to be—like their premises—also false. We are, therefore, not at all surprised to hear him say "we do not pretend to understand the differences between the loyal and disloyal Methodists of Baltimore," and that "it matters very little what the points were." Certainly not, if we wish to remain in the dark ourselves and to blind others; but if we desire to "come to the light" and establish the truth, then it is of much importance "what the points were," and we have honestly attempted to set them forth without indulging in any reproachful or vindictive language. But we may hereafter have more to say on the subject if necessary.

THE CARD OF REV. MR. DASHIELL.

Editors of the American—You have consented to allow me space to correct the errors in your report of my arrest and imprisonment by the military authorities of this Department. I proceed to do so.

1. The charge was stated to be *the tearing down and destroying of the American flag*. I did not tear it down, but removed it and the rude staff together. I did not destroy it. It was not injured, is now in my possession, and was offered to the Provost Marshal in disproof of the charge.

2. It was said the flag was put up by some *Union people*. Who knows this? Did your reporter, or the one who sent the despatch to the Associated Press, *know who put it up?* It was evidently placed upon the building by disorderly mischief-makers. (1.) The flag itself was a small one and cost perhaps fifty cents. (2.) It was put up in the night and hurriedly. (3.) It was nailed to the outside of a second-story window, and the window was nailed fast from the outside. (4.) Major Fish distinctly denied having had it placed there. (5.) I had not received any notification from the authorities, civil or military. (6.) Nobody has a *right* to place a flag upon my premises without my consent. For these reasons I believe no *Union people* put it up. Some rowdies, upon instigation of two or three officeholders, did the deed to provoke disturbance, and to burlesque the orders of this military department about flags upon places of worship. I should be sorry to believe otherwise, or to think that you supposed any respectable man capable of so mean and cowardly a trespass upon the rights of property.

3. It was said that I was the minister of the congregation. This is another error. Whatever I may think of the movement, I have never preached for them, and am not a member.

4. It was said that I was going to the Sunday School. Another error. There was no one present in the building at the time.

5. That I kicked out the glass. This is utterly false. To reach the flag I was compelled to force the window, as it

was nailed from the outside. I broke the glass with my umbrella handle.

6. It is said that I jumped into a carriage, and drove off. The carriage was at my own door, five squares off, in another street, and waiting for me to go with Sterling Thomas, Esq., to the Penitentiary, to preach.

7. Personally, I care very little about such displays of flags. I believe no military or civil officer has a *right* to place them upon private property, and that such petty acts are injurious to any cause, by encouraging the "bad fellows of a baser sort" to imitate the conduct of their superiors, and by creating special distinctions in the community, when each should enjoy unmolested his rights, and if charged with wrong, suffer by law, and not mob rule, after a fair trial by the established courts.

As to my release, you have told your readers that I was "released upon a parole dictated by the Government." The following letter, that tendered the parole which is herewith submitted, w'l prove that it was the second parole offered to me, and that it was carefully accommodated to my sense of right. I assure you that if Major Fish, as Provost Marshal, had not lowered his tone, and urged in respectful language his appeal to sign, I should yet have been in Fort McHenry.

[For the papers referred to, see *ante*.]

This parole must be interpreted by the official document that introduced it. In that document I am told "you said to me it would have been better," &c. In the parole the word "duty" is substituted for "it would have been better." The meaning, as I understood it, is this—that it would have been prudent and expedient, in view of the disturbances about the flag at the New Assembly rooms, to have ascertained with certainty whether the flag was put up by authority. And indeed I am now willing to add that it would have been more becoming in me, as a minister of the Gospel, to have delayed any action until the Sabbath had passed, and then to have notified the police or the military before I removed it. This, however, decides nothing about the right of *putting up* flags on private property without the owner's consent. Yours truly,

JOHN H. DASHIELL.

February 28, 1863.

The Department of Missouri.

THE McPHEETERS CASE.

ORDER OF MAJOR GENERAL CURTIS.

OFFICE PROVOST MARSHAL GENERAL,
DEPARTMENT OF THE MISSOURI,
ST. LOUIS, MO., *December* 19, 1862.

[SPECIAL ORDER NO. 152.]

WHEREAS, On account of unmistakable evidence of sympathy with the rebellion on the part of Rev. Sam'l B. McPheeters, Pastor of the Pine Street Church, certain loyal members of his congregation, about six months since, urged him to avow his sentiments openly, and to take a stand in favor of the Government, which he refused to do, and has also published and circulated two letters within the last two weeks, in which he not only refuses to declare whether he is in favor of the success of the authorities of the nation in their efforts to put down a cruel and desolating rebellion, and has failed to remove a wide-spread and increasing impression, that he desires the success of the rebel cause; and whereas, the said McPheeters, acting with others of the same denomination, has used all the influence of his ministerial character to prevent the body of the Church with which he is connected, from declaring or manifesting its loyalty to the Government, and has refused to observe, in their obvious meaning and intent, the recommendations of the President of the United States to the various churches, and has allowed the influence of his wife, his brothers, and intimate associates, to seduce him from an open and manly support of the Government into active sympathy with the rebellion, whereby the influence of his ministerial position has greatly encouraged the enemies of the Government in their wicked schemes for its overthrow, and is still exerting an injurious influence, especially upon the youth and other members of his congregation, leading them to believe that he sympathizes with the rebels, and justifies their cause, and to adopt sentiments of hostility to the Government and to become active rebels; and whereas, in all his course of unfriendliness to the Government, and sympathy with, and favor to, rebels, the said McPheeters has been stimulated and encouraged, if not led on, by his wife, who openly avows herself a rebel; whereby the said McPheeters and his wife, have forfeited the right to the protection and favor of the Government in their present position, and have become promoters of rebellion and civil discord. Therefore, it is ordered that the said McPheeters and his wife leave the State of Missouri, within ten days after the service of this order, and that they take up their residence within the free States, north of Indianapolis, and west of Pennsylvania, and remain there during the war, and that said McPheeters cease from this date to exercise the functions of his office within the State of Missouri, and that he deliver to the Clerk of Pine Street Church all books, records and papers belonging to that Church.

It is further ordered, that the church edifice, books and papers, at the corner of Eleventh and Pine Streets, be placed under the control of three loyal members of Pine Street Church, namely: George P. Strong, James M. Corbitt and John M. Ferguson, who shall see that its pulpit be filled by a loyal minister of the Gospel, who can invoke the blessing of the head of the Church upon the efforts of the Government to re-establish its authority.

By command of Major General Curtis.

F. A. DICK,
Provost Marshal General Dep't of the Missouri.

LETTER OF DR. M'PHEETERS TO ATTORNEY GENERAL BATES.

ST. LOUIS, MO., *Dec.* 23, 1862.

Hon. EDWARD BATES,
Attorney-General of the United States:

DEAR SIR: Knowing how much your time is occupied in the discharge of the duties of your office, it is with extreme reluctance that I ask your consideration of the case which I have to submit. And if it were an individual or private matter, or one of small moment, I would not trouble you, but it is one so important in the principle involved, and may be so far-reaching in its consequences, that I feel compelled to call your official attention to it.

Inclosed I send you an order of Major General Curtis, and the documents and papers connected with and resulting in this order.

From these papers it will be seen that a question of a purely ecclesiastical nature has been raised between some of the members of my Church and myself as to the rights involved in the relation of a pastor to his people, to wit: whether the members of a Presbyterian Church have a right to demand of their pastor that he should define in writing his views and position on civil and political questions. For the reasons set forth at large in the accompanying documents, I denied and resisted this claim of right. My whole action in this matter has been the result of religious convictions and my life-long views of the nature and duty of the Gospel ministry. The members of my Church who made this demand, at first tried to coerce obedience by ecclesiastical means. They tried to get a majority of the Church to ask for a dissolution of the pastoral relation. In this they utterly failed. Four-fifths of the Church, and all of the Church Session, numbering seven, except one, without distinction of party or opinion, adhered to me. Intimations had been thrown out in conversation, that if, in no other way, the military authorities would be appealed to to enforce their views. I have no positive evidence as to the persons who brought the matter before the military authorities. But the order of General Curtis, on its face, shows that it rests upon this controversy in my Church.

It is proper for me further to state that no notice was given me, nor was I examined, or in any way questioned as to the truth or falsehood of the charges made. Now, the points to which I desire to call your official attention are these:

First. That the military authorities have assumed to decide an ecclesiastical question between me and some of the members of my charge, and that they have construed my denial of the right which they claim to demand of me as their pastor—an answer to civil and political questions—*as an act of disloyalty to the Government.*

Second. That in this order the military authorities have made my action in the Church court upon questions purely ecclesiastical, a matter not only of military review, but of military punishment. The language of the order is: "And whereas the said McPheeters, acting with others of the same denomination, has used all the influence of his ministerial character to prevent the body of the Church with which he is connected from declaring or manifesting its loyalty to the Government." This can only refer to my course in the last General Assembly of the Presbyterian Church; for these questions have not come up in any other Church courts with which I am connected. I did, however, in the General Assembly of May, last, oppose certain resolutions introduced into that body, which I regarded as an indirect violation of the Constitution of the Presbyterian Church, which says: 'Synods or councils are to handle or conclude nothing but what is ecclesiastical, and are not to intermeddle with civil affairs which concern the commonwealth, unless by way of humble petition in cases extraordinary, or by way of advice for satisfaction of countenance, if they be thereunto required by the civil magistrate."—Confession of Faith, Chapter XXXI: § 4. I said nothing as to the merits of the civil question upon which the decision of the Assembly was asked. I only maintained that it had no right to "handle or conclude" such matters. This was certainly no offence for which I should be subjected to military punishment, and, I humbly submit, a subject upon which it was not proper for them to decide.

Third. It will moreover be seen that the military authorities are dealing with me not *as a citizen*, but distinctly and formally as a minister of the Gospel. They commanded me to "cease from this date the functions of" my "office in the State of Missouri." Now, my office as a minister of the Gospel, I do not receive from the State but from the church of Christ, and its functions can only be suspended by those from whom I received my office, and it seems to me that the military authorities should not sit in judgment upon that office, that they should only know me as a citizen, and only deal with me as such.

Fourth. It will be further seen in the order that the military authorities take command not only of the church edifice, but of the books and papers, i. e., the church records, and order them to be given into the hands of three individuals, who, while they are members of the church, and one of them an elder, are not the persons to whom the church has or would commit them if permitted to declare her will; and further still it will be seen from this order, that these same three individuals are appointed by the military to fill the pulpit, and determine what kind of religious instruction the church shall have. All this is not only done, but it is published to the world in an order which will be read through the country.

I have felt it to be my duty, not only as a minister of the Gospel, but as a good citizen, to call the distinct attention of the Government to this matter, and ask if this order is not in accordance with the Constitution, laws, and usages of the United States, that such steps may be taken as shall be necessary to correct it. In the meantime I design to render implicit obedience to all these orders, for while I cannot admit that my ministerial office, or the government and worship of the church, is under the direction of the civil or military authorities, yet I feel it my duty to set an example of obedience, and to wait the correction which I feel convinced will be made by those having the ultimate decision of the matter. And it is, in my esteem, a happy circumstance that I find in the legal adviser of the Government one, who, at the same time, is so well acquainted with the history and constitution of the church in which I am a minister.

I have said nothing of what I consider the cruel personal wrong which is done to me by this order. It can be considered as nothing less than an official endorsement of a letter which appears in the *St. Louis Democrat*, (newspaper) Dec. 13, 1862, signed by the three individuals to whom Gen. Curtis hands over the church to which I minister, which letter I regard as a most shameless and false assault upon my character, so that if this order is permitted to remain, the whole influence of the Government, to which I have a right to look for protection, sends me out branded with crimes which I contemplate with horror, and which I indignantly deny that I have committed.

The only offence, if offence it be, which malice itself can charge against me, is, that being a minister of the Gospel, I have aimed to stand aloof, not only in public, but in private, from the exciting discussions of these unhappy times, and to devote all my energies to the distinctive duties of my calling. But while this has been the course which I have thought proper and becoming me as a man set apart by the church of God, to deal with men about their highest interests, I have at the same time, not forgotten my duty as a citizen. In a formal paper read before the General Assembly of the Presbyterian church, and which is upon its records, and was published through the country, I declared "that true allegiance and lawful subjection and obedience to the civil Government, as an ordinance of God, are among the highest duties of religion," and more recently still, in the public prints and over my own signature, I declared that "as a citizen, I hold it to be a most important and indispensable part of my duty to God, to obey law, to submit to the authorities, to pray for them, to render them the honors due their several stations, and to promote peace and quietness," and what is more, I have not only taught this in words, but by *my example*, I have declared the same thing, by the quiet but unhesitating manner in which I have gone forward in the discharge of every civil duty enjoined upon me either by the word of God or by the laws of the land, and especially by voluntarily taking the following oath, enjoined by the State Convention of Missouri, June 10th, 1862, upon those who solemnize the right of matrimony. [Here the oath was inserted.]

But while I feel that it is hard for a course like this, that I should be driven as a criminal from my home into a climate unfriendly to my impaired health, and among strangers who are by an official paper warned to suspect me, I say, while I feel all this to be a great wrong, *I do not come to make any personal plea.* If the good of the State requires that a quiet and peaceful family should be banished, that an innocent man should be treated as a criminal, let it be done. The man is not worthy the name of a man who is not willing to suffer even wrongfully for the public good. I come to ask that the church may be left to her liberty, that the military authorities be not permitted to judge and decide between me and the members of my church, upon purely ecclesiastical questions; that they be not permitted to assume authority over the government and worship of the Presbyterian church.

Let this be done and I am prepared to show, by patient endurance, the kind and degree of obedience, which, as a Christian citizen, I am ready to render to the "powers that be."

As for the rest, I shall calmly but confidently leave my character and my innocency to be vindicated by that Divine Providence before whom even a sparrow does not fall unobserved, and who can make all things work together for his people's good.

What is proper to be done in this matter is not for me to decide, but I most earnestly and respectfully request that the subject may receive such attention as is proper.

The only personal request I make is, that if the sentence of banishment is carried out, that I may have sufficient time allowed me to make reasonable preparation for my departure, and that I may be permitted to choose what locality I prefer in "the loyal States," or to go to a foreign country, if I shall so elect.

Very respectfully,

SAMUEL B. McPHEETERS.

MODIFICATION OF THE ORDER.

OFFICE OF THE PROVOST MARSHAL GEN'L,
DEPARTMENT OF THE MISSOURI,
ST. LOUIS, MO., *Dec.* 28, 1862.

Rev. S. B. McPHEETERS and WIFE:

The order made against you on the 19th of December, is modified until further orders, to this extent: that you are not required to leave the State.

By order of Major General Curtis:

F. A. DICK,
Lieut. Col., Provost Marshal General.

LETTER OF THE PRESIDENT TO GEN. CURTIS.

EXECUTIVE MANSION,
WASHINGTON, *January* 2, 1863.

Major General CURTIS:

MY DEAR SIR: Yours of December 29th by the hand of Mr. Strong is just received. The day I telegraphed you suspending the order in relation to Dr. McPheeters, he with Mr. Bates, the Attorney General, appeared before me and left with me a copy of the order mentioned. The Dr. also showed me the copy of an oath which he said he had taken, which is indeed very strong, and specific. He also verbally assured me that he had constantly prayed in church for the President and Government, as he had always done before the present war. In looking over the recitals in your order, I do not see that this matter of the prayer, as he states it, is negatived; nor that any violation of his oath is charged, nor in fact that anything specific is alleged against him. The charges are all general, that he has a rebel wife, and rebel relations, that he sympathizes with rebels, and that he exercises rebel influence.

Now after talking with him, I tell you frankly, I believe he does sympathize with the rebels; but the question remains whether such a man of unquestioned good moral character, who has taken such an oath as he has, and cannot even be charged of violating it, and who can be charged with no other specific act or omission, can with safety to this government be exiled upon the suspicion of his secret sympathies. But I agree that this must be left to you who are on the spot; and if, after all, you think the public good requires his removal, my suspension of the order is withdrawn, only with this qualification, that the time during the suspension is not to be counted against him. I have promised him this.

But I must add that the United States Government must not, as by this order, undertake to run the churches. When an individual, in a church or out of it, becomes dangerous to the public interest, he must be checked; but let the churches, as such, take care of themselves.

It will not do for the United States to appoint Trustees, Supervisors, or other agents for the churches.

Yours very truly,

A. LINCOLN.

P. S.—The committee composed of Messrs. Yeatman and Filley, (Mr. Broadhead not attending,) has presented your letter and the memorial of sundry citizens. On the whole subject embraced, exercise your best judgment, with a sole view to the public interest, and I will not interfere without hearing you.

A. LINCOLN.

January 3, 1863.

LETTER FROM GEN. CURTIS TO DR. M'PHEETERS.

HEADQUARTERS DEPARTMENT OF THE MISSOURI,
ST. LOUIS, *March 28th*, 1863.

Rev. S. B. MCPHEETERS, *St. Louis:*

Restraint having been imposed on your exercise of public unctions because of supposed disloyalty, some of your riends have traversed the fact of your being disloyal, and desire my personal intervention. With a view of ascertaining your sentiments, I submit to you the following interrogatories for your answer:

1st, Do you wish the rebellion crushed, and are you in favor of the restoration of the national authority over all our territory?

2d, In the conflict of war now existing do you desire the success of the federal and the defeat of the rebel forces?

I have the honor to be, sir, very respectfully, your obedient servant,

S. R. CURTIS,
Major General.

These questions, Dr. McPheeters declined to answer for reasons given below:

REPLY OF DR. M'PHEETERS.

ST. LOUIS, *March* 31, 1863.

To Major General CURTIS,
Commanding the Department of the Missouri:

GENERAL: I have the honor of acknowledging the receipt of your favor of the 28th instant, the Sabbath intervening between its date and reception.

Allow me, General, to express my thanks for the kind manner in which you received and heard certain friends of mine, and for your further kindness in reviewing your decision in my case.

Under other circumstances than those in which I find myself placed, it might be proper and becoming in me to express freely and fully, both my desires and opinions, as far as I have desire or have formed opinions in relation to our sad national calamities; but the position in which my seemingly hard fate has placed me is peculiar and embarrassing, and my answer to your interrogatories must be determined in view of all the circumstances surrounding me and my conviction of duty. I do not mean that I have or that any citizen ought to have any difficulty in acknowledging his allegiance. Certainly no such difficulty is in my way. When in the General Assembly of my church it was charged that I was "disloyal," defining that word according to the standard authorities, I promptly and thoroughly repelled the charge before the whole country; and when the Convention of this State, by ordinance, required a most carefully prepared oath of allegiance to be taken by those who solemnize the rites of matrimony, in obedience to the teachings of my church on that particular matter, (Directory of Worship, chap. xi, § 1,) and from a sense of duty, I voluntarily subscribed and filed it, as required. And in this connection allow me to say, that one of the things which I have found it hardest to bear in the course of the authorities toward me, is that I have not only been treated as if I had taken that oath without honor of conscience, but whatever influence my office or character give me, is made to encourage and sustain those who are shaking the very foundation of all society by denying the solemn and binding obligations of an oath. But I forbear. I have said so much as due to myself and to my friends who have interposed in my behalf.

As to the particular interrogatories propounded, they are of the same import as those which certain members of my church and congregation demanded that I should answer. I denied their right to require me to give any answer to such questions, and in doing so used this language: "And this position I take, not from any disposition to stand out captiously upon an abstract question of right, nor from any disposition improperly to conceal my views on political questions, but from a conscientious conviction that I cannot yield the thing you claim without, to the full extent of my example, compromising the rights of every minister, and endangering the peace of all the churches." When I refused to answer the questions of the members of my church, they made appeal to the public, and directly or indirectly to the military authorities; the result was that Military Order No. 152 was made and issued, which, for my silence and refusal to answer these gentlemen, banished me from my pulpit, and, as originally made, from the State. This order is, in express terms on its face, based on my position above quoted, taken with these members of my church.

If I was right then, it cannot now be proper that I should give an answer which I then declined on principle, a principle on the maintenance of which I then and now believe depends in a great degree the peace, the purity and the spiritual power of the church. I do not expect you, General, to see all the consequences of the precedent which my answer to the questions proposed would establish, as I think I see them. But this I think I have a right to expect, that you will see that, believing as I do, I cannot answer the questions which you propound, *under the circumstances in which they are propounded*, without abandoning my religious convictions and wounding my conscience. I dare not, then, whatever be the consequences to me personally, make such a reply to your letter as you probably expected.

But I trust I have said enough to satisfy you that all charges of disloyalty against me are without foundation. In this connection I may be pardoned for quoting from your "Circular letter" defining loyalty. You say: "*Prima facie*, an oath of allegiance is evidence of loyalty, and when men have taken upon themselves such obligations, and have lived and acted consistently with them, they should be regarded as loyal." I have taken the oath voluntarily and conscientiously; I have lived in consistency with it; your own words declare the rest, I "should be regarded as loyal." Under your order, and with any construction that can be put upon it, I would be allowed to buy and sell, to practice medicine or to plead law. Why not to preach the gospel?

But I will not weary your patience. I have not believed that in anything that has occurred, *you* have designed to do me injustice, and I hope that you will see your way clear to remove the hindrances to my returning to my work and calling. In any event I shall try and so live and act, that those who know me will be constrained to confess that I am not a bad, much less a dangerous citizen.

I have the honor to be, General,
Your obedient servant,
SAML. B. McPHEETERS.

LETTER OF DR. M'PHEETERS TO MAJOR GENERAL SCHOFIELD.

ST. LOUIS, *June* 2, 1863.

To Major General SCHOFIELD,
Commanding the Department of the Missouri:

GENERAL: The Presbytery of St. Louis, of which I am a member, stands adjourned to meet in this city on to-morrow to hear and consider certain matters in relation to the Church of which I am the pastor. The matters that will be then discussed are of deep personal interest to me. Special Order No. 152, issued on the 19th of December, 1862, prohibits my exercising the functions of my office in the State of Missouri during the present war. One of the functions of my office, as a minister of the Gospel, is to sit in ecclesiastical courts, and my object in addressing you is respectfully to request that under the circumstances which I have stated, you will so far suspend Order No. 152 as not to hold me guilty of its violation if I attend this meeting of my Church court and participate in its deliberations.

I deem it but proper to say that when Presbytery held its meeting in this city on the 15th of last month for the same purpose, that I made a verbal request through Brigadier General Edwards of General Curtis to be allowed to sit in Presbytery without offence to the military authorities, and it was not granted. This I felt to be hard, as my only object in asking a temporary suspension of the order was that I might have an opportunity to defend my ministerial character and conduct before the ecclesiastical court to which I am amenable.

I have the honor to be, General, your obedient servant,
SAMUEL B. McPHEETERS.

REPLY OF GENERAL SCHOFIELD.

HEADQUARTERS DEPARTMENT OF THE MISSOURI,
ST. LOUIS, *June* 3, 1863.

Rev. SAMUEL B. MCPHEETERS:

SIR: I am directed by the Major General commanding to say that you have permission to attend the meeting of the Presbytery of St. Louis for the purpose of defending your ministerial character, but not to act as a member of such body.

I am, sir, very respecfully, your obedient servant,
A. V. COLBURN,
A. A. G.

LETTER OF DR. M'PHEETERS TO GOV. GAMBLE.

ST. LOUIS, *December* 3, 1863.

To Governor GAMBLE:

DEAR SIR: As your time is necessarily occupied by your official duties, it is with reluctance that I trouble you with any matters relating to myself. I know, too, that the removal of the grievance under which I labor is not immediately in your hands. What I wish to ask of you, however, is only your kind offices in suggesting anything that it may be proper for me to do, and any assistance in the premises which you may be disposed to give me. I flatter myself that my intercourse with you in years past has left the impression on you that I will not knowingly make any statement which I do not myself believe to be true.

My case is this: On the 19th day of December, 1862, a military order was issued containing a three-fold sentence. 1st. Myself and wife were to be banished to specified limits in the Northern States. 2d. While I remained in Missouri I was prohibited the exercise of my functions as a minister of the Gospel. 3d. My Church was taken from the control of its ecclesiastical officers, and given in charge of a commission who are directed to provide a preacher and conduct the services. By a subsequent order, dated December 28, 1862, the sentence of banishment was suspended. By a third order, dated March 4, the control of my Church was returned to the church officers. From these several orders (copies of which I inclose, marked A, B, and C) it will be seen that the only part of the original order against me that remains in force, is that which forbids me the exercise of my distinctive functions as a minister of the Gospel. So true is this, that it is known to the entire community that for nearly a year I have been in the full and uninterrupted enjoyment of every right of a citizen, except my ecclesiastical and religious rights. Refusing to receive a salary from my congregation for services I was prevented from rendering, I have been forced to turn to secular pursuits. For many months past I have found employment in a law office. In this position I have not only prepared, but, in person, presented and passed claims before a commission appointed by the President of the United States. If prepared, I might practice law; if disposed, I might publicly lecture on history, art, or science. I have voted without challenge or objection. In short, there is no secular calling which is not as open to me as to any other citizen, and yet it would be a military offence for me to preach a sermon, to administer the Lord's Supper, to officiate at a funeral, or to sit in an Ecclesiastical Court! The simple naked fact is, that as matters now stand, the military authorities have deposed me from the Gospel Ministry, and this is the only grievance under which I labor and from which I seek to be relieved. I could give a very rational explanation of this strange, not to say absurd issue of my case, but it would require more space than I think proper to occupy. Suffice it to say that it is manifest on the face of the original order that it was no part of the purpose of the military authorities, at the time the order was issued, to prohibit the exercise of my ministerial functions for a longer time than the ten days which were to elapse between the order and the banishment. When the order of banishment was suspended it was so worded, however, as to leave the ecclesiastical sentence in force. And there matters have stood to this time. I think I have a right to assume, if there was any valid ground why I should have been punished, that it would have come to light in a year, and I am confident if there had been any evidence against me I would not have been permitted to remain in the State. The truth is, Governor, that the original sentence was hastily issued upon the representation of one or two misguided and prejudiced men, and was pronounced without my having any examination or trial whatwhatever. This I have always regarded as hard treatment. For some months before the order was issued, hearing that charges and insinuations were being made against me privately, I went in person to both the District Provost Marshal and to the Provost Marshal General, and made special request that if charges of any kind were preferred against me that I might have a hearing before sentence was passed. And if this, as it seemed to me, reasonable request had been granted, I firmly believe that no order would ever have been issued. It is most certain that the order of December 19 could not be obtained against me now I believe that those who asked and procured it then, would not ask it to-day. I am much mistaken if they are glad to-day of what they did a year ago.

I have not, up to this time, presented my case to the General now commanding this Department, nor asked him to review it, mainly for two reasons:

1st. It was a case decided by his predecessor.

2d. Friends in whose judgment I relied, thought that in the condition of things in Missouri, it was better for me patiently to wait. I feel that I have now waited long enough, and I think something should be done in my case. I am the only minister, of any denomination in the city, prohibited by the military authorities from preaching. I appeal to you as one acquainted with this community, and acquainted with me, if such a distinction against me makes the impression upon respectable citizens that this sentence is just and right! The question I wish to submit to you is, what should I do to bring my case before the proper authorities? If the sentence can be removed by a simple reversal, giving no reasons, and going into no explanation, I have no objection. If a trial is necessary, then I ask, as a matter of justice, that it may be full and searching, and that I have a fair opportunity of thoroughly vindicating my character and conduct.

Most respectfully, your obedient servant,

SAML. B. McPHEETERS.

LETTER OF PRESIDENT LINCOLN TO O. D. FILLEY.

EXECUTIVE MANSION,
WASHINGTON, *December* 22, 1863.

O. D. FILLEY, Esq., *St. Louis. Mo*:

I have just looked over a petition signed by some three dozen citizens of St. Louis, and the accompanying letters, one by yourself, one by a Mr. Nathan Ranney, and one by a Mr. John D. Coalter, the whole relating to the Rev. Dr. McPheeters. The petition prays in the name of justice and mercy that I will restore Dr. McPheeters to all his ecclesiastical rights.

This gives no intimation as to what ecclesiastical rights are withheld. Your letter states that Provost-Marshal Dick, about a year ago, ordered the arrest of Dr. McPheeters, Pastor of Pine Street Church, prohibited him from officiating, and placed the management of the affairs of the church out of the control of the chosen Trustees; and near the close you state that a certain course "would insure his release." Mr. Ranney's letter says: "Dr. Samuel B. McPheeters is enjoying all the rights of a civilian, but cannot preach the gospel!!!" Mr Coalter, in his letter, asks: "Is it not a strange illustration of the condition of things, that the question who shall be allowed to preach in a church in St. Louis shall be decided by the *President* of the *United States?*"

Now, all this sounds very strangely; and, withal, a little as if you gentlemen, making the application, do not understand the case alike; one affirming that the doctor is enjoying all the rights of a civilian, and another pointing out to me what will secure his *release.* On the 2d of January last, I wrote to General Curtis in relation to Mr. Dick's order upon Doctor McPheeters; and, as I suppose the Doctor is enjoying all the rights of a civilian, I only quote that part of my letter which relates to the Church. It was as follows: "But I must add that the United States Government must not, as by this order, undertake to run the churches. When an individual, in the church or out of it, becomes dangerous to the public interest, he must be checked; but the churches, as such, must take care of themselves. It will not do for the United States to appoint Trustees, Supervisors, or other agents for the churches."

This letter going to General Curtis, then in command there, I supposed, of course, it was obeyed, especially as I heard no further complaint from Doctor McPheeters or his friends for nearly an entire year. I have never interfered, nor thought of interfering as to who shall or shall not preach in any church; nor have I knowingly or believingly tolerated any one else to so interfere by my authority. If any one is so interfering, by color of my authority, I would like to have it specifically made known to me.

If, after all, what is now sought, is to have me put Doctor M. back over the head of a majority of his own congregation, that, too, will be declined. I will not have control of any church on any side.

Yours respectfully,

A. LINCOLN.

LETTER OF ATTORNEY-GENERAL BATES TO DR. M'PHEETERS.

WASHINGTON, *December* 31, 1863.

Rev. SAMUEL B. McPHEETERS, D. D., *St. Louis, Mo.*:

REV. AND DEAR SIR: Governor Gamble transmitted to me (in his letter of December 21) your letter to him of Dec. 3, which contains a lucid statement of the condition in which you suppose yourself to be left, by the various military orders, copies of which accompanied your letter.

Before the receipt of Gov. Gamble's letter I had received a petition in your behalf, addressed to the President, by some twenty or more, among whom I recognize some of the worthiest men in St. Louis. That petition, with several letters of individuals, which were sent with it I laid before the President. He seemed much surprised to find that you were still laboring under any clerical or professional disability, in consequence of those ill advised military orders, which, in all their personal and civil bearings had been superseded long ago. And he answered Mr. O. D. Filley (who wrote one of the letters, above referred to) in a manner which he supposed, would end the question. Again, I brought the matter to his notice, by exhibiting the documents first mentioned in this letter. The President, in substance, answered that it was always his wish and purpose to hold individuals responsible for their own acts, without any reference to the fact that they happened to be members or officers of particular churches—that the fact of being a member or pastor of a church was no excuse for personal misdemeanor. But that he never intended to assume or permit his subordinate officers to assume, any power to govern or control the churches, or in any manner to determine who may or who may not preach and minister in them. You say that you are in the full fruition of your *civil* rights, and the President considers you as free in the enjoyment of your ecclesiastical rights.

I write this with the express permission of the President, and I presume to advise that you quietly resume the exercise of all the rights, duties, and functions of your office, as if no interruption had occurred.

I remain with great respect, your friend and servant,
EDWARD BATES.

THE CHARGE OF THE CHURCH EDIFICE.

Upon the issue of the order of December 19, 1862, the session, (Elders John Whitehill, William T. Wood, Alexander Marshall, David K. Ferguson, and William W. Greene, *present*, and Martin Simpson, and George P. Strong, and the Pastor, *absent*,) at its meeting, Dec. 20, 1862, passed these resolutions unanimously:

1. By the standards and Constitution of the Presbyterian Church, the government and discipline of the Church is in the Session of the Church, composed of the Pastor and Elders, chosen and elected by the people; and the Session only has, or can have, the rightful custody and control of the church edifice, and books and papers of the Church.

2. The Constitution of the Church provides for the selection of Pastors and Ministers, and only in the modes provided can a Pastor or Minister be appointed, or elected, for any church or congregation. All power and control in the selection of Pastors and Ministers, is by our Constitution denied to the civil or other government, or other human power outside of the Church.

3. As members of this Session, we are under solemn vows to obey and maintain the Constitution of the Presbyterian Church, and whilst we yield obedience to said military order, and surrender, so far as we have possession and custody, our church edifice, books and papers, to the control of the individuals indicated, to wit: George P. Strong, James M. Corbitt and John M. Ferguson, a sense of duty constrains us to record our convictions, that the necessary effect of the order is to suspend, while the order is in force, organized church action.

4. We earnestly urge and entreat all the members the of Church not to suffer this sore affliction to scatter our little flock, but to maintain steadfastly their present relations with Pine Street Church, and in faith and trust and Christian patience, await the return of the day when in God's providence, the possession and control of our church edifice, and the government and discipline of the Church, shall be restored to us, to be used and exercised in accordance with the Constitution and Standards of the Presbyterian Church.

5. We know not on what evidence the military authority acted, as their order affects our Pastor, the Rev. Samuel B. McPheeters, and intend no impeachment of their action; but adhering to our Pastor as we do, and as our solemn vows require of us, a sense of duty impels us to bear our testimony to his rare talents and efficiency as a minister, and to his faithfulness as a Pastor. We have been on terms of most familiar intercourse with him. We believe more than four-fifths of the church and congregation would unite with us in this utterance. We commend him to the sympathy and affection of God's people, wherever he may go or sojourn in his involuntary wanderings from the people of his charge, whom he so much loves.

6. We have no purpose in these resolutions to criticise the order of the military, referred to; our only aim has been to declare our views of our powers and duty as a church session in the circumstances that surround us.

REVOCATION OF THE ORDER.

HEADQUARTERS DEPARTMENT OF THE MISSOURI,
OFFICE OF THE PROVOST MARSHAL GEN'L,
ST. LOUIS, *March* 4, 1863.

Special Order No. 25.]

Special Order No. 152, paragraph II, of date of 19th December, 1862, relating to the Pine Street Presbyterian Church, is hereby further modified as follows:

It appearing that Messrs. Strong, Corbitt, and Ferguson have not taken charge of the church edifice, books and papers, so much of said order as directed them so to do is now rescinded.

By command of Maj. Gen. S. R. Curtis.

F. A. DICK,
Lt. Col. and Provost Marshal General.

The case of Dr. McPheeters was before the last General Assembly of the (Old School) Presbyterian Church, on an appeal. A body claiming to be the Presbytery of St. Louis dissolved the pastoral relation between Dr. McPheeters and the Pine Street congregation, and on his resuming service, requested him to desist. The Assembly refused to sustain the complaint of Dr. McPheeters, 47 voting to sustain, 2 to sustain in part, 117 not to sustain, and 1 excused from voting.

THE ANDERSON CASE.

COURT MARTIAL AND SENTENCE OF S. J. P. ANDERSON, D. D.

Before a military commission which convened at St. Louis, Missouri, pursuant to Special Orders No. 97, series of 1863, from Headquarters St. Louis District, and of which Colonel John F. Tyler, 1st regiment of Infantry, M. S. M., is President, was arraigned and tried Rev. S. J. P. Anderson, citizen of St. Louis, Missouri, on the following charge and specifications:

Charge.—Disloyalty to the Federal Government.

First Specification.—Uttering disloyal expressions, and expressions of hostility to the Government of the United States, and manifesting sympathy with rebels and their cause. In that, he has asserted and maintained, avowed and admitted, that rebellion is not a sin; that the South is right; that the war against the rebellion is wrong and unwarrantable; that the South is justified in its course, and that it cannot be subdued by Federal arms; using, also, other language and expressions of similar import and tendency.

Second Specification.—In that he has openly justified the attack on and capture of Fort Sumter, in April, 1861, and at sundry times prior to June 1, 1863.

Third Specification.—In that he did, at his residence at St. Louis, display, or permit to be displayed from his house, the rebel colors, and erect, or permitted to be erected, or to be continued on his premises, a mound or miniature fort or fortification designated as "Fort Sumter," and bearing the rebel flag a considerable time in the spring of 1861.

Fourth Specification.—In that he denounced the capture of Camp Jackson by the Federal forces as a violent outrage on the sovereignty of the State.

Fifth Specification.—Having openly approved of the firing on United States soldiers in the streets of St. Louis on or about the 11th and 13th days of May, 1861, and denounced these soldiers as "home butchers," "murderers," and words of like import.

Sixth Specification.—Evincing pleasure and gratification in rebel successes and Federal reverses, thus signifying his approval of the rebellion.

Seventh Specification.—Openly stating and avowing that the war against the rebels is wrong and unwarrantable, and that he could not pray for its success on the national fast day of September 30, 1861.

Eighth Specification.—At a meeting of several clergymen, held in the city of St. Louis, to concert a union of their several churches in the observance of a national fast day, appointed by the President of the United States for the 30th day of September, 1861, he conditioned his joining in such observance on this, that the success of the Federal arms should not be prayed for, and he refused to join in such observance of a fast day because his conditions were rejected.

Ninth Specification.—That on and after a meeting of the Church Extension Board of the so-called Old School Presbyterian Church in the city of St. Louis, in conversation, argued and spoke in favor of the rebel cause, and against the efforts of the Government of the United States to put down the rebellion, averring that the South was in the right, and could not and ought not to be conquered.

Tenth Specification.—That, as a clergyman and a pastor, he has openly cast his influence in favor of the rebellion, and against the Government of the United States, by his public and private conduct, language and demeanor, in this wise—that he has averred the South to be right, and the Government of the United States to be wrong, in the present conflict, and that rebellion is not a sin; that it could not be put down by the Government of the United States; that it ought to succeed and would succeed; and that loyalty had nothing to do with the qualification for membership in the church, Synod, and other religious bodies.

Eleventh Specification.—In that he had arms concealed in his house for the purpose of resisting the Federal troops known as Home Guards, and which were designated by him as "Dutch rule," and also saying that he would use these arms if his liberties were attempted to be interfered with by them, and using words of like import, intimating that he intended resistance to military law.

The Commission, after mature deliberation and reflection, have found the prisoner guilty of all the above specifications, and also the charge, and have therefore sentenced him to be sent south of the lines of the Federal army at as early a day as practicable.

The proceedings have been disapproved by the Commanding General, on account of a defect in the orders convening the Commission. The number of members in this case was reduced below the minimum prescribed in paragraph 2, in General Orders No. 1, series of 1862, from these headquarters.

The proceedings are therefore inoperative and void.

ORDER RESPECTING RELIGIOUS CONVOCATIONS.

HEADQUARTERS DEPARTMENT OF THE MISSOURI,
ST. LOUIS, MO., *March* 5, 1864.

COLONEL: In the opinion of the General Commanding, the interests of the country require that due protection should be given within the limits of this department to religious convocations, and other religious assemblages of persons whose function it is to teach religion and morality to the people. But at the present time he deems it expedient that the members of such assemblages should be required to give satisfactory evidence of their loyalty to the Government of the United States as a condition precedent to such privilege of assemblage and protection.

The Major General Commanding desires that you take such steps as in your judgment will best secure these objects.

I am, Colonel, very respectfully, your obedient servant,

O. D. GREEN,
Assistant Adjutant General.

To Col. J. P. SANDERSON, *Provost Marshal General, Department of Missouri.*

EXPLANATORY LETTER FROM GEN. ROSECRANS.

HEADQUARTERS DEP'T OF THE MISSOURI,
ST. LOUIS, MO., *April* 29, 1864.

DEAR SIR: Assured by your letter of the 25th that the members of the Presbytery, which were to have met at Booneville, are loyal, I am quite satisfied that nothing but a proper understanding of the origin and purposes of the order is necessary to cause it to meet their hearty approval.

My respect for your body, and for the principles of religious freedom, require that I should give an explanation to you and the religious public.

Loyal church members, both lay and clerical, called my attention to the fact that many assemblages of ministers and teachers of religion of various denominations were to convene during the spring and summer, in which would doubtless be many persons openly and avowedly hostile to the National and State Governments; that in one most of them would be open enemies to the Union. They also prayed me to take such measures as that those assemblages should not be used to concoct treason or injure the national cause.

What was to be done? If all who claim to meet for religious purposes can do so without question, a convocation from Price's army, under the garb of religion, may assemble with impunity and plot treason in our midst.

If, on the contrary, religious assemblies, really such, are scrutinized with the same freedom as political meetings of unknown and doubtful character, not only would it be necessary to inquire into the ministerial character of its members, but their public and private proceedings must be so watched that treason could not be perpetrated without detection and punishment, which would occasion a most irksome interference with personal privacy and the freedom of religious action.

As the General commanding this department, my duty to the country and the people of the State required me to protect them from the machinations of enemies, who, under the cover of the freedom of religion, should attempt to conceal plans and counsels opposed to the interests, peace, and safety of the State and the nation, while, as a Christian, I felt bound to secure religion from the danger and disgrace of being used as the cloak of malice, and its freedom from a surveillance freely exercised over political meetings.

To fulfil these duties the Provost Marshal General was instructed as follows: [See order above.]

Upon these instructions the Provost Marshal General issued the orders to which your letter alludes.

In that order, as now enforced, he protects those meetings, and dispenses with surveillance of the members or proceedings, on the simple and easy conditions that the members will, individually, assure him of their loyalty in either one of the following ways:

First. By certifying on honor that they have sworn to support the Constitution and Government of the United States, and provisional government of this State, as required by the laws thereof, to enable ministers to solemnize marriage, each at the time and place set opposite to his name. Or,

Second. By taking an oath of the form prescribed in that order.

I am quite sure that, upon proper understanding and reflection, the friends of religion and its freedom will thank me as much as do the friends of the Union for this order.

I regret to say that, while I have abundant evidence of their satisfaction, I know of very few who have complained of it who have been remarkable for loyalty. Most of them have been remarkable for their sympathy with the rebellion, and now live in our midst croaking, fault-finding, and even rejoicing in the nation's struggles and reverses, like the impious son of Noah, who uncovered and mocked at the nakedness of his father.

It is very easy to see that such persons injure the cause of religious freedom, as they do that of the country.

From what has been said, it is manifest that the order, while providing against public danger, protects the freedom and purity of religion, on the one hand, from disgraceful complicity with treason, and, on the other, from an irksome surveillance, which would otherwise become necessary in time of public danger.

W. S. ROSECRANS,
Major General.

To the Rev. J. B. FINLEY, *Stated Clerk, Westchester College, Fulton, Missouri.*

THE DEPARTMENT OF MISSISSIPPI.

1864, June 18—Col. B. G. Farrar, commanding at Natchez, issued this order:

ORDER OF COL. B. G. FARRAR.

HEADQUARTERS U. S. FORCES,
NATCHEZ, MISS., *June* 18, 1864.

[SPECIAL ORDER, No. 31.]

Extract.

II. The Colonel commanding this district having been officially notified that the pastors of many churches in this city neglect to make any public recognition of allegiance under which they live, and to which they are indebted for protection, and further, that the regular form of prayer for "the President of the United States, and all others in authority," prescribed by the ritual in some churches, and by established custom in others, has been omitted in the stated services of churches of all denominations, it is hereby

Ordered, That hereafter, the ministers of such churches as may have the prescribed form of prayer for the President of the United States, shall be read at each and every service in which it is required by the rubrics—and that those of other denominations, which have no such form—shall on like occasions pronounce a prayer appropriate to the time, and expressive of a proper spirit toward the Chief Magistrate of the United States. Any minister failing to comply with these orders, will be immediately prohibited from exercising the functions of his office in this city—and render himself liable to be sent beyond the lines of the United States forces—at the discretion of the Colonel commanding.

The Provost Marshal is charged with the execution of this order. By command of

B. G. FARRAR,
Colonel Commanding.

JAMES E. MONTGOMERY,
Capt. and Asst. Adj. Gen.

PROTEST OF THE BISHOP OF NATCHEZ.

To Col. B. G. FARRAR, *Commanding at Natchez:*

RESPECTED SIR: Returning to Natchez from a portion of my visitation, I have had communicated to me your Special Order No. 31, dated June 18th, requiring all pastors of churches to make public recognition of their allegiance to the government under which they live, and to which they are indebted for protection; to pronounce a prayer appropriate to the times, and expressive of a proper spirit towards the Chief Magistrate of the United States. I have had some personal interviews with you in reference to this Order, and so has the Vicar General, Very Rev'd M. Grignon. We both take the occasion to express our thanks for the politeness we have experienced from you on all these occasions.

Indeed, the intercourse of our clergy with the Commanders at Natchez, and the officers associated with them, has been generally agreeable, and we all offer our thanks. I must mention in particular Major General Crocker, for one conspicuous act of his, directing the entire restoration of the fence around our cemetery when it had been destroyed. Our orphans, likewise, have experienced their goodness in receiving supplies from the Commissary stores. It is true that the presence of the army was the very cause of their needing this assistance, because it closed the ordinary channels of their resources; but this does not cancel our obligations of gratitude towards the Commanders here, and the administration at Washington, for thus alleviating the miseries of war towards those helpless children, and the good sisters and others who have kindly come here to take care of them. Their prayers are offered up every night for all their benefactors.

With regard to the subject of this Special Order, I have to state, that the prayers prescribed by our rulers are in the book called the "Roman Missal," and among them there is none that mentions, especially, any civil government. The prayers contained in our various English prayer books are commonly approved of by individual bishops, simply as containing nothing contrary to the teachings of the Church, but they are not part of our prescribed religious service.

In the Catholic Cathedral of Natchez, as I have informed you, every morning we recite in English the Litany of the Saints, wherein we make express supplication for all Christian rulers, for peace and unity among all Christian people, and for eternal good things to our benefactors; among whom, certainly, are to be chiefly reckoned those to whom we are indebted for protection.

Those prayers appear to you to be not sufficient to satisfy the requisitions of this Special Order.

I have further informed you that a somewhat similar order, or request, was made once before by the military Commander at Natchez, that I then referred the matter to higher authority, that the answer given was: That we should not be further molested on the subject, and that, in fact, we were not molested again during the two months which elapsed before the publication of the present Order. I have also told you why the correspondence was not made public.

Having this decision from higher authority, it appears to me that the matter is not exactly open for discussion in Natchez. The evidence I have given of such a decision having been rendered, (though not official,) gives at least a sufficient ground for suspension of any action under the Order, until the same higher authority can be heard from, and its instruction can be received in official form.

My respect, however, for the post you occupy, and your personal claims to my regard, make it agreeable to me to give you all reasonable satisfaction, not by discussing the question, but my making known to you the reasons, and the spirit which actuate me in declining to comply.

I shall be glad, also, if you suffer this letter to be published, to have my neighbors round me, soldiers and civilians, and most of all the flock under my care, to whom I am bound to render good examples—I shall be glad to have them understand the true spirit and motives of my conduct. The more so, because false impressions have prevailed in consequence of false reports having been circulated—some of them intended to be complimentary, concerning my language and conduct on the former occasion, above referred to. I take this opportunity of making it known, whether it be accounted to my credit or my discredit, simply as a fact, that I did not on that occasion use any words of boldness, but I endeavored simply to express, in as pleasant terms as I could command, the reasons why I ought not to be expected to comply.

And I now expressly declare that my declining to submit to this Order is not intended as an expression of disregard, or as dislike, towards any civil or military authority, nor towards any person exercising such authority. It is not intended as a manifestation of disloyalty, nor of loyalty, nor of any person claiming power. It has no political signification. It is simply of the Liberty of the Church to discharge her divine functions, without interference from other persons.

And this, in a country where all religions are equal before the government, amounts to the same thing as the liberty of the people, (not against God, but against the State,) in peace and in war, to choose for themselves their religion, and their religious guides.

If an order like this were made by any other civil or military authority that might be in command at Natchez, it would be my duty to resist then as I resist now.

The chief reasons for resistance may be reduced to these two. One is, that religious worship ought to be directed exclusively by religious authorities. I speak not of the negative right of other powers to suppress acts of intended and unwarranted insult, of which there is no question here, but of the positive ordering of prayers, sermons, ceremonies, &c.

The other reason especial to the present case, is, that Divine Worship being directed to God, it is not proper to introduce anything into it for the purpose of exhibiting our sentiments on temporal matters. This appears to be addressing our devotions to men instead of God.

But as the weight of these two principles depends, with most persons, on the political consequences and collateral bearings of a departure from them, I beg you to have patience if I judge that the interests intrusted to me by God, which are involved in this question, require of me a somewhat lengthy development.

It is to be observed that loyalty or disloyalty are, in truth, personal sentiments. Strictly speaking, they do not belong to aggregate bodies, but to the individuals who constitute the bodies; and a recognition of allegiance uttered by a priest in the presence of the congregation, would not imply any profession made by one individual, which was of no force whatever as regarded any other individual. And why—out of a whole community should one single person be required to make such profession? and the very person, who by his office and his conduct, has the least of all to do with civil, military, or political affairs—the priest.

If it should ever be charged that I, or any priest of the diocese, had in his conduct departed from his office, and done anything injurious to the government, let the charge be stated and examined, let the individual be held responsible for his own conduct like any other citizen, and let not God's solemn worship be altered or interfered with on one man's account.

Catholic Faith teaches that God appointed the Church to direct men in the manner of worshipping Him—to tell them when, and how, they ought to offer their public devotions—what outward forms and ceremonies are suitable and what prayers, and forms of prayer, are appropriate on, public occasions. Whether others regard this as true or false it is the doctrine of the Church, received from God, like the doctrine of the Incarnation, or any other dogma. It is essential to her existence; to renounce it would be to declare herself an impostor. For a Bishop to abandon it would be to betray the solemn trust confided to him by God—to sacrifice the eternal interests of the souls under his care, and to scandalize the whole Catholic Church throughout the world.

Now, any acceptance on my part of this "Special Order" would be, in my judgment, equivalent to abandoning this doctrine, by acknowledging the right of others than the Church to take share in the direction of Divine Worship.

This Order requires us to introduce a totally new element into our Sacred Worship, viz: the public profession of temporal allegiance to the constituted authorities by a prayer to be pronounced professedly for this end.

I have no hesitation to express, not in words only, but in the sincerity of my mind, all respect for his Excellency, the President of the United States, and to profess cheerful obedience to his government in all things lawful while I live under it and enjoy its protection; and this without any questioning as to his personal merits, simply because he is the Chief Magistrate, and my religion teaches me to respect all who are in authority, because authority is from God. Whether the possessor of it be designated by election or any other means, whatever legitimate authority he possesses, it is from God who gives it to him, and my respect for all those who hold authority is a part of my respect for God, and a part of my religion. The same I say of all civil governments in the world.

But the designating of an individual by his name, or by a special title, is not a part of my worship of God. And though if it would assist to excite devotion, it might be done innocently, and even laudably, when there would be no danger of its being misunderstood; yet to do it, not for exciting feelings of devotion, but avowedly for the purpose of making profession of allegiance, and when it would be understood as acknowledging a right on the part of the secular powers, civil or military, to interfere in the arrangement of religious worship—this would, to my mind, be a criminal betrayal of my sacred trust, and a deep injury to the Church, in which alone are my hopes of eternal salvation.

Further, this Order asserts the right of requiring us if necessary, to compose entirely new prayers, "appropriate to the times, and "expressive of a proper spirit towards the Chief Magistrate of the United States."

This necessarily implies a right in the Commander to judge what times, and what emergencies are worthy of new and appropriate prayers, and what spirit our prayers must be expressive of; and consequently, a right to inspect our prayers, and to make such alterations as he judges necessary to render them appropriate and sufficiently expressive. This is no extravagant conclusion of mind. You are in this very case claiming to exercise this right; for I have told you that we are reciting prayers which I, as Bishop, judge to be appropriate, and expressive of the proper spirit towards our rulers.

You, as military Commander, judge that they do not answer the purpose, and you require me to recite new ones, or to add to these in such a way that they may meet your judgment.

I gladly bear testimony that I see in you no desire to embarrass us; on the contrary, you are disposed to be as forbearing as possible, consistently with your claim.

You would be satisfied with very little—a few words—perhaps a single word—but you insist upon that word. Why is so much importance attached to the utterance of a word? Manifestly, because you feel as I do, that the utterance of that word would be the acknowledgement of a principle. That principle would be, that our Divine Worship is a proper occasion for professions of allegiance, and that the military Commander has a right to require the recital of prayers which he judges appropriate to the times, and expressive of the proper spirit.

This right once admitted in a military Commander, he

will himself be the judge of when and how to exercise it. Your good will and moderation will be no rule for another, whether at Natchez or elsewhere. The few words which will satisfy you may appear to him to be an evasion, and if he thinks they are, it will be his duty to require more. Now, if other events arise which he judges of sufficient importance to require new prayers appropriate to the new times, it will be his duty to demand them. There will be still more reason for exercising this right, with regard to our sermons and instructions than with regard to our prayers; and there is nothing to hinder him from applying it, likewise, to our ceremonies.

And there have been already indications of a disposition to extend this interference to the pulpit and the ceremonies. I have heard of the clergy being called on to publish from the pulpit the proclamation of the civil power. Happily the Commander was a gentleman of clear mind, and moderation, and he acquiesced in the reply made to him, that the pulpit was not the organ of communication between the civil powers and the people. But, if he possessed the right which this Special Order implies, he might equally have refused to acquiesce, and have insisted upon the reading of that, or any other civil or military document, which he should judge it suitable to have communicated through the pulpit.

And with regard to the ceremonies, I have been told that some papers were hinting, if not openly declaring, that various clergymen, in different churches, ought to be made to suffer for not celebrating certain feasts and fasts appointed by the Government, or rather, for not holding their Divine Service at the hours, and with the degree of solemnity, which the editor judged suitable.

Progress is very rapid in this country, especially in time of war, and what is thrown out to-day as a hint by a single paper, may in a few months become a common clamor, and an established rule.

And observe that this right of interference with the Church's worship of God, would be exercised in this country by men who acknowledge no responsibility to her rule, and profess no acquaintance with her laws and liturgy.

This consideration is a general answer to all such arguments as might be drawn from any practices in Catholic countries, practices, not imposed by military authority, but dictated by the Church itself, of her own accord, and guarded against danger of abuse by her enactments—enactments which the civil authority engages to enforce.

Still more, a right of this kind can be as sternly claimed, and as rigorously enforced by one military authority as by another. The priests in other parts of this diocese (which comprises the entire State of Mississippi,) or myself, while discharging my Episcopal visitation in those parts, could equally be called on to invoke God's assistance for the enemies of the United States.

And now, in simple, honest truth, what would such contradictory prayers be worth? and what would either or both powers have gained when they had extorted a public pronouncing of them? As prayers to God, they would be a mockery, and as professions of allegiance, I repeat it, they are no part of Catholic worship, and I cannot consent to introduce them into it. The entire freedom of the Church to direct her own Divine worship is not, I believe, a peculiar claim of the Catholic Church. If I am rightly informed, nearly all denominations have likewise claimed it, whether all of them have exercised it at all times or not. It has always been the boast of some of the New England Colonies, that they were founded by men who left their homes rather than brook the interference of the State with their manner of worshipping God; and if some of them are charged with afterwards persecuting men for conscience's sake, even then, it has been said, it was not an exercise of the State's authority over the Church, but rather the Church was directing the State to drive out what the Church believed to be false worship.

And this liberty of the Church to direct Divine worship has always been recognized by the State. I need not quote to you the well known clause of the Constitution of the United States, prohibiting Congress from any interference with the free exercise of religious worship.

The illustrious General Jackson, when President of the United States, determined as he was in the exercise of his authority to its fullest extent, said he had no constitutional power even to invite the people to observe an annual Thanksgiving day. He was to administer the civil government, and to take no cognizance of the religion of the people, except so far as to protect each one in following his own, without molestation from his neighbors.

If later Presidents, exercising their own judgment in the matter, have thought it well on especial emergencies, as in time of pestilence and of war, to call on all the people to offer prayers on certain days, yet, as far as I know, they have confined themselves to a simple invitation, and not pretended to compel any one to comply.

Nor is there any reason in the circumstances, why such a power should be claimed at this particular time. These prayers are no necessity of war—no armies would be strengthened or supplied, no enemy would be weakened or embarrassed, no friends would be encouraged, no opponent would be disheartened.

On the contrary, the effect would be to give pain and alarm to many, and, most of all, to those who have most warmly espoused the cause of the Union, believing that it was the best protection of their religious liberty; for, to a true Christian, who has any faith and manliness in him, the dearest of all liberties must be that of the exercise of his religion. Country, Constitution, Union, Independence, Flag, however warm sentiments any of these may awaken in his heart, after all, they express in themselves but temporal goods. The real value of these things is the protection and security they afford him while he is working out the great end of his creation, the service of God, and the saving of his immortal soul. "*What will it profit him to gain the whole world, if he lose his own soul?*" And what must he care for the power and glory of his country, if purchased at the sacrifice of the means given him to save his soul?

And among those means, in the opinion of most of Christians, and in the absolute conviction, the Divine faith of every Catholic, most conspicuous and efficient is the Church, in the free exercise of all the duties imposed on her by God.

If the country claims a right to interfere with her religious worship, it puts a shackle on her freedom, which every earnest Catholic will feel as a deep wrong and a more grievous injury than iron manacles upon his wrists. It would be felt as an injury by numbers of persons in all the walks of life, whose past and present services to the United States, rendered in various ways, do not deserve an injury at the hands of Government.

I say this, not as a ground for claiming any privilege, nor any exemption from just and reasonable laws, but that you may better understand how widely extended and how deeply unmerited would be the injustice of any interference with our religious worship. Allow me to mention, not in any vain parade, but for the better understanding of the bearing of this question, the Sisters of Charity, of Mercy, of the Holy Cross, and all the other orders of religious ladies, who have been for three years wearing out their willing lives in the military hospitals—ladies from Mississippi, Louisiana, and South Carolina, by the side of ladies from Massachusetts and Illinois—who have saved so many lives, and comforted so many deaths. That pleasant smile of theirs, that cheery word, which lifts up the heart of a poor, suffering soldier, and gives him more strength than medicines or food; it reaches his heart, because it comes from theirs; and what smile can their hearts give, when they know that those very soldiers, whose lives they are saving, may be employed to close their churches, and to conduct their bishops and priests beyond the lines, because they will not acknowledge the right of the civil government to alter their religious worship?

And, in truth, what is it that makes such women? that infuses into their hearts that heroic charity, and that religious tenderness? It is the very freedom which the Church enjoys to train her children with such devotions and religious practices as she judges to be most beneficial to their souls, according to their circumstances and their states of life, without interference from any human power.

Once make the Church a subject of the State in spiritual functions, and she is no longer a living Church of the Holy Ghost, infusing into her children the life of Catholic charity; she becomes a kind of pious branch of police.

And we, the Catholic clergy of this Diocese of Natchez, have done nothing to merit molestation from the United States Government. We have never lent our public advocacy nor our private influence to its injury, neither before nor since the war began. I have never preached a political sermon, and never advised any one, neither in public nor in private, neither directly nor indirectly, to join any army, nor to give a vote for or against any of the measures which led to the present war; and, to the best of my knowledge, all the priests of the Diocese have likewise kept themselves free from political entanglements. Not that we had not the right, like other citizens, to take an active part in politics if we chose, but, having dedicated ourselves primarily to the care of souls, we endeavored to follow the line of conduct recommended to the clergy by all the bishops of this province, in the Council of New Orleans, held in January 1856, in these words of their pastoral letter: "It is hardly necessary for us to remind you that you are to confine yourself to the spiritual guardianship of your respective flocks, and within the line of your ecclesiastical duties. Leave to the politicians the politics of the day. Your business is the salvation of souls and the interests of Jesus Christ." We have tried accordingly to keep ourselves free to render religious services to all who might desire them, whether permanent members of our flocks, those neighbors among whom we have been living, and to whom we are at tached by natural as well as by religious ties, or whether temporary sojourners, soldiers, or civilians, masters and servants, white and colored—all who have immortal souls have had equal claim upon our time and care when they desired our religious services.

I shall conclude by mentioning facts, not for the purpose of courting favor, but to let you understand the spirit which the Church has given to priests, without making professions of allegiance a portion of her religious worship, and that you may judge whether the Government would gain anything of substantial good by interfering with the Church's own way of teaching her children their duties to their fellow-men.

One of the priests of this Diocese, one whom I most esteemed and loved among them all, sacrificed his life for the soldiers of the United States Army, in February of 1863. It was the Rev. Basil Elia. He asked my permission to go to the soldiers at Young's Point, and in that neighborhood, opposite to Vicksburg, because he had heard that many were dying there without a priest. His own statement was that a hundred Catholics were dying in a week. It was outside of my Diocese, and I had use for his services at home; yet I approved of his going, for the same reason he asked to go, simply because there were so many there who wanted his assistance. His incessant fatigues and exposure soon brought the prevailing disease on himself. He could not be induced to abandon those poor souls until he was entirely prostrated. He was carried to Memphis in March, and he died there the 2d of April.

Another priest, now at the Cathedral, is just recovering his strength after four months of sickness, brought on him in spite of a robust constitution, by his attention to the sick, chiefly those dying of the smallpox, almost all of them being either United States soldiers or poor colored people, gathered at Natchez, on account of its occupation by the United States army.

Indeed, ever since the beginning of last August, the chief portion of the labors of the Catholic clergy of Natchez have been absorbed by them. For myself, though my episcopal duties have been urgently demanding my attention, yet I have devoted much more time and labor to the United States soldiers and the colored people, during the last ten months, than I ever gave to any sick before, during all the eighteen years of my sacred ministry.

And there is a collateral point, which, perhaps, it would be more dignified to leave unnoticed; but, in this country, it will be regarded as necessary for a just appreciation. The labors of our priests have been rendered without any chaplain's salaries, or any other temporal remuneration. When we were obliged to keep three horses instead of one, the commanders rendered us some assistance in that regard; but even that only multiplied our expenses, by the necessity of providing for them.

Simply from a sense of religious duty, and in accordance with the spirit of the Church, we have labored along; with the blessing of God we shall continue to labor, if you will suffer us to do so without renouncing the Divine obligations of the Church, from which alone our labors derive their value.

But if you demand of us, in the name of the civil or military government, to alter our religious worship, the care of which is intrusted by God to the Church alone, our line of conduct is simply and clearly marked out by the Divine Author of both Church and State, and with the assistance of His Grace, we hope to adhere to it. "*Render to Cæsar the things that are Cæsar's, and to God the things that are God's.*"

I have the honor to remain, respected Sir, with all consideration, your obedient servant,

†WM. HENRY ELDER,
Bishop of Natchez.

ST. MARY'S CATHEDRAL, NATCHEZ, *July* 13, 1864.

July 22—Brigadier General Mason Brayman issued this order:

HEADQUARTERS UNITED STATES FORCES,
NATCHEZ, MISS., *July* 22, 1864.

[SPECIAL ORDER No. 11.]

Extract.

V.—It appears that while the country was at peace William Henry Elder, Bishop of Natchez, caused to be read as a portion of the proper and recognized religious service of the Roman Catholic Church within his ecclesiastical jurisdiction, the usual prayer for the President of the United States, &c., whereby was signified and taught a true and loyal spirit towards the Government and authorities of the United States, and a pious desire for the prosperity and maintenance thereof.

It further appears, that after the establishment of the pretended Government of the "Confederate" States of America, in violation of the Constitution and laws of the United States, and in treasonable and armed rebellion against the same, the said William Henry Elder, Bishop of Natchez, did cause to be abolished and stricken from the proper and usual service of the Roman Catholic Church, within his ecclesiastical jurisdiction, the prayer for the President of the United States, &c., and did substitute and cause to be read in place thereof a like prayer for the President of the pretended "Confederate" States, &c., whereby he publicly renounced his allegiance to the Government of the United States, and declared allegiance to a power then in armed resistance against the same, and compassing its overthrow: such act being in violation of his duty as a citizen of the United States, and of evil example to them under his ecclesiastical authority, he well knowing that thereby was instigated and promoted rebellion and armed hostility against the lawful authority of the United States.

It furthermore appears, that on the 18th of June *ultimo*, a Special Order (No. 31) was issued by the officer then commanding the United States forces at Natchez, requiring that the prayer for the President of the United States, &c., should be restored and appropriately read as part of Divine Service, (as had been the custom aforetime in the Roman Catholic Church at Natchez.)

The said William Henry Elder, Bishop of Natchez, being still in rebellion against the United States, and ill disposed towards the government thereof—not having repented of nor retracted his treasonable conduct and teachings as aforesaid, but on the contrary repudiating and denying the authority of the Government and its officers in that behalf; and having for a long time, though frequently warned, contumaciously refused, and still utterly refusing obedience to said order, thus encouraging the people under his authority in treasonable practices, and impairing the force of discipline! *It is therefore ordered:*

First. That the said William Henry Elder, Bishop of Natchez, be expelled from the lines of the Army of the United States, not to return without permission, on pain of imprisonment, during the continuance of the rebellion.

Second. That the Provost Marshal close, and hold military possession of, St. Mary's Cathedral, situated in the city of Natchez, and all other houses or places of worship within this command, and under the ecclesiastical jurisdiction of the said Bishop William H. Elder, in which the prayer for the President of the United States has heretofore been, but is not now, read.

Inasmuch, however, as the said William Henry Elder, has requested in a respectful manner, that any action under said order No. 31, be suspended "until communication can be had with the authorities at Washington:" *It is further ordered:*

That action under said order No. 31, and the paragraphs "*First*" and "*Second*" of this order be accordingly suspended until further orders; and that, in the meantime, the Provost Marshal af Natchez, cause the said William H. Elder, Bishop of Natchez, to report in person, within twenty-four (24) hours after receiving a copy of this order, to the Officer commanding the U. S. forces at Vidalia, and remain within his military lines under penalty of the immediate execution of the order before named.

The Provost Marshal at Natchez and Vidalia, respectively, will see to the strict observance of this order.

By order of Brig. Gen. M. Brayman:

J. H. ODLIN,
Captain and Ass't Adjutant General.

August 12—Gen. Brayman issued the following:

HEADQUARTERS UNITED STATES FORCES,
NATCHEZ, MISS., *August* 12, 1864.

[SPECIAL ORDER No. 31.]

Military authority having been for the time vindicated, so much of Special Order No. 11 as requires Rev. William Henry Elder, Bishop of Natchez, to remain within the military lines of the post of Vidalia, (La.,) is suspended, and he may return to his home and duties until the pleasure of the War Department be known in his case.

And as all solemn appeals to the Supreme Being, not proceeding from honest hearts and willing minds, are necessarily offensive to Him, and subversive of sound morality, so much of Special Order No. 31, June 18, 1864, as requires public prayer to be pronounced in behalf of the President of the United States and the Union is suspended until further orders; leaving all persons conducting divine worship at liberty to manifest such measure of hostility as they may feel against the Government and Union of these States, and their sympathy with the rebellion, by omitting such supplication, if so minded.

By order of Brig. Gen. M. Brayman:

J. H. ODLIN,
Assistant Adjutant General.

The case, on reaching Washington, was referred to Major General Canby, Commanding

Department, by whom no further action appears to have been taken.

THE DEPARTMENT OF THE GULF.

ORDERS OF MAJOR GENERAL BUTLER.

NEW ORLEANS, *May* 13, 1862.

[GENERAL ORDER No. 27.]

It having come to the knowledge of the commanding general that Friday next is observed as a day of fasting and prayer, in obedience to some supposed proclamation of one Jefferson Davis, in the several churches of this city, it is ordered that no such observance be had.

Churches and religious houses are to be kept open as in time of profound peace, but no religious exercises are to be had upon the supposed authority above mentioned.

By command of Major General Butler.

OFFICE MILITARY COMMANDANT NEW ORLEANS, CITY HALL, *May* 28, 1862.

[GENERAL ORDERS.]

Hereafter, in the churches in the city of New Orleans, prayer will not be offered up for the destruction of the Union or Constitution of the United States, for the success of rebel armies, for the Confederate States, so-called, or any officers of the same, civil or military, in their official capacity.

While protection will be afforded to all churches, religious houses and establishments, and religious services are to be held as in time of profound peace, this protection will not be allowed to be perverted to the upholding of treason, or advocacy of it in any form. Where thus perverted, it will be withdrawn.

G. F. SHEPLEY, *Military Commandant.*

Rev. Drs. Leacock and Goodrich, and Mr. Fulton, of the Episcopal churches, declined to read the prayer for the President of the United States; and they were sent to New York by the next steamer. Some weeks after, they returned to New Orleans, but, Gen. Banks requiring the oath of allegiance as a condition of landing, they returned to New York.

DEPARTMENT OF THE TENNESSEE.

ORDERS OF MILITARY GOVERNOR ANDREW JOHNSON.

STATE OF TENNESSEE, EXECUTIVE DEPARTMENT, NASHVILLE, *June* 28, 1862.

Lieut.-Col. R. W. MCCLAIN, *Acting Provost Marshal:*

SIR: Rev. Drs. Howell, Ford, Sehon, Sawrie, and Baldwin are under arrest, and they are hereby placed in your custody.

Should they desire to give evidence of their loyalty by taking the oath of allegiance and giving their individual bonds in the sum of $5,000 each for the faithful observance thereof, they will be permitted to do so, and their release ordered accordingly.

If, however, it is their determination not to give such evidence of loyalty, they will be committed to prison, there to remain until arrangements are completed for their transportation South, beyond the Federal lines, there to be left, with the distinct understanding that if they recross or come again within said lines during the existing rebellion, they will be considered spies and dealt with accordingly.

Very respectfully,

ANDREW JOHNSON, *Military Governor.*

EXECUTIVE DEPARTMENT, *June* 28, 1862.

Lieut.-Col. MCCLAIN, *Acting Provost Marshal:*

SIR: I have to request that you will issue stringent orders prohibiting all visitors to the members of the clergy this day sent as prisoners to the penitentiary, except such as have special permission from me for that purpose; and I would add, this privilege should be granted only for good and sufficient reasons. I would suggest that no encouragement should be given to that secession spirit and feeling which are manifested by numerous offerings of delicacies, &c., by sympathizing rebel friends.

These men were not sent to the penitentiary there to be kept as objects of especial attention from traitors, nor to be lionized by a class of people, who, if properly dealt with, would be allowed the privilege of expressing their sympathy only within the same place of confinement.

They are there as enemies of our Government, and as such are entitled and should receive such consideration only as attaches to a person guilty of so infamous a crime.

Very respectfully,

ANDREW JOHNSON, *Military Governor.*

On the 29th of June Rev. C. D. Elliott and Dr. Cheatham were arrested and sent to the penitentiary. All of these ministers, except Dr Howell, were subsequently sent through the lines.

THE DEPARTMENT OF VIRGINIA.

ORDER OF BRIG. GEN. WILD, AT NORFOLK.

NORFOLK, VA., *Feb.* 11, 1864.

[GENERAL ORDERS No. 3.]

All places of public worship in Norfolk and Portsmouth are hereby placed under the control of the provost marshals of Norfolk and Portsmouth respectively, who shall see the pulpits properly filled by displacing, when necessary, the present incumbents, and substituting men of known loyalty and the same sectarian denomination, either military or civil, subject to the approval of the commanding general. They shall see that all churches are open freely to all officers and soldiers, white or colored, at the usual hour of worship, and at other times, if desired; and they shall see that no insult or indignity be offered to them, either by word, look, or gesture on the part of the congregation. The necessary expenses will be levied as far as possible, in accordance with the previous usages or regulations of each congregation respectively.

No property shall be removed, either public or private, without permission from these headquarters.

By command of Brigadier General E. A. Wild.

CASE OF REV. JAMES D. ARMSTRONG.

WAR DEPARTMENT, BUREAU OF MILITARY JUSTICE, *April* 30, 1864.

To Hon. E. M. STANTON, *Secretary of War:*

In the case of Rev. James D. Armstrong, of Norfolk, Va., I have the honor to submit the following report:

This person having been placed at hard labor on the public works by Major General Butler, in March last, as a punishment for his disloyalty, an appeal in his behalf by his sister, residing in Orange Co., New York, was addressed to the Secretary, and the case thereupon, at the suggestion of this office, referred to General Butler for report.

From this report of the 9th inst., it appears that Armstrong, who has been for some years a Presbyterian clergyman at Norfolk, took and subscribed about February last, the oath of allegiance to the United States which is published in General Order No. 49, of Headquarters of Department of Virginia and North Carolina, December 10, 1863; in which he "solemnly swore, in the presence of Almighty God," as follows: That he would "henceforth faithfully support, protect and defend the Constitution of the United States, and the Union of the States thereunder;" that he would "abide by and faithfully support all acts of Congress passed during the existing rebellion with reference to slaves;" also, "all proclamations of the President of the United States made during the rebellion, having reference to slaves."

And further, he gave his "solemn parole of honor (to be enforced according to military law)" that he would "hold no correspondence with or afford any aid or comfort to any enemies or opposers of the United States, save as an act of humanity."

And he further "solemnly declared that this oath and parole were taken and given fully and willingly, and without any mental reservation or evasion whatever, and with full intention to keep the same."

It being suspected however, that he had practically violated this oath, &c., and was a disloyal and dangerous person, Armstrong was summoned before an aide-de-camp of the General commanding, and subsequently before the General himself, and subjected to an examination in regard to his feelings, sympathies and actions as a man of professed loyalty.

From his answers to the questions addressed to him, it fully appears as follows: That he took the oath in accordance with the Scriptural injunction to obey the "powers that be," and with the intention of keeping it as far as his *actions* were concerned; but that at the same time he could not control his *feelings*.

That when a friend of his, in coming out of the Custom House at Norfolk, after both had taken the oath together, exclaimed that he "would like to spit upon the Northern Yankees," he did not rebuke him, because he considered that he took the oath "with the same view as himself."

That his sympathies have always been with the rebels. That he thinks the South entirely justified in beginning and continuing the war; and believes that the Confederacy should be recognized as an independent Government.

That he does not regard Jefferson Davis and his associates as traitors, or as deserving any punishment.

That he believes that human slavery is sanctioned by the Bible.

That he has never opened his church on the days of fast or thanksgiving appointed by the President, but *has* opened it for meetings of prayer on days designated by Davis, of the so-called Southern Confederacy; that he has determined never to pray that the President or the military, &c., authorities may be successful in putting an end to the rebellion; that since the war he has never preached a sermon in his church favorable to the Union cause; and that he would never allow any other minister to pray there for the Union and against the rebels; but that he has himself prayed for "the authorities over us," meaning the President of the United States, &c.

That he did not regret the federal loss at Smithfield a few weeks since.

From these admissions, which constitute the only evidence presented, it would appear that Armstrong, except in the case of calling prayer meetings in his church in obedience to the requirements of the rebel Davis, has not committed what are commonly regarded overt acts of positive disloyalty, but has violated his oath rather in sentiment and feeling than in the open expression, by language or deed, of hostility to our Government. There is, however, doubtless enough in these admissions to convict the party before a military tribunal of a technical violation of his oath, and probably other testimony could be procured which would present his guilt in a still more decided form. As to his perfidy and bitter disloyalty there can be no question.

In regard to Maj. Gen. Butler's manner of treatment in this case, it is to be said, that while a temporary confinement of a suspected party, preparatory to his being brought to trial, or for other necessary purpose, is customary and allowable, there is believed to be no precedent in our service for the imposition by a commanding general of a formal punishment, and especially (as in the present case) of an infamous punishment, without any trial whatever. The military law, in providing a just and summary mode of trial, also provides for the proper punishment of all military offences, and the case must be extremely rare in which this law cannot be more properly appealed to for the infliction of such punishment than the will of the general commanding

It is advised, therefore, that Armstrong either be brought to trial by military commission for a violation of his oath and parole of honor, or sent beyond our lines as a dangerous character. General Butler represents that his society and influence were more prejudicial to the interests of the United States in his neighborhood than a company of rebel cavalry would have been; and his banishment to the enemy's country would be, not a punishment, but a measure of police regulation sanctioned by the exigencies of war, and most proper to be employed in the present instance.

J. HOLT,
Judge Advocate General.

Proposed Action in Congress.

First Session, Thirty-eighth Congress.

1864, March 31—Mr. Powell offered this resolution:

Resolved, That the Secretary of War be directed to transmit to the Senate all orders that have been issued from his department, or by generals of the army of the United States, authorizing any person or persons to take possession of any church or churches, or house dedicated to the worship of God, or house or property belonging to any home or foreign mission society, or houses and property belonging to any denomination of Christians in the United States; and that he inform the Senate how many churches and how much property, and of what kind and description, has been taken possession of in pursuance of said orders, and where the same is situated, and to what denomination of Christians the property so taken belonged.

April 5—The resolution was tabled—yeas 27, nays 11, as follows:

Yeas—Messrs. Anthony, Clark, Collamer, Conness, Dixon, Doolittle, Fessenden, Foot, Grimes, Hale, Harding, Harlan, Harris, Howard, Howe, Lane of Indiana, Lane of Kansas, Morgan, Morrill, Ramsey, Sherman, Sprague, Sumner, Ten Eyck, Trumbull, Wade, Wilson—27.

Nays—Messrs. *Buckalew*, *Carlile*, Cowan, *Davis*, Johnson, Pomeroy, *Powell*, *Riddle*, *Saulsbury*, Van Winkle, Willey—16.

July 1—Mr. Powell introduced this bill, which was referred to the Committee on the Judiciary:

Be it enacted, &c., That it shall not be lawful for the Secretary of War, or any other person who, for the time being, may be acting as Secretary of War, or any officer of the army of the United States, or other person engaged in the military service of the United States, to take charge of any church or house of public worship, in any State or Territory of the United States, with a view of dismissing a minister therefrom, or of appointing a minister thereto, or installing a minister therein; and that it shall not be lawful for the Secretary of War, or any person for the time being who may be acting as Secretary of War, or any officer of the army of the United States, by proclamation, order, or otherwise, to appoint or designate any person or persons to take charge of any church or house of public worship for the purposes aforesaid. And the Secretary of War, or any person who for the time being may be acting as Secretary of War, or any officer of the army of the United States, or other person engaged in the military service of the United States, who violates this act, shall, for every such offence, be liable to indictment as for a misdemeanor, in any court of the United States having jurisdiction to hear, try, and determine cases of misdemeanor; and on conviction thereof shall pay a fine not exceeding ten thousand dollars, and suffer imprisonment in the penitentiary not more than ten years at the discretion of the court trying the same. And any person convicted as aforesaid shall moreover be disqualified from holding any office of honor, profit, or trust under the Government of the United States.

Reconstruction of Churches.

CHURCHES IN NEW ORLEANS.

THE EPISCOPAL CHURCHES.

Headquarters Department of the Gulf,
Office of Provost Marshal General,
New Orleans, *June* 3, 1864.

To the Wardens and Vestrymen of St. Peter's Church:

By orders of the Major General commanding, you will please furnish me as follows:

1st. List of Wardens, Vestrymen, and Trustees, with date and mode of appointment, and present residence.

2d. List of pew-holders, and others who have contributed statedly to the support of the Church, the rector, or the officiating minister, with the amounts contributed by each, and sums yet due; and the names of such other heads of families, or other adults, who by their stated attendance may have been regarded as members of the congregation during the period aforesaid, with their places of residence.

3d. An account in detail of all financial transactions, and the present pecuniary condition of the corporation, with an inventory of church buildings and their valuation.

Very respectfully,

JAMES BOWEN, *Brig. Gen.*,
Provost Marshal General, Department of the Gulf.

Headquarters Department of the Gulf,
Office of Provost Marshal General,
New Orleans, *June* 15, 1864.

Major George B. Drake, *A. A. General:*

In compliance with orders from Department Headquarters, I respectfully report that the Episcopal Churches in which the prayers for the President and Congress were not read prior to 1st March, were, viz:

St. Paul's,
St. Peter's,
Trinity.

On the 1st March, after due notice, I appointed the following Trustees in St. Peter's Church, in place of the Wardens and Vestrymen:

Wm. Lewis,
John Brooks,
James Jackson,
Henry Houlgrone,
John Houlgrone.

By consent of the Post Chaplain, and with my approval, the Rev. Mr. A. Vallas was authorized to act as the officiating clergyman. On the 9th April the Rev. Mr. L. T. Jessup, clergyman of Trinity Church resigned, and the Rev. Mr. Vallas succeeded him. In both of the churches the prayers for the President and for Congress are read. The Rev. Mr. Vallas officiates in one in the morning and the other in the evening.

The prayers for the President and for Congress were omitted in the services of St. Paul's Church till the 10th of April. Since that date they have been read regularly by the officiating clergyman, the Rev. Mr. Guion.

I respectfully submit the papers of the Wardens of St. Paul's and St. Peter's Churches, and the letters of the Rev.

Mr. Vallas in respect to the financial condition of these Churches.

I was informed by the Rev. Dr. Newman, that at a small Episcopal Church in Algiers, conducted by an alien clergyman, the prayers for the President and for Congress were not read, and I directed the church to be closed.

This is the only Episcopal church in New Orleans, or in its vicinity, in which the above-mentioned prayers are not read.

I am, Major, very respectfully, your obedient servant,
JAMES BOWEN, *Brig. Gen.*,
Provost Marshal General, Department of the Gulf.

PRESBYTERIAN CHURCHES.

To Brigadier General JAMES BOWEN, *Provost Marshal General, Department of the Gulf:*

We, the undersigned, a Committee appointed by you to "ascertain and report the names of the trustees of the several Presbyterian and Baptist churches in this city, Algiers, and Carrollton, and whether the trustees of these churches have taken the oath of allegiance to the United States," &c., do respectfully report:

That in accordance with said order, your Committee proceeded to the performance of their duties, the result of which is presented in a tabular form hereto annexed, to which they refer for the particulars connected with said investigation as it respects the officers of said churches, their present residence, their status as to loyalty, oath, &c. That in the investigation which has been made by your Committee, commencing with the First Presbyterian Church, they report that this church was originally incorporated March 1, 1834, under the corporate name of the "Presbyterian Church of the City and Parish of New Orleans;" that on the 28th of February, 1854, an amendment of said act was passed, in which amended act the title of said church was changed to the "First Presbyterian Church and Congregation of the City and Parish of New Orleans," that in said act the second section thereof reads as follows:

"That said corporation shall have power to elect from their own body, who own or rent pews in said church, trustees to represent them in their temporal affairs or concerns, and that the said trustees shall consist of five, and shall have power to make and establish, from time to time, such by-laws and regulations as they shall judge proper for the election of their own officers, and for supplying the vacancies which may occur among the same, for regulating the time and places of meeting of said trustees or members composing said corporation, &c., and for the government and management of the temporal affairs of said corporation, and generally for the transaction of all the temporal concerns of said corporation of every kind: *Provided*, that such by-laws and regulations are not inconsistent with the *Constitution* and *Laws* of the *United States*, or with those of this State, or with the provisions of this act; *and provided, also*, that no sale or other alienation of any of the property of said corporation, except the pews of the church, shall be valid and legal, without the written concurrence and consent of all the then ruling elders of the said First Presbyterian Church.

"SEC. 3. That the said church shall be governed in its ecclesiastical affairs by the doctrine, discipline, rules, and regulations of the Presbyterian Church of the United States, known and designated as the Old School Presbyterian Church, the General Assembly of which held its last annual session in the City of Philadelphia and State of Pennsylvania."

That the Rev. B. M. Palmer, of South Carolina, was installed as the pastor of this church some time in the year 1856, and continued so to act until some time in the year 1861, when he, together with a large number of the members and congregation of said church, left for the Confederacy, and have not since returned; that the relation of said pastor with said church has never been dissolved; that the said Palmer, as late as about the month of May last, attended a meeting of the so-called "General Assembly of the Confederate States," as the representative of said church; that he, together with *six* out of *eight* of the ruling elders of said church are "*rebels*," in the largest sense of that word; that of said elders there is only one reliable Union man, to wit: J. A. Mabin; that of the five trustees, one has resigned; one is said to have acted with the Confederate authorities in their action against northern men; that the remaining trustees, though having taken the oath of allegiance to the United States, covertly act with the enemies of that Government.

The pecuniary condition of the church is as follows:

There is a mortgage debt against the church of $10,000, which is held by the French house of Rochereau & Co., of this city; the interest for the past three years is also due and unpaid. The church property is insured for the sum of $70,000.

Your Committee further report, that the Third Presbyterian Church was incorporated and chartered in the year 1847 or 1848; that your Committee have been unable to obtain the precise date of said charter; that the said charter contains the same provisions in relation to officers, organization and government as that of the First Presbyterian Church; that in regard to said officers and their present position, &c., your Committee refer to the tabular statement hereto annexed.

This church is encumbered with a debt of $10,000, secured by mortgage in favor of the house of Rochereau & Co., above referred to; that there is also a debt of $2,000, due to the Citizen's Bank of this city, secured, as your Committee believe, by a mortgage; that there is also a debt of $1,000, due to a loyal lady named Miss Clark, a resident of New York city; that the said debts, with the interest thereon, amount to about $15,000, most of which is due to disloyal foreigners and citizens.

Your Committee further report that the Fourth Presbyterian Church is an incorporated body under a charter similar in all respects to that of the churches above mentioned. Your Committee have been unable to ascertain the indebtedness of this church, but they are informed that there is a debt existing against it in favor of the same parties who hold the large incumbrances on the other churches above mentioned.

Your Committee further report, that the church known as the Prytania Street Presbyterian Church, in all respects in the particulars above specified, is similarly situated as the other churches mentioned in this report.

Each of these churches, through its officers and a large majority of its members, identified themselves with the existing rebellion, attempting a disseverance from that loyal body of men known as the "General Assembly of the Presbyterian Church," who, at its session in 1861, so nobly and patriotically sustained our glorious Government and its authority; that shortly after that time these churches connected themselves with what has been called the "General Assembly of the Confederate States," a body without any right for its establishment or continuance, or the recognition, if any, of any competent authority, having the power so to do; that since the occupation of the city of New Orleans by the United States Government, these churches, through some chicane and secret action, have each constituted themselves into an independent Presbyterian Church, thus attempting to carry out the false principle of *secession*, and contrary to the charter under which they are severally organized.

Your Committee would also state that these Churches, except the one known as the Second Presbyterian Church, so far as their pulpit supply is concerned, are virtually vacant—that is, they have no regular or stated pastor; that they sometimes have services, conducted by laymen; that there are many members of said churches of undoubted loyalty, who strongly suspect most, if not all, the church officers, who yet remain in this city and have not departed for the Confederacy and elsewhere, of strong sympathies for the rebellion, which has produced so much terrible suffering and devastation throughout our land; that these loyal Presbyterians do not feel at home among these churches, and have often been insulted for their loyalty; that these loyal people are anxious to open these churches to ministers of approved loyalty; that applications have been made to some of the disloyal and unworthy officers now connected with said churches by loyal ministers of the Presbyterian Church to allow them to officiate in their churches, and have been refused.

Your Committee further report that these churches, since their organization, have been connected with and represented in the General Assembly named in their respective charters, until just prior to the breaking out of the said rebellion, when, without the consent or authority of said Assembly, they dissevered themselves therefrom by illegal and unauthorized proceedings on their part; that the said "General Assembly of the Presbyterian Church of the United States of America," as the highest judicatory of said Church, under the 5th article of chapter 12 of the Form of Government of said Church, has the power "of reproving, warning, or bearing testimony against error in doctrine or immorality in practice in any church, presbytery, or synod; of superintending the concerns of the whole Church," &c., of which powers, your Committee believe, they have never been deprived by any action of said churches, and are amply sufficient to enable the said Assembly, at the proper time and through the proper representation, to deal with the recusant members of their body and correct the evils which have existed, and at present exist, but that it is necessary for some other authority to take present action with strong hand in aid of loyalty, so that the necessary proceedings may be initiated by which said Assembly may obtain such information as will enable it to act upon the powers inherent therein, a portion of which are above specified.

Your Committee would also refer to the annexed order of the War Department in relation to the action of the military officers of this and other departments concerning the churches of the Presbyterian denomination, which is believed by your Committee will authorize them to accomplish the result herein proposed, to wit: the immediate occupation of these churches by the persons specified in said order, or any others duly authorized by said General Assembly, through whom these churches may be re-organized by loyal officers, members, and congregations, and thus bring about that consummation so devoutly to be wished, viz: a resumption of the proper and legitimate authority of said denomination, and thereby work a wholesome influence in favor of the noblest Government ever devised by man.

All which is respectfully submitted.

ROBERT H. SHANNON,
CHARLES STRONG,
Committee.

NEW ORLEANS, *August* 7, 1864.

WAR DEPARTMENT,
ASSISTANT ADJUTANT GENERAL'S OFFICE,
WASHINGTON, *March* 10, 1864.

To the Generals commanding the Military Division of the Mississippi and the Departments of the Gulf, of the South, and of Virginia and North Carolina, and all Generals and officers commanding armies, detachments, and posts, and all officers in the service of the United States in the above mentioned Departments. The Board of Domestic Missions of the Presbyterian Church, and the Presbyterian Committee of Home Missions, enjoy the entire confidence of this Department, and no doubt is entertained that all ministers who may be appointed by them will be entirely loyal.

You are expected to permit such ministers of the gospel, bearing a commission of the "Board of Domestic Missions, or of the Presbyterian Committee of Home Missions" of the Presbyterian Church, who may convince you that their commissions are genuine, to exercise the functions of their office within your command, and to give them all the aid, countenance and support which may be practicable, and in your judgment proper, in the execution of their important mission.

By order of the Secretary of War.

E. D. TOWNSEND,
Assistant Adjutant General.

Table referred to in the foregoing Report.

CHURCH AND LOCATION.	NAMES.	OFFICERS, &C.	OATH.	WHERE NOW ARE.	REMARKS.
First Presbyterian Church, opposite Lafayette Square..	B. M. Palmer	Pastor	No	In the Confederacy.	
	Samuel Jones, Jr	Trustee	Yes	New Orleans	Has resigned—resignation not yet accepted.
	J. K. Collins	do	Yes	New Orleans	Secessionist.
	W. H. Thomas	do	Yes	New Orleans	do.
	E. H. Wheeler	do	Yes	New Orleans	do.
	J. A. Mabin	R. Elder	Yes	New Orleans.	
	E. S. Keep	do	Yes	New Orleans	Secessionist.
	Dr. W. Richardson	do	No	In the Confederacy.	
	Wm. Black	do	No	In the Confederacy.	
	W. P. Campbell	do	No	England	By permission of Gen. Butler.
	John T. Hardy	do	No	In the Confederacy.	
	Wm. A. Bartlett	do	No	In the Confederacy.	
	Alfred Hennen	do	No	In the Confederacy.	
Sec'd Presbyterian Church, corner of Calliope and Prytania.	This church is now in possession of the military authorities, and no names could be obtained.				This church belongs to J. W. Stanton, formerly of this city, now in Connecticut.
Third Presbyterian Church, Royal street, opposite Washington Square	Henry Smith	Pastor	No	In the Confederacy.	
	W. C. Raymond	Trustee	Yes	New Orleans	Secessionist
	J. T. Warner	do	Yes	New Orleans.	
	Geo. Heation	do	Neut. Oath.	New Orleans	Secessionist.
	W. C. Raymond	Elder	Yes	New Orleans	Secessionist.
	Frederick Stringer	do	No	In the Confederacy.	
Fourth Presbyterian Church on Gasquet street	G. L. Moore	Pastor	No	In the Confederacy.	Supposed to be preaching in Mobile.
	J. R. Young	Trustee & Elder.	Yes	New Orleans.	
	Alex. McVicker	do	Yes	New Orleans.	
	James Causley	do	Yes	New Orleans.	
	George Waterman	do	Yes	New Orleans.	
	Wm. Wilson	do	Yes	New Orleans.	
	John Hayes	do			Could not obtain any information about him.
Prytania St. Church, corner of Prytania and Josephine	Isaac Henderson	Pastor	Yes	Gone North some weeks since.	It is supposed will not return.
	F. Wing, President	Trustee	No	In the Confederacy.	
	A. B. Griswold, Secretary	do	Yes	New Orleans	Secessionist.
	Lewis Elkin	do	No	Said to be in Paris	Runaway Englishman.
	Samuel E. Moore	do	Yes	New Orleans	Secessionist.
	S. B. Newman	Elder	Yes	New Orleans	Rebel Sympathizer.
	D. Hadden	do	No	In the Confederacy.	
	Elijah Peale	do	Yes	New York.	
	Moses Greenwood	do	Yes	New York.	

CHURCHES IN EAST TENNESSEE.

On the 2d of September, 1864, a meeting of the Union Presbytery was held in Knox county, attended by three ministers and the lay representatives of twelve congregations, and it was unanimously resolved to dissolve their connection with the "United Synod of the Presbyterian Church," a pro-slavery denomination which originated, in 1857, by secession from the New School Presbyterians, and to reconnect themselves with the New School Presbyterian General Assembly. This Presbytery embraces about 30 churches with 2,400 communicants, of which 20 are in the counties of Blount, Knox, and Jefferson. The majority of the ministers of the Presbytery had, in 1857, effected an ecclesiastical secession without consulting the congregations, and all of them who had advocated church secession, with but one exception, plunged into rebellion. In May, 1863, the disloyal majority, at a meeting of the Presbytery, passed a resolution, neither to license, nor to ordain, nor to receive from another Presbytery, any man not sympathizing with the rebel Confederacy, or opposed to slaveholding. There were then only four Union and loyal ministers belonging to the Presbytery, all of whom were absent from the meeting, and two of whom soon after died. The two others, together with one who has recanted his rebel sentiments, were the ministers present at this year's meeting of the Presbytery. Two new clerical members were added to the Presbytery, one by ordination, and the other on letter of dismission from a Congregational Association in Michigan.

At a convention of loyal ministers and laymen of the Holston Annual Conference of the Methodist Episcopal Church South, held at Knoxville on August 17, 1864, it was resolved that the loyal members of the Conference have a just claim to all the church property; that they really constitute the Southern Methodist Church within the bounds of the Holston Conference; that they propose at the earliest day practicable, to transfer the same to the Methodist Episcopal Church in the United States; and that the ministers be instructed to propose to their congregations to go *en masse* to the Methodist Episcopal Church in the United States. There are in the bounds of the Holston Conference one hundred and twenty preachers known to be loyal, and forty others supposed to be true to the Union; and it is thought, therefore, that the work of reconstruction will be easily accomplished.

The Cumberland Presbyterians of the rebellious States, though very numerous, have never succeeded in effecting a separate church organization. The delegates from East Tennessee, at the General Assembly of the present year, voted with the majority for resolutions demanding the cessation of slavery in both Church and State.

WESLEYAN METHODIST.

GENERAL CONFERENCE OF THE WESLEYAN METHODIST CONNECTION, 1864.

June 1—The body met at Adrian, Michigan.

June 4—The Report of the Committee on the State of the Country, Revs. W. H. Brewster and A. Crooks, and E. Starbuck, layman, was adopted, as follows:

Meeting as we do, a national body, at a time when a civil war of unequalled magnitude, and fraught with consequences, not only to this nation, but the world, without a parallel, is raging; when the telegraphic wires stretching through this vast republic seem so many nerves of sensation uniting us with the fields of conflict where the nation's life seems to depend upon success, or defeat, we should be justly charged with indifference—with want of patriotism, did we give no expression of views and feelings upon the subject.

We desire humbly and gratefully to confess that, as a *nation*, we are in the hands of a merciful and just God, who is dealing with us in the way of judgment for our sins, tempered with mercy, extorting from the nation the confession, "How unsearchable are his judgments and his ways past finding out."

He who does not see that God is dealing with this nation, is blind indeed. So striking are the evidences of the Divine hand—so has God conducted us and overruled the plans and purposes of men, bringing about results we all desired but which we should have failed to achieve had our wished for success in the earlier struggles been realized, that in our reverses, not less than in our victories, we recognize the unsearchable wisdom, justice and goodness of God. His justice afflicts us, that we may humble ourselves and repent of our sins, and be willing to surrender the hateful cause of this rebellion, while his mercy spares us, that we may yet be a people to his praise.

We rejoice, that contrary to the wishes of the President—in spite of political parties—in spite of the influence of the border States, the war has become a war for freedom on the one hand, and for the establishment of slavery on the other; and before the nations of the earth, and before God we are obliged to accept this issue. We bow with adoring wonder before the sublimity and grandeur of the onward sweep of Divine Providence in the events now transpiring among us.

We recognize with gratitude to Almighty God the remarkable change of national sentiment upon the subject of slavery, and the rights of colored persons. "It is the Lord's doings and marvelous in our eyes," and one of those results reconciling us to the sacrifices of life, and the other evils incident to this war. Every blow struck by the Union army, is a blow for liberty, every victory over the rebels, is a victory in behalf of liberty; and the advance of our army, is the onward march of freedom into the heart of despotism, and our success is a triumph in behalf of liberty for all races of men.

Resolved,—That the war being a judgment of God upon the nation for national sins, pride, infidelity, and oppression, the only way to permanent peace and prosperity, is through national repentance.

Resolved,—That we accept civil war in the course of Divine Providence as a result of national crimes, while its horrors of bloodshed and savage cruelty have deepened our purpose to labor and pray for that period when the nations of the earth shall learn war no more.

Resolved,—That in the spirit of patriots and christians, we affirm for ourselves and our churches, our *unqualified* loyalty to the Government, and our readiness to endure and make all the sacrifices necessary to the overthrow of the rebellion, and the destruction of slavery, its guilty cause.

W. H. BREWSTER,
ADAM CROOKS,
EDWARD STARBUCK,
Committee.

Rev. J. Watson, voting against, in brief remarks stated that he was opposed to war at any time.

June 7—The Report of the Committee to draft an address to the President of the United States—Revs. W. H. Brewster, Henry Norton, and W. W. Lyle, and Joseph Parrish, and C. G. Case, laymen—was adopted as follows:

ADRIAN COLLEGE, ADRIAN, MICH., *June* 6, 1864.

To His Excellency ABRAHAM LINCOLN, *President of the United States:*

The General Conference of the Wesleyan Methodist Connection of America, convened at Adrian, Michigan, in its Quadrennial Assembly deems it fit and proper in its associated capacity, to extend to you its christian greeting.

And first of all, as an assembly of christian ministers and laymen, we desire to say to you as the Chief Magistrate of the Nation, "*May grace, mercy, and peace from God our Father, and from the Lord Jesus Christ rest upon you.*" In common with all the truly loyal of our citizens we have felt the deepest interest in the great struggle now going on to maintain the integrity of the nation, and to protect and perpetuate those institutions of freedom so dear to every American heart, and which have been threatened by the wicked rebellion which now rages. And we have not ceased to pray that God, in his adorable Providence, would not only incline the hearts of his people to true repentance on account of our national sins, and especially of the great sin of the nation, human bondage; but that He would graciously vouchsafe to our army and navy such victories over armed traitors as that this most wicked and causeless of rebellions might be speedily crushed, and the nation be restored to peace and tranquillity. Aside from the general principles of loyalty and genuine patriotism, there are very special reasons why we, as a connection of christian churches, should be more than ordinarily interested in our country's severe struggle for the maintenance of righteous government.

Taking as one of the cardinal truths of christianity, that God hath made of one blood all nations of men that dwell on the face of the earth, and being convinced that it was a duty we owed to God and humanity to protest by word and deed against the fearful crime of American slavery, which was sanctioned and protected by the leading christian denominations of the land!

The denomination which we represent, and which is known as the "Wesleyan Methodist Connection of America," organized twenty-one years ago. Holding with a firm grasp the doctrines of grace taught by the Methodist Episcopal Church, from which we seceded on account of her then notoriously pro-slavery principles and practice. We differed from the church of our early choice only on matters of ecclesiastical polity, and the great distinctive principle of holding no fellowship with the slaveholder, his aider, or apologist.

During these twenty-one years no slaveholder, nor sympathizer with slavery, has ever been received into the membership of our churches, and since this wicked rebellion has raged, a single disloyal Wesleyan Methodist has been unknown throughout our entire connection.

We have watched with anxious solicitude and prayerful interest the course which you, as the Chief Executive of the nation, have pursued in these days of commotion and bloodshed. And realizing the unspeakable importance of the issues at stake, and the difficulties by which your administration has been surrounded, and the conflicting elements that have conspired to trammel or thwart some of the most obviously correct, and, as the results show, the wisest and most successful measures you have from time to time adopted to crush the rebellion; we have not withheld from you our heartfelt sympathy, nor ceased to pray that

God would vouchsafe to you the guidance of Divine wisdom, the gracious care of His Almighty arm, and the comforts of His grace.

We would not conceal the fact that we have not been always free from anxiety, and even fear regarding some of the measures adopted by your administration; neither can we refrain from frankly stating that we have often felt grieved and disappointed at the apparent reluctance exhibited in adopting such measures as would ere now have struck a fatal blow at the very heart of the rebellion. We believe that righteousness exalteth a nation, but sin is not only the reproach of any people, but must, sooner or later, result in the withdrawal of the Divine blessing. The crying sin of slavery has been at once our national reproach and the cause of our national troubles; and, aside entirely from any political or military necessity, it ought to have been destroyed as a moral duty, and as one of the evidences of a genuine national repentance, without which we have no claims on the Divine mercy. We would by no means forget or ignore the advanced, and we would add, noble position you occupy on this all important question, though we thus speak.

We thank you for your edict of emancipation. We thank you in the name of that God who has revealed himself as the friend, and protector, and avenger of the poor and needy. We thank you in the name of the millions of the oppressed of our land. We thank you in the name of universal humanity, and we only regret that that document, noble as it is, is too partial and discriminating in favor of those States, and parts of States not in open rebellion, but whose treason against God's moral government only the more clearly shows that their treasonable proclivities are but scarcely concealed; and their protestations of loyalty are but for the basest and most selfish of purposes.

That you. Sir, may be guided by more than human wisdom in your onerous and responsible position, and that every spiritual and temporal blessing may be yours, that our noble soldiers and sailors, so heroically and nobly fighting the battles of liberty may be abundantly successful, and that that day may speedily dawn when the bow of peace shall again be seen in our heavens, and we be a united and happy people, with the dear old flag waving over a redeemed and regenerated nation, is our earnest and devout prayer.

With feelings of the highest esteem and regard. tendered you by this Conference, the undersigned are authorized in its behalf to sign and forward to you this epistle.

Respectfully, &c., LUTHER LEE, *President*.
JOHN McELDOWNEY, *Secretary*.

Same day—The report of the committee to draft an Address to the Churches—Luther Lee, D. D., Revs. W. W. Crane and M. Q. McFarland—was adopted, as follows:

To the members of the Wesleyan Methodist Connection of America, the General Conference in session at Adrian, Michigan, June, 1864, sendeth greeting: Grace and peace be multiplied unto you, through the knowledge of God the Father, and our Lord. Jesus Christ, in the comfort of the Holy Spirit. It gives us great pleasure to be able to assure you that our coming together has been in peace, and that we have been much refreshed in meeting once more as your representatives, to take each other by the hand of christian fellowship, and to look upon each others' faces once more in the flesh, many of us having long been endeared to each other, in common with you, by common labors, sacrifices, and sufferings in the cause of God and humanity.

The times are portentous, and wrath has fallen upon our beloved country, fearful in extent, though it be less than our national sins deserve.

The fearful evil of slavery, which our nation so long cherished in its bosom, has at last stung it like a viper, and convulsed our whole commonwealth. This evil has culminated in rebellion and war, which has filled our land with weeping and sorrow for the thousands slain. But amid the evils that oppress us, our confidence remains unshaken in the Providence of God, as all-wise, gracious, and efficient; and we exhort you all to maintain the same confidence, as we trust you have done, and will continue to do. It is no doubt a consolation to you, as it is to us, to know that we foresaw these evils as the probable retribution for the national sin of slavery, and faithfully warned our fellow-citizens of the same, and did what we could to remove the evil and avert the gathering storm; but our words were not heeded, only so far as to be requited with opposition, slander, hatred, and persecution; yet all we suffered is now more than compensated in knowing that we did our duty in the premises; that as a denomination we never had a slaveholder in our communion, and never disgraced the religion we profess by giving its sanction in any form or degree to the crime of human bondage, and never opposed those who opposed slavery. It gives us great satisfaction to know that on the breaking out of the pro-slavery rebellion, the position we had occupied for twenty years is the one the government and the nation has been compelled to assume, so that when they wheeled to face the foe we found ourselves already in line, without having to right about face.

We exhort you, brethren, still to adhere to the great principles of freedom and human right that gave us existence as a religious organization, and to remain true to your God and your country; and be sure to maintain constant and earnest prayer to God that He will render the war the instrument of the entire removal of slavery, and give it a speedy termination in the triumph of the authority of the government over rebellion, and in the return of peace and prosperity to our suffering country. We have great confidence in God, that he will in his Providence make an end of slavery by the means of the war, and bring our nation through the dreadful trial, purified and redeemed from the reign of oppression.

The war has very materially impeded our religious progress, it having made large drafts upon our membership, and even taken numbers of our ministers for the defence of our common country against the most wicked rebellion and war that ever disgraced humanity. The excitement which has pervaded the public mind has also diverted attention from the subject of religion, and tended to render the moral power of the ministry and churches unavailing for the promotion of revivals; yet we have reason to thank God and take courage in view of the progress that has been made. We have been favored with many gracious revivals, which have resulted in the enlargement of some of the churches and in the organization of new ones, and in the erection of new houses of worship. Our progress, if not rapid, has been steadily onward, and we have been strengthened in all the elements that give efficiency to our connection; and we are most happy to be able to state that since our last quadrennial gathering, we have been blessed with greater internal peace and harmony than has marked any former period of our history. We cannot forbear to congratulate you in regard to two achievements of the last four years.

* * * * * * * *

5. The missionary cause is the last object we will name as presenting special claims to your benevolence. This is very important in our circumstances, as we have many feeble churches, who must receive help from stronger churches, or soon be erased from our records.

This aid can be most effectually rendered through a well devised home missionary system, into which we exhort all the churches to enter with zeal and large benevolence.

There is yet another field of missionary enterprise, calling loudly for our most enlarged christian benevolence. It is the freedmen of the southern States. These victims of oppression are now being thrown upon their own resources by the convulsions of the war, and demand aid, which they must have or suffer, if not perish. Voluntary emancipation upon the soil by slaveholders, would have been attended by far less evil consequences, as then the resources of the country would not have been impaired, and they would have found employment in the fields of their former bondage. But the war has desolated the country, consumed its supplies of food and clothing, while the slaves have broken away and rushed by thousands to our lines for protection, in the most destitute and pitiable condition. We may suppose that Government is now doing what it can to elevate their condition, but that is not sufficient to meet their circumstances; they need not only food and clothing, but advice, instruction, schools, and the gospel in its purity, which they have never had. It will require years of benevolent effort to elevate this degraded people, after so many generations of dark bondage, and it is a work which must be done, not by Government but by religious communities, and while others enter into it with zeal, let us not be found wanting.

And now, brethren, remember that we have a great work to do, and that time is short. Years rush along, and hasten us all onward to our final account. Up, then, and be at the appropriate work of life, which is not to hoard up a little of this world for others to quarrel over when we are gone, but to do good, to bless mankind, to spread the gospel of salvation, to glorify God here in our bodies and our spirits, which are his, and to win a throne and a crown of glory in immortality. Remember that it is in this life that eternal destinies are settled; it is on the moral battle-fields of earth that immortal crowns, and thorns, and kingdoms are won. The day of judgment will declare our destiny, and mete out our reward; but here amid the activities of life, we determine for ourselves what they shall be. May the God of all truth and grace administer unto you abundantly the aid and consolation of the Holy Spirit, and fill you with zeal, and love, and power to do His will, and make you perfect in Christ Jesus, to whom, with the Father and the Holy Ghost, be ascribed everlasting praises. Amen.

LUTHER LEE
WM. W. CRANE,
M. Q. McFARLAND.
Committee.

The Wesleyan Church has always been anti-slavery, in its organic law. At its Quadrennial Convention of 1860, an address to the churches was adopted, in which this language is used concerning their "testimonies:"

Slavery, that great crime against humanity and sin against God, has always been, and is universally prohibited. All slave-buying and slave-holding, all apology for either, and all political support of slavery, are made criminal offences.

In the Report on Reforms, then made by Revs. D. Worth and H. Norton, and M. Merrick, layman, this language is used:

Resolved, That this General Conference regards slavery with the most inexpressible loathing and detestation. We regard it as a system of unparalleled wickedness and infamy, whose component parts are theft, adultery, piracy, man-stealing and murder; and whose atrocious character was well defined by the great and good John Wesley, when he pronounced American slavery as the vilest that ever saw the sun. We believe that its utter extinction should be sought by every friend of God and humanity, by all the means which God has put in our power, civil, political and religious—by "pen and tongue, by vote and prayer"—and all those parties or organizations, political or religious, whose motto is not the immediate death of this terrific curse and dishonor, are unworthy of the fellowship or support of the true disciples of Christ.

Resolved, 2. That immediate emancipation is the right of the slave and the duty of the master; and that we are not at liberty to demand, or receive less than this full measure of justice and restitution; and to the accomplishment of this purpose we bend all our efforts, and we cannot turn aside from our holy purpose at the suggestions of a worldly policy, which would mingle sordid expediency with the pure and noble counsels of our Lord Jesus Christ. We cannot act upon the policy of choosing the least of two evils; but we must treat all such suggestions of a compromising policy, as the offspring of that wisdom which is earthly, sensual, devilish.

UNITARIAN.

Additional to the memoranda given on page 504, respecting the Unitarian Church, are the resolutions passed at a Convention of the Unitarian Church, held at Springfield, Massachusetts, October 14, 1863:

Rev. Dr. Hill, of Worcester, Mass., now moved a series of patriotic resolutions:

Whereas, individuals and ecclesiastical bodies have, at different times and in different places, published opinions on the duties of religious men, that have served to awaken doubts in the minds of the conscientious and weaken the hands of the Government; therefore—

Resolved, By members of the Unitarian body assembled in convention in Springfield, Massachusetts, that we tender to the President of the United States our sympathy and our prayers in this great day of the country's peril and his responsibility; that while as christians we are peacemakers, and labor for the spread of peace, we cheerfully offer our own life, and that of our children for the perilled life of the nation; that, while we owe allegiance to the constituted authorities at all times, we hold it now, when treason and rebellion are abroad, an especial duty, both by word and act, to express it, and that while the privilege of individual freedom is vouchsafed to all, irrespective of color, as a religious right sanctioned by the spirit and letter of the scriptures, we cannot refrain from the expression of our satisfaction at the proclamation of freedom by the Chief Magistrate to millions now in bondage, and the indulgence of the hope that the tremendous scenes through which we are passing will result in the liberty and christian progress of all.

Rev. Dr. Farley, of Brooklyn, New York, seconded the resolutions with a brief but forcible speech. He thought if ever a man demanded, and needed, and deserved the cordial co-operation, and sympathy, and prayers of a people, Abraham Lincoln was that man.

The resolutions were unanimously adopted, and the Convention then adjourned.

Religious Duties of Masters to Servants.

The following paragraphs are from recent secular papers:

The Episcopal Convention of South Carolina has declared that the marriage relation binds slave and master equally; that every Christian master should so regulate the sale or disposal of a married slave as not to infringe the Divine injunction forbidding the separation of husband and wife; that where an involuntary and final separation of married slaves has occurred the case of the sufferers is to be distinguished from any human agency which has separated them. The master is responsible to God for disregarding his commands; the slaves are entitled to sympathy and consideration; that in such cases of separation where neither party is at fault, and where separation appears to be permanent and final, the refusal to allow a second marriage would often produce much evil and hardship, and this Convention, in giving its judgment in favor of such marriages, would do so in the qualified language applied by the Apostles in cases of self restraint: "If they cannot contain, let them marry; for it is better to marry than to burn."

The Protestant and Catholic clergy of the Confederacy are calling attention to the duty of enforcing the sanctity of the marriage relation among slaves. The Baptist Convention of Georgia has adopted an emphatic resolution upon the subject. The Southern Churchman quotes various religious authorities, setting forth the sinfulness of any neglect by masters of this Christian duty; among them Bishop Verot, (Roman Catholic Bishop of Savannah,) who says: "Slavery, to become a permanent institution of the South, must be made to conform to the law of God; a Southern Confederacy will never thrive unless it rests upon morality and order; the Supreme Arbiter of nations will not bless with stability and prosperity a state of things which would be a flagrant violation of His holy commandments."

In this connection, this paragraph from Dr. Jacob Cooper's Article on Slavery in the Church Courts, *Danville Review,* December, 1864, p 521, has interest:

In Transylvania Presbytery, at its spring meeting in April, 1861, a resolution was introduced by Rev S. B. Cheek, to memorialize the Legislature for the passage of a law permitting church members and others who had a conscience in the matter, to have the marriages of their slaves legally solemnized. By this the master would voluntarily submit to the pecuniary loss incurred by making it impossible to sell either one of a married couple without the other. This resolution contemplated no compulsory action on any, save those who felt scandalized that Christian masters must, by existing laws, see members of their own households and churches living in a state of concubinage, and who chose to avail themselves of its provisions to put away this sin. Though it was introduced in the most Christian spirit, and embraced a case where the consciences of believers ought, if ever, to be bound, yet this resolution was laid on the table, nearly every member of Presbytery voting against it. For it was argued by an eminent man, himself *once* an emancipationist, that though the matter presented was one of undoubted grievance, involving a sin which ought to be purged away, yet, to prevent agitation in the Church at such a time of intense political strife, there must be no intermeddling; and so, with a few words of caution, spoken in a whisper, against drawing upon the church the suspicion of sharing in the Abolition crusade, this paper was secretly buried like an untimely birth.

Valuable Records from the Bureau of Military Justice.

As illustrating the slave system, and the action of the Administration in the enforcement of the Proclamation of Emancipation, as well as the character of the war waged against the national authority, the following original records from the Bureau of Military Justice possess historic value:

CASE OF ROBERT TAYLOR, OF TENNESSEE.

WAR DEPARTMENT, ADJUTANT GENERAL'S OFFICE,
WASHINGTON, *May* 9, 1864.

[General Court Martial Orders, No. 88.]

I...Before a Military Commission, consisting of Captain C. Thompson, 19th Michigan Volunteers; Captain Owen Griffith, 22d Wisconsin Volunteers; Captain James Nutt, 9th Indiana Volunteers; Captain D. R. May, 22d Wisconsin

Volunteers; First Lieutenant George Banman, 22d Wisconsin Volunteers; and which convened at Murfreesboro', Tennessee, September 14, 1863, pursuant to Special Orders, No. 8, dated Post Headquarters, Murfreesboro', September 9, 1863, was arraigned and tried—

Robert Taylor, a citizen.

CHARGE—"Murder."

Specification—"In this: that he, the said *Robert Taylor*, a citizen of Coffee county, in the State of Tennessee, did beat a negro woman named 'Retter,' in such manner that she died from the effects of the wounds thus inflicted. This on or about the 31st day of August, 1863, at or near the residence of said *Robert Taylor*, about three miles from the town of Hillsboro', in Coffee county, Tennessee."

To which charge and specification the accused, *Robert Taylor*, a citizen, pleaded "Not Guilty."

FINDING.—The Commission having maturely considered the evidence adduced, finds the accused, Robert Taylor, a citizen, as follows:

Of the Specification, "Guilty."

Of the Charge, "Not Guilty as charged, but 'Guilty of manslaughter.'"

SENTENCE.—And the Commission does therefore sentence him, Robert Taylor, a citizen, "To be confined in the State Penitentiary for the period of five years."

II. The proceedings, findings, and sentence in the foregoing case having been approved by the Major General commanding the Department, and laid before the President of the United States, the following are his orders:

The testimony in the case, as found in the record, is brief and free from all discrepancy or contradiction. The prisoner, it seems, alleged that an amount of money had been stolen from him—how much was not stated—but there was no proof of any such theft, still less anything tending to connect with it the murdered woman, on whom his suspicions fell. Probably, however, from apprehension of punishment, this woman—whom he claimed to own—made an attempt to run away, was pursued by the prisoner and his neighbors, captured, and brought back. The prisoner then procured a rope, and, addressing himself to the bystanders, asked if there was any one present who could tie "a hang knot," when a man named Womack stepped forward and tied it. The prisoner then adjusted it around the neck of the woman, and, throwing it over the limb of a tree, in the sight of his own dwelling, where were his wife and daughters, the work of murder began. Finding that the woman protected herself by seizing the rope with her hands, it was slackened and her hands tied, and again she was drawn up so that her toes barely touched the ground, and in this position she was held by the prisoner until, from suffocation and exhaustion, her head fell on one side. Through the interposition of the prisoner's wife and the bystanders, the rope was then loosened, and an opportunity given the woman to revive. While this torture was going on, the prisoner declared his object to be to compel the woman to confess the theft charged upon her, but she stoutly denied any knowledge of the money alleged to have been lost. She was now taken by the prisoner to his tanyard, distant 200 or 250 yards, and was then stripped by him of all her clothes except her chemise. In the language of one of the witnesses, she was then "confined by crossing her hands and tying them together, then putting them over her knees with a stick thrust under, holding them in that position." Thus pinioned, and lying alternately on her face and on her side, as the purposes of her tormentor required, for some two hours and a half, with brief intervals, she was whipped by the prisoner with a leather thong, two inches wide and three feet long, having a knot at the end. At the expiration of this time, "some neighbors present said they thought he had whipped her about enough for that time," and he thereupon desisted. She was then untied and assisted by one of the neighbors towards the kitchen, staggering and falling several times from exhaustion on the way. She succeeded, however, in reaching the kitchen, on the threshold of which she fell, in the presence of the prisoner's wife, and a few minutes thereafter expired.

The shameless character of the defence was in keeping with the crime.

It was insisted in the defence that the woman's death was produced by some cold water, of which, in her heated and exhausted condition, she had drunk; and in attempted palliation of the prisoner's murderous brutality, it was proved by several of his neighbors that he bore a good moral character, and clothed and fed his slaves well; and for himself, he stated that he had once before, on a similar charge, given the woman even a worse whipping than that of which she died!

That a body of officers holding commissions in the Army of the United States, and acting under the responsibility of an oath, should deal thus lightly with so shocking a sacrifice of human life, cannot but excite sentiments of mingled surprise and regret. Every circumstance surrounding the crime aggravates its enormity—among which may be named the absence of all provocation; the prolonged torture to which the wretched sufferer was subjected, thus affording ample time for all human passion, had any existed, to have cooled; but above all, the sex and utter helplessness of the bound and unresisting victim.

The President directs that the sentence, inadequate as it is, shall, except as to the place of confinement, be carried into execution, and Albany, New York, is designated as the Penitentiary where he shall be confined. But while doing so, he feels it incumbent upon him to call the attention of the Army, and especially of those charged with the administration of military justice, to the insensibility displayed by this Commission, and to express the disapprobation with which it is regarded. The members of the Commission, in thus lightly dealing with one of the most revolting murders on record, have done no honor to themselves, and afforded an example which it is hoped will never again be witnessed in the service.

The prisoner will be sent, under proper guard, to Albany, New York, and delivered to the warden of the Penitentiary at that place, for confinement for the period of five years, in accordance with the sentence.

By order of the Secretary of War:

E. D. TOWNSEND,
Assistant Adjutant General.

CASE OF REV. FOUNTAIN BROWN, OF ARKANSAS.

WAR DEPARTMENT, BUREAU OF MILITARY JUSTICE,
May 24th, 1864.

To the PRESIDENT:

In the case of *Fountain Brown*, a citizen of Arkansas, referred to this office by order of your Excellency, May 23d, 1864, the following report is respectfully submitted:

This is an application for the pardon of a man convicted by a military commission of selling into slavery, and running beyond the Union lines, colored persons who had been made free by the President's proclamation of emancipation.

The facts proved are briefly these: The prisoner, who is a preacher and presiding elder of the Methodist Church, in the State of Arkansas, resided at or near Flat Bayou, and, at the date of the President's proclamation, held as slaves two families of negroes, numbering about ten persons, old and young, of both sexes These families consisted of—1st, Lucy and her husband, John, two children that she had by him, and two that she had by another person, supposed to have been one McAfee, a white man; and 2d, Delia, with her husband, Horton, and two children, one by him and the other by an unknown father. After the occupation of the district, including Flat Bayou, by the Union forces, the prisoner informed these people, or at least the men, that they were free, and, if they wished, could leave—thus recognizing the proclamation and renouncing his claim to their services. They did not then leave him. In the course of last year, (1863,) the white man McAfee, who had been cohabiting with the woman Lucy, who was a light mulatto, frequently besought the prisoner to assist him in getting her and her children away with him to Texas. This arrangement the prisoner claims to have declined to enter into, on the ground that it was contrary to existing law. McAfee then proposed to buy them, but the prisoner refused to make the sale; yet, after much solicitation and the offer of seven thousand dollars for the lot, he finally yielded. The bargain was struck; he received four thousand dollars cash in hand, and the purchaser's promise to pay the balance; and McAfee carried off the women and children, eight in number, beyond the lines, and, as it is supposed, to Texas. One of the colored men, the husband of Lucy, left his wife at home on Monday morning, and, returning on Tuesday evening, found no trace of her or her children. Powerless to assert their rights, or ignorant of them, they had been abducted by McAfee, who abandoned his own wife at Flat Bayou, where she still resides.

The men both testify that their wives did not want to go away, and it would appear that they contemplated with aversion and terror the probability of being compelled by McAfee to accompany him.

It seems that the conscience of the prisoner, or his fear of the vengeance of the outraged law, would not let him rest. He made his appearance at the Headquarters at Pine Bluff, and, relating his story, solicited exemption from prosecution. He was, however, arraigned before a military commission for kidnapping and for selling into slavery persons of African descent made free by the President's proclamation, found guilty, and sentenced to confinement in a military prison for five years. Major General Steele, commanding the Department, approved the finding and sentence, and forwarded the proceedings for the action of the President, which has not yet been had.

In the opinion of this officer, it was not requisite that the confirmation of the President should be obtained; but, as it is presumable that the execution of the sentence will not commence until directed by him, it is expedient and proper that action should be taken, and it is recommended that the sentence be confirmed.

The pardon of the prisoner is now applied for by citizens of Arkansas, who sign a petition averring that he has subscribed the oath prescribed by the proclamation of amnesty, and has always heretofore been a good and influential man in the church and the community. The paper sets forth no other proof of loyalty. This petition is favorably recommended by Colonel Powell Clayton, commanding at Pine Bluff. It is presented by Mr. A. A. C. Rogers, who claims to be a member of Congress elect from the Second District of Arkansas, and who says that he believes the prisoner intended no wrong; that the act for which he was tried occurred soon after the Federal occupation of that section, "whilst all was confusion, doubt, and uncertainty;" that the husband and father of the negroes sold had been taken to Texas, the owner wanted the wife and children, they wanted to go, and the prisoner sold them, in ignorance of the nature of the offence. He adds that he thinks the pardon, if granted, would strengthen the good feeling of his district toward the government.

Mr. Rogers has fallen into several serious errors in his version of the case. He states that the husband and father of the negroes sold had been taken to Texas. So far from this being true, it is in evidence that the husbands of both the women are still at Flat Bayou; and so far from the woman Lucy wanting to go, her husband testifies that she begged him to remove her from the custody of the prisoner, and of McAfee, lest she should be taken away by force.

Besides, whether the wishes of the adults about going or remaining were consulted or not, it is a mockery of truth, as shallow as it is wicked, to attribute consent to the six helpless and mindless children, the oldest of whom was a boy of seven, and the youngest a baby but a few months old. It would require a rule of law as repugnant to reason as the extinct slave-code of Arkansas was revolting to humanity, to impute the exercise of volition to the unhappy little beings, whom his barbarous avarice, proving stronger than his sense of the obligations of law, human or divine, impelled a presiding elder of the Methodist Church to sell into a life of hopeless bondage in a distant State.

Moreover, whatever "confusion" may, as Mr. Rogers avers, have attended the advent of the Union troops at Flat Bayou, it does not appear to have unsettled the perceptions of the prisoner, who, so far from being in "doubt and uncertainty," as to the law by which he was bound, expressly told McAfee that a sale would be illegal, and only forgot his scruples and his renunciation of the authority of a master, when the tempting bid of seven thousand dollars was finally offered.

The crime of the prisoner was a deliberate and wilful violation of law. It set at naught the proclamation of emancipation. It snatched two wretched females, free by that charter, away from their husbands and surrendered them to a thraldom of lust and violence, to end only with their lives. It consigned six unoffending children, free by that charter, to perpetual servitude, in a region deemed by the purchaser (who was also the father of at least two of them) safely remote from the influences of liberty and the restraints of law.

All the features of the offence are so brutal and so depraved, that to be abhorred they need only to be recited; but when it is considered that the perpetrator is a presiding elder of the Methodist Church of the State of Arkansas, a man, by his position and his pretensions, the exemplar of public and private morality among the people around him, to whom multitudes looked up as their preceptor and spiritual guide, it must be admitted that the measure of his guilt is incomparably aggravated.

That a criminal of so deep a dye, who has been adjudged to suffer the abridgment of his liberty for five years, for depriving eight human beings of theirs forever, should (with the price of his guilt still in his pocket) ask a pardon from the government he has defied, seems an instance of effrontery scarcely paralleled even in the annals of the present rebellion.

The government, it is conceived, would be recreant to the principles which it has been forced by treason to inaugurate, if it were to treat their flagrant violation with lenity.

The proclamation of emancipation is nothing, or it is an irrevocable decree of freedom to all within its terms.

It is a solemn law of the land, upheld by the inherent war-powers of a nation struggling for self-preservation, sanctioned by reason and sanctified by precious blood. Violations of it should be punished in proportion to the magnitude of their consequences, and the importance of sustaining it by warning examples.

The absence of prohibitory sanctions in the proclamation itself, furnishes no pretext for the misinterpretation which would exempt the prisoner from punishment for his crime. These persons stood before the law disenthralled of the shackles of slavery and absolutely free, and so the prisoner had recognized them to be. He, having, with a full knowledge of their emancipation, deliberately re-enslaved them, wilfully incurred all the penalties denounced against the most atrocious species of kidnapping.

The crime of the prisoner, by reason of his conspicuous social and religious position, has doubtless attracted the notice of a large number of the people of his State. His pardon, obtaining equal publicity, would, it is believed, be taken by the traitorous adherents of slavery as a tacit official declaration that the Government did not seriously intend to maintain the most momentous and vital of its war measures, and that the President consented to be understood as permitting to pass into a mockery that proclamation upon which, on the 1st day of January, 1863, he solemnly invoked "the considerate judgment of mankind, and the gracious favor of Almighty God."

This is believed to be the first case in which a violation of the Proclamation of Emancipation has been brought to the notice of the President. It is deemed fortunate for the great purposes of justice that the proof is so strong and the circumstances so marked. The offender is a prominent personage; the victims young and weak; the sale made with full knowledge of the law and the rights of freedom it bestowed; the transaction notorious and basely mercenary. It is fit to be made a test case, in which the Government may distinctly re-assure the South of its unalterable purpose to enforce the decree which it has deliberately promulgated. If, while the able-bodied freedmen, attracted and encouraged by that decree, are enrolling themselves as soldiers under the standard which they recognize as the symbol and the guaranty of freedom, and are exposing themselves to the perils of battle on the field, and to the horrors of massacre if captured, their late masters are suffered to sell and transport their helpless wives and children into renewed servitude, without encountering the inflexible severity of adequate punishment, the Government cannot fail to stand before the world dishonored by such breach of a faith which, on the part of the unhappy race with whom it has been plighted, is being everywhere bravely and loyally kept with their blood. If the Government could pardon this outrage upon its laws, or mitigate its punishment, how can it forget the wretched victims of the crime? The conviction is fully entertained that the question of pardon or mitigation should not even be considered until these victims shall have been returned to within our military lines, and thus restored to the status of freedom which they there occupied.

J. HOLT,
Judge Advocate General.

Application denied and sentence approved.

A. LINCOLN.

AUGUST 9, 1864.

CASE OF WEST BOGAN, OF ARKANSAS.

JUDGE ADVOCATE GENERAL'S OFFICE,
May 30, 1864.

To the PRESIDENT:

West Bogan, a negro, was tried February 1st before a military Commission, sitting at Helena, Ark., on the charge of "murder."

In this that the said West Bogan on or about the 15th of December, 1863, killed Munroe Bogan, a citizen of Phillips Co., Arkansas, by striking him with an axe upon the head and neck.

The court found him guilty and sentenced him to be hung; General Buford approves the findings and sentence, and recommends that it be commuted to imprisonment at hard labor in some Northern penitentiary for such length of time as the Commanding General shall judge proper. Gen. Steele suspends execution in consequence of this suggestion, and forwards the proceedings for the action of the President.

The proceedings were strictly regular. The evidence showed that prisoner was and had long been a slave of Munroe Bogan, the deceased, and was still held by him as such despite the Proclamation of Emancipation. It was testified by numerous witnesses that prisoner was in general of an obedient and submissive nature, though when thwarted and irritated by oppression, reckless of what he did.

His master, on the other hand, was shown to have been cruel and exacting, forcing his slaves by constant punishments, to labor night and day and frequently on Sundays, giving them no holiday or resting time, and, as one witness testified, whipping some one every day—and this last too, not as a passionate man might do, by snatching the first weapon at hand and with it punishing a fault, but with a deliberate coolness, as shown by his regularly sending for the driver with his whip, which denoted that his temper was fully under his control.

The homicide took place in the early morning, near the prisoner's quarters, and when he was on his way to his day's task. Of the immediate cause of the difficulty, there is no evidence; but Tom, a negro at work in an adjoining field, had his attention drawn to the struggle by hearing his master's call to him, and, on looking round, saw the deceased fall, and the prisoner deal upon his prostrate body two blows with the axe in his hand, which nearly severed the head from the shoulders. It was testified by a negro witness for the prosecution, that he had heard the prisoner declare his intention to kill his master, "because his master was going to kill him for running about and going away from home." It was in evidence that the deceased had expressed, only the night before, his intention to whip the prisoner on the following day.

The negro Tom, also testified that Clarence Bogan, another field hand who was at work at his side, first heard the alarm, and said he believed that master Munroe and West were fighting.

Maria Bogan, a slave of deceased, testifies that she was sitting in her own cabin at the time of the homicide, and that her children cried out that "master was trying to whip Uncle West:" whereupon she went the door, and saw West give two blows with the axe upon her master's neck.

It can scarcely be doubted, therefore, that Munroe Bogan, at the moment of his death, was in the act of inflicting corporeal punishment upon the prisoner, which, under the changed relations of the white and black populations of the Southern States, he had no right to do,—and that roused by pain and by a sense of wrong, the generally willing and submissive slave turned upon him, and took his life—converting, for the moment, into a weapon of revenge, the implement with which he was quietly going to his unrecompensed toil.

The case would, therefore, seem to be divested of those elements of malice and deliberate purpose, which alone can constitute the crime of murder; while the provocation under which prisoner was driven to take the life of his oppressor was great and not to be excused.

The administration of the Government must and does recognize the colored population of the rebellious States, as occupying the *status* of freedmen. This office in considering the present and kindred cases, necessarily accepts this recognition with all its legitimate consequences.

It is, therefore, held that Munroe Bogan, when he met his death, was in violation of law and right holding the prisoner in absolute slavery—not only holding him in slavery but also imposing upon him ceaseless toil and cruel punishments. It is a conclusion, justified by the record, that it was in resistance to an attempt by deceased to inflict such punishment, in accordance with threats previously made, that the fatal blow was struck by the prisoner, who had doubtless borne the oppressions of his task master till endurance seemed to him no longer possible.

That in these circumstances, ground is found for mitigation, and much mitigation, of the sentence pronounced, will scarcely be questioned.

It is for the President to determine how far this mitigation shall extend.

J. HOLT,
Judge Advocate General.

Sentence disapproved.

A. LINCOLN.

JULY 8, 1864.

CASE OF JOHN J. GLOVER, OF ARKANSAS.

WAR DEPARTMENT, BUREAU OF MILITARY JUSTICE,
June 6th, 1864.

To the PRESIDENT:

John J. Glover, alias Jake, a negro, was tried September 18th, 1863, before a military commission sitting at Memphis, Tennessee, on the charge of "murder in the first degree," under which he was accused of the murder of one George Redman, a citizen of Arkansas, in the month of August preceding. He was found guilty and sentenced to be hung.

The sentence was approved by General Hurlbut and General Sherman, and the day of execution fixed for January 29, 1864. Prisoner could not be found on that day, and subsequently General Sherman ascertained that he could not legally carry out the sentence without reference to the President, and the record has in consequence been sent to this office.

The evidence by no means warrants the sentence awarded by the court. There can be no doubt that prisoner discharged a pistol at Redman, the result of which was his death; but the circumstances under which the homicide occurred would appear to extenuate if not entirely remove the prisoner's guilt. The evidence showed that prisoner went across the Mississippi river from Tennessee to Arkansas with another negro called "Dave" at his request, for the purpose of rescuing the two young daughters of the latter from Redman's hands. This Dave was tried and convicted about the same time for the same murder; and on his trial it was testified that Redman, an old man of seventy-two years of age, was retaining the two girls in slavery against their father's will and in violation of the President's emancipation proclamation, and had declared to Dave his intention to keep them. On Dave's trial it was further shown, by the testimony of his daughter, that Redman had sworn to shoot any man that came after them. Dave and Jake, the prisoner, crossed the river together in a skiff to effect the girls' release, and about two o'clock in the morning succeeded in getting one of the girls and taking her to the boat. They went back for the other, and while reconnoitering the premises, were pursued by old Redman with a pistol, and at once took to flight. It does not appear however, that they knew that he had this pistol at the time. They ran towards the river, and being closely followed and in fact stumbled upon by Redman, Jake in his excitement drew his pistol and fired, wounding Redman so that he died a few days afterwards. Redman, Jake in his excitement drew his pistol and fired, wounding Redman so that he died a few days afterwards. Redman, it was testified, was a kind and indulgent master to his slaves, and had taken the oath of allegiance. On the same evening, some hours previously, Jake had caught a horse belonging to Redman's son, and had taken it across the river into Tennessee, afterwards returning to help Dave obtain his children. When captured, he confessed that he shot the deceased.

Much doubt cannot but be felt whether prisoner merits any punishment for the part he took in the transaction which led to the death of the deceased. It is true that he had no personal interest in the rescue of the two girls, such as his companion "Dave" had; but that rescue was a lawful and justifiable act on the part of his companion, and the prisoner's participation in it must be held to be no less justifiable and lawful.

It does not appear that he went to Redman's plantation with a purpose of murder, but rather with a single view to the assistance of his friend in the delivery of his children from bondage; and the agitation caused by the pursuit of the master, and the imagined peril of his own life, led him involuntarily into the commission of the deed for which he has already suffered an imprisonment of nine weary months

It is true he was engaged in a business for which he could offer no excuse but that of friendship, and a wish to extend to the family of his comrade the benefits of the same freedom which he himself enjoyed; and with a knowledge of the dangers of the enterprise in which a fellow-feeling led him to take a part, and of the extreme severity with which offenders of his race are treated by their white masters, it can scarcely be imputed to him as a crime that he took with him a weapon of defence, nor that in his great and natural terror under the close and armed pursuit to which he was subjected, he should have instinctively made use of it.

It is believed to be a case in which a strong and armed man has rashly thrown away his life in an endeavor to enslave a feeble young woman in defiance of the proclamation of the President which had declared her free.

J. HOLT,
Judge Advocate General.

Sentence disapproved.

A. LINCOLN.

JULY 8, 1864.

CASE OF JOHN Y. BEALL.

HEADQUARTERS DEPARTMENT OF THE EAST,
NEW YORK CITY, *Feb. 21st*, 1865.

[General Orders, No. 17.]

I. The following General Order will replace General Order No. 14, from these Headquarters:

II. Before a Military Commission which convened at Fort Lafayette, New York Harbor, and at New York City, by virtue of Special Orders Nos. 14 and 42, current series, from these Headquarters, of Jan. 17th and Feb. 17th, 1865, and of which Brig. Gen. Fitz Henry Warren, United States Volunteers, is President, was arraigned and tried—

John Y. Beall.

CHARGE I.—"Violation of the law of war."

Specification 1st.—"In this: that John Y. Beall, a citizen of the insurgent State of Virginia, did, on or about the 19th day of September, 1864, at or near Kelly's Island, in the State of Ohio, without lawful authority, and by force of arms, seize and capture the steamboat 'Philo Parsons.'"

Specification 2d.—"In this: that John Y. Beall, a citizen of the insurgent State of Virginia, did, on or about the 19th day of September, 1864, at or near Middle Bass Island, in the State of Ohio, without lawful authority, and by force of arms, seize, capture, and sink the steamboat 'Island Queen.'"

Specification 3d.—"In this: that John Y. Beall, a citizen of the insurgent State of Virginia, was found acting as a spy, at or near Kelly's Island, in the State of Ohio, on or about the 19th day of September, 1864."

Specification 4th.—"In this: that John Y. Beall, a citizen of the insurgent State of Virginia, was found acting as a spy, on or about the 19th day of September, 1864, at or near Middle Bass Island, in the State of Ohio."

Specification 5th.—"In this: that John Y. Beall, a citizen of the insurgent State of Virginia, was found acting as a spy, on or about the 16th day of December, 1864, at or near Suspension Bridge, in the State of New York."

Specification 6th.—"In this: that John Y. Beall, a citizen of the insurgent State of Virginia, being without lawful authority, and for unlawful purposes, in the State of New York, did, in said State of New York, undertake to carry on irregular and unlawful warfare as a guerrilla, and, in the execution of said undertaking, attempted to destroy the lives and property of the peaceable and unoffending inhabitants of said State, and of persons therein travelling, by throwing a train of cars, and the passengers in said cars, from the railroad track, on the railroad between Dunkirk and Buffalo, by placing obstructions across the said track."

All this in said State of New York, and on or about the 15th day of December, 1864, at or near Buffalo.

CHARGE II.—"Acting as a spy."

Specification 1st.—"In this: that John Y. Beall, a citizen of the insurgent State of Virginia, was found acting as a spy in the State of Ohio, at or near Kelley's Island, on or about the 19th day of September, 1864."

Specification 2d.—"In this: that John Y. Beall, a citizen of the insurgent State of Virginia, was found acting as a spy in the State of Ohio, on or about the 19th day of September, 1864, at or near Middle Bass Island."

Specification 3d.—"In this: that John Y. Beall, a citizen of the insurgent State of Virginia, was found acting as a spy, in the State of New York, at or near Suspension Bridge, on or about the 16th day of September, 1864."

To which charges and specifications the accused pleaded "Not Guilty."

FINDING.—Of the 1st specification, 1st charge, "Guilty."
Of the 2d specification, 1st charge, "Guilty."
Of the 3d specification, 1st charge, "Guilty."
Of the 4th specification, 1st charge, "Guilty."
Of the 5th specification, 1st charge, "Guilty."
Of the 6th specification, 1st charge, "Guilty."
Of the 1st charge, "Guilty."
Of the 1st specification, 2d charge, "Guilty."
Of the 2d specification, 2d charge, "Guilty."
Of the 3d specification, 2d charge, "Not Guilty," as to the day averred, but guilty of acting as a spy, at or near Suspension Bridge, in the State of New York, on or about December 16th, 1864.
Of the 2d charge, "Guilty."

SENTENCE.—And the Commission does therefore sentence him, the said John Y. Beall, "To be hanged by the neck until dead, at such time and place as the General in command of the Department may direct," two-thirds of the members concurring therein.

III. In reviewing the proceedings of the Court, the circumstances on which the charges are founded, and the questions of law raised on the trial, the Major General Commanding has given the most earnest and careful consideration to them all.

The testimony shows that the accused, while holding a commission from the authorities at Richmond as Acting Master in the navy of the insurgent States, embarked at Sandwich, in Canada, on board the "Philo Parsons," an unarmed steamer, while on one of her regular trips, carrying passengers and freight from Detroit, in the State of Michigan, to Sandusky, in the State of Ohio. The captain had been induced by Burley, one of the confederates of the accused, to land at Sandwich, which was not one of the regular stopping places of the steamer, for the purpose of receiving them. Here the accused and two others took passage. At Malden, another Canadian port, and one of the regular stopping places, about twenty-five more came on board. The accused was in citizen's dress, showing no insignia of his rank or profession, embarking as an ordinary passenger, and representing himself to be on a pleasure trip to Kelley's Island, in Lake Erie, within the jurisdiction of the State of Ohio.

After eight hours, he and his associates, arming themselves with revolvers and hand-axes, brought surreptitiously on board. rose on the crew, took possession of the steamer, threw overboard part of the freight, and robbed the clerk of the money in his charge—putting all on board under duress. Later in the evening he and his party took possession of another unarmed steamer, (the "Island Queen,") scuttled her, and set her adrift on the lake. These transactions occurred within the jurisdiction of the State of Ohio, on the 19th day of September, 1864.

On the 16th day of December, 1864, the accused was arrested near the Suspension Bridge over the Niagara River, within the State of New York. The testimony shows that he and two officers of the army of the insurgent States—Col. Martin and Lieut. Headley—with two other confederates, had made an unsuccessful attempt, under the direction of the first-named officer, to throw the passenger train, coming from the West to Buffalo, off the railroad track, for the purpose of robbing the express company. It is further shown that this was the third attempt in which the accused was concerned to accomplish the same object; that between two of these attempts the party, including the accused, went to Canada and returned, and that they were on their way back to Canada when he was arrested. In these transactions, as in that on Lake Erie, the accused, though holding a commission from the insurgent authorities at Richmond, was in disguise, procuring information with the intention of using it, as he subsequently did, to inflict injury upon unarmed citizens of the United States, and their private property.

The substance of the charges against the accused is that he was acting as a spy, and carrying on irregular or guerrilla warfare against the United States; in other words, that he was acting in the two-fold character of a spy and a guerrillero. He was found guilty on both charges, and sentenced to death; and the Major General Commanding fully concurs in the judgment of the Court. In all the transactions with which he was implicated—in one as a chief, and in the other as a subordinate agent—he was not only acting the part of a spy in procuring information to be used for hostile purposes, but he was also committing acts condemned by the common judgment and the common conscience of all civilized states, except when done in open warfare by avowed enemies. Throughout these transactions he was not only in disguise, but personating a false character.

It is not at all essential to the purpose of sustaining the finding of the Court, and yet it is not inappropriate, to state, as an indication of the *animus* of the accused and his confederates, that the attempts to throw the railroad train off the track were made at night, when the obstruction would be less likely than in the daytime to be noticed by the engineer or conductor, thus putting in peril the lives of hundreds of men, women, and children. In these attempts three officers, holding commissions in the military service of the insurgent States, were concerned. The accused is shown by the testimony to be a man of education and refinement, and it is difficult to account for his agency in transactions so abhorent to the moral sense, and so inconsistent with all the rules of honorable warfare.

The accused, in justification of the transaction on Lake Erie, produced the manifesto of Jefferson Davis, assuming the responsibility of the act, and declaring that it was done by his authority. It is hardly necessary to say that no such assumption can sanction an act not warranted by the laws of civilized warfare. If Mr. Davis were at the head of an independent government, recognized as such by other nations, he would have no power to sanction what the usage of civilized states has condemned. The Government of the United States, from a desire to mitigate the asperities of war, has given to the insurgents of the South the benefit of the rules which govern sovereign states in the conduct of hostilities with each other; and any violation of those rules should, for the sake of good order here and the cause of humanity throughout the world, be visited with the severest penalty. War, under its mildest aspects, is the heaviest calamity that can befall our race; and he who, in a spirit of revenge or with lawless violence, transcends the limits to which it is restricted by the common behest of all Christian communities, should receive the punishment which the common voice has declared to be due to the crime. The Major General Commanding feels that a want of firmness and inflexibility on his part, in executing the sentence of death in such a case, would be an offence against the outraged civilization and humanity of the age.

It is hereby ordered that John Y. Beall be hanged by the neck till he is dead, on Governor's Island, on Friday, the 24th day of February, inst., between the hours of 12 M. and 2 in the afternoon.*

The commanding officer at Fort Columbus is charged with the execution of this order.

By command of Major General DIX:

D. T. VAN BUREN,
Colonel and Assistant Adjutant General.

CASE OF ROBERT C. KENNEDY.

HEADQUARTERS DEPARTMENT OF THE EAST,
NEW YORK CITY, *March 20th*, 1865.

[General Orders, No. 24.]

1. Before a Military Commission, which convened at Fort Lafayette, New York Harbor, and at New York City, by virtue of Special Orders, No. 14, current series, from these Headquarters, of January 17th, 1865, and of which Brig.-Gen. Fitz Henry Warren, United States Volunteers, is President, was arraigned and tried:

Robert C. Kennedy.

CHARGE I.—"Acting as a spy."

---

*In the Virginia Senate, March 3, 1865, joint resolutions were unanimously adopted expressing the sentiments of the General Assembly in regard to the execution of John Yates Beall, and recommending the adoption of such steps as may be necessary in retaliation for the offence committed by the authorities of the United States.

Specification 1st.—"In this, that Robert C. Kennedy, a captain in the military service of the insurgent States, was found acting as a spy in the City of New York, in the State of New York, on or about the first day of November, 1864."

Specification 2d.—"In this, that Robert C. Kennedy, a captain in the military service of the insurgent States, was found acting as a spy in the City of Detroit, in the State of Michigan, on or about the 29th day of December, 1864."

CHARGE II.—"Violation of the laws of war."

Specification.—"In this, that Robert C. Kennedy, a captain in the military service of the insurgent States, undertook to carry on irregular and unlawful warfare in the City and State of New York, and, in the execution of said undertaking, attempted to burn and destroy said city of New York, by setting fire thereto. All this in said city of New York on or about the 25th day of November, 1864."

To which charges and specifications the accused pleaded "Not Guilty."

FINDING.—Of specification 1st, charge I, "Guilty."
Of specification 2d, charge I, "Guilty."
Of charge I, "Guilty."
Of specification, charge II, "Guilty."
Of charge II, "Guilty."

SENTENCE.—And, thereupon, the Commission sentence him, said Robert C. Kennedy, Captain in the military service of the insurgent States, "to be hanged by the neck until dead, at such time and place as the General in command of the Department may direct," two-thirds of the members concurring therein.

II. The Major-General Commanding approves the proceedings, finding and sentence of the court. It is shown by the testimony:

1. That the accused has been an officer in the service of the insurgent States since August, 1861.

2. That he was in the City of New York in disguise, and under a false name, in the month of November, several weeks immediately preceding the attempt to set the city on fire.

3. That he was here for a purpose which he refused to disclose, and that he returned hastily by night to Canada.

4. That he stated, in the presence of several persons, that he set fire to Barnum's Museum, and to one of the "down town" hotels; and

5. That he was arrested at Detroit in disguise, armed with a revolver, travelling under a false name, and with a passport representing himself to be a loyal citizen.

On proof of these facts, he was convicted of acting as a spy and carrying on irregular and illegal warfare. The person who testified to his confession of having set on fire Barnum's Museum and one of the hotels in the lower part of the city, was not under duress or an accomplice, was a reluctant witness, and could have had no motive to make a false statement. He is corroborated by other testimony.

The attempt to set fire to the city of New York is one of the greatest atrocities of the age. There is nothing in the annals of barbarism, which evinces greater vindictiveness. It was not a mere attempt to destroy the city, but to set fire to crowded hotels and places of public resort, in order to secure the greatest possible destruction of human life. The evidence shows that Barnum's Museum and ten hotels were fired on the evening of the 25th of November, the fires in most of them breaking out in quick succession, and indicating not only deliberate and complex design and concert on the part of the incendiaries, but a cool calculation to create so many conflagrations at the same time as to baffle the efforts of the Fire Department to extinguish them. In all the buildings fired, not only non-combatant men, but women and children, were congregated in great numbers; and nothing but the most diabolical spirit of revenge could have impelled the incendiaries to acts so revolting.

The participation of the accused in this inhuman enterprise is a crime, which follows him, and his liability to answer for it is not to be cast off by withdrawing for a time from the jurisdiction within which it was committed. He has not only been guilty of carrying on irregular warfare, in violation of the usages of civilized States in the conduct of war, but he has, by outraging every principle of humanity, incurred the highest penalty known to the law.

His escape to Canada was followed in a few days by his return to the United States, again in disguise, with a new name, and personating a loyal citizen, while holding a commission in the service of the insurgents, thus furnishing the highest *prima facie* evidence that he was acting as a spy. No rebutting evidence was produced on the trial, although it continued twenty-three days, of which fifteen were given to the accused, by adjournments, to procure testimony and prepare his defence. Two papers were read as a part of his address to the Court; one a pledge given to the transportation agent in Canada, to return with all due diligence "to the Confederacy," and the other, a certificate made by him that he was a citizen of the State of Louisiana, with a request that he might be provided with means to return "to the Confederacy." Admitting their genuineness, they do not repel the presumption raised by the circumstances attending his arrest—the disguise and the false pretences, with which he was found within our lines. His flight to Canada was not a return within the lines of his own army. If he had found his way back to the insurgent States, and had been subsequently captured in battle, he could not have been convicted under the first specification of the first charge. But neither of these facts exists to remove or terminate his liability to conviction under that specification.

Whatever question may exist as to the effect of his return to Canada, after having lurked as a spy, as charged in the first specification, no such question can arise as to his guilt as a spy, as charged in the second specification, which sets forth an offence entirely distinct from the first, of which he has been convicted on full proof.

The Major General Commanding considers his duty as clear in this case as in that of Beall. The lives, the property, the domestic security of non-combatant citizens must be protected against all invasion not in strict accordance with the laws and usages of civilized States in the conduct of war. Crimes, which outrage and shock the moral sense by their atrocity, must not only be punished and the perpetrators be deprived of the power of repeating them, but the sternest condemnation of the law must be presented to others to deter them from the commission of similar enormities.

Robert C. Kennedy will be hanged by the neck till he is dead, at Fort Lafayette, New York Harbor, on Saturday, the twenty-fifth day of March instant, between the hours of twelve, noon, and two in the afternoon.

The Commanding Officer of Fort Lafayette is charged with the execution of this order.

By command of Major General DIX:

D. T. VAN BUREN,
Colonel and Ass't Adj't Gen.

The Military and Rev. S. H. Wingfield.

HEADQUARTERS NORFOLK AND PORTSMOUTH,
NORFOLK, VA., *February* 25, '64.

[Special Orders No. 44.]

IV.—It having been reported to the General Commanding that *S. H. Wingfield*, of Portsmouth, is an avowed secessionist, and that he takes every opportunity to disseminate his traitorous dogmas, much to the annoyance of his loyal neighbors, and that on one occasion at a place of worship, while the prayer for the President of the United States was being read, his conduct was such as to annoy and disgust the loyal portion of the congregation; and believing a wholesome example is necessary for the benefit of Mr. *Wingfield* in particular, and the class in this community he represents in general—men of education and ability, who use the talents God has given them for the purpose of stirring up strife against the Government of the United States;

It is therefore ordered that the *Provost Marshal* arrest Mr. *S. H. Wingfield*, and that he be turned over to Col. *Sawtelle* to work for three (3) months cleaning the streets of Norfolk and Portsmouth, thus employing his time for the benefit of the Government he has abused, and in a small way atone for his disloyalty and treason.

By order of Brig. Gen'l E. A. WILD:

GEORGE H. JOHNSTON,
Capt. and Asst. Adjt. Gen'l.

[By Telegram from Fort Monroe, dated March 1st, '64.]

To Brig. Gen'l WILD:

The remainder of the sentence imposed by Brig. Gen'l Wild on the Rev. Mr. Wingfield is remitted; he will be sent to Capt. Cassells at Fort Monroe for custody. His punishment is remitted, not from respect for the man or his acts, or because it is unjust, but because its nature may be supposed to reflect upon the Christian Church, which, by his connection with it, has been already too much disgraced.

By command of Maj. Gen'l BUTLER:

A. F. PUFFER,
Capt. and A. D. C.

[By Telegram from Fort Monroe, dated March 4th, '64.]

To Brig. Gen'l WILD:

Did you receive my order of the 1st inst., by telegraph, concerning Wingfield?

BENJ. F. BUTLER, *Maj. Gen'l.*

[By Telegram from Fort Monroe, dated March 4th, '64.]

To Brig. Gen'l WILD:

The order concerning Wingfield was sent you by telegraph, but by the blindness of the operators did not reach you.

BENJ. F. BUTLER,
Major Gen'l Com'd'

[By Telegram from Fort Monroe, dated March 12th, '64.]

To Brig. Gen'l WILD:

Wrote you this A. M. about Wingfield.

BENJ. F. BUTLER, *Maj. Gen'l.*

—

[By Telegram from Fort Monroe, dated March 29th, '64.]

To Brig. Gen'l WILD:

It is complained to me that no hearing was had by Wingfield previous to his sentence; if so, is there any objection to a hearing before me?

BENJ. F. BUTLER, *Maj. Gen'l.*

Gen'l Pope's Modification of Gen. Rosecrans's Order respecting Religious Convocations.

Paragraph 3, of Special Order No. 62, from the office of Provost Marshal General, of date March 8, 1864, prescribing rules to be observed by religious convocations, is hereby so modified as to read as follows:

"It is hereby made the duty of all such assemblages to submit the roll of the members of their organization to the Provost Marshal of the district in which the assemblage has convened, before proceeding to the transaction of business.

"The Provost Marshal to whom the roll is submitted will thereupon proceed to ascertain from the records of his office whether any of the members of said assemblage have failed to take and subscribe to the oath prescribed by said Special Orders No. 62, and any person found to have so failed will be by him at once forbidden to participate in the business of the assembly, until such time as he has complied with the requirements of said order; and should any person so forbidden meet with or attempt in any manner to participate in the doings of said assembly, he will be immediately arrested and sent to this office, with a statement of the facts in his case."

J. H. BAKER,
Provost Marshal General.

PROCEEDINGS

OF THE

SECOND SESSION OF THE THIRTY-EIGHTH CONGRESS OF THE UNITED STATES, AND THE SECOND SESSION OF THE SECOND CONGRESS OF THE REBEL STATES.

Second Session, Thirty-Eighth Congress.

PRESIDENT LINCOLN'S FOURTH ANNUAL MESSAGE, DECEMBER 5, 1864.

Fellow-Citizens of the Senate and House of Representatives:

Again the blessings of health and abundant harvests claim our profoundest gratitude to Almighty God.

The condition of our foreign affairs is reasonably satisfactory.

Mexico continues to be a theatre of civil war. While our political relations with that country have undergone no change, we have, at the same time, strictly maintained neutrality between the belligerents.

At the request of the States of Costa Rica and Nicaragua, a competent engineer has been authorized to make a survey of the river San Juan and the port of San Juan. It is a source of much satisfaction that the difficulties which for a moment excited some political apprehensions, and caused a closing of the inter-oceanic transit route, have been amicably adjusted, and that there is a good prospect that the route will soon be reopened with an increase of capacity and adaptation. We could not exaggerate either the commercial or the political importance of that great improvement.

It would be doing injustice to an important South American State not to acknowledge the directness, frankness, and cordiality with which the United States of Colombia have entered into intimate relations with this Government. A claims convention has been constituted to complete the unfinished work of the one which closed its session in 1861.

The new liberal constitution of Venezuela having gone into effect with the universal acquiesence of the people, the Government under it has been recognized, and diplomatic intercourse with it has opened in a cordial and friendly spirit. The long-deferred Aves Island claim has been satisfactorily paid and discharged.

Mutual payments have been made of the claims awarded by the late joint commission for the settlement of claims between the United States and Peru. An earnest and cordial friendship continues to exist between the two countries, and such efforts as were in my power have been used to remove misunderstanding and avert a threatened war between Peru and Spain.

Our relations are of the most friendly nature with Chili, the Argentine Republic, Bolivia, Costa Rica, Paraguay, San Salvador, and Hayti.

During the past year no differences of any kind have arisen with any of those republics, and, on the other hand, their sympathies with the United States are constantly expressed with cordiality and earnestness.

The claim arising from the seizure of the cargo of the brig Macedonian in 1821 has been paid in full by the government of Chili.

Civil war continues in the Spanish part of San Domingo, apparently without prospect of an early close.

Official correspondence has been freely opened with Liberia, and it gives us a pleasing view of social and political progress in that republic. It may be expected to derive new vigor from American influence, improved by the rapid disappearance of slavery in the United States.

I solicit your authority to furnish to the republic a gunboat at moderate cost, to be reimbursed to the United States by installments. Such a vessel is needed for the safety of that State against the native African races; and in Liberian hands it would be more effective in arresting the African slave trade than a squadron in our own hands. The possession of the least organized naval force would stimulate a generous ambition in the republic, and the confidence which we should manifest by furnishing it would win forbearance and favor towards the colony from all civilized nations.

The proposed overland telegraph between America and Europe, by the way of Behring's Straits and Asiatic Russia, which was sanctioned by Congress at the last session, has been undertaken, under very favorable circumstances, by an association of American citizens, with the cordial good-will and support as well of this government as of those of Great Britain and Russia. Assurances have been received from most of the South American States of their high appreciation of the enterprise, and their readiness to co-operate in constructing lines tributary to that world-encircling communication. I learn with much satisfaction that the noble design of a telegraphic communication between the eastern coast of America and Great Britain has been renewed with full expectation of its early accomplishment.

Thus it is hoped that with the return of domestic peace the country will be able to resume with energy and advantage its former high career of commerce and civilization.

Our very popular and estimable representative in Egypt died in April last. An unpleasant altercation which arose between the temporary incumbent of the office and the government of the Pasha resulted in a suspension of intercourse. The evil was promptly corrected on the arrival of the successor in the consulate, and our relations with Egypt, as well as our relations with the Barbary Powers, are entirely satisfactory.

The rebellion which has so long been flagrant in China, has at last been suppressed, with the coöperating good offices of this government and of the other western commercial States. The judicial consular establishment there has become very difficult and onerous, and it will need legislative revision to adapt it to the extension of our commerce and to the more intimate intercourse which has been instituted with the government and people of that vast empire. China seems to be accepting with hearty good-will the conventional laws which regulate commercial and social intercourse among the western nations.

Owing to the peculiar situation of Japan, and the anomalous form of its government, the action of that empire in performing treaty stipulations is inconstant and capricious. Nevertheless, good progress has been effected by the western powers, moving with enlightened concert. Our own pecuniary claims have been allowed, or put in course of settlement, and the inland sea has been reopened to commerce. There is reason also to believe that these proceedings have increased rather than diminished the friendship of Japan towards the United States.

The ports of Norfolk, Fernandina, and Pensacola have been opened by proclamation. It is hoped that foreign merchants will now consider whether it is not safer and more profitable to themselves, as well as just to the United States, to resort to these and other open ports, than it is to pursue, through many hazards, and at vast cost, a contraband trade with the other ports which are closed, if not by actual military occupation, at least by a lawful and effective blockade.

For myself, I have no doubt of the power and duty of the Executive, under the law of nations, to exclude enemies of the human race from an asylum in the United States. If Congress should think that proceedings in such cases lack the authority of law, or ought to be further regulated by it, I recommend that provision be made for effectually preventing foreign slave-traders from acquiring domicile and facilities for their criminal occupation in our country.

It is possible that, if it were a new and open question, the maritime powers, with the lights they now enjoy, would not concede the privileges of a naval belligerent to the insurgents of the United States, destitute, as they are, and always have been, equally of ships-of-war and of ports and harbors. Disloyal emissaries have been neither less assiduous nor more successful during the last year than they were before that time in their efforts, under favor of that privilege, to embroil our country in foreign wars. The desire and determination of the governments of the maritime States to defeat that design are believed to be as sincere as, and cannot be more earnest than, our own. Nevertheless, unforeseen political difficulties have arisen, especially in Brazilian and British ports, and on the northern boundary of the United States, which have required, and are likely to continue to require, the practice of constant vigilance, and a just and conciliatory spirit on the part of the United States, as well as of the nations concerned and their governments.

Commissioners have been appointed under the treaty with Great Britain on the adjustment of the claims of the Hudson's Bay and Puget Sound Agricultural Companies, in Oregon, and are now proceeding to the execution of the trust assigned to them.

In view of the insecurity of life and property in the region adjacent to the Canadian border, by reason of recent assaults and depredations committed by inimical and desperate persons who are harbored there, it has been thought proper to give notice that after the expiration of six months, the period conditionally stipulated in the existing arrangement with Great Britain, the United States must hold themselves at liberty to increase their naval armament upon the lakes if they shall find that proceeding necessary. The condition of the border will necessarily come into consideration in connection with the question of continuing or modifying the rights of transit from Canada through the United States, as well as the regulation of imposts, which were temporarily established by the reciprocity treaty of the 5th June, 1854.

I desire, however, to be understood, while making this statement, that the colonial authorities of Canada are not deemed to be intentionally unjust or unfriendly toward the United States; but, on the contrary, there is every reason to expect that, with the approval of the imperial government, they will take the necessary measures to prevent new incursions across the border.

The act passed at the last session for the encouragement of emigration has, so far as was possible, been put into operation. It seems to need amendment which will enable the officers of the government to prevent the practice of frauds against the immigrants while on their way and on their arrival in the ports, so as to secure them here a free choice of avocations and places of settlement. A liberal disposition toward this great national policy is manifested by most of the European States, and ought to be reciprocated on our part by giving the immigrants effective national protection. I regard our emigrants as one of the principal replenishing streams which are appointed by Providence to repair the ravages of internal war and its wastes of national strength and health. All that is necessary is to secure the flow of that stream in its present fullness, and to that end the government must in every way make it manifest that it neither needs nor designs to impose involuntary military service upon those who come from other lands to cast their lot in our country.

The financial affairs of the government have been successfully administered during the last year. The legislation of the last session of Congress has beneficially affected the revenues, although sufficient time has not yet elapsed to experience the full effect of several of the provisions of the acts of Congress imposing increased taxation.

The receipts during the year, from all sources, upon the basis of warrants signed by the Secretary of the Treasury, including loans and the balance in the Treasury on the 1st day of July, 1863, were $1,394,796,007 62; and the aggregate disbursements, upon the same basis, were $1,298,056,-101 89, leaving a balance in the Treasury, as shown by warrants, of $96,739,905 73.

Deduct from these amounts the amount of the principal of the public debt redeemed, and the amount of issues in substitution therefor, and the actual cash operations of the Treasury were: receipts, $884,076,646 57; disbursements, $865,234,087 86; which leaves a cash balance in the Treasury of $18,842,558 71.

Of the receipts, there were derived from customs, $102,316,152 99; from lands, $588,333 29; from direct taxes, $475,648 96; from internal revenue, $109,741,134 10; from miscellaneous sources, $47,511,448 10; and from loans applied to actual expenditures, including former balance, $623,443,929 13.

There were disbursed, for the civil service, $27,505,599 46; for pensions and Indians, $7,517,930 97; for the War Department, $690,791,842 97; for the Navy Department, $85,733,292 77; for interest of the public debt, $53,685,421 69 —making an aggregate of $865,234,087 86, and leaving a balance in the Treasury of $18,842,558 71, as before stated.

For the actual receipts and disbursements for the first quarter, and the estimated receipts and disbursements for the three remaining quarters of the current fiscal year, and the general operations of the Treasury in detail, I refer you to the report of the Secretary of the Treasury. I concur with him in the opinion that the proportion of moneys required to meet the expenses consequent upon the war derived from taxation should be still further increased; and I earnestly invite your attention to this subject, to the end that there may be such additional legislation as shall be required to meet the just expectations of the Secretary.

The public debt on the 1st day of July last, as appears by the books of the Treasury, amounted to $1,740,690,489 49. Probably, should the war continue for another year, that amount may be increased by not far from $500,000,000. Held, as it is for the most part, by our own people, it has become a substantial branch of national, though private, property. For obvious reasons, the more nearly this property can be distributed among all the people the better. To favor such general distribution, greater inducements to become owners might, perhaps, with good effect and without injury, be presented to persons of limited means. With this view, I suggest whether it might not be both competent and expedient for Congress to provide that a limited amount of some future issue of public securities might be held by any *bona fide* purchaser exempt from taxation and from seizure for debt, under such restrictions and limitations as might be necessary to guard against abuse of so important a privilege. This would enable every prudent person to set aside a small annuity against a possible day of want.

Privileges like these would render the possession of such securities, to the amount limited, most desirable to every person of small means who might be able to save enough for the purpose. The great advantage of citizens being creditors as well as debtors, with relation to the public debt, is obvious. Men readily perceive that they cannot be much oppressed by a debt which they owe to themselves.

The public debt on the 1st day of July last, although somewhat exceeding the estimate of the Secretary of the Treasury made to Congress at the commencement of the last session, falls short of the estimate of that officer made in the preceding December, as to its probable amount at the beginning of this year, by the sum of $3,995,097 31. This fact exhibits a satisfactory condition and conduct of the operations of the Treasury.

The national banking system is proving to be acceptable to capitalists and to the people. On the 25th day of November five hundred and eighty-four national banks had been organized, a considerable number of which were conversions from State banks. Changes from State systems to the national system are rapidly taking place, and it is hoped that very soon there will be in the United States no banks of issue not authorized by Congress, and no bank-note circulation not secured by the Government. That the Government and the people will derive great benefit from this change in the banking systems of the country can hardly be questioned. The national system will create a reliable and permanent influence in support of the national credit, and protect the people against losses in the use of paper money. Whether or not any further legislation is advisable for the suppression of State bank issues it will be for Congress to determine. It seems quite clear that the Treasury cannot be satisfactorily conducted unless the Government can exercise a restraining power over the bank-note circulation of the country.

The report of the Secretary of War and the accompanying documents will detail the campaigns of the armies in the field since the date of the last annual message, and also the operations of the several administrative bureaus of the War Department during the last year. It will also specify the measures deemed essential for the national defence, and to keep up and supply the requisite military force.

The report of the Secretary of the Navy presents a comprehensive and satisfactory exhibit of the affairs of that Department and of the naval service. It is a subject of congratulation and laudable pride to our countrymen that a navy of such vast proportions has been organized in so brief a period, and conducted with so much efficiency and success.

The general exhibit of the Navy, including vessels under construction on the 1st of December, 1864, shows a total of 671 vessels, carrying 4,610 guns, and of 510,396 tons, being an actual increase during the year, over and above all losses by shipwreck or in battle, of 83 vessels, 167 guns, and 42,427 tons.

The total number of men at this time in the naval service, including officers, is about 51,000.

There have been captured by the Navy during the year 324 vessels, and the whole number of naval captures since hostilities commenced is 1,379, of which 267 are steamers.

The gross proceeds arising from the sale of condemned

prize property, thus far reported, amount to $14,396.250 51. A large amount of such proceeds is still under adjudication, and yet to be reported.

The total expenditure of the Navy Department of every description, including the cost of the immense squadrons that have been called into existence from the 4th of March, 1861, to the 1st of November, 1864, are $238,647,262 35.

Your favorable consideration is invited to the various recommendations of the Secretary of the Navy, especially in regard to a navy-yard and suitable establishment for the construction and repair of iron vessels, and the machinery and armature for our ships, to which reference was made in my last annual message.

Your attention is also invited to the views expressed in the report in relation to the legislation of Congress at its last session in respect to prize on our inland waters.

I cordially concur in the recommendation of the Secretary as to the propriety of creating the new rank of vice admiral in our naval service.

Your attention is invited to the report of the Postmaster General for a detailed account of the operations and financial condition of the Post Office Department.

The postal revenues for the year ending June 30, 1864, amounted to $12,438,253 78, and the expenditures to $12,644,786 20; the excess of expenditures over receipts being $206,532 42.

The views presented by the Postmaster General on the subject of special grants by the government in aid of the establishment of new lines of ocean mail steamships and the policy he recommends for the development of increased commercial intercourse with adjacent and neighboring countries, should receive the careful consideration of Congress.

It is of noteworthy interest that the steady expansion of population, improvement, and governmental institutions over the new and unoccupied portions of our country has scarcely been checked, much less impeded or destroyed, by our great civil war, which at first glance would seem to have absorbed almost the entire energies of the nation.

The organization and admission of the State of Nevada has been completed in conformity with law, and thus our excellent system is firmly established in the mountains which once seemed a barren and uninhabitable waste between the Atlantic States and those which have grown up on the coast of the Pacific ocean.

The Territories of the Union are generally in a condition of prosperity and rapid growth. Idaho and Montana, by reason of their great distance and the interruption of communication with them by Indian hostilities, have been only partially organized; but it is understood that these difficulties are about to disappear, which will permit their governments, like those of the others, to go into speedy and full operation.

As intimately connected with and promotive of this material growth of the nation, I ask the attention of Congress to the valuable information and important recommendations relating to the public lands, Indian affairs, the Pacific railroad, and mineral discoveries contained in the report of the Secretary of the Interior, which is herewith transmitted, and which report also embraces the subjects of patents, pensions, and other topics of public interest pertaining to his Department.

The quantity of public land disposed of during the five quarters ending on the 30th of September last was 4,221,342 acres, of which 1,538,614 acres were entered under the homestead law. The remainder was located with military land warrants, agricultural scrip certified to States for railroads, and sold for cash. The cash received from sales and location fees was $1,019,446.

The income from sales during the fiscal year ending the 30th of June, 1864, was $678,007 21, against $136,077 95 received during the preceding year. The aggregate number of acres surveyed during the year has been equal to the quantity disposed of; and there is open to settlement about 133,000,000 acres of surveyed land.

The great enterprise of connecting the Atlantic with the Pacific States by railways and telegraph lines has been entered upon with a vigor that gives assurance of success, notwithstanding the embarrassments arising from the prevailing high prices of materials and labor. The route of the main line of the road has been definitely located for one hundred miles westward from the initial point at Omaha City, Nebraska, and a preliminary location of the Pacific railroad of California has been made from Sacramento eastward to the great bend of the Truckee river in Nevada.

Numerous discoveries of gold, silver, and cinnabar mines have been added to the many heretofore known, and the country occupied by the Sierra Nevada and Rocky mountains, and the subordinate ranges, now teems with enterprising labor, which is richly remunerative. It is believed that the product of the mines of precious metals in that region has, during the year, reached, if not exceeded, one hundred millions in value.

It was recommended in my last annual message that our Indian system be remodeled. Congress, at its last session, acting upon the recommendation, did provide for reorganizing the system in California, and it is believed that under the present organization the mangement of the Indians there will be attended with reasonable success. Much yet remains to be done to provide for the proper government of the Indians in other parts of the country to render it secure for the advancing settler and to provide for the welfare of the Indian. The Secretary reiterates his recommendations, and to them the attention of Congress is invited.

The liberal provisions made by Congress for paying pensions to invalid soldiers and sailors of the Republic, and to the widows, orphans, and dependent mothers of those who have fallen in battle, or died of disease contracted or of wounds received in the service of their country, have been diligently administered. There have been added to the pension rolls, during the year ending the 30th day of June last, the names of 16,770 invalid soldiers and of 271 disabled seamen, making the present number of army invalid pensioners 22,767, and of navy invalid pensioners 712.

Of widows, orphans, and mothers, 22,198 have been placed on the army pension rolls, and 248 on the navy rolls. The present number of army pensioners of this class is 25,433, and of the navy pensioners 793. At the beginning of the year the number of revolutionary pensioners was 1,430; only twelve of them were soldiers, of whom seven have since died. The remainder are those who, under the law, receive pensions because of relationship to revolutionary soldiers. During the year ending the 30th of June, 1864, $4,504,616 92 have been paid to pensioners of all classes.

I cheerfully commend to your continued patronage the benevolent institutions of the District of Columbia which have hitherto been established or fostered by Congress, and respectfully refer, for information concerning them, and in relation to the Washington aqueduct, the Capitol, and other matters of local interest, to the report of the Secretary.

The Agricultural Department, under the supervision of its present energetic and faithful head, is rapidly commending itself to the great and vital interest it was created to advance. It is peculiarly the people's Department, in which they feel more directly concerned than in any other. I commend it to the continued attention and fostering care of Congress.

The war continues. Since the last annual message all the important lines and positions then occupied by our forces have been maintained, and our arms have steadily advanced; thus liberating the regions left in the rear, so that Missouri, Kentucky, Tennessee, and parts of other States have again produced reasonably fair crops.

The most remarkable feature in the military operations of the year is General Sherman's attempted march of three hundred miles directly through the insurgent region. It tends to show a great increase of our relative strength that our General-in-Chief should feel able to confront and hold in check every active force of the enemy, and yet to detach a well appointed large army to move on such an expedition. The result not yet being known, conjecture in regard to it is not here indulged.

Important movements have also occurred during the year to the effect of moulding society for durability in the Union. Although short of complete success, it is much in the right direction that twelve thousand citizens in each of the States of Arkansas and Louisiana have organized loyal State governments, with free constitutions, and are earnestly struggling to maintain and administer them. The movements in the same direction, more extensive though less definite, in Missouri, Kentucky, and Tennessee, should not be overlooked. But Maryland presents the example of complete success. Maryland is secure to liberty and Union for all the future. The genius of rebellion will no more claim Maryland. Like another foul spirit, being driven out, it may seek to tear her, but it will woo her no more.

At the last session of Congress a proposed amendment of the Constitution abolishing slavery throughout the United States passed the Senate, but failed for lack of the requisite two-thirds vote in the House of Representatives. Although the present is the same Congress, and nearly the same members, and without questioning the wisdom or patriotism of those who stood in opposition, I venture to recommend the reconsideration and passage of the measure at the present session. Of course the abstract question is not changed; but an intervening election shows, almost certainly, that the next Congress will pass the measure if this does not. Hence there is only a question of *time* as to when the proposed amendment will go to the States for their action. And as it is to so go, at all events, may we not agree that the sooner the better? It is not claimed that the election has imposed a duty on members to change their views or their votes, any further than, as an additional element to be considered, their judgment may be affected by it. It is the voice of the people now, for the first time, heard upon the question. In a great national crisis like ours, unanimity of action among those seeking a common end is very desirable—almost indispensable. And yet no approach to such unanimity is attainable unless some deference shall be paid to the will of the majority simply because it is the will of the majority. In this case the common end is the maintenance of the Union; and, among the means to secure that end, such will, through the election, is most clearly declared in favor of such constitutional amendment.

The most reliable indication of public purpose in this country is derived through our popular elections. Judging by the recent canvass and its result, the purpose of the people within the loyal States to maintain the integrity of the Union was never more firm nor more nearly unanimous than now. The extraordinary calmness and good order with which the millions of voters met and mingled at the polls give strong assurance of this. Not only all those who supported the Union ticket, so-called, but a great majority of the opposing party also, may be fairly claimed to entertain and to be actuated by the same purpose. It is an unanswerable argument to this effect, that no candidate for any office whatever, high or low, has ventured to seek votes on the avowal that he was for giving up the Union. There have been much impugning of motives, and much heated controversy as to the proper means and best mode of advancing the Union cause; but on the distinct issue of Union or no Union the politicians have shown their instinctive knowledge that there is no diversity among the people. In affording the people the fair opportunity of showing, one to another and to the world, this firmness and unanimity of purpose, the election has been of vast value to the national cause.

The election has exhibited another fact not less valuable to be known—the fact that we do not approach exhaustion in the most important branch of national resources—that of living men. While it is melancholy to reflect that the war has filled so many graves and carried mourning to so many hearts, it is some relief to know that, compared with the surviving, the fallen have been so few. While corps and divisions and brigades and regiments have formed and fought and dwindled and gone out of existence, a great majority of the men who composed them are still living. The same is true of the naval service. The election returns prove this. So many voters could not else be found. The States regularly holding elections both now and four years ago, to wit: California, Connecticut, Delaware, Illinois, Indiana, Iowa, Kentucky, Maine, Maryland, Massachusetts, Michigan, Minnesota, Missouri, New Hampshire, New Jersey, New York, Ohio, Oregon, Pennsylvania, Rhode Island, Vermont, West Virginia, and Wisconsin, cast 3,982,011 votes now against 3,870,222 cast then, showing an aggregate now of 3,982,011. To this is to be added 33,762 cast now in the new States of Kansas and Nevada, which States did not vote in 1860, thus swelling the aggregate to 4,015,773 and the net increase during the three years and a half of war to 145,551. A table is appended showing particulars. To this again should be added the number of all soldiers in the field from Massachusetts, Rhode Island, New Jersey, Delaware, Indiana, Illinois, and California, who, by the laws of those States, could not vote away from their homes, and which number cannot be less than 90,000. Nor yet is this all. The number in organized Territories is triple now what it was four years ago, while thousands, white and black, join us as the national arms press back the insurgent lines. So much is shown affirmatively and negatively by the election. It is not material to inquire *how* the increase has been produced or to show that it would have been *greater* but for the war, which is probably true. The important fact remains demonstrated that we have *more* men *now* than we had when the war *began;* that we are not exhausted nor in process of exhaustion; that we are *gaining* strength, and may if need be maintain the contest indefinitely. This as to men. Material resources are now more complete and abundant than ever.

The national resources, then, are unexhausted, and, as we believe, inexhaustible. The public purpose to re-establish and maintain the national authority is unchanged, and, as we believe, unchangeable. The manner of continuing the effort remains to choose. On careful consideration of all the evidence accessible, it seems to me that no attempt at negotiation with the insurgent leader could result in any good. He would accept nothing short of severance of the Union—precisely what we will not and cannot give. His declarations to this effect are explicit and oft repeated. He does not attempt to deceive us. He affords us no excuse to deceive ourselves. He cannot voluntarily reaccept the Union; we cannot voluntarily yield it. Between him and us the issue is distinct, simple, and inflexible. It is an issue which can only be tried by war, and decided by victory. If we yield, we are beaten; if the Southern people fail him, he is beaten. Either way, it would be the victory and defeat following war. What is true, however, of him who heads the insurgent cause is not necessarily true of those who follow. Although he cannot reaccept the Union, they can. Some of them, we know, already desire peace and reunion. The number of such may increase. They can at any moment have peace simply by laying down their arms and submitting to the national authority under the Constitution. After so much, the Government could not, if it would, maintain war against them. The loyal people would not sustain or allow it. If questions should remain, we would adjust them by the peaceful means of legislation, conference, courts, and votes, operating only in constitutional and lawful channels. Some certain, and other possible, questions are, and would be, beyond the executive power to adjust; as, for instance, the admission of members into Congress, and whatever might require the appropriation of money. The executive power itself would be greatly diminished by the cessation of actual war. Pardons and remissions of forfeitures, however, would still be within executive control. In what spirit and temper this control would be exercised can be fairly judged of by the past.

A year ago general pardon and amnesty, upon specified terms, were offered to all, except certain designated classes; and it was, at the same time, made known that the excepted classes were still within contemplation of special clemency. During the year many availed themselves of the general provision, and many more would, only that the signs of bad faith in some, led to such precautionary measures as rendered the practical process less easy and certain. During the same time also special pardons have been granted to individuals of the excepted classes, and no voluntary application has been denied. Thus, practically, the door has been, for a full year, open to all, except such as were not in condition to make free choice—that is, such as were in custody or under constraint. It is still so open to all. But the time may come—probably will come—when public duty shall demand that it be closed; and that, in lieu, more rigorous measures than heretofore shall be adopted.

In presenting the abandonment of armed resistance to the national authority on the part of the insurgents, as the only indispensable condition to ending the war on the part of the Government, I retract nothing heretofore said as to slavery. I repeat the declaration made a year ago, that "while I remain in my present position I shall not attempt to retract or modify the emancipation proclamation, nor shall I return to slavery any person who is free by the terms of that proclamation, or by any of the acts of Congress." If the people should, by whatever mode or means, make it an executive duty to re-enslave such persons, another, and not I, must be their instrument to perform it.

In stating a single condition of peace, I mean simply to say that the war will cease on the part of the Government whenever it shall have ceased on the part of those who began it. ABRAHAM LINCOLN.

DECEMBER 6, 1864.

Table showing the Aggregate Votes in the States named, at the Presidential Elections respectively in 1860 *and* 1864.

	1860.	1864.
California	118,840	*110,000
Connecticut	77,246	86,616
Delaware	16,039	16,924
Illinois	339,693	348,235
Indiana	272,143	280,645
Iowa	128,331	143,331
Kentucky	146,216	*91,300
Maine	97,918	115,141
Maryland	92,502	72,703
Massachusetts	169,533	175,487
Michigan	154,747	162,413
Minnesota	34,799	42,534
Missouri	165,538	*90,000
New Hampshire	65,953	69,111
New Jersey	121,125	128,680
New York	675,156	730,664
Ohio	442,441	470,745
Oregon	14,410	†14,410
Pennsylvania	476,442	572,697
Rhode Island	19,931	22,187
Vermont	42,844	55,811
West Virginia	46,195	33,874
Wisconsin	152,180	148,513
	3,870,222	3,982,011
Kansas	17,234	
Nevada	16,528	
		33,762
Total		4,015,773
		3,870,222
Net increase		145,551

* Nearly. † Estimated.

Memorandum of Changes in List of Senators and Representatives.

The following changes occurred from the last session:

IN SENATE.

1864, December 5—Nathan A. Farwell, of Maine, qualified as successor of William Pitt Fessenden, resigned to become Secretary of the Treasury. Mr. Fessenden, having been re-elected, resumed his seat March 4, 1865.

1865, February 1—William M. Stewart and James W. Nye took their seats as Senators from Nevada—the former drawing the term to expire March 3, 1867, the latter the term to expire March 3, 1869.

1865, February 13—Thomas Holliday Hicks, of Maryland, died. His successor, John A. J. Creswell, was not qualified until March 10, during the Special Executive Session of the Senate.

IN HOUSE OF REPRESENTATIVES.

1864, December 5—Dwight Townsend, of New York, qualified as successor of Henry G. Stebbins, resigned.

1864, December 21—Henry G. Worthington, of Nevada, qualified.

Arrests of Citizens, and the Writ of Habeas Corpus.

ARRESTS OF CITIZENS.

1865, February 18—The Secretary of War, in reply to a resolution of the Senate, of February 14,* sent a report to that body of his action under the act referred to, (see p. 183,) of which these extracts give the substance:

Shortly after the passage of said act, viz, on the 23d of March, 1863, Colonel Holt, Judge Advocate General, the chief law officer of the Department, was, by an order of that date, charged with the execution of the provisions of that act in the following instructions:

War Department,
Washington City, *March* 23, 1863.

Colonel: I beg you to direct your attention to the provision of the late act of Congress requiring prisoners held under military authority to be released within a certain time, and to ask that proceedings may be taken against such as are not proper to be released, and that you will see that the provisions of that law are observed in regard to all persons held in military custody.

Very respectfully, your obedient servant,

EDWIN M. STANTON,
Secretary of War.

Hon. J. Holt, *Judge Advocate General.*

After these instructions, the Judge Advocate General made report, transmitting to this department a list of political prisoners, and reported that "duplicates had been furnished to the judges of the circuit and district courts of the United States, in compliance with the requirements of the act of Congress." His report is as follows:

Judge Advocate General's Office,
Washington, *June* 9, 1863.

Sir: Pursuant to instructions received from you under date of March 23, 1863, I have the honor to transmit herewith lists of political prisoners, of which duplicates have been furnished to the judges of the circuit and district courts of the United States, in compliance with the requirements of the act of Congress of March 3 last, entitled "An act relating to habeas corpus, and regulating judicial proceedings in certain cases."

Your instructions to me were, "to see that the provisions of that law are observed in regard to all persons held in military custody." For the preparation of the lists required by those provisions, there were furnished me by you rolls of prisoners confined in the Government prisons at St. Louis, Alton, Louisville, Sandusky, Wheeling, Camp Chase, Ohio, Fort Lafayette, Fort McHenry, Fort Delaware, and in the Old Capitol Prison at Washington. In consequence of the late date of your letter of instruction, and of the receipt of the rolls, as well as on account of the pressure of business, the lists have not been furnished within the twenty days specified in the act. This delay, however, cannot affect the privileges of the prisoners in question, as will be seen by a reference to the third section of the act alluded to at the end of this communication.

Most of the rolls furnished are incomplete in view of the requirements of the act, in that they do not state where the offences were committed, or by whose authority the arrests were made, and some of them do not specify, in many cases, what was the offence or charge. The residence of prisoners, however, is generally given, and this, in nearly every case, affords a venue for trial, according to the terms of the act.

It not being generally stated in the rolls by whose authority the arrests which are the subject of this communication were made, it has been presumed (for the purposes of the present lists) that all were made by the authority, either directly or indirectly, of the President, acting through the Secretary of War. In point of fact, however, it is believed that these arrests were generally made by military commanders and provost marshals, without any intervention on the part of the President or Secretary.

A considerable number of the prisoners enumerated in some of the rolls, especially those from the prisons of St. Louis and Alton, are not included in the lists prepared by me for the United States judges. The act does not appear to have been carefully framed, and has been found to be extremely difficult of construction. In view of this fact and of the deficiencies in the rolls, as well as in consideration of the exigencies of the service, the act has been strictly construed by me; and those cases which are clearly *triable by court-martial or military commission*, and which are being every day thus tried, and readily and summarily disposed of, are not generally included in the lists.

Such are cases of prisoners arrested as "guerrillas" or "bushwhackers," or as being connected with or aiding these. So, too, of those arrested for communicating intelligence to the enemy in the sense of the 57th article of war, and of those taken as spies. It is not believed that it was intended in the act to invite attention to cases of persons charged with *purely military offences*, or of persons suffering *under sentences of military tribunals.*

The cases of parties confined under sentences pronounced by military courts previous to the date of the act are, therefore, not contained in the present lists. But the large class of prisoners, in whose case no charge or offence is set forth in the rolls, or who are noted as "awaiting charges," and the numerous class of those who are specified as "confined during the war," (without it being added that they are under sentence,) are both included. The lists also embrace those cases in which the charge is stated in general terms, as by the words "rebel," "disloyal," &c., &c., and further comprise prisoners held as "hostages" merely, or as "refugees."

The construction of the act which has been adopted by me is supported by the consideration that, under its provisions, such construction cannot impair the rights of any prisoner not placed in the lists; for it is provided, in the third section, that in case a prisoner is omitted to be presented by the Secretary to the Judge in the formal list, he may obtain, by a process therein prescribed, the judge's order for his discharge upon the same terms as those which govern the case of the prisoners whose names, &c., have been furnished in the list by the Secretary.

Very respectfully, your obedient servant,

J. HOLT,
Judge Advocate General.

Hon. E. M. Stanton, *Secretary of War.*

I have no knowledge or information of any other persons held as State or political prisoners of the United States, by order or authority of the President of the United States, or of the Secretary of State, or of the Secretary of War, in any fort, arsenal, or other place, since the date of the report of the Judge Advocate General.

Prior to the passage of the act approved March 3, 1863, measures had been taken by the Secretary of War to examine and determine the cases of State and political prisoners, by the appointment of commissioners to visit, from time to time, the military prisons, with authority to discharge all cases proper to be discharged. Since the passage of the act, the same course has been pursued in regard to persons arrested by State authorities or subordinate military com-

---

* On motion of Mr. Powell, unanimously adopted:

Resolved, That the Secretary of War be directed to inform the Senate whether or not he has furnished the judges of the circuit and district courts of the United States, and of the District of Columbia, a list of the names of the persons held as "State or political prisoners, or otherwise than as prisoners of war, as required by the second section of the act entitled 'An act relating to habeas corpus and regulating judicial proceedings in certain cases,'" approved March 3, 1863.

manders, without authority from the President, Secretary of State, or Secretary of War.

In some of the military departments persons were occasionally arrested and held in military prisons as State or political prisoners, by order of State executives or local military commanders, without any authority from the President, Secretary of State, or Secretary of War. Although those persons did not come within the terms of the act of Congress, measures were from time to time taken to have all such cases promptly investigated, and the parties released, whenever it could be done without prejudice to the public safety. To that end a commissioner was appointed to investigate all cases of imprisonment at Camp Chase; and a special commission, charged with similar duty, consisting of the honorables Benjamin S. Cowan, Roswell Marsh, and Samuel W. Bostwick, visited the State prisons at Alton, St. Louis, Camp Douglas, and elsewhere in the department of the Missouri. * * * * *

A special commission, consisting of Judge King and Judge Bond, was also appointed for the examination of prisoners confined at Fort Delaware or elsewhere in the Middle department. General Dix was also directed, by an order, dated the 12th of January, 1864, to investigate the cases of persons arrested and detained in Fort Lafayette and other military prisons in the Eastern department, which have been used, by direction of the President, for the custody of persons seized by naval officers while engaged in blockade running or illicit trade, and which class of prisoners is not specified in the act of Congress of March 3, 1863. * * * * *

The military prisons in the District of Columbia have been used for the custody of prisoners arrested by the military commanders of this and other Departments, as well as by the Navy Department. On the 1st of February, 1864, Major Turner, Judge Advocate, was directed to investigate all cases of persons arrested and imprisoned in the military prisons of the District of Columbia, and has continued charged with that special duty until the present time. * * * * * *

Frequent inspections of military prisons, in addition to the foregoing measures, have also been made by officers specially assigned to that duty. * * *

I have the honor to be, very respectfully, your obedient servant, EDWIN M. STANTON, *Secretary of War.*

The PRESIDENT OF THE SENATE.

IN SENATE.

1864, December 19—Mr. POWELL submitted the following resolution, and asked for its present consideration:

Resolved, That the President be requested to communicate to the Senate all information in his possession bearing on the arrest and imprisonment of Colonel Richard J. Jacob, Lieutenant Governor of the State of Kentucky, and Col. Frank Woolford, one of the Presidential electors of that State; particularly by whose order they were arrested and imprisoned, where they are at present confined, and what offences are charged against them.

December 20—Resolution amended by inserting after the word "Senate," the words "if not in his opinion incompatible with the public interest," and adopted.

1865, January 31—The President responded, giving papers on the subject.

IN HOUSE OF REPRESENTATIVES.

1864, De[illegible]mber 15—Mr. MALLORY offered a similar resolution, but, being objected to, it went over under the rules.

1865, January 10—Mr. KERNAN, by unanimous consent, introduced the following resolution, which was agreed to:

Resolved, That the Committee on Military Affairs be, and the same is, directed to inquire and report to the House what legislation or action, if any, is necessary to secure to persons arrested and imprisoned by military authority a prompt examination into the cause of their arrest, and their discharge if there be no adequate cause for their detention, and a speedy trial where there is such cause.

1865, January 18—Mr. GANSON, by unanimous consent, introduced the following resolution, which was agreed to:

Resolved, That the Military Committee be, and they are hereby, directed to ascertain and report to this House as soon as possible the number of persons now confined in the Old Capitol and Carroll prisons; when such persons were respectively arrested and confined, and upon what charges their arrests were made; whether any of such persons are officers of the Army, and have been confined without a trial beyond the time in that respect prescribed by law or by the regulations in the military service; and whether any persons so in prison are confined without any written charges made against them; and whether there are any persons now in said prisons who have not had any trial; if so, report the names of such persons, the time when they were arrested, and the alleged cause of their arrest respectively; and that the said committee be, and they are hereby, authorized to send for persons and papers.

Mr. STEVENS subsequently moved to reconsider the vote by which the resolution was adopted. Mr. GARFIELD moved to lay this motion on the table, which was agreed to—yeas, 136, nays 5, as follows:

YEAS—Messrs. Alley, Allison, Ames, *Ancona*, Arnold, Ashley, *Baily*, *Augustus C. Baldwin*, John D. Baldwin, Baxter, Beaman, Blaine, Blair, *Bliss*, Boutwell, Boyd, Brandegee, *Brooks*, Broomall, *James S. Brown*, William G. Brown, Freeman Clarke, *Clay*, *Coffroth*, Cole, *Cox*, *Cravens*, Creswell, Henry Winter Davis, Thomas T. Davis, Dawes, *Dawson*, Deming, *Denison*, Dixon, Donnelly, Driggs, *Eden*, *Edgerton*, *Eldridge*, Eliot, *English*, Farnsworth, *Finck*, Frank, *Ganson*, Garfield, *Grider*, Griswold, Hale, *Hall*, *Harrington*, *Charles M. Harris*, *Herrick*, Higby, *Holman*, Hotchkiss, Asahel W. Hubbard, John H. Hubbard, Ingersoll, *William Johnson*, *Kalbfleisch*, Kasson, Kelley, Francis W. Kellogg, *Kernan*, *King*, Knox, *Law*, *Lazear*, *Le Blond*, *Long*, Longyear, *Mallory*, *Marcy*, McClurg, *McDowell*, Samuel F. Miller, Moorhead, Morrill, Daniel Morris, *James R. Morris*, *Morrison*, Amos Myers, Leonard Myers, *Noble*, Norton, Charles O'Neill, *John O'Neill*, Orth, Patterson, *Pendleton*, Perham, *Perry*, Pike, Price, *Samuel J. Randall*, William H. Randall, Alexander H. Rice, John H. Rice, *Robinson*, *Rogers*, Edward H. Rollins, *James S. Rollins*, *Ross*, Scofield, *Scott*, Shannon, Sloan, Smith, Smithers, Starr, *John B. Steele*, *Stiles*, *Strouse*, *Stuart*, *Sweat*, Thayer, *Townsend*, Tracy, Upson, Van Valkenburgh, *Wadsworth*, *Ward*, Ellihu B. Washburne, William B. Washburn, Webster, *Wheeler*, *Chilton A. White*, *Joseph W. White*, Williams, Wilder, Wilson, Windom, *Fernando Wood*, *Yeaman*—136.

NAYS—Messrs. Cobb, Eckley, McBride, Spalding, Stevens—5.

No report appears to have been made.

1865, January 30—Mr. ELDRIDGE asked, but failed to obtain, leave to offer this resolution:

Resolved, That the President of the United States be respectfully requested, and the Secretary of State and Secretary of War be directed, to report and furnish to this House the names of the persons, if any there are, who have been arrested and are now held in imprisonment or confinement in any prison, fort, or other place whatsoever, for political offences, or any other alleged offence against the Government or authority of the United States by the order, command, consent, or knowledge of any of them, or either of them respectively, and who have not been charged, tried, or convicted before any civil or criminal (not military) court of the land, together with the charge against such person, or cause for such arrest and imprisonment, excepting only such persons as may, at the time of their arrest, have been in the military or naval service of the United States, together with the name of the prison, fort, or place where they are severally kept or confined: also whether any person or persons, for any alleged like offence, have been banished or sent from the United States, or those not in rebellion to the rebellious States, the names, times, alleged offences, and causes thereof; and whether with or without trial; and if tried, before what court.

February 20—It being before the House, a motion to table it was lost—yeas 54, nays 58, as follows:

YEAS—Messrs. Ames, Ashley, Baxter, Beaman, Blair, Boutwell, Broomall, Ambrose W. Clark, Freeman Clarke, Cobb, Cole, Thomas T. Davis, Deming, Dixon, Dumont, Eckley, Eliot, Farnsworth, Grinnell, Higby, Hooper, John H. Hubbard, Hulburd, Julian, Kasson, Kelley, Francis W. Kellogg, Knox, Littlejohn, Loan, Longyear, Marvin, McBride, McClurg, Samuel F. Miller, Morrill, Daniel Morris, Amos Myers, Norton, Patterson, Perham, Pomeroy, William H. Randall, John H. Rice, Edward H. Rollins, Shannon, Sloan, Smith, Smithers, Starr, Tracy, Upson, William B. Washburn, Worthington—54.

NAYS—Messrs. *James C. Allen*, Allison, *Ancona*, *Baily*, *Augustus C. Baldwin*, John D. Baldwin, *Bliss*, Brandegee,

James S. Brown, William G. Brown, *Chanler*, *Clay*, *Coffroth*, *Cox*, *Dawson*, *Denison*, Donnelly, Driggs, *Eden*, *Edgerton*, *Eldridge*, *Finck*, *Ganson*, Griswold, *Harrington*, *Charles M. Harris*, *Herrick*, *Holman*, *Hutchins*, Ingersoll, *Kalbfleisch*, Orlando Kellogg, *Kernan*, *Knapp*, *Le Blond*, *Long*, *Mallory*, *Marcy*, *McKinney*, *William H. Miller*, *James R. Morris*, *Nelson*, *Noble*, *Odell*, *Pendleton*, *Pruyn*, *Radford*, *Ross*, *John B. Steele*, *William G. Steele*, Thayer, *Townsend*, *Wadsworth*, Whaley, *Wheeler*, Wilson, *Winfield*, *Fernando Wood*—58.

A decisive vote upon it was not taken—other business having intervened.

1865, March 2—The Miscellaneous Appropriation bill being before the Committee of the Whole,

Mr. DAVIS, of Maryland, moved the following amendment as an additional section:

SEC. —. *And be it further enacted*, That no person shall be tried by court-martial, or military commission, in any State or Territory where the courts of the United States are open, except persons actually mustered, or commissioned, or appointed in the military or naval service of the United States, or rebel enemies charged with being spies; and all proceedings heretofore had contrary to this provision are vacated; and all persons not subject to trial, under this act, by court-martial or military commission, now held under sentence thereof, shall be forthwith discharged or delivered to the civil authorities to be proceeded against before the courts of the United States according to law; and all acts inconsistent herewith are hereby repealed.

Mr. SCHENCK moved to amend by striking out all after the word "spies," as follows:

And all proceedings heretofore had contrary to this provision are vacated; and all persons not subject to trial, under this act, by court-martial or military commission, now held under sentence thereof, shall be forthwith discharged or delivered to the civil authorities to be proceeded against before the courts of the United States according to law; and all acts inconsistent herewith are hereby repealed.

Mr. YEAMAN. I ask my friend from Ohio [Mr. Schenck] to accept the following as an addition to his amendment, to be inserted in lieu of what he proposes to strike out:

Or enemies charged with a violation of the laws of war.

Mr. SCHENCK. That is for guerrillas?

Mr. YEAMAN. Yes, sir.

Mr. SCHENCK. I will modify my amendment so as to make it to strike out all of the amendment of the gentleman from Maryland [Mr. Davis] after the word "spies," and insert what the gentleman from Kentucky [Mr. Yeaman] has proposed.

Mr. KASSON suggested this substitute, which Mr. Davis declined to accept:

That no person shall hereafter be tried by court-martial or military commission in any State or Territory where the courts of the United States are open for any charge not specified as an offence by military or civil law, nor for offences cognizable in said courts and punishable by existing civil law, except they are persons actually mustered or commissioned or appointed in the military or naval service of the United States, or rebel enemies, or spies, or conspirators in aid of the rebellion against the United States who are charged with being spies, or with being the violators of military law.

Mr. DAVIS subsequently consented to strike from his amendment the words, "discharged or."

Mr. SCHENCK'S amendment was rejected—ayes 53, nays 71.

Mr. DAVIS'S amendment was agreed to—yeas 75, nays 64.

Mr. YEAMAN moved to add this proviso to Mr. Davis's amendment, but withdrew it on being refused permission to explain it:

Provided, That in cases of murder, arson, larceny, robbery, malicious arrest, false imprisonment, assault and battery, maiming, shooting, or stabbing with intent to kill, done by the enemies of the United States, or those in armed hostility to the laws thereof, the circuit and district courts of the United States, and commissioners of the United States, shall have as full and complete jurisdiction as the several courts of the States where any of said crimes may be done, with power to inflict the same punishments: *And provided further*, That nothing in this act shall be construed to prevent or restrict courts-martial of their jurisdiction of offenses against the laws and usages of war, committed by persons in armed rebellion to the laws of the United States.

Mr. JENCKES moved to add after the word "spies," the words "or guerrillas;" which was agreed to.

The bill having been reported from the Committee of the Whole with sundry amendments, Mr. DAVIS moved to amend the amendment adopted on his motion by the Committee of the Whole on the state of the Union, by striking out all after the word "spies," as follows:

Or guerrillas; and all proceedings heretofore had contrary to this provision are vacated, and all persons not subject to trial under this act by courts-martial or military commissions now held under sentence thereof, shall be forthwith delivered to the civil authorities to be proceeded against before the courts of the United States according to law; and all acts inconsistent herewith are hereby repealed.

So that the clause will read:

And be it further enacted, That no person shall be tried by court-martial or military commission in any State or Territory where the courts of the United States are open, except persons actually mustered, or commissioned, or appointed in the military or naval service of the United States, or rebel emissaries charged with being spies.

Which was agreed to—yeas 73, nays 71, as follows:

YEAS—Messrs. *James C. Allen*, *Ancona*, *Augustus C. Baldwin*, Beaman, *Bliss*, Boutwell, Brandegee, *Brooks*, Broomall, *Coffroth*, *Cox*, *Cravens*, Henry Winter Davis, Dawes, *Dawson*, Deming, Dixon, *Eden*, *Eldridge*, Eliot, *English*, *Ganson*, Garfield, Gooch, *Grider*, Griswold, Hale, *Harding*, *Benjamin G. Harris*, *Herrick*, *Holman*, Hotchkiss, *Hutchins*, *Kernan*, *King*, *Knapp*, *Law*, *Lazear*, *Marcy*, *McKinney*, *Middleton*, *James R. Morris*, *Morrison*, *Nelson*, *Noble*, *Odell*, *John O'Neill*, *Pendleton*, Perham, *Perry*, Price, *Radford*, Alexander H. Rice, *Rogers*, *Ross*, Schenck, Scofield, *Scott*, Smithers, *John B. Steele*, *William G. Steele*, *Strouse*, *Stuart*, *Townsend*, Tracy, Upson, *Ward*, William B. Washburn, Webster, *Wheeler*, *Chilton A. White*, *Joseph W. White*, *Winfield*—73.

NAYS—Messrs. Allison, Arnold, Ashley, John D. Baldwin, Baxter, Blaine, Blow, Boyd, *Chanler*, Ambrose W. Clark, Freeman Clarke, Cobb, Cole, *Denison*, Driggs, Eckley, *Edgerton*, Farnsworth, *Finck*, Grinnell, Higby, Hooper, Asahel W. Hubbard, John H. Hubbard, Hulburd, Ingersoll, Jenckes, *Philip Johnson*, *Kalbfleisch*, Kelley, Francis W. Kellogg, Orlando Kellogg, Knox, Littlejohn, Loan, *Long*, Longyear, Marvin, McBride, McClurg, Samuel F. Miller, *William H. Miller*, Moorhead, Morrill, Daniel Morris, Amos Myers, Leonard Myers, Norton, Charles O'Neill, Orth, Patterson, Pike, Pomeroy, *Pruyn*, *Samuel J. Randall*, William H. Randall, John H. Rice, Edward H. Rollins, Shannon, Sloan, Spalding, Stevens, *Stiles*, Thayer, Thomas, Elihu B. Washburne, Wilson, Windom, Woodbridge, Worthington, *Yeaman*—71.

The amendment as amended was then agreed to—yeas 80, nays 64, as follows:

YEAS—Messrs. *James C. Allen*, *Ancona*, *Augustus C. Baldwin*, *Bliss*, Boutwell, Brandegee, *Brooks*, Broomall, *James S. Brown*, *Chanler*, *Coffroth*, *Cox*, *Cravens*, Henry Winter Davis, Dawes, *Dawson*, Deming, *Denison*, Dixon, *Eden*, *Edgerton*, *Eldridge*, *English*, *Finck*, *Ganson*, Garfield, Gooch, *Grider*, Griswold, Hale, *Harding*, *Benjamin G. Harris*, *Herrick*, *Holman*, Hotchkiss, *Hutchins*, *Philip Johnson*, *Kalbfleisch*, *Kernan*, *King*, *Knapp*, *Law*, *Lazear*, *Le Blond*, *Long*, *McKinney*, *Middleton*, *William H Miller*, *James R. Morris*, *Morrison*, *Nelson*, *Noble*, *Odell*, *John O'Neill*, *Pendleton*, *Perry*, *Pruyn*, *Radford*, *Samuel J. Randall*, Alexander H Rice, *Rogers*, *James S. Rollins*, *Ross*, Schenck, *Scott*, Smithers, *John B. Steele*, *William G. Steele*, *Stiles*, *Strouse*, *Stuart*, *Townsend*, Tracy, *Ward*, Webster, *Wheeler*, *Chilton A. White*, *Joseph W. White*, *Winfield*, *Yeaman*—80.

NAYS—Messrs. Ames, Arnold, Ashley, John D. Baldwin,

Baxter, Beaman, Blow, Boyd, Ambrose W. Clark, Freeman Clarke, Cobb, Cole, Eckley, Eliot, Farnsworth, Frank, Grinnell, Higby, Hooper, Asahel W. Hubbard, John H. Hubbard, Hulburd, Ingersoll, Jenckes, Kasson, Kelley, Francis W. Kellogg, Orlando Kellogg, Knox, Littlejohn, Loan, Longyear, Marvin, McBride, McClurg, Samuel F. Miller, Moorhead, Morrill, Daniel Morris, Amos Myers, Leonard Myers, Norton, Charles O'Neill, Orth, Patterson, Perham, Pike, Pomeroy, William H. Randall, John H. Rice, Scofield, Shannon, Sloan, Spalding, Stevens, Thayer, Thomas, Upson, Ellihu B. Washburne, William B. Washburn, Wilson, Windom, Woodbridge, Worthington—64.

The Appropriation bill then passed the House—yeas 92, nays 41.

IN SENATE.

March 3—Mr. Trumbull moved to amend the amendment so that it would read:

That no person shall be tried by court-martial or military commission in any State or Territory where the courts of the United States are open, except persons employed, drafted, enlisted, or actually mustered or commissioned or appointed in the military or naval service of the United States, or rebel enemies charged with being spies.

Which was agreed to—yeas 25, nays 4 as follows:

Yeas—Messrs. Anthony, *Buckalew*, Clark, Cowan, *Davis*, Farwell, Foster, Grimes, Hale, *Hendricks*, *Johnson*, Lane of Indiana, *McDougall*, Morgan, Morrill, *Nesmith*, *Powell*, Ramsey, *Riddle*, Sprague, Sumner, Trumbull, Van Winkle, Wade, Wilson—25.

Nays—Messrs. Conness, Howard, Nye, Stewart—4.

Mr. Lane, of Indiana, moved to strike out the section as amended, which was agreed to—yeas 20, nays 14, as follows:

Yeas—Messrs. Anthony, Brown, Chandler, Clark, Conness, Farwell, Foster, Grimes, Harlan, Howard, Howe, Lane of Indiana, Morgan, Morrill, Nye, Ramsey, Stewart, Sumner, Wilkinson, Wilson—20.

Nays—Messrs. *Buckalew*, Cowan, *Davis*, Hale, *Hendricks*, *Johnson*, *McDougall*, *Nesmith*, *Powell*, *Riddle*, Sprague, Trumbull, Van Winkle, Wade—14.

The bill then passed—yeas 26, nays 5.

The House insisted on its action; and a Committee of Conference reported an agreement upon all the points of disagreement, except with regard to arrests; but the hour of adjournment arrived before either House acted on the report, and the bill fell.

BAIL IN CERTAIN CASES OF ARREST.

February 24—Mr. Trumbull moved to take up Senate bill providing for bail in certain cases of military arrests.

It provides that contractors, who, by the sixteenth section of the act of July 17, 1862, are made subject to trial by military tribunals, should be allowed bail when arrested.

Mr. Powell offered this as a new section:

That any officer in the executive, military, or naval service of the United States, who shall arrest or cause to be arrested, any person or persons not engaged in the military or naval service of the United States, and who is not engaged in the rebellion against the United States, shall immediately hand the person or persons so arrested over to the civil authorities to have the case investigated and the parties so arrested tried according to law. Any officer engaged in the executive, naval, or military service of the United States, who shall violate this section, shall be deemed guilty of a felony, and, upon indictment and conviction thereof in any court of the United States having jurisdiction to try and punish such cases, shall be punished by a fine of not less than $500 and not exceeding $10,000, and confinement in the penitentiary of not less than one year, nor more than five years, in the discretion of the court trying the same: *Provided*, That nothing in this section shall be so construed as to prevent any officer who shall make an unlawful arrest from being prosecuted in a civil suit for damages for such unlawful arrest.

The subject was debated and laid aside, and not again reached.

HABEAS CORPUS.

1865, February 11—Before the Supreme Court of the District of Columbia, in the case of Christopher V. Hogan, confined in the Old Capitol prison, (upon charges of implication in the robbery of a paymaster,) on whose behalf a writ of *habeas corpus* was issued, the following return was made by William P. Wood, the keeper of the prison:

That the body of Hogan is in my possession; that he was arrested and imprisoned by authority of the President of the United States; and that I do not produce this body by reason of the order of the President of the United States, endorsed upon said writ, to which reference is hereby respectfully made.

The endorsement of the President is:

The within-named Christopher Hogan was arrested and is imprisoned by my authority. This writ of habeas corpus is suspended, and the officer having Hogan in custody is directed not to produce his body, but hold him in custody until further order, giving this order in your return to the court. A. LINCOLN.

January 23, 1865.

In the argument it was contended that the 2d section of the act of March 3, 1863, contained restrictions on the power of suspension, one of which was that if a regular term of the proper United States court should come and go without an indictment being found against the prisoner, he was entitled to discharge on *habeas corpus*. The Court unanimously overruled the point, Justice Olin delivering the opinion. Justice Wylie dissented from the reasoning of the opinion, though concurring in the opinion.

IN HOUSE.

1865, February 11—Mr. Le Blond introduced a bill to repeal "An act relating to *habeas corpus*, and regulating judicial proceedings in certain cases;" which was referred to the Committee on the Judiciary.

February 16—Reported unfavorably from the Committee, by Mr. Wilson.

PUNISHMENT OF AN EDITOR.

The following paragraph appeared in the public papers, telegraphed from Trenton, N. J., February 15, 1865:

In the United States Court, E. N. Fuller, editor of *The Newark Journal*, was fined $100 for publishing articles against the United States Enrollment Law. He pleaded guilty and made a statement to the Court which mitigated his offence.

Confiscation.

In continuation of the record on pages 195—203, and 260, it should be stated that the proposition to repeal the clause limiting confiscation to life-estate was a part of the first report of the Committee of Conference on the Freedmen's bill; which was rejected in the Senate, February 22, 1865, (for which, see beyond.) There was no direct vote on the naked proposition in the Senate, and no other vote involving it in the second session of the Thirty-eighth Congress; but these proceedings took place:

IN HOUSE OF REPRESENTATIVES.

1865, February 22—Mr. Williams, from the Judiciary Committee, reported this bill:

That so much of the joint resolution explanatory of "An act to suppress insurrection, to punish treason and rebellion, to seize and confiscate the property of rebels, and for other purposes," approved July seventeenth, eighteen hundred and sixty-two, as prohibits the forfeiture of the real estate of rebels beyond their natural lives, be, and the same is hereby, repealed.

SEC. 2. That this act shall take effect and be in force from and after its passage.

February 23—Mr. HOLMAN moved that it be tabled; which was lost—yeas 52, nays 61. On ordering it to be engrossed and read a third time, the yeas were 67, nays 54. A motion by Mr. Cox to table it, when on final passage, was lost—yeas 68, nays 68, the Speaker voting nay. The bill then passed—yeas 73, nays 72, as follows:

YEAS—Messrs. Allison, Ames, Ashley, John D. Baldwin, Baxter, Beaman, Blaine, Boutwell, Boyd, Brandegee, Broomall, Ambrose W. Clark, Freeman Clarke, Cobb, Cole, Thomas T. Davis, Dawes, Deming, Dixon, Donnelly, Driggs, Dumont, Eckley, Eliot, Frank, Garfield, Gooch, Grinnell, Higby, Hooper, Asahel W. Hubbard, John H. Hubbard, Hulburd, Ingersoll, Jenckes, Kelley, Orlando Kellogg, Knox, Littlejohn, Loan, Longyear, Marvin, McBride, McClurg, Samuel F. Miller, Moorhead, Morrill, Daniel Morris, Leonard Myers, Norton, Orth, Patterson, Pike, Pomeroy, Price, Alexander H. Rice, John H. Rice, Edward H. Rollins, Schenck, Shannon, Sloan, Smithers, Starr, Stevens, Thayer, Upson, Van Valkenburgh, Ellihu B. Washburne, William B. Washburn, Wilder, Wilson, Woodbridge, Worthington—73.

NAYS—Messrs. *James C. Allen, Ancona, Baily, Augustus C. Baldwin*, Blair, *Bliss, Brooks, James S. Brown, Chanler, Clay, Coffroth, Cox, Cravens, Dawson, Denison, Eden, Edgerton, Eldridge, English, Finck, Ganson*, Griswold, Hale, *Hall, Harding, Benjamin G. Harris, Holman, Hutchins, Philip Johnson, Kalbfleisch, Kernan, King, Law, Lazear, Le Blond, Long, Mallory, Marcy, McAllister, William H. Miller, James R. Morris, Morrison, Nelson, Noble, Odell, John O'Neill, Pendleton, Perry, Pruyn, Radford, Samuel J. Randall*, Wm. H. Randall, *Rogers, James S. Rollins, Ross, John B. Steele, William G. Steele, Stiles, Strouse, Stuart, Sweat, Townsend*, Tracy, *Voorhees, Wadsworth*, Webster, Whaley, *Wheeler, Joseph W. White, Winfield, Fernando Wood, Yeaman*—72.

This bill was not reached in the Senate.

Military Legislation.

AMENDMENT TO THE ENROLLMENT BILL.

The Enrollment Act of March 3, 1865, though lengthy, contains no new principle, and is devoted to details. One section (the 22d) repeals the 3d section of the act of July 4, 1864, which authorized the Governors of loyal States to send recruiting agents to certain of the rebellious States,* (see p. 117.) It passed as reported from the Committee of Conference:

IN SENATE,

Without a division.

IN HOUSE OF REPRESENTATIVES,

The vote was—yeas 72, nays 56, as follows:

YEAS—Messrs. Allison, Ames, Arnold, Ashley, *Baily*, John D. Baldwin, Baxter, Beaman, Blow, Boutwell, Broomall, Ambrose W. Clark, Freeman Clarke, Cobb, Cole, Creswell, Henry Winter Davis, Thomas T. Davis, Dawes, Dixon, Driggs, Eckley, Eliot, Garfield, Gooch, Griswold, Higby, Asahel W. Hubbard, John H. Hubbard, Hulburd, Jenckes, Kasson, Kelley, Orlando Kellogg, *King*, Littlejohn, Longyear, Marvin, *McAllister*, McClurg, Samuel F. Miller, Moorhead, Morrill, Amos Myers, Leonard Myers, *Odell*, Charles O'Neill, Orth, Patterson, Perham, Pike, Pomeroy, Price, William H. Randall, Alexander H. Rice, John H. Rice, *James S. Rollins*, Schenck, Scofield, Shannon, Sloan, Smith, Smithers, Upson, Van Valkenburgh, William B. Washburn, Williams, Wilder, Wilson, Windom, Woodbridge, Worthington—72.

NAYS—Messrs. *James C. Allen, Ancona, Augustus C. Baldwin, Bliss*, Boyd, *Brooks, James S. Brown, Chanler, Coffroth, Cravens, Dawson, Edgerton, Eldridge, English*, Farnsworth, *Finck*, Grinnell, Hale, *Charles M Harris, Herrick, Holman*, Hotchkiss, Ingersoll, *Philip Johnson, Kalbfleisch*, Francis W. Kellogg, *Knapp, Le Blond, Long, Mallory, Marcy, McKinney, William H. Miller, James R. Morris, Morrison, Nelson, Noble*, Norton, *John O'Neill, Pendleton, Perry, Radford, Samuel J. Randall, Ross, Scott, John B. Steele*, Stevens, *Stiles, Strouse, Stuart*, Tracy, *Voorhees, Ward*, Ellihu B. Washburne, Whaley, *Chilton A. White*—56.

During the consideration of the general question, these votes were taken:

IN SENATE.

CIVIL INSTEAD OF MILITARY COURTS.

February 7—Mr. COWAN offered an amendment to the effect that recruiting agents, substitute brokers, or other persons enlisting any insane person, &c., shall be fined and imprisoned upon conviction by any "court of the United States having competent jurisdiction," instead of by a "court martial or military commission," as the section was reported from the Military Committee; which was agreed to—yeas 29, nays 14, as follows:

YEAS—Messrs. *Buckalew, Carlile*, Cowan, *Davis*, Dixon, Doolittle, Farwell, Foot, Foster, Hale, Harlan, Harris, Henderson, *Hendricks*, Howe, *Johnson*, Lane of Kansas, Morgan, *Nesmith*, Pomeroy, *Powell, Richardson Riddle, Saulsbury*, Ten Eyck, Trumbull, Van Winkle, Willey, *Wright*—29.

NAYS—Messrs. Anthony, Brown, Chandler, Clark, Conness, Grimes, Howard, Morrill, Nye, Ramsey, Sherman, Stewart, Sumner, Wilson—14.

NO SUBSTITUTION.

Mr. LANE, of Kansas, moved as a substitute for the first section:

That all acts and parts of acts now in force providing for substitutions, or regulating the substitution of another for a person drafted into the military service, be, and the same are hereby, repealed.

Which was rejected—yeas 7, nays 31, as follows:

YEAS—Messrs. Brown, Doolittle, Grimes, Howe, Lane of Indiana, Lane of Kansas, Ramsey—7.

NAYS—Messrs. Anthony, *Buckalew*, Clark, Collamer, Conness, Cowan, *Davis*, Dixon, Farwell, Foot, Foster, Hale, Harlan, Harris, Henderson, *Hendricks, Johnson*, Morgan, Morrill, Pomeroy, *Powell, Riddle*, Sherman, Stewart, Sumner, Ten Eyck, Trumbull, Van Winkle, Willey, Wilson, *Wright*—31.

EXEMPTION OF OFFICIALS.

Mr. HENDRICKS offered an additional section:

That the heads of Executive Departments, judges of the courts of the United States, and members of Congress, during their term of service, shall be exempt from military duty.

Which was rejected—yeas 9, nays 27, as follows:

YEAS—Messrs. Brown, *Buckalew, Davis, Hendricks*, Pomeroy, *Powell, Riddle*, Trumbull. *Wright*—9.

NAYS—Messrs. Anthony, Chandler, Clark, Conness, Cowan, Dixon, Farwell, Foot, Foster, Grimes, Harlan, Harris, Henderson, Howard, *Johnson*, Lane of Indiana, Lane of Kansas, Morgan, Morrill, Ramsey, Sherman, Stewart, Sumner, Ten Eyck, Van Winkle, Willey, Wilson—27.

IN HOUSE OF REPRESENTATIVES.

TO REPEAL ALL CONSCRIPTION LAWS.

February 27—Mr. CHANLER, of New York, offered this section as an addition to the 13th section of the House bill:

That so much of all acts or parts of acts entitled acts to regulate and provide for enrolling and calling out the national forces, and for other purposes, as authorize the President of the United States to raise troops by conscription

---

*February 6—On an Enrollment bill, Mr. BUCKALEW offered a repealing clause, which was agreed to—yeas 28, nays 12, as follows:

YEAS—Messrs. Brown, *Buckalew, Carlile*, Chandler, Collamer, Cowan, *Davis*, Doolittle, Grimes, Harlan, Harris, Henderson, *Hendricks*, Howard, Howe, *Johnson*, Lane of Indiana, *Nesmith, Powell*, Ramsey, *Richardson, Saulsbury*, Sherman, Ten Eyck, Trumbull, Van Winkle, Willey, *Wright*—28.

NAYS—Messrs. Anthony, Clark, Conness, Dixon, Farwell, Foster, Hale, Morgan, Morrill, Nye, Sumner, Wilson—12.

be, and hereby are, repealed; and that all acts and parts of acts inconsistent with this section be, and the same are hereby, repealed.

Which was not agreed to—yeas 27, nays 95, as follows:

YEAS—Messrs. *Ancona, Brooks, Chanler, Clay, Denison, Eden, Edgerton, Eldridge, Benjamin G. Harris, Le Blond, Long, Mallory, William H. Miller, Morrison, Noble, John O'Neill, Pendleton, Perry, Pruyn, Rogers, Ross, Stiles, Strouse, Townsend, Wadsworth, Chilton A. White, Joseph W. White*—27.

NAYS—Messrs. *James C. Allen*, Allison, Ames, Ashley, *Baily*, John D. Baldwin, Baxter, Beaman, Blaine, Boyd, Brandegee, Broomall, Cobb, Cole, *Cravens*, Henry Winter Davis, Thomas T. Davis, Dawes, Deming, Dixon, Donnelly, Driggs, Dumont, Eckley, Eliot, *English*, Farnsworth, Frank, *Ganson*, Garfield, Gooch, *Grider*, Griswold, Hale, Higby, Hooper, Hotchkiss, Asahel W. Hubbard, John H. Hubbard, Hulburd, Ingersoll, Jenckes, Kelley, Francis W. Kellogg, Orlando Kellogg, *King*, Knox, *Lazear*, Littlejohn, Loan, Longyear, *Marcy*, Marvin, McBride, McClurg, Samuel F. Miller, Moorhead, Morrill, Daniel Morris, Amos Myers, Leonard Myers, Norton, *Odell*, Charles O'Neill, Orth, Patterson, Perham, Pomeroy, Price, William H. Randall, Alexander H. Rice, John H. Rice, Edward H. Rollins, Schenck, *Scott*, Shannon, Sloan, Smithers, Spalding, Stevens, Thayer, Tracy, Upson, Van Valkenburgh, Elihu B. Washburne, William B. Washburn, Webster, Whaley, *Wheeler*, Williams, Wilder, Wilson, Windom, Woodbridge, Worthington—95.

RESOLUTIONS CONCERNING ENROLLMENT.

IN SENATE.

1864, December 15—Mr. BROWN offered the following, which was agreed to:

Resolved, That the Committee on Military Affairs and the Militia be, and they are hereby, instructed to inquire into the expediency of so amending the act of Congress of March 8, 1792, entitled "An act more effectually to provide for the national defence by establishing a uniform militia throughout the United States," and also the several acts amendatory of the same, as shall provide for the enrollment of all male citizens between the ages of eighteen and forty-five, resident in the respective States, without respect to color; and also to submit such other provisions as may tend more efficiently to organize the militia system of the United States, and report by bill or otherwise.

IN HOUSE OF REPRESENTATIVES.

EXEMPTION OF THE CLERGY.

1865, February 6—Mr. PRICE, by unanimous consent, introduced the following, which was adopted:

Whereas the genius and policy of our Government is opposed to making distinctions between religious denominations, but guarantees equal protection to all and exclusive privileges to none; and whereas it is alleged that certain preachers of the gospel, belonging to some of the churches whose religious tenets do not bring them within the scope of the act of February, 1864, for "enrolling and calling out the national forces," have, since the passage of said act, been exempted from military duty after being drafted, without complying with section seventeen of said law: Therefore,

Be it resolved, That the Secretary of War be, and he is hereby, directed to inform this House whether any privileges have been granted to the preachers of any denomination of professing Christians which have been denied to others, and if so, what denomination those persons belonged to, and also their names and place of residence, with the reasons for making such distinction.

February 8—The Secretary of War sent this reply:

WAR DEPARTMENT,
WASHINGTON CITY, *February* 7, 1865.

SIR: I have the honor to transmit herewith the report of the Provost Marshal General in answer to the resolution of the House of Representatives of the 6th instant, in relation to preachers of the gospel. I have no information upon the subject referred to in the resolution except that contained in the report of the Provost Marshal General, and do not know of any privileges having been granted to preachers of one denomination of professing Christians that have been denied to other denominations.

Very respectfully, your obedient servant,
EDWIN M. STANTON,
Secretary of War.

WAR DEPARTMENT,
PROVOST MARSHAL GENERAL'S BUREAU,
WASHINGTON, D. C., *February* 7, 1865.

SIR: I have the honor to acknowledge the receipt of a resolution of the House of Representatives, dated February 6, 1865, wherein the Secretary of War is "directed to inform this House whether any privileges have been granted to the preachers of any denomination of professing Christians which have been denied to others, and if so, what denomination these persons belonged to, and also their names and place of residence, with the reasons for making such distinction."

In reply I have the honor to state that I know of no instance in which boards of enrollment have exempted preachers of the gospel belonging to churches "whose religious tenets do not bring them within the scope of the act of February, 1864, for enrolling and calling out the national forces," nor do I know of any "privileges having been granted to the preachers of any denomination of professing Christians which have been denied to others."

I have the honor to be, sir, very respectfully, your obedient servant,
JAMES B. FRY,
Provost Marshal General.

CONFISCATION OF PROPERTY OF DESERTERS.

1864, December 21—Mr. GRINNELL asked, but failed to obtain, leave to offer this:

Resolved, That the Committee on Military Affairs be instructed to report at an early day upon the expediency of a law to confiscate for the Government, when practicable, so much of the property of conscripts who have failed to report for duty as may be required to secure the services of a soldier in their stead.

1865, January 7—Mr. G. offered the resolution, and it was passed.

FREEDOM OF SOLDIERS' FAMILIES.

IN SENATE.

1865, January 9—A joint resolution passed,* with these provisions:

That the wife and children, if any he have, of any person that has been, or may be, mustered into the military or naval service of the United States, shall, from and after its passage, be forever free, any law, usage, or custom whatsoever to the contrary notwithstanding; and in determining who is or was the wife and who are the children of an enlisted person, evidence that he and the woman claimed to be his wife have cohabited together, or associated as husband and wife, and so continued to cohabit or associate at the time of the enlistment, or evidence that a form or ceremony of marriage (whether such marriage was or was not authorized or recognized by law) has been entered into or celebrated by them, and that the parties thereto thereafter lived together, or associated or cohabited as husband and wife, and so continued to live, cohabit or associate at the time of the enlistment, shall be deemed sufficient proof of marriage, and the children born of any such marriage shall be deemed and taken to be the children embraced within the provisions of the act, whether such marriage shall or shall not have been dissolved at the time of such enlistment.

---

* HEADQUARTERS DEPARTMENT OF KENTUCKY,
LOUISVILLE, KY., *March* 12, 1865.

[General Orders No. 10.]

The General commanding announces to the colored men of Kentucky that, by an act of Congress passed on the 3d day of March, 1865, the wives and children of all colored men who have heretofore enlisted, or who may hereafter enlist, in the military service of the Government, are made free.

This act of justice to the soldiers claims from them renewed efforts, by courage, fortitude, and discipline, to win a good name, to be shared by a free wife and free children. To colored men not in the army it offers an opportunity to coin freedom for themselves and their posterity.

The rights secured to colored soldiers under this law will, if necessary, be enforced by the military authorities of this Department; and it is expected that the loyal men and women of Kentucky will encourage colored men to enlist in the army, and, after they have done so, recognize them as upholders of their government and defenders of their homes, and exercise towards the helpless women and children made free by this law that benevolence and charity which has always characterized the people of the State.

By command of Major General PALMER:
J. P. WATSON,
Capt. and A. A. A. G.

The vote was—yeas 27, nays 10, as follows:

YEAS—Messrs. Anthony, Brown, Chandler, Clark, Conness, Dixon, Farwell, Foot, Foster, Grimes, Hale, Harlan, Harris, Hicks, Howe, Lane of Indiana, Morgan, Morrill, Pomeroy, Ramsey, Sherman, Sprague, Sumner, Van Winkle, Wade, Willey, Wilson—27.

NAYS—Messrs. *Buckalew*, *Carlile*, Cowan, *Davis*, *Hendricks*, *Johnson*, *Nesmith*, *Powell*, *Saulsbury*, Trumbull—10.

February 22—The House passed it—yeas 74, nays 63 as follows:

YEAS—Messrs. Allison, Ames, Anderson, Arnold, Ashley, *Baily*, John D. Baldwin, Baxter, Beaman, Blaine, Blow, Boutwell, Boyd, Broomall, Ambrose W. Clark, Cobb, Cole, Dawes, Dixon, Donnelly, Driggs, Dumont, Eckley, Eliot, Garfield, Gooch, Grinnell, Higby, Hooper, Asahel W. Hubbard, John H. Hubbard, Hulburd, Ingersoll, Jenckes, Kasson, Kelley, Orlando Kellogg, Knox, Littlejohn, Loan, Longyear, Marvin, McClurg, Samuel F. Miller, Moorhead, Morrill, Daniel Morris, Amos Myers, Leonard Myers, Norton, Charles O'Neill, Orth, Perham, Pike, Pomeroy, Price, Alexander H. Rice, John H. Rice, Edward H. Rollins, Schenck, Scofield, Shannon, Sloan, Stevens, Thayer, Tracy, Upson, Van Valkenburgh, Ellihu B. Washburne, William B. Washburn, Williams, Wilder, Wilson, Worthington—74.

NAYS—Messrs. *James C. Allen*, *Ancona*, *Augustus C. Baldwin*, *Bliss*, *Brooks*, *Chanler*, *Clay*, *Coffroth*, *Cox*, *Cravens*, Henry Winter Davis, *Dawson*, *Denison*, *Eden*, *Edgerton*, *Eldridge*, *Finck*, *Ganson*, *Grider*, Griswold, Hale, *Hall*, *Harding*, *Harrington*, *Charles M. Harris*, *Herrick*, *Kalbfleisch*, *Kernan*, *Knapp*, *Law*, *Le Blond*, *Long*, *Mallory*, McBride, *McKinney*, *William H. Miller*, *James R. Morris*, *Morrison*, *Nelson*, *Noble*, *Odell*, *Pendleton*, *Perry*, *Pruyn*, *Radford*, *Samuel J. Randall*, William H. Randall, *Ross*, Smith, Smithers, *John B. Steele*, *William G. Steele*, *Stiles*, *Strouse*, *Stuart*, *Sweat*, *Townsend*, *Voorhees*, *Wadsworth*, Whaley, *Winfield*, *Fernando Wood*, *Yeaman*—63.

During the pendency of the resolution in the SENATE:

1865, January 9—Mr. DAVIS, of Kentucky, proposed to amend so as to make it read:

The wife and children, if any he have, of any person who may be hereafter mustered into the military or naval service of the United States, shall, from and after the passage of this act, be forever free.

Which was rejected—yeas 6, (Messrs *Buckalew*, *Davis*, *Hendricks*, *Powell*, *Saulsbury*, Trumbull,) nays, 32.

Mr. POWELL offered a proviso:

Provided, That no slave shall be emancipated by virtue of this resolution until the owner of the slave or slaves so emancipated shall be paid a just compensation.

Which was rejected—yeas 7, nays 30:

YEAS—Messrs. *Buckalew*, *Davis*, *Hendricks*, *Johnson*, *Nesmith*, *Powell*, *Saulsbury*—7.

NAYS—Messrs. Anthony, Brown, *Carlile*, Chandler, Clark, Collamer, Conness, Cowan, Dixon, Farwell, Foot, Foster, Grimes, Hale, Harlan, Harris, Henderson, Hicks, Lane of Indiana, Morgan, Pomeroy, Ramsey, Sherman, Sprague, Sumner, Trumbull, Van Winkle, Wade, Willey, Wilson—30.

Mr. SAULSBURY offered this proviso, which was rejected:

Provided, That the provisions of this resolution shall not apply to or be operative in any State that has not assumed to secede from the Union.

COMPENSATION FOR ENLISTED SLAVES.

IN SENATE.

1865, January 25—The following resolution, offered by Mr. POWELL, was adopted:

Resolved, That the Secretary of War be directed to inform the Senate whether or not he has appointed a commission in each of the slave States represented in Congress "charged to award to each loyal person to whom a colored volunteer may owe service a just compensation, not exceeding $300, for each colored volunteer," as required by the twenty-fourth section of the act approved February 24, 1864, entitled "An act to amend an act entitled 'An act for enrolling and calling out the national forces, and for other purposes,' approved March 3, 1863;" and if he has not appointed said commission, that he inform the Senate why he has not done so.

IN HOUSE OF REPRESENTATIVES.

1865. January 17—Mr. GRIDER submitted the following resolution, which was agreed to:

Resolved, That the Secretary of War is respectfully requested to communicate to this House whether he has, according to the law approved February 24, 1864, appointed a commissioner in each of the slave States represented in Congress, to be charged with the duty to award to each loyal person, to whom a colored volunteer may owe service, "a just compensation, not exceeding $300," for each such colored volunteer, to be paid out of the fund derived from commutation money.

Resolved further, That he state as near as may be, the amount of said fund, and what further sum will probably be necessary to meet the requisitions of said law.

January 25—The Secretary replied:

WAR DEPARTMENT,
WASHINGTON CITY, *January* 25, 1865.

SIR: In answer to the resolution of the House of Representatives dated the 17th instant, in relation to the appointment of commissioners in the slave States, to award to the owners of slaves enlisted as volunteers compensation for their services, I have the honor to say, in reply to the first branch of the inquiry, that commissioners have been appointed in the States of Maryland and Delaware, and that in the other slave States, by the President's direction, no appointments have yet been made.

In answer to the second branch of the resolution, I have the honor to state that the amount of the commutation fund is reported by the provost marshal to be $12,170,663 45, a portion of which has been assigned for the payment of bounties required in raising new troops. It is believed, however, that there will be sufficient to pay to the owners of slaves the sum allowed by the act of Congress.

Very respectfully, your obedient servant,

EDWIN M. STANTON,
Secretary of War.

1865, February 16—Mr. GRIDER asked unanimous consent to introduce the following resolution:

Resolved, That the President of the United States be respectfully requested, if not inconsistent with the public interest, to communicate to the House why commissioners have not been appointed by the Secretary of War, according to the provisions of a bill approved July, 1864, providing for the valuation of slaves enlisted in the United States army in the States of Kentucky and Missouri.

Mr. STEVENS objected.

UNEMPLOYED GENERALS.

1864, December 14—The House passed a bill similar to that mentioned on page 285, with the addition of a section providing that, during the war, the provisions of the section shall be applied each month to the general officers—yeas 99, nays 38, as follows:

YEAS—Messrs. Allison, Ames, *Ancona*, Arnold, Ashley, *Baily*, John D. Baldwin, Baxter, Beaman, Blaine, Blair, Blow, Boutwell, Boyd, Brandegee, Broomall, Ambrose W. Clark, Freeman Clarke, Cobb, Cole, *Cravens*, Thomas T. Davis, Dawes, *Dawson*, Deming, Dixon, Donnelly, Driggs, Eckley, *Edgerton*, Eliot, *English*, Farnsworth, *Finck*, Garfield, Grinnell, Griswold, Hale, *Harrington*, Higby, *Holman*, Hooper, Hotchkiss, Asahel W. Hubbard, John H. Hubbard, Hulburd, Ingersoll, Jenckes, Kasson, Francis W. Kellogg, Orlando Kellogg, Knox, *Law*, *Lazear*, *Le Blond*, Littlejohn, Longyear, Marvin, *McAllister*, McClurg, McIndoe, Moorhead, Morrill, Daniel Morris, Amos Myers, Leonard Myers, Charles O'Neill, Orth, Patterson, Perham, Pike, Pomeroy, Price, Alexander H. Rice, John H. Rice, Edward H Rollins, *James S. Rollins*, Schenck, Scofield, Shannon, Sloan, Smith, Smithers, Spalding, Starr, *Stuart*, Thayer, Thomas, Upson, Van Valkenburgh, Ellihu B. Washburne, William B. Washburn, Whaley, Williams, Wilder, Wilson, Windom, *Benjaman Wood*, *Yeaman*—99.

NAYS—Messrs. *James C. Allen*, *Augustus C. Baldwin*, *Brooks*, *James S. Brown*, *Chanler*, *Cox*, *Denison*, *Eden*, *Eldridge*, *Ganson*, *Grider*, *Harding*, *Herrick*, *Kalbfleisch*, *Kernan*, *King*, *Knapp*, *Long*, *Mallory*, *Marcy*, *McDowell*, *McKinney*, *William H. Miller*, *James R. Morris*, *Morrison*, *Noble*, Norton, *John O'Neill*, *Pendleton*, *Samuel J. Randall*, *Ross*, *Scott*, *John B. Steele*, *William G. Steele*, Stevens, *Stiles*, *Townsend*, *Wadsworth*—38.

1865, January 6—In Senate, the bill was indefinitely postponed—yeas 28, nays 8, as follows:

YEAS—Messrs. Brown, *Buckalew*, *Carlile*, Clark, Dixon, Doolittle, Foot, Foster, Grimes, *Harding*, Harris, Henderson, *Hendricks*, Hicks, *Johnson*, Lane of Indiana, Morgan, Morrill, *Nesmith*, *Powell*, Ramsey, *Richardson*, *Saulsbury*, Sherman, Sumner, Van Winkle, Willey, Wilson—28.

NAYS—Messrs. Conness, *Davis*, Farwell, Harlan, Howe, Pomeroy, Trumbull, Wade—8.

VOTES OF THANKS.

Congress passed several joint resolutions, tendering thanks to army and navy officers commanding, and to officers and men under their command, upon which there was generally no division called. But in the House, January 25, 1865, on a resolution thanking Major General Philip H. Sheridan, and the officers and men under his command, for the gallantry, military skill, and courage displayed in the then recent battles in the Shenandoah Valley, and especially for their services at Cedar Run, October 19, 1864, which retrieved the fortunes of the day, the yeas and nays were called, and were—yeas 131, nays 2, as follows:

YEAS—Messrs. *James C. Allen*, *William J. Allen*, Allison, Ames, *Ancona*, Anderson, Arnold, Ashley, *Augustus C. Baldwin*, John D. Baldwin, Baxter, Beaman, Blaine, Blair, Blow, Boutwell, Boyd, *Brooks*, Broomall, *James S. Brown*, William G. Brown, Ambrose W. Clark, Cobb, *Coffroth*, Cole, *Cox*, *Cravens*, Henry Winter Davis, Thomas T. Davis, Dawes, Deming, *Denison*, Dixon, Donnelly, Driggs, Eckley, *Edgerton*, Eliot, Farnsworth, *Finck*, Frank, *Ganson*, Garfield, Gooch, *Grider*, Grinnell, Griswold, Hale, *Harding*, *Charles M. Harris*, Higby, *Holman*, Hooper, Hotchkiss, Asahel W. Hubbard, John H. Hubbard, Ingersoll, Jenckes, Julian, *Kalbfleisch*, Kasson, Kelley, *Kernan*, *King*, Knox, *Lazear*, Littlejohn, Loan, Longyear, *Mallory*, Marvin, *McAllister*, McBride, McClurg, *McDowell*, McIndoe, Samuel F. Miller, *William H. Miller*, Moorhead, Morrill, Daniel Morris, *Morrison*, Amos Myers, Leonard Myers, *Noble*, Norton, Charles O'Neill, *John O'Neill*, Orth, Patterson, Perham, Pike, Price, *Radford*, *Samuel J. Randall*, William H. Randall, Alexander H. Rice, John H. Rice, *Robinson*, *Rogers*, Edward H. Rollins, *James S. Rollins*, *Ross*, Schenck, Scofield, *Scott*, Shannon, Sloan, Smith, Smithers, Spalding, *John B. Steele*, *William G. Steele*, Stevens, *Strouse*, *Stuart*, Thayer, Thomas, *Townsend*, Upson, Van Valkenburgh, *Wadsworth*, Ellihu B. Washburne, William B. Washburn, Webster, Whaley, *Wheeler*, *Joseph W. White*, Wilson, Windom, *Yeaman*—131.

NAYS—Messrs. *Benjamin G. Harris*, *Chilton A. White*—2.

MILITARY INTERFERENCE IN ELECTIONS.

IN HOUSE OF REPRESENTATIVES.

1865, February 22—The bill of the Senate, referred to on pages 315 and 316, passed the House—yeas 113, nays 19:

YEAS—Messrs. *James C. Allen*, Ames, *Ancona*, Anderson, Arnold, *Baily*, *Augustus C. Baldwin*, Baxter, Blaine, *Bliss*, Blow, Boutwell, *Brooks*, Broomall, *Chanler*, Ambrose W. Clark, *Clay*, *Coffroth*, *Cox*, *Cravens*, Dawes, *Dawson*, *Denison*, Donnelly, Dumont, Eckley, *Eden*, *Edgerton*, *Eldridge*, Eliot, *English*, *Finck*, *Ganson*, Gooch, *Grider*, Grinnell, Griswold, Hale, *Hall*, *Harding*, *Benjamin G. Harris*, *Charles M. Harris*, *Herrick*, Higby, *Holman*, Hooper, Asahel W. Hubbard, John H. Hubbard, Hulburd, Ingersoll, Jenckes, *Kalbfleisch*, Kasson, *Kernan*, *Knapp*, *Law*, *Le Blond*, Littlejohn, *Long*, Longyear, *Mallory*, Marvin, McBride, *McKinney*, Samuel F. Miller, *William H. Miller*, Moorhead, Daniel Morris, *James R. Morris*, *Morrison*, Amos Myers, Leonard Myers, *Nelson*, *Noble*, *Odell*, Charles O'Neill, Patterson, *Pendleton*, Perham, *Perry*, Pomeroy, Price, *Pruyn*, *Radford*, *Samuel J. Randall*, William H. Randall, Alexander H. Rice, Edward H. Rollins, *Ross*, Scofield, Smith, *John B. Steele*, *William G. Steele*, *Stiles*, *Strouse*, *Stuart*, *Sweat*, Thayer, *Townsend*, Tracy, Van Valkenburgh, *Voorhees*, *Wadsworth*, Ellihu B. Washburne, William B. Washburn, Webster, Whaley, Williams, Wilson, *Winfield*, *Fernando Wood*, Woodbridge, *Yeaman*—113.

NAYS—Messrs. Ashley, Beaman, Boyd, Cobb, Cole, Henry Winter Davis, Thomas T. Davis, Garfield, Kelley, Knox, John H. Rice, Schenck, Shannon, Sloan, Smithers, Stevens, Upson, Wilder, Worthington—19.

Peace.

THE HAMPTON ROADS CONFERENCE.

1865, February 10—These messages from President LINCOLN were received and read:

MESSAGE TO THE HOUSE.

To the Honorable the House of Representatives:

In response to your resolution of the 8th instant,* requesting information in relation to a conference recently held in Hampton Roads, I have the honor to state, that on the day of the date I gave Francis P. Blair, Senior, a card, written on as follows, to wit:

Allow the bearer, F. P. Blair, Senior, to pass our lines, go south, and return. A. LINCOLN.
December 28, 1864.

That at the time I was informed that Mr. Blair sought the card as a means of getting to Richmond, Virginia; but he was given no authority to speak or act for the government, nor was I informed of anything he would say or do on his own account, or otherwise. Afterwards Mr. Blair told me that he had been to Richmond, and had seen Mr. Jefferson Davis; and he (Mr. B.) at the same time left with me a manuscript letter, as follows, to wit:

RICHMOND, *Va., January* 12, 1865.

SIR: I have deemed it proper, and probably desirable to you, to give you, in this form the substance of remarks made by me, to be repeated by you to President Lincoln, &c., &c.

I have no disposition to find obstacles in forms, and am willing, now as heretofore, to enter into negotiations for the restoration of peace; and am ready to send a commission whenever I have reason to suppose it will be received, or to receive a commission, if the United States Government shall choose to send one. That, notwithstanding the rejection of our former offers, I would, if you could promise that a commissioner, minister, or other agent would be received, appoint one immediately, and renew the effort to enter into conference, with a view to secure peace to the two countries.

Yours, &c., JEFFERSON DAVIS.
F. P. BLAIR, Esq.

Afterwards, and with the view that it should be shown to Mr. Davis, I wrote and delivered to Mr. Blair a letter, as follows, to wit:

WASHINGTON, *January* 18, 1865.

SIR: Your having shown me Mr. Davis's letter to you of the 12th instant, you may say to him that I have constantly been, am now, and shall continue ready to receive any agent whom he, or any other influential person now resisting the national authority, may informally send to me, with the view of securing peace to the people of our one common country.

Yours, &c., A. LINCOLN.
F. P. BLAIR, Esq.

Afterwards Mr. Blair dictated for and authorized me to make an entry on the back of my retained copy of the letter last above recited, which entry is as follows:

JANUARY 28, 1865.

To-day Mr. Blair tells me that on the 21st instant he delivered to Mr. Davis the original, of which the within is a copy, and left it with him; that at the time of delivering it Mr. Davis read it over twice in Mr. Blair's presence, at the close of which he (Mr. Blair) remarked that the part about "our one common country" related to the part of Mr. Davis's letter about "the two countries," to which Mr. Davis replied that he so understood it.

A. LINCOLN.

Afterwards the Secretary of War placed in

* The resolution was offered by Mr. STEVENS, and is as follows:

Resolved, That the President be requested to communicate to this House such information as he may deem not incompatible with the public interest relative to the recent conference between himself and the Secretary of State and Messrs. Stephens, Hunter, and Campbell, in Hampton Roads.

my hands the following telegram, indorsed by him as appears:

[Cipher.]

OFFICE UNITED STATES MILITARY TELEGRAPH,
WAR DEPARTMENT.

The following telegram received at Washington, January 29, 1865, from headquarters Army of James, 6.30 P. M., January 29, 1865:

The following despatch just received from Major General Parke, who refers it to me for my action. I refer it to you in Lieutenant General Grant's absence.

E. O. C. ORD,
Major General Commanding.

Hon. EDWIN M. STANTON, *Secretary of War.*

HEADQUARTERS ARMY OF POTOMAC,
4 P. M., *January* 29, 1865.

The following despatch is forwarded to you for your action. Since I have no knowledge of General Grant's having had any understanding of this kind, I refer the matter to you as the ranking officer present in the two armies.

JNO. G. PARKE,
Major General Commanding.

Major General E. O. C. ORD,
Headquarters Army of the James.

FROM HEADQUARTERS NINTH ARMY CORPS, 29*th.*

Alex. H. Stephens, R. M. T. Hunter, and J. A. Campbell desire to cross my lines, in accordance with an understanding claimed to exist with Lieutenant General Grant, on their way to Washington as peace commissioners. Shall they be admitted? They desire an early answer, to come through immediately. Would like to reach City Point to-night, if they can. If they cannot do this, they would like to come through at 10 A. M. to-morrow morning.

O. B. WILCOX,
Major General Commanding 9th Corps.

Major General JNO. G. PARKE,
Headquarters Army of Potomac.

Respectfully referred to the President for such instructions as he may be pleased to give.

EDWIN M. STANTON,
Secretary of War.

January 29—8.30 P. M.

It appears that about the time of placing the foregoing telegram in my hands, the Secretary of War despatched General Ord, as follows, to wit:

[Sent in cipher at 2 A. M., 30th.]

WAR DEPARTMENT,
WASHINGTON CITY, *January* 29, 1865—10 *P. M.*

SIR: This Department has no knowledge of any understanding by General Grant to allow any person to come within his lines as commissioner of any sort. You will therefore allow no one to come into your lines under such character or profession, until you receive the President's instructions, to whom your telegram will be submitted for his directions.

EDWIN M. STANTON,
Secretary of War.

Major General ORD.

Afterwards, by my direction, the Secretary of War telegraphed General Ord as follows, to wit:

WAR DEPARTMENT,
WASHINGTON, D. C., 10.30 A. M., *January* 30, 1865.

SIR: By direction of the President, you are instructed to inform the three gentlemen, Messrs. Stephens, Hunter, and Campbell, that a messenger will be despatched to them at or near where they now are without unnecessary delay.

EDWIN M. STANTON,
Secretary of War.

Major General E. O. C. ORD,
Headquarters Army of the James.

Afterwards I prepared and put into the hands of Major Thomas T. Eckert the following instructions and message:

EXECUTIVE MANSION,
WASHINGTON, *January* 30, 1865.

SIR: You will proceed with the documents placed in your hands, and, on reaching General Ord, will deliver him the letter addressed to him by the Secretary of War; then, by General Ord's assistance, procure an interview with Messrs. Stephens, Hunter, and Campbell, or any of them. Deliver to him or them the paper on which your own letter is written. Note on the copy which you retain the time of delivery, and to whom delivered. Receive their answer in writing, waiting a reasonable time for it, and which, if it contain their decision to come through, without further condition, will be your warrant to ask General Ord to pass them through, as directed in the letter of the Secretary of War to him. If, by their answer, they decline to come, or propose other terms, do not have them passed through. And this being your whole duty, return and report to me.

Yours truly, A. LINCOLN.

Major T. T. ECKERT.

—

Messrs. ALEX. H. STEPHENS, J. A. CAMPBELL, and R. M. T. HUNTER:

GENTLEMEN: I am instructed by the President of the United States to place this paper in your hands, with the information that if you pass through the United States military lines, it will be understood that you do so for the purpose of an informal conference, on the basis of the letter, a copy of which is on the reverse side of this sheet, and that, if you choose to pass on such understanding, and so notify me in writing, I will procure the commanding general to pass you through the lines and to Fortress Monroe, under such military precautions as he may deem prudent, and at which place you will be met in due time by some person or persons, for the purpose of such informal conference; and, further, that you shall have protection, safe conduct, and safe return in all events.

THOMAS T. ECKERT,
Major and Aide-de-Camp.

CITY POINT, *Va., February* 1, 1865.

WASHINGTON, *January* 18, 1865.

SIR: Your having shown me Mr. Davis's letter to you of the 12th instant, you may say to him that I have constantly been, am now, and shall continue ready to receive any agent whom he, or any other influential person now resisting the national authority, may informally send to me, with the view of securing peace to the people of our one common country.

Yours, &c.,
A. LINCOLN.

F. P. BLAIR, Esq.

Afterwards, but before Major Eckert had departed, the following despatch was received from General Grant:

[Cipher.]

OFFICE UNITED STATES MILITARY TELEGRAPH,
WAR DEPARTMENT.

The following telegram, received at Washington, January 31, 1865. From City Point, Va., 10.30 A. M., January 30, 1865.

His Excellency ABRAHAM LINCOLN,
President of the United States:

The following communication was received here last evening:

PETERSBURG, VIRGINIA, *January* 30, 1865.

SIR: We desire to pass your lines under safe conduct, and to proceed to Washington, to hold a conference with President Lincoln upon the subject of the existing war, and with a view of ascertaining upon what terms it may be terminated, in pursuance of the course indicated by him in his letter to Mr. Blair of January 18, 1865, of which we presume you have a copy, and if not we wish to see you in person, if convenient, and to confer with you upon the subject. Very respectfully yours,

ALEXANDER H. STEPHENS.
J. A. CAMPBELL.
R. M. T. HUNTER.

Lieutenant General U. S. GRANT,
Commanding Armies United States.

I have sent directions to receive these gentlemen, and expect to have them at my quarters this evening, awaiting your instructions.

U. S. GRANT,
Lieut. Gen'l Commanding Armies U. S.

This, it will be perceived, transferred General Ord's agency in the matter to General Grant. I resolved, however, to send Major Eckert forward with his message, and accordingly telegraphed General Grant as follows, to wit:

EXECUTIVE MANSION,
WASHINGTON, *January*, 31, 1865.

Lieutenant General GRANT, *City Point, Va.:*

A messenger is coming to you on the business contained in your despatch. Detain the gentlemen in comfortable quarters until he arrives, and then act upon the message he brings as far as applicable, it having been made up to pass through General Ord's hands, and when the gentlemen were supposed to be beyond our lines. A. LINCOLN.

Sent in cipher at 1.30 P. M.

When Major Eckert departed, he bore with

him a letter of the Secretary of War to General Grant, as follows, to wit:

WAR DEPARTMENT,
WASHINGTON, D. C., *January* 30, 1865.

GENERAL: The President desires that you will please procure for the bearer, Major Thomas T. Eckert, an interview with Messrs. Stephens, Hunter, and Campbell, and if, on his return to you, he request it, pass them through our lines to Fortress Monroe, by such route and under such military precautions as you may deem prudent, giving them protection and comfortable quarters while there, and that you let none of this have any effect upon your movements or plans.

By order of the President:

EDWIN M. STANTON,
Secretary of War.

Lieutenant General GRANT, *Commanding, &c.*

Supposing the proper point to be then reached, I despatched the Secretary of State with the following instructions, Major Eckert, however, going ahead of him:

EXECUTIVE MANSION,
WASHINGTON, *January* 31, 1865.

You will proceed to Fortress Monroe, Virginia, there to meet and informally confer with Messrs. Stephens, Hunter, and Campbell, on the basis of my letter to F. P. Blair, Esq., of January 18, 1865, a copy of which you have. You will make known to them that three things are indispensable, to wit:

1. The restoration of the national authority throughout all the States.

2. No receding, by the Executive of the United States, on the slavery question, from the position assumed thereon in the late annual message to Congress, and in preceding documents.

3. No cessation of hostilities short of an end of the war and the disbanding of all forces hostile to the government.

You will inform them that all propositions of theirs, not inconsistent with the above, will be considered and passed upon in a spirit of sincere liberality. You will hear all they may choose to say, and report it to me. You will not assume to definitely consummate anything.

Yours, &c., ABRAHAM LINCOLN.

Hon. WILLIAM H. SEWARD, *Secretary of State.*

On the day of its date, the following telegram was sent to General Grant:

[Sent in cipher at 9.30 A. M.]
WAR DEPARTMENT,
WASHINGTON, D. C., *February* 1, 1865.

Lieutenant General GRANT, *City Point, Va.:*

Let nothing which is transpiring change, hinder, or delay your military movements or plans.

A. LINCOLN.

Afterwards the following despatch was received from General Grant:

[In cipher.]
OFFICE U. S. MILITARY TELEGRAPH,
WAR DEPARTMENT.

The following telegram received at Washington 2.30 P. M. February 1, 1865, from City Point, Virginia, February 1, 12.30 P. M., 1865:

Your despatch received. There will be no armistice in consequence of the presence of Mr. Stephens and others within our lines. The troops are kept in readiness to move at the shortest notice, if occasion should justify it.

U. S. GRANT,
Lieut. General.

His Excellency A. LINCOLN, *President United States.*

To notify Major Eckert that the Secretary of State would be at Fortress Monroe, and to put them in communication, the following despatch was sent:

WAR DEPARTMENT,
WASHINGTON, D. C., *February* 1, 1865.

Call at Fortress Monroe, and put yourself under direction of Mr. S., whom you will find there.

A. LINCOLN.

Major T. T. ECKERT, care of General Grant,
City Point, Va.

On the morning of the 2d instant, the following telegrams were received by me, respectively, from the Secretary of State and Major Eckert:

FORT MONROE, VA., 11.30 P. M., *February* 1, 1865.

Arrived at ten this evening. Richmond party not here. I remain here. WILLIAM H. SEWARD.

The PRESIDENT of the United States.

CITY POINT, VA., 10 P. M., *February* 1, 1865.

His Excellency A. LINCOLN, *President of the United States:*

I have the honor to report the delivery of your communication and my letter at 4.15 this afternoon, to which I received a reply at 6 P. M., but not satisfactory.

At 8 P. M. the following note, addressed to General Grant, was received:

CITY POINT, VA., *February* 1, 1865.

SIR: We desire to go to Washington city, to confer informally with the President, personally, in reference to the matters mentioned in his letter to Mr. Blair, of the 18th January, ultimo, without any personal compromise on any question in the letter. We have the permission to do so from the authorities in Richmond.

Very respectfully yours,

ALEX. H. STEPHENS.
R. M. T. HUNTER.
J. A. CAMPBELL.

Lieutenant General GRANT.

At 9.30 P. M., I notified them that they could not proceed further, unless they complied with the terms expressed in my letter. The point of meeting designated in the above note would not, in my opinion, be insisted upon. Think Fort Monroe would be acceptable. Having complied with my instructions, I will return to Washington to-morrow, unless otherwise ordered.

THOS. T. ECKERT, *Major, &c.*

On reading this despatch of Major Eckert, I was about to recall him and the Secretary of State, when the following telegram of General Grant to the Secretary of War was shown me:

[In cipher.]
OFFICE UNITED STATES MILITARY TELEGRAPH,
WAR DEPARTMENT.

The following telegram received at Washington 4.35 A. M., February 2, 1865. From City Point, Va., February 1, 10.30 P. M., 1865:

Now that the interview between Major Eckert, under his written instructions, and Mr. Stephens and party has ended, I will state confidentially, but not officially, to become a matter of record, that I am convinced, upon conversation with Messrs. Stephens and Hunter, that their intentions are good and their desire sincere to restore peace and union. I have not felt myself at liberty to express even views of my own, or to account for my reticency. This has placed me in an awkward position, which I could have avoided by not seeing them in the first instance. I fear now their going back without any expression from any one in authority will have a bad influence. At the same time I recognize the difficulties in the way of receiving these informal commissioners at this time, and do not know what to recommend. I am sorry, however, that Mr. Lincoln cannot have an interview with the two named in this despatch, if not all three now within our lines. Their letter to me was all that the President's instructions contemplated to secure their safe conduct, if they had used the same language to Major Eckert.

U. S. GRANT,
Lieutenant General.

Hon. EDWIN M. STANTON, *Secretary of War.*

This dispatch of General Grant changed my purpose; and accordingly I telegraphed him and the Secretary of State respectively as follows:

[Sent in cipher at 9 A. M.]
WAR DEPARTMENT,
WASHINGTON, D. C., *February* 2, 1865.

Lieut. Gen. GRANT, *City Point, Virginia:*

Say to the gentlemen I will meet them personally at Fortress Monroe as soon as I can get there.

A. LINCOLN.

[Sent in cipher at 9 A. M.]
WAR DEPARTMENT,
WASHINGTON, D. C., *February* 2, 1865.

Hon. WM. H. SEWARD, *Fortress Monroe, Virginia:*

Induced by a dispatch from General Grant, I join you at Fort Monroe as soon as I can come.

A. LINCOLN.

Before starting the following dispatch was shown me. I proceeded, nevertheless:

[Cipher.]
OFFICE U. S. MILITARY TELEGRAPH,
WAR DEPARTMENT.

The following telegram, received at Washington, Feb-

ruary 2, 1865. From City Point, Virginia, 9 A. M., February 2, 1865:
[Copy to Hon. Edwin M. Stanton, Secretary of War, Washington.]

Hon. WM. H. SEWARD, *Secretary of State, Fort Monroe:*

The gentlemen here have accepted the proposed terms, and will leave for Fort Monroe at 9.30 A. M.

U. S. GRANT,
Lieutenant General.

On the night of the 2d I reached Hampton Roads, found the Secretary of State and Major Eckert on a steamer anchored off shore, and learned of them that the Richmond gentlemen were on another steamer also anchored off shore, in the Roads, and that the Secretary of State had not yet seen or communicated with them. I ascertained that Major Eckert had literally complied with his instructions, and I saw, for the first time, the answer of the Richmond gentlemen to him, which, in his despatch to me of the 1st, he characterizes as "not satisfactory." That answer is as follows, to wit:

CITY POINT, VIRGINIA, *February* 1, 1865.

MAJOR: Your note, delivered by yourself this day, has been considered. In reply, we have to say that we were furnished with a copy of the letter of President Lincoln to Francis P. Blair, Esq., of the 18th of January ultimo, another copy of which is appended to your note. Our instructions are contained in a letter, of which the following is a copy:

RICHMOND, *January* 28, 1865.

In conformity with the letter of Mr. Lincoln, of which the foregoing is a copy, you are to proceed to Washington city for informal conference with him upon the issues involved in the existing war, and for the purpose of securing peace to the two countries.

With great respect, your obedient servant,
JEFFERSON DAVIS.

The substantial object to be obtained by the informal conference is, to ascertain upon what terms the existing war can be terminated honorably.

Our instructions contemplate a personal interview between President Lincoln and ourselves at Washington city, but with this explanation we are ready to meet any person or persons that President Lincoln may appoint, at such place as he may designate. Our earnest desire is, that a just and honorable peace may be agreed upon, and we are prepared to receive or to submit propositions which may, possibly, lead to the attainment of that end.

Very respectfully yours,
ALEXANDER H. STEPHENS.
R. M. T. HUNTER.
JNO. A. CAMPBELL.

THOMAS T. ECKERT, *Major, and A. D. C.*

A note of these gentlemen, subsequently addressed to General Grant, has already been given in Major Eckert's despatch of the 1st instant.

I also here saw, for the first time, the following note, addressed by the Richmond gentlemen to Major Eckert:

CITY POINT, VA., *February* 2, 1865.

MAJOR: In reply to your verbal statement, that your instructions did not allow you to alter the conditions upon which a passport could be given to us, we say that we are willing to proceed to Fortress Monroe, and there to have an informal conference, with any person or persons that President Lincoln may appoint, on the basis of his letter to Francis P. Blair of the 18th of January ultimo, or upon any other terms or conditions that he may hereafter propose, not inconsistent with the essential principles of self-government and popular rights upon which our institutions are founded.

It is our earnest wish to ascertain, after a free interchange of ideas and information, upon what principles and terms, if any, a just and honorable peace can be established without the further effusion of blood, and to contribute our utmost efforts to accomplish such a result.

We think it better to add, that, in accepting your passport we are not to be understood as committing ourselves to anything, but to carry to this informal conference the views and feelings above expressed.

Very respectfully yours, &c.,
ALEXANDER H. STEPHENS.
J. A. CAMPBELL.
R. M. T. HUNTER.

THOMAS T. ECKERT, *Major, and A. D. C.*

NOTE.—The above communication was delivered to me at Fort Monroe at 4.30 P. M., February 2d, by Lieutenant Colonel Babcock, of General Grant's staff.

THOMAS T. ECKERT,
Major, and A. D. C.

On the morning of the 3d, the three gentlemen, Messrs. Stephens, Hunter, and Campbell, came aboard of our steamer, and had an interview with the Secretary of State and myself, of several hours' duration. No question of preliminaries to the meeting was then and there made or mentioned. No other person was present; no papers were exchanged or produced; and it was, in advance, agreed that the conversation was to be informal and verbal merely.

On our part, the whole substance of the instructions to the Secretary of State, hereinbefore recited, was stated and insisted upon, and nothing was said inconsistent therewith; while, by the other party, it was not said that in any event or on any condition, they *ever* would consent to re-union; and yet they equally omitted to declare that they *never* would so consent. They seemed to desire a postponement of that question, and the adoption of some other course first which, as some of them seemed to argue, might or might not lead to re-union; but which course, we thought, would amount to an indefinite postponement. The conference ended without result.

The foregoing, containing as is believed all the information sought, is respectfully submitted.

ABRAHAM LINCOLN.

EXECUTIVE MANSION, *February* 10, 1865.

MESSAGE TO THE SENATE.

To the Senate of the United States:

In answer to the resolution of the Senate, of the 8th instant,* requesting information concerning recent conversations or communications with insurgents, under executive sanction, I transmit a report from the Secretary of State, to whom the resolution was referred.

ABRAHAM LINCOLN.

WASHINGTON, *February* 10, 1865.

—

To the PRESIDENT:

The Secretary of State, to whom was referred a resolution of the Senate of the 8th instant, requesting "the President of the United States, if, in his opinion, not incompatible with the public interests, to furnish to the Senate any

* The resolution was offered by Mr. SUMNER, and is as follows:

Resolved, That the President of the United States be requested, if in his opinion not incompatible with the public interest, to furnish to the Senate any information in his possession concerning recent conversations or communications with certain rebels, said to have been under executive sanction, including communications with the rebel Jefferson Davis, and any correspondence relative thereto.

This amendment, offered by Mr. SAULSBURY, was rejected:

And that he be also requested to inform the Senate whether he, or others acting under his authority, did not require, as a condition to reunion, the acquiescence of said persons mentioned in said resolution, or of the public authorities of the so-called Confederate States, in the abolition of slavery in said States; and also, whether he, or those acting by his authority, did not require as a condition to negotiation that the said confederates should lay down their arms. And that he be requested to inform the Senate fully in reference to everything connected with or occurring in said conference or conferences in relation to the subject matter of said conferences. And also that he be requested to state whether or not an armistice was not asked for by Messrs. Stephens, Hunter, and Campbell, with the view to prepare the minds of the Southern people for peace and reunion of the States.

information in his possession concerning recent conversations or communications with certain rebels, said to have taken place under executive sanction, including communications with the rebel Jefferson Davis, and any correspondence relating thereto," has the honor to report that the Senate may properly be referred to a special message of the President bearing upon the subject of the resolution, and transmitted to the House this day. Appended to this report is a copy of an instruction which has been addressed to Charles Francis Adams, Esq., envoy extraordinary and minister plenipotentiary of the United States at London, and which is the only correspondence found in this department touching the subject referred to in the resolution.

Respectfully submitted.

WILLIAM H. SEWARD.

DEPARTMENT OF STATE,
WASHINGTON, *February* 10, 1865.

MR. SEWARD TO MR. ADAMS.

No. 1258.] DEPARTMENT OF STATE,
WASHINGTON, *February* 7, 1865.

SIR: It is a truism that in times of peace there are always instigators of war. So soon as a war begins there are citizens who impatiently demand negotiations for peace. The advocates of war, after an agitation, longer or shorter, generally gain their fearful end, though the war declared is not unfrequently unnecessary and unwise. So peace agitators in time of war ultimately bring about an abandonment of the conflict, sometimes without securing the advantages which were originally expected from the conflict.

The agitators for war in time of peace, and for peace in time of war, are not necessarily, or perhaps ordinarily, unpatriotic in their purposes or motives. Results alone determine whether they are wise or unwise. The treaty of peace concluded at Guadalupe Hidalgo was secured by an irregular negotiator, under the ban of the government. Some of the efforts which have been made to bring about negotiations with a view to end our civil war are known to the whole world, because they have employed foreign as well as domestic agents. Others, with whom you have had to deal confidentially, are known to yourself, although they have not publicly transpired. Other efforts have occurred here which are known only to the persons actually moving in them and to this government. I am now to give, for your information, an account of an affair, of the same general character, which recently received much attention here, and which, doubtless, will excite inquiry abroad.

A few days ago Francis P. Blair, Esq., of Maryland, obtained from the President a simple leave to pass through our military lines, without definite views known to the government. Mr. Blair visited Richmond, and on his return he showed to the President a letter which Jefferson Davis had written to Mr. Blair, in which Davis wrote that Mr. Blair was at liberty to say to President Lincoln that Davis was now, as he always had been, willing to send commissioners, if assured they would be received, or to receive any that should be sent; that he was not disposed to find obstacles in forms. He would send commissioners to confer with the President, with a view to a restoration of peace between the two countries, if he could be assured they would be received. The President thereupon, on the 18th of January, addressed a note to Mr. Blair, in which the President, after acknowledging that he had read the note of Mr. Davis, said that he was, is, and always should be willing to receive any agents that Mr. Davis or any other influential person now actually resisting the authority of the government might send to confer informally with the President, with a view to the restoration of peace to the people of our one common country. Mr. Blair visited Richmond with this letter, and then again came back to Washington. On the 29th instant we were advised from the camp of Lieutenant General Grant that Alexander H. Stephens, R. M. T. Hunter, and John A. Campbell were applying for leave to pass through the lines to Washington, as peace commissioners, to confer with the President. They were permitted by the Lieutenant General to come to his headquarters, to await there the decision of the President. Major Eckert was sent down to meet the party from Richmond at General Grant's headquarters. The major was directed to deliver to them a copy of the President's letter to Mr. Blair, with a note to be addressed to them, and signed by the major, in which they were directly informed that if they should be allowed to pass our lines they would be understood as coming for an informal conference, upon the basis of the aforenamed letter of the 18th of January to Mr. Blair. If they should express their assent to this condition in writing, then Major Eckert was directed to give them safe conduct to Fortress Monroe, where a person coming from the President would meet them. It being thought probable, from a report of their conversation with Lieutenant General Grant, that the Richmond party would, in the manner prescribed, accept the condition mentioned, the Secretary of State was charged by the President with the duty of representing this government in the expected informal conference. The Secretary arrived at Fortress Monroe in the night of the first day of February. Major Eckert met him in the morning of the second of February with the information that the persons who had come from Richmond had not accepted, in writing, the condition upon which he was allowed to give them conduct to Fortress Monroe. The major had given the same information by telegraph to the President, at Washington. On receiving this information, the President prepared a telegram directing the Secretary to return to Washington. The Secretary was preparing, at the same moment, to so return, without waiting for instructions from the President; but at this juncture Lieutenant General Grant telegraphed to the Secretary of War, as well as to the Secretary of State, that the party from Richmond had reconsidered and accepted the conditions tendered them through Major Eckert, and General Grant urgently advised the President to confer in person with the Richmond party. Under these circumstances, the Secretary, by the President's direction, remained at Fortress Monroe, and the President joined him there on the night of the 2d of February. The Richmond party was brought down the James river in a United States steam transport during the day, and the transport was anchored in Hampton Roads.

On the morning of the 3d the President, attended by the Secretary, received Messrs. Stephens, Hunter, and Campbell on board the United States steam transport River Queen, in Hampton Roads. The conference was altogether informal. There was no attendance of secretaries, clerks, or other witnesses. Nothing was written or read. The conversation, although earnest and free, was calm, and courteous, and kind on both sides. The Richmond party approached the discussion rather indirectly, and at no time did they either make categorical demands, or tender formal stipulations, or absolute refusals. Nevertheless, during the conference, which lasted four hours, the several points at issue between the government and the insurgents were distinctly raised, and discussed fully, intelligently, and in an amicable spirit. What the insurgent party seemed chiefly to favor was a postponement of the question of separation, upon which the war is waged, and a mutual direction of efforts of the government, as well as those of the insurgents, to some extrinsic policy or scheme for a season, during which passions might be expected to subside, and the armies be reduced, and trade and intercourse between the people of both sections resumed. It was suggested by them that through such postponement we might now have immediate peace, with some not very certain prospect of an ultimate satisfactory adjustment of political relations between this government and the States, section, or people now engaged in conflict with it.

This suggestion, though deliberately considered, was nevertheless regarded by the President as one of armistice or truce, and he announced that we can agree to no cessation or suspension of hostilities, except on the basis of the disbandment of the insurgent forces, and the restoration of the national authority throughout all the States in the Union. Collaterally, and in subordination to the proposition which was thus announced, the anti-slavery policy of the United States was reviewed in all its bearings, and the President announced that he must not be expected to depart from the positions he had heretofore assumed in his proclamation of emancipation and other documents, as these positions were reiterated in his last annual message. It was further declared by the President that the complete restoration of the national authority everywhere was an indispensable condition of any assent on our part to whatever form of peace might be proposed. The President assured the other party that, while he must adhere to these positions, he would be prepared, so far as power is lodged with the Executive, to exercise liberality. His power, however, is limited by the Constitution; and when peace should be made, Congress must necessarily act in regard to appropriations of money and to the admission of representatives from the insurrectionary States. The Richmond party were then informed that Congress had, on the 31st ultimo, adopted by a constitutional majority a joint resolution submitting to the several States the proposition to abolish slavery throughout the Union, and that there is every reason to expect that it will be soon accepted by three-fourths of the States, so as to become a part of the national organic law.

The conference came to an end by mutual acquiesence, without producing an agreement of views upon the several matters discussed, or any of them. Nevertheless, it is perhaps of some importance that we have been able to submit our opinions and views directly to prominent insurgents, and to hear them in answer in a courteous and not unfriendly manner.

I am, sir, your obedient servant,

WILLIAM H. SEWARD.

DAVIS'S ACCOUNT OF THE CONFERENCE.

To the Senate and House of Representatives of the Confederate States of America:

Having recently received a written notification which satisfied me that the President of the United States was disposed to confer informally with unofficial agents which might be sent by me, with a view to the restoration of peace, I requested the Hon. Alexander H. Stephens, the Hon. R. M. T. Hunter, and the Hon. John A. Campbell to proceed through our lines and to hold conference with Mr. Lincoln, or any one he might depute to represent him.

I herewith transmit, for the information of Congress, the report of the eminent citizens above named, showing that the enemy refused to enter into negotiations with the Confederate States, or any one of them separately, or to give to our people any other terms or guaranties than those which the conqueror may grant, or to permit us to have peace on any other basis than our unconditional submission to their rule, coupled with the acceptance of their recent legislation on the subject of the relations between the white and black population of each State. Such is, as I understand, the effect of the amendment to the Constitution which has been adopted by the Congress of the United States. JEFFERSON DAVIS.

EXECUTIVE OFFICE, RICHMOND, *Feb.* 6, 1865.

RICHMOND, VA., *Feb.* 5, 1865.

To the PRESIDENT OF THE CONFEDERATE STATES:

SIR: Under your letter of appointment of the 28th ult., we proceeded to seek an "informal conference" with Abraham Lincoln, President of the United States, upon the subject mentioned in the letter. The conference was granted, and took place on the 3d instant, on board of a steamer in Hampton Roads, where we met President Lincoln and the Hon. Mr. Seward, Secretary of State of the United States. It continued for several hours, and was both full and explicit.

We learned from them that the message of President Lincoln to the Congress of the United States in December last explains clearly and distinctly his sentiments as to the terms, conditions, and method of proceeding by which peace can be secured to the people, and we were not informed that they would be modified or altered to obtain that end. We understand from him that no terms or proposals of any treaty or agreement looking to an ultimate settlement would be entertained or made by him with the Confederate States, because that would be a recognition of their existence as a separate power, which, under no circumstances, would be done; and for like reasons that no such terms would be entertained by him from the States separately; that no extended truce or armistice (as at present advised) would be granted, without a satisfactory assurance in advance of a complete restoration of the authority of the United States over all places within the States of the Confederacy.

That whatever consequence may follow from the reestablishment of that authority must be accepted; but that individuals subject to pains and penalties under the laws of the United States might rely upon a very liberal use of the power confided to him to remit those pains and penalties if peace be restored.

During the conference the proposed amendment to the Constitution of the United States, adopted by Congress on the 31st ultimo, was brought to our notice. This amendment declares that neither slavery nor involuntary servitude, except for crimes, should exist within the United States, or any place within their jurisdiction, and that Congress should have power to enforce this amendment by appropriate legislation.*

Of all the correspondence that preceded the conference herein mentioned, and leading to the same, you have heretofore been informed.

Very respectfully, your obedient servants,

ALEX. H. STEPHENS,
R. M. T. HUNTER,
JOHN A. CAMPBELL.†

DAVIS AND THE RICHMOND ADMINISTRATION ON PEACE.

February 6—A public meeting was held in Richmond, to respond to the terms of peace offered by Davis. Rev. Dr. Burrows, of the Baptist Church, made an opening prayer. Governor Smith spoke, followed by Jefferson Davis, whose speech is thus reported in the Richmond *Dispatch* of the 7th:

Upon the subject of the recent Peace Commission, President Davis said that for himself he had never entertained much hope of effecting honorable terms so long as our cause was meeting with reverses; but under the circumstances, when semi-official representation had so frequently visited our government, intimating that negotiations might result in a satisfactory adjustment of our difficulties, when it was plain that the sufferings of the people dictated that every effort on his part should be made to bring about a cessation of hostilities, he felt it his duty, as he had always done, to appoint those whom he regarded as among the best men we had, who were most calculated to heal the existing breach which severed us, and obtain that independence for the Confederacy from the Federal government which no other power on the face of earth but Yankees would think of denying. As to conditions of peace, President Davis emphatically asserted that none save the independence of the Confederacy could ever receive his sanction. He had embarked in the cause with a full knowledge of the tremendous odds against us. But with the approval of a just Providence, which he conscienticusly believed was on our side, and a united resolve of our people, he doubted not that victory would yet crown our labors. In his correspondence with Mr. Lincoln, that functionary had always spoken of the United States and Confederacy as our afflicted country; but in his replies he —the speaker—had never failed to refer to them as separate

---

* Letter from General Grant in 1862, on reconstruction:

VICKSBURG, MISSISSIPPI, *August* 30, 1862.

Hon. E. B. WASHBURNE:

DEAR SIR: * * * The people of the North need not quarrel over the institution of slavery. What Vice President Stephens acknowledges the corner-stone of the Confederacy is already knocked out. Slavery is already dead and cannot be resurrected. It would take a standing army to maintain slavery in the South, if we were to make peace to-day, guaranteeing to the South all their former constitutional privileges. I never was an abolitionist; not even what could be called anti-slavery; but I try to judge fairly and honestly, and it became patent to my mind early in the rebellion, that the North and South could never live at peace with each other except as one nation, and that without slavery. As anxious as I am to see peace established, I would not, therefore, be willing to see any settlement until this question is forever settled.

Your sincere friend,

U. S. GRANT.

† Intercepted letter of John A. Campbell:

CONFEDERATE STATES OF AMERICA,
WAR DEPARTMENT, RICHMOND, VA.,
September 13, 1864.

DEAR SIR: Your letter of the 31st ultimo, was received to-day. Your appointment has been made, and the commission sent to Madison, Georgia. It is difficult to form any opinion as to prospects before us. It is very apparent that the people in both sections of the late Union earnestly desire peace, and that the principal difficulty lies in the settlement of the terms. The sentiment of the Northern people in favor of a restoration of the Union has been constantly growing, especially among the better classes of the population. They have discovered that alone they will be the victims of a turbulent Democracy, who have no control over themselves and will exact no responsibility from their leaders as rulers. They are not willing to rely upon their own capacity to govern themselves. With Union this class would make peace on any terms and would modify their Constitution to meet our views. But this is not the governing class at the North, and I do not see that any modification of their Constitution can be made, nor how any guaranties can be given. Any peace on the terms of Union will have to be made on the terms of their present Union. No administration at the North can offer more or could fulfill any agreement to do more. The issue, therefore, that is presented to us, is a return to the conditions of 1860, or independence. In my judgment all discussion of the question in any other form is a useless, if not a pernicious discussion. I do not think that any considerable party at the North is prepared to adopt the alternative we propose, and no considerable party at the South is prepared to adopt the alternative proposed by our enemies. I am not, therefore, yet hopeful of peace. But events seem to be hastening onward towards a termination of the war, and in the termination of the war, a solution of the terms of a settlement must take place. I do not venture to predict what that settlement will be. A civil commotion at the North—defeats of our armies—defeats of the Northern armies will affect these. None can decide when any of these events may occur. I fear that my answer will not be very satisfactory. But I cannot reduce the question of peace to the category of the "How."

Respectfully yours,

J. A. CAMPBELL.

Mr. JOEL A. BELLUPS.

and distinct governments, and sooner than we should ever be united again he would be willing to yield up everything he had on earth, and if it were possible would sacrifice a thousand lives before he would succumb.

He concluded by exhorting those at home who are able to bear arms to unite with those already in the army in repelling the foe, believing that thereby we would compel the Yankees in less than twelve months to petition us for peace upon our own terms.

These resolutions were adopted:

Whereas, The Commonwealth of Virginia, in concert with other American States, did, in the year 1776, solemnly set forth that when any form of government becomes destructive of the happiness or dangerous to the liberties of the people, it is the right and the duty of the people to alter or abolish it, in pursuance whereof they did declare themselves independent States; *and whereas,* her separate independence, and that of the co-acting States, was afterwards acknowledged by the world; *and whereas,* Virginia did subsequently form with other States a common Government or agency for the management of their foreign affairs and other specified general purposes, which said common Government or agency, received no other or further recognition by foreign powers than as representatives of the several State sovereignties already recognized; *and whereas,* Virginia, in entering into this association of federation, did expressly reserve for herself, and therefore for her co-States, co-States' rights which attached to the act itself of resuming the powers whensoever the same might be perverted to their injury or oppression; *and whereas,* the Commonwealth of Virginia did in sovereign convention, in April, 1861, decide and determine that circumstances had arrived which made it her imperative duty, as it was her indisputable right, to withdraw from the association known as the United States of America, and resume her separate sovereignty; *and whereas,* this legitimate act has been followed by an atrocious war upon her and upon the States with which she subsequently formed a new confederation, by the States from which she and they withdrew, for the purpose of subjecting her and them to the absolute and tyrannical domination of the United States; *and whereas,* after four years of hostilities, conducted on the part of our enemies with a barbarity equalled only by the wickedness of their designs, their authorities did invite a conference with a view to the establishment of peace, which invitation was responded to by the Confederate authorities; *and whereas,* it appears from the report of the Confederate Commissioners to said conference that it was declared on the part of our enemy that nothing should terminate the existing war *but our unconditional submission to their yoke,* and the acknowledgment of their absolute authority; that their laws for the confiscation of our property and execution of our citizens should be enforced by the judges and other officers whom they would appoint for that purpose; that the only palliation of our wretchedness should be the voluntary mercy of those who for four years have murdered our people and ravaged our homes; that our social system shall be immediately upturned and hereafter regulated at their will; that the uniform which our soldiers have made so honorable must be stripped from their persons, and the flag under which they have so often marched to victory must be trailed in the dust and thrown away forever; therefore be it

Resolved, That we, the citizens here assembled, do spurn with the indignation due to so gross an insult, the terms on which the President of the United States has proffered peace to the people of the Confederate States.

Resolved, That the circumstances under which that proffer has been made add to the outrage, and stamp it as a designed and premeditated indignity to our people.

Resolved, That our profoundest gratitude is due to the soldiers who for four years have maintained our liberties against the utmost efforts of our enemies, and that while we look to them to illustrate in future feats of the past, we will sustain their efforts by every means and resource at our command.

Resolved, That in His presence, and in the face of the world, reverently invoking thereto the aid of Almighty God, we renew our resolve to maintain our liberties and independence; and to this we mutually pledge our lives, our fortunes, and our sacred honor.

February 9—A war meeting was held in Richmond, at which R. M. T. Hunter presided. Secretary Benjamin, Hugh W. Sheffey, and others spoke. The following resolutions were adopted:

Whereas, While the existing war between the United States and the Confederate States has been and still is a war of conquest on the part of the former, it has been waged by the latter in defence of life, liberty, and property, and to secure the right of self-government for the people; and

Whereas, The President of the United States has recently declared that there is no government or authority, either State or Confederate, within the Confederate States, with which he can make any terms, and that there can be no peace until the Confederate States shall lay down their arms and submit to the authority of the Government of the United States, and accept the laws of the same, some of which threaten our people with all that is degrading in subjugation, and all that is cruel in conquest; now, therefore, be it

Resolved, First, That the events which have occurred during the progress of the war have but confirmed our original determination to strike for our independence, and that, with the blessing of God, we will never lay down our arms until it shall have been won. [Wild and long continued cheering followed the reading of this resolution.]

Secondly, That as we believe our resources to be sufficient for the purpose, we do not doubt that we shall conduct the war successfully, and to that issue, and we hereby invoke the people, in the name of the holiest of all causes, to spare neither their blood nor their treasure in its maintenance and support.

Thirdly, That we tender our thanks to our soldiers in the field for their noble efforts in behalf of the country, its rights and its liberties, and take this occasion to assure them that no effort of ours shall be spared to assist them in maintaining the great cause to which we hereby devote ourselves and our all.

CORRESPONDENCE OF GENS. LEE AND GRANT, ON A MILITARY CONVENTION.

RICHMOND, VA., *March* 13, 1865.

To the Senate and House of Representatives:

I herewith transmit for your information copies of the correspondence referred to in my message of this date, in regard to the proposed conference to adjust terms of peace by means of a military convention.

JEFFERSON DAVIS.

HEADQUARTERS C. S. ARMIES, *March* 2, 1865.

Lieut. Gen. U. S. GRANT,
Commanding United States Armies:

GENERAL: Lieut. Gen. Longstreet has informed me that, in a recent conversation between himself and Maj. Gen. Ord, as to the possibility of arriving at a satisfactory adjustment of the present unhappy difficulties by means of a military convention, Gen. Ord stated that if I desired to have an interview with you on the subject, you would not decline, provided I had authority to act. Sincerely desiring to leave nothing untried which may put an end to the calamities of war, I propose to meet you at such convenient time and place as you may designate, with the hope that, upon an interchange of views, it may be found practicable to submit the subjects of controversy between the belligerents to a convention of the kind mentioned.

In such event, I am authorized to do whatever the result of the proposed interview may render necessary or advisable. Should you accede to this proposition, I would suggest that, if agreeable to you, we meet at the place selected by Gens. Ord and Longstreet for the interview, at 11 A. M. on Monday next.

Very respectfully your obedient servant,

R. E. LEE, *General.*

HEADQUARTERS ARMIES U. S., *March* 4, 1865.

Gen. R. E. LEE,
Commanding C. S. Armies:

GENERAL: Your two letters of the 2d instant were received yesterday. In regard to any apprehended misunderstanding in reference to the exchange of political prisoners, I think there need be none. Gen. Ord or Gen. Longstreet has probably misunderstood what I said to the former on the subject, or I may have failed to make myself understood, possibly. A few days before the interview between Generals Longstreet and Ord, I had received a despatch from Gen. Hoffman, Commissary General of Prisoners, stating in substance that all prisoners of war who were or had been in close confinement or irons, whether under charges or sentences, had been ordered to City Point for exchange. I forwarded the substance of that despatch to Lieut. Col. Mulford, Assistant Agent of Exchange, and presumed it probable that he had communicated it to Col. Robert Ould. A day or two after, an offender, who was neither a prisoner of war nor a political prisoner, was executed, after a fair and impartial trial, and in accordance with the laws of war and the usage of civilized nations. It was in explanation of this class of cases I told Gen. Ord to speak to Gen. Longstreet.

Reference to my letter of February 16 will show my understanding on the subject of releasing political or citizen prisoners.

In regard to meeting you on the 6th inst., I would state

that I have no authority to accede to your proposition for a conference on the subject proposed. Such authority is vested in the President of the United States alone.

Gen. Ord could only have meant that I would not refuse an interview on any subject on which I have a right to act; which, of course, would be such as are purely of a military character, and on the subject of exchange, which has been entrusted to me.

I have the honor to be, very respectfully, your obedient servant, U. S. GRANT, *Lieut. Gen.*

RICHMOND, VA., *Feb.* 28.

Gen. R. E. LEE, *Commanding, &c.:*

GENERAL: You will learn by the letter of Gen. Longstreet the result of his second interview with Gen. Ord. The points as to whether yourself or Gen. Grant should invite the other to a conference is not worth discussing. If you think the statements of Gen. Ord render it probably useful that the conference suggested should be had, you will proceed as you may prefer, and are clothed with all the supplemental authority you may need in the consideration of any proposition for a military convention, or the appointment of a commissioner to enter into such an arrangement as will cause at least temporary suspension of hostilities.

Very truly, yours,

JEFFERSON DAVIS.

RESOLUTION ON CONSTITUTIONAL POWERS.

1865, February 6—Mr. EDGERTON submitted the following resolution, and demanded the previous question on its adoption:

Whereas the *Daily Morning Chronicle*, of this city, the reputed political organ of the President, in recent editorials upon the subject of negotiations for peace, has referred to the President of the United States as having gone "in his sovereign capacity" to treat with the commissioners from Richmond, and has further described the President as "the sovereign head of the greatest Government on earth;" and whereas the supreme court of the District of Columbia has, by a late solemn adjudication, affirmed principles as the law of the land which recognized arbitrary dictatorial powers in the President, not only as to military but as to civil offenders, which are subversive of civil liberty and of the public welfare: therefore,

Resolved, (as the judgment of this House,) That the President of the United States is in no constitutional sense the sovereign thereof, but that all his governmental powers are derived from the Constitution and constitutional laws of the United States, and are limited by them; and this House sincerely deprecate all political teachings and judicial decisions having a tendency to exalt the President above the Constitution and laws, or to clothe him with attributes unknown to them, or to derogate from the powers of Congress; and they affirm that the principle that the people are sovereign, and that all departments of the Government are their agents or servants, and should be kept in strict subordination to the Constitution and laws, is essential to the permanence of republican government and to civil liberty.

Mr. BALDWIN (of Mass.) proposing to debate it, the resolution went over.

PROPOSITIONS FOR "PEACE."

IN SENATE.

1864, December 12—Mr. GARRETT DAVIS offered this resolution, which was ordered to be printed:

Joint resolution for the restoration of peace and the Union, the vindication of the Constitution, and the construction of additional and adequate guaranties of the rights and liberties of the people of the United States.

Resolved by the Senate and House of Representatives of the United States of America in Congress assembled, That a convention of all the States is the most appropriate agency by which to bring about the restoration of peace and the Union, the vindication of the Constitution, and the construction of additional and adequate guaranties of the rights and liberties of the people of the United States; and to promote these great ends, such a convention should be held, and should consider the following propositions as the basis of a lasting settlement of all difficulties between the belligerent States and people, and as amendments of the Constitution of the United States:

First. The States of Maine, New Hampshire, and Vermont to be formed into one State; the States of Massachusetts, Connecticut, and Rhode Island to be formed into one State; and the States of Maryland, Delaware, and the Eastern shore of Virginia to be formed into one State. But this consolidation of States to be for federal and national purposes only, unless the respective States to be formed into one shall otherwise determine.

Second. The President and the Vice President to be taken alternately from the free and slave States, and for the term of four years; but both not to be at the same time citizens of the free or slave states. No person who may have filled the office of President ever again to be eligible to it.

Third. The President and Vice President to be chosen in this manner: In the month of January next before the expiration of the presidential term for the time being, each State to select one of its own citizens, who shall be a native-born citizen of the United States, for the presidency or the vice presidency, the ensuing term, as such State may be a free or a slave State, and as the free or slave States may be entitled to the presidency or the vice presidency; and shall certify under the seal of State, by the governor thereof, to each house of Congress and to the Supreme Court of the United States, severally, the name of such citizen, and for which office he has been selected; and the two houses of Congress shall convene in the hall of the House the first Monday of February ensuing, and request the attendance of the Supreme Court, and when it shall be present, the certificates of the names of all the persons for the presidency that have been received shall be opened, and from those certified as herein directed the Supreme Court shall, in the presence of the two houses of Congress, choose a President, and then a Vice President, from the names so certified for that office. Whenever the office of President shall become vacant during the term, it shall devolve on the Vice President; and when the vice presidency so becomes vacant, the Senate shall, from its own body, and from the senators representing the free or the slave States, as they may differ on this point from the incumbent of the presidency, select a Vice President, to continue in office for the occasion; and thereupon the seat of the senator thus becoming Vice President shall be vacant. No justice of the Supreme Court to be eligible to any other office whatever.

Fourth. The President to have the power to remove from office the head of the Department of State; of the Treasury, War, Navy, and Interior Departments; the Attorney General; all diplomatic officers, whether of the grade of embassadors, commissioners, or charge d'affaires, and secretaries of legation. All other officers, except those holding office during good behaivior, whom the President is required to nominate to the Senate, he may suspend from their offices; but in making such suspensions he shall report each case, with the cause thereof, to the Senate, if it be in session, and if not, at its next session. In all cases where the Senate shall concur with the President, the suspension shall become an absolute removal; but as to those in which it does not concur before the end of the sssion to which the President is required to report them, the officers shall then, ipso facto, be reinstated in their respective offices. The President also to have power to remove all other civil officers, appointed by executive power, for incompetency to discharge their duties; for want of fidelity to the Constitution and laws of the United States, or for gross and habitual immorality; but to each officer thus removed he shall cause to be delivered a written statement of the cause of his removal, the truth and sufficiency of which the officer may try in the United States court held in the district in which he may have been performing his duties, on writ of quo warranto sued out against his successor in office, and a judgment thereon in his favor to have the effect to restore him to office.

Fifth. The absolute right, at all times, and under all conditions, of the people to the writ of habeas corpus, and to trial by jury in the mode prescribed by the Constitution, for capital or other offences, being indispensable to secure to them personal liberty, the freedom of religious opinion and worship, and the sanctity of church edifices, the freedom of speech and the press, and the right of the people at their elections to vote for those whom they prefer, without constraint, intimidation, and in faithful conformity to the laws, and under the exclusive direction of the proper officers of such elections; their right peaceably to assemble and freely to discuss and pronounce their opinions on all public measures, and the conduct of public officers; and to purchase and keep arms and munitions for their own defence; the exemption of all persons not in the military or naval service of the United States, or in the militia when in actual service in time of war or public danger, from military arrest, except when they are within the actual lines of some corps in time of war or public danger, and when arrested under such circumstances to be at once handed over to the proper civil authorities; and the absolute immunity of such persons from trial or examination, under martial or military law, by military tribunals of any kind, or by any other law or courts than the civil contra-distinguished from the military; and of their persons, houses, papers, and effects from searches and seizures, without warrant or other process of law; the military power never to be brought into conflict with the civil authorities, but in all times where it is necessary and proper, to be employed to uphold the civil law and courts. The Constitution and laws of the United States made in pursuance of it, being the supreme law of the land, and continuously and under all circumstances of unimpaired validity, no other law or authority can have any effect to nullify, suspend, or limit their operation. And all acts of Congress not authorized by the Constitution, and all edicts and proclamations of the President, or orders of any military officer, in derogation of the Constitution or laws, being utterly null and void, the President having no power whatever that is not conferred by an express provision of the Constitution, or by some law of Congress passed in pursuance of it. And the only localities and conditions in which the Constitution, laws, and courts of the United States can be suspended, being when a portion of the country is occupied by a dominating hostile army; and as its rule is removed, theirs being resumed, the right of the people to all the sources of information, by the purchase of and transmission to them of all books, newspapers, and so forth, without any obstruction, and to free trade and commerce with their fellow-citizens of all the States, except so far as restricted by law. The personal rights, privileges, and liberties here set forth being the inheritance of the people of the United States, and the chief and inestimable fruits of human government, they shall always be held to be inviolable, and their infraction to be both a grievous private wrong to every person thereby injured, and also a public crime; and all persons who may commit it to become infamous, and to be further punished by laws to be passed for that purpose, without pardon or commutation.

Sixth. Each State to have the exclusive right and power to declare and establish, within its own limits, every subject of property and its local and domestic institutions, and to make all laws and regulations concerning them.

Seventh. Private property not to be taken for the United States, except to subserve some operation of the federal government authorized by the Constitution, and not until full and fair compensation shall have been made to its owner, or secured to him in a mode to be provided by law.

Eighth. No military necessity ever to originate or confer any power whatever, except with and for armed forces in the field or in garrison, and within their present actual lines, to supply the ordinary and necessary military wants of each force essential to the public service, immediate or impending, and so urgent as not to allow the delay which would be required for the action of the civil authority; and all power created or authorized by any military necessity to be exercised exclusively by the officer present and in the actual command of the force in which and where it arises. The United States to be bound to make full indemnity for the damage sustained by all persons from any acts done by any of its military officers under a real or supposed military necessity, and the officer to be also responsible to all persons injured by his abuse of power.

Ninth. No negro, or person whose mother or grandmother is or was a negro, to be a citizen of the United States.

Tenth. The enumeration in this proposition of certain rights and liberties of the people, and powers of the States, and of denials, restrictions, and limitations of powers to the United States, the federal government or its officers, not to be held to deny, or disparage any of the other rights and liberties of the people or powers of the States; and as to the United States, the federal government or any of its officers to confer or enlarge any power whatever.

Eleventh. In giving construction to the Constitution, this rule shall be inflexibly adhered to. All rights, liberties, or privileges assured by it to the people, or powers reserved to the States; and all denials, restrictions, or limitations of power to the United States, the federal government, or any of its officers, provided for by its particular, or express language, not to be abrogated, impaired, or in any way affected, by any of its general language or provisions, or by any implication resulting from it, or by any other law or laws whatsoever.

IN HOUSE OF REPRESENTATIVES.

1865, January 16—Mr. Cox offered the following resolution:

Whereas the country hails with manifestations of patriotic joy and congratulation the victories recently achieved by our brave armies; and whereas "the recognized object of war, at least among civilized and Christian nations, is an honorable and satisfactory peace; and that although we do not know that the insurgents are yet prepared to agree to any terms of pacification that our Government would or should deem acceptable, yet as there can be no possible harm resulting from ascertaining precisely what they are ready to do, and in order to refute the imputation that the Administration contemplates with satisfaction a continuance of hostilities for their own sake, on any ground of mere punctilio, or for any reason than because it is compelled by an absorbing regard for the very end of its existence;" and whereas "an established and rightly constituted Government," combating armed and menacing rebellion, should strain every nerve to overcome at the earliest moment the resistance it encounters, and should not merely welcome, but seek satisfactory (however informal) assurances that its end has been attained:" Therefore,

Resolved, That now, in this hour of victory, which is the hour of magnanimity, it is eminently the duty of the President, on the basis of the present "rightfully constituted Government," either to send or receive commissioners or agents with a view to national pacification and tranquillity, or by some other rational means known to civilized or Christian nations, secure the cessation of hostilities and the Union of the States.

Which was laid on the table—yeas 84, nays 51, as follows:

YEAS—Messrs. Alley, Allison, Ames, Anderson, Arnold, Ashley, *Baily*, John D. Baldwin, Baxter, Beaman, Boutwell, Boyd, Brandegee, Broomall, Ambrose W. Clark, Freeman Clarke, Cobb, Cole, Henry Winter Davis, Thomas T. Davis, Dawes, Deming, Dixon, Donnelly, Eckley, Eliot, Frank, Garfield, Gooch, Grinnell, Griswold, Higby, Hooper, Asahel W. Hubbard, John H. Hubbard, Ingersoll, Jenckes, Julian, Kasson, Kelley, Francis W. Kellogg, Knox, Littlejohn, Loan, Longyear, Marvin, McClurg, McIndoe, Samuel F. Miller, Morrill, Daniel Morris, Amos Myers, Leonard Myers, Norton, Orth, Patterson, Perham, Pike, Price, William H. Randall, Alexander H. Rice, John H. Rice, Edward H. Rollins, Schenck, Scofield, Sloan, Smith, Smithers, Spalding, Starr, Stevens, Thayer, Thomas, Upson, Van Valkenburgh, Ellihu B. Washburne, William B. Washburn, Webster, *Wheeler*, Williams, Wilder, Wilson, Windom, Worthington—84.

NAYS—Messrs. *Ancona*, *Augustus C. Baldwin*, *Bliss*, *Brooks*, *James S. Brown*, *Chanler*, *Coffroth*, *Cox*, *Cravens*, *Denison*, *Eden*, *Edgerton*, *Eldridge*, *English*, *Finck*, Hale, *Hall*, *Harrington*, *Charles M. Harris*, *Holman*, *William Johnson*, Orlando Kellogg, *Kernan*, *King*, *Law*, *Lazear*, *Le Blond*, *Long*, *Mallory*, *Marcy*, *McAllister*, *McDowell*, *McKinney*, *James R. Morris*, *Morrison*, *Noble*, *Pendleton*, *Radford*, *Samuel J. Randall*, *Robinson*, *Rogers*, *Ross*, *Scott*, *John B. Steele*, *Stiles*, *Townsend*, *Wadsworth*, *Chilton A. White*, *Joseph W. White*, *Fernando Wood*, *Yeaman*—51.

January 31—FERNANDO WOOD offered the following resolution, which was objected to, and laid over under the rule; and, February 6, was adopted without a division:

Resolved, That it is the duty of the President to maintain, in every constitutional and legal manner, the integrity of the American Union as formed by the fathers of the Republic, and in no event, and under no circumstances, to proffer or accept negotiations which shall admit by the remotest implication the existence of any other federal or confederate government within the territory of the United States.

February 4—Mr. INGERSOLL offered the following resolution, which was laid over, under the rule:

Whereas it is alleged that informal negotiations are now pending between the United States and the so-called Confederate States with a view to a restoration of peace: Therefore,

Be it resolved, That it is the deliberate and emphatic opinion of this House that no enduring peace can or should be made which shall ever recognize the traitorous leaders of this rebellion as citizens of the United States, entitled to equal rights, privileges and immunities with the loyal people thereof under the Constitution of the United States.

February 6—Mr Cox offered the following resolution:

Resolved, That the President of the United States, in endeavoring to ascertain the disposition of the insurgents in arms against the authority of the Federal Government, with a view to negotiations for peace and the restoration of the Union, is entitled to the gratitude of a suffering and distracted country; and that with a similar view he be respectfully requested to omit no reasonable exertions hereafter which may lead to the desired object, to wit, peace and Union.

Resolved, That, if not incompatible with the above object and the public interests, he be requested to communicate to this House all information leading to and connected with the recent negotiations.

He afterwards withdrew the second resolution. The House refused to lay the first reso-

lution on the table—yeas 30, nays 108, as follows:

YEAS—Messrs. Allison, *Augustus C. Baldwin*, Beaman, Brandegee, Freeman Clarke, Henry Winter Davis, Dawes, Driggs, *Edgerton*, Higby, John H. Hubbard, Jenckes, *William Johnson*, Julian, Francis W. Kellogg, Knox, Loan, L ng, Longyear, Marvin, McClurg, Morrill, *Rogers*, Sloan, Smithers, Stevens, Thomas, Upson, *Wadsworth*, Windom, —30.

NAYS—Messrs. *James C. Allen*, *William J. Allen*, Alley, Ames, *Ancona*, Arnold, Ashley, John D. Baldwin, Baxter, Blair, Blow, Boutwell, Boyd, Broomall, *James S. Brown*, William G. Brown, *Chanler*, Ambrose W. Clark, Clay, Cobb, *Coffroth*, *Cox*, *Cravens*, Thomas T. Davis, *Dawson*, Deming, Dumont, Eckley, *Eldridge*, Eliot, Farnsworth, *Finck*, Frank, *Ganson*, Garfield, Gooch, Grinnell, Hale, *Hall*, *Harding*, *Harrington*, *Benjamin G. Harris*, *Charles M. Harris*, *Herrick*, *Holman*, Hooper, Asahel W. Hubbard, Hulburd, *Hutchins*, Ingersoll, *Philip Johnson*, Kelley, Orlando Kellogg, *Law*, *Lazear*. *Le Blond*, McBride, McIndoe, *McKinney*, *Middleton*, Samuel F. Miller, Daniel Morris, *Morrison*, Amos Myers, *Noble*, Norton, *Odell*, Charles O'Neill, *John O'Neill*, Orth, Patterson, *Pendleton*, Perham, *Perry*, Pike, Pomeroy, Price, *Pruyn*, William H. Randall, Alexander H. Rice, John H. Rice, Edward H. Rollins, *James S. Rollins*, *Ross*, Schenck, Scofield, *Scott*, Shannon, Spalding, *John B. Steele*, *Stiles*, *Strouse*, *Sweat*, *Townsend*, Tracy, Van Valkenburgh, *Ward*, Elihu B. Washburne, William B. Washburn, Whaley, Williams, Wilder, Wilson, *Winfield*, *Fernando Wood*, Woodbridge, Worthington, *Yeaman*—108.

The resolution went over, and was afterwards withdrawn.

1865, February 8—Mr. TOWNSEND offered the following resolution, which was objected, and was laid over, under the rule:

Resolved, That we hail with profound emotions of satisfaction the disposition of the Southern people to submit the questions that have so long drenched our land in blood to the arbitrament of reason rather than the sword; and we pledge our earnest efforts to sustain all measures looking to a settlement that an honorable Government, seeking to sustain its integrity, can offer.

1865, February 13—Mr. DAWSON offered the following resolution:

Whereas the American people have now been engaged in a civil war of gigantic dimensions for nearly four years, which has resulted in frightful destruction of life, property, and treasure, creating an enormous public debt, imposing the most oppressive taxes, covering the land with affliction, corrupting the general morals, and putting in peril the liberties of the nation; and whereas, on the part of the United States and the people of the States which adhere to this government, this is, and ought to be, a war solely to vindicate the Constitution and restore the laws to their just supremacy, and to that we are bound by our oaths and by our solemn pledges made in the face of the world when the war commenced: Therefore,

Resolved, That the President of the United States be requested to use all honorable and just means to bring about a lasting peace and the re-establishment of fraternal relations among all the people by a restoration of the Union upon the simple and just basis of the Constitution and laws, with every proper gurantee to the southern States that they shall be protected in the full enjoyment of their rights, and that undisturbed control of their own local affairs which the Federal Constitution was intended to secure to them and to us.

Which was laid on the table—yeas 73, nays 47, as follows:

YEAS—Messrs. Alley, Anderson, Ashley, *Baily*, John D. Baldwin, Beaman, Blaine, Boutwell, Boyd, Brandegee, Broomall, Ambrose W. Clark, Freeman Clarke, Cobb, Cole, Dawes, Deming, Dixon, Donnelly, Driggs, Eckley, Eliot, Garfield, Hale, Higby, Hooper, Asahel W. Hubbard, John H. Hubbard, Hulburd, Ingersoll, Julian, Kasson, Kelley, Francis W. Kellogg, Orlando Kellogg, Knox, Littlejohn, Longyear, Marvin, McBride, McClurg, McIndoe, Samuel F. Miller, Moorhead, Morrill, Daniel Morris, Amos Myers, Charles O'Neill, Orth, Perham, Pomeroy, William H. Randall, Alexander H. Rice, John H. Rice, Edward H. Rollins, Schenck, Scofield, Shannon, Smithers, Thayer, Thomas, Tracy, Upson, Van Valkenburgh, William B. Washburn, Webster, Whaley, Williams, Wilder, Wilson, Windom, Woodbridge, Worthington—73.

NAYS—Messrs. *James C. Allen*, *Ancona*, *Bliss*, *Brooks*, William G. Brown, *Chanler*, *Clay*, *Coffroth*, *Cox*, *Cravens*, *Dawson*, *Denison*, *Edgerton*, *Eldridge*, *Finck*, *Grider*, *Hall*, *Harding*, *Charles M. Harris*, *Herrick*, *Holman*, *Philip Johnson*, *William Johnson*, *Kalbfleisch*, *King*, *Lazear*, *Le Blond*, *Mallory*, *McAllister*, *Middleton*, *William H. Miller*, *James R. Morris*, *Morrison*, *Nelson*, *John O'Neill*, *Pendleton*, *Pruyn*, *James S. Rollins*, *Ross*, *William G. Steele*, *Stiles*, *Strouse*, *Sweat*, *Townsend*, *Wadsworth*, *Joseph W. White*, *Yeaman*—47.

1865, February 13—Mr. WILLIAMS offered the following resolutions:

Resolved, 1. That there is no power under the Constitution, in any branch of this Government, to treat with the States confederated in rebellion against it, either for the severance of this Union or for the abrogation of any article of its fundamental law.

Resolved, 2. That inasmuch as the said confederated States have taken up arms against the Government of the United States without any just provocation, and for the avowed purpose of asserting and establishing their independence thereof, and still persist in maintaining that position by armed resistance to its authority: and inasmuch also as the public authorities of this nation have not only declared, as was their duty, that they can accept no terms and entertain no propositions for anything short of absolute and unconditional submission to its laws, and with a clemency and magnanimity almost without example in history have proclaimed a general amnesty, without limits as to time, to such of the malefactors as shall return to their duty, with the exception only of the chief conspirators:

It is hereby declared to be the sense of this House that this Government has already exhausted all the resources of a just and wise statesmanship—except so far as regards the further earnest and vigorous prosecution of the war for the enforcement of the laws—in the effort to restore peace to this nation, and has, to this end, done all that a proper regard for its own interests can allow and all that a decent respect for the opinions of the world could demand of it; and that therefore any further overtures through embassies, public or private, official or unofficial, looking to treaty or compromise with the usurpers at Richmond, would be not only unprofitable, as they would be inconsistent with the rights and dignity of this nation, but are to be deprecated as absolutely mischievous, in giving encouragement to the insurgents and protracting their resistance, by exposing us to misconstruction, and giving color to the delusion that we mistrust our ability to subdue them to obedience, and are ready to accept something short of the restoration of the Union and the unconditional submission of those who have rebelled against it.

Which were laid on the table—yeas 72, nays 52, as follows:

YEAS—Messrs. *James C. Allen*. *William J. Allen*, Alley, Ames, *Ancona*, Anderson, *Baily*, Blair, *Bliss*, Boutwell, Brandegee, *Brooks*, *James S. Brown*, William G. Brown, *Chanler*, Ambrose W. Clark, *Clay*, *Coffroth*, *Cox*, *Cravens*, Dawes, *Dawson*, *Denison*, Dumont, Eckley, *Edgerton*, *Eldridge*, Eliot, *Finck*, Frank, Gooch, *Grider*, Hale, *Harding*, *Benjamin G. Harris*, *Charles M. Harris*, *Herrick*, *Holman*, Hooper, John H. Hubbard, *Hutchins*, *Philip Johnson*, *William Johnson*, *Kalbfleisch*, Kasson, Orlando Kellogg, *Law*, *Lazear*, *Le Blond*, *Long*, *Mallory*, *McKinney*, *Middleton*, *William H. Miller*, Morrill, *James R. Morris*, *Morrison*, *Nelson*, *Pendleton*, Pike, Pomeroy, *Pruyn*, Alexander H. Rice, *James S. Rollins*, *Ross*, Spalding, *William G. Steele*, *Stiles*, *Townsend*, *Wadsworth*, Webster, *Joseph W. White*—72.

NAYS—Messrs. Ashley, John D. Baldwin, Baxter, Beaman, Blaine, Boyd, Broomall, Freeman Clarke, Cobb, Cole, Dixon, Donnelly, Driggs, Higby, Asahel W. Hubbard, Hulburd, Ingersoll, Julian, Kelley, Francis W. Kellogg, Knox, Loan, Longyear, Marvin, McClurg, McIndoe, Moorhead, Daniel Morris, Amos Myers, Charles O'Neill, Orth, Patterson, Perham, Wm. H. Randall, John H. Rice, Edward H. Rollins, Schenck, Scofield, Shannon, Smithers, Starr, Thayer, Tracy, Upson, Van Valkenburgh, William B. Washburn, Williams, Wilder, Wilson, Windom, Woodbridge, Worthington—52.

REPUDIATION OF REBEL DEBT.

IN SENATE.

1865, February 17—Mr. SUMNER submitted the following resolution, which was objected to, but adopted at the evening session without a division:

Whereas certain persons have put in circulation the report that on the suppression of the rebellion the rebel debt or loan may be recognized in whole or in part by the United States; and whereas such a report is calculated to give a false value to such rebel debt or loan: Therefore,

Resolved by the Senate, (the House of Representatives concurring,) That Congress hereby declares that the rebel debt or loan is simply an agency of the rebellion which the United States can never, under any circumstances, recognize in any part or in any way.

IN HOUSE OF REPRESENTATIVES.

March 3, 1865—It passed. There were a few voices in the negative, but no division was called.

Reconstruction of States.

(See pages 317—332, 436—441.)

IN HOUSE OF REPRESENTATIVES.

1864, December 20—Mr. Ashley reported from the Select Committee a bill to guarantee to certain States whose governments have been usurped or overthrown, a republican form of government; which was reported modified January 16, 1865. It authorized the appointment by the President, with the consent of the Senate, in each State declared in rebellion a provisional governor, with the pay and emoluments of a brigadier general, to be charged with the civil administration prior to the recognition of a State government, and with the execution of the laws of the United States and the laws in force when the State government was overthrown; but no law or usage whereby any person was heretofore held in involuntary servitude shall be recognized or enforced by any court or officer in such State; and the laws for the trial and punishment of white persons shall extend to all persons, and jurors shall have the qualifications of voters under this law for delegates to the convention. The appointment by the President of other necessary officers is authorized. The expenses of the civil government to be borne by taxes laid in conformity with prior State laws. Sections 4, 5, 6, and 15 are as follows:

That all persons held to involuntary servitude or labor in the States or parts of States in which such persons have been declared free by any proclamation of the President, are hereby emancipated and discharged therefrom, and they and their posterity shall be forever free. And if any such person or their posterity shall be restrained of liberty, under pretence of any claim to such service or labor, the courts of the United States shall, on *habeas corpus*, discharge them.

That if any person declared free by this act, or any law of the United States, or any proclamation of the President, be restrained of liberty, with intent to be held in or reduced to involuntary servitude or labor, the person convicted before a court of competent jurisdiction of such act shall be punished by fine of not less than $1,500, and be imprisoned not less than five nor more than twenty years.

That every person who shall hereafter hold or exercise any office, civil or military, except offices merely ministerial and military offices below the grade of colonel in the rebel service, State or confederate, is hereby declared not to be a citizen of the United States.

That the United States, in Congress assembled, do hereby recognize the government of the State of Louisiana, inaugurated under and by the convention which assembled on the 6th day of April, A. D. 1864, at the city of New Orleans; and the government of the State of Arkansas, inaugurated under and by the convention which assembled on the 8th day of January, 1864, at the city of Little Rock: *Provided*, That the same or other conventions, duly assembled, shall first have incorporated into the constitutions of those States, respectively, the conditions prescribed in the twelfth section of this act, and the marshal of the United States shall have returned to the President of the United States the enrollment directed by the seventh section to be made and returned to the provisional governor, and it shall appear thereby that the persons taking the oath to support the Constitution of the United States, together with the citizens of the United States from such State in the military or naval service of the United States, amount to a majority of the persons enrolled in the State. And the President shall, thereupon, by proclamation, declare the recognition by the United States, in Congress assembled, of the said government of such State; and from the date of such proclamation the said government shall be entitled to the guarantee and all other rights of a State government under the Constitution of the United States; but this act shall not operate a recognition of a State government in either of said States till the conditions aforesaid are complied with, and till that time those States shall be subject to this law.

Other sections provide for an enrollment, on the sufficient return of the people of any State to their obedience to the Constitution, of all white male citizens of the United States resident in the State in their respective counties, and upon a majority (including those in the United States military and naval service) taking the oath of allegiance, the loyal people are to elect delegates equal in number to the number of both houses of the State Legislature. The voters are the loyal male citizens of the United States, of the age of twenty-one years, and enrolled and resident at the time in the district in which they offer to vote, and those absent in the military service of the United States. "No person who has held or exercised any office, civil or military, State or confederate, under the rebel usurpation, or who has voluntarily borne arms against the United States, shall vote or be eligible to be elected as delegate at such election." If the Convention shall declare, on behalf of the people of the State, their submission to the Constitution and laws of the United States, and shall incorporate the following provisions into the Constitution of the State:

First. No person who has held or exercised any office, civil or military, except civil offices merely ministerial and military offices below the grade of colonel, State or confederate, under the usurping power, shall vote for or be a member of the legislature or governor.

Second. Involuntary servitude is forever prohibited, and the freedom of all persons is guaranteed in said State.

Third. No debt or confederate, created by or under the sanction of the usurping power, or in any manner in aid thereof, shall be recognized or paid by the State.

And the Constitution be then ratified by a majority of the voters qualified as aforesaid, the President shall, by proclamation, recognize the State government thus established, and from that date, senators and representatives, and presidential electors may be chosen.

1865, January 16—Mr. Kelley moved to amend by adding to the white citizens enrolled, "and all other male citizens of the United States who may be able to read the Constitution thereof."

Mr. Eliot moved the following as a substitute, the third section having been accepted by him when offered, as a separate proposition, by Mr. Arnold:

That the States declared to be in rebellion against the United States, and within which the authority of the Constitution and laws of the United States has been overthrown, shall not be permitted to resume their political relations with the government of the United States until, by action of the loyal citizens within such States, respectively, a State constitution shall be ordained and established, republican in form, forever prohibiting involuntary servitude within such State, and guaranteeing to all persons freedom and equality of rights before the law.

Sec. 2. That the State of Louisiana is hereby permitted to resume its political relations with the government of the United States under the constitution adopted by the convention which assembled on the sixth day of April, anno Domini eighteen hundred and sixty-four, at New Orleans.

Sec. 3. That in all that portion of the United States heretofore declared to be in rebellion against the United States, and enumerated in the President's proclamation of

January 1, 1863, slavery and involuntary servitude, otherwise than in the punishment of crime whereof the accused shall have been duly convicted, shall be, and the same hereby is, abolished and prohibited forever, and the reenslavement, or holding, or attempting to hold in slavery or involuntary servitude, any person within such States made free by this act, or declared to be free by the proclamation of the President of the United States, dated January 1, 1863, or of any of their descendants, otherwise than in the punishment of crime whereof the accused shall have been duly convicted, is and shall be forever prohibited, any law or regulation of either of said States to the contrary notwithstanding.

Mr. WILSON moved to substitute the following:

Senators and Representatives shall not be received from any State heretofore declared in rebellion against the United States until by an act or joint resolution of Congress, approved by the President, or passed notwithstanding his objections, such State shall have been first declared to have organized a just local government, republican in form, and to be entitled to representation in the respective Houses of Congress.

January 17—The bill was postponed to February,—yeas 103, nays 34.

February 21—Mr. ASHLEY offered, on behalf of the committee, a substitute, which differed chiefly in this respect from the original bill. The section recognizing the State governments of Louisiana and Arkansas was omitted, and this substituted for it:

That if the persons exercising the functions of Governor and Legislature under the rebel usurpation in any State heretofore declared to be in rebellion shall, before armed resistance to the national Government is suppressed in such State, submit to the authority of the United States, and take the oath to support the Constitution of the United States, and adopt by law the third provision prescribed in the eighth section of this act, and ratify the amendment to the Constitution of the United States proposed by Congress to the Legislatures of the several States on the 31st day of January, A. D. 1865, it shall be lawful for the President of the United States to recognize the said Governor and Legislature as the lawful State government of such State, and to certify the fact to Congress for its recognition: *Provided*, That nothing herein contained shall operate to disturb the boundary lines of any States heretofore recognized by and now represented in the Congress of the United States.

Mr. KELLEY's amendment was modified so as to provide for striking out the word "white" in the enrollment section.

Mr. WILSON modified his substitute, so as to make it read:

That Senators and Representatives shall not be received from any State heretofore declared in rebellion against the United States until Congress, by concurrent action of both Houses, shall have first declared a just local government, republican in form, to have been organized therein, and such State to be entitled to representation in the respective Houses of Congress.

Mr. ELIOT modified his, so as to make it read:

That the States declared to be in rebellion against the United States, and within which the authority of the Constitution and laws of the United States has been overthrown, shall not be permitted to resume their political relations with the Government of the United States, until, by action of the loyal citizens within such States respectively, a State constitution shall be ordained and established, republican in form, forever prohibiting involuntary servitude within said State, and guaranteeing to all persons freedom and equal rights before the law.

On motion of Mr. MALLORY, the bill was laid on the table—yeas 92, nays 64, as follows:

YEAS—Messrs. *James C. Allen*, *Ancona*, Anderson, *Baily*, *Augustus C. Baldwin*, Blair, *Bliss*, Boyd, William G. Brown, *Chanler*, *Clay*, Cobb, *Coffroth*, *Cox*, *Cravens*, Thomas T. Davis, Dawes, *Dawson*, *Denison*, Eckley, *Eden*, *Edgerton*, *Eldridge*, *English*, *Finck*, *Ganson*, Gooch, *Grider*, Griswold, Hale, *Hall*, *Harding*, *Harrington*, *Benjamin G. Harris*, *Charles M. Harris*, *Herrick*, *Holman*, Hulburd, *Hutchins*, Julian, *Kalbfleisch*, *Kernan*, *King*, *Knapp*, *Law*, *Lazear*, *Le Blond*, Littlejohn, *Long*, *Mallory*, *Marcy*, Marvin, *McAllister*, *McKinney*, *William H. Miller*, *James R. Morris*, *Morrison*, *Nelson*, *Noble*, *Odell*, *Pendleton*, Pike, Pomeroy, *Pruyn*, *Radford*, *Samuel J. Randall*, William H. Randall, Alexander H. Rice, *Rogers*, *James S. Rollins*, *Ross*, Smith, *John B. Steele*, *William G. Steele*, Stevens, *Stiles*, *Strouse*, *Stuart*, *Sweat*, Thomas, *Townsend*, Tracy, Van Valkenburgh, *Wadsworth*, William B. Washburn, Webster, Whaley, *Wheeler*, *Joseph W. White*, *Winfield*, *Fernando Wood*, *Yeaman*—92.

NAYS—Messrs. Allison, Ames, Arnold, Ashley, John D. Baldwin, Baxter, Beaman, Blaine, Blow, Boutwell, Brandegee, Broomall, Ambrose W. Clark, Cole, Henry Winter Davis, Deming, Dixon, Donnelly, Driggs, Dumont, Eliot, Farnsworth, Garfield, Grinnell, Higby, Hooper, Asahel W. Hubbard, John H. Hubbard, Ingersoll, Jenckes, Kelley, Francis W. Kellogg, Orlando Kellogg, Knox, Loan, Longyear, McBride, McClurg, Samuel F. Miller, Moorhead, Morrill, Daniel Morris, Amos Myers, Leonard Myers, Norton, Charles O'Neill, Orth, Patterson, Perham, Price, John H. Rice, Edward H. Rollins, Schenck, Scofield, Shannon, Sloan, Smithers, Starr, Thayer, Upson, Williams, Wilson, Woodbridge, Worthington—64.

February 22—Mr. WILSON, from the Judiciary Committee, reported this bill:

That neither the people nor the Legislature of any State, the people of which were declared to be in insurrection against the United States by the proclamation of the President, dated August 16, 1861, shall hereafter elect Representatives or Senators to the Congress of the United States until the President, by proclamation, shall have declared that armed hostility to the Government of the United States within such State has ceased; nor until the people of such State shall have adopted a constitution of government not repugnant to the Constitution and laws of the United States; nor until, by a law of Congress, such State shall have been declared to be entitled to representation in the Congress of the United States of America.

Mr. ASHLEY offered, as a substitute, the bill offered by him yesterday.

Mr. KELLEY moved to strike out the word "white" from the Enrollment section.

Mr. BLAIR moved that the bill be tabled; which was agreed to—yeas 80, nays 65, as follows:

YEAS—Messrs. *James C. Allen*, *Ancona*, Anderson, *Baily*, Blair, *Bliss*, *Brooks*, William G. Brown, *Chanler*, *Clay*, Cobb, *Cox*, *Cravens*, Dawes, *Dawson*, *Denison*, *Eden*, *Edgerton*, *Eldridge*, *English*, *Finck*, *Ganson*, Gooch, *Grider*, Griswold, *Hall*, *Harding*, *Harrington*, *Benjamin G. Harris*, *Charles M. Harris*, *Herrick*, *Holman*, *Hutchins*, *Kalbfleisch*, Kasson, *Kernan*, *Knapp*, *Law*, *Lazear*, *Le Blond*, *Long*, *Mallory*, *Marcy*, Marvin, *McAllister*, *McKinney*, *William H. Miller*, *James R. Morris*, *Morrison*, *Nelson*, *Noble*, *Odell*, *Pendleton*, *Perry*, Pike, Pomeroy, *Pruyn*, *Radford*, *Samuel J. Randall*, William H. Randall, Alexander H. Rice, *Rogers*, *James S. Rollins*, *Ross*, Smith, *John B. Steele*, *William G. Steele*, *Stiles*, *Strouse*, *Stuart*, *Townsend*, Tracy, *Voorhees*, *Wadsworth*, William B. Washburn, Whaley, *Wheeler*, *Winfield*, *Fernando Wood*, *Yeaman*—80.

NAYS—Messrs. Allison, Ames, Ashley, John D. Baldwin, Baxter, Beaman, Blow, Boutwell, Boyd, Brandegee, Broomall, Ambrose W. Clark, Cole, Henry Winter Davis, Deming, Dixon, Donnelly, Driggs, Dumont, Eckley, Eliot, Garfield, Grinnell, Higby, Hooper, Asahel W. Hubbard, John H. Hubbard, Hulburd, Ingersoll, Jenckes, Kelley, Orlando Kellogg, Knox, Littlejohn, Loan, Longyear, McBride, McClurg, Samuel F. Miller, Moorhead, Morrill, Daniel Morris, Amos Myers, Leonard Myers, Charles O'Neill, Orth, Perham, Price, John H. Rice, Edward H. Rollins, Schenck, Scofield, Shannon, Sloan, Smithers, Starr, Stevens, Thayer, Upson, Van Valkenburgh, Ellihu B. Washburne, Williams, Wilder, Wilson, Woodbridge—65.

REPRESENTATION IN THE ELECTORAL COLLEGE.

IN HOUSE OF REPRESENTATIVES.

1865, January 30—Mr. WILSON reported from the Committee on the Judiciary this resolution, which was passed without a division:

Joint resolution declaring certain States not entitled to representation in the electoral college.

Whereas the inhabitants and local authorities of the States of Virginia, North Carolina, South Carolina, Georgia, Florida, Alabama, Mississippi, Louisiana, Texas, Arkansas, and Tennessee rebelled against the government of the United States, and have continued in a state of armed rebellion for more than three years, and were in said state of armed rebellion on the eighth day of November, eighteen hundred and sixty-four: Therefore,

Be it resolved, &c., That the States mentioned in the preamble to this joint resolution are not entitled to representation in the electoral college for the choice of President and Vice-President of the United States for the term of office commencing on the fourth day of March, eighteen hundred and sixty-five; and no electoral votes shall be received or counted from said States concerning the choice of President and Vice-President for said term of office.

IN SENATE.

February 1—Mr. TRUMBULL reported it from the Judiciary Committee, with this amendment:

To strike from the preamble these words: "And have continued in a state of armed rebellion for more than three years, and were in said state of armed rebellion on the 8th day of November, 1864."

And substitute these: "And were in such state of rebellion on the 8th day of November, 1864, that no valid election for President and Vice President of the United States according to the Constitution and laws thereof was held therein on said day."

Which was agreed to, in Committee of the Whole.

Mr. TEN EYCK moved to strike from the preamble the word "Louisiana."

Mr. COLLAMER moved this as a substitute for the preamble and resolution:

That the people of no State, the inhabitants whereof have been declared in a State of insurrection by virtue of the fifth section of the act entitled "An act further to provide for the collection of duties on imports, and for other purposes," approved March July 13, 1861, shall be regarded as empowered to elect electors of President and Vice President of the United States until said condition of insurrection shall cease and be so declared by virtue of a law of the United States, or until they shall be represented in both houses of Congress.

Nor shall any vote cast by any such electors elected by the votes of the inhabitants of any such State, or the Legislature thereof, be received or counted.

Mr. LANE, of Indiana, moved to postpone the resolution indefinitely, which was lost—yeas 11, nays 26, as follows:

YEAS—Messrs. Cowan, Doolittle, Farwell, Harlan, Harris, Howe, Lane of Indiana, *Nesmith*, Ten Eyck, Van Winkle, Willey—11.

NAYS—Messrs. Anthony, *Buckalew*, Clark, Collamer, Conness, *Davis*, Dixon, Foster, Hale, Henderson, Howard, *Johnson*, Lane of Kansas, Morgan, Morrill, Nye, *Powell*, Sherman, Sprague, Stewart, Sumner, Trumbull, Wade, Wilkinson, Wilson, *Wright*—26.

1865, February 3—Mr. TEN EYCK'S amendment was not agreed to—yeas 15, nays 22, as follows:

YEAS—Messrs. Cowan, Dixon, Doolittle, Farwell, Harlan, Harris, Howe, Lane of Indiana, Lane of Kansas, *Nesmith*, Pomeroy, Ramsey, Ten Eyck, Van Winkle, Willey—15.

NAYS—Messrs. Brown, *Buckalew*, Clark, Collamer, Conness, *Davis*, Foster, Henderson, *Hendricks*, Howard, *Johnson*, Morgan, Morrill, *Powell*, *Saulsbury*, Sherman, Sprague, Sumner, Trumbull, Wade, Wilkinson, *Wright*—22.

Mr. LANE, of Kansas, moved to strike out the preamble, which was not agreed to—yeas 12, nays 30, as follows:

YEAS—Messrs. Cowan, Doolittle, Harlan, Harris, Howe, Lane of Indiana, Lane of Kansas, *Nesmith*, Pomeroy, Ten Eyck, Van Winkle, Willey—12.

NAYS—Messrs. Brown, *Buckalew*, Chandler, Clark, Conness, *Davis*, Dixon, Farwell, Foster, Grimes, Hale, Henderson, *Hendricks*, Howard, *Johnson*, Morgan, Morrill, Nye, *Powell*, Ramsey, *Saulsbury*, Sherman, Sprague, Stewart, Sumner, Trumbull, Wade, Wilkinson, Wilson, *Wright*—30.

Mr. HARRIS moved to amend by substituting as follows:

Whereas in pursuance of an act of Congress approved on the 13th day of July, 1861, the President did, on the 16th day of August, 1861, declare the inhabitants of certain States, and among others the States of Tennessee and Louisiana, to be in a state of insurrection against the United States; and whereas, with a view to encourage the inhabitants of such States to resume their allegiance to the United States and to reinaugurate loyal State governments, the President, on the 8th day of December, 1863, issued his proclamation, whereby it was declared, among other things, that in case a State Government should be re-established in any of said States, in a manner therein specified, such government should be recognized as the true government of the State; and whereas the loyal inhabitants of the States of Tennessee and Louisiana, invited so to do by the said last mentioned proclamation, have in good faith established State governments loyal to the United States, or attempted so to do; and whereas such loyal inhabitants at the recent presidential election have chosen electors of President and Vice-President, who have in pursuance of the requirement of the Constitution, cast their votes for the President and Vice-President; and whereas doubts exist as to the validity of such election of presidential electors in the said States of Tennessee and Louisiana; and whereas it is well understood that the result of the presidential election could in no way be affected by the votes of the said States, whether the same be counted or not: Therefore,

Be it resolved, &c., That it is inexpedient to determine the question as to the validity of the election of electors in the said States of Tennessee and Louisiana, and that in counting the votes for President and Vice President the result be declared as it would stand if the votes of the said States were counted, and also as it would stand if the votes of the said States were excluded, such result being the same in either case.

Which was rejected—yeas 12, nays 31, as follows:

YEAS—Messrs. Cowan, Doolittle, Farwell, Harris, Howe, Lane of Indiana, Lane of Kansas, *Nesmith*, Pomeroy, Ten Eyck, Van Winkle, Willey—12.

NAYS—Messrs. Brown, *Buckalew*, Chandler, Clark, Collamer, Conness, *Davis*, Dixon, Foster, Grimes, Hale, Harlan, Henderson, *Hendricks*, Howard, *Johnson*, Morgan, Morrill, Nye, *Powell*, Ramsey, *Saulsbury*, Sherman, Sprague, Stewart, Sumner, Trumbull, Wade, Wilkinson, Wilson, *Wright*—31.

February 4—Mr. COLLAMER'S amendment was rejected—yeas 13, nays 27, as follows:

YEAS—Messrs. Anthony, Brown, Clark, Collamer, Dixon, Farwell, Foot, Harlan, Howard, Lane of Kansas, Ramsey, Sumner, Wilson—13.

NAYS—Messrs. *Buckalew*, Chandler, Conness, Cowan, *Davis*, Doolittle, Foster, Hale, Harris, Henderson, *Hendricks*, Howe, *Johnson*, Lane of Indiana, Morgan, Morrill, Nye, Pomeroy, *Powell*, *Saulsbury*, Sherman, Stewart, Ten Eyck, Trumbull, Van Winkle, Willey, *Wright*—27.

The joint resolution as amended being reported to the Senate,

Mr. POMEROY moved to strike out the words "state of rebellion" and insert in lieu thereof the word "condition;" which was adopted—yeas 26, nays 13, as follows:

YEAS—Messrs. Anthony, Brown, *Buckalew*, Chandler, Clark, Conness, *Davis*, Dixon, Doolittle, Farwell, Foot, Harlan, Harris, Henderson, *Hendricks*, Lane of Kansas, Morgan, Pomeroy, *Powell*, Ramsey, *Saulsbury*, Sherman, Trumbull, Van Winkle, Willey, Wilson—26.

NAYS—Messrs. Collamer, Cowan, Foster, Grimes, Hale, Howard, *Johnson*, Morrill, Nye, Stewart, Ten Eyck, Wade, *Wright*—13.

The amendment as amended was then agreed to—yeas 32, nays 6, (Messrs. Cowan, Foot, *Johnson*, Ten Eyck, Van Winkle, Willey.)

Mr. LANE, of Kansas, moved to strike out the preamble, and to strike out after the word "States," in the first line of the resolution, the words "mentioned in the preamble," and to insert in lieu of them "of Virginia, North Carolina, South Carolina, Georgia, Florida, Alabama, Mississippi, Louisiana, Texas, Arkansas, and Tennessee."

Which was rejected—yeas 7, nays 30, as follows:

YEAS—Messrs. Cowan, Doolittle, Harris, Lane of Kansas, Nesmith, Van Winkle, Willey—7.

NAYS—Messrs. Anthony, Brown, *Buckalew*, Chandler, Clark, Collamer, Conness, *Davis*, Dixon, Farwell, Foster, Grimes, Hale, Harlan, Henderson, *Hendricks*, Howard, *Johnson*, Morgan, Morrill, Nye, *Powell*, Ramsey, *Saulsbury*, Sherman, Sumner, Ten Eyck, Trumbull, Wade, *Wright*—30.

And the resolution passed—yeas 29, nays 10:

YEAS—Messrs. Anthony, Brown, *Buckalew*, Chandler, Clark, Collamer, Conness, *Davis*, Dixon, Farwell, Foster, Grimes, Hale, Harlan, Henderson, *Hendricks*, Howard, *Johnson*, Morgan, Morrill, Nye, *Powell*, Ramsey, Sherman, Stewart, Sumner, Trumbull, Wade, *Wright*—29.

NAYS—Messrs. Cowan, Doolittle, Harris, Howe, Lane of Kansas, *Nesmith*, *Saulsbury*, Ten Eyck, Van Winkle, Willey—10.

February 4—The House concurred in the amendments.

Pending this question, Mr. YEAMAN proposed to offer this substitute for the resolution, but, on the point being raised, it was ruled out of order at that stage:

That the votes of the Presidential electors of any State shall be counted when presented and verified in the ordinary and legal method; and it is incompetent and immaterial for Congress to go behind such verification, and inquire whether a part of the citizens of such State may have been in rebellion; and all laws and parts of laws and joint resolutions incompatible with this are hereby repealed.

February 10—This message from the PRESIDENT was laid before the Senate:

To the honorable the Senate and
House of Representatives:

The joint resolution entitled "Joint resolution declaring certain States not entitled to representation in the Electoral College" has been signed by the Executive, in deference to the view of Congress implied in its passage and presentation to him. In his own view, however, the two Houses of Congress, convened under the twelfth article of the Constitution, have complete power to exclude from counting all electoral votes deemed by them to be illegal; and it is not competent for the Executive to defeat or obstruct that power by a veto, as would be the case if his action were at all essential in the matter. He disclaims all right of the Executive to interfere in any way in the matter of canvassing or counting electoral votes, and he also disclaims that, by signing said resolution, he has expressed any opinion on the recitals of the preamble, or any judgment of his own upon the subject of the resolution.

ABRAHAM LINCOLN.

EXECUTIVE MANSION, *February* 8, 1865.

THE LOUISIANA QUESTION.

IN SENATE.

1864, December 7—The credentials of Charles Smith and R. King Cutler, as Senators, were presented, and referred to the Committee on the Judiciary.

1865, February 18—Mr. TRUMBULL made this written report:

The Committee on the Judiciary, to whom were referred the credentials of R. King Cutler and Charles Smith, claiming seats from the State of Louisiana, report:

That in the early part of eighteen hundred and sixty-one the constituted authorities of the State of Louisiana undertook to withdraw that State from the Union, and so far succeeded in the attempt as by force of arms to expel from the State for a time the authority of the United States, and set up a government in hostility thereto.

Since that time the United States, as a necessity to the maintaining of its legitimate authority in Louisiana as one of the States of the Union, has been compelled to take possession thereof by its military forces, and, in the absence of any local organizations or civil magistrates loyal to the Union, temporarily to govern the same by military power.

While a large portion of the State, embracing more than two-thirds of its population, was thus under the control of the military power, steps were taken, with its sanction, and to some extent under its direction, for the reorganization of a State government loyal to the government of the United States. The first action had looking to such reorganization was a registration of the loyal persons within the limits of military control entitled to vote under the constitution and laws of Louisiana at the beginning of the rebellion. The lists thus made up contain the names of between fifteen and eighteen thousand voters, which is represented to be more than half the number of voters in the same parishes previous to the rebellion, and more than two-thirds of the voting population within the same localities at the time the registry was taken. The next step taken in the reorganization of the State government was the election of State officers on the 22d of February, 1864, under the auspices of the military authority acting in conjunction with prominent and influential citizens. At this election 11,414 votes were polled, 808 of which were cast by soldiers and sailors—citizens of Louisiana, who would not have been entitled to vote under the constitution of Louisiana as it existed prior to the rebellion, for the sole reason that they were in the military service, but who possessed in other respects all the qualifications of voters required by that instrument. The balance, 10,606, were legal voters under the constitution of the State prior to the rebellion. The third step in the reorganization of the State government was to call a convention for the amendment of the constitution of the State. Delegates to this convention were elected March 28, 1864, under the joint and harmonious direction of the military authorities, and the State officers who had been elected on the 22d February previous. In a paper submitted to the committee by Major General Banks he states that delegates were apportioned to every election district in the State, both within and beyond the lines, so that if beyond the lines of the army the people of the State had chosen to participate in that election, the delegates might have been received if they had shown themselves loyal to the government. They were about 150 in number. All elections subsequent to that for delegates have been ordered and controlled by the representatives of the people.

In the organization of the convention it was provided that a majority of the whole number apportioned to the State, if every district within and beyond the lines had been represented, should constitute a quorum for the transaction of business. Every vote in the convention, from a question of order to the ratification of the constitution, was conducted under this rule, and was approved by a majority of all the delegates apportioned to the State if every district had been represented.

The delegates met in convention, in the city of New Orleans, on the 6th day of April, 1864, remained in session till July 23, 1864, and adopted a constitution, republican in form, and in entire harmony with the Constitution of the United States and the great principles of human liberty.

This constitution was submitted, by the convention which adopted it, to the people for ratification, on the first Monday of September, 1864, and adopted by a vote of 6.836 for, to 1,566 against it.

At the same time the vote was taken on the adoption of the constitution, a legislature was elected, representing all those parishes of the State reclaimed from insurgent control, and embracing about two thirds of its population. This legislature assembled at New Orleans on the 3d day of October, 1864, and proceeded to put in operation a State government by providing for levying and collecting taxes, the establishment of tribunals for the administration of justice, the adoption of a system of education, and such other measures as were necessary to the re-establishment of a State government in harmony with the Constitution and laws of the United States. The State government thus inaugurated has been in successful operation since the period of its establishment, and your committee are assured that if no exterior hostile force is permitted to enter the State, the local State government is fully equal to the maintaining of peace and tranquillity throughout the State, in subordination to the Constitution and laws of the United States.

The manner in which the new State government was inaugurated is not wholly free from objection. The local State authorities having rebelled against the government, and there being no State or local officers in existence loyal to its authority, in taking the initiatory steps for a reorganization, some irregularities were unavoidable, and the number of voters participating in this reorganization is less than would have been desirable. Yet, when we take into consideration the large number of voters who had left the State in consequence of the rebellion, who had fallen in battle, or were absent at the time of the election, both in the Union and rebel armies, and the difficulties attending the obtaining of a full vote from those remaining, in consequence of the unsettled condition of affairs in the State, and the further fact that the adoption of the amended constitution was not seriously opposed, and therefore the question of its ratification not calculated to call out a full vote, the number of votes cast is perhaps as large as could have been expected, and the State government which has been reorganized, as your committee believe, fairly represents a majority of the loyal voters of the State.

Appended hereto is a copy of the various orders and proclamations issued in regard to the election of State officers, delegates to the Constitutional convention, and members of the legislature, and also a copy of election laws and instructions relative to the duties of commissioners of elections, issued for the guidance of officers in conducting said election.

Messrs. Cutler and Smith, the claimants for seats, were duly elected senators by the legislature which convened on the third day of October, 1864, and but for the fact that, in pursuance of an act of Congress passed on the 13th day of July, 1861, the inhabitants of the State of Louisiana were declared to be in a state of insurrection against the United States, and all commercial intercourse between them and the citizens of other States declared to be unlawful, which condition of things had not ceased at the time of the reorganization of the State government and the election of Messrs. Cutler and Smith, your committee would recommend their immediate admission to seats.

The persons in possession of the local authorities of Louisiana having rebelled against the authority of the United States, and her inhabitants having been declared to be in a state of insurrection in pursuance of a law passed by the two Houses of Congress, your committee deem it improper for this body to admit to seats senators from Louisiana, till by some joint action of both Houses there shall be some recognition of an existing State government acting in harmony with the government of the United States, and recognizing its authority.

Your committee therefore recommend for adoption, before taking definite action upon the right of the claimants to seats, the accompanying joint resolution.

The joint resolution is as follows:

Resolved, &c., That the United States do hereby recognize the government of the State of Louisiana, inaugurated under and by the convention which assembled on the 6th day of April, A. D. 1864, at the city of New Orleans, as the legitimate government of the said State, and entitled to the guaranties and all other rights of a State government under the Constitution of the United States.

February 23—Mr. SUMNER moved this substitute:

That neither the people nor the Legislature of any State, the people of which were declared to be in insurrection against the United States by the proclamation of the President, dated August 16, 1861, shall hereafter elect Representatives or Senators to the Congress of the United States until the President, by proclamation, shall have declared that armed hostility to the Government of the United States within such State has ceased; nor until the people of such State shall have adopted a constitution of government not repugnant to the Constitution and laws of the United States; nor until, by a law of Congress, such State shall have been declared to be entitled to representation in the Congress of the United States of America.

Which was not agreed to—yeas 8, nays 29, as follows:

YEAS—Messrs. Brown, Conness, Grimes, Howard, Sprague, Stewart, Sumner, Wade—8.

NAYS—Messrs. Anthony, *Buckalew*, *Carlile*, Collamer, Cowan, Dixon, Doolittle, Farwell, Foster, Hale, Harlan, Harris, *Hendricks*, *Johnson*, Lane of Indiana, Lane of Kansas, Morgan, Morrill, *Nesmith*, Nye, Pomeroy, *Powell*, Ramsey, *Richardson*, *Riddle*, Ten Eyck, Trumbull, Willey, *Wright*—29.

February 25—Mr. SUMNER gave notice of his intention to offer this substitute at the proper time:

That it is the duty of the United States, at the earliest practicable moment consistent with the common defence and the general walfare, to re-establish by act of Congress republican governments in those States where loyal governments have been vacated by the existing rebellion, and thus, to the full extent of their power, fulfil the requirement of the Constitution, that "the United States shall guarantee to every State in this Union a republican form of government."

SEC. 2. That this important duty is imposed by the Constitution in express terms on "the United States," and not on individuals or classes of individuals, or on any military commander or executive officer, and cannot be intrusted to any such persons, acting, it may be, for an oligarchical class, and in disregard of large numbers of loyal people; but it must be performed by the United States, represented by the President and both Houses of Congress, acting for the whole people thereof.

SEC. 3. That, in determining the extent of this duty, and in the absence of any precise definition of the term "republican form of government," we cannot err, if, when called to perform this guarantee under the Constitution, we adopt the self-evident truths of the Declaration of Independence as an authoritative rule, and insist that in every re-established State the consent of the governed shall be the only just foundation of government, and all men shall be equal before the law.

SEC. 4. That, independent of the Declaration of Independence, it is plain that any duty imposed by the Constitution must be performed in conformity with justice and reason, and in the light of existing facts; that, therefore, in the performance of this guarantee, there can be no power under the Constitution to disfranchise loyal people, or to recognize any such disfranchisement, especially when it may hand over the loyal majority to the government of the disloyal minority; nor can there be any power under the Constitution to discriminate in favor of the rebellion by admitting to the electoral franchise rebels who have forfeited all rights and by excluding loyal persons who have never forfeited any right.

SEC. 5. That the United States, now called at a crisis of history to perform this guarantee, will fail in duty under the Constitution, should they allow the re-establishment of any State without proper safeguards for the rights of all the citizens, and especially without making it impossible for rebels now in arms against the national government to trample upon the rights of those who are now fighting the battles of the Union.

SEC. 6. That the path of justice is also the path of peace, and that for the sake of peace it is better to obey the Constitution, and, in conformity with its requirements in the performance of the guarantee, to re-establish State governments on the consent of the governed and the equality of all persons before the law, to the end that the foundations thereof may be permanent, and that no loyal majorities may be again overthrown or ruled by any oligarchical class.

SEC. 7. That a government founded on military power, or having its origin in military orders, cannot be a "republican form of government" according to the requirement of the Constitution; and that its recognition will be contrary not only to the Constitution, but also to that essential principal of our government which, in the language of Jefferson, establishes "the supremacy of the civil over the military authority."

SEC. 8. That in the States whose governments have been already vacated, a government founded on an oligarchical class, even if erroneously recognized as a "republican form of government" under the guarantee of the Constitution, cannot sustain itself securely without national support; that such an oligarchical government is not competent at this moment to discharge the duties and execute the powers of a State; and that its recognition as a legitimate government will tend to enfeeble the Union, to postpone the day of reconciliation, and to endanger the national tranquillity.

SEC. 9. That considerations of expediency are in harmony with the requirements of the Constitution and the dictates of justice and reason, especially now, when colored soldiers have shown their military value; that as their muskets are needed for the national defence against rebels in the field, so are their ballots yet more needed against the subtle enemies of the Union at home; and that without their support at the ballot-box the cause of human rights and of the Union itself will be in constant peril.

February 25—Mr. SUMNER offered this proviso to be added to the resolution:

Provided, That this shall not take effect except upon the fundamental condition that within the State there shall be no denial of the electoral franchise, or of any other rights on account of color or race, but all persons shall be equal before the law. And the Legislature of the State, by a solemn public act, shall declare the assent of the State to this fundamental condition, and shall transmit to the President of the United States an authentic copy of such assent whenever the same shall be adopted, upon the receipt whereof he shall, by proclamation, announce the fact; whereupon, without any further proceedings on the part of Congress, this joint resolution shall take effect.

Mr HENDERSON moved to insert after the word "race," the words "or sex."

After debate, Mr. WADE moved the postponement of the further consideration of the subject until the first Monday of December next; which was not agreed to—yeas 12, nays 17, as follows:

YEAS—Messrs. Brown, *Buckalew*, *Carlile*, Chandler, *Davis*, *Hendricks*, Howard, *Powell*, *Riddle*, Sumner, Wade, *Wright*—12.

NAYS—Messrs. Clark, Dixon, Doolittle, Foot, Foster, Harlan, Henderson, Howe, Lane of Indiana, Lane of Kansas, Morgan, Pomeroy, Ramsey, Ten Eyck, Trumbull, Willey, Wilson—17.

The remainder of the sitting was consumed

in formal motions to adjourn, and in debate; and the subject was not again reached during the session.

IN HOUSE OF REPRESENTATIVES.

1864, December 13—Mr. Eliot offered a joint resolution declaring that the State of Louisiana may resume its political relations with the Government of the United States. Referred to the Committee on the Judiciary.

1865, February 11—Mr. Dawes, from the Committee on Elections, made this report:

The Committee of Elections, to whom were referred the credentials of M. F. Bonzano, claiming a seat in this house as a representative from the first congressional district in Louisiana, submit the following report:

The election upon which Mr. Bonzano claims the seat was held on the 5th of September, 1864. The number of votes cast was—

For Mr. Bonzano	1,609
For all others	1,456
Total	3,065

This election derives its authority from the constitutional convention which commenced its session in New Orleans, April 6, 1864, which amended essentially and adopted anew the constitution of Louisiana, and, among other things, did on the 22d of July, 1864, divide the State into five congressional districts, in accordance with the number of representatives assigned to that State in the apportionment under the census of 1860, and ordered an election to be held on the first Monday of September, 1864, to fill the vacancies caused by the failure of the State hitherto to elect representatives to the present Congress. As the election under consideration derives its authority from this convention, a recital of the main facts connected with the origin and action of that convention becomes necessary to a proper understanding of the subject.

From nearly the commencement of the rebellion till the appearance of the federal fleet under Commodore Farragut before the city of New Orleans in April, 1862, the State had been overrun by the rebel armies, and the governor had traitorously abandoned his duty and post, leaving the people without loyal government, and delivered over to the rebellion. Upon the taking possession of New Orleans by General Butler on the 1st of May following, he issued a proclamation, in which, among other things, he invited "all persons well disposed towards the government of the United States" to renew their oath of allegiance, and promised to such the protection of the armies of the United States. Under this proclamation sixty-one thousand three hundred and eighty-two (61,382) citizens took the oath of allegiance before the close of the following October. Subsequently, as the rebel army retired from other portions of the State, and the federal army advanced and extended its lines, the citizens of the districts or parishes thus delivered from the restraint of the rebellion also promptly came forward and renewed their allegiance to the government of the Union. Soldiers, white and black, enlisted into the armies of the Union, and in New Orleans many of the citizens formed themselves into home-guards, to assist the federal authorities in case of an attack by the rebels.

As fast as new parishes were brought into the federal lines and the people in sufficiently large numbers renewed their allegiance, and recognized the authority of the United States, the military governor of the State appointed judges, justices of the peace, clerks of courts, sheriffs, constables, and other civil officers, and performed all the acts which legally and constitutionally devolve upon the governor of Louisiana. In all of which her loyal citizens acquiesced and rendered an unquestioned obedience.

Under a proclamation issued by the then military governor, November 14, 1862, an election was held December 3, 1862, for representatives in the 37th Congress from the first and second congressional districts of the State, under the old apportionment and the law of Louisiana as it existed before the rebellion. In the first, 2,643 votes, and in the second 5,117 votes were cast at this election. And the gentlemen claiming to have been thus duly elected presented their credentials to the last Congress, which, after careful examination and full discussion, admitted them to seats as members. The admission of these representatives to seats, and the opportunity which it gave to the loyal sentiment of the State to be heard and make itself manifest, had a most salutary effect upon the people of that State, and from that time the desire for a new State government and a resumption of State functions rapidly increased throughout all that portion of the State within our lines.

The major general commanding in the department of the Gulf, yielding to the pressure from all sides that he would give direction to some practical end to the efforts which this desire on the part of the people was prompting to reorganize and re-establish their State government, did, under the direction of the President, issue on January 11, 1864, a proclamation which is annexed to this report, inviting the people of Louisiana to participate in an election on the 22d of February of State officers under the constitution and laws of the State, except so far as they related to the subject of slavery, which were declared to be to that extent suspended and inoperative. Several orders intended to secure freedom of election and conformity as far as possible to the laws of Louisiana previous to the rebellion were issued by the general commanding, and the evidence is satisfactory to the committee that to the extent of the federal lines this election was general, conducted in good order, free from military or other control, and largely participated in by the people.

It resulted in the election of State officers by a vote of 11,414. At this election no person voted who was not by the constitution and laws of Louisiana a voter, except soldiers and sailors in the service of the United States who were citizens of Louisiana and in the State at the time of the election, to the number of 808. All who voted took the oath prescribed by the President in his proclamation of December 8, 1863.

These officers were installed on the 4th of March following at New Orleans, in presence and with the acclaim of a large concourse of people, estimated at 50,000. On the eleventh of the same month the commanding general issued another order, which accompanies this report, calling for an election of delegates to a convention for the revision and amendment of the constitution of the State. The governor by a proclamation joined in this call. All parties were consulted in reference to this election, and differed only as to the time of holding it.

This convention commenced its sessions at New Orleans, April 6, 1864, and adjourned on the 25th of July. The entire proceedings and debates of this body have been laid upon the tables of the members of this house. The most important changes in the constitution of the State proposed by it were those in relation to slavery. The following were adopted by it, as the first and second articles of the constitution:

TITLE I.

EMANCIPATION.

Article 1. Slavery and involuntary servitude, except as a punishment for crime, whereof the party shall have been duly convicted, are hereby forever abolished and prohibited throughout the State.

Article 2. The legislature shall make no law recognizing the right of property in man.

The proceedings of the convention were, by proclamation of the governor, submitted to the people for ratification or rejection on September 5, 1864, and were ratified without material opposition. The whole number of votes was over 9,000.

This constitutional convention, by an ordinance adopted, divided the State into five Congressional districts, and directed elections for representatives to the present Congress to be held in them on the 5th September, 1864. And in accordance with said ordinance, the governor issued his proclamation directing elections to be held in accordance with it. In pursuance of this ordinance of the convention and proclamation of the governor, elections were held in these several districts for representatives in this Congress; and in the first, M. F. Bonzano received 1,609 votes out of 3,065 cast. The governor gave him, accordingly, a certificate of his election, which has been presented to the House and referred to this committee.

The committee have heard Mr. Bonzano in his own behalf, as also Mr. Field, who claims to have been elected at the same time in the second district, General Banks, and others. The information and arguments submitted by them accompany this report.

This election depends for its validity upon the effect which the House is disposed to give to the efforts to reorganize a State government in Louisiana, which have here been briefly recited. The districting of the State for representatives, and the fixing of the time for holding the election, were the act of the convention. Indeed, the election of Governor and other State officers, as well as the existence of the convention itself, as well as its acts, are all parts of the same movements.

It is objected to their validity, that they neither originated in nor followed any pre-existing law of the State or nation. But the answer to this objection lies in the fact that in the nature of the case, neither a law of the State or nation to meet the case was a possibility. The State was attempting to rise out of the ruin caused by an armed *overthrow* of its laws. They had been trampled in the dust; and there existed nobody in the State to make an enabling act. Congress cannot pass an enabling act for a

State. It is neither one of the powers granted by the several States to the general government, nor necessary to the carrying out of any of those powers; and all "the powers not delegated to the United States by the Constitution, nor prohibited by it to the States, are reserved to the States respectively, *or the people.*" It is preposterous to have expected at the hands of the rebel authorities in Louisiana that, previous to the overthrow of the State government, they should prepare a legal form of proceeding for its restoration. In the absence of any such legal form prepared beforehand in the State, and like absence of power on the part of the general government under the delegated powers of the Constitution, it follows, that the power to restore a lost State government in Louisiana existed nowhere, or in "the people," the original source of all political power in this country. The people, in the exercise of that power, cannot be required to conform to any particular mode, for that presupposes a power to prescribe outside of themselves, which it has been seen does not exist. The *result* must be republican; for the people and the States have surrendered to the United States, to that extent, the power over their form of government in this, that "the United States shall guarantee to every State a republican form of government."

It follows, therefore, that if this work of reorganizing and re-establishing a State government was the work of the people, it was the legitimate exercise of an inalienable and inherent right, and, if republican in form, is entitled not only to recognition but to the "guaranty" of the Constitution.

The attention of the committee has therefore been directed to the inquiry how far this effort to restore constitutional government in Louisiana has been the work of the people. Those engaged in the traitorous attempt to destroy the government form no part of that people engaged in the patriotic effort to restore it. The government is to be made, if at all, for and by patriots and not by traitors. In answering another and essential question, whether a government once erected in that State will be able to maintain itself against domestic violence, traitors must be counted, but not for their voice in making the government itself. As well might the inmates of a State prison be enumerated and consulted upon determining the character of a code of laws designed for their government.

The evidence before the committee, and all the information they could obtain, satisfied them that the movement which resulted in the election of State officers, the calling of a convention to revise and amend the constitution, the ratification of such revisal and amendment by a popular vote, and the subsequent election of representatives in Congress, was not only participated in by a large majority, almost approaching to unanimity, of the loyal people of the State, but that that loyal people constituted a majority of all the people of the State. Making proper allowance for those who have been driven out by the rebellion, have gone into its ranks, or perished at its hands, and also for the sparsely settled and in some parts barren character of nearly all that portion of the State still outside of the federal lines compared with the populous and rich and fertile portions within, there can be but little doubt of the correctness of these conclusions. The committee refer to the accompanying statements for the extent, character, and population of the portions of the State within and outside the federal lines.

The committee find from all the facts that this election was held under the auspices of a new State organization which has arisen upon the ruins of the old, in as much conformity to law as the nature of the case would permit—in which the loyal people throughout the State acquiesce—and at this moment in the full discharge of all the functions of a State government. They entertain no doubt of the ability of this government to maintain itself against domestic violence if protected from enemies without. About forty thousand loyal Louisianians, white and black, are now in the armies of the Union, a force amply sufficient to overawe any lurking discontent, or punish any open resistance within its borders. The committee cannot doubt that it is the duty of Congress to encourage this effort to restore law and order in Louisiana. The precedents are many since the rebellion commenced, of the admission of members where greater irregularities existed than in the present case. In the Louisiana case, in the last House, the committee held the following language, which was sustained by a very large vote in the House:

"Representation is one of the very essentials of a republican form of government, and no one doubts that the United States cannot fulfil this obligation without guaranteeing that representation here. It was in fulfilment of this obligation that the army of the Union entered New Orleans, drove out the rebel usurpation, and restored to the discharge of its appropriate functions the civil authority there. Its work is not ended till there is representation here. It cannot secure that representation through the aid of a rebel governor. Hence the necessity for a military governor to discharge such functions, both military and civil, which necessity imposes in the interim between the absolute reign of rebellion and the complete restoration of law. Suppose Governor Moore to be the only traitor in Louisiana: one of two things must take place. The people must remain unrepresented, or some one must *assume* to fix a time to hold these elections. Which alternative approaches nearest to republicanism, nearest to the fulfilment of our obligations to guarantee a republican form of government to that people—closing the door of representation, or recognizing as valid the time fixed by the military governor? Are this people to wait for representation here till their rebel governor returns to his loyalty and appoints a day for an election, or is the government to guarantee that representation as best it may? The committee cannot distinguish between this act of the military governor and the many civil functions he is performing every day, acquiesced in by everybody. To pronounce this illegal and refuse to recognize it, is to pronounce his whole administration void and a usurpation. But necessity put him there and keeps him there."

In another case, that of Andrew J. Clements, of Tennessee, the committee of the last House, after a careful examination of the whole subject, submitted a resolution, which was unanimously adopted by the House, in favor of his right to the seat he claimed, based upon the following conclusion:

"In conclusion, the committee, upon the whole evidence, find that on the day of election no armed force prevented any considerable number of voters in any part of the district from going to the polls, and that on that day, in conformity with the forms of law, two thousand votes at least were cast for the memorialist as a representative to this Congress, and none, so far as the committee know, for any other person. They therefore report the following resolution, and recommend its adoption."

The committee of the present House have had occasion repeatedly to state the same positions in coming to conclusions upon similar cases, in which they have been sustained by the House. They are strengthened in these conclusions upon a re-examination of them in the present case, and they therefore submit the following resolution:

Resolved, That M. F. Bonzano is entitled to a seat in this House as a representative from the first congressional district in Louisiana.

Messrs. SMITHERS and UPSON presented this minority report:

The undersigned, minority of the Committee of Elections, to which was referred a certain paper, purporting to be the credentials of M. F. Bonzano as representative from the first congressional district of the State of Louisiana, beg leave to submit the following views, dissenting from the report of the said committee as presented by the majority thereof:

Before proceeding to consider the facts presented by the meagre and unsatisfactory testimony produced before them, the undersigned deem it proper to suggest, briefly, their views of the condition of Louisiana, the true issue proposed for the consideration of this House, and the nature and amount of proof requisite to its proper determination.

The people of Louisiana, acting through their regularly constituted authorities, on the 11th day of December, 1860, ordered a convention and appointed the 23d day of January, 1861, for its assemblage. Pursuant to the act of the legislature an election for delegates was held and the convention met on the day fixed. On the 25th of the same month an ordinance of secession was adopted by a vote of 113 yeas to 17 nays, which, by authority of the convention, was submitted for ratification and subsequently ratified by a vote of 20,448 to 17,296,* and afterward, on the 21st day of March, the same convention ratified the confederate constitution by a vote of 101 to 7.

In these proceedings, not only the regular authorities, but the people of Louisiana participated. In pursuance of the resolution of the people of that State acting through approved and organized bodies, the whole public property of the United States, including great treasure and vast quantities of munitions of war, was seized by public functionaries and transferred to the political organization styling itself "the Confederate States of America."

By official acts and resolutions the authorities of Louisiana, acting by force of the powers with which they were invested by the positive sanction of the people, declared the bonds which had theretofore attached that people to the Government of the United States to be disrupted and their allegiance to be transferred to another sovereignty. The government created by them went into existence and

* This erroneous statement was taken from the first edition of this work. See page 4 of this volume, and the votes given at the close of this chapter.

full operation, and there was no other government in the State of Louisiana nor any other organized body assuming or pretending to exercise civil functions, executive, legislative, or judicial. Thus was established a government *de facto*.

The operation of this act was very different as affecting the people and Government of the United States and the people and government of Louisiana. So far as the United States was concerned, and so far as her rights were to be affected, the act was wholly unconstitutional and void. It changed no relation of citizenship or allegiance, and her rights of jurisdiction and sovereignty remained unimpaired, only suspended in their exercise by the presence of a military power which prevented the operation of civil sovereignty and the enforcement of the laws through the civil magistracy. The necessity for the assertion of these rights by the suppression of armed resistance to her authority required a resort to force, and a manifestation of opposition by organized rebellion developed a condition of civil war, which to the ordinary incidents of sovereignty superadded the rights of a belligerent power. Thus the State of Louisiana became subject to the laws of war, and, rebellion in that State being yet unsuppressed, there has hitherto been no government there recognized by the United States, except the commander-in-chief of the army, and no law except the military code.

Though thus inoperative and ineffectual against the government and people of the Union, the acts of the people of Louisiana were sufficient to work a radical change in their relations to their former State government. By their revolutionary but voluntary actions they disorganized their own political society, abrogated their former political institutions, and erected in their stead a government operated by a magistracy acknowledging no allegiance to our Constitution, but holding and administering their offices in derogation of and in hostility to the authority and laws of the United States.

By these disorganizing acts the sovereign power of Louisiana reverted to the loyal people of that State, and was held in abeyance until such time as by the suppression of the rebellion and the overthrow of the usurping authority they should be rendered capable to resume the functions of government through the organic action of the people, manifesting their will by their voluntary choice of a government republican in form, and subordinate to the Constitution and laws of the United States.

Whether this has been accomplished is the primary question to be determined, for until there is an organized State, there is no right or capacity to be represented in the Congress of the United States.

In the determination of this question the burden of proof is on those who seek for admission, or claim any benefit under or by force of the establishment of such pretended government. It is matter of public history, recognized and certified by the official acts and declarations of this government, that the inhabitants of the State of Louisiana were in insurrection against the United States, and that such condition still remains wholly unchanged or unaffected by any rescission or modification thereof.

Has evidence been presented which authorizes this house to declare that the people of Louisiana, by any proper mode of expression, have changed the status in which they were placed by their own acts and established a republican government? Such only is the form contemplated by the Constitution; such only has any title to representation on this floor; such only is the United States bound to guarantee or authorized to recognize.

The indispensable quality of such government is that it shall emanate from the people, and not only must it be derived from the great body, but their agency in its organization must have been voluntary. The idea of restraint is incompatible with volition. The government must not only rest on the consent of the governed, but that consent must not be procured by force or intimidation.

It is not sufficient that the result may show that a government apparently republican has been created, but the creation must be the exercise of a will unaffected by the presence of an overawing power.

The erection of a State government is a purely civil act. It has no affinity or connection with martial law. The civil power is alone capable to distinguish or declare the fact of its establishment or the essential conditions of its existence. The Congress of the United States is the only body having authority, primarily, to recognize the government of a State. Neither the Executive nor any subordinate military commander has capacity to incept or consummate its creation. The undersigned do not insist that an act of Congress is necessary as a prerequisite to enable the people of Louisiana to form a government, but the judgment of Congress must be passed on the result of the action of the people, in the recognition of their act, before representatives can be entitled to admission on this floor. This house must be satisfied that their constitution is ordained in accordance with their deliberate and unforced will, before it it can lend its sanction to the act or recognize its validity. Two questions, therefore, are presented for consideration:

1. Did the great body of the loyal people of Louisiana, in fact, participate or clearly concur in the establishment of the government offered for recognition?

2. Was their act the result of their deliberate will and voluntary choice, unprocured by military interference?

If both these questions are affirmatively answered, then the State government set up by the convention of 1864 is entitled to be recognized; if either is negatived, then there can be no pretence of right to such recognition, or to the admission of representatives from the State of Louisiana.

In considering these questions, it is matter of regret that the testimony before the committee was so limited, being confined to the statements of Major General Banks and A. P. Field, and the evidence of R. V. Montague and Luther V. Parker, all produced by and in support of the right of the claimants.

No one appeared to contest the recognition of the State government, or to dispute the validity of the credentials of the proposed members. The committee had, therefore, no opportunity to examine witnesses adverse to them, although it is well understood that there are many who dissent from the action pretended to have been had in Louisiana, and we are compelled to decide this grave matter upon the *ex parte* declarations of persons interested in, or manifestly strongly affected toward, the recognition of the government inaugurated by the convention. With circumstances so unfavorable to a proper exhibition of the facts attending its organization, the undersigned proceed to consider the two material questions proposed:

1. Did the great body of the loyal people of Louisiana concur in the establishment of the State government demanding our recognition?

There are forty-eight parishes in the State of Louisiana, including the city of New Orleans. Of these, nineteen, to wit: Orleans, Ascension, Assumption, Avoyelles, East Baton Rouge, West Baton Rouge, Concordia, East Feliciana, Jefferson, Lafourche, Madison, Plaquemines, St. Bernard, St. James, St. John the Baptist, St. Mary, Terrebonne, Iberville, and Rapides, sent delegates by a total vote of about 6,500, leaving the residue of the State, or twenty-nine parishes, unrepresented; and at the election for the ratification of the constitution, held on the 5th of September, 1864, being also the day on which representatives to Congress were voted for, the number polled, as returned to the committee, was about 8,000, of which some 6,500 were cast in the city of New Orleans alone, the votes in the fourth and fifth congressional districts amounting, in the aggregate, to 676.

This convention was composed of ninety-five delegates, of which number the parish of Orleans was represented by sixty-three, leaving to the country parishes the residue of thirty-two. The undersigned have no definite information of the number of votes polled in each parish, either at the election of delegates, or on the question of ratification, nor the number cast for the constitution, nor, if any, against it, but they are enabled to furnish some indication of the vote outside of New Orleans by the sparse returns which they gather from the journal of the convention.

It appears that the parish of Ascension, within our lines and neighboring to New Orleans, and which in 1860 had a white population of 3,940, elected her delegates by 61 votes; that Plaquemines, with a white population in 1860 of 2,529, cast 246; and in the parish of Madison, the witness Montague was elected by a vote of 28.

It is admitted that elections were held only in the parishes included within our lines, and that these lines were the Têche on the one side and the Amite on the other, comprehending the parish or city of Orleans, and the neighboring parishes on the Mississippi. To a question propounded to General Banks as to what portion of the State voted, his reply was:

"All as far up as Point Coupeè, and there were some men from the Red river who voted at Vidalia."

And in his statement he announces that—

"The city of New Orleans is really the State of Louisiana."

In 1860 there were 357,629 whites in the State, of whom 149,063, or much less than one-half, were in New Orleans, so that in no legitimate sense can it be said that it constitutes the State. It is incredible that there are not many loyal men, the test of loyalty being the willingness to take an oath of allegiance, who were entitled to suffrage upon the question of the formation of their government, but who, from the control of the public enemy, had no opportunity to vote. But assume the statement to be true, it is in evidence that there are not less than 13,000 registered and qualified voters in the city of New Orleans alone who have taken the oath prescribed by the proclamation of the President, and the vote cast at the ratification and the election for members of Congress demonstrates that not more than one-half the number of those entitled to vote in that city voted at that election, to say nothing of the residue of the State.

In the suggestions presented by General Banks to the Judiciary Committee of the Senate, he attempts to account for the meagre vote by the operation of three causes:

"1st. By the fact that no opposition to the constitution was manifested in public or private, and no special effort on the part of its friends was required to secure its adoption.

"2d. That the fact that much uncertainty existed as to the probable ratification of the form of government by the Congress of the United States, deterred many persons from supporting it who would gladly have done so had they known it to be in accordance with the wishes of the government; and,

"3d. From the belief that it was possible that the rebel authority in this State might hereafter be established, when persons participating in the reorganization would suffer in consequence of that act.

"These last considerations affected many perfectly well disposed and naturally loyal but timid persons.

"Had a contest upon the constitution been made by the opponents of emancipation, and had it been generally understood that the authority for organization would have been approved by the government of the United States, the vote in this election would not have been less than 15,000."

As to the cause first assigned, without intimating that General Banks does not speak according to his belief, in view of the testimony of Messrs. Field and Parker, who were doubtless better informed, the undersigned must be permitted to doubt the accuracy or extent of his knowledge; for it is unquestionable that there was much private if not public hostility to its ratification.

The other causes alleged are very striking, as demonstrating not the concurrence of the people, but exactly the reverse, and indicating a settled purpose not to have anything to do with the election. They found very sufficient grounds for not participating, and the undersigned suggest that they are fatal to the reasoning of General Banks.

Mr. Field felt the force of the objection on that point and endeavored to avoid it. In accounting for the paucity of the vote, he says:

"It may be asked, and with some propriety too, why did we not poll a larger vote? That was beyond our control. You see, the party representing the McClellan interest refused to vote. They would have no participation in the election. The party representing the interest of Mr. Durant would not vote for what they called a bogus government. We could not force them to vote. They were qualified, for they had taken the oath of allegiance."

Luther V. Parker, also, speaking in relation to the canvass, gives his experience and the result of his observation:

"The election was as fully canvassed as any, and those who wanted to speak and oppose the adoption of the constitution, spoke as freely as they would at any other time or place. I was one of the speakers at the election for members of Congress, and I know the contest was a sharp one. There were all the elements of opposition brought to bear that could be and in every shape and form. The only thing that we had trouble with was, that there were certain parties there who would not vote either one way or the other.

"Question. By Mr. Dawes Why?

"Answer. They would not give any reason why.

"Question. Were they parties professing to be loyal?

"Answer. Parties reputed to be loyal, and we had no reason to believe them to be disloyal.

"Question. By Mr. Smithers. What proportion of such men was there?

"Answer. I cannot tell.

"Question. Was the number large or small?

"Answer. Pretty large.

"Question. By Mr. Dawes. Who represented those men who declined to participate in the election?

"Answer. I understood Durant and Fellows, and a few such men."

It is true that General Banks, in his statement, says, in reply to the question as to what portion of the loyal people of Louisiana are represented by the views which Mr. Durant entertains:

"There are not enough to appear at the polls. It is a party of chieftains without an army."

But it is manifest that those who are better acquainted with the facts place a higher estimate on their numerical strength, since they allege their defection as one of the chief reasons for the smallness of the vote.

General Banks, in his statement to the Senate Committee, estimates the number of registered voters within the Union lines at from 15,000 to 18,000; so that not more than one-half participated in the erection of the new government, even of those within the lines actually held by the army, to say nothing of those who lived in all the State of Louisiana lying without our occupancy, and this, too, upon the supposition that every vote that was cast was in favor of ratification.

But it is argued that having an opportunity to vote, their refusal to avail themselves of the privilege was the fault of the recusants, and that they are bound by the acts of those who exercise the power of suffrage.

From this proposition the undersigned wholly dissent. Whatever force the suggestion might have in the case of the choice of representatives or other officers chosen at an election established by and held in conformity with an existing law prescribing such election, they are unable to perceive its application to the creation of a government and the adoption of a constitution emanating and deriving its sanction from the original action of the people, much less to an election ordered by the military power without warrant of law. On the contrary, it was, in their judgment, requisite to the establishment of such government that it should have received the support and sanction of a majority of the loyal people of Louisiana.

In his statement to the committee, General Banks directs attention to the topography of the State of Louisiana, for the purpose of establishing the fact that the lands capable of production are along the river banks, and that the larger portion of arable and therefore inhabited lands are within the Union lines, suggesting thereby the presence of population.

Unless he intended this inference, it is difficult to discover the pertinency of the allusion or the value of his observations in this behalf. In this suggestion he has been even more unfortunate than in relation to the number of votes.

By computation from the photographed map furnished to the committee, it appears that within the lines nominally held by the Union arms, there are 982,714 acres of improved lands, while in the parishes wholly outside, and over which there is no pretence of control, there are 1,574,307 acres. This result is produced upon a calculation most favorable to the claimants, since it embraces parishes, such as Rapides, Concordia, Avoyelles, and St. Martin's, which, while nominally within our lines of control, are really abandoned. From this computation the parishes of Bienville without and Assumption and St. Bernard within our lines are excluded, no data concerning them being furnished by the map.

Without pursuing this branch of the investigation further, the undersigned suggest that the first question should be negatively answered, and that, in view of the facts, it may be truly averred that the people of Louisiana did not participate or concur in the establishment of the government presented for recognition.

The second question is whether the government pretended to be formed was the result of the voluntary act of the people of Louisiana, unprocured by military interference.

This will be best answered by the history of its establishment, by the views of its authors, and its actual capability to effect the purposes for which civil governments are created.

It is testified by Major General Banks, and admitted, that the duty of organizing a Government in the State of Louisiana was committed by the President to General Shepley, then military governor of New Orleans, and to Thomas J. Durant, an eminent citizen of that city; that, in pursuance of the power thus vested in them, they proceeded to some extent in the enrollment of voters and in developing sentiments of loyalty among the inhabitants. The work of reorganization not proceeding with sufficient rapidity to satisfy the Executive, in December, 1863, General Banks received a letter from that functionary, expressing his disappointment at the development of loyal feeling, and calling upon him to communicate the reason. To this letter General Banks replied that he could not explain the cause, but that if the President desired an enrollment of the loyal people, or a government organized, it could be done, and if the Executive would give him directions he would do it immediately. In answer to this proffer authority was conferred upon him to take such measures as he thought necessary to organize a loyal free State government by the people of Louisiana, without other suggestion or limitation.

The authority committed to the former agents of the President was revoked, and the trust was broadly and unrestrictedly confided to the major general commanding the department of the Gulf, the military representative of the commander-in-chief, ruling with absolute authority over the State to be re organized, and of which State he declared that "the fundamental law was martial law." In pursuance of the authority, in execution of the trust, and in assurance of a complete redemption of the pledge made to the President, General Banks, on the 11th of January, 1864, issued an order for the election of State officers and indicated the 22d of February as the day of election, and subsequently, in consummation of the object with which he was charged, issued another order to which the undersigned call attention. In that order the following language is used:

"Those who have exercised or are entitled to the rights of citizens of the United States will be required to participate in the measures necessary for the re-establishment of civil government." "It is therefore a solemn duty resting upon all persons to assist in the earliest possible restoration of civil government. Let them participate in the measures suggested for this purpose. Opinion is free and candidates are numerous. Open hostility cannot be permitted—indifference will be treated as crime and faction as treason."

The undersigned regret that they have not a copy of the official order, but they have no doubt of the correctness of the quotation, as it is fully confirmed by the statement of Major General Banks before the committee. He thus speaks in relation to the election, and the orders issued by him relative thereto:

"I appealed very strongly to the people to take a part in the election. I thought it was necessary, and I said what I thought was right—that the loyal citizen who refused to take any part in the measures necessary for re-establishing the authority of the Government of the United States, or in its political institutions, could not be considered loyal, and had not an absolute claim to remain there. But it was never said to any man, 'You must vote;' 'You shall vote; if you do not you shall be sent away.' That idea never was enforced."

Let it be remembered that the question was not concerning the enforcement of obedience to the laws of the United States, it was not concerning the repression of hostility against its authority, but concerning the re-organization of their State government and the election of their municipal officers, which they had the absolute right to determine, and to which freedom of opinion and action was essential.

Let it also be remembered that, in his letter to the President, General Banks had declared that he could and promised that he would re-organize a State government in Louisiana; and that the purpose being so declared, the agent to effect it was the military commander, vested with complete control over the lives and fortunes of the voter, and holding in his hands the terrible enginery of martial law.

In view of these facts, it appears to the undersigned to be the veriest sophistry to declare that "it was never said to any man, 'You must vote.'"

The order finds its counterpart in the letter of Mason to the Virginia electors, with the additional incentive to obedience that the major general had at his command all the machinery of military commissions, provost marshals, and files of bayonets, to enable him to carry his threat of banishment into speedy and unappealable execution.

It is no answer that he did not do it—it is no palliation that he did not mean to do it—the threat was clear and unequivocal, the power to enforce it was present, and no man but the major general himself could venture to determine that he would not execute it. The invitation was irresistible; the effect, invincible: people voted; Hahn was declared elected, and the promise of the major general thus far redeemed.

Immediately following the gubernatorial election, an order issued from the same inexorable authority, commanding the choice of delegates to a convention, appointing the day of election and the time and place of its assemblage. In pursuance of this command, delegates were chosen, and the first paragraph of the record of the debates indicates their judgment as to the source of their power. This journal commences by the statement:

"This day being fixed by the general order of Major General Nathaniel P. Banks, commanding the United States forces in the department of the Gulf."

At a subsequent stage of their proceedings, on page 614 of the same journal, one of the most active and apparently influential members, afterwards elected a senator and now applying for admission, arguing their capacity to punish for an alleged contempt, thus defines the origin and power of the convention:

"We are not only a convention of the State of Louisiana, but a military power—created and emanating from no other source than the military power, and existing by virtue of civil authority of the Government of the United States."

With such high origin and unlimited power, it is somewhat ludicrous that it was powerless to arrest a simple citizen, but was compelled to request of General Banks to issue his order directing his provost marshal to take measures necessary to enable the sergeant-at-arms to bring a newspaper editor before the convention. So wholly dependent were they on the military authority, and so open in their acknowledgment, that they assembled at the command and sat in the shadow of the sword of the major general commanding the department of the Gulf.

Such and so directly under the instigation of General Banks being the reorganization of the pretended government, the undersigned invite attention to the question whether it is capable to fulfil the legitimate objects of its creation—the protection of the citizen in the enjoyment of his civil rights, in the maintenance of commercial intercourse, and the punishment of offenders against its own laws.

How far it is effective for the former will be manifest from an order issued by command of Major General Hurlbut, so late as December 21, 1864, and signed by Harai Robinson, colonel 1st Louisiana cavalry and provost marshal general. The order is in these words:

["Special Order No. 145.]

"1. The military approval on permits for plantation, family, and trade store supplies, when such permits do not exceed two hundred and fifty dollars, will in future be signed by order of the provost marshal general, by a commissioned officer on duty at this office. This signature shall be valid for all military posts and for the following parishes: St. Bernard, Plaquemines, Orleans, Jefferson, St. Charles, St. John Baptist, St. James, Lafourche, Terrebonne, and as much of Assumption and St. Mary as may be within our military lines."

So utterly unready are the people of Louisiana for civil government, that it is not permitted to the inhabitants to traffic even for family stores, without a military permit, within the parishes considered most loyal, and of these parishes there are only nine within the whole State in which such permit is available.

If such be its condition as to commercial intercourse among its own citizens, the undersigned suggest that the government is placed in even a more absurd view as to its helplessness in assuring protection by the punishment of offenders against its own laws. In proof of this they ask attention to the following order issued by Major General Hurlbut, dated December 27, 1864:

["Special Order No. 349.]

"3. Upon the official report of the attorney general of the State of Louisiana that the ordinary courts of justice are insufficient to punish the offenders named by him, and in consideration that the State government and courts of Louisiana owe their present existence to military authority, it is ordered that Michael De Courcey, Benjamin Orr, E. McShane, Y. M. Robinson, A. G. Pierson, and B. Wadsworth, for peculation and other offences, be sent for trial before the military commission now in session in the city of New Orleans, and of which Brigadier General B. S. Roberts, United States volunteers, is president, and that the attorney general of the State of Louisiana be admitted to appear before said commission as public prosecutor."

What a conclusive refutation of the allegation of the existence of a government capable to maintain itself, and to fulfil the conditions of its establishment, and how absolute the proof as to the regard in which it is held by the military authorities! The attorney general of the State supplicates the major general to supplant the majesty of the law, and to erect a military commission to try offences properly cognizable by the ordinary criminal tribunals; and with cool complacency General Hurlbut accedes to the request, in consideration that the State government and courts owe their existence to military authority, and graciously permits the law officer to appear before the military commission to prosecute offences against the municipal code of Louisiana!

Surely it is mockery to designate such a government by the name of republic, or to dignify such a community with the title of a State.

Two points are pressed by General Banks with much earnestness as inducements to recognition:

1. The propriety of recognition as tending to develop loyal sentiments.

2. The danger that the inhabitants will invite French intervention.

With due respect, the undersigned fail to perceive the force of these suggestions.

Loyalty in Louisiana, in the main, consists of mere submission to the power having the present ascendency. It is clearly and truly stated by General Banks that little reliance is to be placed on an oath of allegiance as a test of fidelity, and it is notorious that the major portion of those within the Union lines, and nearly all the delegates to the convention, took the oath of allegiance to "the Confederate States," and so long as their power was maintained in Louisiana, either voluntarily or compulsorily, demonstrated their faithfulness by obedience. Upon the occupation of New Orleans by the Union forces the same persons, with equal readiness, took the oath prescribed by the President's proclamation, and so long as we hold occupancy and control will remain faithful—but no longer. Should the rebel arms again prevail there, the great body will succumb and relapse into acquiescence in its supremacy.

The only effective mode is to suppress the rebellion in the State—to destroy the government at Shreveport—to take permanent occupancy of the country, and give such assurance of protection as will enable the people to rest secure in their demonstrations of fidelity. This is not to be done by the creation or recognition of improvised or impotent civil governments, but by the steady advance of the army, bringing the inhabitants under our permanent control.

When this shall have been done, the work of restoration and reorganization will be desirable and easy of attainment. Until it shall have been accomplished all schemes of reconstruction are futile, resulting only in the creation of *quasi* civil governments wholly subject to military authority, and incapable of furnishing protection or insuring respect.

The suggestion of French interference and apprehension for the safety of New Orleans savors of the argument *ad captandum*.

The undersigned will be permitted to observe that France is affected by no consideration of the presence or absence of civil government in Louisiana. Without underrating the importance of the city of New Orleans or the navigation of the Mississippi, they suggest that their safety is better insured by naval armaments, well appointed fortifications, and the bayonets of our gallant soldiers, than by the unsubstantial sovereignty vested in Governor Hahn. Foreign intervention has been prevented, not by considerations of national morality or the arts of diplomacy, but by the manifestation of the power and energy of the people of the United States, by her stupendous resources, by her wonderful invention in the perfection of the enginery of war, and by the prowess of her army and navy, rendering doubtful, if not desperate, the issue of any conflict on land or sea.

These are the instrumentalities upon which we must rely, not only for the safety of New Orleans but for the final suppression of the rebellion, until which time the question should be, not how soon States shall be reorganized and members be admitted on this floor, but how they shall be restrained from setting up governments without a people and proposing representatives without constituencies, to the danger of feeble legislation and the detriment of the republic.

In view of the facts elicited by the investigation of the matter committed to them, the undersigned submit the following resolution, dissenting from the vote of the majority of the committee:

Resolved, That M. F. Bonzano, claiming to be a representative from the first congressional district of Louisiana, is not entitled to a seat in this House as a member thereof.

N. B. SMITHERS,
CHAS. UPSON.

February 17—An affirmative report was presented in the cases of A. P. Field and W. D. Mann, claiming seats from the second and third congressional districts in Louisiana, based upon the reasoning and facts stated in the preceding report.

No votes were taken.

THE ARKANSAS QUESTION.

IN SENATE.

1865, January 27—Mr. POMEROY introduced this joint resolution, which was referred to the Committee on the Judiciary:

FOR THE RETURN OF ARKANSAS TO THE UNION.

Whereas the President of the United States, by a proclamation bearing date the sixteenth day of August, one thousand eight hundred and sixty-one, did, among other things, declare that the inhabitants of the State of Arkansas were in a condition of insurrection against the United States, and that all commercial intercourse between the said State, and the inhabitants thereof, and the citizens of other States, and other parts of the United States, was and would remain unlawful, until such insurrection should cease or be suppressed; and whereas, by their own act, the citizens of a portion of the said State met in convention, at Fort Smith, on the thirtieth day of October, anno Domini eighteen hundred and sixty-three, and passed resolutions recommending the choosing of delegates to a State convention; the vigorous prosecution of the war, as long as rebels in arms against the government of the United States could be found, and the abolition of the institution of slavery, and announcing further the determination to support the administration in its efforts to suppress the existing rebellion; and which movement was heartily seconded by thousands of the loyal citizens of the State, who, without knowledge that an amnesty proclamation was about to be promulgated, were earnestly desirous of being recognized again by the general government; and whereas, under the President's proclamation of December eight, eighteen hundred and sixty-three, and his instructions to Major General Steele, then commanding the department of Arkansas, bearing date January twenty, eighteen hundred and sixty-four, a State government was duly, and without military restraint, organized on the fourteenth, fifteenth, and sixteenth days of March, anno Domini eighteen hundred and sixty-four, and a constitution republican in form and forever prohibiting slavery and involuntary servitude, except for the punishment of crime, was ratified by a vote of twelve thousand two hundred and twenty-six for, to one hundred and seventy-seven against it; and whereas the progress of our arms has been such in Arkansas as to justify the re-establishment of a State government therein, and the evidences of the loyalty of the people of this State, evinced by their united and cordial support and adherence to this constitution and the laws made under it, and by furnishing over six full regiments and a battery for the cause of the Union in this national conflict are sufficient to entitle their claim for the recognition of their present State government to the favorable action of Congress: Therefore,

Be it resolved, &c., That the President of the United States be, and he is hereby, authorized and requested to issue his proclamation declaring the inhabitants of Arkansas no longer in a state of insurrection against the United States, and relieving them from the restriction upon their commercial intercourse with the "citizens of other States, and other parts of the United States," created by the said proclamation.

SEC. 2. That the senators and members of the House of Representatives from the said State elected under and by virtue of the new constitution thereof, to represent the said State in the Congress of the United States be permitted to take their seats upon presentation of the usual and proper credentials.

IN HOUSE OF REPRESENTATIVES.

1865, February 17—Mr. DAWES, from the Committee on Elections, made this report:

The Committee of Elections, to whom were referred the credentials of T. M. Jacks and J. M. Johnson, claiming seats in this House as representatives from the first and third congressional districts of Arkansas, submit the following report:

There seems in Arkansas at all times to have been a large number of unconditional Union men. It is evident that the so-called secession ordinance was not passed in accordance with the wishes of the people of the State. The convention elected in 1861 was largely Union, but, without instructions from the people, passed the ordinance of secession.

After three years of war and desolation, the loyal people of Arkansas assembled in convention at Little Rock in January, 1864. The result of the convention's deliberations was the amending of the State constitution, the appointment of a provisional governor, lieutenant governor, and secretary of state, and the designation of the 14th, 15h, and 16th days of March as the time for holding a general election throughout the State.

The acts of this convention, judging from the statements of its members, were rather suggestive than obligatory. Indeed it did not claim its acts as binding until they were ratified by the people, which was done with a unanimity seldom met with. At the election on the 14th, 15th, and 16th of March the acts of the convention were approved by 12,177 voters, while they were disapproved by only 226. At that election the people of more than forty counties elected State and county officers necessary to set to work again the machinery of a loyal State government which had been overthrown by the rebellion in the month of May, 1861.

On the 18th of April, 1864, the State government was formally inaugurated, since which time it has been struggling for an existence under difficulties which those who are strangers to its trials cannot properly appreciate.

The amended constitution differs from the constitution of the State before the rebellion in but a few important particulars.

1st. It forever prohibits slavery or involuntary servitude which it does in the following words, viz:

[Extract from the present Constitution of the State of Arkansas.]

ARTICLE V.

Abolishment of Slavery.

SEC. 1. "Neither slavery nor involuntary servitude shall hereafter exist in this State, otherwise than for the punishment of crime, whereof the party shall have been convicted by due process of law; nor shall any male person arrived at the age of twenty-one years, nor female arrived at the age of eighteen years, be held to serve any person as a servant, under any indenture or contract hereafter made, unless such person shall enter into such indenture or contract while in a state of perfect freedom, and on condition of a *bona fide* consideration received, or to be received" for their services.

"Nor shall any indenture of any negro or mulatto hereafter made and executed out of this State, or, if made in this State, when the term of service exceeds one year, be of the least validity, except those given in case of apprenticeship, which shall not be for a longer term than until the apprentice shall arrive at the age of twenty-one years, if a male, or the age of eighteen years, if a female"

It also provides for the office of lieutenant governor, an office not known to the old State constitution.

The supreme judges of the State are, under the amended constitution elected by the people; under the old they were chosen by the legislature. There are some other trifling differences relating to the trial for cases of assault and battery, the amount of claims that may be tried before a justice's court, &c.

The preamble to the Constitution repudiates emphatically the rebel debt of the State, and declares null and void all acts of rebel magistrates done under the authority of the rebellion, save the solemnization of matrimony, the act of conveyancing, and others of similar nature provided for under like circumstances under the common law. The convention also provided that all laws and parts of laws in force in the State prior to the sixth day of May, A. D. 1861, and not inconsistent with the amended constitution, should be in full force and effect as before the rebellion.

The governor elect was duly and formally inaugurated on the 18th April. The legislature, composed of senators and representatives from more than forty of fifty-five counties in the State, met at the State capitol, on the 11th of April, and each house organized with a quorum present during the first week of the session.

The legislature remained in session to the 1st of June, when they adjourned until the first Monday in November, at which time they again met, and continued in session to the 1st of January of the present year, when they again adjourned until the 1st January, A. D., 1866.

During the session of April and May, 1864, the legislature elected two United States senators, to fill the unexpired terms of Wm. K. Sebastian and Dr. Mitchel, senators from that State previous to the commencement of the rebellion.

During the said session of the legislature they passed an act defining the qualification of voters, which shows most clearly that they entertain no sympathy or fellowship with the rebellion. The sixth section of that act is in the following words:

"*And be it further enacted by the general assembly of the State of Arkansas,* That each voter shall, before depositing his vote at any election in this State, take an oath that he will support the Constitution of the United States and of this State, and that he has not voluntarily borne arms against the United States, or this State, nor aided, directly or indirectly, the so-called confederate authorities, since the eighteenth day of April, A. D. 1864, (the day the governor was inaugurated,) said oath to be administered by one of the judges of the election; and this act shall take effect from and after its passage."

This act shows a commendable prudence on the part of the legislature to guard the ballot-box against the disloyal part of the people. While the constitution makes no provision against returned rebels who were once citizens of the State, this prompt legislation shows that the people are determined to guard themselves in the future against those who have well nigh ruined their State in the past.

Arkansas has given another proof of her loyalty and devotion to the United States, which should not be overlooked. From evidence which your committee have no disposition to discredit, it appears that Arkansas has furnished at least ten thousand volunteer soldiers for the United States armies. These men are to-day either filling a soldier's grave, or the ranks of their country's armies.

At the election in March, 1864, the people of the 1st congressional district elected T. M. Jacks as their representative in Congress, by a vote of about three thousand. The 2d district elected A. A. C. Rogers by a large majority over his competitor. The 3d district, J. M. Johnson, by a very large majority.

The first district is composed of the following named counties: Arkansas, Conway, Crittenden, Craighead, Fulton, Greene, Independence, Izard, Jackson, Lawrence, Mississippi, Monroe, Philips, Poinsett, Prairie, Randolph, St. Francis, Searcy, Van Buren, and White. These counties by their returns show that in the Presidential election in 1860 they cast 16,841 votes. Fourteen of these counties, viz: Arkansas, Conway, Crittenden, Fulton, Independence, Izard, Jackson, Lawrence, Monroe, Philips, Prairie, Randolph, and Van Buren, which participated pretty fully in the election of March, cast the aggregate vote of 3,000. These counties in 1860 gave 14,005 votes—the six counties not voting, or voting to only a very limited extent, in the election of March, to wit: Craighead, Greene, Mississippi, Poinsett, Searcy, and St. Francis gave in 1860 2,836 votes; these, under the ratio of the vote cast in the eleven counties that did vote, should have given about 537 votes at the March election. Of the 3,000 votes cast in this district for member of Congress, T. M. Jacks received all but *fifteen*.

In the second district, composed of the counties of Ashley, Bradley, Calhoun, Chicot, Clark, Columbia, Dallas, Desha, Drew, Hempstead, Hot Springs, Jefferson, Lafayette, Ouachita, Pulaski, Saline, and Union, your committee have not been able to satisfy themselves as to the vote cast; the evidence going to show that in this district the vote was respectable as compared to the whole vote of the State—that some four or five counties did not vote in the election, and that the vote of the counties of Jefferson and Pulaski was relatively large.

In the third district, composed of the counties of Benton, Carroll, Crawford, Franklin, Johnson, Madison, Marion, Montgomery, Newton, Perry, Pike, Polk, Pope, Scott, Clark, Sebastian, Sevier, Washington, and Yell, the vote in March was a tolerably full one, all except the county of Perry participating in the election.

In this district the vote for representative in Congress was nearly five thousand, of which vote J. M. Johnson received over four thousand. These counties in 1860 gave an aggregate vote of 16,932.

The position taken by the committee in the case of Mr. Bonzano, of Louisiana, will apply with equal force to these cases from Arkansas. In the report in that case the committee say:

"This election depends for its validity upon the effect which the House is disposed to give to the efforts to reorganize a State government in Louisiana, which have here been briefly recited. The districting of the State for representatives, and the fixing of the time for holding the election, were the act of the convention. Indeed, the election of governor and other State officers, as well as the existence of the convention itself, as well as its acts, are all parts of the same movements.

"It is objected to their validity, that they neither originated in nor followed any pre-existing law of the State or nation. But the answer to this objection lies in the fact that, in the nature of the case, neither a law of the State nor nation to meet the case was a possibility. The State was attempting to rise out of the ruin caused by an armed *overthrow* of its laws. They had been trampled in the dust; and there existed no body in the State to make an enabling act. Congress cannot pass an enabling act for a State. It is neither one of the powers granted by the several States to the general government, nor necessary to the carrying out of any of those powers; and all 'the powers not delegated to the United States by the Constitution, nor prohibited by it to the States, are reserved to the States respectively, *or the people.*' It is preposterous to have expected at the hands of the rebel authorities in Louisiana that, previous to the overthrow of the State government, they should prepare a legal form of proceeding for its restoration. In the absence of any such legal form prepared beforehand in the State, and like absence of power on the part of the general government, under the delegated powers of the Constitution, it follows, that the power to restore a lost State government in Louisiana existed nowhere, or in 'the people,' the original source of all political power in this country. The people, in the exercise of that power, cannot be required to conform to any particular mode, for that presupposes a power to prescribe outside of themselves, which it has been seen does not exist. The *result* must be republican; for the people and the States have surrendered to the United States, to that extent, the power over their form of government in this, that 'the United States shall guarantee to every State a republican form of government.'

"It follows, therefore, that if this work of reorganizing and re-establishing a State government was the work of the people, it was the legitimate exercise of an inalienable and inherent right, and, if republican in form, is entitled not only to recognition, but to the 'guaranty' of the Constitution."

The committee recommend to the House for its adoption the subjoined resolutions:

Resolved, That T. M. Jacks is entitled to a seat in this House as a representative from the first congressional district in Arkansas.

Resolved, That J. M. Johnson is entitled to a seat in this House as a representative from the third congressional district in Arkansas.

No vote was reached upon the question.

SENATORS FROM INSURRECTIONARY STATES.

SENATOR FROM VIRGINIA.

1865, February 17—Mr. Willey offered the credentials of Joseph Segar, Senator elect from the State of Virginia, to supply the vacancy occasioned by the death of Lemuel J. Bowden.

Mr. SUMNER moved their reference to the Committee on the Judiciary. Mr. SHERMAN moved that the credentials do lie upon the table, which was agreed to—yeas 29, nays 13:

YEAS—Messrs. Anthony, Brown, *Buckalew*, Chandler, Clark, Collamer, Conness, Cowan, Davis, Doolittle, Farwell, Foster, Hale, Harlan, Howard, Howe, Morgan, Morrill, Nye, *Powell*, Ramsey, Sherman, Sprague, Sumner, Ten Eyck, Trumbull, Wade, Wilkinson, Wilson—29.

NAYS—Messrs. Dixon, *Hendricks*, *Johnson*, Lane of Indiana, Lane of Kansas, *McDougall*, *Nesmith*, Pomeroy, *Richardson*, *Saulsbury*, Van Winkle, Willey, *Wright*—13.

Subsequently—at the special session—they were withdrawn, re-presented, and postponed until the next session.

SENATOR FROM LOUISIANA.

March 2—Mr. DOOLITTLE offered the credentials of Michael Hahn as a Senator from Louisiana for six years. Mr. DAVIS objected to the reception of the paper. On motion of Mr. TRUMBULL, the motion of Mr. DOOLITTLE to receive it was laid on the table. Subsequently—at the special session—they were withdrawn, re-presented, and postponed until the next December.

IN SENATE—SPECIAL SESSION.

SENATOR FROM ARKANSAS.

1865, March 7—Mr. LANE, of Kansas, offered the credentials of William D. Snow, as Senator from Arkansas, which were referred to the Committee on the Judiciary.

March 9—Mr. TRUMBULL made this report, which was agreed to:

In the year 1861 the constituted authorities of the State of Arkansas undertook to withdraw that State from the Union, and so far succeeded in the attempt as by force of arms to expel from the State for a time the authorities of the United States, and set up a government in hostility thereto; and in pursuance of an act of Congress, the inhabitants of said State have since been declared to be in a state of insurrection against the United States. The committee, therefore, recommend that the question of the admission of Mr. Snow to a seat be postponed till the next session of Congress, and until Congress shall take action in regard to the recognition of the alleged existing State government in Arkansas.

SENATOR FROM VIRGINIA.

March 9—Mr. DOOLITTLE offered the credentials of John C. Underwood, as Senator from Virginia for six years; which were postponed until the next session.

PREREQUISITES FOR REPRESENTATION IN THE SENATE.

March 8—Mr. SUMNER proposed to offer and have this resolution referred to the Committee on the Judiciary, but objection was made:

Resolved, That where a State has been declared to be in insurrection, no person can be recognized as Senator from such State, or as claimant of a seat as Senator from such State, until after the occurrence of three several conditions: first, the cessation of all armed hostility to the United States within the limits of such State; secondly, the adoption by such State of a constitution of government, republican in form, and not repugnant to the Constitution and laws of the United States; and thirdly, an act of Congress declaring that the people of such State are entitled to representation in the Congress of the United States.

THE SECESSION OF LOUISIANA.

I have recently obtained the journal of the Convention of Louisiana which passed the Ordinance of Secession, and, in view of the interest attaching to these proceedings, subjoin these facts:

1861, January 23—Convention met at Baton Rouge, and provided for the appointment of this Committee of Fifteen "to prepare and report as soon as possible an ordinance providing for the withdrawal of the State of Louisiana from the present Federal Union:" J. Perkins, jr., of Madison, A. Declouet, A. B. Roman, Edward Sparrow, I. Garrett, T. J. Semmes, L. J. Dupre, A. Provosty, W. R. Miles, J. L. Lewis, A. Talbot, W. R. Barrow, J. K. Elgee, C. Roselius, G. M. Williamson.

January 24—Mr. Perkins reported a Secession Ordinance, and a resolution relative to the navigation of the Mississippi river. Mr. Rozier and Mr. Fuqua presented each a substitute for the report. The action of Governor Moore in seizing the forts, arsenals, and munitions of war within the State was approved—yeas 119, nays 5, (Cicero C. Meredith, David Pierson, Joseph A. Rozier, W. T. Stocker, James G. Taliaferro.)

January 25—J. L. Manning, Commissioner from South Carolina, and J. A. Winston, from Alabama, received and heard; and January 30, W. J. Vason, from Georgia, and February 12, John Robertson, from Virginia. An address was received from U. S. Senators Slidell and Benjamin, and Representatives Landrum and Davidson. January 31—George Williamson appointed Commissioner to Texas.

VOTES ON ORDINANCE.

January 25—The question was first taken on Mr. Rozier's substitute, which proposed a Convention of the slaveholding States at Nashville, February 25th next, to determine what amendments of the Constitution are necessary and proper, in case of the failure of the prompt adoption of which said Convention to be reassembled and forthwith organize a separate Confederacy of slaveholding States. The vote was yeas 24, nays 106. The YEAS were:

Messrs. Bermudez, Bienvenu, Clark, Cook, Connelly, Conner of St. Tammany, Cottman, Davidson of Sabine, Duffel, Garrett, Gill, Hough, Lewis of Orleans, Meredith, McCollom, Patterson, Pierson of Winn, Roselius, Rozier, Smart, Stocker, Taliaferro, Verret, Williams—24.

The question was next taken on Mr. Fuqua's substitute, declaring that Louisiana cannot and will not submit to the administration of Lincoln and Hamlin upon the "principles that the Constitution does not recognize property in slaves, that the Government should prevent the extension of slavery into the common territory, and that all the powers of the Government should be so exercised as in time to abolish this institution wherever it exists;" announcing that any attempt to coerce any seceding State will absolve Louisiana from all allegiance to the Federal Government, and that Louisiana in that event would make common cause with the State attacked; and declaring for a Convention of slaveholding States at Montgomery, Alabama, February 4, 1861, as requested by that State, for the formation by said Convention of a Federal Union of the slaveholding States, and the freedom of the navigation of the Mississippi and its tributaries; and for an adjournment until February 28, 1861, to hear the report of the action of the Montgomery Convention. Which was lost—yeas 47, nays 73. The YEAS were:

Messrs. Bermudez, Bienvenu, Bush, Clark, Cook, Connelly, Conner of St. Tammany, Cottman, Davidson of Sabine, Duffel, Fuqua, Gardère, Garrett, Gaudet, Herron, Hough, Hollinsworth, Lagroue, LeBlanc, LeBourgeois, Lewis of Claiborne, Lewis of Orleans, Martin of Assumption, Magee, Melançon, Meredith, McCollom, Patterson, Perkins of Lafourche, Pierson of Winn, Pike, Polk, Pope, Pugh, Roman, Roselius, Rozier, Sompayrac, Scott of Claiborne, Scott of East Feliciana, Stocker, Thomasson, Tucker, Verret, Walker, Williams of East Baton Rouge, Williams of St. Helena —47.

The Ordinance of Secession, as reported from the committee, was then passed—yeas 113, nays 17, as follows:

YEAS—Messrs. W. R. Adams, Wm. Dumont Anderson, Bernard Avegno, A. Barbin, Wm. Ruffin Barrow, E. Bermudez, P. E. Bonford, A. Bonner, C. C. Briscoe, Walthal Burton, Louis Bush, E. G. W. Butler, Thos. J. Caldwell, Fenelon Cannon, Wm. C. Carr, George Clark, Thomas A. Cooke, G. F. Connelly, Lemuel P. Conner, Sidney S. Conner, Wm. Alex. Davidson, E. C. Davidson, Alex. Declouet, Alcibiade DeBlanc, Samuel W. Dorsey, Ed. Duffel, Lucius J. Dupre, J. B. Elam, J. K. Elgee, Ro. W. Estlin, G. L. Fuselier, James O. Fuqua, A. H. Gladden, Y. W. Graves, A. M. Gray, Wm. E. Gill, M. E. Girard, Sid. H. Griffin, J. Hernandez, Andrew S. Herron, B. L. Hodge, Robert Hodges, S. Hollinsworth, Theodore Johnson, Thomas H. Kennedy, Wilson M. Kidd, Felix Labatut, E. Lawrence, Chas. T. Lagroue, Chas. O. LeBlanc, Felix Lewis, John L. Lewis, Th. C. Manning, Henry Marshall, Antoine Marrero, Leon D. Marks, J. N. Marks, Robt. Campbell Martin, John H. Martin, Nehemiah Magee, W. R. Miles, J. J. Michel, Jo. E. Miller, John Moore, Jas. McCloskey, Andrew McCollom, Henderson McFarland, jr., Sam'l Washington McKneely, A. Mouton, M. O. H. Norton, Jules G. Olivier, D. O'Bryan, Wm. Patterson, J. Scudday Perkins, John Perkins, jr., W. M. Perkins, Wm. R. Peck, John Pemberton, Aaron H. Pierson, Wm. S. Pike, H. M. Polk, N. W. Pope, Aug. Provosty, Walter Pugh, Hardy Richardson, J. B. Slawson, W. W. Smart, C. L. Swayze, Thos. J. Semmes, Chas. D. Stewart, Edward Sparrow, J. Sompayrac, Nelson J. Scott, Tho. W. Scott, Washington M. Smith, Benjamin S. Tappan, Augustus Talbot, R. Taylor, of St. Charles, J. A. Taylor, of St. Landry, Louis Texada, J. M. Thomasson, Robert B. Todd, John T. Towles, Caleb J. Tucker, Mark Valentine, W. B. Warren, Alexander Walker, J. A. Williams, James A. Williams, George Williamson, Joseph Biddle Wilkinson, P. S. Wiltz, Zebulon York—113.

NAYS—Messrs. Charles Bienvenu, Thomas E. H. Cottman, Fergus Gardère, Isaiah Garrett, J. K. Gaudet, Wade H. Hough, Louis S. LeBourgeois, George W. Lewis, E. O. Melançon, Cicero C. Meredith, David Pierson, A. B. Roman, Christian Roselius, Joseph A. Rozier, W. T. Stocker, James G. Taliaferro, A. Verret—17.

Upon the announcement of this vote, the President declared the connection between the State of Louisiana and the Federal Union dissolved; the flag of the State was placed on the platform; prayer was pronounced by Rev. W. E. N. Lingfield, and the flag blessed, according to the rites and forms of the Roman Catholic Church, by Father Hubert.

The accompanying resolution recognizing the right of the free navigation of the Mississippi river and its tributaries by all friendly States bordering thereon, the right of egress and ingress of the mouths of the Mississippi by all friendly States and Powers, and declaring "our willingness to enter into any stipulations to guarantee the exercise of said rights," was unanimously adopted.

The ordinance was then signed by 121 members, being all of those who voted above, except Messrs. Garrett, Hough, George W. Lewis, Meredith, D. Pierson, Roselius, Rozier, Stocker, and Taliaferro.

ON SUBMITTING THE ORDINANCE AND CONSTITUTION TO POPULAR VOTE.

Pending the final vote above taken,

A resolution of Mr. Bienvenu that, whatever be the action of the Convention on Secession, it shall have no effect until the same shall have been ratified by a vote of the majority of the people at the ballot-box, on the 25th of February, 1861, was disagreed to—yeas 45, nays 84. The affirmative vote was the same as on Mr. Fuqua's substitute, except that Messrs. Cook, Hollinsworth, Pope, and Walker, then in the affirmative, were now in the negative, and Mr. A. H. Pierson, then not voting, was now in the affirmative, and Mr. Taliaferro, then in the negative, was now in the affirmative.

March 16—Mr. Bienvenu offered an ordinance requesting the President of the Convention to lay before it the official returns at the election for the delegates; but a motion to suspend the rules for the purpose was lost—yeas 23, nays 73.

An ordinance offered by Mr. Cannon, to submit the permanent constitution of the Confederate States adopted by the Confederate Congress, March 11, to the qualified voters of the State for their ratification or rejection, on the 6th of May, was rejected—yeas 26, nays 74. The YEAS were:

Messrs. Bienvenu, Bush, Cannon, Clark, Connelly, Cottman, Davidson of Sabine, Duffel, Fuqua, Herron, Hough, Johnson, Lagroue, Lewis of Claiborne, Lewis of Orleans, McCollom, Melançon, Meredith, Pike, Roselius, Rozier, Scott of East Feliciana, Sompayrac, Stocker, Taliaferro, Thomasson, Tucker—26.

March 21—An ordinance offered by Mr. Rozier, to provide for the election of a convention "to adopt or reject the Confederate Constitution," was laid on the table—yeas 94, nays 10, (Messrs. Bienvenu, Connelly, Duffel, Garrett, Lewis of Orleans, Meredith, Roselius, Rozier, Stocker, Taliaferro.)

The constitution was then ratified, and declared binding upon the people of the State of Louisiana—yeas 101, nays 7, (Messrs. Bienvenu, Garrett, Lewis of Orleans, Roselius, Rozier, Stocker, Taliaferro).

RIGHT OF SECEDING FROM THE CONFEDERACY.

Mr. Rozier offered an amendment to the ratifying ordinance, declaring that in adopting the constitution, the State "expressly reserves to herself the right, peaceably to withdraw from the Union created by that constitution, whenever, in the judgment of her citizens, her paramount interest may require it;" which was laid on the table—yeas 92, nays 11, (Messrs. Bienvenu, Connelly, Duffel, Garrett, Lewis of Orleans, Martin of Assumption, Melançon, Roselius, Rozier, Stocker, Taliaferro.)

PUBLIC PROPERTY SEIZED.

February 5, 1861—A committee reported that "this public property was in the hands of the officers of the late Federal Government, within the parish of Orleans, February 1, 1861:"

In Sub-Treasurer's vault at the Mint, in gold and silver coin	$483,983 98
In Treasury of the Mint, in gold, silver, and copper	101,745 81
In Dr. M. F. Bonzano's possession, melter and refiner	143,689 85
In B. F. Taylor's possession, coiner	172,875 86
Of this sum	$902,295 50

$389,267 46 belong to "permanent bullion fund."
249,926 68 belong to "individual depositors."
4,051 38 "accumulated profit on coinage."

$643,245 52

The amount of "import duties assessed on merchandise in warehouse, entered for warehousing to 31st January, 1861," was reported, February 11, by Collector F. H. Hatch, at $734,336.

March 7—An ordinance passed transferring the "Bullion fund" ($389,267 46) to the "Government of the Confederate States of America," and the sum of $147,519 66, being the balance received by the State depositary from the customs since January 31st. This ordinance passed without a division, several amendments intended to reduce the amount transferred having failed by decided votes.

OFFICERS OF THE CONVENTION.

The officers of the convention were: J. Thomas Wheat, *Secretary;* E. E. Kidd, *Assistant Secretary;* J. O. Nixon, of the New Orleans *Crescent, Printer;* A. M. Perrault, *Sergeant-at-Arms;* J. R. T. Hyams, *Warrant Clerk;* Emile Wilz and Albert Fabre, *Translating Clerks;* William Simmons, *Doorkeeper;* James Kirby, *Page.*

Constitutional Amendment for the Extinction of Slavery, and Kindred Subjects.

THE ANTI-SLAVERY AMENDMENT.

1865, January 6—Mr. ASHLEY called up the motion to reconsider the vote taken June 15, 1864, (see page 258,) when the whole subject was discussed.

January 31—Mr. STILES moved to lay on the table the motion to reconsider, which was not agreed to—yeas 57, nays 111, as follows:

YEAS—Messrs. *James C. Allen, William J. Allen, Ancona, Bliss, Brooks, James S. Brown, Chanler, Clay, Cox, Cravens, Dawson, Denison, Eden, Edgerton, Eldridge, Finck, Ganson, Grider, Hall, Harding, Harrington, Benjamin G. Harris, Charles M. Harris, Holman, Philip Johnson, William Johnson, Kalbfleisch, Kernan, Knapp, Law, Long, Mallory, William H. Miller, Jas. R. Morris, Morrison, Noble, John O'Neill, Pendleton, Perry, Pruyn, Samuel J. Randall, Robinson, Ross, Scott, William G. Steele, Stiles, Strouse, Stuart, Sweat, Townsend, Wadsworth, Ward, Chilton A. White, Joseph W. White, Winfield, Benjamin Wood, Fernando Wood*—57.

NAYS—Messrs. Alley, Allison, Ames, Anderson, Arnold, Ashley, *Baily, Augustus C. Baldwin*, John D. Baldwin, Baxter, Beaman, Blaine, Blair, Blow, Boutwell, Boyd, Brandegee, Broomall, William G. Brown, Ambrose W. Clark, Freeman Clarke, Cobb, *Coffroth*, Cole, Creswell, Henry Winter Davis, Thomas T. Davis, Dawes, Deming, Dixon, Donnelly, Driggs, Dumont, Eckley, Eliot, Farnsworth, Frank, Garfield, Gooch, Grinnell, Griswold, Hale, *Herrick*, Higby, Hooper, Hotchkiss, A. W. Hubbard, John H. Hubbard, Hulburd, Ingersoll, Jenckes, Julian, Kasson, Kelley, Francis W. Kellogg, Orlando Kellogg, *King*, Knox, Littlejohn, Loan, Longyear, Marvin, *McAllister*, McBride, McClurg, McIndoe, Samuel F. Miller, Moorhead, Morrill, Dan'l Morris, Amos Myers, Leonard Myers, Norton, *Odell*, Charles O'Neill, Orth, Patterson, Perham, Pike, Pomeroy, Price, William H. Randall, Alexander H. Rice, John H. Rice, Edward H. Rollins, *James S. Rollins*, Schenck, Scofield, Shannon, Sloan, Smith, Smithers, Spalding, Starr, Stevens, Thayer, Thomas, Tracy, Upson, Van Valkenburgh, Ellihu B. Washburne, William B. Washburn, Webster, *Wheeler*, Williams, Wilder, Wilson, Windom, Woodbridge, Worthington, *Yeaman*—111.

The motion to reconsider was then agreed to—yeas 112, nays 57, as follows:

YEAS—Messrs. Alley, Allison, Ames, Anderson, Arnold, Ashley, *Baily*, John D. Baldwin, Baxter, Beaman, Blaine, Blair, Blow, Boutwell, Boyd, Brandegee, Broomall, William G. Brown, Ambrose W. Clark, Freeman Clarke, Cobb, *Coffroth*, Cole, Creswell, Henry Winter Davis, Thomas T. Davis, Dawes, Deming, Dixon, Donnelly, Driggs, Dumont, Eckley, Eliot, *English*, Farnsworth, Frank, Garfield, Gooch, Grinnell, Griswold, Hale, *Herrick*, Higby, Hooper, Hotchkiss, A. W. Hubbard, John H. Hubbard, Hulburd, Ingersoll, Jenckes, Julian, Kasson, Kelley, Francis W. Kellogg, Orlando Kellogg, *King*, Knox, Littlejohn, Loan, Longyear, Marvin, *McAllister*, McBride, McClurg, McIndoe, Samuel F. Miller, Moorhead, Morrill, Daniel Morris, Amos Myers, Leonard Myers, Norton, *Odell*, Charles O'Neill, Orth, Patterson, Perham, Pike, Pomeroy, Price, William H. Randall, Alexander H. Rice, John H. Rice, Edward H. Rollins, *James S. Rollins*, Schenck, Scofield, Shannon, Sloan, Smith, Smithers, Spalding, Starr, Stevens, Thayer, Thomas, Tracy, Upson, Van Valkenburgh, Ellihu B. Washburne, William B. Washburn, Webster, Whaley, *Wheeler*, Williams, Wilder, Wilson, Windom, Woodbridge, Worthington, *Yeaman*—112.

NAYS—Messrs. *James C. Allen, William J. Allen, Ancona, Bliss, Brooks, James S. Brown, Chanler, Clay, Cox, Cravens, Dawson, Denison, Eden, Edgerton, Eldridge, Finck, Ganson, Grider, Hall, Harding, Harrington, Benjamin G. Harris, Charles M. Harris, Holman, Philip Johnson, William Johnson, Kalbfleisch, Kernan, Knapp, Law, Long, Mallory, William H. Miller, James R. Morris, Morrison, Noble, John O'Neill, Pendleton, Perry, Pruyn, Samuel J. Randall, Robinson, Ross, Scott, William G. Steele, Stiles, Strouse, Stuart, Sweat, Townsend, Wadsworth, Ward, Chilton A. White, Joseph W. White, Winfield, Benjamin Wood, Fernando Wood*—57.

The resolution, as given on page 256, then passed*—yeas 119, nays 56, 8 absent,† as follows:

YEAS—Messrs. Alley, Allison, Ames, Anderson, Arnold, Ashley, *Baily, Augustus C. Baldwin*, John D. Baldwin, Baxter, Beaman, Blaine, Blair, Blow, Boutwell, Boyd, Brandegee, Broomall, William G. Brown, Ambrose W. Clark, Freeman Clarke, Cobb, *Coffroth*, Cole, Colfax, (*Speaker*,) Creswell, Henry Winter Davis, Thomas T. Davis, Dawes, Deming, Dixon, Donnelly, Driggs, Dumont, Eckley, Eliot, *English*, Farnsworth, Frank, *Ganson*, Garfield, Gooch, Grinnell, Griswold, Hale, *Herrick*, Higby, Hooper, Hotchkiss, Asahel W. Hubbard, John H. Hubbard, Hulburd, *Hutchins*, Ingersoll, Jenckes, Julian, Kasson, Kelley, Francis W. Kellogg, Orlando Kellogg, *King*, Knox, Littlejohn, Loan, Longyear, Marvin, *McAllister*, McBride, McClurg, McIndoe, Samuel F. Miller, Moorhead, Morrill, Daniel Morris, Amos Myers, Leonard Myers, *Nelson*, Norton, *Odell*, Charles O'Neill, Orth, Patterson, Perham, Pike, Pomeroy, Price, *Radford*, William H. Randall, Alexander H. Rice, John H. Rice, Edward H. Rollins, *James S. Rollins*, Schenck, Scofield, Shannon, Sloan, Smith, Smithers, Spalding, Starr, *John B. Steele*, Stevens, Thayer, Thomas, Tracy, Upson, Van Valkenburgh, Ellihu B. Washburne, William B. Washburn, Webster, Whaley, *Wheeler*, Williams, Wilder, Wilson, Windom, Woodbridge, Worthington, *Yeaman*—119.

NAYS—Messrs. *James C. Allen, William J. Allen, Ancona, Bliss, Brooks, James S. Brown, Chanler, Clay, Cox, Cravens, Dawson, Denison, Eden, Edgerton, Eldridge, Finck, Grider, Hall, Harding, Harrington, Benjamin G. Harris, Charles M. Harris, Holman, Philip Johnson, William Johnson, Kalbfleisch, Kernan, Knapp, Law, Long, Mallory, William H. Miller, James R. Morris, Morrison, Noble, John O'Neill, Pendleton, Perry, Pruyn, Samuel J. Randall, Robinson, Ross, Scott, William G. Steele, Stiles, Strouse, Stuart, Sweat, Townsend, Wadsworth, Ward, Chilton A. White, Joseph W. White, Winfield, Benjamin Wood, Fernando Wood*—56.

THE PRESIDENT'S APPROVAL.

The joint resolution was approved by the

---

*1865, February 4—The delegates from certain Territories obtained permission to enter this paper upon the Journal of the House:

HOUSE OF REPRESENTATIVES,
WASHINGTON, *February* 1, 1865.

Representing Territories which must soon become States, as Delegates deprived of the inestimable privilege of voting in this House, and feeling a deep interest in the proposition to amend the Federal Constitution forever prohibiting slavery within the jurisdiction of the United States, demanded alike by the exigencies of the times, the voice of the loyal people, and by our efforts in the field to suppress a rebellion inaugurated and sustained for the purpose of perpetuating slavery, we cannot do less than state that the measure meets our unqualified approbation.

H. P. BENNET, Colorado.
J. F. KINNEY, Utah.
S. G. DAILY, Nebraska.
CHARLES D. POSTON, Arizona.
J. B. S. TODD, Dacotah.
W. H. WALLACE, Idaho.
FRANCISCO PEREA, New Mexico.

†ABSENT—Messrs. *Lazear, Le Blond, Marcy, McDowell, McKinney, Middleton, Rogers, Voorhees*—8.

PRESIDENT February 1, respecting which, the Senate, February 7, passed this resolution :

Resolved, That the article of amendment proposed by Congress to be added to the Constitution of the United States respecting the extinction of slavery therein, having been inadvertently presented to the President for his approval, it is hereby declared that such approval was unnecessary to give effect to the action of Congress in proposing said amendment, inconsistent with the former practice in reference to all amendments to the Constitution heretofore adopted,* and being inadvertently done, should not constitute a precedent for the future; and the Secretary is hereby instructed not to communicate the notice of the approval of said proposed amendment by the President to the House of Representatives.

A concurrent resolution was passed, requesting the PRESIDENT to transmit to the Executives of the several States the above amendment.

THE RULE OF RATIFICATION.

IN SENATE.

1865, February 4—Mr. SUMNER submitted the following resolutions, which were ordered to be printed:

Concurrent resolutions declaring the rule in ascertaining the three-fourths of the several States required in the ratification of a constitutional amendment.

Whereas Congress, by a vote of two-thirds of both houses, has proposed an amendment to the Constitution prohibiting slavery throughout the United States, which, according to the existing requirement of the Constitution, will be valid to all intents and purposes as part of the Constitution, when ratified by the legislatures of three-fourths of the several States; and whereas, in the present condition of the country, with certain States in arms against the national government, it becomes necessary to determine what number of States constitutes the three-fourths required by the Constitution; therefore,

Resolved by the Senate, (the House of Representatives concurring,) That the rule followed in ascertaining the *two-thirds of both houses* proposing the amendment to the Constitution should be followed in ascertaining the *three-fourths of the several States* ratifying the amendment; that, as in the first case, the two-thirds are founded on the simple fact of representation in the two houses, so in the second case, the three-fourths must be founded on the simple fact of representation in the government of the country, and the support thereof, and that any other rule establishes one basis for the proposition of the amendment and another for its ratification, placing one on a simple fact and the other on a claim of right, while it also recognizes the power of rebels in arms to interpose a veto upon the national government in one of its highest functions.

Resolved, That all acts, executive and legislative, in pursuance of the Constitution, and all treaties made under the authority of the United States, are valid to all intents and purposes throughout the United States, although certain rebel States fail to participate therein; and that the same rule is equally applicable to an amendment of the Constitution.

Resolved, That the amendment of the Constitution, prohibiting slavery throughout the United States, will be valid, to all intents and purposes, as part of the Constitution whenever ratified by three-fourths of the States *de facto* exercising the powers and prerogatives of the United States under the Constitution thereof.

Resolved, That any other rule, requiring the participation of the rebel States, while illogical and unreasonable, is dangerous in its consequences, inasmuch as all recent Presidential proclamations, including that of emancipation, also, all recent acts of Congress, including those creating the national debt and establishing a national currency; and also all recent treaties, including the treaty with Great Britain for the extinction of the slave trade, have been made, enacted, or ratified respectively without any participation of the rebel States.

Resolved, That any other rule must tend to postpone the great day when the prohibition of slavery will be valid to all intents and purposes as part of the Constitution of the United States; but the rule herewith declared will assure the immediate ratification of the prohibition and the consummation of the national desires.

*The amendment *proposed* by the 36th Congress was *approved* by President Buchanan, March 2, 1861. See *Statutes at Large*, vol. 12, p. 251.

PROPOSED COMPENSATION TO LOYAL SLAVE OWNERS.

IN HOUSE OF REPRESENTATIVES.

1865, February 6—Mr. ROLLINS, of Missouri, introduced the following joint resolution, which was laid over:

Whereas the Senate and House of Representatives of the Congress of the United States having passed, on the 31st day of January, 1865, a joint resolution to submit to the Legislatures of the several States an amendment to the Constitution of the United States, which joint resolution is as follows:

"*Resolved by the Senate and House of Representatives of the United States of America in Congress assembled*, That the following article be proposed to the Legislatures of the several States as an amendment to the Constitution of the United States, which, when ratified by three-fourths of said Legislatures, shall be valid, to all intents and purposes, as a part of the said Constitution, namely:

"ART. XIII. SEC. 1. Neither slavery nor involuntary servitude, except as a punishment for crime, whereof the party shall have been duly convicted, shall exist within the United States, or any place subject to their jurisdiction.

"SEC. 2. Congress shall have power to enforce this article by appropriate legislation."

And whereas by the ratification of this amendment by three-fourths of the several States all persons heretofore held as slaves under the laws of certain States of the Union will be made free; and in consequence thereof a large number of citizens, (among them many widows and orphans,) their former owners, who are, have always been, or may be willing to again become faithful to the Government of the United States, and who have not been in the civil or military service of the so-called Confederate States, will be subjected to heavy pecuniary losses; and whereas this being a measure necessary to "form a more perfect Union, establish justice" to all men, "insure domestic tranquillity," "promote the general welfare, and secure the blessings of liberty to ourselves" and future generations, in the attainment of which great objects the people of all the States have a common interest and for their establishment should make mutual sacrifices;

Be it therefore resolved, &c., That all persons faithful to the Constitution and obedient to the laws of the United States, residents of any State that shall ratify the amendment to the Constitution of the United States proposed to the Legislatures of the several States by the Congress of the United States on the 31st day of January, 1865, who have not been in the civil or military service of the so-called Confederate States, and who have been deprived of the services of these slaves, heretofore recognized by law as property by said amendment, or by any act or ordinance of emancipation of any State of the United States, shall receive therefor a just and reasonable compensation; said compensation to be provided for by the United States Government without unreasonable delay.

OTHER PROPOSITIONS FOR AMENDMENT.

APPORTIONMENT OF REPRESENTATION.*

IN SENATE.

1865, February 5—Mr. SUMNER offered the

*Letter of Prof. Francis Lieber, LL. D., Columbia College, New York, to Senator Morgan:

SIR: As the election, on the 8th of November last, has added one of the highest national acts to the history of our kind, so the amendment of the Constitution which yesterday passed the House of Representatives, will be the greatest effect of the present revolt, if, as we all hope, three-fourths of the State Legislatures shall give their assent.

The same year, 1788, saw the framing of our Constitution and the first cultivation of the cotton-plant in Georgia; and in course of time this textile plant gave renewed vitality and expansion to slavery, festering in our great polity, until the gangrene broke out in the deep woe of a wide and bitter civil war. The year 1865 will cure our system of this poisonous malady. Seventy-seven years is a long period; the reckless rebellion has brought grief to all and anguish to many hearts, but if the effect of the fevered period be the throwing off of the malignant virus, the Nation will stand purified, and the dire inconsistency which has existed so long between our Bill of Rights of the Fourth of July and our fostering protection of extending bondage, will at last pass away. The sacrifices which we have made will not have been too great.

The amendment which is now offered to the American people runs thus:

"*Neither slavery nor involuntary servitude, except as a*

following, which was referred to the Committee on the Judiciary:

Resolved, (two-thirds of both Houses concurring,) That

---

punishment for crime, whereof the party shall have been duly convicted, shall exist within the United States, or any place subject to their jurisdiction."

These are simple and straightforward words, allowing of no equivocation, yet, considered in connection with some passages of the Constitution, they require some remarks, which I address to you, Sir, as one of the United States Senators from New York, and as my neighbor in this city.

The amendment extinguishes slavery in the whole dominion of the United States. The Constitution as it now stands, (Article 1, section 2, paragraph 3,) however, directs that representatives "shall be apportioned among the several States, which may be included within the Union, according to their respective numbers, which shall be determined by adding to the whole number of free persons, including those bound to service for a term of years, and, excluding Indians not taxed, three-fifths of all other persons."

If, then, "all other persons"—that is, slaves—are declared free, and the foregoing provision of the Constitution is not amended, we simply add two-fifths to the basis of apportionment of Representatives in the Southern States; in other words, the number of Representatives in Congress from the States in which slavery has existed will be increased by the present amendment. As, however, these States, and especially those in which the colored citizens exceed in number the whites, will not give the common suffrage to the citizens of African extraction (as, indeed, many of the Northern States—for instance Pennsylvania—do not give it, and as other States give the right of voting to colored people on the condition of possessing freeholds only,) the result of the amendment as now proposed, without a supplementary amendment, would be an increased number of Southern Representatives in Congress of the same number of white citizens. In this case the Rebellion, though ultimately subdued at the cost of torrents of our blood and streams of our wealth, would be rewarded with an enlarged representation. No loyal citizen can wish for such a consummation. How is the difficulty to be avoided?

Let us first remember the following three points:

1. In the practice of every State of the Union those citizens vote for electors of the President of the United States who have a right to vote for Representatives in Congress. Immediately after the adoption of the Constitution of the United States, the Legislatures of several States elected the electors; but a more national spirit soon prevailed, and in all the different States of the Union the people elected the electors, except in South Carolina. There the Legislature retained the election of electors down to the breaking out of the rebellion, on the avowed ground that thus the State obtained a greater influence, this election of electors in South Carolina always taking place after the election by the people had been consummated in all the other States.

2. In every State those citizens who have a right to vote for the most numerous branch of the State Legislature, have also the right to vote for members of Congress.

3. In every State of the Union it is the State itself which determines by its own Constitution, who shall have the right to vote for members of the State Legislature.

These considerations, then, would lead to the suggestion, that the apportionment of members of Congress ought to be made according to the numbers of citizens who in each State have the right to vote for the State Legislature, or for its most numerous branch.

This suggestion may be expressed in an amendment additional to the one just passed, in such words as these:

"Representatives shall be apportioned among the several States which may be included within this Union, according to the respective numbers of male citizens of age having the qualifications requisite for electing members of the most numerous branch of the respective State Legislatures. The actual enumeration of said citizens shall be regularly made by the census of the United States, but a special census shall take place before the next new apportionment of representatives shall be made by the Congress of the United States."

You will observe that the words used in this proposition of an amendment have been taken, as far as it was feasible, from the Constitution itself. Article 1, section 2, paragraphs 1 and 3.

Believing, as I do, that this subject deserves the attention of the American people, I have not hesitated to make use of your permission to address to you this public letter, and have the honor to be, sir, your very obedient,

FRANCIS LIEBER.

NEW YORK, *Feb.* 1, 1865.

Hon. E. D. MORGAN, *Senator of the United States, Washington, D. C.*

the following article be proposed to the Legislatures of the several States as an amendment to the Constitution of the United States, which, when ratified by three-fourths of such Legislatures, shal become a part of the Constitution, to wit:

Representatives shall be apportioned among the several States which may be included within this Union, according to the number of male citizens of age having in each State the qualifications requisite for electors of the most numerous branch of the State Legislature. The actual enumeration of such citizens shall be made by the census of the United States.

February 22—Mr. TRUMBULL, from the committee, reported adversely upon it.

IN HOUSE OF REPRESENTATIVES.

1864, December 7—Mr. SLOAN offered the following resolution:

Resolved, That the Judiciary Committee be instructed to inquire into the expediency of so amending section two of article one of the Constitution of the United States, that Representatives in Congress shall be apportioned among the several States which may be included within the Union, according to their respective numbers of qualified electors, and to report by bill or otherwise.

Which was adopted—yeas 60, nays 55, as follows:

YEAS—Messrs. Alley, Allison, Ames, Arnold, *Baily*, John D. Baldwin, Baxter, Beaman, Blow, Boutwell, Boyd, Broomall, Ambrose W. Clark, Cobb, Cole, Donnelly, Driggs, Eckley, Eliot, Farnsworth, Garfield, Grinnell, Hooper, Asahel W. Hubbard, Hulburd, Ingersoll, Julian, Kasson, Kelley, Orlando Kellogg, Longyear, Marvin, McBride, McClurg, Moorhead, Morrill, Daniel Morris, Leonard Myers, Norton, Charles O'Neill, Orth, Patterson, Perham, Price, William H. Randall, Alexander H. Rice, John H. Rice, Schenck, Shannon, Sloan, Spalding, Starr, Stevens, Thomas, Upson, Van Valkenburgh, Ellihu B. Washburne, *Wheeler*, Williams, Wilson—60.

NAYS—Messrs. *James C. Allen*, *Ancona*, *Augustus C. Baldwin*, Blair, *Bliss*, Brandegee, *Brooks*, *James S. Brown*, *Chanler*, *Coffroth*, *Cox*, Dawes, *Dawson*, Deming, *Denison*, Dixon, *Eden*, *English*, *Finck*, Frank, *Ganson*, *Grider*, *Harding*, *Harrington*, *Holman*, J. H. Hubbard, Jenckes, *Kalbfleisch*, *Kernan*, *Law*, *Le Blond*, *Marcy*, *Middleton*, *William H. Miller*, *James R. Morris*, *Morrison*, *Noble*, *Odell*, *John O'Neill*, *Pendleton*, *Pruyn*, *Radford*, *Rogers*, *Scott*, Smith, Smithers, *John B. Steele*, *William G. Steele*, *Stiles*, *Strouse*, *Stuart*, *Sweat*, *Townsend*, Webster, Whaley, *Fernando Wood*—55.

1865, January 16—Mr. SLOAN introduced a bill to submit to the Legislatures of the several States this proposition:

ART. XIII. SEC. 1. Representatives in Congress shall be apportioned among the several States which may be included within this Union, according to their respective numbers of qualified electors. The actual enumeration shall be made in the year 1870, and within every subsequent term of ten years, in such manner as Congress shall by law direct.

SEC. 2. Direct taxes shall be apportioned among the several States according to the appraised value of taxable property therein respectively. The rule of appraisal and taxation shall be uniform.

Referred to the Committee on the Judiciary, and not reported upon.

TO AUTHORIZE THE TAXING OF EXPORTS.

IN SENATE.

1865, January 23—Mr. DIXON offered this joint resolution:

Resolved, &c., (two-thirds of both Houses concurring,) That in lieu of the fifth paragraph of the ninth section of the first article of the Constitution of the United States, the following be proposed as an amendment to the Constitution of the United States, which, when ratified by three-fourths of the legislatures of the several States, shall be valid to all intents and purposes as part of the said Constitution, to wit:

The Congress shall have power to lay a tax or duty on articles exported from any State.

February 22—Mr. TRUMBULL, from the committee, reported adversely, deeming it injudicious and unadvisable at this time to propose that amendment to the Constitution.

IN HOUSE OF REPRESENTATIVES.

1864, December 5—Mr. Davis, of Maryland, offered the following, which was referred to the Committee on Ways and Means:

Resolved, That the Committee on Ways and Means be instructed to report a bill for the amendment of the Constitution, providing that so much of the ninth section of the first article of the Constitution as declares that "no tax or duty shall be laid on articles exported from any State" be, and the same is hereby, annulled.

The Committee made no report. (See page 259 for Mr. Blaine's proposition on same subject)

TO RECOGNIZE THE CHRISTIAN RELIGION.

IN SENATE.

1865, February 22—Mr. Trumbull, from the Judiciary Committee, asked to be discharged from the further consideration of the memorial of the Presbytery of Cincinnati of September 20, 1864, and the petition of citizens for such an amendment to the Constitution as will more fully recognize the obligations of the Christian religion, and of the memorial of the Executive Committee of the Board of Delegates of the American Israelites protesting against said amendment.

—

TRANSFER OF A GUNBOAT TO LIBERIA.

IN SENATE.

1864, December 15—The Senate passed a bill to authorize the President to transfer a gunboat to the government of Liberia, (as recommended in his message,) by a vote of yeas 33, nays 9, as follows:

Yeas—Messrs. Anthony, Brown, Chandler, Clark, Collamer, Conness, Cowan, Dixon, Doolittle, Farwell, Foot, Foster, Grimes, Harlan, Harris, Henderson, Howard, Johnson, Lane of Indiana, Lane of Kansas, Morgan, Pomeroy, Ramsey, Sherman, Sprague, Sumner, Ten Eyck, Trumbull, Van Winkle, Wade, Wilkinson, Willey, Wilson—33.

Nays—Messrs. *Buckalew, Carlile, Davis, Harding, Hendricks, Nesmith, Powell, Riddle, Wright*—9.

The bill was not reached in the House.

TO REMOVE DISQUALIFICATION OF COLOR IN CARRYING THE MAILS.

IN SENATE.

1864, December 19—The following bill, (see p. 240)—

That from and after the passage of this act no person, by reason of color, shall be disqualified from employment in carrying the mails, and all acts and parts of acts establishing such disqualification, including especially the seventh section of the act of March 3, 1825, are hereby repealed—

Passed the Senate—

Yeas—Messrs Anthony, Brown, Clark, Conness, Dixon, Doolittle, Farwell, Foot, Foster, Grimes, Harlan, Harris, Henderson, Howe, Lane of Indiana, Lane of Kansas, Morgan, Pomeroy, Ramsey, Sherman, Sprague, Sumner, Van Winkle, Wilkinson, Willey, Wilson—36.

Nays—Messrs. *Davis, Powell, Richardson, Riddle, Wright*—5.

Mr. Johnson explained that he would have voted "aye" if present in time.

1865, March 3—The House considered the bill. Mr. Eden moved that it be laid on the table, which was lost—yeas 30, nays 65, as follows:

Yeas—Messrs. *Ancona, Bliss, James S. Brown, Chanler, Coffroth, Cox, Cravens, Eden, Edgerton, Eldridge, Finck, Knapp*, Knox, *Le Blond, Long, Marcy, Middleton, James R. Morris, Noble, John O'Neill*, Price, *Pruyn, Samuel J. Randall*, William H. Randall, *Ross, Scott, Stiles, Strouse, Townsend, Chilton A. White*—30.

Nays—Messrs Allison, Ames, Arnold, Ashley, *Baily*, John D. Baldwin, Baxter, Beaman, Blow, Boutwell, Boyd, Broomall, Ambrose W. Clark, Cobb, Cole, Creswell, Henry Winter Davis, Dawes, Dixon, Eckley, Eliot, Farnsworth, Frank, Garfield, Gooch, Grinnell, Griswold, Higby, Asahel W. Hubbard, John H. Hubbard, Hulburd, Ingersoll, Jenckes, Kelley, Littlejohn, Longyear, Marvin, McBride, McClurg, Samuel F. Miller, Moorhead, Morrill, Norton, Charles O'Neill, Orth, Patterson, Perham, Pomeroy, Alexander H. Rice, John H. Rice, Schenck, Scofield, Shannon, Sloan, Smithers, Thayer, Upson, Van Valkenburgh, Ellihu B. Washburne, Williams, Wilder, Wilson, Windom, Woodbridge, Worthington—65.

It then passed without a division.

EXCLUSION OF COLORED PERSONS FROM THE CARS.

IN SENATE.

Pending the bill to incorporate the Baltimore and Washington Depot and Potomac Ferry Railway Company,

1865, January 17—Mr. Sumner moved to add this proviso:

Provided, That no person shall be excluded from any car on account of color.

Which was agreed to—yeas 24, nays 6, as follows:

Yeas—Messrs. Anthony, Brown, Clark, Collamor, Conness, Dixon, Farwell, Foot, Foster, Harlan, Harris, Henderson, Hicks, Howard, Howe, Morgan, Morrill, Ramsey, Sherman, Sprague, Sumner, Van Winkle, Willey, Wilson—24.

Nays—Messrs. *Davis, Hendricks, Powell, Richardson, Riddle, Saulsbury*—6.

This bill did not finally pass.

Pending the supplement to the charter of the Metropolitan Railroad Company in the District of Columbia, (the Senate being in Committee of the Whole,)

1865, February 4—Mr. Sumner moved this new section:

That the provision prohibiting any exclusion from any car on account of color, already applicable to the Metropolitan railroad, is hereby extended to every other railroad in the District of Columbia.

Which was not agreed to—yeas 19, nays 20, as follows:

Yeas—Messrs. Anthony, Brown, Clark, Collamer, Farwell, Foot, Harlan, Harris, Henderson, Howard, Howe, Lane of Kansas, Morgan, Nye, Pomeroy, Ramsey, Stewart, Sumner, Wilson—19.

Nays—Messrs. *Buckalew*, Conness, Cowan, *Davis*, Dixon, Doolittle, Hale, *Hendricks, Johnson*, Lane of Indiana, Morrill, *Nesmith, Powell, Richardson, Saulsbury*, Ten Eyck, Trumbull, Van Winkle, Willey, *Wright*—20.

Immediately after, Mr. Sumner renewed it in open Senate.

February 6—It was agreed to—yeas 26, nays 10, as follows:

Yeas—Messrs. Anthony, Brown, Chandler, Collamer, Conness, Dixon,* Doolittle, Farwell, Foot, Foster, Grimes, Harris, Howard, Johnson, Lane of Indiana, Lane of Kansas, Morgan, Morrill, Nye, Pomeroy, Ramsey, Stewart, Sumner, Wade, Willey, Wilson—26.

Nays—Messrs. Cowan, *Davis*, Henderson, *Hendricks, Nesmith, Powell, Richardson, Saulsbury*, Van Winkle, *Wright*—10.

IN HOUSE OF REPRESENTATIVES.

February 22—Mr. Thomas T. Davis, from the Committee on the District of Columbia, reported the bill with sundry amendments, one of which was to strike out the above section and insert the following:

Sec. 5. That the provision prohibiting any exclusion

---

* Mr. Dixon made this explanation, February 6:

I wish to say in regard to this amendment, that I opposed it on Saturday on the ground that it seemed to conflict with the rights of another company not now before the Senate; but since that time I have seen the managers and controllers of that company, and find that they are unwilling to contend on this subject with what they considered to be the public opinion. They therefore make no objection to it; and I shall make none.

38

from any car on account of color, already applicable to the Metropolitan railroad, is hereby repealed.

March 2—By unanimous consent all the amendments were withdrawn, and the Senate bill passed without a division.

PASSES FOR COLORED PERSONS LEAVING THE DISTRICT OF COLUMBIA.

IN HOUSE OF REPRESENTATIVES.

1865, March 3—Mr. SCHENCK, from the Military Committee, reported this resolution:

Resolved, That in the judgment of this House the order of the major general commanding the department of Washington and the twenty-second Army corps, issued on the 12th day of July, 1864, directing that no colored man should be allowed to leave Washington city going North, without a pass, is a regulation which makes an odious discrimination, in conflict with the law of the United States, which has declared free alike all citizens and residents of the District of Columbia; and that the President is hereby requested to direct said military order to be at once revoked.

Which was adopted, yeas 75, nays 24, as follows:

YEAS—Messrs. Allison, Ames, Arnold, Ashley, *Baily*, John D. Baldwin, Baxter, Beaman, *Bliss*, Blow, Boutwell, Boyd, Broomall, Ambrose W. Clark, Cobb, Cole, Creswell, Henry Winter Davis, Thomas T. Davis, Dixon, Driggs, Eckley, Eliot, Farnsworth, Frank, Garfield, Gooch, Grinnell, Griswold, Hale, Higby, Asahel W. Hubbard, John H. Hubbard, Hulburd, Ingersoll, Kasson, Kelley, Francis W. Kellogg, Littlejohn, Longyear, Marvin, *McAllister*, McBride, McClurg, Samuel F. Miller, Moorhead, Morrill, Daniel Morris, Amos Myers, Norton, *Odell*, Charles O'Neill, Orth, Patterson, Perham, Pike, Pomeroy, Price, Alexander H. Rice, John H. Rice, Schenck, Scofield, Shannon, Smithers, Thayer, Tracy, Upson, Ellihu B. Washburne, William B. Washburn, Williams, Wilder, Wilson, Windom, Woodbridge, Worthington—75.

NAYS—Messrs. *Ancona, Augustus C. Baldwin, Coffroth, Cox, Cravens, Eden, Eldridge, Knapp, McKinney, James R. Morris, Morrison, John O'Neill, Pendleton, Pruyn, Samuel J. Randall, Ross, Scott, John B. Steele, Stiles, Strouse, Townsend, Voorhees*, Whaley, *Wheeler*—24.

BUREAU OF FREEDMEN'S AFFAIRS.

The condition of this bill at the close of the first session of the Thirty-eighth Congress is stated on page 260.

1864, December 20—The House disagreed to the Senate amendments, and requested a committee of conference, to which the Senate assented. The committee consisted of Messrs. Eliot of Mass., Kelley of Penna., and *Noble* of Ohio, on the part of the House, and Messrs. Sumner of Mass., Howard of Michigan, and *Buckalew* of Penna., on the part of the Senate.

1865, February 2—The Committee reported a bill with these features:

A department of freedmen and abandoned lands is established, to be administered by a commissioner to be appointed by the President with the consent of the Senate, at an annual salary of $4 000, with prescribed subordinates. The commissioner is authorized to create districts, not to exceed two in each rebel State, when sufficiently brought under the military power of the United States, each to be under the supervision of an assistant commissioner, at an annual salary of $2.500, who is to appoint four local superintendents and clerks in each district at an annual salary of $1,500. The commissioner to have the general superintendence of all freedmen; to watch over the execution of all laws, proclamations, and military orders of emancipation, or in any way concerning freedmen; to establish necessary regulations to protect in their rights the freedmen, who are to be treated in all respects as free men, with all proper remedies in courts of justice, &c. The assistant commissioners are to take possession of all abandoned real estate belonging to disloyal persons, and all real estate to which the United States have title. or of which the United States have possession, and not already appropriated to government uses, and all property found on and belonging to such estate, and to lease them to freedmen on such terms as may be agreed upon, or to others if not required for freedmen, the leases to be for one year. Existing leases made by special agents of the Treasury Department are confirmed. Whenever the commissioner cannot otherwise employ any of the freedmen who may come under his care, he shall, so far as practicable, make provision for them with humane and suitable persons, at a just compensation for their services. The commissioner to report annually to Congress. All assistant quartermasters, local superintendents, and clerks, as well as supervising special agents, are declared to be in the military service of the United States, and liable to trial by court-martial or military commissions. Section 13 applies to confiscation, and is as follows:

That the last clause of a joint resolution explanatory of "An act to suppress insurrection, to punish treason and rebellion, to seize and confiscate the property of rebels, and for other purposes," approved July 17, 1862, be, and the same is hereby, repealed.

A motion to table the report was lost—yeas 67, nays 83.

February 9—The report was adopted—yeas 64, nays 62, as follows:

YEAS—Messrs. Allison, Ames, Arnold, Ashley, John D. Baldwin, Baxter, Beaman, Boutwell, Boyd, Broomall, Ambrose W. Clark, Cobb, Cole, Dawes, Deming, Donnelly, Eckley, Eliot, Frank, Grinnell, Hooper, John H. Hubbard, Hulburd, Ingersoll, Jenckes, Julian, Kasson, Kelley, Orlando Kellogg, Knox, Littlejohn, Loan, Longyear, Marvin, McBride, McClurg, McIndoe, Samuel F. Miller, Morrill, Amos Myers, Leonard Myers, Norton, Charles O'Neill, Orth, Patterson, Pike, Pomeroy, Alexander H. Rice, John H. Rice, Edward H. Rollins, Scofield, Sloan, Spalding, Starr, Stevens, Thayer, Upson, Van Valkenburgh, William B. Washburn, Wilder, Wilson, Windom, Woodbridge, Worthington—64.

NAYS—Messrs. *James C. Allen, Ancona, Baily, Augustus C. Baldwin, Brooks*, William G. Brown, *Chanler, Clay, Coffroth, Cox, Cravens*, Thomas T. Davis, *Dawson, Edgerton, Eldridge, English, Finck, Ganson, Grider, Hall, Harding, Benjamin G. Harris, Charles M. Harris, Holman, Philip Johnson, Kalbfleisch. King, Knapp, Le Blond, Long, Mallory, McAllister, McKinney, Middleton, William H. Miller, James R. Morris, Nelson, Noble, Odell, John O'Neill, Pendleton, Radford*, William H. Randall, *Rogers, Ross*, Schenck, Smithers, *John B. Steele, William G. Steele, Stiles, Strouse, Sweat, Townsend*, Tracy, *Wadsworth, Ward*, Ellihu B. Washburne, Webster, Whaley, *Wheeler, Joseph W. White, Winfield*—62.

1865, February 22—In Senate, it was rejected—yeas 14, nays 24:

YEAS—Messrs. Anthony, Brown, Chandler, Foot, Howard, Morgan, Morrill, Pomeroy, Ramsey, Sprague, Stewart, Sumner, Wade, Wilson—14.

NAYS—Messrs. *Buckalew, Carlile*, Cowan, *Davis*, Dixon, Doolittle, Grimes, Hale, Harlan, Harris, Henderson. Howe, *Johnson*, Lane of Indiana, *McDougall, Nesmith, Powell, Richardson, Riddle*, Ten Eyck, Trumbull, Van Winkle, Willey, *Wright*—24.

February 28—A new committee—Messrs. Wilson, Harlan, and Willey, of the Senate, and Schenck, Boutwell, and *Jas. S Rollins*, of the House, made a report to establish in the War Department, for the war and one year thereafter, a Bureau of Refugees, Freedmen, and Abandoned Lands, for the supervision and management of all abandoned lands, and the control of all subjects relating to refugees and freedmen from rebel States, or from any district of country within the territory embraced in the operations of the army, under rules to be approved by the President. The bureau to have a Commissioner at $3,000 a year, and $50,000 bonds, with an assistant commissioner for each rebel State, not exeeeding ten, at $2,500 a year, and $20,000 bonds. The Assistants to make quarterly reports to the Commissioner, and he a report at each session of Congress.

Section 2 authorizes the Secretary of War to direct such issues of provisions, clothing, and fuel as he may deem needful for the immediate and temporary shelter and supply of destitute and suffering refugees and freedmen, and their wives and children, under such rules and regulations as he may direct.

The bill also gives the Commissioner, under the direction of the President, authority to set apart for the use of loyal refugees and freedmen such tracts of land within the insurrectionary States as shall have been abandoned, or to which the United States shall have acquired title by confiscation, or sale, or otherwise. And to every male citizen, whether refugee or freedman, as aforesaid, there shall be assigned not more than forty acres of such land, and the person to whom it is so assigned shall be protected in the use and enjoyment of the land for the term of three years, at an annual rent not exceeding six per cent upon the value of said land as it was appraised by the State authorities in 1860, for the purpose of taxation, and in case no such appraisal can be found, then the rental shall be based upon the estimated value of the land in said year, to be ascertained in such manner as the Commissioner may, by regulation, prescribe. At the end of said term or at any time during said term, the occupants of any parcels so assigned may purchase the land and receive such title thereto as the United States can convey upon paying therefor the value of the land, as ascertained and fixed for the purpose of determining the annual rent as aforesaid.

The report was adopted in Senate.

March 3—It was adopted in the House without a division, after a motion to lay it on the table, made by Mr. Cox, was rejected—yeas 52, nays 77, as follows:

YEAS—Messrs. *James C. Allen, Ancona, Baily, Bliss, Brooks, Coffroth, Cox, Dawson, Denison, Eden, Edgerton, Eldridge, English, Finck, Ganson, Grider, Harding, Benjamin G. Harris, Charles M. Harris, Herrick, Holman, Philip Johnson, Kalbfleisch, Kernan, Knapp, Law, Le Blond, Long, Marcy, McAllister, McKinney, William H. Miller, James R. Morris, Morrison, Nelson, Odell, John O'Neill, Pendleton, Pruyn, Samuel J. Randall,* William H. Randall, *Ross, Scott, John B. Steele, Stiles, Strouse, Stuart, Townsend, Voorhees, Wheeler, Chilton A. White, Yeaman*—52.

NAYS—Messrs. Alley, Allison, Ames, Arnold, Ashley, John D. Baldwin, Baxter, Beaman, Blaine, Blow, Boutwell, Brandegee, Broomall, Ambrose W. Clark, Freeman Clarke, Cobb, Cole, Henry Winter Davis, Thomas T. Davis, Dawes, Deming, Eliot, Farnsworth, Frank, Garfield, Gooch, Grinnell, Higby, Hotchkiss, Asahel W. Hubbard, John H. Hubbard, Hulburd, Ingersoll, Kasson, Kelley, Francis W. Kellogg, Orlando Kellogg, Knox, Littlejohn, Loan, Longyear, Marvin, McBride, McClurg, Moorhead, Morrill, Daniel Morris, Amos Myers, Leonard Myers, Norton, Charles O'Neill, Orth, Patterson, Perham, Pike, Price, John H. Rice, Edward H. Rollins, *James S. Rollins*, Schenck, Scofield, Shannon, Sloan, Spalding, Thayer, Thomas, Tracy, Upson, Van Valkenburgh, Ellihu B. Washburne, William B. Washburn, Whaley, Williams, Wilder, Wilson, Windom, Woodbridge—77.

Action of State Legislatures on the Anti-Slavery Amendment.

MAINE.

SENATE—FEBRUARY 7, 1865.

YEAS—Messrs. Jeremiah Dingley, jr., Parker P. Burleigh, George W. Woodman, Samuel A. Holbrook, George Pierce, Daniel T. Richardson, Eben M. Harnor, Moses R. Ludwig, John B. Walker, Joseph A. Sanborn, Josiah True, Crosly Hinds, Everett W. Stetson, William Wirt Virgin, Thomas Chase, Elias J. Hale, Augustus D. Manson, Osgood N. Bradbury, Lewis Barker, Thomas J. Southard, John S. Tenney, David D. Stewart, Samuel H. Talbot, Lewis L. Wadsworth, jr., William McGilvery, Elias Milliken, Esreff H. Banks, Luther Sanborn—27.

NAYS—None.

HOUSE—FEBRUARY 7, 1865.

YEAS—Messrs. A. H. Abbot, Freeman Atwood, John Barker, George C. Bartlett, Isaac Beale, William Bean, Calvin Bickford, Gershom Bliss, T. W. Bowman, John H. Bradford, J. D. Bragdon, Lewis Bingham, Alonzo Bryant, Rowland Carlton, Reuben Carver, M. V. B. Chase, William H. Chesley, Cyrus P. Church, Tobias Churchell, S. W. Cleaves, N. O. Crane, Josiah Crosby, Franklin Curtis, W. A. P. Dillingham, N. Dingley, jr., H. M. Eaton, M. M. Eaton, H. A. Ellis, J. W. Fairbanks, D. J. Fisher, John B. Fogg, G. L. Follansbee, Charles Foster, J. B. Foster, A. C. French, John French, Chas. H. Frost, Thomas H. Garnsey, Jesse Gould, George Gower, Joseph Granger, J. A. Gushee, John Haley, Calvin Hall, Timothy Haw, G. W. Hammond, Otis Hathaway, Asa Heath, Samuel F. Hersey, J. U. Hill, N. T. Hill, John D. Hopkins, Reuben S. Hunt, A. F. Hutchinson, I. W. Johnson, A. M. Jones, D. H. Kilbreth, Wm. H. Kilby, Thomas S. Lang, S. W. Larrabee, Thomas Little, Wm. F. Lord, B. Lyford, jr., Gideon Mayo, H. S. McIntire, T. H. McLain, D. Merry, J. F. Miller, Merrick Monroe, N. P. Monroe, John Montgomery, J. S. Moore, Wm. Moore, E. S. F. Nickerson, Lyndon Oak, George F. Patten, Rufus Patten, George W. Perkins, Nathan Philbrick, William J. Phillips, William Poole, Abel Prescott, J. H. Pullen, Francis A. Reed, B. M. Roberts, Spaulding Robinson, William Rogers, J. H. Sanborn, J. H. Sayward, F. A. Simpson, George W. Smith, John L. Stevens, Martin L. Stover, S. H. Sweetzer, Rufus P. Tapley, Joel Valley, A. K. Walker, D. P. Wasgatt, Nathan Webb, E. P. Weston, Joseph H. Williams, William Wilson, Almon Young—103.

NAYS—Messrs. B. M. Baker, Samuel M. Bradbury, Thos. J. Burbank, Joseph Chase, O. G. Hamilton, William B. Higgins, William Hill, Isaac Hobart, James M. Howe, jr., J. D. Lawler, Sewall Lord, Edward Payson, Charles A. Shaw, O. R. Sirois, Joshua Whitney—15.

NEW HAMPSHIRE.

Legislature will meet June 7, 1865.

MASSACHUSETTS.

SENATE—FEBRUARY 3, 1865.

YEAS—Messrs. Charles Adams, jr., Henry Alexander, jr., Eben A. Andrews, Henry Barstow, Josiah C. Blaisdell, Paul A. Chadbourne, Francis Childs, William W. Clapp, jr., Freeman Cobb, Charles R. Codman, James Easton, 2d, James S. Eldridge, Jonathan E. Field, George Foster, George Frost, Martin Griffin, George Heywood, Milo Hildreth, John Hill, Francis A. Hobart, Yorick G. Hurd, Abijah M. Ide, Emerson Johnson, Thomas Kneil, Alden Leland, Jacob H. Loud, Joel Merriam, Francis E. Parker, Albert C. Parsons, Robert C. Pitman, Joseph A. Pond, William L. Reed, Moses D. Southwick, Hiram A. Stevens, Levi Stockbridge, E. B. Stoddard, Darwin Ware, Solomon C. Wells, Tappan Wentworth, Samuel M. Worcester—40.

NAYS—None.

HOUSE—FEBRUARY 3, 1865.

YEAS—Messrs. Augustus O. Allen, Daniel Allen, James H. Allen, Horace J. Adams, Joseph L. Andrews, John F. Arnold, Jonathan Arnold, jr., Joseph T. Bailey, John L. Baker, Charles H. Ballard, J. B. Bancroft, Edward Bangs, Seth Bardwell, George W. Bartlett, James Bartlett, Henry Barton, Emory L. Bates, Horatio Bates, William N. Batchelder, Richard Beeching, Cyrus Bell, Joseph A. Benjamin, Newton J. Benjamin, Joseph D. Billings, Frederick A. Boomer, William Bosworth, Charles M. Bowers, Eleazer Boynton, jr., Reuben Boynton, Prince Brackett, E. S. Bradford, Timothy G. Brainard, Amos F. Breed, Abram Briggs, Edwin Briggs, Charles O. Brown, George A. Brown, Wright Brownell, George F. Brown, John Brown, Ezra P. Brownell, Alexander H. Bullock, Erskine D. Burbank, Charles G. Burnham, Henry M. Burrall, Henry J. Bush, Archibald

Campbell, Levi N. Campbell, George P. Carter, William Carpenter, Horace J. Chapin, John Clark, James W. Clark, William S. Clark, George P. Clapp, Ira N. Conant, David H. Coolidge, Horace H. Coolidge, George W. Copeland, Abiel B. Crane, Tully Crosby, William Cumston, George Dane, William Daniels, William W. Davis, George Davis, George P. Denny, Robert W. Derby, Anson Dexter, Daniel Dewey, Charles C. Doten, Lewis J. Dudley, Theodore Dunn, George N. Dutton, Edwin Draper, Jedediah Dwelley, Jacob S. Eaton, John Eddy, David G. Eldridge, Henry H. Faxon, Beriah W. Fay, Anson D. Fessenden, Zibeon C. Field, Charles Fitz, Samuel J. Fletcher, James J. Flynn, John W. Frederick, Reuben P. Folger, Nelson J. Foss, William Foss, Benadam Gallup, Micajah C. Gaskill, Jarvis W. Gibbs, Amasa Gibson, Nathaniel Gilbert, John Glancey, Charles Goddard, William B. Goodnow, Thomas C. Goodwin, George W. Greene, Henry S. Greene, Daniel R. Haines, Arad Hall, Joseph Hall, George F. Hatch, George L. Hawkes, Joel P. Hewins, Luther Hill, Thomas Hills, Nathaniel J. Holden, William H. Hooper, John C. Houghton, Cornelius Howland, T. W. Horton, Richard A. Hunt, Robert Johnson, Levi F. Jones, Silas Jones, Horace W. Jordan, C. F. Johnson, Calvin Kelton, John W. Kimball, Moses Kimball, Lucius J. Knowles, David Knox, Luke Leach, Job M. Leonard, Simeon L. Leonard, Edward Lewis, Samuel Little, William B. Long, Willard Lovering, Leander F. Lynde, John W. Mahan, John F. Manahan, Elbridge G. Manning, John P. Marble, Lorenzo Marrett, Sylvester S. May, William F. McKinstry, Charles R. McLean, William T. McNeill, A. M. McPhail, jr., Simeon Miller, Joseph Mitchell, 2d, George H. Monroe, Elliot Montague, Henry W. Moulton, John G. Mudge, David C. Murdock, John S. Needham, Henry A. Noyes, Albert Nichols, Charles H. Odell, Caleb W. Osborn, Samuel Osborn, jr., Theodore Otis, Amasa Paine, George W. Patch, Frederick Pease, George S. Pendergast, Benjamin F. Phillips, Avery Plumer, Job Pierce, Joseph G. Pollard, Handel Pond, Ezra T. Pope, Charles P. Preston, Thomas H. Prime, Francis B. Ray, Thomas Rice, jr., Stephen N. Richardson, Edward Riley, John F. Robbins, Edward H. Rogers, Jacob Rogers, Robert B. Rogers, Simon J. Roney, Harrison Root, Amos Rowe, jr., Henry O. Russell, George D. Ryder, George S. Saunders, Ezekiel Sawin, George L. Sawin, Luke Sawyer, Henry A. Scudder, Henry Seymour, Elijah Shaw, Edgar J. Sherman, Henry Shortle, George Soule, Jesse G. D. Stearns, Albert W. Stevens, Charles T. Stevens, Daniel H. Stickney, F. M. Stone, Zina E. Stone, Caleb Swan, Ephraim Snow, Daniel J. Sweeney, Henry Souther, Lewis H. Taylor, Solomon Thatcher, David Thayer, Oakes Tirrell, Joseph Tucker, Nathan Tucker, jr., Calvin K. Turner, 2d, Seth Turner, Robert A. Vinal, William Vinton, Thomas L. Wakefield, Edward P. Wallace, Sullivan L. Ward, T. W. Ward, A. W. Warren, Cephas Washburn, jr., Horace Waters, John Wells, Stephen R. White, Augustine Whitney, Lewis C. Whiton, Crocker Wilder, William F. Wilder, Frederick A Willard, Charles A. Winchester, George C. Winchester, Lyman Woodward —233.

NAYS—None.

RHODE ISLAND.

SENATE—FEBRUARY 2, 1865.

YEAS—Messrs. Seth Padelford, Francis Armington, Nicholas Ball, Thomas T. Barber, Borden Chase, Samuel W. Church, Lyman A. Cook, Frederick N. Cottrell, Lewis Fairbrother, Stephen C. Fisk, Anson Greene, Charles Hart, Job W. Hill, Bradbury C. Hill, Edwin W. Hopkins, William B. Howland, Benedict Lapman, William B. Lawton, Allen C. Matthewson, John W. Morey, Abner W. Peckham, James M. Pendleton, Benjamin Seabury, Samuel Shove, Job S. Steene, Pardon W. Stevens, Enos K. Tifft, Thomas A. Whitman—28.

NAYS—Messrs. Gideon H. Durfee, John C. Ellis, Joseph W. Sweet, Laban C. Wade—4.

HOUSE—FEBRUARY 2 1865.

YEAS—Emor J. Angell, Asa B. Anthony, Smith R. Arnold, Olney H. Austin, Rowse Babcock, William Binney, Ellis L. Blake, William W. Blodgett, Henry D. Brown, Oliver C. Brownell, Hazard A. Burdick, William Butler, Albert W. Carpenter, Hazard E. Champlin, Edmund N. Clark, John H. Clarke, Thomas N. Clarke, Ralph P. Devereaux, Luther Dickens, Herbert E. Dodge, Benjamin F. Drowne, Nathaniel B. Durfee, Alexander Farnum, John S. Fiske, James E. France, Asa M. Gammell, Joseph F. Gilmore, Christopher A. Hall, David S. Harris, Stephen Harris, Thomas G. Hazard, Charles W. Holbrook, Geo. W. Holt, Jefferson S. Howard, Henry Ide, Ephraim S. Jackson, George G. King, Jesse Metcalf, Joseph Olney, George L. Owen, Benjamin G. Pabodie, George W. Payton, Samuel W. Pearce, Abraham Peckham, James D'W. Perry, Daniel B. Pond, William M. Rawson, Stafford W. Razee, William H. Reynolds, Daniel Sayles, William P. Sheffield, George W. Sheldon, William Sheldon, Lemuel M. E. Stone, Lyman A. Taft, Benjamin J. Tilley, James Waterhouse, Henry B. Waterman, Thomas C. Watson, Vernon Weaver, John E. Weeden, Alfred A. Williams—62.

NAYS—Cyrus H. Morse, Amasa Sprague, Henry G. Tucker, Alfred H. Willard—4.

CONNECTICUT.

Legislature will meet May 3, 1865.

VERMONT.

SENATE.

Amendment ratified, but vote not received.

HOUSE—MARCH 9, 1865.

YEAS—*Addison county:* Charles Merrill, Parris Fletcher, Noble F. Dunshee, Henry Lane, Michael Ball, James Carson, William C. Chaffee, A. S. Barker, John W. Stewart, Ira Gifford, L. S. Hemenway, E. Holland, Joseph Smith, A. M. Everts, Lewis Treadway, Thomas Morrison, William S. Hopkins, Edwin Everts, Edwin Lawrence, F. G. Wright. *Bennington county:* J. N. B. Thomas, A. B. Gardner, Welcome Allen, John Elwell, Ambrose Woodward, John C. Roberts, A. G. Bowker, W. B. Arnold, Apollos Bailey, William Sherman, Walter B. Randall, Aaron Pike, P. Shuffleton, Cephas Williams, Obed Eddy. *Caledonia county:* C. A. Sylvester, C. T. A. Humphrey, William J. Stanton, A. P. Renfrew, D. W. Aiken, E. W. Church, M. C. Henderson, Jacob Way, George Cowles, Gates B. Bullard, Joseph Bartlett, Harvey Burbank, J. W. Hastings. *Chittenden county:* Lawrence Barnes, H. H. Newell, A. C. Brownell, D. H. Macomber, M. H. Baldwin, Henry Brewster, L. L. Lane, H. G. Boardman, Safford Bronson, John L. Barstow, Norman Isham, Martin Wires, Alney Stone, D. B. Fay. *Essex county:* Raymond Fuller, W. M. Currier, S. H. Parsons, Levi Howe, O. T. Walter, Philander C. Ford, William H. Meacham, William Sims, William Sewall, Isaac R. Houston. *Franklin county:* William C. Wilson, George C. Ellsworth, W. R. Hutchinson, Anson Soule, A G. Soule, A. E Parker, John Colcord, Hiram H. Hale, Warren Robinson, Columbus Green, Orville J. Smith, John F. Draper, Bradley Barlow, Dennison Dorman. *Grand Isle county:* H. P Kinsley, J. McGowan, S. H. Pike, Joel Town, O. G. Wheeler. *Lamoille county:* Junius Wires, James Brown, Charles S. Parker, R. S. Page, Samuel Belding, Joseph J. Boynton, E. H. Shattuck, Ira D. R. Collins. *Orange county:* J. A. Spear, Ephraim F. Claflin, William Hebard, William H. Kibbey, William R. Shedd, E. C. Camp, L. L. Wheeler, Harry Huntington, S. M. Gleason, William T. George J. M. Whitney, Heman A. White. *Orleans county:* H. P. Cushing, Isaac C. Smith, Daniel Webster, Ira Boynton, Jesse E Merrill, J. H. Skimer, Duron Whittlesey, John M. Smith, George A. Hinman, Silas G. Bean, David Johnson, B F. Paine, Byram Bartlett, Ira A. Adams, Edson H. Lathe, H. C. Wilson, D. H. Buck, I. D. Bemis. *Rutland county:* Daniel Crofoot, G. W. Parmenter, Pitt W. Hyde, L. I. Winslow, Lensey Rownds, jr., H. Fisk, Corrill Reed, B. F. Holmes, Willard Ross, J. C. Thornton, Harley Spaulding, Alfred Crowley, Luther P. Rowe, Ervin Pratt, R. F. Wing, J. C. Wheaton, Charles A. Rann, Seneca M. Dorr, Joseph H. Spofford, H. C. Gleason, Cyrus Cramton, D. E. Nicholson. J. H. Parks, Samuel Adams. *Washington county:* Josiah Benjamin, Edwin Fisher, A. M. Foster, Edwin C. Crossett, T. C. Kelton, George O. Boyce, C. W. H. Dwinell, C. C. Putnam, Whitman G. Ferrin, George Bulkley, Samuel Keith, Willard S. Martin, Edmond Pope, David M. Phelps, John Dolph, William W. Wells, A. W. Nelson, J. E. Macomber. *Windham county:* A. A. Wyman, S. M. Waite, C. W. Stebbins, William H. Jones, Leroy Wilder, Francis Daniels, Samuel L. Hunt, A. H. Tucker, Elijah M. Torrey. Alanson Whitman, Simeon Adams, Austin J. Morse, John Kimball, Albert Blanchard, Jonas H. Smith, O. S. Howard, Lorenzo Brown, A. J. Dexter, L. F. Ward, Waters Gillett, James M. Tyler, Stephen Harris. *Windsor county:* Geo. W Stickney, George Davis, F. W. Anderson, John F. Deane, Wm. Rounds, A. G. Dewey, John Colby, H. W. Albee, A. G. Pease, A. B. Martin, Harvey N. Bruce, Merritt E. Goddard, Wm. M. Huntington, John S. Marcy, A. B. Mosher, C. A. Forbush, J. B. Rogers, Hyren Henry, Lucius A. Gould, M. F. Morrison, Stephen G. Abbott, Lewis Pratt—215.

NAYS—D. H. Shoff of Essex, John Lynde of Orange—2.

NEW YORK.

SENATE—FEBRUARY 2, 1865.

YEAS—Messrs. Norman M. Allen, Cheney Ames, Wilkes Angel, Alexander H. Bailey, James A. Bell, Daniel H. Cole, James M. Cook, Ezra Cornell, John B. Dutcher, Charles J. Folger, Frederick H. Hastings, Palmer E. Havens, Stephen S. Hayt, Albert Hobbs, Frederick Julia d, William Laimbeer, jr., Henry R. Low, Demas Strong, Andrew D. White, Stephen K. Williams—20.

NAYS—Messrs. Orson M. Allaben, George Beach, Robert Christie, jr., Luke F. Cozans, Thomas C. Fields, Henry C. Murphy, Ira Shafer, Christian B. Woodruff—8.

ASSEMBLY—FEBRUARY 3, 1865.

YEAS—Messrs. Charles M. Crandall, Albon A. Lewis, William P. Angel, E. Curtis Topliff, Benjamin M. Close, John L. Parker, Sextus H. Hungerford, Martin Crewell, William T. Post, George W. Sumner, Samuel S. Stafford, Samuel W. Carpenter, Dan'l Squires, Ira E. Sherman, James Oliver, James Howard, Mark D. Wilber, Edwin W. Godfrey, William H. Richardson, John W. Brown, Henry Tillinghast, E. Bradley Lee, James C. Kellogg, Lewis Palmer, Russell B. Biddlecome, John C. Perry, Jacob Worth, Nathan Clark, Hugh D. McCall, Jonathan B. Morey, Alfred A. Brown, Alvin Strong, Fairchild Andrews, William Rankin, Thomas E. Stewart, Samuel C. Reed, Thomas B. Van Buren, Guy C. Humphrey, Lorenzo Rouse, Thomas D. Penfield, George W. Cole, Albert L. Green, Daniel P. Wood, Harvey P. Tolman, Volney Edgerton, Edward Brunson, Ananias B. Hulse, Edmund L. Pitts, Elias Root, Richard K. Sanford, Avery W. Severance, George M. Hollis, Robert M. Hasbrouck, George Parker, James Redington, Daniel Shaw, Edward Edwards, Charles Stanford, Lorenzo Webber, William E. Bonham, Alexander Olcott, Horace Bemis, William H. Gleason, William W. Shepard, Henry B. Lord, Jerome Lapham, Sylvester E. Spoor, Thaddeus W. Collins, William H. Rogers, George A. Brandreth, George G. Hoskins, Eben S. Smith—72.

NAYS—Messrs. Harman Vanderzee, Oliver M. Hungerford, Alexander Robertson, Walter Shultz, Walter W. Stanard, Harman S. Cutting, John G. Langner, Prentiss W. Hallenbeck, William D. Veeder, Patrick Burns, John McConvill, Simeon Sammons, Jacob L. Smith, Bryan Gaughan, George L. Loutrel, James B. Murray, Charles Blauvelt, Edward S. Maloy, Jacob Seebacher, Thomas J. Creamer, John McDonald, Joseph A. Lyons, Alexander Ward, Michael N. Salmon, John Keegan, Sidney P. Ingraham, jr., Abram B. Weaver, Theodore H. Cooper, Luther I. Burditt, Jeremiah Sherwood, William Turner, Charles McNeill, Mathew V. A. Fonda, James Ridgeway, Prince W. Nickerson, Geo. W. Chapman, Edward Eldredge, Jesse F. Bookstaver, Andrew S. Weller, Pierre C. Talman—40.

NEW JERSEY.

SENATE—MARCH 16, 1865.

A joint resolution ratifying the proposed Constitutional Amendment was offered by Hon. James M. Scovel, of Camden county, and, after a prolonged debate, was defeated by the vote given below:

YEAS—Messrs. Richard M. Acton, Benjamin Buckley, George D. Horner, Providence Ludlam, Joseph L. Reeves, James M. Scovel, W. W. Ware, George M. Wright—8.

NAYS—Messrs. Lyman A. Chandler, Joshua Doughty, Daniel Holsman, James Jenkins, Henry B. Kennedy, Henry S. Little, Joseph J. Martin, Theodore F. Randolph, Amos Robins, Edward W. Scudder (President,) John G. Trusdell, Alexander Wurts—12.

HOUSE—MARCH 1, 1865.

YEAS—Messrs. Nathan S. Abbott, John Bates, Thomas Philander C. Brinck, William Callahan, Jas. D. Cleaver, Beesley, Jacob Birdsall, Isaac D. Blauvelt, John F. Bodine, Joseph T. Crowell (Speaker,) A. M. P. V. H. Dickeson, Samuel Fisher, Alexander B. Green, Rufus F. Harrison, Israel Heulings, Henry J. Irick, Levi D. Jarrard, Simon Lake, John N. Landell, Charles C. Lathrop, Charles A. Lighthipe, Robert Moore, Isaac W. Nicholson, James H. Nixon, Thomas B. Peddie, J. B. I. Robison, Ryneir Staats, Samuel Stockton, Garret Van Wagoner, William D. Wilson—30.

NAYS—Messrs. Leon Abbett, Elijah Allen, David Anderson, David B. Boss, William L. Broking, Daniel Cory, Abraham C. Coriell, D. E. Culver, Isaac Demarest, Philip A. Dougherty, Abraham W. Duryee, —— Edsall, Jas. E. Goble, A. B. Haring, Charles G. Hoagland, Jesse Hoffman, Daniel A. Holmes, William J. Iliff, William W Iliff, Bernard Kearney, Aaron Kinter, Geo. Schenck, J. C. Seiffert, Michael Taylor, Alfred M. Treadwell, Hiram Van Buskirk, John Van Vorst, John A. Weart, James J. Willever, Silas Young—30.

DELAWARE.

SENATE—FEBRUARY 8, 1865.

YEAS—Messrs. John P. Belville, John F. Williamson, Isaac S. Elliott—3.

NAYS—Messrs. John H. Bewley, Thomas Cahall, Henry Hickman, William Hitch, James Ponds, Gove Saulsbury—6.

HOUSE—FEBRUARY 8, 1865.

YEAS—Messrs. John Alderdice, John A. Duncan, Andrew Eleasin, James H. Hoffecker, John G. Jackson, Elias N. Moore, Merit H. Paxson—7.

NAYS—Messrs. Charles M. Adams, William F. Carney, Henry C. Douglas, William Dyer, William D. Fowler, Abner Harrington, John Hickman, Benjamin Hitch, Shepard P. Houston, John Jones, Miles Messick, James Stuart, Henry Todd, John C Wilson—12.

PENNSYLVANIA.

SENATE—FEBRUARY 3, 1865.

YEAS—Messrs. T. J. Bigham, B. Champneys, George Connell, J. M. Dunlap, D. Fleming, J. L Graham, Kirk Haines, L. W. Hall, Thomas Hoge, George W. Householder, Morrow B. Lowry, C. McCandless, Jeremiah Nichols, Jacob E. Ridgway, Horace Royer, Thomas St. Clair, S. F. Wilson, W. Worthington, W. J. Turrell, (*Speaker*)—19.

NAYS—Messrs. H. B. Beardslee, George H. Bucher, Hiester Clymer, C. M. Donovan, William Hopkins, O. P. James, John Latta, William McSherry, David B. Montgomery, William M. Randall, J. B. Stark, J. Walls—12.

HOUSE—FEBRUARY 3, 1865.

YEAS—Messrs. William Foster, W. H. Ruddiman, W. W. Watt, Joseph T. Thomas, James Freeborn, Thomas Cochran, S. S. Pancoast, F. D. Sterner, L. V. Sutphin, Francis Hood, William F. Smith, E. G. Lee, James Miller, Alfred Slack, John P. Glass, H. B. Herron, R. A. Colville, Sam'l Chadwick, George Y. McKee, J. H. Marsh, Lorenzo Grinnell, Joseph G. Adlum, Nathan J. Sharpless, N. A. Pennypacker, W. B. Waddell, J. C. Sturtevant, H. C. Alleman, Daniel Keiser, Elwood Tyson, J. R. Cochran, John N. Swoope, John Balsbach, George E. Smith, J. R. McAfee, E. Billingfelt, R. W. Shenk, Day Wood, Charles Denues, Isaac Hoffer, S. H. Orwig, Samuel Alleman, G. B. Manley, Charles Koonce, S. McKinley, William Haslett, J. H. Negley, A. K. McClure, Moses A. Ross, D. B. Armstrong, George H. Wells, P. M. Osterhout, J. W. Guernsey, A. G. Olmstead, William Burgwin, W. D. Brown, James R. Kelley, M. S. Quay—56.

NAYS—Messrs. Samuel Josephs, George A. Quigley, James Donnelly, James H. Marshall, John Missimer, H. B. Rhoads, Fred Harner, Luther Calvin, F. W. Headman, C. L. Pershing, Peter Gilbert, C. T. Alexander, W. W. Barr, T. J. Boyer, E. B. Eldred, W. H. Jacoby, John D. Bowman, T. B. Searight, Thomas Rose, Nelson Weiser, James F. Kline, Harry Hakes, A. D. Markley, E. L. Satterthwait, Owen Rice, T. H. Purdy, J. McDowell Sharpe, Michael Weaver, John Dormer, Joshua Boyer, William H. Nelson, J. F. Spangler, James Cameron—33.

MARYLAND.

SENATE—FEBRUARY 3, 1865.

YEAS—Messrs. James L. Billingslea, Thomas K. Carroll, Curtis Davis, Elias Davis, George C. Maund, James M. McNeal, Charles H. Ohr, Edward P. Philpot, Jacob Tome, Robert Turner, Joseph C. Whitney—11.

NAYS—Messrs. Daniel Clarke, James T. Earle, Sprigg Harwood, John W. Jenkins, Daniel Jones, Thomas B. Lansdale, Richard Mackall, Littleton Maclin, J. T. B. McMaster, Wm. B. Stephenson—10.

HOUSE—FEBRUARY 1, 1865.

YEAS—Messrs. John M. Frazier, (*Speaker*,) David Agnew, E. F. Anderson, John W. Angel, C. Bartol, Upton Buhrman, F. A. Clift, James H. Cook, Benjamin F. Cronise, J. P. Cummins, F. T. Darling, M. G. Dean, Henry S. Eavey, George Everhart, S. C. Garrison, Thomas B. Hambleton, Joseph Harris, Henry G. Hazen, John H. Hodson, William H. Hoffman, Caleb B. Hynes, Henry C. Jones, Samuel Keefer, David King, Jesse A. Kirk, H. B. Laverton, James F. Lee, David K. Lusby, David J. Markey, James McCauley, Jethro J. McCullough, Henry S. Miller, Thomas H. Mules, Nicholas D. Norris, Nicholas H. Parker, George B. Pennington, James F. Pilkinton, Zephaniah Poteet, David Rhinehart, Moses Shaw, Michael Sherry, Michael Showacre, George Slothower, Samuel P. Smith, Thomas A. Smith, Samuel J. Soper, H. J. C. Tarr, Thomas J. Tull, James Valliant, S. W. Wardwell, Arthur J. Willis, William S. Wooden, Frederick K. Zeigler—53.

NAYS—Messrs. Charles B. Calvert, jr., Isaac Cairns, R. B. B. Chew, S. Comegys, Ritchie Fooks, Benjamin Fawcett, Joshua R. Handy, Thomas C. Hopkins, Baker A. Jameson, John Lee, Lemuel Malone, Oliver Miller, Alfred B. Nairne, Thomas F. J. Rider, James S. Robinson, Henry A. Silver, Washington A. Smith, Claudius Stewart, John C. Tolson, Lewis Usilton, Adam C. Warner, G. W. Watkins, Henry Williams, Joshua R. Wilson—24.

VIRGINIA.

SENATE—FEBRUARY 8, 1865.

YEAS—Messrs. T. P. Brown, L. C. P. Cowper, F. W. Lemoly, J. F. Mercier, S. W. Powell, T. S. Tennis, C. H. Whitehurst—7.

NAYS—None.

HOUSE—FEBRUARY 9, 1865.

YEAS—Messrs. J. Madison Downey, J. J. Henshaw, Job Hawxhurst, Enoch Haislip, Reuben Johnston, Allen C. Harmon, J. R. Birch, R. E. Nash, James W. Brownley, Robert Wood, Andrew L. Hill—11.

NAYS—Messrs. William H. Gibbons, Thomas H. Kellam—2.

KENTUCKY.

SENATE—FEBRUARY 22, 1865.

YEAS—Messrs. R. T. Baker, N. R. Bluck, B. H. Bristow, J. H. G. Bush, Milton J. Cook, J. R. Duncan, John F. Fisk, W. W. Gardner, W. H. Grainger, W. C. Grier, J. D. Landrum, Elijah Patrick, John A. Prall—13.

NAYS—Messrs. William S. Botts, John B. Bruner, F. S. Cleveland, Harrison Cockrill, Ben. S. Coffey, Richard H. Field, T. T. Garrard, Asa P. Grover, T. W. Hammond, James Harrison, John J. Landram, H. D. McHenry, William B. Read, Geo. C. Riffe, James F. Robinson, William Sampson, Ben. Spaulding, Cyrenius Wait, Walter C. Whitaker, C. T. Worthington, George Wright—21.

HOUSE—FEBRUARY 23, 1865.

YEAS—Messrs. A. S. Allan, T. J. Birchett, Henry Bohannon, John C. Bolin, E. A. Brown, John W. Campbell, James W. Davis, Sebastian Eifort, John K. Faulkner, Elijah Gabbert, Aaron Gregg, R. A. Hamilton, Jacob Hawthorn, A. H. Herrod, M. E. Ingram, O. P. Johnson, William R. Kinney, Perry S. Layton, J. H. Lowry, William L. Neale, Hiram S. Powell, J. C. Sayers, E. W. Smith, Henry G. Van Seggern, Willie Waller, M. E. White, George H. Whitten, James Wilson, George T. Wood—29.

NAYS—Messrs. H. Taylor, Alfred Allen, William M. Allen, William H. Baker, Joshua F. Bell, William Bell, James T. Bramlette, William A. Brooks, R. J. Brown, Isaac Calhoon, T. P. Cardwell, John B. Carlile, Joseph H. Chandler, John T. Clark, Samuel E. DeHaven, John M. Delph, Edward F. Dulin, William Elliott, J. B. English, W. M. Fisher, Stephen F. Gano, Francis Gardner, Eben M. Garriott, John J. Gatewood, Hiram Hagan, C. M. Hanks, Richard H. Hanson, C. C. Harvey, P. B. Hawkins, Thomas P. Hayes, Samuel Larkins, J. F. Lauck, L. S. Luttrell, Thomas A. Marshall, John S. McFarland, John L. McGinnis, Milton McCrew, H. C. McLoed, W. H. Miller, Thomas W. Owings, William A. Pepper, James T. Pierson, F. M. Ray, John D. Ross, George S. Shanklin, E. H. Smith, R. J. Spurr, Caleb Stinson, T. R. Taylor, John R. Thomas, S. B. Thomas, William R. Thompson, H. W. Tuttle, Thomas W. Varnum, A. G. Waggener, A. H. Ward, Isaac N. Webb—57.

OHIO.

SENATE—FEBRUARY 7, 1865.

YEAS—Messrs. Joshua Bates, J. M. Connell, J. Cranor, William F. Curtis, Joseph C. Devin, Benjamin Eggleston, Isaac Gass, Lewis B. Gunckel, Alphonso Hart, A. P. Howard, William C. Howells, Samuel Humphreville, John C. Jamison, James Loudon, Henry S. Martin, H. G. McBurney, N. K. McKenzie, H. S. Neal, Eben Newton, John F. Patton, William Stanbery, William Stanton, Job E. Stevenson, William H. West, Frederick Wickham, Samuel Williamson—26

NAYS—Messrs. George L. Converse, William Lang, John D. O'Connor, M. R. Willett—4.

HOUSE—FEBRUARY 8, 1865.

YEAS—Messrs Allison, Ayres, Babcock, Bidwell, Branchman, Brinkerhoff, Clark, Cochrane, Davenport, Dawson, Delano, Deford, Dryden, Evans of Brown, Evans of Clinton, Everett, Ferrell, Forbes, Free, Galogly, Glover, Green of Hamilton, Gunsaulus, Harrison, Hayden, Hixon, Hogh, Hoover, Huston, Johnston of Athens, Johnson of Lawrence, Johnson of Summit, Keyser of Noble, Kibbee, Kirby, Knelend, Lindsley, Little, Lockwood, Long, Lyon, McGill, McIntyre, Messenger, Miller, Odlin, Purcell, Randall, Reber, Soot, Scott, Seig, Spahr, Thompson, Warner, Waters, West—57.

NAYS—Messrs. Beer, Desbach, Edwards, Estill, Fielding, Hibbs, Jones, Kyser of Monroe, Putnam, Thornhill—10.

LOUISIANA.

SENATE—FEBRUARY 17, 1865.

YEAS—Messrs. Barnett, Bell, Brownlee, Brown, Boyce, Benson, Gastinel, Hart, Hills, Kavanagh, Lara, Montamat, Newell, Nicolas, Purcell, O'Connell, Sullivan, Walters—18.

NAYS—None.

HOUSE—FEBRUARY 14, 1865.

YEAS—Messrs. G. E. Bovee, E. M. Bouligny, James Buckley, J. V. Bofill, Joseph G. Baum, Lewis Balser, H. Brown, H. Bensell, jr., Joseph S. Badger, Simeon. Belden, D. W. F. Bisbee, Young Burke, F. Boudreaux, G. W. Bangs, L. Bernard, C. G. Breckenridge, H. C. Belden, R. L. Brooks, P. Creigh, F. G. Chamberlain, D. Christie, L. D. Corley, T. Cook, B. Collins, P. L. Dufresne, James Duane, Victor Danel, M. Egan, D. Evans, John Foley, R. Gammon, R. Galligan, H. Griffiths, P. Harnan, G. Howes, J. Haberlin, F. Honratty, J. M. Hawkins, A. Hawthorne, Thomas Ingram, T. F. Kavanagh, Jacob Kleas, T. U. Laster, T. J. Lester, L. E. Laloire, S. W. Lewis, John McCann, W. D. Miller, R. M. Miller, W. R. Meeks, H. Maas, John T. Michel, C. St. Martin, A. B. Mace, T. F. Maguire, T. Marie, P. K. O'Connor, O. H. Poynot, H. G. Pearson, jr., W. M. Prescott, W. A. Riggs, John Rotge, Boyd Robinson, J. A. Spellicy, J. Schillang, W. H. Seymour, M. Senette, P. E. R. Smith, D. W. Shaw, John S. Tully, S. M. Todd, J. T. Van Trump, Thomas J. Wheeler, John J. Woodward, John T. Wood, W. H. Waters, James Walsh—78.

NAYS—None.

INDIANA.

SENATE—FEBRUARY 10, 1865.

YEAS—Messrs. Allison, Beeson, Bennett, Bonham, Brown of Hamilton, Cason, Chapman, Cullen, Davis, Downey, Dunning, Dykes, Hyatt, Milligan, Niles, Noyes, Oyler, Penden, Richmond, Terry, Thompson, Van Buskirk, Ward, Wood, Wright—26.

NAYS—Messrs. Barker, Bowman, Bradley, Brown of Wells, Carson, Cobb, Corbin, Douglass, English, Finch, Fuller, Gaff, Gifford, Hanna, Hord, Jenkins, Marshall, Mason, McClurg, Newlin, Staggs, Vawter, Williams—24.

HOUSE—FEBRUARY 13, 1865.

YEAS—Messrs. Thomas Atkinson, E. Banta, Robert Boyd, David C. Branham, John T. Burns, David M. Chambers, Firman Church, Fred. W. Cook, E. Cox, John Sim, William W. Foulke, Howard Crook, F. M. Emerson, Benj. F. Ferris, Benj. T. Goodman, Samuel Gregory, Francis P. Griffith, Henry Groves, John A. Hendricks, Joseph M. Hershey, J. L. Miller, William H. Bonner, William W. Higgins, John H. Willis, Charles F. Hogate, Jonas Hoover, Henly James, Silas Johnson, Alfred Kilgore, Higgins Lane, Robert M. Lockhart, N. J. Major, F. M. Meredith, J. E. Woodruff, Seymour F. Montgomery, Horatio C. Newcomb, J. H. McVey, Ezra Olleman, Thomas W. Reese, B. E. Rhoads, Joseph Riford, Stephen C. Sabin, Michael T. Shuey, David M. Stewart, William Stivers, Thomas M. Stringer, Edward T. Sullivan, Gilbert Trusler, Harvey W. Upson, Augustus Welch, Thomas C. Whiteside, Bartlett Woods, T. T. Wright, Philip Zeigler, John U. Pettit, (*Speaker*)—56.

NAYS—Messrs. O. Bird, Stephen G. Burton, Newton Burwell, Samuel Buskirk, A. J. Beckett, John R. Coffroth, Philomon N. Collins, Samuel Colover, E. Croan, Cyrus L. Dunham, Lloyd Glasebrook, Richard Gregg, John Hargrove, James Harrison, Jonas G. Howard, John M. Humphreys, Thomas Hunt, Charles R. Lasselle, John P. Lemon, John W. Lopp, Cornelius J. Miller, John B. Milroy, R. Osborn, Robert Perigo, J. W. Richardson, H. L. Roach, Samuel A. Shoaff, John M. Stuckey, John G. Stinger, Elijah M. Spencer, Thomas M. Sullivan, J. T. Shoaff, George C. Thatcher, A. C. Veach, John H. White—36.

ILLINOIS.

SENATE—JANUARY 31, 1865.

YEAS—Messrs. John H. Addams, Edward R. Allen, Washington Bushnell, Francis A. Eastman, Isaac Funk, David K. Green, Cornelius Lansing, John T. Lindsay, Alonzo W. Mack, Albert O. Mason, Andrew W. Metcalf, Murray McConnell, Joseph Peters, Daniel Richards, Bryant T. Schofield, James Strain, Jasper D. Ward, Alfred Webster, Linus E. Worcester—19.

NAYS—Messrs. John B. Cohrs, William H. Green, Andrew J. Hunter, Daniel Reily, Horatio M. Vandeveer, John W. Wescott—6.

HOUSE—FEBRUARY 1, 1865.

YEAS—Messrs. Julius A. Barnsback, Lewis J. Bond, William Brown, Obed W. Bryant, Horatio C. Burchard, —— Childs, Ansel B. Cook, Harry D. Cook, Franklin Corwin, Daniel W. Dame, Andrew H. Dolton, Hiram Dresser, Richard C. Dunn, Milton M. Ford, George D. Henderson, Joseph M. Holyoke, William T. Hopkins, —— Huntley, Edward S. Isham, William Jackson, Oliver C. Johnson, Malden Jones, Meritt L. Joslyn, Chauncey A. Lake, Joseph W. Lloyd, Sylvester

S. Mann, Alexander McCoy, Archibald J. McIntyre, John Miller, Isaac Miller, Nathaniel Niles, Harrison Noble, Eugene B. Payne, Daniel J. Pinckney, John D. Platt, Isaac C. Pugh, Ira V. Randall, Jonathan Simpson, Leander Smith, Solomon L. Spink, William C. Stacy, Alexander F. Stevenson, Jason W. Strevell, George Strong, John Thomas, John L. Tincher, John Warner, Charles H. Wood—48.

NAYS—Messrs. Elisha E. Barrett, Valentine S. Benson. Charles Burnett, Hiram B. Decius, Sargeant Gobble, John Hill, Lawrence W. James, William H. Logan, John McDonald, William Middlesworth, Ambrose M. Miller, Lewis W. Miller, D. H. Morgan, Milton M. Morrill, Timothy M. Morse, William K. Murphy, William H. Neece, Nathaniel M. Perry, Thomas Redmond. Samuel R. Saltonstall, John Sharon, Jonathan Shelby, John T. Springer, Samuel E. Stevenson, John Ward, Henry W. Webb, Scott Wike, William T. Yeargain—28.

MICHIGAN.

SENATE—FEBRUARY 2, 1865.

YEAS—Messrs. Levi Aldrich, S. F. Brown, Warren Chapman, J. Webster Childs, V. P. Collier, J. G. Crawford, R. J. Crego, C. M. Crosswell, Alexander P. Davis, Westbrook Divine, Wilson C. Easell, John H. Forster, Frederick Fowler, Andrew Howell, Giles Hubbard, William Jay, David H. Jerome, Cyrus G. Luce, E. W. Merrill, John M. Nevins, William R. Nims, Henry M. Perrin, Jonathan G. Wait, James B. Walker, M. C. Watkins—25.

NAYS—Joseph Godfrey, Loren L. Treat—2.

HOUSE—FEBRUARY 2, 1865.

YEAS—Messrs. Robert P. Aitken, Abram Allen, George W. Allen, James Bayley, William Ball, Moses Bartow, J. P. Beach, John K. Boies, W. H. Brockway, Horace H. Cady, Levi Camburn, Israel E. Carleton, James B. Cobb, A. B. Copley, A. B. Dunlap, A. L. Green, A. D. Griswold, Harvey Haynes, Ezra Hazen, M. D. Howard, O. F. Howard, John S. Jenness, Edward Jewell, George C. Jones, John H. Jones, Lucius Keeler, M. C. Kenny, John Landon, Leander Lapham, Denison J. Lewis, Henry M. Look, George Luther. C F. Mallary, A. C. Maxwell, George R. McKay, Charles E. Mickley, Darius Monroe, E. G. Morton, O. W. Munger, R. B. C. Newcomb, Robert Nixon, William H. Osborn, Albert Pack, William Packard, N. G. Phillips, Lucien Reed, Gilbert E. Reed, (*Speaker*,) S. W. Rowe, J. G. Runyan, R. Sanderson, Peter Schars, Henry Seymour, Charles Shier, Albert B. Slocum, Luther Smith, William T. Smith, Edwin Stewart, John M. Swift, W. H. Taylor, George W. Thayer, Z. D. Thomas, Myron Tupper, William S. Utley, James Van Vleet, Dean P. Warner, John B. Welsh, William E. White, William S. Wilcox, Baron B. Willits, B. M. Williams, Richard Winsor, J. J. Woodman, N. R. Woodruff, J. D. Woodworth, S. W. Yawkey—75.

NAYS—Messrs. William S. Bond, David G. Colwell, Titus Dort, Victor Dusseau, Joshua Forbes, Paul Gies, Elias Haire, Richard Hawley, Benjamin S. Horton, Benjamin May, J. Q. McKernan, Cyrus Miles, James O'Grady, Charles M. Pitts, J. A. T. Wendell—15.

IOWA.

Legislature will meet on the second Monday of January, 1866.

WISCONSIN.

SENATE—FEBRUARY 21, 1865.

YEAS—Messrs. George S. Barnum, John A. Bently, William Blair, Jonathan Bowman, J. T. Chase, W. H. Chandler, J. A. Chandler, Samuel Cole, G. DeWitt Elwood, Joseph Harris, Thomas Hood, William Ketchum, William A. Lawrence, W. L. Lincoln, N. M. Littlejohn, Carl C. Pope, George Reed, M. H. Sessions, William E. Smith, Anthony Van Wyck, Henry G. Webb, Walter S. Wescott, George F. Wheeler, Smith S. Wilkinson, W. K. Wilson, A. H. Young, M. K. Young—27.

NAYS—Messrs. S. W. Budlong, Satterlee, Fred. S. Ellis, L. Morgan, Hugh P. Reynolds, F. O. Thorpe—6.

HOUSE—FEBRUARY 24, 1865.

YEAS—Messrs. W. J. Abrams, Oscar Babcock, Levi W. Barden, James Berry, A. A. Boyce, W. T. Bonniwell, jr., William Brandon, Lorentus J. Brayton, J. H. Brinkerhoff, John Burgess, J. N. Cadby, Solomon C. Carr, John B. Cassoday, F. R. Church, Nathan Cobb, William M. Colloday, DeWitt Davis, Thomas Davis, Richard Dewhurst, Reuben Doud, David Dunwiddie, H L. Eaton, N. H. Emmons, R. K. Fay, W. W. Field, (*Speaker*,) William P. Forsyth, Henry Fowler, J. S. Frary, M. A. Fulton, Myron Gilbert, Robert Glenn, B. F. Groesbeck, Jackson Hadley, J. F. Hand, T. N. Horton, Daniel Johnson, Stoddard Judd, E. P. King, William A. Knapp, Francis Little, M. F. Lowth, W. W. McLaughlin, M. J. McRaith, E. S. Miner, J. B. Montieth, Daniel Mowe, Jacob Oberman, William H. Officer, S. W. Osborn, William Owen, William Palmer, Alanson Pike, D. A. Reed, Sam. Ryan, Jr., Charles Rogers, James Ross, E. C. Salisbury, James Sawyer, William Simmons, Z. G. Simmons, Edwin Slade, Gardner Spoor, A. W. Starks, Albert C. Stuntz, J. M. Tarr, Allen Taylor, H. C. Tilton, O. B. Thomas, Jared Thompson, jr., Henry Utt, D. C. Van Ostrand, John Vaughan, F. A. Weage, Cephas Whipple, George C. Williams, H. S. Winsor, H. S. Wooster—77.

NAYS—Messrs. Thomas Boyd, Charles B. Daggett, M. L. Delaney, David Ford, Ernst Franckenberg, Ferdinand Gnewuch, E. B. Goodsell, Oscar F. Jones, David Knab, Jonathan Large, Hector McLean, Henry Mulholland, Michael Murphy, S. A. Pease, Peter Peters, Jonathan Piper, Lyman Walker, Joseph Wedig, John W. Weiler, Richard White, Thomas Weaver—21.

MISSOURI.

SENATE —1865.

YEAS—George W. Anderson, Joseph E. Baldwin, John H. Cox, Henry J. Deal, Alexander F. Denny, Cyrus H. Frost, Gist Goebel, J. J. Grovelly, William N. Harrison, William P. Harrison, Charles H. Howland, Frederick Kayser, J. W. D. L. F. Mack, A. C. Marvin, Madison Miller, Frederick Muench, Jewett Norris, J. V. Pratt, M. H. Richey, C. C. Simmons, George R. Smith, Henry S. Stevens, P. A. Thompson, Elias V. Wilson, J. N. Young—25.

NAYS—James M. Gordon, W. W. Mosby—2.

HOUSE—1865.

AYES—Thomas W. Alhed, T. G. Babcoke, Robert Bailey, William N. Beal, J. W. Black, W. F. Bodenhamer, O. S. Brown, T. P. Bruton, Richard Bucham, B. F. Bumpass, D. D. Burns, Enos Claske, Josiah Coleman, Ichabod Comstock, W. H. Coalter, Thomas Crowe, W. H. H. Cundiff, E. W. Decker, Lawrence Dry, Sam. Downey, John Duggie, Thomas A. Eagle, Henry Elliott, J. H. Faulconer, William Fenn, G. A. Finkenburg, J. F. Foster, E. W. Fox, Joseph Gill, James S. Goodson, Clark H. Greene, Albert Griffin, John Grimes, S. C. Hammer, A. J. Harlan, J. B. Hasper, A. G. Hollister, C. H. Howe, George L. Hewitt, Gideon Howell, George W. Houts, E. H. E. Jameson, N. C. Johnson, William Jones, Robert A Keller, Francis Kellerman, D. M. King, P. C. Lane, J. W. Lee, J. R. Legg, A. J. Lloyd, Robert Logan, John B. Logan, Alfred Mathews, J. C. McBride, N. McDonald, John McGoldrick, W. H. McLane, J. W. McMillan, Jas. McMurty, James Means, D. J. Meloy, R. H. Melton, Joseph L. Minor. Alfred Montgomery, John D. Myers, Lewis Myers, J. W. Moreland, C. A. Newcomb, M. J. Payne, Daniel Proctor, John F. Powers, Wm. Ray, Thomas A. Reed, George W. Rinker, Stephen J. Reynolds, P. C. Roberts, Erastus Sackett, Thomas Simms, A. E. Simpson, G. W. Smiley, Reuben Smith, Irwin Z. Smith, James Southard, E. W. Southworth, D. D. Stockton, Joseph Thompson, William Weaver, C. B. Walker, Jeremiah White, B. F. Wilson, B. H. Wilson—92.

NAYS—Boyle Gordon, Thomas C. Gordon, William Spratt —3.

MINNESOTA.

SENATE—FEBRUARY 15, 1865.

YEAS—D. Cameron, J. V. Daniels, G. D. George, B. A. Lowell, D. Morrison, L. Miller, J. McKusick, J. Nicols, L. Nutting, J. S. Pillsbury, E. Rice, D. G. Shillock, B. D. Sprague, Melville C. Smith, H. A. Swift, J. A. Thacher—16.

NAYS—Luther H. Baxter, D. F. Langley, D. S. Norton, J. J. Porter, J. P. Wilson—5.

HOUSE—FEBRUARY 8, 1865.

YEAS—Cyrus Aldrich, A. H. Bullis, Wm. Chalfant, Wm. Colvill, jr., F. R. E. Cornell, Royal Crane, J. B. Crooker, C. F. Davis, J. B. Downer, J. L. Gibbs, Charles D. Gilfillan, John M. Gilman, F. N. Goodrich, Charles Griswold, L. C. Harrington, Stephen Hewson, Henry Hill, L. A. Huntoon, J. B. Locke, W. H. Patten, Henry Poehler, F. A. Renz, L. Z. Rogers, F. E. Shandrew, Ansel Smith, L. J. Stark, F. M. Stowell, Charles Taylor, William Teachout, C. D. Tuthill, E. F. West, Reuben Whittemore, Armstrong, (*Speaker*)—33.

NAYS—Louis A. Evans, K. N. Guiteau W. T. Rigby, Oscar Taylor, Henry W. Tew—5.

KANSAS.

SENATE—FEBRUARY 7, 1865.

YEAS—Messrs. President James McGrew, H. K. W. Bartlett, Oliver Barber, G. A. Colton, A. Danford, F. H. Drenning, C. V. Eskridge, Henry Foote, W. P. Gambell, O. J. Grover, D. W. Houston, D. H. Horne, J. H. Jones, J. F. Legate, J. T. Lane, E. C. Manning, T. E. Milhoan, Thomas

Murphy, F. W. Potter, M. Quigg, S. Speer, A. H. Smith, Charles P. Twiss, William Weer—25.

NAYS—None.

HOUSE—FEBRUARY 7, 1865.

YEAS—Messrs. Speaker Jacob Stotler, R. H. Abraham, Samuel F. Attwood, Milton R. Benton, J. F. Broadhead, O. H. Browne, A. A. Callen, D. G. Campbell, D. L. Campbell, H. Cavender, J. A. Christy, R. Church, L. D. Cleavinger, Charles C. Coffinberry, Hugh A. Cook, Werner Craig, Rufus Darby, D. Detrick, C. L. Dille, William Draper, M. R. Dutton, G. H. Fairchild, Daniel C. Finn, Robert Cole Foster, James Fletcher, Charles S. Glick, G. W. Glick, William Goss, Nelson Griswold Thomas O. Gwartney, James Hanway, James M. Harvey, A B. Hendrick, J. Hodgson, W. L. Houts, N. B. Hughes, Michael Jordan, William Karr, J. R. Kennedy, Lawrence Kennedy, C. Kohler, Cyrus Leland, jr., M. R. Leonard, A. J. Loomis, E. Lowe, S. D. Macdonald, William Martindale, J. McClellan, James R. Mead, Joel Moody, William Morrow, T. M. O'Brien, F. R. Page, D. L. Payne, William B. Perry, N. P. Rawlings, Robert Riddle, H. Rice, H. D. Rogers, Ed. Russell, I. D. Sammons, J. P. Salisbury, E. S. Scudder, H. D. Shepherd, Henry Smith, S. J. H. Snyder, E. Stafford, J. Spencer, Watson Spencer, George Storch, C. H. Stratton, N. Z. Strong, D H. Sutherland, F. B. Swift, Job Throckmorton, John D. Wells, A. G West—77.

NAYS—None.

WEST VIRGINIA.

SENATE—FEBRUARY 3, 1865.

YEAS—Messrs. John H. Atkinson, Aaron Bechtol, John B. Bowen, John J. Brown, James Burley, William F. Chambers, James M. Corley, William S. Dunbar, D. D. T. Dunbar, Aaron Hawkins, Daniel Haymond, B. M. Kitchen, E. S. Mahon, Edwin Maxwell, Daniel Peck, J. M. Phelps, William Price, Greenbury Slack, President W. E. Stevenson—19.

NAYS—None.

HOUSE—FEBRUARY 3, 1865.

YEAS—Messrs. Thomas P. Adams, William Alexander, John S. Barns, John Boggs, Greenberry D. Bonar, Jesse H. Cather, George K. Cox, Horatio N. Crooks, O. D. Downey, Lewis Dyche, James H. Ferguson, Solomon S. Fleming, Jacob T. Galloway, Baptiste Gilmore, Nathan Goff, Theodore N. Gornell, Adam Gregory, Benjamin Hagar, Joseph W. Hall, James H. Hinchman, John Kellar, William H. King, Daniel Lamb, Thomas Little, John B. Lough, William Mairs, John Michael, Joshua S. Morris, James C. McGrew, Henry C. McWhorter, Abel B. Parks, Spicer Patrick, Aaron D. Peterson, Jesse F. Phares, David S. Pinnell, Eli Riddle, Charles F. Scott, Abel Segur, Buckner J. Smith, William Smith, Benjamin L. Stephenson, Thomas H. Trainer, Rathbone Van Winkle, Meredith Wells, William Willen, Lee Roy Kramer, (*Speaker*)—44.

NAYS—None.

NEVADA.

SENATE—FEBRUARY 16, 1865.

YEAS—W. H. Clagett, Lewis Doron, D. L. Hastings, J. W. Haines, Frederick Hutchins, William W. Hobart, John Ives, Alfred James, S. A. Kellogg, Charles Lambert, M. D. Larrowe, A. J. Lockwood, Jonas Seeley, J. S. Slingerland, Chas. A. Sumner, M. S. Thompson, N. W. Winton—16.

NAY—F. M. Proctor—1.

HOUSE—FEBRUARY 16, 1865.

YEAS—A. C. Bearss, H. H. Beck, D. H. Brown, James Bolan, H. M. Bien, W. W. Bishop, Erastus Bond, J. E. W. Cary, W. M. Cutter, S. C. Denson, J. A. Dun, Henry Epstein, A. L. Greely, D. H. Haskell, Cyril Hawkins, J. L. Hinckley, W. G. Lee, J. A. Myrick, John S. Mayhugh, L. C. McKeeby, B. H. Nichols, H. G. Parker, Edwin Patten, M. A. Rosenblatt, James A. Rigbey, James Small, R. M. Shackleford, E. P. Sine, Jacob Smith, W. F. Toombs, D. P. Walter, Daniel Wellington, R. A. Young, C. W. Tozer, (*Speaker*)—34.

NAY—James A. St. Clair—1.

TENNESSEE.

1865, March 4—The amendment was ratified in the Senate, and the House of Representatives, without dissent.

Foreign Policy of the United States.

1864, December 15—Mr. H. WINTER DAVIS, from the Committee on Foreign Affairs, reported this resolution, (being the same as closed his report on page 354:)

Resolved, That Congress has a constitutional right to an authoritative voice in declaring and prescribing the foreign policy of the United States as well in the recognition of new powers as in other matters; and it is the constitutional duty of the President to respect that policy, not less in diplomatic negotiations than in the use of the national force when authorized by law; and the propriety of any declaration of foreign policy by Congress is sufficiently proved by the vote which pronounces it; and such proposition, while pending and undetermined, is not a fit topic of diplomatic explanation with any foreign power.

Which was laid on the table—yeas 70, nays 63, as follows:

YEAS—Messrs. Alley, Ames, Anderson, Arnold, *Baily*, John D. Baldwin, Baxter, Beaman, Blaine, Blair, Boutwell, Boyd, Broomall, Ambrose W. Clark, Cobb, Cole, Thomas T. Davis, Dawes, Deming, Dixon, Donnelly, Driggs, Eckley, Eliot, Farnsworth, Gooch, Grinnell, Hale, Higby, Hotchkiss, John H. Hubbard, Hulburd, Ingersoll, Kelley, Francis W. Kellogg, Orlando Kellogg, Littlejohn, Longyear, Marvin, McBride, McIndoe, Samuel F. Miller, Moorhead, Morrill, Daniel Morris, Amos Myers, Leonard Myers, Norton, Charles O'Neill, Patterson, Perham, Pike, Pomeroy, Price, Alexander H. Rice, Edward H. Rollins, Scofield, Shannon, Smith, Spalding, Thomas, Tracy, Upson, Ellihu B. Washburne, William B. Washburn, Whaley, *Wheeler*, Wilson, Windom, Woodbridge—70.

NAYS—Messrs. *James C. Allen*, *William J. Allen*, Allison, *Ancona*, Ashley, *Augustus C. Baldwin*, *Bliss*, Blow, *Brooks*, *J. S. Brown*, *Chanler*, *Cox*, *Cravens*, Henry Winter Davis, *Dawson*, *Denison*, *Eden*, *Edgerton*, *Eldridge*, *Finck*, *Ganson*, Garfield, Griswold, *Harding*, *Herrick*, *Holman*, Asahel W. Hubbard, Jenckes, *P. Johnson*, *Kalbfleisch*, *Kernan*, *King*, Knox, *Law*, *Le Blond*, Loan, *Mallory*, *Marcy*, *McAllister*, *William H. Miller*, *James R. Morris*, *Morrison*, *Noble*, *Odell*, *John O'Neill*, Orth, *Pendleton*, *Perry*, *Radford*, *Samuel J. Randall*, Schenck, Sloan, Smithers, Starr, *John B. Steele*, *William G. Steele*, Stevens, *Stiles*, *Stuart*, *Sweat*, *Townsend*, *Wadsworth*, *Yeaman*—63.

December 19—A resolution, in same language, was offered by Mr. H. WINTER DAVIS, which the House—yeas 50, nays 73—refused to table. The question being divided, the first branch ending with the word "law," was agreed to—yeas 119, nays 8, (Messrs. Blair, Boutwell, Cole, F. W. Kellogg, Littlejohn, Pomeroy, Smith, and Van Valkenburgh.) The second branch of the resolution, being the remainder of it, was agreed to—yeas 68, nays 59, as follows.

YEAS—Messrs. *William J. Allen*, Allison, Ames, *Ancona*, Anderson, *Augustus C. Baldwin*, Baxter, *Bliss*, Blow, Boyd, *Chanler*, *Coffroth*, *Cox*, *Cravens*, Henry Winter Davis, *Dawson*, *Denison*, *Eden*, *Eldridge*, *Finck*, *Ganson*, Garfield, *Grider*, Griswold, *Harrington*, *Charles M. Harris*, *Herrick*, Higby, *Holman*, Asahel W. Hubbard, Jenckes, *Kernan*, *Knapp*, Knox, *Law*, *Lazear*, *Le Blond*, *Mallory*, *Marcy*, *McDowell*, *McKinney*, Moorhead, Morrill, *James R. Morris*, *Nelson*, *Noble*, *John O'Neill*, Orth, *Pendleton*, *Perry*, Price, *Pruyn*, *Samuel J. Randall*, *Ross*, Schenck, *Scott*, Sloan, Smithers, *John B. Steele*, Stevens, *Strouse*, *Stuart*, *Sweat*, *Townsend*, *Vorhees*, *Wadsworth*, *Joseph W. White*, Williams—68.

NAYS—Messrs. Alley, *Baily*, John D. Baldwin, Beaman, Blair, Boutwell, Brandegee, Broomall, Ambrose W. Clark, Cobb, Cole, Creswell, Thomas T. Davis, Dawes, Dixon, Driggs, Eckley, Eliot, Frank, Grinnell, Hale, Hotchkiss, John H. Hubbard, Hulburd, Kasson, Kelley, Francis W. Kellogg, Orlando Kellogg, Littlejohn, Marvin, McBride, McClurg, McIndoe, Amos Myers, Leonard Myers, Norton, Charles O'Neill, Patterson, Perham, Pike, Pomeroy, Alexander H. Rice, John H. Rice, E. H. Rollins, Scofield, Shannon, Smith, Spalding, Thayer, Thomas, Tracy, Upson, Van Valkenburgh, Ellihu B. Washburne, William B. Washburn, Whaley, Wilson, Windom, *Yeaman*—59.

Financial.

The following bills were passed:

1865, January 28—Authorized, in lieu of any bonds under act of June 30, 1864, Treasury notes of the description and character authorized in second section thereof, limiting the bonds and notes to $400,000,000, exempting the notes from taxation by or under State or municipal authority, and providing that "such Treasury notes may be disposed of for lawful money, or for any other Treasury notes or certificates of indebtedness, or certificates of deposit issued under any previous act of Congress," and that the act shall not be construed to give authority for the issue of any legal-tender notes, in any form, beyond the balance unissued of the amount authorized by the second section of the act of June 30, 1864.

1865, March 3—Authorized $600,000,000 in bonds and Treasury notes—the bonds to be not less than $50 and payable at any period not more than forty years or redeemable after any period not less than five nor more than forty; the Treasury notes to be convertible into the bonds, be of such denominations (not less than $50,) bearing such dates, and be made redeemable or payable at the discretion of the Secretary of the Treasury. Interest on bonds to be payable semi-annually; on Treasury notes semi-annually, annually, or at maturity; and the principal, or interest, or both, may be made payable in coin or other lawful money; the interest, if payable in coin, not to exceed 6 per cent; if not so payable in coin, not to exceed 7.3. Bonds authorized under act of June 30, 1864, may be of the description herein authorized; and any Treasury notes or interest-bearing obligations may be converted into any description of bonds herein authorized, and they shall not be considered a part of the $600,000,000 herein provided for.

No new principle was involved, and it is not considered necessary to trace a struggle upon matters of detail.

Statement of the Public Debt of the United States, March 31, 1865.

DEBT BEARING INTEREST IN COIN.

AUTHORIZING ACTS.	RATE OF INTEREST.	CHARACTER OF ISSUE.	AMOUNT OUTSTANDING.	INTEREST.
January 28, 1847	6 per cent.	Bonds	$9,415,250 00	$564,915 00
March 31, 1848	6 per cent.	Bonds	8,908,341 80	534,500 50
June 14, 1858	5 per cent.	Bonds	20,000,000 00	1,000,000 00
June 22, 1860	5 per cent.	Bonds	7,022,000 00	351.100 00
February 8, 1861	6 per cent.	Bonds	18,415,000 00	1,104,900 00
July 17, and August 5, 1861	6 per cent.	Bonds	50,000,000 00	3,000,000 00
July 17, and August 5, 1861	6 per cent.	Bonds exchanged for 7 3.10	139,146,400 00	8,348,734 00
February 25, 1862	6 per cent.	Bonds, 5-20's	510,756,900 00	30,645,414 00
June 30, 1864	6 per cent.	Bonds, 5-20's	85,789,000 00	5,147,340 00
March 3, 1864	5 per cent.	Bonds, 10-40's	172,770,100 00	8,638,505 00
September 9, 1850	5 per cent.	Bonds, Texas Indemnity	1,507,000 00	75,350 00
March 2, 1861	6 per cent.	Bonds, Oregon War	1,016,000 00	60,960 00
July 17, 1861	7 3-10 pr c.	Notes, Three Years	615,250 00	44,913 25
March 3, 1863	6 per cent.	Bonds	75,000,000 00	4,500,000 00
Aggregate of debt bearing Coin Interest			$1,100,361,241 80	$64,016,631 75

DEBT BEARING INTEREST IN LAWFUL MONEY.

AUTHORIZING ACTS.	RATE OF INTEREST.	CHARACTER OF ISSUE.		AMOUNT OUTSTANDING.	INTEREST.
July 11, 1862	4 per cent.	Temporary Loan		$650,476 56	$26,019 06
July 11, 1862	5 per cent.	Temporary Loan		5,708,262 52	285,413 12
July 11, 1862	6 per cent.	Temporary Loan		46,093,589 21	2,765,615 35
March 1, 1862	6 per cent.	Certificates of Indebtedness		171,790,000 00	10,307,400 00
March 3, 1863	5 per cent.	One and Two Years Notes	$211,000,000 00		
Less withdrawn and destroyed or ready to be destroyed			141,477,650 00	69,522,350 00	3,476,117 50
March 3, 1863	6 per cent.	3 Years Compound Interest Notes	15,000,000 00		
June 30, 1864	6 per cent.	3 Years Compound Interest Notes	141,477,650 00	156,477,650 00	
June 30, 1864	7 3-10 pr c.	3 Years Treasury Notes	230,000,000 00		
March 3, 1865	7 3-10 pr c.	3 Years Treasury Notes	70,812,800 00	300,812,800 00	21,959,334 40
Aggregate of debt bearing Lawful Money Interest				$751,055,128 29	$38,819,899 43

DEBT ON WHICH INTEREST HAS CEASED.

CHARACTER OF ISSUE.	AMOUNT OUTSTANDING.
Bonds	$203,808 45
Treasury Notes	104,511 64
Treasury Notes	8,800 00
Treasury Notes	600 00
Treasury Notes	30,500 00
Temporary Loan Coin	1,200 00
Aggregate of debt on which Interest has ceased	$349,420 09

Statement of the Public Debt—Continued.

DEBT BEARING NO INTEREST.

CHARACTER OF ISSUE.		AMOUNT OUTSTANDING.
United States Notes	$60,030,000 00	
Less amount withdrawn	59,537,896 00	
Amount outstanding	492,104 00	
United States Notes	399,507,896 00	
		$400,000,000 00
United States Notes	49,300,202 00	
Less amount withdrawn	16,139,633 00	
		33,160,569 00
Fractional Currency	10,952,724 76	
Fractional Currency	12,301,369 31	
		24,254,094 07
		457,414,663 07
Unpaid requisitions	114,256,548 93	
Amount in Treasury	56,481,924 84	
		57,774,624 09
Aggregate of debt not bearing Interest		$515,189,287 16

RECAPITULATION.

DEBT.	AMOUNT OUTSTANDING.	INTEREST.	LEGAL TENDER NOTES IN CIRCULATION.	AMOUNT.
Bearing int'rst in Coin	$1,100,361,241 80	$64,016,631 75	One and Two Years 5 per cent. Notes	$69,522,350
Bearing interest in Lawful Money	751,055,128 29	38,819,899 43	United States Notes, old issue	492,104
			United States Notes, new issue	432,668,465
On which interest has ceased	349,420 09		Compound Interest Notes, act of March 3, 1863.	15,000,000
			Compound Interest Notes, act of June 30, 1864.	141,477,650
Bearing no interest	515,189,287 16			
				$659,160,569
	$2,366,955,077 34	$102,836,531 18		

Miscellaneous.

REPEAL OF FISHING BOUNTIES.

IN SENATE.

Pending the Internal Revenue bill,

1865, March 2—This amendment, adopted in Committee of the Whole—

That from and after the abrogation of the reciprocity treaty with Great Britain all acts and parts of acts granting allowances or bounties on the tonnage of vessels engaged in the bank or other cod fisheries be, and the same are hereby, repealed—

Was rejected—yeas 18, nays 20, as follows:

YEAS—Messrs. Brown, *Buckalew*, Chandler, *Davis*, Doolittle, Harlan, Harris, Henderson, *Hendricks*, Lane of Indiana, *Nesmith*, *Powell*, *Riddle*, Sherman, Van Winkle, Wilkinson, Willey, *Wright*—18.

NAYS—Messrs. Anthony, Clark, Conness, Dixon, Farwell, Foster, Howe, *Johnson*, Lane of Kansas, *McDougall*, Morgan, Morrill, Nye, Ramsey, Sprague, Stewart, Sumner, Ten Eyck, Wade, Wilson—20.

Oath of Allegiance for Lawyers.

IN SENATE.

1864, December 21—Mr. HARLAN offered this resolution:

Resolved, That the Committee on the District of Columbia be instructed to inquire into the expediency and propriety of requiring all residents of the District of Columbia to take and file with the provost marshal of said District an oath of allegiance or fidelity to the Government of the United States similar to the oath required by law of Members and Senators in Congress and other officers of the Government; and also the expediency and propriety of prohibiting all persons from doing business in said District or with the several Departments of the Government who have not or may not take and file such oath; and that said committee have leave to report by bill or otherwise.

Which was agreed to—yeas 24, nays 10, as follows:

YEAS—Messrs. Anthony, Clark, Collamer, Conness, Dixon, Farwell, Foot, Foster, Grimes, Hale, Harlan, Howard, Lane of Indiana, Lane of Kansas, Morgan, Pomeroy Sherman, Sprague, Sumner, Ten Eyck, Trumbull, Van Winkle, Wilkinson, Willey—24.

NAYS—Messrs. Brown, *Buckalew*, Cowan, *Davis*, Henderson, *Hendricks*, *Johnson*, *Powell*, *Richardson*, *Saulsbury*—10.

December 22—A bill, described below, and extending the principle indicated on page 376, was passed—yeas 27, nays 4, as follows:

YEAS—Messrs. Anthony, Brown, Clark, Collamer, Conness, Dixon, Doolittle, Farwell, Foot, Foster, Grimes, Harlan, Harris, Henderson, *Johnson*, Lane of Indiana, Lane of Kansas, Morgan, Pomeroy, Ramsey, Sherman, Sprague, Sumner, Ten Eyck, Van Winkle, Willey, Wilson—27.

NAYS—Messrs. *Buckalew*, *Davis*, *Richardson*, *Saulsbury*—4.

1865, January 20—The bill passed the House—ayes 66, noes 26, on a division.

It provides that no person, after the date of this act, shall be admitted to the bar of the Supreme Court of the United States, or at any time after the 4th of March next be admitted to the bar of any circuit court or district court of the United States, or the Court of Claims, as an attorney or counselor, or be allowed to appear by virtue of any previous admission, or any special powers of attorney, unless he first takes and subscribes the oath prescribed in the "Act to prescribe an oath of office," approved July 2, 1862, which said oath so taken and subscribed shall be preserved among the files of such court, and that any person who shall falsely take said oath shall be guilty of per-

jury, and, on conviction, be liable to the pains and penalties of perjury, and the additional pains and penalties prescribed in the said act.*

Abolition of Slavery in West Virginia.

This record completes that made on pages 377, 378:

Both Houses of the Legislature of West Virginia have passed this bill, which has become a law:

Be it enacted by the Legislature of West Virginia:

1. All persons held to service or labor as slaves in this State are hereby declared free.

2. There shall hereafter be neither slavery nor involuntary servitude in this State except in punishment of crime, whereof the party shall have been duly convicted.

The Wheeling *Intelligencer* says: "This bill wipes out the remnant of slavery in West Virginia at a blow. It was not offered or passed as an amendment to the Constitution. The Constitution simply prescribes a limit beyond which certain persons of certain ages shall not be held slaves, and makes no enactment at all in regard to those supposed to be left in slavery for life."

Letter of Horace Greeley to the President, Preceding the Niagara Falls Negotiation.

As part of the history of the negotiation recorded on pages 301-303, this letter of Mr. Greeley, until recently unpublished, is given. It is understood that there are other letters from several parties not yet divulged:

NEW YORK, *July* 7, 1864.

MY DEAR SIR: I venture to inclose you a letter and telegraphic despatch that I received yesterday from our irrepressible friend Colorado Jewett, at Niagara Falls. I think they deserve attention. Of course I do not endorse Jewett's positive averment that his friends at the Falls have "full powers" from J. D., though I do not doubt that he thinks they have. I let that statement stand as simply evidencing the anxiety of the Confederates everywhere for peace. So much is beyond doubt.

And, therefore, I venture to remind you that our bleeding, bankrupt, almost dying country also longs for peace—shudders at the prospect of fresh conscriptions, of further wholesale devastations, and of new rivers of human blood; and a wide-spread conviction that the government and its prominent supporters are not anxious for peace, and do not improve proffered opportunities to achieve it, is doing great harm now, and is morally certain, unless removed, to do far greater in the approaching elections.

It is not enough that we anxiously desire a true and lasting peace; we ought to demonstrate and establish the truth beyond cavil. The fact that A. H. Stephens was not permitted a year ago to visit and confer with the authorities at Washington has done harm, which the tone at the late National Convention at Baltimore is not calculated to counteract.

I entreat you, in your own time and manner, to submit overtures for pacification to the Southern insurgents, which the impartial must pronounce frank and generous. If only with a view to the momentous election soon to occur in North Carolina, and of the draft to be enforced in the free States, this should be done at once. I would give the safe conduct required by the rebel envoys at Niagara upon their parole to avoid observation and to refrain from all communication with their sympathizers in the loyal States; but you may see reasons for declining it. But whether through them or otherwise, do not, I entreat you, fail to make the Southern people comprehend that you, and all of us, are anxious for peace, and prepared to grant liberal terms. I venture to suggest the following

PLAN OF ADJUSTMENT.

1. The Union is restored and declared perpetual.

2. Slavery is utterly and forever abolished throughout the same.

3. A complete amnesty for all political offences, with a restoration of all the inhabitants of each State to the privileges of citizens of the United States.

4. The Union to pay four hundred million dollars in five per cent. United States stock to the late slave States, loyal and secession alike, to be apportioned *pro rata*, according to their slave population respectively, by the census of 1860, in compensation for the losses of their loyal citizens by the abolition of slavery. Each State to be entitled to its quota upon the ratification by its Legislature of this adjustment. The bonds to be at the absolute disposal of the Legislature aforesaid.

5. The said slave States to be entitled henceforth to representation in the House on the basis of their total instead of their Federal population, the whole now being free.

6. A National Convention, to be assembled so soon as may be, to ratify this adjustment, and make such changes in the Constitution as may be deemed advisable.

Mr. President, I fear you do not realize how intently the people desire any peace consistent with the National integrity and honor, and how joyously they would hail its achievement and bless its authors. With United States stocks worth but forty cents in gold per dollar, and drafting about to commence on the third million of Union soldiers, can this be wondered at?

I do not say that a just peace is now attainable, though I believe it to be so. But I do say that a frank offer by you to the insurgents of terms which the impartial say ought to be accepted, will, at the worst, prove an immense and sorely needed advantage to the national cause. It may save us from a Northern insurrection.

Yours, truly, HORACE GREELEY.

Hon. A. LINCOLN, *President, Washington, D. C.*

P. S.—Even though it should be deemed unadvisable to make an offer of terms to the rebels, I insist that, in any possible case, it is desirable that any offer they may be disposed to make should be received, and either accepted or rejected. I beg you to invite those now at Niagara to exhibit their credentials and submit their ultimatum.

H. G.

The Menonites on the War.

The religious society known as the "Menonites," at their annual Conference held at Germantown, Pa., March 6 and 7, 1865, passed a series of resolutions sustaining the government in its efforts to crush the rebellion. Among them are the following:

Resolved, That the success of our arms on sea and land during the last year calls aloud for thanksgiving and praise to Almighty God, who alone is the giver of victory, and in whose hands are the destinies of men and nations.

Resolved, That the present war is a struggle between truth and error, right and wrong, freedom and bondage.

Resolved, That we have unfaltering confidence in the Chief Executive of our nation; in the honest purposes of his heart; in his fidelity to God and the best interests of the whole people, and to the sublime principles of freedom and justice the wide world over.

Resolved, That we pledge him our undivided support and most ardent prayers in his efforts to maintain our national

* These proceedings took place at the First Session of the Thirty-Eighth Congress:

IN SENATE.

1863, December 17—Mr. SUMNER offered this as a new rule for the Senate:

The oath or affirmation prescribed by act of Congress of July 2, 1862, to be taken and subscribed before entering upon the duties of office, shall be taken and subscribed by every Senator, in open Senate, before entering upon his duties. It shall also be taken and subscribed in the same way by the Secretary of the Senate; but the other officers of the Senate may take and subscribe it in the office of the Secretary.

December 18—Mr. SAULSBURY moved this substitute:

That the Committee on the Judiciary be instructed to inquire whether Senators and Representatives in Congress are included within the provisions of the act entitled "An Act to prescribe an oath of office, and for other purposes," approved July 2, 1862, and whether the said act is in accordance or in conflict with the Constitution of the United States.

A motion to refer to the Committee on the Judiciary was lost—yeas 15, nays 26.

1864, January 21—Mr. SAULSBURY's substitute was lost—yeas 12, nays 26. The YEAS were: Messrs. *Buckalew, Carlile,* Cowan, *Davis, Harding,* Henderson, *Hendricks,* Johnson, *Powell, Saulsbury,* Willey, *Wright.*

January 25—The new rule was adopted—yeas 28, nays 11, as follows:

YEAS—Messrs. Anthony, Brown, Chandler, Clark, Collamer, Conness, Dixon, Fessenden, Foster, Grimes, Hale, Harlan, Henderson, Howard, Lane of Kansas, Morgan, Morrill, Ramsey, Sherman, Sprague, Sumner, Ten Eyck, Trumbull, Van Winkle, Wade, Wilkinson, Willey, Wilson—28.

NAYS—Messrs. *Buckalew, Carlile,* Cowan, *Davis,* Doolittle, Harris, Howe, Johnson, *Powell, Saulsbury, Wright*—11.

honor untarnished, and crush out the last vestige of this slaveholders' foul rebellion.

Resolved, That it is the duty of every Christian patriot to pray for the President and all that are high in authority; for our soldiers and seamen, and for the success of our arms; and that he, who in the hour of his country's travail stands not up manfully to vindicate her cause, or witholds his support from the government whose fostering care has guaranteed him all the rights and immunities of citizenship, is recreant to God and false to the highest principles of truth and justice, and unworthy the name of an American citizen.

Additional Proclamations, Orders, Letters, and Addresses of President Lincoln.*

PROCLAMATIONS.

FOR THREE HUNDRED THOUSAND MEN.†

Whereas, by the act approved July 4, 1864, entitled "An act further to regulate and provide for the enrolling and calling out the national forces, and for other purposes," it is provided that the President of the United States may "at his discretion at any time hereafter call for any number of men as volunteers for the respective terms of one, two and three years for military service," and "that in case the quota or any part thereof, of any town, township, ward of a city, precinct or election district, or of a county not so subdivided, shall not be filled within the space of fifty days after such call, then the President shall immediately order a draft for one year, to fill such quota or any part thereof which may be unfilled;" and whereas, by the credits allowed in accordance with the act of Congress on the call for five hundred thousand men, made July 18th, 1864, the number of men to be obtained under that call was reduced to 280,-000; and whereas, the operations of the enemy in certain States have rendered it impracticable to procure from them their full quotas of troops, under said call; and whereas, from the foregoing causes but 250,000 men have been put into the army, navy, and marine corps, under the said call of July 18, 1864, leaving a deficiency on that call of 250,000; now, therefore, I, ABRAHAM LINCOLN, President of the United States of America, in order to supply the aforesaid deficiency, and to provide for casualties in the military and naval service of the United States, do issue this, my call, for Three Hundred Thousand Volunteers to serve for one, two or three years. The quotas of the States, districts and sub-districts under this call will be assigned by the War Department through the Bureau of the Provost Marshal General of the United States, and "in case the quota or any part thereof, of any town, township, ward of a city, precinct or election district, or of a county, not so subdivided, shall not be filled" before the 15th day of February, 1865, then a draft shall be made to fill such quota, or any part thereof under this call, which may be unfilled on said 15th day of February, 1865.

In testimony whereof I have hereunto set my hand and caused the seal of the United States to be affixed.

Done at the city of Washington, this 19th day of December, in the year of our Lord one thousand eight hun-[L. S.] dred and sixty-four, and of the Independence of the United States of America the eighty-ninth.

ABRAHAM LINCOLN.

By the President:
WM. H. SEWARD, *Secretary of State.*

---

*For other Papers, see pages 332–337, and 423–425.

†For other calls, see pages 114, 115, and 270. 1865, April 13—Secretary STANTON sent this telegram to Major General DIX:

WAR DEPARTMENT,
WASHINGTON, D. C., *April* 13, 6 P. M.

Major General DIX, *New York:*

This department, after mature consideration and consultation with the Lieutenant General upon the result of the recent campaign, has come to the following determinations, which will be carried into effect by appropriate orders immediately to be issued:

First. To stop all drafting and recruiting in the loyal States.

Second. To curtail purchases for arms, ammunition, quartermaster and commissary supplies, and reduce the expenses of the military establishment in its several branches.

Third. To reduce the number of general and staff officers to the actual necessities of the service.

Fourth. To remove all military restriction upon trade and commerce, so far as may be consistent with public safety.

As soon as these measures can be put in operation, it will be made known by public orders.

EDWIN M. STANTON,
Secretary of War.

PARDON TO DESERTERS.

Whereas, the twenty-first section of the act of Congress, approved on the third instant, entitled "An act to amend the several acts heretofore passed to provide for the enrolling and calling out the national forces, and for other purposes," requires "that in addition to the other lawful penalties of the crime of desertion from the military and naval service, all persons who have deserted the military or naval service of the United States who shall not return to said service, or report themselves to a provost marshal within sixty days after the proclamation hereinafter mentioned, shall be deemed and taken to have voluntarily relinquished and forfeited their rights of citizenship and their rights to become citizens, and such deserters shall be forever incapable of holding any office of trust or profit under the United States, or of exercising any rights of citizens thereof; and all persons who shall hereafter desert the military or naval service, and all persons who, being duly enrolled, shall depart the jurisdiction of the district in which he is enrolled, or go beyond the limits of the United States with intent to avoid any draft into the military or naval service, duly ordered, shall be liable to the penalties of this section. And the President is hereby authorized and required forthwith, on the passage of this act, to issue his proclamation setting forth the provisions of this section, in which proclamation the President is requested to notify all deserters returning within sixty days, as aforesaid, that they shall be pardoned on condition of returning to their regiments and companies, or to such other organizations as they may be assigned to, until they shall have served for a period of time equal to their original term of enlistment."

Now, therefore, be it known that I, ABRAHAM LINCOLN, President of the United States, do issue this my proclamation, as required by said act, ordering and requiring all deserters to return to their proper posts; and I do hereby notify them that all deserters who shall, within sixty days from the date of this proclamation, viz: on or before the 10th day of May, 1865, return to service, or report themselves to a provost marshal, shall be pardoned, on condition that they return to their regiments and companies, or to such other organizations as they may be assigned to, and serve the remainder of their original terms of enlistment, and, in addition thereto, a period equal to the time lost by desertion.

In testimony whereof, I have hereunto set my hand, and caused the seal of the United States to be affixed.

Done at the city of Washington, this eleventh day of March, in the year of our Lord one thousand eight [L. S.] hundred and sixty-five, and of the Independence of the United States, the eighty-ninth.

ABRAHAM LINCOLN.

By the President:
WILLIAM H. SEWARD, *Secretary of State.*

A WARNING TO BLOCKADE-RUNNERS AND OTHERS.

DEPARTMENT OF STATE,
WASHINGTON, *March* 14, 1865.

The President directs that all persons who now are, or hereafter shall be, found within the United States, and who have been engaged in holding intercourse or trade with the insurgents by sea, if they are citizens of the United States or domiciled aliens, be arrested and held as prisoners of war until the war shall close, subject, nevertheless, to prosecution, trial, and conviction for any offence committed by them as spies, or otherwise against the laws of war.

The President further directs that all non-resident foreigners who now are, or hereafter shall be, found in the United States, and who have been or shall hereafter be engaged in violating the blockade of the insurgent ports, shall leave the United States within twelve days from the publication of this order, or from their subsequent arrival in the United States, if on the Atlantic side, and forty days if on the Pacific side of the country. And such persons shall not return to the United States during the continuance of the war.

Provost Marshals and Marshals of the United States will arrest and commit to military custody all such offenders as shall disregard this order, whether they have passports or not, and they will be detained in such custody until the end of the war, or until discharged by subsequent order of the President.

WILLIAM H. SEWARD,
Secretary of State.

A REWARD OFFERED FOR THE ARREST OF RAIDERS.

The following has been promulgated by the Secretary of State:

To all whom these presents may concern:

Whereas for some time past evil disposed persons have crossed the borders of the United States, or entered their ports by sea from countries where they are tolerated, and have committed capital felonies against the property and life of American citizens, as well in the cities as in the rural districts of the country:

Now, therefore, in the name and by the authority of the President of the United States, I do hereby make known that a reward of one thousand dollars will be paid at this Department for the capture of each of such offenders, upon his conviction by a civil or military tribunal, to whomsoever shall arrest and deliver such offenders into the custody of the civil or military authorities of the United States; and the like reward will be paid, upon the same terms, for the capture of any such persons so entering the United States whose offences shall be committed subsequently to the publication of this notice. A reward of five hundred dollars will be paid, upon conviction, for the arrest of any person who shall have aided and abetted offences of the class before named within the territory of the United States.

Given under my hand and the seal of the Department of State, at Washington, this fourth day of April, A. D. 1865.

WILLIAM H. SEWARD,
Secretary of State.

CLOSING CERTAIN PORTS.

Whereas by my proclamations of the nineteenth and twenty-seventh days of April, one thousand eight hundred and sixty-one, the ports of the United States in the States of Virginia, North Carolina, South Carolina, Georgia, Florida, Alabama, Mississippi, Louisiana, and Texas were declared to be subject to blockade; but whereas the said blockade has, in consequence of actual military occupation by this Government, since been conditionally set aside or relaxed in respect to the ports of Norfolk and Alexandria, in the State of Virginia; Beaufort, in the State of North Carolina; Port Royal, in the State of South Carolina; Pensacola and Fernandina, in the State of Florida, and New Orleans, in the State of Louisiana:

And whereas, by the fourth section of the act of Congress, approved on the thirteenth of July, eighteen hundred and sixty-one, entitled "An act further to provide for the collection of duties on imports and for other purposes," the President, for the reasons therein set forth, is authorized to close certain ports of entry:

Now, therefore, be it known that I, ABRAHAM LINCOLN, President of the United States, do hereby proclaim that the ports of Richmond, Tappahannock, Cherrystone, Yorktown, and Petersburg, in Virginia; of Camden, (Elizabeth City,) Edenton, Plymouth, Washington, Newbern, Ocracoke, and Wilmington, in North Carolina; of Charleston, Georgetown, and Beaufort, in South Carolina; of Savannah, St. Mary's, and Brunswick, (Darien,) in Georgia; of Mobile, in Alabama; of Pearl river, (Shieldsborough,) Natchez, and Vicksburg, in Mississippi; of St. Augustine, Key West, St. Marks, (Port Leon,) St. Johns, (Jacksonville,) and Apalachicola, in Florida; of Teche, (Franklin,) in Louisiana; of Galveston, La Salle, Brazos de Santiago, (Point Isabel,) and Brownsville, Texas, are hereby closed, and all right of importation, warehousing, and other privileges shall, in respect to the ports aforesaid, cease until they shall have again been opened by order of the President; and if, while said ports are so closed, any ship or vessel from beyond the United States, or having on board any articles subject to duties, shall attempt to enter any such port, the same, together with its tackle, apparel, furniture, and cargo shall be forfeited to the United States.

In witness whereof, I have hereunto set my hand and caused the seal of the United States to be affixed.

Done at the city of Washington, this eleventh day of April, in the year of our Lord one thousand eight hundred [L. S.] and sixty-five, and of the Independence of the United States of America the eighty-ninth.

ABRAHAM LINCOLN.

By the President:
WILLIAM H. SEWARD, *Secretary of State.*

EQUALITY OF RIGHTS WITH ALL MARITIME NATIONS.

Whereas for some time past vessels of war of the United States have been refused, in certain foreign ports, privileges and immunities to which they were entitled by treaty, public law, or the comity of nations, at the same time that vessels of war of the country wherein the said privileges and immunities have been withheld have enjoyed them fully and uninterruptedly in ports of the United States; which condition of things has not always been forcibly resisted by the United States, although, on the other hand, they have not at any time failed to protest against and declare their dissatisfaction with the same; in the view of the United States no condition any longer exists which can be claimed to justify the denial to them by any one of said nations of customary naval rights such as has heretofore been so unnecessarily persisted in:

Now, therefore, I, ABRAHAM LINCOLN, President of the United States, do hereby make known, that if after a reasonable time shall have elapsed for intelligence of this proclamation to have reached any foreign country in whose ports the said privileges and immunities shall have been refused, as aforesaid, they shall continue to be so refused, then and thenceforth the same privileges and immunities shall be refused to the vessels of war of that country in the ports of the United States; and this refusal shall continue until war vessels of the United States shall have been placed upon an entire equality in the foreign ports aforesaid with similar vessels of other countries. The United States, whatever claim or pretence may have existed heretofore, are now, at least, entitled to claim and concede an entire and friendly equality of rights and hospitalities with all maritime nations.

In witness whereof, I have hereunto set my hand and caused the seal of the United States to be affixed.

Done at the city of Washington, this eleventh day of April, in the year of our Lord one thousand eight [L. S.] hundred and sixty-five, and of the Independence of the United States of America the eighty-ninth.

ABRAHAM LINCOLN.

By the President:
WILLIAM H. SEWARD, *Secretary of State.*

PORT OF KEY WEST.

Whereas, by my proclamation of this date the port of Key West, in the State of Florida, was inadvertently included among those which are not open to commerce:

Now, therefore, be it known that I, ABRAHAM LINCOLN, President of the United States, do hereby declare and make known that the said port of Key West is and shall remain open to foreign and domestic commerce upon the same conditions by which that commerce has there hitherto been governed.

In witness whereof, I have hereunto set my hand and caused the seal of the United States to be affixed.

Done at the city of Washington, this eleventh day of April, in the year of our Lord one thousand eight [L. S.] hundred and sixty-five, and of the Independence of the United States of America the eighty-ninth.

ABRAHAM LINCOLN.

By the President:
WM. H. SEWARD, *Secretary of State.*

OBSERVANCE OF THE SABBATH.

EXECUTIVE MANSION,
WASHINGTON, *Nov.* 16, 1864.

The President, Commander-in-Chief of the Army and Navy, desires and enjoins the orderly observance of the Sabbath by the officers and men in the military and naval service. The importance for man and beast of the prescribed weekly rest, the sacred rights of Christian soldiers and sailors, a becoming deference to the best sentiment of Christian people, and a due regard for the Divine will, demand that Sunday labor in the Army and Navy be reduced to the measure of strict necessity.

The discipline and character of the national forces should not suffer, nor the cause they defend be imperiled, by the profanation of the day or name of the Most High. "At this time of public distress"—adopting the words of Washington in 1776—"men may find enough to do in the service of their God and their country without abandoning themselves to vice and immorality." The first General Order issued by the Father of his Country after the Declaration of Independence, indicates the spirit in which our institutions were founded and should ever be defended: "*The General hopes and trusts that every officer and man will endeavor to live and act as becomes a Christian soldier, defending the dearest rights and liberties of his country.*"

ABRAHAM LINCOLN.

LETTERS.

TO MRS. ELIZA P. GURNEY.

EXECUTIVE MANSION,
WASHINGTON, *September* 30, 1864.

MY ESTEEMED FRIEND: I have not forgotten, probably never shall forget, the very impressive occasion when yourself and friends visited me on a Sabbath forenoon two years ago. Nor had your kind letter, written nearly a year later, ever been forgotten. In all it has been your purpose to strengthen my reliance in God. I am much indebted to the good Christian people of the country for their constant prayers and consolations, and to no one of them more than to yourself. The purposes of the Almighty are perfect and must prevail, though we erring mortals may fail to accurately perceive them in advance. We hoped for a happy termination of this terrible war long before this; but God knows best, and has ruled otherwise. We shall yet acknowledge His wisdom and our own errors therein; meanwhile we must work earnestly in the best light He gives us, trusting that so working still conduces to the great ends He ordains. Surely He intends some great good to follow this mighty convulsion which no mortal could make, and no mortal could stay.

Your people—the Friends—have had, and are having, very great trials, on principles and faith opposed to both war and oppression. They can only practically oppose oppression by war. In this hard dilemma, some have chosen one horn and some the other.

For those appealing to me on conscientious grounds I have done and shall do the best I could and can in my own conscience under my oath to the law. That you believe this I doubt not, and believing it I shall still receive for my country and myself your earnest prayers to our Father in Heaven. Your sincere friend,

A. LINCOLN.

TO DEACON JOHN PHILLIPS.

Deacon John Phillips, of Sturbridge, Massachusetts, whose great age—one hundred and four years—did not prevent him from voting on the 8th of November, received the following letter from the PRESIDENT:

EXECUTIVE MANSION,
WASHINGTON, *Nov.* 21, 1864.

MY DEAR SIR: I have heard of the incident at the polls in your town, in which you acted so honorable a part, and I take the liberty of writing to you to express my personal gratitude for the compliment paid me by the suffrage of a citizen so venerable.

The example of such devotion to civic duties in one whose days have already been extended an average lifetime beyond the Psalmist's limit, cannot but be valuable and fruitful. It is not for myself only, but for the country, which you have in your sphere served so long and so well, that I thank you. Your friend and servant,

A. LINCOLN.

Deacon JOHN PHILLIPS.

TO MRS. BIXBY.

Mrs. Bixby, the recipient of the following letter from President LINCOLN, is a poor widow living in the Eleventh Ward of Boston. Her sixth son was severely wounded in a recent battle:

EXECUTIVE MANSION,
WASHINGTON, *Nov.* 21, 1864.

DEAR MADAM: I have been shown on the file of the War Department a statement of the Adjutant General of Massachusetts, that you are the mother of five sons who have died gloriously on the field of battle.

I feel how weak and fruitless must be any word of mine which should attempt to beguile you from the grief of a loss so overwhelming; but I cannot refrain from tendering to you the consolation that may be found in the thanks of the Republic they died to save.

I pray that our Heavenly Father may assuage the anguish of your bereavements, and leave only the cherished memory of the loved and lost, and the solemn pride that must be yours to have laid so costly a sacrifice upon the altar of freedom.

Yours, very sincerely and respectfully,

A. LINCOLN.

To Mrs. BIXBY, *Boston, Mass.*

TO THE NEW ENGLAND SOCIETY.

EXECUTIVE MANSION,
WASHINGTON, *December* 19, 1864.

MY DEAR SIR: I have the honor to acknowledge the reception of your kind invitation to be present at the annual festival of the New England Society to commemorate the landing of the Pilgrims, on Thursday, the 22d of this month.

My duties will not allow me to avail myself of your kindness.

I cannot but congratulate you and the country, however, upon the spectacle of devoted unanimity, presented by the people at home, the citizens that form our marching columns, and the citizens that fill our squadrons on the sea, all animated by the same determination to complete the work our fathers began and transmitted.

The work of the Plymouth emigrants was the glory of their age. While we reverence their memory, let us not forget how vastly greater is our opportunity. I am, very truly, your obedient servant, A. LINCOLN.

JOSEPH H. CHOATE, Esq.

TO A SOLDIERS' FAIR.

EXECUTIVE MANSION,
WASHINGTON, *December* 19, 1864.

To the Ladies managing the Soldiers' Fair at Springfield, Mass.:

Your kind invitation to be present at the opening of your fair is duly received by the hand of Mr. Ashmun. Grateful for the compliment, and ever anxious to aid the good cause in which you are engaged, I yet am compelled, by public duties here, to decline. The recent good news from Generals Sherman, Thomas, and, indeed, from nearly all quarters, will be far better than my presence, and will afford all the impulse and enthusiasm you will need.

Your obedient servant, A. LINCOLN.

ON AFFAIRS IN MISSOURI.

EXECUTIVE MANSION,
WASHINGTON, *February* 20, 1865.

His Excellency Governor Fletcher:

It seems that there is now no organized military force of the enemy in Missouri, and yet that destruction of property and life is rampant everywhere. Is not the cure for this within easy reach of the people themselves? It cannot but be that every man, not naturally a robber or cut-throat, would gladly put an end to this state of things. A large majority in every locality must feel alike upon this subject; and if so, they only need to reach an understanding, one with another. Each leaving all others alone solves the problem; and surely each would do this but for his apprehension that others will not leave him alone. Cannot this mischievous distrust be removed? Let neighborhood meetings be everywhere called and held of all entertaining a sincere purpose for mutual security in the future, whatever they may heretofore have thought, said, or done about the war or about anything else. Let all such meet, and, waiving all else, pledge each to cease harassing others, and to make common cause against whoever persists in making, aiding, or encouraging further disturbance. The practical means they will best know how to adopt and apply. At such meetings old friendships will cross the memory, and honor and Christian charity will come in to help.

Please consider whether it may not be well to suggest this to the now afflicted people of Missouri.

Yours, truly,

A. LINCOLN.

ON EMPLOYING DISABLED SOLDIERS.

EXECUTIVE MANSION,
WASHINGTON, *March* 1, 1865.

GENTLEMEN: I have received your address, on the part of the Bureau for the Employment of Disabled and Discharged Soldiers, which has recently been established in connection with the Protective War Claim Association of the Sanitary Commission.

It gives me pleasure to assure you of my hearty concurrence with the purposes you announce, and I shall at all times be ready to recognize the paramount claims of the soldiers of the nation in the disposition of public trusts. I shall be glad, also, to make these suggestions to the several heads of departments.

I am, very truly, your obedient servant,

A. LINCOLN

To Lieut. Gen. WINFIELD SCOTT, *President;* HOWARD POTTER, WM. E. DODGE, JR., THEO. ROOSEVELT, Esqs.

ADDRESSES.

AT THE CONSECRATION OF THE NATIONAL CEMETERY, GETTYSBURG, NOVEMBER 19, 1863.

FOURSCORE and seven years ago our fathers brought forth upon this continent a new nation, conceived in Liberty, and dedicated to the proposition that all men are created equal.

Now we are engaged in a great civil war, testing whether that nation, or any nation so conceived and so dedicated, can long endure. We are met on a great battle-field of that war. We are met to dedicate a portion of it as the final resting place of those who here gave their lives that that nation might live. It is altogether fitting and proper that we should do this.

But in a larger sense we cannot dedicate, we cannot consecrate, we cannot hallow this ground. The brave men, living and dead, who struggled here, have consecrated it far above our power to add or detract. The world will little note nor long remember what we say here, but it can never forget what they did here. It is for us, the living, rather to be dedicated here to the unfinished work that they have thus far so nobly carried on. It is rather for us to be here dedicated to the great task remaining before us, – that from these honored dead we take increased devotion to the cause for which they here gave the last full measure of devotion,—that we here highly resolve that the dead shall not have died in vain, that the nation shall, under God, have a new birth of freedom, and that the government of the people, by the people, and for the people, shall not perish from the earth.

TO A COMMITTEE OF THE NEW YORK WORKINGMEN'S REPUBLICAN ASSOCIATION.

1864, March 21—The PRESIDENT, replying to their address, said:

GENTLEMEN OF THE COMMITTEE: The honorary membership in your association so generously tendered is gratefully accepted. You comprehend, as your address shows, that the existing rebellion means more and tends to more than the perpetuation of African slavery; that it is in fact a war upon the rights of all working people. Partly to show that the view has not escaped my attention, and partly that I cannot better express myself, I read a passage from the message to Congress in December, 1861. (See pages 135, 136.)

The views then expressed remain unchanged, nor have I much to add. None are so deeply interested to resist the present rebellion as the working people. Let them beware of prejudices working disunion and hostility among themselves. The most notable feature of a disturbance in your city last summer was the hanging of some working people by other working people. It should never be so. The strongest bond of human sympathy, outside of the family relation, should be one uniting all working people, of all nations, tongues, and kindreds. Nor should this lead to a war upon property or the owners of property. Property is the fruit of labor; property is desirable; is a positive good in the world. That some should be rich shows that others may become rich, and hence is just encouragement to industry and enterprise. Let not him who is houseless pull down the house of another, but let him labor diligently and build one for himself; thus by example assuring that his own shall be safe from violence when built.

TO A CLUB OF PENNSYLVANIANS.

November 8—The President, at a late hour in the night, was serenaded by a club of Pennsylvanians, and spoke as follows:

Friends and Fellow-Citizens: Even before I had been informed by you that this compliment was paid me by loyal citizens of Pennsylvania friendly to me, I had inferred that you were of that portion of my countrymen who think that the best interests of the nation are to be subserved by the support of the present Administration. I do not pretend to say that you who think so embrace all the patriotism and loyalty of the country; but I do believe, and, I trust, without personal interest, that the welfare of the country *does* require that such support and endorsement be given.

I earnestly believe that the consequences of this day's work (if it be as you assure, and as now seems probable) will be to the lasting advantage, if not to the very salvation, of the country. I cannot at this hour say what has been the result of the election. But whatever it may be, I have no desire to modify this opinion, that all who have labored to-day in behalf of the Union organization have wrought for the best interests of their country and the world, not only for the present but for all future ages.

I am thankful to God for this approval of the people; but, while deeply gratified for this mark of their confidence in me, if I know my heart, my gratitude is free from any taint of personal triumph. I do not impugn the motives of any one opposed to me. It is no pleasure to me to triumph over any one; but I give thanks to the Almighty for this evidence of the people's resolution to stand by free government and the rights of humanity.

TO SUNDRY POLITICAL CLUBS.

November 10—The several Lincoln and Johnson Clubs of the District of Columbia called on the President, and gave him a serenade in honor of his re-election. There was, in addition, an immense concourse of spectators of both sexes in front of the Executive mansion.

The President appeared at an upper window, and when the cheers with which he was greeted had ceased, he spoke as follows:

It has long been a grave question whether any Government, not too strong for the liberties of its people, can be strong enough to maintain its existence in great emergencies.

On this point the present rebellion has brought our Republic to a severe test, and a Presidential election, occurring in regular course during the rebellion, has added not a little to the strain. If the loyal people, united, were put to the utmost of their strength by the rebellion, must they not fail when divided, and partially paralyzed by a political war among themselves?

But the election was a necessity. We cannot have a free Government without elections; and if the rebellion could force us to forego or postpone a national election, it might fairly claim to have already conquered and ruined us.

The strife of the election is but human nature practically applied to the facts in the case. What has occurred in this case must ever recur in similar cases. Human nature will not change. In any future great national trial, compared with the men who have passed through this, we shall have as weak and as strong, as silly and as wise, as bad and as good. Let us therefore study the incidents of this as philosophy to learn wisdom from, and none of them as wrongs to be revenged. [Cheers.]

But the election, along with its incidental and undesired strife, has done good, too. It has demonstrated that a people's Government can sustain a national election in the midst of a great civil war. [Renewed cheers.] Until now it has not been known to the world that this was a possibility. It shows, also, how sound and how strong we still are. It shows that, even among candidates of the same party, he who is most devoted to the Union, and most opposed to treason, can receive most of the people's vote. [Applause.]

It shows, also, to the extent yet unknown, that we have more men now than we had when the war began. Gold is good in its place, but living, brave, patriotic men, are better than gold. [Cheers and other demonstrations of applause.]

But the rebellion continues; and now that the election is over, may not all having a common interest re-unite in a common effort to save our common country? [Cheers.]

For my own part, I have striven, and shall strive, to avoid placing any obstacle in the way. [Cheers.] So long as I have been here I have not willingly planted a thorn in any man's bosom. While I am deeply sensible to the high compliment of a re-election, and duly grateful, as I trust, to Almighty God for having directed my countrymen to a right conclusion, as I think, for their own good, it adds nothing to my satisfaction that any other man may be disappointed or pained by the result. [Cheers.] May I ask those who have not differed with me to join with me in this same spirit towards those who have?

And now let me close by asking three hearty cheers for our brave soldiers and seamen, and their gallant and skilful commanders.

TO A MARYLAND COMMITTEE.

November 17—A committee of Maryland Union men called upon the President.

W. H. Purnell, Esq., in behalf of the Committee, delivered an address, in which he said they rejoiced that the people, by such an overwhelming and unprecedented majority, had again re-elected Mr. Lincoln to the Presidency and endorsed his course—elevating him to the proudest and most honorable position on earth. They felt under deep obligation to him, because he had appreciated their condition as a Slave State. It was not too much to say that by the exercise of rare discretion on his part, Maryland to-day occupies her position in favor of freedom. Slavery has been abolished therefrom by the sovereign decree of the people. With deep and lasting gratitude they desired that his Administration, as it had been approved in the past, might also be successful in the future, and result in the restoration of the Union, with freedom as its immutable basis. They trusted that on retiring from his high and honorable position the universal verdict might be that he deserved well of mankind, and that favoring heaven might "crown his days with loving kindness and tender mercies."

The President, in reply, said he had to confess he had been duly notified of the intention to make this friendly call some days ago, and in this he had had a fair opportunity afforded to be ready with a set speech; but he had not prepared one, being too busy for that purpose. He would say, however, that he was gratified with the result of the Presidential election. He had kept as near as he could to the exercise of his best judgment for the interest of the whole country, and to have the seal of approbation stamped on the course he had pursued was exceedingly grateful to his feelings. He thought he could say, in as large a sense as any other man, that his pleasure consisted in belief that the policy he had pursued was the best, if not the only one, for the safety of the country.

He had said before, and now repeated, that he indulged in no feeling of triumph over any man who thought or acted differently from himself. He had no such feeling towards any living man. When he thought of Maryland, in particular, he was of the opinion that she had more than double her share in what had occurred in the recent elections. The adoption of a free State constitution was a greater thing than the part taken by the people of the State in the Presidential election. He would any day have stipulated to lose Maryland in the Presidential election to save it by the adoption of a free State constitution, because the Presidential election comes every four years, while that is a thing which, being done, cannot be undone. He therefore thought that in that they had a victory for the right, worth a great deal more than their part in the Presidential election, though of the latter he thought highly. He had once before said, but would say again, that those who have differed with us and opposed us will see that the result of the

Presidential election is better for their own good than if they had been successful.

Thanking the Committee for their compliment, he brought his brief speech to a close.

ON THE ADOPTION OF THE ANTI-SLAVERY CONSTITUTIONAL AMENDMENT.

1865, February 1—A large delegation called at the Executive Mansion.

After the band had played one or two favorite airs, the PRESIDENT appeared at the centre upper window, under the portico, and his appearance was greeted with loud cheers, and when they had subsided the PRESIDENT said he supposed the passage through Congress of the constitutional amendment for the abolishment of slavery throughout the United States was the occasion to which he was indebted for the honor of this call. [Applause.] The occasion was one of congratulation to the country and the whole world. But there is a task yet before us—to go forward and have consummated by the votes of the States that which Congress had so nobly begun yesterday. [Applause, and cries of "They will do it," &c.] He had the honor to inform those present that Illinois had already to-day done the work. [Applause.] Maryland was about half through, but he felt proud that Illinois was a little ahead. He thought the measure was a very fitting, if not an indispensable, adjunct to the winding up of this great difficulty. [Applause.] He wished the reunion of all the States perfected, and so effected as to remove all cause of disturbance in the future; and to attain this end it was necessary that the original disturbing cause should, if possible, be rooted out.

He thought all would bear him witness that he had never shrunk from doing all that he could to eradicate slavery by issuing an emancipation proclamation. [Applause.] But that proclamation falls far short of what the amendment will be when fully consummated. A question might be raised whether the proclamation was legally valid. It might be urged that it only aided those who came into our lines, and that it was inoperative as to those who did not give themselves up; or that it would have no effect upon the children of slaves born hereafter; in fact, it would be urged that it did not meet the evil. But the amendment is a king's cure-all for all the evils. [Applause.] It winds the whole thing up. He would repeat that it was the fitting, if not the indispensable, adjunct to the consummation of the great game we are playing. He could not but congratulate all present, himself, the country, and the whole world upon this great moral victory. In conclusion, he thanked those present for the call.

ON BEING OFFICIALLY NOTIFIED OF RE-ELECTION.

Having served four years in the depths of a great and yet unended national peril, I can view this call to a second term in nowise more flattering to myself than as an expression of the public judgment that I may better finish a difficult work, in which I have labored from the first, than could any one less severely schooled to the task. In this view and with assured reliance on that Almighty Ruler who has so graciously sustained us thus far, and with increased gratitude to the generous people for their continued confidence, I accept the renewed trust with its yet onerous and perplexing duties and responsibilities.

PRESIDENT LINCOLN'S SECOND INAUGURAL ADDRESS, MARCH 4, 1865.

FELLOW-COUNTRYMEN: At this second appearing to take the oath of the presidential office, there is less occasion for an extended address than there was at the first. Then, a statement, somewhat in detail, of a course to be pursued, seemed fitting and proper. Now, at the expiration of four years, during which public declarations have been constantly called forth on every point and phase of the great contest which still absorbs the attention and engrosses the energies of the nation, little that is new could be presented. The progress of our arms, upon which all else chiefly depends, is as well known to the public as to myself; and it is, I trust, reasonably satisfactory and encouraging to all. With high hope for the future, no prediction in regard to it is ventured.

On the occasion corresponding to this four years ago, all thoughts were anxiously directed to an impending civil war. All dreaded it—all sought to avert it. While the inaugural address was being delivered from this place, devoted altogether to *saving* the Union without war, insurgent agents were in the city seeking to *destroy* it without war—seeking to dissolve the Union, and divide effects, by negotiation. Both parties deprecated war; but one of them would *make* war rather than let the nation survive; and the other would *accept* war rather than let it perish. And the war came.

One-eighth of the whole population were colored slaves, not distributed generally over the Union, but localized in the southern part of it. These slaves constituted a peculiar and powerful interest. All knew that this interest was, somehow, the cause of the war. To strengthen, perpetuate and extend this interest was the object for which the insurgents would rend the Union, even by war; while the government claimed no right to do more than to restrict the territorial enlargement of it. Neither party expected for the war the magnitude or the duration which it has already attained. Neither anticipated that the *cause* of the conflict might cease with, or even before, the conflict itself should cease. Each looked for an easier triumph, and a result less fundamental and astounding. Both read the same Bible, and pray to the same God; and each invokes His aid against the other. It may seem strange that any men should dare to ask a just God's assistance in wringing their bread from the sweat of other men's faces; but let us judge not, that we be not judged. The prayers of both could not be answered—that of neither has been answered fully. The Almighty has His own purposes. "Woe unto the world because of offences! for it must needs be that offences come; but woe to that man by whom the offence cometh." If we shall suppose that American slavery is one of those offences which, in the providence of God, must needs come, but which, having continued through His appointed time, He now wills to remove, and that He gives to both north and south this terrible war, as the woe due to those by whom the offence came, shall we discern therein any departure from those divine attributes which the believers in a living God always ascribe to Him? Fondly do we hope—fervently do we pray—that this mighty scourge of war may speedily pass away. Yet, if God wills that it continue until all the wealth piled by the bondman's two hundred and fifty years of unrequited toil shall be sunk, and until every drop of blood drawn with the lash shall be paid by another drawn with the sword, as was said three thousand years ago, so still it must be said, "The judgments of the Lord are true and righteous altogether."

With malice toward none; with charity for all; with firmness in the right, as God gives us to see the right, let us strive on to finish the work we are in; to bind up the nation's wounds, to care for him who shall have borne the battle, and for his widow, and his orphan—to do all which may achieve and cherish a just and a lasting peace among ourselves, and with all nations.

ON THE SLAVES FIGHTING FOR THE REBELS.

1865, March 17—On the occasion of the presentation of a captured rebel flag to Gov. Morton, of Indiana, President LINCOLN made these remarks:

FELLOW-CITIZENS: A few words only. I was born in Kentucky, raised in Indiana, reside in Illinois, and now here, it is my duty to care equally for the good people of all the States. I am to-day glad of seeing it in the power of an Indiana regiment to present this captured flag to the good Governor of their State. And yet I would not wish to compliment Indiana above other States, remembering that all have done so well.

There are but few aspects of this great war on which I have not already expressed my views by speaking or writing. *There is one*—the recent effort of "our erring brethren," sometimes so called, to employ the slaves in their armies. The great question with them has been, "will the negro fight for them?" They ought to know better than we, and doubtless do know better than we. I may incidentally remark, however, that having in my life heard many arguments—or strings of words meant to pass for arguments—intended to show that the negro ought to be a slave; that if he shall now really fight to keep himself a slave, it will be a far better argument why he should remain a slave than I have ever before heard.

He, perhaps, ought to be a slave, if he desires it ardently enough to fight for it. Or, if one out of four will, for his own freedom, fight to keep the other three in slavery, he ought to be a slave for his selfish meanness. I have always thought that all men should be free; but if any should be slaves, it should be first those who desire it for *themselves*, and secondly those who desire it for *others*. Whenever I hear any one arguing for slavery, I feel a strong impulse to see it tried on him personally.

There is one thing about the negro's fighting for the rebels which we can know as well as they can; and that is that they cannot at the same time fight in their armies and stay at home and make bread for them. And this being known and remembered, we can have but little concern whether they become soldiers or not. I am rather in favor of the measure, and would at any time, if I could, have loaned them a vote to carry it. We have to reach the bottom of the insurgent resources; and that they employ, or seriously think of employing the slaves as soldiers, gives us glimpses of the bottom. Therefore I am glad of what we learn on this subject.

ON VICTORY AND RECONSTRUCTION.

1865, April 11—After the fall of Richmond and the surrender of the Army of Northern Virginia, President Lincoln was called upon in Washington, and made these remarks:

We meet this evening not in sorrow, but in gladness of heart. The evacuation of Petersburg and Richmond, and the surrender of the principal insurgent army, give hope of a righteous and speedy peace, whose joyous expression cannot be restrained. In the midst of this, however, He from whom all blessings flow must not be forgotten. A call for a national thanksgiving is being prepared, and will be duly promulgated. Nor must those whose harder part give us the cause of rejoicing be overlooked. Their honors must not be parcelled out with others. I myself was near the front, and had the high pleasure of transmitting much of the good news to you; but no part of the honor, for plan or execution, is mine. To Gen. Grant, his skilful officers and brave men, all belongs. The gallant navy stood ready, but was not in reach to take active part.

By these recent successes, the re-inauguration of the national authority, reconstruction, which has had a large share of thought from the first, is pressed much more closely upon our attention. It is fraught with great difficulty. Unlike the case of a war between independent nations, there is no authorized organ for us to treat with. No one man has authority to give up the rebellion for any other man. We simply must begin with and mould from disorganized and discordant elements. Nor is it a small additional embarrassment that we, the loyal people, differ among ourselves as to the mode, manner, and means of reconstruction.

As a general rule, I abstain from reading the reports of attacks upon myself, wishing not to be provoked by that to which I cannot properly offer an answer. In spite of this precaution, however, it comes to my knowledge that I am much censured from some supposed agency in setting up and seeking to sustain the new State government of Louisiana. In this I have done just so much as, and no more than, the public knows. In the annual message of December, 1863, and accompanying proclamation, I presented a plan of reconstruction (as the phrase goes) which I promised, if adopted by any State, should be acceptable to, and sustained by the Executive Government of the nation. I distinctly stated that this was not the only plan which might possibly be acceptable; and I also distinctly protested that the Executive claimed no right to say when or whether members should be admitted to seats in Congress from such States. This plan was, in advance, submitted to the then Cabinet, and distinctly approved by every member of it. One of them suggested that I should then, and in that connection, apply the Emancipation Proclamation to the theretofore excepted parts of Virginia and Louisiana; that I should drop the suggestion about apprenticeship for freed people, and that I should omit the protest against my own power, in regard to the admission of members of Congress; but even he approved every part and parcel of the plan which has since been employed or touched by the action of Louisiana.

The new Constitution of Louisiana, declaring emancipation for the whole State, practically applies the proclamation to the part previously excepted. It does not adopt apprenticeship for freed people, and it is silent, as it could not well be otherwise, about the admission of members to Congress. So that, as it applies to Louisiana, every member of the Cabinet fully approved the plan. The message went to Congress, and I received many commendations of the plan, written and verbal; and not a single objection to it, from any professed emancipationist, came to my knowledge, until after the news reached Washington that the people of Louisiana had begun to move in accordance with it. From about July, 1862, I had corresponded with different persons supposed to be interested, seeking a reconstruction of a State government for Louisiana. When the message of 1863, with the plan before mentioned, reached New Orleans, Gen. Banks wrote me he was confident that the people, with his military co-operation, would reconstruct substantially on that plan. I wrote him and some of them to try it. They tried it, and the result is known. Such only has been my agency in getting up the Louisiana government. As to sustaining it, my promise is out, as before stated. But as bad promises are better broken than kept, I shall treat this as a bad promise and break it whenever I shall be convinced that keeping it is adverse to the public interest. But I have not yet been so convinced.

I have been shown a letter on this subject, supposed to be an able one, in which the writer expresses regret that my mind has not seemed to be definitely fixed on the question whether the seceded States, so-called, are in the Union or out of it. It would, perhaps, add astonishment to his regret were he to learn that, since I have found professed Union men endeavoring to make that question, I have *purposely* forborne any public expression upon it. As appears to me, that question has not been, nor yet is, a practically material one, and that any discussion of it, while it thus remains practically immaterial, could have no effect other than the mischievous one of dividing our friends. As yet, whatever it may hereafter become, that question is bad, as the basis of a controversy, and good for nothing at all—a merely pernicious abstraction. We all agree that the seceded States, so-called, are out of their proper practical relation with the Union, and that the sole object of the Government, civil and military, in regard to those States, is to again get them into that proper practical relation. I believe it is not only possible, but in fact easier to do this without deciding, or even considering, whether these States have ever been out of the Union, than with it. Finding themselves safely at home, it would be utterly immaterial whether they had ever been abroad. Let us all join in doing the acts necessary to restoring the proper practical relations between these States and the Union, and each forever after innocently indulge his own opinion whether, in doing the acts, he brought the States from without into the Union, or only gave them proper assistance, they never having been out of it.

The amount of constituency, so to speak, on which the new Louisiana government rests, would be more satisfactory to all if it contained fifty, thirty, or even twenty thousand, instead of only about twelve thousand, as it really does. It is also unsatisfactory to some that the elective franchise is not given to the colored man. I would myself prefer that it were now conferred on the very intelligent, and on those who serve our cause as soldiers. Still the question is not whether the Louisiana government, as it stands, is quite all that is desirable. The question is: "Will it be wiser, take it as it is, and help to improve it, or to reject and disperse it?" "Can Louisiana be brought into proper practical relation with the Union *sooner* by *sustaining* or by *discarding* her new State government?"

Some twelve thousand voters in the heretofore slave State of Louisiana have sworn allegiance to the Union, assumed to be the rightful political power of the State, held elections, organized a State government, adopted a free State constitution, giving the benefit of public schools equally to black and white, and empowering the Legislature to confer the elective franchise upon the colored man. Their Legislature has already voted to ratify the constitutional amendment recently passed by Congress, abolishing slavery throughout the nation. These twelve thousand persons are thus fully committed to the Union, and to perpetual freedom in the State; committed to the very things and nearly all the things the nation wants, and they ask the nation's recognition and its assistance to make good that committal. Now, if we reject and spurn them, we do our utmost to disorganize and disperse them. We, in effect, say to the white men, "You are worthless, or worse; we will neither help you, nor be helped by you." To the blacks we say, "This cup of Liberty which these, your old masters, hold to your lips, we will dash from you, and leave you to the chances of gathering the spilled and scattered contents in some vague and undefined when, where, and how." If this course, discouraging and paralyzing both white and black, has any tendency to bring Louisiana into proper practical relations with the Union, I have, so far, been unable to perceive it. If, on the contrary, we recognize and sustain the new government of Louisiana, the converse of all this is made true.

We encourage the hearts and nerve the arms of the twelve thousand to adhere to their work and argue for it, and proselyte for it, and fight for it, and feed it, and grow it, and ripen it to a complete success. The colored man, too, seeing all united for him, is inspired with vigilance, and energy, and daring to the same end. Grant that he desires the elective franchise, will he not attain it sooner by saving the already advanced steps toward it than by running backward over them? Concede that the new government of Louisiana is only to what it should be as the egg is to the fowl; we shall sooner have the fowl by hatching the egg than by smashing it. Again, if we reject Louisiana, we also reject one vote in favor of the proposed amendment to the National Constitution. To meet this proposition it has been argued that no more than three-fourths of those States which have not attempted secession are necessary to validly ratify the amendment. I do not commit myself against this further than to say that such a ratification would be questionable, and sure to be persistently questioned; whilst a ratification by three-fourths of all the States would be unquestioned and unquestionable.

I repeat the question, "Can Louisiana be brought into proper practical relation with the Union *sooner* by *sustaining* or by *discarding* her new State government?" What has been said of Louisiana will apply generally to other States. And yet so great peculiarities pertain to each State, and such important and sudden changes occur in the same State, and, withal, so new and unprecedented is the whole case, that no exclusive and inflexible plan can safely be prescribed as to details and collaterals. Such exclusive and inflexible plan would surely become a new entanglement. Important principles may, and must, be inflexible.

In the present situation, as the phrase goes, it may be my duty to make some new announcement to the people of the South. I am considering, and shall not fail to act when satisfied that action will be proper.*

PRESIDENT LINCOLN'S SECOND CABINET.

Secretary of State—WILLIAM H. SEWARD, of New York.

Secretary of the Treasury—HUGH McCULLOCH, of Indiana.

Secretary of War—EDWIN M. STANTON, of Ohio.

Secretary of the Navy—GIDEON WELLES, of Connecticut.

Secretary of the Interior—JOHN P. USHER, of Indiana; to be succeeded, May 15, by JAMES HARLAN, of Iowa.

Attorney General—JAMES SPEED, of Kentucky.

Postmaster General—WILLIAM DENNISON, of Ohio.

DEATH OF PRESIDENT LINCOLN.

1865, April 15—President LINCOLN died in Washington city, at twenty-two minutes past seven o'clock, A. M., of wounds inflicted the night before by an assassin, supposed to be John Wilkes Booth.

Same day—ANDREW JOHNSON, Vice President, qualified as President, Chief Justice Chase having administered the oath of office.

Second Rebel Congress--Second Session.

Met in Richmond Monday, November 7, 1864.

JEFFERSON DAVIS'S MESSAGE.

* * * * * * *

EMPLOYMENT OF SLAVES.

The employment of slaves for service with the army as teamsters or cooks, or in the way of work upon fortifications, or in the Government work shops, or in hospitals, and other similar duties, was authorized by the act of 17th February last, and provision was made for their impressment to a number not exceeding twenty thousand, if it should be found impracticable to obtain them by contract with the owners. The law contemplated the hiring only of the labor of these slaves, and imposed on the Government the liability to pay for the value of such as might be lost to the owners from casualties resulting from their employment in the service.

This act has produced less result than was anticipated, and further provision is required to render it efficacious. But my present purpose is to invite your consideration to the propriety of a radical modification in the theory of the law.

THE LAW ON THE SUBJECT.

Viewed merely as property, and therefore as the subject of impressment, the service or labor of the slave has been frequently claimed for short periods in the construction of defensive works. The slave, however, bears another relation to the State—that of a person. The law of last February contemplates only the relation of the slave to the master, and limits the impressment to a certain term of service. But for the purposes enumerated in the act, instruction in the manner of encamping, marching, and parking trains is needful, so that, even in this limited employment, length of service adds greatly to the value of the negro's labor. Hazard is also encountered in all the positions to which the negroes can be assigned for service with the army, and the duties required of them demand loyalty and zeal

In this aspect the relation of person predominates so far as to render it doubtful whether the private right of property can consistently and beneficially be continued, and it would seem proper to acquire for the public service the entire property in the labor of the slave, and to pay therefor due compensation, rather than to impress his labor for short terms; and this the more especially as the effect of the present law would vest this entire property in all cases where the slave might be recaptured after compensation for his loss had been paid to the private owner

Whenever the entire property in the service of a slave is thus acquired by the Government, the question is presented by what tenure he should be held. Should he be retained in servitude, or should his emancipation be held out to him as a reward for faithful service, or should it be granted at once on the promise of such service? and if emancipated, what action should be taken to secure for the freedman the permission of the State from which he was drawn to reside within its limits after the close of his public service? The permission would doubtless be more readily accorded as a reward for past faithful service, and a double motive for zealous discharge of duty would thus be offered to those employed by the Government, their freedom, and the gratification of the local attachment which is so marked a characteristic of the negro, and forms so powerful an incentive to his action.

DAVIS OPPOSED TO IMMEDIATE EMANCIPATION.

The policy of engaging to liberate the negro on his discharge after service faithfully rendered seems to me preferable to that of granting immediate manumission, or that of retaining him in servitude. If this policy should recommend itself to the judgment of Congress, it is suggested that, in addition to the duties heretofore performed by the slave, he might be advantageously employed as pioneer and engineer laborer, and in that event, that the number should be augmented to forty thousand.

A DISTINCTION DRAWN.

Beyond this limit and these employments, it does not seem to me desirable, under existing circumstances, to go. A broad, moral distinction exists between the use of slaves as soldiers in defence of their homes and the incitement of the same persons to insurrection against their masters. The one is justifiable, if necessary: the other is iniquitous and unworthy of a civilized people; and such is the judgment of all writers on public law, as well as that expressed and insisted on by our enemies in all wars prior to that now waged against us. By none have the practices, of which they are now guilty, been denounced with greater severity than by themselves in the two wars with Great Britain in the last and in the present century; and in the Declaration of Independence of 1776, when enumeration was made of the wrongs which justified the revolt from Great Britain, the climax of atrocity was deemed to be reached only when the English monarch was denounced as having "excited domestic insurrection amongst us."

EMPLOYMENT OF SLAVES AS SOLDIERS—DAVIS OPPOSES A GENERAL LAW.

The subject is to be viewed by us, therefore, solely in the light of policy and our social economy. When so regarded, I must dissent from those who advise a general levy and arming of the slaves for the duty of soldiers. Until our white population shall prove insufficient for the armies we require and can afford to have in the field, to employ, as a soldier, the negro who has merely been trained to labor, and as a laborer, the white man, accustomed from his youth to the use of fire-arms, would scarcely be deemed wise or advantageous by any; and this is the question now before us. But should the alternative ever be presented of subju-

*For this corrected copy of his last speech I am indebted, through a mutual friend, to President LINCOLN, who frequently rendered me essential service by giving facilities for obtaining accurate copies of important papers.

gation or of the employment of the slave as a soldier, there seems no reason to doubt what should then be our decision.

Whether our view embraces what would, in so extreme a case, be the sum of misery entailed by the dominion of the enemy or to be restricted solely to the welfare and happiness of the negro population themselves, the result would be the same. The appalling demoralization, suffering, disease and death which have been caused by partially substituting the invader's system of policy for the kind relation previously subsisting between the master and slave, have been a sufficient demonstration that external interference with our institution of domestic slavery is productive of evil only. If the subject involved no other consideration than the mere right of property, the sacrifices heretofore made by our people have been such as to permit no doubt of their readiness to surrender every possession in order to secure their independence.

REBEL CARE OF THE AFRICAN.

But the social and political question, which is exclusively under the control of the several States, has a far wider and more enduring importance than that of pecuniary interest. In its manifold phase, it embraces the stability of our republican institutions, resting on the actual political equality of all its citizens, and includes the fulfillment of the task which has been so happily begun, that of Christianizing and improving the condition of the Africans who have, by the will of Providence, been placed in our charge. Comparing the results of our own experience with those of the experiments of others, who have borne similar relation to the African race, the people of the several States of the Confederacy have abundant reason to be satisfied with the past, and to use the greatest circumspection in determining their course.

These considerations, however, are rather applicable to the improbable contingency of our need of resorting to this element of resistance than to our present condition. If the recommendation above made, for the training of forty thousand negroes for the service indicated shall meet your approbation, it is certain that even this limited number, by their preparatory training in intermediate duties, would form a more valuable reserve force, in case of urgency, than threefold their number suddenly called from field labor; while a fresh levy could, to a certain extent, supply their places in the special service for which they are now employed.

NEGOTIATIONS FOR PEACE.

The disposition of this government for a peaceful solution of the issues which the enemy has referred to the arbitrament of arms has been too often manifested and is too well known to need new assurances. But while it is true that individuals and parties in the United States have indicated a desire to substitute reason for force, and by negotiation to stop the further sacrifice of human life, and to arrest the calamities which now afflict both countries, the authorities who control the government of our enemies have too often and too clearly expressed their resolution to make no peace except on terms of our unconditional submission and degradation, to leave us any hope of the cessation of hostilities until the delusion of their ability to conquer us is dispelled. Among those who are already disposed for peace, many are actuated by principle and by disapproval and abhorrence of the iniquitous warfare that their government is waging, while others are moved by the conviction that it is no longer to the interest of the United States to continue a struggle in which success is unattainable.

Whenever this fast growing conviction shall have taken firm root in the minds of a majority of the Northern people, there will be produced that willingness to negotiate for peace which is now confined to our side. Peace is manifestly impossible unless desired by both parties to this war, and the disposition for it among our enemies will be best and most certainly evoked by the demonstration on our part of ability and unshaken determination to defend our rights, and to hold no earthly price too dear for their purchase. Whenever there shall be, on the part of our enemies, a desire for peace, there will be no difficulty in finding means by which negotiation can be opened; but it is obvious that no agency can be called into action until this desire shall be mutual. When that contingency shall happen, the government, to which is confided the treaty-making power, can be at no loss for means adapted to accomplish so desirable an end.

In the hope that the day will soon be reached when, under Divine favor, these States may be allowed to enter on their former peaceful pursuits, and to develop the abundant natural resources with which they are blessed, let us then resolutely continue to devote our united and unimpaired energies to the defence of our homes, our lives, and our liberties. This is the true path to peace. Let us tread it with confidence in the assured result.

JEFFERSON DAVIS.

CHANGES IN LIST OF SENATORS AND REPRESENTATIVES.

The changes from the list, as found on page 402, are these:

IN SENATE.

Missouri—George G. Vest, appointed by Gov. Reynolds, in place of L. M. Louis.

North Carolina—The Legislature, at its late session, elected Thomas S. Ashe as successor of Mr. Dortch, for the next Congress.

IN HOUSE OF REPRESENTATIVES.*

Tennessee—Henry S. Foote abandoned his seat, came within our lines, and is now in Europe. He was expelled from the House—yeas 73, nays 0.

Alabama—William R. Smith announced his withdrawal, but the next day withdrew it and resumed his seat. Mr. Cobb has died since expulsion. His vacancy has not been filled.

THE NEGRO SOLDIER BILL.†

The following bill passed both Houses:

A Bill to increase the military forces of the Confederate States.

The Congress of the Confederate States of America do enact, That in order to provide additional forces to repel invasion, maintain the rightful possession of the Confederate States, secure their independence and preserve their institutions, the President be and he is hereby authorized to ask for and accept from the owners of slaves the services of such number of able-bodied negro men as he may

---

* A bill passed the Congress postponing the election for Representatives in Missouri for the next Congress until November next!

† General Lee's letter on the subject:

HEADQUARTERS C. S. ARMIES, *February* 18.

Hon. E. BARKSDALE, *House of Representatives, Richmond:*

SIR: I have the honor to acknowledge the receipt of your letter of the 12th instant, with reference to the employment of negroes as soldiers. I think the measure not only expedient but necessary. The enemy will certainly use them against us, if he can get possession of them; and, as his present numerical superiority will enable him to penetrate many parts of the country, I cannot see the wisdom of the policy of holding them to await his arrival, when we may, by timely action and judicious management, use them to arrest his progress. I do not think that our white population can supply the necessities of a long war, without overtaxing its capacity, and imposing great suffering on our people; and I believe that we should provide for a protracted struggle, not merely for a battle or a campaign. In answer to your second question, I can only say that, in my opinion, the negroes, under proper circumstances, will make efficient soldiers. I think we could at least do as well with them as the enemy, and he attaches great importance to their assistance. Under good officers and good instruction I do not see why they should not become soldiers. They possess all the physical qualification, and their habits of obedience constitute a good foundation for discipline. They furnish more promising material than many armies of which we read in history, which owed their efficiency to discipline alone. I think those who are employed should be freed. It would be neither just nor wise, in my opinion, to require them to remain as slaves. The best course to pursue, it seems to me, would be to call for such as are willing to come with the consent of their owners. An impressment or draft would not be likely to bring out the best class, and this course would make the war more distasteful to them and their owners. I have no doubt that, if Congress would authorize their reception into the service, and empower the President to call upon individuals or States for such as they are willing to contribute, with the condition of emancipation to all enrolled, a sufficient number would be forthcoming to enable us to try the experiment. If it prove successful, most of the objections to the measure would disappear; and if individuals still remained unwilling to send their negroes to the army, the force of public opinion in the States would soon bring about such legislation as would remove all obstacles. I think the matter should be left as far as possible to the people and to the States, which alone can legislate, as the necessities of this particular service may require. As to the mode of organizing them, it should be left as free from restraint as possible. Experience will suggest the best course, and it would be inexpedient to trammel the subject with provisions that might, in the end, prevent the adoption of reforms suggested by actual trial.

With great respect, your obedient servant,

R. E. LEE, *General*.

deem expedient for and during the war, to perform military service in whatever capacity he may direct.

SEC. 2. That the General-in-Chief be authorized to organize the said slaves into companies, battalions, regiments, and brigades, under such rules and regulations as the Secretary of War may prescribe, and to be commanded by such officers as the President may appoint.

SEC. 3. That, while employed in the service, the said troops shall receive the same rations, clothing, and compensation as are allowed to other troops in the same branch of the service.

SEC. 4. That if, under the previous section of this act, the President shall not be able to raise a sufficient number of troops to prosecute the war successfully and maintain the sovereignty of the States, and the independence of the Confederate States, then he is hereby authorized to call on each State, whenever he thinks it expedient, for her quota of 300,000 troops, in addition to those subject to military service under existing laws, or so many thereof as the President may deem necessary, to be raised from such classes of the population, irrespective of color, in each State, as the proper authorities thereof may determine: *Provided*, That not more than 25 per cent. of the male slaves between the ages of 18 and 45 in any State shall be called for under the provisions of this act.

SEC. 5. That nothing in this act shall be construed to authorize a change in the relation of the said slaves.

In Senate† the vote was:

YEAS—Messrs. Brown, Burnett, Caperton, Henry, Hunter, Oldham, Semmes, Simms, Watson—9.

NAYS—Messrs. Barnwell, Graham, Johnson of Georgia, Johnson of Missouri, Maxwell, Orr, Vest, Wigfall—8.

The proviso to the fourth section was added in the Senate. On concurring in it, the vote in the House was—yeas 40, nays 28, as follows:

AYES—Messrs. Anderson, Barksdale, Batson, Baylor, Blandford, Bradley, H. W. Bruce, Carroll, Clark, Clopton, Conrad, Darden, DeJarnette, Dickinson, Dupre, Elliott, Ewing, Funsten, Gaither, Goode, Gray, Hanly, Johnston, Keeble, Lyon, Machen, Marshall, McMullen, Menees, Miller, Moore, Murray, Perkins, Read, Russell, Simpson, Snead, Staples, Triplett, Villere—40.

NAYS—Messrs. Atkins, Baldwin, Branch, Chambers, Colyer, Cruickshank, Fuller, Gholson, Gilmer, Hartridge, Hatcher, Herbert, Holliday, J. M. Leach, J. T. Leach, Logan, McCallum, Ramsay, Rogers, Sexton, J. M. Smith, Wm. N. H. Smith, Turner, Wickham, Wilkes, Witherspoon, Bocock, (*Speaker*)—28.

†February 23—The same bill was indefinitely postponed in the Senate—yeas 11, nays 10, as follows:

YEAS—Messrs. Baker, Barnwell, Caperton, Garland, Graham, Hunter, Johnson of Ga., Johnson of Mo., Maxwell Orr, Wigfall—11.

NAYS—Messrs. Brown, Burnett, Haynes, Henry, Oldham, Semmes, Simms, Vest, Walker, Watson—10.

Subsequently, the Legislature of Virginia instructed their Senators to support it, which they obeyed. February 25—The Senate of Virginia passed this bill, which is presumed to have become a law:

1. *Be it enacted by the General Assembly*, That the Governor of this Commonwealth be and he is hereby authorized and empowered to call for volunteers from among the slaves and free negroes of the State to aid in defence of the capital and such other points as are or may be threatened by the public enemy.

2. That it shall be the duty of the Governor to cause all slaves who may volunteer with the consent of their masters, and all free negroes who shall tender their services, to be organized into infantry companies, of not less than sixty-four, rank and file, under white officers to be appointed by himself, and shall place the same, as fast as so organized, at the disposal of the General-in-Chief of the Confederate armies; or he may order all such volunteers to report immediately to the General-in-Chief, to be organized and officered by him, if thereby time can be saved, and the interests of the service promoted.

3. All laws and parts of laws now in force prohibiting the carrying of arms by slaves or free negroes are hereby suspended, during their terms of service, in favor of such volunteers as may be called to the field under this act.

4. The forces raised and organized under this act shall be enlisted for one year from the date of being mustered into the service of the Confederate States.

5. This act shall be in force from its passage.

The following is the vote:

AYES—Messrs. Alderson, Armstrong, Brannon, Branch, Christian of Augusta, Coghill, Collier, Douglas, Frazier, Garnett, Graham, Hart, Hunter, Jones, Keen, Lewis, Logan, Newton, Newman of Mason, Quesanberry, Stevenson, Spitler, Tayloe, Taylor, Thomas, Wiley, Witten—27.

NOES—Messrs. Dickinson, Dulancy, Saunders—3.

BILL ON EXEMPTIONS AND DETAILS.

A Bill to diminish the number of exemptions and details.

The Congress of the Confederate States of America do enact, That so much of the "Act to organize forces to serve during the war," approved February 17, 1864, as exempts one person as overseer or agriculturist on each farm or plantation upon which there were, at specified times, fifteen able-bodied field hands, between the ages of sixteen and fifty, upon certain conditions, is hereby repealed; *Provided*, that exemptions of persons over forty-five years of age may be granted under the provisions of the act aforesaid; and said persons shall be liable to military service upon the expiration of the time for which they received exemption by reason of having executed bonds for one year from the date thereof.*

SEC. 2. No exemption or detail shall be granted by the President or Secretary of War by virtue of said act, except of persons lawfully reported by a board of surgeons as unable to perform active service in the field; persons over the age of forty years, and of laborers, artisans, mechanics, and persons of scientific skill employed by or working for the Confederate or State Governments, and shown by proper testimony to be such laborers, artisans, mechanics, or persons of scientific skill, and with the same exceptions all exemptions and details heretofore granted by the President or Secretary of War, by virtue of said act, are hereby revoked.

SEC. 3. That all skilled artisans and mechanics who are engaged in the employment of the government of the Confederate States, are hereby exempt from all military service during the time they are so employed; *Provided*, they are persons whose services, labor, or skill may be more usefully employed for the public good at home than in the field, to be determined by the Secretary of War, on the sworn testimony of disinterested witnesses, under such rules and regulations as he may prescribe; and the names of all persons so exempted or detailed, together with the reason for the detail, shall be submitted to Congress at the beginning of each session.

DAVIS'S VETO.

To the Senate and House of Representatives of the Confederate States of America:

I have now under consideration the act entitled "An act to diminish the number of exemptions and details," which has passed both Houses, and presented to me Saturday, the 11th instant.

The act contains two provisions, which would, in practice, so impair the efficiency of the service as to counterbalance, if not outweigh the advantages that would result from the other clauses contained in it.

The third section exempts all skilled artisans and mechanics in the employ of the Government from all military service. A very important and indeed indispensable portion of our local defence troops consists of these mechanics and artisans. They amount to many thousands in the Confederacy; and while they are and should remain exempt from general service, no good cause is perceived why they should not, like all good citizens capable of bearing arms, be organized for local defence, and be ready to defend the localities in which they are respectively employed against sudden raids and incursions. If exempt from this local service, it will be necessary to detach, in many cases, troops

* February 23—This message was received in the House:

I herewith transmit for your information a communication from the Secretary of War relative to the accessions to the army from each State since April 16, 1862, to the number of persons liable to conscription who have been exempted or detailed, and to the number of those between the ages of seventeen and forty-five, and not unfitted for active service in the field, who are employed in the several States in the manner indicated in your inquiry.

JEFFERSON DAVIS.

The message and accompanying documents were laid upon the table and ordered to be printed. The message states that the

Number of conscripts assigned to the army from camps of instruction was	81,995
Deserters returned to the army	21,056
Assignments under section eighth of the act of February 17, 1864	7,733
Approximate estimates of men who have joined the army without passing the camps of instruction	76,206
Total number of exempts	66,586
Agricultural details	2,217
Detailed on account of public necessity	5,803
Details for bureaus and departments, not including artisans and mechanics	4,612
Detail of contractors to furnish supplies	717
Detail of artisans and mechanics	6,960

from the armies in the field. It is believed that if this provision becomes a law, the gain of strength resulting from the repeal of other exemptions enacted by the first sections of the law would be more than counterbalanced by the loss of this local force.

The second provision to which I refer is that which revokes all details and exemptions heretofore granted by the President and Secretary of War, and prohibits the grant of such exemptions and details hereafter. There is little hazard in saying that such a provision could not be executed without so disorganizing the public service as to produce very injurious results. In every department of the Government, in every branch of the service throughout the country, there are duties to be performed which cannot be discharged except by men instructed and trained in their performance. Long experience makes them experts. Their services become in their peculiar sphere of duty worth to the country greatly more than any they could possibly render in the field. Some of them it would be impossible to immediately replace. The Treasury expert who detects a forged note at a glance, the accounting officer whose long experience makes him a living repository of the rules and the precedents which guard the treasury from frauds, the superintendents of the manufacturing establishments of the Government which supply shoes, wagons, harness, ambulances, &c., for the army; the employés who have been especially trained in the distribution and subdivision of mail matter among the various routes by which it is to reach its destination, are among the daily instances which are recorded in the experience of executive officers. To withdraw from the public service at once, and without any means of replacing them, the very limited number of experts—believed to be less than one hundred—who are affected by this bill, is to throw the whole machinery of Government into confusion and disorder at a period when none who are not engaged in executive duties can have an adequate idea of the difficulties by which they are already embarrassed.

The desire of the Executive and Secretary of War to obtain for the army the services of every man available for the public defence can hadly be doubted, and Congress may be assured that nothing but imperative necessity could induce the exercise of any discretion invested in them to retain men out of the army. But no government can be administered without vesting some discretion in the executive officers in the application of general rules to classes of the population. Individual exceptions exist to all such rules; these exceptions cannot be provided for by legislation in advance. I earnestly hope that Congress will pass an amendment to this act now under consideration in accordance with the foregoing recommendation, so that I may be able, by signing both the act and amendment, to secure unimpaired benefit to the proposed legislation.

JEFFERSON DAVIS.

EXECUTIVE OFFICE, RICHMOND, *March* 13, 1865.

I am not aware that this conflict of opinion between the Congress and the Executive was reconciled.

SEQUESTRATION.

1864, December 3—The House considered this bill:

A Bill to be entitled an act to provide for sequestering of the property of persons liable to military service, who have departed, or shall depart, from the Confederate States without permission.

SEC. 1. *The Congress of the Confederate States of America do enact*, That if any person shall voluntarily depart from the Confederate States without the permission of the President or of the general officer commanding the Trans Mississippi department, or of an officer by one of them authorized to grant such permission, and if such person, at the time of such departure, shall be liable to military service, according to the laws of the Confederate States, he shall, from the time of his departure, be treated for the purposes of this act as an alien enemy, and his property shall be liable to sequestration and sale in like manner as the property of other alien enemies. But all proceedings for the sequestration and sale of his property shall cease, and he shall cease to be treated as an alien enemy by reason of such departure, if, during the present war, and before a decree of sequestration shall be pronounced against his property, he shall return and enter upon the performance of military service according to law. But this act shall not apply to persons who at the time of their departure shall bona fide reside within the lines of the enemy, or in a part of the Confederacy in the military occupation of the enemy.

SEC. 2. If any person to whom the preceding section applies shall voluntarily, and without such permission, go within the military lines of the enemy, and remain there more than sixty days, he shall be presumed to have departed from the Confederate States within the meaning of this act.

SEC. 3 If any person has heretofore voluntarily, and without such permission, departed from the Confederate States, or gone within the military lines of the enemy for the purpose of avoiding military service, being at the time liable to military service according to law, or being now liable to military service according to law, such person shall be also treated as an alien enemy, and his property shall be liable to sequestration and sale, according to all the preceding provisions, unless such person shall return and enter upon military service according to law, within six months after the passage of this act.

SEC. 4. All grants, conveyances, sales, gifts, and transfers of property hereafter made by any person who shall be liable to military service at the time of making the same, and whose property shall become liable to sequestration under this act, and all liens and incumbrances hereafter created on this property, when he is liable to military service, shall be void as against the claim of sequestration.

It was repeatedly considered and debated, before being passed.

1865, February 15—The Senate passed the bill—yeas 12, nays 7, as follows:

YEAS—Messrs. Baker, Brown, Burnett, Caperton, Dortch, Garland, Henry, Hill, Johnson of Missouri, Simms, Vest, Wigfall—12.

NAYS—Messrs. Graham, Haynes, Maxwell, Oldham, Semmes, Walker, Watson—7.

THE TAX LAW OF 1865.

[*From the Richmond Sentinel, March* 13.]

We publish in another column the text of the new tax law. It will be acceptable to the reader to have a synopsis of its provisions presented in plainer phrase. We are indebted for the following to a gentleman who had an active part in the passage of the law. The tax law of the present session imposes for the year 1865 taxes as follows:

1. Upon the value of all property, real and personal, not expressly exempted or taxed at a different rate, eight per cent. The property to be assessed on the basis of the market value of the same or similar property in the neighborhood where assessed in the year 1860. The property and assets of corporations, associations, and joint-stock companies, whether incorporated or not, taxed in the same manner and to the same extent as the property and assets of individuals, to be paid by the corporations or joint-stock companies. Banks not to be taxed on deposits of money to the credit of and subject to the checks of others. Stocks or shares in corporations, associations, or joint-stock companies not to be taxed as property, but the dividends to be taxed as income.

2. Upon the amount of all gold and silver coin, and upon the amount of all moneys held abroad, or bills of exchange drawn therefor, promissory notes. rights, credits, and securities, payable in foreign countries, and upon the specie value of all gold dust, or gold and silver bullion, twenty per cent.

3. Upon the amount of all moneys, except those abroad, bank bills, treasury notes, and other paper issued as currency, on hand or on deposit on the day of the approval of the act, five per cent.

4. Upon the amount of all solvent credits, except those held abroad, five per cent. Bonds and stocks issued by the Confederate States, or any State, and all loans to the Government of the Confederate States, are exempted from taxation, except as to the interest thereon, which is taxed as income. This income tax does not apply to bonds or stocks exempted by law from taxation.

5. Upon profits made by buying or selling merchandise, effects, or property of any description, or money, gold or silver, stocks, credits, or obligations of any kind, at any time between January 1, 1865, and January 1, 1866, ten per cent. in addition to the tax on such profits as income. The profits to be ascertained by the difference between the price paid in Confederate treasury notes, including all costs and charges, and the price realized in the same currency. If the objects of the sale were purchased at any time since January 1, 1863, this additional tax to attach on the profits realized on the sale therefor in 1865.

6. Upon the amount of profits exceeding twenty-five per cent., made during the year 1865, by any bank or banking company, insurance or other joint-stock company, a tax of twenty-five per cent. This tax to apply to individuals or partnerships, as well as to corporations—individuals and partnerships that have not been assessed, or have not paid for the year 1864, the tax of twenty-five per cent. imposed on the excess of profits over twenty-five per cent. for that year, to pay the same in 1865.

7. The property, income, and moneys of hospitals, asylums, churches, schools, colleges, and charitable institutions are exempted from taxation so long as it remains

within such lines; but income derived therefrom is taxed as income under existing laws.

8. The following are exempted from taxation: Property of each head of a family to the value of five hundred dollars; for each minor child one hundred dollars; for each son in the army or navy, or who has died in the service, five hundred dollars. The property of every soldier, of a soldier's widow, or orphan family or minors, to the value of one thousand dollars. Said exemptions not to apply where the property, exclusive of household furniture, exceeds one thousand dollars in value. Household furniture, where the value does not exceed three hundred dollars on the basis of the value of 1860, wearing apparel, goods manufactured by any person for the use and consumption of his family, including slaves, poultry, fruit, and products raised for the family of the producer, and not for sale; corn, bacon, and other agricultural products which were produced in 1864, and necessary for the taxpayer's family, including his slaves during the present year, and in his possession on the day of his approval of the act, are exempted from taxation.

9. Taxes on property for the year 1865 are to be assessed as on the day of the passage of this act, and to be due and collected on the 1st of June next, or as soon thereafter as practicable. The additional taxes on profits for 1865 to be assessed and collected according to the provisions of existing laws. All the taxes imposed by this act, as well as the taxes on incomes and profits, and the specific taxes, and taxes on sales, of the existing laws, are to be paid in Confederate treasury notes, or in certificates of indebtedness; provided that at least one-half be paid in the notes.

10. Any tax payer allowed, under regulations to be prescribed by the Secretary of the Treasury, to pay his taxes in advance.

11. The provision of the act of the 17th of February, 1864, which allowed the assessed tax on property employed in agriculture to be credited by the tax in kind, is repealed; that where income from property was taxed the property itself should be exempted, is also repealed.

12. The Secretary of the Treasury, on the recommendation of the boards of police, county courts, or other county, district, or parish tribunals, is authorized to suspend the collection of taxes in those districts where depredations have been committed by the enemy, in cases of individuals whose resources have been so seriously damaged or destroyed as to render the payment of taxes impossible or oppressive. To all the taxes above specified an addition of *one-eighth* of the amount is made, *in each case* to be paid in treasury notes and applied to the payment of the increased compensation of the soldier.

The taxes for 1865 may, therefore, be summed up as follows:

On all property (except foreign credits, coin, &c.,) eight per cent. on the valuation of 1860. On coin and foreign credits twenty per cent., and on bullion, plate, jewelry, &c., ten per cent.

One-tenth of all the productions of the soil, as established by the present law of tax in kind. On the income from property not employed in agriculture, the rates prescribed by the existing laws. No abatement of the property tax in the case of agriculturists because of the tithe tax, and no abatement in the case of other property holders because of the income tax. Agriculturists to pay no income tax.

The present taxes on incomes, salaries, &c., are continued.

Exemptions are specified above.

Five per cent. on all solvent credits, bonds, and stocks. The bonds of States, and the bonds, stocks, and loans to the Confederate States, to be taxed upon the interest as income and not upon principal. Ten per cent. additional to income tax on profits made by dealing in property, money, bonds, stocks, &c., in 1865 or in 1864, which are not already paid. Twenty-five per cent. on property exceeding twenty-five per cent. made in 1865 by banks, corporations, individuals, or partnerships, &c., to be paid in like manner.

This tax to be collected also for 1864 of those who may not have paid the same.

An addition of one-eighth in every case, except that of tax in kind, to be applied to paying the soldiers.

The person who is liable for the taxes and responsible for their payment is the one who holds or owns the property on the day of the passage of the act.

BILL TO DEFINE AND PUNISH CONSPIRACY AGAINST THE CONFEDERATE STATES.

1864, December 15—The Senate passed the following bill:

A Bill to define and punish conspiracy against the Confederate States.

SECTION 1. *The Congress of the Confederate States of America do enact,* That if two or more persons within any State or Territory of the Confederate States shall, with intent to injure the Confederate States, conspire to subvert, overturn or destroy by force the Government of the Confederate States; or to oppose by force the execution of the laws of the Confederate States, or by force to hinder, delay or prevent the execution of any law of the Confederate States, or to seize, take, possess or destroy any property of the Confederate States, against its consent, or to prevent, delay or hinder, by force or fraud, the transportation of supplies of men to, or belonging to the army of the Confederate States, or to destroy or injure any road, boat, engine or work employed in such transportation, or to hold any secret communication or intercourse with an enemy of the Confederate States, or to aid or abet the enemy in his war upon the Confederate States, or persons in rebellion against the same, or to promote disobedience of lawful military orders, mutiny or desertion, or unauthorized absence in the army of the Confederate States or among the soldiers in the military service, each and every person so offending shall be guilty of a high crime, and, upon conviction thereof, shall be punished by fine not exceeding five thousand dollars, and shall be imprisoned, with or without labor, not exceeding five years: *Provided,* That any person charged with any offence mentioned in this act, if such person be in the military or naval service of the Confederate States, may be tried by a military court or court martial, and if found guilty shall be punished by fine and imprisonment as hereinbefore provided, or such other punishment, not capital, as the court shall adjudge; and if the person charged be not in the military or naval service as aforesaid, such person shall be tried in the District Court of the Confederate States for the proper district.

Yeas 10, nays 6, as follows:

YEAS—Messrs. Baker, Barnwell, Caperton, Dortch, Garland, Henry, Hill, Johnson of Mo., Semmes, Sparrow—10.

NAYS—Messrs. Graham, Hunter, Johnson of Ga., Maxwell, Orr, Watson—6.

When Mr. Hunter's name was called, he stated that he believed Congress had the right to pass the bill; but, like the gentleman from Florida, he did not see that there was any necessity for it. He therefore voted against it.

The bill is as it came from the House, with the exception of the proviso added, as recommended by the Senate Judiciary Committee. The House is supposed to have concurred, and the bill to have become a law.

PEACE AND INDEPENDENCE.

Additional to what is stated on pages 456 and 457, are the following facts:

RESOLUTION ON INDEPENDENCE.

IN SENATE.

1864, December 13—On motion of Mr. BARNWELL, a joint resolution defining the position of the Confederate States, and declaring the determination of the Congress and the people thereof to prosecute the war till their independence is acknowledged, was taken up and adopted by an unanimous vote—yeas 16, nays none.

IN HOUSE OF REPRESENTATIVES.

1865, January 13—The resolution was reported favorably from the Committee on Foreign Relations, with a verbal amendment. Mr. HENRY said he preferred the original language of the resolutions; if he recollected aright, it was the language of the Declaration of Independence. Mr. SEMMES said *that was the objection to it.* Mr. HENRY said that was no objection; the Declaration of Independence was a very good document. The amendment was concurred in, and the resolutions passed.

RESOLUTIONS CONCERNING PEACE.

December 16—Mr. TURNER, (N. C.,) under a suspension of the rules, introduced resolutions

that the President, by and with the advice and consent of the Senate, be and he is hereby requested to appoint thirteen commissioners, one from each of the States of the Confederate States, to tender propositions for a conference, in order to negotiate terms of peace, and failing in this, said commissioners shall use all their influence to secure an exchange of prisoners and to mitigate the horrors of the existing war.

Mr. BARKSDALE, (Miss.,) offered the following resolution as a substitute for those presented by the gentleman from North Carolina:

Whereas, the people of the Confederate States having been compelled, by the acts of the non-slaveholding States, to dissolve their connection with those States, and to form a new compact in order to preserve their liberties; and whereas, the efforts made by the Government of the Confederate States, immediately upon its organization, to establish friendly relations between it and the Government of the United States having proved unavailing by reason of the refusal of the Government of the United States to hold intercourse with the Commissioners appointed by this Government for that purpose; and whereas, the Government of the United States having since repeatedly refused to listen to propositions for an honorable peace, and having declared to foreign powers in advance that it would reject any offer of mediation which they might be prompted to make in the interest of humanity for terminating the war; and thus, having manifested their determination to continue it, with a view to the reduction of the people of these States to a degrading bondage, or to their extermination: therefore, be it

Resolved, That while we reiterate our readiness to enter upon negotiations for peace whenever the hearts of our enemies are so inclined, we will pursue without faltering the course we have deliberately chosen, and for the preservation of our liberties will employ whatever means Providence has placed at our disposal.

Resolved, That the mode prescribed in the Constitution of the Confederate States for making treaties of peace afford ample means for the attainment of that end, whenever the Government of the United States abandon their wicked purpose to subjugate them, and evince a willingness to enter upon negotiations for terminating the war.

Pending which, the morning hour having expired, the subject was postponed.

December 17—Mr. MCMULLEN, of Virginia, offered this substitute:

Whereas, according to the Declaration of Independence of the United States, and the Constitution of the Confederate States, the people of each of said States, in their highest sovereign capacity, have a right to alter, amend, or abolish the government under which they live, and establish such other as they may deem most expedient; and whereas, the people of the several Confederate States have thought proper to sever their political connection with the people and government of the United States, for reasons which it is not needful here to state; and whereas, the people of the Confederate States have organized and established a distinct government for themselves; and whereas, because the people of the Confederate States have thus exercised their undoubted right in this respect, the people and government of the United States have thought proper to make war upon them; and whereas, there seems to be a difference of opinion on the part of the respective governments and people as to which of the contending parties is responsible for the commencement of the present war; therefore,

Resolved, That while it is inexpedient, and would be incompatible with the dignity of the Confederate States to send commissioners to Washington city for the purpose of securing a cessation of hostilities, yet it would be, in the judgment of this body, eminently proper that the House of Representatives of the Confederate States should despatch without delay to some convenient point a body of commissioners, thirteen in number, composed of one representative from each of the said States, to meet and confer with such individuals as may be appointed by the government of the United States in regard to all outstanding questions of difference between the two governments, and to agree, if possible, upon terms of a lasting and honorable peace, subject to the ratification of the respective governments and of the sovereign States respectively represented therein.

1865, January 11—Mr. MILES, of South Carolina, introduced a series, of which these are a part:

Resolved, That under the Constitution Congress alone has the right to declare war, and the President, by and with the advice and consent of the Senate, to make a treaty of peace.

Resolved, That all attempts to make peace with the United States by the action or intervention of the separate States composing the Confederacy are unauthorized by the Constitution, in contravention of the supreme law of the land, and therefore revolutionary.

Resolved, That we, the representatives of the Confederate States, are firmly determined to continue the struggle in which we are involved until the United States shall acknowledge our independence; and to this determination, with a sincere conviction of the justice of our cause, and an humble reliance upon the Supreme Ruler of nations, we do solemnly and faithfully pledge ourselves.

1865, January 23—Mr. J. T. LEACH, of North Carolina, offered these resolutions:

Whereas, the protracted struggle on the part of the Confederate States for their constitutional rights against the federal government, who claims the exercise of rights over States and the property of the citizens not guaranteed by the Constitution of the United States nor the laws of Congress is a just cause of alarm to the friends of civil liberty; and

Whereas, the cruel manner in which the war has been conducted on the part of the federal authorities, in the destruction of the private property of non-combatants and other acts of wantonness not tolerated by the usages of civilized nations, justifies the painful apprehension that the federal authorities are blind to their constitutional obligations, deaf to the demands of justice, the appeals of suffering humanity, the groans of the dying, the cries of hapless mothers and weeping orphans:

Resolved, therefore, For the purpose of averting, if possible, further horrors of this bloody, fratricidal strife, revolting alike to the feelings of statesmen, patriots, and Christians, and to add moral to our physical strength, that we, members of the House of Representatives of the Confederate Congress, in behalf of justice and suffering humanity, appeal most earnestly to the President and the Senators of the Confederate Congress to appoint such number of commissioners as, in their judgment, the importance of the occasion demands, to offer an armistice to the federal authorities, preparatory to negotiations for peace.

Resolved, That should the federal authorities agree to an armistice, and consent to negotiate for peace, the President, by and with the advice and consent of the Senate, be requested to appoint commissioners for the purpose of conferring with the federal authorities, and that such terms of peace as may be agreed to by them and certified by the President and Senate—two-thirds of the Senate concurring—shall constitute a bond of peace between the belligerents.

Resolved, That should the federal authorities refuse to entertain terms of peace, by negotiation, and thereby deny us our constitutional rights, for the purpose of more effectually maintaining those rights, and at the same time avert, if possible, the fearful and humiliating fate of subjugation, alike revolting to the feelings of freemen and repugnant to the demands of justice, that we, the representatives of this House, do unanimously pledge the undivided resources of the Confederate States in defence of our inalienable rights as freemen.

Mr. MCMULLEN, of Va., moved that the resolutions be considered in secret session, as the same question was now before the House in another form.

Mr. ATKINS, of Tenn., moved that the resolutions be referred to the Committee on Foreign Relations, which was ordered by an almost unanimous vote.

IN SENATE.

Mr. HENRY, of Tennessee, offered these resolutions, which were taken up November 29, and after debate referred to the Committee on Foreign Relations:

Resolved by the Congress of the Confederate States of America, That the people of the Confederate States are endowed by their Creator with the inalienable rights of life, liberty, and the pursuit of happiness; that to secure these rights governments were instituted among men, deriving their just powers from the consent of the governed; and whenever any government becomes destructive of these ends, it is the right of the people to alter or abolish it, and to institute a new government, laying its foundation on such principles, and organizing its powers in such form, as to them shall seem most likely to effect their safety and happiness; that on these principles, embodied in the Declaration of American Independence, the United Colonies, in 1776, dissolved the connection that bound them to the Government of Great Britain, and on them the Confederate States have severed the bonds of that political union which connected them with the people of the government of the United States of America, rather than submit to the repeated injuries inflicted upon them by that people, and to the usurpations of that government, all of which had the direct object to deprive them of their rights, rob them of their property, secured to them by constitutional guaranty, and to establish an absolute tyranny over these States.

Resolved, That the Confederate States appealed to arms in defence of these rights and to establish these principles only after they had in vain conjured the people of the government of the United States, by all the ties of a common kindred, to discountenance and discontinue these injuries and usurpations, and after they had petitioned for redress, in the most appropriate terms, and received in answer only a repetition of insults and injuries, which foreshadowed usurpations still more dangerous to liberty.

Resolved, That, after nearly four years of cruel, devastating, and unnatural war, in which the people of the Confederate States have unquestionably established their capacity for self-government, and their ability to resist the attempts of the enemy to subjugate them, this Congress does not hesitate to avow its sincere desire for peace, and to that end proclaim to the world the readiness of the government of the Confederate States to open negotiations to establish a permanent and honorable peace between the Confederate States and the United States, upon the basis of the separate independence of the former.

Resolved, That the time has come when the Confederate Congress, in the name of the people of the Confederate States, deem it proper again to proclaim to the world their unalterable determination to be free; and that they do not abate one jot of their high resolve to die freemen rather than live slaves; and, further, if the people of the United States, by re-electing Abraham Lincoln, mean to tender to them four years more of war or re-union with them on any terms, deeply deprecating the dire necessity so wantonly thrust upon them, and relying upon the justice of their cause and the gallantry of their soldiers, they accept the gauge of battle, and leave the result to the righteous arbitrament of Heaven.

Resolved, That in view of the determination of the enemy to prosecute this horrid war still further, against which the Confederate States have at all times protested, and which the enemy have waged with extraordinary vigor, and which has been marked by acts of extraordinary atrocity, in violation of all the usages of civilized warfare, the Congress of the Confederate States will from this hour dedicate themselves anew to the great cause of self-defence against the combined tyranny of the enemy; that it shall no longer be the momentary occupation of the Congress and the people of the Confederate States, but the business of their lives, to gather together the entire strength of the country in men and material of war, and put it forth, as with the will of one man, and with an unconquerable determination to defend their altars and their firesides till the last votary of freedom falls around them.

Mr. Henry did not desire to discuss the resolutions at this time. He merely wished to have them printed and placed upon the calendar. At the proper time he trusted that Senators would express their sentiments on this question, and a spirit would go out to the country that we are fully up to the mark, and intend to achieve our independence or die in the good fight.

January 30—Mr. Oldham (Texas) offered a series of resolutions, passed by the Legislature of Texas, declaring the determination of that State to accept no terms of peace which did not guarantee the independence of the Confederacy. Mr. Oldham said that he offered these resolutions, passed by the Legislature of his State, with peculiar satisfaction and pleasure. He referred briefly to the course pursued by one State since the commencement of this war. Her sons did not wait for the enemy to invade her borders; but when the tocsin of war was first sounded they rushed to the defence of glorious Old Virginia, and they were always to be found where the battle raged the fiercest. He alluded to the peace propositions, and to the call for a convention of States. He believed a convention of the States impracticable at this time. A majority of the States would not send delegates to such a convention. His State had spoken out; she wanted no peace which did not bring independence with it. We Texans, who had been for four years battling for our liberties, would be satisfied with nothing short of independence. He did not question the patriotism of those who believed in any other association than that prescribed by the Constitution. We must keep our people united; that was the sure road to peace and independence. He did not deny that our people were depressed, but it was caused by the dispelling of the illusions of peace, by the triumphant march of Sherman through Georgia, and his capture of the city of Savannah.

Mr. Brown said that nothing had fallen so gratefully upon his ears as the heroic resolutions passed by the Legislature of the heroic State of Texas. He did not believe that we could get honesty and fair dealing from the Yankees until we had thrashed it into them. In his opinion we would have peace when we conquered it at the point of the bayonet and the mouth of the cannon.

Mr. Wigfall was at the seat of government of his State when these resolutions were introduced, and he informed the Senate that they expressed the sentiment of his people. The resolutions were ordered to be printed.

JEFFERSON DAVIS ON STATE NEGOTIATION FOR PEACE.

Richmond, Va., *November* 17, 1864.

To the Hons. Senators of Georgia—Messrs. A. R. Wright, (President Senate,) Y. L. Guerry, J. M. Chambers, Thomas E. Lloyd, Frederick K. West, Robert B. Nesbit:

Gentlemen: I answered by telegraph this morning your letter of the 11th inst., as requested, and now respectfully comply with your desire that I should express my views on the subject to which you invite my attention.

In forwarding to me the resolutions introduced into the House of Representatives of Georgia by Mr. Stephens, of Hancock, you state that you are not inclined to favor the passage of these or any similar resolutions, believing them to have a tendency to create divisions among ourselves, and to unite and strengthen our enemies, but that it is asserted in Milledgeville that I favor such action on the part of the States, and would be pleased to see Georgia cast her influence in that way. You are kind enough to say that if this be true, and if the passage of these or similar resolutions would in the slightest degree aid or assist me in bringing the war to a successful and speedy close, you will give them your earnest and hearty support.

I return you my cordial thanks for this expression of confidence, but assure you that there is no truth in the assertions which you mention, and I presume that you will already have seen by the closing part of my annual message, which must have reached you since the date of your letter, that I have not contemplated the use of any other agency in treating for peace than that established by the Constitution of the Confederate States.

That agency seems to me to be well adapted to its purpose, and free from the injurious consequences that would follow any other means that have been suggested.

The objection to separate State action which you present in your letter, appears to be so conclusive as to admit no reply. The immediate and inevitable tendency of such distinct action in each State is to create discordant instead of united counsels, to suggest to our enemies the possibility of a dissolution of the Confederacy, and to encourage them, by the spectacle of our divisions, to more determined action against us.

They would readily adopt the false idea that some of the States of the Confederacy are disposed to abandon their sister States and make separate terms of peace for themselves, and if such a suspicion, however unfounded, were once engendered among our own people, it would be destructive of that spirit of mutual confidence and support which forms our chief reliance for success in the maintenance of our cause.

When the proposal of separate State action was first mooted, it appeared to me so impracticable, so void of any promise of good, that I gave no heed to the proposal; but upon its adoption by citizens, whose position and ability give weight to the expression of their opinions, I was led to a serious consideration of the subject. My first impressions have not been changed by reflection.

If all the States of the two hostile Federations are to meet in Convention, it is plain that such a meeting can only take place *after* an agreement as to the time, place, and terms on which they are to meet. Now, without discussing the minor although not trifling difficulties of agreeing as to time and place, it is certain that the States would never consent to a Convention without a previous agreement as to the *terms* on which they were to meet.

The proposed Convention must meet on the basis either that no State should, against its own will, be bound by the decision of the Convention, or that it should be so bound. But it is plain that an agreement on the basis that no State should be bound, without its consent, by the result of the deliberations, would be an abandonment on the part of the North of the pretended right of coercion; would be an absolute recognition of the independence of the several States of the Confederacy; would be, in a word, so complete a concession of the rightfulness of our cause that the most visionary cannot hope for such an agreement in advance of the meeting of a Convention.

The only other possible basis of meeting is that each State should agree, beforehand, to be bound by the decision of the Convention, and such agreement is but another form of submission to Northern dominion, as we well know that in such a Convention we should be outnumbered nearly two to one. On the very threshold of the scheme proposed, therefore, we are met by an obstacle which cannot be removed. Is not the impracticable character of the project apparent?

You will observe that I leave entirely out of view the suggestion that a Convention of all the States of both Federations should be held by common consent without any previous understanding as to the effect of its decisions—should meet merely in debate and pass resolutions that are to bind no one. It is not supposed that this can really be the meaning attached to the proposal by those who are active in its support, although the resolutions to which you invite my attention declare that the function of such a Convention would be simply to *propose* a plan of peace, with the *consent* of the two belligerents; or, in other words, to act as negotiators in treating for peace.

This part of the scheme is not intelligible to me. If the Convention is only to be held with the consent of the two belligerents, that consent cannot be obtained without negotiation. The plan then would resolve itself into a scheme that the two Governments should negotiate an agreement for the appointment of negotiators to make proposals for a treaty. It seems much more prompt and simple to negotiate for peace at once than to negotiate for the appointment of negotiators, who are to meet without power to do anything but make proposals.

If the Government of the United States is willing to make peace, it will treat for peace directly. If unwilling, it will refuse to consent to the Convention of States. The author of these resolutions and those who concur in his views appear to me to commit the radical error of supposing that the obstacle to obtaining the peace which we all desire consists in the difficulty of finding proper agencies for negotiating, so that the whole scope of the resolutions ends in nothing but suggesting that, if the enemy will treat, the best agency would be State Delegates to a Convention, whereas the whole and only obstacle is that the enemy will not treat at all, or entertain any other proposition than that we should submit to their yoke, acknowledge that we are criminals, and appeal to their mercy for pardon.

After this statement of objections, it may appear superfluous to add others of less gravity; but as you invite a full expression of my views, I will add that history is replete with instances of the interminable difficulties and delays which attend the attempt to negotiate on great and conflicting interests, when the parties to the negotiation are numerous. If this has been the case where the parties possessed full powers to conclude a treaty, what can we hope from an assembly of negotiators from thirty or forty States, who, in the midst of an exasperating warfare, are to meet without power to conclude anything?

In the history of our own country we find that in the time of profound peace, when the most cordial brotherhood of sentiment existed, and when a long and bloody war had been brought to a triumphant close, it required two years to assemble a Convention and bring its deliberations to an end, and another year to procure the ratification of their labors. With such a war as the present in progress, the views of the large assemblage of negotiators proposed would undergo constant change, according to the vicissitude of the struggle, and the attempt to secure concordant views would soon be abandoned, and leave the parties more embittered than ever—less hopeful of the possibility of successful negotiation.

Again, how is the difficulty resulting from the conflicting pretensions of the two belligerents in regard to several of the States to be overcome? Is it supposed that Virginia would enter into a convention with a delegation from what our enemies choose to term the "State" of "West Virginia," and thus recognize an insolent and violent dismemberment of her territory? Or would the United States consent that "West Virginia" should be deprived of her pretensions to equal rights, after having formally admitted her as a State, and allowed her to vote at a Presidential election? Who would send a delegation from Louisiana, Tennessee, Kentucky, Missouri?

The enemy claim to hold the governments of these States, while we assert them to be members of the Confederacy. Would delegates be received from both sides? If so, there would soon be a disruption of the Convention. If delegates are received from neither side, then a number of the States most vitally interested in the result would remain unrepresented, and what value could be attached to the mere representations of a body of negotiators under such circumstances?

Various other considerations suggest themselves, but enough has been said to justify my conclusion that the proposal of separate State action is unwise, impracticable and offers no prospect of good to counterbalance its manifold injurious consequences to the cause of our country.

Very respectfully, yours, &c.,

JEFFERSON DAVIS.

CONVENTION OF THE STATES.

In December, 1864, Mr. FOOTE of Tennessee, introduced two resolutions looking towards a conference of States. The first declares it unpatriotic for any of the rebel States to withdraw from the Confederacy, but allowable for them to confer in their sovereign capacity on the prosecution of the war and the attainment of peace. The second is as follows:

Resolved, That the present condition of the country is such as to render it eminently desirable that, for the purposes specified, a convention of these States, in their highest sovereign capacity, should be convoked without delay, and that if such convocation should be judged for the present impracticable, it would be desirable that each of said States should, "with as little delay as possible," appoint a limited number of commissioners with power to confer freely and fraternally with each other touching the present condition of the country, and of offering such advisory suggestions to said Confederate Government as might be calculated to prove advantageous in the further prosecution of the existing war, or conducive to the establishment of an early and honorable peace.

These resolutions were laid on the table by a vote of 63 to 13. Those who voted in the negative were:

Messrs. Bell of Georgia, Boyce of South Carolina, Colyar of Tennessee, Cruickshank of Alabama, Foote of Tennessee, Fuller of North Carolina, Gilmer of North Carolina, Lumpkin of Georgia, J. M. Leach of North Carolina, Logan of North Carolina, McMullen of Virginia, Ramsay of North Carolina, Smith of North Carolina.

THE MEXICAN QUESTION.

1864, November 7—Mr. MURRAY, of Tennessee, introduced the following joint resolution:

The Congress of the Confederate States do resolve, That we have no sympathy with the efforts to establish a monarchy in Mexico, and that we will not, directly or indirectly, aid in the establishment of a monarchy on the Continent of America.

Referred to the Committee on Foreign Affairs.

1865, January 30—Mr. DEJARNETTE, of Virginia, offered the following preamble and joint resolution, and the House suspended the five minute rule to allow him to speak to the merits of the resolution:

Whereas all nations have seen with alarm the establishment of any formidable power in their vicinity; and

Whereas the people of the Confederate States, as well as the people of the United States, have ever cherished the resolve that any further acquisition of territory in North America by any foreign power would be inconsistent with their prosperity and development; and

Whereas the invasion of Mexico by France has resulted, as is alleged, in the establishment of a government founded on the consent of the governed; nevertheless, we have reasons to believe that ulterior designs are entertained against California and the Pacific States, which we do not regard as parties to the war now waged against us, as they have furnished neither men nor money for its prosecution: therefore

The Congress of the Confederate States of America do resolve, That the time may not be distant when we will be prepared to unite, on the basis of the independence of the Confederate States, with those most interested in the vindication of the principles of the Monroe doctrine, for their mediation to the exclusion of all seeming violations of those principles on the continent of North America.

Mr. DeJarnette said that if England and France saw that we intended to pursue the policy indicated in the resolution, they would give us all we wanted and more than we hoped for.

On motion of Mr. Atkins, (Tenn.,) the preamble and resolution were referred to the Committee on Foreign Affairs.

DAVIS'S LAST MESSAGE.

Both Houses of the Rebel Congress had agreed to adjourn *sine die*, March 9th; but Mr. Davis requested them to remain in session a few days longer. On the 13th, he sent them a message on the state of the Confederacy, in which allusion is made to the perils surrounding it, and these recommendations are made:

That means be devised for securing to the officers of the supply departments two millions of dollars in coin, to supply the Virginia and North Carolina armies for one year. That the impressment law be modified so as not to allow public officers to impress supplies without making payment of the valuation at the time of impressment. That more efficient revenue measures be passed; that more rigorous military bills be passed, and that a general militia law be enacted. Respecting the suspension of the privilege of the writ of *habeas corpus*, he used this language:

I have heretofore, in a confidential message to the two Houses, stated the facts which induced me to consider it necessary that the privilege of the writ of *habeas corpus* should be suspended. The conviction of the necessity of this measure has become deeper, as the events of the struggle have been developed. Congress has not concurred with me in opinion. It is my duty to say that the time has arrived when the suspension of the writ is not simply advisable and expedient, but almost indispensable to the successful conduct of the war. On Congress must rest the responsibility of declining to exercise a power conferred by the Constitution as a means of public safety to be used in periods of national peril resulting from foreign invasion. If our present circumstances are not such as were contemplated when this power was conferred, I confess myself at a loss to imagine any contingency in which this clause of the Constitution will not remain a dead letter.

ON PEACE.

Congress will remember that in the conference above referred to our commissioners were informed that the Government of the United States would not enter into any agreement or treaty whatever with the Confederate States, nor with any single State; and that the only possible mode of obtaining peace was by laying down our arms, disbanding our forces, and yielding unconditional obedience to the laws of the United States, including those passed for the confiscation of our property, and the constitutional amendment for the abolition of slavery. It will further be remembered that Mr. Lincoln declares that the only terms on which hostilities would cease, were those stated in his message of December last, in which we were informed that in the event of our penitent submission, he would temper justice with mercy; and that the question whether we would be governed as dependent territories, or permitted to have a representation in their Congress, was one on which he could promise nothing, but which would be decided by their Congress, after our submission had been accepted.

It has not, however, been hitherto stated to you that in the course of the conference at Fortress Monroe, a suggestion was made by one of our commissioners that the objections entertained by Mr. Lincoln to treating with the government of the Confederacy or with any separate State might be avoided by substituting for the usual mode of negotiating through commissioners or other diplomatic agents, the method sometimes employed of a military convention to be entered into by the Commanding Generals of the armies of the two belligerents. This, he admitted, was a power possessed by him, though it was not thought commensurate with all the questions involved. As he did not accept the suggestion when made, he was afterwards requested to reconsider his conclusion upon the subject of a suspension of hostilities, which he agreed to do, but said that he had maturely considered of the plan, and had determined that it could not be done.

Subsequently, however, an interview with Gen. Longstreet was asked for by Gen. Ord, commanding the enemy's army of the James, during which Gen. Longstreet was informed by him that there was a possibility of arriving at a satisfactory adjustment of the present unhappy difficulties, by means of a military convention, and that if Gen. Lee desired an interview on the subject, it would not be declined, provided Gen. Lee had authority to act. This communication was supposed to be the consequence of the suggestion above referred to, and Gen. Lee, according to instructions, wrote to Gen. Grant on the 2d of this month, proposing to meet him for conference on the subject, and stating that he was vested with the requisite authority. Gen. Grant's reply stated that he had no authority to accede to the proposed conference; that his powers extended only to making a convention on subjects purely of a military character, and that Gen. Ord could only have meant that an interview would not be refused on any subject of which he, Gen. Grant, had the right to act.

It thus appears that neither with the Confederate authorities, nor the authorities of any State, nor through the Commanding Generals, will the Government of the United States treat or make any terms or agreement whatever for the cessation of hostilities. There remains, then, for us no choice but to continue this contest to a final issue; for the people of the Confederacy can be but little known to him who supposes it possible they would ever consent to purchase, at the cost of degradation and slavery, permission to live in a country garrisoned by their own negroes, and governed by officers sent by the conqueror to rule over them.

WRIT OF HABEAS CORPUS.

1865, January 20—Mr. J. M. Leach, of N. C., offered the following:

Resolved, That the privilege of the writ of *habeas corpus* is one of the great bulwarks of freedom, and that it ought not to be suspended except in extreme cases where the public safety imperatively demands it; that the people of this Confederacy are united in a great struggle for liberty, and that no exigency exists justifying its suspension.

The resolution was lost by the following vote:

Yeas—Messrs Anderson, Bell, Boyce, Branch, Clopton, Colyar, Cruickshank, Darden, Foster, Fuller, Garland, Gilmer, Lumpkin, J. M. Leach, J. T. Leach, Lester, Logan, Marshall, Miles, Murray, Orr, Ramsay, J. M. Smith, W. E. Smith, Turner, Wickham—26.

Nays—Messrs. Aiken, Baldwin, Barksdale, Batson, Blanford, Baylor, Bradley, H. W. Bruce, Chrisman, Clark, Cluskey, Conrow, DeJarnette, Dupre, Ewing, Farrow, Gaither, Gholson, Goode, Gray, Hanley, Hatcher, Herbert, Hilton, Holder, Johnson, Keeble, Lyon, Machen, Moore, Norton, Perkins, Read, Russell, Sexton, Shewmake, Simpson, Snead, Staples, Triplett, Villere, Wilkes, Mr. Speaker—43.

On motion of Mr. Russell, of Va., it was referred to the Committee on the Judiciary.

1864, December 24—The same resolution was negatived—yeas 31, nays 41, as follows:

Yeas—Messrs. Anderson, Atkins, Ayer, Baldwin, Boyce,

Branch, Clopton, Colyar, Cruickshank, Darden, Echols, Farrow, Foster, Gaither, Garland, Hanley, Herbert, Holden, Lumpkin, Lester, Marshall, Menees, Miles, Simpson, J. M. Smith, W. E. Smith, Smith, (Ala.,) Smith, (N. C.,) Wickham, Witherspoon—31.

NAYS—Messrs. Aiken, Barksdale, Batson, Blanford, E. M. Bruce, H. W. Bruce, Chilton, Chrisman, Clark, Cluskey, Conrad, Conrow, Dickenson, Dupre, Elliott, Ewing, Funsten, Gholson, Goode, Hartridge, Hatcher, Holliday, Johnson, Keeble, Kenner, Lyon, Machen, Norton, Perkins, Pugh, Sexton, Shewmake, Snead, Swan, Triplett, Vest, Villere, Welsh, Wilkes, Mr. Speaker—41.

1865, March 15—The House passed a bill—yeas 36, nays 32—suspending the privilege, but the Senate—yeas 6, nays 9—at first refused to concur, but subsequently passed it, as follows:

Whereas the Confederate States are invaded, and the public safety requires a suspension of the privilege of the writ of habeas corpus,

The Congress of the Confederate States of America do enact, That the privilege of the writ of habeas corpus is hereby suspended until otherwise provided by law, in all cases of arrest or detention by order of the President, the Secretary of War, or the general officer commanding the Trans-Mississippi Military Department.

SEC. 2. Until otherwise provided by law, the said privilege shall be suspended for sixty days from the time of arrest, in every case of arrest or detention by order of a general officer commanding an army, or a military department or district.

SEC. 3. Every such order shall be in writing, signed by the officer making the same, and shall name or describe the person to be arrested or detained.

SEC. 4. No military officer, detaining a person by virtue of any such order, shall be compelled, in answer to any writ of habeas corpus, to appear in person, or to return the body of the person so detained; but upon his certificate, under oath, that such person is detained by him under such an order, accompanied with a copy of the order, further proceedings under the writ shall cease and remain suspended according to the provisions of the preceding sections.

FINANCIAL.

1865, March 17—A law was enacted "to raise coin for the purpose of furnishing necessary supplies to the army," which imposes a tax of twenty-five per cent. on coin in the hands of individuals or banks in excess of $200, and authorizing in lieu thereof a loan from the banks, to the extent of $2,000,000, if made by the 17th of April. A supplementary act commuted this tax where the owners of coin would exchange it for cotton at the rate of fifteen cents per pound. Before March 28, the State of Virginia advanced $300,000 in coin for the use of the Commissary Department, for which an order was signed by the rebel Secretary of the Treasury for 2,000,000 pounds of cotton, "with the right to export the same free of all conditions except the payment of the (export) duty of seventy-five cents per pound." About that time, William W. Crump, Assistant Secretary of the Treasury, was sent to the banks of North and South Carolina and Georgia, to negotiate for their share of the loan. These facts are obtained from official documents found in Richmond, and published recently in the New York and other papers.

GENERAL MILITIA LAW.

The general militia law recommended above is said to have been passed.

CHANGE IN MR. DAVIS'S CABINET.

Secretary of War—John C. Breckinridge appointed, January 6, 1865, in place of James A. Seddon, resigned.

Peace Movements in the States.

NORTH CAROLINA.

Several resolutions on the subject of peace were offered.

In November, 1864, Mr. POOL proposed these in the Senate:

Resolved, That five commissioners be appointed by this General Assembly, to act with Commissioners from the other States of the Confederacy as a medium for negotiating a peace with the United States.

Resolved, That each of the other States of the Confederacy be requested to create a similar commission, with as little delay as practicable, and to co-operate with North Carolina in requesting of President Davis, in the name of these sovereign States, that he tender the United States a condition for negotiating a peace through the medium of these commissioners.

Resolved, That the Governor make known to each of the other States of the Confederacy this action of the General Assembly of North Carolina, and endeavor to secure their co-operation.

Resolved, That whenever any five States shall have responded by the appointment of commissioners, the Governor shall communicate the proceeding officially to President Davis, and request his prompt action upon the proposition.

In December, resolutions were introduced recommending the appointment of a delegation from that body to represent all parts of the State, to proceed to Washington to secure terms of peace. Laid over.

The following is the report of a majority of the Committee of the North Carolina Legislature, to whom were referred a series of resolutions entitled "resolutions to initiate negotiations for an honorable peace:"

The majority of the "joint select committee of the two Houses," to which were referred Senate resolutions No. 4, entitled "resolutions to initiate negotiations for an honorable peace," report the same back to the Senate without amendment, and recommend that they pass.

The majority of the committee believe that while every effort is being made to increase and strengthen the army by the most severe drain upon the people, for men and means, these extreme requirements should be accompanied by some manifestations of an effort and desire to secure an honorable peace by all other legitimate measures.

Commissioners heretofore tendered have been refused by the United States upon the pretext that their reception would imply a recognition of the Confederate Government, as preliminary, and that in case of a failure to agree upon a treaty such recognition would nevertheless stand. These resolutions seek to remove this objection by appointing commissioners on the part of the States, whose civil existence and authority have never been denied; but, at the same time, to make their tender and all powers dependent on the action and adoption of the President. It is not proposed that these commissioners derive any powers from the States, but only that they be tendered by the President for a peace conference, he giving to them such powers and instructions as he may deem necessary and proper.

JOHN POOL, *Chairman.*
A. C. COWLE.
D. F. CALDWELL.

1865, January 11—In the House of Commons, Mr. SHARPE introduced the following resolutions:

Resolved, That State sovereignty is the principle on which North Carolina and the other States withdrew from the United States Government; and, therefore, the States comprising the Southern Confederacy are sovereigns, and that the Confederate Government is only the agent of the States, and subject to their control.

Resolved, further, That the States in their sovereign capacity have the right to take up the question of peace or war, and settle it without consultation with the President of the Southern Confederacy or of the so-called United States.

On motion of Mr. CRAWFORD, of Rowan, these resolutions were laid on the table—ayes 52, nays 50.

January 19—In the House of Commons, Mr. HANES submitted a preamble and resolution on the subject of a general convention of the Confederate States, the former attributing oppressive and unconstitutional laws, which have been passed from time to time to irresponsible representatives from States which have no constituents upon whom the laws passed by them can operate; the latter reading as follows:

Resolved, That the joint select Committee on Confederate Relations be instructed to frame and bring in a bill forthwith, calling a convention of the people of this State, or submitting the question to them, so as to enable them to assemble in convention should a majority of them desire to do so, for the purpose of so amending the Constitution as to provide that hereafter the representatives of any State or States whose territory is in the hands of the enemy, so that the Confederate laws cannot be enforced therein, shall not, during the continuance of such occupation by the enemy, be permitted to vote upon any question of legislation, but shall have only such rights as are allowed to delegates in the territories of the Confederate States, and of considering such other amendments as said three States shall concur on suggestion.

Resolved, further, That State sovereignty being the principle on which North Carolina and other States withdrew from the Federal Union, the States comprising the Southern Confederacy are sovereigns, and the Confederate Government is only their agent and subject to their control, and the States in their sovereign capacity in general convention assembled have a right to negotiate peace with the Government of the United States without consultation with the President of the Confederate States.

Mr. HANES followed in a long argument in support of his resolutions, at the close of which, on motion of Mr. PERSON, they were laid upon the table—yeas 58, nays 39.

Mr. SMITH, of Johnston, introduced a bill to call a convention of the people, which passed its first reading and was referred to the Judiciary Committee. It declares that the present condition of the country demands that the sovereign people of this State should assemble in convention to effect, if possible, an honorable termination of the present war, and provides that an election shall be held on the 13th of February, 1865, the vote to be "convention," or "no convention;" that if the majority of the votes cast be for the convention, such convention shall be held in the city of Raleigh on the second Monday of March, and consist of one hundred and twenty delegates.

VIRGINIA.

[*From the Richmond Examiner, Jan.* 13.]

1865, January 12—In the House of Delegates, Mr. MILLER introduced a long series of peace resolutions for the appointment of five commissioners, and to declare for an armistice, a national convention, and an honorable peace through State action. The following debate took place:

Mr. TOMLIN moved to indefinitely postpone.

Mr. MILLER. I would ask the yeas and nays on that motion. I hope the House will come to the record on this question. I do not commit the House in this proposition to the policy of reconstruction, to which I am opposed, as is to be seen by the resolutions. The question is an important one, and its discussion now was not contemplated. I think it would be more appropriate to consider it in secret session.

Mr. PENDLETON. I hope the gentleman from King William [Mr. Tomlin] will modify his motion to the simple proposition to lay the preamble and resolution on the table. There are some things in the resolutions I am not prepared to vote against; such, for instance, as that which proposes to mitigate the horrors of war. But, at the same time, I denounce the cardinal objects of the resolutions as foreign to the honor, welfare, and dignity of Virginia, putting, as it does, the State in a revolutionary position, severing her connection from that of the Confederate States. The proposition is, in fact, that she secedes.

Mr. MILLER. The gentleman is mistaken as to any such proposition being in them.

Mr. PENDLETON. I would be glad, then, if the gentleman will state their meaning. To my mind they are firebrands, thrown into our midst at one of the closest and most critical periods of the war, and I denounce them as unworthy of Virginia; yet I prefer that they be laid upon the table, in order to see what in them is good and what evil, and to see if the good may not be put to some account, and the bad, which forms the spirit of them, and for which I denounce them, eliminated.

Mr. MILLER. Upon conference with gentlemen not entirely opposed to the resolutions, I will consent to withdraw them.

[Numerous objections to permit their withdrawal were made, and the expression "dispose of them at once and forever" was repeated in various parts of the House.]

Mr. ANDERSON. If this was the first movement of the kind which that gentleman [Mr. Miller] has made in this House, I would consent to let him withdraw his resolutions. But a year ago he threw a similar firebrand into this House; and when the motion was made to dispose of it, as is proposed to dispose of this, even the gentleman himself [Mr. Miller] did not have the hardihood to vote against its indefinite postponement. His name cannot be found, sir, on record against the postponement of his own proposition. What is his object now, after his first effort met with such a signal repulse that he himself shrank from resistance? These resolutions are similar and responsive to propositions which have been made in other States by the party which, under the cloak of peace, are attempting to destroy the Confederacy. Every man who, under the cloak of peace, comes forward with propositions of that kind, must be viewed as prepared to submit. Yes, sir, submit. For there can be no other terms. The Secretary of State of the United States has said that the South can only have peace by laying down its arms; and as to this favorite proposition of State conventions, he, the United States Secretary, has said, we cannot open communications with you, because we would sacrifice our position in regard to your doctrine of the superiority of State sovereignty over the Constitution of the United States. It is important to act promptly in this matter, and to give no countenance to this mischievous, and, I believe, treasonable party.

The yeas and nays being called, the motion to indefinitely postpone was adopted. Yeas, 101; nays, 2—Messrs. Miller of Lee, and Smith of Russell.

January 20—In the House of Delegates Mr. DOUGLAS offered the following joint resolutions:

Resolved by the Senate and House of Delegates of Virginia in General Assembly convened, That the State of Virginia, having entered into the present contest with the United States, and made common cause with the confederates to uphold and defend their rights and liberties from a common danger, is ready and anxious for the return of peace whenever the same can be obtained on terms honorable and just alike to herself and them, and in a manner calculated to secure for all time the precious objects for which we are contending.

Resolved, That the Legislature, representing the sentiment of Virginia, desires the constitutional department of the confederate government to avail itself of every favorable indication to negotiate for terms of peace; yet we solemnly deprecate any irregular action in the premises, either in the shape of a congressional commission, or other way, as revolutionary and dangerous in character, violative of the faith mutually pledged by the States to each other in the adoption of the confederate constitution, by distracting and dividing the minds of the people, to weaken our power of resistance, disintegrate these States, and place the people of this State especially at the mercy of the common enemy.

Mr. MARSHALL moved that the rules be suspended in order that the resolutions might be placed on the secret calendar. He thought the resolutions should be considered in secret session. In reference to these resolutions he had something to say which he would not like to say in open session.

Mr. DOUGLAS opposed the motion to place the resolutions on the secret calendar. Such a disposition of them would defeat the object which he had in view. He wished to see the resolutions adopted, and go forth as the views of this Legislature. He desired to put his heel on every irregular attempt to negotiate terms of peace either in the shape of a congressional commission, by separate State action, or otherwise. Such schemes, in his estimation, would lead to a disintegration of States and the overthrow of the government which the people have instituted.

Mr. ARMSTRONG thought it best that the resolutions should be considered in secret session.

Mr. COLLIER was in favor of discussing the resolutions in open session. He wanted the people to know what their representatives were doing, and what were our opinions.

The motion to suspend the rule with a view of transferring the resolutions to the secret calendar was disagreed to, and it was laid aside.

January 26—In the House of Delegates,

Mr. SMITH, of Russell, sent to the clerk's desk and caused to be read a series of resolutions deploring the war and looking to the attainment of peace by the arbitrament of diplomacy and negotiation, the sword having failed. The resolutions, after much discussion, were indefinitely postponed.

March 9—In the House of Delegates, the following debate occurred on the proposition for a State Convention:

On motion to suspend the rules for the reconsideration of the vote by which the bill conferring conventional power upon the General Assembly was lost, Mr. HUNTER, of Berkeley, obtained the floor in opposition to the proposition to reconsider the vote.

The discussion already had upon the subject had had, he thought, dangerous and pernicious effects. He hoped the vote would not be reconsidered; that the bill would be left to sleep the sleep of death. Mr. BUFORD, of Pittsylvania, hoped the House would arraign itself upon the question fair and square without prejudice; he thought no harm could come of a Convention. The time might come when legislators would not find themselves behind the people in this matter. He was willing to trust the people and the people should be willing to trust their legislators. Mr. SHEFFEY, (*Speaker*,) with Mr. Kelley in the Chair, spoke in opposition to the motion to reconsider the vote by which the bill to clothe the Constitutional Assembly with constitutional powers was lost. If two evils were proposed, he would choose the least—the straight-out Convention. He did not understand that there was to be any difference in powers to be conferred upon either body. True, the legislature could not touch the bill of rights nor unite the powers of legislature, executive and judicial. If anything was contemplated by a convention, it was looking to the severance of Virginia's connection with the Confederacy and opening of new and separate negotiations with the treaty-making power of the North. Once open this flood-gate and you will let loose a current that will sweep with desolation the last hope of freedom from this continent. Had we not rather bear those ills we have than fly to others that we know not of? How long will it be after this convention is called before a cry will go forth and reconstruction or no reconstruction become the watchword of these dangerous times? No harm to trust the people, as gentlemen say, but it is a terrible harm for Virginia to lead off in the expression of distrust for the general government. People will say, if the army will say it, that Virginia is preparing to cast loose from the body of her Confederate Union. Our enemy will say that Virginia is preparing to leave the sinking ship and to take to her jolly-boat. The speaker never would with his voice advocate a call for a convention, legislative or straight-out. If other States fly madly from their sphere like erratic rockets to blaze a while, and then die out in eternal night forever, let them fly; but let Virginia be one of those calm, fixed stars, veiled sometimes in cloud and tempest, but indestructible as the firmament from which it shines. Virginia must never perish thus.

Mr. STAPLES, of Patrick, interrupting the Speaker, appealed to the House. He had never said that a convention was to prepare Virginia for the dissolution of her copartnership in the Confederate Union.

Mr. SHEFFEY, continuing, said it was now too late to do this thing. The ship of State is upon the rapids, and if the helmsman cannot guide the ship she must be dashed to pieces. It was no time now to change front; no time to seek a hiding-place from the tempest of war. If we are to sink, let us sink where we stand, and go down with our ship with one triumphant shout of defiance, with the flag of Virginia—"*Sic Semper Tyrannis*"—floating over us.

Mr. BURWELL, of Bedford, was going to stick to the ship till she struck or run ashore; then he would build a raft of the fragments and see what could be done. He favored a convention, vested in the Legislature.

Mr. ROBERTSON, of Richmond, said that only when our armies were overthrown, the Confederacy torn limb from limb and State from State, would he give his vote or consent to go into convention. Even up to to the last extremity, the honor and integrity of Virginia demanded that she should stand firm. If legislators be of the opinion that a convention is demanded, they should withdraw themselves from the possible imputation of being candidates for its membership.

Mr. STAPLES obtained the floor, when Mr. BOULDIN called for the order of the day. The consideration of the tax bill and the question under debate was postponed, and a resolution from the Senate extending the session twenty-two days from Tuesday next taken up.

ALABAMA.

November, 1864—This preamble and resolution were submitted by Mr. PARSONS and debated:

Whereas ABRAHAM LINCOLN, as President of the United States, and commander-in-chief of the army and navy thereof, and the friends and supporters of his administration, have declared that negotiations for peace cannot be entertained except on a basis of restoration of the Union in its territorial integrity and the abolition of slavery, and that the existing war must be prosecuted until the men of these Confederate States are compelled to submit to these terms or are subjugated, and, if necessary to secure this end, exterminated, their lands confiscated, and their women and children driven forth as wanderers on the face of the earth:

And whereas the re-election of ABRAHAM LINCOLN to the office of President of the United States is advocated by many, if not all of his supporters upon these grounds, and that there is no other way to terminate the war, insisting that there is no disposition on the part of the people of these States to enter into negotiations for peace, except on the distinct admission of the separate independence of these States as a basis:

And whereas, at a recent Convention held in the city of Chicago, a numerous and powerful party has declared its willingness, if successful, to stop fighting and open negotiations with us on the basis of the Federal Constitution as it is, and the restoration of the Union under it: now, therefore—

Be it resolved by the Senate and House of Representatives of the State of Alabama in General Assembly convened, That we sincerely desire peace. If the aforesaid party is successful, we are willing and ready to open negotiations for peace on the basis indicated in the platform adopted by said Convention—our sister States of this Confederacy being willing thereto.

For further action, see page 456.

GEORGIA.

In November, 1864, these resolutions were offered by Mr. LINTON STEPHENS:

The General Assembly of the State of Georgia do resolve that the independence of the Southern Confederate States of America, based upon the constitutional compact between the sovereign States composing the Confederacy, and maintained through nearly four years of gigantic war, justly claims from the world its recognition as a rightful fact.

2. That all the States which composed the late American Union, as well those embraced within the present United States as those embraced within the Southern Confederacy, are what the original thirteen States were declared to be by our fathers of 1776, and acknowledged to be by George the Third of England—independent and sovereign; not as one political community, but as States, each one of them constituting such a "people" as have the inalienable right to terminate any Government of their former choice, by withdrawing from it their consent, just as the original thirteen States, through their common agent, acting for and in the name of each one of them, by the withdrawal of their consent, put a rightful termination to the British Government, which has been established over them with their consent.

3. That the sovereignty of the individual States is the only basis of permanent peace on the American continent, and will, if the voice of passion and war can once be hushed, and reason allowed to resume her sway, lead us to an easy and lasting solution of all the matters of controversy involved in the present lamentable war, by simply leaving all the States free to form their political associations with one another, not by force of arms, which excludes the idea of "consent," but by a rational consideration of their respective interests growing out of their natural considerations.

4. That as the very point of controversy in the present war is the settlement of the political association of the States, no treaty of peace can be perfected consistently with the sovereignty of the individual States, without State action on the part of at least those States whose preference may justly be regarded as doubtful, and have not yet been expressed through the appropriate organs; and therefore opposition to all State co-operation in perfecting a peace cannot be consistent with a desire for its establishment on a basis of the sovereignty of the States.

5. That we hail with gratification the just and sound sentiment coming from a large and growing party in the North, that all associations of these American States must be voluntary, and not forcible, and we give a hearty response to their proposition to suspend the conflict of arms, and hold a convention of States to inaugurate a plan for permanent peace.

6. That the appropriate action of such a convention would be not to perform any agreement or compact between States, but only to frame and propose a plan of peace; and the assembling of such a convention, for such a purpose, would be relieved from all possible constitutional objection by the consent of the two Governments; and with such consent, the proposed Convention would but act as com-

missioners for the negotiation of peace, subject to the ratification of both Governments, and in all points involving the sovereignty or integrity of the States, subject also to the ratification of the particular States whose sovereignty might be so involved.

7. That we respectfully, but most earnestly, urge upon our own Government the propriety and wisdom of not only expressing a desire for peace, through the Presidential messages and Congressional manifestoes, but of making, on all suitable occasions, and especially just after signal successes of our arms, official, open, and unequivocal offers to treat for peace, through the medium of a convention of States, leaving our adversary to accept our offers, or by rejecting them, to prove to his own people that he is waging this unnatural war, not for peace nor the good of his country, but for purposes of the most unholy and dangerous ambition.

On motion, two hundred copies were ordered to be printed.

RESULT OF THE PRESIDENTIAL ELECTION OF 1864.

[This table includes the Home Vote and the Army Vote.]

STATES.	ELECTORAL VOTE.		POPULAR VOTE.		TOTALS.
	Lincoln.	McClellan.	Lincoln.	McClellan.	
Maine	7	....	72,278	47,736	120,014
New Hampshire	5	....	36,595	33,034	69,629
Massachusetts	12	....	126,742	48,745	175,487
Rhode Island	4	....	14,343	8,718	23,061
Connecticut	6	....	44,693	42,288	86,981
Vermont	5	....	42,422	13,325	55,747
New York	33	....	368,726	361,986	730,712
New Jersey	....	7	60,723	68,014	128,737
Pennsylvania	26	....	296,389	276,308	572,697
Delaware	....	3	8,155	8,767	16,922
Maryland	7	....	40,153	32,739	72,892
Virginia					
North Carolina					
South Carolina					
Georgia					
Kentucky	....	11	27,786	64,301	92,087
Tennessee					
Ohio	21	....	265,154	205,568	470,722
Louisiana					
Mississippi					
Indiana	13	....	150,422	130,233	280,655
Illinois	16	....	189,487	158,349	347,836
Alabama					
Missouri	11	....	72,991	31,026	104,017
Arkansas					
Michigan	8	....	85,352	67,370	152,722
Florida					
Texas					
Iowa	8	....	87,331	49,260	136,591
Wisconsin*	8	....	79,564	63,875	143,439
Minnesota	4	....	25,060	17,375	42,435
California	5	....	62,134	43,841	105,975
Oregon	3	....	9,888	8,457	18,345
Kansas	3	....	14,228	3,871	18,099
West Virginia	5	....	23,223	10,457	33,680
Nevada†	2	....	9,826	6,594	16,420
	212	21	2,213,665	1,802,237	4,015,902

ARMY VOTE FOR PRESIDENT, 1864.

STATES.	Lincoln.	McClellan.	Totals.
Maine	4,174	741	4,915
New Hampshire	2,066	690	2,756
Vermont ‡	243	49	292
Pennsylvania	26,712	12,349	39,061
Maryland	2,800	321	3,121
Kentucky §	1,194	2,823	4,017
Ohio	41,146	9,757	50,903
Michigan	9,402	2,959	12,361
Iowa	15,178	1,364	16,542
Wisconsin	11,372	2,458	13,830
California	2,600	237	2,837
Minnesota ‖			
Kansas ¶			
	116,887	33,748	150,635

* In Wisconsin, 3,163 votes for Lincoln, and 1,729 votes for McClellan electors were rejected for informality, and 418 scattering votes were cast, so that the total vote should have been 148,749.

† This State was entitled to three electors, but one dying before the canvass was concluded, but two votes were cast in the Electoral College.

‡ In Vermont, a large army vote was returned too late to be counted.

§ In the camps of Kentucky soldiers within that State, the army vote was included in the general canvass.

‖ No army vote was received until too late for the canvass.

¶ The Kansas soldiers' vote was 2,867 for Lincoln and 543 for McClellan; not canvassed on account of being received too late.

☞ President LINCOLN's estimate, page 558, was but 129 less than the exact result!

INDEX.

A

B

C

D

E

I

L

M

N

O

P

S

T

U

V

W

Y

Z